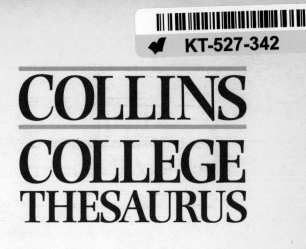

COLLINS
COLLEGE
THESAURUS

BANK *of* ENGLISH

This thesaurus has been compiled by referring to the Bank of English – a unique database of the English language with examples of over 200 million words enabling Collins lexicographers to analyse how English is actually used today and how it is changing. This is the evidence on which the changes in this thesaurus are based.

The Bank of English was set up as a joint initiative by HarperCollins Publishers and Birmingham University to be a resource for language research and lexicography. It contains a very wide range of material from books, newspapers, radio, TV, magazines, letters, and talks reflecting the whole spectrum of English today. Its size and range make it an unequalled resource and the purpose-built software for its analysis is unique to Collins Dictionaries.

This ensures that Collins Dictionaries accurately reflect English as it is used today in a way that is most helpful to both the dictionary and thesaurus user as well as including the full range of rarer and historical words and meanings.

COLLINS

COLLEGE
THESAURUS

HarperCollins*Publishers*

First Edition 1995
Reprinted 1995

2 3 4 5 6 7 8 9

© 1995 HarperCollins Publishers
ISBN 0 00 470900 4

A catalogue record for this book is
available from the British Library.

NOTE
Entered words that we have reason to believe
constitute trademarks have been designated as such.
However, neither the presence nor absence of
such designation should be regarded as affecting the
legal status of any trademark.

Typeset by Morton Word Processing Ltd.
Scarborough, England

Printed and bound in Great Britain by
HarperCollins Manufacturing
P.O. Box, Glasgow G4 0NB

FOREWORD

The name "Thesaurus" comes from a Greek word meaning treasure or treasury, and COLLINS COLLEGE THESAURUS is a treasury of words. In it you will find a rich collection of synonyms, words or expressions of similar meaning, arranged in a straightforward alphabetical list so that you can easily find an apt alternative for the word or idea you have in mind.

Suppose that you want to find another word for *difficult*. Perhaps you have used this word already, or you feel that it is not quite suited to the tone of what you want to write or say. When you look up *difficult* you will find alternative words, covering the various contexts in which *difficult* might occur: for example, from the many alternatives given, you could substitute an *onerous* task; a *knotty* problem; an *obstreperous* child; *straitened* circumstances.

In addition, many entries are followed by lists of antonyms, words or expressions of opposite meaning. These can be used to express a meaning by denying the opposite. Instead of "the situation is difficult", the antonym list at *difficult* may suggest to you "the situation is by no means *straightforward*".

COLLINS COLLEGE THESAURUS is arranged, like a dictionary, in a single alphabetical listing of main entry words. You go straight to the word that is your starting point, and there you find the synonyms. No matter how many meanings a word has, synonyms for all of them will be found at the one entry, as will the antonyms, where included.

The English language today is changing more rapidly than at any time in the past. New words, new ways of expressing old ideas, are continually coming into existence, and these are recorded and monitored by the Collins English Dictionaries language-monitoring programme. This new edition of COLLINS COLLEGE THESAURUS draws on the Bank of English to ensure that the very latest new synonyms and antonyms have been included.

COLLINS COLLEGE THESAURUS is a comprehensive and up-to-date treasury of words. It will enable you to choose exactly the right word for any occasion, as well as being simply a pleasure for you to browse through, marvelling at the richness and the variety of the English language.

EXPLANATORY NOTES

1. Under each main entry word, the synonyms are arranged alphabetically. When a word has distinctly separate meanings, separate numbered lists are given for the different senses.

2. Where it is desirable to distinguish between different parts of speech, labels have been added as follows: *n.* (noun), *v.* (verb), *adj.* (adjective), *adv.* (adverb), *pron.* (pronoun), *conj.* (conjunction), *prep.* (preposition), *interj.* (interjection). See entries for *living, loaf, loan, local.*

3. Usually the synonyms for a particular part of speech are grouped together. Thus, in the entry *catch* synonyms for all the verb senses are given first, followed by synonyms for all the noun senses. Sometimes, however, noun and verb functions are very closely associated in specific meanings, and where this is the case the synonyms are grouped by meanings, as in the entry for *cover*.

4. When a headword has more than one meaning *and* can function as more than one part of speech, a new part-of-speech function is shown by a large swung dash (~), as in the entry for *glance* or *grasp*.

5. Much-used phrases appear as main entries; for instance, *act for* comes after *act*. Expressions such as *a priori* or *en route* are also given as main entries within the alphabetical listing. Short idiomatic phrases are entered under their key word and are to be found either at the end of the entry or immediately following the sense with which they are associated. Thus, the phrase, *take a dim view* appears as sense 7 of the entry *dim*, since the synonyms in sense 6 most closely approximate to the meaning of the phrase.

6. Plural forms that have a distinctly separate meaning, such as *provisions*, are entered at their own alphabetical position, while those with a less distinct difference, such as *appurtenances*, are given as a separate sense under the singular form, e.g. *appurtenance* ... 2. *Plural* ...

7. The antonym lists which follow many entries are arranged alphabetically, and, where appropriate, treated according to the rules given above for synonyms.

8. A label in brackets applies only to the synonym preceding it while one which is not bracketed relates to the whole of that particular sense. Labels have been abbreviated when a readily understandable shortened form exists, such as *Sl.* (Slang), *Inf.* (Informal), and *Fig.* (Figurative).

9. The small swung dash symbol (~) is used to show that a word has been broken merely because it happens to fall at the end of a line, while the conventional sign (–) is used to distinguish a word which is always written with a hyphen, as in the entry for *ancient*.

> **ancient** aged, age-old, antediluvian, anti~ quated, antique, archaic, bygone, early, hoary, obsolete, old, olden, old-fashioned, outmoded, out-of-date, primeval, primordial, superannuated, timeworn
> **Antonyms** current, fresh, in vogue, late, modern, modish, new, newfangled, new-fashioned, novel, recent, state-of-the-art, up-to-date, with it (*Inf.*), young

EDITORIAL STAFF

A

abaft *Nautical* aft, astern, behind

abandon *v.* **1.** desert, forsake, jilt, leave, leave behind **2.** evacuate, quit, vacate, withdraw/from **3.** abdicate, cede, give up, relinquish, renounce, resign, surrender, waive, yield **4.** desist, discontinue, drop, forgo, kick (*Inf.*) ~*n.* **5.** careless freedom, dash, recklessness, unrestraint, wantonness, wild impulse, wildness
Antonyms *v.* claim, continue, defend, hold, keep, maintain, take, uphold ~*n.* control, moderation, restraint

abandoned 1. cast aside, cast away, cast out, derelict, deserted, discarded, dropped, forlorn, forsaken, jilted, left, neglected, outcast, rejected, relinquished, unoccupied, vacant **2.** corrupt, debauched, depraved, dissipated, dissolute, profligate, reprobate, sinful, wanton, wicked **3.** uncontrolled, uninhibited, unrestrained, wild
Antonyms (*sense 1*) claimed, kept, maintained, occupied (*sense 2*) good, high-principled, honest, moral, pure, reputable, righteous, upright, virtuous, worthy (*sense 3*) conscious, restrained

abandonment 1. dereliction, desertion, forsaking, jilting, leaving **2.** evacuation, quitting, withdrawal from **3.** abdication, cession, giving up, relinquishment, renunciation, resignation, surrender, waiver **4.** desistance, discontinuation, dropping

abase belittle, bring low, cast down, debase, degrade, demean, demote, depress, disgrace, dishonour, downgrade, humble, humiliate, lower, mortify, reduce
Antonyms advance, aggrandize, dignify, elevate, exalt, glorify, honour, prefer, promote, raise, upgrade

abasement belittlement, debasement, degradation, demotion, depression, disgrace, dishonour, downgrading, humbling, humiliation, lowering, mortification, reduction, shame

abashed affronted, ashamed, astounded, bewildered, chagrined, confounded, confused, discomfited, discomposed, disconcerted, discountenanced, dismayed, embarrassed, humbled, humiliated, mortified, perturbed, shamefaced, taken aback
Antonyms at ease, blatant, bold, brazen, composed, confident, unashamed, undaunted, undismayed, unperturbed

abate 1. alleviate, appease, attenuate, decline, decrease, diminish, dull, dwindle, ease, ebb, fade, lessen, let up, mitigate, moderate, quell, reduce, relax, relieve, sink, slacken, slake, slow, subside, taper off, wane, weaken **2.** deduct, discount, subtract
Antonyms add to, amplify, augment, boost, enhance, escalate, increase, intensify, magnify, multiply, strengthen

abatement 1. alleviation, allowance, attenuation, cessation, decline, decrease, diminution, dulling, dwindling, easing, extenuation, fading, lessening, let-up (*Inf.*), mitigation, moderation, quelling, reduction, relief, remission, slackening, slaking, slowing, tapering off, waning, weakening **2.** deduction, discount, subtraction

abbey cloister, convent, friary, monastery, nunnery, priory

abbreviate abridge, abstract, clip, compress, condense, contract, curtail, cut, digest, epitomize, précis, reduce, shorten, summarize, trim, truncate
Antonyms amplify, draw out, elongate, expand, extend, increase, lengthen, prolong, protract, spin out, stretch out

abbreviation abridgment, abstract, clipping, compendium, compression, condensation, conspectus, contraction, curtailment, digest, epitome, précis, reduction, résumé, shortening, summary, synopsis, trimming, truncation

abdicate abandon, abjure, abnegate, cede, forgo, give up, quit, relinquish, renounce, resign, retire, step down (*Inf.*), surrender, vacate, waive, yield

abdication abandonment, abjuration, abnegation, cession, giving up, quitting, relinquishment, renunciation, resignation, retiral (*esp. Scot.*), retirement, surrender, waiver, yielding

abdominal gastric, intestinal, stomachic, stomachical, visceral

abduct carry off, kidnap, make off with, run away with, run off with, seize, snatch (*Sl.*)

abduction carrying off, kidnapping, seizure

aberration 1. aberrancy, abnormality, anomaly, defect, deviation, divergence, eccentricity, irregularity, lapse, oddity, peculiarity, quirk, rambling, straying, wandering **2.** delusion, hallucination, illusion, instability, mental disorder, vagary

abet 1. aid, assist, back, condone, connive at, help, promote, sanction, second, succour, support, sustain, uphold **2.** egg on, encourage, incite, prompt, spur, urge

abeyance 1. adjournment, deferral, dis~

continuation, inactivity, intermission, post~
ponement, recess, reservation, suspense,
suspension, waiting **2. in abeyance** hang~
ing fire, on ice (*Inf.*), pending, shelved, sus~
pended

abhor abominate, detest, execrate, hate,
loathe, recoil from, regard with repugnance
or horror, shrink from, shudder at
Antonyms admire, adore, cherish, covet,
delight in, desire, enjoy, like, love, relish

abhorrent abominable, detestable, disgust~
ing, distasteful, execrable, hated, hateful,
heinous, horrible, horrid, loathsome, ob~
noxious, obscene, odious, offensive, repel~
lent, repugnant, repulsive, revolting, yucky
or yukky (*Sl.*)

abide 1. accept, bear, brook, endure, put up
with, stand, stomach, submit to, suffer, tol~
erate **2.** dwell, linger, live, lodge, reside,
rest, sojourn, stay, stop, tarry, wait **3.** con~
tinue, endure, last, persist, remain, survive

abide by 1. acknowledge, agree to, comply
with, conform to, follow, obey, observe,
submit to **2.** adhere to, carry out, dis~
charge, fulfil, hold to, keep to, persist in,
stand by

abiding constant, continuing, durable, en~
during, eternal, everlasting, fast, firm, im~
mortal, immutable, indissoluble, lasting,
permanent, persistent, persisting, steadfast,
surviving, tenacious, unchanging, unending
Antonyms brief, ephemeral, evanescent,
fleeting, momentary, passing, short, short-
lived, temporary, transient, transitory

ability adeptness, aptitude, capability, ca~
pacity, competence, competency, craft, dex~
terity, endowment, energy, expertise, ex~
pertness, facility, faculty, flair, force, gift,
knack, know-how (*Inf.*), potentiality, power,
proficiency, qualification, skill, talent
Antonyms inability, incapability, incapac~
ity, incompetence, powerlessness, weakness

abject 1. base, contemptible, cringing, de~
based, degraded, despicable, dishonourable,
fawning, grovelling, humiliating, ignoble,
ignominious, low, mean, servile, slavish,
sordid, submissive, vile, worthless **2.** de~
plorable, forlorn, hopeless, miserable, out~
cast, pitiable, wretched
Antonyms august, dignified, distinguished,
elevated, eminent, exalted, grand, great, high,
lofty, noble, patrician, worthy

abjectness 1. abjection, baseness, con~
temptibleness, debasement, degradation,
dishonour, humbleness, humiliation, igno~
miny, lowness, meanness, servility, slav~
ishness, sordidness, submissiveness, vile~
ness, worthlessness **2.** destitution, forlorn~
ness, hopelessness, misery, pitiableness,
pitifulness, squalor, wretchedness

ablaze 1. afire, aflame, alight, blazing,
burning, fiery, flaming, ignited, lighted, on
fire **2.** aglow, brilliant, flashing, gleaming,
glowing, illuminated, incandescent, lumi~
nous, radiant, sparkling **3.** angry, aroused,
enthusiastic, excited, fervent, frenzied,
fuming, furious, impassioned, incensed,
passionate, raging, stimulated

able accomplished, adept, adequate, adroit,
capable, clever, competent, effective,
efficient, experienced, expert, fit, fitted,
gifted, highly endowed, masterful, masterly,
powerful, practised, proficient, qualified,
skilful, skilled, strong, talented
Antonyms amateurish, inadequate, inca~
pable, incompetent, ineffective, inefficient,
inept, mediocre, unfit, unskilful, weak

able-bodied firm, fit, hale, hardy, healthy,
hearty, lusty, powerful, robust, sound,
staunch, stout, strapping, strong, sturdy,
vigorous
Antonyms ailing, debilitated, feeble, fragile,
frail, sickly, tender, weak

ablution bath, bathing, cleansing, lavation,
purification, shower, wash, washing

abnegation abandonment, abjuration, ab~
stinence, continence, disallowance, eschew~
al, forbearance, giving up, refusal, rejection,
relinquishment, renunciation, sacrifice,
self-denial, surrender, temperance

abnormal aberrant, anomalous, atypical,
curious, deviant, eccentric, erratic, excep~
tional, extraordinary, irregular, monstrous,
odd, oddball (*Inf.*), off-the-wall (*Sl.*), outré,
peculiar, queer, singular, strange, uncom~
mon, unexpected, unnatural, untypical, un~
usual, wacko (*Sl.*), weird
Antonyms common, conventional, custom~
ary, familiar, natural, normal, ordinary,
regular, unexceptional, usual

abnormality aberration, anomaly, atypi~
calness, bizarreness, deformity, deviation,
eccentricity, exception, extraordinariness,
flaw, irregularity, monstrosity, oddity, pe~
culiarity, queerness, singularity, strange~
ness, uncommonness, unexpectedness, un~
naturalness, untypicalness, unusualness,
weirdness

abode domicile, dwelling, dwelling-place,
habitat, habitation, home, house, lodging,
pad (*Sl.*), quarters, residence

abolish abrogate, annihilate, annul, axe
(*Inf.*), blot out, cancel, destroy, do away
with, eliminate, end, eradicate, expunge,
exterminate, extinguish, extirpate, invali~
date, nullify, obliterate, overthrow, over~
turn, put an end to, quash, repeal, repudi~
ate, rescind, revoke, stamp out, subvert,
suppress, terminate, vitiate, void, wipe out
Antonyms authorize, continue, create, es~
tablish, found, institute, introduce, legalize,

promote, reinstate, reintroduce, restore, re~ vive, sustain

abolition abrogation, annihilation, annul~ ment, blotting out, cancellation, destruction, elimination, end, ending, eradication, ex~ punction, extermination, extinction, extir~ pation, invalidation, nullification, oblitera~ tion, overthrow, overturning, quashing, re~ peal, repudiation, rescission, revocation, stamping out, subversion, suppression, ter~ mination, vitiation, voiding, wiping out, withdrawal

abominable abhorrent, accursed, atro~ cious, base, contemptible, despicable, de~ testable, disgusting, execrable, foul, godawful (Sl.), hateful, heinous, hellish, horrible, horrid, loathsome, nauseous, ob~ noxious, obscene, odious, repellent, repre~ hensible, repugnant, repulsive, revolting, terrible, vile, villainous, wretched, yucky or yukky (Sl.)
Antonyms admirable, agreeable, charming, commendable, delightful, desirable, good, laudable, likable or likeable, lovable, pleasant, pleasing, wonderful

abominate abhor, detest, execrate, hate, loathe, recoil from, regard with repugnance, shudder at
Antonyms admire, adore, cherish, dote on, esteem, idolize, love, revere, treasure, wor~ ship

abomination 1. abhorrence, antipathy, aversion, detestation, disgust, distaste, ex~ ecration, hate, hatred, horror, loathing, odium, repugnance, revulsion **2.** anathema, bête noire, bugbear, curse, disgrace, evil, horror, plague, shame, torment

aboriginal ancient, autochthonous, earliest, first, indigenous, native, original, primary, primeval, primitive, primordial, pristine

abort 1. miscarry, terminate (a pregnancy) **2.** arrest, axe (Inf.), call off, check, end, fail, halt, stop, terminate

abortion 1. aborticide, deliberate miscar~ riage, feticide, miscarriage, termination **2.** disappointment, failure, fiasco, misadven~ ture, monstrosity, vain effort

abortive adj. **1.** bootless, failed, failing, fruitless, futile, idle, ineffectual, miscarried, unavailing, unsuccessful, useless, vain **2.** Biol. imperfectly developed, incomplete, ru~ dimentary, stunted ~n. **3.** Medical abortifa~ cient

abound be jammed with, be packed with, be plentiful, crowd, flourish, increase, infest, luxuriate, overflow, proliferate, super~ abound, swarm, swell, teem, thrive

abounding abundant, bountiful, copious, filled, flourishing, flowing, flush, full, lav~ ish, luxuriant, overflowing, plenteous, plentiful, profuse, prolific, rank, replete, rich, superabundant, teeming

about prep. **1.** anent (Scot.), as regards, concerned with, concerning, connected with, dealing with, on, re, referring to, re~ garding, relating to, relative to, respecting, touching, with respect to **2.** adjacent, be~ side, circa (used with dates), close to, near, nearby **3.** around, encircling, on all sides, round, surrounding **4.** all over, over, through, throughout ~adv. **5.** almost, ap~ proaching, approximately, around, close to, more or less, nearing, nearly, roughly **6.** from place to place, here and there, hither and thither, to and fro ~adj. **7.** active, around, astir, in motion, present, stirring

about to intending to, on the point of, on the verge or brink of, ready to

above prep. **1.** atop, beyond, exceeding, higher than, on top of, over, upon **2.** before, beyond, exceeding, prior to, superior to, surpassing ~adv. **3.** aloft, atop, in heaven, on high, overhead ~adj. **4.** aforementioned, aforesaid, earlier, foregoing, preceding, previous, prior
Antonyms prep. (sense 1) below, beneath, under, underneath (sense 2) inferior, lesser, less than, lower than, subordinate

aboveboard 1. adv. candidly, forthrightly, frankly, honestly, honourably, openly, overtly, straightforwardly, truly, truthfully, uprightly, veraciously, without guile **2.** adj. candid, fair and square, forthright, frank, guileless, honest, honourable, kosher (Inf.), legitimate, on the up and up, open, overt, square, straight, straightforward, true, trustworthy, truthful, upfront (Inf.), upright, veracious
Antonyms adj. clandestine, crooked, deceit~ ful, deceptive, devious, dishonest, fraudulent, furtive, secret, secretive, shady, sly, sneaky, underhand

abracadabra 1. chant, charm, conjuration, hocus-pocus, incantation, invocation, magic, mumbo jumbo, sorcery, spell, voodoo, witchcraft **2.** babble, balderdash, blather, drivel, gibberish, gobbledegook, jabber, jar~ gon, nonsense, pap, twaddle

abrade erase, erode, file, grind, rub off, scour, scrape away, scrape out, wear away, wear down, wear off

abrasion 1. Medical chafe, graze, scrape, scratch, scuff, surface injury **2.** abrading, chafing, erosion, friction, grating, rubbing, scouring, scraping, scratching, scuffing, wearing away, wearing down

abrasive adj. **1.** chafing, erosive, frictional, grating, rough, scraping, scratching, scratchy, scuffing **2.** annoying, biting, caustic, cutting, galling, grating, hurtful, irritating, nasty, rough, sharp, unpleasant,

vitriolic ~*n.* **3.** abradant, burnisher, grind~
er, scarifier, scourer

abreast 1. alongside, beside, level, shoulder
to shoulder, side by side **2.** acquainted, *au
courant,* au fait, conversant, familiar, in~
formed, in touch, knowledgeable, up to date

abridge abbreviate, abstract, clip, compress,
concentrate, condense, contract, curtail, cut,
cut down, decrease, digest, diminish, epito~
mize, lessen, précis, reduce, shorten, sum~
marize, synopsize (*U.S.*), trim
   Antonyms amplify, augment, enlarge, ex~
pand, extend, go into detail, lengthen, prolong,
protract, spin out, stretch out

abridgment abbreviation, abstract, com~
pendium, condensation, conspectus, con~
traction, curtailment, cutting, decrease, di~
gest, diminishing, diminution, epitome,
lessening, limitation, outline, précis, reduc~
tion, restraint, restriction, résumé, short~
ening, summary, synopsis

abroad 1. beyond the sea, in foreign lands,
out of the country, overseas **2.** about, at
large, away, circulating, current, elsewhere,
extensively, far, far and wide, forth, in cir~
culation, out, out-of-doors, outside, publicly,
widely, without

abrupt 1. blunt, brisk, brusque, curt, direct,
discourteous, gruff, impatient, impolite,
rough, rude, short, snappish, snappy, terse,
unceremonious, uncivil, ungracious **2.** pre~
cipitous, sharp, sheer, steep, sudden **3.**
hasty, headlong, hurried, precipitate, quick,
sudden, surprising, swift, unanticipated,
unexpected, unforeseen **4.** broken, discon~
nected, discontinuous, irregular, jerky, un~
even
   Antonyms (*sense 1*) civil, courteous, gra~
cious, polite (*sense 2*) gradual (*sense 3*) easy,
leisurely, slow, thoughtful, unhurried

abscond bolt, clear out, decamp, disappear,
do a bunk (*Brit. sl.*), do a runner (*Sl.*), es~
cape, flee, flit (*Inf.*), fly, fly the coop (*U.S. &
Canad. inf.*), make off, run off, skedaddle
(*Inf.*), slip away, sneak away, steal away,
take a powder (*U.S. & Canad. sl.*), take it on
the lam (*U.S. & Canad. sl.*)

absence 1. absenteeism, nonappearance,
nonattendance, truancy **2.** default, defect,
deficiency, lack, need, nonexistence, omis~
sion, privation, unavailability, want **3.**
absent-mindedness, abstraction, distraction,
inattention, preoccupation, reverie

absent *adj.* **1.** away, elsewhere, gone, lack~
ing, missing, nonattendant, nonexistent, not
present, out, truant, unavailable, wanting
2. absent-minded, absorbed, abstracted, be~
mused, blank, daydreaming, distracted,
dreamy, empty, faraway, heedless, inatten~
tive, musing, oblivious, unheeding, unthinking,

vacant, vague ~*v.* **3. absent oneself** ab~
scond, depart, keep away, play truant, re~
move, slope off (*Inf.*), stay away, truant,
withdraw
   Antonyms *adj.* (*sense 1*) attendant, in at~
tendance, present (*sense 2*) alert, attentive,
aware, conscious, thoughtful ~*v.* attend, show
up (*Inf.*)

absently absent-mindedly, abstractedly, be~
musedly, blankly, distractedly, dreamily,
emptily, heedlessly, inattentively, oblivi~
ously, on automatic pilot, unconsciously,
unheedingly, vacantly, vaguely

absent-minded absent, absorbed, ab~
stracted, bemused, distracted, dreaming,
dreamy, engrossed, faraway, forgetful,
heedless, in a brown study, inattentive,
musing, oblivious, preoccupied, unaware,
unconscious, unheeding, unthinking
   Antonyms alert, awake, observant, on one's
toes, on the ball, perceptive, quick, vigilant,
wary, wide-awake

absolute 1. arrant, complete, consummate,
deep-dyed (*Usually derogatory*), downright,
entire, out-and-out, outright, perfect, pure,
sheer, thorough, total, unadulterated, unal~
loyed, unmitigated, unmixed, unqualified,
utter **2.** actual, categorical, certain, conclu~
sive, decided, decisive, definite, exact,
genuine, infallible, positive, precise, sure,
unambiguous, unequivocal, unquestionable
3. absolutist, arbitrary, autarchical, auto~
cratic, autonomous, despotic, dictatorial,
full, peremptory, sovereign, supreme, ty~
rannical, unbounded, unconditional, unlim~
ited, unqualified, unquestionable, unre~
strained, unrestricted

absolutely 1. completely, consummately,
entirely, fully, perfectly, purely, thoroughly,
totally, unmitigatedly, utterly, wholly **2.**
actually, categorically, certainly, conclu~
sively, decidedly, decisively, definitely, ex~
actly, genuinely, infallibly, positively, pre~
cisely, surely, truly, unambiguously, un~
equivocally, unquestionably **3.** arbitrarily,
autocratically, autonomously, despotically,
dictatorially, fully, peremptorily, sover~
eignly, supremely, tyrannically, uncondi~
tionally, unquestionably, unrestrainedly,
without qualification
   Antonyms conditionally, fairly, probably,
reasonably, somewhat

absoluteness 1. consummateness, en~
tirety, perfection, purity, thoroughness, to~
tality, unmitigatedness, wholeness **2.** as~
suredness, certainty, certitude, conclusive~
ness, correctness, decidedness, decisiveness,
definiteness, exactitude, genuineness, infal~
libility, positiveness, precision, sureness,
surety, truth, unambiguousness, unequivo~
calness **3.** arbitrariness, autonomy, despot~
ism, dictatorialness, fullness, peremptori~

ness, supremacy, tyranny, unboundedness, unquestionability, unrestrainedness, unrestrictedness

absolution acquittal, amnesty, deliverance, discharge, dispensation, exculpation, exemption, exoneration, forgiveness, freeing, indulgence, liberation, mercy, pardon, release, remission, setting free, shriving, vindication

absolutism absoluteness, arbitrariness, autarchy, authoritarianism, autocracy, despotism, dictatorship, totalitarianism, tyranny

absolutist arbiter, authoritarian, autocrat, despot, dictator, totalitarian, tyrant

absolve acquit, clear, deliver, discharge, exculpate, excuse, exempt, exonerate, forgive, free, let off, liberate, loose, pardon, release, remit, set free, shrive, vindicate
Antonyms blame, censure, charge, condemn, convict, damn, denounce, excoriate, pass sentence on, reprehend, reproach, reprove, sentence, upbraid

absorb 1. assimilate, consume, devour, digest, drink in, exhaust, imbibe, incorporate, ingest, osmose, receive, soak up, suck up, take in 2. captivate, engage, engross, enwrap, fascinate, fill, fill up, fix, hold, immerse, monopolize, occupy, preoccupy, rivet

absorbed 1. captivated, concentrating, engaged, engrossed, fascinated, fixed, held, immersed, involved, lost, occupied, preoccupied, rapt, riveted, wrapped up 2. assimilated, consumed, devoured, digested, exhausted, imbibed, incorporated, received

absorbing arresting, captivating, engrossing, fascinating, gripping, interesting, intriguing, preoccupying, riveting, spellbinding
Antonyms boring, dreary, dull, humdrum, mind-numbing, monotonous, tedious, tiresome, unexciting

absorption 1. assimilation, consumption, digestion, exhaustion, incorporation, osmosis, soaking up, sucking up 2. captivation, concentration, engagement, fascination, holding, immersion, intentness, involvement, occupation, preoccupation, raptness

abstain avoid, cease, decline, deny (oneself), desist, forbear, forgo, give up, keep from, kick (*Inf.*), refrain, refuse, renounce, shun, stop, withhold
Antonyms abandon oneself, give in, indulge, partake, yield

abstemious abstinent, ascetic, austere, continent, frugal, moderate, self-denying, sober, sparing, temperate
Antonyms gluttonous, greedy, immoderate, incontinent, intemperate, self-indulgent

abstention abstaining, abstinence, avoid-

ance, desistance, eschewal, forbearance, nonindulgence, refraining, refusal, self-control, self-denial, self-restraint

abstinence abstemiousness, asceticism, avoidance, continence, forbearance, moderation, refraining, self-denial, self-restraint, soberness, sobriety, teetotalism, temperance
Antonyms abandon, acquisitiveness, covetousness, excess, gluttony, greediness, indulgence, self-indulgence, wantonness

abstinent abstaining, abstemious, continent, forbearing, moderate, self-controlled, self-denying, self-restraining, sober, temperate

abstract *adj.* 1. abstruse, arcane, complex, conceptual, deep, general, generalized, hypothetical, indefinite, intellectual, nonconcrete, notional, occult, philosophical, profound, recondite, separate, subtle, theoretic, theoretical, unpractical, unrealistic ~*n.* 2. abridgment, compendium, condensation, digest, epitome, essence, outline, précis, recapitulation, résumé, summary, synopsis ~*v.* 3. abbreviate, abridge, condense, digest, epitomize, outline, précis, shorten, summarize, synopsize (*U.S.*) 4. detach, dissociate, extract, isolate, remove, separate, steal, take away, take out, withdraw
Antonyms *adj.* actual, concrete, definite, factual, material, real, specific ~*n.* enlargement, expansion ~*v.* (*sense 4*) add, combine, inject

abstracted 1. absent, absent-minded, bemused, daydreaming, dreamy, faraway, inattentive, preoccupied, remote, withdrawn, woolgathering 2. abbreviated, abridged, condensed, digested, epitomized, shortened, summarized, synopsized (*U.S.*)

abstraction 1. absence, absent-mindedness, bemusedness, dreaminess, inattention, pensiveness, preoccupation, remoteness, woolgathering 2. concept, formula, generality, generalization, hypothesis, idea, notion, theorem, theory, thought

abstruse abstract, arcane, complex, dark, deep, Delphic, enigmatic, esoteric, hidden, incomprehensible, mysterious, mystical, obscure, occult, perplexing, profound, puzzling, recondite, subtle, unfathomable, vague
Antonyms apparent, clear, conspicuous, evident, manifest, open, overt, patent, perceptible, plain, self-evident, transparent, unsubtle

absurd crazy (*Inf.*), daft (*Inf.*), farcical, foolish, idiotic, illogical, inane, incongruous, irrational, laughable, ludicrous, meaningless, nonsensical, preposterous, ridiculous, senseless, silly, stupid, unreasonable

Antonyms intelligent, logical, prudent, ra~ tional, reasonable, sagacious, sensible, smart, wise

absurdity bêtise (*Rare*), craziness (*Inf.*), daftness (*Inf.*), farce, farcicality, farcical~ ness, folly, foolishness, idiocy, illogicality, illogicalness, incongruity, irrationality, joke, ludicrousness, meaninglessness, non~ sense, preposterousness, ridiculousness, senselessness, silliness, stupidity, unrea~ sonableness

abundance 1. affluence, ampleness, boun~ ty, copiousness, exuberance, fullness, heap (*Inf.*), plenitude, plenteousness, plenty, pro~ fusion **2.** affluence, big bucks (*Inf., chiefly U.S.*), big money, fortune, megabucks (*U.S. & Canad. sl.*), opulence, pretty penny (*Inf.*), riches, tidy sum (*Inf.*), wad (*U.S. & Canad. sl.*), wealth
Antonyms dearth, deficiency, lack, need, paucity, scantiness, scarcity, sparseness

abundant ample, bounteous, bountiful, co~ pious, exuberant, filled, full, lavish, luxuri~ ant, overflowing, plenteous, plentiful, pro~ fuse, rank, rich, teeming, well-provided, well-supplied
Antonyms deficient, few, few and far be~ tween, inadequate, in short supply, insufficient, lacking, rare, scant, scanty, scarce, short, sparse

abuse *v.* **1.** damage, exploit, harm, hurt, ill-treat, impose upon, injure, maltreat, manhandle, mar, misapply, misuse, oppress, spoil, take advantage of, wrong **2.** calumni~ ate, castigate, curse, defame, disparage, in~ sult, inveigh against, libel, malign, revile, scold, slander, smear, swear at, traduce, upbraid, vilify, vituperate ~*n.* **3.** damage, exploitation, harm, hurt, ill-treatment, im~ position, injury, maltreatment, man~ handling, misapplication, misuse, oppres~ sion, spoiling, wrong **4.** blame, calum~ niation, castigation, censure, character as~ sassination, contumely, curses, cursing, defamation, derision, disparagement, in~ sults, invective, libel, opprobrium, re~ proach, revilement, scolding, slander, swearing, tirade, traducement, upbraiding, vilification, vituperation **5.** corruption, crime, delinquency, fault, injustice, mis~ conduct, misdeed, offence, sin, wrong, wrongdoing
Antonyms *v.* (*sense 1*) care for, protect (*sense 2*) acclaim, commend, compliment, extol, flatter, praise, respect

abusive 1. calumniating, castigating, cen~ sorious, contumelious, defamatory, derisive, disparaging, insulting, invective, libellous, maligning, offensive, opprobrious, re~ proachful, reviling, rude, scathing, scolding, slanderous, traducing, upbraiding, vilifying,

vituperative **2.** brutal, cruel, destructive, harmful, hurtful, injurious, rough
Antonyms (*sense 1*) approving, compliment~ tary, eulogistic, flattering, laudatory, pan~ egyrical, praising

abysmal bottomless, boundless, complete, deep, endless, extreme, immeasurable, in~ calculable, infinite, profound, thorough, unending, unfathomable, vast

abyss abysm, bottomless depth, chasm, cre~ vasse, fissure, gorge, gulf, pit, void

academic *adj.* **1.** bookish, campus, college, collegiate, erudite, highbrow, learned, let~ tered, literary, scholarly, scholastic, school, studious, university **2.** abstract, conjectur~ al, hypothetical, impractical, notional, speculative, theoretical ~*n.* **3.** academician, don, fellow, lecturer, master, professor, pu~ pil, scholar, scholastic, schoolman, student, tutor

accede 1. accept, acquiesce, admit, agree, assent, comply, concede, concur, consent, endorse, grant, own, yield **2.** assume, at~ tain, come to, enter upon, inherit, succeed, succeed to (*as heir*)

accelerate advance, expedite, forward, fur~ ther, hasten, hurry, pick up speed, precipi~ tate, quicken, speed, speed up, spur, step up (*Inf.*), stimulate
Antonyms decelerate, delay, hinder, im~ pede, obstruct, slow down

acceleration expedition, hastening, hurry~ ing, quickening, speeding up, spurring, stepping up (*Inf.*), stimulation

accent *n.* **1.** beat, cadence, emphasis, force, pitch, rhythm, stress, timbre, tonality **2.** articulation, enunciation, inflection, into~ nation, modulation, pronunciation, tone ~*v.* **3.** accentuate, emphasize, stress, underline, underscore

accentuate accent, draw attention to, em~ phasize, highlight, stress, underline, under~ score
Antonyms gloss over, make light of, make little of, minimize, play down, soft-pedal (*Inf.*), underplay

accept 1. acquire, gain, get, have, obtain, receive, secure, take **2.** accede, acknowl~ edge, acquiesce, admit, adopt, affirm, agree to, approve, believe, buy (*Sl.*), concur with, consent to, cooperate with, recognize, swal~ low (*Inf.*) **3.** bear, bow to, brook, defer to, put up with, stand, submit to, suffer, take, yield to **4.** acknowledge, admit, assume, avow, bear, take on, undertake
Antonyms decline, deny, disown, rebut, ref~ use, reject, repudiate, spurn

acceptable 1. agreeable, delightful, grate~ ful, gratifying, pleasant, pleasing, welcome **2.** adequate, admissible, all right, fair,

moderate, passable, satisfactory, so-so (*Inf.*), standard, tolerable
Antonyms unacceptable, unsatisfactory, unsuitable

acceptance 1. accepting, acquiring, gaining, getting, having, obtaining, receipt, securing, taking **2.** accedence, accession, acknowledgment, acquiescence, admission, adoption, affirmation, agreement, approbation, approval, assent, belief, compliance, concession, concurrence, consensus, consent, cooperation, credence, O.K. *or* okay (*Inf.*), permission, recognition, stamp *or* seal of approval **3.** deference, standing, submission, taking, yielding **4.** acknowledgment, admission, assumption, avowal, taking on, undertaking

accepted acceptable, acknowledged, admitted, agreed, agreed upon, approved, authorized, common, confirmed, conventional, customary, established, normal, received, recognized, regular, sanctioned, standard, time-honoured, traditional, universal, usual
Antonyms abnormal, irregular, unconventional, uncustomary, unorthodox, unusual, unwonted

access 1. admission, admittance, approach, avenue, course, door, entering, entrance, entrée, entry, gateway, key, passage, passageway, path, road **2.** *Medical* attack, fit, onset, outburst, paroxysm

accessibility 1. approachability, attainability, availability, handiness, nearness, obtainability, possibility, readiness **2.** affability, approachability, conversableness, cordiality, friendliness, informality **3.** exposedness, openness, susceptibility

accessible 1. achievable, at hand, attainable, available, get-at-able (*Inf.*), handy, near, nearby, obtainable, on hand, possible, reachable, ready **2.** affable, approachable, available, conversable, cordial, friendly, informal **3.** exposed, liable, open, subject, susceptible, vulnerable, wide-open
Antonyms far-off, hidden, inaccessible, secreted, unapproachable, unavailable, unobtainable, unreachable

accession 1. addition, augmentation, enlargement, extension, increase **2.** assumption, attaining to, attainment of, entering upon, succession (*to a throne, dignity, or office*), taking on, taking over **3.** accedence, acceptance, acquiescence, agreement, assent, concurrence, consent

accessory *n.* **1.** abettor, accomplice, assistant, associate (*in crime*), colleague, confederate, helper, partner **2.** accent, accompaniment, addition, add-on, adjunct, adornment, aid, appendage, attachment, component, convenience, decoration, extension, extra, frill, help, supplement, trim, trim-

ming ~*adj.* **3.** abetting, additional, aiding, ancillary, assisting in, auxiliary, contributory, extra, secondary, subordinate, supplemental, supplementary

accident 1. blow, calamity, casualty, chance, collision, crash, disaster, misadventure, mischance, misfortune, mishap, pile-up (*Inf.*) **2.** chance, fate, fluke, fortuity, fortune, hazard, luck

accidental adventitious, casual, chance, contingent, fortuitous, haphazard, inadvertent, incidental, inessential, nonessential, random, uncalculated, uncertain, unessential, unexpected, unforeseen, unintended, unintentional, unlooked-for, unplanned, unpremeditated, unwitting
Antonyms calculated, designed, expected, foreseen, intended, intentional, planned, prepared

accidentally adventitiously, by accident, by chance, by mistake, casually, fortuitously, haphazardly, inadvertently, incidentally, randomly, unconsciously, undesignedly, unexpectedly, unintentionally, unwittingly
Antonyms by design, consciously, deliberately, designedly, on purpose, wilfully

acclaim 1. *v.* applaud, approve, celebrate, cheer, clap, commend, crack up (*Inf.*), eulogize, exalt, extol, hail, honour, laud, praise, salute, welcome **2.** *n.* acclamation, applause, approbation, approval, celebration, cheering, clapping, commendation, eulogizing, exaltation, honour, laudation, plaudits, praise, welcome
Antonyms *n.* bad press, brickbats, censure, criticism, disparagement, fault-finding, flak (*Inf.*), panning (*Inf.*), stick (*Sl.*), vituperation

acclamation acclaim, adulation, approbation, cheer, cheering, cheers, enthusiasm, laudation, loud homage, ovation, plaudit, praise, salutation, shouting, tribute

acclimatization acclimation, accommodation, acculturation, adaptation, adjustment, habituation, inurement, naturalization

acclimatize accommodate, acculture, accustom, adapt, adjust, become seasoned to, get used to, habituate, inure, naturalize

accommodate 1. billet, board, cater for, entertain, harbour, house, lodge, put up, quarter, shelter **2.** afford, aid, assist, furnish, help, oblige, provide, purvey, serve, supply **3.** accustom, adapt, adjust, comply, compose, conform, fit, harmonize, modify, reconcile, settle

accommodating complaisant, considerate, cooperative, friendly, helpful, hospitable, kind, obliging, polite, unselfish, willing
Antonyms disobliging, inconsiderate, rude, uncooperative, unhelpful

accommodation 1. adaptation, adjust-

ment, compliance, composition, compro~
mise, conformity, fitting, harmony,
modification, reconciliation, settlement **2.**
board, digs (*Brit. inf.*), harbouring, house,
housing, lodging(s), quartering, quarters,
shelter, sheltering **3.** aid, assistance, help,
provision, service, supply

accompany 1. attend, chaperon, conduct,
convoy, escort, go with, squire, usher **2.**
belong to, coexist with, coincide with, come
with, follow, go together with, join with,
occur with, supplement

accompanying accessory, added, addi~
tional, appended, associate, associated, at~
tached, attendant, complementary, con~
comitant, concurrent, connected, fellow,
joint, related, supplemental, supplementary

accomplice abettor, accessory, ally, assis~
tant, associate, coadjutor, collaborator, col~
league, confederate, helper, henchman,
partner

accomplish achieve, attain, bring about,
bring off (*Inf.*), carry out, complete, con~
clude, consummate, do, effect, effectuate,
execute, finish, fulfil, manage, perform,
produce, realize
Antonyms fail, fall short, forsake, give up

accomplished 1. achieved, attained,
brought about, carried out, completed, con~
cluded, consummated, done, effected, ex~
ecuted, finished, fulfilled, managed, per~
formed, produced, realized **2.** adept, con~
summate, cultivated, expert, gifted, master~
ly, polished, practised, proficient, skilful,
skilled, talented
Antonyms (*sense 2*) amateurish, incapable,
incompetent, inexpert, unestablished, un~
proven, unrealized, unskilled, untalented

accomplishment 1. achievement, attain~
ment, bringing about, carrying out, com~
pletion, conclusion, consummation, doing,
effecting, execution, finishing, fulfilment,
management, performance, production, re~
alization **2.** achievement, act, attainment,
coup, deed, exploit, feat, stroke, triumph **3.**
ability, achievement, art, attainment, capa~
bility, craft, gift, proficiency, skill, talent

accord *v.* **1.** agree, assent, be in tune (*Inf.*),
concur, conform, correspond, fit, harmo~
nize, match, suit, tally **2.** allow, bestow,
concede, confer, endow, give, grant, present,
render, tender, vouchsafe ~*n.* **3.** accord~
ance, agreement, concert, concurrence,
conformity, congruence, correspondence,
harmony, rapport, sympathy, unanimity,
unison
Antonyms *v.* (*sense 1*) conflict, contrast, dif~
fer, disagree, discord (*sense 2*) hold back, ref~
use, withhold ~*n.* conflict, contention, dis~
agreement, discord

accordance 1. accord, agreement, assent,

concert, concurrence, conformity, congru~
ence, correspondence, harmony, rapport,
sympathy, unanimity **2.** according, allow~
ance, bestowal, concession, conferment,
conferral, endowment, gift, giving, granting,
presentation, rendering, tendering

accordingly 1. appropriately, correspond~
ingly, fitly, properly, suitably **2.** as a result,
consequently, ergo, hence, in consequence,
so, therefore, thus

according to 1. commensurate with, in
proportion, in relation **2.** as believed by, as
maintained by, as stated by, in the light of,
on the authority of, on the report of **3.** af~
ter, after the manner of, consistent with, in
accordance with, in compliance with, in
conformity with, in harmony with, in
keeping with, in line with, in obedience to,
in step with, in the manner of, obedient to

account *n.* **1.** chronicle, description, detail,
explanation, history, narration, narrative,
recital, record, relation, report, statement,
story, tale, version **2.** *Commerce* balance,
bill, book, books, charge, computation, in~
ventory, invoice, ledger, reckoning, register,
score, statement, tally **3.** advantage, benefit,
consequence, distinction, esteem, honour,
import, importance, merit, note, profit,
rank, repute, significance, standing, use,
value, worth **4.** basis, cause, consideration,
ground, grounds, interest, motive, reason,
regard, sake, score ~*v.* **5.** appraise, assess,
believe, calculate, compute, consider, count,
deem, esteem, estimate, explain, gauge,
hold, judge, rate, reckon, regard, think,
value, weigh

accountability 1. answerability, charge~
ability, culpability, liability, responsibility
2. comprehensibility, explainability, expli~
cability, intelligibility, understandability

accountable 1. amenable, answerable,
charged with, liable, obligated, obliged, re~
sponsible **2.** comprehensible, explainable,
explicable, intelligible, understandable

account for 1. answer for, clarify, clear
up, elucidate, explain, illuminate, justify,
rationalize **2.** destroy, incapacitate, kill, put
out of action

accredit 1. appoint, authorize, certify, com~
mission, depute, empower, endorse, entrust,
guarantee, license, recognize, sanction,
vouch for **2.** ascribe, assign, attribute,
credit

accredited appointed, authorized, certified,
commissioned, deputed, deputized, empow~
ered, endorsed, guaranteed, licensed,
official, recognized, sanctioned, vouched for

accrue accumulate, amass, arise, be added,
build up, collect, enlarge, ensue, flow, fol~
low, grow, increase, issue, spring up

accumulate accrue, amass, build up, col~

lect, cumulate, gather, grow, hoard, in~
crease, pile up, stockpile, store
Antonyms diffuse, disperse, disseminate,
dissipate, distribute, propagate, scatter

accumulation aggregation, augmentation,
build-up, collection, conglomeration, gath~
ering, growth, heap, hoard, increase, mass,
pile, stack, stock, stockpile, store

accuracy accurateness, authenticity, care~
fulness, closeness, correctness, exactitude,
exactness, faithfulness, faultlessness,
fidelity, meticulousness, niceness, nicety,
precision, strictness, truth, truthfulness,
veracity, verity
Antonyms carelessness, erroneousness,
imprecision, inaccuracy, incorrectness, in~
exactitude, laxity, laxness

accurate authentic, careful, close, correct,
exact, faithful, faultless, just, meticulous,
nice, precise, proper, regular, right, scru~
pulous, spot-on (*Brit. inf.*), strict, true,
truthful, unerring, veracious
Antonyms careless, defective, faulty, im~
perfect, imprecise, inaccurate, incorrect, in~
exact, slovenly, wrong

accurately authentically, carefully, closely,
correctly, exactly, faithfully, faultlessly,
justly, meticulously, nicely, precisely, prop~
erly, regularly, rightly, scrupulously,
strictly, truly, truthfully, unerringly, vera~
ciously

accursed 1. bedevilled, bewitched, con~
demned, cursed, damned, doomed, hopeless,
ill-fated, ill-omened, jinxed, luckless, ruined,
undone, unfortunate, unlucky, wretched **2.**
abominable, despicable, detestable, ex~
ecrable, hateful, hellish, horrible
Antonyms (*sense 1*) blessed, charmed, fa~
voured, fortunate, lucky

accusation allegation, arraignment, at~
tribution, charge, citation, complaint, de~
nunciation, impeachment, imputation, in~
crimination, indictment, recrimination

accuse allege, arraign, attribute, blame,
censure, charge, cite, denounce, impeach,
impute, incriminate, indict, recriminate,
tax
Antonyms absolve, answer, defend, deny,
exonerate, plea, reply, vindicate

accustom acclimatize, acquaint, adapt, dis~
cipline, exercise, familiarize, habituate, in~
ure, season, train

accustomed 1. acclimatized, acquainted,
adapted, disciplined, exercised, familiar, fa~
miliarized, given to, habituated, in the hab~
it of, inured, seasoned, trained, used **2.**
common, conventional, customary, estab~
lished, everyday, expected, fixed, general,
habitual, normal, ordinary, regular, rou~
tine, set, traditional, usual, wonted
Antonyms (*sense 1*) unaccustomed, unfa~

miliar, unused (*sense 2*) abnormal, infrequent,
occasional, odd, peculiar, rare, strange, unac~
customed, uncommon, unfamiliar, unusual

ace *n.* **1.** *Cards, dice, etc.* one, single point **2.**
Inf. adept, buff (*Inf.*), champion, dab hand
(*Brit. inf.*), expert, genius, hotshot (*Inf.*),
master, maven (*U.S.*), star, virtuoso, whiz
(*Inf.*), winner, wizard (*Inf.*) ~*adj.* **3.** *Inf.*
brilliant, champion, excellent, expert, fine,
great, masterly, outstanding, superb, vir~
tuoso

ache *v.* **1.** hurt, pain, pound, smart, suffer,
throb, twinge **2.** agonize, eat one's heart
out, grieve, mourn, sorrow, suffer **3.** covet,
crave, desire, eat one's heart out over,
hanker, hope, hunger, long, need, pine,
thirst, yearn ~*n.* **4.** hurt, pain, pang,
pounding, smart, smarting, soreness, suf~
fering, throb, throbbing **5.** anguish, grief,
mourning, sorrow, suffering **6.** craving, de~
sire, hankering, hope, hunger, longing,
need, pining, thirst, yearning

achievable accessible, accomplishable, ac~
quirable, attainable, feasible, obtainable,
possible, practicable, reachable, realizable,
winnable, within one's grasp

achieve accomplish, acquire, attain, bring
about, carry out, complete, consummate, do,
earn, effect, execute, finish, fulfil, gain, get,
obtain, perform, procure, reach, realize, win

achievement 1. accomplishment, acquire~
ment, attainment, completion, execution,
fulfilment, performance, production, reali~
zation **2.** accomplishment, act, deed, effort,
exploit, feat, stroke

acid 1. acerb, acerbic, acetic, acidulous, ac~
rid, biting, pungent, sharp, sour, tart, vin~
egarish, vinegary **2.** acerbic, biting, bitter,
caustic, cutting, harsh, hurtful, mordacious,
mordant, pungent, sharp, stinging, trench~
ant, vitriolic
Antonyms (*sense 1*) alkaline, bland, mild,
pleasant, sweet (*sense 2*) benign, bland, gentle,
kindly, mild, pleasant, sweet

acidity 1. acerbity, acidulousness, acridity,
acridness, bitterness, pungency, sharpness,
sourness, tartness, vinegariness, vin~
egarishness **2.** acerbity, acridity, acridness,
bitterness, causticity, causticness, harsh~
ness, hurtfulness, mordancy, pungency,
sharpness, trenchancy

acknowledge 1. accede, accept, acquiesce,
admit, allow, concede, confess, declare,
grant, own, profess, recognize, yield **2.** ad~
dress, greet, hail, notice, recognize, salute
3. answer, notice, react to, recognize, reply
to, respond to, return
Antonyms (*sense 1*) contradict, deny, dis~
claim, discount, reject, renounce, repudiate
(*senses 2 & 3*) deny, disavow, disdain, disre~
gard, ignore, rebut, reject, snub, spurn

acknowledged accepted, accredited, ad~ mitted, answered, approved, conceded, con~ fessed, declared, professed, recognized, re~ turned

acknowledgment 1. acceptance, acces~ sion, acquiescence, admission, allowing, confession, declaration, profession, realiza~ tion, yielding **2.** addressing, greeting, hail, hailing, notice, recognition, salutation, sa~ lute **3.** answer, appreciation, Brownie points, credit, gratitude, reaction, recogni~ tion, reply, response, return, thanks

acme apex, climax, crest, crown, culmina~ tion, height, high point, optimum, peak, pinnacle, summit, top, vertex, zenith
Antonyms bottom, depths, low point, mini~ mum, nadir, rock bottom, zero

acquaint advise, announce, apprise, dis~ close, divulge, enlighten, familiarize, in~ form, let (someone) know, notify, reveal, tell

acquaintance 1. associate, colleague, con~ tact **2.** association, awareness, cognizance, companionship, conversance, conversancy, experience, familiarity, fellowship, intima~ cy, knowledge, relationship, social contact, understanding
Antonyms (*sense 1*) buddy, good friend, inti~ mate, stranger (*sense 2*) ignorance, unfamili~ arity

acquainted alive to, apprised of, *au fait*, aware of, cognizant of, conscious of, con~ versant with, experienced in, familiar with, informed of, in on, knowledgeable about, privy to, versed in

acquiesce accede, accept, agree, allow, ap~ prove, assent, bow to, comply, concur, con~ form, consent, give in, go along with, sub~ mit, yield
Antonyms balk at, contest, demur, disagree, dissent, fight, object, protest, refuse, resist, veto

acquiescence acceptance, accession, agreement, approval, assent, compliance, concurrence, conformity, consent, giving in, obedience, submission, yielding

acquiescent acceding, accepting, agreeable, agreeing, approving, assenting, compliant, concurrent, conforming, consenting, obedi~ ent, submissive, yielding

acquire achieve, amass, attain, buy, collect, earn, gain, gather, get, obtain, pick up, pro~ cure, realize, receive, score (*Sl.*), secure, win
Antonyms be deprived of, forfeit, forgo, give up, lose, relinquish, renounce, surrender, waive

acquirement accomplishment, achieve~ ment, acquisition, attainment, gathering, knowledge, learning, mastery, mental gains, qualification, skill

acquisition 1. buy, gain, possession, prize, property, purchase **2.** achievement, ac~ quirement, attainment, gaining, learning, obtainment, procurement, pursuit

acquisitive avaricious, avid, covetous, grabbing, grasping, greedy, predatory, ra~ pacious
Antonyms bounteous, bountiful, generous, lavish, liberal, munificent, open-handed, unselfish, unstinting

acquisitiveness avarice, avidity, avidness, covetousness, graspingness, greed, predato~ riness, rapaciousness, rapacity

acquit 1. absolve, clear, deliver, discharge, exculpate, exonerate, free, fulfil, liberate, release, relieve, vindicate **2.** discharge, pay, pay off, repay, satisfy, settle **3.** bear, be~ have, comport, conduct, perform
Antonyms (*sense 1*) blame, charge, condemn, convict, damn, find guilty, sentence

acquittal absolution, clearance, deliverance, discharge, exculpation, exoneration, freeing, liberation, release, relief, vindication

acquittance acknowledgment, discharge, payment, receipt, release, settlement, set~ tling

acrid 1. acerb, acid, astringent, biting, bit~ ter, burning, caustic, harsh, irritating, pungent, sharp, stinging, vitriolic **2.** acri~ monious, biting, bitter, caustic, cutting, harsh, mordacious, mordant, nasty, sarcas~ tic, sharp, trenchant, vitriolic

acrimonious acerbic, astringent, biting, bitter, caustic, censorious, churlish, crab~ bed, cutting, irascible, mordacious, mor~ dant, peevish, petulant, pungent, rancorous, sarcastic, severe, sharp, spiteful, splenetic, tart, testy, trenchant, vitriolic
Antonyms affable, benign, forgiving, good-tempered

acrimony acerbity, asperity, astringency, bitterness, churlishness, harshness, ill will, irascibility, mordancy, peevishness, ran~ cour, sarcasm, spleen, tartness, trenchancy, virulence
Antonyms amity, friendliness, friendship, good feelings, goodwill, liking, warmth

act *n.* **1.** accomplishment, achievement, ac~ tion, blow, deed, doing, execution, exertion, exploit, feat, move, operation, performance, step, stroke, undertaking **2.** bill, decree, edict, enactment, law, measure, ordinance, resolution, statute **3.** affectation, attitude, counterfeit, dissimulation, fake, feigning, front, performance, pose, posture, pretence, sham, show, stance **4.** performance, rou~ tine, show, sketch, turn ~*v.* **5.** acquit, bear, behave, carry, carry out, comport, conduct, do, enact, execute, exert, function, go about, make, move, operate, perform, react, serve, strike, take effect, undertake, work **6.** af~

fect, assume, counterfeit, dissimulate, feign, imitate, perform, pose, posture, pretend, put on, seem, sham **7.** act out, characterize, en~ act, impersonate, mime, mimic, perform, personate, personify, play, play *or* take the part of, portray, represent

act for cover for, deputize for, fill in for, function in place of, replace, represent, serve, stand in for, substitute for, take the place of

acting *adj.* **1.** interim, *pro tem*, provisional, substitute, surrogate, temporary ~*n.* **2.** characterization, dramatics, enacting, im~ personation, performance, performing, playing, portrayal, portraying, stagecraft, theatre **3.** assuming, counterfeiting, dis~ simulation, feigning, imitating, imitation, imposture, play-acting, posing, posturing, pretence, pretending, putting on, seeming, shamming

action 1. accomplishment, achievement, act, blow, deed, exercise, exertion, exploit, feat, move, operation, performance, step, stroke, undertaking **2.** activity, energy, force, live~ liness, spirit, vigour, vim, vitality **3.** activ~ ity, effect, effort, exertion, force, function~ ing, influence, motion, movement, opera~ tion, power, process, work, working **4.** bat~ tle, combat, conflict, fighting, warfare **5.** af~ fray, battle, clash, combat, contest, encoun~ ter, engagement, fight, fray, skirmish, sortie **6.** case, cause, lawsuit, litigation, proceed~ ing, prosecution, suit

actions bearing, behaviour, comportment, conduct, demeanour, deportment, manners, ways

activate actuate, animate, arouse, energize, galvanize, get going, impel, initiate, kick~ start, mobilize, motivate, move, prod, prompt, propel, rouse, set going, set in mo~ tion, set off, start, stimulate, stir, switch on, trigger (off), turn on
Antonyms arrest, check, deactivate, halt, impede, stall, stop, terminate, turn off

active 1. acting, astir, at work, doing, effec~ tual, functioning, in action, in force, in op~ eration, live, moving, operative, running, stirring, working **2.** bustling, busy, en~ gaged, full, hard-working, involved, occu~ pied, on the go (*Inf.*), on the move, strenu~ ous **3.** alert, animated, diligent, energetic, industrious, lively, nimble, on the go (*Inf.*), quick, spirited, sprightly, spry, vibrant, vigorous, vital, vivacious **4.** activist, ag~ gressive, ambitious, assertive, committed, devoted, energetic, engaged, enterprising, enthusiastic, forceful, forward, hard-working, industrious, militant, zealous
Antonyms dormant, dull, idle, inactive, in~ operative, lazy, sedentary, slow, sluggish, tor~ pid, unimaginative, unoccupied

activity 1. action, activeness, animation, bustle, enterprise, exercise, exertion, hurly-burly, hustle, labour, life, liveliness, motion, movement, stir, work **2.** act, avo~ cation, deed, endeavour, enterprise, hobby, interest, job, labour, occupation, pastime, project, pursuit, scheme, task, undertaking, venture, work
Antonyms (*sense 1*) dullness, idleness, im~ mobility, inaction, inactivity, indolence, in~ ertia, lethargy, passivity, sluggishness, torpor

act on, act upon 1. act in accordance with, carry out, comply with, conform to, follow, heed, obey, yield to **2.** affect, alter, change, influence, modify, sway, transform

actor 1. actress, dramatic artist, leading man, performer, play-actor, player, Thes~ pian, tragedian, trouper **2.** agent, doer, ex~ ecutor, factor, functionary, operative, op~ erator, participant, participator, performer, perpetrator, practitioner, worker

actress actor, dramatic artist, leading lady, performer, play-actor, player, starlet, Thes~ pian, tragedienne, trouper

actual 1. absolute, categorical, certain, con~ crete, corporeal, definite, factual, indisput~ able, indubitable, physical, positive, real, substantial, tangible, undeniable, unques~ tionable **2.** authentic, confirmed, genuine, real, realistic, true, truthful, verified **3.** current, existent, extant, live, living, pres~ ent, present-day, prevailing
Antonyms (*senses 1 & 2*) fictitious, hypo~ thetical, made-up, probable, supposed, theo~ retical, unreal, untrue

actually absolutely, as a matter of fact, de facto, essentially, indeed, in fact, in point of fact, in reality, in truth, literally, really, truly, veritably

actuate animate, arouse, cause, dispose, drive, excite, get going, impel, incite, in~ duce, influence, inspire, instigate, motivate, move, prompt, quicken, rouse, set off, spur, stimulate, stir, urge

act up be naughty, carry on, cause trouble, give bother, give trouble, horse around (*Inf.*), malfunction, mess about, misbehave, piss about (*Taboo sl.*), piss around (*Taboo sl.*), play up (*Brit. inf.*)

act upon *see* ACT ON

acumen acuteness, astuteness, cleverness, discernment, ingenuity, insight, intelli~ gence, judgment, keenness, penetration, perception, perspicacity, perspicuity, sa~ gacity, sharpness, shrewdness, smartness, smarts (*Sl., chiefly U.S.*), wisdom, wit

acute 1. astute, canny, clever, discerning, discriminating, incisive, ingenious, insight~ ful, intuitive, keen, observant, penetrating, perceptive, perspicacious, piercing, sensi~ tive, sharp, smart, subtle **2.** critical, cru~

cial, dangerous, decisive, essential, grave, important, serious, severe, sudden, urgent, vital **3.** cutting, distressing, excruciating, exquisite, fierce, harrowing, intense, overpowering, overwhelming, piercing, poignant, powerful, racking, severe, sharp, shooting, shrill, stabbing, sudden, violent **4.** cuspate, needle-shaped, peaked, pointed, sharp, sharpened
Antonyms (*sense 1*) dense, dim, dim-witted, dull, obtuse, slow, stupid, unintelligent (*sense 4*) blunt, blunted, dull, obtuse, unsharpened

acuteness 1. acuity, astuteness, canniness, cleverness, discernment, discrimination, ingenuity, insight, intuition, intuitiveness, keenness, perception, perceptiveness, perspicacity, sensitivity, sharpness, smartness, subtleness, subtlety, wit **2.** criticality, criticalness, cruciality, danger, dangerousness, decisiveness, essentiality, gravity, importance, seriousness, severity, suddenness, urgency, vitalness **3.** distressingness, exquisiteness, fierceness, intenseness, intensity, poignancy, powerfulness, severity, sharpness, shrillness, suddenness, violence **4.** pointedness, sharpness

adage aphorism, apophthegm, axiom, byword, dictum, maxim, motto, precept, proverb, saw, saying

adamant 1. determined, firm, fixed, immovable, inexorable, inflexible, insistent, intransigent, obdurate, relentless, resolute, rigid, set, stiff, stubborn, unbending, uncompromising, unrelenting, unshakable, unyielding **2.** adamantine, flinty, hard, impenetrable, indestructible, rock-hard, rocky, steely, stony, tough, unbreakable
Antonyms (*sense 1*) compliant, compromising, easy-going, flexible, lax, pliant, receptive, responsive, susceptible, tensile, tractable, yielding (*sense 2*) bendy, ductile, flexible, pliable, pliant, yielding

adapt acclimatize, accommodate, adjust, alter, apply, change, comply, conform, convert, familiarize, fashion, fit, habituate, harmonize, make, match, modify, prepare, qualify, remodel, shape, suit, tailor

adaptability adaptableness, adjustability, alterability, changeability, compliancy, convertibility, flexibility, malleability, modifiability, plasticity, pliability, pliancy, resilience, variability, versatility

adaptable adjustable, alterable, changeable, compliant, conformable, convertible, easygoing, easy-oasy (*Sl.*), flexible, malleable, modifiable, plastic, pliant, resilient, variable, versatile

adaptation 1. adjustment, alteration, change, conversion, modification, refitting, remodelling, reworking, shift, transformation, variation, version **2.** acclimatization,

accustomedness, familiarization, habituation, naturalization

add 1. adjoin, affix, amplify, annex, append, attach, augment, enlarge by, include, increase by, supplement **2.** add up, compute, count up, reckon, sum up, total, tot up
Antonyms deduct, diminish, lessen, reduce, remove, subtract, take away, take from

addendum addition, adjunct, affix, appendage, appendix, attachment, augmentation, codicil, extension, extra, postscript, supplement

addict 1. dope-fiend (*Sl.*), fiend (*Inf.*), freak (*Inf.*), head (*Sl.*), junkie (*Inf.*), user (*Inf.*) **2.** adherent, buff (*Inf.*), devotee, enthusiast, fan, follower, freak (*Inf.*), nut (*Sl.*)

addicted absorbed, accustomed, dedicated, dependent, devoted, disposed, fond, habituated, hooked (*Sl.*), inclined, obsessed, prone

addiction craving, dependence, enslavement, habit, obsession

addition 1. accession, adding, adjoining, affixing, amplification, annexation, attachment, augmentation, enlargement, extension, inclusion, increasing **2.** addendum, additive, adjunct, affix, appendage, appendix, extension, extra, gain, increase, increment, supplement **3.** adding up, computation, counting up, reckoning, summation, summing up, totalling, totting up **4. in addition (to)** additionally, also, as well (as), besides, into the bargain, moreover, over and above, to boot, too, withal
Antonyms deduction, detachment, diminution, lessening, reduction, removal, subtraction

additional added, add-on, affixed, appended, extra, fresh, further, increased, more, new, other, over-and-above, spare, supplementary

address *n.* **1.** abode, domicile, dwelling, home, house, location, lodging, pad (*Sl.*), place, residence, situation, whereabouts **2.** direction, inscription, superscription **3.** discourse, disquisition, dissertation, harangue, lecture, oration, sermon, speech, talk **4.** adroitness, art, dexterity, discretion, expertness, ingenuity, skilfulness, skill, tact ~*v.* **5.** accost, apostrophize, approach, greet, hail, invoke, salute, speak to, talk to **6.** discourse, give a speech, give a talk, harangue, lecture, orate, sermonize, speak, spout, talk **7. address (oneself) to** apply (oneself) to, attend to, concentrate on, devote (oneself) to, engage in, focus on, knuckle down to, look to, take care of, take up, turn to, undertake

adduce advance, allege, cite, designate, mention, name, offer, present, quote

add up 1. add, compute, count, count up, reckon, sum up, total, tot up **2.** amount, come to, imply, indicate, mean, reveal, sig~

nify **3.** be plausible, be reasonable, hold water, make sense, ring true, stand to rea~ son

adept 1. *adj.* able, accomplished, adroit, dexterous, expert, masterful, masterly, practised, proficient, skilful, skilled, versed **2.** *n.* buff (*Inf.*), dab hand (*Brit. inf.*), expert, genius, hotshot (*Inf.*), master, maven (*U.S.*), whiz (*Inf.*)
Antonyms *adj.* amateurish, awkward, clumsy, inept, unskilled

adequacy capability, commensurateness, competence, fairness, requisiteness, satis~ factoriness, sufficiency, suitability, toler~ ability

adequate capable, commensurate, compe~ tent, enough, fair, passable, requisite, satis~ factory, sufficient, suitable, tolerable
Antonyms deficient, inadequate, insufficient, lacking, meagre, scant, short, unsatisfactory, unsuitable

adhere 1. attach, cement, cleave, cling, co~ here, fasten, fix, glue, glue on, hold fast, paste, stick, stick fast, unite **2.** abide by, be attached, be constant, be devoted, be faith~ ful, be loyal, be true, cleave to, cling, follow, fulfil, heed, keep, keep to, maintain, mind, obey, observe, respect, stand by, support

adherent 1. *n.* admirer, advocate, devotee, disciple, fan, follower, hanger-on, hench~ man, partisan, protagonist, sectary, sup~ porter, upholder, votary **2.** *adj.* adhering, adhesive, clinging, gluey, glutinous, gum~ my, holding, mucilaginous, sticking, sticky, tacky, tenacious
Antonyms *n.* adversary, antagonist, dispu~ tant, dissentient, enemy, foe, opponent, op~ poser, opposition, rival

adhesive 1. *adj.* adhering, attaching, cling~ ing, cohesive, gluey, glutinous, gummy, holding, mucilaginous, sticking, sticky, tacky, tenacious **2.** *n.* cement, glue, gum, mucilage, paste

adieu congé, farewell, goodbye, leave-taking, parting, valediction

adipose fat, fatty, greasy, obese, oily, oleaginous, sebaceous

adjacent abutting, adjoining, alongside, be~ side, bordering, close, contiguous, near, neighbouring, next door, proximate, touch~ ing, within sniffing distance (*Inf.*)
Antonyms distant, far away, remote, sepa~ rated

adjoin abut, add, affix, annex, append, ap~ proximate, attach, border, combine, com~ municate with, connect, couple, impinge, interconnect, join, link, neighbour, touch, unite, verge

adjoining abutting, adjacent, bordering, connecting, contiguous, impinging, inter~

connecting, joined, joining, near, neigh~ bouring, next door, touching, verging

adjourn defer, delay, discontinue, interrupt, postpone, prorogue, put off, put on the back burner (*Inf.*), recess, stay, suspend, take a rain check on (*U.S. & Canad. inf.*)
Antonyms assemble, continue, convene, gather, open, remain, reopen, stay

adjournment deferment, deferral, delay, discontinuation, interruption, postpone~ ment, prorogation, putting off, recess, stay, suspension

adjudge adjudicate, allot, apportion, assign, award, decide, declare, decree, determine, distribute, judge, order, pronounce

adjudicate adjudge, arbitrate, decide, de~ termine, judge, mediate, referee, settle, um~ pire

adjudication adjudgment, arbitration, con~ clusion, decision, determination, finding, judgment, pronouncement, ruling, settle~ ment, verdict

adjunct accessory, addendum, addition, add-on, appendage, appurtenance, auxiliary, complement, supplement

adjure 1. appeal to, beg, beseech, entreat, implore, invoke, pray, supplicate **2.** charge, command, direct, enjoin, order

adjust acclimatize, accommodate, accustom, adapt, alter, arrange, compose, convert, dispose, fit, fix, harmonize, make conform, measure, modify, order, reconcile, rectify, redress, regulate, remodel, set, settle, suit, tune (up)

adjustable adaptable, alterable, flexible, malleable, modifiable, mouldable, movable, tractable

adjustment 1. adaptation, alteration, ar~ rangement, arranging, fitting, fixing, modification, ordering, rectification, re~ dress, regulation, remodelling, setting, tun~ ing **2.** acclimatization, harmonization, ori~ entation, reconciliation, settlement, settling in

ad-lib 1. *v.* busk, extemporize, improvise, make up, speak extemporaneously, speak impromptu, speak off the cuff, vamp, wing it (*Inf.*) **2.** *adj.* extemporaneous, extempore, extemporized, impromptu, improvised, made up, off-the-cuff (*Inf.*), unprepared, un~ rehearsed **3.** *adv.* extemporaneously, ex~ tempore, impromptu, off the cuff, off the top of one's head (*Inf.*), without preparation, without rehearsal

administer 1. conduct, control, direct, govern, handle, manage, oversee, run, superintend, supervise **2.** apply, contribute, dispense, distribute, execute, give, impose, mete out, perform, provide

administration 1. administering, applica~

tion, conduct, control, direction, dispensa~
tion, distribution, execution, governing,
government, management, overseeing, per~
formance, provision, running, superintend~
ence, supervision **2.** executive, governing
body, government, management, ministry,
term of office

administrative directorial, executive, gov~
ernmental, gubernatorial (*Chiefly U.S.*),
management, managerial, organizational,
regulatory, supervisory

admirable choice, commendable, estimable,
excellent, exquisite, fine, laudable, merito~
rious, praiseworthy, rare, sterling, superior,
valuable, wonderful, worthy
Antonyms bad, commonplace, deplorable,
disappointing, displeasing, mediocre, worth~
less

admiration adoration, affection, amaze~
ment, appreciation, approbation, approval,
astonishment, delight, esteem, pleasure,
praise, regard, respect, surprise, veneration,
wonder, wonderment

admire 1. adore, appreciate, approve, es~
teem, idolize, look up to, praise, prize, re~
spect, think highly of, value, venerate, wor~
ship **2.** appreciate, delight in, marvel at,
take pleasure in, wonder at
Antonyms contemn, deride, despise, look
down on, look down one's nose at (*Inf.*), mis~
prize, scorn, sneer at, spurn, undervalue

admirer 1. beau, boyfriend, lover, suitor,
sweetheart, wooer **2.** adherent, buff (*Inf.*),
devotee, disciple, enthusiast, fan, follower,
partisan, protagonist, supporter, votary,
worshipper

admissible acceptable, allowable, allowed,
passable, permissible, permitted, tolerable,
tolerated
Antonyms disallowed, inadmissible, intol~
erable, unacceptable

admission 1. acceptance, access, admit~
tance, entrance, entrée, entry, ingress, ini~
tiation, introduction **2.** acknowledgment,
admitting, affirmation, allowance, avowal,
concession, confession, declaration, disclo~
sure, divulgence, profession, revelation

admit 1. accept, allow, allow to enter, give
access, initiate, introduce, let in, receive,
take in **2.** acknowledge, affirm, avow, con~
cede, confess, declare, disclose, divulge,
own, profess, reveal **3.** agree, allow, grant,
let, permit, recognize
Antonyms (*sense 1*) exclude, keep out (*senses
2 & 3*) deny, dismiss, forbid, negate, prohibit,
reject

admittance acceptance, access, admitting,
allowing, entrance, entry, letting in, pas~
sage, reception

admonish advise, bawl out (*Inf.*), berate,
carpet (*Inf.*), caution, censure, check, chew

out (*U.S. & Canad. inf.*), chide, counsel, en~
join, exhort, forewarn, give a rocket (*Brit.
& N.Z. inf.*), read the riot act, rebuke, rep~
rimand, reprove, scold, tear into (*Inf.*), tear
(someone) off a strip (*Brit. inf.*), tell off
(*Inf.*), upbraid, warn
Antonyms applaud, commend, compliment,
congratulate, praise

admonition advice, berating, caution,
chiding, counsel, rebuke, remonstrance,
reprimand, reproach, reproof, scolding,
telling off (*Inf.*), upbraiding, warning

admonitory admonishing, advisory, cau~
tionary, rebuking, reprimanding, reproach~
ful, reproving, scolding, warning

ado agitation, bother, bustle, commotion,
confusion, delay, disturbance, excitement,
flurry, fuss, pother, stir, to-do, trouble

adolescence 1. boyhood, girlhood, ju~
venescence, minority, teens, youth **2.** boy~
ishness, childishness, girlishness, immatu~
rity, juvenility, puerility, youthfulness

adolescent 1. *adj.* boyish, girlish, growing,
immature, juvenile, puerile, teenage, young,
youthful **2.** *n.* juvenile, minor, teenager,
youngster, youth

adopt 1. accept, appropriate, approve, as~
sume, choose, embrace, endorse, espouse,
follow, maintain, ratify, select, support, take
on, take over, take up **2.** foster, take in
Antonyms (*sense 1*) abandon, abnegate, cast
aside, cast off, disavow, disclaim, disown, for~
swear, give up, reject, renounce, repudiate,
spurn, wash one's hands of

adoption 1. acceptance, approbation, ap~
propriation, approval, assumption, choice,
embracing, endorsement, espousal, follow~
ing, maintenance, ratification, selection,
support, taking on, taking over, taking up
2. adopting, fosterage, fostering, taking in

adorable appealing, attractive, captivating,
charming, cute, darling, dear, delightful,
fetching, lovable, pleasing, precious
Antonyms despicable, displeasing, hateful,
unlikable *or* unlikeable, unlovable

adoration admiration, esteem, estimation,
exaltation, glorification, honour, idolatry,
idolization, love, reverence, veneration,
worship, worshipping

adore admire, bow to, cherish, dote on, es~
teem, exalt, glorify, honour, idolize, love,
revere, reverence, venerate, worship
Antonyms abhor, abominate, despise, de~
test, execrate, hate, loathe

adorn array, beautify, bedeck, deck, deco~
rate, embellish, emblazon, enhance, enrich,
festoon, garnish, grace, ornament, trim

adornment 1. accessory, decoration, em~
bellishment, festoon, frill, frippery, orna~
ment, trimming **2.** beautification, decorat~

ing, decoration, embellishment, ornamenta~
tion, trimming

adrift 1. afloat, drifting, unanchored, un~
moored **2.** aimless, directionless, goalless,
purposeless **3.** amiss, astray, off course,
wrong

adroit able, adept, apt, artful, clever, cun~
ning, deft, dexterous, expert, ingenious,
masterful, neat, nimble, proficient, quick-
witted, skilful, skilled
Antonyms awkward, blundering, bungling,
cack-handed (*Inf.*), clumsy, ham-fisted (*Inf.*),
inept, inexpert, maladroit, uncoordinated,
unhandy, unskilful

adroitness ability, ableness, address,
adeptness, aptness, artfulness, cleverness,
craft, cunning, deftness, dexterity, expert~
ise, ingeniousness, ingenuity, masterful~
ness, mastery, nimbleness, proficiency,
quick-wittedness, skilfulness, skill

adulation blandishment, bootlicking (*Inf.*),
extravagant flattery, fawning, fulsome
praise, servile flattery, sycophancy, worship
Antonyms abuse, calumniation, censure,
condemnation, disparagement, revilement,
ridicule, vilification, vituperation

adulatory blandishing, bootlicking (*Inf.*),
fawning, flattering, obsequious, praising,
servile, slavish, sycophantic, worshipping

adult 1. *adj.* full grown, fully developed,
fully grown, grown-up, mature, of age, ripe
2. *n.* grown *or* grown-up person (man *or*
woman), grown-up, person of mature age

adulterate 1. *v.* attenuate, bastardize, con~
taminate, corrupt, debase, depreciate, de~
teriorate, devalue, make impure, mix with,
thin, vitiate, water down, weaken **2.** *adj.*
adulterated, attenuated, bastardized, con~
taminated, corrupt, debased, depreciated,
deteriorated, devalued, mixed, thinned, vi~
tiated, watered down, weakened

adumbrate 1. delineate, indicate, outline,
silhouette, sketch, suggest **2.** augur, fore~
cast, foreshadow, foretell, portend, predict,
prefigure, presage, prognosticate, prophesy
3. bedim, darken, eclipse, obfuscate, ob~
scure, overshadow

adumbration 1. delineation, draft, indica~
tion, outline, rough, silhouette, sketch, sug~
gestion **2.** augury, forecast, foreshadowing,
foretelling, omen, portent, prediction,
prefiguration, prefigurement, presage, prog~
nostication, prophecy, sign **3.** bedimming,
cloud, darkening, darkness, eclipse, eclips~
ing, obfuscation, obscuring, overshadowing,
shadow

advance *v.* **1.** accelerate, bring forward,
bring up, come forward, elevate, go ahead,
go forward, go on, hasten, move onward,
move up, press on, proceed, progress, pro~
mote, send forward, send up, speed, up~

grade **2.** benefit, further, grow, improve,
multiply, prosper, thrive **3.** adduce, allege,
cite, offer, present, proffer, put forward,
submit, suggest **4.** increase (*price*), lend,
pay beforehand, raise (*price*), supply on
credit ~*n.* **5.** advancement, development,
forward movement, headway, inroad, on~
ward movement, progress **6.** advancement,
amelioration, betterment, breakthrough,
furtherance, gain, growth, improvement,
progress, promotion, step **7.** appreciation,
credit, deposit, down payment, increase (*in
price*), loan, prepayment, retainer, rise (*in
price*) **8.** advances approach, approaches,
moves, overtures, proposals, proposition
~*adj.* **9.** beforehand, early, foremost, for~
ward, in front, leading, prior **10. in ad~
vance** ahead, beforehand, earlier, in the
forefront, in the lead, in the van, previously
Antonyms *v.* (*sense 1*) demote, hold back,
impede, move back, regress, retard, retreat,
set back, withdraw (*sense 2*) decrease, dimin~
ish, lessen, weaken (*sense 3*) hide, hold back,
suppress, withhold (*sense 4*) defer payment,
withhold payment

advanced ahead, avant-garde, extreme,
foremost, forward, higher, late, leading,
precocious, progressive
Antonyms backward, behind, retarded,
underdeveloped, undeveloped

advancement 1. advance, forward move~
ment, headway, onward movement, pro~
gress **2.** advance, amelioration, betterment,
gain, growth, improvement, preferment,
progress, promotion, rise

advantage aid, ascendancy, asset, assis~
tance, avail, benefit, blessing, boon, con~
venience, dominance, edge, gain, good, help,
interest, lead, precedence, pre-eminence,
profit, service, start, superiority, sway,
upper hand, use, utility, welfare
Antonyms curse, difficulty, disadvantage,
downside, drawback, handicap, hindrance,
inconvenience, snag

advantageous 1. dominant, dominating,
favourable, superior **2.** beneficial, conveni~
ent, expedient, helpful, of service,
profitable, useful, valuable, worthwhile
Antonyms detrimental, unfavourable, un~
fortunate, unhelpful, useless

advent appearance, approach, arrival, com~
ing, entrance, occurrence, onset, visitation

adventitious accidental, casual, chance,
extraneous, foreign, fortuitous, incidental,
nonessential, unexpected

adventure 1. *n.* chance, contingency, en~
terprise, escapade, experience, exploit, haz~
ard, incident, occurrence, risk, speculation,
undertaking, venture **2.** *v.* dare, endanger,
hazard, imperil, jeopardize, risk, venture

adventurer 1. daredevil, hero, heroine,

knight-errant, soldier of fortune, swash~
buckler, traveller, venturer, voyager, wan~
derer **2.** charlatan, fortune-hunter, gambler,
mercenary, opportunist, rogue, speculator

adventurous adventuresome, audacious,
bold, dangerous, daredevil, daring, enter~
prising, foolhardy, have-a-go (*Inf.*), hazard~
ous, headstrong, intrepid, rash, reckless,
risky, temerarious (*Rare*), venturesome
Antonyms careful, cautious, chary, circum~
spect, hesitant, prudent, safe, tentative, timid,
timorous, unadventurous, wary

adversary antagonist, competitor, contest~
ant, enemy, foe, opponent, opposer, rival
Antonyms accomplice, ally, associate, col~
laborator, colleague, confederate, co-worker,
friend, helper, partner, supporter

adverse antagonistic, conflicting, contrary,
detrimental, disadvantageous, hostile, inex~
pedient, inimical, injurious, inopportune,
negative, opposing, opposite, reluctant, re~
pugnant, unfavourable, unfortunate, un~
friendly, unlucky, unpropitious, unwilling
Antonyms advantageous, auspicious,
beneficial, favourable, fortunate, helpful,
lucky, opportune, promising, propitious,
suitable

adversity affliction, bad luck, calamity, ca~
tastrophe, disaster, distress, hardship, hard
times, ill-fortune, ill-luck, misery, misfor~
tune, mishap, reverse, sorrow, suffering,
trial, trouble, woe, wretchedness

advertise advise, announce, apprise, bla~
zon, crack up (*Inf.*), declare, display, flaunt,
inform, make known, notify, plug (*Inf.*),
praise, proclaim, promote, promulgate,
publicize, publish, puff, push (*Inf.*), tout

advertisement ad (*Inf.*), advert (*Brit. inf.*),
announcement, bill, blurb, circular, com~
mercial, display, notice, placard, plug (*Inf.*),
poster, promotion, publicity, puff

advice 1. admonition, caution, counsel,
guidance, help, injunction, opinion, recom~
mendation, suggestion, view **2.** information,
instruction, intelligence, notice, notifica~
tion, warning, word

advisability appropriateness, aptness, de~
sirability, expediency, fitness, judicious~
ness, profitability, propriety, prudence,
seemliness, soundness, suitability, wisdom

advisable appropriate, apt, desirable, ex~
pedient, fit, fitting, judicious, politic,
profitable, proper, prudent, recommended,
seemly, sensible, sound, suggested, suitable,
wise
Antonyms ill-advised, impolitic, improper,
imprudent, inappropriate, inexpedient, inju~
dicious, silly, stupid, undesirable, unfitting,
unprofitable, unseemly, unsound, unsuitable,
unwise

advise 1. admonish, caution, commend,

counsel, enjoin, prescribe, recommend,
suggest, urge **2.** acquaint, apprise, inform,
make known, notify, report, tell, warn

adviser aide, authority, coach, confidant,
consultant, counsel, counsellor, guide, help~
er, lawyer, mentor, right-hand man, solici~
tor, teacher, tutor

advisory advising, consultative, counsel~
ling, helping, recommending

advocacy advancement, argument for,
backing, campaigning for, championing,
defence, encouragement, espousal,
justification, pleading for, promotion,
promulgation, propagation, proposal, rec~
ommendation, spokesmanship, support,
upholding, urging

advocate *v.* **1.** advise, argue for, campaign
for, champion, countenance, defend, en~
courage, espouse, favour, hold a brief for
(*Inf.*), justify, plead for, prescribe, press for,
promote, propose, recommend, speak for,
support, uphold, urge ~*n.* **2.** apologist,
apostle, backer, campaigner, champion,
counsellor, defender, pleader, promoter,
proponent, proposer, speaker, spokesman,
supporter, upholder **3.** *Law* attorney, bar~
rister, counsel, lawyer, solicitor
Antonyms *v.* contradict, oppose, resist,
speak against, take a stand against, take issue
with

aegis advocacy, auspices, backing, favour,
guardianship, patronage, protection, shel~
ter, sponsorship, support, wing

affability amiability, amicability, approach~
ability, benevolence, benignity, civility,
congeniality, cordiality, courtesy, friendli~
ness, geniality, good humour, good nature,
graciousness, kindliness, mildness, oblig~
ingness, pleasantness, sociability, urbanity,
warmth

affable amiable, amicable, approachable,
benevolent, benign, civil, congenial, cordial,
courteous, friendly, genial, good-humoured,
good-natured, gracious, kindly, mild, oblig~
ing, pleasant, sociable, urbane, warm
Antonyms brusque, cold, discourteous, dis~
tant, haughty, rude, stand-offish, surly, unap~
proachable, uncivil, unfriendly, ungracious,
unpleasant, unsociable

affair 1. activity, business, circumstance,
concern, episode, event, happening, inci~
dent, interest, matter, occurrence, proceed~
ing, project, question, subject, transaction,
undertaking **2.** amour, intrigue, liaison, re~
lationship, romance

affect 1. act on, alter, bear upon, change,
concern, impinge upon, influence, interest,
involve, modify, prevail over, regard, relate
to, sway, transform **2.** disturb, impress,
move, overcome, perturb, stir, touch, upset
3. adopt, aspire to, assume, contrive,

counterfeit, feign, imitate, pretend, put on, sham, simulate

affectation act, affectedness, appearance, artificiality, assumed manners, façade, fak~ery, false display, insincerity, mannerism, pose, pretence, pretension, pretentiousness, sham, show, simulation, unnatural imitation

affected 1. afflicted, altered, changed, concerned, damaged, deeply moved, distressed, hurt, impaired, impressed, influenced, injured, melted, stimulated, stirred, touched, troubled, upset **2.** artificial, assumed, camp (*Inf.*), conceited, contrived, counterfeit, feigned, insincere, la-di-da (*Inf.*), mannered, mincing, phoney *or* phony (*Inf.*), pompous, precious, pretended, pretentious, put-on, sham, simulated, spurious, stiff, studied, unnatural
Antonyms (*sense 1*) cured, unaffected, un~concerned, unharmed, uninjured, unmoved, untouched (*sense 2*) genuine, natural, real, unaffected

affecting moving, pathetic, piteous, pitiable, pitiful, poignant, sad, saddening, touching

affection amity, attachment, care, desire, feeling, fondness, friendliness, goodwill, inclination, kindness, liking, love, passion, propensity, tenderness, warmth

affectionate attached, caring, devoted, doting, fond, friendly, kind, loving, tender, warm, warm-hearted
Antonyms cold, cool, glacial, indifferent, stony, uncaring, undemonstrative, unfeeling, unresponsive

affiliate ally, amalgamate, annex, associate, band together, combine, confederate, con~nect, incorporate, join, unite

affiliation alliance, amalgamation, associa~tion, banding together, coalition, combina~tion, confederation, connection, incorpora~tion, joining, league, merging, relationship, union

affinity 1. alliance, analogy, closeness, compatibility, connection, correspondence, kinship, likeness, relation, relationship, re~semblance, similarity **2.** attraction, fond~ness, inclination, leaning, liking, partiality, rapport, sympathy
Antonyms (*sense 1*) difference, disparity, dissimilarity (*sense 2*) abhorrence, animosity, antipathy, aversion, dislike, hatred, hostility, loathing, repugnance, revulsion

affirm assert, asseverate, attest, aver, avouch, avow, certify, confirm, declare, maintain, pronounce, ratify, state, swear, testify
Antonyms deny, disallow, rebut, refute, re~ject, renounce, repudiate, rescind, retract

affirmation assertion, asseveration, attes~tation, averment, avouchment, avowal, certification, confirmation, declaration, oath, pronouncement, ratification, state~ment, testimony

affirmative agreeing, approving, assenting, concurring, confirming, consenting, cor~roborative, favourable, positive
Antonyms denying, disagreeing, disap~proving, dissenting, negating, negative

affix add, annex, append, attach, bind, fas~ten, glue, join, paste, put on, stick, subjoin, tack, tag
Antonyms detach, disconnect, remove, take off, unfasten, unglue

afflict beset, burden, distress, grieve, harass, hurt, oppress, pain, plague, rack, smite, torment, trouble, try, wound

affliction adversity, calamity, cross, curse, depression, disease, distress, grief, hard~ship, misery, misfortune, ordeal, pain, plague, scourge, sickness, sorrow, suffering, torment, trial, tribulation, trouble, woe, wretchedness

affluence abundance, big bucks (*Inf., chiefly U.S.*), big money, exuberance, fortune, megabucks (*U.S. & Canad. sl.*), opulence, plenty, pretty penny (*Inf.*), profusion, pros~perity, riches, tidy sum (*Inf.*), wad (*U.S. & Canad. sl.*), wealth

affluent 1. loaded (*Sl.*), moneyed, opulent, prosperous, rich, wealthy, well-heeled (*Inf.*), well-off, well-to-do **2.** abundant, copious, exuberant, plenteous, plentiful
Antonyms (*sense 1*) broke (*Inf.*), destitute, hard-up (*Inf.*), impecunious, impoverished, indigent, penniless, penurious, poor, poverty-stricken, skint (*Brit. sl.*), stony-broke (*Brit. sl.*)

afford 1. bear, spare, stand, sustain **2.** be~stow, furnish, give, grant, impart, offer, produce, provide, render, supply, yield

affray *bagarre*, brawl, contest, disturbance, dogfight, encounter, feud, fight, fracas, free-for-all (*Inf.*), mêlée, outbreak, quarrel, scrap, scrimmage, scuffle, set-to (*Inf.*), shin~dig (*Inf.*), shindy (*Inf.*), skirmish, tumult

affront 1. *v.* abuse, anger, annoy, displease, insult, offend, outrage, pique, provoke, slight, vex **2.** *n.* abuse, indignity, injury, insult, offence, outrage, provocation, slap in the face (*Inf.*), slight, slur, vexation, wrong

afire 1. ablaze, aflame, alight, blazing, burn~ing, fiery, flaming, ignited, lighted, lit, on fire **2.** aglow, aroused, excited, fervent, im~passioned, passionate, stimulated

aflame 1. ablaze, afire, alight, blazing, burning, fiery, flaming, ignited, lighted, lit, on fire **2.** afire, aroused, excited, fervent, impassioned, passionate, stimulated **3.** aglow, flushed, inflamed, red, ruddy

afoot about, abroad, afloat, astir, brewing,

circulating, current, going on, hatching, in preparation, in progress, in the wind, on the go (*Inf.*), operating, up (*Inf.*)

afraid 1. alarmed, anxious, apprehensive, cowardly, faint-hearted, fearful, frightened, intimidated, nervous, reluctant, scared, suspicious, timid, timorous **2.** regretful, sorry, unhappy
Antonyms audacious, bold, fearless, happy, inapprehensive, indifferent, pleased, unafraid

afresh again, anew, newly, once again, once more, over again

after afterwards, behind, below, following, later, subsequently, succeeding, thereafter
Antonyms before, earlier, in advance, in front, previously, prior to, sooner

aftermath after-effects, consequences, effects, end, outcome, results, sequel, upshot

again 1. afresh, anew, another time, once more **2.** also, besides, furthermore, in addition, moreover, on the contrary, on the other hand

against 1. anti (*Inf.*), averse to, contra (*Inf.*), counter, hostile to, in contrast to, in defiance of, in opposition to, in the face of, opposed to, opposing, resisting, versus **2.** abutting, close up to, facing, fronting, in contact with, on, opposite to, touching, upon **3.** in anticipation of, in expectation of, in preparation for, in provision for

age *n.* **1.** date, day(s), duration, epoch, era, generation, lifetime, period, span, time **2.** advancing years, decline (*of life*), majority, maturity, old age, senescence, senility, seniority ~*v.* **3.** decline, deteriorate, grow old, mature, mellow, ripen
Antonyms *n.* (*sense 2*) adolescence, boyhood, childhood, girlhood, immaturity, juvenescence, salad days, young days, youth

aged age-old, ancient, antiquated, antique, elderly, getting on, grey, hoary, old, senescent, superannuated
Antonyms adolescent, boyish, childish, girlish, immature, juvenile, young, youthful

agency 1. action, activity, auspices, efficiency, force, influence, instrumentality, intercession, intervention, means, mechanism, mediation, medium, operation, power, work **2.** bureau, business, department, office, organization

agenda calendar, diary, list, plan, programme, schedule, timetable

agent 1. advocate, deputy, emissary, envoy, factor, go-between, negotiator, rep (*Inf.*), representative, substitute, surrogate **2.** actor, author, doer, executor, mover, officer, operative, operator, performer, worker **3.** agency, cause, force, instrument, means, power, vehicle

aggravate 1. exacerbate, exaggerate,

heighten, increase, inflame, intensify, magnify, make worse, worsen **2.** *Inf.* annoy, be on one's back (*Sl.*), bother, exasperate, gall, get in one's hair (*Inf.*), get on one's nerves (*Inf.*), hassle (*Inf.*), irk, irritate, nark (*Brit., Aust., & N.Z. sl.*), needle (*Inf.*), nettle, pester, piss one off (*Taboo sl.*), provoke, tease, vex
Antonyms (*sense 1*) alleviate, assuage, calm, diminish, ease, improve, lessen, mitigate, smooth (*sense 2*) assuage, calm, pacify, please

aggravation 1. exacerbation, exaggeration, heightening, increase, inflaming, intensification, magnification, worsening **2.** *Inf.* annoyance, exasperation, gall, hassle (*Inf.*), irksomeness, irritation, provocation, teasing, vexation

aggregate 1. *v.* accumulate, amass, assemble, collect, combine, heap, mix, pile **2.** *n.* accumulation, agglomeration, amount, assemblage, body, bulk, collection, combination, heap, lump, mass, mixture, pile, sum, total, whole **3.** *adj.* accumulated, added, assembled, collected, collective, combined, composite, corporate, cumulative, mixed, total

aggression 1. assault, attack, encroachment, injury, invasion, offence, offensive, onslaught, raid **2.** aggressiveness, antagonism, belligerence, destructiveness, hostility, pugnacity

aggressive 1. belligerent, destructive, hostile, offensive, pugnacious, quarrelsome **2.** assertive, bold, dynamic, energetic, enterprising, forceful, militant, pushing, pushy (*Inf.*), vigorous, zealous
Antonyms friendly, mild, peaceful, quiet, retiring, submissive

aggressor assailant, assaulter, attacker, invader

aggrieved afflicted, distressed, disturbed, harmed, hurt, ill-used, injured, peeved (*Inf.*), saddened, unhappy, woeful, wronged

aghast afraid, amazed, appalled, astonished, astounded, awestruck, confounded, frightened, horrified, horror-struck, shocked, startled, stunned, thunder-struck

agile active, acute, alert, brisk, clever, limber, lissom(e), lithe, lively, nimble, prompt, quick, quick-witted, sharp, sprightly, spry, supple, swift
Antonyms awkward, clumsy, heavy, lumbering, ponderous, slow, slow-moving, stiff, ungainly, unsupple

agility activity, acuteness, alertness, briskness, cleverness, litheness, liveliness, nimbleness, promptitude, promptness, quickness, quick-wittedness, sharpness, sprightliness, spryness, suppleness, swiftness

agitate 1. beat, churn, convulse, disturb, rock, rouse, shake, stir, toss **2.** alarm,

arouse, confuse, disconcert, disquiet, dis~
tract, disturb, excite, faze, ferment, fluster,
incite, inflame, perturb, rouse, ruffle,
stimulate, trouble, unnerve, upset, work up,
worry **3.** argue, debate, discuss, dispute,
examine, ventilate
Antonyms (*sense 2*) appease, assuage, calm,
calm down, mollify, pacify, placate, quiet,
quieten, soothe, still, tranquillize

agitation 1. churning, convulsion, disturb~
ance, rocking, shake, shaking, stir, stirring,
tossing, turbulence, upheaval **2.** alarm,
arousal, clamour, commotion, confusion,
discomposure, disquiet, distraction, dis~
turbance, excitement, ferment, flurry,
fluster, incitement, lather (*Inf.*), outcry,
stimulation, trouble, tumult, turmoil,
upheaval, upset, worry **3.** argument, con~
troversy, debate, discussion, disputation,
dispute, ventilation

agitator agent provocateur, demagogue,
firebrand, inciter, instigator, rabble-rouser,
revolutionary, stirrer (*Inf.*), troublemaker

agog avid, curious, eager, enthralled, en~
thusiastic, excited, expectant, impatient, in
suspense, keen
Antonyms apathetic, incurious, indifferent,
unconcerned, uninterested

agonize afflict, be in agony, be in anguish,
distress, harrow, labour, pain, rack, strain,
strive, struggle, suffer, torment, torture,
worry, writhe

agony affliction, anguish, distress, misery,
pain, pangs, suffering, throes, torment, tor~
ture, woe

agree 1. accede, acquiesce, admit, allow,
assent, be of the same mind, comply, con~
cede, concur, consent, engage, grant, per~
mit, see eye to eye, settle **2.** accord, answer,
chime, coincide, conform, correspond, fit,
get on (together), harmonize, match, square,
suit, tally
Antonyms contradict, deny, differ, disagree,
dispute, dissent, rebut, refute, retract

agreeable 1. acceptable, congenial, de~
lightful, enjoyable, gratifying, likable *or*
likeable, pleasant, pleasing, pleasurable,
satisfying, to one's liking, to one's taste **2.**
appropriate, befitting, compatible, consist~
ent, fitting, in keeping, proper, suitable **3.**
acquiescent, amenable, approving, comply~
ing, concurring, consenting, in accord, re~
sponsive, sympathetic, well-disposed, will~
ing
Antonyms (*sense 1*) disagreeable, displeas~
ing, horrid, offensive, unlikable *or* unlikeable,
unpleasant (*sense 2*) inappropriate, unaccep~
table, unfitting, unsuitable

agreement 1. accord, accordance, affinity,
analogy, compatibility, compliance, concert,
concord, concurrence, conformity, congru~
ity, consistency, correspondence, harmony,
similarity, suitableness, union, unison **2.**
arrangement, bargain, compact, contract,
covenant, deal (*Inf.*), pact, settlement, trea~
ty, understanding
Antonyms (*sense 1*) altercation, argument,
clash, conflict, difference, discord, discrepan~
cy, disparity, dispute, dissent, dissimilarity,
diversity, division, falling-out, incompatibil~
ity, incongruity, quarrel, row, squabble,
strife, tiff, wrangle

agriculture agronomics, agronomy, culti~
vation, culture, farming, husbandry, tillage

aground ashore, beached, foundered,
grounded, high and dry, on the rocks,
stranded, stuck

ahead along, at an advantage, at the head,
before, forwards, in advance, in front, in
the foreground, in the lead, in the van~
guard, leading, on, onwards, to the fore,
winning

aid *v.* **1.** abet, assist, befriend, encourage, fa~
vour, help, promote, relieve, second, serve,
subsidize, succour, support, sustain ~*n.* **2.**
assistance, benefit, encouragement, favour,
help, promotion, relief, service, succour,
support **3.** abettor, adjutant, aide, aide-de-
camp, assistant, helper, second, supporter
Antonyms *v.* detract from, harm, hinder,
hurt, impede, obstruct, oppose, thwart ~*n.*
hindrance

aim 1. *v.* aspire, attempt, design, direct,
draw a bead (on), endeavour, intend, level,
mean, plan, point, propose, purpose, re~
solve, seek, set one's sights on, sight, strive,
take aim (at), train, try, want, wish **2.** *n.*
ambition, aspiration, course, design, desire,
direction, end, goal, intent, intention, mark,
object, objective, plan, purpose, scheme,
target, wish

aimless chance, directionless, erratic,
frivolous, goalless, haphazard, pointless,
purposeless, random, stray, undirected, un~
guided, unpredictable, vagrant, wayward
Antonyms decided, deliberate, determined,
firm, fixed, positive, purposeful, resolute, re~
solved, settled, single-minded

air *n.* **1.** atmosphere, heavens, sky **2.** blast,
breath, breeze, draught, puff, waft, whiff,
wind, zephyr **3.** ambience, appearance, at~
mosphere, aura, bearing, character, de~
meanour, effect, feeling, flavour, impres~
sion, look, manner, mood, quality, style,
tone, vibes (*Sl.*) **4.** circulation, display, dis~
semination, exposure, expression, publicity,
utterance, vent, ventilation **5.** aria, lay,
melody, song, tune ~*v.* **6.** aerate, expose,
freshen, ventilate **7.** circulate, communi~
cate, declare, disclose, display, disseminate,
divulge, exhibit, expose, express, give vent

to, make known, make public, proclaim, publicize, reveal, tell, utter, ventilate, voice

airily 1. animatedly, blithely, breezily, buoyantly, gaily, happily, high-spiritedly, jauntily, light-heartedly **2.** daintily, delicately, ethereally, gracefully, lightly

airiness 1. breeziness, draughtiness, freshness, gustiness, lightness, openness, windiness **2.** ethereality, immateriality, incorporeality, insubstantiality, lightness, weightlessness **3.** animation, blitheness, breeziness, buoyancy, gaiety, happiness, high spirits, jauntiness, light-heartedness, lightness of heart

airing 1. aeration, drying, freshening, ventilation **2.** excursion, jaunt, outing, promenade, stroll, walk **3.** circulation, display, dissemination, exposure, expression, publicity, utterance, vent, ventilation

airless breathless, close, heavy, muggy, oppressive, stale, stifling, stuffy, suffocating, sultry, unventilated
Antonyms airy, blowy, breezy, draughty, fresh, gusty, light, open, spacious, well-ventilated

airs affectation, affectedness, arrogance, haughtiness, hauteur, pomposity, pretensions, superciliousness, swank (*Inf.*)

airy 1. blowy, breezy, draughty, fresh, gusty, light, lofty, open, spacious, uncluttered, well-ventilated, windy **2.** aerial, delicate, ethereal, fanciful, flimsy, illusory, imaginary, immaterial, incorporeal, insubstantial, light, vaporous, visionary, weightless, wispy **3.** animated, blithe, buoyant, cheerful, cheery, chirpy (*Inf.*), debonair, frolicsome, gay, genial, graceful, happy, high-spirited, jaunty, light, light-hearted, lively, merry, nonchalant, sprightly, upbeat (*Inf.*)
Antonyms (*sense 1*) airless, close, heavy, muggy, oppressive, stale, stifling, stuffy, suffocating, unventilated (*sense 2*) concrete, corporeal, material, real, realistic, substantial, tangible (*sense 3*) cheerless, dismal, gloomy, glum, melancholy, miserable, morose, sad

aisle alley, corridor, gangway, lane, passage, passageway, path

alacrity alertness, avidity, briskness, cheerfulness, dispatch, eagerness, enthusiasm, gaiety, hilarity, joyousness, liveliness, promptness, quickness, readiness, speed, sprightliness, willingness, zeal
Antonyms apathy, dullness, inertia, lethargy, reluctance, slowness, sluggishness, unconcern, unwillingness

alarm v. **1.** daunt, dismay, distress, frighten, give (someone) a turn (*Inf.*), panic, put the wind up (someone) (*Inf.*), scare, startle, terrify, unnerve **2.** alert, arouse, signal, warn ~n. **3.** anxiety, apprehension, consternation, dismay, distress, fear, fright, nervous-

ness, panic, scare, terror, trepidation, unease, uneasiness **4.** alarm-bell, alert, bell, danger signal, distress signal, siren, tocsin, warning **5.** *Archaic* call to arms, summons to arms
Antonyms v. (*sense 1*) assure, calm, comfort, reassure, relieve, soothe ~n. (*sense 3*) calm, calmness, composure, sang-froid, serenity

alarming daunting, dismaying, distressing, disturbing, dreadful, frightening, scaring, shocking, startling, terrifying, unnerving

alcoholic 1. *adj.* brewed, distilled, fermented, hard, inebriant, inebriating, intoxicating, spirituous, strong, vinous **2.** *n.* bibber, boozer (*Inf.*), dipsomaniac, drunk, drunkard, hard drinker, inebriate, soak (*Sl.*), sot, sponge (*Inf.*), tippler, toper, tosspot (*Inf.*), wino (*Inf.*)

alcove bay, bower, compartment, corner, cubbyhole, cubicle, niche, nook, recess

alert 1. *adj.* active, agile, attentive, brisk, careful, circumspect, heedful, lively, nimble, observant, on guard, on one's toes, on the ball (*Inf.*), on the lookout, on the watch, perceptive, quick, ready, spirited, sprightly, vigilant, wary, watchful, wide-awake **2.** *n.* alarm, signal, siren, warning **3.** *v.* alarm, forewarn, inform, notify, signal, warn
Antonyms *adj.* careless, heedless, inactive, languid, lethargic, listless, oblivious, slow, unaware, unconcerned, unwary ~n. all clear ~v. lull

alertness activeness, agility, attentiveness, briskness, carefulness, circumspection, heedfulness, liveliness, nimbleness, perceptiveness, promptitude, quickness, readiness, spiritedness, sprightliness, vigilance, wariness, watchfulness

alias 1. *adv.* also called, also known as, otherwise, otherwise known as **2.** *n.* assumed name, nom de guerre, nom de plume, pen name, pseudonym, stage name

alibi defence, excuse, explanation, justification, plea, pretext, reason

alien 1. *adj.* adverse, conflicting, contrary, estranged, exotic, foreign, inappropriate, incompatible, incongruous, not native, not naturalized, opposed, outlandish, remote, repugnant, separated, strange, unfamiliar **2.** *n.* foreigner, newcomer, outsider, stranger
Antonyms *adj.* affiliated, akin, alike, allied, analogous, cognate, connected, corresponding, kindred, like, parallel, related, similar ~n. citizen, countryman, dweller, inhabitant, national, resident

alienate 1. break off, disaffect, divert, divorce, estrange, make unfriendly, separate, set against, turn away, withdraw **2.** *Law* abalienate, convey, transfer

alienation 1. breaking off, disaffection, diversion, divorce, estrangement, indiffer~ ence, remoteness, rupture, separation, set~ ting against, turning away, withdrawal **2.** *Law* abalienation, conveyance, transfer

alight[1] *v.* come down, come to rest, descend, disembark, dismount, get down, get off, land, light, perch, settle, touch down
Antonyms ascend, climb, float up, fly up, go up, lift off, mount, move up, rise, scale, soar, take off

alight[2] *adj.* **1.** ablaze, aflame, blazing, burn~ ing, fiery, flaming, flaring, ignited, lighted, lit, on fire **2.** bright, brilliant, illuminated, lit up, shining

align 1. arrange in line, coordinate, even, even up, line up, make parallel, order, range, regulate, straighten **2.** affiliate, agree, ally, associate, cooperate, join, side, sympathize

alignment 1. adjustment, arrangement, co~ ordination, evening, evening up, line, lining up, order, ranging, regulating, sequence, straightening up **2.** affiliation, agreement, alliance, association, cooperation, sympa~ thy, union

alike 1. *adj.* akin, analogous, corresponding, duplicate, equal, equivalent, even, identical, parallel, resembling, similar, the same, uniform **2.** *adv.* analogously, correspond~ ingly, equally, evenly, identically, similarly, uniformly
Antonyms *adj.* different, dissimilar, di~ verse, separate, unlike ~*adv.* differently, dis~ tinctly, unequally

alive 1. animate, breathing, having life, in the land of the living (*Inf.*), living, subsist~ ing **2.** active, existent, existing, extant, functioning, in existence, in force, opera~ tive, unquenched **3.** active, alert, animated, awake, brisk, cheerful, chirpy (*Inf.*), eager, energetic, full of life, lively, quick, spirited, sprightly, spry, vigorous, vital, vivacious, zestful
Antonyms (*sense 1*) dead, deceased, depart~ ed, expired, extinct, gone, inanimate, lifeless (*sense 2*) extinct, inactive, inoperative, lost (*sense 3*) apathetic, dull, inactive, lifeless, spiritless

alive to alert to, awake to, aware of, cogni~ zant of, eager for, sensible of, sensitive to, susceptible to

alive with abounding in, bristling with, bustling with, buzzing with, crawling with, hopping with, infested with, jumping with, lousy with (*Sl.*), overrun by, packed with, swarming with, teeming with, thronged with

all *adj.* **1.** every bit of, the complete, the en~ tire, the sum of, the totality of, the total of, the whole of **2.** each, each and every, every, every one of, every single **3.** complete, en~

tire, full, greatest, perfect, total, utter ~*n.* **4.** aggregate, entirety, everything, sum, sum total, total, total amount, totality, utmost, whole, whole amount ~*adv.* **5.** altogether, completely, entirely, fully, totally, utterly, wholly

allegation accusation, affirmation, asser~ tion, asseveration, averment, avowal, char~ ge, claim, declaration, deposition, plea, pro~ fession, statement

allege advance, affirm, assert, asseverate, aver, avow, charge, claim, declare, depose, maintain, plead, profess, put forward, state
Antonyms abjure, contradict, deny, dis~ agree with, disavow, disclaim, gainsay (*Ar~ chaic or literary*), oppose, refute, renounce, repudiate

alleged 1. affirmed, asserted, averred, de~ clared, described, designated, stated **2.** doubtful, dubious, ostensible, professed, purported, so-called, supposed, suspect, suspicious

allegiance adherence, constancy, devotion, duty, faithfulness, fealty, fidelity, homage, loyalty, obedience, obligation, troth (*Archa~ ic*)
Antonyms disloyalty, faithlessness, false~ ness, inconstancy, infidelity, perfidy, treach~ ery, treason, unfaithfulness

allegorical emblematic, figurative, parabol~ ic, symbolic, symbolizing

allegory apologue, emblem, fable, myth, parable, story, symbol, symbolism, tale

allergic 1. affected by, hypersensitive, sen~ sitive, sensitized, susceptible **2.** *Inf.* antipa~ thetic, averse, disinclined, hostile, loath, opposed

allergy 1. antipathy, hypersensitivity, sen~ sitivity, susceptibility **2.** *Inf.* antipathy, aversion, disinclination, dislike, hostility, loathing, opposition

alley alleyway, backstreet, lane, passage, passageway, pathway, walk

alliance affiliation, affinity, agreement, as~ sociation, coalition, combination, compact, concordat, confederacy, confederation, con~ nection, federation, league, marriage, pact, partnership, treaty, union
Antonyms alienation, breach, break, disaf~ fection, dissociation, disunion, disunity, di~ vision, rupture, separation, severance, split, split-up

allied affiliated, amalgamated, associated, bound, combined, confederate, connected, hand in glove (*Inf.*), in cahoots (*U.S. inf.*), in league, joined, joint, kindred, leagued, linked, married, related, unified, united, wed

allocate allot, apportion, appropriate, as~

sign, budget, designate, earmark, mete, set aside, share out

allocation allotment, allowance, apportion~ ment, appropriation, grant, lot, measure, portion, quota, ration, share, stint, stipend

allot allocate, apportion, appropriate, assign, budget, designate, earmark, mete, set aside, share out

allotment 1. allocation, allowance, appor~ tionment, appropriation, grant, lot, meas~ ure, portion, quota, ration, share, stint, sti~ pend **2.** kitchen garden, patch, plot, tract

all-out complete, determined, exhaustive, full, full-scale, maximum, optimum, out~ right, resolute, supreme, thorough, thoroughgoing, total, undivided, unlimited, unremitting, unrestrained, unstinted, utmost

Antonyms careless, cursory, half-hearted, negligent, off-hand, perfunctory, unenthusi~ astic

allow 1. acknowledge, acquiesce, admit, concede, confess, grant, own **2.** approve, authorize, bear, brook, endure, give leave, let, permit, put up with (*Inf.*), sanction, stand, suffer, tolerate **3.** allocate, allot, as~ sign, deduct, give, grant, provide, remit, spare

Antonyms (*sense 1*) contradict, deny, dis~ agree with, gainsay (*Archaic or literary*), op~ pose (*sense 2*) ban, disallow, forbid, prohibit, proscribe, refuse (*sense 3*) deny, forbid, refuse

allowable acceptable, admissible, all right, appropriate, approved, permissible, sanc~ tionable, sufferable, suitable, tolerable

allowance 1. allocation, allotment, amount, annuity, apportionment, grant, lot, meas~ ure, pension, portion, quota, ration, remit~ tance, share, stint, stipend, subsidy **2.** ad~ mission, concession, sanction, sufferance, toleration **3.** concession, deduction, dis~ count, rebate, reduction

allow for arrange for, consider, foresee, keep in mind, make allowances for, make concessions for, make provision for, plan for, provide for, set (something) aside for, take into account, take into consideration

alloy *n.* **1.** admixture, amalgam, blend, com~ bination, composite, compound, hybrid, meld, mixture ~*v.* **2.** admix, amalgamate, blend, combine, compound, fuse, meld, mix **3.** adulterate, debase, devalue, diminish, impair

all right *adj.* **1.** acceptable, adequate, aver~ age, fair, O.K. *or* okay (*Inf.*), passable, sat~ isfactory, standard, unobjectionable **2.** hale, healthy, safe, sound, unharmed, unim~ paired, uninjured, well, whole ~*adv.* **3.** ac~ ceptably, adequately, O.K. *or* okay (*Inf.*), passably, satisfactorily, unobjectionably, well enough

Antonyms *adj.* (*sense 1*) bad, inadequate, not good enough, not up to scratch (*Inf.*), objec~ tionable, poor, unacceptable, unsatisfactory (*sense 2*) ailing, bad, ill, injured, off colour, out of sorts, poorly, sick, sickly, unhealthy, un~ well

allure 1. *v.* attract, beguile, cajole, captivate, charm, coax, decoy, enchant, entice, invei~ gle, lead on, lure, persuade, seduce, tempt, win over **2.** *n.* appeal, attraction, charm, enchantment, enticement, glamour, lure, persuasion, seductiveness, temptation

alluring attractive, beguiling, bewitching, captivating, come-hither, enchanting, fasci~ nating, fetching, glamorous, intriguing, se~ ductive, sexy, tempting

Antonyms abhorrent, off-putting (*Brit. inf.*), repellent, repugnant, repulsive, unattractive

allusion casual remark, glance, hint, impli~ cation, indirect reference, innuendo, insin~ uation, intimation, mention, suggestion

ally 1. *n.* abettor, accessory, accomplice, as~ sociate, coadjutor, collaborator, colleague, confederate, co-worker, friend, helper, part~ ner **2.** *v.* affiliate, associate, band together, collaborate, combine, confederate, connect, join, join forces, league, marry, unify, unite

Antonyms *n.* adversary, antagonist, com~ petitor, enemy, foe, opponent, rival ~*v.* alien~ ate, disaffect, disunite, divide, drive apart, separate, set at odds

almighty 1. absolute, all-powerful, invin~ cible, omnipotent, supreme, unlimited **2.** *Inf.* awful, desperate, enormous, excessive, great, intense, loud, severe, terrible

Antonyms (*sense 1*) helpless, impotent, pow~ erless, weak (*sense 2*) feeble, insignificant, paltry, poor, slight, tame, weak

almost about, all but, approximately, as good as, close to, just about, nearly, not far from, not quite, on the brink of, practically, virtually, well-nigh

alone 1. abandoned, apart, by itself, by oneself, deserted, desolate, detached, for~ lorn, forsaken, isolated, lonely, lonesome, only, separate, single, single-handed, sole, solitary, unaccompanied, unaided, unas~ sisted, unattended, uncombined, uncon~ nected, unescorted **2.** incomparable, matchless, peerless, singular, unequalled, unique, unparalleled, unsurpassed

Antonyms (*sense 1*) accompanied, aided, among others, assisted, escorted, helped, jointly, together (*sense 2*) equalled, surpassed

aloof 1. chilly, cold, cool, detached, distant, forbidding, formal, haughty, indifferent, re~ mote, reserved, standoffish, supercilious, unapproachable, unfriendly, uninterested, unresponsive, unsociable, unsympathetic **2.** above, apart, at a distance, away, distanced, distant

Antonyms (*sense 1*) friendly, gregarious, neighbourly, open, sociable, sympathetic, warm

aloud 1. audibly, clearly, distinctly, intelligibly, out loud, plainly **2.** clamorously, loudly, noisily, vociferously

already as of now, at present, before now, by now, by that time, by then, by this time, even now, heretofore, just now, previously

also additionally, along with, and, as well, as well as, besides, further, furthermore, in addition, including, into the bargain, moreover, on top of that, plus, to boot, too

alter adapt, adjust, amend, change, convert, diversify, metamorphose, modify, recast, reform, remodel, reshape, revise, shift, transform, transmute, turn, vary

alteration adaptation, adjustment, amendment, change, conversion, difference, diversification, metamorphosis, modification, reformation, remodelling, reshaping, revision, shift, transformation, transmutation, variance, variation

alternate *v.* **1.** act reciprocally, alter, change, fluctuate, follow in turn, follow one another, interchange, intersperse, oscillate, rotate, substitute, take turns, vary ~*adj.* **2.** alternating, every other, every second, interchanging, rotating **3.** alternative, another, different, second, substitute

alternative 1. *n.* choice, option, other (*of two*), preference, recourse, selection, substitute **2.** *adj.* alternate, another, different, other, second, substitute

alternatively as an alternative, by way of alternative, if not, instead, on the other hand, or, otherwise

although albeit, despite the fact that, even if, even supposing, even though, notwithstanding, tho' (*U.S. or poetic*), though, while

altitude elevation, height, loftiness, peak, summit

altogether 1. absolutely, completely, fully, perfectly, quite, thoroughly, totally, utterly, wholly **2.** all in all, all things considered, as a whole, collectively, generally, in general, *in toto*, on the whole **3.** all told, everything included, in all, in sum, *in toto*, taken together
Antonyms (*sense 1*) halfway, incompletely, in part, in some measure, not fully, partially, relatively, slightly, somewhat, to a certain degree *or* extent, up to a certain point

altruistic benevolent, charitable, considerate, generous, humanitarian, philanthropic, public-spirited, self-sacrificing, unselfish
Antonyms egoistic, egoistical, egotistic, egotistical, greedy, looking out for number one (*Inf.*), mean, self-centred, self-interested, selfish, self-seeking, ungenerous

always aye (*Scot.*), consistently, constantly, continually, eternally, ever, everlastingly, evermore, every time, forever, *in perpetuum*, invariably, perpetually, repeatedly, unceasingly, without exception
Antonyms hardly, hardly ever, infrequently, once in a blue moon, once in a while, only now and then, on rare occasions, rarely, scarcely ever, seldom

amalgamate alloy, ally, blend, coalesce, combine, commingle, compound, fuse, incorporate, integrate, intermix, meld, merge, mingle, unite
Antonyms disunite, divide, part, separate, split, split up

amalgamation admixture, alliance, alloy, amalgam, amalgamating, blend, coalition, combination, commingling, composite, compound, fusion, incorporation, integration, joining, meld, merger, mingling, mixing, mixture, union

amass accumulate, aggregate, assemble, collect, compile, garner, gather, heap up, hoard, pile up, rake up, scrape together

amateur dabbler, dilettante, layman, nonprofessional

amateurish amateur, bungling, clumsy, crude, inexpert, unaccomplished, unprofessional, unskilful
Antonyms experienced, expert, practised, professional, skilled

amaze alarm, astonish, astound, bewilder, bowl over (*Inf.*), confound, daze, dumbfound, electrify, flabbergast, shock, stagger, startle, stun, stupefy, surprise

amazement admiration, astonishment, bewilderment, confusion, marvel, perplexity, shock, stupefaction, surprise, wonder

ambassador agent, consul, deputy, diplomat, emissary, envoy, legate, minister, plenipotentiary, representative

ambiguity doubt, doubtfulness, dubiety, dubiousness, enigma, equivocacy, equivocality, equivocation, inconclusiveness, indefiniteness, indeterminateness, obscurity, puzzle, tergiversation, uncertainty, unclearness, vagueness

ambiguous cryptic, Delphic, doubtful, dubious, enigmatic, enigmatical, equivocal, inconclusive, indefinite, indeterminate, obscure, oracular, puzzling, uncertain, unclear, vague
Antonyms clear, definite, explicit, obvious, plain, simple, specific, unequivocal, unmistakable, unquestionable

ambition 1. aspiration, avidity, desire, drive, eagerness, enterprise, get-up-and-go (*Inf.*), hankering, longing, striving, yearning, zeal **2.** aim, aspiration, desire, dream, end, goal, hope, intent, objective, purpose, wish

ambitious 1. aspiring, avid, desirous, driving, eager, enterprising, hopeful, intent, purposeful, striving, zealous **2.** arduous, bold, challenging, demanding, difficult, elaborate, energetic, exacting, formidable, grandiose, hard, impressive, industrious, pretentious, severe, strenuous
Antonyms apathetic, easy, lazy, modest, simple, unambitious, unaspiring

ambivalence clash, conflict, contradiction, doubt, equivocation, fluctuation, hesitancy, indecision, irresolution, opposition, uncer~ tainty, vacillation, wavering

ambivalent clashing, conflicting, contra~ dictory, debatable, doubtful, equivocal, fluctuating, hesitant, inconclusive, in two minds, irresolute, mixed, opposed, uncer~ tain, undecided, unresolved, unsure, vacil~ lating, warring, wavering
Antonyms certain, clear, conclusive, con~ vinced, decided, definite, free from doubt, positive, sure, unwavering

amble dawdle, meander, mosey (*Inf.*), ram~ ble, saunter, stroll, walk, wander

ambush 1. *n.* ambuscade, concealment, cover, hiding, hiding place, lying in wait, retreat, shelter, trap, waylaying **2.** *v.* am~ buscade, bushwhack (*U.S.*), ensnare, sur~ prise, trap, waylay

amenable 1. able to be influenced, acqui~ escent, agreeable, open, persuadable, re~ sponsive, susceptible, tractable **2.** account~ able, answerable, chargeable, liable, re~ sponsible
Antonyms inflexible, intractable, mulish, obdurate, obstinate, pig-headed, recalcitrant, stiff-necked, stubborn, unbending, unyielding

amend alter, ameliorate, better, change, correct, enhance, fix, improve, mend, modi~ fy, rectify, reform, remedy, repair, revise

amendment 1. alteration, amelioration, betterment, change, correction, emendation, enhancement, improvement, mending, modification, rectification, reform, remedy, repair, revision **2.** addendum, addition, ad~ junct, alteration, attachment, clarification

amends apology, atonement, compensation, expiation, indemnity, recompense, redress, reparation, requital, restitution, restoration, satisfaction

amenity 1. advantage, comfort, conveni~ ence, facility, service **2.** affability, agree~ ableness, amiability, complaisance, cour~ tesy, mildness, pleasantness (*of situation*), politeness, refinement, suavity
Antonyms (*sense 2*) bad manners, discour~ tesy, impoliteness, incivility, rudeness, ungraciousness

amiability affability, agreeableness, ami~ ableness, attractiveness, benignity, charm, cheerfulness, delightfulness, engagingness, friendliness, friendship, geniality, good hu~ mour, good nature, kindliness, kindness, lovableness, pleasantness, pleasingness, so~ ciability, sweetness, sweetness and light (*Inf.*), sweet temper, winsomeness

amiable affable, agreeable, attractive, be~ nign, charming, cheerful, congenial, de~ lightful, engaging, friendly, genial, good-humoured, good-natured, kind, kindly, lik~ able *or* likeable, lovable, obliging, pleasant, pleasing, sociable, sweet-tempered, winning, winsome
Antonyms disagreeable, displeasing, hos~ tile, ill-natured, loathsome, repellent, sour, unfriendly, unpleasant

amicable amiable, brotherly, civil, cordial, courteous, fraternal, friendly, good-humoured, harmonious, kind, kindly, neighbourly, peaceable, peaceful, polite, so~ ciable
Antonyms antagonistic, bellicose, belliger~ ent, disagreeable, hostile, ill-disposed, impo~ lite, inimical, pugnacious, quarrelsome, un~ civil, unfriendly, unkind, unsociable

amid amidst, among, amongst, in the middle of, in the midst of, in the thick of, sur~ rounded by

amiss 1. *adj.* awry, confused, defective, er~ roneous, fallacious, false, faulty, improper, inaccurate, inappropriate, incorrect, mis~ taken, out of order, unsuitable, untoward, wrong **2.** *adv.* as an insult, as offensive, er~ roneously, faultily, improperly, inappropri~ ately, incorrectly, mistakenly, out of turn, unsuitably, wrongly
Antonyms *adj.* accurate, appropriate, cor~ rect, in order, O.K. *or* okay (*Inf.*), perfect, proper, right, suitable, true ~*adv.* appropri~ ately, correctly, properly, rightly, suitably, well

ammunition armaments, cartridges, ex~ plosives, materiel, munitions, powder, rounds, shells, shot, shot and shell

amnesty absolution, condonation, dispen~ sation, forgiveness, general pardon, im~ munity, oblivion, remission (*of penalty*), re~ prieve

amok *see* AMUCK

among, amongst 1. amid, amidst, in as~ sociation with, in the middle of, in the midst of, in the thick of, midst, surrounded by, together with, with **2.** between, to each of **3.** in the class of, in the company of, in the group of, in the number of, out of **4.** by all of, by the joint action of, by the whole of, mutually, with one another

amorous affectionate, amatory, ardent, at~ tached, doting, enamoured, erotic, fond,

impassioned, in love, lovesick, loving, lust~
ful, passionate, tender
Antonyms aloof, cold, distant, frigid, frosty,
indifferent, passionless, stand-offish, unde~
monstrative, unfeeling, unloving

amorphous characterless, formless, incho~
ate, indeterminate, irregular, nebulous,
nondescript, shapeless, unformed, un~
shaped, unshapen, unstructured, vague
Antonyms definite, distinct, regular,
shaped, structured

amount 1. bulk, expanse, extent, lot, mag~
nitude, mass, measure, number, quantity,
supply, volume **2.** addition, aggregate, en~
tirety, extent, lot, sum, sum total, total,
whole **3.** full effect, full value, import, re~
sult, significance

amount to add up to, aggregate, become,
come to, develop into, equal, grow, mean,
purport, total

ample abounding, abundant, big, bountiful,
broad, capacious, commodious, copious,
enough and to spare, expansive, extensive,
full, generous, great, large, lavish, liberal,
plenteous, plentiful, plenty, profuse, rich,
roomy, spacious, substantial, unrestricted,
voluminous, wide
Antonyms inadequate, insufficient, little,
meagre, restricted, scant, skimpy, small,
sparse, unsatisfactory

amplification augmentation, boosting,
deepening, development, dilation, elabora~
tion, enlargement, expansion, expatiation,
extension, fleshing out, heightening, in~
crease, intensification, lengthening,
magnification, raising, rounding out,
strengthening, stretching, supplementing,
widening

amplify augment, boost, deepen, develop,
dilate, elaborate, enlarge, expand, expatiate,
extend, flesh out, go into detail, heighten,
increase, intensify, lengthen, magnify,
raise, round out, strengthen, stretch, sup~
plement, widen
Antonyms abbreviate, abridge, boil down,
condense, curtail, cut down, decrease, reduce,
simplify

amply abundantly, bountifully, capaciously,
completely, copiously, extensively, fully,
generously, greatly, lavishly, liberally,
plenteously, plentifully, profusely, richly,
substantially, thoroughly, unstintingly,
well, with a blank cheque, with a free hand,
without stinting
Antonyms inadequately, insufficiently,
meagrely, poorly, scantily, skimpily, sparsely,
thinly

amputate curtail, cut off, lop, remove,
separate, sever, truncate

amuck, amok berserk, destructively, fero~
ciously, frenziedly, in a frenzy, insanely,

madly, maniacally, murderously, savagely,
uncontrollably, violently, wildly

amuse beguile, charm, cheer, delight, di~
vert, enliven, entertain, gladden, gratify,
interest, occupy, please, recreate, regale,
tickle
Antonyms be tedious, bore, jade, pall on,
send to sleep, tire, weary

amusement 1. beguilement, cheer, delight,
diversion, enjoyment, entertainment, fun,
gladdening, gratification, hilarity, interest,
jollies (*Sl.*), laughter, merriment, mirth,
pleasing, pleasure, recreation, regalement,
sport **2.** distraction, diversion, entertain~
ment, game, hobby, joke, lark, pastime,
prank, recreation, sport
Antonyms boredom, displeasure, monoto~
ny, sadness, tedium

amusing charming, cheerful, cheering,
comical, delightful, diverting, droll, enjoy~
able, entertaining, facetious, funny, glad~
dening, gratifying, humorous, interesting,
jocular, laughable, lively, merry, pleasant,
pleasing, rib-tickling, witty
Antonyms boring, dead, dull, flat, hum~
drum, monotonous, stale, tedious, tiresome,
unamusing, unexciting, unfunny, uninter~
esting, wearisome

anaemic ashen, bloodless, characterless,
colourless, dull, enervated, feeble, frail,
infirm, pale, pallid, sickly, wan, weak
Antonyms blooming, florid, full-blooded,
glowing, hearty, radiant, rosy, rosy-cheeked,
rubicund, ruddy, sanguine

anaesthetic 1. *n.* analgesic, anodyne, nar~
cotic, opiate, painkiller, sedative, soporific,
stupefacient, stupefactive **2.** *adj.* analgesic,
anodyne, deadening, dulling, narcotic,
numbing, opiate, pain-killing, sedative,
sleep-inducing, soporific, stupefacient,
stupefactive

analogous agreeing, akin, alike, compa~
rable, corresponding, equivalent, homolo~
gous, like, parallel, related, resembling,
similar
Antonyms contrasting, different, discrep~
ant, disparate, dissimilar, diverse, unlike

analogy agreement, comparison, correla~
tion, correspondence, equivalence, homol~
ogy, likeness, parallel, relation, resem~
blance, similarity, similitude

analyse 1. assay, estimate, evaluate, exam~
ine, interpret, investigate, judge, research,
test, work over **2.** anatomize, break down,
consider, dissect, dissolve, divide, resolve,
separate, study, think through

analysis 1. anatomization, anatomy, assay,
breakdown, dissection, dissolution, division,
enquiry, examination, investigation, perus~
al, resolution, scrutiny, separation, sifting,
test **2.** estimation, evaluation, finding, in~

terpretation, judgment, opinion, reasoning, study

analytic, analytical detailed, diagnostic, discrete, dissecting, explanatory, expository, inquiring, inquisitive, interpretative, inter~ pretive, investigative, logical, organized, problem-solving, questioning, rational, searching, studious, systematic, testing

anarchic chaotic, confused, disordered, dis~ organized, lawless, misgoverned, misruled, rebellious, revolutionary, rioting, riotous, ungoverned
Antonyms controlled, decorous, disciplined, law-abiding, ordered, peaceable, peaceful, quiet, restrained, well-behaved

anarchist insurgent, nihilist, rebel, revolu~ tionary, terrorist

anarchy chaos, confusion, disorder, disor~ ganization, lawlessness, misgovernment, misrule, rebellion, revolution, riot
Antonyms control, discipline, government, law, law and order, order, peace, rule

anathema 1. ban, condemnation, curse, damnation, denunciation, excommunica~ tion, execration, imprecation, malediction, proscription, taboo **2.** abomination, bane, *bête noire*, bugbear, enemy, pariah

anathematize abominate, ban, condemn, curse, damn, denounce, excommunicate, execrate, imprecate, proscribe

anatomize analyse, break down, dissect, dissolve, divide, examine, resolve, scruti~ nize, separate, study

anatomy 1. analysis, dismemberment, dis~ section, division, enquiry, examination, in~ vestigation, study **2.** build, composition, frame, framework, make-up, structure

ancestor forebear, forefather, forerunner, precursor, predecessor, progenitor
Antonyms descendant, inheritor, issue, off~ spring, progeny, successor

ancestry ancestors, antecedents, blood, derivation, descent, extraction, family, forebears, forefathers, genealogy, house, line, lineage, origin, parentage, pedigree, progenitors, race, stock

ancient aged, age-old, antediluvian, anti~ quated, antique, archaic, bygone, early, hoary, obsolete, old, olden, old-fashioned, outmoded, out-of-date, primeval, primordial, superannuated, timeworn
Antonyms current, fresh, in vogue, late, modern, modish, new, newfangled, new-fashioned, novel, recent, state-of-the-art, up-to-date, with it (*Inf.*), young

ancillary accessory, additional, auxiliary, contributory, extra, secondary, subordinate, subsidiary, supplementary
Antonyms cardinal, chief, main, major, premier, primary, prime, principal

and along with, also, as well as, further~ more, in addition to, including, moreover, plus, together with

anecdote reminiscence, short story, sketch, story, tale, urban legend, yarn

anew afresh, again, another time, from scratch, from the beginning, once again, once more, over again

angel 1. archangel, cherub, divine messen~ ger, guardian spirit, seraph, spiritual being **2.** *Inf.* beauty, darling, dear, dream, gem, ideal, jewel, paragon, saint, treasure

angelic 1. celestial, cherubic, ethereal, heavenly, seraphic **2.** adorable, beatific, beautiful, entrancing, innocent, lovely, pure, saintly, virtuous
Antonyms (*sense 1*) demonic, devilish, dia~ bolic, diabolical, fiendish, hellish, infernal, satanic

anger 1. *n.* annoyance, antagonism, choler, displeasure, exasperation, fury, ill humour, ill temper, indignation, ire, irritability, ir~ ritation, outrage, passion, pique, rage, re~ sentment, spleen, temper, vexation, wrath **2.** *v.* affront, aggravate (*Inf.*), annoy, an~ tagonize, be on one's back (*Sl.*), displease, enrage, exasperate, excite, fret, gall, get in one's hair (*Inf.*), get on one's nerves (*Inf.*), hassle (*Inf.*), incense, infuriate, irritate, madden, nark (*Brit., Aust., & N.Z. sl.*), net~ tle, offend, outrage, pique, piss one off (*Ta~ boo sl.*), provoke, rile, vex
Antonyms *n.* acceptance, amiability, ap~ proval, calmness, forgiveness, goodwill, gratification, liking, patience, peace, pleasure ~*v.* appease, calm, pacify, placate, please, soothe

angle *n.* **1.** bend, corner, crook, crotch, cusp, edge, elbow, intersection, knee, nook, point **2.** approach, aspect, outlook, perspec~ tive, point of view, position, side, slant, standpoint, viewpoint ~*v.* **3.** cast, fish

angle for aim for, be after (*Inf.*), cast about for, contrive, fish for, hunt, invite, look for, scheme, seek, solicit, try for

angry annoyed, antagonized, choleric, cross, displeased, enraged, exasperated, furious, hacked (off) (*U.S. sl.*), heated, hot, hot under the collar (*Inf.*), ill-tempered, incensed, in~ dignant, infuriated, irascible, irate, ireful, irritable, irritated, mad (*Inf.*), nettled, out~ raged, passionate, piqued, pissed off (*Taboo sl.*), provoked, raging, resentful, riled, sple~ netic, tumultuous, uptight (*Inf.*), wrathful
Antonyms agreeable, amiable, calm, con~ genial, friendly, gratified, happy, loving, mild, peaceful, pleasant, pleased

anguish agony, distress, grief, heartache, heartbreak, misery, pain, pang, sorrow, suffering, throe, torment, torture, woe

anguished afflicted, agonized, broken~

hearted, distressed, grief-stricken, suffering, tormented, tortured, wounded, wretched

angular bony, gaunt, lank, lanky, lean, macilent (*Rare*), rangy, rawboned, scrawny, skinny, spare

animal *n.* **1.** beast, brute, creature **2.** *Applied to a person* barbarian, beast, brute, monster, savage, wild man ~*adj.* **3.** bestial, bodily, brutish, carnal, fleshly, gross, physical, sensual

animate *v.* **1.** activate, embolden, encourage, energize, enliven, excite, fire, gladden, impel, incite, inspire, inspirit, instigate, invigorate, kindle, move, prod, quicken, revive, rouse, spark, spur, stimulate, stir, urge, vitalize, vivify ~*adj.* **2.** alive, breathing, live, living, moving **3.** gay, lively, spirited, vivacious
Antonyms *v.* check, curb, deaden, deter, devitalize, discourage, dull, inhibit, kill, make lifeless, put a damper on, restrain

animated active, airy, ardent, brisk, buoyant, dynamic, ebullient, elated, energetic, enthusiastic, excited, fervent, gay, lively, passionate, quick, sparky, spirited, sprightly, vibrant, vigorous, vital, vivacious, vivid, zealous, zestful
Antonyms apathetic, boring, dejected, depressed, dull, inactive, lethargic, lifeless, listless, monotonous, passive

animation action, activity, airiness, ardour, brio, briskness, buoyancy, dynamism, ebullience, elation, energy, enthusiasm, excitement, exhilaration, fervour, gaiety, high spirits, life, liveliness, passion, pep, pizzazz *or* pizazz (*Inf.*), sparkle, spirit, sprightliness, verve, vibrancy, vigour, vitality, vivacity, zeal, zest, zing (*Inf.*)

animosity acrimony, animus, antagonism, antipathy, bad blood, bitterness, enmity, hate, hatred, hostility, ill will, malevolence, malice, malignity, rancour, resentment, virulence
Antonyms amity, benevolence, congeniality, friendliness, friendship, goodwill, harmony, kindness, love, rapport, sympathy

annals accounts, archives, chronicles, history, journals, memorials, records, registers

annex 1. add, adjoin, affix, append, attach, connect, fasten, join, subjoin, tack, unite **2.** acquire, appropriate, arrogate, conquer, expropriate, occupy, seize, take over
Antonyms (*sense 1*) detach, disconnect, disengage, disjoin, disunite, remove, separate, unfasten

annexation annexing, appropriation, arrogation, conquest, expropriation, occupation, seizure, takeover

annexe 1. ell, extension, supplementary building, wing **2.** addendum, addition, adjunct, affix, appendix, attachment, supplement

annihilate abolish, destroy, eradicate, erase, exterminate, extinguish, extirpate, liquidate, nullify, obliterate, root out, wipe out

annihilation abolition, destruction, eradication, erasure, extermination, extinction, extinguishing, extirpation, liquidation, nullification, obliteration, rooting out, wiping out

annotate commentate, comment on, elucidate, explain, footnote, gloss, illustrate, interpret, make observations, note

annotation comment, commentary, elucidation, exegesis, explanation, explication, footnote, gloss, illustration, interpretation, note, observation

announce 1. advertise, blow wide open (*Sl.*), broadcast, declare, disclose, divulge, give out, intimate, make known, proclaim, promulgate, propound, publish, report, reveal, tell **2.** augur, betoken, foretell, harbinger, herald, portend, presage, signal, signify
Antonyms (*sense 1*) bury, conceal, cover up, hide, hold back, hush, hush up, keep back, keep quiet, keep secret, suppress, withhold

announcement advertisement, broadcast, bulletin, communiqué, declaration, disclosure, divulgence, intimation, proclamation, promulgation, publication, report, revelation, statement

announcer anchor man, broadcaster, commentator, master of ceremonies, newscaster, news reader, reporter

annoy aggravate (*Inf.*), anger, badger, bedevil, be on one's back (*Sl.*), bore, bother, bug (*Inf.*), displease, disturb, exasperate, gall, get (*Inf.*), get in one's hair (*Inf.*), get on one's nerves (*Inf.*), harass, harry, hassle (*Inf.*), incommode, irk, irritate, madden, molest, nark (*Brit., Aust., & N.Z. sl.*), needle (*Inf.*), nettle, peeve, pester, piss one off (*Taboo sl.*), plague, provoke, rile, ruffle, tease, trouble, vex
Antonyms appease, calm, comfort, console, mollify, solace, soothe

annoyance 1. aggravation, anger, bedevilment, bother, displeasure, disturbance, exasperation, harassment, hassle (*Inf.*), irritation, nuisance, provocation, trouble, vexation **2.** bind (*Inf.*), bore, bother, drag (*Inf.*), gall, nuisance, pain (*Inf.*), pain in the arse (*Taboo inf.*), pain in the neck (*Inf.*), pest, plague, tease

annoying aggravating, bedevilling, boring, bothersome, displeasing, disturbing, exasperating, galling, harassing, irksome, irritating, maddening, peeving (*Inf.*), provoking, teasing, troublesome, vexatious

Antonyms agreeable, amusing, charming, delightful, diverting, enjoyable, entertaining, gratifying, pleasant

annual once a year, yearlong, yearly

annually by the year, each year, every year, once a year, per annum, per year, year af~ ter year, yearly

annul abolish, abrogate, cancel, counter~ mand, declare *or* render null and void, in~ validate, negate, nullify, obviate, recall, re~ peal, rescind, retract, reverse, revoke, void
Antonyms bring back, re-enforce, re~ establish, reimpose, reinstate, reintroduce, restore

annulment abolition, abrogation, cancella~ tion, countermanding, invalidation, nega~ tion, nullification, recall, repeal, rescind~ ment, rescission, retraction, reversal, revo~ cation, voiding

anodyne 1. *n.* analgesic, narcotic, pain~ killer, painreliever, palliative **2.** *adj.* an~ algesic, deadening, dulling, narcotic, numb~ ing, pain-killing, pain-relieving, palliative

anoint 1. daub, embrocate, grease, oil, rub, smear, spread over **2.** anele (*Archaic*), bless, consecrate, hallow, sanctify

anomalous aberrant, abnormal, atypical, bizarre, deviating, eccentric, exceptional, incongruous, inconsistent, irregular, odd, oddball (*Inf.*), off-the-wall (*Sl.*), outré, pecu~ liar, rare, unusual
Antonyms common, customary, familiar, natural, normal, ordinary, regular, typical, usual

anomaly aberration, abnormality, depar~ ture, deviation, eccentricity, exception, in~ congruity, inconsistency, irregularity, odd~ ity, peculiarity, rarity

anon before long, betimes (*Archaic*), erelong (*Archaic or poetic*), forthwith, presently, promptly, shortly, soon

anonymous 1. incognito, innominate, nameless, unacknowledged, unattested, un~ authenticated, uncredited, unidentified, un~ known, unnamed, unsigned **2.** character~ less, nondescript, unexceptional
Antonyms (*sense 1*) accredited, acknowl~ edged, attested, authenticated, credited, identified, known, named, signed

answer *n.* **1.** acknowledgment, comeback, counterattack, defence, explanation, plea, reaction, refutation, rejoinder, reply, report, resolution, response, retort, return, riposte, solution, vindication ~*v.* **2.** acknowledge, explain, react, refute, rejoin, reply, resolve, respond, retort, return, solve **3.** conform, correlate, correspond, do, fill, fit, fulfil, measure up, meet, pass, qualify, satisfy, serve, suffice, suit, work
Antonyms *n.* inquiry, interrogation, query,

question ~*v.* (*sense 2*) ask, inquire, interro~ gate, query, question

answerable 1. accountable, amenable, chargeable, liable, responsible, subject, to blame **2.** explainable, refutable, resolvable, solvable

answer back argue, be cheeky, be imper~ tinent, cheek (*Inf.*), contradict, disagree, dispute, rebut, retort, talk back

answer for 1. be accountable for, be an~ swerable for, be chargeable for, be liable for, be responsible for, be to blame for, take the rap for (*Sl.*) **2.** atone for, make amends for, pay for, suffer for

answer to 1. be accountable to, be an~ swerable to, be responsible to, be ruled by, obey **2.** agree, confirm, correspond, fit, match, meet

antagonism antipathy, competition, conflict, contention, discord, dissension, friction, hostility, opposition, rivalry
Antonyms accord, agreement, amity, friendship, harmony, love, peacefulness, sympathy

antagonist adversary, competitor, con~ tender, enemy, foe, opponent, opposer, rival

antagonistic adverse, antipathetic, at odds, at variance, averse, conflicting, contentious, hostile, ill-disposed, incompatible, in dis~ pute, inimical, opposed, unfriendly

antagonize 1. aggravate (*Inf.*), alienate, anger, annoy, be on one's back (*Sl.*), disaf~ fect, estrange, gall, get in one's hair (*Inf.*), get on one's nerves (*Inf.*), hassle (*Inf.*), in~ sult, irritate, nark (*Brit., Aust., & N.Z. sl.*), offend, piss one off (*Taboo sl.*), repel, rub (someone) up the wrong way (*Inf.*) **2.** con~ tend with, counteract, neutralize, oppose, struggle with, work against
Antonyms (*sense 1*) appease, calm, concili~ ate, disarm, mollify, pacify, placate, propiti~ ate, soothe, win over

antecedent anterior, earlier, foregoing, former, preceding, precursory, preliminary, previous, prior
Antonyms after, coming, consequent, ensu~ ing, following, later, posterior, subsequent, succeeding, successive

antecedents 1. ancestors, ancestry, blood, descent, extraction, family, forebears, fore~ fathers, genealogy, line, progenitors, stock **2.** background, history, past

antediluvian 1. prehistoric, primeval, primitive, primordial **2.** ancient, antiquat~ ed, antique, archaic, obsolete, old-fashioned, out-of-date, out of the ark (*Inf.*), passé

anteroom antechamber, foyer, lobby, outer room, reception room, vestibule, waiting room

anthem 1. canticle, chant, chorale, hymn, psalm **2.** paean, song of praise

anthology analects, choice, collection, compendium, compilation, digest, garland, miscellany, selection, treasury

anticipate 1. apprehend, await, count upon, expect, forecast, foresee, foretell, hope for, look for, look forward to, predict, prepare for **2.** antedate, beat (someone) to it (*Inf.*), forestall, intercept, prevent

anticipation apprehension, awaiting, expectancy, expectation, foresight, foretaste, forethought, hope, preconception, premonition, prescience, presentiment

anticlimax bathos, comedown (*Inf.*), disappointment, letdown
Antonyms climax, culmination, height, highlight, high point, peak, summit, top, zenith

antics buffoonery, capers, clowning, escapades, foolishness, frolics, larks, mischief, monkey tricks, playfulness, pranks, silliness, skylarking, stunts, tomfoolery, tricks

antidote antitoxin, antivenin, corrective, counteragent, countermeasure, cure, neutralizer, nostrum, preventive, remedy, specific

antipathetic abhorrent, antagonistic, averse, disgusting, distasteful, hateful, hostile, incompatible, invidious, loathsome, obnoxious, odious, offensive, repellent, repugnant, repulsive, revolting, yucky *or* yukky (*Sl.*)

antipathy abhorrence, animosity, animus, antagonism, aversion, bad blood, contrariety, disgust, dislike, distaste, enmity, hatred, hostility, ill will, incompatibility, loathing, odium, opposition, rancour, repugnance, repulsion
Antonyms affection, affinity, attraction, bond, empathy, fellow-feeling, goodwill, harmony, partiality, rapport, sympathy, tie

antiquated 1. antediluvian, antique, archaic, dated, obsolete, old-fashioned, old hat, outmoded, out-of-date, outworn, passé **2.** aged, ancient, elderly, hoary, old, superannuated
Antonyms all-singing, all-dancing, current, fashionable, fresh, modern, modish, new, state-of-the-art, stylish, up-to-date, young

antique *adj.* **1.** aged, ancient, elderly, old, superannuated **2.** archaic, obsolete, old-fashioned, outdated **3.** antiquarian, classic, olden, vintage ~*n.* **4.** bygone, heirloom, object of virtu, relic

antiquity 1. age, ancientness, elderliness, old age, oldness **2.** ancient times, distant past, olden days, time immemorial **3.** antique, relic, ruin

antiseptic 1. *adj.* aseptic, clean, germ-free, hygienic, pure, sanitary, sterile, uncontaminated, unpolluted **2.** *n.* bactericide, disinfectant, germicide, purifier
Antonyms *adj.* contaminated, dirty, impure, infected, insanitary, polluted, septic, unhygienic

antisocial 1. alienated, asocial, misanthropic, reserved, retiring, uncommunicative, unfriendly, unsociable, withdrawn **2.** antagonistic, belligerent, disorderly, disruptive, hostile, menacing, rebellious
Antonyms (*sense 1*) companionable, friendly, gregarious, philanthropic, sociable, social

antithesis 1. antipode, contrary, contrast, converse, inverse, opposite, reverse **2.** contradiction, contraposition, contrariety, contrast, inversion, opposition, reversal

anxiety angst, apprehension, care, concern, disquiet, disquietude, distress, foreboding, fretfulness, misgiving, nervousness, restlessness, solicitude, suspense, tension, trepidation, unease, uneasiness, watchfulness, worry
Antonyms assurance, calmness, confidence, contentment, relief, security, serenity

anxious 1. apprehensive, careful, concerned, disquieted, distressed, disturbed, fearful, fretful, in suspense, nervous, overwrought, restless, solicitous, taut, tense, troubled, twitchy (*Inf.*), uneasy, unquiet (*Chiefly literary*), watchful, wired (*Sl.*), worried **2.** ardent, avid, desirous, eager, expectant, impatient, intent, itching, keen, yearning
Antonyms (*sense 1*) assured, calm, certain, collected, composed, confident, cool, nonchalant, unfazed (*Inf.*), unperturbed (*sense 2*) disinclined, hesitant, loath, nonchalant, reluctant

apart 1. afar, alone, aloof, aside, away, by itself, by oneself, cut off, distant, distinct, divorced, excluded, independent, independently, isolated, piecemeal, separate, separated, separately, singly, to itself, to oneself, to one side **2.** asunder, in bits, in pieces, into parts, to bits, to pieces **3. apart from** aside from, besides, but, except for, excluding, not counting, other than, save

apartment accommodation, chambers, compartment, flat, living quarters, penthouse, quarters, room, rooms, suite

apathetic cold, cool, emotionless, impassive, indifferent, insensible, listless, passive, phlegmatic, sluggish, stoic, stoical, torpid, unconcerned, unemotional, unfeeling, uninterested, unmoved, unresponsive
Antonyms active, anxious, aroused, bothered, caring, committed, concerned, emotional, enthusiastic, excited, interested, moved, passionate, responsive, troubled, worried, zealous

apathy coldness, coolness, emotionlessness, impassibility, impassivity, indifference, inertia, insensibility, listlessness, nonchalance, passiveness, passivity, phlegm, sluggishness, stoicism, torpor, unconcern, unfeelingness, uninterestedness, unresponsiveness
Antonyms anxiety, attention, concern, emotion, enthusiasm, feeling, interest, zeal

ape affect, caricature, copy, counterfeit, echo, imitate, mimic, mirror, mock, parody, parrot

aperture breach, chink, cleft, crack, eye, eyelet, fissure, gap, hole, interstice, opening, orifice, passage, perforation, rent, rift, slit, slot, space, vent

apex acme, apogee, climax, crest, crown, culmination, height, high point, peak, pinnacle, point, summit, tip, top, vertex, zenith
Antonyms base, bottom, depths, lowest point, nadir, perigee, rock bottom

aphorism adage, apothegm, axiom, dictum, gnome, maxim, precept, proverb, saw, saying

apiece each, for each, from each, individually, respectively, separately, severally, to each
Antonyms all together, as a group, collectively, en masse, overall, together

aplomb balance, calmness, composure, confidence, coolness, equanimity, levelheadedness, poise, sang-froid, self-assurance, self-confidence, self-possession, stability
Antonyms awkwardness, chagrin, confusion, discomfiture, discomposure, embarrassment, self-consciousness

apocryphal doubtful, dubious, equivocal, fictitious, legendary, mythical, questionable, spurious, unauthenticated, uncanonical, unsubstantiated, unverified
Antonyms attested, authentic, authenticated, authorized, canonical, credible, factual, substantiated, true, undisputed, unquestionable, verified

apologetic contrite, penitent, regretful, remorseful, rueful, sorry

apologist advocate, arguer, champion, defender, justifier, maintainer, pleader, spokesman, supporter, vindicator

apologize ask forgiveness, beg pardon, express regret, say one is sorry, say sorry

apology 1. acknowledgment, confession, defence, excuse, explanation, extenuation, justification, plea, vindication **2.** caricature, excuse, imitation, makeshift, mockery, stopgap, substitute, travesty

apostate 1. *n.* backslider, defector, deserter, heretic, recreant (*Archaic*), renegade, traitor, turncoat **2.** *adj.* backsliding, disloy-al, faithless, false, heretical, perfidious, recreant, traitorous, treacherous, unfaithful, untrue

apostle 1. evangelist, herald, messenger, missionary, preacher, proselytizer **2.** advocate, champion, pioneer, propagandist, propagator, proponent

apotheosis deification, elevation, exaltation, glorification, idealization, idolization

apotheosize deify, elevate, exalt, glorify, idealize, idolize

appal alarm, astound, daunt, dishearten, dismay, frighten, harrow, horrify, intimidate, outrage, petrify, scare, shock, terrify, unnerve

appalling alarming, astounding, awful, daunting, dire, disheartening, dismaying, dreadful, fearful, frightening, frightful, ghastly, godawful (*Sl.*), grim, harrowing, hellacious (*U.S. sl.*), hideous, horrible, horrid, horrific, horrifying, intimidating, petrifying, scaring, shocking, terrible, terrifying, unnerving
Antonyms comforting, consolatory, consoling, encouraging, heartening, reassuring

apparatus 1. appliance, contraption (*Inf.*), device, equipment, gear, implements, machine, machinery, materials, means, mechanism, outfit, tackle, tools, utensils **2.** bureaucracy, chain of command, hierarchy, network, organization, setup (*Inf.*), structure, system

apparel accoutrements, array (*Poetic*), attire, clothes, clothing, costume, dress, equipment, garb, garments, gear (*Inf.*), habiliments, habit, outfit, raiment (*Archaic or poetic*), robes, trappings, vestments

apparent 1. blatant, clear, conspicuous, discernible, distinct, evident, indubitable, manifest, marked, obvious, open, overt, patent, plain, understandable, unmistakable, visible **2.** ostensible, outward, seeming, specious, superficial
Antonyms (*sense 1*) ambiguous, doubtful, dubious, hazy, indefinite, indistinct, obscure, uncertain, unclear, vague (*sense 2*) actual, authentic, bona fide, genuine, honest, intrinsic, real, sincere, true

apparently it appears that, it seems that, on the face of it, ostensibly, outwardly, seemingly, speciously, superficially

apparition 1. appearance, manifestation, materialization, presence, vision, visitation **2.** chimera, eidolon, ghost, phantom, revenant, shade (*Literary*), spectre, spirit, spook (*Inf.*), visitant, wraith

appeal *n.* **1.** adjuration, application, entreaty, invocation, petition, plea, prayer, request, solicitation, suit, supplication **2.** allure, attraction, attractiveness, beauty,

charm, engagingness, fascination, interest~
ingness, pleasingness ~*v.* **3.** adjure, apply,
ask, beg, beseech, call, call upon, entreat,
implore, petition, plead, pray, refer, re~
quest, resort to, solicit, sue, supplicate **4.**
allure, attract, charm, engage, entice, fasci~
nate, interest, invite, please, tempt
Antonyms *n.* (*sense 1*) denial, refusal, rejec~
tion, repudiation (*sense 2*) repulsiveness ~*v.*
(*sense 3*) deny, refuse, reject, repudiate, re~
pulse (*sense 4*) alienate, bore, repulse, revolt

appear 1. arise, arrive, attend, be present,
come forth, come into sight, come into
view, come out, come to light, crop up
(*Inf.*), develop, emerge, issue, loom, materi~
alize, occur, show (*Inf.*), show up (*Inf.*),
surface, turn out, turn up **2.** look (like *or* as
if), occur, seem, strike one as **3.** be appar~
ent, be clear, be evident, be manifest, be
obvious, be patent, be plain **4.** become
available, be created, be developed, be in~
vented, be published, come into being, come
into existence, come out **5.** act, be exhibit~
ed, come on, come onstage, enter, perform,
play, play a part, take part
Antonyms be doubtful, be unclear, disap~
pear, vanish

appearance 1. advent, appearing, arrival,
coming, debut, emergence, introduction,
presence, showing up (*Inf.*), turning up **2.**
air, aspect, bearing, demeanour, expression,
face, figure, form, image, look, looks, man~
ner, mien (*Literary*) **3.** front, guise, illusion,
image, impression, outward show, pretence,
semblance

appease allay, alleviate, assuage, blunt,
calm, compose, conciliate, diminish, ease,
lessen, lull, mitigate, mollify, pacify, pla~
cate, quell, quench, quiet, satisfy, soften,
soothe, subdue, tranquillize
Antonyms aggravate (*Inf.*), anger, annoy,
antagonize, arouse, be on one's back (*Sl.*), dis~
turb, enrage, get in one's hair (*Inf.*), get on
one's nerves (*Inf.*), hassle (*Inf.*), incense,
inflame, infuriate, irritate, madden, nark
(*Brit., Aust., & N.Z. sl.*), piss one off (*Taboo sl.*),
provoke, rile, upset

appeasement 1. acceding, accommoda~
tion, compromise, concession, conciliation,
placation, propitiation **2.** abatement, alle~
viation, assuagement, blunting, easing,
lessening, lulling, mitigation, mollification,
pacification, quelling, quenching, quieting,
satisfaction, softening, solace, soothing,
tranquillization

appellation address, description, designa~
tion, epithet, name, sobriquet, style, term,
title

append add, adjoin, affix, annex, attach,
fasten, hang, join, subjoin, tack on, tag on

Antonyms detach, disconnect, disengage,
remove, separate, take off

appendage 1. accessory, addendum, addi~
tion, adjunct, affix, ancillary, annexe, ap~
pendix, appurtenance, attachment, auxilia~
ry, supplement **2.** *Zool.* extremity, limb,
member, projection, protuberance

appendant *adj.* **1.** added, additional, ad~
joined, affixed, annexed, appended, at~
tached, auxiliary, fastened, joined, sub~
joined, supplementary, tacked on, tagged on
2. accompanying, associated, attendant,
concomitant, connected, consequential, fol~
lowing, related, resulting ~*n.* **3.** addition,
adjunct, affix, annexe, appendage, appendix,
attachment, supplement

appendix addendum, addition, add-on, ad~
junct, appendage, codicil, postscript, sup~
plement

appertain *Usually with* **to** apply, bear
upon, be characteristic of, be connected,
belong, be part of, be pertinent, be proper,
be relevant, have to do with, inhere in,
pertain, refer, relate, touch upon

appetence, appetency 1. appetite, crav~
ing, desire, hankering, hunger, longing,
need, yearning **2.** bent, drive, inclination,
instinct, leaning, penchant, propensity **3.**
affection, affinity, allurement, attraction,
fondness, liking, partiality

appetite appetence, appetency, craving, de~
mand, desire, hankering, hunger, inclina~
tion, liking, longing, passion, proclivity,
propensity, relish, stomach, taste, willing~
ness, yearning, zeal, zest
Antonyms abhorrence, aversion, disgust,
disinclination, dislike, distaste, loathing, re~
pugnance, repulsion, revulsion

appetizer 1. antipasto, canapé, cocktail,
hors d'oeuvre, titbit **2.** apéritif, cocktail **3.**
foretaste, sample, taste

appetizing appealing, delicious, inviting,
mouthwatering, palatable, savoury,
scrumptious (*Inf.*), succulent, tasty, tempt~
ing
Antonyms distasteful, nauseating, unappe~
tizing, unpalatable, unsavoury

applaud acclaim, approve, cheer, clap,
commend, compliment, crack up (*Inf.*), en~
courage, eulogize, extol, laud, magnify (*Ar~
chaic*), praise
Antonyms blast, boo, censure, condemn,
criticize, decry, deprecate, deride, disparage,
excoriate, hiss, lambast(e), pan (*Inf.*), put
down, ridicule, run down, slag (off) (*Sl.*), tear
into (*Inf.*), vilify

applause acclaim, acclamation, accolade,
approbation, approval, cheering, cheers,
commendation, eulogizing, hand, hand~
clapping, laudation, ovation, plaudit, praise

appliance apparatus, device, gadget, imple~
ment, instrument, machine, mechanism,
tool

applicable apposite, appropriate, apropos,
apt, befitting, fit, fitting, germane, pertinent,
relevant, suitable, suited, to the point, to
the purpose, useful
Antonyms inapplicable, inappropriate, ir~
relevant, unsuitable, wrong

applicant aspirant, candidate, claimant, in~
quirer, petitioner, postulant, suitor, suppli~
ant

application 1. appositeness, exercise,
function, germaneness, pertinence, practice,
purpose, relevance, use, value **2.** appeal,
claim, inquiry, petition, request, requisi~
tion, solicitation, suit **3.** assiduity, atten~
tion, attentiveness, commitment, dedication,
diligence, effort, hard work, industry, per~
severance, study **4.** balm, cream, dressing,
emollient, lotion, ointment, poultice, salve,
unguent

apply 1. administer, assign, bring into play,
bring to bear, carry out, employ, engage,
execute, exercise, exert, implement, prac~
tise, put to use, use, utilize **2.** appertain, be
applicable, be appropriate, bear upon, be
fitting, be relevant, fit, pertain, refer, relate,
suit **3.** anoint, bring into contact with, cov~
er with, lay on, paint, place, put on, smear,
spread on, touch to **4.** appeal, claim, in~
quire, make application, petition, put in,
request, requisition, solicit, sue **5.** address,
be assiduous, be diligent, be industrious,
buckle down (*Inf.*), commit, concentrate,
dedicate, devote, direct, give, make an ef~
fort, pay attention, persevere, study, try,
work hard

appoint 1. allot, arrange, assign, choose,
decide, designate, determine, establish, fix,
set, settle **2.** assign, choose, commission,
delegate, elect, install, name, nominate, se~
lect **3.** command, decree, direct, enjoin, or~
dain **4.** equip, fit out, furnish, provide,
supply
Antonyms (*sense 1*) cancel (*sense 2*) dis~
charge, dismiss, fire, give the sack (*Inf.*), sack
(*Inf.*) (*sense 4*) dismantle, divest, strip

appointed 1. allotted, arranged, assigned,
chosen, decided, designated, determined,
established, fixed, set, settled **2.** assigned,
chosen, commissioned, delegated, elected,
installed, named, nominated, selected **3.**
commanded, decreed, directed, enjoined,
ordained **4.** equipped, fitted out, furnished,
provided, supplied

appointment 1. arrangement, assignation,
consultation, date, engagement, interview,
meeting, rendezvous, session, tryst (*Archa~
ic*) **2.** allotment, assignment, choice, choos~
ing, commissioning, delegation, designation,

election, installation, naming, nomination,
selection **3.** assignment, berth (*Inf.*), job,
office, place, position, post, situation, sta~
tion **4.** appointee, candidate, delegate,
nominee, office-holder, representative **5.**
Usually plural accoutrements, appurte~
nances, equipage, fittings, fixtures, furnish~
ings, gear, outfit, paraphernalia, trappings

apportion allocate, allot, assign, deal, dis~
pense, distribute, divide, dole out, measure
out, mete out, parcel out, ration out, share

apportionment allocation, allotment, as~
signment, dealing out, dispensing, distribu~
tion, division, doling out, measuring out,
meting out, parcelling out, rationing out,
sharing

apposite appertaining, applicable, appro~
priate, apropos, apt, befitting, fitting, ger~
mane, pertinent, proper, relevant, suitable,
suited, to the point, to the purpose
Antonyms inapplicable, inappropriate, in~
apt, irrelevant, unsuitable, unsuited

appraisal 1. assessment, estimate, estima~
tion, evaluation, judgment, opinion, recce
(*Sl.*), sizing up (*Inf.*) **2.** assay, pricing, rat~
ing, reckoning, survey, valuation

appraise assay, assess, estimate, evaluate,
eye up, gauge, inspect, judge, price, rate,
recce (*Sl.*), review, size up (*Inf.*), survey,
value

appreciable ascertainable, clear-cut, con~
siderable, definite, detectable, discernible,
distinguishable, evident, marked, material,
measurable, noticeable, obvious, perceiv~
able, perceptible, pronounced, recognizable,
significant, substantial, visible
Antonyms immaterial, imperceptible, in~
appreciable, indiscernible, indistinguishable,
insignificant, invisible, minor, minute, negli~
gible, small, trivial, undetectable, unnotice~
able, unsubstantial

appreciate 1. be appreciative, be grateful
for, be indebted, be obliged, be thankful for,
give thanks for **2.** acknowledge, be alive to,
be aware (cognizant, conscious) of, compre~
hend, estimate, know, perceive, realize,
recognize, sympathize with, take account of,
understand **3.** admire, cherish, enjoy, es~
teem, like, prize, rate highly, regard, relish,
respect, savour, treasure, value **4.** enhance,
gain, grow, improve, increase, inflate, raise
the value of, rise
Antonyms (*sense 1*) be ungrateful (*sense 2*) be
unaware, misunderstand, underrate (*sense 3*)
belittle, disdain, disparage, scorn (*sense 4*)
deflate, depreciate, devaluate, fall

appreciation 1. acknowledgment, grateful~
ness, gratitude, indebtedness, obligation,
thankfulness, thanks **2.** admiration, ap~
praisal, assessment, awareness, cognizance,
comprehension, enjoyment, esteem, estima~

tion, knowledge, liking, perception, realiza~ tion, recognition, regard, relish, respect, responsiveness, sensitivity, sympathy, understanding, valuation **3.** enhancement, gain, growth, improvement, increase, inflation, rise **4.** acclamation, criticism, critique, notice, praise, review, tribute
Antonyms (*sense 1*) ingratitude (*sense 2*) an~ tipathy, dislike, ignorance, incomprehension (*sense 3*) decline, depreciation, devaluation, fall

appreciative 1. beholden, grateful, indebt~ ed, obliged, thankful **2.** admiring, aware, cognizant, conscious, enthusiastic, in the know (*Inf.*), knowledgeable, mindful, per~ ceptive, pleased, regardful, respectful, re~ sponsive, sensitive, supportive, sympathet~ ic, understanding

apprehend 1. arrest, bust (*Inf.*), capture, catch, collar (*Inf.*), feel one's collar (*Sl.*), lift (*Sl.*), nab (*Inf.*), nail (*Inf.*), nick (*Sl., chiefly Brit.*), pinch (*Inf.*), run in (*Sl.*), seize, take, take prisoner **2.** appreciate, believe, com~ prehend, conceive, grasp, imagine, know, perceive, realize, recognize, think, under~ stand **3.** be afraid of, dread, fear
Antonyms (*sense 1*) discharge, free, let go, liberate, release (*sense 2*) be unaware of, be unconscious of, misapprehend, misconceive, miss, misunderstand

apprehension 1. alarm, anxiety, appre~ hensiveness, concern, disquiet, doubt, dread, fear, foreboding, misgiving, mistrust, premonition, suspicion, trepidation, unease, uneasiness, worry **2.** arrest, capture, catch~ ing, seizure, taking **3.** awareness, compre~ hension, grasp, intellect, intelligence, ken, knowledge, perception, understanding **4.** belief, concept, conception, conjecture, idea, impression, notion, opinion, sentiment, thought, view
Antonyms (*sense 1*) assurance, composure, confidence, nonchalance, serenity, unconcern (*sense 2*) discharge, liberation, release (*sense 3*) incomprehension

apprehensive afraid, alarmed, anxious, concerned, disquieted, doubtful, fearful, foreboding, mistrustful, nervous, suspi~ cious, twitchy (*Inf.*), uneasy, worried
Antonyms assured, at ease, composed, confident, nonchalant, unafraid

apprentice beginner, learner, neophyte, novice, probationer, pupil, student, trainee, tyro
Antonyms ace (*Inf.*), adept, dab hand (*Brit. inf.*), expert, master, past master, pro

approach *v.* **1.** advance, catch up, come close, come near, come to, draw near, gain on, meet, move towards, near, push for~ ward, reach **2.** appeal to, apply to, broach the matter with, make advances to, make a proposal to, make overtures to, sound out **3.** begin, begin work on, commence, em~ bark on, enter upon, make a start, set about, undertake **4.** approximate, be com~ parable to, be like, come close to, come near to, compare with, resemble ~*n.* **5.** access, advance, advent, arrival, avenue, coming, drawing near, entrance, nearing, passage, road, way **6.** approximation, likeness, sem~ blance **7.** *Often plural* advance, appeal, ap~ plication, invitation, offer, overture, propo~ sal, proposition **8.** attitude, course, manner, means, method, mode, modus operandi, procedure, style, technique, way

approachable 1. accessible, attainable, come at able (*Inf.*), get-at-able (*Inf.*), reach able **2.** affable, congenial, cordial, friendly, open, sociable
Antonyms (*sense 1*) inaccessible, out of reach, out-of-the-way, remote, un-get-at-able (*Inf.*), unreachable (*sense 2*) aloof, chilly, cool, distant, frigid, remote, reserved, standoffish, unfriendly, unsociable, withdrawn

approbation acceptance, acclaim, ap~ plause, approval, assent, commendation, congratulation, encouragement, endorse~ ment, favour, laudation, praise, ratification, recognition, sanction, support
Antonyms blame, censure, condemnation, disapprobation, disapproval, disfavour, dis~ like, displeasure, dissatisfaction, reproof, stricture

appropriate *adj.* **1.** adapted, applicable, apposite, appurtenant, apropos, apt, becom~ ing, befitting, belonging, congruous, correct, felicitous, fit, fitting, germane, meet (*Ar~ chaic*), opportune, pertinent, proper, rel~ evant, right, seemly, suitable, to the point, to the purpose, well-suited, well-timed ~*v.* **2.** allocate, allot, apportion, assign, devote, earmark, set apart **3.** annex, arrogate, as~ sume, commandeer, confiscate, expropriate, impound, pre-empt, seize, take, take over, take possession of, usurp **4.** embezzle, filch, misappropriate, pilfer, pocket, steal
Antonyms *adj.* improper, inappropriate, in~ compatible, incorrect, inopportune, irrel~ evant, unfitting, unsuitable, untimely ~*v.* cede, donate, give, relinquish, withhold

appropriateness applicability, apposite~ ness, aptness, becomingness, congruous~ ness, correctness, felicitousness, felicity, fitness, fittingness, germaneness, oppor~ tuneness, pertinence, properness, relevance, rightness, seemliness, suitability, timeli~ ness, well-suitedness

appropriation 1. allocation, allotment, ap~ portionment, assignment, earmarking, set~ ting apart **2.** annexation, arrogation, as~ sumption, commandeering, confiscation, expropriation, impoundment, pre-emption, seizure, takeover, taking, usurpation

approval 1. acquiescence, agreement, assent, authorization, blessing, compliance, concurrence, confirmation, consent, countenance, endorsement, imprimatur, leave, licence, mandate, O.K. *or* okay (*Inf.*), permission, ratification, recommendation, sanction, the go-ahead (*Inf.*), the green light, validation **2.** acclaim, admiration, applause, appreciation, approbation, commendation, esteem, favour, good opinion, liking, praise, regard, respect
Antonyms disapproval, dislike, disparagement, displeasure, dissatisfaction, objection

approve 1. acclaim, admire, applaud, appreciate, be pleased with, commend, esteem, favour, have a good opinion of, like, praise, regard highly, respect, think highly of **2.** accede to, accept, advocate, agree to, allow, assent to, authorize, bless, concur in, confirm, consent to, countenance, endorse, give the go-ahead (*Inf.*), give the green light, go along with, mandate, O.K. *or* okay (*Inf.*), pass, permit, ratify, recommend, sanction, second, subscribe to, uphold, validate
Antonyms (*sense 1*) blame, censure, condemn, deplore, deprecate, disapprove, dislike, find unacceptable, frown on, look down one's nose at (*Inf.*), object to, take exception to (*sense 2*) disallow, discountenance, veto

approximate *adj.* **1.** almost accurate, almost exact, close, near **2.** estimated, inexact, loose, rough **3.** analogous, close, comparable, like, near, relative, similar, verging on **4.** adjacent, bordering, close together, contiguous, near, nearby, neighbouring ~*v.* **5.** approach, border on, come close, come near, reach, resemble, touch, verge on
Antonyms *adj.* (*senses 1 & 2*) accurate, correct, definite, exact, precise, specific

approximately about, almost, around, circa (*used with dates*), close to, generally, in the neighbourhood of, in the region of, in the vicinity of, just about, loosely, more or less, nearly, not far off, relatively, roughly

approximation 1. conjecture, estimate, estimation, guess, guesswork, rough calculation, rough idea **2.** approach, correspondence, likeness, resemblance, semblance

appurtenance 1. accessory, accompaniment, adjunct, annexe, appendage, appurtenant, attachment, auxiliary, concomitant, incidental, piece of equipment, subordinate, subsidiary, supplement **2.** *Plural* accessories, accompaniments, accoutrements, appendages, equipment, impedimenta, paraphernalia, trappings

a priori 1. deduced, deductive, from cause to effect, inferential **2.** conjectural, postulated, postulational, presumptive, self-evident, suppositional, theoretical

apron pinafore, pinny (*Inf.*)

apropos *adj.* **1.** applicable, apposite, appropriate, apt, befitting, belonging, correct, fit, fitting, germane, meet (*Archaic*), opportune, pertinent, proper, related, relevant, right, seemly, suitable, to the point, to the purpose ~*adv.* **2.** appropriately, aptly, opportunely, pertinently, relevantly, suitably, timely, to the point, to the purpose **3.** by the bye, by the way, incidentally, in passing, parenthetically, while on the subject

apropos of *prep.* in respect of, on the subject of, re, regarding, respecting, with reference to, with regard to, with respect to

apt 1. applicable, apposite, appropriate, apropos, befitting, correct, fit, fitting, germane, meet (*Archaic*), pertinent, proper, relevant, seemly, suitable, timely, to the point, to the purpose **2.** disposed, given, inclined, liable, likely, of a mind, prone, ready **3.** astute, bright, clever, expert, gifted, ingenious, intelligent, prompt, quick, sharp, skilful, smart, talented, teachable
Antonyms (*sense 1*) ill-fitted, ill-suited, ill-timed, improper, inapplicable, inapposite, inappropriate, infelicitous, inopportune, irrelevant, unsuitable, untimely (*sense 3*) awkward, clumsy, dull, gauche, incompetent, inept, inexpert, maladroit, slow, stupid

aptitude 1. bent, disposition, inclination, leaning, predilection, proclivity, proneness, propensity, tendency **2.** ability, aptness, capability, capacity, cleverness, faculty, flair, gift, giftedness, intelligence, knack, proficiency, quickness, talent **3.** applicability, appositeness, appropriateness, fitness, relevance, suitability, suitableness

aptness 1. applicability, appositeness, appropriateness, becomingness, congruousness, correctness, felicitousness, felicity, fitness, fittingness, germaneness, opportuneness, pertinence, properness, relevance, rightness, seemliness, suitability, timeliness, well-suitedness **2.** aptitude, bent, disposition, inclination, leaning, liability, likelihood, likeliness, predilection, proclivity, proneness, propensity, readiness, tendency **3.** ability, capability, capacity, cleverness, faculty, fitness, flair, gift, giftedness, intelligence, knack, proficiency, quickness, suitability, talent

arable cultivable, farmable, fecund, fertile, fruitful, ploughable, productive, tillable

arbiter 1. adjudicator, arbitrator, judge, referee, umpire **2.** authority, controller, dictator, expert, governor, lord, master, pundit, ruler

arbitrariness 1. capriciousness, fancifulness, inconsistency, randomness, subjectivity, unreasonableness, whimsicality, wilfulness **2.** absoluteness, despotism, dictatorialness, dogmatism, domineeringness, high-

handedness, imperiousness, magisterial~
ness, overbearingness, peremptoriness,
summariness, tyrannicalness, tyrannous~
ness, tyranny, uncontrolledness, unlimited~
ness, unrestrainedness

arbitrary 1. capricious, chance, discretion~
ary, erratic, fanciful, inconsistent, optional,
personal, random, subjective, unreasonable,
whimsical, wilful **2.** absolute, autocratic,
despotic, dictatorial, dogmatic, domineer~
ing, high-handed, imperious, magisterial,
overbearing, peremptory, summary, tyran~
nical, tyrannous, uncontrolled, unlimited,
unrestrained
Antonyms (*sense 1*) consistent, judicious,
logical, objective, rational, reasonable, rea~
soned, sensible, sound

arbitrate adjudge, adjudicate, decide, deter~
mine, judge, mediate, pass judgment, ref~
eree, settle, sit in judgment, umpire

arbitration adjudication, arbitrament, de~
cision, determination, judgment, settlement

arbitrator adjudicator, arbiter, judge, ref~
eree, umpire

arc arch, bend, bow, crescent, curve, half-
moon

arcane cabbalistic, esoteric, hidden, mys~
terious, occult, recondite, secret

arch¹ *n.* **1.** archway, curve, dome, span,
vault **2.** arc, bend, bow, curvature, curve,
hump, semicircle ~*v.* **3.** arc, bend, bow,
bridge, curve, embow, span

arch² **1.** accomplished, chief, consummate,
expert, finished, first, foremost, greatest,
head, highest, lead, leading, main, major,
master, pre-eminent, primary, principal, top
2. artful, frolicsome, knowing, mischievous,
pert, playful, roguish, saucy, sly, waggish,
wily

archaic ancient, antiquated, antique, behind
the times, bygone, obsolete, old, olden (*Ar~
chaic*), old-fashioned, old hat, outmoded, out
of date, passé, primitive, superannuated
Antonyms contemporary, current, fresh,
latest, modern, modish, new, newfangled,
novel, present, recent, state-of-the-art, up-to-
date, up-to-the-minute, with it (*Inf.*)

arched curved, domed, embowed, vaulted

archer bowman (*Archaic*), toxophilite (*For~
mal*)

archetype classic, exemplar, form, ideal,
model, norm, original, paradigm, pattern,
prime example, prototype, standard

architect 1. designer, master builder,
planner **2.** author, contriver, creator, de~
viser, engineer, founder, instigator, inven~
tor, maker, originator, planner, prime mov~
er, shaper

architecture 1. architectonics, building,
construction, design, planning **2.** construc~

tion, design, framework, make-up, struc~
ture, style

archives 1. annals, chronicles, documents,
papers, records, registers, rolls **2.** museum,
record office, registry, repository

arctic 1. far-northern, hyperborean, polar **2.**
Inf. chilly, cold, freezing, frigid, frost-bound,
frosty, frozen, gelid, glacial, icy

ardent avid, eager, enthusiastic, fervent,
fervid, fierce, fiery, flaming, hot, hot-
blooded, impassioned, intense, keen, lusty,
passionate, spirited, vehement, warm,
warm-blooded, zealous
Antonyms apathetic, cold, cool, frigid, im~
passive, indifferent, lukewarm, unenthusias~
tic, unloving

ardour avidity, devotion, eagerness, ear~
nestness, enthusiasm, feeling, fervour,
fierceness, fire, heat, intensity, keenness,
passion, spirit, vehemence, warmth, zeal

arduous backbreaking, burdensome,
difficult, exhausting, fatiguing, formidable,
gruelling, hard, harsh, heavy, laborious,
onerous, painful, punishing, rigorous, se~
vere, steep, strenuous, taxing, tiring, toil~
some, tough, troublesome, trying
Antonyms child's play (*Inf.*), easy, easy-
peasy (*Sl.*), effortless, facile, light, no bother,
no trouble, painless, simple, undemanding

area 1. district, domain, locality, neigh~
bourhood, patch, plot, realm, region, sector,
sphere, stretch, territory, tract, turf (*U.S.
sl.*), zone **2.** ambit, breadth, compass, ex~
panse, extent, range, scope, size, width **3.**
arena, department, domain, field, province,
realm, sphere, territory **4.** part, portion,
section, sector **5.** sunken space, yard

arena 1. amphitheatre, bowl, coliseum, field,
ground, park (*U.S. & Canad.*), ring, sta~
dium, stage **2.** area, battlefield, battle~
ground, domain, field, field of conflict, lists,
province, realm, scene, scope, sector,
sphere, territory, theatre

argot cant, dialect, idiom, jargon, lingo
(*Inf.*), parlance, patois, slang, vernacular

argue 1. altercate, bandy words, bicker,
disagree, dispute, fall out (*Inf.*), feud, fight,
have an argument, quarrel, squabble,
wrangle **2.** assert, claim, contend, contro~
vert, debate, discuss, dispute, expostulate,
hold, maintain, plead, question, reason, re~
monstrate **3.** convince, persuade, prevail
upon, talk into, talk round **4.** demonstrate,
denote, display, evince, exhibit, imply, in~
dicate, manifest, point to, show, suggest

argument 1. altercation, barney (*Inf.*),
bickering, clash, controversy, difference of
opinion, disagreement, dispute, falling out
(*Inf.*), feud, fight, quarrel, row, squabble,
wrangle **2.** assertion, claim, contention, de~
bate, discussion, dispute, expostulation,

plea, pleading, questioning, remonstrance, remonstration **3.** argumentation, case, defence, dialectic, ground(s), line of reasoning, logic, polemic, reason, reasoning **4.** abstract, gist, outline, plot, story, story line, subject, summary, synopsis, theme
Antonyms (*senses 1 & 2*) accord, agreement, concurrence, rebuttal, refutation, response

argumentative 1. belligerent, combative, contentious, contrary, disputatious, litigious, opinionated, quarrelsome **2.** contentious, controversial, disputed, polemic
Antonyms (*sense 1*) accommodating, amenable, complaisant, compliant, conciliatory, easy-going, obliging

arid 1. barren, desert, dried up, dry, moistureless, parched, sterile, torrid, waterless **2.** boring, colourless, dreary, dry, dull, flat, jejune, lifeless, spiritless, tedious, uninspired, uninteresting, vapid
Antonyms (*sense 1*) fertile, fruitful, lush, rich, verdant (*sense 2*) exciting, interesting, lively, sexy (*Inf.*), spirited, stimulating, vivacious

aridity, aridness 1. barrenness, dryness, moisturelessness, parchedness, sterility, waterlessness **2.** boredom, colourlessness, dreariness, dryness, dullness, flatness, jejuneness, jejunity, lifelessness, spiritlessness, tediousness, tedium, uninspiredness, uninterestingness, vapidity, vapidness

aright accurately, appropriately, aptly, correctly, duly, exactly, fitly, in due order, justly, properly, rightly, suitably, truly, without error

arise 1. appear, begin, come into being, come to light, commence, crop up (*Inf.*), emanate, emerge, ensue, follow, happen, issue, occur, originate, proceed, result, set in, spring, start, stem **2.** get to one's feet, get up, go up, rise, stand up, wake up **3.** ascend, climb, lift, mount, move upward, rise, soar, tower

aristocracy body of nobles, elite, gentry, *haut monde*, nobility, noblesse (*Literary*), patricians, patriciate, peerage, ruling class, upper class, upper crust (*Inf.*)
Antonyms commoners, common people, hoi polloi, lower classes, masses, plebeians, plebs, proles (*Derogatory sl., chiefly Brit.*), proletariat, working classes

aristocrat aristo (*Inf.*), grandee, lady, lord, noble, nobleman, noblewoman, patrician, peer, peeress

aristocratic 1. blue-blooded, elite, gentle (*Archaic*), gentlemanly, highborn, lordly, noble, patrician, titled, upper-class, wellborn **2.** courtly, dignified, elegant, fine, haughty, polished, refined, snobbish, stylish, well-bred
Antonyms (*sense 1*) common, lower-class,

plebeian, proletarian, working-class (*sense 2*) boorish, coarse, common, crass, crude, ill-bred, uncouth, unrefined, vulgar

arm¹ *n.* **1.** appendage, limb, upper limb **2.** bough, branch, department, detachment, division, extension, offshoot, projection, section, sector **3.** branch, channel, estuary, firth, inlet, sound, strait, tributary **4.** authority, command, force, might, potency, power, strength, sway

arm² *v.* **1.** *Esp. with weapons* accoutre, array, deck out, equip, furnish, issue with, outfit, provide, rig, supply **2.** mobilize, muster forces, prepare for war, take up arms **3.** brace, equip, forearm, fortify, gird one's loins, guard, make ready, outfit, prepare, prime, protect, strengthen

armada fleet, flotilla, navy, squadron

armaments ammunition, arms, guns, materiel, munitions, ordnance, weaponry, weapons

armed accoutred, arrayed, carrying weapons, equipped, fitted out, forearmed, fortified, furnished, girded, guarded, in arms, prepared, primed, protected, provided, ready, rigged out, strengthened, supplied, under arms

armistice ceasefire, peace, suspension of hostilities, truce

armour armour plate, covering, protection, sheathing, shield

armoured armour-plated, bombproof, bulletproof, ironclad, mailed, protected, steel-plated

armoury ammunition dump, arms depot, arsenal, magazine, ordnance depot

arms 1. armaments, firearms, guns, instruments of war, ordnance, weaponry, weapons **2.** blazonry, crest, escutcheon, heraldry, insignia

army 1. armed force, host (*Archaic*), land forces, legions, military, military force, soldiers, soldiery, troops **2.** *Fig.* array, horde, host, multitude, pack, swarm, throng, vast number

aroma bouquet, fragrance, odour, perfume, redolence, savour, scent, smell

aromatic balmy, fragrant, odoriferous, perfumed, pungent, redolent, savoury, spicy, sweet-scented, sweet-smelling
Antonyms acrid, bad-smelling, fetid, foul, foul-smelling, malodorous, niffy (*Brit. sl.*), noisome, offensive, olid, rank, reeking, smelly, stinking, whiffy (*Brit. sl.*)

around *prep.* **1.** about, encircling, enclosing, encompassing, environing, on all sides of, on every side of, surrounding **2.** about, approximately, circa (*used with dates*), roughly ~*adv.* **3.** about, all over, everywhere, here and there, in all directions, on all sides, throughout, to and fro **4**. at hand, close, close at hand, close by, near, nearby, nigh (*Archaic or dialect*)

arouse agitate, animate, awaken, call forth, enliven, excite, foment, foster, goad, incite, inflame, instigate, kindle, move, prod, pro~ voke, quicken, rouse, sharpen, spark, spur, stimulate, stir up, summon up, waken, wake up, warm, whet, whip up
Antonyms allay, alleviate, assuage, calm, dampen, dull, end, lull, pacify, quell, quench, still

arrange 1. align, array, class, classify, dis~ pose, file, form, group, line up, marshal, or~ der, organize, position, put in order, range, rank, set out, sort, sort out (*Inf.*), systema~ tize, tidy **2**. adjust, agree to, come to terms, compromise, construct, contrive, determine, devise, fix up, organize, plan, prepare, proj~ ect, schedule, settle **3**. adapt, instrument, orchestrate, score
Antonyms (*senses 1 & 2*) disarrange, disor~ ganize, disturb, mess up, scatter

arrangement 1. alignment, array, classification, design, display, disposition, form, grouping, line-up, marshalling, order, ordering, organization, ranging, rank, setup (*Inf.*), structure, system **2**. *Often plural* ad~ justment, agreement, compact, compromise, construction, deal, devising, organization, plan, planning, preparation, provision, schedule, settlement, terms **3**. adaptation, instrumentation, interpretation, orchestra~ tion, score, version

arrant absolute, atrocious, blatant, complete, deep-dyed (*Usually derogatory*), downright, egregious, extreme, flagrant, gross, infa~ mous, monstrous, notorious, out-and-out, outright, rank, thorough, thoroughgoing, undisguised, unmitigated, utter, vile

array *n*. **1**. arrangement, collection, display, disposition, exhibition, formation, line-up, marshalling, muster, order, parade, show, supply **2**. *Poetic* apparel, attire, clothes, dress, finery, garb, garments, raiment (*Ar~ chaic or poetic*), regalia ~*v*. **3**. align, ar~ range, display, dispose, draw up, exhibit, form up, group, line up, marshal, muster, order, parade, place in order, range, set in line (*Military*), show **4**. accoutre, adorn, apparel (*Archaic*), attire, bedeck, caparison, clothe, deck, decorate, dress, equip, festoon, fit out, garb, get ready, outfit, robe, supply, wrap

arrest *v*. **1**. apprehend, bust (*Inf.*), capture, catch, collar (*Inf.*), detain, feel one's collar (*Sl.*), lay hold of, lift (*Sl.*), nab (*Inf.*), nail (*Inf.*), nick (*Sl., chiefly Brit.*), pinch (*Inf.*), run in (*Sl.*), seize, take, take into custody, take prisoner **2**. block, check, delay, end, halt, hinder, hold, inhibit, interrupt, ob~ struct, restrain, retard, slow, stall, stay, stop, suppress **3**. absorb, catch, engage, en~ gross, fascinate, grip, hold, intrigue, occupy ~*n*. **4**. apprehension, bust (*Inf.*), capture, cop (*Sl.*), detention, seizure **5**. blockage, check, delay, end, halt, hindrance, inhibi~ tion, interruption, obstruction, restraint, stalling, stay, stoppage, suppression
Antonyms *v*. (*sense 1*) free, let go, release, set free (*sense 2*) accelerate, encourage, precipi~ tate, promote, quicken, speed up ~*n*. (*sense 4*) freeing, release (*sense 5*) acceleration, encour~ agement, precipitation, promotion, quicken~ ing

arresting conspicuous, engaging, extraordi~ nary, impressive, noticeable, outstanding, remarkable, striking, stunning, surprising
Antonyms inconspicuous, unimpressive, unnoticeable, unremarkable

arrival 1. advent, appearance, arriving, coming, entrance, happening, occurrence, taking place **2**. arriver, caller, comer, en~ trant, incomer, newcomer, visitant, visitor

arrive 1. appear, attain, befall, come, enter, get to, happen, occur, reach, show up (*Inf.*), take place, turn up **2**. *Inf.* achieve recogni~ tion, become famous, make good, make it (*Inf.*), make the grade (*Inf.*), reach the top, succeed
Antonyms (*sense 1*) depart, disappear, exit, go, go away, leave, retire, take (one's) leave, vanish, withdraw

arrogance bluster, conceit, conceitedness, contemptuousness, disdainfulness, haughti~ ness, hauteur, high-handedness, imperious~ ness, insolence, loftiness, lordliness, over~ weeningness, pomposity, pompousness, presumption, pretension, pretentiousness, pride, scornfulness, superciliousness, swag~ ger, uppishness (*Brit. inf.*)
Antonyms bashfulness, diffidence, humil~ ity, meekness, modesty, politeness, shyness

arrogant assuming, blustering, conceited, contemptuous, disdainful, haughty, high and mighty (*Inf.*), high-handed, imperious, insolent, lordly, overbearing, overweening, pompous, presumptuous, pretentious, proud, scornful, supercilious, swaggering, uppish (*Brit. inf.*)
Antonyms bashful, deferential, diffident, humble, modest, polite, servile, shy, unas~ suming

arrogate appropriate, assume, claim undu~ ly, commandeer, demand, expropriate, pre~ sume, seize, usurp

arrogation appropriation, assumption, commandeering, demand, expropriation, presumption, seizure, usurpation

arrow 1. bolt, dart, flight, quarrel, reed (*Archaic*), shaft (*Archaic*) **2**. indicator, pointer

arsenal ammunition dump, armoury, arms depot, magazine, ordnance depot, stock, stockpile, store, storehouse, supply

art 1. adroitness, aptitude, artifice (*Archaic*), artistry, craft, craftsmanship, dexterity, expertise, facility, ingenuity, knack, knowledge, mastery, method, profession, skill, trade, virtuosity **2.** artfulness, artifice, astuteness, craftiness, cunning, deceit, duplicity, guile, trickery, wiliness

artful adept, adroit, clever, crafty, cunning, deceitful, designing, dexterous, foxy, ingenious, intriguing, masterly, politic, proficient, resourceful, scheming, sharp, shrewd, skilful, sly, smart, subtle, tricky, wily
Antonyms artless, clumsy, frank, ingenuous, open, simple, straightforward, unadept, unskilled, untalented

article 1. commodity, item, object, piece, substance, thing, unit **2.** composition, discourse, essay, feature, item, paper, piece, story, treatise **3.** branch, clause, count, detail, division, head, heading, item, matter, paragraph, part, particular, passage, piece, point, portion, section

articulate *adj.* **1.** clear, coherent, comprehensible, eloquent, expressive, fluent, intelligible, lucid, meaningful, understandable, vocal, well-spoken ~*v.* **2.** enounce, enunciate, express, pronounce, say, speak, state, talk, utter, verbalize, vocalize, voice **3.** connect, couple, fit together, hinge, join, joint
Antonyms *adj.* dumb, faltering, halting, hesitant, incoherent, incomprehensible, indistinct, mumbled, mute, poorly-spoken, silent, speechless, stammering, stuttering, tongue-tied, unclear, unintelligible, voiceless

articulation 1. delivery, diction, enunciation, expression, pronunciation, saying, speaking, statement, talking, utterance, verbalization, vocalization, voicing **2.** connection, coupling, hinge, joint, jointing, juncture

artifice 1. contrivance, device, dodge, expedient, hoax, machination, manoeuvre, ruse, stratagem, subterfuge, tactic, trick, wile **2.** artfulness, chicanery, craft, craftiness, cunning, deception, duplicity, guile, scheming, slyness, trickery **3.** adroitness, cleverness, deftness, facility, finesse, ingenuity, invention, inventiveness, skill

artificer 1. artisan, craftsman, mechanic **2.** architect, builder, contriver, creator, designer, deviser, inventor, maker, originator

artificial 1. man-made, manufactured, non-natural, plastic, synthetic **2.** bogus, counterfeit, ersatz, fake, imitation, mock, phoney *or* phony (*Inf.*), sham, simulated, specious, spurious **3.** affected, assumed,

contrived, false, feigned, forced, hollow, insincere, meretricious, phoney *or* phony (*Inf.*), pretended, spurious, unnatural
Antonyms authentic, frank, genuine, honest, natural, sincere, true, unaffected

artillery battery, big guns, cannon, cannonry, gunnery, ordnance

artisan artificer, craftsman, handicraftsman, journeyman, mechanic, skilled workman, technician

artistic aesthetic, beautiful, creative, cultivated, cultured, decorative, elegant, exquisite, graceful, imaginative, ornamental, refined, sensitive, sophisticated, stylish, tasteful
Antonyms inartistic, inelegant, tasteless, unattractive, untalented

artistry accomplishment, art, artistic ability, brilliance, craft, craftsmanship, creativity, finesse, flair, genius, mastery, proficiency, sensibility, skill, style, talent, taste, touch, virtuosity, workmanship

artless 1. candid, direct, fair, frank, genuine, guileless, honest, open, plain, sincere, straightforward, true, undesigning, upfront (*Inf.*) **2.** humble, natural, plain, pure, simple, unadorned, unaffected, uncontrived, unpretentious **3.** awkward, bungling, clumsy, crude, incompetent, inept, maladroit, primitive, rude, unskilled, untalented **4.** childlike, ingenuous, innocent, jejune, naive, trustful, trusting, unsophisticated
Antonyms (*sense 1*) artful, crafty, cunning, designing, dishonest, false, insincere (*sense 2*) affected, artificial, unnatural (*sense 3*) aesthetic, artful, artistic, crafty, cunning, sophisticated (*sense 4*) sophisticated, suspicious

as *conj.* **1.** at the time that, during the time that, just as, when, while **2.** in the manner that, in the way that, like **3.** that which, what **4.** because, considering that, seeing that, since **5.** in the same manner with, in the same way that, like **6.** for instance, like, such as ~*prep.* **7.** being, in the character of, in the role of, under the name of **8. as for** as regards, in reference to, on the subject of, with reference to, with regard to, with respect to **9. as it were** in a manner of speaking, in a way, so to say, so to speak

ascend climb, float up, fly up, go up, lift off, mount, move up, rise, scale, slope upwards, soar, take off, tower
Antonyms alight, descend, dip, drop, fall, go down, incline, move down, plummet, plunge, sink, slant, slope, subside, tumble

ascendancy, ascendency authority, command, control, dominance, domination, dominion, hegemony, influence, mastery, power, predominance, pre-eminence, prevalence, reign, rule, sovereignty, superiority, supremacy, sway, upper hand

Antonyms inferiority, servility, subjection, subordination, weakness

ascendant, ascendent *adj.* **1.** ascending, climbing, going upwards, mounting, rising **2.** authoritative, commanding, controlling, dominant, influential, powerful, predominant, pre-eminent, prevailing, ruling, superior, supreme, uppermost ~*n.* **3. in the ascendant** ascending, climbing, commanding, dominant, dominating, flourishing, growing, increasing, mounting, on the rise, on the way up, prevailing, rising, supreme, up-and-coming, uppermost, winning

ascent **1.** ascending, ascension, clambering, climb, climbing, mounting, rise, rising, scaling, upward movement **2.** acclivity, gradient, incline, ramp, rise, rising ground, upward slope

ascertain confirm, determine, discover, establish, ferret out, find out, fix, identify, learn, make certain, settle, suss (out) (*Sl.*), verify

ascetic **1.** *n.* abstainer, anchorite, hermit, monk, nun, recluse, self-denier **2.** *adj.* abstemious, abstinent, austere, celibate, frugal, harsh, plain, puritanical, rigorous, self-denying, self-disciplined, severe, Spartan, stern
Antonyms *n.* hedonist, sensualist, voluptuary ~*adj.* abandoned, comfortable, luxurious, self-indulgent, sensuous, voluptuous

asceticism abstemiousness, abstinence, austerity, celibacy, frugality, harshness, mortification of the flesh, plainness, puritanism, rigorousness, rigour, self-abnegation, self-denial, self-discipline, self-mortification

ascribe assign, attribute, charge, credit, impute, put down, refer, set down

ashamed abashed, bashful, blushing, chagrined, conscience-stricken, crestfallen, discomfited, distressed, embarrassed, guilty, humbled, humiliated, mortified, prudish, reluctant, remorseful, shamefaced, sheepish, shy, sorry
Antonyms gratified, honoured, pleased, proud, satisfied, unashamed, vain

ashen anaemic, ashy, colourless, grey, leaden, livid, pale, pallid, pasty, wan, white
Antonyms blooming, blushing, florid, flushed, glowing, radiant, red, reddish, rosy, rosy-cheeked, rubicund, ruddy

ashore aground, landwards, on dry land, on land, on the beach, on the shore, shorewards, to the shore

aside **1.** *adv.* alone, alongside, apart, away, beside, in isolation, in reserve, on one side, out of mind, out of the way, privately, separately, to one side, to the side **2.** *n.* departure, digression, excursion, excursus, interpolation, interposition, parenthesis, tangent

asinine braindead (*Inf.*), brainless, daft (*Inf.*), dunderheaded, fatuous, foolish, goofy (*Inf.*), gormless (*Brit. inf.*), halfwitted, idiotic, imbecile, imbecilic, inane, moronic, obstinate, senseless, silly, stupid, thickheaded, thick-witted
Antonyms brainy (*Inf.*), bright, clever, intelligent, quick-witted, sage, sane, sensible, sharp, smart, wise

ask **1.** inquire, interrogate, query, question, quiz **2.** appeal, apply, beg, beseech, claim, crave, demand, entreat, implore, petition, plead, pray, request, seek, solicit, sue, supplicate **3.** bid, invite, summon
Antonyms (*sense 1*) answer, reply, respond

askance **1.** awry, indirectly, obliquely, out of the corner of one's eye, sideways, with a side glance **2.** disapprovingly, distrustfully, doubtfully, dubiously, mistrustfully, sceptically, suspiciously

askew *adv./adj.* aslant, awry, cockeyed (*Inf.*), crooked, crookedly, lopsided, oblique, obliquely, off-centre, skewwhiff (*Brit. inf.*), to one side
Antonyms aligned, even, in line, level, right, square, straight, true

asleep crashed out (*Sl.*), dead to the world (*Inf.*), dormant, dozing, fast asleep, napping, sleeping, slumbering, snoozing (*Inf.*), sound asleep

aspect **1.** air, appearance, attitude, bearing, condition, countenance, demeanour, expression, look, manner, mien (*Literary*) **2.** bearing, direction, exposure, outlook, point of view, position, prospect, scene, situation, view **3.** angle, facet, feature, side

asperity acerbity, acrimony, bitterness, churlishness, crabbedness, crossness, harshness, irascibility, irritability, moroseness, peevishness, roughness, ruggedness, severity, sharpness, sourness, sullenness

asphyxiate choke, smother, stifle, strangle, strangulate, suffocate, throttle

aspirant **1.** *n.* applicant, aspirer, candidate, hopeful, postulant, seeker, suitor **2.** *adj.* ambitious, aspiring, eager, endeavouring, hopeful, longing, striving, wishful

aspiration aim, ambition, craving, desire, dream, eagerness, endeavour, goal, hankering, hope, longing, object, objective, wish, yearning

aspire aim, be ambitious, be eager, crave, desire, dream, hanker, hope, long, pursue, seek, wish, yearn

aspiring *adj.* ambitious, aspirant, eager, endeavouring, hopeful, longing, striving, wishful, would-be

ass **1.** donkey, jennet, moke (*Sl.*) **2.** airhead

(*Sl.*), berk (*Brit. sl.*), blockhead, bonehead (*Sl.*), charlie (*Brit. inf.*), coot, daftie (*Inf.*), dickhead (*Sl.*), dipstick (*Brit. sl.*), divvy (*Brit. sl.*), dolt, dope (*Inf.*), dork (*Sl.*), dunce, dweeb (*U.S. sl.*), fool, fuckwit (*Taboo sl.*), geek (*Sl.*), gonzo (*Sl.*), halfwit, idiot, jackass, jerk (*Sl., chiefly U.S. & Canad.*), nerd *or* nurd (*Sl.*), nincompoop, ninny, nitwit (*Inf.*), numskull *or* numbskull, oaf, pillock (*Brit. sl.*), plank (*Brit. sl.*), plonker (*Sl.*), prat (*Sl.*), prick (*Derogatory sl.*), schmuck (*U.S. sl.*), simpleton, twerp *or* twirp (*Inf.*), twit (*Inf., chiefly Brit.*), wally (*Sl.*)

assail 1. assault, attack, belabour, beset, charge, encounter, fall upon, invade, lay into (*Inf.*), maltreat, set about, set upon **2.** abuse, berate, blast, criticize, impugn, lambast(e), malign, put down, revile, tear into (*Inf.*), vilify

assailant aggressor, assailer, assaulter, attacker, invader

assassin eliminator (*Sl.*), executioner, hatchet man (*Sl.*), hit man (*Sl.*), killer, liquidator, murderer, slayer

assassinate blow away (*Sl., chiefly U.S.*), eliminate (*Sl.*), hit (*Sl.*), kill, liquidate, murder, slay, take out (*Sl.*)

assault 1. *n.* aggression, attack, charge, incursion, inroad, invasion, offensive, onset, onslaught, storm, storming, strike **2.** *v.* assail, attack, belabour, beset, charge, fall upon, invade, lay into (*Inf.*), set about, set upon, storm, strike at
Antonyms *n.* defence, protection, resistance ~*v.* defend, protect, resist

assay *v.* **1.** analyse, appraise, assess, evaluate, examine, inspect, investigate, prove, test, try, weigh ~*n.* **2.** *Archaic* attempt, endeavour, essay, stab (*Inf.*), try, venture **3.** analysis, examination, inspection, investigation, test, trial

assemble 1. accumulate, amass, bring together, call together, collect, come together, congregate, convene, convoke, flock, forgather, gather, marshal, meet, muster, rally, round up, summon **2.** build up, connect, construct, erect, fabricate, fit together, join, make, manufacture, piece together, put together, set up
Antonyms adjourn, break up (*Inf.*), disassemble, disband, dismiss, disperse, distribute, divide, scatter, take apart

assembly 1. accumulation, aggregation, assemblage, body, collection, company, conclave, conference, congregation, congress, convocation, council, crowd, diet, flock, gathering, group, house, mass, meeting, multitude, rally, synod, throng **2.** building up, connecting, construction, erection, fabrication, fitting together, joining,

manufacture, piecing together, putting together, setting up

assent 1. *v.* accede, accept, acquiesce, agree, allow, approve, comply, concur, consent, fall in with, go along with, grant, permit, sanction, subscribe **2.** *n.* acceptance, accession, accord, acquiescence, agreement, approval, compliance, concurrence, consent, permission, sanction
Antonyms *v.* deny, differ, disagree, dissent, object, protest, rebut, reject, retract ~*n.* denial, disagreement, disapproval, dissension, dissent, objection, refusal

assert 1. affirm, allege, asseverate, attest, aver, avouch (*Archaic*), avow, contend, declare, maintain, predicate, profess, pronounce, state, swear **2.** claim, defend, insist upon, press, put forward, stand up for, stress, uphold, vindicate **3. assert oneself** exert one's influence, make one's presence felt, put oneself forward
Antonyms (*senses 1 & 2*) deny, disavow, disclaim, rebut, refute, retract

assertion 1. affirmation, allegation, asseveration, attestation, avowal, contention, declaration, predication, profession, pronouncement, statement **2.** defence, insistence, maintenance, stressing, vindication

assertive aggressive, confident, decided, decisive, demanding, dogmatic, domineering, emphatic, feisty (*Inf., chiefly U.S. & Canad.*), firm, forceful, forward, insistent, overbearing, positive, pushy (*Inf.*), self-assured, strong willed
Antonyms backward, bashful, diffident, hesitant, insecure, meek, modest, reserved, retiring, self-conscious, self-effacing, sheepish, shrinking, shy, timid, timorous, unassertive, unobtrusive

assess 1. appraise, compute, determine, estimate, evaluate, eye up, fix, gauge, judge, rate, size up (*Inf.*), value, weigh **2.** demand, evaluate, fix, impose, levy, rate, tax, value

assessment 1. appraisal, computation, determination, estimate, estimation, evaluation, judgment, rating, valuation **2.** charge, demand, duty, evaluation, fee, impost, levy, rate, rating, tariff, tax, taxation, toll, valuation

asset 1. advantage, aid, benefit, blessing, boon, help, resource, service **2.** *Plural* capital, estate, funds, goods, holdings, means, money, possessions, property, reserves, resources, valuables, wealth
Antonyms (*sense 1*) burden, disadvantage, drag, drawback, encumbrance, handicap, hindrance, impediment, liability, millstone, minus (*Inf.*), nuisance

assiduous attentive, constant, diligent, hard-working, indefatigable, industrious, laborious, persevering, persistent, sedulous,

steady, studious, unflagging, untiring, un~
wearied
Antonyms careless, idle, inattentive, indo~
lent, lax, lazy, negligent, slack

assign 1. appoint, choose, delegate, desig~
nate, name, nominate, select **2.** allocate, al~
lot, apportion, consign, distribute, give, give
out, grant, make over **3.** appoint, appropri~
ate, determine, fix, set apart, stipulate **4.**
accredit, ascribe, attribute, put down

assignation 1. clandestine meeting, illicit
meeting, rendezvous, secret meeting, tryst
(*Archaic*) **2.** allocation, allotment, appoint~
ment, apportionment, appropriation, as~
cription, assignment, attribution, choice,
consignment, delegation, designation, de~
termination, distribution, giving, grant,
nomination, selection, specification, stipu~
lation

assignment 1. appointment, charge, com~
mission, duty, job, mission, position, post,
responsibility, task **2.** allocation, allotment,
appointment, apportionment, appropriation,
ascription, assignation (*Law, chiefly Scot.*),
attribution, choice, consignment, delega~
tion, designation, determination, distribu~
tion, giving, grant, nomination, selection,
specification, stipulation

assimilate 1. absorb, digest, imbibe (*Liter~
ary*), incorporate, ingest, learn, take in **2.**
acclimatize, accommodate, acculturate, ac~
custom, adapt, adjust, become like, become
similar, blend in, conform, fit, homogenize,
intermix, mingle

assist abet, aid, back, benefit, boost, col~
laborate, cooperate, encourage, expedite, fa~
cilitate, further, help, promote, reinforce,
relieve, second, serve, succour, support,
sustain, work for, work with
Antonyms frustrate, hamper, handicap,
hinder, hold back, hold up, impede, obstruct,
resist, thwart, work against

assistance abetment, aid, backing, benefit,
boost, collaboration, cooperation, encour~
agement, furtherance, help, helping hand,
promotion, reinforcement, relief, service,
succour, support, sustenance
Antonyms hindrance, obstruction, opposi~
tion, resistance

assistant abettor, accessory, accomplice,
aide, aider, ally, associate, auxiliary, back~
er, coadjutor (*Rare*), collaborator, colleague,
confederate, cooperator, helper, helpmate,
henchman, partner, protagonist, right-hand
man, second, supporter

associate *v.* **1.** affiliate, ally, combine, con~
federate, conjoin, connect, correlate, couple,
identify, join, league, link, lump together,
mix, pair, relate, think of together, unite,
yoke **2.** accompany, befriend, be friends,
consort, fraternize, hang about, hang out

(*Inf.*), hobnob, mingle, mix, run around
(*Inf.*) ~*n.* **3.** ally, collaborator, colleague,
companion, compeer, comrade, confederate,
confrère, co-worker, follower, friend, mate,
partner
Antonyms (*sense 1*) detach, disconnect, dis~
sociate, distance, distinguish, divorce, isolate,
segregate, separate, set apart (*sense 2*) avoid,
be alienated, be estranged, break off, part
company

association 1. affiliation, alliance, band,
clique, club, coalition, combine, company,
confederacy, confederation, cooperative,
corporation, federation, fraternity, group,
league, order, organization, partnership,
society, syndicate, union **2.** affinity, com~
panionship, comradeship, familiarity, fel~
lowship, fraternization, friendship, intima~
cy, liaison, partnership, relations, relation~
ship **3.** blend, bond, combination, concomi~
tance, connection, correlation, identi~
fication, joining, juxtaposition, linkage,
linking, lumping together, mixing, mixture,
pairing, relation, tie, union, yoking

assort arrange, array, categorize, classify,
dispose, distribute, file, grade, group, range,
rank, sort, type

assorted 1. different, diverse, diversified,
heterogeneous, manifold, miscellaneous,
mixed, motley, sundry, varied, variegated,
various **2.** arranged, arrayed, categorized,
classified, disposed, filed, graded, grouped,
ranged, ranked, sorted, typed
Antonyms (*sense 1*) alike, homogeneous,
identical, like, same, similar, uniform, un~
varied

assortment 1. array, choice, collection,
diversity, farrago, hotchpotch, jumble,
medley, *mélange*, miscellany, mishmash,
mixed bag (*Inf.*), mixture, potpourri, salma~
gundi, selection, variety **2.** arrangement,
categorizing, classification, disposition, dis~
tribution, filing, grading, grouping, ranging,
ranking, sorting, typing

assuage 1. allay, alleviate, calm, ease, less~
en, lighten, mitigate, moderate, palliate,
quench, relieve, soothe, temper **2.** appease,
calm, lull, mollify, pacify, quiet, relax, sat~
isfy, soften, soothe, still, tranquillize
Antonyms (*sense 1*) aggravate, exacerbate,
heighten, increase, intensify, worsen (*sense 2*)
aggravate, embitter, enrage, infuriate, mad~
den, provoke

assume 1. accept, believe, expect, fancy,
guess (*Inf., chiefly U.S. & Canad.*), imagine,
infer, presume, presuppose, suppose, sur~
mise, suspect, take for granted, think **2.**
adopt, affect, counterfeit, feign, imitate, im~
personate, mimic, pretend to, put on, sham,
simulate **3.** accept, acquire, attend to, be~
gin, don, embark upon, embrace, enter

upon, put on, set about, shoulder, take on, take over, take responsibility for, take up, undertake **4.** acquire, appropriate, arrogate, commandeer, expropriate, pre-empt, seize, take, take over, usurp
Antonyms (*sense 1*) know, prove (*senses 3 & 4*) give up, hand over, leave, put aside, relin~ quish

assumed 1. affected, bogus, counterfeit, fake, false, feigned, fictitious, imitation, made-up, make-believe, phoney *or* phony (*Inf.*), pretended, pseudonymous, sham, simulated, spurious **2.** accepted, expected, hypothetical, presumed, presupposed, sup~ posed, surmised, taken for granted **3.** ap~ propriated, arrogated, pre-empted, seized, usurped
Antonyms (*senses 1 & 2*) actual, authentic, known, natural, positive, real, stated, true

assuming *adj.* arrogant, bold, conceited, disdainful, domineering, egotistic, forward, haughty, imperious, overbearing, presump~ tuous, pushy (*Inf.*), rude

assumption 1. acceptance, belief, conjec~ ture, expectation, fancy, guess, hypothesis, inference, postulate, postulation, premise, premiss, presumption, presupposition, sup~ position, surmise, suspicion, theory **2.** ac~ ceptance, acquisition, adoption, embracing, entering upon, putting on, shouldering, takeover, taking on, taking up, undertaking **3.** acquisition, appropriation, arrogation, expropriation, pre-empting, seizure, take~ over, taking, usurpation **4.** arrogance, con~ ceit, imperiousness, presumption, pride, self-importance

assurance 1. affirmation, assertion, decla~ ration, guarantee, oath, pledge, profession, promise, protestation, vow, word, word of honour **2.** assertiveness, assuredness, bold~ ness, certainty, certitude, confidence, con~ viction, coolness, courage, faith, firmness, nerve, poise, positiveness, security, self-confidence, self-reliance, sureness **3.** arro~ gance, brass neck (*Brit. inf.*), chutzpah (*U.S. & Canad. inf.*), effrontery, gall (*Inf.*), impu~ dence, neck (*Inf.*), nerve (*Inf.*), presumption
Antonyms (*sense 1*) falsehood, lie (*sense 2*) apprehension, diffidence, distrust, doubt, self-doubt, self-effacement, shyness, timidity, uncertainty

assure 1. comfort, convince, embolden, en~ courage, hearten, persuade, reassure, soothe **2.** affirm, attest, certify, confirm, declare confidently, give one's word to, guarantee, pledge, promise, swear, vow **3.** clinch, complete, confirm, ensure, guarantee, make certain, make sure, seal, secure

assured 1. beyond doubt, clinched, confirmed, dependable, ensured, fixed, guaranteed, indubitable, irrefutable, made

certain, sealed, secure, settled, sure, un~ questionable **2.** assertive, audacious, bold, brazen, certain, complacent, confident, overconfident, poised, positive, pushy (*Inf.*), self-assured, self-confident, self-possessed, sure of oneself
Antonyms (*sense 1*) ambiguous, doubtful, indefinite, questionable, uncertain, unconfirmed, unsettled, unsure (*sense 2*) bashful, diffident, hesitant, retiring, self-conscious, self-effacing, timid

astonish amaze, astound, bewilder, con~ found, daze, dumbfound, flabbergast (*Inf.*), stagger, stun, stupefy, surprise

astonishing amazing, astounding, bewil~ dering, breathtaking, brilliant, impressive, sensational (*Inf.*), staggering, striking, stunning, stupefying, surprising, wondrous (*Archaic or literary*)
Antonyms anticipated, expected, foreseen

astonishment amazement, awe, bewilder~ ment, confusion, consternation, stupefac~ tion, surprise, wonder, wonderment

astound amaze, astonish, bewilder, con~ found, daze, dumbfound, flabbergast (*Inf.*), overwhelm, stagger, stun, stupefy, surprise

astounding amazing, astonishing, bewil~ dering, breathtaking, brilliant, impressive, sensational (*Inf.*), staggering, striking, stunning, stupefying, surprising, wondrous (*Archaic or literary*)

astray *adj./adv.* **1.** adrift, afield, amiss, lost, off, off course, off the mark, off the right track, off the subject **2.** into error, into sin, to the bad, wrong

astronaut cosmonaut, spaceman, space pi~ lot, space traveller, spacewoman

astute adroit, artful, bright, calculating, canny, clever, crafty, cunning, discerning, foxy, insightful, intelligent, keen, knowing, penetrating, perceptive, politic, sagacious, sharp, shrewd, sly, subtle, wily
Antonyms dull, ingenuous, naive, slow, straightforward, stupid, unintelligent, un~ knowing

astuteness acumen, adroitness, artfulness, brightness, canniness, cleverness, crafti~ ness, cunning, discernment, foxiness, in~ sight, intelligence, keenness, knowledge, penetration, perceptiveness, sagacity, sharpness, shrewdness, slyness, smarts (*Sl., chiefly U.S.*), subtlety, suss (*Sl.*), wiliness

asylum 1. harbour, haven, preserve, refuge, retreat, safety, sanctuary, shelter **2.** *Old-fashioned* funny farm (*Facetious*), hospital, institution, laughing academy (*U.S. sl.*), loony bin (*Sl.*), madhouse (*Inf.*), mental hospital, nuthouse (*Sl.*), psychiatric hospi~ tal, rubber room (*U.S. sl.*)

atheism disbelief, freethinking, godlessness,

heathenism, infidelity, irreligion, nonbelief, paganism, scepticism, unbelief

atheist disbeliever, freethinker, heathen, infidel, irreligionist, nonbeliever, pagan, sceptic, unbeliever

athlete competitor, contender, contestant, games player, gymnast, player, runner, sportsman, sportswoman

athletic 1. *adj.* able-bodied, active, brawny, energetic, fit, herculean, husky (*Inf.*), lusty, muscular, powerful, robust, sinewy, strap~ping, strong, sturdy, vigorous, well-proportioned **2.** *pl. n..* contests, exercises, games of strength, gymnastics, races, sports, track and field events
Antonyms (*sense 1*) delicate, feeble, frail, puny, sickly, weedy (*Inf.*)

atmosphere 1. aerosphere, air, heavens, sky **2.** air, ambience, aura, character, cli~mate, environment, feel, feeling, flavour, mood, quality, spirit, surroundings, tone, vibes (*Sl.*)

atom bit, crumb, dot, fragment, grain, iota, jot, mite, molecule, morsel, mote, particle, scintilla (*Rare*), scrap, shred, speck, spot, tittle, trace, whit

atone 1. *With* **for** answer for, compensate, do penance for, make amends for, make re~dress, make reparation for, make up for, pay for, recompense, redress **2.** appease, expiate, make expiation for, propitiate, rec~oncile, redeem

atonement amends, compensation, expia~tion, payment, penance, propitiation, rec~ompense, redress, reparation, restitution, satisfaction

atrocious 1. barbaric, brutal, cruel, dia~bolical, fiendish, flagrant, godawful (*Sl.*), heinous, hellacious (*U.S. sl.*), infamous, in~fernal, inhuman, monstrous, nefarious, ruthless, savage, vicious, villainous, wicked **2.** appalling, detestable, execrable, grievous, horrible, horrifying, shocking, terrible
Antonyms admirable, civilized, fine, gener~ous, gentle, good, honourable, humane, kind, merciful, tasteful

atrocity 1. abomination, act of savagery, barbarity, brutality, crime, cruelty, enor~mity, evil, horror, monstrosity, outrage, villainy **2.** atrociousness, barbarity, barba~rousness, brutality, cruelty, enormity, fiendishness, grievousness, heinousness, horror, infamy, inhumanity, monstrous~ness, nefariousness, ruthlessness, savagery, shockingness, viciousness, villainousness, wickedness

attach 1. add, adhere, affix, annex, append, bind, connect, couple, fasten, fix, join, link, make fast, secure, stick, subjoin, tie, unite **2.** accompany, affiliate, associate, become associated with, combine, enlist, join, join

forces with, latch on to, sign on with, sign up with, unite with **3.** ascribe, assign, as~sociate, attribute, connect, impute, invest with, lay, place, put **4.** allocate, allot, ap~point, assign, consign, designate, detail, earmark, second, send
Antonyms detach, disconnect, dissociate, loosen, remove, retire, separate, untie, with~draw

attached 1. affectionate towards, devoted, fond of, full of regard for, possessive **2.** ac~companied, engaged, married, partnered, spoken for

attachment 1. adapter, bond, clamp, con~nection, connector, coupling, fastener, fas~tening, joint, junction, link, tie **2.** affection, affinity, attraction, bond, devotion, fidelity, fondness, friendship, liking, love, loyalty, partiality, possessiveness, predilection, re~gard, tenderness **3.** accessory, accoutre~ment, adapter, addition, add-on, adjunct, appendage, appurtenance, auxiliary, exten~sion, extra, fitting, fixture, supplement, supplementary part
Antonyms (*sense 2*) animosity, antipathy, aversion, disinclination, distaste, hatred, hostility, loathing

attack *n.* **1.** aggression, assault, charge, for~ay, incursion, inroad, invasion, offensive, onset, onslaught, raid, rush, strike **2.** abuse, blame, calumny, censure, character assassination, criticism, denigration, im~pugnment, stick (*Sl.*), vilification **3.** access, bout, convulsion, fit, paroxysm, seizure, spasm, spell, stroke ~*v.* **4.** assail, assault, charge, fall upon, invade, lay into (*Inf.*), raid, rush, set about, set upon, storm, strike (at) **5.** abuse, berate, blame, blast, censure, criticize, excoriate, impugn, lambast(e), malign, put down, revile, tear into (*Inf.*), vilify
Antonyms *n.* defence, retreat, support, vin~dication, withdrawal ~*v.* defend, guard, pro~tect, retreat, support, sustain, vindicate, withdraw

attacker aggressor, assailant, assaulter, in~truder, invader, raider

attain accomplish, achieve, acquire, arrive at, bring off, complete, earn, effect, fulfil, gain, get, grasp, obtain, procure, reach, re~alize, reap, score (*Sl.*), secure, win

attainable accessible, accomplishable, achievable, at hand, feasible, gettable, graspable, likely, obtainable, possible, po~tential, practicable, probable, procurable, reachable, realizable, within reach
Antonyms impossible, impracticable, im~probable, inaccessible, out of reach, unattain~able, unfeasible, unlikely, unobtainable, un~procurable, unreachable

attainment 1. accomplishment, achieve~

ment, acquirement, acquisition, arrival at, completion, feat, fulfilment, gaining, getting, obtaining, procurement, reaching, realiza~ tion, reaping, winning **2.** ability, accom~ plishment, achievement, art, capability, competence, gift, mastery, proficiency, skill, talent

attempt 1. *n.* assault, attack, bid, crack (*Inf.*), effort, endeavour, essay, experiment, go (*Inf.*), shot (*Inf.*), stab (*Inf.*), trial, try, undertaking, venture **2.** *v.* endeavour, es~ say, experiment, have a crack (go (*Inf.*), shot (*Inf.*), stab (*Inf.*)) *Inf.*, seek, strive, tackle, take on, try, try one's hand at, undertake, venture

attend 1. appear, be at, be here, be present, be there, frequent, go to, haunt, make one (*Archaic*), put in an appearance, show one~ self, show up (*Inf.*), turn up, visit **2.** care for, look after, mind, minister to, nurse, take care of, tend **3.** follow, hear, hearken (*Archaic*), heed, listen, look on, mark, mind, note, notice, observe, pay attention, pay heed, regard, take to heart, watch **4.** ac~ company, arise from, be associated with, be connected with, be consequent on, follow, go hand in hand with, issue from, occur with, result from **5.** *With* **to** apply oneself to, concentrate on, devote oneself to, get to work on, look after, occupy oneself with, see to, take care of **6.** accompany, chaper~ on, companion, convoy, escort, guard, squire, usher **7.** be in the service of, serve, wait upon, work for
Antonyms (*sense 1*) be absent, miss, play truant (*sense 2*) neglect (*senses 3 & 5*) discount, disregard, ignore, neglect (*sense 4*) dissociate

attendance 1. appearance, attending, be~ ing there, presence **2.** audience, crowd, gate, house, number present, turnout

attendant 1. *n.* aide, assistant, auxiliary, chaperon, companion, custodian, escort, flunky, follower, guard, guide, helper, lack~ ey, menial, servant, steward, underling, usher, waiter **2.** *adj.* accessory, accompa~ nying, associated, concomitant, consequent, related

attention 1. concentration, consideration, contemplation, deliberation, heed, heedful~ ness, intentness, mind, scrutiny, thinking, thought, thoughtfulness **2.** awareness, con~ sciousness, consideration, notice, observa~ tion, recognition, regard **3.** care, concern, looking after, ministration, treatment **4.** *Often plural* assiduities, care, civility, com~ pliment, consideration, courtesy, deference, gallantry, mindfulness, politeness, regard, respect, service
Antonyms carelessness, discourtesy, disre~ gard, disrespect, distraction, impoliteness, inattention, laxity, laxness, negligence, thoughtlessness, unconcern

attentive 1. alert, awake, careful, concen~ trating, heedful, intent, listening, mindful, observant, regardful, studious, watchful **2.** accommodating, civil, conscientious, con~ siderate, courteous, devoted, gallant, gra~ cious, kind, obliging, polite, respectful, thoughtful
Antonyms absent-minded, careless, dis~ tracted, dreamy, heedless, inattentive, ne~ glectful, negligent, preoccupied, remiss, thoughtless, unheeding, unmindful

attest adjure, affirm, assert, authenticate, aver, bear out, bear witness, certify, confirm, corroborate, declare, demonstrate, display, evince, exhibit, give evidence, in~ voke, manifest, prove, ratify, seal, show, substantiate, swear, testify, verify, vouch for, warrant, witness
Antonyms contradict, controvert, deny, disprove, gainsay (*Archaic or literary*), give the lie to, prove false, rebut, refute

attic *n.* garret, loft

attire 1. *n.* accoutrements, apparel, array (*Poetic*), clothes, clothing, costume, dress, garb, garments, gear (*Inf.*), habiliments, habit, outfit, raiment (*Archaic or poetic*), robes, uniform, vestment, wear **2.** *v.* accou~ tre, apparel (*Archaic*), array, clothe, cos~ tume, deck out, dress, equip, fit out, garb, get ready, rig out, robe, turn out

attitude 1. approach, disposition, frame of mind, mood, opinion, outlook, perspective, point of view, position, posture, stance, standing, view **2.** air, aspect, bearing, car~ riage, condition, demeanour, manner, mien (*Literary*), pose, position, posture, stance

attract allure, appeal to, bewitch, captivate, charm, decoy, draw, enchant, endear, enga~ ge, entice, fascinate, incline, induce, inter~ est, invite, lure, pull (*Inf.*), tempt
Antonyms disgust, give one the creeps (*Inf.*), put one off, repel, repulse, revolt, turn one off (*Inf.*)

attraction allure, appeal, attractiveness, bait, captivation, charm, come-on (*Inf.*), draw, enchantment, endearment, entice~ ment, fascination, inducement, interest, in~ vitation, lure, magnetism, pull (*Inf.*), temp~ tation, temptingness

attractive agreeable, alluring, appealing, beautiful, captivating, charming, comely, engaging, enticing, fair, fascinating, fetch~ ing, glamorous, good-looking, gorgeous, handsome, interesting, inviting, likable *or* likeable, lovely, magnetic, pleasant, pleas~ ing, prepossessing, pretty, seductive, tempt~ ing, winning, winsome
Antonyms disagreeable, displeasing, dis~ tasteful, offensive, repulsive, ugly, unappeal~ ing, unbecoming, uninviting, unlikable *or* unlikeable, unpleasant, unsightly

attribute 1. *v.* apply, ascribe, assign, blame, charge, credit, impute, lay at the door of, put down to, refer, set down to, trace to **2.** *n.* aspect, character, characteristic, facet, feature, idiosyncrasy, indication, mark, note, peculiarity, point, property, quality, quirk, sign, symbol, trait, virtue

attrition 1. abrasion, chafing, erosion, friction, grinding, rubbing, scraping, wear, wearing away, wearing down **2.** attenuation, debilitation, harassment, harrying, thinning out, weakening, wearing down

attune acclimatize, accord, accustom, adapt, adjust, coordinate, familiarize, harmonize, modulate, regulate, set, tune

auburn chestnut-coloured, copper-coloured, henna, nutbrown, reddish-brown, russet, rust-coloured, tawny, Titian red

audacious 1. adventurous, bold, brave, courageous, daredevil, daring, dauntless, death-defying, enterprising, fearless, intrepid, rash, reckless, risky, valiant, venturesome **2.** assuming, brazen, cheeky, defiant, disrespectful, forward, fresh (*Inf.*), impertinent, impudent, insolent, pert, presumptuous, rude, sassy (*U.S. inf.*), shameless

Antonyms (*sense 1*) careful, cautious, cowardly, frightened, guarded, prudent, timid, unadventurous, unenterprising (*sense 2*) deferential, gracious, tactful, unassuming

audacity 1. adventurousness, audaciousness, boldness, bravery, courage, daring, dauntlessness, enterprise, fearlessness, front, guts (*Inf.*), intrepidity, nerve, rashness, recklessness, valour, venturesomeness **2.** audaciousness, brass neck (*Brit. inf.*), cheek, chutzpah (*U.S. & Canad. inf.*), defiance, disrespectfulness, effrontery, forwardness, gall (*Inf.*), impertinence, impudence, insolence, neck (*Inf.*), nerve, pertness, presumption, rudeness, shamelessness

audible clear, detectable, discernible, distinct, hearable, perceptible

Antonyms faint, imperceptible, inaudible, indistinct, low, out of earshot

audience 1. assemblage, assembly, congregation, crowd, gallery, gathering, house, listeners, onlookers, spectators, turnout, viewers **2.** devotees, fans, following, market, public **3.** consultation, hearing, interview, meeting, reception

audit *Accounting* **1.** *n.* balancing, check, checking, examination, inspection, investigation, review, scrutiny, verification **2.** *v.* balance, check, examine, go over, go through, inspect, investigate, review, scrutinize, verify

au fait abreast of, *au courant*, clued-up (*Inf.*), conversant, expert, familiar, fully informed, in the know, in touch, knowledgeable, on the ball (*Inf.*), well-acquainted, well up

augment add to, amplify, boost, build up, dilate, enhance, enlarge, expand, extend, grow, heighten, increase, inflate, intensify, magnify, multiply, raise, reinforce, strengthen, swell

Antonyms contract, curtail, cut down, decrease, diminish, lessen, lower, reduce, shrink

augmentation accession, addition, amplification, boost, build-up, dilation, enhancement, enlargement, expansion, extension, growth, heightening, increase, inflation, intensification, magnification, multiplication, reinforcement, rise, strengthening, swelling

augur 1. *n.* auspex, diviner, haruspex, oracle, prophet, seer, soothsayer **2.** *v.* be an omen of, bespeak (*Archaic*), betoken, bode, foreshadow, harbinger, herald, portend, predict, prefigure, presage, promise, prophesy, signify

augury 1. divination, prediction, prophecy, soothsaying, sortilege **2.** auspice, forerunner, forewarning, harbinger, herald, omen, portent, precursor, presage, prognostication, promise, prophecy, sign, token, warning

august dignified, exalted, glorious, grand, high-ranking, imposing, impressive, kingly, lofty, magnificent, majestic, monumental, noble, regal, solemn, stately, superb

aura air, ambience, aroma, atmosphere, emanation, feel, feeling, mood, odour, quality, scent, suggestion, tone, vibes (*Sl.*), vibrations (*Sl.*)

auspice *n.* **1.** *Usually plural* advocacy, aegis, authority, backing, care, championship, charge, control, countenance, guidance, influence, patronage, protection, sponsorship, supervision, support **2.** augury, indication, omen, portent, prognostication, prophecy, sign, token, warning

auspicious bright, encouraging, favourable, felicitous, fortunate, happy, hopeful, lucky, opportune, promising, propitious, prosperous, rosy, timely

Antonyms bad, black, discouraging, ill-omened, inauspicious, infelicitous, ominous, unfavourable, unfortunate, unlucky, unpromising, unpropitious

austere 1. cold, exacting, forbidding, formal, grave, grim, hard, harsh, inflexible, rigorous, serious, severe, solemn, stern, stiff, strict, stringent, unfeeling, unrelenting **2.** abstemious, abstinent, ascetic, chaste, continent, economical, exacting, puritanical, rigid, self-denying, self-disciplined, sober, solemn, Spartan, strait-laced, strict, unrelenting **3.** bleak, economical, harsh,

plain, severe, simple, spare, Spartan, stark, subdued, unadorned, unornamented
Antonyms abandoned, affable, cheerful, comfortable, convivial, flexible, free-and-easy, genial, immoral, indulgent, jovial, kindly, loose, luxurious, permissive, sweet

austerity 1. coldness, exactingness, forbid~ dingness, formality, gravity, grimness, hardness, harshness, inflexibility, rigour, seriousness, severity, solemnity, sternness, stiffness, strictness **2.** abstemiousness, ab~ stinence, asceticism, chasteness, chastity, continence, economy, exactingness, puri~ tanism, rigidity, self-denial, self-discipline, sobriety, solemnity, Spartanism, strictness **3.** economy, plainness, severity, simplicity, spareness, Spartanism, starkness

authentic accurate, actual, authoritative, bona fide, certain, dependable, factual, faithful, genuine, legitimate, original, pure, real, reliable, simon-pure (*Rare*), true, true-to-life, trustworthy, valid, veritable
Antonyms counterfeit, fake, false, fictitious, fraudulent, hypothetical, imitation, mislead~ ing, mock, spurious, supposed, synthetic, un~ faithful, unreal, untrue

authenticate attest, authorize, avouch, certify, confirm, endorse, guarantee, vali~ date, verify, vouch for, warrant
Antonyms annul, invalidate, render null and void

authenticity accuracy, actuality, authori~ tativeness, certainty, dependability, factu~ alness, faithfulness, genuineness, legitima~ cy, purity, realness, reliability, trust~ worthiness, truth, truthfulness, validity, veritableness, verity

author architect, composer, creator, design~ er, doer, fabricator, father, founder, framer, initiator, inventor, maker, mover, origina~ tor, parent, planner, prime mover, produc~ er, writer

authoritarian 1. *adj.* absolute, autocratic, despotic, dictatorial, disciplinarian, doctri~ naire, dogmatic, domineering, harsh, im~ perious, rigid, severe, strict, tyrannical, unyielding **2.** *n.* absolutist, autocrat, despot, dictator, disciplinarian, tyrant
Antonyms *adj.* broad-minded, democratic, flexible, indulgent, lenient, liberal, permis~ sive, tolerant

authoritative 1. accurate, authentic, definitive, dependable, factual, faithful, learned, reliable, scholarly, sound, true, trustworthy, truthful, valid, veritable **2.** assertive, autocratic, commanding, confident, decisive, dictatorial, dogmatic, dominating, imperative, imperious, impos~ ing, lordly, masterly, peremptory, self-assured **3.** approved, authorized, com~

manding, legitimate, official, sanctioned, sovereign
Antonyms (*sense 1*) deceptive, undepend~ able, unreliable (*sense 2*) humble, subservient, timid, weak (*sense 3*) unauthorized, unofficial, unsanctioned

authority 1. ascendancy, charge, command, control, direction, domination, dominion, force, government, influence, jurisdiction, might, power, prerogative, right, rule, say-so, strength, supremacy, sway, weight **2. the authorities** administration, govern~ ment, management, officialdom, police, powers that be, the establishment **3.** authorization, justification, licence, permis~ sion, permit, sanction, say-so, warrant **4.** arbiter, bible, connoisseur, expert, judge, master, professional, scholar, specialist, textbook **5.** attestation, avowal, declaration, evidence, profession, say-so, statement, tes~ timony, word

authorization 1. ability, authority, power, right, say-so, strength **2.** approval, creden~ tials, leave, licence, permission, permit, sanction, say-so, warrant

authorize 1. accredit, commission, empow~ er, enable, entitle, give authority **2.** accred~ it, allow, approve, confirm, countenance, give authority for, give leave, license, per~ mit, ratify, sanction, vouch for, warrant
Antonyms ban, debar, disallow, exclude, forbid, outlaw, preclude, prohibit, proscribe, rule out, veto

autocracy absolutism, despotism, dictator~ ship, tyranny

autocrat absolutist, despot, dictator, tyrant

autocratic absolute, all-powerful, despotic, dictatorial, domineering, imperious, tyran~ nical, tyrannous, unlimited

automatic 1. automated, mechanical, mechanized, push-button, robot, self-acting, self-activating, self-moving, self-propelling, self-regulating **2.** habitual, kneejerk, me~ chanical, perfunctory, routine, unconscious **3.** instinctive, instinctual, involuntary, me~ chanical, natural, reflex, spontaneous, un~ conscious, unwilled **4.** assured, certain, in~ escapable, inevitable, necessary, routine, unavoidable
Antonyms (*sense 1*) done by hand, hand-operated, human, manual, physical (*senses 2 & 3*) conscious, deliberate, intentional, volun~ tary

autonomous free, independent, self-determining, self-governing, self-ruling, sovereign

autonomy freedom, home rule, independ~ ence, self-determination, self-government, self-rule, sovereignty
Antonyms dependency, foreign rule, sub~ jection

autopsy dissection, necropsy, postmortem, postmortem examination

auxiliary 1. *adj.* accessory, aiding, ancil~ lary, assisting, back-up, emergency, fall~ back, helping, reserve, secondary, subsidi~ ary, substitute, supplementary, supporting **2.** *n.* accessory, accomplice, ally, assistant, associate, companion, confederate, helper, henchman, partner, protagonist, reserve, subordinate, supporter
Antonyms *adj.* cardinal, chief, essential, first, leading, main, primary, prime, principal

available accessible, applicable, at hand, at one's disposal, attainable, convenient, free, handy, obtainable, on hand, on tap, ready, ready for use, to hand, vacant
Antonyms busy, engaged, inaccessible, in use, occupied, spoken for, taken, unattain~ able, unavailable, unobtainable

avalanche 1. landslide, landslip, snow- slide, snow-slip **2.** barrage, deluge, flood, inundation, torrent

avant-garde *adj.* experimental, far-out (*Sl.*), ground-breaking, innovative, innova~ tory, pioneering, progressive, unconven~ tional, way-out (*Inf.*)
Antonyms conservative, conventional, hidebound, reactionary, traditional

avarice acquisitiveness, close-fistedness, covetousness, cupidity, graspingness, greed, greediness, meanness, miserliness, niggard~ liness, parsimony, penny-pinching, penuri~ ousness, rapacity, stinginess
Antonyms benevolence, bountifulness, ex~ travagance, generosity, largess *or* largesse, liberality, unselfishness

avaricious acquisitive, close-fisted, covet~ ous, grasping, greedy, mean, miserable, mi~ serly, niggardly, parsimonious, penny- pinching, penurious, rapacious, stingy, tight-arsed (*Taboo sl.*), tight as a duck's arse (*Taboo sl.*), tight-assed (*U.S. taboo sl.*)

avenge even the score for, get even for (*Inf.*), hit back, punish, repay, requite, re~ taliate, revenge, take satisfaction for, take vengeance

avenue access, alley, approach, boulevard, channel, course, drive, driveway, entrance, entry, pass, passage, path, pathway, road, route, street, thoroughfare, way

aver affirm, allege, assert, asseverate, avouch, avow, declare, maintain, proclaim, profess, pronounce, protest, say, state, swear

average *n.* **1.** common run, mean, medium, midpoint, norm, normal, par, rule, run, run of the mill, standard **2. on average** as a rule, for the most part, generally, normally, typically, usually ~*adj.* **3.** banal, common, commonplace, fair, general, indifferent, mediocre, middling, moderate, normal, not bad, ordinary, passable, regular, run-of- the-mill, so-so (*Inf.*), standard, tolerable, typical, undistinguished, unexceptional, usual **4.** intermediate, mean, median, me~ dium, middle ~*v.* **5.** balance out to, be on average, do on average, even out to, make on average
Antonyms *adj.* abnormal, awful, bad, differ~ ent, exceptional, great, maximum, memo~ rable, minimum, notable, outstanding, re~ markable, special, terrible, unusual

averse antipathetic, backward, disinclined, hostile, ill-disposed, indisposed, inimical, loath, opposed, reluctant, unfavourable, un~ willing
Antonyms agreeable, amenable, disposed, eager, favourable, inclined, keen, sympathet~ ic, willing

aversion abhorrence, animosity, antipathy, detestation, disgust, disinclination, dislike, distaste, hate, hatred, horror, hostility, in~ disposition, loathing, odium, opposition, re~ luctance, repugnance, repulsion, revulsion, unwillingness
Antonyms desire, inclination, liking, love, willingness

avert 1. turn, turn aside, turn away **2.** avoid, fend off, forestall, frustrate, preclude, prevent, stave off, ward off

aviation aeronautics, flight, flying, powered flight

aviator aeronaut, airman, flier, pilot

avid 1. ardent, devoted, eager, enthusiastic, fanatical, fervent, intense, keen, passionate, zealous **2.** acquisitive, athirst, avaricious, covetous, grasping, greedy, hungry, insa~ tiable, rapacious, ravenous, thirsty, vora~ cious
Antonyms (*sense 1*) apathetic, impassive, indifferent, lukewarm, unenthusiastic

avidity 1. ardour, devotion, eagerness, en~ thusiasm, fervour, keenness, zeal **2.** ac~ quisitiveness, avarice, covetousness, cupid~ ity, desire, graspingness, greediness, hank~ ering, hunger, insatiability, longing, rapac~ ity, ravenousness, thirst, voracity

avocation 1. diversion, hobby, occupation, pastime, recreation **2.** business, calling, employment, job, occupation, profession, pursuit, trade, vocation, work

avoid avert, body-swerve (*Scot.*), bypass, circumvent, dodge, duck (out of) (*Inf.*), elude, escape, eschew, evade, fight shy of, keep aloof from, keep away from, prevent, refrain from, shirk, shun, sidestep, steer clear of
Antonyms approach, confront, contact, face, find, invite, pursue, seek out, solicit

avoidance body swerve (*Scot.*), circumven~ tion, dodging, eluding, escape, eschewal, evasion, keeping away from, prevention, refraining, shirking, shunning, steering clear of

avowed acknowledged, admitted, confessed, declared, open, professed, self-proclaimed, sworn

await 1. abide, anticipate, expect, look for, look forward to, stay for, wait for **2.** attend, be in readiness for, be in store for, be pre~ pared for, be ready for, wait for

awake v. **1.** awaken, rouse, wake, wake up **2.** activate, alert, animate, arouse, awaken, call forth, enliven, excite, fan, incite, kin~ dle, provoke, revive, stimulate, stir up, vivify ~adj. **3.** alert, alive, aroused, atten~ tive, awakened, aware, conscious, heedful, not sleeping, observant, on guard, on the alert, on the lookout, vigilant, wakeful, waking, watchful, wide-awake
Antonyms adj. asleep, crashed out (Sl.), dead to the world (Inf.), dormant, dozing, in~ attentive, napping, sleeping, unaware, un~ conscious

awaken activate, alert, animate, arouse, awake, call forth, enliven, excite, fan, in~ cite, kindle, provoke, revive, rouse, stimu~ late, stir up, vivify, wake

awakening n. activation, animating, arousal, awaking, birth, enlivening, incite~ ment, kindling, provocation, revival, rous~ ing, stimulation, stirring up, vivification, waking, waking up

award v. **1.** accord, adjudge, allot, appor~ tion, assign, bestow, confer, decree, distrib~ ute, endow, gift, give, grant, hand out, pre~ sent, render ~n. **2.** adjudication, allotment, bestowal, conferment, conferral, decision, decree, endowment, gift, hand-out, order, presentation, stipend **3.** decoration, gift, grant, prize, trophy, verdict

aware acquainted, alive to, appreciative, apprised, attentive, au courant, clued-up (Inf.), cognizant, conscious, conversant, en~ lightened, familiar, hip (Sl.), informed, knowing, knowledgeable, mindful, sensible, sentient, wise (Sl.)
Antonyms ignorant, insensible, oblivious, unaware, unfamiliar with, unknowledgeable

awareness acquaintance, appreciation, at~ tention, cognizance, consciousness, enlight~ enment, familiarity, knowledge, mindful~ ness, perception, realization, recognition, sensibility, sentience, understanding

away adv. **1.** abroad, elsewhere, from here, from home, hence, off **2.** apart, at a dis~ tance, far, remote **3.** aside, out of the way, to one side **4.** continuously, incessantly, interminably, relentlessly, repeatedly, uninterruptedly, unremittingly ~adj. **5.** abroad, absent, elsewhere, gone, not at home, not here, not present, not there, out ~interj. **6.** beat it (Sl.), begone, be off, bug~

ger off (Taboo sl.), fuck off (Offens. taboo sl.), get lost (Inf.), get out, go, go away, on your bike (Sl.), on your way

awe 1. n. admiration, amazement, astonish~ ment, dread, fear, horror, respect, rever~ ence, terror, veneration, wonder **2.** v. amaze, astonish, cow, daunt, frighten, hor~ rify, impress, intimidate, stun, terrify
Antonyms n. arrogance, boldness, con~ tempt, disrespect, fearlessness, irreverence, scorn

awe-inspiring amazing, astonishing, awe~ some, breathtaking, daunting, fearsome, impressive, intimidating, magnificent, striking, stunning (Inf.), wonderful, won~ drous (Archaic or literary)
Antonyms bland, boring, dull, flat, hum~ drum, insipid, prosaic, tame, tedious, unim~ pressive, uninspiring, vapid

awesome alarming, amazing, astonishing, awe-inspiring, awful, breathtaking, daunt~ ing, dreadful, fearful, fearsome, formidable, frightening, horrible, horrifying, imposing, impressive, intimidating, magnificent, ma~ jestic, overwhelming, redoubtable, shock~ ing, solemn, striking, stunning, stupefying, terrible, terrifying, wonderful, wondrous (Archaic or literary)

awe-stricken,   awe-struck   afraid, amazed, astonished, awed, awe-inspired, cowed, daunted, dumbfounded, fearful, frightened, horrified, impressed, intimidat~ ed, shocked, struck dumb, stunned, terrified, wonder-stricken, wonder-struck

awful 1. abysmal, alarming, appalling, de~ plorable, dire, distressing, dreadful, fearful, frightful, ghastly, godawful (Sl.), gruesome, harrowing, hellacious (U.S. sl.), hideous, horrendous, horrible, horrid, horrific, hor~ rifying, nasty, shocking, terrible, tremen~ dous, ugly, unpleasant, unsightly **2.** Archaic amazing, awe-inspiring, awesome, dread, fearsome, majestic, portentous, solemn
Antonyms (sense 1) amazing, brilliant, ex~ cellent, fabulous (Inf.), fantastic, great (Inf.), magnificent, marvellous, miraculous, sensa~ tional (Inf.), smashing (Inf.), super (Inf.), su~ perb, terrific, tremendous, wonderful

awfully 1. badly, disgracefully, disrepu~ tably, dreadfully, inadequately, reprehen~ sibly, shoddily, unforgivably, unpleasantly, wickedly, woefully, wretchedly **2.** Inf. bad~ ly, dreadfully, exceedingly, exceptionally, excessively, extremely, greatly, immensely, quite, terribly, very, very much

awhile briefly, for a little while, for a mo~ ment, for a short time, for a while

awkward 1. all thumbs, artless, blunder~ ing, bungling, clownish, clumsy, coarse, gauche, gawky, graceless, ham-fisted, ham-handed, ill-bred, inelegant, inept, inexpert,

lumbering, maladroit, oafish, rude, skill-
less, stiff, uncoordinated, uncouth, ungainly, ungraceful, unpolished, unrefined, unskilful, unskilled **2.** cumbersome, difficult,
inconvenient, troublesome, unhandy, unmanageable, unwieldy **3.** compromising,
cringe-making (*Brit. inf.*), delicate, difficult,
embarrassed, embarrassing, ill at ease, inconvenient, inopportune, painful, perplexing, sticky (*Inf.*), thorny, ticklish, troublesome, trying, uncomfortable, unpleasant,
untimely **4.** annoying, bloody-minded (*Brit.
inf.*), difficult, disobliging, exasperating,
hard to handle, intractable, irritable, perverse, prickly, stubborn, touchy, troublesome, trying, uncooperative, unhelpful, unpredictable, vexatious, vexing **5.** chancy
(*Inf.*), dangerous, difficult, hazardous, perilous, risky
Antonyms (*sense 1*) adept, adroit, dexterous,
graceful, skilful (*sense 2*) convenient, easy,
handy (*sense 3*) comfortable, pleasant

awkwardness 1. artlessness, clownish-
ness, clumsiness, coarseness, gaucheness,
gaucherie, gawkiness, gracelessness, ill-
breeding, inelegance, ineptness, inexpertness, maladroitness, oafishness, rudeness,
skill-lessness, stiffness, uncoordination, uncouthness, ungainliness, unskilfulness,
unskilledness **2.** cumbersomeness, difficulty, inconvenience, troublesomeness, unhandiness, unmanageability, unwieldiness
3. delicacy, difficulty, discomfort, embarrassment, inconvenience, inopportuneness,
painfulness, perplexingness, stickiness
(*Inf.*), thorniness, ticklishness, unpleasantness, untimeliness **4.** bloody-mindedness

(*Brit. inf.*), difficulty, disobligingness, intractability, irritability, perversity, prickliness, stubbornness, touchiness, uncooperativeness, unhelpfulness, unpredictability
5. chanciness (*Inf.*), danger, difficulty,
hazardousness, peril, perilousness, risk,
riskiness

axe *n.* **1.** adze, chopper, hatchet **2. an axe
to grind** grievance, personal consideration,
pet subject, private ends, private purpose,
ulterior motive **3. the axe** *Inf.* cancellation,
cutback, discharge, dismissal, termination,
the boot (*Sl.*), the chop (*Sl.*), the (old)
heave-ho (*Inf.*), the order of the boot (*Sl.*),
the sack (*Inf.*), wind-up ~*v.* **4.** chop, cut
down, fell, hew **5.** *Inf.* cancel, cut back, discharge, dismiss, dispense with, eliminate,
fire (*Inf.*), get rid of, oust, relegate, remove,
sack (*Inf.*), terminate, throw out, turn off
(*Inf.*), wind up

axiom adage, aphorism, apophthegm, dictum, fundamental, gnome, maxim, postulate, precept, principle, truism

axiomatic 1. absolute, accepted, apodictic,
assumed, certain, fundamental, given,
granted, indubitable, manifest, presupposed,
self-evident, understood, unquestioned **2.**
aphoristic, apophthegmatic, epigrammatic,
gnomic, pithy, terse

axis 1. axle, centre line, pivot, shaft, spindle
2. alliance, bloc, coalition, compact, entente, league, pact

axle arbor, axis, mandrel, pin, pivot, rod,
shaft, spindle

azure blue, cerulean, clear blue, sky-blue,
sky-coloured, ultramarine

B

babble 1. v. blab, burble, cackle, chatter, gabble, gibber, gurgle, jabber, mumble, murmur, mutter, prate, prattle, rabbit (on) (*Brit. inf.*), run off at the mouth (*Sl.*), waffle (*Inf., chiefly Brit.*) **2.** n. burble, clamour, drivel, gabble, gibberish, murmur, waffle (*Inf., chiefly Brit.*)

babe 1. ankle-biter (*Aust. sl.*), baby, bairn (*Scot.*), child, infant, nursling, rug rat (*Sl.*), sprog (*Sl.*), suckling **2.** babe in arms, ingénue, innocent

baby 1. n. ankle-biter (*Aust. sl.*), babe, bairn (*Scot.*), child, infant, newborn child, rug rat (*Sl.*), sprog (*Sl.*) **2.** adj. diminutive, dwarf, little, midget, mini, miniature, minute, pygmy *or* pigmy, small, teensy-weensy, teeny-weeny, tiny, wee **3.** v. coddle, cosset, humour, indulge, mollycoddle, overindulge, pamper, pet, spoil, spoon-feed

babyish baby, childish, foolish, immature, infantile, juvenile, namby-pamby, puerile, silly, sissy, soft (*Inf.*), spoiled
Antonyms adult, grown-up, mature, of age

bacchanal 1. carouser, debauchee, drunkard, reveller, roisterer, winebibber **2.** debauch, debauchery, orgy, revel, revelry

back v. **1.** abet, advocate, assist, champion, countenance, encourage, endorse, espouse, favour, finance, promote, sanction, second, side with, sponsor, subsidize, support, sustain, underwrite **2.** backtrack, go back, move back, regress, retire, retreat, reverse, turn tail, withdraw ~n. **3.** backside, end, far end, hind part, hindquarters, posterior, rear, reverse, stern, tail end ~adj. **4.** end, hind, hindmost, posterior, rear, tail **5.** *From an earlier time* delayed, earlier, elapsed, former, overdue, past, previous **6.** behind one's back covertly, deceitfully, secretly, sneakily, surreptitiously
Antonyms v. (*sense 1*) attack, combat, hinder, thwart, undermine, weaken (*sense 2*) advance, approach, move forward, progress ~n. face, fore, front, head ~adj. advance, fore, front, future, late

backbiting abuse, aspersion, bitchiness (*Sl.*), calumniation, calumny, cattiness (*Inf.*), defamation, denigration, detraction, disparagement, gossip, malice, scandalmongering, slander, spite, spitefulness, vilification, vituperation

backbone 1. *Medical* spinal column, spine, vertebrae, vertebral column **2.** bottle (*Brit. sl.*), character, courage, determination, firmness, fortitude, grit, hardihood, mettle, moral fibre, nerve, pluck, resolution, resolve, stamina, steadfastness, strength of character, tenacity, toughness, will, willpower **3.** basis, foundation, mainstay, support

backbreaking arduous, crushing, exhausting, gruelling, hard, killing, laborious, punishing, strenuous, toilsome, wearing, wearying

back down accede, admit defeat, backpedal, concede, give in, surrender, withdraw, yield

backer advocate, angel (*Inf.*), benefactor, patron, promoter, second, sponsor, subscriber, supporter, underwriter, well-wisher

backfire boomerang, disappoint, fail, flop (*Inf.*), miscarry, rebound, recoil

background breeding, circumstances, credentials, culture, education, environment, experience, grounding, history, milieu, preparation, qualifications, tradition, upbringing

backhanded ambiguous, double-edged, equivocal, indirect, ironic, oblique, sarcastic, sardonic, two-edged

backing abetment, accompaniment, advocacy, aid, assistance, championing, encouragement, endorsement, espousal, funds, grant, moral support, patronage, promotion, sanction, seconding, sponsorship, subsidy, support

backlash backfire, boomerang, counteraction, counterblast, kickback, reaction, recoil, repercussion, resentment, resistance, response, retaliation, retroaction

backlog accumulation, build-up, excess, hoard, reserve, reserves, resources, stock, supply

back out abandon, cancel, chicken out (*Inf.*), cop out (*Sl.*), give up, go back on, recant, renege, resign, retreat, withdraw

backslide fall from grace, go astray, go wrong, lapse, regress, relapse, renege, retrogress, revert, sin, slip, stray, weaken

backslider apostate, deserter, recidivist, recreant, renegade, reneger, turncoat

back up aid, assist, bolster, confirm, corroborate, reinforce, second, stand by, substantiate, support

backward adj. **1.** bashful, diffident, hesitating, late, reluctant, shy, sluggish, tardy, unwilling, wavering **2.** behind, behindhand, braindead (*Inf.*), dense, dozy (*Brit. inf.*), dull, obtuse, retarded, slow, stupid, subnor~

mal, underdeveloped, undeveloped ~*adv.* **3.** aback, behind, in reverse, rearward
Antonyms *adj.* advanced, ahead, bold, brash, eager, forward, pushy (*Inf.*), willing ~*adv.* correctly, forward, frontward, properly

backwoods 1. *adj.* agrestic, hick (*Inf., chiefly U.S. & Canad.*), isolated, remote, rustic, uncouth **2.** *n.* back of beyond, mid~ dle of nowhere, outback, sticks (*Inf.*)

bacteria bacilli, bugs (*Sl.*), germs, microbes, microorganisms, pathogens, viruses

bad 1. chickenshit (*U.S. sl.*), defective, deficient, duff (*Brit. inf.*), erroneous, falla~ cious, faulty, imperfect, inadequate, incor~ rect, inferior, of a sort *or* of sorts, pathetic, poor, poxy (*Sl.*), substandard, unsatisfactory **2.** damaging, dangerous, deleterious, detri~ mental, harmful, hurtful, injurious, ruin~ ous, unhealthy **3.** base, corrupt, criminal, delinquent, evil, immoral, mean, sinful, vile, villainous, wicked, wrong **4.** disobedi~ ent, mischievous, naughty, unruly **5.** de~ cayed, mouldy, off, putrid, rancid, rotten, sour, spoiled **6.** disastrous, distressing, grave, harsh, painful, serious, severe, terri~ ble **7.** ailing, diseased, ill, sick, unwell **8.** apologetic, conscience-stricken, contrite, guilty, regretful, remorseful, sad, sorry, upset **9.** adverse, discouraged, discouraging, distressed, distressing, gloomy, grim, mel~ ancholy, troubled, troubling, unfortunate, unpleasant **10. not bad** all right, average, fair, fair to middling (*Inf.*), moderate (*O.K. or okay*), (*Inf.*), passable, respectable, so-so (*Inf.*), tolerable
Antonyms (*sense 1*) adequate, fair, satisfac~ tory (*sense 2*) agreeable, beneficial, good, healthful, safe, sound, wholesome (*sense 3*) ethical, fine, first-rate, good, moral, righteous, virtuous (*sense 4*) biddable, docile, good, obedient, well-behaved

bad blood acrimony, anger, animosity, an~ tagonism, dislike, enmity, feud, hatred, ill feeling, ill will, malevolence, malice, ran~ cour, resentment

badge brand, device, emblem, identification, insignia, mark, sign, stamp, token

badger bend someone's ear (*Inf.*), bully, chivvy, goad, harass, harry, hound, impor~ tune, nag, pester, plague, torment

badinage banter, chaff, drollery, mockery, persiflage, pleasantry, raillery, repartee, teasing, waggery, wordplay

badly 1. carelessly, defectively, erroneously, faultily, imperfectly, inadequately, incor~ rectly, ineptly, poorly, shoddily, wrong, wrongly **2.** unfavourably, unfortunately, unsuccessfully **3.** criminally, evilly, im~ morally, improperly, naughtily, shamefully, unethically, wickedly **4.** acutely, deeply, desperately, exceedingly, extremely, grave~

ly, greatly, intensely, painfully, seriously, severely
Antonyms ably, competently, correctly, ethically, morally, properly, righteously, rightly, satisfactorily, splendidly, well

bad manners boorishness, churlishness, coarseness, discourtesy, disrespect, impo~ liteness, incivility, inconsideration, indeli~ cacy, rudeness, unmannerliness
Antonyms civility, cordiality, courteous~ ness, courtesy, good manners, graciousness, politeness, urbanity

baffle 1. amaze, astound, bewilder, con~ found, confuse, daze, disconcert, dumb~ found, elude, flummox, mystify, nonplus, perplex, puzzle, stump, stun **2.** balk, check, defeat, foil, frustrate, hinder, thwart, upset
Antonyms (*sense 1*) clarify, clear up, eluci~ date, explain, explicate, interpret, make plain, shed *or* throw light upon, spell out

bag *v.* **1.** balloon, bulge, droop, sag, swell **2.** acquire, capture, catch, gain, get, kill, land, shoot, take, trap

baggage accoutrements, bags, belongings, equipment, gear, impedimenta, luggage, paraphernalia, suitcases, things

baggy billowing, bulging, droopy, floppy, ill-fitting, loose, oversize, roomy, sagging, seated, slack
Antonyms close, close-fitting, constricted, cramped, narrow, snug, stretched, taut, tight, tight-fitting

bail[1] *n.* bond, guarantee, guaranty, pledge, security, surety, warranty

bail[2] **, bale** *v.* dip, drain off, ladle, scoop

bail out, bale out 1. aid, help, relieve, rescue **2.** escape, quit, retreat, withdraw

bait *n.* **1.** allurement, attraction, bribe, de~ coy, enticement, inducement, lure, snare, temptation ~*v.* **2.** aggravate (*Inf.*), annoy, be on one's back (*Sl.*), bother, gall, get in one's hair (*Inf.*), get on one's nerves (*Inf.*), harass, hassle (*Inf.*), hound, irk, irritate, nark (*Brit., Aust., & N.Z. sl.*), needle (*Inf.*), persecute, piss one off (*Taboo sl.*), provoke, tease, torment, wind up (*Brit. sl.*) **3.** allure, beguile, entice, lure, seduce, tempt

baked arid, desiccated, dry, parched, scorched, seared, sun-baked, torrid

balance *v.* **1.** level, match, parallel, poise, stabilize, steady **2.** adjust, compensate for, counteract, counterbalance, counterpoise, equalize, equate, make up for, neutralize, offset **3.** assess, compare, consider, deliber~ ate, estimate, evaluate, weigh **4.** calculate, compute, settle, square, tally, total ~*n.* **5.** correspondence, equilibrium, equipoise, equity, equivalence, evenness, parity, sym~ metry **6.** composure, equanimity, poise, self-control, self-possession, stability,

steadiness **7.** difference, remainder, resi~
due, rest, surplus
Antonyms v. outweigh, overbalance, upset
~n. disproportion, instability, shakiness, un~
balance, uncertainty

balanced disinterested, equitable, even~
handed, fair, impartial, just, unbiased, un~
prejudiced
Antonyms biased, distorted, jaundiced, lop~
sided, one-sided, partial, predisposed, preju~
diced, slanted, unfair, warped, weighted

balance sheet account, budget, credits
and debits, ledger, report, statement

balcony 1. terrace, veranda **2.** gallery,
gods, upper circle

bald 1. baldheaded, baldpated, depilated,
glabrous (*Biol.*), hairless **2.** barren, bleak,
exposed, naked, stark, treeless, uncovered
3. bare, blunt, direct, downright, forthright,
outright, plain, severe, simple, straight,
straightforward, unadorned, unvarnished,
upfront (*Inf.*)

balderdash balls (*Taboo sl.*), bilge (*Inf.*),
bosh (*Inf.*), bull (*Sl.*), bullshit (*Taboo sl.*),
bunk (*Inf.*), bunkum or buncombe (*Chiefly
U.S.*), claptrap (*Inf.*), cobblers (*Brit. taboo
sl.*), crap (*Sl.*), drivel, eyewash (*Inf.*), gar~
bage (*Inf.*), gibberish, guff (*Sl.*), hogwash,
hokum (*Sl., chiefly U.S. & Canad.*),
horsefeathers (*U.S. sl.*), hot air (*Inf.*), moon~
shine, nonsense, pap, piffle (*Inf.*), poppycock
(*Inf.*), rot, rubbish, shit (*Taboo sl.*), tommy~
rot, tosh (*Sl., chiefly Brit.*), trash, tripe
(*Inf.*), twaddle

baldness 1. alopecia (*Pathology*),
baldheadedness, baldpatedness, glabrous~
ness (*Biol.*), hairlessness **2.** barrenness,
bleakness, nakedness, sparseness, stark~
ness, treelessness **3.** austerity, bluntness,
plainness, severity, simplicity, spareness

bale *see* BAIL[2]

baleful calamitous, deadly, evil, harmful,
hurtful, injurious, maleficent, malevolent,
malignant, menacing, mournful, noxious,
ominous, pernicious, ruinous, sad, sinister,
venomous, woeful
Antonyms beneficial, benevolent, benign,
friendly, good, healthy, salubrious

bale out *see* BAIL OUT

balk 1. demur, dodge, evade, flinch, hesitate,
jib, recoil, refuse, resist, shirk, shrink from
2. baffle, bar, check, counteract, defeat, dis~
concert, foil, forestall, frustrate, hinder, ob~
struct, prevent, thwart
Antonyms (*sense 1*) accede, accept, acqui~
esce, comply, relent, submit, yield (*sense 2*)
abet, advance, aid, assist, further, help, pro~
mote, support, sustain

balky intractable, obstinate, stubborn, unco~

operative, unmanageable, unpredictable,
unruly

ball 1. drop, globe, globule, orb, pellet,
sphere, spheroid **2.** ammunition, bullet,
grapeshot, pellet, shot, slug

ballast balance, counterbalance, counter~
weight, equilibrium, sandbag, stability, sta~
bilizer, weight

balloon v. belly, billow, bloat, blow up, di~
late, distend, enlarge, expand, inflate, puff
out, swell

ballot election, poll, polling, vote, voting

ballyhoo 1. babble, commotion, fuss, hub~
bub, hue and cry, hullabaloo, noise, racket,
to-do **2.** advertising, build-up, hype, promo~
tion, propaganda, publicity

balm 1. balsam, cream, embrocation, emol~
lient, lotion, ointment, salve, unguent **2.**
anodyne, comfort, consolation, curative,
palliative, restorative, solace

balmy 1. clement, mild, pleasant, summery,
temperate **2.** *Also* **barmy** crackpot (*Inf.*),
crazy, daft (*Inf.*), foolish, goofy (*Inf.*), idiotic,
insane, loony (*Sl.*), loopy (*Inf.*), nuts (*Sl.*),
nutty (*Sl.*), odd, off one's trolley (*Sl.*), out to
lunch (*Inf.*), silly, stupid, up the pole (*Inf.*)
Antonyms (*sense 1*) annoying, discomfort~
ing, harsh, inclement, intense, irksome,
rough, stormy

bamboozle 1. cheat, con (*Inf.*), deceive,
defraud, delude, dupe, fool, hoax, hoodwink,
skin (*Sl.*), swindle, trick **2.** baffle, befuddle,
confound, confuse, mystify, perplex, puzzle,
stump

ban 1. v. banish, bar, black, blackball, block,
boycott, debar, disallow, disqualify, exclude,
forbid, interdict, outlaw, prohibit, pro~
scribe, restrict, suppress **2.** n. block, boy~
cott, censorship, embargo, interdict, inter~
diction, prohibition, proscription, restric~
tion, stoppage, suppression, taboo
Antonyms v. allow, approve, authorize, let,
permit, sanction ~n. allowance, approval,
permission, sanction

banal clichéd, cliché-ridden, commonplace,
everyday, hackneyed, humdrum, mundane,
old hat, ordinary, pedestrian, platitudinous,
stale, stereotyped, stock, threadbare, tired,
trite, unimaginative, unoriginal, vapid
Antonyms challenging, distinctive, fresh,
imaginative, interesting, new, novel, original,
stimulating, unique, unusual

banality bromide (*Inf.*), cliché, common~
place, platitude, triteness, trite phrase,
triviality, truism, vapidity

band[1] n. bandage, belt, binding, bond, chain,
cord, fetter, fillet, ligature, manacle, ribbon,
shackle, strap, strip, tie

band[2] n. **1.** assembly, association, bevy,
body, camp, clique, club, company, coterie,

crew (*Inf.*), gang, horde, party, posse (*Inf.*), society, troop **2.** combo, ensemble, group, orchestra ~*v.* **3.** affiliate, ally, consolidate, federate, gather, group, join, merge, unite
Antonyms *v.* cleave, disperse, disunite, divide, part, segregate, separate, split, sunder

bandage 1. *n.* compress, dressing, gauze, plaster **2.** *v.* bind, cover, dress, swathe

bandit brigand, crook, desperado, footpad, freebooter, gangster, gunman, highwayman, hijacker, marauder, outlaw, pirate, racketeer, robber, thief

bandy 1. *v.* barter, exchange, interchange, pass, shuffle, swap, throw, toss, trade **2.** *adj.* bandy-legged, bent, bowed, bow-legged, crooked, curved

bane affliction, *bête noire*, blight, burden, calamity, curse, despair, destruction, disaster, downfall, misery, nuisance, pest, plague, ruin, scourge, torment, trial, trouble, woe
Antonyms blessing, comfort, consolation, joy, pleasure, relief, solace, support

baneful baleful, calamitous, deadly, deleterious, destructive, disastrous, fatal, harmful, hurtful, injurious, maleficent, noxious, pernicious, pestilential, ruinous, venomous

bang *n.* **1.** boom, burst, clang, clap, clash, detonation, explosion, peal, pop, report, shot, slam, thud, thump **2.** belt (*Inf.*), blow, box, bump, cuff, hit, knock, punch, smack, stroke, wallop (*Inf.*), whack ~*v.* **3.** bash (*Inf.*), beat, belt (*Inf.*), bump, clatter, crash, hammer, knock, pound, pummel, rap, slam, strike, thump **4.** boom, burst, clang, detonate, drum, echo, explode, peal, resound, thump, thunder ~*adv.* **5.** abruptly, hard, headlong, noisily, precisely, slap, smack, straight, suddenly

banish 1. deport, drive away, eject, evict, exclude, excommunicate, exile, expatriate, expel, ostracize, outlaw, shut out, transport **2.** ban, cast out, discard, dislodge, dismiss, dispel, eliminate, eradicate, get rid of, oust, remove, shake off
Antonyms accept, admit, embrace, hail, invite, offer hospitality to, receive, welcome

banishment deportation, exile, expatriation, expulsion, proscription, transportation

banisters balusters, balustrade, handrail, rail, railing

bank¹ 1. *n.* accumulation, depository, fund, hoard, repository, reserve, reservoir, savings, stock, stockpile, store, storehouse **2.** *v.* deal with, deposit, keep, save, transact business with

bank² ** *n.* **1. banking, embankment, heap, mass, mound, pile, ridge **2.** brink, edge, margin, shore, side ~*v.* **3.** amass, heap,

mass, mound, pile, stack **4.** camber, cant, heel, incline, pitch, slant, slope, tilt, tip

**bank³ ** *n.* array, file, group, line, rank, row, sequence, series, succession, tier, train

bank on assume, believe in, count on, depend on, lean on, look to, rely on, trust

bankrupt broke (*Inf.*), depleted, destitute, exhausted, failed, impoverished, insolvent, lacking, ruined, spent
Antonyms in the money (*Inf.*), on the up and up, prosperous, solvent, sound, wealthy

bankruptcy disaster, exhaustion, failure, indebtedness, insolvency, lack, liquidation, ruin

banner banderole, burgee, colours, ensign, fanion, flag, gonfalon, pennant, pennon, standard, streamer

banquet dinner, feast, meal, repast, revel, treat

banter 1. *v.* chaff, deride, jeer, jest, joke, josh (*Sl., chiefly U.S. & Canad.*), kid (*Inf.*), make fun of, rib (*Inf.*), ridicule, taunt, tease, twit **2.** *n.* badinage, chaff, chaffing, derision, jeering, jesting, joking, kidding (*Inf.*), mockery, persiflage, pleasantry, raillery, repartee, ribbing (*Inf.*), ridicule, wordplay

baptism 1. christening, immersion, purification, sprinkling **2.** beginning, debut, dedication, initiation, introduction, launching, rite of passage

baptize 1. besprinkle, cleanse, immerse, purify **2.** admit, enrol, initiate, recruit **3.** call, christen, dub, name, title

bar *n.* **1.** batten, crosspiece, paling, palisade, pole, rail, rod, shaft, stake, stick **2.** barricade, barrier, block, deterrent, hindrance, impediment, obstacle, obstruction, rail, railing, stop **3.** boozer (*Brit., Aust., & N.Z. inf.*), canteen, counter, inn, lounge, pub (*Inf., chiefly Brit.*), public house, saloon, taproom, tavern, watering hole (*Facetious sl.*) **4.** bench, court, courtroom, dock, law court **5.** *Law* barristers, body of lawyers, counsel, court, judgment, tribunal ~*v.* **6.** barricade, bolt, fasten, latch, lock, secure **7.** ban, black, blackball, exclude, forbid, hinder, keep out, obstruct, prevent, prohibit, restrain
Antonyms *n.* (*sense 2*) aid, benefit, help ~*v.* (*sense 7*) accept, admit, allow, clear, let, open, permit, receive

barb 1. bristle, point, prickle, prong, quill, spike, spur, thorn **2.** affront, cut, dig, gibe, insult, rebuff, sarcasm, scoff, sneer

barbarian *n.* **1.** brute, hooligan, lout, lowbrow, ned (*Sl.*), ruffian, savage, vandal, yahoo **2.** bigot, boor, ignoramus, illiterate, lowbrow, philistine ~*adj.* **3.** boorish, crude, lowbrow, philistine, primitive, rough, un~

couth, uncultivated, uncultured, unsophis~
ticated, vulgar, wild
Antonyms *adj.* civil, civilized, cultured,
genteel, highbrow, refined, sophisticated,
urbane, well-mannered

barbaric 1. primitive, rude, uncivilized,
wild **2.** barbarous, boorish, brutal, coarse,
crude, cruel, fierce, inhuman, savage, un~
couth, vulgar
Antonyms civilized, cultivated, cultured,
gentlemanly, gracious, humane, refined, so~
phisticated, urbane

barbarism 1. coarseness, crudity, savagery,
uncivilizedness **2.** atrocity, barbarity,
enormity, outrage **3.** corruption, misusage,
misuse, solecism, vulgarism

barbarity brutality, cruelty, inhumanity,
ruthlessness, savagery, viciousness

barbarous 1. barbarian, brutish, primitive,
rough, rude, savage, uncivilized, uncouth,
wild **2.** barbaric, brutal, cruel, ferocious,
heartless, inhuman, monstrous, ruthless,
vicious **3.** coarse, crude, ignorant, uncul~
tured, unlettered, unrefined, vulgar

bare 1. buck naked (*Sl.*), denuded, exposed,
in the raw (*Inf.*), naked, naked as the day
one was born (*Inf.*), nude, peeled, shorn,
stripped, unclad, unclothed, uncovered, un~
dressed, without a stitch on (*Inf.*) **2.** barren,
blank, empty, lacking, mean, open, poor,
scanty, scarce, unfurnished, vacant, void,
wanting **3.** austere, bald, basic, cold, essen~
tial, hard, literal, plain, severe, sheer, sim~
ple, spare, spartan, stark, unadorned, un~
embellished, unvarnished
Antonyms abundant, adorned, attired, clad,
clothed, concealed, covered, dressed, full,
hidden, plentiful, profuse, well-stocked

barefaced 1. audacious, bold, brash, bra~
zen, impudent, insolent, shameless **2.** bald,
blatant, flagrant, glaring, manifest, naked,
obvious, open, palpable, patent, transparent,
unconcealed
Antonyms concealed, covered, hidden, in~
conspicuous, masked, obscured, secret,
tucked away, unseen

barely almost, hardly, just, only just,
scarcely
Antonyms amply, completely, fully, pro~
fusely

bargain *n.* **1.** agreement, arrangement,
business, compact, contract, convention,
engagement, negotiation, pact, pledge,
promise, stipulation, transaction, treaty,
understanding **2.** (cheap) purchase, dis~
count, giveaway, good buy, good deal, good
value, reduction, snip (*Inf.*), steal (*Inf.*) ~*v.*
3. agree, contract, covenant, negotiate,
promise, stipulate, transact **4.** barter, buy,
deal, haggle, sell, trade, traffic

bargain for anticipate, contemplate, expect,
foresee, imagine, look for, plan for

bargain on assume, bank on, count on, de~
pend on, plan on, rely on

barge canal boat, flatboat, lighter, narrow
boat, scow

barge in break in, burst in, butt in, in~
fringe, interrupt, intrude, muscle in (*Inf.*)

barge into bump into, cannon into, collide
with, hit, push, shove

bark[1] **1.** *n.* casing, cortex (*Anat., bot.*), cov~
ering, crust, husk, rind, skin **2.** *v.* abrade,
flay, rub, scrape, shave, skin, strip

bark[2] **1.** *n./v.* bay, growl, howl, snarl, woof,
yap, yelp **2.** *v. Fig.* bawl, bawl at, berate,
bluster, growl, shout, snap, snarl, yell

barmy 1. *Also* **balmy** crackpot (*Inf.*), crazy,
daft (*Inf.*), dippy, doolally (*Sl.*), foolish,
goofy (*Inf.*), idiotic, insane, loony (*Sl.*),
loopy (*Inf.*), nuts (*Sl.*), nutty (*Sl.*), odd, off
one's trolley (*Sl.*), out to lunch (*Inf.*), silly,
stupid, up the pole (*Inf.*) **2.** fermenting,
foamy, frothy, spumy, yeasty
Antonyms (*sense 1*) all there (*Inf.*), in one's
right mind, of sound mind, rational, reason~
able, sane, sensible

baroque bizarre, convoluted, elaborate, ex~
travagant, flamboyant, florid, grotesque, or~
nate, overdecorated, rococo

barracks billet, camp, cantonment, casern,
encampment, garrison, quarters

barrage 1. battery, bombardment, cannon~
ade, curtain of fire, fusillade, gunfire, salvo,
shelling, volley **2.** assault, attack, burst,
deluge, hail, mass, onslaught, plethora,
profusion, rain, storm, stream, torrent

barred 1. banded, crosshatched, lined,
marked, ribbed, ridged, streaked, striped,
veined **2.** banned, excluded, forbidden, out~
lawed, prohibited, proscribed, taboo

barren 1. childless, infecund, infertile, ster~
ile, unprolific **2.** arid, desert, desolate, dry,
empty, unfruitful, unproductive, waste **3.**
boring, dull, flat, fruitless, lacklustre, stale,
uninformative, uninspiring, uninstructive,
uninteresting, unrewarding, useless, vapid
Antonyms fecund, fertile, fruitful, instruc~
tive, interesting, lush, productive, profitable,
rich, useful

barricade 1. *n.* barrier, blockade, bulwark,
fence, obstruction, palisade, rampart,
stockade **2.** *v.* bar, block, blockade, defend,
fortify, obstruct, protect, shut in

barrier 1. bar, barricade, block, blockade,
boundary, ditch, fence, fortification, obsta~
cle, obstruction, pale, railing, rampart, stop,
wall **2.** *Fig.* check, difficulty, drawback,
handicap, hindrance, hurdle, impediment,
limitation, obstacle, restriction, stumbling
block

barter bargain, exchange, haggle, sell, swap, trade, traffic

base[1] *n.* **1.** bed, bottom, foot, foundation, groundwork, pedestal, rest, stand, support **2.** basis, core, essence, essential, fundamental, heart, key, origin, principle, root, source **3.** camp, centre, headquarters, home, post, settlement, starting point, sta~ tion ~*v.* **4.** build, construct, depend, derive, establish, found, ground, hinge, locate, station
Antonyms (*sense 1*) apex, crest, crown, peak, summit, top, vertex

base[2] **1.** abject, contemptible, corrupt, de~ praved, despicable, dishonourable, disrepu~ table, evil, ignoble, immoral, infamous, scandalous, shameful, sordid, vile, villain~ ous, vulgar, wicked **2.** downtrodden, grov~ elling, low, lowly, mean, menial, miserable, paltry, pitiful, poor, servile, slavish, sorry, subservient, worthless, wretched **3.** adul~ terated, alloyed, counterfeit, debased, fake, forged, fraudulent, impure, inferior, pinch~ beck, spurious
Antonyms admirable, good, honest, hon~ ourable, just, lofty, moral, noble, pure, rare, righteous, unalloyed, upright, valuable, vir~ tuous

baseless groundless, unconfirmed, uncor~ roborated, unfounded, ungrounded, unjustifiable, unjustified, unsubstantiated, unsupported
Antonyms authenticated, confirmed, cor~ roborated, proven, substantiated, supported, validated, verified, well-founded

baseness 1. contemptibility, degradation, depravation, depravity, despicability, dis~ grace, ignominy, infamy, notoriety, oblo~ quy, turpitude **2.** lowliness, meanness, misery, poverty, servility, slavishness, sub~ servience, vileness, worthlessness, wretch~ edness **3.** adulteration, debasement, fraudulence, phoneyness *or* phoniness (*Inf.*), pretence, speciousness, spuriousness

bash 1. *v.* belt (*Inf.*), biff (*Sl.*), break, chin (*Sl.*), crash, crush, deck (*Sl.*), hit, lay one on (*Sl.*), punch, slosh (*Brit. sl.*), smash, sock (*Sl.*), strike, wallop (*Inf.*) **2.** *n.* attempt, crack (*Inf.*), go (*Inf.*), shot (*Inf.*), stab (*Inf.*), try

bashful abashed, blushing, confused, con~ strained, coy, diffident, easily embarrassed, nervous, overmodest, reserved, reticent, re~ tiring, self-conscious, self-effacing, shame~ faced, sheepish, shrinking, shy, timid, tim~ orous
Antonyms aggressive, arrogant, bold, brash, conceited, confident, egoistic, fearless, for~ ward, immodest, impudent, intrepid, pushy (*Inf.*), self-assured

bashfulness constraint, coyness, diffidence,

embarrassment, hesitation, modesty, re~ serve, self-consciousness, sheepishness, shyness, timidity, timorousness

basic bog-standard (*Inf.*), central, elementa~ ry, essential, fundamental, indispensable, inherent, intrinsic, key, necessary, primary, radical, underlying, vital
Antonyms complementary, minor, periph~ eral, secondary, supplementary, supporting, trivial, unessential

basically at bottom, at heart, *au fond*, es~ sentially, firstly, fundamentally, inherently, in substance, intrinsically, mostly, primari~ ly, radically

basics brass tacks (*Inf.*), core, essentials, facts, fundamentals, hard facts, necessaries, nitty-gritty (*Inf.*), nuts and bolts (*Inf.*), practicalities, principles, rudiments

basis 1. base, bottom, footing, foundation, ground, groundwork, support **2.** chief in~ gredient, core, essential, fundamental, heart, premise, principal element, principle, theory

bask 1. laze, lie in, loll, lounge, relax, sun~ bathe, swim in, toast oneself, warm oneself **2.** delight in, enjoy, indulge oneself, luxuri~ ate, relish, revel, savour, take pleasure, wallow

bass deep, deep-toned, grave, low, low-pitched, resonant, sonorous

bastard 1. *n.* illegitimate (child), love child, natural child, whoreson (*Archaic*) **2.** *adj.* adulterated, baseborn, counterfeit, false, il~ legitimate, imperfect, impure, inferior, ir~ regular, misbegotten, sham, spurious

bastion bulwark, citadel, defence, fastness, fortress, mainstay, prop, rock, stronghold, support, tower of strength

bat bang, hit, punch, rap, smack, strike, swat, thump, wallop (*Inf.*), whack

batch accumulation, aggregation, amount, assemblage, bunch, collection, crowd, group, lot, pack, quantity, set

bath 1. *n.* ablution, cleansing, douche, douse, scrubbing, shower, soak, soaping, sponging, tub, wash, washing **2.** *v.* bathe, clean, douse, lave (*Archaic*), scrub down, shower, soak, soap, sponge, tub, wash

bathe 1. *v.* cleanse, cover, dunk, flood, im~ merse, moisten, rinse, soak, steep, suffuse, wash, wet **2.** *n.* dip, dook (*Scot.*), swim, wash

bathing costume bathing suit, bikini, swimming costume, swimsuit, trunks

bathos anticlimax, false pathos, letdown, mawkishness, sentimentality

baton club, crook, mace, rod, sceptre, staff, stick, truncheon, wand

battalion army, brigade, company, contin~

gent, division, force, horde, host, legion, multitude, regiment, squadron, throng

batten¹ board up, clamp down, cover up, fasten, fasten down, fix, nail down, secure, tighten

batten² fatten, flourish, gain, grow, increase, prosper, thrive, wax

batter 1. assault, bash (*Inf.*), beat, belabour, break, buffet, clobber (*Sl.*), dash against, lambast(e), lash, pelt, pound, pummel, smash, smite, thrash, wallop (*Inf.*) **2.** bruise, crush, deface, demolish, destroy, disfigure, hurt, injure, mangle, mar, maul, ruin, shatter, shiver, total (*Sl.*), trash (*Sl.*)

battered beaten, beat-up (*Inf.*), broken-down, bruised, crushed, damaged, dilapidated, injured, ramshackle, squashed, weather-beaten

battery 1. chain, ring, sequence, series, set, suite **2.** assault, attack, beating, mayhem, onslaught, physical violence, thumping **3.** artillery, cannon, cannonry, gun emplacements, guns

battle *n.* **1.** action, attack, combat, encounter, engagement, fight, fray, hostilities, skirmish, war, warfare **2.** agitation, campaign, clash, conflict, contest, controversy, crusade, debate, disagreement, dispute, head-to-head, strife, struggle ~*v.* **3.** agitate, argue, clamour, combat, contend, contest, dispute, feud, fight, strive, struggle, war
Antonyms *n.* accord, agreement, armistice, ceasefire, concord, entente, peace, suspension of hostilities, truce

battle-axe ballbreaker (*Sl.*), disciplinarian, fury, harridan, scold, shrew, tartar, termagant, virago, vixen

battle cry catchword, motto, slogan, war cry, war whoop, watchword

battlefield battleground, combat zone, field, field of battle, front

battlement barbican, bartizan, bastion, breastwork, bulwark, crenellation, fortification, parapet, rampart

battleship capital ship, gunboat, man-of-war, ship of the line, warship

batty barking (*Sl.*), barking mad (*Sl.*), barmy (*Sl.*), bats (*Sl.*), bonkers (*Sl., chiefly Brit.*), cracked (*Sl.*), crackers (*Brit. sl.*), crackpot (*Inf.*), cranky (*Inf.*), crazy, daft (*Inf.*), dotty (*Sl., chiefly Brit.*), eccentric, insane, loony (*Sl.*), loopy (*Inf.*), lunatic, mad, not the full shilling (*Inf.*), nuts (*Sl.*), nutty (*Sl.*), odd, oddball (*Inf.*), off one's rocker (*Sl.*), off one's trolley (*Sl.*), off-the-wall (*Sl.*), outré, out to lunch (*Inf.*), peculiar, potty (*Brit. inf.*), queer (*Inf.*), screwy (*Inf.*), touched, up the pole (*Inf.*), wacko (*Sl.*)

bauble bagatelle, gewgaw, gimcrack, kick-shaw, knick-knack, plaything, toy, trifle, trinket

bawd brothel-keeper, madam, pimp, procuress, prostitute, whore, working girl (*Facetious sl.*)

bawdy blue, coarse, dirty, erotic, gross, indecent, indecorous, indelicate, lascivious, lecherous, lewd, libidinous, licentious, lustful, obscene, prurient, ribald, risqué, rude, salacious, smutty, steamy (*Inf.*), suggestive, vulgar
Antonyms chaste, clean, decent, good, modest, moral, respectable, seemly, undefiled, upright, virtuous

bawl 1. bellow, call, clamour, halloo, howl, roar, shout, vociferate, yell **2.** blubber, cry, sob, squall, wail, weep

bay¹ bight, cove, gulf, inlet, natural harbour, sound

bay² alcove, compartment, embrasure, niche, nook, opening, recess

bay³ 1. *v./n.* bark, bell, clamour, cry, growl, howl, yelp **2.** *n.* **at bay** caught, cornered, trapped

bayonet *v.* impale, knife, run through, spear, stab, stick, transfix

bays chaplet, garland, glory, laurel crown, praise, prize, renown, trophy

bazaar 1. exchange, market, marketplace, mart **2.** bring-and-buy, fair, fête, sale of work

be 1. be alive, breathe, exist, inhabit, live **2.** befall, come about, come to pass, happen, occur, take place, transpire (*Inf.*) **3.** abide, continue, endure, last, obtain, persist, prevail, remain, stand, stay, survive

beach coast, lido, littoral, margin, plage, sands, seaboard (*Chiefly U.S.*), seashore, seaside, shingle, shore, strand, water's edge

beachcomber forager, loafer, scavenger, scrounger, tramp, vagabond, vagrant, wanderer

beached abandoned, aground, ashore, deserted, grounded, high and dry, marooned, stranded, wrecked

beacon beam, bonfire, flare, lighthouse, pharos, rocket, sign, signal, signal fire, smoke signal, watchtower

bead blob, bubble, dot, drop, droplet, globule, pellet, pill, spherule

beads chaplet, choker, necklace, necklet, pearls, pendant, rosary

beak 1. bill, mandible, neb (*Archaic or dialect*), nib **2.** nose, proboscis, snout **3.** *Nautical* bow, prow, ram, rostrum, stem

beam *n.* **1.** girder, joist, plank, rafter, spar, support, timber **2.** bar, emission, gleam, glimmer, glint, glow, radiation, ray, shaft, streak, stream ~*v.* **3.** broadcast, emit, glare, gleam, glitter, glow, radiate, shine, transmit **4.** grin, laugh, smile

beaming 1. beautiful, bright, brilliant, flashing, gleaming, glistening, glittering, radiant, scintillating, shining, sparkling **2.** cheerful, grinning, happy, joyful, smiling, sunny

bear 1. bring, carry, convey, hump (*Brit. sl.*), move, take, tote (*Inf.*), transport **2.** cherish, entertain, exhibit, harbour, have, hold, maintain, possess, shoulder, support, sustain, uphold, weigh upon **3.** abide, admit, allow, brook, endure, permit, put up with (*Inf.*), stomach, suffer, tolerate, undergo **4.** beget, breed, bring forth, develop, engender, generate, give birth to, produce, yield
Antonyms abandon, cease, desert, discontinue, drop, give up, leave, put down, quit, relinquish, shed

bearable admissible, endurable, manageable, passable, sufferable, supportable, sustainable, tolerable
Antonyms insufferable, insupportable, intolerable, oppressive, too much (*Inf.*), unacceptable, unbearable, unendurable

beard 1. *n.* bristles, five-o'clock shadow, stubble, whiskers **2.** *v.* brave, confront, dare, defy, face, oppose, tackle

bearded bewhiskered, bristly, bushy, hairy, hirsute, shaggy, stubbly, unshaven, whiskered

beardless 1. barefaced, clean-shaven, hairless, smooth, smooth-faced **2.** callow, fresh, green, immature, inexperienced

bear down 1. burden, compress, encumber, press down, push, strain, weigh down **2.** advance on, approach, attack, close in, converge on, move in

bearer 1. agent, carrier, conveyor, messenger, porter, runner, servant **2.** beneficiary, consignee, payee

bearing 1. air, aspect, attitude, behaviour, carriage, demeanour, deportment, manner, mien, posture **2.** *Nautical* course, direction, point of compass **3.** application, connection, import, pertinence, reference, relation, relevance, significance
Antonyms (*sense 3*) inappositeness, inappropriateness, inaptness, inconsequence, irrelevance, irrelevancy, non sequitur

bearings aim, course, direction, location, orientation, position, situation, track, way, whereabouts

bear on affect, appertain to, belong to, concern, involve, pertain to, refer to, relate to, touch upon

bear out confirm, corroborate, endorse, justify, prove, substantiate, support, uphold, vindicate

bear up bear the brunt, carry on, endure, grin and bear it (*Inf.*), persevere, suffer, withstand

bear with be patient, forbear, make allowances, put up with (*Inf.*), suffer, tolerate, wait

beast 1. animal, brute, creature **2.** barbarian, brute, fiend, ghoul, monster, ogre, sadist, savage, swine

beastly 1. animal, barbarous, bestial, brutal, brutish, coarse, cruel, depraved, inhuman, monstrous, repulsive, sadistic, savage **2.** awful, disagreeable, foul, horrid, mean, nasty, rotten, shitty (*Taboo sl.*), terrible, unpleasant
Antonyms agreeable, fine, good, humane, pleasant, sensitive

beat *v.* **1.** bang, batter, belt (*Inf.*), break, bruise, buffet, cane, chin (*Sl.*), clobber (*Sl.*), cudgel, deck (*Sl.*), drub, flog, hit, knock, lambast(e), lash, lay one on (*Sl.*), lick (*Inf.*), maul, pelt, pound, punch, strike, thrash, thwack, whip **2.** best, blow out of the water (*Sl.*), clobber (*Sl.*), conquer, defeat, excel, lick (*Inf.*), master, outdo, outrun, outstrip, overcome, overwhelm, run rings around (*Inf.*), subdue, surpass, tank (*Sl.*), undo, vanquish, wipe the floor with (*Inf.*) **3.** fashion, forge, form, hammer, model, shape, work **4.** flap, flutter, palpitate, pound, pulsate, pulse, quake, quiver, shake, throb, thump, tremble, vibrate **5. beat it** bugger off (*Taboo sl.*), depart, exit, fuck off (*Offens. taboo sl.*), get lost (*Inf.*), go away, hook it (*Sl.*), hop it (*Sl.*), leave, piss off (*Taboo sl.*), scarper (*Brit. sl.*), scram (*Inf.*), shoo, skedaddle (*Inf.*), vamoose (*Sl., chiefly U.S.*) ~*n.* **6.** belt (*Inf.*), blow, hit, lash, punch, shake, slap, strike, swing, thump **7.** flutter, palpitation, pulsation, pulse, throb **8.** accent, cadence, measure (*Prosody*), metre, rhythm, stress, time **9.** circuit, course, path, rounds, route, way ~*adj.* **10.** *Sl.* clapped out (*Aust. & N.Z. inf.*), exhausted, fatigued, tired, wearied, worn out, zonked (*Sl.*)

beaten 1. baffled, cowed, defeated, disappointed, disheartened, frustrated, overcome, overwhelmed, thwarted, vanquished **2.** forged, formed, hammered, shaped, stamped, worked **3.** much travelled, trampled, trodden, well-trodden, well-used, worn **4.** blended, foamy, frothy, mixed, stirred, whipped, whisked

beating 1. belting (*Inf.*), caning, chastisement, corporal punishment, flogging, pasting (*Sl.*), slapping, smacking, thrashing, whipping **2.** conquest, defeat, downfall, overthrow, pasting (*Sl.*), rout, ruin

beatitude beatification, blessedness, bliss, ecstasy, exaltation, felicity, happiness, holy joy, saintliness

beat up assault, attack, batter, beat the liv~ ing daylights out of (*Inf.*), clobber (*Sl.*), do over (*Brit., Aust., & N.Z. sl.*), duff up (*Brit. sl.*), fill in (*Brit. sl.*), knock about or around, lambast(e), put the boot in (*Sl.*), thrash

beau 1. admirer, boyfriend, escort, fancy man (*Sl.*), fiancé, guy (*Inf.*), leman (*Archa~ ic*), lover, suitor, swain, sweetheart **2.** cavalier, coxcomb, dandy, fop, gallant, ladies' man, popinjay, swell (*Inf.*)

beautiful alluring, appealing, attractive, charming, comely, delightful, drop-dead (*Sl.*), exquisite, fair, fine, glamorous, good-looking, gorgeous, graceful, handsome, lovely, pleasing, radiant, ravishing, stun~ ning (*Inf.*)
Antonyms awful, bad, hideous, repulsive, terrible, ugly, unattractive, unpleasant, un~ sightly

beautify adorn, array, bedeck, deck, deco~ rate, embellish, enhance, festoon, garnish, gild, glamorize, grace, ornament

beauty 1. allure, attractiveness, bloom, charm, comeliness, elegance, exquisiteness, fairness, glamour, grace, handsomeness, loveliness, pulchritude, seemliness, symme~ try **2.** belle, charmer, cracker (*Sl.*), goddess, good-looker, lovely (*Sl.*), stunner (*Inf.*), Ve~ nus **3.** advantage, asset, attraction, benefit, blessing, boon, excellence, feature, good thing
Antonyms detraction, disadvantage, flaw, repulsiveness, ugliness, unpleasantness, un~ seemliness

beaver away exert oneself, graft (*Inf.*), hammer away, peg away, persevere, persist, plug away (*Inf.*), slog, work

becalmed motionless, settled, still, strand~ ed, stuck

because as, by reason of, in that, on ac~ count of, owing to, since, thanks to

beckon 1. bid, gesticulate, gesture, motion, nod, signal, summon, wave at **2.** allure, at~ tract, call, coax, draw, entice, invite, lure, pull, tempt

becloud bedim, befog, complicate, confuse, darken, muddle, obfuscate, obscure, over~ cast, screen, veil

become 1. alter to, be transformed into, change into, develop into, evolve into, grow into, mature into, metamorphose into, ripen into **2.** embellish, enhance, fit, flatter, grace, harmonize, ornament, set off, suit

becoming 1. attractive, comely, enhancing, flattering, graceful, neat, pretty, tasteful **2.** appropriate, befitting, *comme il faut*, com~ patible, congruous, decent, decorous, fit, fitting, in keeping, meet (*Archaic*), proper, seemly, suitable, worthy

Antonyms improper, ugly, unattractive, unbecoming, unfit, unsuitable, unworthy

bed *n.* **1.** bedstead, berth, bunk, cot, couch, divan, pallet **2.** area, border, garden, patch, plot, row, strip **3.** base, bottom, foundation, groundwork, substratum ~*v.* **4.** base, em~ bed, establish, fix, found, implant, insert, plant, settle, set up

bedaub besmear, smear, smirch, soil, spat~ ter, splash, stain

bedazzle amaze, astound, bewilder, blind, captivate, confuse, daze, dazzle, dumbfound, enchant, overwhelm, stagger, stun

bedclothes bedding, bed linen, blankets, coverlets, covers, duvets, eiderdowns, pillowcases, pillows, quilts, sheets

bed down lie, retire, settle down, sleep, turn in (*Inf.*)

bedeck adorn, array, bedight (*Archaic*), be~ dizen (*Archaic*), decorate, embellish, fes~ toon, garnish, ornament, trim

bedevil afflict, aggravate (*Inf.*), annoy, be on one's back (*Sl.*), confound, distress, fret, frustrate, get in one's hair (*Inf.*), get on one's nerves (*Inf.*), harass, hassle (*Inf.*), irk, irritate, pester, plague, torment, torture, trouble, vex, worry

bedlam chaos, clamour, commotion, confu~ sion, furore, hubbub, hullabaloo, madhouse (*Inf.*), noise, pandemonium, tumult, turmoil, uproar

bedraggled dirty, dishevelled, disordered, drenched, dripping, messy, muddied, mud~ dy, sodden, soiled, stained, sullied, un~ kempt, untidy

bedridden confined, confined to bed, flat on one's back, incapacitated, laid up (*Inf.*)

bedrock 1. bed, bottom, foundation, nadir, rock bottom, substratum, substructure **2.** basics, basis, core, essentials, fundamentals, roots

beef 1. *Inf.* brawn, flesh, heftiness, muscle, physique, robustness, sinew, strength **2.** *Sl.* complaint, criticism, dispute, grievance, gripe (*Inf.*), grouch (*Inf.*), grouse, grumble, objection, protest, protestation

beefy *Inf.* **1.** brawny, bulky, burly, hulking, muscular, stalwart, stocky, strapping, stur~ dy, thickset **2.** chubby, corpulent, fat, fleshy, heavy, obese, overweight, paunchy, plump, podgy, portly, pudgy, rotund
Antonyms feeble, frail, puny, scrawny, skinny, weak

beetle, beetling *adj.* hanging over, jut~ ting, leaning over, overhanging, pendent, projecting, prominent, protruding, sticking out, swelling over

befall bechance, betide, chance, come to pass, ensue, fall, follow, happen, material~

ize, occur, supervene, take place, transpire (*Inf.*)

befitting apposite, appropriate, becoming, fit, fitting, meet (*Archaic*), proper, right, seemly, suitable
Antonyms improper, inappropriate, irrelevant, unbecoming, unfit, unsuitable, wrong

before 1. *adv.* ahead, earlier, formerly, in advance, in front, previously, sooner **2.** *prep.* earlier than, in advance of, in front of, in the presence of, prior to
Antonyms *adv.* after, afterwards, behind, later, subsequently, thereafter ~*prep.* after, behind, following, succeeding

beforehand ahead of time, already, before, before now, earlier, in advance, in anticipation, previously, sooner

befriend advise, aid, assist, back, benefit, encourage, favour, help, patronize, side with, stand by, succour, support, sustain, uphold, welcome

befuddle baffle, bewilder, confuse, daze, disorient, intoxicate, muddle, puzzle, stupefy
Antonyms clarify, clear up, elucidate, explicate, illuminate, interpret, make clear, make plain, resolve, simplify, throw *or* shed light on

befuddled confused, dazed, fuddled, groggy (*Inf.*), inebriated, intoxicated, muddled, woozy (*Inf.*)

beg 1. beseech, crave, desire, entreat, implore, importune, petition, plead, pray, request, solicit, supplicate **2.** blag (*Sl.*), cadge, call for alms, mooch (*Sl.*), scrounge, seek charity, solicit charity, sponge on, touch (someone) for (*Sl.*) **3.** *As in* **beg the question** avoid, dodge, duck (*Inf.*), equivocate, eschew, evade, fend off, flannel (*Brit. inf.*), hedge, parry, shirk, shun, sidestep
Antonyms (*sense 1*) apportion, award, bestow, commit, confer, contribute, donate, give, grant, impart, present (*sense 2*) claim, demand, exact, extort, insist on

beget 1. breed, father, generate, get, procreate, propagate, sire **2.** bring, bring about, cause, create, effect, engender, give rise to, occasion, produce, result in

beggar *n.* **1.** bag lady (*Chiefly U.S.*), bum (*Inf.*), cadger, mendicant, scrounger (*Inf.*), sponger (*Inf.*), supplicant, tramp, vagrant **2.** bankrupt, down-and-out, pauper, starveling ~*v.* **3.** *As in* **beggar description** baffle, challenge, defy, surpass

beggarly abject, base, contemptible, despicable, destitute, impoverished, inadequate, indigent, low, meagre, mean, miserly, needy, niggardly, pitiful, poor, poverty-stricken, stingy, vile, wretched

beggary bankruptcy, destitution, indigence,

need, pauperism, poverty, vagrancy, want, wretchedness

begin 1. commence, embark on, inaugurate, initiate, instigate, institute, prepare, set about, set on foot, start **2.** appear, arise, be born, come into being, come into existence, commence, crop up (*Inf.*), dawn, emerge, happen, originate, spring, start
Antonyms cease, complete, end, finish, stop, terminate

beginner amateur, apprentice, cub, fledgling, freshman, greenhorn (*Inf.*), initiate, learner, neophyte, novice, recruit, starter, student, tenderfoot, trainee, tyro
Antonyms authority, expert, master, old hand, old stager, old-timer, past master, past mistress, pro (*Inf.*), professional, trouper, veteran

beginning 1. birth, commencement, inauguration, inception, initiation, onset, opening, opening move, origin, outset, overture, preface, prelude, rise, rudiments, source, start, starting point **2.** embryo, fount, fountainhead, germ, root, seed
Antonyms (*sense 1*) closing, completion, conclusion, end, ending, finish, termination

begrime besmirch, blacken, dirty, muddy, smear, smirch, soil, spatter, stain, sully, tarnish

begrudge be jealous, be reluctant, be stingy, envy, grudge, resent

beguile 1. befool, cheat, deceive, delude, dupe, fool, hoodwink, impose on, mislead, trick **2.** amuse, charm, cheer, delight, distract, divert, engross, entertain, occupy, solace, tickle the fancy of
Antonyms alarm, alert, enlighten, put right

beguiling alluring, attractive, bewitching, captivating, charming, diverting, enchanting, entertaining, enthralling, interesting, intriguing

behalf account, advantage, benefit, defence, good, interest, part, profit, sake, side, support

behave 1. act, function, operate, perform, run, work **2.** act correctly, conduct oneself properly, mind one's manners
Antonyms act up (*Inf.*), be bad, be insubordinate, be naughty, carry on (*Inf.*), get up to mischief (*Inf.*), misbehave, muck about (*Brit. sl.*)

behaviour 1. actions, bearing, carriage, comportment, conduct, demeanour, deportment, manner, manners, ways **2.** action, functioning, operation, performance

behest bidding, charge, command, commandment, decree, dictate, direction, expressed desire, injunction, instruction, mandate, order, precept, wish

behind *prep.* **1.** after, at the back of, at the

rear of, following, later than **2.** at the bot~
tom of, causing, initiating, instigating, re~
sponsible for **3.** backing, for, in agreement,
on the side of, supporting ~*adv.* **4.** after,
afterwards, following, in the wake (of), next,
subsequently **5.** behindhand, in arrears, in
debt, overdue ~*n.* **6.** arse (*Taboo sl.*), ass
(*U.S. & Canad. taboo sl.*), bottom, bum (*Brit.
sl.*), buns (*U.S. sl.*), butt (*U.S. & Canad. inf.*),
buttocks, derrière (*Euphemistic*), jacksy
(*Brit. sl.*), posterior, rump, seat, tail (*Inf.*)
Antonyms (*sense 1*) earlier than, in advance
of, in front of, in the presence of, prior to (*sense
4*) ahead, earlier, formerly, in advance, previ~
ously, sooner

behindhand backward, behind time, dila~
tory, late, remiss, slow, tardy

behind the times antiquated, dated, *dé~
modé*, obsolete, old-fashioned, old hat, out~
moded, out of date, passé
Antonyms advanced, avant-garde, experi~
mental, far-out (*Sl.*), ground-breaking, inno~
vative, pioneering, progressive, trendy (*Brit.
inf.*), unconventional, way-out (*Inf.*)

behold 1. *v.* check, check out (*Inf.*), clock
(*Brit. sl.*), consider, contemplate, discern,
eye, eyeball (*U.S. sl.*), get a load of (*Inf.*),
look at, observe, perceive, recce (*Sl.*), re~
gard, scan, survey, take a dekko at (*Brit.
sl.*), view, watch, witness **2.** *interj.* lo, look,
mark, observe, see, watch

beholden bound, grateful, indebted, obli~
gated, obliged, owing, under obligation

beige biscuit, buff, *café au lait*, camel, cin~
namon, coffee, cream, ecru, fawn, khaki,
mushroom, neutral, oatmeal, sand, tan

being 1. actuality, animation, existence,
life, living, reality **2.** entity, essence, na~
ture, soul, spirit, substance **3.** animal,
beast, body, creature, human being, indi~
vidual, living thing, mortal, thing
Antonyms nihility, nonbeing, nonexistence,
nothingness, nullity, oblivion

belabour 1. batter, beat, clobber (*Sl.*), flog,
lambast(e), thrash, whip **2.** attack, berate,
blast, castigate, censure, criticize, excoriate,
flay, lambast(e), lay into (*Inf.*), put down,
tear into (*Inf.*)

belated behindhand, behind time, delayed,
late, overdue, tardy

belch 1. burp (*Inf.*), eruct, eructate, hiccup
2. discharge, disgorge, emit, erupt, give off,
gush, spew forth, vent, vomit

beleaguered badgered, beset, besieged,
bothered, harassed, nagged, persecuted,
plagued, put upon, set upon, vexed

belie 1. confute, contradict, deny, disprove,
gainsay (*Archaic or literary*), give the lie to,
negate, rebut, repudiate **2.** conceal, deceive,

disguise, falsify, gloss over, mislead, mis~
represent

belief 1. admission, assent, assurance,
confidence, conviction, credit, feeling, im~
pression, judgment, notion, opinion, per~
suasion, presumption, reliance, theory,
trust, view **2.** credence, credo, creed, doc~
trine, dogma, faith, ideology, principles,
tenet
Antonyms disbelief, distrust, doubt, dubi~
ety, incredulity, mistrust, scepticism

believable acceptable, authentic, credible,
creditable, imaginable, likely, plausible,
possible, probable, reliable, trustworthy,
verisimilar
Antonyms doubtful, dubious, fabulous, im~
plausible, incredible, questionable, unaccep~
table, unbelievable

believe 1. accept, be certain of, be con~
vinced of, buy (*Sl.*), count on, credit, depend
on, have faith in, hold, place confidence in,
presume true, rely on, swallow (*Inf.*), swear
by, trust **2.** assume, conjecture, consider,
gather, guess (*Inf., chiefly U.S. & Canad.*),
imagine, judge, maintain, postulate, pre~
sume, reckon, speculate, suppose, think
Antonyms disbelieve, distrust, doubt, know,
question

believer adherent, convert, devotee, disci~
ple, follower, proselyte, protagonist, sup~
porter, upholder, zealot
Antonyms agnostic, atheist, disbeliever,
doubting Thomas, infidel, sceptic, unbeliever

belittle decry, deprecate, depreciate, deride,
derogate, detract, diminish, disparage,
downgrade, minimize, scoff at, scorn, sneer
at, underestimate, underrate, undervalue
Antonyms boast about, elevate, exalt, mag~
nify, praise, vaunt

belligerent 1. *adj.* aggressive, antagonistic,
argumentative, bellicose, combative, con~
tentious, hostile, litigious, pugnacious,
quarrelsome, unfriendly, warlike, warring
2. *n.* combatant, fighter, warring nation
Antonyms amicable, benign, conciliatory,
friendly, harmonious, nonviolent, without
hostility

bellow *n./v.* bawl, bell, call, clamour, cry,
howl, roar, scream, shout, shriek, yell

belly 1. *n.* abdomen, breadbasket (*Sl.*), cor~
poration (*Inf.*), gut, insides (*Inf.*), paunch,
potbelly, stomach, tummy, vitals **2.** *v.* bil~
low, bulge, fill, spread, swell, swell out

belong 1. *With* **to** be at the disposal of, be
held by, be owned by, be the property of **2.**
With **to** be affiliated to, be allied to, be a
member of, be associated with, be included
in **3.** attach to, be connected with, be
fitting, be part of, fit, go with, have as a
proper place, pertain to, relate to

belonging acceptance, affiliation, affinity,

association, attachment, fellowship, inclu~
sion, kinship, loyalty, rapport, relationship

belongings accoutrements, chattels, effects,
gear, goods, paraphernalia, personal prop~
erty, possessions, stuff, things

beloved admired, adored, cherished, dar~
ling, dear, dearest, loved, pet, precious,
prized, revered, sweet, treasured, wor~
shipped

below *adv.* **1.** beneath, down, lower, under,
underneath ~*prep.* **2.** inferior, lesser, lesser
than, subject, subordinate, unworthy of **3.**
below par below average, imperfect, infe~
rior, off colour, off form, poor, second-rate,
unfit

belt 1. band, cincture, cummerbund, girdle,
girth, sash, waistband **2.** *Geog.* area, dis~
trict, layer, region, stretch, strip, tract, zone
3. below the belt cowardly, foul, not
playing the game (*Inf.*), unfair, unjust, un~
scrupulous, unsporting, unsportsmanlike

bemoan bewail, deplore, express sorrow,
grieve for, lament, moan over, mourn, re~
gret, rue, weep for

bemuse amaze, bewilder, confuse, daze,
flummox, muddle, nonplus, overwhelm,
perplex, puzzle, stun

bemused absent-minded, at sea, bewil~
dered, confused, dazed, engrossed,
flummoxed, fuddled, half-drunk, muddled,
nonplussed, perplexed, preoccupied,
stunned, stupefied, tipsy

bench 1. form, pew, seat, settle, stall **2.**
board, counter, table, trestle table, work~
bench, worktable **3.** court, courtroom,
judge, judges, judiciary, magistrate, magis~
trates, tribunal

benchmark criterion, example, gauge, lev~
el, measure, model, norm, par, reference,
reference point, standard, touchstone,
yardstick

bend *v.* **1.** arc, arch, bow, buckle, contort,
crouch, curve, deflect, diverge, flex, incline,
incurvate, lean, stoop, swerve, turn, twist,
veer, warp **2.** compel, direct, influence,
mould, persuade, shape, subdue, submit,
sway, yield ~*n.* **3.** angle, arc, arch, bow,
corner, crook, curve, hook, loop, turn, twist,
zigzag

beneath 1. *adv.* below, in a lower place,
underneath **2.** *prep.* below, inferior to, less
than, lower than, unbefitting, underneath,
unworthy of
Antonyms (*sense 2*) above, atop, beyond, ex~
ceeding, higher than, on top of, over, upon

benediction beatitude, *benedictus*, benison,
blessing, consecration, favour, grace, grati~
tude, invocation, orison, prayer, thankful~
ness, thanksgiving

benefactor angel (*Inf.*), backer, contributor,

donor, helper, patron, philanthropist, pro~
moter, sponsor, subscriber, subsidizer, sup~
porter, well-wisher

beneficial advantageous, benign, expedient,
favourable, gainful, healthful, helpful,
profitable, salubrious, salutary, serviceable,
useful, valuable, wholesome
Antonyms detrimental, disadvantageous,
harmful, pernicious, useless

beneficiary assignee, heir, inheritor, lega~
tee, payee, receiver, recipient, successor

benefit 1. *n.* advantage, aid, asset, assis~
tance, avail, betterment, blessing, boon, fa~
vour, gain, good, help, interest, profit, use
2. *v.* advance, advantage, aid, ameliorate,
assist, avail, better, enhance, further, im~
prove, profit, promote, serve
Antonyms *n.* damage, detriment, disad~
vantage, downside, harm, impairment, inju~
ry, loss ~*v.* damage, deprive, detract from,
harm, impair, injure, worsen

benevolence altruism, charity, compas~
sion, fellow feeling, generosity, goodness,
goodwill, humanity, kind-heartedness,
kindness, sympathy
Antonyms ill will, malevolence, selfishness,
stinginess, unkindness

benevolent affable, altruistic, beneficent,
benign, bounteous, bountiful, caring, chari~
table, compassionate, considerate, generous,
humane, humanitarian, kind, kind-hearted,
liberal, philanthropic, tender-hearted,
warm-hearted, well-disposed

benighted backward, crude, ignorant, illit~
erate, primitive, uncivilized, uncultivated,
unenlightened

benign 1. affable, amiable, complaisant,
friendly, generous, genial, gracious, kind,
kindly, liberal, obliging, sympathetic **2.**
balmy, gentle, healthful, mild, refreshing,
temperate, warm, wholesome **3.** advanta~
geous, auspicious, beneficial, encouraging,
favourable, good, lucky, propitious, salutary
4. *Medical* curable, harmless, limited, re~
mediable, slight, superficial
Antonyms bad, disobliging, harsh, hateful,
inhumane, malicious, malign, severe, stern,
unfavourable, unkind, unlucky, unpleasant,
unsympathetic

bent *adj.* **1.** angled, arched, bowed, crooked,
curved, hunched, stooped, twisted **2.** *With*
on determined, disposed, fixed, inclined,
insistent, predisposed, resolved, set ~*n.* **3.**
ability, aptitude, bag (*Sl.*), cup of tea (*Inf.*),
facility, faculty, flair, forte, inclination,
knack, leaning, penchant, preference, pro~
clivity, propensity, talent, tendency
Antonyms (*sense 1*) aligned, erect, even,
horizontal, in line, level, perpendicular,
plumb, smooth, square, straight, true,
upright, vertical

bequeath bestow, commit, endow, entrust, give, grant, hand down, impart, leave to by will, pass on, transmit, will

bequest bequeathal, bestowal, dower, en~ dowment, estate, gift, heritage, inheritance, legacy, settlement, trust

berate bawl out (*Inf.*), blast, carpet (*Inf.*), castigate, censure, chew out (*U.S. & Canad. inf.*), chide, criticize, excoriate, give a rock~ et (*Brit. & N.Z. inf.*), lambast(e), put down, rail at, read the riot act, rebuke, reprimand, reproach, reprove, revile, scold, tear into (*Inf.*), tear (someone) off a strip (*Brit. inf.*), tell off (*Inf.*), upbraid, vituperate
Antonyms acclaim, admire, applaud, ap~ prove, cheer, commend, compliment, con~ gratulate, extol, laud, praise

bereave afflict, deprive of kindred, dispos~ sess, divest, make destitute, strip, take away from, widow

bereavement affliction, death, deprivation, loss, misfortune, tribulation

bereft cut off, deprived, destitute, devoid, lacking, minus, parted from, robbed of, shorn, wanting

berserk amok, ape (*Sl.*), apeshit (*Sl.*), crazy, enraged, frantic, frenzied, insane, mad, ma~ niacal, manic, rabid, raging, uncontrollable, violent, wild

berth *n.* **1.** bed, billet, bunk, cot (*Nautical*), hammock **2.** anchorage, dock, harbour, ha~ ven, pier, port, quay, slip, wharf **3.** ap~ pointment, employment, job, living, posi~ tion, post, situation ~*v.* **4.** *Nautical* anchor, dock, drop anchor, land, moor, tie up

beseech adjure, ask, beg, call upon, crave, entreat, implore, importune, petition, plead, pray, solicit, sue, supplicate

beset 1. assail, attack, besiege, encircle, en~ close, encompass, environ, hem in, sur~ round **2.** *Fig.* badger, bedevil, embarrass, entangle, harass, perplex, pester, plague

besetting habitual, harassing, inveterate, persistent, prevalent, troublesome

beside 1. abreast of, adjacent to, alongside, at the side of, close to, near, nearby, neigh~ bouring, next door to, next to, overlooking **2. beside oneself** apoplectic, berserk crazed, delirious, demented, deranged, des~ perate, distraught, frantic, frenzied, insane, mad, out of one's mind, unbalanced, uncon~ trolled, unhinged

besides 1. *adv.* also, as well, further, furthermore, in addition, moreover, other~ wise, too, what's more **2.** *prep.* apart from, barring, excepting, excluding, in addition to, other than, over and above, without

beside the point extraneous, immaterial, inapplicable, inapposite, inappropriate, in~ consequent, irrelevant, neither here nor there, unconnected
Antonyms admissible, applicable, apposite, appropriate, appurtenant, apt, fitting, ger~ mane, pertinent, relevant, significant, to the point

besiege 1. beleaguer, beset, blockade, confine, encircle, encompass, environ, hedge in, hem in, invest (*Rare*), lay siege to, shut in, surround **2.** badger, bend someone's ear (*Inf.*), bother, harass, harry, hassle (*Inf.*), hound, importune, nag, pester, plague, trouble

besotted 1. befuddled, bevvied (*Dialect*), blitzed (*Sl.*), blotto (*Sl.*), bombed (*Sl.*), drunk, intoxicated, legless (*Inf.*), lit up (*Sl.*), out of it (*Sl.*), out to it (*Aust. & N.Z. sl.*), paralytic (*Inf.*), pissed (*Taboo sl.*), smashed (*Sl.*), steamboats (*Sl.*), steaming (*Sl.*), stupefied, wasted (*Sl.*), wrecked (*Sl.*), zonked (*Sl.*) **2.** doting, hypnotized, infatuated, smitten, spellbound **3.** confused, foolish, muddled, witless

bespatter bedaub, befoul, begrime, be~ smirch, besprinkle, muddy, smear, spatter, splatter, sully

best *adj.* **1.** chief, finest, first, first-class, first-rate, foremost, highest, leading, most excellent, outstanding, perfect, pre-eminent, principal, superlative, supreme, unsur~ passed **2.** advantageous, apt, correct, gold~ en, most desirable, most fitting, right **3.** greatest, largest, most ~*adv.* **4.** advanta~ geously, attractively, excellently, most for~ tunately **5.** extremely, greatly, most deeply, most fully, most highly ~*n.* **6.** choice, cream, elite, favourite, finest, first, flower, pick, prime, top **7.** hardest, highest en~ deavour, utmost ~*v.* **8.** beat, blow out of the water (*Sl.*), conquer, defeat, get the better of, lick (*Inf.*), master, outclass, outdo, run rings around (*Inf.*), surpass, tank (*Sl.*), thrash, triumph over, trounce, undo, wipe the floor with (*Inf.*)

bestial animal, barbaric, barbarous, beast~ like, beastly, brutal, brutish, carnal, de~ graded, depraved, gross, inhuman, low, savage, sensual, sordid, vile

bestow accord, allot, apportion, award, commit, confer, donate, entrust, give, grant, hand out, honour with, impart, lavish, pre~ sent, render to
Antonyms acquire, attain, come by, earn, gain, get, make, net, obtain, procure, secure

bestride bestraddle, bridge, dominate, ex~ tend, mount, span, step over, straddle, tow~ er over

bet 1. *n.* ante, gamble, hazard, long shot, pledge, risk, speculation, stake, venture, wager **2.** *v.* chance, gamble, hazard, pledge, punt (*Chiefly Brit.*), put money on, risk, speculate, stake, venture, wager

bête noire abomination, anathema, aver~ sion, bane, bugbear, curse, pet hate

betide bechance, befall, chance, come to pass, crop up (*Inf.*), ensue, happen, occur, overtake, supervene, take place, transpire (*Inf.*)

betimes anon, beforehand, before long, early, erelong (*Archaic or poetic*), first thing, in good time, punctually, seasonably, soon

betoken augur, bespeak, bode, declare, de~ note, evidence, indicate, manifest, mark, portend, presage, prognosticate, promise, represent, signify, suggest, typify

betray 1. be disloyal (treacherous, unfaith~ ful), break one's promise, break with, double-cross (*Inf.*), inform on *or* against, sell down the river (*Inf.*), sell out (*Inf.*), shop (*Sl., chiefly Brit.*) **2.** blurt out, disclose, divulge, evince, expose, give away, lay bare, let slip, manifest, reveal, show, tell, tell on, uncover, unmask **3.** beguile, corrupt, de~ ceive, delude, dupe, ensnare, entrap, lead astray, mislead, undo **4.** abandon, desert, forsake, jilt, walk out on

betrayal 1. deception, disloyalty, double-cross (*Inf.*), double-dealing, duplicity, false~ ness, perfidy, sell-out (*Inf.*), treachery, trea~ son, trickery, unfaithfulness **2.** blurting out, disclosure, divulgence, giving away, revelation, telling
Antonyms (*sense 1*) allegiance, constancy, devotion, faithfulness, fealty, fidelity, loyalty, steadfastness, trustiness, trustworthiness (*sense 2*) guarding, keeping, keeping secret, preserving, safeguarding

betrayer apostate, conspirator, deceiver, renegade, traitor

betrothal affiancing, betrothing, engage~ ment, espousal (*Archaic*), marriage compact, plight, promise, troth, vow

better *adj.* **1.** bigger, excelling, finer, fitter, greater, higher-quality, larger, more appro~ priate (desirable, expert, fitting, suitable, useful, valuable), preferable, superior, sur~ passing, worthier **2.** cured, fitter, fully re~ covered, healthier, improving, less ill, mending, more healthy, on the mend (*Inf.*), progressing, recovering, stronger, well **3.** bigger, greater, larger, longer ~*adv.* **4.** in a more excellent manner, in a superior way, more advantageously (attractively, compe~ tently, completely, effectively, thoroughly), to a greater degree ~*v.* **5.** advance, amelio~ rate, amend, correct, enhance, forward, further, improve, meliorate, mend, promote, raise, rectify, reform **6.** beat, cap (*Inf.*), clobber (*Sl.*), exceed, excel, improve on *or* upon, lick (*Inf.*), outdo, outstrip, run rings around (*Inf.*), surpass, top ~*n.* **7. get the**

better of beat, best, defeat, get the upper hand, outdo, outsmart (*Inf.*), outwit, prevail over, score off, surpass, triumph over, worst
Antonyms *adj.* inferior, lesser, smaller, substandard, worse ~*adv.* worse ~*v.* depress, devaluate, go downhill, impoverish, lessen, lower, weaken, worsen

between amidst, among, betwixt, halfway, in the middle of, mid

beverage bevvy (*Dialect*), draught, drink, libation (*Facetious*), liquid, liquor, potable, potation, refreshment

bevy 1. band, bunch (*Inf.*), collection, com~ pany, crowd, gathering, group, pack, troupe **2.** covey, flight, flock

bewail bemoan, cry over, deplore, express sorrow, grieve for, keen, lament, moan, mourn, regret, repent, rue, wail, weep over

beware avoid, be careful (cautious, wary), guard against, heed, look out, mind, refrain from, shun, steer clear of, take heed, watch out

bewilder baffle, befuddle, bemuse, con~ found, confuse, daze, flummox, mix up, mystify, nonplus, perplex, puzzle, stupefy

bewildered at sea, awed, baffled, bamboo~ zled (*Inf.*), confused, disconcerted, dizzy, flummoxed, giddy, mystified, nonplussed, perplexed, puzzled, speechless, startled, stunned, surprised, taken aback, uncertain

bewitch absorb, allure, attract, beguile, captivate, charm, enchant, enrapture, en~ trance, fascinate, hypnotize, ravish, spell~ bind
Antonyms disgust, give one the creeps (*Inf.*), make one sick, offend, repel, repulse, sicken, turn off (*Inf.*)

bewitched charmed, enchanted, entranced, mesmerized, possessed, spellbound, trans~ formed, under a spell, unrecognizable

beyond above, apart from, at a distance, away from, before, farther, out of range, out of reach, outwith (*Scot.*), over, past, remote, superior to, yonder

bias *n.* **1.** bent, bigotry, favouritism, incli~ nation, intolerance, leaning, narrow-mindedness, one-sidedness, partiality, pen~ chant, predilection, predisposition, preju~ dice, proclivity, proneness, propensity, ten~ dency, turn, unfairness **2.** angle, cross, di~ agonal line, slant ~*v.* **3.** distort, influence, predispose, prejudice, slant, sway, twist, warp, weight
Antonyms (*sense 1*) equality, equity, fair~ ness, impartiality, neutrality, objectivity, open-mindedness

biased distorted, embittered, jaundiced, one-sided, partial, predisposed, prejudiced, slanted, swayed, twisted, warped, weighted

bicker argue, disagree, dispute, fight, quar~
rel, row (*Inf.*), scrap (*Inf.*), spar, squabble,
wrangle
Antonyms accord, acquiesce, agree, assent,
concur, cooperate, get on, harmonize

bid *v.* **1.** offer, proffer, propose, submit, ten~
der **2.** call, greet, say, tell, wish **3.** ask, call,
charge, command, desire, direct, enjoin, in~
struct, invite, require, solicit, summon, tell
~*n.* **4.** advance, amount, offer, price, pro~
posal, proposition, submission, sum, tender
5. attempt, crack (*Inf.*), effort, endeavour,
go (*Inf.*), stab (*Inf.*), try, venture

biddable amenable, complaisant, coopera~
tive, docile, obedient, teachable, tractable
Antonyms awkward, difficult, disobedient,
intractable, petulant, querulous, refractory,
unruly

bidding **1.** beck, behest, call, canon, charge,
command, demand, direction, injunction,
instruction, invitation, order, request, sum~
mons **2.** auction, offer, offers, proposal,
tender

big **1.** bulky, burly, colossal, considerable,
elephantine, enormous, extensive, gigantic,
great, huge, hulking, humongous *or* hu~
mungous (*U.S. sl.*), immense, large, mam~
moth, massive, ponderous, prodigious, siz~
able, spacious, substantial, vast, volumi~
nous **2.** big-time (*Inf.*), eminent, important,
influential, leading, main, major league
(*Inf.*), momentous, paramount, powerful,
prime, principal, prominent, serious,
significant, valuable, weighty **3.** adult, el~
der, grown, grown-up, mature **4.** altruistic,
benevolent, generous, gracious, heroic,
magnanimous, noble, princely, unselfish **5.**
arrogant, boastful, bragging, conceited,
haughty, inflated, pompous, pretentious,
proud
Antonyms (*senses 1 & 3*) diminutive, imma~
ture, insignificant, little, mini, miniature, pe~
tite, pint-sized (*Inf.*), pocket-sized, pygmy *or*
pigmy, small, tiny, wee, young (*sense 2*) hum~
ble, ignoble, insignificant, minor, modest, or~
dinary, unimportant, unknown

bigot dogmatist, fanatic, persecutor, sectar~
ian, zealot

bigoted biased, dogmatic, illiberal, intoler~
ant, narrow-minded, obstinate, opinionated,
prejudiced, sectarian, twisted, warped
Antonyms broad-minded, equitable, open-
minded, tolerant, unbiased, unbigoted, un~
prejudiced

bigotry bias, discrimination, dogmatism,
fanaticism, ignorance, injustice, intoler~
ance, mindlessness, narrow-mindedness,
pig-ignorance (*Sl.*), prejudice, provincialism,
racialism, racism, sectarianism, sexism,
unfairness

Antonyms broad-mindedness, forbearance,
open-mindedness, permissiveness, tolerance

bigwig big cheese (*Sl., old-fashioned*), big
gun (*Inf.*), big noise (*Inf.*), big shot (*Inf.*),
celeb (*Inf.*), celebrity, dignitary, heavy~
weight (*Inf.*), mogul, nob (*Sl.*), notability,
notable, panjandrum, personage, somebody,
V.I.P.
Antonyms cipher, lightweight (*Inf.*), no~
body, nonentity, nothing, zero

bile anger, bitterness, churlishness, ill hu~
mour, irascibility, irritability, nastiness,
peevishness, rancour, spleen

bilious **1.** liverish, nauseated, out of sorts,
queasy, sick **2.** bad-tempered, cantanker~
ous, crabby, cross, crotchety, edgy, grouchy
(*Inf.*), grumpy, ill-humoured, ill-tempered,
irritable, nasty, peevish, ratty (*Brit. & N.Z.
inf.*), short-tempered, testy, tetchy, touchy

bilk bamboozle (*Inf.*), cheat, con (*Inf.*), cozen,
deceive, defraud, do (*Sl.*), fleece, rook (*Sl.*),
skin (*Sl.*), stiff (*Sl.*), swindle, trick

bill[1] *n.* **1.** account, charges, invoice, note of
charge, reckoning, score, statement, tally **2.**
advertisement, broadsheet, bulletin, circu~
lar, handbill, handout, leaflet, notice, plac~
ard, playbill, poster **3.** agenda, card, cata~
logue, inventory, list, listing, programme,
roster, schedule, syllabus **4.** measure, piece
of legislation, projected law, proposal ~*v.* **5.**
charge, debit, figure, invoice, reckon, record
6. advertise, announce, give advance notice
of, post

bill[2] beak, mandible, neb (*Archaic or dialect*),
nib

billet **1.** *n.* accommodation, barracks, lodg~
ing, quarters **2.** *v.* accommodate, berth,
quarter, station

billow *n.* **1.** breaker, crest, roller, surge,
swell, tide, wave **2.** cloud, deluge, flood,
outpouring, rush, surge, wave ~*v.* **3.** bal~
loon, belly, puff up, rise up, roll, surge,
swell

billowy heaving, rippling, rolling, surging,
swelling, swirling, undulating, waving,
wavy

bind *v.* **1.** attach, fasten, glue, hitch, lash,
paste, rope, secure, stick, strap, tie, tie up,
truss, wrap **2.** compel, constrain, engage,
force, necessitate, obligate, oblige, pre~
scribe, require **3.** confine, detain, hamper,
hinder, restrain, restrict **4.** bandage, cover,
dress, encase, swathe, wrap **5.** border, edge,
finish, hem, trim ~*n.* **6.** *Inf.* bore, difficulty,
dilemma, drag (*Inf.*), hot water (*Inf.*), nui~
sance, pain in the arse (*Taboo inf.*), pre~
dicament, quandary, spot (*Inf.*), tight spot
Antonyms (*senses 1 & 3*) free, loosen, release,
unbind, undo, unfasten, untie

binding *adj.* compulsory, conclusive, im~

perative, indissoluble, irrevocable, manda~
tory, necessary, obligatory, unalterable
Antonyms discretionary, free, noncompul~
sory, optional, uncompelled, unconstrained,
unforced, voluntary

binge beano (*Brit. sl.*), bender (*Inf.*), blind
(*Sl.*), bout, feast, fling, jag (*Sl.*), orgy, spree

biography account, curriculum vitae, CV,
life, life history, life story, memoir, mem~
oirs, profile, record

birth 1. childbirth, delivery, nativity, partu~
rition **2.** beginning, emergence, fountain~
head, genesis, origin, rise, source **3.** ances~
try, background, blood, breeding, deriva~
tion, descent, extraction, forebears, geneal
ogy, line, lineage, nobility, noble extraction,
parentage, pedigree, race, stock, strain
Antonyms (*senses 1 & 2*) death, demise, end,
extinction, passing, passing away *or* on

bisect bifurcate, cross, cut across, cut in
half, cut in two, divide in two, halve, inter~
sect, separate, split, split down the middle

bisexual AC/DC (*Sl.*), ambidextrous (*Sl.*),
androgyne, androgynous, bi (*Sl.*), epicene,
gynandromorphic *or* gynandromorphous
(*Entomology*), gynandrous, hermaphrodite,
hermaphroditic, monoclinous (*Botany*),
swinging both ways (*Sl.*)

bishopric diocese, episcopacy, episcopate,
primacy, see

bit¹ 1. atom, chip, crumb, fragment, grain,
iota, jot, mite, morsel, mouthful, part, piece,
remnant, scrap, segment, slice, small piece,
speck, tittle, whit **2.** instant, jiffy (*Inf.*), lit~
tle while, minute, moment, period, second,
spell, tick (*Brit. inf.*), time

bit² 1. brake, check, curb, restraint, snaffle
2. take the bit in *or* **between one's teeth**
defy, disobey, get stuck into (*Inf.*), get to
grips with, rebel, resist, revolt, run amok,
rush into, set about

bitchy backbiting, catty (*Inf.*), cruel, mali~
cious, mean, nasty, rancorous, shrewish,
snide, spiteful, venomous, vicious, vindic~
tive, vixenish
Antonyms charitable, generous, gracious,
kindly, magnanimous, nice

bite *v.* **1.** champ, chew, clamp, crunch,
crush, cut, gnaw, grip, hold, masticate, nib~
ble, nip, pierce, pinch, rend, seize, snap,
tear, wound **2.** burn, corrode, eat away, eat
into, erode, smart, sting, tingle, wear away
~*n.* **3.** itch, nip, pinch, prick, smarting,
sting, tooth marks, wound **4.** food, light
meal, morsel, mouthful, piece, refreshment,
snack, taste **5.** edge, kick (*Inf.*), piquancy,
punch (*Inf.*), pungency, spice

biting 1. bitter, blighting, cold, cutting,
freezing, harsh, nipping, penetrating, pierc~
ing, sharp **2.** caustic, cutting, incisive,

mordacious, mordant, sarcastic, scathing,
severe, sharp, stinging, trenchant, vitriolic,
withering

bitter 1. acerb, acid, acrid, astringent,
sharp, sour, tart, unsweetened, vinegary **2.**
acrimonious, begrudging, crabbed, embit~
tered, hostile, morose, rancorous, resentful,
sore, sour, sullen, with a chip on one's
shoulder **3.** calamitous, cruel, dire, dis~
tressing, galling, grievous, harsh, heart~
breaking, merciless, painful, poignant,
ruthless, savage, vexatious **4.** biting, fierce,
freezing, intense, severe, stinging
Antonyms appreciative, balmy, bland, for~
tunate, friendly, gentle, grateful, happy, mel~
low, mild, pleasant, sugary, sweet, thankful

bitterness 1. acerbity, acidity, sharpness,
sourness, tartness, vinegariness **2.** animos~
ity, grudge, hostility, pique, rancour, re~
sentment **3.** acrimoniousness, asperity,
sarcasm, venom, virulence

bizarre abnormal, comical, curious, eccen~
tric, extraordinary, fantastic, freakish, gro~
tesque, ludicrous, odd, oddball (*Inf.*), off~
beat, off-the-wall (*Sl.*), outlandish, outré,
peculiar, queer, ridiculous, rum (*Brit. sl.*),
strange, unusual, wacko (*Sl.*), way-out (*Inf.*),
weird, zany
Antonyms common, customary, normal,
ordinary, regular, routine, standard, typical

blab blow wide open (*Sl.*), blurt out, disclose,
divulge, gossip, let slip, reveal, shop (*Sl.*,
chiefly Brit.), sing (*Sl., chiefly U.S.*), spill
one's guts (*Sl.*), tattle, tell, tell all, tell on

blabber 1. *n.* busybody, gossip, informer,
rumour-monger, scandalmonger, talebearer,
tattler, telltale **2.** *v.* blather, blether (*Scot.*),
chatter, gab (*Inf.*), jabber, prattle

black *adj.* **1.** coal-black, dark, dusky, ebony,
inky, jet, murky, pitchy, raven, sable, star~
less, stygian, swarthy **2.** *Fig.* atrocious, de~
pressing, dismal, distressing, doleful, fore~
boding, funereal, gloomy, hopeless, horrible,
lugubrious, mournful, ominous, sad, sombre
3. dingy, dirty, filthy, grimy, grubby, soiled,
sooty, stained **4.** angry, furious, hostile,
menacing, resentful, sullen, threatening **5.**
bad, evil, iniquitous, nefarious, villainous,
wicked ~*v.* **6.** ban, bar, blacklist, boycott
~*n.* **7. in the black** in credit, in funds, sol~
vent, without debt
Antonyms amicable, bright, cheerful,
friendly, good, happy, honourable, illuminat~
ed, light, lighted, lit, moonlit, moral, pleased,
pure, sunny, warm, white, whitish

blackball *v.* ban, bar, blacklist, debar, drum
out, exclude, expel, ostracize, oust, repudi~
ate, snub, vote against

blacken 1. befoul, begrime, cloud, darken,
grow black, make black, smudge, soil **2.**
bad-mouth (*Sl., chiefly U.S. & Canad.*), ca~

lumniate, decry, defame, defile, denigrate, dishonour, knock (*Inf.*), malign, rubbish (*Inf.*), slag (off) (*Sl.*), slander, smear, smirch, stain, sully, taint, tarnish, traduce, vilify

blackguard bad egg (*Old-fashioned inf.*), bastard (*Offens.*), blighter (*Brit. inf.*), bounder (*Old-fashioned Brit. sl.*), bugger (*Taboo sl.*), miscreant, rascal, rogue, scoun~ drel, scumbag (*Sl.*), shit (*Taboo sl.*), son-of-a-bitch (*Sl., chiefly U.S. & Canad.*), swine, villain, wretch

blacklist *v.* ban, bar, blackball, boycott, de~ bar, exclude, expel, ostracize, preclude, proscribe, reject, repudiate, snub, vote against

black magic black art, diabolism, necro~ mancy, sorcery, voodoo, witchcraft, wizard~ ry

blackmail 1. *n.* bribe, exaction, extortion, hush money (*Sl.*), intimidation, milking, pay-off (*Inf.*), protection (*Inf.*), ransom, shakedown (*U.S. sl.*), slush fund **2.** *v.* bleed (*Inf.*), bribe, coerce, compel, demand, exact, extort, force, hold to ransom, milk, squeeze, threaten

blackness darkness, duskiness, gloom, inkiness, melanism, murkiness, nigres~ cence, nigritude (*Rare*), swarthiness
Antonyms brightness, brilliance, efful~ gence, incandescence, lambency, light, light~ ness, luminescence, luminosity, phosphores~ cence, radiance

blackout *n.* **1.** coma, faint, loss of con~ sciousness, oblivion, swoon, syncope (*Pa~ thology*), unconsciousness **2.** power cut, power failure **3.** censorship, noncommuni~ cation, radio silence, secrecy, suppression, withholding news

black out *v.* **1.** conceal, cover, darken, eclipse, obfuscate, shade **2.** collapse, faint, flake out (*Inf.*), lose consciousness, pass out, swoon

black sheep disgrace, dropout, ne'er-do-well, outcast, prodigal, renegade, reprobate, wastrel

blame *n.* **1.** accountability, culpability, fault, guilt, incrimination, liability, onus, rap (*Sl.*), responsibility **2.** accusation, cas~ tigation, censure, charge, complaint, con~ demnation, criticism, recrimination, re~ proach, reproof, stick (*Sl.*) ~*v.* **3.** accuse, admonish, blast, censure, charge, chide, condemn, criticize, disapprove, express dis~ approbation, find fault with, hold respon~ sible, lambast(e), put down, reprehend, re~ proach, reprove, tax, tear into (*Inf.*), up~ braid
Antonyms *n.* absolution, acclaim, alibi, Brownie points, commendation, credit, ex~ cuse, exoneration, honour, praise, tribute, vindication ~*v.* absolve, acclaim, acquit, ap~

prove of, clear, commend, compliment, ex~ cuse, exonerate, forgive, praise, vindicate

blameless above suspicion, clean, faultless, guiltless, immaculate, impeccable, innocent, in the clear, irreproachable, perfect, squeaky-clean, stainless, unblemished, un~ impeachable, unoffending, unspotted, un~ sullied, untarnished, upright, virtuous
Antonyms at fault, censurable, culpable, guilty, reprovable, responsible, to blame

blameworthy discreditable, disreputable, indefensible, inexcusable, iniquitous, rep~ rehensible, reproachable, shameful

bland 1. boring, dull, flat, humdrum, insip~ id, monotonous, tasteless, tedious, undistinctive, unexciting, uninspiring, un~ interesting, unstimulating, vapid, weak **2.** affable, amiable, congenial, courteous, debonair, friendly, gentle, gracious, smooth, suave, unemotional, urbane **3.** balmy, calm, mild, mollifying, nonirritant *or* nonirritating (*Medical*), soft, soothing, tem~ perate
Antonyms (*sense 1*) distinctive, exciting, in~ spiring, interesting, rousing, stimulating, turbulent, volatile (*sense 3*) annoying, harsh, irritating, rough, severe

blandishments blarney, cajolery, coaxing, compliments, fawning, flattery, ingratiation, inveiglement, soft soap (*Inf.*), soft words, sweet talk (*Inf.*), wheedling, winning ca~ resses

blank *adj.* **1.** bare, clean, clear, empty, plain, spotless, uncompleted, unfilled, un~ marked, void, white **2.** deadpan, dull, emp~ ty, expressionless, hollow, impassive, inane, lifeless, poker-faced (*Inf.*), vacant, vacuous, vague **3.** at a loss, at sea, bewildered, con~ founded, confused, disconcerted, dumb~ founded, flummoxed, muddled, nonplussed, uncomprehending **4.** absolute, complete, outright, thorough, unqualified, utter ~*n.* **5.** emptiness, empty space, gap, nothing~ ness, space, tabula rasa, vacancy, vacuity, vacuum, void
Antonyms alert, busy, completed, expres~ sive, filled in, full, intelligent, interested, live~ ly, marked, productive, profitable, rewarding, significant, thoughtful, useful, valuable

blanket *n.* **1.** afghan, cover, coverlet, rug **2.** carpet, cloak, coat, coating, covering, en~ velope, film, layer, mantle, sheet, wrapper, wrapping ~*adj.* **3.** across-the-board, all-inclusive, comprehensive, overall, sweep~ ing, wide-ranging ~*v.* **4.** cloak, cloud, coat, conceal, cover, eclipse, hide, mask, obscure, suppress, surround

blankness abstraction, fatuity, inanity, in~ difference, no recollection, obliviousness, vacancy, vacuity

blare blast, boom, clamour, clang, honk,

hoot, peal, resound, roar, scream, sound out, toot, trumpet

blarney blandishment, cajolery, coaxing, exaggeration, flattery, honeyed words, overpraise, soft soap (*Inf.*), spiel, sweet talk (*Inf.*), wheedling

blasé apathetic, bored, cloyed, glutted, in~ different, jaded, lukewarm, nonchalant, off~ hand, satiated, surfeited, unconcerned, un~ excited, uninterested, unmoved, weary, world-weary
Antonyms affected, caring, enthusiastic, excited, interested, responsive, stimulated

blaspheme abuse, anathematize, curse, damn, desecrate, execrate, profane, revile, swear

blasphemous godless, impious, irreli~ gious, irreverent, profane, sacrilegious, un~ godly
Antonyms devout, God-fearing, godly, pi~ ous, religious, respectful, reverent, reveren~ tial

blasphemy cursing, desecration, execra~ tion, impiety, impiousness, indignity (*to God*), irreverence, profanation, profaneness, profanity, sacrilege, swearing

blast n./v. **1.** blare, blow, clang, honk, peal, scream, toot, wail ~n. **2.** bang, blow-up, burst, crash, detonation, discharge, erup~ tion, explosion, outburst, salvo, volley **3.** gale, gust, squall, storm, strong breeze, tempest ~v. **4.** blow up, break up, burst, demolish, destroy, explode, ruin, shatter **5.** blight, kill, shrivel, wither **6.** attack, casti~ gate, criticize, flay, lambast(e), put down, rail at, tear into (*Inf.*)

blasted blighted, desolated, destroyed, dev~ astated, ravaged, ruined, shattered, spoiled, wasted, withered

blastoff n. discharge, expulsion, firing, launch, launching, liftoff, projection, shot

blatant **1.** bald, brazen, conspicuous, flagrant, flaunting, glaring, naked, obtru~ sive, obvious, ostentatious, outright, overt, prominent, pronounced, sheer, unmitigated **2.** clamorous, deafening, ear-splitting, harsh, loud, noisy, piercing, strident
Antonyms agreeable, cultured, dignified, hidden, inconspicuous, quiet, refined, soft, subtle, tasteful, unnoticeable, unobtrusive, well-mannered

blather claptrap (*Inf.*), drivel, gibberish, gobbledegook, jabber, jabbering, moonshine, pap, twaddle

blaze n. **1.** bonfire, conflagration, fire, flame, flames **2.** beam, brilliance, flare, flash, glare, gleam, glitter, glow, light, radiance **3.** blast, burst, eruption, flare-up, fury, out~ break, outburst, rush, storm, torrent ~v. **4.** beam, burn, fire, flame, flare, flash, glare,

gleam, glow, shine **5.** boil, explode, flare up, fume, seethe

blazon broadcast, celebrate, flourish, make known, proclaim, renown, trumpet

bleach blanch, etiolate, fade, grow pale, lighten, peroxide, wash out, whiten

bleached achromatic, etiolated, faded, lightened, peroxided, stone-washed, washed-out

bleak **1.** bare, barren, chilly, cold, desolate, exposed, gaunt, open, raw, unsheltered, weather-beaten, windswept, windy **2.** cheerless, comfortless, depressing, discour~ aging, disheartening, dismal, dreary, gloomy, grim, hopeless, joyless, sombre, unpromising
Antonyms cheerful, cosy, encouraging, promising, protected, sheltered, shielded

bleary blurred, blurry, dim, fogged, foggy, fuzzy, hazy, indistinct, misty, murky, rheumy, watery

bleed **1.** exude, flow, gush, lose blood, ooze, run, seep, shed blood, spurt, trickle, weep **2.** deplete, drain, draw *or* take blood, ex~ haust, extort, extract, fleece, leech, milk, phlebotomize (*Medical*), reduce, sap, squeeze **3.** ache, agonize, feel for, grieve, pity, suffer, sympathize

blemish **1.** n. blot, blotch, blur, defect, de~ merit, disfigurement, disgrace, dishonour, fault, flaw, imperfection, mark, scar, smirch, smudge, speck, spot, stain, taint **2.** v. blot, blotch, blur, damage, deface, disfigure, flaw, impair, injure, mar, mark, smirch, smudge, spoil, spot, stain, sully, taint, tarnish
Antonyms n. enhancement, improvement, ornament, perfection, purity, refinement ~v. correct, enhance, improve, perfect, purify, refine, restore

blend v. **1.** amalgamate, coalesce, combine, compound, fuse, intermix, meld, merge, mingle, mix, synthesize, unite **2.** comple~ ment, fit, go well, go with, harmonize, suit ~n. **3.** alloy, amalgam, amalgamation, com~ bination, composite, compound, concoction, fusion, meld, mix, mixture, synthesis, union

bless **1.** anoint, consecrate, dedicate, exalt, extol, give thanks to, glorify, hallow, invoke happiness on, magnify, ordain, praise, sanctify, thank **2.** bestow, endow, favour, give, grace, grant, provide
Antonyms (*sense 1*) accuse, anathematize, curse, damn, excommunicate, execrate, ful~ minate, imprecate (*sense 2*) afflict, blight, bur~ den, curse, destroy, doom, plague, scourge, torment, trouble, vex

blessed **1.** adored, beatified, divine, hal~ lowed, holy, revered, sacred, sanctified **2.** endowed, favoured, fortunate, granted, jam~

my (*Brit. sl.*), lucky **3.** blissful, contented, glad, happy, joyful, joyous

blessedness beatitude, bliss, blissfulness, content, felicity, happiness, heavenly joy, pleasure, sanctity, state of grace, *summum bonum*

blessing 1. benediction, benison, commen~ dation, consecration, dedication, grace, in~ vocation, thanksgiving **2.** approbation, ap~ proval, backing, concurrence, consent, fa~ vour, good wishes, leave, permission, re~ gard, sanction, support **3.** advantage, benefit, boon, bounty, favour, gain, gift, godsend, good fortune, help, kindness, profit, service, windfall
Antonyms condemnation, curse, damage, deprivation, disadvantage, disapproval, dis~ favour, drawback, harm, malediction, mis~ fortune, objection, reproof

blight *n.* **1.** canker, decay, disease, fungus, infestation, mildew, pest, pestilence, rot **2.** affliction, bane, contamination, corruption, curse, evil, plague, pollution, scourge, woe ~*v.* **3.** blast, destroy, injure, nip in the bud, ruin, shrivel, taint with mildew, wither **4.** *Fig.* annihilate, crush, dash, disappoint, frustrate, mar, nullify, ruin, spoil, undo, wreck
Antonyms *n.* benefaction, blessing, boon, bounty, favour, godsend, help, service

blind *adj.* **1.** destitute of vision, eyeless, sightless, stone-blind, unseeing, unsighted, visionless **2.** *Fig.* careless, heedless, igno~ rant, inattentive, inconsiderate, indifferent, indiscriminate, injudicious, insensitive, morally darkened, neglectful, oblivious, prejudiced, thoughtless, unaware of, uncon~ scious of, uncritical, undiscerning, un~ mindful of, unobservant, unreasoning **3.** hasty, impetuous, irrational, mindless, rash, reckless, senseless, uncontrollable, uncon~ trolled, unthinking, violent, wild **4.** closed, concealed, dark, dead-end, dim, hidden, leading nowhere, obscured, obstructed, without exit ~*n.* **5.** camouflage, cloak, cov~ er, façade, feint, front, mask, masquerade, screen, smoke screen
Antonyms *adj.* alive to, attentive, aware, concerned, conscious, discerning, heedful, knowledgeable, noticeable, observant, obvi~ ous, open, seeing, sighted

blindly 1. aimlessly, at random, confusedly, frantically, indiscriminately, instinctively, madly, purposelessly, wildly **2.** carelessly, heedlessly, impulsively, inconsiderately, passionately, recklessly, regardlessly, senselessly, thoughtlessly, unreasonably, wilfully

blink 1. bat, flutter, glimpse, nictate, nicti~ tate, peer, squint, wink **2.** flash, flicker, gleam, glimmer, scintillate, shine, sparkle,

twinkle, wink **3.** *Fig.* condone, connive at, disregard, ignore, overlook, pass by, turn a blind eye to **4. on the blink** *Sl.* faulty, malfunctioning, not working (properly), on the fritz (*U.S. sl.*), out of action, out of or~ der, playing up

bliss beatitude, blessedness, blissfulness, ec~ stasy, euphoria, felicity, gladness, happi~ ness, heaven, joy, paradise, rapture
Antonyms affliction, anguish, distress, grief, heartbreak, misery, mourning, regret, sadness, sorrow, unhappiness, woe, wretch~ edness

blissful cock-a-hoop, delighted, ecstatic, elated, enchanted, enraptured, euphoric, happy, heavenly (*Inf.*), in ecstasies, joyful, joyous, over the moon (*Inf.*), rapt, rapturous

blister abscess, blain, bleb, boil, bubble, canker, carbuncle, cyst, furuncle (*Pathol~ ogy*), pimple, pustule, sore, swelling, ulcer, welt, wen

blithe 1. animated, buoyant, carefree, cheerful, cheery, chirpy (*Inf.*), debonair, gay, genial, gladsome (*Archaic*), happy, jaunty, light-hearted, merry, mirthful, sprightly, sunny, upbeat (*Inf.*), vivacious **2.** careless, casual, heedless, indifferent, non~ chalant, thoughtless, unconcerned, untrou~ bled
Antonyms concerned, dejected, depressed, gloomy, kind-hearted, melancholy, morose, preoccupied, sad, thoughtful, unhappy

blitz assault, attack, blitzkrieg, bombard~ ment, offensive, onslaught, raid, strike

blizzard blast, gale, snowstorm, squall, storm, tempest

bloat balloon, blow up, dilate, distend, en~ large, expand, inflate, puff up, swell
Antonyms contract, deflate, shrink, shrivel, wither, wrinkle

blob ball, bead, bubble, dab, dewdrop, drop, droplet, glob, globule, lump, mass, pearl, pellet, pill

bloc alliance, axis, cabal, clique, coalition, combine, entente, faction, group, league, ring, schism, union, wing

block *n.* **1.** bar, brick, cake, chunk, cube, hunk, ingot, lump, mass, piece, square **2.** bar, barrier, blockage, hindrance, impedi~ ment, jam, obstacle, obstruction, occlusion, stoppage ~*v.* **3.** bung up (*Inf.*), choke, clog, close, obstruct, plug, stop up **4.** arrest, bar, check, deter, halt, hinder, impede, obstruct, stop, thwart
Antonyms *v.* (*sense 3*) clear, open, unblock, unclog (*sense 4*) advance, aid, expedite, facili~ tate, foster, further, lend support to, promote, push, support

blockade barricade, barrier, block, closure, encirclement, hindrance, impediment, ob~

stacle, obstruction, restriction, siege, stop~
page

blockage block, blocking, impediment, ob~
struction, occlusion, stoppage, stopping up

blockhead berk (*Brit. sl.*), bonehead (*Sl.*),
charlie (*Brit. inf.*), chump (*Inf.*), coot, dick~
head (*Sl.*), dipstick (*Brit. sl.*), divvy (*Brit.
sl.*), dolt, dork (*Sl.*), dullard, dunce, dweeb
(*U.S. sl.*), fool, fuckwit (*Taboo sl.*), geek (*Sl.*),
gonzo (*Sl.*), idiot, ignoramus, jerk (*Sl.,
chiefly U.S. & Canad.*), nerd *or* nurd (*Sl.*),
noodle, numskull *or* numbskull, pillock
(*Brit. sl.*), plank (*Brit. sl.*), plonker (*Sl.*), prat
(*Sl.*), prick (*Derogatory sl.*), schmuck (*U.S.
sl.*), thickhead, twit (*Inf., chiefly Brit.*), wally
(*Sl.*)

block out chart, map out, outline, plan,
sketch

bloke bastard (*Inf.*), bod (*Inf.*), body, boy,
bugger (*Sl.*), chap, character (*Inf.*), customer
(*Inf.*), fellow, guy (*Inf.*), individual, man,
person, punter (*Inf.*)

blond, blonde fair, fair-haired, fair-
skinned, flaxen, golden-haired, light, light-
coloured, light-complexioned, tow-headed

blood 1. gore, lifeblood, vital fluid **2.** an~
cestry, birth, consanguinity, descendants,
descent, extraction, family, kindred, kin~
ship, lineage, noble extraction, relations **3.**
Fig. anger, disposition, feeling, passion,
spirit, temper

bloodcurdling appalling, chilling, dread~
ful, fearful, frightening, hair-raising, hor~
rendous, horrifying, scaring, spine-chilling,
terrifying

bloodless 1. cold, languid, lifeless, listless,
passionless, spiritless, torpid, unemotional,
unfeeling **2.** anaemic, ashen, chalky, col~
ourless, pale, pallid, pasty, sallow, sickly,
wan

bloodshed blood bath, bloodletting, butch~
ery, carnage, gore, killing, massacre, mur~
der, slaughter, slaying

bloodthirsty barbarous, brutal, cruel, fe~
rocious, inhuman, murderous, ruthless,
savage, vicious, warlike

bloody 1. bleeding, blood-soaked, blood-
spattered, bloodstained, gaping, raw,
unstaunched **2.** cruel, ferocious, fierce,
sanguinary, savage

bloom *n.* **1.** blossom, blossoming, bud,
efflorescence, flower, opening (*of flowers*) **2.**
Fig. beauty, blush, flourishing, flush, fresh~
ness, glow, health, heyday, lustre, perfec~
tion, prime, radiance, rosiness, vigour ~*v.*
3. blossom, blow, bud, burgeon, open,
sprout **4.** develop, fare well, flourish, grow,
prosper, succeed, thrive, wax

Antonyms *n.* (*sense 2*) bloodlessness, pale~
ness, pallor, wanness, whiteness ~*v.* (*senses 3*

& 4) decay, decline, die, droop, fade, fail, lan~
guish, perish, shrink, shrivel, wane, waste,
wilt, wither

blossom *n.* **1.** bloom, bud, floret, flower,
flowers ~*v.* **2.** bloom, burgeon, flower **3.**
Fig. bloom, develop, flourish, grow, mature,
progress, prosper, thrive

blot *n.* **1.** blotch, mark, patch, smear,
smudge, speck, splodge, spot **2.** blemish,
blur, defect, demerit, disgrace, fault, flaw,
scar, smirch, spot, stain, taint ~*v.* **3.** be~
spatter, disfigure, disgrace, mark, smirch,
smudge, spoil, spot, stain, sully, tarnish **4.**
absorb, dry, soak up, take up **5. blot out**
cancel, darken, destroy, efface, erase, ex~
punge, obliterate, obscure, shadow

blotch blemish, blot, mark, patch, scar,
smirch, smudge, smutch, splash, splodge,
spot, stain

blotchy blemished, macular, patchy, red~
dened, scurvy, spotty, uneven

blow¹ *v.* **1.** blast, breathe, exhale, fan, pant,
puff, waft **2.** flow, rush, stream, whirl **3.**
bear, buffet, drive, fling, flutter, sweep,
waft, whirl, whisk **4.** blare, mouth, pipe,
play, sound, toot, trumpet, vibrate ~*n.* **5.**
blast, draught, flurry, gale, gust, puff,
strong breeze, tempest, wind

blow² *n.* **1.** bang, bash (*Inf.*), belt (*Inf.*), buf~
fet, clomp (*Sl.*), clout (*Inf.*), clump (*Sl.*),
knock, punch, rap, slosh (*Brit. sl.*), smack,
sock (*Sl.*), stroke, thump, wallop (*Inf.*),
whack **2.** *Fig.* affliction, bolt from the blue,
bombshell, bummer (*Sl.*), calamity, catas~
trophe, comedown (*Inf.*), disappointment,
disaster, jolt, misfortune, reverse, setback,
shock, upset

blowout 1. blast, detonation, eruption, ex~
plosion **2.** break, burst, escape, flat, flat
tyre, fuse, leak, puncture, rupture, tear **3.**
beano (*Brit. sl.*), binge (*Inf.*), carousal, ca~
rouse, feast, party, rave (*Brit. sl.*), rave-up
(*Brit. sl.*), spree

blow out 1. extinguish, put out, snuff **2.**
burst, erupt, explode, rupture, shatter

blow over be forgotten, cease, die down,
disappear, end, finish, pass, pass away,
subside, vanish

blow up 1. bloat, distend, enlarge, expand,
fill, inflate, puff up, pump up, swell **2.** blast,
bomb, burst, detonate, dynamite, explode,
go off, rupture, shatter **3.** enlarge, enlarge
on, exaggerate, heighten, magnify, overstate
4. *Inf.* become angry, become enraged, blow
a fuse (*Sl., chiefly U.S.*), crack up (*Inf.*),
erupt, fly off the handle (*Inf.*), go off the
deep end (*Inf.*), go up the wall (*Sl.*), hit the
roof (*Inf.*), lose one's temper, rage, see red
(*Inf.*)

blowzy, blowsy 1. bedraggled, dishev~

elled, frowzy, slatternly, slipshod, sloppy, slovenly, sluttish, tousled, unkempt, untidy **2.** florid, red-faced, ruddy

bludgeon n. **1.** club, cosh (*Brit.*), cudgel, shillelagh, truncheon ~v. **2.** beat, beat up, club, cosh (*Brit.*), cudgel, knock down, strike **3.** browbeat, bulldoze (*Inf.*), bully, coerce, dragoon, force, hector, railroad (*Inf.*), steamroller

blue 1. azure, cerulean, cobalt, cyan, navy, sapphire, sky-coloured, ultramarine **2.** *Fig.* dejected, depressed, despondent, dismal, downcast, down-hearted, down in the dumps (*Inf.*), fed up, gloomy, glum, low, melancholy, sad, unhappy **3.** *Inf.* bawdy, dirty, indecent, lewd, naughty, near the knuckle (*Inf.*), obscene, risqué, smutty, vulgar

Antonyms (*sense 2*) blithe, cheerful, cheery, chirpy (*Inf.*), elated, genial, happy, jolly, merry, optimistic, sunny (*sense 3*) decent, respectable

blueprint design, draft, layout, norm, outline, pattern, pilot scheme, plan, project, prototype, scheme, sketch

blues dejection, depression, despondency, doldrums, dumps (*Inf.*), gloom, gloominess, glumness, low spirits, melancholy, moodiness, the hump (*Brit. inf.*)

bluff[1] **1.** v. deceive, defraud, delude, fake, feign, humbug, lie, mislead, pretend, sham **2.** n. bluster, boast, braggadocio, bragging, bravado, deceit, deception, fake, feint, fraud, humbug, idle boast, lie, mere show, pretence, sham, show, subterfuge

bluff[2] n. **1.** bank, cliff, crag, escarpment, headland, peak, precipice, promontory, ridge, scarp ~adj. **2.** abrupt, blunt, blustering, downright, frank, genial, good-natured, hearty, open, outspoken, plain-spoken **3.** abrupt, perpendicular, precipitous, sheer, steep, towering

Antonyms (*sense 2*) delicate, diplomatic, discreet, judicious, sensitive, tactful, thoughtful

blunder n. **1.** error, fault, inaccuracy, mistake, oversight, slip, slip-up (*Inf.*) **2.** bloomer (*Brit. inf.*), boob (*Brit. sl.*), boo-boo (*Inf.*), clanger (*Inf.*), faux pas, gaffe, gaucherie, howler (*Inf.*), impropriety, indiscretion, mistake ~v. **3.** bodge (*Inf.*), botch, bungle, err, slip up (*Inf.*) **4.** bumble, confuse, flounder, misjudge, stumble

Antonyms n. accuracy, achievement, correctness, success ~v. be correct, be exact, get it right, go alertly

blunt adj. **1.** dull, dulled, edgeless, pointless, rounded, unsharpened **2.** *Fig.* bluff, brusque, discourteous, downright, explicit, forthright, frank, impolite, outspoken, plain-spoken, rude, straightforward, tact-

less, trenchant, uncivil, unpolished, upfront (*Inf.*) ~v. **3.** dampen, deaden, dull, numb, soften, take the edge off, water down, weaken

Antonyms adj. acute, courteous, diplomatic, keen, pointed, sensitive, sharp, subtle, tactful ~v. animate, put an edge on, sharpen, stimulate, vitalize

blur v. **1.** becloud, bedim, befog, cloud, darken, dim, fog, make hazy, make indistinct, make vague, mask, obscure, soften **2.** blot, smear, smudge, spot, stain ~n. **3.** blear, blurredness, cloudiness, confusion, dimness, fog, haze, indistinctness, obscurity **4.** blot, smear, smudge, spot, stain

blurred bleary, blurry, faint, foggy, fuzzy, hazy, ill-defined, indistinct, lacking definition, misty, nebulous, out of focus, unclear, vague

blurt out babble, blab, cry, disclose, exclaim, gush, reveal, run off at the mouth (*Sl.*), spill, spill one's guts (*Sl.*), spill the beans (*Inf.*), spout (*Inf.*), sputter, tattle, tell all, utter suddenly

blush 1. v. colour, crimson, flush, redden, turn red, turn scarlet **2.** n. colour, flush, glow, pink tinge, reddening, rosiness, rosy tint, ruddiness

Antonyms v. blanch, blench, drain, fade, pale, turn pale, whiten

bluster 1. v. boast, brag, bulldoze, bully, domineer, hector, rant, roar, roister, storm, swagger, swell, vaunt **2.** n. bluff, boasting, boisterousness, bombast, bragging, bravado, crowing, swagger, swaggering

blustery blusterous, boisterous, gusty, inclement, squally, stormy, tempestuous, violent, wild

board n. **1.** panel, piece of timber, plank, slat, timber **2.** daily meals, food, meals, provisions, victuals **3.** advisers, advisory group, committee, conclave, council, directorate, directors, panel, trustees ~v. **4.** embark, embus, enplane, enter, entrain, mount **5.** accommodate, feed, house, lodge, put up, quarter, room

Antonyms (*sense 4*) alight, arrive, disembark, dismount, get off, go ashore, land

boast v. **1.** blow one's own trumpet, bluster, brag, crow, exaggerate, puff, strut, swagger, talk big (*Sl.*), vaunt **2.** be proud of, congratulate oneself on, exhibit, flatter oneself, possess, pride oneself on, show off ~n. **3.** avowal, brag, gasconade (*Rare*), rodomontade (*Literary*), swank (*Inf.*), vaunt **4.** gem, joy, pride, pride and joy, source of pride, treasure

Antonyms v. cover up, depreciate, disavow, disclaim ~n. disavowal, disclaimer

boastful bragging, cocky, conceited, crowing, egotistical, puffed-up, swaggering,

swanky (*Inf.*), swollen-headed, vainglorious, vaunting
Antonyms deprecating, humble, modest, self-belittling, self-effacing, unassuming

bob bounce, duck, hop, jerk, leap, nod, oscillate, quiver, skip, waggle, weave, wobble

bode augur, betoken, forebode, foreshadow, foretell, forewarn, impart, omen, portend, predict, presage, prophesy, signify, threaten

bodiless disembodied, ghostly, immaterial, incorporeal, insubstantial, spectral, spiritual, supernatural

bodily 1. *adj.* actual, carnal, corporal, corporeal, fleshly, material, physical, substantial, tangible **2.** *adv.* altogether, as a body, as a group, collectively, completely, en masse, entirely, fully, totally, wholly

body 1. build, figure, form, frame, physique, shape, torso, trunk **2.** cadaver, carcass, corpse, dead body, relics, remains, stiff (*Sl.*) **3.** being, creature, human, human being, individual, mortal, person **4.** bulk, essence, main part, mass, material, matter, substance **5.** association, band, bloc, collection, company, confederation, congress, corporation, society **6.** crowd, horde, majority, mass, mob, multitude, throng **7.** consistency, density, firmness, richness, solidity, substance

boffin authority, brain(s) (*Inf.*), brainbox, egghead, genius, intellect, intellectual, inventor, mastermind, maven (*U.S.*), planner, thinker, virtuoso, wizard

bog fen, marsh, marshland, mire, morass, moss (*Scot. & Northern English dialect*), peat bog, quagmire, slough, swamp, wetlands

bog down delay, halt, impede, sink, slow down, slow up, stall, stick

bogey 1. apparition, bogeyman, goblin, hobgoblin, imp, spectre, spirit, spook (*Inf.*), sprite **2.** *bête noire*, bugaboo, bugbear, nightmare

boggle 1. be alarmed (confused, surprised, taken aback), shy, stagger, startle, take fright **2.** demur, dither (*Chiefly Brit.*), doubt, equivocate, falter, hang back, hesitate, hover, jib, shillyshally (*Inf.*), shrink from, vacillate, waver

boggy fenny, marshy, miry, muddy, oozy, quaggy, soft, spongy, swampy, waterlogged, yielding

bogus artificial, counterfeit, dummy, ersatz, fake, false, forged, fraudulent, imitation, phoney *or* phony (*Inf.*), pseudo (*Inf.*), sham, spurious
Antonyms actual, authentic, genuine, real, true

bohemian 1. *adj.* alternative, artistic, arty (*Inf.*), avant-garde, eccentric, exotic, left bank, nonconformist, oddball (*Inf.*), offbeat, off-the-wall (*Sl.*), outré, unconventional, unorthodox, way-out (*Inf.*) **2.** *n.* beatnik, dropout, hippie, iconoclast, nonconformist
Antonyms *adj.* bourgeois, conservative, conventional, square (*Inf.*), straight (*Sl.*), straight-laced, stuffy

boil¹ *v.* **1.** agitate, bubble, churn, effervesce, fizz, foam, froth, seethe **2.** be angry, be indignant, blow a fuse (*Sl., chiefly U.S.*), crack up (*Inf.*), fly off the handle (*Inf.*), foam at the mouth (*Inf.*), fulminate, fume, go off the deep end (*Inf.*), go up the wall (*Sl.*), rage, rave, see red (*Inf.*), storm

boil² *n.* blain, blister, carbuncle, furuncle (*Pathology*), gathering, pustule, tumour, ulcer

boil down come down, condense, decrease, reduce, summarize

boiling 1. baking, blistering, hot, roasting, scorching, tropical, very hot **2.** angry, cross, enraged, fuming, furious, incensed, indignant, infuriated

boisterous 1. bouncy, clamorous, disorderly, impetuous, loud, noisy, obstreperous, riotous, rollicking, rowdy, rumbustious, unrestrained, unruly, uproarious, vociferous, wild **2.** blustery, gusty, raging, rough, squally, stormy, tempestuous, tumultuous, turbulent
Antonyms calm, controlled, peaceful, quiet, restrained, self-controlled, subdued

bold 1. adventurous, audacious, brave, courageous, daring, dauntless, enterprising, fearless, gallant, gritty, heroic, intrepid, lion-hearted, valiant, valorous **2.** barefaced, brash, brazen, cheeky, confident, feisty (*Inf., chiefly U.S. & Canad.*), forward, fresh (*Inf.*), impudent, insolent, pert, pushy (*Inf.*), rude, sassy (*U.S. inf.*), saucy, shameless **3.** bright, colourful, conspicuous, eye-catching, flashy, forceful, lively, loud, prominent, pronounced, showy, spirited, striking, strong, vivid
Antonyms conservative, cool, courteous, cowardly, dull, faint-hearted, fearful, meek, modest, ordinary, pale, polite, retiring, shy, soft, tactful, timid, timorous, unimaginative

bolster aid, assist, augment, boost, brace, buoy up, buttress, cushion, help, hold up, maintain, pillow, prop, reinforce, shore up, stay, strengthen, support

bolt *n.* **1.** bar, catch, fastener, latch, lock, sliding bar **2.** peg, pin, rivet, rod **3.** bound, dart, dash, escape, flight, rush, spring, sprint **4.** arrow, dart, missile, projectile, shaft, thunderbolt ~*v.* **5.** bar, fasten, latch, lock, secure **6.** cram, devour, gobble, gorge, gulp, guzzle, stuff, swallow whole, wolf **7.** abscond, bound, dash, decamp, do a runner (*Sl.*), escape, flee, fly, fly the coop (*U.S. &*

Canad. inf.), hurtle, jump, leap, make a break (for it), run, run for it, rush, skedad~ dle (*Inf.*), spring, sprint, take a powder (*U.S. & Canad. sl.*), take it on the lam (*U.S. & Canad. sl.*)

bomb 1. *n.* bombshell, charge, device, ex~ plosive, grenade, mine, missile, projectile, rocket, shell, torpedo **2.** *v.* attack, blow up, bombard, destroy, shell, strafe, torpedo

bombard 1. assault, blast, blitz, bomb, cannonade, fire upon, open fire, pound, shell, strafe **2.** assail, attack, barrage, bat~ ter, beset, besiege, harass, hound, pester

bombardment assault, attack, barrage, blitz, bombing, cannonade, fire, flak, fusil~ lade, shelling, strafe

bombast bluster, brag, braggadocio, ex~ travagant boasting, fustian, gasconade (*Rare*), grandiloquence, grandiosity, mag~ niloquence, pomposity, rant, rodomontade (*Literary*)

bombastic declamatory, fustian, grandilo~ quent, grandiose, high-flown, histrionic, inflated, magniloquent, pompous, ranting, turgid, verbose, windy, wordy

bona fide actual, authentic, genuine, hon~ est, kosher (*Inf.*), lawful, legal, legitimate, real, true
Antonyms bogus, counterfeit, ersatz, fake, false, imitation, phoney *or* phony (*Inf.*), sham

bond *n.* **1.** band, binding, chain, cord, fas~ tening, fetter, ligature, link, manacle, shackle, tie **2.** affiliation, affinity, attach~ ment, connection, link, relation, tie, union **3.** agreement, compact, contract, covenant, guarantee, obligation, pledge, promise, word ~*v.* **4.** bind, connect, fasten, fix together, fuse, glue, gum, paste

bonny 1. beautiful, comely, fair, handsome, lovely, pretty, sweet **2.** bouncing, buxom, chubby, fine, plump, rounded, shapely **3.** blithe, cheerful, cheery, gay, joyful, merry, sunny, winsome

bonus benefit, bounty, commission, divi~ dend, extra, gift, gratuity, hand-out, hono~ rarium, icing on the cake, perk (*Brit. inf.*), plus, premium, prize, reward

bon viveur *bon vivant*, epicure, epicurean, foodie, gastronome, gourmet, hedonist, luxurist, pleasure-seeker, voluptuary
Antonyms abstainer, ascetic, celibate, self-denier

bony angular, emaciated, gangling, gaunt, lanky, lean, macilent (*Rare*), rawboned, scrawny, skinny, thin

book *n.* **1.** hardback, manual, paperback, publication, roll, scroll, textbook, title, tome, tract, volume, work **2.** album, diary, exercise book, jotter, notebook, pad ~*v.* **3.** arrange for, bill, charter, engage, line up,

make reservations, organize, procure, pro~ gramme, reserve, schedule **4.** enrol, enter, insert, list, log, mark down, note, post, put down, record, register, write down

bookish academic, donnish, erudite, intel~ lectual, learned, literary, pedantic, scholar~ ly, studious, well-read

boom *v.* **1.** bang, blast, crash, explode, re~ sound, reverberate, roar, roll, rumble, thunder **2.** develop, expand, flourish, gain, grow, increase, intensify, prosper, spurt, strengthen, succeed, swell, thrive ~*n.* **3.** bang, blast, burst, clap, crash, explosion, roar, rumble, thunder **4.** advance, boost, development, expansion, gain, growth, im~ provement, increase, jump, push, spurt, upsurge, upswing, upturn
Antonyms *v.* (*sense 2*) crash, fail, fall, slump ~*n.* (*sense 4*) bust (*Inf.*), collapse, crash, de~ cline, depression, downturn, failure, hard times, recession, slump

boomerang backfire, come back, come home to roost, rebound, recoil, return, re~ verse, ricochet

boon[1] *n.* advantage, benefaction, benefit, blessing, donation, favour, gift, godsend, grant, gratuity, hand-out, present, windfall

boon[2] *adj.* close, intimate, special

boor barbarian, brute, bumpkin, churl, clodhopper (*Inf.*), clodpole, hayseed (*U.S. & Canad. inf.*), hick (*Inf., chiefly U.S. & Canad.*), lout, oaf, peasant, philistine, red~ neck (*U.S. sl.*), vulgarian

boorish awkward, barbaric, bearish, churl~ ish, clownish, coarse, crude, gross, gruff, hick (*Inf., chiefly U.S. & Canad.*), ill-bred, loutish, lubberly, oafish, rude, rustic, un~ civilized, uncouth, uneducated, unrefined, vulgar
Antonyms cultured, gallant, genteel, polite, refined, sophisticated, urbane

boost *n.* **1.** encouragement, help, hype, im~ provement, praise, promotion **2.** heave, hoist, lift, push, raise, shove, thrust **3.** ad~ dition, expansion, improvement, increase, increment, jump, rise ~*v.* **4.** advance, ad~ vertise, assist, crack up (*Inf.*), encourage, foster, further, hype, improve, inspire, plug (*Inf.*), praise, promote, support, sustain **5.** elevate, heave, hoist, lift, push, raise, shove, thrust **6.** add to, amplify, develop, enlarge, expand, heighten, hoick, increase, jack up, magnify, raise
Antonyms *n.* condemnation, criticism, cut~ back, decline, decrease, deterioration, fall, knock (*Inf.*), reduction ~*v.* condemn, criticize, cut, decrease, diminish, drop, hinder, hold back, knock (*Inf.*), lessen, let down, lower, moderate, pare, reduce, scale down

boot *v.* **1.** drive, drop-kick, kick, knock, punt, shove **2.** *Inf.* dismiss, eject, expel, give the bum's rush (*Sl.*), give the heave *or* push (*Inf.*), kick out, kiss off (*Sl., chiefly U.S. & Canad.*), oust, relegate, sack (*Inf.*), show one the door, throw out, throw out on one's ear (*Inf.*)

bootless fruitless, futile, ineffective, profitless, unavailing, unsuccessful, useless, vain

booty boodle (*Sl., chiefly U.S.*), gains, haul, loot, pillage, plunder, prey, spoil, spoils, swag (*Sl.*), takings, winnings

border *n.* **1.** bound, boundary, bounds, brim, brink, confine, confines, edge, flange, hem, limit, limits, lip, margin, pale, rim, skirt, verge **2.** borderline, boundary, frontier, line, march ~*v.* **3.** bind, decorate, edge, fringe, hem, rim, trim

borderline *adj.* ambivalent, doubtful, equivocal, indecisive, indefinite, indeterminate, inexact, marginal, unclassifiable

border on 1. abut, adjoin, connect, contact, impinge, join, march, neighbour, touch, verge on **2.** approach, approximate, be like, be similar to, come close to, come near, echo, match, parallel, resemble

bore¹ 1. *v.* burrow, drill, gouge out, mine, penetrate, perforate, pierce, sink, tunnel **2.** *n.* borehole, calibre, drill hole, hole, shaft, tunnel

bore² 1. *v.* annoy, be tedious, bother, exhaust, fatigue, jade, pall on, pester, send to sleep, tire, trouble, vex, wear out, weary, worry **2.** *n.* bother, drag (*Inf.*), dullard, dull person, headache (*Inf.*), nuisance, pain (*Inf.*), pain in the arse (*Taboo inf.*), pain in the neck (*Inf.*), pest, tiresome person, wearisome talker, yawn (*Inf.*)
Antonyms *v.* amuse, divert, engross, excite, fascinate, hold the attention of, interest, stimulate

boredom apathy, doldrums, dullness, ennui, flatness, irksomeness, monotony, sameness, tediousness, tedium, weariness, world-weariness
Antonyms amusement, entertainment, excitement, interest, stimulation

boring dead, dull, flat, ho-hum (*Inf.*), humdrum, insipid, mind-numbing, monotonous, repetitious, routine, stale, tedious, tiresome, tiring, unexciting, uninteresting, unvaried, wearisome

borrow 1. blag (*Sl.*), cadge, mooch (*Sl.*), scrounge (*Inf.*), take and return, take on loan, touch (someone) for (*Sl.*), use temporarily **2.** acquire, adopt, appropriate, copy, filch, imitate, obtain, pilfer, pirate, plagiarize, simulate, steal, take, use, usurp
Antonyms advance, give, lend, loan, provide, return, supply

bosom *n.* **1.** breast, bust, chest **2.** affec-

tions, emotions, feelings, heart, sentiments, soul, spirit, sympathies **3.** centre, circle, core, midst, protection, shelter ~*adj.* **4.** boon, cherished, close, confidential, intimate, very dear

boss¹ 1. *n.* administrator, big cheese (*Sl., old-fashioned*), chief, director, employer, executive, foreman, gaffer (*Inf., chiefly Brit.*), governor (*Inf.*), head, kingpin, leader, manager, master, Mister Big (*Sl., chiefly U.S.*), numero uno (*Inf.*), overseer, owner, superintendent, supervisor **2.** *v.* administrate, command, control, direct, employ, manage, oversee, run, superintend, supervise, take charge

boss² knob, nub, nubble, point, protuberance, stud, tip

boss around bully, dominate, domineer, oppress, order, overbear, push around (*Sl.*), put upon, tyrannize

bossy arrogant, authoritarian, autocratic, despotic, dictatorial, domineering, hectoring, high-handed, imperious, lordly, overbearing, tyrannical

botch 1. *v.* balls up (*Taboo sl.*), blunder, bodge (*Inf.*), bungle, butcher, cobble, cock up (*Brit. sl.*), fuck up (*Offens. taboo sl.*), fumble, mar, mend, mess, mismanage, muff, patch, screw up (*Inf.*), spoil **2.** *n.* balls-up (*Taboo sl.*), blunder, bungle, bungling, cock-up (*Brit. sl.*), failure, fuck-up (*Offens. taboo sl.*), fumble, hash, mess, miscarriage, pig's breakfast (*Inf.*), pig's ear (*Inf.*)

bother 1. *v.* alarm, annoy, bend someone's ear (*Inf.*), concern, dismay, distress, disturb, gall, harass, hassle (*Inf.*), inconvenience, irritate, molest, nag, nark (*Brit., Aust., & N.Z. sl.*), pester, plague, put out, trouble, upset, vex, worry **2.** *n.* aggravation, annoyance, bustle, difficulty, flurry, fuss, gall, hassle (*Inf.*), inconvenience, irritation, molestation, nuisance, perplexity, pest, problem, strain, trouble, vexation, worry
Antonyms *v.* aid, assist, facilitate, further, help, relieve, succour, support ~*n.* advantage, aid, benefit, comfort, convenience, help, service, use

bothersome aggravating, annoying, distressing, exasperating, inconvenient, irritating, tiresome, troublesome, vexatious, vexing
Antonyms appropriate, beneficial, commodious, convenient, handy, helpful, serviceable, useful

bottleneck block, blockage, congestion, hold-up, impediment, jam, obstacle, obstruction, snarl-up (*Inf., chiefly Brit.*)

bottle up check, contain, curb, keep back, restrict, shut in, suppress, trap

bottom *n.* **1.** base, basis, bed, deepest part, depths, floor, foot, foundation, groundwork,

lowest part, pedestal, support **2.** lower side, sole, underneath, underside **3.** arse (*Taboo sl.*), ass (*U.S. & Canad. taboo sl.*), backside, behind (*Inf.*), bum (*Brit. sl.*), buns (*U.S. sl.*), butt (*U.S. & Canad. inf.*), buttocks, derrière (*Euphemistic*), fundament, jacksy (*Brit. sl.*), posterior, rear, rear end, rump, seat, tail (*Inf.*) **4.** base, basis, cause, core, essence, ground, heart, mainspring, origin, princi~ ple, root, source, substance ~*adj.* **5.** base, basement, basic, fundamental, ground, last, lowest, undermost
Antonyms *n.* cover, crown, height, lid, peak, summit, surface, top ~*adj.* higher, highest, top, upper

bottomless boundless, deep, fathomless, immeasurable, inexhaustible, infinite, un~ fathomable, unlimited

bounce *v.* **1.** bob, bound, bump, jounce, jump, leap, rebound, recoil, resile, ricochet, spring, thump **2.** *Sl.* boot out (*Inf.*), eject, fire (*Inf.*), kick out (*Inf.*), oust, relegate, throw out ~*n.* **3.** bound, elasticity, give, re~ bound, recoil, resilience, spring, springiness **4.** animation, brio, dynamism, energy, go (*Inf.*), life, liveliness, pep, vigour, vitality, vivacity, zip (*Inf.*)

bouncing blooming, bonny, healthy, robust, thriving, vigorous

bound[1] *adj.* **1.** cased, fastened, fixed, pin~ ioned, secured, tied, tied up **2.** certain, des~ tined, doomed, fated, sure **3.** beholden, committed, compelled, constrained, duty-bound, forced, obligated, obliged, pledged, required

bound[2] *v./n.* bob, bounce, caper, frisk, gambol, hurdle, jump, leap, lope, pounce, prance, skip, spring, vault

bound[3] *n.* **1.** *Usually plural* border, boundary, confine, edge, extremity, fringe, limit, line, march, margin, pale, periphery, rim, termination, verge **2.** out of bounds banned, barred, forbidden, off-limits (*Chiefly U.S. military*), prohibited, taboo ~*v.* **3.** cir~ cumscribe, confine, define, delimit, demar~ cate, encircle, enclose, hem in, limit, re~ strain, restrict, surround, terminate

boundary barrier, border, borderline, bounds, brink, confines, edge, extremity, fringe, frontier, limits, march, margin, pale, precinct, termination, verge

boundless endless, illimitable, immeasur~ able, immense, incalculable, inexhaustible, infinite, limitless, measureless, unbounded, unconfined, unending, unlimited, untold, vast
Antonyms bounded, confined, limited, little, restricted, small

bountiful **1.** abundant, ample, bounteous, copious, exuberant, lavish, luxuriant, plen~ teous, plentiful, prolific **2.** beneficent, bounteous, generous, liberal, magnanimous, munificent, open-handed, princely, prodigal, unstinting

bouquet **1.** boutonniere, bunch of flowers, buttonhole, corsage, garland, nosegay, posy, spray, wreath **2.** aroma, fragrance, per~ fume, redolence, savour, scent

bourgeois conventional, hidebound, ma~ terialistic, middle-class, traditional

bout **1.** course, fit, period, round, run, ses~ sion, spell, spree, stint, stretch, term, time, turn **2.** battle, boxing match, competition, contest, encounter, engagement, fight, head-to-head, match, set-to, struggle

bovine dense, dozy (*Brit. inf.*), dull, slow, sluggish, stolid, stupid, thick

bow[1] *v.* **1.** bend, bob, droop, genuflect, in~ cline, make obeisance, nod, stoop **2.** accept, acquiesce, comply, concede, defer, give in, kowtow, relent, submit, succumb, surren~ der, yield **3.** cast down, conquer, crush, de~ press, overpower, subdue, subjugate, van~ quish, weigh down ~*n.* **4.** bending, bob, genuflexion, inclination, kowtow, nod, obeisance, salaam

bow[2] *Nautical* beak, fore, head, prow, stem

bowdlerize blue-pencil, censor, clean up, expurgate, mutilate

bowels **1.** entrails, guts, innards (*Inf.*), in~ sides (*Inf.*), intestines, viscera, vitals **2.** belly, core, deep, depths, hold, inside, inte~ rior **3.** *Archaic* compassion, mercifulness, mercy, pity, sympathy, tenderness

bower alcove, arbour, grotto, leafy shelter, shady recess, summerhouse

bowl[1] *n.* basin, deep dish, vessel

bowl[2] *v.* fling, hurl, pitch, revolve, roll, ro~ tate, spin, throw, trundle, whirl

bowl over **1.** amaze, astonish, astound, dumbfound, stagger, startle, stun, surprise **2.** bring down, fell, floor, knock down, overthrow, overturn

bow out abandon, back out, cop out (*Sl.*), get out, give up, pull out, quit, resign, re~ tire, step down (*Inf.*), withdraw

box[1] **1.** *n.* ark (*Dialect*), carton, case, casket, chest, container, kist (*Scot. & Northern English dialect*), pack, package, portman~ teau, receptacle, trunk **2.** *v.* pack, package, wrap

box[2] *v.* **1.** exchange blows, fight, spar **2.** belt (*Inf.*), buffet, butt, chin (*Sl.*), clout (*Inf.*), cuff, deck (*Sl.*), hit, lay one on (*Sl.*), punch, slap, sock (*Sl.*), strike, thwack, wallop (*Inf.*), whack ~*n.* **3.** belt (*Inf.*), blow, buffet, clout (*Inf.*), cuff, punch, slap, stroke, thumping, wallop (*Inf.*)

boxer fighter, prizefighter, pugilist, sparrer, sparring partner

box in cage, confine, contain, coop up, en~ close, hem in, isolate, shut in, surround, trap

boxing fisticuffs, prizefighting, pugilism, sparring, the fight game (*Inf.*), the ring

boy fellow, junior, lad, schoolboy, stripling, youngster, youth

boycott ban, bar, black, blackball, blacklist, embargo, exclude, ostracize, outlaw, pro~ hibit, proscribe, refrain from, refuse, reject, spurn
Antonyms accept, advocate, back, champi~ on, defend, espouse, help, patronize, promote, support, welcome

boyfriend admirer, beau, date, follower, le~ man (*Archaic*), lover, man, steady, suitor, swain, sweetheart, toy boy, young man

boyish adolescent, childish, immature, in~ nocent, juvenile, puerile, young, youthful

brace 1. *n.* bolster, bracer, bracket, buttress, prop, reinforcement, stanchion, stay, strut, support, truss **2.** *v.* bandage, bind, bolster, buttress, fasten, fortify, hold up, prop, re~ inforce, shove, shove up, steady, strap, strengthen, support, tie, tighten

bracing brisk, chilly, cool, crisp, energizing, exhilarating, fortifying, fresh, invigorating, lively, refreshing, restorative, reviving, rousing, stimulating, tonic, vigorous
Antonyms debilitating, draining, enervat~ ing, exhausting, fatiguing, sapping, soporific, taxing, tiring, weakening

brackish bitter, briny, saline, salt, salty, undrinkable
Antonyms clean, clear, fresh, pure, sweet, unpolluted

brag blow one's own trumpet, bluster, boast, crow, swagger, talk big (*Sl.*), vaunt

braggart bigmouth (*Sl.*), bluffer, blusterer, boaster, brag, braggadocio, bragger, hot dog (*Chiefly U.S.*), show-off (*Inf.*), swaggerer, swashbuckler

braid entwine, interlace, intertwine, inter~ weave, lace, plait, ravel, twine, weave

brain brainbox, egghead (*Inf.*), genius, high~ brow, intellect, intellectual, mastermind, prodigy, pundit, sage, scholar

brainless braindead (*Inf.*), foolish, idiotic, inane, inept, mindless, senseless, stupid, thoughtless, unintelligent, witless

brains capacity, intellect, intelligence, mind, nous (*Brit. sl.*), reason, sagacity, savvy (*Sl.*), sense, shrewdness, smarts (*Sl., chiefly U.S.*), suss (*Sl.*), understanding, wit

brainwashing alteration, conditioning, in~ doctrination, persuasion, re-education

brainy bright, brilliant, clever, intelligent, smart

brake 1. *n.* check, constraint, control, curb,

rein, restraint **2.** *v.* check, decelerate, halt, moderate, reduce speed, slacken, slow, stop

branch 1. arm, bough, limb, offshoot, prong, ramification, shoot, spray, sprig **2.** chapter, department, division, local office, office, part, section, subdivision, subsection, wing

branch out add to, develop, diversify, en~ large, expand, extend, increase, multiply, proliferate, ramify, spread out

brand *n.* **1.** cast, class, grade, kind, make, quality, sort, species, type, variety **2.** em~ blem, hallmark, label, mark, marker, sign, stamp, symbol, trademark **3.** blot, disgrace, infamy, mark, reproach, slur, smirch, stain, stigma, taint ~*v.* **4.** burn, burn in, label, mark, scar, stamp **5.** censure, denounce, discredit, disgrace, expose, mark, stigmatize

brandish display, exhibit, flaunt, flourish, parade, raise, shake, swing, wield

brash 1. audacious, foolhardy, hasty, im~ petuous, impulsive, indiscreet, precipitate, rash, reckless **2.** bold, brazen, cocky, for~ ward, heedless, impertinent, impudent, in~ solent, pushy (*Inf.*), rude
Antonyms careful, cautious, polite, prudent, reserved, respectful, thoughtful, timid, un~ certain

brass audacity, brass neck (*Brit. inf.*), cheek, chutzpah (*U.S. & Canad. inf.*), effrontery, front, gall, impertinence, impudence, inso~ lence, neck (*Inf.*), nerve (*Inf.*), presumption, rudeness

brassy 1. barefaced, bold, brash, brazen, forward, impudent, insolent, loud-mouthed, pert, pushy (*Inf.*), saucy **2.** blatant, flashy, garish, gaudy, hard, jazzy (*Inf.*), loud, ob~ trusive, showy, vulgar **3.** blaring, cacopho~ nous, dissonant, grating, harsh, jangling, jarring, loud, noisy, piercing, raucous, shrill, strident
Antonyms discreet, low-key, modest, played down, quiet, restrained, subdued, toned down, understated

bravado bluster, boast, boastfulness, boast~ ing, bombast, brag, braggadocio, fanfaro~ nade (*Rare*), swagger, swaggering, swash~ buckling, vaunting

brave 1. *adj.* ballsy (*Taboo sl.*), bold, coura~ geous, daring, dauntless, fearless, gallant, gritty, heroic, intrepid, plucky, resolute, undaunted, valiant, valorous **2.** *v.* bear, beard, challenge, confront, dare, defy, en~ dure, face, stand up to, suffer, tackle, with~ stand
Antonyms *adj.* afraid, chickenshit (*U.S. sl.*), cowardly, craven, faint-hearted, fearful, frightened, scared, shrinking, timid ~*v.* give in to, retreat from, surrender to

bravery balls (*Taboo sl.*), ballsiness (*Taboo sl.*), boldness, bravura, courage, daring, dauntlessness, doughtiness, fearlessness,

fortitude, gallantry, grit, guts (*Inf.*), hardi~
hood, hardiness, heroism, indomitability,
intrepidity, mettle, pluck, pluckiness, spirit,
spunk (*Inf.*), valour
Antonyms cowardice, faint-heartedness,
fearfulness, fright, timidity

bravo assassin, bandit, brigand, cutthroat,
desperado, hired killer, murderer, villain

bravura animation, audacity, boldness,
brilliance, brio, daring, dash, display, élan,
energy, exhibitionism, ostentation, panache,
punch (*Inf.*), spirit, verve, vigour, virtuosity

brawl 1. *n.* affray (*Law*), altercation, argu~
ment, *bagarre*, battle, broil, clash, disorder,
dispute, donnybrook, fight, fracas, fray,
free-for-all (*Inf.*), melee *or* mêlée, punch-up
(*Brit. inf.*), quarrel, row (*Inf.*), ruckus (*Inf.*),
rumpus, scrap (*Inf.*), scrimmage, scuffle,
shindig (*Inf.*), shindy (*Inf.*), skirmish,
squabble, tumult, uproar, wrangle **2.** *v.* al~
tercate, argue, battle, dispute, fight, quarrel,
row (*Inf.*), scrap (*Inf.*), scuffle, tussle, wran~
gle, wrestle

brawn beef (*Inf.*), beefiness (*Inf.*), brawni~
ness, flesh, might, muscle, muscles, muscu~
larity, power, robustness, strength, vigour

brawny athletic, beefy (*Inf.*), bulky, burly,
fleshy, hardy, hefty (*Inf.*), herculean, husky
(*Inf.*), lusty, muscular, powerful, Ramboesque, robust, sinewy, stalwart, strapping,
strong, sturdy, thewy, thickset, vigorous,
well-built, well-knit
Antonyms frail, scrawny, skinny, thin, un~
developed, weak, weakly, weedy (*Inf.*), wimp~
ish *or* wimpy (*Inf.*)

bray 1. *v.* bell, bellow, blare, heehaw, hoot,
roar, screech, trumpet **2.** *n.* bawl, bell, bel~
low, blare, cry, harsh sound, heehaw, hoot,
roar, screech, shout

brazen *adj.* **1.** audacious, barefaced, bold,
brash, brassy (*Inf.*), defiant, forward, im~
modest, impudent, insolent, pert, pushy
(*Inf.*), saucy, shameless, unabashed, un~
ashamed **2.** brass, brassy, bronze, metallic
~*v.* **3.** *With* **out** be impenitent, be un~
ashamed, confront, defy, outface, outstare,
persevere, stare out
Antonyms (*sense 1*) cautious, decorous,
diffident, mannerly, modest, reserved, re~
spectful, reticent, secret, shy, stealthy, timid

breach 1. aperture, break, chasm, cleft,
crack, fissure, gap, hole, opening, rent, rift,
rupture, split **2.** contravention, disobedi~
ence, infraction, infringement, noncompli~
ance, nonobservance, offence, transgression,
trespass, violation **3.** alienation, difference,
disaffection, disagreement, dissension, divi~
sion, estrangement, falling-out (*Inf.*), part~
ing of the ways, quarrel, schism, separa~
tion, severance, variance
Antonyms (*sense 2*) adherence to, attention,

compliance, discharge, fulfilment, heeding,
honouring, observation, performance

bread 1. aliment, diet, fare, food, neces~
sities, nourishment, nutriment, provisions,
subsistence, sustenance, viands, victuals **2.**
Sl. ackers (*Sl.*), brass (*Northern English
dialect*), cash, dibs (*Sl.*), dosh (*Brit. & Aust.
sl.*), dough (*Sl.*), finance, funds, money, nec~
essary (*Inf.*), needful (*Inf.*), rhino (*Brit. sl.*),
shekels (*Inf.*), silver, spondulicks (*Sl.*), tin
(*Sl.*)

breadth 1. beam (*of a ship*), broadness,
latitude, span, spread, wideness, width **2.**
amplitude, area, compass, comprehensive~
ness, dimension, expanse, extensiveness,
extent, magnitude, measure, range, reach,
scale, scope, size, space, spread, sweep,
vastness **3.** broad-mindedness, freedom,
latitude, liberality, open-mindedness, open~
ness, permissiveness

break *v.* **1.** batter, burst, crack, crash, de~
molish, destroy, disintegrate, divide, frac~
ture, fragment, part, rend, separate, sever,
shatter, shiver, smash, snap, splinter, split,
tear, total (*Sl.*), trash (*Sl.*) **2.** breach,
contravene, disobey, disregard, infract
(*Law*), infringe, renege on, transgress, vio~
late **3.** cow, cripple, demoralize, dispirit,
enervate, enfeeble, impair, incapacitate,
subdue, tame, undermine, weaken **4.** aban~
don, cut, discontinue, give up, interrupt,
pause, rest, stop, suspend **5.** bust (*Inf.*), de~
grade, demote, discharge, dismiss, humili~
ate, impoverish, make bankrupt, reduce,
ruin **6.** announce, come out, disclose, di~
vulge, impart, inform, let out, make public,
proclaim, reveal, tell **7.** *Of a record, etc.*
beat, better, cap (*Inf.*), exceed, excel, go be~
yond, outdo, outstrip, surpass, top **8.** ap~
pear, burst out, come forth suddenly,
emerge, erupt, happen, occur **9.** cut and
run (*Inf.*), dash, escape, flee, fly, get away,
hook it (*Sl.*), run away **10.** cushion, dimin~
ish, lessen, lighten, moderate, reduce, sof~
ten, weaken ~*n.* **11.** breach, cleft, crack,
division, fissure, fracture, gap, gash, hole,
opening, rent, rift, rupture, split, tear **12.**
breather (*Inf.*), entr'acte, halt, hiatus, inter~
lude, intermission, interruption, interval,
let-up (*Inf.*), lull, pause, recess, respite, rest,
suspension **13.** alienation, breach, disaffec~
tion, dispute, divergence, estrangement, rift,
rupture, schism, separation, split **14.** *Inf.*
advantage, chance, fortune, opening, oppor~
tunity, stroke of luck
Antonyms (*sense 1*) attach, bind, connect,
fasten, join, repair, unite (*sense 2*) abide by,
adhere to, conform, discharge, follow, obey,
observe

breakable brittle, crumbly, delicate, flimsy,
fragile, frail, frangible, friable
Antonyms durable, indestructible, infran~

gible, lasting, nonbreakable, resistant, rug~
ged, shatterproof, solid, strong, toughened,
unbreakable

break away 1. decamp, escape, flee, fly,
hook it (*Sl.*), make a break for it, make a
run for it (*Inf.*), make off, run away **2.**
break with, detach, part company, secede,
separate

breakdown 1. collapse, crackup (*Inf.*), dis~
integration, disruption, failure, mishap,
stoppage **2.** analysis, categorization,
classification, detailed list, diagnosis, dis~
section, itemization

break down be overcome, collapse, conk
out (*Inf.*), crack up (*Inf.*), fail, give way, go
kaput (*Inf.*), go to pieces, seize up, stop, stop
working

breaker billow, comber, roller, wave,
whitecap, white horse

break-in breaking and entering, burglary,
invasion, robbery

break in 1. barge in, burst in, butt in,
interfere, interject, interpose, interrupt,
intervene, intrude, put one's two cents in
(*U.S. sl.*) **2.** break and enter, burgle, invade,
rob **3.** accustom, condition, get used to, ha~
bituate, initiate, prepare, tame, train

break into begin, burst into, burst out,
commence, dissolve into, give way to,
launch into

break off 1. detach, divide, part, pull off,
separate, sever, snap off, splinter **2.** cease,
desist, discontinue, end, finish, halt, pause,
stop, suspend, terminate

break out 1. appear, arise, begin, com~
mence, emerge, happen, occur, set in,
spring up, start **2.** abscond, bolt, break
loose, burst out, escape, flee, get free **3.**
burst out, erupt

breakthrough advance, development, dis~
covery, find, finding, gain, improvement,
invention, leap, progress, quantum leap,
step forward

break-up breakdown, breaking, crackup
(*Inf.*), disintegration, dispersal, dissolution,
divorce, ending, parting, rift, separation,
split, splitting, termination, wind-up

break up adjourn, disband, dismantle, dis~
perse, disrupt, dissolve, divide, divorce,
end, part, scatter, separate, sever, split,
stop, suspend, terminate

breakwater groyne, jetty, mole, sea wall,
spur

breast 1. boob (*Sl.*), bosom, bust, chest,
front, teat, thorax, tit (*Sl.*), udder **2.** being,
conscience, core, emotions, feelings, heart,
seat of the affections, sentiments, soul,
thoughts

breath 1. air, animation, breathing, exhala~
tion, gasp, gulp, inhalation, pant, respira~

tion, wheeze **2.** aroma, niff (*Brit. sl.*), odour,
smell, vapour, whiff **3.** break, breather,
breathing-space, instant, moment, pause,
respite, rest, second **4.** faint breeze, flutter,
gust, puff, sigh, slight movement, waft,
zephyr **5.** hint, murmur, suggestion, suspi~
cion, undertone, whisper **6.** animation, en~
ergy, existence, life, lifeblood, life force, vi~
tality

breathe 1. draw in, gasp, gulp, inhale and
exhale, pant, puff, respire, wheeze **2.** im~
bue, impart, infuse, inject, inspire, instil,
transfuse **3.** articulate, express, murmur,
say, sigh, utter, voice, whisper

breather break, breathing space, breath of
air, halt, pause, recess, respite, rest

breathless 1. choking, exhausted, gasping,
gulping, out of breath, panting, short-
winded, spent, wheezing, winded **2.** agog,
anxious, astounded, avid, eager, excited,
flabbergasted (*Inf.*), gobsmacked (*Brit. sl.*),
on tenterhooks, open-mouthed, thunder~
struck, with bated breath

breathtaking amazing, astonishing, awe-
inspiring, awesome, brilliant, exciting,
heart-stirring, impressive, magnificent,
moving, overwhelming, sensational, strik~
ing, stunning (*Inf.*), thrilling, wondrous
(*Archaic or literary*)

breed *v.* **1.** bear, beget, bring forth, engen~
der, generate, hatch, multiply, originate,
procreate, produce, propagate, reproduce **2.**
bring up, cultivate, develop, discipline,
educate, foster, instruct, nourish, nurture,
raise, rear **3.** arouse, bring about, cause,
create, generate, give rise to, induce, make,
occasion, originate, produce, stir up ~*n.* **4.**
brand, class, extraction, family, ilk, kind,
line, lineage, pedigree, progeny, race, sort,
species, stamp, stock, strain, type, variety

breeding 1. ancestry, cultivation, develop~
ment, lineage, nurture, raising, rearing, re~
production, training, upbringing **2.** civility,
conduct, courtesy, cultivation, culture, gen~
tility, manners, polish, refinement, sophis~
tication, urbanity

breeze 1. *n.* air, breath of wind, capful of
wind, current of air, draught, flurry, gust,
light wind, puff of air, waft, whiff, zephyr
2. *v.* flit, glide, hurry, move briskly, pass,
sail, sally, sweep, trip

breezy 1. airy, blowing, blowy, blusterous,
blustery, fresh, gusty, squally, windy **2.**
airy, animated, blithe, buoyant, carefree,
casual, cheerful, chirpy (*Inf.*), debonair,
easy-going, free and easy, genial, informal,
jaunty, light, light-hearted, lively, sparkling,
sparky, spirited, sprightly, sunny, upbeat
(*Inf.*), vivacious
Antonyms calm, depressed, dull, heavy,

lifeless, mournful, oppressive, sad, serious, windless

brevity 1. conciseness, concision, conden~ sation, crispness, curtness, economy, pithi~ ness, succinctness, terseness **2.** briefness, ephemerality, impermanence, shortness, transience, transitoriness
Antonyms (*sense 1*) circuity, diffuseness, discursiveness, long-windedness, prolixity, rambling, redundancy, tautology, tedious~ ness, verbiage, verboseness, verbosity, wordiness

brew *v.* **1.** boil, ferment, infuse (*tea*), make (*beer*), prepare by fermentation, seethe, soak, steep, stew **2.** breed, concoct, con~ trive, develop, devise, excite, foment, form, gather, hatch, plan, plot, project, scheme, start, stir up ~*n.* **3.** beverage, blend, con~ coction, distillation, drink, fermentation, infusion, liquor, mixture, preparation

bribe 1. *n.* allurement, backhander (*Sl.*), boodle (*Sl., chiefly U.S.*), corrupting gift, en~ ticement, graft (*Inf.*), hush money (*Sl.*), in~ centive, inducement, kickback (*U.S.*), pay~ off (*Inf.*), payola (*Inf.*), reward for treachery, sop, sweetener (*Sl.*) **2.** *v.* buy off, corrupt, get at, grease the palm *or* hand of (*Sl.*), influence by gifts, lure, oil the palm of (*Inf.*), pay off (*Inf.*), reward, square, suborn

bribery buying off, corruption, graft (*Inf.*), inducement, palm-greasing (*Sl.*), payola (*Inf.*), protection, subornation

bric-a-brac baubles, bibelots, curios, gew~ gaws, kickshaws, knick-knacks, objects of virtu, *objets d'art,* ornaments, trinkets

bridal bride's, conjugal, connubial, hy~ meneal, marital, marriage, matrimonial, nuptial, spousal, wedding

bridge *n.* **1.** arch, flyover, overpass, span, viaduct **2.** band, bond, connection, link, tie ~*v.* **3.** arch over, attach, bind, connect, couple, cross, cross over, extend across, go over, join, link, reach across, span, trav~ erse, unite
Antonyms *v.* cleave, come apart, disjoin, di~ vide, keep apart, separate, sever, split, sunder, widen

bridle *v.* **1.** check, constrain, control, curb, govern, keep in check, master, moderate, rein, repress, restrain, subdue **2.** be indig~ nant, bristle, draw (oneself) up, get angry, get one's back up, raise one's hackles, rear up ~*n.* **3.** check, control, curb, rein, re~ straint, trammels

brief *adj.* **1.** compendious, compressed, con~ cise, crisp, curt, laconic, limited, pithy, short, succinct, terse, thumbnail, to the point **2.** ephemeral, fast, fleeting, hasty, lit~ tle, momentary, quick, quickie (*Inf.*), short, short-lived, swift, temporary, transitory **3.** abrupt, blunt, brusque, curt, sharp, short,

surly ~*n.* **4.** abridgment, abstract, digest, epitome, outline, précis, sketch, summary, synopsis **5.** argument, case, contention, data, defence, demonstration ~*v.* **6.** advise, clue in (*Inf.*), explain, fill in (*Inf.*), gen up (*Brit. inf.*), give (someone) a rundown, give (someone) the gen (*Brit. inf.*), inform, in~ struct, prepare, prime, put (someone) in the picture (*Inf.*)
Antonyms *adj.* circuitous, detailed, diffuse, extensive, lengthy, long, long-drawn-out, long-winded, protracted

briefing conference, directions, guidance, information, instruction, instructions, meeting, preamble, preparation, priming, rundown

briefly abruptly, briskly, casually, concisely, cursorily, curtly, fleetingly, hastily, hur~ riedly, in a few words, in a nutshell, in brief, in outline, in passing, momentarily, precisely, quickly, shortly, temporarily

brigade band, body, camp, company, con~ tingent, corps, crew, force, group, organiza~ tion, outfit, party, squad, team, troop, unit

brigand bandit, desperado, footpad (*Archa~ ic*), freebooter, gangster, highwayman, ma~ rauder, outlaw, plunderer, robber, ruffian

bright 1. beaming, blazing, brilliant, daz~ zling, effulgent, flashing, gleaming, glisten~ ing, glittering, glowing, illuminated, in~ tense, lambent, luminous, lustrous, radiant, resplendent, scintillating, shimmering, shining, sparkling, twinkling, vivid **2.** clear, clement, cloudless, fair, limpid, lucid, pellucid, pleasant, sunny, translucent, transparent, unclouded **3.** acute, astute, aware, brainy, brilliant, clear-headed, clev~ er, ingenious, intelligent, inventive, keen, quick, quick-witted, sharp, smart, wide-awake **4.** auspicious, encouraging, excel~ lent, favourable, golden, good, hopeful, op~ timistic, palmy, promising, propitious, prosperous, rosy **5.** cheerful, chirpy (*Inf.*), gay, genial, glad, happy, jolly, joyful, joy~ ous, light-hearted, lively, merry, sparky, upbeat (*Inf.*), vivacious **6.** distinguished, famous, glorious, illustrious, magnificent, outstanding, remarkable, splendid
Antonyms (*senses 1 & 2*) cloudy, dark, dim, dusky, gloomy, grey, overcast, poorly lit (*sense 3*) dense, dim, dim-witted (*Inf.*), dull, dumb (*Inf.*), foolish, idiotic, ignorant, retarded, sim~ ple, slow, stupid, thick, unintelligent, witless

brighten 1. clear up, enliven, gleam, glow, illuminate, lighten, light up, make brighter, shine **2.** become cheerful, buck up (*Inf.*), buoy up, cheer, encourage, enliven, glad~ den, hearten, make happy, perk up
Antonyms (*sense 1*) becloud, blacken, cloud over *or* up, dim, dull, obscure, overshadow, shade, shadow (*sense 2*) become angry, become

gloomy, blacken, cloud, deject, depress, dis~ pirit, look black, sadden

brilliance, brilliancy 1. blaze, brightness, dazzle, effulgence, gleam, glitter, intensity, luminosity, lustre, radiance, refulgence, re~ splendence, sheen, sparkle, vividness **2.** acuity, aptitude, braininess, cleverness, distinction, excellence, genius, giftedness, greatness, inventiveness, talent, wisdom **3.** éclat, gilt, glamour, gorgeousness, grandeur, illustriousness, magnificence, pizzazz *or* pi~ zazz (*Inf.*), splendour
Antonyms darkness, dimness, dullness, fol~ ly, idiocy, inanity, incompetence, ineptitude, obscurity, paleness, silliness, simple-mindedness, stupidity, thickness

brilliant 1. ablaze, bright, coruscating, daz~ zling, glittering, glossy, intense, luminous, lustrous, radiant, refulgent, resplendent, scintillating, shining, sparkling, vivid **2.** celebrated, eminent, exceptional, famous, glorious, illustrious, magnificent, notable, outstanding, splendid, superb **3.** accom~ plished, acute, astute, brainy, clever, dis~ cerning, expert, gifted, intellectual, intelli~ gent, inventive, masterly, penetrating, pro~ found, quick, talented
Antonyms (*sense 1*) dark, dim, dull, gloomy, obscure (*senses 2 & 3*) dim, dull, ordinary, run-of-the-mill, simple, slow, stupid, unac~ complished, unexceptional, untalented

brim 1. *n.* border, brink, circumference, edge, flange, lip, margin, rim, skirt, verge **2.** *v.* fill, fill up, hold no more, overflow, run over, spill, well over

brimful brimming, filled, flush, full, level with, overflowing, overfull, packed, running over

bring 1. accompany, bear, carry, conduct, convey, deliver, escort, fetch, gather, guide, import, lead, take, transfer, transport, usher **2.** cause, contribute to, create, effect, en~ gender, inflict, occasion, produce, result in, wreak **3.** compel, convince, dispose, force, induce, influence, make, move, persuade, prevail on *or* upon, prompt, sway **4.** com~ mand, earn, fetch, gross, net, produce, re~ turn, sell for, yield

bring about accomplish, achieve, bring to pass, cause, compass, create, effect, effectu~ ate, generate, give rise to, make happen, manage, occasion, produce, realize

bring down abase, cut down, drop, fell, floor, lay low, level, lower, overthrow, overturn, pull down, reduce, shoot down, undermine, upset

bring in accrue, bear, be worth, fetch, gross, produce, profit, realize, return, yield

bring off accomplish, achieve, bring home the bacon (*Inf.*), bring to pass, carry off,

carry out, crack it (*Inf.*), cut it (*Inf.*), dis~ charge, execute, perform, pull off, succeed

bring up 1. breed, develop, educate, form, nurture, raise, rear, support, teach, train **2.** advance, allude to, broach, introduce, men~ tion, move, propose, put forward, submit

brink border, boundary, brim, edge, fringe, frontier, limit, lip, margin, point, rim, skirt, threshold, verge

brisk 1. active, agile, alert, animated, bus~ tling, busy, energetic, lively, nimble, no-nonsense, quick, sparky, speedy, sprightly, spry, vigorous, vivacious **2.** biting, bracing, crisp, exhilarating, fresh, invigorating, keen, nippy, refreshing, sharp, snappy, stimulating
Antonyms boring, dull, enervating, heavy, lazy, lethargic, slow, sluggish, tiring, unenergetic, wearisome

briskly actively, apace, brusquely, coolly, decisively, efficiently, energetically, firmly, incisively, nimbly, pdq (*Sl.*), posthaste, promptly, pronto (*Inf.*), quickly, rapidly, readily, smartly, vigorously

bristle *n.* **1.** barb, hair, prickle, spine, stub~ ble, thorn, whisker ~*v.* **2.** horripilate, prickle, rise, stand on end, stand up **3.** be angry, be infuriated, be maddened, bridle, flare up, get one's dander up (*Sl.*), rage, see red, seethe, spit (*Inf.*) **4.** *With* **with** abound, be alive, be thick, crawl, hum, swarm, teem

bristly bearded, bewhiskered, hairy, prickly, rough, stubbly, unshaven, whiskered

brittle 1. breakable, crisp, crumbling, crumbly, delicate, fragile, frail, frangible, friable, shatterable, shivery **2.** curt, edgy, irritable, nervous, prim, stiff, stilted, tense, wired (*Sl.*)
Antonyms durable, elastic, flexible, infran~ gible, nonbreakable, resistant, rugged, shatterproof, strong, sturdy, toughened

broach 1. approach, bring up, hint at, introduce, mention, open up, propose, raise the subject, speak of, suggest, talk of, touch on **2.** crack, draw off, open, pierce, punc~ ture, start, tap, uncork

broad 1. ample, beamy (*of a ship*), capa~ cious, expansive, extensive, generous, large, roomy, spacious, vast, voluminous, wide, widespread **2.** all-embracing, catholic, com~ prehensive, encyclopedic, far-reaching, gen~ eral, global, inclusive, nonspecific, sweep~ ing, undetailed, universal, unlimited, wide, wide-ranging **3.** *As in* **broad daylight** clear, full, obvious, open, plain, straight~ forward, undisguised **4.** broad-minded, lib~ eral, open, permissive, progressive, toler~ ant, unbiased **5.** blue, coarse, gross, im~ proper, indecent, indelicate, near the knuckle (*Inf.*), unrefined, vulgar
Antonyms close, confined, constricted,

cramped, limited, meagre, narrow, restricted, tight

broadcast v. **1.** air, beam, cable, put on the air, radio, relay, show, televise, transmit **2.** advertise, announce, circulate, disseminate, make public, proclaim, promulgate, publish, report, spread ~n. **3.** programme, show, telecast, transmission

broaden augment, develop, enlarge, expand, extend, fatten, increase, open up, spread, stretch, supplement, swell, widen
Antonyms circumscribe, constrain, diminish, narrow, reduce, restrict, simplify, tighten

broad-minded catholic, cosmopolitan, dispassionate, flexible, free-thinking, indulgent, liberal, open-minded, permissive, responsive, tolerant, unbiased, unbigoted, undogmatic, unprejudiced
Antonyms biased, bigoted, closed-minded, dogmatic, inflexible, intolerant, narrow-minded, prejudiced, uncharitable

broadside abuse, assault, attack, battering, bombardment, censure, criticism, denunciation, diatribe, philippic, stick (Sl.)

brochure advertisement, booklet, circular, folder, handbill, hand-out, leaflet, mailshot, pamphlet

broke bankrupt, bust (Inf.), cleaned out (Sl.), dirt-poor (Inf.), down and out, flat broke (Inf.), impoverished, insolvent, on one's uppers, penniless, penurious, ruined, short, skint (Brit. sl.), stony-broke (Brit. sl.), without two pennies to rub together (Inf.)
Antonyms affluent, comfortable, flush (Inf.), in the money (Inf.), prosperous, rich, solvent, wealthy, well-to-do

broken 1. burst, demolished, destroyed, fractured, fragmented, rent, ruptured, separated, severed, shattered, shivered **2.** defective, exhausted, feeble, imperfect, kaput (Inf.), not functioning, out of order, ruined, run-down, spent, weak **3.** disconnected, discontinuous, disturbed, erratic, fragmentary, incomplete, intermittent, interrupted, spasmodic **4.** beaten, browbeaten, crippled, crushed, defeated, demoralized, humbled, oppressed, overpowered, subdued, tamed, vanquished **5.** dishonoured, disobeyed, disregarded, forgotten, ignored, infringed, isolated, retracted, traduced, transgressed **6.** disjointed, halting, hesitating, imperfect, stammering

broken-down collapsed, dilapidated, in disrepair, inoperative, kaput (Inf.), not functioning, not in working order, old, on the blink (Sl.), on the fritz (U.S. sl.), out of commission, out of order, worn out

brokenhearted crestfallen, desolate, despairing, devastated, disappointed, disconsolate, grief-stricken, heartbroken, heart-sick,

inconsolable, miserable, mournful, prostrated, sorrowful, wretched

broker agent, dealer, factor, go-between, intermediary, middleman, negotiator

bronze brownish, chestnut, copper, copper-coloured, metallic brown, reddish-brown, reddish-tan, rust, tan

brood v. **1.** agonize, dwell upon, eat one's heart out, fret, meditate, mope, mull over, muse, ponder, repine, ruminate, think upon **2.** cover, hatch, incubate, set, sit upon ~n. **3.** breed, chicks, children, clutch, family, hatch, infants, issue, litter, offspring, progeny, young

brook beck, burn, gill (Dialect), rill, rivulet, runnel (Literary), stream, streamlet, watercourse

brothel bagnio, bawdy house (Archaic), bordello, cathouse (U.S. sl.), house of ill fame, house of ill repute, house of prostitution, knocking shop (Sl.), red-light district, stews (Archaic), whorehouse

brother 1. blood brother, kin, kinsman, relation, relative, sibling **2.** associate, chum (Inf.), cock (Brit. inf.), colleague, companion, compeer, comrade, confrère, fellow member, mate, pal (Inf.), partner **3.** cleric, friar, monk, regular, religious

brotherhood 1. brotherliness, camaraderie, companionship, comradeship, fellowship, friendliness, kinship **2.** alliance, association, clan, clique, community, coterie, fraternity, guild, league, order, society, union

brotherly affectionate, altruistic, amicable, benevolent, cordial, fraternal, friendly, kind, neighbourly, philanthropic, sympathetic

brow 1. air, appearance, aspect, bearing, countenance, eyebrow, face, forehead, front, mien, temple **2.** brim, brink, crest, crown, edge, peak, rim, summit, tip, top, verge

browbeat badger, bulldoze (Inf.), bully, coerce, cow, domineer, dragoon, hector, intimidate, lord it over, oppress, overawe, overbear, threaten, tyrannize
Antonyms beguile, cajole, coax, entice, flatter, inveigle, lure, manoeuvre, seduce, sweet-talk (Inf.), tempt, wheedle

brown 1. adj. auburn, bay, brick, bronze, bronzed, browned, brunette, chestnut, chocolate, coffee, dark, donkey brown, dun, dusky, fuscous, ginger, hazel, rust, sunburnt, tan, tanned, tawny, toasted, umber **2.** v. cook, fry, grill, sauté, seal, sear

browned off cheesed off (Brit. sl.), discontented, discouraged, disgruntled, disheartened, fed up, pissed off (Taboo sl.), sick as a parrot (Inf.), weary

brown study absorption, abstractedness,

abstraction, contemplation, meditation, musing, preoccupation, reflection, reverie, rumination

browse 1. dip into, examine cursorily, flip through, glance at, leaf through, look round, look through, peruse, scan, skim, survey **2.** crop, eat, feed, graze, nibble, pas~ture

bruise v. **1.** blacken, blemish, contuse, crush, damage, deface, discolour, injure, mar, mark, pound, pulverize **2.** displease, grieve, hurt, injure, insult, offend, pain, sting, wound ~n. **3.** black-and-blue mark, black mark, blemish, contusion, discolora~tion, injury, mark, swelling

brunt burden, force, full force, impact, pres~sure, shock, strain, stress, thrust, violence

brush[1] n. **1.** besom, broom, sweeper **2.** clash, conflict, confrontation, encounter, fight, fracas, scrap (Inf.), set-to (Inf.), skir~mish, slight engagement, spot of bother (Inf.), tussle ~v. **3.** buff, clean, paint, polish, sweep, wash **4.** caress, contact, flick, glance, graze, kiss, scrape, stroke, sweep, touch

brush[2] n. brushwood, bushes, copse, scrub, shrubs, thicket, undergrowth, underwood

brush aside discount, dismiss, disregard, have no time for, ignore, kiss off (Sl., chiefly U.S. & Canad.), override, sweep aside

brush-off n. cold shoulder, cut, dismissal, go-by (Sl.), kiss-off (Sl., chiefly U.S. & Canad.), knock-back (Sl.), rebuff, refusal, rejection, repudiation, repulse, slight, snub, the (old) heave-ho (Inf.)

brush off v. cold-shoulder, cut, deny, dis~dain, dismiss, disown, disregard, ignore, kiss off (Sl., chiefly U.S. & Canad.), put down, rebuff, refuse, reject, repudiate, scorn, slight, snub, spurn

brush up bone up on (Inf.), cram, go over, polish up, read up, refresh one's memory, relearn, revise, study

brusque abrupt, blunt, curt, discourteous, gruff, hasty, impolite, sharp, short, surly, tart, terse, unmannerly
Antonyms accommodating, civil, courteous, gentle, patient, polite, well-mannered

brutal 1. barbarous, bloodthirsty, cruel, fe~rocious, heartless, inhuman, merciless, pitiless, remorseless, ruthless, savage, un~civilized, vicious **2.** animal, beastly, bestial, brute, brutish, carnal, coarse, crude, sen~sual **3.** bearish, callous, gruff, harsh, impo~lite, insensitive, rough, rude, severe, unciv~il, unfeeling, unmannerly
Antonyms civilized, gentle, humane, kind, merciful, polite, refined, sensitive, soft-hearted

brutally barbarically, barbarously, brutish~

ly, callously, cruelly, ferociously, fiercely, hardheartedly, heartlessly, in cold blood, inhumanly, meanly, mercilessly, murder~ously, pitilessly, remorselessly, ruthlessly, savagely, unkindly, viciously

brute n. **1.** animal, beast, creature, wild animal **2.** barbarian, beast, devil, fiend, ghoul, monster, ogre, sadist, savage, swine ~adj. **3.** bodily, carnal, fleshly, instinctive, mindless, physical, senseless, unthinking **4.** bestial, coarse, depraved, gross, sensual

bubble n. **1.** air ball, bead, blister, blob, drop, droplet, globule, vesicle **2.** bagatelle, delusion, fantasy, illusion, toy, trifle, vanity ~v. **3.** boil, effervesce, fizz, foam, froth, percolate, seethe, sparkle **4.** babble, burble, gurgle, murmur, purl, ripple, trickle, trill

bubbly 1. carbonated, curly, effervescent, fizzy, foamy, frothy, lathery, sparkling, sudsy **2.** animated, bouncy, elated, excited, happy, lively, merry, sparky

buccaneer corsair, freebooter, pirate, pri~vateer, sea-rover

buckle n. **1.** catch, clasp, clip, fastener, hasp **2.** bulge, contortion, distortion, kink, warp ~v. **3.** catch, clasp, close, fasten, hook, se~cure **4.** bend, bulge, cave in, collapse, con~tort, crumple, distort, fold, twist, warp

buckle down apply oneself, exert oneself, launch into, pitch in, put one's shoulder to the wheel, set to

buck up 1. get a move on, hasten, hurry up, shake a leg, speed up **2.** brighten, cheer up, encourage, hearten, inspirit, perk up, rally, take heart

bucolic agrarian, agrestic, agricultural, country, pastoral, rural, rustic

bud 1. n. embryo, germ, shoot, sprout **2.** v. burgeon, burst forth, develop, grow, pullu~late, shoot, sprout

budding beginning, burgeoning, developing, embryonic, fledgling, flowering, germinal, growing, incipient, nascent, potential, promising

budge 1. dislodge, give way, inch, move, propel, push, remove, roll, shift, slide, stir **2.** bend, change, convince, give way, influence, persuade, sway, yield

budget 1. n. allocation, allowance, cost, finances, financial statement, fiscal esti~mate, funds, means, resources **2.** v. allocate, apportion, cost, cost out, estimate, plan, ra~tion

buff[1] **1.** adj. sandy, straw, tan, yellowish, yellowish-brown **2.** n. **in the buff** bare, buck naked (Sl.), in one's birthday suit (Inf.), in the altogether (Inf.), in the raw (Inf.), naked, nude, unclad, unclothed, with bare skin, without a stitch on (Inf.) **3.** v. brush, burnish, polish, rub, shine, smooth

buff[2] *Inf.* addict, admirer, aficionado, con~
noisseur, devotee, enthusiast, expert, fan,
fiend (*Inf.*), freak (*Inf.*), grandmaster, hot~
shot (*Inf.*), maven (*U.S.*), whiz (*Inf.*)

buffer bulwark, bumper, cushion, fender,
intermediary, safeguard, screen, shield,
shock absorber

buffet[1] *n.* café, cafeteria, cold table, counter,
cupboard, refreshment-counter, salad bar,
sideboard, snack bar

buffet[2] **1.** *v.* bang, batter, beat, box, bump,
clobber (*Sl.*), cuff, flail, knock, lambast(e),
pound, pummel, punch, push, rap, shove,
slap, strike, thump, wallop (*Inf.*) **2.** *n.* bang,
blow, box, bump, cuff, jolt, knock, push,
rap, shove, slap, smack, thump, wallop (*Inf.*)

buffoon clown, comedian, comic, droll, fool,
harlequin, jester, joker, merry-andrew, silly
billy (*Inf.*), wag

bug *n.* **1.** *Inf.* bacterium, disease, germ, in~
fection, microorganism, virus **2.** craze, fad,
mania, obsession, rage **3.** blemish, catch,
defect, error, failing, fault, flaw, glitch,
gremlin, imperfection, snarl-up (*Inf., chiefly
Brit.*), virus ~*v.* **4.** *Inf.* aggravate (*Inf.*), an~
noy, badger, be on one's back (*Sl.*), bother,
disturb, gall, get in one's hair (*Inf.*), get on
one's nerves (*Inf.*), get on one's wick (*Brit.
sl.*), harass, hassle (*Inf.*), irk, irritate, nark
(*Brit., Aust., & N.Z. sl.*), needle (*Inf.*), nettle,
pester, piss one off (*Taboo sl.*), plague, vex
5. eavesdrop, listen in, spy, tap, wiretap

bugbear anathema, bane, *bête noire*, bogey,
bugaboo, devil, dread, fiend, horror, night~
mare, pet hate

build *v.* **1.** assemble, construct, erect, fabri~
cate, form, make, put up, raise **2.** base, be~
gin, constitute, establish, formulate, found,
inaugurate, initiate, institute, originate, set
up, start **3.** accelerate, amplify, augment,
develop, enlarge, escalate, extend, improve,
increase, intensify, strengthen ~*n.* **4.** body,
figure, form, frame, physique, shape, struc~
ture
Antonyms *v.* contract, debilitate, decline,
decrease, demolish, dilute, dismantle, end,
finish, harm, impair, lower, reduce, relin~
quish, sap, suspend, tear down, weaken

building 1. domicile, dwelling, edifice, fab~
ric, house, pile, structure **2.** architecture,
construction, erection, fabricating, raising

build-up 1. accumulation, development,
enlargement, escalation, expansion, gain,
growth, increase **2.** ballyhoo (*Inf.*), hype,
plug (*Inf.*), promotion, publicity, puff **3.** ac~
cretion, accumulation, heap, load, mass,
stack, stockpile, store

built-in essential, implicit, in-built, includ~
ed, incorporated, inherent, inseparable, in~
tegral, part and parcel of

bulge *n.* **1.** bump, hump, lump, projection,
protrusion, protuberance, swelling **2.** boost,
increase, intensification, rise, surge ~*v.* **3.**
bag, dilate, distend, enlarge, expand, proj~
ect, protrude, puff out, sag, stand out, stick
out, swell, swell out
Antonyms bowl, cave, cavity, concavity,
crater, dent, depression, hole, hollow, inden~
tation, pit, trough

bulk *n.* **1.** amplitude, bigness, dimensions,
immensity, largeness, magnitude, massive~
ness, size, substance, volume, weight **2.**
better part, body, generality, lion's share,
main part, majority, major part, mass,
most, nearly all, plurality, preponderance
~*v.* **3. bulk large** be important, carry
weight, dominate, loom, loom large, pre~
ponderate, stand out, threaten

bulky big, colossal, cumbersome, elephan~
tine, enormous, ginormous (*Inf.*), heavy,
huge, hulking, humongous *or* humungous
(*U.S. sl.*), immense, mammoth, massive,
massy, mega (*Sl.*), ponderous, substantial,
unmanageable, unwieldy, very large, volu~
minous, weighty
Antonyms convenient, handy, manageable,
neat, slim, small, wieldy

bulldoze 1. demolish, flatten, level, raze **2.**
drive, force, propel, push, shove, thrust **3.**
browbeat, bully, coerce, cow, dragoon, hec~
tor, intimidate, railroad (*Inf.*)

bullet ball, missile, pellet, projectile, shot,
slug

bulletin account, announcement, communi~
cation, communiqué, dispatch, message,
news flash, notification, report, statement

bull-headed headstrong, inflexible, mulish,
obstinate, pig-headed, stiff-necked, stubborn,
stupid, tenacious, uncompromising, un~
yielding, wilful

bullish assured, bold, confident, expectant,
improving, positive, rising

bully 1. *n.* big bully, browbeater, bully boy,
coercer, intimidator, oppressor, persecutor,
ruffian, tormentor, tough **2.** *v.* bluster,
browbeat, bulldoze (*Inf.*), bullyrag, coerce,
cow, domineer, hector, intimidate, oppress,
overbear, persecute, push around (*Sl.*), ride
roughshod over, swagger, terrorize, tyran~
nize **3.** *adj.* admirable, excellent, fine, nifty
(*Inf.*), radical (*Inf.*), very good **4.** *interj.*
bravo, capital, good, grand, great, well done

bulwark 1. bastion, buttress, defence, em~
bankment, fortification, outwork, partition,
rampart, redoubt **2.** buffer, guard, main~
stay, safeguard, security, support

bumbling awkward, blundering, botching,
bungling, clumsy, incompetent, inefficient,
inept, lumbering, maladroit, muddled,
stumbling

Antonyms able, brisk, capable, competent, efficient, equal, fit

bump *v.* **1.** bang, collide (with), crash, hit, knock, slam, smash into, strike **2.** bounce, jar, jerk, jolt, jostle, jounce, rattle, shake **3.** budge, dislodge, displace, move, remove, shift ~*n.* **4.** bang, blow, collision, crash, hit, impact, jar, jolt, knock, rap, shock, smash, thud, thump **5.** bulge, contusion, hump, knob, knot, lump, node, nodule, protuber~ance, swelling

bumper *adj.* abundant, bountiful, excellent, exceptional, jumbo (*Inf.*), massive, mega (*Sl.*), prodigal, spanking (*Inf.*), teeming, un~usual, whacking (*Inf., chiefly Brit.*), whop~ping (*Inf.*)

bump into chance upon, come across, en~counter, happen upon, light upon, meet, meet up with, run across, run into

bumpkin boor, clodhopper, clown, country bumpkin, hayseed (*U.S. & Canad. inf.*), hick (*Inf., chiefly U.S. & Canad.*), hillbilly, lout, lubber, oaf, peasant, rustic, yokel

bump off assassinate, blow away (*Sl., chiefly U.S.*), dispatch, do away with, do in (*Sl.*), eliminate, finish off, kill, knock off (*Sl.*), liquidate, murder, remove, rub out (*U.S. sl.*), take out (*Sl.*), wipe out (*Inf.*)

bumptious arrogant, boastful, brash, cocky, conceited, egotistic, forward, full of oneself, impudent, overbearing, overconfi~dent, presumptuous, pushy (*Inf.*), self-assertive, showy, swaggering, vainglorious, vaunting

bumpy bone-breaking, bouncy, choppy, ir~regular, jarring, jerky, jolting, jolty, knob~by, lumpy, pitted, potholed, rough, rutted, uneven

bunch *n.* **1.** assortment, batch, bouquet, bundle, clump, cluster, collection, heap, lot, mass, number, parcel, pile, quantity, sheaf, spray, stack, tuft **2.** band, bevy, crew (*Inf.*), crowd, flock, gang, gathering, group, knot, mob, multitude, party, posse (*Inf.*), swarm, team, troop ~*v.* **3.** assemble, bundle, clus~ter, collect, congregate, cram together, crowd, flock, group, herd, huddle, mass, pack

bundle *n.* **1.** accumulation, assortment, batch, bunch, collection, group, heap, mass, pile, quantity, stack **2.** bag, bale, box, car~ton, crate, pack, package, packet, pallet, parcel, roll ~*v.* **3.** bale, bind, fasten, pack, package, palletize, tie, tie together, tie up, truss, wrap **4.** *With* out, off, into, *etc.* hurry, hustle, push, rush, shove, throw, thrust **5.** *With* up clothe warmly, muffle up, swathe, wrap up

bungle blow (*Sl.*), blunder, bodge (*Inf.*), botch, butcher, cock up (*Brit. sl.*), foul up, fuck up (*Offens. taboo sl.*), fudge, louse up

(*Sl.*), make a mess of, mar, mess up, mis~calculate, mismanage, muff, ruin, screw up (*Inf.*), spoil
Antonyms accomplish, achieve, carry off, effect, fulfil, succeed, triumph

bungling awkward, blundering, botching, cack-handed (*Inf.*), clumsy, ham-fisted (*Inf.*), ham-handed (*Inf.*), incompetent, inept, maladroit, unskilful

bunk, bunkum balderdash, balls (*Taboo sl.*), baloney (*Inf.*), bilge (*Inf.*), bosh (*Inf.*), bullshit (*Taboo sl.*), cobblers (*Brit. taboo sl.*), crap (*Sl.*), eyewash (*Inf.*), garbage (*Inf.*), guff (*Sl.*), havers (*Scot.*), hogwash, hokum (*Sl., chiefly U.S. & Canad.*), hooey (*Sl.*), horsefeathers (*U.S. sl.*), hot air (*Inf.*), moon~shine, nonsense, piffle (*Inf.*), poppycock (*Inf.*), rot, rubbish, shit (*Taboo sl.*), stuff and nonsense, tarradiddle, tomfoolery, tommyrot, tosh (*Sl., chiefly Brit.*), trash, tripe (*Inf.*), truck (*Inf.*), twaddle

buoy 1. *n.* beacon, float, guide, marker, sig~nal **2.** *v. With* up boost, cheer, cheer up, encourage, hearten, keep afloat, lift, raise, support, sustain

buoyancy 1. floatability, lightness, weight~lessness **2.** animation, bounce (*Inf.*), cheer~fulness, cheeriness, good humour, high spirits, liveliness, pep, spiritedness, sunni~ness, zing (*Inf.*)

buoyant 1. afloat, floatable, floating, light, weightless **2.** animated, blithe, bouncy, breezy, bright, carefree, cheerful, chirpy (*Inf.*), debonair, genial, happy, jaunty, joy~ful, light-hearted, lively, peppy (*Inf.*), sparky, sunny, upbeat (*Inf.*), vivacious
Antonyms (*sense 2*) cheerless, depressed, despairing, dull, forlorn, gloomy, glum, hope~less, melancholy, moody, morose, pessimistic, sad, sullen, unhappy

burden *n.* **1.** affliction, anxiety, care, clog, encumbrance, grievance, load, millstone, obstruction, onus, responsibility, sorrow, strain, stress, trial, trouble, weight, worry **2.** *Nautical* cargo, freight, lading, tonnage ~*v.* **3.** bother, encumber, handicap, load, oppress, overload, overwhelm, saddle with, strain, tax, weigh down, worry

bureau 1. desk, writing desk **2.** agency, branch, department, division, office, service

bureaucracy 1. administration, author~ities, civil service, corridors of power, di~rectorate, government, ministry, official~dom, officials, the system **2.** bumbledom, officialdom, officialese, red tape, regulations

bureaucrat administrator, apparatchik, civil servant, functionary, mandarin, min~ister, office-holder, officer, official, public servant

burglar cat burglar, filcher, housebreaker, picklock, pilferer, robber, sneak thief, thief

burglary break-in, breaking and entering, filching, housebreaking, larceny, pilferage, robbery, stealing, theft, thieving

burial burying, entombment, exequies, funeral, inhumation, interment, obsequies, sepulture

buried 1. coffined, consigned to the grave, entombed, interred, laid to rest **2.** dead and buried, dead and gone, in the grave, long gone, pushing up the daisies, six feet under **3.** covered, forgotten, hidden, repressed, sunk in oblivion, suppressed **4.** cloistered, concealed, hidden, private, sequestered, tucked away **5.** caught up, committed, concentrating, devoted, engrossed, immersed, intent, lost, occupied, preoccupied, rapt

burlesque 1. *n.* caricature, mock, mockery, parody, satire, send-up (*Brit. inf.*), spoof (*Inf.*), takeoff (*Inf.*), travesty **2.** *adj.* caricatural, comic, farcical, hudibrastic, ironical, ludicrous, mock, mock-heroic, mocking, parodic, satirical, travestying **3.** *v.* ape, caricature, exaggerate, imitate, lampoon, make fun of, mock, parody, ridicule, satirize, send up (*Brit. inf.*), spoof (*Inf.*), take off (*Inf.*), take the piss out of (*Taboo sl.*), travesty

burly beefy (*Inf.*), big, brawny, bulky, hefty, hulking, muscular, powerful, Ramboesque, stocky, stout, strapping, strong, sturdy, thickset, well-built
Antonyms lean, puny, scraggy, scrawny, slight, spare, thin, weak, weedy (*Inf.*), wimpish *or* wimpy (*Inf.*)

burn 1. be ablaze, be on fire, blaze, flame, flare, flash, flicker, glow, smoke **2.** brand, calcine, char, ignite, incinerate, kindle, light, parch, reduce to ashes, scorch, set on fire, shrivel, singe, toast, wither **3.** bite, hurt, pain, smart, sting, tingle **4.** be excited (angry, aroused, inflamed, passionate), blaze, desire, fume, seethe, simmer, smoulder, yearn **5.** consume, eat up, expend, use

burning 1. blazing, fiery, flaming, flashing, gleaming, glowing, hot, illuminated, scorching, smouldering **2.** all-consuming, ardent, eager, earnest, fervent, fervid, flaming, frantic, frenzied, impassioned, intense, passionate, vehement, zealous **3.** acrid, biting, caustic, irritating, painful, piercing, prickling, pungent, reeking, smarting, stinging, tingling **4.** acute, compelling, critical, crucial, essential, important, pressing, significant, urgent, vital
Antonyms apathetic, calm, cool, cooling, faint, indifferent, mild, numbing, passive, soothing

burnish 1. *v.* brighten, buff, furbish, glaze, polish, rub up, shine, smooth **2.** *n.* gloss, lustre, patina, polish, sheen, shine
Antonyms *v.* abrade, graze, scratch, scuff

burrow 1. *n.* den, hole, lair, retreat, shelter, tunnel **2.** *v.* delve, dig, excavate, hollow out, scoop out, tunnel

burst *v.* **1.** blow up, break, crack, disintegrate, explode, fly open, fragment, puncture, rend asunder, rupture, shatter, shiver, split, tear apart **2.** barge, break, break out, erupt, gush forth, run, rush, spout ~*n.* **3.** bang, blast, blasting, blowout, blow-up, breach, break, crack, discharge, explosion, rupture, split **4.** eruption, fit, gush, gust, outbreak, outburst, outpouring, rush, spate, spurt, surge, torrent ~*adj.* **5.** flat, punctured, rent, ruptured, split

bury 1. consign to the grave, entomb, inearth, inhume, inter, lay to rest, sepulchre **2.** conceal, cover, cover up, enshroud, hide, secrete, shroud, stash (*Inf.*), stow away **3.** drive in, embed, engulf, implant, sink, submerge **4.** absorb, engage, engross, immerse, interest, occupy
Antonyms (*senses 1 & 2*) bring to light, dig up, discover, disinter, dredge up, exhume, expose, find, reveal, turn up, uncover, unearth

bush 1. hedge, plant, shrub, shrubbery, thicket **2.** backwoods, brush, scrub, scrubland, the wild, woodland

bushy bristling, bristly, fluffy, fuzzy, luxuriant, rough, shaggy, spreading, stiff, thick, unruly, wiry

busily actively, assiduously, briskly, carefully, diligently, earnestly, energetically, industriously, intently, purposefully, speedily, strenuously

business 1. calling, career, craft, employment, function, job, line, métier, occupation, profession, pursuit, trade, vocation, work **2.** company, concern, corporation, enterprise, establishment, firm, organization, venture **3.** bargaining, commerce, dealings, industry, manufacturing, merchandising, selling, trade, trading, transaction **4.** affair, assignment, concern, duty, function, issue, matter, point, problem, question, responsibility, subject, task, topic

businesslike correct, efficient, matter-of-fact, methodical, orderly, organized, practical, professional, regular, routine, systematic, thorough, well-ordered, workaday
Antonyms careless, disorderly, disorganized, frivolous, impractical, inefficient, irregular, sloppy, unprofessional, unsystematic, untidy

businessman, businesswoman capitalist, employer, entrepreneur, executive, financier, *homme d'affaires,* industrialist, merchant, tradesman, tycoon

bust[1] bosom, breast, chest, torso

bust[2] *v.* **1.** break, burst, fracture, rupture **2.** bankrupt, break, crash, fail, impoverish, ruin **3.** arrest, catch, collar (*Inf.*), cop (*Sl.*), feel one's collar (*Sl.*), lift (*Sl.*), nab (*Inf.*), nail (*Inf.*), raid, search ~*adj.* **4. go bust** become insolvent, be ruined, break, fail, go bankrupt ~*n.* **5.** arrest, capture, cop (*Sl.*), raid, search, seizure

bustle 1. *v.* beetle, bestir, dash, flutter, fuss, hasten, hurry, rush, scamper, scramble, scurry, scuttle, stir, tear **2.** *n.* activity, ado, agitation, commotion, excitement, flurry, fuss, haste, hurly-burly, hurry, pother, stir, to-do, tumult
Antonyms *v.* be indolent, idle, laze, lie around, loaf, loiter, loll, relax, rest, take it easy ~*n.* inaction, inactivity, quiet, quietness, stillness, tranquillity

busy *adj.* **1.** active, assiduous, brisk, diligent, employed, engaged, engrossed, hard at work, industrious, in harness, occupied, on duty, persevering, slaving, working **2.** active, energetic, exacting, full, hectic, hustling, lively, on the go (*Inf.*), restless, strenuous, tireless, tiring **3.** fussy, inquisitive, interfering, meddlesome, meddling, nosy, officious, prying, snoopy, stirring, troublesome ~*v.* **4.** absorb, employ, engage, engross, immerse, interest, occupy
Antonyms (*senses 1 & 2*) idle, inactive, indolent, lackadaisical, lazy, off duty, relaxed, shiftless, slothful, unoccupied

busybody eavesdropper, gossip, intriguer, intruder, meddler, nosy parker (*Inf.*), pry, scandalmonger, snoop, snooper, stirrer (*Inf.*), troublemaker

but *conj.* **1.** further, however, moreover, nevertheless, on the contrary, on the other hand, still, yet **2.** bar, barring, except, excepting, excluding, notwithstanding, save, with the exception of ~*adv.* **3.** just, merely, only, simply, singly, solely

butcher *n.* **1.** destroyer, killer, murderer, slaughterer, slayer ~*v.* **2.** carve, clean, cut, cut up, dress, joint, prepare, slaughter **3.** assassinate, cut down, destroy, exterminate, kill, liquidate, massacre, put to the sword, slaughter, slay **4.** bodge (*Inf.*), botch, destroy, mess up, mutilate, ruin, spoil, wreck

butchery blood bath, blood-letting, bloodshed, carnage, killing, massacre, mass murder, murder, slaughter

butt[1] **1.** haft, handle, hilt, shaft, shank, stock **2.** base, end, fag end (*Inf.*), foot, leftover, stub, tail, tip

butt[2] Aunt Sally, dupe, laughing stock, mark, object, point, subject, target, victim

butt[3] *v./n.* **1.** *With or of the head or horns* buck, buffet, bump, bunt, jab, knock, poke, prod, punch, push, ram, shove, thrust ~*v.* **2.** abut, join, jut, meet, project, protrude **3.** *With* **in** *or* **into** chip in (*Inf.*), cut in, interfere, interrupt, intrude, meddle, put one's oar in, put one's two cents in (*U.S. sl.*),

stick one's nose in

butt[4] barrel, cask, pipe

buttonhole *v. Fig.* accost, bore, catch, detain in talk, grab, importune, persuade importunately, take aside, waylay

buttress 1. *n.* abutment, brace, mainstay, pier, prop, reinforcement, shore, stanchion, stay, strut, support **2.** *v.* augment, back up, bolster, brace, prop, prop up, reinforce, shore, shore up, strengthen, support, sustain, uphold

buxom ample, bosomy, busty, comely, curvaceous, debonair, fresh-looking, fullbosomed, healthy, hearty, jocund, jolly, lively, lusty, merry, plump, robust, sprightly, voluptuous, well-rounded, winsome
Antonyms delicate, frail, slender, slight, slim, svelte, sylphlike, thin, trim

buy *v.* **1.** acquire, get, invest in, obtain, pay for, procure, purchase, score (*Sl.*), shop for **2.** *Often with* **off** bribe, corrupt, fix (*Inf.*), grease someone's palm (*Sl.*), square, suborn ~*n.* **3.** acquisition, bargain, deal, purchase
Antonyms *v.* auction, retail, sell, vend

buzz *n.* **1.** bombilation *or* bombination (*Literary*), buzzing, drone, hiss, hum, murmur, purr, ring, ringing, sibilation, susurration *or* susurrus (*Literary*), whir, whisper **2.** dirt (*U.S. sl.*), gen (*Brit. inf.*), gossip, hearsay, latest (*Inf.*), news, report, rumour, scandal, whisper ~*v.* **3.** bombilate *or* bombinate (*Literary*), drone, fizzle, hum, murmur, reverberate, ring, sibilate, susurrate (*Literary*), whir, whisper, whizz **4.** chatter, gossip, natter, rumour, tattle

by *prep.* **1.** along, beside, by way of, close to, near, next to, over, past, via **2.** through, through the agency of, under the aegis of ~*adv.* **3.** aside, at hand, away, beyond, close, handy, near, past, to one side

by and by before long, erelong (*Archaic or poetic*), eventually, in a while, in the course of time, one day, presently, soon

bygone ancient, antiquated, departed, erstwhile, extinct, forgotten, former, gone by, lost, of old, of yore, olden, one-time, past, past recall, previous, sunk in oblivion
Antonyms coming, forthcoming, future, prospective, to be, to come

bypass avoid, body-swerve (*Scot.*), circumvent, depart from, detour round, deviate from, get round, go round, ignore, neglect, outflank, pass round

bystander eyewitness, looker-on, observer, onlooker, passer-by, spectator, viewer, watcher, witness
Antonyms contributor, partaker, participant, party

C

cab hackney, hackney carriage, minicab, taxi, taxicab

cabin 1. berth, bothy, chalet, cot, cottage, crib, hovel, hut, lodge, shack, shanty, shed **2.** berth, compartment, deckhouse, quarters, room

cabinet 1. case, chiffonier, closet, commode, cupboard, dresser, escritoire, locker **2.** administration, assembly, council, counsellors, ministry **3.** apartment, boudoir, chamber (*Archaic*)

cackle babble, blather, chatter, chuckle, cluck, crow, gabble, gibber, giggle, jabber, prattle, snicker, snigger, titter

cad bounder (*Old-fashioned Brit. sl.*), churl, cur, dastard (*Archaic*), heel (*Sl.*), knave, rat (*Inf.*), rotter (*Sl., chiefly Brit.*), scumbag (*Sl.*)

cadaverous ashen, blanched, bloodless, corpselike, deathlike, deathly, emaciated, exsanguinous, gaunt, ghastly, haggard, hollow-eyed, pale, pallid, wan

caddish despicable, ill-bred, low, ungentlemanly, unmannerly
Antonyms gentlemanly, honourable, laudable, mannerly, pleasant, praiseworthy

cadence 1. beat, lilt, measure (*Prosody*), metre, pulse, rhythm, swing, tempo, throb **2.** accent, inflection, intonation, modulation

café cafeteria, coffee bar, coffee shop, lunchroom, restaurant, snack bar, tearoom

cage 1. *v.* confine, coop up, fence in, immure, impound, imprison, incarcerate, lock up, mew, pound, restrain, shut up **2.** *n.* corral (*U.S.*), enclosure, pen, pound

cagey, cagy careful, cautious, chary, discreet, guarded, noncommittal, shrewd, wary, wily
Antonyms careless, dull, imprudent, indiscreet, reckless, stolid, unthinking, unwary

cajole beguile, coax, decoy, dupe, entice, entrap, flatter, inveigle, lure, manoeuvre, mislead, seduce, sweet-talk (*Inf.*), tempt, wheedle

cake 1. *v.* bake, cement, coagulate, congeal, consolidate, dry, encrust, harden, inspissate (*Archaic*), ossify, solidify, thicken **2.** *n.* bar, block, cube, loaf, lump, mass, slab

calamitous blighting, cataclysmic, catastrophic, deadly, devastating, dire, disastrous, fatal, pernicious, ruinous, tragic, woeful
Antonyms advantageous, beneficial, favourable, fortunate, good, helpful

calamity adversity, affliction, cataclysm, catastrophe, disaster, distress, downfall, hardship, misadventure, mischance, misfortune, mishap, reverse, ruin, scourge, tragedy, trial, tribulation, woe, wretchedness
Antonyms advantage, benefit, blessing, boon, good fortune, good luck, help

calculate 1. adjust, compute, consider, count, determine, enumerate, estimate, figure, gauge, judge, rate, reckon, value, weigh, work out **2.** aim, design, intend, plan

calculated considered, deliberate, intended, intentional, planned, premeditated, purposeful
Antonyms haphazard, hasty, heedless, hurried, impetuous, impulsive, rash, spontaneous, unintentional, unplanned, unpremeditated

calculating canny, cautious, contriving, crafty, cunning, designing, devious, Machiavellian, manipulative, politic, scheming, sharp, shrewd, sly
Antonyms blunt, direct, downright, frank, guileless, honest, open, outspoken, sincere, undesigning

calculation 1. answer, computation, estimate, estimation, figuring, forecast, judgment, reckoning, result **2.** caution, circumspection, contrivance, deliberation, discretion, foresight, forethought, planning, precaution

calibre 1. bore, diameter, gauge, measure **2.** *Fig.* ability, capacity, distinction, endowment, faculty, force, gifts, merit, parts, quality, scope, stature, strength, talent, worth

call *v.* **1.** announce, arouse, awaken, cry, cry out, hail, halloo, proclaim, rouse, shout, waken, yell **2.** assemble, bid, collect, contact, convene, convoke, gather, invite, muster, rally, summon **3.** give (someone) a bell (*Brit. sl.*), phone, ring up (*Inf., chiefly Brit.*), telephone **4.** christen, denominate, describe as, designate, dub, entitle, label, name, style, term **5.** announce, appoint, declare, decree, elect, ordain, order, proclaim, set apart **6.** consider, estimate, judge, regard, think ~*n.* **7.** cry, hail, scream, shout, signal, whoop, yell **8.** announcement, appeal, command, demand, invitation, notice, order, plea, request, ring (*Inf., chiefly Brit.*), summons, supplication, visit **9.** cause, claim, excuse, grounds, justification, need, occasion, reason, right, urge

Antonyms v. (sense 1) be quiet, be silent, murmur, mutter, speak softly, whisper (senses 2 & 5) call off, cancel, dismiss, disperse, excuse, release ~n. (sense 7) murmur, mutter, whisper (sense 8) dismissal, release

call for 1. demand, entail, involve, necessitate, need, occasion, require, suggest **2.** collect, fetch, pick up, uplift (Scot.)

calling business, career, employment, life's work, line, métier, mission, occupation, profession, province, pursuit, trade, vocation, walk of life, work
Antonyms affliction, avocation, curse, dislike, hobby

call on 1. drop in on, look in on, look up, see, visit **2.** appeal to, ask, bid, call upon, entreat, invite, invoke, request, summon, supplicate

callous apathetic, case-hardened, cold, hard-bitten, hard-boiled (Inf.), hardened, hardhearted, harsh, heartless, indifferent, indurated (Rare), insensate, insensible, insensitive, inured, obdurate, soulless, thick-skinned, torpid, uncaring, unfeeling, unresponsive, unsusceptible, unsympathetic
Antonyms caring, compassionate, considerate, gentle, sensitive, soft, sympathetic, tender, understanding

calm adj. **1.** balmy, halcyon, mild, pacific, peaceful, placid, quiet, restful, serene, smooth, still, tranquil, windless **2.** collected, composed, cool, dispassionate, equable, impassive, imperturbable, relaxed, sedate, self-possessed, undisturbed, unemotional, unexcitable, unexcited, unfazed (Inf.), unflappable (Inf.), unmoved, unruffled ~v. **3.** hush, mollify, placate, quieten, relax, soothe ~n. **4.** calmness, hush, peace, peacefulness, quiet, repose, serenity, stillness
Antonyms adj. agitated, aroused, discomposed, disturbed, emotional, excited, fierce, frantic, heated, perturbed, rough, shaken, stormy, troubled, wild, worried ~v. aggravate, agitate, arouse, disturb, excite, irritate, stir ~n. agitation, disturbance, wildness

calmness 1. calm, composure, equability, hush, motionlessness, peace, peacefulness, placidity, quiet, repose, restfulness, serenity, smoothness, stillness, tranquillity **2.** composure, cool (Sl.), coolness, dispassion, equanimity, impassivity, imperturbability, poise, sang-froid, self-possession

calumny abuse, aspersion, backbiting, calumniation, defamation, denigration, derogation, detraction, evil-speaking, insult, libel, lying, misrepresentation, obloquy, revilement, slander, smear, stigma, vilification, vituperation

camouflage 1. n. blind, cloak, concealment, cover, deceptive markings, disguise,

false appearance, front, guise, mask, masquerade, mimicry, protective colouring, screen, subterfuge **2.** v. cloak, conceal, cover, disguise, hide, mask, obfuscate, obscure, screen, veil
Antonyms v. bare, display, exhibit, expose, reveal, show, uncover, unmask, unveil

camp[1] bivouac, camping ground, camp site, cantonment (Military), encampment, tents

camp[2] affected, artificial, camped up (Inf.), campy (Inf.), effeminate, mannered, ostentatious, poncy (Sl.), posturing

campaign attack, crusade, drive, expedition, jihad (Rare), movement, offensive, operation, push

cancel 1. abolish, abort, abrogate, annul, blot out, call off, countermand, cross out, delete, do away with, efface, eliminate, erase, expunge, obliterate, obviate, quash, repeal, repudiate, rescind, revoke **2.** balance out, compensate for, counterbalance, make up for, neutralize, nullify, obviate, offset, redeem

cancellation abandoning, abandonment, abolition, annulment, deletion, elimination, quashing, repeal, revocation

cancer blight, canker, carcinoma (Pathology), corruption, evil, growth, malignancy, pestilence, rot, sickness, tumour

candid 1. blunt, downright, fair, forthright, frank, free, guileless, impartial, ingenuous, just, open, outspoken, plain, sincere, straightforward, truthful, unbiased, unequivocal, unprejudiced, upfront (Inf.) **2.** impromptu, informal, uncontrived, unposed
Antonyms biased, complimentary, diplomatic, flattering, kind, subtle

candidate applicant, aspirant, claimant, competitor, contender, contestant, entrant, nominee, possibility, runner, solicitant, suitor

candour artlessness, directness, fairness, forthrightness, frankness, guilelessness, honesty, impartiality, ingenuousness, naïveté, openness, outspokenness, simplicity, sincerity, straightforwardness, truthfulness, unequivocalness
Antonyms bias, cunning, deceit, diplomacy, dishonesty, flattery, insincerity, prejudice, subtlety

canker 1. v. blight, consume, corrode, corrupt, embitter, envenom, inflict, poison, pollute, rot, rust, waste away **2.** n. bane, blight, blister, cancer, corrosion, corruption, infection, lesion, rot, scourge, sore, ulcer

cannon 1. artillery piece, big gun, field gun, gun, mortar **2.** Plural artillery, battery, big guns, cannonry, field guns, guns, ordnance

cannonade barrage, battery, bombardment, broadside, pounding, salvo, shelling, volley

canny acute, artful, astute, careful, cautious, circumspect, clever, judicious, knowing, perspicacious, prudent, sagacious, sharp, shrewd, subtle, wise, worldly-wise
Antonyms bumbling, inept, lumpen (*Inf.*), obtuse, unskilled

canon catalogue, criterion, dictate, formula, list, precept, principle, regulation, roll, rule, standard, statute, yardstick

canopy awning, baldachin, covering, shade, sunshade, tester

cant *n.* **1.** affected piety, humbug, hypocrisy, insincerity, lip service, pious platitudes, pretence, pretentiousness, sanctimonious~ness, sham holiness **2.** argot, jargon, lingo, slang, vernacular ~*v.* **3.** angle, bevel, in~cline, rise, slant, slope, tilt

cantankerous bad-tempered, captious, choleric, contrary, crabby, cranky (*U.S., Canad., & Irish inf.*), crotchety (*Inf.*), crusty, difficult, disagreeable, grouchy (*Inf.*), grumpy, ill-humoured, irascible, irri~table, liverish, peevish, perverse, quarrel~some, ratty (*Brit. & N.Z. inf.*), testy, tetchy
Antonyms agreeable, amiable, breezy, cheerful, complaisant, congenial, genial, good-natured, happy, kindly, merry, placid, pleasant, vivacious

canter *n.* amble, dogtrot, easy gait, jog, lope

canting hypocritical, insincere, Janus-faced, sanctimonious, two-faced

canvass *v.* **1.** analyse, campaign, election~eer, examine, inspect, investigate, poll, scan, scrutinize, sift, solicit, solicit votes, study, ventilate **2.** agitate, debate, discuss, dispute ~*n.* **3.** examination, investigation, poll, scrutiny, survey, tally

canyon coulee (*U.S.*), gorge, gulch (*U.S.*), gulf, gully, ravine

cap *v.* beat, better, clobber (*Sl.*), complete, cover, crown, eclipse, exceed, excel, finish, lick (*Inf.*), outdo, outstrip, overtop, run rings around (*Inf.*), surpass, top, transcend

capability ability, capacity, competence, fa~cility, faculty, means, potential, potentiality, power, proficiency, qualification(s), where~withal
Antonyms inability, incompetence, inef~ficiency, ineptitude, powerlessness

capable able, accomplished, adapted, adept, adequate, apt, clever, competent, efficient, experienced, fitted, gifted, intelligent, mas~terly, proficient, qualified, skilful, suited, susceptible, talented
Antonyms incapable, incompetent, ineffec~tive, inept, inexpert, unqualified, unskilled

capacious ample, broad, comfortable, com~modious, comprehensive, expansive, ex~tended, extensive, generous, liberal, roomy, sizable, spacious, substantial, vast, volumi~nous, wide
Antonyms confined, constricted, cramped, enclosed, incommodious, insubstantial, lim~ited, narrow, poky, restricted, small, tight, tiny, uncomfortable, ungenerous

capacity 1. amplitude, compass, dimen~sions, extent, magnitude, range, room, scope, size, space, volume **2.** ability, apti~tude, aptness, brains, capability, cleverness, competence, competency, efficiency, facility, faculty, forte, genius, gift, intelligence, power, readiness, strength **3.** appointment, function, office, position, post, province, role, service, sphere

cape chersonese (*Poetic*), head, headland, ness (*Archaic*), peninsula, point, promon~tory

caper 1. *v.* bounce, bound, cavort, dance, frisk, frolic, gambol, hop, jump, leap, romp, skip, spring, trip **2.** *n.* antic, dido (*Inf.*), es~capade, gambol, high jinks, hop, jape, jest, jump, lark (*Inf.*), leap, mischief, practical joke, prank, revel, shenanigan (*Inf.*), sport, stunt

capital *adj.* **1.** cardinal, central, chief, con~trolling, essential, foremost, important, leading, main, major, overruling, para~mount, pre-eminent, primary, prime, prin~cipal, prominent, vital **2.** excellent, fine, first, first-rate, prime, splendid, sterling, superb, world-class ~*n.* **3.** assets, cash, finance, finances, financing, funds, invest~ment(s), means, money, principal, property, resources, stock, wealth, wherewithal

capitalism free enterprise, *laissez faire*, private enterprise, private ownership

capitulate come to terms, give in, give up, relent, submit, succumb, surrender, yield
Antonyms beat, conquer, crush, defeat, get the better of, lick (*Inf.*), overcome, overpower, subdue, subjugate, vanquish

capitulation accedence, submission, sur~render, yielding

caprice changeableness, fad, fancy, fickleness, fitfulness, freak, humour, im~pulse, inconstancy, notion, quirk, vagary, whim, whimsy

capricious changeful, crotchety (*Inf.*), er~ratic, fanciful, fickle, fitful, freakish, impul~sive, inconstant, mercurial, odd, queer, quirky, unpredictable, variable, wayward, whimsical
Antonyms certain, consistent, constant, de~cisive, determined, firm, resolute, respon~sible, stable, unchangeable, unmoveable, un~wavering

capsize invert, keel over, overturn, tip over, turn over, turn turtle, upset

capsule 1. bolus, lozenge, pill, tablet, troche (*Medical*) **2.** case, pericarp (*Botany*), pod, receptacle, seed vessel, sheath, shell, vessel

captain boss, chief, chieftain, commander, head, leader, master, number one (*Inf.*), officer, (senior) pilot, skipper

captivate absorb, allure, attract, beguile, bewitch, charm, dazzle, enamour, enchant, enrapture, enslave, ensnare, enthral, entrance, fascinate, hypnotize, infatuate, lure, mesmerize, ravish, seduce, win
Antonyms alienate, disenchant, disgust, repel, repulse

captive 1. *n.* bondservant, convict, detainee, hostage, internee, prisoner, prisoner of war, slave **2.** *adj.* caged, confined, enslaved, ensnared, imprisoned, incarcerated, locked up, penned, restricted, subjugated

captivity bondage, confinement, custody, detention, durance (*Archaic*), duress, enthralment, imprisonment, incarceration, internment, restraint, servitude, slavery, thraldom, vassalage

capture 1. *v.* apprehend, arrest, bag, catch, collar (*Inf.*), feel one's collar (*Sl.*), lift (*Sl.*), nab (*Inf.*), nail (*Inf.*), secure, seize, take, take into custody, take prisoner **2.** *n.* apprehension, arrest, catch, imprisonment, seizure, taking, taking captive, trapping
Antonyms *v.* free, let go, let out, liberate, release, set free, turn loose

car 1. auto (*U.S.*), automobile, jalopy (*Inf.*), machine, motor, motorcar, vehicle **2.** buffet car, cable car, coach, dining car, (railway) carriage, sleeping car, van

carafe decanter, flagon, flask, jug, pitcher

carcass body, cadaver (*Medical*), corpse, corse (*Archaic*), dead body, framework, hulk, remains, shell, skeleton

cardinal capital, central, chief, essential, first, foremost, fundamental, greatest, highest, important, key, leading, main, paramount, pre-eminent, primary, prime, principal
Antonyms dispensable, least important, lowest, secondary, subordinate, unessential

care 1. affliction, anxiety, burden, concern, disquiet, hardship, interest, perplexity, pressure, responsibility, solicitude, stress, tribulation, trouble, vexation, woe, worry **2.** attention, carefulness, caution, circumspection, consideration, direction, forethought, heed, management, meticulousness, pains, prudence, regard, vigilance, watchfulness **3.** charge, control, custody, guardianship, keeping, management, ministration, protection, supervision, ward
Antonyms (*sense 1*) pleasure, relaxation (*sense 2*) abandon, carelessness, heedlessness, inattention, indifference, laxity, laxness, neglect, negligence, unconcern

career *n.* **1.** calling, employment, life work, livelihood, occupation, pursuit, vocation **2.** course, passage, path, procedure, progress, race, walk ~*v.* **3.** barrel (along) (*Inf., chiefly U.S. & Canad.*), bolt, burn rubber (*Inf.*), dash, hurtle, race, rush, speed, tear

care for 1. attend, foster, look after, mind, minister to, nurse, protect, provide for, tend, watch over **2.** be fond of, desire, enjoy, find congenial, like, love, prize, take to, want

carefree airy, blithe, breezy, buoyant, careless, cheerful, cheery, chirpy (*Inf.*), easygoing, happy, happy-go-lucky, insouciant, jaunty, light-hearted, lightsome (*Archaic*), radiant, sunny, untroubled
Antonyms blue, careworn, cheerless, dejected, depressed, desolate, despondent, down, gloomy, melancholy, miserable, sad, unhappy, worried

careful 1. accurate, attentive, cautious, chary, circumspect, conscientious, discreet, fastidious, heedful, painstaking, precise, prudent, punctilious, scrupulous, thoughtful, thrifty **2.** alert, concerned, judicious, mindful, particular, protective, solicitous, vigilant, wary, watchful
Antonyms abandoned, careless, casual, inaccurate, inattentive, inexact, neglectful, negligent, reckless, remiss, slovenly, thoughtless, unconcerned, untroubled

careless 1. absent-minded, cursory, forgetful, hasty, heedless, incautious, inconsiderate, indiscreet, negligent, perfunctory, regardless, remiss, thoughtless, unconcerned, unguarded, unmindful, unthinking **2.** inaccurate, irresponsible, lackadaisical, neglectful, offhand, slapdash, slipshod, sloppy (*Inf.*) **3.** artless, casual, nonchalant, unstudied
Antonyms accurate, alert, anxious, attentive, careful, cautious, concerned, correct, neat, on the ball (*Inf.*), orderly, painstaking, tidy, wary, watchful

carelessness inaccuracy, inattention, inconsiderateness, indiscretion, irresponsibility, laxity, laxness, neglect, negligence, omission, remissness, slackness, sloppiness (*Inf.*), thoughtlessness

caress 1. *v.* cuddle, embrace, fondle, hug, kiss, nuzzle, pet, stroke **2.** *n.* cuddle, embrace, fondling, hug, kiss, pat, stroke

caretaker 1. *n.* concierge, curator, custodian, janitor, keeper, porter, superintendent, warden, watchman **2.** *adj.* holding, interim, short-term, temporary

cargo baggage, consignment, contents, freight, goods, lading, load, merchandise, shipment, tonnage, ware

caricature 1. *n.* burlesque, cartoon, distortion, farce, lampoon, mimicry, parody, pas~

quinade, satire, send-up (*Brit. inf.*), takeoff (*Inf.*), travesty **2.** *v.* burlesque, distort, lampoon, mimic, mock, parody, ridicule, satirize, send up (*Brit. inf.*), take off (*Inf.*)

carnage blood bath, bloodshed, butchery, havoc, holocaust, massacre, mass murder, murder, shambles, slaughter

carnal 1. amorous, animal, erotic, fleshly, impure, lascivious, lecherous, lewd, libidinous, licentious, lustful, prurient, randy (*Inf., chiefly Brit.*), raunchy (*Sl.*), salacious, sensual, sensuous, sexual, sexy (*Inf.*), steamy (*Inf.*), unchaste, voluptuous, wanton **2.** bodily, corporeal, earthly, human, mundane, natural, physical, profane, secular, sublunary, temporal, unregenerate, unspiritual, worldly

carnival celebration, fair, festival, fête, fiesta, gala, holiday, jamboree, jubilee, Mardi Gras, merrymaking, revelry

carol canticle, canzonet, chorus, ditty, hymn, lay, noel, song, strain

carouse bend the elbow (*Inf.*), bevvy (*Dialect*), booze (*Inf.*), drink, imbibe, make merry, quaff, roister, wassail

carp beef (*Sl.*), cavil, censure, complain, criticize, find fault, hypercriticize, knock (*Inf.*), kvetch (*U.S. sl.*), nag, pick holes, quibble, reproach
Antonyms admire, applaud, approve, commend, compliment, extol, laud (*Literary*), pay tribute to, praise, sing the praises of, speak highly of

carpenter cabinet-maker, joiner, woodworker

carping captious, cavilling, critical, faultfinding, grouchy (*Inf.*), hard to please, hypercritical, nagging, nit-picking (*Inf.*), picky (*Inf.*), reproachful

carriage 1. carrying, conveyance, conveying, delivery, freight, transport, transportation **2.** cab, coach, conveyance, vehicle **3.** *Fig.* air, bearing, behaviour, comportment, conduct, demeanour, deportment, gait, manner, mien, posture, presence

carry 1. bear, bring, conduct, convey, fetch, haul, hump (*Brit. sl.*), lift, lug, move, relay, take, tote (*Inf.*), transfer, transmit, transport **2.** accomplish, capture, effect, gain, secure, win **3.** drive, impel, influence, motivate, spur, urge **4.** bear, bolster, hold up, maintain, shoulder, stand, suffer, support, sustain, underpin, uphold **5.** broadcast, communicate, display, disseminate, give, offer, publish, release, stock

carry on 1. continue, endure, keep going, last, maintain, perpetuate, persevere, persist **2.** administer, manage, operate, run **3.** *Inf.* create (*Sl.*), make a fuss, misbehave

carry out accomplish, achieve, carry through, consummate, discharge, effect, execute, fulfil, implement, perform, realize

carton box, case, container, pack, package, packet

cartoon animated cartoon, animated film, animation, caricature, comic strip, lampoon, parody, satire, sketch, takeoff (*Inf.*)

cartridge 1. capsule, case, cassette, container, cylinder, magazine **2.** charge, round, shell

carve chip, chisel, cut, divide, engrave, etch, fashion, form, grave (*Archaic*), hack, hew, incise, indent, inscribe, mould, sculpt, sculpture, slash, slice, whittle

cascade 1. *n.* avalanche, cataract, deluge, falls, flood, fountain, outpouring, shower, torrent, waterfall **2.** *v.* descend, flood, gush, overflow, pitch, plunge, pour, spill, surge, tumble

case 1. box, cabinet, canister, capsule, carton, cartridge, casket, chest, compact, container, crate, holder, receptacle, shell, suitcase, tray, trunk **2.** capsule, casing, cover, covering, envelope, folder, integument, jacket, sheath, wrapper, wrapping **3.** circumstance(s), condition, context, contingency, dilemma, event, plight, position, predicament, situation, state **4.** example, illustration, instance, occasion, occurrence, specimen **5.** *Law* action, cause, dispute, lawsuit, proceedings, process, suit, trial

cash ackers (*Sl.*), banknotes, brass (*Northern English dialect*), bread (*Sl.*), bullion, change, coin, coinage, currency, dibs (*Sl.*), dosh (*Brit. & Aust. sl.*), dough (*Sl.*), funds, money, necessary (*Inf.*), needful (*Inf.*), notes, payment, ready (*Inf.*), ready money, resources, rhino (*Brit. sl.*), shekels (*Inf.*), silver, specie, spondulicks (*Sl.*), tin (*Sl.*), wherewithal

cashier 1. *n.* accountant, bank clerk, banker, bursar, clerk, purser, teller, treasurer **2.** *v.* break, cast off, discard, discharge, dismiss, drum out, expel

casket ark (*Dialect*), box, case, chest, coffer, jewel box, kist (*Scot. & Northern English dialect*)

cast *v.* **1.** chuck (*Inf.*), drive, drop, fling, hurl, impel, launch, lob, pitch, project, shed, shy, sling, throw, thrust, toss **2.** bestow, deposit, diffuse, distribute, emit, give, radiate, scatter, shed, spread **3.** allot, appoint, assign, choose, name, pick, select **4.** add, calculate, compute, figure, forecast, reckon, total **5.** form, found, model, mould, set, shape ~*n.* **6.** fling, lob, throw, thrust, toss **7.** air, appearance, complexion, demeanour, look, manner, mien, semblance, shade, stamp, style, tinge, tone, turn **8.** actors, characters, company, dramatis personae, players, troupe

cast down deject, depress, desolate, discourage, dishearten, dispirit

caste class, estate, grade, lineage, order, race, rank, social order, species, station, status, stratum

castigate bawl out (*Inf.*), beat, berate, blast, cane, carpet (*Inf.*), censure, chasten, chastise, chew out (*U.S. & Canad. inf.*), correct, criticize, discipline, dress down (*Inf.*), excoriate, flail, flay, flog, give a rocket (*Brit. & N.Z. inf.*), haul over the coals (*Inf.*), lambast(e), lash, put down, read the riot act, rebuke, reprimand, scold, scourge, tear into (*Inf.*), tear (someone) off a strip (*Brit. inf.*), whip

castle chateau, citadel, donjon, fastness, fortress, keep, mansion, palace, peel, stronghold, tower

casual 1. accidental, chance, contingent, fortuitous, incidental, irregular, occasional, random, serendipitous, uncertain, unexpected, unforeseen, unintentional, unpremeditated **2.** apathetic, blasé, cursory, indifferent, informal, insouciant, lackadaisical, nonchalant, offhand, perfunctory, relaxed, unconcerned **3.** informal, non-dressy, sporty
Antonyms (*sense 1*) arranged, deliberate, expected, fixed, foreseen, intentional, planned, premeditated (*sense 2*) committed, concerned, direct, enthusiastic, passionate, serious, systematic (*sense 3*) ceremonial, dressy, formal

casualties dead, fatalities, losses, missing, wounded

casualty 1. loss, sufferer, victim **2.** accident, calamity, catastrophe, chance, contingency, disaster, misadventure, misfortune, mishap

cat feline, grimalkin, malkin (*Archaic*), moggy (*Sl.*), mouser, puss (*Inf.*), pussy (*Inf.*), tabby

catalogue 1. *n.* directory, gazetteer, index, inventory, list, record, register, roll, roster, schedule **2.** *v.* accession, alphabetize, classify, file, index, inventory, list, register, tabulate

catapult 1. *n.* ballista, sling, slingshot (*U.S.*), trebuchet **2.** *v.* heave, hurl, hurtle, pitch, plunge, propel, shoot, toss

cataract 1. cascade, deluge, downpour, falls, Niagara, rapids, torrent, waterfall **2.** *Medical* opacity (*of the eye*)

catastrophe 1. adversity, affliction, blow, bummer (*Sl.*), calamity, cataclysm, devastation, disaster, failure, fiasco, ill, meltdown (*Inf.*), mischance, misfortune, mishap, reverse, tragedy, trial, trouble **2.** conclusion, culmination, curtain, debacle, dénouement, end, finale, termination, upshot, winding-up

catcall 1. *v.* boo, deride, gibe, give the bird to (*Inf.*), hiss, jeer, whistle **2.** *n.* boo, gibe, hiss, jeer, raspberry, whistle

catch *v.* **1.** apprehend, arrest, capture, clutch, ensnare, entangle, entrap, feel one's collar (*Sl.*), get, grab, grasp, grip, lay hold of, lift (*Sl.*), nab (*Inf.*), nail (*Inf.*), seize, snare, snatch, take **2.** detect, discover, expose, find out, surprise, take unawares, unmask **3.** bewitch, captivate, charm, delight, enchant, enrapture, fascinate **4.** contract, develop, get, go down with, incur, succumb to, suffer from **5.** apprehend, discern, feel, follow, get, grasp, hear, perceive, recognize, sense, take in, twig (*Brit. inf.*) ~*n.* **6.** bolt, clasp, clip, fastener, hasp, hook, hook and eye, latch, sneck, snib (*Scot.*) **7.** disadvantage, drawback, fly in the ointment, hitch, snag, stumbling block, trap, trick
Antonyms *v.* (*sense 1*) drop, free, give up, liberate, loose, release (*sense 3*) alienate, bore, disenchant, disgust, fail to interest, repel (*sense 4*) avert, avoid, escape, ward off ~*n.* (*sense 7*) advantage, benefit, bonus, boon, reward

catching 1. communicable, contagious, infectious, infective, transferable, transmittable **2.** attractive, captivating, charming, enchanting, fascinating, fetching, taking, winning
Antonyms (*sense 1*) incommunicable, noncatching, non-contagious, non-infectious, non-transmittable

catch on comprehend, find out, grasp, see, see through, twig (*Brit. inf.*), understand

catchword byword, motto, password, refrain, slogan, watchword

catchy captivating, haunting, memorable, popular

catechize cross-examine, drill, examine, grill (*Inf.*), interrogate, question

categorical absolute, direct, downright, emphatic, explicit, express, positive, unambiguous, unconditional, unequivocal, unqualified, unreserved
Antonyms conditional, hesitant, indefinite, qualified, questionable, uncertain, vague

category class, classification, department, division, grade, grouping, head, heading, list, order, rank, section, sort, type

cater furnish, outfit, provide, provision, purvey, supply, victual

catharsis abreaction, cleansing, lustration, purgation, purging, purification, release

catholic all-embracing, all-inclusive, broad-minded, charitable, comprehensive, eclectic, ecumenical, general, global, liberal, tolerant, unbigoted, universal, unsectarian, whole, wide, world-wide

Antonyms bigoted, exclusive, illiberal, limited, narrow-minded, parochial, sectarian

cattle beasts, bovines, cows, kine (*Archaic*), livestock, neat (*Archaic*), stock

catty backbiting, bitchy (*Inf.*), ill-natured, malevolent, malicious, mean, rancorous, shrewish, snide, spiteful, venomous
Antonyms benevolent, charitable, compassionate, considerate, generous, kind, pleasant

caucus assembly, conclave, congress, convention, get-together (*Inf.*), meeting, parley, session

cause *n.* **1.** agent, beginning, creator, genesis, mainspring, maker, origin, originator, prime mover, producer, root, source, spring **2.** account, agency, aim, basis, consideration, end, grounds, incentive, inducement, motivation, motive, object, purpose, reason **3.** attempt, belief, conviction, enterprise, ideal, movement, purpose, undertaking ~*v.* **4.** begin, bring about, compel, create, effect, engender, generate, give rise to, incite, induce, lead to, motivate, occasion, precipitate, produce, provoke, result in
Antonyms *n.* consequence, effect, end, outcome, result ~*v.* deter, foil, inhibit, prevent, stop

caustic 1. acrid, astringent, biting, burning, corroding, corrosive, keen, mordant, vitriolic **2.** acrimonious, cutting, mordacious, pungent, sarcastic, scathing, severe, stinging, trenchant, virulent, vitriolic
Antonyms agreeable, bland, gentle, healing, kind, loving, mild, pleasant, pleasing, soft, soothing, sweet, temperate

caution *n.* **1.** alertness, care, carefulness, circumspection, deliberation, discretion, forethought, heed, heedfulness, prudence, vigilance, watchfulness **2.** admonition, advice, counsel, injunction, warning ~*v.* **3.** admonish, advise, tip off, urge, warn
Antonyms *n.* carelessness, daring, imprudence, rashness, recklessness ~*v.* dare

cautious alert, cagey (*Inf.*), careful, chary, circumspect, discreet, guarded, heedful, judicious, prudent, tentative, vigilant, wary, watchful
Antonyms adventurous, bold, careless, daring, foolhardy, heedless, impetuous, inattentive, incautious, indiscreet, madcap, rash, reckless, unguarded, unheedful, venturesome, venturous

cavalcade array, march-past, parade, procession, spectacle, train

cavalier *n.* **1.** chevalier, equestrian, horseman, knight, royalist **2.** beau, blade (*Archaic*), escort, gallant, gentleman ~*adj.* **3.** arrogant, condescending, curt, disdainful, haughty, insolent, lofty, lordly, offhand, scornful, supercilious

cavalry horse, horsemen, mounted troops

Antonyms foot soldiers, infantrymen

cave cavern, cavity, den, grotto, hollow

caveat admonition, caution, warning

cavern cave, hollow, pothole

cavernous 1. concave, deep-set, hollow, sunken, yawning **2.** echoing, resonant, reverberant, sepulchral

cavil beef (*Sl.*), carp, censure, complain, find fault, hypercriticize, kvetch (*U.S. sl.*), object, quibble

cavity crater, dent, gap, hole, hollow, pit

cease break off, bring *or* come to an end, conclude, culminate, desist, die away, discontinue, end, fail, finish, halt, leave off, refrain, stay, stop, terminate
Antonyms begin, commence, continue, initiate, start

ceaseless constant, continual, continuous, endless, eternal, everlasting, incessant, indefatigable, interminable, never-ending, nonstop, perennial, perpetual, unending, unremitting, untiring
Antonyms broken, erratic, intermittent, irregular, occasional, periodic, spasmodic, sporadic

cede abandon, abdicate, allow, concede, convey, grant, hand over, make over, relinquish, renounce, resign, step down (*Inf.*), surrender, transfer, yield

celebrate bless, commemorate, commend, crack up (*Inf.*), drink to, eulogize, exalt, extol, glorify, honour, keep, laud, observe, perform, praise, proclaim, publicize, rejoice, reverence, solemnize, toast

celebrated acclaimed, distinguished, eminent, famed, famous, glorious, illustrious, lionized, notable, outstanding, popular, pre-eminent, prominent, renowned, revered, well-known
Antonyms dishonoured, forgotten, insignificant, obscure, trivial, unacclaimed, undistinguished, unknown, unnotable, unpopular

celebration 1. beano (*Brit. sl.*), carousal, festival, festivity, gala, jollification, jubilee, junketing, merrymaking, party, rave (*Brit. sl.*), rave-up (*Brit. sl.*), revelry **2.** anniversary, commemoration, honouring, observance, performance, remembrance, solemnization

celebrity 1. big name, big shot (*Inf.*), bigwig (*Inf.*), celeb (*Inf.*), dignitary, lion, luminary, megastar (*Inf.*), name, personage, personality, star, superstar, V.I.P. **2.** distinction, éclat, eminence, fame, glory, honour, notability, popularity, pre-eminence, prestige, prominence, renown, reputation, repute, stardom
Antonyms has-been, nobody, obscurity, unknown

celerity dispatch, expedition, fleetness, haste, promptness, quickness, rapidity, speed, swiftness, velocity, vivacity

celestial angelic, astral, divine, elysian, empyrean (*Poetic*), eternal, ethereal, god~ like, heavenly, immortal, seraphic, spiritu~ al, sublime, supernatural

celibacy chastity, continence, purity, sin~ gleness, virginity

cell 1. cavity, chamber, compartment, cubi~ cle, dungeon, stall **2.** caucus, coterie, group, nucleus, unit

cement 1. *v.* attach, bind, bond, cohere, combine, glue, gum, join, plaster, seal, sol~ der, stick together, unite, weld **2.** *n.* adhe~ sive, binder, glue, gum, paste, plaster, seal~ ant

cemetery burial ground, churchyard, God's acre, graveyard, necropolis

censor blue-pencil, bowdlerize, cut, expur~ gate

censorious captious, carping, cavilling, condemnatory, disapproving, disparaging, fault-finding, hypercritical, scathing, severe

censure 1. *v.* abuse, bawl out (*Inf.*), berate, blame, blast, carpet (*Inf.*), castigate, chew out (*U.S. & Canad. inf.*), chide, condemn, criticize, denounce, excoriate, give (some~ one) a rocket (*Brit. & N.Z. inf.*), lambast(e), put down, read the riot act, rebuke, repre~ hend, reprimand, reproach, reprove, scold, tear into (*Inf.*), tear (someone) off a strip (*Brit. inf.*), upbraid **2.** *n.* blame, castigation, condemnation, criticism, disapproval, dressing down (*Inf.*), obloquy, rebuke, re~ monstrance, reprehension, reprimand, re~ proach, reproof, stick (*Sl.*), stricture
Antonyms *v.* applaud, commend, compli~ ment, laud (*Literary*) ~*n.* approval, commen~ dation, compliment, encouragement

central chief, essential, focal, fundamental, inner, interior, key, main, mean, median, mid, middle, primary, principal
Antonyms exterior, minor, outer, outer~ most, secondary, subordinate, subsidiary

centralize amalgamate, compact, concen~ trate, concentre, condense, converge, incor~ porate, rationalize, streamline, unify

centre 1. *n.* bull's-eye, core, crux, focus, heart, hub, kernel, mid, middle, midpoint, nucleus, pivot **2.** *v.* cluster, concentrate, converge, focus, revolve
Antonyms *n.* border, boundary, brim, cir~ cumference, edge, fringe, limit, lip, margin, perimeter, periphery, rim ~*v.* bestrew, dif~ fuse, disseminate, fling, scatter, spread, sprinkle, strew, toss

centrepiece cynosure, epergne, focus, highlight, hub, star

ceremonial 1. *adj.* formal, liturgical, ritu~ al, ritualistic, solemn, stately **2.** *n.* ceremo~ ny, formality, rite, ritual, solemnity
Antonyms casual, informal, relaxed, simple

ceremonious civil, courteous, courtly, deferential, dignified, exact, formal, precise, punctilious, ritual, solemn, starchy (*Inf.*), stately, stiff

ceremony 1. commemoration, function, observance, parade, rite, ritual, service, show, solemnities **2.** ceremonial, decorum, etiquette, form, formal courtesy, formality, niceties, pomp, propriety, protocol

certain 1. assured, confident, convinced, positive, satisfied, sure **2.** ascertained, con~ clusive, incontrovertible, indubitable, ir~ refutable, known, plain, true, undeniable, undoubted, unequivocal, unmistakable, val~ id **3.** bound, definite, destined, fated, in~ eluctable, inescapable, inevitable, inexo~ rable, sure **4.** decided, definite, established, fixed, settled **5.** assured, constant, depend~ able, reliable, stable, staunch, steady, trust~ worthy, unfailing, unquestionable **6.** ex~ press, individual, particular, precise, spe~ cial, specific
Antonyms disputable, doubtful, dubious, equivocal, fallible, indefinite, questionable, uncertain, unconvinced, undecided, unlikely, unreliable, unsettled, unsure

certainty 1. assurance, authoritativeness, certitude, confidence, conviction, faith, in~ dubitableness, inevitability, positiveness, sureness, trust, validity **2.** fact, reality, sure thing (*Inf.*), surety, truth
Antonyms disbelief, doubt, indecision, qualm, scepticism, uncertainty, unsureness

certificate authorization, credential(s), di~ ploma, document, licence, testimonial, voucher, warrant

certify ascertain, assure, attest, authenti~ cate, aver, avow, confirm, corroborate, de~ clare, endorse, guarantee, notify, show, tes~ tify, validate, verify, vouch, witness

chafe abrade, anger, annoy, exasperate, fret, fume, gall, grate, incense, inflame, irritate, nark (*Brit., Aust., & N.Z. sl.*), offend, pro~ voke, rage, rasp, rub, ruffle, scrape, scratch, vex, worry
Antonyms allay, alleviate, appease, assuage, calm, conciliate, mollify, pacify, placate, please, soothe

chaff *n.* **1.** dregs, glumes, hulls, husks, ref~ use, remains, rubbish, trash, waste **2.** badi~ nage, banter, joking, josh (*Sl., chiefly U.S. & Canad.*), persiflage, raillery, teasing ~*v.* **3.** banter, deride, jeer, josh (*Sl., chiefly U.S. & Canad.*), mock, rib (*Inf.*), ridicule, scoff, take the piss out of (*Taboo sl.*), taunt, tease

chagrin 1. *n.* annoyance, discomfiture, dis~ composure, displeasure, disquiet, dissatis~ faction, embarrassment, fretfulness, hu~

miliation, ill-humour, irritation, mortifica~
tion, peevishness, spleen, vexation **2.** *v.*
annoy, discomfit, discompose, displease,
disquiet, dissatisfy, embarrass, humiliate,
irk, irritate, mortify, peeve, vex

chain *v.* **1.** bind, confine, enslave, fetter,
gyve (*Archaic*), handcuff, manacle, restrain,
shackle, tether, trammel, unite ~*n.* **2.** bond,
coupling, fetter, link, manacle, shackle, un~
ion **3.** concatenation, progression, se~
quence, series, set, string, succession, train

chairman chairperson, chairwoman, direc~
tor, master of ceremonies, president, pre~
sider, speaker, spokesman, toastmaster

chalk up accumulate, achieve, attain, cred~
it, enter, gain, log, mark, record, register,
score, tally, win

challenge 1. *v.* accost, arouse, beard,
brave, call out, claim, confront, dare, defy,
demand, dispute, face off (*Sl.*), impugn, in~
vestigate, object to, provoke, question, re~
quire, stimulate, summon, tackle, tax, test,
throw down the gauntlet, try **2.** *n.* confron~
tation, dare, defiance, face-off (*Sl.*), interro~
gation, provocation, question, summons to
contest, test, trial, ultimatum

chamber 1. apartment, bedroom, cavity,
compartment, cubicle, enclosure, hall, hol~
low, room **2.** assembly, council, legislative
body, legislature

champion 1. *n.* backer, challenger, con~
queror, defender, guardian, hero, nonpareil,
patron, protector, title holder, upholder,
victor, vindicator, warrior, winner **2.** *v.*
advocate, back, defend, encourage, espouse,
fight for, promote, stick up for (*Inf.*), sup~
port, uphold

chance *n.* **1.** liability, likelihood, occasion,
odds, opening, opportunity, possibility,
probability, prospect, scope, time, window
2. accident, casualty, coincidence, contin~
gency, destiny, fate, fortuity, fortune, luck,
misfortune, peril, providence **3.** gamble,
hazard, jeopardy, risk, speculation, uncer~
tainty ~*v.* **4.** befall, betide, come about,
come to pass, fall out, happen, occur **5.** en~
danger, gamble, go out on a limb, hazard,
jeopardize, risk, stake, try, venture, wager
~*adj.* **6.** accidental, casual, contingent, for~
tuitous, inadvertent, incidental, random,
serendipitous, unforeseeable, unforeseen,
unintentional, unlooked-for
Antonyms *n.* certainty, design, impossibil~
ity, improbability, intention, surety, unlike~
lihood ~*adj.* arranged, deliberate, designed,
expected, foreseen, intentional, planned

chancy dangerous, dicey (*Inf., chiefly Brit.*),
dodgy (*Brit., Aust., & N.Z. sl.*), hazardous,
perilous, problematical, risky, speculative,
uncertain

Antonyms certain, reliable, safe, secure,
sound, stable, sure

change *v.* **1.** alter, convert, diversify,
fluctuate, metamorphose, moderate, modify,
mutate, reform, remodel, reorganize, re~
style, shift, transform, transmute, vacillate,
vary, veer **2.** alternate, barter, convert,
displace, exchange, interchange, remove,
replace, substitute, swap (*Inf.*), trade,
transmit ~*n.* **3.** alteration, difference, in~
novation, metamorphosis, modification,
mutation, permutation, revolution, trans~
formation, transition, transmutation, vicis~
situde **4.** conversion, exchange, inter~
change, substitution, trade **5.** break (*Inf.*),
departure, diversion, novelty, variation,
variety
Antonyms *v.* hold, keep, remain, stay ~*n.*
constancy, invariability, monotony, perma~
nence, stability, uniformity

changeable capricious, changeful, cheq~
uered, erratic, fickle, fitful, fluid, incon~
stant, irregular, kaleidoscopic, labile
(*Chem.*), mercurial, mobile, mutable, pro~
tean, shifting, temperamental, uncertain,
uneven, unpredictable, unreliable, unset~
tled, unstable, unsteady, vacillating, vari~
able, versatile, volatile, wavering
Antonyms constant, invariable, irrevers~
ible, regular, reliable, stable, steady, un~
changeable

changeless abiding, consistent, constant,
eternal, everlasting, fixed, immovable, im~
mutable, permanent, perpetual, regular, re~
liable, resolute, settled, stationary, stead~
fast, steady, unalterable, unchanging, uni~
form, unvarying

channel *n.* **1.** canal, chamber, conduit, duct,
fluting, furrow, groove, gutter, main, pas~
sage, route, strait **2.** *Fig.* approach, artery,
avenue, course, means, medium, path,
route, way ~*v.* **3.** conduct, convey, direct,
guide, transmit

chant 1. *n.* carol, chorus, melody, psalm,
song **2.** *v.* carol, chorus, croon, descant, in~
tone, recite, sing, warble

chaos anarchy, bedlam, confusion, disorder,
disorganization, entropy, lawlessness, pan~
demonium, tumult
Antonyms neatness, orderliness, organiza~
tion, tidiness

chaotic anarchic, confused, deranged, dis~
ordered, disorganized, lawless, purposeless,
rampageous, riotous, topsy-turvy, tumultu~
ous, uncontrolled

chap bloke (*Brit. inf.*), character, cove (*Sl.*),
customer (*Inf.*), dude (*U.S. & Canad. inf.*),
fellow, guy (*Inf.*), individual, person, sort,
type

chaperon 1. *n.* companion, duenna, escort,

governess **2.** *v.* accompany, attend, escort, protect, safeguard, shepherd, watch over

chapter clause, division, episode, part, period, phase, section, stage, topic

char carbonize, cauterize, scorch, sear, singe

character 1. attributes, bent, calibre, cast, complexion, constitution, disposition, individuality, kidney, make-up, marked traits, nature, personality, quality, reputation, temper, temperament, type **2.** honour, integrity, rectitude, strength, uprightness **3.** card (*Inf.*), eccentric, nut (*Sl.*), oddball (*Inf.*), odd bod (*Inf.*), oddity, original, queer fish (*Brit. inf.*), wacko (*Sl.*) **4.** cipher, device, emblem, figure, hieroglyph, letter, logo, mark, rune, sign, symbol, type **5.** part, persona, portrayal, role **6.** fellow, guy (*Inf.*), individual, person, sort, type

characteristic 1. *adj.* distinctive, distinguishing, idiosyncratic, individual, peculiar, representative, singular, special, specific, symbolic, symptomatic, typical **2.** *n.* attribute, faculty, feature, idiosyncrasy, mark, peculiarity, property, quality, quirk, trait
Antonyms *adj.* rare, uncharacteristic, unrepresentative, unusual

characterize brand, distinguish, identify, indicate, inform, mark, represent, stamp, typify

charade fake, farce, pantomime, parody, pretence, travesty

charge *v.* **1.** accuse, arraign, blame, impeach, incriminate, indict, involve ~*n.* **2.** accusation, allegation, imputation, indictment ~*v.* **3.** assail, assault, attack, rush, storm ~*n.* **4.** assault, attack, onset, onslaught, rush, sortie ~*v.* **5.** afflict, burden, commit, entrust, tax ~*n.* **6.** burden, care, concern, custody, duty, office, responsibility, safekeeping, trust, ward **7.** amount, cost, damage (*Inf.*), expenditure, expense, outlay, payment, price, rate ~*v.* **8.** fill, instil, lade, load, suffuse **9.** bid, command, demand, enjoin, exhort, instruct, order, require ~*n.* **10.** canon, command, demand, dictate, direction, exhortation, injunction, instruction, mandate, order, precept
Antonyms *v.* (*sense 1*) absolve, acquit, clear, exonerate, pardon ~*n.* (*sense 2*) absolution, acquittal, clearance, exoneration, pardon, reprieve ~*v.* (*sense 3*) retreat, withdraw ~*n.* (*sense 4*) retreat, withdrawal

charitable 1. beneficent, benevolent, bountiful, eleemosynary, generous, kind, lavish, liberal, philanthropic **2.** broad-minded, considerate, favourable, forgiving, gracious, humane, indulgent, kindly, lenient, magnanimous, sympathetic, tolerant, understanding
Antonyms inconsiderate, mean, stingy,

strict, uncharitable, unforgiving, ungenerous, unkind, unsympathetic

charity 1. alms-giving, assistance, benefaction, contributions, donations, endowment, fund, gift, hand-out, largess *or* largesse, philanthropy, relief **2.** affection, Agape, altruism, benevolence, benignity, bountifulness, bounty, compassion, fellow feeling, generosity, goodness, goodwill, humanity, indulgence, love, pity, tenderheartedness
Antonyms (*sense 1*) miserliness, selfishness, stinginess, uncharitableness (*sense 2*) hatred, ill will, intolerance, malice

charlatan cheat, con man (*Inf.*), fake, fraud, impostor, mountebank, phoney *or* phony (*Inf.*), pretender, quack, sham, swindler

charm *v.* **1.** absorb, allure, attract, beguile, bewitch, cajole, captivate, delight, enamour, enchant, enrapture, entrance, fascinate, mesmerize, please, ravish, win, win over ~*n.* **2.** allure, allurement, appeal, attraction, desirability, enchantment, fascination, magic, magnetism, sorcery, spell **3.** amulet, fetish, good-luck piece, lucky piece, periapt (*Rare*), talisman, trinket
Antonyms *v.* alienate, repel, repulse ~*n.* (*sense 2*) repulsiveness, unattractiveness

charming appealing, attractive, bewitching, captivating, delectable, delightful, engaging, eye-catching, fetching, irresistible, likable *or* likeable, lovely, pleasant, pleasing, seductive, winning, winsome
Antonyms disgusting, horrid, repulsive, unappealing, unattractive, unlikable *or* unlikeable, unpleasant, unpleasing

chart 1. *n.* blueprint, diagram, graph, map, plan, table, tabulation **2.** *v.* delineate, draft, graph, map out, outline, plot, shape, sketch

charter 1. *n.* bond, concession, contract, deed, document, franchise, indenture, licence, permit, prerogative, privilege, right **2.** *v.* authorize, commission, employ, hire, lease, rent, sanction

chase 1. *v.* course, drive, drive away, expel, follow, hound, hunt, pursue, put to flight, run after, track **2.** *n.* hunt, hunting, pursuit, race, venery (*Archaic*)

chasm abyss, alienation, breach, cavity, cleft, crater, crevasse, fissure, gap, gorge, gulf, hiatus, hollow, opening, ravine, rent, rift, split, void

chassis anatomy, bodywork, frame, framework, fuselage, skeleton, substructure

chaste austere, decent, decorous, elegant, immaculate, incorrupt, innocent, modest, moral, neat, pure, quiet, refined, restrained, simple, unaffected, uncontaminated, undefiled, unsullied, vestal, virginal, virtuous, wholesome
Antonyms blemished, corrupt, dirty, dishonourable, gaudy, immoral, impure, mar~

ried, ornate, promiscuous, self-indulgent, tainted, unchaste, unclean, unrestrained, wanton

chasten afflict, castigate, chastise, correct, cow, curb, discipline, humble, humiliate, repress, soften, subdue, tame

chastise beat, berate, castigate, censure, correct, discipline, flog, lash, lick (*Inf.*), punish, scold, scourge, upbraid, whip
Antonyms caress, commend, compliment, congratulate, cuddle, embrace, fondle, hug, praise, reward

chastity celibacy, continence, innocence, maidenhood, modesty, purity, virginity, virtue
Antonyms debauchery, immorality, lewd~ ness, licentiousness, profligacy, promiscuity, wantonness

chat 1. *n.* chatter, chinwag (*Brit. inf.*), con~ fab (*Inf.*), gossip, heart-to-heart, natter, talk, tête-à-tête **2.** *v.* chatter, chew the rag *or* fat (*Sl.*), gossip, jaw (*Sl.*), natter, rabbit (on) (*Brit. inf.*), talk

chatter *n./v.* babble, blather, chat, gab (*Inf.*), gossip, jabber, natter, prate, prattle, rabbit (on) (*Brit. inf.*), tattle, twaddle

chatty colloquial, familiar, friendly, gossipy, informal, newsy (*Inf.*), talkative
Antonyms aloof, cold, distant, formal, hos~ tile, quiet, reserved, shy, silent, standoffish, taciturn, timid, unfriendly, unsociable

cheap 1. bargain, cheapo (*Inf.*), cut-price, economical, economy, inexpensive, keen, low-cost, low-priced, reasonable, reduced, sale **2.** bush-league (*Aust. & N.Z. inf.*), chickenshit (*U.S. sl.*), common, crappy (*Sl.*), dime-a-dozen (*Inf.*), inferior, paltry, piss-poor (*U.S. taboo sl.*), poor, poxy (*Sl.*), second-rate, shoddy, tatty, tawdry, tinhorn (*U.S. sl.*), two-bit (*U.S. & Canad. sl.*), worth~ less **3.** base, contemptible, despicable, low, mean, scurvy, sordid, vulgar
Antonyms (*sense 1*) costly, dear, expensive, pricey (*Inf.*), steep (*senses 2 & 3*) admirable, charitable, decent, elegant, generous, good, high-class, honourable, superior, tasteful, valuable

cheapen belittle, debase, degrade, demean, denigrate, depreciate, derogate, devalue, discredit, disparage, lower

cheat *v.* **1.** bamboozle (*Inf.*), beguile, bilk, con (*Inf.*), cozen, deceive, defraud, diddle (*Inf.*), do (*Inf.*), double-cross (*Inf.*), dupe, finagle (*Inf.*), fleece, fool, gull (*Archaic*), hoax, hoodwink, kid (*Inf.*), mislead, rip off (*Sl.*), skin (*Sl.*), stiff (*Sl.*), sting (*Inf.*), swin~ dle, take for a ride (*Inf.*), take in (*Inf.*), thwart, trick, victimize **2.** baffle, check, de~ feat, deprive, foil, frustrate, prevent, thwart ~*n.* **3.** artifice, deceit, deception, fraud, im~ posture, rip-off (*Sl.*), scam (*Sl.*), sting (*Inf.*),

swindle, trickery **4.** charlatan, cheater, chiseller (*Inf.*), con man (*Inf.*), deceiver, dodger, double-crosser (*Inf.*), impostor, knave (*Archaic*), rogue, shark, sharper, swindler, trickster

check *v.* **1.** check out (*Inf.*), compare, confirm, enquire into, examine, inspect, in~ vestigate, look at, look over, make sure, monitor, note, probe, research, scrutinize, study, take a dekko at (*Brit. sl.*), test, tick, verify, vet, work over **2.** arrest, bar, bridle, control, curb, delay, halt, hinder, impede, inhibit, limit, nip in the bud, obstruct, pause, rein, repress, restrain, retard, stop, thwart **3.** admonish, bawl out (*Inf.*), blame, carpet (*Inf.*), chew out (*U.S. & Canad. inf.*), chide, give (someone) a rocket (*Brit. & N.Z. inf.*), give (someone) a row (*Inf.*), rate, read the riot act, rebuff, rebuke, reprimand, re~ prove, scold, tear into (*Inf.*), tear (someone) off a strip (*Brit. inf.*), tell off (*Inf.*), ~*n.* **4.** examination, inspection, investigation, re~ search, scrutiny, test **5.** constraint, control, curb, damper, hindrance, impediment, in~ hibition, limitation, obstacle, obstruction, rein, restraint, stoppage **6.** blow, disap~ pointment, frustration, rejection, reverse, setback
Antonyms *v.* (*sense 1*) disregard, ignore, ne~ glect, overlook, pass over, pay no attention to (*sense 2*) accelerate, advance, begin, encour~ age, further, give free rein, help, release, start

cheek audacity, brass neck (*Brit. inf.*), bra~ zenness, chutzpah (*U.S. & Canad. inf.*), dis~ respect, effrontery, front, gall (*Inf.*), imper~ tinence, impudence, insolence, lip (*Sl.*), neck (*Inf.*), nerve, sauce (*Inf.*), temerity

cheeky audacious, disrespectful, forward, fresh (*Inf.*), impertinent, impudent, insolent, insulting, lippy (*U.S. & Canad. sl.*), pert, sassy (*U.S. inf.*), saucy
Antonyms civil, complaisant, courteous, decorous, deferential, mannerly, polite, re~ spectful, well-behaved, well-mannered

cheer *v.* **1.** animate, brighten, buoy up, cheer up, comfort, console, elate, elevate, encourage, enliven, exhilarate, gladden, hearten, incite, inspirit, solace, uplift, warm **2.** acclaim, applaud, clap, hail, hurrah ~*n.* **3.** animation, buoyancy, cheerfulness, com~ fort, gaiety, gladness, glee, hopefulness, joy, liveliness, merriment, merry-making, mirth, optimism, solace **4.** acclamation, ap~ plause, ovation, plaudits
Antonyms *v.* (*sense 1*) darken, depress, dis~ courage, dishearten, sadden (*sense 2*) blow a raspberry, boo, hiss, jeer, ridicule

cheerful animated, blithe, bright, bucked (*Inf.*), buoyant, cheery, chirpy (*Inf.*), con~ tented, enlivening, enthusiastic, gay, genial, glad, gladsome (*Archaic*), happy, hearty, jaunty, jolly, joyful, light-hearted, lightsome

(*Archaic*), merry, optimistic, pleasant, spar~
kling, sprightly, sunny, upbeat (*Inf.*)
Antonyms cheerless, dejected, depressed,
depressing, despondent, dismal, down, down~
cast, down in the dumps (*Inf.*), dull, gloomy,
lifeless, melancholy, miserable, morose, pen~
sive, sad, unhappy, unpleasant

cheerfulness buoyancy, exuberance, gai~
ety, geniality, gladness, good cheer, good
humour, high spirits, jauntiness, joyous~
ness, light-heartedness

cheering auspicious, bright, comforting,
encouraging, heartening, promising, propi~
tious

cheerless austere, bleak, comfortless, dark,
dejected, depressed, desolate, despondent,
disconsolate, dismal, dolorous, drab, dreary,
dull, forlorn, funereal, gloomy, grim, joy~
less, melancholy, miserable, mournful, sad,
sombre, sorrowful, sullen, unhappy, woebe~
gone, woeful
Antonyms cheerful, cheery, elated, happy,
jolly, joyful, light-hearted, merry

cheer up brighten, buck up (*Inf.*), comfort,
encourage, enliven, gladden, hearten, jolly
along (*Inf.*), perk up, rally, take heart

cheery breezy, carefree, cheerful, chirpy
(*Inf.*), genial, good-humoured, happy, jovial,
lively, pleasant, sunny, upbeat (*Inf.*)

chemical compound, drug, potion, synthetic

cherish care for, cleave to, cling to, comfort,
cosset, encourage, entertain, foster, har~
bour, hold dear, nourish, nurse, nurture,
prize, shelter, support, sustain, treasure
Antonyms abandon, desert, despise, dis~
dain, dislike, forsake, hate, neglect

cherubic adorable, angelic, heavenly, inno~
cent, lovable, seraphic, sweet

chest ark (*Dialect*), box, case, casket, coffer,
crate, kist (*Scot. & Northern English dia~
lect*), strongbox, trunk

chew 1. bite, champ, crunch, gnaw, grind,
masticate, munch **2.** *Fig. Usually with* **over**
consider, deliberate upon, meditate, mull
(over), muse on, ponder, reflect upon, ru~
minate, weigh

chic elegant, fashionable, modish, sexy (*Inf.*),
smart, stylish, trendy (*Brit. inf.*), up-to-date
Antonyms dinosaur, inelegant, naff (*Brit.
sl.*), old-fashioned, outmoded, out-of-date, pas~
sé, shabby, unfashionable

chide admonish, bawl out (*Inf.*), berate,
blame, blast, carpet (*Inf.*), censure, check,
chew out (*U.S. & Canad. inf.*), criticize, find
fault, give (someone) a rocket (*Brit. & N.Z.
inf.*), give (someone) a row (*Inf.*), lambast(e),
lecture, put down, read the riot act, rebuke,
reprehend, reprimand, reproach, reprove,
scold, tear into (*Inf.*), tear (someone) off a
strip (*Brit. inf.*), tell off (*Inf.*), upbraid

chief 1. *adj.* big-time (*Inf.*), capital, cardinal,
central, especial, essential, foremost, grand,
highest, key, leading, main, major league
(*Inf.*), most important, outstanding, para~
mount, predominant, pre-eminent, premier,
prevailing, primary, prime, principal, su~
perior, supreme, uppermost, vital **2.** *n.* boss
(*Inf.*), captain, chieftain, commander, direc~
tor, governor, head, leader, lord, manager,
master, principal, ringleader, ruler, super~
intendent, suzerain
Antonyms *adj.* least, minor, subordinate,
subsidiary ~*n.* follower, subject, subordinate

chiefly above all, especially, essentially, in
general, in the main, largely, mainly, most~
ly, on the whole, predominantly, primarily,
principally, usually

child ankle-biter (*Aust. sl.*), babe, baby, bairn
(*Scot.*), brat, chit, descendant, infant, issue,
juvenile, kid (*Inf.*), little one, minor, nipper
(*Inf.*), nursling, offspring, progeny, rug rat
(*Sl.*), sprog (*Sl.*), suckling, toddler, tot, wean
(*Scot.*), youngster

childbirth accouchement, child-bearing,
confinement, delivery, labour, lying-in, par~
turition, travail

childhood boyhood, girlhood, immaturity,
infancy, minority, schooldays, youth

childish boyish, foolish, frivolous, girlish,
immature, infantile, juvenile, puerile, silly,
simple, trifling, weak, young
Antonyms adult, grown-up, manly, mature,
sensible, sophisticated, womanly

childlike artless, credulous, guileless, in~
genuous, innocent, naive, simple, trustful,
trusting, unfeigned

chill *adj.* **1.** biting, bleak, chilly, cold, freez~
ing, frigid, parky (*Brit. inf.*), raw, sharp,
wintry **2.** *Fig.* aloof, cool, depressing, dis~
tant, frigid, hostile, stony, unfriendly,
ungenial, unresponsive, unwelcoming ~*v.*
3. congeal, cool, freeze, refrigerate **4.** *Fig.*
dampen, deject, depress, discourage, dis~
hearten, dismay ~*n.* **5.** bite, cold, coldness,
coolness, crispness, frigidity, nip, rawness,
sharpness

chilly 1. blowy, breezy, brisk, cool, crisp,
draughty, fresh, nippy, parky (*Brit. inf.*),
penetrating, sharp **2.** frigid, hostile, un~
friendly, unresponsive, unsympathetic,
unwelcoming
Antonyms (*sense 1*) balmy, hot, mild,
scorching, sunny, sweltering, warm (*sense 2*)
affable, chummy (*Inf.*), congenial, cordial,
friendly, responsive, sociable, sympathetic,
warm, welcoming

chime boom, clang, dong, jingle, peal, ring,
sound, strike, tinkle, tintinnabulate, toll

china ceramics, crockery, porcelain, pottery,
service, tableware, ware

chink aperture, cleft, crack, cranny, crevice, cut, fissure, flaw, gap, opening, rift

chip 1. *n.* dent, flake, flaw, fragment, nick, notch, paring, scrap, scratch, shard, shav~ ing, sliver, wafer **2.** *v.* chisel, damage, gash, nick, whittle

chip in contribute, donate, go Dutch (*Inf.*), interpose, interrupt, pay, subscribe

chivalrous bold, brave, courageous, cour~ teous, courtly, gallant, gentlemanly, heroic, high-minded, honourable, intrepid, knight~ ly, magnanimous, true, valiant
Antonyms boorish, cowardly, cruel, dis~ honourable, disloyal, rude, uncourtly, ungal~ lant, unmannerly

chivalry courage, courtesy, courtliness, gal~ lantry, gentlemanliness, knight-errantry, knighthood, politeness

chivvy annoy, badger, bend someone's ear (*Inf.*), bug (*Inf.*), harass, hassle (*Inf.*), hound, nag, pester, plague, pressure (*Inf.*), prod, torment

choice 1. *n.* alternative, discrimination, election, option, pick, preference, say, se~ lection, variety **2.** *adj.* bad (*Sl.*), best, cru~ cial (*Sl.*), dainty, def (*Sl.*), elect, elite, excel~ lent, exclusive, exquisite, hand-picked, nice, precious, prime, prize, rare, select, special, superior, uncommon, unusual, valuable

choke asphyxiate, bar, block, bung, clog, close, congest, constrict, dam, gag, obstruct, occlude, overpower, smother, stifle, stop, strangle, suffocate, suppress, throttle

choleric angry, bad-tempered, cross, fiery, hasty, hot, hot-tempered, ill-tempered, iras~ cible, irritable, passionate, petulant, quick-tempered, ratty (*Brit. & N.Z. inf.*), testy, tetchy, touchy

choose adopt, cull, designate, desire, elect, espouse, fix on, opt for, pick, predestine, prefer, see fit, select, settle upon, single out, take, wish
Antonyms decline, dismiss, exclude, forgo, leave, refuse, reject, throw aside

choosy discriminating, exacting, faddy, fas~ tidious, finicky, fussy, particular, picky (*Inf.*), selective
Antonyms easy (*Inf.*), easy to please, indis~ criminate, undemanding, unselective

chop 1. *v.* axe, cleave, cut, fell, hack, hew, lop, sever, shear, slash, truncate **2.** *n.* **the chop** *Sl.* dismissal, one's cards, sacking (*Inf.*), termination, the axe (*Inf.*), the boot (*Sl.*), the (old) heave-ho (*Inf.*), the order of the boot (*Sl.*), the sack (*Inf.*)

choppy blustery, broken, rough, ruffled, squally, tempestuous
Antonyms calm, smooth, windless

chop up cube, dice, divide, fragment, mince

chore burden, duty, errand, fag (*Inf.*), job, task

chortle cackle, chuckle, crow, guffaw

chorus 1. choir, choristers, ensemble, sing~ ers, vocalists **2.** burden, refrain, response, strain **3.** accord, concert, harmony, unison

christen baptize, call, designate, dub, name, style, term, title

chronic 1. confirmed, deep-rooted, deep-seated, habitual, incessant, incurable, in~ eradicable, ingrained, inveterate, persistent **2.** *Inf.* abysmal, appalling, atrocious, awful, dreadful
Antonyms infrequent, occasional, tempo~ rary

chronicle 1. *n.* account, annals, diary, his~ tory, journal, narrative, record, register, story **2.** *v.* enter, narrate, put on record, record, recount, register, relate, report, set down, tell

chronicler annalist, diarist, historian, his~ toriographer, narrator, recorder, reporter, scribe

chronological consecutive, historical, in sequence, ordered, progressive, sequential
Antonyms haphazard, intermittent, irregu~ lar, out-of-order, random

chubby buxom, flabby, fleshy, plump, podgy, portly, rotund, round, stout, tubby
Antonyms lean, skinny, slender, slight, slim, sylphlike, thin

chuck cast, discard, fling, heave, hurl, pitch, shy, sling, throw, toss

chuckle chortle, crow, exult, giggle, laugh, snigger, titter

chum cock (*Brit. inf.*), companion, comrade, crony, friend, mate (*Inf.*), pal (*Inf.*)

chunk block, dollop (*Inf.*), hunk, lump, mass, piece, portion, slab, wad, wodge (*Brit. inf.*)

chunky beefy (*Inf.*), dumpy, stocky, stubby, thickset

churl 1. boor, lout, oaf **2.** bumpkin, clod~ hopper (*Inf.*), clown, hayseed (*U.S. & Canad. inf.*), hick (*Inf., chiefly U.S. & Canad.*), hillbilly, peasant, rustic, yokel **3.** curmudgeon, miser, niggard, skinflint

churlish 1. boorish, brusque, crabbed, harsh, ill-tempered, impolite, loutish, mo~ rose, oafish, rude, sullen, surly, uncivil, uncouth, unmannerly, vulgar **2.** close-fisted, illiberal, inhospitable, mean, miserly, nig~ gardly, unneighbourly, unsociable
Antonyms admirable, agreeable, amiable, civil, courteous, cultivated, generous, good-tempered, mannerly, noble, pleasant, polite, well-bred

churlishness boorishness, crassness, crudeness, loutishness, oafishness, rude~ ness, surliness, uncouthness

churn agitate, beat, boil, convulse, foam, froth, seethe, stir up, swirl, toss

cigarette cancer stick (*Sl.*), ciggy (*Inf.*), coffin nail (*Sl.*), fag (*Brit. sl.*), gasper (*Sl.*), smoke

cinema big screen (*Inf.*), films, flicks (*Sl.*), motion pictures, movies, pictures

cipher 1. nil, nothing, nought, zero 2. nobody, nonentity 3. character, digit, figure, number, numeral, symbol 4. code, cryptograph 5. device, logo, mark, monogram

circle *n.* 1. band, circumference, coil, cordon, cycle, disc, globe, lap, loop, orb, perimeter, periphery, revolution, ring, round, sphere, turn 2. area, bounds, circuit, compass, domain, enclosure, field, orbit, province, range, realm, region, scene, sphere 3. assembly, class, clique, club, company, coterie, crowd, fellowship, fraternity, group, order, school, set, society ~*v.* 4. belt, circumnavigate, circumscribe, coil, compass, curve, encircle, enclose, encompass, envelop, gird, hem in, pivot, revolve, ring, rotate, surround, tour, whirl

circuit 1. area, compass, course, journey, lap, orbit, perambulation, revolution, round, route, tour, track 2. boundary, bounding line, bounds, circumference, compass, district, limit, pale, range, region, tract

circuitous ambagious (*Archaic*), devious, indirect, labyrinthine, meandering, oblique, rambling, roundabout, tortuous, winding **Antonyms** as the crow flies, direct, straight, undeviating, unswerving

circulate 1. broadcast, diffuse, disseminate, distribute, issue, make known, promulgate, propagate, publicize, publish, spread 2. flow, gyrate, radiate, revolve, rotate

circulation 1. currency, dissemination, distribution, spread, transmission, vogue 2. circling, flow, motion, rotation

circumference border, boundary, bounds, circuit, edge, extremity, fringe, limits, outline, pale, perimeter, periphery, rim, verge

circumscribe bound, confine, define, delimit, delineate, demarcate, encircle, enclose, encompass, environ, hem in, limit, mark off, restrain, restrict, straiten, surround

circumspect attentive, canny, careful, cautious, deliberate, discreet, discriminating, guarded, heedful, judicious, observant, politic, prudent, sagacious, sage, vigilant, wary, watchful **Antonyms** bold, careless, daring, foolhardy, heedless, imprudent, rash, venturous

circumstance accident, condition, contingency, detail, element, event, fact, factor, happening, incident, item, occurrence, particular, position, respect, situation

circumstances life style, means, position, resources, situation, state, state of affairs, station, status, times

circumstantial conjectural, contingent, detailed, founded on circumstances, hearsay, incidental, indirect, inferential, particular, presumptive, provisional, specific

cistern basin, reservoir, sink, tank, vat

citadel bastion, fastness, fortification, fortress, keep, stronghold, tower

citation 1. commendation, excerpt, illustration, passage, quotation, quote, reference, source 2. award, commendation, mention

cite 1. adduce, advance, allude to, enumerate, evidence, extract, mention, name, quote, specify 2. *Law* call, subpoena, summon

citizen burgess, burgher, denizen, dweller, freeman, inhabitant, ratepayer, resident, subject, townsman

city 1. *n.* conurbation, megalopolis, metropolis, municipality 2. *adj.* civic, metropolitan, municipal, urban

civic borough, communal, community, local, municipal, public

civil 1. civic, domestic, home, interior, municipal, political 2. accommodating, affable, civilized, complaisant, courteous, courtly, obliging, polished, polite, refined, urbane, well-bred, well-mannered **Antonyms** (*sense 1*) military, religious, state (*sense 2*) discourteous, ill-mannered, impolite, rude, uncivil, unfriendly, ungracious, unpleasant

civility affability, amiability, breeding, complaisance, cordiality, courteousness, courtesy, good manners, graciousness, politeness, politesse, tact, urbanity

civilization 1. advancement, cultivation, culture, development, education, enlightenment, progress, refinement, sophistication 2. community, nation, people, polity, society 3. customs, mores, way of life

civilize cultivate, educate, enlighten, humanize, improve, polish, refine, sophisticate, tame

civilized cultured, educated, enlightened, humane, polite, sophisticated, tolerant, urbane **Antonyms** barbarous, green, ignorant, naive, primitive, simple, uncivilized, uncultivated, uncultured, undeveloped, uneducated, unenlightened, unsophisticated, untutored, wild

claim 1. *v.* allege, ask, assert, call for, challenge, collect, demand, exact, hold, insist, maintain, need, pick up, profess, require, take, uphold 2. *n.* affirmation, allegation,

application, assertion, call, demand, peti~
tion, pretension, privilege, protestation, re~
quest, requirement, right, title

clamber claw, climb, scale, scrabble,
scramble, shin

clamorous blaring, deafening, insistent,
lusty, noisy, riotous, strident, tumultuous,
uproarious, vehement, vociferous

clamour agitation, babel, blare, brouhaha,
commotion, din, exclamation, hubbub, hul~
labaloo, noise, outcry, racket, shout, shout~
ing, uproar, vociferation

clamp 1. *n.* bracket, fastener, grip, press,
vice **2.** *v.* brace, clinch, fasten, fix, impose,
make fast, secure

clan band, brotherhood, clique, coterie, fac~
tion, family, fraternity, gens, group, house,
order, race, schism, sect, sept, set, society,
sodality, tribe

clang 1. *v.* bong, chime, clank, clash, jangle,
resound, reverberate, ring, toll **2.** *n.* clang~
our, ding-dong, knell, reverberation

clap 1. acclaim, applaud, cheer **2.** bang, pat,
punch, slap, strike gently, thrust, thwack,
wallop (*Inf.*), whack
Antonyms (*sense 1*) blow a raspberry, boo,
catcall, hiss, jeer

claptrap affectation, balls (*Taboo sl.*), bilge
(*Inf.*), blarney, bombast, bosh (*Inf.*), bull
(*Sl.*), bullshit (*Taboo sl.*), bunk (*Inf.*), bun~
kum *or* buncombe (*Chiefly U.S.*), cobblers
(*Brit. taboo sl.*), crap (*Sl.*), drivel, eyewash
(*Inf.*), flannel (*Brit. inf.*), garbage (*Inf.*), guff
(*Sl.*), hogwash, hokum (*Sl., chiefly U.S. &
Canad.*), horsefeathers (*U.S. sl.*), hot air
(*Inf.*), humbug, insincerity, moonshine,
nonsense, pap, piffle (*Inf.*), poppycock (*Inf.*),
rodomontade (*Literary*), rot, rubbish, shit
(*Taboo sl.*), tommyrot, tosh (*Sl., chiefly
Brit.*), tripe (*Inf.*)

clarification elucidation, explanation, ex~
position, illumination, interpretation, sim~
plification

clarify 1. clear up, elucidate, explain, expli~
cate, illuminate, interpret, make plain, re~
solve, simplify, throw *or* shed light on **2.**
cleanse, purify, refine

clarity clearness, comprehensibility,
definition, explicitness, intelligibility, lim~
pidity, lucidity, obviousness, precision,
simplicity, transparency
Antonyms cloudiness, complexity, compli~
cation, dullness, haziness, imprecision, intri~
cacy, murkiness, obscurity

clash *v.* **1.** bang, clang, clank, clatter, crash,
jangle, jar, rattle **2.** conflict, cross swords,
feud, grapple, quarrel, war, wrangle ~*n.* **3.**
brush, collision, conflict, confrontation, dif~
ference of opinion, disagreement, fight,
showdown (*Inf.*)

clasp *v.* **1.** attack, clutch, concatenate, con~
nect, embrace, enfold, fasten, grapple, grasp,
grip, hold, hug, press, seize, squeeze ~*n.* **2.**
brooch, buckle, catch, clip, fastener, fasten~
ing, grip, hasp, hook, pin, press stud, snap
3. embrace, grasp, grip, hold, hug

class 1. *n.* caste, category, classification,
collection, denomination, department, divi~
sion, genre, genus, grade, group, grouping,
kind, league, order, rank, set, sort, species,
sphere, stamp, status, type, value **2.** *v.*
brand, categorize, classify, codify, designate,
grade, group, label, rank, rate

classic *adj.* **1.** best, consummate, finest,
first-rate, masterly, world-class **2.** arche~
typal, definitive, exemplary, ideal, master,
model, paradigmatic, quintessential, stand~
ard **3.** characteristic, regular, standard,
time-honoured, typical, usual **4.** abiding,
ageless, deathless, enduring, immortal,
lasting, undying ~*n.* **5.** exemplar, master~
piece, masterwork, model, paradigm, proto~
type, standard
Antonyms *adj.* inferior, modern, poor,
second-rate, terrible, unrefined, unrepre~
sentative ~*n.* trash

classical 1. chaste, elegant, harmonious,
pure, refined, restrained, symmetrical,
understated, well-proportioned **2.** Attic,
Augustan, Grecian, Greek, Hellenic, Latin,
Roman

classification analysis, arrangement, cata~
loguing, categorization, codification, grad~
ing, sorting, taxonomy

classify arrange, catalogue, categorize,
codify, dispose, distribute, file, grade,
pigeonhole, rank, sort, systematize, tabulate

clause 1. article, chapter, condition, para~
graph, part, passage, section **2.** heading,
item, point, provision, proviso, rider,
specification, stipulation

claw 1. *n.* nail, nipper, pincer, talon, tenta~
cle, unguis **2.** *v.* dig, graze, lacerate, man~
gle, maul, rip, scrabble, scrape, scratch,
tear

clean *adj.* **1.** faultless, flawless, fresh, hy~
gienic, immaculate, impeccable, laundered,
pure, sanitary, spotless, squeaky-clean, un~
blemished, unsoiled, unspotted, unstained,
unsullied, washed **2.** antiseptic, clarified,
decontaminated, natural, purified, sterile,
sterilized, unadulterated, uncontaminated,
unpolluted **3.** chaste, decent, exemplary,
good, honourable, impeccable, innocent,
moral, pure, respectable, undefiled, upright,
virtuous **4.** delicate, elegant, graceful, neat,
simple, tidy, trim, uncluttered **5.** complete,
conclusive, decisive, entire, final, perfect,
thorough, total, unimpaired, whole ~*v.* **6.**
bath, cleanse, deodorize, disinfect, do up,
dust, launder, lave, mop, purge, purify,

rinse, sanitize, scour, scrub, sponge, swab, sweep, vacuum, wash, wipe

Antonyms *adj.* (*sense 1*) dirty, filthy, mucky, scuzzy (*Sl., chiefly U.S.*), soiled, sullied, un~washed (*sense 2*) adulterated, contaminated, infected, polluted (*sense 3*) dishonourable, immoral, impure, indecent, unchaste (*sense 4*) chaotic, disorderly, disorganized, higgledy-piggledy (*Inf.*), shambolic (*Inf.*), untidy ~*v.* adulterate, defile, dirty, disorder, disorganize, infect, mess up, pollute, soil, stain

clean-cut chiselled, clear, definite, etched, neat, outlined, sharp, trim, well-defined

cleanse absolve, clean, clear, lustrate, purge, purify, rinse, scour, scrub, wash

cleanser detergent, disinfectant, purifier, scourer, soap, soap powder, solvent

clear[1] *adj.* **1.** bright, cloudless, fair, fine, halcyon, light, luminous, shining, sunny, unclouded, undimmed **2.** apparent, articulate, audible, blatant, coherent, comprehensible, conspicuous, definite, distinct, evident, explicit, express, incontrovertible, intelligible, lucid, manifest, obvious, palpable, patent, perceptible, plain, pronounced, recognizable, unambiguous, unequivocal, unmistakable, unquestionable **3.** empty, free, open, smooth, unhampered, unhindered, unimpeded, unlimited, unobstructed **4.** crystalline, glassy, limpid, pellucid, see-through, translucent, transparent **5.** certain, convinced, decided, definite, positive, resolved, satisfied, sure **6.** clean, guiltless, immaculate, innocent, pure, sinless, stainless, unblemished, undefiled, untarnished, untroubled

Antonyms (*sense 1*) cloudy, dark, dull, foggy, hazy, misty, murky, overcast, stormy (*sense 2*) ambiguous, confused, doubtful, equivocal, hidden, inarticulate, inaudible, incoherent, indistinct, inexplicit, obscured, unrecognizable (*sense 3*) barricaded, blocked, closed, engaged, hampered, impeded, obstructed (*sense 4*) cloudy, muddy, non-translucent, non-transparent, opaque, turbid

clear[2] *v.* **1.** clean, cleanse, erase, purify, refine, sweep away, tidy (up) **2.** break up, brighten, clarify, lighten **3.** absolve, acquit, excuse, exonerate, justify, vindicate **4.** emancipate, free, liberate, set free **5.** disengage, disentangle, extricate, free, loosen, open, rid, unblock, unclog, unload, unpack **6.** jump, leap, miss, pass over, vault **7.** acquire, earn, gain, make, reap, secure

Antonyms (*sense 3*) accuse, blame, charge, condemn, convict, find guilty

clearance 1. authorization, consent, endorsement, go-ahead (*Inf.*), green light, leave, O.K. *or* okay (*Inf.*), permission, sanction **2.** allowance, gap, headroom, margin

3. depopulation, emptying, evacuation, eviction, removal, unpeopling, withdrawal

clear-cut definite, explicit, plain, precise, specific, straightforward, unambiguous, unequivocal

clearly beyond doubt, distinctly, evidently, incontestably, incontrovertibly, markedly, obviously, openly, overtly, undeniably, undoubtedly

clear out 1. empty, exhaust, get rid of, sort, tidy up **2.** beat it (*Sl.*), decamp, depart, hook it (*Sl.*), leave, make oneself scarce, retire, slope off, take oneself off, withdraw

clear up 1. answer, clarify, elucidate, explain, resolve, solve, straighten out, unravel **2.** order, rearrange, tidy (up)

cleave[1] abide by, adhere, agree, attach, be devoted to, be true, cling, cohere, hold, remain, stand by, stick

cleave[2] crack, dissever, disunite, divide, hew, open, part, rend, rive, sever, slice, split, sunder, tear asunder

clergy churchmen, clergymen, clerics, ecclesiastics, first estate, holy orders, ministry, priesthood, the cloth

clergyman chaplain, cleric, curate, divine, father, man of God, man of the cloth, minister, padre, parson, pastor, priest, rabbi, rector, reverend (*Inf.*), vicar

clerical 1. ecclesiastical, pastoral, priestly, sacerdotal **2.** book-keeping, clerkish, clerkly, office, secretarial, stenographic

clever able, adroit, apt, astute, brainy (*Inf.*), bright, canny, capable, cunning, deep, dexterous, discerning, expert, gifted, ingenious, intelligent, inventive, keen, knowing, knowledgeable, quick, quick-witted, rational, resourceful, sagacious, sensible, shrewd, skilful, smart, talented, witty

Antonyms awkward, boring, clumsy, dense, dull, ham-fisted (*Inf.*), inept, inexpert, maladroit, slow, stupid, thick, unaccomplished, unimaginative, witless

cleverness ability, adroitness, astuteness, brains, brightness, canniness, dexterity, flair, gift, gumption (*Brit. inf.*), ingenuity, intelligence, nous (*Brit. sl.*), quickness, quick wits, resourcefulness, sagacity, sense, sharpness, shrewdness, smartness, smarts (*Sl., chiefly U.S.*), suss (*Sl.*), talent, wit

cliché banality, bromide, chestnut (*Inf.*), commonplace, hackneyed phrase, old saw, platitude, stereotype, truism

click *n./v.* **1.** beat, clack, snap, tick ~*v.* **2.** *Inf.* become clear, come home (to), fall into place, make sense **3.** *Sl.* be compatible, be on the same wavelength, feel a rapport, get on, go over, hit it off (*Inf.*), make a hit, succeed, take to each other

client applicant, buyer, consumer, customer,

dependant, habitué, patient, patron, protégé, shopper

clientele business, clients, customers, following, market, patronage, regulars, trade

cliff bluff, crag, escarpment, face, overhang, precipice, rock face, scar, scarp

climactic climactical, critical, crucial, decisive, paramount, peak

climate 1. clime, country, region, temperature, weather **2.** ambience, disposition, feeling, mood, temper, tendency, trend

climax 1. *n.* acme, apogee, crest, culmination, head, height, highlight, high spot (*Inf.*), *ne plus ultra*, pay-off (*Inf.*), peak, summit, top, zenith **2.** *v.* come to a head, culminate, peak

climb ascend, clamber, mount, rise, scale, shin up, soar, top

climb down 1. descend, dismount **2.** back down, eat crow (*U.S. inf.*), eat one's words, retract, retreat

clinch 1. assure, cap, conclude, confirm, decide, determine, seal, secure, set the seal on, settle, sew up (*Inf.*), verify **2.** bolt, clamp, fasten, fix, make fast, nail, rivet, secure **3.** clutch, cuddle, embrace, grasp, hug, squeeze

cling adhere, attach to, be true to, clasp, cleave to, clutch, embrace, fasten, grasp, grip, hug, stick, twine round

clip¹ 1. *v.* crop, curtail, cut, cut short, dock, pare, prune, shear, shorten, snip, trim **2.** *n./v. Inf.* belt (*Inf.*), box, clout (*Inf.*), cuff, knock, punch, skelp (*Dialect*), smack, thump, wallop (*Inf.*), whack **3.** *n. Inf.* gallop, lick (*Inf.*), rate, speed, velocity

clip² *v.* attach, fasten, fix, hold, pin, staple

clique cabal, circle, clan, coterie, crew (*Inf.*), crowd, faction, gang, group, mob, pack, posse (*Inf.*), schism, set

cloak 1. *v.* camouflage, conceal, cover, disguise, hide, mask, obscure, screen, veil **2.** *n.* blind, cape, coat, cover, front, mantle, mask, pretext, shield, wrap

clodhopper booby, boor, bumpkin, clown, galoot (*Sl., chiefly U.S.*), loon (*Inf.*), lout, oaf, yokel

clog 1. *v.* block, bung, burden, congest, dam up, hamper, hinder, impede, jam, obstruct, occlude, shackle, stop up **2.** *n.* burden, dead weight, drag, encumbrance, hindrance, impediment, obstruction

cloistered cloistral, confined, hermitic, insulated, reclusive, restricted, secluded, sequestered, sheltered, shielded, shut off, withdrawn
Antonyms extrovert, genial, gregarious, outgoing, public, sociable, social

close¹ *v.* **1.** bar, block, bung, choke, clog,

confine, cork, fill, lock, obstruct, plug, seal, secure, shut, shut up, stop up **2.** axe (*Inf.*), cease, complete, conclude, culminate, discontinue, end, finish, mothball, shut down, terminate, wind up **3.** come together, connect, couple, fuse, grapple, join, unite
Antonyms (*sense 1*) clear, free, open, release, unblock, unclog, uncork, unstop, widen (*sense 2*) begin, commence, initiate, open, start (*sense 3*) disconnect, disjoin, disunite, divide, part, separate, split, uncouple

close² 1. adjacent, adjoining, approaching, at hand, handy, hard by, imminent, impending, near, nearby, neighbouring, nigh, proximate, upcoming, within sniffing distance (*Inf.*) **2.** compact, congested, cramped, cropped, crowded, dense, impenetrable, jam-packed, packed, short, solid, thick, tight **3.** accurate, conscientious, exact, faithful, literal, precise, strict **4.** alert, assiduous, attentive, careful, concentrated, detailed, dogged, earnest, fixed, intense, intent, keen, minute, painstaking, rigorous, searching, thorough **5.** attached, confidential, dear, devoted, familiar, inseparable, intimate, loving **6.** airless, confined, frowsty, fuggy, heavy, humid, muggy, oppressive, stale, stifling, stuffy, suffocating, sweltering, thick, unventilated **7.** hidden, private, reticent, retired, secluded, secret, secretive, taciturn, uncommunicative, unforthcoming **8.** illiberal, mean, mingy (*Brit. inf.*), miserly, near, niggardly, parsimonious, penurious, stingy, tight as a duck's arse (*Taboo sl.*), tight-fisted, ungenerous
Antonyms (*sense 1*) distant, far, far away, far off, future, outlying, remote (*sense 2*) dispersed, empty, free, loose, penetrable, porous, uncongested, uncrowded (*sense 5*) alienated, aloof, chilly, cold, cool, distant, indifferent, standoffish, unfriendly (*sense 6*) airy, fresh, refreshing, roomy, spacious (*sense 8*) charitable, extravagant, generous, lavish, liberal, magnanimous, unstinting

close³ cessation, completion, conclusion, culmination, denouement, end, ending, finale, finish, termination

closed 1. fastened, locked, out of business, out of service, sealed, shut **2.** concluded, decided, ended, finished, over, resolved, settled, terminated **3.** exclusive, restricted
Antonyms (*sense 1*) ajar, open, unclosed, unfastened, unlocked, unsealed

cloth dry goods, fabric, material, stuff, textiles

clothe accoutre, apparel, array, attire, bedizen (*Archaic*), caparison, cover, deck, doll up (*Sl.*), drape, dress, endow, enwrap, equip, fit out, garb, get ready, habit, invest, outfit, rig, robe, swathe
Antonyms disrobe, divest, expose, strip, strip off, unclothe, uncover, undress

clothes, clothing apparel, attire, clobber (*Brit. sl.*), costume, dress, duds (*Inf.*), ensemble, garb, garments, gear (*Inf.*), get-up (*Inf.*), glad rags (*Inf.*), habits, outfit, raiment (*Archaic or poetic*), rigout (*Inf.*), togs (*Inf.*), vestments, vesture, wardrobe, wear

cloud *n.* **1.** billow, darkness, fog, gloom, haze, mist, murk, nebula, nebulosity, obscurity, vapour **2.** crowd, dense mass, flock, horde, host, multitude, shower, swarm, throng ~*v.* **3.** becloud, darken, dim, eclipse, obfuscate, obscure, overcast, overshadow, shade, shadow, veil **4.** confuse, disorient, distort, impair, muddle

cloudy blurred, confused, dark, dim, dismal, dull, dusky, emulsified, gloomy, hazy, indistinct, leaden, louring *or* lowering, muddy, murky, nebulous, obscure, opaque, overcast, sombre, sullen, sunless
Antonyms bright, clear, distinct, fair, obvious, plain, sunny, uncloudy

clout 1. *v.* box, chin (*Sl.*), clobber (*Sl.*), cuff, deck (*Sl.*), hit, lay one on (*Sl.*), punch, skelp (*Dialect*), sock (*Sl.*), strike, thump, wallop (*Inf.*), wham **2.** *n.* authority, bottom, influence, power, prestige, pull, standing, weight

clown *n.* **1.** buffoon, comedian, dolt, fool, harlequin, jester, joker, merry-andrew, mountebank, pierrot, prankster, punchinello **2.** boor, clodhopper (*Inf.*), hind (*Obsolete*), peasant, swain (*Archaic*), yahoo, yokel ~*v.* **3.** act the fool, act the goat, jest, mess about, piss about (*Taboo sl.*), piss around (*Taboo sl.*)

club 1. *n.* bat, bludgeon, cosh (*Brit.*), cudgel, stick, truncheon **2.** *v.* bash, baste, batter, beat, bludgeon, clobber (*Sl.*), clout (*Inf.*), cosh (*Brit.*), hammer, pommel (*Rare*), pummel, strike **3.** *n.* association, circle, clique, company, fraternity, group, guild, lodge, order, set, society, sodality, union

clue evidence, hint, indication, inkling, intimation, lead, pointer, sign, suggestion, suspicion, tip, tip-off, trace

clump 1. *n.* bunch, bundle, cluster, mass, shock **2.** *v.* bumble, clomp, lumber, plod, stamp, stomp, stump, thud, thump, tramp

clumsy accident-prone, awkward, blundering, bumbling, bungling, butterfingered (*Inf.*), cack-handed (*Inf.*), gauche, gawky, ham-fisted (*Inf.*), ham-handed (*Inf.*), heavy, ill-shaped, inept, inexpert, klutzy (*U.S. & Canad. sl.*), lumbering, maladroit, ponderous, uncoordinated, uncouth, ungainly, unhandy, unskilful, unwieldy
Antonyms adept, adroit, competent, deft, dexterous, expert, graceful, handy, proficient, skilful

cluster 1. *n.* assemblage, batch, bunch, clump, collection, gathering, group, knot **2.**

v. assemble, bunch, collect, flock, gather, group

clutch catch (up), clasp, cling to, embrace, fasten, grab, grapple, grasp, grip, seize, snatch

clutches claws, control, custody, grasp, grip, hands, keeping, possession, power, sway

clutter 1. *n.* confusion, disarray, disorder, hotchpotch, jumble, litter, mess, muddle, untidiness **2.** *v.* litter, scatter, strew
Antonyms *n.* neatness, order, organization, tidiness ~*v.* arrange, order, organize, straighten, tidy

coach *n.* **1.** bus, car, carriage, charabanc, vehicle **2.** handler, instructor, teacher, trainer, tutor ~*v.* **3.** cram, drill, exercise, instruct, prepare, train, tutor

coalesce amalgamate, blend, cohere, combine, come together, commingle, commix, consolidate, fraternize, fuse, incorporate, integrate, meld, merge, mix, unite

coalition affiliation, alliance, amalgam, amalgamation, association, bloc, combination, compact, confederacy, confederation, conjunction, fusion, integration, league, merger, union

coarse 1. boorish, brutish, coarse-grained, foul-mouthed, gruff, loutish, rough, rude, uncivil **2.** bawdy, earthy, immodest, impolite, improper, impure, indelicate, inelegant, mean, offensive, raunchy (*Sl.*), ribald, rude, smutty, vulgar **3.** coarse-grained, crude, homespun, impure, rough-hewn, unfinished, unpolished, unprocessed, unpurified, unrefined
Antonyms (*senses 1 & 2*) civilized, cultured, elegant, fine, genteel, inoffensive, pleasant, polished, polite, proper, refined, sophisticated, urbane, well-bred, well-mannered (*sense 3*) fine-grained, polished, purified, refined, smooth, soft

coarsen anaesthetize, blunt, callous, deaden, desensitize, dull, harden, indurate, roughen

coarseness bawdiness, boorishness, crudity, earthiness, indelicacy, offensiveness, poor taste, ribaldry, roughness, smut, smuttiness, uncouthness, unevenness

coast 1. *n.* beach, border, coastline, littoral, seaboard, seaside, shore, strand **2.** *v.* cruise, drift, freewheel, get by, glide, sail, taxi

coat *n.* **1.** fleece, fur, hair, hide, pelt, skin, wool **2.** coating, covering, layer, overlay ~*v.* **3.** apply, Artex (*Trademark*), cover, plaster, smear, spread

coating blanket, coat, covering, dusting, film, finish, glaze, lamination, layer, membrane, patina, sheet, skin, varnish, veneer

coax allure, beguile, cajole, decoy, entice,

flatter, inveigle, persuade, prevail upon, soft-soap (*Inf.*), soothe, sweet-talk (*Inf.*), talk into, wheedle
Antonyms browbeat, bully, coerce, force, harass, intimidate, pressurize, threaten

cock 1. *n.* chanticleer, cockerel, rooster **2.** *v.* perk up, prick, raise, stand up

cockeyed absurd, askew, asymmetrical, awry, crazy, crooked, lopsided, ludicrous, nonsensical, preposterous, skewwhiff (*Brit. inf.*), squint (*Inf.*)

cocky arrogant, brash, cocksure, conceited, egotistical, lordly, swaggering, swollen-headed, vain
Antonyms hesitant, lacking confidence, modest, self-effacing, uncertain, unsure

coddle baby, cosset, humour, indulge, mollycoddle, nurse, pamper, pet, spoil, wet-nurse (*Inf.*)

code 1. cipher, cryptograph **2.** canon, convention, custom, ethics, etiquette, manners, maxim, regulations, rules, system

cogency conviction, force, potency, power, strength

cogent compelling, conclusive, convincing, effective, forceful, forcible, influential, irresistible, potent, powerful, strong, urgent, weighty

cogitate consider, contemplate, deliberate, meditate, mull over, muse, ponder, reflect, ruminate, think

cogitation consideration, contemplation, deliberation, meditation, reflection, rumination, thought

cognate affiliated, akin, alike, allied, analogous, associated, connected, kindred, related, similar

cognition apprehension, awareness, comprehension, discernment, insight, intelligence, perception, reasoning, understanding

coherent articulate, comprehensible, consistent, intelligible, logical, lucid, meaningful, orderly, organized, rational, reasoned, systematic
Antonyms confusing, disjointed, illogical, incomprehensible, inconsistent, meaningless, rambling, unintelligible, vague

coil convolute, curl, entwine, loop, snake, spiral, twine, twist, wind, wreathe, writhe

coin 1. *v.* conceive, create, fabricate, forge, formulate, frame, invent, make up, mint, mould, originate, think up **2.** *n.* cash, change, copper, dosh (*Brit. & Aust. sl.*), money, silver, specie

coincide 1. be concurrent, coexist, occur simultaneously, synchronize **2.** accord, harmonize, match, quadrate, square, tally **3.** acquiesce, agree, concur, correspond
Antonyms be inconsistent, be unlike,

contradict, differ, disagree, diverge, divide, part, separate

coincidence 1. accident, chance, eventuality, fluke, fortuity, happy accident, luck, stroke of luck **2.** concomitance, concurrence, conjunction, correlation, correspondence, synchronism

coincident coinciding, concomitant, concurring, consonant, contemporaneous, coordinate, correspondent, synchronous

coincidental 1. accidental, casual, chance, fluky (*Inf.*), fortuitous, unintentional, unplanned **2.** coincident, concomitant, concurrent, simultaneous, synchronous
Antonyms (*sense 1*) calculated, deliberate, done on purpose, intentional, planned, prearranged

cold *adj.* **1.** arctic, biting, bitter, bleak, brumal, chill, chilly, cool, freezing, frigid, frosty, frozen, gelid, harsh, icy, inclement, parky (*Brit. inf.*), raw, wintry **2.** benumbed, chilled, chilly, freezing, frozen to the marrow, numbed, shivery **3.** aloof, apathetic, cold-blooded, dead, distant, frigid, glacial, indifferent, inhospitable, lukewarm, passionless, phlegmatic, reserved, spiritless, standoffish, stony, undemonstrative, unfeeling, unmoved, unresponsive, unsympathetic ~*n.* **4.** chill, chilliness, coldness, frigidity, frostiness, iciness, inclemency
Antonyms (*sense 1*) balmy, heated, hot, mild, sunny, warm (*sense 3*) alive, animated, caring, compassionate, conscious, demonstrative, emotional, friendly, loving, open, passionate, responsive, spirited, sympathetic, warm

cold-blooded barbarous, brutal, callous, cruel, dispassionate, heartless, inhuman, merciless, pitiless, Ramboesque, ruthless, savage, steely, stony-hearted, unemotional, unfeeling, unmoved
Antonyms caring, charitable, civilized, concerned, emotional, feeling, friendly, humane, involved, kind, kind-hearted, merciful, open, passionate, sensitive, warm

cold-hearted callous, detached, frigid, hardhearted, harsh, heartless, indifferent, inhuman, insensitive, stony-hearted, uncaring, unfeeling, unkind, unsympathetic

collaborate 1. cooperate, coproduce, join forces, participate, team up, work together **2.** collude, conspire, cooperate, fraternize

collaboration alliance, association, concert, cooperation, partnership, teamwork

collaborator 1. associate, colleague, confederate, co-worker, partner, team-mate **2.** collaborationist, fraternizer, quisling, traitor, turncoat

collapse 1. *v.* break down, cave in, come to nothing, crack up (*Inf.*), crumple, fail, faint, fall, fold, founder, give way, subside **2.** *n.* breakdown, cave-in, disintegration, down~

fall, exhaustion, failure, faint, flop, prostra~ tion, subsidence

collar *v.* apprehend, appropriate, capture, catch, grab, lay hands on, nab (*Inf.*), nail (*Inf.*), seize

colleague aider, ally, assistant, associate, auxiliary, coadjutor (*Rare*), collaborator, companion, comrade, confederate, confrère, fellow worker, helper, partner, team-mate, workmate

collect 1. accumulate, aggregate, amass, as~ semble, gather, heap, hoard, save, stockpile **2.** assemble, cluster, congregate, convene, converge, flock together, rally **3.** acquire, muster, obtain, raise, secure, solicit
Antonyms disperse, distribute, scatter, spread, strew

collected calm, composed, confident, cool, placid, poised, sedate, self-possessed, serene, together (*Sl.*), unfazed (*Inf.*), unperturbable, unperturbed, unruffled
Antonyms agitated, distressed, emotional, excitable, irritable, nervous, perturbed, ruffled, shaky, troubled, twitchy (*Inf.*), un~ poised, unsteady

collection 1. accumulation, anthology, compilation, congeries, heap, hoard, mass, pile, set, stockpile, store **2.** assemblage, as~ sembly, assortment, cluster, company, con~ gregation, convocation, crowd, gathering, group **3.** alms, contribution, offering, offer~ tory

collective aggregate, combined, common, composite, concerted, cooperative, corpo~ rate, cumulative, joint, shared, unified, united
Antonyms divided, individual, piecemeal, split, uncombined, uncooperative

collide clash, come into collision, conflict, crash, meet head-on

collision 1. accident, bump, crash, impact, pile-up (*Inf.*), prang (*Inf.*), smash **2.** clash, clashing, conflict, confrontation, encounter, opposition, skirmish

colloquial conversational, demotic, every~ day, familiar, idiomatic, informal, vernacu~ lar

collusion cahoots (*Inf.*), complicity, conniv~ ance, conspiracy, craft, deceit, fraudulent artifice, intrigue, secret understanding

colonist colonial, colonizer, frontiersman, homesteader (*U.S.*), immigrant, pioneer, planter, settler

colonize open up, people, pioneer, populate, settle

colonnade arcade, cloisters, covered walk, peristyle, portico

colony community, dependency, dominion, outpost, possession, province, satellite state, settlement, territory

colossal Brobdingnagian, elephantine, enormous, gargantuan, gigantic, ginormous (*Inf.*), herculean, huge, humongous *or* hu~ mungous (*U.S. sl.*), immense, mammoth, massive, monstrous, monumental, moun~ tainous, prodigious, titanic, vast
Antonyms average, diminutive, little, miniature, minute, ordinary, pygmy *or* pig~ my, slight, small, tiny, weak, wee

colour *n.* **1.** colorant, coloration, complex~ ion, dye, hue, paint, pigment, pigmentation, shade, tincture, tinge, tint **2.** animation, bloom, blush, brilliance, flush, glow, liveli~ ness, rosiness, ruddiness, vividness **3.** *Fig.* appearance, disguise, excuse, façade, false show, guise, plea, pretence, pretext, sem~ blance ~*v.* **4.** colourwash, dye, paint, stain, tinge, tint **5.** *Fig.* disguise, distort, embroi~ der, exaggerate, falsify, garble, gloss over, misrepresent, pervert, prejudice, slant, taint **6.** blush, burn, crimson, flush, go crimson, redden

colourful 1. bright, brilliant, Day-glo (*Trademark*), intense, jazzy (*Inf.*), kaleido~ scopic, motley, multicoloured, psychedelic, rich, variegated, vibrant, vivid **2.** charac~ terful, distinctive, graphic, interesting, lively, picturesque, rich, stimulating, un~ usual, vivid
Antonyms (*sense 1*) colourless, dark, drab, dreary, dull, faded, pale, washed out (*sense 2*) boring, characterless, dull, flat, lifeless, mo~ notonous, unexciting, uninteresting, unvar~ ied

colourless 1. achromatic, achromic, anaemic, ashen, bleached, drab, faded, neu~ tral, sickly, wan, washed out **2.** character~ less, dreary, insipid, lacklustre, tame, unin~ teresting, unmemorable, vacuous, vapid
Antonyms (*sense 1*) blooming, flushed, glowing, healthy, radiant, robust, ruddy (*sense 2*) animated, bright, colourful, compelling, distinctive, exciting, interesting, unusual

colours 1. banner, emblem, ensign, flag, standard **2.** *Fig.* aspect, breed, character, identity, nature, stamp, strain

column 1. cavalcade, file, line, list, proces~ sion, queue, rank, row, string, train **2.** caryatid, obelisk, pilaster, pillar, post, shaft, support, upright

columnist correspondent, critic, editor, gossip columnist, journalist, journo (*Sl.*), reporter, reviewer

coma drowsiness, insensibility, lethargy, oblivion, somnolence, stupor, torpor, trance, unconsciousness

comatose drowsy, drugged, insensible, le~ thargic, sleepy, sluggish, somnolent, soporose (*Medical*), stupefied, torpid, un~ conscious

comb *v.* **1.** arrange, curry, dress, groom,

untangle **2.** *Of flax, wool, etc.* card, hackle, hatchel, heckle, tease, teasel, teazle **3.** *Fig.* go through with a fine-tooth comb, hunt, rake, ransack, rummage, scour, screen, search, sift, sweep

combat 1. *n.* action, battle, conflict, contest, encounter, engagement, fight, skirmish, struggle, war, warfare **2.** *v.* battle, contend, contest, cope, defy, do battle with, engage, fight, oppose, resist, strive, struggle, withstand
Antonyms *n.* agreement, armistice, peace, surrender, truce ~*v.* accept, acquiesce, declare a truce, give up, make peace, support, surrender

combatant 1. *n.* adversary, antagonist, belligerent, contender, enemy, fighter, fighting man, gladiator, opponent, serviceman, soldier, warrior **2.** *adj.* battling, belligerent, combating, conflicting, contending, fighting, opposing, warring

combative aggressive, antagonistic, bellicose, belligerent, contentious, militant, pugnacious, quarrelsome, truculent, warlike
Antonyms nonaggressive, nonbelligerent, nonviolent, pacific, pacifist, peaceable, peaceful, peace-loving

combination 1. amalgam, amalgamation, blend, coalescence, composite, connection, meld, mix, mixture **2.** alliance, association, cabal, cartel, coalition, combine, compound, confederacy, confederation, consortium, conspiracy, federation, merger, syndicate, unification, union

combine amalgamate, associate, bind, blend, bond, compound, connect, cooperate, fuse, incorporate, integrate, join (together), link, marry, meld, merge, mix, pool, put together, synthesize, unify, unite
Antonyms detach, dissociate, dissolve, disunite, divide, part, separate, sever

combustible explosive, flammable, incendiary, inflammable

come 1. advance, appear, approach, arrive, become, draw near, enter, happen, materialize, move, move towards, near, occur, originate, show up (*Inf.*), turn out, turn up (*Inf.*) **2.** appear, arrive, attain, enter, materialize, reach, show up (*Inf.*), turn up (*Inf.*) **3.** fall, happen, occur, take place **4.** arise, emanate, emerge, end up, flow, issue, originate, result, turn out **5.** extend, reach **6.** be available (made, offered, on offer, produced)

come about arise, befall, come to pass, happen, occur, result, take place, transpire (*Inf.*)

come across bump into (*Inf.*), chance upon, discover, encounter, find, happen upon, hit upon, light upon, meet, notice, stumble upon, unearth

come along develop, improve, mend, perk up, pick up, progress, rally, recover, recuperate

come apart break, come unstuck, crumble, disintegrate, fall to pieces, give way, separate, split, tear

come at 1. attain, discover, find, grasp, reach **2.** assail, assault, attack, charge, fall upon, fly at, go for, light into, rush, rush at

comeback 1. rally, rebound, recovery, resurgence, return, revival, triumph **2.** rejoinder, reply, response, retaliation, retort, riposte

come back reappear, recur, re-enter, return

come between alienate, divide, estrange, interfere, meddle, part, separate, set at odds

come by acquire, get, lay hold of, obtain, procure, score (*Sl.*), secure, take possession of, win

come clean acknowledge, admit, confess, make a clean breast of, own up, reveal, sing (*Sl., chiefly U.S.*), spill one's guts (*Sl.*)

comedian card (*Inf.*), clown, comic, funny man, humorist, jester, joker, laugh (*Inf.*), wag, wit

comedown anticlimax, blow, decline, deflation, demotion, disappointment, humiliation, letdown, reverse

come down 1. decline, degenerate, descend, deteriorate, fall, go downhill, reduce, worsen **2.** choose, decide, favour, recommend

come down on bawl out (*Inf.*), blast, carpet (*Inf.*), chew out (*U.S. & Canad. inf.*), criticize, dress down (*Inf.*), give (someone) a rocket (*Brit. & N.Z. inf.*), jump on (*Inf.*), lambast(e), put down, read the riot act, rebuke, reprimand, tear into (*Inf.*), tear (someone) off a strip (*Brit. inf.*)

come down to amount to, boil down to, end up as, result in

come down with ail, be stricken with, catch, contract, fall ill, fall victim to, get, sicken, take, take sick

comedy chaffing, drollery, facetiousness, farce, fun, hilarity, humour, jesting, joking, light entertainment, sitcom (*Inf.*), slapstick, wisecracking, witticisms
Antonyms high drama, melancholy, melodrama, opera, sadness, seriousness, serious play, soap opera, solemnity, tragedy

come forward offer one's services, present *or* proffer oneself, volunteer

come in appear, arrive, cross the threshold, enter, finish, reach, show up (*Inf.*)

come in for acquire, bear the brunt of, endure, get, receive, suffer

comely 1. attractive, beautiful, becoming,

blooming, bonny, buxom, fair, good-looking, graceful, handsome, lovely, pleasing, pretty, wholesome, winsome **2.** *Archaic* decent, decorous, fit, fitting, proper, seemly, suit~ able

Antonyms affected, disagreeable, distaste~ ful, faded, homely, improper, indecorous, mumsy, plain, repulsive, ugly, unattractive, unbecoming, unfitting, unnatural, unpleas~ ant, unseemly

come off go off, happen, occur, succeed, take place, transpire (*Inf.*)

come on 1. advance, develop, improve, make headway, proceed, progress **2.** ap~ pear, begin, take place

come out 1. appear, be published (an~ nounced, divulged, issued, released, report~ ed, revealed) **2.** conclude, end, result, ter~ minate

come out with acknowledge, come clean, declare, disclose, divulge, lay open, own, own up, say

come round 1. accede, acquiesce, allow, concede, grant, mellow, relent, yield **2.** come to, rally, recover, regain conscious~ ness, revive **3.** call, drop in, pop in, stop by, visit

come through 1. accomplish, achieve, prevail, succeed, triumph **2.** endure, sur~ vive, weather the storm, withstand

come up arise, crop up, happen, occur, rise, spring up, turn up

comeuppance chastening, deserts, due reward, dues, merit, punishment, recom~ pense, requital, retribution

come up to admit of comparison with, ap~ proach, compare with, equal, match, meas~ ure up to, meet, resemble, rival, stand *or* bear comparison with

come up with advance, create, discover, furnish, offer, present, produce, propose, provide, submit, suggest

comfort *v.* **1.** alleviate, assuage, cheer, commiserate with, compassionate (*Archaic*), console, ease, encourage, enliven, gladden, hearten, inspirit, invigorate, reassure, re~ fresh, relieve, solace, soothe, strengthen ~*n.* **2.** aid, alleviation, cheer, compensation, consolation, ease, encouragement, enjoy~ ment, help, relief, satisfaction, succour, support **3.** cosiness, creature comforts, ease, luxury, opulence, snugness, wellbeing **Antonyms** *v.* aggravate (*Inf.*), agitate, annoy, bother, depress, discomfort, distress, excite, hassle (*Inf.*), irk, irritate, rile, ruffle, sadden, trouble ~*n.* aggravation, annoyance, discour~ agement, displeasure, hassle (*Inf.*), inconven~ ience, irritation

comfortable 1. adequate, agreeable, ample, commodious, convenient, cosy, delightful,

easy, enjoyable, homely, loose, loose-fitting, pleasant, relaxing, restful, roomy, snug **2.** at ease, contented, gratified, happy, relaxed, serene **3.** affluent, prosperous, well-off, well-to-do

Antonyms (*sense 1*) disagreeable, inad~ equate, skin-tight, tight, tight-fitting, uncom~ fortable, unpleasant (*sense 2*) distressed, dis~ turbed, ill at ease, miserable, nervous, on tenterhooks, tense, troubled, uncomfortable, uneasy

comforting cheering, consolatory, consol~ ing, encouraging, heart-warming, inspirit~ ing, reassuring, soothing

Antonyms alarming, dismaying, disturbing, perplexing, upsetting, worrying

comfortless 1. bleak, cheerless, cold, desolate, dismal, dreary **2.** disconsolate, forlorn, inconsolable, miserable, sick at heart, woebegone, wretched

comic 1. *adj.* amusing, comical, droll, fa~ cetious, farcical, funny, humorous, jocular, joking, light, rich, waggish, witty **2.** *n.* buf~ foon, clown, comedian, funny man, humor~ ist, jester, wag, wit

Antonyms depressing, melancholy, pathet~ ic, sad, serious, solemn, touching, tragic

comical absurd, amusing, comic, diverting, droll, entertaining, farcical, funny, hilari~ ous, humorous, laughable, ludicrous, price~ less, ridiculous, risible, side-splitting, silly, whimsical

coming *adj.* **1.** approaching, at hand, due, en route, forthcoming, future, imminent, impending, in store, in the wind, near, next, nigh, upcoming **2.** aspiring, future, promising, up-and-coming ~*n.* **3.** accession, advent, approach, arrival

command *v.* **1.** bid, charge, compel, de~ mand, direct, enjoin, order, require **2.** ad~ minister, control, dominate, govern, handle, head, lead, manage, reign over, rule, super~ vise, sway ~*n.* **3.** behest, bidding, canon, commandment, decree, demand, direction, directive, edict, fiat, injunction, instruction, mandate, order, precept, requirement, ulti~ matum **4.** authority, charge, control, direc~ tion, domination, dominion, government, grasp, management, mastery, power, rule, supervision, sway, upper hand

Antonyms (*sense 1*) appeal (to), ask, beg, be~ seech, plead, request, supplicate (*sense 2*) be inferior, be subordinate, follow

commandeer appropriate, confiscate, ex~ propriate, hijack, requisition, seize, seques~ ter, sequestrate, usurp

commander boss, captain, chief, C in C, C.O., commander-in-chief, commanding officer, director, head, leader, officer, ruler

commanding 1. advantageous, control~ ling, decisive, dominant, dominating, su~

perior **2.** assertive, authoritative, autocrat~
ic, compelling, forceful, imposing, impres~
sive, peremptory
Antonyms retiring, shrinking, shy, submis~
sive, timid, unassertive, unimposing, weak

commemorate celebrate, honour, immor~
talize, keep, memorialize, observe, pay trib~
ute to, remember, salute, solemnize
Antonyms disregard, forget, ignore, omit,
overlook, pass over, take no notice of

commemoration ceremony, honouring,
memorial service, observance, remem~
brance, tribute

commemorative celebratory, dedicatory,
in honour, in memory, in remembrance,
memorial

commence begin, embark on, enter upon,
inaugurate, initiate, open, originate, start
Antonyms bring or come to an end, cease,
complete, conclude, desist, end, finish, halt,
stop, terminate, wind up

commend 1. acclaim, applaud, approve,
compliment, crack up (Inf.), eulogize, extol,
praise, recommend, speak highly of **2.**
commit, confide, consign, deliver, entrust,
hand over, yield
Antonyms (sense 1) attack, blast, censure,
condemn, criticize, denounce, disapprove,
knock (Inf.), lambast(e), put down, slam, tear
into (Inf.), (sense 2) hold back, keep, keep back,
retain, withdraw, withhold

commendable admirable, creditable, de~
serving, estimable, exemplary, laudable,
meritorious, praiseworthy, worthy

commendation acclaim, acclamation, ap~
probation, approval, Brownie points, credit,
encomium, encouragement, good opinion,
panegyric, praise, recommendation

commensurate adequate, appropriate, co~
extensive, comparable, compatible, consist~
ent, corresponding, due, equivalent, fit,
fitting, in accord, proportionate, sufficient

comment v. **1.** animadvert, interpose,
mention, note, observe, opine, point out,
remark, say, utter **2.** annotate, criticize,
elucidate, explain, interpret ~n. **3.** animad~
version, observation, remark, statement **4.**
annotation, commentary, criticism, eluci~
dation, explanation, exposition, illustration,
note

commentary analysis, critique, descrip~
tion, exegesis, explanation, narration, notes,
review, treatise, voice-over

commentator 1. commenter, reporter,
special correspondent, sportscaster **2.** an~
notator, critic, expositor, interpreter, scho~
liast

commerce 1. business, dealing, exchange,
merchandising, trade, traffic **2.** communi~

cation, dealings, intercourse, relations, so~
cializing

commercial 1. business, mercantile,
profit-making, sales, trade, trading **2.** in
demand, marketable, popular, profitable,
saleable **3.** exploited, materialistic, merce~
nary, monetary, pecuniary, profit-making,
venal

commingle amalgamate, blend, combine,
commix, intermingle, intermix, join, meld,
mingle, unite

commission n. **1.** appointment, authority,
charge, duty, employment, errand, function,
mandate, mission, task, trust, warrant **2.**
allowance, brokerage, compensation, cut,
fee, percentage, rake-off (Sl.), royalties **3.**
board, body of commissioners, commission~
ers, committee, delegation, deputation, rep~
resentative ~v. **4.** appoint, authorize, con~
tract, delegate, depute, empower, engage,
nominate, order, select, send

commit 1. carry out, do, enact, execute,
perform, perpetrate **2.** commend, confide,
consign, deliver, deposit, engage, entrust,
give, hand over **3.** align, bind, compromise,
endanger, make liable, obligate, pledge,
rank **4.** confine, imprison, put in custody
Antonyms (sense 1) omit (sense 2) receive,
withhold (sense 3) disavow, vacillate, waver
(sense 4) free, let out, release, set free

commitment 1. duty, engagement, liabil~
ity, obligation, responsibility, tie **2.** adher~
ence, dedication, devotion, involvement,
loyalty **3.** assurance, guarantee, pledge,
promise, undertaking, vow, word
Antonyms disavowal, indecisiveness, nega~
tion, vacillation, wavering

common 1. average, commonplace, con~
ventional, customary, daily, everyday, fa~
miliar, frequent, general, habitual, hum~
drum, obscure, ordinary, plain, regular,
routine, run-of-the-mill, simple, standard,
stock, usual, workaday **2.** accepted, general,
popular, prevailing, prevalent, universal,
widespread **3.** collective, communal, com~
munity, popular, public, social **4.** coarse,
hackneyed, inferior, low, pedestrian, ple~
beian, stale, trite, undistinguished, vulgar
Antonyms (sense 1) abnormal, distin~
guished, famous, formal, important, infre~
quent, noble, outstanding, rare, scarce, so~
phisticated, strange, superior, uncommon,
unknown, unpopular, unusual (sense 3) per~
sonal, private (sense 4) cultured, gentle,
refined, sensitive

commonplace 1. adj. banal, common,
customary, everyday, humdrum, mundane,
obvious, ordinary, pedestrian, stale,
threadbare, trite, uninteresting, widespread,
worn out **2.** n. banality, cliché, platitude,
truism

Antonyms *adj.* exciting, extraordinary, in~
frequent, interesting, new, novel, original,
rare, strange, uncommon, unfamiliar, unique,
unusual

common-sense, common-sensical
adj. astute, down-to-earth, hard-headed, ju~
dicious, level-headed, matter-of-fact, practi~
cal, realistic, reasonable, sane, sensible,
shrewd, sound
Antonyms airy-fairy (*Inf.*), daft (*Inf.*), fool~
ish, impractical, irrational, unrealistic, un~
reasonable, unthinking, unwise

common sense good sense, gumption
(*Brit. inf.*), horse sense, level-headedness,
mother wit, native intelligence, nous (*Brit.
sl.*), practicality, prudence, reasonableness,
smarts (*Sl., chiefly U.S.*), sound judgment,
soundness, wit

commotion ado, agitation, brouhaha, bus~
tle, disorder, disturbance, excitement, fer~
ment, furore, fuss, hubbub, hullabaloo,
hurly-burly, perturbation, racket, riot,
rumpus, to-do, tumult, turmoil, upheaval,
uproar

communal collective, communistic, com~
munity, general, joint, neighbourhood, pub~
lic, shared
Antonyms exclusive, individual, personal,
private, single, unshared

commune[1] *v.* **1.** communicate, confer,
confide in, converse, discourse, discuss,
parley **2.** contemplate, meditate, muse,
ponder, reflect

commune[2] *n.* collective, community, co~
operative, kibbutz

communicable catching, contagious, in~
fectious, taking, transferable, transmittable

communicate acquaint, announce, be in
contact, be in touch, connect, convey, cor~
respond, declare, disclose, disseminate, di~
vulge, impart, inform, make known, pass
on, phone, proclaim, publish, report, reveal,
ring up (*Inf., chiefly Brit.*), signify, spread,
transmit, unfold
Antonyms conceal, cover up, hold back,
hush up, keep back, keep secret, keep under
wraps, repress, sit on (*Inf.*), suppress, whitewash (*Inf.*), withhold

communication 1. connection, contact,
conversation, correspondence, dissemina~
tion, intercourse, link, transmission **2.** an~
nouncement, disclosure, dispatch, informa~
tion, intelligence, message, news, report,
statement, word

communications 1. routes, transport,
travel **2.** information technology, media,
publicity, public relations, telecommunica~
tions

communicative candid, chatty, convers~
able, expansive, forthcoming, frank, in~

formative, loquacious, open, outgoing,
talkative, unreserved, voluble
Antonyms quiet, reserved, reticent, secre~
tive, taciturn, uncommunicative, uninforma~
tive, untalkative

communion 1. accord, affinity, agreement,
closeness, communing, concord, consensus,
converse, fellowship, harmony, intercourse,
participation, rapport, sympathy, together~
ness, unity **2.** *Church* Eucharist, Lord's
Supper, Mass, Sacrament

communiqué announcement, bulletin,
dispatch, news flash, official communica~
tion, report

communism Bolshevism, collectivism,
Marxism, socialism, state socialism

communist Bolshevik, collectivist, Marx~
ist, Red (*Inf.*), socialist

community 1. association, body politic,
brotherhood, commonwealth, company, dis~
trict, general public, locality, people, popu~
lace, population, public, residents, society,
state **2.** affinity, agreement, identity, like~
ness, sameness, similarity

commute 1. barter, exchange, interchange,
substitute, switch, trade **2.** *Law: of penal~
ties, etc.* alleviate, curtail, mitigate, modify,
reduce, remit, shorten, soften

commuter 1. *n.* daily traveller, strap~
hanger (*Inf.*), suburbanite **2.** *adj.* suburban

compact[1] *adj.* **1.** close, compressed, con~
densed, dense, firm, impenetrable, imper~
meable, pressed together, solid, thick **2.**
brief, compendious, concise, epigrammatic,
laconic, pithy, pointed, succinct, terse, to
the point ~*v.* **3.** compress, condense, cram,
pack down, stuff, tamp
Antonyms *adj.* (*sense 1*) dispersed, large,
loose, roomy, scattered, spacious, sprawling
(*sense 2*) circumlocutory, garrulous, lengthy,
long-winded, prolix, rambling, verbose,
wordy ~*v.* disperse, loosen, separate

compact[2] *n.* agreement, alliance, arrange~
ment, bargain, bond, concordat, contract,
covenant, deal, entente, pact, stipulation,
treaty, understanding

companion 1. accomplice, ally, associate,
buddy (*Inf.*), colleague, comrade, confeder~
ate, consort, crony, friend, mate (*Inf.*), part~
ner **2.** aide, assistant, attendant, chaperon,
duenna, escort, squire **3.** complement,
counterpart, fellow, match, mate, twin

companionable affable, congenial, con~
versable, convivial, cordial, familiar,
friendly, genial, gregarious, neighbourly,
outgoing, sociable

companionship amity, camaraderie, com~
pany, comradeship, conviviality, esprit de
corps, fellowship, fraternity, friendship,
rapport, togetherness

company 1. assemblage, assembly, band, bevy, body, camp, circle, collection, community, concourse, convention, coterie, crew, crowd, ensemble, gathering, group, league, party, set, throng, troop, troupe, turnout **2.** association, business, concern, corporation, establishment, firm, house, partnership, syndicate **3.** callers, companionship, fellowship, guests, party, presence, society, visitors

comparable 1. a match for, as good as, commensurate, equal, equivalent, in a class with, on a par, proportionate, tantamount **2.** akin, alike, analogous, cognate, corresponding, related, similar
Antonyms different, dissimilar, incommensurable, incomparable, unequal

comparative approximate, by comparison, qualified, relative

compare 1. *With* **with** balance, collate, contrast, juxtapose, set against, weigh **2.** *With* **to** correlate, equate, identify with, liken, parallel, resemble **3.** *Be the equal of* approach, approximate to, bear comparison, be in the same class as, be on a par with, come up to, compete with, equal, hold a candle to, match, vie

comparison 1. collation, contrast, distinction, juxtaposition **2.** analogy, comparability, correlation, likeness, resemblance, similarity

compartment 1. alcove, bay, berth, booth, carrel, carriage, cell, chamber, cubbyhole, cubicle, locker, niche, pigeonhole, section **2.** area, category, department, division, section, subdivision

compass *n.* **1.** area, bound, boundary, circle, circuit, circumference, enclosure, extent, field, limit, range, reach, realm, round, scope, sphere, stretch, zone ~*v.* **2.** beset, besiege, blockade, circumscribe, encircle, enclose, encompass, environ, hem in, invest (*Rare*), surround **3.** accomplish, achieve, attain, bring about, effect, execute, fulfil, perform, procure, realize

compassion charity, clemency, commiseration, compunction, condolence, fellow feeling, heart, humanity, kindness, mercy, pity, quarter, ruth (*Archaic*), softheartedness, sorrow, sympathy, tenderheartedness, tenderness
Antonyms apathy, cold-heartedness, indifference, mercilessness, unconcern

compassionate benevolent, charitable, humane, humanitarian, indulgent, kindhearted, kindly, lenient, merciful, pitying, sympathetic, tender, tender-hearted, understanding
Antonyms callous, harsh, heartless, inhumane, pitiless, uncaring, unfeeling, unmerciful, unsympathetic

compatibility affinity, agreement, amity, concord, congeniality, empathy, harmony, like-mindedness, rapport, singlemindedness, sympathy

compatible accordant, adaptable, agreeable, congenial, congruent, congruous, consistent, consonant, harmonious, in harmony, in keeping, like-minded, reconcilable, suitable
Antonyms contradictory, inappropriate, inapt, incompatible, unfitting, unharmonious, unsuitable

compatriot countryman, fellow citizen, fellow countryman

compel bulldoze (*Inf.*), coerce, constrain, dragoon, drive, enforce, exact, force, hustle (*Sl.*), impel, make, necessitate, oblige, railroad (*Inf.*), restrain, squeeze, urge

compelling 1. cogent, conclusive, convincing, forceful, irrefutable, powerful, telling, weighty **2.** enchanting, enthralling, gripping, hypnotic, irresistible, mesmeric, spellbinding **3.** binding, coercive, imperative, overriding, peremptory, pressing, unavoidable, urgent
Antonyms (*sense 1*) boring, dull, humdrum, monotonous, ordinary, repetitious, tiresome, uneventful, uninteresting, wearisome

compensate 1. atone, indemnify, make good, make restitution, recompense, refund, reimburse, remunerate, repay, requite, reward, satisfy **2.** balance, cancel (out), counteract, counterbalance, countervail, make amends, make up for, offset, redress

compensation amends, atonement, damages, indemnification, indemnity, meed (*Archaic*), payment, recompense, reimbursement, remuneration, reparation, requital, restitution, reward, satisfaction

compete be in the running, challenge, contend, contest, emulate, fight, pit oneself against, rival, strive, struggle, vie

competence ability, adequacy, appropriateness, capability, capacity, competency, craft, expertise, fitness, proficiency, skill, suitability
Antonyms inability, inadequacy, incompetence

competent able, adapted, adequate, appropriate, capable, clever, endowed, equal, fit, pertinent, proficient, qualified, sufficient, suitable
Antonyms cowboy (*Inf.*), inadequate, incapable, incompetent, inexperienced, inexpert, undependable, unqualified, unskilled

competition 1. contention, contest, emulation, one-upmanship (*Inf.*), opposition, rivalry, strife, struggle **2.** championship, contest, event, head-to-head, puzzle, quiz, tournament **3.** challengers, field, opposition, rivals

competitive aggressive, ambitious, an~ tagonistic, at odds, combative, cutthroat, dog-eat-dog, emulous, opposing, rival, vying

competitor adversary, antagonist, chal~ lenger, competition, contestant, emulator, opponent, opposition, rival

compile accumulate, amass, anthologize, collect, cull, garner, gather, marshal, or~ ganize, put together

complacency contentment, gratification, pleasure, satisfaction, self-satisfaction, smugness

complacent contented, gratified, pleased, pleased with oneself, satisfied, self-assured, self-contented, self-righteous, self-satisfied, serene, smug, unconcerned
Antonyms discontent, dissatisfied, in~ secure, rude, troubled, uneasy, unsatisfied

complain beef (*Sl.*), bellyache (*Sl.*), bemoan, bewail, bitch (*Sl.*), bleat, carp, deplore, find fault, fuss, grieve, gripe (*Inf.*), groan, grouch (*Inf.*), grouse, growl, grumble, kick up a fuss (*Inf.*), kvetch (*U.S. sl.*), lament, moan, whine, whinge (*Inf.*)

complaint 1. accusation, annoyance, beef (*Sl.*), bitch (*Sl.*), charge, criticism, dissatis~ faction, fault-finding, grievance, gripe (*Inf.*), grouch (*Inf.*), grouse, grumble, lament, moan, plaint, protest, remonstrance, trou~ ble, wail **2.** affliction, ailment, disease, dis~ order, illness, indisposition, malady, sick~ ness, upset

complement *n.* **1.** companion, completion, consummation, correlative, counterpart, finishing touch, rounding-off, supplement **2.** aggregate, capacity, entirety, quota, total, totality, wholeness ~*v.* **3.** cap (*Inf.*), com~ plete, crown, round off, set off

complementary companion, completing, correlative, corresponding, fellow, interde~ pendent, interrelating, matched, reciprocal
Antonyms contradictory, different, incom~ patible, incongruous, uncomplementary

complete *adj.* **1.** all, entire, faultless, full, intact, integral, plenary, unabridged, un~ broken, undivided, unimpaired, whole **2.** accomplished, achieved, concluded, ended, finished **3.** absolute, consummate, deep-dyed (*Usually derogatory*), dyed-in-the-wool, outright, perfect, thorough, thoroughgoing, total, utter ~*v.* **4.** accomplish, achieve, cap, close, conclude, crown, discharge, do, end, execute, fill in, finalize, finish, fulfil, perfect, perform, realize, round off, settle, termi~ nate, wrap up (*Inf.*)
Antonyms *adj.* deficient, imperfect, incom~ plete, inconclusive, partial, spoilt, unaccom~ plished, unfinished, unsettled ~*v.* begin, com~ mence, initiate, mar, spoil, start

completely absolutely, altogether, down to the ground, en masse, entirely, from A to Z,

from beginning to end, fully, heart and soul, hook, line and sinker, in full, *in toto*, perfectly, quite, root and branch, solidly, thoroughly, totally, utterly, wholly

completion accomplishment, attainment, close, conclusion, consummation, culmina~ tion, end, expiration, finalization, fruition, fulfilment, realization

complex *adj.* **1.** circuitous, complicated, convoluted, Daedalian (*Literary*), intricate, involved, knotty, labyrinthine, mingled, mixed, tangled, tortuous **2.** composite, compound, compounded, heterogeneous, manifold, multifarious, multiple ~*n.* **3.** ag~ gregate, composite, network, organization, scheme, structure, synthesis, system **4.** fixation, fixed idea, *idée fixe*, obsession, phobia, preoccupation
Antonyms (*sense 1*) clear, easy, easy-peasy (*Sl.*), elementary, obvious, simple, straight~ forward, uncomplicated

complexion 1. colour, colouring, hue, pig~ mentation, skin, skin tone **2.** appearance, aspect, cast, character, countenance, dispo~ sition, guise, light, look, make-up, nature, stamp

complexity complication, convolution, elaboration, entanglement, intricacy, in~ volvement, multiplicity, ramification

compliance acquiescence, agreement, as~ sent, complaisance, concession, concur~ rence, conformity, consent, deference, obedience, observance, passivity, submis~ sion, submissiveness, yielding
Antonyms defiance, disobedience, non~ compliance, nonconformity, opposition, re~ fusal, resistance, revolt

complicate confuse, entangle, interweave, involve, make intricate, muddle, ravel, snarl up
Antonyms clarify, clear up, disentangle, elucidate, explain, facilitate, simplify, spell out, unsnarl

complicated 1. Byzantine (*of attitudes, etc.*), complex, convoluted, elaborate, inter~ laced, intricate, involved, labyrinthine **2.** difficult, involved, perplexing, problematic, puzzling, troublesome
Antonyms clear, easy, easy-peasy (*Sl.*), sim~ ple, straightforward, uncomplicated, unde~ manding, understandable, uninvolved, user-friendly

complication 1. combination, complexity, confusion, entanglement, intricacy, mix~ ture, web **2.** aggravation, difficulty, draw~ back, embarrassment, factor, obstacle, problem, snag

complicity abetment, collaboration, collu~ sion, concurrence, connivance

compliment 1. *n.* admiration, bouquet, commendation, congratulations, courtesy,

eulogy, favour, flattery, honour, praise, tribute **2.** *v.* commend, congratulate, crack up (*Inf.*), extol, felicitate, flatter, laud, pay tribute to, praise, salute, sing the praises of, speak highly of, wish joy to
Antonyms *n.* complaint, condemnation, criticism, disparagement, insult, reproach ~*v.* blast, condemn, criticize, decry, disparage, insult, lambast(e), put down, reprehend, reproach, tear into (*Inf.*)

complimentary 1. appreciative, approving, commendatory, congratulatory, eulogistic, flattering, laudatory, panegyrical **2.** courtesy, donated, free, free of charge, gratis, gratuitous, honorary, on the house
Antonyms (*sense 1*) abusive, critical, disparaging, fault-finding, insulting, scathing, uncomplimentary, unflattering

compliments good wishes, greetings, regards, remembrances, respects, salutation

comply abide by, accede, accord, acquiesce, adhere to, agree to, conform to, consent to, defer, discharge, follow, fulfil, obey, observe, perform, respect, satisfy, submit, yield
Antonyms break, defy, disobey, disregard, fight, ignore, oppose, refuse to obey, reject, repudiate, resist, spurn, violate

component 1. *n.* constituent, element, ingredient, item, part, piece, unit **2.** *adj.* composing, constituent, inherent, intrinsic

compose 1. build, compound, comprise, constitute, construct, fashion, form, make, make up, put together **2.** contrive, create, devise, frame, imagine, indite, invent, produce, write **3.** adjust, arrange, reconcile, regulate, resolve, settle **4.** appease, assuage, calm, collect, control, pacify, placate, quell, quiet, soothe, still, tranquillize
Antonyms (*sense 1*) bulldoze, demolish, destroy, dismantle, obliterate, raze (*sense 4*) agitate, disturb, excite, perturb, trouble, unsettle, upset

composed at ease, calm, collected, confident, cool, imperturbable, laid-back (*Inf.*), level-headed, poised, relaxed, sedate, self-possessed, serene, together (*Sl.*), tranquil, unfazed (*Inf.*), unflappable, unruffled, unworried
Antonyms agitated, anxious, disturbed, excited, nervous, ruffled, twitchy (*Inf.*), uncontrolled, uneasy, unpoised, upset

composite 1. *adj.* blended, combined, complex, compound, conglomerate, mixed, synthesized **2.** *n.* amalgam, blend, compound, conglomerate, fusion, meld, synthesis

composition 1. arrangement, configuration, constitution, design, form, formation, layout, make-up, organization, structure **2.** compilation, creation, fashioning, forma-

tion, formulation, invention, making, mixture, production **3.** creation, essay, exercise, literary work, opus, piece, study, treatise, work, writing **4.** arrangement, balance, concord, consonance, harmony, placing, proportion, symmetry

compost humus, mulch, organic fertilizer

composure aplomb, calm, calmness, collectedness, cool (*Sl.*), coolness, dignity, ease, equanimity, imperturbability, placidity, poise, sang-froid, sedateness, self-assurance, self-possession, serenity, tranquillity
Antonyms agitation, discomposure, excitability, impatience, nervousness, perturbation, uneasiness

compound *v.* **1.** amalgamate, blend, coalesce, combine, concoct, fuse, intermingle, meld, mingle, mix, synthesize, unite **2.** add to, aggravate, augment, complicate, exacerbate, heighten, intensify, magnify, worsen **3.** *Used of a dispute, difference, etc.* adjust, arrange, compose, settle ~*n.* **4.** alloy, amalgam, blend, combination, composite, composition, conglomerate, fusion, medley, meld, mixture, synthesis ~*adj.* **5.** complex, composite, conglomerate, intricate, multiple, not simple
Antonyms *v.* decrease, divide, lessen, minimize, moderate, modify, part, segregate ~*n.* element ~*adj.* pure, simple, single, unmixed

comprehend 1. apprehend, assimilate, conceive, discern, fathom, grasp, know, make out, perceive, see, take in, understand **2.** comprise, contain, embody, embrace, enclose, encompass, include, involve, take in
Antonyms (*sense 1*) get (it) wrong, get the wrong end of the stick, misapprehend, misconceive, misconstrue, misinterpret, miss the point of, mistake, misunderstand, pervert

comprehensible clear, coherent, conceivable, explicit, graspable, intelligible, plain, understandable, user-friendly

comprehension 1. conception, discernment, grasp, intelligence, judgment, knowledge, perception, realization, sense, understanding **2.** compass, domain, field, limits, province, range, reach, scope
Antonyms (*sense 1*) incomprehension, misapprehension, misunderstanding, unawareness

comprehensive all-embracing, all-inclusive, blanket, broad, catholic, complete, encyclopedic, exhaustive, extensive, full, inclusive, sweeping, thorough, umbrella, wide
Antonyms incomplete, limited, narrow, restricted, specialized, specific

compress abbreviate, compact, concentrate, condense, constrict, contract, cram, crowd, crush, knit, press, pucker, shorten, squash, squeeze, summarize, wedge

compressed abridged, compact, compact~ed, concentrated, concise, consolidated, constricted, flattened, reduced, shortened, squashed, squeezed

compression condensation, consolidation, constriction, crushing, pressure, squeezing, wedging

comprise 1. be composed of, comprehend, consist of, contain, embrace, encompass, include, take in **2.** compose, constitute, form, make up

compromise v. **1.** adjust, agree, arbitrate, compose, compound, concede, give and take, go fifty-fifty (Inf.), meet halfway, settle, strike a balance ~n. **2.** accommodation, ac~cord, adjustment, agreement, concession, give-and-take, half measures, middle ground, settlement, trade-off ~v. **3.** dis~credit, dishonour, embarrass, endanger, ex~pose, hazard, imperil, implicate, jeopardize, prejudice, weaken
Antonyms v. argue, assure, boost, contest, differ, disagree, enhance, support ~n. conten~tion, controversy, difference, disagreement, dispute, quarrel

compulsion 1. coercion, constraint, de~mand, duress, force, obligation, pressure, urgency **2.** drive, necessity, need, obses~sion, preoccupation, urge

compulsive besetting, compelling, driving, irresistible, obsessive, overwhelming, un~controllable, urgent

compulsory binding, de rigueur, forced, imperative, mandatory, obligatory, re~quired, requisite
Antonyms discretionary, non-obligatory, non-requisite, optional, unimperative, un~necessary, voluntary

compute add up, calculate, cast up, cipher, count, enumerate, estimate, figure, figure out, measure, rate, reckon, sum, tally, total

comrade ally, associate, buddy (Inf.), cock (Brit. inf.), colleague, companion, compatri~ot, compeer, confederate, co-worker, crony, fellow, friend, mate (Inf.), pal (Inf.), partner

concave cupped, depressed, excavated, hol~low, hollowed, incurved, indented, scooped, sunken
Antonyms bulging, convex, curving, protu~berant, rounded

conceal bury, camouflage, cover, disguise, dissemble, hide, keep dark, keep secret, mask, obscure, screen, secrete, shelter, stash (Inf.)
Antonyms disclose, display, divulge, expose, lay bare, reveal, show, uncover, unmask, un~veil

concealed covered, hidden, inconspicuous, masked, obscured, screened, secret, secret~ed, tucked away, unseen

concealment camouflage, cover, disguise, hideaway, hide-out, hiding, secrecy
Antonyms disclosure, display, exposure, give-away, leak, revelation, showing, uncov~ering

concede 1. accept, acknowledge, admit, al~low, confess, grant, own **2.** cede, give up, hand over, relinquish, surrender, yield
Antonyms (sense 1) contest, deny, disclaim, dispute, protest, refute, reject (sense 2) beat, conquer, defeat, fight to the bitter end, make a stand

conceit 1. amour-propre, arrogance, com~placency, egotism, narcissism, pride, self-importance, self-love, swagger, vainglory, vanity **2.** Archaic belief, fancy, fantasy, idea, image, imagination, judgment, notion, opinion, quip, thought, vagary, whim, whimsy

conceited arrogant, bigheaded (Inf.), cocky, egotistical, immodest, narcissistic, over~weening, puffed up, self-important, stuck up (Inf.), swollen-headed, vain, vainglorious
Antonyms humble, modest, self-effacing, unassuming

conceivable believable, credible, imagi~nable, possible, thinkable
Antonyms inconceivable, incredible, unbe~lievable, unimaginable, unthinkable

conceive 1. appreciate, apprehend, believe, comprehend, envisage, fancy, grasp, imag~ine, realize, suppose, understand **2.** con~trive, create, design, develop, devise, form, formulate, produce, project, purpose, think up **3.** become impregnated, become preg~nant

concentrate 1. be engrossed in, consider closely, focus attention on, give all one's attention to, put one's mind to, rack one's brains **2.** bring to bear, centre, cluster, converge, focus **3.** accumulate, cluster, col~lect, congregate, gather, huddle
Antonyms (sense 1) disregard, let one's mind wander, lose concentration, pay no attention to, pay no heed to (senses 2 & 3) deploy, diffuse, disperse, dissipate, scatter, spread out

concentrated 1. all-out (Inf.), deep, hard, intense, intensive **2.** boiled down, con~densed, evaporated, reduced, rich, thick~ened, undiluted

concentration 1. absorption, application, heed, single-mindedness **2.** bringing to bear, centralization, centring, combination, compression, consolidation, convergence, focusing, intensification **3.** accumulation, aggregation, cluster, collection, conver~gence, horde, mass
Antonyms (sense 1) absent-mindedness, dis~regard, distraction, inattention (senses 2 & 3) diffusion, dispersion, scattering, spreading-out

concept abstraction, conception, conceptu~ alization, hypothesis, idea, image, impres~ sion, notion, theory, view

conception 1. concept, design, idea, image, notion, plan **2.** beginning, birth, formation, inception, initiation, invention, launching, origin, outset **3.** appreciation, clue, com~ prehension, impression, inkling, perception, picture, understanding **4.** fertilization, ger~ mination, impregnation, insemination

concern *v.* **1.** affect, apply to, bear on, be relevant to, interest, involve, pertain to, re~ gard, touch ~*n.* **2.** affair, business, charge, department, field, interest, involvement, job, matter, mission, occupation, responsibility, task, transaction **3.** bearing, importance, interest, reference, relation, relevance ~*v.* **4.** bother, disquiet, distress, disturb, make anxious, make uneasy, perturb, trouble, worry ~*n.* **5.** anxiety, apprehension, atten~ tion, burden, care, consideration, disquiet, disquietude, distress, heed, responsibility, solicitude, worry **6.** business, company, corporation, enterprise, establishment, firm, house, organization

concerned 1. active, implicated, interested, involved, mixed up, privy to **2.** anxious, bothered, distressed, disturbed, exercised, troubled, uneasy, upset, worried **3.** atten~ tive, caring, interested, solicitous
Antonyms aloof, carefree, detached, indif~ ferent, neglectful, unconcerned, uninterested, untroubled, without a care

concerning about, anent (*Scot.*), apropos of, as regards, as to, in the matter of, on the subject of, re, regarding, relating to, re~ specting, touching, with reference to

concert *n.* **1.** accord, agreement, concord, concordance, harmony, unanimity, union, unison **2. in concert** concertedly, in col~ laboration, in league, in unison, jointly, shoulder to shoulder, together, unanimous~ ly

concerted agreed upon, collaborative, combined, coordinated, joint, planned, pre~ arranged, united
Antonyms disunited, separate, uncontrived, uncooperative, unplanned

concession 1. acknowledgment, admission, assent, confession, surrender, yielding **2.** adjustment, allowance, boon, compromise, grant, indulgence, permit, privilege, sop

conciliate appease, disarm, mediate, molli~ fy, pacify, placate, propitiate, reconcile, re~ store harmony, soothe, win over

conciliation appeasement, disarming, mollification, pacification, placation, propi~ tiation, reconciliation, soothing

conciliatory appeasing, disarming, irenic, mollifying, pacific, peaceable, placatory, propitiative

concise brief, compact, compendious, com~ pressed, condensed, epigrammatic, laconic, pithy, short, succinct, summary, synoptic, terse, to the point
Antonyms diffuse, discursive, garrulous, lengthy, long-winded, prolix, rambling, ver~ bose, wordy

conclave assembly, cabinet, conference, congress, council, parley, secret *or* private meeting, session

conclude 1. bring down the curtain, cease, close, come to an end, complete, draw to a close, end, finish, round off, terminate, wind up **2.** assume, decide, deduce, gather, infer, judge, reckon (*Inf.*), sum up, suppose, surmise **3.** accomplish, bring about, carry out, clinch, decide, determine, effect, estab~ lish, fix, pull off, resolve, settle, work out
Antonyms (*sense 1*) begin, commence, ex~ tend, initiate, open, protract, start

conclusion 1. close, completion, end, finale, finish, result, termination **2.** conse~ quence, culmination, issue, outcome, result, sequel, upshot **3.** agreement, conviction, decision, deduction, inference, judgment, opinion, resolution, settlement, verdict **4. in conclusion** finally, in closing, lastly, to sum up

conclusive clinching, convincing, decisive, definite, definitive, final, irrefutable, ulti~ mate, unanswerable, unarguable
Antonyms contestable, disputable, doubtful, dubious, impeachable, inconclusive, indeci~ sive, indefinite, questionable, refutable, un~ convincing, vague

concoct brew, contrive, cook up (*Inf.*), de~ sign, devise, fabricate, formulate, hatch, in~ vent, make up, manufacture, mature, plot, prepare, project, think up, trump up

concoction blend, brew, combination, compound, contrivance, creation, mixture, preparation

concrete *adj.* **1.** actual, definite, explicit, factual, material, real, sensible, specific, substantial, tangible **2.** calcified, compact, compressed, conglomerated, consolidated, firm, petrified, solid, solidified ~*n.* **3.** ce~ ment (*Not in technical usage*), concretion
Antonyms (*sense 1*) abstract, immaterial, indefinite, insubstantial, intangible, notional, theoretical, unspecified, vague

concubine courtesan, kept woman, leman (*Archaic*), mistress, odalisque, paramour

concupiscence appetite, desire, horniness (*Sl.*), lasciviousness, lechery, libidinousness, libido, lickerishness (*Archaic*), lust, lustful~ ness, randiness (*Inf., chiefly Brit.*)

concur accede, accord, acquiesce, agree, ap~ prove, assent, coincide, combine, consent, cooperate, harmonize, join

concurrent 1. coexisting, coincident, con~ certed, concomitant, contemporaneous, simultaneous, synchronous **2.** confluent, convergent, converging, uniting **3.** agree~ ing, at one, compatible, consentient, con~ sistent, cooperating, harmonious, in agree~ ment, in rapport, like-minded, of the same mind

concussion clash, collision, crash, impact, jarring, jolt, jolting, shaking, shock

condemn 1. blame, censure, damn, de~ nounce, disapprove, excoriate, reprehend, reproach, reprobate, reprove, upbraid **2.** convict, damn, doom, pass sentence on, proscribe, sentence
Antonyms (*sense 1*) acclaim, applaud, ap~ prove, commend, compliment, condone, praise (*sense 2*) acquit, free, liberate

condemnation 1. blame, censure, de~ nouncement, denunciation, disapproval, re~ proach, reprobation, reproof, stricture **2.** conviction, damnation, doom, judgment, proscription, sentence

condensation 1. abridgment, contraction, digest, précis, synopsis **2.** condensate, deli~ quescence, distillation, liquefaction, pre~ cipitate, precipitation **3.** compression, con~ centration, consolidation, crystallization, curtailment, reduction

condense 1. abbreviate, abridge, compact, compress, concentrate, contract, curtail, encapsulate, epitomize, précis, shorten, summarize **2.** boil down, coagulate, con~ centrate, decoct, precipitate (*Chem.*), reduce, solidify, thicken
Antonyms (*sense 1*) elaborate, enlarge, ex~ pand, expatiate, increase, lengthen, pad out, spin out (*sense 2*) dilute, make thinner, thin (out), water down, weaken

condensed 1. abridged, compressed, con~ centrated, curtailed, shortened, shrunken, slimmed down, summarized **2.** boiled down, clotted, coagulated, concentrated, precipi~ tated (*Chem.*), reduced, thickened

condescend 1. be courteous, bend, come down off one's high horse (*Inf.*), deign, humble *or* demean oneself, lower oneself, see fit, stoop, submit, unbend (*Inf.*), vouch~ safe **2.** patronize, talk down to

condescending disdainful, lofty, lordly, patronizing, snobbish, snooty (*Inf.*), super~ cilious, superior, toffee-nosed (*Sl., chiefly Brit.*)

condition *n.* **1.** case, circumstances, plight, position, predicament, shape, situation, state, state of affairs, *status quo* **2.** arrange~ ment, article, demand, limitation, modifi~ cation, prerequisite, provision, proviso, qualification, requirement, requisite, re~ striction, rider, rule, stipulation, terms **3.** fettle, fitness, health, kilter, order, shape,

state of health, trim **4.** ailment, complaint, infirmity, malady, problem, weakness **5.** caste, class, estate, grade, order, position, rank, status, stratum ~*v.* **6.** accustom, adapt, educate, equip, habituate, inure, make ready, prepare, ready, tone up, train, work out

conditional contingent, dependent, limited, provisional, qualified, subject to, with res~ ervations
Antonyms absolute, categorical, uncondi~ tional, unrestricted

conditioned acclimatized, accustomed, adapted, adjusted, familiarized, habituated, inured, made ready, prepared, seasoned, trained, used

conditioning *n.* **1.** grooming, preparation, readying, training **2.** accustoming, famil~ iarization, hardening, inurement, reorien~ tation, seasoning ~*adj.* **3.** astringent, ton~ ing

conditions circumstances, environment, milieu, situation, surroundings, way of life

condom flunky (*Sl.*), Frenchie (*Sl.*), French letter (*Sl.*), French tickler (*Sl.*), rubber (*U.S. sl.*), rubber johnny (*Brit. sl.*), scumbag (*U.S. sl.*), sheath

condone disregard, excuse, forgive, let pass, look the other way, make allowance for, overlook, pardon, turn a blind eye to, wink at
Antonyms censure, condemn, denounce, disapprove, punish

conduct *n.* **1.** administration, control, di~ rection, guidance, leadership, management, organization, running, supervision ~*v.* **2.** administer, carry on, control, direct, gov~ ern, handle, lead, manage, organize, preside over, regulate, run, supervise **3.** accompa~ ny, attend, chair, convey, escort, guide, pi~ lot, preside over, steer, usher ~*n.* **4.** atti~ tude, bearing, behaviour, carriage, com~ portment, demeanour, deportment, man~ ners, mien (*Literary*), ways ~*v.* **5.** acquit, act, behave, carry, comport, deport

confederacy alliance, bund, coalition, compact, confederation, conspiracy, cov~ enant, federation, league, union

confederate 1. *adj.* allied, associated, combined, federal, federated, in alliance **2.** *n.* abettor, accessory, accomplice, ally, as~ sociate, colleague, partner **3.** *v.* ally, amal~ gamate, associate, band together, combine, federate, merge, unite

confer 1. accord, award, bestow, give, grant, hand out, present, vouchsafe **2.** consult, converse, deliberate, discourse, parley, talk

conference colloquium, congress, consul~ tation, convention, convocation, discussion, forum, meeting, seminar, symposium, teach-in

confess 1. acknowledge, admit, allow, blurt out, come clean (*Inf.*), concede, confide, disclose, divulge, grant, make a clean breast of, own, own up, recognize, sing (*Sl., chiefly U.S.*), spill one's guts (*Sl.*) **2.** affirm, assert, attest, aver, confirm, declare, evince, manifest, profess, prove, reveal
Antonyms button one's lips, conceal, cover, deny, hide, hush up, keep mum, keep secret, keep under wraps, repudiate, suppress, withhold

confession acknowledgment, admission, avowal, disclosure, divulgence, exposure, revelation, unbosoming

confidant, confidante alter ego, bosom friend, close friend, crony, familiar, intimate

confide 1. admit, breathe, confess, disclose, divulge, impart, reveal, whisper **2.** commend, commit, consign, entrust

confidence 1. belief, credence, dependence, faith, reliance, trust **2.** aplomb, assurance, boldness, courage, firmness, nerve, self-possession, self-reliance **3. in confidence** between you and me (and the gatepost), confidentially, in secrecy, privately
Antonyms (*sense 1*) disbelief, distrust, doubt, misgiving, mistrust (*sense 2*) apprehension, fear, self-doubt, shyness, uncertainty

confident 1. certain, convinced, counting on, positive, satisfied, secure, sure **2.** assured, bold, dauntless, fearless, self-assured, self-reliant
Antonyms (*sense 1*) doubtful, dubious, not sure, tentative, uncertain, unconvinced, unsure (*sense 2*) afraid, hesitant, insecure, jittery, lacking confidence, mousy, nervous, scared, self-doubting, unsure

confidential 1. classified, hush-hush (*Inf.*), intimate, off the record, private, privy, secret **2.** faithful, familiar, trusted, trustworthy, trusty

confidentially behind closed doors, between ourselves, in camera, in confidence, in secret, personally, privately, sub rosa

confine 1. *v.* bind, bound, cage, circumscribe, enclose, hem in, hold back, immure, imprison, incarcerate, intern, keep, limit, repress, restrain, restrict, shut up, straiten **2.** *n.* border, boundary, frontier, limit, precinct

confined 1. enclosed, limited, restricted **2.** in childbed, in childbirth, lying-in

confinement 1. custody, detention, imprisonment, incarceration, internment, porridge (*Sl.*) **2.** *accouchement,* childbed, childbirth, labour, lying-in, parturition, time, travail

confines boundaries, bounds, circumference, edge, limits, pale, precincts

confirm 1. assure, buttress, clinch, establish, fix, fortify, reinforce, settle, strengthen **2.** approve, authenticate, bear out, corroborate, endorse, ratify, sanction, substantiate, validate, verify

confirmation 1. authentication, corroboration, evidence, proof, substantiation, testimony, validation, verification **2.** acceptance, agreement, approval, assent, endorsement, ratification, sanction
Antonyms (*sense 1*) contradiction, denial, disavowal, repudiation (*sense 2*) annulment, cancellation, disapproval, refusal, rejection

confirmed chronic, dyed-in-the-wool, habitual, hardened, ingrained, inured, inveterate, long-established, rooted, seasoned

confiscate appropriate, commandeer, expropriate, impound, seize, sequester, sequestrate
Antonyms free, give, give back, hand back, release, restore, return

confiscation appropriation, expropriation, forfeiture, impounding, seizure, sequestration, takeover

conflict *n.* **1.** battle, clash, collision, combat, contention, contest, encounter, engagement, fight, fracas, head-to-head, set-to (*Inf.*), strife, war, warfare **2.** antagonism, bad blood, difference, disagreement, discord, dissension, divided loyalties, friction, hostility, interference, opposition, strife, variance ~*v.* **3.** be at variance, clash, collide, combat, contend, contest, differ, disagree, fight, interfere, strive, struggle
Antonyms *n.* accord, agreement, harmony, peace, treaty, truce ~*v.* agree, coincide, harmonize, reconcile

conflicting antagonistic, clashing, contradictory, contrary, discordant, inconsistent, opposed, opposing, paradoxical
Antonyms accordant, agreeing, compatible, congruous, consistent, harmonious, similar, unopposing

conform 1. adapt, adjust, comply, fall in with, follow, follow the crowd, obey, run with the pack, yield **2.** accord, agree, assimilate, correspond, harmonize, match, square, suit, tally

conformation anatomy, arrangement, build, configuration, form, framework, outline, shape, structure

conformist *n.* Babbitt (*U.S.*), conventionalist, stick-in-the-mud (*Inf.*), traditionalist, yes man

conformity 1. allegiance, Babbittry (*U.S.*), compliance, conventionality, observance, orthodoxy **2.** affinity, agreement, conformance, congruity, consonance, correspondence, harmony, likeness, resemblance, similarity

confound 1. amaze, astonish, astound, baffle, bewilder, confuse, dumbfound, flabbergast (*Inf.*), flummox, mix up, mystify, nonplus, perplex, startle, surprise **2.** annihilate, contradict, demolish, destroy, explode, overthrow, overwhelm, refute, ruin

confront accost, beard, brave, bring face to face with, challenge, defy, encounter, face, face off (*Sl.*), face up to, oppose, stand up to, tackle
Antonyms avoid, body-swerve (*Scot.*), circumvent, dodge, evade, flee, give a wide berth to, keep clear of, sidestep, steer clear of

confrontation conflict, contest, crisis, encounter, face-off (*Sl.*), head-to-head, set-to (*Inf.*), showdown (*Inf.*)

confuse 1. baffle, bemuse, bewilder, darken, faze, flummox, mystify, nonplus, obscure, perplex, puzzle **2.** blend, confound, disarrange, disorder, intermingle, involve, jumble, mingle, mistake, mix up, muddle, ravel, snarl up (*Inf.*), tangle **3.** abash, addle, demoralize, discomfit, discompose, disconcert, discountenance, disorient, embarrass, fluster, mortify, nonplus, rattle (*Inf.*), shame, throw off balance, unnerve, upset

confused 1. at a loss, at sea, at sixes and sevens, baffled, bewildered, dazed, discombobulated (*Inf., chiefly U.S. & Canad.*), disorganized, disorientated, flummoxed, muddled, muzzy (*U.S. inf.*), nonplussed, not with it (*Inf.*), perplexed, puzzled, taken aback, thrown off balance, upset **2.** at sixes and sevens, chaotic, disarranged, disarrayed, disordered, disorderly, disorganized, higgledy-piggledy (*Inf.*), hugger-mugger (*Archaic*), in disarray, jumbled, mistaken, misunderstood, mixed up, out of order, topsy-turvy, untidy
Antonyms arranged, aware, enlightened, informed, in order, on the ball (*Inf.*), ordered, orderly, organized, tidy, with it (*Inf.*)

confusing ambiguous, baffling, complicated, contradictory, disconcerting, inconsistent, misleading, muddling, perplexing, puzzling, unclear
Antonyms clear, definite, explicit, plain, simple, straightforward, uncomplicated, understandable

confusion 1. befuddlement, bemusement, bewilderment, disorientation, mystification, perplexity, puzzlement **2.** bustle, chaos, clutter, commotion, disarrangement, disarray, disorder, disorganization, hodgepodge (*U.S.*), hotchpotch, jumble, mess, muddle, pig's breakfast (*Inf.*), shambles, state, tangle, turmoil, untidiness, upheaval **3.** abashment, chagrin, demoralization, discom-

fiture, distraction, embarrassment, fluster, perturbation
Antonyms (*sense 1*) clarification, composure, enlightenment, explanation, solution (*sense 2*) arrangement, neatness, order, organization, tidiness

congenial adapted, affable, agreeable, companionable, compatible, complaisant, favourable, fit, friendly, genial, kindly, kindred, like-minded, pleasant, pleasing, suitable, sympathetic, well-suited

congenital 1. constitutional, inborn, inbred, inherent, innate, natural **2.** *Inf.* complete, deep-dyed (*Usually derogatory*), inveterate, thorough, utter

congested blocked-up, clogged, crammed, crowded, jammed, overcrowded, overfilled, overflowing, packed, stuffed, stuffed-up, teeming
Antonyms clear, empty, free, half-full, uncongested, uncrowded, unhampered, unhindered, unimpeded, unobstructed

congestion bottleneck, clogging, crowding, jam, mass, overcrowding, snarl-up (*Inf., chiefly Brit.*), surfeit

conglomerate 1. *adj.* amassed, clustered, composite, heterogeneous, massed **2.** *v.* accumulate, agglomerate, aggregate, cluster, coalesce, snowball **3.** *n.* agglomerate, aggregate, multinational

conglomeration accumulation, aggregation, assortment, combination, composite, hotchpotch, mass, medley, miscellany, mishmash, potpourri

congratulate compliment, felicitate, wish joy to

congratulations best wishes, compliments, felicitations, good wishes, greetings

congregate assemble, collect, come together, concentrate, convene, converge, convoke, flock, forgather, gather, mass, meet, muster, rally, rendezvous, throng
Antonyms break up, dispel, disperse, dissipate, part, scatter, separate, split up

congregation assembly, brethren, crowd, fellowship, flock, host, laity, multitude, parish, parishioners, throng

congress assembly, chamber of deputies, conclave, conference, convention, convocation, council, delegates, diet, house, legislative assembly, legislature, meeting, parliament, representatives

conic, conical cone-shaped, conoid, funnel-shaped, pointed, pyramidal, tapered, tapering

conjecture 1. *v.* assume, fancy, guess, hypothesize, imagine, infer, suppose, surmise, suspect, theorize **2.** *n.* assumption, conclusion, fancy, guess, guesstimate (*Inf.*), guesswork, hypothesis, inference, notion, presumption, shot in the dark, speculation, supposition, surmise, theorizing, theory

conjugal bridal, connubial, hymeneal, marital, married, matrimonial, nuptial, spousal, wedded

conjunction association, coincidence, combination, concurrence, juxtaposition, union

conjure 1. juggle, play tricks **2.** bewitch, call upon, cast a spell, charm, enchant, fascinate, invoke, raise, rouse, summon up **3.** adjure, appeal to, beg, beseech, crave, entreat, implore, importune, pray, supplicate

conjurer, conjuror magician, miracle-worker, sorcerer, thaumaturge (*Rare*), wizard

conjure up bring to mind, contrive, create, evoke, produce as by magic, recall, recollect

connect affix, ally, associate, cohere, combine, couple, fasten, join, link, relate, unite
Antonyms detach, disconnect, dissociate, divide, part, separate, sever, unfasten

connected 1. affiliated, akin, allied, associated, banded together, bracketed, combined, coupled, joined, linked, related, united **2.** *Of speech* coherent, comprehensible, consecutive, intelligible

connection 1. alliance, association, attachment, coupling, fastening, junction, link, tie, union **2.** affiliation, affinity, association, bond, commerce, communication, correlation, correspondence, intercourse, interrelation, liaison, link, marriage, relation, relationship, relevance, tie-in **3.** context, frame of reference, reference **4.** acquaintance, ally, associate, contact, friend, sponsor **5.** kin, kindred, kinsman, kith, relation, relative

connivance abetment, abetting, collusion, complicity, conspiring, tacit consent

connive 1. cabal, collude, conspire, cook up (*Inf.*), intrigue, plot, scheme **2.** *With* **at** abet, aid, be an accessory to, be a party to, be in collusion with, blink at, disregard, lend oneself to, let pass, look the other way, overlook, pass by, shut one's eyes to, turn a blind eye to, wink at

connoisseur aficionado, appreciator, arbiter, authority, buff (*Inf.*), cognoscente, devotee, expert, judge, maven (*U.S.*), savant, specialist, whiz (*Inf.*)

conquer 1. beat, blow out of the water (*Sl.*), checkmate, clobber (*Sl.*), crush, defeat, discomfit, get the better of, humble, lick (*Inf.*), master, overcome, overpower, overthrow, prevail, quell, rout, run rings around (*Inf.*), subdue, subjugate, succeed, surmount, tank (*Sl.*), triumph, undo, vanquish, wipe the floor with (*Inf.*) **2.** acquire, annex, obtain, occupy, overrun, seize, win
Antonyms (*sense 1*) be defeated, capitulate,

give in, give up, lose, quit, submit, surrender, throw in the towel, yield

conqueror champion, conquistador, defeater, hero, lord, master, subjugator, vanquisher, victor, winner

conquest 1. defeat, discomfiture, mastery, overthrow, pasting (*Sl.*), rout, triumph, vanquishment, victory **2.** acquisition, annexation, appropriation, coup, invasion, occupation, subjection, subjugation, takeover **3.** captivation, enchantment, enthralment, enticement, seduction **4.** acquisition, adherent, admirer, catch, fan, feather in one's cap, follower, prize, supporter, worshipper

conscience 1. moral sense, principles, scruples, sense of right and wrong, still small voice **2. in all conscience** assuredly, certainly, fairly, honestly, in truth, rightly, truly

conscience-stricken ashamed, compunctious, contrite, disturbed, guilty, penitent, remorseful, repentant, sorry, troubled

conscientious 1. careful, diligent, exact, faithful, meticulous, painstaking, particular, punctilious, thorough **2.** high-minded, high-principled, honest, honourable, incorruptible, just, moral, responsible, scrupulous, straightforward, strict, upright
Antonyms careless, irresponsible, negligent, remiss, slack, thoughtless, unconscientious, unprincipled, unreliable, unscrupulous, untrustworthy

conscious 1. alert, alive to, awake, aware, clued-up (*Inf.*), cognizant, percipient, responsive, sensible, sentient, wise to (*Sl.*) **2.** calculated, deliberate, intentional, knowing, premeditated, rational, reasoning, reflective, responsible, self-conscious, studied, wilful
Antonyms (*sense 1*) ignorant, insensible, oblivious, unaware, unconscious (*sense 2*) accidental, uncalculated, unintended, unintentional, unplanned, unpremeditated, unwitting

consciousness apprehension, awareness, knowledge, realization, recognition, sensibility

consecrate dedicate, devote, exalt, hallow, ordain, sanctify, set apart, venerate

consecutive chronological, following, in sequence, in turn, running, sequential, seriatim, succeeding, successive, uninterrupted

consensus agreement, assent, common consent, concord, concurrence, general agreement, harmony, unanimity, unity

consent 1. *v.* accede, acquiesce, agree, allow, approve, assent, comply, concede, concur, permit, yield **2.** *n.* acquiescence, agreement, approval, assent, compliance,

concession, concurrence, go-ahead (*Inf.*), O.K. *or* okay (*Inf.*), permission, sanction
Antonyms *v.* decline, demur, disagree, dis~ approve, dissent, refuse, resist ~*n.* disagree~ ment, disapproval, dissent, refusal, unwill~ ingness

consequence 1. effect, end, event, issue, outcome, repercussion, result, sequel, upshot 2. account, concern, import, impor~ tance, interest, moment, note, portent, significance, value, weight 3. bottom, dis~ tinction, eminence, notability, rank, repute, standing, status 4. **in consequence** as a result, because, following

consequent ensuing, following, resultant, resulting, sequential, subsequent, succes~ sive

consequently accordingly, ergo, hence, necessarily, subsequently, therefore, thus

conservation custody, economy, guardian~ ship, husbandry, maintenance, preserva~ tion, protection, safeguarding, safekeeping, saving, upkeep

conservative 1. *adj.* cautious, convention~ al, die-hard, guarded, hidebound, middle-of-the-road, moderate, quiet, reactionary, right-wing, sober, tory, traditional 2. *n.* middle-of-the-roader, moderate, reactionary, right-winger, stick-in-the-mud (*Inf.*), tory, traditionalist
Antonyms *adj.* imaginative, innovative, liberal, progressive, radical ~*n.* changer, in~ novator, progressive, radical

conservatory glasshouse, greenhouse, hot~ house

conserve go easy on, hoard, husband, keep, nurse, preserve, protect, save, store up, take care of, use sparingly
Antonyms be extravagant, blow (*Sl.*), dissi~ pate, fritter away, misspend, misuse, spend, spend like water, squander, use up, waste

consider 1. chew over, cogitate, consult, contemplate, deliberate, discuss, examine, eye up, meditate, mull over, muse, ponder, reflect, revolve, ruminate, study, think about, turn over in one's mind, weigh, work over 2. believe, deem, hold to be, judge, rate, regard as, think 3. bear in mind, care for, keep in view, make allowance for, reckon with, regard, remember, respect, take into account

considerable 1. abundant, ample, appreci~ able, comfortable, goodly, great, large, lav~ ish, marked, much, noticeable, plentiful, reasonable, sizable, substantial, tidy, toler~ able 2. distinguished, important, in~ fluential, noteworthy, renowned, significant, venerable
Antonyms insignificant, insubstantial, meagre, ordinary, paltry, small, unimportant, unremarkable

considerably appreciably, greatly, mark~ edly, noticeably, remarkably, significantly, substantially, very much

considerate attentive, charitable, circum~ spect, concerned, discreet, forbearing, kind, kindly, mindful, obliging, patient, tactful, thoughtful, unselfish
Antonyms heedless, inconsiderate, selfish, thoughtless

consideration 1. analysis, attention, cogi~ tation, contemplation, deliberation, discus~ sion, examination, perusal, reflection, re~ gard, review, scrutiny, study, thought 2. concern, factor, issue, point 3. concern, considerateness, friendliness, kindliness, kindness, respect, solicitude, tact, thought~ fulness 4. fee, payment, perquisite, recom~ pense, remuneration, reward, tip 5. **take into consideration** bear in mind, make al~ lowance for, take into account, weigh

considering all in all, all things consid~ ered, insomuch as, in the light of, in view of

consignment 1. *Act of consigning* assign~ ment, committal, dispatch, distribution, en~ trusting, handing over, relegation, sending, shipment, transmittal 2. *Something con~ signed* batch, delivery, goods, shipment

consist 1. *With* of amount to, be composed of, be made up of, comprise, contain, em~ body, include, incorporate, involve 2. *With* in be expressed by, be found *or* contained in, inhere, lie, reside

consistent 1. constant, dependable, persis~ tent, regular, steady, true to type, unchang~ ing, undeviating 2. accordant, agreeing, all of a piece, coherent, compatible, congruous, consonant, harmonious, logical
Antonyms (*sense 1*) changing, deviating, er~ ratic, inconsistent, irregular (*sense 2*) contra~ dictory, contrary, discordant, incompatible, incongruous, inconsistent, inharmonious

consolation alleviation, assuagement, cheer, comfort, ease, easement, encourage~ ment, help, relief, solace, succour, support

console assuage, calm, cheer, comfort, en~ courage, express sympathy for, relieve, sol~ ace, soothe
Antonyms aggravate (*Inf.*), agitate, annoy, discomfort, distress, hassle (*Inf.*), hurt, sad~ den, torment, trouble, upset

consolidate 1. amalgamate, cement, com~ bine, compact, condense, conjoin, federate, fuse, harden, join, solidify, thicken, unite 2. fortify, reinforce, secure, stabilize, strengthen

consolidation alliance, amalgamation, as~ sociation, compression, condensation, fed~ eration, fortification, fusion, reinforcement, strengthening

consort *n.* **1.** associate, companion, fellow, husband, partner, significant other (*U.S. inf.*), spouse (*of a reigning monarch*), wife ~*v.* **2.** associate, fraternize, go around with, hang about, around *or* out with, keep company, mingle, mix **3.** accord, agree, correspond, harmonize, square, tally

conspicuous 1. apparent, blatant, clear, discernible, easily seen, evident, manifest, noticeable, obvious, patent, perceptible, visible **2.** celebrated, distinguished, eminent, famous, illustrious, notable, outstanding, prominent, remarkable, signal, striking **3.** blatant, flagrant, flashy, garish, glaring, showy
Antonyms (*sense 1*) concealed, hidden, imperceptible, inconspicuous, indiscernible, invisible, obscure, unnoticeable (*sense 2*) humble, inconspicuous, insignificant, ordinary, unacclaimed, undistinguished, unmemorable, unnotable

conspiracy cabal, collusion, confederacy, frame-up (*Sl.*), intrigue, league, machination, plot, scheme, treason

conspirator cabalist, conspirer, intriguer, plotter, schemer, traitor

conspire 1. cabal, confederate, contrive, devise, hatch treason, intrigue, machinate, manoeuvre, plot, scheme **2.** combine, concur, conduce, contribute, cooperate, tend, work together

constancy decision, determination, devotion, fidelity, firmness, fixedness, permanence, perseverance, regularity, resolution, stability, steadfastness, steadiness, tenacity, uniformity

constant 1. continual, even, firm, fixed, habitual, immovable, immutable, invariable, permanent, perpetual, regular, stable, steadfast, steady, unalterable, unbroken, uniform, unvarying **2.** ceaseless, continual, continuous, endless, eternal, everlasting, incessant, interminable, never-ending, nonstop, perpetual, persistent, relentless, sustained, uninterrupted, unrelenting, unremitting **3.** determined, dogged, persevering, resolute, unflagging, unshaken, unwavering **4.** attached, dependable, devoted, faithful, loyal, stalwart, staunch, tried-and-true, true, trustworthy, trusty, unfailing
Antonyms (*senses 1 & 2*) changeable, changing, deviating, erratic, inconstant, intermittent, irregular, occasional, random, uneven, unstable, unsustained, variable (*sense 4*) disloyal, fickle, irresolute, undependable

constantly all the time, always, aye (*Scot.*), continually, continuously, endlessly, everlastingly, incessantly, interminably, invariably, morning, noon and night, night and day, nonstop, perpetually, persistently, relentlessly

Antonyms (every) now and then, every so often, from time to time, intermittently, irregularly, now and again, occasionally, off and on, periodically, sometimes

consternation alarm, amazement, anxiety, awe, bewilderment, confusion, dismay, distress, dread, fear, fright, horror, panic, shock, terror, trepidation

constituent *adj.* **1.** basic, component, elemental, essential, integral ~*n.* **2.** component, element, essential, factor, ingredient, part, principle, unit **3.** elector, voter

constitute 1. compose, comprise, create, enact, establish, fix, form, found, make, make up, set up **2.** appoint, authorize, commission, delegate, depute, empower, name, nominate, ordain

constitution 1. composition, establishment, formation, organization **2.** build, character, composition, disposition, form, habit, health, make-up, nature, physique, structure, temper, temperament

constitutional *adj.* **1.** congenital, inborn, inherent, intrinsic, organic **2.** chartered, statutory, vested ~*n.* **3.** airing, stroll, turn, walk

constrain 1. bind, coerce, compel, drive, force, impel, necessitate, oblige, pressure, pressurize, urge **2.** chain, check, confine, constrict, curb, hem in, rein, restrain, straiten

constrained embarrassed, forced, guarded, inhibited, reserved, reticent, subdued, unnatural

constraint 1. coercion, compulsion, force, necessity, pressure, restraint **2.** bashfulness, diffidence, embarrassment, inhibition, repression, reservation, restraint, timidity **3.** check, curb, damper, deterrent, hindrance, limitation, rein, restriction

construct assemble, build, compose, create, design, elevate, engineer, erect, establish, fabricate, fashion, form, formulate, found, frame, make, manufacture, organize, put up, raise, set up, shape
Antonyms bulldoze, demolish, destroy, devastate, dismantle, flatten, knock down, level, pull down, raze, tear down

construction 1. assembly, building, composition, creation, edifice, erection, fabric, fabrication, figure, form, formation, shape, structure **2.** explanation, inference, interpretation, reading, rendering

constructive helpful, positive, practical, productive, useful, valuable
Antonyms destructive, futile, ineffective, limp-wristed, negative, unhelpful, unproductive, useless, vain, worthless

consult 1. ask, ask advice of, commune, compare notes, confer, consider, debate, deliberate, interrogate, question, refer to, take counsel, turn to **2.** consider, have regard for, regard, respect, take account of, take into consideration

consultant adviser, authority, specialist

consultation appointment, conference, council, deliberation, dialogue, discussion, examination, hearing, interview, meeting, seminar, session

consume 1. absorb, deplete, dissipate, drain, eat up, employ, exhaust, expend, finish up, fritter away, lavish, lessen, spend, squander, use, use up, utilize, vanish, waste, wear out **2.** devour, eat, eat up, gob~ ble (up), guzzle, polish off (*Inf.*), put away, swallow **3.** annihilate, decay, demolish, de~ stroy, devastate, lay waste, ravage **4.** *Often passive* absorb, devour, dominate, eat up, engross, monopolize, obsess, preoccupy

consumer buyer, customer, purchaser, shopper, user

consuming absorbing, compelling, devour~ ing, engrossing, excruciating, gripping, im~ moderate, overwhelming, tormenting

consummate 1. *v.* accomplish, achieve, carry out, compass, complete, conclude, crown, effectuate, end, finish, perfect, per~ form **2.** *adj.* absolute, accomplished, com~ plete, conspicuous, deep-dyed (*Usually de~ rogatory*), finished, matchless, perfect, pol~ ished, practised, skilled, superb, supreme, total, transcendent, ultimate, unqualified, utter
Antonyms *v.* begin, commence, conceive, get under way, inaugurate, initiate, originate, start

consumption 1. consuming, decay, de~ crease, depletion, destruction, diminution, dissipation, drain, exhaustion, expenditure, loss, use, using up, utilization, waste **2.** *Medical* atrophy, emaciation, phthisis, T.B., tuberculosis

contact *n.* **1.** association, communication, connection **2.** approximation, contiguity, junction, juxtaposition, touch, union **3.** ac~ quaintance, connection ~*v.* **4.** approach, call, communicate with, get *or* be in touch with, get hold of, phone, reach, ring (up) (*Inf., chiefly Brit.*), speak to, write to

contagious catching, communicable, epi~ demic, epizootic (*Veterinary medicine*), in~ fectious, pestiferous, pestilential, spreading, taking (*Inf.*), transmissible

contain 1. accommodate, enclose, have ca~ pacity for, hold, incorporate, seat **2.** com~ prehend, comprise, embody, embrace, in~ clude, involve **3.** control, curb, hold back, hold in, repress, restrain, stifle

container holder, receptacle, repository, vessel

contaminate adulterate, befoul, corrupt, defile, deprave, infect, pollute, radioactivate, smirch, soil, stain, sully, taint, tarnish, vi~ tiate
Antonyms clean, cleanse, decontaminate, deodorize, disinfect, fumigate, purify, sani~ tize, sterilize

contamination adulteration, contagion, corruption, decay, defilement, dirtying, filth, foulness, impurity, infection, poison~ ing, pollution, radioactivation, rottenness, taint

contemplate 1. brood over, consider, de~ liberate, meditate, meditate on, mull over, muse over, observe, ponder, reflect upon, revolve *or* turn over in one's mind, rumi~ nate (upon), study **2.** behold, check out (*Inf.*), examine, eye, eye up, gaze at, inspect, recce (*Sl.*), regard, scrutinize, stare at, sur~ vey, view, weigh **3.** aspire to, consider, de~ sign, envisage, expect, foresee, have in view *or* in mind, intend, mean, plan, propose, think of

contemplation 1. cogitation, considera~ tion, deliberation, meditation, musing, pon~ dering, reflection, reverie, rumination, thought **2.** examination, gazing at, inspec~ tion, looking at, observation, recce (*Sl.*), scrutiny, survey, viewing

contemplative deep *or* lost in thought, in a brown study, intent, introspective, medi~ tative, musing, pensive, rapt, reflective, ru~ minative, thoughtful

contemporary *adj.* **1.** coetaneous (*Rare*), coeval, coexistent, coexisting, concurrent, contemporaneous, synchronous **2.** à la mode, current, happening (*Inf.*), in fashion, latest, modern, newfangled, present, present-day, recent, trendy (*Brit. inf.*), ultramodern, up-to-date, up-to-the-minute, with it (*Inf.*) ~*n.* **3.** compeer, fellow, peer
Antonyms *adj.* antecedent, antique, early, obsolete, old, old-fashioned, out-of-date, passé, succeeding

contempt 1. condescension, contumely, derision, despite (*Archaic*), disdain, disre~ gard, disrespect, mockery, neglect, scorn, slight **2.** *A state of contempt* disgrace, dis~ honour, humiliation, shame
Antonyms admiration, esteem, honour, lik~ ing, regard, respect

contemptible abject, base, cheap, degen~ erate, despicable, detestable, ignominious, low, low-down (*Inf.*), mean, measly, paltry, pitiful, scurvy, shabby, shameful, vile, worthless
Antonyms admirable, attractive, honour~ able, laudable, pleasant, praiseworthy

contemptuous arrogant, cavalier, conde~ scending, contumelious, derisive, disdain~ ful, haughty, high and mighty, insolent, in~

sulting, scornful, sneering, supercilious, withering

Antonyms civil, courteous, deferential, gracious, humble, mannerly, obsequious, polite, respectful

contend 1. clash, compete, contest, cope, emulate, grapple, jostle, litigate, skirmish, strive, struggle, vie **2.** affirm, allege, argue, assert, aver, avow, debate, dispute, hold, maintain

content¹ 1. *v.* appease, delight, gladden, gratify, humour, indulge, mollify, placate, please, reconcile, sate, satisfy, suffice **2.** *n.* comfort, contentment, ease, gratification, peace, peace of mind, pleasure, satisfaction **3.** *adj.* agreeable, at ease, comfortable, contented, fulfilled, satisfied, willing to accept

content² 1. burden, essence, gist, ideas, matter, meaning, significance, substance, text, thoughts **2.** capacity, load, measure, size, volume

contented at ease, at peace, cheerful, comfortable, complacent, content, glad, gratified, happy, pleased, satisfied, serene, thankful

Antonyms annoyed, discontented, displeased, dissatisfied, pissed off (*Taboo sl.*), troubled, uncomfortable, uneasy

contention 1. competition, contest, discord, dispute, dissension, enmity, feuding, hostility, rivalry, row, strife, struggle, wrangling **2.** affirmation, allegation, argument, assertion, asseveration, belief, claim, declaration, ground, idea, maintaining, opinion, position, profession, stand, thesis, view

contentious argumentative, bickering, captious, cavilling, combative, controversial, cross, disputatious, factious, litigious, peevish, perverse, pugnacious, quarrelsome, querulous, wrangling

contentment comfort, complacency, content, contentedness, ease, equanimity, fulfilment, gladness, gratification, happiness, peace, pleasure, repletion, satisfaction, serenity

Antonyms discomfort, discontent, discontentment, displeasure, dissatisfaction, uneasiness, unhappiness

contents 1. constituents, elements, ingredients, load **2.** chapters, divisions, subject matter, subjects, themes, topics

contest *n.* **1.** competition, game, head-to-head, match, tournament, trial **2.** affray, altercation, battle, combat, conflict, controversy, debate, discord, dispute, encounter, fight, shock, struggle ~*v.* **3.** compete, contend, fight, fight over, strive, vie **4.** argue, call in *or* into question, challenge, debate, dispute, doubt, litigate, object to, oppose, question

contestant aspirant, candidate, competitor, contender, entrant, participant, player

context 1. background, connection, frame of reference, framework, relation **2.** ambience, circumstances, conditions, situation

continent abstemious, abstinent, ascetic, austere, celibate, chaste, self-restrained, sober

contingency accident, chance, emergency, event, eventuality, fortuity, happening, incident, juncture, possibility, uncertainty

contingent *adj.* **1.** *With* **on** *or* **upon** conditional, controlled by, dependent, subject to **2.** accidental, casual, fortuitous, haphazard, random, uncertain ~*n.* **3.** batch, body, bunch (*Inf.*), deputation, detachment, group, mission, quota, section, set

continual constant, continuous, endless, eternal, everlasting, frequent, incessant, interminable, oft-repeated, perpetual, recurrent, regular, repeated, repetitive, unceasing, uninterrupted, unremitting

Antonyms broken, ceasing, erratic, fluctuating, fragmentary, infrequent, intermittent, interrupted, irregular, occasional, periodic, spasmodic, sporadic, terminable

continually all the time, always, aye (*Scot.*), constantly, endlessly, eternally, everlastingly, forever, incessantly, interminably, nonstop, persistently, repeatedly

continuance continuation, duration, period, protraction, term

continuation 1. addition, extension, furtherance, postscript, sequel, supplement **2.** maintenance, perpetuation, prolongation, resumption

continue 1. abide, carry on, endure, last, live on, persist, remain, rest, stay, stay on, survive **2.** go on, keep at, keep on, keep the ball rolling, keep up, maintain, persevere, persist in, prolong, pursue, stick at, stick to, sustain **3.** draw out, extend, lengthen, project, prolong, reach **4.** carry on, pick up where one left off, proceed, recommence, resume, return to, take up

Antonyms (*sense 1*) abdicate, leave, quit, resign, retire, step down (*senses 2 & 4*) break off, call it a day, cease, discontinue, give up, leave off, pack in (*Brit. inf.*), quit, stop

continuing enduring, in progress, lasting, ongoing, sustained

continuity cohesion, connection, flow, interrelationship, progression, sequence, succession, whole

continuous connected, constant, continued, extended, prolonged, unbroken, unceasing, undivided, uninterrupted

Antonyms broken, disconnected, ending, inconstant, intermittent, interrupted, occasional, passing, severed, spasmodic

contour curve, figure, form, lines, outline, profile, relief, shape, silhouette

contraband 1. *n.* black-marketing, boot~ legging, moonshine (*U.S.*), rum-running, smuggling, trafficking **2.** *adj.* banned, black-market, bootleg, bootlegged, forbid~ den, hot (*Inf.*), illegal, illicit, interdicted, prohibited, smuggled, unlawful

contract *v.* **1.** abbreviate, abridge, com~ press, condense, confine, constrict, curtail, dwindle, epitomize, knit, lessen, narrow, pucker, purse, reduce, shrink, shrivel, tighten, wither, wrinkle **2.** agree, arrange, bargain, clinch, close, come to terms, com~ mit oneself, covenant, engage, enter into, negotiate, pledge, stipulate **3.** acquire, be afflicted with, catch, develop, get, go down with, incur ~*n.* **4.** agreement, arrangement, bargain, bond, commission, commitment, compact, concordat, convention, covenant, deal (*Inf.*), engagement, pact, settlement, stipulation, treaty, understanding
Antonyms (*sense 1*) broaden, develop, dis~ tend, enlarge, expand, grow, increase, inflate, multiply, spread, stretch, swell, widen (*sense 2*) decline, disagree, refuse, turn down (*sense 3*) avert, avoid, escape, ward off

contraction abbreviation, compression, constriction, diminution, drawing in, eli~ sion, narrowing, reduction, shortening, shrinkage, shrivelling, tensing, tightening

contradict be at variance with, belie, chal~ lenge, contravene, controvert, counter, counteract, deny, dispute, gainsay (*Archaic or literary*), impugn, negate, oppose, rebut
Antonyms affirm, agree, authenticate, confirm, defend, endorse, support, verify

contradiction conflict, confutation, contravention, denial, incongruity, incon~ sistency, negation, opposite

contradictory antagonistic, antithetical, conflicting, contrary, discrepant, incompat~ ible, inconsistent, irreconcilable, opposed, opposite, paradoxical, repugnant

contraption apparatus, contrivance, de~ vice, gadget, instrument, mechanism, rig

contrary *adj.* **1.** adverse, antagonistic, clashing, contradictory, counter, discordant, hostile, inconsistent, inimical, opposed, op~ posite, paradoxical **2.** awkward, balky, can~ tankerous, cussed (*Inf.*), difficult, disoblig~ ing, froward, intractable, obstinate, per~ verse, stroppy (*Brit. sl.*), thrawn (*Northern English dialect*), unaccommodating, way~ ward, wilful ~*n.* **3.** antithesis, converse, opposite, reverse **4. on the contrary** con~ versely, in contrast, not at all, on the other hand, quite the opposite *or* reverse
Antonyms (*sense 1*) accordant, congruous, consistent, harmonious, in agreement, paral~ lel, unopposed (*sense 2*) accommodating,

agreeable, amiable, cooperative, eager to please, helpful, obliging, tractable, willing

contrast 1. *n.* comparison, contrariety, dif~ ference, differentiation, disparity, dissimi~ larity, distinction, divergence, foil, opposi~ tion **2.** *v.* compare, differ, differentiate, dis~ tinguish, oppose, set in opposition, set off

contribute 1. add, afford, bestow, chip in (*Inf.*), donate, furnish, give, provide, sub~ scribe, supply **2.** be conducive, be instru~ mental, be partly responsible for, conduce, help, lead, tend

contribution addition, bestowal, donation, gift, grant, input, offering, stipend, sub~ scription

contributor 1. backer, bestower, conferrer, donor, giver, patron, subscriber, supporter **2.** correspondent, freelance, freelancer, journalist, journo (*Sl.*), reporter

contrite chastened, conscience-stricken, humble, in sackcloth and ashes, penitent, regretful, remorseful, repentant, sorrowful, sorry

contrivance 1. artifice, design, dodge, ex~ pedient, fabrication, formation, intrigue, inventiveness, machination, measure, plan, plot, project, ruse, scheme, stratagem, trick **2.** apparatus, appliance, contraption, device, equipment, gadget, gear, implement, in~ strument, invention, machine, mechanism

contrive 1. concoct, construct, create, de~ sign, devise, engineer, fabricate, frame, im~ provise, invent, manufacture, wangle (*Inf.*) **2.** arrange, bring about, effect, hit upon, manage, manoeuvre, plan, plot, scheme, succeed

contrived artificial, elaborate, forced, la~ boured, overdone, planned, recherché, strained, unnatural
Antonyms genuine, natural, relaxed, spon~ taneous, unaffected, unconstrained, un~ feigned, unforced, unpretentious

control *v.* **1.** administer, boss (*Inf.*), call the tune, command, conduct, direct, dominate, govern, handle, have charge of, hold the purse strings, lead, manage, manipulate, oversee, pilot, reign over, rule, steer, superintend, supervise **2.** bridle, check, constrain, contain, curb, hold back, limit, master, rein in, repress, restrain, subdue **3.** *Used of a machine, an experiment, etc.* counteract, determine, monitor, regulate, verify ~*n.* **4.** authority, charge, command, direction, discipline, government, guidance, jurisdiction, management, mastery, over~ sight, rule, superintendence, supervision, supremacy **5.** brake, check, curb, limita~ tion, regulation, restraint

controls console, control panel, dash, dash~ board, dials, instruments

controversial at issue, contended, contentious, controvertible, debatable, disputable, disputed, open to question, polemic, under discussion

controversy altercation, argument, contention, debate, discussion, dispute, dissension, polemic, quarrel, row, squabble, strife, wrangle, wrangling

convalescence improvement, recovery, recuperation, rehabilitation, return to health

convalescent *adj.* getting better, improving, mending, on the mend, recovering, recuperating

convene assemble, bring together, call, come together, congregate, convoke, gather, meet, muster, rally, summon

convenience 1. accessibility, appropriateness, availability, fitness, handiness, opportuneness, serviceability, suitability, usefulness, utility **2.** *A convenient time or situation* chance, leisure, opportunity, spare moment, spare time **3.** accommodation, advantage, benefit, comfort, ease, enjoyment, satisfaction, service, use **4.** *A useful device* amenity, appliance, comfort, facility, help, labour-saving device
Antonyms discomfort, hardship, inconvenience, uselessness

convenient 1. adapted, appropriate, beneficial, commodious, fit, fitted, handy, helpful, labour-saving, opportune, seasonable, serviceable, suitable, suited, timely, useful, well-timed **2.** accessible, at hand, available, close at hand, handy, just round the corner, nearby, within reach
Antonyms awkward, distant, inaccessible, inconvenient, out-of-the-way, unsuitable, useless

convent convent school, nunnery, religious community

convention 1. assembly, conference, congress, convocation, council, delegates, meeting, representatives **2.** code, custom, etiquette, formality, practice, propriety, protocol, tradition, usage **3.** agreement, bargain, compact, concordat, contract, pact, protocol, stipulation, treaty

conventional 1. accepted, common, correct, customary, decorous, expected, formal, habitual, normal, ordinary, orthodox, prevailing, prevalent, proper, regular, ritual, standard, traditional, usual, wonted **2.** banal, bourgeois, commonplace, hackneyed, hidebound, pedestrian, prosaic, routine, run-of-the-mill, stereotyped, unoriginal
Antonyms abnormal, off-the-wall (*Sl.*), uncommon, unconventional, unorthodox

converge coincide, combine, come together, concentrate, focus, gather, join, meet, merge, mingle

conversant *Usually with* **with** acquainted, *au fait*, experienced, familiar, knowledgeable, practised, proficient, skilled, versed, well-informed, well up in (*Inf.*)

conversation chat, chinwag (*Brit. inf.*), colloquy, communication, communion, confab (*Inf.*), confabulation, conference, converse, dialogue, discourse, discussion, exchange, gossip, intercourse, powwow, talk, tête-à-tête

conversational chatty, colloquial, communicative, informal

converse 1. *n.* antithesis, contrary, obverse, opposite, other side of the coin, reverse **2.** *adj.* contrary, counter, opposite, reverse, reversed, transposed

conversion 1. change, metamorphosis, transfiguration, transformation, transmogrification (*Jocular*), transmutation **2.** adaptation, alteration, modification, reconstruction, remodelling, reorganization **3.** change of heart, proselytization, rebirth, reformation, regeneration

convert[1] *v.* **1.** alter, change, interchange, metamorphose, transform, transmogrify (*Jocular*), transmute, transpose, turn **2.** adapt, apply, appropriate, modify, remodel, reorganize, restyle, revise **3.** baptize, bring to God, convince, proselytize, reform, regenerate, save

convert[2] *n.* catechumen, disciple, neophyte, proselyte

convex bulging, gibbous, outcurved, protuberant, rounded
Antonyms concave, cupped, depressed, excavated, hollowed, indented, sunken

convey 1. bear, bring, carry, conduct, fetch, forward, grant, guide, move, send, support, transmit, transport **2.** communicate, disclose, impart, make known, relate, reveal, tell **3.** *Law* bequeath, cede, deliver, demise, devolve, grant, lease, transfer, will

conveyance 1. carriage, movement, transfer, transference, transmission, transport, transportation **2.** transport, vehicle

convict 1. *v.* condemn, find guilty, imprison, pronounce guilty, sentence **2.** *n.* con (*Sl.*), criminal, culprit, felon, jailbird, lag (*Sl.*), malefactor, prisoner, villain

conviction 1. assurance, certainty, certitude, confidence, earnestness, fervour, firmness, reliance **2.** belief, creed, faith, opinion, persuasion, principle, tenet, view

convince assure, bring round, gain the confidence of, persuade, prevail upon, prove to, satisfy, sway, win over

convincing cogent, conclusive, credible, impressive, incontrovertible, likely, persuasive, plausible, powerful, probable, telling, verisimilar

Antonyms beyond belief, dubious, far-fetched, implausible, improbable, inconclusive, incredible, unconvincing, unlikely

convoy 1. *n.* armed guard, attendance, attendant, escort, guard, protection **2.** *v.* accompany, attend, escort, guard, pilot, protect, shepherd, usher

convulse agitate, churn up, derange, disorder, disturb, shake, shatter, twist, work

convulsion 1. agitation, commotion, disturbance, furore, shaking, tumult, turbulence, upheaval **2.** contortion, contraction, cramp, fit, paroxysm, seizure, spasm, throe (*Rare*), tremor

cook up concoct, contrive, devise, dream up, fabricate, improvise, invent, manufacture, plot, prepare, scheme, trump up

cool *adj.* **1.** chilled, chilling, chilly, coldish, nippy, refreshing **2.** calm, collected, composed, deliberate, dispassionate, imperturbable, laid-back (*Inf.*), level-headed, placid, quiet, relaxed, sedate, self-controlled, self-possessed, serene, together (*Sl.*), unemotional, unexcited, unfazed (*Inf.*), unruffled **3.** aloof, apathetic, distant, frigid, incurious, indifferent, lukewarm, offhand, reserved, standoffish, uncommunicative, unconcerned, unenthusiastic, unfriendly, uninterested, unresponsive, unwelcoming **4.** audacious, bold, brazen, cheeky, impertinent, impudent, presumptuous, shameless **5.** *Inf.* cosmopolitan, elegant, sophisticated, urbane ~*v.* **6.** chill, cool off, freeze, lose heat, refrigerate **7.** abate, allay, assuage, calm (down), dampen, lessen, moderate, quiet, temper ~*n.* **8.** *Sl.* calmness, composure, control, poise, self-control, self-discipline, self-possession, temper

Antonyms *adj.* (*sense 1*) lukewarm, moderately hot, sunny, tepid, warm (*sense 2*) agitated, delirious, excited, impassioned, nervous, overwrought, perturbed, tense, troubled, twitchy (*Inf.*) (*sense 3*) amiable, chummy (*Inf.*), cordial, friendly, outgoing, receptive, responsive, sociable, warm ~*v.* (*sense 6*) heat, reheat, take the chill off, thaw, warm, warm up

coop 1. *n.* box, cage, enclosure, hutch, pen, pound **2.** *v.* cage, confine, immure, impound, imprison, pen, pound, shut up

cooperate abet, aid, assist, collaborate, combine, concur, conduce, conspire, contribute, coordinate, go along with, help, join forces, pitch in, play ball (*Inf.*), pool resources, pull together, work together

Antonyms conflict, contend with, fight, hamper, hamstring, hinder, impede, obstruct, oppose, prevent, put the mockers on (*Inf.*), resist, struggle against, stymie, thwart

cooperation assistance, collaboration, combined effort, concert, concurrence, esprit de corps, give-and-take, helpfulness, participation, responsiveness, teamwork, unity

Antonyms discord, dissension, hindrance, opposition, rivalry

cooperative 1. accommodating, helpful, obliging, responsive, supportive **2.** coactive, collective, combined, concerted, coordinated, joint, shared, unified, united

coordinate 1. *v.* correlate, harmonize, integrate, match, mesh, organize, relate, synchronize, systematize **2.** *adj.* coequal, correlative, correspondent, equal, equivalent, parallel, tantamount

cope 1. carry on, get by (*Inf.*), hold one's own, make out (*Inf.*), make the grade, manage, rise to the occasion, struggle through, survive **2. cope with** contend, deal, dispatch, encounter, grapple, handle, struggle, tangle, tussle, weather, wrestle

copious abundant, ample, bounteous, bountiful, extensive, exuberant, full, generous, lavish, liberal, luxuriant, overflowing, plenteous, plentiful, profuse, rich, superabundant

copulate ball (*Taboo sl., chiefly U.S.*), bonk (*Inf.*), fuck (*Taboo sl.*), have intercourse, have sex, hump (*Taboo sl.*), screw (*Taboo sl.*), shag (*Taboo sl., chiefly Brit.*)

copy *n.* **1.** archetype, carbon copy, counterfeit, duplicate, facsimile, fake, fax, forgery, image, imitation, likeness, model, pattern, photocopy, Photostat (*Trademark*), print, replica, replication, representation, reproduction, transcription, Xerox (*Trademark*) ~*v.* **2.** counterfeit, duplicate, photocopy, Photostat (*Trademark*), replicate, reproduce, transcribe, Xerox (*Trademark*) **3.** ape, echo, emulate, follow, follow suit, follow the example of, imitate, mimic, mirror, parrot, repeat, simulate

Antonyms *n.* model, original, pattern, prototype, the real thing ~*v.* create, originate

cord line, rope, string, twine

cordial affable, affectionate, agreeable, cheerful, congenial, earnest, friendly, genial, heartfelt, hearty, invigorating, sociable, warm, warm-hearted, welcoming, whole-hearted

Antonyms aloof, cold, distant, formal, frigid, reserved, unfriendly, ungracious

cordiality affability, amiability, friendliness, geniality, heartiness, sincerity, warmth, wholeheartedness

cordon 1. *n.* barrier, chain, line, ring **2.** *v.* **cordon off** close off, encircle, enclose, fence off, isolate, picket, separate, surround

core centre, crux, essence, gist, heart, kernel, nub, nucleus, pith

corner *n.* **1.** angle, bend, crook, joint **2.** cavity, cranny, hideaway, hide-out, hidey-hole (*Inf.*), hole, niche, nook, recess, retreat **3.** hole (*Inf.*), hot water (*Inf.*), pickle (*Inf.*), predicament, spot (*Inf.*), tight spot ~*v.* **4.** bring to bay, run to earth, trap **5.** *As in* **corner the market** dominate, engross, hog (*Sl.*), monopolize

cornerstone 1. quoin **2.** basis, bedrock, key, premise, starting point

corny banal, commonplace, dull, feeble, hackneyed, maudlin, mawkish, old-fashioned, old hat, sentimental, stale, stereotyped, trite

corporal anatomical, bodily, carnal, corporeal (*Archaic*), fleshly, material, physical, somatic

corporate allied, collaborative, collective, combined, communal, joint, merged, pooled, shared, united

corporation 1. association, corporate body, society **2.** civic authorities, council, municipal authorities, town council **3.** *Inf.* beer belly (*Inf.*), paunch, pod, pot, potbelly, spare tyre, spread (*Inf.*)

corps band, body, company, contingent, crew, detachment, division, regiment, squad, squadron, team, troop, unit

corpse body, cadaver, carcass, remains, stiff (*Sl.*)

corpulent beefy (*Inf.*), bulky, burly, fat, fattish, fleshy, large, lusty, obese, overweight, plump, portly, roly-poly, rotund, stout, tubby, well-padded
Antonyms anorexic, bony, emaciated, gaunt, scrawny, skin and bones (*Inf.*), skinny, slim, thin, thin as a rake, underweight

correct *v.* **1.** adjust, amend, cure, emend, improve, rectify, redress, reform, regulate, remedy, right **2.** admonish, chasten, chastise, chide, discipline, punish, reprimand, reprove ~*adj.* **3.** accurate, equitable, exact, faultless, flawless, just, O.K. *or* okay (*Inf.*), precise, regular, right, strict, true **4.** acceptable, appropriate, diplomatic, fitting, kosher (*Inf.*), O.K. *or* okay (*Inf.*), proper, seemly, standard
Antonyms *v.* (*sense 1*) damage, harm, impair, ruin, spoil (*sense 2*) compliment, excuse, praise ~*adj.* (*sense 3*) false, inaccurate, incorrect, untrue, wrong (*sense 4*) improper, inappropriate, unacceptable, unfitting, unsuitable

correction 1. adjustment, alteration, amendment, emendation, improvement, modification, rectification, righting **2.** admonition, castigation, chastisement, discipline, punishment, reformation, reproof

corrective *adj.* **1.** palliative, rehabilitative, remedial, restorative, therapeutic **2.** disciplinary, penal, punitive, reformatory

correctly accurately, aright, perfectly, precisely, properly, right, rightly

correctness 1. accuracy, exactitude, exactness, faultlessness, fidelity, preciseness, precision, regularity, truth **2.** *bon ton*, civility, decorum, good breeding, propriety, seemliness

correlate associate, compare, connect, co-ordinate, correspond, equate, interact, parallel, tie in

correlation alternation, correspondence, equivalence, interaction, interchange, interdependence, interrelationship, reciprocity

correspond 1. accord, agree, be consistent, coincide, complement, conform, correlate, dovetail, fit, harmonize, match, square, tally **2.** communicate, exchange letters, keep in touch, write
Antonyms be at variance, be dissimilar, be inconsistent, belie, be unlike, differ, disagree, diverge, vary

correspondence 1. agreement, analogy, coincidence, comparability, comparison, concurrence, conformity, congruity, correlation, fitness, harmony, match, relation, similarity **2.** communication, letters, mail, post, writing

correspondent *n.* **1.** letter writer, pen friend *or* pal **2.** contributor, gazetteer (*Archaic*), journalist, journo (*Sl.*), reporter, special correspondent ~*adj.* **3.** analogous, comparable, like, parallel, reciprocal, similar

corresponding analogous, answering, complementary, correlative, correspondent, equivalent, identical, interrelated, matching, reciprocal, similar, synonymous

corridor aisle, alley, hallway, passage, passageway

corroborate authenticate, back up, bear out, confirm, document, endorse, establish, ratify, substantiate, support, sustain, validate
Antonyms contradict, disprove, invalidate, negate, rebut, refute

corrode canker, consume, corrupt, deteriorate, eat away, erode, gnaw, impair, oxidize, rust, waste, wear away

corrosive 1. acrid, biting, caustic, consuming, corroding, erosive, virulent, vitriolic, wasting, wearing **2.** caustic, cutting, incisive, mordant, sarcastic, trenchant, venomous, vitriolic

corrugated channelled, creased, crinkled, fluted, furrowed, grooved, puckered, ridged, rumpled, wrinkled

corrupt *adj.* **1.** bent (*Sl.*), bribable, crooked (*Inf.*), dishonest, fraudulent, rotten, shady (*Inf.*), unethical, unprincipled, unscrupulous, venal **2.** abandoned, debased, defiled, degenerate, demoralized, depraved, dishon-

oured, dissolute, profligate, vicious ~v. **3.** bribe, buy off, debauch, demoralize, deprave, entice, fix (*Inf.*), grease (someone's) palm (*Sl.*), lure, pervert, square, suborn, subvert ~adj. **4.** adulterated, altered, contaminated, decayed, defiled, distorted, doctored, falsified, infected, polluted, putrescent, putrid, rotten, tainted ~v. **5.** adulterate, contaminate, debase, defile, doctor, infect, putrefy, spoil, taint, tamper with, vitiate
Antonyms adj. (*senses 1 & 2*) ethical, honest, honourable, moral, noble, principled, righteous, scrupulous, straight, undefiled, upright, virtuous ~v. (*sense 3*) correct, purify, reform

corruption 1. breach of trust, bribery, bribing, crookedness (*Inf.*), demoralization, dishonesty, extortion, fiddling (*Inf.*), fraud, fraudulency, graft (*Inf.*), jobbery, profiteering, shadiness, shady dealings (*Inf.*), unscrupulousness, venality **2.** baseness, decadence, degeneration, degradation, depravity, evil, immorality, impurity, iniquity, perversion, profligacy, sinfulness, turpitude, vice, viciousness, wickedness **3.** adulteration, debasement, decay, defilement, distortion, doctoring, falsification, foulness, infection, pollution, putrefaction, putrescence, rot, rottenness

corset 1. belt, bodice, corselet, foundation garment, girdle, panty girdle, stays (*Rare*) **2.** *Fig.* check, curb, limitation, restriction

cosmetic adj. beautifying, nonessential, superficial, surface, touching-up

cosmic grandiose, huge, immense, infinite, limitless, measureless, universal, vast

cosmonaut astronaut, spaceman, space pilot

cosmopolitan 1. adj. broad-minded, catholic, open-minded, sophisticated, universal, urbane, well-travelled, worldly, worldly-wise **2.** n. cosmopolite, jetsetter, man or woman of the world, sophisticate
Antonyms adj. hidebound, illiberal, insular, limited, narrow-minded, parochial, provincial, restricted, rustic, unsophisticated

cost n. **1.** amount, charge, damage (*Inf.*), expenditure, expense, figure, outlay, payment, price, rate, worth **2.** damage, deprivation, detriment, expense, harm, hurt, injury, loss, penalty, sacrifice, suffering ~v. **3.** come to, command a price of, sell at, set (someone) back (*Inf.*) **4.** *Fig.* do disservice to, harm, hurt, injure, lose, necessitate

costly 1. dear, excessive, exorbitant, expensive, extortionate, highly-priced, steep (*Inf.*), stiff, valuable **2.** gorgeous, lavish, luxurious, opulent, precious, priceless, rich, splendid, sumptuous **3.** *Entailing loss or sacrifice* catastrophic, damaging, deleteri-

ous, disastrous, harmful, loss-making, ruinous, sacrificial
Antonyms (*sense 1*) cheap, cheapo (*Inf.*), dirt-cheap, economical, fair, inexpensive, low-priced, reasonable, reduced

costs 1. budget, expenses, outgoings **2. at all costs** at any price, no matter what, regardless, without fail

costume apparel, attire, clothing, dress, ensemble, garb, get-up (*Inf.*), livery, national dress, outfit, robes, uniform

cosy comfortable, comfy (*Inf.*), cuddled up, homely, intimate, secure, sheltered, snug, snuggled down, tucked up, warm

cottage but-and-ben (*Scot.*), cabin, chalet, cot, hut, lodge, shack

couch 1. v. express, frame, phrase, set forth, utter, word **2.** n. bed, chaise longue, chesterfield, daybed, divan, ottoman, settee, sofa

cough 1. n. bark, frog or tickle in one's throat, hack **2.** v. bark, clear one's throat, hack, hawk, hem

cough up ante up (*Inf., chiefly U.S.*), come across, deliver, fork out (*Sl.*), give up, hand over, shell out (*Inf.*), surrender

council assembly, board, cabinet, chamber, committee, conclave, conference, congress, convention, convocation, diet, governing body, house, ministry, panel, parliament, synod

counsel n. **1.** admonition, advice, caution, consideration, consultation, deliberation, direction, forethought, guidance, information, recommendation, suggestion, warning **2.** advocate, attorney, barrister, lawyer, legal adviser, solicitor ~v. **3.** admonish, advise, advocate, caution, exhort, instruct, prescribe, recommend, urge, warn

count v. **1.** add (up), calculate, cast up, check, compute, enumerate, estimate, number, reckon, score, tally, tot up **2.** consider, deem, esteem, impute, judge, look upon, rate, regard, think **3.** carry weight, cut any ice (*Inf.*), enter into consideration, matter, rate, signify, tell, weigh **4.** include, number among, take into account or consideration ~n. **5.** calculation, computation, enumeration, numbering, poll, reckoning, sum, tally

countenance n. **1.** appearance, aspect, expression, face, features, look, mien, physiognomy, visage **2.** aid, approval, assistance, backing, endorsement, favour, sanction, support ~v. **3.** abet, aid, approve, back, champion, condone, encourage, endorse, help, sanction, support **4.** brook, endure, put up with (*Inf.*), stand for (*Inf.*), tolerate

counter 1. adv. against, at variance with, contrarily, contrariwise, conversely, in defiance of, versus **2.** adj. adverse, against,

conflicting, contradictory, contrary, con~
trasting, obverse, opposed, opposing, oppo~
site **3.** *v.* answer, hit back, meet, offset,
parry, resist, respond, retaliate, return,
ward off
Antonyms *adj.* accordant, parallel, similar
~*v.* accept, give in, surrender, take, yield

counteract annul, check, contravene,
counterbalance, countervail, cross, defeat,
foil, frustrate, hinder, invalidate, negate,
neutralize, obviate, offset, oppose, resist,
thwart

counterbalance balance, compensate,
counterpoise, countervail, make up for, off~
set, set off

counterfeit 1. *v.* copy, fabricate, fake,
feign, forge, imitate, impersonate, pretend,
sham, simulate **2.** *adj.* bogus, copied, ersatz,
faked, false, feigned, forged, fraudulent,
imitation, phoney *or* phony (*Inf.*), pseud
(*Inf.*), pseudo (*Inf.*), sham, simulated, spuri~
ous, suppositious **3.** *n.* copy, fake, forgery,
fraud, imitation, phoney *or* phony (*Inf.*), re~
production, sham
Antonyms authentic, genuine, good, origi~
nal, real, the real thing

countermand annul, cancel, override, re~
peal, rescind, retract, reverse, revoke

counterpart complement, copy, correlative,
duplicate, equal, fellow, match, mate, oppo~
site number, supplement, tally, twin

countless endless, immeasurable, incalcu~
lable, infinite, innumerable, legion, limit~
less, measureless, multitudinous, myriad,
numberless, uncounted, untold
Antonyms finite, limited, restricted

count on *or* **upon** bank on, believe (in),
depend on, lean on, pin one's faith on,
reckon on, rely on, take for granted, take
on trust, trust

count out disregard, except, exclude, leave
out, leave out of account, pass over

country *n.* **1.** commonwealth, kingdom, na~
tion, people, realm, sovereign state, state **2.**
fatherland, homeland, motherland, nation~
ality, native land, *patria* **3.** land, part, re~
gion, terrain, territory **4.** citizenry, citizens,
community, electors, grass roots, inhabit~
ants, nation, people, populace, public, soci~
ety, voters **5.** backwoods, boondocks (*U.S.
sl.*), countryside, farmland, green belt, out~
back (*Aust. & N.Z.*), outdoors, provinces,
rural areas, sticks (*Inf.*), the back of be~
yond, the middle of nowhere, wide open
spaces (*Inf.*) ~*adj.* **6.** agrarian, agrestic,
Arcadian, bucolic, georgic (*Literary*), land~
ed, pastoral, provincial, rural, rustic
Antonyms *n.* (*sense 5*) city, metropolis, town
~*adj.* city, cosmopolitan, sophisticated,
urban, urbane

countryman 1. bumpkin, country dweller,

farmer, hayseed (*U.S. & Canad. inf.*), hick
(*Inf., chiefly U.S. & Canad.*), hind (*Obsolete*),
husbandman, peasant, provincial, rustic,
swain, yokel **2.** compatriot, fellow citizen

countryside country, farmland, green belt,
outback (*Aust. & N.Z.*), outdoors, panorama,
sticks (*Inf.*), view, wide open spaces (*Inf.*)

count up add, reckon up, sum, tally, total

county 1. *n.* province, shire **2.** *adj.* green~
wellie, huntin', shootin', and fishin' (*Inf.*),
plummy (*Inf.*), tweedy, upper-class, upper-
crust (*Inf.*)

coup accomplishment, action, deed, exploit,
feat, manoeuvre, masterstroke, stratagem,
stroke, stroke of genius, stunt, *tour de force*

couple 1. *n.* brace, duo, item, pair, span (*of
horses or oxen*), twain (*Archaic*), twosome **2.**
v. buckle, clasp, conjoin, connect, hitch,
join, link, marry, pair, unite, wed, yoke

coupon card, certificate, detachable portion,
slip, ticket, token, voucher

courage balls (*Taboo sl.*), ballsiness (*Taboo
sl.*), boldness, bottle (*Brit. sl.*), bravery, dar~
ing, dauntlessness, fearlessness, firmness,
fortitude, gallantry, grit, guts (*Inf.*), hardi~
hood, heroism, intrepidity, lion-heartedness,
mettle, nerve, pluck, resolution, spunk
(*Inf.*), valour
Antonyms cowardice, faint-heartedness,
fear, timidity

courageous audacious, ballsy (*Taboo sl.*),
bold, brave, daring, dauntless, fearless, gal~
lant, gritty, hardy, heroic, indomitable, in~
trepid, lion-hearted, plucky, resolute, stal~
wart, stouthearted, valiant, valorous
Antonyms chicken (*Sl.*), chicken-hearted,
chickenshit (*U.S. sl.*), cowardly, craven, das~
tardly, faint-hearted, gutless (*Inf.*), lily-
livered, pusillanimous, scared, spineless,
timid, timorous, yellow (*Inf.*)

course *n.* **1.** advance, advancement, conti~
nuity, development, flow, furtherance,
march, movement, order, progress, pro~
gression, sequence, succession, unfolding **2.**
channel, direction, line, orbit, passage,
path, road, route, tack, track, trail, trajec~
tory, way **3.** duration, lapse, passage, pass~
ing, sweep, term, time **4.** behaviour, con~
duct, manner, method, mode, plan, policy,
procedure, programme, regimen **5.** cinder
track, circuit, lap, race, racecourse, round
6. classes, course of study, curriculum, lec~
tures, programme, schedule, studies ~*v.* **7.**
dash, flow, gush, move apace, race, run,
scud, scurry, speed, stream, surge, tumble
8. chase, follow, hunt, pursue **9. in due
course** eventually, finally, in the course of
time, in the end, in time, sooner or later
10. of course certainly, definitely, indubi~
tably, naturally, obviously, undoubtedly,
without a doubt

court *n.* **1.** cloister, courtyard, piazza, plaza, quad (*Inf.*), quadrangle, square, yard **2.** hall, manor, palace **3.** attendants, cortege, entourage, retinue, royal household, suite, train **4.** bar, bench, court of justice, lawcourt, seat of judgment, tribunal **5.** ad~ dresses, attention, homage, respects, suit ~*v.* **6.** chase, date, go (out) with, go steady with (*Inf.*), keep company with, make love to, pay court to, pay one's addresses to, pursue, run after, serenade, set one's cap at, sue (*Archaic*), take out, walk out with, woo **7.** cultivate, curry favour with, fawn upon, flatter, pander to, seek, solicit **8.** attract, bring about, incite, invite, prompt, provoke, seek

courteous affable, attentive, ceremonious, civil, courtly, elegant, gallant, gracious, mannerly, polished, polite, refined, respect~ ful, urbane, well-bred, well-mannered
Antonyms discourteous, disrespectful, ill- mannered, impolite, insolent, rude, uncivil, ungracious, unkind

courtesy 1. affability, civility, courteous~ ness, courtliness, elegance, gallantness, gal~ lantry, good breeding, good manners, gra~ ciousness, polish, politeness, urbanity **2.** benevolence, consent, consideration, favour, generosity, indulgence, kindness

courtier attendant, follower, henchman, liegeman, pursuivant (*History*), squire, train-bearer

courtly affable, aristocratic, ceremonious, chivalrous, civil, decorous, dignified, el~ egant, flattering, formal, gallant, highbred, lordly, obliging, polished, refined, stately, urbane

courtship courting, engagement, keeping company, pursuit, romance, suit, wooing

courtyard area, enclosure, peristyle, play~ ground, quad, quadrangle, yard

cove anchorage, bay, bayou, creek, firth *or* frith (*Scot.*), inlet, sound

covenant *n.* **1.** arrangement, bargain, com~ mitment, compact, concordat, contract, convention, pact, promise, stipulation, trea~ ty, trust **2.** bond, deed ~*v.* **3.** agree, bar~ gain, contract, engage, pledge, stipulate, undertake

cover *v.* **1.** camouflage, cloak, conceal, cover up, curtain, disguise, eclipse, enshroud, hide, hood, house, mask, obscure, screen, secrete, shade, shroud, veil ~*n.* **2.** cloak, cover-up, disguise, façade, front, mask, pre~ tence, screen, smoke screen, veil, window- dressing ~*v.* **3.** defend, guard, protect, re~ inforce, shelter, shield, watch over ~*n.* **4.** camouflage, concealment, defence, guard, hiding place, protection, refuge, sanctuary, shelter, shield, undergrowth, woods ~*v.* **5.** canopy, clothe, coat, daub, dress, encase,

envelop, invest, layer, mantle, overlay, overspread, put on, wrap ~*n.* **6.** binding, canopy, cap, case, clothing, coating, cover~ ing, dress, envelope, jacket, lid, sheath, top, wrapper ~*v.* **7.** comprehend, comprise, consider, contain, deal with, embody, em~ brace, encompass, examine, include, incor~ porate, involve, provide for, refer to, sur~ vey, take account of **8.** double for, fill in for, relieve, stand in for, substitute, take over, take the rap for (*Sl.*) **9.** describe, de~ tail, investigate, narrate, recount, relate, report, tell of, write up **10.** balance, com~ pensate, counterbalance, insure, make good, make up for, offset ~*n.* **11.** compensation, indemnity, insurance, payment, protection, reimbursement ~*v.* **12.** cross, pass through *or* over, range, travel over, traverse **13.** engulf, flood, overrun, submerge, wash over
Antonyms *v.* exclude, exhibit, expose, omit, reveal, show, unclothe, uncover, unmask, un~ wrap ~*n.* base, bottom

covering 1. *n.* blanket, casing, clothing, coating, cover, housing, layer, overlay, pro~ tection, shelter, top, wrap, wrapper, wrap~ ping **2.** *adj.* accompanying, descriptive, ex~ planatory, introductory

cover-up complicity, concealment, con~ spiracy, front, smoke screen, whitewash (*Inf.*)

cover up 1. conceal, cover one's tracks, feign ignorance, hide, hush up, keep dark, keep secret, keep silent about, keep under one's hat (*Inf.*), repress, stonewall, suppress, whitewash (*Inf.*) **2.** Artex (*Trademark*), coat, cover, encrust, envelop, hide, plaster, slather (*U.S. sl.*), swathe

covet aspire to, begrudge, crave, desire, envy, fancy (*Inf.*), hanker after, have one's eye on, long for, lust after, thirst for, yearn for

covetous acquisitive, avaricious, close- fisted, envious, grasping, greedy, jealous, mercenary, rapacious, yearning

cow awe, browbeat, bully, daunt, dishearten, dismay, frighten, intimidate, overawe, psych out (*Inf.*), scare, subdue, terrorize, unnerve

coward caitiff (*Archaic*), chicken (*Sl.*), cra~ ven, dastard (*Archaic*), faint-heart, funk (*Inf.*), poltroon, recreant (*Archaic*), ren~ egade, scaredy-cat (*Inf.*), skulker, sneak, wimp (*Inf.*), yellow-belly (*Sl.*)

cowardly abject, base, caitiff (*Archaic*), chicken (*Sl.*), chicken-hearted, chickenshit (*U.S. sl.*), craven, dastardly, faint-hearted, fearful, gutless (*Inf.*), lily-livered, pusillani~ mous, recreant (*Archaic*), scared, shrinking, soft, spineless, timorous, weak, weak-kneed (*Inf.*), white-livered, yellow (*Inf.*)
Antonyms audacious, bold, brave, coura~

geous, daring, dauntless, doughty, intrepid, plucky, valiant

cowboy broncobuster (*U.S.*), cattleman, cowhand, cowpuncher (*U.S. inf.*), drover, gaucho (*S. American*), herder, herdsman, rancher, ranchero (*U.S.*), stockman, wran~ gler (*U.S.*)

cower cringe, crouch, draw back, fawn, flinch, grovel, quail, shrink, skulk, sneak, tremble, truckle

coy arch, backward, bashful, coquettish, de~ mure, evasive, flirtatious, kittenish, modest, overmodest, prudish, reserved, retiring, self-effacing, shrinking, shy, skittish, timid
Antonyms bold, brash, brass-necked (*Brit. inf.*), brassy (*Inf.*), brazen, flip (*Inf.*), forward, impertinent, impudent, pert, pushy (*Inf.*), saucy, shameless

crabbed 1. acrid, acrimonious, captious, churlish, cross, cynical, difficult, fretful, harsh, ill-tempered, irritable, morose, per~ verse, petulant, prickly, ratty (*Brit. & N.Z. inf.*), sour, splenetic, surly, tart, testy, tetchy, tough, trying **2.** *Of handwriting* awkward, cramped, hieroglyphical, illegible, indecipherable, laboured, squeezed, un~ readable

crack v. **1.** break, burst, chip, chop, cleave, crackle, craze, fracture, rive, snap, splinter, split ~n. **2.** breach, break, chink, chip, cleft, cranny, crevice, fissure, fracture, gap, interstice, rift ~v. **3.** burst, crash, detonate, explode, pop, ring, snap ~n. **4.** burst, clap, crash, explosion, pop, report, snap ~v. **5.** break down, collapse, give way, go to pieces, lose control, succumb, yield ~v./n. **6.** *Inf.* buffet, clip (*Inf.*), clout (*Inf.*), cuff, slap, thump, wallop (*Inf.*), whack ~v. **7.** de~ cipher, fathom, get the answer to, solve, work out ~n. **8.** *Inf.* attempt, go (*Inf.*), op~ portunity, stab (*Inf.*), try **9.** *Sl.* dig, funny remark, gag (*Inf.*), insult, jibe, joke, quip, smart-alecky remark, wisecrack, witticism ~*adj.* **10.** *Sl.* ace, choice, elite, excellent, first-class, first-rate, hand-picked, superior, world-class

cracked 1. broken, chipped, crazed, dam~ aged, defective, faulty, fissured, flawed, im~ perfect, split **2.** *Sl.* bats (*Sl.*), batty (*Sl.*), crackbrained, crackpot (*Inf.*), crazy (*Inf.*), daft (*Inf.*), eccentric, insane, loony (*Sl.*), loopy (*Inf.*), nuts (*Sl.*), nutty (*Sl.*), oddball (*Inf.*), off one's head *or* nut (*Sl.*), off one's trolley (*Sl.*), off-the-wall (*Sl.*), out of one's mind, outré, out to lunch (*Inf.*), round the bend (*Sl.*), touched, up the pole (*Inf.*), wacko (*Sl.*)

cracked up blown up, exaggerated, hyped (up), overpraised, overrated, puffed up

crack up break down, collapse, come apart at the seams (*Inf.*), freak out (*Inf.*), go ape

(*Sl.*), go apeshit (*Sl.*), go berserk, go crazy (*Inf.*), go off one's rocker (*Sl.*), go out of one's mind, go to pieces, have a breakdown, throw a wobbly (*Sl.*)

cradle n. **1.** bassinet, cot, crib, Moses basket **2.** *Fig.* beginning, birthplace, fount, fountainhead, origin, source, spring, well~ spring ~v. **3.** hold, lull, nestle, nurse, rock, support **4.** nourish, nurture, tend, watch over

craft 1. ability, aptitude, art, artistry, clev~ erness, dexterity, expertise, expertness, in~ genuity, knack, know-how (*Inf.*), skill, tech~ nique, workmanship **2.** artfulness, artifice, contrivance, craftiness, cunning, deceit, duplicity, guile, ruse, scheme, shrewdness, stratagem, subterfuge, subtlety, trickery, wiles **3.** business, calling, employment, handicraft, handiwork, line, occupation, pursuit, trade, vocation, work **4.** aircraft, barque, boat, plane, ship, spacecraft, vessel

craftiness artfulness, astuteness, canniness, cunning, deviousness, duplicity, foxiness, guile, shrewdness, slyness, subtlety, tricki~ ness, wiliness

craftsman artificer, artisan, maker, master, skilled worker, smith, technician, wright

craftsmanship artistry, expertise, mas~ tery, technique, workmanship

crafty artful, astute, calculating, canny, cunning, deceitful, designing, devious, du~ plicitous, foxy, fraudulent, guileful, insidi~ ous, knowing, scheming, sharp, shrewd, sly, subtle, tricksy, tricky, wily
Antonyms candid, ethical, frank, honest, ingenuous, innocent, naive, open, simple

crag aiguille, bluff, peak, pinnacle, rock, tor

cram 1. compact, compress, crowd, crush, fill to overflowing, force, jam, overcrowd, overfill, pack, pack in, press, ram, shove, squeeze, stuff **2.** glut, gorge, gormandize, guzzle, overeat, overfeed, pig out (*Sl.*), put *or* pack away, satiate, stuff **3.** *Inf.* bone up on (*Inf.*), con, grind, mug up (*Sl.*), revise, study, swot, swot up

cramp[1] v. check, circumscribe, clog, confine, constrain, encumber, hamper, hamstring, handicap, hinder, impede, inhibit, obstruct, restrict, shackle, stymie, thwart

cramp[2] n. ache, contraction, convulsion, crick, pain, pang, shooting pain, spasm, stiffness, stitch, twinge

cramped 1. awkward, circumscribed, closed in, confined, congested, crowded, hemmed in, jammed in, narrow, over~ crowded, packed, restricted, squeezed, un~ comfortable **2.** *Esp. of handwriting* crabbed, indecipherable, irregular, small
Antonyms (*sense 1*) capacious, commodious,

large, open, roomy, sizable, spacious, uncongested, uncrowded

crank case (*Inf.*), character (*Inf.*), freak (*Inf.*), kook (*U.S. & Canad. inf.*), nut (*Sl.*), oddball (*Inf.*), odd fish (*Inf.*), queer fish (*Brit. inf.*), rum customer (*Brit. sl.*), screwball (*Sl., chiefly U.S. & Canad.*), wacko (*Sl.*), weirdo *or* weirdie (*Inf.*)

cranky bizarre, capricious, eccentric, errat~ ic, freakish, freaky (*Sl.*), funny (*Inf.*), idio~ syncratic, odd, oddball (*Inf.*), off-the-wall (*Sl.*), outré, peculiar, queer, quirky, rum (*Brit. sl.*), strange, wacko (*Sl.*), wacky (*Sl.*)

cranny breach, chink, cleft, crack, crevice, fissure, gap, hole, interstice, nook, opening, rift

crash *n.* **1.** bang, boom, clang, clash, clatter, clattering, din, racket, smash, smashing, thunder ~*v.* **2.** break, break up, dash to pieces, disintegrate, fracture, fragment, shatter, shiver, smash, splinter **3.** come a cropper (*Inf.*), dash, fall, fall headlong, give way, hurtle, lurch, overbalance, pitch, plunge, precipitate oneself, sprawl, topple **4.** bang, bump (into), collide, crash-land (*an aircraft*), drive into, have an accident, hit, hurtle into, plough into, run together, wreck ~*n.* **5.** accident, bump, collision, jar, jolt, pile-up (*Inf.*), prang (*Inf.*), smash, smash-up, thud, thump, wreck **6.** bank~ ruptcy, collapse, debacle, depression, down~ fall, failure, ruin, smash ~*v.* **7.** be ruined, collapse, fail, fold, fold up, go broke (*Inf.*), go bust (*Inf.*), go to the wall, go under, smash ~*adj.* **8.** *Of a course of studies, etc.* emergency, immediate, intensive, round- the-clock, speeded-up, telescoped, urgent

crass asinine, blundering, boorish, bovine, coarse, dense, doltish, gross, indelicate, in~ sensitive, lumpish, oafish, obtuse, stupid, unrefined, witless
Antonyms brainy (*Inf.*), bright, clever, el~ egant, intelligent, polished, refined, sensitive, sharp, smart

crate **1.** *n.* box, case, container, packing case, tea chest **2.** *v.* box, case, encase, en~ close, pack, pack up

crater depression, dip, hollow, shell hole

crave **1.** be dying for, cry out for (*Inf.*), de~ sire, eat one's heart out over, fancy (*Inf.*), hanker after, hope for, hunger after, long for, lust after, need, pant for, pine for, re~ quire, sigh for, thirst for, want, yearn for **2.** ask, beg, beseech, entreat, implore, petition, plead for, pray for, seek, solicit, supplicate

craven **1.** *adj.* abject, caitiff (*Archaic*), chicken-hearted, chickenshit (*U.S. sl.*), cow~ ardly, dastardly, fearful, lily-livered, mean- spirited, niddering (*Archaic*), pusillanimous, scared, timorous, weak, yellow (*Inf.*) **2.** *n.* base fellow (*Archaic*), caitiff (*Archaic*), cow~

ard, dastard (*Archaic*), niddering (*Archaic*), poltroon, recreant (*Archaic*), renegade, wheyface, yellow-belly (*Sl.*)

craving appetite, cacoethes, desire, hanker~ ing, hope, hunger, longing, lust, thirst, urge, yearning, yen (*Inf.*)

crawl **1.** advance slowly, creep, drag, go on all fours, inch, move at a snail's pace, move on hands and knees, pull *or* drag oneself along, slither, worm one's way, wriggle, writhe **2.** be overrun (alive, full of, lousy (*Sl.*)), swarm, teem **3.** abase oneself, brown-nose (*Taboo sl.*), cringe, fawn, grovel, humble oneself, kiss ass (*U.S. & Canad. taboo sl.*), pander to, toady, truckle
Antonyms (*sense 1*) dart, dash, fly, hasten, hurry, race, run, rush, sprint, step on it (*Inf.*), walk

craze **1.** *n.* enthusiasm, fad, fashion, infat~ uation, mania, mode, novelty, passion, pre~ occupation, rage, the latest (*Inf.*), thing, trend, vogue **2.** *v.* bewilder, confuse, de~ ment, derange, distemper, drive mad, en~ rage, infatuate, inflame, madden, make in~ sane, send crazy *or* berserk, unbalance, un~ hinge

crazy **1.** *Inf.* a bit lacking upstairs (*Inf.*), barking (*Sl.*), barking mad (*Sl.*), barmy (*Sl.*), batty (*Sl.*), berserk, bonkers (*Sl., chiefly Brit.*), cracked (*Sl.*), crackpot (*Inf.*), crazed, cuckoo (*Inf.*), daft (*Inf.*), delirious, dement~ ed, deranged, idiotic, insane, loopy (*Inf.*), lunatic, mad, mad as a hatter, mad as a March hare, maniacal, mental (*Sl.*), not all there (*Inf.*), not the full shilling (*Inf.*), nuts (*Sl.*), nutty (*Sl.*), nutty as a fruitcake (*Sl.*), off one's head (*Sl.*), off one's trolley (*Sl.*), off-the-wall (*Sl.*), of unsound mind, out to lunch (*Inf.*), potty (*Brit. inf.*), round the bend (*Sl.*), touched, unbalanced, unhinged, up the pole (*Inf.*) **2.** bizarre, eccentric, fan~ tastic, odd, oddball (*Inf.*), outrageous, pecu~ liar, ridiculous, rum (*Brit. sl.*), silly, strange, wacko (*Sl.*), weird **3.** absurd, bird- brained (*Inf.*), cockeyed (*Inf.*), derisory, fatuous, foolhardy, foolish, half-baked (*Inf.*), idiotic, ill-conceived, impracticable, impru~ dent, inane, inappropriate, irresponsible, ludicrous, nonsensical, potty (*Brit. inf.*), preposterous, puerile, quixotic, senseless, short-sighted, unrealistic, unwise, unwork~ able, wild **4.** *Inf.* ardent, beside oneself, de~ voted, eager, enamoured, enthusiastic, fa~ natical, hysterical, infatuated, into (*Inf.*), mad, passionate, smitten, very keen, wild (*Inf.*), zealous
Antonyms (*sense 1*) all there (*Inf.*), *compos mentis*, down-to-earth, in one's right mind, in~ telligent, mentally sound, practical, prudent, rational, reasonable, sane, sensible, smart, wise (*sense 2*) common, conventional, normal, ordinary, orthodox, regular, usual (*sense 3*)

appropriate, brilliant, feasible, possible, practicable, prudent, realistic, responsible, sensible, wise, workable (*sense 4*) cool, indif~ ferent, uncaring, unenthusiastic, uninterest~ ed

creak *v.* grate, grind, groan, rasp, scrape, scratch, screech, squeak, squeal

cream *n.* **1.** cosmetic, emulsion, essence, liniment, lotion, oil, ointment, paste, salve, unguent **2.** best, *crème de la crème*, elite, flower, pick, prime ~*adj.* **3.** off-white, yellowish-white

creamy buttery, creamed, lush, milky, oily, rich, smooth, soft, velvety

crease 1. *v.* corrugate, crimp, crinkle, crumple, double up, fold, pucker, ridge, ruck up, rumple, screw up, wrinkle **2.** *n.* bulge, corrugation, fold, groove, line, over~ lap, pucker, ridge, ruck, tuck, wrinkle

create 1. beget, bring into being *or* exist~ ence, coin, compose, concoct, design, devel~ op, devise, dream up (*Inf.*), form, formulate, generate, give birth to, give life to, hatch, initiate, invent, make, originate, produce, spawn **2.** appoint, constitute, establish, found, install, invest, make, set up **3.** bring about, cause, lead to, occasion
Antonyms annihilate, close, demolish, de~ stroy

creation 1. conception, formation, genera~ tion, genesis, making, procreation, siring **2.** constitution, development, establishment, formation, foundation, inception, institu~ tion, laying down, origination, production, setting up **3.** achievement, brainchild (*Inf.*), *chef-d'oeuvre*, concept, concoction, handi~ work, invention, *magnum opus, pièce de ré~ sistance*, production **4.** all living things, cosmos, life, living world, natural world, nature, universe, world

creative artistic, clever, fertile, gifted, im~ aginative, ingenious, inspired, inventive, original, productive, stimulating, visionary

creativity cleverness, fecundity, fertility, imagination, imaginativeness, ingenuity, inspiration, inventiveness, originality, productivity, talent

creator architect, author, begetter, designer, father, framer, God, initiator, inventor, maker, originator, prime mover

creature 1. animal, beast, being, brute, critter (*U.S. dialect*), dumb animal, living thing, lower animal, quadruped **2.** body, character, fellow, human being, individual, man, mortal, person, soul, wight (*Archaic*), woman **3.** dependant, hanger-on, hireling, instrument (*Inf.*), lackey, minion, puppet, retainer, tool, wretch

credentials attestation, authorization, card, certificate, deed, diploma, docket, letter of

recommendation *or* introduction, letters of credence, licence, missive, passport, recom~ mendation, reference(s), testament, testi~ monial, title, voucher, warrant

credibility believability, believableness, in~ tegrity, plausibility, reliability, tenability, trustworthiness

credible 1. believable, conceivable, imagi~ nable, likely, plausible, possible, probable, reasonable, supposable, tenable, thinkable, verisimilar **2.** dependable, honest, reliable, sincere, trustworthy, trusty
Antonyms (*sense 1*) doubtful, implausible, inconceivable, incredible, questionable, un~ believable, unlikely (*sense 2*) dishonest, insin~ cere, not dependable, unreliable, untrustwor~ thy

credit *n.* **1.** acclaim, acknowledgment, ap~ proval, Brownie points, commendation, fame, glory, honour, kudos, merit, praise, recognition, thanks, tribute **2.** character, clout (*Inf.*), esteem, estimation, good name, influence, position, prestige, regard, repu~ tation, repute, standing, status **3.** belief, confidence, credence, faith, reliance, trust **4.** *As in* be a credit to feather in one's cap, honour, source of satisfaction *or* pride **5.** on credit by deferred payment, by instal~ ments, on account, on hire-purchase, on (the) H.P., on the slate (*Inf.*), on tick (*Inf.*) ~*v.* **6.** *With* with accredit, ascribe to, as~ sign to, attribute to, chalk up to (*Inf.*), im~ pute to, refer to **7.** accept, bank on, believe, buy (*Sl.*), depend on, fall for, have faith in, rely on, swallow (*Inf.*), trust

creditable admirable, commendable, de~ serving, estimable, exemplary, honourable, laudable, meritorious, praiseworthy, repu~ table, respectable, worthy

credulity blind faith, credulousness, gulli~ bility, naiveté, silliness, simplicity, stupid~ ity

credulous born yesterday (*Inf.*), dupable, green, gullible, naive, overtrusting, trustful, uncritical, unsuspecting, unsuspicious
Antonyms cynical, incredulous, sceptical, suspecting, unbelieving, wary

creed articles of faith, belief, canon, cat~ echism, confession, credo, doctrine, dogma, persuasion, principles, profession (*of faith*), tenet

creek 1. bay, bight, cove, firth *or* frith (*Scot.*), inlet **2.** *U.S., Canad., & Aust.* bayou, brook, rivulet, runnel, stream, streamlet, tributary, watercourse

creep *v.* **1.** crawl, crawl on all fours, glide, insinuate, slither, squirm, worm, wriggle, writhe **2.** approach unnoticed, skulk, slink, sneak, steal, tiptoe **3.** crawl, dawdle, drag, edge, inch, proceed at a snail's pace **4.** bootlick (*Inf.*), brown-nose (*Taboo sl.*), cow~

er, cringe, fawn, grovel, kiss (someone's) ass (*U.S. & Canad. taboo sl.*), kowtow, pan~ der to, scrape, suck up to (*Inf.*), toady, truckle ~*n.* **5.** *Sl.* ass-kisser (*U.S. & Canad. taboo sl.*), bootlicker (*Inf.*), brown-noser (*Taboo sl.*), sneak, sycophant, toady **6. give one the creeps** *or* **make one's flesh creep** disgust, frighten, horrify, make one flinch (quail, shrink, squirm, wince), make one's hair stand on end (*Inf.*), repel, repulse, scare, terrify, terrorize

creeper climber, climbing plant, rambler, runner, trailing plant, vine (*Chiefly U.S.*)

creepy awful, direful, disgusting, disturbing, eerie, forbidding, frightening, ghoulish, goose-pimply (*Inf.*), gruesome, hair-raising, horrible, macabre, menacing, nightmarish, ominous, scary (*Inf.*), sinister, terrifying, threatening, unpleasant, weird

crescent *n.* **1.** half-moon, meniscus, new moon, old moon, sickle, sickle-shape ~*adj.* **2.** arched, bow-shaped, curved, falcate, semicircular, sickle-shaped **3.** *Archaic* growing, increasing, waxing

crest 1. apex, crown, head, height, highest point, peak, pinnacle, ridge, summit, top **2.** aigrette, caruncle (*Zoology*), cockscomb, comb, crown, mane, panache, plume, tassel, topknot, tuft **3.** *Heraldry* badge, bearings, charge, device, emblem, insignia, symbol

crestfallen chapfallen, dejected, depressed, despondent, disappointed, disconsolate, dis~ couraged, disheartened, downcast, down~ hearted, sick as a parrot (*Inf.*)
Antonyms cock-a-hoop, elated, encouraged, exuberant, happy, in seventh heaven, joyful, on cloud nine (*Inf.*), over the moon (*Inf.*)

crevice chink, cleft, crack, cranny, fissure, fracture, gap, hole, interstice, opening, rent, rift, slit, split

crew 1. hands, (ship's) company, (ship's) complement **2.** company, corps, gang, party, posse, squad, team, working party **3.** *Inf.* assemblage, band, bunch (*Inf.*), camp, com~ pany, crowd, gang, herd, horde, lot, mob, pack, posse (*Inf.*), set, swarm, troop

crib *n.* **1.** bassinet, bed, cot, cradle **2.** bin, box, bunker, manger, rack, stall **3.** *Inf.* key, translation, trot (*U.S. sl.*) ~*v.* **4.** *Inf.* cheat, pass off as one's own work, pilfer, pirate, plagiarize, purloin, steal **5.** box up, cage, confine, coop, coop up, enclose, fence, im~ prison, limit, pen, rail, restrict, shut in

crime 1. atrocity, fault, felony, job (*Inf.*), malfeasance, misdeed, misdemeanour, of~ fence, outrage, transgression, trespass, un~ lawful act, violation, wrong **2.** corruption, delinquency, guilt, illegality, iniquity, law~ breaking, malefaction, misconduct, sin, un~ righteousness, vice, villainy, wickedness, wrong, wrongdoing

criminal *n.* **1.** con (*Sl.*), con man (*Inf.*), con~ vict, crook (*Inf.*), culprit, delinquent, evil~ doer, felon, jailbird, lag (*Sl.*), lawbreaker, malefactor, offender, sinner, transgressor, villain ~*adj.* **2.** bent (*Sl.*), corrupt, crooked (*Inf.*), culpable, felonious, illegal, illicit, im~ moral, indictable, iniquitous, lawless, ne~ farious, peccant (*Rare*), under-the-table, un~ lawful, unrighteous, vicious, villainous, wicked, wrong **3.** *Inf.* deplorable, foolish, preposterous, ridiculous, scandalous, sense~ less
Antonyms commendable, honest, honour~ able, innocent, law-abiding, lawful, legal, right

criminality corruption, culpability, delin~ quency, depravity, guiltiness, illegality, sinfulness, turpitude, villainy, wickedness

cringe 1. blench, cower, dodge, draw back, duck, flinch, quail, quiver, recoil, shrink, shy, start, tremble, wince **2.** bend, bootlick (*Inf.*), bow, brown-nose (*Taboo sl.*), crawl, creep, crouch, fawn, grovel, kiss ass (*U.S. & Canad. taboo sl.*), kneel, kowtow, pander to, sneak, stoop, toady, truckle

cripple *v.* **1.** debilitate, disable, enfeeble, hamstring, incapacitate, lame, maim, muti~ late, paralyse, weaken **2.** bring to a stand~ still, cramp, damage, destroy, halt, impair, put out of action, ruin, spoil, vitiate
Antonyms advance, aid, assist, assist the progress of, ease, expedite, facilitate, further, help, promote

crippled bedridden, deformed, disabled, en~ feebled, handicapped, housebound, inca~ pacitated, laid up (*Inf.*), lame, paralysed

crisis 1. climacteric, climax, confrontation, critical point, crunch (*Inf.*), crux, culmina~ tion, height, moment of truth, point of no return, turning point **2.** catastrophe, criti~ cal situation, dilemma, dire straits, disaster, emergency, exigency, extremity, meltdown (*Inf.*), mess, panic stations (*Inf.*), plight, predicament, quandary, strait, trouble

crisp 1. brittle, crispy, crumbly, crunchy, firm, fresh, unwilted **2.** bracing, brisk, fresh, invigorating, refreshing **3.** brief, brusque, clear, incisive, pithy, short, suc~ cinct, tart, terse **4.** clean-cut, neat, orderly, smart, snappy, spruce, tidy, trig (*Archaic or dialect*), well-groomed, well-pressed
Antonyms (*sense 1*) drooping, droopy, flaccid, floppy, limp, soft, wilted, withered (*sense 2*) balmy, clement, mild, pleasant, warm

criterion bench mark, canon, gauge, meas~ ure, norm, par, principle, proof, rule, standard, test, touchstone, yardstick

critic 1. analyst, arbiter, authority, com~ mentator, connoisseur, expert, expositor, judge, pundit, reviewer **2.** attacker, carper, caviller, censor, censurer, detractor, fault-

critical

134

critical

finder, knocker (*Inf.*), Momus, reviler, vilifier

critical 1. captious, carping, cavilling, censorious, derogatory, disapproving, disparaging, fault-finding, nagging, niggling, nitpicking (*Inf.*), scathing **2.** accurate, analytical, diagnostic, discerning, discriminating, fastidious, judicious, penetrating, perceptive, precise **3.** all-important, crucial, dangerous, deciding, decisive, grave, hairy (*Sl.*), high-priority, momentous, perilous, pivotal, precarious, pressing, psychological, risky, serious, urgent, vital
Antonyms appreciative, approving, complimentary, permissive, safe, secure, settled, uncritical, undiscriminating, unimportant

criticism 1. animadversion, bad press, brickbats (*Inf.*), censure, character assassination, critical remarks, disapproval, disparagement, fault-finding, flak (*Inf.*), knocking (*Inf.*), panning (*Inf.*), slam (*Sl.*), slating (*Inf.*), stick (*Sl.*), stricture **2.** analysis, appraisal, appreciation, assessment, comment, commentary, critique, elucidation, evaluation, judgment, notice, review

criticize 1. animadvert on *or* upon, blast, carp, censure, condemn, disapprove of, disparage, excoriate, find fault with, give (someone *or* something) a bad press, knock (*Inf.*), lambast(e), nag at, pan (*Inf.*), pass strictures upon, pick to pieces, put down, slam (*Sl.*), slate (*Inf.*), tear into (*Inf.*) **2.** analyse, appraise, assess, comment upon, evaluate, give an opinion, judge, pass judgment on, review
Antonyms commend, compliment, extol, laud (*Literary*), praise

critique analysis, appraisal, assessment, commentary, essay, examination, review, treatise

croak *v.* **1.** caw, gasp, grunt, squawk, utter *or* speak harshly (huskily, throatily), wheeze **2.** *Inf.* complain, groan, grouse, grumble, moan, murmur, mutter, repine **3.** *Sl.* buy it (*U.S. sl.*), check out (*U.S. sl.*), die, expire, go belly-up (*Sl.*), hop the twig (*Inf.*), kick it (*Sl.*), kick the bucket (*Inf.*), pass away, peg it (*Inf.*), peg out (*Inf.*), perish, pop one's clogs (*Inf.*)

crook 1. *n. Inf.* cheat, chiseller (*Inf.*), criminal, knave (*Archaic*), lag (*Sl.*), racketeer, robber, rogue, shark, swindler, thief, villain **2.** *v.* angle, bend, bow, curve, flex, hook

crooked 1. anfractuous, bent, bowed, crippled, curved, deformed, deviating, disfigured, distorted, hooked, irregular, meandering, misshapen, out of shape, tortuous, twisted, twisting, warped, winding, zigzag **2.** angled, askew, asymmetric, at an angle, awry, lopsided, off-centre, skewwhiff (*Brit. inf.*), slanted, slanting, squint, tilted,

to one side, uneven, unsymmetrical **3.** *Inf.* bent (*Sl.*), corrupt, crafty, criminal, deceitful, dishonest, dishonourable, dubious, fraudulent, illegal, knavish, nefarious, questionable, shady (*Inf.*), shifty, treacherous, underhand, under-the-table, unlawful, unprincipled, unscrupulous
Antonyms (*sense 1*) flat, straight (*sense 3*) ethical, fair, honest, honourable, lawful, legal, straight, upright

croon breathe, hum, purr, sing, warble

crop *n.* **1.** fruits, gathering, harvest, produce, reaping, season's growth, vintage, yield ~*v.* **2.** clip, curtail, cut, dock, lop, mow, pare, prune, reduce, shear, shorten, snip, top, trim **3.** bring home, bring in, collect, garner, gather, harvest, mow, pick, reap **4.** browse, graze, nibble

crop up appear, arise, emerge, happen, occur, spring up, turn up

cross *adj.* **1.** angry, annoyed, cantankerous, captious, churlish, crotchety (*Inf.*), crusty, disagreeable, fractious, fretful, grouchy (*Inf.*), grumpy, hacked (off) (*U.S. sl.*), ill-humoured, ill-tempered, impatient, in a bad mood, irascible, irritable, liverish, out of humour, peeved (*Inf.*), peevish, pettish, petulant, pissed off (*Taboo sl.*), put out, querulous, ratty (*Brit. & N.Z. inf.*), shirty (*Sl., chiefly Brit.*), short, snappish, snappy, splenetic, sullen, surly, testy, tetchy, vexed, waspish ~*v.* **2.** bridge, cut across, extend over, ford, meet, pass over, ply, span, traverse, zigzag **3.** crisscross, intersect, intertwine, lace, lie athwart of **4.** blend, crossbreed, cross-fertilize, cross-pollinate, hybridize, interbreed, intercross, mix, mongrelize **5.** block, deny, foil, frustrate, hinder, impede, interfere, obstruct, oppose, resist, thwart ~*n.* **6.** affliction, burden, grief, load, misery, misfortune, trial, tribulation, trouble, woe, worry **7.** crucifix, rood **8.** crossing, crossroads, intersection, junction **9.** amalgam, blend, combination, crossbreed, cur, hybrid, hybridization, mixture, mongrel, mutt (*Sl.*) ~*adj.* **10.** crosswise, intersecting, oblique, transverse **11.** adverse, contrary, opposed, opposing, unfavourable **12.** *Involving an interchange* opposite, reciprocal
Antonyms (*sense 1*) affable, agreeable, calm, cheerful, civil, congenial, even-tempered, genial, good-humoured, good-natured, nice, placid, pleasant, sweet

cross-examine catechize, grill (*Inf.*), interrogate, pump, question, quiz

cross out *or* **off** blue-pencil, cancel, delete, eliminate, strike off *or* out

crotch crutch, groin

crotchet caprice, fad, fancy, quirk, vagary, whim, whimsy

crotchety awkward, bad-tempered, cantan~ kerous, contrary, crabby, cross, crusty, curmudgeonly, difficult, disagreeable, frac~ tious, grumpy, irritable, liverish, obstrep~ erous, peevish, ratty (*Brit. & N.Z. inf.*), sur~ ly, testy, tetchy

crouch 1. bend down, bow, duck, hunch, kneel, squat, stoop **2.** abase oneself, cower, cringe, fawn, grovel, pander to, truckle

crow bluster, boast, brag, drool, exult, flourish, gloat, glory in, strut, swagger, tri~ umph, vaunt

crowd *n.* **1.** army, assembly, bevy, compa~ ny, concourse, flock, herd, horde, host, mass, mob, multitude, pack, press, rabble, swarm, throng, troupe **2.** bunch (*Inf.*), cir~ cle, clique, group, lot, set **3.** attendance, audience, gate, house, spectators ~*v.* **4.** cluster, congregate, cram, flock, forgather, gather, huddle, mass, muster, press, push, stream, surge, swarm, throng **5.** bundle, congest, cram, pack, pile, squeeze **6.** batter, butt, elbow, jostle, shove **7. the crowd** hoi polloi, masses, mob, people, populace, pro~ letariat, public, rabble, rank and file, riff~ raff, vulgar herd

crowded busy, congested, cramped, crushed, full, huddled, jam-packed, mobbed, overflowing, packed, populous, swarming, teeming, thronged

crown *n.* **1.** chaplet, circlet, coronal (*Poetic*), coronet, diadem, tiara **2.** bays, distinction, garland, honour, kudos, laurels, laurel wreath, prize, trophy **3.** emperor, empress, king, monarch, monarchy, queen, *rex*, roy~ alty, ruler, sovereign, sovereignty **4.** acme, apex, crest, head, perfection, pinnacle, summit, tip, top, ultimate, zenith ~*v.* **5.** adorn, dignify, festoon, honour, invest, re~ ward **6.** be the climax *or* culmination of, cap, complete, consummate, finish, fulfil, perfect, put the finishing touch to, round off, surmount, terminate, top **7.** *Sl.* belt (*Inf.*), biff (*Sl.*), box, cuff, hit over the head, punch

crowning *adj.* climactic, consummate, cul~ minating, final, paramount, sovereign, su~ preme, ultimate

crucial 1. central, critical, decisive, pivotal, psychological, searching, testing, trying **2.** *Inf.* essential, high-priority, important, mo~ mentous, pressing, urgent, vital

crucify 1. execute, harrow, persecute, rack, torment, torture **2.** *Sl.* lampoon, pan (*Inf.*), ridicule, tear to pieces, wipe the floor with (*Inf.*)

crude 1. boorish, coarse, crass, dirty, gross, indecent, lewd, obscene, smutty, tactless, tasteless, uncouth, vulgar **2.** natural, raw, unmilled, unpolished, unprepared, unpro~ cessed, unrefined **3.** clumsy, makeshift, outline, primitive, rough, rough-hewn, rude, rudimentary, sketchy, undeveloped, unfin~ ished, unformed, unpolished

Antonyms (*sense 1*) genteel, polished, refined, subtle, tasteful (*sense 2*) fine, fine-grained, polished, prepared, processed, refined

crudely bluntly, clumsily, coarsely, impo~ litely, indecently, pulling no punches (*Inf.*), roughly, rudely, sketchily, tastelessly, vul~ garly

crudity 1. coarseness, crudeness, impropri~ ety, indecency, indelicacy, lewdness, loud~ ness, lowness, obscenity, obtrusiveness, smuttiness, vulgarity **2.** clumsiness, crude~ ness, primitiveness, roughness, rudeness

cruel 1. atrocious, barbarous, bitter, blood~ thirsty, brutal, brutish, callous, cold-blooded, depraved, excruciating, fell (*Ar~ chaic*), ferocious, fierce, flinty, grim, hard, hard-hearted, harsh, heartless, hellish, im~ placable, inclement, inexorable, inhuman, inhumane, malevolent, murderous, painful, poignant, Ramboesque, ravening, raw, re~ lentless, remorseless, sadistic, sanguinary, savage, severe, spiteful, stony-hearted, un~ feeling, unkind, unnatural, vengeful, vi~ cious **2.** merciless, pitiless, ruthless, unre~ lenting

Antonyms benevolent, caring, compassion~ ate, gentle, humane, kind, merciful, sympa~ thetic, warm-hearted

cruelly 1. barbarously, brutally, brutishly, callously, ferociously, fiercely, heartlessly, in cold blood, mercilessly, pitilessly, sadis~ tically, savagely, spitefully, unmercifully, viciously **2.** bitterly, deeply, fearfully, grievously, monstrously, mortally, severely

cruelty barbarity, bestiality, bloodthirsti~ ness, brutality, brutishness, callousness, depravity, ferocity, fiendishness, hard~ heartedness, harshness, heartlessness, in~ humanity, mercilessness, murderousness, ruthlessness, sadism, savagery, severity, spite, spitefulness, venom, viciousness

cruise *v.* **1.** coast, sail, voyage **2.** coast, drift, keep a steady pace, travel along ~*n.* **3.** boat trip, sail, sea trip, voyage

crumb atom, bit, grain, mite, morsel, parti~ cle, scrap, shred, sliver, snippet, *soupçon*, speck

crumble 1. bruise, crumb, crush, fragment, granulate, grind, pound, powder, pulverize, triturate **2.** break up, collapse, come to dust, decay, decompose, degenerate, de~ teriorate, disintegrate, fall apart, go to pieces, go to wrack and ruin, moulder, per~ ish, tumble down

crumple 1. crease, crush, pucker, rumple, screw up, wrinkle **2.** break down, cave in, collapse, fall, give way, go to pieces

crunch 1. *v.* champ, chew noisily, chomp, grind, masticate, munch **2.** *n. Inf.* crisis, critical point, crux, emergency, hour of de~cision, moment of truth, test

crusade campaign, cause, drive, holy war, jihad, movement, push

crusader advocate, campaigner, champion, reformer

crush *v.* **1.** bray, break, bruise, comminute, compress, contuse, crease, crumble, crum~ple, crunch, mash, pound, pulverize, rum~ple, smash, squeeze, wrinkle **2.** conquer, extinguish, overcome, overpower, over~whelm, put down, quell, stamp out, subdue, vanquish **3.** abash, browbeat, chagrin, dis~pose of, humiliate, mortify, put down (*Sl.*), quash, shame **4.** embrace, enfold, hug, press, squeeze ~*n.* **5.** crowd, huddle, jam, party

crust caking, coat, coating, concretion, cov~ering, film, incrustation, layer, outside, scab, shell, skin, surface

crusty 1. brittle, crisp, crispy, friable, hard, short, well-baked, well-done **2.** brusque, cantankerous, captious, choleric, crabby, cross, curt, gruff, ill-humoured, irritable, peevish, prickly, ratty (*Brit. & N.Z. inf.*), short, short-tempered, snappish, snarling, splenetic, surly, testy, tetchy, touchy

cry *v.* **1.** bawl, bewail, blubber, boohoo, greet (*Scot. or archaic*), howl one's eyes out, keen, lament, mewl, pule, shed tears, snivel, sob, wail, weep, whimper, whine, whinge (*Inf.*), yowl ~*n.* **2.** bawling, blubbering, crying, greet (*Scot. or archaic*), howl, keening, la~ment, lamentation, plaint (*Archaic*), snivel, snivelling, sob, sobbing, sorrowing, wailing, weep, weeping ~*v.* **3.** bawl, bell, bellow, call, call out, ejaculate, exclaim, hail, hal~loo, holler (*Inf.*), howl, roar, scream, screech, shout, shriek, sing out, vociferate, whoop, yell ~*n.* **4.** bawl, bell, bellow, call, ejaculation, exclamation, holler (*Inf.*), hoot, howl, outcry, roar, scream, screech, shriek, squawk, whoop, yell, yelp, yoo-hoo ~*v.* **5.** advertise, announce, bark (*Inf.*), broadcast, bruit, hawk, noise, proclaim, promulgate, publish, trumpet ~*n.* **6.** announcement, barking (*Inf.*), noising, proclamation, publi~cation ~*v.* **7.** beg, beseech, clamour, en~treat, implore, plead, pray ~*n.* **8.** appeal, entreaty, petition, plea, prayer, supplication **Antonyms** (*sense 1*) chortle, chuckle, giggle, laugh, snicker, snigger, twitter (*sense 3*) drone, mumble, murmur, mutter, speak in hushed tones, speak softly, utter indistinctly, whisper

cry down asperse, bad-mouth (*Sl., chiefly U.S. & Canad.*), belittle, decry, denigrate, disparage, knock (*Inf.*), rubbish (*Inf.*), run down, slag (off) (*Sl.*)

cry off back out, beg off, cop out (*Sl.*), ex~cuse oneself, quit, withdraw, withdraw from

crypt catacomb, tomb, undercroft, vault

cub 1. offspring, whelp, young **2.** babe (*Inf.*), beginner, fledgling, greenhorn (*Inf.*), lad, learner, puppy, recruit, tenderfoot, trainee, whippersnapper, youngster

cubbyhole 1. den, hideaway, hole, snug **2.** compartment, niche, pigeonhole, recess, slot

cuddle canoodle (*Sl.*), clasp, cosset, embrace, fondle, hug, nestle, pet, snuggle

cuddly buxom, cuddlesome, curvaceous, huggable, lovable, plump, soft, warm

cudgel 1. *n.* bastinado, baton, bludgeon, club, cosh (*Brit.*), shillelagh, stick, trun~cheon **2.** *v.* bang, baste, batter, beat, bludg~eon, cane, cosh (*Brit.*), drub, maul, pound, pummel, thrash, thump, thwack

cue catchword, hint, key, nod, prompting, reminder, sign, signal, suggestion

cuff off the cuff ad lib, extempore, im~promptu, improvised, offhand, off the top of one's head, on the spur of the moment, spontaneous, spontaneously, unrehearsed

cul-de-sac blind alley, dead end

culminate climax, close, come to a climax, come to a head, conclude, end, end up, finish, rise to a crescendo, terminate, wind up

culmination acme, apex, apogee, climax, completion, conclusion, consummation, crown, crowning touch, finale, height, *ne plus ultra*, peak, perfection, pinnacle, punch line, summit, top, zenith

culpable answerable, at fault, blamable, blameworthy, censurable, found wanting, guilty, in the wrong, liable, reprehensible, sinful, to blame, wrong
Antonyms blameless, clean (*Sl.*), guiltless, innocent, in the clear, not guilty, squeaky-clean

culprit criminal, delinquent, evildoer, felon, guilty party, malefactor, miscreant, offend~er, person responsible, rascal, sinner, transgressor, villain, wrongdoer

cult 1. body, church, clique, denomination, faction, faith, following, party, religion, school, sect **2.** admiration, craze, devotion, idolization, reverence, veneration, worship

cultivate 1. bring under cultivation, farm, fertilize, harvest, plant, plough, prepare, tend, till, work **2.** ameliorate, better, bring on, cherish, civilize, develop, discipline, el~evate, enrich, foster, improve, polish, pro~mote, refine, train **3.** aid, devote oneself to, encourage, forward, foster, further, help, patronize, promote, pursue, support **4.** as~sociate with, butter up, consort with, court, dance attendance upon, run after, seek out, seek someone's company *or* friendship, take trouble *or* pains with

cultivation 1. agronomy, farming, garden~ ing, husbandry, planting, ploughing, tillage, tilling, working **2.** breeding, civility, civili~ zation, culture, discernment, discrimina~ tion, education, enlightenment, gentility, good taste, learning, letters, manners, pol~ ish, refinement, sophistication, taste **3.** ad~ vancement, advocacy, development, en~ couragement, enhancement, fostering, fur~ therance, help, nurture, patronage, promo~ tion, support **4.** devotion to, pursuit, study

cultural artistic, broadening, civilizing, de~ velopmental, edifying, educational, educa~ tive, elevating, enlightening, enriching, hu~ mane, humanizing, liberal, liberalizing

culture 1. civilization, customs, life style, mores, society, stage of development, the arts, way of life **2.** accomplishment, breed~ ing, education, elevation, enlightenment, erudition, gentility, good taste, improve~ ment, polish, politeness, refinement, so~ phistication, urbanity **3.** agriculture, agronomy, cultivation, farming, husbandry

cultured accomplished, advanced, educated, enlightened, erudite, genteel, highbrow, knowledgeable, polished, refined, scholarly, urbane, versed, well-bred, well-informed, well-read
Antonyms coarse, common, inelegant, un~ cultivated, uneducated, unpolished, unre~ fined, vulgar

culvert channel, conduit, drain, gutter, watercourse

cumbersome awkward, bulky, burden~ some, clumsy, cumbrous, embarrassing, heavy, hefty (*Inf.*), incommodious, incon~ venient, oppressive, unmanageable, un~ wieldy, weighty
Antonyms compact, convenient, easy to use, handy, manageable, practical, serviceable, wieldy

cumulative accruing, accumulative, aggre~ gate, amassed, collective, heaped, increas~ ing, snowballing

cunning *adj.* **1.** artful, astute, canny, crafty, devious, foxy, guileful, knowing, Machia~ vellian, sharp, shifty, shrewd, subtle, tricky, wily ~*n.* **2.** artfulness, astuteness, crafti~ ness, deceitfulness, deviousness, foxiness, guile, shrewdness, slyness, trickery, wili~ ness ~*adj.* **3.** adroit, deft, dexterous, imagi~ native, ingenious, skilful ~*n.* **4.** ability, adroitness, art, artifice, cleverness, craft, deftness, dexterity, finesse, ingenuity, skill, subtlety
Antonyms *adj.* artless, dull, ethical, frank, honest, ingenuous, maladroit ~*n.* candour, clumsiness, ingenuousness, sincerity

cup beaker, cannikin, chalice, cupful, demi~

tasse, draught, drink, goblet, potion, teacup, trophy

cupboard ambry (*Obsolete*), cabinet, closet, locker, press

Cupid amoretto, Eros, god of love, love

curb 1. *v.* bite back, bridle, check, constrain, contain, control, hinder, impede, inhibit, moderate, muzzle, repress, restrain, restrict, retard, subdue, suppress **2.** *n.* brake, bridle, check, control, deterrent, limitation, rein, restraint

curdle clot, coagulate, condense, congeal, curd, solidify, thicken, turn sour
Antonyms deliquesce, dissolve, liquefy, melt, soften, thaw

cure *v.* **1.** alleviate, correct, ease, heal, help, make better, mend, rehabilitate, relieve, remedy, restore, restore to health ~*n.* **2.** alleviation, antidote, corrective, healing, medicine, nostrum, panacea, recovery, remedy, restorative, specific, treatment ~*v.* **3.** dry, kipper, pickle, preserve, salt, smoke

cure-all catholicon, elixir, *elixir vitae*, nos~ trum, panacea

curiosity 1. inquisitiveness, interest, nosi~ ness (*Inf.*), prying, snooping (*Inf.*) **2.** celeb~ rity, freak, marvel, novelty, oddity, phe~ nomenon, rarity, sight, spectacle, wonder **3.** bibelot, bygone, curio, knickknack, *objet d'art*, trinket

curious 1. inquiring, inquisitive, interested, puzzled, questioning, searching **2.** inquisi~ tive, meddling, nosy (*Inf.*), peeping, peering, prying, snoopy (*Inf.*) **3.** bizarre, exotic, extraordinary, marvellous, mysterious, novel, odd, peculiar, puzzling, quaint, queer, rare, rum (*Brit. sl.*), singular, strange, unconventional, unexpected, unique, unorthodox, unusual, wonderful
Antonyms (*senses 1 & 2*) incurious, indiffer~ ent, uninquisitive, uninterested (*sense 3*) common, everyday, familiar, ordinary

curl 1. *v.* bend, coil, convolute, corkscrew, crimp, crinkle, crisp, curve, entwine, frizz, loop, meander, ripple, spiral, turn, twine, twirl, twist, wind, wreathe, writhe **2.** *n.* coil, curlicue, kink, ringlet, spiral, twist, whorl

curly corkscrew, crimped, crimpy, crinkly, crisp, curled, curling, frizzy, fuzzy, kinky, permed, spiralled, waved, wavy, winding

currency 1. bills, coinage, coins, dosh (*Brit. & Aust. sl.*), medium of exchange, money, notes **2.** acceptance, circulation, exposure, popularity, prevalence, publicity, transmis~ sion, vogue

current *adj.* **1.** accepted, circulating, com~ mon, common knowledge, customary, gen~ eral, going around, in circulation, in pro~ gress, in the air, in the news, ongoing,

popular, present, prevailing, prevalent, rife, topical, widespread **2.** contemporary, fash~ ionable, happening (*Inf.*), in, in fashion, in vogue, now (*Inf.*), present-day, sexy (*Inf.*), trendy (*Brit. inf.*), up-to-date, up-to-the- minute ~*n.* **3.** course, draught, flow, jet, progression, river, stream, tide, tideway, undertow **4.** atmosphere, drift, feeling, in~ clination, mood, tendency, trend, undercur~ rent, vibes (*Sl.*)
Antonyms (*sense 2*) archaic, obsolete, old- fashioned, outmoded, out-of-date, passé, past

curse *n.* **1.** blasphemy, expletive, oath, ob~ scenity, swearing, swearword **2.** anathema, ban, denunciation, evil eye, excommunica~ tion, execration, hoodoo (*Inf.*), imprecation, jinx, malediction, malison (*Archaic*) **3.** affliction, bane, burden, calamity, cross, disaster, evil, hardship, misfortune, ordeal, plague, scourge, torment, tribulation, trou~ ble, vexation ~*v.* **4.** be foul-mouthed, blas~ pheme, cuss (*Inf.*), swear, take the Lord's name in vain, turn the air blue (*Inf.*), use bad language **5.** accurse, anathematize, damn, excommunicate, execrate, fulminate, imprecate **6.** afflict, blight, burden, destroy, doom, plague, scourge, torment, trouble, vex

cursed 1. accursed, bedevilled, blighted, cast out, confounded, damned, doomed, ex~ communicate, execrable, fey (*Scot.*), fore- doomed, ill-fated, star-crossed, unholy, un~ sanctified, villainous **2.** abominable, damnable, detestable, devilish, fell (*Archa~ ic*), fiendish, hateful, infamous, infernal, loathsome, odious, pernicious, pestilential, vile

curt abrupt, blunt, brief, brusque, concise, gruff, offhand, pithy, rude, sharp, short, snappish, succinct, summary, tart, terse, unceremonious, uncivil, ungracious

curtail abbreviate, abridge, contract, cut, cut back, cut short, decrease, dock, lessen, lop, pare down, reduce, retrench, shorten, trim, truncate

curtailment abbreviation, abridgment, contraction, cutback, cutting, cutting short, docking, retrenchment, truncation

curtain 1. *n.* drape (*Chiefly U.S.*), hanging **2.** *v.* conceal, drape, hide, screen, shroud, shut off, shutter, veil

curve 1. *v.* arc, arch, bend, bow, coil, hook, inflect, spiral, swerve, turn, twist, wind **2.** *n.* arc, bend, camber, curvature, half-moon, loop, trajectory, turn

curved arced, arched, bent, bowed, crooked, humped, rounded, serpentine, sinuous, sweeping, turned, twisted

cushion 1. *n.* beanbag, bolster, hassock, headrest, pad, pillow, scatter cushion, squab **2.** *v.* bolster, buttress, cradle, damp~

en, deaden, muffle, pillow, protect, soften, stifle, support, suppress

custody 1. aegis, auspices, care, charge, custodianship, guardianship, keeping, ob~ servation, preservation, protection, safe- keeping, supervision, trusteeship, tutelage, ward, watch **2.** arrest, confinement, deten~ tion, durance (*Archaic*), duress, imprison~ ment, incarceration

custom 1. habit, habitude (*Rare*), manner, mode, procedure, routine, way, wont **2.** convention, etiquette, fashion, form, for~ mality, matter of course, observance, ob~ servation, policy, practice, praxis, ritual, rule, style, tradition, unwritten law, usage, use **3.** customers, patronage, trade

customarily as a rule, commonly, general~ ly, habitually, in the ordinary way, nor~ mally, ordinarily, regularly, traditionally, usually

customary accepted, accustomed, acknowl~ edged, common, confirmed, conventional, established, everyday, familiar, fashionable, general, habitual, normal, ordinary, popu~ lar, regular, routine, traditional, usual, wonted
Antonyms exceptional, infrequent, irregu~ lar, occasional, rare, uncommon, unusual

customer buyer, client, consumer, habitué, patron, prospect, purchaser, regular (*Inf.*), shopper

customs duty, import charges, tariff, taxes, toll

cut *v.* **1.** chop, cleave, divide, gash, incise, lacerate, nick, notch, penetrate, pierce, score, sever, slash, slice, slit, wound **2.** carve, chip, chisel, chop, engrave, fashion, form, inscribe, saw, sculpt, sculpture, shape, whittle **3.** clip, dock, fell, gather, hack, harvest, hew, lop, mow, pare, prune, reap, saw down, shave, trim **4.** contract, cut back, decrease, ease up on, lower, rational~ ize, reduce, slash, slim (down) **5.** abbrevi~ ate, abridge, condense, curtail, delete, edit out, excise, precis, shorten **6.** *Often with* **through, off,** *or* **across** bisect, carve, cleave, cross, dissect, divide, interrupt, intersect, part, segment, sever, slice, split, sunder **7.** avoid, cold-shoulder, freeze (someone) out (*Inf.*), grieve, hurt, ignore, insult, look straight through (someone), pain, put down, send to Coventry, slight, snub, spurn, sting, turn one's back on, wound ~*n.* **8.** gash, graze, groove, incision, laceration, nick, rent, rip, slash, slit, stroke, wound **9.** cutback, decrease, decrement, diminution, economy, fall, lowering, reduc~ tion, saving **10.** *Inf.* chop (*Sl.*), division, kickback (*Chiefly U.S.*), percentage, piece, portion, rake-off (*Sl.*), section, share, slice **11.** configuration, fashion, form, look,

mode, shape, style **12. a cut above** *Inf.*
better than, higher than, more efficient (ca~
pable, competent, reliable, trustworthy,
useful) than, superior to **13. cut and dried**
Inf. automatic, fixed, organized, pre~
arranged, predetermined, settled, sorted out
(*Inf.*)
Antonyms (*sense 5*) add to, augment, enlarge,
expand, extend, fill out, increase (*sense 7*) ac~
cept gladly, embrace, greet, hail, receive, wel~
come with open arms

cutback cut, decrease, economy, lessening,
reduction, retrenchment

cut back check, curb, decrease, economize,
lessen, lower, prune, reduce, retrench,
slash, trim

cut down 1. fell, hew, level, lop, raze **2.**
Sometimes with on decrease, lessen, lower,
reduce **3.** blow away (*Sl., chiefly U.S.*), dis~
patch, kill, massacre, mow down, slaughter,
slay (*Archaic*), take out (*Sl.*) **4. cut (some~
one) down to size** abash, humiliate, make
(someone) look small, take the wind out of
(someone's) sails

cute appealing, attractive, charming, de~
lightful, engaging, lovable, sweet, winning,
winsome

cut in break in, butt in, interpose, interrupt,
intervene, intrude, move in (*Inf.*)

cut off 1. disconnect, intercept, interrupt,
intersect **2.** bring to an end, discontinue,
halt, obstruct, suspend **3.** isolate, separate,
sever **4.** disinherit, disown, renounce

cut out 1. cease, delete, extract, give up,
kick (*Inf.*), refrain from, remove, sever, stop
2. *Inf.* displace, eliminate, exclude, oust,
supersede, supplant

cut out for adapted, adequate, competent,
designed, equipped, fitted, qualified, suit~
able, suited

cut-price bargain, cheap, cheapo (*Inf.*),
cut-rate (*Chiefly U.S.*), reduced, sale

cut short abort, break off, bring to an end,

check, halt, interrupt, leave unfinished,
postpone, stop, terminate

cutthroat *n.* **1.** assassin, bravo, butcher,
executioner, heavy (*Sl.*), hit man (*Sl.*),
homicide, killer, liquidator, murderer,
slayer (*Archaic*), thug ~*adj.* **2.** barbarous,
bloodthirsty, bloody, cruel, death-dealing,
ferocious, homicidal, murderous, savage,
thuggish, violent **3.** competitive, dog-eat-
dog, fierce, relentless, ruthless, unprinci~
pled

cutting *adj.* **1.** biting, bitter, chill, keen,
numbing, penetrating, piercing, raw, sharp,
stinging **2.** acid, acrimonious, barbed, bit~
ter, caustic, hurtful, malicious, mordacious,
pointed, sarcastic, sardonic, scathing, se~
vere, trenchant, vitriolic, wounding
Antonyms (*sense 1*) balmy, pleasant, sooth~
ing (*sense 2*) consoling, flattering, kind, mild

cut up *v.* **1.** carve, chop, dice, divide, mince,
slice **2.** injure, knife, lacerate, slash, wound
3. *Inf.* blast, criticize, crucify (*Sl.*), give
(someone *or* something) a rough ride, lam~
bast(e), pan (*Inf.*), put down, ridicule, slate
(*Inf.*), tear into (*Inf.*), vilify ~*adj.* **4.** *Inf.*
agitated, dejected, desolated, distressed,
disturbed, heartbroken, stricken, upset,
wretched

cycle aeon, age, circle, era, period, phase,
revolution, rotation, round (*of years*)

cynic doubter, misanthrope, misanthropist,
pessimist, sceptic, scoffer

cynical contemptuous, derisive, distrustful,
ironic, misanthropic, misanthropical,
mocking, mordacious, pessimistic, sarcastic,
sardonic, sceptical, scoffing, scornful,
sneering, unbelieving
Antonyms credulous, green, gullible, hope~
ful, optimistic, trustful, trusting, unsceptical,
unsuspecting

cynicism disbelief, doubt, misanthropy,
pessimism, sarcasm, sardonicism, scepti~
cism

D

dabble 1. dip, guddle (*Scot.*), moisten, pad~ dle, spatter, splash, sprinkle, wet **2.** dally, dip into, play at, potter, tinker, trifle (with)

dabbler amateur, dilettante, potterer, tink~ erer, trifler

dab hand ace (*Inf.*), adept, buff (*Inf.*), dab~ ster (*Dialect*), expert, hotshot (*Inf.*), maven (*U.S.*), past master, whiz (*Inf.*), wizard

daft 1. absurd, asinine, crackpot (*Inf.*), cra~ zy, dopey (*Inf.*), foolish, giddy, goofy (*Inf.*), idiotic, inane, loopy (*Inf.*), off one's trolley (*Sl.*), out to lunch (*Inf.*), scatty (*Brit. inf.*), silly, simple, stupid, up the pole (*Inf.*), wit~ less **2.** barking (*Sl.*), barking mad (*Sl.*), crackers (*Brit. sl.*), crazy, demented, de~ ranged, insane, lunatic, mental (*Sl.*), not the full shilling (*Inf.*), nuts (*Sl.*), nutty (*Sl.*), touched, unhinged **3.** *With* **about** besotted by, crazy (*Inf.*), doting, dotty (*Sl., chiefly Brit.*), infatuated by, mad, nuts (*Sl.*), nutty (*Inf.*), potty (*Brit. inf.*), sweet on

dagger 1. bayonet, dirk, poniard, skean, stiletto **2. at daggers drawn** at enmity, at loggerheads, at odds, at war, on bad terms, up in arms **3. look daggers** frown, glare, glower, look black, lour *or* lower, scowl

daily *adj.* **1.** circadian, diurnal, everyday, quotidian **2.** common, commonplace, day-to-day, everyday, ordinary, quotidian, regu~ lar, routine ~*adv.* **3.** constantly, day after day, day by day, every day, often, once a day, per diem, regularly

dainty *adj.* **1.** charming, delicate, elegant, exquisite, fine, graceful, neat, petite, pretty **2.** choice, delectable, delicious, palatable, savoury, tasty, tender, toothsome **3.** choosy, fastidious, finical, finicky, fussy, mincing, nice, particular, picky (*Inf.*), refined, scru~ pulous ~*n.* **4.** *bonne bouche,* delicacy, fancy, sweetmeat, titbit
Antonyms awkward, clumsy, coarse, gauche, inelegant, maladroit, uncouth, un~ gainly

dale bottom, coomb, dell, dingle, glen, strath (*Scot.*), vale, valley

dally 1. dawdle, delay, dilly-dally (*Inf.*), fool (about *or* around), fritter away, hang about, linger, loiter, procrastinate, tarry, waste time, while away **2.** *Often with* **with** caress, flirt, fondle, fool (about *or* around), frivol (*Inf.*), lead on, play, play fast and loose (*Inf.*), tamper, tease, toy, trifle
Antonyms hasten, hurry (up), make haste, push forward *or* on, run, step on it (*Inf.*)

dam 1. *n.* barrage, barrier, embankment, hindrance, obstruction, wall **2.** *v.* barricade, block, block up, check, choke, confine, hold back, hold in, obstruct, restrict

damage *n.* **1.** destruction, detriment, dev~ astation, harm, hurt, impairment, injury, loss, mischief, mutilation, suffering **2.** *Inf.* bill, charge, cost, expense, total **3.** *Plural* compensation, fine, indemnity, reimburse~ ment, reparation, satisfaction ~*v.* **4.** deface, harm, hurt, impair, incapacitate, injure, mar, mutilate, ruin, spoil, tamper with, undo, weaken, wreck
Antonyms *n.* gain, improvement, reparation ~*v.* better, fix, mend, repair

damages compensation, fine, indemnity, reimbursement, reparation, satisfaction

damaging deleterious, detrimental, disad~ vantageous, harmful, hurtful, injurious, prejudicial, ruinous
Antonyms advantageous, favourable, healthful, helpful, profitable, salutary, useful, valuable, wholesome

dame baroness, dowager, *grande dame,* lady, matron (*Archaic*), noblewoman, peeress

damn *v.* **1.** blast, castigate, censure, con~ demn, criticize, denounce, denunciate, ex~ coriate, inveigle against, lambast(e), pan (*Inf.*), put down, slam (*Sl.*), slate (*Inf.*), tear into (*Inf.*) **2.** abuse, anathematize, blas~ pheme, curse, execrate, imprecate, revile, swear **3.** condemn, doom, sentence ~*n.* **4.** brass farthing, hoot, iota, jot, tinker's curse *or* damn (*Sl.*), two hoots, whit **5. not give a damn** be indifferent, not care, not mind
Antonyms (*sense 1*) acclaim, admire, ap~ plaud, approve, cheer, compliment, congratu~ late, extol, honour, laud, praise (*sense 2*) adore, bless, exalt, glorify, magnify (*Archaic*), pay homage to

damnable abominable, accursed, atrocious, culpable, cursed, despicable, detestable, ex~ ecrable, hateful, horrible, offensive, wicked
Antonyms admirable, commendable, cred~ itable, excellent, exemplary, fine, honourable, laudable, meritorious, praiseworthy, worthy

damnation anathema, ban, condemnation, consigning to perdition, damning, denun~ ciation, doom, excommunication, objurga~ tion, proscription, sending to hell

damned 1. accursed, anathematized, con~ demned, doomed, infernal, lost, reprobate, unhappy **2.** *Sl.* confounded, despicable, de~ testable, hateful, infamous, infernal, loath~ some, revolting

damning accusatorial, condemnatory, dam~

natory, dooming, implicating, implicative, incriminating

damp *n.* **1.** clamminess, dampness, dank~ ness, dew, drizzle, fog, humidity, mist, moisture, mugginess, vapour ~*adj.* **2.** clammy, dank, dewy, dripping, drizzly, hu~ mid, misty, moist, muggy, sodden, soggy, sopping, vaporous, wet ~*v.* **3.** dampen, moisten, wet **4.** *Fig.* allay, check, chill, cool, curb, dash, deaden, deject, depress, dimin~ ish, discourage, dispirit, dull, inhibit, mod~ erate, restrain, stifle ~*n.* **5.** *Fig.* check, chill, cold water (*Inf.*), curb, damper, dis~ couragement, gloom, restraint, wet blanket (*Inf.*)
Antonyms *n.* (*sense 1*) aridity, dryness ~*adj.* arid, dry, watertight ~*v.* (*sense 4*) encourage, hearten, inspire

damper chill, cloud, cold water (*Inf.*), curb, discouragement, gloom, hindrance, kill-joy, pall, restraint, wet blanket (*Inf.*)

dance 1. *v.* bob up and down, caper, cut a rug (*Inf.*), frolic, gambol, hop, jig, prance, rock, skip, spin, sway, swing, trip, whirl **2.** *n.* ball, dancing party, disco, discotheque, hop (*Inf.*), knees-up (*Brit. inf.*), social

dandy 1. *n.* beau, blade (*Archaic*), blood (*Rare*), buck (*Archaic*), coxcomb, dude (*U.S. & Canad. inf.*), exquisite (*Obsolete*), fop, macaroni (*Obsolete*), man about town, pea~ cock, popinjay, swell (*Inf.*), toff (*Brit. sl.*) **2.** *adj. Inf.* capital, excellent, fine, first-rate, great, splendid

danger endangerment, hazard, insecurity, jeopardy, menace, peril, pitfall, precarious~ ness, risk, threat, venture, vulnerability

dangerous alarming, breakneck, chancy (*Inf.*), exposed, hairy (*Sl.*), hazardous, in~ secure, menacing, nasty, parlous (*Archaic*), perilous, precarious, risky, threatening, treacherous, ugly, unchancy (*Scot.*), unsafe, vulnerable
Antonyms harmless, innocuous, O.K. *or* okay (*Inf.*), out of danger, out of harm's way, protected, safe, safe and sound, secure

dangerously 1. alarmingly, carelessly, daringly, desperately, harmfully, hazard~ ously, perilously, precariously, recklessly, riskily, unsafely, unsecurely **2.** critically, gravely, seriously, severely

dangle *v.* **1.** depend, flap, hang, hang down, sway, swing, trail **2.** brandish, entice, flaunt, flourish, lure, tantalize, tempt, wave

dangling disconnected, drooping, hanging, loose, swaying, swinging, trailing, uncon~ nected

dapper active, brisk, chic, dainty, natty (*Inf.*), neat, nice, nimble, smart, soigné *or* soignée, spruce, spry, stylish, trig (*Archaic or dialect*), trim, well-groomed, well turned out

Antonyms disarrayed, dishevelled, dowdy, frowzy, ill-groomed, rumpled, slobby (*Inf.*), sloppy (*Inf.*), slovenly, unkempt, untidy

dapple *v.* bespeckle, dot, fleck, freckle, mottle, speckle, spot, stipple

dappled brindled, checkered, flecked, freckled, mottled, piebald, pied, speckled, spotted, stippled, variegated

dare *v.* **1.** challenge, defy, goad, provoke, taunt, throw down the gauntlet **2.** adven~ ture, brave, endanger, gamble, hazard, make bold, presume, risk, stake, venture ~*n.* **3.** challenge, defiance, provocation, taunt

daredevil 1. *n.* adventurer, desperado, ex~ hibitionist, hot dog (*Chiefly U.S.*), madcap, show-off (*Inf.*), stunt man **2.** *adj.* adventur~ ous, audacious, bold, daring, death-defying, madcap, reckless

daring 1. *adj.* adventurous, audacious, ballsy (*Taboo sl.*), bold, brave, daredevil, fearless, game (*Inf.*), have-a-go (*Inf.*), impul~ sive, intrepid, plucky, rash, reckless, val~ iant, venturesome **2.** *n.* audacity, balls (*Ta~ boo sl.*), ballsiness (*Taboo sl.*), boldness, bottle (*Brit. sl.*), bravery, courage, derring~ do (*Archaic*), fearlessness, grit, guts (*Inf.*), intrepidity, nerve (*Inf.*), pluck, rashness, spirit, spunk (*Inf.*), temerity
Antonyms *adj.* anxious, careful, cautious, cowardly, faint-hearted, fearful, timid, uncourageous, wary ~*n.* anxiety, caution, cowardice, fear, timidity

dark *adj.* **1.** black, brunette, dark-skinned, dusky, ebony, sable, swarthy **2.** cloudy, darksome (*Literary*), dim, dingy, indistinct, murky, overcast, pitch-black, pitchy, shad~ owy, shady, sunless, unlit **3.** abstruse, ar~ cane, concealed, cryptic, deep, Delphic, en~ igmatic, hidden, mysterious, mystic, ob~ scure, occult, puzzling, recondite, secret **4.** bleak, cheerless, dismal, doleful, drab, gloomy, grim, joyless, morbid, morose, mournful, sombre **5.** benighted, ignorant, uncultivated, unenlightened, unlettered **6.** atrocious, damnable, evil, foul, hellish, hor~ rible, infamous, infernal, nefarious, satanic, sinful, sinister, vile, wicked **7.** angry, dour, forbidding, frowning, glowering, glum, ominous, scowling, sulky, sullen, threaten~ ing ~*n.* **8.** darkness, dimness, dusk, gloom, murk, murkiness, obscurity, semi-darkness **9.** evening, night, nightfall, night-time, twi~ light **10.** *Fig.* concealment, ignorance, se~ crecy
Antonyms (*sense 1*) blond, blonde, fair, fair-haired, flaxen-haired, light, light-complexioned, towheaded (*senses 2 & 4*) bright, cheerful, clear, genial, glad, hopeful, pleasant, sunny

darken 1. becloud, blacken, cloud up *or*

over, deepen, dim, eclipse, make dark, make darker, make dim, obscure, overshadow, shade, shadow **2.** become angry, become gloomy, blacken, cast a pall over, cloud, deject, depress, dispirit, grow troubled, look black, sadden

Antonyms (*sense 1*) brighten, clear up, enliven, gleam, glow, illuminate, lighten, light up, make bright, shine (*sense 2*) become cheerful, cheer, encourage, gladden, hearten, make happy, perk up

darkness 1. blackness, dark, dimness, dusk, duskiness, gloom, murk, murkiness, nightfall, obscurity, shade, shadiness, shadows **2.** *Fig.* blindness, concealment, ignorance, mystery, privacy, secrecy, unawareness

darling *n.* **1.** beloved, dear, dearest, love, sweetheart, truelove **2.** apple of one's eye, blue-eyed boy, fair-haired boy (*U.S.*), favourite, pet, spoilt child ~*adj.* **3.** adored, beloved, cherished, dear, precious, treasured **4.** adorable, attractive, captivating, charming, cute, enchanting, lovely, sweet

darn 1. *v.* cobble up, mend, patch, repair, sew up, stitch **2.** *n.* invisible repair, mend, patch, reinforcement

dart 1. bound, dash, flash, flit, fly, race, run, rush, scoot, shoot, spring, sprint, start, tear, whistle, whiz **2.** cast, fling, hurl, launch, propel, send, shoot, sling, throw

dash *v.* **1.** break, crash, destroy, shatter, shiver, smash, splinter **2.** cast, fling, hurl, slam, sling, throw **3.** barrel (along) (*Inf.,* *chiefly U.S. & Canad.*), bolt, bound, burn rubber (*Inf.*), dart, fly, haste, hasten, hurry, race, run, rush, speed, spring, sprint, tear **4.** abash, chagrin, confound, dampen, disappoint, discomfort, discourage **5.** blight, foil, frustrate, ruin, spoil, thwart, undo ~*n.* **6.** bolt, dart, haste, onset, race, run, rush, sortie, sprint, spurt **7.** brio, élan, flair, flourish, panache, spirit, style, verve, vigour, vivacity **8.** bit, drop, flavour, hint, little, pinch, smack, soupçon, sprinkling, suggestion, tinge, touch

Antonyms *v.* crawl, dawdle, enhance, improve, walk ~*n.* lot, much

dashing 1. bold, daring, debonair, exuberant, gallant, lively, plucky, spirited, swashbuckling **2.** dapper, dazzling, elegant, flamboyant, jaunty, showy, smart, sporty, stylish, swish (*Inf., chiefly Brit.*)

Antonyms boring, dreary, dull, lacklustre, stolid, unexciting, uninteresting

data details, documents, dope (*Inf.*), facts, figures, info (*Inf.*), information, input, materials, statistics

date *n.* **1.** age, epoch, era, period, stage, time **2.** appointment, assignation, engagement, meeting, rendezvous, tryst **3.** escort, friend,

partner, steady (*Inf.*) **4. out of date** antiquated, archaic, dated, obsolete, old, old-fashioned, passé **5. to date** now, so far, up to now, up to the present, up to this point, yet **6. up-to-date** à la mode, contemporary, current, fashionable, modern, trendy (*Brit. inf.*), up-to-the-minute ~*v.* **7.** assign a date to, determine the date of, fix the period of, put a date on **8.** bear a date, belong to, come from, exist from, originate in **9.** become obsolete, be dated, obsolesce, show one's age

dated antiquated, archaic, *démodé*, obsolete, old-fashioned, old hat, out, outdated, outmoded, out of date, passé, unfashionable, untrendy (*Brit. inf.*)

Antonyms à la mode, all the rage, chic, cool (*Inf.*), current, hip (*Sl.*), in vogue, latest, modern, modish, popular, stylish, trendy (*Brit. inf.*), up-to-date

daub *v.* **1.** coat, cover, paint, plaster, slap on (*Inf.*), smear **2.** bedaub, begrime, besmear, blur, deface, dirty, grime, smirch, smudge, spatter, splatter, stain, sully ~*n.* **3.** blot, blotch, smear, smirch, splodge, splotch, spot, stain

daunt 1. alarm, appal, cow, dismay, frighten, frighten off, intimidate, overawe, scare, subdue, terrify **2.** deter, discourage, dishearten, dispirit, put off, shake

Antonyms cheer, comfort, encourage, hearten, inspire, inspirit, reassure, spur, support

daunted *adj.* alarmed, cowed, demoralized, deterred, discouraged, disillusioned, dismayed, dispirited, downcast, frightened, hesitant, intimidated, overcome, put off, unnerved

dauntless bold, brave, courageous, daring, doughty, fearless, gallant, gritty, heroic, indomitable, intrepid, lion-hearted, resolute, stouthearted, undaunted, unflinching, valiant, valorous

dawdle dally, delay, dilly-dally (*Inf.*), fritter away, hang about, idle, lag, loaf, loiter, potter, trail, waste time

Antonyms fly, get a move on (*Inf.*), hasten, hurry, lose no time, make haste, rush, scoot, step on it (*Inf.*)

dawn *n.* **1.** aurora (*Poetic*), cockcrow, crack of dawn, dawning, daybreak, daylight, dayspring (*Poetic*), morning, sunrise, sunup ~*v.* **2.** break, brighten, gleam, glimmer, grow light, lighten ~*n.* **3.** advent, beginning, birth, dawning, emergence, genesis, inception, onset, origin, outset, rise, start, unfolding ~*v.* **4.** appear, begin, develop, emerge, initiate, open, originate, rise, unfold **5.** come into one's head, come to mind, cross one's mind, flash across one's mind, hit, occur, register (*Inf.*), strike

day 1. daylight, daylight hours, daytime, twenty-four hours, working day **2.** age, ascendancy, cycle, epoch, era, generation, height, heyday, period, prime, time, zenith **3.** date, particular day, point in time, set time, time **4. call it a day** *Inf.* end, finish, knock off (*Inf.*), leave off, pack it in (*Sl.*), pack up (*Inf.*), shut up shop, stop **5. day after day** continually, monotonously, persistently, regularly, relentlessly **6. day by day** daily, gradually, progressively, steadily

daybreak break of day, cockcrow, crack of dawn, dawn, dayspring (*Poetic*), first light, morning, sunrise, sunup

daydream *n.* **1.** dream, imagining, musing, reverie, stargazing, vision, woolgathering **2.** castle in the air *or* in Spain, dream, fancy, fantasy, figment of the imagination, fond hope, pipe dream, wish ~*v.* **3.** dream, envision, fancy, fantasize, hallucinate, imagine, muse, stargaze

daydreamer castle-builder, dreamer, fantast, pipe dreamer, visionary, Walter Mitty, wishful thinker, woolgatherer

daylight 1. light of day, sunlight, sunshine **2.** broad day, daylight hours, daytime **3.** full view, light of day, openness, public attention

daze *v.* **1.** benumb, numb, paralyse, shock, stun, stupefy **2.** amaze, astonish, astound, befog, bewilder, blind, confuse, dazzle, dumbfound, flabbergast (*Inf.*), flummox, nonplus, perplex, stagger, startle, surprise ~*n.* **3.** bewilderment, confusion, distraction, shock, stupor, trance, trancelike state

dazed at sea, baffled, bemused, bewildered, confused, disorientated, dizzy, dopey (*Sl.*), flabbergasted (*Inf.*), flummoxed, fuddled, groggy (*Inf.*), light-headed, muddled, nonplussed, numbed, perplexed, punch-drunk, shocked, staggered, stunned, stupefied, woozy (*Inf.*)

dazzle *v.* **1.** bedazzle, blind, blur, confuse, daze **2.** amaze, astonish, awe, bowl over (*Inf.*), fascinate, hypnotize, impress, overawe, overpower, overwhelm, strike dumb, stupefy ~*n.* **3.** brilliance, éclat, flash, glitter, magnificence, razzle-dazzle (*Sl.*), razzmatazz (*Sl.*), sparkle, splendour

dazzling brilliant, drop-dead (*Sl.*), glittering, glorious, radiant, ravishing, scintillating, sensational (*Inf.*), shining, sparkling, splendid, stunning, sublime, superb, virtuoso
Antonyms dull, ordinary, tedious, unexceptional, unexciting, uninspiring, uninteresting, unmemorable, unremarkable

dead *adj.* **1.** deceased, defunct, departed, extinct, gone, inanimate, late, lifeless, passed away, perished **2.** apathetic, callous, cold, dull, frigid, glassy, glazed, indifferent, inert, lukewarm, numb, paralysed, spirit-

less, torpid, unresponsive, wooden **3.** barren, inactive, inoperative, not working, obsolete, stagnant, sterile, still, unemployed, unprofitable, useless **4.** boring, dead-and-alive, dull, flat, ho-hum (*Inf.*), insipid, stale, tasteless, uninteresting, vapid **5.** *Fig.* absolute, complete, downright, entire, outright, thorough, total, unqualified, utter **6.** *Inf.* dead beat (*Inf.*), exhausted, spent, tired, worn out ~*n.* **7.** depth, middle, midst ~*adv.* **8.** absolutely, completely, directly, entirely, exactly, totally
Antonyms active, alive, animate, animated, effective, existing, in use, lively, living, operative, productive, responsive, vivacious, working

deaden abate, alleviate, anaesthetize, benumb, blunt, check, cushion, damp, dampen, diminish, dull, hush, impair, lessen, muffle, mute, numb, paralyse, quieten, reduce, smother, stifle, suppress, weaken

deadlock cessation, dead heat, draw, full stop, halt, impasse, stalemate, standoff, standstill, tie

deadly 1. baleful, baneful, dangerous, death-dealing, deathly, destructive, fatal, lethal, malignant, mortal, noxious, pernicious, poisonous, venomous **2.** cruel, grim, implacable, mortal, ruthless, savage, unrelenting **3.** ashen, deathlike, deathly, ghastly, ghostly, pallid, wan, white **4.** accurate, effective, exact, on target, precise, sure, true, unerring, unfailing **5.** *Inf.* boring, dull, ho-hum (*Inf.*), mind-numbing, monotonous, tedious, uninteresting, wearisome

deadpan *adj.* blank, empty, expressionless, impassive, inexpressive, inscrutable, poker-faced, straight-faced

deaf *adj.* **1.** hard of hearing, stone deaf, without hearing **2.** indifferent, oblivious, unconcerned, unhearing, unmoved

deafen din, drown out, make deaf, split *or* burst the eardrums

deafening booming, dinning, ear-piercing, ear-splitting, intense, overpowering, piercing, resounding, ringing, thunderous

deal *v.* **1.** *With* **with** attend to, cope with, handle, manage, oversee, see to, take care of, treat **2.** *With* **with** concern, consider, treat (of) **3.** *With* **with** act, behave, conduct oneself **4.** bargain, buy and sell, do business, negotiate, sell, stock, trade, traffic, treat (with) ~*n.* **5.** *Inf.* agreement, arrangement, bargain, contract, pact, transaction, understanding ~*v.* **6.** allot, apportion, assign, bestow, dispense, distribute, divide, dole out, give, mete out, reward, share ~*n.* **7.** amount, degree, distribution, extent, portion, quantity, share, transaction **8.** cut and shuffle, distribution, hand, round, single game

dealer chandler, marketer, merchandiser, merchant, purveyor, supplier, trader, tradesman, wholesaler

dealings business, business relations, commerce, trade, traffic, transactions, truck

dear *adj.* **1.** beloved, cherished, close, darling, esteemed, familiar, favourite, intimate, precious, prized, respected, treasured **2.** at a premium, costly, expensive, high-priced, overpriced, pricey (*Inf.*), ~*n.* **3.** angel, beloved, darling, loved one, precious, treasure ~*adv.* **4.** at a heavy cost, at a high price, at great cost, dearly
Antonyms cheap, common, disliked, hated, inexpensive, worthless

dearly 1. extremely, greatly, profoundly, very much **2.** affectionately, devotedly, fondly, lovingly, tenderly **3.** at a heavy cost, at a high price, at great cost, dear

death 1. bereavement, cessation, curtains (*Inf.*), decease, demise, departure, dissolution, dying, end, exit, expiration, loss, passing, quietus, release **2.** annihilation, destruction, downfall, eradication, extermination, extinction, finish, grave, obliteration, ruin, ruination, undoing
Antonyms beginning, birth, emergence, genesis, growth, origin, rise, source

deathless eternal, everlasting, immortal, imperishable, incorruptible, timeless, undying
Antonyms corporeal, earthly, ephemeral, human, mortal, passing, temporal, transient, transitory

deathly 1. cadaverous, deathlike, gaunt, ghastly, grim, haggard, pale, pallid, wan **2.** deadly, extreme, fatal, intense, mortal, terrible

debacle catastrophe, collapse, defeat, devastation, disaster, downfall, fiasco, havoc, overthrow, reversal, rout, ruin, ruination

debase 1. abase, cheapen, degrade, demean, devalue, disgrace, dishonour, drag down, humble, humiliate, lower, reduce, shame **2.** adulterate, bastardize, contaminate, corrupt, defile, depreciate, impair, pollute, taint, vitiate
Antonyms elevate, enhance, exalt, improve, purify, uplift

debased 1. adulterated, depreciated, devalued, impure, lowered, mixed, polluted, reduced **2.** abandoned, base, corrupt, debauched, degraded, depraved, fallen, low, perverted, sordid, vile
Antonyms chaste, decent, ethical, good, honourable, incorruptible, innocent, moral, pure, upright, virtuous

debasement 1. adulteration, contamination, depreciation, devaluation, pollution, reduction **2.** abasement, baseness, corruption, degradation, depravation, perversion

debatable arguable, borderline, controversial, disputable, doubtful, dubious, iffy (*Inf.*), in dispute, moot, open to question, problematical, questionable, uncertain, undecided, unsettled

debate *v.* **1.** argue, contend, contest, controvert, discuss, dispute, question, wrangle ~*n.* **2.** altercation, argument, contention, controversy, discussion, disputation, dispute, polemic, row ~*v.* **3.** cogitate, consider, deliberate, meditate upon, mull over, ponder, reflect, revolve, ruminate, weigh ~*n.* **4.** cogitation, consideration, deliberation, meditation, reflection

debauched *adj.* abandoned, corrupt, debased, degenerate, degraded, depraved, dissipated, dissolute, immoral, licentious, perverted, pervy (*Sl.*), profligate, sleazy, wanton

debilitate devitalize, enervate, enfeeble, exhaust, incapacitate, prostrate, relax, sap, undermine, weaken, wear out
Antonyms animate, brighten, energize, enliven, excite, fire, invigorate, pep up, perk up, rouse, stimulate, vitalize, wake up

debility decrepitude, enervation, enfeeblement, exhaustion, faintness, feebleness, frailty, incapacity, infirmity, languor, malaise, sickliness, weakness

debonair affable, buoyant, charming, cheerful, courteous, dashing, elegant, jaunty, light-hearted, refined, smooth, sprightly, suave, urbane, well-bred

debris bits, brash, detritus, dross, fragments, litter, pieces, remains, rubbish, rubble, ruins, waste, wreck, wreckage

debt 1. arrears, bill, claim, commitment, debit, due, duty, liability, obligation, score **2. in debt** accountable, beholden, in arrears, in hock (*Inf., chiefly U.S.*), in the red (*Inf.*), liable, owing, responsible

debtor borrower, defaulter, insolvent, mortgagor

debunk cut down to size, deflate, disparage, expose, lampoon, mock, puncture, ridicule, show up

debut beginning, bow, coming out, entrance, first appearance, inauguration, initiation, introduction, launching, presentation

decadence corruption, debasement, decay, decline, degeneration, deterioration, dissipation, dissolution, fall, perversion, retrogression

decadent corrupt, debased, debauched, decaying, declining, degenerate, degraded, depraved, dissolute, immoral, self-indulgent
Antonyms decent, ethical, good, high-minded, honourable, incorruptible, moral, principled, proper, upright, upstanding, virtuous

decant drain, draw off, pour out, tap

decapitate behead, execute, guillotine

decay v. **1.** atrophy, crumble, decline, de~ generate, deteriorate, disintegrate, dissolve, dwindle, moulder, shrivel, sink, spoil, wane, waste away, wear away, wither **2.** corrode, decompose, mortify, perish, putrefy, rot ~n. **3.** atrophy, collapse, decadence, decline, de~ generacy, degeneration, deterioration, dy~ ing, fading, failing, wasting, withering **4.** caries, cariosity, decomposition, gangrene, mortification, perishing, putrefaction, pu~ trescence, putridity, rot, rotting
Antonyms v. expand, flourish, flower, grow, increase ~n. growth

decayed bad, carious, carrion, corroded, decomposed, perished, putrefied, putrid, rank, rotten, spoiled, wasted, withered

decaying crumbling, deteriorating, disinte~ grating, gangrenous, perishing, putrefa~ cient, rotting, wasting away, wearing away

decease 1. n. death, demise, departure, dissolution, dying, release **2.** v. buy it (U.S. sl.), cease, check out (U.S. sl.), croak (Sl.), die, expire, go belly-up (Sl.), kick it (Sl.), kick the bucket (Sl.), pass away or on or over, peg it (Inf.), peg out (Inf.), perish, pop one's clogs (Inf.)

deceased adj. dead, defunct, departed, ex~ pired, finished, former, gone, late, lifeless, lost

deceit 1. artifice, cheating, chicanery, craftiness, cunning, deceitfulness, decep~ tion, dissimulation, double-dealing, duplic~ ity, fraud, fraudulence, guile, hypocrisy, imposition, pretence, slyness, treachery, trickery, underhandedness **2.** artifice, blind, cheat, chicanery, deception, duplicity, fake, feint, fraud, imposture, misrepresentation, pretence, ruse, scam (Sl.), sham, shift, sting (Inf.), stratagem, subterfuge, swindle, trick, wile
Antonyms candour, frankness, honesty, openness, sincerity, truthfulness

deceitful counterfeit, crafty, deceiving, de~ ceptive, designing, dishonest, disingenuous, double-dealing, duplicitous, fallacious, false, fraudulent, guileful, hypocritical, illusory, insincere, knavish (Archaic), sneaky, treacherous, tricky, two-faced, underhand, untrustworthy

deceive 1. bamboozle (Inf.), beguile, betray, cheat, con (Inf.), cozen, delude, disappoint, double-cross (Inf.), dupe, ensnare, entrap, fool, hoax, hoodwink, impose upon, kid (Inf.), lead (someone) on (Inf.), mislead, outwit, pull a fast one (Sl.), pull the wool over (someone's) eyes, stiff (Sl.), sting (Inf.), swindle, take for a ride (Inf.), take in (Inf.), trick **2. be deceived by** be made a fool of, be taken in (by), be the dupe of, bite, fall

for, fall into a trap, swallow (Inf.), swallow hook, line, and sinker (Inf.), take the bait

decency appropriateness, civility, correct~ ness, courtesy, decorum, etiquette, fitness, good form, good manners, modesty, propri~ ety, respectability, seemliness

decent 1. appropriate, becoming, befitting, chaste, comely, comme il faut, decorous, delicate, fit, fitting, modest, nice, polite, presentable, proper, pure, respectable, seemly, suitable **2.** acceptable, adequate, ample, average, competent, fair, passable, reasonable, satisfactory, sufficient, tolerable **3.** accommodating, courteous, friendly, generous, gracious, helpful, kind, obliging, thoughtful
Antonyms awkward, clumsy, discourteous, immodest, improper, inadequate, incorrect, indecent, inept, unsatisfactory, unseemly, unsuitable

deception 1. craftiness, cunning, deceit, deceitfulness, deceptiveness, dissimulation, duplicity, fraud, fraudulence, guile, hypoc~ risy, imposition, insincerity, legerdemain, treachery, trickery **2.** artifice, bluff, canard, cheat, decoy, feint, fraud, hoax, hokum (Sl., chiefly U.S. & Canad.), illusion, imposture, leg-pull (Brit. inf.), lie, pork pie (Brit. sl.), porky (Brit. sl.), ruse, sham, snare, strata~ gem, subterfuge, trick, wile
Antonyms artlessness, candour, fidelity, frankness, honesty, openness, scrupulous~ ness, straightforwardness, trustworthiness, truthfulness

deceptive ambiguous, deceitful, delusive, dishonest, fake, fallacious, false, fraudulent, illusory, misleading, mock, specious, spuri~ ous, unreliable

decide adjudge, adjudicate, choose, come to a conclusion, commit oneself, conclude, de~ cree, determine, elect, end, make a decision, make up one's mind, purpose, reach or come to a decision, resolve, settle
Antonyms be indecisive, be unable to de~ cide, blow hot and cold (Inf.), dither (Chiefly Brit.), falter, fluctuate, hesitate, hum and haw, seesaw, shillyshally (Inf.), swither (Scot.), vacillate

decided 1. absolute, categorical, certain, clear-cut, definite, distinct, express, indis~ putable, positive, pronounced, unambigu~ ous, undeniable, undisputed, unequivocal, unquestionable **2.** assertive, decisive, de~ liberate, determined, emphatic, firm, reso~ lute, strong-willed, unfaltering, unhesitating
Antonyms doubtful, dubious, hesitant, in~ decisive, irresolute, questionable, undeter~ mined, weak

decidedly absolutely, certainly, clearly, de~ cisively, distinctly, downright, positively, unequivocally, unmistakably

deciding chief, conclusive, critical, crucial, decisive, determining, influential, prime, principal, significant

decipher construe, crack, decode, deduce, explain, figure out (*Inf.*), interpret, make out, read, reveal, solve, suss (out) (*Sl.*), understand, unfold, unravel

decision 1. arbitration, conclusion, finding, judgment, outcome, resolution, result, ruling, sentence, settlement, verdict **2.** decisiveness, determination, firmness, purpose, purposefulness, resoluteness, resolution, resolve, strength of mind *or* will

decisive 1. absolute, conclusive, critical, crucial, definite, definitive, fateful, final, influential, momentous, positive, significant **2.** decided, determined, firm, forceful, incisive, resolute, strong-minded, trenchant
Antonyms doubtful, hesitant, hesitating, indecisive, in two minds (*Inf.*), irresolute, pussy-footing (*Inf.*), uncertain, undecided, vacillating

deck *v.* **1.** adorn, apparel (*Archaic*), array, attire, beautify, bedeck, bedight (*Archaic*), bedizen (*Archaic*), clothe, decorate, dress, embellish, festoon, garland, grace, ornament, trim **2. deck up** *or* **out** doll up (*Sl.*), get ready, prettify, pretty up, prink, rig out, tog up *or* out, trick out

declaim 1. harangue, hold forth, lecture, orate, perorate, proclaim, rant, recite, speak, spiel (*Inf.*) **2. declaim against** attack, decry, denounce, inveigh, rail

declamation address, harangue, lecture, oration, rant, recitation, speech, tirade

declaration 1. acknowledgment, affirmation, assertion, attestation, averment, avowal, deposition, disclosure, protestation, revelation, statement, testimony **2.** announcement, edict, manifesto, notification, proclamation, profession, promulgation, pronouncement, pronunciamento

declarative, declaratory affirmative, definite, demonstrative, enunciatory, explanatory, expository, expressive, positive

declare 1. affirm, announce, assert, asseverate, attest, aver, avow, certify, claim, confirm, maintain, proclaim, profess, pronounce, state, swear, testify, utter, validate **2.** confess, convey, disclose, make known, manifest, reveal, show

decline *v.* **1.** abstain, avoid, deny, forgo, refuse, reject, say 'no', send one's regrets, turn down **2.** decrease, diminish, drop, dwindle, ebb, fade, fail, fall, fall off, flag, lessen, shrink, sink, wane ~*n.* **3.** abatement, diminution, downturn, drop, dwindling, falling off, lessening, recession, slump ~*v.* **4.** decay, degenerate, deteriorate, droop, languish, pine, weaken, worsen ~*n.* **5.** decay, decrepitude, degeneration, deteriora-

tion, enfeeblement, failing, senility, weakening, worsening **6.** *Archaic* consumption, phthisis, tuberculosis ~*v.* **7.** descend, dip, sink, slant, slope ~*n.* **8.** declivity, hill, incline, slope
Antonyms *v.* accept, agree, consent, improve, increase, rise ~*n.* improvement, rise, upswing

decompose 1. break up, crumble, decay, fall apart, fester, putrefy, rot, spoil **2.** analyse, atomize, break down, break up, decompound, disintegrate, dissect, dissolve, distil, separate

decomposition atomization, breakdown, corruption, decay, disintegration, dissolution, division, putrefaction, putrescence, putridity, rot

décor colour scheme, decoration, furnishing style, ornamentation

decorate 1. adorn, beautify, bedeck, deck, embellish, enrich, festoon, grace, ornament, trim **2.** colour, do up (*Inf.*), furbish, paint, paper, renovate, wallpaper **3.** cite, honour, pin a medal on

decoration 1. adornment, beautification, elaboration, embellishment, enrichment, garnishing, ornamentation, trimming **2.** arabesque, bauble, cartouch(e), curlicue, falderal, festoon, flounce, flourish, frill, furbelow, garnish, ornament, scroll, spangle, trimmings, trinket **3.** award, badge, colours, emblem, garter, medal, order, ribbon, star

decorative adorning, arty-crafty, beautifying, enhancing, fancy, nonfunctional, ornamental, pretty

decorous appropriate, becoming, befitting, comely, *comme il faut*, correct, decent, dignified, fit, fitting, mannerly, polite, proper, refined, sedate, seemly, staid, suitable, well-behaved
Antonyms inapposite, inappropriate, malapropos, out of keeping, unbefitting, undignified, unseemly

decorum behaviour, breeding, courtliness, decency, deportment, dignity, etiquette, gentility, good grace, good manners, gravity, politeness, politesse, propriety, protocol, punctilio, respectability, seemliness
Antonyms bad manners, churlishness, impoliteness, impropriety, indecorum, rudeness, unseemliness

decoy 1. *n.* attraction, bait, ensnarement, enticement, inducement, lure, pretence, trap **2.** *v.* allure, bait, deceive, ensnare, entice, entrap, inveigle, lure, seduce, tempt

decrease 1. *v.* abate, contract, curtail, cut down, decline, diminish, drop, dwindle, ease, fall off, lessen, lower, peter out, reduce, shrink, slacken, subside, wane **2.** *n.* abatement, contraction, cutback, decline,

diminution, downturn, dwindling, ebb, fall~ ing off, lessening, loss, reduction, shrink~ age, subsidence
Antonyms *v.* enlarge, expand, extend, in~ crease ~*n.* expansion, extension, growth

decree 1. *n.* act, canon, command, demand, dictum, edict, enactment, law, mandate, or~ der, ordinance, precept, proclamation, regulation, ruling, statute 2. *v.* command, decide, demand, determine, dictate, enact, establish, lay down, ordain, order, pre~ scribe, proclaim, pronounce, rule

decrepit 1. aged, crippled, debilitated, dod~ dering, effete, feeble, frail, incapacitated, infirm, superannuated, wasted, weak 2. antiquated, battered, beat-up (*Inf.*), broken-down, deteriorated, dilapidated, ramshack~ le, rickety, run-down, tumble-down, weather-beaten, worn-out

decry abuse, asperse, belittle, blame, blast, censure, condemn, criticize, cry down, de~ nounce, depreciate, derogate, detract, de~ value, discredit, disparage, excoriate, lam~ bast(e), put down, rail against, run down, tear into (*Inf.*), traduce, underestimate, underrate, undervalue

dedicate 1. commit, devote, give over to, pledge, surrender 2. address, assign, in~ scribe, offer 3. bless, consecrate, hallow, sanctify, set apart

dedicated committed, devoted, enthusias~ tic, given over to, purposeful, single-minded, sworn, wholehearted, zealous
Antonyms indifferent, uncaring, uncom~ mitted, unconcerned, uninterested, unre~ sponsive

dedication 1. adherence, allegiance, com~ mitment, devotedness, devotion, faithful~ ness, loyalty, single-mindedness, whole~ heartedness 2. address, inscription, message 3. consecration, hallowing, sanctification
Antonyms apathy, coolness, indifference, insensibility, torpor, unconcern, uninterest~ edness

deduce conclude, derive, draw, gather, glean, infer, reason, take to mean, under~ stand

deduct decrease by, knock off (*Inf.*), reduce by, remove, subtract, take away, take from, take off, take out, withdraw
Antonyms add, add to, enlarge

deduction 1. assumption, conclusion, con~ sequence, corollary, finding, inference, rea~ soning, result 2. abatement, allowance, de~ crease, diminution, discount, reduction, subtraction, withdrawal

deed 1. achievement, act, action, exploit, fact, feat, performance, reality, truth 2. *Law* contract, document, indenture, instru~ ment, title, title deed, transaction

deem account, believe, conceive, consider, esteem, estimate, hold, imagine, judge, reckon, regard, suppose, think

deep *adj.* 1. abyssal, bottomless, broad, far, profound, unfathomable, wide, yawning 2. abstract, abstruse, arcane, esoteric, hidden, mysterious, obscure, recondite, secret 3. acute, discerning, learned, penetrating, sa~ gacious, wise 4. artful, astute, canny, cun~ ning, designing, devious, insidious, know~ ing, scheming, shrewd 5. extreme, grave, great, intense, profound, unqualified 6. ab~ sorbed, engrossed, immersed, lost, preoccu~ pied, rapt 7. *Of a colour* dark, intense, rich, strong, vivid 8. *Of a sound* bass, booming, full-toned, low, low pitched, resonant, sono~ rous ~*n.* 9. *Usually preceded by* **the** briny (*Inf.*), high seas, main, ocean, sea 10. cul~ mination, dead, middle, mid point ~*adv.* 11. deeply, far down, far into, late
Antonyms high, light, pale, shallow, sharp, simple, superficial

deepen 1. dig out, dredge, excavate, hollow, scoop out, scrape out 2. grow, increase, in~ tensify, magnify, reinforce, strengthen

deeply 1. completely, gravely, profoundly, seriously, severely, thoroughly, to the heart, to the quick 2. acutely, affectingly, distressingly, feelingly, intensely, mourn~ fully, movingly, passionately, sadly

deep-rooted *or* **deep-seated** confirmed, entrenched, fixed, ineradicable, ingrained, inveterate, rooted, settled, subconscious, unconscious
Antonyms eradicable, exterior, external, on the surface, peripheral, shallow, skin-deep, slight, superficial, surface

deface blemish, deform, destroy, disfigure, impair, injure, mar, mutilate, obliterate, spoil, sully, tarnish, total (*Sl.*), trash (*Sl.*), vandalize

defacement blemish, damage, destruction, disfigurement, distortion, impairment, in~ jury, mutilation, vandalism

de facto 1. *adv.* actually, in effect, in fact, in reality, really 2. *adj.* actual, existing, real

defamation aspersion, calumny, character assassination, denigration, disparagement, libel, obloquy, opprobrium, scandal, slan~ der, slur, smear, traducement, vilification

defamatory abusive, calumnious, contu~ melious, denigrating, derogatory, disparag~ ing, injurious, insulting, libellous, slander~ ous, vilifying, vituperative

defame asperse, bad-mouth (*Sl., chiefly U.S. & Canad.*), belie, besmirch, blacken, calum~ niate, cast a slur on, cast aspersions on, denigrate, detract, discredit, disgrace, dis~ honour, disparage, knock (*Inf.*), libel, ma~ lign, rubbish (*Inf.*), slag (off) (*Sl.*), slander, smear, speak evil of, stigmatize, traduce, vilify, vituperate

default 1. *n.* absence, defect, deficiency, dereliction, failure, fault, lack, lapse, ne~ glect, nonpayment, omission, want **2.** *v.* bilk, defraud, dodge, evade, fail, levant (*Brit.*), neglect, rat (*Inf.*), swindle, welsh (*Sl.*)

defaulter delinquent, embezzler, levanter (*Brit.*), nonpayer, offender, peculator, welsher (*Sl.*)

defeat *v.* **1.** beat, blow out of the water (*Sl.*), clobber (*Sl.*), conquer, crush, lick (*Inf.*), master, overpower, overthrow, overwhelm, quell, repulse, rout, run rings around (*Inf.*), subdue, subjugate, tank (*Sl.*), undo, van~ quish, wipe the floor with (*Inf.*) **2.** baffle, balk, confound, disappoint, discomfit, foil, frustrate, get the better of, ruin, thwart ~*n.* **3.** beating, conquest, debacle, overthrow, pasting (*Sl.*), repulse, rout, trouncing, van~ quishment **4.** disappointment, discomfiture, failure, frustration, rebuff, repulse, reverse, setback, thwarting
Antonyms *v.* bow, lose, submit, succumb, surrender, yield ~*n.* success, triumph, victory

defeated balked, beaten, bested, checkmat~ ed, conquered, crushed, licked (*Inf.*), over~ come, overpowered, overwhelmed, routed, thrashed, thwarted, trounced, vanquished, worsted
Antonyms conquering, dominant, glorious, successful, triumphal, triumphant, undefeat~ ed, victorious, winning

defeatist 1. *n.* pessimist, prophet of doom, quitter, submitter, yielder **2.** *adj.* pessimis~ tic

defect *n.* **1.** blemish, blotch, error, failing, fault, flaw, foible, imperfection, mistake, spot, taint, want **2.** absence, default, deficiency, frailty, inadequacy, lack, short~ coming, weakness ~*v.* **3.** abandon, aposta~ tize, break faith, change sides, desert, go over, rebel, revolt, tergiversate, walk out on (*Inf.*)

defection abandonment, apostasy, back~ sliding, dereliction, desertion, rebellion, re~ volt

defective 1. broken, deficient, faulty, flawed, imperfect, inadequate, incomplete, insufficient, not working, out of order, scant, short **2.** abnormal, mentally deficient, retarded, subnormal
Antonyms adequate, intact, normal, perfect, whole, working

defector apostate, deserter, rat (*Inf.*), recre~ ant (*Archaic*), renegade, runagate (*Archaic*), tergiversator, turncoat

defence 1. armament, cover, deterrence, guard, immunity, protection, resistance, safeguard, security, shelter **2.** barricade, bastion, buckler, bulwark, buttress, fast~ ness, fortification, rampart, shield **3.** apolo~ gia, apology, argument, excuse, exoneration, explanation, extenuation, justification, plea, vindication **4.** *Law* alibi, case, declaration, denial, plea, pleading, rebuttal, testimony

defenceless endangered, exposed, helpless, naked, powerless, unarmed, unguarded, unprotected, vulnerable, wide open
Antonyms free from harm, guarded, out of harm's way, protected, safe, safe and sound, secure

defend 1. cover, fortify, guard, keep safe, preserve, protect, safeguard, screen, secure, shelter, shield, ward off, watch over **2.** as~ sert, champion, endorse, espouse, justify, maintain, plead, speak up for, stand by, stand up for, stick up for (*Inf.*), support, sustain, uphold, vindicate

defendant appellant, defence, litigant, of~ fender, prisoner at the bar, respondent, the accused

defender 1. bodyguard, escort, guard, pro~ tector **2.** advocate, champion, patron, spon~ sor, supporter, vindicator

defensible 1. holdable, impregnable, safe, secure, unassailable **2.** justifiable, pardon~ able, permissible, plausible, tenable, valid, vindicable
Antonyms faulty, inexcusable, insupport~ able, unforgivable, unjustifiable, unpardon~ able, untenable, wrong

defensive averting, defending, on the de~ fensive, opposing, protective, safeguarding, uptight (*Inf.*), watchful, withstanding

defensively at bay, in defence, in self-defence, on guard, on the defensive, suspi~ ciously

defer[1] adjourn, delay, hold over, postpone, procrastinate, prorogue, protract, put off, put on ice, put on the back burner (*Inf.*), set aside, shelve, suspend, table, take a rain check on (*U.S. & Canad. inf.*)

defer[2] accede, bow, capitulate, comply, give in, give way to, respect, submit, yield

deference 1. acquiescence, capitulation, complaisance, compliance, obedience, obei~ sance, submission, yielding **2.** attention, ci~ vility, consideration, courtesy, esteem, homage, honour, obeisance, politeness, re~ gard, respect, reverence, thoughtfulness, veneration
Antonyms (*sense 1*) disobedience, insubor~ dination, noncompliance, nonobservance, re~ volt (*sense 2*) contempt, discourtesy, dishon~ our, disregard, disrespect, impertinence, im~ politeness, impudence, incivility, insolence, irreverence, lack of respect, rudeness

deferential civil, complaisant, considerate, courteous, dutiful, ingratiating, obedient,

obeisant, obsequious, polite, regardful, re~
spectful, reverential, submissive

deferment, deferral adjournment, delay,
moratorium, postponement, putting off,
stay, suspension

defiance challenge, confrontation, con~
tempt, contumacy, disobedience, disregard,
insolence, insubordination, opposition,
provocation, rebelliousness, recalcitrance,
spite
Antonyms accordance, acquiescence, com~
pliance, deference, obedience, observance,
regard, respect, subservience

defiant aggressive, audacious, bold, chal~
lenging, contumacious, daring, disobedient,
insolent, insubordinate, mutinous, provoca~
tive, rebellious, recalcitrant, refractory,
truculent
Antonyms cowardly, meek, obedient, re~
spectful, submissive

deficiency 1. defect, demerit, failing, fault,
flaw, frailty, imperfection, shortcoming,
weakness **2.** absence, dearth, deficit, inad~
equacy, insufficiency, lack, scantiness,
scarcity, shortage
Antonyms abundance, adequacy, sufficient,
superfluity, surfeit

deficient 1. defective, faulty, flawed, im~
paired, imperfect, incomplete, inferior, un~
satisfactory, weak **2.** exiguous, inadequate,
insufficient, lacking, meagre, pathetic,
scant, scanty, scarce, short, skimpy, want~
ing

deficit arrears, default, deficiency, loss,
shortage, shortfall

defiled besmirched, desecrated, dishon~
oured, impure, polluted, profaned, ravished,
spoilt, tainted, unclean
Antonyms chaste, clean, immaculate, inno~
cent, spotless, uncontaminated, uncorrupted,
undefiled, unstained, unsullied, untainted

define 1. characterize, describe, designate,
detail, determine, explain, expound, inter~
pret, specify, spell out **2.** bound, circum~
scribe, delimit, delineate, demarcate, limit,
mark out, outline

definite 1. clear, clear-cut, clearly defined,
determined, exact, explicit, express, fixed,
marked, obvious, particular, precise,
specific **2.** assured, certain, decided, guar~
anteed, positive, settled, sure
Antonyms confused, fuzzy, general, hazy,
ill-defined, imprecise, indefinite, indetermi~
nate, indistinct, inexact, loose, obscure, un~
certain, unclear, undetermined, vague

definitely absolutely, beyond any doubt,
categorically, certainly, clearly, decidedly,
easily, far and away, finally, indubitably,
obviously, plainly, positively, surely, unde~
niably, unequivocally, unmistakably, un~

questionably, without doubt, without fail,
without question

definition 1. clarification, description, elu~
cidation, explanation, exposition, statement
of meaning **2.** delimitation, delineation, de~
marcation, determination, fixing, outlining,
settling **3.** clarity, contrast, distinctness,
focus, precision, sharpness

definitive absolute, authoritative, complete,
conclusive, decisive, exhaustive, final, per~
fect, reliable, ultimate

deflate 1. collapse, contract, empty, ex~
haust, flatten, puncture, shrink, void **2.**
chasten, dash, debunk (*Inf.*), disconcert,
dispirit, humble, humiliate, mortify, put
down (*Sl.*), squash, take the wind out of
(someone's) sails **3.** *Economics* decrease,
depreciate, depress, devalue, diminish, re~
duce
Antonyms aerate, amplify, balloon, bloat,
blow up, boost, dilate, distend, enlarge, exag~
gerate, expand, increase, inflate, puff up *or*
out, pump up, swell

deflect bend, deviate, diverge, glance off,
ricochet, shy, sidetrack, slew, swerve, turn,
turn aside, twist, veer, wind

deflection aberration, bend, declination,
deviation, divergence, drift, refraction,
swerve, veer

deform 1. buckle, contort, distort, gnarl,
malform, mangle, misshape, twist, warp **2.**
cripple, deface, disfigure, injure, maim,
mar, mutilate, ruin, spoil

deformed 1. bent, blemished, crippled,
crooked, disfigured, distorted, maimed,
malformed, mangled, marred, misbegotten,
misshapen **2.** depraved, gross, offensive,
perverted, twisted, warped

deformity 1. abnormality, defect,
disfigurement, distortion, irregularity, mal~
formation, misproportion, misshapenness,
ugliness **2.** corruption, depravity, gross~
ness, hatefulness, vileness

defraud beguile, bilk, cheat, con (*Inf.*), co~
zen, delude, diddle (*Inf.*), do (*Sl.*), dupe, em~
bezzle, fleece, gull (*Archaic*), gyp (*Sl.*), out~
wit, pilfer, pull a fast one on (*Inf.*), rip off
(*Sl.*), rob, rook (*Sl.*), skin (*Sl.*), stiff (*Sl.*),
swindle, trick

deft able, adept, adroit, agile, clever, dexter~
ous, expert, handy, neat, nimble, proficient,
skilful
Antonyms awkward, bumbling, cack-
handed (*Inf.*), clumsy, gauche, inept, mala~
droit, unskilful

defunct 1. dead, deceased, departed, ex~
tinct, gone **2.** a dead letter, bygone, expired,
inoperative, invalid, nonexistent, not func~
tioning, obsolete, out of commission

defy 1. beard, brave, challenge, confront,

contemn, dare, despise, disregard, face, flout, hurl defiance at, provoke, scorn, slight, spurn **2.** baffle, defeat, elude, foil, frustrate, repel, repulse, resist, thwart, withstand

degenerate 1. *adj.* base, corrupt, debased, debauched, decadent, degenerated, degraded, depraved, deteriorated, dissolute, fallen, immoral, low, mean, perverted, pervy (*Sl.*) **2.** *v.* decay, decline, decrease, deteriorate, fall off, lapse, regress, retrogress, rot, sink, slip, worsen

degeneration debasement, decline, degeneracy, descent, deterioration, dissipation, dissolution, regression

degradation 1. abasement, debasement, decadence, decline, degeneracy, degeneration, demotion, derogation, deterioration, downgrading, perversion **2.** discredit, disgrace, dishonour, humiliation, ignominy, mortification, shame

degrade 1. cheapen, corrupt, debase, demean, deteriorate, discredit, disgrace, dishonour, humble, humiliate, impair, injure, pervert, shame, vitiate **2.** break, cashier, demote, depose, downgrade, lower, reduce to inferior rank **3.** adulterate, dilute, doctor, mix, thin, water, water down, weaken **Antonyms** dignify, elevate, enhance, ennoble, honour, improve, promote, raise

degraded abandoned, base, corrupt, debased, debauched, decadent, depraved, despicable, disgraced, disreputable, dissolute, low, mean, profligate, sordid, vicious, vile

degrading cheapening, contemptible, debasing, demeaning, disgraceful, dishonourable, humiliating, infra dig (*Inf.*), lowering, shameful, undignified, unworthy

degree 1. class, grade, level, order, position, rank, standing, station, status **2.** division, extent, gradation, grade, interval, limit, mark, measure, notch, point, rung, scale, stage, step, unit **3.** ambit, calibre, extent, intensity, level, measure, proportion, quality, quantity, range, rate, ratio, scale, scope, severity, standard **4. by degrees** bit by bit, gently, gradually, imperceptibly, inch by inch, little by little, slowly, step by step

deign condescend, consent, deem worthy, lower oneself, see fit, stoop, think fit

deity celestial being, divine being, divinity, god, goddess, godhead, idol, immortal, supreme being

dejected blue, cast down, crestfallen, depressed, despondent, disconsolate, disheartened, dismal, doleful, down, downcast, downhearted, gloomy, glum, low, low-spirited, melancholy, miserable, morose, sad, sick as a parrot (*Inf.*), woebegone, wretched **Antonyms** blithe, cheerful, chirpy (*Inf.*), encouraged, genial, happy, joyous, light-hearted, upbeat (*Inf.*)

dejection blues, depression, despair, despondency, doldrums, downheartedness, dumps (*Inf.*), gloom, gloominess, heavyheartedness, low spirits, melancholy, sadness, sorrow, the hump (*Brit. inf.*), unhappiness

de jure according to the law, by right, legally, rightfully

delay *v.* **1.** defer, hold over, postpone, procrastinate, prolong, protract, put off, put on the back burner (*Inf.*), shelve, stall, suspend, table, take a rain check on (*U.S. & Canad. inf.*), temporize ~*n.* **2.** deferment, postponement, procrastination, stay, suspension ~*v.* **3.** arrest, bog down, check, detain, halt, hinder, hold back, hold up, impede, obstruct, retard, set back, slow up, stop ~*n.* **4.** check, detention, hindrance, hold-up, impediment, interruption, interval, obstruction, setback, stoppage, wait ~*v.* **5.** dawdle, dilly-dally (*Inf.*), drag, lag, linger, loiter, tarry ~*n.* **6.** dawdling, dilly-dallying (*Inf.*), lingering, loitering, tarrying **Antonyms** accelerate, advance, dispatch, expedite, facilitate, forward, hasten, hurry, precipitate, press, promote, quicken, rush, speed (up), urge

delectable adorable, agreeable, appetizing, charming, dainty, delicious, delightful, enjoyable, enticing, gratifying, inviting, luscious, lush, pleasant, pleasurable, satisfying, scrumptious (*Inf.*), tasty, toothsome, yummy (*Sl.*) **Antonyms** awful, disagreeable, disgusting, distasteful, dreadful, horrible, horrid, nasty, offensive, terrible, unappetizing, unpleasant, yucky *or* yukky (*Sl.*)

delectation amusement, delight, diversion, enjoyment, entertainment, gratification, happiness, jollies (*Sl.*), pleasure, refreshment, relish, satisfaction

delegate *n.* **1.** agent, ambassador, commissioner, deputy, envoy, legate, representative, vicar ~*v.* **2.** accredit, appoint, authorize, commission, depute, designate, empower, mandate **3.** assign, consign, devolve, entrust, give, hand over, pass on, relegate, transfer

delegation 1. commission, contingent, deputation, embassy, envoys, legation, mission **2.** assignment, commissioning, committal, deputizing, devolution, entrustment, relegation

delete blot out, blue-pencil, cancel, cross out, cut out, dele, edit, edit out, efface, erase, excise, expunge, obliterate, remove, rub out, strike out

deliberate *v.* **1.** cogitate, consider, consult, debate, discuss, meditate, mull over, pon-

der, reflect, think, weigh ~*adj.* **2.** calculat~
ed, conscious, considered, designed, inten~
tional, planned, prearranged, premeditated,
purposeful, studied, thoughtful, wilful **3.**
careful, cautious, circumspect, heedful,
measured, methodical, ponderous, prudent,
slow, thoughtful, unhurried, wary
Antonyms (*sense 2*) accidental, inadvertent,
unconscious, unintended, unpremeditated,
unthinking (*sense 3*) fast, haphazard, hasty,
heedless, hurried, impetuous, impulsive, rash

deliberately by design, calculatingly, con~
sciously, determinedly, emphatically, in
cold blood, intentionally, knowingly, on
purpose, pointedly, resolutely, studiously,
wilfully, wittingly

deliberation 1. calculation, care, careful~
ness, caution, circumspection, cogitation,
consideration, coolness, forethought, medi~
tation, prudence, purpose, reflection,
speculation, study, thought, wariness **2.**
conference, consultation, debate, discussion

delicacy 1. accuracy, daintiness, elegance,
exquisiteness, fineness, lightness, nicety,
precision, subtlety **2.** debility, flimsiness,
fragility, frailness, frailty, infirmity, slen~
derness, tenderness, weakness **3.** discrimi~
nation, fastidiousness, finesse, purity,
refinement, sensibility, sensitiveness, sen~
sitivity, tact, taste **4.** *bonne bouche,* dainty,
luxury, relish, savoury, titbit, treat

delicate 1. ailing, debilitated, flimsy, frag~
ile, frail, sickly, slender, slight, tender,
weak **2.** choice, dainty, delicious, elegant,
exquisite, fine, graceful, savoury, tender **3.**
faint, muted, pastel, soft, subdued, subtle **4.**
accurate, deft, detailed, minute, precise,
skilled **5.** considerate, diplomatic, discreet,
sensitive, tactful **6.** critical, difficult, pre~
carious, sensitive, sticky (*Inf.*), ticklish,
touchy **7.** careful, critical, discriminating,
fastidious, nice, prudish, pure, refined,
scrupulous, squeamish
Antonyms bright, careless, coarse, crude,
harsh, healthy, inconsiderate, indelicate, in~
sensitive, rough, strong, unrefined

delicately carefully, daintily, deftly, el~
egantly, exquisitely, fastidiously, finely,
gracefully, lightly, precisely, sensitively,
skilfully, softly, subtly, tactfully

delicious 1. ambrosial, appetizing, choice,
dainty, delectable, luscious, mouthwatering,
nectareous, palatable, savoury, scrumptious
(*Inf.*), tasty, toothsome, yummy (*Sl.*) **2.**
agreeable, charming, delightful, enjoyable,
entertaining, exquisite, pleasant, pleasing
Antonyms disagreeable, distasteful, un~
pleasant

delight *n.* **1.** ecstasy, enjoyment, felicity,
gladness, gratification, happiness, jollies
(*Sl.*), joy, pleasure, rapture, transport ~*v.* **2.**

amuse, charm, cheer, divert, enchant,
gratify, please, ravish, rejoice, satisfy, thrill
3. *With* **in** appreciate, enjoy, feast on, glory
in, indulge in, like, love, luxuriate in, rel~
ish, revel in, savour
Antonyms *n.* disapprobation, disfavour,
dislike, displeasure, dissatisfaction, distaste
~*v.* disgust, displease, dissatisfy, gall, irk, of~
fend, upset, vex

delighted captivated, charmed, cock-a-hoop,
ecstatic, elated, enchanted, gladdened, hap~
py, joyous, jubilant, overjoyed, over the
moon (*Inf.*), pleased, rapt, thrilled

delightful agreeable, amusing, captivating,
charming, congenial, delectable, enchant~
ing, engaging, enjoyable, entertaining, fas~
cinating, gratifying, heavenly, pleasant,
pleasing, pleasurable, rapturous, ravishing,
thrilling
Antonyms disagreeable, displeasing, dis~
tasteful, horrid, nasty, unpleasant

delinquency crime, fault, misbehaviour,
misconduct, misdeed, misdemeanour, of~
fence, wrongdoing

delinquent criminal, culprit, defaulter, ju~
venile delinquent, lawbreaker, malefactor,
miscreant, offender, villain, wrongdoer,
young offender

delirious 1. crazy, demented, deranged, in~
coherent, insane, light-headed, mad, raving,
unhinged **2.** beside oneself, carried away,
corybantic, ecstatic, excited, frantic, fren~
zied, hysterical, wild
Antonyms calm, clear-headed, coherent,
compos mentis, in one's right mind, lucid, ra~
tional, sane, sensible

delirium 1. aberration, derangement, hal~
lucination, insanity, lunacy, madness, rav~
ing **2.** ecstasy, fever, frenzy, fury, hysteria,
passion, rage

deliver 1. bear, bring, carry, cart, convey,
distribute, transport **2.** cede, commit, give
up, grant, hand over, make over, relin~
quish, resign, surrender, transfer, turn
over, yield **3.** acquit, discharge, emanci~
pate, free, liberate, loose, ransom, redeem,
release, rescue, save **4.** announce, declare,
give, give forth, present, proclaim, pro~
nounce, publish, read, utter **5.** administer,
aim, deal, direct, give, inflict, launch,
strike, throw **6.** discharge, dispense, feed,
give forth, provide, purvey, release, supply

deliverance emancipation, escape, libera~
tion, ransom, redemption, release, rescue,
salvation

delivery 1. consignment, conveyance, dis~
patch, distribution, handing over, surren~
der, transfer, transmission, transmittal **2.**
articulation, elocution, enunciation, intona~
tion, speech, utterance **3.** *Medical* child~
birth, confinement, labour, parturition **4.**

deliverance, escape, liberation, release, res~cue

delude bamboozle (*Inf.*), beguile, cheat, con (*Inf.*), cozen, deceive, dupe, fool, gull (*Archaic*), hoax, hoodwink, impose on, kid (*Inf.*), lead up the garden path (*Inf.*), misguide, mislead, take in (*Inf.*), trick

deluge n. **1.** cataclysm, downpour, flood, inundation, overflowing, spate, torrent **2.** *Fig.* avalanche, barrage, flood, rush, spate, torrent ~v. **3.** douse, drench, drown, flood, inundate, soak, submerge, swamp **4.** *Fig.* engulf, inundate, overload, overrun, overwhelm, swamp

delusion deception, error, fallacy, false impression, fancy, hallucination, illusion, misapprehension, misbelief, misconception, mistake, phantasm, self-deception

de luxe choice, costly, elegant, exclusive, expensive, gorgeous, grand, luxurious, opulent, palatial, plush (*Inf.*), rich, select, special, splendid, splendiferous (*Facetious*), sumptuous, superior

delve burrow, dig into, examine, explore, ferret out, investigate, look into, probe, ransack, research, rummage, search, unearth

demagogue agitator, firebrand, haranguer, rabble-rouser, soapbox orator

demand v. **1.** ask, challenge, inquire, interrogate, question, request **2.** call for, cry out for, entail, involve, necessitate, need, require, take, want **3.** claim, exact, expect, insist on, order ~n. **4.** bidding, charge, inquiry, interrogation, order, question, request, requisition **5.** call, claim, market, necessity, need, requirement, want **6. in demand** fashionable, in vogue, needed, popular, requested, sought after
Antonyms v. come up with, contribute, furnish, give, grant, produce, provide, supply, yield

demanding 1. challenging, difficult, exacting, exhausting, exigent, hard, taxing, tough, trying, wearing **2.** clamorous, imperious, importunate, insistent, nagging, pressing, urgent
Antonyms a piece of cake (*Inf.*), child's play (*Inf.*), easy, easy-peasy (*Sl.*), effortless, facile, no bother, painless, simple, straightforward, uncomplicated, undemanding

demarcate define, delimit, determine, differentiate, distinguish between, fix, mark, separate

demarcation 1. bound, boundary, confine, enclosure, limit, margin, pale **2.** delimitation, differentiation, distinction, division, separation

demean abase, debase, degrade, descend, humble, lower, stoop

demeanour air, bearing, behaviour, carriage, comportment, conduct, deportment, manner, mien

demented barking (*Sl.*), barking mad (*Sl.*), crackbrained, crackpot (*Inf.*), crazed, crazy, daft (*Inf.*), deranged, distraught, dotty (*Sl., chiefly Brit.*), foolish, frenzied, idiotic, insane, loopy (*Inf.*), lunatic, mad, maniacal, manic, *non compos mentis,* not the full shilling (*Inf.*), off one's trolley (*Sl.*), out to lunch (*Inf.*), unbalanced, unhinged, up the pole (*Inf.*)
Antonyms all there (*Inf.*), *compos mentis,* in one's right mind, lucid, mentally sound, normal, of sound mind, rational, reasonable, sensible, sound

democracy commonwealth, government by the people, representative government, republic

democratic autonomous, egalitarian, popular, populist, representative, republican, self-governing

demolish 1. bulldoze, destroy, dismantle, flatten, knock down, level, overthrow, pulverize, raze, ruin, tear down, total (*Sl.*), trash (*Sl.*) **2.** *Fig.* annihilate, blow out of the water (*Sl.*), defeat, destroy, lick (*Inf.*), master, overthrow, overturn, tank (*Sl.*), undo, wipe the floor with (*Inf.*), wreck **3.** consume, devour, eat, gobble up, put away
Antonyms build, construct, create, repair, restore, strengthen

demolition bulldozing, destruction, explosion, knocking down, levelling, razing, wrecking

demon 1. devil, evil spirit, fiend, ghoul, goblin, malignant spirit **2.** *Fig.* devil, fiend, ghoul, monster, rogue, villain **3.** ace (*Inf.*), addict, fanatic, fiend, go-getter (*Inf.*), master, wizard **4.** daemon, daimon, genius, guardian spirit, ministering angel, numen

demonic, demoniac, demoniacal 1. devilish, diabolic, diabolical, fiendish, hellish, infernal, satanic **2.** crazed, frantic, frenetic, frenzied, furious, hectic, like one possessed, mad, maniacal, manic

demonstrable attestable, axiomatic, certain, evident, evincible, incontrovertible, indubitable, irrefutable, obvious, palpable, positive, provable, self-evident, undeniable, unmistakable, verifiable

demonstrate 1. display, establish, evidence, evince, exhibit, indicate, manifest, prove, show, testify to **2.** describe, explain, illustrate, make clear, show how, teach **3.** march, parade, picket, protest, rally

demonstration 1. affirmation, confirmation, display, evidence, exhibition, expression, illustration, manifestation, proof, substantiation, testimony, validation **2.** description, explanation, exposition, presen~

tation, test, trial **3.** march, mass lobby, pa~
rade, picket, protest, rally, sit-in

demonstrative 1. affectionate, effusive,
emotional, expansive, expressive, gushing,
loving, open, unreserved, unrestrained **2.**
evincive, explanatory, expository, illustra~
tive, indicative, symptomatic
Antonyms (*sense 1*) aloof, cold, contained,
distant, formal, impassive, reserved, re~
strained, stiff, unaffectionate, undemonstra~
tive, unemotional, unresponsive

demoralize 1. cripple, daunt, deject, de~
press, disconcert, discourage, dishearten,
dispirit, enfeeble, psych out (*Inf.*), rattle
(*Inf.*), sap, shake, undermine, unnerve,
weaken **2.** corrupt, debase, debauch, de~
prave, lower, pervert, vitiate
Antonyms (*sense 1*) boost, cheer, egg on, en~
courage, hearten, spur

demoralized 1. broken, crushed, de~
pressed, discouraged, disheartened, dispir~
ited, downcast, sick as a parrot (*Inf.*), sub~
dued, unmanned, unnerved, weakened **2.**
bad, base, corrupt, degenerate, depraved,
dissolute, immoral, low, reprobate, sinful,
wicked

demote declass, degrade, disrate (*Naval*),
downgrade, kick downstairs (*Sl.*), lower in
rank, relegate
Antonyms advance, elevate, kick upstairs
(*Inf.*), prefer, raise, upgrade

demur 1. *v.* balk, cavil, disagree, dispute,
doubt, hesitate, object, pause, protest, ref~
use, take exception, waver **2.** *n.* compunc~
tion, demurral, demurrer, dissent, hesita~
tion, misgiving, objection, protest, qualm,
scruple

demure 1. decorous, diffident, grave, mod~
est, reserved, reticent, retiring, sedate, shy,
sober, staid, unassuming **2.** affected, bash~
ful, coy, priggish, prim, prissy (*Inf.*), prud~
ish, strait-laced
Antonyms brash, brazen, forward, immod~
est, impudent, shameless

den 1. cave, cavern, haunt, hide-out, hole,
lair, shelter **2.** cloister, cubbyhole, hide~
away, retreat, sanctuary, sanctum, snug~
gery, study

denial adjuration, contradiction, disavowal,
disclaimer, dismissal, dissent, negation,
prohibition, rebuff, refusal, rejection, re~
nunciation, repudiation, repulse, retraction,
veto
Antonyms acknowledgment, admission,
affirmation, avowal, confession, declaration,
disclosure, divulgence, profession, revelation

denigrate asperse, bad-mouth (*Sl., chiefly
U.S. & Canad.*), belittle, besmirch, blacken,
calumniate, decry, defame, disparage, im~
pugn, knock (*Inf.*), malign, revile, rubbish

(*Inf.*), run down, slag (off) (*Sl.*), slander,
vilify
Antonyms acclaim, admire, approve, cheer,
compliment, eulogize, extol, honour, laud,
praise

denigration aspersion, backbiting, defa~
mation, detraction, disparagement, obloquy,
scandal, scurrility, slander, vilification

denominate call, christen, designate, dub,
entitle, name, phrase, style, term

denomination 1. belief, communion,
creed, persuasion, religious group, school,
sect **2.** grade, size, unit, value **3.** body, cat~
egory, class, classification, group **4.** appel~
lation, designation, label, name, style, term,
title

denote betoken, designate, express, imply,
import, indicate, mark, mean, show, signify,
typify

denounce accuse, arraign, attack, brand,
castigate, censure, condemn, declaim
against, decry, denunciate, excoriate, im~
pugn, proscribe, revile, stigmatize, vilify

dense 1. close, close-knit, compact, com~
pressed, condensed, heavy, impenetrable,
opaque, solid, substantial, thick, thickset **2.**
blockish, braindead (*Inf.*), crass, dozy (*Brit.
inf.*), dull, obtuse, slow, slow-witted, stolid,
stupid, thick, thick-witted
Antonyms alert, bright, clever, intelligent,
light, quick, scattered, sparse, thin, transpar~
ent

density 1. body, bulk, closeness, compact~
ness, consistency, crowdedness, denseness,
impenetrability, mass, solidity, thickness,
tightness **2.** crassness, dullness, obtuseness,
slowness, stolidity, stupidity, thickness

dent 1. *n.* chip, concavity, crater, depres~
sion, dimple, dip, hollow, impression, in~
dentation, pit **2.** *v.* depress, dint, gouge,
hollow, imprint, make a dent in, make con~
cave, press in, push in

denude bare, divest, expose, lay bare, strip,
uncover

deny 1. contradict, disagree with, disprove,
gainsay (*Archaic or literary*), oppose, rebuff,
rebut, refute **2.** abjure, disavow, discard,
disclaim, disown, recant, renege, renounce,
repudiate, retract, revoke **3.** begrudge, de~
cline, disallow, forbid, negative, refuse, re~
ject, turn down, veto, withhold
Antonyms accept, acknowledge, admit,
affirm, agree, allow, concede, confirm, grant,
let, permit, receive, recognize

deodorant air freshener, antiperspirant,
deodorizer, disinfectant, fumigant

depart 1. absent (oneself), decamp, disap~
pear, escape, exit, go, go away, hook it (*Sl.*),
leave, migrate, quit, remove, retire, retreat,
set forth, slope off, start out, take (one's)

leave, vanish, withdraw **2.** deviate, differ, digress, diverge, stray, swerve, turn aside, vary, veer
Antonyms arrive, remain, show up (*Inf.*), stay, turn up

departed dead, deceased, expired, late

department 1. district, division, province, region, sector **2.** branch, bureau, division, office, section, station, subdivision, unit **3.** area, domain, function, line, province, realm, responsibility, speciality, sphere

departure 1. exit, exodus, going, going away, leave-taking, leaving, removal, re~ tirement, withdrawal **2.** abandonment, branching off, deviation, digression, diver~ gence, variation, veering **3.** branching out, change, difference, innovation, novelty, shift
Antonyms advent, appearance, arrival, coming, entrance, return

depend 1. bank on, build upon, calculate on, confide in, count on, lean on, reckon on, rely upon, trust in, turn to **2.** be based on, be contingent on, be determined by, be subject to, be subordinate to, hang on, hinge on, rest on, revolve around

dependable faithful, reliable, reputable, responsible, staunch, steady, sure, trust~ worthy, trusty, unfailing
Antonyms irresponsible, undependable, unreliable, unstable, untrustworthy

dependant *n.* child, client, hanger-on, henchman, minion, minor, protégé, relative, retainer, subordinate, vassal

dependent *adj.* **1.** counting on, defence~ less, helpless, immature, reliant, relying on, vulnerable, weak **2.** conditional, contingent, depending, determined by, liable to, rela~ tive, subject to **3.** feudal, subject, subordi~ nate, tributary
Antonyms autarkic, autonomous, inde~ pendent, self-determining, self-governing, self-reliant

depict 1. delineate, draw, illustrate, limn, outline, paint, picture, portray, render, re~ produce, sculpt, sketch **2.** characterize, de~ scribe, detail, narrate, outline, sketch

deplete bankrupt, consume, decrease, drain, empty, evacuate, exhaust, expend, impoverish, lessen, milk, reduce, use up
Antonyms add to, augment, enhance, ex~ pand, increase, raise, step up (*Inf.*), swell

depleted consumed, decreased, depreciated, devoid of, drained, emptied, exhausted, lessened, out of, reduced, short of, spent, used (up), wasted, weakened, worn out

depletion attenuation, consumption, de~ crease, deficiency, diminution, drain, dwin~ dling, exhaustion, expenditure, lessening, lowering, reduction, using up

deplorable 1. calamitous, dire, disastrous, distressing, grievous, heartbreaking, lam~ entable, melancholy, miserable, pitiable, regrettable, sad, unfortunate, wretched **2.** blameworthy, disgraceful, dishonourable, disreputable, execrable, opprobrious, repre~ hensible, scandalous, shameful
Antonyms A1 or A-one (*Inf.*), admirable, bad (*Sl.*), brilliant, excellent, fantastic, great (*Inf.*), laudable, marvellous, notable, outstanding, praiseworthy, super (*Inf.*), superb

deplore 1. bemoan, bewail, grieve for, la~ ment, mourn, regret, rue, sorrow over **2.** abhor, censure, condemn, denounce, depre~ cate, disapprove of, excoriate, object to

deploy arrange, dispose, extend, position, redistribute, set out, set up, spread out, station, use, utilize

deport 1. banish, exile, expatriate, expel, extradite, oust **2.** *Used reflexively* acquit, act, bear, behave, carry, comport, conduct, hold

deportation banishment, eviction, exile, expatriation, expulsion, extradition, trans~ portation

deportment air, appearance, aspect, bear~ ing, behaviour, carriage, cast, comportment, conduct, demeanour, manner, mien, pos~ ture, stance

depose 1. break, cashier, degrade, demote, dethrone, dismiss, displace, downgrade, oust, remove from office **2.** *Law* avouch, declare, make a deposition, testify

deposit *v.* **1.** drop, lay, locate, place, pre~ cipitate, put, settle, sit down **2.** amass, bank, consign, entrust, hoard, lodge, save, store ~*n.* **3.** down payment, instalment, money (*in bank*), part payment, pledge, re~ tainer, security, stake, warranty **4.** accu~ mulation, alluvium, deposition, dregs, lees, precipitate, sediment, silt

deposition 1. dethronement, dismissal, displacement, ousting, removal **2.** *Law* affidavit, declaration, evidence, sworn statement, testimony

depository depot, repository, safe-deposit box, store, storehouse, warehouse

depot 1. depository, repository, storehouse, warehouse **2.** *Military* arsenal, dump **3.** bus station, garage, terminus

deprave brutalize, corrupt, debase, de~ bauch, degrade, demoralize, lead astray, pervert, seduce, subvert, vitiate

depraved abandoned, corrupt, debased, de~ bauched, degenerate, degraded, dissolute, evil, immoral, lascivious, lewd, licentious, perverted, pervy (*Sl.*), profligate, shameless, sinful, vicious, vile, wicked
Antonyms chaste, decent, ethical, good,

honourable, innocent, moral, principled, proper, pure, upright, virtuous, wholesome

depravity baseness, contamination, corrup~ tion, criminality, debasement, debauchery, degeneracy, depravation, evil, immorality, iniquity, profligacy, sinfulness, turpitude, vice, viciousness, vitiation, wickedness

depreciate 1. decrease, deflate, devaluate, devalue, lessen, lose value, lower, reduce **2.** belittle, decry, denigrate, deride, detract, disparage, look down on, ridicule, run down, scorn, sneer at, traduce, underesti~ mate, underrate, undervalue
Antonyms (*sense 1*) add to, appreciate, aug~ ment, enhance, enlarge, expand, grow, in~ crease, rise (*sense 2*) admire, appreciate, cher~ ish, esteem, like, prize, rate highly, regard, respect, value

depreciation 1. deflation, depression, de~ valuation, drop, fall, slump **2.** belittlement, deprecation, derogation, detraction, dispar~ agement, pejoration

depress 1. cast down, chill, damp, daunt, deject, desolate, discourage, dishearten, dispirit, make despondent, oppress, sadden, weigh down **2.** debilitate, devitalize, drain, enervate, exhaust, lower, sap, slow up, weaken **3.** cheapen, depreciate, devaluate, devalue, diminish, downgrade, impair, less~ en, lower, reduce **4.** flatten, level, lower, press down, push down
Antonyms cheer, elate, hearten, heighten, increase, lift, raise, strengthen, uplift

depressed 1. blue, crestfallen, dejected, despondent, discouraged, dispirited, down, downcast, downhearted, down in the dumps (*Inf.*), fed up, glum, low, low-spirited, mel~ ancholy, moody, morose, pessimistic, sad, unhappy **2.** concave, hollow, indented, re~ cessed, set back, sunken **3.** *Of an area, cir~ cumstances* deprived, destitute, disadvant~ aged, distressed, grey, needy, poor, poverty-stricken, run-down **4.** cheapened, depreciated, devalued, impaired, weakened

depressing black, bleak, daunting, deject~ ing, depressive, discouraging, dishearten~ ing, dismal, dispiriting, distressing, dreary, funereal, gloomy, harrowing, heartbreaking, hopeless, melancholy, sad, saddening, som~ bre

depression 1. dejection, despair, despond~ ency, dolefulness, downheartedness, dumps (*Inf.*), gloominess, hopelessness, low spirits, melancholia, melancholy, sadness, the blues, the hump (*Brit. inf.*) **2.** *Commerce* dullness, economic decline, hard *or* bad times, inactivity, lowness, recession, slump, stagnation **3.** bowl, cavity, concavity, dent, dimple, dip, excavation, hollow, impression, indentation, pit, sag, sink, valley

deprivation 1. denial, deprival, disposses~

sion, divestment, expropriation, removal, withdrawal, withholding **2.** destitution, detriment, disadvantage, distress, hardship, need, privation, want

deprive bereave, despoil, dispossess, divest, expropriate, rob, strip, wrest

deprived bereft, denuded, destitute, disad~ vantaged, forlorn, in need, in want, lacking, necessitous, needy, poor
Antonyms born with a silver spoon in one's mouth, favoured, fortunate, golden, happy, having a charmed life, lucky, prosperous, sit~ ting pretty (*Inf.*), successful, well-off

depth 1. abyss, deepness, drop, extent, measure, profoundness, profundity **2.** *Fig.* astuteness, discernment, insight, penetra~ tion, profoundness, profundity, sagacity, wisdom **3.** abstruseness, complexity, ob~ scurity, reconditeness **4.** intensity, rich~ ness, strength **5.** *Often plural* abyss, bowels of the earth, deepest (furthest, innermost, most intense, remotest) part, middle, midst, slough of despond **6. in depth** comprehen~ sively, extensively, intensively, thoroughly
Antonyms (*sense 1*) apex, apogee, crest, crown, height, peak, pinnacle, summit, top, vertex, zenith (*sense 2*) *Fig.* emptiness, lack of depth *or* substance, superficiality, triviality

deputation 1. commission, delegates, del~ egation, deputies, embassy, envoys, legation **2.** appointment, assignment, commission, designation, nomination

deputize 1. commission, delegate, depute **2.** act for, stand in for, take the place of, understudy

deputy 1. *n.* agent, ambassador, commis~ sioner, delegate, legate, lieutenant, nuncio, proxy, representative, second-in-command, substitute, surrogate, vicegerent **2.** *adj.* as~ sistant, depute (*Scot.*), subordinate

derange 1. confound, confuse, disarrange, disarray, discompose, disconcert, disorder, displace, disturb, ruffle, unsettle, upset **2.** craze, dement (*Rare*), drive mad, madden, make insane, unbalance, unhinge

deranged barking (*Sl.*), barking mad (*Sl.*), berserk, crackpot (*Inf.*), crazed, crazy, de~ lirious, demented, distracted, frantic, fren~ zied, insane, irrational, loopy (*Inf.*), lunatic, mad, maddened, not the full shilling (*Inf.*), off one's trolley (*Sl.*), out to lunch (*Inf.*), unbalanced, unhinged, up the pole (*Inf.*)
Antonyms all there (*Inf.*), calm, *compos mentis*, in one's right mind, lucid, mentally sound, normal, of sound mind

derelict *adj.* **1.** abandoned, deserted, dilapi~ dated, discarded, forsaken, neglected, ruined **2.** careless, irresponsible, lax, negli~ gent, remiss, slack *~n.* **3.** bag lady (*Chiefly U.S.*), bum (*Inf.*), down-and-out, good-for-

nothing, ne'er-do-well, outcast, tramp, va~
grant, wastrel

dereliction 1. delinquency, evasion, fail~
ure, faithlessness, fault, neglect, negligence,
nonperformance, remissness **2.** abandon~
ment, abdication, desertion, forsaking, re~
linquishment, renunciation

deride chaff, contemn, detract, disdain, dis~
parage, flout, gibe, insult, jeer, knock (*Inf.*),
mock, pooh-pooh, ridicule, scoff, scorn,
sneer, take the piss out of (*Taboo sl.*), taunt

derision contempt, contumely, disdain, dis~
paragement, disrespect, insult, laughter,
mockery, raillery, ridicule, satire, scoffing,
scorn, sneering

derisory contemptible, insulting, laughable,
ludicrous, outrageous, preposterous, ridicu~
lous

derivation 1. acquiring, deriving, extrac~
tion, getting, obtaining **2.** ancestry, basis,
beginning, descent, etymology, foundation,
genealogy, origin, root, source

derivative *adj.* **1.** acquired, borrowed, de~
rived, inferred, obtained, procured, trans~
mitted **2.** copied, imitative, plagiaristic,
plagiarized, rehashed, secondary, second-
hand, uninventive, unoriginal ~*n.* **3.** by-
product, derivation, descendant, offshoot,
outgrowth, spin-off
Antonyms *adj.* archetypal, authentic, first-
hand, genuine, master, original, prototypical,
seminal

derive 1. collect, deduce, draw, elicit, ex~
tract, follow, gain, gather, get, glean, infer,
obtain, procure, receive, trace **2.** *With* **from**
arise, descend, emanate, flow, issue, origi~
nate, proceed, spring from, stem from

derogatory belittling, damaging, defama~
tory, depreciative, detracting, discreditable,
dishonouring, disparaging, injurious, offen~
sive, slighting, uncomplimentary, unfa~
vourable, unflattering
Antonyms appreciative, complimentary,
flattering, fulsome, laudatory

descend 1. alight, dismount, drop, fall, go
down, move down, plummet, plunge, sink,
subside, tumble **2.** dip, gravitate, incline,
slant, slope **3.** be handed down, be passed
down, derive, issue, originate, proceed,
spring **4.** abase oneself, condescend, degen~
erate, deteriorate, lower oneself, stoop **5.**
Often with **on** arrive, assail, assault, attack,
come in force, invade, pounce, raid, swoop
Antonyms ascend, climb, go up, mount, rise,
scale, soar

descent 1. coming down, drop, fall, plunge,
swoop **2.** declination, declivity, dip, drop,
incline, slant, slope **3.** ancestry, extraction,
family tree, genealogy, heredity, lineage,
origin, parentage **4.** debasement, decadence,
decline, degradation, deterioration **5.** as~

sault, attack, foray, incursion, invasion,
pounce, raid, swoop

describe 1. characterize, define, depict, de~
tail, explain, express, illustrate, narrate,
portray, recount, relate, report, specify, tell
2. delineate, draw, mark out, outline, trace

description 1. account, characterization,
delineation, depiction, detail, explanation,
narration, narrative, portrayal, report, rep~
resentation, sketch **2.** brand, breed, catego~
ry, class, genre, genus, ilk, kidney, kind,
order, sort, species, type, variety

descriptive circumstantial, depictive, de~
tailed, explanatory, expressive, graphic, il~
lustrative, pictorial, picturesque, vivid

desecrate abuse, blaspheme, commit sacri~
lege, contaminate, defile, despoil, dishonour,
pervert, pollute, profane, violate
Antonyms esteem, exalt, glorify, hallow,
prize, respect, revere, value, venerate, wor~
ship

desert[1] **1.** *n.* solitude, waste, wasteland,
wilderness, wilds **2.** *adj.* arid, bare, barren,
desolate, infertile, lonely, solitary, unculti~
vated, uninhabited, unproductive, untilled,
waste, wild

desert[2] *v.* abandon, abscond, betray, de~
camp, defect, forsake, give up, go over the
hill (*Military sl.*), jilt, leave, leave high and
dry, leave (someone) in the lurch, leave
stranded, maroon, quit, rat (on) (*Inf.*), re~
linquish, renounce, resign, run out on (*Inf.*),
strand, throw over, vacate, walk out on
(*Inf.*)
Antonyms be a source of strength to, look
after, maintain, provide for, succour, sustain,
take care of

deserted abandoned, bereft, cast off, der~
elict, desolate, empty, forlorn, forsaken,
godforsaken, isolated, left in the lurch, left
stranded, lonely, neglected, solitary, un~
friended, unoccupied, vacant

deserter absconder, apostate, defector, es~
capee, fugitive, rat (*Inf.*), renegade, run~
away, traitor, truant

desertion abandonment, absconding, apos~
tasy, betrayal, defection, departure, derelic~
tion, escape, evasion, flight, forsaking, re~
linquishment, truancy

deserve be entitled to, be worthy of, earn,
gain, justify, merit, procure, rate, warrant,
win

deserved appropriate, condign, due,
earned, fair, fitting, just, justifiable,
justified, meet (*Archaic*), merited, proper,
right, rightful, suitable, warranted, well-
earned

deserving commendable, estimable, laud~
able, meritorious, praiseworthy, righteous,
worthy

Antonyms not deserving of, not good enough, not worth, undeserving, unworthy

design v. **1.** delineate, describe, draft, draw, outline, plan, sketch, trace ~n. **2.** blueprint, delineation, draft, drawing, model, outline, plan, scheme, sketch ~v. **3.** conceive, create, fabricate, fashion, invent, originate, think up ~n. **4.** arrangement, configuration, construction, figure, form, motif, organization, pattern, shape, style ~v. **5.** aim, contrive, destine, devise, intend, make, mean, plan, project, propose, purpose, scheme, tailor ~n. **6.** enterprise, plan, project, schema, scheme, undertaking **7.** aim, end, goal, intent, intention, meaning, object, objective, point, purport, purpose, target, view **8.** *Often plural* conspiracy, evil intentions, intrigue, machination, plot, scheme

designate 1. call, christen, dub, entitle, label, name, nominate, style, term **2.** allot, appoint, assign, choose, delegate, depute, nominate, select **3.** characterize, define, denote, describe, earmark, indicate, pinpoint, show, specify, stipulate

designation 1. denomination, description, epithet, label, mark, name, title **2.** appointment, classification, delegation, indication, selection, specification

designer 1. architect, artificer, couturier, creator, deviser, inventor, originator, stylist **2.** conniver, conspirator, intriguer, plotter, schemer

designing artful, astute, conniving, conspiring, crafty, crooked (*Inf.*), cunning, deceitful, devious, intriguing, Machiavellian, plotting, scheming, sharp, shrewd, sly, treacherous, tricky, unscrupulous, wily

desirability advantage, benefit, merit, profit, usefulness, value, worth

desirable 1. advantageous, advisable, agreeable, beneficial, covetable, eligible, enviable, good, pleasing, preferable, profitable, worthwhile **2.** adorable, alluring, attractive, fascinating, fetching, glamorous, seductive, sexy (*Inf.*)
Antonyms disagreeable, distasteful, unacceptable, unappealing, unattractive, undesirable, unpleasant, unpopular, unsexy (*Inf.*)

desire v. **1.** aspire to, covet, crave, desiderate, fancy, hanker after, hope for, long for, set one's heart on, thirst for, want, wish for, yearn for ~n. **2.** appetite, aspiration, craving, hankering, hope, longing, need, thirst, want, wish, yearning, yen (*Inf.*), ~v. **3.** ask, entreat, importune, petition, request, solicit ~n. **4.** appeal, entreaty, importunity, petition, request, solicitation, supplication **5.** appetite, concupiscence, lasciviousness, lechery, libido, lust, lustfulness, passion

desired accurate, appropriate, correct, expected, express, fitting, necessary, particular, proper, required, right

desirous ambitious, anxious, aspiring, avid, craving, desiring, eager, hopeful, hoping, keen, longing, ready, willing, wishing, yearning
Antonyms averse, disinclined, grudging, indisposed, loath, opposed, reluctant, unenthusiastic, unwilling

desist abstain, break off, cease, discontinue, end, forbear, give over (*Inf.*), give up, have done with, kick (*Inf.*), leave off, pause, refrain from, remit, stop, suspend

desolate adj. **1.** bare, barren, bleak, desert, dreary, godforsaken, ruined, solitary, unfrequented, uninhabited, waste, wild ~v. **2.** depopulate, despoil, destroy, devastate, lay low, lay waste, pillage, plunder, ravage, ruin ~adj. **3.** abandoned, bereft, cheerless, comfortless, companionless, dejected, depressing, despondent, disconsolate, dismal, downcast, forlorn, forsaken, gloomy, lonely, melancholy, miserable, wretched ~v. **4.** daunt, deject, depress, discourage, dishearten, dismay, distress, grieve
Antonyms adj. cheerful, happy, inhabited, joyous, light-hearted, populous ~v. cheer, develop, encourage, hearten, nourish

desolation 1. destruction, devastation, havoc, ravages, ruin, ruination **2.** barrenness, bleakness, desolateness, forlornness, isolation, loneliness, solitariness, solitude, wildness **3.** anguish, dejection, despair, distress, gloom, gloominess, melancholy, misery, sadness, unhappiness, woe, wretchedness

despair v. **1.** despond, give up, lose heart, lose hope ~n. **2.** anguish, dejection, depression, desperation, despondency, disheartenment, gloom, hopelessness, melancholy, misery, wretchedness **3.** burden, cross, hardship, ordeal, pain, trial, tribulation

despairing anxious, broken-hearted, dejected, depressed, desperate, despondent, disconsolate, dismal, downcast, frantic, grief-stricken, hopeless, inconsolable, melancholy, miserable, suicidal, wretched

desperado bandit, criminal, cutthroat, gangster, gunman, heavy (*Sl.*), hoodlum (*Chiefly U.S.*), lawbreaker, mugger (*Inf.*), outlaw, ruffian, thug, villain

desperate 1. audacious, dangerous, daring, death-defying, determined, foolhardy, frantic, furious, hasty, hazardous, headstrong, impetuous, madcap, precipitate, rash, reckless, risky, violent, wild **2.** acute, critical, dire, drastic, extreme, great, urgent, very grave **3.** despairing, despondent, forlorn, hopeless, inconsolable, irrecoverable, irremediable, irretrievable, wretched

desperately 1. badly, dangerously, grave~
ly, perilously, seriously, severely **2.** appal~
lingly, fearfully, frightfully, hopelessly,
shockingly

desperation 1. defiance, foolhardiness,
frenzy, heedlessness, impetuosity, madness,
rashness, recklessness **2.** agony, anguish,
anxiety, despair, despondency, distraction,
heartache, hopelessness, misery, pain, sor~
row, torture, trouble, unhappiness, worry

despicable abject, base, beyond contempt,
cheap, contemptible, degrading, detestable,
disgraceful, disreputable, hateful, igno~
minious, infamous, low, mean, pitiful, rep~
rehensible, scurvy, shameful, sordid, vile,
worthless, wretched
Antonyms admirable, estimable, ethical,
exemplary, good, honest, honourable, moral,
noble, praiseworthy, righteous, upright, vir~
tuous, worthy

despise abhor, contemn, deride, detest, dis~
dain, disregard, flout, loathe, look down on,
neglect, revile, scorn, slight, spurn, under~
value
Antonyms admire, adore, be fond of, be keen
on, cherish, dig (*Sl.*), esteem, fancy (*Inf.*), love,
relish, revel in, take to

despite against, even with, in contempt of,
in defiance of, in spite of, in the face of, in
the teeth of, notwithstanding, regardless of,
undeterred by

despoil denude, deprive, destroy, devastate,
dispossess, divest, loot, pillage, plunder,
ravage, rifle, rob, strip, total (*Sl.*), trash
(*Sl.*), vandalize, wreak havoc upon, wreck

despond be cast down, be depressed, des~
pair, give up, lose heart, lose hope, mourn,
sorrow

despondency dejection, depression, des~
pair, desperation, disconsolateness, dis~
couragement, dispiritedness, downhearted~
ness, gloom, hopelessness, low spirits, mel~
ancholy, misery, sadness, the hump (*Brit.
inf.*), wretchedness

despondent blue, dejected, depressed, des~
pairing, disconsolate, discouraged, dis~
heartened, dismal, dispirited, doleful, down,
downcast, downhearted, gloomy, glum,
hopeless, in despair, low, low-spirited, mel~
ancholy, miserable, morose, sad, sick as a
parrot (*Inf.*), sorrowful, woebegone, wretch~
ed
Antonyms buoyant, cheerful, cheery, chirpy
(*Inf.*), genial, glad, happy, hopeful, joyful,
light-hearted, optimistic, upbeat (*Inf.*)

despot autocrat, dictator, monocrat, op~
pressor, tyrant

despotic absolute, arbitrary, arrogant,
authoritarian, autocratic, dictatorial, domi~
neering, imperious, monocratic, oppressive,
tyrannical, unconstitutional

despotism absolutism, autarchy, autocra~
cy, dictatorship, monocracy, oppression, to~
talitarianism, tyranny

destination 1. harbour, haven, journey's
end, landing-place, resting-place, station,
stop, terminus **2.** aim, ambition, design,
end, goal, intention, object, objective, pur~
pose, target

destine allot, appoint, assign, consecrate,
decree, design, devote, doom, earmark, fate,
intend, mark out, ordain, predetermine,
preordain, purpose, reserve

destined 1. bound, certain, designed,
doomed, fated, foreordained, ineluctable,
inescapable, inevitable, intended, meant,
ordained, predestined, unavoidable **2.** as~
signed, booked, bound for, directed, en
route, heading, on the road to, routed,
scheduled

destiny cup, divine decree, doom, fate, for~
tune, karma, kismet, lot, portion

destitute 1. dirt-poor (*Inf.*), distressed,
down and out, flat broke (*Inf.*), impecuni~
ous, impoverished, indigent, insolvent,
moneyless, necessitous, needy, on one's
uppers, on the breadline (*Inf.*), penniless,
penurious, poor, poverty-stricken, short,
without two pennies to rub together (*Inf.*)
2. bereft of, deficient in, depleted, deprived
of, devoid of, drained, empty of, in need of,
lacking, wanting, without

destitution beggary, dire straits, distress,
impecuniousness, indigence, neediness,
pauperism, pennilessness, penury, priva~
tion, utter poverty, want
Antonyms affluence, fortune, good fortune,
life of luxury, luxury, plenty, prosperity,
riches, wealth

destroy annihilate, blow to bits, break
down, crush, demolish, desolate, devastate,
dismantle, dispatch, eradicate, extinguish,
extirpate, gut, kill, ravage, raze, ruin, shat~
ter, slay, smash, torpedo, total (*Sl.*), trash
(*Sl.*), waste, wipe out, wreck

destruction annihilation, crushing, demo~
lition, devastation, downfall, end, eradica~
tion, extermination, extinction, havoc, liq~
uidation, massacre, overthrow, overwhelm~
ing, ruin, ruination, shattering, slaughter,
undoing, wreckage, wrecking

destructive 1. baleful, baneful, calamitous,
cataclysmic, catastrophic, damaging, dead~
ly, deleterious, detrimental, devastating, fa~
tal, harmful, hurtful, injurious, lethal,
maleficent, noxious, pernicious, ruinous **2.**
adverse, antagonistic, contrary, derogatory,
discouraging, discrediting, disparaging,
hostile, invalidating, negative, opposed,
undermining, vicious

detach cut off, disconnect, disengage, dis~
entangle, disjoin, disunite, divide, free, iso~

late, loosen, remove, segregate, separate, sever, tear off, unbridle, uncouple, unfasten, unhitch
Antonyms attach, bind, connect, fasten

detached 1. disconnected, discrete, disjoined, divided, free, loosened, separate, severed, unconnected **2.** aloof, disinterested, dispassionate, impartial, impersonal, neutral, objective, reserved, unbiased, uncommitted, uninvolved, unprejudiced
Antonyms biased, concerned, interested, involved, partisan, prejudiced

detachment 1. aloofness, coolness, indifference, nonchalance, remoteness, unconcern **2.** disinterestedness, fairness, impartiality, neutrality, nonpartisanship, objectivity **3.** disconnection, disengagement, disjoining, separation, severing **4.** *Military* body, detail, force, party, patrol, squad, task force, unit

detail *n.* **1.** aspect, component, count, element, fact, factor, feature, item, particular, point, respect, specific, technicality **2.** *Plural* fine points, minutiae, niceties, particulars, parts, trivia, trivialities **3. in detail** comprehensively, exhaustively, inside out, item by item, point by point, thoroughly **4.** *Military* assignment, body, detachment, duty, fatigue, force, party, squad ~*v.* **5.** catalogue, delineate, depict, describe, enumerate, individualize, itemize, narrate, particularize, portray, recite, recount, rehearse, relate, specify, tabulate **6.** allocate, appoint, assign, charge, commission, delegate, detach, send

detailed blow-by-blow, circumstantial, comprehensive, elaborate, exact, exhaustive, full, intricate, itemized, meticulous, minute, particular, particularized, specific, thorough
Antonyms brief, compact, concise, condensed, limited, pithy, short, slight, succinct, summary, superficial, terse

detain 1. check, delay, hinder, hold up, impede, keep, keep back, retard, slow up (*or* down), stay, stop **2.** arrest, confine, hold, intern, restrain

detect 1. ascertain, catch, descry, distinguish, identify, note, notice, observe, recognize, scent, spot **2.** catch, disclose, discover, expose, find, reveal, track down, uncover, unmask

detection discovery, exposé, exposure, ferreting out, revelation, tracking down, uncovering, unearthing, unmasking

detective bizzy (*Sl.*), C.I.D. man, constable, cop (*Sl.*), copper (*Sl.*), dick (*Sl., chiefly U.S.*), gumshoe (*U.S. sl.*), investigator, private eye, private investigator, sleuth (*Inf.*), tec (*Sl.*)

detention confinement, custody, delay, hindrance, holding back, imprisonment, incarceration, keeping in, porridge (*Sl.*), quarantine, restraint, withholding
Antonyms acquittal, discharge, emancipation, freedom, liberation, liberty, release

deter caution, check, damp, daunt, debar, discourage, dissuade, frighten, hinder, inhibit from, intimidate, prevent, prohibit, put off, restrain, stop, talk out of

detergent 1. *n.* cleaner, cleanser **2.** *adj.* abstergent, cleaning, cleansing, detersive, purifying

deteriorate 1. corrupt, debase, decline, degenerate, degrade, deprave, depreciate, go downhill (*Inf.*), go to pot, go to the dogs (*Inf.*), impair, injure, lower, slump, spoil, worsen **2.** be the worse for wear (*Inf.*), crumble, decay, decline, decompose, disintegrate, ebb, fade, fall apart, lapse, retrogress, weaken, wear away
Antonyms advance, ameliorate, get better, improve, upgrade

deterioration atrophy, corrosion, debasement, decline, degeneration, degradation, depreciation, descent, dilapidation, disintegration, downturn, drop, fall, lapse, retrogression, slump, vitiation, worsening

determination 1. backbone, constancy, conviction, dedication, doggedness, drive, firmness, fortitude, indomitability, perseverance, persistence, resoluteness, resolution, resolve, single-mindedness, steadfastness, tenacity, willpower **2.** conclusion, decision, judgment, purpose, resolve, result, settlement, solution, verdict
Antonyms doubt, hesitancy, hesitation, indecision, instability, irresolution, vacillation

determine 1. arbitrate, conclude, decide, end, finish, fix upon, ordain, regulate, settle, terminate **2.** ascertain, certify, check, detect, discover, find out, learn, verify, work out **3.** choose, decide, elect, establish, fix, make up one's mind, purpose, resolve **4.** affect, condition, control, decide, dictate, direct, govern, impel, impose, incline, induce, influence, lead, modify, regulate, rule, shape

determined bent on, constant, dogged, firm, fixed, immovable, intent, persevering, persistent, purposeful, resolute, set on, single-minded, stalwart, steadfast, strongminded, strong-willed, tenacious, unflinching, unwavering

determining conclusive, critical, crucial, deciding, decisive, definitive, essential, final, important, settling

deterrent *n.* check, curb, defensive measures, determent, discouragement, disincentive, hindrance, impediment, obstacle, restraint
Antonyms bait, carrot (*Inf.*), enticement,

incentive, inducement, lure, motivation, spur, stimulus

detest abhor, abominate, despise, dislike intensely, execrate, feel aversion (disgust, hostility, repugnance) towards, hate, loathe, recoil from
Antonyms adore, cherish, dig (*Sl.*), dote on, love, relish

detonate blast, blow up, discharge, explode, fulminate, set off, touch off, trigger

detonation bang, blast, blow-up, boom, discharge, explosion, fulmination, report

detour bypass, byway, circuitous route, deviation, diversion, indirect course, round~about way

detract 1. devaluate, diminish, lessen, lower, reduce, take away from 2. deflect, distract, divert, shift
Antonyms add to, augment, boost, complement, enhance, improve, reinforce, strengthen

detraction abuse, aspersion, belittlement, calumny, defamation, denigration, deprecation, disparagement, innuendo, insinuation, misrepresentation, muckraking, running down, scandalmongering, scurrility, slander, traducement, vituperation

detractor backbiter, belittler, defamer, denigrator, derogator (*Rare*), disparager, muckraker, scandalmonger, slanderer, traducer

detriment damage, disadvantage, disservice, harm, hurt, impairment, injury, loss, mischief, prejudice

detrimental adverse, baleful, damaging, deleterious, destructive, disadvantageous, harmful, inimical, injurious, mischievous, pernicious, prejudicial, unfavourable
Antonyms advantageous, beneficial, efficacious, favourable, good, helpful, salutary

devastate 1. demolish, desolate, despoil, destroy, lay waste, level, pillage, plunder, ravage, raze, ruin, sack, spoil, total (*Sl.*), trash (*Sl.*), waste, wreck 2. *Inf.* chagrin, confound, discomfit, discompose, disconcert, floor (*Inf.*), nonplus, overpower, overwhelm, take aback

devastating caustic, cutting, deadly, destructive, effective, incisive, keen, mordant, overpowering, overwhelming, ravishing, sardonic, satirical, savage, stunning, trenchant, vitriolic, withering

devastation demolition, depredation, desolation, destruction, havoc, pillage, plunder, ravages, ruin, ruination, spoliation

develop 1. advance, blossom, cultivate, evolve, flourish, foster, grow, mature, progress, promote, prosper, ripen 2. amplify, augment, broaden, dilate upon, elaborate, enlarge, expand, unfold, work out 3. ac-

quire, begin, breed, commence, contract, establish, form, generate, invent, originate, pick up, start 4. be a direct result of, break out, come about, ensue, follow, happen, result

development 1. advance, advancement, evolution, expansion, growth, improvement, increase, maturity, progress, progression, spread, unfolding, unravelling 2. change, circumstance, event, happening, incident, issue, occurrence, outcome, phenomenon, result, situation, turn of events, upshot

deviant 1. *adj.* aberrant, abnormal, bent (*Sl.*), deviate, devious, freaky (*Sl.*), heretical, kinky (*Sl.*), perverse, perverted, pervy (*Sl.*), queer (*Inf., derogatory*), sick (*Inf.*), twisted, warped, wayward 2. *n.* deviate, freak, misfit, odd type, pervert, queer (*Inf., derogatory*)
Antonyms conventional, normal, orthodox, straight, straightforward

deviate avert, bend, deflect, depart, differ, digress, diverge, drift, err, meander, part, stray, swerve, turn, turn aside, vary, veer, wander

deviation aberration, alteration, change, deflection, departure, digression, discrepancy, disparity, divergence, fluctuation, inconsistency, irregularity, shift, variance, variation

device 1. apparatus, appliance, contraption, contrivance, gadget, gimmick, gismo *or* gizmo (*Sl., chiefly U.S. & Canad.*), implement, instrument, invention, tool, utensil 2. artifice, design, dodge, expedient, gambit, improvisation, manoeuvre, plan, ploy, project, purpose, ruse, scheme, shift, stratagem, strategy, stunt, trick, wile 3. badge, colophon, crest, design, emblem, figure, insignia, logo, motif, motto, symbol, token

devil 1. *Sometimes cap.* Apollyon, archfiend, Beelzebub, Belial, Clootie (*Scot.*), demon, fiend, Lucifer, Old Harry (*Inf.*), Old Nick (*Inf.*), Old Scratch (*Inf.*), Prince of Darkness, Satan 2. beast, brute, demon, fiend, ghoul, monster, ogre, rogue, savage, terror, villain 3. imp, monkey (*Inf.*), pickle (*Brit. inf.*), rascal, rogue, scamp, scoundrel 4. beggar, creature, thing, unfortunate, wretch 5. demon, enthusiast, fiend, go-getter (*Inf.*)

devilish accursed, atrocious, damnable, detestable, diabolic, diabolical, execrable, fiendish, hellish, infernal, satanic, wicked

devil-may-care careless, casual, easygoing, flippant, happy-go-lucky, heedless, insouciant, nonchalant, reckless, swaggering, swashbuckling, unconcerned

devilry, deviltry 1. devilment, jiggery-pokery (*Inf., chiefly Brit.*), knavery, mischief, mischievousness, monkey-business (*Inf.*), rascality, roguery 2. cruelty, evil, malevolence, malice, vice, viciousness, villainy, wickedness **3.** black magic, diablerie, diabolism, sorcery

devious 1. calculating, crooked (*Inf.*), deceitful, dishonest, double-dealing, evasive, indirect, insidious, insincere, not straightforward, scheming, sly, surreptitious, treacherous, tricky, underhand, wily **2.** circuitous, confusing, crooked, deviating, erratic, excursive, indirect, misleading, rambling, roundabout, tortuous, wandering **Antonyms** blunt, candid, direct, downright, forthright, frank, honest, straight, straightforward, undeviating, unswerving

devise arrange, conceive, concoct, construct, contrive, design, dream up, form, formulate, frame, imagine, invent, plan, plot, prepare, project, scheme, think up, work out

devoid barren, bereft, deficient, denuded, destitute, empty, free from, lacking, sans (*Archaic*), vacant, void, wanting, without

devolution decentralization, delegation

devolve 1. be transferred, commission, consign, delegate, depute, entrust, fall upon *or* to, rest with, transfer **2.** *Law* alienate, be handed down, convey

devote allot, apply, appropriate, assign, commit, concern oneself, consecrate, dedicate, enshrine, give, occupy oneself, pledge, reserve, set apart

devoted ardent, caring, committed, concerned, constant, dedicated, devout, faithful, fond, loving, loyal, staunch, steadfast, true **Antonyms** disloyal, inconstant, indifferent, uncommitted, undedicated, unfaithful

devotee addict, adherent, admirer, aficionado, buff (*Inf.*), disciple, enthusiast, fan, fanatic, follower, supporter, votary

devotion 1. adherence, allegiance, commitment, consecration, constancy, dedication, faithfulness, fidelity, loyalty **2.** adoration, devoutness, godliness, holiness, piety, prayer, religiousness, reverence, sanctity, spirituality, worship **3.** affection, ardour, attachment, earnestness, fervour, fondness, intensity, love, passion, zeal **4.** *Plural* church service, divine office, prayers, religious observance **Antonyms** (*sense 1*) carelessness, disregard, inattention, indifference, laxity, laxness, neglect, thoughtlessness (*sense 2*) derision, disrespect, impiety, irreverence

devour 1. bolt, consume, cram, dispatch, eat, gobble, gorge, gulp, guzzle, pig out on (*Sl.*), polish off (*Inf.*), stuff, swallow, wolf **2.** annihilate, consume, destroy, ravage, spend, waste, wipe out **3.** absorb, appreciate, be engrossed by, be preoccupied, delight in, drink in, enjoy, feast on, go through, read compulsively *or* voraciously, relish, revel in, take in

devouring consuming, excessive, flaming, insatiable, intense, overwhelming, passionate, powerful

devout 1. godly, holy, orthodox, pious, prayerful, pure, religious, reverent, saintly **2.** ardent, deep, devoted, earnest, fervent, genuine, heartfelt, intense, passionate, profound, serious, sincere, zealous **Antonyms** impious, indifferent, irreligious, irreverent, passive, sacrilegious

devoutly fervently, heart and soul, profoundly, sincerely, with all one's heart

dexterity 1. adroitness, artistry, craft, deftness, effortlessness, expertise, facility, finesse, handiness, knack, mastery, neatness, nimbleness, proficiency, skill, smoothness, touch **2.** ability, address, adroitness, aptitude, aptness, art, cleverness, expertness, ingenuity, readiness, skilfulness, tact **Antonyms** clumsiness, gaucheness, inability, incapacity, incompetence, ineptitude, uselessness

diabolical appalling, atrocious, damnable, difficult, disastrous, dreadful, excruciating, fiendish, hellacious (*U.S. sl.*), hellish, nasty, outrageous, shocking, tricky, unpleasant, vile

diagnose analyse, determine, distinguish, identify, interpret, investigate, pinpoint, pronounce, recognize

diagnosis 1. analysis, examination, investigation, scrutiny **2.** conclusion, interpretation, opinion, pronouncement

diagonal *adj.* angled, cater-cornered (*U.S. inf.*), cornerways, cross, crossways, crosswise, oblique, slanting

diagonally aslant, at an angle, cornerwise, crosswise, obliquely, on the bias, on the cross

diagram chart, drawing, figure, layout, outline, plan, representation, sketch

dialect accent, idiom, jargon, language, lingo (*Inf.*), localism, patois, pronunciation, provincialism, speech, tongue, vernacular

dialectic 1. *adj.* analytic, argumentative, dialectical, logical, polemical, rational, rationalistic **2.** *n. Often plural* argumentation, contention, discussion, disputation, logic, polemics, ratiocination, reasoning

dialogue 1. colloquy, communication, confabulation, conference, conversation, converse, discourse, discussion, duologue, interlocution **2.** conversation, lines, script, spoken part

diametric, diametrical antipodal, antithetical, conflicting, contrary, contrasting, counter, opposed, opposite

diametrically absolutely, completely, entirely, utterly

diarrhoea *n.* dysentery, gippy tummy, holi~
day tummy, looseness, Montezuma's re~
venge (*Inf.*), Spanish tummy, the runs, the
skits (*Inf.*), the skitters (*Inf.*), the trots (*Inf.*)

diary appointment book, chronicle, daily
record, day-to-day account, engagement
book, Filofax (*Trademark*), journal

diatribe abuse, castigation, criticism, de~
nunciation, disputation, harangue, invec~
tive, philippic, reviling, stream of abuse,
stricture, tirade, verbal onslaught, vitu~
peration

dicey chancy (*Inf.*), dangerous, difficult,
hairy (*Sl.*), risky, ticklish, tricky

dicky *adj.* fluttery, queer, shaky, unreliable,
unsound, unsteady, weak

dictate *v.* **1.** read out, say, speak, transmit,
utter **2.** command, decree, demand, direct,
enjoin, establish, impose, lay down, ordain,
order, prescribe, pronounce ~*n.* **3.** behest,
bidding, command, decree, demand, direc~
tion, edict, fiat, injunction, mandate, order,
ordinance, requirement, statute, ultimatum,
word **4.** canon, code, dictum, law, precept,
principle, rule

dictator absolute ruler, autocrat, despot,
oppressor, tyrant

dictatorial 1. absolute, arbitrary, autocrat~
ic, despotic, totalitarian, tyrannical, unlim~
ited, unrestricted **2.** authoritarian, bossy
(*Inf.*), dogmatical, domineering, imperious,
iron-handed, magisterial, oppressive, over~
bearing
Antonyms constitutional, democratic,
egalitarian, humble, restricted, servile, sup~
pliant, tolerant

dictatorship absolute rule, absolutism,
authoritarianism, autocracy, despotism,
reign of terror, totalitarianism, tyranny

diction 1. expression, language, phraseol~
ogy, phrasing, style, usage, vocabulary,
wording **2.** articulation, delivery, elocution,
enunciation, fluency, inflection, intonation,
pronunciation, speech

dictionary concordance, encyclopedia,
glossary, lexicon, vocabulary, wordbook

didactic edifying, educational, enlightening,
homiletic, instructive, moral, moralizing,
pedagogic, pedantic, preceptive

die 1. breathe one's last, buy it (*U.S. sl.*),
check out (*U.S. sl.*), croak (*Sl.*), decease, de~
part, expire, finish, give up the ghost, go
belly-up (*Sl.*), hop the twig (*Sl.*), kick it (*Sl.*),
kick the bucket (*Sl.*), pass away, peg it
(*Inf.*), peg out (*Inf.*), perish, pop one's clogs
(*Inf.*), snuff it (*Sl.*) **2.** decay, decline, disap~
pear, dwindle, ebb, end, fade, lapse, pass,
sink, subside, vanish, wane, wilt, wither **3.**
break down, fade out *or* away, fail, fizzle
out, halt, lose power, peter out, run down,

stop **4.** ache, be eager, desire, hunger, lan~
guish, long, pine for, swoon, yearn **5.**
Usually with **of** be overcome, collapse, suc~
cumb to
Antonyms be born, begin, build, come to life,
exist, flourish, grow, increase, live, survive

die-hard 1. *n.* fanatic, intransigent, old
fogy, reactionary, stick-in-the-mud (*Inf.*),
ultraconservative, zealot **2.** *adj.* dyed-in-
the-wool, immovable, inflexible, intransi~
gent, reactionary, ultraconservative, un~
compromising, unreconstructed (*Chiefly
U.S.*)

diet[1] *n.* **1.** abstinence, dietary, fast, regime,
regimen **2.** aliment, comestibles, commons,
edibles, fare, food, nourishment, nutriment,
provisions, rations, subsistence, sustenance,
viands, victuals ~*v.* **3.** abstain, eat spar~
ingly, fast, lose weight, reduce, slim
Antonyms *v.* get fat, glut, gobble, gormand~
ize, guzzle, indulge, overindulge, pig out (*Sl.*),
stuff oneself

diet[2] chamber, congress, convention, coun~
cil, legislative assembly, legislature, meet~
ing, parliament, sitting

differ 1. be dissimilar, be distinct, contra~
dict, contrast, depart from, diverge, run
counter to, stand apart, vary **2.** clash, con~
tend, debate, demur, disagree, dispute, dis~
sent, oppose, take issue
Antonyms accord, acquiesce, agree, assent,
coincide, concur, cooperate, harmonize

difference 1. alteration, change, contrast,
deviation, differentiation, discrepancy, dis~
parity, dissimilarity, distinction, distinct~
ness, divergence, diversity, unlikeness,
variation, variety **2.** distinction, exception,
idiosyncrasy, particularity, peculiarity,
singularity **3.** argument, clash, conflict,
contention, contrariety, contretemps, con~
troversy, debate, disagreement, discordance,
dispute, quarrel, row, set-to (*Inf.*), strife, tiff,
wrangle **4.** balance, remainder, rest, result
Antonyms (*senses 1, 2 & 3*) affinity, agree~
ment, comparability, concordance, conform~
ity, congruence, likeness, relation, resem~
blance, sameness, similarity, similitude

different 1. altered, at odds, at variance,
changed, clashing, contrasting, deviating,
discrepant, disparate, dissimilar, divergent,
diverse, inconsistent, opposed, unlike **2.**
another, discrete, distinct, individual, other,
separate **3.** assorted, divers (*Archaic*), di~
verse, manifold, many, miscellaneous,
multifarious, numerous, several, some,
sundry, varied, various **4.** another story,
atypical, bizarre, distinctive, extraordinary,
out of the ordinary, peculiar, rare, singular,
something else, special, strange, uncom~
mon, unconventional, unique, unusual

differential 1. *adj.* diacritical, discrimina~

tive, distinctive, distinguishing **2.** *n.* amount of difference, difference, discrepancy, disparity

differentiate 1. contrast, discern, discriminate, distinguish, make a distinction, mark off, separate, set off *or* apart, tell apart **2.** adapt, alter, change, convert, make different, modify, transform

difficult 1. arduous, burdensome, demanding, formidable, hard, laborious, no picnic (*Inf.*), onerous, painful, strenuous, toilsome, uphill, wearisome **2.** abstract, abstruse, baffling, complex, complicated, delicate, enigmatical, intricate, involved, knotty, obscure, perplexing, problematical, thorny, ticklish **3.** demanding, fastidious, fractious, fussy, hard to please, intractable, obstreperous, perverse, refractory, rigid, tiresome, troublesome, trying, unaccommodating, unamenable, unmanageable **4.** dark, full of hardship, grim, hard, straitened, tough, trying
Antonyms accommodating, amenable, cooperative, easy, easy-peasy (*Sl.*), light, manageable, obvious, plain, pleasant, simple, straightforward, uncomplicated

difficulty 1. arduousness, awkwardness, hardship, laboriousness, labour, pain, painfulness, strain, strenuousness, tribulation **2.** deep water, dilemma, distress, embarrassment, fix (*Inf.*), hot water (*Inf.*), jam (*Inf.*), mess, perplexity, pickle (*Inf.*), plight, predicament, quandary, spot (*Inf.*), straits, tight spot, trial, trouble **3.** *Often plural* complication, hassle (*Inf.*), hindrance, hurdle, impediment, objection, obstacle, opposition, pitfall, problem, protest, snag, stumbling block

diffidence backwardness, bashfulness, constraint, doubt, fear, hesitancy, hesitation, humility, insecurity, lack of self-confidence, meekness, modesty, reluctance, reserve, self-consciousness, sheepishness, shyness, timidity, timidness, timorousness, unassertiveness
Antonyms assurance, boldness, confidence, courage, firmness, self-confidence, self-possession

diffident backward, bashful, constrained, distrustful, doubtful, hesitant, insecure, meek, modest, reluctant, reserved, self-conscious, self-effacing, sheepish, shrinking, shy, suspicious, timid, timorous, unassertive, unassuming, unobtrusive, unsure, withdrawn

diffuse *adj.* **1.** circumlocutory, copious, diffusive, digressive, discursive, long-winded, loose, maundering, meandering, prolix, rambling, vague, verbose, waffling (*Inf.*), wordy **2.** dispersed, scattered, spread out, unconcentrated ~*v.* **3.** circulate, dispel,

dispense, disperse, disseminate, dissipate, distribute, propagate, scatter, spread
Antonyms *adj.* apposite, brief, compendious, concentrated, concise, succinct, terse, to the point

diffusion 1. circulation, dispersal, dispersion, dissemination, dissipation, distribution, expansion, propaganda, propagation, scattering, spread **2.** circuitousness, diffuseness, digressiveness, discursiveness, long-windedness, prolixity, rambling, verbiage, verbosity, wandering, wordiness

dig *v.* **1.** break up, burrow, delve, excavate, gouge, grub, hoe, hollow out, mine, penetrate, pierce, quarry, scoop, till, tunnel, turn over **2.** drive, jab, poke, prod, punch, thrust **3.** delve, dig down, go into, investigate, probe, research, search **4.** *With* **out** *or* **up** bring to light, come across, come up with, discover, expose, extricate, find, retrieve, root (*Inf.*), rootle, uncover, unearth **5.** *Inf.* appreciate, enjoy, follow, groove (*Dated sl.*), like, understand ~*n.* **6.** jab, poke, prod, punch, thrust **7.** barb, crack (*Sl.*), cutting remark, gibe, insult, jeer, quip, sneer, taunt, wisecrack (*Inf.*)

digest *v.* **1.** absorb, assimilate, concoct, dissolve, incorporate, macerate **2.** absorb, assimilate, con, consider, contemplate, grasp, master, meditate, ponder, study, take in, understand **3.** arrange, classify, codify, dispose, methodize, systematize, tabulate **4.** abridge, compress, condense, reduce, shorten, summarize ~*n.* **5.** abridgment, abstract, compendium, condensation, epitome, précis, résumé, summary, synopsis

digestion absorption, assimilation, conversion, incorporation, ingestion, transformation

dig in 1. defend, entrench, establish, fortify, maintain **2.** *Inf.* begin, set about, start eating, tuck in (*Inf.*)

dignified august, decorous, distinguished, exalted, formal, grave, honourable, imposing, lofty, lordly, noble, reserved, solemn, stately, upright
Antonyms crass, inelegant, unbecoming, undignified, unseemly, vulgar

dignify adorn, advance, aggrandize, distinguish, elevate, ennoble, exalt, glorify, grace, honour, promote, raise

dignitary *n.* bigwig (*Inf.*), celeb (*Inf.*), high-up (*Inf.*), notability, notable, personage, pillar of society (the church, the state), public figure, V.I.P., worthy

dignity 1. courtliness, decorum, grandeur, gravity, hauteur, loftiness, majesty, nobility, propriety, solemnity, stateliness **2.** elevation, eminence, excellence, glory, greatness, honour, importance, nobleness, rank, respectability, standing, station, status **3.**

amour-propre, pride, self-esteem, self-importance, self-possession, self-regard, self-respect

digress be diffuse, depart, deviate, diverge, drift, expatiate, get off the point *or* subject, go off at a tangent, meander, ramble, stray, turn aside, wander

digression apostrophe, aside, departure, detour, deviation, divergence, diversion, footnote, obiter dictum, parenthesis, straying, wandering

dilapidated battered, beat-up (*Inf.*), broken-down, crumbling, decayed, decaying, decrepit, fallen in, falling apart, gone to rack and ruin, in ruins, neglected, ramshackle, rickety, ruined, ruinous, run-down, shabby, shaky, tumbledown, uncared for, worn-out

dilate 1. broaden, distend, enlarge, expand, extend, puff out, stretch, swell, widen **2.** amplify, be profuse, be prolix, descant, detail, develop, dwell on, enlarge, expand, expatiate, expound, spin out
Antonyms compress, constrict, contract, narrow, shrink

dilation broadening, dilatation, distension, enlargement, expansion, extension, increase, spread

dilatory backward, behindhand, dallying, delaying, laggard, lingering, loitering, procrastinating, putting off, slack, slow, sluggish, snail-like, tardy, tarrying, time-wasting
Antonyms on-the-ball (*Inf.*), prompt, punctual, sharp (*Inf.*)

dilemma 1. difficulty, embarrassment, fix (*Inf.*), jam (*Inf.*), mess, perplexity, pickle (*Inf.*), plight, predicament, problem, puzzle, quandary, spot (*Inf.*), strait, tight corner *or* spot **2. on the horns of a dilemma** between a rock and a hard place (*Inf.*), between Scylla and Charybdis, between the devil and the deep blue sea

dilettante aesthete, amateur, dabbler, nonprofessional, trifler

diligence activity, application, assiduity, assiduousness, attention, attentiveness, care, constancy, earnestness, heedfulness, industry, intentness, laboriousness, perseverance, sedulousness

diligent active, assiduous, attentive, busy, careful, conscientious, constant, earnest, hard-working, indefatigable, industrious, laborious, painstaking, persevering, persistent, sedulous, studious, tireless
Antonyms careless, dilatory, inconstant, indifferent, lazy

dilly-dally dally, dawdle, delay, dither (*Chiefly Brit.*), falter, fluctuate, hesitate,

hover, linger, loiter, potter, procrastinate, shillyshally (*Inf.*), trifle, vacillate, waver

dilute *v.* **1.** adulterate, cut, make thinner, thin (out), water down, weaken **2.** *Fig.* attenuate, decrease, diffuse, diminish, lessen, mitigate, reduce, temper, weaken
Antonyms concentrate, condense, intensify, strengthen, thicken

dim *adj.* **1.** caliginous (*Archaic*), cloudy, dark, darkish, dusky, grey, overcast, poorly lit, shadowy, tenebrous, unilluminated **2.** bleary, blurred, faint, fuzzy, ill-defined, indistinct, obscured, shadowy, unclear **3.** braindead (*Inf.*), dense, doltish, dozy (*Brit. inf.*), dull, dumb (*Inf.*), obtuse, slow, slow on the uptake (*Inf.*), stupid, thick **4.** confused, hazy, imperfect, indistinct, intangible, obscure, remote, shadowy, vague **5.** dingy, dull, feeble, lacklustre, muted, opaque, pale, sullied, tarnished, weak **6.** dashing, depressing, discouraging, gloomy, sombre, unfavourable, unpromising **7. take a dim view** be displeased, be sceptical, disapprove, look askance, reject, suspect, take exception, view with disfavour ~*v.* **8.** bedim, blur, cloud, darken, dull, fade, lower, obscure, tarnish, turn down
Antonyms (*sense 1*) bright, clear, cloudless, fair, limpid, pleasant, sunny, unclouded (*sense 2*) bright, brilliant, clear, distinct, limpid, palpable (*sense 3*) acute, astute, aware, brainy, bright, clever, intelligent, keen, quick-witted, sharp, smart

dimension *Often plural* **1.** amplitude, bulk, capacity, extent, measurement, proportions, size, volume **2.** bigness, extent, greatness, importance, largeness, magnitude, measure, range, scale, scope

diminish 1. abate, contract, curtail, cut, decrease, lessen, lower, reduce, retrench, shrink, weaken **2.** decline, die out, dwindle, ebb, fade away, peter out, recede, shrivel, slacken, subside, wane **3.** belittle, cheapen, demean, depreciate, devalue
Antonyms amplify, augment, enhance, enlarge, expand, grow, heighten, increase

diminution abatement, contraction, curtailment, cut, cutback, decay, decline, decrease, deduction, lessening, reduction, retrenchment, weakening

diminutive *adj.* bantam, Lilliputian, little, midget, mini, miniature, minute, petite, pocket(-sized), pygmy *or* pigmy, small, teensy-weensy, teeny-weeny, tiny, under-sized, wee
Antonyms big, colossal, enormous, giant, gigantic, great, immense, jumbo (*Inf.*), king-size, massive (*Inf.*)

din 1. *n.* babel, clamour, clangour, clash, clatter, commotion, crash, hubbub, hullabaloo, noise, outcry, pandemonium, racket,

row, shout, uproar **2.** *v. Usually with* **into** drum into, go on at, hammer into, incul~ cate, instil, instruct, teach
Antonyms *n.* calm, calmness, hush, peace, quiet, quietness, silence, tranquillity

dine 1. banquet, chow down (*Sl.*), eat, feast, lunch, sup **2.** *Often with* **on, off** *or* **upon** consume, eat, feed on

dingy bedimmed, colourless, dark, dim, dirty, discoloured, drab, dreary, dull, dusky, faded, gloomy, grimy, murky, obscure, seedy, shabby, soiled, sombre, tacky (*Inf.*)

dinky cute, dainty, mini, miniature, natty (*Inf.*), neat, petite, small, trim

dinner banquet, beanfeast (*Brit. inf.*), blow~ out (*Sl.*), collation, feast, main meal, meal, refection, repast, spread (*Inf.*)

dip *v.* **1.** bathe, douse, duck, dunk, immerse, plunge, rinse, souse **2.** decline, descend, disappear, droop, drop (down), fade, fall, lower, sag, set, sink, slope, slump, subside, tilt **3.** ladle, scoop, spoon **4.** *With* **in** *or* **into** browse, dabble, glance at, peruse, play at, run over, sample, skim, try **5.** *With* **in** *or* **into** draw upon, reach into ~*n.* **6.** douche, drenching, ducking, immersion, plunge, soaking **7.** bathe, dive, plunge, swim **8.** concoction, dilution, infusion, mixture, preparation, solution, suspension **9.** basin, concavity, depression, hole, hollow, incline, slope **10.** decline, drop, fall, lowering, sag, slip, slump

diplomacy 1. international negotiation, statecraft, statesmanship **2.** artfulness, craft, delicacy, discretion, finesse, savoir-faire, skill, subtlety, tact
Antonyms awkwardness, clumsiness, in~ eptness, tactlessness, thoughtlessness

diplomat conciliator, go-between, mediator, moderator, negotiator, politician, public re~ lations expert, tactician

diplomatic adept, discreet, polite, politic, prudent, sensitive, subtle, tactful
Antonyms impolitic, insensitive, rude, tact~ less, thoughtless, undiplomatic, unsubtle

dire 1. alarming, appalling, awful, calami~ tous, cataclysmic, catastrophic, cruel, dis~ astrous, godawful (*Sl.*), horrible, horrid, ru~ inous, terrible, woeful **2.** dismal, dreadful, fearful, gloomy, grim, ominous, portentous **3.** critical, crucial, crying, desperate, dras~ tic, exigent, extreme, pressing, urgent

direct[1] *v.* **1.** administer, advise, conduct, control, dispose, govern, guide, handle, lead, manage, mastermind, oversee, preside over, regulate, rule, run, superintend, supervise **2.** bid, charge, command, demand, dictate, enjoin, instruct, order **3.** guide, indicate, lead, point in the direction of, point the way, show **4.** address, aim, cast, fix, focus, intend, level, mean, point, train, turn **5.**

address, label, mail, route, send, super~ scribe

direct[2] *adj.* **1.** candid, downright, frank, honest, man-to-man, matter-of-fact, open, outspoken, plain-spoken, sincere, straight, straightforward, upfront (*Inf.*) **2.** absolute, blunt, categorical, downright, explicit, ex~ press, plain, point-blank, unambiguous, un~ equivocal **3.** nonstop, not crooked, shortest, straight, through, unbroken, undeviating, uninterrupted **4.** face-to-face, first-hand, head-on, immediate, personal
Antonyms ambiguous, circuitous, crooked, devious, indirect, mediated, sly, subtle

direction 1. administration, charge, com~ mand, control, government, guidance, lead~ ership, management, order, oversight, superintendence, supervision **2.** aim, bear~ ing, course, line, path, road, route, track, way **3.** bent, bias, current, drift, end, lean~ ing, orientation, proclivity, tack, tendency, tenor, trend **4.** address, label, mark, super~ scription

directions briefing, guidance, guidelines, indication, instructions, plan, recommen~ dation, regulations

directive *n.* charge, command, decree, dic~ tate, edict, fiat, imperative, injunction, in~ struction, mandate, notice, order, ordi~ nance, regulation, ruling

directly 1. by the shortest route, exactly, in a beeline, precisely, straight, unswervingly, without deviation **2.** as soon as possible, at once, dead, due, forthwith, immediately, in a second, instantaneously, instantly, pdq (*Sl.*), posthaste, presently, promptly, pronto (*Inf.*), quickly, right away, soon, speedily, straightaway **3.** candidly, face-to-face, hon~ estly, in person, openly, overtly, personally, plainly, point-blank, straightforwardly, truthfully, unequivocally, without prevari~ cation

director administrator, boss (*Inf.*), chair~ man, chief, controller, executive, governor, head, leader, manager, organizer, principal, producer, supervisor

dirge coronach (*Scot. & Irish*), dead march, elegy, funeral song, lament, requiem, threnody

dirt 1. crap (*Sl.*), crud (*Sl.*), dust, excrement, filth, grime, grot (*Sl.*), impurity, mire, muck, mud, shit (*Taboo sl.*), slime, smudge, stain, tarnish **2.** clay, earth, loam, soil **3.** indecency, obscenity, pornography, sleaze, smut

dirty *adj.* **1.** begrimed, filthy, foul, grimy, grotty (*Sl.*), grubby, grungy (*Sl., chiefly U.S.*), messy, mucky, muddy, nasty, pollut~ ed, scuzzy (*Sl., chiefly U.S.*), soiled, sullied, unclean **2.** blue, indecent, obscene, off-colour, pornographic, risqué, salacious,

sleazy, smutty, vulgar **3.** clouded, dark, dull, miry, muddy, not clear **4.** corrupt, crooked, dishonest, fraudulent, illegal, treacherous, unfair, unscrupulous, unsport~ ing **5.** base, beggarly, contemptible, cow~ ardly, despicable, ignominious, low, low-down (*Inf.*), mean, nasty, scurvy, shabby, sordid, squalid, vile **6.** angry, annoyed, bit~ ter, indignant, offended, resentful, scorch~ ing **7.** *Of weather* gusty, louring *or* lower~ ing, rainy, squally, stormy ~*v.* **8.** begrime, blacken, defile, foul, mess up, muddy, pol~ lute, smear, smirch, smudge, soil, spoil, stain, sully
Antonyms *adj.* clean, decent, honest, moral, pleasant, pure, reputable, respectable, upright ~*v.* clean, tidy up

disability 1. affliction, ailment, complaint, defect, disablement, disorder, handicap, im~ pairment, infirmity, malady **2.** disqualification, impotency, inability, inca~ pacity, incompetency, unfitness, weakness

disable 1. cripple, damage, debilitate, en~ feeble, hamstring, handicap, immobilize, impair, incapacitate, paralyse, prostrate, put out of action, render *hors de combat*, render inoperative, unfit, unman, weaken **2.** disenable, disqualify, invalidate, render *or* declare incapable

disabled bedridden, crippled, handicapped, incapacitated, infirm, lame, maimed, man~ gled, mutilated, paralysed, weak, weakened, wrecked
Antonyms able-bodied, fit, hale, healthy, hearty, robust, sound, strong, sturdy

disadvantage 1. damage, detriment, dis~ service, harm, hurt, injury, loss, prejudice **2.** *Often plural* burden, downside, draw~ back, flaw, fly in the ointment (*Inf.*), handi~ cap, hardship, hindrance, impediment, in~ convenience, liability, minus (*Inf.*), nui~ sance, privation, snag, trouble, weakness, weak point **3. at a disadvantage** boxed in, cornered, handicapped, in a corner, vulner~ able
Antonyms advantage, aid, benefit, conveni~ ence, gain, help, merit, profit

disadvantageous adverse, damaging, del~ eterious, detrimental, harmful, hurtful, ill-timed, inconvenient, inexpedient, injurious, inopportune, prejudicial, unfavourable

disaffected alienated, antagonistic, discon~ tented, disloyal, dissatisfied, estranged, hostile, mutinous, rebellious, seditious, un~ compliant, unsubmissive

disaffection alienation, animosity, antago~ nism, antipathy, aversion, breach, dis~ agreement, discontent, dislike, disloyalty, dissatisfaction, estrangement, hostility, ill will, repugnance, resentment, unfriendli~ ness

disagree 1. be discordant, be dissimilar, conflict, contradict, counter, depart, deviate, differ, diverge, run counter to, vary **2.** ar~ gue, bicker, clash, contend, contest, debate, differ (in opinion), dispute, dissent, fall out (*Inf.*), have words (*Inf.*), object, oppose, quarrel, take issue with, wrangle **3.** be in~ jurious, bother, discomfort, distress, hurt, make ill, nauseate, sicken, trouble, upset
Antonyms accord, agree, coincide, concur, get on (together), harmonize

disagreeable 1. bad-tempered, brusque, churlish, contrary, cross, difficult, disoblig~ ing, ill-natured, irritable, nasty, peevish, ratty (*Brit. & N.Z. inf.*), rude, surly, tetchy, unfriendly, ungracious, unlikable *or* un~ likeable, unpleasant **2.** disgusting, dis~ pleasing, distasteful, horrid, nasty, objec~ tionable, obnoxious, offensive, repellent, re~ pugnant, repulsive, uninviting, unpalatable, unpleasant, unsavoury, yucky *or* yukky (*Sl.*)
Antonyms agreeable, congenial, delightful, enjoyable, friendly, good-natured, lovely, nice, pleasant

disagreement 1. difference, discrepancy, disparity, dissimilarity, dissimilitude, di~ vergence, diversity, incompatibility, incon~ gruity, unlikeness, variance **2.** altercation, argument, clash, conflict, debate, difference, discord, dispute, dissent, division, falling out, misunderstanding, quarrel, row, squabble, strife, wrangle **3. in disagree~ ment** at daggers drawn, at loggerheads, at odds, at variance, disunited, in conflict, in disharmony
Antonyms accord, agreement, assent, con~ sensus, correspondence, harmony, similarity, unison, unity

disallow 1. abjure, disavow, disclaim, dis~ miss, disown, rebuff, refuse, reject, repudi~ ate **2.** ban, boycott, cancel, embargo, forbid, prohibit, proscribe, veto

disappear 1. abscond, be lost to view, de~ part, drop out of sight, ebb, escape, eva~ nesce, fade away, flee, fly, go, pass, recede, retire, vanish from sight, wane, withdraw **2.** cease, cease to be known, die out, dis~ solve, end, evaporate, expire, fade, leave no trace, melt away, pass away, perish, vanish
Antonyms appear, arrive, materialize, re~ appear

disappearance departure, desertion, dis~ appearing, disappearing trick, eclipse, eva~ nescence, evaporation, fading, flight, going, loss, melting, passing, vanishing, vanishing point

disappoint 1. chagrin, dash, deceive, de~ lude, disenchant, disgruntle, dishearten, disillusion, dismay, dissatisfy, fail, let down, sadden, vex **2.** baffle, balk, defeat, disconcert, foil, frustrate, hamper, hinder, thwart

disappointed balked, cast down, depressed, despondent, discontented, discouraged, disenchanted, disgruntled, disillusioned, dissatisfied, distressed, downhearted, foiled, frustrated, let down, saddened, thwarted, upset
Antonyms content, contented, fulfilled, happy, pleased, satisfied

disappointing depressing, disagreeable, disconcerting, discouraging, failing, inadequate, inferior, insufficient, lame, pathetic, sad, second-rate, sorry, unexpected, unhappy, unsatisfactory, unworthy, upsetting

disappointment 1. chagrin, discontent, discouragement, disenchantment, disillusionment, displeasure, dissatisfaction, distress, failure, frustration, ill-success, mortification, regret, unfulfilment 2. blow, calamity, disaster, failure, fiasco, letdown, miscarriage, misfortune, setback, washout (*Inf.*)

disapproval censure, condemnation, criticism, denunciation, deprecation, disapprobation, displeasure, dissatisfaction, objection, reproach, stick (*Sl.*)

disapprove 1. *Often with* of blame, censure, condemn, deplore, deprecate, discountenance, dislike, find unacceptable, frown on, look down one's nose at (*Inf.*), object to, reject, take exception to 2. disallow, set aside, spurn, turn down, veto
Antonyms applaud, approve, commend, compliment, endorse, give the go-ahead (to) (*Inf.*), like, O.K. or okay (*Inf.*)

disarmament arms limitation, arms reduction, de-escalation, demilitarization, demobilization

disarming charming, irresistible, likable or likeable, persuasive, winning

disarrange confuse, derange, discompose, disorder, disorganize, disturb, jumble (up), mess (up), scatter, shake (up), shuffle, unsettle, untidy

disarray 1. confusion, discomposure, disharmony, dismay, disorder, disorderliness, disorganization, disunity, indiscipline, unruliness, upset 2. chaos, clutter, dishevelment, hodgepodge (*U.S.*), hotchpotch, jumble, mess, mix-up, muddle, pig's breakfast (*Inf.*), shambles, state, tangle, untidiness
Antonyms arrangement, harmony, method, neatness, order, orderliness, organization, pattern, plan, regularity, symmetry, system, tidiness

disaster accident, act of God, adversity, blow, bummer (*Sl.*), calamity, cataclysm, catastrophe, misadventure, mischance, misfortune, mishap, reverse, ruin, ruination, stroke, tragedy, trouble

disastrous adverse, calamitous, cataclysmal, cataclysmic, catastrophic, destructive, detrimental, devastating, dire, dreadful, fatal, hapless, harmful, ill-fated, ill-starred, ruinous, terrible, tragic, unfortunate, unlucky, unpropitious, untoward

disbelief distrust, doubt, dubiety, incredulity, mistrust, scepticism, unbelief
Antonyms belief, credence, credulity, faith, trust

disbelieve discount, discredit, give no credence to, mistrust, not accept, not buy (*Sl.*), not credit, not swallow (*Inf.*), reject, repudiate, scoff at, suspect

disbeliever agnostic, atheist, doubter, doubting Thomas, questioner, sceptic, scoffer
Antonyms adherent, believer, devotee, disciple, follower, proselyte, supporter, upholder, zealot

disbelievingly askance, cynically, doubtingly, incredulously, mistrustfully, quizzically, sceptically, suspiciously, with a pinch of salt

discard abandon, axe (*Inf.*), cast aside, chuck (*Inf.*), dispense with, dispose of, ditch (*Sl.*), drop, dump (*Inf.*), get rid of, jettison, junk (*Inf.*), reject, relinquish, remove, repudiate, scrap, shed, throw away or out
Antonyms hang or hold on to, hold back, keep, reserve, retain, save

discerning acute, astute, clear-sighted, critical, discriminating, ingenious, intelligent, judicious, knowing, penetrating, perceptive, percipient, perspicacious, piercing, sagacious, sensitive, sharp, shrewd, subtle, wise

discharge *v.* 1. absolve, acquit, allow to go, clear, exonerate, free, liberate, pardon, release, set free ~*n.* 2. acquittal, clearance, exoneration, liberation, pardon, release, remittance ~*v.* 3. cashier, discard, dismiss, eject, expel, fire (*Inf.*), give (someone) the sack (*Inf.*), oust, remove, sack (*Inf.*), ~*n.* 4. congé, demobilization, dismissal, ejection, the boot (*Sl.*), the (old) heave-ho (*Inf.*), the order of the boot (*Sl.*), the sack (*Inf.*), ~*v.* 5. detonate, explode, fire, let off, set off, shoot ~*n.* 6. blast, burst, detonation, discharging, explosion, firing, fusillade, report, salvo, shot, volley ~*v.* 7. disembogue, dispense, emit, empty, excrete, exude, give off, gush, leak, ooze, pour forth, release, void ~*n.* 8. emission, emptying, excretion, flow, ooze, pus, secretion, seepage, suppuration, vent, voiding ~*v.* 9. disburden, lighten, off-load, remove, unburden, unload ~*n.* 10. disburdening, emptying, unburdening, unloading ~*v.* 11. accomplish, carry out, do, execute, fulfil, observe, perform ~*n.* 12. accomplishment, achievement, execution, ful~

filment, observance, performance ~v. **13.** clear, honour, meet, pay, relieve, satisfy, settle, square up ~n. **14.** payment, satisfac~ tion, settlement

disciple adherent, apostle, believer, cat~ echumen, convert, devotee, follower, learn~ er, partisan, proselyte, pupil, student, sup~ porter, votary
Antonyms guru, leader, master, swami, teacher

disciplinarian authoritarian, despot, drill sergeant, hard master, martinet, stickler, strict teacher, taskmaster, tyrant

discipline n. **1.** drill, exercise, method, practice, regimen, regulation, training **2.** conduct, control, orderliness, regulation, restraint, self-control, strictness **3.** castiga~ tion, chastisement, correction, punishment **4.** area, branch of knowledge, course, cur~ riculum, field of study, speciality, subject ~v. **5.** break in, bring up, check, control, drill, educate, exercise, form, govern, in~ struct, inure, prepare, regulate, restrain, train **6.** castigate, chasten, chastise, correct, penalize, punish, reprimand, reprove

disclaim abandon, abjure, abnegate, decline, deny, disaffirm, disallow, disavow, disown, forswear, rebut, reject, renege, renounce, repudiate, retract

disclose 1. blow wide open (Sl.), broadcast, communicate, confess, divulge, impart, leak, let slip, make known, make public, publish, relate, reveal, spill one's guts about (Sl.), spill the beans about (Inf.), tell, unveil, utter **2.** bring to light, discover, exhibit, expose, lay bare, reveal, show, uncover, unveil
Antonyms conceal, cover, dissemble, hide, keep dark, keep secret, mask, obscure, secrete, veil

disclosure acknowledgment, admission, announcement, broadcast, confession, dec~ laration, discovery, divulgence, exposé, ex~ posure, leak, publication, revelation, un~ covering

discolour fade, mar, mark, rust, soil, stain, streak, tarnish, tinge

discomfort 1. n. ache, annoyance, disquiet, distress, gall, hardship, hurt, inquietude, irritation, malaise, nuisance, pain, soreness, trouble, uneasiness, unpleasantness, vexa~ tion **2.** v. discomfit, discompose, disquiet, distress, disturb, embarrass, make uncom~ fortable
Antonyms n. comfort, ease, reassurance, solace ~v. alleviate, assuage, comfort, ease, reassure, solace, soothe

discomposure agitation, anxiety, confu~ sion, discomfiture, disquiet, disquietude, distraction, disturbance, embarrassment,

fluster, inquietude, malaise, nervousness, perturbation, trepidation, uneasiness

disconcert 1. abash, agitate, bewilder, dis~ compose, disturb, faze, flummox, flurry, fluster, nonplus, perplex, perturb, put out of countenance, rattle (Inf.), ruffle, shake up (Inf.), take aback, throw off balance, trou~ ble, unbalance, unnerve, unsettle, upset, worry **2.** baffle, balk, confuse, defeat, disar~ range, frustrate, hinder, put off, thwart, undo

disconcerted annoyed, at sea, bewildered, caught off balance, confused, distracted, disturbed, embarrassed, fazed, flummoxed, flurried, flustered, mixed-up, nonplussed, out of countenance, perturbed, rattled (Inf.), ruffled, shook up (Inf.), taken aback, thrown (Inf.), troubled, unsettled, upset

disconcerting alarming, awkward, baffling, bewildering, bothersome, confus~ ing, dismaying, distracting, disturbing, em~ barrassing, off-putting (Brit. inf.), perplex~ ing, upsetting

disconnect cut off, detach, disengage, di~ vide, part, separate, sever, take apart, un~ couple

disconnected confused, disjointed, gar~ bled, illogical, incoherent, irrational, jum~ bled, mixed-up, rambling, uncoordinated, unintelligible, wandering

disconnection cessation, cut-off, cutting off, discontinuation, discontinuity, inter~ ruption, separation, severance, stoppage, suspension

disconsolate crushed, dejected, desolate, despairing, dismal, forlorn, gloomy, grief~ stricken, heartbroken, hopeless, inconsol~ able, melancholy, miserable, sad, unhappy, woeful, wretched

discontent n. discontentment, displeasure, dissatisfaction, envy, fretfulness, regret, restlessness, uneasiness, unhappiness, vexation

discontented brassed off (Brit. sl.), cheesed off (Brit. sl.), complaining, disaf~ fected, disgruntled, displeased, dissatisfied, exasperated, fed up, fretful, miserable, pissed off (Taboo sl.), unhappy, vexed, with a chip on one's shoulder (Inf.)
Antonyms cheerful, content, contented, happy, pleased, satisfied

discontinue abandon, axe (Inf.), break off, cease, drop, end, finish, give up, halt, inter~ rupt, kick (Inf.), leave off, pause, put an end to, quit, refrain from, stop, suspend, termi~ nate

discontinued abandoned, ended, finished, given up or over, halted, no longer made, terminated

discord 1. clashing, conflict, contention,

difference, disagreement, discordance, dis~
pute, dissension, disunity, division, friction,
incompatibility, lack of concord, opposition,
row, rupture, strife, variance, wrangling **2.**
cacophony, din, disharmony, dissonance,
harshness, jangle, jarring, racket, tumult
Antonyms accord, agreement, concord,
euphony, friendship, harmony, melody,
peace, tunefulness, understanding, unison,
unity

discordant 1. at odds, clashing, conflicting,
contradictory, contrary, different, disagree~
ing, divergent, incompatible, incongruous,
inconsistent, opposite **2.** cacophonous, dis~
sonant, grating, harsh, inharmonious, jan~
gling, jarring, shrill, strident, unmelodious

discount v. **1.** brush off (Sl.), disbelieve,
disregard, ignore, leave out of account,
overlook, pass over **2.** deduct, lower, mark
down, rebate, reduce, take off ~n. **3.** abate~
ment, allowance, concession, cut, cut price,
deduction, drawback, percentage (Inf.), re~
bate, reduction

discountenance v. **1.** abash, chagrin,
confuse, discompose, disconcert, embarrass,
humiliate, put down (Sl.), shame **2.** con~
demn, disapprove, discourage, disfavour,
frown on, object to, oppose, resist, take ex~
ception to, veto

discourage 1. abash, awe, cast down, cow,
damp, dampen, dash, daunt, deject, demor~
alize, depress, dishearten, dismay, dispirit,
frighten, intimidate, overawe, psych out
(Inf.), put a damper on, scare, unman, un~
nerve **2.** check, curb, deprecate, deter, dis~
countenance, disfavour, dissuade, divert
from, hinder, inhibit, prevent, put off, re~
strain, talk out of, throw cold water on
(Inf.)
Antonyms bid, countenance, embolden, en~
courage, hearten, inspire, urge, welcome

discouraged crestfallen, dashed, daunted,
deterred, disheartened, dismayed, dispirit~
ed, downcast, down in the mouth, glum,
pessimistic, put off, sick as a parrot (Inf.)

discouragement 1. cold feet (Inf.), dejec~
tion, depression, despair, despondency, dis~
appointment, discomfiture, dismay, down~
heartedness, hopelessness, loss of con~
fidence, low spirits, pessimism **2.** con~
straint, curb, damper, deterrent, disincen~
tive, hindrance, impediment, obstacle, op~
position, rebuff, restraint, setback

discouraging dampening, daunting, de~
pressing, disappointing, disheartening, dis~
piriting, off-putting (Brit. inf.), unfavour~
able, unpropitious

discourse n. **1.** chat, communication, con~
versation, converse, dialogue, discussion,
seminar, speech, talk **2.** address, disquisi~
tion, dissertation, essay, homily, lecture,

oration, sermon, speech, talk, treatise ~v.
3. confer, converse, debate, declaim, dis~
cuss, expatiate, hold forth, speak, talk

discourteous abrupt, bad-mannered, boor~
ish, brusque, curt, disrespectful, ill-bred,
ill-mannered, impolite, insolent, offhand,
rude, uncivil, uncourteous, ungentlemanly,
ungracious, unmannerly
Antonyms civil, courteous, courtly, gra~
cious, mannerly, polite, respectful, well-
mannered

discourtesy 1. bad manners, disrespect~
fulness, ill-breeding, impertinence, impo~
liteness, incivility, insolence, rudeness,
ungraciousness, unmannerliness **2.** affront,
cold shoulder, insult, rebuff, slight, snub

discover 1. bring to light, come across,
come upon, dig up, find, light upon, locate,
turn up, uncover, unearth **2.** ascertain, de~
scry, detect, determine, discern, disclose,
espy, find out, get wise to (Inf.), learn, no~
tice, perceive, realize, recognize, reveal, see,
spot, suss (out) (Sl.), turn up, uncover **3.**
conceive, contrive, design, devise, invent,
originate, pioneer

discoverer author, explorer, founder, ini~
tiator, inventor, originator, pioneer

discovery 1. ascertainment, detection, dis~
closure, espial, exploration, finding, intro~
duction, locating, location, origination, rev~
elation, uncovering **2.** bonanza, break~
through, coup, find, findings, godsend, in~
novation, invention, secret

discredit v. **1.** blame, bring into disrepute,
censure, defame, degrade, detract from, dis~
grace, dishonour, disparage, reproach,
slander, slur, smear, vilify ~n. **2.** asper~
sion, censure, disgrace, dishonour, disre~
pute, ignominy, ill-repute, imputation,
odium, reproach, scandal, shame, slur,
smear, stigma ~v. **3.** challenge, deny, dis~
believe, discount, dispute, distrust, doubt,
mistrust, question ~n. **4.** distrust, doubt,
mistrust, question, scepticism, suspicion
Antonyms v. acclaim, applaud, commend,
honour, laud, pay tribute to, praise ~n. ac~
claim, acknowledgment, approval, commen~
dation, credit, honour, merit, praise

discreditable blameworthy, degrading,
disgraceful, dishonourable, humiliating, ig~
nominious, improper, infamous, reprehen~
sible, scandalous, shameful, unprincipled,
unworthy

discredited brought into disrepute, de~
bunked, discarded, exploded, exposed, obso~
lete, outworn, refuted, rejected

discreet careful, cautious, circumspect,
considerate, diplomatic, discerning, guard~
ed, judicious, politic, prudent, reserved, sa~
gacious, sensible, tactful, wary
Antonyms incautious, indiscreet, injudi~

cious, rash, tactless, undiplomatic, unthink~
ing, unwise

discrepancy conflict, contrariety, differ~
ence, disagreement, discordance, disparity,
dissimilarity, dissonance, divergence, in~
congruity, inconsistency, variance, vari~
ation

discretion 1. acumen, care, carefulness,
caution, circumspection, consideration, di~
plomacy, discernment, good sense, heedful~
ness, judgment, judiciousness, maturity,
prudence, sagacity, tact, wariness **2.** choice,
disposition, inclination, liking, mind, op~
tion, pleasure, predilection, preference, re~
sponsibility, volition, will, wish
Antonyms carelessness, indiscretion, in~
sensitivity, rashness, tactlessness, thought~
lessness

discretionary arbitrary (*Law*), elective,
nonmandatory, open, open to choice, op~
tional, unrestricted

discriminate 1. disfavour, favour, show
bias, show prejudice, single out, treat as
inferior, treat differently, victimize **2.** as~
sess, differentiate, discern, distinguish,
draw a distinction, evaluate, segregate,
separate, sift, tell the difference

discriminating acute, astute, critical, cul~
tivated, discerning, fastidious, keen, par~
ticular, refined, selective, sensitive, tasteful
Antonyms careless, desultory, general, hit
or miss (*Inf.*), indiscriminate, random, undis~
criminating, unselective, unsystematic

discrimination 1. bias, bigotry, favourit~
ism, inequity, intolerance, prejudice, un~
fairness **2.** acumen, acuteness, clearness,
discernment, insight, judgment, keenness,
penetration, perception, refinement, sagac~
ity, subtlety, taste

discriminatory, discriminative 1. bi~
ased, favouring, inequitable, one-sided, par~
tial, partisan, preferential, prejudiced,
prejudicial, unjust, weighted **2.** analytical,
astute, differentiating, discerning, discrimi~
nating, perceptive, perspicacious

discuss argue, confer, consider, consult
with, converse, debate, deliberate, examine,
exchange views on, get together, go into,
reason about, review, sift, talk about,
thrash out, ventilate, weigh up the pros and
cons

discussion analysis, argument, colloquy,
confabulation, conference, consideration,
consultation, conversation, debate, delib~
eration, dialogue, discourse, examination,
exchange, review, scrutiny, seminar, sym~
posium

disdain 1. *v.* belittle, contemn, deride, des~
pise, disregard, look down on, look down
one's nose at (*Inf.*), misprize, pooh-pooh,
reject, scorn, slight, sneer at, spurn, under~

value **2.** *n.* arrogance, contempt, contumely,
derision, dislike, haughtiness, hauteur, in~
difference, scorn, sneering, snobbishness,
superciliousness

disdainful aloof, arrogant, contemptuous,
derisive, haughty, high and mighty (*Inf.*),
hoity-toity (*Inf.*), insolent, proud, scornful,
sneering, supercilious, superior

disease 1. affliction, ailment, complaint,
condition, disorder, ill health, illness, in~
disposition, infection, infirmity, malady,
sickness, upset **2.** *Fig.* blight, cancer, can~
ker, contagion, contamination, disorder,
malady, plague

diseased ailing, infected, rotten, sick, sick~
ly, tainted, unhealthy, unsound, unwell,
unwholesome

disembark alight, arrive, get off, go ashore,
land, step out of

disembodied bodiless, ghostly, immaterial,
incorporeal, intangible, phantom, spectral,
spiritual, unbodied

disembowel draw, eviscerate, gut, paunch

disenchanted blasé, cynical, disappointed,
disillusioned, indifferent, jaundiced, let
down, out of love, sick of, soured, unde~
ceived

disenchantment disappointment, disillu~
sion, disillusionment, revulsion, rude
awakening

disengage 1. disentangle, ease, extricate,
free, liberate, loosen, release, set free, un~
bridle, unloose, untie **2.** detach, disconnect,
disjoin, disunite, divide, separate, undo,
withdraw

disengaged 1. apart, detached, free, loose,
out of gear, released, separate, unattached,
unconnected, uncoupled **2.** at ease, at lei~
sure, free, not busy, uncommitted, unoccu~
pied, vacant

disengagement detachment, disconnec~
tion, disentanglement, division, separation,
withdrawal

disentangle 1. detach, disconnect, disen~
gage, extricate, free, loose, separate, sever,
unfold, unravel, unsnarl, untangle, untwist
2. clarify, clear (up), resolve, simplify, sort
out, work out

disfavour 1. disapprobation, disapproval,
dislike, displeasure **2.** *As in* **fall into dis~
favour** bad books (*Inf.*), discredit, dises~
teem, disgrace, doghouse (*Inf.*), shame, un~
popularity **3.** bad turn, discourtesy, disser~
vice

disfigure blemish, damage, deface, deform,
disfeature, distort, injure, maim, make ugly,
mar, mutilate, scar

disfigurement blemish, defacement, de~
fect, deformity, distortion, impairment, in~
jury, mutilation, scar, spot, stain

disgorge 1. barf (*U.S. sl.*), belch, chuck (up) (*Sl., chiefly U.S.*), chunder (*Sl., chiefly Aust.*), discharge, do a technicolour yawn (*Sl.*), eject, empty, expel, regurgitate, spew, spit up, spout, throw up, toss one's cookies (*U.S. sl.*), upchuck (*U.S. sl.*), vomit **2.** cede, give up, relinquish, renounce, resign, surrender, yield

disgrace *n.* **1.** baseness, degradation, dishonour, disrepute, ignominy, infamy, odium, opprobrium, shame **2.** aspersion, blemish, blot, defamation, reproach, scandal, slur, stain, stigma **3.** contempt, discredit, disesteem, disfavour, obloquy ~*v.* **4.** abase, bring shame upon, defame, degrade, discredit, disfavour, dishonour, disparage, humiliate, reproach, shame, slur, stain, stigmatize, sully, taint
Antonyms *n.* credit, esteem, favour, grace, honour, repute ~*v.* credit, grace, honour

disgraced branded, degraded, discredited, dishonoured, humiliated, in disgrace, in the doghouse (*Inf.*), mortified, shamed, stigmatized

disgraceful blameworthy, contemptible, degrading, detestable, discreditable, dishonourable, disreputable, ignominious, infamous, low, mean, opprobrious, scandalous, shameful, shocking, unworthy

disgruntled annoyed, cheesed off (*Brit. sl.*), discontented, displeased, dissatisfied, grumpy, hacked (off) (*U.S. sl.*), huffy, irritated, malcontent, peeved, peevish, petulant, pissed off (*Taboo sl.*), put out, sulky, sullen, testy, vexed

disguise *v.* **1.** camouflage, cloak, conceal, cover, hide, mask, screen, secrete, shroud, veil **2.** deceive, dissemble, dissimulate, fake, falsify, fudge, gloss over, misrepresent ~*n.* **3.** camouflage, cloak, costume, cover, get-up (*Inf.*), mask, screen, veil **4.** deception, dissimulation, façade, front, pretence, semblance, trickery, veneer

disguised camouflaged, cloaked, covert, fake, false, feigned, incognito, in disguise, masked, pretend, undercover, unrecognizable

disgust 1. *v.* cause aversion, displease, fill with loathing, gross out (*U.S. sl.*), nauseate, offend, outrage, put off, repel, revolt, sicken, turn one's stomach **2.** *n.* abhorrence, abomination, antipathy, aversion, detestation, dislike, distaste, hatefulness, hatred, loathing, nausea, odium, repugnance, repulsion, revulsion
Antonyms *v.* delight, impress, please ~*n.* liking, love, pleasure, satisfaction, taste

disgusted appalled, nauseated, offended, outraged, repelled, repulsed, scandalized, sick and tired of (*Inf.*), sickened, sick of (*Inf.*)

disgusting abominable, cringe-making (*Brit. inf.*), detestable, distasteful, foul, gross, grotty (*Sl.*), hateful, loathsome, nasty, nauseating, nauseous, objectionable, obnoxious, odious, offensive, repellent, repugnant, revolting, shameless, sickening, stinking, vile, vulgar, yucky *or* yukky (*Sl.*)

dish *n.* **1.** bowl, plate, platter, salver **2.** fare, food, recipe ~*v.* **3.** *Sl.* finish, muck up (*Sl.*), ruin, spoil, torpedo, wreck

dishearten cast down, crush, damp, dampen, dash, daunt, deject, depress, deter, discourage, dismay, dispirit, put a damper on
Antonyms buck up (*Inf.*), cheer up, encourage, hearten, lift, perk up, rally

disheartened crestfallen, crushed, daunted, dejected, depressed, disappointed, discouraged, dismayed, dispirited, downcast, downhearted, sick as a parrot (*Inf.*)

dishevelled bedraggled, blowzy, disarranged, disarrayed, disordered, frowzy, hanging loose, messy, ruffled, rumpled, tousled, uncombed, unkempt, untidy
Antonyms chic, dapper, neat, smart, soigné *or* soignée, spick-and-span, spruce, tidy, trim, well-groomed

dishonest bent (*Sl.*), cheating, corrupt, crafty, crooked (*Inf.*), deceitful, deceiving, deceptive, designing, disreputable, double-dealing, false, fraudulent, guileful, knavish (*Archaic*), lying, mendacious, perfidious, shady (*Inf.*), swindling, treacherous, unfair, unprincipled, unscrupulous, untrustworthy, untruthful
Antonyms honest, honourable, law-abiding, lawful, principled, true, trustworthy, upright

dishonesty cheating, chicanery, corruption, craft, criminality, crookedness, deceit, duplicity, falsehood, falsity, fraud, fraudulence, graft (*Inf.*), improbity, mendacity, perfidy, sharp practice, stealing, treachery, trickery, unscrupulousness, wiliness

dishonour *v.* **1.** abase, blacken, corrupt, debase, debauch, defame, degrade, discredit, disgrace, shame, sully **2.** defile, deflower, pollute, rape, ravish, seduce ~*n.* **3.** abasement, degradation, discredit, disfavour, disgrace, disrepute, ignominy, infamy, obloquy, odium, opprobrium, reproach, scandal, shame **4.** abuse, affront, discourtesy, indignity, insult, offence, outrage, slight
Antonyms *v.* esteem, exalt, respect, revere, worship ~*n.* decency, goodness, honour, integrity, morality, principles, rectitude

dishonourable 1. base, contemptible, despicable, discreditable, disgraceful, ignoble, ignominious, infamous, scandalous, shameful **2.** blackguardly, corrupt, disreputable, shameless, treacherous, unprincipled, unscrupulous, untrustworthy

dish out allocate, distribute, dole out, hand out, inflict, mete out

dish up hand out, ladle, prepare, present, produce, scoop, serve, spoon

disillusion v. break the spell, bring down to earth, disabuse, disenchant, open the eyes of, shatter one's illusions, undeceive

disillusioned disabused, disappointed, disenchanted, enlightened, indifferent, out of love, sadder and wiser, undeceived

disincentive damper, determent, deterrent, discouragement, dissuasion, impediment

disinclination alienation, antipathy, aversion, demur, dislike, hesitance, lack of desire, lack of enthusiasm, loathness, objection, opposition, reluctance, repugnance, resistance, unwillingness

disinclined antipathetic, averse, balking, hesitating, indisposed, loath, not in the mood, opposed, reluctant, resistant, unwilling

disinfect clean, cleanse, decontaminate, deodorize, fumigate, purify, sanitize, sterilize
Antonyms contaminate, defile, infect, poison, pollute, taint, vitiate

disinfectant antiseptic, germicide, sanitizer, sterilizer

disingenuous artful, cunning, deceitful, designing, dishonest, duplicitous, feigned, guileful, insidious, insincere, shifty, sly, two-faced, uncandid, underhanded, unfair, wily

disinherit cut off, cut off without a penny, disown, dispossess, oust, repudiate

disintegrate break apart, break up, crumble, disunite, fall apart, fall to pieces, reduce to fragments, separate, shatter, splinter

disinterest candidness, detachment, disinterestedness, dispassionateness, equity, fairness, impartiality, justice, neutrality, unbiasedness

disinterested candid, detached, dispassionate, equitable, even-handed, free from self-interest, impartial, impersonal, neutral, outside, unbiased, uninvolved, unprejudiced, unselfish
Antonyms biased, involved, partial, prejudiced, selfish

disjointed 1. aimless, confused, disconnected, disordered, fitful, incoherent, loose, rambling, spasmodic, unconnected **2.** disconnected, dislocated, displaced, disunited, divided, separated, split

dislike 1. n. animosity, animus, antagonism, antipathy, aversion, detestation, disapprobation, disapproval, disgust, disinclination, displeasure, distaste, enmity, hatred, hostility, loathing, odium, repugnance **2.** v. abhor, abominate, be averse to, despise, detest, disapprove, disfavour, disrelish, hate, have no taste or stomach for, loathe, not be able to bear or abide, object to, scorn, shun
Antonyms n. admiration, attraction, delight, esteem, inclination, liking ~v. esteem, favour, like

dislocate 1. disorder, displace, disrupt, disturb, misplace, shift **2.** disarticulate, disconnect, disengage, disjoint, disunite, luxate (*Medical*), put out of joint, unhinge

dislocation 1. disarray, disorder, disorganization, disruption, disturbance, misplacement **2.** disarticulation, disconnection, disengagement, luxation (*Medical*), unhinging

disloyal apostate, disaffected, faithless, false, perfidious, seditious, subversive, traitorous, treacherous, treasonable, two-faced, unfaithful, unpatriotic, untrustworthy
Antonyms constant, dependable, dutiful, faithful, loyal, steadfast, true, trustworthy, trusty

disloyalty betrayal of trust, breach of trust, breaking of faith, deceitfulness, double-dealing, falseness, falsity, inconstancy, infidelity, perfidy, Punic faith, treachery, treason, unfaithfulness

dismal black, bleak, cheerless, dark, depressing, despondent, discouraging, dolorous, dreary, forlorn, funereal, gloomy, gruesome, lonesome, louring or lowering, lugubrious, melancholy, sad, sombre, sorrowful
Antonyms bright, cheerful, cheery, glad, happy, joyful, light-hearted, sunny

dismay v. **1.** affright, alarm, appal, distress, fill with consternation, frighten, horrify, paralyse, scare, terrify, unnerve **2.** daunt, disappoint, discourage, dishearten, disillusion, dispirit, put off ~n. **3.** agitation, alarm, anxiety, apprehension, consternation, distress, dread, fear, fright, horror, panic, terror, trepidation **4.** chagrin, disappointment, discouragement, disillusionment, upset

dismember amputate, anatomize, cut into pieces, disjoint, dislimb, dislocate, dissect, divide, mutilate, rend, sever

dismiss 1. axe (*Inf.*), cashier, discharge, fire (*Inf.*), give notice to, kiss off (*Sl., chiefly U.S. & Canad.*), lay off, oust, remove, sack (*Inf.*), send packing (*Inf.*) **2.** disband, disperse, dissolve, free, let go, release, send away **3.** banish, discard, dispel, disregard, drop, lay aside, pooh-pooh, put out of one's mind, reject, relegate, repudiate, set aside, shelve, spurn

dismissal 1. adjournment, congé, end, freedom to depart, permission to go, release **2.** discharge, expulsion, kiss-off (*Sl., chiefly U.S. & Canad.*), marching orders (*Inf.*), no~

tice, one's books *or* cards (*Inf.*), removal, the boot (*Sl.*), the (old) heave-ho (*Inf.*), the order of the boot (*Sl.*), the push (*Sl.*), the sack (*Inf.*)

disobedience indiscipline, infraction, in~ subordination, mutiny, noncompliance, nonobservance, recalcitrance, revolt, unru~ liness, waywardness

disobedient contrary, contumacious, defiant, disorderly, froward, insubordinate, intractable, mischievous, naughty, noncompliant, nonobservant, obstreperous, refractory, undisciplined, unruly, wayward, wilful
Antonyms biddable, compliant, dutiful, manageable, obedient, submissive, well-behaved

disobey contravene, defy, disregard, flout, go counter to, ignore, infringe, overstep, rebel, refuse to obey, resist, transgress, vio~ late

disorderly 1. chaotic, confused, disorgan~ ized, higgledy-piggledy (*Inf.*), indiscrimi~ nate, irregular, jumbled, messy, shambolic (*Inf.*), unsystematic, untidy **2.** boisterous, disruptive, indisciplined, lawless, obstrep~ erous, rebellious, refractory, riotous, rowdy, stormy, tumultuous, turbulent, ungovern~ able, unlawful, unmanageable, unruly
Antonyms arranged, neat, orderly, organ~ ized, tidy

disorganize break up, confuse, derange, destroy, disarrange, discompose, disorder, disrupt, disturb, jumble, make a shambles of, muddle, turn topsy-turvy, unsettle, upset

disorganized chaotic, confused, disor~ dered, haphazard, jumbled, muddled, shuffled, unmethodical, unorganized, un~ systematic

disown abandon, abnegate, cast off, deny, disallow, disavow, disclaim, rebut, refuse to acknowledge *or* recognize, reject, renounce, repudiate, retract

disparage asperse, bad-mouth (*Sl., chiefly U.S. & Canad.*), belittle, blast, criticize, de~ cry, defame, degrade, denigrate, deprecate, depreciate, deride, derogate, detract from, discredit, disdain, dismiss, knock (*Inf.*), lambast(e), malign, minimize, put down, ridicule, rubbish (*Inf.*), run down, scorn, slag (off) (*Sl.*), slander, tear into (*Inf.*), tra~ duce, underestimate, underrate, undervalue, vilify

disparagement aspersion, belittlement, condemnation, contempt, contumely, criti~ cism, debasement, degradation, denuncia~ tion, depreciation, derision, derogation, de~ traction, discredit, disdain, impairment, lessening, prejudice, reproach, ridicule, scorn, slander, underestimation

dispassionate 1. calm, collected, com~

posed, cool, imperturbable, moderate, quiet, serene, sober, temperate, unemotional, unexcitable, unexcited, unfazed (*Inf.*), un~ moved, unruffled **2.** candid, detached, dis~ interested, fair, impartial, impersonal, in~ different, neutral, objective, unbiased, un~ involved, unprejudiced
Antonyms (*sense 1*) ardent, emotional, ex~ cited, fervent, impassioned, intense, passion~ ate (*sense 2*) biased, concerned, interested, in~ volved, partial, prejudiced

dispatch, despatch *v.* **1.** accelerate, con~ sign, dismiss, express, forward, hasten, hurry, quicken, remit, send, transmit **2.** conclude, discharge, dispose of, expedite, finish, make short work of (*Inf.*), perform, settle **3.** assassinate, blow away (*Sl., chiefly U.S.*), bump off (*Sl.*), butcher, eliminate (*Sl.*), execute, finish off, kill, murder, put an end to, slaughter, slay, take out (*Sl.*), ~*n.* **4.** alacrity, celerity, expedition, haste, precipi~ tateness, promptitude, promptness, quick~ ness, rapidity, speed, swiftness **5.** account, bulletin, communication, communiqué, document, instruction, item, letter, mes~ sage, missive, news, piece, report, story

dispel allay, banish, chase away, dismiss, disperse, dissipate, drive away, eliminate, expel, resolve, rout, scatter

dispensable disposable, expendable, ines~ sential, needless, nonessential, superfluous, unnecessary, unrequired, useless
Antonyms crucial, essential, important, in~ dispensable, necessary, requisite, vital

dispensation 1. allotment, appointment, apportionment, bestowal, conferment, con~ signment, dealing out, disbursement, dis~ tribution, endowment, supplying **2.** award, dole, part, portion, quota, share **3.** admin~ istration, direction, economy, management, plan, regulation, scheme, stewardship, sys~ tem **4.** exception, exemption, immunity, in~ dulgence, licence, permission, privilege, re~ laxation, relief, remission, reprieve

dispense 1. allocate, allot, apportion, as~ sign, deal out, disburse, distribute, dole out, mete out, share **2.** measure, mix, prepare, supply **3.** administer, apply, carry out, di~ rect, discharge, enforce, execute, imple~ ment, operate, undertake **4.** except, excuse, exempt, exonerate, let off (*Inf.*), release, re~ lieve, reprieve **5.** *With* **with** abstain from, do without, forgo, give up, omit, relinquish, waive **6.** *With* **with** abolish, brush aside, cancel, dispose of, disregard, do away with, get rid of, ignore, pass over, render need~ less, shake off

disperse 1. broadcast, circulate, diffuse, disseminate, dissipate, distribute, scatter, spread, strew **2.** break up, disappear, dis~

band, dismiss, dispel, dissolve, rout, scatter, send off, separate, vanish
Antonyms amass, assemble, collect, concentrate, congregate, convene, gather, muster, pool

dispirited crestfallen, dejected, depressed, despondent, discouraged, disheartened, down, downcast, gloomy, glum, in the doldrums, low, morose, sad, sick as a parrot (*Inf.*)

displace 1. derange, disarrange, disturb, misplace, move, shift, transpose 2. cashier, depose, discard, discharge, dismiss, fire (*Inf.*), remove, sack (*Inf.*) 3. crowd out, oust, replace, succeed, supersede, supplant, take the place of 4. dislocate, dislodge, dispossess, eject, evict, force out, unsettle

display *v.* 1. betray, demonstrate, disclose, evidence, evince, exhibit, expose, manifest, open, open to view, present, reveal, show, unveil 2. expand, extend, model, open out, spread out, stretch out, unfold, unfurl 3. boast, flash (*Inf.*), flaunt, flourish, parade, show off, vaunt ~*n.* 4. array, demonstration, exhibition, exposition, exposure, manifestation, presentation, revelation, show 5. flourish, ostentation, pageant, parade, pomp, show, spectacle
Antonyms *v.* conceal, cover, hide, keep dark, keep secret, mask, secrete, veil

displease aggravate (*Inf.*), anger, annoy, disgust, dissatisfy, exasperate, gall, hassle (*Inf.*), incense, irk, irritate, nark (*Brit., Aust., & N.Z. sl.*), nettle, offend, pique, piss one off (*Taboo sl.*), provoke, put out, rile, upset, vex

displeasure anger, annoyance, disapprobation, disapproval, disfavour, disgruntlement, dislike, dissatisfaction, distaste, indignation, irritation, offence, pique, resentment, vexation, wrath
Antonyms approval, endorsement, pleasure, satisfaction

disposable 1. biodegradable, compostable, decomposable, nonreturnable, paper, throwaway 2. at one's service, available, consumable, expendable, free for use, spendable

disposal 1. clearance, discarding, dumping (*Inf.*), ejection, jettisoning, parting with, relinquishment, removal, riddance, scrapping, throwing away 2. arrangement, array, dispensation, disposition, distribution, grouping, placing, position 3. assignment, bequest, bestowal, consignment, conveyance, dispensation, gift, settlement, transfer 4. *As in* **at one's disposal** authority, conduct, control, determination, direction, discretion, government, management, ordering, regulation, responsibility

dispose 1. adjust, arrange, array, determine, distribute, fix, group, marshal, order, place, put, range, rank, regulate, set, settle, stand 2. actuate, adapt, bias, condition, incline, induce, influence, lead, motivate, move, predispose, prompt, tempt

disposed apt, given, inclined, liable, likely, of a mind to, predisposed, prone, ready, subject, tending towards

dispose of 1. deal with, decide, determine, end, finish with, settle 2. bestow, give, make over, part with, sell, transfer 3. bin (*Inf.*), chuck (*Inf.*), destroy, discard, dump (*Inf.*), get rid of, jettison, junk (*Inf.*), scrap, throw out *or* away, unload

disposition 1. character, constitution, make-up, nature, spirit, temper, temperament 2. bent, bias, habit, inclination, leaning, predisposition, proclivity, proneness, propensity, readiness, tendency 3. adjustment, arrangement, classification, disposal, distribution, grouping, ordering, organization, placement 4. control, direction, disposal, management, regulation

disproportion asymmetry, discrepancy, disparity, imbalance, inadequacy, inequality, insufficiency, lopsidedness, unevenness, unsuitableness
Antonyms balance, congruity, harmony, proportion, symmetry

disproportionate excessive, incommensurate, inordinate, out of proportion, too much, unbalanced, unequal, uneven, unreasonable

disprove confute, contradict, controvert, discredit, expose, give the lie to, invalidate, negate, prove false, rebut, refute
Antonyms ascertain, bear out, confirm, evince, prove, show, substantiate, verify

disputation argumentation, controversy, debate, dispute, dissension, polemics

dispute *v.* 1. altercate, argue, brawl, clash, contend, debate, discuss, quarrel, row, spar, squabble, wrangle 2. challenge, contest, contradict, controvert, deny, doubt, impugn, question, rebut ~*n.* 3. altercation, argument, *bagarre*, brawl, conflict, disagreement, discord, disturbance, feud, friction, quarrel, shindig (*Inf.*), shindy (*Inf.*), strife, wrangle 4. argument, contention, controversy, debate, discussion, dissension

disqualification 1. disability, disablement, incapacitation, incapacity, unfitness 2. debarment, disenablement, disentitlement, elimination, exclusion, incompetence, ineligibility, rejection

disqualified debarred, eliminated, ineligible, knocked out, out of the running

disqualify 1. disable, incapacitate, invalidate, unfit (*Rare*) 2. ban, debar, declare ineligible, disentitle, preclude, prohibit, rule out

disquiet 1. *n.* alarm, angst, anxiety, concern, disquietude, distress, disturbance, fear, foreboding, fretfulness, nervousness, restlessness, trepidation, trouble, uneasiness, unrest, worry **2.** *v.* agitate, annoy, bother, concern, discompose, distress, disturb, fret, harass, hassle (*Inf.*), incommode, make uneasy, perturb, pester, plague, trouble, unsettle, upset, vex, worry

disquieting annoying, bothersome, disconcerting, distressing, disturbing, harrowing, irritating, perturbing, troubling, unnerving, unsettling, upsetting, vexing, worrying

disregard *v.* **1.** brush aside *or* away, discount, disobey, ignore, laugh off, leave out of account, make light of, neglect, overlook, pass over, pay no attention to, pay no heed to, take no notice of, turn a blind eye to **2.** brush off (*Sl.*), cold-shoulder, contemn, despise, disdain, disparage, slight, snub ~*n.* **3.** brushoff (*Sl.*), contempt, disdain, disrespect, heedlessness, ignoring, inattention, indifference, neglect, negligence, oversight, slight, the cold shoulder
Antonyms *v.* attend, heed, listen to, mind, note, pay attention to, regard, respect, take into consideration, take notice of

disrepair 1. collapse, decay, deterioration, dilapidation, ruination **2. in disrepair** broken, bust (*Inf.*), decayed, decrepit, kaput (*Inf.*), not functioning, on the blink (*Sl.*), out of commission, out of order, worn-out

disreputable 1. base, contemptible, derogatory, discreditable, disgraceful, dishonourable, disorderly, ignominious, infamous, louche, low, mean, notorious, opprobrious, scandalous, shady (*Inf.*), shameful, shocking, unprincipled, vicious, vile **2.** bedraggled, dilapidated, dingy, dishevelled, down at heel, scruffy, seedy, shabby, threadbare, worn
Antonyms decent, reputable, respectable, respected, upright, worthy

disrepute discredit, disesteem, disfavour, disgrace, dishonour, ignominy, ill favour, ill repute, infamy, obloquy, shame, unpopularity

disrespect contempt, discourtesy, dishonour, disregard, impertinence, impoliteness, impudence, incivility, insolence, irreverence, lack of respect, lese-majesty, rudeness, unmannerliness
Antonyms esteem, regard, respect

disrespectful bad-mannered, cheeky, contemptuous, discourteous, ill-bred, impertinent, impolite, impudent, insolent, insulting, irreverent, misbehaved, rude, uncivil

disrupt 1. agitate, confuse, disorder, disorganize, disturb, spoil, throw into disorder,

upset **2.** break up *or* into, interfere with, interrupt, intrude, obstruct, unsettle, upset

disruption confusion, disarray, disorder, disorderliness, disturbance, interference, interruption, stoppage

disruptive confusing, disorderly, distracting, disturbing, obstreperous, troublemaking, troublesome, unruly, unsettling, upsetting
Antonyms biddable, cooperative, docile, obedient, well-behaved

dissatisfaction annoyance, chagrin, disappointment, discomfort, discontent, dislike, dismay, displeasure, distress, exasperation, frustration, irritation, regret, resentment, unhappiness

dissatisfied disappointed, discontented, disgruntled, displeased, fed up, frustrated, not satisfied, unfulfilled, ungratified, unhappy, unsatisfied
Antonyms content, contented, pleased, satisfied

dissect 1. anatomize, cut up *or* apart, dismember, lay open **2.** analyse, break down, explore, inspect, investigate, research, scrutinize, study

dissection 1. anatomization, anatomy, autopsy, dismemberment, necropsy, postmortem (examination) **2.** analysis, breakdown, examination, inspection, investigation, research, scrutiny

disseminate broadcast, circulate, diffuse, disperse, dissipate, distribute, proclaim, promulgate, propagate, publicize, publish, scatter, sow, spread

dissemination broadcasting, circulation, diffusion, distribution, promulgation, propagation, publication, publishing, spread

dissension conflict, conflict of opinion, contention, difference, disagreement, discord, discordance, dispute, dissent, friction, quarrel, row, strife, variance

dissent 1. *v.* decline, differ, disagree, object, protest, refuse, withhold assent *or* approval **2.** *n.* difference, disagreement, discord, dissension, dissidence, nonconformity, objection, opposition, refusal, resistance
Antonyms *v.* agree, assent, concur ~*n.* accord, agreement, assent, concurrence, consensus

dissenter disputant, dissident, nonconformist, objector, protestant

dissentient *adj.* conflicting, differing, disagreeing, dissenting, dissident, opposing, protesting

dissertation critique, discourse, disquisition, essay, exposition, thesis, treatise

disservice bad turn, disfavour, harm, ill turn, injury, injustice, unkindness, wrong
Antonyms courtesy, good turn, indulgence,

kindness, obligement (*Scot. or archaic*), ser~
vice
dissident 1. *adj.* differing, disagreeing, dis~
cordant, dissentient, dissenting, heterodox,
nonconformist, schismatic **2.** *n.* agitator,
dissenter, protestor, rebel, recusant
dissimilar different, disparate, divergent,
diverse, heterogeneous, manifold, mis~
matched, not alike, not capable of compari~
son, not similar, unlike, unrelated, various
Antonyms alike, comparable, congruous,
corresponding, in agreement, much the same,
resembling, uniform
dissimilarity difference, discrepancy, dis~
parity, dissimilitude, distinction, diver~
gence, heterogeneity, incomparability,
nonuniformity, unlikeness, unrelatedness
dissipate 1. burn up, consume, deplete, ex~
pend, fritter away, indulge oneself, lavish,
misspend, run through, spend, squander,
waste **2.** disappear, dispel, disperse, dis~
solve, drive away, evaporate, scatter, vanish
dissipated 1. abandoned, debauched, dis~
solute, intemperate, profligate, rakish, self-
indulgent **2.** consumed, destroyed, exhaust~
ed, scattered, squandered, wasted
dissipation 1. abandonment, debauchery,
dissoluteness, drunkenness, excess, ex~
travagance, indulgence, intemperance, lav~
ishness, prodigality, profligacy, squander~
ing, wantonness, waste **2.** amusement,
distraction, diversion, entertainment,
gratification **3.** disappearance, disintegra~
tion, dispersion, dissemination, dissolution,
scattering, vanishing
dissociate 1. break off, disband, disrupt,
part company, quit **2.** detach, disconnect,
distance, divorce, isolate, segregate, sepa~
rate, set apart
dissolute abandoned, corrupt, debauched,
degenerate, depraved, dissipated, immoral,
lax, lewd, libertine, licentious, loose,
profligate, rakish, unrestrained, vicious,
wanton, wild
Antonyms chaste, clean-living, good, moral,
squeaky-clean, upright, virtuous
dissolution 1. breaking up, disintegration,
division, divorce, parting, resolution, sepa~
ration **2.** death, decay, decomposition, de~
mise, destruction, dispersal, extinction,
overthrow, ruin **3.** adjournment, conclu~
sion, disbandment, discontinuation, dismis~
sal, end, ending, finish, suspension, termi~
nation **4.** corruption, debauchery, dissipa~
tion, intemperance, wantonness **5.** disap~
pearance, evaporation, liquefaction, melt~
ing, solution
Antonyms (*sense 1*) alliance, amalgamation,
coalition, combination, unification, union
dissolve 1. deliquesce, flux, fuse, liquefy,
melt, soften, thaw **2.** crumble, decompose,

diffuse, disappear, disintegrate, disperse,
dissipate, dwindle, evanesce, evaporate,
fade, melt away, perish, vanish, waste away
3. axe (*Inf.*), break up, destroy, discontinue,
dismiss, end, overthrow, ruin, suspend, ter~
minate, wind up **4.** break into *or* up, col~
lapse, disorganize, disunite, divorce, loose,
resolve into, separate, sever
dissuade advise against, deter, discourage,
disincline, divert, expostulate, persuade not
to, put off, remonstrate, talk out of, urge
not to, warn
Antonyms bring round (*Inf.*), coax, con~
vince, persuade, sway, talk into
distance *n.* **1.** absence, extent, gap, inter~
val, lapse, length, range, reach, remoteness,
remove, separation, space, span, stretch,
width **2.** aloofness, coldness, coolness, fri~
gidity, reserve, restraint, stiffness **3. go
the distance** bring to an end, complete,
finish, see through, stay the course **4. keep
one's distance** avoid, be aloof (indifferent,
reserved), keep (someone) at arm's length,
shun **5. in the distance** afar, far away, far
off, on the horizon, yonder ~*v.* **6.** dissociate
oneself, put in proportion, separate oneself
7. leave behind, outdistance, outdo, outrun,
outstrip, pass
distant 1. abroad, afar, far, faraway, far-
flung, far-off, outlying, out-of-the-way, re~
mote, removed **2.** apart, disparate, dis~
persed, distinct, scattered, separate **3.** aloof,
ceremonious, cold, cool, formal, haughty,
reserved, restrained, reticent, standoffish,
stiff, unapproachable, unfriendly, with~
drawn **4.** faint, indirect, indistinct, obscure,
slight, uncertain
Antonyms (*senses 1 & 2*) adjacent, adjoining,
at hand, close, handy, imminent, near, near~
by, neighbouring, nigh, proximate, within
sniffing distance (*Inf.*), (*sense 3*) close, friendly,
intimate, warm
distaste abhorrence, antipathy, aversion,
detestation, disfavour, disgust, disinclina~
tion, dislike, displeasure, disrelish, dissat~
isfaction, horror, loathing, odium, repug~
nance, revulsion
distasteful abhorrent, disagreeable, dis~
pleasing, loathsome, nauseous, objection~
able, obnoxious, obscene, offensive, repug~
nant, repulsive, undesirable, uninviting,
unpalatable, unpleasant, unsavoury
Antonyms agreeable, charming, enjoyable,
pleasing, pleasurable
distend balloon, bloat, bulge, dilate, enlarge,
expand, increase, inflate, puff, stretch,
swell, widen
distended bloated, dilated, enlarged, ex~
panded, inflated, puffy, stretched, swollen,
tumescent
distil condense, draw out, evaporate, ex~

press, extract, press out, purify, rectify, refine, sublimate, vaporize

distillation elixir, essence, extract, quin~ tessence, spirit

distinct 1. apparent, blatant, clear, clear-cut, decided, definite, evident, lucid, mani~ fest, marked, noticeable, obvious, palpable, patent, plain, recognizable, sharp, unam~ biguous, unmistakable, well-defined 2. de~ tached, different, discrete, dissimilar, indi~ vidual, separate, unconnected
Antonyms common, connected, fuzzy, iden~ tical, indefinite, indistinct, obscure, similar, unclear, vague

distinction 1. differentiation, discernment, discrimination, penetration, perception, separation 2. contrast, difference, differen~ tial, division, separation 3. characteristic, distinctiveness, feature, individuality, mark, particularity, peculiarity, quality 4. account, celebrity, consequence, credit, eminence, excellence, fame, greatness, hon~ our, importance, merit, name, note, promi~ nence, quality, rank, renown, reputation, repute, superiority, worth

distinctive characteristic, different, distin~ guishing, extraordinary, idiosyncratic, in~ dividual, original, peculiar, singular, spe~ cial, typical, uncommon, unique
Antonyms common, ordinary, run-of-the-mill, typical

distinctly clearly, decidedly, definitely, evi~ dently, manifestly, markedly, noticeably, obviously, palpably, patently, plainly, pre~ cisely, sharply

distinctness 1. clarity, lucidity, obvious~ ness, plainness, sharpness, vividness 2. de~ tachment, difference, discreteness, dispar~ ateness, dissimilarity, dissociation, distinc~ tiveness, individuality, separation

distinguish 1. ascertain, decide, determine, differentiate, discriminate, judge, tell apart, tell between, tell the difference 2. catego~ rize, characterize, classify, individualize, make distinctive, mark, separate, set apart, single out 3. discern, know, make out, per~ ceive, pick out, recognize, see, tell 4. cel~ ebrate, dignify, honour, immortalize, make famous, signalize

distinguishable clear, conspicuous, dis~ cernible, evident, manifest, noticeable, ob~ vious, perceptible, plain, recognizable, well-marked

distinguished 1. acclaimed, celebrated, conspicuous, eminent, famed, famous, illus~ trious, notable, noted, renowned, well-known 2. conspicuous, extraordinary, marked, outstanding, signal, striking
Antonyms common, inelegant, inferior, un~ distinguished, unknown

distinguishing characteristic, different, differentiating, distinctive, individualistic, marked, peculiar, typical

distort 1. bend, buckle, contort, deform, disfigure, misshape, twist, warp, wrench, wrest 2. bias, colour, falsify, garble, mis~ represent, pervert, slant, twist

distortion 1. bend, buckle, contortion, crookedness, deformity, malformation, twist, twistedness, warp 2. bias, colouring, falsification, misrepresentation, perversion, slant

distract 1. divert, draw away, sidetrack, turn aside 2. amuse, beguile, engross, en~ tertain, occupy 3. agitate, bewilder, con~ found, confuse, derange, discompose, dis~ concert, disturb, harass, madden, perplex, puzzle, torment, trouble

distracted 1. agitated, at sea, bemused, be~ wildered, confounded, confused, flustered, harassed, in a flap (*Inf.*), perplexed, puzzled, troubled 2. crazy, deranged, desperate, dis~ traught, frantic, frenzied, grief-stricken, in~ sane, mad, overwrought, raving, wild

distracting bewildering, bothering, confus~ ing, disconcerting, dismaying, disturbing, off-putting (*Brit. inf.*), perturbing

distraction 1. abstraction, agitation, be~ wilderment, commotion, confusion, discord, disorder, disturbance 2. amusement, be~ guilement, diversion, divertissement, enter~ tainment, pastime, recreation 3. disturb~ ance, diversion, interference, interruption 4. aberration, alienation, delirium, de~ rangement, desperation, frenzy, hallucina~ tion, incoherence, insanity, mania

distraught agitated, anxious, beside one~ self, crazed, desperate, distracted, dis~ tressed, frantic, hysterical, mad, out of one's mind, overwrought, raving, wild, worked-up, wrought-up

distress *n.* 1. affliction, agony, anguish, anxiety, desolation, discomfort, grief, heartache, misery, pain, sadness, sorrow, suffering, torment, torture, woe, worry, wretchedness 2. adversity, calamity, desti~ tution, difficulties, hardship, indigence, misfortune, need, poverty, privation, straits, trial, trouble ~*v.* 3. afflict, agonize, bother, disturb, grieve, harass, harrow, pain, per~ plex, sadden, torment, trouble, upset, wor~ ry, wound

distressed 1. afflicted, agitated, anxious, distracted, distraught, saddened, tormented, troubled, upset, worried, wretched 2. desti~ tute, indigent, needy, poor, poverty-stricken, straitened

distressing affecting, afflicting, distressful, disturbing, grievous, harrowing, heart-breaking, hurtful, lamentable, nerve-racking, painful, sad, upsetting, worrying

distribute 1. administer, allocate, allot, ap~ portion, assign, deal, dispense, dispose, di~ vide, dole out, give, measure out, mete, share **2.** circulate, convey, deliver, hand out, pass round **3.** diffuse, disperse, dis~ seminate, scatter, spread, strew **4.** arrange, assort, categorize, class, classify, file, group

distribution 1. allocation, allotment, ap~ portionment, dispensation, division, dole, partition, sharing **2.** circulation, diffusion, dispersal, dispersion, dissemination, propa~ gation, scattering, spreading **3.** arrange~ ment, assortment, classification, disposition, grouping, location, organization, placement **4.** *Commerce* dealing, delivery, handling, mailing, marketing, trading, transport, transportation

district area, community, locale, locality, neighbourhood, parish, quarter, region, sector, vicinity, ward

distrust 1. *v.* be sceptical of, be suspicious of, be wary of, disbelieve, discredit, doubt, misbelieve, mistrust, question, smell a rat (*Inf.*), suspect, wonder about **2.** *n.* disbelief, doubt, dubiety, lack of faith, misgiving, mistrust, qualm, question, scepticism, sus~ picion, wariness
Antonyms *v.* believe, depend, have confidence, have faith, trust ~*n.* confidence, faith, reliance, trust

disturb 1. bother, butt in on, disrupt, inter~ fere with, interrupt, intrude on, pester, rouse, startle **2.** confuse, derange, disar~ range, disorder, disorganize, muddle, un~ settle **3.** agitate, alarm, annoy, confound, discompose, distract, distress, excite, fluster, harass, hassle (*Inf.*), perturb, ruffle, shake, trouble, unnerve, unsettle, upset, worry
Antonyms calm, compose, lull, pacify, quiet, quieten, reassure, relax, relieve, settle, soothe

disturbance 1. agitation, annoyance, both~ er, confusion, derangement, disorder, dis~ traction, hindrance, interruption, intrusion, molestation, perturbation, upset **2.** bother (*Inf.*), brawl, commotion, disorder, fracas, fray, hubbub, riot, ruckus (*Inf.*), ruction (*Inf.*), shindig (*Inf.*), shindy (*Inf.*), tumult, turmoil, upheaval, uproar

disturbed 1. *Psychiatry* disordered, malad~ justed, neurotic, troubled, unbalanced, upset **2.** agitated, anxious, apprehensive, bothered, concerned, disquieted, nervous, troubled, uneasy, upset, worried
Antonyms balanced, calm, collected, self-possessed, unfazed (*Inf.*), untroubled

disturbing agitating, alarming, disconcert~ ing, discouraging, dismaying, disquieting, distressing, frightening, harrowing, per~ turbing, startling, threatening, troubling, unsettling, upsetting, worrying

disuse abandonment, decay, desuetude, dis~ continuance, idleness, neglect, non-employment, nonuse
Antonyms application, employment, prac~ tice, service, usage, use

ditch *n.* **1.** channel, drain, dyke, furrow, gully, moat, trench, watercourse ~*v.* **2.** dig, drain, excavate, gouge, trench **3.** *Sl.* aban~ don, axe (*Inf.*), bin (*Inf.*), chuck (*Inf.*), dis~ card, dispose of, drop, dump (*Inf.*), get rid of, jettison, junk (*Inf.*), scrap, throw out *or* overboard

dither 1. *v.* faff about (*Brit. inf.*), falter, ha~ ver, hesitate, oscillate, shillyshally (*Inf.*), swither (*Scot.*), teeter, vacillate, waver **2.** *n.* bother, flap (*Inf.*), fluster, flutter, pother, stew (*Inf.*), tiz-woz (*Inf.*), tizzy (*Inf.*), twitter (*Inf.*)
Antonyms *v.* come to a conclusion, conclude, decide, make a decision, make up one's mind, reach *or* come to a decision, resolve, settle

dive *v.* **1.** descend, dip, disappear, drop, duck, fall, go underwater, jump, leap, nose-dive, pitch, plummet, plunge, sub~ merge, swoop ~*n.* **2.** dash, header (*Inf.*), jump, leap, lunge, nose dive, plunge, spring **3.** *Sl.* honky-tonk (*U.S. sl.*), joint (*Sl.*), sleazy bar

diverge 1. bifurcate, branch, divaricate, di~ vide, fork, part, radiate, separate, split, spread **2.** be at odds, be at variance, conflict, differ, disagree, dissent **3.** depart, deviate, digress, meander, stray, turn aside, wander

divergence branching out, deflection, de~ parture, deviation, difference, digression, disparity, divagation, ramification, separa~ tion, varying

divergent conflicting, deviating, different, differing, disagreeing, dissimilar, diverging, diverse, separate, variant

divers different, manifold, many, multifari~ ous, numerous, several, some, sundry, var~ ied, various

diverse 1. assorted, diversified, manifold, miscellaneous, of every description, several, sundry, varied, various **2.** different, differ~ ing, discrete, disparate, dissimilar, distinct, divergent, separate, unlike, varying

diversify alter, assort, branch out, change, expand, mix, modify, spread out, transform, variegate, vary

diversion 1. alteration, change, deflection, departure, detour, deviation, digression, variation **2.** amusement, beguilement, de~ light, distraction, divertissement, enjoy~ ment, entertainment, game, gratification, jollies (*Sl.*), pastime, play, pleasure, recrea~ tion, relaxation, sport

diversity assortment, difference, dissimi~

larity, distinctiveness, divergence, diverse~
ness, diversification, heterogeneity, medley,
multiplicity, range, unlikeness, variance,
variegation, variety

divert 1. avert, deflect, redirect, switch,
turn aside **2.** amuse, beguile, delight, en~
tertain, gratify, recreate, regale **3.** detract,
distract, draw or lead away from, lead
astray, sidetrack

diverting amusing, beguiling, enjoyable,
entertaining, fun, humorous, pleasant

divest 1. denude, disrobe, doff, remove,
strip, take off, unclothe, undress **2.** deprive,
despoil, dispossess, strip

divide 1. bisect, cleave, cut (up), detach,
disconnect, part, partition, segregate, sepa~
rate, sever, shear, split, subdivide, sunder
2. allocate, allot, apportion, deal out, dis~
pense, distribute, divvy (up) (Inf.), dole out,
measure out, portion, share **3.** alienate,
break up, cause to disagree, come between,
disunite, estrange, set or pit against one
another, set at variance or odds, sow dis~
sension, split **4.** arrange, categorize, classi~
fy, grade, group, put in order, separate, sort
Antonyms (sense 1) combine, come together,
connect, join, knit, marry, splice, unite

dividend bonus, cut (Inf.), divvy (Inf.), ex~
tra, gain, plus, portion, share, surplus

divine adj. **1.** angelic, celestial, godlike,
heavenly, holy, spiritual, superhuman,
supernatural **2.** consecrated, holy, religious,
sacred, sanctified, spiritual **3.** beatific,
blissful, exalted, mystical, rapturous, su~
preme, transcendent, transcendental, trans~
mundane **4.** Inf. beautiful, excellent, glori~
ous, marvellous, perfect, splendid, superla~
tive, wonderful ~n. **5.** churchman, clergy~
man, cleric, ecclesiastic, minister, pastor,
priest, reverend ~v. **6.** apprehend, conjec~
ture, deduce, discern, foretell, guess, infer,
intuit, perceive, prognosticate, suppose,
surmise, suspect, understand **7.** Of water or
minerals dowse

diviner 1. astrologer, augur, oracle, prophet,
seer, sibyl, soothsayer **2.** Of water or min~
erals dowser

divinity 1. deity, divine nature, godhead,
godhood, godliness, holiness, sanctity **2.**
daemon, deity, genius, god, goddess, guard~
ian spirit, spirit **3.** religion, religious stud~
ies, theology

divisible dividable, fractional, separable,
splittable

division 1. bisection, cutting up, detaching,
dividing, partition, separation, splitting up
2. allotment, apportionment, distribution,
sharing **3.** border, boundary, demarcation,
divide, divider, dividing line, partition **4.**
branch, category, class, compartment, de~
partment, group, head, part, portion, sec~

tion, sector, segment **5.** breach, difference
of opinion, disagreement, discord, disunion,
estrangement, feud, rupture, split, variance
Antonyms (sense 5) accord, agreement, con~
cord, harmony, peace, union, unity

divisive alienating, damaging, detrimental,
discordant, disruptive, estranging, inhar~
monious, pernicious, troublesome, unset~
tling

divorce 1. n. annulment, breach, break, de~
cree nisi, dissolution, disunion, rupture,
separation, severance, split-up **2.** v. annul,
disconnect, dissociate, dissolve (marriage),
disunite, divide, part, separate, sever, split
up, sunder

divulge betray, blow wide open (Sl.), com~
municate, confess, declare, disclose, exhibit,
expose, impart, leak, let slip, make known,
proclaim, promulgate, publish, reveal, spill
(Inf.), spill one's guts about (Sl.), tell, un~
cover
Antonyms conceal, hide, keep secret

dizzy 1. faint, giddy, light-headed, off bal~
ance, reeling, shaky, staggering, swimming,
vertiginous, weak at the knees, wobbly,
woozy (Inf.) **2.** at sea, befuddled, bemused,
bewildered, confused, dazed, dazzled, mud~
dled **3.** lofty, steep, vertiginous **4.** Inf. ca~
pricious, fickle, flighty, foolish, frivolous,
giddy, light-headed, scatterbrained, silly

do v. **1.** accomplish, achieve, act, carry out,
complete, conclude, discharge, end, execute,
perform, produce, transact, undertake, work
2. answer, be adequate, be enough, be of
use, be sufficient, pass muster, satisfy,
serve, suffice, suit **3.** arrange, be respon~
sible for, fix, get ready, look after, make,
make ready, organize, prepare, see to, take
on **4.** decipher, decode, figure out, puzzle
out, resolve, solve, work out **5.** adapt, ren~
der, translate, transpose **6.** bear oneself,
behave, carry oneself, comport oneself,
conduct oneself **7.** fare, get along, get on,
make out, manage, proceed **8.** bring about,
cause, create, effect, produce **9.** Of a play,
etc. act, give, perform, present, produce, put
on **10.** Inf. cover, explore, journey through
or around, look at, stop in, tour, travel, vis~
it **11.** Inf. cheat, con (Inf.), cozen, deceive,
defraud, diddle (Inf.), dupe, fleece, hoax,
skin (Sl.), stiff (Sl.), swindle, take (someone)
for a ride (Inf.), trick ~n. **12.** Inf. affair,
event, function, gathering, occasion, party
13. do's and don'ts Inf. code, customs,
etiquette, instructions, regulations, rules,
standards

do away with 1. blow away (Sl., chiefly
U.S.), bump off (Sl.), destroy, do in (Sl.), ex~
terminate, kill, liquidate, murder, slay, take
out (Sl.) **2.** abolish, axe (Inf.), chuck (Inf.),

discard, discontinue, eliminate, get rid of, junk (*Inf.*), put an end to, remove

docile amenable, biddable, compliant, duc~ tile, manageable, obedient, pliant, submis~ sive, teachable (*Rare*), tractable
Antonyms difficult, intractable, obstreper~ ous, troublesome, trying, uncooperative, un~ manageable

docility amenability, biddableness, compli~ ance, ductility, manageability, meekness, obedience, pliancy, submissiveness, trac~ tability

dock¹ *n.* **1.** harbour, pier, quay, waterfront, wharf ~*v.* **2.** anchor, berth, drop anchor, land, moor, put in, tie up **3.** *Of spacecraft* couple, hook up, join, link up, rendezvous, unite

dock² **1.** clip, crop, curtail, cut off, cut short, diminish, lessen, shorten **2.** decrease, de~ duct, diminish, lessen, reduce, subtract, withhold
Antonyms (*sense 2*) augment, boost, in~ crease, raise

docket **1.** *n.* bill, certificate, chit, chitty, counterfoil, label, receipt, tab, tag, tally, ticket **2.** *v.* catalogue, file, index, label, mark, register, tab, tag, ticket

doctor *n.* **1.** general practitioner, G.P., medic (*Inf.*), medical practitioner, physician ~*v.* **2.** apply medication to, give medical treatment to, treat **3.** botch, cobble, do up (*Inf.*), fix, mend, patch up, repair **4.** alter, change, disguise, falsify, fudge, misrepre~ sent, pervert, tamper with **5.** add to, adul~ terate, cut, dilute, mix with, spike, water down

doctrinaire *adj.* **1.** biased, dogmatic, fa~ natical, inflexible, insistent, opinionated, rigid **2.** hypothetical, ideological, impracti~ cal, speculative, theoretical, unpragmatic, unrealistic

doctrine article, article of faith, belief, can~ on, concept, conviction, creed, dogma, opinion, precept, principle, teaching, tenet

document **1.** *n.* certificate, instrument, le~ gal form, paper, record, report **2.** *v.* authenticate, back up, certify, cite, cor~ roborate, detail, give weight to, instance, particularize, substantiate, support, vali~ date, verify

doddering aged, decrepit, doddery, falter~ ing, feeble, floundering, infirm, senile, shaky, shambling, tottery, trembly, un~ steady, weak

doddle cakewalk (*Inf.*), child's play (*Inf.*), cinch (*Sl.*), easy-peasy (*Sl.*), no sweat (*Sl.*), picnic (*Inf.*), piece of cake (*Inf.*), pushover (*Sl.*)

dodge *v.* **1.** body-swerve (*Scot.*), dart, duck, shift, sidestep, swerve, turn aside **2.** avoid,

body-swerve (*Scot.*), deceive, elude, equivo~ cate, evade, fend off, flannel (*Brit. inf.*), fudge, get out of, hedge, parry, shirk, shuffle, trick ~*n.* **3.** contrivance, device, feint, flannel (*Brit. inf.*), machination, ploy, ruse, scheme, stratagem, subterfuge, trick, wheeze (*Brit. sl.*), wile

dodger evader, shifty so-and-so, shirker, slacker, slippery one, slyboots, trickster

doer achiever, active person, activist, bus~ tler, dynamo, go-getter (*Inf.*), live wire (*Sl.*), organizer, powerhouse (*Sl.*), wheeler-dealer (*Inf.*)

doff **1.** *Of a hat* lift, raise, remove, take off, tip, touch **2.** *Of clothing* cast off, discard, remove, shed, slip off, slip out of, take off, throw off, undress

dog *n.* **1.** bitch, canine, cur, hound, man's best friend, mongrel, mutt (*Sl.*), pooch (*Sl.*), pup, puppy, tyke **2.** *Inf.* beast, blackguard, cur, heel (*Sl.*), knave (*Archaic*), scoundrel, villain **3. dog-eat-dog** cutthroat, ferocious, fierce, ruthless, vicious, with no holds barred **4. go to the dogs** *Inf.* degenerate, deteriorate, go down the drain, go to pot, go to ruin ~*v.* **5.** haunt, hound, plague, pur~ sue, shadow, tail (*Inf.*), track, trail, trouble

dogged determined, firm, immovable, inde~ fatigable, obstinate, persevering, persistent, pertinacious, resolute, single-minded, staunch, steadfast, steady, stiff-necked, stubborn, tenacious, unflagging, unshak~ able, unyielding
Antonyms doubtful, half-hearted, hesitant, irresolute, undetermined, unsteady

doggedness bulldog tenacity, determina~ tion, endurance, obstinacy, perseverance, persistence, pertinacity, relentlessness, resolution, single-mindedness, steadfastness, steadiness, stubbornness, tenaciousness, te~ nacity

dogma article, article of faith, belief, credo, creed, doctrine, opinion, precept, principle, teachings, tenet

dogmatic **1.** arbitrary, arrogant, assertive, categorical, dictatorial, doctrinaire, down~ right, emphatic, imperious, magisterial, ob~ durate, opinionated, overbearing, peremp~ tory **2.** authoritative, canonical, categorical, doctrinal, ex cathedra, oracular, positive

dogmatism arbitrariness, arrogance, dic~ tatorialness, imperiousness, opinionated~ ness, peremptoriness, positiveness, pre~ sumption

dogsbody drudge, general factotum, maid *or* man of all work, menial, skivvy (*Chiefly Brit.*), slave

do in **1.** blow away (*Sl., chiefly U.S.*), butch~ er, dispatch, eliminate (*Sl.*), execute, kill, liquidate, murder, slaughter, slay, take out

(*Sl.*) **2.** exhaust, fag (*Inf.*), fatigue, knacker (*Sl.*), shatter (*Inf.*), tire, wear out, weary

doing achievement, act, action, carrying out *or* through, deed, execution, exploit, handi~ work, implementation, performance

doings actions, affairs, concerns, dealings, deeds, events, exploits, goings-on (*Inf.*), handiwork, happenings, proceedings, trans~ actions

doldrums apathy, blues, boredom, depres~ sion, dullness, dumps (*Inf.*), ennui, gloom, inertia, lassitude, listlessness, malaise, stagnation, tedium, the hump (*Brit. inf.*), torpor

dole *n.* **1.** allowance, alms, benefit, donation, gift, grant, gratuity, modicum, parcel, pit~ tance, portion, quota, share **2.** allocation, allotment, apportionment, dispensation, distribution, division ~*v.* **3.** *Usually with* **out** administer, allocate, allot, apportion, assign, deal, dispense, distribute, divide, give, hand out, mete, share

doll up deck out, dress up (like a dog's din~ ner), get ready, gussy up (*Sl.*), preen, primp, prink, tart up (*Sl.*), titivate, trick out

dolt ass, berk (*Brit. sl.*), blockhead, booby, charlie (*Brit. inf.*), chump (*Inf.*), clot (*Brit. inf.*), coot, dimwit (*Inf.*), dipstick (*Brit. sl.*), dope (*Inf.*), dork (*Sl.*), dullard, dunce, dweeb (*U.S. sl.*), fool, fuckwit (*Taboo sl.*), geek (*Sl.*), gonzo (*Sl.*), idiot, ignoramus, jerk (*Sl., chiefly U.S. & Canad.*), lamebrain (*Inf.*), nerd *or* nurd (*Sl.*), nitwit (*Inf.*), numskull *or* numbskull, oaf, plank (*Brit. sl.*), plonker (*Sl.*), prat (*Sl.*), prick (*Derogatory sl.*), schmuck (*U.S. sl.*), simpleton, thickhead, twit (*Inf., chiefly Brit.*), wally (*Sl.*)

domestic *adj.* **1.** domiciliary, family, home, household, private **2.** domesticated, home- loving, homely, housewifely, stay-at-home **3.** domesticated, house, house-trained, pet, tame, trained **4.** indigenous, internal, na~ tive, not foreign ~*n.* **5.** char (*Inf.*), char~ woman, daily, daily help, help, maid, serv~ ant, woman (*Inf.*)

domesticate 1. break, gentle, house-train, tame, train **2.** acclimatize, accustom, famil~ iarize, habituate, naturalize

domesticated 1. *Of plants or animals* broken (in), naturalized, tame, tamed **2.** *Of people* domestic, home-loving, homely, house-trained (*Jocular*), housewifely
Antonyms feral, ferocious, savage, unbro~ ken, undomesticated, untamed, wild

dominant 1. ascendant, assertive, authori~ tative, commanding, controlling, governing, leading, presiding, ruling, superior, su~ preme **2.** chief, influential, main, outstand~ ing, paramount, predominant, pre-eminent, prevailing, prevalent, primary, principal, prominent

Antonyms ancillary, auxiliary, inferior, junior, lesser, lower, minor, secondary, sub~ servient, subsidiary

dominate 1. control, direct, domineer, govern, have the upper hand over, have the whip hand over, keep under one's thumb, lead, lead by the nose (*Inf.*), master, mo~ nopolize, overbear, rule, tyrannize **2.** be~ stride, loom over, overlook, stand head and shoulders above, stand over, survey, tower above **3.** detract from, eclipse, outshine, overrule, overshadow, predominate, prevail over

domination 1. ascendancy, authority, command, control, influence, mastery, power, rule, superiority, supremacy, sway **2.** despotism, dictatorship, oppression, re~ pression, subjection, subordination, sup~ pression, tyranny

domineer bluster, boss around *or* about (*Inf.*), browbeat, bully, hector, intimidate, lord (it) over, menace, overbear, ride roughshod over, swagger, threaten, tyran~ nize

domineering arrogant, authoritarian, autocratic, bossy (*Inf.*), coercive, despotic, dictatorial, high-handed, imperious, iron- handed, magisterial, masterful, oppressive, overbearing, tyrannical
Antonyms meek, obsequious, servile, shy, submissive, subservient

dominion 1. ascendancy, authority, com~ mand, control, domination, government, ju~ risdiction, mastery, power, rule, sovereign~ ty, supremacy, sway **2.** country, domain, empire, kingdom, patch, province, realm, region, territory, turf (*U.S. sl.*)

don clothe oneself in, dress in, get into, pull on, put on, slip on *or* into

donate bequeath, bestow, chip in (*Inf.*), contribute, gift, give, hand out, make a gift of, present, subscribe

donation alms, benefaction, boon, contri~ bution, gift, grant, gratuity, hand-out, lar~ gess *or* largesse, offering, present, stipend, subscription

done *adj.* **1.** accomplished, completed, con~ cluded, consummated, ended, executed, finished, over, perfected, realized, terminat~ ed, through **2.** cooked, cooked enough, cooked sufficiently, cooked to a turn, ready **3.** depleted, exhausted, finished, spent, used up **4.** acceptable, conventional, *de rigueur*, proper **5.** *Inf.* cheated, conned (*Inf.*), duped, taken for a ride (*Inf.*), tricked ~*interj.* **6.** agreed, it's a bargain, O.K. *or* okay (*Inf.*), settled, you're on (*Inf.*) **7. done for** *Inf.* beaten, broken, dashed, defeated, destroyed, doomed, finished, foiled, lost, ruined, un~ done, wrecked **8. done in** *or* **up** *Inf.* all in (*Sl.*), bushed (*Inf.*), clapped out (*Aust. &*

N.Z. inf.), dead (*Inf.*), dead beat (*Inf.*), dog~ tired (*Inf.*), exhausted, fagged out (*Inf.*), knackered (*Sl.*), on one's last legs, ready to drop, tired out, worn out, worn to a frazzle (*Inf.*), zonked (*Sl.*) **9. have done with** be through with, desist, end relations with, finish with, give up, throw over, wash one's hands of

donnish bookish, erudite, formalistic, pedagogic, pedantic, precise, scholarly, scholastic

donor almsgiver, benefactor, contributor, donator, giver, grantor (*Law*), philanthro~ pist
Antonyms assignee, beneficiary, inheritor, legatee, payee, receiver, recipient

doom *n.* **1.** catastrophe, death, destiny, de~ struction, downfall, fate, fortune, lot, por~ tion, ruin **2.** condemnation, decision, de~ cree, judgment, sentence, verdict **3.** Arma~ geddon, Doomsday, end of the world, Judg~ ment Day, the Last Day, the Last Judgment, the last trump ~*v.* **4.** condemn, consign, damn, decree, destine, foreordain, judge, predestine, preordain, sentence, threaten

doomed bedevilled, bewitched, condemned, cursed, fated, hopeless, ill-fated, ill-omened, luckless, star-crossed

door **1.** doorway, egress, entrance, entry, exit, ingress, opening **2. lay at the door of** blame, censure, charge, hold responsible, impute to **3. out of doors** alfresco, in the air, out, outdoors, outside **4. show some~ one the door** ask to leave, boot out (*Inf.*), bounce (*Sl.*), eject, oust, show out

do out of balk, bilk, cheat, con (*Inf.*), co~ zen, deprive, diddle (*Inf.*), swindle, trick

dope *n.* **1.** drugs, narcotic, opiate **2.** berk (*Brit. sl.*), blockhead, charlie (*Brit. inf.*), coot, dickhead (*Sl.*), dimwit (*Inf.*), dipstick (*Brit. sl.*), divvy (*Brit. sl.*), dolt, dork (*Sl.*), dunce, dweeb (*U.S. sl.*), fool, fuckwit (*Taboo sl.*), geek (*Sl.*), gonzo (*Sl.*), idiot, jerk (*Sl., chiefly U.S. & Canad.*), lamebrain (*Inf.*), nerd *or* nurd (*Sl.*), nitwit (*Inf.*), numskull *or* numbskull, oaf, pillock (*Brit. sl.*), plank (*Brit. sl.*), plonker (*Sl.*), prat (*Sl.*), prick (*Derogatory sl.*), schmuck (*U.S. sl.*), simple~ ton, twit (*Inf., chiefly Brit.*), wally (*Sl.*) **3.** details, facts, gen (*Brit. inf.*), info (*Inf.*), in~ formation, inside information, lowdown (*Inf.*), news, tip ~*v.* **4.** anaesthetize, doctor, drug, inject, knock out, narcotize, sedate, stupefy

dormant asleep, comatose, fallow, hiber~ nating, inactive, inert, inoperative, latent, quiescent, sleeping, sluggish, slumbering, suspended, torpid
Antonyms active, alert, aroused, awake, awakened, conscious, wakeful, wide-awake

doe dosage, draught, drench, measure, por~ tion, potion, prescription, quantity

dot *n.* **1.** atom, circle, dab, fleck, full stop, iota, jot, mark, mite, mote, point, speck, speckle, spot **2. on the dot** exactly, on time, precisely, promptly, punctually, to the minute ~*v.* **3.** dab, dabble, fleck, speckle, spot, sprinkle, stipple, stud

dotage **1.** decrepitude, feebleness, imbecil~ ity, old age, second childhood, senility, weakness **2.** doting, foolish fondness, infat~ uation

dote on *or* **upon** admire, adore, hold dear, idolize, lavish affection on, prize, treasure

doting adoring, devoted, fond, foolish, in~ dulgent, lovesick

double *adj.* **1.** binate (*Botany*), coupled, doubled, dual, duplicate, in pairs, paired, twice, twin, twofold **2.** deceitful, dishonest, false, hypocritical, insincere, Janus-faced, knavish (*Archaic*), perfidious, treacherous, two-faced, vacillating ~*v.* **3.** duplicate, en~ large, fold, grow, increase, magnify, multi~ ply, plait, repeat ~*n.* **4.** clone, copy, counterpart, dead ringer (*Sl.*), Doppelgäng~ er, duplicate, fellow, impersonator, look-alike, mate, replica, ringer (*Sl.*), spitting image (*Inf.*), twin **5. at** *or* **on the double** at full speed, briskly, immediately, in double-quick time, pdq (*Sl.*), posthaste, quickly, without delay

double-cross betray, cheat, cozen, defraud, hoodwink, mislead, swindle, trick, two-time (*Inf.*)

double-dealer betrayer, cheat, con man (*Inf.*), cozen, deceiver, dissembler, double-crosser (*Inf.*), fraud, hypocrite, rogue, swin~ dler, traitor, two-timer (*Inf.*)

double-dealing **1.** *n.* bad faith, betrayal, cheating, deceit, deception, dishonesty, du~ plicity, foul play, hypocrisy, mendacity, perfidy, treachery, trickery, two-timing (*Inf.*) **2.** *adj.* cheating, crooked (*Inf.*), de~ ceitful, dishonest, duplicitous, fraudulent, hypocritical, lying, perfidious, sneaky, swindling, treacherous, tricky, two-faced, two-timing (*Inf.*), underhanded, untrust~ worthy, wily

double entendre ambiguity, double meaning, innuendo, play on words, pun

doubt *v.* **1.** discredit, distrust, fear, lack confidence in, misgive, mistrust, query, question, suspect ~*n.* **2.** apprehension, dis~ quiet, distrust, fear, incredulity, lack of faith, misgiving, mistrust, qualm, scepti~ cism, suspicion ~*v.* **3.** be dubious, be un~ certain, demur, fluctuate, hesitate, scruple, vacillate, waver ~*n.* **4.** dubiety, hesitancy, hesitation, indecision, irresolution, lack of conviction, suspense, uncertainty, vacilla~ tion **5.** ambiguity, confusion, difficulty, di~

lemma, perplexity, problem, quandary **6. no doubt** admittedly, assuredly, certainly, doubtless, doubtlessly, probably, surely
Antonyms v. accept, believe, buy (*Sl.*), have faith in, swallow (*Inf.*), trust ~n. belief, certainty, confidence, conviction, trust

doubter agnostic, disbeliever, doubting Thomas, questioner, sceptic, unbeliever

doubtful 1. ambiguous, debatable, dodgy (*Brit., Aust., & N.Z. inf.*), dubious, equivocal, hazardous, iffy (*Inf.*), inconclusive, indefinite, indeterminate, obscure, precarious, problematic(al), questionable, unclear, unconfirmed, unsettled, vague **2.** distrustful, hesitating, in two minds (*Inf.*), irresolute, leery (*Sl.*), perplexed, sceptical, suspicious, tentative, uncertain, unconvinced, undecided, unresolved, unsettled, unsure, vacillating, wavering **3.** disreputable, dodgy (*Brit., Aust., & N.Z. inf.*), dubious, questionable, shady (*Inf.*), suspect, suspicious
Antonyms certain, decided, definite, indubitable, positive, resolute

doubtless 1. assuredly, certainly, clearly, indisputably, of course, precisely, surely, truly, undoubtedly, unquestionably, without doubt **2.** apparently, most likely, ostensibly, presumably, probably, seemingly, supposedly

dour 1. dismal, dreary, forbidding, gloomy, grim, morose, sour, sullen, unfriendly **2.** austere, hard, inflexible, obstinate, rigid, rigorous, severe, strict, uncompromising, unyielding
Antonyms carefree, cheerful, cheery, chirpy (*Inf.*), genial, good-humoured, happy, jovial, pleasant, sunny

dovetail v. **1.** fit, fit together, interlock, join, link, mortise, tenon, unite **2.** accord, agree, coincide, conform, correspond, harmonize, match, tally

dowdy dingy, drab, frowzy, frumpish, frumpy, ill-dressed, old-fashioned, scrubby (*Brit. inf.*), shabby, slovenly, tacky (*U.S. inf.*), unfashionable
Antonyms chic, dressy, fashionable, neat, smart, spruce, trim, well-dressed

dower 1. dowry, inheritance, legacy, portion, provision, share **2.** endowment, faculty, gift, talent

do without abstain from, dispense with, forgo, get along without, give up, kick (*Inf.*), manage without

down adj. **1.** blue, dejected, depressed, disheartened, dismal, downcast, low, miserable, sad, sick as a parrot (*Inf.*), unhappy ~v. **2.** bring down, fell, floor, knock down, overthrow, prostrate, subdue, tackle, throw, trip **3.** *Inf.* drain, drink (down), gulp, put away, swallow, toss off ~n. **4.** decline, descent, drop, dropping, fall, falling, reverse

5. have a down on *Inf.* be antagonistic or hostile to, be anti (*Inf.*), bear a grudge towards, be contra (*Inf.*), be prejudiced against, be set against, feel ill will towards, have it in for (*Sl.*) **6. down with** away with, get rid of, kick out (*Inf.*), oust, push out

down and out 1. adj. derelict, destitute, dirt-poor (*Inf.*), flat broke (*Inf.*), impoverished, penniless, ruined, short, without two pennies to rub together (*Inf.*) **2. down-and-out** n. bag lady (*Chiefly U.S.*), beggar, bum (*Inf.*), derelict, dosser (*Brit. sl.*), loser, outcast, pauper, tramp, vagabond, vagrant

downcast cheerless, crestfallen, daunted, dejected, depressed, despondent, disappointed, disconsolate, discouraged, disheartened, dismal, dismayed, dispirited, miserable, sad, sick as a parrot (*Inf.*), unhappy
Antonyms cheerful, cheery, chirpy (*Inf.*), contented, elated, genial, happy, joyful, lighthearted, optimistic

downfall 1. breakdown, collapse, comedown, comeuppance (*Sl.*), debacle, descent, destruction, disgrace, fall, overthrow, ruin, undoing **2.** cloudburst, deluge, downpour, rainstorm

downgrade 1. degrade, demote, humble, lower or reduce in rank, take down a peg (*Inf.*) **2.** decry, denigrate, detract from, disparage, run down
Antonyms advance, ameliorate, better, elevate, enhance, improve, promote, raise, upgrade

downhearted blue, chapfallen, crestfallen, dejected, depressed, despondent, discouraged, disheartened, dismayed, dispirited, downcast, low-spirited, sad, sick as a parrot (*Inf.*), sorrowful, unhappy

downpour cloudburst, deluge, flood, inundation, rainstorm, torrential rain

downright 1. absolute, arrant, blatant, categorical, clear, complete, deep-dyed (*Usually derogatory*), explicit, out-and-out, outright, plain, positive, simple, thoroughgoing, total, undisguised, unequivocal, unqualified, utter **2.** blunt, candid, forthright, frank, honest, open, outspoken, plain, sincere, straightforward, straight-from-the-shoulder, upfront (*Inf.*)

down-to-earth common-sense, hardheaded, matter-of-fact, mundane, nononsense, plain-spoken, practical, realistic, sane, sensible, unsentimental

downtrodden abused, afflicted, distressed, exploited, helpless, oppressed, subjugated, subservient, tyrannized

downward adj. declining, descending, earthward, heading down, sliding, slipping

doze 1. *v.* catnap, drop off (*Inf.*), drowse, kip (*Brit. sl.*), nap, nod, nod off (*Inf.*), sleep, sleep lightly, slumber, snooze (*Inf.*), zizz (*Brit. inf.*) **2.** *n.* catnap, forty winks (*Inf.*), kip (*Brit. sl.*), little sleep, nap, shuteye (*Sl.*), siesta, snooze (*Inf.*), zizz (*Brit. inf.*)

drab cheerless, colourless, dingy, dismal, dreary, dull, flat, gloomy, grey, lacklustre, shabby, sombre, uninspired, vapid
Antonyms bright, cheerful, colourful, jazzy (*Inf.*), vibrant, vivid

draft *v.* **1.** compose, delineate, design, draw, draw up, formulate, outline, plan, sketch ~*n.* **2.** abstract, delineation, outline, plan, preliminary form, rough, sketch, version **3.** bill (*of exchange*), cheque, order, postal order

drag *v.* **1.** draw, hale, haul, lug, pull, tow, trail, tug, yank **2.** crawl, creep, go slowly, inch, limp along, shamble, shuffle **3.** dawdle, draggle, lag behind, linger, loiter, straggle, trail behind **4.** *With* **on** *or* **out** draw out, extend, keep going, lengthen, persist, prolong, protract, spin out, stretch out **5. drag one's feet** *Inf.* block, hold back, obstruct, procrastinate, stall ~*n.* **6.** *Sl.* annoyance, bore, bother, nuisance, pain (*Inf.*), pain in the arse (*Taboo inf.*), pest

dragging boring, dull, going slowly, humdrum, mind-numbing, monotonous, tedious, tiresome, wearisome

dragoon *v.* browbeat, bully, coerce, compel, constrain, drive, force, impel, intimidate, railroad (*Inf.*), strong-arm (*Inf.*)

drain *v.* **1.** bleed, draw off, dry, empty, evacuate, milk, pump off *or* out, remove, tap, withdraw **2.** consume, deplete, dissipate, empty, exhaust, sap, strain, tax, use up, weary **3.** discharge, effuse, exude, flow out, leak, ooze, seep, trickle, well out **4.** drink up, finish, gulp down, quaff, swallow ~*n.* **5.** channel, conduit, culvert, ditch, duct, outlet, pipe, sewer, sink, trench, watercourse **6.** depletion, drag, exhaustion, expenditure, reduction, sap, strain, withdrawal **7. down the drain** gone, gone for good, lost, ruined, wasted

drainage bilge (water), seepage, sewage, sewerage, waste

dram drop, glass, measure, shot (*Inf.*), slug, snifter (*Inf.*), snort (*Sl.*), tot

drama 1. dramatization, play, show, stage play, stage show, theatrical piece **2.** acting, dramatic art, dramaturgy, stagecraft, theatre, Thespian art **3.** crisis, dramatics, excitement, histrionics, scene, spectacle, theatrics, turmoil

dramatic 1. dramaturgic, dramaturgical, theatrical, Thespian **2.** breathtaking, climactic, electrifying, emotional, exciting, melodramatic, sensational, shock-horror (*Facetious*), startling, sudden, suspenseful, tense, thrilling **3.** affecting, effective, expressive, impressive, moving, powerful, striking, vivid
Antonyms ordinary, run-of-the-mill, undramatic, unexceptional, unmemorable

dramatist dramaturge, playwright, screenwriter, scriptwriter

dramatize act, exaggerate, lay it on (thick) (*Sl.*), make a performance of, overdo, overstate, play-act, play to the gallery

drape 1. adorn, array, cloak, cover, fold, swathe, wrap **2.** dangle, droop, drop, hang, lean over, let fall, suspend

drastic desperate, dire, extreme, forceful, harsh, radical, severe, strong

draught 1. *Of air* current, flow, influx, movement, puff **2.** dragging, drawing, haulage, pulling, traction **3.** cup, dose, drench, drink, potion, quantity

draw *v.* **1.** drag, haul, pull, tow, tug **2.** delineate, depict, design, map out, mark out, outline, paint, portray, sketch, trace **3.** deduce, derive, get, infer, make, take **4.** allure, attract, bring forth, call forth, elicit, engage, entice, evoke, induce, influence, invite, persuade **5.** extort, extract, pull out, take out **6.** attenuate, elongate, extend, lengthen, stretch **7.** breathe in, drain, inhale, inspire, puff, pull, respire, suck **8.** compose, draft, formulate, frame, prepare, write **9.** choose, pick, select, single out, take ~*n.* **10.** *Inf.* attraction, enticement, lure, pull (*Inf.*) **11.** dead heat, deadlock, impasse, stalemate, tie

drawback defect, deficiency, detriment, difficulty, disadvantage, downside, fault, flaw, fly in the ointment (*Inf.*), handicap, hindrance, hitch, impediment, imperfection, nuisance, obstacle, snag, stumbling block, trouble
Antonyms advantage, asset, benefit, gain, help, service, use

draw back recoil, retract, retreat, shrink, start back, withdraw

drawing cartoon, delineation, depiction, illustration, outline, picture, portrayal, representation, sketch, study

drawl *v. Of speech sounds* drag out, draw out, extend, lengthen, prolong, protract

drawling dragging, drawly, droning, dull, twanging, twangy

drawn fatigued, fraught, haggard, harassed, harrowed, pinched, sapped, strained, stressed, taut, tense, tired, worn

draw on employ, exploit, extract, fall back on, have recourse to, make use of, rely on, take from, use

draw out drag out, extend, lengthen, make

longer, prolong, prolongate, protract, spin out, stretch, string out
Antonyms curtail, cut, cut short, dock, pare down, reduce, shorten, trim, truncate

draw up 1. bring to a stop, halt, pull up, run in, stop, stop short **2.** compose, draft, formulate, frame, prepare, write out

dread 1. *v.* anticipate with horror, cringe at, fear, have cold feet (*Inf.*), quail, shrink from, shudder, tremble **2.** *n.* affright, alarm, apprehension, aversion, awe, dismay, fear, fright, funk (*Inf.*), heebie-jeebies (*Sl.*), horror, terror, trepidation **3.** *adj.* alarming, awe-inspiring, awful, dire, dreaded, dreadful, frightening, frightful, horrible, terrible, terrifying

dreadful alarming, appalling, awful, dire, distressing, fearful, formidable, frightful, ghastly, godawful (*Sl.*), grievous, hellacious (*U.S. sl.*), hideous, horrendous, horrible, monstrous, shocking, terrible, tragic, tremendous

dream *n.* **1.** daydream, delusion, fantasy, hallucination, illusion, imagination, pipe dream, reverie, speculation, trance, vagary, vision **2.** ambition, aspiration, design, desire, goal, hope, notion, thirst, wish **3.** beauty, delight, gem, joy, marvel, pleasure, treasure ~*v.* **4.** build castles in the air *or* in Spain, conjure up, daydream, envisage, fancy, fantasize, hallucinate, have dreams, imagine, stargaze, think, visualize

dreamer daydreamer, Don Quixote, fantasist, fantasizer, fantast, idealist, romancer, theorizer, utopian, visionary, Walter Mitty

dreamland cloud-cuckoo-land, cloudland, dream world, fairyland, fantasy, illusion, land of dreams, land of make-believe, land of Nod, never-never land (*Inf.*), sleep

dream up concoct, contrive, cook up (*Inf.*), create, devise, hatch, imagine, invent, spin, think up

dreamy 1. airy-fairy, dreamlike, fanciful, imaginary, impractical, quixotic, speculative, surreal, vague, visionary **2.** chimerical, dreamlike, fantastic, intangible, misty, phantasmagoric, phantasmagorical, shadowy, unreal **3.** absent, abstracted, daydreaming, faraway, in a reverie, musing, pensive, preoccupied, with one's head in the clouds **4.** calming, gentle, lulling, relaxing, romantic, soothing
Antonyms common-sense, down-to-earth, feet-on-the-ground, practical, pragmatic, realistic, unromantic

dreary 1. bleak, cheerless, comfortless, depressing, dismal, doleful, downcast, drear, forlorn, funereal, gloomy, glum, joyless, lonely, lonesome, melancholy, mournful, sad, solitary, sombre, sorrowful, wretched

2. boring, colourless, drab, dull, ho-hum (*Inf.*), humdrum, lifeless, mind-numbing, monotonous, routine, tedious, uneventful, uninteresting, wearisome
Antonyms bright, cheerful, happy, interesting, joyful

dregs 1. deposit, draff, dross, grounds, lees, residue, residuum, scourings, scum, sediment, trash, waste **2.** *Sl.* canaille, down-and-outs, good-for-nothings, outcasts, rabble, ragtag and bobtail, riffraff, scum

drench 1. *v.* drown, duck, flood, imbrue, inundate, saturate, soak, souse, steep, wet **2.** *n. Veterinary* dose, physic, purge

dress *n.* **1.** costume, ensemble, frock, garment, get-up (*Inf.*), gown, outfit, rigout (*Inf.*), robe, suit **2.** apparel, attire, clothes, clothing, costume, garb, garments, gear (*Inf.*), guise, habiliment, raiment (*Archaic or poetic*), togs, vestment ~*v.* **3.** attire, change, clothe, don, garb, put on, robe, slip on *or* into **4.** adorn, apparel (*Archaic*), array, bedeck, deck, decorate, drape, embellish, festoon, furbish, ornament, rig, trim **5.** adjust, align, arrange, comb (out), dispose, do (up), fit, get ready, groom, prepare, set, straighten **6.** bandage, bind up, plaster, treat
Antonyms (*sense 3*) disrobe, divest oneself of, peel off (*Sl.*), shed, strip, take off one's clothes

dress down bawl out (*Inf.*), berate, carpet (*Inf.*), castigate, chew out (*U.S. & Canad. inf.*), give a rocket (*Brit. & N.Z. inf.*), haul over the coals, read the riot act, rebuke, reprimand, reprove, scold, tear into (*Inf.*), tear (someone) off a strip (*Brit. inf.*), tell off (*Inf.*), upbraid

dressmaker couturier, modiste, seamstress, sewing woman, tailor

dress up 1. doll up (*Sl.*), dress for dinner, dress formally, put on one's best bib and tucker (*Inf.*), put on one's glad rags (*Inf.*) **2.** disguise, play-act, put on fancy dress, wear a costume **3.** beautify, do oneself up, embellish, gild, improve, titivate, trick out *or* up

dribble 1. drip, drop, fall in drops, leak, ooze, run, seep, trickle **2.** drip saliva, drivel, drool, slaver, slobber

drift *v.* **1.** be carried along, coast, float, go (aimlessly), meander, stray, waft, wander **2.** accumulate, amass, bank up, drive, gather, pile up ~*n.* **3.** accumulation, bank, heap, mass, mound, pile **4.** course, current, direction, flow, impulse, movement, rush, sweep, trend **5.** *Fig.* aim, design, direction, gist, implication, import, intention, meaning, object, purport, scope, significance, tendency, tenor, thrust

drill *v.* **1.** coach, discipline, exercise, in-

struct, practise, rehearse, teach, train ~*n.*
2. discipline, exercise, instruction, practice,
preparation, repetition, training ~*v.* **3.**
bore, penetrate, perforate, pierce, puncture,
sink in ~*n.* **4.** bit, borer, boring-tool, gim~
let, rotary tool

drink *v.* **1.** absorb, drain, gulp, guzzle, im~
bibe, partake of, quaff, sip, suck, sup, swal~
low, swig (*Inf.*), swill, toss off, wash down,
wet one's whistle (*Inf.*) **2.** bend the elbow
(*Inf.*), bevvy (*Dialect*), booze (*Inf.*), carouse,
go on a binge *or* bender (*Inf.*), hit the bottle
(*Inf.*), indulge, pub-crawl (*Inf., chiefly Brit.*),
revel, tipple, tope, wassail ~*n.* **3.** beverage,
liquid, potion, refreshment, thirst quencher
4. alcohol, booze (*Inf.*), hooch *or* hootch
(*Inf., chiefly U.S. & Canad.*), liquor, spirits,
the bottle (*Inf.*) **5.** cup, draught, glass, gulp,
noggin, sip, snifter (*Inf.*), swallow, swig
(*Inf.*), taste, tipple **6. the drink** *Inf.* the
briny (*Inf.*), the deep, the main, the ocean,
the sea

drinker alcoholic, bibber, boozer (*Inf.*), dip~
somaniac, drunk, drunkard, guzzler, in~
ebriate, lush (*Sl.*), soak (*Sl.*), sot, sponge
(*Inf.*), tippler, toper, wino (*Inf.*)

drink in absorb, assimilate, be all ears (*Inf.*),
be fascinated by, be rapt, hang on
(someone's) words, hang on the lips of, pay
attention

drink to pledge, pledge the health of, salute,
toast

drip *v.* **1.** dribble, drizzle, drop, exude, filter,
plop, splash, sprinkle, trickle ~*n.* **2.** drib~
ble, dripping, drop, leak, trickle **3.** *Inf.*
milksop, mummy's boy (*Inf.*), namby-
pamby, ninny, softy (*Inf.*), weakling, weed
(*Inf.*), wet (*Brit. inf.*)

drive *v.* **1.** herd, hurl, impel, propel, push,
send, urge **2.** direct, go, guide, handle,
manage, motor, operate, ride, steer, travel
3. actuate, coerce, compel, constrain, dra~
goon, force, goad, harass, impel, motivate,
oblige, overburden, overwork, press, prick,
prod, prompt, railroad (*Inf.*), rush, spur **4.**
dash, dig, hammer, plunge, ram, sink, stab,
thrust ~*n.* **5.** excursion, hurl (*Scot.*), jaunt,
journey, outing, ride, run, spin (*Inf.*), trip,
turn **6.** action, advance, appeal, campaign,
crusade, effort, push (*Inf.*), surge **7.** ambi~
tion, effort, energy, enterprise, get-up-and-go
(*Inf.*), initiative, motivation, pep, pressure,
push (*Inf.*), vigour, zip (*Inf.*)

drive at aim, allude to, get at, have in mind,
hint at, imply, indicate, insinuate, intend,
intimate, mean, refer to, signify, suggest

drivel *v.* **1.** dribble, drool, slaver, slobber **2.**
babble, blether, gab (*Inf.*), gas (*Inf.*), maun~
der, prate, ramble, waffle (*Inf., chiefly Brit.*),
~*n.* **3.** balderdash, balls (*Taboo sl.*), bilge
(*Inf.*), blah (*Sl.*), bosh (*Inf.*), bull (*Sl.*), bull~

shit (*Taboo sl.*), bunk (*Inf.*), bunkum *or*
buncombe (*Chiefly U.S.*), cobblers (*Brit. ta~
boo sl.*), crap (*Sl.*), dross, eyewash (*Inf.*), fa~
tuity, garbage (*Inf.*), gibberish, guff (*Sl.*),
hogwash, hokum (*Sl., chiefly U.S. &
Canad.*), horsefeathers (*U.S. sl.*), hot air
(*Inf.*), moonshine, nonsense, pap, piffle
(*Inf.*), poppycock (*Inf.*), prating, rot, rub~
bish, shit (*Taboo sl.*), stuff, tommyrot, tosh
(*Sl., chiefly Brit.*), tripe (*Inf.*), twaddle,
waffle (*Inf., chiefly Brit.*) **4.** saliva, slaver,
slobber

driving compelling, dynamic, energetic,
forceful, galvanic, sweeping, vigorous, vio~
lent

drizzle 1. *n.* fine rain, Scotch mist, smir
(*Scot.*) **2.** *v.* mizzle (*Dialect*), rain, shower,
spot *or* spit with rain, spray, sprinkle

droll amusing, clownish, comic, comical, di~
verting, eccentric, entertaining, farcical,
funny, humorous, jocular, laughable, ludi~
crous, odd, oddball (*Inf.*), off-the-wall (*Sl.*),
quaint, ridiculous, risible, waggish, whim~
sical

drone[1] *n.* couch potato (*Sl.*), idler, leech,
loafer, lounger, parasite, scrounger (*Inf.*),
skiver (*Brit. sl.*), sluggard, sponger (*Inf.*)

drone[2] *v.* **1.** buzz, hum, purr, thrum, vi~
brate, whirr **2.** *Often with* **on** be boring,
chant, drawl, intone, prose about, speak
monotonously, spout, talk interminably ~*n.*
3. buzz, hum, murmuring, purr, thrum, vi~
bration, whirr, whirring

drool 1. *Often with* **over** dote on, fondle,
gloat over, gush, make much of, pet, rave
(*Inf.*), slobber over, spoil **2.** dribble, drivel,
salivate, slaver, slobber, water at the mouth

droop 1. bend, dangle, drop, fall down, hang
(down), sag, sink **2.** decline, diminish, fade,
faint, flag, languish, slump, wilt, wither **3.**
despond, falter, give in, give up, give way,
lose heart *or* hope

drop *n.* **1.** bead, bubble, driblet, drip, drop~
let, globule, pearl, tear **2.** dab, dash,
mouthful, nip, pinch, shot (*Inf.*), sip, spot,
taste, tot, trace, trickle **3.** abyss, chasm, de~
clivity, descent, fall, plunge, precipice, slope
4. cut, decline, decrease, deterioration,
downturn, fall-off, lowering, reduction,
slump ~*v.* **5.** dribble, drip, fall in drops,
trickle **6.** decline, depress, descend, dimin~
ish, dive, droop, fall, lower, plummet,
plunge, sink, tumble **7.** abandon, axe (*Inf.*),
cease, desert, discontinue, forsake, give up,
kick (*Inf.*), leave, quit, relinquish, remit,
terminate **8.** *Inf.* disown, ignore, jilt, reject,
renounce, repudiate, throw over **9.** *Some~
times with* **off** deposit, leave, let off, set
down, unload

drop in (on) blow in (*Inf.*), call, call in, go

and see, look in (on), look up, pop in (*Inf.*), roll up (*Inf.*), stop, turn up, visit

drop off 1. decline, decrease, diminish, dwindle, fall off, lessen, slacken **2.** allow to alight, deliver, leave, let off, set down **3.** *Inf.* catnap, doze (off), drowse, fall asleep, have forty winks (*Inf.*), nod (off), snooze (*Inf.*)

drop out abandon, back out, cop out (*Sl.*), forsake, give up, leave, quit, renege, stop, withdraw

drought 1. aridity, dehydration, drouth (*Scot.*), dryness, dry spell, dry weather, parchedness **2.** dearth, deficiency, insufficiency, lack, need, scarcity, shortage, want
Antonyms abundance, deluge, downpour, flood, flow, inundation, outpouring, profusion, rush, stream, torrent

drove collection, company, crowd, flock, gathering, herd, horde, mob, multitude, press, swarm, throng

drown 1. deluge, drench, engulf, flood, go down, go under, immerse, inundate, sink, submerge, swamp **2.** *Fig.* deaden, engulf, muffle, obliterate, overcome, overpower, overwhelm, stifle, swallow up, wipe out

drowse 1. *v.* be drowsy, be lethargic, be sleepy, doze, drop off (*Inf.*), kip (*Brit. sl.*), nap, nod, sleep, slumber, snooze (*Inf.*), zizz (*Brit. inf.*) **2.** *n.* doze, forty winks (*Inf.*), kip (*Brit. sl.*), nap, sleep, slumber, zizz (*Brit. inf.*)

drowsy 1. comatose, dazed, dopey (*Sl.*), dozy, drugged, half asleep, heavy, lethargic, nodding, sleepy, somnolent, tired, torpid **2.** dreamy, lulling, restful, sleepy, soothing, soporific
Antonyms alert, awake, full of beans (*Inf.*), lively, perky

drubbing beating, clobbering (*Sl.*), defeat, flogging, hammering (*Inf.*), licking (*Inf.*), pasting (*Sl.*), pounding, pummelling, thrashing, trouncing, walloping (*Inf.*), whipping

drudge 1. *n.* dogsbody (*Inf.*), factotum, hack, maid *or* man of all work, menial, plodder, scullion (*Archaic*), servant, skivvy (*Chiefly Brit.*), slave, toiler, worker **2.** *v.* grind (*Inf.*), keep one's nose to the grindstone, labour, moil (*Archaic or dialect*), plod, plug away (*Inf.*), slave, toil, work

drudgery chore, donkey-work, fag (*Inf.*), grind (*Inf.*), hack work, hard work, labour, menial labour, skivvying (*Brit.*), slavery, slog, sweat (*Inf.*), sweated labour, toil

drug *n.* **1.** medicament, medication, medicine, physic, poison, remedy **2.** dope (*Sl.*), narcotic, opiate, stimulant ~*v.* **3.** administer a drug, dope (*Sl.*), dose, medicate, treat

4. anaesthetize, deaden, knock out, numb, poison, stupefy

drug addict *n.* acid head (*Inf.*), crack-head (*Inf.*), dope-fiend (*Sl.*), head (*Inf.*), hop-head (*Inf.*), junkie (*Inf.*), tripper (*Inf.*)

drugged bombed (*Sl.*), comatose, doped (*Sl.*), dopey (*Sl.*), flying (*Sl.*), high (*Inf.*), on a trip (*Inf.*), out of it (*Sl.*), out of one's mind (*Sl.*), out to it (*Aust. & N.Z. sl.*), smashed (*Sl.*), spaced out (*Sl.*), stoned (*Sl.*), stupefied (*Sl.*), turned on (*Sl.*), under the influence (*Inf.*), wasted (*Sl.*), wrecked (*Sl.*), zonked (*Sl.*)

drum *v.* **1.** beat, pulsate, rap, reverberate, tap, tattoo, throb **2.** *With* **into** din into, drive home, hammer away, harp on, instil, reiterate

drum up attract, bid for, canvass, obtain, petition, round up, solicit

drunk 1. *adj.* bacchic, bevvied (*Dialect*), blitzed (*Sl.*), blotto (*Sl.*), bombed (*Sl.*), canned (*Sl.*), drunken, flying (*Sl.*), fu' (*Scot.*), fuddled, half seas over (*Inf.*), inebriated, intoxicated, legless (*Inf.*), lit up (*Sl.*), loaded (*Sl., chiefly U.S. & Canad.*), maudlin, merry (*Brit. inf.*), muddled, out of it (*Sl.*), out to it (*Aust. & N.Z. sl.*), paralytic (*Inf.*), pickled (*Inf.*), pie-eyed (*Sl.*), pissed (*Taboo sl.*), plastered (*Inf.*), sloshed (*Sl.*), smashed (*Sl.*), soaked (*Inf.*), steamboats (*Sl.*), steaming (*Sl.*), stewed (*Sl.*), stoned (*Sl.*), tanked up (*Sl.*), tiddly (*Sl., chiefly Brit.*), tight (*Inf.*), tipsy, tired and emotional (*Euphemistic*), under the influence (*Inf.*), wasted (*Sl.*), well-oiled (*Sl.*), wrecked (*Sl.*), zonked (*Sl.*) **2.** *n.* boozer (*Inf.*), drunkard, inebriate, lush (*Sl.*), soak (*Sl.*), sot, toper, wino (*Inf.*)

drunkard alcoholic, carouser, dipsomaniac, drinker, drunk, lush (*Sl.*), soak (*Sl.*), sot, tippler, toper, wino (*Inf.*)

drunken 1. bevvied (*Dialect*), bibulous, blitzed (*Sl.*), blotto (*Sl.*), bombed (*Sl.*), boozing (*Inf.*), drunk, flying (*Sl.*), (gin-)sodden, inebriate, intoxicated, legless (*Inf.*), lit up (*Sl.*), out of it (*Sl.*), out to it (*Aust. & N.Z. sl.*), paralytic (*Inf.*), pissed (*Taboo sl.*), red-nosed, smashed (*Sl.*), sottish, steamboats (*Sl.*), steaming (*Sl.*), tippling, toping, under the influence (*Inf.*), wasted (*Sl.*), wrecked (*Sl.*), zonked (*Sl.*) **2.** bacchanalian, bacchic, boozy (*Inf.*), debauched, dionysian, dissipated, orgiastic, riotous, saturnalian

drunkenness alcoholism, bibulousness, dipsomania, inebriety, insobriety, intemperance, intoxication, sottishness, tipsiness

dry *adj.* **1.** arid, barren, dehydrated, desiccated, dried up, juiceless, moistureless, parched, sapless, thirsty, torrid, waterless **2.** *Fig.* boring, dreary, dull, ho-hum (*Inf.*), monotonous, plain, tedious, tiresome, uninteresting **3.** *Fig.* cutting, deadpan, droll, keen, low-key, quietly humorous, sarcastic,

sharp, sly ~v. **4.** dehumidify, dehydrate, desiccate, drain, make dry, parch, sear **5.** *With* **out** *or* **up** become dry, become un~ productive, harden, mummify, shrivel up, wilt, wither, wizen
Antonyms *adj.* (*sense 1*) damp, humid, moist, wet (*sense 2*) entertaining, interesting, lively ~v. moisten, wet

dryness aridity, aridness, dehumidification, dehydration, drought, thirst, thirstiness

dual binary, coupled, double, duplex, dupli~ cate, matched, paired, twin, twofold

dubious 1. doubtful, hesitant, iffy (*Inf.*), leery (*Sl.*), sceptical, uncertain, uncon~ vinced, undecided, unsure, wavering **2.** ambiguous, debatable, dodgy (*Brit., Aust., & N.Z. inf.*), doubtful, equivocal, indefinite, indeterminate, obscure, problematical, un~ clear, unsettled **3.** dodgy (*Brit., Aust., & N.Z. inf.*), fishy (*Inf.*), questionable, shady (*Inf.*), suspect, suspicious, undependable, unreliable, untrustworthy
Antonyms certain, definite, dependable, ob~ vious, positive, reliable, sure, trustworthy

duck 1. bend, bob, bow, crouch, dodge, drop, lower, stoop **2.** dip, dive, douse, dunk, im~ merse, plunge, souse, submerge, wet **3.** *Inf.* avoid, body-swerve (*Scot.*), dodge, escape, evade, shirk, shun, sidestep

duct blood vessel, canal, channel, conduit, funnel, passage, pipe, tube

dud 1. *n.* failure, flop (*Inf.*), washout (*Inf.*) **2.** *adj.* broken, bust (*Inf.*), duff (*Brit. inf.*), failed, inoperative, kaput (*Inf.*), not' func~ tioning, valueless, worthless

dudgeon ire, resentment, umbrage, wrath

due *adj.* **1.** in arrears, outstanding, owed, owing, payable, unpaid **2.** appropriate, be~ coming, bounden, deserved, fit, fitting, just, justified, merited, obligatory, proper, requi~ site, right, rightful, suitable, well-earned **3.** adequate, ample, enough, plenty of, sufficient **4.** expected, expected to arrive, scheduled ~n. **5.** comeuppance (*Sl.*), des~ erts, merits, prerogative, privilege, right(s) ~adv. **6.** dead, direct, directly, exactly, straight, undeviatingly

duel *n.* **1.** affair of honour, single combat **2.** clash, competition, contest, encounter, en~ gagement, fight, head-to-head, rivalry ~v. **3.** clash, compete, contend, contest, fight, ri~ val, struggle, vie with

dues charge, charges, fee, levy

duffer blunderer, booby, bungler, clod, clot (*Brit. inf.*), galoot (*Sl., chiefly U.S.*), lubber, lummox (*Inf.*), oaf

dulcet agreeable, charming, delightful, euphonious, harmonious, honeyed, mellifluent, mellifluous, melodious, musical, pleasant, pleasing, soothing, sweet

dull *adj.* **1.** braindead (*Inf.*), dense, dim, dim-witted (*Inf.*), doltish, dozy (*Brit. inf.*), obtuse, slow, stolid, stupid, thick, unintelli~ gent **2.** apathetic, blank, callous, dead, empty, heavy, indifferent, insensible, in~ sensitive, lifeless, listless, passionless, slow, sluggish, unresponsive, unsympathetic, vacuous **3.** banal, boring, commonplace, dozy, dreary, dry, flat, ho-hum (*Inf.*), hum~ drum, mind-numbing, monotonous, plain, prosaic, run-of-the-mill, tedious, tiresome, unimaginative, uninteresting, vapid **4.** blunt, blunted, dulled, edgeless, not keen, not sharp, unsharpened **5.** cloudy, dim, dismal, gloomy, leaden, opaque, overcast, turbid **6.** depressed, inactive, slack, slow, sluggish, torpid, uneventful **7.** drab, faded, feeble, indistinct, lacklustre, muffled, murky, muted, sombre, subdued, subfusc, toned-down ~v. **8.** dampen, deject, depress, discourage, dishearten, dispirit, sadden **9.** allay, alleviate, assuage, blunt, lessen, miti~ gate, moderate, palliate, paralyse, relieve, soften, stupefy, take the edge off **10.** cloud, darken, dim, fade, obscure, stain, sully, tar~ nish
Antonyms *adj.* active, bright, clever, dis~ tinct, exciting, intelligent, interesting, lively, sharp

duly 1. accordingly, appropriately, befit~ tingly, correctly, decorously, deservedly, fittingly, properly, rightfully, suitably **2.** at the proper time, on time, punctually

dumb 1. at a loss for words, inarticulate, mum, mute, silent, soundless, speechless, tongue-tied, voiceless, wordless **2.** *Inf.* asi~ nine, braindead (*Inf.*), dense, dim-witted (*Inf.*), dozy (*Brit. inf.*), dull, foolish, obtuse, stupid, thick, unintelligent
Antonyms (*sense 2*) articulate, bright, clev~ er, intelligent, quick-witted, smart

dumbfounded, dumfounded amazed, astonished, astounded, at sea, bewildered, bowled over (*Inf.*), breathless, confounded, confused, dumb, flabbergasted (*Inf.*), flummoxed, gobsmacked (*Brit. sl.*), knocked for six (*Inf.*), knocked sideways (*Inf.*), non~ plussed, overcome, overwhelmed, speech~ less, staggered, startled, stunned, taken aback, thrown, thunderstruck

dummy *n.* **1.** figure, form, lay figure, mani~ kin, mannequin, model **2.** copy, counterfeit, duplicate, imitation, sham, substitute **3.** *Sl.* berk (*Brit. sl.*), blockhead, charlie (*Brit. inf.*), coot, dickhead (*Sl.*), dimwit (*Inf.*), dip~ stick (*Brit. sl.*), divvy (*Brit. sl.*), dolt, dork (*Sl.*), dullard, dunce, dweeb (*U.S. sl.*), fool, fuckwit (*Taboo sl.*), geek (*Sl.*), gonzo (*Sl.*), jerk (*Sl., chiefly U.S. & Canad.*), lamebrain (*Inf.*), nerd *or* nurd (*Sl.*), nitwit (*Inf.*), num~ skull *or* numbskull, oaf, pillock (*Brit. sl.*), plank (*Brit. sl.*), plonker (*Sl.*), prat (*Sl.*), prick (*Derogatory sl.*), schmuck (*U.S. sl.*), simpleton, wally (*Sl.*), ~*adj.* **4.** artificial, bogus, fake, false, imitation, mock, phoney *or* phony (*Inf.*), sham, simulated **5.** mock, practice, simulated, trial

dump *v.* **1.** deposit, drop, fling down, let fall, throw down **2.** coup (*Scot.*), discharge, dispose of, ditch (*Sl.*), empty out, get rid of, jettison, scrap, throw away *or* out, tip, un~ load ~*n.* **3.** junkyard, refuse heap, rubbish heap, rubbish tip, tip **4.** *Inf.* hole (*Inf.*), hovel, joint (*Sl.*), mess, pigsty, shack, shan~ ty, slum

dumps blues, dejection, depression, de~ spondency, dolour, gloom, gloominess, low spirits, melancholy, mopes, sadness, the hump (*Brit. inf.*), unhappiness, woe

dunce ass, blockhead, bonehead (*Sl.*), dim~ wit (*Inf.*), dolt, donkey, duffer (*Inf.*), dullard, dunderhead, goose (*Inf.*), halfwit, ignora~ mus, lamebrain (*Inf.*), loon (*Inf.*), moron, nincompoop, nitwit (*Inf.*), numskull *or* numbskull, oaf, simpleton, thickhead

dungeon cage, cell, donjon, lockup, oubli~ ette, prison, vault

duplicate **1.** *adj.* corresponding, identical, matched, matching, twin, twofold **2.** *n.* car~ bon copy, clone, copy, double, facsimile, fax, likeness, lookalike, match, mate, photocopy, Photostat (*Trademark*), replica, reproduc~ tion, ringer (*Sl.*), twin, Xerox (*Trademark*) **3.** *v.* clone, copy, double, echo, fax, photo~ copy, Photostat (*Trademark*), repeat, repli~ cate, reproduce, Xerox (*Trademark*)

duplicity artifice, chicanery, deceit, decep~ tion, dishonesty, dissimulation, double~ dealing, falsehood, fraud, guile, hypocrisy, perfidy
Antonyms candour, honesty, straight~ forwardness

durability constancy, durableness, endur~ ance, imperishability, lastingness, perma~ nence, persistence

durable abiding, constant, dependable, en~ during, fast, firm, fixed, hard-wearing, last~ ing, long-lasting, permanent, persistent, re~ liable, resistant, sound, stable, strong, stur~ dy, substantial, tough
Antonyms breakable, brittle, delicate, frag~ ile, impermanent, perishable, weak

duress **1.** coercion, compulsion, constraint, pressure, threat **2.** captivity, confinement, constraint, hardship, imprisonment, incar~ ceration, restraint

dusk **1.** dark, evening, eventide, gloaming (*Scot. or poetic*), nightfall, sundown, sunset, twilight **2.** *Poetic* darkness, gloom, murk, obscurity, shade, shadowiness
Antonyms aurora (*Poetic*), cockcrow, dawn, dawning, daybreak, daylight, morning, sun~ light, sunup

dusky **1.** dark, dark-complexioned, dark~ hued, sable, swarthy **2.** caliginous (*Archa~ ic*), cloudy, crepuscular, darkish, dim, gloomy, murky, obscure, overcast, shadowy, shady, tenebrous, twilight, twilit, veiled

dust *n.* **1.** fine fragments, grime, grit, parti~ cles, powder, powdery dirt **2.** dirt, earth, ground, soil **3.** *Inf.* commotion, disturbance, fuss, racket, row **4. bite the dust** *Inf.* die, drop dead, expire, fall in battle, pass away, perish **5. lick the dust** *Inf.* be servile, bootlick (*Inf.*), demean oneself, grovel, kow~ tow, toady **6. throw dust in the eyes of** con (*Sl.*), confuse, deceive, fool, have (someone) on, hoodwink, mislead, take in (*Inf.*), ~*v.* **7.** cover, dredge, powder, scatter, sift, spray, spread, sprinkle

dusty **1.** dirty, grubby, sooty, unclean, undusted, unswept **2.** chalky, crumbly, fri~ able, granular, powdery, sandy

dutiful compliant, conscientious, deferential, devoted, docile, duteous (*Archaic*), filial, obedient, punctilious, respectful, reveren~ tial, submissive
Antonyms disobedient, disrespectful, in~ subordinate, remiss, uncaring

duty **1.** assignment, business, calling, char~ ge, engagement, function, mission, obliga~ tion, office, onus, province, responsibility, role, service, task, work **2.** allegiance, def~ erence, loyalty, obedience, respect, rever~ ence **3.** customs, due, excise, impost, levy, tariff, tax, toll **4. do duty for** stand in, substitute, take the place of **5. be the duty of** behove (*Archaic*), be incumbent upon, belong to, be (someone's) pigeon (*Brit. inf.*), be up to (*Inf.*), devolve upon, pertain to, rest with **6. off duty** at leisure, free, off, off work, on holiday **7. on duty** at work, busy, engaged

dwarf *n.* **1.** bantam, homunculus, hop-o'- my-thumb, Lilliputian, manikin, midget, pygmy *or* pigmy, Tom Thumb **2.** gnome, goblin ~*adj.* **3.** baby, bonsai, diminutive, dwarfed, Lilliputian, miniature, petite, pocket, small, teensy-weensy, teeny-weeny, tiny, undersized ~*v.* **4.** dim, diminish, dominate, minimize, overshadow, tower above *or* over **5.** check, cultivate by bonsai, lower, retard, stunt

dwell abide, establish oneself, hang out (*Inf.*), inhabit, live, lodge, quarter, remain, reside, rest, settle, sojourn, stay, stop

dwelling abode, domicile, dwelling house, establishment, habitation, home, house, lodging, pad (*Sl.*), quarters, residence

dwell on *or* **upon** be engrossed in, con~ tinue, elaborate, emphasize, expatiate, harp on, linger over, tarry over

dwindle abate, contract, decay, decline, de~ crease, die away (down, out), diminish, ebb,

fade, fall, grow less, lessen, peter out, pine,
shrink, shrivel, sink, subside, taper off,
wane, waste away, weaken, wither
Antonyms advance, amplify, develop, dilate,
enlarge, escalate, expand, grow, heighten, in~
crease, magnify, multiply, swell, wax

dye 1. *n.* colorant, colour, colouring, pig~
ment, stain, tinge, tint **2.** *v.* colour, pig~
ment, stain, tincture, tinge, tint

dyed-in-the-wool complete, confirmed,
deep-dyed (*Usually derogatory*), deep-rooted,
die-hard, entrenched, established, inveter~
ate, through-and-through

dying at death's door, ebbing, expiring, fad~
ing, failing, final, going, *in extremis*, mori~
bund, mortal, passing, perishing, sinking

dynamic active, driving, electric, energetic,
forceful, go-ahead, go-getting (*Inf.*), high-
powered, lively, magnetic, powerful, vigor~
ous, vital, zippy (*Inf.*)
Antonyms apathetic, couldn't-care-less
(*Inf.*), impassive, inactive, listless, sluggish,
torpid, undynamic, unenergetic

dynasty ascendancy, dominion, empire,
government, house, regime, rule, sover~
eignty, sway

E

each 1. *adj.* every **2.** *pron.* each and every one, each one, every one, one and all **3.** *adv.* apiece, for each, from each, individually, per capita, per head, per person, respectively, singly, to each

eager agog, anxious, ardent, athirst, avid, earnest, enthusiastic, fervent, fervid, greedy, hot, hungry, impatient, intent, keen, longing, raring, vehement, yearning, zealous
Antonyms apathetic, blasé, impassive, indifferent, lazy, nonchalant, opposed, unambitious, unconcerned, unenthusiastic, unimpressed, uninterested

eagerness ardour, avidity, earnestness, enthusiasm, fervour, greediness, heartiness, hunger, impatience, impetuosity, intentness, keenness, longing, thirst, vehemence, yearning, zeal

ear *Fig.* **1.** attention, consideration, hearing, heed, notice, regard **2.** appreciation, discrimination, musical perception, sensitivity, taste

early *adj.* **1.** advanced, forward, premature, untimely **2.** primeval, primitive, primordial, undeveloped, young ~*adv.* **3.** ahead of time, beforehand, betimes (*Archaic*), in advance, in good time, prematurely, too soon
Antonyms (*sense 2*) developed, mature, ripe, seasoned (*sense 3*) behind, belated, late, overdue, tardy

earn 1. bring in, collect, draw, gain, get, gross, make, net, obtain, procure, realize, reap, receive **2.** acquire, attain, be entitled to, be worthy of, deserve, merit, rate, warrant, win

earnest *adj.* **1.** close, constant, determined, firm, fixed, grave, intent, resolute, resolved, serious, sincere, solemn, stable, staid, steady, thoughtful **2.** ardent, devoted, eager, enthusiastic, fervent, fervid, heartfelt, impassioned, keen, passionate, purposeful, urgent, vehement, warm, zealous ~*n.* **3.** determination, reality, resolution, seriousness, sincerity, truth **4.** assurance, deposit, down payment, earnest money (*Law*), foretaste, guarantee, pledge, promise, security, token
Antonyms *adj.* apathetic, couldn't-care-less, flippant, frivolous, half-hearted, indifferent, insincere, light, slack, trifling, unconcerned, unenthusiastic, uninterested, unstable ~*n.* apathy, indifference, unconcern

earnings emolument, gain, income, pay, proceeds, profits, receipts, remuneration, return, reward, salary, stipend, takings, wages

earth 1. globe, orb, planet, sphere, terrestrial sphere, world **2.** clay, clod, dirt, ground, land, loam, mould, sod, soil, topsoil, turf

earthenware ceramics, crockery, crocks, pots, pottery, terra cotta

earthly 1. mundane, sublunary, tellurian, telluric, terrene, terrestrial, worldly **2.** human, material, mortal, non-spiritual, profane, secular, temporal, worldly **3.** base, carnal, fleshly, gross, low, materialistic, physical, sensual, sordid, vile **4.** *Inf.* conceivable, feasible, imaginable, likely, possible, practical
Antonyms ethereal, heavenly, immaterial, immortal, otherwordly, spiritual, supernatural, unearthly

ease *n.* **1.** affluence, calmness, comfort, content, contentment, enjoyment, happiness, leisure, peace, peace of mind, quiet, quietude, relaxation, repose, rest, restfulness, serenity, tranquillity **2.** easiness, effortlessness, facility, readiness, simplicity **3.** flexibility, freedom, informality, liberty, naturalness, unaffectedness, unconstraint, unreservedness **4.** aplomb, composure, insouciance, nonchalance, poise, relaxedness ~*v.* **5.** abate, allay, alleviate, appease, assuage, calm, comfort, disburden, lessen, lighten, mitigate, moderate, mollify, pacify, palliate, quiet, relax, relent, relieve, slacken, soothe, still, tranquillize **6.** aid, assist, expedite, facilitate, forward, further, lessen the labour of, make easier, simplify, smooth, speed up **7.** edge, guide, inch, manoeuvre, move carefully, slide, slip, squeeze, steer
Antonyms *n.* agitation, arduousness, awkwardness, clumsiness, concern, constraint, difficulty, discomfort, disturbance, effort, exertion, formality, hardship, irritation, pain, poverty, tension, toil, tribulation ~*v.* aggravate, discomfort, exacerbate, hinder, irritate, make nervous, make uneasy, retard, worsen

easily 1. comfortably, effortlessly, facilely, readily, simply, smoothly, with ease, without difficulty, without trouble **2.** absolutely, beyond question, by far, certainly, clearly, definitely, doubtlessly, far and away, indisputably, indubitably, plainly, surely, undeniably, undoubtedly, unequivocally, unquestionably, without a doubt **3.** almost certainly, probably, well

easy 1. a piece of cake (*Inf.*), a pushover (*Sl.*), child's play (*Inf.*), clear, easy-peasy (*Sl.*), effortless, facile, light, no bother, not difficult, no trouble, painless, simple, smooth, straightforward, uncomplicated, undemanding **2.** calm, carefree, comfort~able, contented, cushy (*Inf.*), easeful, lei~surely, peaceful, pleasant, quiet, relaxed, satisfied, serene, tranquil, undisturbed, un~troubled, unworried, well-to-do **3.** flexible, indulgent, lenient, liberal, light, mild, per~missive, tolerant, unburdensome, unopp~ressive **4.** affable, casual, easy-going, friendly, gentle, graceful, gracious, infor~mal, laid-back (*Inf.*), mild, natural, open, pleasant, relaxed, smooth, tolerant, unaf~fected, unceremonious, unconstrained, un~demanding, unforced, unpretentious **5.** ac~commodating, amenable, biddable, compli~ant, docile, gullible, manageable, pliant, soft, submissive, suggestible, susceptible, tractable, trusting, yielding **6.** comfortable, gentle, leisurely, light, mild, moderate, temperate, undemanding, unexacting, un~hurried

Antonyms affected, anxious, arduous, com~plex, demanding, dictatorial, difficult, exact~ing, exhausting, forced, formal, formidable, hard, harsh, impossible, inflexible, insecure, intolerant, onerous, poor, rigid, self-conscious, stern, stiff, stressful, strict, un~comfortable, unnatural, unyielding, worried

easy-going amenable, calm, carefree, cas~ual, complacent, easy, easy-oasy (*Sl.*), even-tempered, flexible, happy-go-lucky, in~dulgent, insouciant, laid-back (*Inf.*), lenient, liberal, mild, moderate, nonchalant, per~missive, placid, relaxed, serene, tolerant, unconcerned, uncritical, undemanding, un~hurried

Antonyms anxious, edgy, fussy, hung-up (*Sl.*), intolerant, irritated, nervy (*Brit. inf.*), on edge, strict, tense, uptight (*Inf.*)

eat 1. chew, consume, devour, gobble, in~gest, munch, scoff (*Sl.*), swallow **2.** break bread, chow down (*Sl.*), dine, feed, have a meal, take food, take nourishment **3.** cor~rode, crumble, decay, dissolve, erode, rot, waste away, wear away **4. eat one's words** abjure, recant, rescind, retract, take (statement) back

eavesdrop bug (*Inf.*), listen in, monitor, overhear, snoop (*Inf.*), spy, tap

ebb v. **1.** abate, fall away, fall back, flow back, go out, recede, retire, retreat, retro~cede, sink, subside, wane, withdraw ~n. **2.** ebb tide, going out, low tide, low water, reflux, regression, retreat, retrocession, subsidence, wane, waning, withdrawal ~v. **3.** decay, decline, decrease, degenerate, de~teriorate, diminish, drop, dwindle, fade away, fall away, flag, lessen, peter out,

shrink, sink, slacken, weaken ~n. **4.** decay, decline, decrease, degeneration, deteriora~tion, diminution, drop, dwindling, fading away, flagging, lessening, petering out, shrinkage, sinking, slackening, weakening

eccentric 1. *adj.* aberrant, abnormal, anomalous, bizarre, capricious, erratic, freakish, idiosyncratic, irregular, odd, odd~ball (*Inf.*), off-the-wall (*Sl.*), outlandish, outré, peculiar, queer (*Inf.*), quirky, rum (*Brit. sl.*), singular, strange, uncommon, unconventional, wacko (*Sl.*), weird, whim~sical **2.** *n.* card (*Inf.*), case (*Inf.*), character (*Inf.*), crank (*Inf.*), freak (*Inf.*), kook (*U.S. & Canad. inf.*), nonconformist, nut (*Sl.*), odd~ball (*Inf.*), odd fish (*Inf.*), oddity, queer fish (*Brit. inf.*), rum customer (*Brit. sl.*), screw~ball (*Sl., chiefly U.S. & Canad.*), wacko (*Sl.*), weirdo *or* weirdie (*Inf.*)

Antonyms *adj.* average, conventional, nor~mal, ordinary, regular, run-of-the-mill, straightforward, typical

eccentricity aberration, abnormality, anomaly, bizarreness, caprice, capricious~ness, foible, freakishness, idiosyncrasy, ir~regularity, nonconformity, oddity, oddness, outlandishness, peculiarity, queerness (*Inf.*), quirk, singularity, strangeness, unconven~tionality, waywardness, weirdness, whimsi~cality, whimsicalness

ecclesiastic 1. *n.* churchman, clergyman, cleric, divine, holy man, man of the cloth, minister, parson, pastor, priest **2.** *adj.* Also **ecclesiastical** church, churchly, clerical, divine, holy, pastoral, priestly, religious, spiritual

echo v. **1.** repeat, resound, reverberate **2.** ape, copy, imitate, mirror, parallel, parrot, recall, reflect, reiterate, reproduce, resem~ble, ring, second ~n. **3.** answer, repetition, reverberation **4.** copy, imitation, mirror image, parallel, reflection, reiteration, re~production, ringing **5.** allusion, evocation, hint, intimation, memory, reminder, sug~gestion, trace **6.** *Often plural* aftereffect, aftermath, consequence, repercussion

eclipse v. **1.** blot out, cloud, darken, dim, extinguish, obscure, overshadow, shroud, veil **2.** exceed, excel, outdo, outshine, sur~pass, transcend ~n. **3.** darkening, dimming, extinction, obscuration, occultation, shad~ing **4.** decline, diminution, failure, fall, loss

economic 1. business, commercial, financial, industrial, mercantile, trade **2.** money-making, productive, profitable, profit-making, remunerative, solvent, viable **3.** bread-and-butter (*Inf.*), budgetary, financial, fiscal, material, monetary, pecu~niary **4.** *Inf. Also* **economical** cheap, fair, inexpensive, low, low-priced, modest, rea~sonable

economical 1. cost-effective, efficient, money-saving, sparing, time-saving, unwasteful, work-saving **2.** careful, econo~ mizing, frugal, prudent, saving, scrimping, sparing, thrifty **3.** *Also* **economic** cheap, fair, inexpensive, low, low-priced, modest, reasonable
Antonyms exorbitant, expensive, extrava~ gant, generous, imprudent, lavish, loss-making, profligate, spendthrift, uneconomi~ cal, unprofitable, unthrifty, wasteful

economize be economical, be frugal, be sparing, cut back, husband, retrench, save, scrimp, tighten one's belt
Antonyms be extravagant, push the boat out (*Inf.*), spend, splurge, squander

economy frugality, husbandry, parsimony, providence, prudence, restraint, retrench~ ment, saving, sparingness, thrift, thriftiness

ecstasy bliss, delight, elation, enthusiasm, euphoria, exaltation, fervour, frenzy, joy, rapture, ravishment, rhapsody, seventh heaven, trance, transport
Antonyms affliction, agony, anguish, dis~ tress, hell, misery, pain, suffering, torment, torture

ecstatic blissful, cock-a-hoop, delirious, elated, enraptured, enthusiastic, entranced, euphoric, fervent, frenzied, in exaltation, in transports of delight, joyful, joyous, on cloud nine (*Inf.*), overjoyed, over the moon (*Inf.*), rapturous, rhapsodic, transported

eddy 1. *n.* counter-current, counterflow, swirl, tideway, undertow, vortex, whirlpool **2.** *v.* swirl, whirl

edge *n.* **1.** border, bound, boundary, brim, brink, contour, flange, fringe, limit, line, lip, margin, outline, perimeter, periphery, rim, side, threshold, verge **2.** acuteness, animation, bite, effectiveness, force, inci~ siveness, interest, keenness, point, pungen~ cy, sharpness, sting, urgency, zest **3.** ad~ vantage, ascendancy, dominance, lead, su~ periority, upper hand **4. on edge** appre~ hensive, eager, edgy, excited, ill at ease, impatient, irritable, keyed up, nervous, on tenterhooks, tense, tetchy, twitchy (*Inf.*), uptight (*Inf.*), wired (*Sl.*) ~*v.* **5.** bind, bor~ der, fringe, hem, rim, shape, trim **6.** creep, ease, inch, sidle, steal, work, worm **7.** hone, sharpen, strop, whet

edgy anxious, ill at ease, irascible, irritable, keyed up, nervous, nervy (*Brit. inf.*), on edge, restive, tense, tetchy, touchy, twitchy (*Inf.*), uptight (*Inf.*), wired (*Sl.*)

edible comestible (*Rare*), digestible, eatable, esculent, fit to eat, good, harmless, palat~ able, wholesome
Antonyms baneful, harmful, indigestible, inedible, noxious, pernicious, poisonous, un~ eatable

edict act, canon, command, decree, demand, dictate, dictum, enactment, fiat, injunction, law, mandate, manifesto, order, ordinance, proclamation, pronouncement, pronuncia~ mento, regulation, ruling, statute, ukase (*Rare*)

edifice building, construction, erection, fab~ ric (*Rare*), habitation, house, pile, structure

edify educate, elevate, enlighten, guide, im~ prove, inform, instruct, nurture, school, teach, uplift

edit 1. adapt, annotate, censor, check, con~ dense, correct, emend, polish, redact, re~ phrase, revise, rewrite **2.** assemble, com~ pose, put together, rearrange, reorder, se~ lect

edition copy, impression, issue, number, printing, programme (*TV, Radio*), version, volume

educate civilize, coach, cultivate, develop, discipline, drill, edify, enlighten, exercise, foster, improve, indoctrinate, inform, in~ struct, mature, rear, school, teach, train, tutor

educated 1. coached, informed, instructed, nurtured, schooled, taught, tutored **2.** civi~ lized, cultivated, cultured, enlightened, ex~ perienced, informed, knowledgeable, learn~ ed, lettered, literary, polished, refined, tasteful
Antonyms (*sense 1*) ignorant, illiterate, un~ educated, unlettered, unread, unschooled, untaught (*sense 2*) benighted, lowbrow, phil~ istine, uncultivated, uncultured, uneducated

education breeding, civilization, coaching, cultivation, culture, development, disci~ pline, drilling, edification, enlightenment, erudition, improvement, indoctrination, in~ struction, knowledge, nurture, scholarship, schooling, teaching, training, tuition, tutor~ ing

educational cultural, didactic, edifying, educative, enlightening, heuristic, improv~ ing, informative, instructive

educative didactic, edifying, educational, enlightening, heuristic, improving, in~ formative, instructive

eerie awesome, creepy (*Inf.*), eldritch (*Poet~ ic*), fearful, frightening, ghostly, mysterious, scary (*Inf.*), spectral, spooky (*Inf.*), strange, uncanny, unearthly, uneasy, weird

efface 1. annihilate, blot out, cancel, cross out, delete, destroy, dim, eradicate, erase, excise, expunge, extirpate, obliterate, raze, rub out, wipe out **2.** *Of oneself* be modest (bashful, diffident, retiring, timid, unasser~ tive), humble, lower, make inconspicuous, withdraw

effect *n.* **1.** aftermath, conclusion, conse~ quence, event, fruit, issue, outcome, result, upshot **2.** clout (*Inf.*), effectiveness, efficacy, efficiency, fact, force, influence, power, reality, strength, use, validity, vigour, weight **3.** drift, essence, impact, import, impression, meaning, purport, purpose, sense, significance, tenor **4.** action, enforcement, execution, force, implementation, operation **5. in effect** actually, effectively, essentially, for practical purposes, in actuality, in fact, in reality, in truth, really, to all intents and purposes, virtually **6. take effect** become operative, begin, come into force, produce results, work ~*v.* **7.** accomplish, achieve, actuate, bring about, carry out, cause, complete, consummate, create, effectuate, execute, fulfil, give rise to, initiate, make, perform, produce

effective 1. able, active, adequate, capable, competent, effectual, efficacious, efficient, energetic, operative, productive, serviceable, useful **2.** cogent, compelling, convincing, emphatic, forceful, forcible, impressive, moving, persuasive, potent, powerful, striking, telling **3.** active, actual, current, in effect, in execution, in force, in operation, operative, real
Antonyms feeble, futile, inactive, inadequate, incompetent, ineffective, ineffectual, inefficient, inoperative, insufficient, powerless, tame, unimpressive, unproductive, useless, vain, weak, worthless

effectiveness bottom, capability, clout (*Inf.*), cogency, effect, efficacy, efficiency, force, influence, potency, power, strength, success, use, validity, vigour, weight

effects belongings, chattels, furniture, gear, goods, movables, paraphernalia, possessions, property, things, trappings

effeminacy delicacy, femininity, softness, tenderness, unmanliness, weakness, womanishness, womanliness

effeminate camp (*Inf.*), delicate, feminine, poofy (*Sl.*), sissy, soft, tender, unmanly, weak, wimpish *or* wimpy (*Inf.*), womanish, womanlike, womanly
Antonyms butch (*Sl.*), he-man (*Inf.*), macho, manly, virile

effervesce bubble, ferment, fizz, foam, froth, sparkle

effervescence 1. bubbling, ferment, fermentation, fizz, foam, foaming, froth, frothing, sparkle **2.** animation, brio, buoyancy, ebullience, enthusiasm, excitedness, excitement, exhilaration, exuberance, gaiety, high spirits, liveliness, pizzazz *or* pizazz (*Inf.*), vim (*Sl.*), vitality, vivacity, zing (*Inf.*)

effervescent 1. bubbling, bubbly, carbonated, fermenting, fizzing, fizzy, foaming, foamy, frothing, frothy, sparkling **2.** animated, bubbly, buoyant, ebullient, enthusiastic, excited, exhilarated, exuberant, gay,

in high spirits, irrepressible, lively, merry, vital, vivacious, zingy (*Inf.*)
Antonyms boring, dull, flat, flavourless, insipid, jejune, lacklustre, lifeless, spiritless, stale, unexciting, vapid, watery, weak

effete 1. corrupt, debased, decadent, decayed, decrepit, degenerate, dissipated, enervated, enfeebled, feeble, ineffectual, overrefined, spoiled, weak **2.** burnt out, drained, enervated, exhausted, played out, spent, used up, wasted, worn out **3.** barren, fruitless, infecund, infertile, sterile, unfruitful, unproductive, unprolific

efficacious active, adequate, capable, competent, effective, effectual, efficient, energetic, operative, potent, powerful, productive, serviceable, successful, useful
Antonyms abortive, futile, ineffective, ineffectual, inefficacious, unavailing, unproductive, unsuccessful, useless

efficacy ability, capability, competence, effect, effectiveness, efficaciousness, efficiency, energy, force, influence, potency, power, strength, success, use, vigour, virtue, weight

efficiency ability, adeptness, capability, competence, economy, effectiveness, efficacy, power, productivity, proficiency, readiness, skilfulness, skill

efficient able, adept, businesslike, capable, competent, economic, effective, effectual, organized, powerful, productive, proficient, ready, skilful, well-organized, workmanlike
Antonyms cowboy (*Inf.*), disorganized, incompetent, ineffectual, inefficient, inept, slipshod, sloppy, unbusinesslike, unproductive, wasteful

effigy dummy, figure, guy, icon, idol, image, likeness, picture, portrait, representation, statue

effluent *n.* **1.** effluvium, pollutant, sewage, waste **2.** discharge, effluence, efflux, emanation, emission, exhalation, flow, issue, outflow, outpouring ~*adj.* **3.** discharged, emanating, emitted, outflowing

effort 1. application, endeavour, energy, exertion, force, labour, pains, power, strain, stress, stretch, striving, struggle, toil, travail (*Literary*), trouble, work **2.** attempt, endeavour, essay, go (*Inf.*), shot (*Inf.*), stab (*Inf.*), try **3.** accomplishment, achievement, act, creation, deed, feat, job, product, production

effortless easy, easy-peasy (*Sl.*), facile, painless, simple, smooth, uncomplicated, undemanding, untroublesome
Antonyms demanding, difficult, formidable, hard, onerous, uphill

effulgent beaming, blazing, bright, brilliant, dazzling, flaming, fluorescent, fulgent (*Poetic*), glowing, incandescent, lucent, luminous, lustrous, radiant, refulgent (*Liter~ary*), resplendent, shining, splendid, vivid

effusion 1. discharge, effluence, efflux, emission, gush, issue, outflow, outpouring, shedding, stream **2.** address, outpouring, speech, talk, utterance, writing

effusive demonstrative, ebullient, enthusi~astic, expansive, extravagant, exuberant, free-flowing, fulsome, gushing, lavish, overflowing, profuse, talkative, unreserved, unrestrained, wordy

egg on encourage, exhort, goad, incite, prod, prompt, push, spur, urge
Antonyms deter, discourage, dissuade, hold back, put off, talk out of

egocentric egoistic, egoistical, egotistic, egotistical, self-centred, selfish

egoism egocentricity, egomania, egotism, narcissism, self-absorption, self-centredness, self-importance, self-interest, selfishness, self-love, self-regard, self-seeking

egoist egomaniac, egotist, narcissist, self-seeker

egoistic, egoistical egocentric, egoma~niacal, egotistic, egotistical, full of oneself, narcissistic, self-absorbed, self-centred, self-important, self-seeking

egotism conceitedness, egocentricity, ego~ism, egomania, narcissism, self-admiration, self-centredness, self-conceit, self-esteem, self-importance, self-love, self-praise, su~periority, vainglory, vanity

egotist bighead (*Inf.*), blowhard (*Inf.*), boaster, braggadocio, braggart, egoist, ego~maniac, self-admirer, swaggerer

egotistic, egotistical boasting, bragging, conceited, egocentric, egoistic, egoistical, egomaniacal, full of oneself, narcissistic, opinionated, self-admiring, self-centred, self-important, superior, vain, vainglorious

egress departure, emergence, escape, exit, exodus, issue, outlet, passage out, vent, way out, withdrawal

eject 1. cast out, discharge, disgorge, emit, expel, spew, spout, throw out, vomit **2.** banish, boot out (*Inf.*), bounce (*Sl.*), deport, dispossess, drive out, evacuate, evict, exile, expel, give the bum's rush (*Sl.*), oust, rel~egate, remove, show one the door, throw out, throw out on one's ear (*Inf.*), turn out **3.** discharge, dislodge, dismiss, fire (*Inf.*), get rid of, kick out (*Inf.*), oust, sack (*Inf.*), throw out

ejection 1. casting out, disgorgement, ex~pulsion, spouting, throwing out **2.** banish~ment, deportation, dispossession, evacu~ation, eviction, exile, expulsion, ouster (*Law*), removal **3.** discharge, dislodgement, dismissal, firing (*Inf.*), sacking (*Inf.*), the boot (*Sl.*), the sack (*Inf.*)

eke out 1. be economical with, be frugal with, be sparing with, economize on, hus~band, stretch out **2.** add to, enlarge, in~crease, make up (with), supplement

elaborate *adj.* **1.** careful, detailed, exact, intricate, laboured, minute, painstaking, perfected, precise, skilful, studied, thorough **2.** complex, complicated, decorated, de~tailed, extravagant, fancy, fussy, involved, ornamented, ornate, ostentatious, showy ~*v.* **3.** add detail, amplify, complicate, decorate, develop, devise, embellish, en~hance, enlarge, expand (upon), flesh out, garnish, improve, ornament, polish, prod~uce, refine, work out
Antonyms *adj.* basic, minimal, modest, plain, simple, unadorned, unembellished, unfussy ~*v.* abbreviate, condense, put in a nutshell, reduce to essentials, simplify, streamline, summarize, truncate

elapse glide by, go, go by, lapse, pass, pass by, roll by, roll on, slip away, slip by

elastic 1. ductile, flexible, plastic, pliable, pliant, resilient, rubbery, springy, stretch~able, stretchy, supple, tensile, yielding **2.** accommodating, adaptable, adjustable, complaisant, compliant, flexible, supple, tolerant, variable, yielding **3.** bouncy, buoyant, irrepressible, resilient
Antonyms firm, immovable, inflexible, in~tractable, obdurate, resolute, rigid, set, stiff, strict, stringent, unyielding

elated animated, blissful, cheered, cock-a-hoop, delighted, ecstatic, elevated, euphoric, excited, exhilarated, exultant, gleeful, in high spirits, joyful, joyous, jubilant, over~joyed, over the moon (*Inf.*), proud, puffed up, rapt, roused
Antonyms dejected, depressed, discouraged, dispirited, downcast, down in the dumps (*Inf.*), miserable, sad, unhappy, woebegone

elation bliss, delight, ecstasy, euphoria, ex~altation, exhilaration, exultation, glee, high spirits, joy, joyfulness, joyousness, jubila~tion, rapture

elbow *n.* **1.** angle, bend, corner, joint, turn **2. at one's elbow** at hand, close by, handy, near, to hand, within reach **3. out at elbow(s)** beggarly, down at heel, impov~erished, in rags, ragged, seedy, shabby, tat~tered **4. rub elbows with** associate, frat~ernize, hang out (*Inf.*), hobnob, mingle, mix, socialize **5. up to the elbows** absorbed, busy, engaged, engrossed, immersed, occu~pied, tied up, up to the ears, wrapped up ~*v.* **6.** bump, crowd, hustle, jostle, knock, nudge, push, shoulder, shove

elbowroom freedom, latitude, leeway, play, room, scope, space

elder *adj.* **1.** ancient, earlier born, first-born, older, senior ~*n.* **2.** older person, senior **3.**

Presbyterianism church official, office bear~
er, presbyter

elect 1. *v.* appoint, choose, decide upon,
designate, determine, opt for, pick, pick out,
prefer, select, settle on, vote **2.** *adj.* choice,
chosen, elite, hand-picked, picked, pref~
erred, select, selected

election appointment, choice, choosing, de~
cision, determination, judgment, preference,
selection, vote, voting

elector chooser, constituent, selector, voter

electric *Fig.* charged, dynamic, exciting,
rousing, stimulating, stirring, tense, thrill~
ing

electrify *Fig.* amaze, animate, astonish,
astound, excite, fire, galvanize, invigorate,
jolt, rouse, shock, startle, stimulate, stir,
take one's breath away, thrill
Antonyms be tedious, bore, fatigue, jade,
send to sleep, weary

elegance, elegancy 1. beauty, courtli~
ness, dignity, exquisiteness, gentility, grace,
gracefulness, grandeur, luxury, polish, po~
liteness, refinement, sumptuousness **2.** dis~
cernment, distinction, propriety, style, taste

elegant 1. à la mode, artistic, beautiful,
chic, choice, comely, courtly, cultivated,
delicate, exquisite, fashionable, fine, gen~
teel, graceful, handsome, luxurious, modish,
nice, polished, refined, stylish, sumptuous,
tasteful **2.** appropriate, apt, clever, effec~
tive, ingenious, neat, simple
Antonyms (*sense 1*) awkward, clumsy,
coarse, gauche, graceless, inelegant, mis~
shapen, plain, tasteless, tawdry, ugly, un~
couth, undignified, ungraceful, unrefined

elegy coronach (*Scot. & Irish*), dirge, keen,
lament, plaint (*Archaic*), requiem, threnody

element 1. basis, component, constituent,
essential factor, factor, feature, hint, ingre~
dient, member, part, section, subdivision,
trace, unit **2.** domain, environment, field,
habitat, medium, milieu, sphere

elementary 1. clear, easy, facile, plain, ru~
dimentary, simple, straightforward, un~
complicated **2.** basic, bog-standard (*Inf.*),
elemental, fundamental, initial, introduc~
tory, original, primary, rudimentary
Antonyms advanced, complex, complicated,
higher, highly-developed, progressive, sec~
ondary, sophisticated

elements 1. basics, essentials, foundations,
fundamentals, principles, rudiments **2.** at~
mospheric conditions, atmospheric forces,
powers of nature, weather

elevate 1. heighten, hoist, lift, lift up, raise,
uplift, upraise **2.** advance, aggrandize, ex~
alt, prefer, promote, upgrade **3.** animate,
boost, brighten, buoy up, cheer, elate, ex~
cite, exhilarate, hearten, lift up, perk up,

raise, rouse, uplift **4.** augment, boost,
heighten, increase, intensify, magnify, swell

elevated 1. dignified, exalted, grand, high,
high-flown, high-minded, inflated, lofty, no~
ble, sublime **2.** animated, bright, cheerful,
cheery, elated, excited, exhilarated, gleeful,
in high spirits, overjoyed
Antonyms (*sense 1*) humble, lowly, modest,
simple

elevation 1. altitude, height **2.** acclivity,
eminence, height, hill, hillock, mountain,
rise, rising ground **3.** exaltedness, gran~
deur, loftiness, nobility, nobleness, sublim~
ity **4.** advancement, aggrandizement, exal~
tation, preferment, promotion, upgrading

elicit bring forth, bring out, bring to light,
call forth, cause, derive, draw out, educe,
evoke, evolve, exact, extort, extract, give
rise to, obtain, wrest

eligible acceptable, appropriate, desirable,
fit, preferable, proper, qualified, suitable,
suited, worthy
Antonyms inappropriate, ineligible, unac~
ceptable, unqualified, unsuitable, unsuited

eliminate 1. cut out, dispose of, do away
with, eradicate, exterminate, get rid of, re~
move, stamp out, take out **2.** axe (*Inf.*), dis~
pense with, disregard, drop, eject, exclude,
expel, ignore, knock out, leave out, omit,
put out, reject, throw out **3.** *Sl.* annihilate,
blow away (*Sl., chiefly U.S.*), bump off (*Sl.*),
kill, liquidate, murder, rub out (*U.S. sl.*),
slay, take out (*Sl.*), terminate, waste (*Inf.*)

elite 1. *n.* aristocracy, best, cream, *crème de
la crème*, elect, flower, gentry, high society,
nobility, pick, upper class **2.** *adj.* aristo~
cratic, best, choice, crack (*Sl.*), elect, exclu~
sive, first-class, noble, pick, selected,
upper-class
Antonyms *n.* dregs, hoi polloi, rabble, riff~
raff

elocution articulation, declamation, deliv~
ery, diction, enunciation, oratory, pronun~
ciation, public speaking, rhetoric, speech,
speechmaking, utterance, voice production

elongate draw out, extend, lengthen, make
longer, prolong, protract, stretch

elope abscond, bolt, decamp, disappear, es~
cape, leave, run away, run off, slip away,
steal away

eloquence expression, expressiveness,
fluency, forcefulness, oratory, persuasive~
ness, rhetoric, way with words

eloquent 1. articulate, fluent, forceful,
graceful, moving, persuasive, silver-
tongued, stirring, well-expressed **2.** expres~
sive, meaningful, pregnant, revealing, sug~
gestive, telling, vivid
Antonyms faltering, halting, hesitant, inar~

ticulate, speechless, stumbling, tongue-tied, wordless

elsewhere abroad, absent, away, hence (*Archaic*), in *or* to another place, not here, not present, somewhere else

elucidate annotate, clarify, clear up, explain, explicate, expound, gloss, illuminate, illustrate, interpret, make plain, shed *or* throw light upon, spell out, unfold

elucidation annotation, clarification, comment, commentary, explanation, explication, exposition, gloss, illumination, illustration, interpretation

elude 1. avoid, body-swerve (*Scot.*), circumvent, dodge, duck (*Inf.*), escape, evade, flee, get away from, outrun, shirk, shun **2.** baffle, be beyond (someone), confound, escape, foil, frustrate, puzzle, stump, thwart

elusive 1. difficult to catch, shifty, slippery, tricky **2.** baffling, fleeting, indefinable, intangible, puzzling, subtle, transient, transitory **3.** ambiguous, deceitful, deceptive, elusory, equivocal, evasive, fallacious, fraudulent, illusory, misleading, oracular, unspecific

emaciated atrophied, attenuate, attenuated, cadaverous, gaunt, haggard, lank, lean, macilent (*Rare*), meagre, pinched, scrawny, skeletal, thin, undernourished, wasted

emaciation atrophy, attenuation, gauntness, haggardness, leanness, meagreness, scrawniness, thinness, wasting away

emanate 1. arise, come forth, derive, emerge, flow, issue, originate, proceed, spring, stem **2.** discharge, emit, exhale, give off, give out, issue, radiate, send forth

emanation 1. arising, derivation, emergence, flow, origination, proceeding **2.** discharge, effluent, efflux, effusion, emission, exhalation, radiation

emancipate deliver, discharge, disencumber, disenthral, enfranchise, free, liberate, manumit, release, set free, unbridle, unchain, unfetter, unshackle
Antonyms bind, capture, enchain, enslave, enthral, fetter, shackle, subjugate, yoke

emancipation deliverance, discharge, enfranchisement, freedom, liberation, liberty, manumission, release
Antonyms bondage, captivity, confinement, detention, enthralment, imprisonment, servitude, slavery, thraldom

embalm 1. mummify, preserve **2.** *Of memories* cherish, consecrate, conserve, enshrine, immortalize, store, treasure **3.** *Poetic* make fragrant, perfume, scent

embargo 1. *n.* ban, bar, barrier, block, blockage, boycott, check, hindrance, impediment, interdict, interdiction, prohibition, proscription, restraint, restriction,

stoppage **2.** *v.* ban, bar, block, boycott, check, impede, interdict, prohibit, proscribe, restrict, stop

embark 1. board ship, go aboard, put on board, take on board, take ship **2.** *With on or* **upon** begin, broach, commence, engage, enter, initiate, launch, plunge into, set about, set out, start, take up, undertake
Antonyms (*sense 1*) alight, arrive, get off, go ashore, land, step out of

embarrass abash, chagrin, confuse, discomfit, discompose, disconcert, discountenance, distress, faze, fluster, mortify, put out of countenance, shame, show up (*Inf.*)

embarrassing awkward, blush-making, compromising, cringe-making (*Brit. inf.*), discomfiting, disconcerting, distressing, humiliating, mortifying, sensitive, shameful, shaming, touchy, tricky, uncomfortable

embarrassment 1. awkwardness, bashfulness, chagrin, confusion, discomfiture, discomposure, distress, humiliation, mortification, self-consciousness, shame, showing up (*Inf.*) **2.** bind (*Inf.*), difficulty, mess, pickle (*Inf.*), predicament, scrape (*Inf.*) **3.** excess, overabundance, superabundance, superfluity, surfeit, surplus

embellish adorn, beautify, bedeck, deck, decorate, dress up, elaborate, embroider, enhance, enrich, exaggerate, festoon, garnish, gild, grace, ornament, tart up (*Sl.*), varnish

embellishment adornment, decoration, elaboration, embroidery, enhancement, enrichment, exaggeration, gilding, ornament, ornamentation, trimming

embezzle abstract, appropriate, defalcate (*Law*), filch, have one's hand in the till (*Inf.*), misapply, misappropriate, misuse, peculate, pilfer, purloin, rip off (*Sl.*), steal

embezzlement abstraction, appropriation, defalcation (*Law*), filching, fraud, larceny, misapplication, misappropriation, misuse, peculation, pilferage, pilfering, purloining, stealing, theft, thieving

embitter 1. alienate, anger, disaffect, disillusion, envenom, make bitter *or* resentful, poison, sour **2.** aggravate, exacerbate, exasperate, worsen

emblazon 1. adorn, blazon, colour, decorate, embellish, illuminate, ornament, paint **2.** crack up (*Inf.*), extol, glorify, laud (*Literary*), praise, proclaim, publicize, publish, trumpet

emblem badge, crest, device, figure, image, insignia, mark, representation, sigil (*Rare*), sign, symbol, token, type

embodiment 1. bodying forth, epitome, example, exemplar, exemplification, expression, incarnation, incorporation, manifesta~

tion, personification, realization, reification, representation, symbol, type **2.** bringing together, codification, collection, combina~ tion, comprehension, concentration, con~ solidation, inclusion, incorporation, inte~ gration, organization, systematization

embolden animate, cheer, encourage, fire, hearten, inflame, inspirit, invigorate, nerve, reassure, rouse, stimulate, stir, strengthen, vitalize

embrace *v.* **1.** clasp, cuddle, encircle, en~ fold, grasp, hold, hug, seize, squeeze, take *or* hold in one's arms **2.** accept, adopt, avail oneself of, espouse, grab, make use of, re~ ceive, seize, take up, welcome **3.** compre~ hend, comprise, contain, cover, deal with, embody, enclose, encompass, include, in~ volve, provide for, subsume, take in, take into account ~*n.* **4.** canoodle (*Sl.*), clasp, clinch (*Sl.*), cuddle, hug, squeeze

embroil complicate, compromise, confound, confuse, disorder, disturb, encumber, en~ mesh, ensnare, entangle, implicate, in~ criminate, involve, mire, mix up, muddle, perplex, trouble

embryo beginning, germ, nucleus, root, ru~ diment

embryonic beginning, early, germinal, im~ mature, inchoate, incipient, primary, rudi~ mentary, seminal, undeveloped
Antonyms advanced, developed, progres~ sive

emend amend, correct, edit, improve, recti~ fy, redact, revise

emendation amendment, correction, edit~ ing, improvement, rectification, redaction, revision

emerge **1.** appear, arise, become visible, come forth, come into view, come out, come up, emanate, issue, proceed, rise, spring up, surface **2.** become apparent, become known, come out, come to light, crop up, develop, materialize, transpire, turn up
Antonyms depart, disappear, enter, fade, fall, recede, retreat, sink, submerge, vanish from sight, wane, withdraw

emergence advent, apparition, appearance, arrival, coming, dawn, development, disclo~ sure, emanation, issue, materialization, rise

emergency crisis, danger, difficulty, exi~ gency, extremity, necessity, panic stations (*Inf.*), pass, pinch, plight, predicament, quandary, scrape (*Inf.*), strait

emigrate migrate, move, move abroad, re~ move

emigration departure, exodus, migration, removal

eminence **1.** celebrity, dignity, distinction, esteem, fame, greatness, illustriousness, importance, notability, note, pre-eminence,

prestige, prominence, rank, renown, repu~ tation, repute, superiority **2.** elevation, height, high ground, hill, hillock, knoll, rise, summit

eminent big-time (*Inf.*), celebrated, con~ spicuous, distinguished, elevated, esteemed, exalted, famous, grand, great, high, high-ranking, illustrious, important, major league (*Inf.*), notable, noted, noteworthy, outstanding, paramount, pre-eminent, pres~ tigious, prominent, renowned, signal, su~ perior, well-known
Antonyms anonymous, commonplace, infa~ mous, lowly, ordinary, undistinguished, unheard-of, unimportant, unknown, unre~ markable, unsung

eminently conspicuously, exceedingly, ex~ ceptionally, extremely, greatly, highly, no~ tably, outstandingly, prominently, remark~ ably, signally, strikingly, surpassingly, well

emission diffusion, discharge, ejaculation, ejection, emanation, exhalation, exudation, issuance, issue, radiation, shedding, trans~ mission, utterance, venting

emit breathe forth, cast out, diffuse, dis~ charge, eject, emanate, exhale, exude, give off, give out, give vent to, issue, radiate, send forth, send out, shed, throw out, transmit, utter, vent
Antonyms absorb, assimilate, consume, de~ vour, digest, drink in, incorporate, ingest, re~ ceive, soak up, suck up, take in

emolument benefit, compensation, earn~ ings, fee, gain, hire, pay, payment, profits, recompense, remuneration, return, reward, salary, stipend, wages

emotion agitation, ardour, excitement, feeling, fervour, passion, perturbation, sen~ sation, sentiment, vehemence, warmth

emotional **1.** demonstrative, excitable, feeling, hot-blooded, passionate, responsive, sensitive, sentimental, susceptible, tem~ peramental, tender, warm **2.** affecting, emotive, exciting, heart-warming, moving, pathetic, poignant, sentimental, stirring, tear-jerking (*Inf.*), thrilling, touching **3.** ar~ dent, enthusiastic, fervent, fervid, fiery, flaming, heated, impassioned, passionate, roused, stirred, zealous
Antonyms apathetic, cold, detached, dis~ passionate, insensitive, phlegmatic, unde~ monstrative, unemotional, unenthusiastic, unexcitable, unfeeling, unmoved, unruffled, unsentimental

emotive **1.** argumentative, controversial, delicate, sensitive, touchy **2.** affecting, emotional, exciting, heart-warming, moving, pathetic, poignant, sentimental, stirring, tear-jerking (*Inf.*), thrilling, touching **3.** ar~ dent, emotional, enthusiastic, fervent, fer~

vid, fiery, heated, impassioned, passionate, roused, stirred, zealous

emphasis accent, accentuation, attention, decidedness, force, importance, impressive~ ness, insistence, intensity, moment, posi~ tiveness, power, pre-eminence, priority, prominence, significance, strength, stress, underscoring, weight

emphasize accent, accentuate, dwell on, give priority to, highlight, insist on, lay stress on, play up, press home, put the ac~ cent on, stress, underline, underscore, weight
Antonyms gloss over, make light of, make little of, minimize, play down, soft-pedal (*Inf.*), underplay

emphatic absolute, categorical, certain, de~ cided, definite, direct, distinct, earnest, en~ ergetic, forceful, forcible, important, im~ pressive, insistent, marked, momentous, positive, powerful, pronounced, resounding, significant, striking, strong, telling, un~ equivocal, unmistakable, vigorous
Antonyms commonplace, equivocal, hesi~ tant, insignificant, tame, tentative, uncertain, undecided, unremarkable, unsure, weak

empire 1. commonwealth, domain, im~ perium (*Rare*), kingdom, realm 2. author~ ity, command, control, dominion, govern~ ment, power, rule, sovereignty, supremacy, sway

empirical, empiric experiential, experi~ mental, first-hand, observed, practical, pragmatic
Antonyms academic, assumed, conjectural, hypothetical, putative, speculative, theoretic, theoretical

emplacement 1. location, lodgment, plat~ form, position, site, situation, station 2. placement, placing, positioning, putting in place, setting up, stationing

employ *v.* 1. commission, engage, enlist, hire, retain, take on 2. engage, fill, keep busy, make use of, occupy, spend, take up, use up 3. apply, bring to bear, exercise, ex~ ert, make use of, ply, put to use, use, utilize ~*n.* 4. employment, engagement, hire, ser~ vice

employed active, busy, engaged, in a job, in employment, in work, occupied, working
Antonyms idle, jobless, laid off, on the dole (*Brit. inf.*), out of a job, out of work, redundant, unoccupied

employee hand, job-holder, staff member, wage-earner, worker, workman

employer boss (*Inf.*), business, company, establishment, firm, gaffer (*Inf., chiefly Brit.*), organization, outfit (*Inf.*), owner, pat~ ron, proprietor

employment 1. engagement, enlistment,

hire, retaining, taking on 2. application, exercise, exertion, use, utilization 3. avo~ cation (*Archaic*), business, calling, craft, employ, job, line, métier, occupation, pro~ fession, pursuit, service, trade, vocation, work

emporium bazaar, market, mart, shop, sto~ re, warehouse

empower allow, authorize, commission, delegate, enable, entitle, license, permit, qualify, sanction, warrant

emptiness 1. bareness, blankness, desertedness, desolation, destitution, va~ cancy, vacuum, void, waste 2. aimlessness, banality, barrenness, frivolity, futility, hol~ lowness, inanity, ineffectiveness, meaning~ lessness, purposelessness, senselessness, silliness, unreality, unsatisfactoriness, un~ substantiality, vainness, valuelessness, vanity, worthlessness 3. cheapness, hol~ lowness, idleness, insincerity, triviality, trivialness 4. absentness, blankness, expressionlessness, unintelligence, vacancy, vacantness, vacuity, vacuousness 5. *Inf.* desire, hunger, ravening

empty *adj.* 1. bare, blank, clear, deserted, desolate, destitute, hollow, unfurnished, uninhabited, unoccupied, untenanted, va~ cant, void, waste 2. aimless, banal, bootless, frivolous, fruitless, futile, hollow, inane, in~ effective, meaningless, purposeless, sense~ less, silly, unreal, unsatisfactory, unsub~ stantial, vain, valueless, worthless 3. cheap, hollow, idle, insincere, trivial 4. absent, blank, expressionless, unintelligent, vacant, vacuous 5. *Inf.* famished, hungry, ravenous, starving (*Inf.*), unfed, unfilled ~*v.* 6. clear, consume, deplete, discharge, drain, dump, evacuate, exhaust, gut, pour out, unburden, unload, use up, vacate, void
Antonyms *adj.* busy, fulfilled, full, inhabit~ ed, interesting, meaningful, occupied, packed, purposeful, satisfying, serious, significant, stuffed, useful, valuable, worthwhile ~*v.* cram, fill, pack, replenish, stock, stuff

empty-headed brainless, dizzy (*Inf.*), featherbrained, flighty, frivolous, giddy, goofy (*Inf.*), harebrained, inane, scatter~ brained, silly, skittish, vacuous

emulate challenge, compete with, contend with, copy, echo, follow, follow suit, follow the example of, imitate, mimic, rival, take after, vie with

enable allow, authorize, capacitate, com~ mission, empower, entitle, facilitate, fit, li~ cense, permit, prepare, qualify, sanction, warrant
Antonyms bar, block, hinder, impede, ob~ struct, prevent, stop, thwart

enact 1. authorize, command, decree, estab~ lish, legislate, ordain, order, pass, proclaim, ratify, sanction **2.** act, act out, appear as, depict, perform, personate, play, play the part of, portray, represent

enactment 1. authorization, command, commandment, decree, dictate, edict, law, legislation, order, ordinance, proclamation, ratification, regulation, statute **2.** acting, depiction, performance, personation, play-acting, playing, portrayal, representation

enamour absorb, bewitch, captivate, charm, enchant, endear, enrapture, entrance, fascinate, infatuate

enamoured bewitched, captivated, charmed, crazy about (*Inf.*), enchanted, enraptured, entranced, fascinated, fond, infatuated, in love, nuts on *or* about (*Sl.*), smitten, swept off one's feet, taken, wild about (*Inf.*)

encampment base, bivouac, camp, camping ground, campsite, cantonment, quarters, tents

encapsulate, incapsulate abridge, compress, condense, digest, epitomize, précis, summarize, sum up

enchant beguile, bewitch, captivate, cast a spell on, charm, delight, enamour, enrapture, enthral, fascinate, hypnotize, mesmerize, ravish, spellbind

enchanter conjurer, magician, magus, necromancer, sorcerer, spellbinder, warlock, witch, wizard

enchanting alluring, appealing, attractive, bewitching, captivating, charming, delightful, endearing, entrancing, fascinating, lovely, pleasant, ravishing, winsome

enchantment 1. allure, allurement, beguilement, bliss, charm, delight, fascination, hypnotism, mesmerism, rapture, ravishment, transport **2.** charm, conjuration, incantation, magic, necromancy, sorcery, spell, witchcraft, wizardry

enchantress 1. conjurer, lamia, magician, necromancer, sorceress, spellbinder, witch **2.** charmer, *femme fatale*, seductress, siren, vamp (*Inf.*)

enclose, inclose 1. bound, circumscribe, cover, encase, encircle, encompass, environ, fence, hedge, hem in, impound, pen, pound, shut in, wall in, wrap **2.** include, insert, put in, send with **3.** comprehend, contain, embrace, hold, include, incorporate

encompass 1. circle, circumscribe, encircle, enclose, envelop, environ, girdle, hem in, ring, surround **2.** bring about, cause, contrive, devise, effect, manage **3.** admit, comprehend, comprise, contain, cover, embody, embrace, hold, include, incorporate, involve, subsume, take in

encounter *v.* **1.** bump into (*Inf.*), chance upon, come upon, confront, experience,

face, happen on *or* upon, meet, run across, run into (*Inf.*) **2.** attack, clash with, combat, come into conflict with, contend, cross swords with, do battle with, engage, face off (*Sl.*), fight, grapple with, strive, struggle ~*n.* **3.** brush, confrontation, meeting, rendezvous **4.** action, battle, clash, collision, combat, conflict, contest, dispute, engagement, face-off (*Sl.*), fight, head-to-head, run-in (*Inf.*), set to (*Inf.*), skirmish

encourage 1. animate, buoy up, cheer, comfort, console, embolden, hearten, incite, inspire, inspirit, rally, reassure, rouse, stimulate **2.** abet, advance, advocate, aid, boost, egg on, favour, forward, foster, further, help, promote, prompt, spur, strengthen, succour, support, urge
Antonyms daunt, depress, deter, discourage, dishearten, dispirit, dissuade, hinder, inhibit, intimidate, prevent, retard, scare, throw cold water on (*Inf.*)

encouragement advocacy, aid, boost, cheer, consolation, favour, help, incitement, inspiration, inspiritment, promotion, reassurance, security blanket (*Inf.*), stimulation, stimulus, succour, support, urging

encouraging bright, cheerful, cheering, comforting, good, heartening, hopeful, promising, reassuring, rosy, satisfactory, stimulating
Antonyms daunting, depressing, disappointing, discouraging, disheartening, dispiriting, offputting (*Inf.*), unfavourable, unpropitious

encroach appropriate, arrogate, impinge, infringe, intrude, invade, make inroads, overstep, trench, trespass, usurp

encroachment appropriation, arrogation, impingement, incursion, infringement, inroad, intrusion, invasion, trespass, usurpation, violation

encumber burden, clog, cramp, embarrass, hamper, handicap, hinder, impede, incommode, inconvenience, make difficult, obstruct, oppress, overload, retard, saddle, slow down, trammel, weigh down

encumbrance burden, clog, difficulty, drag, embarrassment, handicap, hindrance, impediment, inconvenience, liability, load, millstone, obstacle, obstruction

end *n.* **1.** bound, boundary, edge, extent, extreme, extremity, limit, point, terminus, tip **2.** attainment, cessation, close, closure, completion, conclusion, consequence, consummation, culmination, denouement, ending, expiration, expiry, finale, finish, issue, outcome, resolution, result, sequel, stop, termination, upshot, wind-up **3.** aim, aspiration, design, drift, goal, intent, intention, object, objective, point, purpose, reason **4.** part, piece, portion, responsibility, share,

side **5.** bit, butt, fragment, leftover, odd~ment, remainder, remnant, scrap, stub, tag end, tail end **6.** annihilation, death, demise, destruction, dissolution, doom, extermina~tion, extinction, ruin, ruination **7. the end** *Sl.* beyond endurance, insufferable, intoler~able, the final blow, the last straw, the limit (*Inf.*), the worst, too much (*Inf.*), unbear~able, unendurable ~*v.* **8.** axe (*Inf.*), bring to an end, cease, close, complete, conclude, culminate, dissolve, expire, finish, resolve, stop, terminate, wind up **9.** abolish, anni~hilate, destroy, exterminate, extinguish, kill, put to death, ruin
Antonyms *n.* beginning, birth, commence~ment, inception, launch, opening, origin, out~set, prelude, source, start ~*v.* begin, come into being, commence, initiate, launch, originate, start

endanger compromise, hazard, imperil, jeopardize, put at risk, put in danger, risk, threaten
Antonyms defend, guard, preserve, protect, safeguard, save, secure

endear attach, attract, bind, captivate, charm, engage, win

endearing adorable, attractive, captivating, charming, cute, engaging, lovable, sweet, winning, winsome

endearment 1. affectionate utterance, lov~ing word, sweet nothing **2.** affection, at~tachment, fondness, love

endeavour 1. *n.* aim, attempt, crack (*Inf.*), effort, enterprise, essay, go (*Inf.*), shot (*Inf.*), stab (*Inf.*), trial, try, undertaking, venture **2.** *v.* aim, aspire, attempt, bend over back~wards (*Inf.*), break one's neck (*Inf.*), bust a gut (*Inf.*), do one's best, do one's damnedest (*Inf.*), essay, give it one's all (*Inf.*), give it one's best shot (*Inf.*), go for broke (*Sl.*), go for it (*Inf.*), have a go (crack (*Inf.*), shot (*Inf.*), stab (*Inf.*)) (*Inf.*), knock oneself out (*Inf.*), labour, make an all-out effort (*Inf.*), make an effort, rupture oneself (*Inf.*), strive, struggle, take pains, try, undertake

ending catastrophe, cessation, close, com~pletion, conclusion, consummation, culmi~nation, denouement, end, finale, finish, resolution, termination, wind-up
Antonyms birth, commencement, inaugu~ration, inception, onset, opening, origin, pref~ace, source, start, starting point

endless 1. boundless, ceaseless, constant, continual, eternal, everlasting, immortal, incessant, infinite, interminable, limitless, measureless, perpetual, unbounded, unbro~ken, undying, unending, uninterrupted, un~limited **2.** interminable, monotonous, over~long **3.** continuous, unbroken, undivided, whole
Antonyms bounded, brief, circumscribed,

finite, limited, passing, restricted, temporary, terminable, transient, transitory

endorse, indorse 1. advocate, affirm, ap~prove, authorize, back, champion, confirm, espouse, favour, prescribe, promote, ratify, recommend, sanction, subscribe to, support, sustain, vouch for, warrant **2.** countersign, sign, superscribe, undersign

endorsement, indorsement 1. com~ment, countersignature, qualification, sig~nature, superscription **2.** advocacy, affir~mation, approbation, approval, authori~zation, backing, championship, confirma~tion, espousal, favour, fiat, O.K. *or* okay (*Inf.*), promotion, ratification, recommenda~tion, sanction, seal of approval, subscrip~tion to, support, warrant

endow award, bequeath, bestow, confer, donate, endue, enrich, favour, finance, fund, furnish, give, grant, invest, leave, make over, provide, purvey, settle on, supply, will

endowment 1. award, benefaction, be~quest, bestowal, boon, donation, fund, gift, grant, hand-out, income, largess *or* largesse, legacy, presentation, property, provision, revenue, stipend **2.** *Often plural* ability, ap~titude, attribute, capability, capacity, facul~ty, flair, genius, gift, power, qualification, quality, talent

end up 1. become eventually, finish as, finish up, pan out (*Inf.*), turn out to be **2.** arrive finally, come to a halt, fetch up (*Inf.*), finish up, stop, wind up

endurable acceptable, bearable, sufferable, supportable, sustainable, tolerable
Antonyms insufferable, insupportable, in~tolerable, too much (*Inf.*), unbearable, unen~durable

endurance 1. bearing, fortitude, patience, perseverance, persistence, pertinacity, res~ignation, resolution, stamina, staying pow~er, strength, submission, sufferance, tenac~ity, toleration **2.** continuation, continuity, durability, duration, immutability, lasting~ness, longevity, permanence, stability

endure 1. bear, brave, cope with, experi~ence, go through, stand, stick it out (*Inf.*), suffer, support, sustain, take it (*Inf.*), thole (*Scot.*), undergo, weather, withstand **2.** abide, allow, bear, brook, countenance, per~mit, put up with, stand, stick (*Sl.*), stomach, submit to, suffer, swallow, take patiently, tolerate **3.** abide, be durable, continue, hold, last, live, live on, persist, prevail, re~main, stand, stay, survive, wear well

enduring abiding, continuing, durable, eternal, firm, immortal, immovable, imper~ishable, lasting, living, long-lasting, peren~nial, permanent, persistent, persisting, pre~vailing, remaining, steadfast, steady, sur~viving, unfaltering, unwavering

Antonyms brief, ephemeral, fleeting, mo~ mentary, passing, short, short-lived, tempo~ rary, transient, transitory

enemy adversary, antagonist, competitor, foe, opponent, rival, the opposition, the other side
Antonyms ally, confederate, friend, sup~ porter

energetic active, animated, brisk, dynamic, forceful, forcible, high-powered, indefati~ gable, lively, potent, powerful, spirited, strenuous, strong, tireless, vigorous, zippy (*Inf.*)
Antonyms debilitated, dull, enervated, in~ active, lazy, lethargic, lifeless, listless, slow, sluggish, torpid, weak

energy activity, animation, ardour, brio, drive, efficiency, élan, exertion, fire, force, forcefulness, get-up-and-go (*Inf.*), go (*Inf.*), intensity, life, liveliness, pep, pluck, power, spirit, stamina, strength, strenuousness, verve, vigour, vim (*Sl.*), vitality, vivacity, zeal, zest, zip (*Inf.*)

enfold, infold clasp, embrace, enclose, en~ compass, envelop, enwrap, fold, hold, hug, shroud, swathe, wrap, wrap up

enforce administer, apply, carry out, co~ erce, compel, constrain, exact, execute, im~ plement, impose, insist on, oblige, pros~ ecute, put in force, put into effect, reinforce, require, urge

enforced compelled, compulsory, con~ strained, dictated, imposed, involuntary, necessary, ordained, prescribed, required, unavoidable, unwilling

enforcement 1. administration, applica~ tion, carrying out, exaction, execution, im~ plementation, imposition, prosecution, re~ inforcement 2. coercion, compulsion, con~ straint, insistence, obligation, pressure, re~ quirement

enfranchise 1. give the vote to, grant suf~ frage to, grant the franchise to, grant voting rights to 2. emancipate, free, liberate, manumit, release, set free

enfranchisement 1. giving the vote, granting suffrage *or* the franchise, granting voting rights 2. emancipation, freedom, freeing, liberating, liberation, manumission, release, setting free

engage 1. appoint, commission, employ, enlist, enrol, hire, retain, take on 2. be~ speak, book, charter, hire, lease, prear~ range, rent, reserve, secure 3. absorb, busy, engross, grip, involve, occupy, preoccupy, tie up 4. allure, arrest, attach, attract, cap~ tivate, catch, charm, draw, enamour, en~ chant, fascinate, fix, gain, win 5. embark on, enter into, join, partake, participate, practise, set about, take part, undertake 6. affiance, agree, betroth (*Archaic*), bind,

commit, contract, covenant, guarantee, ob~ ligate, oblige, pledge, promise, undertake, vouch, vow 7. *Military* assail, attack, com~ bat, come to close quarters with, encounter, face off (*Sl.*), fall on, fight with, give battle to, join battle with, meet, take on 8. acti~ vate, apply, bring into operation, energize, set going, switch on 9. dovetail, interact, interconnect, interlock, join, mesh
Antonyms (*sense 1*) axe (*Inf.*), discharge, dismiss, fire (*Inf.*), give notice to, lay off, oust, remove, sack (*Inf.*)

engaged 1. affianced, betrothed (*Archaic*), pledged, promised, spoken for 2. absorbed, busy, committed, employed, engrossed, in use, involved, occupied, preoccupied, tied up, unavailable
Antonyms available, fancy-free, free, unat~ tached, uncommitted, unengaged

engagement 1. assurance, betrothal, bond, compact, contract, oath, obligation, pact, pledge, promise, troth (*Archaic*), undertaking, vow, word 2. appointment, arrangement, commitment, date, meeting 3. commission, employment, gig (*Inf.*), job, post, situation, stint, work 4. action, battle, combat, conflict, confrontation, contest, en~ counter, face-off (*Sl.*), fight

engaging agreeable, appealing, attractive, captivating, charming, enchanting, fasci~ nating, fetching (*Inf.*), likable *or* likeable, lovable, pleasant, pleasing, winning, win~ some
Antonyms disagreeable, objectionable, ob~ noxious, offensive, repulsive, unattractive, unlikable *or* unlikeable, unlovely, unpleasant

engender 1. beget, breed, bring about, cause, create, excite, foment, generate, give rise to, hatch, incite, induce, instigate, lead to, make, occasion, precipitate, produce, provoke 2. beget, breed, bring forth, father, generate, give birth to, procreate, propa~ gate, sire, spawn

engine 1. machine, mechanism, motor 2. agency, agent, apparatus, appliance, con~ trivance, device, implement, instrument, means, tool, weapon

engineer 1. *n.* architect, contriver, design~ er, deviser, director, inventor, manager, manipulator, originator, planner, schemer 2. *v.* bring about, cause, concoct, contrive, control, create, devise, effect, encompass, finagle (*Inf.*), manage, manoeuvre, master~ mind, originate, plan, plot, scheme, wangle (*Inf.*)

engrave 1. carve, chase, chisel, cut, en~ chase (*Rare*), etch, grave (*Archaic*), inscribe 2. impress, imprint, print 3. embed, fix, impress, imprint, infix, ingrain, lodge

engraving 1. carving, chasing, chiselling, cutting, dry point, enchasing (*Rare*), etch~

ing, inscribing, inscription **2.** block, carv~
ing, etching, inscription, plate, woodcut **3.**
etching, impression, print

engross 1. absorb, arrest, engage, engulf,
hold, immerse, involve, occupy, preoccupy
2. corner, monopolize, sew up (*U.S.*)

engrossed absorbed, captivated, caught up,
deep, enthralled, fascinated, gripped, im~
mersed, intent, intrigued, lost, preoccupied,
rapt, riveted

engrossing absorbing, captivating, com~
pelling, enthralling, fascinating, gripping,
interesting, intriguing, riveting

enhance add to, augment, boost, comple~
ment, elevate, embellish, exalt, heighten,
improve, increase, intensify, lift, magnify,
raise, reinforce, strengthen, swell
Antonyms debase, decrease, depreciate, de~
value, diminish, lower, minimize, reduce,
spoil

enigma conundrum, mystery, problem,
puzzle, riddle, teaser

enigmatic, enigmatical ambiguous,
cryptic, Delphic, doubtful, equivocal, in~
comprehensible, indecipherable, inexpli~
cable, inscrutable, mysterious, obscure,
oracular, perplexing, puzzling, recondite,
sphinxlike, uncertain, unfathomable, unin~
telligible
Antonyms clear, comprehensible, simple,
straightforward, uncomplicated

enjoin 1. advise, bid, call upon, charge,
command, counsel, demand, direct, instruct,
order, prescribe, require, urge, warn **2.**
Law ban, bar, disallow, forbid, interdict,
place an injunction on, preclude, prohibit,
proscribe, restrain

enjoy 1. appreciate, be entertained by, be
pleased with, delight in, like, rejoice in,
relish, revel in, take joy in, take pleasure in
or from **2.** be blessed *or* favoured with, ex~
perience, have, have the benefit of, have the
use of, own, possess, reap the benefits of,
use **3. enjoy oneself** have a ball (*Inf.*),
have a good time, have fun, make merry
Antonyms (*sense 1*) abhor, despise, detest,
dislike, hate, have no taste *or* stomach for,
loathe

enjoyable agreeable, amusing, delectable,
delicious, delightful, entertaining, gratify~
ing, pleasant, pleasing, pleasurable, satisfy~
ing, to one's liking
Antonyms despicable, disagreeable, dis~
pleasing, hateful, loathsome, obnoxious, of~
fensive, repugnant, unenjoyable, unpleasant,
unsatisfying, unsavoury

enjoyment 1. amusement, delectation, de~
light, diversion, entertainment, fun, glad~
ness, gratification, gusto, happiness, indul~
gence, joy, pleasure, recreation, relish, sat~

isfaction, zest **2.** advantage, benefit, exer~
cise, ownership, possession, use

enlarge 1. add to, amplify, augment, blow
up (*Inf.*), broaden, diffuse, dilate, distend,
elongate, expand, extend, grow, heighten,
increase, inflate, lengthen, magnify, make
or grow larger, multiply, stretch, swell,
wax, widen **2.** amplify, descant, develop,
dilate, elaborate, expand, expatiate, give
details
Antonyms abbreviate, abridge, compress,
condense, curtail, decrease, diminish, lessen,
narrow, reduce, shorten, shrink, trim, trun~
cate

enlighten advise, apprise, cause to under~
stand, civilize, counsel, edify, educate, in~
form, instruct, make aware, teach

enlightened aware, broad-minded, civi~
lized, cultivated, educated, informed,
knowledgeable, liberal, literate, open-
minded, reasonable, refined, sophisticated
Antonyms ignorant, narrow-minded,
short-sighted, small-minded, unaware, un~
educated, unenlightened

enlightenment awareness, broad-minded~
ness, civilization, comprehension, cultiva~
tion, edification, education, information,
insight, instruction, knowledge, learning,
literacy, open-mindedness, refinement,
sophistication, teaching, understanding,
wisdom

enlist engage, enrol, enter (into), gather,
join, join up, muster, obtain, procure, re~
cruit, register, secure, sign up, volunteer

enliven animate, brighten, buoy up, cheer,
cheer up, excite, exhilarate, fire, gladden,
hearten, inspire, inspirit, invigorate, pep
up, perk up, quicken, rouse, spark, stimu~
late, vitalize, vivify, wake up
Antonyms chill, dampen, deaden, depress,
put a damper on, repress, subdue

enmity acrimony, animosity, animus, an~
tagonism, antipathy, aversion, bad blood,
bitterness, hate, hatred, hostility, ill will,
malevolence, malice, malignity, rancour,
spite, venom
Antonyms affection, amity, cordiality,
friendliness, friendship, geniality, goodwill,
harmony, love, warmth

ennoble aggrandize, dignify, elevate, en~
hance, exalt, glorify, honour, magnify, raise

ennui boredom, dissatisfaction, lassitude,
listlessness, tedium, the doldrums

enormity 1. atrociousness, atrocity, de~
pravity, disgrace, evilness, heinousness,
monstrousness, nefariousness, outrageous~
ness, turpitude, viciousness, vileness, vil~
lainy, wickedness **2.** abomination, atrocity,
crime, disgrace, evil, horror, monstrosity,
outrage, villainy **3.** *Inf.* enormousness,

greatness, hugeness, immensity, magnitude, massiveness, vastness

enormous 1. astronomic, Brobdingnagian, colossal, elephantine, excessive, gargantuan, gigantic, gross, huge, humongous *or* humungous (*U.S. sl.*), immense, jumbo (*Inf.*), mammoth, massive, monstrous, mountainous, prodigious, titanic, tremendous, vast **2.** *Archaic* abominable, atrocious, depraved, disgraceful, evil, heinous, monstrous, nefarious, odious, outrageous, vicious, vile, villainous, wicked

Antonyms diminutive, dwarf, infinitesimal, insignificant, Lilliputian, little, meagre, microscopic, midget, minute, petite, pint-sized (*Inf.*), small, tiny, trivial, wee

enough 1. *adj.* abundant, adequate, ample, plenty, sufficient **2.** *n.* abundance, adequacy, ample supply, plenty, right amount, sufficiency **3.** *adv.* abundantly, adequately, amply, fairly, moderately, passably, reasonably, satisfactorily, sufficiently, tolerably

enquire 1. ask, query, question, request information, seek information **2.** *Also in~ quire* conduct an inquiry, examine, explore, inspect, investigate, look into, make inquiry, probe, research, scrutinize, search

enquiry 1. query, question **2.** *Also* **inquiry** examination, exploration, inquest, inspection, investigation, probe, research, scrutiny, search, study, survey

enrage aggravate (*Inf.*), anger, exasperate, gall, incense, incite, inflame, infuriate, irritate, madden, make one's blood boil, make one see red (*Inf.*), nark (*Brit., Aust., & N.Z. sl.*), provoke

Antonyms appease, assuage, calm, conciliate, mollify, pacify, placate, soothe

enraged aggravated (*Inf.*), angered, angry, boiling mad, cross, exasperated, fuming, furious, incensed, inflamed, infuriated, irate, irritated, livid (*Inf.*), mad (*Inf.*), raging, raging mad, wild

enrich 1. make rich, make wealthy **2.** aggrandize, ameliorate, augment, cultivate, develop, endow, enhance, improve, refine, supplement **3.** adorn, decorate, embellish, grace, ornament

enrol 1. chronicle, inscribe, list, note, record **2.** accept, admit, engage, enlist, join up, matriculate, recruit, register, sign up *or* on, take on

enrolment acceptance, admission, engagement, enlistment, matriculation, recruitment, registration

en route in transit, on *or* along the way, on the road

ensemble *n.* **1.** aggregate, assemblage, collection, entirety, set, sum, total, totality, whole, whole thing **2.** costume, get-up (*Inf.*), outfit, suit **3.** band, cast, chorus, company, group, supporting cast, troupe ~*adv.* **4.** all at once, all together, as a group, as a whole, at once, at the same time, en masse, in concert

enshrine apotheosize, cherish, consecrate, dedicate, embalm, exalt, hallow, preserve, revere, sanctify, treasure

enshroud cloak, cloud, conceal, cover, enclose, enfold, envelop, enwrap, hide, obscure, pall, shroud, veil, wrap

ensign badge, banner, colours, flag, jack, pennant, pennon, standard, streamer

enslave bind, dominate, enchain, enthral, reduce to slavery, subjugate, yoke

ensue arise, attend, be consequent on, befall, come after, come next, come to pass (*Archaic*), derive, flow, follow, issue, proceed, result, stem, succeed, supervene, turn out *or* up

Antonyms antecede, come first, forerun, go ahead of, go before, introduce, lead, pave the way, precede, usher

ensure, insure 1. certify, confirm, effect, guarantee, make certain, make sure, secure, warrant **2.** guard, make safe, protect, safeguard, secure

entail bring about, call for, cause, demand, encompass, give rise to, impose, involve, lead to, necessitate, occasion, require, result in

entangle 1. catch, compromise, embroil, enmesh, ensnare, entrap, foul, implicate, involve, knot, mat, mix up, ravel, snag, snare, tangle, trammel, trap **2.** bewilder, complicate, confuse, jumble, mix up, muddle, perplex, puzzle, snarl, twist

Antonyms (*sense 1*) detach, disconnect, disengage, disentangle, extricate, free, loose, separate, sever, unfold, unravel, unsnarl, untangle, untwist (*sense 2*) clarify, clear (up), resolve, simplify, work out

entanglement 1. complication, confusion, ensnarement, entrapment, imbroglio (*Obsolete*), involvement, jumble, knot, mesh, mess, mix-up, muddle, snare, snarl-up (*Inf., chiefly Brit.*), tangle, toils, trap **2.** difficulty, embarrassment, imbroglio, involvement, liaison, predicament, tie

enter 1. arrive, come *or* go in *or* into, insert, introduce, make an entrance, pass into, penetrate, pierce **2.** become a member of, begin, commence, commit oneself to, embark upon, enlist, enrol, join, participate in, set about, set out on, sign up, start, take part in, take up **3.** inscribe, list, log, note, record, register, set down, take down **4.** offer, present, proffer, put forward, register, submit, tender

Antonyms depart, drop out, exit, go, issue

from, leave, pull out, resign, retire, take one's leave, withdraw

enterprise 1. adventure, effort, endeavour, essay, operation, plan, programme, project, undertaking, venture **2.** activity, adventurousness, alertness, audacity, bold~ness, daring, dash, drive, eagerness, energy, enthusiasm, get-up-and-go (*Inf.*), gumption (*Inf.*), initiative, pep, push (*Inf.*), readiness, resource, resourcefulness, spirit, vigour, zeal **3.** business, company, concern, estab~lishment, firm, operation

enterprising active, adventurous, alert, audacious, bold, daring, dashing, eager, en~ergetic, enthusiastic, go-ahead, intrepid, keen, ready, resourceful, spirited, stirring, up-and-coming, venturesome, vigorous, zealous

entertain 1. amuse, charm, cheer, delight, divert, occupy, please, recreate (*Rare*), re~gale **2.** accommodate, be host to, harbour, have company, have guests *or* visitors, lodge, put up, show hospitality to, treat **3.** cherish, cogitate on, conceive, consider, contemplate, foster, harbour, hold, imagine, keep in mind, maintain, muse over, ponder, support, think about, think over

entertaining amusing, charming, cheering, delightful, diverting, funny, humorous, in~teresting, pleasant, pleasing, pleasurable, recreative (*Rare*), witty

entertainment amusement, cheer, dis~traction, diversion, enjoyment, fun, good time, leisure activity, pastime, play, pleas~ure, recreation, satisfaction, sport, treat

enthral absorb, beguile, captivate, charm, enchant, enrapture, entrance, fascinate, grip, hold spellbound, hypnotize, intrigue, mesmerize, ravish, rivet, spellbind

enthralling beguiling, captivating, charm~ing, compelling, compulsive, enchanting, entrancing, fascinating, gripping, hypnotiz~ing, intriguing, mesmerizing, riveting, spellbinding

enthusiasm 1. ardour, avidity, devotion, eagerness, earnestness, excitement, fervour, frenzy, interest, keenness, passion, relish, vehemence, warmth, zeal, zest **2.** craze, fad (*Inf.*), hobby, hobbyhorse, interest, mania, passion, rage

enthusiast admirer, aficionado, buff (*Inf.*), devotee, fan, fanatic, fiend (*Inf.*), follower, freak (*Inf.*), lover, supporter, zealot

enthusiastic ardent, avid, devoted, eager, earnest, ebullient, excited, exuberant, fer~vent, fervid, forceful, hearty, keen, lively, passionate, spirited, unqualified, unstinting, vehement, vigorous, warm, wholehearted, zealous
Antonyms apathetic, blasé, bored, cool, dis~passionate, half-hearted, indifferent, noncha~lant, unconcerned, unenthusiastic, uninter~ested

entice allure, attract, beguile, cajole, coax, decoy, draw, inveigle, lead on, lure, per~suade, prevail on, seduce, tempt, wheedle

entire 1. complete, full, gross, total, whole **2.** absolute, full, outright, thorough, total, undiminished, unmitigated, unreserved, unrestricted **3.** intact, perfect, sound, un~broken, undamaged, unmarked, unmarred, whole, without a scratch **4.** continuous, in~tegrated, unbroken, undivided, unified

entirely 1. absolutely, altogether, complete~ly, fully, in every respect, perfectly, thor~oughly, totally, unreservedly, utterly, whol~ly, without exception, without reservation **2.** exclusively, only, solely
Antonyms incompletely, moderately, par~tially, partly, piecemeal, slightly, somewhat, to a certain extent *or* degree

entirety 1. absoluteness, completeness, fullness, totality, undividedness, unity, wholeness **2.** aggregate, sum, total, unity, whole

entitle 1. accredit, allow, authorize, em~power, enable, enfranchise, fit for, license, make eligible, permit, qualify for, warrant **2.** call, characterize, christen, denominate, designate, dub, label, name, style, term, title

entity 1. being, body, creature, existence, individual, object, organism, presence, quantity, substance, thing **2.** essence, es~sential nature, quiddity (*Philosophy*), quin~tessence, real nature

entourage 1. associates, attendants, com~panions, company, cortege, court, escort, followers, following, retainers, retinue, staff, suite, train **2.** ambience, environment, environs, milieu, surroundings

entrails bowels, guts, innards (*Inf.*), insides (*Inf.*), intestines, offal, viscera

entrance[1] *n.* **1.** access, avenue, door, door~way, entry, gate, ingress, inlet, opening, passage, portal, way in **2.** appearance, arri~val, coming in, entry, ingress, introduction **3.** access, admission, admittance, entrée, entry, ingress, permission to enter **4.** be~ginning, commencement, debut, initiation, introduction, outset, start
Antonyms departure, egress, exit, exodus, leave-taking, outlet, way out

entrance[2] *v.* **1.** absorb, bewitch, captivate, charm, delight, enchant, enrapture, enthral, fascinate, gladden, ravish, spellbind, trans~port **2.** hypnotize, mesmerize, put in a trance
Antonyms bore, disenchant, irritate, offend, put off, turn off (*Inf.*)

entrant 1. beginner, convert, initiate, neo~phyte, newcomer, new member, novice, probationer, tyro **2.** candidate, competitor, contestant, entry, participant, player

entreaty appeal, earnest request, exhorta~ tion, importunity, petition, plea, prayer, re~ quest, solicitation, suit, supplication

entrench, intrench 1. construct defences, dig in, dig trenches, fortify **2.** anchor, dig in, embed, ensconce, establish, fix, implant, ingrain, install, lodge, plant, root, seat, set, settle **3.** encroach, impinge, infringe, interlope, intrude, make inroads, trespass

entrenched, intrenched deep-rooted, deep-seated, firm, fixed, indelible, ineradi~ cable, ingrained, rooted, set, unshakable, well-established

entrepreneur businessman, business~ woman, contractor, director, financier, im~ presario, industrialist, magnate, tycoon

entrust, intrust assign, authorize, charge, commend, commit, confide, consign, del~ egate, deliver, give custody of, hand over, invest, trust, turn over

entry 1. appearance, coming in, entering, entrance, initiation, introduction **2.** access, avenue, door, doorway, entrance, gate, in~ gress, inlet, opening, passage, passageway, portal, way in **3.** access, admission, en~ trance, entrée, free passage, permission to enter **4.** account, item, jotting, listing, memo, memorandum, minute, note, record, registration **5.** attempt, candidate, competi~ tor, contestant, effort, entrant, participant, player, submission
Antonyms departure, egress, exit, leave, leave-taking, withdrawal

entwine, intwine braid, embrace, encir~ cle, entwist (*Archaic*), interlace, intertwine, interweave, knit, plait, ravel, surround, twine, twist, weave, wind
Antonyms disentangle, extricate, free, separate, straighten out, undo, unravel, un~ tangle, unwind

enumerate 1. cite, detail, itemize, list, mention, name, quote, recapitulate, recite, recount, rehearse, relate, specify, spell out, tell **2.** add up, calculate, compute, count, number, reckon, sum up, tally, total

enunciate 1. articulate, enounce, pro~ nounce, say, sound, speak, utter, vocalize, voice **2.** declare, proclaim, promulgate, pronounce, propound, publish, state

envelop blanket, cloak, conceal, cover, em~ brace, encase, encircle, enclose, encompass, enfold, engulf, enwrap, hide, obscure, sheathe, shroud, surround, swaddle, swathe, veil, wrap

envelope case, casing, coating, cover, cov~ ering, jacket, sheath, shell, skin, wrapper, wrapping

enviable advantageous, blessed, covetable,

desirable, favoured, fortunate, lucky, much to be desired, privileged
Antonyms disagreeable, painful, thankless, uncomfortable, undesirable, unenviable, un~ pleasant

envious begrudging, covetous, green-eyed, green with envy, grudging, jaundiced, jeal~ ous, malicious, resentful, spiteful

environ beset, besiege, encircle, enclose, encompass, engird, envelop, gird, hem, in~ vest (*Rare*), ring, surround

environment atmosphere, background, conditions, context, domain, element, habi~ tat, locale, medium, milieu, scene, setting, situation, surroundings, territory

environmentalist conservationist, ecolo~ gist, friend of the earth, green

environs district, locality, neighbourhood, outskirts, precincts, purlieus, suburbs, sur~ rounding area, vicinity

envisage 1. conceive (of), conceptualize, contemplate, fancy, imagine, picture, think up, visualize **2.** anticipate, envision, fore~ see, predict, see

envision anticipate, conceive of, contem~ plate, envisage, foresee, predict, see, visual~ ize

envoy agent, ambassador, courier, delegate, deputy, diplomat, emissary, intermediary, legate, messenger, minister, plenipotenti~ ary, representative

envy 1. *n.* covetousness, enviousness, grudge, hatred, ill will, jealousy, malice, malignity, resentfulness, resentment, spite, the green-eyed monster (*Inf.*) **2.** *v.* be envi~ ous (of), begrudge, be jealous (of), covet, grudge, resent

ephemeral brief, evanescent, fleeting, flitting, fugacious, fugitive, impermanent, momentary, passing, short, short-lived, temporary, transient, transitory
Antonyms abiding, durable, enduring, eter~ nal, immortal, lasting, long-lasting, persist~ ing, steadfast

epicure 1. *bon vivant*, epicurean, foodie, gastronome, gourmet **2.** glutton, gourmand, hedonist, sensualist, sybarite, voluptuary

epicurean 1. *adj.* gluttonous, gour~ mandizing, hedonistic, libertine, luscious, lush, luxurious, pleasure-seeking, self-indulgent, sensual, sybaritic, voluptuous **2.** *n. bon vivant*, epicure, foodie, gastronome, gourmet

epidemic 1. *adj.* general, pandemic, pre~ vailing, prevalent, rampant, rife, sweeping, wide-ranging, widespread **2.** *n.* contagion, growth, outbreak, plague, rash, spread, upsurge, wave

epigram aphorism, *bon mot*, quip, witticism

epilogue afterword, coda, concluding speech, conclusion, postscript
Antonyms exordium, foreword, introduction, preamble, preface, prelude, prologue

episode 1. adventure, affair, business, circumstance, escapade, event, experience, happening, incident, matter, occurrence **2.** chapter, instalment, part, passage, scene, section

epistle communication, letter, message, missive, note

epithet appellation, description, designation, moniker *or* monicker (*Sl.*), name, nickname, sobriquet, tag, title

epitome 1. archetype, embodiment, essence, exemplar, norm, personification, quintessence, representation, type, typical example **2.** abbreviation, abridgment, abstract, compendium, condensation, conspectus, contraction, digest, précis, résumé, summary, syllabus, synopsis

epitomize 1. embody, exemplify, illustrate, incarnate, personify, represent, symbolize, typify **2.** abbreviate, abridge, abstract, condense, contract, curtail, cut, encapsulate, précis, reduce, shorten, summarize, synopsize

epoch age, date, era, period, time

equable 1. agreeable, calm, composed, easy-going, even-tempered, imperturbable, level-headed, placid, serene, temperate, unexcitable, unfazed (*Inf.*), unflappable (*Inf.*), unruffled **2.** consistent, constant, even, regular, smooth, stable, steady, temperate, tranquil, unchanging, uniform, unvarying
Antonyms changeable, excitable, fitful, inconsistent, irregular, nervous, temperamental, uneven, unpredictable, unstable, volatile

equal *adj.* **1.** alike, commensurate, equivalent, identical, like, one and the same, proportionate, tantamount, the same, uniform **2.** balanced, corresponding, egalitarian, even, evenly balanced, evenly matched, evenly proportioned, fifty-fifty (*Inf.*), level pegging (*Brit. inf.*), matched, regular, symmetrical, uniform, unvarying **3.** able, adequate, capable, competent, fit, good enough, ready, strong enough, suitable, up to **4.** egalitarian, equable, even-handed, fair, impartial, just, unbiased ~*n.* **5.** brother, compeer, counterpart, equivalent, fellow, match, mate, parallel, peer, rival, twin ~*v.* **6.** agree with, amount to, balance, be equal to, be even with, be level with, be tantamount to, come up to, correspond to, equalize, equate, even, level, match, parallel, rival, square with, tally with, tie with
Antonyms *adj.* different, disproportionate, dissimilar, diverse, inadequate, inequitable, irregular, unbalanced, unequal, uneven, un-

like, unmatched ~*v.* be different, be unequal, disagree

equality balance, coequality, correspondence, egalitarianism, equal opportunity, equatability, equivalence, evenness, fairness, identity, likeness, parity, sameness, similarity, uniformity
Antonyms bias, discrimination, disparity, imparity, inequality, lack of balance, prejudice, unevenness, unfairness

equalize balance, equal, equate, even up, level, make equal, match, regularize, smooth, square, standardize

equate agree, balance, be commensurate, compare, correspond with *or* to, equalize, liken, make *or* be equal, match, offset, pair, parallel, square, tally, think of together

equation agreement, balancing, comparison, correspondence, equality, equalization, equating, equivalence, likeness, match, pairing, parallel

equestrian 1. *adj.* in the saddle, mounted, on horseback **2.** *n.* cavalier (*Archaic*), horseman, knight, rider

equilibrium 1. balance, counterpoise, equipoise, evenness, rest, stability, steadiness, symmetry **2.** calm, calmness, collectedness, composure, coolness, equanimity, poise, self-possession, serenity, stability, steadiness

equip accoutre, arm, array, attire, deck out, dress, endow, fit out, fit up, furnish, kit out, outfit, prepare, provide, rig, stock, supply

equipment accoutrements, apparatus, appurtenances, baggage, equipage, furnishings, furniture, gear, materiel, outfit, paraphernalia, rig, stuff, supplies, tackle, tools

equitable candid, disinterested, dispassionate, due, even-handed, fair, honest, impartial, just, nondiscriminatory, proper, proportionate, reasonable, right, rightful, unbiased, unprejudiced

equity disinterestedness, equitableness, even-handedness, fair-mindedness, fairness, fair play, honesty, impartiality, integrity, justice, reasonableness, rectitude, righteousness, uprightness
Antonyms bias, discrimination, injustice, partiality, preference, prejudice, unfairness

equivalence agreement, alikeness, conformity, correspondence, equality, evenness, identity, interchangeableness, likeness, match, parallel, parity, sameness, similarity, synonymy

equivalent 1. *adj.* alike, commensurate, comparable, correspondent, corresponding, equal, even, homologous, interchangeable, of a kind, same, similar, synonymous, tantamount **2.** *n.* correspondent, counterpart,

equal, match, opposite number, parallel, peer, twin
Antonyms *adj.* different, dissimilar, incom~ parable, unequal, unlike

equivocal ambiguous, ambivalent, doubtful, dubious, evasive, indefinite, indeterminate, misleading, oblique, obscure, oracular, pre~ varicating, questionable, suspicious, uncer~ tain, vague
Antonyms absolute, certain, clear, clear-cut, decisive, definite, evident, explicit, incontro~ vertible, indubitable, manifest, plain, posi~ tive, straight, unambiguous, unequivocal

equivocate avoid the issue, beat about the bush (*Inf.*), dodge, evade, fence, flannel (*Brit. inf.*), fudge, hedge, parry, prevaricate, pussyfoot (*Inf.*), quibble, shuffle, sidestep, tergiversate, waffle (*Inf., chiefly Brit.*)

equivocation ambiguity, double talk, doubtfulness, evasion, hedging, prevarica~ tion, quibbling, shuffling, tergiversation, waffle (*Inf., chiefly Brit.*), weasel words (*Inf., chiefly U.S.*)

era aeon, age, cycle, date, day *or* days, epoch, generation, period, stage, time

eradicate abolish, annihilate, deracinate, destroy, efface, eliminate, erase, excise, ex~ punge, exterminate, extinguish, extirpate, obliterate, remove, root out, stamp out, uproot, weed out, wipe out

eradication abolition, annihilation, deraci~ nation, destruction, effacement, elimination, erasure, expunction, extermination, extinc~ tion, extirpation, obliteration, removal

erase blot, cancel, delete, efface, excise, ex~ punge, obliterate, remove, rub out, scratch out, wipe out

erect *adj.* **1.** elevated, firm, perpendicular, pricked-up, raised, rigid, standing, stiff, straight, upright, vertical ~*v.* **2.** build, con~ struct, elevate, lift, mount, pitch, put up, raise, rear, set up, stand up **3.** create, es~ tablish, form, found, initiate, institute, or~ ganize, set up
Antonyms *adj.* bent, flaccid, horizontal, leaning, limp, prone, recumbent, relaxed, su~ pine ~*v.* demolish, destroy, dismantle, raze, tear down

erection 1. assembly, building, construc~ tion, creation, elevation, establishment, fabrication, manufacture **2.** building, con~ struction, edifice, pile, structure

erode abrade, consume, corrode, destroy, deteriorate, disintegrate, eat away, grind down, spoil, wear down *or* away

erosion abrasion, attrition, consumption, corrasion, corrosion, destruction, deterio~ ration, disintegration, eating away, grind~ ing down, spoiling, wear, wearing down *or* away

erotic amatory, aphrodisiac, carnal, erog~ enous, lustful, rousing, seductive, sensual, sexy (*Inf.*), steamy (*Inf.*), stimulating, sug~ gestive, titillating, voluptuous

err 1. be inaccurate, be incorrect, be in er~ ror, blunder, go astray, go wrong, make a mistake, misapprehend, miscalculate, mis~ judge, mistake, slip up (*Inf.*) **2.** be out of order, deviate, do wrong, fall, go astray, lapse, misbehave, offend, sin, transgress, trespass

errand charge, commission, job, message, mission, task

errant 1. *Archaic* itinerant, journeying, peripatetic, rambling, roaming, roving, wandering **2.** aberrant, deviant, erring, of~ fending, sinning, straying, wayward, wrong

erratic 1. aberrant, abnormal, capricious, changeable, desultory, eccentric, fitful, in~ consistent, inconstant, irregular, shifting, uneven, unpredictable, unreliable, unstable, variable, wayward **2.** directionless, me~ andering, planetary, wandering
Antonyms certain, consistent, constant, de~ pendable, invariable, natural, normal, pre~ dictable, regular, reliable, stable, steady, straight, unchanging, undeviating

erroneous amiss, fallacious, false, faulty, flawed, inaccurate, incorrect, inexact, inva~ lid, mistaken, spurious, unfounded, un~ sound, untrue, wrong
Antonyms accurate, correct, factual, fault~ less, flawless, precise, right, true, veracious

error 1. bloomer (*Brit. inf.*), blunder, boner (*Sl.*), boob (*Brit. sl.*), delusion, erratum, fal~ lacy, fault, flaw, howler (*Inf.*), inaccuracy, misapprehension, miscalculation, miscon~ ception, mistake, oversight, slip, solecism **2.** delinquency, deviation, fault, lapse, mis~ deed, offence, sin, transgression, trespass, wrong, wrongdoing

erstwhile bygone, ex (*Inf.*), former, late, old, once, one-time, past, previous, quon~ dam, sometime

erudite cultivated, cultured, educated, knowledgeable, learned, lettered, literate, scholarly, well-educated, well-read
Antonyms ignorant, illiterate, shallow, un~ educated, uninformed, unlettered, un~ schooled, untaught, unthinking

erupt 1. be ejected, belch forth, blow up, break out, burst forth, burst into, burst out, discharge, explode, flare up, gush, pour forth, spew forth *or* out, spit out, spout, throw off, vent, vomit **2.** *Medical* appear, break out

eruption 1. discharge, ejection, explosion, flare-up, outbreak, outburst, sally, venting **2.** *Medical* inflammation, outbreak, rash

escalate amplify, ascend, be increased, en~

large, expand, extend, grow, heighten, in~ crease, intensify, magnify, mount, raise, rise, step up
Antonyms abate, contract, decrease, de~ scend, diminish, fall, lessen, limit, lower, shrink, wane, wind down

escapade adventure, antic, caper, fling, lark (*Inf.*), mischief, prank, romp, scrape (*Inf.*), spree, stunt, trick

escape *v.* **1.** abscond, bolt, break free *or* out, decamp, do a bunk (*Brit. sl.*), do a run~ ner (*Sl.*), flee, fly, fly the coop (*U.S. & Canad. inf.*), get away, hook it (*Sl.*), make *or* effect one's escape, make one's getaway, run away *or* off, skedaddle (*Inf.*), skip, slip away, take a powder (*U.S. & Canad. sl.*), take it on the lam (*U.S. & Canad. sl.*), ~*n.* **2.** bolt, break, break-out, decampment, flight, getaway ~*v.* **3.** avoid, body-swerve (*Scot.*), circumvent, dodge, duck, elude, evade, pass, shun, slip ~*n.* **4.** avoidance, circumvention, elusion, evasion ~*v.* **5.** dis~ charge, drain, emanate, exude, flow, gush, issue, leak, pour forth, seep, spurt ~*n.* **6.** discharge, drain, effluence, efflux, emana~ tion, emission, gush, leak, leakage, outflow, outpour, seepage, spurt ~*v.* **7.** baffle, be be~ yond (someone), be forgotten by, elude, puzzle, stump ~*n.* **8.** distraction, diversion, pastime, recreation, relief

eschew abandon, abjure, abstain from, avoid, elude, fight shy of, forgo, forswear, give up, have nothing to do with, keep *or* steer clear of, kick (*Inf.*), refrain from, re~ nounce, shun, swear off

escort *n.* **1.** bodyguard, company, convoy, cortege, entourage, guard, protection, reti~ nue, safeguard, train **2.** attendant, beau, chaperon, companion, guide, partner, pro~ tector, squire (*Rare*) ~*v.* **3.** accompany, chaperon, conduct, convoy, guard, guide, lead, partner, protect, shepherd, squire, usher

especial 1. chief, distinguished, exception~ al, extraordinary, marked, notable, note~ worthy, outstanding, principal, signal, spe~ cial, uncommon, unusual **2.** exclusive, ex~ press, individual, particular, peculiar, per~ sonal, private, singular, special, specific, unique

especially 1. chiefly, conspicuously, excep~ tionally, extraordinarily, largely, mainly, markedly, notably, outstandingly, princi~ pally, remarkably, signally, specially, strik~ ingly, supremely, uncommonly, unusually **2.** exclusively, expressly, particularly, pe~ culiarly, singularly, specifically, uniquely

espionage counter-intelligence, intelli~ gence, spying, surveillance, undercover work

espousal 1. adoption, advocacy, backing,

championing, championship, defence, em~ bracing, maintenance, promotion, support, taking up **2.** *Archaic* affiancing, betrothal, betrothing (*Archaic*), engagement, espousing (*Archaic*), marriage, nuptials, plighting, wedding

espouse 1. adopt, advocate, back, champi~ on, defend, embrace, maintain, promote, stand up for, support, take up **2.** *Archaic* betroth (*Archaic*), marry, take as spouse, take to wife, wed

essay article, composition, discourse, dis~ quisition, dissertation, paper, piece, tract, treatise

essence 1. being, core, crux, entity, heart, kernel, life, lifeblood, meaning, nature, pith, principle, quiddity, quintessence, signifi~ cance, soul, spirit, substance **2.** concen~ trate, distillate, elixir, extract, spirits, tinc~ ture **3.** *Rare* cologne, fragrance, perfume, scent **4. in essence** basically, essentially, fundamentally, in effect, in substance, in the main, materially, substantially, to all intents and purposes, virtually **5. of the essence** crucial, essential, indispensable, of the utmost importance, vital, vitally important

essential *adj.* **1.** crucial, important, indis~ pensable, necessary, needed, requisite, vital **2.** basic, cardinal, constitutional, elemental, elementary, fundamental, inherent, innate, intrinsic, key, main, principal, radical **3.** absolute, complete, ideal, perfect, quintes~ sential **4.** concentrated, distilled, extracted, rectified, refined, volatile ~*n.* **5.** basic, fun~ damental, must, necessity, prerequisite, principle, requisite, rudiment, *sine qua non,* vital part
Antonyms accessory, dispensable, expend~ able, extra, extraneous, incidental, inessen~ tial, lesser, minor, nonessential, option, sec~ ondary, superfluous, surplus, trivial, unim~ portant, unnecessary

establish 1. base, constitute, create, decree, enact, ensconce, entrench, fix, form, found, ground, implant, inaugurate, install, insti~ tute, organize, plant, root, secure, settle, set up, start **2.** authenticate, certify, confirm, corroborate, demonstrate, prove, ratify, show, substantiate, validate, verify

establishment 1. creation, enactment, formation, foundation, founding, inaugura~ tion, installation, institution, organization, setting up **2.** business, company, concern, corporation, enterprise, firm, house, insti~ tute, institution, organization, outfit (*Inf.*), setup (*Inf.*), structure, system **3.** building, factory, house, office, plant, quarters **4.** abode, domicile, dwelling, home, house, household, pad (*Sl.*), residence **5. the Es~ tablishment** established order, institution~

alized authority, ruling class, the powers that be, the system

estate 1. area, demesne, domain, holdings, lands, manor, property **2.** *Property law* as~ sets, belongings, effects, fortune, goods, possessions, property, wealth **3.** caste, class, order, rank **4.** condition, lot, period, place, position, quality, rank, situation, standing, state, station, status

esteem *v.* **1.** admire, be fond of, cherish, honour, like, love, prize, regard highly, re~ spect, revere, reverence, think highly of, treasure, value, venerate **2.** *Formal* ac~ count, believe, calculate, consider, deem, estimate, hold, judge, rate, reckon, regard, think, view ~*n.* **3.** admiration, Brownie points, consideration, credit, estimation, good opinion, honour, regard, respect, rev~ erence, veneration

estimate *v.* **1.** appraise, assess, calculate roughly, evaluate, gauge, guess, judge, number, reckon, value **2.** assess, believe, conjecture, consider, form an opinion, guess, judge, rank, rate, reckon, surmise, think ~*n.* **3.** appraisal, appraisement, ap~ proximate calculation, assessment, evalu~ ation, guess, guesstimate (*Inf.*), judgment, reckoning, valuation **4.** appraisal, ap~ praisement, assessment, belief, conjecture, educated guess, estimation, judgment, opin~ ion, surmise, thought(s)

estimation 1. appraisal, appreciation, as~ sessment, belief, consideration, considered opinion, estimate, evaluation, judgment, opinion, view **2.** admiration, Brownie points, credit, esteem, good opinion, hon~ our, regard, respect, reverence, veneration

estrange alienate, antagonize, disaffect, disunite, divide, drive apart, lose *or* destroy the affection of, make hostile, part, sepa~ rate, set at odds, withdraw, withhold
Antonyms ally, associate, coalesce, couple, fuse, join, link, marry, unite

estrangement alienation, antagonization, breach, break-up, disaffection, dissociation, disunity, division, hostility, parting, sepa~ ration, split, withdrawal, withholding

estuary creek, firth, fjord, inlet, mouth

et cetera and others, and so forth, and so on, and the like, and the rest, et al.

etch carve, corrode, cut, eat into, engrave, furrow, impress, imprint, incise, ingrain, inscribe, stamp

etching carving, engraving, impression, imprint, inscription, print

eternal 1. abiding, ceaseless, constant, deathless, endless, everlasting, immortal, infinite, interminable, never-ending, peren~ nial, perpetual, sempiternal (*Literary*), timeless, unceasing, undying, unending,

unremitting, without end **2.** deathless, en~ during, everlasting, immortal, immutable, imperishable, indestructible, lasting, per~ manent
Antonyms changing, ephemeral, evanes~ cent, finite, fleeting, infrequent, irregular, mortal, occasional, perishable, random, rare, temporal, transient, transitory

eternity 1. age, ages, endlessness, for ever, immortality, infinitude, infinity, perpetuity, timelessness, time without end **2.** *Theology* heaven, paradise, the afterlife, the here~ after, the next world

ethical conscientious, correct, decent, fair, fitting, good, honest, honourable, just, mor~ al, principled, proper, right, righteous, upright, virtuous
Antonyms dishonourable, disreputable, immoral, improper, indecent, low-down (*Inf.*), underhand, unethical, unfair, unscrupulous, unseemly

ethics conscience, moral code, morality, moral philosophy, moral values, principles, rules of conduct, standards

ethnic cultural, folk, indigenous, national, native, racial, traditional

etiquette civility, code, convention, cour~ tesy, customs, decorum, formalities, good *or* proper behaviour, manners, politeness, politesse, propriety, protocol, rules, usage

eulogize acclaim, applaud, commend, com~ pliment, crack up (*Inf.*), cry up, exalt, extol, glorify, laud, magnify (*Archaic*), panegyrize, pay tribute to, praise, sing *or* sound the praises of

eulogy acclaim, acclamation, accolade, ap~ plause, commendation, compliment, enco~ mium, exaltation, glorification, laudation, paean, panegyric, plaudit, praise, tribute

euphoria bliss, ecstasy, elation, exaltation, exhilaration, exultation, glee, high spirits, intoxication, joy, joyousness, jubilation, rapture, transport
Antonyms depression, despair, desponden~ cy, dolefulness, downheartedness, dumps (*Inf.*), gloominess, hopelessness, low spirits, melancholia, melancholy, sadness, the blues

evacuate 1. abandon, clear, decamp, de~ part, desert, forsake, leave, move out, pull out, quit, relinquish, remove, vacate, with~ draw **2.** crap (*Taboo sl.*), defecate, dis~ charge, eject, eliminate, empty, excrete, ex~ pel, shit (*Taboo sl.*), void

evade 1. avoid, body-swerve (*Scot.*), cir~ cumvent, decline, dodge, duck, elude, es~ cape, escape the clutches of, eschew, get away from, shirk, shun, sidestep, steer clear of **2.** balk, circumvent, cop out (*Sl.*), equivocate, fence, fend off, flannel (*Brit. inf.*), fudge, hedge, parry, prevaricate, quib~ ble, waffle (*Inf., chiefly Brit.*)

Antonyms brave, confront, encounter, face, meet, meet face to face

evaluate appraise, assay, assess, calculate, estimate, gauge, judge, rank, rate, reckon, size up (*Inf.*), value, weigh

evaluation appraisal, assessment, calcula~ tion, estimate, estimation, judgment, opin~ ion, rating, valuation

evanescent brief, ephemeral, fading, fleeting, fugacious, fugitive, impermanent, momentary, passing, short-lived, transient, transitory, vanishing

evangelical, evangelistic crusading, missionary, propagandizing, proselytizing, zealous

evaporate 1. dehydrate, desiccate, dry, dry up, vaporize **2.** dematerialize, disappear, dispel, disperse, dissipate, dissolve, eva~ nesce, fade, fade away, melt, melt away, vanish

evaporation 1. dehydration, desiccation, drying, drying up, vaporization **2.** dema~ terialization, disappearance, dispelling, dis~ persal, dissipation, dissolution, evanes~ cence, fading, fading away, melting, melting away, vanishing

evasion artifice, avoidance, circumvention, cop-out (*Sl.*), cunning, dodge, elusion, equivocation, escape, evasiveness, excuse, fudging, obliqueness, pretext, prevarication, ruse, shift, shirking, shuffling, sophism, sophistry, subterfuge, trickery, waffle (*Inf., chiefly Brit.*)

evasive cagey (*Inf.*), casuistic, casuistical, cunning, deceitful, deceptive, devious, dis~ sembling, elusive, elusory, equivocating, indirect, misleading, oblique, prevaricating, shifty, shuffling, slippery, sophistical, tricky **Antonyms** candid, direct, frank, guileless, honest, open, straight, straightforward, truthful, unequivocating

eve 1. day before, night before, vigil **2.** brink, edge, point, threshold, verge

even *adj.* **1.** flat, flush, horizontal, level, parallel, plane, plumb, smooth, steady, straight, true, uniform **2.** constant, metri~ cal, regular, smooth, steady, unbroken, uniform, uninterrupted, unvarying, unwa~ vering **3.** calm, composed, cool, equable, equanimous, even-tempered, imperturbable, peaceful, placid, serene, stable, steady, tranquil, undisturbed, unexcitable, unruffled, well-balanced **4.** coequal, com~ mensurate, comparable, drawn, equal, equalized, equally balanced, fifty-fifty (*Inf.*), identical, level, level pegging (*Brit. inf.*), like, matching, neck and neck, on a par, parallel, similar, square, the same, tied, uniform **5.** balanced, disinterested, dispas~ sionate, equitable, fair, fair and square, im~ partial, just, unbiased, unprejudiced **6. get**

even (with) *Inf.* be revenged *or* revenge oneself, even the score, give tit for tat, pay back, reciprocate, repay, requite, return like for like, settle the score, take an eye for an eye, take vengeance ~*adv.* **7.** all the more, much, still, yet **8.** despite, disregard~ ing, in spite of, notwithstanding **9. even as** at the same time as, at the time that, dur~ ing the time that, exactly as, just as, while, whilst **10. even so** all the same, be that as it may, despite (that), however, in spite of (that), nevertheless, nonetheless, notwith~ standing (that), still, yet ~*v.* **11.** *Often fol~ lowed by* **out** *or* **up** align, balance, become level, equal, equalize, flatten, level, match, regularize, smooth, square, stabilize, steady **12. even the score** be revenged *or* revenge oneself, equalize, get even (*Inf.*), give tit for tat, pay (someone) back, reciprocate, repay, requite, return like for like, settle the score, take an eye for an eye, take vengeance **Antonyms** (*senses 1 & 2*) asymmetrical, awry, broken, bumpy, changeable, changing, curving, different, fluctuating, irregular, odd, rough, twisting, undulating, uneven, variable, wavy (*sense 3*) agitated, changeable, emotion~ al, excitable, quick-tempered, unpredictable (*sense 4*) disproportionate, ill-matched, imbalanced, irregular, unequal, uneven (*sense 5*) biased, partial, prejudiced, unbalanced, unequal, unfair

even-handed balanced, disinterested, equitable, fair, fair and square, impartial, just, unbiased, unprejudiced

evening crepuscule, dusk, e'en (*Archaic or poetic*), eve, even (*Archaic*), eventide (*Ar~ chaic or poetic*), gloaming (*Scot. or poetic*), twilight, vesper (*Archaic*)

event 1. adventure, affair, business, cir~ cumstance, episode, escapade, experience, fact, happening, incident, matter, milestone, occasion, occurrence **2.** conclusion, conse~ quence, effect, end, issue, outcome, result, termination, upshot **3.** bout, competition, contest, game, tournament **4. at all events** at any rate, come what may, in any case, in any event, regardless, whatever happens

even-tempered calm, composed, cool, cool-headed, equable, imperturbable, level-headed, peaceful, placid, serene, steady, tranquil, unexcitable, unruffled **Antonyms** emotional, excitable, hasty, highly-strung, hot-headed, hot-tempered, irascible, quick-tempered, temperamental, touchy, volatile

eventful active, busy, consequential, criti~ cal, crucial, decisive, dramatic, exciting, fateful, full, historic, important, lively, memorable, momentous, notable, note~ worthy, remarkable, significant **Antonyms** commonplace, dull, humdrum, insignificant, ordinary, trivial, uneventful,

unexceptional, unexciting, unimportant, un~
interesting, unremarkable

eventual concluding, consequent, ensuing,
final, future, later, overall, prospective, re~
sulting, ultimate

eventuality case, chance, contingency,
event, likelihood, possibility, probability

eventually after all, at the end of the day,
finally, in the course of time, in the end, in
the long run, one day, some day, some time,
sooner or later, ultimately, when all is said
and done

ever 1. at all, at any time (period, point), by
any chance, in any case, on any occasion **2.**
always, at all times, aye (*Scot.*), constantly,
continually, endlessly, eternally, ever~
lastingly, evermore, for ever, incessantly,
perpetually, relentlessly, to the end of time,
unceasingly, unendingly

everlasting 1. abiding, deathless, endless,
eternal, immortal, imperishable, inde~
structible, infinite, interminable, never-
ending, perpetual, timeless, undying **2.**
ceaseless, constant, continual, continuous,
endless, incessant, interminable, never-
ending, unceasing, uninterrupted, unremit~
ting
Antonyms brief, ephemeral, fleeting, im~
permanent, passing, short-lived, temporary,
transient, transitory

evermore always, eternally, ever, for ever,
in perpetuum, to the end of time

every all, each, each one, the whole number

everybody all and sundry, each one, each
person, everyone, every person, one and all,
the whole world

everyday 1. daily, quotidian **2.** accus~
tomed, banal, common, common or garden
(*Inf.*), commonplace, conventional, custom~
ary, dull, familiar, frequent, habitual, in~
formal, mundane, ordinary, routine, run-
of-the-mill, stock, unexceptional, unimagi~
native, usual, wonted, workaday
Antonyms best, exceptional, exciting,
extraordinary, incidental, individual, infre~
quent, interesting, irregular, now and then,
occasional, original, outlandish, periodic,
special, uncommon, unusual

everyone all and sundry, each one, each
person, everybody, every person, one and
all, the whole world

everything all, each thing, the aggregate,
the entirety, the lot, the sum, the total, the
whole caboodle (*Inf.*), the whole lot

everywhere all around, all over, far and
wide *or* near, high and low, in each place,
in every place, omnipresent, the world over,
to *or* in all places, ubiquitous, ubiquitously

evict boot out (*Inf.*), chuck out (*Inf.*), dis~
lodge, dispossess, eject, expel, kick out

(*Inf.*), oust, put out, remove, show the door
(to), throw on to the streets, throw out, turf
out (*Inf.*), turn out

eviction clearance, dislodgement, dispos~
session, ejection, expulsion, ouster (*Law*),
removal

evidence 1. *n.* affirmation, attestation,
averment, confirmation, corroboration,
data, declaration, demonstration, deposi~
tion, grounds, indication, manifestation,
mark, proof, sign, substantiation, testimo~
ny, token, witness **2.** *v.* demonstrate, de~
note, display, evince, exhibit, indicate,
manifest, prove, reveal, show, signify, testi~
fy to, witness

evident apparent, blatant, clear, conspicu~
ous, incontestable, incontrovertible, indis~
putable, manifest, noticeable, obvious, pal~
pable, patent, perceptible, plain, tangible,
unmistakable, visible
Antonyms ambiguous, concealed, doubtful,
dubious, hidden, imperceptible, obscure,
questionable, secret, uncertain, unclear, un~
known, vague

evidently 1. clearly, doubtless, doubtlessly,
incontestably, incontrovertibly, indisput~
ably, manifestly, obviously, patently, plain~
ly, undoubtedly, unmistakably, without
question **2.** apparently, it seems, it would
seem, ostensibly, outwardly, seemingly, to
all appearances

evil *adj.* **1.** bad, base, corrupt, depraved,
heinous, immoral, iniquitous, maleficent,
malevolent, malicious, malignant, nefari~
ous, reprobate, sinful, vicious, vile, villain~
ous, wicked, wrong ~*n.* **2.** badness, base~
ness, corruption, curse, depravity, heinous~
ness, immorality, iniquity, maleficence,
malignity, sin, sinfulness, turpitude, vice,
viciousness, villainy, wickedness, wrong,
wrongdoing ~*adj.* **3.** baneful (*Archaic*), ca~
lamitous, catastrophic, deleterious, destruc~
tive, detrimental, dire, disastrous, harmful,
hurtful, inauspicious, injurious, mischie~
vous, painful, pernicious, ruinous, sorrow~
ful, unfortunate, unlucky, woeful ~*n.* **4.**
affliction, calamity, catastrophe, disaster,
harm, hurt, ill, injury, mischief, misery,
misfortune, pain, ruin, sorrow, suffering,
woe ~*adj.* **5.** foul, mephitic, noxious, offen~
sive, pestilential, putrid, unpleasant, vile

evoke 1. arouse, awaken, call, excite, give
rise to, induce, recall, rekindle, stimulate,
stir up, summon up **2.** call forth, educe
(*Rare*), elicit, produce, provoke **3.** arouse,
call, call forth, conjure up, invoke, raise,
summon
Antonyms contain, hold in check, inhibit,
muffle, repress, restrain, smother, stifle, sup~
press

evolution development, enlargement,

evolvement, expansion, growth, increase, maturation, progress, progression, unfolding, unrolling, working out

evolve develop, disclose, educe, elaborate, enlarge, expand, grow, increase, mature, open, progress, unfold, unroll, work out

exact *adj.* **1.** accurate, careful, correct, definite, explicit, express, faithful, faultless, identical, literal, methodical, orderly, particular, precise, right, specific, true, unequivocal, unerring, veracious, very **2.** careful, exacting, meticulous, painstaking, punctilious, rigorous, scrupulous, severe, strict ~*v.* **3.** call for, claim, command, compel, demand, extort, extract, force, impose, insist upon, require, squeeze, wrest, wring
Antonyms *adj.* approximate, careless, imprecise, inaccurate, incorrect, indefinite, inexact, loose, rough, slovenly

exacting demanding, difficult, hard, harsh, imperious, oppressive, painstaking, rigid, rigorous, severe, stern, strict, stringent, taxing, tough, unsparing
Antonyms easy, easy-peasy (*Sl.*), effortless, no bother, simple, undemanding

exactly *adv.* **1.** accurately, carefully, correctly, definitely, explicitly, faithfully, faultlessly, literally, methodically, precisely, rigorously, scrupulously, severely, strictly, truly, truthfully, unequivocally, unerringly, veraciously **2.** absolutely, bang, explicitly, expressly, indeed, in every respect, just, particularly, precisely, quite, specifically **3. not exactly** *Ironical* by no means, certainly not, hardly, in no manner, in no way, not at all, not by any means, not quite, not really ~*interj.* **4.** absolutely, assuredly, as you say, certainly, indeed, just so, of course, precisely, quite, quite so, spot-on (*Brit. inf.*), truly

exactness accuracy, carefulness, correctness, exactitude, faithfulness, faultlessness, nicety, orderliness, painstakingness, preciseness, precision, promptitude, regularity, rigorousness, rigour, scrupulousness, strictness, truth, unequivocalness, veracity
Antonyms imprecision, inaccuracy, incorrectness, inexactness, unfaithfulness

exaggerate amplify, embellish, embroider, emphasize, enlarge, exalt, hyperbolize, inflate, lay it on thick (*Inf.*), magnify, make a federal case of (*U.S. inf.*), make a production (out) of (*Inf.*), overdo, overemphasize, overestimate, overstate

exaggerated amplified, exalted, excessive, extravagant, highly coloured, hyped, hyperbolic, inflated, overblown, overdone, overestimated, overstated, over the top (*Inf.*), pretentious, tall (*Inf.*)

exaggeration amplification, embellish-

ment, emphasis, enlargement, exaltation, excess, extravagance, hyperbole, inflation, magnification, overemphasis, overestimation, overstatement, pretension, pretentiousness
Antonyms litotes, meiosis, restraint, underplaying, understatement

exalt 1. advance, aggrandize, dignify, elevate, ennoble, honour, promote, raise, upgrade **2.** acclaim, apotheosize, applaud, bless, crack up (*Inf.*), extol, glorify, idolize, laud, magnify (*Archaic*), pay homage to, pay tribute to, praise, reverence, set on a pedestal, worship **3.** animate, arouse, electrify, elevate, excite, fire the imagination (of), heighten, inspire, inspirit, stimulate, uplift **4.** delight, elate, exhilarate, fill with joy, thrill

exaltation 1. advancement, aggrandizement, dignity, elevation, eminence, ennoblement, grandeur, high rank, honour, loftiness, prestige, promotion, rise, upgrading **2.** acclaim, acclamation, apotheosis, applause, blessing, extolment, glorification, glory, homage, idolization, laudation, lionization, magnification, panegyric, plaudits, praise, reverence, tribute, worship **3.** animation, elevation, excitement, inspiration, stimulation, uplift **4.** bliss, delight, ecstasy, elation, exhilaration, exultation, joy, joyousness, jubilation, rapture, transport

exalted 1. august, dignified, elevated, eminent, grand, high, high-ranking, honoured, lofty, prestigious **2.** elevated, high-minded, ideal, intellectual, lofty, noble, sublime, superior, uplifting **3.** *Inf.* elevated, exaggerated, excessive, inflated, overblown, pretentious **4.** animated, blissful, cock-a-hoop, ecstatic, elated, elevated, excited, exhilarated, exultant, in high spirits, in seventh heaven, inspired, inspirited, joyous, jubilant, on cloud nine (*Inf.*), over the moon (*Inf.*), rapturous, stimulated, transported, uplifted

examination analysis, assay, catechism, checkup, exploration, inquiry, inquisition, inspection, interrogation, investigation, observation, perusal, probe, questioning, quiz, recce (*Sl.*), research, review, scrutiny, search, study, survey, test, trial

examine 1. analyse, appraise, assay, check, check out, consider, explore, go over *or* through, inspect, investigate, look over, peruse, ponder, pore over, probe, recce (*Sl.*), research, review, scan, scrutinize, sift, study, survey, take stock of, test, vet, weigh, work over **2.** catechize, cross-examine, grill (*Inf.*), inquire, interrogate, question, quiz

example 1. case, case in point, exemplification, illustration, instance, sample, specimen **2.** archetype, exemplar, ideal,

illustration, model, norm, paradigm, para~
gon, pattern, precedent, prototype, standard
3. admonition, caution, lesson, warning **4.**
for example as an illustration, by way of
illustration, e.g., *exempli gratia*, for in~
stance, to cite an instance, to illustrate

exasperate aggravate (*Inf.*), anger, annoy,
bug (*Inf.*), embitter, enrage, exacerbate, ex~
cite, gall, get (*Inf.*), get in one's hair (*Inf.*),
get on one's nerves (*Inf.*), hassle (*Inf.*), in~
cense, inflame, infuriate, irk, irritate, mad~
den, nark (*Brit., Aust., & N.Z. sl.*), needle
(*Inf.*), nettle, peeve (*Inf.*), pique, piss one off
(*Taboo sl.*), provoke, rankle, rile (*Inf.*),
rouse, try the patience of, vex
Antonyms appease, assuage, calm, concili~
ate, mollify, pacify, placate, soothe

exasperation aggravation (*Inf.*), anger,
annoyance, exacerbation, fury, ire (*Liter~
ary*), irritation, passion, pique, provocation,
rage, vexation, wrath

excavate burrow, cut, delve, dig, dig out,
dig up, gouge, hollow, mine, quarry, scoop,
trench, tunnel, uncover, unearth

excavation burrow, cavity, cut, cutting,
dig, diggings, ditch, dugout, hole, hollow,
mine, pit, quarry, shaft, trench, trough

exceed 1. beat, be superior to, better, cap
(*Inf.*), eclipse, excel, go beyond, outdistance,
outdo, outreach, outrun, outshine, outstrip,
overtake, pass, run rings around (*Inf.*), sur~
mount, surpass, top, transcend **2.** go be~
yond the bounds of, go over the limit of, go
over the top, overstep

exceeding enormous, exceptional, exces~
sive, extraordinary, great, huge, pre~
eminent, superior, superlative, surpassing,
vast

exceedingly enormously, especially, ex~
ceptionally, excessively, extraordinarily,
extremely, greatly, highly, hugely, inordi~
nately, superlatively, surpassingly, unusu~
ally, vastly, very

excel 1. beat, be superior, better, cap (*Inf.*),
eclipse, exceed, go beyond, outdo, outrival,
outshine, pass, run rings around (*Inf.*), sur~
mount, surpass, top, transcend **2.** be good,
be master of, be proficient, be skilful, be
talented, predominate, shine, show talent,
take precedence

excellence distinction, eminence, fineness,
goodness, greatness, high quality, merit,
perfection, pre-eminence, purity, superior~
ity, supremacy, transcendence, virtue,
worth

excellent A1 *or* A-one (*Inf.*), admirable,
boffo (*Sl.*), brill (*Inf.*), brilliant, capital,
champion, chillin' (*U.S. sl.*), choice, crack~
ing (*Brit. inf.*), crucial (*Sl.*), def (*Sl.*), distin~
guished, estimable, exemplary, exquisite,
fine, first-class, first-rate, good, great, jim-

dandy (*Sl.*), mean (*Sl.*), mega (*Sl.*), merito~
rious, notable, noted, outstanding, prime,
select, sovereign, sterling, superb, superior,
superlative, tiptop, top-notch (*Inf.*), topping
(*Brit. sl.*), world-class, worthy
Antonyms abysmal, bad, dreadful, faulty,
imperfect, incompetent, inexpert, inferior,
lousy (*Sl.*), mediocre, piss-poor (*Taboo sl.*),
poor, rotten (*Inf.*), second-class, second-rate,
substandard, terrible, unskilled

except 1. *prep.* Also **except for** apart
from, bar, barring, besides, but, excepting,
excluding, exclusive of, omitting, other
than, save (*Archaic*), saving, with the ex~
ception of **2.** *v.* ban, bar, disallow, exclude,
leave out, omit, pass over, reject, rule out

exception 1. debarment, disallowment, ex~
cepting, exclusion, leaving out, omission,
passing over, rejection **2.** anomaly, depar~
ture, deviation, freak, inconsistency, ir~
regularity, oddity, peculiarity, quirk, spe~
cial case **3. take exception** be offended, be
resentful, demur, disagree, object, quibble,
take offence, take umbrage

exceptional 1. aberrant, abnormal,
anomalous, atypical, deviant, extraordinary,
inconsistent, irregular, odd, peculiar, rare,
singular, special, strange, uncommon, un~
usual **2.** excellent, extraordinary, marvel~
lous, notable, outstanding, phenomenal,
prodigious, remarkable, special, superior
Antonyms average, awful, bad, common,
customary, familiar, lousy (*Sl.*), mediocre,
normal, ordinary, regular, second-rate,
straightforward, typical, unexceptional, un~
remarkable, usual

excess *n.* **1.** glut, leftover, overabundance,
overdose, overflow, overload, plethora, re~
mainder, superabundance, superfluity, sur~
feit, surplus, too much **2.** debauchery, dis~
sipation, dissoluteness, exorbitance, ex~
travagance, immoderation, intemperance,
overindulgence, prodigality, unrestraint
~*adj.* **3.** extra, leftover, redundant, remain~
ing, residual, spare, superfluous, surplus
Antonyms (*sense 1*) dearth, deficiency,
insufficiency, lack, shortage, want (*sense 2*)
moderation, restraint, self-control, self-
discipline, self-restraint, temperance

excessive disproportionate, enormous, ex~
aggerated, exorbitant, extravagant, extreme,
immoderate, inordinate, intemperate, need~
less, O.T.T. (*Sl.*), overdone, overmuch, over
the top (*Sl.*), prodigal, profligate, super~
fluous, too much, unconscionable, undue,
unreasonable

exchange *v.* **1.** bandy, barter, change,
commute, convert into, interchange, recip~
rocate, swap (*Inf.*), switch, trade, truck ~*n.*
2. barter, dealing, interchange, quid pro
quo, reciprocity, substitution, swap (*Inf.*),

switch, tit for tat, trade, traffic, truck **3.** Bourse, market

excitable edgy, emotional, hasty, highly strung, hot-headed, hot-tempered, irascible, mercurial, nervous, passionate, quick-tempered, sensitive, susceptible, temperamental, testy, touchy, uptight (*Inf.*), violent, volatile
Antonyms calm, cool, cool-headed, even-tempered, imperturbable, laid-back (*Inf.*), placid, unexcitable, unruffled

excite agitate, animate, arouse, awaken, discompose, disturb, electrify, elicit, evoke, fire, foment, galvanize, incite, inflame, inspire, instigate, kindle, move, provoke, quicken, rouse, stimulate, stir up, thrill, titillate, waken, whet

excited aflame, agitated, animated, aroused, awakened, discomposed, disturbed, enthusiastic, feverish, flurried, high (*Inf.*), hot and bothered (*Inf.*), moved, nervous, overwrought, roused, stimulated, stirred, thrilled, tumultuous, wild, worked up

excitement 1. action, activity, ado, adventure, agitation, animation, commotion, discomposure, elation, enthusiasm, ferment, fever, flurry, furore, heat, kicks (*Inf.*), passion, perturbation, thrill, tumult, warmth **2.** impulse, incitement, instigation, motivation, motive, provocation, stimulation, stimulus, urge

exciting dramatic, electrifying, exhilarating, inspiring, intoxicating, moving, provocative, rip-roaring (*Inf.*), rousing, sensational, sexy (*Inf.*), stimulating, stirring, thrilling, titillating
Antonyms boring, dreary, dull, flat, humdrum, mind-numbing, monotonous, unexciting, uninspiring, uninteresting

exclaim call, call out, cry, cry out, declare, ejaculate, proclaim, shout, utter, vociferate, yell

exclamation call, cry, ejaculation, expletive, interjection, outcry, shout, utterance, vociferation, yell

exclude 1. ban, bar, black, blackball, boycott, debar, disallow, embargo, forbid, interdict, keep out, ostracize, prohibit, proscribe, refuse, shut out, veto **2.** count out, eliminate, except, ignore, leave out, omit, pass over, preclude, reject, repudiate, rule out, set aside **3.** bounce (*Sl.*), drive out, eject, evict, expel, force out, get rid of, oust, remove, throw out
Antonyms accept, admit, allow, count, include, let in, permit, receive, welcome

exclusion 1. ban, bar, boycott, debarment, embargo, forbiddance, interdict, nonadmission, preclusion, prohibition, proscription, refusal, veto **2.** elimination, exception,

omission, rejection, repudiation **3.** eviction, expulsion, removal

exclusive 1. absolute, complete, entire, full, only, private, single, sole, total, undivided, unique, unshared, whole **2.** aristocratic, chic, choice, clannish, classy (*Sl.*), cliquish, closed, discriminative, elegant, fashionable, high-toned, limited, narrow, posh (*Inf., chiefly Brit.*), private, restricted, restrictive, ritzy (*Sl.*), select, selfish, snobbish, swish (*Inf., chiefly Brit.*), top-drawer, up-market **3.** confined, limited, peculiar, restricted, unique **4.** debarring, except for, excepting, excluding, leaving aside, not counting, omitting, restricting, ruling out
Antonyms common, communal, inclusive, nonexclusive, open, partial, popular, public, shared, sociable, unrestricted

excommunicate anathematize, ban, banish, cast out, denounce, eject, exclude, expel, proscribe, remove, repudiate, unchurch

excruciating acute, agonizing, burning, exquisite, extreme, harrowing, insufferable, intense, piercing, racking, searing, severe, tormenting, torturous, unbearable, unendurable, violent

exculpate absolve, acquit, clear, discharge, dismiss, excuse, exonerate, free, justify, pardon, release, vindicate

excursion 1. airing, day trip, expedition, jaunt, journey, outing, pleasure trip, ramble, tour, trip **2.** detour, deviation, digression, episode, excursus, wandering

excusable allowable, defensible, forgivable, justifiable, minor, pardonable, permissible, slight, understandable, venial, warrantable

excuse *v.* **1.** absolve, acquit, bear with, exculpate, exonerate, extenuate, forgive, indulge, make allowances for, overlook, pardon, pass over, tolerate, turn a blind eye to, wink at **2.** apologize for, condone, defend, explain, justify, mitigate, vindicate **3.** absolve, discharge, exempt, free, let off, liberate, release, relieve, spare ~*n.* **4.** apology, defence, explanation, grounds, justification, mitigation, plea, pretext, reason, vindication **5.** cop-out (*Sl.*), disguise, evasion, expedient, makeshift, pretence, pretext, semblance, shift, subterfuge **6.** *Inf.* apology, makeshift, mockery, substitute, travesty
Antonyms *v.* accuse, arraign, blame, censure, charge, chasten, chastise, compel, condemn, convict, correct, criticize, hold responsible, indict, oblige, punish, sentence ~*n.* (*sense 4*) accusation, charge, imputation, indictment

execrate abhor, abominate, anathematize, condemn, curse, damn, denounce, deplore, despise, detest, excoriate, hate, imprecate, loathe, revile, slam (*Sl.*), vilify

execration abhorrence, abomination,

anathema, condemnation, contempt, curse, damnation, detestation, excoriation, hate, hatred, imprecation, loathing, malediction, odium, vilification

execute 1. behead, electrocute, guillotine, hang, kill, put to death, shoot **2.** accom~ plish, achieve, administer, bring off, carry out, complete, consummate, discharge, do, effect, enact, enforce, finish, fulfil, imple~ ment, perform, prosecute, put into effect, realize, render **3.** *Law* deliver, seal, serve, sign, validate

execution 1. accomplishment, achieve~ ment, administration, carrying out, com~ pletion, consummation, discharge, effect, enactment, enforcement, implementation, operation, performance, prosecution, reali~ zation, rendering **2.** capital punishment, hanging, killing **3.** delivery, manner, mode, performance, rendition, style, technique **4.** *Law* warrant, writ

executioner 1. hangman, headsman **2.** as~ sassin, exterminator, hit man (*Sl.*), killer, liquidator, murderer, slayer

executive *n.* **1.** administrator, director, manager, official **2.** administration, direc~ torate, directors, government, hierarchy, leadership, management ~*adj.* **3.** adminis~ trative, controlling, decision-making, di~ recting, governing, managerial

exemplary 1. admirable, commendable, correct, estimable, excellent, fine, good, honourable, ideal, laudable, meritorious, model, praiseworthy, punctilious, sterling **2.** admonitory, cautionary, monitory, warning **3.** characteristic, illustrative, rep~ resentative, typical

exemplify demonstrate, depict, display, embody, evidence, exhibit, illustrate, in~ stance, manifest, represent, serve as an ex~ ample of, show

exempt 1. *v.* absolve, discharge, except, ex~ cuse, exonerate, free, grant immunity, let off, liberate, release, relieve, spare **2.** *adj.* absolved, clear, discharged, excepted, ex~ cused, favoured, free, immune, liberated, not liable, not subject, privileged, released, spared
Antonyms *adj.* accountable, answerable, chargeable, liable, obligated, responsible, subject

exemption absolution, discharge, dispen~ sation, exception, exoneration, freedom, immunity, privilege, release

exercise *v.* **1.** apply, bring to bear, employ, enjoy, exert, practise, put to use, use, utilize, wield **2.** discipline, drill, habituate, inure, practise, train, work out **3.** afflict, agitate, annoy, burden, distress, disturb, occupy, pain, perturb, preoccupy, trouble, try, vex, worry ~*n.* **4.** action, activity, dis~ cipline, drill, drilling, effort, labour, toil, training, work, work-out **5.** accomplish~ ment, application, discharge, employment, enjoyment, exertion, fulfilment, implemen~ tation, practice, use, utilization **6.** drill, lesson, practice, problem, schooling, schoolwork, task, work

exert 1. bring into play, bring to bear, em~ ploy, exercise, expend, make use of, put forth, use, utilize, wield **2. exert oneself** apply oneself, bend over backwards (*Inf.*), break one's neck (*Inf.*), bust a gut (*Inf.*), do one's best, do one's damnedest (*Inf.*), en~ deavour, give it one's all (*Inf.*), give it one's best shot (*Inf.*), go for broke (*Sl.*), go for it (*Inf.*), knock oneself out (*Inf.*), labour, make an all-out effort (*Inf.*), make an effort, rup~ ture oneself (*Inf.*), spare no effort, strain, strive, struggle, toil, try hard, work

exertion action, application, attempt, effort, employment, endeavour, exercise, industry, labour, pains, strain, stretch, struggle, toil, travail (*Literary*), trial, use, utilization

exhaust 1. bankrupt, cripple, debilitate, disable, drain, enervate, enfeeble, fatigue, impoverish, prostrate, sap, tire, tire out, weaken, wear out **2.** consume, deplete, dis~ sipate, expend, finish, run through, spend, squander, use up, waste **3.** drain, dry, empty, strain, void **4.** be emitted, dis~ charge, emanate, escape, issue

exhausted 1. all in (*Sl.*), beat (*Sl.*), clapped out (*Aust. & N.Z. inf.*), crippled, dead (*Inf.*), dead beat (*Inf.*), dead tired, debilitated, dis~ abled, dog-tired (*Inf.*), done in (*Inf.*), drained, enervated, enfeebled, fatigued, jad~ ed, knackered (*Sl.*), out on one's feet (*Inf.*), prostrated, ready to drop, sapped, spent, tired out, wasted, weak, worn out, zonked (*Sl.*) **2.** at an end, consumed, depleted, dis~ sipated, done, expended, finished, gone, spent, squandered, used up, wasted **3.** bare, drained, dry, empty, void
Antonyms active, animated, conserved, en~ livened, invigorated, kept, preserved, re~ freshed, rejuvenated, replenished, restored, revived, stimulated

exhausting arduous, backbreaking, crip~ pling, debilitating, difficult, draining, ener~ vating, fatiguing, gruelling, hard, laborious, punishing, sapping, strenuous, taxing, test~ ing, tiring

exhaustion 1. debilitation, enervation, fa~ tigue, feebleness, lassitude, prostration, tiredness, weariness **2.** consumption, de~ pletion, emptying

exhaustive all-embracing, all-inclusive, all-out (*Inf.*), complete, comprehensive, en~ cyclopedic, extensive, far-reaching, full, full-scale, in-depth, intensive, sweeping, thorough, thoroughgoing, total

exhibit 217 **expand**

Antonyms casual, cursory, desultory, in~
complete, perfunctory, sketchy, superficial

exhibit 1. *v.* air, demonstrate, disclose, dis~
play, evidence, evince, expose, express,
flaunt, indicate, make clear *or* plain, mani~
fest, offer, parade, present, put on view, re~
veal, show **2.** *n.* display, exhibition, illus~
tration, model, show

exhibition airing, demonstration, display,
exhibit, expo (*Inf.*), exposition, fair, mani~
festation, performance, presentation, repre~
sentation, show, showing, spectacle

exhilarating breathtaking, cheering, enliv~
ening, exalting, exciting, exhilarant, exhila~
rative, exhilaratory, gladdening, invigorat~
ing, stimulating, thrilling, vitalizing

exhilaration animation, cheerfulness, de~
light, elation, exaltation, excitement, gaiety,
gladness, gleefulness, high spirits, hilarity,
joy, joyfulness, liveliness, mirth, sprightli~
ness, vivacity
Antonyms dejection, depression, despond~
ency, gloom, low spirits, melancholy, misery,
sadness

exhort admonish, advise, beseech, bid, call
upon, caution, counsel, encourage, enjoin,
entreat, goad, incite, persuade, press,
prompt, spur, urge, warn

exhortation admonition, advice, beseech~
ing, bidding, caution, counsel, encourage~
ment, enjoinder (*Rare*), entreaty, goading,
incitement, lecture, persuasion, sermon,
urging, warning

exhume dig up, disentomb, disinter,
unbury, unearth
Antonyms bury, entomb, inearth, inhume,
inter

exigency, exigence 1. acuteness, con~
straint, criticalness, demandingness, diffi~
culty, distress, emergency, imperativeness,
necessity, needfulness, pressingness, pres~
sure, stress, urgency **2.** constraint, demand,
necessity, need, requirement, wont **3.** cri~
sis, difficulty, emergency, extremity, fix
(*Inf.*), hardship, jam (*Inf.*), juncture, panic
stations (*Inf.*), pass, pickle (*Inf.*), pinch,
plight, predicament, quandary, scrape (*Inf.*),
strait

exigent 1. acute, constraining, critical,
crucial, imperative, importunate, insistent,
necessary, needful, pressing, urgent **2.** ar~
duous, demanding, difficult, exacting, hard,
harsh, rigorous, severe, stiff, strict, strin~
gent, taxing, tough

exile *n.* **1.** banishment, deportation, expat~
riation, expulsion, ostracism, proscription,
separation **2.** deportee, émigré, expatriate,
outcast, refugee ~*v.* **3.** banish, deport, drive
out, eject, expatriate, expel, ostracize, oust,
proscribe

exist 1. abide, be, be extant, be living, be
present, breathe, continue, endure, happen,
last, live, obtain, occur, prevail, remain,
stand, survive **2.** eke out a living, get along
or by, stay alive, subsist, survive

existence 1. actuality, animation, being,
breath, continuance, continuation, duration,
endurance, life, subsistence, survival **2.** be~
ing, creature, entity, thing **3.** creation, life,
reality, the world

existent abiding, around, current, endur~
ing, existing, extant, in existence, living,
obtaining, present, prevailing, remaining,
standing, surviving

exit *n.* **1.** door, egress, gate, outlet, passage
out, vent, way out **2.** adieu, departure,
evacuation, exodus, farewell, going, good~
bye, leave-taking, retirement, retreat, with~
drawal **3.** death, decease, demise, expiry,
passing away ~*v.* **4.** bid farewell, depart, go
away, go offstage (*Theatre*), go out, issue,
leave, retire, retreat, say goodbye, take
one's leave, withdraw
Antonyms (*sense 1*) entrance, entry, ingress,
inlet, opening, way in (*sense 4*) arrive, come *or*
go in *or* into, enter, make an entrance

exodus departure, evacuation, exit, flight,
going out, leaving, migration, retirement,
retreat, withdrawal

exonerate 1. absolve, acquit, clear, dis~
charge, dismiss, exculpate, excuse, justify,
pardon, vindicate **2.** discharge, dismiss, ex~
cept, excuse, exempt, free, let off, liberate,
release, relieve

exorbitant enormous, excessive, extortion~
ate, extravagant, extreme, immoderate, in~
ordinate, outrageous, preposterous, ridicu~
lous, unconscionable, undue, unreasonable,
unwarranted
Antonyms cheap, fair, moderate, reasonable

exorcise adjure, cast out, deliver (from),
drive out, expel, purify

exorcism adjuration, casting out, deliver~
ance, driving out, expulsion, purification

exotic 1. alien, external, extraneous, ex~
trinsic, foreign, imported, introduced, natu~
ralized, not native **2.** bizarre, colourful, cu~
rious, different, extraordinary, fascinating,
glamorous, mysterious, outlandish, pecu~
liar, strange, striking, unfamiliar, unusual
Antonyms (*sense 2*) conventional, familiar,
ordinary, pedestrian, plain, run-of-the-mill,
unmemorable, unremarkable

expand 1. amplify, augment, bloat, blow up,
broaden, develop, dilate, distend, enlarge,
extend, fatten, fill out, grow, heighten, in~
crease, inflate, lengthen, magnify, multiply,
prolong, protract, swell, thicken, wax, wid~
en **2.** diffuse, open (out), outspread, spread
(out), stretch (out), unfold, unfurl, unravel,
unroll **3.** amplify, develop, dilate, elaborate,

embellish, enlarge, expatiate, expound, flesh out, go into detail

Antonyms abbreviate, close, condense, con~ tract, decrease, reduce, shorten, shrink

expanse area, breadth, extent, field, plain, range, space, stretch, sweep, tract

expansion amplification, augmentation, development, diffusion, dilatation, disten~ sion, enlargement, expanse, growth, in~ crease, inflation, magnification, multiplica~ tion, opening out, spread, swelling, unfold~ ing, unfurling

expansive 1. dilating, distending, elastic, enlargeable, expanding, extendable, inflat~ able, stretching, stretchy, swelling **2.** all~ embracing, broad, comprehensive, exten~ sive, far-reaching, inclusive, thorough, vo~ luminous, wide, wide-ranging, widespread **3.** affable, communicative, easy, effusive, free, friendly, garrulous, genial, loquacious, open, outgoing, sociable, talkative, unre~ served, warm

expatiate amplify, descant, develop, dilate, dwell on, elaborate, embellish, enlarge, ex~ pound, go into detail

expatriate 1. *adj.* banished, emigrant, émigré, exiled, refugee **2.** *n.* emigrant, émi~ gré, exile **3.** *v.* banish, exile, expel, ostra~ cize, proscribe

expect 1. assume, believe, calculate, con~ jecture, forecast, foresee, imagine, presume, reckon, suppose, surmise, think, trust **2.** anticipate, await, bargain for, contemplate, envisage, hope for, look ahead to, look for, look forward to, predict, watch for **3.** call for, count on, demand, insist on, look for, rely upon, require, want, wish

expectancy 1. anticipation, assumption, belief, conjecture, expectation, hope, look~ ing forward, prediction, presumption, prob~ ability, supposition, surmise, suspense, waiting **2.** likelihood, outlook, prospect

expectant 1. anticipating, anxious, appre~ hensive, awaiting, eager, expecting, hopeful, in suspense, ready, watchful **2.** enceinte, expecting (*Inf.*), gravid, pregnant

expectation 1. assumption, assurance, be~ lief, calculation, confidence, conjecture, forecast, likelihood, presumption, probabil~ ity, supposition, surmise, trust **2.** anticipa~ tion, apprehension, chance, expectancy, fear, hope, looking forward, outlook, pos~ sibility, prediction, promise, prospect, sus~ pense **3.** demand, insistence, reliance, re~ quirement, trust, want, wish

expecting enceinte, expectant, gravid, in the club (*Brit. sl.*), in the family way (*Inf.*), pregnant, with child

expediency, expedience 1. advanta~ geousness, advisability, appropriateness,

aptness, benefit, convenience, desirability, effectiveness, fitness, helpfulness, judi~ ciousness, meetness, practicality, pragma~ tism, profitability, properness, propriety, prudence, suitability, usefulness, utili~ tarianism, utility **2.** contrivance, device, expedient, makeshift, manoeuvre, means, measure, method, resort, resource, scheme, shift, stopgap, stratagem, substitute

expedient 1. *adj.* advantageous, advisable, appropriate, beneficial, convenient, desir~ able, effective, fit, helpful, judicious, meet, opportune, politic, practical, pragmatic, profitable, proper, prudent, suitable, useful, utilitarian, worthwhile **2.** *n.* contrivance, device, expediency, makeshift, manoeuvre, means, measure, method, resort, resource, scheme, shift, stopgap, stratagem, substitute

Antonyms *adj.* detrimental, disadvanta~ geous, futile, harmful, ill-advised, impracti~ cal, imprudent, inadvisable, inappropriate, ineffective, inexpedient, unwise, wrong

expedite accelerate, advance, assist, dis~ patch, facilitate, forward, hasten, hurry, precipitate, press, promote, quicken, rush, speed (up), urge

Antonyms block, curb, decelerate, delay, handicap, hold up, obstruct, restrict, slow up *or* down

expedition 1. enterprise, excursion, explo~ ration, journey, mission, quest, safari, tour, trek, trip, undertaking, voyage **2.** company, crew, explorers, team, travellers, voyagers, wayfarers **3.** alacrity, celerity, dispatch, expeditiousness, haste, hurry, promptness, quickness, rapidity, readiness, speed, swift~ ness

expeditious active, alert, brisk, diligent, efficient, fast, hasty, immediate, instant, nimble, prompt, quick, rapid, ready, speedy, swift

expel 1. belch, cast out, discharge, dislodge, drive out, eject, remove, spew, throw out **2.** ban, banish, bar, black, blackball, dis~ charge, dismiss, drum out, evict, exclude, exile, expatriate, give the bum's rush (*Sl.*), oust, proscribe, relegate, send packing, show one the door, throw out, throw out on one's ear (*Inf.*), turf out (*Inf.*)

Antonyms (*sense 2*) admit, allow to enter, give access, let in, receive, take in, welcome

expend consume, disburse, dissipate, em~ ploy, exhaust, fork out (*Sl.*), go through, lay out (*Inf.*), pay out, shell out (*Inf.*), spend, use (up)

expendable dispensable, inessential, non~ essential, replaceable, unimportant, unnec~ essary

Antonyms crucial, essential, indispensable, key, necessary, vital

expenditure application, charge, con~

sumption, cost, disbursement, expense, out~
goings, outlay, output, payment, spending,
use

expense charge, consumption, cost, dis~
bursement, expenditure, loss, outlay, out~
put, payment, sacrifice, spending, toll, use

expensive costly, dear, excessive, exorbi~
tant, extravagant, high-priced, inordinate,
lavish, overpriced, rich, steep (*Inf.*), stiff
Antonyms bargain, budget, cheap, cut-price,
economical, inexpensive, low-cost, low-
priced, reasonable

experience n. **1.** contact, doing, evidence,
exposure, familiarity, involvement, know-
how (*Inf.*), knowledge, observation, partici~
pation, practice, proof, training, trial,
understanding **2.** adventure, affair, en~
counter, episode, event, happening, inci~
dent, occurrence, ordeal, test, trial ~v. **3.**
apprehend, become familiar with, behold,
encounter, endure, face, feel, go through,
have, know, live through, meet, observe,
participate in, perceive, sample, sense, suf~
fer, sustain, taste, try, undergo

experienced 1. accomplished, adept, ca~
pable, competent, expert, familiar, knowl~
edgeable, master, practised, professional,
qualified, seasoned, skilful, tested, trained,
tried, veteran, well-versed **2.** knowing, ma~
ture, sophisticated, wise, worldly, worldly-
wise
Antonyms apprentice, green, incompetent,
inexperienced, new, unqualified, unskilled,
untrained, untried

experiment 1. n. assay, attempt, examina~
tion, experimentation, investigation, pro~
cedure, proof, research, test, trial, trial and
error, trial run, venture **2.** v. assay, exam~
ine, investigate, put to the test, research,
sample, test, try, verify

experimental empirical, exploratory, pilot,
preliminary, probationary, provisional,
speculative, tentative, test, trial, trial-and-
error

expert 1. n. ace (*Inf.*), adept, authority, buff
(*Inf.*), connoisseur, dab hand (*Brit. inf.*),
hotshot (*Inf.*), master, maven (*U.S.*), past
master, pro (*Inf.*), professional, specialist,
virtuoso, whiz (*Inf.*), wizard **2.** adj. able,
adept, adroit, apt, clever, deft, dexterous,
experienced, facile, handy, knowledgeable,
master, masterly, practised, professional,
proficient, qualified, skilful, skilled, trained,
virtuoso
Antonyms n. amateur, dabbler, ham, lay~
man, nonprofessional, novice ~adj. amateur~
ish, cack-handed (*Inf.*), clumsy, incompetent,
inexperienced, unpractised, unqualified, un~
skilled, untrained

expertise ableness, adroitness, aptness,
cleverness, command, craft, deftness, dex~

terity, expertness, facility, judgment, knack,
know-how (*Inf.*), knowledge, masterliness,
mastery, proficiency, skilfulness, skill

expertness ableness, adroitness, aptness,
command, craft, deftness, dexterity, expert~
ise, facility, judgment, know-how (*Inf.*),
knowledge, masterliness, mastery, profi~
ciency, skilfulness, skill

expire 1. cease, close, come to an end, con~
clude, end, finish, lapse, run out, stop, ter~
minate **2.** breathe out, emit, exhale, expel
3. buy it (*U.S. sl.*), check out (*U.S. sl.*),
croak (*Sl.*), decease, depart, die, go belly-up
(*Sl.*), kick it (*Sl.*), kick the bucket (*Inf.*),
pass away or on, peg it (*Inf.*), peg out (*Inf.*),
perish, pop one's clogs (*Inf.*)

explain 1. clarify, clear up, define, demon~
strate, describe, disclose, elucidate, expli~
cate (*Formal*), expound, illustrate, interpret,
make clear or plain, resolve, solve, teach,
unfold **2.** account for, excuse, give an ex~
planation for, give a reason for, justify

explanation 1. clarification, definition,
demonstration, description, elucidation, ex~
plication, exposition, illustration, interpre~
tation, resolution **2.** account, answer, cause,
excuse, justification, meaning, mitigation,
motive, reason, sense, significance, vindi~
cation

explanatory demonstrative, descriptive,
elucidatory, explicative, expository, illumi~
native, illustrative, interpretive, justifying

explicit absolute, categorical, certain, clear,
definite, direct, distinct, exact, express,
frank, open, outspoken, patent, plain, posi~
tive, precise, specific, stated, straight~
forward, unambiguous, unequivocal, un~
qualified, unreserved, upfront (*Inf.*)
Antonyms ambiguous, cryptic, general, im~
plicit, implied, indefinite, indirect, inexact,
obscure, oracular, suggested, uncertain,
vague

explode 1. blow up, burst, detonate, dis~
charge, erupt, go off, set off, shatter, shiver
2. belie, debunk, discredit, disprove, give
the lie to, invalidate, refute, repudiate

exploit n. **1.** accomplishment, achievement,
adventure, attainment, deed, escapade, feat,
stunt ~v. **2.** abuse, impose upon, manipu~
late, milk, misuse, play on or upon, take
advantage of **3.** capitalize on, cash in on
(*Inf.*), make capital out of, make use of,
profit by or from, put to use, turn to ac~
count, use, use to advantage, utilize

exploration 1. analysis, examination, in~
quiry, inspection, investigation, probe, re~
search, scrutiny, search, study **2.** expedi~
tion, recce (*Sl.*), reconnaissance, survey,
tour, travel, trip

exploratory analytic, experimental, fact-finding, investigative, probing, searching, trial

explore 1. analyse, examine, inquire into, inspect, investigate, look into, probe, prospect, research, scrutinize, search, work over **2.** case (*Sl.*), have *or* take a look around, range over, recce (*Sl.*), reconnoitre, scout, survey, tour, travel, traverse

explosion 1. bang, blast, burst, clap, crack, detonation, discharge, outburst, report **2.** eruption, fit, outbreak, outburst, paroxysm

explosive 1. unstable, volatile **2.** fiery, stormy, touchy, vehement, violent **3.** charged, dangerous, hazardous, over~ wrought, perilous, tense, ugly

exponent 1. advocate, backer, champion, defender, promoter, propagandist, propo~ nent, spokesman, spokeswoman, supporter, upholder **2.** commentator, demonstrator, elucidator, expositor, expounder, illustrator, interpreter **3.** example, exemplar, illustra~ tion, indication, model, norm, sample, specimen, type **4.** executant, interpreter, performer, player, presenter

expose 1. display, exhibit, manifest, pres~ ent, put on view, reveal, show, uncover, unveil **2.** air, betray, blow wide open (*Sl.*), bring to light, denounce, detect, disclose, divulge, lay bare, let out, make known, re~ veal, show up, smoke out, uncover, unearth, unmask **3.** endanger, hazard, imperil, jeop~ ardize, lay open, leave open, make vulner~ able, risk, subject **4.** *With* **to** acquaint with, bring into contact with, familiarize with, introduce to, make conversant with
Antonyms conceal, cover, hide, keep secret, mask, protect, screen, shelter, shield

exposed 1. bare, exhibited, laid bare, made manifest, made public, on display, on show, on view, revealed, shown, unconcealed, un~ covered, unveiled **2.** open, open to the el~ ements, unprotected, unsheltered **3.** in danger, in peril, laid bare, laid open, left open, liable, open, susceptible, vulnerable

exposition 1. account, commentary, cri~ tique, description, elucidation, exegesis, ex~ planation, explication, illustration, inter~ pretation, presentation **2.** demonstration, display, exhibition, expo (*Inf.*), fair, presen~ tation, show

expostulate argue (with), dissuade, pro~ test, reason (with), remonstrate (with)

exposure 1. baring, display, exhibition, manifestation, presentation, publicity, rev~ elation, showing, uncovering, unveiling **2.** airing, betrayal, denunciation, detection, disclosure, divulgence, divulging, exposé, revelation, unmasking **3.** danger, hazard, jeopardy, risk, vulnerability **4.** acquaint~ ance, contact, conversancy, experience, fa~ miliarity, introduction, knowledge **5.** as~

pect, frontage, location, outlook, position, setting, view

expound describe, elucidate, explain, ex~ plicate (*Formal*), illustrate, interpret, set forth, spell out, unfold

express *v.* **1.** articulate, assert, asseverate, communicate, couch, declare, enunciate, phrase, pronounce, put, put across, put into words, say, speak, state, tell, utter, verbal~ ize, voice, word **2.** bespeak, convey, denote, depict, designate, disclose, divulge, embody, evince, exhibit, indicate, intimate, make known, manifest, represent, reveal, show, signify, stand for, symbolize, testify **3.** ex~ tract, force out, press out, squeeze out ~*adj.* **4.** accurate, categorical, certain, clear, definite, direct, distinct, exact, explicit, out~ right, plain, pointed, precise, unambiguous **5.** clear-cut, especial, particular, singular, special **6.** direct, fast, high-speed, nonstop, quick, quickie (*Inf.*), rapid, speedy, swift

expression 1. announcement, assertion, asseveration, communication, declaration, enunciation, mention, pronouncement, speaking, statement, utterance, verbaliza~ tion, voicing **2.** demonstration, embodi~ ment, exhibition, indication, manifestation, representation, show, sign, symbol, token **3.** air, appearance, aspect, countenance, face, look, mien (*Literary*) **4.** choice of words, delivery, diction, emphasis, execu~ tion, intonation, language, phraseology, phrasing, speech, style, wording **5.** idiom, locution, phrase, remark, set phrase, term, turn of phrase, word

expressive 1. eloquent, emphatic, energet~ ic, forcible, lively, mobile, moving, poign~ ant, striking, strong, sympathetic, telling, vivid **2.** allusive, demonstrative, indicative, meaningful, pointed, pregnant, revealing, significant, suggestive, thoughtful
Antonyms blank, dead-pan, dull, empty, im~ passive, inscrutable, poker-faced (*Inf.*), straight-faced, vacuous, wooden

expressly 1. especially, exactly, intention~ ally, on purpose, particularly, precisely, purposely, specially, specifically **2.** abso~ lutely, categorically, clearly, decidedly, definitely, distinctly, explicitly, in no un~ certain terms, manifestly, outright, plainly, pointedly, positively, unambiguously, un~ equivocally, unmistakably

expropriate appropriate, arrogate, assume, commandeer, confiscate, impound, requisi~ tion, seize, take, take over

expulsion banishment, debarment, dis~ charge, dislodgment, dismissal, ejection, eviction, exclusion, exile, expatriation, ex~ trusion, proscription, removal

expurgate blue-pencil, bowdlerize, censor, clean up (*Inf.*), cut, purge, purify

exquisite 1. beautiful, dainty, delicate, el~
egant, fine, lovely, precious **2.** attractive,
beautiful, charming, comely, lovely, pleas~
ing, striking **3.** admirable, choice, consum~
mate, delicious, excellent, fine, flawless, in~
comparable, matchless, outstanding, peer~
less, perfect, rare, select, splendid, superb,
superlative **4.** appreciative, consummate,
cultivated, discerning, discriminating, fas~
tidious, impeccable, meticulous, polished,
refined, selective, sensitive **5.** acute, excru~
ciating, intense, keen, piercing, poignant,
sharp
Antonyms flawed, ill-favoured, imperfect,
ugly, unattractive, unlovely, unsightly

extempore *adv./adj.* ad lib, extempora~
neous, extemporary, freely, impromptu, im~
provised, offhand, off the cuff (*Inf.*), off the
top of one's head, on the spot, spontaneous~
ly, unplanned, unpremeditated, unprepared

extemporize ad-lib, busk, improvise, make
up, play (it) by ear, vamp, wing it (*Inf.*)

extend 1. carry on, continue, drag out,
draw out, elongate, lengthen, make longer,
prolong, protract, spin out, spread out,
stretch, unfurl, unroll **2.** carry on, con~
tinue, go on, last, take **3.** amount to, attain,
go as far as, reach, spread **4.** add to, ampli~
fy, augment, broaden, develop, dilate, en~
hance, enlarge, expand, increase, spread,
supplement, widen **5.** advance, bestow,
confer, give, grant, hold out, impart, offer,
present, proffer, put forth, reach out,
stretch out, yield
Antonyms abbreviate, abridge, condense,
contract, curtail, cut, decrease, limit, reduce,
restrict, shorten, take back, withdraw

extended 1. continued, drawn-out, elon~
gated, enlarged, lengthened, long, pro~
longed, protracted, spread (out), stretched
out, unfolded, unfurled, unrolled **2.** broad,
comprehensive, enlarged, expanded, exten~
sive, far-reaching, large-scale, sweeping,
thorough, wide, widespread **3.** conferred,
outstretched, proffered, stretched out

extension 1. amplification, augmentation,
broadening, continuation, delay, develop~
ment, dilatation, distension, elongation, en~
largement, expansion, extent, increase,
lengthening, postponement, prolongation,
protraction, spread, stretching, widening **2.**
addendum, addition, add-on, adjunct, an~
nexe, appendage, appendix, branch, ell,
supplement, wing

extensive all-inclusive, broad, capacious,
commodious, comprehensive, expanded, ex~
tended, far-flung, far-reaching, general,
great, huge, humongous *or* humungous
(*U.S. sl.*), large, large-scale, lengthy, long,
pervasive, prevalent, protracted, spacious,
sweeping, thorough, universal, vast, volu~
minous, wholesale, wide, widespread
Antonyms circumscribed, confined, con~
stricted, limited, narrow, restricted, tight

extent 1. ambit, bounds, compass, play,
range, reach, scope, sphere, sweep **2.**
amount, amplitude, area, breadth, bulk, de~
gree, duration, expanse, expansion, length,
magnitude, measure, quantity, size, stretch,
term, time, volume, width

extenuating justifying, mitigating, moder~
ating, qualifying, serving as an excuse

exterior *n.* **1.** appearance, aspect, coating,
covering, façade, face, finish, outside, shell,
skin, surface ~*adj.* **2.** external, outer,
outermost, outside, outward, superficial,
surface **3.** alien, exotic, external, extra~
neous, extrinsic, foreign, outside
Antonyms *n.* inner, inside, interior ~*adj.*
domestic, inherent, inside, interior, internal,
intrinsic

exterminate abolish, annihilate, destroy,
eliminate, eradicate, extirpate

external 1. apparent, exterior, outer,
outermost, outside, outward, superficial,
surface, visible **2.** alien, exotic, exterior,
extramural, extraneous, extrinsic, foreign,
independent, outside
Antonyms inherent, inner, inside, interior,
internal, intrinsic

extinct 1. dead, defunct, gone, lost, van~
ished **2.** doused, extinguished, inactive, out,
quenched, snuffed out **3.** abolished, defunct,
ended, obsolete, terminated, void
Antonyms active, existing, extant,
flourishing, living, surviving, thriving

extinction abolition, annihilation, death,
destruction, dying out, eradication, exci~
sion, extermination, extirpation, oblitera~
tion, oblivion

extinguish 1. blow out, douse, put out,
quench, smother, snuff out, stifle **2.** abolish,
annihilate, destroy, eliminate, end, eradi~
cate, erase, expunge, exterminate, extirpate,
kill, obscure, remove, suppress, wipe out

extol acclaim, applaud, celebrate, commend,
crack up (*Inf.*), cry up, eulogize, exalt, glo~
rify, laud, magnify (*Archaic*), panegyrize,
pay tribute to, praise, sing the praises of

extort blackmail, bleed (*Inf.*), bully, coerce,
exact, extract, force, squeeze, wrest, wring

extortion 1. blackmail, coercion, compul~
sion, demand, exaction, force, oppression,
rapacity, shakedown (*U.S. sl.*) **2.** enormity,
exorbitance, expensiveness, overcharging

extortionate 1. excessive, exorbitant, ex~
travagant, immoderate, inflated, inordinate,
outrageous, preposterous, sky-high, unrea~
sonable **2.** blood-sucking (*Inf.*), exacting,

grasping, hard, harsh, oppressive, rapa~
cious, rigorous, severe, usurious
Antonyms (*sense 1*) fair, inexpensive, mod~
erate, modest, reasonable

extra *adj.* **1.** accessory, added, additional,
add-on, ancillary, auxiliary, fresh, further,
more, new, other, supplemental, sup~
plementary **2.** excess, extraneous, inessen~
tial, leftover, needless, redundant, reserve,
spare, supererogatory, superfluous, super~
numerary, surplus, unnecessary, unneeded,
unused ~*n.* **3.** accessory, addendum, addi~
tion, add-on, adjunct, affix, appendage, ap~
purtenance, attachment, bonus, comple~
ment, extension, supernumerary, sup~
plement ~*adv.* **4.** especially, exceptionally,
extraordinarily, extremely, particularly, re~
markably, uncommonly, unusually
Antonyms *adj.* (*sense 2*) compulsory, essen~
tial, mandatory, necessary, needed, obliga~
tory, required, requisite, vital ~*n.* essential,
must, necessity, precondition, prerequisite,
requirement, requisite

extract *v.* **1.** draw, extirpate, pluck out,
pull, pull out, remove, take out, uproot,
withdraw **2.** bring out, derive, draw, elicit,
evoke, exact, gather, get, glean, obtain,
reap, wrest, wring **3.** deduce, derive, devel~
op, educe, elicit, evolve **4.** distil, draw out,
express, obtain, press out, separate out,
squeeze, take out **5.** abstract, choose, cite,
copy out, cull, cut out, quote, select ~*n.* **6.**
concentrate, decoction, distillate, distilla~
tion, essence, juice **7.** abstract, citation,
clipping, cutting, excerpt, passage, quota~
tion, selection

extraction 1. drawing, extirpation, pulling,
removal, taking out, uprooting, withdrawal
2. derivation, distillation, separation **3.** an~
cestry, birth, blood, derivation, descent,
family, lineage, origin, parentage, pedigree,
race, stock

extraneous 1. accidental, additional, ad~
ventitious, extra, incidental, inessential,
needless, nonessential, peripheral, redun~
dant, superfluous, supplementary, unessen~
tial, unnecessary, unneeded **2.** beside the
point, immaterial, impertinent, inadmissi~
ble, inapplicable, inapposite, inappropriate,
inapt, irrelevant, off the subject, uncon~
nected, unrelated **3.** adventitious, alien, ex~
otic, external, extrinsic, foreign, out of
place, strange

extraordinary amazing, bizarre, curious,
exceptional, fantastic, marvellous, notable,
odd, outstanding, particular, peculiar, phe~
nomenal, rare, remarkable, singular, spe~
cial, strange, surprising, uncommon, unfa~
miliar, unheard-of, unique, unprecedented,
unusual, unwonted, weird, wonderful, won~
drous (*Archaic or literary*)
Antonyms banal, common, commonplace,

customary, everyday, ordinary, unexception~
al, unremarkable, usual

extravagance 1. improvidence, lavishness,
overspending, prodigality, profligacy, pro~
fusion, squandering, waste, wastefulness **2.**
absurdity, dissipation, exaggeration, excess,
exorbitance, folly, immoderation, outra~
geousness, preposterousness, recklessness,
unreasonableness, unrestraint, wildness

extravagant 1. excessive, improvident,
imprudent, lavish, prodigal, profligate,
spendthrift, wasteful **2.** absurd, exaggerat~
ed, excessive, exorbitant, fanciful, fantastic,
foolish, immoderate, inordinate, O.T.T. (*Sl.*),
outrageous, over the top (*Sl.*), preposterous,
reckless, unreasonable, unrestrained, wild
3. fancy, flamboyant, flashy, garish, gaudy,
grandiose, ornate, ostentatious, pretentious,
showy **4.** costly, excessive, exorbitant, ex~
pensive, extortionate, inordinate, over~
priced, steep (*Inf.*), unreasonable
Antonyms careful, close, conservative,
down-to-earth, economical, frugal, miserly,
moderate, prudent, realistic, reasonable, re~
strained, sensible, sober, sparing, thrifty,
tight-fisted (*Inf.*)

extreme *adj.* **1.** acute, great, greatest, high,
highest, intense, maximum, severe, su~
preme, ultimate, utmost, uttermost, worst
2. downright, egregious, exaggerated, ex~
ceptional, excessive, extraordinary, ex~
travagant, fanatical, immoderate, inordi~
nate, intemperate, O.T.T. (*Sl.*), out-and-out,
outrageous, over the top (*Sl.*), radical, re~
markable, sheer, uncommon, unconven~
tional, unreasonable, unusual, utter, zealous
3. dire, Draconian, drastic, harsh, radical,
rigid, severe, stern, strict, unbending, un~
compromising **4.** faraway, far-off, farthest,
final, last, most distant, outermost, remot~
est, terminal, ultimate, utmost, uttermost
~*n.* **5.** acme, apex, apogee, boundary, cli~
max, consummation, depth, edge, end, ex~
cess, extremity, height, limit, maximum,
minimum, nadir, pinnacle, pole, termina~
tion, top, ultimate, zenith
Antonyms *adj.* average, common, mild,
moderate, modest, nearest, ordinary, reason~
able, traditional, unremarkable

extremely acutely, awfully (*Inf.*), exceed~
ingly, exceptionally, excessively, extraordi~
narily, greatly, highly, inordinately, in~
tensely, markedly, quite, severely, terribly,
to or in the extreme, ultra, uncommonly,
unusually, utterly, very

extremist die-hard, fanatic, radical, ultra,
zealot

extremity 1. acme, apex, apogee, border,
bound, boundary, brim, brink, edge, end,
extreme, frontier, limit, margin, maximum,
minimum, nadir, pinnacle, pole, rim, ter~

minal, termination, terminus, tip, top, ulti~ mate, verge, zenith **2.** acuteness, climax, consummation, depth, excess, height **3.** ad~ versity, crisis, dire straits, disaster, emer~ gency, exigency, hardship, pinch, plight, setback, trouble **4.** *Plural* fingers and toes, hands and feet, limbs

extricate clear, deliver, disembarrass, dis~ engage, disentangle, free, get out, get (someone) off the hook (*Sl.*), liberate, re~ lease, relieve, remove, rescue, withdraw, wriggle out of

extrovert amiable, exuberant, gregarious, hearty, out-going, sociable, social
Antonyms introspective, introverted, inward-looking, self-contained, withdrawn

exuberance 1. animation, brio, buoyancy, cheerfulness, eagerness, ebullience, effer~ vescence, energy, enthusiasm, excitement, exhilaration, high spirits, life, liveliness, pep, spirit, sprightliness, vigour, vitality, vivacity, zest **2.** effusiveness, exaggeration, excessiveness, fulsomeness, lavishness, prodigality, superfluity **3.** abundance, copi~ ousness, lavishness, lushness, luxuriance, plenitude, profusion, rankness, richness, superabundance, teemingness

exuberant 1. animated, buoyant, cheerful, chirpy (*Inf.*), eager, ebullient, effervescent, elated, energetic, enthusiastic, excited, ex~ hilarated, full of life, high-spirited, in high spirits, lively, sparkling, spirited, sprightly, upbeat (*Inf.*), vigorous, vivacious, zestful **2.** effusive, exaggerated, excessive, fulsome, lavish, overdone, prodigal, superfluous **3.** abundant, copious, lavish, lush, luxuriant, overflowing, plenteous, plentiful, profuse, rank, rich, superabundant, teeming
Antonyms (*sense 1*) apathetic, dull, lifeless, subdued, unenthusiastic

exult 1. be delighted, be elated, be in high spirits, be joyful, be jubilant, be overjoyed, celebrate, jubilate, jump for joy, make mer~ ry, rejoice **2.** boast, brag, crow, drool, gloat, glory (in), revel, take delight in, taunt, tri~ umph, vaunt

exultant cock-a-hoop, delighted, elated, ex~ ulting, flushed, gleeful, joyful, joyous, jubi~ lant, overjoyed, over the moon (*Inf.*), rapt,

rejoicing, revelling, transported, trium~ phant

exultation 1. celebration, delight, elation, glee, high spirits, joy, joyousness, jubila~ tion, merriness, rejoicing, transport **2.** boasting, bragging, crowing, gloating, glory, glorying, revelling, triumph

eye *n.* **1.** eyeball, optic (*Inf.*), orb (*Poetic*), peeper (*Sl.*) **2.** appreciation, discernment, discrimination, judgment, perception, rec~ ognition, taste **3.** *Often plural* belief, judg~ ment, mind, opinion, point of view, view~ point **4. keep an** *or* **one's eye on** guard, keep in view, keep tabs on (*Inf.*), keep un~ der surveillance, look after, look out for, monitor, observe, pay attention to, regard, scrutinize, supervise, survey, watch, watch over **5. an eye for an eye** justice, reprisal, requital, retaliation, retribution, revenge, vengeance **6. lay, clap** *or* **set eyes on** be~ hold, come across, encounter, meet, notice, observe, run into, see **7. see eye to eye** accord, agree, back, be in unison, coincide, concur, fall in, get on, go along, harmonize, jibe (*Inf.*), subscribe to **8. up to one's eyes** busy, caught up, engaged, flooded out, fully occupied, inundated, overwhelmed, up to here, up to one's elbows, wrapped up in ~*v.* **9.** check, check out (*Inf.*), clock (*Brit. sl.*), contemplate, eyeball (*U.S. sl.*), gaze at, get a load of (*Inf.*), glance at, have *or* take a look at, inspect, look at, peruse, recce (*Sl.*), re~ gard, scan, scrutinize, stare at, study, sur~ vey, take a dekko at (*Brit. sl.*), view, watch **10.** eye up, give (someone) the (glad) eye, leer at, make eyes at, ogle

eyeful 1. butcher's (*Brit. sl.*), gander (*Inf.*), gaze, glance, look, shufti (*Brit. sl.*), sight, view **2.** beauty, dazzler, knockout (*Inf.*), show, sight, sight for sore eyes (*Inf.*), spec~ tacle, stunner (*Inf.*), vision

eyesight observation, perception, range of vision, sight, vision

eyesore atrocity, blemish, blight, blot, disfigurement, disgrace, horror, mess, mon~ strosity, sight (*Inf.*), ugliness

eyewitness bystander, looker-on, observer, onlooker, passer-by, spectator, viewer, watcher, witness

F

fable 1. allegory, apologue, legend, myth, parable, story, tale **2.** fabrication, fairy story (*Inf.*), falsehood, fantasy, fib, fiction, figment, invention, lie, romance, tall story (*Inf.*), untruth, urban legend, white lie, yarn (*Inf.*)
Antonyms actuality, certainty, fact, reality, truth, verity

fabric 1. cloth, material, stuff, textile, web **2.** constitution, construction, foundations, framework, infrastructure, make-up, organization, structure

fabricate 1. assemble, build, construct, erect, fashion, form, frame, make, manufacture, shape **2.** coin, concoct, devise, fake, falsify, feign, forge, form, invent, make up, trump up

fabrication 1. assemblage, assembly, building, construction, erection, manufacture, production **2.** cock-and-bull story (*Inf.*), concoction, fable, fairy story (*Inf.*), fake, falsehood, fiction, figment, forgery, invention, lie, myth, pork pie (*Brit. sl.*), porky (*Brit. sl.*), untruth

fabulous 1. amazing, astounding, breathtaking, fictitious, immense, inconceivable, incredible, legendary, phenomenal, unbelievable **2.** *Inf.* brilliant, fantastic (*Inf.*), magic (*Inf.*), marvellous, out-of-this-world (*Inf.*), sensational (*Inf.*), spectacular, superb, wonderful **3.** apocryphal, fantastic, fictitious, imaginary, invented, legendary, made-up, mythical, unreal
Antonyms actual, common, commonplace, credible, genuine, natural, ordinary, real

façade appearance, exterior, face, front, frontage, guise, mask, pretence, semblance, show, veneer

face *n.* **1.** clock (*Brit. sl.*), countenance, dial (*Brit. sl.*), features, kisser (*Sl.*), lineaments, mug (*Sl.*), phiz *or* phizog (*Sl.*), physiognomy, visage **2.** appearance, aspect, expression, frown, grimace, look, *moue*, pout, scowl, smirk **3.** air, appearance, disguise, display, exterior, façade, front, mask, pretence, semblance, show **4.** authority, dignity, honour, image, prestige, reputation, self-respect, standing, status **5.** *Inf.* assurance, audacity, boldness, brass neck (*Brit. inf.*), cheek (*Inf.*), chutzpah (*U.S. & Canad. inf.*), confidence, effrontery, front, gall (*Inf.*), impudence, neck (*Inf.*), nerve, presumption, sauce (*Inf.*) **6.** aspect, cover, exterior, facet, front, outside, right side, side, surface **7. face to face** *à deux*, confronting, eyeball to

eyeball, in confrontation, opposite, tête-à-tête, vis-à-vis **8. fly in the face of** act in defiance of, defy, disobey, go against, oppose, rebel against, snap one's fingers at (*Inf.*) **9. on the face of it** apparently, at first sight, seemingly, to all appearances, to the eye **10. pull (**or** make) a long face** frown, grimace, knit one's brows, look black (disapproving, displeased, put out, stern), lour *or* lower, pout, scowl, sulk **11. show one's face** approach, be seen, come, put in *or* make an appearance, show up (*Inf.*), turn up **12. to one's face** directly, in one's presence, openly, straight ~*v.* **13.** be confronted by, brave, come up against, confront, cope with, deal with, defy, encounter, experience, face off (*Sl.*), meet, oppose, tackle **14.** be opposite, front onto, give towards *or* onto, look onto, overlook **15.** clad, coat, cover, dress, finish, level, line, overlay, sheathe, surface, veneer

facet angle, aspect, face, part, phase, plane, side, slant, surface

facetious amusing, comical, droll, flippant, frivolous, funny, humorous, jesting, jocose, jocular, merry, playful, pleasant, tongue in cheek, unserious, waggish, witty
Antonyms earnest, genuine, grave, lugubrious, pensive, sedate, serious, sincere, sober, thoughtful

face up to accept, acknowledge, come to terms with, confront, cope with, deal with, meet head-on, tackle

facile 1. adept, adroit, dexterous, easy, effortless, fluent, light, proficient, quick, ready, simple, skilful, smooth, uncomplicated **2.** cursory, glib, hasty, shallow, slick, superficial
Antonyms awkward, careful, clumsy, difficult, intractable, maladroit, slow, thoughtful, unskilful

facilitate assist the progress of, ease, expedite, forward, further, help, make easy, promote, smooth the path of, speed up
Antonyms delay, encumber, frustrate, hamper, handicap, hinder, hold up *or* back, impede, obstruct, prevent, restrain, thwart

facility 1. ability, adroitness, craft, dexterity, ease, efficiency, effortlessness, expertness, fluency, gift, knack, proficiency, quickness, readiness, skilfulness, skill, smoothness, talent **2.** *Often plural* advantage, aid, amenity, appliance, convenience, equipment, means, opportunity, resource
Antonyms awkwardness, clumsiness,

difficulty, hardship, ineptness, maladroit~ness, pains

facing 1. *adj.* fronting, opposite, partnering **2.** *n.* cladding, coating, façade, false front, front, overlay, plaster, reinforcement, re~vetment, stucco, surface, trimming, veneer

facsimile carbon, carbon copy, copy, dupli~cate, fax (*Trademark*), photocopy, Photostat (*Trademark*), print, replica, reproduction, transcript, Xerox (*Trademark*)

fact 1. act, deed, event, *fait accompli,* hap~pening, incident, occurrence, performance **2.** actuality, certainty, gospel (truth), naked truth, reality, truth **3.** circumstance, detail, feature, item, particular, point, specific **4. in fact** actually, indeed, in point of fact, in reality, in truth, really, truly
Antonyms delusion, fable, fabrication, falsehood, fiction, invention, lie, tall story, untruth, yarn (*Inf.*)

faction 1. bloc, cabal, camp, caucus, clique, coalition, combination, confederacy, con~tingent, coterie, division, gang, ginger group, group, junta, lobby, minority, party, pressure group, schism, section, sector, set, splinter group **2.** conflict, disagreement, discord, disharmony, dissension, disunity, division, divisiveness, friction, infighting, rebellion, sedition, strife, tumult, turbu~lence
Antonyms (*sense 2*) accord, agreement, am~ity, assent, concord, consensus, friendship, goodwill, harmony, peace, rapport, unanim~ity, unity

factious conflicting, contentious, disputa~tious, dissident, divisive, insurrectionary, litigious, malcontent, mutinous, partisan, rebellious, refractory, rival, sectarian, sedi~tious, troublemaking, tumultuous, turbu~lent, warring

factor 1. aspect, cause, circumstance, com~ponent, consideration, determinant, el~ement, influence, item, part, point, thing **2.** *Scot.* agent, deputy, estate manager, middleman, reeve, steward

factory manufactory (*Obsolete*), mill, plant, works

factotum Girl Friday, handyman, jack of all trades, Man Friday, man of all work, odd job man

facts data, details, gen (*Brit. inf.*), info (*Inf.*), information, the lowdown (*Inf.*), the score (*Inf.*), the whole story

factual accurate, authentic, circumstantial, close, correct, credible, exact, faithful, genuine, literal, matter-of-fact, objective, precise, real, sure, true, true-to-life, un~adorned, unbiased, veritable
Antonyms embellished, fanciful, fictitious, fictive, figurative, imaginary, unreal

faculties capabilities, intelligence, powers, reason, senses, wits

faculty 1. ability, adroitness, aptitude, bent, capability, capacity, cleverness, dexterity, facility, gift, knack, power, propensity, readiness, skill, talent, turn **2.** branch of learning, department, discipline, profession, school, teaching staff (*Chiefly U.S.*) **3.** authorization, licence, prerogative, privi~lege, right
Antonyms (*sense 1*) failing, inability, short~coming, unskilfulness, weak point, weakness

fad affectation, craze, fancy, fashion, mania, mode, rage, trend, vogue, whim

fade 1. blanch, bleach, blench, dim, discol~our, dull, grow dim, lose colour, lose lustre, pale, wash out **2.** decline, die away, die out, dim, disappear, disperse, dissolve, droop, dwindle, ebb, etiolate, evanesce, fail, fall, flag, languish, melt away, perish, shrivel, vanish, vanish into thin air, wane, waste away, wilt, wither

faded bleached, dim, discoloured, dull, etio~lated, indistinct, lustreless, pale, washed out

fading declining, decreasing, disappearing, dying, on the decline, vanishing

faeces bodily waste, droppings, dung, ex~crement, excreta, ordure, stools

fag bender (*Sl.*), catamite, dyke (*Sl.*), fairy (*Sl.*), gay, homo (*Inf.*), homosexual, lesbian, nancy boy (*Sl.*), poof (*Sl.*), poofter (*Sl.*), queen (*Sl.*), queer (*Inf., derogatory*), woofter (*Sl.*)

fail 1. be defeated, be found lacking *or* want~ing, be in vain, be unsuccessful, break down, come a cropper (*Inf.*), come to grief, come to naught, come to nothing, fall, fall short, fall short of, fall through, fizzle out (*Inf.*), flop (*Inf.*), founder, go astray, go belly-up (*Sl.*), go down, go down like a lead balloon (*Inf.*), go up in smoke, meet with disaster, miscarry, misfire, miss, not make the grade (*Inf.*), run aground, turn out bad~ly **2.** abandon, break one's word, desert, disappoint, forget, forsake, let down, ne~glect, omit **3.** be on one's last legs (*Inf.*), cease, conk out (*Inf.*), cut out, decline, die, disappear, droop, dwindle, fade, give out, give up, gutter, languish, peter out, sicken, sink, stop working, wane, weaken **4.** be~come insolvent, close down, crash, fold (*Inf.*), go bankrupt, go broke (*Inf.*), go bust (*Inf.*), go into receivership, go out of busi~ness, go to the wall, go under, smash **5. without fail** conscientiously, constantly, dependably, like clockwork, punctually, regularly, religiously, without exception
Antonyms bloom, flourish, grow, pass, prosper, strengthen, succeed, thrive, triumph

failing 1. *n.* blemish, blind spot, defect, deficiency, drawback, error, failure, fault, flaw, foible, frailty, imperfection, lapse, miscarriage, misfortune, shortcoming, weakness **2.** *prep.* in default of, in the ab~ sence of, lacking

Antonyms *(sense 1)* advantage, asset, forte, metier, speciality, strength, strong suit

failure 1. abortion, breakdown, collapse, de~ feat, downfall, fiasco, frustration, lack of success, miscarriage, overthrow, wreck **2.** black sheep, dead duck *(Sl.)*, disappoint~ ment, dud *(Inf.)*, flop *(Inf.)*, incompetent, loser, ne'er-do-well, no-good, no-hoper *(Chiefly Aust.)*, nonstarter, washout *(Inf.)* **3.** default, deficiency, dereliction, neglect, negligence, nonobservance, nonperfor~ mance, nonsuccess, omission, remissness, shortcoming, stoppage **4.** breakdown, decay, decline, deterioration, failing, loss **5.** bank~ ruptcy, crash, downfall, folding *(Inf.)*, insol~ vency, ruin

Antonyms adequacy, care, effectiveness, fortune, observance, prosperity, strengthen~ ing, success, triumph

faint *adj.* **1.** bleached, delicate, dim, distant, dull, faded, faltering, feeble, hazy, hushed, ill-defined, indistinct, light, low, muffled, muted, soft, subdued, thin, vague, whis~ pered **2.** feeble, remote, slight, unenthusi~ astic, weak **3.** dizzy, drooping, enervated, exhausted, faltering, fatigued, giddy, lan~ guid, lethargic, light-headed, muzzy, ver~ tiginous, weak, woozy *(Inf.)* **4.** faint-hearted, lily-livered, spiritless, timid, tim~ orous ~*v.* **5.** black out, collapse, fade, fail, flake out *(Inf.)*, keel over *(Inf.)*, languish, lose consciousness, pass out, swoon *(Liter~ ary)*, weaken ~*n.* **6.** blackout, collapse, swoon *(Literary)*, syncope *(Pathology)*, un~ consciousness

Antonyms *adj.* bold, brave, bright, clear, conspicuous, courageous, distinct, energetic, fresh, hearty, loud, powerful, strong, vigorous

faint-hearted chickenshit *(U.S. sl.)*, cow~ ardly, diffident, half-arsed, half-assed *(U.S. & Canad. sl.)*, half-hearted, irresolute, spineless, timid, timorous, weak, yellow

faintly 1. feebly, in a whisper, indistinctly, softly, weakly **2.** a little, dimly, slightly, somewhat

Antonyms audacious, bold, brave, coura~ geous, daring, dauntless, fearless, game *(Inf.)*, intrepid, plucky, stouthearted

fair[1] *adj.* **1.** above board, according to the rules, clean, disinterested, dispassionate, equal, equitable, even-handed, honest, hon~ ourable, impartial, just, lawful, legitimate, objective, on the level *(Inf.)*, proper, square, trustworthy, unbiased, unprejudiced, upright **2.** blond, blonde, fair-haired, flaxen-haired, light, light-complexioned, tow-haired, towheaded **3.** adequate, all right, average, decent, mediocre, middling,

moderate, not bad, O.K. *or* okay *(Inf.)*, passable, reasonable, respectable, satisfac~ tory, so-so *(Inf.)*, tolerable **4.** beauteous, beautiful, bonny, comely, handsome, lovely, pretty, well-favoured **5.** bright, clear, clem~ ent, cloudless, dry, favourable, fine, sunny, sunshiny, unclouded

Antonyms *(sense 1)* bad, biased, bigoted, dis~ criminatory, dishonest, inequitable, one-sided, partial, partisan, prejudiced, unfair, unjust *(sense 4)* homely, plain, ugly

fair[2] *n.* bazaar, carnival, expo *(Inf.)*, exposi~ tion, festival, fête, gala, market, show

fair-and-square above board, correct, honest, just, kosher *(Inf.)*, on the level *(Inf.)*, straight

fairly 1. adequately, moderately, pretty well, quite, rather, reasonably, somewhat, toler~ ably **2.** deservedly, equitably, honestly, im~ partially, justly, objectively, properly, with~ out fear or favour **3.** absolutely, in a man~ ner of speaking, positively, really, veritably

fair-minded disinterested, even-handed, impartial, just, open-minded, unbiased, un~ prejudiced

fairness decency, disinterestedness, equi~ tableness, equity, impartiality, justice, le~ gitimacy, rightfulness, uprightness

fairy brownie, elf, hob, leprechaun, peri, pixie, Robin Goodfellow, sprite

fairy tale *or* **fairy story 1.** folk tale, ro~ mance **2.** cock-and-bull story *(Inf.)*, fabrica~ tion, fantasy, fiction, invention, lie, pork pie *(Brit. sl.)*, porky *(Brit. sl.)*, tall story, un~ truth

faith 1. assurance, confidence, conviction, credence, credit, dependence, reliance, trust **2.** belief, church, communion, creed, de~ nomination, dogma, persuasion, religion **3.** allegiance, constancy, faithfulness, fealty, fidelity, loyalty, troth *(Archaic)*, truth, truthfulness **4.** *As in* keep faith, in good faith honour, pledge, promise, sincerity, vow, word, word of honour

Antonyms agnosticism, apprehension, de~ nial, disbelief, distrust, doubt, incredulity, infidelity, misgiving, mistrust, rejection, scepticism, suspicion, uncertainty

faithful 1. attached, constant, dependable, devoted, immovable, loyal, reliable, staunch, steadfast, true, true-blue, trusty, truthful, unswerving, unwavering **2.** accu~ rate, close, exact, just, precise, strict, true **3. the faithful** adherents, believers, breth~ ren, communicants, congregation, followers, the elect

Antonyms disloyal, doubting, faithless, false, false-hearted, fickle, inconstant, perfidious, recreant *(Archaic)*, traitorous, treacherous, unbelieving, unfaithful, unreli~ able, untrue, untrustworthy, untruthful

faithfulness 1. adherence, constancy, dependability, devotion, fealty, fidelity, loyalty, trustworthiness **2.** accuracy, closeness, exactness, justice, strictness, truth

faithless disloyal, doubting, false, fickle, inconstant, perfidious, traitorous, treacherous, unbelieving, unfaithful, unreliable, untrue, untrustworthy, untruthful

faithlessness betrayal, disloyalty, fickleness, inconstancy, infidelity, perfidy, treachery, unfaithfulness

fake 1. *v.* affect, assume, copy, counterfeit, fabricate, feign, forge, pretend, put on, sham, simulate **2.** *n.* charlatan, copy, forgery, fraud, hoax, imitation, impostor, mountebank, phoney *or* phony (*Inf.*), reproduction, sham **3.** *adj.* affected, artificial, assumed, counterfeit, false, forged, imitation, mock, phoney *or* phony (*Inf.*), pinchbeck, pseudo (*Inf.*), reproduction, sham
Antonyms *adj.* actual, authentic, bona fide, faithful, genuine, honest, legitimate, real, true, veritable

fall *v.* **1.** be precipitated, cascade, collapse, crash, descend, dive, drop, drop down, go head over heels, keel over, nose-dive, pitch, plummet, plunge, settle, sink, stumble, subside, topple, trip, trip over, tumble **2.** abate, become lower, decline, decrease, depreciate, diminish, drop, dwindle, ebb, fall off, flag, go down, lessen, slump, subside **3.** be overthrown, be taken, capitulate, give in *or* up, give way, go out of office, pass into enemy hands, resign, succumb, surrender, yield **4.** be a casualty, be killed, be lost, be slain, die, meet one's end, perish **5.** become, befall, chance, come about, come to pass, fall out, happen, occur, take place **6. fall foul of** brush with, come into conflict with, cross swords with, have trouble with, make an enemy of **7. fall in love (with)** become attached to, become enamoured of, become fond of, become infatuated (with), be smitten by, conceive an affection for, fall (for), lose one's heart (to), take a fancy to **8.** fall away, incline, incline downwards, slope **9.** backslide, err, go astray, lapse, offend, sin, transgress, trespass, yield to temptation ~*n.* **10.** descent, dive, drop, nose dive, plummet, plunge, slip, spill, tumble **11.** cut, decline, decrease, diminution, dip, drop, dwindling, falling off, lessening, lowering, reduction, slump **12.** capitulation, collapse, death, defeat, destruction, downfall, failure, overthrow, resignation, ruin, surrender **13.** declivity, descent, downgrade, incline, slant, slope **14.** degradation, failure, lapse, sin, slip, transgression
Antonyms (*sense 1*) ascend, climb, go up, increase, mount, rise, scale, soar, wax (*sense 2*) advance, appreciate, climb, escalate, extend, heighten, increase (*senses 3 & 4*) endure, hold out, prevail, survive, triumph

fallacious deceptive, delusive, delusory, erroneous, false, fictitious, illogical, illusory, incorrect, misleading, mistaken, sophistic, sophistical, spurious, untrue, wrong

fallacy casuistry, deceit, deception, delusion, error, falsehood, faultiness, flaw, illusion, inconsistency, misapprehension, misconception, mistake, sophism, sophistry, untruth

fall apart break up, crumble, disband, disintegrate, disperse, dissolve, fall to bits, go *or* come to pieces, lose cohesion, shatter

fall asleep doze off, drop off (*Inf.*), go to sleep, nod off (*Inf.*)

fall back on call upon, employ, have recourse to, make use of, press into service, resort to

fall behind be in arrears, drop back, get left behind, lag, lose one's place, trail

fall down disappoint, fail, fail to make the grade, fall short, go wrong, prove unsuccessful

fallen *adj.* **1.** collapsed, decayed, flat, on the ground, ruinous, sunken **2.** disgraced, dishonoured, immoral, loose, lost, ruined, shamed, sinful, unchaste **3.** dead, killed, lost, perished, slain, slaughtered

fall for 1. become infatuated with, desire, fall in love with, lose one's head over, succumb to the charms of **2.** accept, be deceived (duped, fooled, taken in) by, buy (*Sl.*), give credence to, swallow (*Inf.*)

fallible erring, frail, ignorant, imperfect, mortal, prone to error, uncertain, weak
Antonyms divine, faultless, impeccable, infallible, omniscient, perfect, superhuman, unerring, unimpeachable

fall in cave in, collapse, come down about one's ears, sink

falling off *n.* deceleration, decline, decrease, deterioration, downward trend, drop, slackening, slowing down, slump, waning, worsening

fall in with accept, agree with, assent, concur with, cooperate with, go along with, support

fall out 1. altercate, argue, clash, differ, disagree, fight, quarrel, squabble **2.** chance, come to pass, happen, occur, pan out (*Inf.*), result, take place, turn out

fallow dormant, idle, inactive, inert, resting, uncultivated, undeveloped, unplanted, untilled, unused

fall short be deficient (lacking, wanting), fail, miss, prove inadequate

fall through come to nothing, fail, fizzle out (*Inf.*), miscarry

false 1. concocted, erroneous, faulty, fictitious, improper, inaccurate, incorrect, inexact, invalid, mistaken, unfounded, un~ real, wrong **2.** lying, mendacious, truthless, unreliable, unsound, untrue, untrustworthy, untruthful **3.** artificial, bogus, counterfeit, ersatz, fake, feigned, forged, imitation, mock, pretended, sham, simulated, spuri~ ous, synthetic **4.** deceitful, deceiving, de~ ceptive, delusive, fallacious, fraudulent, hypocritical, misleading, trumped up **5.** dishonest, dishonourable, disloyal, double-dealing, duplicitous, faithless, false-hearted, hypocritical, perfidious, treacherous, trea~ sonable, two-faced, unfaithful, untrustwor~ thy **6. play (someone) false** betray, cheat, deceive, double-cross, give the Judas kiss to, sell down the river (*Inf.*), stab in the back

Antonyms authentic, bona fide, correct, ex~ act, faithful, genuine, honest, kosher (*Inf.*), loyal, real, right, sincere, sound, true, trust~ worthy, valid

falsehood 1. deceit, deception, dishonesty, dissimulation, inveracity (*Rare*), mendacity, perjury, prevarication, untruthfulness **2.** fabrication, fib, fiction, lie, misstatement, pork pie (*Brit. sl.*), porky (*Brit. sl.*), story, untruth

falsification adulteration, deceit, dissimu~ lation, distortion, forgery, misrepresenta~ tion, perversion, tampering with

falsify alter, belie, cook (*Sl.*), counterfeit, distort, doctor, fake, forge, garble, misrep~ resent, misstate, pervert, tamper with

falter break, hesitate, shake, speak haltingly, stammer, stumble, stutter, totter, tremble, vacillate, waver

Antonyms continue, endure, keep going, last, persevere, persist, proceed, stand firm, stick at, survive

faltering broken, hesitant, irresolute, stam~ mering, tentative, timid, uncertain, weak

fame celebrity, credit, eminence, glory, honour, illustriousness, name, prominence, public esteem, renown, reputation, repute, stardom

Antonyms disgrace, dishonour, disrepute, ignominy, infamy, oblivion, obscurity, shame

familiar 1. accustomed, common, common or garden (*Inf.*), conventional, customary, domestic, everyday, frequent, household, mundane, ordinary, recognizable, repeated, routine, stock, well-known **2. familiar with** abreast of, acquainted with, at home with, *au courant, au fait*, aware of, conscious of, conversant with, introduced, knowledge~ able, no stranger to, on speaking terms with, versed in, well up in **3.** amicable, buddy-buddy (*Sl., chiefly U.S. & Canad.*), chummy (*Inf.*), close, confidential, cordial, easy, free, free-and-easy, friendly, hail-fellow-well-met, informal, intimate, near, open, palsy-walsy (*Inf.*), relaxed, unceremo~ nious, unconstrained, unreserved **4.** bold, disrespectful, forward, impudent, intrusive, overfree, presuming, presumptuous

Antonyms aloof, cold, detached, distant, formal, ignorant, infrequent, unaccustomed, unacquainted, uncommon, unfamiliar, un~ friendly, uninformed, unknown, unskilled, unusual

familiarity 1. acquaintance, acquaintance~ ship, awareness, experience, grasp, under~ standing **2.** absence of reserve, closeness, ease, fellowship, freedom, friendliness, friendship, informality, intimacy, natural~ ness, openness, sociability, unceremonious~ ness **3.** boldness, disrespect, forwardness, liberties, liberty, presumption

Antonyms constraint, decorum, distance, formality, ignorance, inexperience, propriety, reserve, respect, unfamiliarity

familiarize accustom, bring into common use, coach, get to know (about), habituate, instruct, inure, make conversant, make used to, prime, school, season, train

family 1. brood, children, descendants, folk (*Inf.*), household, issue, kin, kindred, kins~ folk, kinsmen, kith and kin, ménage, off~ spring, one's nearest and dearest, one's own flesh and blood, people, progeny, relations, relatives **2.** ancestors, ancestry, birth, blood, clan, descent, dynasty, extraction, forebears, forefathers, genealogy, house, line, lineage, parentage, pedigree, race, sept, stemma, stirps, strain, tribe **3.** class, classification, genre, group, kind, network, subdivision, system

family tree ancestry, extraction, genealogy, line, lineage, line of descent, pedigree, stemma, stirps

famine dearth, destitution, hunger, scarcity, starvation

famished ravening, ravenous, ready to eat a horse (*Inf.*), starved, starving, voracious

famous acclaimed, celebrated, conspicuous, distinguished, eminent, excellent, far-famed, glorious, honoured, illustrious, legendary, lionized, much-publicized, notable, noted, prominent, remarkable, renowned, signal, well-known

Antonyms forgotten, mediocre, obscure, uncelebrated, undistinguished, unexception~ al, unknown, unremarkable

fan¹ *v.* **1.** *Often fig.* add fuel to the flames, agitate, arouse, enkindle, excite, impassion, increase, provoke, rouse, stimulate, stir up, whip up, work up **2.** air-condition, air-cool, blow, cool, refresh, ventilate, winnow (*Rare*), ~*n.* **3.** air conditioner, blade, blow~

er, propeller, punkah (*In India*), vane, ven~
tilator

fan² adherent, admirer, aficionado, buff
(*Inf.*), devotee, enthusiast, fiend (*Inf.*), fol~
lower, freak (*Inf.*), groupie (*Sl.*), lover, root~
er (*U.S.*), supporter, zealot

fanatic *n.* activist, addict, bigot, buff (*Inf.*),
devotee, enthusiast, extremist, militant, vi~
sionary, zealot

fanatical bigoted, burning, enthusiastic, ex~
treme, fervent, frenzied, immoderate, mad,
obsessive, overenthusiastic, passionate,
rabid, visionary, wild, zealous

fanciful capricious, chimerical, curious, ex~
travagant, fabulous, fairy-tale, fantastic,
ideal, imaginary, imaginative, mythical,
poetic, romantic, unreal, visionary, whim~
sical, wild
Antonyms conventional, dry, dull, literal,
matter of fact, ordinary, pedestrian, predict~
able, routine, sensible, sober, unimaginative,
uninspired

fancy *v.* **1.** be inclined to think, believe,
conceive, conjecture, guess (*Inf., chiefly U.S.
& Canad.*), imagine, infer, reckon, suppose,
surmise, think, think likely **2.** be attracted
to, crave, desire, dream of, hanker after,
have a yen for, hope for, long for, relish,
thirst for, wish for, would like, yearn for **3.**
Inf. be attracted to, be captivated by, desire,
favour, go for, have an eye for, like, lust af~
ter, prefer, take a liking to, take to ~*n.* **4.**
caprice, desire, humour, idea, impulse, in~
clination, notion, thought, urge, whim **5.**
fondness, hankering, inclination, liking,
partiality, predilection, preference, relish,
thirst **6.** conception, image, imagination,
impression **7.** chimera, daydream, delusion,
dream, fantasy, nightmare, phantasm, vi~
sion ~*adj.* **8.** baroque, decorated, decora~
tive, elaborate, elegant, embellished, ex~
travagant, fanciful, intricate, ornamental,
ornamented, ornate **9.** capricious, chimeri~
cal, delusive, fanciful, fantastic, far-fetched,
illusory, whimsical
Antonyms (*sense 5*) aversion, disinclination,
dislike (*sense 8*) basic, cheap, common, inferi~
or, ordinary, plain, simple, unadorned, un~
decorated

fanfare ballyhoo, fanfaronade, flourish,
trump (*Archaic*), trumpet call, tucket (*Ar~
chaic*)

fantastic 1. comical, eccentric, exotic, fan~
ciful, freakish, grotesque, imaginative, odd,
oddball (*Inf.*), off-the-wall (*Sl.*), outlandish,
outré, peculiar, phantasmagorical, quaint,
queer, rococo, strange, unreal, weird,
whimsical **2.** ambitious, chimerical, ex~
travagant, far-fetched, grandiose, illusory,
ludicrous, ridiculous, unrealistic, visionary,
wild **3.** absurd, capricious, implausible, in~

credible, irrational, mad, preposterous, un~
likely **4.** *Inf.* enormous, extreme, great,
overwhelming, severe, tremendous **5.** *Inf.*
boffo (*Sl.*), brill (*Inf.*), chillin' (*U.S. sl.*),
cracking (*Brit. inf.*), crucial (*Sl.*), def (*Sl.*),
excellent, first-rate, jim-dandy (*Sl.*), marvel~
lous, mean (*Sl.*), mega (*Sl.*), out of this
world (*Inf.*), sensational (*Inf.*), sovereign,
superb, topping (*Brit. sl.*), wonderful,
world-class
Antonyms common, credible, everyday,
moderate, normal, ordinary, poor, rational,
realistic, sensible, typical

fantasy, phantasy 1. creativity, fancy,
imagination, invention, originality **2.** appa~
rition, daydream, delusion, dream, fancy,
figment of the imagination, flight of fancy,
hallucination, illusion, mirage, nightmare,
pipe dream, reverie, vision

far *adv.* **1.** afar, a good way, a great distance,
a long way, deep, miles **2.** considerably,
decidedly, extremely, greatly, incomparably,
much, very much **3. by far** by a long chalk
(*Inf.*), by a long shot, by a long way, easily,
far and away, immeasurably, incomparably,
to a great degree, very much **4. far and
wide** broadly, everywhere, extensively, far
and near, here, there, and everywhere,
widely, worldwide **5. so far** thus far, to
date, until now, up to now, up to the pres~
ent ~*adj.* **6.** distant, faraway, far-flung,
far-off, far-removed, long, outlying, out-of-
the-way, remote, removed
Antonyms adjacent, adjoining, alongside, at
close quarters, beside, bordering, close, con~
tiguous, near, nearby, neighbouring, proxi~
mate, within sniffing distance (*Inf.*)

faraway 1. beyond the horizon, distant, far,
far-flung, far-off, far-removed, outlying, re~
mote **2.** absent, abstracted, distant, dreamy,
lost

farce 1. broad comedy, buffoonery, bur~
lesque, comedy, satire, slapstick **2.** absurd~
ity, joke, mockery, nonsense, parody, ri~
diculousness, sham, travesty

farcical absurd, amusing, comic, custard-pie,
derisory, diverting, droll, funny, laughable,
ludicrous, nonsensical, preposterous, ri~
diculous, risible, slapstick

fare *n.* **1.** charge, passage money, price,
ticket money, transport cost **2.** passenger,
pick-up (*Inf.*), traveller **3.** commons, diet,
eatables, feed, food, meals, menu, nosebag
(*Sl.*), provisions, rations, sustenance, table,
tack (*Inf.*), victuals, vittles (*Obs. or dialect*)
~*v.* **4.** do, get along, get on, make out,
manage, prosper **5.** *Used impersonally* go,
happen, pan out (*Inf.*), proceed, turn out

farewell adieu, adieux *or* adieus, departure,
goodbye, leave-taking, parting, sendoff
(*Inf.*), valediction

far-fetched doubtful, dubious, fantastic, hard to swallow (*Inf.*), implausible, improbable, incredible, preposterous, strained, unbelievable, unconvincing, unlikely, unnatural, unrealistic
Antonyms acceptable, authentic, believable, credible, feasible, imaginable, likely, plausible, possible, probable, realistic, reasonable

farm 1. *n.* acreage, acres, croft (*Scot.*), farmstead, grange, holding, homestead, land, plantation, ranch (*Chiefly North American*), smallholding, station (*Aust. & N.Z.*) **2.** *v.* bring under cultivation, cultivate, operate, plant, practise husbandry, till the soil, work

farmer agriculturist, agronomist, husbandman, smallholder, yeoman

farming agriculture, agronomy, husbandry

far-reaching broad, extensive, important, momentous, pervasive, significant, sweeping, widespread

far-sighted acute, canny, cautious, discerning, far-seeing, judicious, politic, prescient, provident, prudent, sage, shrewd, wise

fascinate absorb, allure, beguile, bewitch, captivate, charm, delight, enamour, enchant, engross, enrapture, enravish, enthral, entrance, hold spellbound, hypnotize, infatuate, intrigue, mesmerize, ravish, rivet, spellbind, transfix
Antonyms alienate, bore, disenchant, disgust, irritate, jade, put one off, sicken, turn one off (*Inf.*)

fascinated absorbed, beguiled, bewitched, captivated, charmed, engrossed, enthralled, entranced, hooked on, hypnotized, infatuated, smitten, spellbound, under a spell

fascinating alluring, bewitching, captivating, compelling, enchanting, engaging, engrossing, enticing, gripping, intriguing, irresistible, ravishing, riveting, seductive
Antonyms boring, dull, mind-numbing, unexciting, uninteresting

fascination allure, attraction, charm, enchantment, glamour, lure, magic, magnetism, pull, sorcery, spell

fascism *n.* absolutism, authoritarianism, autocracy, dictatorship, Hitlerism, totalitarianism

fashion *n.* **1.** convention, craze, custom, fad, latest, latest style, look, mode, prevailing taste, rage, style, trend, usage, vogue **2.** attitude, demeanour, manner, method, mode, style, way **3.** appearance, configuration, cut, figure, form, guise (*Archaic*), line, make, model, mould, pattern, shape, stamp **4.** description, kind, sort, stamp, type **5.** beau monde, fashionable society, high society, jet set **6. after a fashion** in a manner of speaking, in a way, moderately, somehow, somehow or other, to a degree, to some extent ~*v.* **7.** construct, contrive, create, design, forge, form, make, manufacture, mould, shape, work **8.** accommodate, adapt, adjust, fit, suit, tailor

fashionable à la mode, all the go (*Inf.*), all the rage, chic, cool (*Sl.*), current, customary, genteel, happening (*Inf.*), hip (*Sl.*), in (*Inf.*), in vogue, latest, modern, modish, popular, prevailing, smart, stylish, trendsetting, trendy (*Brit. inf.*), up-to-date, up-to-the-minute, usual, voguish (*Inf.*), with it (*Inf.*)
Antonyms behind the times, dated, frumpy, obsolete, old-fashioned, old-hat, outmoded, out of date, uncool (*Sl.*), unfashionable, unpopular, unstylish, untrendy (*Brit. inf.*)

fast¹ *adj.* **1.** accelerated, brisk, fleet, flying, hasty, hurried, mercurial, nippy (*Brit. inf.*), quick, quickie (*Inf.*), rapid, speedy, swift, winged ~*adv.* **2.** apace, hastily, hell for leather (*Inf.*), hotfoot, hurriedly, in haste, like a bat out of hell (*Sl.*), like a flash, like a shot (*Inf.*), pdq (*Sl.*), posthaste, presto, quickly, rapidly, speedily, swiftly, with all haste ~*adj.* **3.** close, constant, fastened, firm, fixed, fortified, immovable, impregnable, lasting, loyal, permanent, secure, sound, stalwart, staunch, steadfast, tight, unwavering ~*adv.* **4.** deeply, firmly, fixedly, securely, soundly, tightly ~*adj.* **5.** dissipated, dissolute, extravagant, gadabout (*Inf.*), giddy, immoral, intemperate, licentious, loose, profligate, promiscuous, rakish, reckless, self-indulgent, wanton, wild ~*adv.* **6.** extravagantly, intemperately, loosely, promiscuously, rakishly, recklessly, wildly **7. pull a fast one** bamboozle (*Inf.*), cheat, con (*Inf.*), deceive, defraud, hoodwink, put one over on (*Inf.*), swindle, take advantage of, take for a ride (*Inf.*), trick
Antonyms (*sense 1*) leisurely, plodding, slow, slow moving, unhurried (*sense 2*) at a snail's pace, at one's leisure, gradually, leisurely, slowly, steadily, unhurriedly (*sense 3*) inconstant, irresolute, unfaithful, unreliable, unstable, wavering, weak

fast² **1.** *v.* abstain, deny oneself, go hungry, go without food, practise abstention, refrain from food *or* eating **2.** *n.* abstinence, fasting

fasten 1. affix, anchor, attach, bind, bolt, chain, connect, fix, grip, join, lace, link, lock, make fast, make firm, seal, secure, tie, unite **2.** *Fig.* aim, bend, concentrate, direct, fix, focus, rivet

fastidious choosey, choosy, critical, dainty, difficult, discriminating, finicky, fussy, hard to please, hypercritical, meticulous, nice, overdelicate, overnice, particular, pernickety, picky (*Inf.*), punctilious, squeamish
Antonyms careless, casual, disorderly,

easygoing, lenient, slack, slipshod, sloppy, slovenly, unsystematic

fat *adj.* **1.** beefy (*Inf.*), broad in the beam (*Inf.*), corpulent, elephantine, fleshy, gross, heavy, obese, overweight, plump, podgy, portly, roly-poly, rotund, solid, stout, tubby **2.** adipose, fatty, greasy, lipid, oily, oleaginous, suety **3.** affluent, cushy (*Sl.*), fertile, flourishing, fruitful, jammy (*Brit. sl.*), lucrative, lush, productive, profitable, prosperous, remunerative, rich, thriving ~*n.* **4.** adipose tissue, beef (*Inf.*), blubber, bulk, cellulite, corpulence, fatness, flab, flesh, obesity, overweight, paunch, weight problem
Antonyms angular, barren, bony, empty, gaunt, lank, lean, poor, scanty, scarce, scrawny, skinny, slender, slight, slim, spare, thin, unproductive, unprofitable, unrewarding

fatal **1.** deadly, destructive, final, incurable, killing, lethal, malignant, mortal, pernicious, terminal **2.** baleful, baneful, calamitous, catastrophic, disastrous, lethal, ruinous **3.** critical, crucial, decisive, destined, determining, doomed, fateful, final, foreordained, inevitable, predestined
Antonyms beneficial, benign, harmless, inconsequential, innocuous, inoffensive, minor, non-lethal, non-toxic, salutary, vitalizing, wholesome

fatalism acceptance, determinism, necessitarianism, passivity, predestinarianism, resignation, stoicism

fatality casualty, deadliness, death, disaster, fatal accident, lethalness, loss, mortality

fate **1.** chance, destiny, divine will, fortune, kismet, nemesis, predestination, providence, weird (*Archaic*) **2.** cup, fortune, horoscope, lot, portion, stars **3.** end, future, issue, outcome, upshot **4.** death, destruction, doom, downfall, end, ruin

fated destined, doomed, foreordained, ineluctable, inescapable, inevitable, marked down, predestined, pre-elected, preordained, sure, written

fateful **1.** critical, crucial, decisive, important, portentous, significant **2.** deadly, destructive, disastrous, fatal, lethal, ominous, ruinous
Antonyms inconsequential, insignificant, nugatory, ordinary, unimportant

father *n.* **1.** begetter, dad (*Inf.*), daddy (*Inf.*), governor (*Inf.*), old boy (*Inf.*), old man (*Inf.*), pa (*Inf.*), papa (*Old-fashioned inf.*), pater, paterfamilias, patriarch, pop (*Inf.*), sire **2.** ancestor, forebear, forefather, predecessor, progenitor **3.** architect, author, creator, founder, inventor, maker, originator, prime mover **4.** city father, elder, leader, patriarch, patron, senator **5.** abbé, confessor,

curé, padre (*Inf.*), pastor, priest ~*v.* **6.** beget, get, procreate, sire **7.** create, engender, establish, found, institute, invent, originate

fatherland homeland, land of one's birth, land of one's fathers, motherland, native land, old country

fatherly affectionate, benevolent, benign, forbearing, indulgent, kind, kindly, paternal, patriarchal, protective, supportive, tender

fathom **1.** divine, estimate, gauge, measure, penetrate, plumb, probe, sound **2.** comprehend, get to the bottom of, grasp, interpret, understand

fathomless abysmal, bottomless, deep, immeasurable, impenetrable, incomprehensible, profound, unfathomable, unplumbed

fatigue **1.** *v.* drain, drain of energy, exhaust, fag (out) (*Inf.*), jade, knacker (*Sl.*), overtire, poop (*Inf.*), take it out of (*Inf.*), tire, weaken, wear out, weary, whack (*Brit. inf.*) **2.** *n.* debility, ennui, heaviness, languor, lethargy, listlessness, overtiredness, tiredness
Antonyms *n.* alertness, animation, energy, freshness, get-up-and-go (*Inf.*), go, indefatigability, life, vigour, zest ~*v.* refresh, rejuvenate, relieve, rest, revive, stimulate

fatten **1.** broaden, coarsen, expand, gain weight, grow fat, put on weight, spread, swell, thicken, thrive **2.** *Often with* **up** bloat, build up, cram, distend, feed, feed up, nourish, overfeed, stuff

fatty adipose, fat, greasy, oily, oleaginous, rich

fatuous absurd, asinine, brainless, dense, dull, foolish, idiotic, inane, ludicrous, lunatic, mindless, moronic, puerile, silly, stupid, vacuous, weak-minded, witless

fault *n.* **1.** blemish, defect, deficiency, demerit, drawback, failing, flaw, imperfection, infirmity, lack, shortcoming, snag, weakness, weak point **2.** blunder, boob (*Brit. sl.*), error, error of judgment, inaccuracy, indiscretion, lapse, mistake, negligence, offence, omission, oversight, slip, slip-up **3.** accountability, culpability, liability, responsibility **4.** delinquency, frailty, lapse, misconduct, misdeed, misdemeanour, offence, peccadillo, sin, transgression, trespass, wrong **5. at fault** answerable, blamable, culpable, guilty, in the wrong, responsible, to blame **6. find fault with** carp at, complain, criticize, pick holes in, pull to pieces, quibble, take to task **7. to a fault** excessively, immoderately, in the extreme, needlessly, out of all proportion, overly (*U.S.*), overmuch, preposterously, ridiculously, unduly ~*v.* **8.** blame, call to account, censure, criticize, find fault with, find lacking, hold (someone) accountable (responsible, to blame), impugn

Antonyms (*sense 1*) asset, attribute, credit, goodness, merit, perfection, strength, virtue

fault-finding 1. *n.* carping, hairsplitting, nagging, niggling, nit-picking (*Inf.*) **2.** *adj.* captious, carping, censorious, critical, hypercritical, pettifogging

Antonyms complimentary, easily pleased, indiscriminate, uncritical, undiscerning, unexacting, unfussy, unperceptive

faultless 1. accurate, classic, correct, ex~ emplary, faithful, flawless, foolproof, im~ peccable, model, perfect, unblemished **2.** above reproach, blameless, guiltless, im~ maculate, impeccable, innocent, irre~ proachable, pure, sinless, spotless, stainless, unblemished, unspotted, unsullied

faulty bad, blemished, broken, damaged, de~ fective, erroneous, fallacious, flawed, im~ paired, imperfect, imprecise, inaccurate, incorrect, invalid, malfunctioning, not working, out of order, unsound, weak, wrong

faux pas bloomer (*Brit. inf.*), blunder, boob (*Brit. sl.*), breach of etiquette, clanger (*Inf.*), gaffe, gaucherie, impropriety, indiscretion, solecism

favour *n.* **1.** approbation, approval, backing, bias, championship, espousal, esteem, fa~ vouritism, friendliness, good opinion, good~ will, grace, kindness, kind regard, partial~ ity, patronage, promotion, support **2.** benefit, boon, courtesy, good turn, indul~ gence, kindness, obligement (*Scot. or Ar~ chaic*), service **3. in favour of** all for (*Inf.*), backing, for, on the side of, pro, supporting, to the benefit of **4.** gift, keepsake, love-token, memento, present, souvenir, token **5.** badge, decoration, knot, ribbons, rosette ~*v.* **6.** be partial to, esteem, have in one's good books, indulge, pamper, pull strings for (*Inf.*), reward, side with, smile upon, spoil, treat with partiality, value **7.** advocate, ap~ prove, back, be in favour of, champion, choose, commend, countenance, encourage, espouse, fancy, incline towards, like, opt for, patronize, prefer, single out, support **8.** abet, accommodate, advance, aid, assist, befriend, do a kindness to, facilitate, help, oblige, promote, succour **9.** *Inf.* be the im~ age *or* picture of, look like, resemble, take after **10.** ease, extenuate, spare

Antonyms *n.* animosity, antipathy, disap~ proval, disfavour, disservice, harm, ill will, injury, malevolence, wrong ~*v.* disapprove, disdain, dislike, inconvenience, object to, op~ pose, thwart

favourable 1. advantageous, appropriate, auspicious, beneficial, convenient, encour~ aging, fair, fit, good, helpful, hopeful, op~ portune, promising, propitious, suitable, timely **2.** affirmative, agreeable, amicable, approving, benign, encouraging, enthusias~ tic, friendly, kind, positive, reassuring, sympathetic, understanding, welcoming, well-disposed

Antonyms disadvantageous, disapproving, ill-disposed, inauspicious, unfavourable, un~ friendly, unhelpful, unpromising, unsympa~ thetic, useless

favourably 1. advantageously, auspicious~ ly, conveniently, fortunately, opportunely, profitably, to one's advantage, well **2.** agreeably, approvingly, enthusiastically, genially, graciously, helpfully, in a kindly manner, positively, with approval (appro~ bation, cordiality), without prejudice

favourite 1. *adj.* best-loved, choice, dearest, esteemed, favoured, preferred **2.** *n.* beloved, blue-eyed boy (*Inf.*), choice, darling, dear, idol, pet, pick, preference, teacher's pet, the apple of one's eye

favouritism bias, jobs for the boys (*Inf.*), nepotism, one-sidedness, partiality, parti~ sanship, preference, preferential treatment

Antonyms equality, equity, evenhanded~ ness, fairness, impartiality, neutrality, objec~ tivity, open-mindedness

fawn[1] *adj.* beige, buff, greyish-brown, neu~ tral

fawn[2] *v. Often with* **on** *or* **upon** be obsequi~ ous, be servile, bow and scrape, brown-nose (*Taboo sl.*), court, crawl, creep, cringe, cur~ ry favour, dance attendance, flatter, grovel, ingratiate oneself, kiss ass (*U S. & Canad. taboo sl.*), kneel, kowtow, lick (someone's) boots, pander to, pay court, toady, truckle

fawning abject, bootlicking (*Inf.*), bowing and scraping, crawling, cringing, deferen~ tial, flattering, grovelling, obsequious, prostrate, servile, slavish, sycophantic

fear *n.* **1.** alarm, apprehensiveness, awe, blue funk (*Inf.*), consternation, cravenness, dismay, dread, fright, horror, panic, qualms, terror, timidity, tremors, trepida~ tion **2.** bête noire, bogey, bugbear, horror, nightmare, phobia, spectre **3.** agitation, anxiety, apprehension, concern, disqui~ etude, distress, doubt, foreboding(s), mis~ giving(s), solicitude, suspicion, unease, un~ easiness, worry **4.** awe, reverence, venera~ tion, wonder ~*v.* **5.** apprehend, be appre~ hensive (afraid, frightened, scared), be in a blue funk (*Inf.*), dare not, dread, have a horror of, have a phobia about, have butterflies in one's stomach (*Inf.*), have qualms, live in dread of, shake in one's shoes, shudder at, take fright, tremble at **6.** anticipate, apprehend, be afraid, expect, foresee, suspect **7.** *With* **for** be anxious (concerned, distressed) about, be disquieted over, feel concern for, tremble for, worry about **8.** respect, revere, reverence, stand in awe of, venerate

fearful 1. afraid, alarmed, anxious, appre~ hensive, diffident, faint-hearted, frightened, hellacious (*U.S. sl.*), hesitant, intimidated, jittery (*Inf.*), jumpy, nervous, nervy (*Brit. inf.*), panicky, pusillanimous, scared, shrinking, tense, timid, timorous, uneasy, wired (*Sl.*) **2.** appalling, atrocious, awful, dire, distressing, dreadful, frightful, ghastly, grievous, grim, gruesome, hair-raising, harrowing, hideous, horrendous, horrible, horrific, monstrous, shocking, terrible, un~ speakable

Antonyms (*sense 1*) ballsy (*Taboo sl.*), bold, brave, confident, courageous, daring, daunt~ less, doughty, gallant, game (*Inf.*), gutsy (*Sl.*), heroic, indomitable, intrepid, lion-hearted, plucky, unabashed, unafraid, undaunted, unflinching, valiant, valorous

fearfully 1. apprehensively, diffidently, in fear and trembling, nervously, timidly, timorously, uneasily, with many misgivings *or* forebodings, with one's heart in one's mouth **2.** awfully, exceedingly, excessively, frightfully, terribly, tremendously, very

fearless bold, brave, confident, courageous, daring, gallant, heroic, indomitable, intrep~ id, plucky, unafraid, valiant, valorous

fearlessness balls (*Taboo sl.*), ballsiness (*Taboo sl.*), boldness, bravery, confidence, courage, dauntlessness, guts (*Inf.*), indomi~ tability, intrepidity, lion-heartedness, nerve, pluckiness

fearsome alarming, appalling, awe-inspiring, awesome, awful, baleful, daunt~ ing, dismaying, formidable, frightening, hair-raising, hellacious (*U.S. sl.*), horren~ dous, horrifying, menacing, unnerving

feasibility expediency, practicability, usefulness, viability, workability

feasible achievable, attainable, likely, pos~ sible, practicable, realizable, reasonable, viable, workable

Antonyms impossible, impracticable, in~ conceivable, unreasonable, untenable, unvi~ able, unworkable

feast n. **1.** banquet, barbecue, beanfeast (*Brit. inf.*), beano (*Brit. sl.*), blowout (*Sl.*), carousal, carouse, dinner, entertainment, festive board, jollification, junket, repast, revels, slap-up meal (*Brit. inf.*), spread (*Inf.*), treat **2.** celebration, festival, fête, gala day, holiday, holy day, saint's day **3.** de~ light, enjoyment, gratification, pleasure, treat ~v. **4.** eat one's fill, eat to one's heart's content, fare sumptuously, gorge, gormandize, indulge, overindulge, pig out (*Sl.*), stuff, stuff one's face (*Sl.*), wine and dine **5.** entertain, hold a reception for, kill

the fatted calf for, regale, treat, wine and dine **6.** delight, gladden, gratify, rejoice, thrill

feat accomplishment, achievement, act, at~ tainment, deed, exploit, performance

feathers down, plumage, plumes

feathery downy, feathered, fluffy, plumate *or* plumose (*Botany & Zool.*), plumed, plumy, wispy

feature n. **1.** aspect, attribute, characteris~ tic, facet, factor, hallmark, mark, peculiar~ ity, point, property, quality, trait **2.** attrac~ tion, crowd puller (*Inf.*), draw, highlight, innovation, main item, special, special at~ traction, speciality, specialty **3.** article, col~ umn, comment, item, piece, report, story ~v. **4.** accentuate, call attention to, empha~ size, give prominence to, give the full works (*Sl.*), headline, play up, present, promote, set off, spotlight, star

features countenance, face, lineaments, physiognomy

feckless aimless, feeble, futile, hopeless, in~ competent, ineffectual, irresponsible, shift~ less, useless, weak, worthless

federate v. amalgamate, associate, combine, confederate, integrate, syndicate, unify, unite

federation alliance, amalgamation, asso~ ciation, *Bund*, coalition, combination, con~ federacy, copartnership, entente, federacy, league, syndicate, union

fed up (with) annoyed, blue, bored, brassed off (*Brit. sl.*), browned-off (*Inf.*), de~ pressed, discontented, dismal, dissatisfied, down, gloomy, glum, hacked (off) (*U.S. sl.*), pissed off (*Taboo sl.*), sick and tired of (*Inf.*), tired of, weary of

fee account, bill, charge, compensation, emolument, hire, honorarium, meed (*Ar~ chaic*), pay, payment, recompense, remu~ neration, reward, toll

feeble 1. debilitated, delicate, doddering, effete, enervated, enfeebled, etiolated, ex~ hausted, failing, faint, frail, infirm, languid, powerless, puny, shilpit (*Scot.*), sickly, weak, weakened, weedy (*Inf.*) **2.** flat, flimsy, inadequate, incompetent, indecisive, inef~ fective, ineffectual, inefficient, insignificant, insufficient, lame, paltry, pathetic, poor, slight, tame, thin, unconvincing, weak

Antonyms ardent, effective, energetic, forceful, hale, healthy, hearty, lusty, robust, stalwart, strong, sturdy, successful, vigorous

feeble-minded addle-pated, bone-headed (*Sl.*), braindead (*Inf.*), deficient, dim-witted (*Inf.*), dozy (*Brit. inf.*), dull, dumb (*Inf.*), half-witted, idiotic, imbecilic, lacking, mo~ ronic, obtuse, retarded, simple, slow on the

uptake, slow-witted, soft in the head (*Inf.*), stupid, vacant, weak-minded
Antonyms astute, aware, bright, clear-headed, clever, intelligent, keen, quick-witted, smart

feebleness 1. debility, delicacy, effeteness, enervation, etiolation, exhaustion, frailness, frailty, incapacity, infirmity, lack of strength, languor, lassitude, sickliness, weakness **2.** flimsiness, inadequacy, incompetence, indecisiveness, ineffectualness, insignificance, insufficiency, lameness, weakness

feed *v.* **1.** cater for, nourish, provide for, provision, supply, sustain, victual, wine and dine **2.** *Sometimes with* **on** devour, eat, exist on, fare, graze, live on, nurture, partake of, pasture, subsist, take nourishment **3.** augment, bolster, encourage, foster, fuel, minister to, strengthen, supply ~*n.* **4.** fodder, food, forage, pasturage, provender, silage **5.** *Inf.* feast, meal, nosh (*Sl.*), nosh-up (*Brit. sl.*), repast, spread (*Inf.*), tuck-in (*Inf.*)

feel *v.* **1.** caress, finger, fondle, handle, manipulate, maul, paw, run one's hands over, stroke, touch **2.** be aware of, be sensible of, endure, enjoy, experience, go through, have, have a sensation of, know, notice, observe, perceive, suffer, take to heart, undergo **3.** explore, fumble, grope, sound, test, try **4.** be convinced, feel in one's bones, have a hunch, have the impression, intuit, sense **5.** believe, be of the opinion that, consider, deem, hold, judge, think **6.** appear, resemble, seem, strike one as **7.** *With* **for** be moved by, be sorry for, bleed for, commiserate, compassionate, condole with, empathize, feel compassion for, pity, sympathize with **8. feel like** could do with, desire, fancy, feel inclined, feel the need for, feel up to, have the inclination, want ~*n.* **9.** finish, surface, texture, touch **10.** air, ambience, atmosphere, feeling, impression, quality, sense, vibes (*Sl.*)

feeler 1. antenna, tentacle, whisker **2.** advance, approach, probe, trial balloon

feeling 1. feel, perception, sensation, sense, sense of touch, touch **2.** apprehension, consciousness, hunch, idea, impression, inkling, notion, presentiment, sense, suspicion **3.** affection, ardour, emotion, fervour, fondness, heat, intensity, passion, sentiment, sentimentality, warmth **4.** appreciation, compassion, concern, empathy, pity, sensibility, sensitivity, sympathy, understanding **5.** inclination, instinct, opinion, point of view, view **6.** air, ambience, atmosphere, aura, feel, mood, quality, vibes (*Sl.*) **7. bad feeling** anger, dislike, distrust, enmity, hostility, upset

feelings ego, emotions, self-esteem, sensitivities, susceptibilities

feline 1. catlike, leonine **2.** graceful, sinuous, sleek, slinky, smooth, stealthy

fell *v.* cut, cut down, demolish, flatten, floor, hew, knock down, level, prostrate, raze, strike down

fellow *n.* **1.** bloke (*Brit. inf.*), boy, chap (*Inf.*), character, customer (*Inf.*), guy (*Inf.*), individual, man, person, punter (*Inf.*) **2.** associate, colleague, companion, compeer, comrade, co-worker, equal, friend, member, partner, peer **3.** brother, counterpart, double, duplicate, match, mate, twin ~*adj.* **4.** affiliated, akin, allied, associate, associated, co-, like, related, similar

fellowship 1. amity, brotherhood, camaraderie, communion, companionability, companionship, familiarity, fraternization, intercourse, intimacy, kindliness, sociability **2.** association, brotherhood, club, fraternity, guild, league, order, sisterhood, society, sodality

feminine 1. delicate, gentle, girlish, graceful, ladylike, modest, soft, tender, womanly **2.** camp (*Inf.*), effeminate, effete, unmanly, unmasculine, weak, womanish
Antonyms Amazonian, butch, indelicate, manly, mannish, masculine, rough, unfeminine, unladylike, unwomanly, virile

femme fatale charmer, Circe, enchantress, seductress, siren, vamp (*Inf.*)

fen bog, holm (*Dialect*), marsh, morass, moss (*Scot.*), quagmire, slough, swamp

fence *n.* **1.** barbed wire, barricade, barrier, defence, guard, hedge, paling, palisade, railings, rampart, shield, stockade, wall **2. on the fence** between two stools, irresolute, uncertain, uncommitted, undecided, vacillating ~*v.* **3.** *Often with* **in** *or* **off** bound, circumscribe, confine, coop, defend, encircle, enclose, fortify, guard, hedge, impound, pen, pound, protect, restrict, secure, separate, surround **4.** beat about the bush, cavil, dodge, equivocate, evade, flannel (*Brit. inf.*), hedge, parry, prevaricate, quibble, shift, stonewall, tergiversate

fencing *Fig.* beating about the bush, double talk, equivocation, evasiveness, hedging, parrying, prevarication, quibbling, stonewalling, tergiversation, weasel words (*Inf., chiefly U.S.*)

ferment *v.* **1.** boil, brew, bubble, concoct, effervesce, foam, froth, heat, leaven, rise, seethe, work ~*n.* **2.** bacteria, barm, fermentation agent, leaven, leavening, mother, mother-of-vinegar, yeast ~*v.* **3.** *Fig.* agitate, boil, excite, fester, foment, heat, incite, inflame, provoke, rouse, seethe, smoulder, stir up ~*n.* **4.** *Fig.* agitation, brouhaha, commotion, disruption, excitement, fever,

frenzy, furore, glow, heat, hubbub, imbro~
glio, state of unrest, stew, stir, tumult, tur~
bulence, turmoil, unrest, uproar
Antonyms *n.* calmness, hush, peacefulness,
quiet, restfulness, stillness, tranquillity

ferocious 1. feral, fierce, predatory, rapa~
cious, ravening, savage, violent, wild **2.**
barbaric, barbarous, bloodthirsty, brutal,
brutish, cruel, merciless, pitiless, relentless,
ruthless, tigerish, vicious
Antonyms calm, docile, gentle, mild, sub~
dued, submissive, tame

ferocity barbarity, bloodthirstiness, brutal~
ity, cruelty, ferociousness, fierceness, inhu~
manity, rapacity, ruthlessness, savageness,
savagery, viciousness, wildness

ferret out bring to light, dig up, disclose,
discover, drive out, elicit, get at, nose out,
root out, run to earth, search out, smell out,
trace, track down, unearth

ferry 1. *n.* ferryboat, packet, packet boat **2.**
v. carry, chauffeur, convey, run, ship, shut~
tle, transport

fertile abundant, fat, fecund, flowering,
flowing with milk and honey, fruit-bearing,
fruitful, generative, luxuriant, plenteous,
plentiful, productive, prolific, rich, teeming,
yielding
Antonyms barren, dry, impotent, infecund,
infertile, poor, sterile, unfruitful, unimagina~
tive, uninventive, unproductive

fertility abundance, fecundity, fruitfulness,
luxuriance, productiveness, richness

fertilize 1. fecundate, fructify, impregnate,
inseminate, make fruitful, make pregnant,
pollinate **2.** compost, dress, enrich, feed,
manure, mulch, top-dress

fertilizer compost, dressing, dung, guano,
manure, marl

fervent, fervid animated, ardent, devout,
eager, earnest, ecstatic, emotional, enthusi~
astic, excited, fiery, flaming, heartfelt, im~
passioned, intense, perfervid (*Literary*), ve~
hement, warm, zealous
Antonyms apathetic, cold, cool, detached,
dispassionate, frigid, impassive, unfeeling,
unimpassioned

fervour animation, ardour, eagerness, ear~
nestness, enthusiasm, excitement, fervency,
intensity, passion, vehemence, warmth, zeal

fester 1. become inflamed, decay, gather,
maturate, putrefy, suppurate, ulcerate **2.**
Fig. aggravate, chafe, gall, intensify, irk,
rankle, smoulder

festival 1. anniversary, commemoration,
feast, fête, fiesta, holiday, holy day, saint's
day **2.** carnival, celebration, entertainment,
festivities, fête, field day, jubilee, treat

festive back-slapping, carnival, celebratory,
cheery, Christmassy, convivial, festal, gala,

gay, gleeful, happy, hearty, holiday, jolly,
jovial, joyful, joyous, jubilant, light-hearted,
merry, mirthful, sportive
Antonyms depressing, drab, dreary, fu~
nereal, gloomy, lugubrious, mournful, sad

festivity 1. amusement, conviviality, fun,
gaiety, jollification, joviality, joyfulness,
merriment, merrymaking, mirth, pleasure,
revelry, sport **2.** *Often plural* beano (*Brit.
sl.*), carousal, celebration, entertainment,
festival, festive event, festive proceedings,
fun and games, jollification, party, rave
(*Brit. sl.*), rave-up (*Brit. sl.*)

festoon 1. *n.* chaplet, garland, lei, swag,
swathe, wreath **2.** *v.* array, bedeck,
beribbon, deck, decorate, drape, garland,
hang, swathe, wreathe

fetch 1. bring, carry, conduct, convey, de~
liver, escort, get, go for, lead, obtain, re~
trieve, transport **2.** draw forth, elicit, give
rise to, produce **3.** bring in, earn, go for,
make, realize, sell for, yield

fetching alluring, attractive, captivating,
charming, cute, enchanting, enticing, fasci~
nating, intriguing, sweet, taking, winsome

fête, fete 1. *n.* bazaar, fair, festival, gala,
garden party, sale of work **2.** *v.* bring out
the red carpet for (someone), entertain re~
gally, hold a reception for (someone), hon~
our, kill the fatted calf for (someone), lion~
ize, make much of, treat, wine and dine

fetish 1. amulet, cult object, talisman **2.**
fixation, *idée fixe*, mania, obsession, thing
(*Inf.*)

feud 1. *n.* argument, bad blood, bickering,
broil, conflict, contention, disagreement,
discord, dissension, enmity, estrangement,
faction, falling out, grudge, hostility, quar~
rel, rivalry, row, strife, vendetta **2.** *v.* be at
daggers drawn, be at odds, bicker, brawl,
clash, contend, dispute, duel, fall out, quar~
rel, row, squabble, war

fever *Fig.* agitation, delirium, ecstasy, ex~
citement, ferment, fervour, flush, frenzy,
heat, intensity, passion, restlessness, tur~
moil, unrest

feverish 1. burning, febrile, fevered,
flaming, flushed, hectic, hot, inflamed, py~
retic (*Medical*) **2.** agitated, desperate, dis~
tracted, excited, frantic, frenetic, frenzied,
impatient, obsessive, overwrought, restless
Antonyms calm, collected, composed, cool,
dispassionate, nonchalant, offhand, serene,
tranquil, unemotional, unexcitable, unfazed
(*Inf.*), unruffled

few *adj.* **1.** hardly any, inconsiderable, in~
frequent, insufficient, meagre, negligible,
not many, rare, scant, scanty, scarce,
scarcely any, scattered, sparse, sporadic,
thin **2. few and far between** at great in~
tervals, hard to come by, infrequent, in

short supply, irregular, rare, scarce, scat~ tered, seldom met with, uncommon, un~ usual, widely spaced ~*pron.* **3.** handful, scarcely any, scattering, small number, some
Antonyms *adj.* (*senses 1 & 2*) abundant, bounteous, divers (*Archaic*), inexhaustible, manifold, many, multifarious, plentiful, sun~ dry

fiancé, fiancée betrothed, intended, pro~ spective spouse, wife- *or* husband-to-be

fiasco balls-up (*Taboo sl.*), catastrophe, cock-up (*Brit. sl.*), debacle, disaster, failure, flap (*Inf.*), fuck-up (*Offens. taboo sl.*), mess, rout, ruin, washout (*Inf.*)

fib *n.* fiction, lie, pork pie (*Brit. sl.*), porky (*Brit. sl.*), prevarication, story, untruth, white lie, whopper (*Inf.*)

fibre 1. fibril, filament, pile, staple, strand, texture, thread, wisp **2.** *Fig.* essence, na~ ture, quality, spirit, substance **3.** *Fig. As in* **moral fibre** resolution, stamina, strength, strength of character, toughness

fickle blowing hot and cold, capricious, changeable, faithless, fitful, flighty, incon~ stant, irresolute, mercurial, mutable, quicksilver, temperamental, unfaithful, un~ predictable, unstable, unsteady, vacillating, variable, volatile
Antonyms changeless, constant, faithful, firm, invariable, loyal, reliable, resolute, set~ tled, stable, staunch, steadfast, true, trust~ worthy

fickleness capriciousness, fitfulness, flightiness, inconstancy, mutability, un~ faithfulness, unpredictability, unsteadiness, volatility

fiction 1. fable, fantasy, legend, myth, novel, romance, story, storytelling, tale, urban legend, work of imagination, yarn (*Inf.*) **2.** cock and bull story (*Inf.*), concoction, fabri~ cation, falsehood, fancy, fantasy, figment of the imagination, imagination, improvisa~ tion, invention, lie, pork pie (*Brit. sl.*), porky (*Brit. sl.*), tall story, untruth

fictional imaginary, invented, legendary, made-up, nonexistent, unreal

fictitious apocryphal, artificial, assumed, bogus, counterfeit, fabricated, false, fanci~ ful, feigned, imaginary, imagined, impro~ vised, invented, made-up, make-believe, mythical, spurious, unreal, untrue
Antonyms actual, authentic, genuine, le~ gitimate, real, true, truthful, veracious, veri~ table

fiddle *v.* **1.** *Often with* **with** fidget, finger, interfere with, mess about *or* around, play, tamper with, tinker, toy, trifle **2.** *Inf.* cheat, cook the books (*Inf.*), diddle (*Inf.*), finagle (*Inf.*), fix, gerrymander, graft (*Inf.*), ma~ noeuvre, racketeer, sting (*Inf.*), swindle,

wangle (*Inf.*), ~*n.* **3.** violin **4. fit as a fid~ dle** blooming, hale and hearty, healthy, in fine fettle, in good form, in good shape, in rude health, in the pink, sound, strong **5.** *Inf.* fix, fraud, graft (*Inf.*), piece of sharp practice, racket, scam (*Sl.*), sting (*Inf.*), swindle, wangle (*Inf.*)

fiddling futile, insignificant, nickel-and-dime (*U.S. sl.*), pettifogging, petty, trifling, trivial

fidelity 1. allegiance, constancy, depend~ ability, devotedness, devotion, faith, faith~ fulness, fealty, integrity, lealty (*Archaic or Scot.*), loyalty, staunchness, troth (*Archaic*), true-heartedness, trustworthiness **2.** accu~ racy, adherence, closeness, correspondence, exactitude, exactness, faithfulness, precise~ ness, precision, scrupulousness
Antonyms disloyalty, faithlessness, false~ ness, inaccuracy, inexactness, infidelity, perfidiousness, treachery, unfaithfulness, untruthfulness

fidget 1. *v.* be like a cat on hot bricks (*Inf.*), bustle, chafe, fiddle (*Inf.*), fret, jiggle, jitter (*Inf.*), move restlessly, squirm, twitch, wor~ ry **2.** *n. Usually* **the fidgets** fidgetiness, jit~ ters (*Inf.*), nervousness, restlessness, un~ ease, uneasiness

fidgety impatient, jerky, jittery (*Inf.*), jumpy, nervous, on edge, restive, restless, twitchy (*Inf.*), uneasy

field *n.* **1.** grassland, green, greensward (*Ar~ chaic or literary*), lea (*Poetic*), mead (*Archa~ ic*), meadow, pasture **2.** applicants, candi~ dates, competition, competitors, contestants, entrants, possibilities, runners **3.** area, bailiwick, bounds, confines, department, discipline, domain, environment, limits, line, metier, pale, province, purview, range, scope, speciality, specialty, sphere of influence (activity, interest, study), terri~ tory ~*v.* **4.** catch, pick up, retrieve, return, stop **5.** *Fig.* deal with, deflect, handle, turn aside

fiend 1. demon, devil, evil spirit, hellhound **2.** barbarian, beast, brute, degenerate, ghoul, monster, ogre, savage **3.** *Inf.* addict, enthusiast, fanatic, freak (*Inf.*), maniac

fiendish accursed, atrocious, black-hearted, cruel, demonic, devilish, diabolical, hell~ ish, implacable, infernal, inhuman, malevo~ lent, malicious, malignant, monstrous, sa~ tanic, savage, ungodly, unspeakable, wicked

fierce 1. baleful, barbarous, brutal, cruel, dangerous, fell (*Archaic*), feral, ferocious, fiery, menacing, murderous, passionate, savage, threatening, tigerish, truculent, un~ controllable, untamed, vicious, wild **2.** blustery, boisterous, furious, howling, in~ clement, powerful, raging, stormy, strong, tempestuous, tumultuous, uncontrollable,

violent **3.** cutthroat, intense, keen, relent~
less, strong
Antonyms affectionate, calm, civilized, cool,
docile, domesticated, gentle, harmless, kind,
mild, peaceful, submissive, tame, temperate,
tranquil

fiercely ferociously, frenziedly, furiously, in
a frenzy, like cat and dog, menacingly, pas~
sionately, savagely, tempestuously, tiger~
ishly, tooth and nail, uncontrolledly, vi~
ciously, with bared teeth, with no holds
barred

fight _v._ **1.** assault, battle, bear arms against,
box, brawl, carry on war, clash, close, com~
bat, come to blows, conflict, contend, cross
swords, do battle, engage, engage in hostil~
ities, exchange blows, feud, go to war,
grapple, joust, row, scrap (_Inf._), spar, strug~
gle, take the field, take up arms against,
tilt, tussle, wage war, war, wrestle **2.** con~
test, defy, dispute, make a stand against,
oppose, resist, stand up to, strive, struggle,
withstand **3.** argue, bicker, dispute, fall out
(_Inf._), squabble, wrangle **4.** carry on, con~
duct, engage in, prosecute, wage **5. fight
shy of** avoid, duck out of (_Inf._), keep aloof
from, keep at arm's length, shun, steer
clear of ~_n._ **6.** action, affray (_Law_), alter~
cation, _bagarre_, battle, bout, brawl, brush,
clash, combat, conflict, contest, dispute,
dissension, dogfight, duel, encounter, en~
gagement, exchange of blows, fracas, fray,
free-for-all (_Inf._), head-to-head, hostilities,
joust, melee _or_ mêlée, passage of arms, riot,
row, rumble (_U.S. & N.Z. sl._), scrap (_Inf._),
scrimmage, scuffle, set-to (_Inf._), shindig
(_Inf._), shindy (_Inf._), skirmish, sparring
match, struggle, tussle, war **7.** _Fig._ bellig~
erence, gameness, mettle, militancy, pluck,
resistance, spirit, will to resist

fight back 1. defend oneself, give tit for
tat, hit back, put up a fight, reply, resist,
retaliate **2.** bottle up, contain, control, curb,
hold back, hold in check, restrain

fight down bottle up, control, curb, hold
back, repress, restrain, suppress

fighter 1. fighting man, man-at-arms, sol~
dier, warrior **2.** boxer, bruiser (_Inf._), prize
fighter, pugilist **3.** antagonist, battler, bel~
ligerent, combatant, contender, contestant,
disputant, militant

fighting 1. _adj._ aggressive, argumentative,
bellicose, belligerent, combative, conten~
tious, disputatious, hawkish, martial, mili~
tant, pugnacious, sabre-rattling, truculent,
warlike **2.** _n._ battle, bloodshed, blows
struck, combat, conflict, hostilities, warfare

fight off beat off, keep _or_ hold at bay, repel,
repress, repulse, resist, stave off, ward off

figurative 1. allegorical, emblematical,
metaphorical, representative, symbolical,

typical **2.** descriptive, fanciful, florid,
flowery, ornate, pictorial, poetical, tropical
(_Rhetoric_)
Antonyms accurate, exact, factual, faithful,
literal, prosaic, simple, true, unpoetical, un~
varnished

figure _n._ **1.** character, cipher, digit, number,
numeral, symbol **2.** amount, cost, price,
sum, total, value **3.** form, outline, shadow,
shape, silhouette **4.** body, build, chassis
(_Sl._), frame, physique, proportions, shape,
torso **5.** depiction, design, device, diagram,
drawing, emblem, illustration, motif, pat~
tern, representation, sketch **6.** celebrity,
character, dignitary, force, leader, notabil~
ity, notable, personage, personality, pres~
ence, somebody, worthy ~_v._ **7.** _Often with_
up add, calculate, compute, count, reckon,
sum, tally, tot up, work out **8.** _Usually with_
in act, appear, be conspicuous, be featured,
be included, be mentioned, contribute to,
feature, have a place in, play a part **9. it
figures** it follows, it goes without saying, it
is to be expected

figurehead cipher, dummy, front man
(_Inf._), leader in name only, man of straw,
mouthpiece, name, nonentity, puppet, straw
man (_Chiefly U.S._), titular _or_ nominal head,
token

figure of speech conceit, image, trope,
turn of phrase

figure out 1. calculate, compute, reckon,
work out **2.** comprehend, decipher, fathom,
make head or tail of (_Inf._), make out, re~
solve, see, suss (out) (_Sl._), understand

filament cilium (_Biol. & Zool._), fibre, fibril,
pile, staple, strand, string, thread, wire,
wisp

filch abstract, cabbage (_Brit. sl._), crib (_Inf._),
embezzle, half-inch (_Old-fashioned sl._), lift
(_Inf._), misappropriate, nick (_Sl., chiefly
Brit._), pilfer, pinch (_Inf._), purloin, rip off
(_Sl._), snaffle (_Brit. inf._), steal, swipe (_Sl._),
take, thieve, walk off with

file¹ _v._ abrade, burnish, furbish, polish, rasp,
refine, rub, rub down, scrape, shape,
smooth

file² _n._ **1.** case, data, documents, dossier,
folder, information, portfolio ~_v._ **2.** docu~
ment, enter, pigeonhole, put in place, rec~
ord, register, slot in (_Inf._), ~_n._ **3.** column,
line, list, queue, row, string ~_v._ **4.** march,
parade, troop

filibuster _n._ **1.** _Chiefly U.S., with reference to
legislation_ delay, hindrance, obstruction,
postponement, procrastination ~_v._ **2.**
Chiefly U.S., with reference to legislation de~
lay, hinder, obstruct, prevent, procrastinate,
put off ~_n._ **3.** adventurer, buccaneer, cor~
sair, freebooter, pirate, sea robber, sea rov~
er, soldier of fortune

fill 1. brim over, cram, crowd, furnish, glut, gorge, inflate, pack, pervade, replenish, sate, satiate, satisfy, stock, store, stuff, supply, swell **2.** charge, imbue, impregnate, overspread, pervade, saturate, suffuse **3.** block, bung, close, cork, plug, seal, stop **4.** assign, carry out, discharge, engage, execute, fulfil, hold, occupy, officiate, perform, take up **5. one's fill** all one wants, ample, a sufficiency, enough, plenty, sufficient
Antonyms diminish, drain, empty, exhaust, shrink, subside, vacate, void

fill in 1. answer, complete, fill out (*U.S.*), fill up **2.** *Inf.* acquaint, apprise, bring up to date, give the facts *or* background, inform, put wise (*Sl.*) **3.** deputize, replace, represent, stand in, sub, substitute, take the place of

filling 1. *n.* contents, filler, innards (*Inf.*), inside, insides, padding, stuffing, wadding **2.** *adj.* ample, heavy, satisfying, square, substantial

film *n.* **1.** coat, coating, covering, dusting, gauze, integument, layer, membrane, pellicle, scum, skin, tissue **2.** blur, cloud, haze, haziness, mist, mistiness, opacity, veil **3.** flick (*Sl.*), motion picture, movie (*U.S. inf.*), ~*v.* **4.** photograph, shoot, take, video, videotape **5.** *Often with* **over** blear, blur, cloud, dull, haze, mist, veil

filmy 1. chiffon, cobwebby, delicate, diaphanous, fine, finespun, flimsy, floaty, fragile, gauzy, gossamer, insubstantial, seethrough, sheer, transparent **2.** bleared, bleary, blurred, blurry, cloudy, dim, hazy, membranous, milky, misty, opalescent, opaque, pearly

filter *v.* **1.** clarify, filtrate, purify, refine, screen, sieve, sift, strain, winnow **2.** *Often with* **through** *or* **out** dribble, escape, exude, leach, leak, ooze, penetrate, percolate, seep, trickle, well ~*n.* **3.** gauze, membrane, mesh, riddle, sieve, strainer

filth 1. carrion, contamination, crap (*Sl.*), crud (*Sl.*), defilement, dirt, dung, excrement, excreta, faeces, filthiness, foul matter, foulness, garbage, grime, grot (*Sl.*), muck, nastiness, ordure, pollution, putrefaction, putrescence, refuse, sewage, shit (*Taboo sl.*), slime, sludge, squalor, uncleanness **2.** corruption, dirty-mindedness, impurity, indecency, obscenity, pornography, smut, vileness, vulgarity

filthy 1. dirty, faecal, feculent, foul, nasty, polluted, putrid, scummy, scuzzy (*Sl., chiefly U.S.*), slimy, squalid, unclean, vile **2.** begrimed, black, blackened, grimy, grubby, miry, mucky, muddy, mud-encrusted, scuzzy (*Sl., chiefly U.S.*), smoky, sooty, unwashed **3.** bawdy, coarse, corrupt, depraved, dirty-minded, foul, foul-mouthed,

impure, indecent, lewd, licentious, obscene, pornographic, smutty, suggestive **4.** base, contemptible, despicable, low, mean, offensive, scurvy, vicious, vile

final 1. closing, concluding, end, eventual, last, last-minute, latest, terminal, terminating, ultimate **2.** absolute, conclusive, decided, decisive, definite, definitive, determinate, finished, incontrovertible, irrevocable, settled
Antonyms earliest, first, initial, introductory, maiden, opening, original, precursory, prefatory, premier, preparatory

finale climax, close, conclusion, crowning glory, culmination, dénouement, epilogue, finis, last act
Antonyms commencement, exordium, foreword, intro (*Inf.*), lead-in, opening, overture, preamble, preface, preliminaries, prelude, proem, prolegomenon, prologue

finality certitude, conclusiveness, decidedness, decisiveness, definiteness, inevitableness, irrevocability, resolution, unavoidability

finalize agree, clinch, complete, conclude, decide, settle, sew up (*Inf.*), tie up, work out, wrap up (*Inf.*)

finally 1. at last, at length, at long last, at the last, at the last moment, eventually, in the end, in the long run, lastly, ultimately, when all is said and done **2.** in conclusion, in summary, to conclude **3.** beyond the shadow of a doubt, completely, conclusively, convincingly, decisively, for all time, for ever, for good, inescapably, inexorably, irrevocably, once and for all, permanently

finance 1. *n.* accounts, banking, business, commerce, economics, financial affairs, investment, money, money management **2.** *v.* back, bankroll (*U.S.*), float, fund, guarantee, pay for, provide security for, set up in business, subsidize, support, underwrite

finances affairs, assets, capital, cash, financial condition, funds, money, resources, wherewithal

financial budgeting, economic, fiscal, monetary, money, pecuniary

find *v.* **1.** catch sight of, chance upon, come across, come up with, descry, discover, encounter, espy, expose, ferret out, hit upon, lay one's hand on, light upon, locate, meet, recognize, run to earth, spot, stumble upon, track down, turn up, uncover, unearth **2.** achieve, acquire, attain, earn, gain, get, obtain, procure, win **3.** get back, recover, regain, repossess, retrieve **4.** arrive at, ascertain, become aware, detect, discover, experience, learn, note, notice, observe, perceive, realise, remark **5.** be responsible for, bring, contribute, cough up (*Inf.*), furnish,

provide, purvey, supply ~*n.* **6.** acquisition, asset, bargain, catch, discovery, good buy
Antonyms (*sense 1*) lose, mislay, misplace, miss, overlook

finding award, conclusion, decision, decree, judgment, pronouncement, recommenda~ tion, verdict

find out 1. detect, discover, learn, note, ob~ serve, perceive, realize **2.** bring to light, catch, detect, disclose, expose, reveal, rum~ ble (*Brit. inf.*), suss (out) (*Sl.*), uncover, un~ mask

fine¹ *adj.* **1.** accomplished, admirable, beau~ tiful, choice, excellent, exceptional, exquis~ ite, first-class, first-rate, great, magnificent, masterly, ornate, outstanding, rare, select, showy, skilful, splendid, sterling, superior, supreme, world-class **2.** balmy, bright, clear, clement, cloudless, dry, fair, pleasant, sunny **3.** dainty, delicate, elegant, expen~ sive, exquisite, fragile, quality **4.** abstruse, acute, critical, discriminating, fastidious, hairsplitting, intelligent, keen, minute, nice, precise, quick, refined, sensitive, sharp, subtle, tasteful, tenuous **5.** delicate, di~ aphanous, fine-grained, flimsy, gauzy, gos~ samer, light, lightweight, powdered, pow~ dery, pulverized, sheer, slender, small, thin **6.** clear, pure, refined, solid, sterling, un~ adulterated, unalloyed, unpolluted **7.** at~ tractive, bonny, good-looking, handsome, lovely, smart, striking, stylish, well- favoured **8.** acceptable, agreeable, all right, convenient, good, hunky-dory (*Inf.*), O.K. or okay (*Inf.*), satisfactory, suitable **9.** bril~ liant, cutting, honed, keen, polished, razor- sharp, sharp
Antonyms (*sense 1*) indifferent, inferior, poor, second rate, substandard (*sense 2*) cloudy, dull, overcast, unpleasant (*senses 3 & 4*) blunt, coarse, crude, dull, heavy, rough, un~ cultured, unfinished, unrefined

fine² **1.** *v.* amerce (*Archaic*), mulct, penalize, punish **2.** *n.* amercement (*Obsolete*), dam~ ages, forfeit, penalty, punishment

finery best bib and tucker (*Inf.*), decorations, frippery, gear (*Inf.*), gewgaws, glad rags (*Inf.*), ornaments, showiness, splendour, Sunday best, trappings, trinkets

finesse *n.* **1.** adeptness, adroitness, artful~ ness, cleverness, craft, delicacy, diplomacy, discretion, know-how (*Inf.*), polish, quick~ ness, savoir-faire, skill, sophistication, sub~ tlety, tact **2.** artifice, bluff, feint, manoeu~ vre, ruse, stratagem, trick, wile ~*v.* **3.** bluff, manipulate, manoeuvre

finger *v.* **1.** feel, fiddle with (*Inf.*), handle, manipulate, maul, meddle with, paw (*Inf.*), play about with, touch, toy with **2. put one's finger on** bring to mind, discover, find out, hit the nail on the head, hit upon,

identify, indicate, locate, pin down, place, recall, remember

finicky choosy (*Inf.*), critical, dainty, difficult, fastidious, finicking, fussy, hard to please, nit-picking (*Inf.*), overnice, overpar~ ticular, particular, picky (*Inf.*), scrupulous, squeamish

finish *v.* **1.** accomplish, achieve, bring to a close *or* conclusion, carry through, cease, close, complete, conclude, culminate, deal with, discharge, do, end, execute, finalize, fulfil, get done, get out of the way, make short work of, put the finishing touch(es) to, round off, settle, stop, terminate, wind up, wrap up (*Inf.*) **2.** *Sometimes with* **up** *or* **off** consume, deplete, devour, dispatch, dis~ pose of, drain, drink, eat, empty, exhaust, expend, spend, use, use up **3.** *Often with* **off** administer *or* give the coup de grâce, anni~ hilate, best, bring down, defeat, destroy, dispose of, drive to the wall, exterminate, get rid of, kill, overcome, overpower, put an end to, rout, ruin, worst ~*n.* **4.** cessation, close, closing, completion, conclusion, cul~ mination, dénouement, end, ending, finale, last stage(s), termination, winding up (*Inf.*), wind-up **5.** annihilation, bankruptcy, cur~ tains (*Inf.*), death, defeat, end, end of the road, liquidation, ruin ~*v.* **6.** elaborate, perfect, polish, refine ~*n.* **7.** cultivation, culture, elaboration, perfection, polish, refinement, sophistication ~*v.* **8.** coat, face, gild, lacquer, polish, smooth off, stain, tex~ ture, veneer, wax ~*n.* **9.** appearance, grain, lustre, patina, polish, shine, smoothness, surface, texture
Antonyms *v.* begin, commence, create, em~ bark on, instigate, start, undertake ~*n.* begin~ ning, birth, commencement, conception, gen~ esis, inauguration, inception, instigation, preamble, preface, prologue

finished 1. accomplished, classic, consum~ mate, cultivated, elegant, expert, flawless, impeccable, masterly, perfected, polished, professional, proficient, refined, skilled, smooth, urbane **2.** accomplished, achieved, closed, complete, completed, concluded, done, ended, entire, final, finalized, full, in the past, over, over and done with, sewed up (*Inf.*), shut, terminated, through, tied up, wrapped up (*Inf.*) **3.** done, drained, empty, exhausted, gone, played out (*Inf.*), spent, used up **4.** bankrupt, defeated, devastated, done for (*Inf.*), doomed, gone, liquidated, lost, ruined, through, undone, washed up (*Inf., chiefly U.S.*), wiped out, wound up, wrecked
Antonyms basic, begun, coarse, crude, im~ perfect, inartistic, incomplete, inelegant, in~ experienced, raw, rough, unfinished, unre~ fined, unskilled, unsophisticated

finite bounded, circumscribed, conditioned,

delimited, demarcated, limited, restricted, subject to limitations, terminable
Antonyms boundless, endless, eternal, everlasting, immeasurable, infinite, intermi~ nable, limitless, perpetual, unbounded
fire *n.* **1.** blaze, combustion, conflagration, flames, inferno **2.** barrage, bombardment, cannonade, flak, fusillade, hail, salvo, shell~ ing, sniping, volley **3.** *Fig.* animation, ar~ dour, brio, burning passion, dash, eager~ ness, élan, enthusiasm, excitement, ferven~ cy, fervour, force, heat, impetuosity, inten~ sity, life, light, lustre, passion, pizzazz *or* pizazz (*Inf.*), radiance, scintillation, sparkle, spirit, splendour, verve, vigour, virtuosity, vivacity **4. hanging fire** delayed, in abey~ ance, pending, postponed, put back, put off, shelved, suspended, undecided **5. on fire a.** ablaze, aflame, alight, blazing, burning, fiery, flaming, in flames **b.** ardent, eager, enthusiastic, excited, inspired, passionate ~*v.* **6.** enkindle, ignite, kindle, light, put a match to, set ablaze, set aflame, set alight, set fire to, set on fire **7.** detonate, discharge, eject, explode, hurl, launch, let off, loose, pull the trigger, set off, shell, shoot, touch off **8.** *Fig.* animate, arouse, electrify, enliv~ en, excite, galvanize, impassion, incite, inflame, inspire, inspirit, irritate, quicken, rouse, stir **9.** *Inf.* cashier, discharge, dis~ miss, give marching orders, kiss off (*Sl., chiefly U.S. & Canad.*), make redundant, sack (*Inf.*), show the door

firebrand *Fig.* agitator, demagogue, fo~ menter, incendiary, instigator, rabble-rouser, soapbox orator, tub-thumper

fireworks 1. illuminations, pyrotechnics **2.** *Fig.* fit of rage, hysterics, paroxysms, rage, rows, storm, temper, trouble, uproar

firm[1] *adj.* **1.** close-grained, compact, com~ pressed, concentrated, congealed, dense, hard, inelastic, inflexible, jelled, jellified, rigid, set, solid, solidified, stiff, unyielding **2.** anchored, braced, cemented, embedded, fast, fastened, fixed, immovable, motionless, riveted, robust, rooted, secure, secured, stable, stationary, steady, strong, sturdy, taut, tight, unfluctuating, unmoving, un~ shakable **3.** adamant, constant, definite, fixed, immovable, inflexible, obdurate, resolute, resolved, set on, settled, stalwart, staunch, steadfast, strict, true, unalterable, unbending, unfaltering, unflinching, un~ shakable, unshaken, unswerving, unwaver~ ing, unyielding
Antonyms flabby, flaccid, flimsy, incon~ stant, insecure, irresolute, limp, loose, shaky, soft, unreliable, unstable, unsteady, wavering

firm[2] *n.* association, business, company, concern, conglomerate, corporation, enter~ prise, house, organization, outfit (*Inf.*), partnership

firmament empyrean (*Poetic*), heaven, heavens, sky, the blue, the skies, vault, vault of heaven, welkin (*Archaic*)

firmly 1. enduringly, immovably, like a rock, motionlessly, securely, steadily, tight~ ly, unflinchingly, unshakably **2.** deter~ minedly, resolutely, staunchly, steadfastly, strictly, through thick and thin, unchange~ ably, unwaveringly, with a rod of iron, with decision

firmness 1. compactness, density, fixedness, hardness, inelasticity, inflexibil~ ity, resistance, rigidity, solidity, stiffness **2.** immovability, soundness, stability, steadi~ ness, strength, tautness, tensile strength, tension, tightness **3.** constancy, fixedness, fixity of purpose, inflexibility, obduracy, resolution, resolve, staunchness, steadfast~ ness, strength of will, strictness

first *adj.* **1.** chief, foremost, head, highest, leading, pre-eminent, prime, principal, rul~ ing **2.** earliest, initial, introductory, maid~ en, opening, original, premier, primeval, primitive, primordial, pristine **3.** basic, cardinal, elementary, fundamental, key, primary, rudimentary ~*adv.* **4.** at the be~ ginning, at the outset, before all else, beforehand, firstly, initially, in the first place, to begin with, to start with ~*n.* **5.** *As in* **from the first** beginning, commence~ ment, inception, introduction, outset, start, starting point, word 'go' (*Inf.*)

first-hand direct, straight from the horse's mouth

first-rate admirable, A1 *or* A-one (*Inf.*), bof~ fo (*Sl.*), brill (*Inf.*), chillin' (*U.S. sl.*), crack (*Sl.*), cracking (*Brit. inf.*), crucial (*Sl.*), def (*Sl.*), elite, excellent, exceptional, exclusive, first class, jim-dandy (*Sl.*), mean (*Sl.*), mega (*Sl.*), outstanding, prime, second to none, sovereign, superb, superlative, tiptop, top, topnotch (*Inf.*), topping (*Brit. sl.*), tops (*Sl.*), world-class

fish out extract, extricate, find, haul out, produce, pull out

fishy 1. *Inf.* dodgy (*Brit., Aust., & N.Z. inf.*), doubtful, dubious, funny (*Inf.*), implausible, improbable, odd, queer, questionable, rum (*Brit. sl.*), suspect, suspicious, unlikely **2.** blank, deadpan, dull, expressionless, glassy, glassy-eyed, inexpressive, lacklustre, life~ less, vacant, wooden **3.** fishlike, piscatorial, piscatory, piscine

fissure breach, break, chink, cleavage, cleft, crack, cranny, crevice, fault, fracture, gap, hole, interstice, opening, rent, rift, rupture, slit, split

fit[1] *adj.* **1.** able, adapted, adequate, apposite, appropriate, apt, becoming, capable, com~ petent, convenient, correct, deserving, equipped, expedient, fitted, fitting, good

enough, meet (*Archaic*), prepared, proper, qualified, ready, right, seemly, suitable, trained, well-suited, worthy **2.** able-bodied, hale, healthy, in good condition, in good shape, in good trim, robust, strapping, toned up, trim, well ~*v.* **3.** accord, agree, be consonant, belong, concur, conform, corre~ spond, dovetail, go, interlock, join, match, meet, suit, tally **4.** *Often with* **out** *or* **up** accommodate, accoutre, arm, equip, fit out, kit out, outfit, prepare, provide, rig out **5.** adapt, adjust, alter, arrange, dispose, fash~ ion, modify, place, position, shape
Antonyms (*sense 1*) amiss, ill-fitted, ill-suited, improper, inadequate, inappropriate, unfit, unprepared, unseemly, unsuitable, un~ timely (*sense 2*) flabby, in poor condition, out of shape, out of trim, unfit, unhealthy

fit² *n.* **1.** attack, bout, convulsion, paroxysm, seizure, spasm **2.** caprice, fancy, humour, mood, whim **3.** bout, burst, outbreak, out~ burst, spell **4. by fits and starts** erratical~ ly, fitfully, intermittently, irregularly, on and off, spasmodically, sporadically, unsystematically

fitful broken, desultory, disturbed, erratic, flickering, fluctuating, haphazard, impul~ sive, inconstant, intermittent, irregular, spasmodic, sporadic, uneven, unstable, variable
Antonyms constant, equable, even, orderly, predictable, regular, steady, systematic, un~ changing, uniform

fitfully desultorily, erratically, in fits and starts, in snatches, intermittently, inter~ ruptedly, irregularly, off and on, spasmodi~ cally, sporadically

fitness 1. adaptation, applicability, appro~ priateness, aptness, competence, eligibility, pertinence, preparedness, propriety, qualifications, readiness, seemliness, suit~ ability **2.** good condition, good health, health, robustness, strength, vigour

fitted 1. adapted, cut out for, equipped, fit, qualified, right, suitable, tailor-made **2.** *Of~ ten with* **with** accoutred, appointed, armed, equipped, furnished, outfitted, provided, rigged out, set up, supplied **3.** built-in, per~ manent

fitting 1. *adj.* apposite, appropriate, becom~ ing, *comme il faut*, correct, decent, deco~ rous, desirable, meet (*Archaic*), proper, right, seemly, suitable **2.** *n.* accessory, at~ tachment, component, connection, part, piece, unit
Antonyms ill-suited, improper, unfitting, unseemly, unsuitable

fix *v.* **1.** anchor, embed, establish, implant, install, locate, place, plant, position, root, set, settle **2.** attach, bind, cement, connect, couple, fasten, glue, link, make fast, pin,

secure, stick, tie **3.** agree on, appoint, ar~ range, arrive at, conclude, decide, define, determine, establish, limit, name, resolve, set, settle, specify **4.** adjust, correct, mend, patch up, put to rights, regulate, repair, see to, sort **5.** congeal, consolidate, harden, ri~ gidify, set, solidify, stiffen, thicken **6.** di~ rect, focus, level at, rivet **7.** *Inf.* bribe, fiddle (*Inf.*), influence, manipulate, ma~ noeuvre, pull strings (*Inf.*), rig **8.** *Sl.* cook (someone's) goose (*Inf.*), get even with (*Inf.*), get revenge on, pay back, settle (someone's) hash (*Inf.*), sort (someone) out (*Inf.*), take retribution on, wreak vengeance on ~*n.* **9.** *Inf.* difficult situation, difficulty, dilemma, embarrassment, hole (*Sl.*), hot water (*Inf.*), jam (*Inf.*), mess, pickle (*Inf.*), plight, pre~ dicament, quandary, spot (*Inf.*), ticklish situation, tight spot

fixation complex, hang-up (*Inf.*), *idée fixe*, infatuation, mania, obsession, preoccupa~ tion, thing (*Inf.*)

fixed 1. anchored, attached, established, im~ movable, made fast, permanent, rigid, root~ ed, secure, set **2.** intent, level, resolute, steady, unbending, unblinking, undeviating, unflinching, unwavering **3.** agreed, ar~ ranged, decided, definite, established, planned, resolved, settled **4.** going, in working order, mended, put right, repaired, sorted **5.** *Inf.* framed, manipulated, packed, put-up, rigged
Antonyms bending, inconstant, mobile, motile, moving, pliant, unfixed, varying, wa~ vering

fix up 1. agree on, arrange, fix, organize, plan, settle, sort out **2.** *Often with* **with** ac~ commodate, arrange for, bring about, fur~ nish, lay on, provide

fizz bubble, effervesce, fizzle, froth, hiss, sparkle, sputter

fizzle out abort, collapse, come to nothing, die away, end in disappointment, fail, fall through, fold (*Inf.*), miss the mark, peter out

fizzy bubbling, bubbly, carbonated, efferves~ cent, gassy, sparkling

flabbergasted abashed, amazed, aston~ ished, astounded, bowled over (*Inf.*), con~ founded, dazed, disconcerted, dumbfounded, gobsmacked (*Brit. sl.*), nonplussed, over~ come, overwhelmed, rendered speechless, speechless, staggered, struck dumb, stunned

flabby 1. baggy, drooping, flaccid, floppy, hanging, lax, limp, loose, pendulous, sag~ ging, slack, sloppy, toneless, unfit, yielding **2.** effete, enervated, feeble, impotent, inef~ fective, ineffectual, nerveless, spineless, weak, wimpish *or* wimpy (*Inf.*)
Antonyms firm, hard, solid, strong, taut, tense, tight, tough

flag¹ v. abate, decline, die, droop, ebb, fade, fail, faint, fall, fall off, feel the pace, lan~ guish, peter out, pine, sag, sink, slump, succumb, taper off, wane, weaken, weary, wilt

flag² n. **1.** banderole, banner, colours, en~ sign, gonfalon, jack, pennant, pennon, standard, streamer ~v. **2.** *Sometimes with* **down** hail, salute, signal, warn, wave **3.** docket, indicate, label, mark, note, tab

flagging declining, decreasing, deteriorat~ ing, ebbing, fading, failing, faltering, giving up, sinking, slowing down, tiring, waning, weakening, wilting

flagrant arrant, atrocious, awful, barefaced, blatant, bold, brazen, crying, dreadful, egregious, enormous, flagitious, flaunting, glaring, heinous, immodest, infamous, no~ torious, open, ostentatious, out-and-out, outrageous, scandalous, shameless, undis~ guised
Antonyms delicate, faint, implied, indirect, insinuated, slight, subtle, understated

flagstone block, flag, paving stone, slab

flail v. beat, thrash, thresh, windmill

flair **1.** ability, accomplishment, aptitude, faculty, feel, genius, gift, knack, mastery, talent **2.** chic, dash, discernment, elegance, panache, style, stylishness, taste

flake **1.** n. disk, lamina, layer, peeling, scale, shaving, sliver, squama (*Biol.*), wafer **2.** v. blister, chip, desquamate, peel (off), scale (off)

flake out collapse, faint, keel over, lose consciousness, pass out, swoon (*Literary*)

flamboyant **1.** actorly, baroque, camp (*Inf.*), elaborate, extravagant, florid, ornate, ostentatious, over the top (*Inf.*), rich, roco~ co, showy, theatrical **2.** brilliant, colourful, dashing, dazzling, exciting, glamorous, glitzy (*Sl.*), swashbuckling

flame v. **1.** blaze, burn, flare, flash, glare, glow, shine ~n. **2.** blaze, brightness, fire, light **3.** *Fig.* affection, ardour, enthusiasm, fervency, fervour, fire, intensity, keenness, passion, warmth **4.** *Inf.* beau, beloved, boy~ friend, girlfriend, heart-throb (*Brit.*), lady~ love, lover, sweetheart

flameproof fire-resistant, incombustible, nonflammable, non-inflammable

flaming **1.** ablaze, afire, blazing, brilliant, burning, fiery, glowing, ignited, in flames, raging, red, red-hot **2.** angry, ardent, aroused, frenzied, hot, impassioned, intense, raging, scintillating, vehement, vivid

flank n. **1.** ham, haunch, hip, loin, quarter, side, thigh **2.** side, wing ~v. **3.** border, bound, edge, fringe, line, screen, skirt, wall

flannel *Fig.* **1.** n. baloney (*Inf.*), blarney, equivocation, flattery, hedging, prevarica~ tion, soft soap (*Inf.*), sweet talk (*U.S. inf.*), waffle (*Inf., chiefly Brit.*), weasel words (*Inf., chiefly U.S.*) **2.** v. blarney, butter up, equivocate, flatter, hedge, prevaricate, pull the wool over (someone's) eyes, soft-soap (*Inf.*), sweet-talk (*Inf.*), waffle (*Inf., chiefly Brit.*)

flap v. **1.** agitate, beat, flail, flutter, shake, swing, swish, thrash, thresh, vibrate, wag, wave ~n. **2.** bang, banging, beating, flutter, shaking, swinging, swish, waving ~v. **3.** *Inf.* dither (*Chiefly Brit.*), fuss, panic ~n. **4.** *Inf.* agitation, commotion, fluster, panic, state (*Inf.*), stew (*Inf.*), sweat (*Inf.*), tizzy (*Inf.*), twitter (*Inf.*) **5.** apron, cover, fly, fold, lapel, lappet, overlap, skirt, tab, tail

flare v. **1.** blaze, burn up, dazzle, flicker, flutter, glare, waver **2.** *Often with* **out** broaden, spread out, widen ~n. **3.** blaze, burst, dazzle, flame, flash, flicker, glare

flare up blaze, blow one's top (*Inf.*), boil over, break out, explode, fire up, fly off the handle (*Inf.*), lose control, lose one's cool (*Inf.*), lose one's temper, throw a tantrum

flash v. **1.** blaze, coruscate, flare, flicker, glare, gleam, glint, glisten, glitter, light, scintillate, shimmer, sparkle, twinkle ~n. **2.** blaze, burst, coruscation, dazzle, flare, flicker, gleam, ray, scintillation, shaft, shimmer, spark, sparkle, streak, twinkle ~v. **3.** barrel (along) (*Inf., chiefly U.S. & Canad.*), bolt, burn rubber (*Inf.*), dart, dash, fly, race, shoot, speed, sprint, streak, sweep, whistle, zoom ~n. **4.** instant, jiffy (*Inf.*), moment, second, shake, split second, trice, twinkling, twinkling of an eye, two shakes of a lamb's tail (*Inf.*), ~v. **5.** display, exhib~ it, expose, flaunt, flourish, show ~n. **6.** burst, demonstration, display, manifesta~ tion, outburst, show, sign, touch ~adj. **7.** *Inf.* cheap, glamorous, naff (*Brit. sl.*), osten~ tatious, tacky (*Inf.*), tasteless, vulgar

flashy brash, cheap, cheap and nasty, flamboyant, flaunting, garish, gaudy, glit~ tery, glitzy (*Sl.*), in poor taste, jazzy (*Inf.*), loud, meretricious, naff (*Brit. sl.*), ostenta~ tious, over the top (*Inf.*), showy, snazzy (*Inf.*), tacky (*Inf.*), tasteless, tawdry, tinselly
Antonyms downbeat, low-key, modest, natural, plain, unaffected, understated

flat¹ adj. **1.** even, horizontal, level, levelled, low, planar, plane, smooth, unbroken **2.** laid low, lying full length, outstretched, prone, prostrate, reclining, recumbent, su~ pine **3.** boring, dead, dull, flavourless, ho-hum (*Inf.*), insipid, jejune, lacklustre, life~ less, monotonous, pointless, prosaic, spirit~ less, stale, tedious, uninteresting, vapid, watery, weak **4.** absolute, categorical, di~ rect, downright, explicit, final, fixed, out-and-out, peremptory, plain, positive,

straight, unconditional, unequivocal, un~
mistakable, unqualified **5.** blown out, burst,
collapsed, deflated, empty, punctured ~*n.* **6.**
Often plural lowland, marsh, mud flat,
plain, shallow, shoal, strand, swamp ~*adv.*
7. absolutely, categorically, completely, ex~
actly, point blank, precisely, utterly **8. flat
out** all out, at full gallop, at full speed, at
full tilt, for all one is worth, hell for leather
(*Inf.*), posthaste, under full steam
Antonyms (*sense 1*) broken, hilly, irregular,
rolling, rough, rugged, slanting, sloping, un~
even, up and down (*sense 2*) on end, perpen~
dicular, straight, upright, vertical (*sense 3*)
bubbly, effervescent, exciting, fizzy, palatable,
sparkling, tasty, zestful

flat² apartment, rooms

flatly absolutely, categorically, completely,
positively, unhesitatingly

flatness 1. evenness, horizontality, level~
ness, smoothness, uniformity **2.** dullness,
emptiness, insipidity, monotony, staleness,
tedium, vapidity

flatten 1. compress, even out, iron out, lev~
el, plaster, raze, roll, smooth off, squash,
trample **2.** bowl over, crush, fell, floor,
knock down, knock off one's feet, prostrate,
subdue

flatter 1. blandish, butter up, cajole, com~
pliment, court, fawn, flannel (*Brit. inf.*), hu~
mour, inveigle, lay it on (thick) (*Sl.*), pan~
der to, praise, puff, soft-soap (*Inf.*), sweet-
talk (*Inf.*), wheedle **2.** become, do something
for, enhance, set off, show to advantage,
suit

flattering 1. becoming, effective, enhanc~
ing, kind, well-chosen **2.** adulatory, compli~
mentary, fawning, fulsome, gratifying, hon~
eyed, honey-tongued, ingratiating, lauda~
tory, sugary
Antonyms (*sense 1*) not shown in the best
light, not shown to advantage, plain, unat~
tractive, unbecoming, unflattering (*sense 2*)
blunt, candid, honest, straight, uncompli~
mentary, warts and all

flattery adulation, blandishment, blarney,
cajolery, false praise, fawning, flannel (*Brit.
inf.*), fulsomeness, honeyed words, obsequi~
ousness, servility, soft-soap (*Inf.*), sweet-talk
(*Inf.*), sycophancy, toadyism

flaunt boast, brandish, display, disport, ex~
hibit, flash about, flourish, make an exhibi~
tion of, make a (great) show of, parade,
show off, sport (*Inf.*), vaunt

flavour *n.* **1.** aroma, essence, extract,
flavouring, odour, piquancy, relish, savour,
seasoning, smack, tang, taste, zest, zing
(*Inf.*) **2.** aspect, character, essence, feel,
feeling, property, quality, soupçon, stamp,
style, suggestion, tinge, tone, touch ~*v.* **3.**

ginger up, imbue, infuse, lace, leaven, sea~
son, spice
Antonyms (*sense 1*) blandness, flatness, in~
sipidity, odourlessness, tastelessness, vapid~
ity

flavouring essence, extract, spirit, tincture,
zest

flaw 1. blemish, defect, disfigurement, fail~
ing, fault, imperfection, scar, speck, spot,
weakness, weak spot **2.** breach, break, cleft,
crack, crevice, fissure, fracture, rent, rift,
scission, split, tear

flawed blemished, broken, chipped, cracked,
damaged, defective, erroneous, faulty, im~
perfect, unsound

flawless 1. faultless, impeccable, perfect,
spotless, unblemished, unsullied **2.** intact,
sound, unbroken, undamaged, whole

fleabite drop in the ocean, nothing, piddling
amount, pinprick, trifle

flea-bitten crawling, decrepit, fetid, flea-
ridden, frowsty, grotty (*Sl.*), grubby, infest~
ed, insalubrious, lousy, mean, mucky, pe~
diculous (*Medical*), run-down, scabby,
scruffy, scurfy, sleazy, slummy, sordid,
squalid, tatty, unhygienic

flee abscond, avoid, beat a hasty retreat,
bolt, cut and run (*Inf.*), decamp, depart, do
a runner (*Sl.*), escape, fly, fly the coop (*U.S.
& Canad. inf.*), get away, hook it (*Sl.*), leave,
make a quick exit, make off, make oneself
scarce (*Inf.*), make one's escape, make one's
getaway, run away, scarper (*Brit. sl.*), shun,
skedaddle (*Inf.*), slope off, split (*Sl.*), take a
powder (*U.S. & Canad. sl.*), take flight, take
it on the lam (*U.S. & Canad. sl.*), take off
(*Inf.*), take to one's heels, vanish

fleece 1. *Fig.* bleed (*Inf.*), cheat, con (*Inf.*),
cozen, defraud, despoil, diddle (*Inf.*), mulct,
overcharge, plunder, rifle, rip off (*Sl.*), rob,
rook (*Sl.*), skin (*Sl.*), soak (*U.S. & Canad.
sl.*), steal, stiff (*Sl.*), swindle, take for a ride
(*Inf.*), take to the cleaners (*Sl.*) **2.** clip,
shear

fleet *n.* argosy, armada, flotilla, naval force,
navy, sea power, squadron, task force, ves~
sels, warships

fleeting brief, ephemeral, evanescent, flit~
ting, flying, fugacious, fugitive, here today,
gone tomorrow, momentary, passing, short,
short-lived, temporary, transient, transitory
Antonyms abiding, continuing, durable,
enduring, eternal, imperishable, lasting,
long-lasting, long-lived, permanent

fleetness celerity, lightning speed, nimble-
footedness, nimbleness, quickness, rapidity,
speed, speediness, swiftness, velocity

flesh 1. beef (*Inf.*), body, brawn, fat, fatness,
food, meat, tissue, weight **2.** animality,
body, carnality, flesh and blood, human na~

ture, physicality, physical nature, sensual~ ity **3.** homo sapiens, humankind, human race, living creatures, man, mankind, mor~ tality, people, race, stock, world **4. one's own flesh and blood** blood, family, kin, kindred, kinsfolk, kith and kin, relations, relatives

flex v. angle, bend, contract, crook, curve, tighten

flexibility adaptability, adjustability, com~ plaisance, elasticity, give (*Inf.*), pliability, pliancy, resilience, springiness, tensility

flexible 1. bendable, ductile, elastic, limber, lissom(e), lithe, mouldable, plastic, pliable, pliant, springy, stretchy, supple, tensile, whippy, willowy, yielding **2.** adaptable, ad~ justable, discretionary, open, variable **3.** amenable, biddable, complaisant, compliant, docile, gentle, manageable, responsive, tractable
Antonyms absolute, determined, fixed, im~ movable, inexorable, inflexible, intractable, obdurate, rigid, staunch, stiff, tough, unyield~ ing

flick v. **1.** dab, fillip, flip, hit, jab, peck, rap, strike, tap, touch **2.** *With* **through** browse, flip, glance, skim, skip, thumb ~n. **3.** fillip, flip, jab, peck, rap, tap, touch

flicker v. **1.** flare, flash, glimmer, gutter, shimmer, sparkle, twinkle **2.** flutter, quiv~ er, vibrate, waver ~n. **3.** flare, flash, gleam, glimmer, spark **4.** atom, breath, drop, glimmer, iota, spark, trace, vestige

flickering fitful, guttering, twinkling, un~ steady, wavering

flight[1] **1.** flying, mounting, soaring, winging **2.** *Of air travel* journey, trip, voyage **3.** aerial navigation, aeronautics, air trans~ port, aviation, flying **4.** cloud, flock, forma~ tion, squadron, swarm, unit, wing

flight[2] **1.** departure, escape, exit, exodus, fleeing, getaway, retreat, running away **2. put to flight** chase off, disperse, drive off, rout, scare off, scatter, send packing, stam~ pede **3. take (to) flight** abscond, beat a re~ treat, bolt, decamp, do a bunk (*Brit. sl.*), do a runner (*Sl.*), flee, fly the coop (*U.S. & Canad. inf.*), light out (*Inf.*), make a hasty retreat, run away *or* off, skedaddle (*Inf.*), take a powder (*U.S. & Canad. sl.*), take it on the lam (*U.S. & Canad. sl.*), withdraw hastily

flimsy 1. delicate, fragile, frail, gimcrack, insubstantial, makeshift, rickety, shaky, shallow, slight, superficial, unsubstantial **2.** chiffon, gauzy, gossamer, light, sheer, thin, transparent **3.** feeble, frivolous, implau~ sible, inadequate, pathetic, poor, thin, transparent, trivial, unconvincing, unsatis~ factory, weak

Antonyms durable, heavy, robust, serious, solid, sound, stout, strong, sturdy, substantial

flinch baulk, blench, cower, cringe, draw back, duck, flee, quail, recoil, retreat, shirk, shrink, shy away, start, swerve, wince, withdraw

fling v. **1.** cast, catapult, chuck (*Inf.*), heave, hurl, jerk, let fly, lob (*Inf.*), pitch, precipi~ tate, propel, send, shy, sling, throw, toss ~n. **2.** cast, lob, pitch, shot, throw, toss **3.** bash, beano (*Brit. sl.*), binge (*Inf.*), bit of fun, good time, indulgence, party, rave (*Brit. sl.*), rave-up (*Brit. sl.*), spree **4.** at~ tempt, bash (*Inf.*), crack (*Inf.*), gamble, go (*Inf.*), shot (*Inf.*), stab (*Inf.*), trial, try, ven~ ture, whirl (*Inf.*)

flip v./n. cast, flick, jerk, pitch, snap, spin, throw, toss, twist

flippancy cheek (*Inf.*), cheekiness, disre~ spectfulness, frivolity, impertinence, irrev~ erence, levity, pertness, sauciness

flippant cheeky, disrespectful, flip (*Inf.*), frivolous, glib, impertinent, impudent, ir~ reverent, offhand, pert, rude, saucy, superficial
Antonyms gracious, mannerly, polite, re~ spectful, serious, sincere, solicitous, well-mannered

flirt v. **1.** chat up (*Inf.*), coquet, dally, lead on, make advances, make eyes at, philander **2.** *Usually with* **with** consider, dabble in, entertain, expose oneself to, give a thought to, play with, toy with, trifle with ~n. **3.** coquette, heart-breaker, philanderer, tease, trifler, wanton

flirtation coquetry, dalliance, intrigue, phi~ landering, teasing, toying, trifling

flirtatious amorous, arch, come-hither, come-on (*Inf.*), coquettish, coy, enticing, flirty, provocative, sportive, teasing

flirting amorous play, chatting up (*Inf.*), co~ quetry, dalliance, sport

float v. **1.** be *or* lie on the surface, be buoy~ ant, displace water, hang, hover, poise, rest on water, stay afloat **2.** bob, drift, glide, move gently, sail, slide, slip along **3.** get going, launch, promote, push off, set up
Antonyms (*senses 1 & 2*) dip, drown, founder, go down, settle, sink, submerge (*sense 3*) abol~ ish, annul, cancel, dissolve, terminate

floating 1. afloat, buoyant, buoyed up, nonsubmersible, ocean-going, sailing, swimming, unsinkable **2.** fluctuating, free, migratory, movable, unattached, uncom~ mitted, unfixed, variable, wandering

flock v. **1.** collect, congregate, converge, crowd, gather, group, herd, huddle, mass, throng, troop ~n. **2.** colony, drove, flight, gaggle, herd, skein **3.** assembly, bevy, col~ lection, company, congregation, convoy, crowd, gathering, group, herd, host, mass, multitude, throng

flog 1. beat, castigate, chastise, flagellate, flay, lambast(e), lash, scourge, thrash, trounce, whack, whip **2.** drive, oppress, overexert, overtax, overwork, punish, push, strain, tax

flogging beating, caning, flagellation, hid~ing (*Inf.*), horsewhipping, lashing, scourg~ing, thrashing, trouncing, whipping

flood v. **1.** brim over, deluge, drown, im~merse, inundate, overflow, pour over, sub~merge, swamp **2.** engulf, flow, gush, over~whelm, rush, surge, swarm, sweep **3.** choke, fill, glut, oversupply, saturate ~n. **4.** deluge, downpour, flash flood, freshet, in~undation, overflow, spate, tide, torrent **5.** abundance, flow, glut, multitude, outpour~ing, profusion, rush, stream, torrent

floor 1. n. level, stage, storey, tier **2.** v. *Fig.* baffle, beat, bewilder, bowl over (*Inf.*), bring up short, confound, conquer, defeat, dis~comfit, disconcert, dumbfound, faze, knock down, nonplus, overthrow, perplex, pros~trate, puzzle, stump, throw (*Inf.*)

flop v. **1.** collapse, dangle, droop, drop, fall, hang limply, sag, slump, topple, tumble **2.** *Inf.* bomb (*U.S. & Canad. sl.*), close, come to nothing, fail, fall flat, fall short, fold (*Inf.*), founder, go belly-up (*Sl.*), go down like a lead balloon (*Inf.*), misfire ~n. **3.** *Inf.* cock~up (*Brit. sl.*), debacle, disaster, failure, fiasco, loser, nonstarter, washout (*Inf.*)
Antonyms v. flourish, make a hit, make it (*Inf.*), prosper, succeed, triumph, work ~n. hit, success, triumph

floral flower-patterned, flowery

florid 1. blowzy, flushed, high-coloured, high-complexioned, rubicund, ruddy **2.** ba~roque, busy, embellished, euphuistic, figurative, flamboyant, flowery, fussy, grandiloquent, high-flown, ornate, over~elaborate
Antonyms anaemic, bare, bloodless, dull, pale, pallid, pasty, plain, unadorned, wan, washed out

flotsam debris, detritus, jetsam, junk, odds and ends, sweepings, wreckage

flounder v. be in the dark, blunder, fumble, grope, muddle, plunge, struggle, stumble, thrash, toss, tumble, wallow

flourish v. **1.** bear fruit, be in one's prime, be successful, be vigorous, bloom, blossom, boom, burgeon, develop, do well, flower, get ahead, get on, go great guns (*Sl.*), go up in the world, grow, grow fat, increase, prosper, succeed, thrive **2.** brandish, display, flaunt, flutter, shake, sweep, swing, swish, twirl, vaunt, wag, wave, wield ~n. **3.** brandish~ing, dash, display, fanfare, parade, shaking, show, showy gesture, twirling, wave **4.**

curlicue, decoration, embellishment, orna~mentation, plume, sweep
Antonyms decline, diminish, dwindle, fade, fail, grow less, pine, shrink, wane

flourishing blooming, burgeoning, doing well, going strong, in the pink, in top form, lush, luxuriant, mushrooming, on the up and up (*Inf.*), prospering, rampant, success~ful, thriving

flout defy, deride, gibe at, insult, jeer at, laugh in the face of, mock, outrage, ridi~cule, scoff at, scorn, scout (*Archaic*), show contempt for, sneer at, spurn, take the piss out of (*Taboo sl.*), taunt, treat with disdain
Antonyms attend, esteem, heed, honour, mind, note, pay attention to, regard, respect, revere, value

flow v. **1.** circulate, course, glide, gush, move, pour, purl, ripple, roll, run, rush, slide, surge, sweep, swirl, whirl **2.** cascade, deluge, flood, inundate, issue, overflow, pour, run, run out, spew, spill, spurt, squirt, stream, teem, well forth **3.** arise, emanate, emerge, issue, pour, proceed, re~sult, spring ~n. **4.** course, current, drift, flood, flux, gush, issue, outflow, outpouring, spate, stream, tide, tideway, undertow **5.** abundance, deluge, effusion, emanation, outflow, outpouring, plenty, plethora, suc~cession, train

flower n. **1.** bloom, blossom, efflorescence **2.** *Fig.* best, choicest part, cream, elite, freshness, greatest *or* finest point, height, pick, vigour ~v. **3.** bloom, blossom, blow, burgeon, effloresce, flourish, mature, open, unfold

flowering adj. abloom, blooming, blossom~ing, florescent, in bloom, in blossom, in flower, open, out, ready

flowery baroque, embellished, euphuistic, fancy, figurative, florid, high-flown, ornate, overwrought, rhetorical
Antonyms austere, bare, basic, modest, muted, plain, restrained, simple, spartan, un~adorned, unembellished

flowing 1. falling, gushing, rolling, rushing, smooth, streaming, sweeping **2.** continuous, cursive, easy, fluent, smooth, unbroken, uninterrupted **3.** abounding, brimming over, flooded, full, overrun, prolific, rich, teeming

fluctuate alter, alternate, change, ebb and flow, go up and down, hesitate, oscillate, rise and fall, seesaw, shift, swing, undulate, vacillate, vary, veer, waver

fluctuation alternation, change, fickleness, inconstancy, instability, oscillation, shift, swing, unsteadiness, vacillation, variation, wavering

fluency articulateness, assurance, com~

mand, control, ease, facility, glibness, readiness, slickness, smoothness, volubility

fluent articulate, easy, effortless, facile, flowing, glib, natural, ready, smooth, smooth-spoken, voluble, well-versed
Antonyms faltering, halting, hesitant, hesi~ tating, inarticulate, stammering, stumbling, terse, tongue-tied

fluff 1. *n.* down, dust, dustball, fuzz, lint, nap, oose (*Scot.*), pile **2.** *v. Inf.* bungle, cock up (*Brit. sl.*), foul up (*Inf.*), fuck up (*Offens. taboo sl.*), make a mess off, mess up (*Inf.*), muddle, screw up (*Inf.*), spoil

fluid *adj.* **1.** aqueous, flowing, in solution, liquefied, liquid, melted, molten, running, runny, watery **2.** adaptable, adjustable, changeable, flexible, floating, fluctuating, indefinite, mercurial, mobile, mutable, pro~ tean, shifting **3.** easy, elegant, feline, flowing, graceful, sinuous, smooth ~*n.* **4.** liquid, liquor, solution
Antonyms *adj.* definite, firm, fixed, hard, immobile, immutable, rigid, set, solid

fluke accident, blessing, break, chance, chance occurrence, coincidence, fortuity, freak, lucky break, quirk, quirk of fate, serendipity, stroke, stroke of luck, windfall

flunky 1. assistant, drudge, hanger-on, me~ nial, minion, slave, toady, tool, underling, yes man **2.** footman, lackey, manservant, valet

flurry *n.* **1.** *Fig.* ado, agitation, bustle, com~ motion, disturbance, excitement, ferment, flap, fluster, flutter, furore, fuss, hurry, stir, to-do, tumult, whirl **2.** flaw, gust, squall **3.** burst, outbreak, spell, spurt ~*v.* **4.** agitate, bewilder, bother, bustle, confuse, discon~ cert, disturb, faze, fluster, flutter, fuss, has~ sle (*Inf.*), hurry, hustle, rattle (*Inf.*), ruffle, unnerve, unsettle, upset

flush[1] *v.* **1.** blush, burn, colour, colour up, crimson, flame, glow, go red, redden, suf~ fuse ~*n.* **2.** bloom, blush, colour, freshness, glow, redness, rosiness ~*v.* **3.** cleanse, douche, drench, eject, expel, flood, hose down, rinse out, swab, syringe, wash out

flush[2] *adj.* **1.** even, flat, level, plane, square, true **2.** abundant, affluent, full, generous, lavish, liberal, overflowing, prodigal **3.** *Inf.* in funds, in the money (*Inf.*), moneyed, rich, rolling (*Sl.*), wealthy, well-heeled (*Inf.*), well-off, well-supplied ~*adv.* **4.** even with, hard against, in contact with, level with, squarely, touching

flushed 1. blushing, burning, crimson, em~ barrassed, feverish, glowing, hot, red, rosy, rubicund, ruddy **2.** *Often with* **with** ablaze, animated, aroused, elated, enthused, excit~ ed, exhilarated, high (*Inf.*), inspired, intoxi~ cated, thrilled

fluster 1. *v.* agitate, bother, bustle, con~ found, confuse, disturb, excite, flurry, has~ sle (*Inf.*), heat, hurry, make nervous, per~ turb, rattle (*Inf.*), ruffle, throw off balance, unnerve, upset **2.** *n.* agitation, bustle, com~ motion, disturbance, dither (*Chiefly Brit.*), flap (*Inf.*), flurry, flutter, furore, perturba~ tion, ruffle, state (*Inf.*), turmoil

flutter *v.* **1.** agitate, bat, beat, flap, flicker, flit, flitter, fluctuate, hover, palpitate, quiv~ er, ripple, ruffle, shiver, tremble, vibrate, waver ~*n.* **2.** palpitation, quiver, quivering, shiver, shudder, tremble, tremor, twitching, vibration **3.** agitation, commotion, confu~ sion, dither (*Chiefly Brit.*), excitement, flur~ ry, fluster, perturbation, state (*Inf.*), state of nervous excitement, tremble, tumult

fly *v.* **1.** flit, flutter, hover, mount, sail, soar, take to the air, take wing, wing **2.** aviate, be at the controls, control, manoeuvre, op~ erate, pilot **3.** display, flap, float, flutter, show, wave **4.** elapse, flit, glide, pass, pass swiftly, roll on, run its course, slip away **5.** barrel (along) (*Inf., chiefly U.S. & Canad.*), be off like a shot (*Inf.*), bolt, burn rubber (*Inf.*), career, dart, dash, hare (*Brit. inf.*), hasten, hurry, race, rush, scamper, scoot, shoot, speed, sprint, tear, whiz (*Inf.*), zoom **6.** abscond, avoid, beat a retreat, clear out (*Inf.*), cut and run (*Inf.*), decamp, disappear, do a runner (*Sl.*), escape, flee, fly the coop (*U.S. & Canad. inf.*), get away, hasten away, hightail (*Inf., chiefly U.S.*), light out (*Inf.*), make a getaway, make a quick exit, make one's escape, run, run for it, run from, show a clean pair of heels, shun, skedaddle (*Inf.*), take a powder (*U.S. & Canad. sl.*), take flight, take it on the lam (*U.S. & Canad. sl.*), take off, take to one's heels **7. fly in the ointment** difficulty, drawback, flaw, hitch, problem, rub, small problem, snag **8. fly off the handle** blow one's top, explode, flip one's lid (*Sl.*), fly into a rage, have a tantrum, hit *or* go through the roof (*Inf.*), let fly (*Inf.*), lose one's cool (*Sl.*), lose one's temper (*Sl.*) **9. let fly a.** burst forth, give free reign, keep nothing back, lash out, let (someone) have it, lose one's temper, tear into (*Inf.*), vent **b.** cast, chuck (*Inf.*), fire, fling, heave, hurl, hurtle, launch, let off, lob (*Inf.*), shoot, sling, throw

fly at assail, assault, attack, belabour, fall upon, get stuck into (*Inf.*), go for, have a go at (*Inf.*), lay about, pitch into (*Inf.*), rush at

fly-by-night *adj.* **1.** cowboy (*Inf.*), dubious, questionable, shady, undependable, unreli~ able, untrustworthy **2.** brief, here today, gone tomorrow, impermanent, short-lived

flying *adj.* **1.** brief, fleeting, fugacious, has~ ty, hurried, rushed, short-lived, transitory **2.** express, fast, fleet, mercurial, mobile, rapid, speedy, winged **3.** airborne, flapping, floating, fluttering, gliding, hovering, in the air, soaring, streaming, volitant, waving, wind-borne, winging

foam 1. *n.* bubbles, froth, head, lather, spray, spume, suds **2.** *v.* boil, bubble, effervesce, fizz, froth, lather

fob off 1. appease, deceive, equivocate with, flannel (*Brit. inf.*), give (someone) the runaround (*Inf.*), put off, stall **2.** dump, foist, get rid of, inflict, palm off, pass off, unload

focus *n.* **1.** bull's eye, centre, centre of activity, centre of attraction, core, cynosure, focal point, headquarters, heart, hub, meeting place, target **2. in focus** clear, distinct, sharp-edged, sharply defined **3. out of focus** blurred, fuzzy, ill-defined, indistinct, muzzy, unclear ~*v.* **4.** aim, bring to bear, centre, concentrate, converge, direct, fix, join, meet, pinpoint, rivet, spotlight, zero in (*Inf.*), zoom in

foe adversary, antagonist, enemy, foeman (*Archaic*), opponent, rival
Antonyms ally, companion, comrade, confederate, friend, partner

fog *n.* **1.** gloom, miasma, mist, murk, murkiness, peasouper (*Inf.*), smog **2.** *Fig.* blindness, confusion, daze, haze, mist, obscurity, perplexity, stupor, trance ~*v.* **3.** becloud, bedim, befuddle, bewilder, blind, cloud, confuse, darken, daze, dim, muddle, obfuscate, obscure, perplex, stupefy **4.** cloud, mist over *or* up, steam up

foggy 1. blurred, brumous (*Rare*), cloudy, dim, grey, hazy, indistinct, misty, murky, nebulous, obscure, smoggy, soupy, vaporous **2.** *Fig.* befuddled, bewildered, clouded, cloudy, confused, dark, dazed, dim, indistinct, muddled, obscure, stupefied, stupid, unclear, vague
Antonyms accurate, alert, awake, bright, clear, decisive, distinct, lucid, palpable, sharp, shrewd, undimmed

foil¹ *v.* baffle, balk, check, checkmate, circumvent, counter, defeat, disappoint, elude, frustrate, nip in the bud, nullify, outwit, put a spoke in (someone's) wheel (*Brit.*), stop, thwart

foil² antithesis, background, complement, contrast, setting

foist fob off, get rid of, impose, insert, insinuate, interpolate, introduce, palm off, pass off, put over, sneak in, unload

fold *v.* **1.** bend, crease, crumple, dog-ear, double, double over, gather, intertwine, overlap, pleat, tuck, turn under ~*n.* **2.** bend, crease, double thickness, folded portion, furrow, knife-edge, layer, overlap, pleat, turn, wrinkle ~*v.* **3.** do up, enclose, enfold, entwine, envelop, wrap, wrap up **4.** *Inf.* be ruined, close, collapse, crash, fail, go bankrupt, go belly-up (*Sl.*), go bust (*Inf.*), go

down like a lead balloon (*Inf.*), go to the wall, go under, shut down

folder binder, envelope, file, portfolio

folk clan, ethnic group, family, kin, kindred, people, race, tribe

follow 1. come after, come next, step into the shoes of, succeed, supersede, supplant, take the place of **2.** chase, dog, hound, hunt, pursue, run after, shadow, stalk, tail (*Inf.*), track, trail **3.** accompany, attend, bring up the rear, come *or* go with, come after, escort, tag along, tread on the heels of **4.** act in accordance with, be guided by, comply, conform, give allegiance to, heed, mind, note, obey, observe, regard, watch **5.** appreciate, catch, catch on (*Inf.*), comprehend, fathom, get, get the picture, grasp, keep up with, realize, see, take in, understand **6.** arise, be consequent, develop, emanate, ensue, flow, issue, proceed, result, spring, supervene **7.** adopt, copy, emulate, imitate, live up to, pattern oneself upon, take as example **8.** be a devotee *or* supporter of, be devoted to, be interested in, cultivate, keep abreast of, support
Antonyms abandon, avoid, desert, disobey, elude, escape, flout, forsake, give up, guide, ignore, lead, precede, reject, renounce, shun, steer

follower 1. adherent, admirer, apostle, backer, believer, convert, devotee, disciple, fan, fancier, habitué, henchman, partisan, protagonist, pupil, representative, supporter, votary, worshipper **2.** attendant, companion, hanger-on, helper, henchman, lackey, minion, retainer (*History*), sidekick (*Sl.*)
Antonyms (*sense 1*) guru, leader, mentor, svengali, swami, teacher, tutor (*sense 2*) antagonist, contender, enemy, foe, opponent, rival

following 1. *adj.* coming, consequent, consequential, ensuing, later, next, specified, subsequent, succeeding, successive **2.** *n.* audience, circle, clientele, coterie, entourage, fans, patronage, public, retinue, suite, support, supporters, train

follow up 1. check out, find out about, investigate, look into, make inquiries, pursue, research **2.** consolidate, continue, make sure, reinforce

folly absurdity, bêtise (*Rare*), daftness (*Inf.*), fatuity, foolishness, idiocy, imbecility, imprudence, indiscretion, irrationality, lunacy, madness, nonsense, preposterousness, rashness, recklessness, silliness, stupidity
Antonyms judgment, level-headedness, moderation, prudence, rationality, reason, sanity, sense, wisdom

fond 1. *With* **of** addicted to, attached to, enamoured of, have a liking (fancy, taste, soft spot) for, hooked on, into (*Inf.*), keen on,

partial to, predisposed towards **2.** adoring, affectionate, amorous, caring, devoted, dot~ ing, indulgent, loving, tender, warm **3.** ab~ surd, credulous, deluded, delusive, delusory, empty, foolish, indiscreet, naive, overopti~ mistic, vain
Antonyms (senses 1 & 2) aloof, austere, averse, disinterested, indifferent, rational, sensible, unaffectionate, unconcerned, unde~ monstrative

fondle caress, cuddle, dandle, pat, pet, stroke

fondly 1. affectionately, dearly, indulgently, lovingly, possessively, tenderly, with affec~ tion **2.** credulously, foolishly, naively, stu~ pidly, vainly

fondness 1. attachment, fancy, liking, love, partiality, penchant, predilection, prefer~ ence, soft spot, susceptibility, taste, weak~ ness **2.** affection, attachment, devotion, kindness, love, tenderness
Antonyms antagonism, antipathy, aversion, coldness, contempt, dislike, enmity, harsh~ ness, hatred, hostility, loathing, repugnance, repulsion

food 1. aliment, board, bread, chow (Inf.), comestibles, commons, cooking, cuisine, diet, eatables (Sl.), eats (Sl.), edibles, fare, feed, foodstuffs, grub (Sl.), larder, meat, menu, nosebag (Sl.), nosh (Sl.), nourish~ ment, nutriment, nutrition, pabulum (Rare), provender, provisions, rations, refreshment, scoff (Sl.), stores, subsistence, sustenance, table, tack (Inf.), tuck (Inf.), viands, vict~ uals, vittles (Obs. or dialect) **2.** Cattle, etc. feed, fodder, forage, provender

foodie bon vivant, bon viveur, connoisseur, epicure, gastronome, gourmet

fool n. **1.** ass, berk (Brit. sl.), bird-brain (Inf.), blockhead, bonehead (Sl.), charlie (Brit. inf.), chump (Inf.), clodpate (Archaic), clot (Brit. inf.), coot, dickhead (Sl.), dimwit (Inf.), dipstick (Brit. sl.), divvy (Brit. sl.), dolt, dope (Inf.), dork (Sl.), dunce, dunder~ head, dweeb (U.S. sl.), fathead (Inf.), fuckwit (Taboo sl.), geek (Sl.), gonzo (Sl.), goose (Inf.), halfwit, idiot, ignoramus, illiterate, imbecile (Inf.), jackass, jerk (Sl., chiefly U.S. & Canad.), lamebrain (Inf.), loon, mooncalf, moron, nerd or nurd (Sl.), nincompoop, ninny, nit (Inf.), nitwit (Inf.), numskull or numbskull, oaf, pillock (Brit. sl.), plank (Brit. sl.), plonker (Sl.), prat (Sl.), prick (Derogatory sl.), sap (Sl.), schmuck (U.S. sl.), silly, simpleton, twerp or twirp (Inf.), twit (Inf., chiefly Brit.), wally (Sl.) **2.** butt, chump (Inf.), dupe, easy mark (Inf.), fall guy (Inf.), greenhorn (Inf.), gull (Archaic), laughing stock, mug (Brit. sl.), stooge (Sl.), sucker (Sl.) **3.** buffoon, clown, comic, har~ lequin, jester, merry-andrew, motley, pier~

rot, punchinello **4. act** or **play the fool** act up, be silly, cavort, clown, cut capers, frol~ ic, lark about (Inf.), mess about, piss about (Taboo sl.), piss around (Taboo sl.), play the goat, show off (Inf.), ~v. **5.** bamboozle, be~ guile, bluff, cheat, con (Inf.), deceive, de~ lude, dupe, gull (Archaic), have (someone) on, hoax, hoodwink, kid (Inf.), make a fool of, mislead, play a trick on, put one over on (Inf.), stiff (Sl.), take in, trick **6.** act the fool, cut capers, feign, jest, joke, kid (Inf.), make believe, piss about (Taboo sl.), piss around (Taboo sl.), pretend, tease **7.** With **with, around with,** or **about with** fiddle (Inf.), meddle, mess, monkey, piss about (Taboo sl.), piss around (Taboo sl.), play, tamper, toy, trifle
Antonyms (senses 1 & 2) expert, genius, master, sage, savant, scholar, wise man

foolery antics, capers, carry-on (Inf., chiefly Brit.), childishness, clowning, folly, fooling, horseplay, larks, mischief, monkey tricks (Inf.), nonsense, practical jokes, pranks, shenanigans (Inf.), silliness, tomfoolery

foolhardy adventurous, bold, hot-headed, impetuous, imprudent, incautious, irre~ sponsible, madcap, precipitate, rash, reck~ less, temerarious, venturesome, venturous
Antonyms alert, careful, cautious, chary, circumspect, heedful, judicious, prudent, shrewd, solicitous, thoughtful, wary, watchful

foolish 1. absurd, asinine, ill-advised, ill-considered, ill-judged, imprudent, inane, incautious, indiscreet, injudicious, nonsen~ sical, senseless, short-sighted, silly, unin~ telligent, unreasonable, unwise **2.** brain~ dead (Inf.), brainless, crackpot (Inf.), crazy, daft (Inf.), doltish, fatuous, goofy (Inf.), half-baked (Inf.), half-witted, harebrained, idiotic, imbecilic, inane, loopy (Inf.), ludi~ crous, mad, moronic, potty (Brit. inf.), ri~ diculous, senseless, silly, simple, stupid, weak, witless
Antonyms bright, cautious, clever, commonsensical, intelligent, judicious, pru~ dent, rational, sagacious, sane, sensible, sharp, smart, sound, thoughtful, wise

foolishly absurdly, idiotically, ill-advisedly, imprudently, incautiously, indiscreetly, in~ judiciously, like a fool, mistakenly, short~ sightedly, stupidly, unwisely, without due consideration

foolishness 1. absurdity, bêtise (Rare), folly, idiocy, imprudence, inanity, indiscre~ tion, irresponsibility, silliness, stupidity, weakness **2.** bunk (Inf.), bunkum or bun~ combe (Chiefly U.S.), carrying-on (Inf., chiefly Brit.), claptrap (Inf.), foolery, non~ sense, rigmarole, rubbish

foolproof certain, guaranteed, infallible,

never-failing, safe, sure-fire (*Inf.*), unassail~
able, unbreakable

footing 1. basis, establishment, foot-hold,
foundation, ground, groundwork, installa~
tion, settlement **2.** condition, grade, posi~
tion, rank, relations, relationship, standing,
state, status, terms

footling fiddling, fussy, hairsplitting, im~
material, insignificant, irrelevant, minor,
nickel-and-dime (*U.S. sl.*), niggly, petty,
pointless, silly, time-wasting, trifling, triv~
ial, unimportant

footstep 1. footfall, step, tread **2.** footmark,
footprint, trace, track

forage 1. *n. Cattle, etc.* feed, fodder, food,
foodstuffs, provender **2.** *v.* cast about, ex~
plore, hunt, look round, plunder, raid, ran~
sack, rummage, scavenge, scour, scrounge
(*Inf.*), search, seek

forbear abstain, avoid, cease, decline, desist,
eschew, hold back, keep from, omit, pause,
refrain, resist the temptation to, restrain
oneself, stop, withhold

forbearance 1. indulgence, leniency, len~
ity, longanimity (*Rare*), long-suffering,
mildness, moderation, patience, resignation,
restraint, self-control, temperance, tolerance
2. abstinence, avoidance, refraining
Antonyms anger, impatience, impetuosity,
intolerance, irritability, shortness

forbearing clement, easy, forgiving, indul~
gent, lenient, long-suffering, merciful, mild,
moderate, patient, tolerant

forbid ban, debar, disallow, exclude, hinder,
inhibit, interdict, outlaw, preclude, prohib~
it, proscribe, rule out, veto
Antonyms allow, approve, authorize, bid,
endorse, grant, let, license, O.K. *or* okay (*Inf.*),
order, permit, sanction

forbidden banned, outlawed, out of bounds,
prohibited, proscribed, taboo, *verboten,* ve~
toed

forbidding 1. abhorrent, disagreeable, odi~
ous, offensive, off-putting (*Brit. inf.*), repel~
lent, repulsive **2.** baleful, daunting, fore~
boding, frightening, grim, hostile, menac~
ing, ominous, sinister, threatening, un~
friendly
Antonyms alluring, attractive, beguiling,
enticing, inviting, magnetic, tempting, wel~
coming, winning

force *n.* **1.** dynamism, energy, impact, im~
pulse, life, might, momentum, muscle, po~
tency, power, pressure, stimulus, strength,
stress, vigour **2.** arm-twisting (*Inf.*), coer~
cion, compulsion, constraint, duress, en~
forcement, pressure, violence **3.** bite, co~
gency, effect, effectiveness, efficacy,
influence, persuasiveness, power, punch
(*Inf.*), strength, validity, weight **4.** drive,

emphasis, fierceness, intensity, persistence,
vehemence, vigour **5.** army, battalion, body,
corps, detachment, division, host, legion,
patrol, regiment, squad, squadron, troop,
unit **6. in force a.** binding, current, effec~
tive, in operation, on the statute book, op~
erative, valid, working **b.** all together, in
full strength, in great numbers ~*v.* **7.** bring
pressure to bear upon, coerce, compel, con~
strain, dragoon, drive, impel, impose, make,
necessitate, obligate, oblige, overcome,
press, press-gang, pressure, pressurize, put
the squeeze on (*Inf.*), railroad (*Inf.*),
strong-arm (*Inf.*), urge **8.** blast, break open,
prise, propel, push, thrust, use violence on,
wrench, wrest **9.** drag, exact, extort, wring
Antonyms *n.* debility, enervation, feeble~
ness, fragility, frailty, impotence, ineffective~
ness, irresolution, powerlessness, weakness
~*v.* coax, convince, induce, persuade, prevail,
talk into

forced 1. compulsory, conscripted, enforced,
involuntary, mandatory, obligatory, slave,
unwilling **2.** affected, artificial, contrived,
false, insincere, laboured, stiff, strained,
unnatural, wooden
Antonyms easy, natural, simple, sincere,
spontaneous, unforced, unpretending, volun~
tary

forceful cogent, compelling, convincing, dy~
namic, effective, persuasive, pithy, potent,
powerful, telling, vigorous, weighty
Antonyms enervated, exhausted, faint, fee~
ble, frail, powerless, spent, weak

forcible 1. active, cogent, compelling, effec~
tive, efficient, energetic, forceful, impres~
sive, mighty, potent, powerful, strong, tell~
ing, valid, weighty **2.** aggressive, armed,
coercive, compulsory, drastic, violent

forcibly against one's will, by force, by
main force, compulsorily, under compul~
sion, under protest, willy-nilly

forebear ancestor, father, forefather, fore~
runner, predecessor, progenitor

forebode augur, betoken, foreshadow, fore~
show, foretell, foretoken, forewarn, indicate,
portend, predict, presage, prognosticate,
promise, vaticinate (*Rare*), warn of

foreboding 1. anxiety, apprehension, ap~
prehensiveness, chill, dread, fear, misgiv~
ing, premonition, presentiment **2.** augury,
foreshadowing, foretoken, omen, portent,
prediction, presage, prognostication, sign,
token, warning

forecast 1. *v.* anticipate, augur, calculate,
divine, estimate, foresee, foretell, plan, pre~
dict, prognosticate, prophesy, vaticinate
(*Rare*) **2.** *n.* anticipation, conjecture, fore~
sight, forethought, guess, outlook, planning,
prediction, prognosis, projection, prophecy

forefather ancestor, father, forebear, fore~

runner, predecessor, primogenitor, pro~ creator, progenitor

forefront centre, fore, foreground, front, lead, prominence, spearhead, van, vanguard

foregoing above, antecedent, anterior, for~ mer, preceding, previous, prior

foreground centre, forefront, front, lime~ light, prominence

foreign 1. alien, borrowed, distant, exotic, external, imported, outlandish, outside, overseas, remote, strange, unfamiliar, un~ known **2.** extraneous, extrinsic, incongru~ ous, irrelevant, unassimilable, uncharac~ teristic, unrelated
Antonyms applicable, characteristic, cus~ tomary, domestic, familiar, intrinsic, native, pertinent, relevant, suited, well-known

foreigner alien, immigrant, incomer, new~ comer, outlander, stranger

foremost chief, first, front, headmost, highest, inaugural, initial, leading, para~ mount, pre-eminent, primary, prime, prin~ cipal, supreme

foreordain doom, fate, foredoom, prear~ range, predestine, predetermine, preordain, reserve

forerunner 1. ancestor, announcer, envoy, forebear, foregoer, harbinger, herald, pre~ cursor, predecessor, progenitor, prototype **2.** augury, foretoken, indication, omen, portent, premonition, prognostic, sign, to~ ken

foresee anticipate, divine, envisage, fore~ bode, forecast, foretell, predict, prophesy, vaticinate (*Rare*)

foreshadow adumbrate, augur, betoken, bode, forebode, imply, indicate, portend, predict, prefigure, presage, promise, proph~ esy, signal

foresight anticipation, care, caution, cir~ cumspection, far-sightedness, forethought, precaution, premeditation, preparedness, prescience, prevision (*Rare*), provision, prudence
Antonyms carelessness, hindsight, impru~ dence, inconsideration, lack of foresight, ne~ glect, retrospection, thoughtlessness, unpre~ paredness

forestry arboriculture, dendrology (*Botany*), silviculture, woodcraft, woodmanship

foretell adumbrate, augur, bode, forebode, forecast, foreshadow, foreshow, forewarn, portend, predict, presage, prognosticate, prophesy, signify, soothsay, vaticinate (*Rare*)

forethought anticipation, far-sightedness, foresight, precaution, providence, provision, prudence
Antonyms carelessness, imprudence, im~

pulsiveness, inconsideration, neglect, unpre~ paredness

forever 1. always, evermore, for all time, for good and all (*Inf.*), for keeps, in perpe~ tuity, till Doomsday, till the cows come home (*Inf.*), till the end of time, world without end **2.** all the time, constantly, continually, endlessly, eternally, ever~ lastingly, incessantly, interminably, perpet~ ually, unremittingly

forewarn admonish, advise, alert, apprise, caution, dissuade, give fair warning, put on guard, put on the qui vive, tip off

foreword introduction, preamble, preface, preliminary, prolegomenon, prologue

forfeit 1. *n.* amercement (*Obsolete*), dam~ ages, fine, forfeiture, loss, mulct, penalty **2.** *v.* be deprived of, be stripped of, give up, lose, relinquish, renounce, surrender

forfeiture confiscation, giving up, loss, re~ linquishment, sequestration (*Law*), surren~ der

forge *v.* **1.** construct, contrive, create, de~ vise, fabricate, fashion, form, frame, ham~ mer out, invent, make, mould, shape, work **2.** coin, copy, counterfeit, fake, falsify, feign, imitate

forger coiner, counterfeiter, falsifier

forgery 1. coining, counterfeiting, falsification, fraudulence, fraudulent imita~ tion **2.** counterfeit, fake, falsification, imi~ tation, phoney *or* phony (*Inf.*), sham

forget 1. consign to oblivion, dismiss from one's mind, let bygones be bygones, let slip from the memory **2.** leave behind, lose sight of, omit, overlook
Antonyms bring to mind, mind, recall, rec~ ollect, remember, retain

forgetful absent-minded, apt to forget, careless, dreamy, heedless, inattentive, lax, neglectful, negligent, oblivious, slapdash, slipshod, unmindful
Antonyms attentive, careful, mindful, re~ tentive, unforgetful, unforgetting

forgetfulness absent-mindedness, abstrac~ tion, carelessness, dreaminess, heedless~ ness, inattention, lapse of memory, laxity, laxness, oblivion, obliviousness, wool~ gathering

forgive absolve, accept (someone's) apology, acquit, bear no malice, condone, excuse, exonerate, let bygones be bygones, let off (*Inf.*), pardon, remit
Antonyms blame, censure, charge, con~ demn, find fault with, reproach, reprove

forgiveness absolution, acquittal, amnesty, condonation, exoneration, mercy, overlook~ ing, pardon, remission

forgiving clement, compassionate, forbear~

ing, humane, lenient, magnanimous, merci~ ful, mild, soft-hearted, tolerant

forgo, forego abandon, abjure, cede, do without, give up, kick (*Inf.*), leave alone *or* out, relinquish, renounce, resign, sacrifice, surrender, waive, yield

forgotten blotted out, buried, bygone, con~ signed to oblivion, gone (clean) out of one's mind, left behind *or* out, lost, obliterated, omitted, past, past recall, unremembered

fork *v.* bifurcate, branch, branch off, diverge, divide, go separate ways, part, split

forked angled, bifurcate(d), branched, branching, divided, pronged, split, tined, zigzag

forlorn abandoned, bereft, cheerless, com~ fortless, deserted, desolate, destitute, dis~ consolate, forgotten, forsaken, friendless, helpless, homeless, hopeless, lonely, lost, miserable, pathetic, pitiable, pitiful, unhap~ py, woebegone, wretched
Antonyms busy, cheerful, happy, hopeful, optimistic, thriving

form[1] *v.* **1.** assemble, bring about, build, concoct, construct, contrive, create, devise, establish, fabricate, fashion, forge, found, invent, make, manufacture, model, mould, produce, put together, set up, shape, stamp **2.** arrange, combine, design, dispose, draw up, frame, organize, pattern, plan, think up **3.** accumulate, appear, become visible, come into being, crystallize, grow, materi~ alize, rise, settle, show up (*Inf.*), take shape **4.** acquire, contract, cultivate, develop, get into (*Inf.*), pick up **5.** compose, comprise, constitute, make, make up, serve as **6.** bring up, discipline, educate, instruct, rear, school, teach, train

form[2] *n.* **1.** appearance, cast, configuration, construction, cut, fashion, formation, mod~ el, mould, pattern, shape, stamp, structure **2.** anatomy, being, body, build, figure, frame, outline, person, physique, shape, sil~ houette **3.** arrangement, character, descrip~ tion, design, guise, kind, manifestation, manner, method, mode, order, practice, semblance, sort, species, stamp, style, sys~ tem, type, variety, way **4.** format, frame~ work, harmony, order, orderliness, organi~ zation, plan, proportion, structure, symme~ try **5.** condition, fettle, fitness, good condi~ tion, good spirits, health, shape, trim **6. off form** below par, not in the pink (*Inf.*), not up to the mark, out of condition, stale, un~ der the weather (*Inf.*), unfit **7.** behaviour, ceremony, conduct, convention, custom, done thing, etiquette, formality, manners, procedure, protocol, ritual, rule **8.** applica~ tion, document, paper, sheet **9.** class, grade, rank

formal 1. approved, ceremonial, explicit,

express, fixed, lawful, legal, methodical, official, prescribed, *pro forma*, regular, rig~ id, ritualistic, set, solemn, strict **2.** affected, aloof, ceremonious, conventional, correct, exact, precise, prim, punctilious, reserved, starched, stiff, unbending
Antonyms casual, easy-going, informal, laid-back (*Inf.*), relaxed, unceremonious, unofficial

formality 1. ceremony, convention, con~ ventionality, custom, form, gesture, matter of form, procedure, red tape, rite, ritual **2.** ceremoniousness, correctness, decorum, etiquette, politesse, protocol, punctilio

formation 1. accumulation, compilation, composition, constitution, crystallization, development, establishment, evolution, forming, generation, genesis, manufacture, organization, production **2.** arrangement, configuration, design, disposition, figure, grouping, pattern, rank, structure

formative 1. impressionable, malleable, mouldable, pliant, sensitive, susceptible **2.** determinative, developmental, influential, moulding, shaping

former 1. antecedent, anterior, *ci-devant*, earlier, erstwhile, ex-, late, one-time, previ~ ous, prior, quondam, whilom (*Archaic*) **2.** ancient, bygone, departed, long ago, long gone, of yore, old, old-time, past **3.** above, aforementioned, aforesaid, first mentioned, foregoing, preceding
Antonyms coming, current, ensuing, fol~ lowing, future, latter, modern, present, present-day, subsequent, succeeding

formerly aforetime (*Archaic*), already, at one time, before, heretofore, lately, once, previously

formidable 1. appalling, baleful, danger~ ous, daunting, dismaying, dreadful, fearful, frightful, horrible, intimidating, menacing, shocking, terrifying, threatening **2.** ardu~ ous, challenging, colossal, difficult, mam~ moth, onerous, overwhelming, staggering, toilsome **3.** awesome, great, impressive, in~ domitable, mighty, powerful, puissant, re~ doubtable, terrific, tremendous
Antonyms cheering, comforting, easy, en~ couraging, genial, heartening, pleasant, re~ assuring

formula 1. form of words, formulary, rite, ritual, rubric **2.** blueprint, method, modus operandi, precept, prescription, principle, procedure, recipe, rule, way

formulate 1. codify, define, detail, express, frame, give form to, particularize, set down, specify, systematize **2.** coin, develop, de~ vise, evolve, forge, invent, map out, origi~ nate, plan, work out

forsake 1. abandon, cast off, desert, disown, jettison, jilt, leave, leave in the lurch, quit, repudiate, throw over **2.** abdicate, forgo, forswear, give up, have done with, kick (*Inf.*), relinquish, renounce, set aside, sur~ render, turn one's back on, yield

forsaken abandoned, cast off, deserted, des~ titute, disowned, forlorn, friendless, ig~ nored, isolated, jilted, left behind, left in the lurch, lonely, marooned, outcast, solitary

fort 1. blockhouse, camp, castle, citadel, fastness, fortification, fortress, garrison, re~ doubt, station, stronghold **2. hold the fort** carry on, keep things moving, keep things on an even keel, maintain the status quo, stand in, take over the reins

forte gift, long suit (*Inf.*), métier, speciality, strength, strong point, talent
Antonyms Achilles heel, chink in one's ar~ mour, defect, failing, imperfection, short~ coming, weak point

forth ahead, away, forward, into the open, onward, out, out of concealment, outward

forthcoming 1. approaching, coming, ex~ pected, future, imminent, impending, pro~ spective, upcoming **2.** accessible, at hand, available, in evidence, obtainable, on tap (*Inf.*), ready **3.** chatty, communicative, ex~ pansive, free, informative, open, sociable, talkative, unreserved

forthright above-board, blunt, candid, di~ rect, downright, frank, open, outspoken, plain-spoken, straightforward, straight from the shoulder (*Inf.*), upfront (*Inf.*)
Antonyms dishonest, furtive, secret, secre~ tive, sneaky, underhand, untruthful

forthwith at once, directly, immediately, instantly, quickly, right away, straight~ away, *tout de suite*, without delay

fortification 1. bastion, bulwark, castle, citadel, defence, fastness, fort, fortress, keep, protection, stronghold **2.** embattle~ ment, reinforcement, strengthening

fortify 1. augment, brace, buttress, embattle, garrison, protect, reinforce, secure, shore up, strengthen, support **2.** brace, cheer, confirm, embolden, encourage, hearten, in~ vigorate, reassure, stiffen, strengthen, sus~ tain
Antonyms debilitate, demoralize, dilute, dishearten, impair, reduce, sap the strength of, weaken

fortitude backbone, braveness, courage, dauntlessness, determination, endurance, fearlessness, firmness, grit, guts (*Inf.*), har~ dihood, intrepidity, patience, perseverance, pluck, resolution, staying power, stout~ heartedness, strength, strength of mind, valour

fortress castle, citadel, fastness, fort, re~ doubt, stronghold

fortunate 1. born with a silver spoon in one's mouth, bright, favoured, golden, hap~ py, having a charmed life, in luck, jammy (*Brit. sl.*), lucky, prosperous, rosy, sitting pretty (*Inf.*), successful, well-off **2.** advanta~ geous, auspicious, convenient, encouraging, expedient, favourable, felicitous, fortuitous, helpful, opportune, profitable, promising, propitious, providential, timely
Antonyms disastrous, hapless, ill-fated, ill-starred, miserable, poor, unfortunate, unhap~ py, unlucky, unsuccessful, wretched

fortunately by a happy chance, by good luck, happily, luckily, providentially

fortune 1. affluence, big bucks (*Inf., chiefly U.S.*), big money, gold mine, megabucks (*U.S. & Canad. sl.*), opulence, possessions, pretty penny (*Inf.*), property, prosperity, riches, tidy sum (*Inf.*), treasure, wad (*U.S. & Canad. sl.*), wealth **2.** accident, chance, contingency, destiny, fate, fortuity, hap (*Archaic*), hazard, kismet, luck, providence **3.** *Often plural* adventures, circumstances, destiny, doom, expectation, experience(s), history, life, lot, portion, star, success **4.** bomb (*Brit. sl.*), bundle (*Sl.*), king's ransom, mint, packet (*Sl.*), pile (*Inf.*), wealth
Antonyms (*sense 1*) destitution, hardship, indigence, penury, poverty, privation

forward *adj.* **1.** advanced, advancing, early, forward-looking, onward, precocious, premature, progressive, well-developed **2.** advance, first, fore, foremost, front, head, leading **3.** assuming, bare-faced, bold, brash, brass-necked (*Brit. inf.*), brazen, brazen-faced, cheeky, confident, familiar, fresh (*Inf.*), impertinent, impudent, overas~ sertive, overweening, pert, presuming, pre~ sumptuous, pushy (*Inf.*), sassy (*U.S. inf.*), ~*adv.* **4.** *Also* **forwards** ahead, forth, on, onward **5.** into consideration, into promi~ nence, into the open, into view, out, to light, to the fore, to the surface ~*v.* **6.** ad~ vance, aid, assist, back, encourage, ex~ pedite, favour, foster, further, hasten, help, hurry, promote, speed, support **7.** *Com~ merce* dispatch, freight, post, route, send, send on, ship, transmit
Antonyms *adj.* backward, diffident, modest, regressive, retiring, shy ~*adv.* backward(s) ~*v.* bar, block, hinder, hold up, impede, ob~ struct, retard, thwart

forward-looking dynamic, enlightened, enterprising, go-ahead, go-getting (*Inf.*), lib~ eral, modern, progressive, reforming

forwardness boldness, brashness, brazen~ ness, cheek (*Inf.*), cheekiness, chutzpah (*U.S. & Canad. inf.*), impertinence, impu~ dence, overconfidence, pertness, presump~ tion

foster 1. cultivate, encourage, feed, foment, nurture, promote, stimulate, support,

uphold **2.** bring up, mother, nurse, raise, rear, take care of **3.** accommodate, cherish, entertain, harbour, nourish, sustain
Antonyms combat, curb, curtail, hold out against, inhibit, oppose, resist, restrain, sub~ due, suppress, withstand

foul *adj.* **1.** contaminated, dirty, disgusting, fetid, filthy, grotty (*Sl.*), grungy (*Sl., chiefly U.S.*), impure, loathsome, malodorous, me~ phitic, nasty, nauseating, noisome, offen~ sive, olid, polluted, putrid, rank, repulsive, revolting, rotten, scuzzy (*Sl., chiefly U.S.*), squalid, stinking, sullied, tainted, unclean, yucky *or* yukky (*Sl.*) **2.** abusive, blasphe~ mous, blue, coarse, dirty, filthy, foul-mouthed, gross, indecent, lewd, low, ob~ scene, profane, scatological, scurrilous, smutty, vulgar **3.** abhorrent, abominable, base, despicable, detestable, disgraceful, dishonourable, egregious, hateful, heinous, infamous, iniquitous, nefarious, notorious, offensive, scandalous, shameful, shitty (*Ta~ boo sl.*), vicious, vile, wicked **4.** crooked, dirty, dishonest, fraudulent, inequitable, shady (*Inf.*), underhand, unfair, unjust, un~ scrupulous, unsportsmanlike **5.** bad, blus~ tery, disagreeable, foggy, murky, rainy, rough, stormy, wet, wild ~*v.* **6.** begrime, besmear, besmirch, contaminate, defile, dirty, pollute, smear, smirch, soil, stain, sully, taint **7.** block, catch, choke, clog, en~ snare, entangle, jam, snarl, twist
Antonyms *adj.* admirable, attractive, clean, clear, decent, fair, fragrant, fresh, pleasant, pure, respectable, spotless, undefiled ~*v.* clean, cleanse, clear, honour, purge, purify, sanitize

foul play chicanery, corruption, crime, de~ ception, dirty work, double-dealing, duplic~ ity, fraud, perfidy, roguery, sharp practice, skulduggery, treachery, villainy

found 1. bring into being, constitute, con~ struct, create, endow, erect, establish, fix, inaugurate, institute, organize, originate, plant, raise, settle, set up, start **2.** base, bottom, build, ground, rest, root, sustain

foundation 1. base, basis, bedrock, bottom, footing, groundwork, substructure, under~ pinning **2.** endowment, establishment, in~ auguration, institution, organization, set~ ting up, settlement

founder[1] *n.* architect, author, beginner, benefactor, builder, constructor, designer, establisher, father, framer, generator, ini~ tiator, institutor, inventor, maker, organiz~ er, originator, patriarch

founder[2] *v.* **1.** be lost, go down, go to the bottom, sink, submerge **2.** *Fig.* abort, break down, collapse, come to grief, come to nothing, fail, fall through, go belly-up (*Sl.*), go down like a lead balloon (*Inf.*), miscarry,

misfire **3.** collapse, fall, go lame, lurch, sprawl, stagger, stumble, trip

foundling orphan, outcast, stray, waif

fountain 1. font, fount, jet, reservoir, spout, spray, spring, well **2.** *Fig.* beginning, cause, commencement, derivation, fount, foun~ tainhead, genesis, origin, rise, source, well~ head, wellspring

fountainhead *fons et origo*, fount, inspira~ tion, mainspring, origin, source, spring, well, wellspring

foxy artful, astute, canny, crafty, cunning, devious, guileful, knowing, sharp, shrewd, sly, tricky, wily

foyer antechamber, anteroom, entrance hall, lobby, reception area, vestibule

fracas affray (*Law*), aggro (*Sl.*), *bagarre*, brawl, disturbance, donnybrook, fight, free-for-all (*Inf.*), melee *or* mêlée, quarrel, riot, row, rumpus, scrimmage, scuffle, shindig (*Inf.*), shindy (*Inf.*), skirmish, trou~ ble, uproar

fractious awkward, captious, crabby, cross, fretful, froward, grouchy (*Inf.*), irritable, peevish, pettish, petulant, querulous, ratty (*Brit. & N.Z. inf.*), recalcitrant, refractory, testy, tetchy, touchy, unruly
Antonyms affable, agreeable, amiable, bid~ dable, complaisant, genial, good-natured, good-tempered, tractable

fracture 1. *n.* breach, break, cleft, crack, fissure, gap, opening, rent, rift, rupture, schism, split **2.** *v.* break, crack, rupture, splinter, split

fragile breakable, brittle, dainty, delicate, feeble, fine, flimsy, frail, frangible, infirm, slight, weak
Antonyms durable, elastic, flexible, hardy, lasting, reliable, resilient, robust, strong, sturdy, tough

fragility brittleness, delicacy, feebleness, frailty, frangibility, infirmity, weakness

fragment 1. *n.* bit, chip, fraction, morsel, oddment, part, particle, piece, portion, remnant, scrap, shiver, sliver **2.** *v.* break, break up, come apart, come to pieces, crumble, disintegrate, disunite, divide, shatter, shiver, splinter, split, split up
Antonyms *v.* bond, combine, compound, fuse, join together, link, marry, merge, syn~ thesize, unify

fragmentary bitty, broken, disconnected, discrete, disjointed, incoherent, incomplete, partial, piecemeal, scattered, scrappy, sketchy, unsystematic

fragrance aroma, balm, bouquet, fragrancy, perfume, redolence, scent, smell, sweet odour
Antonyms effluvium, miasma, niff (*Brit. sl.*),

offensive smell, pong (*Brit. inf.*), reek, smell, stink, whiff (*Brit. sl.*)

fragrant ambrosial, aromatic, balmy, odor~ iferous, odorous, perfumed, redolent, sweet-scented, sweet-smelling
Antonyms fetid, foul-smelling, malodorous, niffy (*Brit. sl.*), noisome, olid, pongy (*Brit. inf.*), reeking, smelling, smelly, stinking

frail breakable, brittle, decrepit, delicate, feeble, flimsy, fragile, frangible, infirm, in~ substantial, puny, slight, tender, unsound, vulnerable, weak, wispy
Antonyms hale, healthy, robust, sound, stalwart, strong, sturdy, substantial, tough, vigorous

frailty 1. fallibility, feebleness, frailness, infirmity, peccability, puniness, suscep~ tibility, weakness **2.** blemish, defect, deficiency, failing, fault, flaw, foible, imper~ fection, peccadillo, shortcoming, vice, weak point
Antonyms asset, fortitude, might, robust~ ness, strength, strong point, virtue

frame *v.* **1.** assemble, build, constitute, con~ struct, fabricate, fashion, forge, form, insti~ tute, invent, make, manufacture, model, mould, put together, set up **2.** block out, compose, conceive, concoct, contrive, cook up, devise, draft, draw up, form, formulate, hatch, map out, plan, shape, sketch **3.** case, enclose, mount, surround ~*n.* **4.** casing, construction, fabric, form, framework, scheme, shell, structure, system **5.** anato~ my, body, build, carcass, morphology, phy~ sique, skeleton **6.** mount, mounting, setting **7. frame of mind** attitude, disposition, fet~ tle, humour, mood, outlook, spirit, state, temper

frame-up fabrication, fit-up (*Sl.*), put-up job, trumped-up charge

framework core, fabric, foundation, frame, frame of reference, groundwork, plan, schema, shell, skeleton, structure, the bare bones

franchise authorization, charter, exemp~ tion, freedom, immunity, prerogative, privilege, right, suffrage, vote

frank artless, blunt, candid, direct, down~ right, forthright, free, honest, ingenuous, open, outright, outspoken, plain, plain- spoken, sincere, straightforward, straight from the shoulder (*Inf.*), transparent, truth~ ful, unconcealed, undisguised, unreserved, unrestricted, upfront (*Inf.*)
Antonyms artful, crafty, cunning, evasive, indirect, inscrutable, reserved, reticent, se~ cretive, shifty, shy, underhand

frankly 1. candidly, honestly, in truth, to be honest **2.** bluntly, directly, freely, openly, overtly, plainly, straight, without reserve

frankness absence of reserve, bluntness,

candour, forthrightness, ingenuousness, openness, outspokenness, plain speaking, truthfulness

frantic at one's wits' end, berserk, beside oneself, desperate, distracted, distraught, fraught (*Inf.*), frenetic, frenzied, furious, hectic, mad, overwrought, raging, raving, uptight (*Inf.*), wild
Antonyms calm, collected, composed, cool, laid-back, poised, self-possessed, together (*Sl.*), unfazed (*Inf.*), unruffled

fraternity association, brotherhood, cama~ raderie, circle, clan, club, companionship, company, comradeship, fellowship, guild, kinship, league, order, set, sodality, union

fraternize associate, concur, consort, co~ operate, go around with, hang out (*Inf.*), hobnob, keep company, mingle, mix, social~ ize, sympathize, unite
Antonyms avoid, eschew, keep away from, shun, steer clear of

fraud 1. artifice, canard, cheat, chicane, chicanery, craft, deceit, deception, double- dealing, duplicity, guile, hoax, humbug, im~ posture, scam (*Sl.*), sharp practice, spuri~ ousness, sting (*Inf.*), stratagems, swindling, treachery, trickery **2.** bluffer, charlatan, cheat, counterfeit, double-dealer, fake, for~ gery, hoax, hoaxer, impostor, mountebank, phoney *or* phony (*Inf.*), pretender, quack, sham, swindler
Antonyms (*sense 1*) fairness, good faith, honesty, integrity, probity, rectitude, trust~ worthiness, virtue

fraudulent counterfeit, crafty, criminal, crooked (*Inf.*), deceitful, deceptive, dishon~ est, double-dealing, duplicitous, false, knav~ ish, phoney *or* phony (*Inf.*), sham, spurious, swindling, treacherous
Antonyms above board, genuine, honest, honourable, lawful, principled, reputable, true, trustworthy, upright

fray *v.* become threadbare, chafe, fret, rub, wear, wear away, wear thin

frayed frazzled, out at elbows, ragged, tat~ tered, threadbare, worn

freak *n.* **1.** aberration, abnormality, abor~ tion, anomaly, grotesque, malformation, monster, monstrosity, mutant, oddity, queer fish (*Brit. inf.*), rara avis, sport (*Biol.*), tera~ tism, weirdo *or* weirdie (*Inf.*) **2.** caprice, crotchet, fad, fancy, folly, humour, irregu~ larity, quirk, turn, twist, vagary, whim, whimsy **3.** *Sl.* addict, aficionado, buff (*Inf.*), devotee, enthusiast, fan, fanatic, fiend (*Inf.*), nut (*Sl.*), ~*adj.* **4.** aberrant, abnormal, atypical, bizarre, erratic, exceptional, fluky (*Inf.*), fortuitous, odd, queer, unaccountable, unexpected, unforeseen, unparalleled, un~ predictable, unusual

free *adj.* **1.** buckshee (*Brit. sl.*), complimen~

tary, for free (*Inf.*), for nothing, free of charge, gratis, gratuitous, on the house, unpaid, without charge **2.** at large, at lib~ erty, footloose, independent, liberated, loose, off the hook (*Sl.*), on the loose, un~ committed, unconstrained, unengaged, un~ fettered, unrestrained **3.** able, allowed, clear, disengaged, loose, open, permitted, unattached, unengaged, unhampered, un~ impeded, unobstructed, unregulated, unre~ stricted, untrammelled **4.** *With* of above, beyond, deficient in, devoid of, exempt from, immune to, lacking (in), not liable to, safe from, sans (*Archaic*), unaffected by, unencumbered by, untouched by, without **5.** autarchic, autonomous, democratic, emancipated, independent, self-governing, self-ruling, sovereign **6.** at leisure, avail~ able, empty, extra, idle, not tied down, spare, unemployed, uninhabited, unoccu~ pied, unused, vacant **7.** casual, easy, fa~ miliar, forward, frank, free and easy, infor~ mal, laid-back (*Inf.*), lax, liberal, loose, natural, open, relaxed, spontaneous, unbid~ den, unceremonious, unconstrained, un~ forced, uninhibited **8.** big (*Inf.*), bounteous, bountiful, charitable, eager, generous, hos~ pitable, lavish, liberal, munificent, open-handed, prodigal, unsparing, unstinting, willing **9. free and easy** casual, easy-going, informal, laid-back (*Inf.*), lax, lenient, liberal, relaxed, tolerant, unceremonious ~*adv.* **10.** at no cost, for love, gratis, with~ out charge **11.** abundantly, copiously, freely, idly, loosely ~*v.* **12.** deliver, dis~ charge, disenthrall, emancipate, let go, let out, liberate, loose, manumit, release, set at liberty, set free, turn loose, unbridle, uncage, unchain, unfetter, unleash, untie **13.** clear, cut loose, deliver, disengage, dis~ entangle, exempt, extricate, ransom, re~ deem, relieve, rescue, rid, unburden, undo, unshackle
Antonyms (*senses 2 & 3*) bound, captive, confined, dependent, fettered, immured, in~ carcerated, occupied, restrained, restricted, secured (*sense 7*) constrained, formal, official, stiff, unnatural (*sense 8*) close, mean, mingy (*Inf.*), stingy, tight, ungenerous (*senses 12 & 13*) confine, imprison, incarcerate, inhibit, limit, restrain, restrict, straiten

freedom 1. autonomy, deliverance, eman~ cipation, home rule, independence, liberty, manumission, release, self-government **2.** exemption, immunity, impunity, privilege **3.** ability, blank cheque, carte blanche, dis~ cretion, elbowroom, facility, flexibility, free rein, latitude, leeway, licence, opportunity, play, power, range, scope **4.** abandon, can~ dour, directness, ease, familiarity, frank~ ness, informality, ingenuousness, lack of restraint *or* reserve, openness, unconstraint

5. boldness, brazenness, disrespect, for~ wardness, impertinence, laxity, licence, overfamiliarity, presumption
Antonyms bondage, captivity, caution, de~ pendence, imprisonment, limitation, respect~ fulness, restraint, restriction, servitude, slavery, thraldom

free-for-all affray (*Law*), *bagarre,* brawl, donnybrook, dust-up (*Inf.*), fight, fracas, melee *or* mêlée, riot, row, scrimmage, shin~ dig (*Inf.*), shindy (*Inf.*)

free hand *n.* authority, blank cheque, carte blanche, discretion, freedom, latitude, lib~ erty, scope

freely 1. of one's own accord, of one's own free will, spontaneously, voluntarily, will~ ingly, without prompting **2.** candidly, frankly, openly, plainly, unreservedly, without reserve **3.** as you please, unchal~ lenged, without let or hindrance, without restraint **4.** abundantly, amply, bountifully, copiously, extravagantly, lavishly, liberally, like water, open-handedly, unstintingly, with a free hand **5.** cleanly, easily, loosely, readily, smoothly

freethinker agnostic, deist, doubter, infidel, sceptic, unbeliever

freeze 1. benumb, chill, congeal, glaciate, harden, ice over *or* up, stiffen **2.** fix, hold up, inhibit, peg, stop, suspend

freezing arctic, biting, bitter, chill, chilled, cutting, frost-bound, frosty, glacial, icy, numbing, parky (*Brit. inf.*), penetrating, po~ lar, raw, Siberian, wintry

freight *n.* **1.** carriage, conveyance, ship~ ment, transportation **2.** bales, bulk, burden, cargo, consignment, contents, goods, haul, lading, load, merchandise, payload, tonnage

French Gallic

frenzied agitated, all het up (*Inf.*), convul~ sive, distracted, distraught, excited, fever~ ish, frantic, frenetic, furious, hysterical, mad, maniacal, rabid, uncontrolled, wild

frenzy 1. aberration, agitation, delirium, derangement, distraction, fury, hysteria, insanity, lunacy, madness, mania, parox~ ysm, passion, rage, seizure, transport, tur~ moil **2.** bout, burst, convulsion, fit, out~ burst, paroxysm, spasm
Antonyms calm, collectedness, composure, coolness, sanity

frequency constancy, frequentness, perio~ dicity, prevalence, recurrence, repetition

frequent[1] *adj.* common, constant, continual, customary, everyday, familiar, habitual, in~ cessant, numerous, persistent, recurrent, recurring, reiterated, repeated, usual
Antonyms few, few and far between, infre~ quent, occasional, rare, scanty, sporadic

frequent[2] *v.* attend, be a regular customer

of, be found at, hang out at (*Inf.*), haunt, patronize, resort, visit
Antonyms avoid, keep away, shun, spurn

frequently commonly, customarily, habitu~ ally, many a time, many times, much, not infrequently, oft (*Archaic or poetic*), often, oftentimes (*Archaic*), over and over again, repeatedly, thick and fast, very often
Antonyms hardly ever, infrequently, occa~ sionally, once in a blue moon (*Inf.*), rarely, seldom

fresh 1. different, latest, modern, modernis~ tic, new, new-fangled, novel, original, re~ cent, this season's, unconventional, un~ usual, up-to-date **2.** added, additional, aux~ iliary, extra, further, more, other, renewed, supplementary **3.** bracing, bright, brisk, clean, clear, cool, crisp, invigorating, pure, refreshing, spanking, sparkling, stiff, sweet, unpolluted **4.** alert, bouncing, bright, bright-eyed and bushy-tailed (*Inf.*), chipper (*Inf.*), energetic, full of vim and vigour (*Inf.*), invigorated, keen, like a new man, lively, refreshed, rested, restored, revived, sprightly, spry, vigorous, vital **5.** blooming, clear, fair, florid, glowing, good, hardy, healthy, rosy, ruddy, wholesome **6.** dewy, undimmed, unfaded, unwearied, unwith~ ered, verdant, vivid, young **7.** artless, cal~ low, green, inexperienced, natural, new, raw, uncultivated, untrained, untried, youthful **8.** crude, green, natural, raw, un~ cured, undried, unprocessed, unsalted **9.** *Inf.* bold, brazen, cheeky, disrespectful, fa~ miliar, flip (*Inf.*), forward, impudent, inso~ lent, pert, presumptuous, sassy (*U.S. inf.*), saucy, smart-alecky (*Inf.*)
Antonyms (*sense 1*) dull, old, ordinary, ste~ reotyped, trite (*sense 3*) impure, musty, stale, warm (*sense 4*) exhausted, weary (*sense 5*) pal~ lid, sickly (*sense 6*) old, weary (*sense 7*) experi~ enced, old (*sense 8*) preserved, salted, tinned (*sense 9*) well-mannered

freshen 1. enliven, freshen up, liven up, refresh, restore, revitalize, rouse, spruce up, titivate **2.** air, purify, ventilate

freshness 1. innovativeness, inventiveness, newness, novelty, originality **2.** bloom, brightness, cleanness, clearness, dewiness, glow, shine, sparkle, vigour, wholesomeness

fret 1. affront, agonize, anguish, annoy, brood, chagrin, goad, grieve, harass, irri~ tate, lose sleep over, provoke, ruffle, tor~ ment, upset *or* distress oneself, worry **2.** agitate, bother, distress, disturb, gall, irk, nag, nettle, peeve (*Inf.*), pique, rankle with, rile, trouble, vex

fretful captious, complaining, cross, crotch~ ety (*Inf.*), edgy, fractious, irritable, out of sorts, peevish, petulant, querulous, ratty

(*Brit. & N.Z. inf.*), short-tempered, splenetic, testy, tetchy, touchy, uneasy

friction 1. abrasion, attrition, chafing, ero~ sion, fretting, grating, irritation, rasping, resistance, rubbing, scraping, wearing away **2.** animosity, antagonism, bad blood, bad feeling, bickering, conflict, disagreement, discontent, discord, disharmony, dispute, dissension, hostility, incompatibility, oppo~ sition, resentment, rivalry, wrangling

friend 1. Achates, alter ego, boon compan~ ion, bosom friend, buddy (*Inf.*), china (*Brit. sl.*), chum (*Inf.*), cock (*Brit. inf.*), compan~ ion, comrade, confidant, crony, familiar, intimate, mate (*Inf.*), pal, partner, playmate, soul mate **2.** adherent, advocate, ally, asso~ ciate, backer, benefactor, partisan, patron, protagonist, supporter, well-wisher
Antonyms adversary, antagonist, competi~ tor, enemy, foe, opponent, rival

friendless abandoned, alienated, all alone, alone, cut off, deserted, estranged, forlorn, forsaken, isolated, lonely, lonesome, ostra~ cized, shunned, solitary, unattached, with no one to turn to, without a friend in the world, without ties

friendliness affability, amiability, compan~ ionability, congeniality, conviviality, geni~ ality, kindliness, mateyness *or* matiness (*Brit. inf.*), neighbourliness, open arms, so~ ciability, warmth

friendly affable, affectionate, amiable, ami~ cable, attached, attentive, auspicious, beneficial, benevolent, benign, buddy-buddy (*Sl., chiefly U.S. & Canad.*), chummy (*Inf.*), close, clubby, companionable, comradely, conciliatory, confiding, convivial, cordial, familiar, favourable, fond, fraternal, genial, good, helpful, intimate, kind, kindly, matey *or* maty (*Brit. inf.*), neighbourly, on good terms, on visiting terms, outgoing, palsy-walsy (*Inf.*), peaceable, propitious, recep~ tive, sociable, sympathetic, thick (*Inf.*), welcoming, well-disposed
Antonyms antagonistic, belligerent, cold, contentious, distant, inauspicious, sinister, uncongenial, unfriendly

friendship affection, affinity, alliance, am~ ity, attachment, benevolence, closeness, concord, familiarity, fondness, friendliness, good-fellowship, goodwill, harmony, inti~ macy, love, rapport, regard
Antonyms animosity, antagonism, antipa~ thy, aversion, conflict, enmity, hatred, hostil~ ity, resentment, strife, unfriendliness

fright 1. alarm, apprehension, (blue) funk (*Inf.*), cold sweat, consternation, dismay, dread, fear, fear and trembling, horror, panic, quaking, scare, shock, terror, the shivers, trepidation **2.** *Inf.* eyesore, frump, mess (*Inf.*), scarecrow, sight (*Inf.*)

Antonyms boldness, bravery, courage, pluck, valor

frighten affright (*Archaic*), alarm, appal, cow, daunt, dismay, freeze one's blood, in~ timidate, make one's blood run cold, make one's hair stand on end (*Inf.*), make (some~ one) jump out of his skin (*Inf.*), petrify, put the wind up (someone) (*Inf.*), scare, scare (someone) stiff, scare the living daylights out of (someone) (*Inf.*), shock, startle, terri~ fy, terrorize, throw into a fright, throw into a panic, unman, unnerve

Antonyms allay, assuage, calm, comfort, encourage, hearten, reassure, soothe

frightened abashed, affrighted (*Archaic*), afraid, alarmed, cowed, dismayed, frozen, in a cold sweat, in a panic, in fear and trepi~ dation, numb with fear, panicky, petrified, scared, scared shitless (*Taboo sl.*), scared stiff, shit-scared (*Taboo sl.*), startled, terrified, terrorized, terror-stricken, un~ nerved

frightening alarming, appalling, baleful, bloodcurdling, daunting, dismaying, dread~ ful, fearful, fearsome, hair-raising, horrify~ ing, intimidating, menacing, scary (*Inf.*), shocking, spooky (*Inf.*), terrifying, unnerv~ ing

frightful 1. alarming, appalling, awful, dire, dread, dreadful, fearful, ghastly, godawful (*Sl.*), grim, grisly, gruesome, harrowing, hellacious (*U.S. sl.*), hideous, horrendous, horrible, horrid, lurid, macabre, petrifying, shocking, terrible, terrifying, traumatic, unnerving, unspeakable **2.** annoying, awful, disagreeable, dreadful, extreme, great, in~ sufferable, terrible, terrific, unpleasant

Antonyms attractive, beautiful, calming, lovely, moderate, nice, pleasant, slight, sooth~ ing

frigid 1. arctic, chill, cold, cool, frost-bound, frosty, frozen, gelid, glacial, hyperboreal, icy, Siberian, wintry **2.** aloof, austere, cold-hearted, forbidding, formal, icy, life~ less, passionless, passive, repellent, rigid, stiff, unapproachable, unbending, unfeeling, unloving, unresponsive

Antonyms ardent, cordial, friendly, hospi~ table, hot, impassioned, passionate, respon~ sive, sensual, stifling, sweltering, warm

frigidity aloofness, austerity, chill, cold-heartedness, coldness, frostiness, iciness, impassivity, lack of response, lifelessness, passivity, touch-me-not attitude, unap~ proachability, unresponsiveness, wintriness

frill *n.* flounce, furbelow, gathering, purfle, ruche, ruching, ruff, ruffle, tuck

frills additions, affectation(s), bits and pieces, decoration(s), dressing up, embellish~ ment(s), extras, fanciness, fandangles, finery, frilliness, frippery, fuss, gewgaws,

jazz (*Sl.*), mannerisms, nonsense, ornamen~ tation, ostentation, superfluities, tomfool~ ery, trimmings

fringe *n.* **1.** binding, border, edging, hem, tassel, trimming **2.** borderline, edge, limits, march, marches, margin, outskirts, perim~ eter, periphery ~*adj.* **3.** unconventional, unofficial, unorthodox ~*v.* **4.** border, edge, enclose, skirt, surround, trim

frisk 1. bounce, caper, cavort, curvet, dance, frolic, gambol, hop, jump, play, prance, rol~ lick, romp, skip, sport, trip **2.** *Inf.* check, inspect, run over, search, shake down (*U.S. sl.*)

frisky bouncy, coltish, frolicsome, full of beans (*Inf.*), full of joie de vivre, high-spirited, in high spirits, kittenish, lively, playful, rollicking, romping, spirited, spor~ tive

Antonyms demure, dull, lacklustre, pensive, sedate, stodgy, stolid, wooden

fritter (away) dally away, dissipate, fool away, idle (away), misspend, run through, spend like water, squander, waste

frivolity childishness, flightiness, flippancy, flummery, folly, frivolousness, fun, gaiety, giddiness, jest, levity, light-heartedness, lightness, nonsense, puerility, shallowness, silliness, superficiality, trifling, triviality

Antonyms earnestness, gravity, humour~ lessness, importance, sedateness, serious~ ness, significance, soberness, sobriety

frivolous 1. childish, dizzy, empty-headed, flighty, flip (*Inf.*), flippant, foolish, giddy, idle, ill-considered, juvenile, light-minded, nonserious, puerile, silly, superficial **2.** ex~ travagant, footling (*Inf.*), impractical, light, minor, nickel-and-dime (*U.S. sl.*), niggling, paltry, peripheral, petty, pointless, shallow, trifling, trivial, unimportant

Antonyms earnest, important, mature, practical, responsible, sensible, serious, sol~ emn, vital

frizzle crisp, fry, hiss, roast, scorch, sizzle, sputter

frolic *v.* **1.** caper, cavort, cut capers, frisk, gambol, lark, make merry, play, rollick, romp, sport ~*n.* **2.** antic, escapade, gamba~ do, gambol, game, lark, prank, revel, romp, spree **3.** amusement, drollery, fun, fun and games, gaiety, high jinks, merriment, sky~ larking (*Inf.*), sport

frolicsome coltish, frisky, gay, kittenish, lively, merry, playful, rollicking, sportive, sprightly, wanton (*Archaic*)

front *n.* **1.** anterior, exterior, façade, face, facing, foreground, forepart, frontage, ob~ verse **2.** beginning, fore, forefront, front line, head, lead, top, van, vanguard **3.** air, appearance, aspect, bearing, countenance, demeanour, expression, exterior, face, manner, mien, show **4.** blind, cover, cover-up, disguise, façade, mask, pretext, show **5. in front** ahead, before, first, in ad~ vance, in the lead, in the van, leading, pre~ ceding, to the fore ~*adj.* **6.** first, foremost, head, headmost, lead, leading, topmost ~*v.* **7.** face (onto), look over *or* onto, overlook **Antonyms** (*senses 1 & 2*) aft, back, back end, behind, hindmost, nethermost, rear

frontier borderland, borderline, bound, boundary, confines, edge, limit, marches, perimeter, verge

frost freeze, freeze-up, hoarfrost, Jack Frost, rime

frosty 1. chilly, cold, frozen, hoar (*Rare*), ice-capped, icicled, icy, parky (*Brit. inf.*), rimy, wintry **2.** discouraging, frigid, off-putting (*Brit. inf.*), standoffish, unenthusi~ astic, unfriendly, unwelcoming

froth 1. *n.* bubbles, effervescence, foam, head, lather, scum, spume, suds **2.** *v.* bub~ ble over, come to a head, effervesce, fizz, foam, lather

frothy 1. foaming, foamy, spumescent, spu~ mous, spumy, sudsy **2.** *Fig.* empty, frilly, frivolous, light, petty, slight, trifling, trivial, trumpery, unnecessary, unsubstantial, vain

frown 1. give a dirty look, glare, glower, knit one's brows, look daggers, lour *or* low~ er, scowl **2.** *With* **on** *or* **upon** disapprove of, discountenance, discourage, dislike, look askance at, not take kindly to, show disap~ proval *or* displeasure, take a dim view of, view with disfavour

frowsty close, fuggy, fusty, ill-smelling, musty, stale, stuffy

frowzy blowzy, dirty, draggletailed (*Archa~ ic*), frumpish, messy, slatternly, sloppy, slovenly, sluttish, ungroomed, unkempt, untidy, unwashed

frozen 1. arctic, chilled, chilled to the mar~ row, frigid, frosted, icebound, ice-cold, ice-covered, icy, numb **2.** fixed, pegged (*of prices*), petrified, rooted, stock-still, stopped, suspended, turned to stone

frugal abstemious, careful, cheeseparing, economical, meagre, niggardly, parsimoni~ ous, penny-wise, provident, prudent, saving, sparing, thrifty **Antonyms** excessive, extravagant, impru~ dent, lavish, luxurious, prodigal, profligate, spendthrift, wasteful

fruit 1. crop, harvest, produce, product, yield **2.** advantage, benefit, consequence, effect, outcome, profit, result, return, reward

fruitful 1. fecund, fertile, fructiferous **2.** abundant, copious, flush, plenteous, plenti~ ful, productive, profuse, prolific, rich, spawning **3.** advantageous, beneficial, ef~ fective, gainful, productive, profitable, re~

warding, successful, useful, well-spent, worthwhile **Antonyms** barren, fruitless, futile, ineffec~ tual, infertile, pointless, scarce, sterile, un~ fruitful, unproductive, useless, vain

fruition actualization, attainment, comple~ tion, consummation, enjoyment, fulfilment, materialization, maturation, maturity, per~ fection, realization, ripeness

fruitless abortive, barren, bootless, futile, idle, ineffectual, in vain, pointless, profitless, to no avail, to no effect, unavail~ ing, unfruitful, unproductive, unprofitable, unprolific, unsuccessful, useless, vain **Antonyms** abundant, effective, fecund, fer~ tile, fruitful, productive, profitable, prolific, useful

fruity 1. full, mellow, resonant, rich **2.** *Inf.* bawdy, blue, hot, indecent, indelicate, juicy, near the knuckle (*Inf.*), racy, ripe, risqué, salacious, sexy, smutty, spicy (*Inf.*), sugges~ tive, titillating, vulgar

frumpish, frumpy badly-dressed, dated, dingy, dowdy, drab, dreary, mumsy, out of date

frustrate 1. baffle, balk, block, check, cir~ cumvent, confront, counter, defeat, disap~ point, foil, forestall, inhibit, neutralize, nullify, render null and void, stymie, thwart **2.** depress, discourage, dishearten **Antonyms** advance, cheer, encourage, en~ dorse, forward, further, hearten, promote, satisfy, stimulate

frustrated carrying a chip on one's shoul~ der (*Inf.*), disappointed, discontented, dis~ couraged, disheartened, embittered, foiled, irked, resentful, sick as a parrot (*Inf.*)

frustration 1. blocking, circumvention, contravention, curbing, failure, foiling, nonfulfilment, nonsuccess, obstruction, thwarting **2.** annoyance, disappointment, dissatisfaction, grievance, irritation, re~ sentment, vexation

fuddled bevvied (*Dialect*), blitzed (*Sl.*), blot~ to (*Sl.*), bombed (*Sl.*), confused, drunk, flying (*Sl.*), inebriated, intoxicated, legless (*Inf.*), lit up (*Sl.*), muddled, muzzy, out of it (*Sl.*), out to it (*Aust. & N.Z. sl.*), paralytic (*Inf.*), pissed (*Taboo sl.*), smashed (*Sl.*), soz~ zled (*Inf.*), steamboats (*Sl.*), steaming (*Sl.*), stupefied, tipsy, wasted (*Sl.*), woozy (*Inf.*), wrecked (*Sl.*), zonked (*Sl.*)

fuddy-duddy *n.* back number (*Inf.*), con~ servative, dinosaur, dodo (*Inf.*), fossil, mu~ seum piece, (old) fogy, square (*Inf.*), stick-in-the-mud (*Inf.*), stuffed shirt (*Inf.*)

fudge *v.* avoid, cook (*Sl.*), dodge, equivocate, evade, fake, falsify, flannel (*Brit. inf.*), hedge, misrepresent, patch up, shuffle, slant, stall

fuel 1. *n. Fig.* ammunition, encouragement, fodder, food, incitement, material, means, nourishment, provocation **2.** *v.* charge, fan, feed, fire, incite, inflame, nourish, stoke up, sustain

fugitive 1. *n.* deserter, escapee, refugee, runagate (*Archaic*), runaway **2.** *adj.* brief, ephemeral, evanescent, fleeing, fleeting, flitting, flying, fugacious, momentary, passing, short, short-lived, temporary, transient, transitory, unstable

fulfil accomplish, achieve, answer, bring to completion, carry out, complete, comply with, conclude, conform to, discharge, effect, execute, fill, finish, keep, meet, obey, observe, perfect, perform, realise, satisfy
Antonyms disappoint, dissatisfy, fail in, fail to meet, fall short of, neglect

fulfilment accomplishment, achievement, attainment, carrying out *or* through, completion, consummation, crowning, discharge, discharging, effecting, end, implementation, observance, perfection, realization

full 1. brimful, brimming, complete, entire, filled, gorged, intact, loaded, replete, sated, satiated, satisfied, saturated, stocked, sufficient **2.** abundant, adequate, all-inclusive, ample, broad, comprehensive, copious, detailed, exhaustive, extensive, generous, maximum, plenary, plenteous, plentiful, thorough, unabridged **3.** chock-a-block, chock-full, crammed, crowded, in use, jammed, occupied, packed, taken **4.** clear, deep, distinct, loud, resonant, rich, rounded **5.** baggy, balloonlike, buxom, capacious, curvaceous, large, loose, plump, puffy, rounded, voluminous, voluptuous **6. in full** completely, in its entirety, in total, *in toto*, without exception **7. to the full** completely, entirely, fully, thoroughly, to the utmost, without reservation
Antonyms abridged, blank, devoid, empty, exhausted, faint, incomplete, limited, partial, restricted, thin, tight, vacant, void

full-blooded ballsy (*Taboo sl.*), gutsy (*Sl.*), hearty, lusty, mettlesome, red-blooded, vigorous, virile

full-bodied fruity, full-flavoured, heady, heavy, mellow, redolent, rich, strong, well-matured

full-grown adult, developed, full-fledged, grown-up, in one's prime, marriageable, mature, nubile, of age, ripe
Antonyms adolescent, green, premature, undeveloped, unfledged, unformed, unripe, untimely, young

fullness 1. abundance, adequateness, ampleness, copiousness, fill, glut, plenty, profusion, repletion, satiety, saturation, sufficiency **2.** broadness, completeness, comprehensiveness, entirety, extensiveness, plenitude, totality, vastness, wealth, wholeness **3.** clearness, loudness, resonance, richness, strength **4.** curvaceousness, dilation, distension, enlargement, roundness, swelling, tumescence, voluptuousness

full-scale all-encompassing, all-out, comprehensive, exhaustive, extensive, full-dress, in-depth, major, proper, sweeping, thorough, thoroughgoing, wide-ranging

fully 1. absolutely, altogether, completely, entirely, every inch, from first to last, heart and soul, in all respects, intimately, perfectly, positively, thoroughly, totally, utterly, wholly **2.** abundantly, adequately, amply, comprehensively, enough, plentifully, satisfactorily, sufficiently **3.** at least, quite, without (any) exaggeration, without a word of a lie (*Inf.*)

fully-fledged experienced, mature, professional, proficient, qualified, senior, time-served, trained

fulmination condemnation, denunciation, diatribe, excoriation, invective, obloquy, philippic, reprobation, tirade

fulsome adulatory, cloying, excessive, extravagant, fawning, gross, immoderate, ingratiating, inordinate, insincere, nauseating, overdone, saccharine, sickening, smarmy (*Brit. inf.*), sycophantic, unctuous

fumble 1. bumble, feel around, flounder, grope, paw (*Inf.*), scrabble **2.** bodge (*Inf.*), botch, bungle, cock up (*Brit. sl.*), fuck up (*Offens. taboo sl.*), make a hash of (*Inf.*), mess up, misfield, mishandle, mismanage, muff, spoil

fume *Fig.* **1.** *v.* blow a fuse (*Sl., chiefly U.S.*), boil, chafe, champ at the bit (*Inf.*), crack up (*Inf.*), fly off the handle (*Inf.*), get hot under the collar (*Inf.*), get steamed up about (*Sl.*), go off the deep end (*Inf.*), go up the wall (*Sl.*), rage, rant, rave, see red (*Inf.*), seethe, smoulder, storm **2.** *n.* agitation, dither (*Chiefly Brit.*), fit, fret, fury, passion, rage, stew (*Inf.*), storm

fumes effluvium, exhalation, exhaust, gas, haze, miasma, pollution, reek, smog, smoke, stench, vapour

fumigate clean out *or* up, cleanse, disinfect, purify, sanitize, sterilize

fuming all steamed up (*Sl.*), angry, at boiling point (*Inf.*), enraged, foaming at the mouth, in a rage, incensed, raging, roused, seething, up in arms

fun *n.* **1.** amusement, cheer, distraction, diversion, enjoyment, entertainment, frolic, gaiety, good time, high jinks, jollification, jollity, joy, junketing, living it up, merriment, merrymaking, mirth, pleasure, recreation, romp, sport, treat, whoopee (*Inf.*) **2.**

buffoonery, clowning, foolery, game, horse~
play, jesting, jocularity, joking, nonsense,
play, playfulness, skylarking (*Inf.*), sport,
teasing, tomfoolery **3. in** *or* **for fun** fa~
cetiously, for a joke, for a laugh, in jest,
jokingly, light-heartedly, mischievously,
playfully, roguishly, teasingly, tongue in
cheek, with a gleam *or* twinkle in one's eye,
with a straight face **4. make fun of** deride,
hold up to ridicule, lampoon, laugh at,
make a fool of, make game of, make sport
of, make the butt of, mock, parody, poke
fun at, rag, rib (*Inf.*), ridicule, satirize, scoff
at, send up (*Brit. inf.*), sneer at, take off,
take the piss out of (*Taboo sl.*), taunt ~*adj.*
5. amusing, convivial, diverting, enjoyable,
entertaining, lively, witty
Antonyms (*sense 1*) depression, desolation,
despair, distress, gloom, grief, melancholy,
misery, sadness, sorrow, unhappiness, woe

function *n.* **1.** activity, business, capacity,
charge, concern, duty, employment, exer~
cise, job, mission, occupation, office, opera~
tion, part, post, province, purpose, raison
d'être, responsibility, role, situation, task
~*v.* **2.** act, act the part of, behave, be in
commission, be in operation *or* action, be in
running order, do duty, go, officiate, oper~
ate, perform, run, serve, serve one's turn,
work ~*n.* **3.** affair, do (*Inf.*), gathering, re~
ception, social occasion

functional hard-wearing, operative, practi~
cal, serviceable, useful, utilitarian, utility,
working

fund *n.* **1.** capital, endowment, fall-back,
foundation, kitty, pool, reserve, stock, store,
supply **2.** hoard, mine, repository, reserve,
reservoir, source, storehouse, treasury, vein
~*v.* **3.** capitalize, endow, finance, float, pay
for, promote, stake, subsidize, support

fundamental 1. *adj.* basic, bog-standard
(*Inf.*), cardinal, central, constitutional, cru~
cial, elementary, essential, first, important,
indispensable, integral, intrinsic, key, nec~
essary, organic, primary, prime, principal,
radical, rudimentary, underlying, vital **2.** *n.*
axiom, basic, cornerstone, essential, first
principle, law, principle, rudiment, rule,
sine qua non
Antonyms advanced, back-up, extra, inci~
dental, lesser, secondary, subsidiary,
superfluous

fundamentally at bottom, at heart, basi~
cally, essentially, intrinsically, primarily,
radically

funds 1. ackers (*Sl.*), brass (*Northern Eng~
lish dialect*), bread (*Sl.*), capital, cash, dibs
(*Sl.*), dosh (*Brit. & Aust. sl.*), dough (*Sl.*),
finance, hard cash, money, necessary (*Inf.*),
needful (*Inf.*), ready money, resources, rhi~
no (*Brit. sl.*), savings, shekels (*Inf.*), silver,

spondulicks (*Sl.*), the ready (*Inf.*), the
wherewithal, tin (*Sl.*) **2. in funds** flush
(*Inf.*), in the black, solvent, well-off, well-
supplied

funeral burial, inhumation, interment, ob~
sequies

funnel *v.* channel, conduct, convey, direct,
filter, move, pass, pour

funny *adj.* **1.** absurd, amusing, a scream
(card (*Inf.*), caution (*Inf.*)) (*Inf.*), comic,
comical, diverting, droll, entertaining, fa~
cetious, farcical, hilarious, humorous, jo~
cose, jocular, jolly, killing (*Inf.*), laughable,
ludicrous, rich, ridiculous, riotous, risible,
side-splitting, silly, slapstick, waggish, witty
2. curious, dubious, mysterious, odd, pecu~
liar, perplexing, puzzling, queer, remark~
able, rum (*Brit. sl.*), strange, suspicious,
unusual, weird ~*n.* **3.** *Inf.* crack (*Sl.*), jest,
joke, play on words, pun, quip, wisecrack,
witticism
Antonyms (*sense 1*) grave, humourless, mel~
ancholy, serious, sober, solemn, stern, unfun~
ny

furious 1. angry, beside oneself, boiling,
cross, enraged, frantic, frenzied, fuming,
incensed, infuriated, in high dudgeon, livid
(*Inf.*), mad, maddened, on the warpath
(*Inf.*), raging, up in arms, wrathful, wroth
(*Archaic*) **2.** agitated, boisterous, fierce, im~
petuous, intense, savage, stormy, tempestu~
ous, tumultuous, turbulent, ungovernable,
unrestrained, vehement, violent, wild
Antonyms calm, dispassionate, impassive,
imperturbable, mild, placated, pleased, se~
rene, tranquil

furnish 1. appoint, decorate, equip, fit (out,
up), outfit, provide, provision, purvey, rig,
stock, store, supply **2.** afford, bestow, en~
dow, give, grant, hand out, offer, present,
provide, reveal, supply

furniture appliances, appointments, chat~
tels, effects, equipment, fittings, furnish~
ings, goods, household goods, movable
property, movables, possessions, things
(*Inf.*)

furore 1. commotion, disturbance, excite~
ment, flap (*Inf.*), frenzy, fury, hullabaloo,
outburst, outcry, stir, to-do, uproar **2.**
craze, enthusiasm, mania, rage

furrow 1. *n.* channel, corrugation, crease,
crow's-foot, fluting, groove, hollow, line,
rut, seam, trench, wrinkle **2.** *v.* corrugate,
crease, draw together, flute, knit, seam,
wrinkle

further 1. *adj.* additional, extra, fresh,
more, new, other, supplementary **2.** *adv.*
additionally, also, as well as, besides,
furthermore, in addition, moreover, on top
of, over and above, to boot, what's more,
yet **3.** *v.* advance, aid, assist, champion,

contribute to, encourage, expedite, facili~
tate, forward, foster, hasten, help, lend sup~
port to, patronize, plug (*Inf.*), promote,
push, speed, succour, work for
Antonyms *v.* foil, frustrate, hinder, impede,
obstruct, oppose, prevent, retard, stop, thwart

furtherance advancement, advocacy, back~
ing, boosting, carrying-out, championship,
promotion, prosecution, pursuit

furthermore additionally, as well, besides,
further, in addition, into the bargain,
moreover, not to mention, to boot, too,
what's more

furthest extreme, farthest, furthermost,
most distant, outermost, outmost, remotest,
ultimate, uttermost

furtive clandestine, cloaked, conspiratorial,
covert, hidden, secret, secretive, skulking,
slinking, sly, sneaking, sneaky, stealthy,
surreptitious, underhand, under-the-table
Antonyms above-board, candid, forthright,
frank, open, public, straightforward, undis~
guised, unreserved

fury 1. anger, frenzy, impetuosity, ire, mad~
ness, passion, rage, wrath **2.** ferocity,
fierceness, force, intensity, power, savagery,
severity, tempestuousness, turbulence, ve~
hemence, violence **3.** bacchante, hag, hell~
cat, shrew, spitfire, termagant, virago, vix~
en
Antonyms calm, calmness, composure,
equanimity, hush, peace, peacefulness, se~
renity, stillness, tranquillity

fuse *v.* agglutinate, amalgamate, blend, coa~
lesce, combine, commingle, dissolve, feder~
ate, integrate, intermingle, intermix, join,
meld, melt, merge, run together, smelt, sol~
der, unite, weld
Antonyms diffuse, dispense, disseminate,
dissipate, disunite, scatter, separate, spread,
strew

fuss *n.* **1.** ado, agitation, bother, bustle,
commotion, confusion, excitement, fidget,
flap (*Inf.*), flurry, fluster, flutter, hurry, pa~
laver, pother, stir, storm in a teacup (*Brit.*),

to-do, upset, worry **2.** altercation, argu~
ment, bother, complaint, difficulty, display,
furore, hassle (*Inf.*), objection, row, squab~
ble, trouble, unrest, upset ~*v.* **3.** bustle,
chafe, fidget, flap (*Inf.*), fret, fume, get in a
stew (*Inf.*), get worked up, labour over,
make a meal of (*Inf.*), make a thing of (*Inf.*),
niggle, take pains, worry

fussy 1. choosy (*Inf.*), dainty, difficult, dis~
criminating, exacting, faddish, faddy, fas~
tidious, finicky, hard to please, nit-picking
(*Inf.*), old-maidish, old womanish, overpar~
ticular, particular, pernickety, picky (*Inf.*),
squeamish **2.** busy, cluttered, overdecorat~
ed, overelaborate, overembellished, over~
worked, rococo

futile 1. abortive, barren, bootless, empty,
forlorn, fruitless, hollow, ineffectual, in
vain, nugatory, profitless, sterile, to no
avail, unavailing, unproductive, unprofit~
able, unsuccessful, useless, vain, valueless,
worthless **2.** idle, pointless, trifling, trivial,
unimportant
Antonyms constructive, effective, fruitful,
profitable, purposeful, significant, successful,
useful, valuable, worthwhile

futility 1. bootlessness, emptiness, fruitless~
ness, hollowness, ineffectiveness, useless~
ness **2.** pointlessness, triviality, unim~
portance, vanity

future 1. *n.* expectation, hereafter, outlook,
prospect, time to come **2.** *adj.* approaching,
coming, destined, eventual, expected, fated,
forthcoming, impending, in the offing, later,
prospective, subsequent, to be, to come, ul~
timate, unborn
Antonyms *adj.* bygone, erstwhile, ex-, for~
mer, late, past, preceding, previous, quondam

fuzzy 1. down-covered, downy, flossy, fluffy,
frizzy, linty, napped, woolly. **2.** bleary,
blurred, distorted, faint, ill-defined, indis~
tinct, muffled, out of focus, shadowy, un~
clear, unfocused, vague
Antonyms clear, defined, detailed, distinct,
in focus, precise

G

gabble 1. *v.* babble, blab, blabber, cackle, chatter, gaggle, gibber, gush, jabber, prattle, rabbit (*Brit. inf.*), rattle, run off at the mouth (*Sl.*), splutter, spout, sputter, waffle (*Inf., chiefly Brit.*) **2.** *n.* babble, blabber, cackling, chatter, drivel, gibberish, jargon, pap, prattle, twaddle, waffle (*Inf., chiefly Brit.*)

gad (about *or* **around)** gallivant, ramble, range, roam, rove, run around, stravaig (*Scot. & northern English dialect*), stray, traipse (*Inf.*), wander

gadabout gallivanter, pleasure-seeker, rambler, rover, wanderer

gadget appliance, contraption (*Inf.*), contrivance, device, gimmick, gizmo (*Sl., chiefly U.S.*), instrument, invention, novelty, thing, tool

gaffe bloomer (*Inf.*), blunder, boob (*Brit. sl.*), boo-boo (*Inf.*), clanger (*Inf.*), faux pas, gaucherie, howler, indiscretion, mistake, slip, solecism

gaffer 1. granddad, greybeard, old boy (*Inf.*), old fellow, old man, old-timer (*U.S.*) **2.** *Inf.* boss (*Inf.*), foreman, ganger, manager, overseer, superintendent, supervisor

gag^1 *v.* **1.** curb, muffle, muzzle, quiet, silence, stifle, still, stop up, suppress, throttle **2.** *Sl.* barf (*Sl.*), disgorge, heave, puke (*Sl.*), retch, spew, throw up (*Inf.*), vomit **3.** *Sl.* choke, gasp, pant, struggle for breath

gag^2 crack (*Sl.*), funny (*Inf.*), hoax, jest, joke, wisecrack (*Inf.*), witticism

gaiety 1. animation, blitheness, blithesomeness (*Literary*), cheerfulness, effervescence, elation, exhilaration, glee, good humour, high spirits, hilarity, *joie de vivre*, jollity, joviality, joyousness, light-heartedness, liveliness, merriment, mirth, sprightliness, vivacity **2.** celebration, conviviality, festivity, fun, jollification, merrymaking, revelry, revels **3.** brightness, brilliance, colour, colourfulness, gaudiness, glitter, show, showiness, sparkle
Antonyms despondency, gloom, melancholy, misery, sadness

gaily 1. blithely, cheerfully, gleefully, happily, joyfully, light-heartedly, merrily **2.** brightly, brilliantly, colourfully, flamboyantly, flashily, gaudily, showily

gain *v.* **1.** achieve, acquire, advance, attain, bag, build up, capture, collect, enlist, gather, get, glean, harvest, improve, increase, net, obtain, pick up, procure, profit, realize, reap, score (*Sl.*), secure, win, win over **2.** acquire, bring in, clear, earn, get, make, net, obtain, produce, realize, win, yield **3.** *Usually with* **on a.** approach, catch up with, close with, get nearer, narrow the gap, overtake **b.** draw *or* pull away from, get farther away, leave behind, outdistance, recede, widen the gap **4.** arrive at, attain, come to, get to, reach **5. gain time** delay, procrastinate, stall, temporize, use delaying tactics ~*n.* **6.** accretion, achievement, acquisition, advance, advancement, advantage, attainment, benefit, dividend, earnings, emolument, growth, headway, improvement, income, increase, increment, lucre, proceeds, produce, profit, progress, return, rise, winnings, yield
Antonyms *v.* fail, forfeit, lose, worsen ~*n.* damage, forfeiture, injury, loss, privation

gainful advantageous, beneficial, expedient, fruitful, lucrative, moneymaking, paying, productive, profitable, remunerative, rewarding, useful, worthwhile

gains booty, earnings, gainings, pickings, prize, proceeds, profits, revenue, takings, winnings

gainsay contradict, contravene, controvert, deny, disaffirm, disagree with, dispute, rebut, retract
Antonyms agree with, back, confirm, support

gait bearing, carriage, pace, step, stride, tread, walk

gala 1. *n.* beano (*Brit. sl.*), carnival, celebration, festival, festivity, fête, jamboree, pageant, party, rave (*Brit. sl.*), rave-up (*Brit. sl.*) **2.** *adj.* celebratory, convivial, festal, festive, gay, jovial, joyful, merry

gale 1. blast, cyclone, hurricane, squall, storm, tempest, tornado, typhoon **2.** *Inf.* burst, eruption, explosion, fit, howl, outbreak, outburst, peal, shout, shriek

gall^1 1. *Inf.* brass (*Inf.*), brass neck (*Brit. inf.*), brazenness, cheek (*Inf.*), chutzpah (*U.S. & Canad. inf.*), effrontery, impertinence, impudence, insolence, neck (*Inf.*), nerve (*Inf.*), sauciness **2.** acrimony, animosity, animus, antipathy, bad blood, bile, bitterness, enmity, hostility, malevolence, malice, malignity, rancour, sourness, spite, spleen, venom

gall^2 *n.* **1.** abrasion, chafe, excoriation, raw spot, scrape, sore, sore spot, wound **2.** aggravation (*Inf.*), annoyance, bother, botheration (*Inf.*), exasperation, harassment, irritant, irritation, nuisance, pest, provoca~

tion, vexation ~*v.* **3.** abrade, bark, chafe, excoriate, fret, graze, irritate, rub raw, scrape, skin **4.** aggravate (*Inf.*), annoy, be on one's back (*Sl.*), bother, exasperate, fret, get in one's hair (*Inf.*), get on one's nerves (*Inf.*), harass, hassle (*Inf.*), irk, irritate, nag, nark (*Brit., Aust., & N.Z. sl.*), nettle, peeve (*Inf.*), pester, piss one off (*Taboo sl.*), plague, provoke, rankle, rile (*Inf.*), rub up the wrong way, ruffle, vex

gallant *adj.* **1.** bold, brave, courageous, dar~ing, dashing, dauntless, doughty, fearless, game (*Inf.*), heroic, high-spirited, honour~able, intrepid, lion-hearted, manful, manly, mettlesome, noble, plucky, valiant, valorous **2.** attentive, chivalrous, courteous, courtly, gentlemanly, gracious, magnanimous, no~ble, polite **3.** august, dignified, elegant, glo~rious, grand, imposing, lofty, magnificent, noble, splendid, stately ~*n.* **4.** admirer, beau, boyfriend, escort, leman (*Archaic*), lover, paramour, suitor, wooer **5.** beau, blade (*Archaic*), buck (*Inf.*), dandy, fop, ladies' man, lady-killer (*Inf.*), man about town, man of fashion **6.** adventurer, cava~lier, champion, daredevil, hero, knight, man of mettle, *preux chevalier*
Antonyms churlish, cowardly, discour~teous, fearful, ignoble, ill-mannered, impolite, rude

gallantry **1.** audacity, boldness, bravery, courage, courageousness, daring, daunt~lessness, derring-do (*Archaic*), fearlessness, heroism, intrepidity, manliness, mettle, nerve, pluck, prowess, spirit, valiance, val~our **2.** attentiveness, chivalry, courteous~ness, courtesy, courtliness, elegance, gentlemanliness, graciousness, nobility, po~liteness
Antonyms churlishness, cowardice, dis~courtesy, irresolution, rudeness, ungra~ciousness

galling aggravating (*Inf.*), annoying, bitter, bothersome, exasperating, harassing, hu~miliating, irksome, irritating, nettlesome, plaguing, provoking, rankling, vexatious, vexing

gallop barrel (along) (*Inf., chiefly U.S. & Canad.*), bolt, career, dart, dash, fly, hasten, hie (*Archaic*), hurry, race, run, rush, scud, shoot, speed, sprint, tear along, zoom

galore à gogo (*Inf.*), all over the place, aplenty, everywhere, in abundance, in great quantity, in numbers, in profusion, to spare

galvanize arouse, awaken, electrify, excite, fire, inspire, invigorate, jolt, kick-start, move, prod, provoke, quicken, shock, spur, startle, stimulate, stir, thrill, vitalize, wake

gamble *v.* **1.** back, bet, game, have a flutter (*Inf.*), lay *or* make a bet, play, punt, stake, try one's luck, wager **2.** back, chance, haz~

ard, put one's faith *or* trust in, risk, specu~late, stake, stick one's neck out (*Inf.*), take a chance, venture ~*n.* **3.** chance, leap in the dark, lottery, risk, speculation, uncertainty, venture **4.** bet, flutter (*Inf.*), punt, wager
Antonyms (*sense 3*) certainty, foregone con~clusion, safe bet, sure thing

gambol **1.** *v.* caper, cavort, curvet, cut a caper, frisk, frolic, hop, jump, prance, rol~lick, skip **2.** *n.* antic, caper, frolic, gambado, hop, jump, prance, skip, spring

game¹ *n.* **1.** amusement, distraction, diver~sion, entertainment, frolic, fun, jest, joke, lark, merriment, pastime, play, recreation, romp, sport **2.** competition, contest, event, head-to-head, match, meeting, round, tour~nament **3.** adventure, business, enterprise, line, occupation, plan, proceeding, scheme, undertaking **4.** chase, prey, quarry, wild animals **5.** *Inf.* design, device, plan, plot, ploy, scheme, stratagem, strategy, tactic, trick **6. make (a) game of** deride, make a fool of, make a laughing stock, make fun of, make sport of, mock, poke fun at, ridicule, send up (*Brit. inf.*)
Antonyms business, chore, duty, job, la~bour, toil, work

game² *adj.* **1.** ballsy (*Taboo sl.*), bold, brave, courageous, dauntless, dogged, fearless, feisty (*Inf., chiefly U.S. & Canad.*), gallant, gritty, have-a-go (*Inf.*), heroic, intrepid, persevering, persistent, plucky, resolute, spirited, unflinching, valiant, valorous **2.** desirous, disposed, eager, inclined, inter~ested, prepared, ready, willing
Antonyms cowardly, fearful, irresolute

gamut area, catalogue, compass, field, range, scale, scope, series, sweep

gang band, bevy, camp, circle, clique, club, company, coterie, crew (*Inf.*), crowd, group, herd, horde, lot, mob, pack, party, posse (*Sl.*), ring, set, shift, squad, team, troupe

gangling, gangly angular, awkward, lanky, loose-jointed, rangy, rawboned, skin~ny, spindly, tall

gangster bandit, brigand, crook (*Inf.*), des~perado, gang member, heavy (*Sl.*), hood (*U.S. sl.*), hoodlum (*Chiefly U.S.*), mobster (*U.S. sl.*), racketeer, robber, ruffian, thug, tough

gap **1.** blank, breach, break, chink, cleft, crack, cranny, crevice, discontinuity, di~vide, entr'acte, hiatus, hole, interlude, intermission, interruption, interstice, in~terval, lacuna, lull, opening, pause, recess, rent, respite, rift, space, vacuity, void **2.** difference, disagreement, disparity, diver~gence, inconsistency

gape **1.** gawk, gawp (*Brit. sl.*), goggle, stare, wonder **2.** crack, open, split, yawn

gaping broad, cavernous, great, open, vast, wide, wide open, yawning

garb *n.* **1.** apparel, array, attire, clothes, clothing, costume, dress, garment, gear (*Sl.*), habiliment, habit, outfit, raiment (*Archaic*), robes, uniform, vestments, wear **2.** cut, fashion, look, mode, style **3.** appear~ ance, aspect, attire, covering, guise, out~ ward form ~*v.* **4.** apparel, attire, clothe, cover, dress, rig out, robe

garbage **1.** bits and pieces, debris, detritus, junk, litter, odds and ends, rubbish, scraps **2.** dreck (*Sl., chiefly U.S.*), dross, filth, muck, offal, refuse, rubbish, scourings, slops, sweepings, swill, trash (*Chiefly U.S.*), waste **3.** balderdash, balls (*Taboo sl.*), bilge (*Inf.*), bosh (*Inf.*), bull (*Sl.*), bullshit (*Taboo sl.*), bunkum *or* buncombe (*Chiefly U.S.*), claptrap (*Inf.*), cobblers (*Brit. taboo sl.*), codswallop (*Brit. sl.*), crap (*Sl.*), drivel, eye~ wash (*Inf.*), flapdoodle (*Sl.*), gibberish, guff (*Sl.*), havers (*Scot.*), hogwash, hokum (*Sl., chiefly U.S. & Canad.*), horsefeathers (*U.S. sl.*), hot air (*Inf.*), moonshine, nonsense, pap, piffle (*Inf.*), poppycock (*Inf.*), rot, shit (*Taboo sl.*), stuff and nonsense, tommyrot, tosh (*Inf.*), tripe (*Inf.*), twaddle

garble **1.** confuse, jumble, mix up **2.** cor~ rupt, distort, doctor, falsify, misinterpret, misquote, misreport, misrepresent, mis~ state, mistranslate, mutilate, pervert, slant, tamper with, twist
Antonyms clarify, decipher, make intelligi~ ble

gargantuan big, Brobdingnagian, colossal, elephantine, enormous, giant, gigantic, huge, humongous *or* humungous (*U.S. sl.*), immense, mammoth, massive, monstrous, monumental, mountainous, prodigious, ti~ tanic, towering, tremendous, vast
Antonyms little, meagre, miniature, paltry, puny, pygmy *or* pigmy, small, tiny

garish brash, brassy, brummagem, cheap, flash (*Inf.*), flashy, flaunting, gaudy, glaring, glittering, loud, meretricious, naff (*Brit. sl.*), raffish, showy, tacky (*Inf.*), tasteless, taw~ dry, vulgar
Antonyms conservative, elegant, modest, plain, refined, sedate, sombre, unobtrusive

garland **1.** *n.* bays, chaplet, coronal, crown, festoon, honours, laurels, wreath **2.** *v.* adorn, crown, deck, festoon, wreathe

garments apparel, array, articles of cloth~ ing, attire, clothes, clothing, costume, dress, duds (*Inf.*), garb, gear (*Sl.*), habiliment, habit, outfit, raiment (*Archaic*), robes, togs, uniform, vestments, wear

garner **1.** *v.* accumulate, amass, assemble, collect, deposit, gather, hoard, husband, lay in *or* up, put by, reserve, save, stockpile,

store, stow away, treasure **2.** *n. Literary* depository, granary, store, storehouse, vault

garnish **1.** *v.* adorn, beautify, bedeck, deck, decorate, embellish, enhance, festoon, grace, ornament, set off, trim **2.** *n.* adornment, decoration, embellishment, enhancement, festoon, garniture, ornament, ornamenta~ tion, trim, trimming
Antonyms denude, spoil, strip

garrison *n.* **1.** armed force, command, de~ tachment, troops, unit **2.** base, camp, en~ campment, fort, fortification, fortress, post, station, stronghold ~*v.* **3.** assign, mount, position, post, put on duty, station **4.** de~ fend, guard, man, occupy, protect, supply with troops

garrulity **1.** babble, babbling, chatter, chat~ tering, chattiness, effusiveness, gabbiness (*Inf.*), garrulousness, gift of the gab (*Inf.*), glibness, loquacity, mouthiness, prating, prattle, talkativeness, verbosity, volubility **2.** diffuseness, long-windedness, prolixity, prosiness, verbosity, windiness, wordiness

garrulous **1.** babbling, chattering, chatty, effusive, gabby (*Inf.*), glib, gossiping, gush~ ing, loquacious, mouthy, prating, prattling, talkative, verbose, voluble **2.** diffuse, gassy (*Sl.*), long-winded, prolix, prosy, verbose, windy, wordy
Antonyms concise, reserved, reticent, suc~ cinct, taciturn, terse, tight-lipped, uncommu~ nicative

gash **1.** *v.* cleave, cut, gouge, incise, lacer~ ate, rend, slash, slit, split, tear, wound **2.** *n.* cleft, cut, gouge, incision, laceration, rent, slash, slit, split, tear, wound

gasp **1.** *v.* blow, catch one's breath, choke, fight for breath, gulp, pant, puff **2.** *n.* blow, ejaculation, exclamation, gulp, pant, puff

gate access, barrier, door, doorway, egress, entrance, exit, gateway, opening, passage, port (*Scot.*), portal

gather **1.** accumulate, amass, assemble, bring *or* get together, collect, congregate, convene, flock, forgather, garner, group, heap, hoard, marshal, mass, muster, pile up, round up, stack up, stockpile **2.** assume, be led to believe, conclude, deduce, draw, hear, infer, learn, make, surmise, under~ stand **3.** clasp, draw, embrace, enfold, hold, hug **4.** crop, cull, garner, glean, harvest, pick, pluck, reap, select **5.** build, deepen, enlarge, expand, grow, heighten, increase, intensify, rise, swell, thicken, wax **6.** fold, pleat, pucker, ruffle, shirr, tuck
Antonyms diffuse, disperse, dissipate, scat~ ter, separate

gathering **1.** assemblage, assembly, com~ pany, conclave, concourse, congregation, congress, convention, convocation, crowd, flock, get-together (*Inf.*), group, knot, meet~

ing, muster, party, rally, throng, turnout **2.** accumulation, acquisition, aggregate, collecting, collection, concentration, gain, heap, hoard, mass, pile, procuring, round~up, stock, stockpile **3.** *Inf.* abscess, boil, carbuncle, pimple, pustule, sore, spot, tumour, ulcer

gauche awkward, clumsy, graceless, ignorant, ill-bred, ill-mannered, inelegant, inept, insensitive, lacking in social graces, maladroit, tactless, uncultured, unpolished, unsophisticated
Antonyms elegant, gracious, polished, polite, refined, sophisticated, tasteful, well-mannered

gaudy brash, bright, brilliant, brummagem, flash (*Inf.*), flashy, florid, garish, gay, glaring, loud, meretricious, naff (*Brit. sl.*), ostentatious, raffish, showy, tacky (*Inf.*), tasteless, tawdry, vulgar
Antonyms colourless, conservative, dull, elegant, modest, quiet, refined, sedate, subtle, tasteful

gauge *v.* **1.** ascertain, calculate, check, compute, count, determine, measure, weigh **2.** adjudge, appraise, assess, estimate, evaluate, guess, judge, rate, reckon, value ~*n.* **3.** basis, criterion, example, exemplar, guide, guideline, indicator, measure, meter, model, par, pattern, rule, sample, standard, test, touchstone, yardstick **4.** bore, capacity, degree, depth, extent, height, magnitude, measure, scope, size, span, thickness, width

gaunt **1.** angular, attenuated, bony, cadaverous, emaciated, haggard, lank, lean, macilent (*Rare*), meagre, pinched, raw-boned, scraggy, scrawny, skeletal, skinny, spare, thin, wasted **2.** bare, bleak, desolate, dismal, dreary, forbidding, forlorn, grim, harsh
Antonyms (*sense 1*) chubby, corpulent, fat, lush, obese, plump, stout, well-fed (*sense 2*) inviting, lush, luxurious

gawk **1.** *n.* boor, churl, clod, clodhopper (*Inf.*), dolt, dunderhead, galoot (*Sl.*), ignoramus, lout, lubber, lummox (*Inf.*), oaf **2.** *v.* gape, gawp (*Sl.*), gaze open-mouthed, goggle, stare

gawky awkward, clownish, clumsy, gauche, loutish, lumbering, lumpish, maladroit, oafish, uncouth, ungainly
Antonyms elegant, graceful, self-assured, well-coordinated

gay *adj.* **1.** homosexual, lesbian, poofy (*Offens. sl.*), queer (*Offens. sl.*) **2.** animated, blithe, carefree, cheerful, debonair, glad, gleeful, happy, hilarious, insouciant, jolly, jovial, joyful, joyous, light-hearted, lively, merry, sparkling, sunny, vivacious **3.** bright, brilliant, colourful, flamboyant, flashy, fresh, garish, gaudy, rich, showy,

vivid **4.** convivial, festive, frivolous, frolicsome, fun-loving, gamesome, merry, playful, pleasure-seeking, rakish, rollicking, sportive, waggish ~*n.* **5.** dyke (*Offens. sl.*), faggot (*U.S. offens. sl.*), fairy (*Offens. sl.*), homosexual, invert, lesbian, poof (*Offens. sl.*), queer (*Offens. sl.*)
Antonyms (*senses 1 & 5*) heterosexual, straight (*sense 2*) cheerless, colourless, conservative, drab, dull, grave, grim, melancholy, miserable, sad, sedate, serious, sober, solemn, sombre, unhappy

gaze **1.** *v.* contemplate, eyeball (*U.S. sl.*), gape, look, look fixedly, regard, stare, view, watch, wonder **2.** *n.* fixed look, look, stare

gazette journal, newspaper, news-sheet, organ, paper, periodical

gear *n.* **1.** cog, cogwheel, gearwheel, toothed wheel **2.** cogs, gearing, machinery, mechanism, works **3.** accessories, accoutrements, apparatus, equipment, harness, instruments, outfit, paraphernalia, rigging, supplies, tackle, tools, trappings **4.** baggage, belongings, effects, kit, luggage, stuff, things **5.** *Sl.* apparel, array, attire, clothes, clothing, costume, dress, garb, garments, habit, outfit, rigout (*Inf.*), togs, wear ~*v.* **6.** adapt, adjust, equip, fit, rig, suit, tailor

gelatinous gluey, glutinous, gummy, jelly-like, mucilaginous, sticky, viscid, viscous

gelid arctic, chilly, cold, freezing, frigid, frosty, frozen, glacial, ice-cold, icy, polar
Antonyms hot, red-hot, scorching, sweltering, torrid

gem **1.** jewel, precious stone, semiprecious stone, stone **2.** flower, jewel, masterpiece, pearl, pick, prize, treasure

genealogy ancestry, blood line, derivation, descent, extraction, family tree, line, lineage, pedigree, progeniture, stemma, stirps, stock, strain

general **1.** accepted, broad, common, extensive, popular, prevailing, prevalent, public, universal, widespread **2.** accustomed, conventional, customary, everyday, habitual, normal, ordinary, regular, typical, usual **3.** approximate, ill-defined, imprecise, inaccurate, indefinite, inexact, loose, undetailed, unspecific, vague **4.** across-the-board, all-inclusive, blanket, broad, catholic, collective, comprehensive, encyclopedic, generic, indiscriminate, miscellaneous, panoramic, sweeping, total, universal
Antonyms definite, distinctive, exact, exceptional, extraordinary, individual, infrequent, particular, peculiar, precise, rare, special, specific, unusual

generality **1.** abstract principle, generalization, loose statement, sweeping statement, vague notion **2.** acceptedness, commonness, extensiveness, popularity, prevalence, uni~

versality **3.** approximateness, imprecise~ ness, indefiniteness, inexactness, lack of detail, looseness, vagueness **4.** breadth, catholicity, comprehensiveness, miscel~ laneity, sweepingness, universality

generally 1. almost always, as a rule, by and large, conventionally, customarily, for the most part, habitually, in most cases, largely, mainly, normally, on average, on the whole, ordinarily, regularly, typically, usually **2.** commonly, extensively, popular~ ly, publicly, universally, widely **3.** approxi~ mately, broadly, chiefly, for the most part, in the main, largely, mainly, mostly, on the whole, predominantly, principally
Antonyms especially, individually, occa~ sionally, particularly, rarely, unusually

generate beget, breed, bring about, cause, create, engender, form, give rise to, initiate, make, originate, procreate, produce, propa~ gate, spawn, whip up
Antonyms annihilate, crush, destroy, end, extinguish, kill, terminate

generation 1. begetting, breeding, crea~ tion, engenderment, formation, genesis, origination, procreation, production, propa~ gation, reproduction **2.** age group, breed, crop **3.** age, day, days, epoch, era, period, time, times

generic all-encompassing, blanket, collec~ tive, common, comprehensive, general, in~ clusive, sweeping, universal, wide
Antonyms individual, particular, precise, specific

generosity 1. beneficence, benevolence, bounteousness, bounty, charity, kindness, largess *or* largesse, liberality, munificence, open-handedness **2.** disinterestedness, goodness, high-mindedness, magnanimity, nobleness, unselfishness

generous 1. beneficent, benevolent, boun~ teous, bountiful, charitable, free, hospitable, kind, lavish, liberal, munificent, open~ handed, princely, prodigal, ungrudging, unstinting **2.** big-hearted, disinterested, good, high-minded, lofty, magnanimous, noble, unselfish **3.** abundant, ample, copi~ ous, full, lavish, liberal, overflowing, plen~ tiful, rich, unstinting
Antonyms avaricious, cheap, close-fisted, greedy, mean, minimal, miserly, parsimoni~ ous, scanty, selfish, small, stingy, tight, tiny

genesis beginning, birth, commencement, creation, dawn, engendering, formation, generation, inception, origin, outset, propa~ gation, root, source, start
Antonyms completion, conclusion, end, finish, termination

genial affable, agreeable, amiable, cheerful, cheery, congenial, convivial, cordial, easygoing, enlivening, friendly, glad, good-natured, happy, hearty, jolly, jovial, joyous, kind, kindly, merry, pleasant, sunny, warm, warm-hearted
Antonyms cheerless, cool, discourteous, frigid, morose, rude, sardonic, sullen, un~ friendly, ungracious, unpleasant

geniality affability, agreeableness, amiabil~ ity, cheerfulness, cheeriness, congenialness, conviviality, cordiality, friendliness, glad~ ness, good cheer, good nature, happiness, heartiness, jollity, joviality, joy, joyousness, kindliness, kindness, mirth, pleasantness, sunniness, warm-heartedness, warmth

genitals genitalia, loins, private parts, pu~ denda, reproductive organs, sex organs

genius 1. adept, brain (*Inf.*), brainbox, buff (*Inf.*), expert, hotshot (*Inf.*), intellect (*Inf.*), maestro, master, master-hand, mastermind, maven (*U.S.*), virtuoso, whiz (*Inf.*) **2.** abil~ ity, aptitude, bent, brilliance, capacity, creative power, endowment, faculty, flair, gift, inclination, knack, propensity, talent, turn
Antonyms dolt, dunce, fool, half-wit, idiot, imbecile, nincompoop, simpleton

genre brand, category, character, class, fashion, genus, group, kind, school, sort, species, stamp, style, type

genteel aristocratic, civil, courteous, court~ ly, cultivated, cultured, elegant, fashionable, formal, gentlemanly, ladylike, mannerly, polished, polite, refined, respectable, so~ phisticated, stylish, urbane, well-bred, well-mannered
Antonyms discourteous, ill-bred, impolite, inelegant, low-bred, natural, plebeian, rude, unaffected, uncultured, unmannerly, unpol~ ished, unrefined

gentility 1. breeding, civility, courtesy, courtliness, cultivation, culture, decorum, elegance, etiquette, formality, good breed~ ing, good manners, mannerliness, polish, politeness, propriety, refinement, respect~ ability, sophistication, urbanity **2.** blue blood, gentle birth, good family, high birth, nobility, rank **3.** aristocracy, elite, gentle~ folk, gentry, nobility, nobles, ruling class, upper class

gentle 1. amiable, benign, bland, compas~ sionate, dove-like, humane, kind, kindly, lenient, meek, merciful, mild, pacific, peaceful, placid, quiet, soft, sweet-tempered, tender **2.** balmy, calm, clement, easy, light, low, mild, moderate, muted, placid, quiet, serene, slight, smooth, soft, soothing, tem~ perate, tranquil, untroubled **3.** easy, grad~ ual, imperceptible, light, mild, moderate, slight, slow **4.** biddable, broken, docile, manageable, placid, tame, tractable **5.** *Ar~ chaic* aristocratic, civil, courteous, cultured, elegant, genteel, gentlemanlike, gentleman-

ly, high-born, ladylike, noble, polished, po~
lite, refined, upper-class, well-born, well-
bred
Antonyms aggressive, cruel, fierce, hard,
harsh, heartless, impolite, powerful, rough,
savage, sharp, strong, sudden, unkind, un~
manageable, violent, wild

gentlemanly civil, civilized, courteous,
cultivated, debonair, gallant, genteel,
gentlemanlike, honourable, mannerly, no~
ble, obliging, polished, polite, refined, repu~
table, suave, urbane, well-bred, well-
mannered

genuine 1. actual, authentic, bona fide,
honest, legitimate, natural, original, pure,
real, sound, sterling, true, unadulterated,
unalloyed, veritable **2.** artless, candid, ear~
nest, frank, heartfelt, honest, sincere, unaf~
fected, unfeigned
Antonyms affected, artificial, bogus,
counterfeit, fake, false, feigned, fraudulent,
hypocritical, imitation, insincere, phoney,
sham, simulated, spurious

germ 1. bacterium, bug (*Inf.*), microbe,
microorganism, virus **2.** beginning, bud,
cause, embryo, origin, root, rudiment, seed,
source, spark **3.** bud, egg, embryo, nucleus,
ovule, ovum, seed, spore, sprout

germane akin, allied, apposite, appropriate,
apropos, apt, cognate, connected, fitting,
kindred, material, pertinent, proper, relat~
ed, relevant, suitable, to the point *or* pur~
pose
Antonyms extraneous, foreign, immaterial,
inappropriate, irrelevant, unrelated

germinate bud, develop, generate, grow,
originate, pullulate, shoot, sprout, swell,
vegetate

gestation development, evolution, incuba~
tion, maturation, pregnancy, ripening

gesticulate gesture, indicate, make a sign,
motion, sign, signal, wave

gesture 1. *n.* action, gesticulation, indica~
tion, motion, sign, signal **2.** *v.* gesticulate,
indicate, motion, sign, signal, wave

get 1. achieve, acquire, attain, bag, bring,
come by, come into possession of, earn, fall
heir to, fetch, gain, glean, inherit, make,
net, obtain, pick up, procure, realize, reap,
receive, score (*Sl.*), secure, succeed to, win
2. be afflicted with, become infected with,
be smitten by, catch, come down with, con~
tract, fall victim to, take **3.** arrest, capture,
collar (*Inf.*), grab, lay hold of, nab (*Inf.*),
nail (*Inf.*), seize, take, trap **4.** become, come
to be, grow, turn, wax **5.** catch, compre~
hend, fathom, follow, hear, notice, perceive,
see, suss (out) (*Sl.*), take in, understand,
work out **6.** arrive, come, make it (*Inf.*),
reach **7.** arrange, contrive, fix, manage,
succeed, wangle (*Inf.*) **8.** coax, convince,

induce, influence, persuade, prevail upon,
sway, talk into, wheedle, win over **9.** com~
municate with, contact, get in touch with,
reach **10.** *Inf.* affect, arouse, excite, have an
effect on, impress, move, stimulate, stir,
touch **11.** *Inf.* annoy, bother, bug (*Inf.*),
gall, get (someone's) goat (*Sl.*), irk, irritate,
nark (*Brit., Aust., & N.Z. sl.*), pique, rub
(someone) up the wrong way, upset, vex **12.**
baffle, confound, mystify, nonplus, perplex,
puzzle, stump

get across 1. cross, ford, negotiate, pass
over, traverse **2.** bring home to, communi~
cate, convey, get (something) through to,
impart, make clear *or* understood, put over,
transmit

get ahead 1. advance, be successful, cut it
(*Inf.*), do well, flourish, get on, make good,
progress, prosper, succeed, thrive **2.** excel,
leave behind, outdo, outmanoeuvre, over~
take, surpass

get along 1. agree, be compatible, be
friendly, get on, harmonize, hit it off (*Inf.*)
2. cope, develop, fare, get by (*Inf.*), make
out (*Inf.*), manage, progress, shift **3.** be off,
depart, go, go away, leave, move off, slope
off

get at 1. acquire, attain, come to grips
with, gain access to, get, get hold of, reach
2. hint, imply, intend, lead up to, mean,
suggest **3.** annoy, attack, be on one's back
(*Sl.*), blame, carp, criticize, find fault with,
hassle (*Inf.*), irritate, nag, nark (*Brit., Aust.,
& N.Z. sl.*), pick on, taunt **4.** bribe, buy off,
corrupt, influence, suborn, tamper with

getaway break, break-out, decampment,
escape, flight

get away abscond, break free, break out,
decamp, depart, disappear, escape, flee,
leave, make good one's escape, slope off

get back 1. recoup, recover, regain, repos~
sess, retrieve **2.** arrive home, come back *or*
home, return, revert, revisit **3.** *With* **at** be
avenged, get even with, give tit for tat, hit
back, retaliate, settle the score with, take
vengeance on

get by 1. circumvent, get ahead of, go
around, go past, overtake, pass, round **2.**
Inf. contrive, cope, exist, fare, get along,
make both ends meet, manage, subsist, sur~
vive

get down 1. alight, bring down, climb
down, descend, disembark, dismount, get
off, lower, step down **2.** bring down, de~
press, dishearten, dispirit

get in alight, appear, arrive, collect, come,
embark, enter, include, infiltrate, insert,
interpose, land, mount, penetrate

get off 1. alight, depart, descend, disem~

bark, dismount, escape, exit, leave **2.** de~
tach, remove, shed, take off

get on 1. ascend, board, climb, embark,
mount **2.** advance, cope, cut it (*Inf.*), fare,
get along, make out (*Inf.*), manage, pro~
gress, prosper, succeed **3.** agree, be com~
patible, be friendly, concur, get along, har~
monize, hit it off (*Inf.*)

get out alight, break out, clear out (*Inf.*),
decamp, escape, evacuate, extricate oneself,
free oneself, leave, vacate, withdraw

get out of avoid, body-swerve (*Scot.*),
dodge, escape, evade, shirk

get over 1. cross, ford, get across, pass,
pass over, surmount, traverse **2.** come
round, get better, mend, pull through, rally,
recover from, revive, survive **3.** defeat, get
the better of, master, overcome, shake off **4.**
communicate, convey, get *or* put across,
impart, make clear *or* understood

get round 1. bypass, circumvent, edge,
evade, outmanoeuvre, skirt **2.** *Inf.* cajole,
coax, convert, persuade, prevail upon, talk
round, wheedle, win over

get together accumulate, assemble, col~
lect, congregate, convene, converge, gather,
join, meet, muster, rally, unite

get up arise, ascend, climb, increase,
mount, rise, scale, stand

ghastly ashen, cadaverous, deathlike,
deathly pale, dreadful, frightful, godawful
(*Sl.*), grim, grisly, gruesome, hideous, hor~
rendous, horrible, horrid, livid, loathsome,
pale, pallid, repellent, shocking, spectral,
terrible, terrifying, wan
Antonyms appealing, attractive, beautiful,
blooming, charming, healthy, lovely, pleasing

ghost 1. apparition, eidolon, manes, phan~
tasm, phantom, revenant, shade (*Literary*),
soul, spectre, spirit, spook (*Inf.*), wraith **2.**
glimmer, hint, possibility, semblance, shad~
ow, suggestion, trace

ghostly eerie, ghostlike, illusory, insub~
stantial, phantasmal, phantom, spectral,
spooky (*Inf.*), supernatural, uncanny, un~
earthly, weird, wraithlike

ghoulish disgusting, grisly, gruesome, ma~
cabre, morbid, sick (*Inf.*), unwholesome

giant 1. *n.* behemoth, colossus, Hercules, le~
viathan, monster, ogre, titan **2.** *adj.* Brob~
dingnagian, colossal, elephantine, enor~
mous, gargantuan, gigantic, huge, humong~
ous *or* humungous (*U.S. sl.*), immense,
jumbo (*Inf.*), large, mammoth, monstrous,
prodigious, titanic, vast
Antonyms (*sense 2*) dwarf, Lilliputian,
miniature, pygmy *or* pigmy, tiny

gibberish babble, balderdash, balls (*Taboo
sl.*), bilge (*Inf.*), blather, bosh (*Inf.*), bull
(*Sl.*), bullshit (*Taboo sl.*), bunkum *or* bun~

combe (*Chiefly U.S.*), cobblers (*Brit. taboo
sl.*), crap (*Sl.*), double talk, drivel, eyewash
(*Inf.*), gabble, garbage (*Inf.*), gobbledegook
(*Inf.*), guff (*Sl.*), hogwash, hokum (*Sl., chiefly
U.S. & Canad.*), horsefeathers (*U.S. sl.*), hot
air (*Inf.*), jabber, jargon, moonshine, mum~
bo jumbo, nonsense, pap, piffle (*Inf.*),
poppycock (*Inf.*), prattle, shit (*Taboo sl.*),
tommyrot, tosh (*Sl., chiefly Brit.*), tripe
(*Inf.*), twaddle, yammer (*Inf.*)

gibe, jibe 1. *v.* deride, flout, jeer, make fun
of, mock, poke fun at, ridicule, scoff, scorn,
sneer, take the piss out of (*Sl.*), taunt, twit
2. *n.* barb, crack (*Sl.*), cutting remark, deri~
sion, dig, jeer, mockery, ridicule, sarcasm,
scoffing, sneer, taunt

giddiness dizziness, faintness, lightheadedness, vertigo

giddy 1. dizzy, dizzying, faint, light-headed,
reeling, unsteady, vertiginous **2.** capricious,
careless, changeable, changeful, erratic,
fickle, flighty, frivolous, heedless, impul~
sive, inconstant, irresolute, irresponsible,
reckless, scatterbrained, silly, thoughtless,
unbalanced, unstable, unsteady, vacillating,
volatile, wild
Antonyms calm, constant, determined, ear~
nest, resolute, serious, steady

gift 1. benefaction, bequest, bonus, boon,
bounty, contribution, donation, grant, gra~
tuity, hand-out, largess *or* largesse, legacy,
offering, present **2.** ability, aptitude, attrib~
ute, bent, capability, capacity, endowment,
faculty, flair, genius, knack, power, talent,
turn

gifted able, accomplished, adroit, brilliant,
capable, clever, expert, ingenious, intelli~
gent, masterly, skilled, talented
Antonyms amateur, backward, dull, inca~
pable, inept, retarded, slow, talentless, un~
skilled

gigantic Brobdingnagian, colossal, Cyclo~
pean, elephantine, enormous, gargantuan,
giant, herculean, huge, humongous *or* hu~
mungous (*U.S. sl.*), immense, mammoth,
monstrous, prodigious, stupendous, titanic,
tremendous, vast
Antonyms diminutive, insignificant, little,
miniature, puny, small, tiny, weak

giggle *v./n.* cackle, chortle, chuckle, laugh,
snigger, tee-hee, titter, twitter

gild adorn, beautify, bedeck, brighten, coat,
deck, dress up, embellish, embroider, en~
hance, enrich, garnish, grace, ornament

gimmick contrivance, device, dodge, gadget,
gambit, gizmo (*Sl., chiefly U.S.*), ploy,
scheme, stratagem, stunt, trick

gingerly 1. *adv.* carefully, cautiously,
charily, circumspectly, daintily, delicately,
fastidiously, hesitantly, reluctantly,
squeamishly, suspiciously, timidly, warily

2. *adj.* careful, cautious, chary, circum~ spect, dainty, delicate, fastidious, hesitant, reluctant, squeamish, suspicious, timid, wary
Antonyms boldly, carelessly, confidently, rashly

gird 1. belt, bind, girdle **2.** blockade, encir~ cle, enclose, encompass, enfold, engird, en~ viron, hem in, pen, ring, surround **3.** brace, fortify, make ready, prepare, ready, steel

girdle 1. *n.* band, belt, cincture, cummer~ bund, fillet, sash, waistband **2.** *v.* bind, bound, encircle, enclose, encompass, engird, environ, gird, hem, ring, surround

girl bird (*Sl.*), chick (*Sl.*), colleen (*Irish*), damsel (*Archaic*), daughter, female child, lass, lassie (*Inf.*), maid (*Archaic*), maiden (*Archaic*), miss, wench

girth bulk, circumference, measure, size

gist core, drift, essence, force, idea, import, marrow, meaning, nub, pith, point, quin~ tessence, sense, significance, substance

give 1. accord, administer, allow, award, bestow, commit, confer, consign, contribute, deliver, donate, entrust, furnish, grant, hand over *or* out, make over, permit, pres~ ent, provide, purvey, supply, vouchsafe **2.** announce, be a source of, communicate, emit, impart, issue, notify, pronounce, pub~ lish, render, transmit, utter **3.** demonstrate, display, evidence, indicate, manifest, offer, proffer, provide, set forth, show **4.** allow, cede, concede, devote, grant, hand over, lend, relinquish, surrender, yield **5.** cause, do, engender, lead, make, occasion, per~ form, produce **6.** bend, break, collapse, fall, recede, retire, sink
Antonyms accept, get, hold, keep, receive, take, withdraw

give away betray, disclose, divulge, expose, inform on, leak, let out, let slip, reveal, shop (*Sl., chiefly Brit.*), uncover

give in admit defeat, capitulate, collapse, comply, concede, quit, submit, succumb, surrender, yield

given addicted, apt, disposed, inclined, lia~ ble, likely, prone

give off discharge, emit, exhale, exude, produce, release, send out, smell of, throw out, vent

give out 1. discharge, emit, exhale, exude, produce, release, send out, smell of, throw out, vent **2.** announce, broadcast, commu~ nicate, disseminate, impart, make known, notify, publish, transmit, utter

give up abandon, capitulate, cease, cede, cut out, desist, despair, forswear, hand over, kick (*Inf.*), leave off, quit, relinquish, re~ nounce, resign, step down (*Inf.*), stop, sur~ render, throw in the towel, waive

glacial 1. arctic, biting, bitter, chill, chilly, cold, freezing, frigid, frosty, frozen, gelid, icy, piercing, polar, raw, wintry **2.** antago~ nistic, cold, frigid, hostile, icy, inimical, unfriendly

glad 1. blithesome (*Literary*), cheerful, chuffed (*Sl.*), contented, delighted, gay, gleeful, gratified, happy, jocund, jovial, joy~ ful, overjoyed, pleased, willing **2.** animated, cheerful, cheering, cheery, delightful, felici~ tous, gratifying, joyous, merry, pleasant, pleasing
Antonyms depressed, discontented, dis~ pleased, melancholy, miserable, sad, sorrow~ ful, unhappy

gladden cheer, delight, elate, enliven, ex~ hilarate, gratify, hearten, please, rejoice

gladly cheerfully, freely, gaily, gleefully, happily, jovially, joyfully, joyously, lief (*Rare*), merrily, readily, willingly, with (a) good grace, with pleasure
Antonyms dolefully, grudgingly, reluctant~ ly, sadly, unenthusiastically, unwillingly

gladness animation, blitheness, cheerful~ ness, delight, felicity, gaiety, glee, happi~ ness, high spirits, hilarity, jollity, joy, joy~ ousness, mirth, pleasure

glamorous alluring, attractive, beautiful, bewitching, captivating, charming, dazzling, elegant, enchanting, entrancing, exciting, fascinating, glittering, glitzy (*Sl.*), glossy, lovely, prestigious, smart
Antonyms colourless, dull, unattractive, unexciting, unglamorous

glamour allure, appeal, attraction, beauty, bewitchment, charm, enchantment, fascina~ tion, magnetism, prestige, ravishment, witchery

glance *v.* **1.** check, check out (*Inf.*), clock (*Brit. inf.*), gaze, glimpse, look, peek, peep, scan, take a dekko at (*Brit. sl.*), view **2.** flash, gleam, glimmer, glint, glisten, glitter, reflect, shimmer, shine, twinkle **3.** bounce, brush, graze, rebound, ricochet, skim **4.** *With* **over, through,** *etc.* browse, dip into, flip through, leaf through, riffle through, run over *or* through, scan, skim through, thumb through ~*n.* **5.** brief look, butcher's (*Brit. sl.*), dekko (*Sl.*), gander (*Inf.*), glimpse, look, peek, peep, quick look, shufti (*Brit. sl.*), squint, view **6.** flash, gleam, glimmer, glint, reflection, sparkle, twinkle **7.** allu~ sion, passing mention, reference
Antonyms (*sense 1*) peruse, scrutinize, study (*sense 5*) examination, good look, inspection, perusal

glare *v.* **1.** frown, give a dirty look, glower, look daggers, lour *or* lower, scowl, stare angrily **2.** blaze, dazzle, flame, flare ~*n.* **3.** angry stare, black look, dirty look, frown, glower, lour *or* lower, scowl **4.** blaze, bril~

liance, dazzle, flame, flare, glow **5.** flashiness, floridness, gaudiness, loudness, meretriciousness, showiness, tawdriness

glaring 1. audacious, blatant, conspicuous, egregious, flagrant, gross, manifest, obvi~ ous, open, outrageous, outstanding, overt, patent, rank, unconcealed, visible **2.** blaz~ ing, bright, dazzling, flashy, florid, garish, glowing, loud
Antonyms concealed, hidden, inconspicu~ ous, obscure, soft, subdued, subtle

glassy 1. clear, glossy, icy, shiny, slick, slippery, smooth, transparent **2.** blank, cold, dazed, dull, empty, expressionless, fixed, glazed, lifeless, vacant

glaze 1. *v.* burnish, coat, enamel, furbish, gloss, lacquer, polish, varnish **2.** *n.* coat, enamel, finish, gloss, lacquer, lustre, patina, polish, shine, varnish

gleam *n.* **1.** beam, flash, glimmer, glow, ray, sparkle **2.** brightness, brilliance, corusca~ tion, flash, gloss, lustre, sheen, splendour **3.** flicker, glimmer, hint, inkling, ray, sugges~ tion, trace ~*v.* **4.** coruscate, flare, flash, glance, glimmer, glint, glisten, glitter, glow, scintillate, shimmer, shine, sparkle

glee cheerfulness, delight, elation, exhilara~ tion, exuberance, exultation, fun, gaiety, gladness, hilarity, jocularity, jollity, jovial~ ity, joy, joyfulness, joyousness, liveliness, merriment, mirth, sprightliness, triumph, verve
Antonyms depression, gloom, melancholy, misery, sadness

gleeful cheerful, chirpy (*Inf.*), cock-a-hoop, delighted, elated, exuberant, exultant, gay, gratified, happy, jocund, jovial, joyful, joy~ ous, jubilant, merry, mirthful, overjoyed, over the moon (*Inf.*), pleased, rapt, trium~ phant

glib artful, easy, fast-talking, fluent, garru~ lous, insincere, plausible, quick, ready, slick, slippery, smooth, smooth-tongued, suave, talkative, voluble
Antonyms halting, hesitant, implausible, sincere, tongue-tied

glide coast, drift, float, flow, fly, roll, run, sail, skate, skim, slide, slip, soar

glimmer *v.* **1.** blink, flicker, gleam, glisten, glitter, glow, shimmer, shine, sparkle, twinkle ~*n.* **2.** blink, flicker, gleam, glow, ray, shimmer, sparkle, twinkle **3.** flicker, gleam, grain, hint, inkling, ray, suggestion, trace

glimpse 1. *n.* brief view, butcher's (*Brit. sl.*), gander (*Inf.*), glance, look, peek, peep, quick look, shufti (*Brit. sl.*), sight, sighting, squint **2.** *v.* catch sight of, clock (*Brit. inf.*), descry, espy, sight, spot, spy, view

glint 1. *v.* flash, gleam, glimmer, glitter,

shine, sparkle, twinkle **2.** *n.* flash, gleam, glimmer, glitter, shine, sparkle, twinkle, twinkling

glisten coruscate, flash, glance, glare, gleam, glimmer, glint, glitter, scintillate, shimmer, shine, sparkle, twinkle

glitter *v.* **1.** coruscate, flare, flash, glare, gleam, glimmer, glint, glisten, scintillate, shimmer, shine, sparkle, twinkle ~*n.* **2.** beam, brightness, brilliance, flash, glare, gleam, lustre, radiance, scintillation, sheen, shimmer, shine, sparkle **3.** display, gaudi~ ness, gilt, glamour, pageantry, show, showiness, splendour, tinsel

gloat crow, drool, exult, glory, relish, revel in, rub it in (*Inf.*), triumph, vaunt

global 1. international, pandemic, plan~ etary, universal, world, worldwide **2.** all-encompassing, all-inclusive, all-out, com~ prehensive, encyclopedic, exhaustive, gen~ eral, thorough, total, unbounded, unlimited
Antonyms (*sense 2*) limited, narrow, paro~ chial, restricted, sectional

globe ball, earth, orb, planet, round, sphere, world

globule bead, bubble, drop, droplet, particle, pearl, pellet

gloom 1. blackness, cloud, cloudiness, dark, darkness, dimness, dullness, dusk, duski~ ness, gloominess, murk, murkiness, obscu~ rity, shade, shadow, twilight **2.** blues, de~ jection, depression, desolation, despair, de~ spondency, downheartedness, low spirits, melancholy, misery, sadness, sorrow, the hump (*Brit. inf.*), unhappiness, woe
Antonyms brightness, cheerfulness, day~ light, delight, happiness, high spirits, jollity, joy, light, mirth, radiance

gloomy 1. black, crepuscular, dark, dim, dismal, dreary, dull, dusky, murky, ob~ scure, overcast, shadowy, sombre, Stygian, tenebrous **2.** bad, black, cheerless, comfort~ less, depressing, disheartening, dismal, dis~ piriting, dreary, funereal, joyless, sad, sad~ dening, sombre **3.** blue, chapfallen, cheer~ less, crestfallen, dejected, despondent, dis~ mal, dispirited, down, downcast, down~ hearted, down in the dumps (*Inf.*), down in the mouth, glum, in low spirits, melan~ choly, miserable, moody, morose, pessimis~ tic, sad, saturnine, sullen
Antonyms blithe, bright, brilliant, cheerful, chirpy (*Inf.*), happy, high-spirited, jolly, jo~ vial, light, merry, radiant, sunny, upbeat (*Inf.*)

glorify 1. add lustre to, adorn, aggrandize, augment, dignify, elevate, enhance, ennoble, illuminate, immortalize, lift up, magnify, raise **2.** adore, apotheosize, beatify, bless, canonize, deify, enshrine, exalt, honour, idolize, pay homage to, revere, sanctify, venerate, worship **3.** celebrate, crack up

(*Inf.*), cry up (*Inf.*), eulogize, extol, hymn, laud, lionize, magnify, panegyrize, praise, sing *or* sound the praises of
Antonyms condemn, debase, defile, degrade, desecrate, dishonour, humiliate, mock

glorious 1. celebrated, distinguished, elevated, eminent, excellent, famed, famous, grand, honoured, illustrious, magnificent, majestic, noble, noted, renowned, sublime, triumphant **2.** beautiful, bright, brilliant, dazzling, divine, effulgent, gorgeous, radiant, resplendent, shining, splendid, splendiferous (*Facetious*), superb **3.** *Inf.* delightful, enjoyable, excellent, fine, gorgeous, great, heavenly (*Inf.*), marvellous, pleasurable, splendid, splendiferous (*Facetious*), wonderful
Antonyms awful, dreary, dull, gloomy, horrible, minor, ordinary, trivial, unimportant, unimpressive, unknown, unpleasant

glory *n.* **1.** celebrity, dignity, distinction, eminence, exaltation, fame, honour, illustriousness, immortality, kudos, praise, prestige, renown **2.** adoration, benediction, blessing, gratitude, homage, laudation, praise, thanksgiving, veneration, worship **3.** éclat, grandeur, greatness, magnificence, majesty, nobility, pageantry, pomp, splendour, sublimity, triumph **4.** beauty, brilliance, effulgence, gorgeousness, lustre, radiance, resplendence ~*v.* **5.** boast, crow, drool, exult, gloat, pride oneself, relish, revel, take delight, triumph
Antonyms blasphemy, condemnation, disgrace, dishonour, disrepute, infamy, shame, triviality, ugliness

gloss¹ *n.* **1.** brightness, brilliance, burnish, gleam, lustre, polish, sheen, shine, varnish, veneer **2.** appearance, façade, front, mask, semblance, show, surface ~*v.* **3.** burnish, finish, furbish, glaze, lacquer, polish, shine, varnish, veneer **4.** camouflage, conceal, cover up, disguise, hide, mask, smooth over, veil, whitewash (*Inf.*)

gloss² **1.** *n.* annotation, comment, commentary, elucidation, explanation, footnote, interpretation, note, scholium, translation **2.** *v.* annotate, comment, construe, elucidate, explain, interpret, translate

glossy bright, brilliant, burnished, glassy, glazed, lustrous, polished, sheeny, shining, shiny, silken, silky, sleek, smooth
Antonyms drab, dull, mat *or* matt, subfusc

glow *n.* **1.** burning, gleam, glimmer, incandescence, lambency, light, luminosity, phosphorescence **2.** brightness, brilliance, effulgence, radiance, splendour, vividness **3.** ardour, earnestness, enthusiasm, excitement, fervour, gusto, impetuosity, intensity, passion, vehemence, warmth **4.** bloom, blush, flush, reddening, rosiness ~*v.* **5.**

brighten, burn, gleam, glimmer, redden, shine, smoulder **6.** be suffused, blush, colour, fill, flush, radiate, thrill, tingle
Antonyms chill, coolness, dullness, greyness, half-heartedness, iciness, indifference, paleness, pallor, wanness

glower 1. *v.* frown, give a dirty look, glare, look daggers, lour *or* lower, scowl **2.** *n.* angry stare, black look, dirty look, frown, glare, lour *or* lower, scowl

glowing 1. aglow, beaming, bright, flaming, florid, flushed, lambent, luminous, radiant, red, rich, ruddy, suffused, vibrant, vivid, warm **2.** adulatory, complimentary, ecstatic, enthusiastic, eulogistic, laudatory, panegyrical, rave (*Inf.*), rhapsodic
Antonyms colourless, cool, cruel, dispassionate, dull, grey, pale, pallid, scathing, unenthusiastic, wan

glue 1. *n.* adhesive, cement, gum, mucilage, paste **2.** *v.* affix, agglutinate, cement, fix, gum, paste, seal, stick

glum chapfallen, churlish, crabbed, crestfallen, crusty, dejected, doleful, down, gloomy, gruff, grumpy, huffy, ill-humoured, low, moody, morose, pessimistic, saturnine, sour, sulky, sullen, surly
Antonyms cheerful, cheery, chirpy (*Inf.*), jolly, joyful, merry, upbeat (*Inf.*)

glut *n.* **1.** excess, overabundance, oversupply, plethora, saturation, superabundance, superfluity, surfeit, surplus ~*v.* **2.** cram, fill, gorge, overfeed, satiate, stuff **3.** choke, clog, deluge, flood, inundate, overload, oversupply, saturate
Antonyms dearth, lack, paucity, scarcity, shortage, want

glutinous adhesive, cohesive, gluey, gooey, gummy, mucilaginous, sticky, viscid, viscous

glutton gannet (*Sl.*), gobbler, gorger, gormandizer, gourmand, pig (*Inf.*)

gluttony gormandizing, gourmandism, greed, greediness, piggishness, rapacity, voraciousness, voracity

gnarled contorted, knotted, knotty, knurled, leathery, rough, rugged, twisted, weather-beaten, wrinkled

gnaw 1. bite, chew, munch, nibble, worry **2.** consume, devour, eat away *or* into, erode, fret, wear away *or* down **3.** distress, fret, harry, haunt, nag, plague, prey on one's mind, trouble, worry

go *v.* **1.** advance, decamp, depart, fare (*Archaic*), journey, leave, make for, move, move out, pass, proceed, repair, set off, slope off, travel, withdraw **2.** function, move, operate, perform, run, work **3.** connect, extend, fit, give access, lead, reach, run, span, spread, stretch **4.** avail, concur,

conduce, contribute, incline, lead to, serve, tend, work towards **5.** develop, eventuate, fall out, fare, happen, pan out (*Inf.*), proceed, result, turn out, work out **6.** accord, agree, blend, chime, complement, correspond, fit, harmonize, match, suit **7.** buy it (*U.S. sl.*), check out (*U.S. sl.*), croak (*Sl.*), die, expire, give up the ghost, go belly-up (*Sl.*), kick it (*Sl.*), kick the bucket (*Sl.*), pass away, peg it (*Inf.*), peg out (*Inf.*), perish, pop one's clogs (*Inf.*) **8.** elapse, expire, flow, lapse, pass, slip away ~*n.* **9.** attempt, bid, crack (*Inf.*), effort, essay, shot (*Inf.*), stab (*Inf.*), try, turn, whack (*Inf.*), whirl (*Inf.*) **10.** *Inf.* activity, animation, brio, drive, energy, force, get-up-and-go (*Inf.*), life, oomph (*Inf.*), pep, spirit, verve, vigour, vitality, vivacity
Antonyms (*sense 1*) arrive, halt, reach, remain, stay, stop (*sense 2*) break (down), fail, malfunction, stop

go about 1. circulate, move around, pass around, wander **2.** approach, begin, set about, tackle, undertake **3.** busy *or* occupy oneself with, devote oneself to

goad 1. *n.* impetus, incentive, incitement, irritation, motivation, pressure, spur, stimulation, stimulus, urge **2.** *v.* annoy, arouse, be on one's back (*Sl.*), drive, egg on, exhort, harass, hassle (*Inf.*), hound, impel, incite, instigate, irritate, lash, nark (*Brit., Aust., & N.Z. sl.*), prick, prod, prompt, propel, spur, stimulate, sting, urge, worry

go-ahead 1. *n. Inf.* assent, authorization, consent, green light, leave, O.K. *or* okay (*Inf.*), permission **2.** *adj.* ambitious, enterprising, go-getting (*Inf.*), pioneering, progressive, up-and-coming

go ahead advance, begin, continue, go forward, go on, proceed, progress

goal aim, ambition, design, destination, end, intention, limit, mark, object, objective, purpose, target

go along 1. acquiesce, agree, assent, concur, cooperate, follow **2.** accompany, carry on, escort, join, keep up, move, pass, travel

go away decamp, depart, exit, hook it (*Sl.*), leave, move out, recede, slope off, withdraw

go back 1. retrocede, return, revert **2.** change one's mind, desert, forsake, renege, repudiate, retract

gobble bolt, cram, devour, gorge, gulp, guzzle, pig out on (*U.S. & Canad. sl.*), stuff, swallow, wolf

go-between agent, broker, dealer, factor, intermediary, liaison, mediator, medium, middleman

go by 1. elapse, exceed, flow on, move onward, pass, proceed **2.** adopt, be guided by,

follow, heed, judge from, observe, take as guide

godforsaken abandoned, backward, bleak, deserted, desolate, dismal, dreary, forlorn, gloomy, lonely, neglected, remote, wretched

godless atheistic, depraved, evil, impious, irreligious, profane, ungodly, unprincipled, unrighteous, wicked

godlike celestial, deific, deiform, divine, heavenly, superhuman, transcendent

godly devout, god-fearing, good, holy, pious, religious, righteous, saintly

go down 1. be beaten, collapse, decline, decrease, drop, fall, founder, go under, lose, set, sink, submerge, submit, suffer defeat **2.** be commemorated (recalled, recorded, remembered)

godsend blessing, boon, manna, stroke of luck, windfall

go far advance, be successful, cut it (*Inf.*), do well, get ahead (*Inf.*), get on (*Inf.*), make a name for oneself, progress, succeed

go for 1. clutch at, fetch, obtain, reach, seek, stretch for **2.** admire, be attracted to, be fond of, choose, favour, hold with, like, prefer **3.** assail, assault, attack, launch oneself at, rush upon, set about *or* upon, spring upon

go in (for) adopt, embrace, engage in, enter, espouse, practise, pursue, take up, undertake

go into 1. begin, develop, enter, participate in, undertake **2.** analyse, consider, delve into, discuss, examine, inquire into, investigate, look into, probe, pursue, research, review, scrutinize, study, work over

golden 1. blond *or* blonde, bright, brilliant, flaxen, resplendent, shining, yellow **2.** best, blissful, delightful, flourishing, glorious, happy, joyful, joyous, precious, prosperous, rich, successful **3.** advantageous, auspicious, excellent, favourable, opportune, promising, propitious, rosy, valuable
Antonyms (*sense 1*) black, brunette, dark, dull (*sense 2*) poorest, sad, unfavourable, worst (*sense 3*) black, dark, sad, unfavourable, untimely, wretched

gone 1. elapsed, ended, finished, over, past **2.** absent, astray, away, lacking, lost, missing, vanished **3.** dead, deceased, defunct, departed, extinct, no more **4.** consumed, done, finished, spent, used up

good *adj.* **1.** acceptable, admirable, agreeable, bad (*Sl.*), capital, choice, commendable, crucial (*Sl.*), excellent, fine, first-class, first-rate, great, hunky-dory (*Inf.*), pleasant, pleasing, positive, precious, satisfactory, splendid, super (*Inf.*), superior, tiptop, valuable, wicked (*Sl.*), world-class, worthy **2.** admirable, estimable, ethical, exemplary,

honest, honourable, moral, praiseworthy, right, righteous, trustworthy, upright, virtuous, worthy **3.** able, accomplished, adept, adroit, capable, clever, competent, dexterous, efficient, expert, first-rate, proficient, reliable, satisfactory, serviceable, skilled, sound, suitable, talented, thorough, useful **4.** adequate, advantageous, auspicious, beneficial, convenient, favourable, fit, fitting, healthy, helpful, opportune, profitable, propitious, salubrious, salutary, suitable, useful, wholesome **5.** eatable, fit to eat, sound, uncorrupted, untainted, whole **6.** altruistic, approving, beneficent, benevolent, charitable, friendly, gracious, humane, kind, kind-hearted, kindly, merciful, obliging, well-disposed **7.** authentic, bona fide, dependable, genuine, honest, legitimate, proper, real, reliable, sound, true, trustworthy, valid **8.** decorous, dutiful, mannerly, obedient, orderly, polite, proper, seemly, well-behaved, well-mannered **9.** agreeable, cheerful, congenial, convivial, enjoyable, gratifying, happy, pleasant, pleasing, pleasurable, satisfying **10.** adequate, ample, complete, considerable, entire, extensive, full, large, long, sizable, solid, substantial, sufficient, whole **11.** best, fancy, finest, newest, nicest, precious, smartest, special, valuable **12.** *Of weather* balmy, bright, calm, clear, clement, cloudless, fair, halcyon, mild, sunny, sunshiny, tranquil ~*n.* **13.** advantage, avail, behalf, benefit, gain, interest, profit, service, use, usefulness, welfare, wellbeing, worth **14.** excellence, goodness, merit, morality, probity, rectitude, right, righteousness, uprightness, virtue, worth **15. for good** finally, for ever, irrevocably, never to return, once and for all, permanently, *sine die*
Antonyms *adj. (sense 1)* awful, bad, boring, disagreeable, dull, inadequate, rotten, tedious, unpleasant *(sense 2)* bad, base, corrupt, dishonest, dishonourable, evil, immoral, improper, sinful *(sense 3)* bad, incompetent, inefficient, unsatisfactory, unskilled *(sense 4)* inappropriate, unbecoming, unbefitting, unfavourable, unfitting, unsuitable, useless *(sense 5)* bad, decayed, mouldy, off, rotten, unsound *(sense 6)* cruel, evil, mean *(Inf.)*, selfish, unkind, vicious, wicked *(sense 7)* counterfeit, false, fraudulent, invalid, phoney *(sense 8)* ill-mannered, mischievous, naughty, rude, unkind *(sense 10)* scant, short ~*n. (sense 13)* detriment, disadvantage, failure, ill-fortune, loss *(sense 14)* badness, baseness, corruption, cruelty, dishonesty, evil, immorality, meanness, wickedness

goodbye adieu, farewell, leave-taking, parting

good-for-nothing 1. *n.* black sheep, idler, layabout, ne'er-do-well, profligate. rapscal-

lion, scapegrace, skiver *(Brit. sl.)*, waster, wastrel **2.** *adj.* feckless, idle, irresponsible, useless, worthless

good-humoured affable, amiable, cheerful, congenial, genial, good-tempered, happy, pleasant

good-looking attractive, comely, fair, handsome, personable, pretty, well-favoured

goodly 1. ample, considerable, large, significant, sizable, substantial, tidy *(Inf.)* **2.** agreeable, attractive, comely, desirable, elegant, fine, good-looking, graceful, handsome, personable, pleasant, pleasing, well-favoured

good-natured agreeable, benevolent, friendly, good-hearted, helpful, kind, kindly, tolerant, warm-hearted, well-disposed, willing to please

goodness 1. excellence, merit, quality, superiority, value, worth **2.** beneficence, benevolence, friendliness, generosity, goodwill, graciousness, humaneness, kind-heartedness, kindliness, kindness, mercy, obligingness **3.** honesty, honour, integrity, merit, morality, probity, rectitude, righteousness, uprightness, virtue **4.** advantage, benefit, nourishment, nutrition, salubriousness, wholesomeness
Antonyms badness, corruption, detriment, disadvantage, dishonesty, evil, immorality, wickedness, worthlessness

goods 1. appurtenances, belongings, chattels, effects, furnishings, furniture, gear, movables, paraphernalia, possessions, property, things, trappings **2.** commodities, merchandise, stock, stuff, wares

goodwill amity, benevolence, favour, friendliness, friendship, heartiness, kindliness, zeal

go off 1. blow up, detonate, explode, fire **2.** happen, occur, take place **3.** decamp, depart, go away, hook it *(Sl.)*, leave, move out, part, quit, slope off **4.** *Inf.* go bad, go stale, rot

go on 1. continue, endure, happen, last, occur, persist, proceed, stay **2.** blether, carry on, chatter, prattle, rabbit *(Brit. inf.)*, ramble on, waffle *(Inf., chiefly Brit.)*, witter (on) *(Inf.)*

go out 1. depart, exit, leave **2.** be extinguished, die out, expire, fade out

go over 1. examine, inspect, rehearse, reiterate, review, revise, study, work over **2.** peruse, read, scan, skim

gore[1] *n.* blood, bloodshed, butchery, carnage, slaughter

gore[2] *v.* impale, pierce, spit, stab, transfix, wound

gorge[1] *n.* canyon, cleft, clough *(Dialect)*, defile, fissure, pass, ravine

gorge² v. bolt, cram, devour, feed, fill, glut, gobble, gormandize, gulp, guzzle, overeat, pig out (*U.S. & Canad. sl.*), raven, sate, satiate, stuff, surfeit, swallow, wolf

gorgeous 1. beautiful, brilliant, dazzling, drop-dead (*Sl.*), elegant, glittering, grand, luxuriant, magnificent, opulent, ravishing, resplendent, showy, splendid, splendiferous (*Facetious*), stunning (*Inf.*), sumptuous, superb **2.** *Inf.* attractive, bright, delightful, enjoyable, exquisite, fine, glorious, good, good-looking, lovely, pleasing
Antonyms cheap, dismal, dreary, dull, gloomy, homely, plain, repulsive, shabby, shoddy, sombre, ugly, unattractive, unsightly

gory blood-soaked, bloodstained, bloodthirsty, bloody, ensanguined (*Literary*), murderous, sanguinary

gospel 1. certainty, fact, the last word, truth, verity **2.** credo, creed, doctrine, message, news, revelation, tidings

gossamer adj. airy, delicate, diaphanous, fine, flimsy, gauzy, light, sheer, silky, thin, transparent

gossip n. **1.** blether, chinwag (*Brit. inf.*), chitchat, clishmaclaver (*Scot.*), dirt (*U.S. sl.*), gen (*Brit. inf.*), hearsay, idle talk, jaw (*Sl.*), latest (*Inf.*), newsmongering (*Old-fashioned*), prattle, scandal, small talk, tittle-tattle **2.** babbler, blatherskite, blether, busybody, chatterbox (*Inf.*), chatterer, flibbertigibbet, gossipmonger, newsmonger (*Old-fashioned*), prattler, quidnunc, scandalmonger, tattler, telltale ~v. **3.** blather, blether, chat, gabble, jaw (*Sl.*), prate, prattle, tattle

go through 1. bear, brave, endure, experience, suffer, tolerate, undergo, withstand **2.** consume, exhaust, squander, use **3.** check, examine, explore, hunt, look, search, work over

go under default, die, drown, fail, fold (*Inf.*), founder, go down, sink, submerge, succumb

gourmet bon vivant, connoisseur, epicure, foodie (*Inf.*), gastronome

govern 1. administer, be in power, command, conduct, control, direct, guide, handle, hold sway, lead, manage, order, oversee, pilot, reign, rule, steer, superintend, supervise **2.** bridle, check, contain, control, curb, direct, discipline, get the better of, hold in check, inhibit, master, regulate, restrain, subdue, tame **3.** decide, determine, guide, influence, rule, sway, underlie

government 1. administration, authority, dominion, execution, governance, law, polity, rule, sovereignty, state, statecraft **2.** administration, executive, ministry, powers-that-be, regime **3.** authority, command, control, direction, domination, guidance, management, regulation, restraint, superintendence, supervision, sway

governor administrator, boss (*Inf.*), chief, commander, comptroller, controller, director, executive, head, leader, manager, overseer, ruler, superintendent, supervisor

go with accompany, agree, blend, complement, concur, correspond, fit, harmonize, match, suit

go without abstain, be denied, be deprived of, deny oneself, do without, go short, lack, want

gown costume, dress, frock, garb, garment, habit, robe

grab bag, capture, catch (up), catch *or* take hold of, clutch, grasp, grip, latch on to, nab (*Inf.*), nail (*Inf.*), pluck, seize, snap up, snatch

grace n. **1.** attractiveness, beauty, charm, comeliness, ease, elegance, finesse, gracefulness, loveliness, pleasantness, poise, polish, refinement, shapeliness, tastefulness **2.** benefaction, beneficence, benevolence, favour, generosity, goodness, goodwill, kindliness, kindness **3.** breeding, consideration, cultivation, decency, decorum, etiquette, mannerliness, manners, propriety, tact **4.** charity, clemency, compassion, forgiveness, indulgence, leniency, lenity, mercy, pardon, quarter, reprieve **5.** benediction, blessing, prayer, thanks, thanksgiving ~v. **6.** adorn, beautify, bedeck, deck, decorate, dignify, distinguish, elevate, embellish, enhance, enrich, favour, garnish, glorify, honour, ornament, set off
Antonyms n. awkwardness, bad manners, clumsiness, condemnation, disfavour, harshness, ill will, inelegance, stiffness, tactlessness, tastelessness, ugliness, ungainliness ~v. desecrate, dishonour, insult, ruin, spoil

graceful agile, beautiful, becoming, charming, comely, easy, elegant, fine, flowing, gracile (*Rare*), natural, pleasing, smooth, symmetrical, tasteful
Antonyms awkward, clumsy, gawky, inelegant, plain, ponderous, stiff, ugly, ungainly, ungraceful

gracious accommodating, affable, amiable, beneficent, benevolent, benign, benignant, charitable, chivalrous, civil, compassionate, considerate, cordial, courteous, courtly, friendly, hospitable, indulgent, kind, kindly, lenient, loving, merciful, mild, obliging, pleasing, polite, well-mannered
Antonyms brusque, cold, discourteous, gruff, haughty, impolite, mean, remote, rude, surly, unfriendly, ungracious, unpleasant

grade n. **1.** brand, category, class, condition, degree, echelon, group, level, mark, notch, order, place, position, quality, rank, rung, size, stage, station, step **2. make the grade**

Inf. come through with flying colours, come up to scratch (*Inf.*), measure up, measure up to expectations, pass muster, prove acceptable, succeed, win through **3.** acclivity, bank, declivity, gradient, hill, incline, rise, slope ~*v.* **4.** arrange, brand, class, classify, evaluate, group, order, range, rank, rate, sort, value

gradient acclivity, bank, declivity, grade, hill, incline, rise, slope

gradual continuous, even, gentle, graduated, moderate, piecemeal, progressive, regular, slow, steady, successive, unhurried
Antonyms abrupt, broken, instantaneous, overnight, sudden

gradually bit by bit, by degrees, drop by drop, evenly, gently, little by little, moderately, piece by piece, piecemeal, progressively, slowly, steadily, step by step, unhurriedly

graduate *v.* **1.** calibrate, grade, mark off, measure out, proportion, regulate **2.** arrange, classify, grade, group, order, range, rank, sort

graft 1. *n.* bud, implant, scion, shoot, splice, sprout **2.** *v.* affix, implant, ingraft, insert, join, splice, transplant

grain 1. cereals, corn **2.** grist, kernel, seed **3.** atom, bit, crumb, fragment, granule, iota, jot, mite, modicum, molecule, morsel, mote, ounce, particle, piece, scintilla (*Rare*), scrap, scruple, spark, speck, suspicion, trace, whit **4.** fibre, nap, pattern, surface, texture, weave **5.** character, disposition, humour, inclination, make-up, temper

grand 1. ambitious, august, dignified, elevated, eminent, exalted, fine, glorious, gorgeous, grandiose, great, haughty, illustrious, imposing, impressive, large, lofty, lordly, luxurious, magnificent, majestic, monumental, noble, opulent, ostentatious, palatial, pompous, pretentious, princely, regal, splendid, splendiferous (*Facetious*), stately, striking, sublime, sumptuous, superb **2.** admirable, excellent, fine, first-class, first-rate, great (*Inf.*), hunky-dory (*Inf.*), marvellous (*Inf.*), outstanding, smashing (*Inf.*), splendid, splendiferous (*Facetious*), super (*Inf.*), superb, terrific (*Inf.*), very good, wonderful, world-class **3.** big-time (*Inf.*), chief, head, highest, lead, leading, main, major league (*Inf.*), preeminent, principal, supreme
Antonyms awful, bad, base, chickenshit (*U.S. sl.*), common, contemptible, crappy (*Sl.*), inferior, insignificant, little, mean, petty, poor, poxy (*Sl.*), secondary, small, terrible, trivial, undignified, unimportant, unimposing, worthless

grandeur augustness, dignity, greatness, importance, loftiness, magnificence, majes-

ty, nobility, pomp, splendour, state, stateliness, sublimity
Antonyms commonness, inferiority, insignificance, lowliness, pettiness, smallness, triviality, unimportance

grandiose 1. affected, ambitious, bombastic, extravagant, flamboyant, high-flown, ostentatious, pompous, pretentious, showy **2.** ambitious, grand, imposing, impressive, lofty, magnificent, majestic, monumental, stately
Antonyms down-to-earth, humble, modest, small-scale, unpretentious

grant *v.* **1.** accede to, accord, acknowledge, admit, agree to, allocate, allot, allow, assign, award, bestow, cede, concede, confer, consent to, donate, give, hand out, impart, permit, present, vouchsafe, yield **2.** *Law* assign, convey, transfer, transmit ~*n.* **3.** admission, allocation, allotment, allowance, award, benefaction, bequest, boon, bounty, concession, donation, endowment, gift, hand-out, present, stipend, subsidy

granule atom, crumb, fragment, grain, iota, jot, molecule, particle, scrap, speck

graphic 1. clear, descriptive, detailed, explicit, expressive, forcible, illustrative, lively, lucid, picturesque, striking, telling, vivid, well-drawn **2.** delineated, diagrammatic, drawn, illustrative, pictorial, representational, seen, visible, visual
Antonyms (*sense 1*) generalized, imprecise, impressionistic, unspecific, vague, woolly

grapple 1. catch, clasp, clutch, come to grips, fasten, grab, grasp, grip, hold, hug, lay *or* take hold, make fast, seize, wrestle **2.** address oneself to, attack, battle, clash, combat, confront, contend, cope, deal with, do battle, encounter, engage, face, fight, struggle, tackle, take on, tussle, wrestle

grasp *v.* **1.** catch (up), clasp, clinch, clutch, grab, grapple, grip, hold, lay *or* take hold of, seize, snatch **2.** catch *or* get the drift of, catch on, comprehend, follow, get, realize, see, take in, understand ~*n.* **3.** clasp, clutches, embrace, grip, hold, possession, tenure **4.** capacity, compass, control, extent, mastery, power, range, reach, scope, sway, sweep **5.** awareness, comprehension, ken, knowledge, mastery, perception, realization, understanding

grasping acquisitive, avaricious, closefisted, covetous, greedy, mean, miserly, niggardly, penny-pinching (*Inf.*), rapacious, selfish, stingy, tight-arsed (*Taboo sl.*), tight as a duck's arse (*Sl.*), tight-assed (*U.S. taboo sl.*), tightfisted, usurious, venal
Antonyms altruistic, generous, unselfish

grate *v.* **1.** mince, pulverize, shred, triturate **2.** creak, grind, rasp, rub, scrape, scratch **3.** aggravate (*Inf.*), annoy, chafe, exasperate, fret, gall, get one down, get on one's nerves (*Inf.*), irk, irritate, jar, nark (*Brit., Aust., & N.Z. sl.*), nettle, peeve, rankle, rub one up the wrong way, set one's teeth on edge, vex

grateful 1. appreciative, beholden, indebt~ ed, obliged, thankful **2.** acceptable, agree~ able, favourable, gratifying, nice, pleasing, refreshing, restful, satisfactory, satisfying, welcome

gratification delight, enjoyment, fruition, fulfilment, glee, indulgence, joy, kick *or* kicks (*Inf.*), pleasure, recompense, relish, reward, satisfaction, thrill
Antonyms control, denial, disappointment, discipline, dissatisfaction, frustration, pain, restraint, sorrow

gratify cater to, delight, favour, feed, fulfil, give pleasure, gladden, humour, indulge, pander to, please, recompense, requite, sat~ isfy, thrill

grating[1] *adj.* annoying, disagreeable, dis~ cordant, displeasing, grinding, harsh, irk~ some, irritating, jarring, offensive, rasping, raucous, scraping, squeaky, strident, un~ pleasant, vexatious
Antonyms agreeable, calming, mellifluous, musical, pleasing, soft, soothing

grating[2] grate, grid, gridiron, grille, lattice, trellis

gratis buckshee (*Brit. sl.*), for nothing, free, freely, free of charge, gratuitously, on the house, unpaid

gratitude appreciation, gratefulness, in~ debtedness, obligation, recognition, sense of obligation, thankfulness, thanks
Antonyms ingratitude, ungratefulness, unthankfulness

gratuitous 1. buckshee (*Brit. sl.*), compli~ mentary, free, spontaneous, unasked-for, unpaid, unrewarded, voluntary **2.** assumed, baseless, causeless, groundless, irrelevant, needless, superfluous, uncalled-for, un~ founded, unjustified, unmerited, unneces~ sary, unprovoked, unwarranted, wanton
Antonyms compulsory, involuntary, justifiable, paid, provoked, relevant, well-founded

gratuity baksheesh, benefaction, bonus, boon, bounty, donation, gift, largess *or* lar~ gesse, perquisite, *pourboire*, present, rec~ ompense, reward, tip

grave[1] *n.* burying place, crypt, last resting place, mausoleum, pit, sepulchre, tomb, vault

grave[2] **1.** dignified, dour, dull, earnest, gloomy, grim-faced, heavy, leaden, long-faced, muted, quiet, sage (*Obsolete*), sedate, serious, sober, solemn, sombre, staid, sub~ dued, thoughtful, unsmiling **2.** acute, criti~ cal, crucial, dangerous, exigent, hazardous,

important, life-and-death, momentous, of great consequence, perilous, pressing, seri~ ous, severe, significant, threatening, urgent, vital, weighty
Antonyms carefree, exciting, flippant, frivolous, happy, insignificant, joyous, merry, mild, trifling, undignified, unimportant

graveyard boneyard (*Inf.*), burial ground, cemetery, charnel house, churchyard, God's acre (*Literary*), necropolis

gravitas gravity, seriousness, solemnity

gravitate 1. *With* **to** *or* **towards** be influenced (attracted, drawn, pulled), in~ cline, lean, move, tend **2.** be precipitated, descend, drop, fall, precipitate, settle, sink

gravity 1. acuteness, consequence, exigency, hazardousness, importance, moment, mo~ mentousness, perilousness, pressingness, seriousness, severity, significance, urgency, weightiness **2.** demureness, dignity, ear~ nestness, gloom, gravitas, grimness, re~ serve, sedateness, seriousness, sobriety, so~ lemnity, thoughtfulness
Antonyms flippancy, frivolity, gaiety, hap~ piness, inconsequentiality, insignificance, joy, levity, merriment, thoughtlessness, triviality, unimportance

graze *v.* **1.** brush, glance off, kiss, rub, scrape, shave, skim, touch **2.** abrade, bark, chafe, scrape, scratch, skin ~*n.* **3.** abrasion, scrape, scratch

greasy 1. fatty, oily, slick, slimy, slippery **2.** fawning, glib, grovelling, ingratiating, oily, slick, smarmy (*Brit. inf.*), smooth, sycophantish, toadying, unctuous

great 1. big, bulky, colossal, elephantine, enormous, extensive, gigantic, huge, hu~ mongous *or* humungous (*U.S. sl.*), immense, large, mammoth, prodigious, stupendous, tremendous, vast, voluminous **2.** extended, lengthy, long, prolonged, protracted **3.** big-time (*Inf.*), capital, chief, grand, head, lead, leading, main, major, major league (*Inf.*), paramount, primary, principal, prominent, superior **4.** considerable, decided, exces~ sive, extravagant, extreme, grievous, high, inordinate, prodigious, pronounced, strong **5.** consequential, critical, crucial, grave, heavy, important, momentous, serious, significant, weighty **6.** celebrated, distin~ guished, eminent, exalted, excellent, famed, famous, glorious, illustrious, notable, note~ worthy, outstanding, prominent, remark~ able, renowned, superb, superlative, talent~ ed, world-class **7.** august, chivalrous, dignified, distinguished, exalted, fine, glori~ ous, grand, heroic, high-minded, idealistic, impressive, lofty, magnanimous, noble, princely, sublime **8.** active, devoted, enthu~ siastic, keen, zealous **9.** able, adept, adroit, crack (*Sl.*), expert, good, masterly,

proficient, skilful, skilled **10.** *Inf.* admirable, boffo (*Sl.*), brill (*Inf.*), chillin' (*U.S. sl.*), cracking (*Brit. inf.*), crucial (*Sl.*), def (*Inf.*), excellent, fantastic (*Inf.*), fine, first-rate, good, hunky-dory (*Inf.*), jim-dandy (*Sl.*), marvellous (*Inf.*), mean (*Sl.*), mega (*Sl.*), sovereign, superb, terrific (*Inf.*), topping (*Brit. sl.*), tremendous (*Inf.*), wonderful **11.** absolute, arrant, complete, consummate, downright, egregious, flagrant, out-and-out, perfect, positive, thoroughgoing, thundering (*Inf.*), total, unmitigated, unqualified, utter
Antonyms average, bad, base, diminutive, hateful, ignoble, inconsequential, inconsiderable, inferior, inhumane, insignificant, little, mean, mild, petty, poor, secondary, second-rate, small, terrible, trivial, undistinguished, unimportant, unkind, unnotable, unskilled, weak

greatly abundantly, by leaps and bounds, by much, considerably, enormously, exceedingly, extremely, highly, hugely, immensely, markedly, mightily, much, notably, powerfully, remarkably, tremendously, vastly, very much

greatness 1. bulk, enormity, hugeness, immensity, largeness, length, magnitude, mass, prodigiousness, size, vastness **2.** amplitude, force, high degree, intensity, potency, power, strength **3.** gravity, heaviness, import, importance, moment, momentousness, seriousness, significance, urgency, weight **4.** celebrity, distinction, eminence, fame, glory, grandeur, illustriousness, lustre, note, renown **5.** chivalry, dignity, disinterestedness, generosity, grandeur, heroism, high-mindedness, idealism, loftiness, majesty, nobility, nobleness, stateliness, sublimity

greed, greediness 1. edacity, esurience, gluttony, gormandizing, hunger, insatiableness, ravenousness, voracity **2.** acquisitiveness, avarice, avidity, covetousness, craving, cupidity, desire, eagerness, graspingness, longing, rapacity, selfishness
Antonyms altruism, benevolence, generosity, largess *or* largesse, munificence, self-restraint, unselfishness

greedy 1. edacious, esurient, gluttonous, gormandizing, hoggish, hungry, insatiable, piggish, ravenous, voracious **2.** acquisitive, avaricious, avid, covetous, craving, desirous, eager, grasping, hungry, impatient, rapacious, selfish
Antonyms altruistic, apathetic, benevolent, full, generous, indifferent, munificent, self-restrained, unselfish

Greek 1. *n.* Hellene **2.** *adj.* Hellenic

green *adj.* **1.** blooming, budding, flourishing, fresh, grassy, leafy, new,

undecayed, verdant, verdurous **2.** fresh, immature, new, raw, recent, unripe **3.** conservationist, ecological, environment-friendly, non-polluting **4.** callow, credulous, gullible, ignorant, immature, inexperienced, inexpert, ingenuous, innocent, naive, new, raw, unpolished, unpractised, unskilful, unsophisticated, untrained, unversed, wet behind the ears (*Inf.*) **5.** covetous, envious, grudging, jealous, resentful **6.** ill, nauseous, pale, sick, unhealthy, wan **7.** immature, pliable, supple, tender, undried, unseasoned, young ~*n.* **8.** common, grassplot, lawn, sward, turf

green light approval, authorization, blessing, clearance, confirmation, go-ahead (*Inf.*), imprimatur, O.K. *or* okay (*Inf.*), permission, sanction

greet accost, address, compliment, hail, meet, nod to, receive, salute, tip one's hat to, welcome

greeting 1. address, hail, reception, salutation, salute, welcome **2.** *Plural* best wishes, compliments, devoirs, good wishes, regards, respects, salutations

gregarious affable, companionable, convivial, cordial, friendly, outgoing, sociable, social
Antonyms antisocial, reserved, solitary, standoffish, unsociable, withdrawn

grey 1. ashen, bloodless, colourless, livid, pale, pallid, wan **2.** cheerless, cloudy, dark, depressing, dim, dismal, drab, dreary, dull, foggy, gloomy, misty, murky, overcast, sunless **3.** anonymous, characterless, colourless, dull, indistinct, neutral, unclear, unidentifiable **4.** aged, ancient, elderly, experienced, hoary, mature, old, venerable

grief 1. affliction, agony, anguish, bereavement, dejection, distress, grievance, hardship, heartache, heartbreak, misery, mournfulness, mourning, pain, regret, remorse, sadness, sorrow, suffering, trial, tribulation, trouble, woe **2. come to grief** *Inf.* come unstuck, fail, meet with disaster, miscarry
Antonyms cheer, comfort, consolation, delight, gladness, happiness, joy, rejoicing, solace

grievance affliction, beef (*Sl.*), complaint, damage, distress, grief, gripe (*Inf.*), hardship, injury, injustice, protest, resentment, sorrow, trial, tribulation, trouble, unhappiness, wrong

grieve 1. ache, bemoan, bewail, complain, deplore, lament, mourn, regret, rue, sorrow, suffer, wail, weep **2.** afflict, agonize, break the heart of, crush, distress, hurt, injure, make one's heart bleed, pain, sadden, wound

Antonyms cheer, comfort, console, ease, gladden, please, rejoice, solace

grievous 1. afflicting, calamitous, damag~ ing, distressing, dreadful, grave, harmful, heavy, hurtful, injurious, lamentable, op~ pressive, painful, severe, wounding **2.** ap~ palling, atrocious, deplorable, dreadful, egregious, flagrant, glaring, heinous, intol~ erable, lamentable, monstrous, offensive, outrageous, shameful, shocking, unbearable **3.** agonized, grief-stricken, heart-rending, mournful, pitiful, sorrowful, tragic
Antonyms delightful, glad, happy, insignificant, joyous, mild, pleasant, trivial, unimportant

grim cruel, ferocious, fierce, forbidding, for~ midable, frightful, ghastly, godawful (*Sl.*), grisly, gruesome, hard, harsh, hideous, horrible, horrid, implacable, merciless, mo~ rose, relentless, resolute, ruthless, severe, shocking, sinister, stern, sullen, surly, ter~ rible, unrelenting, unyielding
Antonyms amiable, attractive, benign, cheerful, easy, genial, gentle, happy, kind, pleasant, soft, sympathetic

grimace 1. *n.* face, frown, mouth, scowl, sneer, wry face **2.** *v.* frown, lour *or* lower, make a face *or* faces, mouth, scowl, sneer

grime dirt, filth, grot (*Sl.*), smut, soot

grimy begrimed, besmeared, besmirched, dirty, filthy, foul, grubby, scuzzy (*Sl.*), smutty, soiled, sooty, unclean

grind *v.* **1.** abrade, comminute, crush, granulate, grate, kibble, mill, pound, pow~ der, pulverize, triturate **2.** file, polish, sand, sharpen, smooth, whet **3.** gnash, grate, grit, scrape **4.** *With* **down** afflict, harass, hold down, hound, oppress, persecute, plague, trouble, tyrannize (over) ~*n.* **5.** *Inf.* chore, drudgery, hard work, labour, sweat (*Inf.*), task, toil

grip *n.* **1.** clasp, handclasp (*U.S.*), purchase **2.** clutches, comprehension, control, domi~ nation, grasp, hold, influence, keeping, mastery, perception, possession, power, tenure, understanding **3. come** *or* **get to grips (with)** close with, confront, contend with, cope with, deal with, encounter, face up to, grapple with, grasp, handle, meet, tackle, take on, undertake ~*v.* **4.** clasp, clutch, grasp, hold, latch on to, seize, take hold of **5.** absorb, catch up, compel, en~ gross, enthral, entrance, fascinate, hold, in~ volve, mesmerize, rivet, spellbind

gripping compelling, compulsive, engross~ ing, enthralling, entrancing, exciting, fasci~ nating, riveting, spellbinding, thrilling, un~ putdownable (*Inf.*)

grisly abominable, appalling, awful, dread~ ful, frightful, ghastly, grim, gruesome, hellacious (*U.S. sl.*), hideous, horrible, hor~

rid, macabre, shocking, sickening, terrible, terrifying
Antonyms agreeable, attractive, charming, innocuous, nice, pleasant

grit *n.* **1.** dust, gravel, pebbles, sand **2.** backbone, balls (*Taboo sl.*), courage, deter~ mination, doggedness, fortitude, gameness, guts (*Inf.*), hardihood, mettle, nerve, per~ severance, pluck, resolution, spirit, tenac~ ity, toughness ~*v.* **3.** clench, gnash, grate, grind

gritty 1. abrasive, dusty, grainy, granular, gravelly, rasping, rough, sandy **2.** ballsy (*Taboo sl.*), brave, courageous, determined, dogged, feisty (*Inf., chiefly U.S. & Canad.*), game, hardy, mettlesome, plucky, resolute, spirited, steadfast, tenacious, tough

groan *n.* **1.** cry, moan, sigh, whine **2.** *Inf.* beef (*Sl.*), complaint, gripe (*Inf.*), grouse, grumble, objection, protest ~*v.* **3.** cry, moan, sigh, whine **4.** *Inf.* beef (*Sl.*), be~ moan, bitch (*Sl.*), complain, gripe (*Inf.*), grouse, grumble, lament, object

groggy befuddled, confused, dazed, dizzy, faint, muzzy, punch-drunk, reeling, shaky, staggering, stunned, stupefied, unsteady, weak, wobbly, woozy (*Inf.*)

groom *n.* **1.** currier (*Rare*), hostler *or* ostler (*Archaic*), stableboy, stableman ~*v.* **2.** clean, dress, get up (*Inf.*), preen, primp, smarten up, spruce up, tidy, turn out **3.** brush, clean, curry, rub down, tend **4.** coach, drill, educate, make ready, nurture, prepare, prime, ready, train

groove channel, cut, cutting, flute, furrow, gutter, hollow, indentation, rebate, rut, score, trench

grope cast about, feel, finger, fish, flounder, fumble, grabble, scrabble, search

gross *adj.* **1.** big, bulky, corpulent, dense, fat, great, heavy, hulking, large, lumpish, massive, obese, overweight, thick **2.** aggre~ gate, before deductions, before tax, entire, total, whole **3.** coarse, crude, improper, im~ pure, indecent, indelicate, lewd, low, ob~ scene, offensive, ribald, rude, sensual, smutty, unseemly, vulgar **4.** apparent, ar~ rant, blatant, downright, egregious, flagrant, glaring, grievous, heinous, mani~ fest, obvious, outrageous, plain, rank, seri~ ous, shameful, sheer, shocking, unmitigat~ ed, unqualified, utter **5.** boorish, callous, coarse, crass, dull, ignorant, imperceptive, insensitive, tasteless, uncultured, undis~ criminating, unfeeling, unrefined, unso~ phisticated ~*v.* **6.** bring in, earn, make, rake in (*Inf.*), take
Antonyms *adj.* (*sense 1*) delicate, little, pe~ tite, slim, small, svelte, thin (*sense 2*) net (*sense 3*) decent, delicate, proper, pure (*sense 4*) par~

tial, qualified (*sense 5*) cultivated, elegant ~*v.* clear, net

grotesque absurd, bizarre, deformed, dis~ torted, extravagant, fanciful, fantastic, freakish, incongruous, ludicrous, mal~ formed, misshapen, odd, outlandish, pre~ posterous, ridiculous, strange, unnatural, weird, whimsical
Antonyms average, classic, graceful, natu~ ral, normal, realistic

ground *n.* **1.** clod, dirt, dry land, dust, earth, field, land, loam, mould, sod, soil, terra firma, terrain, turf **2.** *Often plural* area, country, district, domain, estate, fields, gardens, habitat, holding, land, prop~ erty, realm, terrain, territory, tract **3.** *Usually plural* account, argument, base, ba~ sis, call, cause, excuse, factor, foundation, inducement, justification, motive, occasion, premise, pretext, rationale, reason **4.** *Usually plural* deposit, dregs, grouts, lees, sediment, settlings **5.** arena, field, park (*Inf.*), pitch, stadium ~*v.* **6.** base, establish, fix, found, set, settle **7.** acquaint with, coach, familiarize with, inform, initiate, in~ struct, prepare, teach, train, tutor

groundless baseless, chimerical, empty, false, idle, illusory, imaginary, unauthor~ ized, uncalled-for, unfounded, unjustified, unprovoked, unsupported, unwarranted
Antonyms justified, logical, proven, real, reasonable, substantial, supported, true, well-founded

groundwork base, basis, cornerstone, footing, foundation, fundamentals, prelimi~ naries, preparation, spadework, underpin~ nings

group *n.* **1.** aggregation, assemblage, asso~ ciation, band, batch, bevy, bunch, camp, category, circle, class, clique, clump, clus~ ter, collection, company, congregation, co~ terie, crowd, faction, formation, gang, gath~ ering, organization, pack, party, posse (*Sl.*), set, troop ~*v.* **2.** arrange, assemble, associ~ ate, assort, bracket, class, classify, dispose, gather, marshal, order, organize, put to~ gether, range, sort **3.** associate, band to~ gether, cluster, congregate, consort, frater~ nize, gather, get together

grouse 1. *v.* beef (*Sl.*), bellyache (*Sl.*), bitch (*Sl.*), bleat, carp, complain, find fault, gripe (*Inf.*), grouch (*Inf.*), grumble, kvetch (*U.S. sl.*), moan, whine, whinge (*Inf.*) **2.** *n.* beef (*Sl.*), complaint, grievance, gripe (*Inf.*), grouch (*Inf.*), grumble, moan, objection, protest

grovel abase oneself, bootlick (*Inf.*), bow and scrape, brown-nose (*Taboo sl.*), cower, crawl, creep, cringe, crouch, demean one~ self, fawn, flatter, humble oneself, kiss ass (*Taboo sl.*), kowtow, pander to, sneak, toady

Antonyms be proud, domineer, face, hold one's head high, intimidate

grow 1. develop, enlarge, expand, extend, fill out, get bigger, get taller, heighten, in~ crease, multiply, spread, stretch, swell, thicken, widen **2.** develop, flourish, germi~ nate, shoot, spring up, sprout, vegetate **3.** arise, issue, originate, spring, stem **4.** ad~ vance, expand, flourish, improve, progress, prosper, succeed, thrive **5.** become, come to be, develop (into), get, turn, wax **6.** breed, cultivate, farm, nurture, produce, propa~ gate, raise
Antonyms decline, decrease, die, diminish, dwindle, fail, lessen, shrink, subside, wane

grown-up 1. *adj.* adult, fully-grown, ma~ ture, of age **2.** *n.* adult, man, woman

growth 1. aggrandizement, augmentation, development, enlargement, evolution, ex~ pansion, extension, growing, heightening, increase, multiplication, proliferation, stretching, thickening, widening **2.** crop, cultivation, development, germination, pro~ duce, production, shooting, sprouting, veg~ etation **3.** advance, advancement, expan~ sion, improvement, progress, prosperity, rise, success **4.** *Medicine* excrescence, lump, tumour
Antonyms decline, decrease, dwindling, failure, lessening, retreat, shrinkage, slack~ ening, subsiding

grub *v.* **1.** burrow, dig up, probe, pull up, root (*Inf.*), rootle (*Brit.*), search for, uproot **2.** ferret, forage, hunt, rummage, scour, search, uncover, unearth **3.** drudge, grind (*Inf.*), labour, plod, slave, slog, sweat, toil ~*n.* **4.** caterpillar, larva, maggot **5.** *Sl.* eats (*Sl.*), feed, food, nosebag (*Sl.*), nosh (*Sl.*), ra~ tions, sustenance, tack (*Inf.*), victuals, vit~ tles (*Obs. or dialect*)

grubby besmeared, dirty, filthy, frowzy, grimy, manky (*Scot. dialect*), mean, messy, mucky, scruffy, scuzzy (*Sl.*), seedy, shabby, slovenly, smutty, soiled, sordid, squalid, unkempt, untidy, unwashed

grudge 1. *n.* animosity, animus, antipathy, aversion, bitterness, dislike, enmity, griev~ ance, hard feelings, hate, ill will, malevo~ lence, malice, pique, rancour, resentment, spite, venom **2.** *v.* begrudge, be reluctant, complain, covet, envy, hold back, mind, re~ sent, stint
Antonyms *n.* appreciation, goodwill, liking, thankfulness ~*v.* be glad for, celebrate, wel~ come

gruelling arduous, backbreaking, brutal, crushing, demanding, difficult, exhausting, fatiguing, fierce, grinding, hard, harsh, la~ borious, punishing, severe, stiff, strenuous, taxing, tiring, trying

Antonyms cushy (*Inf.*), easy, enjoyable, light, pleasant, undemanding

gruesome abominable, awful, fearful, ghastly, grim, grisly, hellacious (*U.S. sl.*), hideous, horrendous, horrible, horrid, horrific, horrifying, loathsome, macabre, obscene, repugnant, repulsive, shocking, spine-chilling, terrible
Antonyms appealing, benign, cheerful, pleasant, sweet

gruff 1. bad-tempered, bearish, blunt, brusque, churlish, crabbed, crusty, curt, discourteous, grouchy (*Inf.*), grumpy, ill-humoured, ill-natured, impolite, rough, rude, sour, sullen, surly, uncivil, ungracious, unmannerly **2.** croaking, guttural, harsh, hoarse, husky, low, rasping, rough, throaty
Antonyms courteous, good-tempered, gracious, kind, mellifluous, pleasant, polite, smooth, sweet

grumble *v.* **1.** beef (*Sl.*), bellyache (*Sl.*), bitch (*Sl.*), bleat, carp, complain, find fault, gripe (*Inf.*), grouch (*Inf.*), grouse, kvetch (*U.S. sl.*), moan, repine, whine, whinge (*Inf.*) **2.** growl, gurgle, murmur, mutter, roar, rumble ~*n.* **3.** beef (*Sl.*), complaint, grievance, gripe (*Inf.*), grouch (*Inf.*), grouse, moan, objection, protest **4.** growl, gurgle, murmur, muttering, roar, rumble

guarantee 1. *n.* assurance, bond, certainty, collateral, covenant, earnest, guaranty, pledge, promise, security, surety, undertaking, warranty, word, word of honour **2.** *v.* answer for, assure, certify, ensure, insure, maintain, make certain, pledge, promise, protect, secure, stand behind, swear, vouch for, warrant

guarantor backer, bailsman (*Rare*), bondsman (*Law*), guarantee, sponsor, supporter, surety, underwriter, voucher, warrantor

guard *v.* **1.** cover, defend, escort, keep, mind, oversee, patrol, police, preserve, protect, safeguard, save, screen, secure, shelter, shield, supervise, tend, watch, watch over ~*n.* **2.** custodian, defender, lookout, picket, protector, sentinel, sentry, warder, watch, watchman **3.** convoy, escort, patrol **4.** buffer, bulwark, bumper, defence, pad, protection, rampart, safeguard, screen, security, shield **5.** attention, care, caution, heed, vigilance, wariness, watchfulness **6. off (one's) guard** napping, unprepared, unready, unwary, with one's defences down **7. on (one's) guard** alert, cautious, circumspect, on the alert, on the lookout, on the qui vive, prepared, ready, vigilant, wary, watchful

guarded cagey (*Inf.*), careful, cautious, circumspect, discreet, leery (*Sl.*), noncommit-tal, prudent, reserved, restrained, reticent, suspicious, wary

guardian attendant, champion, curator, custodian, defender, escort, guard, keeper, preserver, protector, trustee, warden, warder

guerrilla freedom fighter, irregular, member of the underground *or* resistance, partisan, underground fighter

guess *v.* **1.** conjecture, estimate, fathom, hypothesize, penetrate, predict, solve, speculate, work out **2.** believe, conjecture, dare say, deem, divine, fancy, hazard, imagine, judge, reckon, suppose, surmise, suspect, think ~*n.* **3.** conjecture, feeling, hypothesis, judgment, notion, prediction, reckoning, speculation, supposition, surmise, suspicion, theory
Antonyms *v.* be certain, be sure, know, prove, show ~*n.* certainty, fact

guesswork conjecture, estimation, presumption, speculation, supposition, surmise, suspicion, theory

guest boarder, caller, company, lodger, visitant, visitor

guidance advice, auspices, conduct, control, counsel, counselling, direction, government, help, instruction, intelligence, leadership, management, teaching

guide *v.* **1.** accompany, attend, conduct, convoy, direct, escort, lead, pilot, shepherd, show the way, steer, usher **2.** command, control, direct, handle, manage, manoeuvre, steer **3.** advise, counsel, educate, govern, influence, instruct, oversee, regulate, rule, superintend, supervise, sway, teach, train ~*n.* **4.** adviser, attendant, chaperon, cicerone, conductor, controller, counsellor, director, dragoman, escort, leader, mentor, monitor, pilot, steersman, teacher, usher **5.** criterion, example, exemplar, ideal, inspiration, lodestar, master, model, par, paradigm, standard **6.** beacon, clue, guiding light, key, landmark, lodestar, mark, marker, pointer, sign, signal, signpost **7.** catalogue, directory, guidebook, handbook, instructions, key, manual, vade mecum

guild association, brotherhood, club, company, corporation, fellowship, fraternity, league, lodge, order, organization, society, union

guile art, artfulness, artifice, cleverness, craft, craftiness, cunning, deceit, deception, duplicity, gamesmanship (*Inf.*), knavery, ruse, sharp practice, slyness, treachery, trickery, trickiness, wiliness
Antonyms candour, frankness, honesty, sincerity, truthfulness

guileful artful, clever, crafty, cunning, deceitful, duplicitous, foxy, sly, sneaky, treacherous, tricky, underhand, wily

guilt 1. blame, blameworthiness, criminal~ity, culpability, delinquency, guiltiness, in~iquity, misconduct, responsibility, sinful~ness, wickedness, wrong, wrongdoing 2. bad conscience, contrition, disgrace, dis~honour, guiltiness, guilty conscience, infa~my, regret, remorse, self-condemnation, self-reproach, shame, stigma
Antonyms blamelessness, honour, inno~cence, pride, righteousness, self-respect, sin~lessness, virtue

guiltless blameless, clean (*Sl.*), clear, im~maculate, impeccable, innocent, irre~proachable, pure, sinless, spotless, squeaky-clean, unimpeachable, unsullied, untainted, untarnished

guilty 1. at fault, blameworthy, convicted, criminal, culpable, delinquent, erring, evil, felonious, iniquitous, offending, reprehen~sible, responsible, sinful, to blame, wicked, wrong 2. ashamed, conscience-stricken, contrite, hangdog, regretful, remorseful, rueful, shamefaced, sheepish, sorry
Antonyms blameless, innocent, moral, proud, righteous, virtuous

gulf 1. bay, bight, sea inlet 2. abyss, breach, chasm, cleft, gap, opening, rent, rift, sepa~ration, split, void, whirlpool

gullibility credulity, innocence, naiveté, simplicity, trustingness

gullible born yesterday, credulous, easily taken in, foolish, green, innocent, naive, silly, simple, trusting, unsceptical, unso~phisticated, unsuspecting
Antonyms cynical, sophisticated, suspi~cious, untrusting, worldly

gully channel, ditch, gutter, watercourse

gulp *v.* 1. bolt, devour, gobble, guzzle, knock back (*Inf.*), quaff, swallow, swig (*Inf.*), swill, toss off, wolf 2. choke, gasp, stifle, swallow ~*n.* 3. draught, mouthful, swallow, swig (*Inf.*)

gum 1. *n.* adhesive, cement, exudate, glue, mucilage, paste, resin 2. *v.* affix, cement, clog, glue, paste, stick, stiffen

gumption ability, acumen, astuteness, cleverness, common sense, discernment, enterprise, get-up-and-go (*Inf.*), horse sense, initiative, mother wit, nous (*Brit. sl.*), re~sourcefulness, sagacity, savvy (*Sl.*), shrewdness, spirit, wit(s)

gunman assassin, bandit, bravo, desperado, gangster, gunslinger (*U.S. sl.*), heavy (*Sl.*), hit man (*Sl.*), killer, mobster (*U.S. sl.*), murderer, terrorist, thug

gurgle 1. *v.* babble, bubble, burble, crow, lap, murmur, plash, purl, ripple, splash 2. *n.* babble, murmur, purl, ripple

guru authority, guiding light, leader, maha~rishi, mahatma, master, mentor, sage, swa~mi, teacher, tutor

gush *v.* 1. burst, cascade, flood, flow, issue, jet, pour, run, rush, spout, spurt, stream 2. babble, blather, chatter, effervesce, effuse, enthuse, jabber, overstate, spout ~*n.* 3. burst, cascade, flood, flow, issue, jet, out~burst, outflow, rush, spout, spurt, stream, torrent 4. babble, blather, chatter, effusion, exuberance

gust *n.* 1. blast, blow, breeze, flurry, gale, puff, rush, squall 2. burst, eruption, explo~sion, fit, gale, outburst, paroxysm, passion, storm, surge ~*v.* 3. blast, blow, puff, squall

gusto appetite, appreciation, brio, delight, enjoyment, enthusiasm, exhilaration, fer~vour, liking, pleasure, relish, savour, verve, zeal, zest
Antonyms apathy, coolness, disinterest, distaste, inertia

gusty blowy, blustering, blustery, breezy, inclement, squally, stormy, tempestuous, windy

gut *n.* 1. *Often plural* belly, bowels, entrails, innards (*Inf.*), insides (*Inf.*), intestines, in~wards, paunch, stomach, viscera 2. *Plural Inf.* audacity, backbone, boldness, bottle (*Sl.*), courage, daring, forcefulness, grit, hardihood, mettle, nerve, pluck, spirit, spunk (*Inf.*), willpower ~*v.* 3. clean, disem~bowel, draw, dress, eviscerate 4. clean out, despoil, empty, pillage, plunder, ransack, ravage, rifle, sack, strip ~*adj.* 5. *Inf.* basic, deep-seated, emotional, heartfelt, innate, instinctive, intuitive, involuntary, natural, spontaneous, unthinking, visceral

gutless abject, chicken (*Sl.*), chickenshit (*U.S. sl.*), cowardly, craven, faint-hearted, feeble, irresolute, lily-livered, spineless, submissive, timid, weak
Antonyms bold, brave, courageous, deter~mined, resolute

gutter channel, conduit, ditch, drain, duct, pipe, sluice, trench, trough, tube

guttersnipe gamin, mudlark (*Sl.*), ragamuffin, street Arab (*Offens.*), street urchin, waif

guttural deep, gravelly, gruff, hoarse, husky, low, rasping, rough, thick, throaty

guy 1. *n. Inf.* bloke (*Brit. inf.*), cat (*Sl.*), chap, fellow, lad, man, person, youth 2. *v.* caricature, make (a) game of, make fun of, mock, poke fun at, rib (*Inf.*), ridicule, send up (*Brit inf.*), take off (*Inf.*), take the piss out of (*Sl.*)

guzzle bolt, carouse, cram, devour, drink, gobble, gorge, gormandize, knock back (*Inf.*), pig out (*U.S. & Canad. sl.*), quaff, stuff (oneself), swill, tope, wolf

Gypsy, Gipsy Bohemian, nomad, rambler,

roamer, Romany, rover, traveller, vaga~
bond, vagrant, wanderer

gyrate circle, pirouette, revolve, rotate,
spin, spiral, twirl, whirl

gyration convolution, pirouette, revolution,
rotation, spin, spinning, spiral, whirl,
whirling

H

habit *n.* **1.** bent, custom, disposition, manner, mannerism, practice, proclivity, propensity, quirk, tendency, way **2.** convention, custom, mode, practice, routine, rule, second nature, tradition, usage, wont **3.** constitution, disposition, frame of mind, make-up, nature **4.** addiction, dependence, fixation, obsession, weakness **5.** apparel, dress, garb, garment, habiliment, riding dress ~*v.* **6.** array, attire, clothe, dress, equip

habitation **1.** abode, domicile, dwelling, dwelling house, home, house, living quarters, lodging, pad (*Sl.*), quarters, residence **2.** inhabitance, inhabitancy, occupancy, occupation, tenancy

habitual **1.** accustomed, common, customary, familiar, fixed, natural, normal, ordinary, regular, routine, standard, traditional, usual, wonted **2.** chronic, confirmed, constant, established, frequent, hardened, ingrained, inveterate, persistent, recurrent
Antonyms abnormal, exceptional, extraordinary, infrequent, irregular, occasional, rare, strange, uncommon, unusual

habituate acclimatize, accustom, break in, condition, discipline, familiarize, harden, inure, make used to, school, season, train

habituated acclimatized, accustomed, adapted, broken in, conditioned, disciplined, familiarized, hardened, inured, schooled, seasoned, trained, used (to)
Antonyms unaccustomed, unfamiliar, unused (to)

habitué constant customer, frequenter, frequent visitor, regular (*Inf.*), regular patron

hack[1] *v.* **1.** chop, cut, gash, hew, kick, lacerate, mangle, mutilate, notch, slash ~*n.* **2.** chop, cut, gash, notch, slash ~*v./n.* **3.** *Inf.* bark, cough, rasp

hack[2] *adj.* **1.** banal, mediocre, pedestrian, poor, stereotyped, tired, undistinguished, uninspired, unoriginal ~*n.* **2.** Grub Street writer, literary hack, penny-a-liner, scribbler **3.** drudge, plodder, slave **4.** crock, hired horse, horse, jade, nag, poor old tired horse

hackles **make one's hackles rise** anger, annoy, bridle at, cause resentment, get one's dander up (*Sl.*), infuriate, make one see red (*Inf.*)

hackneyed banal, clichéd, common, commonplace, overworked, pedestrian, played out (*Inf.*), run-of-the-mill, stale, stereotyped, stock, threadbare, timeworn, tired, trite, unoriginal, worn-out
Antonyms fresh, imaginative, new, novel, original, striking, unusual

hag ballbreaker (*Sl.*), beldam (*Archaic*), crone, fury, harridan, Jezebel, shrew, termagant, virago, vixen, witch

haggard careworn, drawn, emaciated, gaunt, ghastly, hollow-eyed, pinched, shrunken, thin, wan, wasted, wrinkled
Antonyms bright-eyed, brisk, energetic, fresh, hale, robust, sleek, vigorous

haggle **1.** bargain, barter, beat down, chaffer, dicker (*Chiefly U.S.*), higgle, palter **2.** bicker, dispute, quarrel, squabble, wrangle

hail[1] *Fig.* **1.** *n.* barrage, bombardment, pelting, rain, shower, storm, volley **2.** *v.* barrage, batter, beat down upon, bombard, pelt, rain, rain down on, shower, storm, volley

hail[2] **1.** acclaim, acknowledge, applaud, cheer, exalt, glorify, greet, honour, salute, welcome **2.** accost, address, call, flag down, halloo, shout to, signal to, sing out, speak to, wave down **3.** *With* **from** be a native of, be born in, come from, originate in
Antonyms (*sense 1*) boo, condemn, criticize, hiss, insult, jeer (*sense 2*) avoid, cut (*Inf.*), ignore, snub

hair **1.** head of hair, locks, mane, mop, shock, tresses **2. by a hair** by a fraction of an inch, by a hair's-breadth, by a narrow margin, by a split second, by a whisker, by the skin of one's teeth **3. get in one's hair** aggravate (*Inf.*), annoy, be on one's back (*Sl.*), exasperate, get on one's nerves (*Inf.*), harass, hassle (*Inf.*), irritate, nark (*Brit., Aust., & N.Z. sl.*), pester, piss one off (*Taboo sl.*), plague **4. let one's hair down** chill out (*Sl., chiefly U.S.*), let it all hang out (*Inf.*), let off steam (*Inf.*), let oneself go, relax, veg out (*Sl., chiefly U.S.*) **5. not turn a hair** keep one's cool (*Sl.*), keep one's hair on (*Brit. inf.*), not bat an eyelid, remain calm **6. split hairs** cavil, find fault, overrefine, pettifog, quibble

hairless bald, baldheaded, beardless, cleanshaven, depilated, glabrous *or* glabrate (*Biol.*), shorn, tonsured

hair-raising alarming, bloodcurdling, breathtaking, creepy, exciting, frightening, horrifying, petrifying, scary, shocking, spine-chilling, startling, terrifying, thrilling

hair's-breadth **1.** *n.* fraction, hair, jot, narrow margin, whisker **2.** *adj.* close, hazardous, narrow

hairsplitting *adj.* captious, carping, cavil~ ling, fault-finding, fine, finicky, nice, nig~ gling, nit-picking (*Inf.*), overrefined, petti~ fogging, quibbling, subtle

hairy 1. bearded, bewhiskered, bushy, fleecy, furry, hirsute, pileous (*Biol.*), pilose (*Biol.*), shaggy, stubbly, unshaven, woolly **2.** *Sl.* dangerous, difficult, hazardous, perilous, risky, scaring

halcyon 1. calm, gentle, mild, pacific, peaceful, placid, quiet, serene, still, tran~ quil, undisturbed, unruffled **2.** *Fig.* care~ free, flourishing, golden, happy, palmy, prosperous

hale able-bodied, blooming, fit, flourishing, healthy, hearty, in fine fettle, in the pink, robust, sound, strong, vigorous, well

half 1. *n.* bisection, division, equal part, fifty per cent, fraction, hemisphere, portion, section **2.** *adj.* divided, fractional, halved, incomplete, limited, moderate, partial **3.** *adv.* after a fashion, all but, barely, inad~ equately, incompletely, in part, partially, partly, pretty nearly, slightly **4. by half** considerably, excessively, very much

half-baked 1. brainless, crackpot (*Inf.*), crazy, foolish, harebrained, inane, loopy (*Inf.*), senseless, silly, stupid **2.** ill- conceived, ill-judged, impractical, poorly planned, short-sighted, unformed, un~ thought out *or* through

half-hearted apathetic, cool, half-arsed, half-assed (*U.S. & Canad. sl.*), indifferent, lacklustre, listless, lukewarm, neutral, pas~ sive, perfunctory, spiritless, tame, unen~ thusiastic, uninterested
Antonyms ambitious, animated, avid, con~ cerned, determined, eager, emotional, ener~ getic, enthusiastic, excited, spirited, warm, wholehearted, zealous

halfway *adv.* **1.** midway, to *or* in the mid~ dle, to the midpoint **2.** incompletely, mod~ erately, nearly, partially, partly, rather **3. meet halfway** accommodate, come to terms, compromise, concede, give and take, strike a balance, trade off ~*adj.* **4.** central, equidistant, intermediate, mid, middle, midway **5.** imperfect, incomplete, moderate, partial, part-way

halfwit airhead (*Sl.*), berk (*Brit. sl.*), charlie (*Brit. inf.*), coot, dickhead (*Sl.*), dimwit (*Inf.*), dipstick (*Brit. sl.*), divvy (*Brit. sl.*), dolt, dork (*Sl.*), dullard, dunce, dunderhead, dweeb (*U.S. sl.*), fool, fuckwit (*Taboo sl.*), geek (*Sl.*), gonzo (*Sl.*), idiot, imbecile (*Inf.*), jerk (*Sl., chiefly U.S. & Canad.*), lamebrain (*Inf.*), mental defective, moron, nerd *or* nurd (*Sl.*), nitwit (*Inf.*), numskull *or* numb~ skull, oaf, pillock (*Brit. sl.*), plank (*Brit. sl.*), plonker (*Sl.*), prat (*Sl.*), prick (*Derogatory*

sl.), schmuck (*U.S. sl.*), simpleton, twit (*Inf., chiefly Brit.*), wally (*Sl.*)

half-witted addle-brained, barmy (*Sl.*), bat~ ty (*Sl.*), crazy, doltish, dull, dull-witted, feeble-minded, flaky (*U.S. sl.*), foolish, goofy (*Inf.*), idiotic, moronic, nerdish *or* nurdish (*Sl.*), obtuse, silly, simple, simple-minded, stupid

hall 1. corridor, entrance hall, entry, foyer, hallway, lobby, passage, passageway, vesti~ bule **2.** assembly room, auditorium, cham~ ber, concert hall, meeting place

hallmark 1. authentication, device, en~ dorsement, mark, seal, sign, signet, stamp, symbol **2.** badge, emblem, indication, sure sign, telltale sign

hallucination aberration, apparition, delu~ sion, dream, fantasy, figment of the imagi~ nation, illusion, mirage, phantasmagoria, vision

halo aura, aureole *or* aureola, corona, hala~ tion (*Photog.*), nimbus, radiance, ring of light

halt[1] *v.* **1.** break off, call it a day, cease, close down, come to an end, desist, draw up, pull up, rest, stand still, stop, wait **2.** arrest, block, bring to an end, check, curb, cut short, end, hold back, impede, obstruct, staunch, stem, terminate ~*n.* **3.** arrest, break, close, end, impasse, interruption, pause, stand, standstill, stop, stoppage, ter~ mination
Antonyms *v.* aid, begin, boost, commence, continue, encourage, forward, go ahead, maintain, proceed, resume, start ~*n.* begin~ ning, commencement, continuation, resump~ tion, start

halt[2] *v.* **1.** be defective, falter, hobble, limp, stumble **2.** be unsure, boggle, dither (*Chiefly Brit.*), haver, hesitate, pause, stam~ mer, swither (*Scot.*), think twice, waver ~*adj.* **3.** *Archaic* crippled, lame, limping

halting awkward, faltering, hesitant, imper~ fect, laboured, stammering, stumbling, stuttering

halve 1. *v.* bisect, cut in half, divide equally, reduce by fifty per cent, share equally, split in two **2.** *n. Plural* **by halves** imperfectly, incompletely, scrappily, skimpily

hammer *v.* **1.** bang, beat, drive, hit, knock, lambast(e), strike, tap **2.** beat out, fashion, forge, form, make, shape **3.** *Often with* **into** din into, drive home, drub into, drum into, grind into, impress upon, instruct, repeat **4.** *Often with* **away (at)** beaver away (*Brit. inf.*), drudge, grind, keep on, peg away (*Chiefly Brit.*), persevere, persist, plug away (*Inf.*), pound away, stick at, work **5.** *Inf.* beat, blow out of the water (*Sl.*), clobber (*Sl.*), defeat, drub, lick (*Inf.*), master, run rings around (*Inf.*), slate (*Inf.*), tank (*Sl.*), thrash, trounce, undo, wipe the floor with (*Inf.*), worst

hammer out accomplish, bring about, come to a conclusion, complete, excogitate, finish, form a resolution, make a decision, negotiate, produce, settle, sort out, thrash out, work out

hamper *v.* bind, cramp, curb, embarrass, encumber, entangle, fetter, frustrate, ham~ string, handicap, hinder, hold up, impede, interfere with, obstruct, prevent, restrain, restrict, slow down, thwart, trammel
Antonyms aid, assist, boost, encourage, ex~ pedite, forward, further, help, promote, speed

hamstring 1. cripple, disable, hock, injure, lame **2.** balk, foil, frustrate, prevent, ruin, stop, thwart

hamstrung at a loss, crippled, disabled, helpless, *hors de combat*, incapacitated, paralysed

hand *n.* **1.** fist, hook, meathook (*Sl.*), mitt (*Sl.*), palm, paw (*Inf.*) **2.** agency, direction, influence, part, participation, share **3.** aid, assistance, help, support **4.** artificer, arti~ san, craftsman, employee, hired man, la~ bourer, operative, worker, workman **5.** cal~ ligraphy, chirography, handwriting, long~ hand, penmanship, script **6.** clap, ovation, round of applause **7.** ability, art, artistry, skill **8. at** *or* **on hand** approaching, avail~ able, close, handy, imminent, near, nearby, on tap (*Inf.*), ready, within reach **9. from hand to mouth** by necessity, improvident~ ly, in poverty, insecurely, on the breadline (*Inf.*), precariously, uncertainly **10. hand in glove** allied, in cahoots (*Inf.*), in league, in partnership **11. hand over fist** by leaps and bounds, easily, steadily, swiftly **12. in hand a.** in order, receiving attention, under control **b.** available for use, in reserve, put by, ready ~*v.* **13.** deliver, hand over, pass **14.** aid, assist, conduct, convey, give, guide, help, lead, present, transmit

handbook Baedeker, guide, guidebook, in~ struction book, manual, vade mecum

handcuff 1. *v.* fetter, manacle, shackle **2.** *n.* *Plural* bracelets (*Sl.*), cuffs (*Inf.*), fetters, manacles, shackles

hand down *or* **on** bequeath, give, grant, pass on *or* down, transfer, will

handful few, small number, small quantity, smattering, sprinkling
Antonyms a lot, crowd, heaps, horde, large number, large quantity, loads (*Inf.*), masses (*Inf.*), mob, plenty, scores, stacks

handicap *n.* **1.** barrier, block, disadvantage, drawback, encumbrance, hindrance, im~ pediment, limitation, millstone, obstacle, restriction, shortcoming, stumbling block **2.** advantage, edge, head start, odds, penalty, upper hand **3.** defect, disability, impair~

ment ~*v.* **4.** burden, encumber, hamper, hamstring, hinder, hold back, impede, limit, place at a disadvantage, restrict, retard
Antonyms *n.* (*sense 1*) advantage, asset, benefit, boost, edge ~*v.* aid, assist, benefit, boost, forward, further, help, promote

handicraft art, artisanship, craft, crafts~ manship, handiwork, skill, workmanship

handiwork 1. craft, handicraft, handwork **2.** achievement, artefact, creation, design, invention, product, production, result

handle *n.* **1.** grip, haft, handgrip, helve, hilt, knob, stock ~*v.* **2.** feel, finger, fondle, grasp, hold, maul, paw (*Inf.*), pick up, poke, touch **3.** control, direct, guide, manage, manipu~ late, manoeuvre, operate, steer, use, wield **4.** administer, conduct, cope with, deal with, manage, supervise, take care of, treat **5.** discourse, discuss, treat **6.** carry, deal in, market, sell, stock, trade, traffic in

handling administration, approach, con~ duct, direction, management, manipulation, running, treatment

hand-me-down *adj.* cast-off, handed down, inherited, passed on, reach-me-down (*Inf.*), second-hand, used, worn

hand-out 1. alms, charity, dole **2.** bulletin, circular, free sample, leaflet, literature (*Inf.*), mailshot, press release

hand out deal out, disburse, dish out (*Inf.*), dispense, disseminate, distribute, give out, mete

hand over deliver, donate, fork out *or* up (*Sl.*), present, release, surrender, transfer, turn over, yield

hand-picked choice, chosen, elect, elite, recherché, select, selected
Antonyms haphazard, indiscriminate, ran~ dom, run-of-the-mill, wholesale

hands 1. authority, care, charge, command, control, custody, disposal, guardianship, keeping, possession, power, supervision **2. hands down** easily, effortlessly, with no contest, with no trouble

handsome 1. admirable, attractive, be~ coming, comely, dishy (*Inf., chiefly Brit.*), elegant, fine, good-looking, gorgeous, grace~ ful, majestic, personable, stately, well-proportioned **2.** abundant, ample, bountiful, considerable, generous, gracious, large, lib~ eral, magnanimous, plentiful, sizable
Antonyms base, cheap, inelegant, meagre, mean, miserly, selfish, small, stingy, tasteless, ugly, unattractive, ungenerous, unprepos~ sessing, unsightly

handsomely abundantly, amply, bounti~ fully, generously, liberally, magnanimously, munificently, plentifully, richly

handwriting calligraphy, chirography, fist, hand, longhand, penmanship, scrawl, script

handy 1. accessible, at or on hand, avail~ able, close, convenient, near, nearby, within reach **2.** convenient, easy to use, helpful, manageable, neat, practical, serviceable, useful, user-friendly **3.** adept, adroit, clever, deft, dexterous, expert, nimble, proficient, ready, skilful, skilled
Antonyms awkward, clumsy, ham-fisted, inaccessible, incompetent, inconvenient, in~ ept, inexpert, maladroit, out of the way, unac~ complished, unavailable, unskilful, unskilled, unwieldy, useless

hang v. **1.** be pendent, dangle, depend, droop, incline, suspend **2.** execute, gibbet, send to the gallows, string up (Inf.) **3.** ad~ here, cling, hold, rest, stick **4.** attach, cover, deck, decorate, drape, fasten, fix, furnish **5.** be poised, drift, float, hover, remain, swing **6.** bend downward, bend forward, bow, dangle, drop, incline, lean over, let droop, loll, lower, sag, trail **7. hang fire** be slow, be suspended, delay, hang back, procrasti~ nate, stall, stick, vacillate ~n. **8. get the hang of** comprehend, get the knack or technique, grasp, understand

hang about or **around 1.** dally, linger, loiter, roam, tarry, waste time **2.** associate with, frequent, hang out (Inf.), haunt, resort

hang back be backward, be reluctant, de~ mur, hesitate, hold back, recoil

hangdog adj. abject, browbeaten, cowed, cringing, defeated, downcast, furtive, guilty, shamefaced, sneaking, wretched

hanger-on dependant, follower, freeloader (Sl.), lackey, leech, ligger (Sl.), minion, parasite, sponger (Inf.), sycophant

hanging adj. **1.** dangling, drooping, flapping, flopping, floppy, loose, pendent, suspended, swinging, unattached, unsup~ ported **2.** undecided, unresolved, unsettled, up in the air (Inf.) **3.** beetle, beetling, jut~ ting, overhanging, projecting, prominent

hang on 1. carry on, continue, endure, go on, hold on, hold out, persevere, persist, re~ main **2.** cling, clutch, grasp, grip, hold fast **3.** be conditional upon, be contingent on, be dependent on, be determined by, depend on, hinge, rest, turn on **4.** Also **hang onto, hang upon** be rapt, give ear, listen atten~ tively **5.** Inf. hold on, hold the line, remain, stop, wait

hangover aftereffects, crapulence, head (Inf.), morning after (Inf.)

hang over be imminent, impend, loom, menace, threaten

hang-up block, difficulty, inhibition, obses~ sion, preoccupation, problem, thing (Inf.)

hank coil, length, loop, piece, roll, skein

hanker With **for** or **after** covet, crave, de~ sire, eat one's heart out over, hope, hunger, itch, long, lust, pine, thirst, want, wish, yearn, yen (Inf.)

hankering craving, desire, hope, hunger, itch, longing, pining, thirst, urge, wish, yearning, yen (Inf.)

haphazard 1. accidental, arbitrary, chance, fluky (Inf.), random **2.** aimless, careless, casual, disorderly, disorganized, hit or miss (Inf.), indiscriminate, slapdash, slipshod, unmethodical, unsystematic
Antonyms arranged, careful, considered, deliberate, methodical, orderly, organized, planned, systematic, thoughtful

happen 1. appear, arise, come about, come off (Inf.), come to pass, crop up (Inf.), de~ velop, ensue, eventuate, follow, materialize, occur, present itself, result, take place, transpire (Inf.) **2.** become of, befall, betide **3.** chance, fall out, have the fortune to be, pan out (Inf.), supervene, turn out

happening accident, adventure, affair, case, chance, episode, escapade, event, ex~ perience, incident, occasion, occurrence, phenomenon, proceeding, scene

happily 1. agreeably, contentedly, delight~ edly, enthusiastically, freely, gladly, hearti~ ly, lief (Rare), willingly, with pleasure **2.** blithely, cheerfully, gaily, gleefully, joyfully, joyously, merrily **3.** auspiciously, favour~ ably, fortunately, luckily, opportunely, pro~ pitiously, providentially, seasonably **4.** ap~ propriately, aptly, felicitously, gracefully, successfully

happiness beatitude, blessedness, bliss, cheer, cheerfulness, cheeriness, content~ ment, delight, ecstasy, elation, enjoyment, exuberance, felicity, gaiety, gladness, high spirits, joy, jubilation, light-heartedness, merriment, pleasure, prosperity, satisfac~ tion, wellbeing
Antonyms annoyance, bane, depression, despondency, distress, grief, low spirits, mis~ ery, misfortune, sadness, sorrow, unhappi~ ness

happy 1. blessed, blest, blissful, blithe, cheerful, cock-a-hoop, content, contented, delighted, ecstatic, elated, glad, gratified, jolly, joyful, joyous, jubilant, merry, over~ joyed, over the moon (Inf.), pleased, rapt, sunny, thrilled, walking on air (Inf.) **2.** ad~ vantageous, appropriate, apt, auspicious, befitting, convenient, enviable, favourable, felicitous, fortunate, lucky, opportune, promising, propitious, satisfactory, season~ able, successful, timely, well-timed
Antonyms depressed, despondent, discon~ tented, displeased, down in the dumps, for~ lorn, gloomy, inapt, joyless, melancholy, mis~ erable, mournful, sad, sombre, sorrowful, sorry, unfortunate, unhappy, unlucky

happy-go-lucky blithe, carefree, casual,

devil-may-care, easy-going, heedless, im~
provident, insouciant, irresponsible, light-
hearted, nonchalant, unconcerned, untrou~
bled
Antonyms careworn, cheerless, gloomy,
melancholy, morose, sad, serious, unhappy

harangue 1. *n.* address, declamation, dia~
tribe, exhortation, lecture, oration, philip~
pic, screed, speech, spiel (*Inf.*), tirade **2.** *v.*
address, declaim, exhort, hold forth, lecture,
rant, spout (*Inf.*)

harass annoy, badger, bait, beleaguer, be on
one's back (*Sl.*), bother, chivvy (*Brit.*), devil
(*Inf.*), disturb, exasperate, exhaust, fatigue,
harry, hassle (*Inf.*), hound, perplex, per~
secute, pester, plague, tease, tire, torment,
trouble, vex, weary, worry

harassed careworn, distraught, harried,
hassled (*Inf.*), plagued, strained, tormented,
troubled, under pressure, under stress,
vexed, worried

harassment aggravation (*Inf.*), annoyance,
badgering, bedevilment, bother, hassle
(*Inf.*), irritation, molestation, nuisance, per~
secution, pestering, torment, trouble, vexa~
tion

harbour *n.* **1.** anchorage, destination, ha~
ven, port **2.** asylum, covert, haven, refuge,
retreat, sanctuary, sanctum, security, shel~
ter ~*v.* **3.** conceal, hide, lodge, protect, pro~
vide refuge, relieve, secrete, shelter, shield
4. believe, brood over, cherish, cling to, en~
tertain, foster, hold, imagine, maintain,
nurse, nurture, retain

hard *adj.* **1.** compact, dense, firm, impen~
etrable, inflexible, rigid, rocklike, solid,
stiff, stony, strong, tough, unyielding **2.** ar~
duous, backbreaking, burdensome, exacting,
exhausting, fatiguing, formidable, Hercu~
lean, laborious, rigorous, strenuous, toil~
some, tough, uphill, wearying **3.** baffling,
complex, complicated, difficult, intricate,
involved, knotty, perplexing, puzzling, tan~
gled, thorny, unfathomable **4.** callous, cold,
cruel, exacting, grim, hardhearted, harsh,
implacable, obdurate, pitiless, ruthless, se~
vere, stern, strict, stubborn, unfeeling, un~
just, unkind, unrelenting, unsparing, un~
sympathetic **5.** calamitous, dark, disagree~
able, disastrous, distressing, grievous, grim,
intolerable, painful, unpleasant **6.** driving,
fierce, forceful, heavy, powerful, strong,
violent **7.** *Of feelings or words* acrimonious,
angry, antagonistic, bitter, hostile, rancor~
ous, resentful **8.** *Of truth or facts* actual,
bare, cold, definite, indisputable, plain, un~
deniable, unvarnished, verified ~*adv.* **9.**
energetically, fiercely, forcefully, forcibly,
heavily, intensely, powerfully, severely,
sharply, strongly, vigorously, violently,
with all one's might, with might and main

10. assiduously, determinedly, diligently,
doggedly, earnestly, industriously, intently,
persistently, steadily, strenuously, untir~
ingly **11.** agonizingly, badly, distressingly,
harshly, laboriously, painfully, roughly, se~
verely, with difficulty **12.** bitterly, hardly,
keenly, rancorously, reluctantly, resentful~
ly, slowly, sorely
Antonyms *adj.* agreeable, amiable, careless,
clear, direct, easy, easy-peasy (*Sl.*), flexible,
friendly, gentle, good, humane, kind, lazy, le~
nient, light, malleable, merciful, mild, per~
missive, pleasant, pliable, simple, soft,
straightforward, uncomplicated, weak ~*adv.*
calmly, easily, gently, lazily, lightly, loosely,
mildly, serenely, softly, weakly

hard and fast binding, immutable, incon~
trovertible, inflexible, invariable, rigid, set,
strict, stringent, unalterable

hard-bitten *or* **hard-boiled** case-
hardened, cynical, down-to-earth, hard-
headed, hard-nosed (*Inf.*), matter-of-fact,
practical, realistic, shrewd, tough, unsenti~
mental
Antonyms benign, compassionate, gentle,
humane, idealistic, merciful, mild, romantic,
sympathetic

hard-core 1. dedicated, die-hard, dyed-in-
the-wool, extreme, intransigent, obstinate,
rigid, staunch, steadfast **2.** explicit, obscene

harden 1. anneal, bake, cake, freeze, set,
solidify, stiffen **2.** brace, buttress, fortify,
gird, indurate, nerve, reinforce, steel,
strengthen, toughen **3.** accustom, brutalize,
case-harden, habituate, inure, season, train

hardened 1. chronic, fixed, habitual, in~
corrigible, inveterate, irredeemable, repro~
bate, set, shameless **2.** accustomed, habitu~
ated, inured, seasoned, toughened
Antonyms infrequent, irregular, occasional,
rare, unaccustomed

hard-headed astute, cool, hard-boiled
(*Inf.*), level-headed, practical, pragmatic, re~
alistic, sensible, shrewd, tough, unsenti~
mental
Antonyms idealistic, impractical, senti~
mental, unrealistic

hardhearted callous, cold, cruel, hard,
heartless, indifferent, inhuman, insensitive,
intolerant, merciless, pitiless, stony,
uncaring, unfeeling, unkind, unsympathetic
Antonyms compassionate, forgiving, gentle,
humane, kind, loving, merciful, sensitive,
soft-hearted, sympathetic, understanding,
warm, warm-hearted

hard-hitting critical, no holds barred,
pulling no punches, strongly worded, tough,
uncompromising, unsparing, vigorous

hardiness boldness, courage, fortitude, in~
trepidity, resilience, resolution, robustness,
ruggedness, sturdiness, toughness, valour

hardline definite, inflexible, intransigent, tough, uncompromising, undeviating, un~ yielding

hardly almost not, barely, by no means, faintly, infrequently, just, not at all, not quite, no way, only, only just, scarcely, with difficulty
Antonyms abundantly, amply, by all means, certainly, completely, easily, fully, indubi~ tably, more than, really, truly, undoubtedly, well over

hard-pressed harried, hotly pursued, in difficulties, pushed (*Inf.*), under attack, un~ der pressure, up against it (*Inf.*), with one's back to the wall

hardship adversity, affliction, austerity, burden, calamity, destitution, difficulty, fa~ tigue, grievance, labour, misery, misfor~ tune, need, oppression, persecution, priva~ tion, suffering, toil, torment, trial, tribula~ tion, trouble, want
Antonyms aid, blessing, boon, comfort, ease, good fortune, happiness, help, prosperity, re~ lief

hard up bankrupt, broke (*Inf.*), bust (*Inf.*), cleaned out (*Sl.*), dirt-poor (*Inf.*), down and out, flat broke (*Inf.*), impecunious, impov~ erished, in the red (*Inf.*), on one's uppers (*Inf.*), out of pocket, penniless, poor, short, short of cash *or* funds, skint (*Brit. sl.*), without two pennies to rub together (*Inf.*)
Antonyms affluent, comfortable (*Inf.*), for~ tunate, loaded (*Sl.*), rich, wealthy, well-heeled (*Inf.*), well-off

hard-wearing durable, resilient, rugged, stout, strong, tough, well-made

hard-working assiduous, busy, conscien~ tious, diligent, energetic, indefatigable, in~ dustrious, sedulous, zealous
Antonyms careless, dilatory, inconstant, indifferent, lazy

hardy 1. firm, fit, hale, healthy, hearty, in fine fettle, lusty, robust, rugged, sound, stalwart, stout, strong, sturdy, tough, vig~ orous 2. bold, brave, courageous, daring, feisty (*Inf., chiefly U.S. & Canad.*), gritty, heroic, intrepid, manly, plucky, resolute, stouthearted, valiant, valorous 3. auda~ cious, brazen, foolhardy, headstrong, impu~ dent, rash, reckless
Antonyms delicate, faint-hearted, feeble, fragile, frail, sickly, soft, weak, weedy (*Inf.*), wimpish *or* wimpy (*Inf.*)

hark back look back, recall, recollect, re~ gress, remember, revert, think back

harlot call girl, fallen woman, hussy, loose woman, pro (*Sl.*), prostitute, scrubber (*Brit. & Aust. sl.*), slag (*Brit. sl.*), streetwalker, strumpet, tart (*Inf.*), tramp (*Sl.*), whore, working girl (*Facetious sl.*)

harm *n.* 1. abuse, damage, detriment, dis~ service, hurt, ill, impairment, injury, loss, mischief, misfortune 2. evil, immorality, iniquity, sin, sinfulness, vice, wickedness, wrong ~*v.* 3. abuse, blemish, damage, hurt, ill-treat, ill-use, impair, injure, maltreat, mar, molest, ruin, spoil, wound
Antonyms *n.* aid, assistance, benefit, bless~ ing, boon, gain, good, goodness, help, im~ provement, reparation, righteousness ~*v.* aid, alleviate, ameliorate, assist, benefit, better, cure, heal, help, improve, repair

harmful baleful, baneful, damaging, del~ eterious, destructive, detrimental, disad~ vantageous, evil, hurtful, injurious, maleficent, noxious, pernicious
Antonyms beneficial, good, harmless, healthy, helpful, innocuous, safe, wholesome

harmless gentle, innocent, innocuous, in~ noxious, inoffensive, nontoxic, not danger~ ous, safe, unobjectionable
Antonyms dangerous, destructive, harmful, unhealthy, unsafe, unwholesome

harmonious 1. agreeable, compatible, concordant, congruous, consonant, coordi~ nated, correspondent, dulcet, euphonic, euphonious, harmonic, harmonizing, matching, mellifluous, melodious, musical, sweet-sounding, symphonious (*Literary*), tuneful 2. agreeable, amicable, compatible, concordant, congenial, cordial, *en rapport*, fraternal, friendly, in accord, in harmony, in unison, of one mind, sympathetic
Antonyms cacophonous, contrasting, dis~ cordant, grating, harsh, incompatible, incon~ sistent, unfriendly, unlike, unmelodious

harmonize accord, adapt, agree, arrange, attune, be in unison, be of one mind, blend, chime with, cohere, compose, coordinate, correspond, match, reconcile, suit, tally, tone in with

harmony 1. accord, agreement, amicability, amity, assent, compatibility, concord, con~ formity, consensus, cooperation, friendship, goodwill, like-mindedness, peace, rapport, sympathy, unanimity, understanding, unity 2. balance, compatibility, concord, congru~ ity, consistency, consonance, coordination, correspondence, fitness, parallelism, suit~ ability, symmetry 3. euphony, melodious~ ness, melody, tune, tunefulness, unison
Antonyms antagonism, cacophony, conflict, contention, disagreement, dissension, hostil~ ity, incongruity, inconsistency, opposition, unsuitability

harness *n.* 1. equipment, gear, tack, tackle, trappings 2. **in harness** active, at work, busy, in action, working ~*v.* 3. couple, hitch up, put in harness, saddle, yoke 4. apply, channel, control, employ, exploit, make productive, mobilize, render useful, turn to account, utilize

harp *With* **on** *or* **upon** dwell on, go on, labour, press, reiterate, renew, repeat

harrowing agonizing, alarming, chilling, distressing, disturbing, excruciating, frightening, heartbreaking, heart-rending, nerve-racking, painful, racking, scaring, terrifying, tormenting, traumatic

harry 1. annoy, badger, bedevil, be on one's back (*Sl.*), bother, chivvy, disturb, fret, get in one's hair (*Inf.*), harass, hassle (*Inf.*), molest, persecute, pester, plague, tease, tor~ment, trouble, vex, worry **2.** depredate (*Rare*), despoil, devastate, pillage, plunder, raid, ravage, rob, sack

harsh 1. coarse, croaking, crude, discordant, dissonant, glaring, grating, guttural, jar~ring, rasping, raucous, rough, strident, un~melodious **2.** abusive, austere, bitter, bleak, brutal, comfortless, cruel, dour, Draconian, drastic, grim, hard, pitiless, punitive, re~lentless, ruthless, severe, sharp, Spartan, stern, stringent, unfeeling, unkind, un~pleasant, unrelenting
Antonyms agreeable, gentle, harmonious, kind, loving, mellifluous, merciful, mild, pleasant, smooth, soft, soothing, sweet

harshly brutally, cruelly, grimly, roughly, severely, sharply, sternly, strictly

harshness acerbity, acrimony, asperity, austerity, bitterness, brutality, churlish~ness, coarseness, crudity, hardness, ill-temper, rigour, roughness, severity, sour~ness, sternness

harvest *n.* **1.** harvesting, harvest-time, in~gathering, reaping **2.** crop, produce, yield **3.** *Fig.* consequence, effect, fruition, prod~uct, result, return ~*v.* **4.** gather, mow, pick, pluck, reap **5.** accumulate, acquire, amass, collect, garner

hash 1. balls-up (*Taboo sl.*), cock-up (*Brit. sl.*), confusion, fuck-up (*Offens. taboo sl.*), hodgepodge (*U.S.*), hotchpotch, jumble, mess, mishmash, mix-up, muddle, pig's breakfast (*Inf.*), pig's ear (*Inf.*), shambles, state **2. make a hash of** *Inf.* bodge (*Inf.*), botch, bungle, cock up (*Brit. sl.*), fuck up (*Offens. taboo sl.*), jumble, mess up, mis~handle, mismanage, mix, muddle

hassle *n.* **1.** altercation, argument, bicker~ing, disagreement, dispute, fight, quarrel, row, squabble, tussle, wrangle **2.** bother, difficulty, inconvenience, problem, struggle, trial, trouble, upset ~*v.* **3.** annoy, badger, be on one's back (*Sl.*), bother, bug (*Inf.*), get in one's hair (*Inf.*), get on one's nerves (*Inf.*), harass, harry, hound, pester

haste 1. alacrity, briskness, celerity, dis~patch, expedition, fleetness, nimbleness, promptitude, quickness, rapidity, rapidness, speed, swiftness, urgency, velocity **2.** bus~tle, hastiness, helter-skelter, hurry, hustle,

impetuosity, precipitateness, rashness, recklessness, rush
Antonyms calmness, care, delay, delibera~tion, leisureliness, slowness, sluggishness, sureness

hasten 1. barrel (along) (*Inf., chiefly U.S. & Canad.*), beetle, bolt, burn rubber (*Inf.*), dash, fly, haste, hurry (up), make haste, race, run, rush, scurry, scuttle, speed, sprint, step on it (*Inf.*), tear (along) **2.** ac~celerate, advance, dispatch, expedite, goad, hurry (up), precipitate, press, push forward, quicken, speed (up), step up (*Inf.*), urge
Antonyms crawl, creep, dawdle, decelerate, delay, hinder, impede, move slowly, retard, slow, slow down

hastily 1. apace, double-quick, fast, hotfoot, pdq (*Sl.*), posthaste, promptly, pronto (*Inf.*), quickly, rapidly, speedily, straightaway **2.** heedlessly, hurriedly, impetuously, impul~sively, on the spur of the moment, precipi~tately, rashly, recklessly, too quickly

hasty 1. brisk, eager, expeditious, fast, fleet, hurried, prompt, rapid, speedy, swift, urgent **2.** brief, cursory, fleeting, passing, perfunctory, rushed, short, superficial **3.** foolhardy, headlong, heedless, impetuous, impulsive, indiscreet, precipitate, rash, reckless, thoughtless, unduly quick **4.** brusque, excited, fiery, hot-headed, hot-tempered, impatient, irascible, irritable, passionate, quick-tempered, snappy
Antonyms careful, cautious, detailed, dis~passionate, leisurely, long, protracted, slow, thorough, thoughtful

hatch 1. breed, bring forth, brood, incubate **2.** *Fig.* conceive, concoct, contrive, cook up (*Inf.*), design, devise, dream up (*Inf.*), manufacture, plan, plot, project, scheme, think up, trump up

hatchet man assassin, bravo, calumniator, cutthroat, debunker, defamer, destroyer, detractor, gunman, heavy (*Sl.*), hired assas~sin, hit man (*Sl.*), killer, murderer, smear campaigner, thug, traducer

hate *v.* **1.** abhor, abominate, be hostile to, be repelled by, be sick of, despise, detest, dis~like, execrate, have an aversion to, loathe, recoil from **2.** be loath, be reluctant, be sorry, be unwilling, dislike, feel disinclined, have no stomach for, shrink from ~*n.* **3.** abhorrence, abomination, animosity, ani~mus, antagonism, antipathy, aversion, de~testation, dislike, enmity, execration, ha~tred, hostility, loathing, odium
Antonyms *v.* be fond of, cherish, dote on, en~joy, esteem, fancy, like, love, relish, treasure, wish ~*n.* affection, amity, devotion, fondness, goodwill, liking, love

hateful abhorrent, abominable, despicable, detestable, disgusting, execrable, forbidding,

foul, heinous, horrible, loathsome, obnox~
ious, obscene, odious, offensive, repellent,
repugnant, repulsive, revolting, vile
Antonyms affectionate, attractive, beauti~
ful, charming, desirable, devoted, friendly,
good, kind, likable or likeable, lovable, loving,
pleasant, wonderful

hatred abomination, animosity, animus,
antagonism, antipathy, aversion, detesta~
tion, dislike, enmity, execration, hate, ill
will, odium, repugnance, revulsion
Antonyms affection, amity, attachment, de~
votion, fondness, friendliness, goodwill, lik~
ing, love

haughty arrogant, assuming, conceited,
contemptuous, disdainful, high, high and
mighty (*Inf.*), hoity-toity (*Inf.*), imperious,
lofty, overweening, proud, scornful, snob~
bish, snooty (*Inf.*), stuck-up (*Inf.*), supercili~
ous, uppish (*Brit. inf.*)
Antonyms humble, meek, mild, modest,
self-effacing, subservient, wimpish or wimpy
(*Inf.*)

haul v. **1.** drag, draw, hale, heave, lug, pull,
tow, trail, tug **2.** carry, cart, convey, hump
(*Brit. sl.*), move, transport ~n. **3.** drag,
heave, pull, tug **4.** booty, catch, find, gain,
harvest, loot, spoils, takings, yield

haunt v. **1.** visit, walk **2.** beset, come back,
obsess, plague, possess, prey on, recur, stay
with, torment, trouble, weigh on **3.** fre~
quent, hang around or about, repair, resort,
visit ~n. **4.** den, gathering place, hangout
(*Inf.*), meeting place, rendezvous, resort,
stamping ground

haunted 1. cursed, eerie, ghostly, jinxed,
possessed, spooky (*Inf.*) **2.** obsessed,
plagued, preoccupied, tormented, troubled,
worried

haunting disturbing, eerie, evocative, in~
delible, nostalgic, persistent, poignant, re~
current, recurring, unforgettable

have 1. hold, keep, obtain, occupy, own,
possess, retain **2.** accept, acquire, gain, get,
obtain, procure, receive, secure, take **3.**
comprehend, comprise, contain, embody,
include, take in **4.** endure, enjoy, experi~
ence, feel, meet with, suffer, sustain,
undergo **5.** *Sl.* cheat, deceive, dupe, fool,
outwit, stiff (*Sl.*), swindle, take in (*Inf.*),
trick **6.** *Usually* **have to** be bound, be com~
pelled, be forced, be obliged, have got to,
must, ought, should **7.** allow, consider, en~
tertain, permit, put up with (*Inf.*), think
about, tolerate **8.** bear, beget, bring forth,
bring into the world, deliver, give birth to
9. have had it *Inf.* be defeated, be ex~
hausted, be finished, be out, be past it (*Inf.*),
be pooped (*U.S. sl.*), be stonkered (*Sl.*)

haven 1. anchorage, harbour, port, roads

(*Nautical*) **2.** *Fig.* asylum, refuge, retreat,
sanctum, shelter

have on 1. be clothed in, be dressed in,
wear **2.** be committed to, be engaged to,
have on the agenda, have planned **3.** *Of a
person* deceive, kid (*Inf.*), play a joke on,
tease, trick, wind up (*Brit. sl.*)

havoc 1. carnage, damage, desolation, de~
spoliation, destruction, devastation, rack
and ruin, ravages, ruin, slaughter, waste,
wreck **2.** *Inf.* chaos, confusion, disorder,
disruption, mayhem, shambles **3. play
havoc (with)** bring into chaos, confuse, de~
molish, destroy, devastate, disorganize, dis~
rupt, wreck

hawk v. **1.** bark (*Inf.*), cry, market, peddle,
sell, tout (*Inf.*), vend **2.** *Often with* **about**
bandy about (*Inf.*), bruit about, buzz, noise
abroad, put about, retail, rumour

hawker barrow boy (*Brit.*), cheap-jack (*Inf.*),
colporteur, crier, huckster, pedlar, vendor

hazardous 1. dangerous, dicey (*Inf., chiefly
Brit.*), difficult, fraught with danger, hairy
(*Sl.*), insecure, perilous, precarious, risky,
unsafe **2.** chancy (*Inf.*), haphazard, precari~
ous, uncertain, unpredictable
Antonyms reliable, safe, secure, sound, sta~
ble, sure

haze cloud, dimness, film, fog, mist, obscu~
rity, smog, smokiness, steam, vapour

hazy 1. blurry, cloudy, dim, dull, faint, fog~
gy, misty, nebulous, obscure, overcast,
smoky, veiled **2.** *Fig.* fuzzy, ill-defined,
indefinite, indistinct, loose, muddled, muz~
zy, nebulous, uncertain, unclear, vague
Antonyms bright, certain, clear, detailed,
light, sunny, well-defined

head n. **1.** bean (*U.S. & Canad. sl.*), conk
(*Sl.*), cranium, crown, loaf (*Sl.*), noddle (*Inf.,
chiefly Brit.*), noggin, nut (*Sl.*), pate, skull **2.**
boss (*Inf.*), captain, chief, chieftain, com~
mander, director, headmaster, head~
mistress, head teacher, leader, manager,
master, principal, superintendent, supervi~
sor **3.** apex, crest, crown, height, peak,
pitch, summit, tip, top, vertex **4.** cutting
edge, first place, fore, forefront, front, van,
vanguard **5.** beginning, commencement,
origin, rise, source, start **6.** ability, apti~
tude, brain, brains (*Inf.*), capacity, faculty,
flair, intellect, intelligence, mentality, mind,
talent, thought, understanding **7.** branch,
category, class, department, division, head~
ing, section, subject, topic **8.** climax, con~
clusion, crisis, culmination, end, turning
point **9.** *Geog.* cape, foreland, headland,
point, promontory **10. go to one's head**
dizzy, excite, intoxicate, make conceited,
puff up **11. head over heels** completely,
intensely, thoroughly, uncontrollably,
utterly, wholeheartedly **12. put (our, their,**

etc.) **heads together** *Inf.* confab (*Inf.*), con~
fabulate, confer, consult, deliberate, discuss,
palaver, powwow, talk over ~*adj.* **13.** arch,
chief, first, foremost, front, highest, leading,
main, pre-eminent, premier, prime, principal, supreme, topmost ~*v.* **14.** be *or* go first,
cap, crown, lead, lead the way, precede, top
15. be in charge of, command, control, di~
rect, govern, guide, lead, manage, rule, run,
supervise **16.** *Often with* **for** aim, go to,
make a beeline for, make for, point, set off
for, set out, start towards, steer, turn

headache 1. cephalalgia (*Medical*), head
(*Inf.*), migraine, neuralgia **2.** *Inf.* bane,
bother, inconvenience, nuisance, problem,
trouble, vexation, worry

headfirst 1. *adj./adv.* diving, headlong,
head-on **2.** *adv.* carelessly, hastily, head
over heels, precipitately, rashly, recklessly

heading 1. caption, headline, name, rubric,
title **2.** category, class, division, section

headlong 1. *adj./adv.* headfirst, headfore~
most, head-on **2.** *adj.* breakneck, dangerous,
hasty, impetuous, impulsive, inconsiderate,
precipitate, reckless, thoughtless **3.** *adv.*
hastily, heedlessly, helter-skelter, hurriedly,
pell-mell, precipitately, rashly, thoughtless~
ly, wildly

head off 1. block off, cut off, deflect, divert,
intercept, interpose, intervene **2.** avert,
fend off, forestall, parry, prevent, stop, ward
off

headstrong contrary, foolhardy, froward,
heedless, imprudent, impulsive, intractable,
mulish, obstinate, perverse, pig-headed,
rash, reckless, self-willed, stiff-necked,
stubborn, ungovernable, unruly, wilful
Antonyms cautious, impressionable, man~
ageable, pliant, subservient, tractable

headway 1. advance, improvement, pro~
gress, progression, way **2. make headway**
advance, come *or* get on, cover ground, de~
velop, gain, gain ground, make strides, pro~
gress

heady 1. inebriating, intoxicating, potent,
spirituous, strong **2.** exciting, exhilarating,
intoxicating, overwhelming, stimulating,
thrilling **3.** hasty, impetuous, impulsive,
inconsiderate, precipitate, rash, reckless,
thoughtless

heal 1. cure, make well, mend, regenerate,
remedy, restore, treat **2.** alleviate, ameliorate, compose, conciliate, harmonize, patch
up, reconcile, settle, soothe
Antonyms aggravate, exacerbate, harm,
hurt, inflame, injure, make worse, reopen,
wound

healing 1. analeptic, curative, medicinal,
remedial, restorative, restoring, sanative,
therapeutic **2.** assuaging, comforting, emol~

lient, gentle, lenitive, mild, mitigative, pal~
liative, soothing

health 1. fitness, good condition, haleness,
healthiness, robustness, salubrity, sound~
ness, strength, vigour, wellbeing **2.** condition, constitution, fettle, form, shape, state,
tone
Antonyms (*sense 1*) debility, disease, frailty,
illness, sickness, weakness

healthy 1. active, blooming, fit, flourishing,
hale, hale and hearty, hardy, hearty, in fine
feather, in fine fettle, in fine form, in good
condition, in good shape (*Inf.*), in the pink,
physically fit, robust, sound, strong, sturdy,
vigorous, well **2.** beneficial, bracing, good
for one, healthful, health-giving, hygienic,
invigorating, nourishing, nutritious, salu~
brious, salutary, wholesome
Antonyms ailing, debilitated, delicate, dis~
eased, feeble, fragile, frail, ill, infirm, poorly
(*Inf.*), sick, sickly, unfit, unhealthy, unsound,
unwell, unwholesome, weak, weedy (*Inf.*)

heap *n.* **1.** accumulation, aggregation, col~
lection, hoard, lot, mass, mound, mountain,
pile, stack, stockpile, store **2.** *Often plural
Inf.* abundance, a lot, great deal, lashings
(*Brit. inf.*), load(s) (*Inf.*), lots (*Inf.*), mass,
mint, ocean(s), oodles (*Inf.*), plenty, pot(s)
(*Inf.*), quantities, stack(s), tons ~*v.* **3.** accu~
mulate, amass, augment, bank, collect,
gather, hoard, increase, mound, pile, stack,
stockpile, store **4.** assign, bestow, burden,
confer, load, shower upon

hear 1. attend, be all ears (*Inf.*), catch,
eavesdrop, give attention, hark, hearken
(*Archaic*), heed, listen in, listen to, overhear
2. ascertain, be informed, be told of, dis~
cover, find out, gather, get wind of (*Inf.*),
hear tell (*Dialect*), learn, pick up, under~
stand **3.** *Law* examine, investigate, judge,
try

hearing 1. audition, auditory, ear, percep~
tion **2.** audience, audition, chance to speak,
interview **3.** auditory range, earshot, hear~
ing distance, range, reach, sound **4.** industrial tribunal, inquiry, investigation, re~
view, trial

hearsay buzz, dirt (*U.S. sl.*), gossip, grape~
vine (*Inf.*), idle talk, mere talk, *on dit*, re~
port, rumour, scuttlebutt (*Sl., chiefly U.S.*),
talk, talk of the town, tittle-tattle, word of
mouth

heart 1. character, disposition, emotion,
feeling, inclination, nature, sentiment, soul,
sympathy, temperament **2.** affection, be~
nevolence, compassion, concern, humanity,
love, pity, tenderness, understanding **3.**
balls (*Taboo sl.*), boldness, bravery, courage,
fortitude, guts (*Inf.*), mettle, mind, nerve,
pluck, purpose, resolution, spirit, spunk
(*Inf.*), will **4.** central part, centre, core,

crux, essence, hub, kernel, marrow, middle, nucleus, pith, quintessence, root **5. at heart** *au fond*, basically, essentially, funda~ mentally, in essence, in reality, really, truly **6. by heart** by memory, by rote, off pat, parrot-fashion (*Inf.*), pat, word for word **7. eat one's heart out** agonize, brood, grieve, mope, mourn, pine, regret, repine, sorrow **8. from (the bottom of) one's heart** deeply, devoutly, fervently, heart and soul, heartily, sincerely, with all one's heart **9. heart and soul** absolutely, completely, de~ votedly, entirely, gladly, wholeheartedly **10. take heart** be comforted, be encouraged, be heartened, brighten up, buck up (*Inf.*), cheer up, perk up, revive

heartbreaking agonizing, bitter, desolat~ ing, disappointing, distressing, grievous, harrowing, heart-rending, pitiful, poignant, sad, tragic
Antonyms cheerful, cheery, comic, glorious, happy, jolly, joyful, joyous, light-hearted

heartbroken brokenhearted, crestfallen, crushed, dejected, desolate, despondent, disappointed, disconsolate, disheartened, dismal, dispirited, downcast, grieved, heartsick, miserable, sick as a parrot (*Inf.*)
Antonyms cheerful, cock-a-hoop, elated, exuberant, happy, in seventh heaven, joyful, joyous, on cloud nine, over the moon (*Inf.*)

heartfelt ardent, cordial, deep, devout, ear~ nest, fervent, genuine, hearty, honest, pro~ found, sincere, unfeigned, warm, whole~ hearted
Antonyms false, feigned, flippant, fraudu~ lent, frivolous, half-hearted, hypocritical, in~ sincere, phoney *or* phony (*Inf.*), pretended, put on, reserved, unenthusiastic, unimpassioned

heartily 1. cordially, deeply, feelingly, genuinely, profoundly, sincerely, unfeign~ edly, warmly **2.** eagerly, earnestly, enthu~ siastically, resolutely, vigorously, zealously **3.** absolutely, completely, thoroughly, total~ ly, very

heartless brutal, callous, cold, cold-blooded, cold-hearted, cruel, hard, hardhearted, harsh, inhuman, merciless, pitiless, un~ caring, unfeeling, unkind
Antonyms compassionate, generous, hu~ mane, kind, merciful, sensitive, sympathetic, warm-hearted

heart-rending affecting, distressing, har~ rowing, heartbreaking, moving, pathetic, piteous, pitiful, poignant, sad, tragic

heartsick dejected, despondent, dispirited, downcast, heartsore, heavy-hearted, sick at heart

heart-to-heart 1. *adj.* candid, intimate, open, personal, sincere, unreserved **2.** *n.* cosy chat, tête-à-tête

heart-warming 1. gratifying, pleasing,

rewarding, satisfying **2.** affecting, cheering, encouraging, heartening, moving, touching, warming

hearty 1. affable, ardent, back-slapping, cordial, eager, ebullient, effusive, enthusi~ astic, friendly, generous, genial, jovial, un~ reserved, warm **2.** earnest, genuine, heart~ felt, honest, real, sincere, true, unfeigned, wholehearted **3.** active, energetic, hale, hardy, healthy, robust, sound, strong, vig~ orous, well **4.** ample, filling, nourishing, sizable, solid, square, substantial
Antonyms cold, cool, delicate, feeble, frail, half-hearted, insincere, mild, sickly, un~ healthy, weak

heat *n.* **1.** calefaction, fever, fieriness, high temperature, hotness, hot spell, sultriness, swelter, torridity, warmness, warmth **2.** *Fig.* agitation, ardour, earnestness, excite~ ment, fervour, fever, fury, impetuosity, in~ tensity, passion, vehemence, violence, warmth, zeal ~*v.* **3.** become warm, chafe, flush, glow, grow hot, make hot, reheat, warm up **4.** animate, excite, impassion, inflame, inspirit, rouse, stimulate, stir, warm
Antonyms *n.* calmness, cold, coldness, com~ posure, coolness ~*v.* chill, cool, cool off, freeze

heated angry, bitter, excited, fierce, fiery, frenzied, furious, impassioned, intense, passionate, raging, stormy, tempestuous, vehement, violent
Antonyms calm, civilized, dispassionate, friendly, half-hearted, mellow, mild, peaceful, quiet, rational, reasoned, serene, subdued, unemotional, unfazed (*Inf.*), unruffled

heathen *n.* **1.** idolater, idolatress, infidel, pagan, unbeliever **2.** barbarian, philistine, savage ~*adj.* **3.** godless, heathenish, idola~ trous, infidel, irreligious, pagan **4.** barbaric, philistine, savage, uncivilized, unenlight~ ened

heave 1. drag (up), elevate, haul (up), heft (*Inf.*), hoist, lever, lift, pull (up), raise, tug **2.** cast, fling, hurl, pitch, send, sling, throw, toss **3.** breathe heavily, groan, puff, sigh, sob, suspire (*Archaic*), utter wearily **4.** bil~ low, breathe, dilate, exhale, expand, palpi~ tate, pant, rise, surge, swell, throb **5.** barf (*U.S. sl.*), be sick, chuck (up) (*Sl., chiefly U.S.*), chunder (*Sl., chiefly Aust.*), do a tech~ nicolour yawn (*Sl.*), gag, retch, spew, throw up (*Inf.*), toss one's cookies (*U.S. sl.*), upchuck (*U.S. sl.*), vomit

heaven 1. abode of God, bliss, Elysium *or* Elysian fields (*Greek myth*), happy hunting ground (*Amerind legend*), hereafter, life everlasting, life to come, next world, nirva~ na (*Buddhism, Hinduism*), paradise, Valhal~ la (*Norse myth*), Zion (*Christianity*) **2.** *Usually plural* empyrean (*Poetic*), ether, firmament, sky, welkin (*Archaic*) **3.** *Fig.* bliss, dreamland, ecstasy, enchantment, felicity, happiness, paradise, rapture, seventh heaven, sheer bliss, transport, utopia

heavenly 1. *Inf.* alluring, beautiful, blissful, delightful, divine (*Inf.*), entrancing, exquisite, glorious, lovely, rapturous, ravishing, sublime, wonderful **2.** angelic, beatific, blessed, blest, celestial, cherubic, divine, empyrean (*Poetic*), extraterrestrial, godlike, holy, immortal, paradisaical, seraphic, superhuman, supernal (*Literary*), supernatural

Antonyms (*sense 1*) abominable, appalling, awful, bad, depressing, dire, disagreeable, dreadful, dreary, dull, frightful, gloomy, grim, hellacious (*U.S. sl.*), horrible, horrid, lousy (*Sl.*), miserable, rotten (*Inf.*), terrible, unpleasant, vile (*sense 2*) earthly, human, secular, worldly

heavily 1. awkwardly, clumsily, ponderously, weightily **2.** laboriously, painfully, with difficulty **3.** completely, decisively, roundly, thoroughly, utterly **4.** dejectedly, dully, gloomily, sluggishly, woodenly **5.** closely, compactly, densely, fast, hard, thick, thickly **6.** deep, deeply, profoundly, sound, soundly **7.** a great deal, considerably, copiously, excessively, frequently, to excess, very much

heaviness 1. gravity, heftiness, ponderousness, weight **2.** arduousness, burdensomeness, grievousness, onerousness, oppressiveness, severity, weightiness **3.** deadness, dullness, languor, lassitude, numbness, sluggishness, torpor **4.** dejection, depression, despondency, gloom, gloominess, glumness, melancholy, sadness, seriousness

heavy 1. bulky, hefty, massive, ponderous, portly, weighty **2.** burdensome, difficult, grievous, hard, harsh, intolerable, laborious, onerous, oppressive, severe, tedious, vexatious, wearisome **3.** apathetic, drowsy, dull, inactive, indolent, inert, listless, slow, sluggish, stupid, torpid, wooden **4.** crestfallen, dejected, depressed, despondent, disconsolate, downcast, gloomy, grieving, melancholy, sad, sorrowful **5.** complex, deep, difficult, grave, profound, serious, solemn, weighty **6.** abundant, considerable, copious, excessive, large, profuse **7.** burdened, encumbered, laden, loaded, oppressed, weighted **8.** boisterous, rough, stormy, tempestuous, turbulent, violent, wild **9.** dull, gloomy, leaden, louring *or* lowering, overcast

Antonyms agile, alert, bearable, brisk, calm, cheerful, compact, easy, exciting, gentle, handy, happy, inconsequential, joyful, light, mild, moderate, quick, slight, small, soft, sparse, trivial, unimportant, weak

heavy-handed 1. awkward, bungling, clumsy, graceless, ham-fisted (*Inf.*), ham-handed (*Inf.*), inept, inexpert, like a bull in a china shop (*Inf.*), maladroit, unhandy **2.** bungling, inconsiderate, insensitive, tactless, thoughtless **3.** autocratic, domineering, harsh, oppressive, overbearing

Antonyms adept, adroit, competent, considerate, considered, dexterous, diplomatic, effectual, efficient, gentle, graceful, intelligent, prudent, sensible, skilful, smart, smooth, submissive, subservient, suitable, tactful, well-advised, well-thought-out, wise

heckle bait, barrack (*Inf.*), boo, disrupt, interrupt, jeer, pester, shout down, taunt

hectic animated, boisterous, chaotic, excited, fevered, feverish, flurrying, flustering, frantic, frenetic, frenzied, furious, heated, riotous, rumbustious, tumultuous, turbulent, wild

Antonyms calm, peaceful, relaxing, tranquil

hector bluster, boast, browbeat, bully, bullyrag, harass, huff and puff, intimidate, menace, provoke, ride roughshod over, roister, threaten, worry

hedge *n.* **1.** hedgerow, quickset **2.** barrier, boundary, screen, windbreak **3.** compensation, counterbalance, guard, insurance cover, protection ~*v.* **4.** border, edge, enclose, fence, surround **5.** block, confine, hem in (about, around), hinder, obstruct, restrict **6.** beg the question, be noncommittal, dodge, duck, equivocate, evade, flannel (*Brit. inf.*), prevaricate, pussyfoot (*Inf.*), quibble, sidestep, temporize, waffle (*Inf., chiefly Brit.*) **7.** cover, fortify, guard, insure, protect, safeguard, shield

heed 1. *n.* attention, care, caution, consideration, ear, heedfulness, mind, note, notice, regard, respect, thought, watchfulness **2.** *v.* attend, bear in mind, be guided by, consider, follow, give ear to, listen to, mark, mind, note, obey, observe, pay attention to, regard, take notice of, take to heart

Antonyms *n.* carelessness, disregard, inattention, laxity, laxness, neglect, thoughtlessness ~*v.* be inattentive to, discount, disobey, disregard, flout, ignore, neglect, overlook, reject, shun, turn a deaf ear to

heedful attentive, careful, cautious, chary, circumspect, mindful, observant, prudent, vigilant, wary, watchful

heedless careless, foolhardy, imprudent, inattentive, incautious, neglectful, negligent, oblivious, precipitate, rash, reckless, thoughtless, unmindful, unobservant, unthinking

Antonyms attentive, aware, careful, cautious, concerned, heedful, mindful, observant, thoughtful, vigilant, wary, watchful

heel¹ *n.* **1.** crust, end, remainder, rump, stub, stump **2.** *Sl.* blackguard, bounder (*Old-fashioned Brit. sl.*), cad (*Brit inf.*), cocksucker (*Taboo sl.*), rotter (*Sl., chiefly Brit.*), scally (*Northwest English dialect*), scoundrel, scumbag (*Sl.*), swine **3. down at heel** dowdy, impoverished, out at elbows, run-down, seedy, shabby, slipshod, slovenly, worn **4. take to one's heels** escape, flee, hook it (*Sl.*), run away *or* off, show a clean pair of heels, skedaddle (*Inf.*), take flight, vamoose (*Sl., chiefly U.S.*) **5. well-heeled** affluent, flush (*Inf.*), moneyed, prosperous, rich, wealthy, well-off, well-to-do

heel² cant, careen, incline, keel over, lean over, list, tilt

hefty 1. beefy (*Inf.*), big, brawny, burly, hulking, husky (*Inf.*), massive, muscular, Ramboesque, robust, strapping, strong **2.** forceful, heavy, powerful, thumping (*Sl.*), vigorous **3.** ample, awkward, bulky, colossal, cumbersome, heavy, large, massive, ponderous, substantial, tremendous, unwieldy, weighty
Antonyms agile, diminutive, feeble, frail, inconsequential, ineffectual, infinitesimal, insignificant, light, little, mild, minute, narrow, petty, pocket-sized, scanty, short, slight, slim, small, soft, thin, tiny, trivial, weak, weedy (*Inf.*), wimpish *or* wimpy (*Inf.*)

height 1. altitude, elevation, highness, loftiness, stature, tallness **2.** apex, apogee, crest, crown, elevation, hill, mountain, peak, pinnacle, summit, top, vertex, zenith **3.** acme, dignity, eminence, exaltation, grandeur, loftiness, prominence **4.** climax, culmination, extremity, limit, maximum, *ne plus ultra*, ultimate, utmost degree, uttermost
Antonyms abyss, base, bottom, canyon, chasm, depth, lowland, lowness, low point, minimum, moderation, nadir, ravine, shortness, smallness, tininess, triviality, valley

heighten 1. add to, aggravate, amplify, augment, enhance, improve, increase, intensify, magnify, sharpen, strengthen **2.** elevate, enhance, ennoble, exalt, magnify, raise, uplift

heir beneficiary, heiress (*Fem.*), inheritor, inheritress *or* inheritrix (*Fem.*), next in line, scion, successor

hell 1. Abaddon, abode of the damned, abyss, Acheron (*Greek myth*), bottomless pit, fire and brimstone, Gehenna (*New Testament, Judaism*), Hades (*Greek myth*), hellfire, infernal regions, inferno, lower world, nether world, Tartarus (*Greek myth*), underworld **2.** affliction, agony, anguish, martyrdom, misery, nightmare, ordeal, suffering, torment, trial, wretchedness **3. hell for leather** at the double, full-tilt, headlong, hotfoot, hurriedly, like a bat out of hell (*Sl.*), pell-mell, posthaste, quickly, speedily, swiftly

hellish 1. damnable, damned, demoniacal,

devilish, diabolical, fiendish, infernal **2.** abominable, accursed, atrocious, barbarous, cruel, detestable, execrable, inhuman, monstrous, nefarious, vicious, wicked
Antonyms admirable, agreeable, benevolent, delightful, fine, gentle, good, harmless, honourable, humane, innocuous, kind, merciful, noble, pleasant, virtuous, wonderful

helm 1. *Nautical* rudder, steering gear, tiller, wheel **2.** *Fig.* command, control, direction, leadership, rule **3. at the helm** at the wheel, directing, in charge, in command, in control, in the driving seat, in the saddle

help v. **1.** abet, aid, assist, back, befriend, cooperate, encourage, lend a hand, promote, relieve, save, second, serve, stand by, succour, support **2.** alleviate, ameliorate, cure, ease, facilitate, heal, improve, mitigate, relieve, remedy, restore **3.** abstain, avoid, control, eschew, forbear, hinder, keep from, prevent, refrain from, resist, shun, withstand ~*n.* **4.** advice, aid, assistance, avail, benefit, cooperation, guidance, helping hand, promotion, service, support, use, utility **5.** assistant, employee, hand, helper, worker **6.** balm, corrective, cure, relief, remedy, restorative, salve, succour
Antonyms v. aggravate, bar, block, discourage, fight, foil, frustrate, harm, hinder, hurt, impede, injure, irritate, make worse, obstruct, oppose ~*n.* aggravation, bane, block, discouragement, hindrance, irritant, obstruction, opposition

helper abettor, adjutant, aide, aider, ally, assistant, attendant, auxiliary, coadjutor, collaborator, colleague, deputy, helpmate, henchman, mate, partner, protagonist, right-hand man, second, subsidiary, supporter

helpful 1. advantageous, beneficial, constructive, favourable, fortunate, practical, productive, profitable, serviceable, timely, useful **2.** accommodating, beneficent, benevolent, caring, considerate, cooperative, friendly, kind, neighbourly, supportive, sympathetic

helping *n.* dollop (*Inf.*), piece, plateful, portion, ration, serving

helpless 1. abandoned, defenceless, dependent, destitute, exposed, forlorn, unprotected, vulnerable **2.** debilitated, disabled, feeble, impotent, incapable, incompetent, infirm, paralysed, powerless, unfit, weak
Antonyms able, capable, competent, equipped, fit, hardy, healthy, hearty, invulnerable, mighty, powerful, robust, safe, secure, solid, strong, sturdy, thriving, tough, well-protected

helter-skelter 1. *adv.* carelessly, hastily, headlong, hurriedly, pell-mell, rashly, recklessly, wildly **2.** *adj.* anyhow, confused, disordered, haphazard, higgledy-piggledy (*Inf.*), hit-or-miss, jumbled, muddled, random, topsy-turvy

hem 1. *n.* border, edge, fringe, margin, trimming **2.** *v. Usually with* **in** beset, border, circumscribe, confine, edge, enclose, environ, hedge in, restrict, shut in, skirt, surround

hence ergo, for this reason, on that account, therefore, thus

henceforth from now on, from this day forward, hence, hereafter, hereinafter, in the future

henpecked browbeaten, bullied, cringing, dominated, led by the nose, meek, subject, subjugated, timid, treated like dirt
Antonyms aggressive, assertive, bossy (*Inf.*), dominating, domineering, forceful, macho, overbearing, Ramboesque, self-assertive, spirited, wilful

herald *n.* **1.** bearer of tidings, crier, messenger **2.** forerunner, harbinger, indication, omen, precursor, sign, signal, token ~*v.* **3.** advertise, announce, broadcast, proclaim, publicize, publish, trumpet **4.** foretoken, harbinger, indicate, pave the way, portend, precede, presage, promise, show, usher in

herd *n.* **1.** assemblage, collection, crowd, crush, drove, flock, horde, mass, mob, multitude, press, swarm, throng **2.** mob, populace, rabble, riffraff, the hoi polloi, the masses, the plebs ~*v.* **3.** assemble, associate, collect, congregate, flock, gather, huddle, muster, rally **4.** drive, force, goad, guide, lead, shepherd, spur

hereafter 1. *adv.* after this, from now on, hence, henceforth, henceforward, in future **2.** *n.* afterlife, future life, life after death, next world, the beyond

hereditary 1. family, genetic, inborn, inbred, inheritable, transmissible **2.** ancestral, bequeathed, handed down, inherited, patrimonial, traditional, transmitted, willed

heredity congenital traits, constitution, genetic make-up, genetics, inheritance

heresy apostasy, dissidence, error, heterodoxy, iconoclasm, impiety, revisionism, schism, unorthodoxy

heretic apostate, dissenter, dissident, nonconformist, renegade, revisionist, schismatic, sectarian, separatist

heretical freethinking, heterodox, iconoclastic, idolatrous, impious, revisionist, schismatic, unorthodox

heritage bequest, birthright, endowment, estate, inheritance, legacy, lot, patrimony, portion, share, tradition

hermit anchoret, anchorite, eremite, monk, recluse, solitary, stylite

hero 1. celeb (*Inf.*), celebrity, champion,

conqueror, exemplar, great man, heart-throb (*Brit.*), idol, man of the hour, megastar (*Inf.*), popular figure, star, superstar, victor **2.** lead actor, leading man, male lead, principal male character, protagonist

heroic 1. bold, brave, courageous, daring, dauntless, doughty, fearless, gallant, intrepid, lion-hearted, stouthearted, undaunted, valiant, valorous **2.** classical, Homeric, legendary, mythological **3.** classic, elevated, epic, exaggerated, extravagant, grand, grandiose, high-flown, inflated
Antonyms (*sense 1*) base, chicken (*Sl.*), cowardly, craven, faint-hearted, ignoble, irresolute, mean, timid (*sense 3*) lowbrow, simple, unadorned

heroine 1. celeb (*Inf.*), celebrity, goddess, ideal, megastar (*Inf.*), woman of the hour **2.** diva, female lead, lead actress, leading lady, prima donna, principal female character, protagonist

heroism boldness, bravery, courage, courageousness, daring, fearlessness, fortitude, gallantry, intrepidity, prowess, spirit, valour

hero worship admiration, adoration, adulation, idealization, idolization, putting on a pedestal, veneration

hesitant diffident, doubtful, half-arsed, half-assed (*U.S. & Canad. sl.*), half-hearted, halting, hanging back, hesitating, irresolute, lacking confidence, reluctant, sceptical, shy, timid, uncertain, unsure, vacillating, wavering
Antonyms arrogant, avid, clear, confident, definite, determined, dogmatic, eager, enthusiastic, firm, forceful, keen, positive, resolute, self-assured, spirited, sure, unhesitating, unwavering

hesitate 1. be uncertain, delay, dither (*Chiefly Brit.*), doubt, haver (*Brit.*), pause, shillyshally (*Inf.*), swither (*Scot.*), vacillate, wait, waver **2.** balk, be reluctant, be unwilling, boggle, demur, hang back, scruple, shrink from, think twice **3.** falter, fumble, hem and haw, stammer, stumble, stutter
Antonyms (*sense 1*) be confident, be decisive, be firm, continue, decide (*sense 2*) be determined, resolve, welcome

hesitation 1. delay, doubt, dubiety, hesitancy, indecision, irresolution, uncertainty, vacillation **2.** demurral, misgiving(s), qualm(s), reluctance, scruple(s), unwillingness **3.** faltering, fumbling, hemming and hawing, stammering, stumbling, stuttering

hew 1. axe, chop, cut, hack, lop, split **2.** carve, fashion, form, make, model, sculpt, sculpture, shape, smooth

heyday bloom, flowering, pink, prime, prime of life, salad days

hiatus aperture, blank, breach, break,

chasm, discontinuity, entr'acte, gap, inter~
ruption, interval, lacuna, lapse, opening,
respite, rift, space

hibernate hole up, lie dormant, overwinter,
remain torpid, sleep snug, vegetate, winter

hidden abstruse, clandestine, close, con~
cealed, covered, covert, cryptic, dark, her~
metic, hermetical, masked, mysterious,
mystic, mystical, obscure, occult, recondite,
secret, shrouded, ulterior, unrevealed, un~
seen, veiled

hide¹ 1. cache, conceal, go into hiding, go to
ground, go underground, hole up, lie low,
secrete, stash (*Inf.*), take cover **2.** blot out,
bury, camouflage, cloak, conceal, cover,
disguise, eclipse, mask, obscure, screen,
shelter, shroud, veil **3.** hush up, keep se~
cret, suppress, withhold
Antonyms admit, bare, confess, disclose,
display, divulge, exhibit, expose, find, flaunt,
reveal, show, uncover, unveil

hide² fell, pelt, skin

hidebound brassbound, conventional, nar~
row, narrow-minded, rigid, set, set in one's
ways, strait-laced, ultraconservative
Antonyms broad-minded, flexible, liberal,
open, receptive, tolerant, unconventional,
unorthodox

hideous 1. ghastly, grim, grisly, grotesque,
gruesome, monstrous, repulsive, revolting,
ugly, unsightly **2.** abominable, appalling,
awful, detestable, disgusting, dreadful,
godawful (*Sl.*), horrendous, horrible, horrid,
loathsome, macabre, obscene, odious,
shocking, sickening, terrible, terrifying
Antonyms appealing, beautiful, captivating,
charming, entrancing, lovely, pleasant,
pleasing

hide-out den, hideaway, hiding place, lair,
secret place, shelter

hiding *n.* beating, caning, drubbing,
flogging, larruping (*Brit. dialect*), lathering
(*Inf.*), licking (*Inf.*), spanking, tanning (*Sl.*),
thrashing, walloping (*Inf.*), whaling, whip~
ping

hierarchy grading, pecking order, ranking

hieroglyphic *adj.* enigmatical, figurative,
indecipherable, obscure, runic, symbolical

high *adj.* **1.** elevated, lofty, soaring, steep,
tall, towering **2.** excessive, extraordinary,
extreme, great, intensified, sharp, strong **3.**
arch, big-time (*Inf.*), chief, consequential,
distinguished, eminent, exalted, important,
influential, leading, major league (*Inf.*), no~
table, powerful, prominent, ruling,
significant, superior **4.** arrogant, boastful,
bragging, despotic, domineering, haughty,
lofty, lordly, ostentatious, overbearing,
proud, tyrannical, vainglorious **5.** capital,
extreme, grave, important, serious **6.** bois~

terous, bouncy (*Inf.*), cheerful, elated, excit~
ed, exhilarated, exuberant, joyful, light-
hearted, merry, strong, tumultuous, turbu~
lent **7.** *Inf.* delirious, euphoric, freaked out
(*Inf.*), hyped up (*Sl.*), inebriated, intoxicat~
ed, on a trip (*Inf.*), spaced out (*Sl.*), stoned
(*Sl.*), tripping (*Inf.*), turned on (*Sl.*), zonked
(*Sl.*) **8.** costly, dear, exorbitant, expensive,
high-priced, steep (*Inf.*), stiff **9.** acute,
high-pitched, penetrating, piercing, piping,
sharp, shrill, soprano, strident, treble **10.**
extravagant, grand, lavish, luxurious, rich
11. gamy, niffy (*Brit. sl.*), pongy (*Brit. inf.*),
strong-flavoured, tainted, whiffy (*Brit. sl.*)
12. high and dry abandoned, bereft, desti~
tute, helpless, stranded **13. high and low**
all over, everywhere, exhaustively, far and
wide, in every nook and cranny **14. high
and mighty** *Inf.* arrogant, cavalier, con~
ceited, disdainful, haughty, imperious,
overbearing, self-important, snobbish,
stuck-up (*Inf.*), superior ~*adv.* **15.** aloft, at
great height, far up, way up ~*n.* **16.** apex,
crest, height, peak, record level, summit,
top **17.** *Inf.* delirium, ecstasy, euphoria, in~
toxication, trip (*Inf.*)
Antonyms (*sense 1*) dwarfed, low, short,
stunted (*sense 2*) average, low, mild, moderate,
reduced, restrained, routine, suppressed
(*sense 3*) average, common, degraded, ignoble,
inconsequential, insignificant, low, lowly,
low-ranking, menial, routine, secondary, un~
distinguished, unimportant (*sense 6*) angry,
dejected, depressed, gloomy, low, melancholy,
sad (*sense 9*) alto, bass, deep, gruff, low, low-
pitched

highbrow 1. *n.* aesthete, Brahmin (*U.S.*),
brain (*Inf.*), brainbox (*Sl.*), egghead (*Inf.*),
intellectual, mastermind, savant, scholar **2.**
adj. bookish, brainy (*Inf.*), cultivated, cul~
tured, deep, highbrowed, intellectual, so~
phisticated
Antonyms *n.* idiot, ignoramus, illiterate,
imbecile (*Inf.*), lowbrow, moron, philistine
~*adj.* ignorant, lowbrow, philistine, shallow,
uncultivated, uninformed, unintellectual,
unlearned, unsophisticated

high-class A1 *or* A-one (*Inf.*), choice, classy
(*Sl.*), elite, exclusive, first-rate, high-quality,
high-toned, posh (*Inf., chiefly Brit.*), ritzy
(*Sl.*), select, superior, swish (*Inf., chiefly
Brit.*), tip-top, top-drawer, top-flight, tops
(*Sl.*), U (*Brit. inf.*), up-market, upper-class
Antonyms cheap, cheapo (*Inf.*), common,
inferior, mediocre, ordinary, run-of-the-mill

highfalutin, highfaluting big, bombastic,
florid, grandiose, high-flown, high-sounding,
lofty, magniloquent, pompous, pretentious,
supercilious, swanky (*Inf.*)

high-flown elaborate, exaggerated, ex~
travagant, florid, grandiose, high-falutin

(*Inf.*), inflated, lofty, magniloquent, over~ blown, pretentious

Antonyms down-to-earth, moderate, mod~ est, practical, pragmatic, realistic, reason~ able, restrained, sensible, simple, straight~ forward, unpretentious

high-handed arbitrary, autocratic, bossy (*Inf.*), despotic, dictatorial, domineering, imperious, inconsiderate, oppressive, over~ bearing, peremptory, self-willed, tyrannical, wilful

highlands heights, hill country, hills, mesa, mountainous region, plateau, tableland, uplands

highlight 1. *n.* best part, climax, feature, focal point, focus, high point, high spot, main feature, memorable part, peak **2.** *v.* accent, accentuate, bring to the fore, em~ phasize, feature, focus attention on, give prominence to, play up, set off, show up, spotlight, stress, underline

Antonyms *n.* disappointment, low point ~*v.* de-emphasize, gloss over, neglect, overlook, play down

highly 1. decidedly, eminently, exceptional~ ly, extraordinarily, extremely, greatly, im~ mensely, supremely, tremendously, vastly, very, very much **2.** appreciatively, approvingly, enthusiastically, favourably, warmly, well

highly strung easily upset, edgy, excitable, irascible, irritable, nervous, nervy (*Brit. inf.*), neurotic, restless, sensitive, stressed, taut, temperamental, tense, tetchy, twitchy (*Inf.*), wired (*Sl.*)

Antonyms calm, collected, easy-going, even-tempered, laid-back (*Inf.*), placid, re~ laxed, serene, unfazed (*Inf.*)

high-minded elevated, ethical, fair, good, honourable, idealistic, magnanimous, mor~ al, noble, principled, pure, righteous, upright, virtuous, worthy

Antonyms dishonest, dishonourable, un~ ethical, unfair

high-powered aggressive, driving, dy~ namic, effective, energetic, enterprising, fast-track, forceful, go-ahead, go-getting (*Inf.*), highly capable, vigorous

high-pressure *Of salesmanship* aggressive, bludgeoning, coercive, compelling, forceful, high-powered, importunate, insistent, in~ tensive, persistent, persuasive, pushy (*Inf.*)

high-sounding affected, artificial, bom~ bastic, extravagant, flamboyant, florid, grandiloquent, grandiose, high-flown, im~ posing, magniloquent, ostentatious, over~ blown, pompous, pretentious, stilted, strained

high-speed brisk, express, fast, hotted-up (*Inf.*), quick, rapid, souped-up (*Inf.*), streamlined, swift

high-spirited animated, boisterous, bold, bouncy, daring, dashing, ebullient, effer~ vescent, energetic, exuberant, frolicsome, full of life, fun-loving, gallant, lively, met~ tlesome, sparky, spirited, spunky (*Inf.*), vi~ brant, vital, vivacious

high spirits abandon, boisterousness, ex~ hilaration, exuberance, good cheer, hilarity, *joie de vivre*, rare good humour

hijack commandeer, expropriate, seize, sky~ jack, take over

hike *v.* **1.** back-pack, hoof it (*Sl.*), leg it (*Inf.*), ramble, tramp, walk **2.** *Usually with* **up** hitch up, jack up, lift, pull up, raise ~*n.* **3.** journey on foot, march, ramble, tramp, trek, walk

hilarious amusing, comical, convivial, en~ tertaining, exhilarated, funny, gay, happy, humorous, jolly, jovial, joyful, joyous, mer~ ry, mirthful, noisy, rollicking, side-splitting, uproarious

Antonyms dull, gloomy, quiet, sad, sedate, serious

hilarity amusement, boisterousness, cheer~ fulness, conviviality, exhilaration, exuber~ ance, gaiety, glee, high spirits, jollification, jollity, joviality, joyousness, laughter, lev~ ity, merriment, mirth

hill 1. brae (*Scot.*), down (*Archaic*), elevation, eminence, fell, height, hillock, hilltop, knoll, mound, mount, prominence, tor **2.** drift, heap, hummock, mound, pile, stack **3.** ac~ clivity, brae (*Scot.*), climb, gradient, incline, rise, slope

hillock barrow, hummock, knap (*Dialect*), knoll, monticule, mound, tump (*Western Brit. dialect*)

hilt 1. grip, haft, handgrip, handle, helve **2. to the hilt** completely, entirely, fully, total~ ly, wholly

hind after, back, caudal (*Anat.*), hinder, pos~ terior, rear

hinder arrest, block, check, debar, delay, deter, encumber, frustrate, hamper, ham~ string, handicap, hold up *or* back, impede, interrupt, obstruct, oppose, prevent, retard, slow down, stop, stymie, thwart, trammel

Antonyms accelerate, advance, aid, benefit, encourage, expedite, facilitate, further, help, hurry, promote, quicken, speed, support

hindmost concluding, final, furthest, fur~ thest behind, last, most remote, rearmost, terminal, trailing, ultimate

hindrance bar, barrier, block, check, deter~ rent, difficulty, drag, drawback, encum~ brance, handicap, hitch, impediment, inter~ ruption, limitation, obstacle, obstruction, restraint, restriction, snag, stoppage, stum~ bling block, trammel

Antonyms advancement, advantage, aid,

asset, assistance, benefit, boon, boost, en~
couragement, furtherance, help, support

hinge v. be contingent, be subject to, de~
pend, hang, pivot, rest, revolve around,
turn

hint n. **1.** allusion, clue, implication, indica~
tion, inkling, innuendo, insinuation, inti~
mation, mention, reminder, suggestion,
tip-off, word to the wise **2.** advice, help,
pointer, suggestion, tip, wrinkle (*Inf.*) **3.**
breath, dash, *soupçon*, speck, suggestion,
suspicion, taste, tinge, touch, trace, under~
tone, whiff, whisper ~v. **4.** allude, cue, im~
ply, indicate, insinuate, intimate, let it be
known, mention, prompt, suggest, tip off

hippie beatnik, bohemian, dropout, flower
child

hire v. **1.** appoint, commission, employ, en~
gage, sign up, take on **2.** charter, engage,
lease, let, rent ~n. **3.** charge, cost, fee,
price, rent, rental

hiss n. **1.** buzz, hissing, sibilance, sibilation
2. boo, catcall, contempt, derision, jeer,
raspberry ~v. **3.** rasp, shrill, sibilate,
wheeze, whirr, whistle, whiz **4.** blow a
raspberry, boo, catcall, condemn, damn, de~
cry, deride, hoot, jeer, mock, revile, ridicule

historian annalist, biographer, chronicler,
historiographer, recorder

historic celebrated, consequential, epoch-
making, extraordinary, famous, momen~
tous, notable, outstanding, red-letter, re~
markable, significant
Antonyms ordinary, uncelebrated, unim~
portant, unknown

historical actual, archival, attested,
authentic, chronicled, documented, factual,
real, verifiable
Antonyms contemporary, current, fabulous,
fictional, legendary, mythical, present-day

history **1.** account, annals, autobiography,
biography, chronicle, memoirs, narration,
narrative, recapitulation, recital, record,
relation, saga, story **2.** ancient history, an~
tiquity, bygone times, days of old, days of
yore, olden days, the good old days, the old
days, the past, yesterday, yesteryear

hit v. **1.** bang, bash (*Inf.*), batter, beat, belt
(*Inf.*), chin (*Sl.*), clip (*Inf.*), clobber (*Sl.*),
clout (*Inf.*), cuff, deck (*Sl.*), flog, knock,
lambast(e), lay one on (*Sl.*), lob, punch, slap,
smack, smite (*Archaic*), sock (*Sl.*), strike,
swat, thump, wallop (*Inf.*), whack **2.** bang
into, bump, clash with, collide with, crash
against, meet head-on, run into, smash into
3. accomplish, achieve, arrive at, attain,
gain, reach, secure, strike, touch **4.** affect,
damage, devastate, impinge on, influence,
leave a mark on, make an impact *or* im~
pression on, move, overwhelm, touch ~n.
5. belt (*Inf.*), blow, bump, clash, clout (*Inf.*),

collision, cuff, impact, knock, rap, shot,
slap, smack, stroke, swipe (*Inf.*), wallop
(*Inf.*) **6.** *Inf.* sellout, sensation, smash (*Inf.*),
success, triumph, winner

hitch v. **1.** attach, connect, couple, fasten,
harness, join, make fast, tether, tie, unite,
yoke **2.** *Often with* up hoick, jerk, pull, tug,
yank **3.** *Inf.* hitchhike, thumb a lift ~n. **4.**
catch, check, delay, difficulty, drawback,
hassle (*Inf.*), hindrance, hold-up, impedi~
ment, mishap, obstacle, problem, snag,
stoppage, trouble

hither close, closer, here, near, nearer, nigh
(*Archaic*), over here, to this place

hitherto heretofore, previously, so far, thus
far, till now, until now, up to now

hit off **1.** capture, catch, impersonate, mim~
ic, represent, take off (*Inf.*) **2. hit it off** *Inf.*
be on good terms, click (*Sl.*), get on (well)
with, take to, warm to

hit on *or* **upon** arrive at, chance upon,
come upon, discover, guess, invent, light
upon, realize, strike upon, stumble on,
think up

hit or miss aimless, casual, cursory, disor~
ganized, haphazard, indiscriminate, per~
functory, random, undirected, uneven
Antonyms arranged, deliberate, organized,
planned, systematic

hit out (at) assail, attack, castigate, con~
demn, denounce, inveigh against, lash out,
rail against, strike out at

hoard **1.** n. accumulation, cache, fall-back,
fund, heap, mass, pile, reserve, stockpile,
store, supply, treasure-trove **2.** v. accumu~
late, amass, buy up, cache, collect, deposit,
garner, gather, hive, lay up, put away, put
by, save, stash away (*Inf.*), stockpile, store,
treasure

hoarder collector, magpie (*Brit.*), miser,
niggard, saver, squirrel (*Inf.*), tight-arse
(*Taboo sl.*), tight-ass (*U.S. taboo sl.*)

hoarse croaky, discordant, grating, gravelly,
growling, gruff, guttural, harsh, husky,
rasping, raucous, rough, throaty
Antonyms harmonious, mellifluous, mel~
low, melodious, smooth

hoary **1.** frosty, grey, grey-haired, grizzled,
hoar, silvery, white, white-haired **2.** aged,
ancient, antiquated, antique, old, venerable

hoax **1.** n. canard, cheat, con (*Inf.*), decep~
tion, fast one (*Inf.*), fraud, imposture, joke,
practical joke, prank, ruse, spoof (*Inf.*),
swindle, trick **2.** v. bamboozle (*Inf.*), befool,
bluff, con (*Sl.*), deceive, delude, dupe, fool,
gammon (*Brit. inf.*), gull (*Archaic*), hood~
wink, hornswoggle (*Sl.*), kid (*Inf.*), swindle,
take in (*Inf.*), take (someone) for a ride
(*Inf.*), trick, wind up (*Brit. sl.*)

hobby diversion, favourite occupation, (lei~

sure) activity, leisure pursuit, pastime, re~laxation, sideline

hobnob associate, consort, fraternize, hang about, hang out (*Inf.*), keep company, min~gle, mix, socialize

hogwash balderdash, balls (*Taboo sl.*), bilge (*Inf.*), bosh (*Inf.*), bull (*Sl.*), bullshit (*Taboo sl.*), bunk (*Inf.*), bunkum *or* bun~combe (*Chiefly U.S.*), cobblers (*Brit. taboo sl.*), crap (*Sl.*), drivel, eyewash (*Inf.*), gar~bage (*Inf.*), guff (*Sl.*), hokum (*Sl., chiefly U.S. & Canad.*), hooey (*Sl.*), horsefeathers (*U.S. sl.*), hot air (*Inf.*), moonshine, nonsense, pap, piffle (*Inf.*), poppycock (*Inf.*), rot, rub~bish, shit (*Taboo sl.*), tommyrot, tosh (*Sl., chiefly Brit.*), trash, tripe (*Inf.*), twaddle

hoi polloi admass, *canaille,* commonalty, riffraff, the (common) herd, the common people, the great unwashed (*Inf. & deroga~tory*), the lower orders, the masses, the plebs, the populace, the proles (*Derogatory sl., chiefly Brit.*), the proletariat, the rabble, the third estate, the underclass

hoist 1. *v.* elevate, erect, heave, lift, raise, rear, upraise **2.** *n.* crane, elevator, lift, tackle, winch

hold *v.* **1.** have, keep, maintain, occupy, own, possess, retain **2.** adhere, clasp, cleave, clinch, cling, clutch, cradle, em~brace, enfold, grasp, grip, stick **3.** arrest, bind, check, confine, curb, detain, impound, imprison, pound, restrain, stay, stop, sus~pend **4.** assume, believe, consider, deem, entertain, esteem, judge, maintain, pre~sume, reckon, regard, think, view **5.** con~tinue, endure, last, persevere, persist, re~main, resist, stay, wear **6.** assemble, call, carry on, celebrate, conduct, convene, have, officiate at, preside over, run, solemnize **7.** bear, brace, carry, prop, shoulder, support, sustain, take **8.** accommodate, comprise, contain, have a capacity for, seat, take **9.** apply, be in force, be the case, exist, hold good, operate, remain true, remain valid, stand up **10. hold one's own** do well, hold fast, hold out, keep one's head above water, keep pace, keep up, maintain one's position, stand firm, stand one's ground, stay put, stick to one's guns (*Inf.*) ~*n.* **11.** clasp, clutch, grasp, grip **12.** anchorage, foothold, footing, leverage, prop, purchase, stay, sup~port, vantage **13.** ascendancy, authority, clout (*Inf.*), control, dominance, dominion, influence, mastery, pull (*Inf.*), sway
Antonyms bestow, break, call off, cancel, come undone, deny, disavow, disclaim, free, give, give up, give way, hand over, let go, let loose, loosen, offer, postpone, put down, re~fute, reject, release, turn over

hold back 1. check, control, curb, inhibit,

rein, repress, restrain, suppress **2.** desist, forbear, keep back, refuse, withhold

holder 1. bearer, custodian, incumbent, keeper, occupant, owner, possessor, propri~etor, purchaser **2.** case, container, cover, housing, receptacle, sheath

hold forth declaim, descant, discourse, go on, harangue, lecture, orate, preach, speak, speechify, spiel (*Inf.*), spout (*Inf.*)

hold off 1. avoid, defer, delay, keep from, postpone, put off, refrain **2.** fend off, keep off, rebuff, repel, repulse, stave off

hold out 1. extend, give, offer, present, proffer **2.** carry on, continue, endure, hang on, last, persevere, persist, stand fast, with~stand

hold over adjourn, defer, delay, postpone, put off, suspend, waive

hold-up 1. bottleneck, delay, difficulty, hitch, obstruction, setback, snag, stoppage, traffic jam, trouble, wait **2.** burglary, mug~ging (*Inf.*), robbery, steaming (*Inf.*), stick-up (*Sl., chiefly U.S.*), theft

hold up 1. delay, detain, hinder, impede, retard, set back, slow down, stop **2.** bolster, brace, buttress, jack up, prop, shore up, support, sustain **3.** mug (*Inf.*), rob, stick up (*Sl., chiefly U.S.*), waylay **4.** display, exhibit, flaunt, present, show **5.** bear up, endure, last, survive, wear

hold with agree to *or* with, approve of, be in favour of, countenance, subscribe to, support, take kindly to
Antonyms be against, disagree with, disap~prove of, hold out against, oppose

hole 1. aperture, breach, break, crack, fissure, gap, opening, orifice, outlet, perfo~ration, puncture, rent, split, tear, vent **2.** cave, cavern, cavity, chamber, depression, excavation, hollow, pit, pocket, scoop, shaft **3.** burrow, covert, den, earth, lair, nest, re~treat, shelter **4.** *Inf.* dive (*Sl.*), dump (*Inf.*), hovel, joint (*Sl.*), slum **5.** *Inf.* cell, dungeon, oubliette, prison **6.** defect, discrepancy, er~ror, fallacy, fault, flaw, inconsistency, loop~hole **7.** *Sl.* dilemma, fix (*Inf.*), hot water (*Inf.*), imbroglio, jam (*Inf.*), mess, predica~ment, quandary, scrape (*Inf.*), spot (*Inf.*), tangle, tight spot **8. pick holes in** asperse, bad-mouth (*Sl., chiefly U.S. & Canad.*), cavil, crab (*Inf.*), criticize, denigrate, disparage, disprove, find fault, knock (*Inf.*), niggle, pull to pieces, put down, rubbish (*Inf.*), run down, slag (off) (*Sl.*), slate (*Inf.*)

hole-and-corner backstairs, clandestine, furtive, secret, secretive, sneaky (*Inf.*), stealthy, surreptitious, underhand, under the counter (*Inf.*)
Antonyms above-board, candid, frank, open, public

holiday 1. break, leave, recess, time off, va~ cation **2.** anniversary, bank holiday, cel~ ebration, feast, festival, festivity, fête, gala, public holiday, saint's day

holier-than-thou goody-goody (*Inf.*), pi~ etistic, pietistical, priggish, religiose, sanc~ timonious, self-righteous, self-satisfied, smug, squeaky-clean, unctuous

holiness blessedness, devoutness, divinity, godliness, piety, purity, religiousness, righteousness, sacredness, saintliness, sanctity, spirituality, virtuousness

hollow *adj.* **1.** empty, not solid, unfilled, vacant, void **2.** cavernous, concave, deep-set, depressed, indented, sunken **3.** deep, dull, expressionless, flat, low, muffled, mut~ ed, reverberant, rumbling, sepulchral, toneless **4.** empty, fruitless, futile, mean~ ingless, pointless, Pyrrhic, specious, un~ availing, useless, vain, worthless **5.** empty, famished, hungry, ravenous, starved **6.** artificial, cynical, deceitful, faithless, false, flimsy, hollow-hearted, hypocritical, insin~ cere, treacherous, unsound, weak **7. beat (someone) hollow** *Inf.* defeat, hammer (*Inf.*), outdo, overcome, rout, thrash, trounce, worst ~*n.* **8.** basin, bowl, cave, cavern, cavity, concavity, crater, cup, den, dent, depression, dimple, excavation, hole, indentation, pit, trough **9.** bottom, dale, dell, dingle, glen, valley ~*v.* **10.** channel, dig, dish, excavate, furrow, gouge, groove, pit, scoop
Antonyms *adj.* (*sense 1*) full, occupied, solid (*sense 2*) convex, rounded (*sense 3*) expressive, vibrant (*sense 4*) gratifying, meaningful, pleasing, satisfying, valuable, worthwhile (*sense 6*) genuine ~*n.* (*sense 8*) bump, mound, projection (*sense 9*) bluff, height, hill, knoll, mountain, rise

holocaust annihilation, carnage, conflagra~ tion, destruction, devastation, fire, geno~ cide, inferno, massacre, mass murder

holy 1. devout, divine, faithful, god-fearing, godly, hallowed, pious, pure, religious, righteous, saintly, sublime, virtuous **2.** blessed, consecrated, dedicated, hallowed, sacred, sacrosanct, sanctified, venerable, venerated
Antonyms blasphemous, corrupt, desecrat~ ed, earthly, evil, human, immoral, impious, irreligious, sacrilegious, secular, sinful, un~ consecrated, unhallowed, unholy, unsancti~ fied, wicked, worldly

homage 1. admiration, adoration, adula~ tion, awe, deference, devotion, duty, esteem, honour, respect, reverence, worship **2.** al~ legiance, devotion, faithfulness, fealty, fidelity, loyalty, obeisance, service, tribute, troth (*Archaic*)

Antonyms condemnation, contempt, dis~ dain, disregard, disrespect, irreverence, scorn

home *n.* **1.** abode, domicile, dwelling, dwelling place, habitation, house, pad (*Sl.*), residence **2.** birthplace, family, fireside, hearth, homestead, home town, household **3.** abode, element, environment, habitat, habitation, haunt, home ground, range, stamping ground, territory **4. at home a.** available, in, present **b.** at ease, comfort~ able, familiar, relaxed **c.** entertaining, giv~ ing a party, having guests, receiving **d.** *As a noun* party, reception, soirée **5. at home in, on,** *or* **with** conversant with, familiar with, knowledgeable, proficient, skilled, well-versed **6. bring home to** drive home, emphasize, impress upon, make clear, press home ~*adj.* **7.** central, domestic, familiar, family, household, inland, internal, local, national, native

homeland country of origin, fatherland, mother country, motherland, native land

homeless 1. *adj.* abandoned, destitute, dis~ placed, dispossessed, down-and-out, exiled, forlorn, forsaken, outcast, unsettled **2.** *n.* **the homeless** dossers (*Brit. sl.*), squatters, vagrants

homelike cheerful, comfortable, cosy, easy, familiar, homy, informal, intimate, relax~ ing, snug

homely comfortable, comfy (*Inf.*), cosy, do~ mestic, downhome (*Sl., chiefly U.S.*), every~ day, familiar, friendly, homelike, home~ spun, homy, informal, modest, natural, or~ dinary, plain, simple, unaffected, unassum~ ing, unpretentious, welcoming
Antonyms affected, elaborate, elegant, grand, ostentatious, pretentious, refined, re~ gal, sophisticated, splendid

homespun artless, coarse, homely, home~ made, inelegant, plain, rough, rude, rustic, unpolished, unsophisticated

homicidal deadly, death-dealing, lethal, maniacal, mortal, murderous

homicide 1. bloodshed, killing, man~ slaughter, murder, slaying **2.** killer, mur~ derer, slayer

homily address, discourse, lecture, preach~ ing, preachment, sermon

homogeneity analogousness, comparabil~ ity, consistency, correspondence, identical~ ness, oneness, sameness, similarity, uni~ formity

homogeneous akin, alike, analogous, cognate, comparable, consistent, identical, kindred, similar, uniform, unvarying
Antonyms different, disparate, dissimilar, divergent, diverse, heterogeneous, manifold, mixed, unlike, unrelated, varied, various, varying

homosexual *adj.* bent (*Sl.*), camp (*Inf.*), gay, homoerotic, lesbian, queer (*Inf., derogatory*), sapphic

honest 1. conscientious, decent, ethical, high-minded, honourable, law-abiding, reliable, reputable, scrupulous, trustworthy, trusty, truthful, upright, veracious, virtuous **2.** above board, authentic, bona fide, genuine, honest to goodness, on the level (*Inf.*), on the up and up, proper, real, straight, true **3.** equitable, fair, fair and square, impartial, just **4.** candid, direct, forthright, frank, ingenuous, open, outright, plain, sincere, straightforward, undisguised, unfeigned, upfront (*Inf.*)
Antonyms bad, corrupt, counterfeit, crooked, deceitful, disguised, dishonest, false, fraudulent, guilty, illegitimate, immoral, insincere, secretive, treacherous, unethical, unfair, unfaithful, unlawful, unprincipled, unreliable, unrighteous, unscrupulous, untrustworthy, untruthful

honestly 1. by fair means, cleanly, ethically, honourably, in good faith, lawfully, legally, legitimately, on the level (*Inf.*), with clean hands **2.** candidly, frankly, in all sincerity, in plain English, plainly, straight (out), to one's face, truthfully

honesty 1. faithfulness, fidelity, honour, incorruptibility, integrity, morality, probity, rectitude, reputability, scrupulousness, straightness, trustworthiness, truthfulness, uprightness, veracity, virtue **2.** bluntness, candour, equity, even-handedness, fairness, frankness, genuineness, openness, outspokenness, plainness, sincerity, straightforwardness

honorary complimentary, ex officio, formal, *honoris causa*, in name *or* title only, nominal, titular, unofficial, unpaid

honour *n.* **1.** credit, dignity, distinction, elevation, eminence, esteem, fame, glory, high standing, prestige, rank, renown, reputation, repute **2.** acclaim, accolade, adoration, Brownie points, commendation, deference, homage, kudos, praise, recognition, regard, respect, reverence, tribute, veneration **3.** decency, fairness, goodness, honesty, integrity, morality, principles, probity, rectitude, righteousness, trustworthiness, uprightness **4.** compliment, credit, favour, pleasure, privilege, source of pride *or* satisfaction **5.** chastity, innocence, modesty, purity, virginity, virtue ~*v.* **6.** admire, adore, appreciate, esteem, exalt, glorify, hallow, prize, respect, revere, reverence, value, venerate, worship **7.** be as good as (*Inf.*), be faithful to, be true to, carry out, discharge, fulfil, keep, live up to, observe **8.** acclaim, celebrate, commemorate, commend, compliment, crack up (*Inf.*), decorate, dignify, exalt, glorify, laud, lionize, praise **9.** accept, acknowledge, cash, clear, credit, pass, pay, take
Antonyms *n.* condemnation, contempt, degradation, disfavour, disgrace, dishonesty, dishonour, disrepute, disrespect, infamy, insincerity, insult, lowness, meanness, scorn, shame, slight, unscrupulousness ~*v.* condemn, defame, degrade, dishonour, disobey, insult, offend, refuse, scorn, slight

honourable 1. ethical, fair, high-minded, honest, just, moral, principled, true, trustworthy, trusty, upright, upstanding, virtuous **2.** distinguished, eminent, great, illustrious, noble, notable, noted, prestigious, renowned, venerable **3.** creditable, estimable, proper, reputable, respectable, respected, right, righteous, virtuous

honours adornments, awards, decorations, dignities, distinctions, laurels, titles

hoodwink bamboozle (*Inf.*), befool, cheat, con (*Inf.*), cozen, deceive, delude, dupe, fool, gull (*Archaic*), hoax, impose, kid (*Inf.*), lead up the garden path (*Inf.*), mislead, pull a fast one on (*Inf.*), rook (*Sl.*), swindle, trick

hook *n.* **1.** catch, clasp, fastener, hasp, holder, link, lock, peg **2.** noose, snare, springe, trap **3. by hook or by crook** by any means, by fair means or foul, somehow, somehow or other, someway **4. hook, line, and sinker** *Inf.* completely, entirely, thoroughly, through and through, totally, utterly, wholly **5. off the hook** *Sl.* acquitted, cleared, exonerated, in the clear, let off, under no obligation, vindicated ~*v.* **6.** catch, clasp, fasten, fix, hasp, secure **7.** catch, enmesh, ensnare, entrap, snare, trap

hooligan casual, delinquent, hoodlum (*Chiefly U.S.*), lager lout, ned (*Sl.*), rowdy, ruffian, tough, vandal, yob *or* yobbo (*Brit. sl.*)

hoop band, circlet, girdle, loop, ring, wheel

hoot *n.* **1.** call, cry, toot **2.** boo, catcall, hiss, jeer, yell **3.** *Inf.* card (*Inf.*), caution (*Inf.*), laugh (*Inf.*), scream (*Inf.*), ~*v.* **4.** boo, catcall, condemn, decry, denounce, execrate, hiss, howl down, jeer, yell at **5.** cry, scream, shout, shriek, toot, whoop, yell

hop 1. *v.* bound, caper, dance, jump, leap, skip, spring, trip, vault **2.** *n.* bounce, bound, jump, leap, skip, spring, step, vault

hope 1. *n.* ambition, anticipation, assumption, belief, confidence, desire, dream, expectancy, expectation, faith, longing **2.** *v.* anticipate, aspire, await, believe, contemplate, count on, desire, expect, foresee, long, look forward to, rely, trust
Antonyms despair, distrust, doubt, dread, hopelessness

hopeful 1. anticipating, assured, buoyant, confident, expectant, looking forward to, optimistic, sanguine **2.** auspicious, bright,

cheerful, encouraging, heartening, promis~
ing, propitious, reassuring, rosy
Antonyms (*sense 1*) cheerless, dejected, des~
pairing, hopeless, pessimistic (*sense 2*) de~
pressing, discouraging, disheartening, un~
promising

hopefully 1. confidently, expectantly, opti~
mistically, sanguinely **2.** *Inf.* all being well,
conceivably, expectedly, feasibly, probably

hopeless 1. defeatist, dejected, demoral~
ized, despairing, desperate, despondent,
disconsolate, downhearted, forlorn, in des~
pair, pessimistic, woebegone **2.** helpless,
incurable, irremediable, irreparable, irre~
versible, lost, past remedy, remediless **3.**
forlorn, futile, impossible, impracticable,
pointless, unachievable, unattainable, use~
less, vain **4.** *Inf.* inadequate, incompetent,
ineffectual, inferior, no good, pathetic, poor,
useless (*Inf.*)
Antonyms (*sense 1*) assured, cheerful,
confident, expectant, happy, heartened, hope~
ful, optimistic, uplifted (*sense 2*) curable, en~
couraging, favourable, heartening, promis~
ing, reassuring, remediable

horde band, crew, crowd, drove, gang, host,
mob, multitude, pack, press, swarm, throng,
troop

horizon 1. field of vision, skyline, vista **2.**
ambit, compass, ken, perspective, prospect,
purview, range, realm, scope, sphere,
stretch

horrible 1. abhorrent, abominable, appall~
ing, awful, dreadful, fearful, frightful,
ghastly, grim, grisly, gruesome, heinous,
hellacious (*U.S. sl.*), hideous, horrid, loath~
some, obscene, repulsive, revolting, shame~
ful, shocking, terrible, terrifying **2.** *Inf.*
awful, beastly (*Inf.*), cruel, disagreeable,
dreadful, ghastly (*Inf.*), horrid, mean, nasty,
terrible, unkind, unpleasant
Antonyms agreeable, appealing, attractive,
charming, delightful, enchanting, fetching,
lovely, pleasant, wonderful

horrid 1. awful, disagreeable, disgusting,
dreadful, horrible, nasty, obscene, offensive,
terrible, unpleasant, yucky *or* yukky (*Sl.*) **2.**
abominable, alarming, appalling, formi~
dable, frightening, hair-raising, harrowing,
hideous, horrific, odious, repulsive, revolt~
ing, shocking, terrifying, terrorizing **3.** *Inf.*
beastly (*Inf.*), cruel, mean, nas' ·, unkind

horrify 1. affright, alarm, frighten, intimi~
date, petrify, scare, terrify, terrorize **2.** ap~
pal, disgust, dismay, gross out (*U.S. sl.*),
outrage, shock, sicken
Antonyms comfort, delight, enchant, en~
courage, gladden, hearten, please, reassure,
soothe

horror 1. alarm, apprehension, awe, con~
sternation, dismay, dread, fear, fright, pan~

ic, terror **2.** abhorrence, abomination, an~
tipathy, aversion, detestation, disgust, ha~
tred, loathing, odium, repugnance, revul~
sion
Antonyms affinity, approval, attraction, de~
light, liking, love

horror-struck *or* **horror-stricken**
aghast, appalled, awe-struck, frightened to
death, horrified, petrified, scared out of
one's wits, shocked

horseman cavalier, cavalryman, dragoon,
equestrian, horse-soldier, rider

horseplay buffoonery, clowning, fooling
around, high jinks, pranks, romping,
rough-and-tumble, roughhousing (*Sl.*), sky~
larking (*Inf.*)

horse sense common sense, gumption
(*Brit. inf.*), judgment, mother wit, nous
(*Brit. sl.*), practicality

hospitable 1. amicable, bountiful, cordial,
friendly, generous, genial, gracious, kind,
liberal, sociable, welcoming **2.** accessible,
amenable, open-minded, receptive, respon~
sive, tolerant
Antonyms (*sense 1*) inhospitable, parsimo~
nious (*sense 2*) inhospitable, intolerant,
narrow-minded, unapproachable, unrecep~
tive

hospitality cheer, conviviality, cordiality,
friendliness, heartiness, hospitableness,
neighbourliness, sociability, warmth, wel~
come

host[1] *n.* **1.** entertainer, innkeeper, landlord,
master of ceremonies, proprietor **2.** anchor
man, compere (*Brit.*), presenter ~*v.* **3.**
compere (*Brit.*), front (*Inf.*), introduce, pre~
sent

host[2] army, array, drove, horde, legion,
multitude, myriad, swarm, throng

hostage captive, gage, pawn, pledge, pris~
oner, security, surety

hostile 1. antagonistic, anti (*Inf.*), bellicose,
belligerent, contrary, ill-disposed, inimical,
malevolent, opposed, opposite, rancorous,
unkind, warlike **2.** adverse, alien, inhospi~
table, unfriendly, unpropitious, unsympa~
thetic, unwelcoming
Antonyms affable, agreeable, amiable, ap~
proving, congenial, cordial, friendly, kind,
peaceful, sympathetic, warm

hostilities conflict, fighting, state of war,
war, warfare
Antonyms alliance, peace, treaty, truce

hostility abhorrence, animosity, animus,
antagonism, antipathy, aversion, detesta~
tion, enmity, hatred, ill will, malevolence,
malice, opposition, resentment, unfriendli~
ness
Antonyms agreement, amity, approval,

congeniality, cordiality, friendliness, good~ will, sympathy

hot 1. blistering, boiling, burning, fiery, flaming, heated, piping hot, roasting, scald~ ing, scorching, searing, steaming, sultry, sweltering, torrid, warm **2.** acrid, biting, peppery, piquant, pungent, sharp, spicy **3.** *Fig.* animated, ardent, excited, fervent, fer~ vid, fierce, fiery, flaming, impetuous, inflamed, intense, irascible, lustful, pas~ sionate, raging, stormy, touchy, vehement, violent **4.** fresh, just out, latest, new, re~ cent, up to the minute **5.** approved, fa~ voured, in demand, in vogue, popular, sought-after **6.** close, following closely, in hot pursuit, near
Antonyms (*sense 1*) chilly, cold, cool, freez~ ing, frigid, frosty, icy, parky (*Brit. inf.*), (*sense 2*) mild (*sense 3*) apathetic, calm, dispassion~ ate, half-hearted, indifferent, mild, moderate (*sense 4*) old, stale, trite (*sense 5*) out of favour, unpopular (*sense 6*) cold

hot air blather, blether, bombast, bosh (*Inf.*), bunkum *or* buncombe (*Chiefly U.S.*), clap~ trap (*Inf.*), empty talk, gas (*Inf.*), guff (*Sl.*), rant, tall talk (*Inf.*), verbiage, wind

hotbed breeding ground, den, forcing house, nest, nursery, seedbed

hot-blooded ardent, excitable, fervent, fiery, heated, impulsive, passionate, rash, spirited, temperamental, wild
Antonyms apathetic, calm, cold, cool, frigid, impassive, restrained, unenthusiastic

hotchpotch conglomeration, farrago, galli~ maufry, hash, hodgepodge (*U.S.*), jumble, medley, *mélange*, mess, miscellany, mish~ mash, mixture, olio, olla podrida, potpourri

hotfoot hastily, helter-skelter, hurriedly, pell-mell, posthaste, quickly, speedily

hothead daredevil, desperado, hotspur, madcap, tearaway

hot-headed fiery, foolhardy, hasty, hot-tempered, impetuous, precipitate, quick-tempered, rash, reckless, unruly, volatile

hothouse 1. *n.* conservatory, glasshouse, greenhouse **2.** *adj.* coddled, dainty, delicate, exotic, fragile, frail, overprotected, pam~ pered, sensitive

hound *v.* **1.** chase, drive, give chase, hunt, hunt down, pursue **2.** badger, goad, harass, harry, impel, persecute, pester, prod, pro~ voke

house *n.* **1.** abode, building, domicile, dwelling, edifice, habitation, home, home~ stead, pad (*Sl.*), residence **2.** family, house~ hold, ménage **3.** ancestry, clan, dynasty, family tree, kindred, line, lineage, race, tribe **4.** business, company, concern, estab~ lishment, firm, organization, outfit (*Inf.*), partnership **5.** assembly, Commons, legis~ lative body, parliament **6.** hotel, inn, public house, tavern **7. on the house** for nothing, free, gratis, without expense ~*v.* **8.** accom~ modate, billet, board, domicile, harbour, lodge, put up, quarter, take in **9.** contain, cover, keep, protect, sheathe, shelter, store

household 1. *n.* family, home, house, mé~ nage **2.** *adj.* domestic, domiciliary, family, ordinary, plain

householder homeowner, occupant, resi~ dent, tenant

housekeeping home economy, home~ making (*U.S.*), housecraft, household man~ agement, housewifery

housing 1. accommodation, dwellings, homes, houses **2.** case, casing, container, cover, covering, enclosure, sheath

hovel cabin, den, hole, hut, shack, shanty, shed

hover 1. be suspended, drift, float, flutter, fly, hang, poise **2.** hang about, linger, wait nearby **3.** alternate, dither (*Chiefly Brit.*), falter, fluctuate, haver (*Brit.*), oscillate, pause, seesaw, swither (*Scot. dialect*), vacil~ late, waver

however after all, anyhow, be that as it may, but, even though, nevertheless, none~ theless, notwithstanding, on the other hand, still, though, yet

howl 1. *n.* bawl, bay, bell, bellow, clamour, cry, groan, hoot, outcry, roar, scream, shriek, ululation, wail, yelp, yowl **2.** *v.* bawl, bell, bellow, cry, cry out, lament, quest (*used of hounds*), roar, scream, shout, shriek, ululate, wail, weep, yell, yelp

howler bloomer (*Brit. inf.*), blunder, boner (*Sl.*), boob (*Brit. sl.*), booboo (*Inf.*), bull (*Sl.*), clanger (*Inf.*), error, malapropism, mistake, schoolboy howler

hub centre, core, focal point, focus, heart, middle, nerve centre, pivot

huddle *n.* **1.** confusion, crowd, disorder, heap, jumble, mass, mess, muddle **2.** *Inf.* confab (*Inf.*), conference, discussion, meet~ ing, powwow ~*v.* **3.** cluster, converge, crowd, flock, gather, press, throng **4.** crouch, cuddle, curl up, hunch up, make oneself small, nestle, snuggle

hue 1. colour, dye, shade, tincture, tinge, tint, tone **2.** aspect, cast, complexion, light

hue and cry brouhaha, clamour, furore, hullabaloo, much ado, outcry, ruction (*Inf.*), rumpus, uproar

huffy, huffish angry, crabbed, cross, crotchety (*Inf.*), crusty, curt, disgruntled, edgy, grumpy, irritable, moody, moping, of~ fended, peevish, pettish, petulant, queru~ lous, ratty (*Brit. & N.Z. inf.*), resentful, shirty (*Sl., chiefly Brit.*), short, snappy,

sulky, sullen, surly, testy, tetchy, touchy, waspish
Antonyms amiable, calm, cheerful, friendly, gay, good-humoured, happy, pleasant, sunny

hug v. **1.** clasp, cuddle, embrace, enfold, hold close, squeeze, take in one's arms **2.** cling to, follow closely, keep close, stay near **3.** cherish, cling, hold onto, nurse, retain ~n. **4.** bear hug, clasp, clinch (Sl.), embrace, squeeze

huge Brobdingnagian, bulky, colossal, el~ephantine, enormous, extensive, gargan~tuan, giant, gigantic, ginormous (Inf.), great, humongous or humungous (U.S. sl.), immense, jumbo (Inf.), large, mammoth, massive, mega (Sl.), monumental, moun~tainous, prodigious, stupendous, titanic, tremendous, vast
Antonyms insignificant, little, microscopic, minute, petty, puny, small, tiny

hulk 1. derelict, frame, hull, shell, ship~wreck, wreck **2.** lout, lubber, lump (Inf.), oaf

hull n. **1.** body, casing, covering, frame, framework, skeleton **2.** husk, peel, pod, rind, shell, shuck, skin ~v. **3.** husk, peel, shell, shuck, skin, trim

hullabaloo babel, bedlam, brouhaha, clam~our, commotion, confusion, din, disturb~ance, furore, hubbub, hue and cry, hurly-burly, noise, outcry, pandemonium, racket, ruckus (Inf.), ruction (Inf.), rumpus, to-do, tumult, turmoil, upheaval, uproar

hum 1. bombinate or bombilate (Literary), buzz, croon, drone, mumble, murmur, purr, sing, throb, thrum, vibrate, whir **2.** be ac~tive, be busy, bustle, buzz, move, pulsate, pulse, stir, vibrate

human adj. **1.** anthropoid, fleshly, manlike, mortal **2.** approachable, compassionate, considerate, fallible, forgivable, humane, kind, kindly, natural, understandable, understanding, vulnerable ~n. **3.** body, child, creature, human being, individual, man, mortal, person, soul, wight (Archaic), woman
Antonyms adj. (sense 1) animal, nonhuman (sense 2) beastly, brutish, cruel, inhuman, un~sympathetic ~n. animal, god, nonhuman

humane benevolent, benign, charitable, clement, compassionate, forbearing, forgiv~ing, gentle, good, good-natured, kind, kind-hearted, kindly, lenient, merciful, mild, sympathetic, tender, understanding
Antonyms barbarous, brutal, cruel, inhu~man, inhumane, ruthless, uncivilized, un~kind, unmerciful, unsympathetic

humanitarian 1. adj. altruistic, beneficent, benevolent, charitable, compassionate, hu~mane, philanthropic, public-spirited **2.** n.

altruist, benefactor, Good Samaritan, phi~lanthropist

humanitarianism beneficence, benevo~lence, charity, generosity, goodwill, hu~manism, philanthropy

humanities classical studies, classics, lib~eral arts, literae humaniores

humanity 1. flesh, Homo sapiens, human~kind, human race, man, mankind, men, mortality, people **2.** human nature, hu~manness, mortality **3.** benevolence, benig~nity, brotherly love, charity, compassion, fellow feeling, kind-heartedness, kindness, mercy, philanthropy, sympathy, tenderness, tolerance, understanding

humanize civilize, cultivate, educate, en~lighten, improve, mellow, polish, reclaim, refine, soften, tame

humble adj. **1.** meek, modest, self-effacing, submissive, unassuming, unostentatious, unpretentious **2.** common, commonplace, insignificant, low, low-born, lowly, mean, modest, obscure, ordinary, plebeian, poor, simple, undistinguished, unimportant, un~pretentious **3.** courteous, deferential, oblig~ing, obsequious, polite, respectful, servile, subservient ~v. **4.** abase, abash, break, bring down, chagrin, chasten, crush, de~base, degrade, demean, disgrace, humiliate, lower, mortify, put down (Sl.), reduce, shame, sink, subdue, take down a peg (Inf.) **5. humble oneself** abase oneself, eat crow (U.S. inf.), eat humble pie, go on bended knee, grovel, swallow one's pride
Antonyms adj. (senses 1 & 3) arrogant, as~suming, conceited, haughty, immodest, lord~ly, ostentatious, overbearing, pompous, pre~sumptuous, pretentious, proud, snobbish, su~perior, vain (sense 2) aristocratic, distin~guished, elegant, famous, glorious, high, im~portant, rich, significant, superior, wealthy ~v. elevate, exalt, magnify, raise

humbug n. **1.** bluff, canard, cheat, deceit, deception, dodge, feint, fraud, hoax, impo~sition, imposture, ruse, sham, swindle, trick, trickery, wile **2.** charlatan, cheat, con man (Inf.), faker, fraud, inpostor, phoney or phony (Inf.), quack, swindler, trickster **3.** baloney (Inf.), cant, charlatanry, claptrap (Inf.), eyewash (Inf.), gammon (Brit. inf.), hypocrisy, nonsense, quackery, rubbish ~v. **4.** bamboozle (Inf.), befool, beguile, cheat, con (Inf.), cozen, deceive, delude, dupe, fool, gull (Archaic), hoax, hoodwink, impose, mislead, swindle, take in (Inf.), trick

humdrum banal, boring, commonplace, dreary, dull, ho-hum (Inf.), mind-numbing, monotonous, mundane, ordinary, repeti~tious, routine, tedious, tiresome, unevent~ful, uninteresting, unvaried, wearisome
Antonyms dramatic, entertaining, exciting,

extraordinary, interesting, lively, sexy (*Inf.*), stimulating

humid clammy, damp, dank, moist, muggy, steamy, sticky, sultry, watery, wet
Antonyms arid, dry, sunny, torrid

humidity clamminess, damp, dampness, dankness, dew, humidness, moistness, moisture, mugginess, sogginess, wetness

humiliate abase, abash, bring low, chagrin, chasten, crush, debase, degrade, discomfit, disgrace, embarrass, humble, make (some~ one) eat humble pie, mortify, put down, shame, subdue, take down a peg (*Inf.*)
Antonyms elevate, honour, magnify, make proud

humiliating cringe-making (*Brit. inf.*), crushing, degrading, disgracing, embar~ rassing, humbling, ignominious, mortifying, shaming

humiliation abasement, affront, chagrin, condescension, degradation, disgrace, dis~ honour, embarrassment, humbling, igno~ miny, indignity, loss of face, mortification, put-down, resignation, self-abasement, shame, submission, submissiveness

humility diffidence, humbleness, lack of pride, lowliness, meekness, modesty, self-abasement, servility, submissiveness, unpretentiousness
Antonyms arrogance, conceit, disdain, haughtiness, pomposity, presumption, pre~ tentiousness, pride, snobbishness, supercili~ ousness, superiority, vanity

humorist card (*Inf.*), comedian, comic, ec~ centric, funny man, jester, joker, wag, wit

humorous amusing, comic, comical, droll, entertaining, facetious, farcical, funny, hi~ larious, jocose, jocular, laughable, ludi~ crous, merry, playful, pleasant, side-splitting, waggish, whimsical, witty
Antonyms earnest, grave, sad, serious, so~ ber, solemn

humour *n.* **1.** amusement, comedy, drollery, facetiousness, fun, funniness, jocularity, lu~ dicrousness, wit **2.** comedy, farce, gags (*Inf.*), jesting, jests, jokes, joking, pleasant~ ry, wisecracks (*Inf.*), wit, witticisms, witti~ ness **3.** disposition, frame of mind, mood, spirits, temper **4.** bent, bias, fancy, freak, mood, propensity, quirk, vagary, whim ~*v.* **5.** accommodate, cosset, favour, feed, flatter, go along with, gratify, indulge, mollify, pamper, pander to, spoil
Antonyms *n.* gravity, grief, melancholy, sadness, seriousness, sobriety, solemnity, sorrow ~*v.* aggravate, excite, oppose, rouse, stand up to

hump *n.* **1.** bulge, bump, hunch, knob, lump, mound, projection, protrusion, pro~ tuberance, swelling **2. the hump** *Brit. inf.* megrims (*Rare*), the blues, the doldrums,

the dumps (*Inf.*), the grumps (*Inf.*), the mopes, the sulks ~*v.* **3.** arch, curve, form a hump, hunch, lift, tense **4.** *Sl.* carry, heave, hoist, lug, shoulder

hunch 1. *n.* feeling, idea, impression, ink~ ling, intuition, premonition, presentiment, suspicion **2.** *v.* arch, bend, crouch, curve, draw in, huddle, hump, squat, stoop, tense

hunchback crookback (*Rare*), crouch-back (*Archaic*), humpback, kyphosis (*Pathology*), Quasimodo

hunger *n.* **1.** appetite, emptiness, esurience, famine, hungriness, ravenousness, starva~ tion, voracity **2.** appetence, appetite, crav~ ing, desire, greediness, itch, lust, thirst, yearning, yen (*Inf.*), ~*v.* **3.** crave, desire, hanker, hope, itch, long, pine, starve, thirst, want, wish, yearn

hungry 1. empty, famished, famishing, hol~ low, peckish (*Inf., chiefly Brit.*), ravenous, sharp-set, starved, starving, voracious **2.** athirst, avid, covetous, craving, desirous, eager, greedy, keen, yearning

hunk block, chunk, gobbet, lump, mass, piece, slab, wedge, wodge (*Brit. inf.*)

hunt *v.* **1.** chase, gun for, hound, pursue, stalk, track, trail **2.** ferret about, forage, go in quest of, look, look high and low, rum~ mage through, scour, search, seek, try to find ~*n.* **3.** chase, hunting, investigation, pursuit, quest, search

hunted careworn, desperate, distraught, gaunt, haggard, harassed, harried, per~ secuted, stricken, terror-stricken, torment~ ed, worn

hurdle *n.* **1.** barricade, barrier, block, fence, hedge, wall **2.** barrier, block, complication, difficulty, handicap, hindrance, impedi~ ment, obstacle, obstruction, snag, stumbling block

hurl cast, chuck (*Inf.*), fire, fling, heave, launch, let fly, pitch, project, propel, send, shy, sling, throw, toss

hurly-burly bedlam, brouhaha, chaos, com~ motion, confusion, disorder, furore, hub~ bub, pandemonium, tumult, turbulence, turmoil, upheaval, uproar
Antonyms composure, order, organization, tidiness

hurricane cyclone, gale, storm, tempest, tornado, twister (*U.S. inf.*), typhoon, willy-willy (*Aust.*), windstorm

hurried breakneck, brief, cursory, hasty, hectic, perfunctory, precipitate, quick, quickie (*Inf.*), rushed, short, slapdash, speedy, superficial, swift

hurry *v.* **1.** barrel (along) (*Inf., chiefly U.S. & Canad.*), burn rubber (*Inf.*), dash, fly, get a move on (*Inf.*), lose no time, make haste, rush, scoot, scurry, step on it (*Inf.*) **2.** ac~

celerate, expedite, goad, hasten, hustle, push on, quicken, speed (up), urge ~*n.* **3.** bustle, celerity, commotion, dispatch, ex~ pedition, flurry, haste, precipitation, promptitude, quickness, rush, speed, urgency
Antonyms *v.* crawl, creep, dawdle, delay, move slowly, retard, slow, slow down ~*n.* calmness, slowness

hurt *v.* **1.** bruise, damage, disable, harm, impair, injure, mar, spoil, wound **2.** ache, be sore, be tender, burn, pain, smart, sting, throb **3.** afflict, aggrieve, annoy, cut to the quick, distress, grieve, pain, sadden, sting, upset, wound ~*n.* **4.** discomfort, distress, pain, pang, soreness, suffering **5.** bruise, sore, wound **6.** damage, detriment, disad~ vantage, harm, injury, loss, mischief, wrong ~*adj.* **7.** bruised, cut, damaged, ˙grazed, harmed, injured, scarred, scraped, scratched, wounded **8.** aggrieved, crushed, injured, miffed (*Inf.*), offended, pained, piqued, rueful, sad, wounded
Antonyms *v.* aid, alleviate, benefit, calm, compensate, compliment, console, cure, for~ ward, heal, heighten, help, increase, please, relieve, repair, restore, soothe ~*n.* delight, happiness, joy, pleasure, pride, satisfaction ~*adj.* alleviated, assuaged, calmed, consoled, healed, placated, relieved, repaired, restored, soothed

hurtful cruel, cutting, damaging, destruc~ tive, detrimental, disadvantageous, dis~ tressing, harmful, injurious, maleficent, malicious, mean, mischievous, nasty, per~ nicious, prejudicial, spiteful, unkind, upsetting, wounding

husband *v.* budget, conserve, economize, hoard, manage thriftily, save, store, use sparingly
Antonyms be extravagant, fritter away, spend, splash out (*Inf., chiefly Brit.*), squander

husbandry 1. agriculture, agronomy, cul~ tivation, farming, land management, tillage **2.** careful management, economy, frugality, good housekeeping, thrift

hush *v.* **1.** mute, muzzle, quieten, shush, si~ lence, still, suppress **2.** allay, appease, calm, compose, mollify, soothe ~*n.* **3.** calm, peace, peacefulness, quiet, silence, still (*Po~ etic*), stillness, tranquillity

hush-hush classified, confidential, restrict~ ed, secret, top-secret

husk bark, chaff, covering, glume, hull, rind, shuck

huskiness dryness, harshness, hoarseness, raspingness, roughness

husky 1. croaking, croaky, gruff, guttural, harsh, hoarse, rasping, raucous, rough, throaty **2.** *Inf.* beefy (*Inf.*), brawny, burly,

hefty, muscular, powerful, Ramboesque, rugged, stocky, strapping, thickset

hussy baggage (*Inf., old-fashioned*), floozy (*Sl.*), jade, minx, quean (*Archaic*), scrubber (*Brit. & Aust. sl.*), slut, strumpet, tart (*Inf.*), tramp (*Sl.*), trollop, wanton, wench (*Archa~ ic*)

hustle bustle, crowd, elbow, force, haste, hasten, hurry, impel, jog, jostle, push, rush, shove, thrust

hut cabin, den, hovel, lean-to, refuge, shanty, shed, shelter

hybrid *n.* amalgam, composite, compound, cross, crossbreed, half-blood, half-breed, mixture, mongrel, mule

hygiene cleanliness, hygienics, sanitary measures, sanitation

hygienic aseptic, clean, disinfected, germ-free, healthy, pure, salutary, sanitary, ster~ ile
Antonyms dirty, filthy, germ-ridden, harm~ ful, insanitary, polluted, unhealthy, unhy~ gienic, unwholesome

hymn anthem, canticle, carol, chant, doxol~ ogy, paean, psalm, song of praise

hype ballyhoo (*Inf.*), brouhaha, build-up, plugging (*Inf.*), promotion, publicity, puffing, racket, razzmatazz (*Sl.*)

hypnotic mesmeric, mesmerizing, narcotic, opiate, sleep-inducing, somniferous, sooth~ ing, soporific, spellbinding

hypnotize 1. mesmerize, put in a trance, put to sleep **2.** absorb, entrance, fascinate, magnetize, spellbind

hypochondriac *adj./n.* valetudinarian

hypocrisy cant, deceit, deceitfulness, de~ ception, dissembling, duplicity, falsity, im~ posture, insincerity, pharisaism, pharisee~ ism, phoneyness *or* phoniness (*Inf.*), pre~ tence, sanctimoniousness, speciousness, two-facedness
Antonyms honesty, sincerity, truthfulness

hypocrite charlatan, deceiver, dissembler, fraud, Holy Willie, impostor, Pecksniff, pharisee, phoney *or* phony (*Inf.*), pretender, Tartuffe, whited sepulchre

hypocritical canting, deceitful, deceptive, dissembling, duplicitous, false, fraudulent, hollow, insincere, Janus-faced, pharisaical, phoney *or* phony (*Inf.*), sanctimonious, spe~ cious, spurious, two-faced

hypothesis assumption, postulate, premise, premiss, proposition, supposition, theory, thesis

hypothetical academic, assumed, conjec~ tural, imaginary, putative, speculative, supposed, theoretical
Antonyms actual, confirmed, established, known, proven, real, true

hysteria agitation, delirium, frenzy, hyster~
ics, madness, panic, unreason

hysterical 1. berserk, beside oneself, con~
vulsive, crazed, distracted, distraught, fran~
tic, frenzied, mad, overwrought, raving,
uncontrollable. **2.** *Inf.* comical, farcical, hi~
larious, screaming, side-splitting, uproari~
ous, wildly funny

Antonyms calm, composed, grave, melan~
choly, poised, sad, self-possessed, serious, un~
fazed (*Inf.*)

I

ice 1. break the ice begin, initiate the pro~ceedings, kick off (*Inf.*), lead the way, make a start, start *or* set the ball rolling (*Inf.*), take the plunge (*Inf.*) **2. on thin ice** at risk, in jeopardy, open to attack, out on a limb, sticking one's neck out (*Inf.*), unsafe, vul~nerable

ice-cold arctic, biting, bitter, chilled to the bone *or* marrow, freezing, frozen, glacial, icy, raw, refrigerated, shivering

icy 1. arctic, biting, bitter, chill, chilling, chilly, cold, freezing, frost-bound, frosty, frozen over, ice-cold, parky (*Brit. inf.*), raw **2.** glacial, glassy, like a sheet of glass, rimy, slippery, slippy (*Inf. or dialect*) **3. *Fig.*** aloof, cold, distant, forbidding, frigid, frosty, gla~cial, hostile, indifferent, steely, stony, un~friendly, unwelcoming
Antonyms (*sense 1*) blistering, boiling, hot, sizzling, warm (*sense 3*) cordial, friendly, gra~cious, warm

idea 1. abstraction, concept, conception, conclusion, fancy, impression, judgment, perception, thought, understanding **2.** be~lief, conviction, doctrine, interpretation, notion, opinion, teaching, view, viewpoint **3.** approximation, clue, estimate, guess, hint, impression, inkling, intimation, no~tion, suspicion **4.** aim, end, import, inten~tion, meaning, object, objective, plan, pur~pose, *raison d'être*, reason, sense, significance **5.** design, hypothesis, plan, recommendation, scheme, solution, sugges~tion, theory **6.** archetype, essence, form, pattern

ideal *n.* **1.** archetype, criterion, epitome, ex~ample, exemplar, last word, model, nonpa~reil, paradigm, paragon, pattern, perfection, prototype, standard, standard of perfection **2.** *Often plural* moral value, principle, standard ~*adj.* **3.** archetypal, classic, com~plete, consummate, model, optimal, perfect, quintessential, supreme **4.** abstract, con~ceptual, hypothetical, intellectual, mental, notional, theoretical, transcendental **5.** fan~ciful, imaginary, impractical, ivory-tower, unattainable, unreal, Utopian, visionary
Antonyms *adj.* (*sense 3*) deficient, flawed, impaired, imperfect, unsuitable (*sense 5*) ac~tual, factual, literal, mundane, ordinary, real

idealist *n.* dreamer, romantic, Utopian, vi~sionary

idealistic impracticable, optimistic, perfec~tionist, quixotic, romantic, starry-eyed, Utopian, visionary

Antonyms down-to-earth, practical, prag~matic, realistic, sensible

ideally all things being equal, if one had one's way, in a perfect world, under the best of circumstances

identical alike, corresponding, duplicate, equal, equivalent, indistinguishable, inter~changeable, like, matching, selfsame, the same, twin
Antonyms different, disparate, distinct, di~verse, separate, unlike

identification 1. cataloguing, classifying, establishment of identity, labelling, naming, pinpointing, recognition **2.** association, connection, empathy, fellow feeling, in~volvement, rapport, relationship, sympathy **3.** credentials, ID, identity card, letters of introduction, papers

identify 1. catalogue, classify, diagnose, flag, label, make out, name, pick out, pin~point, place, put one's finger on (*Inf.*), rec~ognize, single out, spot, tag **2. *Often with with*** ally, associate, empathize, feel for, put in the same category, put oneself in the place *or* shoes of, relate to, respond to, see through another's eyes, think of in connec~tion (with)

identity 1. distinctiveness, existence, indi~viduality, oneness, particularity, personal~ity, self, selfhood, singularity, uniqueness **2.** accord, correspondence, empathy, rap~port, sameness, unanimity, unity

idiocy abject stupidity, asininity, cretinism, fatuity, fatuousness, foolishness, imbecility, inanity, insanity, lunacy, senselessness, tomfoolery
Antonyms acumen, sagacity, sanity, sense, soundness, wisdom

idiom 1. expression, locution, phrase, set phrase, turn of phrase **2.** jargon, language, mode of expression, parlance, style, talk, usage, vernacular

idiomatic dialectal, native, vernacular

idiosyncrasy affectation, characteristic, eccentricity, habit, mannerism, oddity, pe~culiarity, personal trait, quirk, singularity, trick

idiot airhead (*Sl.*), ass, berk (*Brit. sl.*), blockhead, booby, charlie (*Brit. inf.*), coot, cretin, dickhead (*Sl.*), dimwit (*Inf.*), dipstick (*Brit. sl.*), divvy (*Brit. sl.*), dork (*Sl.*), dunderhead, dweeb (*U.S. sl.*), fool, fuckwit (*Taboo sl.*), geek (*Sl.*), gonzo (*Sl.*), halfwit, imbecile, jerk (*Sl., chiefly U.S. & Canad.*), lamebrain (*Inf.*), mooncalf, moron, nerd *or* nurd (*Sl.*), nincompoop, nitwit (*Inf.*), num~ skull *or* numbskull, oaf, pillock (*Brit. sl.*), plank (*Brit. sl.*), plonker (*Sl.*), prat (*Sl.*), prick (*Derogatory sl.*), schmuck (*U.S. sl.*), simpleton, twit (*Inf., chiefly Brit.*), wally (*Sl.*)

idiotic asinine, braindead (*Inf.*), crackpot (*Inf.*), crazy, daft (*Inf.*), dumb (*Inf.*), fatuous, foolhardy, foolish, halfwitted, harebrained, imbecile, imbecilic, inane, insane, loopy (*Inf.*), lunatic, moronic, senseless, stupid, unintelligent
Antonyms brilliant, commonsensical, in~ telligent, sensible, thoughtful, wise

idle *adj.* **1.** dead, empty, gathering dust, in~ active, jobless, mothballed, out of action *or* operation, out of work, redundant, station~ ary, ticking over, unemployed, unoccupied, unused, vacant **2.** indolent, lackadaisical, lazy, shiftless, slothful, sluggish **3.** frivo~ lous, insignificant, irrelevant, nugatory, superficial, trivial, unhelpful, unnecessary **4.** abortive, bootless, fruitless, futile, groundless, ineffective, of no avail, otiose, pointless, unavailing, unproductive, unsuc~ cessful, useless, vain, worthless ~*v.* **5.** *Of~ ten with* **away** dally, dawdle, fool, fritter, hang out (*Inf.*), kill time, laze, loiter, lounge, potter, waste, while **6.** bob off (*Brit. sl.*), coast, drift, mark time, shirk, sit back and do nothing, skive (*Brit. sl.*), slack, slow down, take it easy, vegetate, veg out (*Sl.*)
Antonyms (*senses 1 & 2*) active, busy, em~ ployed, energetic, functional, industrious, oc~ cupied, operative, working (*sense 3*) impor~ tant, meaningful (*sense 4*) advantageous, ef~ fective, fruitful, profitable, useful, worthwhile

idleness 1. inaction, inactivity, leisure, time on one's hands, unemployment **2.** hi~ bernation, inertia, laziness, shiftlessness, sloth, sluggishness, torpor, vegetating **3.** dilly-dallying (*Inf.*), lazing, loafing, potter~ ing, skiving (*Brit. sl.*), time-wasting, trifling

idling *adj.* dawdling, drifting, loafing, pot~ tering, resting, resting on one's oars, taking it easy, ticking over

idol 1. deity, god, graven image, image, pa~ gan symbol **2.** *Fig.* beloved, darling, fa~ vourite, hero, pet, pin-up (*Sl.*), superstar

idolater 1. heathen, idol-worshipper, pagan **2.** admirer, adorer, devotee, idolizer, vota~ ry, worshipper

idolatrous adoring, adulatory, reverential, uncritical, worshipful

idolatry adoration, adulation, apotheosis, deification, exaltation, glorification, hero worship, idolizing

idolize admire, adore, apotheosize, bow down before, deify, dote upon, exalt, glorify, hero-worship, look up to, love, revere, rev~

erence, venerate, worship, worship to ex~ cess

if 1. *conj.* admitting, allowing, assuming, granting, in case, on condition that, on the assumption that, provided, providing, sup~ posing, though, whenever, wherever, whether **2.** *n.* condition, doubt, hesitation, stipulation, uncertainty

ignite burn, burst into flames, catch fire, fire, flare up, inflame, kindle, light, put a match to (*Inf.*), set alight, set fire to, take fire, touch off

ignominious abject, despicable, discredit~ able, disgraceful, dishonourable, disrepu~ table, humiliating, indecorous, inglorious, mortifying, scandalous, shameful, sorry, undignified
Antonyms creditable, honourable, repu~ table, worthy

ignominy bad odour, contempt, discredit, disgrace, dishonour, disrepute, humiliation, infamy, mortification, obloquy, odium, op~ probrium, reproach, shame, stigma
Antonyms credit, honour, repute

ignorance 1. greenness, inexperience, in~ nocence, nescience (*Literary*), oblivion, un~ awareness, unconsciousness, unfamiliarity **2.** benightedness, blindness, illiteracy, lack of education, mental darkness, unenlight~ enment, unintelligence
Antonyms (*sense 2*) comprehension, en~ lightenment, insight, intelligence, knowledge, understanding, wisdom

ignorant 1. benighted, blind to, inexperi~ enced, innocent, in the dark about, oblivi~ ous, unaware, unconscious, unenlightened, uninformed, uninitiated, unknowing, un~ schooled, unwitting **2.** green, illiterate, na~ ive, unaware, uncultivated, uneducated, unknowledgeable, unlearned, unlettered, unread, untaught, untrained, untutored **3.** crass, crude, gross, half-baked (*Inf.*), insen~ sitive, rude, shallow, superficial, uncom~ prehending, unscholarly
Antonyms astute, aware, brilliant, con~ scious, cultured, educated, informed, knowl~ edgeable, learned, literate, sagacious, wise

ignore be oblivious to, bury one's head in the sand, cold-shoulder, cut (*Inf.*), discount, disregard, give the cold shoulder to, neglect, overlook, pass over, pay no attention to, re~ ject, send (someone) to Coventry, shut one's eyes to, take no notice of, turn a blind eye to, turn a deaf ear to, turn one's back on
Antonyms acknowledge, heed, note, pay at~ tention to, recognize, regard

ill *adj.* **1.** ailing, dicky (*Brit. inf.*), diseased, funny (*Inf.*), indisposed, infirm, laid up (*Inf.*), not up to snuff (*Inf.*), off-colour, on the sick list (*Inf.*), out of sorts (*Inf.*), poorly (*Inf.*), queasy, queer, seedy (*Inf.*), sick, un~

der the weather (*Inf.*), unhealthy, unwell, valetudinarian **2.** bad, damaging, deleterious, detrimental, evil, foul, harmful, iniquitous, injurious, ruinous, unfortunate, unlucky, vile, wicked, wrong **3.** acrimonious, adverse, antagonistic, cantankerous, cross, harsh, hateful, hostile, hurtful, inimical, malevolent, malicious, sullen, surly, unfriendly, unkind **4.** disturbing, foreboding, inauspicious, ominous, sinister, threatening, unfavourable, unhealthy, unlucky, unpromising, unpropitious, unwholesome ~*n.* **5.** affliction, hardship, harm, hurt, injury, misery, misfortune, pain, trial, tribulation, trouble, unpleasantness, woe **6.** ailment, complaint, disease, disorder, illness, indisposition, infirmity, malady, malaise, sickness **7.** abuse, badness, cruelty, damage, depravity, destruction, evil, ill usage, malice, mischief, suffering, wickedness ~*adv.* **8.** badly, hard, inauspiciously, poorly, unfavourably, unfortunately, unluckily **9.** barely, by no means, hardly, insufficiently, scantily **10.** *As in* **ill-gotten** criminally, dishonestly, foully, fraudulently, illegally, illegitimately, illicitly, unlawfully, unscrupulously

Antonyms *adj.* (*sense 1*) hale, healthy, strong, well (*sense 2*) favourable, good (*sense 3*) generous, kind ~*n.* good, honour, kindness ~*adv.* easily, well

ill-advised foolhardy, foolish, ill-considered, ill-judged, impolitic, imprudent, inappropriate, incautious, indiscreet, injudicious, misguided, overhasty, rash, reckless, short-sighted, thoughtless, unseemly, unwise, wrong-headed

Antonyms appropriate, cautious, discreet, judicious, politic, prudent, seemly, sensible, wise

ill-assorted incompatible, incongruous, inharmonious, mismatched, uncongenial, unsuited

ill at ease anxious, awkward, disquieted, disturbed, edgy, faltering, fidgety, hesitant, nervous, on edge, on pins and needles (*Inf.*), on tenterhooks, out of place, restless, self-conscious, strange, tense, twitchy (*Inf.*), uncomfortable, uneasy, unquiet, unrelaxed, unsettled, unsure, wired (*Sl.*)

Antonyms at ease, comfortable, easy, quiet, relaxed, settled, sure

ill-bred bad-mannered, boorish, churlish, coarse, crass, discourteous, ill-mannered, impolite, indelicate, rude, uncivil, uncivilized, uncouth, ungallant, ungentlemanly, unladylike, unmannerly, unrefined, vulgar

Antonyms civil, courteous, delicate, mannerly, refined, urbane, well-bred

ill-defined blurred, dim, fuzzy, indistinct, nebulous, shadowy, unclear, vague, woolly

Antonyms apparent, clear, conspicuous, distinct, evident, manifest, obvious, plain

ill-disposed against, antagonistic, anti (*Inf.*), antipathetic, averse, disobliging, down on (*Inf.*), hostile, inimical, opposed, uncooperative, unfriendly, unwelcoming

Antonyms cooperative, friendly, obliging, welcoming, well-disposed

illegal actionable (*Law*), banned, black-market, bootleg, criminal, felonious, forbidden, illicit, lawless, outlawed, prohibited, proscribed, unauthorized, unconstitutional, under-the-counter, under-the-table, unlawful, unlicensed, unofficial, wrongful

Antonyms lawful, legal, licit, permissible

illegality crime, criminality, felony, illegitimacy, illicitness, lawlessness, unlawfulness, wrong, wrongness

illegible crabbed, faint, hard to make out, hieroglyphic, indecipherable, obscure, scrawled, undecipherable, unreadable

Antonyms clear, decipherable, legible, plain, readable

illegitimate 1. illegal, illicit, improper, unauthorized, unconstitutional, under-the-table, unlawful, unsanctioned **2.** baseborn (*Archaic*), bastard, born on the wrong side of the blanket, born out of wedlock, fatherless, misbegotten (*Literary*), natural, spurious (*Rare*) **3.** illogical, incorrect, invalid, spurious, unsound

Antonyms (*sense 1*) authorized, constitutional, lawful, legal, legitimate, proper, sanctioned

ill-fated blighted, doomed, hapless, ill-omened, ill-starred, luckless, star-crossed, unfortunate, unhappy, unlucky

ill feeling animosity, animus, antagonism, bad blood, bitterness, disgruntlement, dissatisfaction, dudgeon (*Archaic*), enmity, frustration, hard feelings, hostility, ill will, indignation, offence, rancour, resentment

Antonyms amity, benevolence, favour, friendship, goodwill, satisfaction

ill-founded baseless, empty, groundless, idle, unjustified, unproven, unreliable, unsubstantiated, unsupported

ill-humoured acrimonious, bad-tempered, crabbed, crabby, cross, disagreeable, grumpy, huffy, impatient, irascible, irritable, like a bear with a sore head (*Inf.*), liverish, mardy (*Dialect*), moody, morose, out of sorts, out of temper, petulant, ratty (*Brit. & N.Z. inf.*), sharp, snappish, snappy, sulky, sullen, tart, testy, tetchy, thin-skinned, touchy, waspish

Antonyms affable, agreeable, amiable, charming, congenial, delightful, genial, good-humoured, good-natured, pleasant

illiberal 1. bigoted, hidebound, intolerant, narrow-minded, prejudiced, reactionary,

small-minded, uncharitable, ungenerous **2.** close-fisted, mean, miserly, niggardly, parsimonious, selfish, sordid, stingy, tight, tight-arsed (*Taboo sl.*), tight as a duck's arse (*Taboo sl.*), tight-assed (*U.S. taboo sl.*), tightfisted, ungenerous
Antonyms (*sense 1*) broad-minded, charitable, generous, liberal, open-minded, right-on (*Inf.*), tolerant

illicit 1. black-market, bootleg, contraband, criminal, felonious, illegal, illegitimate, prohibited, unauthorized, unlawful, unlicensed **2.** clandestine, forbidden, furtive, guilty, immoral, improper, wrong
Antonyms above-board, lawful, legal, legitimate, licit, permissible, proper

illiteracy benightedness, ignorance, illiterateness, lack of education

illiterate benighted, ignorant, uncultured, uneducated, unlettered, untaught, untutored
Antonyms cultured, educated, lettered, literate, taught, tutored

ill-judged foolish, ill-advised, ill-considered, injudicious, misguided, overhasty, rash, short-sighted, unwise, wrong-headed

ill-mannered badly behaved, boorish, churlish, coarse, discourteous, ill-behaved, ill-bred, impolite, insolent, loutish, rude, uncivil, uncouth, unmannerly
Antonyms civil, courteous, cultivated, mannerly, polished, polite, refined, well-mannered

ill-natured bad-tempered, catty (*Inf.*), churlish, crabbed, cross, cross-grained, disagreeable, disobliging, malevolent, malicious, mean, nasty, perverse, petulant, spiteful, sulky, sullen, surly, unfriendly, unkind, unpleasant
Antonyms agreeable, amiable, cheerful, congenial, friendly, good-natured, kind, obliging, pleasant

illness affliction, ailment, attack, complaint, disability, disease, disorder, ill health, indisposition, infirmity, malady, malaise, poor health, sickness

illogical absurd, fallacious, faulty, inconclusive, inconsistent, incorrect, invalid, irrational, meaningless, senseless, sophistical, specious, spurious, unreasonable, unscientific, unsound
Antonyms coherent, consistent, correct, logical, rational, reasonable, scientific, sound, valid

ill-starred doomed, ill-fated, ill-omened, inauspicious, star-crossed, unfortunate, unhappy, unlucky

ill temper annoyance, bad temper, crossness, curtness, impatience, irascibility, irritability, petulance, sharpness, spitefulness, tetchiness

ill-tempered annoyed, bad-tempered, choleric, cross, curt, grumpy, ill-humoured, impatient, irascible, irritable, liverish, ratty (*Brit. & N.Z. inf.*), sharp, spiteful, testy, tetchy, touchy
Antonyms benign, cheerful, good-natured, mild-mannered, patient, pleasant, sweet-tempered

ill-timed awkward, inappropriate, inconvenient, inept, inopportune, unseasonable, untimely, unwelcome
Antonyms appropriate, convenient, opportune, seasonable, timely, well-timed

ill-treat abuse, damage, handle roughly, harass, harm, harry, ill-use, injure, knock about *or* around, maltreat, mishandle, misuse, oppress, wrong

ill-treatment abuse, damage, harm, ill-use, injury, mistreatment, misuse, rough handling

illuminate 1. brighten, illumine (*Literary*), irradiate, light, light up **2.** clarify, clear up, elucidate, enlighten, explain, explicate, give insight into, instruct, interpret, make clear, shed light on **3.** adorn, decorate, illustrate, ornament
Antonyms (*sense 1*) black out, darken, dim, obscure, overshadow (*sense 2*) befog, cloud, dull, obfuscate, overcast, shade, veil

illuminating enlightening, explanatory, helpful, informative, instructive, revealing
Antonyms confusing, obscuring, puzzling, unhelpful

illumination 1. beam, brightening, brightness, light, lighting, lighting up, lights, radiance, ray **2.** awareness, clarification, edification, enlightenment, insight, inspiration, instruction, perception, revelation, understanding

illusion 1. chimera, daydream, fantasy, figment of the imagination, hallucination, ignis fatuus, mirage, mockery, phantasm, semblance, will-o'-the-wisp **2.** deception, delusion, error, fallacy, false impression, fancy, misapprehension, misconception
Antonyms actuality, reality, truth

illusory *or* **illusive** apparent, Barmecide, beguiling, chimerical, deceitful, deceptive, delusive, fallacious, false, hallucinatory, misleading, mistaken, seeming, sham, unreal, untrue
Antonyms authentic, down-to-earth, factual, genuine, real, reliable, solid, true

illustrate 1. bring home, clarify, demonstrate, elucidate, emphasize, exemplify, exhibit, explain, explicate, instance, interpret, make clear, make plain, point up, show **2.** adorn, decorate, depict, draw, ornament, picture, sketch

illustrated decorated, embellished, graphic,

illustration 312 **imitative**

illuminated, pictorial, picture, pictured, with illustrations

illustration 1. analogy, case, case in point, clarification, demonstration, elucidation, example, exemplification, explanation, instance, interpretation, specimen **2.** adornment, decoration, figure, picture, plate, sketch

illustrious brilliant, celebrated, distinguished, eminent, exalted, famed, famous, glorious, great, noble, notable, noted, prominent, remarkable, renowned, resplendent, signal, splendid
Antonyms humble, ignoble, infamous, lowly, meek, notorious, obscure, unassuming

ill will acrimony, animosity, animus, antagonism, antipathy, aversion, bad blood, dislike, enmity, envy, grudge, hard feelings, hatred, hostility, malevolence, malice, no love lost, rancour, resentment, spite, unfriendliness, venom
Antonyms amiability, amity, charity, congeniality, cordiality, friendship, goodwill

image 1. appearance, effigy, figure, icon, idol, likeness, picture, portrait, reflection, representation, statue **2.** chip off the old block (*Inf.*), counterpart, (dead) ringer (*Sl.*), Doppelgänger, double, facsimile, replica, similitude, spit (*Inf., chiefly Brit.*), spitting image *or* spit and image (*Inf.*) **3.** conceit, concept, conception, figure, idea, impression, mental picture, perception, trope

imaginable believable, comprehensible, conceivable, credible, likely, plausible, possible, supposable, thinkable, under the sun, within the bounds of possibility
Antonyms impossible, incomprehensible, inconceivable, incredible, unbelievable, unimaginable, unlikely, unthinkable

imaginary assumed, chimerical, dreamlike, fancied, fanciful, fictional, fictitious, hallucinatory, hypothetical, ideal, illusive, illusory, imagined, invented, legendary, made-up, mythological, nonexistent, phantasmal, shadowy, supposed, supposititious, supposititious, unreal, unsubstantial, visionary
Antonyms actual, factual, genuine, known, proven, real, substantial, tangible, true

imagination 1. creativity, enterprise, fancy, ingenuity, insight, inspiration, invention, inventiveness, originality, resourcefulness, vision, wit, wittiness **2.** chimera, conception, idea, ideality, illusion, image, invention, notion, supposition, unreality

imaginative clever, creative, dreamy, enterprising, fanciful, fantastic, ingenious, inspired, inventive, original, poetical, visionary, vivid, whimsical
Antonyms literal, mundane, ordinary, uncreative, unimaginative, uninspired, unoriginal, unpoetical, unromantic

imagine 1. conceive, conceptualize, conjure up, create, devise, dream up (*Inf.*), envisage, fantasize, form a mental picture of, frame, invent, picture, plan, project, scheme, see in the mind's eye, think of, think up, visualize **2.** apprehend, assume, believe, conjecture, deduce, deem, fancy, gather, guess (*Inf., chiefly U.S. & Canad.*), infer, realize, suppose, surmise, suspect, take for granted, take it, think

imbecile 1. *n.* berk (*Brit. sl.*), bungler, charlie (*Brit. inf.*), coot, cretin, dickhead (*Sl.*), dipstick (*Brit. sl.*), divvy (*Brit. sl.*), dolt, dork (*Sl.*), dotard, dweeb (*U.S. sl.*), fool, fuckwit (*Taboo sl.*), geek (*Sl.*), gonzo (*Sl.*), halfwit, idiot, jerk (*Sl., chiefly U.S. & Canad.*), moron, nerd *or* nurd (*Sl.*), numskull *or* numbskull, pillock (*Brit. sl.*), plank (*Brit. sl.*), plonker (*Sl.*), prat (*Sl.*), prick (*Derogatory sl.*), schmuck (*U.S. sl.*), thickhead, tosser (*Brit. sl.*), twit (*Inf., chiefly Brit.*), wally (*Sl.*) **2.** *adj.* asinine, braindead (*Inf.*), fatuous, feeble-minded, foolish, idiotic, imbecilic, inane, ludicrous, moronic, simple, stupid, thick, witless

imbecility asininity, childishness, cretinism, fatuity, foolishness, idiocy, inanity, incompetency, stupidity
Antonyms comprehension, intelligence, perspicacity, reasonableness, sagacity, sense, soundness, wisdom

imbibe 1. consume, drink, knock back (*Inf.*), quaff, sink (*Inf.*), suck, swallow, swig (*Inf.*) **2.** *Literary* absorb, acquire, assimilate, gain, gather, ingest, receive, take in

imbroglio complexity, complication, embarrassment, entanglement, involvement, misunderstanding, quandary

imitate affect, ape, burlesque, caricature, copy, counterfeit, do (*Inf.*), do an impression of, duplicate, echo, emulate, follow, follow in the footsteps of, follow suit, impersonate, mimic, mirror, mock, parody, personate, repeat, send up (*Brit. inf.*), simulate, spoof (*Inf.*), take a leaf out of (someone's) book, take off (*Inf.*), travesty

imitation *n.* **1.** aping, copy, counterfeit, counterfeiting, duplication, echoing, likeness, mimicry, resemblance, simulation **2.** fake, forgery, impersonation, impression, mockery, parody, reflection, replica, reproduction, sham, substitution, takeoff (*Inf.*), travesty ~*adj.* **3.** artificial, dummy, ersatz, man-made, mock, phoney *or* phony (*Inf.*), pseudo (*Inf.*), repro, reproduction, sham, simulated, synthetic
Antonyms *adj.* authentic, genuine, original, real, true, valid

imitative copied, copycat (*Inf.*), copying, derivative, echoic, mimetic, mimicking, mock, onomatopoeic, parrotlike, plagiarized, pseudo (*Inf.*), put-on, second-hand, simulated, unoriginal

imitator aper, copier, copycat (*Inf.*), echo, epigone (*Rare*), follower, impersonator, im~ pressionist, mimic, parrot, shadow

immaculate 1. clean, impeccable, neat, neat as a new pin, spick-and-span, spruce, squeaky-clean, trim, unexceptionable **2.** above reproach, faultless, flawless, guiltless, impeccable, incorrupt, innocent, perfect, pure, sinless, spotless, squeaky-clean, stain~ less, unblemished, uncontaminated, unde~ filed, unpolluted, unsullied, untarnished, virtuous
Antonyms contaminated, corrupt, dirty, filthy, impeachable, impure, polluted, stained, tainted, unclean

immaterial 1. a matter of indifference, extraneous, impertinent, inapposite, incon~ sequential, inconsiderable, inessential, insignificant, irrelevant, of little account, of no consequence, of no importance, trifling, trivial, unimportant, unnecessary **2.** airy, disembodied, ethereal, ghostly, incorporeal, metaphysical, spiritual, unembodied, un~ substantial
Antonyms (*sense 1*) crucial, essential, ger~ mane, important, material, relevant, significant, substantial (*sense 2*) earthly, physical, real, tangible

immature 1. adolescent, crude, green, im~ perfect, premature, raw, undeveloped, unfinished, unfledged, unformed, unripe, unseasonable, untimely, young **2.** babyish, callow, childish, inexperienced, infantile, jejune, juvenile, puerile, wet behind the ears (*Inf.*)
Antonyms adult, developed, fully-fledged, mature, mellow, responsible, ripe

immaturity 1. crudeness, crudity, green~ ness, imperfection, rawness, unprepared~ ness, unripeness **2.** babyishness, callow~ ness, childishness, inexperience, juvenility, puerility

immeasurable bottomless, boundless, endless, illimitable, immense, incalculable, inestimable, inexhaustible, infinite, limit~ less, measureless, unbounded, unfathom~ able, unlimited, vast
Antonyms bounded, calculable, estimable, exhaustible, fathomable, finite, limited, measurable

immediate 1. instant, instantaneous **2.** adjacent, close, contiguous, direct, near, nearest, next, primary, proximate, recent **3.** actual, current, existing, extant, on hand, present, pressing, up to date, urgent
Antonyms delayed, distant, far, late, later, leisurely, postponed, remote, slow, tardy

immediately 1. at once, before you could say Jack Robinson (*Inf.*), directly, forth~ with, instantly, now, posthaste, promptly, pronto (*Inf.*), right away, right now, straight away, this instant, this very minute, *tout de suite*, unhesitatingly, without delay, without hesitation **2.** at first hand, closely, directly, nearly

immemorial age-old, ancient, archaic, fixed, long-standing, of yore, olden (*Archa~ ic*), rooted, time-honoured, traditional

immense Brobdingnagian, colossal, el~ ephantine, enormous, extensive, giant, gi~ gantic, ginormous (*Inf.*), great, huge, hu~ mongous *or* humungous (*U.S. sl.*), illimit~ able, immeasurable, infinite, interminable, jumbo (*Inf.*), large, mammoth, massive, mega (*Sl.*), monstrous, monumental, prodi~ gious, stupendous, titanic, tremendous, vast
Antonyms infinitesimal, little, microscopic, minuscule, minute, puny, small, tiny

immensity bulk, enormity, expanse, extent, greatness, hugeness, infinity, magnitude, massiveness, scope, size, sweep, vastness

immersion 1. baptism, bathe, dip, dipping, dousing, ducking, dunking, plunging, sub~ merging **2.** *Fig.* absorption, concentration, involvement, preoccupation

immigrant incomer, newcomer, settler

imminent at hand, brewing, close, coming, fast-approaching, forthcoming, gathering, impending, in the air, in the offing, loom~ ing, menacing, near, nigh (*Archaic*), on the horizon, on the way, threatening, upcoming
Antonyms delayed, distant, far-off, remote

immobile at a standstill, at rest, fixed, fro~ zen, immobilized, immotile, immovable, like a statue, motionless, rigid, riveted, rooted, stable, static, stationary, stiff, still, stock-still, stolid, unmoving
Antonyms active, mobile, movable, on the move, pliant, portable, vigorous

immobility absence of movement, firmness, fixity, immovability, inertness, motionless~ ness, stability, steadiness, stillness

immobilize bring to a standstill, cripple, disable, freeze, halt, lay up (*Inf.*), paralyse, put out of action, render inoperative, stop, transfix

immoderate egregious, enormous, exag~ gerated, excessive, exorbitant, extravagant, extreme, inordinate, intemperate, O.T.T. (*Sl.*), over the odds (*Inf.*), over the top (*Sl.*), profligate, steep (*Inf.*), uncalled-for, uncon~ scionable, uncontrolled, undue, unjustified, unreasonable, unrestrained, unwarranted, wanton
Antonyms controlled, judicious, mild, mod~ erate, reasonable, restrained, temperate

immodesty 1. bawdiness, coarseness, im~ purity, indecorousness, indelicacy, lewd~ ness, obscenity **2.** audacity, balls (*Taboo*

sl.), boldness, brass neck (*Brit. inf.*), for~ wardness, gall (*Inf.*), impudence, shame~ lessness, temerity
Antonyms (*sense 1*) decency, decorousness, delicacy, modesty, restraint, sobriety

immoral abandoned, bad, corrupt, de~ bauched, degenerate, depraved, dishonest, dissolute, evil, impure, indecent, iniquitous, lewd, licentious, nefarious, obscene, of easy virtue, pornographic, profligate, reprobate, sinful, unchaste, unethical, unprincipled, vicious, vile, wicked, wrong
Antonyms conscientious, good, honourable, inoffensive, law-abiding, moral, pure, upright, virtuous

immorality badness, corruption, debauch~ ery, depravity, dissoluteness, evil, iniquity, licentiousness, profligacy, sin, turpitude, vice, wickedness, wrong
Antonyms goodness, honesty, lawfulness, morality, purity

immortal *adj.* **1.** abiding, constant, death-defying, deathless, endless, enduring, eter~ nal, everlasting, imperishable, incorrupt~ ible, indestructible, lasting, perennial, per~ petual, sempiternal (*Literary*), timeless, un~ dying, unfading ~*n.* **2.** god, goddess, Olym~ pian **3.** genius, great (*Usually plural*), hero, paragon
Antonyms *adj.* ephemeral, fading, fleeting, mortal, passing, perishable, temporary, tran~ sitory

immortality 1. deathlessness, endlessness, eternity, everlasting life, incorruptibility, indestructibility, perpetuity, timelessness **2.** celebrity, fame, glorification, gloriousness, glory, greatness, renown

immortalize apotheosize, celebrate, com~ memorate, enshrine, eternalize, eternize, exalt, glorify, memorialize, perpetuate, sol~ emnize

immovable 1. fast, firm, fixed, immutable, jammed, rooted, secure, set, stable, station~ ary, stuck, unbudgeable **2.** adamant, con~ stant, impassive, inflexible, obdurate, reso~ lute, steadfast, stony-hearted, unchangeable, unimpressionable, unshakable, unshaken, unwavering, unyielding
Antonyms (*sense 2*) changeable, flexible, im~ pressionable, movable, shakable, wavering, yielding

immune clear, exempt, free, insusceptible, invulnerable, let off (*Inf.*), not affected, not liable, not subject, proof (against), protect~ ed, resistant, safe, unaffected
Antonyms exposed, liable, prone, suscep~ tible, unprotected, vulnerable

immunity 1. amnesty, charter, exemption, exoneration, franchise, freedom, indemnity, invulnerability, liberty, licence, preroga~

tive, privilege, release, right **2.** immuniza~ tion, protection, resistance
Antonyms (*sense 1*) exposure, liability, openness, proneness, susceptibility, vulner~ ability

immunize inoculate, protect, safeguard, vaccinate

imp brat, demon, devil, gamin, minx, pickle (*Brit. inf.*), rascal, rogue, scamp, sprite, urchin

impact *n.* **1.** bang, blow, bump, collision, concussion, contact, crash, force, jolt, knock, shock, smash, stroke, thump **2.** brunt, burden, consequences, effect, full force, impression, influence, meaning, pow~ er, repercussions, significance, thrust, weight ~*v.* **3.** clash, collide, crash, crush, hit, strike

impair blunt, damage, debilitate, decrease, deteriorate, diminish, enervate, enfeeble, harm, hinder, injure, lessen, mar, reduce, spoil, undermine, vitiate, weaken, worsen
Antonyms ameliorate, amend, better, en~ hance, facilitate, improve, strengthen

impaired damaged, defective, faulty, flawed, imperfect, unsound

impart 1. communicate, convey, disclose, discover, divulge, make known, pass on, relate, reveal, tell **2.** accord, afford, bestow, confer, contribute, give, grant, lend, offer, yield

impartial detached, disinterested, equal, equitable, even-handed, fair, just, neutral, nondiscriminating, nonpartisan, objective, open-minded, unbiased, unprejudiced, without fear or favour
Antonyms biased, bigoted, influenced, par~ tial, prejudiced, swayed, unfair, unjust

impartiality detachment, disinterest, disin~ terestedness, dispassion, equality, equity, even-handedness, fairness, lack of bias, neutrality, nonpartisanship, objectivity, open-mindedness
Antonyms bias, favouritism, partiality, partisanship, subjectivity, unfairness

impassable blocked, closed, impenetrable, obstructed, pathless, trackless, unnavigable

impasse blind alley (*Inf.*), dead end, dead~ lock, stalemate, standoff, standstill

impassioned animated, ardent, blazing, excited, fervent, fervid, fiery, flaming, furi~ ous, glowing, heated, inflamed, inspired, intense, passionate, rousing, stirring, vehe~ ment, violent, vivid, warm, worked up
Antonyms apathetic, cool, impassive, indif~ ferent, objective, reasoned

impatience 1. haste, hastiness, heat, im~ petuosity, intolerance, irritability, irri~ tableness, quick temper, rashness, short~ ness, snappiness, vehemence, violence **2.**

agitation, anxiety, avidity, disquietude, eagerness, edginess, fretfulness, nervous~ ness, restiveness, restlessness, uneasiness
Antonyms (*sense 2*) calm, composure, con~ trol, forbearance, patience, restraint, seren~ ity, tolerance

impatient 1. abrupt, brusque, curt, de~ manding, edgy, hasty, hot-tempered, indig~ nant, intolerant, irritable, quick-tempered, snappy, sudden, testy, vehement, violent **2.** agog, athirst, chafing, eager, fretful, head~ long, impetuous, like a cat on hot bricks (*Inf.*), restless, straining at the leash
Antonyms (*sense 1*) calm, composed, cool, easy-going, imperturbable, patient, quiet, se~ rene, tolerant

impeach 1. accuse, arraign, blame, cen~ sure, charge, criminate (*Rare*), denounce, indict, tax **2.** call into question, cast asper~ sions on, cast doubt on, challenge, dispar~ age, impugn, question

impeachment accusation, arraignment, indictment

impeccable above suspicion, blameless, exact, exquisite, faultless, flawless, im~ maculate, incorrupt, innocent, irreproach~ able, perfect, precise, pure, sinless, stain~ less, unblemished, unerring, unimpeachable
Antonyms blameworthy, corrupt, cursory, defective, deficient, faulty, flawed, shallow, sinful, superficial

impecunious broke (*Inf.*), cleaned out (*Sl.*), destitute, dirt-poor (*Inf.*), down and out, flat broke (*Inf.*), indigent, insolvent, penniless, poverty-stricken, short, skint (*Brit. sl.*), stony (*Brit. sl.*), strapped (*Sl.*), without two pennies to rub together (*Inf.*)
Antonyms affluent, prosperous, rich, wealthy, well-off, well-to-do

impede bar, block, brake, check, clog, curb, delay, disrupt, hamper, hinder, hold up, obstruct, restrain, retard, slow (down), stop, throw a spanner in the works (*Brit. inf.*), thwart
Antonyms advance, aid, assist, further, help, promote

impediment bar, barrier, block, check, clog, curb, defect, difficulty, encumbrance, hindrance, obstacle, obstruction, snag, stumbling block
Antonyms advantage, aid, assistance, ben~ efit, encouragement, relief, support

impedimenta accoutrements, baggage, be~ longings, effects, equipment, gear, junk (*Inf.*), luggage, movables, odds and ends, paraphernalia, possessions, stuff, things, trappings, traps

impel actuate, chivy, compel, constrain, drive, force, goad, incite, induce, influence, inspire, instigate, motivate, move, oblige, power, prod, prompt, propel, push, require, spur, stimulate, urge
Antonyms check, discourage, dissuade, re~ buff, repulse, restrain

impending approaching, brewing, coming, forthcoming, gathering, hovering, immi~ nent, in the offing, looming, menacing, near, nearing, on the horizon, threatening, upcoming

impenetrable 1. dense, hermetic, impass~ able, impermeable, impervious, inviolable, solid, thick, unpierceable **2.** arcane, baffling, cabbalistic, dark, enigmatic, enig~ matical, hidden, incomprehensible, indis~ cernible, inexplicable, inscrutable, mysteri~ ous, obscure, unfathomable, unintelligible
Antonyms (*sense 1*) accessible, enterable, passable, penetrable, pierceable, vulnerable (*sense 2*) clear, explicable, obvious, soluble, understandable

imperative 1. compulsory, crucial, essen~ tial, exigent, indispensable, insistent, ob~ ligatory, pressing, urgent, vital **2.** authori~ tative, autocratic, commanding, dictatorial, domineering, high-handed, imperious, lord~ ly, magisterial, peremptory
Antonyms (*sense 1*) avoidable, discretional, nonessential, optional, unimportant, unnec~ essary

imperceptible faint, fine, gradual, impal~ pable, inappreciable, inaudible, indiscern~ ible, indistinguishable, infinitesimal, insen~ sible, invisible, microscopic, minute, shad~ owy, slight, small, subtle, teensy-weensy, teeny-weeny, tiny, undetectable, unnotice~ able
Antonyms audible, detectable, discernible, distinguishable, noticeable, perceptible, vis~ ible

imperceptibly by a hair's-breadth, inap~ preciably, indiscernibly, invisibly, little by little, slowly, subtly, unnoticeably, unob~ trusively, unseen

imperfect broken, damaged, defective, deficient, faulty, flawed, immature, im~ paired, incomplete, inexact, limited, partial, patchy, rudimentary, sketchy, undeveloped, unfinished
Antonyms complete, developed, exact, finished, flawless, perfect

imperfection blemish, defect, deficiency, failing, fallibility, fault, flaw, foible, frailty, inadequacy, incompleteness, infirmity, insufficiency, peccadillo, scar, shortcoming, stain, taint, weakness, weak point
Antonyms adequacy, completeness, con~ summation, excellence, faultlessness, flawlessness, perfection, sufficiency

imperial 1. kingly, majestic, princely, queenly, regal, royal, sovereign **2.** august, exalted, grand, great, high, imperious, lofty, magnificent, noble, superior, supreme

imperil endanger, expose, hazard, jeopard~ ize, risk
Antonyms care for, guard, protect, safe~ guard, secure

imperishable abiding, enduring, eternal, everlasting, immortal, indestructible, per~ ennial, permanent, perpetual, undying, un~ fading, unforgettable
Antonyms destructible, dying, fading, for~ gettable, mortal, perishable

impermeable hermetic, impassable, im~ penetrable, impervious, nonporous, proof, resistant

impersonal aloof, bureaucratic, business~ like, cold, detached, dispassionate, formal, inhuman, neutral, remote
Antonyms friendly, intimate, outgoing, personal, warm

impersonate act, ape, caricature, do (*Inf.*), do an impression of, enact, imitate, mas~ querade as, mimic, parody, pass oneself off as, personate, pose as (*Inf.*), take off (*Inf.*)

impersonation caricature, imitation, im~ pression, mimicry, parody, takeoff (*Inf.*)

impertinence assurance, audacity, back~ chat (*Inf.*), boldness, brass neck (*Brit. inf.*), brazenness, cheek (*Inf.*), chutzpah (*U.S. & Canad. inf.*), disrespect, effrontery, for~ wardness, front, impudence, incivility, in~ solence, neck (*Inf.*), nerve (*Inf.*), pertness, presumption, rudeness, sauce (*Inf.*)

impertinent 1. bold, brazen, cheeky (*Inf.*), discourteous, disrespectful, flip (*Inf.*), for~ ward, fresh (*Inf.*), impolite, impudent, inso~ lent, interfering, lippy (*U.S. & Canad. sl.*), pert, presumptuous, rude, sassy (*U.S. inf.*), saucy (*Inf.*), uncivil, unmannerly **2.** inap~ plicable, inappropriate, incongruous, irrel~ evant
Antonyms (*sense 1*) mannerly, polite, re~ spectful (*sense 2*) appropriate, germane, im~ portant, pertinent, relevant, vital

imperturbable calm, collected, compla~ cent, composed, cool, equanimous, nerve~ less, sedate, self-possessed, serene, stoical, tranquil, undisturbed, unexcitable, unfazed (*Inf.*), unflappable (*Inf.*), unmoved, unruffled
Antonyms agitated, excitable, frantic, jit~ tery (*Inf.*), nervous, panicky, ruffled, touchy, upset

impervious 1. hermetic, impassable, im~ penetrable, impermeable, imperviable, in~ vulnerable, resistant, sealed **2.** closed to, immune, invulnerable, proof against, unaf~ fected by, unmoved by, unreceptive, unswayable, untouched by

impetuosity haste, hastiness, impulsive~

ness, precipitancy, precipitateness, rash~ ness, vehemence, violence

impetuous ardent, eager, fierce, furious, hasty, headlong, impassioned, impulsive, passionate, precipitate, rash, spontaneous, spur-of-the-moment, unbridled, unplanned, unpremeditated, unreflecting, unrestrained, unthinking, vehement, violent
Antonyms cautious, leisurely, mild, slow, wary

impetuously helter-skelter, impulsively, in the heat of the moment, on the spur of the moment, passionately, rashly, recklessly, spontaneously, unthinkingly, vehemently, without thinking

impetus 1. catalyst, goad, impulse, impul~ sion, incentive, motivation, push, spur, stimulus **2.** energy, force, momentum, power

impiety godlessness, iniquity, irreligion, ir~ reverence, profaneness, profanity, sacrilege, sinfulness, ungodliness, unholiness, un~ righteousness, wickedness
Antonyms devoutness, godliness, holiness, piety, respect, reverence, righteousness

impinge 1. encroach, invade, make inroads, obtrude, trespass, violate **2.** affect, bear upon, have a bearing on, influence, in~ fringe, relate to, touch, touch upon **3.** clash, collide, dash, strike

impious blasphemous, godless, iniquitous, irreligious, irreverent, profane, sacri~ legious, sinful, ungodly, unholy, unright~ eous, wicked
Antonyms devout, godly, holy, pious, reli~ gious, reverent, righteous

impish devilish, elfin, mischievous, prank~ ish, puckish, rascally, roguish, sportive, waggish

implacability implacableness, inexorabil~ ity, inflexibility, intractability, merciless~ ness, pitilessness, relentlessness, ruthless~ ness, unforgivingness, vengefulness

implacable cruel, inexorable, inflexible, intractable, merciless, pitiless, rancorous, relentless, remorseless, ruthless, unappeas~ able, unbending, uncompromising, unfor~ giving, unrelenting, unyielding
Antonyms appeasable, flexible, lenient, merciful, reconcilable, relenting, tolerant, yielding

implant 1. inculcate, infix, infuse, insemi~ nate, instil, sow **2.** embed, fix, graft, ingraft, insert, place, plant, root, sow

implement 1. *n.* agent, apparatus, appli~ ance, device, gadget, instrument, tool, utensil **2.** *v.* bring about, carry out, com~ plete, effect, enforce, execute, fulfil, per~ form, put into action *or* effect, realize

Antonyms *v.* delay, hamper, hinder, impede, weaken

implementation accomplishment, carry~ing out, discharge, effecting, enforcement, execution, fulfilment, performance, per~forming, realization

implicate associate, compromise, concern, embroil, entangle, imply, include, incrimi~nate, inculpate, involve, mire, tie up with
Antonyms acquit, disentangle, dissociate, eliminate, exclude, exculpate, rule out

implicated incriminated, involved, sus~pected, under suspicion

implication 1. association, connection, en~tanglement, incrimination, involvement **2.** conclusion, inference, innuendo, meaning, overtone, presumption, ramification, significance, signification, suggestion

implicit 1. contained, implied, inferred, in~herent, latent, tacit, taken for granted, un~declared, understood, unspoken **2.** absolute, constant, entire, firm, fixed, full, steadfast, total, unhesitating, unqualified, unreserved, unshakable, unshaken, wholehearted
Antonyms (*sense 1*) declared, explicit, ex~pressed, obvious, patent, spoken, stated

implicitly absolutely, completely, firmly, unconditionally, unhesitatingly, unreserv~edly, utterly, without reservation

implied hinted at, implicit, indirect, inher~ent, insinuated, suggested, tacit, undeclared, unexpressed, unspoken, unstated

implore beg, beseech, conjure, crave, en~treat, go on bended knee to, importune, plead with, pray, solicit, supplicate

imply 1. connote, give (someone) to under~stand, hint, insinuate, intimate, signify, suggest **2.** betoken, denote, entail, evidence, import, include, indicate, involve, mean, point to, presuppose

impolite bad-mannered, boorish, churlish, discourteous, disrespectful, ill-bred, ill-mannered, indecorous, indelicate, insolent, loutish, rough, rude, uncivil, uncouth, un~gallant, ungentlemanly, ungracious, un~ladylike, unmannerly, unrefined
Antonyms courteous, decorous, gallant, gracious, mannerly, polite, refined, respect~ful, well-bred

impoliteness bad manners, boorishness, churlishness, discourtesy, disrespect, inci~vility, indelicacy, insolence, rudeness, un~mannerliness
Antonyms civility, courtesy, delicacy, man~nerliness, politeness, respect

impolitic ill-advised, ill-judged, imprudent, indiscreet, inexpedient, injudicious, mala~droit, misguided, undiplomatic, untimely, unwise

Antonyms diplomatic, discreet, expedient, judicious, politic, prudent, timely, wise

import *n.* **1.** bearing, drift, gist, implication, intention, meaning, message, purport, sense, significance, thrust **2.** bottom, con~sequence, importance, magnitude, moment, significance, substance, weight ~*v.* **3.** bring in, introduce, land

importance 1. concern, consequence, im~port, interest, moment, momentousness, significance, substance, value, weight **2.** bottom, distinction, eminence, esteem, influence, mark, pre-eminence, prestige, prominence, standing, status, usefulness, worth

important 1. far-reaching, grave, large, material, meaningful, momentous, of sub~stance, primary, salient, serious, signal, significant, substantial, urgent, weighty **2.** big-time (*Inf.*), eminent, foremost, high-level, high-ranking, influential, leading, major league (*Inf.*), notable, noteworthy, of note, outstanding, powerful, pre-eminent, prominent, seminal **3.** *Usually with* **to** ba~sic, essential, of concern *or* interest, rel~evant, valuable, valued
Antonyms inconsequential, insignificant, minor, needless, negligible, secondary, triv~ial, undistinctive, unimportant, unnecessary

importunate burning, clamant, clamorous, demanding, dogged, earnest, exigent, insist~ent, persistent, pertinacious, pressing, so~licitous, troublesome, urgent

impose 1. decree, establish, exact, fix, in~stitute, introduce, lay, levy, ordain, place, promulgate, put, set **2.** appoint, charge with, dictate, enforce, enjoin, inflict, pre~scribe, saddle (someone) with **3.** *With* **on** *or* **upon** butt in, encroach, foist, force oneself, gate-crash (*Inf.*), horn in (*Inf.*), intrude, ob~trude, presume, take liberties, trespass **4.** *With* **on** *or* **upon a.** abuse, exploit, play on, take advantage of, use **b.** con (*Inf.*), deceive, dupe, hoodwink, pull the wool over (somebody's) eyes, trick

imposing august, commanding, dignified, effective, grand, impressive, majestic, state~ly, striking
Antonyms insignificant, mean, modest, or~dinary, petty, poor, unimposing

imposition 1. application, decree, intro~duction, laying on, levying, promulgation **2.** cheek (*Inf.*), encroachment, intrusion, lib~erty, presumption **3.** artifice, cheating, con (*Inf.*), deception, dissimulation, fraud, hoax, imposture, stratagem, trickery **4.** burden, charge, constraint, duty, levy, tax

impossibility hopelessness, impracticabil~ity, inability, inconceivability

impossible 1. beyond one, beyond the bounds of possibility, hopeless, impracti~

cable, inconceivable, not to be thought of, out of the question, unachievable, unat~ tainable, unobtainable, unthinkable **2.** ab~ surd, inadmissible, insoluble, intolerable, ludicrous, outrageous, preposterous, unac~ ceptable, unanswerable, ungovernable, un~ reasonable, unsuitable, unworkable
Antonyms (*sense 1*) conceivable, imaginable, likely, plausible, possible, reasonable

impostor charlatan, cheat, deceiver, fake, fraud, hypocrite, impersonator, knave (*Ar~ chaic*), phoney *or* phony (*Inf.*), pretender, quack, rogue, sham, trickster

impotence disability, enervation, feeble~ ness, frailty, helplessness, inability, inad~ equacy, incapacity, incompetence, ineffec~ tiveness, inefficacy, inefficiency, infirmity, paralysis, powerlessness, uselessness, weakness
Antonyms ability, adequacy, competence, effectiveness, efficacy, efficiency, powerful~ ness, strength, usefulness

impotent disabled, emasculate, enervated, feeble, frail, helpless, incapable, incapaci~ tated, incompetent, ineffective, infirm, nerveless, paralysed, powerless, unable, unmanned, weak
Antonyms able, capable, competent, effec~ tive, manned, potent, powerful, strong

impoverish 1. bankrupt, beggar, break, ruin **2.** deplete, diminish, drain, exhaust, pauperize, reduce, sap, use up, wear out

impoverished 1. bankrupt, destitute, dis~ tressed, impecunious, indigent, in reduced *or* straitened circumstances, necessitous, needy, on one's uppers, penurious, poverty-stricken, ruined, straitened **2.** bar~ ren, denuded, depleted, drained, empty, ex~ hausted, played out, reduced, spent, sterile, worn out
Antonyms (*sense 1*) affluent, rich, wealthy, well-off (*sense 2*) fecund, fertile, productive

impracticability futility, hopelessness, impossibility, impracticality, unsuitable~ ness, unworkability, uselessness

impracticable 1. impossible, out of the question, unachievable, unattainable, un~ feasible, unworkable **2.** awkward, imprac~ tical, inapplicable, inconvenient, unservice~ able, unsuitable, useless
Antonyms feasible, possible, practicable, practical, serviceable, suitable

impractical 1. impossible, impracticable, inoperable, nonviable, unrealistic, unser~ viceable, unworkable, visionary, wild **2.** idealistic, romantic, starry-eyed, un~ businesslike, unrealistic, visionary
Antonyms (*sense 1*) possible, practical, ser~ viceable, viable, workable (*sense 2*) down-to-earth, realistic, sensible

impracticality hopelessness, impossibility, inapplicability, romanticism, unworkability

imprecise ambiguous, blurred round the edges, careless, equivocal, estimated, fluctuating, hazy, ill-defined, inaccurate, indefinite, indeterminate, inexact, inexplic~ it, loose, rough, sloppy (*Inf.*), vague, wide of the mark, woolly
Antonyms accurate, careful, definite, deter~ minate, exact, explicit, precise

impregnable immovable, impenetrable, indestructible, invincible, invulnerable, se~ cure, strong, unassailable, unbeatable, unconquerable, unshakable
Antonyms destructible, exposed, insecure, movable, open, pregnable, shakable, vulner~ able

impregnate 1. fill, imbrue (*Rare*), imbue, infuse, percolate, permeate, pervade, satu~ rate, seep, soak, steep, suffuse **2.** fecundate, fertilize, fructify, get with child, inseminate, make pregnant

impress 1. affect, excite, grab (*Inf.*), influence, inspire, make an impression, move, stir, strike, sway, touch **2.** *Often with* **on** *or* **upon** bring home to, emphasize, fix, inculcate, instil into, stress **3.** emboss, en~ grave, imprint, indent, mark, print, stamp

impression 1. effect, feeling, impact, influence, reaction, sway **2. make an im~ pression** arouse comment, be conspicuous, cause a stir, excite notice, find favour, make a hit (*Inf.*), make an impact, stand out **3.** belief, concept, conviction, fancy, feeling, funny feeling (*Inf.*), hunch, idea, memory, notion, opinion, recollection, sense, suspi~ cion **4.** brand, dent, hollow, impress, im~ print, indentation, mark, outline, stamp, stamping **5.** edition, imprinting, issue, printing **6.** imitation, impersonation, paro~ dy, send-up (*Brit. inf.*), takeoff (*Inf.*)

impressionable feeling, gullible, ingenu~ ous, open, receptive, responsive, sensitive, suggestible, susceptible, vulnerable
Antonyms blasé, hardened, insensitive, jaded, unresponsive

impressive affecting, exciting, forcible, moving, powerful, stirring, striking, touch~ ing
Antonyms ordinary, unimposing, unim~ pressive, uninspiring, unmemorable, weak

imprint 1. *n.* impression, indentation, mark, print, sign, stamp **2.** *v.* engrave, es~ tablish, etch, fix, impress, print, stamp

imprison confine, constrain, detain, im~ mure, incarcerate, intern, jail, lock up, put away, put under lock and key, send down (*Inf.*), send to prison
Antonyms discharge, emancipate, free, lib~ erate, release

imprisoned behind bars, captive, confined,

immured, incarcerated, in irons, in jail, in~ side (*Sl.*), interned, jailed, locked up, put away, under lock and key

imprisonment confinement, custody, de~ tention, durance (*Archaic*), duress, incar~ ceration, internment, porridge (*Sl.*)

improbability doubt, doubtfulness, dubi~ ety, uncertainty, unlikelihood

improbable doubtful, dubious, fanciful, far-fetched, implausible, questionable, un~ believable, uncertain, unconvincing, un~ likely, weak
Antonyms certain, convincing, doubtless, likely, plausible, probable, reasonable

impromptu 1. *adj.* ad-lib, extemporaneous, extempore, extemporized, improvised, off~ hand, off the cuff (*Inf.*), spontaneous, un~ premeditated, unprepared, unrehearsed, unscripted, unstudied **2.** *adv.* ad lib, off the cuff (*Inf.*), off the top of one's head (*Inf.*), on the spur of the moment, spontaneously, without preparation
Antonyms *adj.* considered, planned, pre~ meditated, prepared, rehearsed

improper 1. impolite, indecent, indecorous, indelicate, off-colour, risqué, smutty, sug~ gestive, unbecoming, unfitting, unseemly, untoward, vulgar **2.** ill-timed, inapplicable, inapposite, inappropriate, inapt, incongru~ ous, infelicitous, inopportune, malapropos, out of place, uncalled-for, unfit, unseason~ able, unsuitable, unsuited, unwarranted **3.** abnormal, erroneous, false, inaccurate, in~ correct, irregular, wrong
Antonyms (*sense 1*) becoming, decent, deco~ rous, delicate, fitting, proper, seemly (*sense 2*) apposite, appropriate, apt, felicitous, oppor~ tune, seasoned, suitable

impropriety 1. bad taste, immodesty, in~ congruity, indecency, indecorum, unsuit~ ability, vulgarity **2.** bloomer (*Brit. inf.*), blunder, faux pas, gaffe, gaucherie, mistake, slip, solecism
Antonyms (*sense 1*) decency, decorum, deli~ cacy, modesty, propriety, suitability

improve 1. advance, ameliorate, amend, augment, better, correct, face-lift, help, mend, polish, rectify, touch up, upgrade **2.** develop, enhance, gain strength, increase, look up (*Inf.*), make strides, perk up, pick up, progress, rally, reform, rise, take a turn for the better (*Inf.*), take on a new lease of life (*Inf.*) **3.** convalesce, gain ground, gain strength, grow better, make progress, mend, recover, recuperate, turn the corner **4.** clean up one's act (*Inf.*), get it together (*Inf.*), get one's act together (*Inf.*), pull one's socks up (*Brit. inf.*), reform, shape up (*Inf.*), turn over a new leaf
Antonyms damage, harm, impair, injure, mar, worsen

improvement 1. advancement, ameliora~ tion, amendment, augmentation, better~ ment, correction, face-lift, gain, rectification **2.** advance, development, enhancement, furtherance, increase, progress, rally, re~ covery, reformation, rise, upswing

improvident careless, heedless, imprudent, inconsiderate, negligent, prodigal, prof~ ligate, reckless, shiftless, short-sighted, spendthrift, thoughtless, thriftless, uneco~ nomical, unthrifty, wasteful
Antonyms careful, considerate, economical, heedful, provident, prudent, thrifty

improvisation ad-lib, ad-libbing, expedient, extemporizing, impromptu, invention, makeshift, spontaneity

improvise 1. ad-lib, busk, coin, extempo~ rize, invent, play it by ear (*Inf.*), speak off the cuff (*Inf.*), vamp, wing it (*Inf.*) **2.** con~ coct, contrive, devise, make do, throw to~ gether

improvised ad-lib, extemporaneous, ex~ tempore, extemporized, makeshift, off the cuff (*Inf.*), spontaneous, spur-of-the-moment, unprepared, unrehearsed

imprudent careless, foolhardy, foolish, heedless, ill-advised, ill-considered, ill~ judged, impolitic, improvident, incautious, inconsiderate, indiscreet, injudicious, irre~ sponsible, overhasty, rash, reckless, temer~ arious, unthinking, unwise
Antonyms careful, cautious, considerate, discreet, judicious, politic, provident, pru~ dent, responsible, wise

impudence assurance, audacity, backchat (*Inf.*), boldness, brass neck (*Brit. inf.*), bra~ zenness, bumptiousness, cheek (*Inf.*), chutz~ pah (*U.S. & Canad. inf.*), effrontery, face (*Inf.*), front, impertinence, insolence, lip (*Sl.*), neck (*Inf.*), nerve (*Inf.*), pertness, pre~ sumption, rudeness, sauciness, shameless~ ness

impudent audacious, bold, bold-faced, bra~ zen, bumptious, cheeky (*Inf.*), cocky (*Inf.*), forward, fresh (*Inf.*), immodest, impertinent, insolent, lippy (*U.S. & Canad. sl.*), pert, presumptuous, rude, sassy (*U.S. inf.*), saucy (*Inf.*), shameless
Antonyms courteous, modest, polite, re~ spectful, retiring, self-effacing, timid, well~ behaved

impulse 1. catalyst, force, impetus, mo~ mentum, movement, pressure, push, stimu~ lus, surge, thrust **2.** *Fig.* caprice, drive, feeling, incitement, inclination, influence, instinct, motive, notion, passion, resolve, urge, whim, wish

impulsive devil-may-care, emotional, hasty, headlong, impetuous, instinctive, intuitive, passionate, precipitate, quick, rash, sponta~

neous, unconsidered, unpredictable, unpre~
meditated
Antonyms arresting, calculating, cautious,
considered, cool, deliberate, halting, planned,
premeditated, rehearsed, restrained

impunity dispensation, exemption, freedom,
immunity, liberty, licence, nonliability,
permission, security

impure 1. admixed, adulterated, alloyed,
debased, mixed, unrefined **2.** contaminated,
defiled, dirty, filthy, foul, infected, polluted,
sullied, tainted, unclean, unwholesome, vi~
tiated **3.** carnal, coarse, corrupt, gross, im~
modest, immoral, indecent, indelicate, las~
civious, lewd, licentious, lustful, obscene,
prurient, ribald, salacious, smutty, un~
chaste, unclean
Antonyms (*sense 2*) clean, immaculate, spot~
less, squeaky-clean, undefiled, unsullied
(*sense 3*) chaste, decent, delicate, modest,
moral, pure, wholesome

impurity 1. admixture, adulteration, mix~
ture **2.** befoulment, contamination,
defilement, dirtiness, filth, foulness, infec~
tion, pollution, taint, uncleanness **3.** *Often
plural* bits, contaminant, dirt, dross, foreign
body, foreign matter, grime, marks, pollu~
tant, scum, spots, stains **4.** carnality,
coarseness, corruption, grossness, immod~
esty, immorality, indecency, lasciviousness,
lewdness, licentiousness, obscenity, pruri~
ence, salaciousness, smuttiness, unchastity,
vulgarity

imputation accusation, ascription, asper~
sion, attribution, blame, censure, charge,
insinuation, reproach, slander, slur

impute accredit, ascribe, assign, attribute,
credit, lay at the door of, refer, set down to

inability disability, disqualification, impo~
tence, inadequacy, incapability, incapacity,
incompetence, ineptitude, powerlessness
Antonyms ability, adequacy, capability, ca~
pacity, competence, potential, power, talent

inaccessible impassable, out of reach, out
of the way, remote, unapproachable, unat~
tainable, un-get-at-able (*Inf.*), unreachable
Antonyms accessible, approachable, attain~
able, reachable

inaccuracy 1. erroneousness, imprecision,
incorrectness, inexactness, unfaithfulness,
unreliability **2.** blunder, boob (*Brit. sl.*),
corrigendum, defect, erratum, error, fault,
howler (*Inf.*), literal (*Printing*), miscalcula~
tion, mistake, slip, typo (*Inf., printing*)

inaccurate careless, defective, discrepant,
erroneous, faulty, imprecise, incorrect, in
error, inexact, mistaken, out, unfaithful,
unreliable, unsound, wide of the mark,
wild, wrong
Antonyms accurate, correct, exact, precise,
reliable, sound

inaccurately carelessly, clumsily, impre~
cisely, inexactly, unfaithfully, unreliably

inaction dormancy, idleness, immobility,
inactivity, inertia, rest, torpidity, torpor

inactive 1. abeyant, dormant, idle, immo~
bile, inert, inoperative, jobless, kicking
one's heels, latent, mothballed, out of ser~
vice, out of work, unemployed, unoccupied,
unused **2.** dull, indolent, lazy, lethargic,
low-key (*Inf.*), passive, quiet, sedentary,
slothful, slow, sluggish, somnolent, torpid
Antonyms (*sense 1*) employed, mobile, occu~
pied, operative, running, used, working (*sense
2*) active, busy, diligent, energetic, industri~
ous, vibrant

inactivity 1. dormancy, hibernation, im~
mobility, inaction, passivity, unemployment
2. dilatoriness, *dolce far niente*, dullness,
heaviness, indolence, inertia, inertness,
lassitude, laziness, lethargy, quiescence,
sloth, sluggishness, stagnation, torpor, veg~
etation
Antonyms action, activeness, bustle, em~
ployment, exertion, mobility, movement

inadequacy 1. dearth, deficiency,
inadequateness, incompleteness, insuffi~
ciency, meagreness, paucity, poverty,
scantiness, shortage, skimpiness **2.** defec~
tiveness, faultiness, inability, inaptness, in~
capacity, incompetence, incompetency, in~
effectiveness, inefficacy, unfitness, unsuit~
ableness **3.** defect, failing, imperfection,
lack, shortage, shortcoming, weakness

inadequate 1. defective, deficient, faulty,
imperfect, incommensurate, incomplete, in~
substantial, insufficient, meagre, niggardly,
scant, scanty, short, sketchy, skimpy,
sparse **2.** found wanting, inapt, incapable,
incompetent, not up to scratch (*Inf.*), un~
equal, unfitted, unqualified
Antonyms (*sense 1*) adequate, ample, com~
plete, perfect, satisfactory, substantial,
sufficient (*sense 2*) apt, capable, competent,
equal, fit, qualified

inadequately imperfectly, insufficiently,
meagrely, poorly, scantily, sketchily,
skimpily, sparsely, thinly

inadmissible immaterial, improper, inap~
propriate, incompetent, irrelevant, unac~
ceptable, unallowable, unqualified, unrea~
sonable

inadvertently 1. carelessly, heedlessly, in
an unguarded moment, negligently,
thoughtlessly, unguardedly, unthinkingly **2.**
accidentally, by accident, by mistake, in~
voluntarily, mistakenly, unintentionally,
unwittingly
Antonyms carefully, consciously, deliber~
ately, heedfully, intentionally

inadvisable ill-advised, impolitic, impru~
dent, inexpedient, injudicious, unwise

inane asinine, daft (*Inf.*), devoid of intelli~
gence, empty, fatuous, frivolous, futile,
goofy (*Inf.*), idiotic, imbecilic, mindless, pu~
erile, senseless, silly, stupid, trifling, unin~
telligent, vacuous, vain, vapid, worthless
Antonyms meaningful, profound, sensible,
serious, significant, weighty, worthwhile

inanimate cold, dead, defunct, extinct, in~
active, inert, insensate, insentient, lifeless,
quiescent, soulless, spiritless
Antonyms active, alive, animate, lively, liv~
ing, moving

inanity asininity, bêtise (*Rare*), daftness
(*Inf.*), emptiness, fatuity, folly, frivolity,
imbecility, puerility, senselessness, silli~
ness, vacuity, vapidity, worthlessness

inapplicable inapposite, inappropriate, in~
apt, irrelevant, unsuitable, unsuited
Antonyms applicable, apposite, appropri~
ate, apt, fitting, pertinent, relevant, suitable

inappropriate disproportionate, ill-fitted,
ill-suited, ill-timed, improper, incongruous,
malapropos, out of place, tasteless, unbe~
coming, unbefitting, unfit, unfitting, un~
seemly, unsuitable, untimely
Antonyms appropriate, becoming, congru~
ous, fitting, proper, seemly, suitable, timely

inapt 1. ill-fitted, ill-suited, inapposite, in~
appropriate, infelicitous, unsuitable, un~
suited **2.** awkward, clumsy, dull, gauche,
incompetent, inept, inexpert, maladroit,
slow, stupid
Antonyms (*sense 1*) apposite, appropriate,
apt, felicitous, fitting, suitable, suited

inarticulate 1. blurred, incoherent, incom~
prehensible, indistinct, muffled, mumbled,
unclear, unintelligible **2.** dumb, mute, si~
lent, speechless, tongue-tied, unspoken, un~
uttered, unvoiced, voiceless, wordless **3.**
faltering, halting, hesitant, poorly spoken
Antonyms (*senses 1 & 3*) articulate, clear,
coherent, comprehensible, intelligible, well-
spoken

inattention absent-mindedness, careless~
ness, daydreaming, disregard, forgetfulness,
heedlessness, inadvertence, inattentiveness,
indifference, neglect, preoccupation,
thoughtlessness, woolgathering

inattentive absent-minded, careless, dis~
tracted, distrait, dreamy, heedless, inad~
vertent, neglectful, negligent, preoccupied,
regardless, remiss, slapdash, slipshod,
thoughtless, unheeding, unmindful, unob~
servant, vague
Antonyms attentive, aware, careful, con~
siderate, heeding, mindful, observant,
thoughtful

inaudible indistinct, low, mumbling, out of
earshot, stifled, unheard
Antonyms audible, clear, discernible, dis~
tinct, perceptible

inaugural dedicatory, first, initial, intro~
ductory, maiden, opening

inaugurate 1. begin, commence, get under
way, initiate, institute, introduce, kick off
(*Inf.*), launch, originate, set in motion, set
up, usher in **2.** induct, install, instate, in~
vest **3.** commission, dedicate, open, ordain

inauguration 1. initiation, institution,
launch, launching, opening, setting up **2.**
induction, installation, investiture

inauspicious bad, black, discouraging, ill-
omened, ominous, unfavourable, unfortu~
nate, unlucky, unpromising, unpropitious,
untoward
Antonyms auspicious, encouraging, fa~
vourable, fortunate, good, lucky, promising,
propitious

inborn congenital, connate, hereditary, in~
bred, ingrained, inherent, inherited, innate,
instinctive, intuitive, native, natural

inbred constitutional, deep-seated, in~
grained, inherent, innate, native, natural

incalculable boundless, countless, enor~
mous, immense, incomputable, inestimable,
infinite, innumerable, limitless, measure~
less, numberless, uncountable, untold, vast,
without number

incantation abracadabra, chant, charm,
conjuration, formula, hex (*U.S. & Canad.
inf.*), invocation, spell

incapable 1. feeble, inadequate, incompe~
tent, ineffective, inept, inexpert,
insufficient, not equal to, not up to, unfit,
unfitted, unqualified, weak **2.** helpless, im~
potent, powerless, unable, unfit **3.** *With* **of**
impervious, not admitting of, not suscep~
tible to, resistant
Antonyms (*sense 1*) adequate, capable, com~
petent, efficient, expert, fit, qualified,
sufficient

incapacitate cripple, disable, disqualify,
immobilize, lay up (*Inf.*), paralyse, pros~
trate, put out of action (*Inf.*), scupper (*Brit.
sl.*), unfit (*Rare*)

incapacitated disqualified, *hors de combat*,
immobilized, indisposed, laid up (*Inf.*), out
of action (*Inf.*), unfit

incapacity disqualification, feebleness, im~
potence, inability, inadequacy, incapability,
incompetency, ineffectiveness, powerless~
ness, unfitness, weakness

incarcerate commit, confine, coop up, de~
tain, gaol, immure, impound, imprison, in~
tern, jail, lock up, put under lock and key,
restrain, restrict, send down (*Brit.*), throw
in jail

incarceration bondage, captivity, confine~
ment, detention, imprisonment, internment,
porridge (*Sl.*), restraint

incarnate 1. in bodily form, in human

form, in the flesh, made flesh **2.** embodied, personified, typified

incarnation avatar, bodily form, embodi~ ment, epitome, exemplification, impersona~ tion, manifestation, personification, type

incautious careless, hasty, heedless, ill-advised, ill-judged, improvident, imprudent, impulsive, inconsiderate, indiscreet, injudi~ cious, negligent, precipitate, rash, reckless, thoughtless, unguarded, unthinking, un~ wary
Antonyms careful, cautious, considerate, discreet, guarded, heedful, judicious, prudent, thoughtful, wary

incautiously imprudently, impulsively, in~ discreetly, precipitately, rashly, recklessly, thoughtlessly, unthinkingly

incendiary *adj.* **1.** dissentious, inflam~ matory, provocative, rabble-rousing, sed~ itious, subversive ~*n.* **2.** arsonist, firebug (*Inf.*), fire raiser, pyromaniac **3.** agitator, demagogue, firebrand, insurgent, rabble-rouser, revolutionary

incense[1] *v.* anger, enrage, exasperate, ex~ cite, gall, get one's hackles up, inflame, in~ furiate, irritate, madden, make one's blood boil (*Inf.*), make one see red (*Inf.*), make one's hackles rise, nark (*Brit., Aust., & N.Z. sl.*), provoke, raise one's hackles, rile (*Inf.*)

incense[2] *n.* aroma, balm, bouquet, fra~ grance, perfume, redolence, scent

incensed angry, cross, enraged, exasperat~ ed, fuming, furious, indignant, infuriated, irate, ireful (*Literary*), mad (*Inf.*), mad~ dened, on the warpath (*Inf.*), steamed up (*Sl.*), up in arms, wrathful

incentive bait, carrot (*Inf.*), encourage~ ment, enticement, goad, impetus, impulse, in~ ducement, lure, motivation, motive, spur, stimulant, stimulus
Antonyms deterrent, discouragement, dis~ incentive, dissuasion, warning

inception beginning, birth, commencement, dawn, inauguration, initiation, kickoff (*Inf.*), origin, outset, rise, start
Antonyms completion, conclusion, end, ending, finish, termination

incessant ceaseless, constant, continual, continuous, endless, eternal, everlasting, interminable, never-ending, nonstop, per~ petual, persistent, relentless, unbroken, un~ ceasing, unending, unrelenting, unremitting
Antonyms infrequent, intermittent, occa~ sional, periodic, rare, sporadic

incessantly all the time, ceaselessly, con~ stantly, continually, endlessly, eternally, everlastingly, interminably, nonstop, per~ petually, persistently, without a break

incidence amount, degree, extent, frequen~ cy, occurrence, prevalence, rate

incident 1. adventure, circumstance, epi~ sode, event, fact, happening, matter, occa~ sion, occurrence **2.** brush, clash, commo~ tion, confrontation, contretemps, disturb~ ance, mishap, scene, skirmish

incidental 1. accidental, casual, chance, fortuitous, odd, random **2.** *With* **to** accom~ panying, attendant, by-the-way, concomi~ tant, contingent, contributory, related **3.** ancillary, minor, nonessential, occasional, secondary, subordinate, subsidiary
Antonyms (*sense 3*) crucial, essential, im~ portant, necessary, vital

incidentally 1. accidentally, by chance, casually, fortuitously **2.** by the bye, by the way, in passing, parenthetically

incidentals contingencies, extras, minutiae, odds and ends

incinerate burn up, carbonize, char, con~ sume by fire, cremate, reduce to ashes

incipient beginning, commencing, develop~ ing, embryonic, inceptive, inchoate, nas~ cent, originating, starting

incise carve, chisel, cut (into), engrave, etch, inscribe

incision cut, gash, notch, opening, slash, slit

incisive 1. acute, keen, penetrating, perspi~ cacious, piercing, trenchant **2.** acid, biting, caustic, cutting, mordacious, mordant, sar~ castic, sardonic, satirical, severe, sharp, vitriolic
Antonyms (*sense 1*) dense, dull, superficial, vague, woolly

incisiveness 1. keenness, penetration, perspicacity, sharpness, trenchancy **2.** acidity, pungency, sarcasm

incite agitate for *or* against, animate, drive, egg on, encourage, excite, foment, goad, im~ pel, inflame, instigate, prod, prompt, pro~ voke, put up to, rouse, set on, spur, stimu~ late, stir up, urge, whip up
Antonyms dampen, deter, discourage, dis~ hearten, dissuade, restrain

incitement agitation, encouragement, goad, impetus, impulse, inducement, instigation, motivation, motive, prompting, provocation, spur, stimulus

incivility bad manners, boorishness, dis~ courteousness, discourtesy, disrespect, ill-breeding, impoliteness, rudeness, unman~ nerliness
Antonyms civility, courteousness, courtesy, good manners, mannerliness, politeness, re~ spect

inclemency 1. bitterness, boisterousness, rawness, rigour, roughness, severity, storminess **2.** callousness, cruelty, harsh~ ness, mercilessness, severity, tyranny, un~ feelingness

inclement 1. bitter, boisterous, foul, harsh,

intemperate, rigorous, rough, severe, stormy, tempestuous **2.** callous, cruel, draconian, harsh, intemperate, merciless, pitiless, rigorous, severe, tyrannical, unfeeling, unmerciful
Antonyms (*sense 1*) balmy, calm, clement, fine, mild, pleasant, temperate (*sense 2*) compassionate, gentle, humane, kind, merciful, tender

inclination 1. affection, aptitude, bent, bias, desire, disposition, fancy, fondness, leaning, liking, partiality, penchant, predilection, predisposition, prejudice, proclivity, proneness, propensity, stomach, taste, tendency, thirst, turn, turn of mind, wish **2.** bending, bow, bowing, nod **3.** angle, bend, bending, deviation, gradient, incline, leaning, pitch, slant, slope, tilt
Antonyms (*sense 1*) antipathy, aversion, disinclination, dislike, revulsion

incline *v.* **1.** be disposed *or* predisposed, bias, influence, persuade, predispose, prejudice, sway, tend, turn **2.** bend, bow, lower, nod, nutate (*Rare*), stoop **3.** bend, bevel, cant, deviate, diverge, heel, lean, slant, slope, tend, tilt, tip, veer ~*n.* **4.** acclivity, ascent, declivity, descent, dip, grade, gradient, ramp, rise, slope

inclined apt, disposed, given, liable, likely, minded, of a mind (*Inf.*), predisposed, prone, willing

inclose *see* ENCLOSE

include 1. comprehend, comprise, contain, cover, embody, embrace, encompass, incorporate, involve, subsume, take in, take into account **2.** add, allow for, build in, count, enter, insert, introduce, number among
Antonyms eliminate, exclude, leave out, omit, rule out

including as well as, containing, counting, inclusive of, plus, together with, with

inclusion addition, incorporation, insertion
Antonyms exception, exclusion, omission, rejection

inclusive across-the-board, all-embracing, all in, all together, blanket, catch-all (*Chiefly U.S.*), comprehensive, full, general, global, *in toto*, overall, sweeping, umbrella, without exception
Antonyms confined, exclusive, limited, narrow, restricted, unique

incognito disguised, in disguise, under an assumed name, unknown, unrecognized

incoherence disconnectedness, disjointedness, inarticulateness, unintelligibility

incoherent confused, disconnected, disjointed, disordered, inarticulate, inconsistent, jumbled, loose, muddled, rambling, stammering, stuttering, unconnected, uncoordinated, unintelligible, wandering, wild

Antonyms coherent, connected, intelligible, logical, rational

incombustible fireproof, flameproof, noncombustible, nonflammable, noninflammable

income earnings, gains, interest, means, pay, proceeds, profits, receipts, revenue, salary, takings, wages

incoming approaching, arriving, entering, homeward, landing, new, returning, succeeding
Antonyms departing, exiting, leaving, outgoing

incomparable beyond compare, inimitable, matchless, paramount, peerless, superlative, supreme, transcendent, unequalled, unmatched, unparalleled, unrivalled

incomparably beyond compare, by far, easily, eminently, far and away, immeasurably

incompatibility antagonism, conflict, discrepancy, disparateness, incongruity, inconsistency, irreconcilability, uncongeniality

incompatible antagonistic, antipathetic, conflicting, contradictory, discordant, discrepant, disparate, ill-assorted, incongruous, inconsistent, inconsonant, irreconcilable, mismatched, uncongenial, unsuitable, unsuited
Antonyms alike, appropriate, compatible, congenial, consistent, harmonious, reconcilable, suitable, suited

incompetence inability, inadequacy, incapability, incapacity, incompetency, ineffectiveness, ineptitude, ineptness, insufficiency, skill-lessness, unfitness, uselessness

incompetent bungling, cowboy (*Inf.*), floundering, incapable, incapacitated, ineffectual, inept, inexpert, insufficient, skill-less, unable, unfit, unfitted, unskilful, useless
Antonyms able, capable, competent, expert, fit, proficient, skilful

incomplete broken, defective, deficient, fragmentary, imperfect, insufficient, lacking, partial, short, unaccomplished, undeveloped, undone, unexecuted, unfinished, wanting
Antonyms accomplished, complete, developed, finished, perfect, unified, whole

incomprehensible above one's head, all Greek to (*Inf.*), baffling, beyond comprehension, beyond one's grasp, enigmatic, impenetrable, inconceivable, inscrutable, mysterious, obscure, opaque, perplexing, puzzling, unfathomable, unimaginable, unintelligible, unthinkable
Antonyms apparent, clear, comprehensible,

conceivable, evident, intelligible, manifest, obvious, understandable

inconceivable beyond belief, impossible, incomprehensible, incredible, mind-boggling (*Inf.*), not to be thought of, out of the question, staggering (*Inf.*), unbelievable, unheard-of, unimaginable, unknowable, unthinkable
Antonyms believable, comprehensible, conceivable, credible, imaginable, likely, plausible, possible, reasonable

inconclusive ambiguous, indecisive, indeterminate, open, uncertain, unconvincing, undecided, unsettled, up in the air (*Inf.*), vague

incongruity conflict, discrepancy, disparity, inappropriateness, inaptness, incompatibility, inconsistency, inharmoniousness, unsuitability

incongruous absurd, conflicting, contradictory, contrary, disconsonant, discordant, extraneous, improper, inappropriate, inapt, incoherent, incompatible, inconsistent, out of keeping, out of place, unbecoming, unsuitable, unsuited
Antonyms appropriate, becoming, compatible, consistent, harmonious, suitable, suited

inconsiderable exiguous, inconsequential, insignificant, light, minor, negligible, petty, slight, small, small-time (*Inf.*), trifling, trivial, unimportant

inconsiderate careless, indelicate, insensitive, intolerant, rude, self-centred, selfish, tactless, thoughtless, uncharitable, ungracious, unkind, unthinking
Antonyms attentive, careful, considerate, gracious, kind, sensitive, tactful, thoughtful, tolerant

inconsistency 1. contrariety, disagreement, discrepancy, disparity, divergence, incompatibility, incongruity, inconsonance, paradox, variance 2. fickleness, instability, unpredictability, unreliability, unsteadiness

inconsistent 1. at odds, at variance, conflicting, contradictory, contrary, discordant, discrepant, incoherent, incompatible, in conflict, incongruous, inconstant, irreconcilable, out of step 2. capricious, changeable, erratic, fickle, inconstant, irregular, uneven, unpredictable, unstable, unsteady, vagarious (*Rare*), variable
Antonyms (*sense 1*) coherent, compatible, homogenous, orderly, reconcilable, uniform (*sense 2*) consistent, constant, predictable, reliable, stable, steady, unchanging

inconsistently contradictorily, differently, eccentrically, erratically, inequably, randomly, unequally, unfairly, unpredictably, variably

inconsolable brokenhearted, desolate, des-

pairing, heartbroken, heartsick, prostrate with grief, sick at heart

inconspicuous camouflaged, hidden, insignificant, modest, muted, ordinary, plain, quiet, retiring, unassuming, unnoticeable, unobtrusive, unostentatious
Antonyms conspicuous, noticeable, obtrusive, obvious, significant, visible

incontestable beyond doubt, beyond question, certain, incontrovertible, indisputable, indubitable, irrefutable, self-evident, sure, undeniable, unquestionable

incontinent 1. unbridled, unchecked, uncontrollable, uncontrolled, ungovernable, ungoverned, unrestrained 2. debauched, lascivious, lecherous, lewd, loose, lustful, profligate, promiscuous, unchaste, wanton

incontrovertible beyond dispute, certain, established, incontestable, indisputable, indubitable, irrefutable, positive, sure, undeniable, unquestionable, unshakable

inconvenience *n.* 1. annoyance, awkwardness, bother, difficulty, disadvantage, disruption, disturbance, downside, drawback, fuss, hassle (*Inf.*), hindrance, nuisance, trouble, uneasiness, upset, vexation 2. awkwardness, cumbersomeness, unfitness, unhandiness, unsuitableness, untimeliness, unwieldiness ~*v.* 3. bother, discommode, disrupt, disturb, give (someone) bother *or* trouble, hassle (*Inf.*), irk, make (someone) go out of his way, put out, put to trouble, trouble, upset

inconvenient 1. annoying, awkward, bothersome, disadvantageous, disturbing, embarrassing, inopportune, tiresome, troublesome, unseasonable, unsuitable, untimely, vexatious 2. awkward, cumbersome, difficult, unhandy, unmanageable, unwieldy
Antonyms (*sense 1*) convenient, handy, opportune, seasonable, suitable, timely

incorporate absorb, amalgamate, assimilate, blend, coalesce, combine, consolidate, embody, fuse, include, integrate, meld, merge, mix, subsume, unite

incorrect erroneous, false, faulty, flawed, improper, inaccurate, inappropriate, inexact, mistaken, out, specious, unfitting, unsuitable, untrue, wide of the mark (*Inf.*), wrong
Antonyms accurate, correct, exact, faultless, fitting, flawless, right, suitable, true

incorrectness erroneousness, error, fallacy, faultiness, impreciseness, imprecision, impropriety, inaccuracy, inexactness, speciousness, unsoundness, unsuitability, wrongness

incorrigible hardened, hopeless, incurable, intractable, inveterate, irredeemable, unreformed

incorruptibility honesty, honour, integrity, justness, uprightness

incorruptible 1. above suspicion, honest, honourable, just, straight, trustworthy, un~ bribable, upright **2.** everlasting, imperish~ able, undecaying

increase *v.* **1.** add to, advance, aggrandize, amplify, augment, boost, build up, develop, dilate, enhance, enlarge, escalate, expand, extend, grow, heighten, inflate, intensify, magnify, mount, multiply, proliferate, pro~ long, raise, snowball, spread, step up (*Inf.*), strengthen, swell, wax ~*n.* **2.** addition, augmentation, boost, development, enlarge~ ment, escalation, expansion, extension, gain, growth, increment, intensification, rise, upsurge, upturn **3. on the increase** developing, escalating, expanding, growing, increasing, multiplying, on the rise, prolif~ erating, spreading
Antonyms *v.* abate, abbreviate, abridge, condense, curtail, decline, decrease, deflate, diminish, dwindle, lessen, reduce, shorten, shrink

increasingly more and more, progressively, to an increasing extent

incredible 1. absurd, beyond belief, far~ fetched, implausible, impossible, improb~ able, inconceivable, preposterous, unbeliev~ able, unimaginable, unthinkable **2.** *Inf.* ace (*Inf.*), amazing, astonishing, astounding, awe-inspiring, brilliant, def (*Sl.*), extraordi~ nary, far-out (*Sl.*), great, marvellous, mega (*Sl.*), prodigious, rad (*Inf.*), sensational (*Inf.*), superhuman, wonderful

incredulity disbelief, distrust, doubt, scep~ ticism, unbelief

incredulous disbelieving, distrustful, doubtful, doubting, dubious, mistrustful, sceptical, suspicious, unbelieving, uncon~ vinced
Antonyms believing, credulous, gullible, naive, trusting, unsuspecting

increment accretion, accrual, accrument, addition, advancement, augmentation, en~ largement, gain, increase, step (up), sup~ plement

incriminate accuse, arraign, blacken the name of, blame, charge, impeach, implicate, inculpate, indict, involve, point the finger at (*Inf.*), stigmatize

incumbent binding, compulsory, manda~ tory, necessary, obligatory

incur arouse, bring (upon oneself), contract, draw, earn, expose oneself to, gain, induce, lay oneself open to, meet with, provoke

incurable *adj.* **1.** dyed-in-the-wool, hopeless, incorrigible, inveterate **2.** fatal, inoperable, irrecoverable, irremediable, remediless, terminal

indebted beholden, grateful, in debt, obli~ gated, obliged, under an obligation

indecency bawdiness, coarseness, crudity, foulness, grossness, immodesty, impropri~ ety, impurity, indecorum, indelicacy, lewd~ ness, licentiousness, obscenity, outrageous~ ness, pornography, smut, smuttiness, un~ seemliness, vileness, vulgarity
Antonyms decency, decorum, delicacy, modesty, propriety, purity, seemliness

indecent 1. blue, coarse, crude, dirty, filthy, foul, gross, immodest, improper, im~ pure, indelicate, lewd, licentious, porno~ graphic, salacious, scatological, smutty, vile **2.** ill-bred, improper, in bad taste, indeco~ rous, offensive, outrageous, tasteless, unbe~ coming, unseemly, vulgar
Antonyms decent, decorous, delicate, mod~ est, proper, pure, respectable, seemly, tasteful

indecipherable crabbed, illegible, indis~ tinguishable, unintelligible, unreadable

indecision ambivalence, dithering (*Chiefly Brit.*), doubt, hesitancy, hesitation, indeci~ siveness, irresolution, shilly-shallying (*Inf.*), uncertainty, vacillation, wavering

indecisive 1. dithering (*Chiefly Brit.*), doubtful, faltering, hesitating, in two minds (*Inf.*), irresolute, pussyfooting (*Inf.*), tenta~ tive, uncertain, undecided, undetermined, vacillating, wavering **2.** inconclusive, in~ definite, indeterminate, unclear, undecided
Antonyms (*sense 1*) certain, decided, deter~ mined, positive, resolute, unhesitating (*sense 2*) clear, conclusive, decisive, definite, deter~ minate, final

indeed actually, certainly, doubtlessly, in point of fact, in truth, positively, really, strictly, to be sure, truly, undeniably, un~ doubtedly, verily (*Archaic*), veritably

indefensible faulty, inexcusable, insup~ portable, unforgivable, unjustifiable, unpar~ donable, untenable, unwarrantable, wrong
Antonyms defensible, excusable, forgivable, justifiable, legitimate, pardonable, support~ able, tenable, warrantable

indefinable dim, hazy, impalpable, inde~ scribable, indistinct, inexpressible, name~ less, obscure, unrealized, vague

indefinite ambiguous, confused, doubtful, equivocal, evasive, general, ill-defined, im~ precise, indeterminate, indistinct, inexact, loose, obscure, oracular, uncertain, unclear, undefined, undetermined, unfixed, un~ known, unlimited, unsettled, vague
Antonyms certain, clear, definite, determi~ nate, distinct, exact, fixed, settled, specific

indefinitely ad infinitum, continually, end~ lessly, for ever, *sine die*

indelible enduring, indestructible, ineffac~

able, ineradicable, inexpungible, inextir~ pable, ingrained, lasting, permanent
Antonyms eradicable, erasable, imperma~ nent, removable, short-lived, temporary, washable

indelicacy bad taste, coarseness, crudity, grossness, immodesty, impropriety, inde~ cency, obscenity, offensiveness, rudeness, smuttiness, suggestiveness, tastelessness, vulgarity

indelicate blue, coarse, crude, embarrass~ ing, gross, immodest, improper, indecent, indecorous, low, near the knuckle (*Inf.*), obscene, off-colour, offensive, risqué, rude, suggestive, tasteless, unbecoming, unseem~ ly, untoward, vulgar
Antonyms becoming, decent, decorous, delicate, modest, proper, refined, seemly

indemnify 1. endorse, guarantee, insure, protect, secure, underwrite **2.** compensate, pay, reimburse, remunerate, repair, repay, requite, satisfy

indemnity 1. guarantee, insurance, protec~ tion, security **2.** compensation, redress, re~ imbursement, remuneration, reparation, requital, restitution, satisfaction **3.** *Law* exemption, immunity, impunity, privilege

indent *v.* **1.** ask for, order, request, requisi~ tion **2.** cut, dint, mark, nick, notch, pink, scallop, score, serrate

independence autarchy, autonomy, free~ dom, home rule, liberty, self-determination, self-government, self-reliance, self-rule, self-sufficiency, separation, sovereignty
Antonyms bondage, dependence, subjec~ tion, subjugation, subordination, subservi~ ence

independent 1. absolute, free, liberated, separate, unconnected, unconstrained, un~ controlled, unrelated **2.** autarchic, autar~ chical, autonomous, decontrolled, non~ aligned, self-determining, self-governing, separated, sovereign **3.** bold, individualis~ tic, liberated, self-contained, self-reliant, self-sufficient, self-supporting, unaided, un~ conventional
Antonyms (*sense 2*) aligned, controlled, de~ pendent, restrained, subject, submissive, subordinate, subservient, subsidiary

independently alone, autonomously, by oneself, individually, on one's own, sepa~ rately, solo, unaided

indescribable beggaring description, be~ yond description, beyond words, incommu~ nicable, indefinable, ineffable, inexpressible, unutterable

indestructible abiding, durable, enduring, everlasting, immortal, imperishable, incor~ ruptible, indelible, indissoluble, lasting, nonperishable, permanent, unbreakable, unfading

Antonyms breakable, corruptible, destruct~ ible, fading, impermanent, mortal, perishable

indeterminate imprecise, inconclusive, indefinite, inexact, uncertain, undefined, undetermined, unfixed, unspecified, unstipulated, vague
Antonyms certain, clear, conclusive, definite, determinate, exact, fixed, precise, specified, stipulated

index 1. clue, guide, indication, mark, sign, symptom, token **2.** director, forefinger, hand, indicator, needle, pointer

indicate 1. add up to (*Inf.*), bespeak, be symptomatic of, betoken, denote, evince, imply, manifest, point to, reveal, show, sig~ nify, suggest **2.** designate, point out, point to, specify **3.** display, express, mark, read, record, register, show

indication clue, evidence, explanation, forewarning, hint, index, inkling, intima~ tion, manifestation, mark, note, omen, por~ tent, sign, signal, suggestion, symptom, warning

indicative exhibitive, indicatory, indicial, pointing to, significant, suggestive, sympto~ matic

indicator display, gauge, guide, index, mark, marker, meter, pointer, sign, signal, signpost, symbol

indict accuse, arraign, charge, impeach, prosecute, serve with a summons, summon, summons, tax

indictment accusation, allegation, charge, impeachment, prosecution, summons

indifference 1. absence of feeling, aloof~ ness, apathy, callousness, carelessness, coldness, coolness, detachment, disregard, heedlessness, inattention, lack of interest, negligence, nonchalance, stoicalness, un~ concern **2.** disinterestedness, dispassion, equity, impartiality, neutrality, objectivity **3.** insignificance, irrelevance, triviality, unimportance
Antonyms (*sense 1*) attention, care, commit~ ment, concern, enthusiasm, heed, regard

indifferent 1. aloof, apathetic, callous, careless, cold, cool, detached, distant, heed~ less, impervious, inattentive, regardless, uncaring, unconcerned, unimpressed, unin~ terested, unmoved, unresponsive, unsym~ pathetic **2.** immaterial, insignificant, of no consequence, unimportant **3.** average, fair, mediocre, middling, moderate, ordinary, passable, perfunctory, so-so (*Inf.*), undistin~ guished, uninspired **4.** disinterested, dis~ passionate, equitable, impartial, neutral, nonaligned, nonpartisan, objective, unbi~ ased, uninvolved, unprejudiced
Antonyms (*sense 1*) avid, compassionate, concerned, eager, enthusiastic, interested, keen, responsive, sensitive, susceptible, sym~

pathetic (*sense 3*) excellent, exceptional, fine, first-class, notable, remarkable

indigent destitute, dirt-poor (*Inf.*), down and out, flat broke (*Inf.*), impecunious, impoverished, in want, necessitous, needy, on one's uppers (*Inf.*), penniless, penurious, poor, poverty-stricken, short, straitened, without two pennies to rub together (*Inf.*)
Antonyms affluent, prosperous, rich, wealthy, well-off, well-to-do

indigestion dyspepsia, dyspepsy, heart~burn, upset stomach

indignant angry, annoyed, disgruntled, exasperated, fuming (*Inf.*), furious, hacked (off) (*U.S. sl.*), heated, huffy (*Inf.*), in a huff, incensed, in high dudgeon, irate, livid (*Inf.*), mad (*Inf.*), miffed (*Inf.*), narked (*Brit., Aust., & N.Z. sl.*), peeved (*Inf.*), pissed off (*Taboo sl.*), provoked, resentful, riled, scornful, seeing red (*Inf.*), sore (*Inf.*), up in arms (*Inf.*), wrathful

indignation anger, exasperation, fury, ire (*Literary*), pique, rage, resentment, right~eous anger, scorn, umbrage, wrath

indignity abuse, affront, contumely, dis~honour, disrespect, humiliation, injury, in~sult, obloquy, opprobrium, outrage, re~proach, slap in the face (*Inf.*), slight, snub

indirect 1. backhanded, circuitous, circum~locutory, crooked, devious, long-drawn-out, meandering, oblique, periphrastic, ram~bling, roundabout, tortuous, wandering, winding, zigzag **2.** ancillary, collateral, contingent, incidental, secondary, subsidi~ary, unintended
Antonyms (*sense 1*) clear-cut, direct, straight, straightforward, undeviating, unin~terrupted (*sense 2*) direct, explicit, express, intended

indirectly by implication, circumlocutorily, in a roundabout way, obliquely, periphras~tically, second-hand

indiscernible hidden, impalpable, imper~ceptible, indistinct, indistinguishable, in~visible, unapparent, undiscernible
Antonyms apparent, clear, discernible, dis~tinct, distinguishable, perceptible, visible

indiscreet foolish, hasty, heedless, ill-advised, ill-considered, ill-judged, impolitic, imprudent, incautious, injudicious, naive, rash, reckless, tactless, undiplomatic, un~thinking, unwise
Antonyms cautious, diplomatic, discreet, judicious, politic, prudent, tactful, wise

indiscretion bloomer (*Brit. inf.*), boob (*Brit. sl.*), error, faux pas, folly, foolishness, gaffe, gaucherie, imprudence, mistake, rashness, recklessness, slip, slip of the tongue, tact~lessness

indiscriminate 1. aimless, careless, desul~tory, general, hit or miss (*Inf.*), random, sweeping, uncritical, undiscriminating, un~methodical, unselective, unsystematic, wholesale **2.** chaotic, confused, haphazard, higgledy-piggledy (*Inf.*), jumbled, mingled, miscellaneous, mixed, mongrel, motley, promiscuous, undistinguishable
Antonyms (*sense 1*) deliberate, discriminat~ing, exclusive, methodical, selective, system~atic

indispensable crucial, essential, impera~tive, key, necessary, needed, needful, requi~site, vital
Antonyms dispensable, disposable, nones~sential, superfluous, unimportant, unneces~sary

indisposed 1. ailing, confined to bed, ill, laid up (*Inf.*), on the sick list (*Inf.*), poorly (*Inf.*), sick, unwell **2.** averse, disinclined, loath, reluctant, unwilling
Antonyms (*sense 1*) fine, fit, hardy, healthy, sound, well

indisposition 1. ailment, ill health, illness, sickness **2.** aversion, disinclination, dislike, distaste, hesitancy, reluctance, unwilling~ness

indisputable absolute, beyond doubt, cer~tain, evident, incontestable, incontrovert~ible, indubitable, irrefutable, positive, sure, unassailable, undeniable, unquestionable
Antonyms assailable, disputable, doubtful, indefinite, questionable, refutable, uncertain, vague

indissoluble abiding, binding, enduring, eternal, fixed, imperishable, incorruptible, indestructible, inseparable, lasting, perma~nent, solid, unbreakable

indistinct ambiguous, bleary, blurred, con~fused, dim, doubtful, faint, fuzzy, hazy, ill-defined, indefinite, indeterminate, indis~cernible, indistinguishable, misty, muffled, obscure, out of focus, shadowy, unclear, undefined, unintelligible, vague, weak
Antonyms clear, defined, determinate, dis~cernible, distinct, distinguishable, evident, intelligible

indistinguishable 1. alike, identical, like as two peas in a pod (*Inf.*), (the) same, twin **2.** imperceptible, indiscernible, invisible, obscure

individual 1. *adj.* characteristic, discrete, distinct, distinctive, exclusive, identical, idiosyncratic, own, particular, peculiar, personal, personalized, proper, respective, separate, several, single, singular, special, specific, unique **2.** *n.* being, body (*Inf.*), character, creature, mortal, party, person, personage, soul, type, unit
Antonyms *adj.* collective, common, conven~tional, general, indistinct, ordinary, universal

individualism egocentricity, egoism, free~

thinking, independence, originality, self-direction, self-interest, self-reliance

individualist freethinker, independent, loner, lone wolf, maverick, nonconformist, original

individuality character, discreteness, distinction, distinctiveness, originality, peculiarity, personality, separateness, singularity, uniqueness

individually apart, independently, one at a time, one by one, personally, separately, severally, singly

indoctrinate brainwash, drill, ground, imbue, initiate, instruct, school, teach, train

indoctrination brainwashing, drilling, grounding, inculcation, instruction, schooling, training

indolent fainéant, idle, inactive, inert, lackadaisical, languid, lazy, lethargic, listless, lumpish, slack, slothful, slow, sluggish, torpid, workshy
Antonyms active, assiduous, busy, conscientious, diligent, energetic, industrious, vigorous

indomitable bold, invincible, resolute, staunch, steadfast, unbeatable, unconquerable, unflinching, untameable, unyielding
Antonyms cowardly, faltering, feeble, shrinking, wavering, weak, yielding

indubitable certain, evident, incontestable, incontrovertible, indisputable, irrefutable, obvious, sure, unarguable, undeniable, undoubted, unquestionable, veritable

induce 1. actuate, convince, draw, encourage, get, impel, incite, influence, instigate, move, persuade, press, prevail upon, prompt, talk into **2.** bring about, cause, effect, engender, generate, give rise to, lead to, occasion, produce, set in motion, set off
Antonyms curb, deter, discourage, dissuade, hinder, prevent, restrain, stop, suppress

inducement attraction, bait, carrot (*Inf.*), cause, come-on (*Inf.*), consideration, encouragement, impulse, incentive, incitement, influence, lure, motive, reward, spur, stimulus, urge

indulge 1. cater to, feed, give way to, gratify, pander to, regale, satiate, satisfy, treat oneself to, yield to **2.** *With* **in** bask in, give free rein to, give oneself up to, luxuriate in, revel in, wallow in **3.** baby, coddle, cosset, favour, foster, give in to, go along with, humour, mollycoddle, pamper, pet, spoil

indulgence 1. excess, fondness, immoderation, intemperance, intemperateness, kindness, leniency, pampering, partiality, permissiveness, profligacy, profligateness, spoiling **2.** appeasement, fulfilment, gratification, satiation, satisfaction **3.** ex-

travagance, favour, luxury, privilege, treat **4.** courtesy, forbearance, goodwill, patience, tolerance, understanding
Antonyms (*sense 1*) moderation, strictness, temperance, temperateness

indulgent compliant, easy-going, favourable, fond, forbearing, gentle, gratifying, kind, kindly, lenient, liberal, mild, permissive, tender, tolerant, understanding
Antonyms austere, demanding, harsh, intolerant, rigorous, stern, strict, stringent, unmerciful

industrialist baron, big businessman, boss, capitalist, captain of industry, financier, magnate, manufacturer, producer, tycoon

industrious active, assiduous, busy, conscientious, diligent, energetic, hardworking, laborious, persevering, persistent, productive, purposeful, sedulous, steady, tireless, zealous
Antonyms idle, indolent, lackadaisical, lazy, shiftless, slothful

industriously assiduously, conscientiously, diligently, doggedly, hard, like a Trojan, nose to the grindstone (*Inf.*), perseveringly, sedulously, steadily, without slacking

industry 1. business, commerce, commercial enterprise, manufacturing, production, trade **2.** activity, application, assiduity, determination, diligence, effort, labour, perseverance, persistence, tirelessness, toil, vigour, zeal

inebriated befuddled, bevvied (*Dialect*), blind drunk, blitzed (*Sl.*), blotto (*Sl.*), bombed (*Sl.*), drunk, flying (*Sl.*), fou *or* fu' (*Scot.*), half-cut (*Inf.*), half seas over (*Inf.*), high (*Inf.*), high as a kite (*Inf.*), inebriate, in one's cups, intoxicated, legless (*Inf.*), lit up (*Sl.*), merry (*Brit. inf.*), out of it (*Sl.*), out to it (*Aust. & N.Z. sl.*), paralytic (*Inf.*), pie-eyed (*Sl.*), pissed (*Taboo sl.*), plastered (*Sl.*), smashed (*Sl.*), sozzled (*Inf.*), steamboats (*Sl.*), steaming (*Sl.*), stoned (*Sl.*), the worse for drink, three sheets in the wind (*Inf.*), tight (*Inf.*), tipsy, under the influence (*Inf.*), under the weather (*Inf.*), wasted (*Sl.*), wrecked (*Sl.*), zonked (*Sl.*)

ineffective barren, bootless, feeble, fruitless, futile, idle, impotent, inadequate, ineffectual, inefficacious, inefficient, unavailing, unproductive, useless, vain, weak, worthless
Antonyms effective, efficacious, efficient, fruitful, potent, productive, useful, worthwhile

ineffectual abortive, bootless, emasculate, feeble, fruitless, futile, idle, impotent, inadequate, incompetent, ineffective, inefficacious, inefficient, inept, lame, powerless, unavailing, useless, vain, weak

inefficiency carelessness, disorganization,

incompetence, muddle, slackness, sloppi~
ness

inefficient cowboy (*Inf.*), disorganized, fee~
ble, incapable, incompetent, ineffectual,
inefficacious, inept, inexpert, slipshod,
sloppy, wasteful, weak
Antonyms able, capable, competent, effec~
tive, efficient, expert, organized, skilled

ineligible disqualified, incompetent (*Law*),
objectionable, ruled out, unacceptable, un~
desirable, unequipped, unfit, unfitted,
unqualified, unsuitable

inept 1. awkward, bumbling, bungling,
cack-handed (*Inf.*), clumsy, cowboy (*Inf.*),
gauche, incompetent, inexpert, maladroit,
unhandy, unskilful, unworkmanlike **2.** ab~
surd, improper, inappropriate, inapt, infe~
licitous, malapropos, meaningless, out of
place, pointless, ridiculous, unfit, unsuitable
Antonyms able, adroit, appropriate, apt,
competent, dexterous, effectual, efficient,
germane, qualified, sensible, skilful, suitable,
talented

ineptitude 1. clumsiness, gaucheness, in~
capacity, incompetence, inexpertness,
unfitness, unhandiness **2.** absurdity, inap~
propriateness, pointlessness, uselessness

inequality bias, difference, disparity, dis~
proportion, diversity, imparity, irregularity,
lack of balance, preferentiality, prejudice,
unevenness

inequitable biased, discriminatory, one-
sided, partial, partisan, preferential, preju~
diced, unfair, unjust
Antonyms even-handed, fair, impartial,
just, unbiased, unprejudiced

inert dead, dormant, dull, idle, immobile,
inactive, inanimate, indolent, lazy, leaden,
lifeless, motionless, passive, quiescent,
slack, slothful, sluggish, slumberous (*Chiefly
poetic*), static, still, torpid, unmoving,
unreactive, unresponsive
Antonyms active, alive, animated, energet~
ic, living, mobile, moving, reactive, respon~
sive, vital

inertia apathy, deadness, disinclination to
move, drowsiness, dullness, idleness, im~
mobility, inactivity, indolence, languor,
lassitude, laziness, lethargy, listlessness,
passivity, sloth, sluggishness, stillness, stu~
por, torpor, unresponsiveness
Antonyms action, activity, animation, brio,
energy, liveliness, vigour, vitality

inescapable certain, destined, fated, in~
eluctable, ineludible (*Rare*), inevitable, in~
exorable, sure, unavoidable

inestimable beyond price, immeasurable,
incalculable, invaluable, precious, priceless,
prodigious

inevitable assured, certain, decreed, des~

tined, fixed, ineluctable, inescapable, inexo~
rable, necessary, ordained, settled, sure,
unavoidable, unpreventable
Antonyms avoidable, escapable, evadable,
preventable, uncertain

inevitably as a necessary consequence, as a
result, automatically, certainly, necessarily,
of necessity, perforce, surely, unavoidably,
willy-nilly

inexcusable indefensible, inexpiable, out~
rageous, unforgivable, unjustifiable, unpar~
donable, unwarrantable
Antonyms defensible, excusable, forgivable,
justifiable, pardonable

inexhaustible 1. bottomless, boundless,
endless, illimitable, infinite, limitless,
measureless, never-ending, unbounded **2.**
indefatigable, tireless, undaunted, unfailing,
unflagging, untiring, unwearied, unweary~
ing
Antonyms (*sense 1*) bounded, exhaustible,
finite, limitable, limited, measurable (*sense 2*)
daunted, enervated, failing, flagging, tiring,
wearied

inexorable adamant, cruel, hard, harsh,
immovable, implacable, ineluctable, ines~
capable, inflexible, merciless, obdurate,
pitiless, relentless, remorseless, severe, un~
appeasable, unbending, unrelenting, un~
yielding
Antonyms bending, flexible, lenient, mov~
able, relenting, yielding

inexorably implacably, inevitably, irresist~
ibly, relentlessly, remorselessly, unrelent~
ingly

inexpensive bargain, budget, cheap, eco~
nomical, low-cost, low-priced, modest, rea~
sonable
Antonyms costly, dear, exorbitant, expen~
sive, high-priced, pricey, uneconomical

inexperience callowness, greenness, igno~
rance, newness, rawness, unexpertness, un~
familiarity

inexperienced amateur, callow, fresh,
green, immature, new, raw, unaccustomed,
unacquainted, unfamiliar, unfledged, un~
practised, unschooled, unseasoned, un~
skilled, untrained, untried, unused, un~
versed, wet behind the ears (*Inf.*)
Antonyms experienced, familiar, knowl~
edgeable, practised, seasoned, skilled,
trained, versed

inexpert amateurish, awkward, bungling,
cack-handed (*Inf.*), clumsy, inept, maladroit,
skill-less, unhandy, unpractised, unprofes~
sional, unskilful, unskilled, unworkmanlike

inexplicable baffling, beyond comprehen~
sion, enigmatic, incomprehensible, inscru~
table, insoluble, mysterious, mystifying,
strange, unaccountable, unfathomable, un~
intelligible

Antonyms comprehensible, explainable, explicable, fathomable, intelligible, soluble, understandable

inexpressible incommunicable, indefin~ able, indescribable, ineffable, unspeakable, unutterable

inexpressive bland, blank, cold, dead, deadpan, emotionless, empty, expression~ less, impassive, inanimate, inscrutable, lifeless, stony, vacant

inextinguishable enduring, eternal, im~ mortal, imperishable, indestructible, irre~ pressible, undying, unquenchable, unsuppressible

inextricably indissolubly, indistinguish~ ably, inseparably, intricately, irretrievably, totally

infallibility 1. faultlessness, impeccability, irrefutability, omniscience, perfection, su~ premacy, unerringness **2.** dependability, reliability, safety, sureness, trustworthiness

infallible 1. faultless, impeccable, omnisci~ ent, perfect, unerring, unimpeachable **2.** certain, dependable, foolproof, reliable, sure, sure-fire (*Inf.*), trustworthy, unbeat~ able, unfailing
Antonyms (*sense 1*) errant, fallible, human, imperfect, mortal (*sense 2*) doubtful, dubious, uncertain, undependable, unreliable, unsure

infamous abominable, atrocious, base, de~ testable, disgraceful, dishonourable, dis~ reputable, egregious, flagitious, hateful, heinous, ignominious, ill-famed, iniquitous, loathsome, monstrous, nefarious, notorious, odious, opprobrious, outrageous, scandal~ ous, scurvy, shameful, shocking, vile, vil~ lainous, wicked
Antonyms esteemed, glorious, honourable, noble, reputable, virtuous

infancy 1. babyhood, early childhood **2.** be~ ginnings, cradle, dawn, early stages, emer~ gence, inception, origins, outset, start
Antonyms (*sense 2*) close, conclusion, death, end, expiration, finish, termination

infant 1. *n.* ankle-biter (*Aust. sl.*), babe, baby, bairn (*Scot.*), child, little one, neonate, newborn child, rug rat (*Sl.*), sprog (*Sl.*), suckling, toddler, tot, wean (*Scot.*) **2.** *adj.* baby, dawning, developing, early, emergent, growing, immature, initial, nascent, new~ born, unfledged, young

infantile babyish, childish, immature, puer~ ile, tender, weak, young
Antonyms adult, developed, mature

infatuate befool, beguile, besot, bewitch, captivate, delude, enchant, enrapture, enravish, fascinate, make a fool of, mislead, obsess, stupefy, sweep one off one's feet, turn (someone's) head

infatuated beguiled, besotted, bewitched, captivated, carried away, crazy about (*Inf.*), enamoured, enraptured, fascinated, head over heels in love with, inflamed, intoxi~ cated, obsessed, possessed, smitten (*Inf.*), spellbound, swept off one's feet, under the spell of

infatuation crush (*Inf.*), fixation, folly, foolishness, madness, obsession, passion, thing (*Inf.*)

infect affect, blight, contaminate, corrupt, defile, influence, poison, pollute, spread to *or* among, taint, touch, vitiate

infection contagion, contamination, cor~ ruption, defilement, poison, pollution, sep~ ticity, virus

infectious catching, communicable, conta~ gious, contaminating, corrupting, defiling, infective, pestilential, poisoning, polluting, spreading, transmittable, virulent, vitiating

infer conclude, conjecture, deduce, derive, gather, presume, read between the lines, surmise, understand

inference assumption, conclusion, conjec~ ture, consequence, corollary, deduction, il~ lation (*Rare*), presumption, reading, sur~ mise

inferior *adj.* **1.** junior, lesser, lower, menial, minor, secondary, subordinate, subsidiary, under, underneath **2.** bad, bush-league (*Aust. & N.Z. inf.*), chickenshit (*U.S. sl.*), crappy (*Sl.*), dime-a-dozen (*Inf.*), duff (*Brit. inf.*), imperfect, indifferent, low-grade, mean, mediocre, of a sort *or* of sorts, piss-poor (*Taboo sl.*), poor, poorer, poxy (*Sl.*), second-class, second-rate, shoddy, sub~ standard, tinhorn (*U.S. sl.*), two-bit (*U.S. & Canad. sl.*), worse ~*n.* **3.** junior, menial, subordinate, underling
Antonyms (*sense 1*) greater, higher, senior, superior, top (*sense 2*) excellent, fine, first-class

inferiority 1. badness, deficiency, imper~ fection, inadequacy, insignificance, mean~ ness, mediocrity, shoddiness, unimportance, worthlessness **2.** abasement, inferior status *or* standing, lowliness, subordination, sub~ servience
Antonyms advantage, ascendancy, domi~ nance, eminence, excellence, superiority

infernal 1. chthonian, Hadean, hellish, low~ er, nether, Plutonian, Stygian, Tartarean (*Literary*), underworld **2.** accursed, dam~ nable, damned, demonic, devilish, diaboli~ cal, fiendish, hellish, malevolent, malicious, satanic
Antonyms angelic, celestial, glorious, god~ like, heavenly, seraphic

infertile barren, infecund, nonproductive, sterile, unfruitful, unproductive
Antonyms fecund, fertile, fruitful, genera~ tive, productive

infertility barrenness, infecundity, sterility, unfruitfulness, unproductiveness

infest beset, flood, invade, overrun, penetrate, permeate, ravage, swarm, throng

infested alive, beset, crawling, lousy (*Sl.*), overrun, pervaded, plagued, ravaged, ridden, swarming, teeming

infiltrate creep in, filter through, insinuate oneself, penetrate, percolate, permeate, pervade, sneak in (*Inf.*), work *or* worm one's way into

infinite absolute, all-embracing, bottomless, boundless, enormous, eternal, everlasting, illimitable, immeasurable, immense, inestimable, inexhaustible, interminable, limitless, measureless, never-ending, numberless, perpetual, stupendous, total, unbounded, uncounted, untold, vast, wide, without end, without number
Antonyms bounded, circumscribed, finite, limited, measurable, restricted

infinitesimal atomic, inappreciable, insignificant, microscopic, minuscule, minute, negligible, teensy-weensy, teeny, teeny-weeny, tiny, unnoticeable, wee
Antonyms enormous, great, huge, infinite, large, vast

infinity boundlessness, endlessness, eternity, immensity, infinitude, perpetuity, vastness

infirm 1. ailing, debilitated, decrepit, doddering, doddery, enfeebled, failing, feeble, frail, lame, weak 2. faltering, indecisive, insecure, irresolute, shaky, unsound, unstable, vacillating, wavering, weak, wobbly
Antonyms (*sense 1*) healthy, hearty, robust, sound, strong, sturdy, vigorous

infirmity 1. debility, decrepitude, deficiency, feebleness, frailty, ill health, imperfection, sickliness, vulnerability 2. ailment, defect, disorder, failing, fault, malady, sickness, weakness
Antonyms health, soundness, stability, strength, vigour

inflame 1. agitate, anger, arouse, embitter, enrage, exasperate, excite, fire, foment, heat, ignite, impassion, incense, infuriate, intoxicate, kindle, madden, provoke, rile, rouse, stimulate 2. aggravate, exacerbate, exasperate, fan, increase, intensify, worsen
Antonyms allay, calm, cool, discourage, extinguish, pacify, quench, quiet, soothe, suppress

inflamed angry, chafing, festering, fevered, heated, hot, infected, red, septic, sore, swollen

inflammable combustible, flammable, incendiary

inflammation burning, heat, painfulness, rash, redness, sore, soreness, tenderness

inflammatory anarchic, demagogic, explosive, fiery, incendiary, inflaming, instigative, insurgent, intemperate, provocative, rabble-rousing, rabid, riotous, seditious

inflate aerate, aggrandize, amplify, balloon, bloat, blow up, boost, dilate, distend, enlarge, escalate, exaggerate, expand, increase, puff up *or* out, pump up, swell
Antonyms collapse, compress, contract, deflate, diminish, lessen, shrink

inflated bombastic, exaggerated, grandiloquent, ostentatious, overblown, swollen

inflation aggrandizement, blowing up, distension, enhancement, enlargement, escalation, expansion, extension, increase, intensification, puffiness, rise, spread, swelling, tumefaction

inflection 1. accentuation, bend, bow, crook, curvature, intonation, modulation 2. *Gram.* conjugation, declension 3. angle, arc, arch

inflexibility 1. hardness, immovability, inelasticity, rigidity, stiffness, stringency 2. fixity, intransigence, obduracy, obstinacy, steeliness

inflexible 1. adamant, brassbound, dyed-in-the-wool, firm, fixed, hard and fast, immovable, immutable, implacable, inexorable, intractable, iron, obdurate, obstinate, relentless, resolute, rigorous, set, set in one's ways, steadfast, steely, stiff-necked, strict, stringent, stubborn, unadaptable, unbending, unchangeable, uncompromising, unyielding 2. hard, hardened, inelastic, nonflexible, rigid, stiff, taut
Antonyms elastic, flexible, irresolute, lissom(e), movable, pliable, pliant, supple, variable, yielding

inflict administer, apply, deliver, exact, impose, levy, mete *or* deal out, visit, wreak

infliction 1. administration, exaction, imposition, perpetration, wreaking 2. affliction, penalty, punishment, trouble, visitation, worry

influence *n.* 1. agency, ascendancy, authority, control, credit, direction, domination, effect, guidance, magnetism, mastery, power, pressure, rule, spell, sway, weight 2. bottom, clout (*Inf.*), connections, good offices, hold, importance, leverage, power, prestige, pull (*Inf.*), weight ~*v.* 3. act *or* work upon, affect, arouse, bias, control, count, direct, dispose, guide, impel, impress, incite, incline, induce, instigate, lead to believe, manipulate, modify, move, persuade, predispose, prompt, rouse, sway 4. bring pressure to bear upon, carry weight with, make oneself felt, pull strings (*Inf.*)

influential authoritative, controlling, effective, efficacious, forcible, guiding, important, instrumental, leading, meaningful,

momentous, moving, persuasive, potent, powerful, significant, telling, weighty
Antonyms impotent, ineffective, ineffectual, powerless, unimportant, uninfluential, un~ persuasive, weak

influx arrival, convergence, flow, incursion, inflow, inrush, inundation, invasion, rush

inform 1. acquaint, advise, apprise, clue in (*Inf.*), communicate, enlighten, give (some~ one) to understand, instruct, leak to, let know, make conversant (with), notify, put (someone) in the picture (*Inf.*), send word to, teach, tell, tip off **2.** *Often with* **against** *or on* betray, blab, blow the whistle on (*Inf.*), clype (*Scot.*), denounce, grass (*Brit. sl.*), incriminate, inculpate, nark (*Brit., Aust., & N.Z. sl.*), peach (*Sl.*), rat (*Inf.*), shop (*Sl., chiefly Brit.*), sing (*Sl., chiefly U.S.*), snitch (*Sl.*), spill one's guts (*Sl.*), squeal (*Sl.*), tell all, tell on (*Inf.*) **3.** animate, char~ acterize, illuminate, imbue, inspire, perme~ ate, suffuse, typify

informal casual, colloquial, cosy, easy, fa~ miliar, natural, relaxed, simple, unceremo~ nious, unconstrained, unofficial
Antonyms ceremonious, constrained, con~ ventional, formal, official, stiff

informality casualness, ease, familiarity, lack of ceremony, naturalness, relaxation, simplicity

information advice, blurb, counsel, data, dope (*Inf.*), facts, gen (*Brit. inf.*), info (*Inf.*), inside story, instruction, intelligence, knowledge, latest (*Inf.*), lowdown (*Inf.*), ma~ terial, message, news, notice, report, tid~ ings, word

informative chatty, communicative, edify~ ing, educational, enlightening, forthcoming, gossipy, illuminating, instructive, newsy, revealing

informed abreast, acquainted, *au courant*, *au fait*, briefed, conversant, enlightened, erudite, expert, familiar, genned up (*Brit. inf.*), in the know (*Inf.*), knowledgeable, learned, posted, primed, reliable, up, up to date, versed, well-read

informer accuser, betrayer, grass (*Brit. sl.*), Judas, nark (*Brit., Aust., & N.Z. sl.*), sneak, squealer (*Sl.*), stool pigeon

infrequent few and far between, occasional, rare, sporadic, uncommon, unusual
Antonyms common, customary, frequent, habitual, often, regular, usual

infringe 1. break, contravene, disobey, transgress, violate **2.** *With on or upon* en~ croach, intrude, trespass

infringement breach, contravention, in~ fraction, noncompliance, nonobservance, transgression, trespass, violation

infuriate anger, be like a red rag to a bull, enrage, exasperate, gall, get one's back up, get one's goat (*Sl.*), incense, irritate, mad~ den, make one's blood boil, make one see red (*Inf.*), make one's hackles rise, nark (*Brit., Aust., & N.Z. sl.*), provoke, raise one's hackles, rile
Antonyms appease, calm, mollify, pacify, placate, propitiate, soothe

infuriating aggravating (*Inf.*), annoying, exasperating, galling, irritating, maddening, mortifying, pestilential, provoking, vexa~ tious

ingenious adroit, bright, brilliant, clever, crafty, creative, dexterous, fertile, inven~ tive, masterly, original, ready, resourceful, shrewd, skilful, subtle
Antonyms artless, clumsy, unimaginative, uninventive, unoriginal, unresourceful, un~ skilful

ingenuity adroitness, cleverness, faculty, flair, genius, gift, ingeniousness, inventive~ ness, knack, originality, resourcefulness, sharpness, shrewdness, skill, turn
Antonyms clumsiness, dullness, incompe~ tence, ineptitude, ineptness

ingenuous artless, candid, childlike, frank, guileless, honest, innocent, naive, open, plain, simple, sincere, trustful, trusting, unreserved, unsophisticated, unstudied
Antonyms artful, crafty, devious, insincere, reserved, sly, sophisticated, subtle, wily

ingenuousness artlessness, candour, frankness, guilelessness, innocence, naive~ ty, openness, trustingness, unsuspicious~ ness
Antonyms artfulness, craftiness, insincer~ ity, slyness, sophistication, subterfuge, sub~ tlety

inglorious discreditable, disgraceful, dis~ honourable, disreputable, failed, humiliat~ ing, ignoble, ignominious, infamous, ob~ scure, shameful, unheroic, unknown, un~ successful, unsung

ingratiate be a yes man, blandish, brown-nose (*Taboo sl.*), crawl, curry favour, fawn, flatter, get in with, get on the right side of, grovel, insinuate oneself, kiss (someone's) ass (*U.S. & Canad. taboo sl.*), lick (someone's) boots, pander to, play up to, rub (someone) up the right way (*Inf.*), seek the favour (of someone), suck up to (*Inf.*), toady, worm oneself into (someone's) favour

ingratiating bootlicking (*Inf.*), crawling, fawning, flattering, humble, obsequious, servile, sycophantic, timeserving, toadying, unctuous

ingratitude thanklessness, unappreciative~ ness, ungratefulness
Antonyms appreciation, gratefulness, gratitude, thankfulness, thanks, thanksgiving

ingredient component, constituent, element, part

inhabit abide, dwell, live, lodge, make one's home, occupy, people, populate, possess, reside, take up residence in, tenant

inhabitant aborigine, citizen, denizen, dweller, indigene, indweller, inmate, native, occupant, occupier, resident, tenant

inhabited colonized, developed, held, occupied, peopled, populated, settled, tenanted

inhale breathe in, draw in, gasp, respire, suck in
Antonyms blow, breathe out, exhale, expire

inherent basic, congenital, connate, essential, hereditary, inborn, inbred, inbuilt, ingrained, inherited, innate, instinctive, intrinsic, native, natural
Antonyms alien, extraneous, extrinsic, imposed, superficial, supplementary

inherit accede to, be bequeathed, be left, come into, fall heir to, succeed to

inheritance bequest, birthright, heritage, legacy, patrimony

inhibit arrest, bar, bridle, check, constrain, cramp (someone's) style (*Inf.*), curb, debar, discourage, forbid, frustrate, hinder, hold back *or* in, impede, obstruct, prevent, prohibit, restrain, stop
Antonyms abet, allow, encourage, further, let, permit, support

inhibited constrained, frustrated, guarded, repressed, reserved, reticent, self-conscious, shy, subdued, uptight (*Inf.*), withdrawn
Antonyms free, natural, outgoing, relaxed, spontaneous, uninhibited, unreserved

inhibition bar, block, check, embargo, hang-up (*Inf.*), hindrance, interdict, mental blockage, obstacle, prohibition, reserve, restraint, restriction, reticence, self-consciousness, shyness

inhospitable 1. cool, uncongenial, unfriendly, ungenerous, unkind, unreceptive, unsociable, unwelcoming, xenophobic **2.** bare, barren, bleak, desolate, empty, forbidding, godforsaken, hostile, lonely, sterile, unfavourable, uninhabitable
Antonyms (*sense 1*) amicable, friendly, generous, genial, gracious, hospitable, sociable, welcoming

inhuman animal, barbaric, barbarous, bestial, brutal, cold-blooded, cruel, diabolical, fiendish, heartless, merciless, pitiless, remorseless, ruthless, savage, unfeeling, vicious
Antonyms charitable, compassionate, feeling, humane, merciful, sensitive, tender, warmhearted

inhumane brutal, cruel, heartless, pitiless, uncompassionate, unfeeling, unkind, unsympathetic

inhumanity atrocity, barbarism, brutality, brutishness, cold-bloodedness, cold-heartedness, cruelty, hardheartedness, heartlessness, pitilessness, ruthlessness, unkindness, viciousness

inhume bury, entomb, inter, lay to rest, sepulchre

inimical adverse, antagonistic, antipathetic, contrary, destructive, disaffected, harmful, hostile, hurtful, ill-disposed, injurious, noxious, opposed, oppugnant (*Rare*), pernicious, repugnant, unfavourable, unfriendly, unwelcoming
Antonyms affable, amicable, congenial, favourable, friendly, good, helpful, kindly, sympathetic, welcoming

inimitable consummate, incomparable, matchless, nonpareil, peerless, supreme, unequalled, unexampled, unique, unmatched, unparalleled, unrivalled, unsurpassable

iniquitous abominable, accursed, atrocious, base, criminal, evil, heinous, immoral, infamous, nefarious, reprehensible, reprobate, sinful, unjust, unrighteous, vicious, wicked

iniquity abomination, baseness, crime, evil, evildoing, heinousness, infamy, injustice, misdeed, offence, sin, sinfulness, unrighteousness, wickedness, wrong, wrongdoing
Antonyms fairness, goodness, honesty, integrity, justice, morality, righteousness, uprightness, virtue

initial *adj.* beginning, commencing, early, first, inaugural, inceptive, inchoate, incipient, introductory, opening, primary
Antonyms closing, concluding, ending, final, last, terminal, ultimate

initially at *or* in the beginning, at first, at the outset, at the start, first, firstly, in the early stages, originally, primarily, to begin with

initiate *v.* **1.** begin, break the ice, commence, get under way, inaugurate, institute, kick off (*Inf.*), kick-start, launch, lay the foundations of, open, originate, pioneer, set going, set in motion, set the ball rolling, start **2.** coach, familiarize with, indoctrinate, induct, instate, instruct, introduce, invest, teach, train ~*n.* **3.** beginner, convert, entrant, learner, member, novice, probationer, proselyte, tyro

initiation admission, commencement, debut, enrolment, entrance, inauguration, inception, induction, installation, instatement, introduction, investiture

initiative 1. advantage, beginning, commencement, first move, first step, lead **2.** ambition, drive, dynamism, enterprise, get-up-and-go (*Inf.*), inventiveness, leadership, originality, push (*Inf.*), resource, resourcefulness

inject 1. inoculate, jab (*Inf.*), shoot (*Inf.*), vaccinate **2.** bring in, infuse, insert, instil, interject, introduce

injection 1. inoculation, jab (*Inf.*), shot (*Inf.*), vaccination, vaccine **2.** dose, infu~ sion, insertion, interjection, introduction

injudicious foolish, hasty, ill-advised, ill-judged, ill-timed, impolitic, imprudent, in~ cautious, inconsiderate, indiscreet, inexpe~ dient, rash, unthinking, unwise
Antonyms cautious, considerate, discreet, expedient, judicious, polite, prudent, well-timed, wise

injunction admonition, command, dictate, exhortation, instruction, mandate, order, precept, ruling

injure abuse, blemish, blight, break, damage, deface, disable, harm, hurt, impair, mal~ treat, mar, ruin, spoil, tarnish, undermine, vitiate, weaken, wound, wrong

injured 1. broken, disabled, hurt, lamed, undermined, weakened, wounded **2.** cut to the quick, disgruntled, displeased, hurt, long-suffering, put out, reproachful, stung, unhappy, upset, wounded **3.** abused, black~ ened, blemished, defamed, ill-treated, ma~ ligned, maltreated, offended, tarnished, vilified, wronged

injury abuse, damage, detriment, disservice, evil, grievance, harm, hurt, ill, injustice, mischief, ruin, wound, wrong

injustice bias, discrimination, favouritism, inequality, inequity, iniquity, one-sidedness, oppression, partiality, partisan~ ship, prejudice, unfairness, unjustness, un~ lawfulness, wrong
Antonyms equality, equity, fairness, im~ partiality, justice, lawfulness, rectitude, right

inkling clue, conception, faintest *or* foggiest idea, glimmering, hint, idea, indication, in~ timation, notion, suggestion, suspicion, whisper

inland *adj.* domestic, interior, internal, up~ country

inlet arm (of the sea), bay, bight, cove, creek, entrance, firth *or* frith (*Scot.*), in~ gress, passage, sea loch (*Scot.*)

inmost *or* **innermost** basic, buried, cen~ tral, deep, deepest, essential, intimate, per~ sonal, private, secret

innate congenital, connate, constitutional, essential, inborn, inbred, indigenous, in~ grained, inherent, inherited, instinctive, intrinsic, intuitive, native, natural
Antonyms accidental, acquired, affected, assumed, cultivated, fostered, incidental, learned, nurtured, unnatural

inner 1. central, essential, inside, interior, internal, intestinal, inward, middle **2.** eso~ teric, hidden, intimate, personal, private,

repressed, secret, unrevealed **3.** emotional, mental, psychological, spiritual
Antonyms (*sense 1*) exterior, external, outer, outside, outward (*sense 2*) exposed, obvious, overt, revealed, surface, unconcealed, unrepressed, visible

innkeeper host, hostess, hotelier, landlady, landlord, mine host, publican

innocence 1. blamelessness, chastity, clean hands, guiltlessness, incorruptibility, pro~ bity, purity, righteousness, sinlessness, stainlessness, uprightness, virginity, virtue **2.** harmlessness, innocuousness, innoxious~ ness, inoffensiveness **3.** artlessness, credu~ lousness, freshness, guilelessness, gullibil~ ity, inexperience, ingenuousness, naiveté, simplicity, unsophistication, unworldliness **4.** ignorance, lack of knowledge, nescience (*Literary*), unawareness, unfamiliarity
Antonyms (*sense 1*) corruption, guilt, impu~ rity, offensiveness, sinfulness, wrongness (*sense 3*) artfulness, cunning, disingenuous~ ness, guile, wiliness, worldliness

innocent *adj.* **1.** blameless, clear, faultless, guiltless, honest, in the clear, not guilty, uninvolved, unoffending **2.** chaste, im~ maculate, impeccable, incorrupt, pristine, pure, righteous, sinless, spotless, stainless, unblemished, unsullied, upright, virgin, virginal **3.** *With of* clear of, empty of, free from, ignorant, lacking, nescient, unac~ quainted with, unaware, unfamiliar with, untouched by **4.** harmless, innocuous, inof~ fensive, unmalicious, unobjectionable, well-intentioned, well-meant **5.** artless, childlike, credulous, frank, guileless, gul~ lible, ingenuous, naive, open, simple, unsuspicious, unworldly, wet behind the ears (*Inf.*), ~*n.* **6.** babe (in arms) (*Inf.*), child, greenhorn (*Inf.*), ingénue (*fem.*)
Antonyms (*sense 1*) blameworthy, culpable, dishonest, guilty, responsible (*sense 2*) cor~ rupt, immoral, impure, sinful, wrong (*sense 4*) evil, harmful, iniquitous, malicious, offen~ sive, wicked (*sense 5*) artful, disingenuous, so~ phisticated, worldly

innovation alteration, change, departure, introduction, modernism, modernization, newness, novelty, variation

innuendo aspersion, hint, implication, im~ putation, insinuation, intimation, overtone, suggestion, whisper

innumerable beyond number, countless, incalculable, infinite, many, multitudinous, myriad, numberless, numerous, unnum~ bered, untold
Antonyms calculable, computable, finite, limited, measurable, numbered

inoffensive harmless, humble, innocent, innocuous, innoxious, mild, neutral,

nonprovocative, peaceable, quiet, retiring,
unobjectionable, unobtrusive, unoffending
Antonyms abrasive, harmful, irksome, irri~
tating, malicious, objectionable, offensive,
provocative

inoperative broken, broken-down, defec~
tive, *hors de combat*, ineffective, ineffectual,
inefficacious, invalid, nonactive, null and
void, on the fritz (*U.S. sl.*), out of action, out
of commission, out of order, out of service,
unserviceable, unworkable, useless

inopportune ill-chosen, ill-timed, inappro~
priate, inauspicious, inconvenient, malap~
ropos, mistimed, unfavourable, unfortunate,
unpropitious, unseasonable, unsuitable,
untimely
Antonyms appropriate, auspicious, con~
venient, favourable, fortunate, opportune,
seasonable, suitable, timely, well-timed

inordinate disproportionate, excessive, ex~
orbitant, extravagant, immoderate, intem~
perate, preposterous, unconscionable, un~
due, unreasonable, unrestrained, unwar~
ranted
Antonyms inhibited, moderate, reasonable,
restrained, rightful, sensible, temperate

inorganic artificial, chemical, man-made,
mineral

inquest inquiry, inquisition, investigation,
probe

inquire 1. examine, explore, inspect, inves~
tigate, look into, make inquiries, probe, re~
search, scrutinize, search 2. *Also* **enquire**
ask, query, question, request information,
seek information

inquiring analytical, curious, doubtful, in~
quisitive, interested, investigative, nosy
(*Inf.*), outward-looking, probing, question~
ing, searching, wondering

inquiry 1. examination, exploration, in~
quest, interrogation, investigation, probe,
research, scrutiny, search, study, survey 2.
Also **enquiry** query, question

inquisition cross-examination, examina~
tion, grilling (*Inf.*), inquest, inquiry, inves~
tigation, question, quizzing, third degree
(*Inf.*)

inquisitive curious, inquiring, intrusive,
nosy (*Inf.*), nosy-parkering (*Inf.*), peering,
probing, prying, questioning, scrutinizing,
snooping (*Inf.*), snoopy (*Inf.*)
Antonyms apathetic, incurious, indifferent,
unconcerned, uninterested, unquestioning

inroad 1. advance, encroachment, foray, in~
cursion, intrusion, invasion, irruption, on~
slaught, raid 2. **make inroads upon** con~
sume, eat away, eat up *or* into, encroach
upon, use up

insane 1. barking (*Sl.*), barking mad (*Sl.*),
crackpot (*Inf.*), crazed, crazy, demented, de~

ranged, loopy (*Inf.*), mad, mentally disor~
dered, mentally ill, *non compos mentis*, not
the full shilling (*Inf.*), off one's trolley (*Sl.*),
of unsound mind, out of one's mind, out to
lunch (*Inf.*), unhinged, up the pole (*Inf.*) 2.
barking (*Sl.*), barking mad (*Sl.*), barmy (*Sl.*),
batty (*Sl.*), bonkers (*Sl., chiefly Brit.*),
cracked (*Sl.*), crackers (*Brit. sl.*), cuckoo
(*Inf.*), loony (*Sl.*), loopy (*Inf.*), mental (*Sl.*),
nuts (*Sl.*), nutty (*Sl.*), off one's chump (*Sl.*),
off one's head (*Sl.*), off one's nut (*Sl.*), off
one's rocker (*Sl.*), round the bend (*Inf.*),
round the twist (*Inf.*), screwy (*Inf.*) 3. bi~
zarre, daft (*Inf.*), fatuous, foolish, idiotic,
impractical, inane, irrational, irresponsible,
lunatic, preposterous, senseless, stupid
Antonyms logical, lucid, normal, practical,
rational, reasonable, reasoned, sane, sensible,
sound

insanitary contaminated, dirtied, dirty,
disease-ridden, feculent, filthy, impure, in~
fected, infested, insalubrious, noxious, pol~
luted, unclean, unhealthy, unhygienic
Antonyms clean, healthy, hygienic, pure,
salubrious, unpolluted

insanity 1. aberration, craziness, delirium,
dementia, frenzy, madness, mental de~
rangement, mental disorder, mental illness
2. folly, irresponsibility, lunacy, preposter~
ousness, senselessness, stupidity
Antonyms logic, lucidity, normality, ra~
tionality, reason, sanity, sense, soundness,
wisdom

insatiable gluttonous, greedy, insatiate, in~
temperate, quenchless, rapacious, ravenous,
unappeasable, unquenchable, voracious
Antonyms appeasable, limited, quenchable,
satiable, temperate

inscribe 1. carve, cut, engrave, etch, im~
press, imprint 2. engross, enlist, enrol, en~
ter, record, register, write 3. address, dedi~
cate

inscription dedication, engraving, label,
legend, lettering, saying, words

inscrutable 1. blank, deadpan, enigmatic,
impenetrable, poker-faced (*Inf.*), sphinxlike,
unreadable 2. hidden, incomprehensible,
inexplicable, mysterious, undiscoverable,
unexplainable, unfathomable, unintelligible
Antonyms clear, comprehensible, evident,
explainable, explicable, intelligible, lucid,
manifest, obvious, open, palpable, patent,
penetrable, plain, readable, revealing, trans~
parent, understandable

insecure 1. afraid, anxious, uncertain,
unconfident, unsure 2. dangerous, defence~
less, exposed, hazardous, ill-protected, open
to attack, perilous, unguarded, unprotected,
unsafe, unshielded, vulnerable 3. built
upon sand, flimsy, frail, insubstantial,
loose, on thin ice, precarious, rickety,

rocky, shaky, unreliable, unsound, unstable, unsteady, weak, wobbly
Antonyms (*sense 1*) assured, certain, confident, decisive, secure (*senses 2 & 3*) firm, protected, reliable, safe, secure, sound, stable, steady, substantial, sure

insecurity 1. anxiety, fear, uncertainty, unsureness, worry **2.** danger, defenceless~ ness, hazard, peril, risk, uncertainty, vul~ nerability, weakness **3.** dubiety, frailness, instability, precariousness, shakiness, un~ certainty, unreliability, unsteadiness, weakness
Antonyms (*sense 1*) assurance, certainty, confidence, security (*senses 2 & 3*) dependabil~ ity, firmness, reliability, safety, security, sta~ bility, steadiness

insensibility 1. apathy, callousness, dull~ ness, indifference, inertia, insensitivity, lethargy, thoughtlessness, torpor **2.** inert~ ness, numbness, unconsciousness

insensible 1. anaesthetized, benumbed, dull, inert, insensate, numbed, senseless, stupid, torpid **2.** apathetic, callous, cold, deaf, hard-hearted, impassive, impervious, indifferent, oblivious, unaffected, unaware, unconscious, unfeeling, unmindful, un~ moved, unresponsive, unsusceptible, un~ touched **3.** imperceivable, imperceptible, minuscule, negligible, unnoticeable
Antonyms (*sense 2*) affected, aware, con~ scious, feeling, mindful, responsive, sensible

insensitive 1. callous, crass, hardened, im~ perceptive, indifferent, obtuse, tactless, thick-skinned, tough, uncaring, uncon~ cerned, unfeeling, unresponsive, unsuscep~ tible **2.** *With* **to** dead to, immune to, im~ pervious to, nonreactive, proof against, un~ affected by, unmoved by
Antonyms (*sense 1*) caring, concerned, per~ ceptive, responsive, sensitive, sentient, sus~ ceptible, tactful, tender

inseparable 1. conjoined, inalienable, in~ dissoluble, indivisible, inseverable **2.** bos~ om, close, devoted, intimate

insert embed, enter, implant, infix, interject, interpolate, interpose, introduce, place, pop in (*Inf.*), put, set, stick in, tuck in, work in
Antonyms delete, extract, pull out, remove, take out, withdraw

insertion addition, implant, inclusion, in~ sert, inset, interpolation, introduction, sup~ plement

inside *n.* **1.** contents, inner part, interior **2.** *Often plural Inf.* belly, bowels, entrails, gut, guts, innards (*Inf.*), internal organs, stom~ ach, viscera, vitals ~*adv.* **3.** indoors, under cover, within ~*adj.* **4.** inner, innermost, interior, internal, intramural, inward **5.** classified, confidential, esoteric, exclusive, internal, limited, private, restricted, secret

Antonyms (*sense 4*) exterior, external, extramural, outer, outermost, outside, out~ ward

insidious artful, crafty, crooked, cunning, deceitful, deceptive, designing, disingenu~ ous, duplicitous, guileful, intriguing, Machiavellian, slick, sly, smooth, sneaking, stealthy, subtle, surreptitious, treacherous, tricky, wily
Antonyms artless, conspicuous, forthright, harmless, honest, ingenuous, obvious, open, sincere, straightforward, upright

insight acumen, awareness, comprehension, discernment, intuition, intuitiveness, judg~ ment, observation, penetration, perception, perspicacity, understanding, vision

insignia badge, crest, decoration, distin~ guishing mark, earmark, emblem, ensign, symbol

insignificance immateriality, incon~ sequence, irrelevance, meaninglessness, negligibility, paltriness, pettiness, triviality, unimportance, worthlessness
Antonyms consequence, importance, mat~ ter, meaningfulness, relevance, significance, weight, worth

insignificant flimsy, immaterial, incon~ sequential, inconsiderable, irrelevant, mea~ gre, meaningless, measly, minor, negligible, nickel-and-dime (*U.S. sl.*), nondescript, non~ essential, not worth mentioning, nugatory, of no account (consequence, moment), paltry, petty, scanty, trifling, trivial, unim~ portant, unsubstantial
Antonyms consequential, considerable, es~ sential, important, meaningful, momentous, relevant, significant, substantial, vital, weighty

insincere deceitful, deceptive, devious, dis~ honest, disingenuous, dissembling, dis~ simulating, double-dealing, duplicitous, evasive, faithless, false, hollow, hypocriti~ cal, Janus-faced, lying, mendacious, perfidious, pretended, two-faced, unfaithful, untrue, untruthful
Antonyms direct, earnest, faithful, genuine, honest, sincere, straightforward, true, truth~ ful

insincerity deceitfulness, deviousness, dis~ honesty, disingenuousness, dissimulation, duplicity, faithlessness, hypocrisy, lip ser~ vice, mendacity, perfidy, pretence, untruth~ fulness
Antonyms directness, faithfulness, honesty, sincerity, truthfulness

insinuate 1. allude, hint, imply, indicate, intimate, suggest **2.** infiltrate, infuse, inject, instil, introduce **3.** curry favour, get in with, ingratiate, worm *or* work one's way in

insinuation 1. allusion, aspersion, hint,

implication, innuendo, slur, suggestion **2.** infiltration, infusion, ingratiating, injection, instillation, introduction

insipid 1. anaemic, banal, bland, character~ less, colourless, drab, dry, dull, flat, ho-hum (*Inf.*), jejune, lifeless, limp, pointless, prosa~ ic, prosy, spiritless, stale, stupid, tame, te~ dious, trite, unimaginative, uninteresting, vapid, weak, wearisome, wishy-washy (*Inf.*) **2.** bland, flavourless, savourless, tasteless, unappetizing, watered down, watery, wishy-washy (*Inf.*)
Antonyms (*sense 1*) colourful, engaging, ex~ citing, interesting, lively, provocative, spirit~ ed, stimulating (*sense 2*) appetizing, fiery, pal~ atable, piquant, pungent, savoury, tasteful

insipidity, insipidness 1. banality, col~ ourlessness, dullness, flatness, lack of im~ agination, pointlessness, staleness, tame~ ness, tediousness, triteness, uninteresting~ ness, vapidity **2.** blandness, flavourlessness, lack of flavour, tastelessness
Antonyms (*sense 1*) animation, character, dynamism, gaiety, liveliness, spirit, vitality, vivacity

insist 1. be firm, brook no refusal, demand, lay down the law, not take no for an an~ swer, persist, press (someone), require, stand firm, stand one's ground, take *or* make a stand, urge **2.** assert, asseverate, aver, claim, contend, hold, maintain, reit~ erate, repeat, swear, urge, vow

insistence assertion, contention, demands, emphasis, importunity, insistency, persis~ tence, pressing, reiteration, stress, urging

insistent demanding, dogged, emphatic, exigent, forceful, importunate, incessant, peremptory, persevering, persistent, press~ ing, unrelenting, urgent

insolence abuse, audacity, backchat (*Inf.*), boldness, cheek (*Inf.*), chutzpah (*U.S. & Canad. inf.*), contemptuousness, contumely, disrespect, effrontery, front, gall (*Inf.*), im~ pertinence, impudence, incivility, insubor~ dination, offensiveness, pertness, rudeness, sauce (*Inf.*), uncivility
Antonyms civility, courtesy, deference, es~ teem, mannerliness, politeness, respect, sub~ mission

insolent abusive, bold, brazen-faced, con~ temptuous, fresh (*Inf.*), impertinent, impu~ dent, insubordinate, insulting, pert, rude, saucy, uncivil
Antonyms civil, courteous, deferential, mannerly, polite, respectful, submissive

insoluble baffling, impenetrable, indeci~ pherable, inexplicable, mysterious, mystify~ ing, obscure, unaccountable, unfathomable, unsolvable
Antonyms accountable, comprehensible,

explicable, fathomable, penetrable, soluble, solvable

insolvency bankruptcy, failure, liquidation, ruin

insolvent bankrupt, broke (*Inf.*), failed, gone bust (*Inf.*), gone to the wall, in queer street (*Inf.*), in receivership, in the hands of the receivers, on the rocks (*Inf.*), ruined

insomnia sleeplessness, wakefulness

inspect audit, check, check out (*Inf.*), ex~ amine, eyeball (*U.S. sl.*), give (something *or* someone) the once-over (*Inf.*), go over *or* through, investigate, look over, oversee, recce (*Sl.*), research, scan, scrutinize, search, superintend, supervise, survey, take a dekko at (*Brit. sl.*), vet, work over

inspection check, checkup, examination, investigation, look-over, once-over (*Inf.*), recce (*Sl.*), review, scan, scrutiny, search, superintendence, supervision, surveillance, survey

inspector censor, checker, critic, examiner, investigator, overseer, scrutineer, scruti~ nizer, superintendent, supervisor

inspiration 1. arousal, awakening, encour~ agement, influence, muse, spur, stimulus **2.** afflatus, creativity, elevation, enthusiasm, exaltation, genius, illumination, insight, revelation, stimulation
Antonyms depressant, deterrent, discour~ agement, disenchantment

inspire 1. animate, be responsible for, en~ courage, enliven, fire *or* touch the imagina~ tion of, galvanize, hearten, imbue, influence, infuse, inspirit, instil, rouse, spark off, spur, stimulate **2.** arouse, enkin~ dle, excite, give rise to, produce, quicken, rouse, stir
Antonyms daunt, deflate, depress, discour~ age, disenchant, dishearten, dispirit

inspired 1. brilliant, dazzling, enthralling, exciting, impressive, memorable, of genius, outstanding, superlative, thrilling, wonder~ ful **2.** *Of a guess* instinctive, instinctual, intuitive **3.** aroused, elated, enthused, ex~ alted, exhilarated, galvanized, possessed, stimulated, stirred up, uplifted

inspiring affecting, encouraging, exciting, exhilarating, heartening, moving, rousing, stimulating, stirring, uplifting
Antonyms boring, depressing, discourag~ ing, disheartening, dispiriting, dull, unin~ spiring

instability capriciousness, changeableness, disequilibrium, fickleness, fitfulness, fluctuation, fluidity, frailty, imbalance, im~ permanence, inconstancy, insecurity, ir~ resolution, mutability, oscillation, precari~ ousness, restlessness, shakiness, transience,

unpredictability, unsteadiness, vacillation, variability, volatility, wavering, weakness
Antonyms balance, constancy, equilibrium, permanence, predictability, resolution, security, stability, steadiness, strength

install, instal 1. fix, lay, lodge, place, position, put in, set up, station **2.** establish, inaugurate, induct, instate, institute, introduce, invest, set up **3.** ensconce, position, settle

installation 1. establishment, fitting, instalment, placing, positioning, setting up **2.** inauguration, induction, instatement, investiture **3.** equipment, machinery, plant, system **4.** *Military* base, establishment, post, station

instalment chapter, division, episode, part, portion, repayment, section

instance *n.* **1.** case, case in point, example, illustration, occasion, occurrence, precedent, situation, time **2.** application, behest, demand, entreaty, importunity, impulse, incitement, insistence, instigation, pressure, prompting, request, solicitation, urging ~*v.* **3.** adduce, cite, mention, name, quote, specify

instant *n.* **1.** flash, jiffy (*Inf.*), moment, second, shake (*Inf.*), split second, tick (*Brit. inf.*), trice, twinkling, twinkling of an eye (*Inf.*), two shakes of a lamb's tail (*Inf.*) **2. on the instant** forthwith, immediately, instantly, now, right away, without delay **3.** juncture, moment, occasion, point, time ~*adj.* **4.** direct, immediate, instantaneous, on-the-spot, prompt, quick, quickie (*Inf.*), split-second, urgent **5.** convenience, fast, precooked, ready-mixed **6.** burning, exigent, imperative, importunate, pressing, urgent

instantaneous direct, immediate, instant, on-the-spot

instantaneously at once, forthwith, immediately, in a fraction of a second, instantly, in the same breath, in the twinkling of an eye (*Inf.*), like greased lightning (*Inf.*), on the instant, on the spot, posthaste, promptly, pronto (*Inf.*), quick as lightning, straight away, then and there

instantly at once, directly, forthwith, immediately, instantaneously, instanter (*Law*), now, on the spot, posthaste, pronto (*Inf.*), right away, right now, straight away, there and then, this minute, *tout de suite*, without delay

instead 1. alternatively, in lieu, in preference, on second thoughts, preferably, rather **2.** *With* **of** as an alternative *or* equivalent to, in lieu of, in place of, rather than

instigate actuate, bring about, encourage, foment, get going, impel, incite, influence, initiate, kick-start, kindle, move, persuade, prod, prompt, provoke, rouse, set off, set on,

spur, start, stimulate, stir up, trigger, urge, whip up
Antonyms discourage, repress, restrain, stop, suppress

instigation behest, bidding, encouragement, incentive, incitement, prompting, urging

instigator agitator, firebrand, fomenter, goad, incendiary, inciter, leader, mischiefmaker, motivator, prime mover, ringleader, spur, stirrer (*Inf.*), troublemaker

instil, instill engender, engraft, imbue, implant, impress, inculcate, infix, infuse, insinuate, introduce

instinct aptitude, faculty, feeling, gift, gut feeling (*Inf.*), gut reaction (*Inf.*), impulse, intuition, knack, natural inclination, predisposition, proclivity, sixth sense, talent, tendency, urge

instinctive automatic, inborn, inherent, innate, instinctual, intuitional, intuitive, involuntary, mechanical, native, natural, reflex, spontaneous, unlearned, unpremeditated, unthinking, visceral
Antonyms acquired, calculated, considered, learned, mindful, premeditated, thinking, voluntary, willed

instinctively automatically, by instinct, intuitively, involuntarily, naturally, without thinking

institute[1] *v.* appoint, begin, bring into being, commence, constitute, enact, establish, fix, found, induct, initiate, install, introduce, invest, launch, ordain, organize, originate, pioneer, put into operation, set in motion, settle, set up, start
Antonyms abandon, abolish, cancel, cease, discontinue, end, stop, suspend, terminate

institute[2] *n.* **1.** academy, association, college, conservatory, foundation, guild, institution, school, seat of learning, seminary, society **2.** custom, decree, doctrine, dogma, edict, law, maxim, precedent, precept, principle, regulation, rule, tenet

institution 1. constitution, creation, enactment, establishment, formation, foundation, initiation, introduction, investiture, investment, organization **2.** academy, college, establishment, foundation, hospital, institute, school, seminary, society, university **3.** convention, custom, fixture, law, practice, ritual, rule, tradition

institutional 1. accepted, bureaucratic, conventional, established, establishment (*Inf.*), formal, organized, orthodox, societal **2.** cheerless, clinical, cold, drab, dreary, dull, forbidding, formal, impersonal, monotonous, regimented, routine, uniform, unwelcoming

instruct 1. bid, canon, charge, command,

direct, enjoin, order, tell **2.** coach, disci~
pline, drill, educate, enlighten, ground,
guide, inform, school, teach, train, tutor **3.**
acquaint, advise, apprise, brief, counsel, in~
form, notify, tell

instruction 1. apprenticeship, coaching,
discipline, drilling, education, enlighten~
ment, grounding, guidance, information,
lesson(s), preparation, schooling, teaching,
training, tuition, tutelage **2.** briefing, com~
mand, demand, direction, directive, injunc~
tion, mandate, order, ruling

instructions advice, directions, guidance,
information, key, orders, recommendations,
rules

instructive cautionary, didactic, edifying,
educational, enlightening, helpful, illumi~
nating, informative, instructional, reveal~
ing, useful

instructor adviser, coach, demonstrator,
exponent, guide, handler, master, mentor,
mistress, pedagogue, preceptor (*Rare*),
schoolmaster, schoolmistress, teacher,
trainer, tutor

instrument 1. apparatus, appliance, con~
traption (*Inf.*), contrivance, device, gadget,
implement, mechanism, tool, utensil **2.**
agency, agent, channel, factor, force, means,
mechanism, medium, organ, vehicle **3.** *Inf.*
cat's-paw, dupe, pawn, puppet, tool

instrumental active, assisting, auxiliary,
conducive, contributory, helpful, helping,
influential, involved, of help *or* service,
subsidiary, useful

insubordinate contumacious, defiant, dis~
obedient, disorderly, fractious, insurgent,
mutinous, rebellious, recalcitrant, refrac~
tory, riotous, seditious, turbulent, undisci~
plined, ungovernable, unruly
Antonyms compliant, deferential, disci~
plined, docile, obedient, orderly, submissive,
subservient

insubordination defiance, disobedience,
indiscipline, insurrection, mutinousness,
mutiny, rebellion, recalcitrance, revolt, ri~
otousness, sedition, ungovernability
Antonyms acquiescence, compliance, def~
erence, discipline, docility, obedience, sub~
mission, subordination

insubstantial 1. feeble, flimsy, frail, poor,
slight, tenuous, thin, weak **2.** chimerical,
ephemeral, false, fanciful, idle, illusory, im~
aginary, immaterial, incorporeal, unreal
Antonyms (*sense 1*) firm, solid, strong, sub~
stantial, weighty

insufferable detestable, dreadful, enough to
test the patience of a saint, enough to try
the patience of Job, impossible, insupport~
able, intolerable, more than flesh and blood
can stand, outrageous, past bearing, too

much, unbearable, unendurable, unspeak~
able
Antonyms appealing, attractive, bearable,
charming, disarming, pleasant

insufficient deficient, inadequate, inca~
pable, incommensurate, incompetent, lack~
ing, scant, short, unfitted, unqualified
Antonyms adequate, ample, commensurate,
competent, enough, plentiful, qualified,
sufficient

insular *Fig.* blinkered, circumscribed,
closed, contracted, cut off, illiberal,
inward-looking, isolated, limited, narrow,
narrow-minded, parish-pump, parochial,
petty, prejudiced, provincial
Antonyms broad-minded, cosmopolitan,
experienced, liberal, open-minded, tolerant,
worldly

insulate *Fig.* close off, cocoon, cushion, cut
off, isolate, protect, sequester, shield, wrap
up in cotton wool

insult 1. *n.* abuse, affront, aspersion, contu~
mely, indignity, insolence, offence, outrage,
put-down, rudeness, slap in the face (*Inf.*),
slight, snub **2.** *v.* abuse, affront, call names,
give offence to, injure, miscall (*Dialect*), of~
fend, outrage, put down, revile, slag (off)
(*Sl.*), slander, slight, snub
Antonyms *n.* compliment, flattery, honour
~*v.* flatter, please, praise

insulting abusive, affronting, contemptuous,
degrading, disparaging, insolent, offensive,
rude, scurrilous, slighting
Antonyms complimentary, deferential,
flattering, laudatory, respectful

insuperable impassable, insurmountable,
invincible, unconquerable
Antonyms conquerable, possible, sur~
mountable

insupportable 1. insufferable, intolerable,
past bearing, unbearable, unendurable **2.**
indefensible, unjustifiable, untenable

insurance assurance, cover, coverage,
guarantee, indemnification, indemnity, pro~
tection, provision, safeguard, security,
something to fall back on (*Inf.*), warranty

insure assure, cover, guarantee, indemnify,
underwrite, warrant

insurgent 1. *n.* insurrectionist, mutineer,
rebel, resister, revolter, revolutionary,
revolutionist, rioter **2.** *adj.* disobedient, in~
subordinate, insurrectionary, mutinous, re~
bellious, revolting, revolutionary, riotous,
seditious

insurmountable hopeless, impassable,
impossible, insuperable, invincible, over~
whelming, unconquerable

insurrection coup, insurgency, mutiny,
putsch, rebellion, revolt, revolution, riot,
rising, sedition, uprising

intact all in one piece, complete, entire, perfect, scatheless, sound, together, unbro~ ken, undamaged, undefiled, unharmed, un~ hurt, unimpaired, uninjured, unscathed, untouched, unviolated, virgin, whole
Antonyms broken, damaged, harmed, im~ paired, injured

integral 1. basic, component, constituent, elemental, essential, fundamental, indis~ pensable, intrinsic, necessary, requisite **2.** complete, entire, full, intact, undivided, whole
Antonyms fractional, inessential, unimpor~ tant, unnecessary

integrate accommodate, amalgamate, as~ similate, blend, coalesce, combine, fuse, harmonize, incorporate, intermix, join, knit, meld, merge, mesh, unite
Antonyms disperse, divide, segregate, sepa~ rate

integration amalgamation, assimilation, blending, combining, commingling, fusing, harmony, incorporation, mixing, unification

integrity 1. candour, goodness, honesty, honour, incorruptibility, principle, probity, purity, rectitude, righteousness, upright~ ness, virtue **2.** coherence, cohesion, com~ pleteness, soundness, unity, wholeness
Antonyms (*sense 1*) corruption, deceit, dis~ honesty, disrepute, duplicity, faultiness, flimsiness, fragility, immorality, uncertainty, unsoundness

intellect 1. brains (*Inf.*), intelligence, judg~ ment, mind, reason, sense, understanding **2.** *Inf.* brain (*Inf.*), egghead (*Inf.*), genius, intellectual, intelligence, mind, thinker

intellectual 1. *adj.* bookish, cerebral, high~ brow, intelligent, mental, rational, scholar~ ly, studious, thoughtful **2.** *n.* academic, egghead (*Inf.*), highbrow, thinker
Antonyms *adj.* ignorant, illiterate, material, physical, stupid, unintellectual, unlearned ~*n.* idiot, moron

intelligence 1. acumen, alertness, aptitude, brain power, brains (*Inf.*), brightness, ca~ pacity, cleverness, comprehension, discern~ ment, grey matter (*Inf.*), intellect, mind, nous (*Brit. sl.*), penetration, perception, quickness, reason, smarts (*Sl., chiefly U.S.*), understanding **2.** advice, data, disclosure, facts, findings, gen (*Brit. inf.*), information, knowledge, low-down (*Inf.*), news, notice, notification, report, rumour, tidings, tip-off, word
Antonyms (*sense 1*) dullness, ignorance, stupidity (*sense 2*) concealment, misinforma~ tion

intelligent acute, alert, apt, brainy (*Inf.*), bright, clever, discerning, enlightened, in~ structed, knowing, penetrating, perspica~ cious, quick, quick-witted, rational, sharp, smart, thinking, well-informed
Antonyms dim-witted, dull, foolish, igno~ rant, obtuse, stupid, unintelligent

intelligentsia eggheads (*Inf.*), highbrows, illuminati, intellectuals, literati, master~ minds, the learned

intelligibility clarity, clearness, compre~ hensibility, distinctness, explicitness, lu~ cidity, plainness, precision, simplicity

intelligible clear, comprehensible, distinct, lucid, open, plain, understandable
Antonyms confused, garbled, incompre~ hensible, puzzling, unclear, unintelligible

intemperate excessive, extravagant, ex~ treme, immoderate, incontinent, inordinate, intoxicated, O.T.T. (*Sl.*), over the top (*Sl.*), passionate, prodigal, profligate, self- indulgent, severe, tempestuous, unbridled, uncontrollable, ungovernable, unrestrained, violent, wild
Antonyms continent, disciplined, moderate, restrained, self-controlled, temperate

intend 1. aim, be resolved *or* determined, contemplate, determine, have in mind *or* view, mean, meditate, plan, propose, pur~ pose, scheme **2.** *Often with* for aim, con~ sign, design, destine, earmark, mark out, mean, set apart

intense 1. acute, agonizing, close, concen~ trated, deep, drastic, excessive, exquisite, extreme, fierce, forceful, great, harsh, in~ tensive, powerful, profound, protracted, se~ vere, strained, unqualified **2.** ardent, burn~ ing, consuming, eager, earnest, energetic, fanatical, fervent, fervid, fierce, flaming, forcible, heightened, impassioned, keen, passionate, speaking, vehement
Antonyms (*sense 1*) easy, gentle, mild, mod~ erate, relaxed, slight (*sense 2*) casual, cool, in~ different, subdued, weak

intensely deeply, extremely, fiercely, pas~ sionately, profoundly, strongly

intensify add fuel to the flames (*Inf.*), add to, aggravate, augment, boost, concentrate, deepen, emphasize, enhance, escalate, exac~ erbate, heighten, increase, magnify, quick~ en, redouble, reinforce, set off, sharpen, step up (*Inf.*), strengthen, whet
Antonyms damp down, decrease, dilute, di~ minish, dull, lessen, minimize, weaken

intensity ardour, concentration, depth, ear~ nestness, emotion, energy, excess, extrem~ ity, fanaticism, fervency, fervour, fierceness, fire, force, intenseness, keenness, passion, potency, power, severity, strain, strength, tension, vehemence, vigour

intensive all-out, comprehensive, concen~ trated, demanding, exhaustive, in-depth, thorough, thoroughgoing

Antonyms apathetic, careless, feeble, hit-or-miss, superficial, weakened

intent *adj.* **1.** absorbed, alert, attentive, committed, concentrated, determined, eager, earnest, engrossed, fixed, industrious, intense, occupied, piercing, preoccupied, rapt, resolute, resolved, steadfast, steady, watchful, wrapped up **2.** bent, hellbent (*Inf.*), set ~*n.* **3.** aim, design, end, goal, intention, meaning, object, objective, plan, purpose **4. to all intents and purposes** as good as, practically, virtually
Antonyms *adj.* (*sense 1*) casual, indifferent, irresolute, unsteady, wavering ~*n.* chance, fortune

intention aim, design, end, end in view, goal, idea, intent, meaning, object, objective, point, purpose, scope, target, view

intentional calculated, deliberate, designed, done on purpose, intended, meant, planned, prearranged, preconcerted, premeditated, purposed, studied, wilful
Antonyms accidental, inadvertent, unintentional, unplanned

intentionally by design, deliberately, designedly, on purpose, wilfully

intently attentively, closely, fixedly. hard, keenly, searchingly, steadily, watchfully

inter bury, entomb, inhume, inurn, lay to rest, sepulchre

intercede advocate, arbitrate, interpose, intervene, mediate, plead, speak

intercept arrest, block, catch, check, cut off, deflect, head off, interrupt, obstruct, seize, stop, take

intercession advocacy, entreaty, good offices, intervention, mediation, plea, pleading, prayer, solicitation, supplication

interchange 1. *v.* alternate, bandy, barter, exchange, reciprocate, swap (*Inf.*), switch, trade **2.** *n.* alternation, crossfire, exchange, give and take, intersection, junction, reciprocation

interchangeable commutable, equivalent, exchangeable, identical, reciprocal, synonymous, the same, transposable

intercourse 1. association, commerce, communication, communion, connection, contact, converse, correspondence, dealings, intercommunication, trade, traffic, truck **2.** carnal knowledge, coition, coitus, congress, copulation, intimacy, nookie (*Sl.*), rumpy-pumpy (*Sl.*), sex (*Inf.*), sexual act, sexual intercourse, sexual relations, the other (*Inf.*)

interest *n.* **1.** affection, attention, attentiveness, attraction, concern, curiosity, notice, regard, suspicion, sympathy **2.** concern, consequence, importance, moment, note, relevance, significance, weight **3.** activity, diversion, hobby, leisure activity, pastime, preoccupation, pursuit, relaxation **4.** advantage, benefit, gain, good, profit **5. in the interest of** for the sake of, on behalf of, on the part of, profitable to, to the advantage of **6.** authority, claim, commitment, influence, investment, involvement, participation, portion, right, share, stake **7.** *Often plural* affair, business, care, concern, matter ~*v.* **8.** amuse, arouse one's curiosity, attract, divert, engross, fascinate, hold the attention of, intrigue, move, touch **9.** affect, concern, engage, involve
Antonyms *n.* (*sense 1*) boredom, coolness, disinterest, dispassion, disregard, unconcern (*sense 2*) inconsequence, insignificance, irrelevance, worthlessness ~*v.* bore, burden, irk, repel, tire, weary

interested 1. affected, attentive, attracted, curious, drawn, excited, fascinated, intent, into (*Inf.*), keen, moved, responsive, stimulated **2.** biased, concerned, implicated, involved, partial, partisan, predisposed, prejudiced
Antonyms (*sense 1*) apathetic, bored, detached, inattentive, indifferent, unconcerned, uninterested, wearied

interesting absorbing, amusing, appealing, attractive, compelling, curious, engaging, engrossing, entertaining, gripping, intriguing, pleasing, provocative, stimulating, suspicious, thought-provoking, unusual
Antonyms boring, dull, mind-numbing, tedious, uninteresting

interfere 1. butt in, get involved, intermeddle, intervene, intrude, meddle, poke one's nose in (*Inf.*), put one's two cents in (*U.S. sl.*), stick one's oar in (*Inf.*), tamper **2.** *Often with* with be a drag upon (*Inf.*), block, clash, collide, conflict, cramp, frustrate, get in the way of, hamper, handicap, hinder, impede, inhibit, obstruct, trammel

interference 1. intermeddling, intervention, intrusion, meddlesomeness, meddling, prying **2.** clashing, collision, conflict, impedance, obstruction, opposition

interim 1. *adj.* acting, caretaker, improvised, intervening, makeshift, pro tem, provisional, stopgap, temporary **2.** *n.* entr'acte, interregnum, interval, meantime, meanwhile, respite

interior *adj.* **1.** inner, inside, internal, inward **2.** *Geog.* central, inland, remote, up-country **3.** *Politics* domestic, home **4.** hidden, inner, intimate, mental, personal, private, secret, spiritual ~*n.* **5.** bosom, centre, contents, core, heart, innards (*Inf.*), inside **6.** *Geog.* centre, heartland, upcountry
Antonyms (*sense 1*) exposed, exterior, external, outer, outside, outward

interjection cry, ejaculation, exclamation, interpolation, interposition

interloper gate-crasher (*Inf.*), intermeddler, intruder, meddler, trespasser, uninvited guest, unwanted visitor

interlude break, breathing space, delay, entr'acte, episode, halt, hiatus, intermission, interval, pause, respite, rest, spell, stop, stoppage, wait

intermediary *n.* agent, broker, entrepreneur, go-between, mediator, middleman

intermediate halfway, in-between (*Inf.*), intermediary, interposed, intervening, mean, mid, middle, midway, transitional

interment burial, burying, funeral, inhumation, sepulture

interminable boundless, ceaseless, dragging, endless, everlasting, immeasurable, infinite, limitless, long, long-drawn-out, long-winded, never-ending, perpetual, protracted, unbounded, unlimited, wearisome
Antonyms bounded, finite, limited, measurable, restricted, temporary

intermingle amalgamate, blend, combine, commingle, commix, fuse, interlace, intermix, interweave, meld, merge, mix

intermission break, cessation, entr'acte, interlude, interruption, interval, let-up (*Inf.*), lull, pause, recess, respite, rest, stop, stoppage, suspense, suspension

intermittent broken, discontinuous, fitful, irregular, occasional, periodic, punctuated, recurrent, recurring, spasmodic, sporadic, stop-go (*Inf.*)
Antonyms continuous, steady, unceasing

intern confine, detain, hold, hold in custody

internal 1. inner, inside, interior, intimate, private, subjective **2.** civic, domestic, home, in-house, intramural
Antonyms (*sense 1*) exposed, exterior, external, outer, outermost, outside, revealed, unconcealed

international cosmopolitan, ecumenical (*Rare*), global, intercontinental, universal, worldwide

interpolate add, insert, intercalate, introduce

interpolation addition, aside, insert, insertion, intercalation, interjection, introduction

interpose 1. come *or* place between, intercede, interfere, intermediate, intervene, intrude, mediate, step in **2.** insert, interject, interrupt (with), introduce, put forth

interpret adapt, clarify, construe, decipher, decode, define, elucidate, explain, explicate, expound, make sense of, paraphrase, read, render, solve, spell out, take, throw light on, translate, understand

interpretation analysis, clarification, construction, diagnosis, elucidation, exegesis, explanation, explication, exposition, meaning, performance, portrayal, reading, rendering, rendition, sense, signification, translation, understanding, version

interpreter annotator, commentator, exponent, scholiast, translator

interrogate ask, catechize, cross-examine, cross-question, enquire, examine, give (someone) the third degree (*Inf.*), grill (*Inf.*), inquire, investigate, pump, put the screws on (*Inf.*), question, quiz

interrogation cross-examination, cross-questioning, enquiry, examination, grilling (*Inf.*), inquiry, inquisition, probing, questioning, third degree (*Inf.*)

interrogative curious, inquiring, inquisitive, inquisitorial, questioning, quizzical

interrupt barge in (*Inf.*), break, break in, break off, break (someone's) train of thought, butt in, check, cut, cut off, cut short, delay, disconnect, discontinue, disjoin, disturb, disunite, divide, heckle, hinder, hold up, interfere (with), intrude, lay aside, obstruct, punctuate, separate, sever, stay, stop, suspend

interrupted broken, cut off, disconnected, discontinuous, disturbed, incomplete, intermittent, uneven

interruption break, cessation, disconnection, discontinuance, disruption, dissolution, disturbance, disuniting, division, halt, hiatus, hindrance, hitch, impediment, intrusion, obstacle, obstruction, pause, separation, severance, stop, stoppage, suspension

intersect bisect, crisscross, cross, cut, cut across, divide, meet

intersection crossing, crossroads, interchange, junction

interval break, delay, distance, entr'acte, gap, hiatus, interim, interlude, intermission, meantime, meanwhile, opening, pause, period, playtime, respite, rest, season, space, spell, term, time, wait

intervene 1. arbitrate, intercede, interfere, interpose oneself, intrude, involve oneself, mediate, put one's two cents in (*U.S. sl.*), step in (*Inf.*), take a hand (*Inf.*) **2.** befall, come to pass, ensue, happen, occur, succeed, supervene, take place

intervention agency, intercession, interference, interposition, intrusion, mediation

interview 1. *n.* audience, conference, consultation, dialogue, evaluation, meeting, oral (examination), press conference, talk **2.** *v.* examine, interrogate, question, sound out, talk to

interviewer examiner, interlocutor, inter~ rogator, investigator, questioner, reporter

interwoven blended, connected, entwined, inmixed, interconnected, interlaced, inter~ locked, intermingled, knit

intestinal abdominal, coeliac, duodenal, gut (*Inf.*), inner, stomachic, visceral

intestines bowels, entrails, guts, innards (*Inf.*), insides (*Inf.*), internal organs, viscera, vitals

intimacy closeness, confidence, confiden~ tiality, familiarity, fraternization, under~ standing
Antonyms alienation, aloofness, coldness, detachment, distance, estrangement, remote~ ness, separation

intimate¹ *adj.* **1.** bosom, cherished, close, confidential, dear, friendly, near, nearest and dearest, thick (*Inf.*), warm **2.** confidential, personal, private, privy, secret **3.** deep, detailed, exhaustive, experienced, first-hand, immediate, in-depth, penetrating, personal, profound, thorough **4.** comfy (*Inf.*), cosy, friendly, informal, snug, tête-à-tête, warm ~*n.* **5.** bosom friend, buddy (*Inf.*), china (*Brit. sl.*), chum (*Inf.*), close friend, cock (*Brit. inf.*), comrade, confidant, confidante, (constant) companion, crony, familiar, friend, mate (*Inf.*), mucker (*Brit. sl.*), pal
Antonyms *n.* (*sense 1*) distant, remote, superficial (*sense 2*) known, open, public ~*n.* enemy, foe, stranger

intimate² *v.* allude, announce, communi~ cate, declare, drop a hint, give (someone) to understand, hint, impart, imply, indicate, insinuate, let it be known, make known, remind, state, suggest, tip (someone) the wink (*Brit. inf.*), warn

intimately **1.** affectionately, closely, confidentially, confidingly, familiarly, per~ sonally, tenderly, very well, warmly **2.** ful~ ly, in detail, inside out, thoroughly, through and through, to the core, very well

intimation **1.** allusion, hint, indication, inkling, insinuation, reminder, suggestion, warning **2.** announcement, communication, declaration, notice

intimidate affright (*Archaic*), alarm, appal, browbeat, bully, coerce, cow, daunt, dis~ hearten, dismay, dispirit, frighten, lean on (*Inf.*), overawe, scare, scare off (*Inf.*), sub~ due, terrify, terrorize, threaten, twist someone's arm (*Inf.*)

intimidation arm-twisting (*Inf.*), browbeat~ ing, bullying, coercion, fear, menaces, pres~ sure, terror, terrorization, threat(s)

intolerable beyond bearing, excruciating, impossible, insufferable, insupportable,

more than flesh and blood can stand, not to be borne, painful, unbearable, unendurable
Antonyms bearable, endurable, painless, possible, sufferable, supportable, tolerable

intolerance bigotry, chauvinism, discrimi~ nation, dogmatism, fanaticism, illiberality, impatience, jingoism, narrow-mindedness, narrowness, prejudice, racialism, racism, xenophobia
Antonyms broad-mindedness, liberality, open-mindedness, patience, tolerance, under~ standing

intolerant bigoted, chauvinistic, dictatorial, dogmatic, fanatical, illiberal, impatient, narrow, narrow-minded, one-sided, preju~ diced, racialist, racist, small-minded, un~ charitable, xenophobic
Antonyms broad-minded, charitable, leni~ ent, liberal, open-minded, patient, tolerant, understanding

intonation **1.** accentuation, cadence, inflection, modulation, tone **2.** chant, in~ cantation

intone chant, croon, intonate, recite, sing

intoxicate **1.** addle, befuddle, fuddle, go to one's head, inebriate, put (someone) under the table (*Inf.*), stupefy **2.** *Fig.* elate, excite, exhilarate, inflame, make one's head spin, stimulate

intoxicated **1.** bevvied (*Dialect*), blitzed (*Sl.*), blotto (*Sl.*), bombed (*Sl.*), canned (*Sl.*), cut (*Brit. sl.*), drunk, drunken, flying (*Sl.*), fuddled, half seas over (*Brit. inf.*), high (*Inf.*), inebriated, in one's cups (*Inf.*), legless (*Inf.*), lit up (*Sl.*), out of it (*Sl.*), out to it (*Aust. & N.Z. sl.*), paralytic (*Inf.*), pissed (*Taboo sl.*), plastered (*Sl.*), smashed (*Sl.*), sozzled (*Inf.*), steamboats (*Sl.*), steaming (*Sl.*), stewed (*Sl.*), stiff (*Sl.*), stoned (*Sl.*), the worse for drink, three sheets in the wind (*Inf.*), tight (*Inf.*), tipsy, under the influence, wasted (*Sl.*), wrecked (*Sl.*), zonked (*Sl.*) **2.** *Fig.* dizzy, elated, enraptured, euphoric, ex~ cited, exhilarated, high (*Inf.*), infatuated, sent (*Sl.*), stimulated

intoxicating **1.** alcoholic, inebriant, in~ toxicant, spirituous, strong **2.** *Fig.* exciting, exhilarating, heady, sexy (*Inf.*), stimulating, thrilling

intoxication **1.** drunkenness, inebriation, inebriety, insobriety, tipsiness **2.** *Fig.* de~ lirium, elation, euphoria, exaltation, excite~ ment, exhilaration, infatuation

intransigent hardline, immovable, intrac~ table, obdurate, obstinate, stiff-necked, stubborn, tenacious, tough, unbending, unbudgeable, uncompromising, unyielding
Antonyms acquiescent, compliant, compro~ mising, flexible, open-minded

intrepid audacious, bold, brave, courageous, daring, dauntless, doughty, fearless, gallant,

game (*Inf.*), have-a-go (*Inf.*), heroic, lion-hearted, nerveless, plucky, resolute, stalwart, stouthearted, unafraid, undaunted, unflinching, valiant, valorous
Antonyms afraid, cautious, cowardly, craven, daunted, faint-hearted, fearful, flinching, irresolute, timid

intricacy complexity, complication, convolutions, elaborateness, entanglement, intricateness, involution, involvement, knottiness, obscurity

intricate baroque, Byzantine, complex, complicated, convoluted, daedal (*Literary*), difficult, elaborate, fancy, involved, knotty, labyrinthine, obscure, perplexing, rococo, sophisticated, tangled, tortuous
Antonyms clear, easy, obvious, plain, simple, straightforward

intrigue *v.* **1.** arouse the curiosity of, attract, charm, fascinate, interest, pique, rivet, tickle one's fancy, titillate **2.** connive, conspire, machinate, manoeuvre, plot, scheme ~*n.* **3.** cabal, chicanery, collusion, conspiracy, double-dealing, knavery, machination, manipulation, manoeuvre, plot, ruse, scheme, sharp practice, stratagem, trickery, wile **4.** affair, amour, intimacy, liaison, romance

intriguing beguiling, compelling, diverting, exciting, fascinating, interesting, tantalizing, titillating

intrinsic basic, built-in, central, congenital, constitutional, elemental, essential, fundamental, genuine, inborn, inbred, inherent, native, natural, radical, real, true, underlying
Antonyms acquired, added, appended, artificial, extraneous, extrinsic, incidental

introduce 1. acquaint, do the honours, familiarize, make known, make the introduction, present **2.** begin, bring in, commence, establish, found, inaugurate, initiate, institute, launch, organize, pioneer, set up, start, usher in **3.** advance, air, bring up, broach, moot, offer, propose, put forward, recommend, set forth, submit, suggest, ventilate **4.** announce, lead into, lead off, open, preface **5.** add, inject, insert, interpolate, interpose, put in, throw in (*Inf.*)

introduction 1. baptism, debut, establishment, first acquaintance, inauguration, induction, initiation, institution, launch, pioneering, presentation **2.** commencement, exordium, foreword, intro (*Inf.*), lead-in, opening, opening passage, opening remarks, overture, preamble, preface, preliminaries, prelude, proem, prolegomena, prolegomenon, prologue **3.** addition, insertion, interpolation
Antonyms (*sense 1*) completion, elimination, termination (*sense 2*) afterward, conclusion,

end, epilogue (*sense 3*) extraction, removal, withdrawal

introductory early, elementary, first, inaugural, initial, initiatory, opening, precursory, prefatory, preliminary, preparatory, starting
Antonyms closing, concluding, final, last, terminating

introspective brooding, contemplative, inner-directed, introverted, inward-looking, meditative, pensive, subjective

introverted indrawn, inner-directed, introspective, inward-looking, self-centred, self-contained, withdrawn

intrude butt in, encroach, infringe, interfere, interrupt, meddle, obtrude, push in, put one's two cents in (*U.S. sl.*), thrust oneself in *or* forward, trespass, violate

intruder burglar, gate-crasher (*Inf.*), infiltrator, interloper, invader, prowler, raider, snooper (*Inf.*), squatter, thief, trespasser

intrusion encroachment, infringement, interference, interruption, invasion, trespass, violation

intrusive disturbing, forward, impertinent, importunate, interfering, invasive, meddlesome, nosy (*Inf.*), officious, presumptuous, pushy (*Inf.*), uncalled-for, unwanted

intuition discernment, hunch, insight, instinct, perception, presentiment, sixth sense

intuitive innate, instinctive, instinctual, involuntary, spontaneous, unreflecting, untaught

inundate deluge, drown, engulf, flood, glut, immerse, overflow, overrun, overwhelm, submerge, swamp

inundation deluge, flood, overflow, tidal wave, torrent

invade 1. assail, assault, attack, burst in, descend upon, encroach, infringe, make inroads, occupy, raid, violate **2.** infect, infest, overrun, overspread, penetrate, permeate, pervade, swarm over

invader aggressor, alien, attacker, looter, plunderer, raider, trespasser

invalid¹ 1. *adj.* ailing, bedridden, disabled, feeble, frail, ill, infirm, poorly (*Inf.*), sick, sickly, valetudinarian, weak **2.** *n.* convalescent, patient, valetudinarian

**invalid² ** *adj.* baseless, fallacious, false, ill-founded, illogical, inoperative, irrational, not binding, nugatory, null, null and void, unfounded, unscientific, unsound, untrue, void, worthless
Antonyms logical, operative, rational, solid, sound, true, valid, viable

invalidate abrogate, annul, cancel, nullify, overrule, overthrow, quash, render null and void, rescind, undermine, undo, weaken

Antonyms authorize, empower, ratify, sanction, strengthen, validate

invaluable beyond price, costly, inesti~ mable, precious, priceless, valuable
Antonyms cheap, rubbishy, valueless, worthless

invariable changeless, consistent, constant, fixed, immutable, inflexible, regular, rigid, set, unalterable, unchangeable, unchanging, unfailing, uniform, unvarying, unwavering
Antonyms alterable, changeable, changing, differing, flexible, inconsistent, irregular, uneven, variable, varying

invariably always, consistently, customari~ ly, day in, day out, ever, every time, ha~ bitually, inevitably, on every occasion, per~ petually, regularly, unfailingly, without ex~ ception

invasion 1. aggression, assault, attack, for~ ay, incursion, inroad, irruption, offensive, onslaught, raid **2.** breach, encroachment, infiltration, infraction, infringement, intru~ sion, overstepping, usurpation, violation

invective abuse, berating, billingsgate, cas~ tigation, censure, contumely, denunciation, diatribe, obloquy, philippic(s), reproach, revilement, sarcasm, tirade, tongue-lashing, vilification, vituperation

invent 1. coin, come up with (*Inf.*), con~ ceive, contrive, create, design, devise, dis~ cover, dream up (*Inf.*), formulate, imagine, improvise, originate, think up **2.** concoct, cook up (*Inf.*), fabricate, feign, forge, make up, manufacture, trump up

invention 1. brainchild (*Inf.*), contraption, contrivance, creation, design, development, device, discovery, gadget, instrument **2.** coinage, creativeness, creativity, genius, imagination, ingenuity, inspiration, inven~ tiveness, originality, resourcefulness **3.** de~ ceit, fabrication, fake, falsehood, fantasy, fib (*Inf.*), fiction, figment *or* product of (someone's) imagination, forgery, lie, pre~ varication, sham, story, tall story (*Inf.*), un~ truth, yarn

inventive creative, fertile, gifted, ground-breaking, imaginative, ingenious, innova~ tive, inspired, original, resourceful
Antonyms imitative, pedestrian, trite, un~ imaginative, uninspired, uninventive

inventor architect, author, coiner, creator, designer, father, framer, maker, originator

inventory *n.* account, catalogue, file, list, record, register, roll, roster, schedule, stock book

inverse *adj.* contrary, converse, inverted, opposite, reverse, reversed, transposed

inversion antipode, antithesis, contraposi~ tion, contrariety, contrary, opposite, rever~ sal, transposal, transposition

invert capsize, introvert, intussuscept (*Pa~ thology*), invaginate (*Pathology*), overset, overturn, reverse, transpose, turn inside out, turn turtle, turn upside down, upset, upturn

invest 1. advance, devote, lay out, put in, sink, spend **2.** endow, endue, provide, sup~ ply **3.** authorize, charge, empower, license, sanction, vest **4.** adopt, consecrate, en~ throne, establish, inaugurate, induct, in~ stall, ordain **5.** *Military* beleaguer, beset, besiege, enclose, lay siege to, surround **6.** *Archaic* array, bedeck, bedizen (*Archaic*), clothe, deck, drape, dress, robe

investigate consider, enquire into, exam~ ine, explore, go into, inquire into, inspect, look into, make enquiries, probe, put to the test, recce (*Sl.*), research, scrutinize, search, sift, study, work over

investigation analysis, enquiry, examina~ tion, exploration, fact finding, hearing, in~ quest, inquiry, inspection, probe, recce (*Sl.*), research, review, scrutiny, search, study, survey

investigator dick (*Sl., chiefly U.S.*), exam~ iner, gumshoe (*U.S. sl.*), inquirer, (private) detective, private eye (*Inf.*), researcher, re~ viewer, sleuth *or* sleuthhound (*Inf.*)

investiture admission, enthronement, in~ auguration, induction, installation, instate~ ment, investing, investment, ordination

investment 1. asset, investing, specula~ tion, transaction, venture **2.** ante (*Inf.*), contribution, stake **3.** *Military* beleaguer~ ing, besieging, blockading, siege, surround~ ing

inveterate chronic, confirmed, deep-dyed (*Usually derogatory*), deep-rooted, deep-seated, dyed-in-the-wool, entrenched, estab~ lished, habitual, hard-core, hardened, in~ corrigible, incurable, ineradicable, in~ grained, long-standing, obstinate

invidious discriminatory, envious (*Obso~ lete*), hateful, obnoxious, odious, offensive, repugnant, slighting, undesirable
Antonyms benevolent, desirable, generous, gratifying, kind, pleasant, pleasing

invigorate animate, brace, buck up (*Inf.*), energize, enliven, exhilarate, fortify, fresh~ en (up), galvanize, harden, liven up, nerve, pep up, perk up, put new heart into, quick~ en, refresh, rejuvenate, revitalize, stimulate, strengthen

invincible impregnable, indestructible, in~ domitable, inseparable, insuperable, invul~ nerable, unassailable, unbeatable, uncon~ querable, unsurmountable, unyielding
Antonyms assailable, beatable, conquer~ able, defenceless, fallible, powerless, unpro~ tected, vulnerable, weak, yielding

inviolable hallowed, holy, inalienable, sa~ cred, sacrosanct, unalterable

inviolate entire, intact, pure, sacred, stain~ less, unbroken, undefiled, undisturbed, un~ hurt, unpolluted, unstained, unsullied, un~ touched, virgin, whole
Antonyms abused, broken, defiled, polluted, stained, sullied, touched, violated

invisible 1. imperceptible, indiscernible, out of sight, unperceivable, unseen **2.** con~ cealed, disguised, hidden, inappreciable, in~ conspicuous, infinitesimal, microscopic
Antonyms (*sense 1*) discernible, distinct, ob~ vious, perceptible, seen, visible

invitation 1. asking, begging, bidding, call, invite (*Inf.*), request, solicitation, summons, supplication **2.** allurement, challenge, come-on (*Inf.*), coquetry, enticement, glad eye (*Inf.*), incitement, inducement, open door, overture, provocation, temptation

invite 1. ask, beg, bid, call, request, request the pleasure of (someone's) company, solic~ it, summon **2.** allure, ask for (*Inf.*), attract, bring on, court, draw, encourage, entice, lead, leave the door open to, provoke, solic~ it, tempt, welcome

inviting alluring, appealing, attractive, be~ guiling, captivating, delightful, engaging, enticing, fascinating, intriguing, magnetic, mouthwatering, pleasing, seductive, tempt~ ing, warm, welcoming, winning
Antonyms disagreeable, offensive, off~ putting (*Brit. inf.*), repellent, unappealing, unattractive, undesirable, uninviting, un~ pleasant

invocation appeal, beseeching, entreaty, petition, prayer, supplication

invoke 1. adjure, appeal to, beg, beseech, call upon, conjure, entreat, implore, peti~ tion, pray, solicit, supplicate **2.** apply, call in, have recourse to, implement, initiate, put into effect, resort to, use

involuntary 1. compulsory, forced, obliga~ tory, reluctant, unwilling **2.** automatic, blind, conditioned, instinctive, instinctual, reflex, spontaneous, unconscious, uncon~ trolled, unintentional, unthinking
Antonyms (*sense 1*) optional, unconstrained, volitional, voluntary, willing (*sense 2*) calcu~ lated, deliberate, intentional, planned, pur~ posed, wilful

involve 1. entail, imply, mean, necessitate, presuppose, require **2.** affect, associate, compromise, concern, connect, draw in, implicate, incriminate, inculpate, mix up (*Inf.*), touch **3.** comprehend, comprise, con~ tain, cover, embrace, include, incorporate, number among, take in **4.** absorb, bind, commit, engage, engross, grip, hold, preoc~ cupy, rivet, wrap up **5.** complicate, embroil, enmesh, entangle, link, mire, mix up, snarl up, tangle

involved 1. Byzantine, complex, complicat~ ed, confusing, convoluted, difficult, elabo~ rate, intricate, knotty, labyrinthine, sophis~ ticated, tangled, tortuous **2.** caught (up), concerned, implicated, in on (*Inf.*), mixed up in *or* with, occupied, participating, tak~ ing part
Antonyms (*sense 1*) easy, easy-peasy (*Sl.*), elementary, simple, simplified, straight~ forward, uncomplicated, unsophisticated

involvement 1. association, commitment, concern, connection, dedication, interest, participation, responsibility **2.** complexity, complication, difficulty, embarrassment, entanglement, imbroglio, intricacy, prob~ lem, ramification

invulnerable impenetrable, indestructible, insusceptible, invincible, proof against, safe, secure, unassailable
Antonyms assailable, defenceless, insecure, susceptible, unprotected, vulnerable, weak

inward *adj.* **1.** entering, inbound, incoming, inflowing, ingoing, inpouring, penetrating **2.** confidential, hidden, inmost, inner, innermost, inside, interior, internal, per~ sonal, private, privy, secret
Antonyms (*sense 2*) exterior, external, open, outer, outermost, outside, outward, public

inwardly at heart, deep down, in one's head, in one's inmost heart, inside, pri~ vately, secretly, to oneself, within

Irish green, Hibernian

irksome aggravating, annoying, boring, bothersome, burdensome, disagreeable, ex~ asperating, irritating, tedious, tiresome, troublesome, uninteresting, unwelcome, vexatious, vexing, wearisome
Antonyms agreeable, enjoyable, gratifying, interesting, pleasant, pleasing, welcome

iron *adj.* **1.** chalybeate, ferric, ferrous, irony **2.** *Fig.* adamant, cruel, hard, heavy, im~ movable, implacable, indomitable, inflexible, obdurate, rigid, robust, steel, steely, strong, tough, unbending, unyielding
Antonyms (*sense 2*) bending, easy, flexible, light, malleable, pliable, soft, weak, yielding

ironic, ironical 1. double-edged, mocking, mordacious, sarcastic, sardonic, satirical, scoffing, sneering, wry **2.** incongruous, paradoxical

iron out clear up, eliminate, eradicate, erase, expedite, get rid of, harmonize, put right, reconcile, resolve, settle, simplify, smooth over, sort out, straighten out, un~ ravel

irons bonds, chains, fetters, gyves (*Archaic*), manacles, shackles

irony 1. mockery, sarcasm, satire **2.** con~ trariness, incongruity, paradox

irrational 1. absurd, crackpot (*Inf.*), crazy, foolish, illogical, injudicious, loopy (*Inf.*), nonsensical, preposterous, silly, unreason~ able, unreasoning, unsound, unthinking, unwise **2.** aberrant, brainless, crazy, de~ mented, insane, mindless, muddle-headed, raving, senseless, unstable, wild
Antonyms (*sense 1*) circumspect, judicious, logical, rational, reasonable, sensible, sound, wise

irrationality absurdity, brainlessness, il~ logicality, insanity, lack of judgment, luna~ cy, madness, preposterousness, senseless~ ness, unreasonableness, unsoundness

irreconcilable 1. hardline, implacable, in~ exorable, inflexible, intransient, unap~ peasable, uncompromising **2.** clashing, conflicting, diametrically opposed, incom~ patible, incongruous, inconsistent, opposed

irrecoverable gone for ever, irreclaimable, irredeemable, irremediable, irreparable, ir~ retrievable, lost, unregainable, unsalvage~ able, unsavable

irrefutable apodeictic, apodictic, beyond question, certain, incontestable, incontro~ vertible, indisputable, indubitable, invin~ cible, irrefragable, irresistible, sure, unan~ swerable, unassailable, undeniable, un~ questionable

irregular *adj.* **1.** desultory, disconnected, eccentric, erratic, fitful, fluctuating, frag~ mentary, haphazard, inconstant, intermit~ tent, nonuniform, occasional, out of order, patchy, random, shifting, spasmodic, spo~ radic, uncertain, uneven, unmethodical, unpunctual, unsteady, unsystematic, vari~ able, wavering **2.** abnormal, anomalous, capricious, disorderly, eccentric, exception~ al, extraordinary, immoderate, improper, inappropriate, inordinate, odd, peculiar, queer, quirky, rum (*Brit. sl.*), unconven~ tional, unofficial, unorthodox, unsuitable, unusual **3.** asymmetrical, broken, bumpy, craggy, crooked, elliptic, elliptical, holey, jagged, lopsided, lumpy, pitted, ragged, rough, serrated, unequal, uneven, unsym~ metrical ~*n.* **4.** guerrilla, partisan, volun~ teer
Antonyms (*sense 1*) certain, invariable, me~ thodical, punctual, reliable, steady, systemat~ ic (*sense 2*) appropriate, conventional, normal, orthodox, proper, regular, usual (*sense 3*) bal~ anced, equal, even, regular, smooth, symmet~ rical

irregularity 1. asymmetry, bumpiness, crookedness, jaggedness, lack of symmetry, lopsidedness, lumpiness, patchiness, rag~ gedness, roughness, spottiness, unevenness **2.** aberration, abnormality, anomaly,

breach, deviation, eccentricity, freak, mal~ function, malpractice, oddity, peculiarity, singularity, unconventionality, unorthodoxy **3.** confusion, desultoriness, disorderliness, disorganization, haphazardness, lack of method, randomness, uncertainty, unpunctuality, unsteadiness

irregularly anyhow, by fits and starts, dis~ connectedly, eccentrically, erratically, fitfully, haphazardly, in snatches, intermit~ tently, jerkily, now and again, occasionally, off and on, out of sequence, spasmodically, unevenly, unmethodically, unpunctually

irrelevance, irrelevancy inappositeness, inappropriateness, inaptness, incon~ sequence, non sequitur
Antonyms appositeness, appropriateness, aptness, consequence, pertinence, point, rel~ evance, suitability

irrelevant beside the point, extraneous, im~ material, impertinent, inapplicable, inappo~ site, inappropriate, inapt, inconsequent, neither here nor there, unconnected, unre~ lated
Antonyms applicable, apposite, appropri~ ate, apt, connected, fitting, pertinent, related, relevant, suitable

irreparable beyond repair, incurable, irre~ coverable, irremediable, irreplaceable, irre~ trievable, irreversible

irreplaceable indispensable, invaluable, priceless, unique, vital

irrepressible boisterous, bubbling over, buoyant, ebullient, effervescent, insup~ pressible, uncontainable, uncontrollable, unmanageable, unquenchable, unrestrain~ able, unstoppable

irreproachable beyond reproach, blame~ less, faultless, guiltless, impeccable, incul~ pable, innocent, irreprehensible, irreprov~ able, perfect, pure, unblemished, unim~ peachable

irresistible 1. compelling, imperative, overmastering, overpowering, overwhelm~ ing, potent, urgent **2.** ineluctable, inescap~ able, inevitable, inexorable, unavoidable **3.** alluring, beckoning, enchanting, fascinat~ ing, ravishing, seductive, tempting

irresolute doubtful, fickle, half-arsed, half-assed (*U.S. & Canad. sl.*), half-hearted, hesitant, hesitating, indecisive, infirm, in two minds, tentative, undecided, undeter~ mined, unsettled, unstable, unsteady, vacil~ lating, wavering, weak
Antonyms decisive, determined, firm, fixed, resolute, resolved, settled, stable, stalwart, steadfast, steady, strong

irrespective of apart from, despite, dis~ counting, in spite of, notwithstanding, re~ gardless of, without reference to, without regard to

irresponsible careless, featherbrained, flighty, giddy, harebrained, harum-scarum, ill-considered, immature, reckless, scatterbrained, shiftless, thoughtless, undependable, unreliable, untrustworthy, wild
Antonyms careful, dependable, levelheaded, mature, reliable, responsible, sensible, trustworthy

irreverence cheek (*Inf.*), cheekiness (*Inf.*), chutzpah (*U.S. & Canad. inf.*), derision, disrespect, flippancy, impertinence, impudence, lack of respect, mockery, sauce (*Inf.*)

irreverent cheeky (*Inf.*), contemptuous, derisive, disrespectful, flip (*Inf.*), flippant, fresh (*Inf.*), iconoclastic, impertinent, impious, impudent, mocking, sassy (*U.S. inf.*), saucy, tongue-in-cheek
Antonyms awed, deferential, meek, pious, respectful, reverent, submissive

irreversible final, incurable, irreparable, irrevocable, unalterable

irrevocable changeless, fated, fixed, immutable, invariable, irremediable, irretrievable, irreversible, predestined, predetermined, settled, unalterable, unchangeable, unreversible

irrigate flood, inundate, moisten, water, wet

irritability bad temper, ill humour, impatience, irascibility, peevishness, petulance, prickliness, testiness, tetchiness, touchiness
Antonyms bonhomie, cheerfulness, complacence, good humour, patience

irritable bad-tempered, cantankerous, choleric, crabbed, crabby, cross, crotchety (*Inf.*), dyspeptic, edgy, exasperated, fiery, fretful, hasty, hot, ill-humoured, ill-tempered, irascible, narky (*Brit. sl.*), out of humour, oversensitive, peevish, petulant, prickly, ratty (*Brit. & N.Z. inf.*), snappish, snappy, snarling, tense, testy, tetchy, touchy
Antonyms agreeable, calm, cheerful, complacent, composed, even-tempered, goodnatured, imperturbable, patient, unexcitable

irritate 1. aggravate (*Inf.*), anger, annoy, bother, drive one up the wall (*Sl.*), enrage, exasperate, fret, gall, get in one's hair (*Inf.*), get one's back up, get one's hackles up, get on one's nerves (*Inf.*), harass, incense, inflame, infuriate, nark (*Brit., Aust., & N.Z. sl.*), needle (*Inf.*), nettle, offend, pester, piss one off (*Taboo sl.*), provoke, raise one's hackles, rankle with, rub up the wrong way (*Inf.*), ruffle, try one's patience, vex 2. aggravate, chafe, fret, inflame, intensify, pain, rub
Antonyms (*sense 1*) calm, comfort, gratify, mollify, placate, please, soothe

irritated angry, annoyed, bothered, cross, displeased, exasperated, flustered, hacked (off) (*U.S. sl.*), harassed, impatient, irritable, nettled, out of humour, peeved (*Inf.*),

piqued, pissed off (*Taboo sl.*), put out, ruffled, vexed

irritating aggravating (*Inf.*), annoying, displeasing, disquieting, disturbing, galling, infuriating, irksome, maddening, nagging, pestilential, provoking, thorny, troublesome, trying, upsetting, vexatious, worrisome
Antonyms agreeable, assuaging, calming, comforting, mollifying, pleasant, pleasing, quieting, soothing

irritation 1. anger, annoyance, crossness, displeasure, exasperation, ill humour, ill temper, impatience, indignation, irritability, resentment, shortness, snappiness, testiness, vexation, wrath 2. aggravation (*Inf.*), annoyance, drag (*Inf.*), gall, goad, irritant, nuisance, pain (*Inf.*), pain in the arse (*Taboo inf.*), pain in the neck (*Inf.*), pest, provocation, tease, thorn in one's flesh
Antonyms (*sense 1*) calm, composure, ease, pleasure, quietude, satisfaction, serenity, tranquillity

isolate cut off, detach, disconnect, divorce, insulate, quarantine, segregate, separate, sequester, set apart

isolated 1. backwoods, hidden, incommunicado, in the middle of nowhere, lonely, off the beaten track, outlying, out-of-the-way, remote, retired, secluded, unfrequented 2. abnormal, anomalous, exceptional, freak, random, single, solitary, special, unique, unrelated, untypical, unusual

isolation aloofness, detachment, disconnection, exile, insularity, insulation, loneliness, quarantine, remoteness, retirement, seclusion, segregation, self-sufficiency, separation, solitude, withdrawal

issue *n.* 1. affair, argument, concern, controversy, matter, matter of contention, point, point in question, problem, question, subject, topic 2. **at issue** at variance, controversial, in disagreement, in dispute, to be decided, under discussion, unsettled 3. **take issue** challenge, disagree, dispute, object, oppose, raise an objection, take exception 4. conclusion, consequence, culmination, effect, end, finale, outcome, pay-off (*Inf.*), result, termination, upshot 5. copy, edition, impression, instalment, number, printing 6. circulation, delivery, dispersion, dissemination, distribution, granting, issuance, issuing, publication, sending out, supply, supplying 7. children, descendants, heirs, offspring, progeny, scions, seed (*Chiefly biblical*), ~*v.* 8. announce, broadcast, circulate, deliver, distribute, emit, give out, promulgate, publish, put in circulation, put out, release 9. arise, be a consequence of, come forth, emanate, emerge, flow, originate, proceed, rise, spring, stem

Antonyms *n.* (*sense 4*) beginning, cause, in~ ception, start (*sense 6*) cancellation, recall (*sense 7*) parent, sire ~*v.* cause, revoke, with~ draw

itch *v.* **1.** crawl, irritate, prickle, tickle, tin~ gle **2.** ache, burn, crave, hanker, hunger, long, lust, pant, pine, yearn ~*n.* **3.** irrita~ tion, itchiness, prickling, tingling **4.** crav~ ing, desire, hankering, hunger, longing, lust, passion, restlessness, yearning, yen (*Inf.*)

itching agog, aquiver, atremble, avid, burn~ ing, consumed with curiosity, eager, impa~ tient, inquisitive, longing, mad keen (*Inf.*), raring, spoiling for

itchy eager, edgy, fidgety, impatient, restive, restless, unsettled

item 1. article, aspect, component, consid~ eration, detail, entry, matter, particular, point, thing **2.** account, article, bulletin, dispatch, feature, note, notice, paragraph, piece, report

itemize count, detail, document, enumerate, instance, inventory, list, number, particu~ larize, record, set out, specify

itinerant *adj.* ambulatory, Gypsy, journey~ ing, migratory, nomadic, peripatetic, roam~ ing, roving, travelling, unsettled, vagabond, vagrant, wandering, wayfaring

Antonyms established, fixed, resident, root~ ed, settled, stable

itinerary 1. circuit, journey, line, pro~ gramme, route, schedule, timetable, tour **2.** Baedeker, guide, guidebook

J

jab *v./n.* dig, lunge, nudge, poke, prod, punch, stab, tap, thrust

jacket case, casing, coat, covering, envelope, folder, sheath, skin, wrapper, wrapping

jackpot award, bonanza, kitty, pool, pot, prize, reward, winnings

jack up 1. elevate, heave, hoist, lift, lift up, raise, rear **2.** accelerate, augment, boost, escalate, increase, inflate, put up, raise

jade harridan, hussy, nag, shrew, slattern, slut, trollop, vixen, wench

jaded 1. clapped out (*Aust. & N.Z. inf.*), exhausted, fagged (out) (*Inf.*), fatigued, spent, tired, tired-out, weary, zonked (*Sl.*) **2.** bored, cloyed, dulled, glutted, gorged, sated, satiated, surfeited, tired
Antonyms eager, enthusiastic, fresh, keen, life-loving, naive, refreshed

jagged barbed, broken, cleft, craggy, denticulate, indented, notched, pointed, ragged, ridged, rough, serrated, snaggy, spiked, toothed, uneven
Antonyms glassy, level, regular, rounded, smooth

jail, gaol 1. *n.* borstal, brig (*Chiefly U.S.*), can (*Sl.*), clink (*Sl.*), cooler (*Sl.*), inside (*Sl.*), jailhouse (*Southern U.S.*), jug (*Sl.*), lockup, nick (*Brit. sl.*), penitentiary (*U.S.*), poky *or* pokey (*U.S. & Canad. sl.*), prison, quod (*Sl.*), reformatory, slammer (*Sl.*), stir (*Sl.*) **2.** *v.* confine, detain, immure, impound, imprison, incarcerate, lock up, send down

jailer, gaoler captor, guard, keeper, screw (*Sl.*), turnkey (*Archaic*), warden, warder

jam *v.* **1.** cram, crowd, crush, force, pack, press, ram, squeeze, stuff, throng, wedge **2.** block, cease, clog, congest, halt, obstruct, stall, stick ~*n.* **3.** crowd, crush, horde, mass, mob, multitude, pack, press, swarm, throng **4.** bind, dilemma, fix (*Inf.*), hole (*Sl.*), hot water, pickle (*Inf.*), plight, predicament, quandary, scrape (*Inf.*), spot (*Inf.*), strait, tight spot, trouble

jamboree beano (*Brit. sl.*), carnival, carousal, carouse, celebration, festival, festivity, fête, frolic, jubilee, merriment, party, rave (*Brit. sl.*), rave-up (*Brit. sl.*), revelry, spree

jangle 1. *v.* chime, clank, clash, clatter, jingle, rattle, vibrate **2.** *n.* cacophony, clang, clangour, clash, din, dissonance, jar, racket, rattle, reverberation
Antonyms (*sense 2*) harmoniousness, mellifluousness, quiet, silence

janitor caretaker, concierge, custodian, doorkeeper, porter

jar¹ amphora, carafe, container, crock, flagon, jug, pitcher, pot, receptacle, urn, vase, vessel

jar² *v.* **1.** bicker, clash, contend, disagree, interfere, oppose, quarrel, wrangle **2.** agitate, convulse, disturb, grate, irritate, jolt, offend, rasp, rattle (*Inf.*), rock, shake, vibrate **3.** annoy, clash, discompose, gall, get on one's nerves (*Inf.*), grate, grind, irk, irritate, nark (*Brit., Aust., & N.Z. sl.*), nettle, piss one off (*Taboo sl.*), ~*n.* **4.** agitation, altercation, bickering, disagreement, discord, grating, irritation, jolt, quarrel, rasping, wrangling

jargon 1. argot, cant, dialect, idiom, lingo (*Inf.*), parlance, patois, slang, tongue, usage **2.** balderdash, bunkum *or* buncombe (*Chiefly U.S.*), drivel, gabble, gibberish, gobbledegook, mumbo jumbo, nonsense, palaver, rigmarole, twaddle

jaundiced 1. cynical, preconceived, sceptical **2.** biased, bigoted, bitter, distorted, envious, hostile, jealous, partial, prejudiced, resentful, spiteful, suspicious
Antonyms credulous, ingenuous, naive, open-minded, optimistic, trusting, unbiased

jaunt airing, excursion, expedition, outing, promenade, ramble, stroll, tour, trip

jaunty airy, breezy, buoyant, carefree, dapper, gay, high-spirited, lively, perky, self-confident, showy, smart, sparky, sprightly, spruce, trim
Antonyms dignified, dull, lifeless, sedate, serious, staid

jaw *v.* **1.** babble, chat, chatter, gossip, lecture, spout, talk **2.** abuse, censure, criticize, revile, scold ~*n.* **3.** chat, chinwag (*Brit. inf.*), conversation, gabfest (*Inf., chiefly U.S. & Canad.*), gossip, natter, talk

jaws abyss, aperture, entrance, gates, ingress, maw, mouth, opening, orifice

jazz up animate, enhance, enliven, heighten, improve

jazzy animated, fancy, flashy, gaudy, lively, smart, snazzy (*Inf.*), spirited, vivacious, wild, zestful

jealous 1. covetous, desirous, emulous, envious, green, green-eyed, grudging, intolerant, invidious, resentful, rival **2.** anxious, apprehensive, attentive, guarded, mistrustful, protective, solicitous, suspicious, vigilant, wary, watchful, zealous

Antonyms carefree, indifferent, satisfied, trusting

jealousy covetousness, distrust, envy, heart-burning, ill-will, mistrust, possessive~ ness, resentment, spite, suspicion

jeer 1. *v.* banter, barrack, cock a snook at (*Brit.*), contemn (*Formal*), deride, flout, gibe, heckle, hector, knock (*Inf.*), mock, ridicule, scoff, sneer, taunt 2. *n.* abuse, as~ persion, boo, catcall, derision, gibe, hiss, hoot, obloquy, ridicule, scoff, sneer, taunt
Antonyms (*sense 1*) acclaim, applaud, cheer, clap, praise (*sense 2*) adulation, applause, cheers, encouragement, praise

jell 1. congeal, harden, set, solidify, thicken 2. come together, crystallize, finalize, form, materialize, take shape

jeopardize chance, endanger, expose, gam~ ble, hazard, imperil, risk, stake, venture

jeopardy danger, endangerment, exposure, hazard, insecurity, liability, peril, pitfall, precariousness, risk, venture, vulnerability

jeremiad complaint, groan, keen, lament, lamentation, moan, plaint, wail

jerk *v./n.* jolt, lurch, pull, throw, thrust, tug, tweak, twitch, wrench, yank

jerky bouncy, bumpy, convulsive, fitful, jolt~ ing, jumpy, rough, shaky, spasmodic, tremulous, twitchy, uncontrolled
Antonyms flowing, frictionless, gliding, smooth

jerry-built cheap, defective, faulty, flimsy, ramshackle, rickety, shabby, slipshod, thrown together, unsubstantial
Antonyms sturdy, substantial, well-built, well-constructed

jest 1. *n.* banter, bon mot, crack (*Sl.*), fun, gag (*Inf.*), hoax, jape, joke, josh (*Sl., chiefly U.S. & Canad.*), play, pleasantry, prank, quip, sally, sport, wisecrack (*Inf.*), witticism 2. *v.* banter, chaff, deride, gibe, jeer, joke, josh (*Sl., chiefly U.S. & Canad.*), kid (*Inf.*), mock, quip, scoff, sneer, tease

jester 1. comedian, comic, humorist, joker, quipster, wag, wit 2. buffoon, clown, fool, harlequin, madcap, mummer, pantaloon, prankster, zany

jet[1] *adj.* black, coal-black, ebony, inky, pitch-black, raven, sable

jet[2] *n.* 1. flow, fountain, gush, spout, spray, spring, stream 2. atomizer, nose, nozzle, rose, spout, sprayer, sprinkler ~*v.* 3. flow, gush, issue, rush, shoot, spew, spout, squirt, stream, surge 4. fly, soar, zoom

jettison abandon, discard, dump, eject, ex~ pel, heave, scrap, throw overboard, unload

jetty breakwater, dock, groyne, mole, pier, quay, wharf

jewel 1. brilliant, gemstone, ornament, pre~ cious stone, rock (*Sl.*), sparkler (*Inf.*), trin~ ket 2. charm, find, gem, humdinger (*Sl.*), masterpiece, paragon, pearl, prize, rarity, treasure, wonder

jewellery finery, gems, jewels, ornaments, precious stones, regalia, treasure, trinkets

Jezebel harlot, harridan, hussy, jade, vira~ go, wanton, witch

jib balk, recoil, refuse, retreat, shrink, stop short

jig *v.* bob, bounce, caper, jiggle, jounce, prance, shake, skip, twitch, wiggle, wobble

jingle *v.* 1. chime, clatter, clink, jangle, rat~ tle, ring, tinkle, tintinnabulate ~*n.* 2. clang, clangour, clink, rattle, reverberation, ring~ ing, tinkle 3. chorus, ditty, doggerel, limer~ ick, melody, song, tune

jinx 1. *n.* black magic, curse, evil eye, hex (*U.S. & Canad. inf.*), hoodoo (*Inf.*), nemesis, plague, voodoo 2. *v.* bewitch, curse, hex (*U.S. & Canad. inf.*)

jitters anxiety, fidgets, heebie-jeebies (*Sl.*), nerves, nervousness, tenseness, the shakes (*Inf.*), the willies (*Inf.*)

jittery agitated, anxious, fidgety, hyper (*Inf.*), jumpy, nervous, quivering, shaky, trembling, twitchy (*Inf.*), wired (*Sl.*)
Antonyms calm, composed, laid-back (*Inf.*), relaxed, together (*Sl.*), unfazed (*Inf.*), unflustered

job 1. affair, assignment, charge, chore, concern, contribution, duty, enterprise, er~ rand, function, pursuit, responsibility, role, stint, task, undertaking, venture, work 2. activity, business, calling, capacity, career, craft, employment, function, livelihood, métier, occupation, office, position, post, profession, situation, trade, vocation 3. al~ lotment, assignment, batch, commission, consignment, contract, lot, output, piece, portion, product, share

jobless idle, inactive, out of work, unem~ ployed, unoccupied

jockey *v.* 1. bamboozle, cheat, con (*Inf.*), de~ ceive, dupe, fool, hoax, hoodwink, trick 2. cajole, engineer, finagle (*Inf.*), ingratiate, insinuate, manage, manipulate, manoeuvre, negotiate, trim, wheedle

jocular amusing, comical, droll, facetious, frolicsome, funny, humorous, jesting, jo~ cose, jocund, joking, jolly, jovial, playful, roguish, sportive, teasing, waggish, whim~ sical, witty
Antonyms earnest, humourless, serious, solemn

jog 1. activate, arouse, nudge, prod, prompt, push, remind, shake, stimulate, stir, suggest 2. bounce, jar, jerk, jiggle, joggle, jolt, jos~ tle, jounce, rock, shake 3. canter, dogtrot, lope, run, trot 4. lumber, plod, traipse (*Inf.*), tramp, trudge

joie de vivre ebullience, enjoyment, en~
thusiasm, gaiety, gusto, joy, joyfulness,
pleasure, relish, zest
Antonyms apathy, depression, distaste

join 1. accompany, add, adhere, annex, ap~
pend, attack, cement, combine, connect,
couple, fasten, knit, link, marry, splice, tie,
unite, yoke **2.** affiliate with, associate with,
enlist, enrol, enter, sign up **3.** adjoin, bor~
der, border on, butt, conjoin, extend, meet,
reach, touch, verge on
Antonyms detach, disconnect, disengage,
disentangle, divide, leave, part, quit, resign,
separate, sever, unfasten

joint *n.* **1.** articulation, connection, hinge,
intersection, junction, juncture, knot, nex~
us, node, seam, union ~*adj.* **2.** collective,
combined, communal, concerted, consoli~
dated, cooperative, joined, mutual, shared,
united ~*v.* **3.** connect, couple, fasten, fit,
join, unite **4.** carve, cut up, dismember,
dissect, divide, segment, sever, sunder

jointly as one, collectively, in common, in
conjunction, in league, in partnership, mu~
tually, together, unitedly
Antonyms individually, separately, singly

joke *n.* **1.** frolic, fun, gag (*Inf.*), jape, jest,
josh (*Sl., chiefly U.S. & Canad.*), lark, play,
prank, pun, quip, quirk, sally, sport, whim~
sy, wisecrack (*Inf.*), witticism, yarn **2.** buf~
foon, butt, clown, laughing stock, simpleton,
target ~*v.* **3.** banter, chaff, deride, frolic,
gambol, jest, josh (*Sl., chiefly U.S. &
Canad.*), kid (*Inf.*), mock, quip, ridicule,
taunt, tease, wind up (*Brit. sl.*)

joker buffoon, clown, comedian, comic, hu~
morist, jester, kidder (*Inf.*), prankster,
trickster, wag, wit

jolly blithesome, carefree, cheerful, chirpy
(*Inf.*), convivial, festive, frolicsome, funny,
gay, genial, gladsome (*Archaic*), hilarious,
jocund, jovial, joyful, joyous, jubilant, mer~
ry, mirthful, playful, sportive, sprightly,
upbeat (*Inf.*)
Antonyms doleful, gaunt, grave, lugubrious,
miserable, morose, saturnine, serious, solemn

jolt *v.* **1.** jar, jerk, jog, jostle, knock, push,
shake, shove **2.** astonish, discompose, dis~
turb, perturb, stagger, startle, stun, sur~
prise, upset ~*n.* **3.** bump, jar, jerk, jog,
jump, lurch, quiver, shake, start **4.** blow,
bolt from the blue, bombshell, reversal, set~
back, shock, surprise, thunderbolt

jostle bump, butt, crowd, elbow, hustle, jog,
joggle, jolt, press, push, scramble, shake,
shove, squeeze, throng, thrust

jot 1. *n.* ace, atom, bit, detail, fraction, grain,
iota, mite, morsel, particle, scintilla, scrap,
smidgen *or* smidgin (*Inf., chiefly U.S. &
Canad.*), speck, tittle, trifle, whit **2.** *v.* list,

note, note down, record, register, scribble,
tad (*Inf., chiefly U.S.*), tally

journal 1. chronicle, daily, gazette, maga~
zine, monthly, newspaper, paper, periodical,
record, register, review, tabloid, weekly **2.**
chronicle, commonplace book, daybook,
diary, log, record

journalist broadcaster, columnist, com~
mentator, contributor, correspondent, hack,
journo (*Sl.*), newsman, newspaperman,
pressman, reporter, scribe (*Inf.*), stringer

journey 1. *n.* excursion, expedition, jaunt,
odyssey, outing, passage, peregrination,
pilgrimage, progress, ramble, tour, travel,
trek, trip, voyage **2.** *v.* fare, fly, go, peregri~
nate, proceed, ramble, range, roam, rove,
tour, travel, traverse, trek, voyage, wander,
wend

jovial airy, animated, blithe, buoyant,
cheery, convivial, cordial, gay, glad, happy,
hilarious, jocose, jocund, jolly, jubilant,
merry, mirthful
Antonyms antisocial, doleful, grumpy, mo~
rose, solemn, unfriendly

joy 1. bliss, delight, ecstasy, elation, exalta~
tion, exultation, felicity, festivity, gaiety,
gladness, glee, hilarity, pleasure, rapture,
ravishment, satisfaction, transport **2.**
charm, delight, gem, jewel, pride, prize,
treasure, treat, wonder
Antonyms bane, despair, grief, misery, sor~
row, tribulation, unhappiness

joyful blithesome, cock-a-hoop, delighted,
elated, enraptured, glad, gladsome (*Archa~
ic*), gratified, happy, jocund, jolly, jovial, ju~
bilant, light-hearted, merry, over the moon
(*Inf.*), pleased, rapt, satisfied

joyless cheerless, dejected, depressed, dis~
mal, dispirited, downcast, dreary, gloomy,
miserable, sad, unhappy

joyous cheerful, festive, heartening, joyful,
merry, rapturous

jubilant cock-a-hoop, elated, enraptured,
euphoric, excited, exuberant, exultant, glad,
joyous, overjoyed, over the moon (*Inf.*), re~
joicing, rhapsodic, thrilled, triumphal, tri~
umphant
Antonyms despondent, doleful, downcast,
melancholy, sad, sorrowful

jubilation celebration, ecstasy, elation, ex~
citement, exultation, festivity, jamboree,
joy, jubilee, triumph

jubilee carnival, celebration, festival, festiv~
ity, fête, gala, holiday

judge *n.* **1.** adjudicator, arbiter, arbitrator,
moderator, referee, umpire **2.** appraiser,
arbiter, assessor, authority, connoisseur,
critic, evaluator, expert **3.** beak (*Brit. sl.*),
justice, magistrate ~*v.* **4.** adjudge, adjudi~
cate, arbitrate, ascertain, conclude, decide,

determine, discern, distinguish, mediate, referee, umpire **5.** appraise, appreciate, assess, consider, criticize, esteem, estimate, evaluate, examine, rate, review, value **6.** adjudge, condemn, decree, doom, find, pass sentence, pronounce sentence, rule, sentence, sit, try

judgment 1. acumen, common sense, discernment, discrimination, intelligence, penetration, percipience, perspicacity, prudence, sagacity, sense, shrewdness, smarts (*Sl., chiefly U.S.*), taste, understanding, wisdom **2.** arbitration, award, conclusion, decision, decree, determination, finding, order, result, ruling, sentence, verdict **3.** appraisal, assessment, belief, conviction, deduction, diagnosis, estimate, finding, opinion, valuation, view **4.** damnation, doom, fate, misfortune, punishment, retribution

judicial 1. judiciary, juridical, legal, official **2.** discriminating, distinguished, impartial, judgelike, magisterial, magistral

judicious acute, astute, careful, cautious, circumspect, considered, diplomatic, discerning, discreet, discriminating, enlightened, expedient, informed, politic, prudent, rational, reasonable, sagacious, sage, sane, sapient, sensible, shrewd, skilful, sober, sound, thoughtful, well-advised, well-judged, wise
Antonyms imprudent, indiscreet, injudicious, tactless, thoughtless

jug carafe, container, crock, ewer, jar, pitcher, urn, vessel

juggle alter, change, disguise, doctor (*Inf.*), falsify, fix (*Inf.*), manipulate, manoeuvre, misrepresent, modify, tamper with

juice extract, fluid, liquid, liquor, nectar, sap, secretion, serum

juicy 1. lush, moist, sappy, succulent, watery **2.** colourful, interesting, provocative, racy, risqué, sensational, spicy (*Inf.*), suggestive, vivid

jumble 1. *v.* confound, confuse, disarrange, dishevel, disorder, disorganize, entangle, mistake, mix, muddle, ravel, shuffle, tangle **2.** *n.* chaos, clutter, confusion, disarrangement, disarray, disorder, farrago, gallimaufry, hodgepodge, hotchpotch (*U.S.*), litter, medley, *mélange*, mess, miscellany, mishmash, mixture, muddle, pig's breakfast (*Inf.*)

jumbo elephantine, giant, gigantic, ginormous (*Inf.*), huge, humongous *or* humungous (*U.S. sl.*), immense, large, mega (*Inf.*), oversized
Antonyms baby, dwarf, micro, mini, pocket, tiny, wee

jump *v.* **1.** bounce, bound, caper, clear, gambol, hop, hurdle, leap, skip, spring, vault **2.** flinch, jerk, recoil, start, wince **3.**

avoid, digress, evade, miss, omit, overshoot, skip, switch **4.** advance, ascend, boost, escalate, gain, hike, increase, mount, rise, surge ~*n.* **5.** bound, buck, caper, hop, leap, skip, spring, vault **6.** barricade, barrier, fence, hurdle, impediment, obstacle, rail **7.** breach, break, gap, hiatus, interruption, lacuna, space **8.** advance, augmentation, boost, increase, increment, rise, upsurge, upturn **9.** jar, jerk, jolt, lurch, shock, start, swerve, twitch, wrench

jumper jersey, pullover, sweater, woolly

jumpy agitated, anxious, apprehensive, fidgety, hyper (*Inf.*), jittery (*Inf.*), nervous, on edge, restless, shaky, tense, timorous, twitchy (*Inf.*), wired (*Sl.*)
Antonyms calm, composed, laid-back (*Inf.*), nerveless, together (*Sl.*), unfazed (*Inf.*), unflustered

junction alliance, combination, connection, coupling, joint, juncture, linking, seam, union

juncture 1. conjuncture, contingency, crisis, crux, emergency, exigency, moment, occasion, point, predicament, strait, time **2.** bond, connection, convergence, edge, intersection, junction, link, seam, weld

junior inferior, lesser, lower, minor, secondary, subordinate, younger
Antonyms elder, higher-ranking, older, senior, superior

junk clutter, debris, dreck (*Sl., chiefly U.S.*), leavings, litter, oddments, odds and ends, refuse, rubbish, rummage, scrap, trash, waste

jurisdiction 1. authority, command, control, dominion, influence, power, prerogative, rule, say, sway **2.** area, bounds, circuit, compass, district, dominion, field, orbit, province, range, scope, sphere, zone

just *adj.* **1.** blameless, conscientious, decent, equitable, fair, fairminded, good, honest, honourable, impartial, lawful, pure, right, righteous, unbiased, upright, virtuous **2.** accurate, correct, exact, faithful, normal, precise, proper, regular, sound, true **3.** appropriate, apt, condign, deserved, due, fitting, justified, legitimate, merited, proper, reasonable, rightful, suitable, well-deserved ~*adv.* **4.** absolutely, completely, entirely, exactly, perfectly, precisely **5.** hardly, lately, only now, recently, scarcely **6.** at most, but, merely, no more than, nothing but, only, simply, solely
Antonyms *adj.* corrupt, devious, dishonest, inappropriate, inequitable, prejudiced, undeserved, unfair, unfit, unjust, unlawful, unreasonable, untrue

just about all but, almost, around, close to, nearly, not quite, practically, well-nigh

justice 1. equity, fairness, honesty, impar~

tiality, integrity, justness, law, legality, le~ gitimacy, reasonableness, rectitude, right **2.** amends, compensation, correction, penalty, recompense, redress, reparation **3.** judge, magistrate

Antonyms dishonesty, favouritism, inequi~ ty, injustice, partiality, unfairness, unlawful~ ness, unreasonableness, untruth, wrong

justifiable acceptable, defensible, excusable, fit, lawful, legitimate, proper, reasonable, right, sound, tenable, understandable, valid, vindicable, warrantable, well-founded

Antonyms arbitrary, capricious, indefen~ sible, inexcusable, unreasonable, unwarrant~ ed

justification 1. absolution, apology, ap~ proval, defence, exculpation, excuse, exon~ eration, explanation, extenuation, plea, ra~ tionalization, vindication **2.** basis, defence, grounds, plea, reason, warrant

justify absolve, acquit, approve, confirm, defend, establish, exculpate, excuse, exon~ erate, explain, legalize, legitimize, maintain, substantiate, support, sustain, uphold, vali~ date, vindicate, warrant

justly accurately, correctly, equally, equi~ tably, fairly, honestly, impartially, lawfully, properly

jut bulge, extend, impend, overhang, poke, project, protrude, stick out

juvenile 1. *n.* adolescent, boy, child, girl, infant, minor, youth **2.** *adj.* babyish, boy~ ish, callow, childish, girlish, immature, in~ experienced, infantile, jejune, puerile, un~ developed, unsophisticated, young, youthful

Antonyms *n.* adult, grown-up ~*adj.* adult, grown-up, mature, responsible

juxtaposition adjacency, closeness, con~ tact, contiguity, nearness, propinquity, proximity, vicinity

K

kaleidoscopic 1. changeable, fluctuating, fluid, many-coloured, mobile, motley, mutable, unstable, variegated **2.** complex, complicated, confused, convoluted, disordered, intricate, jumbled, varied

kamikaze *adj.* foolhardy, self-destructive, suicidal

keel over black out (*Inf.*), capsize, collapse, faint, founder, overturn, pass out, swoon (*Literary*), topple over, upset

keen 1. ardent, avid, devoted to, eager, earnest, ebullient, enthusiastic, fervid, fierce, fond of, impassioned, intense, into (*Inf.*), zealous **2.** acid, acute, biting, caustic, cutting, edged, finely honed, incisive, penetrating, piercing, pointed, razorlike, sardonic, satirical, sharp, tart, trenchant, vitriolic **3.** astute, brilliant, canny, clever, discerning, discriminating, perceptive, perspicacious, quick, sagacious, sapient, sensitive, shrewd, wise
Antonyms (*sense 1*) apathetic, half-hearted, indifferent, laodicean, lukewarm, unenthusiastic, uninterested (*sense 2*) blunt, dull (*sense 3*) dull, obtuse, unperceptive

keenness 1. ardour, avidity, avidness, diligence, eagerness, earnestness, ebullience, enthusiasm, fervour, impatience, intensity, passion, zeal, zest **2.** acerbity, harshness, incisiveness, mordancy, penetration, pungency, rigour, severity, sharpness, sternness, trenchancy, unkindness, virulence **3.** astuteness, canniness, cleverness, discernment, insight, sagacity, sapience, sensitivity, shrewdness, wisdom

keep *v.* **1.** conserve, control, hold, maintain, possess, preserve, retain **2.** accumulate, amass, carry, deal in, deposit, furnish, garner, heap, hold, pile, place, stack, stock, store, trade in **3.** care for, defend, guard, look after, maintain, manage, mind, operate, protect, safeguard, shelter, shield, tend, watch over **4.** board, feed, foster, maintain, nourish, nurture, provide for, provision, subsidize, support, sustain, victual **5.** accompany, associate with, consort with, fraternize with **6.** arrest, block, check, constrain, control, curb, delay, detain, deter, hamper, hamstring, hinder, hold, hold back, impede, inhibit, keep back, limit, obstruct, prevent, restrain, retard, shackle, stall, withhold **7.** adhere to, celebrate, commemorate, comply with, fulfil, hold, honour, obey, observe, perform, respect, ritualize, solemnize ~*n.* **8.** board, food, livelihood, living, maintenance, means, nourishment,

subsistence, support **9.** castle, citadel, donjon, dungeon, fastness, stronghold, tower
Antonyms abandon, discard, disregard, expedite, free, give up, ignore, liberate, lose, release, speed

keep at be steadfast, carry on, complete, continue, drudge, endure, finish, grind, labour, last, maintain, persevere, persist, remain, slave, stay, stick, toil

keep back 1. check, constrain, control, curb, delay, hold back, limit, prohibit, restrain, restrict, retard, withhold **2.** censor, conceal, hide, reserve, suppress, withhold

keeper attendant, caretaker, curator, custodian, defender, gaoler, governor, guard, guardian, jailer, overseer, preserver, steward, superintendent, warden, warder

keeping 1. aegis, auspices, care, charge, custody, guardianship, keep, maintenance, patronage, possession, protection, safekeeping, trust **2.** accord, agreement, balance, compliance, conformity, congruity, consistency, correspondence, harmony, observance, proportion

keep on carry on, continue, endure, last, persevere, persist, prolong, remain

keepsake emblem, favour, memento, relic, remembrance, reminder, souvenir, symbol, token

keep up balance, compete, contend, continue, emulate, keep pace, maintain, match, persevere, preserve, rival, sustain, vie

keg barrel, cask, drum, firkin, hogshead, tun, vat

kernel core, essence, germ, gist, grain, marrow, nub, pith, seed, substance

key *n.* **1.** latchkey, opener **2.** *Fig.* answer, clue, cue, explanation, guide, indicator, interpretation, lead, means, pointer, sign, solution, translation ~*adj.* **3.** basic, chief, crucial, decisive, essential, fundamental, important, leading, main, major, pivotal, principal
Antonyms (*sense 3*) minor, secondary, subsidiary, superficial

key in enter, input, keyboard, type

keynote centre, core, essence, gist, heart, kernel, marrow, pith, substance, theme

kick *v.* **1.** boot, punt **2.** *Fig.* complain, gripe (*Inf.*), grumble, object, oppose, protest, rebel, resist, spurn **3.** *Inf.* abandon, desist from, give up, leave off, quit, stop ~*n.* **4.** force, intensity, pep, power, punch, pungency, snap (*Inf.*), sparkle, strength, tang, verve, vitality, zest **5.** buzz (*Sl.*), enjoyment, excitement, fun, gratification, jollies (*Sl.*), pleasure, stimulation, thrill

kickoff *n.* beginning, commencement, open~ ing, outset, start

kick off *v.* begin, commence, get under way, initiate, kick-start, open, start

kick out discharge, dismiss, eject, evict, ex~ pel, get rid of, give the bum's rush (*Sl.*), kiss off (*Sl., chiefly U.S. & Canad.*), oust, reject, remove, sack (*Inf.*), show one the door, throw out on one's ear (*Inf.*), toss out

kid 1. *n.* ankle-biter (*Aust. sl.*), baby, bairn, boy, child, girl, infant, lad, lass, little one, rug rat (*Sl.*), sprog (*Sl.*), stripling, teenager, tot, youngster, youth **2.** *v.* bamboozle, be~ guile, cozen, delude, fool, gull (*Archaic*), hoax, hoodwink, jest, joke, mock, plague, pretend, rag (*Brit.*), ridicule, tease, trick, wind up (*Brit. sl.*)

kidnap abduct, capture, hijack, hold to ran~ som, remove, seize, steal

kill 1. annihilate, assassinate, blow away (*Sl., chiefly U.S.*), bump off (*Sl.*), butcher, destroy, dispatch, do away with, do in (*Sl.*), eradicate, execute, exterminate, extirpate, knock off (*Sl.*), liquidate, massacre, murder, neutralize, obliterate, slaughter, slay, take out (*Sl.*), take (someone's) life, waste (*Inf.*) **2.** *Fig.* cancel, cease, deaden, defeat, extin~ guish, halt, quash, quell, ruin, scotch, smother, stifle, still, stop, suppress, veto

killer assassin, butcher, cutthroat, destroyer, executioner, exterminator, gunman, hit man (*Sl.*), liquidator, murderer, slaughterer, slayer

killing *n.* **1.** bloodshed, carnage, execution, extermination, fatality, homicide, man~ slaughter, massacre, murder, slaughter, slaying **2.** *Inf.* bomb (*Sl.*), bonanza, cleanup (*Inf.*), coup, gain, profit, success, windfall ~*adj.* **3.** deadly, death-dealing, deathly, fa~ tal, lethal, mortal, murderous **4.** *Inf.* debili- tating, enervating, exhausting, fatiguing, punishing, tiring **5.** *Inf.* absurd, amusing, comical, hilarious, ludicrous, uproarious

kill-joy dampener, damper, spoilsport, wet blanket (*Inf.*)

kin *n.* **1.** affinity, blood, connection, consan~ guinity, extraction, kinship, lineage, rela~ tionship, stock **2.** connections, family, kin~ dred, kinsfolk, kinsmen, kith, people, rela~ tions, relatives ~*adj.* **3.** akin, allied, close, cognate, consanguine, consanguineous, kin~ dred, near, related

kind¹ *n.* **1.** brand, breed, class, family, ge~ nus, ilk, race, set, sort, species, stamp, va~ riety **2.** character, description, essence, habit, manner, mould, nature, persuasion, sort, style, temperament, type

kind² *adj.* affectionate, amiable, amicable, beneficent, benevolent, benign, bounteous, charitable, clement, compassionate, con~ genial, considerate, cordial, courteous, friendly, generous, gentle, good, gracious, humane, indulgent, kind-hearted, kindly, lenient, loving, mild, neighbourly, obliging, philanthropic, propitious, sympathetic, tender-hearted, thoughtful, understanding
Antonyms cruel, hard-hearted, harsh, heartless, merciless, severe, unkind, unsym~ pathetic, vicious

kind-hearted altruistic, amicable, compas~ sionate, considerate, generous, good- natured, gracious, helpful, humane, kind, sympathetic, tender-hearted
Antonyms cold, cold-hearted, cruel, hard- hearted, harsh, heartless, selfish, severe, un~ kind, unsympathetic

kindle 1. fire, ignite, inflame, light, set fire to **2.** *Fig.* agitate, animate, arouse, awaken, bestir, enkindle, exasperate, excite, foment, incite, induce, inflame, inspire, provoke, rouse, sharpen, stimulate, stir, thrill
Antonyms douse, extinguish, quell, quench

kindliness amiability, beneficence, benevo~ lence, benignity, charity, compassion, friendliness, gentleness, humanity, kind- heartedness, kindness, sympathy

kindly 1. *adj.* affable, beneficial, benevolent, benign, compassionate, cordial, favourable, genial, gentle, good-natured, hearty, helpful, kind, mild, pleasant, polite, sympathetic, warm **2.** *adv.* agreeably, cordially, gra~ ciously, politely, tenderly, thoughtfully
Antonyms *adj.* cruel, harsh, malevolent, malicious, mean, severe, spiteful, unkindly, unsympathetic ~*adv.* cruelly, harshly, ma~ levolently, maliciously, meanly, spitefully, unkindly, unsympathetically

kindness 1. affection, amiability, benefi~ cence, benevolence, charity, clemency, compassion, decency, fellow-feeling, gener~ osity, gentleness, goodness, goodwill, grace, hospitality, humanity, indulgence, kindli~ ness, magnanimity, patience, philanthropy, tenderness, tolerance, understanding **2.** aid, assistance, benefaction, bounty, favour, generosity, good deed, help, service
Antonyms (*sense 1*) animosity, callousness, cold-heartedness, cruelty, hard-heartedness, heartlessness, ill will, inhumanity, malevo~ lence, malice, misanthropy, viciousness

kindred *n.* **1.** affinity, consanguinity, rela~ tionship **2.** connections, family, flesh, kin, kinsfolk, kinsmen, lineage, relations, rela~ tives ~*adj.* **3.** affiliated, akin, allied, cog~ nate, congenial, corresponding, kin, like, matching, related, similar

king crowned head, emperor, majesty, mon~ arch, overlord, prince, ruler, sovereign

kingdom 1. dominion, dynasty, empire, monarchy, realm, reign, sovereignty **2.** commonwealth, county, division, nation, province, state, territory, tract **3.** area, domain, field, province, sphere, territory

kink 1. bend, coil, corkscrew, crimp, entanglement, frizz, knot, tangle, twist, wrinkle **2.** cramp, crick, pang, pinch, spasm, stab, tweak, twinge **3.** complication, defect, difficulty, flaw, hitch, imperfection, knot, tangle **4.** crotchet, eccentricity, fetish, foible, idiosyncrasy, quirk, singularity, vagary, whim

kinky 1. bizarre, eccentric, odd, oddball (*Inf.*), off-the-wall (*Sl.*), outlandish, outré, peculiar, queer, quirky, strange, unconventional, wacko (*Sl.*), weird **2.** degenerated, depraved, deviant, licentious, perverted, pervy (*Sl.*), unnatural, warped **3.** coiled, crimped, curled, curly, frizzled, frizzy, tangled, twisted

kinsfolk connections, family, kin, kindred, kinsmen, relations, relatives

kinship 1. blood relationship, consanguinity, kin, relation, ties of blood **2.** affinity, alliance, association, bearing, connection, correspondence, relationship, similarity

kinsman blood relative, fellow clansman, fellow tribesman, relation, relative

kiosk bookstall, booth, counter, newsstand, stall, stand

kiss *v.* **1.** buss (*Archaic*), canoodle (*Sl.*), greet, neck (*Inf.*), osculate, peck (*Inf.*), salute, smooch (*Inf.*) **2.** brush, caress, glance, graze, scrape, touch ~*n.* **3.** buss (*Archaic*), osculation, peck (*Inf.*), smacker (*Sl.*)

kit accoutrements, apparatus, effects, equipment, gear, impedimenta, implements, instruments, outfit, paraphernalia, provisions, rig, supplies, tackle, tools, trappings, utensils

kitchen cookhouse, galley, kitchenette

kit out *or* **up** accoutre, arm, deck out, equip, fit out, fix up, furnish, outfit, provide with, supply

knack ability, adroitness, aptitude, bent, capacity, dexterity, expertise, expertness, facility, flair, forte, genius, gift, handiness, ingenuity, propensity, quickness, skilfulness, skill, talent, trick
Antonyms awkwardness, clumsiness, disability, ineptitude

knave blackguard, bounder (*Old-fashioned Brit. sl.*), cheat, cocksucker (*Taboo sl.*), rapscallion, rascal, reprobate, rogue, rotter (*Sl., chiefly Brit.*), scally (*Northwest English dialect*), scallywag (*Inf.*), scamp, scapegrace, scoundrel, scumbag (*Sl.*), swindler, varlet (*Archaic*), villain

knavery chicanery, corruption, deceit, deception, dishonesty, double-dealing, duplicity, fraud, imposture, rascality, roguery, trickery, villainy

knavish deceitful, deceptive, dishonest, dishonourable, fraudulent, lying, rascally, roguish, scoundrelly, tricky, unprincipled, unscrupulous, villainous
Antonyms honest, honourable, noble, principled, trustworthy

knead blend, form, manipulate, massage, mould, press, rub, shape, squeeze, stroke, work

kneel bow, bow down, curtsey, curtsy, genuflect, get down on one's knees, kowtow, make obeisance, stoop

knell 1. *v.* announce, chime, herald, peal, resound, ring, sound, toll **2.** *n.* chime, peal, ringing, sound, toll

knickers bloomers, briefs, drawers, panties, smalls, underwear

knick-knack bagatelle, bauble, bibelot, bric-a-brac, gewgaw, gimcrack, kickshaw, plaything, trifle, trinket

knife 1. *n.* blade, cutter, cutting tool **2.** *v.* cut, impale, lacerate, pierce, slash, stab, wound

knit 1. affix, ally, bind, connect, contract, fasten, heal, interlace, intertwine, join, link, loop, mend, secure, tie, unite, weave **2.** crease, furrow, knot, pucker, wrinkle

knob boss, bulk, bump, bunch, hump, knot, knurl, lump, nub, projection, protrusion, protuberance, snag, stud, swell, swelling, tumour

knock *v.* **1.** belt (*Inf.*), buffet, chin (*Sl.*), clap, cuff, deck (*Sl.*), hit, lay one on (*Sl.*), punch, rap, slap, smack, smite (*Archaic*), strike, thump, thwack ~*n.* **2.** belt (*Inf.*), blow, box, clip, clout (*Inf.*), cuff, hammering, rap, slap, smack, thump ~*v.* **3.** *Inf.* abuse, asperse, belittle, carp, cavil, censure, condemn, criticize, deprecate, disparage, find fault, lambast(e), run down, slag (off) (*Sl.*), slam (*Sl.*), ~*n.* **4.** blame, censure, condemnation, criticism, defeat, failure, heat (*Sl., chiefly U.S. & Canad.*), rebuff, rejection, reversal, setback, slagging (off) (*Sl.*), stick (*Sl.*), stricture

knock about *or* **around 1.** ramble, range, roam, rove, traipse, travel, wander **2.** abuse, batter, beat up (*Inf.*), bruise, buffet, clobber (*Sl.*), damage, hit, hurt, lambast(e), maltreat, manhandle, maul, mistreat, strike, wound

knock down batter, clout (*Inf.*), demolish, destroy, fell, floor, level, pound, raze, smash, wallop (*Inf.*), wreck

knock off 1. clock off, clock out, complete, conclude, finish, stop work, terminate **2.** blag (*Sl.*), cabbage (*Brit. sl.*), filch, nick (*Sl.*, *chiefly Brit.*), pilfer, pinch, purloin, rob, steal, thieve **3.** assassinate, blow away (*Sl.*, *chiefly U.S.*), bump off (*Sl.*), do away with, do in (*Sl.*), kill, liquidate, murder, slay, take out (*Sl.*), waste (*Inf.*)

knockout 1. *coup de grâce,* kayo (*Sl.*), KO or K.O. (*Sl.*) **2.** hit, sensation, smash, smash-hit, stunner (*Inf.*), success, triumph, winner
Antonyms (*sense 2*) failure, flop (*Inf.*), turkey (*Inf.*)

knot *v.* **1.** bind, complicate, entangle, knit, loop, secure, tether, tie, weave ~*n.* **2.** bond, bow, braid, connection, joint, ligature, loop, rosette, tie **3.** aggregation, bunch, clump, cluster, collection, heap, mass, pile, tuft **4.** assemblage, band, circle, clique, company, crew (*Inf.*), crowd, gang, group, mob, pack, set, squad

know 1. apprehend, comprehend, experi~ ence, fathom, feel certain, ken (*Scot.*), learn, notice, perceive, realize, recognize, see, undergo, understand **2.** associate with, be acquainted with, be familiar with, frater~ nize with, have dealings with, have knowl~ edge of, recognize **3.** differentiate, discern, distinguish, identify, make out, perceive, recognize, see, tell
Antonyms be ignorant, be unfamiliar with, misunderstand

know-how ability, adroitness, aptitude, capability, craft, dexterity, experience, ex~ pertise, faculty, flair, ingenuity, knack, knowledge, proficiency, savoir-faire, skill, talent

knowing 1. astute, clever, clued-up (*Inf.*), competent, discerning, experienced, expert, intelligent, qualified, skilful, well-informed **2.** acute, cunning, eloquent, expressive, meaningful, perceptive, sagacious, shrewd, significant **3.** aware, conscious, deliberate, intended, intentional
Antonyms accidental, ignorant, ingenuous, naive, obtuse, unintentional

knowingly consciously, deliberately, inten~ tionally, on purpose, purposely, wilfully, wittingly

knowledge 1. education, enlightenment, erudition, instruction, intelligence, learn~ ing, scholarship, schooling, science, tuition, wisdom **2.** ability, apprehension, cognition, comprehension, consciousness, discern~ ment, grasp, judgment, recognition, under~ standing **3.** acquaintance, cognizance, fa~ miliarity, information, intimacy, notice
Antonyms ignorance, illiteracy, misunder~ standing, unawareness, unfamiliarity

knowledgeable 1. acquainted, *au courant*, *au fait*, aware, clued-up (*Inf.*), cognizant, conscious, conversant, experienced, famili~ ar, in the know (*Inf.*), understanding, well-informed **2.** educated, erudite, intelligent, learned, lettered, scholarly

known acknowledged, admitted, avowed, celebrated, common, confessed, familiar, famous, manifest, noted, obvious, patent, plain, popular, published, recognized, well-known
Antonyms closet (*Inf.*), concealed, hidden, secret, unfamiliar, unknown, unrecognized, unrevealed

knuckle under *v.* accede, acquiesce, ca~ pitulate, give in, give way, submit, suc~ cumb, surrender, yield
Antonyms be defiant, hold out (against), kick up (a fuss *or* stink), rebel, resist

L

label *n.* **1.** docket (*Chiefly Brit.*), flag, mark~ er, sticker, tag, tally, ticket **2.** characteriza~ tion, classification, description, epithet **3.** brand, company, mark, trademark ~*v.* **4.** docket (*Chiefly Brit.*), flag, mark, stamp, sticker, tag, tally **5.** brand, call, character~ ize, class, classify, define, describe, desig~ nate, identify, name

laborious 1. arduous, backbreaking, bur~ densome, difficult, exhausting, fatiguing, hard, herculean, onerous, strenuous, tire~ some, tiring, toilsome, tough, uphill, wear~ ing, wearisome **2.** assiduous, diligent, hard-working, indefatigable, industrious, painstaking, persevering, sedulous, tireless, unflagging **3.** *Of literary style, etc.* forced, laboured, not fluent, ponderous, strained **Antonyms** easy, easy-peasy (*Sl.*), effortless, light, natural, simple

labour *n.* **1.** industry, toil, work **2.** em~ ployees, hands, labourers, workers, work~ force, workmen **3.** donkey-work, drudgery, effort, exertion, grind (*Inf.*), industry, pains, painstaking, sweat (*Inf.*), toil, travail **4.** chore, job, task, undertaking **5.** childbirth, contractions, delivery, labour pains, pains, parturition, throes, travail ~*v.* **6.** drudge, endeavour, grind (*Inf.*), peg along *or* away (*Chiefly Brit.*), plod, plug along *or* away (*Inf.*), slave, strive, struggle, sweat (*Inf.*), toil, travail, work **7.** *Usually with* **under** be a victim of, be burdened by, be disadvant~ aged, suffer **8.** dwell on, elaborate, make a federal case of (*U.S. inf.*), make a produc~ tion (out) of (*Inf.*), overdo, overemphasize, strain **9.** *Of a ship* heave, pitch, roll, toss **Antonyms** *n.* ease, idleness, leisure, relaxa~ tion, repose, respite, rest ~*v.* relax, rest

laboured 1. awkward, difficult, forced, heavy, stiff, strained **2.** affected, contrived, overdone, overwrought, ponderous, studied, unnatural

labourer blue-collar worker, drudge, hand, labouring man, manual worker, navvy (*Brit. inf.*), unskilled worker, worker, work~ ing man, workman

labyrinth coil, complexity, complication, convolution, entanglement, intricacy, jun~ gle, knotty problem, maze, perplexity, puz~ zle, riddle, snarl, tangle, windings

lace *n.* **1.** filigree, netting, openwork, tatting **2.** bootlace, cord, shoelace, string, thong, tie ~*v.* **3.** attach, bind, close, do up, fasten, intertwine, interweave, thread, tie, twine **4.** add to, fortify, mix in, spike

lacerate 1. claw, cut, gash, jag, maim, mangle, rend, rip, slash, tear, wound **2.** *Fig.* afflict, distress, harrow, rend, torment, tor~ ture, wound

laceration cut, gash, injury, mutilation, rent, rip, slash, tear, wound

lachrymose crying, dolorous, lugubrious, mournful, sad, tearful, weeping, weepy (*Inf.*), woeful

lack 1. *n.* absence, dearth, deficiency, depri~ vation, destitution, insufficiency, need, pri~ vation, scantiness, 'scarcity, shortage, shortcoming, shortness, want **2.** *v.* be deficient in, be short of, be without, miss, need, require, want **Antonyms** *n.* abundance, adequacy, excess, plentifulness, sufficiency, surplus ~*v.* enjoy, have, own, possess

lackadaisical 1. apathetic, dull, enervated, half-arsed, half-assed (*U.S. & Canad. sl.*), half-hearted, indifferent, languid, languor~ ous, lethargic, limp, listless, spiritless **2.** abstracted, dreamy, idle, indolent, inert, lazy **Antonyms** ambitious, diligent, excited, in~ spired, spirited

lackey 1. ass-kisser (*U.S. & Canad. taboo sl.*), brown-noser (*Taboo sl.*), creature, fawner, flatterer, flunky, hanger-on, instru~ ment, menial, minion, parasite, pawn, sycophant, toady, tool, yes man **2.** attend~ ant, flunky, footman, manservant, valet, varlet (*Archaic*)

lacking defective, deficient, flawed, im~ paired, inadequate, minus (*Inf.*), missing, needing, sans (*Archaic*), wanting, without

lacklustre boring, dim, drab, dry, dull, flat, leaden, lifeless, lustreless, muted, prosaic, sombre, unimaginative, uninspired, vapid

laconic brief, compact, concise, crisp, curt, pithy, sententious, short, succinct, terse, to the point **Antonyms** long-winded, loquacious, ram~ bling, verbose, voluble, wordy

lad boy, chap (*Inf.*), fellow, guy (*Inf.*), ju~ venile, kid (*Inf.*), laddie (*Scot.*), schoolboy, shaver (*Inf.*), stripling, youngster, youth

laden burdened, charged, encumbered, fraught, full, hampered, loaded, oppressed, taxed, weighed down, weighted

lady-killer Casanova, Don Juan, heart~ breaker, ladies' man, libertine, Lothario, philanderer, rake, roué, wolf (*Inf.*), woman~ izer

ladylike courtly, cultured, decorous, elegant, genteel, modest, polite, proper, refined, re~ spectable, well-bred
Antonyms discourteous, ill-bred, ill-mannered, impolite, rude, uncultured, un~ ladylike, unmannerly, unrefined

lag 1. be behind, dawdle, delay, drag (be~ hind), drag one's feet (*Inf.*), hang back, idle, linger, loiter, saunter, straggle, tarry, trail **2.** decrease, diminish, ebb, fail, fall off, flag, lose strength, slacken, wane

laggard dawdler, idler, lingerer, loafer, loi~ terer, lounger, saunterer, skiver (*Brit. sl.*), slowcoach (*Brit. inf.*), slowpoke (*U.S. & Canad. inf.*), sluggard, snail, straggler

laid-back at ease, casual, easy-going, easy-oasy (*Sl.*), free and easy, relaxed, together (*Sl.*), unflappable (*Inf.*), unhurried
Antonyms edgy, jittery (*Inf.*), jumpy, keyed-up, nervous, on edge, tense, twitchy (*Inf.*), uptight (*Inf.*), wound-up (*Inf.*)

laid up bedridden, disabled, housebound, ill, immobilized, incapacitated, injured, on the sick list, out of action (*Inf.*), sick

lair 1. burrow, den, earth, form, hole, nest, resting place **2.** *Inf.* den, hide-out, refuge, retreat, sanctuary

laissez faire *n.* free enterprise, free trade, individualism, live and let live, non~ intervention

lame 1. crippled, defective, disabled, game, halt (*Archaic*), handicapped, hobbling, limping **2.** *Fig.* feeble, flimsy, inadequate, insufficient, pathetic, poor, thin, uncon~ vincing, unsatisfactory, weak

lament *v.* **1.** bemoan, bewail, complain, de~ plore, grieve, mourn, regret, sorrow, wail, weep ~*n.* **2.** complaint, keening, lamenta~ tion, moan, moaning, plaint, ululation, wail, wailing **3.** coronach (*Scot. & Irish*), dirge, elegy, monody, requiem, threnody

lamentable 1. deplorable, distressing, grievous, harrowing, mournful, regrettable, sorrowful, tragic, unfortunate, woeful **2.** low, meagre, mean, miserable, pitiful, poor, unsatisfactory, wretched

lamentation dirge, grief, grieving, keening, lament, moan, mourning, plaint, sobbing, sorrow, ululation, wailing, weeping

lampoon 1. *n.* burlesque, caricature, paro~ dy, pasquinade, satire, send-up (*Brit. inf.*), skit, squib, takeoff (*Inf.*) **2.** *v.* burlesque, caricature, make fun of, mock, parody, pas~ quinade, ridicule, satirize, send up (*Brit. inf.*), squib, take off (*Inf.*)

land *n.* **1.** dry land, earth, ground, terra firma **2.** dirt, ground, loam, soil **3.** countryside, farming, farmland, rural dis~ tricts **4.** acres, estate, grounds, property, real property, realty **5.** country, district,

fatherland, motherland, nation, province, region, territory, tract ~*v.* **6.** alight, arrive, berth, come to rest, debark, disembark, dock, touch down **7.** *Sometimes with* **up** ar~ rive, bring, carry, cause, end up, lead, turn up, wind up **8.** *Inf.* acquire, gain, get, ob~ tain, score (*Sl.*), secure, win

landlord 1. host, hotelier, hotel-keeper, innkeeper **2.** freeholder, lessor, owner, pro~ prietor

landmark 1. feature, monument **2.** crisis, milestone, turning point, watershed **3.** benchmark, boundary, cairn, milepost, signpost

landscape countryside, outlook, panorama, prospect, scene, scenery, view, vista

landslide 1. *n.* avalanche, landslip, rockfall **2.** *adj.* decisive, overwhelming, runaway

language 1. communication, conversation, discourse, expression, interchange, par~ lance, speech, talk, utterance, verbalization, vocalization **2.** argot, cant, dialect, idiom, jargon, lingo (*Inf.*), lingua franca, patois, speech, terminology, tongue, vernacular, vocabulary **3.** diction, expression, phra~ seology, phrasing, style, wording

languid 1. drooping, faint, feeble, languor~ ous, limp, pining, sickly, weak, weary **2.** indifferent, lackadaisical, languorous, lazy, listless, spiritless, unenthusiastic, uninter~ ested **3.** dull, heavy, inactive, inert, lethar~ gic, sluggish, torpid
Antonyms active, energetic, strong, tireless, vigorous

languish 1. decline, droop, fade, fail, faint, flag, sicken, waste, weaken, wilt, wither **2.** *Often with* **for** desire, eat one's heart out over, hanker, hunger, long, pine, sigh, want, yearn **3.** be abandoned, be disregard~ ed, be neglected, rot, suffer, waste away **4.** brood, despond, grieve, repine, sorrow
Antonyms bloom, flourish, prosper, thrive

languishing 1. declining, deteriorating, drooping, droopy, fading, failing, flagging, sickening, sinking, wasting away, weak, weakening, wilting, withering **2.** dreamy, longing, lovelorn, lovesick, melancholic, nostalgic, pensive, pining, soulful, tender, wistful, woebegone, yearning

lank 1. dull, lifeless, limp, long, lustreless, straggling **2.** attenuated, emaciated, gaunt, lanky, lean, rawboned, scraggy, scrawny, skinny, slender, slim, spare, thin

lanky angular, bony, gangling, gaunt, loose-jointed, rangy, rawboned, scraggy, scrawny, spare, tall, thin, weedy (*Inf.*)
Antonyms brawny, burly, chubby, fat, mus~ cular, plump, portly, rotund, rounded, short, sinewy, stocky, stout

lap[1] **1.** *n.* circle, circuit, course, distance,

loop, orbit, round, tour **2.** _v._ cover, enfold, envelop, fold, swaddle, swathe, turn, twist, wrap

lap² **1.** gurgle, plash, purl, ripple, slap, splash, swish, wash **2.** drink, lick, sip, sup

lapse _n._ **1.** error, failing, fault, indiscretion, mistake, negligence, omission, oversight, slip **2.** break, gap, intermission, interrup~ tion, interval, lull, passage, pause **3.** back~ sliding, decline, descent, deterioration, drop, fall, relapse ~_v._ **4.** decline, degener~ ate, deteriorate, drop, fail, fall, sink, slide, slip **5.** become obsolete, become void, end, expire, run out, stop, terminate

lapsed **1.** discontinued, ended, expired, finished, invalid, out of date, run out, unre~ newed **2.** backsliding, lacking faith, non~ practising

larceny burglary, misappropriation, pilfer~ ing, purloining, robbery, stealing, theft

large **1.** big, bulky, colossal, considerable, elephantine, enormous, giant, gigantic, gi~ normous (_Inf._), goodly, great, huge, hu~ mongous _or_ humungous (_U.S. sl._), immense, jumbo (_Inf._), king-size, man-size, massive, mega (_Sl._), monumental, sizable, substan~ tial, tidy (_Inf._), vast **2.** abundant, ample, broad, capacious, comprehensive, copious, extensive, full, generous, grand, grandiose, liberal, plentiful, roomy, spacious, sweep~ ing, wide **3.** **at large a.** at liberty, free, on the loose, on the run, roaming, unconfined **b.** as a whole, chiefly, generally, in general, in the main, mainly **c.** at length, consider~ ably, exhaustively, greatly, in full detail **Antonyms** brief, inconsiderable, infinitesi~ mal, little, minute, narrow, petty, scanty, scarce, short, slender, slight, slim, small, sparse, thin, tiny, trivial

largely as a rule, by and large, chiefly, con~ siderably, extensively, generally, mainly, mostly, predominantly, primarily, princi~ pally, to a great extent, widely

large-scale broad, extensive, far-reaching, global, sweeping, vast, wholesale, wide, wide-ranging

largess, largesse **1.** alms-giving, benefac~ tion, bounty, charity, generosity, liberality, munificence, open-handedness, philanthro~ py **2.** bequest, bounty, donation, endow~ ment, gift, grant, present

lark **1.** _n._ antic, caper, escapade, fling, frolic, fun, gambol, game, jape, mischief, prank, revel, rollick, romp, skylark, spree **2.** _v._ ca~ per, cavort, cut capers, frolic, gambol, have fun, make mischief, play, rollick, romp, sport

lash¹ _n._ **1.** blow, hit, stripe, stroke, swipe (_Inf._), ~_v._ **2.** beat, birch, chastise, flagellate, flog, horsewhip, lam (_Sl._), lambast(e), scourge, thrash, whip **3.** beat, buffet, dash,

drum, hammer, hit, knock, lambast(e), lar~ rup (_Dialect_), pound, punch, smack, strike **4.** attack, belabour, berate, blast, castigate, censure, criticize, flay, lambast(e), lampoon, put down, ridicule, satirize, scold, tear into (_Inf._), upbraid

lash² bind, fasten, join, make fast, rope, se~ cure, strap, tie

lass bird (_Sl._), chick (_Sl._), colleen (_Irish_), damsel, girl, lassie (_Inf._), maid, maiden, miss, schoolgirl, wench (_Facetious_), young woman

last¹ _adj._ **1.** aftermost, at the end, hindmost, rearmost **2.** latest, most recent **3.** closing, concluding, extreme, final, furthest, remot~ est, terminal, ultimate, utmost ~_adv._ **4.** af~ ter, behind, bringing up the rear, in _or_ at the end, in the rear ~_n._ **5.** close, comple~ tion, conclusion, end, ending, finale, finish, termination **6.** **at last** at length, eventually, finally, in conclusion, in the end, ultimately **Antonyms** (_sense 1_) first, foremost, leading (_sense 3_) earliest, first, initial, introductory, opening

last² _v._ abide, carry on, continue, endure, hold on, hold out, keep, keep on, persist, remain, stand up, survive, wear **Antonyms** cease, depart, die, end, expire, fade, fail, stop, terminate

last-ditch all-out (_Inf._), desperate, final, frantic, heroic, straining, struggling

lasting abiding, continuing, deep-rooted, durable, enduring, eternal, indelible, life~ long, long-standing, long-term, perennial, permanent, perpetual, unceasing, undying, unending **Antonyms** ephemeral, fleeting, momentary, passing, short-lived, transient, transitory

lastly after all, all in all, at last, finally, in conclusion, in the end, to conclude, to sum up, ultimately

last word, the **1.** final say, finis, summa~ tion, ultimatum **2.** best, cream, _crème de la crème_, crown, epitome, _ne plus ultra_, per~ fection, quintessence, ultimate **3.** _dernier cri_, fashion, latest, newest, rage, vogue

latch **1.** _n._ bar, bolt, catch, clamp, fastening, hasp, hook, lock, sneck (_Dialect_) **2.** _v._ bar, bolt, fasten, lock, make fast, secure, sneck (_Dialect_)

late _adj._ **1.** behind, behindhand, belated, de~ layed, last-minute, overdue, slow, tardy, unpunctual **2.** advanced, fresh, modern, new, recent **3.** dead, deceased, defunct, de~ parted, ex-, former, old, past, preceding, previous ~_adv._ **4.** at the last minute, behindhand, behind time, belatedly, dilato~ rily, slowly, tardily, unpunctually **Antonyms** _adj._ (_sense 1_) beforehand, early, prompt, punctual, seasoned, timely (_sense 2_) old (*sense 3*) alive, existing ~*adv.* beforehand, early, in advance

lately in recent times, just now, latterly, not long ago, of late, recently

lateness advanced hour, belatedness, delay, late date, retardation, tardiness, unpunctuality

latent concealed, dormant, hidden, inherent, invisible, lurking, potential, quiescent, secret, undeveloped, unexpressed, unrealized, unseen, veiled
Antonyms apparent, conspicuous, developed, evident, expressed, manifest, obvious, realized

later *adv.* after, afterwards, by and by, in a while, in time, later on, next, subsequently, thereafter

lateral edgeways, flanking, side, sideward, sideways

latest *adj.* current, fashionable, happening (*Inf.*), in, modern, most recent, newest, now, up-to-date, up-to-the-minute, with it (*Inf.*)

lather *n.* **1.** bubbles, foam, froth, soap, soapsuds, suds **2.** *Inf.* dither (*Chiefly Brit.*), fever, flap (*Inf.*), fluster, fuss, pother, state (*Inf.*), stew (*Inf.*), sweat, tizzy (*Inf.*), twitter (*Inf.*), ~*v.* **3.** foam, froth, soap **4.** *Inf.* beat, cane, drub, flog, lambast(e), strike, thrash, whip

lathery bubbly, foamy, frothy, soapy, sudsy

latitude 1. breadth, compass, extent, range, reach, room, scope, space, span, spread, sweep, width **2.** elbowroom, freedom, indulgence, laxity, leeway, liberty, licence, play, unrestrictedness

latter closing, concluding, last, last-mentioned, later, latest, modern, recent, second
Antonyms antecedent, earlier, foregoing, former, preceding, previous, prior

latterly hitherto, lately, of late, recently

lattice fretwork, grating, grid, grille, latticework, mesh, network, openwork, reticulation, tracery, trellis, web

laudable admirable, commendable, creditable, estimable, excellent, meritorious, of note, praiseworthy, worthy
Antonyms base, blameworthy, contemptible, ignoble, lowly, unworthy

laudatory acclamatory, adulatory, approbatory, approving, commendatory, complimentary, eulogistic, panegyrical

laugh *v.* **1.** be convulsed (*Inf.*), be in stitches, bust a gut (*Inf.*), chortle, chuckle, crack up (*Inf.*), crease up (*Inf.*), giggle, guffaw, roar with laughter, snigger, split one's sides, titter **2.** laugh at belittle, deride, jeer, lampoon, make a mock of, make fun of, mock, ridicule, scoff at, take the mickey (out of) (*Inf.*), taunt ~*n.* **3.** belly laugh

(*Inf.*), chortle, chuckle, giggle, guffaw, roar *or* shriek of laughter, snigger, titter **4.** *Inf.* card (*Inf.*), caution (*Inf.*), clown, comedian, comic, entertainer, hoot (*Inf.*), humorist, joke, lark, scream (*Inf.*), wag, wit

laughable 1. absurd, derisive, derisory, ludicrous, nonsensical, preposterous, ridiculous, worthy of scorn **2.** amusing, comical, diverting, droll, farcical, funny, hilarious, humorous, mirthful, risible

laughing stock Aunt Sally (*Brit.*), butt, everybody's fool, fair game, figure of fun, target, victim

laugh off brush aside, dismiss, disregard, ignore, minimize, pooh-pooh, shrug off

laughter 1. cachinnation, chortling, chuckling, giggling, guffawing, laughing, tittering **2.** amusement, glee, hilarity, merriment, mirth

launch 1. cast, discharge, dispatch, fire, project, propel, send off, set afloat, set in motion, throw **2.** begin, commence, embark upon, inaugurate, initiate, instigate, introduce, open, start

laurels acclaim, awards, bays, Brownie points, commendation, credit, distinction, fame, glory, honour, kudos, praise, prestige, recognition, renown, reward

lavatory bathroom, bog (*Sl.*), can (*U.S. & Canad. sl.*), cloakroom (*Brit.*), crapper (*Taboo sl.*), Gents, head(s) (*Nautical sl.*), john (*Sl., chiefly U.S. & Canad.*), khazi (*Sl.*), Ladies, latrine, little boy's room (*Inf.*), little girl's room (*Inf.*), loo (*Brit. inf.*), pissoir, powder room, (public) convenience, toilet, washroom, water closet, W.C.

lavish *adj.* **1.** abundant, copious, exuberant, lush, luxuriant, opulent, plentiful, profuse, prolific, sumptuous **2.** bountiful, effusive, free, generous, liberal, munificent, openhanded, unstinting **3.** exaggerated, excessive, extravagant, immoderate, improvident, intemperate, prodigal, thriftless, unreasonable, unrestrained, wasteful, wild ~*v.* **4.** deluge, dissipate, expend, heap, pour, shower, spend, squander, waste
Antonyms *adj.* cheap, frugal, meagre, miserly, parsimonious, scanty, sparing, stingy, thrifty, tight-fisted ~*v.* begrudge, economize, stint, withhold

law 1. charter, code, constitution, jurisprudence **2.** act, canon, code, command, commandment, covenant, decree, demand, edict, enactment, order, ordinance, rule, statute **3.** axiom, canon, criterion, formula, precept, principle, regulation, standard **4. lay down the law** dictate, dogmatize, emphasize, pontificate

law-abiding compliant, dutiful, good, honest, honourable, lawful, obedient, orderly, peaceable, peaceful

lawbreaker convict, criminal, crook (*Inf.*), culprit, delinquent, felon (*Formerly criminal law*), miscreant, offender, sinner, trans~ gressor, trespasser, villain, violater, wrong~ doer

lawful allowable, authorized, constitutional, just, legal, legalized, legitimate, licit, per~ missible, proper, rightful, valid, warranted
Antonyms banned, forbidden, illegal, il~ legitimate, illicit, prohibited, unauthorized, unlawful

lawless anarchic, chaotic, disorderly, in~ subordinate, insurgent, mutinous, rebel~ lious, reckless, riotous, seditious, ungov~ erned, unrestrained, unruly, wild
Antonyms civilized, compliant, disciplined, law-abiding, lawful, legitimate, licit, obedient, orderly, regimented, restrained, well-governed

lawsuit action, argument, case, cause, con~ test, dispute, industrial tribunal, litigation, proceedings, prosecution, suit, trial

lawyer advocate, attorney, barrister, coun~ sel, counsellor, legal adviser, solicitor

lax 1. careless, casual, easy-going, easy-oasy (*Sl.*), lenient, neglectful, negligent, overin~ dulgent, remiss, slack, slapdash, slipshod **2.** broad, general, imprecise, inaccurate, indefinite, inexact, nonspecific, shapeless, vague **3.** flabby, flaccid, loose, slack, soft, yielding
Antonyms (*sense 1*) conscientious, disci~ plined, firm, heedful, moral, rigid, scrupulous, severe, stern, strict, stringent (*sense 3*) firm, rigid

lay[1] **1.** deposit, establish, leave, place, plant, posit, put, set, set down, settle, spread **2.** arrange, dispose, locate, organize, position, set out **3.** bear, deposit, produce **4.** ad~ vance, bring forward, lodge, offer, present, put forward, submit **5.** allocate, allot, as~ cribe, assign, attribute, charge, impute **6.** concoct, contrive, design, devise, hatch, plan, plot, prepare, work out **7.** apply, as~ sess, burden, charge, encumber, impose, saddle, tax **8.** bet, gamble, give odds, haz~ ard, risk, stake, wager **9.** allay, alleviate, appease, assuage, calm, quiet, relieve, soothe, still, suppress **10. lay bare** disclose, divulge, explain, expose, reveal, show, un~ veil **11. lay hands on a.** acquire, get, get hold of, grab, grasp, seize **b.** assault, attack, beat up, lay into (*Inf.*), set on **c.** discover, find, unearth **d.** *Christianity* bless, confirm, consecrate, ordain **12. lay hold of** get, get hold of, grab, grasp, grip, seize, snatch

lay[2] **1.** laic, laical, nonclerical, secular **2.** amateur, inexpert, nonprofessional, non~ specialist

layabout beachcomber, couch potato (*Sl.*), good-for-nothing, idler, laggard, loafer,
lounger, ne'er-do-well, shirker, skiver (*Brit. sl.*), slubberdegullion (*Archaic*), vagrant, wastrel

lay aside abandon, cast aside, dismiss, postpone, put aside, put off, reject, shelve

lay down 1. discard, drop, give, give up, relinquish, surrender, yield **2.** affirm, as~ sume, establish, formulate, ordain, postu~ late, prescribe, stipulate

layer 1. bed, ply, row, seam, stratum, thick~ ness, tier **2.** blanket, coat, coating, cover, covering, film, mantle, sheet

lay in accumulate, amass, build up, collect, hoard, stockpile, stock up, store (up)

lay into assail, attack, belabour, hit out at, lambast(e), let fly at, pitch into (*Inf.*), set about

layman amateur, lay person, nonprofes~ sional, outsider

lay-off discharge, dismissal, unemployment

lay off 1. discharge, dismiss, drop, let go, make redundant, oust, pay off **2.** *Inf.* cease, desist, give it a rest (*Inf.*), give over (*Inf.*), give up, leave alone, leave off, let up, quit, stop

lay on 1. cater (for), furnish, give, provide, purvey, supply **2. lay it on** *Sl.* butter up, exaggerate, flatter, overdo it, overpraise, soft-soap (*Inf.*)

layout arrangement, design, draft, forma~ tion, geography, outline, plan

lay out 1. arrange, design, display, exhibit, plan, spread out **2.** *Inf.* disburse, expend, fork out (*Sl.*), invest, pay, shell out (*Inf.*), spend **3.** *Inf.* kayo (*Sl.*), knock for six (*Inf.*), knock out, knock unconscious, KO *or* K.O. (*Sl.*)

laziness dilatoriness, do-nothingness, faine~ ance, faineancy, idleness, inactivity, indo~ lence, lackadaisicalness, slackness, sloth, slothfulness, slowness, sluggishness, tardi~ ness

lazy 1. idle, inactive, indolent, inert, remiss, shiftless, slack, slothful, slow, workshy **2.** drowsy, languid, languorous, lethargic, sleepy, slow-moving, sluggish, somnolent, torpid
Antonyms active, assiduous, diligent, ener~ getic, industrious, quick, stimulated

leach drain, extract, filter, filtrate, lixiviate (*Chem.*), percolate, seep, strain

lead *v.* **1.** conduct, escort, guide, pilot, pre~ cede, show the way, steer, usher **2.** cause, dispose, draw, incline, induce, influence, persuade, prevail, prompt **3.** command, di~ rect, govern, head, manage, preside over, supervise **4.** be ahead (of), blaze a trail, come first, exceed, excel, outdo, outstrip, surpass, transcend **5.** experience, have, live, pass, spend, undergo **6.** bring on, cause, conduce, contribute, produce, result in, serve, tend ~n. **7.** advance, advantage, cutting edge, edge, first place, margin, precedence, primacy, priority, start, su~premacy, van, vanguard **8.** direction, ex~ample, guidance, leadership, model **9.** clue, guide, hint, indication, suggestion, tip, trace **10.** leading role, principal, protagonist, star part, title role ~adj. **11.** chief, first, fore~most, head, leading, main, most important, premier, primary, prime, principal

leader bellwether, boss (*Inf.*), captain, chief, chieftain, commander, conductor, counsel~lor, director, guide, head, number one, principal, ringleader, ruler, superior
Antonyms adherent, disciple, follower, hanger-on, henchman, sidekick (*Sl.*), sup~porter

leadership 1. administration, direction, directorship, domination, guidance, man~agement, running, superintendency **2.** authority, command, control, influence, initiative, pre-eminence, supremacy, sway

leading chief, dominant, first, foremost, governing, greatest, highest, main, number one, outstanding, pre-eminent, primary, principal, ruling, superior
Antonyms following, hindmost, incidental, inferior, lesser, minor, secondary, subordi~nate, superficial

lead on beguile, deceive, draw on, entice, inveigle, lure, seduce, string along (*Inf.*), tempt

lead up to approach, intimate, introduce, make advances, make overtures, pave the way, prepare for, prepare the way, work round to

leaf *n.* **1.** blade, bract, flag, foliole, frond, needle, pad **2.** folio, page, sheet **3. turn over a new leaf** amend, begin anew, change, change one's ways, improve, reform ~v. **4.** bud, green, put out leaves, turn green **5.** browse, flip, glance, riffle, skim, thumb (through)

leaflet advert (*Brit. inf.*), bill, booklet, bro~chure, circular, handbill, mailshot, pam~phlet

league *n.* **1.** alliance, association, band, coalition, combination, combine, compact, confederacy, confederation, consortium, federation, fellowship, fraternity, group, guild, order, partnership, union **2.** ability group, category, class, level **3. in league (with)** allied, collaborating, hand in glove, in cahoots (*Inf.*), leagued ~v. **4.** ally, amal~gamate, associate, band, collaborate, com~bine, confederate, join forces, unite

leak *n.* **1.** aperture, chink, crack, crevice, fissure, hole, opening, puncture **2.** drip, leakage, leaking, oozing, percolation, seep~age **3.** disclosure, divulgence ~v. **4.** dis~

charge, drip, escape, exude, ooze, pass, per~colate, seep, spill, trickle **5.** blow wide open (*Sl.*), disclose, divulge, give away, let slip, let the cat out of the bag, make known, make public, pass on, reveal, spill the beans (*Inf.*), tell

leaky cracked, holey, leaking, not water~tight, perforated, porous, punctured, split, waterlogged

lean¹ *v.* **1.** be supported, prop, recline, re~pose, rest **2.** bend, heel, incline, slant, slope, tilt, tip **3.** be disposed to, be prone to, favour, gravitate towards, have a propen~sity, prefer, tend **4.** confide, count on, de~pend, have faith in, rely, trust

lean² *adj.* **1.** angular, bony, emaciated, gaunt, lank, macilent (*Rare*), rangy, scrag~gy, scrawny, skinny, slender, slim, spare, thin, unfatty, wiry **2.** bare, barren, inad~equate, infertile, meagre, pitiful, poor, scanty, sparse, unfruitful, unproductive
Antonyms abundant, ample, brawny, burly, fat, fertile, full, obese, plentiful, plump, portly, profuse, rich

leaning aptitude, bent, bias, disposition, in~clination, liking, partiality, penchant, pre~dilection, proclivity, proneness, propensity, taste, tendency

leap *v.* **1.** bounce, bound, caper, cavort, frisk, gambol, hop, jump, skip, spring **2.** *Fig.* arrive at, come to, form hastily, hasten, hurry, jump, reach, rush **3.** clear, jump (over), vault **4.** advance, become prominent, escalate, gain attention, increase, rocket, soar, surge ~n. **5.** bound, caper, frisk, hop, jump, skip, spring, vault **6.** escalation, in~crease, rise, surge, upsurge, upswing

learn 1. acquire, attain, become able, grasp, imbibe, master, pick up **2.** commit to memory, con (*Archaic*), get off pat, get (something) word-perfect, learn by heart, memorize **3.** ascertain, detect, determine, discern, discover, find out, gain, gather, hear, suss (out) (*Sl.*), understand

learned academic, cultured, erudite, experi~enced, expert, highbrow, intellectual, let~tered, literate, scholarly, skilled, versed, well-informed, well-read
Antonyms ignorant, illiterate, uneducated, unlearned

learner 1. apprentice, beginner, neophyte, novice, tyro **2.** disciple, pupil, scholar, stu~dent, trainee
Antonyms (*sense 1*) adept, expert, grand~master, master, maven, pastmaster, virtuoso, wizard (*sense 2*) coach, instructor, mentor, teacher, tutor

learning acquirements, attainments, cul~ture, education, erudition, information, knowledge, letters, literature, lore, re~

search, scholarship, schooling, study, tui~
tion, wisdom

lease *v.* charter, hire, let, loan, rent

leash *n.* **1.** lead, rein, tether **2.** check, con~
trol, curb, hold, restraint ~*v.* **3.** fasten, se~
cure, tether, tie up **4.** check, control, curb,
hold back, restrain, suppress

least feeblest, fewest, last, lowest, meanest,
minimum, minutest, poorest, slightest,
smallest, tiniest

leathery coriaceous, durable, hard, hard~
ened, leatherlike, leathern (*Archaic*), rough,
rugged, tough, wrinkled

leave[1] *v.* **1.** abandon, abscond, decamp, de~
part, desert, disappear, do a bunk (*Brit. sl.*),
exit, flit (*Inf.*), forsake, go, go away, hook it
(*Sl.*), move, pull out, quit, relinquish, retire,
set out, slope off, take off (*Inf.*), withdraw **2.**
forget, lay down, leave behind, mislay **3.**
cause, deposit, generate, produce, result in
4. abandon, cease, desert, desist, drop,
evacuate, forbear, give up, refrain, relin~
quish, renounce, stop, surrender **5.** allot,
assign, cede, commit, consign, entrust, give
over, refer **6.** bequeath, demise, devise
(*Law*), hand down, transmit, will
Antonyms appear, arrive, assume, come,
continue, emerge, hold, persist, remove, re~
tain, stay

leave[2] *n.* **1.** allowance, authorization, con~
cession, consent, dispensation, freedom,
liberty, permission, sanction **2.** furlough,
holiday, leave of absence, sabbatical, time
off, vacation **3.** adieu, departure, farewell,
goodbye, leave-taking, parting, retirement,
withdrawal
Antonyms (*sense 1*) denial, prohibition, re~
fusal, rejection (*sense 2*) duty (*sense 3*) arrival,
stay

leaven *n.* **1.** barm, ferment, leavening, yeast
2. *Fig.* catalyst, influence, inspiration ~*v.*
3. ferment, lighten, raise, work **4.** *Fig.* el~
evate, imbue, inspire, permeate, pervade,
quicken, stimulate, suffuse

leave off abstain, break off, cease, desist,
discontinue, end, give over (*Inf.*), give up,
halt, kick (*Inf.*), knock off (*Inf.*), refrain,
stop

leave out bar, cast aside, count out, disre~
gard, except, exclude, ignore, neglect, omit,
overlook, reject

leavings bits, dregs, fragments, leftovers,
orts (*Archaic or dialect*), pieces, refuse, re~
mains, remnants, residue, scraps, spoil,
sweepings, waste

lecherous carnal, concupiscent, goatish
(*Archaic or literary*), lascivious, lewd, li~
bidinous, licentious, lubricious (*U.S. sl.*),
lubricous, lustful, prurient, randy (*Inf.,*
chiefly Brit.), raunchy (*Sl.*), ruttish, sala~
cious, unchaste, wanton
Antonyms prim, proper, prudish, puritani~
cal, strait-laced, virginal, virtuous

lechery carnality, concupiscence, debauch~
ery, lasciviousness, lecherousness, leching
(*Inf.*), lewdness, libertinism, libidinousness,
licentiousness, lubricity, lust, lustfulness,
profligacy, prurience, rakishness, randiness
(*Inf., chiefly Brit.*), salaciousness, sensuality,
wantonness, womanizing

lecture *n.* **1.** address, discourse, disquisi~
tion, harangue, instruction, lesson, speech,
talk ~*v.* **2.** address, discourse, expound,
give a talk, harangue, hold forth, speak,
spout, talk, teach ~*n.* **3.** castigation, cen~
sure, chiding, dressing-down (*Inf.*), going-
over (*Inf.*), heat (*Sl., chiefly U.S. & Canad.*),
rebuke, reprimand, reproof, scolding,
talking-to (*Inf.*), telling off (*Inf.*), wigging
(*Brit. sl.*) ~*v.* **4.** admonish, bawl out (*Inf.*),
berate, carpet (*Inf.*), castigate, censure,
chew out (*U.S. & Canad. inf.*), chide, give a
rocket (*Brit. & N.Z. inf.*), rate, read the riot
act, reprimand, reprove, scold, tear into
(*Inf.*), tear (someone) off a strip (*Brit. inf.*),
tell off (*Inf.*)

ledge mantle, projection, ridge, shelf, sill,
step

leech *Fig.* bloodsucker (*Inf.*), freeloader (*Sl.*),
hanger-on, ligger (*Sl.*), parasite, sponger
(*Inf.*), sycophant

leer *n./v.* drool, eye, gloat, goggle, grin, ogle,
smirk, squint, stare, wink

lees deposit, dregs, grounds, precipitate, ref~
use, sediment, settlings

leeway elbowroom, latitude, margin, play,
room, scope, space

left *adj.* **1.** larboard (*Nautical*), left-hand,
port, sinistral **2.** *Of politics* leftist, left-wing,
liberal, progressive, radical, socialist

left-handed 1. *Archaic* awkward, cack-
handed (*Inf.*), careless, clumsy, fumbling,
gauche, maladroit **2.** ambiguous, back~
handed, double-edged, enigmatic, equivocal,
indirect, ironic, sardonic

leftover *n.* **1.** legacy, remainder, residue,
surplus, survivor **2.** *Plural* leavings, odd~
ments, odds and ends, remains, remnants,
scraps ~*adj.* **3.** excess, extra, remaining,
surplus, uneaten, unused, unwanted

leg *n.* **1.** limb, lower limb, member, pin
(*Inf.*), stump (*Inf.*) **2.** brace, prop, support,
upright **3.** lap, part, portion, section, seg~
ment, stage, stretch **4. a leg up** assistance,
boost, help, helping hand, push, support **5.**
not have a leg to stand on *Inf.* be de~
fenceless, be full of holes, be illogical, be
invalid, be undermined, be vulnerable, lack
support **6. on one's (its) last legs** about to

break down, about to collapse, at death's door, dying, exhausted, failing, giving up the ghost, worn out **7. pull someone's leg** *Inf.* chaff, deceive, fool, kid (*Inf.*), make fun of, tease, trick, wind up (*Brit. sl.*) **8. shake a leg** *Sl.* **a.** get a move on (*Inf.*), get crack~ ing (*Inf.*), hasten, hurry, look lively (*Inf.*), rush, stir one's stumps **b.** boogie (*Sl.*), dance, get down (*Inf., chiefly U.S.*), hoof it (*Sl.*), trip the light fantastic **9. stretch one's legs** exercise, go for a walk, move about, promenade, stroll, take a walk, take the air ~*v.* **10. leg it** *Inf.* go on foot, hot~ foot, hurry, run, skedaddle (*Inf.*), walk

legacy 1. bequest, devise (*Law*), estate, gift, heirloom, inheritance **2.** birthright, endow~ ment, heritage, inheritance, patrimony, throwback, tradition

legal 1. allowable, allowed, authorized, con~ stitutional, lawful, legalized, legitimate, lic~ it, permissible, proper, rightful, sanctioned, valid **2.** forensic, judicial, juridical

legality accordance with the law, admis~ sibleness, lawfulness, legitimacy, permis~ sibility, rightfulness, validity

legalize allow, approve, authorize, decrimi~ nalize, legitimate, legitimatize, license, per~ mit, sanction, validate

legatee beneficiary, heir, inheritor, recipi~ ent

legation consulate, delegation, diplomatic mission, embassy, envoys, ministry, repre~ sentation

legend 1. fable, fiction, folk tale, myth, narrative, saga, story, tale, urban legend **2.** celeb (*Inf.*), celebrity, luminary, marvel, megastar (*Inf.*), phenomenon, prodigy, spectacle, wonder **3.** caption, device, in~ scription, motto **4.** cipher, code, key, table of symbols

legendary 1. apocryphal, fabled, fabulous, fanciful, fictitious, mythical, romantic, sto~ ried, traditional **2.** celebrated, famed, fa~ mous, illustrious, immortal, renowned, well-known
Antonyms (*sense 1*) factual, genuine, his~ torical (*sense 2*) unknown

legibility clarity, decipherability, ease of reading, legibleness, neatness, plainness, readability, readableness

legible clear, decipherable, distinct, easily read, easy to read, neat, plain, readable

legion *n.* **1.** army, brigade, company, divi~ sion, force, troop **2.** drove, horde, host, mass, multitude, myriad, number, throng ~*adj.* **3.** countless, multitudinous, myriad, numberless, numerous, very many

legislate codify, constitute, enact, establish, make laws, ordain, pass laws, prescribe, put in force

legislation 1. codification, enactment, lawmaking, prescription, regulation **2.** act, bill, charter, law, measure, regulation, rul~ ing, statute

legislative *adj.* congressional, judicial, ju~ ridical, jurisdictive, lawgiving, lawmaking, ordaining, parliamentary

legislator lawgiver, lawmaker, parliamen~ tarian

legislature assembly, chamber, congress, diet, house, lawmaking body, parliament, senate

legitimate *adj.* **1.** acknowledged, authentic, authorized, genuine, kosher (*Inf.*), lawful, legal, legit (*Sl.*), licit, proper, real, rightful, sanctioned, statutory, true **2.** admissible, correct, just, justifiable, logical, reasonable, sensible, valid, warranted, well-founded ~*v.* **3.** authorize, legalize, legitimatize, legiti~ mize, permit, pronounce lawful, sanction
Antonyms *adj.* false, fraudulent, illegal, il~ legitimate, unfair, unfounded, unjustified, unlawful, unreasonable, unsound

legitimatize, legitimize authorize, legal~ ize, legitimate, permit, pronounce lawful, sanction

leisure 1. breathing space, ease, freedom, free time, holiday, liberty, opportunity, pause, quiet, recreation, relaxation, respite, rest, retirement, spare moments, spare time, time off, vacation **2. at leisure a.** available, free, not booked up, on holiday, unengaged, unoccupied **b.** *Also* **at one's leisure** at an unhurried pace, at one's con~ venience, deliberately, in one's own (good) time, unhurriedly, when it suits one, when one gets round to it (*Inf.*), without hurry
Antonyms business, duty, employment, la~ bour, obligation, occupation, work

leisurely 1. *adj.* comfortable, easy, gentle, laid-back (*Inf.*), lazy, relaxed, restful, slow, unhurried **2.** *adv.* at one's convenience, at one's leisure, comfortably, deliberately, easily, indolently, lazily, lingeringly, slowly, unhurriedly, without haste
Antonyms *adj.* brisk, fast, hasty, hectic, hurried, quick, rapid, rushed ~*adv.* briskly, hastily, hurriedly, quickly, rapidly

lend 1. accommodate one with, advance, loan **2.** add, afford, bestow, confer, contrib~ ute, furnish, give, grant, hand out, impart, present, provide, supply **3. lend an ear** give ear, hearken (*Archaic*), heed, listen, take notice **4. lend a hand** aid, assist, give a (helping) hand, help, help out **5. lend it~ self to** be adaptable, be appropriate, be serviceable, fit, present opportunities of, suit **6. lend oneself to** agree, consent, co~ operate, countenance, espouse, support

length 1. *Of linear extent* distance, extent, longitude, measure, reach, span **2.** *Of time* duration, period, space, span, stretch, term **3.** measure, piece, portion, section, segment **4.** elongation, extensiveness, lengthiness, protractedness **5. at length a.** completely, fully, in depth, in detail, thoroughly, to the full **b.** for ages, for a long time, for hours, interminably **c.** at last, at long last, eventually, finally, in the end

lengthen continue, draw out, elongate, expand, extend, increase, make longer, prolong, protract, spin out, stretch
Antonyms abbreviate, abridge, curtail, cut, cut down, diminish, shorten, trim

lengthy diffuse, drawn-out, extended, interminable, lengthened, long, long-drawn-out, long-winded, overlong, prolix, prolonged, protracted, tedious, verbose, very long
Antonyms brief, concise, condensed, limited, short, succinct, terse, to the point

leniency, lenience clemency, compassion, forbearance, gentleness, indulgence, lenity, mercy, mildness, moderation, pity, quarter, tenderness, tolerance

lenient clement, compassionate, forbearing, forgiving, gentle, indulgent, kind, merciful, mild, sparing, tender, tolerant
Antonyms harsh, merciless, rigid, rigorous, severe, stern, strict, stringent

lesbian 1. *n.* butch (*Sl.*), dyke (*Sl.*), sapphist, tribade **2.** *adj.* butch (*Sl.*), gay, homosexual, sapphic, tribadic

less *adj.* **1.** shorter, slighter, smaller **2.** inferior, minor, secondary, subordinate ~*adv.* **3.** barely, little, meagerly, to a smaller extent ~*prep.* **4.** excepting, lacking, minus, subtracting, without

lessen abate, abridge, contract, curtail, decrease, de-escalate, degrade, die down, diminish, dwindle, ease, erode, grow less, impair, lighten, lower, minimize, moderate, narrow, reduce, relax, shrink, slacken, slow down, weaken, wind down
Antonyms add to, augment, boost, enhance, enlarge, expand, increase, magnify, multiply, raise

lessening abatement, contraction, curtailment, decline, decrease, de-escalation, diminution, dwindling, ebbing, erosion, let-up (*Inf.*), minimization, moderation, petering out, reduction, shrinkage, slackening, slowing down, waning, weakening

lesser inferior, less important, lower, minor, secondary, slighter, subordinate, under-
Antonyms greater, higher, major, primary, superior

lesson 1. class, coaching, instruction, period, schooling, teaching, tutoring **2.** assignment, drill, exercise, homework, lecture, practice, reading, recitation, task **3.** deterrent, example, exemplar, message, model, moral, precept **4.** admonition, censure, chiding, punishment, rebuke, reprimand, reproof, scolding, warning

let¹ *v.* **1.** allow, authorize, entitle, give leave, give permission, give the go-ahead (green light, O.K. *or* okay (*Inf.*)) (*Inf.*), grant, permit, sanction, suffer (*Archaic*), tolerate, warrant **2.** hire, lease, rent **3.** allow, cause, enable, grant, make, permit

let² *n.* constraint, hindrance, impediment, interference, obstacle, obstruction, prohibition, restriction

letdown anticlimax, bitter pill, blow, comedown (*Inf.*), disappointment, disgruntlement, disillusionment, frustration, setback, washout (*Inf.*)

let down disappoint, disenchant, disillusion, dissatisfy, fail, fall short, leave in the lurch, leave stranded

lethal baneful, dangerous, deadly, deathly, destructive, devastating, fatal, mortal, murderous, noxious, pernicious, poisonous, virulent
Antonyms harmless, healthy, innocuous, safe, wholesome

lethargic apathetic, comatose, debilitated, drowsy, dull, enervated, heavy, inactive, indifferent, inert, languid, lazy, listless, sleepy, slothful, slow, sluggish, somnolent, stupefied, torpid
Antonyms active, alert, animated, energetic, responsive, spirited, stimulated, vigorous

lethargy apathy, drowsiness, dullness, hebetude (*Rare*), inaction, indifference, inertia, languor, lassitude, listlessness, sleepiness, sloth, slowness, sluggishness, stupor, torpidity, torpor
Antonyms animation, brio, energy, life, liveliness, spirit, verve, vigour, vim, vitality, vivacity, zeal, zest

let in admit, allow to enter, give access to, greet, include, incorporate, receive, take in, welcome

let off 1. detonate, discharge, emit, explode, exude, fire, give off, leak, release **2.** absolve, discharge, dispense, excuse, exempt, exonerate, forgive, pardon, release, spare

let out 1. emit, give vent to, produce **2.** discharge, free, let go, liberate, release **3.** betray, blow wide open (*Sl.*), disclose, leak, let fall, let slip, make known, reveal

letter 1. character, sign, symbol **2.** acknowledgment, answer, billet (*Archaic*), communication, dispatch, epistle, line, message, missive, note, reply **3. to the letter** accurately, exactly, literally, precisely, strictly, word for word

letters belles-lettres, culture, erudition, humanities, learning, literature, scholarship

let-up abatement, break, cessation, interval,

lessening, lull, pause, recess, remission, respite, slackening

let up abate, decrease, diminish, ease (up), moderate, relax, slacken, stop, subside

level *adj.* **1.** consistent, even, flat, horizon~ tal, plain, plane, smooth, uniform **2.** aligned, balanced, commensurate, compa~ rable, equal, equivalent, even, flush, in line, neck and neck, on a line, on a par, propor~ tionate **3.** calm, equable, even, even-tempered, stable, steady ~*v.* **4.** even off *or* out, flatten, make flat, plane, smooth **5.** bulldoze, demolish, destroy, devastate, equalize, flatten, knock down, lay low, pull down, raze, smooth, tear down, wreck **6.** aim, beam, direct, focus, point, train **7.** *Inf.* be above board, be frank, be honest, be open, be straightforward, be up front (*Sl.*), come clean (*Inf.*), keep nothing back ~*n.* **8.** altitude, elevation, height, vertical position **9.** achievement, degree, grade, position, rank, stage, standard, standing, status **10.** bed, floor, layer, storey, stratum, zone **11.** flat surface, horizontal, plain, plane **12. on the level** *Inf.* above board, fair, genuine, honest, open, sincere, square, straight, straightforward, up front (*Sl.*)
Antonyms *adj.* (*sense 1*) bumpy, hilly, slant~ ed, tilted, uneven, vertical, warped (*sense 2*) above, below ~*v.* (*sense 5*) build, erect, raise, roughen

level-headed balanced, calm, collected, composed, cool, dependable, even-tempered, reasonable, sane, self-possessed, sensible, steady, together (*Sl.*), unflappable (*Inf.*)

lever **1.** *n.* bar, crowbar, handle, handspike, jemmy **2.** *v.* force, jemmy, move, prise, pry (*U.S.*), purchase, raise

leverage ascendancy, authority, clout (*Inf.*), influence, pull (*Inf.*), purchasing power, rank, weight

levity buoyancy, facetiousness, fickleness, flightiness, flippancy, frivolity, giddiness, light-heartedness, light-mindedness, silli~ ness, skittishness, triviality
Antonyms earnestness, gravity, serious~ ness, solemnity

levy *v.* **1.** charge, collect, demand, exact, gather, impose, tax **2.** call, call up, con~ script, mobilize, muster, press, raise, sum~ mon ~*n.* **3.** assessment, collection, exaction, gathering, imposition **4.** assessment, duty, excise, fee, imposition, impost, tariff, tax, toll

lewd bawdy, blue, dirty, impure, indecent, lascivious, libidinous, licentious, loose, lustful, obscene, pornographic, profligate, salacious, smutty, unchaste, vile, vulgar, wanton, wicked

lewdness bawdiness, carnality, crudity, debauchery, depravity, impurity, indecency,

lasciviousness, lechery, licentiousness, lu~ bricity, obscenity, pornography, profligacy, salaciousness, smut, smuttiness, unchastity, vulgarity, wantonness

liability **1.** accountability, answerability, culpability, duty, obligation, onus, respon~ sibility **2.** arrear, debit, debt, indebtedness, obligation **3.** burden, disadvantage, drag, drawback, encumbrance, handicap, hin~ drance, impediment, inconvenience, mill~ stone, minus (*Inf.*), nuisance **4.** likelihood, probability, proneness, susceptibility, ten~ dency

liable **1.** accountable, amenable, answerable, bound, chargeable, obligated, responsible **2.** exposed, open, subject, susceptible, vulner~ able **3.** apt, disposed, inclined, likely, prone, tending **4. render oneself liable to** expose oneself to, incur, lay oneself open to, run the risk of

liaison **1.** communication, connection, con~ tact, go-between, hook-up, interchange, intermediary **2.** affair, amour, entangle~ ment, illicit romance, intrigue, love affair, romance

liar fabricator, falsifier, fibber, perjurer, pre~ varicator, storyteller (*Inf.*)

libel **1.** *n.* aspersion, calumny, defamation, denigration, obloquy, slander, smear, vitu~ peration **2.** *v.* blacken, calumniate, defame, derogate, drag (someone's) name through the mud, malign, revile, slander, slur, smear, traduce, vilify

libellous aspersive, calumniatory, calumni~ ous, defamatory, derogatory, false, injuri~ ous, malicious, maligning, scurrilous, slan~ derous, traducing, untrue, vilifying, vitu~ perative

liberal **1.** advanced, humanistic, latitudi~ narian, libertarian, progressive, radical, re~ formist, right-on (*Inf.*) **2.** altruistic, beneficent, bounteous, bountiful, charitable, free-handed, generous, kind, open-handed, open-hearted, prodigal, unstinting **3.** ad~ vanced, broad-minded, catholic, enlight~ ened, high-minded, humanitarian, indul~ gent, magnanimous, permissive, right-on (*Inf.*), tolerant, unbiased, unbigoted, un~ prejudiced **4.** abundant, ample, bountiful, copious, handsome, lavish, munificent, plentiful, profuse, rich **5.** broad, flexible, free, general, inexact, lenient, loose, not close, not literal, not strict
Antonyms biased, bigoted, cheap, con~ servative, fixed, inadequate, inflexible, intol~ erant, left-wing, limited, literal, prejudiced, reactionary, right-wing, skimpy, small, stin~ gy, strict

liberality **1.** altruism, beneficence, benevo~ lence, bounty, charity, free-handedness, generosity, kindness, largess *or* largesse,

munificence, open-handedness, philanthro~
py **2.** breadth, broad-mindedness, candour,
catholicity, impartiality, latitude, liberal~
ism, libertarianism, magnanimity, permis~
siveness, progressivism, toleration

liberalize ameliorate, broaden, ease, ex~
pand, extend, loosen, mitigate, moderate,
modify, relax, slacken, soften, stretch

liberate deliver, discharge, disenthral,
emancipate, free, let loose, let out, manu~
mit, redeem, release, rescue, set free
Antonyms confine, detain, immure, impris~
on, incarcerate, intern, jail, lock up, put away

liberation deliverance, emancipation, en~
franchisement, freedom, freeing, liberating,
liberty, manumission, redemption, release,
unfettering, unshackling

liberator deliverer, emancipator, freer,
manumitter, redeemer, rescuer, saviour

libertine 1. *n.* debauchee, lech *or* letch
(*Inf.*), lecher, loose liver, profligate, rake,
reprobate, roué, seducer, sensualist, volup~
tuary, womanizer **2.** *adj.* abandoned, cor~
rupt, debauched, decadent, degenerate, de~
praved, dissolute, immoral, licentious,
profligate, rakish, reprobate, voluptuous,
wanton

liberty 1. autonomy, emancipation, freedom,
immunity, independence, liberation, re~
lease, self-determination, sovereignty **2.**
authorization, blank cheque, carte blanche,
dispensation, exemption, franchise, free~
dom, leave, licence, permission, preroga~
tive, privilege, right, sanction **3.** *Often plu~
ral* disrespect, familiarity, forwardness, im~
pertinence, impropriety, impudence, inso~
lence, overfamiliarity, presumption, pre~
sumptuousness **4. at liberty** free, not
confined, on the loose, unlimited, unoccu~
pied, unrestricted
Antonyms captivity, compulsion, con~
straint, duress, enslavement, imprisonment,
restraint, restriction, slavery, tyranny

libidinous carnal, concupiscent, debauched,
impure, incontinent, lascivious, lecherous,
lickerish (*Archaic*), loose, lustful, prurient,
randy (*Inf., chiefly Brit.*), ruttish, salacious,
sensual, unchaste, wanton, wicked

licence *n.* **1.** authority, authorization, carte
blanche, certificate, charter, dispensation,
entitlement, exemption, immunity, leave,
liberty, permission, permit, privilege, right,
warrant **2.** freedom, independence, latitude,
liberty, self-determination **3.** abandon, an~
archy, disorder, excess, immoderation, im~
propriety, indulgence, irresponsibility, law~
lessness, laxity, profligacy, unruliness
Antonyms constraint, denial, moderation,
prohibition, restraint, restriction, strictness

license *v.* accredit, allow, authorize, certify,

commission, empower, entitle, permit,
sanction, warrant
Antonyms ban, debar, disallow, forbid, out~
law, prohibit, proscribe, rule out, veto

licentious abandoned, debauched, disor~
derly, dissolute, immoral, impure, lascivi~
ous, lax, lewd, libertine, libidinous, lubri~
cious, lubricous, lustful, profligate, promis~
cuous, sensual, uncontrollable, uncon~
trolled, uncurbed, unruly, wanton
Antonyms chaste, law-abiding, lawful, mor~
al, principled, proper, scrupulous, virtuous

licentiousness abandon, debauchery, dis~
sipation, dissoluteness, lechery, lewdness,
libertinism, libidinousness, lubricity, lust,
lustfulness, profligacy, promiscuity, pruri~
ence, salaciousness, salacity, wantonness

lick *v.* **1.** brush, lap, taste, tongue, touch,
wash **2.** *Of flames* dart, flick, flicker, ignite,
kindle, play over, ripple, touch **3.** *Inf.* **a.**
blow out of the water (*Sl.*), clobber (*Sl.*),
defeat, master, overcome, rout, run rings
around (*Inf.*), tank (*Sl.*), trounce, undo,
vanquish, wipe the floor with (*Inf.*), **b.** beat,
clobber (*Sl.*), flog, lambast(e), slap, spank,
strike, thrash, wallop (*Inf.*), **c.** beat, best,
blow out of the water (*Sl.*), clobber (*Sl.*), ex~
cel, outdo, outstrip, run rings around (*Inf.*),
surpass, tank (*Sl.*), top, wipe the floor with
(*Inf.*), ~*n.* **4.** bit, brush, dab, little, sample,
speck, stroke, taste, touch **5.** *Inf.* clip (*Inf.*),
pace, rate, speed

licking 1. beating, drubbing, flogging, hid~
ing (*Inf.*), spanking, tanning (*Sl.*), thrashing,
whipping **2.** beating, defeat, drubbing,
pasting (*Sl.*), trouncing

lie[1] 1. *v.* dissimulate, equivocate, fabricate,
falsify, fib, forswear oneself, invent, mis~
represent, perjure, prevaricate, tell a lie,
tell untruths **2.** *n.* deceit, fabrication, false~
hood, falsification, falsity, fib, fiction, in~
vention, mendacity, pork pie (*Brit. sl.*),
porky (*Brit. sl.*), prevarication, untruth,
white lie

lie[2] *v.* **1.** be prone, be prostrate, be recum~
bent, be supine, couch, loll, lounge, recline,
repose, rest, sprawl, stretch out **2.** be, be
buried, be found, be interred, be located,
belong, be placed, be situated, exist, extend,
remain **3.** *Usually with* **on** *or* **upon** burden,
oppress, press, rest, weigh **4.** *Usually with*
in be present, consist, dwell, exist, inhere,
pertain **5. lie low** conceal oneself, go to
earth, go underground, hide, hide away,
hide out, hole up, keep a low profile, keep
out of sight, lurk, skulk, take cover

liege chieftain, feudal lord, master, overlord,
seigneur, sovereign, superior, suzerain

life 1. animation, being, breath, entity,
growth, sentience, viability, vitality **2.** be~
ing, career, continuance, course, duration,

existence, lifetime, span, time **3.** human, human being, individual, mortal, person, soul **4.** autobiography, biography, career, confessions, history, life story, memoirs, story **5.** behaviour, conduct, life style, way of life **6.** the human condition, the times, the world, this mortal coil, trials and tribu~ lations, vicissitudes **7.** activity, animation, brio, energy, get-up-and-go (*Inf.*), go (*Inf.*), high spirits, liveliness, oomph (*Inf.*), pep, sparkle, spirit, verve, vigour, vitality, vi~ vacity, zest **8.** animating spirit, *élan vital*, essence, heart, lifeblood, soul, spirit, vital spark **9.** creatures, living beings, living things, organisms, wildlife **10. come to life** awaken, become animate, revive, rouse, show signs of life **11. for dear life** *Inf.* desperately, for all one is worth, intensely, quickly, urgently, vigorously

lifeblood animating force, driving force, essence, guts (*Inf.*), heart, inspiration, life, stimulus, vital spark

lifeless 1. cold, dead, deceased, defunct, ex~ tinct, inanimate, inert **2.** bare, barren, des~ ert, empty, sterile, uninhabited, unproduc~ tive, waste **3.** cold, colourless, dull, flat, heavy, hollow, lacklustre, lethargic, listless, passive, pointless, slow, sluggish, spent, spiritless, static, stiff, torpid, wooden **4.** co~ matose, dead to the world (*Inf.*), in a faint, inert, insensate, insensible, out cold, out for six, unconscious

Antonyms active, alive, animate, animated, live, lively, living, spirited, vital

lifelike authentic, exact, faithful, graphic, natural, photographic, real, realistic, true-to-life, undistorted, vivid

lifelong constant, deep-rooted, enduring, for all one's life, for life, lasting, lifetime, long-lasting, long-standing, perennial, per~ manent, persistent

lifetime all one's born days, career, course, day(s), existence, life span, one's natural life, period, span, time

life work business, calling, career, interest, mission, occupation, profession, purpose, pursuit, vocation, work

lift *v.* **1.** bear aloft, buoy up, draw up, el~ evate, heft (*Inf.*), hoist, pick up, raise, raise high, rear, upheave, uplift, upraise **2.** ad~ vance, ameliorate, boost, dignify, elevate, enhance, exalt, improve, promote, raise, upgrade **3.** annul, cancel, countermand, end, relax, remove, rescind, revoke, stop, terminate **4.** ascend, be dispelled, climb, disappear, disperse, dissipate, mount, rise, vanish **5.** *Inf.* appropriate, blag (*Sl.*), cab~ bage (*Brit. sl.*), copy, crib (*Inf.*), half-inch (*Old-fashioned sl.*), nick (*Sl., chiefly Brit.*), pilfer, pinch (*Inf.*), pirate, plagiarize, pocket, purloin, steal, take, thieve ~*n.* **6.** car ride,

drive, ride, run, transport **7.** boost, encour~ agement, fillip, pick-me-up, reassurance, shot in the arm (*Inf.*), uplift **8.** elevator (*Chiefly U.S.*)

Antonyms *v.* (*sense 1*) dash, depress, drop, hang, lower (*sense 3*) establish, impose (*sense 4*) descend, drop, fall, lower ~*n.* (*sense 7*) blow, letdown

light¹ *n.* **1.** blaze, brightness, brilliance, ef~ fulgence, flash, glare, gleam, glint, glow, il~ lumination, incandescence, lambency, lu~ minescence, luminosity, lustre, phospho~ rescence, radiance, ray, refulgence, scintil~ lation, shine, sparkle **2.** beacon, bulb, can~ dle, flare, lamp, lantern, lighthouse, star, taper, torch, windowpane **3.** broad day, cockcrow, dawn, daybreak, daylight, day~ time, morn (*Poetic*), morning, sun, sun~ beam, sunrise, sunshine **4.** *Fig.* angle, ap~ proach, aspect, attitude, context, interpre~ tation, point of view, slant, vantage point, viewpoint **5.** awareness, comprehension, elucidation, explanation, illustration, infor~ mation, insight, knowledge, understanding **6.** example, exemplar, guiding light, model, paragon, shining example **7.** flame, lighter, match **8. bring to light** disclose, discover, expose, reveal, show, uncover, unearth, un~ veil **9. come to light** appear, be disclosed, be discovered, be revealed, come out, tran~ spire, turn up **10. in (the) light of** bearing in mind, because of, considering, in view of, taking into account, with knowledge of **11. shed** *or* **throw light on** clarify, clear up, elucidate, explain, simplify ~*adj.* **12.** aglow, bright, brilliant, glowing, illuminated, lu~ minous, lustrous, shining, sunny, well-lighted, well-lit **13.** bleached, blond, faded, fair, light-hued, light-toned, pale, pastel ~*v.* **14.** fire, ignite, inflame, kindle, set a match to **15.** brighten, clarify, floodlight, flood with light, illuminate, illumine, irradiate, lighten, light up, put on, switch on, turn on **16.** animate, brighten, cheer, irradiate, lighten

Antonyms *n.* cloud, dark, darkness, dusk, mystery, obscurity, shade, shadow ~*adj.* dark, deep, dim, dusky, gloomy ~*v.* cloud, darken, douse, dull, extinguish, put out, quench

light² *adj.* **1.** airy, buoyant, delicate, easy, flimsy, imponderous, insubstantial, light~ some, lightweight, portable, slight, under~ weight **2.** faint, gentle, indistinct, mild, moderate, slight, soft, weak **3.** incon~ sequential, inconsiderable, insignificant, minute, scanty, slight, small, thin, tiny, trifling, trivial, unsubstantial, wee **4.** cushy (*Inf.*), easy, effortless, manageable, moder~ ate, simple, undemanding, unexacting, untaxing **5.** agile, airy, graceful, light-footed, lithe, nimble, sprightly, sylphlike **6.**

amusing, diverting, entertaining, frivolous, funny, gay, humorous, light-hearted, pleas~ ing, superficial, trifling, trivial, witty **7.** airy, animated, blithe, carefree, cheerful, cheery, fickle, frivolous, gay, lively, merry, sunny **8.** dizzy, giddy, light-headed, reeling, unsteady, volatile **9.** digestible, frugal, modest, not heavy, not rich, restricted, small **10.** crumbly, friable, loose, porous, sandy, spongy ~*v.* **11.** alight, land, perch, settle **12.** *With* **on** *or* **upon** chance, come across, discover, encounter, find, happen upon, hit upon, stumble on
Antonyms *adj.* burdensome, clumsy, deep, forceful, hard, heavy, intense, profound, rich, serious, sombre, strenuous, strong, substan~ tial, weighty

lighten[1] become light, brighten, flash, gleam, illuminate, irradiate, light up, make bright, shine

lighten[2] **1.** disburden, ease, make lighter, reduce in weight, unload **2.** allay, alleviate, ameliorate, assuage, ease, facilitate, lessen, mitigate, reduce, relieve **3.** brighten, buoy up, cheer, elate, encourage, gladden, heart~ en, inspire, lift, perk up, revive
Antonyms (*sense 1*) burden, encumber, handicap (*sense 2*) aggravate, heighten, in~ crease, intensify, make worse, worsen (*sense 3*) depress, oppress, sadden, weigh down

light-fingered crafty, crooked (*Inf.*), dis~ honest, furtive, pilfering, pinching (*Inf.*), shifty, sly, stealing, thieving, underhand

light-headed 1. bird-brained (*Inf.*), featherbrained, fickle, flighty, flippant, fool~ ish, frivolous, giddy, inane, rattlebrained (*Sl.*), shallow, silly, superficial, trifling **2.** delirious, dizzy, faint, giddy, hazy, vertigi~ nous, woozy (*Inf.*)

light-hearted blithe, blithesome (*Literary*), bright, carefree, cheerful, chirpy (*Inf.*), ef~ fervescent, frolicsome, gay, genial, glad, gleeful, happy-go-lucky, insouciant, jocund, jolly, jovial, joyful, joyous, merry, playful, sunny, untroubled, upbeat (*Inf.*)
Antonyms cheerless, dejected, depressed, despondent, gloomy, heavy-hearted, melan~ choly, morose, sad

lightless caliginous (*Archaic*), dark, dim, dusky, gloomy, inky, jet black, murky, pitch-black, pitch-dark, pitchy, Stygian, sunless, tenebrous, unilluminated, unlight~ ed, unlit

lightly 1. airily, delicately, faintly, gently, gingerly, slightly, softly, timidly **2.** moder~ ately, sparingly, sparsely, thinly **3.** easily, effortlessly, readily, simply **4.** breezily, carelessly, flippantly, frivolously, heedless~ ly, indifferently, slightingly, thoughtlessly
Antonyms abundantly, arduously, awk~ wardly, carefully, earnestly, firmly, forceful~

ly, heavily, ponderously, seriously, slowly, thickly, with difficulty

lightweight *adj.* inconsequential, insignificant, nickel-and-dime (*U.S. sl.*), of no account, paltry, petty, slight, trifling, trivial, unimportant, worthless
Antonyms important, momentous, serious, significant, substantial, weighty

likable, likeable agreeable, amiable, ap~ pealing, attractive, charming, engaging, friendly, genial, nice, pleasant, pleasing, sympathetic, winning, winsome

like[1] **1.** *adj.* akin, alike, allied, analogous, approximating, cognate, corresponding, equivalent, identical, parallel, relating, re~ sembling, same, similar **2.** *n.* counterpart, equal, fellow, match, parallel, twin
Antonyms *adj.* contrasted, different, dis~ similar, divergent, diverse, opposite, unlike ~*n.* opposite

like[2] *v.* **1.** adore (*Inf.*), be fond of, be keen on, be partial to, delight in, dig (*Sl.*), enjoy, go for, love, relish, revel in **2.** admire, appre~ ciate, approve, cherish, esteem, hold dear, prize, take a shine to (*Inf.*), take to **3.** care to, choose, choose to, desire, fancy, feel in~ clined, prefer, select, want, wish ~*n.* **4.** *Usually plural* cup of tea (*Inf.*), favourite, liking, partiality, predilection, preference
Antonyms *v.* abominate, despise, detest, dislike, hate, loathe

likelihood chance, good chance, liability, likeliness, possibility, probability, prospect, reasonableness, strong possibility

likely *adj.* **1.** anticipated, apt, disposed, ex~ pected, in a fair way, inclined, liable, on the cards, possible, probable, prone, tending, to be expected **2.** be *or* seem likely be in the running for, bid fair, incline towards, promise, stand a good chance, suggest, tend **3.** believable, credible, feasible, plausible, reasonable, verisimilar **4.** acceptable, agreeable, appropriate, befitting, fit, pleas~ ing, proper, qualified, suitable **5.** fair, fa~ vourite, hopeful, odds-on, promising, up~ and-coming ~*adv.* **6.** doubtlessly, in all probability, like as not (*Inf.*), like enough (*Inf.*), no doubt, presumably, probably

liken compare, equate, juxtapose, match, parallel, relate, set beside

likeness 1. affinity, correspondence, resem~ blance, similarity, similitude **2.** copy, counterpart, delineation, depiction, effigy, facsimile, image, model, photograph, pic~ ture, portrait, replica, representation, re~ production, study **3.** appearance, form, guise, semblance

liking affection, affinity, appreciation, at~ traction, bent, bias, desire, fondness, incli~ nation, love, partiality, penchant, predilec~ tion, preference, proneness, propensity, soft spot, stomach, taste, tendency, thirst, weakness

Antonyms abhorrence, aversion, dislike, hatred, loathing, repugnance

limb 1. appendage, arm, extension, extrem~ity, leg, member, part, wing **2.** bough, branch, offshoot, projection, spur

limelight attention, celebrity, fame, glare of publicity, prominence, public eye, publicity, public notice, recognition, stardom, the spotlight

limit n. **1.** bound, breaking point, cutoff point, deadline, end, end point, furthest bound, greatest extent, termination, the bitter end, ultimate, utmost **2.** *Often plural* border, boundary, confines, edge, end, ex~tent, frontier, pale, perimeter, periphery, precinct **3.** ceiling, check, curb, limitation, maximum, obstruction, restraint, restric~tion **4. the limit** *Inf.* enough, it (*Inf.*), the end, the last straw ~v. **5.** bound, check, circumscribe, confine, curb, delimit, de~marcate, fix, hem in, hinder, ration, re~strain, restrict, specify, straiten

limitation block, check, condition, con~straint, control, curb, disadvantage, draw~back, impediment, obstruction, qualifica~tion, reservation, restraint, restriction, snag

limited 1. bounded, checked, circumscribed, confined, constrained, controlled, curbed, defined, finite, fixed, hampered, hemmed in, restricted **2.** cramped, diminished, inad~equate, insufficient, minimal, narrow, re~duced, restricted, scant, short, unsatisfac~tory

Antonyms boundless, limitless, unlimited, unrestricted

limitless boundless, countless, endless, il~limitable, immeasurable, immense, inex~haustible, infinite, measureless, never-ending, numberless, unbounded, uncalcu~lable, undefined, unending, unlimited, un~told, vast

limp[1] **1.** *v.* falter, halt (*Archaic*), hobble, hop, shamble, shuffle **2.** *n.* hobble, lameness

limp[2] *adj.* **1.** drooping, flabby, flaccid, flexible, floppy, lax, limber, loose, pliable, relaxed, slack, soft **2.** debilitated, enervated, exhausted, lethargic, spent, tired, weak, worn out

Antonyms (*sense 1*) firm, hard, rigid, solid, stiff, taut, tense, unyielding (*sense 2*) hardy, powerful, robust, strong, sturdy, tough

line[1] *n.* **1.** band, bar, channel, dash, groove, mark, rule, score, scratch, streak, stripe, stroke, underline **2.** crease, crow's foot, furrow, mark, wrinkle **3.** border, border~line, boundary, demarcation, edge, frontier, limit, mark **4.** configuration, contour, fea~tures, figure, outline, profile, silhouette **5.** cable, cord, filament, rope, strand, string,

thread, wire, wisp **6.** axis, course, direction, path, route, track, trajectory **7.** approach, avenue, belief, course, course of action, ideology, method, policy, position, practice, procedure, scheme, system **8.** activity, area, bag (*Sl.*), business, calling, department, em~ployment, field, forte, interest, job, occupa~tion, profession, province, pursuit, speciali~zation, trade, vocation **9.** column, crocodile (*Brit.*), file, procession, queue, rank, row, sequence, series **10.** ancestry, breed, fami~ly, lineage, race, stock, strain, succession **11.** card, letter, message, note, postcard, report, word **12.** clue, hint, indication, in~formation, lead **13.** *Military* disposition, firing line, formation, front, front line, po~sition, trenches **14. draw the line** lay down the law, object, prohibit, put one's foot down, restrict, set a limit **15. in line a.** in alignment, in a row, plumb, straight, true **b.** in accord, in agreement, in con~formity, in harmony, in step **16. in line for** a candidate for, being considered for, due for, in the running for, next in succession to, on the short list for ~v. **17.** crease, cut, draw, furrow, inscribe, mark, rule, score, trace, underline **18.** border, bound, edge, fringe, rank, rim, skirt, verge

line[2] *v.* ceil, cover, face, fill, interline

lineaments configuration, countenance, face, features, line, outline, phiz *or* phizog (*Sl., chiefly Brit.*), physiognomy, trait, vis~age

lined 1. feint, ruled **2.** furrowed, wizened, worn, wrinkled

lines 1. appearance, configuration, contour, cut, outline, shape, style **2.** convention, ex~ample, model, pattern, plan, principle, pro~cedure **3.** part, script, words

line-up arrangement, array, row, selection, team

line up 1. fall in, form ranks, queue up **2.** assemble, come up with, lay on, obtain, or~ganize, prepare, procure, produce, secure **3.** align, arrange, array, marshal, order, range, regiment, straighten

linger 1. hang around, loiter, remain, stay, stop, tarry, wait **2.** dally, dawdle, delay, idle, lag, procrastinate, take one's time **3.** cling to life, die slowly, hang on, last, sur~vive **4.** abide, continue, endure, persist, re~main, stay

lingering dragging, long-drawn-out, persis~tent, protracted, remaining, slow

link n. **1.** component, constituent, division, element, member, part, piece **2.** affiliation, affinity, association, attachment, bond, con~nection, joint, knot, liaison, relationship, tie, tie-up, vinculum ~v. **3.** attach, bind, connect, couple, fasten, join, tie, unite, yoke

4. associate, bracket, connect, identify, re~late
Antonyms v. detach, disconnect, divide, separate, sever, split, sunder

lion *Fig.* **1.** brave man, champion, conquer~or, fighter, hero, warrior **2.** big name, celeb (*Inf.*), celebrity, idol, luminary, megastar (*Inf.*), notable, prodigy, star, superstar, V.I.P., wonder **3. beard the lion in his den** brave, confront, court destruction, defy danger, face, stand up to, tempt providence

lion-hearted bold, brave, courageous, dar~ing, dauntless, heroic, intrepid, resolute, stalwart, valiant, valorous
Antonyms chicken-hearted, chickenshit (*U.S. sl.*), cowardly, craven, faint-hearted, gutless (*Inf.*), lily-livered, pusillanimous, spineless, timorous, wimpish *or* wimpy (*Inf.*), yellow (*Inf.*)

lionize acclaim, adulate, aggrandize, cel~ebrate, crack up (*Inf.*), eulogize, exalt, fête, glorify, hero-worship, honour, idolize, make much of, mob, sing *or* sound the praises of

lip 1. brim, brink, edge, flange, margin, rim **2.** *Sl.* backchat (*Inf.*), cheek (*Inf.*), effron~tery, impertinence, insolence, rudeness, sauce (*Inf.*) **3.** *Music* control, embouchure **4. smack** *or* **lick one's lips** anticipate, de~light in, drool over, enjoy, gloat over, rel~ish, savour over

liquid *n.* **1.** fluid, juice, liquor, solution ~*adj.* **2.** aqueous, flowing, fluid, liquefied, melted, molten, running, runny, thawed, wet **3.** bright, brilliant, clear, limpid, shin~ing, translucent, transparent **4.** dulcet, fluent, mellifluent, mellifluous, melting, smooth, soft, sweet **5.** *Of assets* convertible, negotiable

liquidate 1. clear, discharge, honour, pay, pay off, settle, square **2.** abolish, annul, cancel, dissolve, terminate **3.** cash, convert to cash, realize, sell off, sell up **4.** annihi~late, blow away (*Sl., chiefly U.S.*), bump off (*Sl.*), destroy, dispatch, do away with, do in (*Sl.*), eliminate, exterminate, finish off, get rid of, kill, murder, remove, rub out (*U.S. sl.*), silence, take out (*Sl.*), wipe out (*Inf.*)

liquor 1. alcohol, booze (*Inf.*), drink, grog, hard stuff (*Inf.*), hooch *or* hootch (*Inf., chiefly U.S. & Canad.*), intoxicant, juice (*Inf.*), spirits, strong drink **2.** broth, extract, gravy, infusion, juice, liquid, stock

list¹ 1. *n.* catalogue, directory, file, index, inventory, invoice, leet (*Scot.*), listing, rec~ord, register, roll, schedule, series, syllabus, tabulation, tally **2.** *v.* bill, book, catalogue, enrol, enter, enumerate, file, index, itemize, note, record, register, schedule, set down, tabulate, write down

list² 1. *v.* cant, careen, heel, heel over, in~cline, lean, tilt, tip **2.** *n.* cant, leaning, slant, tilt

listen 1. attend, be all ears, be attentive, give ear, hang on (someone's) words, hark, hear, hearken (*Archaic*), keep one's ears open, lend an ear, pin back one's ears (*Inf.*), prick up one's ears **2.** concentrate, do as one is told, give heed to, heed, mind, obey, observe, pay attention, take notice

listless apathetic, enervated, heavy, impas~sive, inattentive, indifferent, indolent, inert, languid, languishing, lethargic, lifeless, limp, lymphatic, mopish, sluggish, spirit~less, supine, torpid, vacant
Antonyms active, alert, attentive, energetic, lively, sparky, spirited, wide-awake

literacy ability, articulacy, articulateness, cultivation, education, knowledge, learning, proficiency, scholarship

literal 1. accurate, close, exact, faithful, strict, verbatim, word for word **2.** boring, colourless, down-to-earth, dull, factual, matter-of-fact, prosaic, prosy, unimagina~tive, uninspired **3.** actual, bona fide, genu~ine, gospel, plain, real, simple, true, unex~aggerated, unvarnished

literally actually, exactly, faithfully, plainly, precisely, really, simply, strictly, to the let~ter, truly, verbatim, word for word

literary bookish, erudite, formal, learned, lettered, literate, scholarly, well-read

literate cultivated, cultured, educated, eru~dite, informed, knowledgeable, learned, let~tered, scholarly, well-informed, well-read

literature 1. belles-lettres, letters, lore, writings, written works **2.** brochure, infor~mation, leaflet, mailshot, pamphlet

lithe flexible, limber, lissom(e), loose-jointed, loose-limbed, pliable, pliant, supple

litigant claimant, contestant, disputant, liti~gator, party, plaintiff

litigate contest at law, file a suit, go to court, go to law, institute legal proceedings, press charges, prosecute, sue

litigation action, case, contending, disput~ing, lawsuit, process, prosecution

litigious argumentative, belligerent, con~tentious, disputatious, quarrelsome

litter *n.* **1.** debris, detritus, fragments, gar~bage (*Chiefly U.S.*), grot (*Sl.*), muck, refuse, rubbish, shreds **2.** clutter, confusion, disar~ray, disorder, jumble, mess, scatter, untidi~ness **3.** brood, family, offspring, progeny, young **4.** bedding, couch, floor cover, mulch, straw-bed **5.** palanquin, stretcher ~*v.* **6.** clutter, derange, disarrange, disor~der, mess up, scatter, strew

little *adj.* **1.** diminutive, dwarf, elfin, infinitesimal, Lilliputian, mini, miniature, minute, petite, pygmy *or* pigmy, short, slender, small, teensy-weensy, teeny-weeny, tiny, wee **2.** babyish, immature, infant, junior, undeveloped, young **3.** hardly any, insufficient, meagre, measly, scant, skimpy, small, sparse **4.** brief, fleeting, hasty, pass~ ing, short, short-lived **5.** inconsiderable, insignificant, minor, negligible, paltry, trifling, trivial, unimportant **6.** base, cheap, illiberal, mean, narrow-minded, petty, small-minded ~*adv.* **7.** barely, hardly, not much, not quite, only just **8.** hardly ever, not often, rarely, scarcely, seldom **9. little by little** bit by bit, by degrees, gradually, imperceptibly, piecemeal, progressively, slowly, step by step ~*n.* **10.** bit, dab, dash, fragment, hint, modicum, particle, pinch, small amount, snippet, speck, spot, tad (*Inf., chiefly U.S.*), taste, touch, trace, trifle

Antonyms *adj.* abundant, ample, big, colos~ sal, considerable, enormous, giant, ginor~ mous (*Inf.*), grave, great, huge, immense, im~ portant, large, long, major, mega (*Sl.*), mo~ mentous, much, plentiful, serious, significant ~*adv.* always, certainly, much, surely ~*n.* lot, many, much

live[1] *v.* **1.** be, be alive, breathe, draw breath, exist, have life **2.** be permanent, be re~ membered, last, persist, prevail, remain alive **3.** *Sometimes with* **in** abide, dwell, hang out (*Inf.*), inhabit, lodge, occupy, re~ side, settle, stay (*Chiefly Scot.*) **4.** abide, continue, earn a living, endure, fare, feed, get along, lead, make ends meet, pass, re~ main, subsist, support oneself, survive **5.** be happy, enjoy life, flourish, luxuriate, make the most of life, prosper, thrive **6. live it up** *Inf.* celebrate, enjoy oneself, have a ball (*Inf.*), have fun, make whoopee (*Inf.*), paint the town red, push the boat out (*Brit. inf.*), revel

live[2] *adj.* **1.** alive, animate, breathing, exist~ ent, living, quick (*Archaic*), vital **2.** active, burning, controversial, current, hot, perti~ nent, pressing, prevalent, topical, unsettled, vital **3.** *Inf.* active, alert, brisk, dynamic, earnest, energetic, lively, sparky, vigorous, vivid, wide-awake **4.** active, alight, blazing, burning, connected, glowing, hot, ignited, smouldering, switched on

livelihood employment, job, living, mainte~ nance, means, (means of) support, occupa~ tion, (source of) income, subsistence, suste~ nance, work

liveliness activity, animation, boisterous~ ness, brio, briskness, dynamism, energy, gaiety, quickness, smartness, spirit, sprightliness, vitality, vivacity

lively 1. active, agile, alert, brisk, chipper (*Inf.*), chirpy (*Inf.*), energetic, full of pep (*Inf.*), keen, nimble, perky, quick, sprightly, spry, vigorous **2.** animated, blithe, blithe~ some, cheerful, chirpy (*Inf.*), frisky, frolic~

some, gay, merry, sparkling, sparky, spirit~ ed, upbeat (*Inf.*), vivacious **3.** astir, bus~ tling, busy, buzzing, crowded, eventful, moving, stirring **4.** bright, colourful, excit~ ing, forceful, invigorating, racy, refreshing, stimulating, vivid

Antonyms apathetic, debilitated, disabled, dull, inactive, lifeless, listless, slow, sluggish, torpid

liven (up) animate, brighten, buck up (*Inf.*), enliven, hot up (*Inf.*), pep up, perk up, put life into, rouse, stir, vitalize, vivify

liverish 1. bilious, queasy, sick **2.** crotchety (*Inf.*), crusty, disagreeable, fratchy (*Inf.*), grumpy, ill-humoured, irascible, irritable, peevish, ratty (*Brit. & N.Z. inf.*), snappy, splenetic, tetchy

livery attire, clothing, costume, dress, garb, raiment (*Archaic or poetic*), regalia, suit, uniform, vestments

live wire ball of fire (*Inf.*), dynamo, go-getter (*Inf.*), hustler (*U.S. & Canad. sl.*), life and soul of the party, self-starter

livid 1. angry, black-and-blue, bruised, con~ tused, discoloured, purple **2.** ashen, blanched, bloodless, doughy, greyish, lead~ en, pale, pallid, pasty, wan, waxen **3.** *Inf.* angry, beside oneself, boiling, cross, en~ raged, exasperated, fuming, furious, in~ censed, indignant, infuriated, mad (*Inf.*), outraged

Antonyms (*sense 3*) assuaged, blissful, con~ tent, delighted, enchanted, forgiving, happy, mollified, overjoyed, pleased

living *adj.* **1.** active, alive, animated, breathing, existing, in the land of the living (*Inf.*), lively, quick (*Archaic*), strong, vigor~ ous, vital **2.** active, contemporary, continu~ ing, current, developing, extant, in use, on~ going, operative, persisting ~*n.* **3.** anima~ tion, being, existence, existing, life, subsist~ ence **4.** life style, mode of living, way of life **5.** job, livelihood, maintenance, (means of) support, occupation, (source of) income, subsistence, sustenance, work **6.** *Church of England* benefice, incumbency, stipend **7. the living** flesh and blood, the quick (*Ar~ chaic*)

Antonyms *adj.* (*sense 1*) dead, deceased, de~ funct, departed, expired, late, lifeless, per~ ished (*sense 2*) obsolescent, obsolete, out-of-date, vanishing

load *n.* **1.** bale, cargo, consignment, freight, lading, shipment **2.** affliction, burden, en~ cumbrance, incubus, millstone, onus, op~ pression, pressure, trouble, weight, worry ~*v.* **3.** cram, fill, freight, heap, lade, pack, pile, stack, stuff **4.** burden, encumber, hamper, oppress, saddle with, trouble, weigh down, worry **5.** *Of firearms* charge, make ready, prepare to fire, prime **6. load the dice** fix, rig, set up

loaded 1. burdened, charged, freighted, full, laden, weighted **2.** biased, distorted, weighted **3.** artful, insidious, manipulative, prejudicial, tricky **4.** at the ready, charged, primed, ready to shoot *or* fire **5.** *Sl.* affluent, flush (*Inf.*), moneyed, rich, rolling (*Sl.*), wealthy, well-heeled (*Inf.*), well off, well-to-do

loaf *n.* **1.** block, cake, cube, lump, slab **2.** *Sl.* block (*Inf.*), chump (*Brit. sl.*), gumption (*Brit. inf.*), head, noddle (*Inf., chiefly Brit.*), nous (*Brit. sl.*), sense

loan 1. *n.* accommodation, advance, allow~ ance, credit, mortgage, touch (*Sl.*) **2.** *v.* ac~ commodate, advance, allow, credit, lend, let out

loath, loth against, averse, backward, counter, disinclined, indisposed, opposed, reluctant, resisting, unwilling
Antonyms anxious, avid, desirous, eager, enthusiastic, keen, willing

loathing abhorrence, abomination, antipa~ thy, aversion, detestation, disgust, execra~ tion, hatred, horror, odium, repugnance, repulsion, revulsion

loathsome abhorrent, abominable, detest~ able, disgusting, execrable, hateful, horri~ ble, nasty, nauseating, obnoxious, obscene, odious, offensive, repugnant, repulsive, re~ volting, vile, yucky *or* yukky (*Sl.*)
Antonyms adorable, attractive, charming, delightful, enchanting, engaging, fetching, likable *or* likeable, lovable, lovely

lobby *n.* **1.** corridor, entrance hall, foyer, hall, hallway, passage, passageway, porch, vestibule **2.** pressure group ~*v.* **3.** bring pressure to bear, campaign for, exert influence, influence, persuade, press for, pressure, promote, pull strings (*Brit. inf.*), push for, solicit votes, urge

local *adj.* **1.** community, district, neigh~ bourhood, parish, provincial, regional **2.** confined, limited, narrow, parish pump, pa~ rochial, provincial, restricted, small-town ~*n.* **3.** character (*Inf.*), inhabitant, local yo~ kel (*Disparaging*), native, resident

locality 1. area, district, neck of the woods (*Inf.*), neighbourhood, region, vicinity **2.** locale, location, place, position, scene, set~ ting, site, spot

localize 1. circumscribe, concentrate, confine, contain, delimit, delimitate, limit, restrain, restrict **2.** ascribe, assign, narrow down, pinpoint, specify

locate 1. come across, detect, discover, find, lay one's hands on, pin down, pinpoint, run to earth, track down, unearth **2.** establish, fix, place, put, seat, set, settle, situate

location bearings, locale, locus, place, point, position, site, situation, spot, venue, where~ abouts

lock[1] *n.* **1.** bolt, clasp, fastening, padlock ~*v.* **2.** bolt, close, fasten, latch, seal, secure, shut, sneck (*Dialect*) **3.** clench, engage, en~ tangle, entwine, join, link, mesh, unite **4.** clasp, clutch, embrace, encircle, enclose, grapple, grasp, hug, press

lock[2] curl, ringlet, strand, tress, tuft

lock out ban, bar, debar, exclude, keep out, refuse admittance to, shut out

lockup can (*Sl.*), cell, cooler (*Sl.*), gaol, jail, jug (*Sl.*), police cell

lock up cage, confine, detain, imprison, in~ carcerate, jail, put behind bars, shut up

locution 1. collocation, expression, idiom, phrase, term, turn of speech, wording **2.** accent, articulation, diction, inflection, in~ tonation, manner of speech, phrasing, style

lodge *n.* **1.** cabin, chalet, cottage, gatehouse, house, hunting lodge, hut, shelter **2.** as~ semblage, association, branch, chapter, club, group, society **3.** den, haunt, lair, re~ treat ~*v.* **4.** accommodate, billet, board, en~ tertain, harbour, put up, quarter, room, shelter, sojourn, stay, stop **5.** become fixed, catch, come to rest, imbed, implant, stick **6.** deposit, file, lay, place, put, put on record, register, set, submit

lodger boarder, guest, paying guest, P.G., resident, roomer, tenant

lodging *Often plural* abode, accommodation, apartments, boarding, digs (*Brit. inf.*), dwelling, habitation, quarters, residence, rooms, shelter

lofty 1. elevated, high, raised, sky-high, soaring, tall, towering **2.** dignified, distin~ guished, elevated, exalted, grand, illustri~ ous, imposing, majestic, noble, renowned, stately, sublime, superior **3.** arrogant, con~ descending, disdainful, haughty, high and mighty (*Inf.*), lordly, patronizing, proud, snooty (*Inf.*), supercilious, toffee-nosed (*Sl., chiefly Brit.*)
Antonyms debased, degraded, dwarfed, friendly, humble, low, lowly, mean, modest, short, stunted, unassuming, warm

log *n.* **1.** block, bole, chunk, piece of timber, stump, trunk ~*v.* **2.** chop, cut, fell, hew ~*n.* **3.** account, chart, daybook, journal, listing, logbook, record, tally ~*v.* **4.** book, chart, make a note of, note, record, register, re~ port, set down, tally

loggerhead at loggerheads at daggers drawn, at each other's throats, at enmity, at odds, estranged, feuding, in dispute, op~ posed, quarrelling

logic 1. argumentation, deduction, dialec~ tics, ratiocination, science of reasoning, syllogistic reasoning **2.** good reason, good sense, reason, sense, sound judgment **3.** chain of thought, coherence, connection, link, rationale, relationship

logical 1. clear, cogent, coherent, consistent, deducible, pertinent, rational, reasonable, relevant, sound, valid, well-organized **2.** judicious, most likely, necessary, obvious, plausible, reasonable, sensible, wise
Antonyms illogical, implausible, instinc~ tive, irrational, unlikely, unorganized, un~ reasonable

logistics coordination, engineering, man~ agement, masterminding, orchestration, or~ ganization, plans, strategy

loiter dally, dawdle, delay, dilly-dally (*Inf.*), hang about *or* around, idle, lag, linger, loaf, loll, saunter, skulk, stroll

loll 1. flop, lean, loaf, lounge, recline, relax, slouch, slump, sprawl **2.** dangle, droop, drop, flap, flop, hang, hang loosely, sag

lone by oneself, deserted, isolated, lonesome, one, only, separate, separated, single, sole, solitary, unaccompanied

loneliness aloneness, desertedness, desola~ tion, dreariness, forlornness, isolation, lonesomeness, seclusion, solitariness, soli~ tude

lonely 1. abandoned, destitute, estranged, forlorn, forsaken, friendless, lonesome, out~ cast **2.** alone, apart, by oneself, companion~ less, isolated, lone, single, solitary, with~ drawn **3.** deserted, desolate, godforsaken, isolated, off the beaten track (*Inf.*), out-of-the-way, remote, secluded, sequestered, solitary, unfrequented, uninhabited
Antonyms (*sense 1*) accompanied, befriend~ ed, popular, together (*sense 2*) bustling, crowded, frequented, populous, teeming

long¹ *adj.* **1.** elongated, expanded, extended, extensive, far-reaching, lengthy, spread out, stretched **2.** dragging, interminable, late, lengthy, lingering, long-drawn-out, pro~ longed, protracted, slow, sustained, tardy
Antonyms abbreviated, abridged, brief, compressed, contracted, little, momentary, quick, short, short-lived, small

long² *v.* covet, crave, desire, dream of, eat one's heart out over, hanker, hunger, itch, lust, pine, want, wish, yearn

longing 1. *n.* ambition, aspiration, coveting, craving, desire, hankering, hope, hunger~ ing, itch, thirst, urge, wish, yearning, yen (*Inf.*) **2.** *adj.* anxious, ardent, avid, craving, desirous, eager, hungry, languishing, pin~ ing, wishful, wistful, yearning
Antonyms *n.* abhorrence, antipathy, apathy, disgust, indifference, loathing, revulsion, un~ concern ~*adj.* apathetic, cold, disgusted, hateful, indifferent, loathing, unconcerned, uninterested

long-lived enduring, full of years, lon~ gevous, long-lasting, old as Methuselah

long-standing abiding, enduring, estab~ lished, fixed, hallowed by time, long-established, long-lasting, long-lived, time-honoured

long-suffering easygoing, forbearing, for~ giving, patient, resigned, stoical, tolerant, uncomplaining

long-winded diffuse, discursive, garrulous, lengthy, long-drawn-out, overlong, prolix, prolonged, rambling, repetitious, tedious, verbose, wordy
Antonyms brief, concise, crisp, curt, lacon~ ic, pithy, sententious, short, succinct, terse, to the point

look *v.* **1.** behold (*Archaic*), check, check out (*Inf.*), clock (*Brit. sl.*), consider, contem~ plate, examine, eye, eyeball (*U.S. sl.*), feast one's eyes upon, gaze, get a load of (*Inf.*), glance, inspect, observe, peep, recce (*Sl.*), regard, scan, scrutinize, see, study, survey, take a dekko at (*Brit. sl.*), take a gander at (*Inf.*), view, watch **2.** appear, display, evi~ dence, exhibit, look like, make clear, mani~ fest, present, seem, seem to be, show, strike one as **3.** face, front, front on, give onto, overlook **4.** anticipate, await, expect, hope, reckon on **5.** forage, hunt, search, seek **6.** gape, gawk, gawp (*Brit. sl.*), glower, goggle, ogle, rubberneck (*Sl.*), stare **7. look like** be the image of, favour, make one think of, put one in mind of, remind one of, resemble, take after ~*n.* **8.** butcher's (*Brit. sl.*), ex~ amination, eyeful (*Inf.*), gander (*Inf.*), gaze, glance, glimpse, inspection, look-see (*Sl.*), observation, once-over (*Inf.*), peek, recce (*Sl.*), review, shufti (*Brit. sl.*), sight, squint (*Inf.*), survey, view **9.** air, appearance, as~ pect, bearing, cast, complexion, counte~ nance, demeanour, effect, expression, face, fashion, guise, manner, mien (*Literary*), semblance

look after attend to, care for, guard, keep an eye on, mind, nurse, protect, sit with, supervise, take care of, take charge of, tend, watch

look down on *or* **upon** contemn, despise, disdain, hold in contempt, look down one's nose at (*Inf.*), misprize, scorn, sneer, spurn, treat with contempt, turn one's nose up (at) (*Inf.*)

look forward to anticipate, await, count on, count the days until, expect, hope for, long for, look for, wait for

look into check out, delve into, examine, explore, follow up, go into, inquire about, inspect, investigate, look over, make en~ quiries, make inquiries, probe, research, scrutinize, study

lookout 1. guard, qui vive, readiness, vigil,

watch **2.** guard, sentinel, sentry, vedette (*Military*), watchman **3.** beacon, citadel, observation post, observatory, post, tower, watchtower **4.** *Inf.* business, concern, funeral (*Inf.*), pigeon (*Brit. inf.*), worry **5.** chances, future, likelihood, outlook, prospect, view

look out be alert, be careful, be on guard, be on the qui vive, be vigilant, beware, keep an eye out, keep one's eyes open (peeled, skinned), pay attention, watch out

look over cast an eye over, check, check out (*Inf.*), examine, eyeball (*U.S. sl.*), flick through, inspect, look through, monitor, peruse, scan, take a dekko at (*Brit. sl.*), view, work over

look up 1. find, hunt for, research, search for, seek out, track down **2.** ameliorate, come along, get better, improve, perk up, pick up, progress, shape up (*Inf.*), show improvement **3.** *With* to admire, defer to, esteem, have a high opinion of, honour, regard highly, respect, revere **4.** call (on), drop in on (*Inf.*), go to see, look in on, pay a visit to, visit

loom 1. appear, become visible, be imminent, bulk, emerge, hover, impend, menace, take shape, threaten **2.** dominate, hang over, mount, overhang, overshadow, overtop, rise, soar, tower

loop 1. *n.* bend, circle, coil, convolution, curl, curve, eyelet, hoop, kink, loophole, noose, ring, spiral, twirl, twist, whorl **2.** *v.* bend, braid, circle, coil, connect, curl, curve round, encircle, fold, join, knot, roll, spiral, turn, twist, wind round

loophole 1. aperture, knothole, opening, slot **2.** *Fig.* avoidance, escape, evasion, excuse, let-out, means of escape, plea, pretence, pretext, subterfuge

loose *adj.* **1.** floating, free, insecure, movable, released, unattached, unbound, unconfined, unfastened, unfettered, unrestricted, unsecured, untied, wobbly **2.** baggy, easy, hanging, loosened, not fitting, not tight, relaxed, slack, slackened, sloppy **3.** diffuse, disconnected, disordered, ill-defined, imprecise, inaccurate, indefinite, indistinct, inexact, rambling, random, vague **4.** abandoned, debauched, disreputable, dissipated, dissolute, fast, immoral, lewd, libertine, licentious, profligate, promiscuous, unchaste, wanton **5.** careless, heedless, imprudent, lax, negligent, rash, thoughtless, unmindful ~*v.* **6.** detach, disconnect, disengage, ease, free, let go, liberate, loosen, release, set free, slacken, unbind, unbridle, undo, unfasten, unleash, unloose, untie

Antonyms *adj.* (*sense 1*) bound, curbed, fastened, fettered, restrained, secured, tethered, tied (*sense 2*) tight (*sense 3*) accurate, clear,

concise, exact, precise (*sense 4*) chaste, disciplined, moral, virtuous ~*v.* bind, cage, capture, fasten, fetter, imprison, tether

loosen 1. detach, let out, separate, slacken, unbind, undo, unloose, unstick, untie, work free, work loose **2.** deliver, free, let go, liberate, release, set free **3.** *Often with* up ease up *or* off, go easy (*Inf.*), lessen, let up, lighten up (*Sl.*), mitigate, moderate, relax, soften, weaken

loot 1. *n.* booty, goods, haul, plunder, prize, spoils, swag (*Sl.*) **2.** *v.* despoil, pillage, plunder, raid, ransack, ravage, rifle, rob, sack

lopsided askew, asymmetrical, awry, cockeyed, crooked, disproportionate, off balance, one-sided, out of shape, out of true, skewwhiff (*Brit. inf.*), squint, tilting, unbalanced, unequal, uneven, warped

lord 1. commander, governor, king, leader, liege, master, monarch, overlord, potentate, prince, ruler, seigneur, sovereign, superior **2.** earl, noble, nobleman, peer, viscount **3.** **lord it over** act big (*Sl.*), be overbearing, boss around (*Inf.*), domineer, order around, play the lord, pull rank, put on airs, swagger

Lord, Our *or* **The** Christ, God, Jehovah, Jesus Christ, the Almighty

lordly 1. arrogant, condescending, despotic, dictatorial, disdainful, domineering, haughty, high and mighty (*Inf.*), high-handed, hoity-toity (*Inf.*), imperious, lofty, overbearing, patronizing, proud, stuck-up (*Inf.*), supercilious, toffee-nosed (*Sl., chiefly Brit.*), tyrannical **2.** aristocratic, dignified, exalted, gracious, grand, imperial, lofty, majestic, noble, princely, regal, stately

lore 1. beliefs, doctrine, experience, folkwisdom, mythos, saws, sayings, teaching, traditional wisdom, traditions, wisdom **2.** erudition, knowhow (*Inf.*), knowledge, learning, letters, scholarship

lose 1. be deprived of, displace, drop, fail to keep, forget, mislay, misplace, miss, suffer loss **2.** capitulate, default, fail, fall short, forfeit, lose out on (*Inf.*), miss, pass up (*Inf.*), yield **3.** be defeated, be the loser, be worsted, come a cropper (*Inf.*), come to grief, get the worst of, lose out, suffer defeat, take a licking (*Inf.*) **4.** consume, deplete, dissipate, drain, exhaust, expend, lavish, misspend, squander, use up, waste **5.** confuse, miss, stray from, wander from **6.** lap, leave behind, outdistance, outrun, outstrip, overtake, pass **7.** dodge, duck, elude, escape, evade, give someone the slip, shake off, slip away, throw off

loser also-ran, dud (*Inf.*), failure, flop (*Inf.*), lemon (*Sl.*), no-hoper (*Aust. sl.*), underdog, washout (*Inf.*)

loss 1. bereavement, deprivation, disap~ pearance, drain, failure, forfeiture, losing, misfortune, mislaying, privation, squander~ ing, waste **2.** cost, damage, defeat, destruc~ tion, detriment, disadvantage, harm, hurt, impairment, injury, ruin **3.** *Plural* casual~ ties, dead, death toll, fatalities, number killed (captured, injured, missing, wounded) **4.** *Sometimes plural* debit, debt, deficiency, deficit, depletion, losings, shrinkage **5. at a loss** at one's wits' end, baffled, bewildered, confused, helpless, nonplussed, perplexed, puzzled, stuck (*Inf.*), stumped
Antonyms acquisition, advantage, finding, gain, preservation, recovery, reimbursement, restoration, saving, winning

lost 1. disappeared, forfeited, mislaid, mis~ placed, missed, missing, strayed, vanished, wayward **2.** adrift, astray, at sea, disorient~ ed, off-course, off-track **3.** baffled, bewil~ dered, clueless (*Sl.*), confused, helpless, ig~ norant, mystified, perplexed, puzzled **4.** abolished, annihilated, demolished, de~ stroyed, devastated, eradicated, exterminat~ ed, obliterated, perished, ruined, wasted, wiped out, wrecked **5.** absent, absorbed, abstracted, distracted, dreamy, engrossed, entranced, preoccupied, rapt, spellbound, taken up **6.** consumed, dissipated, frittered away, misapplied, misdirected, misspent, misused, squandered, wasted **7.** bygone, dead, extinct, forgotten, gone, lapsed, obso~ lete, out-of-date, past, unremembered **8.** abandoned, corrupt, damned, depraved, dissolute, fallen, irreclaimable, licentious, profligate, unchaste, wanton

lot 1. assortment, batch, bunch (*Inf.*), collec~ tion, consignment, crowd, group, quantity, set **2.** accident, chance, destiny, doom, fate, fortune, hazard, plight, portion **3.** allow~ ance, cut (*Inf.*), parcel, part, percentage, piece, portion, quota, ration, share **4. a lot** *or* **lots** abundance, a great deal, heap(s), large amount, load(s) (*Inf.*), masses (*Inf.*), numbers, ocean(s), oodles (*Inf.*), piles (*Inf.*), plenty, quantities, reams (*Inf.*), scores, stack(s) **5. draw lots** choose, cut for aces, cut straws (*Inf.*), decide, pick, select, spin a coin, toss up **6. throw in one's lot with** ally *or* align oneself with, join, join forces with, join fortunes with, make common cause with, support

lotion balm, cream, embrocation, liniment, salve, solution

lottery 1. draw, raffle, sweepstake **2.** chance, gamble, hazard, risk, toss-up (*Inf.*), venture

loud 1. blaring, blatant, boisterous, boom~ ing, clamorous, deafening, ear-piercing, ear-splitting, forte (*Music*), high-sounding, noisy, obstreperous, piercing, resounding, rowdy, sonorous, stentorian, strident,

strong, thundering, tumultuous, turbulent, vehement, vociferous **2.** *Fig.* brash, brassy, flamboyant, flashy, garish, gaudy, glaring, lurid, naff (*Brit. sl.*), ostentatious, showy, tacky (*Inf.*), tasteless, tawdry, vulgar **3.** brash, brazen, coarse, crass, crude, loud-mouthed (*Inf.*), offensive, raucous, vulgar
Antonyms (*sense 1*) gentle, inaudible, low, low-pitched, quiet, silent, soft, soundless, subdued (*sense 2*) conservative, dull, sober, sombre (*sense 3*) quiet, reserved, retiring, shy, unassuming

loudly at full volume, at the top of one's voice, clamorously, deafeningly, fortissimo (*Music*), lustily, noisily, shrilly, uproarious~ ly, vehemently, vigorously, vociferously

lounge *v.* **1.** laze, lie about, loaf, loiter, loll, recline, relax, saunter, sprawl, take it easy **2.** dawdle, fritter time away, hang out (*Inf.*), idle, kill time, pass time idly, potter, veg out (*Sl., chiefly U.S.*), waste time

lout bear, boor, bumpkin, churl, clod, clum~ sy idiot, dolt, gawk, lubber, lummox (*Inf.*), ned (*Sl.*), oaf, yahoo, yob *or* yobbo (*Brit. sl.*)

lovable adorable, amiable, attractive, capti~ vating, charming, cuddly, cute, delightful, enchanting, endearing, engaging, fetching (*Inf.*), likable *or* likeable, lovely, pleasing, sweet, winning, winsome
Antonyms abhorrent, abominable, detest~ able, hateful, loathsome, obnoxious, odious, offensive, revolting

love *v.* **1.** adore, adulate, be attached to, be in love with, cherish, dote on, have affec~ tion for, hold dear, idolize, prize, think the world of, treasure, worship **2.** appreciate, delight in, desire, enjoy, fancy, have a weakness for, like, relish, savour, take pleasure in **3.** canoodle (*Sl.*), caress, cuddle, embrace, fondle, kiss, neck (*Inf.*), pet ~*n.* **4.** adoration, adulation, affection, amity, ar~ dour, attachment, devotion, fondness, friendship, infatuation, liking, passion, rapture, regard, tenderness, warmth **5.** de~ light, devotion, enjoyment, fondness, incli~ nation, liking, partiality, relish, soft spot, taste, weakness **6.** angel, beloved, darling, dear, dearest, dear one, inamorata, inamo~ rato, leman (*Archaic*), loved one, lover, sweet, sweetheart, truelove **7. for love** for nothing, freely, free of charge, gratis, pleas~ urably, without payment **8. for love or money** by any means, ever, under any conditions **9. in love** besotted, charmed, enamoured, enraptured, infatuated, smitten **10. fall in love (with)** bestow one's affec~ tions on, be taken with, fall for, lose one's heart (to), take a shine to (*Inf.*)
Antonyms *v.* (*senses 1 & 2*) abhor, abominate, detest, dislike, hate, scorn ~*n.* (*senses 4 & 5*) abhorrence, abomination, animosity, antago~ nism, antipathy, aversion, bitterness, detes~

tation, disgust, dislike, hate, hatred, hostility, ill will, incompatibility, loathing, malice, re~ pugnance, resentment, scorn (sense 6) enemy, foe

love affair 1. affair, *affaire de coeur*, amour, intrigue, liaison, relationship, ro~ mance **2.** appreciation, devotion, enthusi~ asm, love, mania, passion

lovely 1. admirable, adorable, amiable, at~ tractive, beautiful, charming, comely, ex~ quisite, graceful, handsome, pretty, sweet, winning **2.** agreeable, captivating, delight~ ful, enchanting, engaging, enjoyable, grati~ fying, nice, pleasant, pleasing
Antonyms abhorrent, detestable, hateful, hideous, loathsome, odious, repellent, repug~ nant, revolting, ugly, unattractive

lover admirer, beau, beloved, boyfriend, fancy man (*Sl.*), fancy woman (*Sl.*), fiancé, fiancée, flame (*Inf.*), girlfriend, inamorata, inamorato, leman (*Archaic*), mistress, par~ amour, suitor, swain (*Archaic*), sweetheart, toy boy

loving affectionate, amorous, ardent, cor~ dial, dear, demonstrative, devoted, doting, fond, friendly, kind, solicitous, tender, warm, warm-hearted
Antonyms aloof, cold, contemptuous, cruel, detached, distasteful, hateful, hostile, indif~ ferent, mean, scornful, unconcerned, unlov~ ing

low 1. fubsy (*Archaic or dialect*), little, short, small, squat, stunted **2.** deep, depressed, ground-level, low-lying, shallow, subsided, sunken **3.** depleted, insignificant, little, meagre, measly, paltry, reduced, scant, small, sparse, trifling **4.** deficient, inad~ equate, inferior, low-grade, mediocre, pa~ thetic, poor, puny, second-rate, shoddy, substandard, worthless **5.** coarse, common, crude, disgraceful, dishonourable, disrepu~ table, gross, ill-bred, obscene, rough, rude, unbecoming, undignified, unrefined, vulgar **6.** humble, lowborn, lowly, meek, obscure, plain, plebeian, poor, simple, unpretentious **7.** blue, brassed off (*Brit. sl.*), dejected, de~ pressed, despondent, disheartened, dismal, down, downcast, down in the dumps (*Inf.*), fed up, forlorn, gloomy, glum, miserable, morose, sad, sick as a parrot (*Inf.*), unhappy **8.** debilitated, dying, exhausted, feeble, frail, ill, prostrate, reduced, sinking, strick~ en, weak **9.** gentle, hushed, muffled, muted, quiet, soft, subdued, whispered **10.** cheap, economical, inexpensive, moderate, modest, reasonable **11.** abject, base, contemptible, dastardly, degraded, depraved, despicable, ignoble, mean, menial, nasty, scurvy, ser~ vile, sordid, unworthy, vile, vulgar
Antonyms admirable, alert, brave, cheerful, elated, elevated, eminent, energetic, enthusi~ astic, exalted, fine, grand, happy, high, high-

ranking, honourable, important, laudable, lofty, loud, noisy, praiseworthy, significant, strong, superior, tall, towering, worthy

lowdown *Inf.* dope (*Inf.*), gen (*Brit. inf.*), info (*Inf.*), information, inside story, intelli~ gence

lower *adj.* **1.** inferior, junior, lesser, low-level, minor, secondary, second-class, smaller, subordinate, under **2.** curtailed, decreased, diminished, lessened, pared down, reduced ~*v.* **3.** depress, drop, fall, let down, make lower, sink, submerge, take down **4.** abase, belittle, condescend, debase, degrade, deign, demean, devalue, disgrace, downgrade, humble, humiliate, stoop **5.** abate, curtail, cut, decrease, diminish, less~ en, minimize, moderate, prune, reduce, slash **6.** soften, tone down
Antonyms *adj.* enlarged, higher, increased ~*v.* amplify, augment, boost, elevate, enlarge, extend, hoist, increase, inflate, lift, magnify, raise

low-key low-pitched, muffled, muted, played down, quiet, restrained, subdued, toned down, understated

low-spirited apathetic, blue, dejected, de~ pressed, despondent, down, gloomy, low, miserable, moody, sad, unhappy

loyal attached, constant, dependable, devot~ ed, dutiful, faithful, immovable, patriotic, staunch, steadfast, tried and true, true, true-blue, true-hearted, trustworthy, trusty, unswerving, unwavering
Antonyms disloyal, false, perfidious, trai~ torous, treacherous, unfaithful, untrustwor~ thy

loyalty allegiance, constancy, dependability, devotion, faithfulness, fealty, fidelity, patri~ otism, reliability, staunchness, steadfast~ ness, troth (*Archaic*), true-heartedness, trueness, trustiness, trustworthiness

lubricate grease, make slippery, make smooth, oil, oil the wheels, smear, smooth the way

lucid 1. clear, clear-cut, comprehensible, crystal clear, distinct, evident, explicit, in~ telligible, limpid, obvious, pellucid, plain, transparent **2.** beaming, bright, brilliant, effulgent, gleaming, luminous, radiant, re~ splendent, shining **3.** clear, crystalline, di~ aphanous, glassy, limpid, pellucid, pure, translucent, transparent **4.** all there, clear-headed, *compos mentis*, in one's right mind, rational, reasonable, sane, sensible, sober, sound
Antonyms (*sense 1*) ambiguous, confused, equivocal, incomprehensible, indistinct, muddled, unclear, unintelligible, vague (*sense 2*) dull (*sense 3*) unclear (*sense 4*) confused, ir~ rational, muddled, unclear, unperceptive, vague

luck 1. accident, chance, destiny, fate, fortu~ity, fortune, hap (*Archaic*), hazard **2.** advantage, blessing, break (*Inf.*), fluke, godsend, good fortune, good luck, prosperity, serendipity, stroke, success, windfall

luckily 1. favourably, fortunately, happily, opportunely, propitiously, providentially **2.** as it chanced, as luck would have it, by chance, fortuitously

luckless calamitous, cursed, disastrous, doomed, hapless, hopeless, ill-fated, ill-starred, jinxed, star-crossed, unfortunate, unhappy, unlucky, unpropitious, unsuc~cessful

lucky 1. advantageous, blessed, charmed, favoured, fortunate, jammy (*Brit. sl.*), pros~perous, serendipitous, successful **2.** adven~titious, auspicious, fortuitous, opportune, propitious, providential, timely
Antonyms bad, detrimental, ominous, un~favourable, unfortunate, unhappy, unlucky, unpromising, untimely

lucrative advantageous, fat, fruitful, gainful, high-income, money-making, paying, pro~ductive, profitable, remunerative, well-paid

lucre gain, mammon, money, profit, riches, spoils, wealth

ludicrous absurd, burlesque, comic, comi~cal, crazy, droll, farcical, funny, incongru~ous, laughable, nonsensical, odd, outland~ish, preposterous, ridiculous, silly, zany
Antonyms grave, logical, sad, sensible, seri~ous, solemn

luggage baggage, bags, cases, gear, impedi~menta, paraphernalia, suitcases, things, trunks

lugubrious dirgelike, dismal, doleful, dreary, funereal, gloomy, melancholy, mo~rose, mournful, sad, serious, sombre, sor~rowful, woebegone, woeful

lukewarm 1. blood-warm, tepid, warm **2.** *Fig.* apathetic, cold, cool, half-arsed, half-assed (*U.S. & Canad. sl.*), half-hearted, in~different, laodicean, phlegmatic, uncon~cerned, unenthusiastic, uninterested, unre~sponsive

lull *v.* **1.** allay, calm, compose, hush, lullaby, pacify, quell, quiet, rock to sleep, soothe, still, subdue, tranquillize **2.** abate, cease, decrease, diminish, dwindle, ease off, let up, moderate, quieten down, slacken, subside, wane ~*n.* **3.** calm, calmness, hush, let-up (*Inf.*), pause, quiet, respite, silence, stillness, tranquillity

lullaby berceuse, cradlesong

lumber[1] **1.** *n.* castoffs, clutter, discards, jumble, junk, refuse, rubbish, trash, trump~ery, white elephants **2.** *v. Brit. sl.* burden, encumber, impose upon, land, load, saddle

lumber[2] *v.* clump, plod, shamble, shuffle, stump, trudge, trundle

lumbering awkward, blundering, bovine, bumbling, clumsy, elephantine, heavy, heavy-footed, hulking, lubberly, overgrown, ponderous, ungainly, unwieldy

luminary big name, celeb (*Inf.*), celebrity, dignitary, leading light, lion, megastar (*Inf.*), notable, personage, somebody, star, V.I.P., worthy

luminous 1. bright, brilliant, glowing, illu~minated, lighted, lit, luminescent, lustrous, radiant, resplendent, shining, vivid **2.** clear, evident, intelligible, lucid, obvious, perspicuous, plain, transparent

lump *n.* **1.** ball, bunch, cake, chunk, clod, cluster, dab, gob, gobbet, group, hunk, mass, nugget, piece, spot, wedge **2.** bulge, bump, growth, hump, protrusion, protuber~ance, swelling, tumescence, tumour ~*v.* **3.** agglutinate, aggregate, batch, bunch, coa~lesce, collect, combine, conglomerate, con~solidate, group, mass, pool, unite

lunacy 1. dementia, derangement, idiocy, insanity, madness, mania, psychosis **2.** ab~erration, absurdity, craziness, folly, fool~hardiness, foolishness, idiocy, imbecility, madness, senselessness, stupidity, tomfool~ery
Antonyms prudence, reason, sanity, sense

lunatic 1. *adj.* barking (*Sl.*), barking mad (*Sl.*), barmy (*Sl.*), bonkers (*Sl., chiefly Brit.*), crackbrained, crackpot (*Inf.*), crazy, daft, demented, deranged, insane, irrational, loopy (*Inf.*), mad, maniacal, not the full shilling (*Inf.*), nuts (*Sl.*), off one's trolley (*Sl.*), out to lunch (*Inf.*), psychotic, un~hinged, up the pole (*Inf.*) **2.** *n.* headbanger (*Inf.*), headcase (*Inf.*), loony (*Sl.*), madman, maniac, nut (*Sl.*), nutcase (*Sl.*), nutter (*Brit. sl.*), psychopath

lunge 1. *n.* charge, cut, jab, pass, pounce, spring, stab, swing, swipe (*Inf.*), thrust **2.** *v.* bound, charge, cut, dash, dive, fall upon, hit at, jab, leap, pitch into (*Inf.*), plunge, poke, pounce, set upon, stab, strike at, thrust

lure 1. *v.* allure, attract, beckon, decoy, draw, ensnare, entice, inveigle, invite, lead on, seduce, tempt **2.** *n.* allurement, attrac~tion, bait, carrot (*Inf.*), come-on (*Inf.*), de~coy, enticement, inducement, magnet, siren song, temptation

lurid 1. exaggerated, graphic, melodramatic, sensational, shock-horror (*Facetious*), shocking, startling, unrestrained, vivid, yellow (*of journalism*) **2.** disgusting, ghast~ly, gory, grim, grisly, gruesome, macabre, revolting, savage, violent **3.** ashen, ghastly, pale, pallid, sallow, wan **4.** bloody, fiery, flaming, glaring, glowering, intense, livid, overbright, sanguine

Antonyms (*senses 1 & 2*) breezy, bright, carefree, controlled, factual, jaunty, light-hearted, mild (*sense 4*) pale, pastel, watery

lurk conceal oneself, crouch, go furtively, hide, lie in wait, move with stealth, prowl, skulk, slink, sneak, snoop

luscious appetizing, delectable, delicious, honeyed, juicy, mouth-watering, palatable, rich, savoury, scrumptious (*Inf.*), succulent, sweet, toothsome, yummy (*Sl.*)

lush 1. abundant, dense, flourishing, green, lavish, overgrown, prolific, rank, teeming, verdant **2.** fresh, juicy, ripe, succulent, tender **3.** elaborate, extravagant, grand, lavish, luxurious, opulent, ornate, palatial, plush (*Inf.*), ritzy (*Sl.*), sumptuous

lust *n.* **1.** carnality, concupiscence, lasciviousness, lechery, lewdness, libido, licentiousness, pruriency, randiness (*Inf., chiefly Brit.*), salaciousness, sensuality, the hots (*Sl.*), wantonness **2.** appetence, appetite, avidity, covetousness, craving, cupidity, desire, greed, longing, passion, thirst ~*v.* **3.** be consumed with desire for, covet, crave, desire, hunger for *or* after, lech after (*Inf.*), need, slaver over, want, yearn

lustre 1. burnish, gleam, glint, glitter, gloss, glow, sheen, shimmer, shine, sparkle **2.** brightness, brilliance, dazzle, lambency, luminousness, radiance, resplendence **3.** distinction, fame, glory, honour, illustriousness, prestige, renown

lusty brawny, energetic, hale, healthy, hearty, in fine fettle, powerful, Ramboesque, red-blooded (*Inf.*), robust, rugged, stalwart, stout, strapping, strong, sturdy, vigorous, virile

luxuriant 1. abundant, ample, copious, excessive, lavish, plenteous, plentiful, prodigal, profuse, superabundant **2.** baroque, corinthian, decorated, elaborate, extravagant, fancy, festooned, flamboyant, florid, flowery, ornate, rococo, sumptuous **3.** dense, exuberant, fecund, fertile, flourishing, fruitful, lush, overflowing, productive, prolific, rank, rich, riotous, teeming, thriving

Antonyms barren, meagre, plain, scanty, simple, sparse, thin, unadorned

luxurious 1. comfortable, costly, de luxe, expensive, lavish, magnificent, opulent, plush (*Inf.*), rich, ritzy (*Sl.*), splendid, sumptuous, well-appointed **2.** epicurean, pampered, pleasure-loving, self-indulgent, sensual, sybaritic, voluptuous

Antonyms ascetic, austere, deprived, economical, plain, poor, sparing, Spartan, squalid, thrifty

luxury 1. affluence, hedonism, opulence, richness, splendour, sumptuousness, voluptuousness **2.** bliss, comfort, delight, enjoyment, gratification, indulgence, pleasure, satisfaction, wellbeing **3.** extra, extravagance, frill, indulgence, nonessential, treat

Antonyms austerity, burden, deprivation, destitution, difficulty, discomfort, hardship, infliction, misery, necessity, need, poverty, privation, want

lying 1. *n.* deceit, dishonesty, dissimulation, double-dealing, duplicity, fabrication, falsity, fibbing, guile, mendacity, perjury, prevarication, untruthfulness **2.** *adj.* deceitful, dishonest, dissembling, double-dealing, false, guileful, mendacious, perfidious, treacherous, two-faced, untruthful

Antonyms *adj.* candid, forthright, frank, honest, reliable, sincere, straight, straightforward, truthful, veracious

lyrical carried away, ecstatic, effusive, emotional, enthusiastic, expressive, impassioned, inspired, poetic, rapturous, rhapsodic

M

macabre cadaverous, deathlike, deathly, dreadful, eerie, frightening, frightful, ghastly, ghostly, ghoulish, grim, grisly, gruesome, hideous, horrid, morbid, un~ earthly, weird
Antonyms appealing, beautiful, charming, delightful, lovely, pleasant

machination artifice, cabal, conspiracy, design, device, dodge, intrigue, manoeuvre, plot, ploy, ruse, scheme, stratagem, trick

machine 1. apparatus, appliance, contrap~ tion, contrivance, device, engine, instru~ ment, mechanism, tool **2.** agency, machin~ ery, organization, party, setup (*Inf.*), struc~ ture, system **3.** *Fig.* agent, automaton, me~ chanical man, puppet, robot, zombie

machinery 1. apparatus, equipment, gear, instruments, mechanism, tackle, tools, works **2.** agency, channels, machine, or~ ganization, procedure, structure, system

mad 1. aberrant, bananas (*Sl.*), barking (*Sl.*), barking mad (*Sl.*), barmy (*Sl.*), batty (*Sl.*), bonkers (*Sl., chiefly Brit.*), crackers (*Brit. sl.*), crackpot (*Inf.*), crazed, crazy (*Inf.*), cuckoo (*Inf.*), delirious, demented, deranged, distracted, flaky (*U.S. sl.*), frantic, frenzied, insane, loony (*Sl.*), loopy (*Inf.*), lu~ natic, mental (*Sl.*), *non compos mentis,* not the full shilling (*Inf.*), nuts (*Sl.*), nutty (*Sl.*), off one's chump (*Sl.*), off one's head (*Sl.*), off one's nut (*Sl.*), off one's rocker (*Sl.*), off one's trolley (*Sl.*), of unsound mind, out of one's mind, out to lunch (*Inf.*), psychotic, rabid, raving, round the bend (*Brit. sl.*), round the twist (*Brit. sl.*), screwy (*Inf.*), un~ balanced, unhinged, unstable, up the pole (*Inf.*) **2.** absurd, asinine, daft (*Inf.*), fool~ hardy, foolish, imprudent, inane, irrational, ludicrous, nonsensical, preposterous, sense~ less, unreasonable, unsafe, unsound, wild **3.** *Inf.* angry, ape (*Sl.*), apeshit (*Sl.*), berserk, cross, enraged, exasperated, fuming, furi~ ous, in a wax (*Inf., chiefly Brit.*), incensed, infuriated, irate, irritated, livid (*Inf.*), rag~ ing, resentful, seeing red (*Inf.*), wild, wrathful **4.** ardent, avid, crazy, daft (*Inf.*), devoted, dotty (*Sl., chiefly Brit.*), enamoured, enthusiastic, fanatical, fond, hooked, im~ passioned, infatuated, in love with, keen, nuts (*Sl.*), wild, zealous **5.** abandoned, agi~ tated, boisterous, ebullient, energetic, excit~ ed, frenetic, frenzied, gay, riotous, uncon~ trolled, unrestrained, wild **6. like mad** *Inf.* energetically, enthusiastically, excitedly, furiously, madly, quickly, rapidly, speedily, unrestrainedly, violently, wildly, with might and main
Antonyms appeased, calm, composed, cool, mollified, nonchalant, rational, sane, sensible, sound, uncaring

madden aggravate (*Inf.*), annoy, craze, de~ range, drive one crazy (off one's head (*Sl.*), out of one's mind, round the bend (*Brit. sl.*), round the twist (*Brit. sl.*), to distraction) (*Inf.*), enrage, exasperate, gall, get one's hackles up, incense, inflame, infuriate, irri~ tate, make one's blood boil, make one see red (*Inf.*), make one's hackles rise, nark (*Brit., Aust., & N.Z. sl.*), piss one off (*Taboo sl.*), provoke, raise one's hackles, unhinge, upset, vex
Antonyms appease, calm, mollify, pacify, soothe

made-up fabricated, false, fictional, imagi~ nary, invented, make-believe, mythical, specious, trumped-up, unreal, untrue

madly 1. crazily, deliriously, dementedly, distractedly, frantically, frenziedly, hysteri~ cally, insanely, rabidly **2.** absurdly, fool~ ishly, irrationally, ludicrously, nonsensi~ cally, senselessly, unreasonably, wildly **3.** energetically, excitedly, furiously, hastily, hotfoot, hurriedly, like mad (*Inf.*), quickly, rapidly, recklessly, speedily, violently, wildly **4.** *Inf.* desperately, devotedly, ex~ ceedingly, excessively, extremely, intensely, passionately, to distraction

madman *or* **madwoman** headbanger (*Inf.*), headcase (*Inf.*), loony (*Sl.*), lunatic, maniac, mental case (*Sl.*), nut (*Sl.*), nutcase (*Sl.*), nutter (*Brit. sl.*), psycho (*Sl.*), psycho~ path, psychotic

madness 1. aberration, craziness, delusion, dementia, derangement, distraction, insan~ ity, lunacy, mania, mental illness, psy~ chopathy, psychosis **2.** absurdity, daftness (*Inf.*), folly, foolhardiness, foolishness, idio~ cy, nonsense, preposterousness, wildness **3.** anger, exasperation, frenzy, fury, ire, rage, raving, wildness, wrath **4.** ardour, craze, enthusiasm, fanaticism, fondness, infatua~ tion, keenness, passion, rage, zeal **5.** aban~ don, agitation, excitement, frenzy, furore, intoxication, riot, unrestraint, uproar

magazine 1. journal, pamphlet, paper, pe~ riodical **2.** ammunition dump, arsenal, de~ pot, powder room (*Obsolete*), store, store~ house, warehouse

magic *n.* **1.** black art, enchantment, necro~ mancy, occultism, sorcery, sortilege, spell, theurgy, witchcraft, wizardry **2.** conjuring, hocus-pocus, illusion, jiggery-pokery (*Inf., chiefly Brit.*), jugglery, legerdemain, presti~ digitation, sleight of hand, trickery **3.** al~ lurement, charm, enchantment, fascination, glamour, magnetism, power ~*adj.* **4.** *Also* **magical** bewitching, charismatic, charm~ ing, enchanting, entrancing, fascinating, magnetic, marvellous, miraculous, sorcer~ ous, spellbinding

magician 1. archimage (*Rare*), conjurer, conjuror, enchanter, enchantress, illusion~ ist, necromancer, sorcerer, thaumaturge (*Rare*), theurgist, warlock, witch, wizard **2.** genius, marvel, miracle-worker, spellbinder, virtuoso, wizard, wonder-worker

magisterial arrogant, assertive, authorita~ tive, bossy (*Inf.*), commanding, dictatorial, domineering, high-handed, imperious, lord~ ly, masterful, overbearing, peremptory **Antonyms** deferential, diffident, humble, servile, shy, submissive, subservient, wimp~ ish *or* wimpy (*Inf.*)

magistrate bailie (*Scot.*), J.P., judge, jus~ tice, justice of the peace, provost (*Scot.*)

magnanimity beneficence, big-heartedness, bountifulness, charitableness, generosity, high-mindedness, largess *or* largesse, munificence, nobility, open-handedness, selflessness, unselfishness

magnanimous beneficent, big, big-hearted, bountiful, charitable, free, generous, great-hearted, handsome, high-minded, kind, kindly, munificent, noble, open-handed, selfless, ungrudging, unselfish, unstinting **Antonyms** miserly, petty, resentful, selfish, small, unforgiving, vindictive

magnate 1. baron, big cheese (*Sl., old-fashioned*), big noise (*Inf.*), big shot (*Inf.*), big wheel (*Sl.*), bigwig (*Inf.*), captain of in~ dustry, chief, fat cat (*Sl., chiefly U.S.*), lead~ er, Mister Big (*Sl., chiefly U.S.*), mogul, na~ bob (*Inf.*), notable, plutocrat, tycoon, V.I.P. **2.** aristo (*Inf.*), aristocrat, baron, bashaw, grandee, magnifico, merchant, noble, no~ table, personage, prince

magnetic alluring, attractive, captivating, charismatic, charming, enchanting, en~ trancing, fascinating, hypnotic, irresistible, mesmerizing, seductive **Antonyms** disagreeable, offensive, repel~ lent, repulsive, unappealing, unattractive, unlikable *or* unlikeable, unpleasant

magnetism allure, appeal, attraction, at~ tractiveness, captivatingness, charisma, charm, draw, drawing power, enchantment, fascination, hypnotism, magic, mesmerism, power, pull, seductiveness, spell

magnification aggrandizement, am~ plification, augmentation, blow-up (*Inf.*), boost, build-up, deepening, dilation, en~

hancement, enlargement, exaggeration, ex~ pansion, heightening, increase, inflation, intensification

magnificence brilliance, éclat, glory, gor~ geousness, grandeur, luxuriousness, luxury, majesty, nobility, opulence, pomp, re~ splendence, splendour, stateliness, sublim~ ity, sumptuousness

magnificent august, brilliant, elegant, el~ evated, exalted, excellent, fine, glorious, gorgeous, grand, grandiose, imposing, im~ pressive, lavish, luxurious, majestic, noble, opulent, outstanding, princely, regal, re~ splendent, rich, splendid, splendiferous (*Facetious*), stately, striking, sublime, sumptuous, superb, superior, transcendent **Antonyms** bad, humble, ignoble, lowly, mean, modest, ordinary, petty, poor, trivial, undistinguished, unimposing

magnify 1. aggrandize, amplify, augment, blow up (*Inf.*), boost, build up, deepen, di~ late, enlarge, expand, heighten, increase, intensify **2.** aggravate, blow up, blow up out of all proportion, dramatize, enhance, exaggerate, inflate, make a federal case of (*U.S. inf.*), make a mountain out of a mole~ hill, make a production (out) of (*Inf.*), over~ do, overemphasize, overestimate, overplay, overrate, overstate **Antonyms** belittle, decrease, deflate, depre~ cate, diminish, disparage, lessen, lower, minimize, reduce, shrink, understate

magniloquent bombastic, declamatory, el~ evated, exalted, grandiloquent, high-flown, high-sounding, lofty, orotund, overblown, pompous, pretentious, rhetorical, sonorous, stilted, turgid

magnitude 1. consequence, eminence, grandeur, greatness, importance, mark, moment, note, significance, weight **2.** amount, amplitude, bigness, bulk, capacity, dimensions, enormity, expanse, extent, hugeness, immensity, intensity, largeness, mass, measure, proportions, quantity, size, space, strength, vastness, volume **Antonyms** insignificance, meanness, small~ ness, triviality, unimportance

maid 1. damsel, girl, lass, lassie (*Inf.*), maiden, miss, nymph (*Poetic*), wench **2.** abigail (*Archaic*), handmaiden (*Archaic*), housemaid, maidservant, servant, serving-maid

maiden *n.* **1.** damsel, girl, lass, lassie (*Inf.*), maid, miss, nymph (*Poetic*), virgin, wench ~*adj.* **2.** chaste, intact, pure, undefiled, un~ married, unwed, virgin, virginal **3.** first, inaugural, initial, initiatory, introductory **4.** fresh, new, unbroached, untapped, un~ tried, unused

maidenly chaste, decent, decorous, demure, gentle, girlish, modest, pure, reserved, undefiled, unsullied, vestal, virginal, virtu~ous

Antonyms brazen, corrupt, defiled, de~praved, dirty, immodest, immoral, impure, indecent, loose, promiscuous, shameless, sin~ful, unchaste, wanton, wicked

mail n. **1.** correspondence, letters, packages, parcels, post **2.** post, postal service, postal system ~v. **3.** dispatch, forward, post, send, send by mail or post

maim cripple, disable, hamstring, hurt, im~pair, incapacitate, injure, lame, mangle, mar, mutilate, put out of action, wound

main adj. **1.** capital, cardinal, central, chief, critical, crucial, essential, foremost, head, leading, necessary, outstanding, paramount, particular, predominant, pre-eminent, premier, primary, prime, principal, special, supreme, vital **2.** absolute, brute, direct, downright, entire, mere, pure, sheer, un~disguised, utmost, utter ~n. **3.** cable, chan~nel, conduit, duct, line, pipe **4.** effort, force, might, potency, power, puissance, strength **5. in** (or **for**) **the main** for the most part, generally, in general, mainly, mostly, on the whole

Antonyms adj. auxiliary, dependent, insignificant, least, lesser, minor, secondary, subordinate, trivial, unimportant

mainly above all, chiefly, first and foremost, for the most part, generally, in general, in the main, largely, mostly, most of all, on the whole, overall, predominantly, primari~ly, principally, substantially, to the greatest extent, usually

mainstay anchor, backbone, bulwark, but~tress, chief support, linchpin, pillar, prop

maintain **1.** care for, carry on, conserve, continue, finance, keep, keep up, look after, nurture, perpetuate, preserve, prolong, pro~vide, retain, supply, support, sustain, take care of, uphold **2.** affirm, allege, assert, as~severate, aver, avow, claim, contend, de~clare, hold, insist, profess, state **3.** advo~cate, argue for, back, champion, defend, fight for, justify, plead for, stand by, take up the cudgels for, uphold, vindicate

Antonyms (sense 1) abolish, break off, con~clude, discontinue, drop, end, finish, give up, relinquish, suspend, terminate (sense 2) dis~avow (sense 3) abandon, desert

maintenance **1.** care, carrying-on, conser~vation, continuance, continuation, keeping, nurture, perpetuation, preservation, pro~longation, provision, repairs, retainment, supply, support, sustainment, sustention, upkeep **2.** aliment, alimony, allowance, food, keep, livelihood, living, subsistence, support, sustenance, upkeep

majestic august, awesome, dignified, el~evated, exalted, grand, grandiose, imperial, imposing, impressive, kingly, lofty, magnificent, monumental, noble, pompous, princely, regal, royal, splendid, splendifer~ous (Facetious), stately, sublime, superb

Antonyms humble, ignoble, lowly, mean, modest, ordinary, unassuming, undistin~guished, unimposing

majesty augustness, awesomeness, dignity, exaltedness, glory, grandeur, imposingness, impressiveness, kingliness, loftiness, magnificence, nobility, pomp, queenliness, royalty, splendour, state, stateliness, sub~limity

Antonyms disgrace, meanness, shame, triviality

major **1.** better, bigger, chief, elder, greater, head, higher, larger, lead, leading, main, most, senior, superior, supreme, uppermost **2.** critical, crucial, grave, great, important, mega (Sl.), notable, outstanding, pre~eminent, radical, serious, significant, vital, weighty

Antonyms auxiliary, inconsequential, insignificant, lesser, minor, secondary, smaller, subordinate, trivial, unimportant

majority **1.** best part, bulk, greater number, mass, more, most, plurality, preponderance, superiority **2.** adulthood, manhood, matur~ity, seniority, womanhood

make v. **1.** assemble, build, compose, con~stitute, construct, create, fabricate, fashion, forge, form, frame, manufacture, mould, originate, produce, put together, shape, synthesize **2.** accomplish, beget, bring about, cause, create, effect, engender, gen~erate, give rise to, lead to, occasion, prod~uce **3.** cause, coerce, compel, constrain, dragoon, drive, force, impel, induce, oblige, press, pressurize, prevail upon, railroad (Inf.), require **4.** appoint, assign, create, designate, elect, install, invest, nominate, ordain **5.** draw up, enact, establish, fix, form, frame, pass **6.** add up to, amount to, compose, constitute, embody, form, repre~sent **7.** act, carry out, do, effect, engage in, execute, perform, practise, prosecute **8.** calculate, estimate, gauge, judge, reckon, suppose, think **9.** acquire, clear, earn, gain, get, net, obtain, realize, secure, take in, win **10.** arrive at, arrive in time for, attain, catch, get to, meet, reach **11. make it** Inf. arrive (Inf.), be successful, come through, crack it (Inf.), cut it (Inf.), get on, get some~where, prosper, pull through, succeed, sur~vive ~n. **12.** brand, build, character, com~position, constitution, construction, cut, designation, form, kind, make-up, mark, model, shape, sort, structure, style, type, variety **13.** cast of mind, character, dispo~sition, frame of mind, humour, kidney, make-up, nature, stamp, temper, tempera~ment

make as if *or* **though** act as if *or* though, affect, feign, feint, give the impression that, make a show of, pretend

make away 1. abscond, beat a hasty re~ treat, clear out (*Inf.*), cut and run (*Inf.*), de~ camp, depart, do a runner (*Sl.*), flee, fly, fly the coop (*U.S. & Canad. inf.*), hook it (*Sl.*), make off, run away *or* off, run for it (*Inf.*), scoot, skedaddle (*Inf.*), slope off, take a powder (*U.S. & Canad. sl.*), take it on the lam (*U.S. & Canad. sl.*), take to one's heels **2.** *With* **with** abduct, cabbage (*Brit. sl.*), carry off, filch, kidnap, knock off (*Sl.*), make off with, nab (*Inf.*), nick (*Sl., chiefly Brit.*), pilfer, pinch (*Inf.*), purloin, steal, swipe (*Sl.*) **3.** *With* **with** blow away (*Sl., chiefly U.S.*), bump off (*Sl.*), destroy, dispose of, do away with, do in (*Sl.*), eliminate, get rid of, kill, murder, rub out (*U.S. sl.*)

make-believe 1. *n.* charade, dream, fanta~ sy, imagination, play-acting, pretence, un~ reality **2.** *adj.* dream, fantasized, fantasy, imaginary, imagined, made-up, mock, pre~ tend, pretended, sham, unreal
Antonyms *n.* actuality, fact, reality, truth~ fulness ~*adj.* authentic, genuine, real, un~ feigned

make believe act as if *or* though, dream, enact, fantasize, imagine, play, play-act, pretend

make do cope, get along *or* by, improvise, manage, muddle through, scrape along *or* by

make for 1. aim for, be bound for, head for *or* towards, proceed towards, steer (a course) for **2.** assail, assault, attack, fall on, fly at, go for, have a go at (*Inf.*), lunge at, set upon **3.** be conducive to, conduce to, contribute to, facilitate, favour, promote

make off 1. abscond, beat a hasty retreat, bolt, clear out (*Inf.*), cut and run (*Inf.*), de~ camp, do a runner (*Sl.*), flee, fly, fly the coop (*U.S. & Canad. inf.*), hook it (*Sl.*), make away, run away *or* off, run for it (*Inf.*), skedaddle (*Inf.*), slope off, take a powder (*U.S. & Canad. sl.*), take it on the lam (*U.S. & Canad. sl.*), take to one's heels **2.** *With* **with** abduct, cabbage (*Brit. sl.*), carry off, filch, kidnap, knock off (*Sl.*), make away with, nab (*Inf.*), nick (*Sl., chiefly Brit.*), pilfer, pinch (*Inf.*), purloin, run away *or* off with, steal, swipe (*Sl.*)

make out 1. descry, detect, discern, dis~ cover, distinguish, espy, perceive, recog~ nize, see **2.** comprehend, decipher, fathom, follow, grasp, perceive, realize, see, suss (out) (*Sl.*), understand, work out **3.** com~ plete, draw up, fill in *or* out, inscribe, write (out) **4.** demonstrate, describe, prove, rep~ resent, show **5.** assert, claim, let on, make

as if *or* though, pretend **6.** fare, get on, manage, prosper, succeed, thrive

maker author, builder, constructor, director, fabricator, framer, manufacturer, producer
Maker Creator, God

makeshift 1. *adj.* expedient, jury (*Chiefly nautical*), make-do, provisional, rough and ready, stopgap, substitute, temporary **2.** *n.* expedient, shift, stopgap, substitute

make-up 1. cosmetics, face (*Inf.*), grease~ paint (*Theatre*), *maquillage,* paint (*Inf.*), powder, war paint (*Inf., humorous*) **2.** arrangement, assembly, composition, configuration, constitution, construction, form, format, formation, organization, structure **3.** build, cast of mind, character, constitution, disposition, figure, frame of mind, make, nature, stamp, temper, tem~ perament

make up 1. compose, comprise, constitute, form **2.** coin, compose, concoct, construct, cook up (*Inf.*), create, devise, dream up, fabricate, formulate, frame, hatch, invent, manufacture, originate, trump up, write **3.** complete, fill, meet, supply **4.** *With* **for** atone, balance, compensate, make amends, offset, recompense, redeem, redress, requite **5.** bury the hatchet, call it quits, come to terms, compose, forgive and forget, make peace, mend, reconcile, settle, shake hands **6. make up one's mind** choose, come to a decision, decide, determine, make a deci~ sion, reach a decision, resolve, settle **7. make up to** *Inf.* chat up (*Inf.*), court, curry favour with, flirt with, make overtures to, woo

making 1. assembly, building, composition, construction, creation, fabrication, forging, manufacture, production **2. in the making** budding, coming, emergent, growing, nas~ cent, potential

makings 1. beginnings, capability, capac~ ity, ingredients, materials, potentiality, po~ tential(s), qualities **2.** earnings, income, proceeds, profits, returns, revenue, takings

maladjusted alienated, disturbed, es~ tranged, hung-up (*Sl.*), neurotic, unstable

maladministration blundering, bungling, corruption, dishonesty, incompetence, inefficiency, malfeasance (*Law*), malprac~ tice, misgovernment, mismanagement, mis~ rule

malady affliction, ailment, complaint, dis~ ease, disorder, ill, illness, indisposition, infirmity, sickness

malaise angst, anxiety, depression, discom~ fort, disquiet, doldrums, enervation, illness, lassitude, melancholy, sickness, unease, weakness

malcontent 1. *adj.* disaffected, discontent~

ed, disgruntled, disgusted, dissatisfied, dis~ sentious, factious, ill-disposed, rebellious, resentful, restive, unhappy, unsatisfied **2.** *n.* agitator, complainer, fault-finder, grouch (*Inf.*), grouser, grumbler, mischief-maker, rebel, stirrer (*Inf.*), troublemaker

male manful, manlike, manly, masculine, virile
Antonyms camp (*Inf.*), effeminate, female, feminine, unmanly, wimpish *or* wimpy (*Inf.*), womanish, womanly

malefactor convict, criminal, crook (*Inf.*), culprit, delinquent, evildoer, felon, law~ breaker, miscreant, offender, outlaw, trans~ gressor, villain, wrongdoer

malevolence hate, hatred, ill will, malice, maliciousness, malignity, rancour, spite, spitefulness, vengefulness, vindictiveness

malevolent baleful, evil-minded, hateful (*Archaic*), hostile, ill-natured, maleficent, malicious, malign, malignant, pernicious, rancorous, spiteful, vengeful, vicious, vin~ dictive
Antonyms amiable, benevolent, benign, friendly, gracious, kind, warm-hearted

malformation crookedness, deformity, distortion, misshape, misshapenness

malformed abnormal, contorted, crooked, deformed, distorted, irregular, misshapen, twisted

malfunction 1. *v.* break down, develop a fault, fail, go wrong **2.** *n.* breakdown, de~ fect, failure, fault, flaw, glitch, impairment

malice animosity, animus, bad blood, bit~ terness, enmity, evil intent, hate, hatred, ill will, malevolence, maliciousness, malignity, rancour, spite, spitefulness, spleen, venge~ fulness, venom, vindictiveness

malicious baleful, bitchy (*Inf.*), bitter, catty (*Inf.*), evil-minded, hateful, ill-disposed, ill-natured, injurious, malevolent, malignant, mischievous, pernicious, rancorous, resent~ ful, shrewish, spiteful, vengeful, vicious
Antonyms amiable, benevolent, friendly, kind, warm-hearted

malign 1. *adj.* bad, baleful, baneful, del~ eterious, destructive, evil, harmful, hostile, hurtful, injurious, maleficent, malevolent, malignant, pernicious, vicious, wicked **2.** *v.* abuse, asperse, bad-mouth (*Sl., chiefly U.S. & Canad.*), blacken (someone's name), ca~ lumniate, defame, denigrate, derogate, dis~ parage, do a hatchet job on (*Inf.*), harm, in~ jure, knock (*Inf.*), libel, revile, rubbish (*Inf.*), run down, slag (off) (*Sl.*), slander, smear, speak ill of, traduce, vilify
Antonyms *adj.* agreeable, amiable, beneficial, benevolent, benign, friendly, good, harmless, honourable, innocuous, kind, mor~ al, virtuous, warm-hearted, wholesome ~*v.* commend, compliment, extol, praise

malignant 1. baleful, bitter, destructive, harmful, hostile, hurtful, inimical, injuri~ ous, maleficent, malevolent, malicious, ma~ lign, of evil intent, pernicious, spiteful, vi~ cious **2.** *Medical* cancerous, dangerous, deadly, evil, fatal, irremediable, metastatic, uncontrollable, virulent
Antonyms (*sense 1*) amicable, benign, friendly, kind, warm-hearted (*sense 2*) benign

malpractice 1. abuse, dereliction, misbe~ haviour, misconduct, mismanagement, neg~ ligence **2.** abuse, misdeed, offence, trans~ gression

maltreat abuse, bully, damage, handle roughly, harm, hurt, ill-treat, injure, mis~ treat

mammoth Brobdingnagian, colossal, el~ ephantine, enormous, gargantuan, giant, gigantic, ginormous (*Inf.*), huge, humongous *or* humungous (*U.S. sl.*), immense, jumbo (*Inf.*), massive, mega (*Sl.*), mighty, monu~ mental, mountainous, prodigious, stupen~ dous, titanic, vast
Antonyms diminutive, insignificant, little, miniature, minute, puny, small, tiny, trivial

man *n.* **1.** bloke (*Brit. inf.*), chap (*Inf.*), gentleman, guy (*Inf.*), male **2.** adult, being, body, human, human being, individual, one, person, personage, somebody, soul **3.** Homo sapiens, humanity, humankind, human race, mankind, mortals, people **4.** attend~ ant, employee, follower, hand, hireling, liegeman, manservant, retainer, servant, soldier, subject, subordinate, valet, vassal, worker, workman **5.** beau, boyfriend, hus~ band, lover, partner, significant other (*U.S. inf.*), spouse **6. to a man** bar none, every one, one and all, unanimously, without ex~ ception ~*v.* **7.** crew, fill, furnish with men, garrison, occupy, people, staff

manacle 1. *n.* bond, chain, fetter, gyve (*Ar~ chaic*), handcuff, iron, shackle, tie **2.** *v.* bind, chain, check, clap *or* put in irons, confine, constrain, curb, fetter, hamper, handcuff, inhibit, put in chains, restrain, shackle, tie one's hands

manage 1. administer, be in charge (of), command, concert, conduct, direct, govern, handle, manipulate, oversee, preside over, rule, run, superintend, supervise **2.** accom~ plish, arrange, bring about *or* off, contrive, cope with, crack it (*Inf.*), cut it (*Inf.*), deal with, effect, engineer, succeed **3.** control, dominate, govern, guide, handle, influence, manipulate, operate, pilot, ply, steer, train, use, wield **4.** carry on, cope, fare, get along, get by (*Inf.*), get on, make do, make out, muddle through, shift, survive
Antonyms bodge (*Inf.*), botch, fail, follow, make a mess of, mismanage, muff, spoil, starve

manageable amenable, compliant, controllable, convenient, docile, easy, governable, handy, submissive, tamable, tractable, user-friendly, wieldy
Antonyms demanding, difficult, disobedient, hard, headstrong, obstinate, refractory, stubborn, ungovernable, unruly, unyielding, wild

management 1. administration, board, bosses (*Inf.*), directorate, directors, employers, executive(s) **2.** administration, care, charge, command, conduct, control, direction, governance, government, guidance, handling, manipulation, operation, rule, running, superintendence, supervision

manager administrator, boss (*Inf.*), comptroller, conductor, controller, director, executive, gaffer (*Inf., chiefly Brit.*), governor, head, organizer, overseer, proprietor, superintendent, supervisor

mandate authority, authorization, bidding, charge, command, commission, decree, directive, edict, fiat, injunction, instruction, order, precept, sanction, warrant

mandatory binding, compulsory, obligatory, required, requisite
Antonyms discretionary, nonbinding, noncompulsory, nonobligatory, optional, unnecessary, voluntary

manful bold, brave, courageous, daring, determined, gallant, hardy, heroic, indomitable, intrepid, manly, noble, powerful, resolute, stalwart, stout, stout-hearted, strong, valiant, vigorous

manfully boldly, bravely, courageously, desperately, determinedly, gallantly, hard, heroically, intrepidly, like a Trojan, like one possessed, like the devil, nobly, powerfully, resolutely, stalwartly, stoutly, strongly, to the best of one's ability, valiantly, vigorously, with might and main

mangle butcher, cripple, crush, cut, deform, destroy, disfigure, distort, hack, lacerate, maim, mar, maul, mutilate, rend, ruin, spoil, tear, total (*Sl.*), trash (*Sl.*), wreck

mangy dirty, grungy (*Sl., chiefly U.S.*), mean, moth-eaten, scabby (*Inf.*), scruffy, scuzzy (*Sl., chiefly U.S.*), seedy, shabby, shoddy, squalid
Antonyms attractive, choice, clean, de luxe, fine, splendid, spotless, superb, tidy, well-dressed, well-kempt, well-kept

manhandle 1. handle roughly, knock about *or* around, maul, paw (*Inf.*), pull, push, rough up **2.** carry, haul, heave, hump (*Brit. sl.*), lift, manoeuvre, pull, push, shove, tug

manhood bravery, courage, determination, firmness, fortitude, hardihood, manfulness, manliness, masculinity, maturity, mettle, resolution, spirit, strength, valour, virility

mania 1. aberration, craziness, delirium, dementia, derangement, disorder, frenzy, insanity, lunacy, madness **2.** cacoethes, craving, craze, desire, enthusiasm, fad (*Inf.*), fetish, fixation, obsession, partiality, passion, preoccupation, rage, thing (*Inf.*)

maniac 1. headbanger (*Inf.*), headcase (*Inf.*), loony (*Sl.*), lunatic, madman, madwoman, nutcase (*Sl.*), nutter (*Brit. sl.*), psycho (*Sl.*), psychopath **2.** enthusiast, fan, fanatic, fiend (*Inf.*), freak (*Inf.*)

manifest 1. *adj.* apparent, blatant, clear, conspicuous, distinct, evident, glaring, noticeable, obvious, open, palpable, patent, plain, unmistakable, visible **2.** *v.* declare, demonstrate, display, establish, evince, exhibit, expose, express, make plain, prove, reveal, set forth, show
Antonyms *adj.* concealed, disguised, hidden, inconspicuous, indistinct, masked, suppressed, unapparent, vague, veiled ~*v.* conceal, cover, cover up, deny, hide, mask, obscure, refute

manifestation appearance, demonstration, disclosure, display, exhibition, exposure, expression, indication, instance, mark, materialization, revelation, show, sign, symptom, token

manifold abundant, assorted, copious, diverse, diversified, many, multifarious, multifold, multiple, multiplied, multitudinous, numerous, varied, various

manipulate 1. employ, handle, operate, ply, use, wield, work **2.** conduct, control, direct, engineer, guide, influence, manoeuvre, negotiate, steer

mankind Homo sapiens, humanity, humankind, human race, man, people

manliness boldness, bravery, courage, fearlessness, firmness, hardihood, heroism, independence, intrepidity, machismo, manfulness, manhood, masculinity, mettle, resolution, stoutheartedness, valour, vigour, virility

manly bold, brave, butch (*Sl.*), courageous, daring, dauntless, fearless, gallant, hardy, heroic, macho, male, manful, masculine, muscular, noble, powerful, Ramboesque, red-blooded (*Inf.*), resolute, robust, stout-hearted, strapping, strong, valiant, valorous, vigorous, virile, well-built
Antonyms camp (*Inf.*), cowardly, craven, delicate, effeminate, faint-hearted, feeble, feminine, frail, ignoble, irresolute, sickly, soft, timid, unmanly, weak, wimpish *or* wimpy (*Inf.*), womanish

man-made artificial, ersatz, manufactured, plastic (*Sl.*), synthetic

manner 1. air, appearance, aspect, bearing, behaviour, comportment, conduct, demeanour, deportment, look, mien (*Literary*),

presence, tone **2.** approach, custom, fash~
ion, form, genre, habit, line, means, meth~
od, mode, practice, procedure, process, rou~
tine, style, tack, tenor, usage, way, wont **3.**
brand, breed, category, form, kind, nature,
sort, type, variety

mannered affected, artificial, posed, pre~
tentious, pseudo (*Inf.*), put-on, stilted
Antonyms genuine, honest, natural, real,
sincere, unaffected, unpretentious

mannerism characteristic, foible, habit,
idiosyncrasy, peculiarity, quirk, trait, trick

mannerly civil, civilized, courteous, deco~
rous, genteel, gentlemanly, gracious, lady~
like, polished, polite, refined, respectful,
well-behaved, well-bred, well-mannered
Antonyms boorish, discourteous, disre~
spectful, ill-mannered, impertinent, impolite,
impudent, insolent, rude, unmannerly

manners 1. bearing, behaviour, breeding,
carriage, comportment, conduct, demean~
our, deportment **2.** ceremony, courtesy, de~
corum, etiquette, formalities, good form,
polish, politeness, politesse, proprieties,
protocol, refinement, social graces, the done
thing

manoeuvre *n.* **1.** action, artifice, dodge,
intrigue, machination, move, movement,
plan, plot, ploy, ruse, scheme, stratagem,
subterfuge, tactic, trick **2.** deployment,
evolution, exercise, movement, operation
~*v.* **3.** contrive, devise, engineer, intrigue,
machinate, manage, manipulate, plan, plot,
pull strings, scheme, wangle (*Inf.*) **4.** de~
ploy, exercise, move **5.** direct, drive, guide,
handle, navigate, negotiate, pilot, steer

mansion abode, dwelling, habitation, hall,
manor, residence, seat, villa

mantle *n.* **1.** *Archaic* cape, cloak, hood,
shawl, wrap **2.** blanket, canopy, cloud, cov~
er, covering, curtain, envelope, pall, screen,
shroud, veil ~*v.* **3.** blanket, cloak, cloud,
cover, disguise, envelop, hide, mask, over~
spread, screen, shroud, veil, wrap

manual 1. *adj.* done by hand, hand-
operated, human, physical **2.** *n.* bible, en~
chiridion (*Rare*), guide, guidebook, hand~
book, instructions, workbook

manufacture *v.* **1.** assemble, build, com~
pose, construct, create, fabricate, forge,
form, make, mass-produce, mould, process,
produce, put together, shape, turn out **2.**
concoct, cook up (*Inf.*), devise, fabricate,
hatch, invent, make up, think up, trump up
~*n.* **3.** assembly, construction, creation,
fabrication, making, mass-production, pro~
duce, production

manufacturer builder, constructor, crea~
tor, fabricator, factory-owner, industrialist,
maker, producer

manure compost, droppings, dung, excre~
ment, fertilizer, muck, ordure

many *adj.* **1.** abundant, copious, countless,
divers (*Archaic*), frequent, innumerable,
manifold, multifarious, multifold, multitu~
dinous, myriad, numerous, profuse, sundry,
umpteen (*Inf.*), varied, various ~*n.* **2.** a
horde, a lot, a mass, a multitude, a thou~
sand and one, heaps (*Inf.*), large numbers,
lots (*Inf.*), piles (*Inf.*), plenty, scores, tons
(*Inf.*), umpteen (*Inf.*) **3. the many** crowd,
hoi polloi, majority, masses, multitude,
people, rank and file

mar blemish, blight, blot, damage, deface,
detract from, disfigure, harm, hurt, impair,
injure, maim, mangle, mutilate, ruin, scar,
spoil, stain, sully, taint, tarnish, vitiate
Antonyms adorn, ameliorate, better, em~
bellish, improve, ornament

maraud despoil, forage, foray, harry, loot,
pillage, plunder, raid, ransack, ravage,
reive (*Dialect*), sack

marauder bandit, brigand, buccaneer, cat~
eran (*Scot.*), corsair, freebooter, moss~
trooper, outlaw, pillager, pirate, plunderer,
raider, ravager, reiver (*Dialect*), robber

march *v.* **1.** file, footslog, pace, parade,
stalk, stride, strut, tramp, tread, walk ~*n.*
2. hike, routemarch, tramp, trek, walk **3.**
demo (*Inf.*), demonstration, parade, proces~
sion **4.** gait, pace, step, stride **5.** advance,
development, evolution, progress, progres~
sion **6. on the march** advancing, afoot,
astir, en route, marching, on one's way, on
the way, proceeding, progressing, under
way

marches borderland, borders, boundaries,
confines, frontiers, limits, marchlands

margin 1. border, bound, boundary, brim,
brink, confine, edge, limit, perimeter, pe~
riphery, rim, side, verge **2.** allowance,
compass, elbowroom, extra, latitude, lee~
way, play, room, scope, space, surplus

marginal 1. bordering, borderline, on the
edge, peripheral **2.** insignificant, low, mini~
mal, minor, negligible, slight, small

marijuana bhang, cannabis, charas, dope
(*Sl.*), ganja, grass (*Sl.*), hash (*Sl.*), hashish,
hemp, kif, leaf (*Sl.*), mary jane (*U.S. sl.*), pot
(*Sl.*), sinsemilla, smoke (*Inf.*), stuff (*Sl.*), tea
(*U.S. sl.*), weed (*Sl.*)

marine maritime, nautical, naval, ocean-
going, oceanic, pelagic, saltwater, sea, sea~
faring, seagoing, thalassic

mariner bluejacket, gob (*U.S. sl.*), hand,
Jack Tar, matelot (*Sl., chiefly Brit.*.), navi~
gator, sailor, salt, sea dog, seafarer, sea~
faring man, seaman, tar

marital conjugal, connubial, married, mat~
rimonial, nuptial, spousal, wedded

maritime 1. marine, nautical, naval, oceanic, sea, seafaring **2.** coastal, littoral, seaside

mark *n.* **1.** blemish, blot, blotch, bruise, dent, impression, line, nick, pock, scar, scratch, smirch, smudge, splotch, spot, stain, streak **2.** badge, blaze, brand, characteristic, device, earmark, emblem, evidence, feature, flag, hallmark, impression, incision, index, indication, label, note, print, proof, seal, sign, signet, stamp, symbol, symptom, token **3.** criterion, level, measure, norm, par, standard, yardstick **4.** aim, end, goal, object, objective, purpose, target **5.** consequence, dignity, distinction, eminence, fame, importance, influence, notability, note, notice, prestige, quality, regard, standing **6.** footmark, footprint, sign, trace, track, trail, vestige **7. make one's mark** achieve recognition, be a success, find a place in the sun, get on in the world, make a success of oneself, make good, make it (*Inf.*), make something of oneself, prosper, succeed ~*v.* **8.** blemish, blot, blotch, brand, bruise, dent, impress, imprint, nick, scar, scratch, smirch, smudge, splotch, stain, streak **9.** brand, characterize, flag, identify, label, stamp **10.** betoken, denote, distinguish, evince, exemplify, illustrate, show **11.** attend, hearken (*Archaic*), mind, note, notice, observe, pay attention, pay heed, regard, remark, watch **12.** appraise, assess, correct, evaluate, grade

marked apparent, blatant, clear, considerable, conspicuous, decided, distinct, evident, manifest, notable, noted, noticeable, obvious, outstanding, patent, prominent, pronounced, remarkable, salient, signal, striking
Antonyms concealed, doubtful, dubious, hidden, imperceptible, inconspicuous, indistinct, insignificant, obscure, unclear, unnoticeable, vague

markedly clearly, considerably, conspicuously, decidedly, distinctly, evidently, greatly, manifestly, notably, noticeably, obviously, outstandingly, patently, remarkably, signally, strikingly, to a great extent

market 1. *n.* bazaar, fair, mart **2.** *v.* offer for sale, retail, sell, vend

marketable in demand, merchantable, salable, sought after, vendible, wanted

marksman, -woman crack shot (*Inf.*), deadeye (*Inf., chiefly U.S.*), dead shot (*Inf.*), good shot, sharpshooter

maroon abandon, cast ashore, cast away, desert, leave, leave high and dry (*Inf.*), strand

marriage 1. espousal, match, matrimony, nuptial rites, nuptials, wedding, wedding ceremony, wedlock **2.** alliance, amalgamation, association, confederation, coupling, link, merger, union

married 1. hitched (*Sl.*), joined, one, spliced (*Inf.*), united, wed, wedded **2.** conjugal, connubial, husbandly, marital, matrimonial, nuptial, spousal, wifely

marrow core, cream, essence, gist, heart, kernel, pith, quick, quintessence, soul, spirit, substance

marry 1. become man and wife, espouse, get hitched (*Sl.*), get spliced (*Inf.*), take the plunge (*Inf.*), take to wife, tie the knot (*Inf.*), walk down the aisle (*Inf.*), wed, wive (*Archaic*) **2.** ally, bond, join, knit, link, match, merge, splice, tie, unify, unite, yoke

marsh bog, fen, morass, moss (*Scot. & northern English dialect*), quagmire, slough, swamp

marshal 1. align, arrange, array, assemble, collect, deploy, dispose, draw up, gather, group, line up, muster, order, organize, rank **2.** conduct, escort, guide, lead, shepherd, usher

marshy boggy, fenny, miry, quaggy, spongy, swampy, waterlogged, wet

martial bellicose, belligerent, brave, heroic, military, soldierly, warlike

martinet disciplinarian, drillmaster, stickler

martyrdom agony, anguish, ordeal, persecution, suffering, torment, torture
Antonyms bliss, ecstasy, happiness, joy

marvel 1. *v.* be amazed, be awed, be filled with surprise, gape, gaze, goggle, wonder **2.** *n.* genius, miracle, phenomenon, portent, prodigy, whiz (*Inf.*), wonder

marvellous 1. amazing, astonishing, astounding, breathtaking, brilliant, extraordinary, miraculous, phenomenal, prodigious, remarkable, sensational (*Inf.*), singular, spectacular, stupendous, wondrous (*Archaic or literary*) **2.** difficult *or* hard to believe, fabulous, fantastic, implausible, improbable, incredible, surprising, unbelievable, unlikely **3.** *Inf.* bad (*Sl.*), boffo (*Sl.*), brill (*Inf.*), chillin' (*U.S. sl.*), colossal, cracking (*Brit. inf.*), crucial (*Sl.*), def (*Sl.*), excellent, fabulous (*Inf.*), fantastic (*Inf.*), glorious, great (*Inf.*), jim-dandy (*Sl.*), magnificent, mean (*Sl.*), mega (*Sl.*), sensational (*Inf.*), smashing (*Inf.*), sovereign, splendid, stupendous, super (*Inf.*), superb, terrific (*Inf.*), topping (*Brit. sl.*), wicked (*Inf.*), wonderful
Antonyms awful, bad, believable, commonplace, credible, everyday, ordinary, terrible

masculine 1. male, manful, manlike, manly, mannish, virile **2.** bold, brave, butch (*Sl.*), gallant, hardy, macho, muscular, powerful, Ramboesque, red-blooded (*Inf.*), reso~

lute, robust, stout-hearted, strapping, strong, vigorous, well-built

mask n. **1.** domino, false face, visor, vizard (*Archaic*) **2.** blind, camouflage, cloak, concealment, cover, cover-up, disguise, façade, front, guise, screen, semblance, show, veil, veneer ~v. **3.** camouflage, cloak, conceal, cover, disguise, hide, obscure, screen, veil

mass n. **1.** block, chunk, concretion, hunk, lump, piece **2.** aggregate, body, collection, entirety, sum, sum total, totality, whole **3.** accumulation, aggregation, assemblage, batch, bunch, collection, combination, conglomeration, heap, load, lot, pile, quantity, stack **4.** assemblage, band, body, bunch (*Inf.*), crowd, group, horde, host, lot, mob, number, throng, troop **5.** body, bulk, greater part, lion's share, majority, preponderance **6.** bulk, dimension, greatness, magnitude, size **7. the masses** commonalty, common people, crowd, hoi polloi, multitude ~adj. **8.** extensive, general, indiscriminate, large-scale, pandemic, popular, wholesale, widespread ~v. **9.** accumulate, amass, assemble, collect, congregate, forgather, gather, mob, muster, rally, swarm, throng

massacre 1. n. annihilation, blood bath, butchery, carnage, extermination, holocaust, killing, mass slaughter, murder, slaughter **2.** v. annihilate, blow away (*Sl., chiefly U.S.*), butcher, cut to pieces, exterminate, kill, mow down, murder, slaughter, slay, take out (*Sl.*), wipe out

massage 1. n. acupressure, kneading, manipulation, reflexology, rubbing, rub-down, shiatsu **2.** v. knead, manipulate, rub, rub down

massive big, bulky, colossal, elephantine, enormous, extensive, gargantuan, gigantic, ginormous (*Inf.*), great, heavy, hefty, huge, hulking, humongous or humungous (*U.S. sl.*), immense, imposing, impressive, mammoth, mega (*Sl.*), monster, monumental, ponderous, solid, substantial, titanic, vast, weighty, whacking (*Inf.*), whopping (*Inf.*)
Antonyms frail, light, little, minute, petty, slight, small, thin, tiny, trivial

master n. **1.** boss (*Inf.*), captain, chief, commander, controller, director, employer, governor, head, lord, manager, overlord, overseer, owner, principal, ruler, skipper (*Inf.*), superintendent **2.** ace (*Inf.*), adept, dab hand (*Brit. inf.*), doyen, expert, genius, grandmaster, maestro, maven (*U.S.*), past master, pro (*Inf.*), virtuoso, wizard **3.** guide, guru, instructor, pedagogue, preceptor, schoolmaster, spiritual leader, swami, teacher, tutor ~adj. **4.** adept, crack (*Inf.*), expert, masterly, proficient, skilful, skilled **5.** chief, controlling, foremost, grand, great,

leading, main, predominant, prime, principal ~v. **6.** acquire, become proficient in, get the hang of (*Inf.*), grasp, learn **7.** bridle, check, conquer, curb, defeat, lick (*Inf.*), overcome, overpower, quash, quell, subdue, subjugate, suppress, tame, triumph over, vanquish **8.** command, control, direct, dominate, govern, manage, regulate, rule
Antonyms n. (*sense 1*) crew, servant, slave, subject (*sense 2*) amateur, novice (*sense 3*) student ~adj. (*sense 4*) amateurish, clumsy, incompetent, inept, novice, unaccomplished, unskilled, untalented (*sense 5*) lesser, minor ~v. (*sense 7*) give in, surrender, yield

masterful 1. adept, adroit, clever, consummate, crack (*Inf.*), deft, dexterous, excellent, expert, exquisite, fine, finished, first-rate, masterly, skilful, skilled, superior, superlative, supreme, world-class **2.** arrogant, authoritative, bossy (*Inf.*), despotic, dictatorial, domineering, high-handed, imperious, magisterial, overbearing, overweening, peremptory, self-willed, tyrannical
Antonyms (*sense 1*) amateurish, clumsy, incompetent, inept, unaccomplished, unskilled, untalented (*sense 2*) irresolute, meek, spineless, weak, wimpish or wimpy (*Inf.*)

masterly adept, adroit, clever, consummate, crack (*Inf.*), dexterous, excellent, expert, exquisite, fine, finished, first-rate, masterful, skilful, skilled, superior, superlative, supreme, world-class

mastermind 1. v. be the brains behind (*Inf.*), conceive, devise, direct, manage, organize, plan **2.** n. architect, authority, brain(s) (*Inf.*), brainbox, director, engineer, genius, intellect, manager, organizer, planner, virtuoso

masterpiece chef d'oeuvre, classic, jewel, magnum opus, master work, pièce de résistance, tour de force

mastery 1. command, comprehension, familiarity, grasp, knowledge, understanding **2.** ability, acquirement, attainment, cleverness, deftness, dexterity, expertise, finesse, know-how (*Inf.*), proficiency, prowess, skill, virtuosity **3.** ascendancy, authority, command, conquest, control, domination, dominion, pre-eminence, rule, superiority, supremacy, sway, triumph, upper hand, victory, whip hand

match n. **1.** bout, competition, contest, game, head-to-head, test, trial **2.** competitor, counterpart, equal, equivalent, peer, rival **3.** companion, complement, counterpart, equal, equivalent, fellow, mate, tally **4.** copy, dead ringer (*Sl.*), double, duplicate, equal, lookalike, replica, ringer (*Sl.*), spit (*Inf., chiefly Brit.*), spit and image (*Inf.*), spitting image (*Inf.*), twin **5.** affiliation, alliance, combination, couple, duet, item

(*Inf.*), marriage, pair, pairing, partnership, union ~*v.* **6.** ally, combine, couple, join, link, marry, mate, pair, unite, yoke **7.** accompany, accord, adapt, agree, blend, coordinate, correspond, fit, go with, harmonize, suit, tally, tone with **8.** compare, compete, contend, emulate, equal, measure up to, oppose, pit against, rival, vie

matching analogous, comparable, coordinating, corresponding, double, duplicate, equal, equivalent, identical, like, paired, parallel, same, toning, twin
Antonyms different, disparate, dissimilar, distinct, divergent, diverse, nonparallel, other, unequal, unlike

matchless consummate, exquisite, incomparable, inimitable, peerless, perfect, superlative, supreme, unequalled, unique, unmatched, unparalleled, unrivalled, unsurpassed
Antonyms average, cheaper, common, commonplace, comparable, equalled, everyday, excelled, inferior, lesser, mediocre, ordinary, second-class, surpassed

mate *n.* **1.** better half (*Humorous*), husband, partner, significant other (*U.S. inf.*), spouse, wife **2.** *Inf.* buddy (*Inf.*), china (*Brit. sl.*), chum (*Brit. inf.*), cock (*Brit. inf.*), comrade, crony, friend, pal (*Inf.*) **3.** associate, colleague, companion, compeer, co-worker, fellow-worker **4.** assistant, helper, subordinate **5.** companion, double, fellow, match, twin ~*v.* **6.** breed, copulate, couple, pair **7.** marry, match, wed **8.** couple, join, match, pair, yoke

material *n.* **1.** body, constituents, element, matter, stuff, substance **2.** data, evidence, facts, information, notes, work **3.** cloth, fabric, stuff ~*adj.* **4.** bodily, concrete, corporeal, fleshly, nonspiritual, palpable, physical, substantial, tangible, worldly **5.** consequential, essential, grave, important, indispensable, key, meaningful, momentous, serious, significant, vital, weighty **6.** applicable, apposite, apropos, germane, pertinent, relevant

materialize appear, come about, come into being, come to pass, happen, occur, take place, take shape, turn up

materially considerably, essentially, gravely, greatly, much, seriously, significantly, substantially
Antonyms barely, hardly, insignificantly, little, scarcely, superficially, unsubstantially

maternal motherly

maternity motherhood, motherliness

matrimonial conjugal, connubial, hymeneal, marital, married, nuptial, spousal, wedded, wedding

matrimony marital rites, marriage, nuptials, wedding ceremony, wedlock

matrix forge, mould, origin, source, womb

matted knotted, tangled, tousled, uncombed

matter *n.* **1.** body, material, stuff, substance **2.** affair, business, concern, episode, event, incident, issue, occurrence, proceeding, question, situation, subject, thing, topic, transaction **3.** amount, quantity, sum **4.** argument, context, purport, sense, subject, substance, text, thesis **5.** consequence, import, importance, moment, note, significance, weight **6.** complication, difficulty, distress, problem, trouble, upset, worry **7.** *Medical* discharge, purulence, pus, secretion ~*v.* **8.** be important, be of consequence, carry weight, count, have influence, make a difference, mean something, signify

matter-of-fact deadpan, down-to-earth, dry, dull, emotionless, flat, lifeless, mundane, plain, prosaic, sober, unembellished, unimaginative, unsentimental, unvarnished

mature 1. *adj.* adult, complete, fit, full-blown, full-grown, fully fledged, grown, grown-up, matured, mellow, of age, perfect, prepared, ready, ripe, ripened, seasoned **2.** *v.* age, become adult, bloom, blossom, come of age, develop, grow up, maturate, mellow, perfect, reach adulthood, ripen, season
Antonyms adolescent, childish, green, immature, incomplete, juvenile, puerile, undeveloped, unfinished, unperfected, unripe, young, youthful

maturity adulthood, completion, experience, full bloom, full growth, fullness, majority, manhood, maturation, matureness, perfection, ripeness, wisdom, womanhood
Antonyms childishness, excitability, immaturity, imperfection, incompletion, irresponsibility, juvenility, puerility, youthfulness

maudlin lachrymose, mawkish, mushy (*Inf.*), overemotional, sentimental, slushy (*Inf.*), soppy (*Brit. inf.*), tearful, weepy (*Inf.*)

maul 1. abuse, handle roughly, ill-treat, manhandle, molest, paw **2.** batter, beat, beat up (*Inf.*), claw, knock about *or* around, lacerate, lambast(e), mangle, pummel, rough up, thrash

maunder 1. dawdle, dilly-dally (*Inf.*), drift, idle, loaf, meander, mooch (*Sl.*), potter, ramble, straggle, stray, traipse (*Inf.*) **2.** babble, blather, blether, chatter, gabble, prattle, rabbit (on) (*Brit. inf.*), ramble, rattle on, waffle (*Inf., chiefly Brit.*), witter (*Inf.*)

mawkish 1. emotional, feeble, gushy (*Inf.*), maudlin, mushy (*Inf.*), schmaltzy (*Sl.*), sentimental, slushy (*Inf.*), soppy (*Brit. inf.*) **2.** disgusting, flat, foul, insipid, jejune, loathsome, nauseous, offensive, stale, vapid

maxim adage, aphorism, apophthegm, axiom, byword, dictum, gnome, motto, proverb, rule, saw, saying

maximum 1. *n.* apogee, ceiling, crest, ex~
tremity, height, most, peak, pinnacle, sum~
mit, top, upper limit, utmost, uttermost,
zenith **2.** *adj.* greatest, highest, maximal,
most, paramount, supreme, topmost, utmost
Antonyms bottom, least, lowest, minimum

maybe it could be, mayhap (*Archaic*), per~
adventure (*Archaic*), perchance (*Archaic*),
perhaps, possibly

mayhem chaos, commotion, confusion, de~
struction, disorder, fracas, havoc, trouble,
violence

maze 1. convolutions, intricacy, labyrinth,
meander **2.** *Fig.* bewilderment, confusion,
imbroglio, mesh, perplexity, puzzle, snarl,
tangle, uncertainty, web

meadow field, grassland, lea (*Poetic*), ley,
pasture

meagre 1. deficient, exiguous, inadequate,
insubstantial, little, measly, paltry, pathetic,
poor, puny, scanty, scrimpy, short, skimpy,
slender, slight, small, spare, sparse **2.** bony,
emaciated, gaunt, hungry, lank, lean,
scraggy, scrawny, skinny, starved, thin,
underfed **3.** barren, infertile, poor, unfruit~
ful, unproductive, weak

mean[1] *v.* **1.** betoken, connote, convey, de~
note, drive at, express, hint at, imply, indi~
cate, purport, represent, say, signify, spell,
stand for, suggest, symbolize **2.** aim, aspire,
contemplate, design, desire, have in mind,
intend, plan, propose, purpose, set out,
want, wish **3.** design, destine, fate, fit,
make, match, predestine, preordain, suit **4.**
bring about, cause, engender, entail, give
rise to, involve, lead to, necessitate, prod~
uce, result in **5.** adumbrate, augur, betoken,
foreshadow, foretell, herald, portend, pres~
age, promise

mean[2] *adj.* **1.** beggarly, close, mercenary,
mingy (*Brit. inf.*), miserly, near (*Inf.*), nig~
gardly, parsimonious, penny-pinching, pe~
nurious, selfish, skimpy, stingy, tight,
tight-arsed (*Taboo sl.*), tight as a duck's
arse (*Taboo sl.*), tight-assed (*U.S. taboo sl.*),
tight-fisted, ungenerous **2.** bad-tempered,
cantankerous, churlish, disagreeable, hos~
tile, ill-tempered, malicious, nasty, rude,
sour, unfriendly, unpleasant **3.** abject, base,
callous, contemptible, degenerate, degraded,
despicable, disgraceful, dishonourable,
hard-hearted, ignoble, low-minded, narrow-
minded, petty, scurvy, shabby, shameful,
sordid, vile, wretched **4.** beggarly, con~
temptible, down-at-heel, grungy (*Sl., chiefly
U.S.*), insignificant, miserable, paltry, petty,
poor, run-down, scruffy, scuzzy (*Sl., chiefly
U.S.*), seedy, shabby, sordid, squalid, taw~
dry, wretched **5.** base, baseborn (*Archaic*),
common, humble, ignoble, inferior, low,
lowborn, lowly, menial, modest, obscure,

ordinary, plebeian, proletarian, servile, un~
distinguished, vulgar
Antonyms agreeable, altruistic, attractive,
big, bountiful, choice, compassionate, conse~
quential, de luxe, excellent, first-rate, gener~
ous, gentle, good, high, honourable, humane,
important, kind, liberal, munificent, noble,
pleasing, praiseworthy, princely, prodigal,
significant, superb, superior, sympathetic,
unselfish, warm-hearted

mean[3] **1.** *n.* average, balance, compromise,
happy medium, median, middle, middle
course *or* way, mid-point, norm **2.** *adj.* av~
erage, intermediate, medial, median, me~
dium, middle, middling, normal, standard

meander 1. *v.* ramble, snake, stravaig
(*Scot. & northern English dialect*), stray,
stroll, turn, wander, wind, zigzag **2.** *n.*
bend, coil, curve, loop, turn, twist, zigzag

meandering anfractuous, circuitous, con~
voluted, indirect, roundabout, serpentine,
snaking, tortuous, wandering, winding
Antonyms direct, straight, straightforward,
undeviating

meaning *n.* **1.** connotation, denotation,
drift, explanation, gist, implication, import,
interpretation, message, purport, sense,
significance, signification, substance,
upshot, value **2.** aim, design, end, goal,
idea, intention, object, plan, point, purpose,
trend **3.** effect, efficacy, force, point, thrust,
use, usefulness, validity, value, worth ~*adj.*
4. eloquent, expressive, meaningful, point~
ed, pregnant, speaking, suggestive

meaningful 1. important, material, pur~
poseful, relevant, serious, significant,
useful, valid, worthwhile **2.** eloquent, ex~
pressive, meaning, pointed, pregnant,
speaking, suggestive
Antonyms inconsequential, insignificant,
meaningless, senseless, superficial, trivial,
unimportant, useless, worthless

meaningless aimless, empty, futile, hol~
low, inane, inconsequential, insignificant,
insubstantial, nonsensical, nugatory, point~
less, purposeless, senseless, trifling, trivial,
useless, vain, valueless, worthless
Antonyms clear, coherent, comprehensible,
consequential, decipherable, deep, evident,
important, intelligible, legible, meaningful,
obvious, purposeful, sensible, significant,
understandable, useful, valuable, worthwhile

meanness 1. minginess (*Brit. inf.*), miser~
liness, niggardliness, parsimony, penuri~
ousness, selfishness, stinginess, tightfistedness **2.** bad temper, cantankerousness,
churlishness, disagreeableness, hostility, ill
temper, malice, maliciousness, nastiness,
rudeness, sourness, unfriendliness, un~
pleasantness **3.** abjectness, baseness, de~
generacy, degradation, despicableness, dis~

gracefulness, dishonourableness, low-mindedness, narrow-mindedness, pettiness, scurviness, shabbiness, shamefulness, sordidness, vileness, wretchedness **4.** beggarliness, contemptibleness, insignificance, paltriness, pettiness, poorness, scruffiness, seediness, shabbiness, sordidness, squalor, tawdriness, wretchedness **5.** baseness, humbleness, lowliness, obscurity, servility

means 1. agency, avenue, channel, course, expedient, instrument, measure, medium, method, mode, process, way **2.** affluence, capital, estate, fortune, funds, income, money, property, resources, riches, substance, wealth, wherewithal **3. by all means** absolutely, certainly, definitely, doubtlessly, of course, positively, surely **4. by means of** by dint of, by way of, through, using, utilizing, via, with the aid of **5. by no means** absolutely not, definitely not, in no way, not at all, not in the least, not in the slightest, not the least bit, no way, on no account

meantime, meanwhile at the same time, concurrently, for now, for the duration, for the moment, for then, in the interim, in the interval, in the intervening time, in the meantime, in the meanwhile, simultaneously

measurable assessable, computable, determinable, gaugeable, material, mensurable, perceptible, quantifiable, quantitative, significant

measure *n.* **1.** allotment, allowance, amount, amplitude, capacity, degree, extent, magnitude, portion, proportion, quantity, quota, range, ration, reach, scope, share, size **2.** gauge, metre, rule, scale, yardstick **3.** method, standard, system **4.** criterion, example, model, norm, par, standard, test, touchstone, yardstick **5.** bounds, control, limit, limitation, moderation, restraint **6.** act, action, course, deed, expedient, manoeuvre, means, procedure, proceeding, step **7.** act, bill, enactment, law, resolution, statute **8.** beat, cadence, foot, metre, rhythm, verse **9. for good measure** as a bonus, besides, in addition, into the bargain, to boot ~*v.* **10.** appraise, assess, calculate, calibrate, compute, determine, estimate, evaluate, gauge, judge, mark out, quantify, rate, size, sound, survey, value, weigh **11.** adapt, adjust, calculate, choose, fit, judge, tailor

measureless beyond measure, boundless, endless, immeasurable, immense, incalculable, inestimable, infinite, limitless, unbounded, vast

measurement 1. appraisal, assessment, calculation, calibration, computation, estimation, evaluation, judgment, mensuration, metage, survey, valuation **2.** amount, amplitude, area, capacity, depth, dimension, extent, height, length, magnitude, size, volume, weight, width

measure out allot, apportion, assign, deal out, dispense, distribute, divide, dole out, issue, mete out, parcel out, pour out, share out

measure up (to) be adequate, be capable, be equal to, be fit, be suitable, be suited, come up to scratch (*Inf.*), come up to standard, compare, cut the mustard (*U.S. sl.*), equal, fit *or* fill the bill, fulfil the expectations, make the grade (*Inf.*), match, meet, rival

meat 1. aliment, cheer, chow (*Inf.*), comestibles, eats (*Sl.*), fare, flesh, food, grub (*Sl.*), nosh (*Sl.*), nourishment, nutriment, provender, provisions, rations, subsistence, sustenance, viands, victuals **2.** core, essence, gist, heart, kernel, marrow, nub, nucleus, pith, point, substance

meaty 1. hearty, nourishing, rich, substantial **2.** beefy (*Inf.*), brawny, burly, fleshy, heavily built, heavy, husky (*Inf.*), muscular, Ramboesque, solid, strapping, sturdy **3.** interesting, meaningful, pithy, profound, rich, significant, substantial

mechanical 1. automated, automatic, machine-driven **2.** automatic, cold, cursory, dead, emotionless, habitual, impersonal, instinctive, involuntary, lacklustre, lifeless, machine-like, matter-of-fact, perfunctory, routine, spiritless, unconscious, unfeeling, unthinking
Antonyms (*sense 1*) manual (*sense 2*) conscious, genuine, sincere, thinking, voluntary, warm, wholehearted

mechanism 1. apparatus, appliance, contrivance, device, instrument, machine, structure, system, tool **2.** action, components, gears, innards (*Inf.*), machinery, motor, workings, works **3.** agency, execution, functioning, means, medium, method, operation, performance, procedure, process, system, technique, workings

meddle butt in, interfere, intermeddle, interpose, intervene, intrude, pry, put one's oar in, put one's two cents in (*U.S. sl.*), stick one's nose in (*Inf.*), tamper

mediate act as middleman, arbitrate, bring to an agreement, bring to terms, conciliate, intercede, interpose, intervene, make peace between, moderate, reconcile, referee, resolve, restore harmony, settle, step in (*Inf.*), umpire

mediator advocate, arbiter, arbitrator, go-between, honest broker, interceder, intermediary, judge, middleman, moderator, negotiator, peacemaker, referee, umpire

medicinal analeptic, curative, healing,

medical, remedial, restorative, roborant, sanatory, therapeutic

medicine cure, drug, medicament, medica~ tion, nostrum, physic, remedy

medieval 1. Gothic **2.** *Inf.* antediluvian, antiquated, antique, archaic, old-fashioned, primitive, unenlightened

mediocre average, banal, commonplace, fair to middling (*Inf.*), indifferent, inferior, insignificant, mean, medium, middling, or~ dinary, passable, pedestrian, run-of-the-mill, second-rate, so-so (*Inf.*), tolerable, undistin~ guished, uninspired
Antonyms distinctive, distinguished, excel~ lent, extraordinary, fine, incomparable, su~ perb, superior, unexcelled, unique, unri~ valled, unsurpassed

mediocrity 1. commonplaceness, indiffer~ ence, inferiority, insignificance, ordi~ nariness, poorness, unimportance **2.** cipher, lightweight (*Inf.*), nobody, nonentity, second-rater

meditate 1. be in a brown study, cogitate, consider, contemplate, deliberate, muse, ponder, reflect, ruminate, study, think **2.** consider, contemplate, design, devise, have in mind, intend, mull over, plan, purpose, scheme, think over

meditation brown study, cerebration, cogitation, concentration, contemplation, musing, pondering, reflection, reverie, ru~ minating, rumination, study, thought

medium *adj.* **1.** average, fair, intermediate, mean, medial, median, mediocre, middle, middling, midway ~*n.* **2.** average, centre, compromise, mean, middle, middle course (ground, path, way), midpoint **3.** agency, avenue, channel, form, instrument, instru~ mentality, means, mode, organ, vehicle, way **4.** atmosphere, conditions, element, environment, habitat, influences, milieu, setting, surroundings **5.** channeller, spirit~ ist, spiritualist
Antonyms *adj.* distinctive, extraordinary, extreme, uncommon, unique, unusual, utmost

medley assortment, confusion, farrago, gal~ limaufry, hodgepodge, hotchpotch, jumble, *mélange*, miscellany, mishmash, mixed bag (*Inf.*), mixture, olio, omnium-gatherum, pastiche, patchwork, potpourri, salmagundi

meek 1. deferential, docile, forbearing, gen~ tle, humble, long-suffering, mild, modest, patient, peaceful, soft, submissive, unas~ suming, unpretentious, yielding **2.** acquies~ cent, compliant, resigned, spineless, spirit~ less, tame, timid, unresisting, weak, weak-kneed (*Inf.*), wimpish *or* wimpy (*Inf.*)
Antonyms arrogant, bold, bossy, domineer~ ing, feisty (*Inf., chiefly U.S. & Canad.*), for~ ward, immodest, overbearing, presumptuous,

pretentious, proud, self-assertive, spirited, wilful

meekness 1. deference, docility, forbear~ ance, gentleness, humbleness, humility, long-suffering, lowliness, mildness, modes~ ty, patience, peacefulness, resignation, soft~ ness, submission, submissiveness **2.** acqui~ escence, compliance, resignation, spineless~ ness, spiritlessness, tameness, timidity, weakness

meet 1. bump into, chance on, come across, confront, contact, encounter, find, happen on, run across, run into **2.** abut, adjoin, come together, connect, converge, cross, intersect, join, link up, touch, unite **3.** an~ swer, carry out, come up to, comply, cope with, discharge, equal, fulfil, gratify, han~ dle, match, measure up, perform, satisfy **4.** assemble, collect, come together, congre~ gate, convene, forgather, gather, muster, rally **5.** bear, encounter, endure, experi~ ence, face, go through, suffer, undergo
Antonyms (*sense 1*) avoid, elude, escape, miss (*sense 2*) diverge (*sense 3*) fail, fall short, renege (*sense 4*) adjourn, disperse, scatter

meeting 1. assignation, confrontation, en~ counter, engagement, introduction, rendez~ vous, tryst (*Archaic*) **2.** assembly, audience, company, conclave, conference, congrega~ tion, congress, convention, convocation, gathering, get-together (*Inf.*), meet, pow~ wow, rally, reunion, session **3.** concourse, confluence, conjunction, convergence, crossing, intersection, junction, union

melancholy 1. *n.* blues, dejection, depres~ sion, despondency, gloom, gloominess, low spirits, misery, pensiveness, sadness, sor~ row, the hump (*Brit. inf.*), unhappiness, woe **2.** *adj.* blue, dejected, depressed, despond~ ent, disconsolate, dismal, dispirited, doleful, down, downcast, downhearted, down in the dumps (*Inf.*), down in the mouth, gloomy, glum, heavy-hearted, joyless, low, low-spirited, lugubrious, melancholic, miser~ able, moody, mournful, pensive, sad, som~ bre, sorrowful, unhappy, woebegone, woeful
Antonyms *n.* delight, gladness, happiness, joy, pleasure ~*adj.* blithe, bright, cheerful, gay, glad, happy, jolly, joyful, joyous, light-hearted, lively, merry, sunny

mellow *adj.* **1.** delicate, full-flavoured, juicy, mature, perfect, rich, ripe, soft, sweet, well-matured **2.** dulcet, euphonic, full, mellifluous, melodious, rich, rounded, smooth, sweet, tuneful, well-tuned **3.** cheerful, cordial, elevated, expansive, gen~ ial, half-tipsy, happy, jolly, jovial, merry (*Brit. inf.*), relaxed ~*v.* **4.** develop, improve, mature, perfect, ripen, season, soften, sweeten
Antonyms *adj.* green, harsh, immature, raw, sour, unripe ~*v.* brutalize, harden

melodious concordant, dulcet, euphonic, euphonious, harmonious, melodic, musical, silvery, sweet-sounding, sweet-toned, tune~ful
Antonyms cacophonous, discordant, grat~ing, harsh, unharmonious, unmelodic, unme~lodious, unmusical, untuneful

melodramatic actressy, blood-and-thunder, extravagant, hammy (*Inf.*), histrionic, over~dramatic, overemotional, sensational, stagy, theatrical

melody 1. air, descant, music, refrain, song, strain, theme, tune 2. euphony, har~mony, melodiousness, music, musicality, tunefulness

melt 1. deliquesce, diffuse, dissolve, flux, fuse, liquefy, soften, thaw 2. *Often with* **away** disappear, disperse, dissolve, eva~nesce, evaporate, fade, vanish 3. disarm, mollify, relax, soften, touch

member 1. associate, fellow, representative 2. appendage, arm, component, constituent, element, extremity, leg, limb, organ, part, portion

membership 1. associates, body, fellows, members 2. belonging, enrolment, fellow~ship, participation

memento keepsake, memorial, relic, re~membrance, reminder, souvenir, token, trophy

memoir account, biography, essay, journal, life, monograph, narrative, record, register

memoirs 1. autobiography, diary, experi~ences, journals, life, life story, memories, recollections, reminiscences 2. annals, chronicles, records, transactions

memorable catchy, celebrated, distin~guished, extraordinary, famous, historic, il~lustrious, important, impressive, momen~tous, notable, noteworthy, remarkable, sig~nal, significant, striking, unforgettable
Antonyms commonplace, forgettable, insignificant, ordinary, trivial, undistin~guished, unimportant, unimpressive, un~memorable

memorial *adj.* 1. commemorative, monu~mental ~*n.* 2. cairn, memento, monument, plaque, record, remembrance, souvenir 3. address, memorandum, petition, statement

memorize commit to memory, con (*Archa~ic*), get by heart, learn, learn by heart, learn by rote, remember

memory 1. recall, recollection, remem~brance, reminiscence, retention 2. com~memoration, honour, remembrance 3. ce~lebrity, fame, glory, name, renown, reputa~tion, repute

menace *v.* 1. alarm, bode ill, browbeat, bully, frighten, impend, intimidate, loom, lour *or* lower, terrorize, threaten, utter

threats to ~*n.* 2. commination, intimida~tion, scare, threat, warning 3. danger, haz~ard, jeopardy, peril 4. *Inf.* annoyance, nui~sance, pest, plague, troublemaker

menacing alarming, baleful, dangerous, forbidding, frightening, intimidating, intimidatory, looming, louring *or* lowering, minacious, minatory, ominous, threatening
Antonyms auspicious, encouraging, fa~vourable, promising

mend *v.* 1. cure, darn, fix, heal, patch, rec~tify, refit, reform, remedy, renew, renovate, repair, restore, retouch 2. ameliorate, amend, better, correct, emend, improve, rectify, reform, revise 3. convalesce, get better, heal, recover, recuperate ~*n.* 4. darn, patch, repair, stitch 5. **on the mend** convalescent, convalescing, getting better, improving, recovering, recuperating

mendacious deceitful, deceptive, dishon~est, duplicitous, fallacious, false, fraudulent, insincere, lying, perfidious, perjured, un~true, untruthful
Antonyms genuine, honest, true, truthful

menial *adj.* 1. boring, dull, humdrum, low-status, routine, unskilled 2. abject, base, degrading, demeaning, fawning, grovelling, humble, ignoble, ignominious, low, lowly, mean, obsequious, servile, slavish, sorry, subservient, sycophantic, vile ~*n.* 3. atten~dant, dogsbody (*Inf.*), domestic, drudge, flunky, labourer, lackey, serf, servant, skivvy (*Chiefly Brit.*), slave, underling, var~let (*Archaic*), vassal
Antonyms *adj.* aristocratic, autocratic, bossy, dignified, domineering, elevated, haughty, high, noble, overbearing, proud ~*n.* boss, chief, commander, lord, master, superi~or

menstruation catamenia (*Physiology*), courses (*Physiology*), flow (*Inf.*), menses, menstrual cycle, monthly (*Inf.*), period, the curse (*Inf.*)

mental 1. cerebral, intellectual 2. deranged, disturbed, insane, lunatic, mad, mentally ill, psychiatric, psychotic, unbalanced, un~stable

mentality 1. brainpower, brains, compre~hension, grey matter (*Inf.*), intellect, intelli~gence quotient, I.Q., mental age, mind, ra~tionality, understanding, wit 2. attitude, cast of mind, character, disposition, frame of mind, make-up, outlook, personality, psychology, turn of mind, way of thinking

mentally in one's head, intellectually, in the mind, inwardly, psychologically, ra~tionally, subjectively

mention *v.* 1. acknowledge, adduce, allude to, bring up, broach, call attention to, cite, communicate, declare, disclose, divulge, hint at, impart, intimate, make known, name, point out, recount, refer to, report, reveal, speak about *or* of, state, tell, touch upon **2. not to mention** as well as, besides, not counting, to say nothing of ~*n.* **3.** acknowledgement, citation, recognition, tribute **4.** allusion, announcement, indication, notification, observation, reference, remark

mentor adviser, coach, counsellor, guide, guru, instructor, teacher, tutor

menu bill of fare, carte du jour, tariff (*Chiefly Brit.*)

mercantile commercial, marketable, trade, trading

mercenary *adj.* **1.** acquisitive, avaricious, bribable, covetous, grasping, greedy, money-grubbing (*Inf.*), sordid, venal **2.** bought, hired, paid, venal ~*n.* **3.** condottiere (*History*), free companion (*History*), freelance (*History*), hireling, soldier of fortune
Antonyms altruistic, benevolent, generous, idealistic, liberal, munificent, philanthropic, unselfish

merchandise 1. *n.* commodities, goods, produce, products, staples, stock, stock in trade, truck, vendibles, wares **2.** *v.* buy and sell, deal in, distribute, do business in, market, retail, sell, trade, traffic in, vend

merchant broker, dealer, purveyor, retailer, salesman, seller, shopkeeper, supplier, trader, tradesman, trafficker, vendor, wholesaler

merciful beneficent, benignant, clement, compassionate, forbearing, forgiving, generous, gracious, humane, kind, lenient, liberal, mild, pitying, soft, sparing, sympathetic, tender-hearted
Antonyms cruel, hard-hearted, inhumane, merciless, pitiless, uncompassionate, unfeeling

merciless barbarous, callous, cruel, fell (*Archaic*), hard, hard-hearted, harsh, heartless, implacable, inexorable, inhumane, pitiless, relentless, ruthless, severe, unappeasable, unfeeling, unforgiving, unmerciful, unpitying, unsparing, unsympathetic

mercurial active, capricious, changeable, erratic, fickle, flighty, gay, impulsive, inconstant, irrepressible, light-hearted, lively, mobile, quicksilver, spirited, sprightly, temperamental, unpredictable, unstable, variable, volatile
Antonyms consistent, constant, dependable, reliable, stable, steady, unchanging

mercy 1. benevolence, charity, clemency, compassion, favour, forbearance, forgiveness, grace, kindness, leniency, pity, quarter **2.** benison (*Archaic*), blessing, boon, godsend, piece of luck, relief **3. at the mercy of** defenceless against, exposed to, in

the clutches of, in the power of, naked before, open to, prey to, subject to, threatened by, unprotected against, vulnerable to
Antonyms brutality, cruelty, harshness, inhumanity, pitilessness, severity

mere *adj.* absolute, bare, common, complete, entire, nothing more than, plain, pure, pure and simple, sheer, simple, stark, unadulterated, unmitigated, unmixed, utter

merge amalgamate, be swallowed up by, become lost in, blend, coalesce, combine, consolidate, converge, fuse, incorporate, intermix, join, meet, meld, melt into, mingle, mix, tone with, unite
Antonyms detach, diverge, divide, part, separate, sever

merger amalgamation, coalition, combination, consolidation, fusion, incorporation, union

merit *n.* **1.** advantage, asset, excellence, good, goodness, integrity, quality, strong point, talent, value, virtue, worth, worthiness **2.** claim, credit, desert, due, right ~*v.* **3.** be entitled to, be worthy of, deserve, earn, have a claim to, have a right to, have coming to one, incur, rate, warrant

meritorious admirable, commendable, creditable, deserving, excellent, exemplary, good, honourable, laudable, praiseworthy, right, righteous, virtuous, worthy
Antonyms discreditable, dishonourable, ignoble, unchivalrous, undeserving, unexceptional, ungenerous, unpraiseworthy

merriment amusement, conviviality, festivity, frolic, fun, gaiety, glee, hilarity, jocularity, jollity, joviality, laughter, levity, liveliness, merrymaking, mirth, revelry, sport

merry 1. blithe, blithesome, carefree, cheerful, chirpy (*Inf.*), convivial, festive, frolicsome, fun-loving, gay, genial, glad, gleeful, happy, jocund, jolly, joyful, joyous, light-hearted, mirthful, rollicking, sportive, upbeat (*Inf.*), vivacious **2.** amusing, comic, comical, facetious, funny, hilarious, humorous, jocular, mirthful **3.** *Brit. inf.* elevated (*Inf.*), happy, mellow, squiffy (*Brit. inf.*), tiddly (*Sl., chiefly Brit.*), tipsy **4. make merry** carouse, celebrate, enjoy oneself, feast, frolic, have a good time, have fun, make whoopee (*Inf.*), revel
Antonyms dejected, dismal, gloomy, miserable, sad, unhappy

mesh *n.* **1.** net, netting, network, plexus, reticulation, tracery, web **2.** entanglement, snare, tangle, toils, trap, web ~*v.* **3.** catch, enmesh, ensnare, entangle, net, snare, tangle, trap **4.** combine, come together, connect, coordinate, dovetail, engage, fit together, harmonize, interlock, knit

mesmerize absorb, captivate, enthral, en~

trance, fascinate, grip, hold spellbound, hypnotize, magnetize, spellbind

mess *n.* **1.** balls-up (*Taboo sl.*), bodge (*Inf.*), botch, chaos, clutter, cock-up (*Brit. sl.*), confusion, dirtiness, disarray, disorder, disorganization, fuck-up (*Offens. taboo sl.*), grot (*Sl.*), hash, hodgepodge (*U.S.*), hotch~ potch, jumble, litter, mishmash, pig's breakfast (*Inf.*), shambles, state, turmoil, untidiness **2.** difficulty, dilemma, fine kettle of fish (*Inf.*), fix (*Inf.*), hot water (*Inf.*), im~ broglio, jam (*Inf.*), mix-up, muddle, per~ plexity, pickle (*Inf.*), plight, predicament, spot (*Inf.*), stew (*Inf.*), tight spot ~*v.* **3.** *Of~ ten with* **up** befoul, besmirch, botch, bungle, clutter, cock up (*Brit. sl.*), dirty, disarrange, dishevel, foul, fuck up (*Offens. taboo sl.*), litter, make a hash of (*Inf.*), muck up (*Brit. sl.*), muddle, pollute, scramble **4.** *Often with* **with** fiddle (*Inf.*), interfere, meddle, play, tamper, tinker

mess about *or* **around 1.** amuse oneself, dabble, fool (about *or* around), footle (*Inf.*), muck about (*Inf.*), piss about *or* around (*Taboo sl.*), play about *or* around, potter, trifle **2.** fiddle (*Inf.*), fool (about *or* around), interfere, meddle, piss about *or* around (*Taboo sl.*), play, tamper, tinker, toy

message 1. bulletin, communication, com~ muniqué, dispatch, intimation, letter, memorandum, missive, note, notice, tidings, word **2.** idea, import, meaning, moral, point, purport, theme **3.** commission, er~ rand, job, mission, task **4. get the mes~ sage** catch on (*Inf.*), comprehend, get it, get the point, see, take the hint, twig (*Brit. inf.*), understand

messenger agent, bearer, carrier, courier, delivery boy, emissary, envoy, errand-boy, go-between, harbinger, herald, runner

messy chaotic, cluttered, confused, dirty, dishevelled, disordered, disorganized, grub~ by, littered, muddled, scuzzy (*Sl., chiefly U.S.*), shambolic (*Inf.*), sloppy (*Inf.*), sloven~ ly, unkempt, untidy
Antonyms clean, meticulous, neat, ordered, orderly, shipshape, smart, squeaky-clean, tidy

metaphor allegory, analogy, emblem, figure of speech, image, symbol, trope

metaphorical allegorical, emblematic, em~ blematical, figurative, symbolic, tropical (*Rhetoric*)

metaphysical 1. basic, esoteric, essential, eternal, fundamental, general, ideal, intel~ lectual, philosophical, profound, specula~ tive, spiritual, subjective, universal **2.** ab~ stract, abstruse, deep, high-flown, oversub~ tle, recondite, theoretical, transcendental **3.** immaterial, impalpable, incorporeal, intan~ gible, spiritual, supernatural, unreal, un~ substantial

mete *v.* administer, allot, apportion, assign, deal, dispense, distribute, divide, dole, measure, parcel, portion, ration, share

meteoric brief, brilliant, dazzling, ephem~ eral, fast, flashing, fleeting, momentary, overnight, rapid, spectacular, speedy, sud~ den, swift, transient
Antonyms gradual, lengthy, long, pro~ longed, slow, steady, unhurried

method 1. approach, arrangement, course, fashion, form, manner, mode, modus op~ erandi, plan, practice, procedure, process, programme, routine, rule, scheme, style, system, technique, way **2.** design, form, or~ der, orderliness, organization, pattern, planning, purpose, regularity, structure, system

methodical businesslike, deliberate, disci~ plined, efficient, meticulous, neat, ordered, orderly, organized, painstaking, planned, precise, regular, structured, systematic, tidy, well-regulated
Antonyms casual, chaotic, confused, disor~ dered, disorderly, haphazard, irregular, ran~ dom, unmethodical

meticulous detailed, exact, fastidious, fussy, microscopic, painstaking, particular, perfectionist, precise, punctilious, scrupu~ lous, strict, thorough
Antonyms careless, haphazard, imprecise, inexact, loose, negligent, slapdash, sloppy

métier 1. calling, craft, line, occupation, profession, pursuit, trade, vocation **2.** forte, long suit (*Inf.*), speciality, specialty, strong point, strong suit

metropolis capital, city

mettle 1. ardour, balls (*Taboo sl.*), boldness, bottle (*Brit. sl.*), bravery, courage, daring, fire, fortitude, gallantry, gameness, grit, guts (*Inf.*), hardihood, heart, indomitability, life, nerve, pluck, resolution, resolve, spirit, spunk (*Inf.*), valour, vigour **2.** calibre, character, disposition, kidney, make-up, nature, quality, stamp, temper, tempera~ ment

microbe bacillus, bacterium, bug (*Inf.*), germ, microorganism, virus

microscopic imperceptible, infinitesimal, invisible, minuscule, minute, negligible, teensy-weensy, teeny-weeny, tiny
Antonyms enormous, gigantic, ginormous (*Inf.*), great, huge, immense, large, vast

midday noon, noonday, noontide, noontime, twelve noon, twelve o'clock

middle *adj.* **1.** central, halfway, inner, in~ side, intermediate, intervening, mean, me~ dial, median, medium, mid ~*n.* **2.** centre, focus, halfway point, heart, inside, mean, midpoint, midsection, midst, thick **3.** mid~ riff, midsection, waist

middleman broker, distributor, entrepre~ neur, go-between, intermediary

middling adequate, all right, average, fair, indifferent, mediocre, medium, moderate, modest, O.K. *or* okay (*Inf.*), ordinary, pass~ able, run-of-the-mill, so-so (*Inf.*), tolerable, unexceptional, unremarkable

midget 1. *n.* dwarf, gnome, homuncule, ho~ munculus, manikin, pygmy *or* pigmy, shrimp (*Inf.*), Tom Thumb **2.** *adj.* baby, dwarf, Lilliputian, little, miniature, pocket, pygmy *or* pigmy, small, teensy-weensy, teeny-weeny, tiny

midnight dead of night, middle of the night, the witching hour, twelve o'clock (at night)

midst 1. bosom, centre, core, depths, heart, hub, interior, middle, thick **2. in the midst of** amidst, among, during, enveloped by, in the middle of, in the thick of, surrounded by

midway betwixt and between, halfway, in the middle

might 1. ability, capability, capacity, clout (*Inf.*), efficacy, efficiency, energy, force, po~ tency, power, prowess, puissance, strength, sway, valour, vigour **2. (with) might and main** as hard as one can, as hard as pos~ sible, forcefully, full blast, full force, lustily, manfully, mightily, vigorously, with all one's might *or* strength

mightily 1. decidedly, exceedingly, ex~ tremely, greatly, highly, hugely, intensely, much, very, very much **2.** energetically, forcefully, lustily, manfully, powerfully, strongly, vigorously, with all one's might and main, with all one's strength

mighty 1. doughty, forceful, hardy, indomi~ table, lusty, manful, potent, powerful, puis~ sant, Ramboesque, robust, stalwart, stout, strapping, strong, sturdy, vigorous **2.** bulky, colossal, elephantine, enormous, gi~ gantic, ginormous (*Inf.*), grand, great, huge, humongous *or* humungous (*U.S. sl.*), im~ mense, large, massive, mega (*Sl.*), monu~ mental, prodigious, stupendous, titanic, towering, tremendous, vast
Antonyms feeble, impotent, small, tiny, un~ imposing, unimpressive, weak, weedy (*Inf.*), wimpish *or* wimpy (*Inf.*)

migrant 1. *n.* drifter, emigrant, gypsy, im~ migrant, itinerant, nomad, rover, tinker, transient, traveller, vagrant, wanderer **2.** *adj.* drifting, gypsy, immigrant, itinerant, migratory, nomadic, roving, shifting, tran~ sient, travelling, vagrant, wandering

migrate drift, emigrate, journey, move, roam, rove, shift, travel, trek, voyage, wan~ der

migration emigration, journey, movement, roving, shift, travel, trek, voyage, wander~ ing

migratory gypsy, itinerant, migrant, no~ madic, peripatetic, roving, shifting, transi~ ent, travelling, unsettled, vagrant, wander~ ing

mild 1. amiable, balmy, bland, calm, clem~ ent, compassionate, docile, easy, easy-going, easy-oasy (*Sl.*), equable, forbearing, forgiv~ ing, gentle, indulgent, kind, meek, mellow, merciful, moderate, pacific, peaceable, plac~ id, pleasant, serene, smooth, soft, temperate, tender, tranquil, warm **2.** demulcent, emol~ lient, lenitive, mollifying, soothing
Antonyms (*sense 1*) bitter, cold, fierce, harsh, rough, stormy, unkind, unpleasant, violent, wild (*sense 2*) harsh, powerful, severe, sharp, strong

mildness blandness, calmness, clemency, docility, forbearance, gentleness, indul~ gence, kindness, leniency, lenity, meekness, mellowness, moderation, placidity, smooth~ ness, softness, temperateness, tenderness, tranquillity, warmth

milieu background, element, environment, locale, location, *mise en scène*, scene, set~ ting, sphere, surroundings

militant *adj.* **1.** active, aggressive, assertive, combative, Ramboesque, vigorous **2.** bellig~ erent, combating, contending, embattled, fighting, in arms, warring ~*n.* **3.** activist, partisan **4.** belligerent, combatant, fighter, gladiator, warrior
Antonyms concessive, pacific, pacifist, peaceful

military 1. *adj.* armed, martial, soldierlike, soldierly, warlike **2.** *n.* armed forces, army, forces, services

militate 1. *With* **against** be detrimental to, conflict with, contend, count, counter, counteract, oppose, resist, tell, weigh **2.** *With* **for** advance, aid, further, help, pro~ mote

militia fencibles (*History*), National Guard (*U.S.*), reserve(s), Territorial Army (*Brit.*), trainband (*History*), yeomanry (*History*)

milk *v.* **1.** drain, draw off, express, extract, let out, press, siphon, tap **2.** bleed, drain, exploit, extract, impose on, pump, take ad~ vantage of, use, wring

milk-and-water feeble, innocuous, insipid, jejune, nerdy *or* nurdy (*Sl.*), vapid, weak, weedy (*Inf.*), wimpish *or* wimpy (*Inf.*), wishy-washy (*Inf.*)
Antonyms effective, energetic, forceful, healthy, Ramboesque, strong

milksop chinless wonder (*Brit. inf.*), cow~ ard, dastard (*Archaic*), jessie (*Scot. sl.*), mollycoddle, namby-pamby, sissy, weakling, wimp (*Inf.*)

mill *n.* **1.** factory, foundry, plant, shop, works **2.** crusher, grinder **3. run of the mill** average, commonplace, everyday, fair, middling, ordinary, routine, unexceptional, unremarkable ~*v.* **4.** comminute, crush, granulate, grate, grind, pound, powder, press, pulverize **5.** crowd, seethe, swarm, throng

millstone 1. grindstone, quernstone **2.** affliction, burden, dead weight, drag, en~ cumbrance, load, weight

mime 1. *n.* dumb show, gesture, mummery, pantomime **2.** *v.* act out, gesture, panto~ mime, represent, simulate

mimic *v.* **1.** ape, caricature, do (*Inf.*), imi~ tate, impersonate, parody, take off (*Inf.*) **2.** echo, look like, mirror, resemble, simulate, take on the appearance of ~*n.* **3.** caricatur~ ist, copycat (*Inf.*), imitator, impersonator, impressionist, parodist, parrot ~*adj.* **4.** echoic, imitation, imitative, make-believe, mimetic, mock, sham, simulated

mince 1. chop, crumble, cut, grind, hash **2.** diminish, euphemize, extenuate, hold back, moderate, palliate, soften, spare, tone down, weaken **3.** attitudinize, give oneself airs, ponce (*Sl.*), pose, posture

mincing affected, camp (*Inf.*), dainty, ef~ feminate, foppish, lah-di-dah (*Inf.*), nice, niminy-piminy, poncy (*Sl.*), precious, pre~ tentious, sissy

mind *n.* **1.** brain(s) (*Inf.*), grey matter (*Inf.*), intellect, intelligence, mentality, ratiocina~ tion, reason, sense, spirit, understanding, wits **2.** memory, recollection, remembrance **3.** brain, head, imagination, psyche **4.** brain (*Inf.*), brainbox, genius, intellect, in~ tellectual, thinker **5.** attitude, belief, feel~ ing, judgment, opinion, outlook, point of view, sentiment, thoughts, view, way of thinking **6.** bent, desire, disposition, fancy, inclination, intention, leaning, notion, pur~ pose, tendency, urge, will, wish **7.** atten~ tion, concentration, thinking, thoughts **8.** judgment, marbles (*Inf.*), mental balance, rationality, reason, sanity, senses, wits **9. in** *or* **of two minds** dithering (*Chiefly Brit.*), hesitant, shillyshallying (*Inf.*), swith~ ering (*Scot.*), uncertain, undecided, unsure, vacillating, wavering **10. make up one's mind** choose, come to a decision, decide, determine, reach a decision, resolve **11. bear** *or* **keep in mind** be cognizant of, be mindful of, remember, take note of ~*v.* **12.** be affronted, be bothered, care, disapprove, dislike, look askance at, object, resent, take offence **13.** adhere to, attend, comply with, follow, heed, listen to, mark, note, notice, obey, observe, pay attention, pay heed to, regard, respect, take heed, watch **14.** be sure, ensure, make certain **15.** attend to,

guard, have charge of, keep an eye on, look after, take care of, tend, watch **16.** be care~ ful, be cautious, be on (one's) guard, be wary, take care, watch **17. never mind** disregard, do not concern yourself, don't bother, don't give (it) a second thought, forget (it), it does not matter, it's none of your business, it's nothing to do with you, pay no attention

mindful alert, alive to, attentive, aware, careful, chary, cognizant, conscious, heed~ ful, regardful, respectful, sensible, thought~ ful, wary, watchful
Antonyms heedless, inattentive, incautious, mindless, oblivious, thoughtless, unaware

mindless 1. asinine, braindead (*Inf.*), brut~ ish, careless, foolish, forgetful, gratuitous, heedless, idiotic, imbecilic, inane, inatten~ tive, moronic, neglectful, negligent, oblivi~ ous, obtuse, stupid, thoughtless, unintelli~ gent, unmindful, unthinking, witless **2.** automatic, brainless, mechanical
Antonyms attentive, aware, considerate, intelligent, mindful, reasonable, reasoning, sane, sensitive, thinking

mind out be careful, be on one's guard, be~ ware, keep one's eyes open, look out, pay attention, take care, watch

mine *n.* **1.** coalfield, colliery, deposit, exca~ vation, lode, pit, shaft, vein **2.** abundance, fund, hoard, reserve, source, stock, store, supply, treasury, wealth **3.** sap, trench, tunnel ~*v.* **4.** delve, dig for, dig up, exca~ vate, extract, hew, quarry, unearth **5.** lay mines in *or* under, sow with mines **6.** sap, subvert, tunnel, undermine, weaken

miner coalminer, collier (*Brit.*), pitman (*Brit.*)

mingle 1. alloy, blend, coalesce, combine, commingle, compound, intermingle, inter~ mix, interweave, join, marry, meld, merge, mix, unite **2.** associate, circulate, consort, fraternize, hang about *or* around, hang out (*Inf.*), hobnob, rub shoulders (*Inf.*), socialize
Antonyms avoid, detach, dissociate, dis~ solve, divide, estrange, part, separate

miniature *adj.* baby, diminutive, dwarf, Lilliputian, little, midget, mini, minuscule, minute, pocket, pygmy *or* pigmy, reduced, scaled-down, small, teensy-weensy, teeny-weeny, tiny, toy, wee
Antonyms big, enlarged, enormous, giant, gigantic, ginormous (*Inf.*), great, huge, im~ mense, large, mega (*Sl.*), oversize

minimal least, least possible, littlest, mini~ mum, nominal, slightest, smallest, token

minimize 1. abbreviate, attenuate, curtail, decrease, diminish, miniaturize, prune, re~ duce, shrink **2.** belittle, decry, deprecate, depreciate, discount, disparage, make light

or little of, play down, underestimate, underrate
Antonyms augment, boast about, elevate, enhance, enlarge, exalt, expand, extend, heighten, increase, magnify, praise, vaunt

minimum 1. *n.* bottom, depth, least, lowest, nadir, slightest **2.** *adj.* least, least possible, littlest, lowest, minimal, slightest, smallest
Antonyms greatest, highest, largest, maxi~mum, most

minion bootlicker (*Inf.*), creature, darling, dependant, favourite, flatterer, flunky, fol~lower, hanger-on, henchman, hireling, lackey, lickspittle, myrmidon, parasite, pet, sycophant, toady, underling, yes man

minister *n.* **1.** chaplain, churchman, clergyman, cleric, divine, ecclesiastic, padre (*Inf.*), parson, pastor, preacher, priest, rec~tor, vicar **2.** administrator, ambassador, cabinet member, delegate, diplomat, envoy, executive, office-holder, official, plenipoten~tiary **3.** agent, aide, assistant, lieutenant, servant, subordinate, underling ~*v.* **4.** ac~commodate, administer, answer, attend, be solicitous of, cater to, pander to, serve, take care of, tend

ministration aid, assistance, favour, help, patronage, relief, service, succour, support

ministry 1. administration, bureau, cabinet, council, department, government, office **2.** holy orders, the church, the priesthood, the pulpit

minor inconsequential, inconsiderable, infe~rior, insignificant, junior, lesser, light, neg~ligible, nickel-and-dime (*U.S. sl.*), paltry, petty, secondary, slight, small, smaller, subordinate, trifling, trivial, unimportant, younger
Antonyms appreciable, consequential, con~siderable, essential, grand, great, heavy, im~portant, major, profound, serious, significant, substantial, superior, vital, weighty

minstrel bard, harper, jongleur, musician, singer, songstress, troubadour

mint *n.* **1.** bomb (*Brit. sl.*), bundle (*Sl.*), for~tune, heap (*Inf.*), King's ransom, million, packet (*Sl.*), pile (*Inf.*), ~*adj.* **2.** brand-new, excellent, first-class, fresh, perfect, unblem~ished, undamaged, untarnished ~*v.* **3.** cast, coin, make, produce, punch, stamp, strike **4.** coin, construct, devise, fabricate, fashion, forge, invent, make up, produce, think up

minute[1] *n.* **1.** sixtieth of an hour, sixty sec~onds **2.** flash, instant, jiffy (*Inf.*), moment, second, shake (*Inf.*), tick (*Brit. inf.*), trice **3.** **any minute** any moment, any second, any time, at any time, before long, very soon **4.** **up to the minute** all the rage, in, latest, modish, (most) fashionable, newest, now (*Inf.*), smart, stylish, trendiest, trendy (*Brit. inf.*), up to date, vogue, with it (*Inf.*)

minute[2] *adj.* **1.** diminutive, fine, infinitesimal, Lilliputian, little, microscopic, miniature, minuscule, slender, small, teensy-weensy, teeny-weeny, tiny **2.** incon~siderable, negligible, paltry, petty, picayune (*U.S.*), piddling (*Inf.*), puny, slight, trifling, trivial, unimportant **3.** close, critical, de~tailed, exact, exhaustive, meticulous, pains~taking, precise, punctilious
Antonyms (*senses 1 & 2*) enormous, gener~ous, gigantic, ginormous (*Inf.*), grand, great, huge, immense, important, major, mega (*Sl.*), monstrous, significant, vital (*sense 3*) careless, haphazard, imprecise, inexact, loose, quick, rough, superficial

minutely closely, critically, exactly, ex~haustively, in detail, meticulously, pains~takingly, precisely, with a fine-tooth comb

minutes memorandum, notes, proceedings, record(s), transactions, transcript

minutiae details, finer points, niceties, par~ticulars, subtleties, trifles, trivia

minx baggage (*Inf., old-fashioned*), coquette, flirt, hoyden, hussy, jade, tomboy, wanton

miracle marvel, phenomenon, prodigy, thaumaturgy, wonder

miraculous amazing, astonishing, astound~ing, extraordinary, incredible, inexplicable, magical, marvellous, phenomenal, preter~natural, prodigious, superhuman, super~natural, thaumaturgic, unaccountable, un~believable, wonderful, wondrous (*Archaic or literary*)
Antonyms awful, bad, banal, common, commonplace, everyday, normal, ordinary, run-of-the-mill, terrible, unexceptional, unre~markable, usual

mirage hallucination, illusion, optical illu~sion, phantasm

mire *n.* **1.** bog, marsh, morass, quagmire, swamp **2.** dirt, grot (*Sl.*), muck, mud, ooze, slime **3.** **in the mire** encumbered, entan~gled, in difficulties, in trouble ~*v.* **4.** bog down, flounder, sink, stick in the mud **5.** begrime, besmirch, bespatter, cake, dirty, muddy, soil **6.** catch up, enmesh, entangle, involve

mirror *n.* **1.** glass, looking-glass, reflector, speculum **2.** copy, double, image, likeness, reflection, replica, representation, twin ~*v.* **3.** copy, depict, echo, emulate, follow, reflect, represent, show

mirth amusement, cheerfulness, festivity, frolic, fun, gaiety, gladness, glee, hilarity, jocularity, jollity, joviality, joyousness, laughter, levity, merriment, merrymaking, pleasure, rejoicing, revelry, sport

mirthful amused, amusing, blithe, cheerful, cheery, festive, frolicsome, funny, gay, glad, gladsome (*Archaic*), happy, hilarious, joc~

und, jolly, jovial, laughable, light-hearted, merry, playful, sportive, uproarious, vivacious
Antonyms dejected, depressed, despondent, dismal, gloomy, grave, lugubrious, melancholy, miserable, morose, sad, saturnine, sedate, serious, solemn, sombre, sorrowful, unhappy

misadventure accident, bad break (*Inf.*), bad luck, bummer (*Sl.*), calamity, catastrophe, debacle, disaster, failure, ill fortune, ill luck, mischance, misfortune, mishap, reverse, setback

misanthrope cynic, egoist, egotist, mankind-hater, misanthropist

misapprehend get hold of the wrong end of the stick, get the wrong idea *or* impression, misconceive, misconstrue, misinterpret, misread, mistake, misunderstand

misapprehension delusion, error, fallacy, false belief, false impression, misconception, misconstruction, misinterpretation, misreading, mistake, misunderstanding, wrong idea *or* impression

misappropriate cabbage (*Brit. sl.*), defalcate (*Law*), embezzle, misapply, misspend, misuse, peculate, pocket, steal, swindle

misbegotten 1. dishonest, disreputable, ill-gotten, illicit, purloined, shady (*Inf.*), stolen, unlawful, unrespectable 2. abortive, hare-brained, ill-advised, ill-conceived, poorly thought-out 3. *Literary* bastard, born out of wedlock, illegitimate, natural, spurious (*Rare*)

misbehave act up (*Inf.*), be bad, be insubordinate, be naughty, carry on (*Inf.*), get up to mischief (*Inf.*), muck about (*Brit. sl.*)
Antonyms act correctly, be good, behave, conduct oneself properly, mind one's manners, mind one's p's and q's, toe the line

misbehaviour acting up (*Inf.*), bad behaviour, impropriety, incivility, indiscipline, insubordination, mischief, misconduct, misdeeds, misdemeanour, monkey business (*Inf.*), naughtiness, rudeness, shenanigans (*Inf.*)

misbelief delusion, error, fallacy, false belief, heresy, unorthodoxy

miscalculate blunder, calculate wrongly, err, get (it) wrong, go wrong, make a mistake, misjudge, overestimate, overrate, slip up, underestimate, underrate

miscarriage 1. miss (*Inf.*), spontaneous abortion 2. botch (*Inf.*), breakdown, error, failure, misadventure, mischance, misfire, mishap, mismanagement, nonsuccess, perversion, thwarting, undoing

miscarry 1. abort 2. come to grief, come to nothing, fail, fall through, gang agley

(*Scot.*), go amiss, go astray, go awry, go wrong, misfire

miscellaneous assorted, confused, diverse, diversified, farraginous, heterogeneous, indiscriminate, jumbled, manifold, many, mingled, mixed, motley, multifarious, multiform, promiscuous, sundry, varied, various

miscellany anthology, assortment, collection, diversity, farrago, gallimaufry, hotchpotch, jumble, medley, *mélange*, mixed bag, mixture, omnium-gatherum, potpourri, salmagundi, variety

mischance accident, bad break (*Inf.*), bad luck, bummer (*Sl.*), calamity, contretemps, disaster, ill chance, ill fortune, ill luck, infelicity, misadventure, misfortune, mishap

mischief 1. devilment, impishness, misbehaviour, monkey business (*Inf.*), naughtiness, pranks, roguery, roguishness, shenanigans (*Inf.*), trouble, waywardness 2. damage, detriment, disadvantage, disruption, evil, harm, hurt, injury, misfortune, trouble 3. devil, imp, monkey, nuisance, pest, rascal, rogue, scallywag (*Inf.*), scamp, tyke (*Inf.*), villain

mischievous 1. arch, bad, badly behaved, exasperating, frolicsome, impish, naughty, playful, puckish, rascally, roguish, sportive, teasing, troublesome, vexatious, wayward 2. bad, damaging, deleterious, destructive, detrimental, evil, harmful, hurtful, injurious, malicious, malignant, pernicious, sinful, spiteful, troublesome, vicious, wicked

misconception delusion, error, fallacy, misapprehension, misconstruction, mistaken belief, misunderstanding, wrong end of the stick, wrong idea

misconduct 1. *n.* delinquency, dereliction, immorality, impropriety, malfeasance (*Law*), malpractice, malversation (*Rare*), misbehaviour, misdemeanour, mismanagement, naughtiness, rudeness, transgression, unethical behaviour, wrongdoing 2. *v.* behave badly, botch (up), bungle, err, make a mess of, misdirect, mismanage, sin

misconstrue get a false impression, make a wrong interpretation, misapprehend, misconceive, misinterpret, misjudge, misread, mistake, mistranslate, misunderstand, take the wrong way (*Inf.*)

miscreant 1. *n.* blackguard, caitiff (*Archaic*), criminal, evildoer, knave (*Archaic*), malefactor, rascal, reprobate, rogue, scally (*Northwest English dialect*), scoundrel, sinner, vagabond, villain, wrongdoer 2. *adj.* corrupt, criminal, depraved, evil, iniquitous, nefarious, rascally, reprehensible, reprobate, scoundrelly, unprincipled, vicious, villainous, wicked

misdeed crime, fault, misconduct, misde-

meanour, offence, sin, transgression, tres~
pass, villainy, wrong

misdemeanour fault, infringement, mis~
behaviour, misconduct, misdeed, offence,
peccadillo, transgression, trespass

miser cheapskate (*Inf.*), churl (*Archaic*),
curmudgeon, hunks (*Rare*), niggard,
penny-pincher (*Inf.*), screw (*Sl.*), Scrooge,
skinflint, tight-arse (*Taboo sl.*), tight-ass
(*U.S. taboo sl.*), tightwad (*U.S. & Canad. sl.*)

miserable 1. afflicted, broken-hearted,
crestfallen, dejected, depressed, desolate,
despondent, disconsolate, dismal, distressed,
doleful, down, downcast, down in the mouth
(*Inf.*), forlorn, gloomy, heartbroken, melan~
choly, mournful, sorrowful, unhappy, woe~
begone, wretched 2. destitute, dirt-poor
(*Inf.*), down and out, flat broke (*Inf.*), im~
poverished, indigent, meagre, needy, penni~
less, poor, poverty-stricken, scanty, short,
without two pennies to rub together (*Inf.*)
3. abject, bad, contemptible, deplorable,
despicable, detestable, disgraceful, lamen~
table, low, mean, pathetic, piteous, pitiable,
scurvy, shabby, shameful, sordid, sorry,
squalid, vile, worthless, wretched
Antonyms admirable, cheerful, comfort~
able, good, happy, respectable, rich

miserly avaricious, beggarly, close, close-
fisted, covetous, grasping, illiberal, mean,
mingy (*Brit. inf.*), near, niggardly, parsimo~
nious, penny-pinching (*Inf.*), penurious,
sordid, stingy, tight-arsed (*Taboo sl.*), tight
as a duck's arse (*Taboo sl.*), tight-assed
(*U.S. taboo sl.*), tightfisted, ungenerous
Antonyms charitable, extravagant, gener~
ous, prodigal, unselfish

misery 1. agony, anguish, depression, deso~
lation, despair, discomfort, distress, gloom,
grief, hardship, melancholy, sadness, sor~
row, suffering, torment, torture, unhappi~
ness, woe, wretchedness 2. affliction, bitter
pill (*Inf.*), burden, calamity, catastrophe,
curse, disaster, hardship, load, misfortune,
ordeal, sorrow, trial, tribulation, trouble,
woe 3. destitution, indigence, need, penury,
poverty, privation, sordidness, squalor,
want, wretchedness 4. *Brit. inf.* grouch
(*Inf.*), killjoy, moaner, pessimist, prophet of
doom, sourpuss (*Inf.*), spoilsport, wet blan~
ket (*Inf.*)
Antonyms comfort, contentment, ease, en~
joyment, happiness, joy, luxury, pleasure

misfire fail, fail to go off, fall through, go
phut (*Inf.*), go wrong, miscarry

misfit eccentric, fish out of water (*Inf.*),
nonconformist, oddball (*Inf.*), square peg (in
a round hole) (*Inf.*)

misfortune 1. bad luck, evil fortune, hard
luck, ill luck, infelicity 2. accident, adver~
sity, affliction, blow, bummer (*Sl.*), calam~

ity, disaster, evil chance, failure, hardship,
harm, loss, misadventure, mischance, mis~
ery, mishap, reverse, setback, stroke of bad
luck, tragedy, trial, tribulation, trouble
Antonyms fortune, good luck, relief

misgiving anxiety, apprehension, distrust,
doubt, dubiety, hesitation, qualm, reserva~
tion, scruple, suspicion, trepidation, uncer~
tainty, unease, worry

misguided deluded, erroneous, foolish, ill-
advised, imprudent, injudicious, labouring
under a delusion *or* misapprehension, mis~
led, misplaced, mistaken, uncalled-for, un~
reasonable, unwarranted, unwise

mishandle bodge (*Inf.*), botch, bungle,
make a hash of (*Inf.*), make a mess of, mess
up (*Inf.*), mismanage, muff, screw (up) (*Inf.*)

mishap accident, adversity, bad luck, ca~
lamity, contretemps, disaster, evil chance,
evil fortune, hard luck, ill fortune, ill luck,
infelicity, misadventure, mischance, mis~
fortune

misinform deceive, give (someone) a bum
steer (*Inf., chiefly U.S.*), give (someone) duff
gen (*Brit. inf.*), misdirect, misguide, mislead

misinterpret distort, falsify, get wrong,
misapprehend, misconceive, misconstrue,
misjudge, misread, misrepresent, mistake,
misunderstand, pervert

misjudge be wrong about, get the wrong
idea about, miscalculate, overestimate,
overrate, underestimate, underrate

mislay be unable to find, be unable to put *or*
lay one's hand on, forget the whereabouts
of, lose, lose track of, misplace, miss

mislead beguile, bluff, deceive, delude, fool,
give (someone) a bum steer (*Inf., chiefly
U.S.*), hoodwink, lead astray, misdirect,
misguide, misinform, pull the wool over
(someone's) eyes (*Inf.*), take in (*Inf.*)

misleading ambiguous, casuistical, confus~
ing, deceitful, deceptive, delusive, delusory,
disingenuous, evasive, false, sophistical,
specious, spurious, tricky (*Inf.*),
unstraightforward
Antonyms candid, clear, correct, direct, ex~
plicit, frank, genuine, honest, obvious, open,
plain, simple, sincere, straightforward, true,
truthful

mismanage be incompetent, be inefficient,
bodge (*Inf.*), botch, bungle, make a hash of
(*Inf.*), make a mess of, maladminister, mess
up, misconduct, misdirect, misgovern, mis~
handle

misplace 1. be unable to find, be unable to
put *or* lay one's hand on, forget the where~
abouts of, lose, lose track of, misfile, mislay,
miss, put in the wrong place 2. place un~
wisely, place wrongly

misprint corrigendum, erratum, literal,

mistake, printing error, typo (*Inf.*), typo~
graphical error

misquote distort, falsify, garble, mangle,
misreport, misrepresent, misstate, muddle,
pervert, quote *or* take out of context, twist

misrepresent belie, disguise, distort, falsi~
fy, garble, misinterpret, misstate, pervert,
twist

misrule 1. bad government, maladminis~
tration, misgovernment, mismanagement **2.**
anarchy, chaos, confusion, disorder, law~
lessness, tumult, turmoil

miss[1] *v.* **1.** avoid, be late for, blunder, err,
escape, evade, fail, fail to grasp, fail to no~
tice, forego, lack, leave out, let go, let slip,
lose, miscarry, mistake, omit, overlook,
pass over, pass up, skip, slip, trip **2.** feel
the loss of, hunger for, long for, need, pine
for, want, wish, yearn for ~*n.* **3.** blunder,
error, failure, fault, loss, mistake, omission,
oversight, want

miss[2] damsel, girl, lass, lassie (*Inf.*), maid,
maiden, schoolgirl, spinster, young lady

misshapen contorted, crippled, crooked,
deformed, distorted, grotesque, ill-made,
ill-proportioned, malformed, twisted, ugly,
ungainly, unshapely, unsightly, warped,
wry

missile projectile, rocket, weapon

missing absent, astray, gone, lacking, left
behind, left out, lost, mislaid, misplaced,
not present, nowhere to be found,
unaccounted-for, wanting
Antonyms accounted for, at hand, available,
here, in attendance, on hand, present, there, to
hand

mission 1. aim, assignment, business, call~
ing, charge, commission, duty, errand, goal,
job, office, operation, purpose, pursuit,
quest, task, trust, undertaking, vocation,
work **2.** commission, delegation, deputa~
tion, embassy, legation, ministry, task force

missionary apostle, converter, evangelist,
preacher, propagandist, proselytizer

missive communication, dispatch, epistle,
letter, memorandum, message, note, report

misspent dissipated, idle, imprudent, mis~
applied, prodigal, profitless, squandered,
thrown away, wasted
Antonyms active, fruitful, industrious,
meaningful, profitable, unwasted, useful,
worthwhile

mist 1. *n.* cloud, condensation, dew, drizzle,
film, fog, haar (*Eastern Brit.*), haze, smog,
smur *or* smir (*Scot.*), spray, steam, vapour
2. *v.* becloud, befog, blur, cloud, film, fog,
obscure, steam (up)

mistake *n.* **1.** bloomer (*Brit. inf.*), blunder,
boob (*Brit. sl.*), boo-boo (*Inf.*), clanger (*Inf.*),
erratum, error, error of judgment, false

move, fault, faux pas, gaffe, goof (*Inf.*),
howler (*Inf.*), inaccuracy, miscalculation,
misconception, misstep, misunderstanding,
oversight, slip, slip-up (*Inf.*), solecism ~*v.*
2. get wrong, misapprehend, misconceive,
misconstrue, misinterpret, misjudge, mis~
read, misunderstand **3.** accept as, confound,
confuse with, misinterpret as, mix up with,
take for **4.** be wide of *or* be off the mark, be
wrong, blunder, boob (*Brit. sl.*), drop a
clanger (*Inf.*), err, goof (*Inf.*), miscalculate,
misjudge, put one's foot in it (*Inf.*), slip up
(*Inf.*)

mistaken barking up the wrong tree (*Inf.*),
erroneous, fallacious, false, faulty, inaccu~
rate, inappropriate, incorrect, in the wrong,
labouring under a misapprehension, mis~
guided, misinformed, misled, off target, off
the mark, unfounded, unsound, wide of the
mark, wrong
Antonyms accurate, correct, logical, right,
sound, true

mistakenly by mistake, erroneously, falla~
ciously, falsely, inaccurately, inappropri~
ately, incorrectly, in error, misguidedly,
wrongly

mistimed badly timed, ill-timed, inconven~
ient, inopportune, unseasonable,
unsynchronized, untimely

mistreat abuse, brutalize, handle roughly,
harm, ill-treat, ill-use, injure, knock about
or around, maltreat, manhandle, maul,
misuse, molest, rough up, wrong

mistress concubine, doxy (*Archaic*), fancy
woman (*Sl.*), floozy (*Sl.*), girlfriend, inamo~
rata, kept woman, ladylove (*Rare*), lover,
paramour

mistrust 1. *v.* apprehend, beware, be wary
of, distrust, doubt, fear, have doubts about,
suspect **2.** *n.* apprehension, distrust, doubt,
dubiety, fear, misgiving, scepticism, suspi~
cion, uncertainty, wariness

mistrustful apprehensive, cautious, chary,
cynical, distrustful, doubtful, dubious, fear~
ful, hesitant, leery (*Sl.*), nervous, sceptical,
suspicious, uncertain, wary
Antonyms certain, definite, positive, sure,
unafraid

misty bleary, blurred, cloudy, dark, dim,
foggy, fuzzy, hazy, indistinct, murky, nebu~
lous, obscure, opaque, overcast, unclear,
vague
Antonyms bright, clear, distinct, lucid, ob~
vious, plain, sunny, well-defined

misunderstand get (it) wrong, get the
wrong end of the stick, get the wrong idea
(about), misapprehend, misconceive, mis~
construe, mishear, misinterpret, misjudge,
misread, miss the point (of), mistake

misunderstanding 1. error, false im~
pression, misapprehension, misconception,

misconstruction, misinterpretation, mis~ judgment, misreading, mistake, mix-up, wrong idea **2.** argument, breach, conflict, difference, difficulty, disagreement, discord, dissension, falling-out (*Inf.*), quarrel, rift, rupture, squabble, variance

misunderstood misconstrued, misheard, misinterpreted, misjudged, misread, unap~ preciated, unrecognized

misuse *n.* **1.** abuse, barbarism, catachresis, corruption, desecration, dissipation, mala~ propism, misapplication, misemployment, misusage, perversion, profanation, solecism, squandering, waste **2.** abuse, cruel treat~ ment, exploitation, harm, ill-treatment, ill~ usage, inhumane treatment, injury, mal~ treatment, manhandling, mistreatment, rough handling ~*v.* **3.** abuse, corrupt, des~ ecrate, dissipate, misapply, misemploy, pervert, profane, prostitute, squander, waste **4.** abuse, brutalize, exploit, handle roughly, harm, ill-treat, ill-use, injure, mal~ treat, manhandle, maul, mistreat, molest, wrong
Antonyms *v.* appreciate, cherish, honour, prize, respect, treasure, use

mitigate abate, allay, appease, assuage, blunt, calm, check, diminish, dull, ease, ex~ tenuate, lessen, lighten, moderate, modify, mollify, pacify, palliate, placate, quiet, re~ duce the force of, remit, soften, soothe, subdue, take the edge off, temper, tone down, tranquillize, weaken
Antonyms aggravate, augment, enhance, heighten, increase, intensify, strengthen

mitigation abatement, allaying, alleviation, assuagement, diminution, easement, ex~ tenuation, moderation, mollification, pallia~ tion, relief, remission

mix *v.* **1.** alloy, amalgamate, associate, blend, coalesce, combine, commingle, commix, compound, cross, fuse, incorporate, inter~ mingle, interweave, join, jumble, meld, merge, mingle, put together, unite **2.** asso~ ciate, come together, consort, fraternize, hang out (*Inf.*), hobnob, join, mingle, so~ cialize ~*n.* **3.** alloy, amalgam, assortment, blend, combination, compound, fusion, medley, meld, mixture

mixed 1. alloyed, amalgamated, blended, combined, composite, compound, fused, in~ corporated, joint, mingled, united **2.** as~ sorted, cosmopolitan, diverse, diversified, heterogeneous, manifold, miscellaneous, motley, varied **3.** crossbred, hybrid, inter~ bred, interdenominational, mongrel **4.** am~ bivalent, equivocal, indecisive, uncertain
Antonyms homogeneous, isolated, pure, straight, unmixed

mixed-up at sea, bewildered, confused, dis~

traught, disturbed, maladjusted, muddled, perplexed, puzzled, upset

mixture admixture, alloy, amalgam, amal~ gamation, association, assortment, blend, brew, combine, composite, compound, con~ coction, conglomeration, cross, fusion, hotchpotch, jumble, medley, *mélange*, meld, miscellany, mix, potpourri, salmagundi, union, variety

mix-up confusion, disorder, fankle (*Scot.*), jumble, mess, mistake, misunderstanding, muddle, snarl-up (*Inf., chiefly Brit.*), tangle

mix up 1. blend, combine, commix, mix **2.** confound, confuse, muddle **3.** bewilder, confuse, disturb, fluster, muddle, perplex, puzzle, throw into confusion, unnerve, upset **4.** embroil, entangle, implicate, in~ volve, rope in

moan *n.* **1.** groan, lament, lamentation, sigh, sob, sough, wail, whine **2.** *Inf.* beef (*Sl.*), bitch (*Sl.*), complaint, gripe (*Inf.*), grouch (*Inf.*), grouse, grumble, kvetch (*U.S. sl.*), protest, whine ~*v.* **3.** bemoan, bewail, deplore, grieve, groan, keen, lament, mourn, sigh, sob, sough, whine **4.** *Inf.* beef (*Sl.*), bitch (*Sl.*), bleat, carp, complain, gripe (*Inf.*), groan, grouch (*Inf.*), grouse, grumble, moan and groan, whine, whinge (*Inf.*)

mob *n.* **1.** assemblage, body, collection, crowd, drove, flock, gang, gathering, herd, horde, host, mass, multitude, pack, press, swarm, throng **2.** class, company, crew (*Inf.*), gang, group, lot, set, troop **3.** canaille, commonalty, great unwashed (*Inf. & de~ rogatory*), hoi polloi, masses, rabble, riffraff, scum ~*v.* **4.** crowd around, jostle, overrun, set upon, surround, swarm around **5.** cram into, crowd, crowd into, fill, fill to over~ flowing, jam, pack

mobile 1. ambulatory, itinerant, locomo~ tive, migrant, motile, movable, moving, peripatetic, portable, travelling, wandering **2.** animated, changeable, ever-changing, expressive

mobilize activate, animate, call to arms, call up, get *or* make ready, marshal, mus~ ter, organize, prepare, put in motion, rally, ready

mock *v.* **1.** chaff, deride, flout, insult, jeer, laugh at, laugh to scorn, make fun of, poke fun at, ridicule, scoff, scorn, show contempt for, sneer, take the mickey (out of) (*Inf.*), take the piss (out of) (*Taboo sl.*), taunt, tease, wind up (*Brit. sl.*) **2.** ape, burlesque, caricature, counterfeit, do (*Inf.*), imitate, lampoon, mimic, parody, satirize, send up (*Brit. inf.*), take off (*Inf.*) **3.** belie, cheat, deceive, delude, disappoint, dupe, elude, fool, let down, mislead **4.** defeat, defy, disappoint, foil, frustrate, thwart ~*n.* **5.** banter, derision, gibe, jeering, mockery,

ridicule, scorn, sneer, sneering **6.** Aunt
Sally (*Brit.*), butt, dupe, fool, jest, laughing
stock, sport, travesty **7.** counterfeit, fake,
forgery, fraud, imitation, phoney *or* phony
(*Inf.*), sham *~adj.* **8.** artificial, bogus,
counterfeit, dummy, ersatz, fake, faked,
false, feigned, forged, fraudulent, imitation,
phoney *or* phony (*Inf.*), pretended, pseudo
(*Inf.*), sham, spurious
Antonyms *v.* encourage, praise, respect, re~
vere *~adj.* authentic, genuine, natural, real,
sincere, true, unfeigned

mockery 1. contempt, contumely, derision,
disdain, disrespect, gibes, insults, jeering,
ridicule, scoffing, scorn **2.** burlesque, cari~
cature, deception, farce, imitation, lampoon,
laughing stock, mimicry, parody, pretence,
send-up (*Brit. inf.*), sham, spoof (*Inf.*), takeoff (*Inf.*), travesty **3.** apology, disappoint~
ment, farce, joke, letdown

mocking contemptuous, contumelious, de~
risive, derisory, disdainful, disrespectful,
insulting, irreverent, sarcastic, sardonic,
satiric, satirical, scoffing, scornful, taunting

model *n.* **1.** copy, dummy, facsimile, image,
imitation, miniature, mock-up, replica, rep~
resentation **2.** archetype, design, epitome,
example, exemplar, gauge, ideal, lodestar,
mould, norm, original, par, paradigm,
paragon, pattern, prototype, standard, type
3. poser, sitter, subject **4.** mannequin **5.**
configuration, design, form, kind, mark,
mode, stamp, style, type, variety, version
~v. **6.** base, carve, cast, design, fashion,
form, mould, pattern, plan, sculpt, shape,
stamp **7.** display, show off, sport (*Inf.*),
wear *~adj.* **8.** copy, dummy, facsimile, imi~
tation, miniature **9.** archetypal, exemplary,
ideal, illustrative, paradigmatic, perfect,
standard, typical
Antonyms *adj.* (*sense 9*) deficient, flawed,
impaired, imperfect

moderate *adj.* **1.** calm, controlled, cool,
deliberate, equable, gentle, judicious, limit~
ed, middle-of-the-road, mild, modest, peace~
able, reasonable, restrained, sober, steady,
temperate **2.** average, fair, fairish, fair to
middling (*Inf.*), indifferent, mediocre, me~
dium, middling, ordinary, passable, so-so
(*Inf.*), unexceptional *~v.* **3.** abate, allay, ap~
pease, assuage, calm, control, curb, de~
crease, diminish, ease, lessen, mitigate,
modulate, pacify, play down, quiet, regu~
late, relax, repress, restrain, soften, soft-
pedal (*Inf.*), subdue, tame, temper, tone
down **4.** arbitrate, chair, judge, mediate,
preside, referee, take the chair
Antonyms *adj.* (*sense 1*) extreme, intemper~
ate, ruffled, unreasonable, wild (*sense 2*) ex~
cessive, expensive, extreme, immoderate, in~
ordinate, unusual *~v.* heighten, increase, in~
tensify

moderately fairly, gently, in moderation,
passably, quite, rather, reasonably, slightly,
somewhat, to a degree, tolerably, to some
extent, within limits, within reason

moderation 1. calmness, composure, cool~
ness, equanimity, fairness, judiciousness,
justice, justness, mildness, moderateness,
reasonableness, restraint, sedateness, tem~
perance **2. in moderation** moderately,
within limits, within reason

modern contemporary, current, fresh, late,
latest, neoteric (*Rare*), new, newfangled,
novel, present, present-day, recent,
twentieth-century, up-to-date, up-to-the-
minute, with it (*Inf.*)
Antonyms ancient, antiquated, archaic,
former, obsolete, old, old-fashioned, old hat,
outmoded, passé, past, square (*Inf.*), uncool
(*Sl.*)

modernize bring into the twentieth centu~
ry, bring up to date, face-lift, make over,
rejuvenate, remake, remodel, renew, reno~
vate, revamp, update

modest 1. bashful, blushing, coy, demure,
diffident, discreet, humble, meek, quiet, re~
served, reticent, retiring, self-conscious,
self-effacing, shy, simple, unassuming, un~
pretentious **2.** fair, limited, middling, mod~
erate, ordinary, small, unexceptional

modesty bashfulness, coyness, decency,
demureness, diffidence, discreetness, hum~
bleness, humility, lack of pretension, meek~
ness, propriety, quietness, reserve, reti~
cence, self-effacement, shyness, simplicity,
timidity, unobtrusiveness, unpretentious~
ness
Antonyms arrogance, assurance, boastful~
ness, boldness, conceit, confidence, egotism,
extravagance, forwardness, haughtiness, im~
modesty, indecency, ostentation, presump~
tion, pretentiousness, pride, showiness, van~
ity

modicum atom, bit, crumb, dash, drop,
fragment, grain, inch, iota, little, mite,
ounce, particle, pinch, scrap, shred, small
amount, speck, tad (*Inf., chiefly U.S.*), tinge,
touch

modification adjustment, alteration,
change, modulation, mutation, qualification,
refinement, reformation, restriction, revi~
sion, variation

modify 1. adapt, adjust, alter, change, con~
vert, recast, redo, refashion, reform, re~
model, reorganize, reshape, revise, rework,
transform, vary **2.** abate, ease, lessen, limit,
lower, moderate, qualify, reduce, relax, re~
strain, restrict, soften, temper, tone down

mogul baron, bashaw, big cheese (*Sl., old-
fashioned*), big gun (*Inf.*), big noise (*Inf.*),
big shot (*Inf.*), big wheel (*Sl.*), lord, mag~

nate, nabob (*Inf.*), notable, personage, po~
tentate, tycoon, V.I.P.

moist clammy, damp, dampish, dank, dewy,
dripping, drizzly, humid, not dry, rainy,
soggy, wet, wettish

moisten bedew, damp, dampen, humidify,
lick, moisturize, soak, water, wet

moisture damp, dampness, dankness, dew,
humidity, liquid, perspiration, sweat, water,
wateriness, wetness

molecule atom, iota, jot, mite, mote, parti~
cle, speck

molest 1. abuse, afflict, annoy, badger, be~
set, bother, bug (*Inf.*), disturb, harass, har~
ry, hector, irritate, persecute, pester,
plague, tease, torment, upset, vex, worry **2.**
abuse, accost, assail, attack, harm, hurt,
ill-treat, injure, interfere with, maltreat,
manhandle

moment 1. flash, instant, jiffy (*Inf.*), min~
ute, no time, second, shake (*Inf.*), split sec~
ond, tick (*Brit. inf.*), trice, twinkling, two
shakes (*Inf.*), two shakes of a lamb's tail
(*Inf.*) **2.** hour, instant, juncture, point, point
in time, stage, time **3.** concern, conse~
quence, gravity, import, importance, seri~
ousness, significance, substance, value,
weight, weightiness, worth

momentarily briefly, for a moment (little
while, minute, second, short time, short
while), for an instant, for the nonce, tem~
porarily

momentary brief, ephemeral, evanescent,
fleeting, flying, fugitive, hasty, passing,
quick, short, short-lived, temporary, transi~
tory
Antonyms lasting, lengthy, long-lived, per~
manent

momentous consequential, critical, cru~
cial, decisive, earth-shaking (*Inf.*), fateful,
grave, historic, important, of moment, piv~
otal, serious, significant, vital, weighty
Antonyms inconsequential, insignificant,
trifling, trivial, unimportant

momentum drive, energy, force, impetus,
power, propulsion, push, strength, thrust

monarch crowned head, emperor, empress,
king, potentate, prince, princess, queen,
ruler, sovereign

monarchy 1. absolutism, autocracy, des~
potism, kingship, monocracy, royalism,
sovereignty **2.** empire, kingdom, principal~
ity, realm

monastery abbey, cloister, convent, friary,
house, nunnery, priory, religious commu~
nity

monastic ascetic, austere, celibate, ceno~
bitic, cloistered, cloistral, coenobitic, con~
templative, conventual, eremitic, hermit-

like, monachal, monkish, recluse, reclusive,
secluded, sequestered, withdrawn

monetary budgetary, capital, cash,
financial, fiscal, pecuniary

money 1. ackers (*Sl.*), banknotes, brass
(*Northern English dialect*), bread (*Sl.*), capi~
tal, cash, coin, currency, dibs (*Sl.*), dosh
(*Brit. & Aust. sl.*), dough (*Sl.*), filthy lucre
(*Facetious*), funds, gelt (*Sl., chiefly U.S.*),
green (*Sl.*), hard cash, legal tender, lolly
(*Brit. sl.*), loot (*Inf.*), mazuma (*Sl., chiefly
U.S.*), megabucks (*U.S. & Canad. sl.*), moo~
lah (*Sl.*), necessary (*Inf.*), needful (*Inf.*), pelf
(*Contemptuous*), readies (*Inf.*), rhino (*Brit.
sl.*), riches, shekels (*Inf.*), silver, specie,
spondulicks (*Sl.*), the ready (*Inf.*), the
wherewithal, tin (*Sl.*), wealth **2. in the
money** affluent, flush (*Inf.*), in clover (*Inf.*),
loaded (*Sl.*), on Easy Street (*Inf.*), prosper~
ous, rich, rolling (*Sl.*), wealthy, well-heeled
(*Inf.*), well-off, well-to-do

moneymaking *adj.* gainful, going, lucra~
tive, paying, profitable, remunerative, suc~
cessful, thriving

mongrel 1. *n.* bigener (*Biol.*), cross, cross~
breed, half-breed, hybrid, mixed breed **2.**
adj. bastard, crossbred, half-breed, hybrid,
of mixed breed

monitor 1. *n.* guide, invigilator, overseer,
prefect (*Brit.*), supervisor, watchdog **2.** *v.*
check, follow, keep an eye on, keep track of,
observe, oversee, record, scan, supervise,
survey, watch

monk brother, friar (*loosely*), monastic, reli~
gious

monkey *n.* **1.** primate, simian **2.** devil,
imp, mischief maker, pickle (*Brit. inf.*), ras~
cal, rogue, scamp **3.** *Sl.* ass, butt, dupe, fool,
laughing stock **4. make a monkey of**
make a fool of, make (someone) a laughing
stock, make fun of, make (someone) look
foolish (ridiculous, silly), play a trick on,
ridicule ~*v.* **5.** fiddle (*Inf.*), fool, interfere,
meddle, mess, play, tamper, tinker, trifle

monkey business 1. carry-on (*Inf.,
chiefly Brit.*), clowning, mischief, monkey
tricks, pranks, shenanigans (*Inf.*), skylark~
ing (*Inf.*), tomfoolery **2.** chicanery, dishon~
esty, funny business, hanky-panky (*Inf.*),
skulduggery (*Inf.*), trickery

monolithic colossal, giant, gigantic, huge,
immovable, impenetrable, imposing, intrac~
table, massive, monumental, solid, substan~
tial, undifferentiated, undivided, unitary

monologue harangue, lecture, sermon, so~
liloquy, speech

monopolize control, corner, corner the
market in, dominate, engross, exercise *or*
have a monopoly of, hog (*Sl.*), keep to one~
self, take over, take up

monotonous all the same, boring, colour~
less, droning, dull, flat, ho-hum (*Inf.*), hum~
drum, mind-numbing, plodding, repetitious,
repetitive, samey (*Inf.*), soporific, tedious,
tiresome, toneless, unchanging, uniform,
uninflected, unvaried, wearisome
Antonyms animated, enjoyable, entertain~
ing, enthralling, exciting, exhilarating, inter~
esting, lively, sexy (*Inf.*), stimulating

monotony boredom, colourlessness, dull~
ness, flatness, humdrumness, monotonous~
ness, repetitiousness, repetitiveness, rou~
tine, sameness, tediousness, tedium, tire~
someness, uniformity, wearisomeness

monster *n.* **1.** barbarian, beast, bogeyman,
brute, demon, devil, fiend, ghoul, ogre, sav~
age, villain **2.** abortion, freak, lusus natu~
rae, miscreation, monstrosity, mutant,
teratism **3.** behemoth, Brobdingnagian, co~
lossus, giant, leviathan, mammoth, titan
~*adj.* **4.** Brobdingnagian, colossal, elephan~
tine, enormous, gargantuan, giant, gigantic,
ginormous (*Inf.*), huge, humongous *or* hu~
mungous (*U.S. sl.*), immense, jumbo (*Inf.*),
mammoth, massive, mega (*Sl.*), monstrous,
stupendous, titanic, tremendous

monstrosity **1.** abortion, eyesore, freak,
horror, lusus naturae, miscreation, mon~
ster, mutant, ogre, teratism **2.** abnormality,
atrocity, dreadfulness, evil, frightfulness,
heinousness, hellishness, hideousness, hor~
ror, loathsomeness, obscenity

monstrous **1.** abnormal, dreadful, enor~
mous, fiendish, freakish, frightful, gro~
tesque, gruesome, hellish, hideous, horren~
dous, horrible, miscreated, obscene, tera~
toid, terrible, unnatural **2.** atrocious, cruel,
devilish, diabolical, disgraceful, egregious,
evil, fiendish, foul, heinous, horrifying, in~
famous, inhuman, intolerable, loathsome,
odious, outrageous, satanic, scandalous,
shocking, vicious, villainous **3.** colossal, el~
ephantine, enormous, gargantuan, giant,
gigantic, ginormous (*Inf.*), great, huge, hu~
mongous *or* humungous (*U.S. sl.*), immense,
mammoth, massive, mega (*Sl.*), prodigious,
stupendous, titanic, towering, tremendous,
vast
Antonyms (*sense 1*) appealing, attractive,
beautiful, delightful, lovely, natural, normal,
ordinary, pleasant (*sense 2*) admirable, decent,
fine, good, honourable, humane, kind, merci~
ful, mild (*sense 3*) diminutive, insignificant,
little, meagre, miniature, minute, puny,
slight, small, tiny

month four weeks, moon, thirty days

monument **1.** cairn, cenotaph, commemo~
ration, gravestone, headstone, marker,
mausoleum, memorial, obelisk, pillar,
shrine, statue, tombstone **2.** memento, rec~

ord, remembrance, reminder, testament, to~
ken, witness

monumental **1.** awe-inspiring, awesome,
classic, enduring, enormous, epoch-making,
historic, immortal, important, lasting, ma~
jestic, memorable, outstanding, prodigious,
significant, stupendous, unforgettable **2.**
commemorative, cyclopean, funerary, me~
morial, monolithic, statuary **3.** *Inf.* cata~
strophic, colossal, egregious, gigantic, great,
horrible, immense, indefensible, massive,
staggering, terrible, tremendous, unforgiv~
able, whopping (*Inf.*)
Antonyms (*sense 1*) ephemeral, incon~
sequential, insignificant, modest, negligible,
ordinary, trivial, undistinguished, unimpor~
tant, unimpressive, unremarkable (*sense 3*)
average, insignificant, mild, petty, slight,
small, tiny, trivial

mood **1.** disposition, frame of mind, hu~
mour, spirit, state of mind, temper, tenor,
vein **2.** bad temper, bate (*Brit. sl.*), blues,
depression, doldrums, dumps (*Inf.*), fit of
pique, grumps (*Inf.*), low spirits, melan~
choly, sulk, the hump (*Brit. inf.*), the sulks
3. in the mood disposed (towards), eager,
favourable, inclined, interested, in the
(right) frame of mind, keen, minded, willing

moody **1.** angry, broody, cantankerous,
crabbed, crabby, crestfallen, cross, crotch~
ety (*Inf.*), crusty, curt, dismal, doleful, dour,
downcast, down in the dumps (*Inf.*), down
in the mouth (*Inf.*), frowning, gloomy, glum,
huffish, huffy, ill-humoured, ill-tempered, in
a huff, in the doldrums, introspective, iras~
cible, irritable, lugubrious, melancholy,
miserable, mopish, mopy, morose, offended,
out of sorts (*Inf.*), pensive, petulant, piqued,
sad, saturnine, short-tempered, splenetic,
sulky, sullen, temperamental, testy, tetchy,
touchy, waspish, wounded **2.** capricious,
changeable, erratic, faddish, fickle, fitful,
flighty, impulsive, inconstant, mercurial,
temperamental, unpredictable, unstable,
unsteady, volatile
Antonyms (*sense 1*) amiable, cheerful, com~
patible, gay, happy, optimistic (*sense 2*) con~
stant, stable, steady

moon *n.* **1.** satellite **2. once in a blue
moon** almost never, hardly ever, rarely,
very seldom ~*v.* **3.** daydream, idle, lan~
guish, mooch (*Sl.*), mope, waste time

moor[1] fell (*Brit.*), heath, moorland, muir
(*Scot.*)

moor[2] anchor, berth, dock, fasten, fix, lash,
make fast, secure, tie up

moot **1.** *adj.* arguable, at issue, contestable,
controversial, debatable, disputable, doubt~
ful, open, open to debate, undecided, unre~
solved, unsettled **2.** *v.* bring up, broach,

introduce, propose, put forward, suggest, ventilate

mop *n.* **1.** sponge, squeegee, swab **2.** mane, shock, tangle, thatch ~*v.* **3.** clean, soak up, sponge, swab, wash, wipe

mop up 1. clean up, mop, soak up, sponge, swab, wash, wipe **2.** *Military* account for, clean out, clear, eliminate, finish off, neu~ tralize, pacify, round up, secure

moral *adj.* **1.** ethical **2.** blameless, chaste, decent, ethical, good, high-minded, honest, honourable, incorruptible, innocent, just, meritorious, noble, principled, proper, pure, right, righteous, upright, upstanding, virtu~ ous ~*n.* **3.** lesson, meaning, message, point, significance **4.** adage, aphorism, apo~ phthegm, epigram, gnome, maxim, motto, proverb, saw, saying
Antonyms amoral, dishonest, dishonour~ able, immoral, improper, sinful, unethical, unfair, unjust, wrong

morale confidence, esprit de corps, heart, mettle, self-esteem, spirit, temper

morality 1. chastity, decency, ethicality, ethicalness, goodness, honesty, integrity, justice, principle, rectitude, righteousness, rightness, uprightness, virtue **2.** conduct, ethics, habits, ideals, manners, moral code, morals, mores, philosophy, principles, standards

morals behaviour, conduct, ethics, habits, integrity, manners, morality, mores, prin~ ciples, scruples, standards

moratorium freeze, halt, postponement, respite, standstill, stay, suspension

morbid 1. brooding, funereal, ghoulish, gloomy, grim, melancholy, pessimistic, sick, sombre, unhealthy, unwholesome **2.** dread~ ful, ghastly, grisly, gruesome, hideous, hor~ rid, macabre **3.** ailing, deadly, diseased, in~ fected, malignant, pathological, sick, sickly, unhealthy, unsound
Antonyms bright, cheerful, happy, healthy, salubrious, wholesome

more 1. *adj.* added, additional, extra, fresh, further, new, other, spare, supplementary **2.** *adv.* better, further, longer, to a greater extent

moreover additionally, also, as well, be~ sides, further, furthermore, in addition, into the bargain, likewise, to boot, too, what is more, withal (*Literary*)

morgue mortuary

moribund 1. at death's door, breathing one's last, doomed, dying, fading fast, fail~ ing, (having) one foot in the grave, *in extre~ mis*, near death, near the end, on one's deathbed, on one's last legs **2.** at a stand~ still, declining, forceless, obsolescent, on its

last legs, on the way out, stagnant, stagnat~ ing, standing still, waning, weak

morning a.m., break of day, dawn, day~ break, forenoon, morn (*Poetic*), morrow (*Archaic*), sunrise

moron airhead (*Sl.*), ass, berk (*Brit. sl.*), blockhead, bonehead (*Sl.*), charlie (*Brit. inf.*), coot, cretin, dickhead (*Sl.*), dimwit (*Inf.*), dipstick (*Brit. sl.*), divvy (*Brit. sl.*), dolt, dope (*Inf.*), dork (*Sl.*), dummy (*Sl.*), dunce, dunderhead, dweeb (*U.S. sl.*), fool, fuckwit (*Taboo sl.*), geek (*Sl.*), gonzo (*Sl.*), halfwit, idiot, imbecile, jerk (*Sl., chiefly U.S. & Canad.*), lamebrain (*Inf.*), mental defec~ tive, muttonhead (*Sl.*), nerd *or* nurd (*Sl.*), nitwit (*Inf.*), numskull *or* numbskull, oaf, pillock (*Brit. sl.*), plank (*Brit. sl.*), plonker (*Sl.*), prat (*Sl.*), prick (*Derogatory sl.*), schmuck (*U.S. sl.*), simpleton, thickhead, tosser (*Brit. sl.*), twit (*Inf., chiefly Brit.*), wally (*Sl.*)

morose blue, churlish, crabbed, crabby, cross, crusty, depressed, dour, down, down in the dumps (*Inf.*), gloomy, glum, grouchy (*Inf.*), gruff, ill-humoured, ill-natured, ill-tempered, in a bad mood, low, melancholy, miserable, moody, mournful, perverse, pes~ simistic, saturnine, sour, sulky, sullen, sur~ ly, taciturn
Antonyms amiable, blithe, cheerful, chirpy (*Inf.*), friendly, gay, genial, good-humoured, good-natured, happy, pleasant, sweet

morsel bit, bite, crumb, fraction, fragment, grain, mouthful, nibble, part, piece, scrap, segment, slice, snack, soupçon, tad (*Inf., chiefly U.S.*), taste, titbit

mortal *adj.* **1.** corporeal, earthly, ephemer~ al, human, impermanent, passing, sublu~ nary, temporal, transient, worldly **2.** dead~ ly, death-dealing, destructive, fatal, killing, lethal, murderous, terminal **3.** bitter, dead~ ly, implacable, irreconcilable, out-and-out, remorseless, sworn, to the death, unrelent~ ing **4.** agonizing, awful, dire, enormous, extreme, grave, great, intense, severe, ter~ rible ~*n.* **5.** being, body, earthling, human, human being, individual, man, person, woman

mortality 1. ephemerality, humanity, im~ permanence, temporality, transience **2.** bloodshed, carnage, death, destruction, fa~ tality, killing, loss of life

mortification 1. abasement, annoyance, chagrin, discomfiture, dissatisfaction, em~ barrassment, humiliation, loss of face, shame, vexation **2.** abasement, chastening, control, denial, discipline, subjugation **3.** *Medical* corruption, festering, gangrene, ne~ crosis, putrescence

mortified 1. abashed, affronted, annoyed, ashamed, chagrined, chastened, confounded, crushed, deflated, discomfited, displeased, embarrassed, given a showing-up (*Inf.*), humbled, humiliated, made to eat humble pie (*Inf.*), put down, put out (*Inf.*), put to shame, rendered speechless, shamed, vexed **2.** abased, chastened, conquered, controlled, crushed, disciplined, subdued **3.** *Of flesh* decayed, gangrenous, necrotic, rotted

mortify 1. abase, abash, affront, annoy, chagrin, chasten, confound, crush, deflate, disappoint, discomfit, displease, embarrass, humble, humiliate, make (someone) eat humble pie (*Inf.*), put down, put to shame, shame, take (someone) down a peg (*Inf.*), vex **2.** abase, chasten, control, deny, discipline, subdue **3.** *Of flesh* become gangrenous, corrupt, deaden, die, fester, gangrene, necrose, putrefy

mortuary funeral home (*U.S.*), funeral parlour, morgue

mostly above all, almost entirely, as a rule, chiefly, customarily, for the most part, generally, largely, mainly, most often, on the whole, particularly, predominantly, primarily, principally, usually

moth-eaten antiquated, decayed, decrepit, dilapidated, grungy (*Sl., chiefly U.S.*), obsolete, outdated, outworn, ragged, scuzzy (*Sl., chiefly U.S.*), seedy, shabby, stale, tattered, threadbare, worn-out

mother *n.* **1.** dam, ma (*Inf.*), mater, mom (*U.S. inf.*), mum (*Brit. inf.*), mummy (*Brit. inf.*), old lady (*Inf.*), old woman (*Inf.*), ~*adj.* **2.** connate, inborn, innate, native, natural ~*v.* **3.** bear, bring forth, drop, give birth to, produce **4.** care for, cherish, nurse, nurture, protect, raise, rear, tend **5.** baby, fuss over, indulge, pamper, spoil

motherly affectionate, caring, comforting, fond, gentle, kind, loving, maternal, protective, sheltering, tender, warm

mother wit brains, common sense, gumption (*Brit. inf.*), horse sense, judgment, native intelligence, savvy (*Sl.*), smarts (*Sl., chiefly U.S.*)

motion *n.* **1.** action, change, flow, kinesics, locomotion, mobility, motility, move, movement, passage, passing, progress, travel **2.** gesticulation, gesture, sign, signal, wave **3.** proposal, proposition, recommendation, submission, suggestion **4. in motion** afoot, functioning, going, in progress, moving, on the go (*Inf.*), on the move (*Inf.*), operational, travelling, under way, working ~*v.* **5.** beckon, direct, gesticulate, gesture, nod, signal, wave

motionless at a standstill, at rest, calm, fixed, frozen, halted, immobile, inanimate, inert, lifeless, paralysed, standing, static, stationary, still, stock-still, transfixed, unmoved, unmoving

Antonyms active, agitated, animated, frantic, lively, mobile, moving, restless, travelling

motivate actuate, arouse, bring, cause, draw, drive, get going, give incentive to, impel, induce, inspire, inspirit, instigate, lead, move, persuade, prod, prompt, provoke, set off, set on, stimulate, stir, trigger

motivation 1. ambition, desire, drive, hunger, inspiration, interest, wish **2.** impulse, incentive, incitement, inducement, inspiration, instigation, motive, persuasion, reason, spur, stimulus

motive 1. *n.* cause, design, ground(s), incentive, incitement, inducement, influence, inspiration, intention, mainspring, motivation, object, occasion, purpose, rationale, reason, spur, stimulus, thinking **2.** *adj.* activating, driving, impelling, motivating, moving, operative, prompting

motley 1. assorted, disparate, dissimilar, diversified, heterogeneous, mingled, miscellaneous, mixed, unlike, varied **2.** chequered, multicoloured, particoloured, polychromatic, polychrome, polychromous, rainbow, variegated

Antonyms (*sense 1*) homogeneous, similar, uniform (*sense 2*) monochromatic, plain, self-coloured, solid

mottled blotchy, brindled, chequered, dappled, flecked, freckled, marbled, piebald, pied, speckled, spotted, stippled, streaked, tabby, variegated

motto adage, byword, cry, dictum, formula, gnome, maxim, precept, proverb, rule, saw, saying, slogan, watchword

mould¹ *n.* **1.** cast, die, form, matrix, pattern, shape, stamp **2.** brand, build, configuration, construction, cut, design, fashion, form, format, frame, kind, line, make, pattern, shape, stamp, structure, style **3.** calibre, character, ilk, kidney, kind, nature, quality, sort, stamp, type ~*v.* **4.** carve, cast, construct, create, fashion, forge, form, make, model, sculpt, shape, stamp, work **5.** affect, control, direct, form, influence, make, shape

mould² blight, fungus, mildew, mouldiness, mustiness

mouldy bad, blighted, decaying, fusty, mildewed, musty, rotten, rotting, spoiled, stale

mound 1. bing (*Scot.*), drift, heap, pile, stack **2.** bank, dune, embankment, hill, hillock, knoll, rise **3.** *Archaeology* barrow, tumulus **4.** bulwark, earthwork, motte (*History*), rampart

mount *v.* **1.** ascend, clamber up, climb, escalade, go up, make one's way up, scale **2.** bestride, climb onto, climb up on, get astride, get (up) on, jump on **3.** arise, ascend, rise, soar, tower **4.** accumulate, build,

escalate, grow, increase, intensify, multiply, pile up, swell **5.** display, frame, set, set off **6.** exhibit, get up (*Inf.*), prepare, produce, put on, stage **7.** *Military* deliver, launch, prepare, ready, set in motion, stage **8.** emplace, fit, install, place, position, put in place, set up ~*n.* **9.** backing, base, fixture, foil, frame, mounting, setting, stand, support **10.** horse, steed (*Literary*)
Antonyms (*sense 1*) descend, drop, go down, make one's way down (*sense 2*) climb down from, climb off, dismount, get down from, get off, jump off (*sense 4*) contract, decline, decrease, diminish, dwindle, fall, lessen, lower, reduce, shrink, wane

mountain 1. alp, ben (*Scot.*), elevation, eminence, fell (*Brit.*), height, mount, Munro, peak **2.** abundance, heap, mass, mound, pile, stack, ton

mountainous 1. alpine, high, highland, rocky, soaring, steep, towering, upland **2.** daunting, enormous, gigantic, great, huge, hulking, immense, mammoth, mighty, monumental, ponderous, prodigious
Antonyms (*sense 2*) diminutive, insignificant, little, minute, petty, puny, small, tiny, trivial, weak

mourn bemoan, bewail, deplore, grieve, keen, lament, miss, rue, sorrow, wail, wear black, weep

mournful 1. afflicting, calamitous, deplorable, distressing, grievous, harrowing, lamentable, melancholy, painful, piteous, plaintive, sad, sorrowful, tragic, unhappy, woeful **2.** brokenhearted, cheerless, desolate, disconsolate, dismal, downcast, funereal, gloomy, grief-stricken, grieving, heartbroken, heavy, heavy-hearted, joyless, lugubrious, melancholy, miserable, rueful, sad, sombre, unhappy, woeful
Antonyms (*sense 1*) agreeable, cheerful, fortunate, happy, lucky, pleasant, satisfying (*sense 2*) bright, cheerful, chirpy (*Inf.*), genial, happy, jolly, joyful, light-hearted, sunny, upbeat (*Inf.*)

mourning 1. bereavement, grief, grieving, keening, lamentation, weeping, woe **2.** black, sackcloth and ashes, weeds, widow's weeds

mouth *n.* **1.** chops (*Sl.*), gob (*Sl., esp. Brit.*), jaws, lips, maw, trap (*Sl.*), yap (*Sl.*) **2.** *Inf.* boasting, braggadocio, bragging, empty talk, gas (*Inf.*), hot air (*Sl.*), idle talk **3.** *Inf.* backchat (*Inf.*), cheek (*Inf.*), impudence, insolence, lip (*Sl.*), rudeness, sauce (*Inf.*) **4.** aperture, cavity, crevice, door, entrance, gateway, inlet, lips, opening, orifice, rim **5.** face, grimace, *moue*, pout, wry face **6.**
down in *or* **at the mouth** blue, crestfallen, dejected, depressed, disheartened, dispirited, down, downcast, down in the dumps

(*Inf.*), in low spirits, melancholy, miserable, sad, sick as a parrot (*Inf.*), unhappy

mouthful bit, bite, drop, forkful, little, morsel, sample, sip, spoonful, sup, swallow, taste

mouthpiece 1. agent, delegate, representative, spokesman, spokeswoman **2.** journal, organ, periodical, publication

movable detachable, mobile, not fixed, portable, portative, transferable, transportable

move *v.* **1.** advance, budge, change position, drift, go, march, proceed, progress, shift, stir, walk **2.** carry, change, shift, switch, transfer, transport, transpose **3.** change residence, flit (*Scot. & northern English dialect*), go away, leave, migrate, move house, quit, relocate, remove **4.** activate, drive, impel, motivate, operate, prod, propel, push, set going, shift, shove, start, turn **5.** actuate, affect, agitate, cause, excite, give rise to, impel, impress, incite, induce, influence, inspire, instigate, lead, make an impression on, motivate, persuade, prompt, rouse, stimulate, touch, urge **6.** advocate, propose, put forward, recommend, suggest, urge ~*n.* **7.** act, action, deed, manoeuvre, measure, motion, movement, ploy, shift, step, stratagem, stroke, turn **8.** change of address, flit (*Scot. & northern English dialect*), flitting (*Scot. & northern English dialect*), migration, relocation, removal, shift, transfer **9. get a move on** get cracking (*Inf.*), get going, hurry (up), make haste, shake a leg (*Inf.*), speed up, step on it (*Inf.*), stir oneself **10. on the move** *Inf.* **a.** in transit, journeying, moving, on the road (*Inf.*), on the run, on the wing, travelling, under way, voyaging **b.** active, advancing, astir, going forward, moving, progressing, stirring, succeeding
Antonyms (*sense 5*) deter, discourage, dissuade, prevent, stop

movement 1. act, action, activity, advance, agitation, change, development, displacement, exercise, flow, gesture, manoeuvre, motion, move, moving, operation, progress, progression, shift, steps, stir, stirring, transfer **2.** camp, campaign, crusade, drive, faction, front, group, grouping, organization, party **3.** current, drift, flow, swing, tendency, trend **4.** action, innards (*Inf.*), machinery, mechanism, workings, works **5.** *Music* division, part, passage, section **6.** beat, cadence, measure (*Prosody*), metre, pace, rhythm, swing, tempo

moving 1. affecting, arousing, emotional, emotive, exciting, impelling, impressive, inspiring, pathetic, persuasive, poignant, stirring, touching **2.** mobile, motile, movable, portable, running, unfixed **3.** dynamic,

impelling, inspirational, motivating, pro~
pelling, stimulating, stimulative
Antonyms (*sense 1*) unemotional,
unexciting, unimpressive, uninspiring (*sense
2*) fixed, immobile, immovable, stationary,
still, unmoving

mow crop, cut, scythe, shear, trim

mow down blow away (*Sl., chiefly U.S.*),
butcher, cut down, cut to pieces, massacre,
shoot down, slaughter

much 1. *adj.* abundant, a lot of, ample, con~
siderable, copious, great, plenteous, plenty
of, sizeable, substantial **2.** *adv.* a great deal,
a lot, considerably, decidedly, exceedingly,
frequently, greatly, indeed, often, regularly
3. *n.* a good deal, a great deal, a lot, an ap~
preciable amount, heaps (*Inf.*), loads (*Inf.*),
lots (*Inf.*), plenty
Antonyms *adj.* inadequate, insufficient, lit~
tle, scant ~*adv.* barely, hardly, infrequently,
irregularly, not a lot, not much, occasionally,
only just, rarely, scarcely, seldom, slightly ~*n.*
hardly anything, little, next to nothing, not a
lot, not much, practically nothing, very little

muck 1. crap (*Taboo sl.*), dung, manure, or~
dure, shit (*Taboo sl.*) **2.** crap (*Sl.*), crud
(*Sl.*), dirt, filth, grot (*Sl.*), gunge (*Inf.*), gunk
(*Inf.*), mire, mud, ooze, scum, sewage, shit
(*Taboo sl.*), slime, sludge **3. make a muck
of** *Sl.* blow (*Sl.*), botch, bungle, cock up
(*Brit. sl.*), fuck up (*Offens. taboo sl.*), make a
mess of, mar, mess up, muff, ruin, screw up
(*Inf.*), spoil

muck up blow (*Sl.*), bodge (*Inf.*), botch,
bungle, cock up (*Brit. sl.*), fuck up (*Offens.
taboo sl.*), make a mess of, make a muck of
(*Sl.*), mar, mess up, muff, ruin, screw up
(*Inf.*), spoil

mud clay, dirt, mire, ooze, silt, slime, sludge

muddle *v.* **1.** confuse, disarrange, disorder,
disorganize, jumble, make a mess of, mess,
mix up, ravel, scramble, spoil, tangle **2.** be~
fuddle, bewilder, confound, confuse, daze,
disorient, perplex, stupefy ~*n.* **3.** chaos,
clutter, confusion, daze, disarray, disorder,
disorganization, fankle (*Scot.*), hodgepodge
(*U.S.*), hotchpotch, jumble, mess, mix-up,
perplexity, pig's breakfast (*Inf.*), plight,
predicament, ravel, tangle

muddled 1. chaotic, confused, disarrayed,
disordered, disorganized, higgledy-piggledy
(*Inf.*), jumbled, messy, mixed-up, scrambled,
tangled **2.** at sea, befuddled, bewildered,
confused, dazed, disoriented, perplexed,
stupefied, vague **3.** confused, incoherent,
loose, muddleheaded, unclear, woolly
Antonyms clear, exact, orderly, organized,
precise

muddy *adj.* **1.** bespattered, boggy, clarty
(*Scot., & northern English dialect*), dirty,
grimy, marshy, miry, mucky, mud-caked,

quaggy, soiled, swampy **2.** blurred, dingy,
dull, flat, lustreless, smoky, unclear,
washed-out **3.** cloudy, dirty, foul, impure,
opaque, turbid **4.** confused, fuzzy, hazy, in~
distinct, muddled, unclear, vague, woolly
~*v.* **5.** begrime, bespatter, cloud, dirty,
smear, smirch, soil

muffle 1. cloak, conceal, cover, disguise,
envelop, hood, mask, shroud, swaddle,
swathe, wrap up **2.** deaden, dull, gag, hush,
muzzle, quieten, silence, soften, stifle, sup~
press

muffled dim, dull, faint, indistinct, muted,
stifled, strangled, subdued, suppressed

mug beaker, cup, flagon, jug, pot, tankard,
toby jug

muggy clammy, close, damp, humid, moist,
oppressive, sticky, stuffy, sultry

mug up bone up on (*Inf.*), burn the mid~
night oil (*Inf.*), cram (*Inf.*), get up (*Inf.*),
study, swot (*Brit. inf.*)

mull consider, contemplate, deliberate, ex~
amine, meditate, muse on, ponder, reflect
on, review, ruminate, study, think about,
think over, turn over in one's mind, weigh

multifarious different, diverse, diversified,
legion, manifold, many, miscellaneous,
multiform, multiple, multitudinous, numer~
ous, sundry, varied, variegated

multiple collective, manifold, many, multi~
tudinous, numerous, several, sundry, vari~
ous

multiply accumulate, augment, breed, build
up, expand, extend, increase, proliferate,
propagate, reproduce, spread
Antonyms abate, decline, decrease, dimin~
ish, lessen, reduce

multitude 1. army, assemblage, assembly,
collection, concourse, congregation, crowd,
great number, horde, host, legion, lot, lots
(*Inf.*), mass, mob, myriad, sea, swarm,
throng **2.** commonalty, common people,
herd, hoi polloi, mob, populace, proletariat,
public, rabble

mumsy dowdy, drab, fogyish, frumpish *or*
frumpy, homely, old-fashioned, plain,
square (*Inf.*), unfashionable, unglamorous,
unsophisticated
Antonyms attractive, beautiful, chic, el~
egant, fashionable, glamorous, modern, mod~
ish, smart, sophisticated, well-dressed

munch champ, chew, chomp, crunch, mas~
ticate, scrunch

mundane 1. banal, commonplace, day-to-
day, everyday, humdrum, ordinary, prosaic,
routine, workaday **2.** earthly, fleshly, hu~
man, material, mortal, secular, sublunary,
temporal, terrestrial, worldly
Antonyms (*sense 1*) dramatic, exciting,
extraordinary, imaginative, interesting, nov~

el, original, special, uncommon, unusual (*sense 2*) ethereal, heavenly, spiritual, un~ worldly

municipal borough, city, civic, community, public, town, urban

municipality borough, burgh (*Scot.*), city, district, town, township, urban community

munificence beneficence, benevolence, big-heartedness, bounteousness, bounty, generosity, generousness, largess *or* lar~ gesse, liberality, magnanimousness, open-handedness, philanthropy

munificent beneficent, benevolent, big-hearted, bounteous, bountiful, free-handed, generous, lavish, liberal, magnanimous, open-handed, philanthropical, princely, rich, unstinting
Antonyms cheap, mean, miserly, parsimo~ nious, small, stingy

murder *n.* **1.** assassination, bloodshed, butchery, carnage, homicide, killing, man~ slaughter, massacre, slaying **2.** *Inf.* agony, an ordeal, a trial, danger, difficulty, hell (*Inf.*), misery, trouble ~*v.* **3.** assassinate, blow away (*Sl., chiefly U.S.*), bump off (*Sl.*), butcher, destroy, dispatch, do in (*Inf.*), do to death, eliminate (*Sl.*), hit (*Sl.*), kill, massa~ cre, rub out (*U.S. sl.*), slaughter, slay, take out (*Sl.*), take the life of, waste (*Inf.*) **4.** abuse, butcher, destroy, mangle, mar, mis~ use, ruin, spoil **5.** *Inf.* beat decisively, blow out of the water (*Sl.*), cream (*Sl., chiefly U.S.*), defeat utterly, drub, hammer (*Inf.*), lick (*Inf.*), make mincemeat of (*Inf.*), slaughter, tank (*Sl.*), thrash, wipe the floor with (*Inf.*)

murderer assassin, butcher, cutthroat, hit man (*Sl.*), homicide, killer, slaughterer, slayer

murderous **1.** barbarous, bloodthirsty, bloody, brutal, cruel, deadly, death-dealing, destructive, devastating, fatal, fell (*Archaic*), ferocious, internecine, lethal, sanguinary, savage, slaughterous, withering **2.** *Inf.* ar~ duous, dangerous, difficult, exhausting, harrowing, hellish (*Inf.*), killing (*Inf.*), sap~ ping, strenuous, unpleasant

murky cheerless, cloudy, dark, dim, dismal, dreary, dull, dusky, foggy, gloomy, grey, impenetrable, misty, nebulous, obscure, overcast
Antonyms bright, cheerful, clear, distinct, sunny

murmur *n.* **1.** babble, buzzing, drone, hum~ ming, mumble, muttering, purr, rumble, susurrus (*Literary*), undertone, whisper, whispering ~*v.* **2.** babble, buzz, drone, hum, mumble, mutter, purr, rumble, speak in an undertone, whisper ~*n.* **3.** beef (*Sl.*), complaint, gripe (*Inf.*), grouse, grumble, moan (*Inf.*), word ~*v.* **4.** beef (*Sl.*), carp,

cavil, complain, gripe (*Inf.*), grouse, grum~ ble, moan (*Inf.*)

muscle *n.* **1.** muscle tissue, sinew, tendon, thew **2.** brawn, clout (*Inf.*), force, forceful~ ness, might, potency, power, stamina, strength, sturdiness, weight ~*v.* **3. muscle in** *Inf.* butt in, elbow one's way in, force one's way in, impose oneself

muscular athletic, beefy (*Inf.*), brawny, husky (*Inf.*), lusty, powerful, powerfully built, Ramboesque, robust, sinewy, stalwart, strapping, strong, sturdy, thickset, vigor~ ous, well-knit

muse be in a brown study, be lost in thought, brood, cogitate, consider, contem~ plate, deliberate, dream, meditate, mull over, ponder, reflect, ruminate, speculate, think, think over, weigh

mushroom *v.* boom, burgeon, expand, flourish, grow rapidly, increase, luxuriate, proliferate, shoot up, spread, spring up, sprout

musical dulcet, euphonic, euphonious, har~ monious, lilting, lyrical, melodic, melo~ dious, sweet-sounding, tuneful
Antonyms discordant, grating, harsh, un~ melodious, unmusical

musing *n.* absent-mindedness, abstraction, brown study, cerebration, cogitation, con~ templation, day-dreaming, dreaming, intro~ spection, meditation, reflection, reverie, ru~ mination, thinking, woolgathering

must *n.* duty, essential, fundamental, im~ perative, necessary thing, necessity, obliga~ tion, prerequisite, requirement, requisite, *sine qua non*

muster *v.* **1.** assemble, call together, call up, collect, come together, congregate, convene, convoke, enrol, gather, group, marshal, meet, mobilize, rally, round up, summon ~*n.* **2.** assemblage, assembly, collection, concourse, congregation, convention, con~ vocation, gathering, meeting, mobilization, rally, roundup **3. pass muster** be *or* come up to scratch, be acceptable, fill the bill (*Inf.*), make the grade, measure up, qualify

musty **1.** airless, dank, decayed, frowsty, fusty, mildewed, mildewy, mouldy, old, smelly, stale, stuffy **2.** ancient, antedilu~ vian, antiquated, banal, clichéd, dull, hack~ neyed, hoary, moth-eaten, obsolete, old-fashioned, stale, threadbare, trite, worn-out
Antonyms (*sense 2*) current, exciting, fash~ ionable, fresh, imaginative, interesting, live~ ly, modern, modish, new, novel, original, un~ usual, up-to-date, with it (*Inf.*)

mutability alteration, change, evolution, metamorphosis, transition, variation, vicis~ situde

mutable adaptable, alterable, changeable,

changing, fickle, flexible, immutable, in~
consistent, inconstant, irresolute, uncertain,
undependable, unreliable, unsettled, unsta~
ble, unsteady, vacillating, variable, volatile,
wavering

mutation 1. alteration, change, deviation,
evolution, metamorphosis, modification,
transfiguration, transformation, variation
2. anomaly, deviant, mutant

mute 1. *adj.* aphasiac, aphasic, aphonic,
dumb, mum, silent, speechless, unex~
pressed, unspeaking, unspoken, voiceless,
wordless **2.** *v.* dampen, deaden, lower,
moderate, muffle, soften, soft-pedal, subdue,
tone down, turn down

mutilate 1. amputate, butcher, cripple, cut
to pieces, cut up, damage, disable, disfigure,
dismember, hack, injure, lacerate, lame,
maim, mangle **2.** adulterate, bowdlerize,
butcher, censor, cut, damage, distort, ex~
purgate, hack, mar, spoil

mutinous bolshie (*Brit. inf.*), contumacious,
disobedient, insubordinate, insurgent, re~
bellious, refractory, revolutionary, riotous,
seditious, subversive, turbulent, ungovern~
able, unmanageable, unruly

mutiny 1. *n.* defiance, disobedience, insub~
ordination, insurrection, rebellion, refusal
to obey orders, resistance, revolt, revolu~
tion, riot, rising, strike, uprising **2.** *v.* be
insubordinate, defy authority, disobey, re~
bel, refuse to obey orders, resist, revolt, rise
up, strike

mutter complain, grouch (*Inf.*), grouse,
grumble, mumble, murmur, rumble

mutual common, communal, correlative,
interactive, interchangeable, interchanged,
joint, reciprocal, reciprocated, requited, re~
turned, shared

muzzle *n.* **1.** jaws, mouth, nose, snout **2.**
gag, guard ~*v.* **3.** censor, choke, curb, gag,
restrain, silence, stifle, suppress

myopic near-sighted, short-sighted

myriad 1. *adj.* a thousand and one, count~
less, immeasurable, incalculable, innumer~
able, multitudinous, untold **2.** *n.* a million,
army, a thousand, flood, horde, host, mil~
lions, mountain, multitude, scores, sea,
swarm, thousands

mysterious abstruse, arcane, baffling, con~
cealed, covert, cryptic, curious, dark, Del~
phic, enigmatic, furtive, hidden, impen~
etrable, incomprehensible, inexplicable, in~
scrutable, insoluble, mystical, mystifying,
obscure, perplexing, puzzling, recondite, se~
cret, secretive, sphinxlike, strange, uncan~
ny, unfathomable, unknown, veiled, weird
Antonyms apparent, clear, intelligible,
manifest, open, plain

mystery conundrum, enigma, problem,
puzzle, question, riddle, secrecy, secret,
teaser

mystic, mystical abstruse, arcane, caba~
listic, cryptic, enigmatical, esoteric, hidden,
inscrutable, metaphysical, mysterious, non~
rational, occult, otherworldly, paranormal,
preternatural, supernatural, transcendental

mystify baffle, bamboozle (*Inf.*), beat (*Sl.*),
befog, bewilder, confound, confuse, elude,
escape, flummox, nonplus, perplex, puzzle,
stump

myth 1. allegory, fable, fairy story, fiction,
folk tale, legend, parable, saga, story, tradi~
tion, urban legend **2.** delusion, fancy, fan~
tasy, figment, illusion, imagination, super~
stition, tall story

mythical 1. allegorical, chimerical, fabled,
fabulous, fairy-tale, legendary, mythologi~
cal, storied **2.** fabricated, fanciful, fantasy,
fictitious, imaginary, invented, made-up,
make-believe, nonexistent, pretended, un~
real, untrue

mythology folklore, folk tales, legend, lore,
mythos, myths, stories, tradition

N

nab apprehend, arrest, capture, catch, collar (*Inf.*), feel one's collar (*Sl.*), grab, lift (*Sl.*), nail (*Inf.*), nick (*Sl., chiefly Brit.*), seize, snatch

nadir bottom, depths, lowest point, minimum, rock bottom, zero
Antonyms acme, apex, climax, crest, height, high point, peak, pinnacle, summit, top, vertex, zenith

nag¹ 1. *v.* annoy, badger, bend someone's ear (*Inf.*), be on one's back (*Sl.*), berate, chivvy, goad, harass, harry, hassle (*Inf.*), henpeck, irritate, nark (*Brit., Aust., & N.Z. sl.*), pester, plague, provoke, scold, torment, upbraid, vex, worry **2.** *n.* harpy, scold, shrew, tartar, termagant, virago

nag² hack, horse, jade, plug (*U.S.*)

nagging continuous, critical, distressing, irritating, painful, persistent, scolding, shrewish, worrying

nail *v.* attach, beat, fasten, fix, hammer, join, pin, secure, tack

naive artless, candid, childlike, confiding, frank, guileless, ingenuous, innocent, jejune, natural, open, simple, trusting, unaffected, unpretentious, unsophisticated, unworldly **2.** callow, credulous, green, gullible, unsuspicious
Antonyms artful, disingenuous, experienced, sly, sophisticated, urbane, worldly, worldly-wise

naiveté, naivety 1. artlessness, candour, frankness, guilelessness, inexperience, ingenuousness, innocence, naturalness, openness, simplicity **2.** callowness, credulity, gullibility

naked 1. bare, buck naked (*Sl.*), denuded, disrobed, divested, exposed, in one's birthday suit (*Inf.*), in the altogether (*Inf.*), in the buff (*Inf.*), in the raw (*Inf.*), naked as the day one was born (*Inf.*), nude, starkers (*Inf.*), stripped, unclothed, unconcealed, uncovered, undraped, undressed, without a stitch on (*Inf.*) **2.** blatant, evident, manifest, open, overt, patent, plain, simple, stark, unadorned, undisguised, unexaggerated, unmistakable, unqualified, unvarnished **3.** defenceless, helpless, insecure, unarmed, unguarded, unprotected, vulnerable
Antonyms clothed, concealed, covered, dressed, wrapped up

nakedness 1. baldness, bareness, nudity, undress **2.** openness, plainness, simplicity, starkness

namby-pamby anaemic, colourless, feeble, insipid, mawkish, prim, prissy (*Inf.*), sentimental, spineless, vapid, weak, weedy (*Inf.*), wimpish *or* wimpy (*Inf.*), wishy-washy (*Inf.*)

name *n.* **1.** appellation, cognomen, denomination, designation, epithet, handle (*Sl.*), moniker *or* monicker (*Sl.*), nickname, sobriquet, term, title **2.** distinction, eminence, esteem, fame, honour, note, praise, renown, repute **3.** character, credit, reputation ~*v.* **4.** baptize, call, christen, denominate, dub, entitle, label, style, term **5.** appoint, choose, cite, classify, commission, designate, flag, identify, mention, nominate, select, specify

named 1. baptized, called, christened, denominated, dubbed, entitled, known as, labelled, styled, termed **2.** appointed, chosen, cited, classified, commissioned, designated, identified, mentioned, nominated, picked, selected, singled out, specified

nameless 1. anonymous, innominate, undesignated, unnamed, untitled **2.** incognito, obscure, undistinguished, unheard-of, unknown, unsung **3.** abominable, horrible, indescribable, ineffable, inexpressible, unmentionable, unspeakable, unutterable

namely i.e., specifically, that is to say, to wit, viz.

nap¹ 1. *v.* catnap, doze, drop off (*Inf.*), drowse, kip (*Brit. sl.*), nod, nod off (*Inf.*), rest, sleep, snooze (*Inf.*), zizz (*Brit. inf.*) **2.** *n.* catnap, forty winks (*Inf.*), kip (*Brit. sl.*), rest, shuteye (*Sl.*), siesta, sleep, zizz (*Brit. inf.*)

nap² down, fibre, grain, pile, shag, weave

narcissism egotism, self-admiration, self-love, vanity

narcotic 1. *n.* anaesthetic, analgesic, anodyne, drug, opiate, painkiller, sedative, tranquillizer **2.** *adj.* analgesic, calming, dulling, hypnotic, Lethean, numbing, painkilling, sedative, somnolent, soporific, stupefacient, stupefactive, stupefying

nark aggravate (*Inf.*), annoy, bother, bug, exasperate, gall, get on one's nerves (*Inf.*), irk, irritate, miff (*Inf.*), nettle, peeve, pique, piss one off (*Taboo sl.*), provoke, rile

narrate chronicle, describe, detail, recite, recount, rehearse, relate, repeat, report, set forth, tell, unfold

narration description, explanation, reading, recital, rehearsal, relation, storytelling, telling, voice-over (*in film*)

narrative account, chronicle, detail, history, report, statement, story, tale

narrator annalist, author, bard, chronicler, commentator, raconteur, reciter, relater, reporter, storyteller, writer

narrow *adj.* **1.** circumscribed, close, confined, constricted, contracted, cramped, incapacious, limited, meagre, near, pinched, restricted, scanty, straitened, tight **2.** bi~ased, bigoted, dogmatic, illiberal, intolerant, narrow-minded, partial, prejudiced, reac~tionary, small-minded **3.** attenuated, fine, slender, slim, spare, tapering, thin **4.** ex~clusive, select **5.** *Inf.* avaricious, close (*Inf.*), mean, mercenary, niggardly, ungenerous ~*v.* **6.** circumscribe, constrict, diminish, limit, reduce, simplify, straiten, tighten
Antonyms ample, big, broad, broad-minded, generous, liberal, open, receptive, spacious, tolerant, wide

narrowly **1.** barely, by a whisker *or* hair's-breadth, just, only just, scarcely **2.** carefully, closely, painstakingly, scrutinizingly

narrow-minded biased, bigoted, con~servative, hidebound, illiberal, insular, in~tolerant, opinionated, parochial, petty, prejudiced, provincial, reactionary, short-sighted, small-minded, strait-laced
Antonyms broad-minded, catholic, cosmo~politan, freethinking, indulgent, open-minded, permissive, tolerant, unprejudiced

narrows channel, gulf, passage, sound, straits

nastiness **1.** defilement, dirtiness, filth, filthiness, foulness, impurity, pollution, squalor, uncleanliness **2.** indecency, licen~tiousness, obscenity, pollution, porn (*Inf.*), pornography, ribaldry, smuttiness **3.** dis~agreeableness, malice, meanness, offensive~ness, spitefulness, unpleasantness

nasty **1.** dirty, disagreeable, disgusting, filthy, foul, grotty (*Sl.*), horrible, loathsome, malodorous, mephitic, nauseating, noisome, objectionable, obnoxious, odious, offensive, polluted, repellent, repugnant, sickening, unappetizing, unpleasant, vile, yucky *or* yukky (*Sl.*) **2.** blue, foul, gross, impure, in~decent, lascivious, lewd, licentious, obscene, pornographic, ribald, smutty **3.** abusive, annoying, bad-tempered, despicable, dis~agreeable, distasteful, malicious, mean, spiteful, unpleasant, vicious, vile **4.** bad, critical, dangerous, painful, serious, severe
Antonyms admirable, agreeable, clean, de~cent, enjoyable, kind, nice, pleasant, sweet

nation commonwealth, community, country, people, population, race, realm, society, state, tribe

national *adj.* **1.** civil, countrywide, govern~mental, nationwide, public, state, wide~spread **2.** domestic, internal, social ~*n.* **3.** citizen, inhabitant, native, resident, subject

nationalism allegiance, chauvinism, fealty, jingoism, loyalty, nationality, patriotism

nationality birth, ethnic group, nation, race

nationwide countrywide, general, national, overall, widespread

native *adj.* **1.** built-in, congenital, endemic, hereditary, inborn, inbred, indigenous, in~grained, inherent, inherited, innate, in~stinctive, intrinsic, inveterate, natal, natu~ral **2.** genuine, original, real **3.** domestic, home, home-grown, home-made, indigenous, local, mother, vernacular **4.** aboriginal, autochthonous ~*n.* **5.** aborigine, autoch~thon, citizen, countryman, dweller, inhabit~ant, national, resident

nativity **1.** birth, delivery, parturition **2.** crèche, manger scene
Antonyms (*sense 1*) death, demise, dying, expiration

natter **1.** *v.* blather, blether, chatter, gabble, gossip, jabber, jaw (*Sl.*), palaver, prate, prattle, rabbit (on) (*Brit. inf.*), talk, talk idly, witter (*Inf.*) **2.** *n.* blather, blether, chat, chinwag (*Brit. inf.*), chitchat, confabu~lation, conversation, gab (*Inf.*), gabble, gab~fest (*Inf., chiefly U.S. & Canad.*), gossip, jabber, jaw (*Sl.*), palaver, prattle, talk

natty chic, crucial (*Sl.*), dapper, elegant, fashionable, neat, smart, snazzy (*Inf.*), spruce, stylish, trendy (*Brit. inf.*), trim, well-dressed, well-turned-out

natural **1.** common, everyday, legitimate, logical, normal, ordinary, regular, typical, usual **2.** characteristic, congenital, essen~tial, inborn, indigenous, inherent, innate, instinctive, intuitive, natal, native **3.** art~less, candid, frank, genuine, ingenuous, open, real, simple, spontaneous, unaffected, unpretentious, unsophisticated, unstudied **4.** organic, plain, pure, unbleached, un~mixed, unpolished, unrefined, whole
Antonyms (*sense 1*) abnormal, irregular, out of the ordinary, strange, untypical (*sense 3*) affected, artificial, assumed, counterfeit, feigned, phoney *or* phony (*Inf.*), unnatural (*sense 4*) manufactured, processed, synthetic, unnatural

naturalism factualism, realism, verisimili~tude

naturalist **1.** biologist, botanist, ecologist, zoologist **2.** factualist, realist

naturalize acclimate, acclimatize, accultur~ate, accustom, adapt, adopt, domesticate, enfranchise, familiarize, grant citizenship, habituate

naturally **1.** *adv.* as anticipated, customari~ly, genuinely, informally, normally, simply, spontaneously, typically, unaffectedly, unpretentiously **2.** *interj.* absolutely, as a matter of course, certainly, of course

nature 1. attributes, character, complexion, constitution, essence, features, make-up, quality, traits **2.** category, description, kind, sort, species, style, type, variety **3.** cosmos, creation, earth, environment, universe, world **4.** disposition, humour, mood, outlook, temper, temperament **5.** country, countryside, landscape, natural history, scenery

naturist nudist

naughty 1. annoying, bad, disobedient, exasperating, fractious, impish, misbehaved, mischievous, perverse, playful, refractory, roguish, sinful, teasing, wayward, wicked, worthless **2.** bawdy, blue, improper, lewd, obscene, off-colour, ribald, risqué, smutty, vulgar
Antonyms good, obedient, polite, proper, seemly, well-behaved, well-mannered

nausea 1. biliousness, qualm(s), queasiness, retching, sickness, squeamishness, vomiting **2.** abhorrence, aversion, disgust, loathing, odium, repugnance, revulsion

nauseate disgust, gross out (*U.S. sl.*), horrify, offend, repel, repulse, revolt, sicken, turn one's stomach

nautical marine, maritime, naval, oceanic, seafaring, seagoing, yachting

naval marine, maritime, nautical, oceanic

navel 1. bellybutton (*Inf.*), omphalos (*Literary*), umbilicus **2.** central point, centre, hub, middle

navigable 1. clear, negotiable, passable, traversable, unobstructed **2.** controllable, dirigible, sailable, steerable

navigate con (*Nautical*), cross, cruise, direct, drive, guide, handle, journey, manoeuvre, pilot, plan, plot, sail, skipper, steer, voyage

navigation cruising, helmsmanship, pilotage, sailing, seamanship, steering, voyaging

navigator mariner, pilot, seaman

navvy ganger, labourer, worker, workman

navy argosy (*Archaic*), armada, fleet, flotilla, warships

near *adj.* **1.** adjacent, adjoining, alongside, at close quarters, beside, bordering, close, close by, contiguous, nearby, neighbouring, nigh, proximate, touching, within sniffing distance (*Inf.*) **2.** approaching, forthcoming, imminent, impending, in the offing, looming, near-at-hand, next, on the cards (*Inf.*), upcoming **3.** akin, allied, attached, connected, dear, familiar, intimate, related **4.** *Inf.* close-fisted, mean, miserly, niggardly, parsimonious, stingy, tightfisted, ungenerous
Antonyms (*senses 1, 2 & 3*) distant, far, far-

away, far-flung, far-off, far-removed, long, outlying, out-of-the-way, remote, removed

nearby 1. *adj.* adjacent, adjoining, convenient, handy, neighbouring **2.** *adv.* at close quarters, close at hand, not far away, proximate, within reach, within sniffing distance (*Inf.*)

nearly *adv.* about, all but, almost, approaching, approximately, as good as, closely, just about, not quite, practically, roughly, virtually, well-nigh

nearness 1. accessibility, availability, closeness, contiguity, handiness, juxtaposition, propinquity, proximity, vicinity **2.** immediacy, imminence **3.** dearness, familiarity, intimacy **4.** *Inf.* meanness, niggardliness, parsimony, stinginess

near-sighted myopic, short-sighted

near thing close shave (*Inf.*), narrow escape, near miss

neat 1. accurate, dainty, fastidious, methodical, nice, orderly, shipshape, smart, spick-and-span, spruce, straight, systematic, tidy, trim, uncluttered **2.** adept, adroit, agile, apt, clever, deft, dexterous, efficient, effortless, elegant, expert, graceful, handy, nimble, practised, precise, skilful, stylish, well-judged **3.** *Of alcoholic drinks* pure, straight, undiluted, unmixed
Antonyms (*senses 1 & 2*) awful, bad, clumsy, cluttered, disarrayed, disorderly, disorganized, incompetent, inefficient, inelegant, messy, slobby (*Inf.*), sloppy (*Inf.*), terrible, untidy

neatly 1. accurately, daintily, fastidiously, methodically, nicely, smartly, sprucely, systematically, tidily **2.** adeptly, adroitly, agilely, aptly, cleverly, deftly, dexterously, efficiently, effortlessly, elegantly, expertly, gracefully, handily, nimbly, precisely, skilfully, stylishly

neatness 1. accuracy, daintiness, fastidiousness, methodicalness, niceness, nicety, orderliness, smartness, spruceness, straightness, tidiness, trimness **2.** adeptness, adroitness, agility, aptness, cleverness, deftness, dexterity, efficiency, effortlessness, elegance, expertness, grace, gracefulness, handiness, nimbleness, preciseness, precision, skilfulness, skill, style, stylishness

nebulous ambiguous, amorphous, cloudy, confused, dim, hazy, imprecise, indefinite, indeterminate, indistinct, misty, murky, obscure, shadowy, shapeless, uncertain, unclear, unformed, vague

necessarily accordingly, automatically, axiomatically, by definition, certainly, compulsorily, consequently, incontrovertibly, ineluctably, inevitably, inexorably, irresistibly, naturally, *nolens volens,* of course, of necessity, perforce, undoubtedly, willy-nilly

necessary 1. compulsory, *de rigueur,* essential, imperative, indispensable, mandatory, needed, needful, obligatory, required, requisite, vital **2.** certain, fated, inescapable, inevitable, inexorable, unavoidable
Antonyms dispensable, expendable, inessential, nonessential, superfluous, unnecessary

necessitate call for, coerce, compel, constrain, demand, entail, force, impel, make necessary, oblige, require

necessities essentials, exigencies, fundamentals, indispensables, needs, requirements

necessity 1. demand, exigency, indispensability, need, needfulness, requirement **2.** desideratum, essential, fundamental, necessary, need, prerequisite, requirement, requisite, *sine qua non,* want **3.** destitution, extremity, indigence, need, penury, poverty, privation **4.** compulsion, destiny, fate, inevitability, inexorableness, obligation

necromancy black art, black magic, demonology, divination, enchantment, magic, sorcery, thaumaturgy (*Rare*), voodoo, witchcraft, witchery, wizardry

necropolis burial ground, cemetery, churchyard, God's acre, graveyard

need *v.* **1.** call for, demand, entail, have occasion to *or* for, lack, miss, necessitate, require, want ~*n.* **2.** longing, requisite, want, wish **3.** deprivation, destitution, distress, extremity, impecuniousness, inadequacy, indigence, insufficiency, lack, neediness, paucity, penury, poverty, privation, shortage **4.** emergency, exigency, necessity, obligation, urgency, want **5.** demand, desideratum, essential, requirement, requisite

needed called for, desired, lacked, necessary, required, wanted

needful essential, indispensable, necessary, needed, required, requisite, stipulated, vital

needle *v.* aggravate (*Inf.*), annoy, bait, be on one's back (*Sl.*), gall, get in one's hair (*Inf.*), get on one's nerves (*Inf.*), goad, harass, hassle (*Inf.*), irk, irritate, nag, nark (*Brit., Aust., & N.Z. sl.*), nettle, pester, piss one off (*Taboo sl.*), prick, prod, provoke, rile, ruffle, spur, sting, taunt

needless causeless, dispensable, excessive, expendable, gratuitous, groundless, nonessential, pointless, redundant, superfluous, uncalled-for, undesired, unnecessary, unwanted, useless
Antonyms beneficial, essential, obligatory, required, useful

needlework embroidery, fancywork, needlecraft, sewing, stitching, tailoring

needy deprived, destitute, dirt-poor (*Inf.*), disadvantaged, impecunious, impoverished, indigent, on the breadline (*Inf.*), penniless, poor, poverty-stricken, underprivileged
Antonyms affluent, comfortable, moneyed, prosperous, rich, wealthy, well-off, well-to-do

nefarious abominable, atrocious, base, criminal, depraved, detestable, dreadful, evil, execrable, foul, heinous, horrible, infamous, infernal, iniquitous, monstrous, odious, opprobrious, shameful, sinful, vicious, vile, villainous, wicked
Antonyms admirable, good, honest, honourable, just, noble, praiseworthy, upright, virtuous

negate 1. abrogate, annul, cancel, countermand, invalidate, neutralize, nullify, obviate, repeal, rescind, retract, reverse, revoke, void, wipe out **2.** contradict, deny, disallow, disprove, gainsay (*Archaic or literary*), oppose, rebut, refute
Antonyms affirm, assert, attest, avouch, avow, certify, confirm, declare, maintain, pronounce, ratify, state, swear, testify

negation 1. antithesis, antonym, contradiction, contrary, converse, counterpart, denial, disavowal, disclaimer, inverse, opposite, rejection, renunciation, reverse **2.** opposition, proscription, refusal, repudiation, veto **3.** cancellation, neutralization, nullification **4.** blank, nonexistence, nothingness, nullity, vacuity, void

negative *adj.* **1.** contradictory, contrary, denying, dissenting, opposing, recusant, refusing, rejecting, resisting **2.** annulling, counteractive, invalidating, neutralizing, nullifying **3.** antagonistic, colourless, contrary, cynical, gloomy, jaundiced, neutral, pessimistic, uncooperative, unenthusiastic, uninterested, unwilling, weak ~*n.* **4.** contradiction, denial, refusal
Antonyms *adj.* affirmative, approving, assenting, cheerful, concurring, enthusiastic, optimistic, positive

negativeness, negativity 1. contradiction, contradictoriness, contrariness, denial, dissent, opposition, recusancy, refusal, rejection, resistance **2.** antagonism, colourlessness, contrariness, cynicism, gloom, neutrality, pessimism, uncooperativeness, uninterestedness, unwillingness, weakness

neglect *v.* **1.** contemn, discount, disdain, disregard, ignore, leave alone, overlook, pass by, rebuff, scorn, slight, spurn **2.** be remiss, evade, forget, let slide, omit, pass over, procrastinate, shirk, skimp ~*n.* **3.** disdain, disregard, disrespect, heedlessness, inattention, indifference, slight, unconcern **4.** carelessness, default, dereliction, failure, forgetfulness, laxity, laxness, neglectfulness,

negligence, oversight, remissness, slack~
ness, slovenliness
Antonyms *v.* appreciate, attend to, notice,
observe, regard, remember, value ~*n.* atten~
tion, care, consideration, notice, regard, re~
spect

neglected 1. abandoned, derelict, over~
grown 2. disregarded, unappreciated,
underestimated, undervalued

negligence carelessness, default, derelic~
tion, disregard, failure, forgetfulness, heed~
lessness, inadvertence, inattention, inatten~
tiveness, indifference, laxity, laxness, ne~
glect, omission, oversight, remissness,
shortcoming, slackness, thoughtlessness

negligent careless, cursory, disregardful,
forgetful, heedless, inadvertent, inattentive,
indifferent, neglectful, nonchalant, offhand,
regardless, remiss, slack, slapdash, slip~
shod, thoughtless, unmindful, unthinking
Antonyms attentive, careful, considerate,
mindful, painstaking, rigorous, thorough,
thoughtful

negligible imperceptible, inconsequential,
insignificant, minor, minute, nickel-and-
dime (*U.S. sl.*), petty, small, trifling, trivial,
unimportant
Antonyms important, noteworthy, sig~
nificant, vital

negotiable debatable, discussable *or* dis~
cussible, transactional, transferable, vari~
able

negotiate 1. adjudicate, arbitrate, arrange,
bargain, conciliate, confer, consult, con~
tract, deal, debate, discuss, handle, manage,
mediate, parley, settle, transact, work out
2. clear, cross, get over, get past, get round,
pass, pass through, surmount

negotiation arbitration, bargaining, de~
bate, diplomacy, discussion, mediation,
transaction, wheeling and dealing (*Inf.*)

neighbourhood community, confines,
district, environs, locale, locality, precincts,
proximity, purlieus, quarter, region, sur~
roundings, vicinity

neighbouring abutting, adjacent, adjoin~
ing, bordering, connecting, contiguous,
near, nearby, nearest, next, surrounding
Antonyms distant, far, far-off, remote

nerve *n.* 1. balls (*Taboo sl.*), ballsiness (*Ta~
boo sl.*), bottle (*Brit. sl.*), bravery, coolness,
courage, daring, determination, endurance,
energy, fearlessness, firmness, force, forti~
tude, gameness, grit, guts (*Inf.*), hardihood,
intrepidity, mettle, might, pluck, resolution,
spirit, spunk (*Inf.*), steadfastness, vigour,
will 2. *Inf.* audacity, boldness, brass (*Inf.*),
brass neck (*Brit. inf.*), brazenness, cheek
(*Inf.*), chutzpah (*U.S. & Canad. inf.*), effron~
tery, front, gall, impertinence, impudence,
insolence, neck (*Inf.*), sauce (*Inf.*), temerity

~*v.* 3. brace, embolden, encourage, fortify,
hearten, invigorate, steel, strengthen

nerve-racking annoying, difficult, dis~
tressing, frightening, harassing, harrowing,
maddening, stressful, tense, trying, worry~
ing

nerves anxiety, fretfulness, heebie-jeebies
(*Sl.*), imbalance, nervousness, strain, stress,
tension, worry

nervous agitated, anxious, apprehensive,
edgy, excitable, fearful, fidgety, flustered,
hesitant, highly strung, hyper (*Inf.*), hys~
terical, jittery (*Inf.*), jumpy, nervy (*Brit.
inf.*), neurotic, on edge, ruffled, shaky,
tense, timid, timorous, twitchy (*Inf.*), un~
easy, uptight (*Inf.*), weak, wired (*Sl.*), wor~
ried
Antonyms bold, calm, confident, constant,
cool, equable, even, laid-back (*Inf.*), peaceful,
relaxed, steady, together (*Sl.*), unfazed (*Inf.*)

nervous breakdown breakdown, col~
lapse, crack-up (*Inf.*), nervous disorder,
neurasthenia (*Obsolete*)

nervousness agitation, anxiety, disquiet,
excitability, fluster, perturbation, tension,
timidity, touchiness, tremulousness, worry

nest 1. den, haunt, hideaway, refuge, resort,
retreat, snuggery 2. breeding-ground, den,
hotbed

nest egg cache, deposit, fall-back, fund(s),
reserve, savings, store

nestle cuddle, curl up, huddle, nuzzle,
snuggle

nestling 1. chick, fledgling 2. babe, babe in
arms, baby, infant, suckling

net[1] 1. *n.* lacework, lattice, mesh, netting,
network, openwork, reticulum, tracery, web
2. *v.* bag, capture, catch, enmesh, ensnare,
entangle, nab (*Inf.*), trap

net[2], **nett** *adj.* 1. after taxes, clear, final,
take-home 2. closing, conclusive, final ~*v.*
3. accumulate, bring in, clear, earn, gain,
make, realize, reap

nether basal, below, beneath, bottom, infe~
rior, lower, Stygian, under, underground

nether world Avernus, Hades, hell, infer~
nal regions, nether regions, underworld

nettle aggravate (*Inf.*), annoy, chafe, exas~
perate, fret, gall, get on one's nerves (*Inf.*),
goad, harass, hassle (*Inf.*), incense, irritate,
nark (*Brit., Aust., & N.Z. sl.*), pique, piss
one off (*Taboo sl.*), provoke, ruffle, sting,
tease, vex

nettled aggrieved, angry, annoyed, chafed,
cross, exasperated, galled, goaded, hacked
(off) (*U.S. sl.*), harassed, huffy, incensed, ir~
ritable, irritated, peeved, peevish, piqued,
pissed off (*Taboo sl.*), provoked, put out,
ratty (*Brit. & N.Z. inf.*), riled, ruffled, stung,
teased, tetchy, touchy, vexed

network arrangement, channels, circuitry, complex, convolution, grid, grill, intercon~ nections, labyrinth, maze, mesh, net, nexus, organization, plexus, structure, system, tracks, web

neurosis abnormality, affliction, derange~ ment, deviation, instability, maladjustment, mental disturbance, mental illness, obses~ sion, phobia, psychological *or* emotional disorder

neurotic abnormal, anxious, compulsive, deviant, disordered, distraught, disturbed, hyper (*Inf.*), maladjusted, manic, nervous, obsessive, overwrought, twitchy (*Inf.*), un~ healthy, unstable
Antonyms calm, laid-back (*Inf.*), level-headed, normal, rational, sane, stable, togeth~ er (*Sl.*), well-adjusted, well-balanced

neuter *v.* castrate, doctor (*Inf.*), dress, emasculate, fix (*Inf.*), geld, spay

neutral **1.** disinterested, dispassionate, even-handed, impartial, indifferent, non-aligned, nonbelligerent, noncombatant, noncommittal, nonpartisan, sitting on the fence, unaligned, unbiased, uncommitted, undecided, uninvolved, unprejudiced **2.** achromatic, colourless, dull, expressionless, indeterminate, indistinct, indistinguishable, intermediate, toneless, undefined
Antonyms active, belligerent, biased, de~ cided, interested, interfering, partial, partici~ pating, positive, prejudiced

neutrality detachment, disinterestedness, impartiality, nonalignment, noninterfer~ ence, noninterventionism, noninvolvement, nonpartisanship

neutralize cancel, compensate for, counter~ act, counterbalance, frustrate, invalidate, negate, nullify, offset, undo

never at no time, not at all, not on your life (*Inf.*), not on your nelly (*Brit. sl.*), no way, on no account, under no circumstances
Antonyms always, aye (*Scot.*), constantly, continually, every time, forever, perpetually, without exception

never-ending boundless, ceaseless, con~ stant, continual, continuous, eternal, ever~ lasting, incessant, interminable, nonstop, perpetual, persistent, relentless, unbroken, unceasing, unchanging, uninterrupted, un~ remitting

never-never hire-purchase (*Brit.*), H.P. (*Brit.*)

nevertheless but, even so, (even) though, however, nonetheless, notwithstanding, re~ gardless, still, yet

new **1.** advanced, all-singing, all-dancing, contemporary, current, different, fresh, happening (*Inf.*), latest, modern, modernis~ tic, modish, newfangled, novel, original, re~

cent, state-of-the-art, topical, ultramodern, unfamiliar, unknown, unused, unusual, up-to-date, virgin **2.** added, extra, more, supplementary **3.** altered, changed, im~ proved, modernized, redesigned, renewed, restored
Antonyms aged, ancient, antiquated, an~ tique, experienced, hackneyed, old, old-fashioned, outmoded, passé, stale, trite

newcomer alien, arrival, beginner, for~ eigner, immigrant, incomer, Johnny-come-lately (*Inf.*), novice, outsider, parvenu, set~ tler, stranger

newfangled all-singing, all-dancing, con~ temporary, fashionable, gimmicky, modern, new, new-fashioned, novel, recent, state-of-the-art
Antonyms antiquated, dated, obsolete, old-fashioned, outmoded, out-of-date, passé

newly anew, freshly, just, lately, latterly, recently

news account, advice, bulletin, communi~ qué, dirt (*U.S. sl.*), disclosure, dispatch, ex~ posé, gen (*Brit. inf.*), gossip, hearsay, infor~ mation, intelligence, latest (*Inf.*), leak, news flash, release, report, revelation, rumour, scandal, statement, story, tidings, word

newsworthy arresting, important, inter~ esting, notable, noteworthy, remarkable, significant, stimulating

next *adj.* **1.** consequent, ensuing, following, later, subsequent, succeeding **2.** adjacent, adjoining, closest, nearest, neighbouring ~*adv.* **3.** afterwards, closely, following, lat~ er, subsequently, thereafter

next world afterlife, afterworld, heaven, hereafter, nirvana, paradise

nibble **1.** *n.* bite, crumb, morsel, peck, snack, *soupçon*, taste, titbit **2.** *v.* bite, eat, gnaw, munch, nip, peck, pick at

nice **1.** agreeable, amiable, attractive, charming, commendable, courteous, de~ lightful, friendly, good, kind, likable *or* likeable, pleasant, pleasurable, polite, pre~ possessing, refined, well-mannered **2.** dain~ ty, fine, neat, tidy, trim **3.** accurate, careful, critical, delicate, discriminating, exact, ex~ acting, fastidious, fine, meticulous, precise, rigorous, scrupulous, strict, subtle **4.** cul~ tured, genteel, refined, respectable, virtu~ ous, well-bred
Antonyms awful, careless, coarse, crude, disagreeable, dreadful, ill-bred, mean, miser~ able, rough, shabby, sloppy (*Inf.*), unfriendly, unkind, unpleasant, vague, vulgar

nicely **1.** acceptably, agreeably, amiably, at~ tractively, charmingly, commendably, courteously, delightfully, kindly, likably, pleasantly, pleasingly, pleasurably, politely, prepossessingly, well **2.** daintily, finely, neatly, tidily, trimly **3.** accurately, careful~

ly, critically, delicately, exactingly, exactly, fastidiously, finely, meticulously, precisely, rigorously, scrupulously, strictly, subtly **4.** genteelly, respectably, virtuously
Antonyms carelessly, sloppily (*Inf.*), unattractively, unfortunately, unpleasantly

niceness 1. agreeableness, amiability, attractiveness, charm, courtesy, delightfulness, friendliness, good manners, goodness, kindness, likableness *or* likeableness, pleasantness, pleasurableness, politeness, refinement **2.** daintiness, fineness, neatness, tidiness, trimness **3.** accuracy, care, carefulness, criticalness, delicacy, discrimination, exactingness, exactitude, exactness, fastidiousness, fineness, meticulosity, meticulousness, preciseness, precision, rigorousness, rigour, scrupulosity, scrupulousness, strictness, subtleness, subtlety **4.** gentility, good breeding, refinement, respectability, virtue

nicety 1. accuracy, exactness, fastidiousness, finesse, meticulousness, minuteness, precision **2.** daintiness, delicacy, discrimination, distinction, nuance, refinement, subtlety

niche 1. alcove, corner, hollow, nook, opening, recess **2.** calling, pigeonhole (*Inf.*), place, position, slot (*Inf.*), vocation

nick[1] chip, cut, damage, dent, mark, notch, scar, score, scratch, snick

nick[2] finger (*Sl.*), knock off (*Sl.*), pilfer, pinch (*Inf.*), snitch (*Sl.*), steal, swipe (*Sl.*)

nickname diminutive, epithet, familiar name, handle (*Sl.*), label, moniker *or* monicker (*Sl.*), pet name, sobriquet

nifty agile, apt, attractive, chic, clever, deft, enjoyable, excellent, neat, pleasing, quick, sharp, smart, spruce, stylish

niggard cheapskate (*Inf.*), cheeseparer, churl (*Archaic*), meanie *or* meany (*Inf., chiefly Brit.*), miser, penny-pincher (*Inf.*), screw (*Sl.*), Scrooge, skinflint, tight-arse (*Taboo sl.*), tight-ass (*U.S. taboo sl.*)

niggardliness 1. avarice, avariciousness, closeness, covetousness, frugality, grudgingness, meanness, mercenariness, miserliness, nearness (*Inf.*), parsimony, penuriousness, sordidness, sparingness, stinginess, thrift, tightfistedness, ungenerousness **2.** beggarliness, inadequacy, insufficiency, meagreness, meanness, miserableness, paltriness, scantiness, skimpiness, smallness, wretchedness

niggardly 1. avaricious, close, covetous, frugal, grudging, mean, mercenary, miserly, near (*Inf.*), parsimonious, penurious, Scroogelike, sordid, sparing, stinging, stingy, tight-arse (*Taboo Sl.*), tight-arsed (*Taboo sl.*), tight as a duck's arse (*Taboo sl.*), tight-ass (*U.S. taboo sl.*), tight-assed (*U.S.*

taboo sl.), tightfisted, ungenerous **2.** beggarly, inadequate, insufficient, meagre, mean, measly, miserable, paltry, scant, scanty, skimpy, small, wretched
Antonyms abundant, ample, bountiful, copious, generous, handsome, lavish, liberal, munificent, plentiful, prodigal, profuse

niggle 1. carp, cavil, criticize, find fault, fuss **2.** annoy, irritate, rankle, worry

niggling 1. cavilling, finicky, fussy, insignificant, minor, nit-picking (*Inf.*), pettifogging, petty, picky (*Inf.*), piddling (*Inf.*), quibbling, trifling, unimportant **2.** gnawing, irritating, persistent, troubling, worrying

night dark, darkness, dead of night, hours of darkness, night-time, night watches

night and day all the time, ceaselessly, constantly, continually, continuously, day in, day out, endlessly, incessantly, interminably, unremittingly

nightfall crepuscule, dusk, eve (*Archaic*), evening, eventide, gloaming (*Scot. or poetic*), sundown, sunset, twilight, vespers
Antonyms aurora (*Poetic*), cockcrow, dawn, dawning, daybreak, daylight, morning, sunrise

nightly *adv./adj.* **1.** each night, every night, night after night, nights (*Inf.*) ~*adv.* **2.** after dark, at night, by night, in the night, nights (*Inf.*), nocturnally ~*adj.* **3.** night-time, nocturnal

nightmare 1. bad dream, hallucination, incubus, succubus **2.** horror, ordeal, torment, trial, tribulation

nihilism 1. abnegation, agnosticism, atheism, denial, disbelief, nonbelief, rejection, renunciation, repudiation, scepticism **2.** blank, emptiness, negation, nonexistence, nothingness, nullity, oblivion **3.** anarchy, disorder, lawlessness, terrorism

nil duck, love, naught, *nihil*, none, nothing, zero, zilch (*Sl.*)

nimble active, agile, alert, brisk, deft, dexterous, lively, nippy (*Brit. inf.*), pdq (*Sl.*), proficient, prompt, quick, quick-witted, ready, smart, sprightly, spry, swift
Antonyms awkward, clumsy, dull, heavy, inactive, indolent, lethargic, slow

nimbleness adroitness, agility, alacrity, alertness, dexterity, finesse, grace, lightness, nippiness (*Brit. inf.*), skill, smartness, sprightliness, spryness

nimbly actively, acutely, agilely, alertly, briskly, deftly, dexterously, easily, fast, fleetly, hotfoot, pdq (*Sl.*), posthaste, proficiently, promptly, pronto (*Inf.*), quickly, quick-wittedly, readily, sharply, smartly, speedily, spryly, swiftly

nimbus ambience, atmosphere, aura, aureole, cloud, corona, glow, halo, irradiation

nincompoop berk (*Brit. sl.*), blockhead, charlie (*Brit. inf.*), coot, dickhead (*Sl.*), dimwit (*Inf.*), dipstick (*Brit. sl.*), divvy (*Sl.*), dolt, dork (*Sl.*), dunce, dweeb (*U.S. sl.*), fool, fuckwit (*Taboo sl.*), geek (*Sl.*), gonzo (*Sl.*), idiot, jerk (*Sl., chiefly U.S. & Canad.*), lame~ brain (*Inf.*), nerd *or* nurd (*Sl.*), ninny, nitwit (*Inf.*), noodle, numskull *or* numbskull, oaf, pillock (*Brit. sl.*), plank (*Brit. sl.*), plonker (*Sl.*), prat (*Sl.*), prick (*Derogatory sl.*), schmuck (*U.S. sl.*), simpleton, twit (*Inf., chiefly Brit.*), wally (*Sl.*)

nip¹ *v.* **1.** bite, catch, clip, compress, grip, nibble, pinch, snag, snap, snip, squeeze, tweak, twitch **2.** check, frustrate, thwart

nip² *n.* dram, draught, drop, finger, mouth~ ful, peg (*Brit.*), portion, shot (*Inf.*), sip, snif~ ter (*Inf.*), soupçon, sup, swallow, taste

nipper **1.** claw, pincer **2.** *Inf.* ankle-biter (*Aust. sl.*), baby, boy, child, girl, infant, kid (*Inf.*), little one, rug rat (*Sl.*), sprog (*Sl.*), tot

nipple boob (*Sl.*), breast, dug, mamilla, pap, papilla, teat, tit, udder

nippy **1.** biting, chilly, nipping, sharp, stinging **2.** *Brit. inf.* active, agile, fast, nim~ ble, pdq (*Sl.*), quick, spry

nit-picking captious, carping, cavilling, finicky, fussy, hairsplitting, pedantic, petti~ fogging, quibbling

nitty-gritty basics, brass tacks (*Inf.*), core, crux, essence, essentials, facts, funda~ mentals, gist, heart of the matter, reality, substance

nitwit (*Inf.*), dickhead (*Sl.*), dimwit (*Inf.*), dipstick (*Brit. sl.*), divvy (*Sl.*), dork (*Sl.*), dummy (*Sl.*), fool, fuckwit (*Taboo sl.*), geek (*Sl.*), halfwit, lamebrain (*Inf.*), nincompoop, ninny, oaf, plank (*Brit. sl.*), simpleton

nob aristo (*Inf.*), aristocrat, big shot (*Inf.*), bigwig (*Inf.*), celeb (*Inf.*), fat cat (*Sl., chiefly U.S.*), nabob (*Inf.*), toff (*Brit. sl.*), V.I.P.

nobble **1.** disable, handicap, incapacitate, weaken **2.** bribe, get at, influence, intimi~ date, outwit, win over **3.** filch, knock off (*Sl.*), nick (*Sl., chiefly Brit.*), pilfer, pinch (*Inf.*), purloin, snitch (*Sl.*), steal, swipe (*Sl.*) **4.** get hold of, grab, take

nobility **1.** aristocracy, elite, high society, lords, nobles, patricians, peerage, ruling class, upper class **2.** dignity, eminence, ex~ cellence, grandeur, greatness, illustrious~ ness, loftiness, magnificence, majesty, no~ bleness, stateliness, sublimity, superiority, worthiness **3.** honour, incorruptibility, in~ tegrity, uprightness, virtue

noble *n.* **1.** aristo (*Inf.*), aristocrat, lord, nobleman, peer ~*adj.* **2.** aristocratic, blue-blooded, gentle (*Archaic*), highborn, lordly, patrician, titled **3.** august, dignified, distin~ guished, elevated, eminent, excellent, grand,

great, imposing, impressive, lofty, splendid, stately, superb **4.** generous, honourable, magnanimous, upright, virtuous, worthy
Antonyms *n.* commoner, peasant, serf ~*adj.* base, contemptible, despicable, dishonest, humble, ignoble, insignificant, lowborn, low~ ly, mean, modest, peasant, plain, plebeian, selfish, vulgar

nobody **1.** no-one **2.** cipher, lightweight (*Inf.*), menial, nonentity, nothing (*Inf.*)
Antonyms big noise (*Inf.*), big shot (*Sl.*), ce~ leb (*Inf.*), celebrity, megastar (*Inf.*), personage, star, superstar, V.I.P.

nocturnal night, nightly, night-time, of the night

nod *v.* **1.** acknowledge, bob, bow, dip, duck, gesture, indicate, nutate (*Rare*), salute, sig~ nal **2.** agree, assent, concur, show agree~ ment **3.** be sleepy, doze, droop, drowse, kip (*Brit. sl.*), nap, sleep, slump, zizz (*Brit. inf.*), ~*n.* **4.** acknowledgment, beck, gesture, greeting, indication, salute, sign, signal

noggin **1.** gill, quarter-pint **2.** cup, dram, mug, nip, tot **3.** *Inf.* bean (*U.S. & Canad. sl.*), block (*Inf.*), bonce (*Brit. sl.*), conk (*Sl.*), dome (*Sl.*), head, napper (*Sl.*), noddle (*Inf., chiefly Brit.*), nut (*Sl.*)

no go futile, hopeless, impossible, not on (*Inf.*), vain

noise **1.** *n.* babble, blare, clamour, clatter, commotion, cry, din, fracas, hubbub, out~ cry, pandemonium, racket, row, sound, talk, tumult, uproar **2.** *v.* advertise, bruit, circu~ late, gossip, publicize, repeat, report, ru~ mour

noiseless hushed, inaudible, mute, muted, quiet, silent, soundless, still

noisy boisterous, cacophonous, chattering, clamorous, deafening, ear-splitting, loud, obstreperous, piercing, riotous, strident, tumultuous, turbulent, uproarious, vocifer~ ous
Antonyms hushed, quiet, silent, still, sub~ dued, tranquil, tuneful

nomad drifter, itinerant, migrant, rambler, rover, vagabond, wanderer

nomadic itinerant, migrant, migratory, pastoral, peripatetic, roaming, roving, trav~ elling, vagrant, wandering

nom de plume alias, assumed name, nom de guerre, pen name, pseudonym

nomenclature classification, codification, locution, phraseology, taxonomy, terminol~ ogy, vocabulary

nominal **1.** formal, ostensible, pretended, professed, puppet, purported, self-styled, so-called, *soi-disant*, supposed, theoretical, titular **2.** inconsiderable, insignificant, minimal, small, symbolic, token, trifling, trivial

nominate appoint, assign, choose, commis~ sion, designate, elect, elevate, empower, name, present, propose, recommend, select, submit, suggest, term

nomination appointment, choice, designa~ tion, election, proposal, recommendation, selection, suggestion

nominee aspirant, candidate, contestant, entrant, favourite, protégé, runner

nonaligned impartial, neutral, uncommit~ ted, undecided

nonchalance calm, composure, cool (*Sl.*), equanimity, imperturbability, indifference, sang-froid, self-possession, unconcern

nonchalant airy, apathetic, blasé, calm, careless, casual, collected, cool, detached, dispassionate, indifferent, insouciant, laid~ back (*Inf.*), offhand, unconcerned, unemo~ tional, unfazed (*Inf.*), unperturbed **Antonyms** anxious, caring, concerned, in~ volved, worried

noncombatant civilian, neutral, nonbel~ ligerent

noncommittal ambiguous, careful, cau~ tious, circumspect, discreet, equivocal, eva~ sive, guarded, indefinite, neutral, politic, reserved, tactful, temporizing, tentative, unrevealing, vague, wary

non compos mentis crazy, deranged, insane, mentally ill, of unsound mind, un~ balanced, unhinged **Antonyms** all there (*Inf.*), *compos mentis,* in one's right mind, lucid, mentally sound, rational, sane

nonconformist dissenter, dissentient, ec~ centric, heretic, iconoclast, individualist, maverick, protester, radical, rebel **Antonyms** Babbitt (*U.S.*), conventionalist, stick-in-the-mud (*Inf.*), traditionalist, yes man

nondescript characterless, common or garden (*Inf.*), commonplace, dull, feature~ less, indeterminate, mousy, ordinary, unclassifiable, unclassified, undistin~ guished, unexceptional, uninspiring, unin~ teresting, unmemorable, unremarkable, vague **Antonyms** distinctive, extraordinary, memorable, remarkable, unique, unusual

none bugger all (*Sl.*), f.a. (*Brit. sl.*), fuck all (*Taboo sl.*), nil, nobody, no-one, no part, not a bit, not any, nothing, not one, sweet F.A. (*Brit. sl.*), sweet Fanny Adams (*Brit. sl.*), zero

nonentity cipher, lightweight (*Inf.*), medi~ ocrity, nobody, small fry, unimportant per~ son

nonessential dispensable, excessive, ex~ pendable, extraneous, inessential, peripher~ al, superfluous, unimportant, unnecessary

Antonyms appropriate, essential, impor~ tant, indispensable, significant, vital

nonetheless despite that, even so, how~ ever, in spite of that, nevertheless, yet

nonexistent chimerical, fancied, fictional, hallucinatory, hypothetical, illusory, imagi~ nary, imagined, insubstantial, legendary, missing, mythical, unreal **Antonyms** actual, existent, existing, genu~ ine, real, true, veritable

nonplus astonish, astound, baffle, bewilder, confound, confuse, discomfit, disconcert, discountenance, dismay, dumbfound, em~ barrass, faze, flummox, mystify, perplex, puzzle, stump, stun, take aback

nonsense absurdity, balderdash, balls (*Ta~ boo sl.*), bilge (*Inf.*), blather, bombast, bosh (*Inf.*), bull (*Sl.*), bullshit (*Taboo sl.*), bunk (*Inf.*), bunkum or buncombe (*Chiefly U.S.*), claptrap (*Inf.*), cobblers (*Brit. taboo sl.*), crap (*Sl.*), double Dutch (*Brit. inf.*), drivel, eyewash (*Inf.*), fatuity, folly, foolishness, garbage (*Inf.*), gibberish, guff (*Sl.*), hogwash, hokum (*Sl., chiefly U.S. & Canad.*), horsefeathers (*U.S. sl.*), hot air (*Inf.*), idiocy, inanity, jest, ludicrousness, moonshine, pap, piffle (*Inf.*), poppycock (*Inf.*), ridicu~ lousness, rot, rubbish, senselessness, shit (*Taboo sl.*), silliness, stuff, stupidity, tommyrot, tosh (*Sl., chiefly Brit.*), trash, tripe (*Inf.*), twaddle, waffle (*Inf., chiefly Brit.*) **Antonyms** fact, reality, reason, sense, seri~ ousness, truth, wisdom

nonsensical absurd, asinine, crazy, foolish, inane, incomprehensible, irrational, ludi~ crous, meaningless, ridiculous, senseless, silly

nonstop 1. *adj.* ceaseless, constant, con~ tinuous, direct, endless, incessant, intermi~ nable, relentless, steady, unbroken, unend~ ing, unfaltering, uninterrupted, unremitting **2.** *adv.* ceaselessly, constantly, continuous~ ly, directly, endlessly, incessantly, intermi~ nably, relentlessly, steadily, unbrokenly, unendingly, unfalteringly, uninterruptedly, unremittingly, without stopping **Antonyms** *adj.* broken, discontinuous, fitful, intermittent, irregular, occasional, periodic, punctuated, recurrent, spasmodic, sporadic, stop-go (*Inf.*)

nook alcove, cavity, corner, cranny, crevice, cubbyhole, hide-out, inglenook (*Brit.*), niche, opening, recess, retreat

noon high noon, midday, noonday, noontide, noontime, twelve noon

norm average, benchmark, criterion, mean, measure, model, par, pattern, rule, stand~ ard, type, yardstick

normal 1. accustomed, acknowledged, aver~ age, common, conventional, habitual, natu~

ral, ordinary, popular, regular, routine, run-of-the-mill, standard, typical, usual **2.** rational, reasonable, sane, well-adjusted
Antonyms abnormal, exceptional, irregular, peculiar, rare, remarkable, singular, uncommon, unnatural, unusual

normality 1. accustomedness, averageness, commonness, commonplaceness, conventionality, habitualness, naturalness, ordinariness, popularity, regularity, routineness, typicality, usualness **2.** adjustment, balance, rationality, reason, sanity

normally as a rule, commonly, habitually, ordinarily, regularly, typically, usually

north 1. *adj.* Arctic, boreal, northerly, northern, polar **2.** *adv.* northerly, north~ward(s)

nose *n.* **1.** beak, bill, conk (*Sl.*), hooter (*Sl.*), neb (*Archaic or dialect*), proboscis, schnozzle (*Sl., chiefly U.S.*), snitch (*Sl.*), snout (*Sl.*) ~*v.* **2.** detect, scent, search (for), smell, sniff **3.** ease forward, nudge, nuzzle, push, shove **4.** meddle, pry, snoop (*Inf.*)

nose dive dive, drop, plummet, plunge

nosegay bouquet, posy

nosh 1. *n.* aliment, chow (*Inf.*), comestibles, eats (*Sl.*), fare, feed, food, grub (*Sl.*), meal, nosebag (*Sl.*), repast, scoff (*Sl.*), sustenance, tack (*Inf.*), viands, victuals, vittles (*Obs. or dialect*) **2.** *v.* consume, eat, scoff (*Sl.*)

nostalgia homesickness, longing, pining, regret, regretfulness, remembrance, reminiscence, wistfulness, yearning

nostalgic emotional, homesick, longing, maudlin, regretful, sentimental, wistful

nostrum cure, cure-all, drug, elixir, medicine, panacea, patent medicine, potion, quack medicine, remedy, sovereign cure, specific, treatment

nosy, nosey curious, eavesdropping, inquisitive, interfering, intrusive, meddlesome, prying, snooping (*Inf.*)

notability 1. celebrity, distinction, eminence, esteem, fame, renown **2.** celeb (*Inf.*), celebrity, dignitary, megastar (*Inf.*), notable, personage, V.I.P., worthy

notable 1. *adj.* celebrated, conspicuous, distinguished, eminent, evident, extraordinary, famous, manifest, marked, memorable, noteworthy, noticeable, notorious, outstanding, pre-eminent, pronounced, rare, remarkable, renowned, striking, uncommon, unusual, well-known **2.** *n.* celeb (*Inf.*), celebrity, dignitary, megastar (*Inf.*), notability, personage, V.I.P., worthy
Antonyms anonymous, concealed, hidden, imperceptible, obscure, unknown, vague

notably conspicuously, distinctly, especially, markedly, noticeably, outstandingly,

particularly, remarkably, signally, strikingly, uncommonly

notation 1. characters, code, script, signs, symbols, system **2.** jotting, notating, note, noting, record

notch *n.* **1.** cleft, cut, incision, indentation, mark, nick, score **2.** *Inf.* cut (*Inf.*), degree, grade, level, step ~*v.* **3.** cut, indent, mark, nick, score, scratch

notch up achieve, gain, make, register, score

note *n.* **1.** annotation, comment, communication, epistle, gloss, jotting, letter, memo, memorandum, message, minute, record, remark, reminder **2.** indication, mark, sign, symbol, token **3.** heed, notice, observation, regard **4.** celebrity, character, consequence, distinction, eminence, fame, prestige, renown, reputation ~*v.* **5.** denote, designate, indicate, mark, mention, notice, observe, perceive, record, register, remark, see

notebook commonplace book, diary, exercise book, Filofax (*Trademark*), jotter, journal, memorandum book, notepad, record book

noted acclaimed, celebrated, conspicuous, distinguished, eminent, famous, illustrious, notable, notorious, prominent, recognized, renowned, well-known
Antonyms infamous, obscure, undistinguished, unknown

notes impressions, jottings, outline, record, report, sketch

noteworthy exceptional, extraordinary, important, notable, outstanding, remarkable, significant, unusual
Antonyms commonplace, insignificant, normal, ordinary, pedestrian, run-of-the-mill, unexceptional, unremarkable

nothing bagatelle, cipher, emptiness, naught, nobody, nonentity, nonexistence, nothingness, nought, nullity, trifle, void, zero

nothingness 1. nihility, nonbeing, nonexistence, nullity, oblivion **2.** insignificance, unimportance, worthlessness

notice *v.* **1.** detect, discern, distinguish, heed, mark, mind, note, observe, perceive, remark, see, spot ~*n.* **2.** cognizance, consideration, heed, interest, note, observation, regard **3.** advice, announcement, communication, instruction, intelligence, intimation, news, notification, order, warning **4.** advertisement, comment, criticism, poster, review, sign **5.** attention, civility, respect
Antonyms *v.* disregard, ignore, neglect, over-look ~*n.* disregard, ignorance, neglect, omission, oversight

noticeable appreciable, blatant, clear, conspicuous, distinct, evident, manifest, ob~

servable, obvious, perceptible, plain, strik~
ing, unmistakable

notification advice, alert, announcement,
declaration, information, intelligence, mes~
sage, notice, notifying, publication, state~
ment, telling, warning

notify acquaint, advise, alert, announce, ap~
prise, declare, inform, publish, tell, warn

notion 1. apprehension, belief, concept,
conception, idea, impression, inkling, judg~
ment, knowledge, opinion, sentiment,
understanding, view **2.** caprice, desire, fan~
cy, impulse, inclination, whim, wish

notional abstract, conceptual, fanciful,
hypothetical, ideal, imaginary, speculative,
theoretical, unreal, visionary
Antonyms actual, factual, genuine, real

notoriety dishonour, disrepute, infamy, ob~
loquy, opprobrium, scandal

notorious 1. dishonourable, disreputable,
infamous, opprobrious, scandalous **2.** bla~
tant, flagrant, glaring, obvious, open, overt,
patent, undisputed

notoriously 1. dishonourably, disrepu~
tably, infamously, opprobriously, scandal~
ously **2.** blatantly, flagrantly, glaringly, no~
tably, obviously, openly, overtly, particu~
larly, patently, spectacularly, undisputedly

notwithstanding although, despite, (even)
though, however, nevertheless, nonetheless,
though, yet

nought naught, nil, nothing, nothingness,
zero

nourish 1. attend, feed, furnish, nurse,
nurture, supply, sustain, tend **2.** comfort,
cultivate, encourage, foster, maintain, pro~
mote, support

nourishing alimentative, beneficial,
healthful, health-giving, nutritious, nutri~
tive, wholesome

nourishment aliment, diet, food, nutri~
ment, nutrition, sustenance, tack (*Inf.*), vi~
ands, victuals, vittles (*Obs. or dialect*)

nouveau riche arriviste, new-rich,
parvenu, upstart

novel 1. *adj.* different, fresh, ground-
breaking, innovative, new, original, rare,
singular, strange, uncommon, unfamiliar,
unusual **2.** *n.* fiction, narrative, romance,
story, tale
Antonyms *adj.* ancient, common, custom~
ary, familiar, habitual, old-fashioned, ordi~
nary, run-of-the-mill, traditional, usual

novelty 1. freshness, innovation, newness,
oddity, originality, strangeness, surprise,
unfamiliarity, uniqueness **2.** bagatelle,
bauble, curiosity, gadget, gewgaw, gim~
crack, gimmick, knick-knack, memento,
souvenir, trifle, trinket

novice amateur, apprentice, beginner, con~

vert, learner, neophyte, newcomer, noviti~
ate, probationer, proselyte, pupil, trainee,
tyro
Antonyms ace, doyen, expert, grandmaster,
master, maven, old hand, professional, teach~
er

novitiate 1. apprenticeship, probation,
training **2.** novice

now 1. at once, immediately, instanter
(*Law*), instantly, presently (*Scot. & U.S.*),
promptly, straightaway **2.** any more, at the
moment, nowadays, these days **3. now and
then** *or* **again** at times, from time to time,
infrequently, intermittently, occasionally,
on and off, once in a while, on occasion,
sometimes, sporadically

nowadays any more, at the moment, in
this day and age, now, these days, today

noxious baneful (*Archaic*), corrupting,
deadly, deleterious, destructive, detrimen~
tal, foul, harmful, hurtful, injurious, insa~
lubrious, noisome, pernicious, pestilential,
poisonous, unhealthy, unwholesome
Antonyms innocuous, innoxious, inoffen~
sive, nontoxic, not dangerous, safe, unobjec~
tionable

nucleus basis, centre, core, focus, heart,
kernel, nub, pivot

nude *au naturel,* bare, buck naked (*Sl.*), dis~
robed, exposed, in one's birthday suit (*Inf.*),
in the altogether (*Inf.*), in the buff (*Inf.*), in
the raw (*Inf.*), naked, naked as the day one
was born (*Inf.*), starkers (*Inf.*), stark-naked,
stripped, unclad, unclothed, uncovered, un~
draped, undressed, without a stitch on (*Inf.*)
Antonyms attired, clothed, covered, dressed

nudge *v.* bump, dig, elbow, jog, poke, prod,
push, shove, touch

nudity bareness, dishabille, nakedness,
nudism, undress

nugget chunk, clump, hunk, lump, mass,
piece

nuisance annoyance, bore, bother, drag
(*Inf.*), gall, hassle (*Inf.*), inconvenience,
infliction, irritation, offence, pain in the
arse (*Taboo inf.*), pest, plague, problem,
trouble, vexation
Antonyms benefit, blessing, delight, happi~
ness, joy, pleasure, satisfaction

null characterless, ineffectual, inoperative,
invalid, nonexistent, null and void, power~
less, useless, vain, valueless, void, worth~
less

nullify abolish, abrogate, annul, bring to
naught, cancel, counteract, countervail, in~
validate, negate, neutralize, obviate, quash,
rebut, render null and void, repeal, rescind,
revoke, veto, void
Antonyms authorize, confirm, endorse,
ratify, validate

nullity characterlessness, ineffectualness, invalidity, nonexistence, powerlessness, uselessness, valuelessness, voidness, worth~lessness

numb 1. *adj.* benumbed, dead, deadened, frozen, immobilized, insensible, insensitive, paralysed, stupefied, torpid, unfeeling **2.** *v.* benumb, deaden, dull, freeze, immobilize, paralyse, stun, stupefy
Antonyms *adj.* feeling, responsive, sensi~tive, sentient

number *n.* **1.** character, count, digit, figure, integer, numeral, sum, total, unit **2.** aggre~gate, amount, collection, company, crowd, horde, many, multitude, quantity, throng **3.** copy, edition, imprint, issue, printing ~*v.* **4.** account, add, calculate, compute, count, enumerate, include, reckon, tell, total
Antonyms *n.* insufficiency, lack, scantiness, scarcity, shortage, want ~*v.* conjecture, guess, theorize

numbered categorized, contained, counted, designated, fixed, included, limited, limited in number, specified, totalled

numberless countless, endless, infinite, innumerable, multitudinous, myriad, un~numbered, untold

numbness deadness, dullness, insensibil~ity, insensitivity, paralysis, stupefaction, torpor, unfeelingness

numeral character, cipher, digit, figure, in~teger, number, symbol

numerous abundant, copious, many, plen~tiful, profuse, several
Antonyms few, not many, scarcely any

nuncio ambassador, envoy, legate, messen~ger

nunnery abbey, cloister, convent, house, monastery

nuptial *adj.* bridal, conjugal, connubial, epithalamial (*Poetic*), hymeneal (*Poetic*), marital, matrimonial, wedded, wedding

nuptials espousal (*Archaic*), marriage, mat~rimony, wedding

nurse *v.* **1.** care for, look after, minister to, tend, treat **2.** breast-feed, feed, nourish, nurture, suckle, wet-nurse **3.** *Fig.* cherish, cultivate, encourage, foster, harbour, keep alive, preserve, promote, succour, support

nurture *n.* **1.** diet, food, nourishment **2.** de~velopment, discipline, education, instruc~tion, rearing, training, upbringing ~*v.* **3.** feed, nourish, nurse, support, sustain, tend **4.** bring up, cultivate, develop, discipline, educate, instruct, rear, school, train
Antonyms *v.* deprive, disregard, ignore, ne~glect, overlook

nut 1. kernel, pip, seed, stone **2.** *Sl.* brain, head, mind, reason, senses **3.** *Sl.* crackpot (*Inf.*), crank (*Inf.*), eccentric, headbanger (*Inf.*), headcase (*Inf.*), loony (*Sl.*), lunatic, madman, maniac, nutcase (*Sl.*), nutter (*Brit. sl.*), oddball (*Inf.*), psycho (*Sl.*), wacko (*Sl.*)

nutrition food, nourishment, nutriment, sustenance

nutritious alimental, alimentative, beneficial, healthful, health-giving, invigor~ating, nourishing, nutritive, strengthening, wholesome

nuts bananas (*Sl.*), barking (*Sl.*), barking mad (*Sl.*), batty (*Sl.*), crazy (*Inf.*), demented, deranged, eccentric, insane, irrational, loony (*Sl.*), loopy (*Inf.*), mad, not the full shilling (*Inf.*), nutty (*Sl.*), off one's trolley (*Sl.*), out to lunch (*Inf.*), psycho (*Sl.*), psychopathic, up the pole (*Inf.*)

nymph damsel, dryad, girl, hamadryad, lass, maid, maiden, naiad, Oceanid (*Greek myth.*), oread, sylph

O

oaf airhead (*Sl.*), berk (*Brit. sl.*), blockhead, bonehead (*Sl.*), booby, brute, charlie (*Brit. inf.*), clod, coot, dickhead (*Sl.*), dipstick (*Brit. sl.*), divvy (*Brit. sl.*), dolt, dork (*Sl.*), dullard, dummy (*Sl.*), dunce, dweeb (*U.S. sl.*), fool, fuckwit (*Taboo sl.*), galoot (*Sl., chiefly U.S.*), gawk, geek (*Sl.*), gonzo (*Sl.*), goon, gorilla (*Inf.*), halfwit, idiot, imbecile, jerk (*Sl., chiefly U.S. & Canad.*), lout, lum~ mox (*Inf.*), moron, nerd *or* nurd (*Sl.*), nin~ compoop, nitwit (*Inf.*), numskull *or* numb~ skull, pillock (*Brit. sl.*), plank (*Brit. sl.*), plonker (*Sl.*), prat (*Sl.*), sap (*Sl.*), schmuck (*U.S. sl.*), simpleton, twit (*Inf., chiefly Brit.*), wally (*Sl.*)
Antonyms brain (*Inf.*), egghead (*Inf.*), geni~ us, intellectual, smart aleck (*Inf.*), wiseacre

oafish blockish, Boeotian, boneheaded (*Sl.*), bovine, brutish, dense, dim, dim-witted (*Inf.*), doltish, dozy (*Brit. inf.*), dull, dumb (*Inf.*), heavy, loutish, lubberly, lumbering, moronic, obtuse, slow on the uptake (*Inf.*), stupid, thick
Antonyms acute, brainy (*Inf.*), bright, clev~ er, intelligent, quick-witted, sharp, smart

oasis *Fig.* haven, island, refuge, resting place, retreat, sanctuary, sanctum

oath 1. affirmation, avowal, bond, pledge, promise, sworn statement, vow, word **2.** blasphemy, curse, cuss (*Inf.*), expletive, im~ precation, malediction, profanity, strong language, swearword

obdurate adamant, callous, dogged, firm, fixed, hard, hard-hearted, harsh, immov~ able, implacable, indurate (*Rare*), inexo~ rable, inflexible, iron, mulish, obstinate, perverse, pig-headed, proof against persua~ sion, relentless, stiff-necked, stubborn, un~ bending, unfeeling, unimpressible, unre~ lenting, unshakable, unyielding
Antonyms amenable, biddable, compliant, flexible, malleable, pliant, soft-hearted, sub~ missive, tender, tractable, yielding

obedience accordance, acquiescence, agreement, compliance, conformability, deference, docility, dutifulness, duty, obser~ vance, respect, reverence, submission, sub~ missiveness, subservience, tractability
Antonyms defiance, disobedience, insubor~ dination, obstinacy, recalcitrance, stubborn~ ness, wilfulness

obedient acquiescent, amenable, biddable, compliant, deferential, docile, duteous, du~ tiful, law-abiding, observant, regardful, re~ spectful, submissive, subservient, tractable, under control, well-trained, yielding
Antonyms arrogant, contrary, disobedient, disrespectful, intractable, obdurate, obsti~ nate, rebellious, stubborn, undutiful, ungov~ ernable, unmanageable, unruly, wayward

obelisk column, monolith, monument, nee~ dle, pillar, shaft

obese corpulent, Falstaffian, fat, fleshy, gross, heavy, outsize, overweight, paunchy, plump, podgy, portly, roly-poly, rotund, stout, tubby, well-upholstered (*Inf.*)
Antonyms emaciated, gaunt, lean, scraggy, skeletal, skinny, slender, thin

obesity beef (*Inf.*), bulk, corpulence, *em~ bonpoint*, fatness, fleshiness, grossness, overweight, portliness, stoutness, tubbiness, weight problem
Antonyms emaciation, gauntness, leanness, skinniness, slenderness, thinness

obey 1. abide by, act upon, adhere to, be ruled by, carry out, comply, conform, dis~ charge, do what is expected, embrace, ex~ ecute, follow, fulfil, heed, keep, mind, ob~ serve, perform, respond, serve **2.** bow to, come to heel, do what one is told, get into line, give in, give way, knuckle under (*Inf.*), submit, succumb, surrender (to), take or~ ders from, toe the line, yield
Antonyms contravene, defy, disobey, disre~ gard, ignore, rebel, transgress, violate

object¹ *n.* **1.** article, body, entity, fact, item, phenomenon, reality, thing **2.** aim, butt, fo~ cus, recipient, target, victim **3.** design, end, end in view, end purpose, goal, idea, intent, intention, motive, objective, point, purpose, reason

object² *v.* argue against, demur, expostulate, oppose, protest, raise objections, take ex~ ception
Antonyms accept, acquiesce, admire, agree, approve, assent, compliment, comply, concur, consent, like, relish, welcome

objection cavil, censure, counter-argument, demur, doubt, exception, niggle (*Inf.*), oppo~ sition, protest, remonstrance, scruple
Antonyms acceptance, affirmation, agree~ ment, approbation, assent, concession, en~ dorsement, support

objectionable abhorrent, deplorable, dis~ agreeable, dislikable *or* dislikeable, dis~ pleasing, distasteful, exceptionable, indeco~ rous, insufferable, intolerable, noxious, ob~ noxious, offensive, regrettable, repugnant,

unacceptable, undesirable, unpleasant, un~
seemly, unsociable
Antonyms acceptable, agreeable, desirable,
likable *or* likeable, pleasant, pleasing, wel~
come

objective 1. *adj.* detached, disinterested,
dispassionate, equitable, even-handed, fair,
impartial, impersonal, judicial, just, open-
minded, unbiased, uncoloured, unemotion~
al, uninvolved, unprejudiced **2.** *n.* aim, am~
bition, aspiration, design, end, end in view,
goal, intention, mark, object, purpose, tar~
get
Antonyms (*sense 1*) abstract, biased, per~
sonal, prejudiced, subjective, theoretical, un~
fair, unjust

objectively disinterestedly, dispassionately,
even-handedly, impartially, with an open
mind, with objectivity *or* impartiality,
without fear or favour

objectivity detachment, disinterest, disin~
terestedness, dispassion, equitableness, im~
partiality, impersonality
Antonyms bent, bias, partiality, predisposi~
tion, prejudice, subjectivity

obligation 1. accountability, account~
ableness, burden, charge, compulsion, duty,
liability, must, onus, requirement, respon~
sibility, trust **2.** agreement, bond, commit~
ment, contract, debt, engagement, promise,
understanding **3. under an obligation** be~
holden, duty-bound, grateful, honour-bound,
indebted, in (someone's) debt, obligated,
obliged, owing a favour, thankful

obligatory binding, coercive, compulsory,
de rigueur, enforced, essential, imperative,
mandatory, necessary, required, requisite,
unavoidable
Antonyms discretionary, elective, non~
compulsory, optional, voluntary

oblige 1. bind, coerce, compel, constrain,
dragoon, force, impel, make, necessitate,
obligate, railroad (*Inf.*), require **2.** accom~
modate, benefit, do (someone) a favour *or* a
kindness, favour, gratify, indulge, please,
put oneself out for, serve
Antonyms (*sense 2*) bother, discommode,
disoblige, disrupt, inconvenience, put out,
trouble

obliged 1. appreciative, beholden, grateful,
gratified, indebted, in (someone's) debt,
thankful **2.** bound, compelled, forced, re~
quired, under an obligation, under compul~
sion, without any option

obliging accommodating, agreeable, ami~
able, civil, complaisant, considerate, co~
operative, courteous, eager to please,
friendly, good-natured, helpful, kind, polite,
willing
Antonyms discourteous, disobliging, in~

considerate, rude, sullen, surly, unaccommo~
dating, uncooperative, unhelpful, unobliging

oblique 1. angled, aslant, at an angle, in~
clined, slanted, slanting, sloped, sloping,
tilted **2.** backhanded, circuitous, circum~
locutory, evasive, implied, indirect, round~
about, sidelong
Antonyms (*sense 2*) blunt, candid, direct,
downright, forthright, frank, open, straight~
forward

obliquely 1. aslant, aslope, at an angle, di~
agonally, slantwise **2.** circuitously, eva~
sively, in a roundabout manner *or* way, in~
directly, not in so many words

obliterate annihilate, blot out, cancel, de~
lete, destroy, destroy root and branch, ef~
face, eradicate, erase, expunge, extirpate,
root out, wipe off the face of the earth, wipe
out
Antonyms build, construct, create, estab~
lish, form, formulate, generate, make

obliteration annihilation, deletion, efface~
ment, elimination, eradication, erasure, ex~
punction, extirpation, wiping (blotting,
rooting, sponging) out
Antonyms building, construction, creation,
establishment, formation, generation, mak~
ing

oblivion 1. abeyance, disregard, forgetful~
ness, insensibility, neglect, obliviousness,
unawareness, unconsciousness, (waters of)
Lethe **2.** blackness, darkness, eclipse, ex~
tinction, limbo, nothingness, obscurity, void
Antonyms (*sense 1*) awareness, conscious~
ness, perception, realization, recognition,
sensibility

oblivious blind, careless, deaf, disregardful,
forgetful, heedless, ignorant, inattentive,
insensible, neglectful, negligent, regardless,
unaware, unconcerned, unconscious, un~
mindful, unobservant
Antonyms alert, attentive, aware, con~
scious, heedful, mindful, observant, watchful

obnoxious abhorrent, abominable, detest~
able, disagreeable, disgusting, dislikable *or*
dislikeable, foul, hateable, hateful, horrid,
insufferable, loathsome, nasty, nauseating,
objectionable, obscene, odious, offensive,
repellent, reprehensible, repugnant, repul~
sive, revolting, sickening, unpleasant
Antonyms agreeable, amiable, charming,
congenial, delightful, likable *or* likeable,
pleasant, pleasing

obscene 1. bawdy, blue, coarse, dirty, dis~
gusting, Fescennine (*Rare*), filthy, foul,
gross, immodest, immoral, improper, im~
pure, indecent, lewd, licentious, loose, of~
fensive, pornographic, prurient, ribald, sa~
lacious, scabrous, shameless, smutty, sug~
gestive, unchaste, unwholesome **2.** *Fig.*

atrocious, evil, heinous, loathsome, outra~
geous, shocking, sickening, vile, wicked
Antonyms (*sense 1*) chaste, decent, decorous,
inoffensive, modest, proper, pure, refined, re~
spectable, seemly

obscenity 1. bawdiness, blueness, coarse~
ness, dirtiness, filthiness, foulness, gross~
ness, immodesty, impurity, lewdness, licen~
tiousness, pornography, prurience, salacity,
smuttiness, suggestiveness, vileness **2.**
four-letter word, impropriety, indecency,
indelicacy, profanity, smut, swearword,
vulgarism **3.** abomination, affront, atrocity,
blight, evil, offence, outrage, vileness,
wrong
Antonyms (*sense 1*) chastity, decency, deco~
rum, delicacy, innocence, modesty, propriety,
purity

obscure *adj.* **1.** abstruse, ambiguous, ar~
cane, concealed, confusing, cryptic, deep,
Delphic, doubtful, enigmatic, esoteric, hazy,
hidden, incomprehensible, indefinite, intri~
cate, involved, mysterious, occult, opaque,
recondite, unclear, vague **2.** blurred, cloud~
ed, cloudy, dim, dusky, faint, gloomy, in~
distinct, murky, obfuscated, shadowy,
shady, sombre, tenebrous, unlit, veiled **3.**
humble, inconspicuous, inglorious, little-
known, lowly, minor, nameless, out-of-the-
way, remote, undistinguished, unheard-of,
unhonoured, unimportant, unknown, un~
noted, unseen, unsung ~*v.* **4.** conceal, cov~
er, disguise, hide, muddy, obfuscate, screen,
throw a veil over, veil **5.** adumbrate, be~
dim, befog, block, block out, blur, cloak,
cloud, darken, dim, dull, eclipse, mask,
overshadow, shade, shroud
Antonyms *adj.* (*senses 1 & 2*) apparent,
bright, clear, conspicuous, definite, distinct,
evident, explicit, intelligible, lucid, manifest,
obvious, plain, prominent, sharp, significant,
straightforward, transparent, unmistakable,
well-defined (*sense 3*) celebrated, distin~
guished, eminent, familiar, famous, illustri~
ous, important, major, prominent, renowned,
well-known, widely-known ~*v.* brighten,
clarify, disclose, explain, explicate, expose,
interpret, reveal, show, uncover, unmask,
unveil

obscurity 1. abstruseness, ambiguity, com~
plexity, impenetrableness, incomprehen~
sibility, intricacy, reconditeness, vagueness
2. darkness, dimness, dusk, duskiness,
gloom, haze, haziness, indistinctness,
murkiness, shadowiness, shadows **3.** in~
conspicuousness, ingloriousness, insignifi~
cance, lowliness, namelessness, nonrecog~
nition, unimportance
Antonyms (*sense 1*) clarity, clearness, com~
prehensibility, explicitness, lucidity, obvi~
ousness, transparency

observable apparent, appreciable, blatant,

clear, detectable, discernible, evident, no~
ticeable, obvious, open, patent, perceivable,
perceptible, recognizable, visible

observance 1. adherence to, attention,
carrying out, celebration, compliance, dis~
charge, fulfilment, heeding, honouring, no~
tice, observation, performance **2.** ceremo~
nial, ceremony, custom, fashion, form, for~
mality, practice, rite, ritual, service, tradi~
tion
Antonyms (*sense 1*) disdain, disregard, eva~
sion, heedlessness, inattention, neglect, nonobservance, omission, oversight

observant alert, attentive, eagle-eyed,
heedful, mindful, obedient, perceptive,
quick, sharp-eyed, submissive, vigilant,
watchful, wide-awake
Antonyms distracted, dreamy, heedless, in~
attentive, indifferent, negligent, preoccupied,
unobservant

observation 1. attention, cognition, con~
sideration, examination, experience, infor~
mation, inspection, knowledge, monitoring,
notice, review, scrutiny, study, surveil~
lance, watching **2.** annotation, comment,
finding, note, obiter dictum, opinion, pro~
nouncement, reflection, remark, thought,
utterance

observe 1. detect, discern, discover, espy,
note, notice, perceive, see, spot, witness **2.**
check, check out (*Inf.*), clock (*Brit. sl.*), con~
template, eyeball (*U.S. sl.*), get a load of
(*Inf.*), keep an eye on (*Inf.*), keep under ob~
servation, look at, monitor, pay attention
to, recce (*Sl.*), regard, scrutinize, study,
survey, take a dekko at (*Brit. sl.*), view,
watch **3.** animadvert, comment, declare,
mention, note, opine, remark, say, state **4.**
abide by, adhere to, comply, conform to,
follow, fulfil, heed, honour, keep, mind,
obey, perform, respect **5.** celebrate, com~
memorate, keep, remember, solemnize
Antonyms (*sense 4*) disregard, ignore, miss,
neglect, omit, overlook, violate

observer beholder, bystander, commenta~
tor, eyewitness, looker-on, onlooker, specta~
tor, spotter, viewer, watcher, witness

obsess bedevil, be on one's mind, be
uppermost in one's thoughts, consume,
dominate, engross, grip, haunt, monopolize,
plague, possess, preoccupy, prey on one's
mind, rule, torment

obsessed beset, dominated, gripped, hag-
ridden, haunted, hung up on (*Sl.*), im~
mersed in, infatuated, in the grip of, preoc~
cupied, troubled
Antonyms aloof, apathetic, detached, disin~
terested, impassive, indifferent, uncaring,
unconcerned

obsession bee in one's bonnet (*Inf.*), com~
plex, enthusiasm, fetish, fixation, hang-up

(*Inf.*), *idée fixe*, infatuation, mania, phobia, preoccupation, ruling passion, thing (*Inf.*)

obsessive besetting, compulsive, consuming, fixed, gripping, haunting, tormenting, unforgettable

obsolescent ageing, declining, dying out, not with it (*Inf.*), on the decline, on the wane, on the way out, past its prime, waning

obsolete anachronistic, ancient, antediluvian, antiquated, antique, archaic, bygone, dated, *démodé*, discarded, disused, extinct, musty, old, old-fashioned, old hat, out, outmoded, out of date, out of fashion, out of the ark (*Inf.*), outworn, passé, superannuated, *vieux jeu*
Antonyms à la mode, contemporary, current, fashionable, in, in vogue, modern, new, present day, trendy (*Brit. inf.*), up-to-date

obstacle bar, barrier, block, check, difficulty, hindrance, hitch, hurdle, impediment, interference, interruption, obstruction, snag, stumbling block
Antonyms advantage, aid, asset, assistance, benefit, crutch, help, support

obstinacy doggedness, firmness, inflexibility, intransigence, mulishness, obduracy, perseverance, persistence, pertinacity, pig-headedness, resoluteness, stubbornness, tenacity, wilfulness
Antonyms compliance, cooperativeness, docility, flexibility, meekness, submissiveness, tractability

obstinate contumacious, determined, dogged, firm, headstrong, immovable, inflexible, intractable, intransigent, mulish, opinionated, persistent, pertinacious, perverse, pig-headed, recalcitrant, refractory, self-willed, steadfast, stiff-necked, strong-minded, stubborn, tenacious, unyielding, wilful
Antonyms amenable, biddable, complaisant, compliant, docile, flexible, irresolute, manageable, obedient, submissive, tractable, undecided, wavering

obstreperous boisterous, clamorous, disorderly, loud, noisy, out of control, out of hand, rackety, rambunctious (*Inf.*), rampaging, raucous, restive, riotous, riproaring (*Inf.*), roistering, roisterous, rough, rowdy, stroppy (*Brit. sl.*), tempestuous, tumultuous, turbulent, uncontrolled, undisciplined, unmanageable, unruly, uproarious, vociferous, wild
Antonyms calm, controlled, disciplined, docile, gentle, orderly, peaceful, placid, quiet

obstruct arrest, bar, barricade, block, bring to a standstill, bung, check, choke, clog, cumber, curb, cut off, frustrate, get in the way of, hamper, hamstring, hide, hinder, hold up, impede, inhibit, interfere with, interrupt, mask, obscure, prevent, restrict, retard, shield, shut off, slow down, stop, thwart, trammel
Antonyms abet, advance, aid, assist, encourage, favour, further, help, promote, support

obstruction bar, barricade, barrier, block, blockage, check, difficulty, hindrance, impediment, obstacle, occlusion, snag, stop, stoppage, trammel
Antonyms aid, assistance, cooperation, encouragement, favour, furtherance, help, support

obstructive awkward, blocking, delaying, hindering, inhibiting, preventative, restrictive, stalling, uncooperative, unhelpful
Antonyms cooperative, encouraging, favourable, helpful, obliging, supportive

obtain 1. achieve, acquire, attain, come by, earn, gain, get, get hold of, get one's hands on, procure, score (*Sl.*), secure **2.** be in force, be prevalent, be the case, exist, hold, prevail, stand
Antonyms (*sense 1*) forfeit, forgo, give up, hand over, lose, relinquish, renounce, surrender

obtainable achievable, at hand, attainable, available, on tap (*Inf.*), procurable, ready, realizable, to be had

obtrusive 1. forward, importunate, interfering, intrusive, meddling, nosy, officious, prying, pushy (*Inf.*) **2.** blatant, noticeable, obvious, prominent, protruding, protuberant, sticking out
Antonyms (*sense 1*) bashful, decorous, diffident, modest, reserved, reticent, retiring, shy, unassuming (*sense 2*) concealed, covert, hidden, inconspicuous, low-key, muted, unnoticeable, unobtrusive

obtrusively blatantly, bluntly, boldly, crassly, importunately, obviously, officiously, pushily

obtuse 1. boneheaded (*Sl.*), dense, dopey (*Inf.*), dull, dull-witted, dumb (*Inf.*), heavy, imperceptive, insensitive, muttonheaded (*Sl.*), retarded, slow, slow on the uptake (*Inf.*), stolid, stupid, thick, thick-skinned, uncomprehending, unintelligent **2.** blunt, rounded
Antonyms (*sense 1*) astute, bright, clever, keen, quick, sensitive, sharp, shrewd, smart

obvious apparent, blatant, clear, clear as a bell, conspicuous, distinct, evident, indisputable, manifest, much in evidence, noticeable, open, overt, palpable, patent, perceptible, plain, plain as the nose on your face (*Inf.*), pronounced, recognizable, right under one's nose (*Inf.*), self-evident, self-explanatory, staring one in the face (*Inf.*), sticking out a mile (*Inf.*), straightforward,

transparent, unconcealed, undeniable, un~
disguised, unmistakable, unsubtle, visible
Antonyms ambiguous, concealed, dark,
hidden, imperceptible, inconspicuous, indis~
tinct, invisible, obscure, unapparent, unclear,
vague

obviously certainly, clearly, distinctly,
manifestly, of course, palpably, patently,
plainly, undeniably, unmistakably, unques~
tionably, without doubt

occasion n. **1.** chance, convenience, inci~
dent, moment, occurrence, opening, oppor~
tunity, time, window **2.** affair, celebration,
event, experience, happening, occurrence **3.**
call, cause, excuse, ground(s), inducement,
influence, justification, motive, prompting,
provocation, reason ~v. **4.** bring about,
cause, create, effect, elicit, engender, evoke,
generate, give rise to, induce, influence, in~
spire, lead to, move, originate, persuade,
produce, prompt, provoke

occasional casual, desultory, incidental,
infrequent, intermittent, irregular, odd,
rare, sporadic, uncommon
Antonyms constant, continual, customary,
frequent, habitual, incessant, regular, rou~
tine, usual

occasionally at intervals, at times, (every)
now and then, every so often, from time to
time, irregularly, now and again, off and
on, on and off, once in a while, on occasion,
periodically, sometimes
Antonyms constantly, continually, con~
tinuously, frequently, habitually, often, regu~
larly, routinely

occult abstruse, arcane, cabbalistic, con~
cealed, esoteric, hidden, invisible, magical,
mysterious, mystic, mystical, obscure, pre~
ternatural, recondite, secret, supernatural,
unknown, unrevealed, veiled
Antonyms apparent, blatant, evident, ex~
posed, manifest, obvious, open, overt, plain,
revealed, visible

occultism black magic, diabolism, magic,
sorcery, supernaturalism, the black arts,
witchcraft

occupant addressee, denizen, holder, in~
cumbent, indweller, inhabitant, inmate,
lessee, occupier, resident, tenant, user

occupation **1.** activity, business, calling,
craft, employment, job, line (of work), post,
profession, pursuit, trade, vocation, walk of
life, work **2.** control, holding, occupancy,
possession, residence, tenancy, tenure, use
3. conquest, foreign rule, invasion, seizure,
subjugation

occupied **1.** busy, employed, engaged, hard
at it (*Inf.*), tied up (*Inf.*), working **2.** en~
gaged, full, in use, taken, unavailable **3.**
full, inhabited, lived-in, peopled, settled,
tenanted

Antonyms (*sense 3*) deserted, empty, tenant~
less, uninhabited, unoccupied, untenanted,
vacant, void

occupy **1.** *Often passive* absorb, amuse,
busy, divert, employ, engage, engross, en~
tertain, hold the attention of, immerse, in~
terest, involve, keep busy *or* occupied, mo~
nopolize, preoccupy, take up, tie up **2.** be
established in, be in residence in, dwell in,
ensconce oneself in, establish oneself in,
inhabit, live in, own, possess, reside in,
stay in (*Scot.*), tenant **3.** cover, fill, hold,
permeate, pervade, take up, use, utilize **4.**
capture, garrison, hold, invade, keep, over~
run, seize, take over, take possession of
Antonyms abandon, depart, desert, evacu~
ate, quit, retreat, vacate, withdraw

occur **1.** arise, befall, betide, chance, come
about, come off (*Inf.*), come to pass (*Archa~
ic*), crop up (*Inf.*), eventuate, happen, ma~
terialize, result, take place, turn up (*Inf.*) **2.**
appear, be found, be met with, be present,
develop, exist, manifest itself, obtain, show
itself **3.** *With* **to** come to mind, come to
one, cross one's mind, dawn on, enter one's
head, spring to mind, strike one, suggest
(offer, present) itself

occurrence **1.** adventure, affair, circum~
stance, episode, event, happening, incident,
instance, proceeding, transaction **2.** ap~
pearance, development, existence, manifes~
tation, materialization

odd **1.** abnormal, atypical, bizarre, curious,
deviant, different, eccentric, exceptional,
extraordinary, fantastic, freak, freakish,
freaky (*Sl.*), funny, irregular, kinky (*Inf.*),
oddball (*Inf.*), off-the-wall (*Sl.*), outlandish,
out of the ordinary, outré, peculiar, quaint,
queer, rare, remarkable, rum (*Brit. sl.*),
singular, strange, uncanny, uncommon,
unconventional, unusual, wacko (*Sl.*),
weird, whimsical **2.** casual, fragmentary,
incidental, irregular, miscellaneous, occa~
sional, periodic, random, seasonal, sundry,
varied, various **3.** leftover, lone, remaining,
single, solitary, spare, surplus, un~
consumed, uneven, unmatched, unpaired
Antonyms common, customary, even, fa~
miliar, habitual, matched, natural, normal,
ordinary, paired, permanent, regular, steady,
typical, unexceptional, unremarkable, usual

oddity **1.** abnormality, anomaly, eccentri~
city, freak, idiosyncrasy, irregularity, kink,
peculiarity, phenomenon, quirk, rarity **2.**
card (*Inf.*), crank (*Inf.*), fish out of water,
maverick, misfit, nut (*Sl.*), oddball (*Inf.*),
odd bird (*Inf.*), odd fish (*Brit. inf.*), rara
avis, screwball (*Sl., chiefly U.S. & Canad.*),
wacko (*Sl.*), weirdo *or* weirdie (*Inf.*) **3.**
abnormality, bizarreness, eccentricity,
extraordinariness, freakishness, incongru~
ity, oddness, outlandishness, peculiarity,

queerness, singularity, strangeness, uncon~ ventionality, unnaturalness

odd man out exception, freak, maverick, misfit, nonconformist, outsider

odds 1. advantage, allowance, edge, lead, superiority **2.** balance, chances, likelihood, probability **3.** *Brit.* difference, disparity, dissimilarity, distinction **4. at odds** at daggers drawn, at loggerheads, at sixes and sevens, at variance, in conflict, in disagree~ ment, in opposition to, not in keeping, on bad terms, out of line

odds and ends bits, bits and pieces, de~ bris, leavings, litter, oddments, remnants, rubbish, scraps, sundry *or* miscellaneous items

odious abhorrent, abominable, detestable, disgusting, execrable, foul, hateful, horrible, horrid, loathsome, obnoxious, obscene, of~ fensive, repellent, repugnant, repulsive, re~ volting, unpleasant, vile, yucky *or* yukky (*Sl.*)
Antonyms agreeable, charming, congenial, delightful, enchanting, enjoyable, pleasant, pleasing, winsome

odour 1. aroma, bouquet, essence, fra~ grance, niff (*Brit. sl.*), perfume, redolence, scent, smell, stench, stink **2.** air, atmos~ phere, aura, emanation, flavour, quality, spirit

odyssey crusade, journey, peregrination, pilgrimage, quest, trek, voyage

off *adj.* **1.** absent, cancelled, finished, gone, inoperative, postponed, unavailable **2.** bad, below par, disappointing, disheartening, displeasing, low-quality, mortifying, poor, quiet, slack, substandard, unrewarding, un~ satisfactory **3.** bad, decomposed, high, mouldy, rancid, rotten, sour, turned ~*adv.* **4.** apart, aside, away, elsewhere, out

off and on (every) now and again, every once in a while, from time to time, inter~ mittently, now and then, occasionally, on and off, sometimes, sporadically

offbeat bizarre, Bohemian, eccentric, far-out (*Sl.*), freaky (*Sl.*), idiosyncratic, kinky (*Inf.*), novel, oddball (*Inf.*), off-the-wall (*Sl.*), outré, rum (*Brit. sl.*), strange, uncommon, uncon~ ventional, unorthodox, unusual, wacko (*Sl.*), way-out (*Inf.*), weird
Antonyms common, conventional, normal, ordinary, orthodox, run-of-the-mill, stereo~ typed, traditional, unoriginal, usual

off colour ill, not up to par, off form, out of sorts, peaky, peely-wally (*Scot.*), poorly (*Inf.*), queasy, run down, sick, under par, under the weather (*Inf.*), unwell, washed out

offence 1. breach of conduct, crime, delin~ quency, fault, lapse, misdeed, misdemean~

our, peccadillo, sin, transgression, trespass, wrong, wrongdoing **2.** affront, displeasure, harm, hurt, indignity, injury, injustice, in~ sult, outrage, put-down (*Sl.*), slight, snub **3.** anger, annoyance, displeasure, hard feel~ ings, huff, indignation, ire (*Literary*), needle (*Inf.*), pique, resentment, umbrage, wounded feelings, wrath **4. take offence** be dis~ gruntled, be offended, get riled, go into a huff, resent, take the huff, take the needle (*Inf.*), take umbrage

offend 1. affront, aggravate (*Inf.*), annoy, disgruntle, displease, fret, gall, give offence, hurt (someone's) feelings, insult, irritate, miff (*Inf.*), nark (*Brit., Aust., & N.Z. sl.*), outrage, pain, pique, piss one off (*Taboo sl.*), provoke, put down, put (someone's) back up, rile, slight, snub, tread on (someone's) toes (*Inf.*), upset, vex, wound **2.** be disagreeable to, disgust, gross out (*U.S. sl.*), make (someone) sick, nauseate, repel, repulse, sicken, turn (someone) off (*Inf.*)
Antonyms (*sense 1*) appease, assuage, con~ ciliate, delight, mollify, placate, please, soothe

offended affronted, disgruntled, displeased, huffy, in a huff, miffed (*Inf.*), outraged, pained, piqued, put out (*Inf.*), resentful, smarting, stung, upset

offender criminal, crook, culprit, delin~ quent, lawbreaker, malefactor, miscreant, sinner, transgressor, villain, wrongdoer

offensive *adj.* **1.** abusive, annoying, detest~ able, discourteous, displeasing, disrespect~ ful, embarrassing, impertinent, insolent, insulting, irritating, objectionable, rude, uncivil, unmannerly **2.** abominable, detest~ able, disagreeable, disgusting, grisly, loath~ some, nasty, nauseating, noisome, obnox~ ious, odious, repellent, revolting, sickening, unpalatable, unpleasant, unsavoury, vile, yucky *or* yukky (*Sl.*) **3.** aggressive, attack~ ing, invading ~*n.* **4.** attack, drive, on~ slaught, push (*Inf.*) **5. on the offensive** advancing, aggressive, attacking, invading, invasive, on the warpath (*Inf.*)
Antonyms *adj.* agreeable, attractive, capti~ vating, charming, civil, conciliatory, cour~ teous, defensive, deferential, delightful, pleasant, polite, respectful ~*n.* defensive

offer *v.* **1.** bid, extend, give, hold out, prof~ fer, put on the market, put under the ham~ mer, put up for sale, tender **2.** afford, fur~ nish, make available, place at (someone's) disposal, present, provide, purvey, show **3.** advance, extend, move, propose, put forth, put forward, submit, suggest **4.** be at (someone's) service, come forward, offer one's services, volunteer ~*n.* **5.** attempt, bid, endeavour, essay, overture, proposal, proposition, submission, suggestion, tender
Antonyms (*sense 1*) recant, refuse, retract, revoke, take back, withdraw, withhold

offering contribution, donation, gift, hand-out, oblation (*in religious contexts*), present, sacrifice, subscription, widow's mite

offhand 1. *adj.* abrupt, aloof, brusque, careless, casual, cavalier, couldn't-care-less, curt, glib, informal, offhanded, perfunctory, take-it-or-leave-it (*Inf.*), unceremonious, unconcerned, uninterested **2.** *adv.* ad lib, extempore, impromptu, just like that (*Inf.*), off the cuff (*Inf.*), off the top of one's head (*Inf.*), without preparation
Antonyms attentive, careful, grave, intent, planned, premeditated, prepared, responsible, serious, thoughtful

office 1. appointment, business, capacity, charge, commission, duty, employment, function, obligation, occupation, place, post, responsibility, role, service, situation, station, trust, work **2.** *Plural* advocacy, aegis, aid, auspices, backing, favour, help, intercession, intervention, mediation, patronage, recommendation, referral, support, word

officer agent, appointee, bureaucrat, dignitary, executive, functionary, office-holder, official, public servant, representative

official 1. *adj.* accredited, authentic, authoritative, authorized, bona fide, certified, endorsed, ex cathedra, ex officio, formal, legitimate, licensed, proper, sanctioned, straight from the horse's mouth (*Inf.*) **2.** *n.* agent, bureaucrat, executive, functionary, office bearer, officer, representative
Antonyms (*sense 1*) casual, doubtful, dubious, informal, unauthorized, unofficial, unreliable

officiate chair, conduct, emcee (*Inf.*), manage, oversee, preside, serve, superintend

officious bustling, dictatorial, forward, impertinent, inquisitive, interfering, intrusive, meddlesome, meddling, mischievous, obtrusive, opinionated, overbusy, overzealous, pragmatical (*Rare*), pushy (*Inf.*), self-important
Antonyms aloof, detached, indifferent, reserved, reticent, retiring, shy, taciturn, unforthcoming, withdrawn

offing in the offing close at hand, coming up, hovering, imminent, in prospect, in the immediate future, in the wings, on the horizon, on the way, upcoming

off-load disburden, discharge, dump, get rid of, jettison, lighten, shift, take off, transfer, unburden, unload, unship

off-putting daunting, discomfiting, disconcerting, discouraging, dismaying, dispiriting, disturbing, formidable, frustrating, intimidating, unnerving, unsettling, upsetting

offset 1. *v.* balance out, cancel out, compensate for, counteract, counterbalance, counterpoise, countervail, make up for,

neutralize **2.** *n.* balance, compensation, counterbalance, counterweight, equipoise

offshoot adjunct, appendage, branch, by-product, development, limb, outgrowth, spin-off, sprout

offspring brood, child, children, descendant, descendants, family, fry, heir, heirs, issue, kids (*Inf.*), progeny, scion, seed (*Chiefly biblical*), spawn, successor, successors, young
Antonyms ancestor, begetter, forebear, forefather, forerunner, parent, predecessor, procreator, progenitor

often again and again, frequently, generally, many a time, much, oft (*Archaic or poetic*), oftentimes (*Archaic*), ofttimes (*Archaic*), over and over again, repeatedly, time after time, time and again
Antonyms hardly ever, infrequently, irregularly, never, now and then, occasionally, rarely, scarcely, seldom

ogle eye up (*Inf.*), gawp at (*Brit. sl.*), give the glad eye (*Inf.*), give the once-over (*Inf.*), lech *or* letch after (*Inf.*), leer, make sheep's eyes at (*Inf.*)

ogre bogey, bogeyman, bugbear, demon, devil, giant, monster, spectre

oil *v.* grease, lubricate

ointment balm, cerate, cream, embrocation, emollient, liniment, lotion, salve, unguent

O.K., okay 1. *adj.* acceptable, accurate, adequate, all right, approved, convenient, correct, fair, fine, good, in order, middling, not bad (*Inf.*), passable, permitted, satisfactory, so-so (*Inf.*), tolerable **2.** *n.* agreement, approbation, approval, assent, authorization, consent, endorsement, go-ahead (*Inf.*), green light, permission, sanction, say-so (*Inf.*), seal of approval **3.** *v.* agree to, approve, authorize, consent to, endorse, entitle, give one's consent to, give the go-ahead (green light, thumbs up) to (*Inf.*), pass, rubber-stamp (*Inf.*), sanction, say yes to **4.** *interj.* agreed, all right, right, roger, very good, very well, yes
Antonyms (*sense 1*) displeasing, inaccurate, inadequate, incorrect, not up to scratch (*Inf.*), poor, unacceptable, unsatisfactory, unsuitable

old 1. advanced in years, aged, ancient, decrepit, elderly, full of years, getting on, grey, grey-haired, grizzled, hoary, mature, over the hill (*Inf.*), past one's prime, patriarchal, senescent, senile, venerable **2.** antediluvian, antiquated, antique, cast-off, crumbling, dated, decayed, done, hackneyed, obsolete, old-fashioned, outdated, outmoded, out of date, passé, stale, superannuated, timeworn, unfashionable, unoriginal, worn-out **3.** aboriginal, antique, archaic, bygone, early, immemorial, of old,

of yore, olden (*Archaic*), original, primeval, primitive, primordial, pristine, remote **4.** age-old, experienced, familiar, hardened, long-established, of long standing, practised, skilled, time-honoured, traditional, versed, veteran, vintage **5.** earlier, erstwhile, ex-, former, one-time, previous, quondam
Antonyms current, fashionable, immature, juvenile, modern, modish, new, novel, recent, up-to-date, young, youthful

old age advancing years, age, agedness, Anno Domini (*Inf.*), autumn *or* evening of one's life, declining years, dotage, senes~cence, senility, Third Age
Antonyms adolescence, childhood, early life, immaturity, juvenescence, young days, youth

old-fashioned ancient, antiquated, archa~ic, behind the times, corny (*Sl.*), dated, dead, *démodé*, fusty, musty, not with it (*Inf.*), obsolescent, obsolete, oldfangled, (old-)fogyish, old hat, old-time, outdated, outmoded, out of date, out of style, out of the ark (*Inf.*), passé, past, square (*Inf.*), superannuated, unfashionable
Antonyms chic, contemporary, current, fashionable, happening (*Inf.*), modern, mod~ish, trendy (*Brit. inf.*), up-to-date, voguish, with it (*Inf.*)

old man elder, elder statesman, father, gaf~fer, grandfather, greybeard, O.A.P. (*Brit.*), old codger (*Inf.*), old stager, oldster (*Inf.*), old-timer (*U.S.*), papa (*Old-fashioned inf.*), patriarch, senior citizen

old-time ancient, antique, bygone, former, old-fashioned, past, vintage

old-world archaic, ceremonious, chival~rous, courtly, gallant, old-fashioned, pictur~esque, quaint, traditional

omen augury, foreboding, foretoken, indi~cation, portent, premonition, presage, prog~nostic, prognostication, sign, straw in the wind, warning, writing on the wall

ominous baleful, dark, fateful, forbidding, foreboding, inauspicious, menacing, mina~tory, portentous, premonitory, sinister, threatening, unpromising, unpropitious
Antonyms auspicious, encouraging, fa~vourable, promising, propitious

omission default, exclusion, failure, forget~fulness, gap, lack, leaving out, neglect, non-inclusion, oversight
Antonyms addition, inclusion, incorpora~tion, insertion

omit disregard, drop, eliminate, exclude, fail, forget, give (something) a miss (*Inf.*), leave out, leave (something) undone, let (something) slide, miss (out), neglect, over~look, pass over, skip
Antonyms add, enter, include, incorporate, insert, put in

omnipotence divine right, invincibility, mastery, sovereignty, supremacy, supreme power, undisputed sway
Antonyms frailty, impotence, inability, in~feriority, powerlessness, vulnerability, weakness

omnipotent all-powerful, almighty, su~preme
Antonyms feeble, frail, impotent, incapable, inferior, powerless, vulnerable, weak

on and off discontinuously, (every) now and again, fitfully, from time to time, inter~mittently, now and then, off and on, on oc~casion, sometimes, spasmodically

once 1. at one time, formerly, in the old days, in the past, in times gone by, in times past, long ago, once upon a time, previously **2. at once a.** directly, forthwith, immedi~ately, instantly, now, right away, straight away, straightway (*Archaic*), this (very) minute, without delay, without hesitation **b.** at *or* in one go (*Inf.*), at the same time, simultaneously, together **3. once and for all** conclusively, decisively, finally, for all time, for good, for the last time, perma~nently, positively, with finality **4. once in a while** at intervals, at times, every now and then, from time to time, now and again, occasionally, once in a blue moon (*Inf.*), on occasion, sometimes

one-horse backwoods, inferior, minor, ob~scure, petty, quiet, sleepy, slow, small, small-time (*Inf.*), tinpot (*Brit. inf.*), unim~portant

onerous backbreaking, burdensome, crush~ing, demanding, difficult, exacting, ex~hausting, exigent, formidable, grave, hard, heavy, laborious, oppressive, responsible, taxing, weighty
Antonyms cushy (*Inf.*), easy, effortless, fac~ile, light, painless, simple, trifling, unde~manding, unexacting, untaxing

one-sided biased, coloured, discriminatory, inequitable, lopsided, partial, partisan, prejudiced, unequal, unfair, unjust
Antonyms equal, equitable, fair, impartial, just, unbiased, uncoloured, unprejudiced

one-time erstwhile, ex-, former, late, previ~ous, quondam, sometime

onlooker bystander, eyewitness, looker-on, observer, spectator, viewer, watcher, wit~ness

only 1. *adv.* at most, barely, exclusively, just, merely, purely, simply **2.** *adj.* exclu~sive, individual, lone, one and only, single, sole, solitary, unique

onomatopoeic echoic, imitative, ono~matopoetic

onset 1. assault, attack, charge, onrush,

onslaught **2.** beginning, inception, kick-off (*Inf.*), outbreak, start
Antonyms (*sense 2*) conclusion, culmina~tion, end, ending, finish, outcome, termina~tion, wind-up

onslaught assault, attack, blitz, charge, of~fensive, onrush, onset
Antonyms defensive, escape, flight, reces~sion, retreat, rout, stampede, withdrawal

onus burden, liability, load, obligation, re~sponsibility, task
Antonyms easement, exemption, exonera~tion, liberation, pardon, release, relief, remis~sion

ooze 1. *v.* bleed, discharge, drain, dribble, drip, drop, emit, escape, exude, filter, leach, leak, overflow with, percolate, seep, strain, sweat, weep **2.** *n.* alluvium, mire, muck, mud, silt, slime, sludge

opaque 1. clouded, cloudy, dim, dull, filmy, hazy, impenetrable, lustreless, muddied, muddy, murky, obfuscated, turbid **2.** ab~struse, baffling, cryptic, difficult, enigmatic, incomprehensible, obscure, unclear, un~fathomable, unintelligible
Antonyms bright, clear, crystal clear, lim~pid, lucid, pellucid, transparent, transpicuous

open *adj.* **1.** agape, ajar, expanded, extend~ed, gaping, revealed, spread out, unbarred, unclosed, uncovered, unfastened, unfolded, unfurled, unlocked, unobstructed, unsealed, yawning **2.** airy, bare, clear, exposed, ex~tensive, free, navigable, not built-up, pass~able, rolling, spacious, sweeping, unclut~tered, uncrowded, unenclosed, unfenced, unsheltered, wide, wide-open **3.** accessible, available, free, general, nondiscriminatory, public, unconditional, unengaged, unoccu~pied, unqualified, unrestricted, vacant **4.** apparent, avowed, barefaced, blatant, clear, conspicuous, downright, evident, flagrant, frank, manifest, noticeable, obvious, overt, plain, unconcealed, undisguised, visible **5.** arguable, debatable, moot, undecided, unre~solved, unsettled, up in the air, yet to be decided **6.** disinterested, free, impartial, objective, receptive, unbiased, uncommit~ted, unprejudiced **7.** *With* **to** an easy target for, at the mercy of, defenceless against, disposed, exposed, liable, susceptible, vul~nerable **8.** artless, candid, fair, frank, guileless, honest, ingenuous, innocent, natural, sincere, transparent, unreserved **9.** filigree, fretted, holey, honeycombed, lacy, loose, openwork, porous, spongy **10.** boun~teous, bountiful, generous, liberal, mu~nificent, prodigal **11.** exposed, undefended, unfortified, unprotected ~*v.* **12.** begin, be~gin business, commence, get *or* start the ball rolling, inaugurate, initiate, kick off (*Inf.*), launch, put up one's plate, set in mo~tion, set up shop, start **13.** clear, crack,

throw wide, unbar, unblock, unclose, un~cork, uncover, undo, unfasten, unlock, un~seal, untie, unwrap **14.** expand, spread (out), unfold, unfurl, unroll **15.** come apart, crack, rupture, separate, split **16.** disclose, divulge, exhibit, explain, lay bare, pour out, show, uncover
Antonyms *adj.* (*senses 1 & 2*) bounded, closed, concealed, confined, covered, crowded, enclosed, fastened, limited, locked, obstruct~ed, restricted, sealed, shut (*senses 3 & 4*) cov~ert, disguised, hidden, inaccessible, private, protected, restricted, secret, veiled (*sense 6*) biased, partial, prejudiced (*senses 7 & 11*) de~fended, protected (*sense 8*) artful, cunning, introverted, reserved, secretive, sly, with~drawn ~*v.* (*sense 12*) close, conclude, end, finish, terminate (*sense 13*) block, close, fasten, lock, obstruct, seal, shut (*sense 14*) fold

open-air alfresco, outdoor

open-handed bountiful, free, generous, lavish, liberal, munificent, prodigal, un~stinting
Antonyms avaricious, close-fisted, grasping, grudging, mean, miserly, parsimonious, penny-pinching (*Inf.*), stingy, tight-fisted

opening *n.* **1.** aperture, breach, break, chink, cleft, crack, fissure, gap, hole, inter~stice, orifice, perforation, rent, rupture, slot, space, split, vent **2.** break (*Inf.*), chance, look-in (*Inf.*), occasion, opportunity, place, vacancy, window **3.** beginning, birth, com~mencement, dawn, inauguration, inception, initiation, kickoff (*Inf.*), launch, launching, onset, opening move, outset, overture, start ~*adj.* **4.** beginning, commencing, early, first, inaugural, initial, initiatory, intro~ductory, maiden, primary
Antonyms (*sense 1*) blockage, cessation, closing, closure, obstruction, occlusion, plug, seal, stoppage (*sense 3*) close, completion, con~clusion, culmination, ending, finale, finish, termination, winding up (*Inf.*)

openly 1. candidly, face to face, forthright~ly, frankly, overtly, plainly, straight from the shoulder (*Inf.*), unhesitatingly, unre~servedly **2.** blatantly, brazenly, flagrantly, in full view, in public, publicly, shameless~ly, unabashedly, unashamedly, wantonly, without pretence
Antonyms covertly, furtively, in camera, privately, quietly, secretly, slyly, surrepti~tiously

open-minded broad, broad-minded, catho~lic, dispassionate, enlightened, free, impar~tial, liberal, reasonable, receptive, tolerant, unbiased, undogmatic, unprejudiced
Antonyms assertive, biased, bigoted, dog~matic, intolerant, narrow-minded, opinionat~ed, pig-headed, prejudiced, uncompromising

operate 1. act, be in action, function, go,

perform, run, work **2.** be in charge of, han~ dle, manage, manoeuvre, use, work **3.** per~ form surgery
Antonyms (*sense 1*) break down, conk out (*Inf.*), cut out (*Inf.*), fail, falter, halt, seize up, stall, stop

operation **1.** action, affair, course, exer~ cise, motion, movement, performance, pro~ cedure, process, use, working **2. in opera~ tion** effective, functioning, going, in action, in force, operative **3.** activity, agency, ef~ fect, effort, force, influence, instrumentality, manipulation **4.** affair, business, deal, en~ terprise, proceeding, transaction, undertak~ ing **5.** assault, campaign, exercise, ma~ noeuvre **6.** surgery

operational functional, going, in working order, operative, prepared, ready, usable, viable, workable, working
Antonyms broken, ineffective, inoperative, kaput (*Inf.*), nonfunctional, on the blink (*Sl.*), out of order

operative *adj.* **1.** active, current, effective, efficient, functional, functioning, in force, in operation, operational, serviceable, standing, workable **2.** crucial, important, indicative, influential, key, relevant, significant ~*n.* **3.** artisan, employee, hand, labourer, machinist, mechanic, worker
Antonyms (*sense 1*) ineffective, inefficient, inoperative, nonfunctional, powerless, unus~ able, unworkable

operator **1.** conductor, driver, handler, mechanic, operative, practitioner, skilled employee, technician, worker **2.** adminis~ trator, contractor, dealer, director, manag~ er, speculator, trader **3.** *Inf.* Machiavellian, machinator, manipulator, mover, shyster (*Sl.*, *chiefly U.S.*), smart aleck (*Inf.*), wheeler-dealer (*Inf.*), wirepuller, worker

opinion **1.** assessment, belief, conception, conjecture, estimation, feeling, idea, im~ pression, judgment, mind, notion, persua~ sion, point of view, sentiment, theory, view **2. be of the opinion** be convinced, believe, be under the impression, conclude, consid~ er, hold, judge, reckon, suppose, surmise, think **3. matter of opinion** debatable point, matter of judgment, moot point, open question, open to debate, up to the individ~ ual

opinionated adamant, biased, bigoted, bull-headed, cocksure, dictatorial, doctri~ naire, dogmatic, inflexible, obdurate, obsti~ nate, overbearing, pig-headed, prejudiced, self-assertive, single-minded, stubborn, un~ compromising
Antonyms broad-minded, compliant, com~ promising, dispassionate, flexible, open-minded, receptive, tolerant, unbiased, unbigoted, unprejudiced

opponent adversary, antagonist, challeng~ er, competitor, contestant, disputant, dis~ sentient, enemy, foe, opposer, rival, the op~ position
Antonyms accomplice, ally, associate, col~ league, friend, helper, mate, supporter

opportune advantageous, appropriate, apt, auspicious, convenient, favourable, felici~ tous, fit, fitting, fortunate, happy, lucky, proper, propitious, seasonable, suitable, timely, well-timed
Antonyms inappropriate, inconvenient, in~ opportune, unfavourable, unfortunate, un~ suitable, untimely

opportunism expediency, exploitation, Machiavellianism, making hay while the sun shines (*Inf.*), pragmatism, realism, *Re~ alpolitik*, striking while the iron is hot (*Inf.*), trimming, unscrupulousness

opportunity break (*Inf.*), chance, conveni~ ence, hour, look-in (*Inf.*), moment, occasion, opening, scope, time, window

oppose **1.** bar, block, check, combat, con~ front, contradict, counter, counterattack, defy, face, fight, fly in the face of, hinder, obstruct, prevent, resist, speak against, stand up to, take a stand against, take issue with, take on, thwart, withstand **2.** com~ pare, contrast, counterbalance, match, pit *or* set against, play off
Antonyms advance, advocate, aid, back, de~ fend, espouse, help, promote, support

opposed against, antagonistic, anti (*Inf.*), antipathetic, antithetical, at daggers drawn, averse, clashing, conflicting, contra (*Inf.*), contrary, dissentient, hostile, incompatible, inimical, in opposition, opposing, opposite

opposing antagonistic, antipathetic, clash~ ing, combatant, conflicting, contrary, en~ emy, hostile, incompatible, irreconcilable, opposed, opposite, rival, warring

opposite *adj.* **1.** corresponding, facing, fronting **2.** adverse, antagonistic, antitheti~ cal, conflicting, contradictory, contrary, contrasted, diametrically opposed, different, differing, diverse, hostile, inconsistent, in~ imical, irreconcilable, opposed, reverse, un~ like ~*n.* **3.** antithesis, contradiction, con~ trary, converse, inverse, reverse, the other extreme, the other side of the coin (*Inf.*)
Antonyms (*sense 2*) alike, consistent, corre~ sponding, identical, like, matching, same, similar, uniform

opposition **1.** antagonism, competition, contrariety, counteraction, disapproval, hostility, obstruction, obstructiveness, pre~ vention, resistance, unfriendliness **2.** an~ tagonist, competition, foe, opponent, other side, rival
Antonyms (*sense 1*) agreement, approval,

collaboration, concurrence, cooperation, cor~
respondence, friendliness, responsiveness

oppress 1. afflict, burden, depress, dispirit,
harass, lie *or* weigh heavy upon, sadden,
take the heart out of, torment, vex **2.** abuse,
crush, harry, maltreat, overpower, over~
whelm, persecute, rule with an iron hand,
subdue, subjugate, suppress, trample
underfoot, tyrannize over, wrong
Antonyms deliver, emancipate, free, liber~
ate, loose, release, set free, unburden

oppressed abused, browbeaten, burdened,
disadvantaged, downtrodden, enslaved,
harassed, henpecked, maltreated, misused,
prostrate, slave, subject, troubled, tyran~
nized, underprivileged
Antonyms advantaged, exalted, favoured,
honoured, liberated, privileged

oppression abuse, brutality, calamity, cru~
elty, hardship, harshness, injury, injustice,
iron hand, maltreatment, misery, persecu~
tion, severity, subjection, suffering, tyranny
Antonyms benevolence, clemency, compas~
sion, goodness, humaneness, justice, kind~
ness, mercy, sympathy, tenderness

oppressive 1. brutal, burdensome, cruel,
despotic, grinding, harsh, heavy, inhuman,
onerous, overbearing, overwhelming, re~
pressive, severe, tyrannical, unjust **2.** air~
less, close, heavy, muggy, overpowering,
stifling, stuffy, suffocating, sultry, torrid
Antonyms (*sense 1*) encouraging, gentle, hu~
mane, just, lenient, merciful, propitious, soft

oppressor autocrat, bully, despot, harrier,
intimidator, iron hand, persecutor, scourge,
slave-driver, taskmaster, tormentor, tyrant

opt (for) choose, decide (on), elect, exercise
one's discretion (in favour of), go for, make
a selection, plump for, prefer
Antonyms decide against, dismiss, elimi~
nate, exclude, preclude, reject, rule out, turn
down

optimistic 1. disposed to take a favourable
view, idealistic, seen through rose-coloured
spectacles, Utopian **2.** assured, bright,
buoyant, buoyed up, cheerful, confident,
encouraged, expectant, hopeful, positive,
sanguine
Antonyms bleak, cynical, despairing, de~
spondent, downhearted, fatalistic, gloomy,
glum, hopeless, pessimistic, resigned

optimum *adj.* A1 *or* A-one (*Inf.*), best,
choicest, flawless, highest, ideal, most fa~
vourable *or* advantageous, optimal, peak,
perfect, superlative
Antonyms inferior, least, lowest, minimal,
poorest, worst

option alternative, choice, election, prefer~
ence, selection

optional discretionary, elective, extra,

noncompulsory, open, possible, up to the
individual, voluntary
Antonyms compulsory, de rigeur, manda~
tory, obligatory, required

opulence 1. affluence, big bucks (*Inf.,
chiefly U.S.*), big money, easy circum~
stances, Easy Street (*Inf.*), fortune, lavish~
ness, luxuriance, luxury, megabucks (*U.S.
& Canad. sl.*), plenty, pretty penny (*Inf.*),
prosperity, riches, richness, sumptuousness,
tidy sum (*Inf.*), wad (*U.S. & Canad. sl.*),
wealth **2.** abundance, copiousness, cornu~
copia, fullness, profusion, richness, supera~
bundance
Antonyms dearth, impecuniousness, indi~
gence, lack, paucity, penury, poverty, priva~
tion, scantiness, scarcity, want

opulent 1. affluent, lavish, luxurious, mon~
eyed, prosperous, rich, sumptuous, wealthy,
well-heeled (*Inf.*), well-off, well-to-do **2.**
abundant, copious, lavish, luxuriant, plen~
tiful, profuse, prolific
Antonyms (*sense 1*) broke (*Inf.*), destitute,
down and out, indigent, moneyless, needy, on
the rocks, penurious, poor, poverty-stricken

opus brainchild, composition, creation,
oeuvre, piece, production, work

oracle 1. augur, Cassandra, prophet, seer,
sibyl, soothsayer **2.** answer, augury, divi~
nation, divine utterance, prediction, prog~
nostication, prophecy, revelation, vision **3.**
adviser, authority, guru, high priest,
horse's mouth, mastermind, mentor, pundit,
source, wizard

oral spoken, verbal, viva voce, vocal

oration address, declamation, discourse,
harangue, homily, lecture, speech, spiel
(*Inf.*)

orator Cicero, declaimer, lecturer, public
speaker, rhetorician, speaker, spellbinder,
spieler (*Inf.*)

oratorical bombastic, Ciceronian, declama~
tory, eloquent, grandiloquent, high-flown,
magniloquent, rhetorical, silver-tongued,
sonorous

oratory declamation, elocution, eloquence,
grandiloquence, public speaking, rhetoric,
speechifying, speech-making, spieling (*Inf.*)

orb ball, circle, globe, ring, round, sphere

orbit *n.* **1.** circle, circumgyration, course,
cycle, ellipse, path, revolution, rotation,
track, trajectory **2.** *Fig.* ambit, compass,
course, domain, influence, range, reach,
scope, sphere, sphere of influence, sweep
~*v.* **3.** circle, circumnavigate, encircle, re~
volve around

orchestrate 1. arrange, score **2.** arrange,
concert, coordinate, integrate, organize,
present, put together, set up, stage-manage

ordain 1. anoint, appoint, call, consecrate,

destine, elect, frock, invest, nominate **2.** fate, foreordain, intend, predestine, prede~ termine **3.** decree, demand, dictate, enact, enjoin, establish, fix, lay down, legislate, order, prescribe, pronounce, rule, set, will

ordeal affliction, agony, anguish, hardship, nightmare, suffering, test, torture, trial, tribulation(s), trouble(s)
Antonyms bliss, delight, elation, enjoyment, gladness, happiness, joy, pleasure

order *n.* **1.** arrangement, harmony, method, neatness, orderliness, organization, pattern, plan, propriety, regularity, symmetry, sys~ tem, tidiness **2.** arrangement, array, cat~ egorization, classification, codification, dis~ posal, disposition, grouping, layout, line, line-up, ordering, placement, progression, sequence, series, setup (*Inf.*), structure, succession **3. in order a.** arranged, in se~ quence, neat, orderly, shipshape, tidy **b.** acceptable, appropriate, called for, correct, fitting, O.K. *or* okay (*Inf.*), right, suitable **4. out of order a.** broken, broken-down, bust (*Inf.*), gone haywire (*Inf.*), gone phut (*Inf.*), in disrepair, inoperative, kaput (*Inf.*), non~ functional, not working, on the blink (*Sl.*), on the fritz (*U.S. sl.*), out of commission, U/S (*Inf.*), wonky (*Brit. sl.*) **b.** improper, in~ decorous, not cricket (*Inf.*), not done, not on (*Inf.*), out of place, out of turn, uncalled-for, wrong **5.** calm, control, discipline, law, law and order, peace, quiet, tranquillity **6.** caste, class, degree, grade, hierarchy, peck~ ing order (*Inf.*), position, rank, status **7.** breed, cast, class, family, genre, genus, ilk, kind, sort, species, subclass, taxonomic group, tribe, type **8.** behest, canon, com~ mand, decree, dictate, direction, directive, injunction, instruction, law, mandate, ordi~ nance, precept, regulation, rule, say-so (*Inf.*), stipulation **9.** application, booking, commission, request, requisition, reserva~ tion **10.** association, brotherhood, commu~ nity, company, fraternity, guild, league, lodge, organization, sect, sisterhood, soci~ ety, sodality, union ~*v.* **11.** adjure, bid, charge, command, decree, demand, direct, enact, enjoin, instruct, ordain, prescribe, require **12.** apply for, authorize, book, call for, contract for, engage, prescribe, request, reserve, send away for **13.** adjust, align, arrange, catalogue, class, classify, conduct, control, dispose, group, lay out, manage, marshal, neaten, organize, put to rights, regulate, set in order, sort out, systematize, tabulate, tidy
Antonyms *n.* (*senses 1 & 2*) chaos, clutter, confusion, disarray, disorder, jumble, mess, muddle, pandemonium, shambles ~*v.* (*sense 13*) clutter, confuse, disarrange, disorder, dis~ turb, jumble up, mess up, mix up, muddle, scramble

orderly *adj.* **1.** businesslike, in apple-pie order (*Inf.*), in order, methodical, neat, regular, scientific, shipshape, systematic, systematized, tidy, trim, well-organized, well-regulated **2.** controlled, decorous, dis~ ciplined, law-abiding, nonviolent, peaceable, quiet, restrained, well-behaved
Antonyms chaotic, disorderly, disorgan~ ized, higgledy-piggledy (*Inf.*), messy, riotous, sloppy, uncontrolled, undisciplined, unsys~ tematic

ordinarily as a rule, commonly, customari~ ly, generally, habitually, in general, in the general run (of things), in the usual way, normally, usually
Antonyms hardly ever, infrequently, occa~ sionally, rarely, scarcely, seldom, uncom~ monly

ordinary 1. accustomed, banal, common, customary, established, everyday, habitual, humdrum, mundane, normal, prevailing, quotidian, regular, routine, settled, stand~ ard, stock, typical, usual, wonted **2.** com~ mon or garden (*Inf.*), conventional, familiar, homespun, household, humble, modest, plain, prosaic, run-of-the-mill, simple, un~ memorable, unpretentious, unremarkable, workaday **3.** average, commonplace, fair, indifferent, inferior, mean, mediocre, pe~ destrian, second-rate, stereotyped, undistin~ guished, unexceptional, uninspired, unre~ markable **4. out of the ordinary** atypical, distinguished, exceptional, exciting, extraordinary, high-calibre, imaginative, important, impressive, inspired, note~ worthy, outstanding, rare, remarkable, significant, special, striking, superior, un~ common, unusual
Antonyms consequential, distinguished, exceptional, extraordinary, important, im~ pressive, inspired, notable, novel, outstand~ ing, rare, significant, superior, uncommon, unconventional, unique, unusual

organ 1. device, implement, instrument, tool **2.** element, member, part, process, structure, unit **3.** agency, channel, forum, journal, means, medium, mouthpiece, newspaper, paper, periodical, publication, vehicle, voice

organic 1. animate, biological, biotic, live, living, natural **2.** integrated, methodical, ordered, organized, structured, systematic **3.** anatomical, constitutional, fundamental, inherent, innate, integral, structural

organism animal, being, body, creature, entity, living thing, structure

organization 1. assembling, assembly, construction, coordination, direction, dis~ posal, formation, forming, formulation, making, management, methodology, organ~ izing, planning, regulation, running, stand~

ardization, structuring **2.** arrangement, chemistry, composition, configuration, con~ formation, constitution, design, format, framework, grouping, make-up, method, or~ ganism, pattern, plan, structure, system, unity, whole **3.** association, body, combine, company, concern, confederation, consor~ tium, corporation, federation, group, insti~ tution, league, outfit (*Inf.*), syndicate

organize arrange, be responsible for, cata~ logue, classify, codify, constitute, construct, coordinate, dispose, establish, form, frame, get going, get together, group, lay the foun~ dations of, lick into shape, look after, mar~ shal, pigeonhole, put in order, put together, run, see to (*Inf.*), set up, shape, straighten out, systematize, tabulate, take care of
Antonyms confuse, derange, disorganize, disrupt, jumble, mix up, muddle, scramble, upset

orgy 1. bacchanal, bacchanalia, carousal, carouse, debauch, revel, revelry, Saturnalia **2.** binge (*Inf.*), bout, excess, indulgence, overindulgence, splurge, spree, surfeit

orientation 1. bearings, coordination, di~ rection, location, position, sense of direc~ tion **2.** acclimatization, adaptation, adjust~ ment, assimilation, breaking in, familiari~ zation, introduction, settling in

orifice aperture, cleft, hole, mouth, opening, perforation, pore, rent, vent

origin 1. base, basis, cause, derivation, *fons et origo*, font (*Poetic*), fount, fountain, fountainhead, occasion, provenance, root, roots, source, spring, wellspring **2.** begin~ ning, birth, commencement, creation, dawning, early stages, emergence, founda~ tion, genesis, inauguration, inception, launch, origination, outset, start **3.** ances~ try, beginnings, birth, descent, extraction, family, heritage, lineage, parentage, pedi~ gree, stirps, stock
Antonyms conclusion, culmination, death, end, expiry, finale, finish, outcome, termina~ tion

original *adj.* **1.** aboriginal, autochthonous, commencing, earliest, early, embryonic, first, infant, initial, introductory, opening, primary, primitive, primordial, pristine, rudimentary, starting **2.** creative, fertile, fresh, ground-breaking, imaginative, ingen~ ious, innovative, innovatory, inventive, new, novel, resourceful, seminal, uncon~ ventional, unprecedented, untried, unusual **3.** archetypal, authentic, first, first-hand, genuine, master, primary, prototypical ~*n.* **4.** archetype, master, model, paradigm, pat~ tern, precedent, prototype, standard, type **5.** anomaly, card (*Inf.*), case (*Inf.*), character, eccentric, nonconformist, nut (*Sl.*), oddball

(*Inf.*), oddity, queer fish (*Brit. inf.*), wacko (*Sl.*), weirdo *or* weirdie (*Inf.*)
Antonyms *adj.* antiquated, banal, borrowed, commonplace, conventional, copied, familiar, final, last, latest, normal, old, old-fashioned, ordinary, secondary, stale, standard, stock, traditional, typical, unimaginative, unorigi~ nal, usual ~*n.* copy, imitation, replica, repro~ duction

originality boldness, break with tradition, cleverness, creativeness, creative spirit, creativity, daring, freshness, imagination, imaginativeness, individuality, ingenuity, innovation, innovativeness, inventiveness, new ideas, newness, novelty, resourceful~ ness, unconventionality, unorthodoxy
Antonyms conformity, conventionality, imitativeness, normality, orthodoxy, regu~ larity, staleness, traditionalism

originally at first, at the outset, at the start, by origin (birth, derivation), first, initially, in the beginning, in the first place, to begin with

originate 1. arise, be born, begin, come, derive, emanate, emerge, flow, issue, pro~ ceed, result, rise, spring, start, stem **2.** bring about, conceive, create, develop, dis~ cover, evolve, form, formulate, generate, give birth to, inaugurate, initiate, institute, introduce, invent, launch, pioneer, produce, set in motion, set up
Antonyms cease, conclude, culminate, end, expire, finish, terminate, wind up

originator architect, author, creator, father, founder, generator, innovator, inventor, maker, mother, pioneer, prime mover

ornament *n.* **1.** accessory, adornment, bauble, decoration, embellishment, festoon, frill, furbelow, garnish, gewgaw, knick~ knack, trimming, trinket **2.** flower, honour, jewel, leading light, pride, treasure ~*v.* **3.** adorn, beautify, bedizen (*Archaic*), brighten, deck, decorate, dress up, embellish, festoon, garnish, gild, grace, prettify, prink, trim

ornamental attractive, beautifying, deco~ rative, embellishing, for show, showy

ornamentation adornment, decoration, elaboration, embellishment, embroidery, frills, ornateness

ornate aureate, baroque, beautiful, be~ decked, busy, convoluted, decorated, elabo~ rate, elegant, fancy, florid, flowery, fussy, high-wrought, ornamented, overelaborate, rococo
Antonyms austere, bare, basic, ordinary, plain, severe, simple, spartan, stark, subdued, unadorned, unfussy

orthodox accepted, approved, conformist, conventional, correct, customary, doctrinal, established, kosher (*Inf.*), official, received, sound, traditional, true, well-established

Antonyms eccentric, heretical, liberal, non~
conformist, novel, off-the-wall (*Sl.*), original,
radical, unconventional, unorthodox, un~
usual

orthodoxy authenticity, authoritativeness,
authority, conformism, conformity, conven~
tionality, devotion, devoutness, faithfulness,
inflexibility, received wisdom, soundness,
traditionalism
Antonyms flexibility, heresy, heterodoxy,
impiety, nonconformism, nonconformity,
unconventionality

oscillate fluctuate, seesaw, sway, swing,
vacillate, vary, vibrate, waver
Antonyms commit oneself, decide, deter~
mine, purpose, resolve, settle

oscillation fluctuation, instability, seesaw~
ing, swing, vacillation, variation, wavering

ossify fossilize, freeze, harden, indurate
(*Rare*), petrify, solidify, stiffen

ostensible alleged, apparent, avowed, ex~
hibited, manifest, outward, plausible, pre~
tended, professed, purported, seeming, so-
called, specious, superficial, supposed

ostensibly apparently, for the ostensible
purpose of, on the face of it, on the surface,
professedly, seemingly, supposedly, to all
intents and purposes

ostentation affectation, boasting, display,
exhibitionism, flamboyance, flashiness,
flaunting, flourish, pageantry, parade,
pomp, pretension, pretentiousness, show,
showiness, showing off (*Inf.*), swank (*Inf.*),
vaunting, window-dressing
Antonyms humility, inconspicuousness,
modesty, plainness, reserve, simplicity,
unpretentiousness

ostentatious boastful, brash, conspicuous,
crass, dashing, extravagant, flamboyant,
flash (*Inf.*), flashy, flaunted, gaudy, loud,
obtrusive, pompous, pretentious, showy,
swanky (*Inf.*), vain, vulgar
Antonyms conservative, inconspicuous,
low-key, modest, plain, reserved, simple,
sombre

ostracism avoidance, banishment, boycott,
cold-shouldering, exclusion, exile, expul~
sion, isolation, rejection
Antonyms acceptance, admission, approval,
inclusion, invitation, reception, welcome

ostracize avoid, banish, blackball, blacklist,
boycott, cast out, cold-shoulder, exclude,
excommunicate, exile, expatriate, expel,
give (someone) the cold shoulder, reject,
send to Coventry, shun, snub
Antonyms accept, admit, approve, embrace,
greet, include, invite, receive, welcome

other *adj.* **1.** added, additional, alternative,
auxiliary, extra, further, more, spare, sup~
plementary **2.** contrasting, different, dis~

similar, distinct, diverse, remaining, sepa~
rate, unrelated, variant

otherwise 1. *conj.* if not, or else, or then **2.**
adv. any other way, contrarily, differently

ounce atom, crumb, drop, grain, iota, parti~
cle, scrap, shred, speck, trace, whit

out *adj.* **1.** impossible, not allowed, not on
(*Inf.*), ruled out, unacceptable **2.** abroad,
absent, away, elsewhere, gone, not at home,
outside **3.** antiquated, behind the times,
dated, dead, *démodé*, old-fashioned, old hat,
passé, square (*Inf.*), unfashionable **4.** at an
end, cold, dead, doused, ended, exhausted,
expired, extinguished, finished, used up
Antonyms (*sense 3*) à la mode, fashionable,
in, in fashion, latest, modern, trendy (*Brit.
inf.*), up-to-date, with it (*Inf.*)

out-and-out absolute, arrant, complete,
consummate, deep-dyed (*Usually deroga~
tory*), downright, dyed-in-the-wool, outright,
perfect, thoroughgoing, total, unmitigated,
unqualified, utter

outbreak burst, epidemic, eruption, explo~
sion, flare-up, flash, outburst, rash, spasm,
upsurge

outburst access, attack, discharge, erup~
tion, explosion, fit of temper, flare-up, gush,
outbreak, outpouring, paroxysm, spasm,
storm, surge

outcast *n.* castaway, derelict, displaced
person, exile, leper, pariah, *persona non
grata*, refugee, reprobate, untouchable,
vagabond, wretch

outclass be a cut above (*Inf.*), beat, eclipse,
exceed, excel, leave *or* put in the shade,
leave standing (*Inf.*), outdistance, outdo,
outrank, outshine, outstrip, overshadow,
run rings around (*Inf.*), surpass

outcome aftereffect, aftermath, conclusion,
consequence, end, end result, issue, payoff
(*Inf.*), result, sequel, upshot

outcry clamour, commotion, complaint, cry,
exclamation, howl, hue and cry, hullabal~
loo, noise, outburst, protest, scream,
screech, uproar, yell

outdated antiquated, antique, archaic, be~
hind the times, *démodé*, obsolete, old-
fashioned, outmoded, out of date, out of
style, passé, unfashionable
Antonyms à la mode, all the rage, contem~
porary, current, fashionable, in vogue, mod~
ern, modish, stylish, trendy (*Brit. inf.*), up-to-
date, with it (*Inf.*)

outdistance leave behind, leave standing
(*Inf.*), lose, outrun, outstrip, shake off

outdo beat, be one up on, best, eclipse, ex~
ceed, excel, get the better of, go one better
than (*Inf.*), outclass, outdistance, outfox,
outjockey, outmanoeuvre, outshine, out~

smart (*Inf.*), overcome, run rings around (*Inf.*), surpass, top, transcend

outdoor alfresco, open-air, out-of-door(s), outside
Antonyms indoor, inside, interior, within

outer exposed, exterior, external, outlying, outside, outward, peripheral, remote, superficial, surface
Antonyms central, closer, inner, inside, in~terior, internal, inward, nearer

outfit *n.* **1.** accoutrements, clothes, costume, ensemble, garb, gear (*Inf.*), get-up (*Inf.*), kit, rigout (*Inf.*), suit, togs (*Inf.*), trappings **2.** *Inf.* clique, company, corps, coterie, crew, firm, *galère*, group, organization, set, setup (*Inf.*), squad, team, unit ~*v.* **3.** accoutre, appoint, equip, fit out, furnish, kit out, pro~vision, stock, supply, turn out

outfitter clothier, costumier, couturier, dressmaker, haberdasher (*U.S.*), modiste, tailor

outflow discharge, drainage, effluence, gush, jet, outfall, outpouring, rush, spout

outgoing **1.** departing, ex-, former, last, leaving, past, retiring, withdrawing **2.** ap~proachable, communicative, cordial, de~monstrative, easy, expansive, extrovert, friendly, genial, gregarious, informal, open, sociable, sympathetic, unreserved, warm
Antonyms (*sense 1*) arriving, entering, in~coming (*sense 2*) austere, cold, indifferent, re~served, retiring, withdrawn

outgoings costs, expenditure, expenses, outlay, overheads

outing excursion, expedition, jaunt, pleas~ure trip, spin (*Inf.*), trip

outlandish alien, barbarous, bizarre, ec~centric, exotic, fantastic, far-out (*Sl.*), for~eign, freakish, grotesque, outré, preposter~ous, queer, strange, unheard-of, weird
Antonyms banal, commonplace, everyday, familiar, humdrum, mundane, normal, ordi~nary, usual, well-known

outlaw **1.** *n.* bandit, brigand, desperado, fu~gitive, highwayman, marauder, outcast, pa~riah, robber **2.** *v.* ban, banish, bar, con~demn, disallow, embargo, exclude, forbid, interdict, make illegal, prohibit, proscribe, put a price on (someone's) head
Antonyms (*sense 2*) allow, approve, author~ize, consent, endorse, legalise, permit, sanc~tion, support

outlay *n.* cost, disbursement, expenditure, expenses, investment, outgoings, spending

outlet **1.** avenue, channel, duct, egress, exit, means of expression, opening, orifice, re~lease, safety valve, vent, way out **2.** market, shop, store

outline *n.* **1.** draft, drawing, frame, frame~work, layout, lineament(s), plan, rough,

skeleton, sketch, tracing **2.** bare facts, main features, recapitulation, résumé, rough idea, rundown, summary, synopsis, thumb~nail sketch **3.** configuration, contour, de~lineation, figure, form, profile, shape, sil~houette ~*v.* **4.** adumbrate, delineate, draft, plan, rough out, sketch (in), summarize, trace

outlook **1.** angle, attitude, frame of mind, perspective, point of view, slant, standpoint, viewpoint, views **2.** expectations, forecast, future, prospect **3.** aspect, panorama, pros~pect, scene, view, vista

outlying backwoods, distant, far-flung, in the middle of nowhere, outer, out-of-the-way, peripheral, provincial, remote

outmoded anachronistic, antediluvian, antiquated, antique, archaic, behind the times, bygone, dated, *démodé*, fossilized, ob~solescent, obsolete, olden (*Archaic*), old~fangled, old-fashioned, old-time, out, out of date, out of style, outworn, passé, square (*Inf.*), superannuated, superseded, unfash~ionable, unusable
Antonyms all the rage, fashionable, fresh, in vogue, latest, modern, modish, new, recent, usable

out of date antiquated, archaic, dated, discarded, elapsed, expired, extinct, invalid, lapsed, obsolete, old-fashioned, outmoded, outworn, passé, stale, superannuated, superseded, unfashionable
Antonyms contemporary, current, fashion~able, in, new, now (*Inf.*), trendy (*Brit. inf.*), up to date, valid

out-of-the-way **1.** distant, far-flung, inac~cessible, isolated, lonely, obscure, off the beaten track, outlying, remote, secluded, unfrequented **2.** abnormal, curious, excep~tional, extraordinary, odd, outlandish, out of the ordinary, peculiar, strange, uncom~mon, unusual
Antonyms (*sense 1*) accessible, close, con~venient, frequented, handy, near, nearby, proximate, reachable, within sniffing dis~tance (*Inf.*)

out of work idle, jobless, laid off, on the dole (*Brit.*), out of a job, redundant, unem~ployed

outpouring cascade, debouchment, deluge, effluence, efflux, effusion, emanation, flow, flux, issue, outflow, spate, spurt, stream, torrent

output achievement, manufacture, outturn (*Rare*), product, production, productivity, yield

outrage *n.* **1.** atrocity, barbarism, enormity, evil, inhumanity **2.** abuse, affront, desecra~tion, indignity, injury, insult, offence, profanation, rape, ravishing, shock, viola~tion, violence **3.** anger, fury, hurt, indigna~

tion, resentment, shock, wrath ~v. **4.** af~
front, incense, infuriate, madden, make
one's blood boil, offend, scandalize, shock
5. abuse, defile, desecrate, injure, insult,
maltreat, rape, ravage, ravish, violate

outrageous 1. abominable, atrocious, bar~
baric, beastly, egregious, flagrant, heinous,
horrible, infamous, inhuman, iniquitous,
nefarious, scandalous, shocking, unspeak~
able, villainous, violent, wicked **2.** dis~
graceful, excessive, exorbitant, extravagant,
immoderate, offensive, O.T.T. (*Sl.*), over the
top (*Sl.*), preposterous, scandalous, shock~
ing, steep (*Inf.*), unreasonable
Antonyms equitable, fair, just, mild, minor,
moderate, reasonable, tolerable, trivial

outright *adj.* **1.** absolute, arrant, complete,
consummate, deep-dyed (*Usually deroga~
tory*), downright, out-and-out, perfect, pure,
thorough, thoroughgoing, total, uncondi~
tional, undeniable, unmitigated, un~
qualified, utter, wholesale **2.** definite, di~
rect, flat, straightforward, unequivocal,
unqualified ~*adv.* **3.** absolutely, completely,
explicitly, openly, overtly, straightforward~
ly, thoroughly, to the full, without hesita~
tion, without restraint **4.** at once, cleanly,
immediately, instantaneously, instantly, on
the spot, straight away, there and then,
without more ado

outset beginning, commencement, early
days, inauguration, inception, kickoff (*Inf.*),
onset, opening, start, starting point
Antonyms closing, completion, conclusion,
consummation, end, finale, finish, termina~
tion

outshine be head and shoulders above, be
superior to, eclipse, leave *or* put in the
shade, outclass, outdo, outstrip, overshad~
ow, surpass, top, transcend, upstage

outside *adj.* **1.** exterior, external, extramu~
ral, extraneous, extreme, out, outdoor, out~
er, outermost, outward, surface **2.** distant,
faint, marginal, negligible, remote, slight,
slim, small, unlikely ~*n.* **3.** exterior, façade,
face, front, skin, surface, topside
Antonyms (*sense 1*) in, indoor, inner, inner~
most, inside, interior, internal, intramural,
inward

outsider alien, foreigner, incomer, inter~
loper, intruder, newcomer, nonmember, odd
man out, outlander, stranger

outskirts borders, boundary, edge, envi~
rons, faubourgs, periphery, purlieus, sub~
urbia, suburbs, vicinity

outspoken abrupt, blunt, candid, direct,
downright, explicit, forthright, frank, free,
free-spoken, open, plain-spoken, round, un~
ceremonious, undissembling, unequivocal,
unreserved

Antonyms diplomatic, gracious, judicious,
reserved, reticent, tactful

outspread 1. *adj.* expanded, extended, fan~
like, fanned out, flared, open, opened up,
outstretched, unfolded, unfurled, wide-open
2. *v.* expand, extend, fan out, open, open
wide, outstretch, spread out, unfold, unfurl

outstanding 1. celebrated, distinguished,
eminent, excellent, exceptional, great, im~
portant, impressive, meritorious, pre~
eminent, special, superior, superlative,
well-known **2.** arresting, conspicuous, eye-
catching, marked, memorable, notable,
noteworthy, prominent, salient, signal,
striking **3.** due, ongoing, open, owing, pay~
able, pending, remaining, uncollected, un~
paid, unresolved, unsettled
Antonyms (*senses 1 & 2*) dull, inferior,
insignificant, mediocre, ordinary, pedestrian,
run-of-the-mill, unexceptional, unimpressive

outward *adj.* apparent, evident, exterior,
external, noticeable, observable, obvious,
ostensible, outer, outside, perceptible,
superficial, surface, visible
Antonyms inner, inside, interior, internal,
invisible, inward, obscure, unnoticeable

outwardly apparently, as far as one can
see, externally, officially, on the face of it,
on the surface, ostensibly, professedly,
seemingly, superficially, to all appearances,
to all intents and purposes, to the eye

outweigh cancel (out), compensate for,
eclipse, make up for, outbalance, overcome,
override, predominate, preponderate, pre~
vail over, take precedence over, tip the
scales

outwit cheat, circumvent, deceive, defraud,
dupe, get the better of, gull (*Archaic*), make
a fool *or* monkey of, outfox, outjockey, out~
manoeuvre, outsmart (*Inf.*), outthink, put
one over on (*Inf.*), run rings round (*Inf.*),
swindle, take in (*Inf.*)

outworn abandoned, antiquated, behind the
times, defunct, discredited, disused, ex~
hausted, hackneyed, obsolete, outdated,
outmoded, out of date, overused, rejected,
stale, superannuated, threadbare, tired,
worn-out
Antonyms credited, fresh, modish, new, re~
cent, up to date, used

oval *adj.* egg-shaped, ellipsoidal, elliptical,
ovate, oviform, ovoid

ovation acclaim, acclamation, applause,
cheering, cheers, clapping, laudation, plau~
dits, tribute
Antonyms abuse, booing, catcalls, derision,
heckling, jeers, jibes, mockery, ridicule

over *adj.* **1.** accomplished, ancient history
(*Inf.*), at an end, by, bygone, closed, com~
pleted, concluded, done (with), ended,
finished, gone, past, settled, up (*Inf.*),

~*adj./adv.* **2.** beyond, extra, in addition, in excess, left over, remaining, superfluous, surplus, unused ~*prep.* **3.** above, on, on top of, superior to, upon **4.** above, exceeding, in excess of, more than ~*adv.* **5.** above, aloft, on high, overhead **6. over and above** added to, as well as, besides, in addition to, let alone, not to mention, on top of, plus **7. over and over (again)** ad nauseam, again and again, frequently, often, repeatedly, time and again

overact exaggerate, ham *or* ham up (*Inf.*), overdo, overplay

overall 1. *adj.* all-embracing, blanket, complete, comprehensive, general, global, inclusive, long-range, long-term, total, umbrella **2.** *adv.* generally speaking, in general, in (the) large, in the long term, on the whole

overawe abash, alarm, browbeat, cow, daunt, frighten, intimidate, scare, terrify
Antonyms bolster, buoy up, cheer up, comfort, console, hearten, reassure

overbalance capsize, keel over, lose one's balance, lose one's footing, overset, overturn, slip, take a tumble, tip over, topple over, tumble, turn turtle, upset

overbearing arrogant, autocratic, bossy (*Inf.*), cavalier, despotic, dictatorial, dogmatic, domineering, haughty, high-handed, imperious, lordly, magisterial, officious, oppressive, overweening, peremptory, supercilious, superior, tyrannical
Antonyms deferential, humble, modest, self-effacing, submissive, unassertive, unassuming

overcast clouded, clouded over, cloudy, darkened, dismal, dreary, dull, grey, hazy, leaden, louring *or* lowering, murky, sombre, sunless, threatening
Antonyms bright, brilliant, clear, cloudless, fine, sunny, unclouded

overcharge 1. cheat, clip (*Sl.*), diddle (*Inf.*), do (*Sl.*), fleece, rip off (*Sl.*), rook (*Sl.*), short-change, skin (*Sl.*), sting (*Inf.*), surcharge **2.** burden, oppress, overburden, overload, overtask, overtax, strain, surfeit **3.** *Literary* embellish, embroider, exaggerate, hyperbolize, lay it on thick (*Inf.*), overstate

overcome 1. *v.* beat, best, be victorious, blow out of the water (*Sl.*), clobber (*Sl.*), come out on top (*Inf.*), conquer, crush, defeat, get the better of, lick (*Inf.*), master, overpower, overthrow, overwhelm, prevail, render incapable (helpless, powerless), rise above, subdue, subjugate, surmount, survive, tank (*Sl.*), triumph over, undo, vanquish, weather, wipe the floor with (*Inf.*), worst **2.** *adj.* affected, at a loss for words, bowled over (*Inf.*), overwhelmed, speechless,

swept off one's feet, unable to continue, visibly moved

overconfident brash, cocksure, foolhardy, hubristic, overweening, presumptuous, riding for a fall (*Inf.*), uppish (*Brit. inf.*)
Antonyms cautious, diffident, doubtful, hesitant, insecure, timid, timorous, uncertain, unsure

overcritical captious, carping, cavilling, fault-finding, hairsplitting, hard to please, hypercritical, nit-picking (*Inf.*), overparticular, pedantic, pernickety (*Inf.*), picky (*Inf.*)
Antonyms easily pleased, easy-going, laid-back (*Inf.*), lenient, tolerant, uncritical, undemanding, unfussy

overcrowded choked, congested, crammed full, hoatching (*Scot.*), jam-packed, like the Black Hole of Calcutta, overloaded, overpopulated, packed (out), swarming
Antonyms abandoned, deserted, desolate, empty, forsaken, unoccupied, vacant

overdo 1. be intemperate, belabour, carry too far, do to death (*Inf.*), exaggerate, gild the lily, go overboard (*Inf.*), go to extremes, lay it on thick (*Inf.*), not know when to stop, overindulge, overplay, overreach, overstate, overuse, overwork, run riot **2. overdo it** bite off more than one can chew, burn the candle at both ends (*Inf.*), drive oneself, fatigue, go too far, have too many irons in the fire, overburden, overload, overtax one's strength, overtire, overwork, strain *or* overstrain oneself, wear oneself out
Antonyms (*sense 1*) belittle, disparage, minimize, play down, underplay, underrate, understate, underuse, undervalue

overdone 1. beyond all bounds, exaggerated, excessive, fulsome, hyped, immoderate, inordinate, overelaborate, preposterous, too much, undue, unnecessary **2.** burnt, burnt to a cinder, charred, dried up, overcooked, spoiled
Antonyms (*sense 1*) belittled, minimized, moderated, played down, underdone, underplayed, understated

overdue behindhand, behind schedule, behind time, belated, late, long delayed, not before time (*Inf.*), owing, tardy, unpunctual
Antonyms ahead of time, beforehand, early, in advance, in good time, punctual

overeat binge (*Inf.*), eat like a horse (*Inf.*), gorge, gormandize, guzzle, make a pig of oneself (*Inf.*), overindulge, pack away (*Sl.*), pig away (*Sl.*), pig out (*Sl.*), stuff, stuff oneself

overemphasize belabour, blow up out of all proportion, lay too much stress on, make a big thing of (*Inf.*), make a federal case of (*U.S. inf.*), make a mountain out of a

molehill (*Inf.*), make a production (out) of (*Inf.*), make something out of nothing, make too much of, overdramatize, overstress
Antonyms belittle, downplay, make light of, minimize, play down, underplay, underrate, understate

overflow *v.* **1.** bubble (brim, fall, pour, run, slop, well) over, discharge, pour out, run with, shower, spill, spray, surge **2.** cover, deluge, drown, flood, inundate, soak, sub~ merge, swamp ~*n.* **3.** discharge, flash flood, flood, flooding, inundation, overabundance, spill, spilling over, surplus

overflowing abounding, bountiful, brimful, copious, plentiful, profuse, rife, super~ abundant, swarming, teeming, thronged
Antonyms deficient, inadequate, insuf~ ficient, lacking, missing, scarce, wanting

overhang *v.* beetle, bulge, cast a shadow, extend, impend, jut, loom, project, protrude, stick out, threaten

overhaul *v.* **1.** check, do up (*Inf.*), examine, inspect, recondition, re-examine, repair, re~ store, service, survey ~*n.* **2.** check, check~ up, examination, going-over (*Inf.*), inspec~ tion, reconditioning, service ~*v.* **3.** catch up with, draw level with, get ahead of, over~ take, pass

overhead 1. *adv.* above, aloft, atop, in the sky, on high, skyward, up above, upward **2.** *adj.* aerial, overhanging, roof, upper
Antonyms (*sense 1*) below, beneath, down~ ward, underfoot, underneath

overheads burden, oncosts, operating cost(s), running cost(s)

overheated agitated, fiery, flaming, impas~ sioned, inflamed, overexcited, roused
Antonyms calm, collected, composed, cool, dispassionate, unemotional, unexcited, un~ fazed (*Inf.*), unruffled

overindulge be immoderate *or* intemper~ ate, drink *or* eat too much, have a binge (*Inf.*), live it up (*Inf.*), make a pig of oneself (*Inf.*), overdo it, pig out (*Sl.*)

overindulgence excess, immoderation, intemperance, overeating, surfeit

overjoyed cock-a-hoop, delighted, deliri~ ously happy, elated, euphoric, happy as a lark, in raptures, joyful, jubilant, on cloud nine (*Inf.*), only too happy, over the moon (*Inf.*), rapt, rapturous, thrilled, tickled pink (*Inf.*), transported
Antonyms crestfallen, dejected, disappoint~ ed, downcast, heartbroken, miserable, sad, unhappy, woebegone

overlay 1. *v.* adorn, blanket, cover, inlay, laminate, ornament, overspread, superim~ pose, veneer **2.** *n.* adornment, appliqué, covering, decoration, ornamentation, veneer

overload burden, encumber, oppress, over~ burden, overcharge, overtax, saddle (with), strain, weigh down

overlook 1. disregard, fail to notice, forget, ignore, leave out of consideration, leave undone, miss, neglect, omit, pass, slight, slip up on **2.** blink at, condone, disregard, excuse, forgive, let bygones be bygones, let one off with, let pass, let ride, make allow~ ances for, pardon, turn a blind eye to, wink at **3.** afford a view of, command a view of, front on to, give upon, have a view of, look over *or* out on
Antonyms (*sense 1*) discern, heed, mark, note, notice, observe, perceive, regard, spot

overly exceedingly, excessively, immoder~ ately, inordinately, over, too, unduly, very much

overpower beat, clobber (*Sl.*), conquer, crush, defeat, get the upper hand over, im~ mobilize, knock out, lick (*Inf.*), master, overcome, overthrow, overwhelm, quell, subdue, subjugate, vanquish

overpowering compelling, extreme, force~ ful, invincible, irrefutable, irresistible, nauseating, overwhelming, powerful, sick~ ening, strong, suffocating, telling, unbear~ able, uncontrollable

overrate assess too highly, exaggerate, make too much of, overestimate, overpraise, overprize, oversell, overvalue, rate too highly, think *or* expect too much of, think too highly of

overreach 1. overreach oneself be hoist with one's own petard, bite off more than one can chew, defeat one's own ends, go too far, have one's schemes rebound (backfire, boomerang) on one, try to be too clever **2.** cheat, circumvent, deceive, defraud, dupe, gull (*Archaic*), outsmart (*Inf.*), outwit, swin~ dle, trick, victimize

override annul, cancel, countermand, dis~ count, disregard, ignore, nullify, outweigh, overrule, quash, reverse, ride roughshod over, set aside, supersede, take no account of, trample underfoot, upset, vanquish

overriding cardinal, compelling, determin~ ing, dominant, final, major, number one, overruling, paramount, pivotal, predomi~ nant, prevailing, primary, prime, ruling, supreme, ultimate
Antonyms immaterial, inconsequential, insignificant, irrelevant, minor, negligible, paltry, petty, trifling, trivial, unimportant

overrule 1. alter, annul, cancel, counter~ mand, disallow, invalidate, make null and void, outvote, override, overturn, recall, re~ peal, rescind, reverse, revoke, rule against, set aside, veto **2.** bend to one's will, control, direct, dominate, govern, influence, prevail over, sway

Antonyms (*sense 1*) allow, approve, consent to, endorse, pass, permit, sanction

overrun 1. cut to pieces, invade, massacre, occupy, overwhelm, put to flight, rout, swamp **2.** choke, infest, inundate, overflow, overgrow, permeate, ravage, spread like wildfire, spread over, surge over, swarm over **3.** exceed, go beyond, overshoot, run over *or* on

overseer boss (*Inf.*), chief, foreman, gaffer (*Inf., chiefly Brit.*), manager, master, super (*Inf.*), superintendent, superior, supervisor

overshadow 1. dominate, dwarf, eclipse, excel, leave *or* put in the shade, outshine, outweigh, render insignificant by compari~ son, rise above, steal the limelight from, surpass, take precedence over, throw into the shade, tower above **2.** adumbrate, be~ cloud, bedim, cloud, darken, dim, obfuscate, obscure, veil **3.** blight, cast a gloom upon, mar, ruin, spoil, take the edge off, take the pleasure *or* enjoyment out of, temper

oversight 1. blunder, carelessness, delin~ quency, error, fault, inattention, lapse, lax~ ity, mistake, neglect, omission, slip **2.** ad~ ministration, care, charge, control, custody, direction, handling, inspection, keeping, management, superintendence, supervision, surveillance

overt apparent, blatant, manifest, observ~ able, obvious, open, patent, plain, public, unconcealed, undisguised, visible
Antonyms concealed, covert, disguised, hidden, hush-hush (*Inf.*), invisible, secret, surreptitious, underhand

overtake 1. catch up with, do better than, draw level with, get past, leave behind, outdistance, outdo, outstrip, overhaul, pass **2.** befall, catch unprepared, come upon, en~ gulf, happen, hit, overwhelm, strike, take by surprise

overthrow *v.* **1.** abolish, beat, bring down, conquer, crush, defeat, depose, dethrone, do away with, master, oust, overcome, over~ power, overwhelm, subdue, subjugate, top~ ple, unseat, vanquish **2.** bring to ruin, de~ molish, destroy, knock down, level, over~ turn, put an end to, raze, ruin, subvert, up~ end, upset ~*n.* **3.** defeat, deposition, de~ struction, dethronement, discomfiture, dis~ establishment, displacement, dispossession, downfall, end, fall, ousting, prostration, rout, ruin, subjugation, subversion, sup~ pression, undoing, unseating
Antonyms *v.* defend, guard, keep, maintain, preserve, protect, restore, support, uphold ~*n.* defence, preservation, protection

overtone association, connotation, flavour, hint, implication, innuendo, intimation, nuance, sense, suggestion, undercurrent

overture 1. *Often plural* advance, approach,

conciliatory move, invitation, offer, opening move, proposal, proposition, signal, tender **2.** *Music* introduction, opening, prelude
Antonyms afterword, close, coda, epilogue, finale, rebuke, rejection, withdrawal

overturn 1. capsize, keel over, knock over *or* down, overbalance, reverse, spill, tip over, topple, tumble, upend, upset, upturn **2.** abolish, annul, bring down, counter~ mand, depose, destroy, invalidate, obviate, overthrow, repeal, rescind, reverse, set aside, unseat

overweening 1. arrogant, cavalier, cock~ sure, cocky, conceited, egotistical, haughty, high and mighty (*Inf.*), high-handed, inso~ lent, lordly, opinionated, pompous, pre~ sumptuous, proud, self-confident, supercili~ ous, uppish (*Brit. inf.*), vain, vainglorious **2.** blown up out of all proportion, excessive, extravagant, immoderate
Antonyms (*sense 1*) deferential, diffident, hesitant, modest, self-conscious, self-effacing, timid, unassuming, unobtrusive

overweight *adj.* ample, bulky, buxom, chubby, chunky, corpulent, fat, fleshy, gross, heavy, hefty, huge, massive, obese, on the plump side, outsize, plump, podgy, portly, stout, tubby (*Inf.*), well-padded (*Inf.*), well-upholstered (*Inf.*)
Antonyms emaciated, gaunt, lean, pinched, scraggy, scrawny, skinny, thin, underweight

overwhelm 1. bury, crush, deluge, engulf, flood, inundate, snow under, submerge, swamp **2.** bowl over (*Inf.*), confuse, devas~ tate, knock (someone) for six (*Inf.*), over~ come, overpower, prostrate, render speech~ less, stagger **3.** crush, cut to pieces, destroy, massacre, overpower, overrun, rout

overwhelming breathtaking, crushing, devastating, invincible, irresistible, over~ powering, shattering, stunning, towering, uncontrollable, vast, vastly superior
Antonyms commonplace, incidental, insignificant, negligible, paltry, resistible, trivial, unimportant

overwork be a slave-driver *or* hard task~ master to, burden, burn the midnight oil, drive into the ground, exhaust, exploit, fa~ tigue, oppress, overstrain, overtax, overuse, prostrate, strain, sweat (*Inf.*), wear out, weary, work one's fingers to the bone

overwrought 1. agitated, beside oneself, distracted, excited, frantic, in a state (tizzy (*Inf.*), twitter (*Inf.*)) (*Inf.*), keyed up, on edge, overexcited, overworked, stirred, strung up (*Inf.*), tense, uptight (*Inf.*), wired (*Sl.*), worked up (*Inf.*), wound up (*Inf.*) **2.** baroque, busy, contrived, florid, flowery, fussy, overdone, overelaborate, overembel~ lished, overornate, rococo
Antonyms (*sense 1*) calm, collected, con~

trolled, cool, dispassionate, emotionless, im~ passive, self-contained, unfazed (*Inf.*), un~ moved

owe be beholden to, be in arrears, be in debt, be obligated *or* indebted, be under an obligation to

owing *adj.* due, outstanding, overdue, owed, payable, unpaid, unsettled

owing to *prep.* as a result of, because of, on account of

own *adj.* **1.** individual, particular, personal, private ~*pron.* **2. on one's own** alone, by oneself, by one's own efforts, independently, isolated, left to one's own devices, off one's own bat, on one's tod (*Brit. sl.*), singly, (standing) on one's own two feet, unaided, unassisted **3. hold one's own** compete, keep going, keep one's end up, keep one's head above water, maintain one's position ~*v.* **4.** be in possession of, be responsible for, enjoy, have, hold, keep, possess, retain **5. own up (to)** admit, come clean (about) (*Inf.*), confess, make a clean breast of, tell the truth (about) **6.** acknowledge, admit, allow, allow to be valid, avow, concede, confess, disclose, go along with, grant, rec~ ognize

owner holder, landlord, lord, master, mis~ tress, possessor, proprietor, proprietress, proprietrix

ownership dominion, possession, propri~ etary rights, proprietorship, right of pos~ session, title

P

pace n. **1.** gait, measure, step, stride, tread, walk **2.** clip (*Inf.*), lick (*Inf.*), momentum, motion, movement, progress, rate, speed, tempo, time, velocity ~v. **3.** march, patrol, pound, stride, walk back and forth, walk up and down **4.** count, determine, mark out, measure, step

pacific 1. appeasing, conciliatory, diplomatic, irenic, pacificatory, peacemaking, placatory, propitiatory **2.** dovelike, dovish, friendly, gentle, mild, nonbelligerent, nonviolent, pacifist, peaceable, peace-loving **3.** at peace, calm, halcyon, peaceful, placid, quiet, serene, smooth, still, tranquil, unruffled
Antonyms aggressive, antagonistic, belligerent, hostile, nonconciliatory, pugnacious, Ramboesque, unforgiving, unfriendly, violent, warlike

pacifist conchie (*Inf.*), conscientious objector, dove, passive resister, peace lover, peacemonger, peacenik (*Inf.*), satyagrahi

pack n. **1.** back pack, bale, bundle, burden, fardel (*Archaic*), kit, kitbag, knapsack, load, package, packet, parcel, rucksack, truss **2.** assemblage, band, bunch, collection, company, crew, crowd, deck, drove, flock, gang, group, herd, lot, mob, set, troop ~v. **3.** batch, bundle, burden, load, package, packet, store, stow **4.** charge, compact, compress, cram, crowd, fill, jam, mob, press, ram, stuff, tamp, throng, wedge **5.** *With* **off** bundle out, dismiss, hustle out, send away, send packing (*Inf.*), send someone about his business

package n. **1.** box, carton, container, packet, parcel **2.** amalgamation, combination, entity, unit, whole ~v. **3.** batch, box, pack, packet, parcel (up), wrap, wrap up

packed brimful, chock-a-block, chock-full, congested, cram-full, crammed, crowded, filled, full, hotching (*Scot.*), jammed, jam-packed, loaded *or* full to the gunwales, overflowing, overloaded, packed like sardines, seething, swarming
Antonyms deserted, empty, uncongested, uncrowded

packet 1. bag, carton, container, package, parcel, poke (*Dialect*), wrapper, wrapping **2.** *Sl.* a bob or two (*Brit. inf.*), big bucks (*Inf., chiefly U.S.*), big money, bomb (*Brit. sl.*), bundle (*Sl.*), fortune, king's ransom (*Inf.*), lot(s), megabucks (*U.S. & Canad. sl.*), mint, pile (*Inf.*), pot(s) (*Inf.*), pretty penny (*Inf.*), tidy sum (*Inf.*), wad (*U.S. & Canad. sl.*)

pack in 1. attract, cram, draw, fill to capacity, squeeze in **2.** *Brit. inf.* cease, chuck (*Inf.*), desist, give up *or* over, jack in, kick (*Inf.*), leave off, stop

pack up 1. put away, store, tidy up **2.** *Inf.* call it a day (*Inf.*), finish, give up, pack in (*Brit. inf.*) **3.** break down, conk out (*Inf.*), fail, give out, stall, stop

pact agreement, alliance, arrangement, bargain, bond, compact, concord, concordat, contract, convention, covenant, deal, league, protocol, treaty, understanding

pad n. **1.** buffer, cushion, protection, stiffening, stuffing, wad **2.** block, jotter, notepad, tablet, writing pad **3.** foot, paw, sole **4.** *Sl.* apartment, flat, hang-out (*Inf.*), home, place, quarters, room ~v. **5.** cushion, fill, line, pack, protect, shape, stuff **6.** *Often with* **out** amplify, augment, eke, elaborate, fill out, flesh out, inflate, lengthen, protract, spin out, stretch

padding 1. filling, packing, stuffing, wadding **2.** hot air (*Inf.*), prolixity, verbiage, verbosity, waffle (*Inf., chiefly Brit.*), wordiness

paddle[1] **1.** n. oar, scull, sweep **2.** v. oar, propel, pull, row, scull

paddle[2] dabble, plash, slop, splash (about), stir, wade

pagan 1. n. Gentile, heathen, idolater, infidel, polytheist, unbeliever **2.** adj. Gentile, heathen, heathenish, idolatrous, infidel, irreligious, polytheistic

page[1] n. **1.** folio, leaf, sheet, side **2.** chapter, episode, epoch, era, event, incident, period, phase, point, stage, time ~v. **3.** foliate, number, paginate

page[2] n. **1.** attendant, bellboy (*U.S.*), footboy, pageboy, servant, squire **2.** v. announce, call, call out, preconize, seek, send for, summon

pageant display, extravaganza, parade, procession, ritual, show, spectacle, tableau

pageantry display, drama, extravagance, glamour, glitter, grandeur, magnificence, parade, pomp, show, showiness, spectacle, splash (*Inf.*), splendour, state, theatricality

pain n. **1.** ache, cramp, discomfort, hurt, irritation, pang, smarting, soreness, spasm, suffering, tenderness, throb, throe (*Rare*), trouble, twinge **2.** affliction, agony, anguish, bitterness, distress, grief, hardship, heartache, misery, suffering, torment, torture, tribulation, woe, wretchedness **3.** *Inf.*

aggravation, annoyance, bore, bother, drag (*Inf.*), gall, headache (*Inf.*), irritation, nuisance, pain in the arse (*Taboo inf.*), pain in the neck (*Inf.*), pest, vexation ~*v.* **4.** ail, chafe, discomfort, harm, hurt, inflame, injure, smart, sting, throb **5.** afflict, aggrieve, agonize, cut to the quick, disquiet, distress, grieve, hurt, sadden, torment, torture, vex, worry, wound **6.** *Inf.* annoy, exasperate, gall, harass, irritate, nark (*Brit., Aust., & N.Z. sl.*), rile, vex

pained aggrieved, anguished, distressed, hurt, injured, miffed (*Inf.*), offended, reproachful, stung, unhappy, upset, worried, wounded

painful 1. afflictive, disagreeable, distasteful, distressing, grievous, saddening, unpleasant **2.** aching, agonizing, excruciating, harrowing, hurting, inflamed, raw, smarting, sore, tender, throbbing **3.** arduous, difficult, hard, laborious, severe, tedious, troublesome, trying, vexatious **4.** *Inf.* abysmal, awful, dire, dreadful, excruciating, extremely bad, godawful, terrible
Antonyms (*sense 1*) agreeable, enjoyable, pleasant, satisfying (*sense 2*) comforting, painless, relieving, soothing (*sense 3*) a piece of cake (*Inf.*), easy, effortless, interesting, short, simple, straightforward, undemanding

painfully alarmingly, clearly, deplorably, distressingly, dreadfully, excessively, markedly, sadly, unfortunately, woefully

painkiller anaesthetic, analgesic, anodyne, drug, palliative, remedy, sedative

painless easy, effortless, fast, no trouble, pain-free, quick, simple, trouble-free

pains 1. assiduousness, bother, care, diligence, effort, industry, labour, special attention, trouble **2.** birth-pangs, childbirth, contractions, labour

painstaking assiduous, careful, conscientious, diligent, earnest, exacting, hardworking, industrious, meticulous, persevering, punctilious, scrupulous, sedulous, strenuous, thorough, thoroughgoing
Antonyms careless, half-hearted, haphazard, heedless, lazy, negligent, slapdash, slipshod, thoughtless

paint *n.* **1.** colour, colouring, dye, emulsion, pigment, stain, tint **2.** *Inf.* cosmetics, face (*Inf.*), greasepaint, make-up, *maquillage*, war paint (*Inf.*) ~*v.* **3.** catch a likeness, delineate, depict, draw, figure, picture, portray, represent, sketch **4.** apply, coat, colour, cover, daub, decorate, slap on (*Inf.*) **5.** bring to life, capture, conjure up a vision, depict, describe, evoke, make one see, portray, put graphically, recount, tell vividly **6. paint the town red** *Inf.* carouse, celebrate, go on a binge (*Inf.*), go on a spree,

go on the town, live it up (*Inf.*), make merry, make whoopee (*Inf.*), revel

pair 1. *n.* brace, combination, couple, doublet, duo, match, matched set, span, twins, two of a kind, twosome, yoke **2.** *v.* bracket, couple, join, marry, match, match up, mate, pair off, put together, team, twin, wed, yoke

palatable 1. appetizing, delectable, delicious, luscious, mouthwatering, savoury, tasty, toothsome **2.** acceptable, agreeable, attractive, enjoyable, fair, pleasant, satisfactory
Antonyms (*sense 1*) bland, flat, insipid, stale, tasteless, unappetizing, unpalatable

palate 1. appetite, heart, stomach, taste **2.** appreciation, enjoyment, gusto, liking, relish, zest

palatial de luxe, gorgeous, grand, grandiose, illustrious, imposing, luxurious, magnificent, majestic, opulent, plush (*Inf.*), regal, spacious, splendid, splendiferous (*Facetious*), stately, sumptuous

pale *adj.* **1.** anaemic, ashen, ashy, bleached, bloodless, colourless, faded, light, pallid, pasty, sallow, wan, washed-out, white, whitish **2.** dim, faint, feeble, inadequate, poor, thin, weak ~*v.* **3.** become pale, blanch, go white, lose colour, whiten **4.** decrease, dim, diminish, dull, fade, grow dull, lessen, lose lustre
Antonyms (*sense 1*) blooming, florid, flushed, glowing, rosy-cheeked, rubicund, ruddy, sanguine

pall *v.* become dull *or* tedious, bore, cloy, glut, jade, satiate, sicken, surfeit, tire, weary

palm¹ 1. hand, hook, meathook (*Sl.*), mitt (*Sl.*), paw (*Inf.*) **2. in the palm of one's hand** at one's mercy, in one's clutches (control, power) **3. grease someone's palm** *Sl.* bribe, buy, corrupt, fix (*Inf.*), give a backhander (*Sl.*), induce, influence, pay off (*Inf.*), square, suborn

palm² *Fig.* bays, crown, fame, glory, honour, laurels, merit, prize, success, triumph, trophy, victory

palm off 1. *With* **on** *or* **with** fob off, foist off, pass off **2.** *With* **on** foist on, force upon, impose upon, take advantage of, thrust upon, unload upon

palmy flourishing, fortunate, glorious, golden, halcyon, happy, joyous, luxurious, prosperous, thriving, triumphant

palpable 1. apparent, blatant, clear, conspicuous, evident, manifest, obvious, open, patent, plain, unmistakable, visible **2.** concrete, material, real, solid, substantial, tangible, touchable

palpitate beat, flutter, pitapat, pitter-patter,

pound, pulsate, pulse, quiver, shiver, throb, tremble, vibrate

palsied arthritic, atonic (*Pathology*), crip~ pled, debilitated, disabled, helpless, para~ lysed, paralytic, rheumatic, sclerotic, shak~ ing, shaky, spastic, trembling

palter 1. be evasive, deceive, double-talk, equivocate, flannel (*Brit. inf.*), fudge, hedge, mislead, prevaricate, shuffle, tergiversate, trifle **2.** bargain, barter, chaffer, dicker (*Chiefly U.S.*), haggle, higgle

paltry base, beggarly, chickenshit (*U.S. sl.*), contemptible, crappy (*Sl.*), derisory, despic~ able, inconsiderable, insignificant, low, meagre, mean, measly, Mickey Mouse (*Sl.*), minor, miserable, nickel-and-dime (*U.S. sl.*), petty, picayune (*U.S.*), piddling (*Inf.*), piti~ ful, poor, poxy (*Sl.*), puny, slight, small, sorry, trifling, trivial, twopenny-halfpenny (*Brit. inf.*), unimportant, worthless, wretch~ ed

Antonyms consequential, considerable, es~ sential, grand, important, major, mega (*Sl.*), significant, valuable

pamper baby, cater to one's every whim, coddle, cosset, fondle, gratify, humour, in~ dulge, mollycoddle, pander to, pet, spoil

pamphlet booklet, brochure, circular, fold~ er, leaflet, tract

pan[1] *n.* **1.** container, pot, saucepan, vessel ~*v.* **2.** look for, search for, separate, sift out, wash **3.** *Inf.* blast, censure, criticize, flay, hammer (*Brit. inf.*), knock (*Inf.*), lam~ bast(e), put down, roast (*Inf.*), rubbish (*Inf.*), slag (off) (*Sl.*), slam (*Sl.*), slate (*Inf.*), tear into (*Inf.*), throw brickbats at (*Inf.*)

pan[2] *v.* follow, move, scan, sweep, swing, track, traverse

panacea catholicon, cure-all, elixir, nos~ trum, sovereign remedy, universal cure

panache a flourish, brio, dash, élan, flair, flamboyance, spirit, style, swagger, verve

pandemonium babel, bedlam, chaos, clamour, commotion, confusion, din, hub~ bub, hue and cry, hullabaloo, racket, ruck~ us (*Inf.*), ruction (*Inf.*), rumpus, tumult, turmoil, uproar

Antonyms arrangement, calm, hush, order, peace, peacefulness, quietude, repose, still~ ness, tranquillity

pang ache, agony, anguish, discomfort, dis~ tress, gripe, pain, prick, spasm, stab, sting, stitch, throe (*Rare*), twinge, wrench

panic *n.* **1.** agitation, alarm, consternation, dismay, fear, fright, horror, hysteria, scare, terror ~*v.* **2.** become hysterical, be terror- stricken, go to pieces, lose one's bottle (*Brit. sl.*), lose one's nerve, overreact **3.** alarm, put the wind up (someone) (*Inf.*), scare, startle, terrify, unnerve

panicky afraid, agitated, distressed, fearful, frantic, frenzied, frightened, hysterical, in a flap (*Inf.*), in a tizzy (*Inf.*), jittery (*Inf.*), nervous, windy (*Sl.*), worked up, worried

Antonyms calm, collected, composed, confident, cool, imperturbable, self- controlled, together (*Sl.*), unexcitable, unfazed (*Inf.*), unflappable, unruffled

panic-stricken *or* **panic-struck** aghast, agitated, alarmed, appalled, fearful, fren~ zied, frightened, frightened out of one's wits, frightened to death, horrified, horror- stricken, hysterical, in a cold sweat (*Inf.*), panicky, petrified, scared, scared shitless (*Taboo sl.*), scared stiff, shit-scared (*Taboo sl.*), startled, terrified, terror-stricken, un~ nerved

panoply array, attire, dress, garb, get-up (*Inf.*), insignia, raiment (*Archaic or poetic*), regalia, show, trappings, turnout

panorama 1. bird's-eye view, prospect, scenery, scenic view, view, vista **2.** overall picture, overview, perspective, survey

panoramic all-embracing, bird's-eye, com~ prehensive, extensive, far-reaching, general, inclusive, overall, scenic, sweeping, wide

pant *v.* **1.** blow, breathe, gasp, heave, huff, palpitate, puff, throb, wheeze **2.** *Fig.* ache, covet, crave, desire, eat one's heart out over, hanker after, hunger, long, pine, set one's heart on, sigh, thirst, want, yearn ~*n.* **3.** gasp, huff, puff, wheeze

panting *adj.* **1.** breathless, gasping, out of breath, out of puff, puffed, puffed out, puffing, short of breath, winded **2.** agog, all agog, anxious, champing at the bit (*Inf.*), eager, impatient, raring to go

pants 1. *Brit.* boxer shorts, briefs, drawers, knickers, panties, underpants, Y-fronts (*Trademark*) **2.** *U.S.* slacks, trousers

pap 1. baby food, mash, mush, pulp **2.** driv~ el, rubbish, trash, trivia

paper *n.* **1.** *Often plural* certificate, deed, documents, instrument, record **2.** *Plural* archive, diaries, documents, dossier, file, letters, records **3.** blat, daily, gazette, jour~ nal, news, newspaper, organ, rag (*Inf.*) **4.** analysis, article, assignment, composition, critique, dissertation, essay, examination, monograph, report, script, study, thesis, treatise **5. on paper** ideally, in the ab~ stract, in theory, theoretically ~*adj.* **6.** cardboard, disposable, flimsy, insubstantial, paper-thin, papery, thin ~*v.* **7.** cover with paper, hang, line, paste up, wallpaper

papery flimsy, fragile, frail, insubstantial, light, lightweight, paperlike, paper-thin, thin

par *n.* **1.** average, level, mean, median, norm, standard, usual **2.** balance, equal footing, equality, equilibrium, equivalence, parity **3. above par** excellent, exceptional, first-rate (*Inf.*), outstanding, superior **4. below par a.** below average, bush-league (*Aust. & N.Z. inf.*), dime-a-dozen (*Inf.*), inferior, lacking, not up to scratch (*Inf.*), poor, second-rate, substandard, tinhorn (*U.S. sl.*), two-bit (*U.S. & Canad. sl.*), wanting **b.** not oneself, off colour (*Chiefly Brit.*), off form, poorly (*Inf.*), sick, under the weather (*Inf.*), unfit, unhealthy **5. par for the course** average, expected, ordinary, predictable, standard, typical, usual **6. on a par** equal, much the same, the same, well-matched **7. up to par** acceptable, adequate, good enough, passable, satisfactory, up to scratch (*Inf.*), up to the mark

parable allegory, exemplum, fable, lesson, moral tale, story

parade *n.* **1.** array, cavalcade, ceremony, column, march, pageant, procession, review, spectacle, train **2.** array, display, exhibition, flaunting, ostentation, pomp, show, spectacle, vaunting ~*v.* **3.** defile, march, process **4.** air, brandish, display, exhibit, flaunt, make a show of, show, show off (*Inf.*), strut, swagger, vaunt

paradise 1. City of God, divine abode, Elysian fields, garden of delights (*Islam*), heaven, heavenly kingdom, Olympus (*Poetic*), Promised Land, Zion (*Christianity*) **2.** Eden, Garden of Eden **3.** bliss, delight, felicity, heaven, seventh heaven, utopia

paradox absurdity, ambiguity, anomaly, contradiction, enigma, inconsistency, mystery, oddity, puzzle

paradoxical absurd, ambiguous, baffling, confounding, contradictory, enigmatic, equivocal, illogical, impossible, improbable, inconsistent, oracular, puzzling, riddling

paragon apotheosis, archetype, criterion, cynosure, epitome, exemplar, ideal, jewel, masterpiece, model, nonesuch (*Archaic*), nonpareil, norm, paradigm, pattern, prototype, quintessence, standard

paragraph clause, item, notice, part, passage, portion, section, subdivision

parallel *adj.* **1.** aligned, alongside, coextensive, equidistant, side by side **2.** akin, analogous, complementary, correspondent, corresponding, like, matching, resembling, similar, uniform ~*n.* **3.** analogue, complement, corollary, counterpart, duplicate, equal, equivalent, likeness, match, twin **4.** analogy, comparison, correlation, correspondence, likeness, parallelism, resemblance, similarity ~*v.* **5.** agree, be alike, chime with, compare, complement, conform, correlate, correspond, equal, keep pace (with), match

Antonyms *adj.* different, dissimilar, diver-

gent, non-parallel, unlike ~*n.* difference, dissimilarity, divergence, opposite, reverse ~*v.* be unlike, differ, diverge

paralyse 1. cripple, debilitate, disable, incapacitate, lame **2.** anaesthetize, arrest, benumb, freeze, halt, immobilize, numb, petrify, stop dead, stun, stupefy, transfix

paralysis 1. immobility, palsy, paresis (*Pathology*) **2.** arrest, breakdown, halt, shutdown, stagnation, standstill, stoppage

paralytic *adj.* **1.** crippled, disabled, immobile, immobilized, incapacitated, lame, numb, palsied, paralysed **2.** *Inf.* bevvied (*Dialect*), blitzed (*Sl.*), blotto (*Sl.*), bombed (*Sl.*), canned (*Sl.*), drunk, flying (*Sl.*), inebriated, intoxicated, legless (*Inf.*), lit up (*Sl.*), out of it (*Sl.*), out to it (*Aust. & N.Z. sl.*), pie-eyed (*Sl.*), pissed (*Taboo sl.*), plastered (*Sl.*), sloshed (*Sl.*), smashed (*Sl.*), steamboats (*Sl.*), steaming (*Sl.*), stewed (*Sl.*), stoned (*Sl.*), tired and emotional (*Euphemistic*), wasted (*Sl.*), wrecked (*Sl.*), zonked (*Sl.*)

parameter constant, criterion, framework, guideline, limit, limitation, restriction, specification

paramount capital, cardinal, chief, dominant, eminent, first, foremost, main, outstanding, predominant, pre-eminent, primary, prime, principal, superior, supreme

Antonyms inferior, insignificant, least, minor, negligible, secondary, slight, subordinate, trifling, unimportant

paraphernalia accoutrements, apparatus, appurtenances, baggage, belongings, clobber (*Brit. sl.*), effects, equipage, equipment, gear, impedimenta, material, stuff, tackle, things, trappings

paraphrase 1. *n.* interpretation, rehash, rendering, rendition, rephrasing, restatement, rewording, translation, version **2.** *v.* express in other words *or* one's own words, interpret, rehash, render, rephrase, restate, reword

parasite bloodsucker (*Inf.*), cadger, drone (*Brit.*), hanger-on, leech, scrounger (*Inf.*), sponge (*Inf.*), sponger (*Inf.*)

parasitic, parasitical bloodsucking (*Inf.*), cadging, leechlike, scrounging (*Inf.*), sponging (*Inf.*)

parcel *n.* **1.** bundle, carton, pack, package, packet **2.** band, batch, bunch, collection, company, crew, crowd, gang, group, lot, pack **3.** piece of land, plot, property, tract ~*v.* **4.** *Often with* **up** do up, pack, package, tie up, wrap **5.** *Often with* **out** allocate, allot, apportion, carve up, deal out, dispense, distribute, divide, dole out, mete out, portion, share out, split up

parch blister, burn, dehydrate, desiccate,

dry up, evaporate, make thirsty, scorch, sear, shrivel, wither

parched arid, dehydrated, dried out *or* up, drouthy (*Scot.*), dry, scorched, shrivelled, thirsty, torrid, waterless, withered

parching *adj.* baking, blistering, burning, dry, drying, hot, roasting (*Inf.*), scorching, searing, sweltering, withering

pardon 1. *v.* absolve, acquit, amnesty, con~ done, exculpate, excuse, exonerate, forgive, free, let off (*Inf.*), liberate, overlook, release, remit, reprieve **2.** *n.* absolution, acquittal, allowance, amnesty, condonation, dis~ charge, excuse, exoneration, forgiveness, grace, indulgence, mercy, release, remis~ sion, reprieve
Antonyms *v.* admonish, blame, castigate, censure, chasten, chastise, condemn, disci~ pline, excoriate, fine, penalize, punish, rebuke ~*n.* condemnation, guilt, penalty, punish~ ment, redress, retaliation, retribution, re~ venge, vengeance

pardonable allowable, condonable, excus~ able, forgivable, minor, not serious, per~ missible, understandable, venial

parent 1. begetter, father, guardian, mother, procreator, progenitor, sire **2.** architect, author, cause, creator, forerunner, origin, originator, prototype, root, source, well~ spring

parentage ancestry, birth, derivation, de~ scent, extraction, family, line, lineage, ori~ gin, paternity, pedigree, race, stirps, stock

pariah exile, leper, outcast, outlaw, undesir~ able, unperson, untouchable

parish church, churchgoers, community, congregation, flock, fold, parishioners

parity 1. consistency, equality, equal terms, equivalence, par, parallelism, quits (*Inf.*), uniformity, unity **2.** affinity, agreement, analogy, conformity, congruity, corre~ spondence, likeness, resemblance, same~ ness, similarity, similitude

park 1. *n.* estate, garden, grounds, parkland, pleasure garden, recreation ground, wood~ land **2.** *v.* leave, manoeuvre, position, sta~ tion

parley 1. *n.* colloquy, confab (*Inf.*), confer~ ence, congress, council, dialogue, discus~ sion, meeting, palaver, powwow, seminar, talk(s) **2.** *v.* confabulate, confer, deliberate, discuss, negotiate, palaver, powwow, speak, talk

parliament 1. assembly, congress, convo~ cation, council, diet, legislature, senate, talking shop (*Inf.*) **2. Parliament** Houses of Parliament, Mother of Parliaments, the House, the House of Commons and the House of Lords, Westminster

parliamentary congressional, deliberative,

governmental, lawgiving, lawmaking, legis~ lative

parlour best room, drawing room, front room, lounge, reception room, sitting room

parlous chancy (*Inf.*), dangerous, desperate, difficult, dire, hairy (*Sl.*), hazardous, peri~ lous, risky

parochial insular, inward-looking, limited, narrow, narrow-minded, parish-pump, pet~ ty, provincial, restricted, small-minded
Antonyms all-embracing, broad, broad-minded, cosmopolitan, international, liberal, national, universal, world-wide

parodist burlesquer, caricaturist, humorist, impressionist, ironist, lampooner, mimic, mocker, pasquinader, satirist

parody *n.* **1.** burlesque, caricature, imita~ tion, lampoon, satire, send-up (*Brit. inf.*), skit, spoof (*Inf.*), takeoff (*Inf.*) **2.** apology, caricature, farce, mockery, travesty ~*v.* **3.** burlesque, caricature, do a takeoff of (*Inf.*), lampoon, mimic, poke fun at, satirize, send up (*Brit. inf.*), spoof (*Inf.*), take off (*Inf.*), take the piss out of (*Taboo sl.*), travesty

paroxysm attack, convulsion, eruption, fit, flare-up (*Inf.*), outburst, seizure, spasm

parrot *n.* **1.** *Fig.* copycat (*Inf.*), imitator, (little) echo, mimic ~*adv.* **2. parrot-fashion** *Inf.* by rote, mechanically, mind~ lessly ~*v.* **3.** copy, echo, imitate, mimic, re~ iterate, repeat

parry 1. block, deflect, fend off, hold at bay, rebuff, repel, repulse, stave off, ward off **2.** avoid, circumvent, dodge, duck (*Inf.*), evade, fence, fight shy of, shun, sidestep

parsimonious cheeseparing, close, close-fisted, frugal, grasping, mean, mingy (*Brit. inf.*), miserable, miserly, near (*Inf.*), nig~ gardly, penny-pinching (*Inf.*), penurious, saving, scrimpy, skinflinty, sparing, stingy, stinting, tight-arse (*Taboo sl.*), tight-arsed (*Taboo sl.*), tight as a duck's arse (*Taboo sl.*), tight-ass (*U.S. taboo sl.*), tight-assed (*U.S. taboo sl.*), tightfisted
Antonyms extravagant, generous, lavish, munificent, open-handed, spendthrift, waste~ ful

parsimony frugality, meanness, mingiess (*Brit. inf.*), miserliness, nearness (*Inf.*), nig~ gardliness, penny-pinching (*Inf.*), stinginess, tightness

parson churchman, clergyman, cleric, di~ vine, ecclesiastic, incumbent, man of God, man of the cloth, minister, pastor, preacher, priest, rector, reverend (*Inf.*), vicar

part *n.* **1.** bit, fraction, fragment, lot, parti~ cle, piece, portion, scrap, section, sector, segment, share, slice **2.** branch, component, constituent, department, division, element, ingredient, limb, member, module, organ, piece, unit **3.** behalf, cause, concern, fac~ tion, interest, party, side **4.** bit, business, capacity, charge, duty, function, involve~ ment, office, place, responsibility, role, say, share, task, work **5.** *Theatre* character, lines, role **6.** *Often plural* airt (*Scot.*), area, district, neck of the woods (*Inf.*), neigh~ bourhood, quarter, region, territory, vicin~ ity **7. for the most part** chiefly, generally, in the main, largely, mainly, mostly, on the whole, principally **8. in good part** cheer~ fully, cordially, good-naturedly, well, with~ out offence **9. in part** a little, in some measure, partially, partly, slightly, some~ what, to a certain extent, to some degree **10. on the part of** for the sake of, in sup~ port of, in the name of, on behalf of **11. take part in** associate oneself with, be in~ strumental in, be involved in, have a hand in, join in, partake in, participate in, play a part in, put one's twopence-worth in, take a hand in ~*v.* **12.** break, cleave, come apart, detach, disconnect, disjoin, dismantle, dis~ unite, divide, rend, separate, sever, split, tear **13.** break up, depart, go, go away, go (their) separate ways, leave, part company, quit, say goodbye, separate, split up, take one's leave, withdraw **14. part with** aban~ don, discard, forgo, give up, let go of, relin~ quish, renounce, sacrifice, surrender, yield **Antonyms** *n.* (*senses 1 & 2*) bulk, entirety, mass, totality, whole ~*v.* (*sense 12*) adhere, close, combine, hold, join, stick, unite (*sense 13*) appear, arrive, come, gather, remain, show up (*Inf.*), stay, turn up

partake 1. *With* **in** engage, enter into, par~ ticipate, share, take part **2.** *With* **of** con~ sume, eat, receive, share, take **3.** *With* **of** evince, evoke, have the quality of, show, suggest

partial 1. fragmentary, imperfect, incom~ plete, limited, uncompleted, unfinished **2.** biased, discriminatory, influenced, interest~ ed, one-sided, partisan, predisposed, preju~ diced, tendentious, unfair, unjust **3. be partial to** be fond of, be keen on, be taken with, care for, have a liking (soft spot, weakness) for **Antonyms** (*sense 1*) complete, entire, finished, full, total, whole (*sense 2*) impartial, objective, unbiased, unprejudiced

partiality 1. bias, favouritism, partisanship, predisposition, preference, prejudice **2.** affinity, bag (*Sl.*), cup of tea (*Inf.*), fondness, inclination, liking, love, penchant, predi~ lection, predisposition, preference, procliv~ ity, taste, weakness **Antonyms** (*sense 1*) disinterest, equity, fair~ ness, impartiality, objectivity (*sense 2*) abhor~ rence, antipathy, aversion, disgust, disincli~ nation, dislike, distaste, loathing, revulsion

partially fractionally, halfway, incompletely,

in part, moderately, not wholly, partly, piecemeal, somewhat, to a certain extent *or* degree

participant associate, contributor, member, partaker, participator, party, shareholder

participate be a participant, be a party to, engage in, enter into, get in on the act, have a hand in, join in, partake, perform, share, take part **Antonyms** abstain, boycott, forgo, forsake, forswear, opt out, pass up, refrain from, take no part of

participation assistance, contribution, in~ volvement, joining in, partaking, partner~ ship, sharing in, taking part

particle atom, bit, crumb, grain, iota, jot, mite, molecule, mote, piece, scrap, shred, speck, tittle, whit

particular *adj.* **1.** distinct, exact, express, peculiar, precise, special, specific **2.** espe~ cial, exceptional, marked, notable, note~ worthy, remarkable, singular, uncommon, unusual **3.** blow-by-blow, circumstantial, detailed, itemized, minute, painstaking, precise, selective, thorough **4.** choosy (*Inf.*), critical, dainty, demanding, discriminating, exacting, fastidious, finicky, fussy, meticu~ lous, nice (*Rare*), overnice, pernickety (*Inf.*), picky (*Inf.*) ~*n.* **5.** *Usually plural* circum~ stance, detail, fact, feature, item, specification **6. in particular** distinctly, es~ pecially, exactly, expressly, particularly, specifically **Antonyms** (*sense 1*) general, imprecise, indefinite, indistinct, inexact, unspecified, vague (*sense 4*) casual, easy, easy to please, in~ discriminate, negligent, slack, sloppy, un~ critical

particularly 1. decidedly, especially, ex~ ceptionally, markedly, notably, outstand~ ingly, peculiarly, singularly, surprisingly, uncommonly, unusually **2.** distinctly, espe~ cially, explicitly, expressly, in particular, specifically

parting *n.* **1.** adieu, departure, farewell, go~ ing, goodbye, leave-taking, valediction **2.** breaking, detachment, divergence, division, partition, rift, rupture, separation, split ~*adj.* **3.** departing, farewell, final, last, val~ edictory

partisan *n.* **1.** adherent, backer, champion, devotee, disciple, follower, stalwart, sup~ porter, upholder, votary ~*adj.* **2.** biased, factional, interested, one-sided, partial, prejudiced, sectarian, tendentious ~*n.* **3.** guerrilla, irregular, resistance fighter, underground fighter ~*adj.* **4.** guerrilla, ir~ regular, resistance, underground **Antonyms** *n.* adversary, contender, critic, detractor, foe, knocker (*Inf.*), leader, oppo~ nent, rival ~*adj.* bipartisan, broad-minded, disinterested, impartial, non-partisan, unbi~ased, unprejudiced

partition *n.* **1.** dividing, division, segrega~tion, separation, severance, splitting **2.** barrier, divider, room divider, screen, wall **3.** allotment, apportionment, distribution, portion, rationing out, share ~*v.* **4.** appor~tion, cut up, divide, parcel out, portion, section, segment, separate, share, split up, subdivide **5.** divide, fence off, screen, sepa~rate, wall off

partly halfway, incompletely, in part, in some measure, not fully, partially, relative~ly, slightly, somewhat, to a certain degree *or* extent, up to a certain point
Antonyms completely, entirely, fully, in full, totally, wholly

partner 1. accomplice, ally, associate, bed~fellow, collaborator, colleague, companion, comrade, confederate, copartner, helper, mate, participant, team-mate **2.** bedfellow, consort, helpmate, her indoors (*Brit. sl.*), husband, mate, significant other (*U.S. inf.*), spouse, wife

partnership 1. companionship, connection, cooperation, copartnership, fellowship, in~terest, participation, sharing **2.** alliance, association, combine, company, conglomer~ate, cooperative, corporation, firm, house, society, union

parts 1. ability, accomplishments, attrib~utes, calibre, capabilities, endowments, fac~ulties, genius, gifts, intellect, intelligence, talents **2.** bits and pieces, components, spare parts, spares

party 1. at-home, bash (*Inf.*), beano (*Brit. sl.*), celebration, do (*Inf.*), festivity, function, gathering, get-together (*Inf.*), knees-up (*Brit. inf.*), rave (*Brit. sl.*), rave-up (*Brit. sl.*), re~ception, shindig (*Inf.*), social, social gather~ing, soirée **2.** band, body, bunch (*Inf.*), company, crew, detachment (*Military*), gang, gathering, group, squad, team, unit **3.** alliance, association, cabal, camp, clique, coalition, combination, confederacy, coterie, faction, grouping, league, schism, set, side **4.** individual, person, somebody, someone **5.** *Law* contractor (*Law*), defendant, liti~gant, participant, plaintiff

pass¹ *v.* **1.** depart, elapse, flow, go, go by *or* past, lapse, leave, move, move onwards, proceed, roll, run **2.** beat, exceed, excel, go beyond, outdistance, outdo, outstrip, sur~mount, surpass, transcend **3.** answer, come up to scratch (*Inf.*), do, get through, gradu~ate, pass muster, qualify, succeed, suffice, suit **4.** beguile, devote, employ, experience, fill, occupy, spend, suffer, undergo, while away **5.** befall, come up, develop, fall out, happen, occur, take place **6.** convey, deliv~er, exchange, give, hand, kick, let have,

reach, send, throw, transfer, transmit **7.** accept, adopt, approve, authorize, decree, enact, establish, legislate, ordain, ratify, sanction, validate **8.** declare, deliver, ex~press, pronounce, utter **9.** disregard, ignore, miss, neglect, not heed, omit, overlook, skip (*Inf.*) **10.** crap (*Taboo sl.*), defecate, dis~charge, eliminate, empty, evacuate, excrete, expel, shit (*Taboo sl.*), void **11.** blow over, cease, die, disappear, dissolve, dwindle, ebb, end, evaporate, expire, fade, go, melt away, terminate, vanish, wane **12.** *With* **for** *or* **as** be accepted as, be mistaken for, be regarded as, be taken for, impersonate, serve as
Antonyms (*sense 1*) bring *or* come to a stand~still, cease, halt, pause, stop (*senses 2 & 3*) be inadequate, be inferior to, be unsuccessful, come a cropper (*Inf.*), fail, lose, suffer defeat (*sense 7*) ban, disallow, invalidate, overrule, prohibit, refuse, reject, veto (*sense 9*) ac~knowledge, heed, note, notice, observe, pay attention to

pass² *n.* **1.** canyon, col, defile, gap, gorge, ravine **2.** authorization, identification, identity card, licence, passport, permission, permit, safe-conduct, ticket, warrant **3.** *Inf.* advances, approach, overture, play (*Inf.*), proposition, suggestion **4.** condition, junc~ture, pinch, plight, predicament, situation, stage, state, state of affairs, straits **5.** feint, jab, lunge, push, swing, thrust

passable 1. acceptable, adequate, admis~sible, allowable, all right, average, fair, fair enough, mediocre, middling, moderate, not too bad, ordinary, presentable, so-so (*Inf.*), tolerable, unexceptional **2.** clear, crossable, navigable, open, traversable, unobstructed
Antonyms (*sense 1*) A1 *or* A-one (*Inf.*), excep~tional, extraordinary, first-class, inadequate, inadmissible, marvellous, outstanding, su~perb, tops (*Sl.*), unacceptable, unsatisfactory (*sense 2*) blocked, closed, impassable, ob~structed, sealed off, unnavigable

passage 1. alley, avenue, channel, course, lane, opening, path, road, route, thorough~fare, way **2.** corridor, doorway, entrance, entrance hall, exit, hall, hallway, lobby, passageway, vestibule **3.** clause, excerpt, extract, paragraph, piece, quotation, read~ing, section, sentence, text, verse **4.** cross~ing, journey, tour, trek, trip, voyage **5.** ad~vance, change, conversion, flow, motion, movement, passing, progress, progression, transit, transition **6.** allowance, authoriza~tion, freedom, permission, right, safe-conduct, visa, warrant **7.** acceptance, en~actment, establishment, legalization, legis~lation, passing, ratification

pass away buy it (*U.S. sl.*), check out (*U.S. sl.*), croak (*Sl.*), decease, depart (this life), die, expire, go belly-up (*Sl.*), kick it (*Sl.*), kick the bucket (*Sl.*), pass on, pass over, peg it (*Inf.*), peg out (*Inf.*), pop one's clogs (*Inf.*), shuffle off this mortal coil, snuff it (*Inf.*)

pass by 1. go past, leave, move past, pass **2.** disregard, miss, neglect, not choose, overlook, pass over

passenger fare, hitchhiker, pillion rider, rider, traveller

passer-by bystander, onlooker, witness

passing *adj.* **1.** brief, ephemeral, fleeting, momentary, short, short-lived, temporary, transient, transitory **2.** casual, cursory, glancing, hasty, quick, shallow, short, slight, superficial ~*n.* **3.** death, decease, demise, end, finish, loss, termination **4. in passing** accidentally, by the bye, by the way, en passant, incidentally, on the way

passion 1. animation, ardour, eagerness, emotion, excitement, feeling, fervour, fire, heat, intensity, joy, rapture, spirit, transport, warmth, zeal, zest **2.** adoration, affection, ardour, attachment, concupiscence, desire, fondness, infatuation, itch, keenness, love, lust, the hots (*Sl.*) **3.** bug (*Inf.*), craving, craze, enthusiasm, fancy, fascination, idol, infatuation, mania, obsession **4.** anger, fit, flare-up (*Inf.*), frenzy, fury, indignation, ire, outburst, paroxysm, rage, resentment, storm, vehemence, wrath
Antonyms apathy, calmness, coldness, coolness, frigidity, hate, indifference, uncon~ cern

passionate 1. amorous, ardent, aroused, desirous, erotic, hot, loving, lustful, sensual, sexy (*Inf.*), steamy (*Inf.*), wanton **2.** animated, ardent, eager, emotional, enthusiastic, excited, fervent, fervid, fierce, flaming, frenzied, heartfelt, impassioned, impetuous, impulsive, intense, strong, vehement, warm, wild, zealous **3.** choleric, excitable, fiery, hot-headed, hot-tempered, irascible, irri~ table, peppery, quick-tempered, stormy, tempestuous, violent
Antonyms (*sense 1*) cold, frigid, passionless, unloving, unresponsive (*sense 2*) apathetic, calm, cold, half-hearted, indifferent, languor~ ous, nonchalant, subdued, unemotional, un~ enthusiastic (*sense 3*) agreeable, calm, easy-going, even-tempered, nonviolent, placid, unexcitable

passive acquiescent, compliant, docile, en~ during, inactive, inert, lifeless, long-suffering, nonviolent, patient, quiescent, receptive, resigned, submissive, unasser~ tive, uninvolved, unresisting
Antonyms active, alive, assertive, bossy (*Inf.*), defiant, domineering, energetic, feisty (*Inf., chiefly U.S. & Canad.*), impatient, in~ volved, lively, rebellious, spirited, violent, zippy (*Inf.*)

pass off 1. counterfeit, fake, feign, make a pretence of, palm off **2.** come to an end, die

away, disappear, fade out, vanish **3.** emit, evaporate, give off, send forth, vaporize **4.** be completed, go off, happen, occur, take place, turn out **5.** dismiss, disregard, ig~ nore, pass by, wink at

pass out 1. *Inf.* become unconscious, black out (*Inf.*), drop, faint, flake out (*Inf.*), keel over (*Inf.*), lose consciousness, swoon (*Lit~ erary*) **2.** deal out, distribute, dole out, hand out

pass over discount, disregard, forget, ig~ nore, not dwell on, omit, overlook, pass by, take no notice of

pass up abstain, decline, forgo, give (some~ thing) a miss (*Inf.*), ignore, let go, let slip, miss, neglect, refuse, reject

password countersign, key word, open sesame, signal, watchword

past *adj.* **1.** accomplished, completed, done, elapsed, ended, extinct, finished, forgotten, gone, over, over and done with, spent **2.** ancient, bygone, early, erstwhile, foregoing, former, late, long-ago, olden, preceding, previous, prior, quondam, recent ~*n.* **3. the past** antiquity, days gone by, days of yore, former times, good old days, history, long ago, olden days, old times, times past, yesteryear (*Literary*) **4.** background, ex~ perience, history, life, past life ~*adv.* **5.** across, beyond, by, on, over ~*prep.* **6.** after, beyond, farther than, later than, outside, over, subsequent to
Antonyms *adj.* arrived, begun, coming, fu~ ture, now, present ~*n.* future, now, present, time to come, today, tomorrow

paste 1. *n.* adhesive, cement, glue, gum, mucilage **2.** *v.* cement, fasten, fix, glue, gum, stick

pastel *adj.* delicate, light, muted, pale, soft, soft-hued
Antonyms bright, deep, rich, strong, vi~ brant, vivid

pastiche blend, farrago, gallimaufry, hotch~ potch, medley, *mélange*, miscellany, mix~ ture, motley

pastille cough drop, jujube, lozenge, tablet, troche (*Medical*)

pastime activity, amusement, distraction, diversion, entertainment, game, hobby, lei~ sure, play, recreation, relaxation, sport

past master ace (*Inf.*), artist, dab hand (*Brit. inf.*), expert, old hand, virtuoso, wiz~ ard

pastor churchman, clergyman, divine, ec~ clesiastic, minister, parson, priest, rector, vicar

pastoral *adj.* **1.** agrestic, Arcadian, bucolic, country, georgic (*Literary*), idyllic, rural, rustic, simple **2.** clerical, ecclesiastical, ministerial, priestly

pasture grass, grassland, grazing, grazing land, lea (*Poetic*), meadow, pasturage, shiel~ ing (*Scot.*)

pat v. **1.** caress, dab, fondle, pet, slap, stroke, tap, touch ~n. **2.** clap, dab, light blow, slap, stroke, tap **3.** cake, dab, lump, portion, small piece

patch n. **1.** piece of material, reinforcement **2.** bit, scrap, shred, small piece, spot, stretch **3.** area, ground, land, plot, tract ~v. **4.** cover, fix, mend, reinforce, repair, sew up **5.** *With up* bury the hatchet, conciliate, make friends, placate, restore, settle, settle differences, smooth

patchwork confusion, hash, hotchpotch, jumble, medley, mishmash, mixture, pas~ tiche

patchy bitty, erratic, fitful, inconstant, ir~ regular, random, sketchy, spotty, uneven, variable, varying
Antonyms constant, even, regular, unbro~ ken, unvarying

patent 1. *adj.* apparent, blatant, clear, con~ spicuous, downright, evident, flagrant, glaring, indisputable, manifest, obvious, open, palpable, transparent, unconcealed, unequivocal, unmistakable **2.** n. copyright, invention, licence

paternal 1. benevolent, concerned, fatherlike, fatherly, protective, solicitous, vigilant **2.** patrilineal, patrimonial

paternity 1. fatherhood, fathership **2.** de~ scent, extraction, family, lineage, parentage **3.** authorship, derivation, origin, source

path 1. footpath, footway, pathway, towpath, track, trail, walkway (*Chiefly U.S.*) **2.** av~ enue, course, direction, passage, procedure, road, route, track, walk, way

pathetic 1. affecting, distressing, harrow~ ing, heartbreaking, heart-rending, melting, moving, pitiable, plaintive, poignant, sad, tender, touching **2.** deplorable, feeble, in~ adequate, lamentable, meagre, measly, mis~ erable, paltry, petty, pitiful, poor, puny, sorry, wet (*Brit. inf.*), woeful **3.** *Sl.* chickenshit (*U.S. sl.*), crappy (*Sl.*), crummy (*Sl.*), poxy (*Sl.*), rubbishy, trashy, uninter~ esting, useless, worthless
Antonyms (*sense 1*) amusing, comical, droll, entertaining, funny, laughable, ludicrous, ri~ diculous

pathfinder discoverer, explorer, guide, pio~ neer, scout, trailblazer

pathless impassable, impenetrable, track~ less, uncharted, unexplored, untrodden, waste, wild

pathos pitiableness, pitifulness, plaintive~ ness, poignancy, sadness

patience 1. calmness, composure, cool (*Sl.*), equanimity, even temper, forbearance, im~ perturbability, restraint, serenity, suffer~ ance, tolerance, toleration **2.** constancy, diligence, endurance, fortitude, long-suffering, perseverance, persistence, resig~ nation, stoicism, submission
Antonyms (*sense 1*) agitation, exasperation, excitement, impatience, irritation, nervous~ ness, passion, restlessness (*sense 2*) irresolu~ tion, vacillation

patient *adj.* **1.** calm, composed, enduring, long-suffering, persevering, persistent, philosophical, quiet, resigned, self-possessed, serene, stoical, submissive, un~ complaining, untiring **2.** accommodating, even-tempered, forbearing, forgiving, indul~ gent, lenient, mild, tolerant, understanding ~n. **3.** case, invalid, sick person, sufferer

patriot chauvinist, flag-waver (*Inf.*), jingo, lover of one's country, loyalist, nationalist

patriotic chauvinistic, flag-waving (*Inf.*), jingoistic, loyal, nationalistic

patriotism flag-waving (*Inf.*), jingoism, love of one's country, loyalty, nationalism

patrol n. **1.** guarding, policing, protecting, rounds, safeguarding, vigilance, watching **2.** garrison, guard, patrolman, sentinel, watch, watchman ~v. **3.** cruise, guard, in~ spect, keep guard, keep watch, make the rounds, police, pound, range, safeguard, walk the beat

patron 1. advocate, angel (*Inf.*), backer, benefactor, champion, defender, friend, guardian, helper, philanthropist, protago~ nist, protector, sponsor, supporter **2.** buyer, client, customer, frequenter, habitué, shop~ per

patronage 1. aid, assistance, backing, ben~ efaction, championship, encouragement, es~ pousal, help, promotion, sponsorship, sup~ port **2.** business, clientele, commerce, cus~ tom, trade, trading, traffic **3.** condescen~ sion, deigning, disdain, patronizing, stoop~ ing

patronize 1. be lofty with, look down on, talk down to, treat as inferior, treat conde~ scendingly, treat like a child **2.** assist, back, befriend, foster, fund, help, maintain, pro~ mote, sponsor, subscribe to, support **3.** be a customer *or* client of, buy from, deal with, do business with, frequent, shop at, trade with

patronizing condescending, contemptuous, disdainful, gracious, haughty, lofty, snob~ bish, stooping, supercilious, superior, toffee-nosed (*Sl., chiefly Brit.*)
Antonyms deferential, humble, obsequious, respectful, servile

patter[1] v. **1.** scurry, scuttle, skip, tiptoe, trip, walk lightly **2.** beat, pat, pelt, pitapat, pitter-patter, rat-a-tat, spatter, tap ~n. **3.** pattering, pitapat, pitter-patter, tapping

patter² *n.* **1.** line, monologue, pitch, spiel (*Inf.*) **2.** chatter, gabble, jabber, nattering, prattle, yak (*Sl.*) **3.** argot, cant, jargon, lingo (*Inf.*), patois, slang, vernacular ~*v.* **4.** babble, blab, chatter, hold forth, jabber, prate, rattle off, rattle on, spiel (*Inf.*), spout (*Inf.*), tattle

pattern *n.* **1.** arrangement, decoration, decorative design, design, device, figure, motif, ornament **2.** arrangement, method, order, orderliness, plan, sequence, system **3.** kind, shape, sort, style, type, variety **4.** design, diagram, guide, instructions, original, plan, stencil, template **5.** archetype, criterion, cynosure, example, exemplar, guide, model, norm, original, par, paradigm, paragon, prototype, sample, specimen, standard ~*v.* **6.** copy, emulate, follow, form, imitate, model, mould, order, shape, style **7.** decorate, design, trim

paucity dearth, deficiency, fewness, insufficiency, lack, meagreness, paltriness, poverty, rarity, scantiness, scarcity, shortage, slenderness, slightness, smallness, sparseness, sparsity

paunch abdomen, beer-belly (*Inf.*), belly, corporation (*Inf.*), pot, potbelly, spare tyre (*Brit. sl.*), spread (*Inf.*)

pauper bankrupt, beggar, down-and-out, have-not, indigent, insolvent, mendicant, poor person

pause **1.** *v.* break, cease, delay, deliberate, desist, discontinue, halt, have a breather (*Inf.*), hesitate, interrupt, rest, stop briefly, take a break, wait, waver **2.** *n.* break, breather (*Inf.*), caesura, cessation, delay, discontinuance, entr'acte, gap, halt, hesitation, interlude, intermission, interruption, interval, let-up (*Inf.*), lull, respite, rest, stay, stoppage, wait
Antonyms *v.* advance, continue, proceed, progress ~*n.* advancement, continuance, progression

pave asphalt, concrete, cover, flag, floor, macadamize, surface, tar, tile

paw *v.* grab, handle roughly, manhandle, maul, molest

pawn¹ **1.** *v.* deposit, gage (*Archaic*), hazard, hock (*Inf., chiefly U.S.*), mortgage, pledge, pop (*Inf.*), stake, wager **2.** *n.* assurance, bond, collateral, gage, guarantee, guaranty, pledge, security

pawn² *n.* cat's-paw, creature, dupe, instrument, plaything, puppet, stooge (*Sl.*), tool, toy

pay *v.* **1.** clear, compensate, cough up (*Inf.*), discharge, foot, give, honour, liquidate, meet, offer, recompense, reimburse, remit, remunerate, render, requite, reward, settle, square up **2.** be advantageous, benefit, be worthwhile, repay, serve **3.** bestow, extend,

give, grant, hand out, present, proffer, render **4.** *Often with* **for** answer for, atone, be punished, compensate, get one's deserts, make amends, suffer, suffer the consequences **5.** bring in, produce, profit, return, yield **6.** be profitable, be remunerative, make a return, make money, provide a living **7.** avenge oneself for, get even with (*Inf.*), get revenge on, pay back, punish, reciprocate, repay, requite, settle a score ~*n.* **8.** allowance, compensation, earnings, emoluments, fee, hand-out, hire, income, meed (*Archaic*), payment, recompense, reimbursement, remuneration, reward, salary, stipend, takings, wages

payable due, mature, obligatory, outstanding, owed, owing, receivable, to be paid

pay back **1.** get even with (*Inf.*), get one's own back, hit back, reciprocate, recompense, retaliate, settle a score **2.** refund, reimburse, repay, return, settle up, square

payment **1.** defrayal, discharge, outlay, paying, remittance, settlement **2.** advance, deposit, instalment, portion, premium, remittance **3.** fee, hire, remuneration, reward, wage

pay off **1.** discharge, dismiss, fire, lay off, let go, sack (*Inf.*) **2.** clear, discharge, liquidate, pay in full, settle, square **3.** be effective (profitable, successful), succeed, work **4.** get even with (*Inf.*), pay back, retaliate, settle a score **5.** *Inf.* bribe, buy off, corrupt, get at, grease the palm of (*Sl.*), oil (*Inf.*), suborn

pay out **1.** cough up (*Inf.*), disburse, expend, fork out *or* over *or* up (*Sl.*), lay out (*Inf.*), shell out (*Inf.*), spend **2.** get even with (*Inf.*), pay back, retaliate, settle a score

peace **1.** accord, agreement, amity, concord, harmony **2.** armistice, cessation of hostilities, conciliation, pacification, treaty, truce **3.** calm, composure, contentment, placidity, relaxation, repose, serenity **4.** calm, calmness, hush, peacefulness, quiet, quietude, repose, rest, silence, stillness, tranquillity

peaceable **1.** amiable, amicable, conciliatory, dovish, friendly, gentle, inoffensive, mild, nonbelligerent, pacific, peaceful, peace-loving, placid, unwarlike **2.** balmy, calm, peaceful, quiet, restful, serene, still, tranquil, undisturbed

peaceful **1.** amicable, at peace, free from strife, friendly, harmonious, nonviolent, on friendly *or* good terms, without hostility **2.** calm, gentle, placid, quiet, restful, serene, still, tranquil, undisturbed, unruffled, untroubled **3.** conciliatory, irenic, pacific, peaceable, peace-loving, placatory, unwarlike
Antonyms agitated, antagonistic, belligerent, bitter, disquieted, disturbed, hostile, loud,

nervous, noisy, Ramboesque, raucous, rest~ less, unfriendly, upset, violent, warlike, war~ ring, wartime

peacemaker appeaser, arbitrator, concili~ ator, mediator, pacifier, peacemonger

peak *n.* **1.** aiguille, apex, brow, crest, pinna~ cle, point, summit, tip, top **2.** acme, apogee, climax, crown, culmination, high point, maximum point, *ne plus ultra*, zenith ~*v.* **3.** be at its height, climax, come to a head, culminate, reach its highest point, reach the zenith

peal **1.** *n.* blast, carillon, chime, clamour, clang, clap, crash, resounding, reverbera~ tion, ring, ringing, roar, rumble, sound, tintinnabulation **2.** *v.* chime, crack, crash, resonate, resound, reverberate, ring, roar, roll, rumble, sound, tintinnabulate, toll

peasant **1.** churl (*Archaic*), countryman, hind (*Obsolete*), rustic, son of the soil, swain (*Archaic*) **2.** *Inf.* boor, churl, country bumpkin, hayseed (*U.S. & Canad. inf.*), hick (*Inf., chiefly U.S. & Canad.*), lout, provincial, yokel

peccadillo error, indiscretion, infraction, lapse, misdeed, misdemeanour, petty of~ fence, slip, trifling fault

peck *v./n.* bite, dig, hit, jab, kiss, nibble, pick, poke, prick, strike, tap

peculiar **1.** abnormal, bizarre, curious, ec~ centric, exceptional, extraordinary, far-out (*Sl.*), freakish, funny, odd, offbeat, off-the-wall (*Sl.*), outlandish, out-of-the-way, outré, quaint, queer, singular, strange, uncom~ mon, unconventional, unusual, wacko (*Sl.*), weird **2.** appropriate, characteristic, dis~ tinct, distinctive, distinguishing, endemic, idiosyncratic, individual, local, particular, personal, private, restricted, special, specific, unique
Antonyms (*sense 1*) commonplace, conven~ tional, expected, familiar, ordinary, usual (*sense 2*) common, general, indistinctive, unspecific

peculiarity **1.** abnormality, bizarreness, eccentricity, foible, freakishness, idiosyn~ crasy, mannerism, oddity, odd trait, queer~ ness, quirk **2.** attribute, characteristic, dis~ tinctiveness, feature, mark, particularity, property, quality, singularity, speciality, trait

pedagogue dogmatist, dominie (*Scot.*), educator, instructor, master, mistress, ped~ ant, schoolmaster, schoolmistress, teacher

pedant casuist, doctrinaire, dogmatist, hairsplitter, literalist, nit-picker (*Inf.*), pedagogue, pettifogger, precisian, quibbler, scholastic, sophist

pedantic abstruse, academic, bookish, di~ dactic, donnish, erudite, formal, fussy, hairsplitting, nit-picking (*Inf.*), overnice, particular, pedagogic, picky (*Inf.*), pompous, precise, priggish, punctilious, scholastic, schoolmasterly, sententious, stilted

pedantry bookishness, finicality, hair~ splitting, overnicety, pedagogism, pettifog~ gery, pomposity, punctiliousness, quibbling, sophistry, stuffiness

peddle flog (*Sl.*), hawk, huckster, market, push (*Inf.*), sell, sell door to door, trade, vend

pedestal **1.** base, dado (*Architect.*), foot, foundation, mounting, pier, plinth, socle, stand, support **2. put on a pedestal** apotheosize, deify, dignify, ennoble, exalt, glorify, idealize, worship

pedestrian **1.** *n.* footslogger, foot-traveller, walker **2.** *adj.* banal, boring, commonplace, dull, flat, ho-hum (*Inf.*), humdrum, medio~ cre, mundane, ordinary, plodding, prosaic, run-of-the-mill, unimaginative, uninspired, uninteresting
Antonyms *n.* driver ~*adj.* exciting, fasci~ nating, imaginative, important, interesting, noteworthy, outstanding, remarkable, significant

pedigree **1.** *n.* ancestry, blood, breed, deri~ vation, descent, extraction, family, family tree, genealogy, heritage, line, lineage, race, stemma, stirps, stock **2.** *adj.* full-blooded, purebred, thoroughbred

peek **1.** *v.* glance, keek (*Scot.*), look, peep, peer, snatch a glimpse, sneak a look, spy, squinny, take *or* have a gander (*Inf.*), take a look **2.** *n.* blink, butcher's (*Brit. sl.*), gander (*Inf.*), glance, glim (*Scot.*), glimpse, keek (*Scot.*), look, look-see (*Sl.*), peep, shufti (*Brit. sl.*)

peel **1.** *v.* decorticate, desquamate, flake off, pare, scale, skin, strip off **2.** *n.* epicarp, exocarp, peeling, rind, skin

peep[1] *v.* **1.** keek (*Scot.*), look from hiding, look surreptitiously, peek, peer, sneak a look, spy, steal a look **2.** appear briefly, emerge, peer out, show partially ~*n.* **3.** butcher's (*Brit. sl.*), gander (*Inf.*), glim (*Scot.*), glimpse, keek (*Scot.*), look, look-see (*Sl.*), peek, shufti (*Brit. sl.*)

peep[2] *v./n.* cheep, chirp, chirrup, pipe, squeak, tweet, twitter

peephole aperture, chink, crack, crevice, fissure, hole, keyhole, opening, pinhole, slit, spyhole

peer[1] *n.* **1.** aristo (*Inf.*), aristocrat, baron, count, duke, earl, lord, marquess, marquis, noble, nobleman, viscount **2.** coequal, com~ peer, equal, fellow, like, match

peer[2] *v.* **1.** gaze, inspect, peep, scan, scruti~ nize, snoop, spy, squinny, squint **2.** appear, become visible, emerge, peep out

peerage aristocracy, lords and ladies, no~bility, peers, titled classes

peerless beyond compare, excellent, incom~parable, matchless, nonpareil, outstanding, second to none, superlative, unequalled, unique, unmatched, unparalleled, unri~valled, unsurpassed
Antonyms commonplace, inferior, medio~cre, ordinary, poor, second-rate

peeved annoyed, exasperated, galled, hacked (off) (*U.S. sl.*), irked, irritated, net~tled, piqued, pissed off (*Taboo sl.*), put out, riled, sore, upset, vexed

peevish acrimonious, cantankerous, cap~tious, childish, churlish, crabbed, cross, crotchety (*Inf.*), crusty, fractious, fretful, grumpy, huffy, ill-natured, ill-tempered, ir~ritable, liverish, pettish, petulant, queru~lous, ratty (*Brit. & N.Z. inf.*), short-tempered, shrewish, snappy, splenetic, sulky, sullen, surly, testy, tetchy, touchy, waspish, whingeing (*Inf.*)
Antonyms affable, agreeable, cheerful, cheery, easy-going, even-tempered, genial, good-natured, happy, merry, pleasant, sweet

peg v. **1.** attach, fasten, fix, join, make fast, secure **2.** *With along or away* apply one~self to, beaver away (*Brit. inf.*), keep at it, keep going, keep on, persist, plod along, plug away at (*Inf.*), stick to it, work at, work away **3.** *Of prices, etc.* control, fix, freeze, limit, set

pelt v. **1.** assail, batter, beat, belabour, bom~bard, cast, hurl, pepper, pummel, shower, sling, strike, thrash, throw, wallop (*Inf.*) **2.** barrel (along) (*Inf., chiefly U.S. & Canad.*), belt (*Sl.*), burn rubber (*Inf.*), career, charge, dash, hurry, run fast, rush, shoot, speed, tear, whiz (*Inf.*) **3.** bucket down (*Inf.*), pour, rain cats and dogs (*Inf.*), rain hard, teem

pen[1] v. commit to paper, compose, draft, draw up, jot down, write

pen[2] **1.** *n.* cage, coop, enclosure, fold, hutch, pound, sty **2.** *v.* cage, confine, coop up, en~close, fence in, hedge, hem in, hurdle, im~pound, mew (up), pound, shut up *or* in

penal corrective, disciplinary, penalizing, punitive, retributive

penalize award a penalty against (*Sport*), correct, discipline, handicap, impose a pen~alty on, inflict a handicap on, punish, put at a disadvantage

penalty disadvantage, fine, forfeit, forfei~ture, handicap, mulct, price, punishment, retribution

penance 1. atonement, mortification, pen~alty, punishment, reparation, sackcloth and ashes **2. do penance** accept punishment, atone, make amends, make reparation, mortify oneself, show contrition, suffer

penchant affinity, bent, bias, disposition, fondness, inclination, leaning, liking, par~tiality, predilection, predisposition, procliv~ity, proneness, propensity, taste, tendency, turn

pending awaiting, forthcoming, hanging fire, imminent, impending, in the balance, in the offing, undecided, undetermined, un~settled, up in the air

penetrate 1. bore, enter, go through, im~pale, perforate, pierce, prick, probe, stab **2.** diffuse, enter, get in, infiltrate, permeate, pervade, seep, suffuse **3.** *Fig.* affect, become clear, be understood, come across, get through to, impress, touch **4.** *Fig.* compre~hend, decipher, discern, fathom, figure out (*Inf.*), get to the bottom of, grasp, suss (out) (*Sl.*), understand, unravel, work out

penetrating 1. biting, carrying, harsh, in~trusive, pervasive, piercing, pungent, sharp, shrill, stinging, strong **2.** *Fig.* acute, astute, critical, discerning, discriminating, inci~sive, intelligent, keen, perceptive, perspica~cious, profound, quick, sagacious, search~ing, sharp, sharp-witted, shrewd
Antonyms (*sense 1*) blunt, dull, mild, sweet (*sense 2*) apathetic, dull, indifferent, obtuse, shallow, stupid, uncomprehending, unper~ceptive

penetration 1. entrance, entry, incision, inroad, invasion, perforation, piercing, puncturing **2.** acuteness, astuteness, dis~cernment, insight, keenness, perception, perspicacity, sharpness, shrewdness, wit

penis chopper (*Brit. sl.*), cock (*Taboo sl.*), dick (*Taboo sl.*), dong (*Sl.*), John Thomas (*Taboo sl.*), joystick (*Sl.*), knob (*Brit. taboo sl.*), member, organ, pecker (*U.S. & Canad. taboo sl.*), phallus, pizzle (*Archaic & dialect*), plonker (*Sl.*), prick (*Taboo sl.*), schlong (*U.S. sl.*), tadger (*Brit. sl.*), tool (*Taboo sl.*), wang (*U.S. sl.*), weenie (*U.S. sl.*), whang (*U.S. sl.*), winkle (*Brit. sl.*)

penitence compunction, contrition, regret, remorse, repentance, ruefulness, self-reproach, shame, sorrow

penitent *adj.* abject, apologetic, atoning, conscience-stricken, contrite, regretful, re~morseful, repentant, rueful, sorrowful, sor~ry
Antonyms callous, impenitent, remorseless, unrepentant

penmanship calligraphy, chirography, fist (*Inf.*), hand, handwriting, longhand, script, writing

pen name allonym, nom de plume, pseudonym

pennant banderole, banner, burgee (*Nauti~cal*), ensign, flag, jack, pennon, streamer

penniless bankrupt, broke (*Inf.*), cleaned

out (*Sl.*), destitute, dirt-poor (*Inf.*), down and out, flat broke (*Inf.*), impecunious, impoverished, indigent, moneyless, necessitous, needy, on one's uppers, penurious, poor, poverty-stricken, ruined, short, skint (*Brit. sl.*), stony-broke (*Brit. sl.*), strapped (*Sl.*), without a penny to one's name, without two pennies to rub together (*Inf.*)
Antonyms affluent, filthy rich, loaded (*Sl.*), rich, rolling (*Sl.*), wealthy, well-heeled (*Inf.*)

penny-pinching *adj.* cheeseparing, close, frugal, mean, mingy (*Brit. inf.*), miserly, near (*Inf.*), niggardly, scrimping, Scroogelike, stingy, tight-arse (*Taboo sl.*), tight-arsed (*Taboo sl.*), tight as a duck's arse (*Taboo sl.*), tight-ass (*U.S. taboo sl.*), tight-assed (*U.S. taboo sl.*), tightfisted
Antonyms generous, kind, liberal, munificent, prodigal, unstinting

pennyworth bit, crumb, jot, little, mite, modicum, particle, scrap, small amount, tittle

pension allowance, annuity, benefit, superannuation

pensioner O.A.P., retired person, senior citizen

pensive blue (*Inf.*), cogitative, contemplative, dreamy, grave, in a brown study (*Inf.*), meditative, melancholy, mournful, musing, preoccupied, reflective, ruminative, sad, serious, sober, solemn, sorrowful, thoughtful, wistful
Antonyms active, carefree, cheerful, frivolous, gay, happy, joyous, light-hearted

pent-up bottled up, bridled, checked, constrained, curbed, held back, inhibited, repressed, smothered, stifled, suppressed

penurious 1. cheeseparing, close, closefisted, frugal, grudging, mean, miserly, near (*Inf.*), niggardly, parsimonious, skimping, stingy, tight-arse (*Taboo sl.*), tight-arsed (*Taboo sl.*), tight as a duck's arse (*Taboo sl.*), tight-ass (*U.S. taboo sl.*), tight-assed (*U.S. taboo sl.*), tightfisted, ungenerous **2.** destitute, down and out, impecunious, impoverished, indigent, needy, penniless, poor, poverty-stricken **3.** beggarly, deficient, inadequate, meagre, miserable, miserly, paltry, poor, scanty

penury 1. beggary, destitution, indigence, need, pauperism, poverty, privation, straitened circumstances, want **2.** dearth, deficiency, lack, paucity, scantiness, scarcity, shortage, sparseness

people *n.* **1.** human beings, humanity, humans, mankind, men and women, mortals, persons **2.** citizens, clan, community, family, folk, inhabitants, nation, population, public, race, tribe **3.** commonalty, crowd, general public, grass roots, hoi polloi, masses, mob, multitude, plebs, populace, rabble, rank and file, the herd ~*v.* **4.** colonize, inhabit, occupy, populate, settle

pepper *v.* **1.** flavour, season, spice **2.** bespeckle, dot, fleck, spatter, speck, sprinkle, stipple, stud **3.** bombard, pelt, riddle, scatter, shower

peppery 1. fiery, highly seasoned, hot, piquant, pungent, spicy **2.** choleric, hottempered, irascible, irritable, quicktempered, snappish, testy, touchy, vitriolic, waspish **3.** astringent, biting, caustic, incisive, sarcastic, sharp, stinging, trenchant, vitriolic
Antonyms (*sense 1*) bland, insipid, mild, tasteless, vapid

perceive 1. be aware of, behold, descry, discern, discover, distinguish, espy, make out, note, notice, observe, recognize, remark, see, spot **2.** appreciate, apprehend, comprehend, conclude, deduce, feel, gather, get (*Inf.*), grasp, know, learn, realize, see, sense, suss (out) (*Sl.*), understand

perceptible apparent, appreciable, blatant, clear, conspicuous, detectable, discernible, distinct, evident, noticeable, observable, obvious, palpable, perceivable, recognizable, tangible, visible
Antonyms concealed, hidden, imperceptible, inconspicuous, indiscernible, invisible, unapparent, undetectable, unnoticeable

perception apprehension, awareness, conception, consciousness, discernment, feeling, grasp, idea, impression, insight, notion, observation, recognition, sensation, sense, taste, understanding

perceptive acute, alert, astute, aware, discerning, insightful, intuitive, observant, penetrating, percipient, perspicacious, quick, responsive, sensitive, sharp
Antonyms dull, indifferent, insensitive, obtuse, slow-witted, stupid, thick

perch 1. *n.* branch, pole, post, resting place, roost **2.** *v.* alight, balance, land, rest, roost, settle, sit on

perchance by chance, for all one knows, haply (*Archaic*), maybe, mayhap (*Archaic*), peradventure (*Archaic*), perhaps, possibly, probably

percipient alert, alive, astute, aware, discerning, discriminating, intelligent, penetrating, perceptive, perspicacious, quickwitted, sharp, wide-awake

percolate drain, drip, exude, filter, filtrate, leach, ooze, penetrate, perk (*of coffee, inf.*), permeate, pervade, seep, strain, transfuse

percussion blow, brunt, bump, clash, collision, concussion, crash, impact, jolt, knock, shock, smash, thump

peremptory 1. absolute, binding, categorical, commanding, compelling, decisive,

final, imperative, incontrovertible, irrefu~
table, obligatory, undeniable **2.** arbitrary,
assertive, authoritative, autocratic, bossy
(*Inf.*), dictatorial, dogmatic, domineering,
high-handed, imperious, intolerant, over~
bearing

perennial 1. abiding, chronic, constant,
continual, continuing, enduring, incessant,
inveterate, lasting, lifelong, persistent, re~
current, unchanging **2.** ceaseless, deathless,
eternal, everlasting, immortal, imperish~
able, never-ending, permanent, perpetual,
unceasing, undying, unfailing, uninterrupt~
ed

perfect *adj.* **1.** absolute, complete, complet~
ed, consummate, entire, finished, full, out-
and-out, sheer, unadulterated, unalloyed,
unmitigated, utter, whole **2.** blameless,
clean, excellent, faultless, flawless, ideal,
immaculate, impeccable, pure, splendid,
spotless, sublime, superb, superlative, su~
preme, unblemished, unmarred, untar~
nished **3.** accurate, close, correct, exact,
faithful, precise, right, spot-on (*Brit. inf.*),
strict, true, unerring **4.** accomplished,
adept, experienced, expert, finished, mas~
terly, polished, practised, skilful, skilled ~*v.*
5. accomplish, achieve, carry out, complete,
consummate, effect, finish, fulfil, perform,
realize **6.** ameliorate, cultivate, develop,
elaborate, hone, improve, polish, refine
Antonyms *adj.* bad, damaged, defective,
deficient, faulty, flawed, impaired, imperfect,
impure, incomplete, inferior, partial, poor,
ruined, spoiled, unfinished, unskilled, worth~
less ~*v.* mar

perfection 1. accomplishment, achieve~
ment, achieving, completion, consumma~
tion, evolution, fulfilment, realization **2.**
completeness, exactness, excellence, ex~
quisiteness, faultlessness, integrity, matur~
ity, perfectness, precision, purity, sublim~
ity, superiority, wholeness **3.** acme, crown,
ideal, paragon

perfectionist formalist, precisian, preci~
sionist, purist, stickler

perfectly 1. absolutely, altogether, com~
pletely, consummately, entirely, fully, quite,
thoroughly, totally, utterly, wholly **2.** ad~
mirably, exquisitely, faultlessly, flawlessly,
ideally, impeccably, superbly, superlatively,
supremely, to perfection, wonderfully
Antonyms (*sense 1*) inaccurately, incom~
pletely, mistakenly, partially (*sense 2*) badly,
defectively, faultily, imperfectly, poorly

perfidious corrupt, deceitful, dishonest,
disloyal, double-dealing, double-faced, faith~
less, false, recreant (*Archaic*), traitorous,
treacherous, treasonous, two-faced, unfaith~
ful, untrustworthy

perfidy betrayal, deceit, disloyalty, double-

dealing, duplicity, faithlessness, falsity,
infidelity, perfidiousness, treachery, treason

perforate bore, drill, hole, honeycomb,
penetrate, pierce, punch, puncture

perform 1. accomplish, achieve, act, bring
about, carry out, complete, comply with,
discharge, do, effect, execute, fulfil, func~
tion, observe, pull off, satisfy, transact,
work **2.** act, appear as, depict, enact, play,
present, produce, put on, render, represent,
stage

performance 1. accomplishment, achieve~
ment, act, carrying out, completion, con~
duct, consummation, discharge, execution,
exploit, feat, fulfilment, work **2.** acting, ap~
pearance, exhibition, gig (*Inf.*), interpreta~
tion, play, portrayal, presentation, produc~
tion, representation, show **3.** action, con~
duct, efficiency, functioning, operation,
practice, running, working **4.** *Inf.* act, be~
haviour, bother, business, carry-on (*Inf.*,
chiefly Brit.), fuss, pother, rigmarole, to-do

performer actor, actress, artiste, play-actor,
player, Thespian, trouper

perfume aroma, attar, balminess, bouquet,
cologne, essence, fragrance, incense, niff
(*Brit. sl.*), odour, redolence, scent, smell,
sweetness

perfunctory automatic, careless, cursory,
heedless, inattentive, indifferent, mechani~
cal, negligent, offhand, routine, sketchy,
slipshod, slovenly, stereotyped, superficial,
unconcerned, unthinking, wooden
Antonyms ardent, assiduous, attentive,
careful, diligent, keen, spirited, thorough,
thoughtful, zealous

perhaps as the case may be, conceivably,
feasibly, for all one knows, it may be, may~
be, perchance (*Archaic*), possibly

peril danger, exposure, hazard, insecurity,
jeopardy, menace, pitfall, risk, uncertainty,
vulnerability
Antonyms certainty, impregnability, in~
vulnerability, safety, security, surety

perilous chancy (*Inf.*), dangerous, exposed,
fraught with danger, hairy (*Sl.*), hazardous,
parlous (*Archaic*), precarious, risky, threat~
ening, unsafe, unsure, vulnerable

perimeter ambit, border, borderline,
boundary, bounds, circumference, confines,
edge, limit, margin, periphery
Antonyms central part, centre, core, heart,
hub, middle, nucleus

period 1. interval, season, space, span,
spell, stretch, term, time, while **2.** aeon,
age, course, cycle, date, days, epoch, era,
generation, season, stage, term, time, years

periodic at fixed intervals, cyclic, cyclical,
every once in a while, every so often, infre~
quent, intermittent, occasional, periodical,

recurrent, regular, repeated, seasonal, spasmodic, sporadic

periodical *n.* journal, magazine, monthly, organ, paper, publication, quarterly, review, serial, weekly

perish 1. be killed, be lost, decease, die, expire, lose one's life, pass away **2.** be destroyed, collapse, decline, disappear, fall, go under, vanish **3.** decay, decompose, disintegrate, moulder, rot, waste, wither

perishable decaying, decomposable, destructible, easily spoilt, liable to rot, short-lived, unstable
Antonyms durable, lasting, long-life, long-lived, non-perishable

perjure (oneself) bear false witness, commit perjury, forswear, give false testimony, lie under oath, swear falsely

perjured deceitful, false, forsworn, lying, mendacious, perfidious, traitorous, treacherous, untrue, untruthful

perjury bearing false witness, false oath, false statement, false swearing, forswearing, giving false testimony, lying under oath, oath breaking, violation of an oath, wilful falsehood

perk up brighten, buck up (*Inf.*), cheer up, liven up, look up, pep up, rally, recover, recuperate, revive, take heart

permanence constancy, continuance, continuity, dependability, durability, duration, endurance, finality, fixedness, fixity, immortality, indestructibility, lastingness, perdurability (*Rare*), permanency, perpetuity, stability, survival

permanent abiding, constant, durable, enduring, eternal, everlasting, fixed, immovable, immutable, imperishable, indestructible, invariable, lasting, long-lasting, perennial, perpetual, persistent, stable, steadfast, unchanging, unfading
Antonyms brief, changing, ephemeral, finite, fleeting, impermanent, inconstant, momentary, mortal, passing, short-lived, temporary, transitory, variable

permeate charge, diffuse throughout, fill, filter through, imbue, impregnate, infiltrate, pass through, penetrate, percolate, pervade, saturate, seep through, soak through, spread throughout

permissible acceptable, admissible, allowable, all right, authorized, kosher (*Inf.*), lawful, legal, legit (*Sl.*), legitimate, licit, O.K. *or* okay (*Inf.*), permitted, proper, sanctioned
Antonyms banned, forbidden, illegal, illicit, prohibited, unauthorized, unlawful

permission allowance, approval, assent, authorization, consent, dispensation, freedom, go-ahead (*Inf.*), green light, leave, liberty, licence, permit, sanction, sufferance, tolerance

permissive acquiescent, easy-going, easyoasy (*Sl.*), forbearing, free, indulgent, latitudinarian, lax, lenient, liberal, open-minded, tolerant
Antonyms authoritarian, denying, domineering, forbidding, grudging, rigid, strict

permit 1. *v.* admit, agree, allow, authorize, consent, empower, enable, endorse, endure, entitle, give leave *or* permission, grant, let, license, own, sanction, suffer, tolerate, warrant **2.** *n.* authorization, liberty, licence, pass, passport, permission, sanction, warrant

permutation alteration, change, shift, transformation, transmutation, transposition

pernicious bad, baleful, baneful (*Archaic*), damaging, dangerous, deadly, deleterious, destructive, detrimental, evil, fatal, harmful, hurtful, injurious, maleficent, malevolent, malicious, malign, malignant, noisome, noxious, offensive, pestilent, poisonous, ruinous, venomous, wicked

pernickety 1. careful, carping, difficult to please, exacting, fastidious, finicky, fussy, hairsplitting, nice, nit-picking (*Inf.*), overprecise, painstaking, particular, picky (*Inf.*), punctilious **2.** detailed, exacting, fiddly, fine, tricky
Antonyms (*sense 1*) careless, easy to please, haphazard, heedless, inattentive, lax, slack, slapdash, slipshod, sloppy, uncritical (*sense 2*) easy, simple

peroration closing remarks, conclusion, recapitulation, recapping (*Inf.*), reiteration, summing-up

perpendicular at right angles to, on end, plumb, straight, upright, vertical

perpetrate be responsible for, bring about, carry out, commit, do, effect, enact, execute, inflict, perform, wreak

perpetual 1. abiding, endless, enduring, eternal, everlasting, immortal, infinite, lasting, never-ending, perennial, permanent, sempiternal (*Literary*), unchanging, undying, unending **2.** ceaseless, constant, continual, continuous, endless, incessant, interminable, never-ending, perennial, persistent, recurrent, repeated, unceasing, unfailing, uninterrupted, unremitting
Antonyms brief, ephemeral, fleeting, impermanent, momentary, passing, short-lived, temporary, transitory

perpetuate continue, eternalize, immortalize, keep alive, keep going, keep up, maintain, preserve, sustain
Antonyms abolish, destroy, end, forget, ignore, put an end to, stamp out, suppress

perplex 1. baffle, befuddle, beset, bewilder, confound, confuse, dumbfound, flummox, mix up, muddle, mystify, nonplus, puzzle, stump **2.** complicate, encumber, entangle, involve, jumble, mix up, snarl up, tangle, thicken

perplexing baffling, bewildering, complex, complicated, confusing, difficult, enigmatic, hard, inexplicable, intricate, involved, knotty, labyrinthine, mysterious, mystify~ ing, paradoxical, puzzling, strange, taxing, thorny, unaccountable, weird

perplexity 1. bafflement, bewilderment, confusion, incomprehension, mystification, puzzlement, stupefaction **2.** complexity, difficulty, inextricability, intricacy, in~ volvement, obscurity **3.** difficulty, dilemma, enigma, fix (*Inf.*), knotty problem, mystery, paradox, puzzle, snarl

perquisite benefit, bonus, dividend, extra, fringe benefit, icing on the cake, perk (*Brit. inf.*), plus

persecute 1. afflict, be on one's back (*Sl.*), distress, dragoon, harass, hassle (*Inf.*), hound, hunt, ill-treat, injure, maltreat, martyr, molest, oppress, pursue, torment, torture, victimize **2.** annoy, badger, bait, bother, pester, tease, vex, worry
Antonyms accommodate, back, calm, cod~ dle, comfort, console, cosset, humour, indulge, leave alone, let alone, mollycoddle, pamper, pet, spoil, support

perseverance constancy, dedication, de~ termination, diligence, doggedness, endur~ ance, indefatigability, persistence, pertinac~ ity, purposefulness, resolution, sedulity, stamina, steadfastness, tenacity

persevere be determined *or* resolved, carry on, continue, endure, go on, hang on, hold fast, hold on (*Inf.*), keep going, keep on *or* at, maintain, persist, plug away (*Inf.*), pur~ sue, remain, stand firm, stick at *or* to
Antonyms be irresolute, dither (*Chiefly Brit.*), end, falter, give in, give up, hesitate, quit, shillyshally (*Inf.*), swither (*Scot.*), throw in the towel, vacillate, waver

persist 1. be resolute, continue, hold on (*Inf.*), insist, persevere, stand firm **2.** abide, carry on, continue, endure, keep up, last, linger, remain

persistence constancy, determination, diligence, doggedness, endurance, grit, in~ defatigability, perseverance, pertinacity, pluck, resolution, stamina, steadfastness, tenacity, tirelessness

persistent 1. assiduous, determined, dog~ ged, enduring, fixed, immovable, indefati~ gable, obdurate, obstinate, persevering, pertinacious, resolute, steadfast, steady, stiff-necked, stubborn, tenacious, tireless, unflagging **2.** constant, continual, continu~ ous, endless, incessant, interminable, never-ending, perpetual, relentless, repeat~ ed, unrelenting, unremitting
Antonyms (*sense 1*) changeable, flexible, ir~ resolute, tractable, yielding (*sense 2*) incon~ stant, intermittent, irregular, occasional, off-and-on, periodic

person 1. being, body, human, human be~ ing, individual, living soul, soul **2. in per~ son** bodily, in the flesh, oneself, personally

persona assumed role, character, façade, face, front, mask, part, personality, public face, role

personable affable, agreeable, amiable, at~ tractive, charming, good-looking, handsome, likable *or* likeable, nice, pleasant, pleasing, presentable, winning
Antonyms disagreeable, sullen, surly, ugly, unattractive, unpleasant, unsightly

personage big noise (*Inf.*), big shot (*Inf.*), celeb (*Inf.*), celebrity, dignitary, luminary, megastar (*Inf.*), notable, personality, public figure, somebody, V.I.P., well-known person, worthy

personal 1. exclusive, individual, intimate, own, particular, peculiar, private, privy, special **2.** bodily, corporal, corporeal, exte~ rior, material, physical **3.** derogatory, dis~ paraging, insulting, nasty, offensive, pejo~ rative, slighting

personality 1. character, disposition, iden~ tity, individuality, make-up, nature, psyche, temper, temperament, traits **2.** attraction, attractiveness, character, charisma, charm, dynamism, likableness *or* likeableness, magnetism, pleasantness **3.** celeb (*Inf.*), ce~ lebrity, famous name, household name, megastar (*Inf.*), notable, personage, star, well-known face, well-known person

personally 1. alone, by oneself, indepen~ dently, in person, in the flesh, on one's own, solely **2.** for oneself, for one's part, from one's own viewpoint, in one's own view **3.** individualistically, individually, privately, specially, subjectively

personate act, depict, do (*Inf.*), enact, feign, imitate, impersonate, play-act, portray, rep~ resent

personification embodiment, epitome, im~ age, incarnation, likeness, portrayal, rec~ reation, representation, semblance

personify body forth, embody, epitomize, exemplify, express, image (*Rare*), incarnate, mirror, represent, symbolize, typify

personnel employees, helpers, human re~ sources, liveware, members, men and women, people, staff, workers, workforce

perspective 1. angle, attitude, broad view, context, frame of reference, objectivity, outlook, overview, proportion, relation,

relative importance, relativity, way of look~
ing **2.** outlook, panorama, prospect, scene,
view, vista

perspicacious acute, alert, astute, aware,
clear-sighted, clever, discerning, keen, ob~
servant, penetrating, perceptive, percipient,
sagacious, sharp, sharp-witted, shrewd

perspicacity acumen, acuteness, discern~
ment, discrimination, insight, keenness,
penetration, perceptiveness, percipience,
perspicaciousness, perspicuity, sagacious~
ness, sagacity, sharpness, shrewdness,
smarts (*Sl., chiefly U.S.*), suss (*Sl.*), wit

perspiration exudation, moisture, sweat,
wetness

perspire be damp, be wet, drip, exude, glow,
pour with sweat, secrete, sweat, swelter

persuade 1. actuate, advise, allure, bring
round (*Inf.*), coax, counsel, entice, impel,
incite, induce, influence, inveigle, prevail
upon, prompt, sway, talk into, urge, win
over **2.** cause to believe, convert, convince,
satisfy
Antonyms deter, discourage, dissuade, for~
bid, prohibit

persuasion 1. blandishment, cajolery, con~
version, enticement, exhortation, induce~
ment, influencing, inveiglement, wheedling
2. cogency, force, persuasiveness, potency,
power, pull (*Inf.*) **3.** belief, certitude, con~
viction, credo, creed, faith, firm belief, fixed
opinion, opinion, tenet, views **4.** camp, cult,
denomination, faction, party, school, school
of thought, sect, side

persuasive cogent, compelling, convincing,
credible, effective, eloquent, forceful, im~
pelling, impressive, inducing, influential,
logical, moving, plausible, sound, telling,
touching, valid, weighty, winning
Antonyms feeble, flimsy, illogical, implau~
sible, incredible, ineffective, invalid, uncon~
vincing, unimpressive, weak

pertain appertain, apply, be appropriate,
bear on, befit, belong, be part of, be rel~
evant, concern, refer, regard, relate

pertinacious bull-headed, determined,
dogged, headstrong, inflexible, intractable,
mulish, obdurate, obstinate, persevering,
persistent, perverse, pig-headed, relentless,
resolute, self-willed, stiff-necked, strong-
willed, stubborn, tenacious, unyielding,
wilful

pertinent admissible, *ad rem*, applicable,
apposite, appropriate, apropos, apt, fit,
fitting, germane, material, pat, proper, rel~
evant, suitable, to the point, to the purpose
Antonyms discordant, foreign, immaterial,
inappropriate, incongruous, irrelevant,
unfitting, unrelated, unsuitable

pertness audacity, brashness, brass (*Inf.*),

bumptiousness, cheek (*Inf.*), cheekiness,
chutzpah (*U.S. & Canad. inf.*), cockiness,
effrontery, forwardness, front, imperti~
nence, impudence, insolence, presumption,
rudeness, sauciness

perturb 1. agitate, alarm, bother, discom~
pose, disconcert, discountenance, disquiet,
disturb, faze, fluster, ruffle, trouble, un~
nerve, unsettle, upset, vex, worry **2.** con~
fuse, disarrange, disorder, muddle, unsettle

perturbed agitated, alarmed, anxious, dis~
concerted, disquieted, disturbed, fearful,
flurried, flustered, ill at ease, nervous, rest~
less, shaken, troubled, uncomfortable, un~
easy, upset, worried
Antonyms assured, at ease, comfortable,
composed, cool, impassive, relaxed, unper~
turbed, unruffled

perusal browse, check, examination, in~
spection, look through, read, scrutiny,
study

peruse browse, check, examine, inspect,
look through, read, run one's eye over,
scan, scrutinize, study, work over

pervade affect, charge, diffuse, extend, fill,
imbue, infuse, overspread, penetrate, per~
colate, permeate, spread through, suffuse

pervasive common, extensive, general, in~
escapable, omnipresent, permeating, per~
vading, prevalent, rife, ubiquitous, univer~
sal, widespread

perverse 1. abnormal, contradictory, con~
trary, delinquent, depraved, deviant, dis~
obedient, froward, improper, incorrect,
miscreant, rebellious, refractory, trouble~
some, unhealthy, unmanageable, unreason~
able **2.** contrary, contumacious, cross-
grained, dogged, headstrong, intractable,
intransigent, obdurate, wilful, wrong-
headed **3.** contrary, mulish, obstinate, pig-
headed, stiff-necked, stubborn, unyielding,
wayward **4.** cantankerous, churlish, crab~
bed, cross, fractious, ill-natured, ill-
tempered, peevish, petulant, spiteful, strop~
py (*Brit. sl.*), surly
Antonyms accommodating, agreeable, ami~
able, complaisant, cooperative, flexible,
good-natured, malleable, obedient, obliging

perversion 1. aberration, abnormality, de~
bauchery, depravity, deviation, immorality,
kink (*Brit. inf.*), kinkiness (*Sl.*), unnatural~
ness, vice, vitiation, wickedness **2.** corrup~
tion, distortion, falsification, misinterpreta~
tion, misrepresentation, misuse, twisting

perversity contradictiveness, contradicto~
riness, contrariness, contumacy, froward~
ness, intransigence, obduracy, refractori~
ness, waywardness, wrong-headedness

pervert *v.* **1.** abuse, distort, falsify, garble,
misconstrue, misinterpret, misrepresent,
misuse, twist, warp **2.** corrupt, debase, de~

perverted 463 phantom

bauch, degrade, deprave, desecrate, initiate, lead astray, subvert ~*n*. **3**. debauchee, degenerate, deviant, weirdo *or* weirdie (*Inf.*)

perverted aberrant, abnormal, corrupt, debased, debauched, depraved, deviant, distorted, evil, immoral, impaired, kinky (*Sl.*), misguided, pervy (*Sl.*), sick, twisted, unhealthy, unnatural, vicious, vitiated, warped, wicked

pessimism cynicism, dejection, depression, despair, despondency, distrust, gloom, gloominess, gloomy outlook, glumness, hopelessness, melancholy, the hump (*Brit. inf.*)

pessimist cynic, defeatist, doomster, gloom merchant (*Inf.*), kill-joy, melancholic, misanthrope, prophet of doom, wet blanket (*Inf.*), worrier

pessimistic bleak, cynical, dark, dejected, depressed, despairing, despondent, distrustful, downhearted, fatalistic, foreboding, gloomy, glum, hopeless, melancholy, misanthropic, morose, resigned, sad
Antonyms assured, bright, buoyant, cheerful, cheery, encouraged, exhilarated, hopeful, in good heart, optimistic, sanguine

pest 1. annoyance, bane, bore, bother, drag (*Inf.*), gall, irritation, nuisance, pain (*Inf.*), pain in the arse (*Taboo inf.*), pain in the neck (*Inf.*), thorn in one's flesh, trial, vexation **2**. bane, blight, bug, curse, epidemic, infection, pestilence, plague, scourge

pester aggravate (*Inf.*), annoy, badger, bedevil, bend someone's ear (*Inf.*), be on one's back (*Sl.*), bother, bug (*Inf.*), chivvy, disturb, drive one up the wall (*Sl.*), fret, get at, get in one's hair (*Inf.*), get on one's nerves (*Inf.*), harass, harry, hassle (*Inf.*), irk, nag, pick on, plague, ride (*Inf.*), torment, worry

pestilence 1. Black Death, epidemic, pandemic, plague, visitation **2**. affliction, bane, blight, cancer, canker, curse, scourge

pestilent 1. annoying, bothersome, galling, irksome, irritating, plaguy (*Inf.*), tiresome, vexing **2**. corrupting, deleterious, destructive, detrimental, evil, harmful, injurious, pernicious, ruinous, vicious **3**. catching, contagious, contaminated, diseased, disease-ridden, infected, infectious, plague-ridden, tainted

pestilential 1. annoying, dangerous, deleterious, destructive, detrimental, evil, foul, harmful, hazardous, injurious, pernicious, ruinous, troublesome **2**. catching, contagious, contaminated, deadly, disease-ridden, infectious, malignant, noxious, pestiferous, poisonous, venomous

pet¹ *n*. **1**. apple of one's eye, blue-eyed boy (*Inf.*), darling, favourite, idol, jewel, treasure ~*adj*. **2**. cherished, dearest, dear to one's heart, favoured, favourite, particular,

preferred, special **3**. domesticated, house, house-broken, house-trained (*Brit.*), tame, trained ~*v*. **4**. baby, coddle, cosset, mollycoddle, pamper, spoil **5**. caress, fondle, pat, stroke **6**. *Inf.* canoodle (*Sl.*), cuddle, kiss, neck (*Inf.*), smooch (*Inf.*), snog (*Brit. sl.*)

pet² bad mood, bate (*Brit. sl.*), huff, ill temper, miff (*Inf.*), paddy (*Brit. inf.*), paddywhack (*Brit. inf.*), pique, pout, sulk, sulks, tantrum, temper

peter out come to nothing, die out, dwindle, ebb, evaporate, fade, fail, give out, run dry, run out, stop, taper off, wane

petition 1. *n*. address, appeal, application, entreaty, invocation, memorial, plea, prayer, request, round robin, solicitation, suit, supplication **2**. *v*. adjure, appeal, ask, beg, beseech, call upon, crave, entreat, plead, pray, press, solicit, sue, supplicate, urge

petrified 1. fossilized, ossified, rocklike **2**. aghast, appalled, dazed, dumbfounded, frozen, horrified, numb, scared shitless (*Taboo sl.*), scared stiff, shit-scared (*Taboo sl.*), shocked, speechless, stunned, stupefied, terrified, terror-stricken

petrify 1. calcify, fossilize, harden, set, solidify, turn to stone **2**. amaze, appal, astonish, astound, confound, dumbfound, horrify, immobilize, paralyse, stun, stupefy, terrify, transfix

petty 1. contemptible, inconsiderable, inessential, inferior, insignificant, little, mean (*Inf.*), negligible, nickel-and-dime (*U.S. sl.*), paltry, piddling (*Inf.*), slight, small, trifling, trivial, unimportant **2**. cheap, grudging, mean, mean-minded, shabby, small-minded, spiteful, stingy, ungenerous **3**. inferior, junior, lesser, lower, minor, secondary, subordinate
Antonyms (*sense 1*) consequential, considerable, essential, important, major, momentous, significant (*sense 2*) broad-minded, generous, liberal, magnanimous, open-minded, tolerant

petulance bad temper, crabbiness, ill humour, irritability, peevishness, pettishness, pique, pouts, querulousness, spleen, sulkiness, sullenness, waspishness

petulant bad-tempered, captious, cavilling, crabbed, cross, crusty, fault-finding, fretful, huffy, ill-humoured, impatient, irritable, moody, peevish, perverse, pouting, querulous, ratty (*Brit. & N.Z. inf.*), snappish, sour, sulky, sullen, ungracious, waspish
Antonyms affable, cheerful, congenial, easy-going, even-tempered, good-humoured, good-natured, happy, patient, smiling

phantom 1. apparition, eidolon, ghost, phantasm, revenant, shade (*Literary*), spectre, spirit, spook (*Inf.*), wraith **2**. chimera,

figment, figment of the imagination, hallu~
cination, illusion, vision

pharisee canter, dissembler, dissimulator,
fraud, humbug, hypocrite, phoney *or* phony
(*Inf.*), pietist, whited sepulchre

phase aspect, chapter, condition, develop~
ment, juncture, period, point, position,
stage, state, step, time

phase out axe (*Inf.*), close, deactivate, dis~
pose of gradually, ease off, eliminate, pull
out, remove, replace, run down, taper off,
terminate, wind down, wind up, withdraw
Antonyms activate, begin, create, establish,
form, initiate, open, set up, start

phenomenal exceptional, extraordinary,
fantastic, marvellous, miraculous, notable,
outstanding, prodigious, remarkable, sen~
sational, singular, uncommon, unique, un~
paralleled, unusual, wondrous (*Archaic or
literary*)
Antonyms average, common, mediocre, or~
dinary, poor, run-of-the-mill, second-rate, un~
exceptional, unremarkable, usual

phenomenon 1. circumstance, episode,
event, fact, happening, incident, occurrence
2. exception, marvel, miracle, nonpareil,
prodigy, rarity, sensation, sight, spectacle,
wonder

philander coquet, court, dally, flirt, fool
around (*Inf.*), toy, trifle, womanize (*Inf.*)

philanderer Casanova, dallier, Don Juan,
flirt, gallant, gay dog, ladies' man, lady-
killer (*Inf.*), Lothario, playboy, stud (*Sl.*),
trifler, wolf (*Inf.*), womanizer (*Inf.*)

philanthropic alms-giving, altruistic,
beneficent, benevolent, benignant, chari~
table, eleemosynary, gracious, humane, hu~
manitarian, kind, kind-hearted, munificent,
public-spirited
Antonyms egoistic, mean, miserly, nig~
gardly, penurious, selfish, self-seeking, stingy

philanthropist alms-giver, altruist, ben~
efactor, contributor, donor, giver, humani~
tarian, patron

philanthropy alms-giving, altruism, be~
neficence, benevolence, benignity, bounty,
brotherly love, charitableness, charity, gen~
erosity, humanitarianism, kind-heartedness,
largess *or* largesse, liberality, munificence,
open-handedness, patronage, public-
spiritedness

philistine 1. *n.* barbarian, boor, bourgeois,
Goth, ignoramus, lout, lowbrow, vulgarian,
yahoo **2.** *adj.* anti-intellectual, boorish,
bourgeois, crass, ignorant, lowbrow, taste~
less, uncultivated, uncultured, uneducated,
unrefined

philosopher dialectician, logician, mahat~
ma, metaphysician, sage, seeker after truth,
theorist, thinker, wise man

philosophical, philosophic 1. abstract,
erudite, learned, logical, rational, sagacious,
theoretical, thoughtful, wise **2.** calm, col~
lected, composed, cool, impassive, imper~
turbable, patient, resigned, sedate, serene,
stoical, tranquil, unruffled
Antonyms (*sense 1*) factual, illogical, irra~
tional, practical, pragmatic, scientific (*sense 2*)
emotional, hot-headed, impulsive, perturbed,
rash, restless, upset

philosophy 1. aesthetics, knowledge, logic,
metaphysics, rationalism, reason, reason~
ing, thinking, thought, wisdom **2.** attitude
to life, basic idea, beliefs, convictions, doc~
trine, ideology, principle, tenets, thinking,
values, viewpoint, *Weltanschauung*, world-
view **3.** composure, coolness, dispassion,
equanimity, resignation, restraint, self-
possession, serenity, stoicism

phlegmatic apathetic, bovine, cold, dull,
frigid, heavy, impassive, indifferent, lethar~
gic, listless, lymphatic, matter-of-fact, plac~
id, sluggish, stoical, stolid, undemonstra~
tive, unemotional, unfeeling
Antonyms active, alert, animated, emotion~
al, energetic, excited, hyper (*Inf.*), lively, pas~
sionate

phobia aversion, detestation, dislike, dis~
taste, dread, fear, hatred, horror, irrational
fear, loathing, obsession, overwhelming
anxiety, repulsion, revulsion, terror, thing
(*Inf.*)
Antonyms bent, fancy, fondness, inclina~
tion, liking, love, partiality, passion, pen~
chant, soft spot

phone *n.* **1.** blower (*Inf.*), telephone **2.** bell
(*Brit. sl.*), buzz (*Inf.*), call, ring (*Inf., chiefly
Brit.*), tinkle (*Brit. inf.*) ~*v.* **3.** buzz (*Inf.*),
call, get on the blower (*Inf.*), give someone a
bell (*Brit. sl.*), give someone a buzz (*Inf.*),
give someone a call, give someone a ring
(*Inf., chiefly Brit.*), give someone a tinkle
(*Brit. inf.*), make a call, ring (up) (*Inf.,
chiefly Brit.*), telephone

phoney 1. *adj.* affected, assumed, bogus,
counterfeit, ersatz, fake, false, forged, imi~
tation, pseudo (*Inf.*), put-on, sham, spurious,
trick **2.** *n.* counterfeit, fake, faker, forgery,
fraud, humbug, impostor, pretender, pseud
(*Inf.*), sham
Antonyms authentic, bona fide, genuine,
original, real, sincere, unaffected, unas~
sumed, unfeigned

photograph 1. *n.* image, likeness, photo
(*Inf.*), picture, print, shot, slide, snap (*Inf.*),
snapshot, transparency **2.** *v.* capture on
film, film, get a shot of, record, shoot, snap
(*Inf.*), take, take a picture of, take
(someone's) picture

photographic accurate, cinematic, de~
tailed, exact, faithful, filmic, graphic, life~

like, minute, natural, pictorial, precise, re~ alistic, retentive, visual, vivid

phrase 1. *n.* expression, group of words, idiom, locution, motto, remark, saying, tag, utterance, way of speaking **2.** *v.* couch, ex~ press, formulate, frame, present, put, put into words, say, term, utter, voice, word

phraseology choice of words, diction, ex~ pression, idiom, language, parlance, phrase, phrasing, speech, style, syntax, wording

physical 1. bodily, carnal, corporal, corpo~ real, earthly, fleshly, incarnate, mortal, so~ matic, unspiritual **2.** material, natural, pal~ pable, real, sensible, solid, substantial, tan~ gible, visible

physician doc (*Inf.*), doctor, doctor of medi~ cine, general practitioner, G.P., healer, M.D., medic (*Inf.*), medical practitioner, medico (*Inf.*), sawbones (*Sl.*), specialist

physique body, build, constitution, figure, form, frame, make-up, shape, structure

pick *v.* **1.** choose, decide upon, elect, fix upon, hand-pick, mark out, opt for, select, settle upon, sift out, single out, sort out **2.** collect, cull, cut, gather, harvest, pluck, pull **3.** have no appetite, nibble, peck at, play *or* toy with, push the food round the plate **4.** foment, incite, instigate, provoke, start **5.** break into, break open, crack, force, jemmy, open, prise open **6. pick one's way** be tentative, find *or* make one's way, move cautiously, tread carefully, work through ~*n.* **7.** choice, choosing, decision, option, preference, selection **8.** choicest, *crème de la crème*, elect, elite, flower, pride, prize, the best, the cream, the tops (*Sl.*)
Antonyms (*sense 1*) cast aside, decline, dis~ card, dismiss, reject, spurn, turn down

picket *n.* **1.** pale, paling, palisade, peg, post, stake, stanchion, upright **2.** demonstrator, flying picket, picketer, protester **3.** guard, lookout, patrol, scout, sentinel, sentry, spotter, vedette (*Military*), watch ~*v.* **4.** blockade, boycott, demonstrate **5.** corral (*U.S.*), enclose, fence, hedge in, palisade, pen in, rail in, shut in, wall in

pickle *n.* **1.** *Inf.* bind (*Inf.*), difficulty, dilem~ ma, fix (*Inf.*), hot water (*Inf.*), jam (*Inf.*), predicament, quandary, scrape (*Inf.*), spot (*Inf.*), tight spot **2.** *Brit. inf.* little horror, mischief, mischief maker, monkey, naughty child, rascal ~*v.* **3.** cure, keep, marinade, preserve, steep

pick-me-up bracer (*Inf.*), drink, pick-up (*Sl.*), refreshment, restorative, roborant, shot in the arm (*Inf.*), stimulant, tonic

pick on badger, bait, blame, bully, goad, hector, tease, torment

pick out 1. choose, cull, hand-pick, select, separate the sheep from the goats, single

out, sort out **2.** discriminate, distinguish, make distinct, make out, notice, perceive, recognize, tell apart

pick-up *n.* **1.** acceleration, response, rev~ ving (*Inf.*), speed-up **2.** change for the bet~ ter, gain, improvement, rally, recovery, re~ vival, rise, strengthening, upswing, upturn

pick up *v.* **1.** gather, grasp, hoist, lift, raise, take up, uplift **2.** buy, come across, find, garner, happen upon, obtain, purchase, score (*Sl.*) **3.** gain, gain ground, get better, improve, make a comeback (*Inf.*), mend, perk up, rally, recover, take a turn for the better **4.** call for, collect, get, give someone a lift, go to get, uplift (*Scot.*) **5.** acquire, get the hang of (*Inf.*), learn, master **6.** *Sl.* ap~ prehend, arrest, bust (*Inf.*), collar (*Inf.*), do (*Sl.*), feel one's collar (*Sl.*), lift (*Sl.*), nab (*Inf.*), nail (*Inf.*), nick (*Sl., chiefly Brit.*), pinch (*Inf.*), pull in (*Brit. sl.*), run in (*Sl.*), take into custody

picnic 1. excursion, *fête champêtre*, outdoor meal, outing **2.** *Inf.* breeze (*U.S. & Canad. inf.*), cakewalk (*Inf.*), child's play (*Inf.*), cinch (*Sl.*), duck soup (*U.S. sl.*), piece of cake (*Brit. inf.*), pushover (*Sl.*), snap (*Inf.*), walkover (*Inf.*)

pictorial expressive, graphic, illustrated, picturesque, representational, scenic, strik~ ing, vivid

picture *n.* **1.** delineation, drawing, effigy, engraving, illustration, image, likeness, painting, photograph, portrait, portrayal, print, representation, similitude, sketch **2.** account, depiction, description, image, im~ pression, re-creation, report **3.** carbon copy, copy, dead ringer (*Sl.*), double, duplicate, image, likeness, living image, lookalike, replica, ringer (*Sl.*), spit (*Inf., chiefly Brit.*), spit and image (*Inf.*), spitting image (*Inf.*), twin **4.** archetype, embodiment, epitome, essence, living example, perfect example, personification **5.** film, flick (*Sl.*), motion picture, movie (*U.S. inf.*) ~*v.* **6.** conceive of, envision, image, see, see in the mind's eye, visualize **7.** delineate, depict, describe, draw, illustrate, paint, photograph, portray, render, represent, show, sketch

picturesque attractive, beautiful, charm~ ing, colourful, graphic, pretty, quaint, sce~ nic, striking, vivid
Antonyms commonplace, drab, dull, every~ day, inartistic, unattractive, uninteresting

piddling chickenshit (*U.S. sl.*), crappy (*Sl.*), derisory, fiddling, insignificant, little, mea~ sly (*Inf.*), Mickey Mouse (*Sl.*), nickel-and-dime (*U.S. sl.*), paltry, petty, piffling, poxy (*Sl.*), puny, trifling, trivial, unimportant, useless, worthless
Antonyms considerable, important, major,

significant, sizable, substantial, tidy (*Inf.*), useful, valuable

piebald black and white, brindled, dappled, flecked, mottled, pied, speckled, spotted

piece *n.* **1.** allotment, bit, chunk, division, fraction, fragment, length, morsel, mouth~ ful, part, portion, quantity, scrap, section, segment, share, shred, slice **2.** case, exam~ ple, instance, occurrence, sample, specimen, stroke **3.** article, bit (*Inf.*), composition, creation, item, production, study, work, work of art **4. go to pieces** break down, crack up (*Inf.*), crumple, disintegrate, fall apart, lose control, lose one's head **5. in pieces** broken, bust (*Inf.*), damaged, disin~ tegrated, in bits, in smithereens, ruined, shattered, smashed **6. of a piece** alike, analogous, consistent, identical, of the same kind, similar, the same, uniform ~*v.* **7.** *Of~ ten with* **together** assemble, compose, fix, join, mend, patch, repair, restore, unite

pièce de résistance *chef-d'oeuvre*, jewel, masterpiece, masterwork, showpiece

piecemeal **1.** *adv.* at intervals, bit by bit, by degrees, by fits and starts, fitfully, inter~ mittently, little by little, partially, slowly **2.** *adj.* fragmentary, intermittent, interrupted, partial, patchy, spotty, unsystematic

pied dappled, flecked, irregular, motley, mottled, multicoloured, parti-coloured, pie~ bald, spotted, streaked, varicoloured, varie~ gated

pier *n.* **1.** jetty, landing place, promenade, quay, wharf **2.** buttress, column, pile, pil~ ing, pillar, post, support, upright

pierce **1.** bore, drill, enter, impale, pen~ etrate, perforate, prick, probe, puncture, run through, spike, stab, stick into, transfix **2.** comprehend, discern, discover, fathom, grasp, realize, see, understand **3.** *Fig.* af~ fect, cut, cut to the quick, excite, hurt, move, pain, rouse, sting, stir, strike, thrill, touch, wound

piercing **1.** *Usually of sound* ear-splitting, high-pitched, loud, penetrating, sharp, shattering, shrill **2.** alert, aware, keen, penetrating, perceptive, perspicacious, probing, quick-witted, searching, sharp, shrewd **3.** *Usually of weather* arctic, biting, bitter, cold, freezing, frosty, keen, nipping, nippy, numbing, raw, wintry **4.** acute, ago~ nizing, excruciating, exquisite, fierce, in~ tense, painful, powerful, racking, severe, sharp, shooting, stabbing

Antonyms (*sense 1*) inaudible, low, low-pitched, mellifluous, quiet, soundless (*sense 2*) obtuse, slow, slow-witted, thick, unperceptive

piety devotion, devoutness, dutifulness, duty, faith, godliness, grace, holiness, pi~ ousness, religion, reverence, sanctity, ven~ eration

pig **1.** boar, grunter, hog, piggy, piglet, porker, shoat, sow, swine **2.** *Inf.* animal, beast, boor, brute, glutton, greedy guts (*Sl.*), guzzler, hog (*Inf.*), slob (*Sl.*), sloven, swine

pigeon **1.** bird, culver (*Archaic*), cushat, dove, squab **2.** *Sl.* dupe, fall guy (*Inf.*), gull (*Archaic*), mug (*Brit. sl.*), sitting duck, sucker (*Sl.*), victim **3.** *Brit. inf.* baby (*Sl.*), business, concern, lookout (*Inf.*), respon~ sibility, worry

pigeonhole *n.* **1.** compartment, cubbyhole, cubicle, locker, niche, place, section **2.** *Inf.* category, class, classification, slot (*Inf.*) ~*v.* **3.** defer, file, postpone, put off, shelve **4.** catalogue, characterize, classify, codify, compartmentalize, label, slot (*Inf.*), sort

pig-headed bull-headed, contrary, cross-grained, dense, froward, inflexible, mulish, obstinate, perverse, self-willed, stiff-necked, stubborn, stupid, unyielding, wilful, wrong-headed

Antonyms agreeable, amiable, complaisant, cooperative, flexible, obliging, open-minded, tractable

pigment colorant, colour, colouring, col~ ouring matter, dye, dyestuff, paint, stain, tincture, tint

pile[1] *n.* **1.** accumulation, assemblage, assort~ ment, collection, heap, hoard, mass, mound, mountain, stack, stockpile **2.** *Inf.* big bucks (*Inf., chiefly U.S.*), big money, bomb (*Brit. sl.*), fortune, megabucks (*U.S. & Canad. sl.*), mint, money, packet (*Sl.*), pot, pretty penny (*Inf.*), tidy sum (*Inf.*), wad (*U.S. & Canad. sl.*), wealth **3.** *Often plural Inf.* a lot, great deal, ocean, oodles (*Inf.*), quantity, stacks **4.** building, edifice, erection, structure ~*v.* **5.** accumulate, amass, assemble, collect, gath~ er, heap, hoard, load up, mass, stack, store **6.** charge, crowd, crush, flock, flood, jam, pack, rush, stream

pile[2] beam, column, foundation, pier, piling, pillar, post, support, upright

pile[3] down, fibre, filament, fur, hair, nap, plush, shag, surface

piles haemorrhoids

pile-up accident, collision, crash, multiple collision, smash, smash-up (*Inf.*)

pilfer appropriate, blag (*Sl.*), cabbage (*Brit. sl.*), embezzle, filch, knock off (*Sl.*), lift (*Inf.*), nick (*Sl., chiefly Brit.*), pinch (*Inf.*), purloin, rifle, rob, snaffle (*Brit. inf.*), snitch (*Sl.*), steal, swipe (*Sl.*), take, thieve, walk off with

pilgrim crusader, hajji, palmer, traveller, wanderer, wayfarer

pilgrimage crusade, excursion, expedition, hajj, journey, mission, tour, trip

pill **1.** bolus, capsule, pellet, pilule, tablet **2. the pill** oral contraceptive **3.** *Sl.* bore, drag

(*Inf.*), nuisance, pain (*Inf.*), pain in the neck (*Inf.*), pest, trial

pillage *v.* **1.** depredate (*Rare*), despoil, free~ boot, loot, maraud, plunder, raid, ransack, ravage, reive (*Dialect*), rifle, rob, sack, spoil (*Archaic*), spoliate, strip ~*n.* **2.** depredation, devastation, marauding, plunder, rapine, robbery, sack, spoliation **3.** booty, loot, plunder, spoils

pillar **1.** column, pier, pilaster, piling, post, prop, shaft, stanchion, support, upright **2.** leader, leading light (*Inf.*), mainstay, rock, supporter, tower of strength, upholder, worthy

pillory *v.* brand, cast a slur on, denounce, expose to ridicule, heap *or* pour scorn on, hold up to shame, lash, show up, stigmatize

pilot **1.** *n.* airman, aviator, captain, conduc~ tor, coxswain, director, flier, guide, helms~ man, leader, navigator, steersman **2.** *v.* conduct, control, direct, drive, fly, guide, handle, lead, manage, navigate, operate, shepherd, steer **3.** *adj.* experimental, model, test, trial

pimple boil, papule (*Pathology*), plook (*Scot.*), pustule, spot, swelling, zit (*Sl.*)

pin *v.* **1.** affix, attach, fasten, fix, join, secure **2.** fix, hold down, hold fast, immobilize, pinion, press, restrain

pinch *v.* **1.** compress, grasp, nip, press, squeeze, tweak **2.** chafe, confine, cramp, crush, hurt, pain **3.** afflict, be stingy, dis~ tress, economize, oppress, pinch pennies, press, scrimp, skimp, spare, stint **4.** *Inf.* blag (*Sl.*), cabbage (*Brit. sl.*), filch, knock off (*Sl.*), lift (*Inf.*), nick (*Sl., chiefly Brit.*), pilfer, purloin, rob, snaffle (*Brit. inf.*), snatch, snitch (*Sl.*), steal, swipe (*Sl.*) **5.** *Inf.* appre~ hend, arrest, bust (*Inf.*), collar (*Inf.*), do (*Sl.*), feel one's collar (*Sl.*), lift (*Sl.*), nab (*Inf.*), nail (*Inf.*), nick (*Sl., chiefly Brit.*), pick up (*Sl.*), pull in (*Brit. sl.*), run in (*Sl.*), take into custody ~*n.* **6.** nip, squeeze, tweak **7.** bit, dash, jot, mite, small quantity, *soupçon*, speck, taste **8.** crisis, difficulty, emergency, exigency, hardship, necessity, oppression, pass, plight, predicament, pressure, strait, stress

Antonyms (*sense 3*) be extravagant, blow (*Sl.*), fritter away, spend like water, squander, waste (*sense 5*) free, let go, let out, release, set free

pinched careworn, drawn, gaunt, haggard, peaky, starved, thin, worn

Antonyms blooming, chubby, fat, glowing, hale and hearty, healthy, plump, radiant, ruddy, well-fed

pin down **1.** compel, constrain, force, make, press, pressurize **2.** designate, deter~ mine, home in on, identify, locate, name, pinpoint, specify **3.** bind, confine, constrain,

fix, hold, hold down, immobilize, nail down, tie down

pine **1.** *Often with* **for** ache, carry a torch for, covet, crave, desire, eat one's heart out over, hanker, hunger for, long, lust after, sigh, thirst for, wish, yearn **2.** decay, de~ cline, droop, dwindle, fade, flag, languish, peak, sicken, sink, waste, weaken, wilt, wither

pinion *v.* bind, chain, confine, fasten, fetter, immobilize, manacle, pin down, shackle, tie

pink¹ **1.** *n.* acme, best, height, peak, perfec~ tion, summit **2.** *adj.* flesh, flushed, reddish, rose, roseate, rosy, salmon

pink² incise, notch, perforate, prick, punch, scallop, score

pinnacle **1.** acme, apex, apogee, crest, crown, eminence, height, meridian, peak, summit, top, vertex, zenith **2.** belfry, cone, needle, obelisk, pyramid, spire, steeple

pinpoint define, distinguish, get a fix on, home in on, identify, locate, spot

pint ale, beer, jar (*Brit. inf.*), jug (*Brit. inf.*)

pint-size diminutive, little, midget, minia~ ture, pocket, pygmy *or* pigmy, small, teensy-weensy, teeny-weeny, tiny, wee

pioneer *n.* **1.** colonist, colonizer, explorer, frontiersman, settler **2.** developer, founder, founding father, innovator, leader, trail~ blazer ~*v.* **3.** create, develop, discover, es~ tablish, initiate, instigate, institute, invent, launch, lay the groundwork, map out, open up, originate, prepare, show the way, start, take the lead

pious **1.** dedicated, devoted, devout, God-fearing, godly, holy, religious, reverent, righteous, saintly, spiritual **2.** goody-goody, holier-than-thou, hypocritical, pietistic, re~ ligiose, sanctimonious, self-righteous, unc~ tuous

Antonyms (*sense 1*) impious, irreligious, ir~ reverent, ungodly, unholy (*sense 2*) humble, meek, sincere

pipe *n.* **1.** conduit, conveyor, duct, hose, line, main, passage, pipeline, tube **2.** briar, clay, meerschaum **3.** fife, horn, tooter, whistle, wind instrument ~*v.* **4.** cheep, peep, play, sing, sound, tootle, trill, tweet, twitter, warble, whistle **5.** bring in, chan~ nel, conduct, convey, siphon, supply, trans~ mit

pipe down belt up (*Sl.*), be quiet, button it (*Sl.*), button one's lip (*Sl.*), hold one's tongue, hush, put a sock in it (*Brit. sl.*), quieten down, shush, shut one's mouth, shut up (*Inf.*), silence

pipe dream castle in the air, chimera, daydream, delusion, dream, fantasy, notion, reverie, vagary

pipeline **1.** conduit, conveyor, duct, line,

passage, pipe, tube **2. in the pipeline** brewing, coming, getting ready, in process, in production, on the way, under way

piquancy 1. bite (*Inf.*), edge, flavour, kick (*Inf.*), pungency, relish, sharpness, spice, spiciness, tang, zest **2.** colour, excitement, interest, pep, pizzazz *or* pizazz (*Inf.*), raci~ness, spirit, vigour, vitality, zip (*Inf.*)

piquant 1. acerb, biting, highly-seasoned, peppery, pungent, savoury, sharp, spicy, stinging, tangy, tart, with a kick (*Inf.*), zesty **2.** interesting, lively, provocative, racy, salty, scintillating, sparkling, spirited, stimulating

Antonyms banal, bland, boring, dull, insip~id, mild, tame, uninteresting

pique *n.* **1.** annoyance, displeasure, grudge, huff, hurt feelings, irritation, miff (*Inf.*), of~fence, resentment, umbrage, vexation, wounded pride ~*v.* **2.** affront, annoy, dis~please, gall, get (*Inf.*), incense, irk, irritate, miff (*Inf.*), mortify, nark (*Brit., Aust., & N.Z. sl.*), nettle, offend, peeve (*Inf.*), pro~voke, put out, put someone's nose out of joint (*Inf.*), rile, sting, vex, wound **3.** arouse, excite, galvanize, goad, kindle, pro~voke, rouse, spur, stimulate, stir, whet **4.** *With* **on** *or* **upon** *Of oneself* congratulate, flatter, plume, preen, pride

piracy buccaneering, freebooting, hijacking, infringement, plagiarism, rapine, robbery at sea, stealing, theft

pirate *n.* **1.** buccaneer, corsair, filibuster, freebooter, marauder, raider, rover, sea robber, sea rover, sea wolf **2.** cribber (*Inf.*), infringer, plagiarist, plagiarizer ~*v.* **3.** ap~propriate, borrow, copy, crib (*Inf.*), lift (*Inf.*), plagiarize, poach, reproduce, steal

pit *n.* **1.** abyss, cavity, chasm, coal mine, crater, dent, depression, dimple, excavation, gulf, hole, hollow, indentation, mine, pock~mark, pothole, trench ~*v.* **2.** *Often with* **against** match, oppose, put in opposition, set against **3.** dent, dint, gouge, hole, in~dent, mark, nick, notch, pockmark, scar

pitch *v.* **1.** bung (*Brit. sl.*), cast, chuck (*Inf.*), fling, heave, hurl, launch, lob (*Inf.*), sling, throw, toss **2.** erect, fix, locate, place, plant, put up, raise, settle, set up, station **3.** flounder, lurch, make heavy weather, plunge, roll, toss, wallow, welter **4.** dive, drop, fall headlong, stagger, topple, tumble ~*n.* **5.** angle, cant, dip, gradient, incline, slope, steepness, tilt **6.** degree, height, highest point, level, point, summit **7.** har~monic, modulation, sound, timbre, tone **8.** line, patter, sales talk, spiel (*Inf.*) **9.** field of play, ground, park (*U.S. & Canad.*), sports field

pitch-black dark, ebony, inky, jet, jet-black, pitch-dark, raven, sable, unlit

pitch in 1. chip in (*Inf.*), contribute, co~operate, do one's bit, help, join in, lend a hand, participate **2.** begin, fall to, get busy, get cracking (*Inf.*), plunge into, set about, set to, tackle

piteous affecting, deplorable, dismal, dis~tressing, doleful, grievous, harrowing, heartbreaking, heart-rending, lamentable, miserable, mournful, moving, pathetic, pitiable, pitiful, plaintive, poignant, sad, sorrowful, woeful, wretched

pitfall 1. banana skin (*Inf.*), catch, danger, difficulty, drawback, hazard, peril, snag, trap **2.** deadfall, downfall, pit, snare, trap

pith 1. core, crux, essence, gist, heart, heart of the matter, kernel, marrow, meat, nub, point, quintessence, salient point, the long and the short of it **2.** consequence, depth, force, import, importance, matter, moment, power, significance, strength, substance, value, weight

pithy brief, cogent, compact, concise, epi~grammatic, expressive, finely honed, force~ful, laconic, meaningful, pointed, short, succinct, terse, to the point, trenchant

Antonyms diffuse, garrulous, long, long-winded, loquacious, prolix, verbose, wordy

pitiful 1. deplorable, distressing, grievous, harrowing, heartbreaking, heart-rending, lamentable, miserable, pathetic, piteous, pitiable, sad, woeful, wretched **2.** abject, base, beggarly, contemptible, despicable, dismal, inadequate, insignificant, low, mean, measly, miserable, paltry, scurvy, shabby, sorry, vile, worthless

Antonyms (*sense 1*) amusing, cheerful, cheering, comical, funny, happy, heartening, laughable, merry (*sense 2*) adequate, admi~rable, honourable, laudable, praiseworthy, significant, valuable

pitiless brutal, callous, cold-blooded, cold-hearted, cruel, hardhearted, harsh, heart~less, implacable, inexorable, inhuman, merciless, relentless, ruthless, uncaring, unfeeling, unmerciful, unsympathetic

Antonyms caring, compassionate, kind, merciful, relenting, responsive, soft-hearted, sparing

pittance allowance, chicken feed (*Sl.*), drop, mite, modicum, peanuts (*Sl.*), portion, ra~tion, slave wages, trifle

pity *n.* **1.** charity, clemency, commiseration, compassion, condolence, fellow feeling, for~bearance, kindness, mercy, quarter, sympa~thy, tenderness, understanding **2.** bummer (*Sl.*), crime (*Inf.*), crying shame, misfortune, regret, sad thing, shame, sin **3. take pity on** feel compassion for, forgive, have mercy on, melt, pardon, put out of one's misery, relent, reprieve, show mercy, spare ~*v.* **4.** bleed for, commiserate with, condole with,

feel for, feel sorry for, grieve for, have compassion for, sympathize with, weep for
Antonyms *(sense 1)* anger, apathy, brutality, cruelty, disdain, fury, hard-heartedness, in~ difference, inhumanity, mercilessness, piti~ lessness, ruthlessness, scorn, severity, un~ concern, wrath

pivot *n.* **1.** axis, axle, fulcrum, spindle, swivel **2.** centre, focal point, heart, hinge, hub, kingpin *~v.* **3.** revolve, rotate, spin, swivel, turn, twirl **4.** be contingent, depend, hang, hinge, rely, revolve round, turn

pixie brownie, elf, fairy, peri, sprite

placard advertisement, *affiche*, bill, poster, public notice, sticker

placate appease, assuage, calm, conciliate, humour, mollify, pacify, propitiate, satisfy, soothe, win over

place *n.* **1.** area, location, locus, point, posi~ tion, site, situation, spot, station, venue, whereabouts **2.** city, district, hamlet, locale, locality, neighbourhood, quarter, region, town, vicinity, village **3.** grade, position, rank, station, status **4.** appointment, berth *(Inf.)*, billet *(Inf.)*, employment, job, posi~ tion, post **5.** abode, apartment, domicile, dwelling, flat, home, house, manor, man~ sion, pad *(Sl.)*, property, residence, seat **6.** accommodation, room, space, stead **7.** af~ fair, charge, concern, duty, function, pre~ rogative, responsibility, right, role **8. in place of** as an alternative to, as a substi~ tute for, in exchange for, in lieu of, instead of, taking the place of **9. put (someone) in his place** bring down, cut down to size, humble, humiliate, make (someone) eat humble pie, make (someone) swallow his pride, mortify, take down a peg *(Inf.)* **10. take place** befall, betide, come about, come to pass *(Archaic)*, go on, happen, occur, transpire *(Inf.)* *~v.* **11.** bung *(Brit. sl.)*, de~ posit, dispose, establish, fix, install, lay, lo~ cate, plant, position, put, rest, set, settle, situate, stand, station, stick *(Inf.)* **12.** ar~ range, class, classify, grade, group, order, rank, sort **13.** associate, identify, know, put one's finger on, recognize, remember, set in context **14.** allocate, appoint, assign, char~ ge, commission, entrust, give

placid calm, collected, composed, cool, eq~ uable, even, even-tempered, gentle, halcyon, imperturbable, mild, peaceful, quiet, self~ possessed, serene, still, tranquil, undis~ turbed, unexcitable, unfazed *(Inf.)*, un~ moved, unruffled, untroubled
Antonyms agitated, disturbed, emotional, excitable, impulsive, passionate, rough, tem~ peramental, tempestuous

plagiarize appropriate, borrow, crib *(Inf.)*, infringe, lift *(Inf.)*, pirate, steal, thieve

plague *n.* **1.** contagion, disease, epidemic, infection, pandemic, pestilence **2.** *Fig.* affliction, bane, blight, calamity, cancer, curse, evil, scourge, torment, trial **3.** *Inf.* aggravation *(Inf.)*, annoyance, bother, has~ sle *(Inf.)*, irritant, nuisance, pain *(Inf.)*, pest, problem, thorn in one's flesh, vexation *~v.* **4.** afflict, annoy, badger, bedevil, be on one's back *(Sl.)*, bother, disturb, fret, get in one's hair *(Inf.)*, get on one's nerves *(Inf.)*, harass, harry, hassle *(Inf.)*, haunt, molest, pain, persecute, pester, tease, torment, tor~ ture, trouble, vex

plain *adj.* **1.** apparent, clear, comprehen~ sible, distinct, evident, legible, lucid, mani~ fest, obvious, patent, transparent, unam~ biguous, understandable, unmistakable, visible **2.** artless, blunt, candid, direct, downright, forthright, frank, guileless, hon~ est, ingenuous, open, outspoken, sincere, straightforward, upfront *(Inf.)* **3.** common, commonplace, everyday, frugal, homely, lowly, modest, ordinary, simple, unaffected, unpretentious, workaday **4.** austere, bare, basic, discreet, modest, muted, pure, re~ strained, severe, simple, Spartan, stark, unadorned, unembellished, unornamented, unpatterned, unvarnished **5.** ill-favoured, no oil painting *(Inf.)*, not beautiful, not striking, ordinary, ugly, unalluring, unat~ tractive, unlovely, unprepossessing **6.** even, flat, level, plane, smooth *~n.* **7.** flatland, grassland, llano, lowland, mesa, open coun~ try, plateau, prairie, steppe, tableland
Antonyms *(sense 1)* ambiguous, complex, concealed, deceptive, difficult, disguised, hid~ den, illegible, incomprehensible, inconspicu~ ous, indiscernible, indistinct, obscure, vague, veiled *(sense 2)* circuitous, indirect, meander~ ing, rambling, roundabout *(sense 3)* affected, distinguished, egotistic, ostentatious, preten~ tious, sophisticated, worldly *(sense 4)* adorned, decorated, fancy, ornate *(sense 5)* attractive, beautiful, comely, good-looking, gorgeous, handsome *(sense 6)* bumpy, not level, uneven

plain-spoken blunt, candid, direct, down~ right, explicit, forthright, frank, open, out~ right, outspoken, straightforward, un~ equivocal, upfront *(Inf.)*
Antonyms diplomatic, discreet, evasive, guarded, indirect, reticent, subtle, tactful, thoughtful

plaintive disconsolate, doleful, grief~ stricken, grievous, heart-rending, melan~ choly, mournful, pathetic, piteous, pitiful, rueful, sad, sorrowful, wistful, woebegone, woeful

plan *n.* **1.** contrivance, design, device, idea, method, plot, procedure, programme, proj~ ect, proposal, proposition, scenario, scheme, strategy, suggestion, system **2.** blueprint, chart, delineation, diagram, drawing, illus~ tration, layout, map, representation, scale drawing, sketch ~v. **3.** arrange, concoct, contrive, design, devise, draft, formulate, frame, invent, organize, outline, plot, pre~ pare, represent, scheme, think out **4.** aim, contemplate, envisage, foresee, intend, mean, propose, purpose

plane n. **1.** flat surface, level surface **2.** condition, degree, footing, level, position, stratum **3.** aeroplane, aircraft, jet ~adj. **4.** even, flat, flush, horizontal, level, plain, regular, smooth, uniform ~v. **5.** glide, sail, skate, skim, volplane

plant n. **1.** bush, flower, herb, shrub, veg~ etable, weed **2.** factory, foundry, mill, shop, works, yard **3.** apparatus, equipment, gear, machinery ~v. **4.** implant, put in the ground, scatter, seed, set out, sow, trans~ plant **5.** establish, fix, found, imbed, insert, institute, lodge, root, set, settle

plaque badge, brooch, cartouch(e), medal, medallion, panel, plate, slab, tablet

plaster n. **1.** gypsum, mortar, plaster of Paris, stucco **2.** adhesive plaster, bandage, dressing, Elastoplast (*Trademark*), sticking plaster ~v. **3.** bedaub, besmear, coat, cover, daub, overlay, smear, spread

plastic adj. **1.** compliant, docile, easily influenced, impressionable, malleable, manageable, pliable, receptive, responsive, tractable **2.** ductile, fictile, flexible, mould~ able, pliable, pliant, soft, supple, tensile **3.** *Sl.* artificial, false, meretricious, phoney or phony (*Inf.*), pseudo (*Inf.*), sham, specious, spurious, superficial, synthetic
Antonyms (*sense 1*) intractable, rebellious, recalcitrant, refractory, unmanageable, un~ receptive (*sense 2*) brittle, hard, inflexible, rigid, stiff, unbending, unyielding (*sense 3*) authentic, genuine, natural, real, sincere, true

plate n. **1.** dish, platter, trencher (*Archaic*) **2.** course, dish, helping, portion, serving **3.** layer, panel, sheet, slab **4.** illustration, lithograph, print ~v. **5.** anodize, coat, cov~ er, electroplate, face, gild, laminate, nickel, overlay, platinize, silver

plateau 1. highland, mesa, table, tableland, upland **2.** level, levelling off, stability, stage

platform 1. dais, podium, rostrum, stage, stand **2.** manifesto, objective(s), party line, policy, principle, programme, tenet(s)

platitude 1. banality, bromide, cliché, commonplace, hackneyed saying, inanity, stereotype, trite remark, truism **2.** banality, dullness, inanity, insipidity, triteness, triviality, vapidity, verbiage

platitudinous banal, clichéd, common~ place, corny (*Sl.*), hack, hackneyed, over~ worked, set, stale, stereotyped, stock, tired, trite, truistic, vapid, well-worn

platoon company, group, outfit (*Inf.*), patrol, squad, squadron, team

platter charger, dish, plate, salver, tray, trencher (*Archaic*)

plaudit *Usually plural* acclaim, acclamation, applause, approbation, approval, clapping, commendation, congratulation, hand, ku~ dos, ovation, praise, round of applause

plausible believable, colourable, conceiv~ able, credible, fair-spoken, glib, likely, per~ suasive, possible, probable, reasonable, smooth, smooth-talking, smooth-tongued, specious, tenable, verisimilar
Antonyms genuine, illogical, implausible, impossible, improbable, inconceivable, in~ credible, real, unbelievable, unlikely

play v. **1.** amuse oneself, caper, engage in games, entertain oneself, fool, frisk, frolic, gambol, have fun, revel, romp, sport, trifle **2.** be in a team, challenge, compete, con~ tend against, participate, rival, take on, take part, vie with **3.** act, act the part of, execute, impersonate, perform, personate, portray, represent, take the part of **4.** bet, chance, gamble, hazard, punt (*Chiefly Brit.*), risk, speculate, take, wager **5. play ball** *Inf.* collaborate, cooperate, go along, play along, reciprocate, respond, show willing **6. play by ear** ad lib, extemporize, improvise, rise to the occasion, take it as it comes **7. play for time** delay, drag one's feet (*Inf.*), filibuster, hang fire, procrastinate, stall, temporize **8. play the fool** act the goat (*Inf.*), clown, clown around, horse around (*Inf.*), lark (about) (*Inf.*), mess about, mon~ key around, skylark (*Inf.*) **9. play the game** *Inf.* conform, follow the rules, go along with, keep in step, play by the rules, play fair, toe the line ~n. **10.** comedy, dra~ ma, dramatic piece, entertainment, farce, masque, performance, piece, radio play, show, soap opera, stage show, television drama, tragedy **11.** amusement, caper, di~ version, entertainment, frolic, fun, gambol, game, jest, pastime, prank, recreation, romp, sport **12.** gambling, gaming **13.** ac~ tion, activity, elbowroom, exercise, give (*Inf.*), latitude, leeway, margin, motion, movement, operation, range, room, scope, space, sweep, swing **14.** action, activity, employment, function, operation, transac~ tion, working **15.** foolery, fun, humour, jest, joking, lark (*Inf.*), prank, sport, teasing

play around dally, fool around, mess around, philander, take lightly, trifle, wom~ anize

playboy gay dog, ladies' man, lady-killer (*Inf.*), lover boy (*Sl.*), man about town, phi~ landerer, pleasure seeker, rake, roué, so~ cialite, womanizer

play down gloss over, make light of, make

little of, minimize, set no store by, soft-pedal (*Inf.*), underplay, underrate

player 1. competitor, contestant, partici-pant, sportsman, sportswoman, team mem-ber **2.** actor, actress, entertainer, perform-er, Thespian, trouper **3.** artist, instrumen-talist, musician, music maker, performer, virtuoso

playful 1. cheerful, coltish, frisky, frolic-some, gay, impish, joyous, kittenish, larkish (*Inf.*), lively, merry, mischievous, puckish, rollicking, spirited, sportive, sprightly, vi-vacious **2.** arch, coy, flirtatious, good-natured, humorous, jesting, jokey, joking, roguish, teasing, tongue-in-cheek, waggish
Antonyms despondent, gloomy, grave, mo-rose, sedate, serious

playmate chum (*Inf.*), companion, comrade, friend, neighbour, pal (*Inf.*), playfellow

play on *or* **upon** abuse, capitalize on, ex-ploit, impose on, milk, profit by, take ad-vantage of, trade on, turn to account, utilize

plaything amusement, bauble, game, gew-gaw, gimcrack, pastime, toy, trifle, trinket

play up 1. accentuate, bring to the fore, call attention to, emphasize, highlight, magnify, point up, stress, turn the spotlight on, underline **2.** *Brit. inf.* be painful, be sore, bother, give one gyp (*Brit. & N.Z. sl.*), give one trouble, hurt, pain, trouble **3.** *Brit. inf.* be awkward, be bolshie (*Brit. inf.*), be cuss-ed (*Inf.*), be disobedient, be stroppy (*Brit. sl.*), give trouble, misbehave **4.** *Brit. inf.* be on the blink (*Sl.*), be wonky (*Brit. sl.*), mal-function, not work properly **5. play up to** *Inf.* bootlick (*Inf.*), brown-nose (*Taboo sl.*), butter up, curry favour, fawn, flatter, get in with, ingratiate oneself, kiss (someone's) ass (*U.S. & Canad. taboo sl.*), pander to, suck up to (*Inf.*), toady

play with 1. amuse oneself with, flirt with, string along, toy with, trifle with **2.** fiddle with (*Inf.*), fidget with, fool around, inter-fere with, jiggle, mess about, waggle, wiggle

playwright dramatist, dramaturge, drama-turgist

plea 1. appeal, begging, entreaty, interces-sion, overture, petition, prayer, request, suit, supplication **2.** *Law* action, allegation, cause, suit **3.** apology, claim, defence, ex-cuse, explanation, extenuation, justification, pretext, vindication

plead 1. appeal (to), ask, beg, beseech, crave, entreat, implore, importune, petition, request, solicit, supplicate **2.** adduce, allege, argue, assert, maintain, put forward, use as an excuse

pleasant 1. acceptable, agreeable, amusing, delectable, delightful, enjoyable, fine, grati-fying, lovely, nice, pleasing, pleasurable,

refreshing, satisfying, welcome **2.** affable, agreeable, amiable, charming, cheerful, cheery, congenial, engaging, friendly, gen-ial, good-humoured, likable *or* likeable, nice
Antonyms awful, cold, disagreeable, dis-tasteful, horrible, horrid, impolite, miserable, offensive, repulsive, rude, unfriendly, unlik-able *or* unlikeable, unpleasant

pleasantry badinage, banter, bon mot, good-natured remark, jest, joke, josh (*Sl., chiefly U.S. & Canad.*), quip, sally, witticism

please 1. amuse, charm, cheer, content, de-light, entertain, give pleasure to, gladden, gratify, humour, indulge, rejoice, satisfy, suit, tickle, tickle pink (*Inf.*) **2.** be inclined, choose, desire, like, opt, prefer, see fit, want, will, wish
Antonyms anger, annoy, depress, disgust, displease, dissatisfy, grieve, incense, offend, provoke, sadden, vex

pleased chuffed (*Brit. sl.*), contented, de-lighted, euphoric, glad, gratified, happy, in high spirits, over the moon (*Inf.*), pleased as punch (*Inf.*), rapt, satisfied, thrilled, tickled, tickled pink (*Inf.*)

pleasing agreeable, amiable, amusing, at-tractive, charming, delightful, engaging, enjoyable, entertaining, gratifying, likable *or* likeable, pleasurable, polite, satisfying, winning
Antonyms boring, disagreeable, dull, mo-notonous, rude, unattractive, unlikable *or* unlikeable, unpleasant

pleasure 1. amusement, bliss, comfort, contentment, delectation, delight, diversion, ease, enjoyment, gladness, gratification, happiness, jollies (*Sl.*), joy, recreation, sat-isfaction, solace **2.** choice, command, de-sire, inclination, mind, option, preference, purpose, will, wish
Antonyms abstinence, anger, disinclina-tion, displeasure, duty, labour, misery, neces-sity, obligation, pain, sadness, sorrow, suffer-ing, unhappiness

plebeian 1. *adj.* base, coarse, common, ig-noble, low, lowborn, lower-class, mean, non-U (*Brit. inf.*), proletarian, uncultivated, unrefined, vulgar, working-class **2.** *n.* com-moner, common man, man in the street, peasant, pleb, prole (*Derogatory sl., chiefly Brit.*), proletarian
Antonyms aristocratic, cultivated, high-born, high-class, patrician, polished, refined, upper-class, well-bred

pledge *n.* **1.** assurance, covenant, oath, promise, undertaking, vow, warrant, word, word of honour **2.** bail, bond, collateral, deposit, earnest, gage, guarantee, pawn, se-curity, surety **3.** health, toast ~*v.* **4.** con-tract, engage, give one's oath (word, word of honour), promise, swear, undertake, vouch,

vow **5.** bind, engage, gage (*Archaic*), guar~
antee, mortgage, plight **6.** drink the health
of, drink to, toast

plenteous 1. abundant, ample, bounteous
(*Literary*), bountiful, copious, generous, in~
exhaustible, infinite, lavish, liberal,
overflowing, plentiful, profuse **2.** bumper,
fertile, fruitful, luxuriant, plentiful, produc~
tive, prolific

plentiful 1. abundant, ample, bounteous
(*Literary*), bountiful, complete, copious,
generous, inexhaustible, infinite, lavish,
liberal, overflowing, plenteous, profuse **2.**
bumper, fertile, fruitful, luxuriant, plen~
teous, productive, prolific
Antonyms deficient, inadequate,
insufficient, scant, scarce, skimpy, small,
sparing, sparse

plenty 1. abundance, enough, fund, good
deal, great deal, heap(s) (*Inf.*), lots (*Inf.*),
mass, masses, mine, mountain(s), oodles
(*Inf.*), pile(s) (*Inf.*), plethora, quantities,
quantity, stack(s), store, sufficiency, volume
2. abundance, affluence, copiousness, fertil~
ity, fruitfulness, luxury, opulence, pleni~
tude, plenteousness, plentifulness, profu~
sion, prosperity, wealth

plethora excess, glut, overabundance, pro~
fusion, superabundance, superfluity, surfeit,
surplus
Antonyms dearth, deficiency, lack, scarcity,
shortage, want

pliable 1. bendable, bendy, ductile, flexible,
limber, lithe, malleable, plastic, pliant, sup~
ple, tensile **2.** adaptable, compliant, docile,
easily led, impressionable, influenceable,
manageable, persuadable, pliant, receptive,
responsive, susceptible, tractable, yielding
Antonyms headstrong, inflexible, intrac~
table, obdurate, obstinate, rigid, stiff, stub~
born, unadaptable, unbending, unyielding,
wilful

pliant 1. bendable, bendy, ductile, flexible,
lithe, plastic, pliable, supple, tensile **2.**
adaptable, biddable, compliant, easily led,
impressionable, influenceable, manageable,
persuadable, pliable, susceptible, tractable,
yielding

plight *n.* case, circumstances, condition,
difficulty, dilemma, extremity, hole (*Sl.*),
hot water (*Inf.*), jam (*Inf.*), perplexity, pickle
(*Inf.*), predicament, scrape (*Inf.*), situation,
spot (*Inf.*), state, straits, tight spot, trouble

plod 1. clump, drag, lumber, slog, stomp
(*Inf.*), tramp, tread, trudge **2.** drudge, grind
(*Inf.*), grub, labour, peg away, persevere,
plough through, plug away (*Inf.*), slog, sol~
dier on, toil

plot¹ *n.* **1.** cabal, conspiracy, covin (*Law*),
intrigue, machination, plan, scheme,
stratagem **2.** action, narrative, outline, sce~

nario, story, story line, subject, theme,
thread ~*v.* **3.** cabal, collude, conspire, con~
trive, hatch, intrigue, machinate, manoeu~
vre, plan, scheme **4.** calculate, chart, com~
pute, draft, draw, locate, map, mark, outline
5. brew, conceive, concoct, contrive, cook
up (*Inf.*), design, devise, frame, hatch, im~
agine, lay, project

plot² *n.* allotment, area, ground, lot, parcel,
patch, tract

plough *v.* **1.** break ground, cultivate, dig,
furrow, ridge, till, turn over **2.** *Usually with*
through cut, drive, flounder, forge, plod,
plunge, press, push, stagger, surge, wade **3.**
With **into** bulldoze, career, crash, hurtle,
plunge, shove, smash

pluck¹ *n.* backbone, balls (*Taboo sl.*),
ballsiness (*Taboo sl.*), boldness, bottle (*Brit.
sl.*), bravery, courage, determination, grit,
guts (*Inf.*), hardihood, heart, intrepidity,
mettle, nerve, resolution, spirit, spunk (*Inf.*)

pluck² *v.* **1.** collect, draw, gather, harvest,
pick, pull out *or* off **2.** catch, clutch, jerk,
pull at, snatch, tug, tweak, yank **3.** finger,
pick, plunk, strum, thrum, twang

plucky ballsy (*Taboo sl.*), bold, brave, cou~
rageous, daring, doughty, feisty (*Inf., chiefly
U.S. & Canad.*), game, gritty, gutsy (*Sl.*),
hardy, have-a-go (*Inf.*), heroic, intrepid,
mettlesome, spirited, spunky (*Inf.*), un~
daunted, unflinching, valiant
Antonyms afraid, chicken (*Sl.*), cowardly,
dastardly, dispirited, lifeless, scared, spine~
less, spiritless, timid, weary, yellow (*Inf.*)

plug *n.* **1.** bung, cork, spigot, stopper, stop~
ple **2.** cake, chew, pigtail, quid, twist, wad
3. *Inf.* advert (*Brit. inf.*), advertisement,
good word, hype, mention, publicity, puff,
push ~*v.* **4.** block, bung, choke, close, cork,
cover, fill, pack, seal, stop, stopper, stopple,
stop up, stuff **5.** *Inf.* advertise, build up,
hype, mention, promote, publicize, puff,
push, write up **6.** *Sl.* blow away (*Sl., chiefly
U.S.*), gun down, pick off, pop, pot, put a
bullet in, shoot **7.** *With* **along** *or* **away** *Inf.*
drudge, grind (*Inf.*), labour, peg away, plod,
slog, toil

plum *Fig.* **1.** *n.* bonus, cream, find, pick,
prize, treasure **2.** *adj.* best, choice, first-
class, prize

plumb *n.* **1.** lead, plumb bob, plummet,
weight ~*adv.* **2.** perpendicularly, up and
down, vertically **3.** bang, exactly, precisely,
slap, spot-on (*Brit. inf.*) ~*v.* **4.** delve, ex~
plore, fathom, gauge, go into, measure,
penetrate, probe, search, sound, unravel

plume 1. *n.* aigrette, crest, feather, pinion,
quill **2.** *v.* *With* **on** *or* **upon** congratulate
oneself, pat oneself on the back, pique one~
self, preen oneself, pride oneself

plump *adj.* beefy (*Inf.*), burly, buxom, chub~

by, corpulent, dumpy, fat, fleshy, full, obese, podgy, portly, roly-poly, rotund, round, stout, tubby, well-covered, well-upholstered (*Inf.*)

Antonyms anorexic, bony, emaciated, lanky, lean, scrawny, skinny, slender, slim, sylphlike, thin

plunder 1. *v.* despoil, devastate, loot, pil~ lage, raid, ransack, ravage, rifle, rob, sack, spoil, steal, strip **2.** *n.* booty, ill-gotten gains, loot, pillage, prey, prize, rapine, spoils, swag (*Sl.*)

plunge *v.* **1.** cast, descend, dip, dive, douse, drop, fall, go down, immerse, jump, nose-dive, pitch, plummet, sink, submerge, swoop, throw, tumble **2.** career, charge, dash, hurtle, lurch, rush, tear ~*n.* **3.** de~ scent, dive, drop, fall, immersion, jump, submersion, swoop

plus 1. *prep.* added to, and, coupled with, with, with the addition of **2.** *adj.* added, additional, add-on, extra, positive, sup~ plementary **3.** *n. Inf.* advantage, asset, ben~ efit, bonus, extra, gain, good point, icing on the cake, perk (*Brit. inf.*), surplus

plush costly, de luxe, lavish, luxurious, luxury, opulent, palatial, rich, ritzy (*Sl.*), sumptuous

Antonyms cheap, cheap and nasty, inex~ pensive, ordinary, plain, spartan

plutocrat capitalist, Croesus, Dives, fat cat (*Sl., chiefly U.S.*), magnate, millionaire, moneybags (*Sl.*), rich man, tycoon

ply 1. carry on, exercise, follow, practise, pursue, work at **2.** employ, handle, ma~ nipulate, swing, utilize, wield **3.** assail, be~ set, besiege, bombard, harass, importune, press, urge

poach appropriate, encroach, hunt *or* fish illegally, infringe, intrude, plunder, rob, steal, steal game, trespass

pocket *n.* **1.** bag, compartment, hollow, pouch, receptacle, sack ~*adj.* **2.** abridged, compact, concise, little, miniature, pint-size(d) (*Inf.*), portable, potted (*Inf.*), small ~*v.* **3.** appropriate, cabbage (*Brit. sl.*), filch, help oneself to, lift (*Inf.*), pilfer, purloin, snaffle (*Brit. inf.*), steal, take **4.** accept, bear, brook, endure, put up with (*Inf.*), stomach, swallow, take, tolerate

pod *n./v.* hull, husk, shell, shuck

podgy chubby, chunky, dumpy, fat, fleshy, fubsy (*Archaic or dialect*), plump, roly-poly, rotund, short and fat, squat, stout, stubby, stumpy, tubby

podium dais, platform, rostrum, stage

poem lyric, ode, rhyme, song, sonnet, verse

poet bard, lyricist, maker (*Archaic*), rhymer, versifier

poetic elegiac, lyric, lyrical, metrical, rhythmical, songlike

poetry metrical composition, poems, poesy (*Archaic*), rhyme, rhyming, verse

poignancy 1. emotion, emotionalism, evocativeness, feeling, pathos, piteousness, plaintiveness, sadness, sentiment, tender~ ness **2.** bitterness, intensity, keenness, pi~ quancy, pungency, sharpness

poignant 1. affecting, agonizing, bitter, distressing, harrowing, heartbreaking, heart-rending, intense, moving, painful, pa~ thetic, sad, touching, upsetting **2.** acute, biting, caustic, keen, penetrating, piercing, pointed, sarcastic, severe **3.** acrid, piquant, pungent, sharp, stinging, tangy

point *n.* **1.** dot, full stop, mark, period, speck, stop **2.** location, place, position, site, spot, stage, station **3.** apex, end, nib, prong, sharp end, spike, spur, summit, tine, tip, top **4.** bill, cape, foreland, head, headland, ness (*Archaic*), promontory **5.** circum~ stance, condition, degree, extent, position, stage **6.** instant, juncture, moment, time, very minute **7.** aim, design, end, goal, in~ tent, intention, motive, object, objective, purpose, reason, use, usefulness, utility **8.** burden, core, crux, drift, essence, gist, heart, import, main idea, marrow, matter, meaning, nub, pith, proposition, question, subject, text, theme, thrust **9.** aspect, detail, facet, feature, instance, item, nicety, par~ ticular **10.** aspect, attribute, characteristic, peculiarity, property, quality, respect, side, trait **11.** score, tally, unit **12. beside the point** immaterial, incidental, inconsequen~ tial, irrelevant, not to the purpose, off the subject, out of the way, pointless, unimpor~ tant, without connection **13. to the point** applicable, apposite, appropriate, apropos, apt, brief, fitting, germane, pertinent, pithy, pointed, relevant, short, suitable, terse ~*v.* **14.** bespeak, call attention to, denote, des~ ignate, direct, indicate, show, signify **15.** aim, bring to bear, direct, level, train **16.** barb, edge, sharpen, taper, whet

point-blank 1. *adj.* abrupt, blunt, categori~ cal, direct, downright, explicit, express, plain, straight-from-the-shoulder, unre~ served **2.** *adv.* bluntly, brusquely, candidly, directly, explicitly, forthrightly, frankly, openly, overtly, plainly, straight, straight~ forwardly

pointed 1. acicular, acuminate, acute, barbed, cuspidate, edged, mucronate, sharp **2.** accurate, acute, biting, cutting, incisive, keen, penetrating, pertinent, sharp, telling, trenchant

pointer 1. guide, hand, indicator, needle **2.** advice, caution, hint, information, recom~ mendation, suggestion, tip, warning

pointless absurd, aimless, fruitless, futile, inane, ineffectual, irrelevant, meaningless, nonsensical, senseless, silly, stupid, un~ availing, unproductive, unprofitable, useless, vague, vain, worthless
Antonyms appropriate, beneficial, desir~ able, fitting, fruitful, logical, meaningful, pro~ ductive, profitable, proper, sensible, to the point, useful, worthwhile

point of view 1. angle, orientation, out~ look, perspective, position, standpoint **2.** approach, attitude, belief, judgment, opin~ ion, slant, view, viewpoint, way of looking at it

point out allude to, bring up, call attention to, identify, indicate, mention, remind, re~ veal, show, specify

poise 1. *n.* aplomb, assurance, calmness, composure, cool (*Sl.*), coolness, dignity, el~ egance, equanimity, equilibrium, grace, presence, presence of mind, sang-froid, savoir-faire, self-possession, serenity **2.** *v.* balance, float, hang, hang in midair, hang suspended, hold, hover, position, support, suspend

poised 1. calm, collected, composed, debo~ nair, dignified, graceful, nonchalant, self-confident, self-possessed, serene, suave, to~ gether (*Inf.*), unfazed (*Inf.*), unruffled, urbane **2.** all set, in the wings, on the brink, prepared, ready, standing by, waiting
Antonyms (*sense 1*) agitated, annoyed, dis~ composed, disturbed, excited, irritated, ruffled, worked up

poison *n.* **1.** bane, toxin, venom **2.** bane, blight, cancer, canker, contagion, contami~ nation, corruption, malignancy, miasma, virus ~*v.* **3.** adulterate, contaminate, en~ venom, give (someone) poison, infect, kill, murder, pollute **4.** corrupt, defile, deprave, pervert, subvert, taint, undermine, vitiate, warp ~*adj.* **5.** deadly, lethal, poisonous, toxic, venomous

poisonous 1. baneful (*Archaic*), deadly, fa~ tal, lethal, mephitic, mortal, noxious, toxic, venomous, virulent **2.** baleful, baneful (*Ar~ chaic*), corruptive, evil, malicious, noxious, pernicious, pestiferous, pestilential, vicious

poke *v.* **1.** butt, dig, elbow, hit, jab, nudge, prod, punch, push, shove, stab, stick, thrust **2.** butt in, interfere, intrude, meddle, nose, peek, poke one's nose into (*Inf.*), pry, put one's two cents in (*U.S. sl.*), snoop (*Inf.*), tamper **3. poke fun at** chaff, jeer, make a mock of, make fun of, mock, rib (*Inf.*), ridi~ cule, send up (*Brit. inf.*), take the mickey (*Inf.*), take the piss (out of) (*Taboo sl.*), tease ~*n.* **4.** butt, dig, hit, jab, nudge, prod, punch, thrust

poky confined, cramped, incommodious, narrow, small, tiny

Antonyms capacious, commodious, large, open, roomy, spacious, wide

polar 1. Antarctic, Arctic, cold, extreme, freezing, frozen, furthest, glacial, icy, ter~ minal **2.** beacon-like, cardinal, guiding, leading, pivotal **3.** antagonistic, antipodal, antithetical, contradictory, contrary, dia~ metric, opposed, opposite

polarity ambivalence, contradiction, contrariety, dichotomy, duality, opposition, paradox

pole[1] bar, mast, post, rod, shaft, spar, staff, standard, stick

pole[2] **1.** antipode, extremity, limit, terminus **2. poles apart** at opposite ends of the earth, at opposite extremes, incompatible, irreconcilable, miles apart, widely separat~ ed, worlds apart

police *n.* **1.** boys in blue (*Inf.*), constabulary, fuzz (*Sl.*), law enforcement agency, police force, the law (*Inf.*), the Old Bill (*Sl.*) ~*v.* **2.** control, guard, keep in order, keep the peace, patrol, protect, regulate, watch **3.** *Fig.* check, monitor, observe, oversee, supervise

policeman bobby (*Inf.*), bogey (*Sl.*), consta~ ble, cop (*Sl.*), copper (*Sl.*), flatfoot (*Sl.*), fuzz (*Sl.*), gendarme (*Sl.*), officer, peeler (*Obsolete Brit. sl.*), pig (*Sl.*), rozzer (*Sl.*)

policy 1. action, approach, code, course, custom, guideline, line, plan, practice, pro~ cedure, programme, protocol, rule, scheme, stratagem, theory **2.** discretion, good sense, prudence, sagacity, shrewdness, wisdom

polish *v.* **1.** brighten, buff, burnish, clean, furbish, rub, shine, smooth, wax **2.** brush up, correct, cultivate, emend, enhance, finish, improve, perfect, refine, touch up ~*n.* **3.** brightness, brilliance, finish, glaze, gloss, lustre, sheen, smoothness, sparkle, veneer **4.** varnish, wax **5.** *Fig.* breeding, class (*Inf.*), elegance, finesse, finish, grace, politesse, refinement, style, suavity, urbanity

polished 1. bright, burnished, furbished, glassy, gleaming, glossy, shining, slippery, smooth **2.** *Fig.* civilized, courtly, cultivated, elegant, finished, genteel, polite, refined, sophisticated, urbane, well-bred **3.** accom~ plished, adept, expert, faultless, fine, flawless, impeccable, masterly, outstanding, professional, skilful, superlative
Antonyms (*sense 1*) dark, dull, matt, rough (*sense 2*) inelegant, uncivilized, uncultivated, unrefined, unsophisticated (*sense 3*) amateur~ ish, inept, inexpert, unaccomplished, un~ skilled

polish off 1. consume, down, eat up, finish, put away, shift (*Inf.*), swill, wolf **2.** blow away (*Sl., chiefly U.S.*), bump off (*Inf.*), dis~ pose of, do away with, do in (*Sl.*), eliminate, get rid of, kill, liquidate, murder, take out (*Sl.*)

polite 1. affable, civil, complaisant, courteous, deferential, gracious, mannerly, obliging, respectful, well-behaved, well-mannered **2.** civilized, courtly, cultured, elegant, genteel, polished, refined, urbane, well-bred
Antonyms crude, discourteous, ill-mannered, impertinent, impolite, impudent, insulting, rude, uncultured, unrefined

politic 1. artful, astute, canny, crafty, cunning, designing, ingenious, intriguing, Machiavellian, scheming, shrewd, sly, subtle, unscrupulous **2.** advisable, diplomatic, discreet, expedient, in one's best interests, judicious, prudent, sagacious, sensible, tactful, wise

politician legislator, Member of Parliament, M.P., office bearer, politico (*Inf., chiefly U.S.*), public servant, statesman

politics 1. affairs of state, civics, government, government policy, political science, polity, statecraft, statesmanship **2.** Machiavellianism, machination, power struggle, *Realpolitik*

poll *n.* **1.** figures, returns, tally, vote, voting **2.** ballot, canvass, census, count, Gallup Poll, (public) opinion poll, sampling, survey ~*v.* **3.** register, tally **4.** ballot, canvass, interview, question, sample, survey

pollute 1. adulterate, befoul, contaminate, dirty, foul, infect, make filthy, mar, poison, smirch, soil, spoil, stain, taint **2.** besmirch, corrupt, debase, debauch, defile, deprave, desecrate, dishonour, profane, sully, violate
Antonyms (*sense 1*) clean, cleanse, decontaminate, disinfect, purge, sanitize, sterilize (*sense 2*) esteem, honour

pollution adulteration, contamination, corruption, defilement, dirtying, foulness, impurity, taint, uncleanness, vitiation

pomp 1. ceremony, éclat, flourish, grandeur, magnificence, pageant, pageantry, parade, solemnity, splendour, state **2.** display, grandiosity, ostentation, pomposity, show, vainglory

pomposity 1. affectation, airs, arrogance, flaunting, grandiosity, haughtiness, pompousness, portentousness, presumption, pretension, pretentiousness, self-importance, vainglory, vanity **2.** bombast, fustian, grandiloquence, loftiness, magniloquence, rant, turgidity

pompous 1. affected, arrogant, bloated, grandiose, imperious, magisterial, ostentatious, overbearing, pontifical, portentous, pretentious, puffed up, self-important, showy, supercilious, vainglorious **2.** boastful, bombastic, flatulent, fustian, grandilo-

quent, high-flown, inflated, magniloquent, orotund, overblown, turgid, windy
Antonyms direct, humble, modest, natural, plain-spoken, self-effacing, simple, succinct, unaffected, unpretentious

pond dew pond, duck pond, fish pond, lochan (*Scot.*), millpond, pool, small lake, tarn

ponder brood, cerebrate, cogitate, consider, contemplate, deliberate, examine, excogitate, give thought to, meditate, mull over, muse, puzzle over, reflect, ruminate, study, think, weigh

ponderous 1. bulky, cumbersome, cumbrous, heavy, hefty, huge, massive, unwieldy, weighty **2.** awkward, clumsy, elephantine, graceless, heavy-footed, laborious, lumbering **3.** dreary, dull, heavy, laboured, lifeless, long-winded, pedantic, pedestrian, plodding, prolix, stilted, stodgy, tedious, verbose
Antonyms (*senses 1 & 2*) graceful, handy, light, light-footed, little, small, tiny, weightless

pontificate declaim, dogmatize, expound, hold forth, lay down the law, pontify, preach, pronounce, sound off

pooh-pooh belittle, brush aside, deride, disdain, dismiss, disregard, make little of, play down, scoff, scorn, slight, sneer, sniff at, spurn, turn up one's nose at (*Inf.*)
Antonyms exalt, extol, glorify, praise

pool¹ 1. lake, mere, pond, puddle, splash, tarn **2.** swimming bath, swimming pool

pool² ** *n.* **1. collective, combine, consortium, group, syndicate, team, trust **2.** bank, funds, jackpot, kitty, pot, stakes ~*v.* **3.** amalgamate, combine, join forces, league, merge, put together, share

poor 1. badly off, broke (*Inf.*), destitute, dirt-poor (*Inf.*), down and out, flat broke (*Inf.*), hard up (*Inf.*), impecunious, impoverished, indigent, in need, in want, necessitous, needy, on one's beam-ends, on one's uppers, on the rocks, penniless, penurious, poverty-stricken, short, skint (*Brit. sl.*), stony-broke (*Brit. sl.*), without two pennies to rub together (*Inf.*) **2.** deficient, exiguous, inadequate, incomplete, insufficient, lacking, meagre, measly, miserable, niggardly, pitiable, reduced, scant, scanty, skimpy, slight, sparse, straitened **3.** below par, chickenshit (*U.S. sl.*), crappy (*Sl.*), faulty, feeble, inferior, low-grade, mediocre, pisspoor (*Taboo sl.*), poxy (*Sl.*), rotten (*Inf.*), rubbishy, second-rate, shabby, shoddy, sorry, substandard, unsatisfactory, valueless, weak, worthless **4.** bad, bare, barren, depleted, exhausted, fruitless, impoverished, infertile, sterile, unfruitful, unproductive **5.** hapless, ill-fated, luckless, miserable, pathetic, pitiable, unfortunate, unhappy, un-

lucky, wretched **6.** humble, insignificant, lowly, mean, modest, paltry, plain, trivial
Antonyms (*sense 1*) affluent, comfortable (*Inf.*), prosperous, rich, wealthy, well-heeled (*Inf.*), well-off (*sense 2*) abundant, adequate, ample, complete, dense, plentiful, satisfactory, sufficient, thick (*sense 3*) excellent, exceptional, first-class, first-rate, satisfactory, superior, valuable (*sense 4*) fertile, fruitful, productive, teeming, yielding (*sense 5*) fortunate, happy, lucky, successful

poorly 1. *adv.* badly, crudely, inadequately, incompetently, inexpertly, inferiorly, insufficiently, meanly, shabbily, unsatisfactorily, unsuccessfully **2.** *adj. Inf.* ailing, below par, ill, indisposed, off colour, out of sorts, rotten (*Inf.*), seedy (*Inf.*), sick, under the weather (*Inf.*), unwell
Antonyms (*sense 1*) acceptably, adequately, competently, expertly, satisfactorily, sufficiently, well (*sense 2*) fit, hale and hearty, healthy, in good health, in the pink, well

pop *v.* **1.** bang, burst, crack, explode, go off, report, snap **2.** *Often with* **in, out,** *etc. Inf.* appear, call, come *or* go suddenly, drop in (*Inf.*), leave quickly, nip in (*Brit. inf.*), nip out (*Brit. inf.*), visit **3.** *Esp. of eyes* bulge, protrude, stick out **4.** insert, push, put, shove, slip, stick, thrust, tuck ~*n.* **5.** bang, burst, crack, explosion, noise, report **6.** *Inf.* fizzy drink, lemonade, soda water, soft drink

pope Bishop of Rome, Holy Father, pontiff, Vicar of Christ

populace commonalty, crowd, general public, hoi polloi, inhabitants, Joe (and Eileen) Public (*Sl.*), Joe Six-Pack (*U.S. sl.*), masses, mob, multitude, people, rabble, throng

popular 1. accepted, approved, celebrated, famous, fashionable, favoured, favourite, in, in demand, in favour, liked, sought-after, well-liked **2.** common, conventional, current, general, prevailing, prevalent, public, standard, stock, ubiquitous, universal, widespread
Antonyms (*sense 1*) despised, detested, disliked, hated, loathed, unaccepted, unpopular (*sense 2*) infrequent, rare, uncommon, unusual

popularity acceptance, acclaim, adoration, approval, celebrity, currency, esteem, fame, favour, idolization, lionization, recognition, regard, renown, reputation, repute, vogue

popularize disseminate, familiarize, give currency to, give mass appeal, make available to all, simplify, spread, universalize

popularly commonly, conventionally, customarily, generally, ordinarily, regularly, traditionally, universally, usually, widely

populate colonize, inhabit, live in, occupy, people, settle

population citizenry, community, denizens, folk, inhabitants, natives, people, populace, residents, society

populous crowded, heavily populated, overpopulated, packed, populated, swarming, teeming, thronged

pore[1] *v.* brood, contemplate, dwell on, examine, go over, peruse, ponder, read, scrutinize, study, work over

pore[2] *n.* hole, opening, orifice, outlet, stoma

pornographic blue, dirty, filthy, indecent, lewd, obscene, offensive, prurient, salacious, smutty

pornography dirt, erotica, filth, indecency, obscenity, porn (*Inf.*), porno (*Inf.*), smut

porous absorbent, absorptive, penetrable, permeable, pervious, spongy
Antonyms impenetrable, impermeable, impervious, nonporous

port *Nautical* anchorage, harbour, haven, roads, roadstead, seaport

portable compact, convenient, easily carried, handy, light, lightweight, manageable, movable, portative

portend adumbrate, augur, bespeak, betoken, bode, foreshadow, foretell, foretoken, forewarn, harbinger, herald, indicate, omen, point to, predict, presage, prognosticate, promise, threaten, vaticinate (*Rare*), warn of

portent augury, foreboding, foreshadowing, forewarning, harbinger, indication, omen, premonition, presage, presentiment, prognostic, prognostication, sign, threat, warning

portentous 1. alarming, crucial, fateful, forbidding, important, menacing, minatory, momentous, ominous, significant, sinister, threatening **2.** amazing, astounding, awe-inspiring, extraordinary, miraculous, phenomenal, prodigious, remarkable, wondrous (*Archaic or literary*) **3.** bloated, elephantine, heavy, pompous, ponderous, pontifical, self-important, solemn

porter[1] baggage attendant, bearer, carrier

porter[2] caretaker, concierge, doorman, gatekeeper, janitor

portion *n.* **1.** bit, fraction, fragment, morsel, part, piece, scrap, section, segment **2.** allocation, allotment, allowance, division, lot, measure, parcel, quantity, quota, ration, share **3.** helping, piece, serving **4.** cup, destiny, fate, fortune, lot, luck ~*v.* **5.** allocate, allot, apportion, assign, deal, distribute, divide, divvy up (*Inf.*), dole out, parcel out, partition, share out

portrait 1. image, likeness, painting, photograph, picture, portraiture, representation, sketch **2.** account, characterization, depic~

tion, description, portrayal, profile, thumb~
nail sketch, vignette

portray 1. delineate, depict, draw, figure,
illustrate, limn, paint, picture, render, rep~
resent, sketch **2.** characterize, depict, de~
scribe, paint a mental picture of, put in
words **3.** act the part of, play, represent

portrayal characterization, delineation, de~
piction, description, impersonation, inter~
pretation, performance, picture, rendering,
representation

pose v. **1.** arrange, model, position, sit, sit
for **2.** *Often with* **as** feign, impersonate,
masquerade as, pass oneself off as, pretend
to be, profess to be, sham **3.** affect, attitu~
dinize, posture, put on airs, show off (*Inf.*),
strike an attitude **4.** advance, posit, pres~
ent, propound, put, put forward, set, state,
submit ~n. **5.** attitude, bearing, mien (*Lit~
erary*), position, posture, stance **6.** act, af~
fectation, air, attitudinizing, façade, front,
mannerism, masquerade, posturing, pre~
tence, role

poser brain-teaser (*Inf.*), conundrum, enig~
ma, knotty point, problem, puzzle, question,
riddle, teaser, tough one, vexed question

position n. **1.** area, bearings, locale, local~
ity, location, place, point, post, reference,
site, situation, spot, station, whereabouts **2.**
arrangement, attitude, disposition, pose,
posture, stance **3.** angle, attitude, belief,
opinion, outlook, point of view, slant,
stance, stand, standpoint, view, viewpoint
4. circumstances, condition, pass, plight,
predicament, situation, state, strait(s) **5.**
caste, class, consequence, eminence, impor~
tance, place, prestige, rank, reputation,
standing, station, stature, status **6.** berth
(*Inf.*), billet (*Inf.*), capacity, duty, employ~
ment, function, job, occupation, office,
place, post, role, situation ~v. **7.** arrange,
array, dispose, fix, lay out, locate, place,
put, set, settle, stand, stick (*Inf.*)

positive 1. absolute, actual, affirmative,
categorical, certain, clear, clear-cut, conclu~
sive, concrete, decisive, definite, direct, ex~
plicit, express, firm, incontrovertible, indis~
putable, real, unequivocal, unmistakable **2.**
assured, certain, confident, convinced, sure
3. assertive, cocksure, decided, dogmatic,
emphatic, firm, forceful, opinionated, per~
emptory, resolute, stubborn **4.** beneficial,
constructive, effective, efficacious,
forward-looking, helpful, practical, produc~
tive, progressive, useful **5.** *Inf.* absolute,
complete, consummate, out-and-out, perfect,
rank, thorough, thoroughgoing, unmitigat~
ed, utter

Antonyms (*sense 1*) contestable, disputable,
doubtful, inconclusive, indecisive, indefinite,
uncertain (*sense 2*) not confident, unassured,

uncertain, unconvinced, unsure (*sense 3*)
diffident, open-minded, receptive, retiring,
timid, unassertive, unobtrusive (*sense 4*) con~
servative, detrimental, harmful, impractical,
reactionary, unhelpful, useless

positively absolutely, assuredly, categori~
cally, certainly, definitely, emphatically,
firmly, surely, undeniably, unequivocally,
unmistakably, unquestionably, with cer~
tainty, without qualification

possess 1. be blessed with, be born with,
be endowed with, enjoy, have, have to one's
name, hold, own **2.** acquire, control, domi~
nate, hold, occupy, seize, take over, take
possession of **3.** bewitch, consume, control,
dominate, enchant, fixate, influence, mes~
merize, obsess, put under a spell

possessed bedevilled, berserk, bewitched,
consumed, crazed, cursed, demented, en~
chanted, frenetic, frenzied, hag-ridden,
haunted, maddened, obsessed, raving, under
a spell

possession 1. control, custody, hold, occu~
pancy, occupation, ownership, proprietor~
ship, tenure, title **2.** *Plural* assets, belong~
ings, chattels, effects, estate, goods and
chattels, property, things, wealth **3.** colony,
dominion, protectorate, province, territory

possessive acquisitive, controlling, covet~
ous, dominating, domineering, grasping,
jealous, overprotective, selfish

possibility 1. feasibility, likelihood, plau~
sibility, potentiality, practicability, work~
ableness **2.** chance, hazard, hope, liability,
likelihood, odds, probability, prospect, risk
3. *Often plural* capabilities, potential, po~
tentiality, promise, prospects, talent

possible 1. conceivable, credible, hypo~
thetical, imaginable, likely, potential **2.** at~
tainable, doable, feasible, on (*Inf.*), practi~
cable, realizable, viable, within reach,
workable **3.** hopeful, likely, potential, prob~
able, promising

Antonyms impossible, impracticable, im~
probable, inconceivable, incredible, unfea~
sible, unimaginable, unlikely, unobtainable,
unreasonable, unthinkable

possibly 1. God willing, haply (*Archaic*),
maybe, mayhap (*Archaic*), peradventure
(*Archaic*), perchance (*Archaic*), perhaps **2.**
at all, by any chance, by any means, in any
way

post[1] **1.** n. column, newel, pale, palisade,
picket, pillar, pole, shaft, stake, standard,
stock, support, upright **2.** v. advertise, affix,
announce, display, make known, pin up,
proclaim, promulgate, publicize, publish,
put up, stick up

post[2] n. **1.** appointment, assignment, berth
(*Inf.*), billet (*Inf.*), employment, job, office,
place, position, situation **2.** beat, place, po~

sition, station ~*v.* **3.** assign, establish, lo~ cate, place, position, put, situate, station

post³ *n.* **1.** collection, delivery, mail, postal service ~*v.* **2.** dispatch, mail, send, trans~ mit **3.** advise, brief, fill in on (*Inf.*), inform, notify, report to

poster advertisement, *affiche,* announce~ ment, bill, notice, placard, public notice, sticker

posterity 1. children, descendants, family, heirs, issue, offspring, progeny, scions, seed (*Chiefly biblical*) **2.** future, future genera~ tions, succeeding generations

postmortem *n.* analysis, autopsy, dissec~ tion, examination, necropsy

postpone adjourn, defer, delay, hold over, put back, put off, put on the back burner (*Inf.*), shelve, suspend, table, take a rain check on (*U.S. & Canad. inf.*) **Antonyms** advance, bring forward, call to order, carry out, go ahead with

postponement adjournment, deferment, deferral, delay, moratorium, respite, stay, suspension

postscript addition, afterthought, after~ word, appendix, P.S., supplement

postulate advance, assume, hypothesize, posit, predicate, presuppose, propose, put forward, suppose, take for granted, theorize

posture *n.* **1.** attitude, bearing, carriage, disposition, mien (*Literary*), pose, position, set, stance **2.** circumstance, condition, mode, phase, position, situation, state **3.** attitude, disposition, feeling, frame of mind, inclination, mood, outlook, point of view, stance, standpoint ~*v.* **4.** affect, attitudi~ nize, do for effect, hot-dog (*Chiefly U.S.*), make a show, pose, put on airs, show off (*Inf.*), try to attract attention

potency authority, capacity, control, effec~ tiveness, efficacy, energy, force, influence, might, muscle, potential, power, puissance, strength, sway, vigour

potent 1. efficacious, forceful, mighty, pow~ erful, puissant, strong, vigorous **2.** cogent, compelling, convincing, effective, forceful, impressive, persuasive, telling **3.** authori~ tative, commanding, dominant, dynamic, influential, powerful **Antonyms** impotent, ineffective, uncon~ vincing, weak

potentate emperor, king, mogul, monarch, overlord, prince, ruler, sovereign

potential 1. *adj.* budding, dormant, embry~ onic, future, hidden, inherent, latent, likely, possible, promising, undeveloped, unreal~ ized **2.** *n.* ability, aptitude, capability, ca~ pacity, possibility, potentiality, power, the makings, what it takes (*Inf.*), wherewithal

potion brew, concoction, cup, dose, draught, elixir, mixture, philtre, tonic

potter dabble, fiddle (*Inf.*), footle (*Inf.*), frib~ ble, fritter, mess about, poke along, tinker

pottery ceramics, earthenware, stoneware, terra cotta

pouch bag, container, pocket, poke (*Dialect*), purse, sack

pounce 1. *v.* ambush, attack, bound onto, dash at, drop, fall upon, jump, leap at, snatch, spring, strike, swoop, take by sur~ prise, take unawares **2.** *n.* assault, attack, bound, jump, leap, spring, swoop

pound¹ 1. batter, beat, belabour, clobber (*Sl.*), hammer, pelt, pummel, strike, thrash, thump **2.** bray (*Dialect*), bruise, comminute, crush, powder, pulverize, triturate **3.** din into, drub into, drum into, hammer into **4.** *With* **out** bang, beat, hammer, thump **5.** clomp, march, stomp (*Inf.*), thunder, tramp **6.** beat, palpitate, pitapat, pulsate, pulse, throb

pound² *n.* compound, enclosure, pen, yard

pour 1. decant, let flow, spill, splash **2.** course, emit, flow, gush, run, rush, spew, spout, stream **3.** bucket down (*Inf.*), come down in torrents, pelt (down), rain, rain cats and dogs (*Inf.*), rain hard *or* heavily, sheet, teem **4.** crowd, stream, swarm, teem, throng

pout 1. *v.* glower, look petulant, look sullen, lour *or* lower, make a *moue,* mope, pull a long face, purse one's lips, sulk, turn down the corners of one's mouth **2.** *n.* glower, long face, *moue,* sullen look

poverty 1. beggary, destitution, distress, hand-to-mouth existence, hardship, indi~ gence, insolvency, necessitousness, neces~ sity, need, pauperism, pennilessness, penu~ ry, privation, want **2.** dearth, deficiency, insufficiency, lack, paucity, scarcity, short~ age **3.** aridity, bareness, barrenness, deficiency, infertility, meagreness, poor~ ness, sterility, unfruitfulness **Antonyms** (*sense 1*) affluence, comfort, luxury, opulence, richness, wealth (*sense 2*) abundance, plethora, sufficiency (*sense 3*) fe~ cundity, fertility, fruitfulness, productiveness

poverty-stricken bankrupt, beggared, broke (*Inf.*), destitute, dirt-poor (*Inf.*), dis~ tressed, down and out, flat broke (*Inf.*), im~ pecunious, impoverished, indigent, needy, on one's beam-ends, on one's uppers, pen~ niless, penurious, poor, short, skint (*Brit. sl.*), stony-broke (*Brit. sl.*), without two pen~ nies to rub together (*Inf.*)

powder *n.* **1.** dust, fine grains, loose parti~ cles, pounce, talc ~*v.* **2.** crush, granulate, grind, pestle, pound, pulverize **3.** cover, dredge, dust, scatter, sprinkle, strew

powdery chalky, crumbling, crumbly, dry, dusty, fine, friable, grainy, granular, loose, pulverized, sandy

power 1. ability, capability, capacity, com~ petence, competency, faculty, potential **2.** brawn, energy, force, forcefulness, inten~ sity, might, muscle, potency, strength, vig~ our, weight **3.** ascendancy, authority, bot~ tom, command, control, dominance, domi~ nation, dominion, influence, mastery, rule, sovereignty, supremacy, sway **4.** authority, authorization, licence, prerogative, privi~ lege, right, warrant
Antonyms (*sense 1*) inability, incapability, incapacity, incompetence (*sense 2*) enerva~ tion, feebleness, impotence, listlessness, weakness

powerful 1. energetic, mighty, potent, ro~ bust, stalwart, strapping, strong, sturdy, vigorous **2.** authoritative, commanding, controlling, dominant, influential, prevail~ ing, puissant, sovereign, supreme **3.** cogent, compelling, convincing, effective, effectual, forceful, forcible, impressive, persuasive, striking, telling, weighty

powerfully forcefully, forcibly, hard, mightily, strongly, vigorously, with might and main

powerless 1. debilitated, disabled, etiolat~ ed, feeble, frail, helpless, impotent, inca~ pable, incapacitated, ineffectual, infirm, paralysed, prostrate, weak **2.** defenceless, dependent, disenfranchised, disfranchised, ineffective, subject, tied, unarmed, vulner~ able
Antonyms (*sense 1*) able-bodied, fit, healthy, lusty, powerful, robust, strong, sturdy

practicability advantage, feasibility, oper~ ability, possibility, practicality, use, usefulness, value, viability, workability

practicable achievable, attainable, doable, feasible, performable, possible, viable, within the realm of possibility, workable
Antonyms beyond the bounds of possibility, impossible, out of the question, unachievable, unattainable, unfeasible, unworkable

practical 1. applied, efficient, empirical, experimental, factual, functional, pragmatic, realistic, utilitarian **2.** businesslike, down-to-earth, everyday, hard-headed, matter-of-fact, mundane, ordinary, realistic, sensible, workaday **3.** doable, feasible, practicable, serviceable, sound, useful, workable **4.** ac~ complished, efficient, experienced, proficient, qualified, seasoned, skilled, trained, veteran, working
Antonyms (*senses 1, 2, & 3*) impossible, im~ practicable, impractical, inefficient, specula~ tive, theoretical, unpractical, unrealistic, un~ sound, unworkable, useless (*sense 4*)

inefficient, inexperienced, unaccomplished, unqualified, unskilled, untrained

practically 1. all but, almost, basically, close to, essentially, fundamentally, in ef~ fect, just about, nearly, to all intents and purposes, very nearly, virtually, well-nigh **2.** clearly, matter-of-factly, rationally, real~ istically, reasonably, sensibly, unsentimen~ tally, with common sense

practice 1. custom, habit, method, mode, praxis, routine, rule, system, tradition, usage, use, usual procedure, way, wont **2.** discipline, drill, exercise, preparation, re~ hearsal, repetition, study, training, work~ out **3.** action, application, effect, exercise, experience, operation, use **4.** business, ca~ reer, profession, vocation, work

practise 1. discipline, drill, exercise, go over, go through, polish, prepare, rehearse, repeat, study, train, warm up, work out **2.** apply, carry out, do, follow, live up to, ob~ serve, perform, put into practice **3.** carry on, engage in, ply, pursue, specialize in, undertake, work at

practised able, accomplished, experienced, expert, proficient, qualified, seasoned, skilled, trained, versed
Antonyms amateurish, bungling, incompe~ tent, inexperienced, inexpert, unqualified, unskilled, untrained

pragmatic businesslike, down-to-earth, efficient, hard-headed, matter-of-fact, prac~ tical, realistic, sensible, utilitarian
Antonyms airy-fairy, idealistic, impracti~ cal, inefficient, starry-eyed, stupid, theoreti~ cal, unprofessional, unrealistic

praise *n.* **1.** acclaim, acclamation, accolade, applause, approbation, approval, cheering, commendation, compliment, congratulation, encomium, eulogy, good word, kudos, lau~ dation, ovation, panegyric, plaudit, tribute **2.** adoration, devotion, glory, homage, thanks, worship ~*v.* **3.** acclaim, admire, applaud, approve, cheer, compliment, con~ gratulate, crack up (*Inf.*), cry up, eulogize, extol, honour, laud, pay tribute to, sing the praises of **4.** adore, bless, exalt, give thanks to, glorify, magnify (*Archaic*), pay homage to, worship

praiseworthy admirable, commendable, creditable, estimable, excellent, exemplary, fine, honourable, laudable, meritorious, worthy
Antonyms condemnable, deplorable, des~ picable, discreditable, disgraceful, dishon~ ourable, ignoble, reprehensible

prance 1. bound, caper, cavort, dance, frisk, gambol, jump, leap, romp, skip, spring, trip **2.** parade, show off (*Inf.*), stalk, strut, swagger, swank (*Inf.*)

prank antic, caper, escapade, frolic, jape,

lark (*Inf.*), practical joke, skylarking (*Inf.*), trick

prattle babble, blather, blether, chatter, clack, drivel, gabble, jabber, patter, rabbit (on) (*Brit. inf.*), rattle on, run off at the mouth (*Sl.*), run on, twitter, waffle (*Inf., chiefly Brit.*), witter (*Inf.*)

pray 1. offer a prayer, recite the rosary, say one's prayers **2.** adjure, ask, beg, beseech, call upon, crave, cry for, entreat, implore, importune, invoke, petition, plead, request, solicit, sue, supplicate, urge

prayer 1. communion, devotion, invocation, litany, orison, supplication **2.** appeal, entreaty, petition, plea, request, suit, supplication

preach 1. address, deliver a sermon, evangelize, exhort, orate **2.** admonish, advocate, exhort, harangue, lecture, moralize, sermonize, urge

preacher clergyman, evangelist, minister, missionary, parson, revivalist

preamble exordium, foreword, introduction, opening move, opening statement *or* remarks, overture, preface, prelude, proem, prolegomenon

precarious chancy (*Inf.*), dangerous, dicey (*Inf., chiefly Brit.*), dodgy (*Brit., Aust., & N.Z. inf.*), doubtful, dubious, hairy (*Sl.*), hazardous, insecure, perilous, risky, shaky, slippery, touch and go, tricky, uncertain, unreliable, unsafe, unsettled, unstable, unsteady, unsure
Antonyms certain, dependable, reliable, safe, secure, stable, steady

precaution 1. insurance, preventative measure, protection, provision, safeguard, safety measure **2.** anticipation, care, caution, circumspection, foresight, forethought, providence, prudence, wariness

precede antecede, antedate, come first, forerun, go ahead of, go before, head, herald, introduce, lead, pave the way, preface, take precedence, usher

precedence antecedence, lead, preeminence, preference, primacy, priority, rank, seniority, superiority, supremacy

precedent *n.* antecedent, authority, criterion, example, exemplar, instance, model, paradigm, pattern, previous example, prototype, standard

preceding above, aforementioned, aforesaid, anterior, earlier, foregoing, former, past, previous, prior

precept 1. behest, canon, command, commandment, decree, dictum, direction, instruction, law, mandate, order, ordinance, principle, regulation, rule, statute **2.** axiom, byword, dictum, guideline, maxim, motto, principle, rule, saying

precinct 1. bound, boundary, confine, enclosure, limit **2.** area, district, quarter, section, sector, zone

precincts borders, bounds, confines, district, environs, limits, milieu, neighbourhood, purlieus, region, surrounding area

precious 1. adored, beloved, cherished, darling, dear, dearest, favourite, idolized, loved, prized, treasured, valued **2.** choice, costly, dear, expensive, exquisite, fine, high-priced, inestimable, invaluable, priceless, prized, rare, recherché, valuable **3.** affected, alembicated, artificial, chichi, fastidious, overnice, overrefined, twee (*Brit. inf.*)

precipice bluff, brink, cliff, cliff face, crag, height, rock face, sheer drop, steep

precipitate *v.* **1.** accelerate, advance, bring on, dispatch, expedite, further, hasten, hurry, press, push forward, quicken, speed up, trigger **2.** cast, discharge, fling, hurl, launch, let fly, send forth, throw ~*adj.* **3.** breakneck, headlong, plunging, rapid, rushing, swift, violent **4.** frantic, harum-scarum, hasty, heedless, hurried, ill-advised, impetuous, impulsive, indiscreet, madcap, precipitous, rash, reckless **5.** abrupt, brief, quick, sudden, unexpected, without warning

precipitous 1. abrupt, dizzy, falling sharply, high, perpendicular, sheer, steep **2.** abrupt, careless, harum-scarum, hasty, heedless, hurried, ill-advised, precipitate, rash, reckless, sudden

précis 1. *n.* abridgment, abstract, *aperçu*, compendium, condensation, digest, outline, résumé, rundown, sketch, summary, synopsis **2.** *v.* abridge, abstract, compress, condense, outline, shorten, summarize, sum up

precise 1. absolute, accurate, actual, clear-cut, correct, definite, exact, explicit, express, fixed, literal, particular, specific, strict, unequivocal **2.** careful, ceremonious, exact, fastidious, finicky, formal, inflexible, meticulous, nice, particular, prim, punctilious, puritanical, rigid, scrupulous, stiff, strict
Antonyms (*sense 1*) ambiguous, careless, equivocal, incorrect, indefinite, indistinct, inexact, loose, vague (*sense 2*) flexible, haphazard, inexact, informal, relaxed, unceremonious

precisely absolutely, accurately, bang, correctly, exactly, just, just so, literally, neither more nor less, plumb (*Inf.*), slap (*Inf.*), smack (*Inf.*), square, squarely, strictly

precision accuracy, care, correctness, definiteness, exactitude, exactness, fidelity, meticulousness, nicety, particularity, preciseness, rigour

preclude check, debar, exclude, forestall,

hinder, inhibit, make impossible, make im~ practicable, obviate, prevent, prohibit, put a stop to, restrain, rule out, stop

precocious advanced, ahead, bright, devel~ oped, forward, quick, smart
Antonyms backward, dense, dull, retarded, slow, underdeveloped, unresponsive

preconception bias, notion, preconceived idea *or* notion, predisposition, prejudice, prepossession, presumption, presupposition

precondition essential, must, necessity, prerequisite, requirement, *sine qua non*

precursor 1. forerunner, harbinger, herald, messenger, usher, vanguard **2.** antecedent, forebear, forerunner, originator, pioneer, predecessor

precursory antecedent, introductory, pre~ ceding, prefatory, preliminary, preparatory, previous, prior

predatory 1. carnivorous, hunting, preda~ cious, rapacious, raptorial, ravening **2.** de~ spoiling, greedy, marauding, pillaging, plundering, rapacious, ravaging, thieving, voracious, vulturine, vulturous

predecessor 1. antecedent, forerunner, precursor, previous (former, prior) job holder **2.** ancestor, antecedent, forebear, forefather

predestination destiny, doom, election (*Theology*), fate, foreordainment, foreordi~ nation, lot, necessity, predetermination

predestine doom, fate, foreordain, mean, predestinate, predetermine, pre-elect, pre~ ordain

predetermined agreed, arranged in ad~ vance, cut and dried (*Inf.*), decided before~ hand, fixed, prearranged, preplanned, set, settled, set up

predicament corner, dilemma, emergency, fix (*Inf.*), hole (*Sl.*), hot water (*Inf.*), jam (*Inf.*), mess, pickle (*Inf.*), pinch, plight, quandary, scrape (*Inf.*), situation, spot (*Inf.*), state, tight spot

predicate 1. affirm, assert, aver, avouch, avow, contend, declare, maintain, proclaim, state **2.** connote, imply, indicate, intimate, signify, suggest **3.** *With* **on** *or* **upon** base, build, establish, found, ground, postulate, rest

predict augur, divine, forebode, forecast, foresee, foretell, portend, presage, prognos~ ticate, prophesy, soothsay, vaticinate (*Rare*)

predictable anticipated, calculable, certain, expected, foreseeable, foreseen, likely, reli~ able, sure, sure-fire (*Inf.*)
Antonyms out of the blue, surprising, unex~ pected, unforeseen, unlikely, unpredictable

prediction augury, divination, forecast, prognosis, prognostication, prophecy, soothsaying, sortilege

predilection bag (*Sl.*), bias, cup of tea (*Inf.*), fancy, fondness, inclination, leaning, liking, love, partiality, penchant, predispo~ sition, preference, proclivity, proneness, propensity, taste, tendency, weakness

predispose affect, bias, dispose, incline, induce, influence, lead, make (one) of a mind to, prejudice, prepare, prime, prompt, sway

predisposed agreeable, amenable, given to, inclined, liable, minded, prone, ready, sub~ ject, susceptible, willing

predisposition bent, bias, disposition, in~ clination, likelihood, penchant, potentiality, predilection, proclivity, proneness, propen~ sity, susceptibility, tendency, willingness

predominance ascendancy, control, domi~ nance, dominion, edge, greater number, hold, leadership, mastery, paramountcy, preponderance, supremacy, sway, upper hand, weight

predominant ascendant, capital, chief, controlling, dominant, important, leading, main, notable, paramount, preponderant, prevailing, prevalent, primary, prime, principal, prominent, ruling, sovereign, su~ perior, supreme, top-priority
Antonyms inferior, minor, secondary, sub~ ordinate, unimportant, uninfluential

predominate be most noticeable, carry weight, get the upper hand, hold sway, out~ weigh, overrule, overshadow, preponderate, prevail, reign, rule, tell

pre-eminence distinction, excellence, paramountcy, predominance, prestige, prominence, renown, superiority, suprema~ cy, transcendence

pre-eminent chief, consummate, distin~ guished, excellent, foremost, incomparable, matchless, outstanding, paramount, peer~ less, predominant, renowned, superior, su~ preme, transcendent, unequalled, unri~ valled, unsurpassed

pre-eminently above all, by far, conspicu~ ously, eminently, emphatically, exception~ ally, far and away, incomparably, inimi~ tably, matchlessly, notably, *par excellence*, particularly, second to none, signally, sin~ gularly, strikingly, superlatively, supremely

pre-empt acquire, anticipate, appropriate, arrogate, assume, seize, take over, usurp

preen 1. *Of birds* clean, plume **2.** array, deck out, doll up (*Sl.*), dress up, prettify, primp, prink, spruce up, titivate, trig (*Ar~ chaic or dialect*), trim **3. preen oneself (on)** congratulate oneself, pique oneself, plume oneself, pride oneself

preface 1. *n.* exordium, foreword, introduc~ tion, preamble, preliminary, prelude, pro~ em, prolegomenon, prologue **2.** *v.* begin, introduce, launch, lead up to, open, precede, prefix

prefer 1. adopt, be partial to, choose, desire, elect, fancy, favour, go for, incline towards, like better, opt for, pick, plump for, select, single out, wish, would rather, would sooner **2.** file, lodge, place, present, press, put forward **3.** advance, aggrandize, elevate, move up, promote, raise, upgrade

preferable best, better, choice, chosen, favoured, more desirable, more eligible, superior, worthier
Antonyms average, fair, ineligible, inferior, mediocre, poor, second-rate, undesirable

preferably as a matter of choice, by choice, first, in *or* for preference, much rather, much sooner, rather, sooner, willingly

preference 1. bag (*Sl.*), choice, cup of tea (*Inf.*), desire, election, favourite, first choice, option, partiality, pick, predilection, selection, top of the list **2.** advantage, favoured treatment, favouritism, first place, precedence, pride of place, priority

preferential advantageous, better, favoured, partial, partisan, privileged, special, superior

preferment advancement, dignity, elevation, exaltation, promotion, rise, upgrading

pregnancy gestation, gravidity

pregnant 1. big *or* heavy with child, enceinte, expectant, expecting (*Inf.*), gravid, in the club (*Brit. sl.*), in the family way (*Inf.*), in the pudding club (*Sl.*), preggers (*Brit. inf.*), with child **2.** charged, eloquent, expressive, loaded, meaningful, pointed, significant, suggestive, telling, weighty **3.** creative, imaginative, inventive, original, seminal **4.** abounding in, abundant, fecund, fertile, fraught, fruitful, full, productive, prolific, replete, rich in, teeming

prehistoric 1. earliest, early, primeval, primitive, primordial **2.** ancient, antediluvian, antiquated, archaic, out of date, out of the ark (*Inf.*)

prejudge anticipate, forejudge, jump to conclusions, make a hasty assessment, presume, presuppose

prejudice n. **1.** bias, jaundiced eye, partiality, preconceived notion, preconception, prejudgment, warp **2.** bigotry, chauvinism, discrimination, injustice, intolerance, narrow-mindedness, racism, sexism, unfairness **3.** damage, detriment, disadvantage, harm, hurt, impairment, loss, mischief ~v. **4.** bias, colour, distort, influence, jaundice, poison, predispose, prepossess, slant, sway, warp **5.** damage, harm, hinder, hurt, impair, injure, mar, spoil, undermine

prejudiced biased, bigoted, conditioned, discriminatory, influenced, intolerant,

jaundiced, narrow-minded, one-sided, opinionated, partial, partisan, prepossessed, unfair
Antonyms fair, impartial, just, neutral, not bigoted, not prejudiced, open-minded, unbiased

prejudicial counterproductive, damaging, deleterious, detrimental, disadvantageous, harmful, hurtful, inimical, injurious, undermining, unfavourable

preliminary 1. *adj.* exploratory, first, initial, initiatory, introductory, opening, pilot, precursory, prefatory, preparatory, prior, qualifying, test, trial **2.** *n.* beginning, first round, foundation, groundwork, initiation, introduction, opening, overture, preamble, preface, prelims, prelude, preparation, start

prelude beginning, commencement, curtain-raiser, exordium, foreword, intro (*Inf.*), introduction, overture, preamble, preface, preliminary, preparation, proem, prolegomenon, prologue, start

premature 1. abortive, early, embryonic, forward, green, immature, incomplete, predeveloped, raw, undeveloped, unfledged, unripe, unseasonable, untimely **2.** *Fig.* hasty, ill-considered, ill-timed, impulsive, inopportune, overhasty, precipitate, previous (*Inf.*), rash, too soon, untimely

prematurely 1. before one's time, too early, too soon, untimely **2.** at half-cock, half-cocked, overhastily, precipitately, rashly, too hastily, too soon

premeditated aforethought, calculated, conscious, considered, contrived, deliberate, intended, intentional, planned, prepense, studied, wilful
Antonyms accidental, inadvertent, unintentional, unplanned, unpremeditated, unwitting

premeditation deliberation, design, determination, forethought, intention, malice aforethought, planning, plotting, prearrangement, predetermination, purpose

premier *n.* **1.** chancellor, head of government, P.M., prime minister ~*adj.* **2.** arch, chief, first, foremost, head, highest, leading, main, primary, prime, principal, top **3.** earliest, first, inaugural, initial, original

premiere debut, first night, first performance, first showing, opening

premises building, establishment, place, property, site

premiss, premise argument, assertion, assumption, ground, hypothesis, postulate, postulation, presupposition, proposition, supposition, thesis

premium 1. bonus, boon, bounty, fee, percentage (*Inf.*), perk (*Brit. inf.*), perquisite, prize, recompense, remuneration, reward **2.**

appreciation, regard, stock, store, value **3. at a premium** beyond one's means, costly, expensive, hard to come by, in great demand, in short supply, like gold dust, not to be had for love or money, rare, scarce, valuable

premonition apprehension, feeling, feeling in one's bones, foreboding, forewarning, funny feeling (*Inf.*), hunch, idea, intuition, misgiving, omen, portent, presage, presentiment, sign, suspicion, warning

preoccupation 1. absence of mind, absent-mindedness, absorption, abstraction, brown study, daydreaming, engrossment, immersion, inattentiveness, musing, oblivion, pensiveness, prepossession, reverie, woolgathering **2.** bee in one's bonnet, concern, fixation, hang-up (*Inf.*), hobbyhorse, *idée fixe*, obsession, pet subject

preoccupied absent-minded, absorbed, abstracted, caught up in, distracted, distrait, engrossed, faraway, heedless, immersed, in a brown study, intent, lost in, lost in thought, oblivious, rapt, taken up, unaware, wrapped up

preparation 1. development, getting ready, groundwork, preparing, putting in order **2.** alertness, anticipation, expectation, foresight, precaution, preparedness, provision, readiness, safeguard **3.** *Often plural* arrangement, measure, plan, provision **4.** composition, compound, concoction, medicine, mixture, tincture **5.** homework, prep (*Inf.*), revision, schoolwork, study, swotting (*Brit. inf.*)

preparatory 1. basic, elementary, introductory, opening, prefatory, preliminary, preparative, primary **2. preparatory to** before, in advance of, in anticipation of, in preparation for, prior to

prepare 1. adapt, adjust, anticipate, arrange, coach, dispose, form, groom, make provision, make ready, plan, practise, prime, put in order, train, warm up **2.** brace, fortify, gird, ready, steel, strengthen **3.** assemble, concoct, construct, contrive, draw up, fashion, fix up, get up (*Inf.*), make, produce, put together, turn out **4.** accoutre, equip, fit, fit out, furnish, outfit, provide, supply

prepared 1. all set, arranged, fit, in order, in readiness, planned, primed, ready, set **2.** able, disposed, inclined, minded, of a mind, predisposed, willing

preparedness alertness, fitness, order, preparation, readiness

preponderance ascendancy, bulk, dominance, domination, dominion, extensiveness, greater numbers, greater part, lion's share, mass, power, predominance, prevalence, superiority, supremacy, sway, weight

preponderant ascendant, dominant, extensive, foremost, greater, important, larger, paramount, predominant, prevailing, prevalent, significant

prepossessed biased, inclined, partial, partisan, predisposed, prejudiced

prepossessing alluring, amiable, appealing, attractive, beautiful, bewitching, captivating, charming, engaging, fair, fascinating, fetching, glamorous, good-looking, handsome, inviting, likable *or* likeable, lovable, magnetic, pleasing, striking, taking, winning

Antonyms disagreeable, displeasing, objectionable, offensive, repulsive, ugly, unattractive, uninviting, unlikable *or* unlikeable

preposterous absurd, asinine, bizarre, crazy, excessive, exorbitant, extravagant, extreme, foolish, impossible, incredible, insane, irrational, laughable, ludicrous, monstrous, nonsensical, out of the question, outrageous, ridiculous, senseless, shocking, unreasonable, unthinkable

prerequisite 1. *adj.* called for, essential, imperative, indispensable, mandatory, necessary, needful, obligatory, of the essence, required, requisite, vital **2.** *n.* condition, essential, imperative, must, necessity, precondition, qualification, requirement, requisite, *sine qua non*

prerogative advantage, authority, birthright, choice, claim, droit, due, exemption, immunity, liberty, perquisite, privilege, right, sanction, title

prescient clairvoyant, discerning, divinatory, divining, far-sighted, foresighted, mantic, perceptive, prophetic, psychic

prescribe appoint, assign, command, decree, define, dictate, direct, enjoin, establish, fix, impose, lay down, ordain, order, require, rule, set, specify, stipulate

prescript command, dictate, dictum, direction, directive, edict, instruction, law, mandate, order, ordinance, precept, regulation, requirement, rule

prescription 1. direction, formula, instruction, recipe **2.** drug, medicine, mixture, preparation, remedy

prescriptive authoritarian, dictatorial, didactic, dogmatic, legislating, preceptive, rigid

presence 1. attendance, being, companionship, company, existence, habitation, inhabitance, occupancy, residence **2.** closeness, immediate circle, nearness, neighbourhood, propinquity, proximity, vicinity **3.** air, appearance, aspect, aura, bearing, carriage, comportment, demeanour, ease, mien (*Literary*), personality, poise, self-assurance **4.** apparition, eidolon, ghost, manifestation, revenant, shade (*Literary*), spectre, spirit, supernatural being, wraith

presence of mind alertness, aplomb, calmness, composure, cool (*Sl.*), coolness, imperturbability, level-headedness, phlegm, quickness, sang-froid, self-assurance, self-command, self-possession, wits

present[1] *adj.* **1.** contemporary, current, existent, existing, extant, immediate, instant, present-day **2.** accounted for, at hand, available, here, in attendance, near, nearby, ready, there, to hand ~*n.* **3.** here and now, now, present moment, the time being, this day and age, today **4. at present** at the moment, just now, now, nowadays, right now **5. for the present** for a while, for the moment, for the nonce, for the time being, in the meantime, not for long, provisionally, temporarily

present[2] *v.* **1.** acquaint with, introduce, make known **2.** demonstrate, display, exhibit, give, mount, put before the public, put on, show, stage **3.** adduce, advance, declare, expound, extend, hold out, introduce, offer, pose, produce, proffer, put forward, raise, recount, relate, state, submit, suggest, tender **4.** award, bestow, confer, donate, entrust, furnish, give, grant, hand out, hand over, offer, proffer, put at (someone's) disposal ~*n.* **5.** benefaction, boon, bounty, donation, endowment, favour, gift, grant, gratuity, hand-out, largess *or* largesse, offering, prezzie (*Inf.*)

presentable acceptable, becoming, decent, fit to be seen, good enough, not bad (*Inf.*), O.K. *or* okay (*Inf.*), passable, proper, respectable, satisfactory, suitable, tolerable
Antonyms below par, not good enough, not up to scratch, poor, rubbishy, unacceptable, unpresentable, unsatisfactory

presentation **1.** award, bestowal, conferral, donation, giving, investiture, offering **2.** appearance, arrangement, delivery, exposition, production, rendition, staging, submission **3.** demonstration, display, exhibition, performance, production, representation, show **4.** coming out, debut, introduction, launch, launching, reception

presentiment anticipation, apprehension, expectation, fear, feeling, foreboding, forecast, forethought, hunch, intuition, misgiving, premonition, presage

presently anon (*Archaic*), before long, by and by, erelong (*Archaic or poetic*), in a minute, in a moment, in a short while, pretty soon (*Inf.*), shortly, soon

preservation conservation, defence, keeping, maintenance, perpetuation, protection, safeguarding, safekeeping, safety, salvation, security, storage, support, upholding

preserve *v.* **1.** care for, conserve, defend,

guard, keep, protect, safeguard, save, secure, shelter, shield **2.** continue, keep, keep up, maintain, perpetuate, retain, sustain, uphold **3.** conserve, keep, put up, save, store ~*n.* **4.** area, domain, field, realm, specialism, sphere **5.** *Often plural* confection, confiture, conserve, jam, jelly, marmalade, sweetmeat **6.** game reserve, reservation, reserve, sanctuary
Antonyms (*sense 1*) assail, assault, attack, leave unprotected, turn out (*sense 2*) abandon, discontinue, drop, end, give up (*sense 3*) blow (*Sl.*), consume, fritter away, spend, squander, waste

preside administer, be at the head of, be in authority, chair, conduct, control, direct, govern, head, lead, manage, officiate, run, supervise

press *v.* **1.** bear down on, compress, condense, crush, depress, force down, jam, mash, push, reduce, squeeze, stuff **2.** calender, finish, flatten, iron, mangle, put the creases in, smooth, steam **3.** clasp, crush, embrace, encircle, enfold, fold in one's arms, hold close, hug, squeeze **4.** compel, constrain, demand, enforce, enjoin, force, insist on **5.** beg, entreat, exhort, implore, importune, petition, plead, pressurize, sue, supplicate, urge **6.** afflict, assail, beset, besiege, disquiet, harass, plague, torment, trouble, vex, worry **7. be pressed** be hard put, be pushed (hurried, rushed) (*Inf.*), be short of **8.** cluster, crowd, flock, gather, hasten, herd, hurry, mill, push, rush, seethe, surge, swarm, throng ~*n.* **9. the press a.** Fleet Street, fourth estate, journalism, news media, newspapers, the papers **b.** columnists, correspondents, gentlemen of the press, journalists, journos (*Sl.*), newsmen, photographers, pressmen, reporters **10.** bunch, crowd, crush, flock, herd, horde, host, mob, multitude, pack, push (*Inf.*), swarm, throng **11.** bustle, demand, hassle (*Inf.*), hurry, pressure, strain, stress, urgency

pressing burning, constraining, crucial, exigent, high-priority, imperative, important, importunate, serious, urgent, vital
Antonyms dispensable, regular, routine, unimportant, unnecessary

pressure **1.** compressing, compression, crushing, force, heaviness, squeezing, weight **2.** coercion, compulsion, constraint, force, influence, obligation, power, sway **3.** adversity, affliction, burden, demands, difficulty, distress, exigency, hassle (*Inf.*), heat, hurry, load, press, strain, stress, urgency

prestige authority, bottom, Brownie points, cachet, celebrity, credit, distinction, eminence, esteem, fame, honour, importance, influence, kudos, regard, renown, reputa~ tion, standing, stature, status, weight

prestigious celebrated, eminent, esteemed, exalted, great, illustrious, important, im~ posing, impressive, influential, notable, prominent, renowned, reputable, respected **Antonyms** humble, lowly, minor, obscure, unimportant, unimpressive, unknown

presumably apparently, doubtless, doubtlessly, in all likelihood, in all prob~ ability, it would seem, likely, most likely, on the face of it, probably, seemingly

presume 1. assume, believe, conjecture, guess (*Inf., chiefly U.S. & Canad.*), infer, posit, postulate, presuppose, suppose, sur~ mise, take for granted, take it, think **2.** dare, go so far, have the audacity, make bold, make so bold, take the liberty, under~ take, venture **3.** bank on, count on, depend, rely, trust

presumption 1. assurance, audacity, boldness, brass (*Inf.*), brass neck (*Brit. inf.*), cheek (*Inf.*), chutzpah (*U.S. & Canad. inf.*), effrontery, forwardness, front, gall (*Inf.*), impudence, insolence, neck (*Inf.*), nerve (*Inf.*), presumptuousness, temerity **2.** an~ ticipation, assumption, belief, conjecture, guess, hypothesis, opinion, premiss, pre~ supposition, supposition, surmise **3.** basis, chance, grounds, likelihood, plausibility, probability, reason

presumptive 1. assumed, believed, ex~ pected, hypothetical, inferred, supposed, understood **2.** believable, conceivable, credible, likely, plausible, possible, prob~ able, reasonable, verisimilar

presumptuous arrogant, audacious, big~ headed (*Inf.*), bold, conceited, foolhardy, forward, insolent, overconfident, overfamil~ iar, overweening, presuming, pushy (*Inf.*), rash, too big for one's boots, uppish (*Brit. inf.*) **Antonyms** bashful, humble, modest, retir~ ing, shy, timid, unassuming

presuppose accept, assume, consider, im~ ply, posit, postulate, presume, suppose, take as read, take for granted, take it

presupposition assumption, belief, hy~ pothesis, preconceived idea, preconception, premiss, presumption, supposition, theory

pretence 1. acting, charade, deceit, decep~ tion, fabrication, fakery, faking, falsehood, feigning, invention, make-believe, sham, simulation, subterfuge, trickery **2.** affecta~ tion, appearance, artifice, display, façade, hokum (*Sl., chiefly U.S. & Canad.*), posing, posturing, pretentiousness, show, veneer **3.** claim, cloak, colour, cover, excuse, façade, garb, guise, mask, masquerade, pretext, ruse, semblance, show, veil, wile **Antonyms** (*sense 1*) actuality, fact, reality

(*sense 2*) candour, frankness, honesty, in~ genuousness, openness

pretend 1. affect, allege, assume, counter~ feit, dissemble, dissimulate, fake, falsify, feign, impersonate, make out, pass oneself off as, profess, put on, sham, simulate **2.** act, imagine, make believe, make up, play, play the part of, suppose **3.** allege, aspire, claim, lay claim, profess, purport

pretended alleged, avowed, bogus, counterfeit, fake, false, feigned, fictitious, imaginary, ostensible, phoney *or* phony (*Inf.*), pretend (*Inf.*), professed, pseudo (*Inf.*), purported, sham, so-called, spurious

pretender aspirant, claimant, claimer

pretension 1. aspiration, assertion, as~ sumption, claim, demand, pretence, profes~ sion **2.** affectation, airs, conceit, hypocrisy, ostentation, pomposity, pretentiousness, self-importance, show, showiness, snobbery, snobbishness, vainglory, vanity

pretentious affected, assuming, bombastic, conceited, exaggerated, extravagant, flaunt~ ing, grandiloquent, grandiose, highfalutin (*Inf.*), high-flown, high-sounding, hollow, inflated, magniloquent, mannered, ostenta~ tious, overambitious, pompous, puffed up, showy, snobbish, specious, vainglorious **Antonyms** modest, natural, plain, simple, unaffected, unassuming, unpretentious

pretext affectation, alleged reason, appear~ ance, cloak, cover, device, excuse, guise, mask, ploy, pretence, red herring, ruse, semblance, show, simulation, veil

pretty *adj.* **1.** appealing, attractive, beauti~ ful, bonny, charming, comely, cute, fair, good-looking, graceful, lovely, personable **2.** bijou, dainty, delicate, elegant, fine, neat, nice, pleasing, tasteful, trim ~*adv.* **3.** *Inf.* fairly, kind of (*Inf.*), moderately, quite, ra~ ther, reasonably, somewhat **Antonyms** plain, ugly, unattractive, un~ shapely, unsightly

prevail 1. be victorious, carry the day, gain mastery, overcome, overrule, prove superi~ or, succeed, triumph, win **2.** abound, be current (prevalent, widespread), exist gen~ erally, obtain, predominate, preponderate **3.** *Often with* **on** *or* **upon** bring round, con~ vince, dispose, incline, induce, influence, persuade, prompt, sway, talk into, win over

prevailing 1. common, current, customary, established, fashionable, general, in style, in vogue, ordinary, popular, prevalent, set, usual, widespread **2.** dominant, influential, main, operative, predominating, preponder~ ating, principal, ruling

prevalence 1. acceptance, commonness, common occurrence, currency, frequency, pervasiveness, popularity, profusion, regu~ larity, ubiquity, universality **2.** ascendancy,

hold, mastery, predominance, preponder~
ance, primacy, rule, sway

prevalent 1. accepted, common, common~
place, current, customary, established,
everyday, extensive, frequent, general, ha~
bitual, popular, rampant, rife, ubiquitous,
universal, usual, widespread **2.** ascendant,
compelling, dominant, governing, powerful,
predominant, prevailing, successful, su~
perior
Antonyms (*sense 1*) confined, infrequent,
limited, localized, rare, restricted, uncom~
mon, unusual

prevaricate beat about the bush, beg the
question, cavil, deceive, dodge, equivocate,
evade, flannel (*Brit. inf.*), give a false colour
to, hedge, lie, palter, quibble, shift, shuffle,
stretch the truth, tergiversate
Antonyms be blunt, be direct, be frank, be
straightforward, come straight to the point,
not beat about the bush

prevarication cavilling, deceit, deception,
equivocation, evasion, falsehood, falsifica~
tion, lie, misrepresentation, pretence, quib~
bling, tergiversation, untruth

prevent anticipate, avert, avoid, balk, bar,
block, check, counteract, defend against,
foil, forestall, frustrate, hamper, head off,
hinder, impede, inhibit, intercept, nip in
the bud, obstruct, obviate, preclude, re~
strain, stave off, stop, thwart, ward off
Antonyms allow, encourage, help, incite,
permit, support, urge

prevention 1. anticipation, avoidance, de~
terrence, elimination, forestalling, obvia~
tion, precaution, preclusion, prophylaxis,
safeguard, thwarting **2.** bar, check, deter~
rence, frustration, hindrance, impediment,
interruption, obstacle, obstruction, stoppage

preventive, preventative *adj.* **1.** ham~
pering, hindering, impeding, obstructive **2.**
counteractive, deterrent, inhibitory, pre~
cautionary, prophylactic, protective, shield~
ing ~*n.* **3.** block, hindrance, impediment,
obstacle, obstruction **4.** deterrent, neutral~
izer, prevention, prophylactic, protection,
protective, remedy, safeguard, shield

previous 1. antecedent, anterior, earlier,
erstwhile, ex-, foregoing, former, one-time,
past, preceding, prior, quondam, sometime
2. *Inf.* ahead of oneself, precipitate, prema~
ture, too early, too soon, untimely
Antonyms (*sense 1*) consequent, following,
later, subsequent, succeeding

previously at one time, a while ago, before,
beforehand, earlier, formerly, heretofore,
hitherto, in advance, in anticipation, in
days *or* years gone by, in the past, once,
then, until now

prey *n.* **1.** game, kill, quarry **2.** dupe, fall
guy (*Inf.*), mark, mug (*Brit. sl.*), target, vic~

tim ~*v.* **3.** devour, eat, feed upon, hunt, live
off, seize **4.** blackmail, bleed (*Inf.*), bully,
exploit, intimidate, take advantage of, ter~
rorize, victimize **5.** burden, distress, hang
over, haunt, oppress, trouble, weigh down,
weigh heavily, worry

price *n.* **1.** amount, asking price, assess~
ment, bill, charge, cost, damage (*Inf.*), esti~
mate, expenditure, expense, face value, fee,
figure, outlay, payment, rate, valuation,
value, worth **2.** consequences, cost, penalty,
sacrifice, toll **3.** bounty, compensation, pre~
mium, recompense, reward **4. at any price**
anyhow, cost what it may, expense no ob~
ject, no matter what the cost, regardless,
whatever the cost **5. beyond price** inesti~
mable, invaluable, of incalculable value,
precious, priceless, treasured, without price
~*v.* **6.** assess, cost, estimate, evaluate, put a
price on, rate, value

priceless 1. beyond price, cherished, costly,
dear, expensive, incalculable, incomparable,
inestimable, invaluable, irreplaceable, pre~
cious, prized, rare, rich, treasured, worth a
king's ransom **2.** *Inf.* absurd, amusing,
comic, droll, funny, hilarious, killing (*Inf.*),
rib-tickling, ridiculous, riotous, side-
splitting
Antonyms cheap, cheapo (*Inf.*), common,
inexpensive, worthless

prick *v.* **1.** bore, impale, jab, lance, perforate,
pierce, pink, punch, puncture, stab **2.** bite,
itch, prickle, smart, sting, tingle **3.** cut,
distress, grieve, move, pain, stab, touch,
trouble, wound **4.** *Usually with* **up** point,
raise, rise, stand erect ~*n.* **5.** cut, gash,
hole, perforation, pinhole, puncture, wound
6. gnawing, pang, prickle, smart, spasm,
sting, twinge

prickle *n.* **1.** barb, needle, point, spike,
spine, spur, thorn **2.** chill, formication,
goose flesh, paraesthesia (*Medical*), pins and
needles (*Inf.*), smart, tickle, tingle, tingling
~*v.* **3.** itch, smart, sting, tingle, twitch **4.**
jab, nick, prick, stick

prickly 1. barbed, brambly, briery, bristly,
spiny, thorny **2.** crawling, itchy, pricking,
prickling, scratchy, sharp, smarting, sting~
ing, tingling **3.** bad-tempered, cantanker~
ous, edgy, fractious, grumpy, irritable, liv~
erish, peevish, pettish, petulant, ratty (*Brit.
& N.Z. inf.*), shirty (*Sl., chiefly Brit.*), snap~
pish, stroppy (*Brit. sl.*), tetchy, touchy,
waspish **4.** complicated, difficult, intricate,
involved, knotty, thorny, ticklish, tricky,
troublesome, trying

pride *n.* **1.** amour-propre, dignity, honour,
self-esteem, self-respect, self-worth **2.** arro~
gance, bigheadedness (*Inf.*), conceit, ego~
tism, haughtiness, hauteur, hubris, lofti~
ness, *morgue*, presumption, pretension,

pretentiousness, self-importance, self-love, smugness, snobbery, superciliousness, vainglory, vanity **3.** boast, gem, jewel, pride and joy, prize, treasure **4.** delight, gratification, joy, pleasure, satisfaction **5.** best, choice, cream, elite, flower, glory, pick ~*v.* **6.** be proud of, boast, brag, congratulate oneself, crow, exult, flatter oneself, glory in, pique, plume, preen, revel in, take pride, vaunt
Antonyms (*sense 1*) humility, meekness, modesty

priest churchman, clergyman, cleric, curate, divine, ecclesiastic, father, father confessor, holy man, man of God, man of the cloth, minister, padre (*Inf.*), pastor, vicar

priestly canonical, clerical, ecclesiastic, hieratic, pastoral, priestlike, sacerdotal

prig goody-goody (*Inf.*), Holy Joe (*Inf.*), Holy Willie (*Inf.*), Mrs Grundy, old maid (*Inf.*), pedant, prude, puritan, stuffed shirt (*Inf.*)

priggish goody-goody (*Inf.*), holier-than-thou, narrow-minded, pedantic, prim, prudish, puritanical, self-righteous, self-satisfied, smug, starchy (*Inf.*), stiff, stuffy

prim demure, fastidious, formal, fussy, old-maidish (*Inf.*), particular, precise, priggish, prissy (*Inf.*), proper, prudish, puritanical, schoolmarmish (*Brit. inf.*), starchy (*Inf.*), stiff, strait-laced
Antonyms carefree, casual, easy-going, informal, laid-back, relaxed

prima donna diva, leading lady, star

primarily 1. above all, basically, chiefly, especially, essentially, for the most part, fundamentally, generally, largely, mainly, mostly, on the whole, principally **2.** at first, at *or* from the start, first and foremost, initially, in the beginning, in the first place, originally

primary 1. best, capital, cardinal, chief, dominant, first, greatest, highest, leading, main, paramount, prime, principal, top **2.** aboriginal, earliest, initial, original, primal, primeval, primitive, primordial, pristine **3.** basic, beginning, bog-standard (*Inf.*), elemental, essential, fundamental, radical, ultimate, underlying **4.** elementary, introductory, rudimentary, simple
Antonyms (*sense 1*) inferior, lesser, lowest, subordinate, supplementary, unimportant (*sense 4*) ensuing, following, later, secondary, subsequent, succeeding

prime *adj.* **1.** best, capital, choice, excellent, first-class, first-rate, grade A, highest, quality, select, selected, superior, top **2.** basic, bog-standard (*Inf.*), earliest, fundamental, original, primary, underlying **3.** chief, leading, main, predominant, pre-eminent, primary, principal, ruling, senior ~*n.* **4.** best days, bloom, flower, full flowering,

height, heyday, maturity, peak, perfection, zenith **5.** beginning, morning, opening, spring, start ~*v.* **6.** break in, coach, fit, get ready, groom, make ready, prepare, train **7.** brief, clue in (*Inf.*), clue up (*Inf.*), fill in (*Inf.*), gen up (*Brit. inf.*), give someone the lowdown (*Inf.*), inform, notify, tell

primeval, primaeval ancient, earliest, early, first, old, original, prehistoric, primal, primitive, primordial, pristine

primitive 1. earliest, early, elementary, first, original, primary, primeval, primordial, pristine **2.** barbarian, barbaric, crude, rough, rude, rudimentary, savage, simple, uncivilized, uncultivated, undeveloped, unrefined **3.** childlike, naive, simple, undeveloped, unsophisticated, untrained, untutored
Antonyms (*sense 1*) advanced, later, modern (*sense 2*) civilized, comfortable, developed, elaborate, refined (*sense 3*) adult, developed, mature, sophisticated, trained, tutored

prince lord, monarch, potentate, ruler, sovereign

princely 1. bounteous, bountiful, generous, gracious, lavish, liberal, magnanimous, munificent, open-handed, rich **2.** august, dignified, grand, high-born, imperial, imposing, lofty, magnificent, majestic, noble, regal, royal, sovereign, stately

principal *adj.* **1.** capital, cardinal, chief, controlling, dominant, essential, first, foremost, highest, key, leading, main, most important, paramount, pre-eminent, primary, prime, strongest ~*n.* **2.** boss (*Inf.*), chief, director, head, leader, master, ruler, superintendent **3.** dean, director, head (*Inf.*), headmaster, headmistress, head teacher, master, rector **4.** assets, capital, capital funds, money **5.** first violin, lead, leader, star
Antonyms auxiliary, inferior, minor, subordinate, subsidiary, supplementary, weakest

principally above all, chiefly, especially, first and foremost, for the most part, in the main, largely, mainly, mostly, particularly, predominantly, primarily

principle 1. assumption, axiom, canon, criterion, dictum, doctrine, dogma, ethic, formula, fundamental, golden rule, law, maxim, moral law, precept, proposition, rule, standard, truth, verity **2.** attitude, belief, code, credo, ethic, morality, opinion, tenet **3.** conscience, integrity, morals, probity, rectitude, scruples, sense of duty, sense of honour, uprightness **4. in principle** ideally, in essence, in theory, theoretically

print *v.* **1.** engrave, go to press, impress, imprint, issue, mark, publish, put to bed (*Inf.*), run off, stamp ~*n.* **2.** book, magazine, newspaper, newsprint, periodical, printed matter, publication, typescript **3. in print a.** in black and white, on paper, on the streets, out, printed, published **b.** available, current, in the shops, obtainable, on the market, on the shelves **4. out of print** no longer published, o.p., unavailable, unobtainable **5.** copy, engraving, photo (*Inf.*), photograph, picture, reproduction **6.** characters, face, font (*Chiefly U.S.*), fount, lettering, letters, type, typeface

priority first concern, greater importance, precedence, pre-eminence, preference, prerogative, rank, right of way, seniority, superiority, supremacy, the lead

priory abbey, cloister, convent, monastery, nunnery, religious house

prison can (*Sl.*), choky (*Sl.*), clink (*Sl.*), confinement, cooler (*Sl.*), dungeon, gaol, glasshouse (*Military inf.*), jail, jug (*Sl.*), lockup, nick (*Brit. sl.*), penal institution, penitentiary (*U.S.*), poky or pokey (*U.S. & Canad. sl.*), pound, quod (*Sl.*), slammer (*Sl.*), stir (*Sl.*)

prisoner 1. con (*Sl.*), convict, jailbird, lag (*Sl.*) **2.** captive, detainee, hostage, internee

privacy 1. isolation, privateness, retirement, retreat, seclusion, separateness, sequestration, solitude **2.** clandestineness, concealment, confidentiality, secrecy

private *adj.* **1.** clandestine, closet, confidential, covert, hush-hush (*Inf.*), in camera, inside, off the record, privy (*Archaic*), secret, unofficial **2.** exclusive, individual, intimate, own, particular, personal, reserved, special **3.** independent, nonpublic **4.** concealed, isolated, not overlooked, retired, secluded, secret, separate, sequestered, solitary, withdrawn **5. in private** behind closed doors, confidentially, in camera, in secret, personally, privately ~*n.* **6.** enlisted man (*U.S.*), private soldier, squaddie or squaddy (*Brit. sl.*), tommy (*Brit. inf.*), Tommy Atkins (*Brit. inf.*)
Antonyms (*sense 1*) disclosed, known, official, open, public, revealed (*sense 2*) common, general, open, public, unlimited, unrestricted (*sense 3*) bustling, busy, frequented, outgoing, sociable, unsecluded

privilege advantage, benefit, birthright, claim, concession, due, entitlement, franchise, freedom, immunity, liberty, prerogative, right, sanction

privileged 1. advantaged, elite, entitled, favoured, honoured, indulged, powerful, ruling, special **2.** allowed, empowered, exempt, free, granted, licensed, sanctioned, vested **3.** *Of information* confidential, exceptional, inside, not for publication, off the record, privy, special

prize[1] *n.* **1.** accolade, award, honour, premium, reward, trophy **2.** haul, jackpot,

purse, stakes, windfall, winnings **3.** aim, ambition, conquest, desire, gain, goal, hope **4.** booty, capture, loot, pickings, pillage, plunder, spoil(s), trophy ~*adj.* **5.** award-winning, best, champion, first-rate, outstanding, top, topnotch (*Inf.*), winning

prize[2] *v.* appreciate, cherish, esteem, hold dear, regard highly, set store by, treasure, value

probability chance(s), expectation, liability, likelihood, likeliness, odds, presumption, prospect

probable apparent, credible, feasible, likely, most likely, odds-on, on the cards, ostensible, plausible, possible, presumable, presumed, reasonable, seeming, verisimilar
Antonyms doubtful, improbable, not likely, unlikely

probably as likely as not, doubtless, in all likelihood, in all probability, likely, maybe, most likely, perchance (*Archaic*), perhaps, possibly, presumably

probation apprenticeship, examination, initiation, novitiate, test, trial, trial period

probe *v.* **1.** examine, explore, go into, investigate, look into, query, research, scrutinize, search, sift, sound, test, verify, work over **2.** explore, feel around, poke, prod ~*n.* **3.** detection, examination, exploration, inquest, inquiry, investigation, research, scrutiny, study

problem *n.* **1.** can of worms (*Inf.*), complication, difficulty, dilemma, disagreement, dispute, disputed point, doubt, hard nut to crack (*Inf.*), point at issue, predicament, quandary, trouble **2.** brain-teaser (*Inf.*), conundrum, enigma, poser, puzzle, question, riddle, teaser ~*adj.* **3.** delinquent, difficult, intractable, uncontrollable, unmanageable, unruly

problematic chancy (*Inf.*), debatable, doubtful, dubious, enigmatic, moot, open to doubt, problematical, puzzling, questionable, tricky, uncertain, unsettled
Antonyms beyond question, certain, clear, definite, indisputable, settled, undebatable, unquestionable

procedure action, conduct, course, custom, form, formula, method, modus operandi, operation, performance, plan of action, policy, practice, process, routine, scheme, step, strategy, system, transaction

proceed 1. advance, carry on, continue, get going, get on with, get under way with, go ahead, go on, make a start, move on, press on, progress, set in motion **2.** arise, come, derive, emanate, ensue, flow, follow, issue, originate, result, spring, stem
Antonyms (*sense 1*) break off, cease, discontinue, end, get behind, halt, leave off, pack in (*Brit. inf.*), retreat, stop

proceeding 1. act, action, course of action, deed, measure, move, occurrence, procedure, process, step, undertaking, venture **2.** *Plural* account, affairs, annals, archives, business, dealings, doings, matters, minutes, records, report, transactions

proceeds earnings, gain, income, produce, products, profit, receipts, returns, revenue, takings, yield

process *n.* **1.** action, course, course of action, manner, means, measure, method, mode, operation, performance, practice, procedure, proceeding, system, transaction **2.** advance, course, development, evolution, formation, growth, movement, progress, progression, stage, step, unfolding **3.** *Law* action, case, suit, trial ~*v.* **4.** deal with, dispose of, fulfil, handle, take care of **5.** alter, convert, prepare, refine, transform, treat

procession 1. cavalcade, column, cortege, file, march, motorcade, parade, train **2.** course, cycle, run, sequence, series, string, succession, train

proclaim advertise, affirm, announce, blaze (abroad), blazon (abroad), circulate, declare, enunciate, give out, herald, indicate, make known, profess, promulgate, publish, shout from the housetops (*Inf.*), show, trumpet
Antonyms conceal, hush up, keep back, keep secret, suppress, withhold

proclamation announcement, declaration, decree, edict, manifesto, notice, notification, promulgation, pronouncement, pronunciamento, publication

procrastinate adjourn, be dilatory, dally, defer, delay, drag one's feet (*Inf.*), gain time, play a waiting game, play for time, postpone, prolong, protract, put off, retard, stall, temporize
Antonyms advance, expedite, get on with, hasten, hurry (up), proceed, speed up

procure acquire, appropriate, buy, come by, earn, effect, find, gain, get, get hold of, lay hands on, manage to get, obtain, pick up, purchase, score (*Sl.*), secure, win

prod *v.* **1.** dig, drive, elbow, jab, nudge, poke, prick, propel, push, shove **2.** egg on, goad, impel, incite, motivate, move, prompt, rouse, spur, stimulate, stir up, urge ~*n.* **3.** boost, dig, elbow, jab, nudge, poke, push, shove **4.** goad, poker, spur, stick **5.** boost, cue, prompt, reminder, signal, stimulus

prodigal *adj.* **1.** excessive, extravagant, immoderate, improvident, intemperate, profligate, reckless, spendthrift, squandering, wanton, wasteful **2.** bounteous, bountiful, copious, exuberant, lavish, luxuriant, profuse, sumptuous, superabundant, teeming ~*n.* **3.** big spender, profligate, spendthrift, squanderer, wastrel

Antonyms (*sense 1*) economical, frugal, miserly, parsimonious, sparing, stingy, thrifty, tight (*sense 2*) deficient, lacking, meagre, scanty, scarce, short, sparse

prodigality 1. abandon, dissipation, excess, extravagance, immoderation, intemperance, profligacy, recklessness, squandering, wantonness, waste, wastefulness **2.** abundance, amplitude, bounteousness, bounty, copiousness, cornucopia, exuberance, horn of plenty, lavishness, luxuriance, plenteousness, plenty, profusion, richness, sumptuousness

prodigious 1. colossal, enormous, giant, gigantic, huge, immeasurable, immense, inordinate, mammoth, massive, monstrous, monumental, stupendous, tremendous, vast **2.** abnormal, amazing, astounding, exceptional, extraordinary, fabulous, fantastic (*Inf.*), flabbergasting (*Inf.*), impressive, marvellous, miraculous, phenomenal, remarkable, staggering, startling, striking, stupendous, unusual, wonderful
Antonyms negligible, normal, ordinary, small, tiny, unexceptional, unimpressive, unremarkable, usual

prodigy 1. brainbox, child genius, genius, mastermind, talent, whiz (*Inf.*), whiz kid (*Inf.*), wizard, wonder child, wunderkind **2.** marvel, miracle, one in a million, phenomenon, rare bird (*Inf.*), sensation, wonder **3.** abnormality, curiosity, freak, grotesque, monster, monstrosity, mutation, spectacle

produce *v.* **1.** compose, construct, create, develop, fabricate, invent, make, manufacture, originate, put together, turn out **2.** afford, bear, beget, breed, bring forth, deliver, engender, furnish, give, render, supply, yield **3.** bring about, cause, effect, generate, give rise to, make for, occasion, provoke, set off **4.** advance, bring forward, bring to light, demonstrate, exhibit, offer, present, put forward, set forth, show **5.** direct, do, exhibit, mount, present, put before the public, put on, show, stage **6.** *Geometry* extend, lengthen, prolong, protract ~*n.* **7.** crop, fruit and vegetables, greengrocery, harvest, product, yield

producer 1. director, impresario, *régisseur* **2.** farmer, grower, maker, manufacturer

product 1. artefact, commodity, concoction, creation, goods, invention, merchandise, produce, production, work **2.** consequence, effect, fruit, issue, legacy, offshoot, outcome, result, returns, spin-off, upshot, yield

production 1. assembly, construction, creation, fabrication, formation, making, manufacture, manufacturing, origination, preparation, producing **2.** direction, management, presentation, staging

productive 1. creative, dynamic, energetic, fecund, fertile, fruitful, generative, inven-

tive, plentiful, producing, prolific, rich, teeming, vigorous **2.** advantageous, beneficial, constructive, effective, fruitful, gainful, gratifying, profitable, rewarding, useful, valuable, worthwhile
Antonyms barren, poor, sterile, unfertile, unfruitful, unproductive, unprofitable, useless

productivity abundance, mass production, output, production, productive capacity, productiveness, work rate, yield

profane adj. **1.** disrespectful, godless, heathen, idolatrous, impious, impure, irreligious, irreverent, pagan, sacrilegious, sinful, ungodly, wicked **2.** lay, secular, temporal, unconsecrated, unhallowed, unholy, unsanctified, worldly **3.** abusive, blasphemous, coarse, crude, filthy, foul, obscene, vulgar ~v. **4.** abuse, commit sacrilege, contaminate, debase, defile, desecrate, misuse, pervert, pollute, prostitute, violate, vitiate
Antonyms clean, decorous, holy, proper, religious, respectful, reverent, sacred, spiritual

profanity abuse, blasphemy, curse, cursing, execration, foul language, four-letter word, impiety, imprecation, irreverence, malediction, obscenity, profaneness, sacrilege, swearing, swearword

profess 1. acknowledge, admit, affirm, announce, assert, asseverate, aver, avow, certify, confess, confirm, declare, maintain, own, proclaim, state, vouch **2.** act as if, allege, call oneself, claim, dissemble, fake, feign, let on, make out, pretend, purport, sham

professed 1. avowed, certified, confirmed, declared, proclaimed, self-acknowledged, self-confessed **2.** alleged, apparent, ostensible, pretended, purported, self-styled, so-called, soi-disant, supposed, would-be

professedly 1. allegedly, apparently, by one's own account, falsely, ostensibly, purportedly, supposedly, under the pretext of **2.** admittedly, avowedly, by open declaration, confessedly

profession 1. business, calling, career, employment, line, line of work, métier, occupation, office, position, sphere, vocation, walk of life **2.** acknowledgment, affirmation, assertion, attestation, avowal, claim, confession, declaration, statement, testimony, vow

professional 1. adj. ace (Inf.), adept, competent, crack (Sl.), efficient, experienced, expert, finished, masterly, polished, practised, proficient, qualified, skilled, slick, trained **2.** n. adept, authority, buff (Inf.), dab hand (Brit. inf.), expert, hotshot (Inf.), maestro, master, maven (U.S.), past master, pro (Inf.), specialist, virtuoso, whiz (Inf.), wizard

Antonyms amateurish, incapable, incompetent, inefficient, inept, inexperienced, unpolished, unqualified, unskilled, untrained

professor don (Brit.), fellow (Brit.), head of faculty, prof (Inf.)

proficiency ability, accomplishment, aptitude, competence, craft, dexterity, expertise, expertness, facility, knack, know-how (Inf.), mastery, skilfulness, skill, talent

proficient able, accomplished, adept, apt, capable, clever, competent, conversant, efficient, experienced, expert, gifted, masterly, qualified, skilful, skilled, talented, trained, versed
Antonyms bad, incapable, incompetent, inept, unaccomplished, unskilled

profile n. **1.** contour, drawing, figure, form, outline, portrait, shape, side view, silhouette, sketch **2.** biography, characterization, character sketch, sketch, thumbnail sketch, vignette **3.** analysis, chart, diagram, examination, graph, review, study, survey, table

profit n. **1.** Often plural bottom line, earnings, emoluments, gain, percentage (Inf.), proceeds, receipts, return, revenue, surplus, takings, winnings, yield **2.** advancement, advantage, avail, benefit, gain, good, interest, use, value ~v. **3.** aid, avail, benefit, be of advantage to, better, contribute, gain, help, improve, promote, serve, stand in good stead **4.** capitalize on, cash in on (Inf.), exploit, learn from, make capital of, make good use of, make the most of, put to good use, rake in (Inf.), reap the benefit of, take advantage of, turn to advantage or account, use, utilize **5.** clean up (Inf.), clear, earn, gain, make a good thing of (Inf.), make a killing (Inf.), make money

profitable 1. commercial, cost-effective, fruitful, gainful, lucrative, money-making, paying, remunerative, rewarding, worthwhile **2.** advantageous, beneficial, economic, expedient, fruitful, productive, rewarding, serviceable, useful, valuable, worthwhile
Antonyms disadvantageous, fruitless, unremunerative, unrewarding, useless, vain, worthless

profiteer 1. n. exploiter, racketeer **2.** v. exploit, fleece, make a quick buck (Sl.), make someone pay through the nose, overcharge, racketeer, skin (Sl.), sting (Inf.)

profligate adj. **1.** abandoned, corrupt, debauched, degenerate, depraved, dissipated, dissolute, immoral, iniquitous, libertine, licentious, loose, promiscuous, shameless, unprincipled, vicious, vitiated, wanton, wicked, wild **2.** extravagant, immoderate, improvident, prodigal, reckless, spendthrift, squandering, wasteful ~n. **3.** debauchee,

degenerate, dissipater, libertine, rake, rep~
robate, roué **4.** prodigal, spendthrift,
squanderer, waster, wastrel
Antonyms (*sense 1*) chaste, decent, moral,
principled, pure, upright, virginal, virtuous
profound 1. abstruse, deep, discerning,
erudite, learned, penetrating, philosophical,
recondite, sagacious, sage, serious, skilled,
subtle, thoughtful, weighty, wise **2.** abys~
mal, bottomless, cavernous, deep, fathom~
less, yawning **3.** abject, acute, deeply felt,
extreme, great, heartfelt, heartrending,
hearty, intense, keen, sincere **4.** absolute,
complete, consummate, exhaustive, exten~
sive, extreme, far-reaching, intense, out-
and-out, pronounced, thoroughgoing, total,
unqualified, utter
Antonyms imprudent, insincere, shallow,
slight, stupid, superficial, thoughtless, un~
educated, uninformed, unknowledgeable, un~
wise
profoundly abjectly, acutely, deeply, ex~
tremely, from the bottom of one's heart,
greatly, heartily, intensely, keenly, serious~
ly, sincerely, thoroughly, very
profuse 1. abundant, ample, bountiful, co~
pious, luxuriant, overflowing, plentiful,
prolific, teeming **2.** excessive, extravagant,
exuberant, fulsome, generous, immoderate,
lavish, liberal, open-handed, prodigal,
unstinting
Antonyms (*sense 1*) deficient, inadequate,
meagre, scanty, scarce, skimpy, sparse (*sense
2*) frugal, illiberal, moderate, provident,
thrifty
profusion abundance, bounty, copiousness,
cornucopia, excess, extravagance, exuber~
ance, glut, lavishness, luxuriance, multi~
tude, oversupply, plenitude, plethora,
prodigality, quantity, riot, superabundance,
superfluity, surplus, wealth
progeny breed, children, descendants,
family, issue, lineage, offspring, posterity,
race, scions, seed (*Chiefly biblical*), stock,
young
programme *n.* **1.** agenda, curriculum,
line-up, list, listing, list of players, order of
events, order of the day, plan, schedule,
syllabus, timetable **2.** broadcast, perfor~
mance, presentation, production, show **3.**
design, order of the day, plan, plan of ac~
tion, procedure, project, scheme ~*v.* **4.** ar~
range, bill, book, design, engage, formulate,
itemize, lay on, line up, list, map out, plan,
prearrange, schedule, work out
progress *n.* **1.** advance, course, movement,
onward course, passage, progression, way
2. advance, advancement, amelioration,
betterment, breakthrough, development,
gain, gaining ground, growth, headway,
improvement, increase, progression, pro~

motion, step forward **3. in progress** being
done, going on, happening, occurring, pro~
ceeding, taking place, under way ~*v.* **4.** ad~
vance, come on, continue, cover ground,
forge ahead, gain ground, gather way, get
on, go forward, make headway, make one's
way, make strides, move on, proceed, travel
5. advance, ameliorate, better, blossom, de~
velop, gain, grow, improve, increase, ma~
ture
Antonyms *n.* decline, failure, recession, re~
gression, relapse, retrogression ~*v.* decrease,
get behind, lose, lose ground, recede, regress,
retrogress
progression 1. advance, advancement,
furtherance, gain, headway, movement for~
ward, progress **2.** chain, course, cycle, or~
der, sequence, series, string, succession
progressive 1. accelerating, advancing,
continuing, continuous, developing, esca~
lating, growing, increasing, intensifying,
ongoing **2.** advanced, avant-garde, dynamic,
enlightened, enterprising, forward-looking,
go-ahead, liberal, modern, radical, reform~
ist, revolutionary, up-and-coming
prohibit 1. ban, debar, disallow, forbid,
interdict, outlaw, proscribe, veto **2.** con~
strain, hamper, hinder, impede, make im~
possible, obstruct, preclude, prevent, re~
strict, rule out, stop
Antonyms allow, authorize, command, con~
sent to, endure, further, give leave, let, license,
order, permit, suffer, tolerate
prohibited banned, barred, forbidden, not
allowed, proscribed, taboo, *verboten*, vetoed
prohibition 1. constraint, exclusion, for~
biddance, interdiction, negation, obstruc~
tion, prevention, restriction **2.** ban, bar,
boycott, disallowance, embargo, injunction,
interdict, proscription, veto
prohibitive 1. forbidding, prohibiting, pro~
scriptive, repressive, restraining, restric~
tive, suppressive **2.** *Esp. of prices* beyond
one's means, excessive, exorbitant, extor~
tionate, high-priced, preposterous, sky-high,
steep (*Inf.*)
project *n.* **1.** activity, assignment, design,
enterprise, job, occupation, plan, pro~
gramme, proposal, scheme, task, undertak~
ing, venture, work ~*v.* **2.** contemplate, con~
trive, design, devise, draft, frame, map out,
outline, plan, propose, purpose, scheme **3.**
cast, discharge, fling, hurl, launch, make
carry, propel, shoot, throw, transmit **4.**
beetle, bulge, extend, jut, overhang, pro~
trude, stand out, stick out **5.** calculate, es~
timate, extrapolate, forecast, gauge, prede~
termine, predict, reckon
projectile bullet, missile, rocket, shell
projection 1. bulge, eaves, jut, ledge, over~
hang, protrusion, protuberance, ridge, shelf,

sill **2.** blueprint, diagram, map, outline, plan, representation **3.** calculation, computation, estimate, estimation, extrapolation, forecast, prediction, reckoning

proletarian 1. *adj.* cloth-cap (*Inf.*), common, plebeian, working-class **2.** *n.* commoner, Joe Bloggs (*Brit. inf.*), man of the people, pleb, plebeian, prole (*Derogatory sl., chiefly Brit.*), worker

proletariat commonalty, commoners, hoi polloi, labouring classes, lower classes, lower orders, plebs, proles (*Derogatory sl., chiefly Brit.*), the common people, the great unwashed (*Inf. & derogatory*), the herd, the masses, the rabble, wage-earners, working class
Antonyms aristo (*Inf.*), aristocracy, gentry, nobility, peerage, ruling class, upper class, upper crust (*Inf.*)

proliferate breed, burgeon, escalate, expand, grow rapidly, increase, multiply, mushroom, run riot, snowball

proliferation build-up, concentration, escalation, expansion, extension, increase, intensification, multiplication, spread, step-up (*Inf.*)

prolific abundant, bountiful, copious, fecund, fertile, fruitful, generative, luxuriant, productive, profuse, rank, rich, teeming
Antonyms barren, fruitless, infertile, sterile, unfruitful, unproductive, unprolific

prologue exordium, foreword, introduction, preamble, preface, preliminary, prelude, proem

prolong carry on, continue, delay, drag out, draw out, extend, lengthen, make longer, perpetuate, protract, spin out, stretch
Antonyms abbreviate, abridge, curtail, cut, cut down, shorten, summarize

promenade *n.* **1.** boulevard, esplanade, parade, prom, public walk, walkway **2.** airing, constitutional, saunter, stroll, turn, walk ~*v.* **3.** perambulate, saunter, stretch one's legs, stroll, take a walk, walk **4.** flaunt, parade, strut, swagger

prominence 1. cliff, crag, crest, elevation, headland, height, high point, hummock, mound, pinnacle, projection, promontory, rise, rising ground, spur **2.** bulge, jutting, projection, protrusion, protuberance, swelling **3.** conspicuousness, markedness, outstandingness, precedence, salience, specialness, top billing, weight **4.** celebrity, distinction, eminence, fame, greatness, importance, name, notability, pre-eminence, prestige, rank, reputation, standing

prominent 1. bulging, hanging over, jutting, projecting, protruding, protrusive, protuberant, standing out **2.** blatant, conspicuous, easily seen, eye-catching, in the foreground, noticeable, obtrusive, obvious,

outstanding, pronounced, remarkable, salient, striking, to the fore, unmistakable **3.** big-time (*Inf.*), celebrated, chief, distinguished, eminent, famous, foremost, important, leading, main, major league (*Inf.*), notable, noted, outstanding, popular, pre-eminent, renowned, respected, top, well-known, well-thought-of
Antonyms (*sense 1*) concave, indented, receding (*sense 2*) inconspicuous, indistinct, insignificant, unnoticeable (*sense 3*) insignificant, minor, secondary, undistinguished, unimportant, unknown, unnotable

promiscuous 1. abandoned, debauched, dissipated, dissolute, fast, immoral, lax, libertine, licentious, loose, of easy virtue, profligate, unbridled, unchaste, wanton, wild **2.** chaotic, confused, disordered, diverse, heterogeneous, ill-assorted, indiscriminate, intermingled, intermixed, jumbled, mingled, miscellaneous, mixed, motley **3.** careless, casual, haphazard, heedless, indifferent, indiscriminate, irregular, irresponsible, random, slovenly, uncontrolled, uncritical, undiscriminating, unfastidious, unselective
Antonyms (*sense 1*) chaste, decent, innocent, modest, moral, pure, undefiled, unsullied, vestal, virginal, virtuous (*sense 2*) homogeneous, identical, neat, ordered, orderly, organized, shipshape, uniform, unmixed (*sense 3*) careful, critical, discriminating, fastidious, responsible, selective

promise *v.* **1.** assure, contract, cross one's heart, engage, give an undertaking, give one's word, guarantee, pledge, plight, stipulate, swear, take an oath, undertake, vouch, vow, warrant **2.** augur, bespeak, betoken, bid fair, denote, give hope of, hint at, hold a probability, hold out hopes of, indicate, lead one to expect, look like, seem likely to, show signs of, suggest ~*n.* **3.** assurance, bond, commitment, compact, covenant, engagement, guarantee, oath, pledge, undertaking, vow, word, word of honour **4.** ability, aptitude, capability, capacity, flair, potential, talent

promising 1. auspicious, bright, encouraging, favourable, full of promise, hopeful, likely, propitious, reassuring, rosy **2.** able, gifted, likely, rising, talented, up-and-coming
Antonyms (*sense 1*) discouraging, unauspicious, unfavourable, unpromising

promontory cape, foreland, head, headland, ness (*Archaic*), point, spur

promote 1. advance, aid, assist, back, boost, contribute to, develop, encourage, forward, foster, further, help, nurture, stimulate, support **2.** aggrandize, dignify, elevate, exalt, honour, kick upstairs (*Inf.*), prefer, raise, upgrade **3.** advocate, call at~

tention to, champion, endorse, espouse, popularize, prescribe, push for, recommend, speak for, sponsor, support, urge, work for **4.** advertise, beat the drum for (*Inf.*), hype, plug (*Inf.*), publicize, puff, push, sell
Antonyms (*sense 1*) discourage, hinder, hold back, impede, obstruct, oppose, prevent (*sense 2*) demote, downgrade, lower *or* reduce in rank

promotion 1. advancement, aggrandizement, elevation, ennoblement, exaltation, honour, move up, preferment, rise, upgrading **2.** advancement, advocacy, backing, boosting, cultivation, development, encouragement, espousal, furtherance, progress, support **3.** advertising, advertising campaign, ballyhoo (*Inf.*), hard sell, hype, media hype, plugging (*Inf.*), propaganda, publicity, puffery (*Inf.*), pushing

prompt *adj.* **1.** early, immediate, instant, instantaneous, on time, pdq (*Sl.*), punctual, quick, rapid, speedy, swift, timely, unhesitating **2.** alert, brisk, eager, efficient, expeditious, quick, ready, responsive, smart, willing ~*adv.* **3.** *Inf.* exactly, on the dot, promptly, punctually, sharp ~*v.* **4.** cause, impel, incite, induce, inspire, instigate, motivate, move, provoke, spur, stimulate, urge **5.** assist, cue, help out, jog the memory, prod, refresh the memory, remind **6.** call forth, cause, elicit, evoke, give rise to, occasion, provoke ~*n.* **7.** cue, help, hint, jog, jolt, prod, reminder, spur, stimulus
Antonyms *adj.* hesitating, inactive, inattentive, inefficient, late, remiss, slack, slow, tardy, unresponsive ~*v.* deter, discourage, prevent, restrain, talk out of

prompter 1. autocue, idiot board (*Sl.*), Teleprompter (*Trademark*) **2.** agitator, catalyst, gadfly, inspirer, instigator, moving spirit, prime mover

prompting assistance, encouragement, hint, incitement, influence, jogging, persuasion, pressing, pressure, prodding, pushing, reminder, reminding, suggestion, urging

promptly at once, by return, directly, hotfoot, immediately, instantly, on the dot, on time, pdq (*Sl.*), posthaste, pronto (*Inf.*), punctually, quickly, speedily, swiftly, unhesitatingly

promptness alacrity, alertness, briskness, dispatch, eagerness, haste, promptitude, punctuality, quickness, readiness, speed, swiftness, willingness

promulgate advertise, announce, broadcast, circulate, communicate, declare, decree, disseminate, issue, make known, make public, notify, proclaim, promote, publish, spread

prone 1. face down, flat, horizontal, lying down, procumbent, prostrate, recumbent, supine **2.** apt, bent, disposed, given, in-

clined, liable, likely, predisposed, subject, susceptible, tending
Antonyms (*sense 1*) erect, face up, perpendicular, supine, upright, vertical (*sense 2*) averse, disinclined, indisposed, not likely, unlikely

prong point, projection, spike, tine, tip

pronounce 1. accent, articulate, enunciate, say, sound, speak, stress, utter, vocalize, voice **2.** affirm, announce, assert, declare, decree, deliver, judge, proclaim

pronounced broad, clear, conspicuous, decided, definite, distinct, evident, marked, noticeable, obvious, striking, strong, unmistakable
Antonyms concealed, hidden, imperceptible, inconspicuous, unapparent, unnoticeable, vague

pronouncement announcement, declaration, decree, dictum, edict, judgment, manifesto, notification, proclamation, promulgation, pronunciamento, statement

pronunciation accent, accentuation, articulation, diction, elocution, enunciation, inflection, intonation, speech, stress

proof *n.* **1.** attestation, authentication, certification, confirmation, corroboration, demonstration, evidence, substantiation, testimony, verification **2.** *As in* **put to the proof** assay, examination, experiment, ordeal, scrutiny, test, trial **3.** *Printing* galley, galley proof, page proof, pull, slip, trial impression, trial print ~*adj.* **4.** impenetrable, impervious, repellent, resistant, strong, tight, treated **5. be proof against** hold out against, resist, stand firm against, stand up to, withstand

prop *v.* **1.** bolster, brace, buttress, hold up, maintain, shore, stay, support, sustain, truss, uphold **2.** lean, rest, set, stand ~*n.* **3.** brace, buttress, mainstay, stanchion, stay, support, truss

propaganda advertising, agitprop, ballyhoo (*Inf.*), brainwashing, disinformation, hype, information, newspeak, promotion, publicity

propagate 1. beget, breed, engender, generate, increase, multiply, procreate, produce, proliferate, reproduce **2.** broadcast, circulate, diffuse, disseminate, make known, proclaim, promote, promulgate, publicize, publish, spread, transmit
Antonyms (*sense 2*) cover up, hide, hush up, keep under wraps, stifle, suppress, withhold

propagation 1. breeding, generation, increase, multiplication, procreation, proliferation, reproduction **2.** circulation, communication, diffusion, dissemination, distribution, promotion, promulgation, spread, spreading, transmission

propel drive, force, impel, launch, push, send, set in motion, shoot, shove, start, thrust
Antonyms check, delay, hold back, pull, slow, stop

propensity aptness, bent, bias, disposition, inclination, leaning, liability, penchant, predisposition, proclivity, proneness, susceptibility, tendency, weakness

proper 1. appropriate, apt, becoming, befitting, fit, fitting, legitimate, meet (*Archaic*), right, suitable, suited 2. *comme il faut*, decent, decorous, *de rigueur*, genteel, gentlemanly, ladylike, mannerly, polite, punctilious, refined, respectable, seemly 3. accepted, accurate, conventional, correct, established, exact, formal, kosher (*Inf.*), orthodox, precise, right 4. characteristic, individual, own, particular, peculiar, personal, respective, special, specific
Antonyms (*senses 1, 2, & 3*) coarse, common, crude, discourteous, impolite, improper, inappropriate, indecent, rude, unbecoming, unconventional, ungentlemanly, unladylike, unorthodox, unrefined, unseemly, unsuitable, wrong

property 1. assets, belongings, building(s), capital, chattels, effects, estate, goods, holdings, house(s), means, possessions, resources, riches, wealth 2. acres, estate, freehold, holding, land, real estate, real property, realty, title 3. ability, attribute, characteristic, feature, hallmark, idiosyncrasy, mark, peculiarity, quality, trait, virtue

prophecy augury, divination, forecast, foretelling, prediction, prognosis, prognostication, revelation, second sight, soothsaying, sortilege, vaticination (*Rare*)

prophesy augur, divine, forecast, foresee, foretell, forewarn, predict, presage, prognosticate, soothsay, vaticinate (*Rare*)

prophet augur, Cassandra, clairvoyant, diviner, forecaster, oracle, prognosticator, prophesier, seer, sibyl, soothsayer

prophetic augural, divinatory, fatidic (*Rare*), foreshadowing, mantic, oracular, predictive, presaging, prescient, prognostic, sibylline, vatic (*Rare*)

propitious 1. advantageous, auspicious, bright, encouraging, favourable, fortunate, full of promise, happy, lucky, opportune, promising, prosperous, rosy, timely 2. benevolent, benign, favourably inclined, friendly, gracious, kind, well-disposed

proportion 1. distribution, ratio, relationship, relative amount 2. agreement, balance, congruity, correspondence, harmony, symmetry 3. amount, cut (*Inf.*), division, fraction, measure, part, percentage, quota, segment, share 4. *Plural* amplitude,

breadth, bulk, capacity, dimensions, expanse, extent, magnitude, measurements, range, scope, size, volume

proportional, proportionate balanced, commensurate, comparable, compatible, consistent, correspondent, corresponding, equitable, equivalent, even, in proportion, just
Antonyms different, discordant, disproportionate, dissimilar, incommensurable, incompatible, inconsistent, unequal

proposal bid, design, motion, offer, overture, plan, presentation, proffer, programme, project, proposition, recommendation, scheme, suggestion, tender, terms

propose 1. advance, come up with, present, proffer, propound, put forward, submit, suggest, tender 2. introduce, invite, name, nominate, present, put up, recommend 3. aim, design, have every intention, have in mind, intend, mean, plan, purpose, scheme 4. ask for someone's hand (in marriage), offer marriage, pay suit, pop the question (*Inf.*)

proposition 1. *n.* motion, plan, programme, project, proposal, recommendation, scheme, suggestion 2. *v.* accost, make an improper suggestion, make an indecent proposal, solicit

propound advance, advocate, contend, lay down, postulate, present, propose, put forward, set forth, submit, suggest

proprietor, proprietress deed holder, freeholder, landlady, landlord, landowner, owner, possessor, titleholder

propriety 1. appropriateness, aptness, becomingness, correctness, fitness, rightness, seemliness, suitableness 2. breeding, courtesy, decency, decorum, delicacy, etiquette, good form, good manners, manners, modesty, politeness, protocol, punctilio, rectitude, refinement, respectability, seemliness 3. **the proprieties** accepted conduct, amenities, civilities, etiquette, niceties, rules of conduct, social code, social conventions, social graces, the done thing
Antonyms (*sense 2*) bad form, bad manners, immodesty, impoliteness, indecency, indecorum, indelicacy, vulgarity

propulsion drive, impetus, impulse, impulsion, momentum, motive power, power, pressure, propelling force, push, thrust

prosaic banal, boring, commonplace, dry, dull, everyday, flat, hackneyed, humdrum, matter-of-fact, mundane, ordinary, pedestrian, routine, stale, tame, trite, unimaginative, uninspiring, vapid, workaday
Antonyms entertaining, exciting, extraordinary, fascinating, imaginative, interesting, poetical, unusual

proscribe 1. ban, boycott, censure, con~

demn, damn, denounce, doom, embargo, forbid, interdict, prohibit, reject **2.** attaint (*Archaic*), banish, blackball, deport, exclude, excommunicate, exile, expatriate, expel, os~ tracize, outlaw
Antonyms (*sense 1*) allow, authorize, en~ dorse, give leave, give permission, license, permit, sanction, warrant

proscription 1. ban, boycott, censure, con~ demnation, damning, denunciation, doom~ ing, embargo, interdict, prohibition, rejec~ tion **2.** attainder (*Archaic*), banishment, de~ portation, ejection, eviction, exclusion, ex~ communication, exile, expatriation, expul~ sion, ostracism, outlawry

prosecute 1. *Law* arraign, bring action against, bring suit against, bring to trial, do (*Sl.*), indict, litigate, prefer charges, put in the dock, put on trial, seek redress, sue, summon, take to court, try **2.** carry on, conduct, direct, discharge, engage in, man~ age, perform, practise, work at **3.** carry through, continue, follow through, per~ severe, persist, pursue, see through

prospect *n.* **1.** anticipation, calculation, contemplation, expectation, future, hope, odds, opening, outlook, plan, presumption, probability, promise, proposal, tnought **2.** landscape, outlook, panorama, perspective, scene, sight, spectacle, view, vision, vista **3.** **in prospect** in sight, in store, in the offing, in the wind, in view, on the cards, on the horizon, planned, projected **4.** *Sometimes plural* chance, likelihood, possibility ~*v.* **5.** explore, go after, look for, search, seek, survey

prospective about to be, anticipated, ap~ proaching, awaited, coming, destined, eventual, expected, forthcoming, future, hoped-for, imminent, intended, likely, looked-for, possible, potential, soon-to-be, - to-be, to come, upcoming

prospectus announcement, catalogue, con~ spectus, list, outline, plan, programme, scheme, syllabus, synopsis

prosper advance, be fortunate, bloom, do well, fare well, flourish, flower, get on, grow rich, make good, make it (*Inf.*), progress, succeed, thrive

prosperity affluence, boom, ease, fortune, good fortune, good times, life of luxury, life of Riley (*Inf.*), luxury, plenty, prosperous~ ness, riches, success, the good life, wealth, well-being
Antonyms adversity, depression, destitu~ tion, failure, indigence, misfortune, poverty, shortage, want

prosperous 1. blooming, booming, doing well, flourishing, fortunate, lucky, on the up and up (*Brit.*), palmy, prospering, suc~ cessful, thriving **2.** affluent, in clover (*Inf.*),

in the money (*Inf.*), moneyed, opulent, rich, wealthy, well-heeled (*Inf.*), well-off, well-to-do **3.** advantageous, auspicious, bright, fa~ vourable, good, profitable, promising, pro~ pitious, timely
Antonyms defeated, failing, impoverished, inauspicious, poor, unfavourable, unfortu~ nate, unlucky, unpromising, unsuccessful, untimely

prostitute 1. *n.* bawd (*Archaic*), brass (*Sl.*), call girl, camp follower, cocotte, courtesan, fallen woman, *fille de joie*, harlot, hooker (*U.S. sl.*), hustler (*U.S. & Canad. sl.*), loose woman, moll (*Sl.*), pro (*Sl.*), scrubber (*Brit. & Aust. sl.*), streetwalker, strumpet, tart (*Inf.*), trollop, white slave, whore, working girl (*Facetious sl.*) **2.** *v.* cheapen, debase, degrade, demean, devalue, misapply, per~ vert, profane

prostitution harlotry, harlot's trade, Mrs. Warren's profession, streetwalking, the game (*Sl.*), the oldest profession, vice, whoredom

prostrate *adj.* **1.** abject, bowed low, flat, horizontal, kowtowing, procumbent, prone **2.** at a low ebb, dejected, depressed, deso~ late, drained, exhausted, fagged out (*Inf.*), fallen, inconsolable, overcome, spent, worn out **3.** brought to one's knees, defenceless, disarmed, helpless, impotent, overwhelmed, paralysed, powerless, reduced ~*v.* **4.** *Of oneself* abase, bend the knee to, bow before, bow down to, cast oneself before, cringe, fall at (someone's) feet, fall on one's knees before, grovel, kneel, kowtow, submit **5.** bring low, crush, depress, disarm, lay low, overcome, overthrow, overturn, overwhelm, paralyse, reduce, ruin **6.** drain, exhaust, fag out (*Inf.*), fatigue, sap, tire, wear out, weary

protagonist 1. central character, hero, heroine, lead, leading character, principal **2.** advocate, champion, exponent, leader, mainstay, moving spirit, prime mover, standard-bearer, supporter

protean changeable, ever-changing, many-sided, mercurial, multiform, mutable, poly~ morphous, temperamental, variable, versa~ tile, volatile

protect care for, chaperon, cover, cover up for, defend, foster, give sanctuary, guard, harbour, keep, keep safe, look after, mount *or* stand guard over, preserve, safeguard, save, screen, secure, shelter, shield, stick up for (*Inf.*), support, take under one's wing, watch over
Antonyms assail, assault, attack, betray, endanger, expose, expose to danger, threaten

protection 1. aegis, care, charge, custody, defence, guardianship, guarding, preserva~ tion, protecting, safeguard, safekeeping, safety, security **2.** armour, barrier, buffer, bulwark, cover, guard, refuge, safeguard, screen, shelter, shield

protective careful, covering, defensive, fatherly, insulating, jealous, maternal, motherly, paternal, possessive, protecting, safeguarding, sheltering, shielding, vigilant, warm, watchful

protector advocate, benefactor, bodyguard, champion, counsel, defender, guard, guardian, guardian angel, knight in shining armour, patron, safeguard, tower of strength

protégé, protégée charge, dependant, discovery, pupil, student, ward

protest *n.* **1.** complaint, declaration, demur, demurral, disapproval, dissent, formal complaint, objection, outcry, protestation, remonstrance ~*v.* **2.** complain, cry out, demonstrate, demur, disagree, disapprove, expostulate, express disapproval, kick (against) (*Inf.*), object, oppose, remonstrate, say no to, take exception **3.** affirm, argue, assert, asseverate, attest, avow, contend, declare, insist, maintain, profess, testify, vow

protestation 1. complaint, disagreement, dissent, expostulation, objection, outcry, protest, remonstrance, remonstration **2.** affirmation, asseveration, avowal, declaration, oath, pledge, profession, vow

protester agitator, demonstrator, dissenter, dissident, protest marcher, rebel

protocol 1. code of behaviour, conventions, courtesies, customs, decorum, etiquette, formalities, good form, manners, politesse, propriety, rules of conduct **2.** agreement, compact, concordat, contract, convention, covenant, pact, treaty

prototype archetype, example, first, mock-up, model, norm, original, paradigm, pattern, precedent, standard, type

protract continue, drag on *or* out, draw out, extend, keep going, lengthen, prolong, spin out, stretch out
Antonyms abbreviate, abridge, compress, curtail, reduce, shorten, summarize

protracted dragged out, drawn-out, extended, interminable, lengthy, long, long-drawn-out, never-ending, overlong, prolonged, spun out, time-consuming

protrude bulge, come through, extend, jut, obtrude, point, pop (*of eyes*), project, shoot out, stand out, start (from), stick out

protrusion bulge, bump, hump, jut, lump, outgrowth, projection, protuberance, swelling

protuberance bulge, bump, excrescence, hump, knob, lump, outgrowth, process, projection, prominence, protrusion, swelling, tumour

protuberant beetling, bulbous, bulging,

gibbous, hanging over, jutting, popping (*of eyes*), prominent, protruding, protrusive, proud (*Dialect*), swelling, swollen
Antonyms concave, flat, indented, receding, sunken

proud 1. appreciative, content, contented, glad, gratified, honoured, pleased, satisfied, self-respecting, well-pleased **2.** arrogant, boastful, conceited, disdainful, egotistical, haughty, high and mighty (*Inf.*), imperious, lordly, narcissistic, orgulous (*Archaic*), overbearing, presumptuous, self-important, self-satisfied, snobbish, snooty (*Inf.*), stuck-up (*Inf.*), supercilious, toffee-nosed (*Sl., chiefly Brit.*), vain **3.** exalted, glorious, gratifying, illustrious, memorable, pleasing, red-letter, rewarding, satisfying **4.** august, distinguished, eminent, grand, great, illustrious, imposing, magnificent, majestic, noble, splendid, stately
Antonyms abject, ashamed, base, deferential, discontented, displeased, dissatisfied, humble, ignoble, ignominious, lowly, meek, modest, submissive, unassuming, undignified, unobtrusive

provable attestable, demonstrable, evincible, testable, verifiable

prove 1. ascertain, attest, authenticate, bear out, confirm, corroborate, demonstrate, determine, establish, evidence, evince, justify, show, show clearly, substantiate, verify **2.** analyse, assay, check, examine, experiment, put to the test, put to trial, test, try **3.** be found to be, come out, end up, result, turn out
Antonyms (*sense 1*) discredit, disprove, give the lie to, refute, rule out

proverb adage, aphorism, apophthegm, byword, dictum, gnome, maxim, saw, saying

proverbial accepted, acknowledged, archetypal, axiomatic, conventional, current, customary, famed, famous, legendary, notorious, self-evident, time-honoured, traditional, typical, unquestioned, well-known

provide 1. accommodate, cater, contribute, equip, furnish, outfit, provision, purvey, stock up, supply **2.** add, afford, bring, give, impart, lend, present, produce, render, serve, yield **3.** *With* for *or* against anticipate, arrange for, forearm, get ready, make arrangements, make plans, plan ahead, plan for, prepare for, take measures, take precautions **4.** *With* for care for, keep, look after, maintain, support, sustain, take care of **5.** determine, lay down, require, specify, state, stipulate
Antonyms (*sense 1*) deprive, keep back, refuse, withhold (*sense 3*) disregard, fail to notice, miss, neglect, overlook (*sense 4*) neglect

providence 1. destiny, divine intervention, fate, fortune, God's will, predestination **2.**

care, caution, discretion, far-sightedness, foresight, forethought, perspicacity, pres~ ence of mind, prudence

provident canny, careful, cautious, dis~ creet, economical, equipped, far-seeing, far-sighted, forearmed, foresighted, frugal, prudent, sagacious, shrewd, thrifty, vigi~ lant, well-prepared, wise
Antonyms careless, heedless, improvident, imprudent, negligent, prodigal, profligate, reckless, short-sighted, spendthrift, thought~ less, thriftless, uneconomical, unthrifty, wasteful

providential fortuitous, fortunate, happy, heaven-sent, lucky, opportune, timely, wel~ come

provider 1. benefactor, donor, giver, source, supplier 2. breadwinner, earner, mainstay, supporter, wage earner

providing, provided *conj.* as long as, contingent upon, given, if and only if, in case, in the event, on condition, on the as~ sumption, subject to, upon these terms, with the proviso, with the understanding

province 1. colony, county, department, dependency, district, division, domain, patch, region, section, territory, tract, turf (*U.S. sl.*), zone 2. *Fig.* area, business, ca~ pacity, charge, concern, duty, employment, field, function, line, orbit, part, pigeon (*Brit. inf.*), post, responsibility, role, sphere, turf (*U.S. sl.*)

provincial *adj.* 1. country, hick (*Inf., chiefly U.S. & Canad.*), home-grown, homespun, lo~ cal, rural, rustic 2. insular, inward-looking, limited, narrow, narrow-minded, parish-pump, parochial, small-minded, small-town (*U.S.*), uninformed, unsophisticated, up~ country ~*n.* 3. country cousin, hayseed (*U.S. & Canad. inf.*), hick (*Inf., chiefly U.S. & Canad.*), rustic, yokel
Antonyms cosmopolitan, fashionable, pol~ ished, refined, sophisticated, urban, urbane

provision 1. accoutrement, catering, equipping, fitting out, furnishing, provid~ ing, supplying, victualling 2. arrangement, plan, prearrangement, precaution, prepara~ tion 3. *Fig.* agreement, clause, condition, demand, proviso, requirement, rider, specification, stipulation, term

provisional conditional, contingent, inter~ im, limited, pro tem, provisory, qualified, stopgap, temporary, tentative, transitional
Antonyms definite, fixed, permanent

provisions comestibles, eatables, eats (*Sl.*), edibles, fare, feed, food, foodstuff, groceries, grub (*Sl.*), nosebag (*Sl.*), provender, rations, stores, supplies, sustenance, tack (*Inf.*), vi~ ands, victuals, vittles (*Obs. or dialect*)

proviso clause, condition, limitation, provi~

sion, qualification, requirement, reserva~ tion, restriction, rider, stipulation, strings

provocation 1. *casus belli*, cause, grounds, incitement, inducement, instigation, justification, motivation, reason, stimulus 2. affront, annoyance, challenge, dare, grievance, indignity, injury, insult, offence, red rag, taunt, vexation

provocative 1. aggravating (*Inf.*), annoy~ ing, challenging, disturbing, galling, goad~ ing, incensing, insulting, offensive, outra~ geous, provoking, stimulating 2. alluring, arousing, erotic, exciting, inviting, seduc~ tive, sexy (*Inf.*), stimulating, suggestive, tantalizing, tempting

provoke 1. affront, aggravate (*Inf.*), anger, annoy, chafe, enrage, exasperate, gall, get in one's hair (*Inf.*), get on one's nerves (*Inf.*), hassle (*Inf.*), incense, infuriate, insult, irk, irritate, madden, make one's blood boil, nark (*Brit., Aust., & N.Z. sl.*), offend, pique, piss one off (*Taboo sl.*), put out, rile, try one's patience, vex 2. bring about, bring on *or* down, call forth, cause, draw forth, elicit, evoke, excite, fire, generate, give rise to, incite, induce, inflame, inspire, instigate, kindle, lead to, motivate, move, occasion, precipitate, produce, promote, prompt, rouse, stimulate, stir
Antonyms (*sense 1*) appease, calm, concili~ ate, mollify, pacify, placate, propitiate, quiet, soothe, sweeten (*sense 2*) abate, allay, assuage, blunt, curb, ease, lessen, lull, mitigate, mod~ erate, modify, relieve, temper

provoking aggravating (*Inf.*), annoying, ex~ asperating, galling, irking, irksome, irritat~ ing, maddening, obstructive, offensive, tire~ some, vexatious, vexing

prowess 1. ability, accomplishment, adept~ ness, adroitness, aptitude, attainment, com~ mand, dexterity, excellence, expertise, ex~ pertness, facility, genius, mastery, skill, talent 2. boldness, bravery, courage, daring, dauntlessness, doughtiness, fearlessness, gallantry, hardihood, heroism, intrepidity, mettle, valiance, valour
Antonyms (*sense 1*) clumsiness, inability, incapability, incompetence, ineptitude, in~ eptness, inexpertise (*sense 2*) cowardice, faint-heartedness, fear, gutlessness, timidity

prowl cruise, hunt, lurk, move stealthily, nose around, patrol, range, roam, rove, scavenge, skulk, slink, sneak, stalk, steal

proximity adjacency, closeness, contiguity, juxtaposition, nearness, neighbourhood, propinquity, vicinity

proxy agent, attorney, delegate, deputy, fac~ tor, representative, substitute, surrogate

prude Grundy, old maid (*Inf.*), prig, puritan, schoolmarm (*Brit. inf.*)

prudence 1. canniness, care, caution, cir~

cumspection, common sense, discretion, good sense, heedfulness, judgment, judi~ ciousness, sagacity, vigilance, wariness, wisdom **2.** careful budgeting, economizing, economy, far-sightedness, foresight, fore~ thought, frugality, good management, hus~ bandry, planning, precaution, preparedness, providence, saving, thrift

prudent 1. canny, careful, cautious, cir~ cumspect, discerning, discreet, judicious, politic, sagacious, sage, sensible, shrewd, vigilant, wary, wise **2.** canny, careful, eco~ nomical, far-sighted, frugal, provident, sparing, thrifty
Antonyms careless, extravagant, heedless, improvident, imprudent, inconsiderate, in~ discreet, irrational, rash, thoughtless, un~ wise, wasteful

prudery Grundyism, old-maidishness (*Inf.*), overmodesty, priggishness, primness, prud~ ishness, puritanicalness, squeamishness, starchiness (*Inf.*), strictness, stuffiness

prudish demure, narrow-minded, old-maidish (*Inf.*), overmodest, overnice, prig~ gish, prim, prissy (*Inf.*), proper, puritanical, schoolmarmish (*Brit. inf.*), squeamish, starchy (*Inf.*), strait-laced, stuffy, Victorian
Antonyms broad-minded, liberal, open-minded, permissive

prune clip, cut, cut back, dock, lop, pare down, reduce, shape, shorten, snip, trim

pry be a busybody, be inquisitive, be nosy (*Inf.*), ferret about, interfere, intrude, med~ dle, nose into, peep, peer, poke, poke one's nose in or into (*Inf.*), snoop (*Inf.*)

prying curious, eavesdropping, impertinent, inquisitive, interfering, intrusive, meddle~ some, meddling, nosy (*Inf.*), snooping (*Inf.*), snoopy (*Inf.*), spying

psalm chant, hymn, paean, song of praise

pseudo *adj.* artificial, bogus, counterfeit, ersatz, fake, false, imitation, mock, not genuine, phoney or phony (*Inf.*), pretended, quasi-, sham, spurious
Antonyms actual, authentic, bona fide, genuine, heartfelt, honest, real, sincere, true, unfeigned

pseudonym alias, assumed name, false name, incognito, nom de guerre, nom de plume, pen name, professional name, stage name

psyche anima, essential nature, individual~ ity, inner man, innermost self, mind, per~ sonality, pneuma (*Philosophy*), self, soul, spirit, subconscious, true being

psychiatrist analyst, headshrinker (*Sl.*), psychoanalyser, psychoanalyst, psycholo~ gist, psychotherapist, shrink (*Sl.*), therapist

psychic 1. clairvoyant, extrasensory, mys~ tic, occult, preternatural, supernatural,

telekinetic, telepathic **2.** mental, psycho~ genic, psychological, spiritual

psychological 1. cerebral, cognitive, in~ tellectual, mental **2.** all in the mind, emo~ tional, imaginary, irrational, psychosomat~ ic, subconscious, subjective, unconscious, unreal

psychology 1. behaviourism, science of mind, study of personality **2.** *Inf.* attitude, mental make-up, mental processes, thought processes, way of thinking, what makes one tick

psychopath headbanger (*Inf.*), headcase (*Inf.*), insane person, lunatic, madman, ma~ niac, mental case (*Sl.*), nutcase (*Sl.*), nutter (*Brit. sl.*), psychotic, sociopath

psychotic *adj.* certifiable, demented, de~ ranged, insane, lunatic, mad, mental (*Sl.*), non compos mentis, off one's chump (head (*Sl.*), rocker (*Sl.*), trolley (*Sl.*)) (*Sl.*), psycho~ pathic, unbalanced

pub or **public house** alehouse (*Archaic*), bar, boozer (*Brit., Aust., & N.Z. inf.*), inn, local (*Brit. inf.*), roadhouse, taproom, tav~ ern, watering hole (*Facetious sl.*)

puberty adolescence, awkward age, ju~ venescence, pubescence, teenage, teens, young adulthood

public *adj.* **1.** civic, civil, common, general, national, popular, social, state, universal, widespread **2.** accessible, communal, com~ munity, free to all, not private, open, open to the public, unrestricted **3.** acknowledged, exposed, in circulation, known, notorious, obvious, open, overt, patent, plain, pub~ lished, recognized **4.** important, prominent, respected, well-known ~*n.* **5.** citizens, com~ monalty, community, country, electorate, everyone, hoi polloi, Joe (and Eileen) Public (*Sl.*), Joe Six-Pack (*U.S. sl.*), masses, multi~ tude, nation, people, populace, population, society, voters **6.** audience, buyers, clien~ tele, followers, following, patrons, support~ ers, those interested, trade **7. in public** co~ ram populo, for all to see, in full view, openly, overtly, publicly
Antonyms (*sense 2*) barred, closed, exclu~ sive, inaccessible, personal, private, restrict~ ed, unavailable (*sense 3*) hidden, secluded, se~ cret, unknown, unrevealed

publication 1. advertisement, airing, an~ nouncement, appearance, broadcasting, declaration, disclosure, dissemination, notification, proclamation, promulgation, publishing, reporting **2.** book, booklet, bro~ chure, handbill, hardback, issue, leaflet, magazine, newspaper, pamphlet, paperback, periodical, title

publicity advertising, attention, ballyhoo (*Inf.*), boost, build-up, hype, plug (*Inf.*), press, promotion, public notice, puff, puff~ ery (*Inf.*)

publicize advertise, beat the drum for (*Inf.*), bring to public notice, broadcast, give pub~ licity to, hype, make known, play up, plug (*Inf.*), promote, puff, push, spotlight, spread about, write up
Antonyms conceal, contain, cover up, keep dark, keep secret, smother, stifle, suppress, withhold

public-spirited altruistic, charitable, community-minded, generous, humanitar~ ian, philanthropic, unselfish

publish 1. bring out, issue, print, produce, put out **2.** advertise, announce, blow wide open (*Sl.*), broadcast, circulate, communi~ cate, declare, disclose, distribute, divulge, impart, leak, proclaim, promulgate, publi~ cize, reveal, spread

pudding afters (*Brit. inf.*), dessert, last course, pud (*Inf.*), second course, sweet

puerile babyish, childish, foolish, immature, inane, infantile, irresponsible, jejune, ju~ venile, naive, petty, ridiculous, silly, trivial, weak
Antonyms adult, grown-up, mature, re~ sponsible, sensible

puff *n.* **1.** blast, breath, draught, emanation, flurry, gust, whiff **2.** drag (*Sl.*), pull, smoke **3.** bulge, bunching, swelling **4.** advertise~ ment, commendation, favourable mention, good word, plug (*Inf.*), sales talk ~*v.* **5.** blow, breathe, exhale, gasp, gulp, pant, wheeze **6.** drag (*Sl.*), draw, inhale, pull at *or* on, smoke, suck **7.** *Usually with* **up** bloat, dilate, distend, expand, inflate, swell **8.** crack up (*Inf.*), hype, overpraise, plug (*Inf.*), praise, promote, publicize, push

puffed 1. done in (*Inf.*), exhausted, gasping, out of breath, panting, short of breath, spent, winded **2. puffed up** bigheaded (*Inf.*), full of oneself, high and mighty (*Inf.*), proud, swollen-headed, too big for one's boots
Antonyms (*sense 2*) humble, modest, self-effacing

puffy bloated, distended, enlarged, inflamed, inflated, puffed up, swollen

pugilism boxing, fighting, prizefighting, the noble art *or* science, the prize ring, the ring

pugilist boxer, bruiser (*Inf.*), fighter, prizefighter, pug (*Sl.*)

pugnacious aggressive, antagonistic, argu~ mentative, bellicose, belligerent, choleric, combative, contentious, disputatious, hot-tempered, irascible, irritable, petulant, quarrelsome
Antonyms calm, conciliatory, gentle, irenic, pacific, peaceable, peaceful, peace-loving, placatory, placid, quiet

pull *v.* **1.** drag, draw, haul, jerk, tow, trail, tug, yank **2.** cull, draw out, extract, gather, pick, pluck, remove, take out, uproot, weed **3.** dislocate, rend, rip, sprain, strain, stretch, tear, wrench **4.** *Inf.* attract, draw, entice, lure, magnetize **5. pull apart** *or* **to pieces** attack, blast, criticize, find fault, flay, lambast(e), lay into (*Inf.*), pan (*Inf.*), pick holes in, put down, run down, slam (*Sl.*), slate (*Inf.*), tear into (*Inf.*) **6. pull oneself together** *Inf.* buck up (*Inf.*), get a grip on oneself, get over it, regain compo~ sure, snap out of it (*Inf.*) **7. pull strings** *Brit. inf.* influence, pull wires (*U.S.*), use one's influence **8. pull someone's leg** *Inf.* chaff, have (someone) on, joke, make fun of, poke fun at, rag, rib (*Inf.*), tease, twit, wind up (*Brit. sl.*) ~*n.* **9.** jerk, tug, twitch, yank **10.** attraction, drawing power, effort, exer~ tion, force, forcefulness, influence, lure, magnetism, power **11.** *Inf.* advantage, bot~ tom, clout (*Inf.*), influence, leverage, mus~ cle, weight **12.** drag (*Sl.*), inhalation, puff
Antonyms *v.* (*sense 1*) drive, nudge, push, ram, shove, thrust (*sense 2*) implant, insert, plant (*sense 4*) deter, discourage, put one off, repel ~*n.* (*sense 9*) nudge, push, shove, thrust

pull down bulldoze, demolish, destroy, raze, remove
Antonyms build, construct, erect, put up, raise, set up

pull in 1. arrive, come in, draw in, draw up, reach, stop **2.** attract, bring in, draw **3.** *Brit. sl.* arrest, bust (*Inf.*), collar (*Inf.*), feel one's collar (*Sl.*), lift (*Sl.*), nab (*Inf.*), nail (*Inf.*), pinch (*Inf.*), run in (*Sl.*), take into custody **4.** clear, earn, gain, gross, make, net, pocket, take home

pull off 1. detach, doff, remove, rip off, tear off, wrench off **2.** accomplish, bring off, carry out, crack it (*Inf.*), cut it (*Inf.*), man~ age, score a success, secure one's object, succeed

pull out abandon, depart, evacuate, leave, quit, rat on, retreat, stop participating, withdraw

pull through come through, get better, get over, pull round, rally, recover, survive, weather

pull up 1. dig out, lift, raise, uproot **2.** brake, come to a halt, halt, reach a stand~ still, stop **3.** admonish, bawl out (*Inf.*), car~ pet (*Inf.*), castigate, chew out (*U.S. & Canad. inf.*), dress down (*Inf.*), give a rocket (*Brit. & N.Z. inf.*), read the riot act, rebuke, reprimand, reprove, take to task, tear into (*Inf.*), tear (someone) off a strip (*Brit. inf.*), tell off (*Inf.*), tick off (*Inf.*)

pulp *n.* **1.** flesh, marrow, soft part **2.** mash, mush, pap, paste, pomace, semiliquid, semisolid, triturate ~*v.* **3.** crush, mash, pulverize, squash, triturate ~*adj.* **4.** cheap, lurid, mushy (*Inf.*), rubbishy, sensational, trashy

pulse 1. *n.* beat, beating, oscillation, pulsa~ tion, rhythm, stroke, throb, throbbing, vi~ bration **2.** *v.* beat, pulsate, throb, tick, vi~ brate

pulverize 1. bray, comminute, crush, granulate, grind, levigate (*Chem.*), mill, pestle, pound, triturate **2.** *Fig.* annihilate, blow out of the water (*Sl.*), crush, defeat, demolish, destroy, flatten, lick (*Inf.*), smash, tank (*Sl.*), vanquish, wipe the floor with (*Inf.*), wreck

pump *v.* **1.** *With* **out** bail out, drain, draw off, drive out, empty, force out, siphon **2.** *With* **up** blow up, dilate, inflate **3.** drive, force, inject, pour, push, send, supply **4.** cross-examine, give (someone) the third de~ gree, grill (*Inf.*), interrogate, probe, question closely, quiz, worm out of

pun double entendre, equivoque, paronoma~ sia (*Rhetoric*), play on words, quip, witti~ cism

punch¹ *v.* **1.** bash (*Inf.*), belt (*Inf.*), biff (*Sl.*), bop (*Inf.*), box, clout (*Inf.*), hit, plug (*Sl.*), pummel, slam, slug, smash, sock (*Sl.*), strike, wallop (*Inf.*) ~*n.* **2.** bash (*Inf.*), biff (*Sl.*), blow, bop (*Inf.*), clout (*Inf.*), hit, jab, knock, plug (*Sl.*), sock (*Sl.*), thump, wallop (*Inf.*) **3.** *Inf.* bite, drive, effectiveness, force, forcefulness, impact, point, verve, vigour

punch² *v.* bore, cut, drill, perforate, pierce, pink, prick, puncture, stamp

punch-drunk befuddled, confused, dazed, groggy (*Inf.*), in a daze, knocked silly, punchy (*Inf.*), reeling, slaphappy (*Inf.*), staggering, stupefied, unsteady, woozy (*Inf.*)

punctilio 1. exactitude, finickiness, meticu~ lousness, particularity, precision, punctili~ ousness, scrupulousness, strictness **2.** con~ vention, delicacy, distinction, fine point, formality, nicety, particular, refinement

punctilious careful, ceremonious, consci~ entious, exact, finicky, formal, fussy, me~ ticulous, nice, particular, precise, proper, scrupulous, strict

punctual early, exact, in good time, on the dot, on time, precise, prompt, punctilious, seasonable, strict, timely
Antonyms behind, behindhand, belated, de~ layed, late, overdue, tardy, unpunctual

punctuality promptitude, promptness, readiness, regularity

punctuate 1. break, interject, interrupt, intersperse, pepper, sprinkle **2.** accentuate, emphasize, lay stress on, mark, point up, stress, underline

puncture *n.* **1.** break, cut, damage, hole, leak, nick, opening, perforation, rupture,

slit **2.** flat, flat tyre ~*v.* **3.** bore, cut, impale, nick, penetrate, perforate, pierce, prick, rupture **4.** deflate, go down, go flat **5.** deflate, discourage, disillusion, flatten, humble, take down a peg (*Inf.*)

pundit buff (*Inf.*), maestro, one of the co~ gnoscenti, (self-appointed) authority *or* ex~ pert

pungent 1. acerb, acid, acrid, aromatic, bitter, highly flavoured, hot, peppery, pi~ quant, seasoned, sharp, sour, spicy, sting~ ing, strong, tangy, tart **2.** acrimonious, acute, barbed, biting, caustic, cutting, inci~ sive, keen, mordacious, mordant, penetrat~ ing, piercing, poignant, pointed, sarcastic, scathing, sharp, stinging, stringent, telling, trenchant, vitriolic
Antonyms bland, dull, inane, mild, moder~ ate, tasteless, unsavoury, unstimulating, weak

punish 1. beat, castigate, chasten, chastise, correct, discipline, flog, give a lesson to, give (someone) the works (*Sl.*), lash, penal~ ize, rap someone's knuckles, scourge, sen~ tence, slap someone's wrist, whip **2.** abuse, batter, give (someone) a going-over (*Inf.*), harm, hurt, injure, knock about, maltreat, manhandle, misuse, oppress, rough up

punishable blameworthy, chargeable, con~ victable, criminal, culpable, indictable

punishing arduous, backbreaking, burden~ some, demanding, exhausting, grinding, gruelling, hard, strenuous, taxing, tiring, uphill, wearing
Antonyms cushy (*Inf.*), easy, effortless, light, simple, undemanding, unexacting, untaxing

punishment 1. chastening, chastisement, comeuppance (*Sl.*), correction, discipline, just deserts, penalty, penance, punitive measures, retribution, sanction, what for (*Inf.*) **2.** *Inf.* abuse, beating, hard work, maltreatment, manhandling, pain, rough treatment, slave labour, torture, victimiza~ tion

punitive in reprisal, in retaliation, puni~ tory, retaliative, retaliatory, revengeful, vindictive

punt *v.* **1.** back, bet, gamble, lay, stake, wa~ ger ~*n.* **2.** bet, gamble, stake, wager **3.** backer, better, gambler, punter

punter *n.* **1.** backer, better, gambler, punt (*Chiefly Brit.*) **2.** *Inf.* bloke (*Brit. inf.*), fel~ low, guy (*Inf.*), man in the street, person **3.** *Inf.* client, customer

puny 1. diminutive, dwarfish, feeble, frail, little, pint-sized (*Inf.*), pygmy *or* pigmy, sickly, stunted, tiny, underfed, undersized, undeveloped, weak, weakly **2.** incon~ sequential, inferior, insignificant, minor,

paltry, petty, piddling (*Inf.*), trifling, trivial,
worthless
Antonyms (*sense 1*) brawny, burly, healthy,
hefty (*Inf.*), husky (*Inf.*), powerful, robust,
strong, sturdy, well-built, well-developed

pup *or* **puppy** *Fig.* braggart, cub, jacka~
napes, popinjay, whelp, whippersnapper,
young dog

pupil beginner, catechumen, disciple, learn~
er, neophyte, novice, scholar, schoolboy,
schoolgirl, student, trainee, tyro
Antonyms coach, instructor, master, mis~
tress, schoolmaster, schoolmistress, schoolteacher, teacher, trainer, tutor

puppet 1. doll, marionette **2.** *Fig.* cat's-paw,
creature, dupe, figurehead, gull (*Archaic*),
instrument, mouthpiece, pawn, stooge, tool

purchase *v.* **1.** acquire, buy, come by, gain,
get, get hold of, invest in, make a purchase,
obtain, pay for, pick up, procure, score (*Sl.*),
secure, shop for **2.** achieve, attain, earn,
gain, realize, win ~*n.* **3.** acquisition, asset,
buy, gain, investment, possession, property
4. advantage, edge, foothold, footing, grasp,
grip, hold, influence, lever, leverage, sup~
port, toehold
Antonyms *v.* (*sense 1*) hawk, market, mer~
chandise, peddle, retail, sell, trade in, vend
~*n.* (*sense 3*) marketing, sale, selling, vending

purchaser buyer, consumer, customer,
vendee (*Law*)
Antonyms dealer, merchant, retailer, sales~
man, salesperson, saleswoman, seller, shop~
keeper, tradesman, vendor

pure 1. authentic, clear, flawless, genuine,
natural, neat, perfect, real, simple, straight,
true, unalloyed, unmixed **2.** clean, disin~
fected, germ-free, immaculate, pasteurized,
sanitary, spotless, squeaky-clean, sterile,
sterilized, unadulterated, unblemished, un~
contaminated, unpolluted, untainted,
wholesome **3.** blameless, chaste, guileless,
honest, immaculate, impeccable, innocent,
maidenly, modest, true, uncorrupted,
undefiled, unspotted, unstained, unsullied,
upright, virgin, virginal, virtuous **4.** abso~
lute, complete, mere, outright, sheer, thor~
ough, unmitigated, unqualified, utter **5.** ab~
stract, academic, philosophical, speculative,
theoretical
Antonyms (*senses 1 & 2*) adulterated, con~
taminated, dirty, filthy, flawed, imperfect,
impure, infected, insincere, mixed, polluted,
tainted (*sense 3*) contaminated, corrupt,
defiled, guilty, immodest, immoral, impure,
indecent, obscene, sinful, spoiled, unchaste,
unclean, untrue (*sense 4*) qualified (*sense 5*)
applied, practical

purely absolutely, completely, entirely, ex~
clusively, just, merely, only, plainly, simp~
ly, solely, totally, wholly

purgatory *As used informally* agony, hell
(*Inf.*), hell on earth, misery, murder (*Inf.*),
the rack, torment, torture

purge *v.* **1.** axe (*Inf.*), clean out, dismiss, do
away with, eject, eradicate, expel, extermi~
nate, get rid of, kill, liquidate, oust, remove,
rid of, rout out, sweep out, wipe out **2.** ab~
solve, cleanse, clear, exonerate, expiate,
forgive, pardon, purify, wash ~*n.* **3.** clean~
up, crushing, ejection, elimination, eradica~
tion, expulsion, liquidation, reign of terror,
removal, suppression, witch hunt **4.** aperi~
ent (*Medical*), cathartic, dose of salts, emet~
ic, enema, laxative, physic (*Rare*), purgative
(*Medical*)

purify 1. clarify, clean, cleanse, decontami~
nate, disinfect, filter, fumigate, refine, sani~
tize, wash **2.** absolve, cleanse, exculpate,
exonerate, lustrate, redeem, sanctify, shrive
Antonyms adulterate, befoul, contaminate,
corrupt, defile, foul, infect, pollute, soil, stain,
sully, taint, tarnish, vitiate

purist classicist, formalist, pedant, preci~
sian, stickler

puritan 1. *n.* fanatic, moralist, pietist,
prude, rigorist, zealot **2.** *adj.* ascetic, aus~
tere, hidebound, intolerant, moralistic, nar~
row, narrow-minded, prudish, puritanical,
severe, strait-laced, strict

puritanical ascetic, austere, bigoted, disap~
proving, fanatical, forbidding, narrow,
narrow-minded, prim, proper, prudish, pu~
ritan, rigid, severe, stiff, strait-laced, strict,
stuffy
Antonyms broad-minded, hedonistic, in~
dulgent, latitudinarian, liberal, permissive,
tolerant

purity 1. brilliance, clarity, cleanliness,
cleanness, clearness, faultlessness, fineness,
genuineness, immaculateness, pureness,
untaintedness, wholesomeness **2.** blame~
lessness, chasteness, chastity, decency,
guilelessness, honesty, innocence, integrity,
piety, rectitude, sincerity, virginity, virtue,
virtuousness
Antonyms cloudiness, contamination, im~
modesty, immorality, impurity,
unchasteness, vice, wickedness

purport *v.* **1.** allege, assert, claim, declare,
maintain, pose as, pretend, proclaim, pro~
fess **2.** betoken, convey, denote, express,
imply, import, indicate, intend, mean, point
to, signify, suggest ~*n.* **3.** bearing, drift,
gist, idea, implication, import, meaning,
significance, spirit, tendency, tenor **4.** aim,
design, intent, intention, object, objective,
plan, purpose

purpose *n.* **1.** aim, design, function, idea,
intention, object, point, principle, reason **2.**
aim, ambition, aspiration, design, desire,
end, goal, hope, intention, object, objective,

plan, project, scheme, target, view, wish **3.** constancy, determination, firmness, persis~ tence, resolution, resolve, single- mindedness, steadfastness, tenacity, will **4.** advantage, avail, benefit, effect, gain, good, outcome, profit, result, return, use, utility **5. on purpose** by design, deliberately, de~ signedly, intentionally, knowingly, pur~ posely, wilfully, wittingly ~*v.* **6.** aim, as~ pire, commit oneself, contemplate, decide, design, determine, have a mind to, intend, make up one's mind, mean, meditate, plan, propose, resolve, set one's sights on, think to, work towards

purposeful decided, deliberate, determined, firm, fixed, immovable, positive, resolute, resolved, settled, single-minded, steadfast, strong-willed, tenacious, unfaltering
Antonyms aimless, faltering, irresolute, purposeless, undecided, undetermined, vacil~ lating, wavering

purposeless aimless, empty, goalless, mo~ tiveless, needless, pointless, senseless, uncalled-for, unnecessary, useless, vacuous, wanton

purposely by design, calculatedly, con~ sciously, deliberately, designedly, expressly, intentionally, knowingly, on purpose, wil~ fully, with intent
Antonyms accidentally, by accident, by chance, by mistake, inadvertently, uncon~ sciously, unintentionally, unknowingly, un~ wittingly

purse *n.* **1.** money-bag, pouch, wallet **2.** cof~ fers, exchequer, funds, means, money, re~ sources, treasury, wealth, wherewithal **3.** award, gift, present, prize, reward ~*v.* **4.** close, contract, knit, pout, press together, pucker, tighten, wrinkle

pursuance bringing about, carrying out, discharge, doing, effecting, execution, fol~ lowing, performance, prosecution, pursuing

pursue **1.** accompany, attend, chase, dog, follow, give chase to, go after, harass, har~ ry, haunt, hound, hunt, hunt down, plague, run after, shadow, stalk, tail (*Inf.*), track **2.** aim for, aspire to, desire, have as one's goal, purpose, seek, strive for, try for, work towards **3.** adhere to, carry on, continue, cultivate, hold to, keep on, maintain, per~ severe in, persist in, proceed, see through **4.** apply oneself, carry on, conduct, engage in, perform, ply, practise, prosecute, tackle, wage, work at **5.** chase after, court, make up to (*Inf.*), pay attention to, pay court to, set one's cap at, woo
Antonyms avoid, eschew, fight shy of, flee, give (someone *or* something) a wide berth, keep away from, run away from, shun, steer clear of

pursuit **1.** chase, hunt, hunting, inquiry,

quest, search, seeking, tracking, trail, trail~ ing **2.** activity, hobby, interest, line, occu~ pation, pastime, pleasure, vocation

push *v.* **1.** depress, drive, poke, press, pro~ pel, ram, shove, thrust **2.** elbow, jostle, make *or* force one's way, move, shoulder, shove, squeeze, thrust **3.** egg on, encourage, expedite, hurry, impel, incite, persuade, press, prod, speed (up), spur, urge **4.** ad~ vertise, boost, cry up, hype, make known, plug (*Inf.*), promote, propagandize, publi~ cize, puff **5.** browbeat, coerce, constrain, dragoon, encourage, exert influence on, influence, oblige ~*n.* **6.** butt, jolt, nudge, poke, prod, shove, thrust **7.** *Inf.* ambition, determination, drive, dynamism, energy, enterprise, get-up-and-go (*Inf.*), go (*Inf.*), gumption (*Inf.*), initiative, pep, vigour, vi~ tality **8.** *Inf.* advance, assault, attack, char~ ge, effort, offensive, onset, thrust **9. the push** *Sl.* discharge, dismissal, kiss-off (*Sl., chiefly U.S. & Canad.*), marching orders (*Inf.*), one's books (*Inf.*), one's cards, the boot (*Sl.*), the (old) heave-ho (*Inf.*), the order of the boot (*Sl.*), the sack (*Inf.*)
Antonyms *v.* (*sense 1*) drag, draw, haul, jerk, pull, tow, trail, tug, yank (*sense 3*) deter, dis~ courage, dissuade, put off ~*n.* (*sense 6*) jerk, pull, tug, yank

pushed *Often with* **for** hurried, in difficulty, pressed, rushed, short of, tight, under pres~ sure, up against it (*Inf.*)

pushing **1.** ambitious, determined, driving, dynamic, enterprising, go-ahead, on the go, purposeful, resourceful **2.** assertive, bold, brash, bumptious, forward, impertinent, intrusive, presumptuous, pushy (*Inf.*), self- assertive

push off beat it (*Sl.*), depart, get lost (*Inf.*), go away, hit the road (*Sl.*), hook it (*Sl.*), launch, leave, light out (*Inf.*), make oneself scarce (*Inf.*), shove off (*Inf.*), slope off, take off (*Inf.*)

pushover **1.** breeze (*U.S. & Canad. inf.*), cakewalk (*Inf.*), child's play (*Inf.*), cinch (*Sl.*), doddle (*Brit. sl.*), duck soup (*U.S. sl.*), picnic (*Inf.*), piece of cake (*Brit. inf.*), walk~ over (*Inf.*) **2.** chump (*Inf.*), easy *or* soft mark (*Inf.*), easy game (*Inf.*), mug (*Brit. sl.*), soft touch (*Sl.*), stooge (*Sl.*), sucker (*Sl.*), walkover (*Inf.*)
Antonyms (*sense 1*) challenge, hassle (*Inf.*), ordeal, test, trial, undertaking

pushy aggressive, ambitious, bold, brash, bumptious, forceful, loud, obnoxious, ob~ trusive, offensive, officious, presumptuous, pushing, self-assertive
Antonyms diffident, inoffensive, meek, mousy, quiet, reserved, retiring, self-effacing, shy, timid, unassertive, unassuming, unob~ trusive

pusillanimous abject, chicken-hearted, cowardly, craven, faint-hearted, fearful, feeble, gutless (*Inf.*), lily-livered, recreant (*Archaic*), spineless, timid, timorous, weak, yellow (*Inf.*)
Antonyms bold, brave, courageous, daring, dauntless, fearless, gallant, heroic, intrepid, plucky, valiant, valorous

pussyfoot 1. creep, prowl, slink, steal, tiptoe, tread warily **2.** beat about the bush, be noncommittal, equivocate, flannel (*Brit. inf.*), hedge, hum and haw, prevaricate, sit on the fence, tergiversate

put 1. bring, deposit, establish, fix, lay, place, position, rest, set, settle, situate **2.** commit, condemn, consign, doom, enjoin, impose, inflict, levy, subject **3.** assign, constrain, employ, force, induce, make, oblige, require, set, subject to **4.** express, phrase, pose, set, state, utter, word **5.** advance, bring forward, forward, offer, posit, present, propose, set before, submit, tender **6.** cast, fling, heave, hurl, lob, pitch, throw, toss

put across *or* **over** communicate, convey, explain, get across, get through, make clear, make oneself understood, spell out

put aside *or* **by 1.** cache, deposit, keep in reserve, lay by, salt away, save, squirrel away, stockpile, store, stow away **2.** bury, discount, disregard, forget, ignore

putative alleged, assumed, commonly believed, imputed, presumed, presumptive, reported, reputed, supposed

put away 1. put back, replace, return to (its) place, tidy away **2.** deposit, keep, lay in, put by, save, set aside, store away **3.** certify, commit, confine, institutionalize, lock up **4.** consume, devour, eat up, gobble, gulp down, wolf down **5.** destroy, do away with, put down, put out of its misery, put to sleep

put down 1. enter, inscribe, log, record, set down, take down, transcribe, write down **2.** crush, quash, quell, repress, silence, stamp out, suppress **3.** *With* to ascribe, attribute, impute, set down **4.** destroy, do away with, put away, put out of its misery, put to sleep **5.** *Sl.* condemn, crush, deflate, dismiss, disparage, humiliate, mortify, reject, shame, slight, snub

put forward advance, introduce, move, nominate, prescribe, present, press, proffer, propose, recommend, submit, suggest, tender

put off 1. defer, delay, hold over, postpone, put back, put on the back burner (*Inf.*), reschedule, take a rain check on (*U.S. & Canad. inf.*) **2.** abash, confuse, discomfit, disconcert, dismay, distress, faze, nonplus, perturb, rattle (*Inf.*), throw (*Inf.*), unsettle **3.** discourage, dishearten, dissuade

Antonyms (*sense 3*) egg on, encourage, incite, persuade, prompt, push, spur, urge

put on 1. change into, don, dress, get dressed in, slip into **2.** affect, assume, fake, feign, make believe, play-act, pretend, sham, simulate **3.** do, mount, present, produce, show, stage **4.** add, gain, increase by **5.** back, bet, lay, place, wager
Antonyms (*sense 1*) cast off, doff, remove, shed, slip off, slip out of, take off, throw off, undress

put out 1. anger, annoy, confound, disturb, exasperate, harass, irk, irritate, nettle, perturb, provoke, vex **2.** blow out, douse, extinguish, quench, smother, snuff out, stamp out **3.** bother, discomfit, discommode, discompose, disconcert, discountenance, disturb, embarrass, impose upon, incommode, inconvenience, put on the spot, trouble, upset **4.** bring out, broadcast, circulate, issue, make known, make public, publish, release

putrid bad, contaminated, corrupt, decayed, decomposed, fetid, foul, off, olid, putrefied, rancid, rank, reeking, rotten, rotting, spoiled, stinking, tainted
Antonyms clean, fresh, pure, sweet, uncontaminated, untainted, wholesome

put up 1. build, construct, erect, fabricate, raise **2.** accommodate, board, entertain, give one lodging, house, lodge, take in **3.** float, nominate, offer, present, propose, put forward, recommend, submit **4.** advance, give, invest, pay, pledge, provide, supply **5. put up to** egg on, encourage, goad, incite, instigate, prompt, put the idea into one's head, urge **6. put up with** *Inf.* abide, bear, brook, endure, lump (*Inf.*), pocket, stand, stand for, stomach, suffer, swallow, take, tolerate
Antonyms (*sense 1*) demolish, destroy, flatten, knock down, level, pull down, raze, tear down (*sense 6*) not stand for, object to, oppose, protest against, reject, take exception to

put-upon abused, beset, exploited, harried, imposed upon, inconvenienced, overworked, put-out, saddled, taken advantage of, taken for a fool, taken for granted, troubled

puzzle *v.* **1.** baffle, beat (*Sl.*), bewilder, confound, confuse, flummox, mystify, nonplus, perplex, stump **2.** ask oneself, brood, cudgel *or* rack one's brains, mull over, muse, ponder, study, think about, think hard, wonder **3.** *Usually with* out clear up, crack, crack the code, decipher, figure out, find the key, get it, get the answer, resolve, see, solve, sort out, suss (out) (*Sl.*), think through, unravel, work out ~*n.* **4.** brain-teaser (*Inf.*), conundrum, enigma, labyrinth, maze, mystery, paradox, poser, problem, question, question mark, riddle, teaser **5.** bafflement,

bewilderment, confusion, difficulty, dilem~
ma, perplexity, quandary, uncertainty

puzzled at a loss, at sea, baffled, beaten,
bewildered, clueless, confused, doubtful,
flummoxed, in a fog, lost, mixed up,
mystified, nonplussed, perplexed, stuck,
stumped, without a clue

puzzlement bafflement, bewilderment,
confusion, disorientation, doubt, doubtful~
ness, mystification, perplexity, questioning,
surprise, uncertainty, wonder

puzzling abstruse, ambiguous, baffling,
bewildering, beyond one, enigmatic,
full of surprises, hard, incomprehensible,
inexplicable, involved, knotty, labyrinthine,
misleading, mystifying, oracular, per~
plexing, unaccountable, unclear, unfathom~
able

Antonyms clear, comprehensible, easy, evi~
dent, intelligible, lucid, manifest, obvious,
patent, plain, simple, unambiguous, un~
equivocal, unmistakable

Q

quack 1. *n.* charlatan, fake, fraud, humbug, impostor, mountebank, phoney *or* phony (*Inf.*), pretender, quacksalver (*Archaic*) **2.** *adj.* counterfeit, fake, fraudulent, phoney *or* phony (*Inf.*), pretended, sham

quagmire 1. bog, fen, marsh, mire, morass, quicksand, slough, swamp **2.** difficulty, dilemma, entanglement, fix (*Inf.*), imbroglio, impasse, jam (*Inf.*), muddle, pass, pickle (*Inf.*), pinch, plight, predicament, quandary, scrape (*Inf.*)

quail blanch, blench, cower, cringe, droop, faint, falter, flinch, have cold feet (*Inf.*), quake, recoil, shake, shrink, shudder, tremble

quaint 1. bizarre, curious, droll, eccentric, fanciful, fantastic, odd, old-fashioned, original, peculiar, queer, rum (*Brit. sl.*), singular, strange, unusual, whimsical **2.** antiquated, antique, artful, charming, gothic, ingenious, old-fashioned, old-world, picturesque
Antonyms fashionable, modern, new, normal, ordinary, up-to-date

quake convulse, move, pulsate, quail, quiver, rock, shake, shiver, shudder, throb, totter, tremble, vibrate, waver, wobble

qualification 1. ability, accomplishment, aptitude, attribute, capability, capacity, eligibility, endowment(s), fitness, quality, skill, suitability, suitableness **2.** allowance, caveat, condition, criterion, exception, exemption, limitation, modification, objection, prerequisite, proviso, requirement, reservation, restriction, rider, stipulation

qualified 1. able, accomplished, adept, capable, certificated, competent, efficient, equipped, experienced, expert, fit, knowledgeable, licensed, practised, proficient, skilful, talented, trained **2.** bounded, circumscribed, conditional, confined, contingent, equivocal, guarded, limited, modified, provisional, reserved, restricted
Antonyms (*sense 1*) amateur, apprentice, self-styled, self-taught, trainee, uncertificated, unqualified, untrained (*sense 2*) categorical, outright, unconditional, unequivocal, whole-hearted

qualify 1. capacitate, certify, commission, condition, empower, endow, equip, fit, ground, permit, prepare, ready, sanction, train **2.** abate, adapt, assuage, circumscribe, diminish, ease, lessen, limit, mitigate, moderate, modify, modulate, reduce, regulate, restrain, restrict, soften, temper,

vary **3.** characterize, describe, designate, distinguish, modify, name
Antonyms (*sense 1*) ban, debar, disqualify, forbid, preclude, prevent

quality 1. aspect, attribute, characteristic, condition, feature, mark, peculiarity, property, trait **2.** character, constitution, description, essence, kind, make, nature, sort **3.** calibre, distinction, excellence, grade, merit, position, pre-eminence, rank, standing, status, superiority, value, worth **4.** *Obsolete* aristocracy, gentry, nobility, ruling class, upper class

qualm 1. anxiety, apprehension, compunction, disquiet, doubt, hesitation, misgiving, regret, reluctance, remorse, scruple, twinge *or* pang of conscience, uncertainty, uneasiness **2.** agony, attack, nausea, pang, queasiness, sickness, spasm, throe (*Rare*), twinge

quandary bewilderment, cleft stick, delicate situation, difficulty, dilemma, doubt, embarrassment, impasse, perplexity, plight, predicament, puzzle, strait, uncertainty

quantity 1. aggregate, allotment, amount, lot, number, part, portion, quota, sum, total **2.** bulk, capacity, expanse, extent, greatness, length, magnitude, mass, measure, size, volume

quarrel *n.* **1.** affray, altercation, argument, *bagarre*, brawl, breach, broil, commotion, contention, controversy, difference (of opinion), disagreement, discord, disputation, dispute, dissension, dissidence, disturbance, feud, fight, fracas, fray, misunderstanding, row, scrap (*Inf.*), shindig (*Inf.*), shindy (*Inf.*), skirmish, spat, squabble, strife, tiff, tumult, vendetta, wrangle ~*v.* **2.** altercate, argue, bicker, brawl, clash, differ, disagree, dispute, fall out (*Inf.*), fight, row, spar, squabble, wrangle **3.** carp, cavil, complain, decry, disapprove, find fault, object to, take exception to
Antonyms (*sense 1*) accord, agreement, concord (*sense 2*) agree, get on *or* along (with)

quarrelsome argumentative, belligerent, cat-and-dog (*Inf.*), choleric, combative, contentious, cross, disputatious, fractious, ill-tempered, irascible, irritable, peevish, petulant, pugnacious, querulous
Antonyms easy-going, equable, even-tempered, placid

quarry aim, game, goal, objective, prey, prize, victim

quarter *n.* **1.** area, direction, district, local~

ity, location, neighbourhood, part, place, point, position, province, region, side, spot, station, territory, zone **2.** clemency, com~ passion, favour, forgiveness, leniency, mer~ cy, pity ~*v.* **3.** accommodate, billet, board, house, install, lodge, place, post, put up, station

quarters abode, accommodation, barracks, billet, cantonment (*Military*), chambers, digs (*Brit. inf.*), domicile, dwelling, habita~ tion, lodging, lodgings, post, residence, rooms, shelter, station

quash 1. beat, crush, destroy, extinguish, extirpate, overthrow, put down, quell, quench, repress, squash, subdue, suppress **2.** annul, cancel, declare null and void, in~ validate, nullify, overrule, overthrow, re~ scind, reverse, revoke, set aside, void

quasi- 1. almost, apparently, partly, seem~ ingly, supposedly **2.** apparent, fake, mock, near, nominal, pretended, pseudo-, seeming, semi-, sham, so-called, synthetic, virtual, would-be

quaver 1. *v.* flicker, flutter, oscillate, pul~ sate, quake, quiver, shake, shudder, thrill, tremble, trill, twitter, vibrate, waver **2.** *n.* break, quiver, shake, sob, throb, tremble, trembling, tremor, trill, vibration, warble

queen 1. consort, monarch, ruler, sovereign **2.** diva, doyenne, ideal, idol, mistress, mod~ el, perfection, prima donna, star

queenly grand, imperial, majestic, noble, regal, royal, stately

queer *adj.* **1.** abnormal, anomalous, atypi~ cal, curious, disquieting, droll, eerie, errat~ ic, extraordinary, funny, odd, outlandish, *outré*, peculiar, remarkable, rum (*Brit. sl.*), singular, strange, uncanny, uncommon, unconventional, unnatural, unorthodox, unusual, weird **2.** doubtful, dubious, fishy (*Inf.*), irregular, mysterious, puzzling, ques~ tionable, shady (*Inf.*), suspicious **3.** dizzy, faint, giddy, light-headed, queasy, reeling, uneasy **4.** crazy, demented, eccentric, idio~ syncratic, irrational, mad, odd, touched, unbalanced, unhinged ~*v.* **5.** bodge (*Inf.*), botch, endanger, harm, impair, imperil, in~ jure, jeopardize, mar, ruin, spoil, thwart, wreck

Antonyms *adj.* believable, common, con~ ventional, customary, natural, normal, ordi~ nary, orthodox, rational, regular, straight, unexceptional, unoriginal ~*v.* aid, boost, en~ hance, help

quell 1. conquer, crush, defeat, extinguish, overcome, overpower, put down, quash, squelch, stamp out, stifle, subdue, suppress, vanquish **2.** allay, alleviate, appease, as~ suage, calm, compose, deaden, dull, miti~ gate, moderate, mollify, pacify, quiet, si~ lence, soothe

quench 1. check, crush, destroy, douse, end, extinguish, put out, smother, snuff out, squelch, stifle, suppress **2.** allay, appease, cool, sate, satiate, satisfy, slake

querulous cantankerous, captious, carping, censorious, complaining, critical, cross, discontented, dissatisfied, fault-finding, fretful, grouchy (*Inf.*), grumbling, hard to please, irascible, irritable, murmuring, peevish, petulant, plaintive, ratty (*Brit. & N.Z. inf.*), sour, testy, tetchy, touchy, wasp~ ish, whining

Antonyms contented, easy to please, eq~ uable, placid, uncomplaining, uncritical, un~ demanding

query *v.* **1.** ask, enquire, question **2.** chal~ lenge, disbelieve, dispute, distrust, doubt, mistrust, suspect ~*n.* **3.** demand, doubt, hesitation, inquiry, objection, problem, question, reservation, scepticism, suspicion

quest *n.* adventure, crusade, enterprise, ex~ pedition, exploration, hunt, journey, mis~ sion, pilgrimage, pursuit, search, voyage

question *v.* **1.** ask, catechize, cross- examine, enquire, examine, grill (*Inf.*), in~ terrogate, interview, investigate, probe, pump (*Inf.*), quiz, sound out **2.** call into question, cast doubt upon, challenge, con~ trovert, disbelieve, dispute, distrust, doubt, impugn, mistrust, oppose, query, suspect ~*n.* **3.** examination, inquiry, interrogation, investigation **4.** argument, confusion, con~ tention, controversy, debate, difficulty, dis~ pute, doubt, dubiety, misgiving, problem, query, uncertainty **5.** issue, motion, point, point at issue, proposal, proposition, sub~ ject, theme, topic **6. in question** at issue, in doubt, open to debate, under discussion **7. out of the question** impossible, incon~ ceivable, not to be thought of, unthinkable

Antonyms (*senses 1 & 3*) answer, reply (*sense 2*) accept, believe, buy (*Sl.*), swallow (*Inf.*), take on trust

questionable arguable, controversial, con~ trovertible, debatable, disputable, dodgy (*Brit., Aust., & N.Z. inf.*), doubtful, dubious, dubitable, equivocal, fishy (*Inf.*), iffy (*Inf.*), moot, paradoxical, problematical, shady (*Inf.*), suspect, suspicious, uncertain, un~ proven, unreliable

Antonyms authoritative, certain, incontro~ vertible, indisputable, straightforward, un~ equivocal

queue chain, concatenation, file, line, order, progression, sequence, series, string, suc~ cession, train

quibble 1. *v.* carp, cavil, equivocate, evade, pretend, prevaricate, shift, split hairs **2.** *n.* artifice, cavil, complaint, criticism, duplic~ ity, equivocation, evasion, nicety, niggle, objection, pretence, prevarication, protest, quirk, shift, sophism, subterfuge, subtlety

quick 1. active, brief, brisk, cursory, ex~peditious, express, fast, fleet, hasty, head~long, hurried, pdq (*Sl.*), perfunctory, prompt, quickie (*Inf.*), rapid, speedy, sud~den, swift **2.** agile, alert, animated, ener~getic, flying, keen, lively, nimble, spirited, sprightly, spry, vivacious, winged **3.** able, acute, adept, adroit, all there (*Inf.*), apt, as~tute, bright, clever, deft, dexterous, dis~cerning, intelligent, nimble-witted, percep~tive, quick on the uptake (*Inf.*), quick-witted, receptive, sharp, shrewd, skilful, smart **4.** abrupt, curt, excitable, hasty, im~patient, irascible, irritable, passionate, petulant, testy, touchy **5.** *Archaic* alive, animate, existing, live, living, viable
Antonyms calm, deliberate, dull, gradual, heavy, inactive, inexpert, lazy, lethargic, long, maladroit, patient, restrained, slow, sluggish, stupid, unintelligent, unresponsive, unskilful

quicken 1. accelerate, dispatch, expedite, hasten, hurry, impel, precipitate, speed **2.** activate, animate, arouse, energize, excite, galvanize, incite, inspire, invigorate, kindle, refresh, reinvigorate, resuscitate, revitalize, revive, rouse, stimulate, strengthen, vital~ize, vivify

quickly abruptly, apace, at a rate of knots (*Inf.*), at *or* on the double, at speed, briskly, expeditiously, fast, hastily, hell for leather (*Inf.*), hotfoot, hurriedly, immediately, in~stantly, pdq (*Sl.*), posthaste, promptly, pronto (*Inf.*), quick, rapidly, soon, speedily, swiftly, with all speed
Antonyms carefully, eventually, slowly, sluggishly, unhurriedly

quick-tempered choleric, excitable, fiery, hot-tempered, impatient, impulsive, iras~cible, irritable, petulant, quarrelsome, ratty (*Brit. & N.Z. inf.*), shrewish, splenetic, testy, tetchy, waspish
Antonyms cool, dispassionate, phlegmatic, placid, slow to anger, tolerant

quick-witted alert, astute, clever, keen, perceptive, sharp, shrewd, smart
Antonyms dull, obtuse, slow, slow-witted, stupid, thick (*Inf.*), unperceptive

quid pro quo compensation, equivalent, exchange, interchange, reprisal, retaliation, substitution, tit for tat

quiescent calm, dormant, in abeyance, in~active, latent, motionless, peaceful, placid, quiet, resting, serene, silent, smooth, still, tranquil, unagitated, undisturbed, unmov~ing, unruffled

quiet *adj.* **1.** dumb, hushed, inaudible, low, low-pitched, noiseless, peaceful, silent, soft, soundless **2.** calm, contented, gentle, mild, motionless, pacific, peaceful, placid, restful,

serene, smooth, tranquil, untroubled **3.** isolated, private, retired, secluded, secret, sequestered, undisturbed, unfrequented **4.** conservative, modest, plain, restrained, simple, sober, subdued, unassuming, unob~trusive, unpretentious **5.** collected, docile, even-tempered, gentle, imperturbable, meek, mild, phlegmatic, reserved, retiring, sedate, shy, unexcitable ~*n.* **6.** calmness, ease, peace, quietness, repose, rest, serenity, si~lence, stillness, tranquillity
Antonyms *adj.* (*sense 1*) deafening, ear-splitting, high-decibel, high-volume, loud, noisy, stentorian (*sense 2*) agitated, alert, ex~citable, exciting, frenetic, troubled, turbulent, violent (*sense 3*) bustling, busy, crowded, ex~citing, fashionable, lively, popular, vibrant (*sense 4*) blatant, brash, bright, conspicuous, glaring, loud, obtrusive, ostentatious, preten~tious, showy (*sense 5*) excitable, excited, high-spirited, impatient, loquacious, pas~sionate, restless, talkative, verbose, violent ~*n.* (*sense 6*) activity, bustle, commotion, din, disturbance, noise, racket

quieten *v.* allay, alleviate, appease, assuage, blunt, calm, compose, deaden, dull, hush, lull, mitigate, mollify, muffle, mute, palliate, quell, quiet, shush (*Inf.*), silence, soothe, stifle, still, stop, subdue, tranquillize
Antonyms aggravate, exacerbate, intensify, provoke, upset, worsen

quietly 1. confidentially, dumbly, in a low voice *or* whisper, in an undertone, in~audibly, in hushed tones, in silence, mutely, noiselessly, privately, secretly, silently, softly, without talking **2.** calmly, content~edly, dispassionately, meekly, mildly, pa~tiently, placidly, serenely, undemonstra~tively **3.** coyly, demurely, diffidently, hum~bly, modestly, unassumingly, unobtrusively, unostentatiously, unpretentiously

quietness calm, calmness, hush, peace, placidity, quiescence, quiet, quietude, re~pose, rest, serenity, silence, still, stillness, tranquillity

quilt bedspread, comforter (*U.S.*), counter~pane, coverlet, duvet, eiderdown

quintessence core, distillation, essence, extract, gist, heart, kernel, lifeblood, mar~row, pith, soul, spirit

quip *n.* badinage, *bon mot*, counterattack, gibe, jest, joke, pleasantry, repartee, retort, riposte, sally, wisecrack (*Inf.*), witticism

quirk aberration, caprice, characteristic, ec~centricity, fancy, fetish, foible, habit, *idée fixe*, idiosyncrasy, kink, mannerism, oddity, peculiarity, singularity, trait, vagary, whim

quirky capricious, curious, eccentric, fanci~ful, idiosyncratic, odd, offbeat, peculiar, rum (*Brit. sl.*), singular, unpredictable, un~usual, whimsical

quisling betrayer, collaborator, fifth col~ umnist, Judas, renegade, traitor, turncoat

quit *v.* **1.** abandon, abdicate, decamp, depart, desert, exit, forsake, go, leave, pull out, re~ linquish, renounce, resign, retire, step down (*Inf.*), surrender, take off (*Inf.*), with~ draw **2.** abandon, cease, conclude, discon~ tinue, drop, end, give up, halt, stop, sus~ pend ~*adj.* **3.** absolved, acquitted, clear, discharged, exculpated, exempt, exonerated, free, released, rid of
Antonyms (*sense 2*) complete, continue, finish, go on with, see through

quite 1. absolutely, completely, consider~ ably, entirely, fully, in all respects, largely, perfectly, precisely, totally, wholly, without reservation **2.** fairly, moderately, rather, reasonably, relatively, somewhat, to a cer~ tain extent, to some degree **3.** in fact, in reality, in truth, really, truly

quiver 1. *v.* agitate, convulse, oscillate, pal~ pitate, pulsate, quake, quaver, shake, shiv~ er, shudder, tremble, vibrate **2.** *n.* convul~ sion, oscillation, palpitation, pulsation, shake, shiver, shudder, spasm, throb, tic, tremble, tremor, vibration

quiz 1. *n.* examination, investigation, ques~ tioning, test **2.** *v.* ask, catechize, examine, grill (*Inf.*), interrogate, investigate, pump (*Inf.*), question

quota allocation, allowance, assignment, cut (*Inf.*), part, portion, proportion, ration, share, slice, whack (*Inf.*)

quotation 1. citation, cutting, excerpt, ex~ tract, passage, quote (*Inf.*), reference, selec~ tion **2.** *Commerce* bid price, charge, cost, estimate, figure, price, quote (*Inf.*), rate, tender

quote adduce, attest, cite, detail, extract, instance, name, paraphrase, proclaim, re~ call, recite, recollect, refer to, repeat, retell

R

rabble 1. canaille, crowd, herd, horde, mob, swarm, throng **2.** *Derogatory* canaille, com~ monalty, commoners, common people, crowd, dregs, hoi polloi, lower classes, lumpenproletariat, masses, peasantry, populace, proletariat, riffraff, scum, the great unwashed (*Inf. & derogatory*), trash (*Chiefly U.S. & Canad.*)
Antonyms (*sense 2*) aristocracy, bourgeoisie, elite, gentry, high society, nobility, upper classes

rabid 1. hydrophobic, mad **2.** berserk, crazed, frantic, frenzied, furious, infuriated, mad, maniacal, raging, violent, wild **3.** big~ oted, extreme, fanatical, fervent, intemper~ ate, intolerant, irrational, narrow-minded, zealous
Antonyms (*sense 3*) half-hearted, moderate, wishy-washy (*Inf.*)

race¹ 1. *n.* chase, competition, contention, contest, dash, pursuit, rivalry **2.** *v.* barrel (along) (*Inf., chiefly U.S. & Canad.*), burn rubber (*Inf.*), career, compete, contest, dart, dash, fly, gallop, hare (*Brit. inf.*), hasten, hurry, run, run like mad (*Inf.*), speed, tear, zoom

**race² ** blood, breed, clan, ethnic group, fami~ ly, folk, house, issue, kin, kindred, line, lineage, nation, offspring, people, progeny, seed (*Chiefly biblical*), stock, tribe, type

racial ethnic, ethnological, folk, genealogical, genetic, national, tribal

rack *n.* **1.** frame, framework, stand, struc~ ture **2.** affliction, agony, anguish, misery, pain, pang, persecution, suffering, torment, torture ~*v.* **3.** afflict, agonize, crucify, dis~ tress, excruciate, harass, harrow, oppress, pain, torment, torture **4.** force, pull, shake, strain, stress, stretch, tear, wrench

racket 1. babel, ballyhoo (*Inf.*), clamour, commotion, din, disturbance, fuss, hubbub, hullabaloo, noise, outcry, pandemonium, row, shouting, tumult, uproar **2.** criminal activity, fraud, illegal enterprise, scheme **3.** *Sl.* business, game (*Inf.*), line, occupation

racy 1. animated, buoyant, dramatic, ener~ getic, entertaining, exciting, exhilarating, heady, lively, sexy (*Inf.*), sparkling, spirited, stimulating, vigorous, zestful **2.** distinctive, piquant, pungent, rich, sharp, spicy, strong, tangy, tart, tasty **3.** bawdy, blue, broad, immodest, indecent, indelicate, naughty, near the knuckle (*Inf.*), off colour, risqué, smutty, spicy (*Inf.*), suggestive

radiance 1. brightness, brilliance, efful~ gence, glare, gleam, glitter, glow, incandes~ cence, light, luminosity, lustre, resplend~ ence, shine **2.** delight, gaiety, happiness, joy, pleasure, rapture, warmth

radiant 1. beaming, bright, brilliant, efful~ gent, gleaming, glittering, glorious, glowing, incandescent, luminous, lustrous, resplend~ ent, shining, sparkling, sunny **2.** beaming, beatific, blissful, delighted, ecstatic, gay, glowing, happy, joyful, joyous, rapt, raptur~ ous
Antonyms (*sense 1*) black, dark, dull, gloomy, sombre (*sense 2*) disconsolate, gloomy, joyless, miserable, sad, sombre, sor~ rowful

radiate 1. diffuse, disseminate, emanate, emit, give off *or* out, gleam, glitter, pour, scatter, send out, shed, shine, spread **2.** branch out, diverge, issue, spread out

radiation emanation, emission, rays

radical *adj.* **1.** basic, constitutional, deep~ seated, essential, fundamental, innate, na~ tive, natural, organic, profound, thorough~ going **2.** complete, drastic, entire, excessive, extreme, extremist, fanatical, revolutionary, severe, sweeping, thorough, violent ~*n.* **3.** extremist, fanatic, militant, revolutionary
Antonyms *adj.* insignificant, minor, superficial, token, trivial ~*n.* conservative, moderate, reactionary

raffle draw, lottery, sweep, sweepstake

ragbag 1. confusion, hotchpotch, jumble, medley, miscellany, mixture, omnium-gatherum, potpourri **2.** *Inf.* frump, scare~ crow (*Inf.*), scruff (*Inf.*), slattern, sloven, slut, trollop

rage *n.* **1.** agitation, anger, frenzy, fury, high dudgeon, ire, madness, mania, obsession, passion, rampage, raving, vehemence, vio~ lence, wrath **2.** craze, enthusiasm, fad (*Inf.*), fashion, latest thing, mode, style, vogue ~*v.* **3.** be beside oneself, be furious, blow a fuse (*Sl., chiefly U.S.*), blow one's top, blow up (*Inf.*), chafe, crack up (*Inf.*), fly off the han~ dle (*Inf.*), foam at the mouth, fret, fume, go off the deep end (*Inf.*), go up the wall (*Sl.*), rant and rave, rave, see red (*Inf.*), seethe, storm, throw a fit (*Inf.*) **4.** be at its height, be uncontrollable, rampage, storm, surge
Antonyms *n.* (*sense 1*) acceptance, calmness, equanimity, gladness, good humour, joy, pleasure, resignation ~*v.* (*sense 3*) accept, keep one's cool, remain unruffled, resign oneself to, stay calm

ragged 1. contemptible, down at heel,

frayed, in holes, in rags, in tatters, mean, poor, rent, scraggy, shabby, shaggy, tat~ tered, tatty, threadbare, torn, unkempt, worn-out **2.** crude, jagged, notched, poor, rough, rugged, serrated, uneven, unfinished **3.** broken, desultory, disorganized, frag~ mented, irregular, uneven
Antonyms (*sense 1*) fashionable, smart, well-dressed

raging beside oneself, boiling mad (*Inf.*), doing one's nut (*Brit. sl.*), enraged, fit to be tied (*Sl.*), fizzing (*Scot.*), foaming at the mouth, frenzied, fuming, furious, incensed, infuriated, mad, raving, seething

rags 1. castoffs, old clothes, tattered cloth~ ing, tatters **2. in rags** down at heel, out at elbow, ragged, seedy, shabby, tattered
Antonyms finery, gladrags, Sunday best

raid 1. *n.* attack, break-in, descent, foray, hit-and-run attack, incursion, inroad, inva~ sion, irruption, onset, sally, seizure, sortie, surprise attack **2.** *v.* assault, attack, break into, descend on, fall upon, forage (*Mili~ tary*), foray, invade, pillage, plunder, reive (*Dialect*), rifle, sack, sally forth, swoop down upon

raider attacker, forager (*Military*), invader, marauder, plunderer, reiver (*Dialect*), rob~ ber, thief

railing balustrade, barrier, fence, paling, rails

rain *n.* **1.** cloudburst, deluge, downpour, drizzle, fall, precipitation, raindrops, rain~ fall, showers **2.** deluge, flood, hail, shower, spate, stream, torrent, volley ~*v.* **3.** bucket down (*Inf.*), come down in buckets (*Inf.*), drizzle, fall, pelt (down), pour, rain cats and dogs (*Inf.*), shower, teem **4.** deposit, drop, fall, shower, sprinkle **5.** bestow, lavish, pour, shower

rainy damp, drizzly, showery, wet
Antonyms arid, dry, fine, sunny

raise 1. build, construct, elevate, erect, ex~ alt, heave, hoist, lift, move up, promote, put up, rear, set upright, uplift **2.** advance, ag~ gravate, amplify, augment, boost, enhance, enlarge, escalate, exaggerate, heighten, hike (up) (*Inf.*), increase, inflate, intensify, jack up, magnify, put up, reinforce, strengthen **3.** advance, aggrandize, elevate, exalt, pre~ fer, promote, upgrade **4.** activate, arouse, awaken, cause, evoke, excite, foment, foster, incite, instigate, kindle, motivate, provoke, rouse, set on foot, stir up, summon up, whip up **5.** bring about, cause, create, en~ gender, give rise to, occasion, originate, produce, provoke, start **6.** advance, bring up, broach, introduce, moot, put forward, suggest **7.** assemble, collect, form, gather, get, levy, mass, mobilize, muster, obtain, rally, recruit **8.** breed, bring up, cultivate,

develop, grow, nurture, produce, propagate, rear **9.** abandon, end, give up, lift, relieve, relinquish, remove, terminate
Antonyms begin, calm, cut, decrease, de~ molish, depress, destroy, diminish, drop, es~ tablish, lessen, let down, level, lower, quash, quell, reduce, ruin, sink, soothe, start, sup~ press, wreck

rake¹ *v.* **1.** collect, gather, remove, scrape up **2.** break up, harrow, hoe, scour, scrape, scratch **3.** *With* **up** *or* **together** assemble, collect, dig up, dredge up, gather, scrape together **4.** comb, examine, hunt, ransack, scan, scour, scrutinize, search **5.** graze, scrape, scratch **6.** enfilade, pepper, sweep

rake² *n.* debauchee, dissolute man, lech *or* letch (*Inf.*), lecher, libertine, playboy, profligate, rakehell (*Archaic*), roué, sensu~ alist, voluptuary
Antonyms ascetic, celibate, monk, puritan

rakish breezy, dapper, dashing, debonair, devil-may-care, flashy, jaunty, natty (*Inf.*), raffish, smart, snazzy (*Inf.*), sporty

rally¹ *v.* **1.** bring *or* come to order, reassem~ ble, re-form, regroup, reorganize, unite ~*n.* **2.** regrouping, reorganization, reunion, stand ~*v.* **3.** assemble, bond together, bring *or* come together, collect, convene, gather, get together, marshal, mobilize, muster, or~ ganize, round up, summon, unite ~*n.* **4.** assembly, conference, congregation, con~ gress, convention, convocation, gathering, mass meeting, meeting, muster ~*v.* **5.** come round, get better, get one's second wind, improve, perk up, pick up, pull through, recover, recuperate, regain one's strength, revive, take a turn for the better ~*n.* **6.** comeback (*Inf.*), improvement, recovery, recuperation, renewal, resurgence, revival, turn for the better
Antonyms *v.* (*sense 3*) disband, disperse, separate, split up (*sense 5*) deteriorate, fail, get worse, relapse, take a turn for the worse, worsen ~*n.* (*sense 6*) collapse, deterioration, relapse, turn for the worse

ram *v.* **1.** butt, collide with, crash, dash, drive, force, hit, impact, run into, slam, smash, strike **2.** beat, cram, crowd, drum, force, hammer, jam, pack, pound, stuff, tamp, thrust

ramble *v.* **1.** amble, drift, perambulate, per~ egrinate, range, roam, rove, saunter, strag~ gle, stravaig (*Scot. & northern English dia~ lect*), stray, stroll, traipse (*Inf.*), walk, wan~ der **2.** meander, snake, twist and turn, wind, zigzag **3.** babble, chatter, digress, ex~ patiate, maunder, rabbit (on) (*Brit. inf.*), rattle on, run off at the mouth (*Sl.*), waffle (*Inf., chiefly Brit.*), wander, witter on (*Inf.*), ~*n.* **4.** excursion, hike, perambulation, per~

egrination, roaming, roving, saunter, stroll, tour, traipse (*Inf.*), trip, walk

rambler drifter, hiker, roamer, rover, stroller, walker, wanderer, wayfarer

rambling 1. circuitous, desultory, diffuse, digressive, disconnected, discursive, dis~ jointed, incoherent, irregular, long-winded, periphrastic, prolix, wordy **2.** irregular, sprawling, spreading, straggling, trailing **Antonyms** (*sense 1*) coherent, concise, direct, to the point

ramification 1. branch, development, di~ varication, division, excrescence, extension, forking, offshoot, outgrowth, subdivision **2.** complication, consequence, development, result, sequel, upshot

ramify 1. branch, divaricate, divide, fork, separate, split up **2.** become complicated, multiply, thicken

ramp grade, gradient, incline, inclined plane, rise, slope

rampage *v.* **1.** go ape (*Sl.*), go apeshit (*Sl.*), go berserk, rage, run amuck, run riot, run wild, storm, tear ~*n.* **2.** destruction, frenzy, fury, rage, storm, tempest, tumult, uproar, violence **3. on the rampage** amuck, ber~ serk, destructive, out of control, raging, rampant, riotous, violent, wild

rampant 1. aggressive, dominant, exces~ sive, flagrant, on the rampage, out of con~ trol, out of hand, outrageous, raging, ram~ paging, riotous, unbridled, uncontrollable, ungovernable, unrestrained, vehement, vio~ lent, wanton, wild **2.** epidemic, exuberant, luxuriant, prevalent, profuse, rank, rife, spreading like wildfire, unchecked, uncon~ trolled, unrestrained, widespread **3.** *Her~ aldry* erect, rearing, standing, upright

rampart barricade, bastion, breastwork, bulwark, defence, earthwork, embankment, fence, fort, fortification, guard, parapet, se~ curity, stronghold, wall

ramshackle broken-down, crumbling, de~ crepit, derelict, dilapidated, flimsy, jerry-built, rickety, shaky, tottering, tumbledown, unsafe, unsteady **Antonyms** solid, stable, steady, well-built

rancid bad, fetid, foul, frowsty, fusty, musty, off, putrid, rank, rotten, sour, stale, strong-smelling, tainted **Antonyms** fresh, pure, undecayed

random 1. accidental, adventitious, aim~ less, arbitrary, casual, chance, desultory, fortuitous, haphazard, hit or miss, inciden~ tal, indiscriminate, purposeless, spot, stray, unplanned, unpremeditated **2. at random** accidentally, adventitiously, aimlessly, ar~ bitrarily, by chance, casually, haphazardly, indiscriminately, irregularly, purposelessly, randomly, unsystematically, willy-nilly

Antonyms definite, deliberate, intended, planned, premeditated, specific

range *n.* **1.** ambit, amplitude, area, bounds, compass, confines, distance, domain, extent, field, latitude, limits, orbit, pale, parameters (*Inf.*), province, purview, radius, reach, scope, span, sphere, sweep **2.** chain, file, line, rank, row, sequence, series, string, tier **3.** assortment, class, collection, gamut, kind, lot, order, selection, series, sort, vari~ ety ~*v.* **4.** align, arrange, array, dispose, draw up, line up, order **5.** arrange, bracket, catalogue, categorize, class, classify, file, grade, group, pigeonhole, rank **6.** aim, align, direct, level, point, train **7.** cruise, explore, ramble, roam, rove, straggle, stray, stroll, sweep, traverse, wander **8.** extend, fluctuate, go, reach, run, stretch, vary be~ tween

rank¹ *n.* **1.** caste, class, classification, degree, dignity, division, echelon, grade, level, no~ bility, order, position, quality, sort, stand~ ing, station, status, stratum, type **2.** col~ umn, file, formation, group, line, range, row, series, tier ~*v.* **3.** align, arrange, ar~ ray, class, classify, dispose, grade, line up, locate, marshal, order, position, range, sort

rank² **1.** abundant, dense, exuberant, flourishing, lush, luxuriant, productive, profuse, strong-growing, vigorous **2.** bad, disagreeable, disgusting, fetid, foul, fusty, gamy, mephitic, musty, noisome, noxious, off, offensive, olid, pungent, putrid, rancid, revolting, stale, stinking, strong-smelling, yucky *or* yukky (*Sl.*) **3.** absolute, arrant, blatant, complete, downright, egregious, ex~ cessive, extravagant, flagrant, glaring, gross, rampant, sheer, thorough, total, un~ disguised, unmitigated, utter **4.** abusive, atrocious, coarse, crass, filthy, foul, gross, indecent, nasty, obscene, outrageous, scur~ rilous, shocking, vulgar

rank and file 1. lower ranks, men, other ranks, private soldiers, soldiers, troops **2.** body, general public, Joe (and Eileen) Pub~ lic (*Sl.*), Joe Six-Pack (*U.S. sl.*), majority, mass, masses

rankle anger, annoy, chafe, embitter, fester, gall, get one's goat (*Sl.*), get on one's nerves (*Inf.*), irk, irritate, piss one off (*Taboo sl.*), rile

ransack 1. comb, explore, go through, rake, rummage, scour, search, turn inside out **2.** despoil, gut, loot, pillage, plunder, raid, ravage, rifle, sack, strip

ransom *n.* **1.** deliverance, liberation, re~ demption, release, rescue **2.** money, pay~ ment, payoff, price ~*v.* **3.** buy (someone) out (*Inf.*), buy the freedom of, deliver, lib~ erate, obtain *or* pay for the release of, re~ deem, release, rescue, set free

rant 1. *v.* bellow, bluster, cry, declaim, rave, roar, shout, spout (*Inf.*), vociferate, yell **2.** *n.* bluster, bombast, diatribe, fanfaronade (*Rare*), harangue, philippic, rhetoric, tirade, vociferation

rapacious avaricious, extortionate, grasping, greedy, insatiable, marauding, plundering, predatory, preying, ravenous, usurious, voracious, wolfish

rapacity avarice, avidity, cupidity, graspingness, greed, greediness, insatiableness, predatoriness, rapaciousness, ravenousness, usury, voraciousness, voracity, wolfishness

rape *n.* **1.** outrage, ravishment, sexual assault, violation **2.** depredation, despoilment, despoliation, pillage, plundering, rapine, sack, spoliation **3.** abuse, defilement, desecration, maltreatment, perversion, violation ~*v.* **4.** outrage, ravish, sexually assault, violate **5.** despoil, loot, pillage, plunder, ransack, sack, spoliate

rapid brisk, expeditious, express, fast, fleet, flying, hasty, hurried, pdq (*Sl.*), precipitate, prompt, quick, quickie (*Inf.*), speedy, swift
Antonyms deliberate, gradual, leisurely, slow, tardy, unhurried

rapidity alacrity, briskness, celerity, dispatch, expedition, fleetness, haste, hurry, precipitateness, promptitude, promptness, quickness, rush, speed, speediness, swiftness, velocity

rapidly apace, at speed, briskly, expeditiously, fast, hastily, hotfoot, hurriedly, in a hurry, in a rush, in haste, like a shot, pdq (*Sl.*), posthaste, precipitately, promptly, pronto (*Inf.*), quickly, speedily, swiftly, with dispatch

rapport affinity, bond, empathy, harmony, interrelationship, link, relationship, sympathy, tie, understanding

rapprochement détente, reconcilement, reconciliation, restoration of harmony, reunion, softening
Antonyms antagonism, dissension, exacerbation, falling-out, quarrel, resumption of hostilities, schism

rapt 1. absorbed, carried away, engrossed, enthralled, entranced, fascinated, gripped, held, intent, preoccupied, spellbound **2.** bewitched, blissful, captivated, charmed, delighted, ecstatic, enchanted, enraptured, rapturous, ravished, transported
Antonyms bored, detached, left cold, unaffected, uninterested, uninvolved, unmoved

rapture beatitude, bliss, cloud nine (*Inf.*), delectation, delight, ecstasy, enthusiasm, euphoria, exaltation, felicity, happiness, joy, ravishment, rhapsody, seventh heaven, spell, transport

rapturous blissful, delighted, ecstatic, enthusiastic, euphoric, exalted, happy, in seventh heaven, joyful, joyous, on cloud nine (*Inf.*), overjoyed, over the moon (*Inf.*), rapt, ravished, rhapsodic, transported

rare 1. exceptional, few, infrequent, out of the ordinary, recherché, scarce, singular, sparse, sporadic, strange, thin on the ground, uncommon, unusual **2.** admirable, choice, excellent, exquisite, extreme, fine, great, incomparable, peerless, superb, superlative **3.** invaluable, precious, priceless, rich
Antonyms abundant, bountiful, common, frequent, habitual, manifold, many, plentiful, profuse, regular

rarely 1. almost never, hardly, hardly ever, infrequently, little, once in a blue moon, once in a while, only now and then, on rare occasions, scarcely ever, seldom **2.** exceptionally, extraordinarily, finely, notably, remarkably, singularly, uncommonly, unusually
Antonyms commonly, frequently, often, regularly, usually

rarity 1. curio, curiosity, find, gem, one-off, pearl, treasure **2.** infrequency, scarcity, shortage, singularity, sparseness, strangeness, uncommonness, unusualness **3.** choiceness, excellence, exquisiteness, fineness, incomparability, incomparableness, peerlessness, quality, superbness **4.** invaluableness, preciousness, pricelessness, richness, value, worth

rascal blackguard, caitiff (*Archaic*), devil, disgrace, good-for-nothing, imp, knave (*Archaic*), miscreant, ne'er-do-well, pickle (*Brit. inf.*), rake, rapscallion, reprobate, rogue, scally (*Northwest English dialect*), scallywag (*Inf.*), scamp, scoundrel, varmint (*Inf.*), villain, wastrel, wretch

rash¹ adventurous, audacious, brash, careless, foolhardy, harebrained, harum-scarum, hasty, headlong, headstrong, heedless, helter-skelter, hot-headed, ill-advised, ill-considered, impetuous, imprudent, impulsive, incautious, indiscreet, injudicious, madcap, precipitate, premature, reckless, thoughtless, unguarded, unthinking, unwary, venturesome
Antonyms canny, careful, cautious, considered, premeditated, prudent, well-thought-out

rash² **1.** eruption, outbreak **2.** epidemic, flood, outbreak, plague, series, spate, succession, wave

rashness adventurousness, audacity, brashness, carelessness, foolhardiness, hastiness, heedlessness, indiscretion, precipitation, recklessness, temerity, thoughtlessness

rasp *n.* **1.** grating, grinding, scrape, scratch ~*v.* **2.** abrade, excoriate, file, grind, rub, sand, scour, scrape **3.** grate (upon), irk, ir~ ritate, jar (upon), rub (someone) up the wrong way, set one's teeth on edge, wear upon

rasping or **raspy** creaking, croaking, croaky, grating, gravelly, gruff, harsh, hoarse, husky, jarring, rough, scratchy

rate n. **1.** degree, percentage, proportion, ratio, relation, scale, standard **2.** charge, cost, dues, duty, fee, figure, hire, price, tar~ iff, tax, toll **3.** gait, measure, pace, speed, tempo, time, velocity **4.** class, classification, degree, grade, position, quality, rank, rat~ ing, status, value, worth **5. at any rate** anyhow, anyway, at all events, in any case, nevertheless ~v. **6.** adjudge, appraise, as~ sess, class, classify, consider, count, esteem, estimate, evaluate, grade, measure, rank, reckon, regard, value, weigh **7.** be entitled to, be worthy of, deserve, merit **8.** Sl. ad~ mire, esteem, respect, think highly of, value

rather 1. a bit, a little, fairly, kind of (Inf.), moderately, pretty (Inf.), quite, relatively, slightly, somewhat, sort of (Inf.), to some degree, to some extent **2.** a good bit, no~ ticeably, significantly, very **3.** instead, more readily, more willingly, preferably, sooner

ratify affirm, approve, authenticate, author~ ize, bear out, bind, certify, confirm, consent to, corroborate, endorse, establish, sanction, sign, uphold, validate
Antonyms abrogate, annul, cancel, reject, repeal, repudiate, revoke

rating class, classification, degree, designa~ tion, estimate, evaluation, grade, order, placing, position, rank, rate, standing, sta~ tus

ratio arrangement, correlation, correspond~ ence, equation, fraction, percentage, pro~ portion, rate, relation, relationship

ration n. **1.** allotment, allowance, dole, helping, measure, part, portion, provision, quota, share **2.** Plural commons (Brit.), food, provender, provisions, stores, supplies ~v. **3.** With out allocate, allot, apportion, deal, distribute, dole, give out, issue, meas~ ure out, mete, parcel out **4.** budget, con~ serve, control, limit, restrict, save

rational 1. enlightened, intelligent, judi~ cious, logical, lucid, realistic, reasonable, sagacious, sane, sensible, sound, wise **2.** cerebral, cognitive, ratiocinative, reasoning, thinking **3.** all there (Inf.), balanced, com~ pos mentis, in one's right mind, lucid, nor~ mal, of sound mind, sane
Antonyms insane, irrational, unreasonable, unsound

rationale exposition, grounds, logic, moti~ vation, philosophy, principle, raison d'être, reasons, theory

rationalize 1. account for, excuse, explain

away, extenuate, justify, make allowance for, make excuses for, vindicate **2.** apply logic to, elucidate, reason out, resolve, think through **3.** make cuts, make more efficient, streamline, trim

rattle v. **1.** bang, clatter, jangle **2.** bounce, jar, jiggle, jolt, jounce, shake, vibrate **3.** With on blether, cackle, chatter, gabble, gibber, jabber, prate, prattle, rabbit (on) (Brit. inf.), run on, witter (Inf.), yak (away) (Sl.) **4.** Inf. discomfit, discompose, discon~ cert, discountenance, disturb, faze, frighten, perturb, put (someone) off his stride, put (someone) out of countenance, scare, shake, upset **5.** With off list, recite, reel off, re~ hearse, run through, spiel off (Inf.)

raucous grating, harsh, hoarse, husky, loud, noisy, rasping, rough, strident
Antonyms dulcet, mellifluous, quiet, smooth, sweet

ravage 1. v. demolish, desolate, despoil, de~ stroy, devastate, gut, lay waste, leave in ruins, loot, pillage, plunder, ransack, raze, ruin, sack, shatter, spoil, wreak havoc on, wreck **2.** n. Often plural damage, demoli~ tion, depredation, desolation, destruction, devastation, havoc, pillage, plunder, rapine, ruin, ruination, spoliation, waste

rave v. **1.** babble, be delirious, fume, go mad (Inf.), rage, rant, roar, run amuck, splutter, storm, talk wildly, thunder **2.** With about Inf. be delighted by, be mad about (Inf.), be wild about (Inf.), cry up, enthuse, gush, praise, rhapsodize ~n. **3.** Inf. acclaim, ap~ plause, encomium, praise **4.** Also **rave-up** Brit. sl. affair, bash (Inf.), beano (Brit. sl.), blow-out (Sl.), celebration, do (Inf.), party **5.** Brit. sl. craze, fad, fashion, vogue ~adj. **6.** Inf. ecstatic, enthusiastic, excellent, favour~ able, laudatory

ravenous 1. famished, starved, starving, very hungry **2.** avaricious, covetous, de~ vouring, ferocious, gluttonous, grasping, greedy, insatiable, insatiate, predatory, ra~ pacious, ravening, voracious, wolfish
Antonyms full, glutted, sated, satiated

ravine canyon, clough (Dialect), defile, flume, gap (U.S.), gorge, gulch (U.S.), gully, linn (Scot.), pass

raving berserk, crazed, crazy, delirious, frantic, frenzied, furious, hysterical, insane, irrational, mad, out of one's mind, rabid, raging, wild

ravish 1. captivate, charm, delight, enchant, enrapture, entrance, fascinate, overjoy, spellbind, transport **2.** abuse, outrage, rape, sexually assault, violate

ravishing beautiful, bewitching, charming, dazzling, delightful, drop-dead (Sl.), en~ chanting, entrancing, gorgeous, lovely, ra~ diant, stunning (Inf.)

raw 1. bloody (*of meat*), fresh, natural, un~
cooked, undressed, unprepared **2.** basic,
coarse, crude, green, natural, organic,
rough, unfinished, unprocessed, unrefined,
unripe, untreated **3.** abraded, chafed,
grazed, open, scratched, sensitive, skinned,
sore, tender **4.** callow, green, ignorant, im~
mature, inexperienced, new, undisciplined,
unpractised, unseasoned, unskilled, un~
trained, untried **5.** bare, blunt, brutal, can~
did, frank, naked, plain, realistic, unembel~
lished, unvarnished **6.** biting, bitter, bleak,
chill, chilly, cold, damp, freezing, harsh,
parky (*Brit. inf.*), piercing, unpleasant, wet
Antonyms (*sense 1*) baked, cooked, done
(*sense 2*) finished, prepared, refined (*sense 4*)
experienced, practised, professional, skilled,
trained (*sense 5*) embellished, gilded

ray 1. bar, beam, flash, gleam, shaft **2.**
flicker, glimmer, hint, indication, scintilla,
spark, trace

raze 1. bulldoze, demolish, destroy, flatten,
knock down, level, pull down, remove, ruin,
tear down, throw down **2.** delete, efface,
erase, excise, expunge, extinguish, extir~
pate, obliterate, rub out, scratch out, strike
out, wipe out

reach *v.* **1.** arrive at, attain, get as far as,
get to, land at, make **2.** contact, extend to,
get (a) hold of, go as far as, grasp, stretch
to, touch **3.** amount to, arrive at, attain,
climb to, come to, drop, fall, move, rise,
sink **4.** *Inf.* hand, hold out, pass, stretch **5.**
communicate with, contact, establish con~
tact with, find, get, get hold of, get in touch
with, get through to, make contact with ~*n.*
6. ambit, capacity, command, compass, dis~
tance, extension, extent, grasp, influence,
jurisdiction, mastery, power, range, scope,
spread, stretch, sweep

react 1. acknowledge, answer, reply, re~
spond **2.** act, behave, conduct oneself, func~
tion, operate, proceed, work

reaction 1. acknowledgment, answer, feed~
back, reply, response **2.** compensation,
counteraction, counterbalance, counter~
poise, recoil **3.** conservatism, counter-
revolution, obscurantism, the right

reactionary 1. *adj.* blimpish, conservative,
counter-revolutionary, obscurantist, rightist
2. *n.* Colonel Blimp, conservative, counter-
revolutionary, die-hard, obscurantist, right~
ist, right-winger
Antonyms (*senses 1 & 2*) leftist, progressive,
radical, reformist, revolutionary, socialist

read 1. glance at, look at, peruse, pore over,
refer to, run one's eye over, scan, study **2.**
announce, declaim, deliver, recite, speak,
utter **3.** comprehend, construe, decipher,
discover, interpret, perceive the meaning

of, see, understand **4.** display, indicate,
record, register, show

readable 1. clear, comprehensible, deci~
pherable, intelligible, legible, plain, under~
standable **2.** easy to read, enjoyable, enter~
taining, enthralling, gripping, interesting,
pleasant, worth reading
Antonyms (*sense 1*) illegible, incomprehen~
sible, indecipherable, unintelligible, unread~
able (*sense 2*) badly-written, boring, dull,
heavy, heavy going, pretentious, turgid, un~
readable

readily 1. cheerfully, eagerly, freely, gladly,
lief (*Rare*), promptly, quickly, voluntarily,
willingly, with good grace, with pleasure **2.**
at once, easily, effortlessly, hotfoot, in no
time, pdq (*Sl.*), quickly, right away,
smoothly, speedily, straight away, unhesi~
tatingly, without delay, without demur,
without difficulty, without hesitation
Antonyms hesitatingly, reluctantly, slowly,
unwillingly, with difficulty

readiness 1. fitness, maturity, preparation,
preparedness, ripeness **2.** aptness, eager~
ness, gameness (*Inf.*), inclination, keenness,
willingness **3.** adroitness, dexterity, ease,
facility, handiness, promptitude, prompt~
ness, quickness, rapidity, skill **4. in readi~
ness** all set, at *or* on hand, at the ready, fit,
prepared, primed, ready, set, waiting, wait~
ing in the wings

reading 1. examination, inspection, perusal,
review, scrutiny, study **2.** homily, lecture,
lesson, performance, recital, rendering,
rendition, sermon **3.** conception, construc~
tion, grasp, impression, interpretation,
treatment, understanding, version **4.**
book-learning, edification, education, erudi~
tion, knowledge, learning, scholarship

ready *adj.* **1.** all set, arranged, completed,
fit, in readiness, organized, prepared,
primed, ripe, set **2.** agreeable, apt, disposed,
eager, game (*Inf.*), glad, happy, have-a-go
(*Inf.*), inclined, keen, minded, predisposed,
prone, willing **3.** acute, adroit, alert, apt,
astute, bright, clever, deft, dexterous, ex~
pert, handy, intelligent, keen, perceptive,
prompt, quick, quick-witted, rapid, re~
sourceful, sharp, skilful, smart **4.** about,
close, in danger of, liable, likely, on the
brink of, on the point of, on the verge of **5.**
accessible, at *or* on hand, at one's
fingertips, at the ready, available, close to
hand, convenient, handy, near, on call, on
tap (*Inf.*), present ~*n.* **6. at the ready** in
readiness, poised, prepared, ready for ac~
tion, waiting ~*v.* **7.** arrange, equip, fit out,
get ready, make ready, order, organize,
prepare, set
Antonyms *adj.* disinclined, distant, hesi~
tant, immature, inaccessible, inexpert, late,
loath, reluctant, slow, unavailable, un~

equipped, unfit, unhandy, unprepared, un~
willing

real absolute, actual, authentic, bona fide,
certain, essential, existent, factual, genuine,
heartfelt, honest, intrinsic, legitimate, posi~
tive, right, rightful, sincere, true, unaffect~
ed, unfeigned, valid, veritable
Antonyms affected, counterfeit, fake, faked,
false, feigned, imaginary, imitation, insincere

realistic 1. businesslike, common-sense,
down-to-earth, hard-headed, level-headed,
matter-of-fact, practical, pragmatic, rational,
real, sensible, sober, unromantic, unsenti~
mental **2.** authentic, faithful, genuine,
graphic, lifelike, natural, naturalistic, rep~
resentational, true, true to life, truthful
Antonyms fanciful, idealistic, impractical,
unrealistic

reality 1. actuality, authenticity, certainty,
corporeality, fact, genuineness, materiality,
realism, truth, validity, verisimilitude, ver~
ity **2. in reality** actually, as a matter of
fact, in actuality, in fact, in point of fact, in
truth, really

realization 1. appreciation, apprehension,
awareness, cognizance, comprehension,
conception, consciousness, grasp, imagina~
tion, perception, recognition, understand~
ing **2.** accomplishment, achievement,
carrying-out, completion, consummation,
effectuation, fulfilment

realize 1. appreciate, apprehend, be cogni~
zant of, become aware of, become conscious
of, catch on (*Inf.*), comprehend, conceive,
grasp, imagine, recognize, take in, twig
(*Brit. inf.*), understand **2.** accomplish, actu~
alize, bring about, bring off, bring to frui~
tion, carry out *or* through, complete, con~
summate, do, effect, effectuate, fulfil, incar~
nate, make concrete, make happen, per~
form, reify **3.** acquire, bring *or* take in,
clear, earn, gain, get, go for, make, net, ob~
tain, produce, sell for

really absolutely, actually, assuredly, cat~
egorically, certainly, genuinely, in actual~
ity, indeed, in fact, in reality, positively,
surely, truly, undoubtedly, verily, without a
doubt

realm 1. country, domain, dominion, em~
pire, kingdom, land, monarchy, principal~
ity, province, state **2.** area, branch, depart~
ment, field, orbit, patch, province, region,
sphere, territory, turf (*U.S. sl.*), world, zone

reap acquire, bring in, collect, cut, derive,
gain, garner, gather, get, harvest, obtain,
win

rear¹ **1.** *n.* back, back end, end, rearguard,
stern, tail, tail end **2.** *adj.* aft, after (*Nauti~
cal*), back, following, hind, hindmost, last,
trailing
Antonyms *n.* bow, forward end, front, nose,

stem, vanguard ~*adj.* foremost, forward,
front, leading

rear² *v.* **1.** breed, bring up, care for, culti~
vate, educate, foster, grow, nurse, nurture,
raise, train **2.** elevate, hoist, hold up, lift,
raise, set upright **3.** build, construct, erect,
fabricate, put up **4.** loom, rise, soar, tower

reason *n.* **1.** apprehension, brains, compre~
hension, intellect, judgment, logic, mental~
ity, mind, ratiocination, rationality, rea~
soning, sanity, sense(s), sound mind,
soundness, understanding **2.** aim, basis,
cause, design, end, goal, grounds, impetus,
incentive, inducement, intention, motive,
object, occasion, purpose, target, warrant,
why and wherefore (*Inf.*) **3.** apologia, apol~
ogy, argument, case, defence, excuse, expla~
nation, exposition, ground, justification, ra~
tionale, vindication **4.** bounds, limits, mod~
eration, propriety, reasonableness, sense,
sensibleness, wisdom **5. in** *or* **within rea~
son** in moderation, proper, reasonable,
sensible, warrantable, within bounds, with~
in limits ~*v.* **6.** conclude, deduce, draw
conclusions, infer, make out, ratiocinate,
resolve, solve, syllogize, think, work out **7.**
With **with** argue, bring round (*Inf.*), debate,
dispute, dissuade, expostulate, move, per~
suade, prevail upon, remonstrate, show
(someone) the error of his ways, talk into *or*
out of, urge, win over
Antonyms (*sense 1*) emotion, feeling, in~
stinct, sentiment

reasonable 1. advisable, arguable, believ~
able, credible, intelligent, judicious,
justifiable, logical, plausible, practical, ra~
tional, reasoned, sane, sensible, sober,
sound, tenable, well-advised, well-thought-
out, wise **2.** acceptable, average, equitable,
fair, fit, honest, inexpensive, just, moderate,
modest, O.K. *or* okay (*Inf.*), proper, right,
tolerable, within reason
Antonyms impossible, irrational, unfair,
unintelligent, unreasonable, unsound

reasoned clear, judicious, logical, sensible,
systematic, well expressed, well presented,
well-thought-out

reasoning 1. analysis, cogitation, deduc~
tion, logic, ratiocination, reason, thinking,
thought **2.** argument, case, exposition, hy~
pothesis, interpretation, proof, train of
thought

reassure bolster, buoy up, cheer up, com~
fort, encourage, hearten, inspirit, put *or* set
one's mind at rest, relieve (someone) of
anxiety, restore confidence to

rebel *v.* **1.** man the barricades, mutiny, re~
sist, revolt, rise up, take to the streets, take
up arms **2.** come out against, defy, disobey,
dissent, refuse to obey **3.** flinch, recoil,
show repugnance, shrink, shy away ~*n.* **4.**

insurgent, insurrectionary, mutineer, resis~
tance fighter, revolutionary, revolutionist,
secessionist **5.** apostate, dissenter, heretic,
nonconformist, schismatic ~*adj.* **6.** insub~
ordinate, insurgent, insurrectionary, muti~
nous, rebellious, revolutionary

rebellion 1. insurgence, insurgency, insur~
rection, mutiny, resistance, revolt, revolu~
tion, rising, uprising **2.** apostasy, defiance,
disobedience, dissent, heresy, insubordina~
tion, nonconformity, schism

rebellious 1. contumacious, defiant, disaf~
fected, disloyal, disobedient, disorderly, in~
subordinate, insurgent, insurrectionary, in~
tractable, mutinous, rebel, recalcitrant,
revolutionary, seditious, turbulent, ungov~
ernable, unruly **2.** difficult, incorrigible,
obstinate, recalcitrant, refractory, resistant,
unmanageable
Antonyms dutiful, loyal, obedient, patriotic,
subordinate, subservient

rebirth new beginning, regeneration, re~
incarnation, renaissance, renascence, re~
newal, restoration, resurgence, resurrec~
tion, revitalization, revival

rebound *v.* **1.** bounce, recoil, resound, re~
turn, ricochet, spring back **2.** backfire,
boomerang, misfire, recoil ~*n.* **3.** bounce,
comeback, kickback, repercussion, return,
ricochet

rebuff 1. *v.* brush off (*Sl.*), check, cold-
shoulder, cut, decline, deny, discourage, put
off, refuse, reject, repulse, resist, slight,
snub, spurn, turn down **2.** *n.* brushoff (*Sl.*),
check, cold shoulder, defeat, denial, dis~
couragement, knock-back (*Sl.*), opposition,
refusal, rejection, repulse, slight, snub, the
(old) heave-ho (*Inf.*), thumbs down
Antonyms *v.* encourage, lead on (*Inf.*), sub~
mit to, welcome ~*n.* come-on (*Inf.*), encour~
agement, thumbs up, welcome

rebuke 1. *v.* admonish, bawl out (*Inf.*), be~
rate, blame, carpet (*Inf.*), castigate, censure,
chew out (*U.S. & Canad. inf.*), chide, dress
down (*Inf.*), give a rocket (*Brit. & N.Z. inf.*),
haul (someone) over the coals (*Inf.*), lecture,
read the riot act, reprehend, reprimand, re~
proach, reprove, scold, take to task, tear
into (*Inf.*), tear (someone) off a strip (*Inf.*),
tell off (*Inf.*), tick off (*Inf.*), upbraid **2.** *n.*
admonition, blame, castigation, censure,
dressing down (*Inf.*), lecture, reprimand,
reproach, reproof, reproval, row, telling-off
(*Inf.*), ticking-off (*Inf.*), tongue-lashing, wig~
ging (*Brit. sl.*)
Antonyms *v.* applaud, approve, commend,
compliment, congratulate, laud, praise ~*n.*
commendation, compliment, laudation,
praise

recalcitrant contrary, contumacious,
defiant, disobedient, insubordinate, intrac~

table, obstinate, refractory, stubborn, un~
controllable, ungovernable, unmanageable,
unruly, unwilling, wayward, wilful
Antonyms amenable, compliant, docile,
obedient, submissive

recall *v.* **1.** bring *or* call to mind, call *or*
summon up, evoke, look *or* think back to,
mind (*Dialect*), recollect, remember, remi~
nisce about **2.** abjure, annul, call back, call
in, cancel, countermand, nullify, repeal, re~
scind, retract, revoke, take back, withdraw
~*n.* **3.** annulment, cancellation, nul~
lification, recision, repeal, rescindment, re~
scission, retraction, revocation, withdrawal
4. memory, recollection, remembrance

recant abjure, apostatize, deny, disavow,
disclaim, disown, forswear, recall, renege,
renounce, repudiate, retract, revoke, take
back, unsay, withdraw
Antonyms insist, maintain, profess,
reaffirm, reiterate, repeat, restate, uphold

recapitulate epitomize, go over again, out~
line, recap (*Inf.*), recount, reiterate, repeat,
restate, review, run over, run through
again, summarize, sum up

recede 1. abate, draw back, ebb, fall back,
go back, regress, retire, retreat, retrocede,
retrogress, return, subside, withdraw **2.**
decline, diminish, dwindle, fade, lessen,
shrink, sink, wane

receipt 1. acknowledgment, counterfoil,
proof of purchase, sales slip, stub, voucher
2. acceptance, delivery, receiving, recep~
tion, recipience **3.** *Plural* gains, gate, in~
come, proceeds, profits, return, takings

receive 1. accept, accept delivery of, ac~
quire, be given, be in receipt of, collect, de~
rive, get, obtain, pick up, take **2.** appre~
hend, be informed of, be told, gather, hear,
perceive **3.** bear, be subjected to, encounter,
experience, go through, meet with, suffer,
sustain, undergo **4.** accommodate, admit, be
at home to, entertain, greet, meet, take in,
welcome

recent contemporary, current, fresh, hap~
pening (*Inf.*), late, latter, latter-day, modern,
new, novel, present-day, up-to-date, young
Antonyms ancient, antique, earlier, early,
former, historical, old

recently currently, freshly, lately, latterly,
newly, not long ago, of late

receptacle container, holder, repository

reception 1. acceptance, admission, re~
ceipt, receiving, recipience **2.** acknowledg~
ment, greeting, reaction, recognition, re~
sponse, treatment, welcome **3.** do (*Inf.*), en~
tertainment, function, levee, party, soirée

receptive 1. alert, bright, perceptive, quick
on the uptake (*Inf.*), responsive, sensitive **2.**
accessible, amenable, approachable, favour~

able, friendly, hospitable, interested, open, open-minded, open to suggestions, suscep~ tible, sympathetic, welcoming
Antonyms biased, narrow-minded, preju~ diced, unreceptive, unresponsive

recess 1. alcove, bay, cavity, corner, de~ pression, hollow, indentation, niche, nook, oriel **2.** *Plural* bowels, depths, heart, in~ nards (*Inf.*), innermost parts, penetralia, reaches, retreats, secret places **3.** break, cessation of business, closure, holiday, intermission, interval, respite, rest, vaca~ tion

recession decline, depression, downturn, drop, slump
Antonyms boom, upturn

recipe 1. directions, ingredients, instruc~ tions, receipt (*Obsolete*) **2.** formula, method, modus operandi, prescription, procedure, process, programme, technique

reciprocal alternate, complementary, cor~ relative, corresponding, equivalent, ex~ changed, give-and-take, interchangeable, interdependent, mutual, reciprocative, re~ ciprocatory
Antonyms one-way, unilateral, unrecipro~ cated

reciprocate 1. barter, exchange, feel in re~ turn, interchange, reply, requite, respond, return, return the compliment, swap, trade **2.** be equivalent, correspond, equal, match

recital account, description, detailing, enu~ meration, narration, narrative, perfor~ mance, reading, recapitulation, recitation, rehearsal, relation, rendering, repetition, statement, story, tale, telling

recitation lecture, narration, passage, per~ formance, piece, reading, recital, rendering, telling

recite declaim, deliver, describe, detail, do one's party piece (*Inf.*), enumerate, itemize, narrate, perform, recapitulate, recount, re~ hearse, relate, repeat, speak, tell

reckless careless, daredevil, devil-may-care, foolhardy, harebrained, harum-scarum, hasty, headlong, heedless, ill-advised, im~ prudent, inattentive, incautious, indiscreet, irresponsible, madcap, mindless, negligent, overventuresome, precipitate, rash, regard~ less, thoughtless, wild
Antonyms careful, cautious, heedful, mind~ ful, observant, responsible, thoughtful, wary

reckon 1. add up, calculate, compute, count, enumerate, figure, number, tally, total **2.** account, appraise, consider, count, deem, esteem, estimate, evaluate, gauge, hold, judge, look upon, rate, regard, think of **3.** assume, believe, be of the opinion, conjec~ ture, expect, fancy, guess (*Inf., chiefly U.S. & Canad.*), imagine, suppose, surmise, think **4.** *With* **with** cope, deal, face, handle,

settle accounts, treat **5.** *With* **with** antici~ pate, bargain for, bear in mind, be prepared for, expect, foresee, plan for, take cogni~ zance of, take into account **6.** *With* **on** *or* **upon** bank, calculate, count, depend, hope for, rely, take for granted, trust in **7. to be reckoned with** consequential, considerable, important, influential, powerful, significant, strong, weighty

reckoning 1. adding, addition, calculation, computation, count, counting, estimate, summation, working **2.** account, bill, char~ ge, due, score, settlement **3.** doom, judg~ ment, last judgment, retribution

reclaim get *or* take back, recapture, recover, redeem, reform, regain, regenerate, re~ instate, rescue, restore, retrieve, salvage

recline be recumbent, lay (something) down, lean, lie (down), loll, lounge, repose, rest, sprawl, stretch out
Antonyms get up, rise, sit up, stand, stand up, stand upright

recluse anchoress, anchorite, ascetic, er~ emite, hermit, monk, solitary

reclusive ascetic, cloistered, eremitic, her~ mitic, hermit-like, isolated, monastic, re~ cluse, retiring, secluded, sequestered, soli~ tary, withdrawn
Antonyms gregarious, sociable

recognition 1. detection, discovery, identification, recall, recollection, remem~ brance **2.** acceptance, acknowledgment, ad~ mission, allowance, appreciation, avowal, awareness, cognizance, concession, confes~ sion, notice, perception, realization, respect, understanding **3.** acknowledgment, appre~ ciation, approval, gratitude, greeting, hon~ our, salute

recognize 1. identify, know, know again, make out, notice, place, recall, recollect, re~ member, spot **2.** accept, acknowledge, ad~ mit, allow, appreciate, avow, be aware of, concede, confess, grant, own, perceive, re~ alize, respect, see, understand **3.** acknowl~ edge, appreciate, approve, greet, honour, salute
Antonyms (*sense 2*) be unaware of, forget, ignore, overlook

recoil *v.* **1.** jerk back, kick, react, rebound, resile, spring back **2.** balk at, draw back, falter, flinch, quail, shrink, shy away **3.** backfire, boomerang, go wrong, misfire, re~ bound ~*n.* **4.** backlash, kick, reaction, re~ bound, repercussion

recollect call to mind, mind (*Dialect*), place, recall, remember, reminisce, summon up

recollection impression, memory, mental image, recall, remembrance, reminiscence

recommend 1. advance, advise, advocate, counsel, enjoin, exhort, prescribe, propose, put forward, suggest, urge **2.** approve, commend, endorse, praise, put in a good word for, speak well of, vouch for **3.** make attractive (acceptable, appealing, interest~ ing)

Antonyms argue against, disapprove of, re~ ject, veto

recommendation 1. advice, counsel, pro~ posal, suggestion, urging **2.** advocacy, ap~ probation, approval, blessing, commenda~ tion, endorsement, favourable mention, good word, plug (*Inf.*), praise, reference, sanction, testimonial

reconcile 1. accept, accommodate, get used, make the best of, put up with (*Inf.*), resign, submit, yield **2.** appease, bring to terms, conciliate, make peace between, pacify, pla~ cate, propitiate, re-establish friendly rela~ tions between, restore harmony between, reunite **3.** adjust, compose, harmonize, patch up, put to rights, rectify, resolve, set~ tle, square

reconciliation 1. appeasement, concili~ ation, détente, pacification, propitiation, *rapprochement*, reconcilement, reunion, understanding **2.** accommodation, adjust~ ment, compromise, harmony, rectification, settlement

Antonyms alienation, antagonism, break~ up, estrangement, falling-out, separation

recondite abstruse, arcane, cabbalistic, concealed, dark, deep, difficult, esoteric, hidden, involved, mysterious, mystical, ob~ scure, occult, profound, secret

Antonyms exoteric, simple, straightforward

recondition do up (*Inf.*), fix up (*Inf., chiefly U.S. & Canad.*), overhaul, remodel, renew, renovate, repair, restore, revamp

reconnaissance exploration, inspection, investigation, observation, patrol, recce (*Sl.*), reconnoitring, scan, scouting, scruti~ ny, survey

reconnoitre case (*Sl.*), explore, get the lie of the land, inspect, investigate, make a re~ connaissance (of), observe, patrol, recce (*Sl.*), scan, scout, scrutinize, see how the land lies, spy out, survey

reconsider change one's mind, have second thoughts, reassess, re-evaluate, re-examine, rethink, review, revise, take another look at, think again, think better of, think over, think twice

reconstruct 1. reassemble, rebuild, recre~ ate, re-establish, reform, regenerate, re~ make, remodel, renovate, reorganize, re~ store **2.** build up, build up a picture of, de~ duce, piece together

record *n.* **1.** account, annals, archives, chronicle, diary, document, entry, file, journal, log, memoir, memorandum, memo~ rial, minute, register, report **2.** documenta~ tion, evidence, memorial, remembrance, testimony, trace, witness **3.** background, career, curriculum vitae, history, perfor~ mance, track record (*Inf.*) **4.** album, black disc, disc, EP, forty-five, gramophone rec~ ord, LP, platter (*U.S. sl.*), recording, release, seventy-eight, single, vinyl **5. off the rec~ ord** confidential, confidentially, in confidence, in private, not for publication, private, sub rosa, under the rose, unofficial, unofficially ~*v.* **6.** chalk up (*Inf.*), chronicle, document, enrol, enter, inscribe, log, min~ ute, note, preserve, put down, put on file, put on record, register, report, set down, take down, transcribe, write down **7.** con~ tain, give evidence of, indicate, read, regis~ ter, say, show **8.** cut, lay down (*Sl.*), make a recording of, put on wax (*Inf.*), tape, tape-record, video, video-tape, wax (*Inf.*)

recorder annalist, archivist, chronicler, clerk, diarist, historian, registrar, scorekeeper, scorer, scribe

recording cut (*Inf.*), disc, gramophone rec~ ord, record, tape, video

recount delineate, depict, describe, detail, enumerate, give an account of, narrate, portray, recite, rehearse, relate, repeat, re~ port, tell, tell the story of

recourse alternative, appeal, choice, ex~ pedient, option, refuge, remedy, resort, re~ source, way out

recover 1. find again, get back, make good, recapture, reclaim, recoup, redeem, regain, repair, repossess, restore, retake, retrieve, take back, win back **2.** bounce back, come round, convalesce, feel oneself again, get back on one's feet, get better, get well, heal, improve, mend, pick up, pull through, rally, recuperate, regain one's health *or* strength, revive, take a turn for the better

Antonyms (*sense 1*) abandon, forfeit, lose (*sense 2*) deteriorate, go downhill, relapse, take a turn for the worse, weaken, worsen

recovery 1. convalescence, healing, im~ provement, mending, rally, recuperation, return to health, revival, turn for the better **2.** amelioration, betterment, improvement, rally, rehabilitation, restoration, revival, upturn **3.** recapture, reclamation, redemp~ tion, repair, repossession, restoration, re~ trieval

recreation amusement, distraction, diver~ sion, enjoyment, entertainment, exercise, fun, hobby, leisure activity, pastime, play, pleasure, refreshment, relaxation, relief, sport

recrimination bickering, counterattack, countercharge, mutual accusation, name-calling, quarrel, retaliation, retort, squab~ bling

recruit *v.* **1.** draft, enlist, enrol, impress,

levy, mobilize, muster, raise, strengthen **2.** engage, enrol, gather, obtain, procure, proselytize, round up, take on, win (over) **3.** augment, build up, refresh, reinforce, re~ new, replenish, restore, strengthen, supply ~n. **4.** apprentice, beginner, convert, greenhorn (*Inf.*), helper, initiate, learner, neophyte, novice, proselyte, rookie (*Inf.*), trainee, tyro
Antonyms (*sense 1*) dismiss, fire, lay off, make redundant, sack (*Inf.*)

rectify 1. adjust, amend, correct, emend, fix, improve, make good, mend, put right, re~ dress, reform, remedy, repair, right, square **2.** *Chem.* distil, purify, refine, separate

rectitude 1. correctness, decency, equity, goodness, honesty, honour, incorruptibility, integrity, justice, morality, principle, probity, righteousness, scrupulousness, uprightness, virtue **2.** accuracy, correct~ ness, exactness, justice, precision, right~ ness, soundness, verity
Antonyms (*sense 1*) baseness, corruption, dishonesty, dishonour, immorality, scandal~ ousness

recuperate convalesce, get back on one's feet, get better, improve, mend, pick up, re~ cover, regain one's health

recur 1. come again, come and go, come back, happen again, persist, reappear, re~ peat, return, revert **2.** be remembered, come back, haunt one's thoughts, return to mind, run through one's mind

recurrent continued, cyclical, frequent, ha~ bitual, periodic, recurring, regular, repeat~ ed, repetitive
Antonyms isolated, one-off

recycle reclaim, reprocess, reuse, salvage, save

red *adj.* **1.** cardinal, carmine, cherry, coral, crimson, gules (*Heraldry*), maroon, pink, rose, ruby, scarlet, vermeil, vermilion, wine **2.** bay, carroty, chestnut, flame-coloured, flaming, foxy, reddish, sandy, titian **3.** blushing, embarrassed, florid, flushed, ru~ bicund, shamefaced, suffused **4.** blooming, glowing, healthy, roseate, rosy, ruddy **5.** bloodshot, inflamed, red-rimmed **6.** blood~ stained, bloody, ensanguined (*Literary*), gory, sanguine ~n. **7.** colour, redness **8. in the red** *Inf.* bankrupt, in arrears, in debit, in debt, in deficit, insolvent, on the rocks, overdrawn, owing money, showing a loss **9. see red** *Inf.* be or get very angry, be beside oneself with rage (*Inf.*), become enraged, blow a fuse (*Sl., chiefly U.S.*), blow one's top, boil, crack up (*Inf.*), fly off the handle (*Inf.*), go mad (*Inf.*), go off one's head (*Sl.*), go off the deep end (*Inf.*), go up the wall (*Sl.*), lose one's rag (*Sl.*), lose one's temper, seethe

redden blush, colour (up), crimson, flush, go red, suffuse

redeem 1. buy back, reclaim, recover, re~ cover possession of, regain, repossess, re~ purchase, retrieve, win back **2.** cash (in), change, exchange, trade in **3.** abide by, ac~ quit, adhere to, be faithful to, carry out, discharge, fulfil, hold to, keep, keep faith with, make good, meet, perform, satisfy **4.** absolve, rehabilitate, reinstate, restore to favour **5.** atone for, compensate for, defray, make amends for, make good, make up for, offset, outweigh, redress, save **6.** buy the freedom of, deliver, emancipate, extricate, free, liberate, pay the ransom of, ransom, rescue, save, set free

redemption 1. reclamation, recovery, re~ possession, repurchase, retrieval **2.** dis~ charge, exchange, fulfilment, performance, quid pro quo, trade-in **3.** amends, atone~ ment, compensation, expiation, reparation **4.** deliverance, emancipation, liberation, ransom, release, rescue, salvation

red-handed bang to rights (*Sl.*), (in) flagrante delicto, in the act, with one's fingers or hand in the till (*Inf.*), with one's pants down (*U.S. sl.*)

redound 1. conduce, contribute, effect, lead to, militate for, tend **2.** accrue, come back, ensue, rebound, recoil, reflect, result

redress *v.* **1.** compensate for, make amends (reparation, restitution) for, make up for, pay for, put right, recompense for **2.** adjust, amend, balance, correct, ease, even up, mend, put right, rectify, reform, regulate, relieve, remedy, repair, restore the balance, square ~n. **3.** aid, assistance, correction, cure, ease, help, justice, rectification, relief, remedy, satisfaction **4.** amends, atonement, compensation, payment, quittance, recom~ pense, reparation, requital, restitution

reduce 1. abate, abridge, contract, curtail, cut down, debase, decrease, depress, dilute, diminish, impair, lessen, lower, moderate, shorten, slow down, tone down, truncate, turn down, weaken, wind down **2.** bank~ rupt, break, impoverish, pauperize, ruin **3.** bring, bring to the point of, conquer, drive, force, master, overpower, subdue, vanquish **4.** be or go on a diet, diet, lose weight, shed weight, slenderize (*Chiefly U.S.*), slim, trim **5.** bring down the price of, cheapen, cut, discount, lower, mark down, slash **6.** break, bring low, degrade, demote, downgrade, humble, humiliate, lower in rank, lower the status of, take down a peg (*Inf.*)
Antonyms augment, defend, elevate, en~ hance, enlarge, exalt, extend, heighten, in~ crease, promote

redundant 1. de trop, excessive, extra, inessential, inordinate, supererogatory,

superfluous, supernumerary, surplus, un~
necessary, unwanted **2.** diffuse, padded,
periphrastic, pleonastic, prolix, repetitious,
tautological, verbose, wordy
Antonyms essential, necessary, needed, vi~
tal

reek v. **1.** hum (*Sl.*), pong (*Brit. inf.*), smell,
smell to high heaven, stink **2.** be charac~
terized by, be permeated by, be redolent of
3. *Dialect* fume, give off smoke *or* fumes,
smoke, steam ~n. **4.** effluvium, fetor, me~
phitis, niff (*Brit. sl.*), odour, pong (*Brit. inf.*),
smell, stench, stink **5.** *Dialect* exhalation,
fumes, smoke, steam, vapour

reel 1. falter, lurch, pitch, rock, roll, stagger,
stumble, sway, totter, waver, wobble **2.** go
round and round, revolve, spin, swim,
swirl, twirl, whirl

refer 1. advert, allude, bring up, cite, hint,
invoke, make mention of, make reference,
mention, speak of, touch on **2.** direct,
guide, point, recommend, send **3.** apply,
consult, go, have recourse to, look up, seek
information from, turn to **4.** apply, be di~
rected to, belong, be relevant to, concern,
pertain, relate **5.** accredit, ascribe, assign,
attribute, credit, impute, put down to **6.**
commit, consign, deliver, hand over, pass
on, submit, transfer, turn over

referee 1. *n.* adjudicator, arbiter, arbitrator,
judge, ref (*Inf.*), umpire **2.** *v.* adjudicate,
arbitrate, judge, mediate, umpire

reference 1. allusion, citation, mention,
note, quotation, remark **2.** applicability,
bearing, concern, connection, consideration,
regard, relation, respect **3.** certification,
character, credentials, endorsement, good
word, recommendation, testimonial

referendum plebiscite, popular vote, public
vote

refine 1. clarify, cleanse, distil, filter, pro~
cess, purify, rarefy **2.** civilize, cultivate, el~
evate, hone, improve, perfect, polish, tem~
per

refined 1. civil, civilized, courtly, cultivat~
ed, cultured, elegant, genteel, gentlemanly,
gracious, ladylike, polished, polite, sophis~
ticated, urbane, well-bred, well-mannered **2.**
cultured, delicate, discerning, discriminat~
ing, exact, fastidious, fine, nice, precise,
punctilious, sensitive, sublime, subtle **3.**
clarified, clean, distilled, filtered, processed,
pure, purified
Antonyms boorish, coarse, common, ill-
bred, impure, inelegant, uncultured, ungen~
tlemanly, unladylike, unmannerly, unrefined

refinement 1. clarification, cleansing, dis~
tillation, filtering, processing, purification,
rarefaction, rectification **2.** fine point, fine
tuning, nicety, nuance, subtlety **3.** breed~
ing, civility, civilization, courtesy, courtli~

ness, cultivation, culture, delicacy, dis~
crimination, elegance, fastidiousness,
fineness, finesse, finish, gentility, good
breeding, good manners, grace, gracious~
ness, polish, politeness, politesse, precision,
sophistication, style, taste, urbanity

reflect 1. echo, give back, imitate, mirror,
reproduce, return, throw back **2.** bear out,
bespeak, communicate, demonstrate, dis~
play, evince, exhibit, express, indicate,
manifest, reveal, show **3.** cogitate, consider,
contemplate, deliberate, meditate, mull
over, muse, ponder, ruminate, think, won~
der

reflection 1. counterpart, echo, image,
mirror image **2.** cerebration, cogitation,
consideration, contemplation, deliberation,
idea, impression, meditation, musing, ob~
servation, opinion, perusal, pondering, ru~
mination, study, thinking, thought, view **3.**
aspersion, censure, criticism, derogation,
imputation, reproach, slur

reform v. **1.** ameliorate, amend, better, cor~
rect, emend, improve, mend, rebuild, re~
claim, reconstitute, reconstruct, rectify, re~
generate, rehabilitate, remodel, renovate,
reorganize, repair, restore, revolutionize **2.**
clean up one's act (*Inf.*), get back on the
straight and narrow (*Inf.*), get it together
(*Inf.*), get one's act together (*Inf.*), go
straight (*Inf.*), mend one's ways, pull one's
socks up (*Brit. inf.*), shape up (*Inf.*), turn
over a new leaf ~n. **3.** amelioration,
amendment, betterment, correction, im~
provement, rectification, rehabilitation,
renovation

refrain v. abstain, avoid, cease, desist, do
without, eschew, forbear, give up, kick
(*Inf.*), leave off, renounce, stop

refresh 1. brace, breathe new life into,
cheer, cool, enliven, freshen, inspirit, re~
animate, reinvigorate, rejuvenate, revital~
ize, revive, revivify, stimulate **2.** brush up
(*Inf.*), jog, prod, prompt, renew, stimulate **3.**
renew, renovate, repair, replenish, restore,
top up

refreshing bracing, cooling, different, fresh,
inspiriting, invigorating, new, novel, origi~
nal, revivifying, stimulating, thirst-
quenching
Antonyms enervating, exhausting,
soporific, tiring, wearisome

refreshment 1. enlivenment, freshening,
reanimation, renewal, renovation, repair,
restoration, revival, stimulation **2.** *Plural*
drinks, food and drink, snacks, titbits

refrigerate chill, cool, freeze, keep cold

refuge asylum, bolt hole, harbour, haven,
hide-out, protection, resort, retreat, sanctu~
ary, security, shelter

refugee displaced person, émigré, escapee, exile, fugitive, runaway

refund 1. *v.* give back, make good, pay back, reimburse, repay, restore, return **2.** *n.* reimbursement, repayment, return

refurbish clean up, do up (*Inf.*), fix up (*Inf., chiefly U.S. & Canad.*), mend, overhaul, re~ equip, refit, remodel, renovate, repair, re~ store, revamp, set to rights, spruce up

refusal 1. defiance, denial, knockback (*Sl.*), negation, no, rebuff, rejection, repudiation, thumbs down **2.** choice, consideration, op~ portunity, option

refuse *v.* abstain, decline, deny, reject, repel, repudiate, say no, spurn, turn down, with~ hold
Antonyms accept, agree, allow, approve, consent, give, permit

refute confute, counter, discredit, disprove, give the lie to, negate, overthrow, prove false, rebut, silence
Antonyms confirm, prove, substantiate

regain 1. get back, recapture, recoup, re~ cover, redeem, repossess, retake, retrieve, take back, win back **2.** get back to, reach again, reattain, return to

regal fit for a king *or* queen, kingly, magnificent, majestic, noble, princely, proud, queenly, royal, sovereign

regard *v.* **1.** behold, check, check out (*Inf.*), clock (*Brit. sl.*), eye, eyeball (*U.S. sl.*), gaze at, get a load of (*Inf.*), look closely at, mark, notice, observe, remark, scrutinize, take a dekko at (*Brit. sl.*), view, watch **2.** account, adjudge, believe, consider, deem, esteem, estimate, hold, imagine, judge, look upon, rate, see, suppose, think, treat, value, view **3.** apply to, be relevant to, concern, have a bearing on, have to do with, interest, per~ tain to, relate to **4.** attend, heed, listen to, mind, note, pay attention to, respect, take into consideration, take notice of ~*n.* **5.** at~ tention, heed, interest, mind, notice **6.** ac~ count, affection, attachment, care, concern, consideration, deference, esteem, honour, love, note, reputation, repute, respect, store, sympathy, thought **7.** aspect, detail, feature, item, matter, particular, point, respect **8.** gaze, glance, look, scrutiny, stare **9.** bear~ ing, concern, connection, reference, rela~ tion, relevance **10.** *Plural* best wishes, compliments, devoirs, good wishes, greet~ ings, respects, salutations

regarding about, apropos, as regards, as to, concerning, in *or* with regard to, in re, in respect of, in the matter of, on the subject of, re, respecting, with reference to

regardless 1. *adj.* disregarding, heedless, inattentive, inconsiderate, indifferent, ne~ glectful, negligent, rash, reckless, remiss, unconcerned, unmindful **2.** *adv.* anyway,

come what may, despite everything, for all that, in any case, in spite of everything, nevertheless, no matter what, nonetheless
Antonyms *adj.* heedful, mindful, regardful

regenerate breathe new life into, change, inspirit, invigorate, reawaken, reconstruct, re-establish, reinvigorate, rejuvenate, re~ new, renovate, reproduce, restore, revive, revivify, uplift
Antonyms become moribund, decline, de~ generate, stagnate, stultify

regime administration, establishment, gov~ ernment, leadership, management, reign, rule, system

regiment *v.* bully, control, discipline, order, organize, regulate, systematize

region 1. area, country, district, division, expanse, land, locality, part, patch, place, province, quarter, section, sector, territory, tract, turf (*U.S. sl.*), zone **2.** domain, field, province, realm, sphere, world **3.** area, lo~ cality, neighbourhood, range, scope, vicin~ ity

regional district, local, parochial, provin~ cial, sectional, zonal

register *n.* **1.** annals, archives, catalogue, chronicle, diary, file, ledger, list, log, memorandum, record, roll, roster, schedule ~*v.* **2.** catalogue, check in, chronicle, enlist, enrol, enter, inscribe, list, note, record, set down, sign on *or* up, take down **3.** be shown, bespeak, betray, display, exhibit, express, indicate, manifest, mark, read, record, reflect, reveal, say, show **4.** *Inf.* come home, dawn on, get through, have an effect, impress, make an impression, sink in, tell

regress backslide, degenerate, deteriorate, ebb, fall away *or* off, fall back, go back, lapse, lose ground, recede, relapse, retreat, retrocede, retrogress, return, revert, wane
Antonyms advance, improve, progress, wax

regret 1. *v.* bemoan, be upset, bewail, de~ plore, feel remorse for, feel sorry for, grieve, lament, miss, mourn, repent, rue, weep over **2.** *n.* bitterness, compunction, contrition, disappointment, grief, lamenta~ tion, pang of conscience, penitence, re~ morse, repentance, ruefulness, self-reproach, sorrow
Antonyms *v.* be happy, be satisfied, feel sat~ isfaction, rejoice ~*n.* callousness, content~ ment, impenitence, lack of compassion, pleasure, satisfaction

regrettable deplorable, disappointing, dis~ tressing, ill-advised, lamentable, pitiable, sad, shameful, unfortunate, unhappy, woe~ ful, wrong

regular 1. common, commonplace, custom~ ary, daily, everyday, habitual, normal, or~ dinary, routine, typical, unvarying, usual

2. consistent, constant, established, even, fixed, ordered, periodic, rhythmic, set, stat~ ed, steady, systematic, uniform **3.** depend~ able, efficient, formal, methodical, orderly, standardized, steady, systematic **4.** bal~ anced, even, flat, level, smooth, straight, symmetrical, uniform **5.** approved, bona fide, classic, correct, established, formal, official, orthodox, prevailing, proper, sanc~ tioned, standard, time-honoured, traditional **Antonyms** abnormal, disorderly, erratic, exceptional, inconsistent, inconstant, infre~ quent, irregular, occasional, rare, uncommon, unconventional, uneven, unmethodical, un~ usual, varied

regulate adjust, administer, arrange, bal~ ance, conduct, control, direct, fit, govern, guide, handle, manage, moderate, modulate, monitor, order, organize, oversee, rule, run, settle, superintend, supervise, systematize, tune

regulation n. **1.** adjustment, administra~ tion, arrangement, control, direction, gov~ ernance, government, management, modu~ lation, supervision, tuning **2.** command~ ment, decree, dictate, direction, edict, law, order, ordinance, precept, procedure, re~ quirement, rule, standing order, statute ~adj. **3.** customary, mandatory, normal, official, prescribed, required, standard, usual

rehabilitate 1. adjust, redeem, reform, re~ integrate, save **2.** clear, convert, fix up (Inf., chiefly U.S. & Canad.), make good, mend, rebuild, recondition, reconstitute, recon~ struct, re-establish, reinstate, reinvigorate, renew, renovate, restore

rehearsal 1. drill, going-over (Inf.), prac~ tice, practice session, preparation, reading, rehearsing, run-through **2.** account, cata~ logue, description, enumeration, list, narra~ tion, recital, recounting, relation, telling

rehearse 1. act, drill, go over, practise, prepare, ready, recite, repeat, run through, study, train, try out **2.** delineate, depict, describe, detail, enumerate, go over, list, narrate, recite, recount, relate, review, run through, spell out, tell, trot out (Inf.)

reign n. **1.** ascendancy, command, control, dominion, empire, hegemony, influence, monarchy, power, rule, sovereignty, su~ premacy, sway ~v. **2.** administer, be in power, command, govern, hold sway, influence, occupy or sit on the throne, rule, wear the crown, wield the sceptre **3.** be rampant, be rife, be supreme, hold sway, obtain, predominate, prevail

rein n. **1.** brake, bridle, check, control, curb, harness, hold, restraint, restriction **2. give (a) free rein (to)** free, give a blank cheque (to), give a free hand, give carte blanche,

give (someone) his head, give way to, in~ dulge, let go, remove restraints ~v. **3.** bri~ dle, check, control, curb, halt, hold, hold back, limit, restrain, restrict, slow down

reincarnation metempsychosis, rebirth, transmigration of souls

reinforce augment, bolster, buttress, em~ phasize, fortify, harden, increase, prop, shore up, stiffen, strengthen, stress, sup~ plement, support, toughen, underline **Antonyms** contradict, undermine, weaken

reinforcement 1. addition, amplification, augmentation, enlargement, fortification, increase, strengthening, supplement **2.** brace, buttress, prop, shore, stay, support **3.** Plural additional or fresh troops, aux~ iliaries, reserves, support

reinstate bring back, recall, re-establish, rehabilitate, replace, restore, return

reject 1. v. bin, cast aside, decline, deny, despise, disallow, discard, eliminate, ex~ clude, jettison, jilt, rebuff, refuse, renounce, repel, repudiate, repulse, say no to, scrap, spurn, throw away or out, turn down, veto **2.** n. castoff, discard, failure, flotsam, sec~ ond **Antonyms** v. accept, agree, allow, approve, permit, receive, select ~n. prize, treasure

rejection brushoff (Sl.), denial, dismissal, elimination, exclusion, knock-back (Sl.), re~ buff, refusal, renunciation, repudiation, the (old) heave-ho (Inf.), thumbs down, veto **Antonyms** acceptance, affirmation, approv~ al, selection

rejoice be glad (happy, overjoyed), celebrate, delight, exult, glory, joy, jump for joy, make merry, revel, triumph **Antonyms** be sad (unhappy, upset), lament, mourn

rejoicing celebration, cheer, delight, elation, exultation, festivity, gaiety, gladness, hap~ piness, joy, jubilation, merrymaking, revel~ ry, triumph

relapse v. **1.** backslide, degenerate, fail, fall back, lapse, regress, retrogress, revert, slip back, weaken **2.** deteriorate, fade, fail, sicken, sink, weaken, worsen ~n. **3.** back~ sliding, fall from grace, lapse, recidivism, regression, retrogression, reversion **4.** de~ terioration, recurrence, setback, turn for the worse, weakening, worsening **Antonyms** v. (sense 2) get better, improve, rally, recover ~n. (sense 4) improvement, ral~ ly, recovery, turn for the better

relate 1. chronicle, describe, detail, give an account of, impart, narrate, present, recite, recount, rehearse, report, set forth, tell **2.** ally, associate, connect, coordinate, corre~ late, couple, join, link **3.** appertain, apply, bear upon, be relevant to, concern, have reference to, have to do with, pertain, refer

Antonyms (*sense 2*) detach, disconnect, dis~ sociate, divorce (*sense 3*) be irrelevant to, be unconnected, have nothing to do with

related 1. accompanying, affiliated, agnate, akin, allied, associated, cognate, concomi~ tant, connected, correlated, interconnected, joint, linked **2.** agnate, akin, cognate, con~ sanguineous, kin, kindred
Antonyms separate, unconnected, unrelated

relation 1. affiliation, affinity, consanguin~ ity, kindred, kinship, propinquity, relation~ ship **2.** kin, kinsman, kinswoman, relative **3.** application, bearing, bond, comparison, connection, correlation, interdependence, link, pertinence, reference, regard, similar~ ity, tie-in **4.** account, description, narration, narrative, recital, recountal, report, story, tale

relations 1. affairs, associations, communi~ cations, connections, contact, dealings, interaction, intercourse, liaison, meetings, rapport, relationship, terms **2.** clan, family, kin, kindred, kinsfolk, kinsmen, relatives, tribe

relationship affair, affinity, association, bond, communications, conjunction, con~ nection, correlation, exchange, kinship, liaison, link, parallel, proportion, rapport, ratio, similarity, tie-up

relative *adj.* **1.** allied, associated, compara~ tive, connected, contingent, corresponding, dependent, proportionate, reciprocal, relat~ ed, respective **2.** applicable, apposite, ap~ propriate, appurtenant, apropos, germane, pertinent, relevant **3.** *With* **to** correspond~ ing to, in proportion to, proportional to ~*n.* **4.** connection, kinsman, kinswoman, mem~ ber of one's *or* the family, relation

relatively comparatively, in *or* by compari~ son, rather, somewhat, to some extent

relax 1. abate, diminish, ease, ebb, lessen, let up, loosen, lower, mitigate, moderate, reduce, relieve, slacken, weaken **2.** be *or* feel at ease, calm, chill out (*Sl., chiefly U.S.*), laze, let oneself go (*Inf.*), let one's hair down (*Inf.*), lighten up (*Sl.*), loosen up, put one's feet up, rest, soften, take it easy, take one's ease, tranquillize, unbend, unwind
Antonyms alarm, alert, heighten, increase, intensify, tense, tighten, work

relaxation 1. amusement, enjoyment, en~ tertainment, fun, leisure, pleasure, recrea~ tion, refreshment, rest **2.** abatement, dimi~ nution, easing, lessening, let-up (*Inf.*), mod~ eration, reduction, slackening, weakening

relay *n.* **1.** relief, shift, turn **2.** communica~ tion, dispatch, message, transmission ~*v.* **3.** broadcast, carry, communicate, hand on, pass on, send, spread, transmit

release *v.* **1.** deliver, discharge, disengage, drop, emancipate, extricate, free, let go, let out, liberate, loose, manumit, set free, turn loose, unbridle, unchain, undo, unfasten, unfetter, unloose, unshackle, untie **2.** ab~ solve, acquit, dispense, excuse, exempt, ex~ onerate, let go, let off **3.** break, circulate, disseminate, distribute, issue, launch, make known, make public, present, publish, put out, unveil ~*n.* **4.** acquittal, deliverance, delivery, discharge, emancipation, freedom, liberation, liberty, manumission, relief **5.** absolution, acquittance, dispensation, ex~ emption, exoneration, let-off (*Inf.*) **6.** an~ nouncement, issue, offering, proclamation, publication
Antonyms *v.* detain, engage, fasten, hold, imprison, incarcerate, keep, suppress, with~ hold ~*n.* detention, imprisonment, incar~ ceration, internment

relent 1. acquiesce, be merciful, capitulate, change one's mind, come round, forbear, give in, give quarter, give way, have pity, melt, show mercy, soften, unbend, yield **2.** die down, drop, ease, fall, let up, relax, slacken, slow, weaken
Antonyms (*sense 1*) be unyielding, give no quarter, remain firm, show no mercy (*sense 2*) increase, intensify, strengthen

relentless 1. cruel, fierce, grim, hard, harsh, implacable, inexorable, inflexible, merciless, pitiless, remorseless, ruthless, uncompromising, undeviating, unforgiving, unrelenting, unstoppable, unyielding **2.** in~ cessant, nonstop, persistent, punishing, sustained, unabated, unbroken, unfaltering, unflagging, unrelenting, unrelieved, unre~ mitting, unstoppable
Antonyms (*sense 1*) compassionate, forgiv~ ing, merciful, submissive, yielding

relevant admissible, *ad rem*, applicable, ap~ posite, appropriate, appurtenant, apt, fitting, germane, material, pertinent, prop~ er, related, relative, significant, suited, to the point, to the purpose
Antonyms beside the point, extraneous, ex~ trinsic, immaterial, inapplicable, inappro~ priate, irrelevant, unconnected, unrelated

reliable certain, dependable, faithful, hon~ est, predictable, regular, reputable, respon~ sible, safe, sound, stable, staunch, sure, tried and true, true, trustworthy, trusty, unfailing, upright
Antonyms irresponsible, undependable, unreliable, untrustworthy

relic fragment, keepsake, memento, remem~ brance, remnant, scrap, souvenir, survival, token, trace, vestige

relief 1. abatement, alleviation, assuage~ ment, balm, comfort, cure, deliverance, ease, easement, mitigation, palliation, re~ lease, remedy, solace **2.** aid, assistance, help, succour, support, sustenance **3.** break, breather (*Inf.*), diversion, let-up (*Inf.*), re~ freshment, relaxation, remission, respite, rest

relieve 1. abate, allay, alleviate, appease, assuage, calm, comfort, console, cure, di~ minish, dull, ease, mitigate, mollify, palli~ ate, relax, salve, soften, solace, soothe **2.** aid, assist, bring aid to, help, succour, sup~ port, sustain **3.** give (someone) a break *or* rest, stand in for, substitute for, take over from, take the place of **4.** deliver, dis~ charge, disembarrass, disencumber, exempt, free, release, unburden **5.** break, brighten, interrupt, let up on (*Inf.*), lighten, slacken, vary
Antonyms (*sense 1*) aggravate, exacerbate, heighten, intensify, worsen

religious 1. churchgoing, devotional, de~ vout, divine, doctrinal, faithful, god-fearing, godly, holy, pious, pure, reverent, right~ eous, sacred, scriptural, sectarian, spiritual, theological **2.** conscientious, exact, faithful, fastidious, meticulous, punctilious, rigid, rigorous, scrupulous, unerring, unswerving
Antonyms (*sense 1*) godless, infidel, irreli~ gious, rational, secular, unbelieving

relish *v.* **1.** appreciate, delight in, enjoy, fancy, like, look forward to, luxuriate in, prefer, revel in, savour, taste ~*n.* **2.** appe~ tite, appreciation, enjoyment, fancy, fond~ ness, gusto, liking, love, partiality, pen~ chant, predilection, stomach, taste, zest **3.** appetizer, condiment, sauce, seasoning **4.** flavour, piquancy, savour, smack, spice, tang, taste, trace
Antonyms *v.* be unenthusiastic about, dis~ like, loathe ~*n.* (*sense 2*) dislike, distaste, loathing

reluctance aversion, backwardness, disin~ clination, dislike, disrelish, distaste, hesi~ tancy, indisposition, loathing, repugnance, unwillingness

reluctant averse, backward, disinclined, grudging, hesitant, indisposed, loath, recal~ citrant, slow, unenthusiastic, unwilling
Antonyms eager, enthusiastic, inclined, keen, willing

rely bank, be confident of, be sure of, bet, count, depend, have confidence in, lean, reckon, repose trust in, swear by, trust

remain abide, be left, cling, continue, delay, dwell, endure, go on, last, linger, persist, prevail, rest, stand, stay, stay behind, stay put (*Inf.*), survive, tarry, wait
Antonyms depart, go, leave

remainder balance, butt, dregs, excess, leavings, oddment, relic, remains, remnant, residue, residuum, rest, stub, surplus, tail end, trace, vestige(s)

remaining abiding, extant, lasting, left, lin~ gering, outstanding, persisting, residual, surviving, unfinished

remains 1. balance, crumbs, debris, detri~ tus, dregs, fragments, leavings, leftovers, oddments, odds and ends, pieces, relics, re~ mainder, remnants, residue, rest, scraps, traces, vestiges **2.** body, cadaver, carcass, corpse

remark *v.* **1.** animadvert, comment, declare, mention, observe, pass comment, reflect, say, state **2.** espy, heed, make out, mark, note, notice, observe, perceive, regard, see, take note *or* notice of ~*n.* **3.** assertion, comment, declaration, observation, opinion, reflection, statement, thought, utterance, word **4.** acknowledgment, attention, com~ ment, consideration, heed, mention, notice, observation, recognition, regard, thought

remarkable conspicuous, distinguished, extraordinary, famous, impressive, miracu~ lous, notable, noteworthy, odd, outstanding, phenomenal, pre-eminent, prominent, rare, signal, singular, strange, striking, surpris~ ing, uncommon, unusual, wonderful
Antonyms banal, common, commonplace, everyday, insignificant, mundane, ordinary, unexceptional, unimpressive, unsurprising, usual

remedy *n.* **1.** antidote, counteractive, cure, medicament, medicine, nostrum, panacea, physic (*Rare*), relief, restorative, specific, therapy, treatment **2.** antidote, corrective, countermeasure, panacea, redress, relief, solution ~*v.* **3.** alleviate, assuage, control, cure, ease, heal, help, mitigate, palliate, re~ lieve, restore, soothe, treat **4.** ameliorate, correct, fix, put right, rectify, redress, re~ form, relieve, repair, set to rights, solve

remember bear in mind, call to mind, call up, commemorate, keep in mind, look back (on), recall, recognize, recollect, reminisce, retain, summon up, think back
Antonyms disregard, forget, ignore, neglect, overlook

remind awaken memories of, bring back to, bring to mind, call to mind, call up, jog one's memory, make (someone) remember, prompt, put in mind, refresh one's memory

reminiscence anecdote, memoir, memory, recall, recollection, reflection, remem~ brance, retrospection, review

reminiscent evocative, redolent, remindful, similar, suggestive

remiss careless, culpable, delinquent, der~ elict, dilatory, forgetful, heedless, inatten~ tive, indifferent, lackadaisical, lax, neglect~ ful, negligent, regardless, slack, slapdash, slipshod, sloppy (*Inf.*), slothful, slow, tardy, thoughtless, unmindful
Antonyms attentive, careful, diligent, painstaking, scrupulous

remission 1. absolution, acquittal, amnes~
ty, discharge, excuse, exemption, exonera~
tion, forgiveness, indulgence, pardon, re~
lease, reprieve **2.** abatement, abeyance, al~
leviation, amelioration, decrease, diminu~
tion, ebb, lessening, let-up (*Inf.*), lull, mod~
eration, reduction, relaxation, respite, sus~
pension

remit *v.* **1.** dispatch, forward, mail, post,
send, transmit **2.** cancel, desist, forbear,
halt, repeal, rescind, stop **3.** abate, allevi~
ate, decrease, diminish, dwindle, ease up,
fall away, mitigate, moderate, reduce, relax,
sink, slacken, soften, wane, weaken **4.** def~
er, delay, postpone, put off, put on the back
burner (*Inf.*), shelve, suspend, take a rain
check on (*U.S. & Canad. inf.*) ~*n.* **5.**
authorization, brief, guidelines, instruc~
tions, orders, terms of reference

remittance allowance, consideration, fee,
payment

remnant balance, bit, butt, end, fragment,
hangover, leftovers, oddment, piece, re~
mainder, remains, residue, residuum, rest,
rump, scrap, shred, stub, survival, tail end,
trace, vestige

remonstrate argue, challenge, complain,
dispute, dissent, expostulate, object, protest,
take exception, take issue

remorse anguish, bad *or* guilty conscience,
compassion, compunction, contrition, grief,
guilt, pangs of conscience, penitence, pity,
regret, repentance, ruefulness, self-
reproach, shame, sorrow

remorseful apologetic, ashamed, chastened,
conscience-stricken, contrite, guilt-ridden,
guilty, penitent, regretful, repentant, rueful,
sad, self-reproachful, sorrowful, sorry

remorseless 1. inexorable, relentless, un~
relenting, unremitting, unstoppable **2.** cal~
lous, cruel, hard, hardhearted, harsh, im~
placable, inhumane, merciless, pitiless,
ruthless, savage, uncompassionate, unfor~
giving, unmerciful

remote 1. backwoods, distant, far, faraway,
far-off, godforsaken, inaccessible, in the
middle of nowhere, isolated, lonely, off the
beaten track, outlying, out-of-the-way, se~
cluded **2.** alien, extraneous, extrinsic, for~
eign, immaterial, irrelevant, outside, re~
moved, unconnected, unrelated **3.** doubtful,
dubious, faint, implausible, inconsiderable,
meagre, negligible, outside, poor, slender,
slight, slim, small, unlikely **4.** abstracted,
aloof, cold, detached, distant, faraway, in~
different, introspective, introverted, re~
moved, reserved, standoffish, unapproach~
able, uncommunicative, uninterested, unin~
volved, withdrawn
Antonyms (*sense 1*) adjacent, central, close,
near, nearby, neighbouring (*sense 2*) intrinsic,

related, relevant (*sense 3*) considerable, good,
likely, strong (*sense 4*) alert, attentive, aware,
gregarious, interested, involved, outgoing,
sociable

removal 1. abstraction, dislodgment, dis~
missal, displacement, dispossession, ejec~
tion, elimination, eradication, erasure, ex~
pulsion, expunction, extraction, purging,
stripping, subtraction, taking off, uprooting,
withdrawal **2.** departure, flitting (*Scot. &
northern English dialect*), move, relocation,
transfer

remove 1. abolish, abstract, amputate, car~
ry off *or* away, delete, depose, detach, de~
throne, discharge, dislodge, dismiss, dis~
place, do away with, doff, efface, eject,
eliminate, erase, excise, expel, expunge, ex~
tract, get rid of, give the bum's rush (*Sl.*),
move, oust, purge, relegate, shed, show one
the door, strike out, take away, take off,
take out, throw out, throw out on one's ear
(*Inf.*), transfer, transport, unseat, wipe out,
withdraw **2.** depart, flit (*Scot. & northern
English dialect*), move, move away, quit, re~
locate, shift, transfer, transport, vacate **3.**
Fig. assassinate, bump off (*Sl.*), dispose of,
do away with, do in (*Sl.*), eliminate, ex~
ecute, get rid of, kill, liquidate, murder,
take out (*Sl.*)
Antonyms (*sense 1*) appoint, don, insert, in~
stall, join, link, place, put, put back, put in, put
on, replace, set

remuneration compensation, earnings,
emolument, fee, income, indemnity, meed
(*Archaic*), pay, payment, profit, recompense,
reimbursement, reparation, repayment, re~
tainer, return, reward, salary, stipend,
wages

remunerative economic, gainful, lucrative,
moneymaking, paying, profitable, recom~
pensing, rewarding, rich, worthwhile

renaissance, renascence awakening,
new birth, new dawn, reappearance, re~
awakening, rebirth, re-emergence, regen~
eration, renewal, restoration, resurgence,
resurrection, revival

render 1. contribute, deliver, furnish, give,
hand out, make available, pay, present,
provide, show, submit, supply, tender, turn
over, yield **2.** display, evince, exhibit,
manifest, show **3.** exchange, give, return,
swap, trade **4.** cause to become, leave, make
5. act, depict, do, give, interpret, perform,
play, portray, present, represent **6.** con~
strue, explain, interpret, put, reproduce, re~
state, transcribe, translate **7.** cede, deliver,
give, give up, hand over, relinquish, sur~
render, turn over, yield **8.** give back, make
restitution, pay back, repay, restore, return

renew begin again, breathe new life into,
bring up to date, continue, extend, fix up

(*Inf.*, *chiefly U.S. & Canad.*), mend, modern~ ize, overhaul, prolong, reaffirm, recom~ mence, recreate, re-establish, refit, refresh, refurbish, regenerate, rejuvenate, renovate, reopen, repair, repeat, replace, replenish, restate, restock, restore, resume, revitalize, transform

renounce abandon, abdicate, abjure, abne~ gate, abstain from, cast off, decline, deny, discard, disclaim, disown, eschew, forgo, forsake, forswear, give up, leave off, quit, recant, reject, relinquish, renege, repudiate, resign, retract, spurn, swear off, throw off, waive, wash one's hands of
Antonyms assert, avow, claim, maintain, reassert

renovate do up (*Inf.*), fix up (*Inf.*, *chiefly U.S. & Canad.*), modernize, overhaul, re~ condition, reconstitute, recreate, refit, re~ form, refurbish, rehabilitate, remodel, re~ new, repair, restore, revamp

renowned acclaimed, celebrated, distin~ guished, eminent, esteemed, famed, famous, illustrious, notable, noted, well-known
Antonyms forgotten, little-known, neglect~ ed, obscure, unknown

rent[1] **1.** *n.* fee, hire, lease, payment, rental, tariff **2.** *v.* charter, hire, lease, let

rent[2] **1.** breach, break, chink, crack, flaw, gash, hole, opening, perforation, rip, slash, slit, split, tear **2.** breach, break, cleavage, discord, dissension, disunity, division, fac~ tion, rift, rupture, schism, split

renunciation abandonment, abdication, abjuration, abnegation, abstention, denial, disavowal, disclaimer, eschewal, forswear~ ing, giving up, rejection, relinquishment, repudiation, resignation, spurning, surren~ der, waiver

repair[1] *v.* **1.** compensate for, fix, heal, make good, make up for, mend, patch, patch up, put back together, put right, recover, recti~ fy, redress, renew, renovate, restore, restore to working order, retrieve, square ~*n.* **2.** adjustment, darn, mend, overhaul, patch, restoration **3.** condition, fettle, form, nick (*Inf.*), shape (*Inf.*), state
Antonyms *v.* damage, destroy, harm, ruin, wreck

repair[2] **1.** betake oneself, go, head for, leave for, move, remove, retire, set off for, with~ draw **2.** have recourse, resort, turn

reparation amends, atonement, compensa~ tion, damages, indemnity, propitiation, rec~ ompense, redress, renewal, repair, requital, restitution, satisfaction

repartee badinage, banter, bon mot, persiflage, pleasantry, raillery, riposte, sal~ ly, wit, witticism, wittiness, wordplay

repast collation, food, meal, nourishment, refection, spread (*Inf.*), victuals

repay **1.** compensate, make restitution, pay back, recompense, refund, reimburse, re~ munerate, requite, restore, return, reward, settle up with, square **2.** avenge, even *or* settle the score with, get back at, get even with (*Inf.*), get one's own back on (*Inf.*), hit back, make reprisal, reciprocate, retaliate, return the compliment, revenge

repeal **1.** *v.* abolish, abrogate, annul, cancel, countermand, declare null and void, invali~ date, nullify, obviate, recall, rescind, re~ verse, revoke, set aside, withdraw **2.** *n.* abolition, abrogation, annulment, cancella~ tion, invalidation, nullification, rescinding, rescindment, rescission, revocation, with~ drawal
Antonyms *v.* confirm, enact, introduce, pass, ratify, reaffirm, validate ~*n.* confirmation, enactment, introduction, passing, rati~ fication, reaffirmation, validation

repeat **1.** *v.* duplicate, echo, iterate, quote, recapitulate, recite, redo, rehearse, reiter~ ate, relate, renew, replay, reproduce, rerun, reshow, restate, retell **2.** *n.* duplicate, echo, recapitulation, reiteration, repetition, re~ play, reproduction, rerun, reshowing

repeatedly again and again, frequently, many a time and oft (*Archaic or poetic*), many times, often, over and over, time after time, time and (time) again

repel **1.** beat off, check, confront, decline, drive off, fight, hold off, keep at arm's length, oppose, parry, put to flight, rebuff, refuse, reject, repulse, resist, ward off **2.** disgust, give one the creeps (*Inf.*), gross out (*U.S. sl.*), make one shudder, make one sick, nauseate, offend, put one off, revolt, sicken, turn one off (*Inf.*), turn one's stomach
Antonyms attract, delight, draw, entrance, fascinate, invite, please, submit

repellent **1.** abhorrent, abominable, cringe-making (*Brit. inf.*), discouraging, disgusting, distasteful, hateful, horrid, loathsome, nauseating, noxious, obnoxious, obscene, odious, offensive, off-putting (*Brit. inf.*), repugnant, repulsive, revolting, sick~ ening, yucky *or* yukky (*Sl.*) **2.** imper~ meable, proof, repelling, resistant

repent atone, be ashamed, be contrite, be sorry, deplore, feel remorse, lament, regret, relent, reproach oneself, rue, see the error of one's ways, show penitence, sorrow

repentance compunction, contrition, grief, guilt, penitence, regret, remorse, sackcloth and ashes, self-reproach, sorriness, sorrow

repentant apologetic, ashamed, chastened, contrite, penitent, regretful, remorseful, rueful, self-reproachful, sorry

repercussion backlash, consequence, echo,

rebound, recoil, result, reverberation, se~ quel, side effect

repetition duplication, echo, iteration, re~ appearance, recapitulation, recital, recur~ rence, redundancy, rehearsal, reiteration, relation, renewal, repeat, repetitiousness, replication, restatement, return, tautology

repetitive boring, dull, mechanical, mo~ notonous, recurrent, samey (*Inf.*), tedious, unchanging, unvaried

repine brood, complain, eat one's heart out, fret, grieve, grumble, lament, languish, moan, mope, murmur, sulk

replace follow, oust, put back, re-establish, reinstate, restore, stand in lieu of, substi~ tute, succeed, supersede, supplant, supply, take over from, take the place of

replacement double, fill-in, proxy, stand-in, substitute, successor, surrogate, under~ study

replenish fill, furnish, make up, provide, refill, reload, renew, replace, restock, re~ store, stock, supply, top up
Antonyms consume, drain, empty, exhaust, use up

replete abounding, brimful, brimming, charged, chock-full, crammed, f.lled, full, full to bursting, full up, glutted, gorged, jammed, jam-packed, sated, satiated, stuffed, teeming, well-provided, well-stocked
Antonyms bare, barren, empty, famished, hungry, lacking, starving, wanting

replica carbon copy, copy, duplicate, fac~ simile, imitation, model, reproduction
Antonyms original

reply 1. *v.* acknowledge, answer, come back, counter, echo, make answer, react, recipro~ cate, rejoin, respond, retaliate, retort, re~ turn, riposte, write back 2. *n.* acknowledg~ ment, answer, comeback (*Inf.*), counter, counterattack, echo, reaction, reciprocation, rejoinder, response, retaliation, retort, re~ turn, riposte

report *n.* 1. account, announcement, article, communication, communiqué, declaration, description, detail, dispatch, information, message, narrative, news, note, paper, piece, recital, record, relation, statement, story, summary, tale, tidings, version, word, write-up 2. gossip, hearsay, rumour, talk 3. character, eminence, esteem, fame, regard, reputation, repute 4. bang, blast, boom, crack, crash, detonation, discharge, explosion, noise, reverberation, sound ~*v.* 5. air, announce, bring word, broadcast, circulate, communicate, cover, declare, de~ scribe, detail, document, give an account of, inform of, mention, narrate, note, notify, pass on, proclaim, publish, recite, record, recount, relate, relay, state, tell, write up 6. appear, arrive, be present, clock in *or* on,

come, present oneself, show up (*Inf.*), turn up

reporter announcer, correspondent, hack (*Derogatory*), journalist, journo (*Sl.*), news~ caster, newshound (*Inf.*), newspaperman, newspaperwoman, pressman, writer

repose *n.* 1. ease, inactivity, peace, quiet, quietness, quietude, relaxation, respite, rest, restfulness, sleep, slumber, stillness, tranquillity 2. aplomb, calmness, compo~ sure, dignity, equanimity, peace of mind, poise, self-possession, serenity, tranquillity ~*v.* 3. drowse, lay down, lie, lie down, lie upon, recline, relax, rest, rest upon, sleep, slumber, take it easy, take one's ease

reprehensible bad, blameworthy, censur~ able, condemnable, culpable, delinquent, discreditable, disgraceful, errant, erring, ignoble, objectionable, opprobrious, remiss, shameful, unworthy
Antonyms acceptable, admirable, forgiv~ able, laudable, pardonable, praiseworthy, un~ objectionable

represent 1. act for, be, betoken, corre~ spond to, equal, equate with, express, mean, serve as, speak for, stand for, substitute for, symbolize 2. embody, epitomize, exemplify, personify, symbolize, typify 3. delineate, denote, depict, describe, designate, evoke, express, illustrate, outline, picture, portray, render, reproduce, show, sketch 4. describe as, make out to be, pass off as, pose as, pre~ tend to be 5. act, appear as, assume the role of, enact, exhibit, perform, play the part of, produce, put on, show, stage

representation 1. account, delineation, depiction, description, illustration, image, likeness, model, narration, narrative, pic~ ture, portrait, portrayal, relation, resem~ blance, sketch 2. body of representatives, committee, delegates, delegation, embassy 3. exhibition, performance, play, produc~ tion, show, sight, spectacle 4. *Often plural* account, argument, explanation, exposition, expostulation, remonstrance, statement

representative *n.* 1. agent, commercial traveller, rep, salesman, traveller 2. arche~ type, embodiment, epitome, exemplar, personification, type, typical example 3. agent, commissioner, councillor, delegate, depute (*Scot.*), deputy, member, member of parliament, M.P., proxy, spokesman, spokeswoman ~*adj.* 4. archetypal, charac~ teristic, emblematic, evocative, exemplary, illustrative, symbolic, typical 5. chosen, delegated, elected, elective
Antonyms (*sense 4*) atypical, extraordinary, uncharacteristic

repress bottle up, chasten, check, control, crush, curb, hold back, hold in, inhibit, keep in check, master, muffle, overcome, overpower, quash, quell, restrain, silence, smother, stifle, subdue, subjugate, suppress, swallow

Antonyms encourage, express, free, give free rein to, let out, liberate, release, support

repression authoritarianism, censorship, coercion, constraint, control, despotism, domination, inhibition, restraint, subjuga~ tion, suppression, tyranny

repressive absolute, authoritarian, coer~ cive, despotic, dictatorial, harsh, oppres~ sive, severe, tough, tyrannical

Antonyms democratic, liberal, libertarian

reprieve v. **1.** grant a stay of execution to, let off the hook (Sl.), pardon, postpone or remit the punishment of **2.** abate, allay, al~ leviate, mitigate, palliate, relieve, respite ~n. **3.** abeyance, amnesty, deferment, par~ don, postponement, remission, stay of ex~ ecution, suspension **4.** abatement, allevia~ tion, let-up (Inf.), mitigation, palliation, re~ lief, respite

reprimand 1. n. admonition, blame, casti~ gation, censure, dressing-down (Inf.), flea in one's ear (Inf.), lecture, rebuke, reprehen~ sion, reproach, reproof, row, talking-to (Inf.), telling-off (Inf.), ticking-off (Inf.), tongue-lashing, wigging (Brit. sl.) **2.** v. ad~ monish, bawl out (Inf.), blame, carpet (Inf.), castigate, censure, check, chew out (U.S. & Canad. inf.), chide, dress down (Inf.), give a rocket (Brit. & N.Z. inf.), give (someone) a row (Inf.), haul over the coals (Inf.), lecture, rap over the knuckles, read the riot act, re~ buke, reprehend, reproach, reprove, scold, send one away with a flea in one's ear (Inf.), take to task, tear into (Inf.), tear (someone) off a strip (Brit. inf.), tell off (Inf.), tick off (Inf.), tongue-lash, upbraid

Antonyms n. commendation, compliment, congratulations, praise ~v. applaud, com~ mend, compliment, congratulate, praise

reprisal an eye for an eye, counterstroke, requital, retaliation, retribution, revenge, vengeance

reproach 1. v. abuse, bawl out (Inf.), blame, blast, carpet (Inf.), censure, chew out (U.S. & Canad. inf.), chide, condemn, criticize, defame, discredit, disparage, find fault with, give a rocket (Brit. & N.Z. inf.), lambast(e), read the riot act, rebuke, reprehend, repri~ mand, reprove, scold, take to task, tear into (Inf.), tear (someone) off a strip (Brit. inf.), upbraid **2.** n. abuse, blame, blemish, cen~ sure, condemnation, contempt, disapproval, discredit, disgrace, dishonour, disrepute, ignominy, indignity, obloquy, odium, op~ probrium, scorn, shame, slight, slur, stain, stigma

reproachful abusive, admonitory, castiga~ tory, censorious, condemnatory, contemp~

tuous, critical, disappointed, disapproving, fault-finding, reproving, scolding, upbraid~ ing

reproduce 1. copy, duplicate, echo, emu~ late, imitate, match, mirror, parallel, print, recreate, repeat, replicate, represent, tran~ scribe **2.** breed, generate, multiply, procre~ ate, produce young, proliferate, propagate, spawn

reproduction 1. breeding, generation, in~ crease, multiplication, procreation, prolif~ eration, propagation **2.** copy, duplicate, facsimile, imitation, picture, print, replica

Antonyms (sense 2) original

reproof admonition, blame, castigation, censure, chiding, condemnation, criticism, dressing-down (Inf.), rebuke, reprehension, reprimand, reproach, reproval, scolding, ticking-off (Inf.), tongue-lashing, upbraiding

Antonyms commendation, compliment, en~ couragement, praise

reprove abuse, admonish, bawl out (Inf.), berate, blame, carpet (Inf.), censure, check, chew out (U.S. & Canad. inf.), chide, con~ demn, give a rocket (Brit. & N.Z. inf.), read the riot act, rebuke, reprehend, reprimand, scold, take to task, tear into (Inf.), tear (someone) off a strip (Brit. inf.), tell off (Inf.), tick off (Inf.), upbraid

Antonyms applaud, commend, compliment, encourage, praise

repudiate abandon, abjure, cast off, cut off, deny, desert, disavow, discard, disclaim, disown, forsake, reject, renounce, rescind, retract, reverse, revoke, turn one's back on, wash one's hands of

Antonyms accept, acknowledge, admit, as~ sert, avow, defend, own, proclaim, ratify

repugnance abhorrence, antipathy, aver~ sion, disgust, dislike, disrelish, distaste, hatred, loathing, odium, reluctance, repul~ sion, revulsion

repugnant 1. abhorrent, abominable, dis~ gusting, distasteful, foul, hateful, horrid, loathsome, nauseating, objectionable, ob~ noxious, odious, offensive, repellent, revolt~ ing, sickening, vile, yucky or yukky (Sl.) **2.** adverse, antagonistic, antipathetic, averse, contradictory, hostile, incompatible, incon~ sistent, inimical, opposed

Antonyms agreeable, attractive, compat~ ible, pleasant, unobjectionable

repulsive abhorrent, abominable, disagree~ able, disgusting, distasteful, forbidding, foul, hateful, hideous, horrid, loathsome, nauseating, objectionable, obnoxious, ob~ scene, odious, offensive, repellent, revolting, sickening, ugly, unpleasant, vile

Antonyms appealing, attractive, delightful, enticing, lovely, pleasant

reputable creditable, estimable, excellent,

good, honourable, honoured, legitimate, of good repute, reliable, respectable, trust~ worthy, upright, well-thought-of, worthy

Antonyms cowboy (*Inf.*), disreputable, fly-by-night, shady (*Inf.*), unreliable, untrustworthy

reputation character, credit, distinction, eminence, esteem, estimation, fame, hon~ our, name, opinion, renown, repute, stand~ ing, stature

repute celebrity, distinction, eminence, es~ teem, estimation, fame, name, renown, reputation, standing, stature

reputed accounted, alleged, believed, con~ sidered, deemed, estimated, held, ostensible, putative, reckoned, regarded, rumoured, said, seeming, supposed, thought

reputedly allegedly, apparently, ostensibly, seemingly, supposedly

request 1. *v.* appeal for, apply for, ask (for), beg, beseech, call for, demand, desire, en~ treat, petition, pray, put in for, requisition, seek, solicit, sue for, supplicate **2.** *n.* ap~ peal, application, asking, begging, call, de~ mand, desire, entreaty, petition, prayer, requisition, solicitation, suit, supplication

Antonyms command, order

require 1. crave, depend upon, desire, have need of, lack, miss, need, stand in need of, want, wish **2.** ask, beg, beseech, bid, call upon, command, compel, constrain, de~ mand, direct, enjoin, exact, insist upon, in~ struct, oblige, order, request **3.** call for, de~ mand, entail, involve, necessitate, take

required called for, compulsory, demanded, essential, mandatory, necessary, needed, obligatory, prescribed, recommended, requisite, set, unavoidable, vital

Antonyms elective, noncompulsory, not necessary, not vital, optional, unimportant, voluntary

requirement demand, desideratum, essen~ tial, lack, must, necessity, need, precondi~ tion, prerequisite, qualification, requisite, *sine qua non,* specification, stipulation, want

requisite 1. *adj.* called for, essential, indis~ pensable, mandatory, necessary, needed, needful, obligatory, prerequisite, required, vital **2.** *n.* condition, desideratum, essential, must, necessity, need, precondition, pre~ requisite, requirement, *sine qua non*

requisition *n.* **1.** application, call, demand, request, summons **2.** appropriation, com~ mandeering, occupation, seizure, takeover ~*v.* **3.** apply for, call for, demand, put in for, request **4.** appropriate, commandeer, occupy, seize, take over, take possession of

rescind abrogate, annul, cancel, counter~ mand, declare null and void, invalidate, ob~

viate, overturn, quash, recall, repeal, re~ tract, reverse, revoke, set aside, void

Antonyms confirm, enact, implement, reaffirm, support, uphold, validate

rescue 1. *v.* deliver, extricate, free, get out, liberate, recover, redeem, release, salvage, save, save the life of, set free **2.** *n.* deliver~ ance, extrication, liberation, recovery, re~ demption, release, relief, salvage, salvation, saving

Antonyms (*sense 1*) abandon, desert, leave, leave behind, lose

research 1. *n.* analysis, delving, examina~ tion, experimentation, exploration, fact-finding, groundwork, inquiry, investigation, probe, scrutiny, study **2.** *v.* analyse, consult the archives, do tests, examine, experiment, explore, investigate, look into, make in~ quiries, probe, scrutinize, study, work over

resemblance affinity, analogy, closeness, comparability, comparison, conformity, correspondence, counterpart, facsimile, im~ age, kinship, likeness, parallel, parity, sameness, semblance, similarity, similitude

Antonyms difference, disparity, dissimilar~ ity, heterogeneity, unlikeness, variation

resemble bear a resemblance to, be like, be similar to, duplicate, echo, favour (*Inf.*), look like, mirror, parallel, put one in mind of, remind one of, take after

resent be angry about, bear a grudge about, begrudge, be in a huff about, be offended by, dislike, feel bitter about, grudge, har~ bour a grudge against, have hard feelings about, object to, take amiss, take as an in~ sult, take exception to, take offence at, take umbrage at

Antonyms accept, approve, be content with, be pleased by, feel flattered by, like, welcome

resentful aggrieved, angry, bitter, embit~ tered, exasperated, grudging, huffish, huffy, hurt, in a huff, incensed, indignant, in high dudgeon, irate, jealous, miffed (*Inf.*), of~ fended, peeved (*Inf.*), piqued, put out, re~ vengeful, unforgiving, wounded

Antonyms content, flattered, gratified, pleased, satisfied

resentment anger, animosity, bitterness, displeasure, fury, grudge, huff, hurt, ill feeling, ill will, indignation, ire, irritation, malice, pique, rage, rancour, umbrage, vexation, wrath

reservation 1. condition, demur, doubt, hesitancy, proviso, qualification, rider, scepticism, scruple, stipulation **2.** enclave, homeland, preserve, reserve, sanctuary, territory, tract

reserve *v.* **1.** conserve, hang on to, hoard, hold, husband, keep, keep back, lay up, preserve, put by, retain, save, set aside, stockpile, store, withhold **2.** bespeak, book,

engage, prearrange, pre-engage, retain, se~
cure **3.** defer, delay, keep back, postpone,
put off, withhold ~*n.* **4.** backlog, cache,
capital, fall-back, fund, hoard, reservoir,
savings, stock, stockpile, store, supply **5.**
park, preserve, reservation, sanctuary, tract
6. aloofness, constraint, coolness, formality,
modesty, reluctance, reservation, restraint,
reticence, secretiveness, shyness, silence,
taciturnity ~*adj.* **7.** alternate, auxiliary,
extra, fall-back, secondary, spare, substitute

reserved 1. booked, engaged, held, kept,
restricted, retained, set aside, spoken for,
taken **2.** aloof, cautious, close-mouthed,
cold, cool, demure, formal, modest, prim,
restrained, reticent, retiring, secretive, shy,
silent, standoffish, taciturn, unapproach~
able, uncommunicative, undemonstrative,
unforthcoming, unresponsive, unsociable **3.**
bound, destined, fated, intended, meant,
predestined
Antonyms (*senses 1 & 2*) ardent, demonstra~
tive, forward, open, sociable, uninhibited,
unreserved, warm

reservoir 1. basin, lake, pond, tank **2.** con~
tainer, holder, receptacle, repository, store,
tank **3.** accumulation, fund, pool, reserves,
source, stock, stockpile, store, supply

reshuffle 1. *n.* change, interchange, re~
alignment, rearrangement, redistribution,
regrouping, reorganization, restructuring,
revision, shake-up (*Inf.*) **2.** *v.* change
around, change the line-up of, interchange,
realign, rearrange, redistribute, regroup,
reorganize, restructure, revise, shake up
(*Inf.*)

reside 1. abide, dwell, hang out (*Inf.*), have
one's home, inhabit, live, lodge, remain,
settle, sojourn, stay **2.** abide, be intrinsic
to, be vested, consist, dwell, exist, inhere,
lie, rest with
Antonyms (*sense 1*) holiday in, visit

residence 1. abode, domicile, dwelling, flat,
habitation, home, house, household, lodg~
ing, pad (*Sl.*), place, quarters **2.** hall, man~
or, mansion, palace, seat, villa **3.** occupan~
cy, occupation, sojourn, stay, tenancy

resident 1. *n.* citizen, denizen, indweller,
inhabitant, local, lodger, occupant, tenant
2. *adj.* dwelling, inhabiting, living, local,
neighbourhood, settled
Antonyms *n.* nonresident, visitor ~*adj.*
nonresident, visiting

residue balance, dregs, excess, extra, left~
overs, remainder, remains, remnant, resid~
uum, rest, surplus

resign 1. abandon, abdicate, cede, forgo,
forsake, give in one's notice, give up, hand
over, leave, quit, relinquish, renounce, step
down (*Inf.*), surrender, turn over, vacate,
yield **2. resign oneself** accept, acquiesce,

bow, give in, give up, reconcile, submit,
succumb, yield

resignation 1. abandonment, abdication,
departure, leaving, notice, relinquishment,
renunciation, retirement, surrender **2.** ac~
ceptance, acquiescence, compliance, endur~
ance, forbearing, fortitude, nonresistance,
passivity, patience, submission, sufferance
Antonyms (*sense 2*) defiance, dissent, kick~
ing up a fuss, protest, resistance

resigned acquiescent, compliant, long-
suffering, patient, stoical, subdued, submis~
sive, unprotesting, unresisting

resilient 1. bouncy, elastic, flexible, plastic,
pliable, rubbery, springy, supple, whippy **2.**
bouncy, buoyant, feisty (*Inf., chiefly U.S. &
Canad.*), hardy, irrepressible, quick to re~
cover, strong, tough
Antonyms (*sense 1*) flaccid, inflexible, limp,
rigid, stiff (*sense 2*) delicate, effete, sensitive,
sickly, weak

resist 1. battle, be proof against, check,
combat, confront, contend with, counteract,
countervail, curb, defy, dispute, fight back,
hinder, hold out against, oppose, put up a
fight (against), refuse, repel, stand up to,
struggle against, thwart, weather, withstand
2. abstain from, avoid, forbear, forgo, keep
from, leave alone, prevent oneself from, re~
frain from, refuse, turn down
Antonyms (*sense 1*) accept, acquiesce, give
in, submit, succumb, surrender, welcome,
yield (*sense 2*) enjoy, give in to, indulge in,
surrender to

resistance battle, combat, contention,
counteraction, defiance, fight, fighting, hin~
drance, impediment, intransigence, ob~
struction, opposition, refusal, struggle

resistant 1. hard, impervious, insuscep~
tible, proof against, strong, tough, unaffect~
ed by, unyielding **2.** antagonistic, combat~
ive, defiant, dissident, hostile, intractable,
intransigent, opposed, recalcitrant, unwill~
ing

resolute bold, constant, determined, dogged,
firm, fixed, immovable, inflexible, obstinate,
persevering, purposeful, relentless, set,
stalwart, staunch, steadfast, strong-willed,
stubborn, tenacious, unbending, undaunted,
unflinching, unshakable, unshaken, unwa~
vering
Antonyms doubtful, irresolute, undecided,
undetermined, unresolved, unsteady, weak

resolution 1. boldness, constancy, courage,
dedication, determination, doggedness, ear~
nestness, energy, firmness, fortitude, obsti~
nacy, perseverance, purpose, relentlessness,
resoluteness, resolve, sincerity, staunch~
ness, staying power, steadfastness, stub~
bornness, tenacity, willpower **2.** aim, deci~
sion, declaration, determination, intent, in~

tention, judgment, motion, purpose, resolve, verdict **3.** answer, end, finding, outcome, settlement, solution, solving, sorting out, unravelling, upshot, working out

resolve v. **1.** agree, conclude, decide, design, determine, fix, intend, make up one's mind, purpose, settle, undertake **2.** answer, clear up, crack, elucidate, fathom, find the solution to, suss (out) (*Sl.*), work out **3.** banish, clear up, dispel, explain, remove **4.** analyse, anatomize, break down, clear, disentangle, disintegrate, dissect, dissolve, liquefy, melt, reduce, separate, solve, split up, unravel **5.** alter, change, convert, metamorphose, transform, transmute ~n. **6.** conclusion, decision, design, intention, objective, project, purpose, resolution, undertaking **7.** boldness, courage, determination, earnestness, firmness, resoluteness, resolution, steadfastness, willpower
Antonyms (*sense 7*) cowardice, halfheartedness, indecision, vacillation, wavering

resort v. **1.** avail oneself of, bring into play, employ, exercise, fall back on, have recourse to, look to, make use of, turn to, use, utilize **2.** frequent, go, haunt, head for, repair, visit ~n. **3.** haunt, holiday centre, refuge, retreat, spot, tourist centre, watering place (*Brit.*) **4.** alternative, chance, course, expedient, hope, possibility, recourse, reference

resound echo, fill the air, re-echo, resonate, reverberate, ring

resounding booming, echoing, full, powerful, resonant, reverberating, rich, ringing, sonorous, sounding, vibrant

resource 1. ability, capability, cleverness, ingenuity, initiative, inventiveness, quickwittedness, resourcefulness, talent **2.** hoard, reserve, source, stockpile, supply **3.** appliance, contrivance, course, device, expedient, means, resort

resourceful able, bright, capable, clever, creative, imaginative, ingenious, inventive, quick-witted, sharp, talented
Antonyms fushionless (*Scot.*), gormless (*Brit. inf.*), unimaginative, uninventive

resources assets, capital, funds, holdings, materials, means, money, property, reserves, riches, supplies, wealth, wherewithal

respect n. **1.** admiration, appreciation, approbation, consideration, deference, esteem, estimation, honour, recognition, regard, reverence, veneration **2.** aspect, characteristic, detail, facet, feature, matter, particular, point, sense, way **3.** bearing, connection, reference, regard, relation **4.** *Plural* compliments, devoirs, good wishes, greetings, regards, salutations ~v. **5.** admire,

adore, appreciate, defer to, esteem, have a good *or* high opinion of, honour, look up to, recognize, regard, revere, reverence, set store by, show consideration for, think highly of, value, venerate **6.** abide by, adhere to, attend, comply with, follow, heed, honour, notice, obey, observe, pay attention to, regard, show consideration for
Antonyms n. (*sense 1*) contempt, disdain, disregard, disrespect, irreverence, scorn ~v. abuse, disregard, disrespect, ignore, neglect, scorn

respectable 1. admirable, decent, decorous, dignified, estimable, good, honest, honourable, proper, reputable, respected, upright, venerable, worthy **2.** ample, appreciable, considerable, decent, fair, fairly good, goodly, presentable, reasonable, sizable, substantial, tidy (*Inf.*), tolerable
Antonyms (*sense 1*) dishonourable, disreputable, ignoble, impolite, improper, indecent, unrefined, unworthy (*sense 2*) paltry, poor, small

respective corresponding, individual, own, particular, personal, relevant, separate, several, specific, various

respite 1. break, breather (*Inf.*), breathing space, cessation, halt, hiatus, intermission, interruption, interval, let-up (*Inf.*), lull, pause, recess, relaxation, relief, rest **2.** adjournment, delay, moratorium, postponement, reprieve, stay, suspension

respond acknowledge, act in response, answer, come back, counter, react, reciprocate, rejoin, reply, retort, return
Antonyms ignore, remain silent, turn a blind eye

response acknowledgment, answer, comeback (*Inf.*), counterattack, counterblast, feedback, reaction, rejoinder, reply, retort, return, riposte

responsibility 1. accountability, amenability, answerability, care, charge, duty, liability, obligation, onus, trust **2.** authority, importance, power **3.** blame, burden, culpability, fault, guilt **4.** conscientiousness, dependability, level-headedness, maturity, rationality, reliability, sensibleness, soberness, stability, trustworthiness

responsible 1. at the helm, carrying the can (*Inf.*), in authority, in charge, in control **2.** accountable, amenable, answerable, bound, chargeable, duty-bound, liable, subject, under obligation **3.** authoritative, decision-making, executive, high, important **4.** at fault, culpable, guilty, to blame **5.** adult, conscientious, dependable, levelheaded, mature, rational, reliable, sensible, sober, sound, stable, trustworthy
Antonyms irresponsible, unaccountable,

unconscientious, undependable, unreliable, untrustworthy

responsive alive, awake, aware, forthcom~ ing, impressionable, open, perceptive, quick to react, reactive, receptive, sensitive, sharp, susceptible, sympathetic
Antonyms apathetic, impassive, insensi~ tive, silent, unresponsive, unsympathetic

rest¹ n. **1.** calm, doze, forty winks (*Inf.*), idleness, inactivity, kip (*Brit. sl.*), leisure, lie-down, motionlessness, nap, refreshment, relaxation, relief, repose, siesta, sleep, slumber, snooze (*Inf.*), somnolence, stand~ still, stillness, tranquillity, zizz (*Brit. inf.*) **2. at rest** asleep, at a standstill, at peace, calm, dead, motionless, peaceful, resting, sleeping, still, stopped, tranquil, unmoving **3.** break, breather (*Inf.*), breathing space, cessation, halt, holiday, interlude, inter~ mission, interval, lull, pause, respite, stop, time off, vacation **4.** haven, lodging, refuge, retreat, shelter **5.** base, holder, prop, shelf, stand, support, trestle ~v. **6.** be at ease, be calm, doze, drowse, have a snooze (*Inf.*), have forty winks (*Inf.*), idle, kip (*Brit. sl.*), laze, lie down, lie still, nap, put one's feet up, refresh oneself, relax, sit down, sleep, slumber, snooze (*Inf.*), take a nap, take it easy, take one's ease, zizz (*Brit. inf.*) **7.** be supported, lay, lean, lie, prop, recline, re~ pose, sit, stand, stretch out **8.** break off, cease, come to a standstill, desist, discon~ tinue, halt, have a break, knock off (*Inf.*), stay, stop, take a breather (*Inf.*) **9.** base, be based, be founded, depend, found, hang, hinge, lie, rely, reside, turn
Antonyms v. keep going, slog away (*Inf.*), work ~n. activity, bustle, work

rest² **1.** n. balance, excess, leftovers, others, remainder, remains, remnants, residue, re~ siduum, rump, surplus **2.** v. be left, con~ tinue being, go on being, keep, remain, stay

restful calm, calming, comfortable, languid, pacific, peaceful, placid, quiet, relaxed, re~ laxing, serene, sleepy, soothing, tranquil, tranquillizing, undisturbed, unhurried
Antonyms agitated, busy, disturbing, rest~ less, uncomfortable, unrelaxed

restitution amends, compensation, indemnification, indemnity, recompense, redress, refund, reimbursement, remunera~ tion, reparation, repayment, requital, resto~ ration, return, satisfaction

restive agitated, edgy, fidgety, fractious, fretful, ill at ease, impatient, jittery (*Inf.*), jumpy, nervous, on edge, recalcitrant, re~ fractory, restless, uneasy, unquiet, unruly
Antonyms at ease, calm, content, peaceful, relaxed, satisfied, serene, tranquil

restless **1.** active, bustling, changeable, footloose, hurried, inconstant, irresolute,

moving, nomadic, roving, transient, turbu~ lent, unsettled, unstable, unsteady, wander~ ing **2.** agitated, anxious, disturbed, edgy, fidgeting, fidgety, fitful, fretful, ill at ease, jumpy, nervous, on edge, restive, sleepless, tossing and turning, troubled, uneasy, un~ quiet, unruly, unsettled, worried
Antonyms comfortable, composed, easy, quiet, relaxed, restful, steady, undisturbed

restlessness **1.** activity, bustle, hurry, hurry-scurry, inconstancy, instability, movement, transience, turbulence, turmoil, unrest, unsettledness **2.** agitation, ants in one's pants (*Sl.*), anxiety, disquiet, disturb~ ance, edginess, fitfulness, fretfulness, heebie-jeebies (*Sl.*), inquietude, insomnia, jitters (*Inf.*), jumpiness, nervousness, res~ tiveness, uneasiness, worriedness

restoration **1.** reconstruction, recovery, refreshment, refurbishing, rehabilitation, rejuvenation, renewal, renovation, repair, revitalization, revival **2.** recovery, re~ establishment, reinstallation, reinstatement, replacement, restitution, return
Antonyms (*sense 1*) demolition, scrapping, wrecking (*sense 2*) abolition, overthrow

restore **1.** fix, mend, rebuild, recondition, reconstruct, recover, refurbish, rehabilitate, renew, renovate, repair, retouch, set to rights, touch up **2.** bring back to health, build up, reanimate, refresh, rejuvenate, revitalize, revive, revivify, strengthen **3.** bring back, give back, hand back, recover, re-establish, reinstate, replace, retrocede, return, send back **4.** reconstitute, re~ enforce, reimpose, reinstate, reintroduce
Antonyms (*sense 1*) demolish, scrap, wreck (*sense 2*) make worse, sicken, weaken (*sense 4*) abolish, abrogate, repeal, rescind

restrain **1.** bridle, check, confine, constrain, contain, control, curb, curtail, debar, gov~ ern, hamper, handicap, harness, hinder, hold, hold back, inhibit, keep, keep under control, limit, muzzle, prevent, rein, re~ press, restrict, straiten, subdue, suppress **2.** arrest, bind, chain, confine, detain, fetter, hold, imprison, jail, lock up, manacle, pin~ ion, tie up
Antonyms (*sense 1*) assist, encourage, help, incite, urge on (*sense 2*) free, liberate, release

restrained **1.** calm, controlled, mild, mod~ erate, muted, reasonable, reticent, self-controlled, soft, steady, temperate, unde~ monstrative **2.** discreet, quiet, subdued, tasteful, unobtrusive
Antonyms (*sense 1*) fiery, hot-headed, in~ temperate, unrestrained, wild (*sense 2*) garish, loud, over-the-top, self-indulgent, tasteless

restraint **1.** coercion, command, compul~ sion, confines, constraint, control, curtail~ ment, grip, hindrance, hold, inhibition,

limitation, moderation, prevention, restric~ tion, self-control, self-discipline, self-possession, self-restraint, suppression **2.** arrest, bondage, bonds, captivity, chains, confinement, detention, fetters, imprison~ ment, manacles, pinions, straitjacket **3.** ban, boycott, bridle, check, curb, embargo, interdict, limit, limitation, rein, taboo
Antonyms (*sense 1*) excess, immoderation, intemperance, licence, self-indulgence (*sense 2*) freedom, liberty

restrict bound, circumscribe, confine, con~ tain, cramp, demarcate, hamper, handicap, hem in, impede, inhibit, keep within bounds *or* limits, limit, regulate, restrain, straiten
Antonyms broaden, encourage, foster, free, promote, widen

restriction check, condition, confinement, constraint, containment, control, curb, de~ marcation, handicap, inhibition, limitation, regulation, restraint, rule, stipulation

result *n.* **1.** conclusion, consequence, deci~ sion, development, effect, end, event, fruit, issue, outcome, product, reaction, sequel, termination, upshot ~*v.* **2.** appear, arise, derive, develop, emanate, ensue, eventuate, flow, follow, happen, issue, spring, stem, turn out **3.** *With* in culminate, end, finish, pan out (*Inf.*), terminate, wind up
Antonyms (*sense 1*) beginning, cause, germ, origin, outset, root, source

resume 1. begin again, carry on, continue, go on, proceed, recommence, reinstitute, reopen, restart, take up *or* pick up where one left off **2.** assume again, occupy again, reoccupy, take back, take up again
Antonyms (*sense 1*) cease, discontinue, stop

resumption carrying on, continuation, fresh outbreak, new beginning, re-establishment, renewal, reopening, restart, resurgence

resurrect breathe new life into, bring back, raise from the dead, reintroduce, renew, restore to life, revive

resurrection comeback (*Inf.*), raising *or* rising from the dead, reappearance, rebirth, renaissance, renascence, renewal, restora~ tion, resurgence, resuscitation, return, re~ turn from the dead, revival
Antonyms burial, demise, killing off

resuscitate breathe new life into, bring round, bring to life, give artificial respira~ tion to, give the kiss of life, quicken, reani~ mate, renew, rescue, restore, resurrect, re~ vitalize, revive, revivify, save

retain 1. absorb, contain, detain, grasp, grip, hang *or* hold onto, hold, hold back, hold fast, keep, keep possession of, main~ tain, preserve, reserve, restrain, save **2.** bear in mind, impress on the memory, keep

in mind, memorize, recall, recollect, re~ member **3.** commission, employ, engage, hire, pay, reserve
Antonyms (*sense 1*) let go, lose, release, use up (*sense 2*) forget

retainer 1. attendant, dependant, domestic, flunky, footman, henchman, lackey, serv~ ant, supporter, valet, vassal **2.** advance, de~ posit, fee

retaliate even the score, exact retribution, get back at, get even with (*Inf.*), get one's own back (*Inf.*), give as good as one gets (*Inf.*), give one a taste of one's own medi~ cine, give tit for tat, hit back, make repris~ al, pay one back in one's own coin, recip~ rocate, return like for like, strike back, take an eye for an eye, take revenge, wreak vengeance
Antonyms accept, submit, turn the other cheek

retaliation an eye for an eye, a taste of one's own medicine, counterblow, counterstroke, reciprocation, repayment, reprisal, requital, retribution, revenge, tit for tat, vengeance

retard arrest, brake, check, clog, decelerate, defer, delay, detain, encumber, handicap, hinder, hold back *or* up, impede, obstruct, set back, slow down, stall
Antonyms accelerate, advance, expedite, hasten, speed, speed up, stimulate

retch barf (*U.S. sl.*), be sick, chuck (up) (*Sl., chiefly U.S.*), chunder (*Sl., chiefly Aust.*), disgorge, do a technicolour yawn (*Sl.*), gag, heave, puke (*Sl.*), regurgitate, spew, throw up (*Inf.*), toss one's cookies (*U.S. sl.*), upchuck (*U.S. sl.*), vomit

reticence quietness, reserve, restraint, se~ cretiveness, silence, taciturnity, uncommu~ nicativeness, unforthcomingness

reticent close-mouthed, mum, quiet, re~ served, restrained, secretive, silent, taci~ turn, tight-lipped, uncommunicative, un~ forthcoming, unspeaking
Antonyms candid, communicative, expan~ sive, frank, open, talkative, voluble

retire 1. be pensioned off, (be) put out to grass (*Inf.*), give up work, stop working **2.** absent oneself, betake oneself, depart, exit, go away, leave, remove, withdraw **3.** go to bed, go to one's room, go to sleep, hit the sack (*Sl.*), kip down (*Brit. sl.*), turn in (*Inf.*) **4.** decamp, ebb, fall back, give ground, give way, pull back, pull out, recede, retreat, withdraw

retirement loneliness, obscurity, privacy, retreat, seclusion, solitude, withdrawal

retiring bashful, coy, demure, diffident, humble, meek, modest, quiet, reclusive, re~ served, reticent, self-effacing, shrinking,

shy, timid, timorous, unassertive, unas~
suming
Antonyms audacious, bold, brassy, forward,
gregarious, outgoing, sociable

retouch brush up, correct, finish, improve,
recondition, renovate, restore, touch up

retract 1. draw in, pull back, pull in, reel
in, sheathe **2.** abjure, cancel, deny, dis~
avow, disclaim, disown, recall, recant, re~
nege, renounce, repeal, repudiate, rescind,
reverse, revoke, take back, unsay, withdraw
3. back out of, go back on, renege on

retreat v. **1.** back away, depart, draw back,
ebb, fall back, give ground, go back, leave,
pull back, recede, recoil, retire, shrink, turn
tail, withdraw ~n. **2.** departure, ebb,
evacuation, flight, retirement, withdrawal
3. asylum, den, haunt, haven, hideaway,
privacy, refuge, resort, retirement, sanctu~
ary, seclusion, shelter
Antonyms v. advance, engage, move for~
ward ~n. (sense 2) advance, charge, entrance

retrench curtail, cut, cut back, decrease,
diminish, economize, husband, lessen, limit,
make economies, pare, prune, reduce, save,
tighten one's belt, trim

retrenchment contraction, cost-cutting,
curtailment, cut, cutback, economy, prun~
ing, reduction, rundown, tightening one's
belt
Antonyms expansion, investment

retribution an eye for an eye, compensa~
tion, justice, Nemesis, punishment, reckon~
ing, recompense, redress, repayment, re~
prisal, requital, retaliation, revenge, re~
ward, satisfaction, vengeance

retrieve fetch back, get back, recall, recap~
ture, recoup, recover, redeem, regain, re~
pair, repossess, rescue, restore, salvage,
save, win back

retrospect afterthought, hindsight, recol~
lection, re-examination, remembrance,
reminiscence, review, survey
Antonyms anticipation, foresight

return v. **1.** come back, come round again,
go back, reappear, rebound, recoil, recur,
repair, retreat, revert, turn back **2.** carry
back, convey, give back, put back, re~
establish, reinstate, remit, render, replace,
restore, retrocede, send, send back, take
back, transmit **3.** give back, pay back, re~
ciprocate, recompense, refund, reimburse,
repay, requite **4.** bring in, earn, make, net,
repay, yield **5.** answer, come back (with),
communicate, rejoin, reply, respond, retort
6. choose, elect, pick, vote in **7.** announce,
arrive at, bring in, come to, deliver, render,
report, submit ~n. **8.** homecoming, re~
appearance, rebound, recoil, recrudescence,
recurrence, retreat, reversion **9.** re~
establishment, reinstatement, replacement,

restoration **10.** advantage, benefit, gain, in~
come, interest, proceeds, profit, revenue,
takings, yield **11.** compensation, meed (Ar~
chaic), reciprocation, recompense, reim~
bursement, reparation, repayment, requital,
retaliation, reward **12.** account, form, list,
report, statement, summary **13.** answer,
comeback (Inf.), rejoinder, reply, response,
retort, riposte
Antonyms v. (sense 1) depart, disappear, go
away, leave (senses 2 & 3) hold, keep, leave, re~
move, retain (sense 4) lose ~n. (sense 8) depar~
ture, leaving (sense 9) removal

reveal 1. announce, betray, blow wide open
(Sl.), broadcast, communicate, disclose, di~
vulge, give away, give out, impart, leak, let
on, let out, let slip, make known, make
public, proclaim, publish, tell **2.** bare, bring
to light, display, exhibit, expose to view, lay
bare, manifest, open, show, uncover, un~
earth, unmask, unveil
Antonyms conceal, cover up, hide, keep
quiet about

revel v. **1.** With in bask, crow, delight, drool,
gloat, indulge, joy, lap up, luxuriate, rejoice,
relish, savour, take pleasure, thrive on,
wallow **2.** carouse, celebrate, go on a spree,
live it up (Inf.), make merry, paint the town
red (Inf.), push the boat out (Brit. inf.), rave
(Brit. sl.), roister, whoop it up (Inf.) ~n. **3.**
Often plural bacchanal, beano (Brit. sl.), ca~
rousal, carouse, celebration, debauch, fes~
tivity, gala, jollification, merrymaking, par~
ty, rave (Brit. sl.), rave-up (Brit. sl.), satur~
nalia, spree
Antonyms (sense 1) abhor, be uninterested
in, dislike, hate, have no taste for

revelation announcement, betrayal, broad~
casting, communication, disclosure, discov~
ery, display, exhibition, exposé, exposition,
exposure, giveaway, leak, manifestation,
news, proclamation, publication, telling,
uncovering, unearthing, unveiling

reveller carouser, celebrator, merrymaker,
partygoer, pleasure-seeker, roisterer

revelry beano (Brit. sl.), carousal, carouse,
celebration, debauch, debauchery, festivity,
fun, jollification, jollity, merrymaking, par~
ty, rave (Brit. sl.), rave-up (Brit. sl.), rois~
tering, saturnalia, spree

revenge 1. n. an eye for an eye, reprisal,
requital, retaliation, retribution, satisfac~
tion, vengeance, vindictiveness **2.** v.
avenge, even the score for, get one's own
back for (Inf.), hit back, make reprisal for,
repay, requite, retaliate, take an eye for an
eye for, take revenge for, vindicate

revenue gain, income, interest, proceeds,
profits, receipts, returns, rewards, takings,
yield
Antonyms expenditure, expenses, outgoings

reverberate echo, rebound, recoil, re-echo, resound, ring, vibrate

revere adore, be in awe of, defer to, exalt, have a high opinion of, honour, look up to, put on a pedestal, respect, reverence, think highly of, venerate, worship
Antonyms deride, despise, hold in contempt, scorn, sneer at

reverence 1. *n.* admiration, adoration, awe, deference, devotion, high esteem, homage, honour, respect, veneration, worship **2.** *v.* admire, adore, be in awe of, hold in awe, honour, pay homage to, respect, revere, venerate, worship
Antonyms (*sense 1*) contempt, contumely, derision, disdain, scorn

reverent adoring, awed, decorous, deferential, devout, humble, loving, meek, pious, respectful, reverential, solemn, submissive
Antonyms cheeky, disrespectful, flippant, impious, irreverent, mocking, sacrilegious

reverse *v.* **1.** invert, transpose, turn back, turn over, turn round, turn upside down, upend **2.** alter, annul, cancel, change, countermand, declare null and void, invalidate, negate, obviate, overrule, overset, overthrow, overturn, quash, repeal, rescind, retract, revoke, set aside, undo, upset **3.** back, backtrack, back up, go backwards, move backwards, retreat ~*n.* **4.** antithesis, contradiction, contrary, converse, inverse, opposite **5.** back, flip side, other side, rear, underside, verso, wrong side **6.** adversity, affliction, blow, check, defeat, disappointment, failure, hardship, misadventure, misfortune, mishap, repulse, reversal, setback, trial, vicissitude ~*adj.* **7.** back to front, backward, contrary, converse, inverse, inverted, opposite
Antonyms *v.* (*sense 2*) carry out, enforce, implement, validate (*sense 3*) advance, go forward, move forward ~*n.* (*sense 5*) forward side, front, obverse, recto, right side

revert backslide, come back, go back, hark back, lapse, recur, regress, relapse, resume, return, take up where one left off

review *v.* **1.** go over again, look at again, reassess, recapitulate, reconsider, reevaluate, re-examine, rethink, revise, run over, take another look at, think over **2.** call to mind, look back on, recall, recollect, reflect on, remember, summon up **3.** assess, criticize, discuss, evaluate, examine, give one's opinion of, inspect, judge, read through, scrutinize, study, weigh, write a critique of ~*n.* **4.** analysis, examination, perusal, report, scrutiny, study, survey **5.** commentary, critical assessment, criticism, critique, evaluation, judgment, notice, study **6.** journal, magazine, periodical **7.** another look, fresh look, reassessment, recapitula-

tion, reconsideration, re-evaluation, reexamination, rethink, retrospect, revision, second look **8.** *Military* display, inspection, march past, parade, procession

reviewer arbiter, commentator, connoisseur, critic, essayist, judge

revise 1. alter, amend, change, correct, edit, emend, modify, reconsider, redo, reexamine, revamp, review, rework, rewrite, update **2.** go over, memorize, reread, run through, study, swot up (*Brit. inf.*)

revision 1. alteration, amendment, change, correction, editing, emendation, modification, re-examination, review, rewriting, updating **2.** homework, memorizing, rereading, studying, swotting (*Brit. inf.*)

revival awakening, quickening, reanimation, reawakening, rebirth, recrudescence, refreshment, renaissance, renascence, renewal, restoration, resurgence, resurrection, resuscitation, revitalization, revivification
Antonyms disappearance, extinction, falling off, suppression

revive animate, awaken, breathe new life into, bring back to life, bring round, cheer, come round, comfort, invigorate, quicken, rally, reanimate, recover, refresh, rekindle, renew, renovate, restore, resuscitate, revitalize, rouse, spring up again
Antonyms die out, disappear, enervate, exhaust, tire out, weary

revoke abolish, abrogate, annul, call back, cancel, countermand, declare null and void, disclaim, invalidate, negate, nullify, obviate, quash, recall, recant, renege, renounce, repeal, repudiate, rescind, retract, reverse, set aside, take back, withdraw
Antonyms confirm, endorse, implement, maintain, put into effect, uphold

revolt *n.* **1.** defection, insurgency, insurrection, mutiny, putsch, rebellion, revolution, rising, sedition, uprising ~*v.* **2.** defect, mutiny, rebel, resist, rise, take to the streets, take up arms (against) **3.** disgust, give one the creeps (*Inf.*), gross out (*U.S. sl.*), make one's flesh creep, nauseate, offend, repel, repulse, shock, sicken, turn off (*Inf.*), turn one's stomach

revolting abhorrent, abominable, appalling, cringe-making (*Brit. inf.*), disgusting, distasteful, foul, horrible, horrid, loathsome, nasty, nauseating, nauseous, noisome, obnoxious, obscene, offensive, repellent, repugnant, repulsive, shocking, sickening, yucky *or* yukky (*Sl.*)
Antonyms agreeable, attractive, delightful, fragrant, palatable, pleasant

revolution *n.* **1.** coup, coup d'état, insurgency, mutiny, putsch, rebellion, revolt, rising, uprising **2.** drastic *or* radical change, innovation, metamorphosis, reformation, sea change, shift, transformation, upheaval **3**. circle, circuit, cycle, gyration, lap, orbit, rotation, round, spin, turn, wheel, whirl

revolutionary *n.* **1**. insurgent, insurrectionary, insurrectionist, mutineer, rebel, revolutionist ~*adj.* **2**. extremist, insurgent, insurrectionary, mutinous, radical, rebel, seditious, subversive **3**. avant-garde, different, drastic, experimental, fundamental, ground-breaking, innovative, new, novel, progressive, radical, thoroughgoing
Antonyms (*senses 1 & 2*) counter-revolutionary, loyalist, reactionary (*sense 3*) conservative, conventional, mainstream, minor, traditional, trivial

revolve 1. circle, go round, gyrate, orbit, rotate, spin, turn, twist, wheel, whirl **2**. consider, deliberate, meditate, mull over, ponder, reflect, ruminate, study, think about, think over, turn over (in one's mind)

revulsion abhorrence, abomination, aversion, detestation, disgust, distaste, loathing, odium, recoil, repugnance, repulsion
Antonyms attraction, desire, fascination, liking, pleasure

reward *n.* **1**. benefit, bonus, bounty, compensation, gain, honour, meed (*Archaic*), merit, payment, premium, prize, profit, recompense, remuneration, repayment, requital, return, wages **2**. comeuppance (*Sl.*), desert, just deserts, punishment, requital, retribution ~*v.* **3**. compensate, honour, make it worth one's while, pay, recompense, remunerate, repay, requite
Antonyms *n.* (*sense 1*) fine, penalty, punishment ~*v.* (*sense 3*) fine, penalize, punish

rewarding advantageous, beneficial, economic, edifying, enriching, fruitful, fulfilling, gainful, gratifying, pleasing, productive, profitable, remunerative, satisfying, valuable, worthwhile
Antonyms barren, boring, fruitless, unproductive, unprofitable, unrewarding, vain

rhetoric 1. eloquence, oratory **2**. bombast, fustian, grandiloquence, hot air (*Inf.*), hyperbole, magniloquence, pomposity, rant, verbosity, wordiness

rhetorical 1. bombastic, declamatory, flamboyant, flashy, florid, flowery, grandiloquent, high-flown, high-sounding, hyperbolic, magniloquent, oratorical, pompous, pretentious, showy, silver-tongued, verbose, windy **2**. linguistic, oratorical, stylistic, verbal

rhyme *n.* **1**. ode, poem, poetry, song, verse **2. rhyme or reason** logic, meaning, method, plan, sense ~*v.* **3**. chime, harmonize, sound like

rhythm accent, beat, cadence, flow, lilt,

measure (*Prosody*), metre, movement, pattern, periodicity, pulse, swing, tempo, time

rhythmic, rhythmical cadenced, flowing, harmonious, lilting, melodious, metrical, musical, periodic, pulsating, throbbing

ribald bawdy, blue, broad, coarse, earthy, filthy, gross, indecent, licentious, naughty, near the knuckle (*Inf.*), obscene, off colour, Rabelaisian, racy, raunchy (*Sl.*), risqué, rude, scurrilous, smutty, vulgar
Antonyms chaste, decent, decorous, genteel, inoffensive, polite, proper, refined, tasteful

rich 1. affluent, filthy rich, flush (*Inf.*), loaded (*Sl.*), made of money (*Inf.*), moneyed, opulent, propertied, prosperous, rolling (*Sl.*), stinking rich (*Inf.*), wealthy, well-heeled (*Inf.*), well-off, well-to-do **2**. abounding, full, productive, well-endowed, well-provided, well-stocked, well-supplied **3**. abounding, abundant, ample, copious, exuberant, fecund, fertile, fruitful, full, lush, luxurious, plenteous, plentiful, productive, prolific **4**. beyond price, costly, elaborate, elegant, expensive, exquisite, fine, gorgeous, lavish, palatial, precious, priceless, splendid, sumptuous, superb, valuable **5**. creamy, delicious, fatty, flavoursome, full-bodied, heavy, highly-flavoured, juicy, luscious, savoury, spicy, succulent, sweet, tasty **6**. bright, deep, gay, intense, strong, vibrant, vivid, warm **7**. deep, dulcet, full, mellifluous, mellow, resonant **8**. amusing, comical, funny, hilarious, humorous, laughable, ludicrous, ridiculous, risible, side-splitting
Antonyms (*sense 1*) destitute, impoverished, needy, penniless, poor (*sense 2*) lacking, poor, scarce, wanting (*sense 3*) barren, poor, unfertile, unfruitful, unproductive (*sense 4*) cheap, cheapo (*Inf.*), inexpensive, valueless, worthless (*sense 5*) bland, dull (*sense 6*) dull, insipid, weak (*sense 7*) high-pitched

riches abundance, affluence, assets, fortune, gold, money, opulence, plenty, property, resources, richness, substance, treasure, wealth
Antonyms dearth, indigence, lack, need, paucity, poverty, scantiness, scarcity, want

richly 1. elaborately, elegantly, expensively, exquisitely, gorgeously, lavishly, luxuriously, opulently, palatially, splendidly, sumptuously **2**. amply, appropriately, fully, in full measure, properly, suitably, thoroughly, well

rid 1. clear, deliver, disabuse, disburden, disembarrass, disencumber, free, lighten, make free, purge, relieve, unburden **2. get rid of** dispense with, dispose of, do away with, dump, eject, eliminate, expel, give the bum's rush (*Sl.*), jettison, remove, shake off, throw away *or* out, unload, weed out

riddle brain-teaser (*Inf.*), Chinese puzzle, co~ nundrum, enigma, mystery, poser, problem, puzzle, rebus, teaser

ride v. **1.** control, handle, manage, sit on **2.** be borne (carried, supported), float, go, journey, move, progress, sit, travel **3.** dominate, enslave, grip, haunt, oppress, tyrannize over ~n. **4.** drive, jaunt, journey, lift, outing, spin (*Inf.*), trip, whirl (*Inf.*)

ridicule 1. n. banter, chaff, derision, gibe, irony, jeer, laughter, mockery, raillery, sarcasm, satire, scorn, sneer, taunting **2.** v. banter, caricature, chaff, deride, humiliate, jeer, lampoon, laugh at, laugh out of court, laugh to scorn, make a fool of, make fun of, make one a laughing stock, mock, parody, poke fun at, pooh-pooh, satirize, scoff, send up (*Brit. inf.*), sneer, take the mickey out of (*Inf.*), take the piss (out of) (*Taboo sl.*), taunt

ridiculous absurd, comical, contemptible, derisory, farcical, foolish, funny, hilarious, inane, incredible, laughable, ludicrous, nonsensical, outrageous, preposterous, ris~ ible, silly, stupid, unbelievable
Antonyms bright, clever, intelligent, logical, prudent, rational, reasonable, sagacious, sane, sensible, serious, smart, solemn, well-thought-out, wise

riffraff *canaille*, dregs of society, hoi polloi, rabble, ragtag and bobtail, scum, undesir~ ables

rifle v. burgle, despoil, go through, gut, loot, pillage, plunder, ransack, rob, rummage, sack, strip

rift 1. breach, break, chink, cleavage, cleft, crack, cranny, crevice, fault, fissure, flaw, fracture, gap, opening, space, split **2.** al~ ienation, breach, difference, disagreement, division, estrangement, falling out (*Inf.*), quarrel, schism, separation, split

rig v. **1.** accoutre, equip, fit out, furnish, kit out, outfit, provision, supply, turn out **2.** arrange, doctor, engineer, fake, falsify, fiddle with (*Inf.*), fix (*Inf.*), gerrymander, juggle, manipulate, tamper with, trump up ~n. **3.** accoutrements, apparatus, equipage, equipment, fitments, fittings, fixtures, gear, machinery, outfit, tackle

right adj. **1.** equitable, ethical, fair, good, honest, honourable, just, lawful, moral, proper, righteous, true, upright, virtuous **2.** accurate, admissible, authentic, correct, ex~ act, factual, genuine, precise, satisfactory, sound, spot-on (*Brit. inf.*), true, unerring, valid, veracious **3.** advantageous, appropri~ ate, becoming, *comme il faut*, convenient, deserved, desirable, done, due, favourable, fit, fitting, ideal, opportune, proper, propi~ tious, rightful, seemly, suitable **4.** all there (*Inf.*), balanced, *compos mentis*, fine, fit,

healthy, in good health, in the pink, lucid, normal, rational, reasonable, sane, sound, unimpaired, up to par, well **5.** conservative, reactionary, Tory **6.** absolute, complete, out-and-out, outright, pure, real, thorough, thoroughgoing, utter ~adv. **7.** accurately, aright, correctly, exactly, factually, genu~ inely, precisely, truly **8.** appropriately, apt~ ly, befittingly, fittingly, properly, satisfacto~ rily, suitably **9.** directly, immediately, in~ stantly, promptly, quickly, straight, straightaway, without delay **10.** bang, ex~ actly, precisely, slap-bang (*Inf.*), squarely **11.** absolutely, all the way, altogether, completely, entirely, perfectly, quite, thor~ oughly, totally, utterly, wholly **12.** ethical~ ly, fairly, honestly, honourably, justly, morally, properly, righteously, virtuously **13.** advantageously, beneficially, favour~ ably, for the better, fortunately, to advan~ tage, well ~n. **14.** authority, business, claim, due, freedom, interest, liberty, li~ cence, permission, power, prerogative, privilege, title **15.** equity, good, goodness, honour, integrity, justice, lawfulness, legal~ ity, morality, propriety, reason, rectitude, righteousness, truth, uprightness, virtue **16. by rights** equitably, in fairness, justly, properly **17. to rights** arranged, in order, straight, tidy ~v. **18.** compensate for, cor~ rect, fix, put right, rectify, redress, repair, settle, set upright, sort out, straighten, vin~ dicate
Antonyms adj. (*sense 1*) bad, dishonest, im~ moral, improper, indecent, unethical, unfair, unjust, wrong (*sense 2*) counterfeit, erroneous, fake, false, fraudulent, illegal, illicit, inaccu~ rate, incorrect, inexact, invalid, mistaken, questionable, uncertain, unlawful, untruth~ ful, wrong (*sense 3*) disadvantageous, inap~ propriate, inconvenient, undesirable, unfitting, unseemly, unsuitable, wrong (*sense 4*) abnormal, unsound (*sense 5*) left, leftist, left-wing, liberal, radical, right-on (*Inf.*), so~ cialist ~adv. (*sense 7*) inaccurately, incorrect~ ly (*sense 8*) improperly (*sense 9*) incompletely, indirectly, slowly (*sense 13*) badly, poorly, un~ favourably ~n. (*sense 15*) badness, dishonour, evil, immorality, impropriety ~v. (*sense 18*) make crooked, topple

right away at once, directly, forthwith, immediately, instantly, now, posthaste, promptly, pronto (*Inf.*), right off, straight~ away, straight off (*Inf.*), this instant, with~ out delay, without hesitation

righteous blameless, equitable, ethical, fair, good, honest, honourable, just, law-abiding, moral, pure, squeaky-clean, upright, virtu~ ous
Antonyms bad, corrupt, dishonest, dishon~ ourable, evil, false, guilty, immoral, improper, indecent, insincere, sinful, unethical, unfair,

unjust, unprincipled, unrighteous, unscru~
pulous, unseemly, wicked

righteousness blamelessness, equity,
ethicalness, faithfulness, goodness, honesty,
honour, integrity, justice, morality, probity,
purity, rectitude, uprightness, virtue

rigid adamant, austere, exact, fixed, harsh,
inflexible, intransigent, invariable, rigor~
ous, set, severe, stern, stiff, strict, stringent,
unalterable, unbending, uncompromising,
undeviating, unrelenting, unyielding
Antonyms bending, elastic, flexible, indul~
gent, lax, lenient, limber, lissom(e), merciful,
mobile, pliable, pliant, soft, supple, tolerant,
yielding

rigorous 1. austere, challenging, demand~
ing, exacting, firm, hard, harsh, inflexible,
rigid, severe, stern, strict, stringent, tough
2. accurate, conscientious, exact, meticu~
lous, nice, painstaking, precise, punctilious,
scrupulous, thorough **3.** bad, bleak, ex~
treme, harsh, inclement, inhospitable, se~
vere
Antonyms (*sense 1*) easy, flexible, friendly,
genial, gentle, humane, indulgent, kind, lax,
lenient, loose, merciful, mild, permissive, re~
laxed, soft, sympathetic, tolerant, weak (*sense
2*) careless, half-hearted, haphazard, imper~
fect, inaccurate, incorrect, inexact, loose,
negligent, slapdash, sloppy, slovenly, unscru~
pulous (*sense 3*) agreeable, mild, pleasant

rigour 1. asperity, austerity, firmness,
hardness, hardship, harshness, inflexibility,
ordeal, privation, rigidity, sternness, strict~
ness, stringency, suffering, trial **2.** accura~
cy, conscientiousness, exactitude, exactness,
meticulousness, preciseness, precision,
punctiliousness, thoroughness

rig-out apparel, clobber (*Brit. sl.*), clothing,
costume, dress, garb, gear (*Inf.*), get-up
(*Inf.*), habit, outfit, raiment (*Archaic or po~
etic*), togs

rig out 1. accoutre, equip, fit, furnish, kit
out, outfit, set up **2.** array, attire, clothe,
costume, dress, kit out

rig up arrange, assemble, build, cobble to~
gether, construct, erect, fix up, improvise,
put together, put up, set up, throw together

rim border, brim, brink, circumference, edge,
flange, lip, margin, verge

rind crust, epicarp, husk, integument, outer
layer, peel, skin

ring¹ *n.* **1.** band, circle, circuit, halo, hoop,
loop, round **2.** arena, circus, enclosure,
rink **3.** association, band, cabal, cartel, cell,
circle, clique, combine, coterie, crew (*Inf.*),
gang, group, junta, knot, mob, organization,
syndicate ~*v.* **4.** circumscribe, encircle, en~
close, encompass, gird, girdle, hem in, seal
off, surround

ring² *v.* **1.** chime, clang, peal, resonate, re~
sound, reverberate, sound, toll **2.** buzz
(*Inf.*), call, phone, telephone ~*n.* **3.** chime,
knell, peal **4.** buzz (*Inf.*), call, phone call

rinse 1. *v.* bathe, clean, cleanse, dip, splash,
wash, wash out, wet **2.** *n.* bath, dip, splash,
wash, wetting

riot *n.* **1.** anarchy, commotion, confusion,
disorder, disturbance, donnybrook, fray,
lawlessness, mob violence, quarrel, row,
street fighting, strife, tumult, turbulence,
turmoil, upheaval, uproar **2.** boisterous~
ness, carousal, excess, festivity, frolic, high
jinks, jollification, merrymaking, revelry,
romp **3.** display, extravaganza, flourish,
show, splash **4. run riot a.** be out of con~
trol, break *or* cut loose, go wild, let oneself
go, raise hell, rampage, throw off all re~
straint **b.** grow like weeds, grow profusely,
luxuriate, spread like wildfire ~*v.* **5.** fight
in the streets, go on the rampage, raise an
uproar, rampage, run riot, take to the
streets **6.** carouse, cut loose, frolic, go on a
binge (*Inf.*), go on a spree, make merry,
paint the town red (*Inf.*), revel, roister,
romp

riotous 1. anarchic, disorderly, insubordi~
nate, lawless, mutinous, rampageous, rebel~
lious, refractory, rowdy, tumultuous, un~
governable, unruly, uproarious, violent **2.**
boisterous, loud, luxurious, noisy, orgiastic,
rambunctious (*Inf.*), roisterous, rollicking,
saturnalian, side-splitting, unrestrained,
uproarious, wanton, wild
Antonyms calm, civilized, disciplined, gen~
tle, lawful, mild, obedient, orderly, peaceful,
quiet, restrained, well-behaved

ripe 1. fully developed, fully grown, mature,
mellow, ready, ripened, seasoned **2.** accom~
plished, complete, finished, in readiness,
perfect, prepared, ready **3.** auspicious, fa~
vourable, ideal, opportune, right, suitable,
timely
Antonyms (*sense 1*) green, immature, unde~
veloped, unripe (*sense 2*) imperfect, incom~
plete, unaccomplished, unfinished, unfit, un~
prepared (*sense 3*) disadvantageous, inappro~
priate, inconvenient, inopportune, unfavour~
able, unfitting, unseemly, unsuitable, un~
timely

ripen burgeon, come of age, come to frui~
tion, develop, get ready, grow ripe, make
ripe, mature, prepare, season

riposte 1. *n.* answer, comeback (*Inf.*),
counterattack, rejoinder, repartee, reply,
response, retort, return, sally **2.** *v.* answer,
come back, reciprocate, rejoin, reply, re~
spond, retort, return

rise *v.* **1.** arise, get out of bed, get to one's
feet, get up, rise and shine, stand up, sur~
face **2.** arise, ascend, climb, enlarge, go up,

grow, improve, increase, intensify, levitate, lift, mount, move up, soar, swell, wax **3.** advance, be promoted, climb the ladder, get on, get somewhere, go places (*Inf.*), progress, prosper, work one's way up **4.** appear, become apparent, crop up, emanate, emerge, eventuate, flow, happen, issue, occur, originate, spring, turn up **5.** mount the barricades, mutiny, rebel, resist, revolt, take up arms **6.** ascend, climb, get steeper, go uphill, mount, slope upwards ~*n.* **7.** advance, ascent, climb, improvement, increase, upsurge, upswing, upturn, upward turn **8.** advancement, aggrandizement, climb, progress, promotion **9.** acclivity, ascent, elevation, hillock, incline, rising ground, upward slope **10.** increment, pay increase, raise (*U.S.*) **11. give rise to** bring about, bring on, cause, effect, produce, provoke, result in
Antonyms *v.* abate, abbreviate, abridge, condense, curtail, decline, decrease, descend, diminish, drop, dwindle, fall, lessen, plunge, reduce, shrink, sink, wane ~*n.* blip, decline, decrease, downswing, downturn, drop, fall

risk 1. *n.* chance, danger, gamble, hazard, jeopardy, peril, pitfall, possibility, speculation, uncertainty, venture **2.** *v.* chance, dare, endanger, expose to danger, gamble, hazard, imperil, jeopardize, put in jeopardy, take a chance on, venture

risky chancy (*Inf.*), dangerous, dicey (*Inf., chiefly Brit.*), dodgy (*Brit., Aust., & N.Z. inf.*), fraught with danger, hazardous, perilous, precarious, touch-and-go, tricky, uncertain, unsafe
Antonyms certain, reliable, safe, secure, stable, sure

rite act, ceremonial, ceremony, communion, custom, form, formality, liturgy, mystery, observance, ordinance, practice, procedure, ritual, sacrament, service, solemnity, usage

ritual *n.* **1.** ceremonial, ceremony, communion, liturgy, mystery, observance, rite, sacrament, service, solemnity **2.** convention, custom, form, formality, habit, ordinance, practice, prescription, procedure, protocol, red tape, routine, stereotype, tradition, usage ~*adj.* **3.** ceremonial, ceremonious, conventional, customary, formal, habitual, prescribed, procedural, routine, stereotyped

rival *n.* **1.** adversary, antagonist, challenger, competitor, contender, contestant, emulator, opponent **2.** compeer, equal, equivalent, fellow, match, peer ~*adj.* **3.** competing, competitive, conflicting, emulating, opposed, opposing ~*v.* **4.** be a match for, bear comparison with, come up to, compare with, compete, contend, emulate, equal, match, measure up to, oppose, seek to displace, vie with

Antonyms *n.* (*sense 1*) ally, friend, helper, supporter ~*v.* (*sense 4*) aid, back, help, support

rivalry antagonism, competition, competitiveness, conflict, contention, contest, duel, emulation, opposition, struggle, vying

road 1. avenue, course, direction, highway, lane, motorway, path, pathway, roadway, route, street, thoroughfare, track, way **2.** *Nautical* anchorage, roadstead

roam drift, meander, peregrinate, prowl, ramble, range, rove, stravaig (*Scot. & northern English dialect*), stray, stroll, travel, walk, wander

roar *v.* **1.** bawl, bay, bell, bellow, clamour, crash, cry, howl, rumble, shout, thunder, vociferate, yell **2.** bust a gut (*Inf.*), crack up (*Inf.*), guffaw, hoot, laugh heartily, split one's sides (*Inf.*), ~*n.* **3.** bellow, clamour, crash, cry, howl, outcry, rumble, shout, thunder, yell **4.** belly laugh (*Inf.*), guffaw, hoot

rob bereave, burgle, cheat, con (*Inf.*), defraud, deprive, despoil, dispossess, do out of (*Inf.*), gyp (*Sl.*), hold up, loot, mug (*Inf.*), pillage, plunder, raid, ransack, rifle, rip off (*Sl.*), sack, skin (*Sl.*), steam (*Inf.*), stiff (*Sl.*), strip, swindle

robber bandit, brigand, burglar, cheat, con man (*Inf.*), fraud, highwayman, looter, mugger (*Inf.*), pirate, plunderer, raider, stealer, swindler, thief

robbery burglary, depredation, embezzlement, filching, fraud, hold-up, larceny, mugging (*Inf.*), pillage, plunder, raid, rapine, rip-off (*Sl.*), spoliation, stealing, steaming (*Inf.*), stick-up (*Sl., chiefly U.S.*), swindle, theft, thievery

robe *n.* **1.** costume, gown, habit, vestment **2.** bathrobe, dressing gown, housecoat, negligee, peignoir, wrapper ~*v.* **3.** apparel (*Archaic*), attire, clothe, drape, dress, garb

robot android, automaton, machine, mechanical man

robust 1. able-bodied, athletic, brawny, fit, hale, hardy, healthy, hearty, husky (*Inf.*), in fine fettle, in good health, lusty, muscular, powerful, Ramboesque, rude, rugged, sinewy, sound, staunch, stout, strapping, strong, sturdy, thickset, tough, vigorous, well **2.** boisterous, coarse, earthy, indecorous, raunchy (*Sl.*), raw, roisterous, rollicking, rough, rude, unsubtle **3.** commonsensical, down-to-earth, hard-headed, practical, pragmatic, realistic, sensible, straightforward
Antonyms delicate, feeble, frail, hothouse (*Inf., often disparaging*), infirm, refined, sickly, slender, unfit, unhealthy, unsound, weak, weedy (*Inf.*), wimpish or wimpy (*Inf.*)

rock¹ 1. boulder, stone **2.** anchor, bulwark,

cornerstone, foundation, mainstay, protec~
tion, support, tower of strength

rock² 1. lurch, pitch, reel, roll, sway, swing,
toss, wobble **2.** astonish, astound, daze,
dumbfound, jar, set one back on one's heels
(*Inf.*), shake, shock, stagger, stun, surprise

rocky 1. boulder-strewn, craggy, pebbly,
rough, rugged, stony **2.** adamant, firm,
flinty, hard, rocklike, rugged, solid, steady,
tough, unyielding

rod bar, baton, birch, cane, crook, dowel,
mace, pole, sceptre, shaft, staff, stick,
switch, wand

rogue blackguard, charlatan, cheat, con
man (*Inf.*), crook (*Inf.*), deceiver, devil,
fraud, knave (*Archaic*), mountebank, ne'er-
do-well, rapscallion, rascal, reprobate, scally
(*Northwest English dialect*), scamp, scoun~
drel, scumbag (*Sl.*), sharper, swindler, vil~
lain

role 1. character, impersonation, part, por~
trayal, representation **2.** capacity, duty,
function, job, part, position, post, task

roll *v.* **1.** elapse, flow, go past, go round, gy~
rate, pass, pivot, reel, revolve, rock, rotate,
run, spin, swivel, trundle, turn, twirl, un~
dulate, wheel, whirl **2.** bind, coil, curl, en~
fold, entwine, envelop, furl, swathe, twist,
wind, wrap **3.** even, flatten, level, press,
smooth, spread **4.** boom, drum, echo,
grumble, resound, reverberate, roar, rum~
ble, thunder **5.** billow, lurch, reel, rock,
sway, swing, toss, tumble, wallow, welter **6.**
lumber, lurch, reel, stagger, swagger, sway,
waddle ~*n.* **7.** cycle, gyration, reel, revolu~
tion, rotation, run, spin, turn, twirl, undu~
lation, wheel, whirl **8.** ball, bobbin, cylin~
der, reel, scroll, spool **9.** annals, catalogue,
census, chronicle, directory, index, inven~
tory, list, record, register, roster, schedule,
scroll, table **10.** billowing, lurching, pitch~
ing, rocking, rolling, swell, tossing, undula~
tion, wallowing, waves **11.** boom, drum~
ming, growl, grumble, resonance, rever~
beration, roar, rumble, thunder

rollicking *adj.* boisterous, carefree, cavort~
ing, devil-may-care, exuberant, frisky, frol~
icsome, hearty, jaunty, jovial, joyous, lively,
merry, playful, rip-roaring (*Inf.*), romping,
spirited, sportive, sprightly, swashbuckling
Antonyms cheerless, despondent, dull,
gloomy, lifeless, melancholy, morose, sad, se~
date, serious, unhappy

roly-poly buxom, chubby, fat, overweight,
plump, podgy, pudgy, rotund, rounded, tub~
by

romance *n.* **1.** affair, *affaire (du coeur)*, af~
fair of the heart, amour, attachment, in~
trigue, liaison, love affair, passion, rela~
tionship **2.** adventure, charm, colour, ex~
citement, exoticness, fascination, glamour,

mystery, nostalgia, sentiment **3.** fairy tale,
fantasy, fiction, idyll, legend, love story,
melodrama, novel, story, tale, tear-jerker
(*Inf.*) **4.** absurdity, exaggeration, fabrica~
tion, fairy tale, falsehood, fiction, flight of
fancy, invention, lie, tall story (*Inf.*),
trumped-up story ~*v.* **5.** be economical with
the truth, exaggerate, fantasize, let one's
imagination run away with one, lie, make
up stories, stretch the truth, tell stories

romantic *adj.* **1.** amorous, fond, lovey-
dovey, loving, mushy (*Inf.*), passionate,
sentimental, sloppy (*Inf.*), soppy (*Brit. inf.*),
tender **2.** charming, colourful, exciting, ex~
otic, fascinating, glamorous, mysterious,
nostalgic, picturesque **3.** dreamy, high-
flown, idealistic, impractical, quixotic,
starry-eyed, unrealistic, utopian, visionary,
whimsical **4.** chimerical, exaggerated, ex~
travagant, fabulous, fairy-tale, fanciful, fan~
tastic, fictitious, idyllic, imaginary, imagi~
native, improbable, legendary, made-up,
unrealistic, wild ~*n.* **5.** Don Quixote,
dreamer, idealist, romancer, sentimentalist,
utopian, visionary
Antonyms *adj.* cold-hearted, insensitive,
practical, realistic, unaffectionate, unimpas~
sioned, uninspiring, unloving, unromantic,
unsentimental

rook *v.* bilk, cheat, clip (*Sl.*), cozen, defraud,
diddle (*Inf.*), do (*Sl.*), fleece, gyp (*Sl.*), mulct,
overcharge, rip off (*Sl.*), skin (*Sl.*), stiff (*Sl.*),
sting (*Inf.*), swindle

room 1. allowance, area, capacity, compass,
elbowroom, expanse, extent, latitude, lee~
way, margin, play, range, scope, space, ter~
ritory, volume **2.** apartment, chamber,
office **3.** chance, occasion, opportunity,
scope

roomy ample, broad, capacious, commodi~
ous, extensive, generous, large, sizable,
spacious, wide
Antonyms bounded, confined, cramped,
narrow, small, tiny, uncomfortable

root *n.* **1.** radicle, radix, rhizome, stem, tu~
ber **2.** base, beginnings, bottom, cause,
core, crux, derivation, essence, foundation,
fountainhead, fundamental, germ, heart,
mainspring, nub, nucleus, occasion, origin,
seat, seed, source, starting point **3.** *Plural*
birthplace, cradle, family, heritage, home,
origins, sense of belonging **4. root and
branch** completely, entirely, finally, radi~
cally, thoroughly, totally, to the last man,
utterly, wholly, without exception ~*v.* **5.**
anchor, become established, become settled,
embed, entrench, establish, fasten, fix,
ground, implant, moor, set, stick, take root

rooted confirmed, deep, deeply felt, deep-
seated, entrenched, established, firm, fixed,
ingrained, radical, rigid

root out 1. *Also* **root up** abolish, cut out, destroy, dig up by the roots, do away with, efface, eliminate, eradicate, erase, extermi~ nate, extirpate, get rid of, remove, tear out by the roots, uproot, weed out **2.** bring to light, dig out, discover, dredge up, produce, turn up, unearth

rope *n.* **1.** cable, cord, hawser, line, strand **2. the rope** capital punishment, halter, hanging, lynching, noose **3. know the ropes** be an old hand, be experienced, be knowledgeable, know all the ins and outs, know one's way around, know the score (*Inf.*), know what's what, know where it's at (*Sl.*) ~*v.* **4.** bind, fasten, hitch, lash, lasso, moor, pinion, tether, tie

rope in drag in, engage, enlist, inveigle, in~ volve, persuade, talk into

roster agenda, catalogue, inventory, list, listing, register, roll, rota, schedule, scroll, table

rostrum dais, platform, podium, stage

rosy 1. pink, red, roseate, rose-coloured **2.** blooming, blushing, flushed, fresh, glowing, healthy-looking, radiant, reddish, roseate, rubicund, ruddy **3.** auspicious, bright, cheerful, encouraging, favourable, hopeful, optimistic, promising, reassuring, roseate, rose-coloured, sunny
Antonyms (*sense 2*) ashen, colourless, grey, pale, pallid, sickly, wan, white (*sense 3*) cheer~ less, depressing, discouraging, dismal, dull, gloomy, hopeless, miserable, pessimistic, un~ happy, unpromising

rot *v.* **1.** corrode, corrupt, crumble, decay, decompose, degenerate, deteriorate, disinte~ grate, fester, go bad, moulder, perish, pu~ trefy, spoil, taint **2.** decline, degenerate, de~ teriorate, languish, waste away, wither away ~*n.* **3.** blight, canker, corrosion, cor~ ruption, decay, decomposition, deteriora~ tion, disintegration, mould, putrefaction, putrescence **4.** balderdash, balls (*Taboo sl.*), bilge (*Inf.*), bosh (*Inf.*), bull (*Sl.*), bullshit (*Taboo sl.*), bunk (*Inf.*), bunkum *or* bun~ combe (*Chiefly U.S.*), claptrap (*Inf.*), cob~ blers (*Brit. taboo sl.*), codswallop (*Brit. sl.*), crap (*Sl.*), drivel, eyewash (*Inf.*), flapdoodle (*Sl.*), garbage (*Chiefly U.S.*), guff (*Sl.*), hog~ wash, hokum (*Sl., chiefly U.S. & Canad.*), horsefeathers (*U.S. sl.*), hot air (*Inf.*), moon~ shine, nonsense, pap, piffle (*Inf.*), poppycock (*Inf.*), rubbish, shit (*Taboo sl.*), stuff and nonsense, tommyrot, tosh (*Sl., chiefly Brit.*), tripe (*Inf.*), twaddle

rotary gyratory, revolving, rotating, rota~ tional, rotatory, spinning, turning

rotate 1. go round, gyrate, pirouette, pivot, reel, revolve, spin, swivel, turn, wheel **2.** alternate, follow in sequence, interchange, switch, take turns

rotation 1. gyration, orbit, pirouette, reel, revolution, spin, spinning, turn, turning, wheel **2.** alternation, cycle, interchanging, sequence, succession, switching

rotten 1. bad, corroded, corrupt, crumbling, decayed, decaying, decomposed, decompos~ ing, disintegrating, festering, fetid, foul, mouldering, mouldy, perished, putrescent, putrid, rank, sour, stinking, tainted, un~ sound **2.** bent (*Sl.*), corrupt, crooked (*Inf.*), deceitful, degenerate, dishonest, dishonour~ able, disloyal, faithless, immoral, merce~ nary, perfidious, treacherous, untrustwor~ thy, venal, vicious **3.** *Inf.* base, contempt~ ible, despicable, dirty, disagreeable, filthy, mean, nasty, scurrilous, shitty (*Taboo sl.*), unpleasant, vile, wicked **4.** *Inf.* bad, deplor~ able, disappointing, regrettable, unfortu~ nate, unlucky **5.** *Inf.* chickenshit (*U.S. sl.*), crummy (*Sl.*), duff (*Brit. inf.*), ill-considered, ill-thought-out, inadequate, inferior, lousy (*Sl.*), low-grade, of a sort *or* of sorts, poor, poxy (*Sl.*), punk, ropy *or* ropey (*Brit. inf.*), sorry, substandard, unacceptable, unsatis~ factory **6.** *Inf.* bad, below par, ill, off colour, poorly (*Inf.*), ropy *or* ropey (*Brit. inf.*), rough (*Inf.*), sick, under the weather (*Inf.*), unwell
Antonyms (*sense 1*) fresh, good, pure, wholesome (*sense 2*) decent, honest, honour~ able, moral, scrupulous, trustworthy (*sense 3*) sweet

rotter bad lot, blackguard, blighter (*Brit. inf.*), bounder (*Old-fashioned Brit. sl.*), cad (*Brit. inf.*), cocksucker (*Taboo sl.*), cur, louse (*Sl.*), rat (*Inf.*), scumbag (*Sl.*), stinker (*Sl.*), swine

rotund 1. bulbous, globular, orbicular, round, rounded, spherical **2.** chubby, cor~ pulent, fat, fleshy, heavy, obese, plump, podgy, portly, roly-poly, rounded, stout, tubby **3.** full, grandiloquent, magniloquent, orotund, resonant, rich, round, sonorous
Antonyms (*sense 2*) angular, gaunt, lank, lanky, lean, scrawny, skinny, slender, slight, slim, thin

rough *adj.* **1.** broken, bumpy, craggy, ir~ regular, jagged, rocky, rugged, stony, un~ even **2.** bristly, bushy, coarse, dishevelled, disordered, fuzzy, hairy, shaggy, tangled, tousled, uncut, unshaven, unshorn **3.** agi~ tated, boisterous, choppy, inclement, squal~ ly, stormy, tempestuous, turbulent, wild **4.** bearish, bluff, blunt, brusque, churlish, coarse, curt, discourteous, ill-bred, ill-mannered, impolite, inconsiderate, indeli~ cate, loutish, rude, unceremonious, uncivil, uncouth, uncultured, ungracious, unman~ nerly, unpolished, unrefined, untutored **5.** boisterous, cruel, curt, drastic, extreme, hard, harsh, nasty, rowdy, severe, sharp, tough, unfeeling, unjust, unpleasant, violent

6. *Inf.* below par, ill, not a hundred per cent (*Inf.*), off colour, poorly (*Inf.*), ropy *or* ropey (*Brit. inf.*), rotten (*Inf.*), sick, under the weather (*Inf.*), unwell, upset **7.** cacophonous, discordant, grating, gruff, harsh, husky, inharmonious, jarring, rasping, raucous, unmusical **8.** arduous, austere, hard, rugged, spartan, tough, uncomfortable, unpleasant, unrefined **9.** basic, crude, cursory, formless, hasty, imperfect, incomplete, quick, raw, rough-and-ready, rough-hewn, rudimentary, shapeless, sketchy, unfinished, unpolished, unrefined, untutored **10.** crude, raw, rough-hewn, uncut, undressed, unhewn, unpolished, unprocessed, unwrought **11.** amorphous, approximate, estimated, foggy, general, hazy, imprecise, inexact, sketchy, vague ~*n.* **12.** draft, mock-up, outline, preliminary sketch, suggestion **13.** *Inf.* bruiser, bully boy, casual, lager lout, ned (*Sl.*), roughneck (*Sl.*), rowdy, ruffian, thug, tough ~*v.* **14. rough out** adumbrate, block out, delineate, draft, outline, plan, sketch, suggest **15. rough up** bash up (*Inf.*), batter, beat the living daylights out of (*Inf.*), beat up, do over (*Brit., Aust., & N.Z. sl.*), knock about *or* around, maltreat, manhandle, mistreat, thrash
Antonyms (*sense 1*) even, level, regular, smooth, unbroken (*sense 2*) smooth, soft (*sense 3*) calm, gentle, quiet, smooth, tranquil (*sense 4*) civil, considerate, courteous, courtly, delicate, elegant, graceful, gracious, pleasant, polite, refined, smooth, sophisticated, urbane, well-bred, well-mannered (*sense 5*) gentle, just, kind, mild, pleasant, quiet, soft (*sense 7*) harmonious, smooth (*sense 8*) comfortable, cushy (*Inf.*), easy, pleasant, soft (*sense 9*) complete, detailed, finished, perfected, polished, refined, specific (*sense 10*) smooth (*sense 11*) exact, perfected, specific

rough-and-tumble 1. *n.* affray (*Law*), brawl, donnybrook, dust-up (*Inf.*), fight, fracas, melee *or* mêlée, punch-up (*Brit. inf.*), roughhouse (*Sl.*), scrap (*Inf.*), scrimmage, scuffle, shindig (*Inf.*), shindy (*Inf.*), struggle **2.** *adj.* boisterous, disorderly, haphazard, indisciplined, irregular, rough, rowdy, scrambled, scrambling

round *adj.* **1.** annular, ball-shaped, bowed, bulbous, circular, curved, curvilinear, cylindrical, discoid, disc-shaped, globular, orbicular, ring-shaped, rotund, rounded, spherical **2.** complete, entire, full, solid, unbroken, undivided, whole **3.** ample, bounteous, bountiful, considerable, generous, great, large, liberal, substantial **4.** ample, fleshy, full, full-fleshed, plump, roly-poly, rotund, rounded **5.** full, mellifluous, orotund, resonant, rich, rotund, sonorous **6.** blunt, candid, direct, frank, outspoken, plain, straightforward, unmodified ~*n.* **7.**

ball, band, circle, disc, globe, orb, ring, sphere **8.** bout, cycle, sequence, series, session, succession **9.** division, lap, level, period, session, stage, turn **10.** ambit, beat, circuit, compass, course, routine, schedule, series, tour, turn **11.** bullet, cartridge, discharge, shell, shot ~*v.* **12.** bypass, circle, circumnavigate, encircle, flank, go round, skirt, turn

roundabout *adj.* circuitous, circumlocutory, devious, discursive, evasive, indirect, meandering, oblique, periphrastic, tortuous
Antonyms direct, straight, straightforward

round off bring to a close, cap, close, complete, conclude, crown, finish off, put the finishing touch to, settle
Antonyms begin, commence, initiate, open, start

round up assemble, bring together, collect, drive, gather, group, herd, marshal, muster, rally

rouse 1. arouse, awaken, call, get up, rise, wake, wake up **2.** agitate, anger, animate, arouse, bestir, disturb, excite, exhilarate, galvanize, get going, incite, inflame, instigate, move, prod, provoke, startle, stimulate, stir, whip up

rousing brisk, electrifying, exciting, exhilarating, inflammatory, inspiring, lively, moving, spirited, stimulating, stirring, vigorous
Antonyms boring, dreary, dull, lifeless, sluggish, spiritless, unenergetic, wearisome, wishy-washy (*Inf.*)

rout 1. *n.* beating, debacle, defeat, disorderly retreat, drubbing, headlong flight, hiding (*Inf.*), licking (*Inf.*), overthrow, overwhelming defeat, pasting (*Sl.*), ruin, shambles, thrashing **2.** *v.* beat, chase, clobber (*Sl.*), conquer, crush, cut to pieces, defeat, destroy, dispel, drive off, drub, lick (*Inf.*), overpower, overthrow, put to flight, put to rout, scatter, tank (*Sl.*), thrash, throw back in confusion, wipe the floor with (*Inf.*), worst

route 1. *n.* avenue, beat, circuit, course, direction, itinerary, journey, passage, path, road, round, run, way **2.** *v.* convey, direct, dispatch, forward, send, steer

routine *n.* **1.** custom, formula, grind (*Inf.*), groove, method, order, pattern, practice, procedure, programme, usage, way, wont **2.** *Inf.* act, bit (*Inf.*), line, performance, piece, spiel (*Inf.*) ~*adj.* **3.** conventional, customary, everyday, familiar, habitual, normal, ordinary, standard, typical, usual, wonted, workaday **4.** boring, clichéd, dull, hackneyed, humdrum, mind-numbing, predictable, run-of-the-mill, shtick (*Sl.*), tedious, tiresome, unimaginative, uninspired, unoriginal

Antonyms *adj.* abnormal, different, excep~
tional, irregular, special, unusual

row[1] bank, column, file, line, queue, range,
rank, sequence, series, string, tier

row[2] *n.* **1.** altercation, *bagarre*, brawl, com~
motion, controversy, dispute, disturbance,
falling-out (*Inf.*), fracas, fray, fuss, noise,
quarrel, racket, ruckus (*Inf.*), ruction (*Inf.*),
rumpus, scrap (*Inf.*), shindig (*Inf.*), shindy
(*Inf.*), shouting match (*Inf.*), slanging match
(*Brit.*), squabble, tiff, trouble, tumult,
uproar **2.** castigation, dressing-down (*Inf.*),
flea in one's ear (*Inf.*), lecture, reprimand,
reproof, rollicking (*Brit. inf.*), talking-to
(*Inf.*), telling-off (*Inf.*), ticking-off (*Inf.*),
tongue-lashing ~*v.* **3.** argue, brawl, dispute,
fight, scrap (*Inf.*), spar, squabble, wrangle

rowdy 1. *adj.* boisterous, disorderly, loud,
loutish, noisy, obstreperous, rough, unruly,
uproarious, wild **2.** *n.* brawler, casual, hoo~
ligan, lager lout, lout, ned (*Sl.*), rough (*Inf.*),
ruffian, tearaway (*Brit.*), tough, trouble~
maker, yahoo, yob *or* yobbo (*Brit. sl.*)
Antonyms *adj.* decorous, gentle, law-
abiding, mannerly, orderly, peaceful, refined

royal 1. imperial, kinglike, kingly, monar~
chical, princely, queenly, regal, sovereign
2. august, grand, impressive, magnificent,
majestic, splendid, stately, superb, superior

rub *v.* **1.** abrade, caress, chafe, clean, fray,
grate, knead, massage, polish, scour, scrape,
shine, smooth, stroke, wipe **2.** apply, put,
smear, spread **3. rub up the wrong way**
aggravate (*Inf.*), anger, annoy, bug (*Inf.*), get
in one's hair (*Inf.*), get one's goat (*Sl.*), get
on one's nerves (*Inf.*), get under one's skin
(*Inf.*), irk, irritate, nark (*Brit., Aust., & N.Z.
sl.*), peeve (*Inf.*), piss one off (*Taboo sl.*), vex
~*n.* **4.** caress, kneading, massage, polish,
shine, stroke, wipe **5.** catch, difficulty,
drawback, hindrance, hitch, impediment,
obstacle, problem, snag, trouble

rubbish 1. crap (*Sl.*), debris, dreck (*Sl.*,
chiefly U.S.*), dregs, dross, flotsam and jet~
sam, garbage (*Chiefly U.S.*), grot (*Sl.*), junk
(*Inf.*), litter, lumber, offal, offscourings, ref~
use, scrap, trash, waste **2.** balderdash, balls
(*Taboo sl.*), bilge (*Inf.*), bosh (*Inf.*), bull (*Sl.*),
bullshit (*Taboo sl.*), bunkum *or* buncombe
(*Chiefly U.S.*), claptrap (*Inf.*), cobblers (*Brit.
taboo sl.*), codswallop (*Brit. sl.*), crap (*Sl.*),
drivel, eyewash (*Inf.*), flapdoodle (*Sl.*), gar~
bage (*Chiefly U.S.*), gibberish, guff (*Sl.*), ha~
vers (*Scot.*), hogwash, hokum (*Sl., chiefly
U.S. & Canad.*), horsefeathers (*U.S. sl.*), hot
air (*Inf.*), moonshine, nonsense, pap, piffle
(*Inf.*), poppycock (*Inf.*), rot, shit (*Taboo sl.*),
stuff and nonsense, tommyrot, tosh (*Sl.,
chiefly Brit.*), tripe (*Inf.*), twaddle

rub out 1. cancel, delete, efface, erase, ex~
cise, expunge, obliterate, remove, wipe out

2. *U.S. sl.* assassinate, blow away (*Sl.,
chiefly U.S.*), bump off (*Sl.*), butcher, dis~
patch, do in (*Inf.*), eliminate (*Sl.*), hit (*Sl.*),
kill, knock off (*Sl.*), murder, slaughter, slay,
take out (*Sl.*), waste (*Inf.*)

ruddy 1. blooming, blushing, florid, flushed,
fresh, glowing, healthy, radiant, red, red~
dish, rosy, rosy-cheeked, rubicund, san~
guine, sunburnt **2.** crimson, pink, red, red~
dish, roseate, ruby, scarlet
Antonyms (*sense 1*) anaemic, ashen, colour~
less, grey, pale, pallid, sickly, wan, white

rude 1. abrupt, abusive, blunt, brusque,
cheeky, churlish, curt, discourteous, disre~
spectful, ill-mannered, impertinent, impo~
lite, impudent, inconsiderate, insolent, in~
sulting, offhand, peremptory, short, uncivil,
unmannerly **2.** barbarous, boorish, brutish,
coarse, crude, graceless, gross, ignorant, il~
literate, loutish, low, oafish, obscene, rough,
savage, scurrilous, uncivilized, uncouth,
uncultured, uneducated, ungracious, unpol~
ished, unrefined, untutored, vulgar **3.** art~
less, crude, inartistic, inelegant, makeshift,
primitive, raw, rough, rough-hewn,
roughly-made, simple **4.** abrupt, harsh,
sharp, startling, sudden, unpleasant, violent
Antonyms (*sense 1*) civil, considerate, cor~
dial, courteous, courtly, decent, gentlemanly,
gracious, ladylike, mannerly, polite, respect~
ful, sociable, urbane, well-bred (*sense 2*) artful,
civilized, cultured, educated, elegant, learned,
polished, refined, urbane (*sense 3*) even,
finished, shapely, smooth, well-made

rudimentary basic, early, elementary, em~
bryonic, fundamental, immature, initial,
introductory, primary, primitive, undevel~
oped, vestigial
Antonyms advanced, complete, developed,
higher, later, mature, refined, secondary, so~
phisticated, supplementary

rudiments basics, beginnings, elements,
essentials, first principles, foundation,
fundamentals

rueful conscience-stricken, contrite, dismal,
doleful, grievous, lugubrious, melancholy,
mournful, penitent, pitiable, pitiful, plain~
tive, regretful, remorseful, repentant, sad,
self-reproachful, sorrowful, sorry, woebe~
gone, woeful
Antonyms cheerful, delighted, glad, happy,
joyful, pleased, unrepentant

ruffian bruiser (*Inf.*), brute, bully, bully boy,
casual, heavy (*Sl.*), hoodlum, hooligan, lager
lout, miscreant, ned (*Sl.*), rascal, rogue,
rough (*Inf.*), roughneck (*Sl.*), rowdy, scoun~
drel, thug, tough, villain, wretch, yardie

ruffle 1. derange, disarrange, discompose,
dishevel, disorder, mess up, rumple, tousle,
wrinkle **2.** agitate, annoy, confuse, discon~
cert, disquiet, disturb, faze, fluster, harass,

hassle (*Inf.*), irritate, nettle, peeve (*Inf.*), perturb, put out, rattle (*Inf.*), shake up (*Inf.*), stir, torment, trouble, unnerve, unsettle, upset, vex, worry

Antonyms (*sense 2*) appease, calm, comfort, compose, console, ease, mollify, solace, soothe

rugged 1. broken, bumpy, craggy, difficult, irregular, jagged, ragged, rocky, rough, stark, uneven **2.** furrowed, leathery, lined, rough-hewn, strong-featured, weather-beaten, weathered, worn, wrinkled **3.** austere, crabbed, dour, gruff, hard, harsh, rough, rude, severe, sour, stern, surly **4.** barbarous, blunt, churlish, crude, graceless, rude, uncouth, uncultured, unpolished, unrefined **5.** arduous, demanding, difficult, exacting, hard, harsh, laborious, rigorous, stern, strenuous, taxing, tough, trying, uncompromising **6.** beefy (*Inf.*), brawny, burly, hale, hardy, husky (*Inf.*), muscular, Ramboesque, robust, strong, sturdy, tough, vigorous, well-built

Antonyms (*sense 1*) even, gentle, level, regular, smooth, unbroken (*sense 2*) delicate, pretty, refined, smooth, unmarked, youthful (*sense 4*) civil, courteous, cultivated, cultured, elegant, polished, polite, refined, subtle, urbane, well-bred (*sense 5*) agreeable, easy, gentle, mild, pleasant, simple, soft, tender, uncomplicated, unexacting (*sense 6*) delicate, feeble, fragile, frail, infirm, sickly, skinny, soft, weak

ruin *n.* **1.** bankruptcy, breakdown, collapse, crackup (*Inf.*), crash, damage, decay, defeat, destitution, destruction, devastation, disintegration, disrepair, dissolution, downfall, failure, fall, havoc, insolvency, nemesis, overthrow, ruination, subversion, the end, undoing, Waterloo, wreck, wreckage ~*v.* **2.** bankrupt, break, bring down, bring to nothing, bring to ruin, crush, defeat, demolish, destroy, devastate, impoverish, lay in ruins, lay waste, overthrow, overturn, overwhelm, pauperize, raze, shatter, smash, total (*Sl.*), trash (*Sl.*), wreak havoc upon, wreck **3.** blow (*Sl.*), bodge (*Inf.*), botch, cock up (*Brit. sl.*), damage, disfigure, fuck up (*Offens. taboo sl.*), injure, make a mess of, mangle, mar, mess up, screw up (*Inf.*), spoil, undo

Antonyms *n.* creation, preservation, success, triumph, victory ~*v.* build, construct, create, enhance, enrich, improve, keep, mend, preserve, repair, restore, save, start, strengthen, submit to, succumb to, support, surrender to, yield to

ruinous 1. baleful, baneful (*Archaic*), calamitous, catastrophic, crippling, deadly, deleterious, destructive, devastating, dire, disastrous, extravagant, fatal, immoderate, injurious, murderous, noxious, pernicious, shattering, wasteful, withering **2.** broken-

down, decrepit, derelict, dilapidated, in ruins, ramshackle, ruined

rule *n.* **1.** axiom, canon, criterion, decree, dictum, direction, guide, guideline, law, maxim, order, ordinance, precept, principle, regulation, ruling, standard, tenet **2.** administration, ascendancy, authority, command, control, direction, domination, dominion, empire, government, influence, jurisdiction, leadership, mastery, power, regime, reign, supremacy, sway **3.** condition, convention, custom, form, habit, order *or* way of things, practice, procedure, routine, tradition, wont **4.** course, formula, method, policy, procedure, way **5. as a rule** customarily, for the most part, generally, mainly, normally, on the whole, ordinarily, usually ~*v.* **6.** administer, be in authority, be in power, be number one (*Inf.*), command, control, direct, dominate, govern, guide, hold sway, lead, manage, preside over, regulate, reign, wear the crown **7.** adjudge, adjudicate, decide, decree, determine, establish, find, judge, lay down, pronounce, resolve, settle **8.** be customary (pre-eminent, prevalent, superior), hold sway, obtain, predominate, preponderate, prevail

rule out ban, debar, dismiss, disqualify, eliminate, exclude, forbid, leave out, obviate, preclude, prevent, prohibit, proscribe, reject

Antonyms allow, approve, authorize, let, license, order, permit, sanction

ruler 1. commander, controller, crowned head, emperor, empress, governor, head of state, king, leader, lord, monarch, potentate, prince, princess, queen, sovereign **2.** measure, rule, straight edge, yardstick

ruling *n.* **1.** adjudication, decision, decree, finding, judgment, pronouncement, resolution, verdict ~*adj.* **2.** commanding, controlling, dominant, governing, leading, regnant, reigning, upper **3.** chief, current, dominant, main, predominant, pre-eminent, preponderant, prevailing, prevalent, principal, regnant, supreme

Antonyms (*sense 3*) auxiliary, inferior, least, minor, secondary, subordinate, subsidiary, unimportant

ruminate brood, chew over, cogitate, consider, contemplate, deliberate, meditate, mull over, muse, ponder, reflect, revolve, think, turn over in one's mind, weigh

rumour 1. *n.* bruit (*Archaic*), buzz, canard, dirt (*U.S. sl.*), gossip, hearsay, news, report, story, talk, tidings, whisper, word **2.** *v.* bruit, circulate, gossip, noise abroad, pass around, publish, put about, report, say, tell, whisper

run *v.* **1.** barrel (along) (*Inf., chiefly U.S. &*

Canad.), bolt, career, dart, dash, gallop, hare (*Brit. inf.*), hasten, hie, hotfoot, hurry, jog, leg it (*Inf.*), lope, race, rush, scamper, scramble, scud, scurry, speed, sprint **2.** ab~ scond, beat a retreat, beat it (*Sl.*), bolt, clear out, cut and run (*Inf.*), decamp, depart, do a runner (*Sl.*), escape, flee, fly the coop (*U.S. & Canad. inf.*), leg it (*Inf.*), make a run for it, make off, scarper (*Brit. sl.*), show a clean pair of heels, skedaddle (*Inf.*), slope off, take a powder (*U.S. & Canad. sl.*), take flight, take it on the lam (*U.S. & Canad. sl.*), take off (*Inf.*), take to one's heels **3.** course, glide, go, move, pass, roll, skim, slide **4.** bear, carry, convey, drive, give a lift to, manoeuvre, operate, propel, transport **5.** go, operate, ply **6.** function, go, operate, per~ form, tick, work **7.** administer, be in charge of, boss (*Inf.*), carry on, conduct, control, coordinate, direct, handle, head, lead, look after, manage, mastermind, operate, over~ see, own, regulate, superintend, supervise, take care of **8.** continue, extend, go, last, lie, proceed, range, reach, stretch **9.** cas~ cade, discharge, flow, go, gush, issue, leak, move, pour, proceed, spill, spout, stream **10.** dissolve, fuse, go soft, liquefy, melt, turn to liquid **11.** be diffused, bleed, lose colour, mix, spread **12.** come apart, come undone, ladder, tear, unravel **13.** be cur~ rent, circulate, climb, creep, go round, spread, trail **14.** display, feature, print, publish **15.** be a candidate, challenge, com~ pete, contend, put oneself up for, stand, take part **16.** bootleg, deal in, ship, smuggle, sneak, traffic in **17. run for it** abscond, bolt, cut and run (*Inf.*), decamp, do a bunk (*Brit. sl.*), do a runner (*Sl.*), escape, flee, fly, fly the coop (*U.S. & Canad. inf.*), make a break for it, make off, scarper (*Brit. sl.*), scram (*Inf.*), show a clean pair of heels, skedaddle (*Inf.*), take a powder (*U.S. & Canad. sl.*), take flight, take it on the lam (*U.S. & Canad. sl.*), take off ~*n.* **18.** dash, gallop, jog, race, rush, sprint, spurt **19.** drive, excursion, jaunt, journey, joy ride (*Inf.*), lift, outing, ride, round, spin (*Inf.*), trip **20.** chain, course, cycle, passage, peri~ od, round, season, sequence, series, spell, streak, stretch, string **21.** category, class, kind, order, sort, type, variety **22.** applica~ tion, demand, pressure, rush **23.** ladder, rip, snag, tear **24.** course, current, direc~ tion, drift, flow, motion, movement, pas~ sage, path, progress, stream, tendency, ten~ or, tide, trend, way **25.** coop, enclosure, pen **26. in the long run** at the end of the day, eventually, in the end, in the final analysis, in time, ultimately, when all is said and done **27. on the run a.** at liberty, escaping, fugitive, in flight, on the lam (*U.S. sl.*), on the loose **b.** defeated, falling back, fleeing, in flight, in retreat, retreating, running

away **c.** at speed, hastily, hurriedly, hurry~ ing, in a hurry, in a rush, in haste
Antonyms (*sense 1*) crawl, creep, dawdle, walk (*sense 2*) remain, stay (*sense 8*) cease, stop

run across bump into, chance upon, come across, come upon, encounter, meet, meet with, run into

runaway *n.* **1.** absconder, deserter, escapee, escaper, fugitive, refugee, truant ~*adj.* **2.** escaped, fleeing, fugitive, loose, out of con~ trol, uncontrolled, wild **3.** easily won, easy, effortless

run away 1. abscond, beat it (*Sl.*), bolt, clear out, cut and run (*Inf.*), decamp, do a bunk (*Brit. sl.*), do a runner (*Sl.*), escape, flee, fly the coop (*U.S. & Canad. inf.*), hook it (*Sl.*), make a run for it, run off, scarper (*Brit. sl.*), scram (*Inf.*), show a clean pair of heels, skedaddle (*Inf.*), take a powder (*U.S. & Canad. sl.*), take flight, take it on the lam (*U.S. & Canad. sl.*), take off, take to one's heels **2. With with a.** abduct, abscond, elope **b.** abscond, make off, pinch (*Inf.*), run off, snatch, steal **c.** romp home, walk it (*Inf.*), win by a mile (*Inf.*), win easily, win hands down

rundown briefing, outline, précis, recap (*Inf.*), résumé, review, run-through, sketch, summary, synopsis

run-down 1. below par, debilitated, drained, enervated, exhausted, fatigued, out of condition, peaky, tired, under the weath~ er (*Inf.*), unhealthy, weak, weary, worn-out **2.** broken-down, decrepit, dilapidated, din~ gy, ramshackle, seedy, shabby, tumble~ down, worn-out
Antonyms (*sense 1*) fighting fit, fine, fit, fit as a fiddle, full of beans (*Inf.*), healthy, well

run down 1. curtail, cut, cut back, de~ crease, drop, pare down, reduce, trim **2.** debilitate, exhaust, sap the strength of, tire, undermine the health of, weaken **3.** as~ perse, bad-mouth (*Sl., chiefly U.S. & Canad.*), belittle, criticize adversely, decry, defame, denigrate, disparage, knock (*Inf.*), put down, revile, rubbish (*Inf.*), slag (off) (*Sl.*), speak ill of, vilify **4.** hit, knock down, knock over, run into, run over, strike

run in 1. break in gently, run gently **2.** *Sl.* apprehend, arrest, bust (*Inf.*), collar (*Inf.*), feel one's collar (*Sl.*), jail, lift (*Sl.*), nab (*Inf.*), nail (*Inf.*), pick up, pinch (*Inf.*), pull in (*Brit. sl.*), take into custody, take to jail, throw in jail

run into 1. bump into, collide with, crash into, dash against, hit, ram, strike **2.** be beset by, be confronted by, bump into, chance upon, come across, come upon, en~ counter, meet, meet with, run across

runner 1. athlete, harrier, jogger, miler, sprinter **2.** courier, dispatch bearer, errand boy, messenger **3.** offshoot, shoot, sprig, sprout, stem, stolon (*Botany*), tendril

running *adj.* **1.** constant, continuous, in~ cessant, in succession, on the trot (*Inf.*), perpetual, together, unbroken, unceasing, uninterrupted **2.** flowing, moving, stream~ ing ~*n.* **3.** administration, charge, conduct, control, coordination, direction, leadership, management, organization, regulation, superintendency, supervision **4.** function~ ing, maintenance, operation, performance, working **5.** competition, contention, contest

run off 1. bolt, clear out, cut and run (*Inf.*), decamp, do a runner (*Sl.*), escape, flee, fly the coop (*U.S. & Canad. inf.*), hook it (*Sl.*), make off, run away, scarper (*Brit. sl.*), show a clean pair of heels, skedaddle (*Inf.*), take a powder (*U.S. & Canad. sl.*), take flight, take it on the lam (*U.S. & Canad. sl.*), take to one's heels **2.** churn out (*Inf.*), duplicate, print, produce **3.** bleed, drain, flow away, siphon, tap **4.** *With* **with a.** lift (*Inf.*), make off, pinch (*Inf.*), purloin, run away, steal, swipe (*Sl.*), **b.** abscond, elope, run away

run-of-the-mill average, banal, common, commonplace, fair, mediocre, middling, modest, ordinary, passable, tolerable, un~ distinguished, unexceptional, unexciting, unimpressive
Antonyms excellent, exceptional, extraor~ dinary, marvellous, out of the ordinary, splendid, unusual

run out 1. be exhausted, cease, close, come to a close, dry up, end, expire, fail, finish, give out, peter out, terminate **2.** *With* **of** be cleaned out, be out of, exhaust one's supply of, have no more of, have none left, have no remaining **3.** *With* **on** *Inf.* abandon, desert, forsake, leave high and dry, leave holding the baby, leave in the lurch, rat (*Inf.*), run away from

run over 1. hit, knock down, knock over, run down, strike **2.** brim over, overflow, spill, spill over **3.** check, examine, go over, go through, rehearse, reiterate, review, run through, survey

run through 1. impale, pierce, spit, stab, stick, transfix **2.** blow (*Sl.*), dissipate, ex~ haust, fritter away, spend like water, squander, throw away, waste **3.** go over, practise, read, rehearse, run over **4.** check, examine, go through, look over, review, run over, survey

rupture *n.* **1.** breach, break, burst, cleavage, cleft, crack, fissure, fracture, rent, split, tear **2.** altercation, breach, break, bust-up (*Inf.*), contention, disagreement, disruption, dissolution, estrangement, falling-out (*Inf.*), feud, hostility, quarrel, rift, schism, split **3.** *Medical* hernia ~*v.* **4.** break, burst, cleave, crack, fracture, puncture, rend, separate,

sever, split, tear **5.** break off, cause a breach, come between, disrupt, dissever, divide, split

rural agrarian, agrestic, agricultural, Arca~ dian, bucolic, countrified, country, hick (*Inf., chiefly U.S. & Canad.*), pastoral, rustic, sylvan, upcountry
Antonyms city, cosmopolitan, town, urban

ruse artifice, blind, deception, device, dodge, hoax, imposture, manoeuvre, ploy, sham, stratagem, subterfuge, trick, wile

rush *v.* **1.** accelerate, barrel (along) (*Inf., chiefly U.S. & Canad.*), bolt, burn rubber (*Inf.*), career, dart, dash, dispatch, expedite, fly, hasten, hotfoot, hurry, hustle, lose no time, make haste, make short work of, press, push, quicken, race, run, scramble, scurry, shoot, speed, speed up, sprint, stampede, tear ~*n.* **2.** charge, dash, dis~ patch, expedition, haste, hurry, race, scramble, speed, stampede, surge, swiftness, urgency ~*v.* **3.** attack, capture, charge, overcome, storm, take by storm ~*n.* **4.** as~ sault, charge, onslaught, push, storm, surge ~*adj.* **5.** brisk, cursory, emergency, expedi~ tious, fast, hasty, hurried, prompt, quick, rapid, swift, urgent
Antonyms (*sense 1*) dally, dawdle, delay, procrastinate, slow down, tarry, wait (*sense 5*) careful, detailed, leisurely, not urgent, slow, thorough, unhurried

rust *n.* **1.** corrosion, oxidation ~*v.* **2.** cor~ rode, oxidize ~*n.* **3.** blight, mildew, mould, must, rot ~*v.* **4.** atrophy, decay, decline, deteriorate, go stale, stagnate, tarnish

rustic *adj.* **1.** agrestic, Arcadian, bucolic, countrified, country, pastoral, rural, sylvan, upcountry **2.** artless, homely, homespun, plain, simple, unaffected, unpolished, unrefined, unsophisticated **3.** awkward, boorish, churlish, cloddish, clodhopping (*Inf.*), clownish, coarse, crude, graceless, hick (*Inf., chiefly U.S. & Canad.*), loutish, lumpish, maladroit, rough, uncouth, uncul~ tured, unmannerly ~*n.* **4.** boor, bumpkin, clod, clodhopper (*Inf.*), clown, country boy, country cousin, countryman, country~ woman, hayseed (*U.S. & Canad. inf.*), hick (*Inf., chiefly U.S. & Canad.*), hillbilly, Hodge, peasant, son of the soil, swain (*Archaic*), yokel
Antonyms *adj.* cosmopolitan, courtly, el~ egant, grand, polished, refined, sophisticated, urban, urbane ~*n.* city slicker, cosmopolitan, courtier, sophisticate, townee, townsman

rustle 1. *v.* crackle, crepitate, crinkle, su~ surrate (*Literary*), swish, whish, whisper, whoosh **2.** *n.* crackle, crepitation, crinkling, rustling, susurration *or* susurrus (*Literary*), whisper

rusty 1. corroded, oxidized, rust-covered,

rusted **2.** chestnut, coppery, reddish, reddish-brown, russet, rust-coloured **3.** cracked, creaking, croaking, croaky, hoarse **4.** ancient, antiquated, antique, dated, old-fashioned, outmoded, out of date, passé **5.** deficient, impaired, not what it was, out of practice, sluggish, stale, unpractised, weak

rut *n.* **1.** furrow, gouge, groove, indentation, pothole, score, track, trough, wheelmark **2.** dead end, groove, habit, humdrum exist~ence, pattern, routine, system ~*v.* **3.** cut, furrow, gouge, groove, hole, indent, mark, score

ruthless adamant, barbarous, brutal, cal~lous, cruel, ferocious, fierce, hard, hard-hearted, harsh, heartless, inexorable, inhu~man, merciless, pitiless, relentless, re~morseless, savage, severe, stern, unfeeling, unmerciful, unpitying, unrelenting, without pity

Antonyms compassionate, forgiving, gentle, humane, kind, lenient, merciful, pitying, sparing

S

sabotage 1. *v.* cripple, damage, destroy, disable, disrupt, incapacitate, sap the foun~ dations of, subvert, throw a spanner in the works (*Brit. inf.*), undermine, vandalize, wreck **2.** *n.* damage, destruction, disrup~ tion, subversion, treachery, treason, wreck~ ing

sack¹ 1. *v.* axe (*Inf.*), discharge, dismiss, fire (*Inf.*), give (someone) his books (*Inf.*), give (someone) his cards, give (someone) his marching orders, give (someone) the boot (*Sl.*), give (someone) the elbow, kick out (*Inf.*), kiss off (*Sl., chiefly U.S. & Canad.*) **2.** *n.* **the sack** discharge, dismissal, termina~ tion of employment, the axe (*Inf.*), the boot (*Sl.*), the chop (*Brit. sl.*), the (old) heave-ho (*Inf.*), the order of the boot (*Sl.*), the push (*Sl.*)

sack² 1. *v.* demolish, depredate (*Rare*), de~ spoil, destroy, devastate, lay waste, loot, maraud, pillage, plunder, raid, ravage, rifle, rob, ruin, spoil, strip **2.** *n.* depredation, de~ spoliation, destruction, devastation, looting, pillage, plunder, plundering, rape, rapine, ravage, ruin, waste

sackcloth and ashes compunction, con~ trition, grief, hair shirt, mortification, mourning, penitence, remorse, repentance

sacred 1. blessed, consecrated, divine, hal~ lowed, holy, revered, sanctified, venerable **2.** inviolable, inviolate, invulnerable, pro~ tected, sacrosanct, secure **3.** ecclesiastical, holy, religious, solemn
Antonyms lay, nonspiritual, profane, secu~ lar, temporal, unconsecrated, worldly

sacrifice 1. *v.* forego, forfeit, give up, im~ molate, let go, lose, offer, offer up, surren~ der **2.** *n.* burnt offering, destruction, heca~ tomb, holocaust (*Rare*), immolation, loss, oblation, renunciation, surrender, votive offering

sacrilege blasphemy, desecration, heresy, impiety, irreverence, mockery, profanation, profaneness, profanity, violation
Antonyms piety, respect, reverence

sad 1. blue, cheerless, dejected, depressed, disconsolate, dismal, doleful, down, down~ cast, down in the dumps (*Inf.*), down in the mouth (*Inf.*), gloomy, glum, grief-stricken, grieved, heavy-hearted, low, low-spirited, lugubrious, melancholy, mournful, pensive, sick at heart, sombre, triste (*Archaic*), un~ happy, wistful, woebegone **2.** calamitous, dark, de῀essing, disastrous, dismal, griev~ ous, harrowing, heart-rending, lachrymose,

moving, pathetic, pitiable, pitiful, poignant, sorry, tearful, tragic, upsetting **3.** bad, de~ plorable, dismal, distressing, grave, lamen~ table, miserable, regrettable, serious, shab~ by, sorry, to be deplored, unfortunate, un~ happy, unsatisfactory, wretched
Antonyms blithe, cheerful, cheery, chirpy (*Inf.*), fortunate, glad, good, happy, in good spirits, jolly, joyful, joyous, light-hearted, merry, pleased

sadden aggrieve, bring tears to one's eyes, cast a gloom upon, cast down, dash, deject, depress, desolate, dispirit, distress, grieve, make blue, make one's heart bleed, upset

saddle *v.* burden, charge, encumber, load, lumber (*Brit. inf.*), task, tax

sadistic barbarous, beastly, brutal, cruel, fiendish, inhuman, perverse, perverted, ruthless, savage, vicious

sadness bleakness, cheerlessness, dejection, depression, despondency, dolefulness, dol~ our (*Poetic*), gloominess, grief, heavy heart, melancholy, misery, mournfulness, poign~ ancy, sorrow, sorrowfulness, the blues, the dumps (*Inf.*), the hump (*Brit. inf.*), tragedy, unhappiness, wretchedness

safe *adj.* **1.** all right, free from harm, im~ pregnable, in safety, intact, O.K. *or* okay (*Inf.*), out of danger, out of harm's way, protected, safe and sound, secure, undam~ aged, unharmed, unhurt, unscathed **2.** harmless, innocuous, nonpoisonous, non~ toxic, pure, tame, unpolluted, wholesome **3.** cautious, circumspect, conservative, de~ pendable, discreet, on the safe side, pru~ dent, realistic, reliable, sure, tried and true, trustworthy, unadventurous **4.** certain, im~ pregnable, risk-free, riskless, secure, sound ~*n.* **5.** coffer, deposit box, repository, safe- deposit box, strongbox, vault
Antonyms (*sense 1*) at risk, damaged, en~ dangered, imperiled, insecure, jeopardized, put at risk, put in danger, threatened (*sense 2*) baneful, dangerous, harmful, hazardous, hurtful, injurious, noxious, pernicious, un~ safe (*sense 3*) imprudent, incautious, reckless, risky, unsafe

safeguard 1. *v.* defend, guard, look after, preserve, protect, screen, shield, watch over **2.** *n.* aegis, armour, bulwark, convoy, de~ fence, escort, guard, protection, security, shield, surety

safely in one piece, in safety, safe and sound, securely, with impunity, without risk, with safety

safety assurance, cover, immunity, impreg~ nability, protection, refuge, sanctuary, se~ curity, shelter

sage 1. *adj.* acute, canny, discerning, intel~ ligent, judicious, learned, perspicacious, politic, prudent, sagacious, sapient, sen~ sible, wise **2.** *n.* authority, elder, expert, guru, mahatma, man of learning, master, Nestor, philosopher, pundit, savant, Solo~ mon, Solon, wise man

sail *v.* **1.** cast *or* weigh anchor, embark, get under way, hoist the blue peter, put to sea, set sail **2.** captain, cruise, go by water, navigate, pilot, ride the waves, skipper, steer, voyage **3.** drift, float, fly, glide, scud, shoot, skim, skirr, soar, sweep, wing **4.** *Inf.* With **in** *or* **into** assault, attack, begin, bela~ bour, fall upon, get going, get to work on, lambast(e), set about, tear into (*Inf.*)

sailor hearty (*Inf.*), Jack Tar, lascar, leatherneck (*Sl.*), marine, mariner, matelot (*Sl., chiefly Brit.*), navigator, salt, sea dog, seafarer, seafaring man, seaman, tar (*Inf.*)

saintly angelic, beatific, blameless, blessed, devout, full of good works, god-fearing, godly, holy, pious, religious, righteous, sainted, saintlike, sinless, virtuous, worthy

sake 1. account, advantage, behalf, benefit, consideration, gain, good, interest, profit, regard, respect, welfare, wellbeing **2.** aim, cause, end, motive, objective, principle, purpose, reason

salary earnings, emolument, income, pay, remuneration, stipend, wage, wages

sale 1. auction, deal, disposal, marketing, selling, transaction, vending **2.** buyers, consumers, customers, demand, market, outlet, purchasers **3. for sale** available, in stock, obtainable, on offer, on sale, on the market

salient arresting, conspicuous, important, jutting, marked, noticeable, outstanding, projecting, prominent, pronounced, pro~ truding, remarkable, signal, striking

sallow anaemic, bilious, jaundiced-looking, pale, pallid, pasty, peely-wally (*Scot.*), sick~ ly, unhealthy, wan, yellowish
Antonyms glowing, healthy-looking, radi~ ant, rosy, ruddy

sally *v.* **1.** erupt, go forth, issue, rush, set out, surge ~*n.* **2.** *Military* foray, incursion, offensive, raid, sortie, thrust **3.** *Fig.* bon mot, crack (*Inf.*), jest, joke, quip, retort, ri~ poste, smart remark, wisecrack (*Inf.*), witti~ cism **4.** escapade, excursion, frolic, jaunt, trip

salt *n.* **1.** flavour, relish, savour, seasoning, taste **2. with a grain** *or* **pinch of salt** cynically, disbelievingly, doubtfully, scepti~ cally, suspiciously, with reservations **3.**

Fig. Attic wit, bite, dry humour, liveliness, piquancy, punch, pungency, sarcasm, sharpness, wit, zest, zip (*Inf.*) **4.** mariner, sailor, sea dog, seaman, tar (*Inf.*) ~*adj.* **5.** brackish, briny, saline, salted, salty

salty 1. brackish, briny, over-salted, saline, salt, salted **2.** colourful, humorous, lively, piquant, pungent, racy, sharp, snappy (*Inf.*), spicy, tangy, tart, witty, zestful

salubrious beneficial, good for one, health~ ful, health-giving, healthy, invigorating, salutary, wholesome

salutary 1. advantageous, beneficial, good, good for one, helpful, practical, profitable, timely, useful, valuable **2.** healthful, healthy, salubrious

salutation address, greeting, obeisance, sa~ lute, welcome

salute *v.* **1.** accost, acknowledge, address, doff one's cap to, greet, hail, kiss, pay one's respects to, salaam, welcome **2.** acknowl~ edge, honour, pay tribute *or* homage to, present arms, recognize, take one's hat off to (*Inf.*) ~*n.* **3.** address, greeting, kiss, obei~ sance, recognition, salaam, salutation, trib~ ute

salvage *v.* glean, recover, redeem, rescue, restore, retrieve, save

salvation deliverance, escape, lifeline, preservation, redemption, rescue, restora~ tion, saving
Antonyms condemnation, damnation, doom, downfall, hell, loss, perdition, ruin

same *adj.* **1.** aforementioned, aforesaid, selfsame, very **2.** alike, corresponding, du~ plicate, equal, equivalent, identical, indis~ tinguishable, interchangeable, synonymous, twin **3.** changeless, consistent, constant, invariable, unaltered, unchanged, unfailing, uniform, unvarying **4. all the same a.** af~ ter all, anyhow, be that as it may, in any event, just the same, nevertheless, nonethe~ less, still **b.** immaterial, not worth men~ tioning, of no consequence, unimportant
Antonyms altered, different, dissimilar, di~ verse, inconsistent, miscellaneous, other, variable

sameness consistency, identicalness, iden~ tity, indistinguishability, lack of variety, likeness, monotony, oneness, predictability, repetition, resemblance, similarity, stand~ ardization, tedium, uniformity

sample 1. *n.* cross section, example, exemplification, illustration, indication, in~ stance, model, pattern, representative, sign, specimen **2.** *v.* experience, inspect, partake of, taste, test, try **3.** *adj.* illustrative, pilot, representative, specimen, test, trial

sanctify absolve, anoint, bless, cleanse, consecrate, hallow, purify, set apart

sanctimonious canting, false, goody-goody (*Inf.*), holier-than-thou, hypocritical, pharisaical, pi (*Brit. sl.*), pietistic, pious, priggish, self-righteous, self-satisfied, smug, Tartuffian *or* Tartufian, too good to be true, unctuous

sanction *n.* **1.** allowance, approbation, approval, authority, authorization, backing, confirmation, countenance, endorsement, O.K. *or* okay (*Inf.*), ratification, stamp *or* seal of approval, support **2.** *Often plural* ban, boycott, coercive measures, embargo, penalty ~*v.* **3.** allow, approve, authorize, back, countenance, endorse, entitle, lend one's name to, permit, support, vouch for **4.** confirm, ratify, warrant
Antonyms *n.* (*sense 1*) ban, disapproval, embargo, prohibition, proscription, refusal, veto (*sense 2*) approbation, approval, authority, authorization, dispensation, licence, permission ~*v.* ban, boycott, disallow, forbid, refuse, reject, veto

sanctity **1.** devotion, godliness, goodness, grace, holiness, piety, purity, religiousness, righteousness, sanctitude, spirituality **2.** inviolability, sacredness, solemnity

sanctuary **1.** altar, church, Holy of Holies, sanctum, shrine, temple **2.** asylum, haven, protection, refuge, retreat, shelter **3.** conservation area, national park, nature reserve, reserve

sane **1.** all there (*Inf.*), *compos mentis,* in one's right mind, in possession of all one's faculties, lucid, mentally sound, normal, of sound mind, rational **2.** balanced, judicious, level-headed, moderate, reasonable, sensible, sober, sound
Antonyms bonkers (*Sl., chiefly Brit.*), crackpot (*Inf.*), crazy, daft (*Inf.*), foolish, insane, loony (*Sl.*), loopy (*Inf.*), mad, mentally ill, *non compos mentis,* nuts (*Sl.*), off one's head (*Sl.*), off one's trolley (*Sl.*), out to lunch (*Inf.*), round the bend *or* twist (*Sl.*), stupid, unreasonable, unsound, up the pole (*Inf.*)

sanguine **1.** animated, assured, buoyant, cheerful, confident, hopeful, in good heart, lively, optimistic, spirited **2.** florid, red, rubicund, ruddy
Antonyms (*sense 1*) despondent, dispirited, down, gloomy, heavy-hearted, melancholy, pessimistic (*sense 2*) anaemic, ashen, pale, pallid, peely-wally (*Scot.*)

sanitary clean, germ-free, healthy, hygienic, salubrious, unpolluted, wholesome

sanity **1.** mental health, normality, rationality, reason, right mind (*Inf.*), saneness, stability **2.** common sense, good sense, judiciousness, level-headedness, rationality, sense, soundness of judgment
Antonyms craziness, dementia, folly, in-

sanity, lunacy, madness, mental derangement, mental illness, senselessness, stupidity

sap[1] *n.* **1.** animating force, essence, lifeblood, vital fluid **2.** *Inf.* charlie (*Brit. inf.*), chump (*Inf.*), drip (*Inf.*), dweeb (*U.S. sl.*), fool, gull (*Archaic*), idiot, jerk (*Sl., chiefly U.S. & Canad.*), muggins (*Brit. sl.*), nerd *or* nurd (*Sl.*), nincompoop, ninny, nitwit (*Inf.*), noddy, noodle, numskull *or* numbskull, oaf, plonker (*Sl.*), prat (*Sl.*), Simple Simon, simpleton, twit (*Inf.*), wally (*Sl.*), weakling, wet (*Brit. inf.*)

sap[2] *v.* bleed, deplete, devitalize, drain, enervate, erode, exhaust, rob, undermine, weaken, wear down

sarcasm bitterness, causticness, contempt, cynicism, derision, irony, mockery, mordancy, satire, scorn, sneering, venom, vitriol

sarcastic acerb, acerbic, acid, acrimonious, backhanded, bitchy (*Inf.*), biting, caustic, contemptuous, cutting, cynical, derisive, disparaging, ironical, mocking, mordacious, mordant, sardonic, sarky (*Brit. inf.*), satirical, sharp, sneering, taunting, vitriolic

sardonic bitter, cynical, derisive, dry, ironical, jeering, malevolent, malicious, malignant, mocking, mordacious, mordant, sarcastic, sneering, wry

Satan Apollyon, Beelzebub, Lord of the Flies, Lucifer, Mephistopheles, Old Nick (*Inf.*), Old Scratch (*Inf.*), Prince of Darkness, The Devil, The Evil One

satanic accursed, black, demoniac, demoniacal, demonic, devilish, diabolic, evil, fiendish, hellish, infernal, inhuman, iniquitous, malevolent, malignant, wicked
Antonyms benevolent, benign, divine, godly, holy

satellite *n.* **1.** communications satellite, moon, sputnik **2.** *Fig.* attendant, dependant, follower, hanger-on, lackey, minion, parasite, retainer, sidekick (*Sl.*), sycophant, vassal ~*adj.* **3.** *Fig.* client, dependent, puppet, subordinate, tributary, vassal

satiate **1.** cloy, glut, gorge, jade, nauseate, overfill, stuff **2.** sate, satisfy, slake, surfeit

satire burlesque, caricature, irony, lampoon, parody, pasquinade, raillery, ridicule, sarcasm, send-up (*Brit. inf.*), skit, spoof (*Inf.*), takeoff (*Inf.*), travesty, wit

satirical, satiric biting, bitter, burlesque, caustic, censorious, cutting, cynical, incisive, ironical, mocking, mordacious, mordant, pungent, Rabelaisian, sarcastic, sardonic, taunting, vitriolic

satirize abuse, burlesque, censure, criticize, deride, hold up to ridicule, lampoon, lash, parody, pillory, ridicule, send up (*Brit. inf.*), take off (*Inf.*), travesty

satisfaction 1. comfort, complacency, con~ tent, contentedness, contentment, ease, en~ joyment, gratification, happiness, peace of mind, pleasure, pride, repletion, satiety, well-being **2.** achievement, appeasing, as~ suaging, fulfilment, gratification, resolution, settlement **3.** amends, atonement, compen~ sation, damages, indemnification, justice, recompense, redress, reimbursement, re~ muneration, reparation, requital, restitu~ tion, settlement, vindication
Antonyms (*senses 1 & 2*) annoyance, discon~ tent, displeasure, dissatisfaction, frustration, grief, injury, misgivings, pain, shame, un~ happiness

satisfactory acceptable, adequate, all right, average, competent, fair, good enough, passable, sufficient, suitable, up to stand~ ard, up to the mark
Antonyms bad, below par, inadequate, insufficient, leaving a lot to be desired, me~ diocre, not up to scratch (*Inf.*), poor, sub~ standard, unacceptable, unsatisfactory, un~ suitable

satisfied at ease, complacent, content, con~ tented, convinced, easy in one's mind, hap~ py, like the cat that swallowed the canary (*Inf.*), pacified, positive, smug, sure

satisfy 1. appease, assuage, content, feed, fill, gratify, indulge, mollify, pacify, pander to, please, quench, sate, satiate, slake, sur~ feit **2.** answer, be enough (adequate, sufficient), come up to expectations, do, fill the bill (*Inf.*), fulfil, meet, qualify, serve, serve the purpose, suffice **3.** assure, con~ vince, dispel (someone's) doubts, persuade, put (someone's) mind at rest, quiet, re~ assure **4.** answer, comply with, discharge, fulfil, meet, pay (off), settle, square up **5.** atone, compensate, indemnify, make good, make reparation for, recompense, remuner~ ate, requite, reward
Antonyms (*senses 1, 2, 3 & 4*) annoy, dis~ please, dissatisfy, dissuade, exasperate, fail to meet, fail to persuade, frustrate, give cause for complaint

satisfying cheering, convincing, filling, gratifying, pleasing, pleasurable, satisfac~ tory

saturate douse, drench, drouk (*Scot.*), im~ bue, impregnate, ret (*used of flax, etc.*), seep, soak, souse, steep, suffuse, waterlog, wet through

saturated drenched, dripping, droukit *or* drookit (*Scot.*), soaked, soaked to the skin, soaking (wet), sodden, sopping (wet), waterlogged, wet through, wringing wet

sauce *n.* audacity, backchat (*Inf.*), brass (*Inf.*), brass neck (*Brit. inf.*), cheek (*Inf.*), cheekiness, disrespectfulness, front, imper~

tinence, impudence, insolence, lip (*Sl.*), neck (*Inf.*), nerve (*Inf.*), rudeness

sauciness backchat (*Inf.*), brass (*Inf.*), bra~ zenness, cheek (*Inf.*), flippancy, imperti~ nence, impudence, insolence, lip (*Sl.*), pert~ ness, rudeness, sauce (*Inf.*)

saucy 1. cheeky (*Inf.*), disrespectful, flip (*Inf.*), flippant, forward, fresh (*Inf.*), imper~ tinent, impudent, insolent, lippy (*U.S. & Canad. sl.*), pert, presumptuous, rude, sassy (*U.S. inf.*), smart-alecky (*Inf.*) **2.** dashing, gay, jaunty, natty (*Inf.*), perky, rakish, sporty

saunter 1. *v.* amble, dally, linger, loiter, meander, mosey (*Inf.*), ramble, roam, rove, stravaig (*Scot. & northern English dialect*), stroll, take a stroll, tarry, wander **2.** *n.* air~ ing, amble, breather, constitutional, peram~ bulation, promenade, ramble, stroll, turn, walk

savage *adj.* **1.** feral, rough, rugged, uncivi~ lized, uncultivated, undomesticated, un~ tamed, wild **2.** barbarous, beastly, bestial, bloodthirsty, bloody, brutal, brutish, cruel, devilish, diabolical, ferocious, fierce, harsh, inhuman, merciless, murderous, pitiless, ravening, ruthless, sadistic, vicious **3.** in a state of nature, nonliterate, primitive, rude, unspoilt ~*n.* **4.** autochthon, barbarian, heathen, indigene, native, primitive **5.** bar~ barian, bear, boor, lout, roughneck (*Sl.*), yahoo, yob (*Brit. sl.*), yobbo (*Brit. sl.*) **6.** beast, brute, fiend, monster ~*v.* **7.** attack, lacerate, mangle, maul, tear into (*Inf.*)
Antonyms *adj.* balmy, civilized, cultivated, domesticated, gentle, humane, kind, merciful, mild, refined, restrained, tame ~*v.* acclaim, celebrate, praise, rave about (*Inf.*)

savagery barbarity, bestiality, bloodthirsti~ ness, brutality, cruelty, ferocity, fierceness, inhumanity, ruthlessness, sadism, vicious~ ness

save 1. bail (someone) out, come to (someone's) rescue, deliver, free, liberate, recover, redeem, rescue, salvage, set free **2.** be frugal, be thrifty, collect, economize, gather, hide away, hoard, hold, husband, keep, keep up one's sleeve (*Inf.*), lay by, put aside for a rainy day, put by, reserve, re~ trench, salt away, set aside, store, tighten one's belt (*Inf.*), treasure up **3.** conserve, guard, keep safe, look after, preserve, pro~ tect, safeguard, screen, shield, take care of **4.** hinder, obviate, prevent, rule out, spare
Antonyms (*senses 1 & 3*) abandon, condemn, discard, endanger, expose, imperil, risk, threaten (*sense 2*) be extravagant, blow (*Sl.*), consume, fritter away, spend, splurge, squan~ der, use, use up, waste

saving 1. *adj.* compensatory, extenuating,

qualifying, redeeming **2.** *n.* bargain, dis~
count, economy, reduction

savings fall-back, fund, nest egg, provision
for a rainy day, reserves, resources, store

saviour defender, deliverer, friend in need,
Good Samaritan, guardian, knight in shin~
ing armour, liberator, preserver, protector,
redeemer, rescuer, salvation

Saviour, Our *or* **The** Christ, Jesus, Mes~
siah, Redeemer

savoir-faire accomplishment, address, di~
plomacy, discretion, finesse, poise, social
graces, social know-how (*Inf.*), tact, ur~
banity

savour *n.* **1.** flavour, piquancy, relish,
smack, smell, tang, taste, zest **2.** distinctive
quality, excitement, flavour, interest, salt,
spice, zest ~*v.* **3.** *Often with* **of** bear the
hallmarks, be indicative, be suggestive,
partake, show signs, smack, suggest, verge
on **4.** appreciate, delight in, drool, enjoy,
enjoy to the full, gloat over, like, luxuriate
in, partake, relish, revel in, smack one's
lips over

savoury 1. agreeable, appetizing, dainty,
delectable, delicious, full-flavoured, good,
luscious, mouthwatering, palatable, pi~
quant, rich, scrumptious (*Inf.*), spicy, tangy,
tasty, toothsome **2.** decent, edifying, honest,
reputable, respectable, wholesome
Antonyms disreputable, distasteful, insipid,
nasty, tasteless, unappetizing, unpalatable,
unpleasant, unsavoury, wersh (*Scot.*)

saw adage, aphorism, apophthegm, axiom,
byword, dictum, gnome, maxim, proverb,
saying

saw-toothed crenate (*Botany, Zool.*), den~
tate, denticulate (*Biol.*), notched, serrate,
serrated

say *v.* **1.** add, affirm, announce, assert, as~
severate, come out with (*Inf.*), declare, give
voice *or* utterance to, maintain, mention,
pronounce, put into words, remark, speak,
state, utter, voice **2.** answer, disclose, di~
vulge, give as one's opinion, make known,
reply, respond, reveal, tell **3.** allege, bruit,
claim, noise abroad, put about, report, ru~
mour, suggest **4.** deliver, do, orate, perform,
read, recite, rehearse, render, repeat **5.** as~
sume, conjecture, dare say, estimate, guess,
hazard a guess, imagine, judge, presume,
suppose, surmise **6.** communicate, convey,
express, give the impression that, imply **7.**
go without saying be accepted, be a mat~
ter of course, be obvious, be self-evident, be
taken as read, be taken for granted, be
understood **8. to say the least** at the very
least, to put it mildly, without any exag~
geration ~*n.* **9.** crack (*Inf.*), turn (chance,
opportunity) to speak, voice, vote **10.**

authority, clout (*Inf.*), influence, power,
sway, weight

saying adage, aphorism, apophthegm, axi~
om, byword, dictum, gnome, maxim, prov~
erb, saw, slogan

scale[1] *n.* **1.** calibration, degrees, gamut,
gradation, graduated system, graduation,
hierarchy, ladder, pecking order (*Inf.*), pro~
gression, ranking, register, seniority sys~
tem, sequence, series, spectrum, spread,
steps **2.** proportion, ratio **3.** degree, extent,
range, reach, scope, way ~*v.* **4.** ascend,
clamber, climb, escalade, mount, surmount
5. adjust, proportion, prorate (*Chiefly U.S.*),
regulate

scale[2] *n.* flake, lamina, layer, plate, squama
(*Biol.*)

scaly flaky, furfuraceous (*Medical*), scabrous,
scurfy, squamous *or* squamose (*Biol.*),
squamulose

scamp devil, imp, knave (*Archaic*),
mischief-maker, monkey, pickle (*Brit. inf.*),
prankster, rascal, rogue, scallywag (*Inf.*),
scapegrace, toe-rag (*Sl.*), tyke (*Inf.*), whip~
persnapper, wretch

scamper beetle, dart, dash, fly, hasten, hie
(*Archaic*), hurry, romp, run, scoot, scurry,
scuttle, sprint

scan check, check out (*Inf.*), clock (*Brit. sl.*),
con (*Archaic*), examine, eyeball (*U.S. sl.*),
get a load of (*Inf.*), glance over, investigate,
look one up and down, look through, recce
(*Sl.*), run one's eye over, run over, scour,
scrutinize, search, size up (*Inf.*), skim, sur~
vey, sweep, take a dekko at (*Brit. sl.*), take
stock of

scandal 1. crime, crying shame (*Inf.*), dis~
grace, embarrassment, offence, sin, wrong~
doing **2.** calumny, defamation, detraction,
discredit, disgrace, dishonour, ignominy,
infamy, obloquy, offence, opprobrium, re~
proach, shame, stigma **3.** abuse, aspersion,
backbiting, dirt, dirty linen (*Inf.*), gossip,
rumours, skeleton in the cupboard, slander,
talk, tattle

scandalize affront, appal, cause a few
raised eyebrows (*Inf.*), disgust, horrify, of~
fend, outrage, shock

scandalous 1. atrocious, disgraceful, dis~
reputable, highly improper, infamous,
monstrous, odious, opprobrious, outra~
geous, shameful, shocking, unseemly **2.** de~
famatory, gossiping, libellous, scurrilous,
slanderous, untrue
Antonyms decent, kind, laudatory, proper,
reputable, respectable, seemly, unimpeach~
able, upright

scant bare, barely sufficient, deficient, inad~
equate, insufficient, limited, little, minimal,
sparse

Antonyms abundant, adequate, ample, full, generous, plentiful, satisfactory, sufficient

scanty bare, deficient, exiguous, inadequate, insufficient, meagre, narrow, poor, restrict~ed, scant, short, skimpy, slender, sparing, sparse, thin

scapegoat fall guy (*Inf.*), whipping boy

scar 1. *n.* blemish, cicatrix, injury, mark, wound **2.** *v.* brand, damage, disfigure, mark, traumatize

scarce at a premium, deficient, few, few and far between, infrequent, in short supply, insufficient, rare, seldom met with, uncom~mon, unusual, wanting
Antonyms abundant, ample, common, commonplace, frequent, numerous, plen~teous, plentiful, sufficient

scarcely 1. barely, hardly, only just, scarce (*Archaic*) **2.** by no means, definitely not, hardly, not at all, on no account, under no circumstances

scarcity dearth, deficiency, infrequency, insufficiency, lack, paucity, poverty, rare~ness, shortage, undersupply, want
Antonyms abundance, excess, glut, superfluity, surfeit, surplus

scare 1. *v.* affright (*Archaic*), alarm, daunt, dismay, frighten, give (someone) a fright, give (someone) a turn (*Inf.*), intimidate, panic, put the wind up (someone) (*Inf.*), shock, startle, terrify, terrorize **2.** *n.* alarm, alert, fright, panic, shock, start, terror

scared fearful, frightened, panicky, panic-stricken, petrified, scared shitless (*Taboo sl.*), shaken, shit-scared (*Taboo sl.*), startled, terrified

scary alarming, bloodcurdling, chilling, creepy (*Inf.*), frightening, hair-raising, hairy (*Sl.*), horrendous, horrifying, intimidating, shocking, spine-chilling, spooky (*Inf.*), ter~rifying, unnerving

scathing belittling, biting, brutal, caustic, critical, cutting, harsh, mordacious, mor~dant, sarcastic, savage, scornful, searing, trenchant, vitriolic, withering

scatter 1. broadcast, diffuse, disseminate, fling, litter, shower, sow, spread, sprinkle, strew **2.** disband, dispel, disperse, dissipate, disunite, put to flight, separate
Antonyms assemble, cluster, collect, con~gregate, converge, rally, unite

scatterbrain bird-brain (*Inf.*), butterfly, featherbrain, flibbertigibbet, grasshopper mind, madcap

scattering few, handful, scatter, smatter, smattering, sprinkling

scenario master plan, outline, résumé, run~down, scheme, sequence of events, sketch, story line, summary, synopsis

scene 1. display, drama, exhibition, pag~eant, picture, representation, show, sight, spectacle, tableau **2.** area, locality, place, position, setting, site, situation, spot, whereabouts **3.** backdrop, background, lo~cation, *mise en scène*, set, setting **4.** act, di~vision, episode, incident, part, stage **5.** carry-on (*Inf., chiefly Brit.*), commotion, confrontation, display of emotion, drama, exhibition, fuss, performance, row, tantrum, to-do, upset **6.** landscape, panorama, pros~pect, view, vista **7.** *Inf.* arena, business, en~vironment, field of interest, milieu, world

scenery 1. landscape, surroundings, ter~rain, view, vista **2.** *Theatre* backdrop, dé~cor, flats, *mise en scène*, set, setting, stage set

scenic beautiful, breathtaking, grand, im~pressive, panoramic, picturesque, spectacu~lar, striking

scent *n.* **1.** aroma, bouquet, fragrance, niff (*Brit. sl.*), odour, perfume, redolence, smell **2.** spoor, track, trail ~*v.* **3.** be on the track *or* trail of, detect, discern, get wind of (*Inf.*), nose out, recognize, sense, smell, sniff, sniff out

scented aromatic, fragrant, odoriferous, perfumed, redolent, sweet-smelling

sceptic agnostic, cynic, disbeliever, doubter, doubting Thomas, Pyrrhonist, scoffer, un~believer

sceptical cynical, disbelieving, doubtful, doubting, dubious, hesitating, incredulous, mistrustful, questioning, quizzical, scoffing, unbelieving, unconvinced
Antonyms believing, certain, convinced, credulous, dogmatic, free from doubt, of fixed mind, sure, trusting, undoubting, unques~tioning

scepticism agnosticism, cynicism, disbelief, doubt, incredulity, Pyrrhonism, suspicion, unbelief

schedule 1. *n.* agenda, calendar, catalogue, inventory, itinerary, list, list of appoint~ments, plan, programme, timetable **2.** *v.* appoint, arrange, be due, book, organize, plan, programme, slot (*Inf.*), time

scheme *n.* **1.** contrivance, course of action, design, device, plan, programme, project, proposal, strategy, system, tactics, theory **2.** arrangement, blueprint, chart, codification, diagram, disposition, draft, layout, outline, pattern, schedule, schema, system **3.** con~spiracy, dodge, game (*Inf.*), intrigue, machinations, manoeuvre, plot, ploy, ruse, shift, stratagem, subterfuge ~*v.* **4.** contrive, design, devise, frame, imagine, lay plans, plan, project, work out **5.** collude, conspire, intrigue, machinate, manoeuvre, plot, wheel and deal (*Inf.*)

scheming artful, calculating, conniving, cunning, deceitful, designing, duplicitous,

foxy, Machiavellian, slippery, sly, tricky, underhand, wily
Antonyms above-board, artless, guileless, honest, ingenuous, naive, straightforward, trustworthy, undesigning

schism breach, break, discord, disunion, division, rift, rupture, separation, splinter~ ing, split

scholar 1. academic, bookworm, egghead (*Inf.*), intellectual, man of letters, savant **2.** disciple, learner, pupil, schoolboy, school~ girl, student

scholarly academic, bookish, erudite, intel~ lectual, learned, lettered, scholastic, studi~ ous, well-read
Antonyms lowbrow, middlebrow, philis~ tine, unacademic, uneducated, unintellectual, unlettered

scholarship 1. accomplishments, attain~ ments, book-learning, education, erudition, knowledge, learning, lore **2.** bursary, exhi~ bition, fellowship

scholastic 1. academic, bookish, learned, lettered, literary, scholarly **2.** pedagogic, pedantic, precise

school *n.* **1.** academy, alma mater, college, department, discipline, faculty, institute, institution, seminary **2.** adherents, circle, class, clique, denomination, devotees, disci~ ples, faction, followers, following, group, pupils, schism, sect, set **3.** creed, faith, out~ look, persuasion, school of thought, stamp, way of life ~*v.* **4.** coach, discipline, drill, educate, indoctrinate, instruct, prepare, prime, train, tutor, verse

schooling 1. book-learning, education, for~ mal education, teaching, tuition **2.** coach~ ing, drill, grounding, guidance, instruction, preparation, training

schoolteacher dominie (*Scot.*), instructor, pedagogue, schoolmarm (*Inf.*), schoolmaster, schoolmistress

science 1. body of knowledge, branch of knowledge, discipline **2.** art, skill, tech~ nique

scientific accurate, controlled, exact, math~ ematical, precise, systematic

scintillate blaze, coruscate, flash, give off sparks, gleam, glint, glisten, glitter, sparkle, twinkle

scintillating animated, bright, brilliant, dazzling, ebullient, exciting, glittering, live~ ly, sparkling, stimulating, witty

scoff belittle, deride, despise, flout, gibe, jeer, knock (*Inf.*), laugh at, make light of, make sport of, mock, poke fun at, pooh-pooh, revile, ridicule, scorn, scout (*Archa~ ic*), slag (off) (*Sl.*), sneer, take the piss (out of) (*Taboo sl.*), taunt, twit

scold 1. *v.* bawl out (*Inf.*), berate, blame,

bring (someone) to book, carpet (*Inf.*), cas~ tigate, censure, chew out (*U.S. & Canad. inf.*), chide, find fault with, give a rocket (*Brit. & N.Z. inf.*), give (someone) a dressing-down (row, talking-to (*Inf.*)) (*Inf.*), go on at, haul (someone) over the coals (*Inf.*), have (someone) on the carpet (*Inf.*), lecture, nag, rate, read the riot act, rebuke, remonstrate with, reprimand, reproach, re~ prove, take (someone) to task, tear into (*Inf.*), tear (someone) off a strip (*Brit. inf.*), tell off (*Inf.*), tick off (*Inf.*), upbraid, vitu~ perate **2.** *n.* nag, shrew, termagant (*Rare*), Xanthippe
Antonyms *v.* acclaim, applaud, approve, commend, compliment, extol, laud, praise

scolding dressing-down (*Inf.*), (good) talking-to (*Inf.*), lecture, piece of one's mind, rebuke, row, telling-off (*Inf.*), ticking-off (*Inf.*), tongue-lashing, wigging (*Brit. sl.*)

scoop *n.* **1.** dipper, ladle, spoon **2.** coup, exclusive, exposé, inside story, revelation, sensation ~*v.* **3.** *Often with* **up** clear away, gather up, lift, pick up, remove, sweep up *or* away, take up **4.** bail, dig, dip, empty, excavate, gouge, hollow, ladle, scrape, shovel

scope ambit, area, capacity, compass, confines, elbowroom, extent, field of refer~ ence, freedom, latitude, liberty, opportunity, orbit, outlook, purview, range, reach, room, space, span, sphere

scorch blacken, blister, burn, char, parch, roast, sear, shrivel, singe, wither

scorching baking, boiling, broiling, burn~ ing, fiery, flaming, red-hot, roasting, sear~ ing, sizzling, sweltering, torrid, tropical, unbearably hot

score *n.* **1.** grade, mark, outcome, points, record, result, total **2. the score** *Inf.* the facts, the reality, the setup (*Inf.*), the situa~ tion, the truth **3.** *Plural* a flock, a great number, an army, a throng, crowds, droves, hosts, hundreds, legions, lots, masses, mil~ lions, multitudes, myriads, swarms, very many **4.** account, basis, cause, ground, grounds, reason **5.** a bone to pick, griev~ ance, grudge, injury, injustice, wrong **6. pay off old scores** avenge, get even with (*Inf.*), get one's own back (*Inf.*), give an eye for an eye, give like for like *or* tit for tat, give (someone) a taste of his own medicine, hit back, pay (someone) back (in his own coin), repay, requite, retaliate **7.** account, amount due, bill, charge, debt, obligation, reckoning, tab (*U.S. inf.*), tally, total ~*v.* **8.** achieve, amass, chalk up (*Inf.*), gain, make, notch up (*Inf.*), win **9.** count, keep a tally of, keep count, record, register, tally **10.** crosshatch, cut, deface, gouge, graze, indent, mar, mark, nick, notch, scrape, scratch, slash **11.** *With* **out** *or* **through** cancel, cross out, delete, obliterate, put a line through, strike out **12.** *Music* adapt, ar~ range, orchestrate, set **13.** gain an advan~ tage, go down well with (someone), impress, make a hit (*Inf.*), make an impact *or* im~ pression, make a point, put oneself across, triumph

score off be one up on (*Inf.*), get the better of, have the laugh on, humiliate, make a fool of, make (someone) look silly, worst

scorn 1. *n.* contempt, contemptuousness, contumely, derision, despite, disdain, dis~ paragement, mockery, sarcasm, scornful~ ness, slight, sneer **2.** *v.* be above, consider beneath one, contemn, curl one's lip at, de~ ride, disdain, flout, hold in contempt, look down on, make fun of, reject, scoff at, scout (*Archaic*), slight, sneer at, spurn, turn up one's nose at (*Inf.*)
Antonyms *n.* acceptance, admiration, affec~ tion, esteem, high regard, respect, tolerance, toleration, veneration, worship ~*v.* accept, admire, esteem, look favourably on, respect, revere, tolerate, venerate, worship

scornful contemptuous, contumelious, defiant, derisive, disdainful, haughty, inso~ lent, insulting, jeering, mocking, sarcastic, sardonic, scathing, scoffing, slighting, sneering, supercilious, withering

scornfully contemptuously, disdainfully, dismissively, scathingly, slightingly, with a sneer, with contempt, with disdain, wither~ ingly, with lip curled

Scots Caledonian, Scottish

scoundrel asshole (*U.S. & Canad. taboo sl.*), asswipe (*U.S. & Canad. taboo sl.*), bad egg (*Old-fashioned inf.*), bastard (*Offens.*), black~ guard, bugger (*Taboo sl.*), caitiff (*Archaic*), cheat, cocksucker (*Taboo sl.*), dastard (*Ar~ chaic*), good-for-nothing, heel (*Sl.*), incorri~ gible, knave (*Archaic*), miscreant, mother, motherfucker (*Taboo sl., chiefly U.S.*), ne'er-do-well, rascal, reprobate, rogue, rot~ ter (*Sl., chiefly Brit.*), scally (*Northwest English dialect*), scamp, scapegrace, scum~ bag (*Sl.*), shit (*Taboo sl.*), son-of-a-bitch (*Sl., chiefly U.S. & Canad.*), swine, turd (*Taboo sl.*), vagabond, villain, wretch

scour[1] abrade, buff, burnish, clean, cleanse, flush, furbish, polish, purge, rub, scrub, wash, whiten

scour[2] beat, comb, forage, go over with a fine-tooth comb, hunt, look high and low, rake, ransack, search

scourge *n.* **1.** affliction, bane, curse, infliction, misfortune, penalty, pest, plague, punishment, terror, torment, visitation **2.** cat, cat-o'-nine-tails, lash, strap, switch, thong, whip ~*v.* **3.** beat, belt (*Inf.*), cane, castigate, chastise, discipline, flog, horse~

whip, lash, lather (*Inf.*), leather, punish, take a strap to, tan (someone's) hide (*Sl.*), thrash, trounce, wallop (*Inf.*), whale, whip **4.** afflict, curse, excoriate, harass, plague, terrorize, torment
Antonyms *n.* (*sense 1*) benefit, blessing, boon, favour, gift, godsend

scout *v.* **1.** case (*Sl.*), check out, investigate, make a reconnaissance, nark (*Brit., Aust., & N.Z. sl.*), observe, probe, recce (*Sl.*), rec~ onnoitre, see how the land lies, spy, spy out, survey, watch **2.** *Often with* **out, up,** *or* **around** cast around for, ferret out, hunt for, look for, rustle up, search for, search out, seek, track down ~*n.* **3.** advance guard, escort, lookout, outrider, precursor, reconnoitrer, vanguard **4.** recruiter, talent scout

scowl 1. *v.* frown, glower, grimace, look daggers at, lour *or* lower **2.** *n.* black look, dirty look, frown, glower, grimace

scramble *v.* **1.** clamber, climb, crawl, move with difficulty, push, scrabble, struggle, swarm **2.** contend, hasten, jockey for posi~ tion, jostle, look lively *or* snappy (*Inf.*), make haste, push, run, rush, strive, vie ~*n.* **3.** climb, trek **4.** commotion, competition, confusion, free-for-all (*Inf.*), hassle (*Inf.*), hustle, melee *or* mêlée, muddle, race, rat race, rush, struggle, tussle

scrap[1] *n.* **1.** atom, bit, bite, crumb, frag~ ment, grain, iota, mite, modicum, morsel, mouthful, part, particle, piece, portion, remnant, sliver, snatch, snippet, trace **2.** junk, off cuts, waste **3. on the scrap heap** discarded, ditched (*Sl.*), jettisoned, put out to grass (*Inf.*), redundant, written off **4.** *Plural* bits, leavings, leftovers, remains, scrapings ~*v.* **5.** abandon, break up, chuck (*Inf.*), demolish, discard, dispense with, ditch (*Sl.*), drop, get rid of, jettison, junk (*Inf.*), shed, throw away *or* out, throw on the scrapheap, toss out, trash (*Sl.*), write off
Antonyms *v.* bring back, recall, re-establish, reinstall, reinstate, restore, return

scrap[2] **1.** *n.* argument, *bagarre*, battle, brawl, disagreement, dispute, dust-up (*Inf.*), fight, quarrel, row, scrimmage, scuffle, set-to (*Inf.*), shindig (*Inf.*), shindy (*Inf.*), squab~ ble, tiff, wrangle **2.** *v.* argue, barney (*Inf.*), bicker, come to blows, fall out (*Inf.*), fight, have a shouting match (*Inf.*), have words, row, spar, squabble, wrangle

scrape *v.* **1.** abrade, bark, graze, rub, scratch, scuff, skin **2.** grate, grind, rasp, scratch, screech, set one's teeth on edge, squeak **3.** clean, erase, file, remove, rub, scour **4.** pinch, save, scrimp, skimp, stint **5. scrape by, in,** *or* **through** barely make it, cut it fine (*Inf.*), get by (*Inf.*), have a close shave (*Inf.*), struggle ~*n.* **6.** *Inf.* awk~

ward *or* embarrassing situation, difficulty, dilemma, distress, fix (*Inf.*), mess, plight, predicament, pretty pickle (*Inf.*), spot (*Inf.*), tight spot, trouble

scrappy bitty, disjointed, fragmentary, in~ complete, perfunctory, piecemeal, sketchy, thrown together

scraps bits, leavings, leftovers, remains, scrapings

scratch *v.* **1.** claw, cut, damage, etch, grate, graze, incise, lacerate, make a mark on, mark, rub, score, scrape **2.** annul, cancel, delete, eliminate, erase, pull out, stand down, strike off, withdraw ~*n.* **3.** blemish, claw mark, gash, graze, laceration, mark, scrape **4. up to scratch** acceptable, ad~ equate, capable, competent, satisfactory, sufficient, up to snuff (*Inf.*), up to standard ~*adj.* **5.** haphazard, hastily prepared, im~ promptu, improvised, rough, rough-and-ready

scrawl doodle, scrabble, scratch, scribble, squiggle, writing

scream *v.* **1.** bawl, cry, holler (*Inf.*), screech, shriek, shrill, sing out, squeal, yell **2.** *Fig.* be conspicuous, clash, jar, shriek ~*n.* **3.** howl, outcry, screech, shriek, wail, yell, yelp **4.** *Inf.* card (*Inf.*), caution (*Inf.*), char~ acter (*Inf.*), comedian, comic, entertainer, hoot (*Inf.*), joker, laugh, riot (*Sl.*), sensation, wag, wit

screech cry, scream, shriek, squawk, squeal, yelp

screen *v.* **1.** cloak, conceal, cover, hide, mask, shade, shroud, shut out, veil **2.** de~ fend, guard, protect, safeguard, shelter, shield **3.** cull, evaluate, examine, filter, gauge, grade, process, riddle, scan, sieve, sift, sort, vet **4.** broadcast, present, put on, show ~*n.* **5.** awning, canopy, cloak, con~ cealment, cover, guard, hedge, mantle, shade, shelter, shield, shroud **6.** mesh, net, partition, room divider

screw *v.* **1.** tighten, turn, twist, work in **2.** contort, contract, crumple, distort, pucker, wrinkle **3.** *Inf.* bring pressure to bear on, coerce, constrain, force, hold a knife to (someone's) throat, oppress, pressurize, put the screws on (*Inf.*), squeeze **4.** *Inf. Often with* **out of** bleed, extort, extract, wrest, wring

screw up 1. contort, contract, crumple, distort, knit, knot, pucker, wrinkle **2.** *Inf.* bitch (up) (*Sl.*), bodge (*Inf.*), botch, bungle, cock up (*Brit. sl.*), fuck up (*Offens. taboo sl.*), louse up (*Sl.*), make a hash of (*Inf.*), make a mess *or* muck-up of (*Sl.*), mess up, mishandle, mismanage, queer (*Inf.*), spoil

scribble *v.* dash off, doodle, jot, pen, scratch, scrawl, write

scribe amanuensis, clerk, copyist, notary (*Archaic*), penman (*Rare*), scrivener (*Ar~ chaic*), secretary, writer

script 1. calligraphy, hand, handwriting, letters, longhand, penmanship, writing **2.** book, copy, dialogue, libretto, lines, manu~ script, text, words

Scripture Holy Bible, Holy Scripture, Holy Writ, The Bible, The Book of Books, The Good Book, The Gospels, The Scriptures, The Word, The Word of God

scroll inventory, list, parchment, roll

Scrooge cheapskate (*Inf.*), meanie *or* meany (*Inf., chiefly Brit.*), miser, money-grubber (*Inf.*), niggard, penny-pincher (*Inf.*), skinflint, tight-arse (*Taboo sl.*), tight-ass (*U.S. taboo sl.*), tightwad (*U.S. & Canad. sl.*)

scrounge beg, blag (*Sl.*), bum (*Inf.*), cadge, forage for, freeload (*Sl.*), hunt around (for), mooch (*Sl.*), sorn (*Scot.*), sponge (*Inf.*), touch (someone) for (*Sl.*), wheedle

scrounger bum (*Inf.*), cadger, freeloader (*Sl.*), parasite, sorner (*Scot.*), sponger (*Inf.*)

scrub *v.* **1.** clean, cleanse, rub, scour **2.** *Inf.* abandon, abolish, call off, cancel, delete, discontinue, do away with, drop, forget about, give up

scruffy disreputable, draggletailed (*Archaic*), frowzy, ill-groomed, mangy, messy, ragged, run-down, scrubby (*Brit. inf.*), seedy, shab~ by, slatternly, sloppy (*Inf.*), slovenly, slut~ tish, squalid, tattered, tatty, ungroomed, unkempt, untidy
Antonyms chic, dapper, natty, neat, soigné *or* soignée, spruce, tidy, well-dressed, well-groomed, well-turned-out

scruple 1. *v.* balk at, be loath, be reluctant, demur, doubt, falter, have misgivings about, have qualms about, hesitate, stick at, think twice about, vacillate, waver **2.** *n.* caution, compunction, difficulty, doubt, hesitation, misgiving, perplexity, qualm, reluctance, second thoughts, squeamishness, twinge of conscience, uneasiness

scrupulous careful, conscientious, exact, fastidious, honourable, meticulous, minute, moral, nice, painstaking, precise, princi~ pled, punctilious, rigorous, strict, upright
Antonyms amoral, careless, dishonest, in~ exact, reckless, slapdash, superficial, uncaring, unconscientious, unprincipled, unscrupulous, without scruples

scrutinize analyse, dissect, examine, ex~ plore, inquire into, inspect, investigate, pe~ ruse, pore over, probe, research, scan, search, sift, study, work over

scrutiny analysis, close study, examination, exploration, inquiry, inspection, investiga~ tion, perusal, search, sifting, study

scuffle 1. *v.* clash, come to blows, contend,

exchange blows, fight, grapple, jostle, struggle, tussle **2.** *n.* affray (*Law*), *bagarre,* barney (*Inf.*), brawl, commotion, disturb~ ance, fight, fray, ruck (*Sl.*), ruckus (*Inf.*), ruction (*Inf.*), rumpus, scrap (*Inf.*), scrim~ mage, set-to (*Inf.*), shindig (*Inf.*), shindy (*Inf.*), skirmish, tussle

sculpture *v.* carve, chisel, cut, fashion, form, hew, model, mould, sculp, sculpt, shape

scum 1. algae, crust, dross, film, froth, im~ purities, offscourings, scruff **2.** *Fig. ca~ naille,* dregs of society, dross, lowest of the low, rabble, ragtag and bobtail, riffraff, rubbish, trash (*Chiefly U.S. & Canad.*)

scurrility abusiveness, billingsgate, coarse~ ness, grossness, indecency, infamousness, invective, obloquy, obscenity, offensiveness, scurrilousness, vituperation

scurrilous abusive, coarse, defamatory, foul, foul-mouthed, gross, indecent, infa~ mous, insulting, low, obscene, offensive, Rabelaisian, ribald, salacious, scabrous, scandalous, slanderous, vituperative, vulgar **Antonyms** civilized, decent, polite, proper, refined, respectful

scurry 1. *v.* beetle, dart, dash, fly, hurry, race, scamper, scoot, scud, scuttle, skim, sprint, whisk **2.** *n.* bustle, flurry, scamper~ ing, whirl **Antonyms** *v.* amble, mooch (*Sl.*), mosey (*Inf.*), saunter, stroll, toddle, wander

scuttle beetle, bustle, hare (*Brit. inf.*), has~ ten, hurry, run, rush, scamper, scoot, scramble, scud, scurry, scutter (*Brit. inf.*)

sea *n.* **1.** main, ocean, the briny (*Inf.*), the deep, the drink (*Inf.*), the waves **2.** *Fig.* abundance, expanse, mass, multitude, plethora, profusion, sheet, vast number **3. at sea** adrift, astray, at a loss, at sixes and sevens, baffled, bewildered, confused, dis~ oriented, lost, mystified, puzzled, upset ~*adj.* **4.** aquatic, briny, marine, maritime, ocean, ocean-going, oceanic, pelagic, salt, saltwater, seagoing

seafaring marine, maritime, nautical, na~ val, oceanic

seal *v.* **1.** bung, close, cork, enclose, fasten, make airtight, plug, secure, shut, stop, stopper, stop up, waterproof **2.** assure, at~ test, authenticate, confirm, establish, ratify, stamp, validate **3.** clinch, conclude, con~ summate, finalize, settle, shake hands on (*Inf.*) **4.** *With* **off** board up, fence off, iso~ late, put out of bounds, quarantine, segre~ gate ~*n.* **5.** assurance, attestation, authen~ tication, confirmation, imprimatur, insig~ nia, notification, ratification, stamp

seam *n.* **1.** closure, joint, suture (*Surgery*) **2.** layer, lode, stratum, vein **3.** furrow, line, ridge, scar, wrinkle

search *v.* **1.** cast around, check, comb, ex~ amine, explore, ferret, frisk (*Inf.*), go over with a fine-tooth comb, inquire, inspect, in~ vestigate, leave no stone unturned, look, look high and low, probe, pry, ransack, rifle through, rummage through, scour, scruti~ nize, seek, sift, turn inside out, turn upside down ~*n.* **2.** examination, exploration, going-over (*Inf.*), hunt, inquiry, inspection, investigation, pursuit, quest, researches, rummage, scrutiny **3. in search of** hunting for, in need of, in pursuit of, looking for, making enquiries concerning, on the look~ out for, on the track of, seeking

searching *adj.* close, intent, keen, minute, penetrating, piercing, probing, quizzical, severe, sharp, thorough **Antonyms** cursory, perfunctory, peripheral, sketchy, superficial

seasickness *mal de mer*

season *n.* **1.** division, interval, juncture, occasion, opportunity, period, spell, term, time, time of year ~*v.* **2.** colour, enliven, flavour, lace, leaven, pep up, salt, salt and pepper, spice **3.** acclimatize, accustom, an~ neal, discipline, habituate, harden, inure, mature, prepare, toughen, train **4.** mitigate, moderate, qualify, temper

seasonable appropriate, convenient, fit, opportune, providential, suitable, timely, welcome, well-timed

seasoned battle-scarred, experienced, hardened, long-serving, mature, old, prac~ tised, time-served, veteran, weathered, well-versed **Antonyms** callow, green, inexperienced, new, novice, unpractised, unseasoned, un~ skilled

seasoning condiment, dressing, flavouring, relish, salt and pepper, sauce, spice

seat *n.* **1.** bench, chair, pew, settle, stall, stool, throne **2.** axis, capital, centre, cradle, headquarters, heart, hub, location, place, site, situation, source, station **3.** base, bed, bottom, cause, footing, foundation, ground, groundwork **4.** abode, ancestral hall, house, mansion, residence **5.** chair, constituency, incumbency, membership, place ~*v.* **6.** ac~ commodate, cater for, contain, have room *or* capacity for, hold, sit, take **7.** deposit, fix, install, locate, place, set, settle, sit

seating accommodation, chairs, places, room, seats

secede apostatize, break with, disaffiliate, leave, pull out, quit, resign, retire, separate, split from, withdraw

secluded cloistered, cut off, isolated, lonely, off the beaten track, out-of-the-way, private, reclusive, remote, retired, sequestered, sheltered, solitary, tucked away, unfre~ quented

Antonyms accessible, busy, frequented, open, public, sociable

seclusion concealment, hiding, isolation, privacy, purdah, remoteness, retirement, retreat, shelter, solitude

second¹ *adj.* **1.** following, next, subsequent, succeeding **2.** additional, alternative, extra, further, other, repeated **3.** inferior, lesser, lower, secondary, subordinate, supporting **4.** double, duplicate, reproduction, twin ~*n.* **5.** assistant, backer, helper, supporter ~*v.* **6.** advance, aid, approve, assist, back, encourage, endorse, forward, further, give moral support to, go along with, help, promote, support

second² *n.* flash, instant, jiffy (*Inf.*), minute, moment, sec (*Inf.*), split second, tick (*Brit. inf.*), trice, twinkling, twinkling of an eye, two shakes of a lamb's tail (*Inf.*)

secondary 1. derivative, derived, indirect, resultant, resulting, second-hand **2.** consequential, contingent, inferior, lesser, lower, minor, second-rate, subordinate, unimportant **3.** alternate, auxiliary, backup, extra, fall-back, relief, reserve, second, subsidiary, supporting
Antonyms cardinal, chief, head, larger, main, major, more important, only, original, preceding, primary, prime, principal, superior

second class *adj.* déclassé, indifferent, inferior, mediocre, outclassed, second-best, second-rate, undistinguished, uninspiring

second-hand 1. *adj.* handed down, hand-me-down (*Inf.*), nearly new, reach-me-down (*Inf.*), used **2.** *adv.* at second-hand, indirectly, on the grapevine (*Inf.*)

second in command depute (*Scot.*), deputy, number two, right-hand man, successor designate

secondly in the second place, next, second

second-rate bush-league (*Aust. & N.Z. inf.*), cheap, cheap and nasty (*Inf.*), commonplace, dime-a-dozen (*Inf.*), inferior, low-grade, low-quality, mediocre, piss-poor (*Taboo sl.*), poor, rubbishy, shoddy, substandard, tacky (*Inf.*), tawdry, tinhorn (*U.S. sl.*), two-bit (*U.S. & Canad. sl.*)
Antonyms a cut above (*Inf.*), choice, de luxe, excellent, fine, first-class, first-rate, good quality, high-class, quality, superior

secrecy 1. concealment, confidentiality, huggermugger (*Rare*), mystery, privacy, retirement, seclusion, silence, solitude, surreptitiousness **2.** clandestineness, covertness, furtiveness, secretiveness, stealth

secret *adj.* **1.** backstairs, camouflaged, cloak-and-dagger, close, closet (*Inf.*), concealed, conspiratorial, covered, covert, disguised, furtive, hidden, hole-and-corner (*Inf.*), hush-hush (*Inf.*), reticent, shrouded, undercover, underground, under wraps, undisclosed, unknown, unpublished, unrevealed, unseen **2.** abstruse, arcane, cabbalistic, clandestine, classified, cryptic, esoteric, mysterious, occult, recondite **3.** hidden, out-of-the-way, private, retired, secluded, unfrequented, unknown **4.** close, deep, discreet, reticent, secretive, sly, stealthy, underhand ~*n.* **5.** code, confidence, enigma, formula, key, mystery, recipe, skeleton in the cupboard **6. in secret** behind closed doors, by stealth, huggermugger (*Archaic*), in camera, incognito, secretly, slyly, surreptitiously
Antonyms *adj.* apparent, candid, disclosed, exoteric, frank, manifest, obvious, open, overt, public, straightforward, unconcealed, visible, well-known

secrete bury, cache, conceal, cover, disguise, harbour, hide, screen, secure, shroud, stash (*Inf.*), stash away (*Inf.*), stow, veil
Antonyms bare, display, exhibit, expose to view, leave in the open, reveal, show, uncover, unmask, unveil

secretive cagey (*Inf.*), clamlike, close, cryptic, deep, enigmatic, playing one's cards close to one's chest, reserved, reticent, tight-lipped, uncommunicative, unforthcoming, withdrawn
Antonyms candid, communicative, expansive, forthcoming, frank, open, unreserved

secretly behind closed doors, behind (someone's) back, clandestinely, confidentially, covertly, furtively, in camera, in confidence, in one's heart, in one's inmost thoughts, in secret, on the q.t. (*Inf.*), on the sly, privately, quietly, stealthily, surreptitiously, unobserved

sect camp, denomination, division, faction, group, party, schism, school, school of thought, splinter group, wing

sectarian 1. *adj.* bigoted, clannish, cliquish, doctrinaire, dogmatic, exclusive, factional, fanatic, fanatical, hidebound, insular, limited, narrow-minded, parochial, partisan, rigid **2.** *n.* adherent, bigot, disciple, dogmatist, extremist, fanatic, partisan, true believer, zealot
Antonyms *adj.* broad-minded, catholic, free-thinking, liberal, non-sectarian, open-minded, tolerant, unbigoted, unprejudiced

section *n.* **1.** component, cross section, division, fraction, fragment, instalment, part, passage, piece, portion, sample, segment, slice, subdivision **2.** *Chiefly U.S.* area, department, district, region, sector, zone

sector area, category, district, division, part, quarter, region, stratum, subdivision, zone

secular civil, earthly, laic, laical, lay, non~ spiritual, profane, state, temporal, worldly
Antonyms divine, holy, religious, sacred, spiritual, theological

secure *adj.* **1.** immune, impregnable, out of harm's way, protected, safe, sheltered, shielded, unassailable, undamaged, un~ harmed **2.** dependable, fast, fastened, firm, fixed, fortified, immovable, stable, steady, tight **3.** assured, certain, confident, easy, reassured, sure **4.** absolute, conclusive, definite, in the bag (*Inf.*), reliable, solid, steadfast, tried and true, well-founded ~*v.* **5.** acquire, come by, gain, get, get hold of, land (*Inf.*), make sure of, obtain, pick up, procure, score (*Sl.*), win possession of **6.** attach, batten down, bolt, chain, fasten, fix, lash, lock, lock up, make fast, moor, pad~ lock, rivet, tie up **7.** assure, ensure, guar~ antee, insure
Antonyms *adj.* endangered, ill-at-ease, in~ secure, loose, not fastened, precarious, unassured, uncertain, uneasy, unfixed, un~ protected, unsafe, unsound, unsure ~*v.* en~ danger, give up, imperil, leave unguaranteed, let (something) slip through (one's) fingers, loose, lose, unloose, untie

security 1. asylum, care, cover, custody, immunity, preservation, protection, refuge, retreat, safekeeping, safety, sanctuary **2.** defence, guards, precautions, protection, safeguards, safety measures, surveillance **3.** assurance, certainty, confidence, conviction, ease of mind, freedom from doubt, positive~ ness, reliance, sureness **4.** collateral, gage, guarantee, hostage, insurance, pawn, pledge, surety
Antonyms (*senses 1, 2 & 3*) exposure, insecu~ rity, jeopardy, uncertainty, vulnerability

sedate calm, collected, composed, cool, decorous, deliberate, demure, dignified, earnest, grave, imperturbable, middle-aged, placid, proper, quiet, seemly, serene, seri~ ous, slow-moving, sober, solemn, staid, tranquil, unflappable (*Inf.*), unruffled
Antonyms agitated, excitable, excited, flighty, impassioned, jumpy, nervous, undignified, uninhibited, unsteady, wild

sedative 1. *adj.* allaying, anodyne, calma~ tive, calming, lenitive, relaxing, sleep- inducing, soothing, soporific, tranquillizing **2.** *n.* anodyne, calmative, downer or down (*Sl.*), narcotic, opiate, sleeping pill, tran~ quillizer

sedentary desk, desk-bound, inactive, mo~ tionless, seated, sitting, torpid
Antonyms active, mobile, motile, moving, on the go (*Inf.*)

sediment deposit, dregs, grounds, lees, precipitate, residuum, settlings

sedition agitation, disloyalty, incitement to riot, rabble-rousing, subversion, treason

seditious disloyal, dissident, insubordinate, mutinous, rebellious, refractory, revolu~ tionary, subversive, treasonable

seduce 1. betray, corrupt, debauch, deflower, deprave, dishonour, ruin (*Archa~ ic*) **2.** allure, attract, beguile, deceive, decoy, ensnare, entice, inveigle, lead astray, lure, mislead, tempt

seduction 1. corruption, defloration, ruin (*Archaic*) **2.** allure, enticement, lure, snare, temptation

seductive alluring, attractive, beguiling, bewitching, captivating, come-hither (*Inf.*), come-to-bed (*Inf.*), enticing, flirtatious, in~ viting, irresistible, provocative, ravishing, sexy (*Inf.*), siren, specious, tempting

seductress Circe, enchantress, *femme fa~ tale*, Lorelei, siren, temptress, vamp (*Inf.*)

see *v.* **1.** behold, catch a glimpse of, catch sight of, check, check out (*Inf.*), clock (*Brit. sl.*), descry, discern, distinguish, espy, eye~ ball (*U.S. sl.*), get a load of (*Sl.*), glimpse, heed, identify, lay or clap eyes on (*Inf.*), look, make out, mark, note, notice, observe, perceive, recognize, regard, sight, spot, take a dekko at (*Brit. sl.*), view, witness **2.** ap~ preciate, catch on (*Inf.*), comprehend, fath~ om, feel, follow, get, get the drift of, get the hang of (*Inf.*), grasp, know, make out, real~ ize, take in, understand **3.** ascertain, deter~ mine, discover, find out, investigate, learn, make enquiries, refer to **4.** ensure, guaran~ tee, make certain, make sure, mind, see to it, take care **5.** consider, decide, deliberate, give some thought to, judge, make up one's mind, mull over, reflect, think over **6.** con~ fer with, consult, encounter, interview, meet, receive, run into, speak to, visit **7.** accompany, attend, escort, lead, show, usher, walk **8.** consort or associate with, court, date (*Inf., chiefly U.S.*), go out with, go steady with (*Inf.*), keep company with, walk out with (*Obsolete*) **9.** anticipate, di~ vine, envisage, foresee, foretell, imagine, picture, visualize

see about 1. attend to, consider, deal with, give some thought to, look after, see to, take care of **2.** investigate, look into, make en~ quiries, research

seed 1. egg, egg cell, embryo, germ, grain, kernel, ovule, ovum, pip, spore **2.** begin~ ning, germ, inkling, nucleus, source, start, suspicion **3.** *Fig.* children, descendants, heirs, issue, offspring, progeny, race, sci~ ons, spawn, successors **4. go** or **run to seed** decay, decline, degenerate, deterio~ rate, go downhill (*Inf.*), go to pieces, go to pot, go to rack and ruin, go to waste, let oneself go, retrogress

seedy 1. crummy (*Sl.*), decaying, dilapidat‐ ed, down at heel, faded, grotty (*Sl.*), grubby, mangy, manky (*Scot. dialect*), old, run-down, scruffy, shabby, sleazy, slovenly, squalid, tatty, unkempt, worn **2.** *Inf.* ailing, ill, off colour, out of sorts, peely-wally (*Scot.*), poorly (*Inf.*), sickly, under the weather (*Inf.*), unwell
Antonyms (*sense 1*) classy, elegant, fashion‐ able, high-toned, posh (*Inf., chiefly Brit.*), ritzy (*Sl.*), smart, swanky (*Inf.*), swish (*Inf., chiefly Brit.*), top-drawer, up-market

see eye to eye accord, agree, click, coin‐ cide, concur, correspond, fit, get along, get on (together), harmonize, speak the same language

seeing *conj.* as, inasmuch as, in view of the fact that, since

seek 1. be after, follow, go gunning for, go in pursuit (quest, search) of, hunt, inquire, look for, pursue, search for **2.** aim, aspire to, attempt, endeavour, essay, have a go (*Inf.*), strive, try **3.** ask, beg, entreat, in‐ quire, invite, petition, request, solicit

seem appear, assume, give the impression, have the *or* every appearance of, look, look as if, look like, look to be, pretend, sound like, strike one as being

seemly appropriate, becoming, befitting, *comme il faut*, decent, decorous, fit, fitting, in good taste, meet (*Archaic*), nice, proper, suitable, suited, the done thing
Antonyms improper, inappropriate, in‐ decorous, in poor taste, out of keeping, out of place, unbecoming, unbefitting, unseemly, unsuitable

see over inspect, look round, see round, tour

seer augur, predictor, prophet, sibyl, sooth‐ sayer

seesaw *v.* alternate, fluctuate, go from one extreme to the other, oscillate, pitch, swing, teeter

seethe 1. boil, bubble, churn, ferment, fizz, foam, froth **2.** be in a state (*Inf.*), be livid (furious, incensed), breathe fire and slaughter, foam at the mouth, fume, get hot under the collar (*Inf.*), rage, see red (*Inf.*), simmer, storm **3.** be alive with, swarm, teem

see-through diaphanous, filmy, fine, flimsy, gauzy, gossamer, sheer, thin, trans‐ lucent, transparent

see through *v.* **1.** be undeceived by, be wise to (*Inf.*), fathom, get to the bottom of, have (someone's) number (*Inf.*), not fall for, penetrate **2. see (something *or* someone) through** help out, keep at, persevere (with), persist, see out, stay to the bitter end, stick by, stick out (*Inf.*), support

see to arrange, attend to, be responsible for, do, look after, manage, organize, sort out, take care of, take charge of

segment bit, compartment, division, part, piece, portion, section, slice, wedge

segregate discriminate against, dissociate, isolate, separate, set apart, single out
Antonyms amalgamate, desegregate, join together, mix, unify, unite

segregation apartheid (*formerly in South Africa*), discrimination, isolation, separa‐ tion

seize 1. catch up, clutch, collar (*Inf.*), fasten, grab, grasp, grip, lay hands on, snatch, take **2.** apprehend, catch, get, grasp, nab (*Inf.*), nail (*Inf.*) **3.** abduct, annex, appropriate, arrest, capture, commandeer, confiscate, hijack, impound, take by storm, take cap‐ tive, take possession of
Antonyms free, hand back, let go, let pass, loose, release, relinquish, set free, turn loose

seizure 1. abduction, annexation, appre‐ hension, arrest, capture, commandeering, confiscation, grabbing, taking **2.** attack, convulsion, fit, paroxysm, spasm

seldom hardly ever, infrequently, not often, occasionally, once in a blue moon (*Inf.*), rarely, scarcely ever
Antonyms again and again, frequently, many a time, much, often, over and over again, time after time, time and again

select *v.* **1.** choose, opt for, pick, prefer, single out, sort out ~*adj.* **2.** choice, excel‐ lent, first-class, first-rate, hand-picked, picked, posh (*Inf., chiefly Brit.*), preferable, prime, rare, recherché, selected, special, superior, topnotch (*Inf.*) **3.** cliquish, elite, exclusive, limited, privileged
Antonyms *v.* eliminate, reject, turn down ~*adj.* cheap, indifferent, indiscriminate, in‐ ferior, ordinary, random, run-of-the-mill, second-rate, shoddy, substandard, unre‐ markable

selection 1. choice, choosing, option, pick, preference **2.** anthology, assortment, choice, collection, line-up, medley, miscellany, pot‐ pourri, range, variety

selective careful, discerning, discriminat‐ ing, discriminatory, eclectic, particular
Antonyms all-embracing, careless, desul‐ tory, indiscriminate, unselective

self-assurance assertiveness, confidence, positiveness, self-confidence, self-possession

self-centred egotistic, inward looking, narcissistic, self-absorbed, selfish, self‐ seeking, wrapped up in oneself

self-confidence aplomb, confidence, high morale, nerve, poise, self-assurance, self‐ reliance, self-respect

self-confident assured, confident, fearless,

poised, secure, self-assured, self-reliant, sure of oneself

self-conscious affected, awkward, bashful, diffident, embarrassed, ill at ease, insecure, nervous, out of countenance, shamefaced, sheepish, uncomfortable

self-control calmness, cool, coolness, restraint, self-discipline, self-mastery, self-restraint, strength of mind *or* will, will~power

self-esteem *amour-propre*, confidence, faith in oneself, pride, self-assurance, self-regard, self-respect, vanity

self-evident axiomatic, clear, incontro~vertible, inescapable, manifestly *or* patently true, obvious, undeniable, written all over (something)

self-government autonomy, democracy, home rule, independence, self-deter~mination, self-rule, sovereignty

self-important arrogant, big-headed, bumptious, cocky, conceited, overbearing, pompous, presumptuous, pushy (*Inf.*), strutting, swaggering, swollen-headed

self-indulgence dissipation, excess, ex~travagance, incontinence, intemperance, self-gratification, sensualism

selfish egoistic, egoistical, egotistic, egotis~tical, greedy, looking out for number one (*Inf.*), mean, mercenary, narrow, self-centred, self-interested, self-seeking, ungen~erous
Antonyms altruistic, benevolent, consider~ate, generous, magnanimous, philanthropic, self-denying, selfless, self-sacrificing, un~grudging, unselfish

self-possessed collected, confident, cool, cool as a cucumber (*Inf.*), poised, self-assured, sure of oneself, together (*Sl.*), unruffled

self-reliant able to stand on one's own two feet (*Inf.*), capable, independent, self-sufficient, self-supporting
Antonyms dependent, helpless, reliant, relying on

self-respect *amour-propre*, dignity, faith in oneself, morale, one's own image, pride, self-esteem

self-righteous complacent, goody-goody (*Inf.*), holier-than-thou, hypocritical, phari~saic, pi (*Brit. sl.*), pietistic, pious, priggish, sanctimonious, self-satisfied, smug, superi~or, too good to be true

self-sacrifice altruism, generosity, self-abnegation, self-denial, selflessness

self-satisfaction complacency, content~ment, ease of mind, flush of success, glow of achievement, pride, self-approbation, self-approval, smugness

self-satisfied complacent, flushed with

success, like a cat that has swallowed the cream *or* the canary, pleased with oneself, proud of oneself, puffed up, self-congratulatory, smug, well-pleased

self-seeking *adj.* acquisitive, calculating, careerist, fortune-hunting, gold-digging, looking out for number one (*Inf.*), merce~nary, on the make (*Sl.*), opportunistic, out for what one can get, self-interested, selfish, self-serving

self-willed cussed (*Inf.*), headstrong, in~tractable, obstinate, opinionated, pig-headed, refractory, stiff-necked, stubborn, stubborn as a mule, ungovernable, wilful

sell 1. barter, dispose of, exchange, put up for sale, trade **2.** be in the business of, deal in, handle, hawk, market, merchandise, peddle, retail, stock, trade in, traffic in, vend **3.** gain acceptance for, promote, put across ∧. *Inf. With* **on** convert to, convince of, get (someone) hooked on, persuade of, talk (someone) into, win (someone) over to **5.** betray, deliver up, give up, sell down the river (*Inf.*), sell out (*Inf.*), surrender
Antonyms (*senses 1 & 2*) acquire, get, invest in, obtain, pay for, procure, purchase, shop for

seller agent, dealer, merchant, purveyor, rep, representative, retailer, salesman, saleswoman, shopkeeper, supplier, trades~man, traveller, vendor

selling 1. business, commercial transac~tions, dealing, trading, traffic **2.** marketing, merchandising, promotion, salesmanship

sell out 1. be out of stock of, dispose of, get rid of, run out of, sell up **2.** *Inf.* betray, break faith with, double-cross (*Inf.*), fail, give away, play false, rat on (*Inf.*), sell down the river (*Inf.*), stab in the back

semblance air, appearance, aspect, bear~ing, façade, figure, form, front, guise, image, likeness, mask, mien, pretence, resem~blance, show, similarity, veneer

semidarkness dusk, gloaming (*Scot. or poetic*), gloom, half-light, murk, twilight, waning light

send 1. communicate, consign, convey, di~rect, dispatch, forward, remit, transmit **2.** cast, deliver, fire, fling, hurl, let fly, propel, shoot **3.** *With* **off, out,** *etc.* broadcast, dis~charge, emit, exude, give off, radiate **4.** *Sl.* charm, delight, electrify, enrapture, en~thrall, excite, intoxicate, move, please, rav~ish, stir, thrill, titillate, turn (someone) on (*Sl.*) **5. send (someone) packing** dis~charge, dismiss, give (someone) the bird (*Inf.*), give (someone) the brushoff (*Sl.*), send away, send (someone) about his *or* her business, send (someone) away with a flea in his *or* her ear (*Inf.*)

send for call for, demand, order, request, summon

sendoff departure, farewell, going-away party, leave-taking, start, valediction

send-up imitation, mickey-take (*Inf.*), mockery, parody, satire, skit, spoof (*Inf.*), take-off (*Inf.*)

send up burlesque, imitate, lampoon, make fun of, mimic, mock, parody, satirize, spoof (*Inf.*), take off (*Inf.*), take the mickey out of (*Inf.*), take the piss out of (*Taboo sl.*)

senile decrepit, doddering, doting, failing, imbecile, in one's dotage, in one's second childhood

senior *adj.* elder, higher ranking, major (*Brit.*), older, superior
Antonyms inferior, junior, lesser, lower, minor, subordinate, younger

seniority eldership, longer service, precedence, priority, rank, superiority

sensation 1. awareness, consciousness, feeling, impression, perception, sense, tingle 2. agitation, commotion, crowd puller (*Inf.*), excitement, furore, hit (*Inf.*), scandal, stir, surprise, thrill, vibes (*Sl.*), wow (*Sl., chiefly U.S.*)

sensational 1. amazing, astounding, breathtaking, dramatic, electrifying, exciting, hair-raising, horrifying, lurid, melodramatic, revealing, scandalous, sensationalistic, shock-horror (*Facetious*), shocking, spectacular, staggering, startling, thrilling, yellow (*of the press*) 2. *Inf.* boffo (*Sl.*), brill (*Inf.*), brilliant, chillin' (*U.S. sl.*), cracking (*Brit. inf.*), crucial (*Sl.*), def (*Sl.*), excellent, exceptional, fabulous (*Inf.*), first class, impressive, jim-dandy (*Sl.*), marvellous, mean (*Sl.*), mega (*Sl.*), mind-blowing (*Inf.*), out of this world (*Inf.*), smashing (*Inf.*), sovereign, superb, topping (*Brit. sl.*)
Antonyms boring, commonplace, dull, humdrum, in good taste, mediocre, ordinary, prosaic, run-of-the-mill, understated, undramatic, unexaggerated, unexciting

sense *n.* 1. faculty, feeling, sensation, sensibility 2. appreciation, atmosphere, aura, awareness, consciousness, feel, impression, intuition, perception, premonition, presentiment, sentiment 3. definition, denotation, drift, gist, implication, import, interpretation, meaning, message, nuance, purport, significance, signification, substance 4. *Sometimes plural* brains (*Inf.*), clear-headedness, cleverness, common sense, discernment, discrimination, gumption (*Brit. inf.*), intelligence, judgment, mother wit, nous (*Brit. sl.*), quickness, reason, sagacity, sanity, sharpness, smarts (*Sl., chiefly U.S.*), tact, understanding, wisdom, wit(s) 5. advantage, good. logic, point, purpose, reason, use, value, worth ~*v.* 6. appreciate, apprehend, be aware of, discern, divine, feel, get the impression, grasp, have a feeling in

one's bones (*Inf.*), have a funny feeling (*Inf.*), have a hunch, just know, notice, observe, perceive, pick up, realize, suspect, understand
Antonyms *n.* (*sense 4*) bêtise (*Rare*), folly, foolishness, idiocy, nonsense, silliness, stupidity ~*v.* be unaware of, fail to grasp *or* notice, miss, misunderstand, overlook

senseless 1. absurd, asinine, crazy, daft (*Inf.*), fatuous, foolish, goofy (*Inf.*), half-witted, idiotic, illogical, imbecilic, inane, incongruous, inconsistent, irrational, ludicrous, mad, meaningless, mindless, moronic, nonsensical, pointless, ridiculous, silly, simple, stupid, unintelligent, unreasonable, unwise 2. anaesthetized, cold, deadened, insensate, insensible, numb, numbed, out, out cold, stunned, unconscious, unfeeling
Antonyms conscious, intelligent, meaningful, rational, reasonable, sensible, sensitive, useful, valid, wise, worthwhile

sensibility 1. responsiveness, sensitiveness, sensitivity, susceptibility 2. *Often plural* emotions, feelings, moral sense, sentiments, susceptibilities 3. appreciation, awareness, delicacy, discernment, insight, intuition, perceptiveness, taste
Antonyms deadness, insensibility, insensitivity, lack of awareness, numbness, unconsciousness, unperceptiveness, unresponsiveness

sensible 1. canny, discreet, discriminating, down-to-earth, far-sighted, intelligent, judicious, matter-of-fact, practical, prudent, rational, realistic, reasonable, sagacious, sage, sane, shrewd, sober, sound, well-reasoned, well-thought-out, wise 2. *Usually with* **of** acquainted with, alive to, aware, conscious, convinced, mindful, observant, sensitive to, understanding 3. appreciable, considerable, discernable, noticeable, palpable, perceptible, significant, tangible, visible
Antonyms (*senses 1 & 2*) blind, daft (*Inf.*), foolish, idiotic, ignorant, injudicious, insensible, insensitive, irrational, senseless, silly, stupid, unaware, unmindful, unreasonable, unwise

sensitive 1. acute, delicate, easily affected, fine, impressionable, keen, perceptive, precise, reactive, responsive, sentient, susceptible 2. delicate, easily upset (hurt, offended), irritable, temperamental, tender, thin-skinned, touchy, umbrageous (*Rare*)
Antonyms approximate, callous, hard, hardened, imprecise, inexact, insensitive, obtuse, thick-skinned, tough, uncaring, unfeeling, unperceptive

sensitivity delicacy, reactiveness, reactivity, receptiveness, responsiveness, sensitiveness, susceptibility

sensual 1. animal, bodily, carnal, epicu-

rean, fleshly, luxurious, physical, unspiri~
tual, voluptuous **2.** erotic, lascivious, lech~
erous, lewd, libidinous, licentious, lustful,
randy (*Inf., chiefly Brit.*), raunchy (*Sl.*), sex~
ual, sexy (*Inf.*), steamy (*Inf.*), unchaste

sensuality animalism, carnality, eroticism,
lasciviousness, lecherousness, lewdness, li~
bidinousness, licentiousness, prurience, sa~
laciousness, sexiness (*Inf.*), voluptuousness

sensuous epicurean, gratifying, hedonistic,
lush, pleasurable, rich, sensory, sumptuous,
sybaritic
Antonyms abstemious, ascetic, celibate,
plain, self-denying, Spartan

sentence 1. *n.* condemnation, decision, de~
cree, doom, judgment, order, pronounce~
ment, ruling, verdict **2.** *v.* condemn, doom,
mete out justice to, pass judgment on, pe~
nalize

sententious 1. aphoristic, axiomatic, brief,
compact, concise, epigrammatic, gnomic,
laconic, pithy, pointed, short, succinct, terse
2. canting, judgmental, moralistic, pomp~
ous, ponderous, preachifying (*Inf.*), sancti~
monious

sentiment 1. emotion, sensibility, softheartedness, tender feeling, tenderness **2.**
Often plural attitude, belief, feeling, idea,
judgment, opinion, persuasion, saying,
thought, view, way of thinking **3.** emotion~
alism, mawkishness, overemotionalism, ro~
manticism, sentimentality, slush (*Inf.*)

sentimental corny (*Sl.*), dewy-eyed, drippy
(*Inf.*), emotional, gushy (*Inf.*), impression~
able, maudlin, mawkish, mushy (*Inf.*), nos~
talgic, overemotional, pathetic, romantic,
schmaltzy (*Sl.*), simpering, sloppy (*Inf.*),
slushy (*Inf.*), soft-hearted, tearful, tear-
jerking (*Inf.*), tender, touching, weepy (*Inf.*)
Antonyms commonsensical, dispassionate,
down-to-earth, earthy, hard-headed, practical,
realistic, undemonstrative, unemotional, un~
feeling, unromantic, unsentimental

sentimentality bathos, corniness (*Sl.*),
emotionalism, gush (*Inf.*), mawkishness,
mush (*Inf.*), nostalgia, play on the emotions,
romanticism, schmaltz (*Sl.*), sloppiness
(*Inf.*), slush (*Inf.*), sob stuff (*Inf.*), tenderness

sentinel *or* **sentry** guard, lookout, picket,
watch, watchman

separable detachable, distinguishable, di~
visible, scissile, severable

separate *v.* **1.** break off, cleave, come apart,
come away, come between, detach, discon~
nect, disentangle, disjoin, divide, keep
apart, remove, sever, split, sunder, uncou~
ple **2.** discriminate between, isolate, put on
one side, segregate, single out, sort out **3.**
bifurcate, break up, disunite, diverge, di~
vorce, estrange, go different ways, part,
part company, set at variance *or* at odds,

split up ~*adj.* **4.** detached, disconnected,
discrete, disjointed, divided, divorced, iso~
lated, unattached, unconnected **5.** alone,
apart, autonomous, distinct, independent,
individual, particular, single, solitary
Antonyms *v.* amalgamate, combine, con~
nect, join, link, merge, mix, unite ~*adj.*
affiliated, alike, connected, interdependent,
joined, similar, unified, united

separated apart, broken up, disassociated,
disconnected, disunited, divided, living
apart, parted, put asunder, separate, split
up, sundered

separately alone, apart, independently, in~
dividually, one at a time, one by one, per~
sonally, severally, singly
Antonyms as a group, as one, collectively, in
a body, in concert, in unison, jointly, together

separation 1. break, detachment, discon~
nection, disengagement, disjunction, disso~
ciation, disunion, division, gap, segregation,
severance **2.** break-up, divorce, estrange~
ment, farewell, leave-taking, parting, rift,
split, split-up

septic festering, infected, poisoned, pussy,
putrefactive, putrefying, putrid, suppurat~
ing, toxic

sepulchre burial place, grave, mausoleum,
sarcophagus, tomb, vault

sequel conclusion, consequence, continu~
ation, development, end, follow-up, issue,
outcome, payoff (*Inf.*), result, upshot

sequence arrangement, chain, course, cy~
cle, order, procession, progression, series,
succession

sequestered cloistered, isolated, lonely,
out-of-the-way, private, quiet, remote, re~
tired, secluded, unfrequented

seraphic angelic, beatific, blissful, celestial,
divine, heavenly, holy, pure, sublime

serene 1. calm, composed, imperturbable,
peaceful, placid, sedate, tranquil, undis~
turbed, unruffled, untroubled **2.** bright,
clear, cloudless, fair, halcyon, unclouded
Antonyms (*sense 1*) agitated, anxious, dis~
turbed, excitable, flustered, perturbed, trou~
bled, uptight (*Inf.*)

serenity 1. calm, calmness, composure,
peace, peacefulness, peace of mind, placid~
ity, quietness, quietude, stillness, tranquil~
lity **2.** brightness, clearness, fairness

series arrangement, chain, course, line, or~
der, progression, run, sequence, set, string,
succession, train

serious 1. grave, humourless, long-faced,
pensive, sedate, sober, solemn, stern,
thoughtful, unsmiling **2.** deliberate, deter~
mined, earnest, genuine, honest, in earnest,
resolute, resolved, sincere **3.** crucial, deep,
difficult, far-reaching, fateful, grim, impor~

tant, momentous, no laughing matter, of moment *or* consequence, pressing, sig~ nificant, urgent, weighty, worrying **4.** acute, alarming, critical, dangerous, grave, severe

Antonyms capricious, carefree, flighty, flippant, frivolous, insignificant, insincere, jolly, joyful, light-hearted, minor, slight, smiling, trivial, uncommitted, undecided, unimportant

seriously 1. all joking aside, earnestly, gravely, in all conscience, in earnest, no joking (*Inf.*), sincerely, solemnly, thought~ fully, with a straight face **2.** acutely, badly, critically, · dangerously, distressingly, gravely, grievously, severely, sorely

seriousness 1. earnestness, gravitas, gravity, humourlessness, sedateness, sobri~ ety, solemnity, staidness, sternness **2.** dan~ ger, gravity, importance, moment, sig~ nificance, urgency, weight

sermon 1. address, exhortation, homily **2.** dressing-down (*Inf.*), harangue, lecture, talking-to (*Inf.*)

servant attendant, domestic, drudge, help, helper, lackey, liegeman, maid, menial, re~ tainer, servitor (*Archaic*), skivvy (*Chiefly Brit.*), slave, varlet (*Archaic*), vassal

serve 1. aid, assist, attend to, be in the ser~ vice of, be of assistance, be of use, help, minister to, oblige, succour, wait on, work for **2.** act, attend, complete, discharge, do, fulfil, go through, observe, officiate, pass, perform **3.** answer, answer the purpose, be acceptable, be adequate, be good enough, content, do, do duty as, do the work of, fill the bill (*Inf.*), function as, satisfy, suffice, suit **4.** arrange, deal, deliver, dish up, dis~ tribute, handle, present, provide, purvey, set out, supply

service *n.* **1.** advantage, assistance, avail, benefit, help, ministrations, supply, use, usefulness, utility **2.** check, maintenance, overhaul, servicing **3.** business, duty, em~ ploy, employment, labour, office, work **4.** ceremony, function, observance, rite, wor~ ship ~*v.* **5.** check, fine tune, go over, main~ tain, overhaul, recondition, repair, tune (up)

serviceable advantageous, beneficial, con~ venient, dependable, durable, efficient, functional, hard-wearing, helpful, operative, practical, profitable, usable, useful, utili~ tarian

Antonyms impractical, inefficient, unser~ viceable, unusable, useless, worn-out

serving *n.* helping, plateful, portion

servitude bondage, bonds, chains, enslave~ ment, obedience, serfdom, slavery, subjuga~ tion, thraldom, thrall, vassalage

session assembly, conference, congress,

discussion, get-together (*Inf.*), hearing, meeting, period, seminar, sitting, term

set¹ *v.* **1.** aim, apply, deposit, direct, embed, fasten, fix, install, lay, locate, lodge, mount, park (*Inf.*), place, plant, plonk, plump, posi~ tion, put, rest, seat, situate, station, stick, turn **2.** agree upon, allocate, appoint, ar~ range, assign, conclude, decide (upon), des~ ignate, determine, establish, fix, fix up, name, ordain, regulate, resolve, schedule, settle, specify **3.** arrange, lay, make ready, prepare, spread **4.** adjust, coordinate, recti~ fy, regulate, synchronize **5.** cake, condense, congeal, crystallize, gelatinize, harden, jell, solidify, stiffen, thicken **6.** allot, decree, impose, lay down, ordain, prescribe, specify **7.** decline, dip, disappear, go down, sink, subside, vanish ~*n.* **8.** attitude, bearing, carriage, fit, hang, position, posture, turn **9.** *mise-en-scène*, scene, scenery, setting, stage set, stage setting ~*adj.* **10.** agreed, appoint~ ed, arranged, customary, decided, definite, established, firm, fixed, prearranged, prede~ termined, prescribed, regular, scheduled, settled, usual **11.** artificial, conventional, formal, hackneyed, rehearsed, routine, standard, stereotyped, stock, traditional, unspontaneous **12.** entrenched, firm, hard and fast, hardened, hidebound, immovable, inflexible, rigid, strict, stubborn **13.** *With* **on** *or* **upon** bent, determined, intent, reso~ lute

Antonyms (*sense 12*) flexible, free, open, open-minded, undecided

set² *n.* **1.** band, circle, class, clique, compa~ ny, coterie, crew (*Inf.*), crowd, faction, gang, group, outfit, posse (*Inf.*), schism, sect **2.** assemblage, assortment, batch, collection, compendium, coordinated group, kit, outfit, series

set about 1. address oneself to, attack, be~ gin, get cracking (*Inf.*), get down to, get to work, get weaving (*Inf.*), make a start on, put one's shoulder to the wheel (*Inf.*), roll up one's sleeves, sail into (*Inf.*), set to, start, tackle, take the first step, wade into (*Inf.*) **2.** as~ sail, assault, attack, belabour, lambast(e), mug (*Inf.*), sail into (*Inf.*)

set aside 1. keep, keep back, put on one side, reserve, save, select, separate, set apart, single out **2.** abrogate, annul, cancel, discard, dismiss, nullify, overrule, overturn, quash, reject, render null and void, repudi~ ate, reverse

setback bit of trouble, blow, bummer (*Sl.*), check, defeat, disappointment, hitch, hold- up, misfortune, rebuff, reverse, upset

set back delay, hinder, hold up, impede, retard, slow

set off 1. depart, embark, leave, sally forth, set out, start out **2.** detonate, explode, ig~

nite, kick-start, light, set in motion, touch off, trigger (off) **3.** bring out the highlights in, enhance, show off, throw into relief

set on assail, assault, attack, fall upon, fly at, go for, incite, instigate, let fly at, pitch into (*Inf.*), pounce on, sail into (*Inf.*), set about, sic, spur on, urge

set out 1. arrange, array, describe, detail, display, dispose, elaborate, elucidate, exhibit, explain, expose to view, lay out, present, set forth **2.** begin, embark, get under way, hit the road (*Sl.*), sally forth, set off, start out, take to the road

setting backdrop, background, context, frame, locale, location, *mise en scène*, mounting, perspective, scene, scenery, set, site, surround, surroundings

settle 1. adjust, dispose, order, put into order, regulate, set to rights, straighten out, work out **2.** choose, clear up, complete, conclude, decide, dispose of, put an end to, reconcile, resolve **3.** *Often with* **on** *or* **upon** agree, appoint, arrange, choose, come to an agreement, confirm, decide, determine, establish, fix **4.** allay, calm, compose, lull, pacify, quell, quiet, quieten, reassure, relax, relieve, sedate, soothe, tranquillize **5.** alight, bed down, come to rest, descend, land, light, make oneself comfortable **6.** dwell, inhabit, live, make one's home, move to, put down roots, reside, set up home, take up residence **7.** colonize, found, people, pioneer, plant, populate **8.** acquit oneself of, clear, discharge, liquidate, pay, quit, square (up) **9.** decline, fall, sink, subside
Antonyms (*sense 4*) agitate, bother, discompose, disquieten, disturb, rattle, trouble, unsettle, upset

settlement 1. adjustment, agreement, arrangement, completion, conclusion, confirmation, disposition, establishment, resolution, termination, working out **2.** clearance, clearing, defrayal, discharge, liquidation, payment, satisfaction **3.** colonization, colony, community, encampment, hamlet, outpost, peopling

settler colonist, colonizer, frontiersman, immigrant, pioneer, planter

set-to argument, argy-bargy (*Brit. inf.*), barney (*Inf.*), brush, disagreement, dust-up (*Inf.*), fight, fracas, quarrel, row, scrap (*Inf.*), slanging match (*Brit.*), spat, squabble, wrangle

setup arrangement, circumstances, conditions, organization, regime, structure, system

set up 1. arrange, begin, compose, establish, found, initiate, install, institute, make provision for, organize, prearrange, prepare **2.** back, build up, establish, finance, promote, put some beef into (*Inf.*), strengthen,

subsidize **3.** assemble, build, construct, elevate, erect, put together, put up, raise

set upon ambush, assail, assault, attack, beat up, fall upon, go for, lay into (*Inf.*), mug (*Inf.*), put the boot in (*Sl.*), set about, turn on

sever 1. bisect, cleave, cut, cut in two, detach, disconnect, disjoin, disunite, divide, part, rend, separate, split, sunder **2.** abandon, break off, dissociate, dissolve, put an end to, terminate
Antonyms attach, connect, continue, fix together, join, link, maintain, unite, uphold

several *adj.* assorted, different, disparate, distinct, divers (*Archaic*), diverse, indefinite, individual, manifold, many, particular, respective, single, some, sundry, various

severe 1. austere, cruel, Draconian, drastic, hard, harsh, inexorable, iron-handed, oppressive, pitiless, relentless, rigid, strict, unbending, unrelenting **2.** cold, disapproving, dour, flinty, forbidding, grave, grim, serious, sober, stern, strait-laced, tight-lipped, unsmiling **3.** acute, bitter, critical, dangerous, distressing, extreme, fierce, grinding, inclement, intense, violent **4.** ascetic, austere, chaste, classic, forbidding, functional, plain, restrained, severe, simple, Spartan, unadorned, unembellished, unfussy **5.** arduous, demanding, difficult, exacting, fierce, hard, punishing, rigorous, stringent, taxing, tough, unrelenting **6.** astringent, biting, caustic, cutting, harsh, mordacious, mordant, satirical, scathing, unsparing, vitriolic
Antonyms (*senses 1, 2, 3, 5 & 6*) affable, clement, compassionate, easy, genial, gentle, kind, lax, lenient, manageable, mild, minor, moderate, relaxed, temperate, tractable (*sense 4*) embellished, fancy, ornamental, ornate

severely 1. harshly, rigorously, sharply, sternly, strictly, with an iron hand, with a rod of iron **2.** acutely, badly, critically, dangerously, extremely, gravely, hard, sorely

severity austerity, gravity, hardness, harshness, plainness, rigour, seriousness, severeness, sternness, strictness, stringency, toughness

sex 1. gender **2.** *Inf.* coition, coitus, copulation, fornication, going to bed (with someone), intimacy, lovemaking, nookie (*Sl.*), rumpy-pumpy (*Sl.*), (sexual) intercourse, sexual relations, the other (*Inf.*) **3.** desire, facts of life, libido, reproduction, sexuality, the birds and the bees (*Inf.*)

sexual 1. carnal, coital, erotic, intimate, of the flesh, sensual, sexy **2.** genital, procreative, reproductive, sex, venereal

sexual intercourse bonking (*Inf.*), carnal

knowledge, coition, coitus, commerce (*Ar~chaic*), congress, consummation, copulation, coupling, fucking (*Taboo*), mating, nookie (*Sl.*), penetration, rumpy-pumpy (*Sl.*), screwing (*Taboo*), shagging (*Taboo*), the other (*Inf.*), union

sexuality bodily appetites, carnality, desire, eroticism, lust, sensuality, sexiness (*Inf.*), virility, voluptuousness

sexy arousing, beddable, bedroom, come-hither (*Inf.*), cuddly, erotic, flirtatious, in~viting, kissable, naughty, provocative, pro~voking, seductive, sensual, sensuous, slinky, suggestive, titillating, voluptuous

shabby 1. dilapidated, down at heel, faded, frayed, having seen better days, mean, ne~glected, poor, ragged, run-down, scruffy, seedy, tattered, tatty, the worse for wear, threadbare, worn, worn-out **2.** cheap, con~temptible, despicable, dirty, dishonourable, ignoble, low, low-down (*Inf.*), mean, rotten (*Inf.*), scurvy, shameful, shoddy, ungentle~manly, unworthy
Antonyms fair, generous, handsome, hon~ourable, in mint condition, neat, new, praise~worthy, smart, well-dressed, well-kept, well-kept, well-to-do, worthy

shack cabin, dump (*Inf.*), hovel, hut, lean-to, shanty, shiel (*Scot.*), shieling (*Scot.*)

shackle *n.* **1.** *Often plural* bond, chain, fet~ter, gyve (*Archaic*), handcuff, hobble, iron, leg-iron, manacle, rope, tether ~*v.* **2.** bind, chain, fetter, handcuff, hobble, manacle, pinion, put in irons, secure, tether, tie, trammel **3.** constrain, embarrass, encum~ber, hamper, hamstring, impede, inhibit, limit, obstruct, restrain, restrict, tie (someone's) hands

shade *n.* **1.** coolness, dimness, dusk, gloom, gloominess, obscurity, screen, semidark~ness, shadiness, shadow, shadows **2. put into the shade** eclipse, make pale by com~parison, outclass, outshine, overshadow **3.** blind, canopy, cover, covering, curtain, screen, shield, veil **4.** colour, hue, stain, tinge, tint, tone **5.** amount, dash, degree, difference, gradation, hint, nuance, sem~blance, suggestion, suspicion, trace, variety **6.** apparition, eidolon, ghost, manes, phan~tom, shadow, spectre, spirit ~*v.* **7.** cast a shadow over, cloud, conceal, cover, darken, dim, hide, mute, obscure, protect, screen, shadow, shield, shut out the light, veil

shadow *n.* **1.** cover, darkness, dimness, dusk, gathering darkness, gloaming (*Scot. or poetic*), gloom, obscurity, protection, shade, shelter **2.** hint, suggestion, suspi~cion, trace **3.** eidolon, ghost, image, phan~tom, remnant, representation, spectre, ves~tige **4.** blight, cloud, gloom, sadness ~*v.* **5.** cast a shadow over, darken, overhang,

screen, shade, shield **6.** dog, follow, spy on, stalk, tail (*Inf.*), trail

shadowy 1. crepuscular, dark, dim, dusky, funereal, gloomy, indistinct, murky, ob~scure, shaded, shady, tenebrious, tenebrous **2.** dim, dreamlike, faint, ghostly, illusory, imaginary, impalpable, intangible, nebu~lous, obscure, phantom, spectral, undefined, unreal, unsubstantial, vague, wraithlike

shady 1. bosky (*Literary*), bowery, cool, dim, leafy, shaded, shadowy, umbrageous **2.** *Inf.* crooked, disreputable, dodgy (*Brit., Aust., & N.Z. inf.*), dubious, fishy (*Inf.*), questionable, shifty, slippery, suspect, sus~picious, unethical, unscrupulous, untrust~worthy
Antonyms (*sense 1*) bright, exposed, open, out in the open, sunlit, sunny, unshaded (*sense 2*) above-board, ethical, honest, honourable, reputable, respectable, straight, trustworthy, upright

shaft 1. handle, pole, rod, shank, stem, upright **2.** beam, gleam, ray, streak **3.** barb, cut, dart, gibe, sting, thrust

shaggy hairy, hirsute, long-haired, rough, tousled, unkempt, unshorn
Antonyms close-cropped, crew-cut, cropped, flat-woven, neatly-trimmed, shorn, short-haired, short-piled, smooth

shake *v.* **1.** bump, fluctuate, jar, joggle, jolt, jounce, oscillate, quake, quiver, rock, shiv~er, shudder, sway, totter, tremble, vibrate, waver, wobble **2.** brandish, flourish, wave **3.** *Often with* **up** agitate, churn, convulse, rouse, stir **4.** discompose, distress, disturb, frighten, intimidate, move, rattle (*Inf.*), shock, unnerve, upset **5.** impair, pull the rug out from under (*Inf.*), undermine, weaken ~*n.* **6.** agitation, convulsion, dis~turbance, jar, jerk, jolt, jounce, pulsation, quaking, shiver, shock, shudder, trembling, tremor, vibration **7.** *Inf.* instant, jiffy (*Inf.*), moment, second, tick (*Brit. inf.*), trice

shake off dislodge, elude, get away from, get rid of, get shot of (*Sl.*), give the slip, leave behind, lose, rid oneself of, throw off

shake up agitate, churn (up), disturb, mix, overturn, reorganize, shock, stir (up), turn upside down, unsettle, upset

shaky 1. all of a quiver (*Inf.*), faltering, in~secure, precarious, quivery, rickety, totter~ing, trembling, tremulous, unstable, un~steady, weak, wobbly **2.** dubious, iffy (*Inf.*), questionable, suspect, uncertain, undepend~able, unreliable, unsound, unsupported
Antonyms dependable, firm, secure, stable, steady, strong

shallow 1. *adj. Fig.* empty, flimsy, foolish, frivolous, idle, ignorant, meaningless, puer~ile, simple, skin-deep, slight, superficial, surface, trivial, unintelligent **2.** *n. Often* *plural* bank, flat, sandbank, sand bar, shelf, shoal

Antonyms *adj.* analytical, comprehensive, deep, in-depth, meaningful, penetrating, perceptive, profound, searching, serious, thoughtful, weighty ~*n.* abyss, chasm, deep, depth, gorge, gulf, pit, void

sham 1. *n.* counterfeit, feint, forgery, fraud, hoax, humbug, imitation, impostor, imposture, phoney *or* phony (*Inf.*), pretence, pretender, pseud (*Inf.*), wolf in sheep's clothing **2.** *adj.* artificial, bogus, counterfeit, ersatz, false, feigned, imitation, mock, phoney *or* phony (*Inf.*), pretended, pseud (*Inf.*), pseudo (*Inf.*), simulated, spurious, synthetic **3.** *v.* affect, assume, counterfeit, fake, feign, imitate, play possum, pretend, put on, simulate

Antonyms *n.* master, original, the genuine article, the real McCoy (*or* McKay), the real thing ~*adj.* authentic, bona fide, genuine, legitimate, natural, real, sound, true, unfeigned, veritable

shambles anarchy, chaos, confusion, disarray, disorder, disorganization, havoc, madhouse, mess, muddle

shame *n.* **1.** blot, contempt, degradation, derision, discredit, disgrace, dishonour, disrepute, ill repute, infamy, obloquy, odium, opprobrium, reproach, scandal, skeleton in the cupboard, smear **2.** abashment, chagrin, compunction, embarrassment, humiliation, ignominy, loss of face, mortification, shamefacedness **3. put to shame** disgrace, eclipse, outclass, outdo, outstrip, show up, surpass ~*v.* **4.** abash, confound, disconcert, disgrace, embarrass, humble, humiliate, mortify, reproach, ridicule, take (someone) down a peg (*Inf.*) **5.** blot, debase, defile, degrade, discredit, dishonour, smear, stain

Antonyms *n.* (*sense 1*) credit, distinction, esteem, glory, honour, pride, renown, self-respect (*sense 2*) brass neck (*Brit. inf.*), brazenness, cheek, shamelessness, unabashedness ~*v.* acclaim, credit, do credit to, enhance the reputation of, honour, make proud

shameful 1. atrocious, base, dastardly, degrading, disgraceful, dishonourable, ignominious, indecent, infamous, low, mean, outrageous, reprehensible, scandalous, unbecoming, unworthy, vile, wicked **2.** blush-making (*Inf.*), cringe-making (*Brit. inf.*), degrading, embarrassing, humiliating, mortifying, shaming

Antonyms admirable, creditable, estimable, exemplary, honourable, laudable, right, worthy

shameless abandoned, audacious, barefaced, brash, brazen, corrupt, depraved, dissolute, flagrant, hardened, immodest, improper, impudent, incorrigible, indecent,

insolent, profligate, reprobate, unabashed, unashamed, unblushing, unprincipled, wanton

shanty bothy (*Scot.*), cabin, hovel, hut, lean-to, shack, shed, shiel (*Scot.*), shieling (*Scot.*)

shape *n.* **1.** build, configuration, contours, cut, figure, form, lines, make, outline, profile, silhouette **2.** frame, model, mould, pattern **3.** appearance, aspect, form, guise, likeness, semblance **4.** condition, fettle, health, kilter, state, trim ~*v.* **5.** create, fashion, form, make, model, mould, produce **6.** accommodate, adapt, convert, define, develop, devise, frame, guide, modify, plan, prepare, regulate, remodel

shapeless amorphous, asymmetrical, battered, embryonic, formless, indeterminate, irregular, misshapen, nebulous, undeveloped, unstructured

Antonyms comely, curvaceous, elegant, graceful, neat, trim, well-formed, well-proportioned, well-turned

share 1. *v.* apportion, assign, distribute, divide, go Dutch (*Inf.*), go fifty-fifty (*Inf.*), go halves, parcel out, partake, participate, receive, split, use in common **2.** *n.* allotment, allowance, contribution, cut (*Inf.*), division, due, lot, part, portion, proportion, quota, ration, whack (*Inf.*)

sharp *adj.* **1.** acute, cutting, honed, jagged, keen, knife-edged, knifelike, pointed, razor-sharp, serrated, sharpened, spiky **2.** abrupt, distinct, extreme, marked, sudden **3.** alert, apt, astute, bright, clever, discerning, knowing, long-headed, observant, penetrating, perceptive, quick, quick-witted, ready, subtle **4.** artful, crafty, cunning, dishonest, fly (*Sl.*), shrewd, sly, smart, unscrupulous, wily **5.** acute, distressing, excruciating, fierce, intense, painful, piercing, severe, shooting, sore, stabbing, stinging, violent **6.** clear, clear-cut, crisp, distinct, well-defined **7.** *Inf.* chic, classy (*Sl.*), dressy, fashionable, natty (*Inf.*), smart, snappy, stylish, trendy (*Inf.*) **8.** acerb, acrimonious, barbed, biting, bitter, caustic, cutting, harsh, hurtful, mordacious, mordant, sarcastic, sardonic, scathing, severe, trenchant, vitriolic **9.** acerb, acerbic, acetic, acid, acrid, burning, hot, piquant, pungent, sour, tart, vinegary ~*adv.* **10.** exactly, on the dot, on time, precisely, promptly, punctually **11.** abruptly, suddenly, unexpectedly, without warning

Antonyms *adj.* (*sense 1*) blunt, dull, edgeless, pointed, rounded, unsharpened (*sense 2*) even, gentle, gradual, moderate, progressive (*sense 3*) dim, dull-witted, dumb (*Inf.*), slow, slow-on-the-uptake, stupid (*sense 4*) artless, guileless, ingenuous, innocent, naive, simple, undesigning (*sense 6*) blurred, fuzzy, ill-defined,

indistinct, unclear (*sense 8*) amicable, cour~
teous, friendly, gentle, kindly, mild (*sense 9*)
bland, mild, tasteless ~*adv.* (*sense 10*) ap~
proximately, more or less, roughly, round
about, vaguely (*sense 11*) bit by bit, gently,
gradually, slowly

sharpen edge, grind, hone, put an edge on,
strop, whet

shatter **1.** break, burst, crack, crush, crush
to smithereens, demolish, explode, implode,
pulverize, shiver, smash, split **2.** blast,
blight, bring to nought, demolish, destroy,
disable, exhaust, impair, overturn, ruin,
torpedo, wreck **3.** break (someone's) heart,
crush, devastate, dumbfound, knock the
stuffing out of (someone) (*Inf.*), upset

shattered all in (*Sl.*), clapped out (*Aust. &
N.Z. inf.*), crushed, dead beat (*Inf.*), dead
tired (*Inf.*), devastated, dog-tired (*Inf.*), done
in (*Inf.*), drained, exhausted, jiggered (*Inf.*),
knackered (*Sl.*), ready to drop, spent, tired
out, weary, worn out, zonked (*Sl.*)

shave *v.* **1.** crop, pare, plane, shear, trim **2.**
brush, graze, touch

shed *v.* **1.** afford, cast, diffuse, drop, emit,
give, give forth, pour forth, radiate, scatter,
shower, spill, throw **2.** cast off, discard,
exuviate, moult, slough

sheepish abashed, ashamed, chagrined,
embarrassed, foolish, mortified, self-
conscious, shamefaced, silly, uncomfortable
Antonyms assertive, audacious, bold, brash,
brass-necked (*Brit. inf.*), brazen, confident,
intractable, obdurate, unabashed, unapolo~
getic, unblushing, unembarrassed

sheer **1.** abrupt, headlong (*Archaic*), per~
pendicular, precipitous, steep **2.** absolute,
arrant, complete, downright, out-and-out,
pure, rank, thoroughgoing, total, unadul~
terated, unalloyed, unmitigated, un~
qualified, utter **3.** *Of fabrics* diaphanous,
fine, gauzy, gossamer, seethrough, thin,
transparent
Antonyms (*sense 1*) gentle, gradual, hori~
zontal, moderate, slanting, sloping (*sense 3*)
coarse, heavy, impenetrable, opaque, thick

sheet **1.** coat, film, folio, lamina, layer, leaf,
membrane, overlay, pane, panel, piece,
plate, slab, stratum, surface, veneer **2.** area,
blanket, covering, expanse, stretch, sweep

shell *n.* **1.** carapace, case, husk, pod ~*v.* **2.**
husk, shuck **3.** attack, barrage, blitz, bomb,
bombard, strafe, strike ~*n.* **4.** chassis,
frame, framework, hull, skeleton, structure

shelter **1.** *v.* cover, defend, guard, harbour,
hide, protect, safeguard, seek refuge, shield,
take in, take shelter **2.** *n.* asylum, cover,
covert, defence, guard, haven, protection,
refuge, retreat, roof over one's head, safety,
sanctuary, screen, security, shiel (*Scot.*),
umbrella

Antonyms *v.* endanger, expose, hazard, im~
peril, lay open, leave open, make vulnerable,
risk, subject

sheltered cloistered, conventual, ensconced,
hermitic, isolated, protected, quiet, reclu~
sive, retired, screened, secluded, shaded,
shielded, withdrawn
Antonyms exposed, laid bare, made public,
open, public, unconcealed, unprotected, un~
sheltered

shelve defer, dismiss, freeze, hold in abey~
ance, hold over, lay aside, mothball,
pigeonhole, postpone, put aside, put off, put
on ice, put on the back burner (*Inf.*), sus~
pend, table (*U.S.*), take a rain check on (*U.S.
& Canad. Inf.*)

shepherd *v.* conduct, convoy, guide, herd,
marshal, steer, usher

shield *n.* **1.** buckler, escutcheon (*Heraldry*),
targe (*Archaic*) **2.** aegis, bulwark, cover,
defence, guard, protection, rampart, safe~
guard, screen, shelter, ward (*Archaic*) ~*v.*
3. cover, defend, guard, protect, safeguard,
screen, shelter, ward off

shift *v.* **1.** alter, budge, change, displace,
fluctuate, move, move around, rearrange,
relocate, remove, reposition, swerve,
switch, transfer, transpose, vary, veer **2.** *As
in* **shift for oneself** assume responsibility,
contrive, devise, fend, get along, look after,
make do, manage, plan, scheme, take care
of ~*n.* **3.** about-turn, alteration, change,
displacement, fluctuation, modification,
move, permutation, rearrangement, remov~
al, shifting, switch, transfer, veering **4.**
artifice, contrivance, craft, device, dodge,
equivocation, evasion, expedient, move, re~
source, ruse, stratagem, subterfuge, trick,
wile

shifty contriving, crafty, deceitful, devious,
duplicitous, evasive, fly-by-night (*Inf.*), fur~
tive, scheming, slippery, sly, tricky, under~
hand, unprincipled, untrustworthy, wily
Antonyms dependable, guileless, honest,
honourable, open, reliable, trustworthy,
upright

shimmer **1.** *v.* dance, gleam, glisten, phos~
phoresce, scintillate, twinkle **2.** *n.* diffused
light, gleam, glimmer, glow, incandescence,
iridescence, lustre, phosphorescence, un~
steady light

shine *v.* **1.** beam, emit light, flash, give off
light, glare, gleam, glimmer, glisten, glitter,
glow, radiate, scintillate, shimmer, sparkle,
twinkle **2.** be conspicuous (distinguished,
outstanding, pre-eminent), excel, stand out,
stand out in a crowd, star **3.** brush, buff,
burnish, polish, rub up ~*n.* **4.** brightness,
glare, gleam, lambency, light, luminosity,
radiance, shimmer, sparkle **5.** glaze, gloss,
lustre, patina, polish, sheen

shining 1. beaming, bright, brilliant, efful~ gent, gleaming, glistening, glittering, lumi~ nous, radiant, resplendent, shimmering, sparkling **2.** *Fig.* brilliant, celebrated, con~ spicuous, distinguished, eminent, glorious, illustrious, leading, outstanding, splendid

shiny agleam, bright, burnished, gleaming, glistening, glossy, lustrous, nitid (*Poetic*), polished, satiny, sheeny

shirk avoid, bob off (*Brit. sl.*), body-swerve (*Scot.*), dodge, duck (out of) (*Inf.*), evade, get out of, scrimshank (*Brit. military sl.*), shun, sidestep, skive (*Brit. sl.*), slack

shirker clock-watcher, dodger, gold brick (*U.S. sl.*), idler, malingerer, quitter, scrimshanker (*Brit. military sl.*), shirk, skiver (*Brit. sl.*), slacker

shiver[1] *v.* **1.** palpitate, quake, quiver, shake, shudder, tremble ~*n.* **2.** flutter, *frisson*, quiver, shudder, thrill, tremble, trembling, tremor **3. the shivers** chattering teeth, chill, goose flesh, goose pimples, the shakes (*Inf.*)

shiver[2] *v.* break, crack, fragment, shatter, smash, smash to smithereens, splinter

shivery chilled, chilly, cold, quaking, quiv~ ery, shaking, shuddery, trembly

shoal sandbank, sand bar, shallow, shelf

shock *v.* **1.** agitate, appal, astound, disgust, disquiet, give (someone) a turn (*Inf.*), gross out (*U.S. sl.*), horrify, jar, jolt, nauseate, numb, offend, outrage, paralyse, revolt, scandalize, shake, shake out of one's com~ placency, shake up (*Inf.*), sicken, stagger, stun, stupefy, traumatize, unsettle ~*n.* **2.** blow, bolt from the blue, bombshell, break~ down, collapse, consternation, distress, dis~ turbance, prostration, state of shock, stu~ pefaction, stupor, trauma, turn (*Inf.*), upset **3.** blow, clash, collision, encounter, impact, jarring, jolt

shocking abominable, appalling, atrocious, detestable, disgraceful, disgusting, disquiet~ ing, distressing, dreadful, foul, frightful, ghastly, hellacious (*U.S. sl.*), hideous, hor~ rible, horrifying, loathsome, monstrous, nauseating, obscene, odious, offensive, out~ rageous, repulsive, revolting, scandalous, sickening, stupefying, unspeakable **Antonyms** admirable, decent, delightful, excellent, expected, fine, first-rate, gratifying, honourable, laudable, marvellous, pleasant, praiseworthy, satisfying, unsurprising, won~ derful

shoddy cheap-jack (*Inf.*), cheapo (*Inf.*), infe~ rior, junky (*Inf.*), poor, rubbishy, second- rate, slipshod, tacky (*Inf.*), tatty, tawdry, trashy **Antonyms** accurate, careful, considerate, craftsman-like, excellent, fastidious, fine,

first-rate, meticulous, noble, quality, superla~ tive, well-made

shoemaker bootmaker, cobbler, souter (*Scot.*)

shoot[1] *v.* **1.** bag, blast (*Sl.*), blow away (*Sl., chiefly U.S.*), bring down, hit, kill, open fire, pick off, plug (*Sl.*), pump full of lead (*Sl.*), zap (*Sl.*) **2.** discharge, emit, fire, fling, hurl, launch, let fly, project, propel **3.** barrel (along) (*Inf., chiefly U.S. & Canad.*), bolt, burn rubber (*Inf.*), charge, dart, dash, flash, fly, hurtle, race, rush, scoot, speed, spring, streak, tear, whisk, whiz (*Inf.*)

shoot[2] **1.** *n.* branch, bud, offshoot, scion, slip, sprig, sprout, twig **2.** *v.* bud, burgeon, germinate, put forth new growth, sprout

shop boutique, emporium, hypermarket, market, mart, store, supermarket

shore 1. *n.* beach, coast, foreshore, lakeside, sands, seaboard (*Chiefly U.S.*), seashore, strand (*Poetic*), waterside **2.** *adj.* littoral

short *adj.* **1.** abridged, brief, compendious, compressed, concise, curtailed, laconic, pithy, sententious, succinct, summary, terse **2.** diminutive, dumpy, fubsy (*Archaic or dialect*), little, low, petite, small, squat, wee **3.** brief, fleeting, momentary, short-lived, short-term **4.** *Often with* of deficient, inad~ equate, insufficient, lacking, limited, low (on), meagre, poor, scant, scanty, scarce, short-handed, slender, slim, sparse, tight, wanting **5.** abrupt, blunt, brusque, crusty, curt, discourteous, gruff, impolite, offhand, sharp, terse, testy, uncivil **6.** direct, straight **7.** *Of pastry* brittle, crisp, crumbly, friable ~*adv.* **8.** abruptly, by surprise, sud~ denly, unaware, without warning **9. cut short** abbreviate, arrest, butt in, curtail, cut in on, dock, halt, interrupt, reduce, stop, terminate **10. fall short** be inad~ equate, disappoint, fail, fall down on (*Inf.*), not come up to expectations *or* scratch (*Inf.*) **11. in short** briefly, in a nutshell, in a word, in essence, to come to the point, to cut a long story short, to put it briefly **12. short of a.** apart from, except, other than, unless **b.** deficient in, in need of, lacking, low (on), missing, wanting **Antonyms** *adj.* (*sense 1*) diffuse, lengthy, long, long-drawn-out, long-winded, prolonged, rambling, unabridged, verbose, wordy (*sense 2*) big, high, lanky, lofty, tall (*sense 3*) extended, long, long-term (*sense 4*) abundant, adequate, ample, bountiful, copious, inexhaustible, plentiful, sufficient, well-stocked (*sense 5*) civ~ il, courteous, polite ~*adv.* (*sense 8*) bit by bit, gently, gradually, little by little, slowly

shortage dearth, deficiency, deficit, failure, inadequacy, insufficiency, lack, leanness, paucity, poverty, scarcity, shortfall, want **Antonyms** abundance, adequate amount, excess, overabundance, plethora, profusion, sufficiency, surfeit, surplus

shortcoming defect, drawback, failing, fault, flaw, foible, frailty, imperfection, weakness, weak point

shorten abbreviate, abridge, curtail, cut, cut back, cut down, decrease, diminish, dock, lessen, prune, reduce, trim, truncate, turn up
Antonyms draw out, elongate, expand, extend, increase, lengthen, make longer, prolong, protract, spin out, stretch

short-sighted 1. myopic, near-sighted **2.** careless, ill-advised, ill-considered, impolitic, impractical, improvident, imprudent, injudicious, unthinking

short-staffed below strength, short-handed, undermanned, understaffed

short-tempered choleric, fiery, hot-tempered, impatient, irascible, peppery, quick-tempered, ratty (*Brit. & N.Z. inf.*), testy, touchy

shot *n.* **1.** discharge, lob, pot shot, throw **2.** ball, bullet, lead, pellet, projectile, slug **3.** marksman, shooter **4.** *Inf.* attempt, chance, conjecture, crack (*Inf.*), effort, endeavour, essay, go (*Inf.*), guess, opportunity, stab (*Inf.*), surmise, try, turn **5. by a long shot a.** by far, easily, far and away, indubitably, undoubtedly, without doubt **b.** by any means, in any circumstances, on any account **6. have a shot** *Inf.* attempt, have a go (bash (*Inf.*), crack (*Inf.*), stab (*Inf.*)) (*Inf.*), tackle, try, try one's luck **7. like a shot** at once, eagerly, immediately, like a flash, quickly, unhesitatingly **8. shot in the arm** *Inf.* boost, encouragement, fillip, impetus, lift, stimulus

shoulder *n.* **1. give (someone) the cold shoulder** cut (*Inf.*), ignore, ostracize, put down, rebuff, shun, snub **2. put one's shoulder to the wheel** *Inf.* apply oneself, buckle down to (*Inf.*), exert oneself, get down to, make every effort, set to work, strive **3. rub shoulders with** *Inf.* associate with, consort with, fraternize with, hobnob with, mix with, socialize with **4. shoulder to shoulder** as one, in cooperation, in partnership, in unity, jointly, side by side, together, united **5. straight from the shoulder** candidly, directly, frankly, man to man, outright, plainly, pulling no punches (*Inf.*), straight, unequivocally, with no holds barred ~*v.* **6.** accept, assume, bear, be responsible for, carry, take on, take upon oneself **7.** elbow, jostle, press, push, shove, thrust

shoulder blade scapula

shout 1. *n.* bellow, call, cry, roar, scream, yell **2.** *v.* bawl, bay, bellow, call (out), cry

(out), holler (*Inf.*), hollo, raise one's voice, roar, scream, yell

shout down drown, drown out, overwhelm, silence

shove *v.* crowd, drive, elbow, impel, jostle, press, propel, push, shoulder, thrust

shovel *v.* convey, dredge, heap, ladle, load, move, scoop, shift, spoon, toss

show *v.* **1.** appear, be visible, blow wide open (*Sl.*), disclose, display, divulge, evidence, evince, exhibit, indicate, make known, manifest, present, register, reveal, testify to **2.** assert, clarify, demonstrate, elucidate, evince, explain, instruct, point out, present, prove, teach **3.** accompany, attend, conduct, escort, guide, lead **4.** accord, act with, bestow, confer, grant ~*n.* **5.** array, demonstration, display, exhibition, expo (*Inf.*), exposition, fair, manifestation, pageant, pageantry, parade, representation, sight, spectacle, view **6.** affectation, air, appearance, display, illusion, likeness, ostentation, parade, pose, pretence, pretext, profession, semblance **7.** entertainment, presentation, production
Antonyms (*senses 1 & 2*) be invisible, conceal, deny, disprove, gainsay (*Archaic or literary*), hide, keep secret, mask, obscure, refute, suppress, veil, withhold

showdown breaking point, clash, climax, confrontation, crisis, culmination, *dénouement*, exposé, face-off (*Sl.*), moment of truth

shower *n.* **1.** *Fig.* barrage, deluge, fusillade, plethora, rain, stream, torrent, volley **2.** *Brit. sl.* bunch of layabouts, crew, rabble ~*v.* **3.** deluge, heap, inundate, lavish, load, pour, rain, spray, sprinkle

showing *n.* **1.** demonstration, display, exhibition, presentation, staging **2.** account of oneself, appearance, demonstration, impression, performance, show, track record **3.** evidence, representation, statement

showman entertainer, impresario, performer, publicist, stage manager

show-off boaster, braggadocio, braggart, egotist, exhibitionist, hot dog (*Chiefly U.S.*), peacock, poseur, swaggerer

show off 1. advertise, demonstrate, display, exhibit, flaunt, parade, spread out **2.** boast, brag, hot-dog (*Chiefly U.S.*), make a spectacle of oneself, shoot a line (*Inf.*), swagger

show up 1. expose, highlight, lay bare, pinpoint, put the spotlight on, reveal, unmask **2.** appear, be conspicuous, be visible, catch the eye, leap to the eye, stand out **3.** *Inf.* embarrass, let down, mortify, put to shame, shame, show in a bad light **4.** *Inf.* appear, arrive, come, make an appearance, put in an appearance, turn up

showy brash, flamboyant, flash (*Inf.*), flashy, garish, gaudy, loud, ostentatious, over the top (*Inf.*), pompous, pretentious, splashy (*Inf.*), tawdry, tinselly
Antonyms discreet, low-key, muted, quiet, restrained, subdued, tasteful, unobtrusive

shred *n.* **1.** bit, fragment, piece, rag, ribbon, scrap, sliver, snippet, tatter **2.** *Fig.* atom, grain, iota, jot, particle, scrap, trace, whit

shrewd acute, artful, astute, calculated, calculating, canny, clever, crafty, cunning, discerning, discriminating, far-seeing, far-sighted, fly (*Sl.*), intelligent, keen, knowing, long-headed, perceptive, perspicacious, sagacious, sharp, sly, smart, wily
Antonyms artless, dull, gullible, imprudent, ingenuous, innocent, naive, obtuse, slow-witted, stupid, trusting, undiscerning, unsophisticated, unworldly

shrewdly artfully, astutely, cannily, cleverly, far-sightedly, knowingly, perceptively, perspicaciously, sagaciously, with all one's wits about one, with consummate skill

shrewdness acumen, acuteness, astuteness, canniness, discernment, grasp, judgment, penetration, perspicacity, quick wits, sagacity, sharpness, smartness, suss (*Sl.*)

shriek *v./n.* cry, holler, howl, scream, screech, squeal, wail, whoop, yell

shrill acute, ear-piercing, ear-splitting, high, high-pitched, penetrating, piercing, piping, screeching, sharp
Antonyms deep, dulcet, mellifluous, silver-toned, soft, soothing, sweet-sounding, velvety, well-modulated

shrink 1. contract, decrease, deflate, diminish, drop off, dwindle, fall off, grow smaller, lessen, narrow, shorten, shrivel, wither, wrinkle **2.** cower, cringe, draw back, flinch, hang back, quail, recoil, retire, shy away, wince, withdraw
Antonyms (*sense 1*) balloon, dilate, distend, enlarge, expand, increase, inflate, mushroom, stretch, swell (*sense 2*) attack, challenge, confront, embrace, face, receive, welcome

shrivel 1. burn, dry (up), parch, scorch, sear **2.** dehydrate, desiccate, dwindle, shrink, wilt, wither, wizen, wrinkle

shrivelled desiccated, dried up, dry, sere (*Archaic*), shrunken, withered, wizened, wrinkled

shroud *v.* **1.** blanket, cloak, conceal, cover, envelop, hide, screen, swathe, veil ~*n.* **2.** cerecloth, cerement, covering, grave clothes, winding sheet **3.** cloud, mantle, pall, screen, veil

shudder 1. *v.* convulse, quake, quiver, shake, shiver, tremble **2.** *n.* convulsion, quiver, spasm, trembling, tremor

shuffle 1. drag, scrape, scuff, scuffle, shamble **2.** confuse, disarrange, disorder, intermix, jumble, mix, rearrange, shift **3.** *Usually with* **off** *or* **out of** beat about the bush, beg the question, cavil, dodge, equivocate, evade, flannel (*Brit. inf.*), gloss over, hedge, prevaricate, pussyfoot (*Inf.*), quibble

shun avoid, body-swerve (*Scot.*), cold-shoulder, elude, eschew, evade, fight shy of, give (someone *or* something) a wide berth, have no part in, keep away from, shy away from, steer clear of

shut 1. bar, close, draw to, fasten, push to, seal, secure, slam **2.** *With* **in, out,** *etc.* cage, confine, enclose, exclude, impound, imprison, pound, wall off *or* up
Antonyms open, throw wide, unbar, unclose, undo, unfasten, unlock

shut down cease, cease operating, close, discontinue, halt, shut up, stop, switch off

shut out 1. bar, black, blackball, debar, exclude, keep out, lock out, ostracize **2.** block out, conceal, cover, hide, mask, screen, veil

shuttle *v.* alternate, commute, go back and forth, go to and fro, ply, seesaw, shunt

shut up 1. bottle up, box in, cage, confine, coop up, immure, imprison, incarcerate, intern, keep in **2.** *Inf.* be quiet, button it (*Sl.*), button one's lip (*Sl.*), fall silent, gag, hold one's tongue, hush, keep one's trap shut (*Sl.*), muzzle, pipe down (*Sl.*), put a sock in it (*Brit. sl.*), silence

shy¹ 1. *adj.* backward, bashful, cautious, chary, coy, diffident, distrustful, hesitant, modest, mousy, nervous, reserved, reticent, retiring, self-conscious, self-effacing, shrinking, suspicious, timid, wary **2.** *v.* *Sometimes with* **off** *or* **away** balk, buck, draw back, flinch, quail, rear, recoil, start, swerve, take fright, wince
Antonyms *adj.* assured, bold, brash, cheeky, confident, fearless, forward, pushy (*Inf.*), rash, reckless, self-assured, self-confident, unsuspecting, unwary

shy² *v.* cast, chuck (*Inf.*), fling, hurl, lob (*Inf.*), pitch, propel, send, sling, throw, toss

shyness bashfulness, diffidence, lack of confidence, modesty, mousiness, nervousness, reticence, self-consciousness, timidity, timidness, timorousness

sick 1. green around the gills (*Inf.*), ill, nauseated, nauseous, puking (*Sl.*), qualmish, queasy **2.** ailing, diseased, feeble, indisposed, laid up (*Inf.*), on the sick list (*Inf.*), poorly (*Inf.*), under par (*Inf.*), under the weather, unwell, weak **3.** *Inf.* black, ghoulish, macabre, morbid, sadistic **4.** *Inf. Often with* **of** blasé, bored, disgusted, displeased, fed up, jaded, revolted, satiated, tired, weary

Antonyms (*senses 1 & 2*) able-bodied, fine, fit, fit and well, fit as a fiddle, hale and hearty, healthy, robust, tranquil, untroubled, unworried, up to par, well

sicken 1. disgust, gross out (*U.S. sl.*), make one's gorge rise, nauseate, repel, revolt, turn one's stomach **2.** ail, be stricken by, contract, fall ill, go down with, show symptoms of, take sick

sickening cringe-making (*Brit. inf.*), disgusting, distasteful, foul, loathsome, nauseating, nauseous, noisome, offensive, putrid, repulsive, revolting, stomach-turning (*Inf.*), vile, yucky *or* yukky (*Sl.*)
Antonyms curative, delightful, health-giving, heartening, inviting, marvellous, mouth-watering, pleasant, salutary, tempting, therapeutic, wholesome, wonderful

sickly 1. ailing, bilious, bloodless, delicate, faint, feeble, indisposed, infirm, in poor health, lacklustre, languid, pallid, peaky, pining, unhealthy, wan, weak **2.** bilious (*Inf.*), cloying, mawkish, nauseating, revolting (*Inf.*), syrupy (*Inf.*)

sickness 1. barfing (*U.S. sl.*), (the) collywobbles (*Sl.*), nausea, queasiness, puking (*Sl.*), vomiting **2.** affliction, ailment, bug (*Inf.*), complaint, disease, disorder, illness, indisposition, infirmity, malady

side *n.* **1.** border, boundary, division, edge, limit, margin, part, perimeter, periphery, rim, sector, verge **2.** aspect, face, facet, flank, hand, part, surface, view **3.** angle, light, opinion, point of view, position, slant, stand, standpoint, viewpoint **4.** camp, cause, faction, party, sect, team **5.** *Brit. sl.* airs, arrogance, insolence, pretentiousness *~adj.* **6.** flanking, lateral **7.** ancillary, incidental, indirect, lesser, marginal, minor, oblique, roundabout, secondary, subordinate, subsidiary *~v.* **8.** *Usually with* **with** ally with, associate oneself with, befriend, favour, go along with, join with, second, support, take the part of, team up with (*Inf.*)
Antonyms *n.* (*sense 1*) centre, core, heart, middle *~adj.* central, essential, focal, fundamental, key, main, middle, primary, principal *~v.* counter, oppose, stand against, withstand

sidelong *adj.* covert, indirect, oblique, sideways

sidestep avoid, body-swerve (*Scot.*), bypass, circumvent, dodge, duck (*Inf.*), elude, evade, find a way round, skip, skirt

sidetrack deflect, distract, divert, lead off the subject

sideways 1. *adv.* crabwise, edgeways, laterally, obliquely, sidelong, sidewards, to the side **2.** *adj.* oblique, side, sidelong, slanted

siesta catnap, doze, forty winks (*Inf.*), kip (*Brit. sl.*), nap, rest, sleep, snooze (*Inf.*), zizz (*Brit. inf.*)

sieve 1. *n.* colander, riddle, screen, sifter, strainer, tammy cloth **2.** *v.* bolt, remove, riddle, separate, sift, strain

sift 1. bolt, filter, pan, part, riddle, separate, sieve **2.** analyse, examine, fathom, go through, investigate, pore over, probe, research, screen, scrutinize, work over

sigh *v.* **1.** breathe, complain, grieve, lament, moan, sorrow, sough, suspire (*Archaic*) **2.** *Often with* **for** eat one's heart out over, languish, long, mourn, pine, yearn

sight *n.* **1.** eye, eyes, eyesight, seeing, vision **2.** appearance, apprehension, eyeshot, field of vision, ken, perception, range of vision, view, viewing, visibility **3.** display, exhibition, pageant, scene, show, spectacle, vista **4.** *Inf.* blot on the landscape (*Inf.*), eyesore, fright (*Inf.*), mess, monstrosity, spectacle **5.** **catch sight of** descry, espy, glimpse, recognize, spot, view *~v.* **6.** behold, discern, distinguish, make out, observe, perceive, see, spot

sign *n.* **1.** clue, evidence, gesture, giveaway, hint, indication, manifestation, mark, note, proof, signal, spoor, suggestion, symptom, token, trace, vestige **2.** board, notice, placard, warning **3.** badge, character, cipher, device, emblem, ensign, figure, logo, mark, representation, symbol **4.** augury, auspice, foreboding, forewarning, omen, portent, presage, warning, writing on the wall *~v.* **5.** autograph, endorse, initial, inscribe, set one's hand to, subscribe **6.** beckon, gesticulate, gesture, indicate, signal, use sign language, wave

signal 1. *n.* beacon, cue, flare, gesture, go-ahead (*Inf.*), green light, indication, indicator, mark, sign, token **2.** *adj.* conspicuous, distinguished, eminent, exceptional, extraordinary, famous, memorable, momentous, notable, noteworthy, outstanding, remarkable, significant, striking **3.** *v.* beckon, communicate, gesticulate, gesture, give a sign to, indicate, motion, nod, sign, wave

significance 1. force, implication(s), import, meaning, message, point, purport, sense, signification **2.** consequence, consideration, importance, impressiveness, matter, moment, relevance, weight

significant 1. denoting, eloquent, expressing, expressive, indicative, knowing, meaning, meaningful, pregnant, suggestive **2.** critical, important, material, momentous, noteworthy, serious, vital, weighty
Antonyms immaterial, inconsequential, insignificant, irrelevant, meaningless, nitpicking, nugatory, of no consequence, paltry, petty, trivial, unimportant, worthless

signify 1. announce, be a sign of, betoken,

communicate, connote, convey, denote, evi~
dence, exhibit, express, imply, indicate, in~
timate, matter, mean, portend, proclaim,
represent, show, stand for, suggest, symbol~
ize **2.** *Inf.* be of importance *or* significance,
carry weight, count, matter

silence *n.* **1.** calm, hush, lull, noiselessness,
peace, quiescence, quiet, stillness **2.** dumb~
ness, muteness, reticence, speechlessness,
taciturnity, uncommunicativeness ~*v.* **3.**
cut off, cut short, deaden, extinguish, gag,
muffle, quell, quiet, quieten, stifle, still,
strike dumb, subdue, suppress
Antonyms *n.* babble, bawling, cacophony,
chatter, clamour, din, garrulousness, hubbub,
loquaciousness, murmuring, noise, prattle,
racket, shouting, sound, speech, talk, talking,
tumult, uproar, verbosity, whispering, yelling
~*v.* amplify, broadcast, champion, dissemi~
nate, encourage, foster, make louder, pro~
mote, promulgate, publicize, rouse, spread,
support, ungag

silent 1. hushed, muted, noiseless, quiet,
soundless, still, stilly (*Poetic*) **2.** dumb,
mum, mute, nonvocal, not talkative,
speechless, struck dumb, taciturn, tongue-
tied, uncommunicative, unspeaking, voice~
less, wordless **3.** aphonic (*Phonetics*), im~
plicit, implied, tacit, understood, unex~
pressed, unpronounced, unspoken

silently as quietly as a mouse (*Inf.*), dumbly,
inaudibly, in silence, mutely, noiselessly,
quietly, soundlessly, speechlessly, without a
sound, wordlessly

silhouette 1. *n.* delineation, form, outline,
profile, shape **2.** *v.* delineate, etch, outline,
stand out

silky silken, sleek, smooth, velvety

silly *adj.* **1.** absurd, asinine, brainless,
childish, dopy (*Sl.*), dozy (*Brit. inf.*), fatuous,
foolhardy, foolish, frivolous, giddy, goofy
(*Inf.*), idiotic, immature, imprudent, inane,
inappropriate, irresponsible, meaningless,
pointless, preposterous, puerile, ridiculous,
senseless, stupid, unwise, witless **2.** *Inf.* be~
numbed, dazed, groggy (*Inf.*), in a daze,
muzzy, stunned, stupefied ~*n.* **3.** *Inf.* clot
(*Brit. inf.*), duffer (*Inf.*), dweeb (*U.S. sl.*),
goose (*Inf.*), ignoramus, nerd *or* nurd (*Sl.*),
ninny, nitwit (*Inf.*), plonker (*Sl.*), prat (*Sl.*),
silly-billy (*Inf.*), simpleton, twit (*Inf.*), wally
(*Sl.*)
Antonyms *adj.* acute, aware, bright, clever,
intelligent, mature, perceptive, profound,
prudent, reasonable, sane, sensible, serious,
smart, thoughtful, well-thought-out, wise

silver 1. *adj.* argent (*Poetic*), pearly, sil~
vered, silvery **2.** *n.* silver plate, silverware

similar alike, analogous, close, comparable,
congruous, corresponding, homogeneous,

homogenous, in agreement, much the same,
resembling, uniform
Antonyms antithetical, clashing, contra~
dictory, contrary, different, disparate, dis~
similar, diverse, heterogeneous, irreconcil~
able, opposite, unalike, unrelated, various,
varying

similarity affinity, agreement, analogy,
closeness, comparability, concordance, con~
gruence, correspondence, likeness, point of
comparison, relation, resemblance, same~
ness, similitude
Antonyms antithesis, contradictoriness,
difference, disagreement, discordance, dis~
crepancy, disparity, dissimilarity, diversity,
heterogeneity, incomparability, irreconcil~
ability, unalikeness, variation, variety

similarly by the same token, correspond~
ingly, in like manner, likewise

simmer *v. Fig.* be angry (agitated, tense,
uptight (*Inf.*)), boil, burn, fume, rage, see
red (*Inf.*), seethe, smart, smoulder

simmer down calm down, collect oneself,
contain oneself, control oneself, cool off *or*
down, get down off one's high horse (*Inf.*),
grow quieter, unwind (*Inf.*)

simple 1. clear, easy, easy-peasy (*Sl.*), el~
ementary, intelligible, lucid, manageable,
plain, straightforward, uncomplicated,
understandable, uninvolved **2.** classic,
clean, natural, plain, Spartan, unadorned,
uncluttered, unembellished, unfussy **3.** el~
ementary, pure, single, unalloyed, un~
blended, uncombined, undivided, unmixed
4. artless, childlike, frank, green, guileless,
ingenuous, innocent, naive, natural, sim~
plistic, sincere, unaffected, unpretentious,
unsophisticated **5.** bald, basic, direct, frank,
honest, naked, plain, sincere, stark, unde~
niable, unvarnished **6.** homely, humble,
lowly, modest, rustic, unpretentious **7.**
brainless, credulous, dense, dumb (*Inf.*),
feeble, feeble-minded, foolish, half-witted,
moronic, obtuse, shallow, silly, slow, stupid,
thick
Antonyms (*senses 1 & 3*) advanced, complex,
complicated, convoluted, difficult, elaborate,
highly developed, intricate, involved, refined,
sophisticated (*senses 2, 4 & 6*) artful, contrived,
elaborate, extravagant, fancy, flashy, fussy,
intricate, ornate, smart, sophisticated, world~
ly, worldly-wise (*sense 7*) astute, bright, clever,
intelligent, knowing, on the ball, quick, quick
on the uptake, quick-witted, sharp, smart,
wise

simple-minded 1. a bit lacking (*Inf.*),
addle-brained, backward, brainless, dead
from the neck up (*Inf.*), dim-witted, feeble-
minded, foolish, idiot, idiotic, moronic, re~
tarded, simple, stupid **2.** artless, natural,
unsophisticated

simpleton berk (*Brit. sl.*), blockhead, boo~
by, charlie (*Brit. inf.*), coot, dickhead (*Sl.*),
dipstick (*Brit. sl.*), divvy (*Brit. sl.*), dolt,
dope (*Inf.*), dork (*Sl.*), dullard, dunce, dweeb
(*U.S. sl.*), fool, fuckwit (*Taboo sl.*), geek (*Sl.*),
gonzo (*Sl.*), goose (*Inf.*), greenhorn (*Inf.*),
idiot, imbecile (*Inf.*), jackass, jerk (*Sl.,
chiefly U.S. & Canad.*), moron, nerd *or* nurd
(*Sl.*), nincompoop, ninny, nitwit (*Inf.*),
numskull *or* numbskull, oaf, plank (*Brit.
sl.*), schmuck (*U.S. sl.*), Simple Simon, stu~
pid (*Inf.*), twerp *or* twirp (*Inf.*), twit (*Inf.,
chiefly Brit.*), wally (*Sl.*)

simplicity 1. absence of complications,
clarity, clearness, ease, easiness, elementa~
riness, obviousness, straightforwardness **2.**
clean lines, lack of adornment, modesty,
naturalness, plainness, purity, restraint **3.**
artlessness, candour, directness, guileless~
ness, innocence, lack of sophistication, na~
ivety, openness
Antonyms (*sense 1*) complexity, complicat~
edness, difficulty, intricacy, lack of clarity
(*sense 2*) decoration, elaborateness, embel~
lishment, fanciness, fussiness, ornateness,
ostentation (*sense 3*) brains, craftiness, cun~
ning, deviousness, guile, insincerity, know~
ingness, sharpness, slyness, smartness, so~
phistication, wariness, wisdom, worldliness

simplify abridge, decipher, disentangle, fa~
cilitate, make intelligible, reduce to essen~
tials, streamline

simply 1. clearly, directly, easily, intelli~
gibly, modestly, naturally, plainly, straight~
forwardly, unaffectedly, unpretentiously,
without any elaboration **2.** just, merely,
only, purely, solely **3.** absolutely, altogeth~
er, completely, really, totally, unreservedly,
utterly, wholly

simultaneous at the same time, coinci~
dent, coinciding, concurrent, contempora~
neous, synchronous

simultaneously all together, at the same
time, concurrently, in chorus, in concert, in
the same breath, in unison, together

sin 1. *n.* crime, damnation, error, evil, guilt,
iniquity, misdeed, offence, sinfulness,
transgression, trespass, ungodliness, un~
righteousness, wickedness, wrong, wrong~
doing **2.** *v.* err, fall, fall from grace, go
astray, lapse, offend, transgress, trespass
(*Archaic*)

sincere artless, bona fide, candid, earnest,
frank, genuine, guileless, heartfelt, honest,
natural, no-nonsense, open, real, serious,
straightforward, true, unaffected, unfeigned,
upfront (*Inf.*), wholehearted
Antonyms affected, artful, artificial, deceit~
ful, deceptive, dishonest, false, feigned, hol~
low, insincere, phoney *or* phony (*Inf.*), pre~
tended, put on, synthetic, token, two-faced

sincerely earnestly, genuinely, honestly, in
all sincerity, in earnest, in good faith, real~
ly, seriously, truly, wholeheartedly

sincerity artlessness, bona fides, candour,
frankness, genuineness, good faith, guile~
lessness, honesty, probity, seriousness,
straightforwardness, truth, wholehearted~
ness

sinecure cushy number (*Inf.*), gravy train
(*Sl.*), money for jam *or* old rope (*Inf.*), soft
job (*Inf.*), soft option

sinful bad, corrupt, criminal, depraved, err~
ing, guilty, immoral, iniquitous, irreligious,
morally wrong, ungodly, unholy, unright~
eous, wicked
Antonyms beatified, blessed, chaste, decent,
free from sin, godly, holy, honest, honourable,
immaculate, moral, pure, righteous, sinless,
spotless, unblemished, upright, virtuous,
without sin

sing 1. carol, chant, chirp, croon, make
melody, pipe, trill, vocalize, warble, yodel
2. *Sl., chiefly U.S.* betray, blow the whistle
(on) (*Inf.*), fink (on) (*Sl., chiefly U.S.*), grass
(*Brit. sl.*), inform (on), peach (*Sl.*), rat (on)
(*Inf.*), shop (*Sl., chiefly Brit.*), spill one's guts
(*Sl.*), spill the beans (*Inf.*), squeal (*Sl.*), tell
all, turn in (*Inf.*) **3.** buzz, hum, purr, whine,
whistle

singe burn, char, scorch, sear

singer balladeer, cantor, chanteuse (*Fem.*),
chorister, crooner, minstrel, soloist, song~
ster, songstress, troubadour, vocalist

single *adj.* **1.** distinct, individual, lone, one,
only, particular, separate, singular, sole,
solitary, unique **2.** free, unattached, un~
married, unwed **3.** exclusive, individual,
separate, simple, unblended, uncompound~
ed, undivided, unmixed, unshared ~*v.* **4.**
Usually with **out** choose, cull, distinguish,
fix on, pick, pick on *or* out, put on one side,
select, separate, set apart, winnow

single-handed alone, by oneself, indepen~
dently, on one's own, solo, unaided, unas~
sisted, without help

single-minded dedicated, determined,
dogged, fixed, hellbent (*Inf.*), monomaniacal,
steadfast, stubborn, tireless, undeviating,
unswerving, unwavering

singly individually, one at a time, one by
one, separately

singular 1. conspicuous, eminent, excep~
tional, notable, noteworthy, outstanding,
prodigious, rare, remarkable, uncommon,
unique, unparalleled **2.** atypical, curious,
eccentric, extraordinary, odd, oddball (*Inf.*),
out-of-the-way, outré, peculiar, puzzling,
queer, strange, unusual, wacko (*Sl.*) **3.** in~
dividual, separate, single, sole
Antonyms common, common or garden,

commonplace, conventional, everyday, familiar, normal, routine, run-of-the-mill, unexceptional, unremarkable, usual

sinister baleful, dire, disquieting, evil, forbidding, injurious, malevolent, malign, malignant, menacing, ominous, threatening
Antonyms auspicious, benevolent, benign, calming, encouraging, good, heartening, heroic, honourable, just, noble, promising, propitious, reassuring, righteous, upright, worthy

sink *v.* **1.** cave in, decline, descend, dip, disappear, droop, drop, drown, ebb, engulf, fall, founder, go down, go under, lower, merge, plummet, plunge, sag, slope, submerge, subside **2.** abate, collapse, drop, fall, lapse, relapse, retrogress, slip, slump, subside **3.** decay, decline, decrease, degenerate, depreciate, deteriorate, die, diminish, dwindle, fade, fail, flag, go downhill (*Inf.*), lessen, weaken, worsen **4.** bore, dig, drill, drive, excavate, lay, put down **5.** be the ruin of, defeat, destroy, finish, overwhelm, ruin, scupper (*Brit. sl.*), seal the doom of **6.** be reduced to, debase oneself, lower oneself, stoop, succumb
Antonyms (*senses 1, 2 & 3*) arise, ascend, climb, enlarge, go up, grow, improve, increase, intensify, move up, rise, rise up, swell, wax

sinless faultless, guiltless, immaculate, innocent, pure, unblemished, uncorrupted, undefiled, unsullied, virtuous, without fault, without sin

sinner evildoer, malefactor, miscreant, offender, reprobate, transgressor, trespasser (*Archaic*), wrongdoer

sip 1. *v.* sample, sup, taste **2.** *n.* drop, swallow, taste, thimbleful

siren charmer, Circe, *femme fatale*, Lorelei, seductress, temptress, vamp (*Inf.*), witch

sissy 1. *n.* baby, coward, jessie (*Scot. sl.*), milksop, milquetoast (*U.S.*), mollycoddle, mummy's boy, namby-pamby, pansy, sisspot (*Inf.*), softy (*Inf.*), weakling, wet (*Brit. inf.*), wimp (*Inf.*) **2.** *adj.* cowardly, effeminate, feeble, namby-pamby, sissified (*Inf.*), soft (*Inf.*), unmanly, weak, wet (*Brit. inf.*), wimpish *or* wimpy (*Inf.*)

sit 1. be seated, perch, rest, settle, take a seat, take the weight off one's feet **2.** assemble, be in session, convene, deliberate, meet, officiate, preside **3.** accommodate, contain, have space for, hold, seat

site 1. *n.* ground, location, place, plot, position, setting, spot **2.** *v.* install, locate, place, position, set, situate

sitting *n.* congress, consultation, get-together (*Inf.*), hearing, meeting, period, session

situation 1. locale, locality, location, place, position, seat, setting, site, spot **2.** ball game (*Inf.*), case, circumstances, condition, kettle of fish (*Inf.*), plight, scenario, state, state of affairs, status quo, the picture (*Inf.*) **3.** rank, sphere, station, status **4.** berth (*Inf.*), employment, job, office, place, position, post

size amount, bigness, bulk, dimensions, extent, greatness, hugeness, immensity, largeness, magnitude, mass, measurement(s), proportions, range, vastness, volume

size up appraise, assess, evaluate, eye up, get (something) taped (*Brit. inf.*), get the measure of, take stock of

sizzle crackle, frizzle, fry, hiss, spit, sputter

skeleton *Fig.* bare bones, bones, draft, frame, framework, outline, sketch, structure

sketch 1. *v.* block out, delineate, depict, draft, draw, outline, paint, plot, portray, represent, rough out **2.** *n.* delineation, design, draft, drawing, outline, plan, skeleton

sketchy bitty, cobbled together, crude, cursory, inadequate, incomplete, outline, perfunctory, rough, scrappy, skimpy, slight, superficial, unfinished, vague
Antonyms complete, detailed, full, thorough

skilful able, accomplished, adept, adroit, apt, clever, competent, dexterous, experienced, expert, handy, masterly, practised, professional, proficient, quick, ready, skilled, trained
Antonyms amateurish, awkward, bungling, cack-handed, clumsy, cowboy (*Inf.*), ham-fisted, incompetent, inept, inexperienced, inexpert, maladroit, slapdash, unaccomplished, unqualified, unskilful, unskilled

skill ability, accomplishment, adroitness, aptitude, art, cleverness, competence, craft, dexterity, experience, expertise, expertness, facility, finesse, handiness, ingenuity, intelligence, knack, proficiency, quickness, readiness, skilfulness, talent, technique
Antonyms awkwardness, brute force, cack-handedness, clumsiness, gaucheness, ham-fistedness, inability, incompetence, ineptitude, inexperience, lack of finesse, maladroitness, unhandiness

skilled able, accomplished, a dab hand at (*Brit. inf.*), experienced, expert, masterly, practised, professional, proficient, skilful, trained
Antonyms amateurish, cowboy (*Inf.*), inexperienced, inexpert, uneducated, unprofessional, unqualified, unskilled, untalented, untrained

skim 1. cream, separate **2.** brush, coast, dart, float, fly, glide, sail, soar **3.** *Usually with* **through** glance, run one's eye over, scan, skip (*Inf.*), thumb *or* leaf through

skimp be mean with, be niggardly, be spar~
ing with, cut corners, pinch, scamp, scant,
scrimp, stint, withhold
Antonyms act as if one had money to burn,
be extravagant, be generous with, be prodigal,
blow (*Sl.*), fritter away, lavish, overspend,
pour on, splurge, squander, throw money
away

skin *n.* **1.** fell, hide, integument, pelt, tegu~
ment **2.** casing, coating, crust, film, husk,
membrane, outside, peel, rind **3. by the
skin of one's teeth** by a hair's-breadth, by
a narrow margin, by a whisker (*Inf.*), nar~
rowly, only just **4. get under one's skin**
aggravate (*Inf.*), annoy, get in one's hair
(*Inf.*), get on one's nerves (*Inf.*), grate on,
irk, irritate, needle (*Inf.*), nettle, piss one off
(*Taboo sl.*), rub up the wrong way ~*v.* **5.**
abrade, bark, excoriate, flay, graze, peel,
scrape

skinflint meanie *or* meany (*Inf., chiefly
Brit.*), miser, niggard, penny-pincher (*Inf.*),
Scrooge, tight-arse (*Taboo sl.*), tight-ass
(*U.S. taboo sl.*), tightwad (*U.S. & Canad. sl.*)

skinny emaciated, lean, macilent (*Rare*),
scraggy, skeletal, skin-and-bone (*Inf.*), thin,
twiggy, undernourished
Antonyms beefy (*Inf.*), broad in the beam
(*Inf.*), fat, fleshy, heavy, obese, plump, podgy,
portly, stout, tubby

skip *v.* **1.** bob, bounce, caper, cavort, dance,
flit, frisk, gambol, hop, prance, trip **2.** es~
chew, get (something) a miss, leave out,
miss out, omit, pass over, skim over **3.** *Inf.*
cut (*Inf.*), dog it *or* dog off (*Dialect*), miss,
play truant from, wag (*Dialect*)

skirmish 1. *n.* affair, affray (*Law*), battle,
brush, clash, combat, conflict, contest,
dust-up (*Inf.*), encounter, engagement, fra~
cas, incident, scrap (*Inf.*), scrimmage, set-to
(*Inf.*), spat, tussle **2.** *v.* clash, collide, come
to blows, scrap (*Inf.*), tussle

skirt *v.* **1.** border, edge, flank, lie alongside
2. *Often with* **around** *or* **round** avoid,
body-swerve (*Scot.*), bypass, circumvent,
detour, evade, steer clear of ~*n.* **3.** *Often
plural* border, edge, fringe, hem, margin,
outskirts, periphery, purlieus, rim

skit burlesque, parody, sketch, spoof (*Inf.*),
takeoff (*Inf.*), travesty, turn

skittish excitable, fickle, fidgety, frivolous,
highly strung, jumpy, lively, nervous, play~
ful, restive
Antonyms calm, composed, demure, laid-
back, placid, relaxed, sober, staid, steady,
unexcitable, unfazed (*Inf.*), unflappable,
unruffled

skive *v.* bob off (*Brit. sl.*), dodge, gold-brick
(*U.S. sl.*), idle, malinger, scrimshank (*Brit.
military sl.*), shirk, skulk, slack

skulk creep, lie in wait, loiter, lurk, pad,
prowl, slink, sneak

sky *n.* **1.** azure (*Poetic*), empyrean (*Poetic*),
firmament, heavens, upper atmosphere,
vault of heaven, welkin (*Archaic*) **2. to the
skies** excessively, extravagantly, fulsomely,
highly, immoderately, inordinately, pro~
fusely

slab chunk, hunk, lump, piece, portion, slice,
wedge, wodge (*Brit. inf.*)

slack *adj.* **1.** baggy, easy, flaccid, flexible,
lax, limp, loose, not taut, relaxed **2.** asleep
on the job (*Inf.*), easy-going, idle, inactive,
inattentive, lax, lazy, neglectful, negligent,
permissive, remiss, slapdash, slipshod, tar~
dy **3.** dull, inactive, quiet, slow, slow-
moving, sluggish ~*n.* **4.** excess, give (*Inf.*),
leeway, looseness, play, room ~*v.* **5.** bob off
(*Brit. sl.*), dodge, flag, idle, neglect, relax,
shirk, skive (*Brit. sl.*), slacken
Antonyms *adj.* (*sense 1*) inflexible, rigid,
stiff, strained, stretched, taut, tight (*senses 2 &
3*) active, bustling, busy, concerned, diligent,
exacting, fast-moving, hard, hard-working,
hectic, meticulous, stern, strict

slacken (off) abate, decrease, diminish,
drop off, ease (off), lessen, let up, loosen,
moderate, reduce, relax, release, slack off,
slow down, tire

slacker dodger, do-nothing, gold brick (*U.S.
sl.*), good-for-nothing, idler, layabout, loafer,
passenger, scrimshanker (*Brit. military sl.*),
shirker, skiver (*Brit. sl.*)

slag (off) *v.* abuse, berate, criticise, deride,
insult, lambast(e), malign, mock, slam,
slander, slang, slate

slam 1. bang, crash, dash, fling, hurl,
smash, throw, thump **2.** *Sl.* attack, blast,
castigate, criticize, damn, excoriate, lam~
bast(e), pan (*Inf.*), pillory, shoot down (*Inf.*),
slate (*Inf.*), tear into (*Inf.*), vilify

slander 1. *n.* aspersion, backbiting, calum~
ny, defamation, detraction, libel, misrepre~
sentation, muckraking, obloquy, scandal,
smear **2.** *v.* backbite, blacken (someone's)
name, calumniate, decry, defame, detract,
disparage, libel, malign, muckrake, slur,
smear, traduce, vilify
Antonyms *n.* acclaim, acclamation, approv~
al, laudation, praise, tribute ~*v.* acclaim, ap~
plaud, approve, compliment, eulogize, laud,
praise, sing the praises of

slanderous abusive, calumnious, damag~
ing, defamatory, libellous, malicious

slang *v.* abuse, berate, call names, hurl in~
sults at, insult, inveigh against, malign, rail
against, revile, vilify, vituperate

slant *v.* **1.** angle off, bend, bevel, cant, heel,
incline, lean, list, shelve, skew, slope, tilt
~*n.* **2.** camber, declination, diagonal, gra~

dient, incline, pitch, rake, ramp, slope, tilt ~*v.* **3.** angle, bias, colour, distort, twist, weight ~*n.* **4.** angle, attitude, bias, empha~ sis, leaning, one-sidedness, point of view, prejudice, viewpoint

slanting angled, aslant, asymmetrical, at an angle, bent, canted, cater-cornered (*U.S. inf.*), diagonal, inclined, oblique, on the bias, sideways, slanted, slantwise, sloping, tilted, tilting

slap *n.* **1.** bang, blow, chin (*Sl.*), clout (*Inf.*), cuff, deck (*Sl.*), lay one on (*Sl.*), smack, spank, wallop (*Inf.*), whack **2. a slap in the face** affront, blow, humiliation, insult, put-down, rebuff, rebuke, rejection, repulse, snub ~*v.* **3.** bang, clap, clout (*Inf.*), cuff, hit, spank, strike, whack **4.** *Inf.* daub, plaster, plonk, spread ~*adv.* **5.** *Inf.* bang, directly, exactly, plumb (*Inf.*), precisely, slap-bang (*Inf.*), smack (*Inf.*)

slapdash careless, clumsy, disorderly, hap~ hazard, hasty, hurried, last-minute, messy, negligent, perfunctory, slipshod, sloppy (*Inf.*), slovenly, thoughtless, thrown-together, untidy

Antonyms careful, conscientious, fastidi~ ous, meticulous, ordered, orderly, pains~ taking, precise, punctilious, thoughtful, tidy

slap down bring to heel, put (someone) in his place, rebuke, reprimand, restrain, squash

slapstick *n.* buffoonery, farce, horseplay, knockabout comedy

slash *v.* **1.** cut, gash, hack, lacerate, rend, rip, score, slit ~*n.* **2.** cut, gash, incision, laceration, rent, rip, slit ~*v.* **3.** cut, drop, lower, reduce

slashing aggressive, biting, brutal, fero~ cious, harsh, savage, searing, vicious

slate *v.* berate, blame, blast, castigate, cen~ sure, criticize, excoriate, haul over the coals (*Inf.*), lambast(e), lay into (*Inf.*), pan (*Inf.*), pitch into (*Inf.*), rail against, rap (someone's) knuckles, rebuke, roast (*Inf.*), scold, slam (*Sl.*), slang, take to task, tear into (*Inf.*), tear (someone) off a strip (*Inf.*)

slaughter *n.* **1.** blood bath, bloodshed, butchery, carnage, extermination, holo~ caust, killing, liquidation, massacre, mur~ der, slaying ~*v.* **2.** butcher, destroy, do to death, exterminate, kill, liquidate, massa~ cre, murder, put to the sword, slay, take out (*Sl.*) **3.** *Inf.* blow out of the water (*Sl.*), crush, defeat, hammer (*Inf.*), lick (*Inf.*), overwhelm, rout, tank (*Sl.*), thrash, trounce, undo, vanquish, wipe the floor with (*Inf.*)

slaughterhouse abattoir, butchery, sham~ bles

slave **1.** *n.* bondservant, bondsman, drudge, scullion (*Archaic*), serf, servant, skivvy

(*Chiefly Brit.*), slavey (*Brit. inf.*), varlet (*Ar~ chaic*), vassal, villein **2.** *v.* drudge, grind (*Inf.*), skivvy (*Brit.*), slog, sweat, toil, work one's fingers to the bone

slavery bondage, captivity, enslavement, serfdom, servitude, subjugation, thraldom, thrall, vassalage

Antonyms emancipation, freedom, liberty, manumission, release

slavish **1.** abject, base, cringing, despicable, fawning, grovelling, low, mean, menial, ob~ sequious, servile, submissive, sycophantic **2.** conventional, imitative, second-hand, unimaginative, uninspired, unoriginal

Antonyms assertive, creative, domineering, imaginative, independent, inventive, master~ ful, original, radical, rebellious, revolution~ ary, self-willed, wilful

slay **1.** annihilate, assassinate, butcher, de~ stroy, dispatch, do away with, do in (*Sl.*), eliminate, exterminate, kill, massacre, mow down, murder, rub out (*U.S. sl.*), slaughter **2.** *Inf.* amuse, be the death of (*Inf.*), im~ press, make a hit with (*Inf.*), wow (*Sl., chiefly U.S.*)

sleazy crummy, disreputable, low, run-down, seedy, sordid, squalid, tacky (*Inf.*)

sleek glossy, lustrous, shiny, smooth, well-fed, well-groomed

Antonyms badly groomed, bedraggled, di~ shevelled, frowzy, ill-nourished, in poor con~ dition, ratty (*Inf.*), rough, shaggy, sloppy, slovenly, unkempt

sleep **1.** *v.* be in the land of Nod, catnap, doze, drop off (*Inf.*), drowse, hibernate, kip (*Brit. sl.*), nod off (*Inf.*), rest in the arms of Morpheus, slumber, snooze (*Inf.*), snore, take a nap, take forty winks (*Inf.*), zizz (*Brit. inf.*) **2.** *n.* beauty sleep (*Inf.*), dorman~ cy, doze, forty winks (*Inf.*), hibernation, kip (*Brit. sl.*), nap, repose, rest, shuteye (*Sl.*), siesta, slumber(s), snooze (*Inf.*), zizz (*Brit. inf.*)

sleepiness doziness, drowsiness, heaviness, lethargy, somnolence, torpor

sleepless **1.** disturbed, insomniac, restless, unsleeping, wakeful **2.** alert, unsleeping, vigilant, watchful, wide awake

sleeplessness insomnia, wakefulness

sleepwalker noctambulist, somnambulist

sleepwalking noctambulation, noctambu~ lism, somnambulation, somnambulism

sleepy **1.** drowsy, dull, heavy, inactive, le~ thargic, sluggish, slumbersome, somnolent, torpid **2.** dull, hypnotic, inactive, quiet, sleep-inducing, slow, slumberous, somno~ lent, soporific

Antonyms active, alert, animated, attentive, awake, boisterous, bustling, busy, energetic, lively, restless, thriving, wakeful, wide-awake

slender 1. lean, narrow, slight, slim, svelte, sylphlike, willowy **2.** inadequate, inconsid~ erable, insufficient, little, meagre, scant, scanty, small, spare **3.** faint, feeble, flimsy, fragile, poor, remote, slight, slim, tenuous, thin, weak
Antonyms ample, appreciable, bulky, chub~ by, considerable, fat, generous, good, heavy, large, podgy, solid, stout, strong, substantial, tubby, well-built

sleuth detective, dick (*Sl., chiefly U.S.*), gumshoe (*U.S. sl.*), private eye (*Inf.*), (pri~ vate) investigator, sleuthhound (*Inf.*), tail (*Inf.*)

slice 1. *n.* cut, helping, piece, portion, seg~ ment, share, sliver, wedge **2.** *v.* carve, cut, divide, sever

slick *adj.* **1.** glib, meretricious, plausible, polished, smooth, sophistical, specious **2.** adroit, deft, dexterous, dextrous, polished, professional, sharp, skilful ~*v.* **3.** make glossy, plaster down, sleek, smarm down (*Brit. inf.*), smooth
Antonyms *adj.* amateur, amateurish, clum~ sy, crude, inexpert, unaccomplished, unpol~ ished, unprofessional, unskilful

slide *v.* **1.** coast, glide, glissade, skim, slip, slither, toboggan, veer **2. let slide** forget, gloss over, ignore, let ride, neglect, pass over, push to the back of one's mind, turn a blind eye to

slight *adj.* **1.** feeble, inconsiderable, insignificant, insubstantial, meagre, measly, minor, modest, negligible, paltry, scanty, small, superficial, trifling, trivial, unimpor~ tant, weak **2.** delicate, feeble, fragile, lightly-built, slim, small, spare ~*v.* **3.** af~ front, cold-shoulder, despise, disdain, dis~ parage, give offence *or* umbrage to, ignore, insult, neglect, put down, scorn, show dis~ respect for, snub, treat with contempt ~*n.* **4.** affront, contempt, discourtesy, disdain, disregard, disrespect, inattention, indiffer~ ence, insult, neglect, rebuff, slap in the face (*Inf.*), snub, (the) cold shoulder
Antonyms *adj.* appreciable, considerable, great, heavy, important, large, muscular, no~ ticeable, obvious, significant, solid, strong, sturdy, substantial, well-built ~*v.* compli~ ment, flatter, praise, speak well of, treat con~ siderately ~*n.* compliment, flattery, praise

slighting belittling, derogatory, disdainful, disparaging, disrespectful, insulting, offen~ sive, scornful, supercilious, uncomplimen~ tary

slightly a little, marginally, on a small scale, somewhat, to some extent *or* degree

slim *adj.* **1.** lean, narrow, slender, slight, svelte, sylphlike, thin, trim **2.** faint, poor, remote, slender, slight ~*v.* **3.** diet, lose weight, reduce, slenderize (*Chiefly U.S.*)

Antonyms *adj.* broad, bulky, chubby, fat, good, heavy, muscular, obese, overweight, strong, sturdy, tubby, well-built, wide ~*v.* build oneself up, put on weight

slimy 1. clammy, glutinous, miry, mucous, muddy, oozy, viscous **2.** creeping, grovel~ ling, obsequious, oily, servile, smarmy (*Brit. inf.*), soapy (*Sl.*), sycophantic, toady~ ing, unctuous

sling *v.* **1.** cast, chuck (*Inf.*), fling, heave, hurl, lob (*Inf.*), shy, throw, toss **2.** dangle, hang, suspend, swing

slink creep, prowl, pussyfoot (*Inf.*), skulk, slip, sneak, steal

slinky clinging, close-fitting, feline, figure-hugging, sinuous, skintight, sleek

slip *v.* **1.** glide, skate, slide, slither **2.** fall, lose one's balance, miss *or* lose one's foot~ ing, skid, trip (over) **3.** conceal, creep, hide, insinuate oneself, sneak, steal **4.** *Sometimes with* **up** blunder, boob (*Brit. sl.*), err, go wrong, make a mistake, miscalculate, mis~ judge, mistake **5.** break away from, break free from, disappear, escape, get away, get clear of, take French leave **6. let slip** blurt out, come out with (*Inf.*), disclose, divulge, give away, leak, let out (*Inf.*), let the cat out of the bag, reveal ~*n.* **7.** bloomer (*Brit. inf.*), blunder, boob (*Brit. sl.*), error, failure, fault, faux pas, imprudence, indiscretion, mistake, omission, oversight, slip of the tongue, slip-up (*Inf.*) **8. give (someone) the slip** dodge, elude, escape from, evade, get away from, lose (someone), outwit, shake (someone) off

slippery 1. glassy, greasy, icy, lubricious (*Rare*), perilous, skiddy (*Inf.*), slippy (*Inf. or dialect*), smooth, unsafe, unstable, unsteady **2.** crafty, cunning, devious, dishonest, du~ plicitous, evasive, false, foxy, shifty, sneaky, treacherous, tricky, two-faced, unpredict~ able, unreliable, untrustworthy

slipshod careless, casual, loose, slapdash, sloppy (*Inf.*), slovenly, unsystematic, untidy

slit 1. *v.* cut (open), gash, impale, knife, lance, pierce, rip, slash, split open **2.** *n.* cut, fissure, gash, incision, opening, rent, split, tear

slither *v.* glide, skitter, slide, slink, slip, snake, undulate

slobbish messy, slatternly, sloppy (*Inf.*), slovenly, unclean, unkempt, untidy

slog *v.* **1.** hit, hit for six, punch, slosh (*Brit. sl.*), slug, sock (*Sl.*), strike, thump, wallop (*Inf.*) **2.** apply oneself to, labour, peg away at, persevere, plod, plough through, slave, toil, tramp, trek, trudge, work ~*n.* **3.** effort, exertion, hike, labour, struggle, tramp, trek, trudge

slogan catch-phrase, catchword, jingle, motto, rallying cry

slop v. overflow, slosh (Inf.), spatter, spill, splash, splatter

slope v. **1.** drop away, fall, incline, lean, pitch, rise, slant, tilt ~n. **2.** brae (Scot.), declination, declivity, descent, downgrade (Chiefly U.S.), gradient, inclination, incline, ramp, rise, scarp, slant, tilt ~v. **3.** With **off, away,** etc. creep, make oneself scarce, skulk, slink, slip, steal

sloping bevelled, cant, inclined, inclining, leaning, oblique, slanting

sloppy 1. sludgy, slushy, splashy, watery, wet **2.** Inf. amateurish, careless, clumsy, hit-or-miss (Inf.), inattentive, messy, slipshod, slovenly, unkempt, untidy, weak **3.** banal, gushing, mawkish, mushy (Inf.), overemotional, sentimental, slushy (Inf.), soppy (Brit. inf.), trite, wet (Brit. inf.)

slot n. **1.** aperture, channel, groove, hole, slit, vent **2.** Inf. niche, opening, place, position, space, time, vacancy ~v. **3.** adjust, assign, fit, fit in, insert, pigeonhole

sloth faineance, idleness, inactivity, indolence, inertia, laziness, slackness, slothfulness, sluggishness, torpor

slothful do-nothing (Inf.), fainéant, idle, inactive, indolent, inert, lazy, skiving (Brit. sl.), slack, sluggish, torpid, workshy

slouch v. droop, loll, slump, stoop

slovenly careless, disorderly, heedless, loose, negligent, slack, slapdash, slatternly, slipshod, sloppy (Inf.), unkempt, untidy
Antonyms careful, clean, conscientious, disciplined, methodical, meticulous, neat, orderly, shipshape, smart, soigné or soignée, tidy, trim, well-groomed, well-ordered

slow adj. **1.** creeping, dawdling, deliberate, easy, lackadaisical, laggard, lagging, lazy, leaden, leisurely, loitering, measured, plodding, ponderous, slow-moving, sluggardly, sluggish, tortoise-like, unhurried **2.** backward, behind, behindhand, delayed, dilatory, late, long-delayed, tardy, unpunctual **3.** gradual, lingering, long-drawn-out, prolonged, protracted, time-consuming **4.** behind the times, boring, conservative, dead, dead-and-alive (Brit.), dull, inactive, one-horse (Inf.), quiet, slack, sleepy, sluggish, stagnant, tame, tedious, uneventful, uninteresting, unproductive, unprogressive, wearisome **5.** blockish, bovine, braindead (Inf.), dense, dim, dozy (Brit. inf.), dull, dull-witted, dumb (Inf.), obtuse, retarded, slow on the uptake (Inf.), slow-witted, stupid, thick, unresponsive **6.** With **to** averse, disinclined, hesitant, indisposed, loath, reluctant, unwilling ~v. **7.** Often with **up** or **down** brake, check, curb, decelerate, delay, detain, handicap, hold up, lag, reduce

speed, rein in, relax, restrict, retard, slacken (off), spin out
Antonyms adj. (senses 1, 2, 3 & 4) action-packed, animated, brisk, eager, exciting, fast, hectic, hurried, interesting, lively, precipitate, prompt, quick, quickie (Inf.), quick-moving, sharp, speedy, stimulating, swift (sense 5) bright, clever, intelligent, perceptive, quick, quick-witted, sharp, smart ~v. accelerate, advance, aid, boost, help, pick up speed, quicken, speed up

slowly at a snail's pace, at one's leisure, by degrees, gradually, inchmeal, in one's own (good) time, leisurely, ploddingly, steadily, taking one's time, unhurriedly, with leaden steps

sluggish dull, heavy, inactive, indolent, inert, lethargic, lifeless, listless, phlegmatic, slothful, slow, slow-moving, torpid, unresponsive
Antonyms animated, brisk, dynamic, energetic, enthusiastic, fast, free-flowing, full of life, industrious, lively, swift, vigorous

sluggishness apathy, drowsiness, dullness, heaviness, indolence, inertia, languor, lassitude, lethargy, listlessness, slothfulness, somnolence, stagnation, torpor

slumber v. be inactive, doze, drowse, kip (Brit. sl.), lie dormant, nap, repose, sleep, snooze (Inf.), zizz (Brit. inf.)

slump v. **1.** collapse, crash, decline, deteriorate, fall, fall off, go downhill (Inf.), plummet, plunge, reach a new low, sink, slip ~n. **2.** collapse, crash, decline, depreciation, depression, downturn, drop, failure, fall, falling-off, low, recession, reverse, stagnation, trough ~v. **3.** bend, droop, hunch, loll, sag, slouch
Antonyms v. advance, boom, develop, expand, flourish, grow, increase, prosper, thrive ~n. advance, boom, boost, development, expansion, gain, growth, improvement, increase, upsurge, upswing, upturn

slur n. affront, aspersion, blot, brand, calumny, discredit, disgrace, innuendo, insinuation, insult, reproach, smear, stain, stigma

slut drab (Archaic), scrubber (Brit. & Aust. sl.), slattern, sloven, tart, trollop

sly adj. **1.** artful, astute, clever, conniving, covert, crafty, cunning, devious, foxy, furtive, guileful, insidious, scheming, secret, shifty, stealthy, subtle, underhand, wily **2.** arch, impish, knowing, mischievous, roguish ~n. **3. on the sly** behind (someone's) back, covertly, like a thief in the night, on the q.t. (Inf.), on the quiet, privately, secretly, surreptitiously, underhandedly, under the counter (Inf.)
Antonyms adj. above-board, artless, direct, frank, guileless, honest, ingenuous, open,

straightforward, trustworthy ~n. above-
board, candidly, forthrightly, on the level,
openly, overtly, publicly

smack v. **1.** box, clap, cuff, hit, pat, slap,
sock (Sl.), spank, strike, tap ~n. **2.** blow,
crack, slap **3. smack in the eye** blow, rebuff, repulse, setback, slap in the face, snub
~adv. **4.** Inf. directly, exactly, plumb,
point-blank, precisely, right, slap (Inf.),
squarely, straight

small 1. diminutive, immature, Lilliputian,
little, mini, miniature, minute, petite, pint-
sized (Inf.), pocket-sized, puny, pygmy or
pigmy, slight, teensy-weensy, teeny, teeny-
weeny, tiny, undersized, wee, young **2.**
insignificant, lesser, minor, negligible, paltry, petty, trifling, unimportant **3.**
inadequate, inconsiderable, insufficient,
limited, meagre, measly, scant, scanty **4.**
humble, modest, small-scale, unpretentious
5. base, grudging, illiberal, mean, narrow,
petty, selfish **6. make (someone) feel
small** chagrin, disconcert, humble, humiliate, make (someone) look foolish, mortify,
put down (Sl.), show up (Inf.), take down a
peg or two (Inf.)
Antonyms (sense 1) ample, big, colossal,
enormous, great, huge, immense, massive,
mega (Sl.), sizable, vast (senses 2, 3 & 4) appreciable, considerable, generous, grand, important, large-scale, major, powerful, serious,
significant, substantial, urgent, vital, weighty

small-minded bigoted, envious, grudging,
hidebound, intolerant, mean, narrow-
minded, petty, rigid, ungenerous
Antonyms broad-minded, far-sighted, generous, liberal, open, open-minded, tolerant,
unbigoted

small-time insignificant, minor, no-account
(U.S. inf.), of no account, of no consequence,
petty, piddling (Inf.), unimportant

smarmy bootlicking (Inf.), bowing and
scraping, crawling, fawning, fulsome,
greasy, ingratiating, obsequious, oily, servile, slimy, smooth, soapy (Sl.), suave,
sycophantic, toadying, unctuous

smart¹ adj. **1.** acute, adept, agile, apt, astute, bright, brisk, canny, clever, ingenious,
intelligent, keen, nimble, quick, quick-
witted, ready, sharp, shrewd **2.** chic, elegant, fashionable, fine, modish, natty (Inf.),
neat, snappy, spruce, stylish, trendy (Brit.
inf.), trim, well turned-out **3.** effective, impertinent, nimble-witted, pointed, ready,
saucy, smart-alecky (Inf.), witty **4.** brisk,
cracking (Inf.), jaunty, lively, quick, spanking, spirited, vigorous
Antonyms (sense 1) daft (Inf.), dense, dim-
witted (Inf.), dull, dumb (Inf.), foolish, idiotic,
moronic, slow, stupid, thick, unintelligent
(sense 2) dowdy, dull, fogeyish, naff (Brit. sl.),

old-fashioned, outmoded, out-of-date, passé,
scruffy, sloppy, uncool, unfashionable,
untrendy (Brit. inf.) (sense 3) modest, polite,
respectful, restrained, unobtrusive

smart² **1.** v. burn, hurt, pain, sting, throb,
tingle **2.** adj. hard, keen, painful, piercing,
resounding, sharp, stinging **3.** n. burning
sensation, pain, pang, smarting, soreness,
sting

smash v. **1.** break, collide, crash, crush, demolish, disintegrate, pulverize, shatter,
shiver ~n. **2.** accident, collision, crash,
pile-up (Inf.), smash-up (Inf.) ~v. **3.** defeat,
destroy, lay waste, overthrow, ruin, total
(Sl.), trash (Sl.), wreck ~n. **4.** collapse, defeat, destruction, disaster, downfall, failure,
ruin, shattering

smashing boffo (Sl.), brill (Inf.), brilliant
(Inf.), chillin' (U.S. sl.), cracking (Brit. inf.),
crucial (Sl.), def (Sl.), excellent, exhilarating, fab (Inf., chiefly Brit.), fabulous (Inf.),
fantastic (Inf.), first-class, first-rate, great
(Inf.), jim-dandy (Sl.), magnificent, marvellous, mean (Sl.), mega (Sl.), out of this
world (Inf.), sensational (Inf.), sovereign,
stupendous, super (Inf.), superb, superlative, terrific (Inf.), topping (Brit. sl.), wonderful, world-class
Antonyms appalling, average, awful, bad,
boring, crap (Sl.), disappointing, disgraceful,
disgusting, dreadful, dreary, dull, hideous,
horrible, mediocre, ordinary, rotten, run-of-
the-mill, sickening, terrible, unexciting, uninspired, vile

smattering bit, dash, elements, modicum,
rudiments, smatter, sprinkling

smear v. **1.** bedaub, bedim, besmirch, blur,
coat, cover, daub, dirty, patch, plaster, rub
on, smirch, smudge, soil, spread over, stain,
sully ~n. **2.** blot, blotch, daub, smirch,
smudge, splotch, streak ~v. **3.** asperse,
besmirch, blacken, calumniate, drag
(someone's) name through the mud, malign,
sully, tarnish, traduce, vilify ~n. **4.** calumny, defamation, libel, mudslinging, slander,
vilification, whispering campaign

smell n. **1.** aroma, bouquet, fragrance, niff
(Brit. sl.), odour, perfume, redolence, scent,
whiff ~v. **2.** get a whiff of, nose, scent, sniff
~n. **3.** fetor, niff (Brit. sl.), pong (Brit. inf.),
stench, stink ~v. **4.** be malodorous, hum
(Sl.), niff (Brit. sl.), pong (Brit. inf.), reek,
stink, stink to high heaven (Inf.), whiff
(Brit. sl.)

smelly evil-smelling, fetid, foul, foul-
smelling, high, malodorous, mephitic, niffy
(Brit. sl.), noisome, olid, pongy (Brit. inf.),
putrid, reeking, stinking, stinky (Inf.),
strong, strong-smelling, whiffy (Brit. sl.)

smirk n. grin, leer, simper, smug look, sneer

smitten 1. afflicted, beset, laid low,

plagued, struck **2.** beguiled, bewitched, bowled over (*Inf.*), captivated, charmed, enamoured, infatuated, swept off one's feet

smoky begrimed, black, caliginous (*Archaic*), grey, grimy, hazy, murky, reeky, smoke-darkened, sooty, thick

smooth *adj.* **1.** even, flat, flush, horizontal, level, plain, plane, unwrinkled **2.** glossy, polished, shiny, silky, sleek, soft, velvety **3.** calm, equable, glassy, mirror-like, peaceful, serene, tranquil, undisturbed, unruffled **4.** agreeable, bland, mellow, mild, pleasant, soothing **5.** debonair, facile, glib, ingratiating, persuasive, silky, slick, smarmy (*Brit. inf.*), suave, unctuous, urbane **6.** easy, effortless, flowing, fluent, frictionless, regular, rhythmic, steady, unbroken, uneventful, uniform, uninterrupted, untroubled, well-ordered ~*v.* **7.** flatten, iron, level, plane, polish, press **8.** allay, alleviate, appease, assuage, calm, ease, extenuate, facilitate, iron out the difficulties of, mitigate, mollify, palliate, pave the way, soften
Antonyms *adj.* (*senses 1 & 2*) abrasive, bumpy, coarse, irregular, jagged, lumpy, rough, sharp, uneven (*sense 3*) agitated, disturbed, edgy, excitable, nervous, ruffled, troubled, troublesome, turbulent, uneasy ~*v.* aggravate, exacerbate, hamper, hinder, intensify, make worse, roughen

smoothness **1.** evenness, flushness, levelness, regularity, unbrokenness **2.** silkiness, sleekness, smooth texture, softness, velvetiness **3.** calmness, glassiness, placidity, serenity, stillness, unruffled surface **4.** glibness, oiliness, smarminess (*Brit. inf.*), suavity, urbanity **5.** ease, efficiency, effortlessness, felicity, finish, flow, fluency, polish, rhythm, slickness, smooth running

smother *v.* **1.** choke, extinguish, snuff, stifle, strangle, suffocate **2.** conceal, hide, keep back, muffle, repress, stifle, suppress **3.** be swimming in, cocoon, cover, envelop, heap, inundate, overwhelm, shower, shroud, surround ~*n.* **4.** fug (*Chiefly Brit.*), smog

smoulder *Fig.* be resentful, boil, burn, fester, fume, rage, seethe, simmer, smart under

smudge **1.** *v.* blacken, blur, daub, dirty, mark, smear, smirch, soil **2.** *n.* blemish, blot, blur, smear, smut, smutch

smug complacent, conceited, holier-than-thou, priggish, self-opinionated, self-righteous, self-satisfied, superior

smuggler bootlegger, contrabandist, gentleman, moonshiner (*U.S.*), rum-runner, runner, trafficker, wrecker

smutty bawdy, blue, coarse, crude, dirty, filthy, improper, indecent, indelicate, lewd, obscene, off colour, pornographic, prurient,

racy, raunchy (*U.S. sl.*), risqué, salacious, suggestive, vulgar

snack bite, bite to eat, break, elevenses (*Brit. inf.*), light meal, nibble, refreshment(s), titbit

snag **1.** *n.* catch, complication, difficulty, disadvantage, downside, drawback, hitch, inconvenience, obstacle, problem, stumbling block, the rub **2.** *v.* catch, hole, rip, tear

snap *v.* **1.** break, come apart, crack, give way, separate **2.** bite, bite at, catch, grip, nip, seize, snatch **3.** bark, flare out, flash, fly off the handle at (*Inf.*), growl, jump down (someone's) throat (*Inf.*), lash out at, retort, snarl, speak sharply **4.** click, crackle, pop **5. snap one's fingers at** cock a snook at (*Brit.*), defy, flout, pay no attention to, scorn, set at naught, wave two fingers at (*Sl.*) **6. snap out of it** cheer up, get a grip on oneself, get over, liven up, perk up, pull oneself together (*Inf.*), recover ~*n.* **7.** crackle, fillip, flick, pop **8.** bite, grab, nip **9.** *Inf.* energy, get-up-and-go (*Inf.*), go (*Inf.*), liveliness, pep, pizzazz *or* pizazz (*Inf.*), vigour, zip (*Inf.*) ~*adj.* **10.** abrupt, immediate, instant, on-the-spot, sudden, unpremeditated

snappy **1.** apt to fly off the handle (*Inf.*), cross, edgy, hasty, impatient, irritable, like a bear with a sore head (*Inf.*), quick-tempered, ratty (*Brit. & N.Z. inf.*), snappish, tart, testy, tetchy, touchy, waspish **2.** chic, dapper, fashionable, modish, natty (*Inf.*), smart, stylish, trendy (*Brit. inf.*), up-to-the-minute, voguish **3. look snappy** be quick, buck up (*Inf.*), get a move on (*Inf.*), get one's skates on, hurry (up), look lively, make haste

snap up avail oneself of, grab, grasp, nab (*Inf.*), pounce upon, seize, swoop down on, take advantage of

snare **1.** *v.* catch, entrap, net, seize, springe, trap, trepan (*Archaic*), wire **2.** *n.* catch, gin, net, noose, pitfall, springe, trap, wire

snarl¹ *v.* complain, growl, grumble, mumble, murmur, show its teeth (*of an animal*)

snarl² *v. Often with* **up** complicate, confuse, embroil, enmesh, entangle, entwine, muddle, ravel, tangle

snarl-up confusion, entanglement, muddle, tangle, (traffic) jam

snatch **1.** *v.* catch up, clutch, gain, grab, grasp, grip, make off with, pluck, pull, rescue, seize, take, win, wrench, wrest **2.** *n.* bit, fragment, part, piece, smattering, snippet, spell

sneak *v.* **1.** cower, lurk, pad, sidle, skulk, slink, slip, smuggle, spirit, steal **2.** *Inf.* grass on (*Brit. sl.*), inform on, peach (*Sl.*), shop (*Sl., chiefly Brit.*), sing (*Sl., chiefly U.S.*), spill one's guts (*Sl.*), tell on (*Inf.*), tell tales ~n. **3.** informer, snake in the grass, telltale ~adj. **4.** clandestine, furtive, quick, secret, stealthy, surprise

sneaking 1. hidden, private, secret, sup~ pressed, unavowed, unconfessed, undi~ vulged, unexpressed, unvoiced **2.** intuitive, nagging, niggling, persistent, uncomfort~ able, worrying **3.** contemptible, furtive, mean, sly, sneaky, surreptitious, two-faced, underhand

sneer 1. v. curl one's lip, deride, disdain, gibe, hold in contempt, hold up to ridicule, jeer, laugh, look down on, mock, ridicule, scoff, scorn, sniff at, snigger, turn up one's nose (Inf.) **2.** n. derision, disdain, gibe, jeer, mockery, ridicule, scorn, snidery, snigger

snide cynical, disparaging, hurtful, ill-natured, insinuating, malicious, mean, nas~ ty, sarcastic, scornful, shrewish, sneering, spiteful, unkind

sniff v. breathe, inhale, smell, snuff, snuffle

snigger giggle, laugh, smirk, sneer, snicker, titter

snip v. **1.** clip, crop, cut, dock, nick, nip off, notch, shave, trim ~n. **2.** bit, clipping, fragment, piece, scrap, shred, snippet **3.** Inf. bargain, giveaway, good buy, steal (Inf.)

snippet fragment, part, particle, piece, scrap, shred, snatch

snivel blubber, cry, girn (Scot. & northern English dialect), gripe (Inf.), grizzle (Inf., chiefly Brit.), mewl, moan, sniffle, snuffle, weep, whimper, whine, whinge (Inf.)

snobbery airs, arrogance, condescension, pretension, pride, side (Brit. sl.), snobbish~ ness, snootiness (Inf.), uppishness (Brit. inf.)

snobbish arrogant, condescending, high and mighty (Inf.), high-hat (Inf., chiefly U.S.), hoity-toity (Inf.), patronizing, preten~ tious, snooty (Inf.), stuck-up (Inf.), superior, toffee-nosed (Sl., chiefly Brit.), uppish (Brit. inf.), uppity
Antonyms down to earth, humble, modest, natural, unassuming, unostentatious, unpre~ tentious, without airs

snoop interfere, poke one's nose in (Inf.), pry, spy

snooper busybody, meddler, nosy parker (Inf.), Paul Pry, pry, snoop (Inf.), stickybeak (Aust. inf.)

snooze 1. v. catnap, doze, drop off (Inf.), drowse, kip (Brit. sl.), nap, nod off (Inf.), take forty winks (Inf.) **2.** n. catnap, doze, forty winks (Inf.), kip (Brit. sl.), nap, siesta

snub 1. v. cold-shoulder, cut (Inf.), cut dead (Inf.), give (someone) the brush-off (Sl.), give (someone) the cold shoulder, humble, humiliate, mortify, put down, rebuff, shame, slight **2.** n. affront, brushoff (Sl.),

humiliation, insult, put-down, slap in the face

snug 1. comfortable, comfy (Inf.), cosy, homely, intimate, sheltered, warm **2.** close, compact, neat, trim

snuggle cuddle, nestle, nuzzle

soak v. **1.** bathe, damp, drench, immerse, infuse, marinate (Cookery), moisten, pen~ etrate, permeate, saturate, seep, steep, wet **2.** With **up** absorb, assimilate, drink in, take up or in

soaking drenched, dripping, droukit or drookit (Scot.), saturated, soaked, soaked to the skin, sodden, sopping, streaming, waterlogged, wet through, wringing wet

soar 1. ascend, fly, mount, rise, tower, wing **2.** climb, escalate, rise, rocket, shoot up
Antonyms descend, dive, drop down, fall, nose-dive, plummet, plunge, swoop

sob v. bawl, blubber, boohoo, cry, greet (Scot. or archaic), howl, shed tears, snivel, weep

sober adj. **1.** abstemious, abstinent, moder~ ate, on the wagon (Inf.), temperate **2.** calm, clear-headed, cold, composed, cool, dispas~ sionate, grave, level-headed, lucid, peaceful, practical, rational, realistic, reasonable, se~ date, serene, serious, solemn, sound, staid, steady, unexcited, unruffled **3.** dark, drab, plain, quiet, severe, sombre, subdued ~v. **4.** Usually with **up** bring (someone) back to earth, calm down, clear one's head, come or bring to one's senses, give (someone) pause for thought, make (someone) stop and think
Antonyms adj. (sense 1) bevvied (Dialect), blitzed (Sl.), blotto (Sl.), bombed (Sl.), drunk, flying (Sl.), fu' (Scot.), guttered (Sl.), had one too many, inebriated, intoxicated, merry (Brit. inf.), paralytic (Inf.), pie-eyed (Sl.), pissed (Taboo sl.), plastered, sloshed (Sl.), smashed (Sl.), steamboats (Sl.), steaming (Sl.), tiddly (Sl., chiefly Brit.), tight (Inf.), tipsy, tired and emotional (Euphemistic), wasted (Sl.), wrecked (Sl.), zonked (Sl.), (senses 2 & 3) bright, excessive, flamboyant, flashy, frivo~ lous, garish, gaudy, giddy, happy, immoder~ ate, imprudent, injudicious, irrational, light, lighthearted, lively, sensational, unrealistic ~v. become intoxicated, get drunk

sobriety 1. abstemiousness, abstinence, moderation, nonindulgence, self-restraint, soberness, temperance **2.** calmness, compo~ sure, coolness, gravity, level-headedness, reasonableness, restraint, sedateness, seri~ ousness, solemnity, staidness, steadiness

so-called alleged, ostensible, pretended, professed, self-styled, soi-disant, supposed

sociability affability, companionability, congeniality, conviviality, cordiality, friendliness, gregariousness, neighbourli~ ness

sociable accessible, affable, approachable, companionable, conversable, convivial, cordial, familiar, friendly, genial, gregarious, neighbourly, outgoing, social, warm
Antonyms antisocial, boorish, businesslike, cold, distant, formal, introverted, reclusive, standoffish, stiff, tense, uncommunicative, unfriendly, unsociable, withdrawn

social *adj.* **1.** collective, common, communal, community, general, group, organized, public, societal **2.** companionable, friendly, gregarious, neighbourly, sociable ~*n.* **3.** do (*Inf.*), gathering, get-together (*Inf.*), party

socialize be a good mixer, entertain, fraternize, get about *or* around, get together, go out, mix

society 1. civilization, culture, humanity, mankind, people, population, social order, the community, the general public, the public, the world at large **2.** camaraderie, companionship, company, fellowship, friendship **3.** association, brotherhood, circle, club, corporation, fellowship, fraternity, group, guild, institute, league, order, organization, sisterhood, union **4.** beau monde, elite, gentry, *haut monde,* high society, polite society, the country set, the nobs (*Sl.*), the smart set, the swells (*Inf.*), the toffs (*Brit. sl.*), the top drawer, upper classes, upper crust (*Inf.*)

sodden boggy, drenched, drookit *or* drookit (*Scot.*), marshy, miry, saturated, soaked, soggy, sopping, waterlogged

soft 1. creamy, cushioned, cushiony, doughy, elastic, gelatinous, pulpy, quaggy, spongy, squashy, swampy, yielding **2.** bendable, ductile (*of metals*), elastic, flexible, impressible, malleable, mouldable, plastic, pliable, supple, tensile **3.** downy, feathery, fleecy, flowing, fluid, furry, like a baby's bottom (*Inf.*), rounded, silky, smooth, velvety **4.** balmy, bland, caressing, delicate, diffuse, dim, dimmed, dulcet, faint, gentle, light, low, mellifluous, mellow, melodious, mild, murmured, muted, pale, pastel, pleasing, quiet, restful, shaded, soft-toned, soothing, subdued, sweet, temperate, twilight, understated, whispered **5.** compassionate, gentle, kind, pitying, sensitive, sentimental, sympathetic, tender, tenderhearted **6.** easy-going, indulgent, lax, lenient, liberal, overindulgent, permissive, spineless, weak **7.** *Inf.* comfortable, cushy (*Inf.*), easy, easy-peasy (*Sl.*), undemanding **8.** effeminate, flabby, flaccid, limp, namby-pamby, out of condition, out of training, overindulged, pampered, podgy, weak **9.** *Inf.* a bit lacking (*Inf.*), daft (*Inf.*), feeble-minded, foolish, silly, simple, soft in the head (*Inf.*), soppy (*Brit. inf.*)
Antonyms (*senses 1, 2 & 3*) abrasive, coarse, firm, grating, hard, inflexible, irritating, rigid, rough, solid, stiff, tough, unyielding (*sense 4*) bright, garish, gaudy, glaring, hard, harsh, loud, noisy, strident, unpleasant (*sense 6*) austere, harsh, no-nonsense, stern, strict

soften abate, allay, alleviate, appease, assuage, calm, cushion, diminish, ease, lessen, lighten, lower, melt, mitigate, moderate, modify, mollify, muffle, palliate, quell, relax, soothe, still, subdue, temper, tone down, turn down

soften up conciliate, disarm, melt, soft-soap (*Inf.*), weaken, win over, work on

softhearted charitable, compassionate, generous, indulgent, kind, sentimental, sympathetic, tender, tenderhearted, warmhearted
Antonyms callous, cold, cruel, hard, hardhearted, heartless, insensitive, uncaring, unkind, unsympathetic

soil[1] *n.* **1.** clay, dirt, dust, earth, ground, loam **2.** country, land, region, terra firma

soil[2] *v.* bedraggle, befoul, begrime, besmirch, defile, dirty, foul, maculate (*Literary*), muddy, pollute, smear, smirch, spatter, spot, stain, sully, tarnish

sojourn 1. *n.* rest, stay, stop, stopover, visit **2.** *v.* abide, dwell, lodge, reside, rest, stay, stop, tarry

solace 1. *n.* alleviation, assuagement, comfort, consolation, relief **2.** *v.* allay, alleviate, comfort, console, mitigate, soften, soothe

soldier enlisted man (*U.S.*), fighter, GI (*U.S. inf.*), man-at-arms, military man, redcoat, serviceman, squaddie *or* squaddy (*Brit. sl.*), Tommy (*Brit. inf.*), trooper, warrior

sole alone, exclusive, individual, one, one and only, only, single, singular, solitary

solecism bloomer (*Brit. inf.*), blunder, booboo (*Inf.*), breach of etiquette, cacology, faux pas, gaffe, gaucherie, impropriety, incongruity, indecorum, lapse, mistake

solely alone, completely, entirely, exclusively, merely, only, single-handedly, singly

solemn 1. earnest, glum, grave, portentous, sedate, serious, sober, staid, thoughtful **2.** august, awe-inspiring, ceremonial, ceremonious, dignified, formal, grand, grave, imposing, impressive, majestic, momentous, stately **3.** devotional, hallowed, holy, religious, reverential, ritual, sacred, sanctified, venerable
Antonyms (*senses 1 & 2*) bright, cheerful, chirpy (*Inf.*), comical, frivolous, genial, happy, informal, jovial, light-hearted, merry, relaxed, unceremonious (*sense 3*) irreligious, irreverent, unholy

solemnity 1. earnestness, grandeur, gravitas, gravity, impressiveness, momentousness, portentousness, sacredness, sanctity, seriousness **2.** *Often plural* celebration,

ceremonial, ceremony, formalities, obser~
vance, proceedings, rite, ritual

solemnize celebrate, commemorate, hon~
our, keep, observe

solicit ask, beg, beseech, canvass, crave, en~
treat, implore, importune, petition, plead
for, pray, seek, supplicate

solicitous anxious, apprehensive, attentive,
careful, caring, concerned, eager, earnest,
troubled, uneasy, worried, zealous

solicitude anxiety, attentiveness, care, con~
cern, considerateness, consideration, re~
gard, worry

solid *adj.* **1.** compact, concrete, dense, firm,
hard, massed, stable, strong, sturdy, sub~
stantial, unshakable **2.** genuine, good, pure,
real, reliable, sound **3.** agreed, complete,
continuous, unalloyed, unanimous, unbro~
ken, undivided, uninterrupted, united, un~
mixed **4.** constant, decent, dependable, esti~
mable, law-abiding, level-headed, reliable,
sensible, serious, sober, trusty, upright,
upstanding, worthy
Antonyms (*sense 1*) broken, crumbling, de~
caying, flimsy, gaseous, hollow, liquid, per~
meable, precarious, shaky, unstable, un~
steady, unsubstantial (*sense 2*) impure, unre~
liable, unsound (*sense 3*) at odds, divided,
mixed, split, undecided (*sense 4*) flighty, irre~
sponsible, unreliable, unsound, unstable, un~
steady

solidarity accord, camaraderie, cohesion,
community of interest, concordance, esprit
de corps, harmony, like-mindedness, sin~
gleness of purpose, soundness, stability,
team spirit, unanimity, unification, unity

solidify cake, coagulate, cohere, congeal,
harden, jell, set

solitary *adj.* **1.** desolate, hidden, isolated,
lonely, out-of-the-way, remote, retired, se~
cluded, sequestered, unfrequented, unvisit~
ed **2.** alone, lone, single, sole **3.** cloistered,
companionless, friendless, hermitical, lone~
ly, lonesome, reclusive, unsociable, unsocial
~*n.* **4.** hermit, introvert, loner (*Inf.*), lone
wolf, recluse
Antonyms *adj.* (*sense 1*) bustling, busy, fre~
quented, public, well-frequented (*senses 2 & 3*)
companionable, convivial, cordial, gregari~
ous, one of a group, outgoing, sociable, social
~*n.* extrovert, mixer, socialite

solitude 1. isolation, loneliness, privacy,
reclusiveness, retirement, seclusion **2.** *Po~
etic* desert, emptiness, waste, wasteland,
wilderness

solution 1. answer, clarification, elucida~
tion, explanation, explication, key, resolu~
tion, result, solving, unfolding, unravelling
2. blend, compound, emulsion, mix, mix~
ture, solvent, suspension (*Chem.*) **3.** discon~
nection, dissolution, liquefaction, melting

solve answer, clarify, clear up, crack, deci~
pher, disentangle, elucidate, explain, ex~
pound, get to the bottom of, interpret, re~
solve, suss (out) (*Sl.*), unfold, unravel, work
out

sombre dark, dim, dismal, doleful, drab,
dull, dusky, funereal, gloomy, grave, joy~
less, lugubrious, melancholy, mournful, ob~
scure, sad, sepulchral, shadowy, shady, so~
ber
Antonyms bright, cheerful, chirpy (*Inf.*),
colourful, dazzling, effusive, full of beans,
garish, gaudy, genial, happy, lively, sunny,
upbeat (*Inf.*)

somebody *n.* big noise (*Inf.*), big shot
(*Inf.*), big wheel (*Sl.*), bigwig (*Inf.*), celeb
(*Inf.*), celebrity, dignitary, heavyweight
(*Inf.*), household name, luminary, megastar
(*Inf.*), name, notable, personage, person of
note, public figure, star, superstar, V.I.P.
Antonyms also-ran, cipher, lightweight
(*Inf.*), menial, nobody, nonentity, nothing
(*Inf.*)

someday eventually, one day, one of these
(fine) days, sooner or later, ultimately

somehow by fair means or foul, by hook
or (by) crook, by some means or other,
come hell or high water (*Inf.*), come what
may, one way or another

sometimes at times, every now and then,
every so often, from time to time, now and
again, now and then, occasionally, off and
on, once in a while, on occasion
Antonyms always, consistently, constantly,
continually, eternally, ever, everlastingly,
evermore, forever, invariably, perpetually,
unceasingly, without exception

somnolent comatose, dozy, drowsy, half-
awake, heavy-eyed, nodding off (*Inf.*),
sleepy, soporific, torpid

song air, anthem, ballad, canticle, canzonet,
carol, chant, chorus, ditty, hymn, lay, lyric,
melody, number, pop song, psalm, shanty,
strain, tune

song and dance ado, commotion, flap
(*Inf.*), fuss, hoo-ha, kerfuffle (*Inf.*), perfor~
mance (*Inf.*), pother, shindig (*Inf.*), shindy
(*Inf.*), stir, to-do

soon anon (*Archaic*), any minute now, be~
fore long, betimes (*Archaic*), erelong (*Ar~
chaic or poetic*), in a little while, in a min~
ute, in a short time, in the near future,
shortly

soothe allay, alleviate, appease, assuage,
calm, calm down, compose, ease, hush, lull,
mitigate, mollify, pacify, quiet, relieve, set~
tle, smooth down, soften, still, tranquillize
Antonyms aggravate (*Inf.*), agitate, annoy,
disquiet, disturb, exacerbate, excite, get on
one's nerves (*Inf.*), hassle (*Inf.*), increase,

inflame, irritate, rouse, stimulate, upset, vex, worry

soothing balsamic, calming, demulcent, easeful, emollient, lenitive, palliative, relaxing, restful

soothsayer augur, diviner, foreteller, prophet, seer, sibyl

sophisticated 1. blasé, citified, cosmopolitan, cultivated, cultured, jet-set, refined, seasoned, urbane, worldly, worldly-wise, world-weary **2.** advanced, complex, complicated, delicate, elaborate, highly-developed, intricate, multifaceted, refined, subtle **Antonyms** basic, naive, old-fashioned, plain, primitive, simple, uncomplicated, unrefined, unsophisticated, unsubtle, unworldly

sophistication finesse, poise, savoir-faire, *savoir-vivre*, urbanity, worldliness, worldly wisdom

sophistry casuistry, fallacy, quibble, sophism

soporific 1. *adj.* hypnotic, sedative, sleep-inducing, sleepy, somniferous (*Rare*), somnolent, tranquillizing **2.** *n.* anaesthetic, hypnotic, narcotic, opiate, sedative, tranquillizer

soppy corny (*Sl.*), daft (*Inf.*), drippy (*Inf.*), gushy (*Inf.*), lovey-dovey, mawkish, over-emotional, schmaltzy (*Sl.*), sentimental, silly, slushy (*Inf.*), soft (*Inf.*), weepy (*Inf.*)

sorcerer enchanter, mage (*Archaic*), magician, magus, necromancer, sorceress, warlock, witch, wizard

sorcery black art, black magic, charm, divination, enchantment, incantation, magic, necromancy, spell, witchcraft, witchery, wizardry

sordid 1. dirty, filthy, foul, mean, seamy, seedy, sleazy, slovenly, slummy, squalid, unclean, wretched **2.** backstreet, base, debauched, degenerate, degraded, despicable, disreputable, low, shabby, shameful, vicious, vile **3.** avaricious, corrupt, covetous, grasping, mercenary, miserly, niggardly, selfish, self-seeking, ungenerous, venal **Antonyms** blameless, clean, decent, fresh, honourable, noble, pure, spotless, squeaky-clean, unblemished, undefiled, unsullied, upright

sore *adj.* **1.** angry, burning, chafed, inflamed, irritated, painful, raw, reddened, sensitive, smarting, tender **2.** annoying, distressing, grievous, harrowing, severe, sharp, troublesome **3.** acute, critical, desperate, dire, extreme, pressing, urgent **4.** afflicted, aggrieved, angry, annoyed, cross, grieved, hurt, irked, irritated, pained, peeved (*Inf.*), resentful, stung, upset, vexed ~*n.* **5.** abscess, boil, chafe, gathering, inflammation, ulcer

sorrow *n.* **1.** affliction, anguish, distress, grief, heartache, heartbreak, misery, mourning, regret, sadness, unhappiness, woe **2.** affliction, blow, bummer (*Sl.*), hardship, misfortune, trial, tribulation, trouble, woe, worry ~*v.* **3.** agonize, bemoan, be sad, bewail, eat one's heart out, grieve, lament, moan, mourn, weep **Antonyms** *n.* bliss, delight, elation, exaltation, exultation, gladness, good fortune, happiness, joy, lucky break, pleasure ~*v.* celebrate, delight, exult, jump for joy, rejoice, revel

sorrowful affecting, afflicted, dejected, depressed, disconsolate, dismal, distressing, doleful, grievous, harrowing, heartbroken, heart-rending, heavy-hearted, lamentable, lugubrious, melancholy, miserable, mournful, painful, piteous, rueful, sad, sick at heart, sorry, tearful, unhappy, woebegone, woeful, wretched

sorry 1. apologetic, conscience-stricken, contrite, guilt-ridden, in sackcloth and ashes, penitent, regretful, remorseful, repentant, self-reproachful, shamefaced **2.** disconsolate, distressed, grieved, melancholy, mournful, sad, sorrowful, unhappy **3.** commiserative, compassionate, full of pity, moved, pitying, sympathetic **4.** abject, base, deplorable, dismal, distressing, mean, miserable, paltry, pathetic, piteous, pitiable, pitiful, poor, sad, shabby, vile, wretched **Antonyms** (*sense 1*) impenitent, not contrite, shameless, unapologetic, unashamed, unremorseful, unrepentant (*sense 2*) cheerful, delighted, elated, happy, joyful (*sense 3*) compassionless (*Rare*), heartless, indifferent, uncompassionate, unconcerned, unmoved, unpitying, unsympathetic

sort *n.* **1.** brand, breed, category, character, class, denomination, description, family, genus, group, ilk, kind, make, nature, order, quality, race, species, stamp, style, type, variety **2. out of sorts** crotchety, down in the dumps (*Inf.*), down in the mouth (*Inf.*), grouchy (*Inf.*), in low spirits, mopy, not up to par, not up to snuff (*Inf.*), off colour, poorly (*Inf.*), under the weather (*Inf.*) **3. sort of** as it were, in part, moderately, rather, reasonably, slightly, somewhat, to some extent ~*v.* **4.** arrange, assort, catalogue, categorize, choose, class, classify, distribute, divide, file, grade, group, order, put in order, rank, select, separate, systematize, tabulate

sort out 1. clarify, clear up, organize, put *or* get straight, resolve, tidy up **2.** pick out, put on one side, segregate, select, separate, sift

soul 1. animating principle, essence, intellect, life, mind, psyche, reason, spirit, vital force **2.** being, body, creature, individual,

man, mortal, person, woman **3.** embodi~
ment, epitome, essence, incarnation,
personification, quintessence, type **4.** ani~
mation, ardour, courage, energy, feeling,
fervour, force, inspiration, nobility, vitality,
vivacity

sound[1] *n.* **1.** din, noise, report, resonance,
reverberation, tone, voice **2.** drift, idea, im~
plication(s), impression, look, tenor **3.** ear~
shot, hearing, range ~*v.* **4.** echo, resonate,
resound, reverberate **5.** appear, give the
impression of, look, seem, strike one as be~
ing **6.** announce, articulate, declare, enun~
ciate, express, pronounce, signal, utter

sound[2] *adj.* **1.** complete, entire, firm, fit,
hale, hale and hearty, healthy, intact, per~
fect, robust, solid, sturdy, substantial, un~
damaged, unhurt, unimpaired, uninjured,
vigorous, well-constructed, whole **2.** cor~
rect, fair, just, level-headed, logical, ortho~
dox, proper, prudent, rational, reasonable,
reliable, responsible, right, right-thinking,
sensible, true, trustworthy, valid, well-
founded, well-grounded, wise **3.** established,
orthodox, proven, recognized, reliable,
reputable, safe, secure, solid, solvent, stable,
tried-and-true **4.** deep, peaceful, unbroken,
undisturbed, untroubled
Antonyms (*sense 1*) ailing, damaged, flimsy,
frail, light, shaky, sketchy, superficial, unbal~
anced, unstable, weak (*senses 2 & 3*) fallacious,
faulty, flawed, incompetent, irrational, irre~
sponsible, specious, unreliable, unsound, un~
stable (*sense 4*) broken, fitful, shallow, trou~
bled

sound[3] *v.* **1.** fathom, plumb, probe **2.** exam~
ine, inspect, investigate, test

sound out canvass, examine, probe, pump,
question, see how the land lies

sour *adj.* **1.** acerb, acetic, acid, acidulated,
bitter, pungent, sharp, tart, unpleasant **2.**
bad, curdled, fermented, gone off, rancid,
turned, unsavoury, unwholesome **3.** acrid,
acrimonious, churlish, crabbed, cynical,
disagreeable, discontented, embittered,
grouchy (*Inf.*), grudging, ill-natured, ill-
tempered, jaundiced, peevish, tart, ungen~
erous, waspish ~*v.* **4.** alienate, disenchant,
embitter, envenom, exacerbate, exasperate,
turn off (*Inf.*)
Antonyms *adj.* (*sense 1*) agreeable, bland,
mild, pleasant, savoury, sugary, sweet (*sense
2*) fresh, unimpaired, unspoiled (*sense 3*) af~
fable, amiable, congenial, friendly, genial,
good-humoured, good-natured, good-
tempered, pleasant, warm-hearted ~*v.* en~
hance, improve, strengthen

source 1. author, begetter, beginning,
cause, commencement, derivation, fount,
fountainhead, origin, originator, rise,
spring, wellspring **2.** authority, informant

souse drench, dunk, immerse, marinate
(*Cookery*), pickle, soak, steep

souvenir keepsake, memento, relic, re~
membrancer (*Archaic*), reminder, token

sovereign *n.* **1.** chief, emperor, empress,
king, monarch, potentate, prince, queen,
ruler, shah, supreme ruler, tsar ~*adj.* **2.**
absolute, chief, dominant, imperial, kingly,
monarchal, paramount, predominant, prin~
cipal, queenly, regal, royal, ruling, su~
preme, unlimited **3.** effectual, efficacious,
efficient, excellent

sovereignty ascendancy, domination,
kingship, primacy, supremacy, supreme
power, suzerainty, sway

sow broadcast, disseminate, implant, in~
seminate, lodge, plant, scatter, seed

space 1. amplitude, capacity, elbowroom,
expanse, extension, extent, leeway, margin,
play, room, scope, spaciousness, volume **2.**
blank, distance, gap, interval, lacuna, omis~
sion **3.** duration, interval, period, span,
time, while **4.** accommodation, berth, place,
seat

spaceman *or* **spacewoman** astronaut,
cosmonaut

spacious ample, broad, capacious, comfort~
able, commodious, expansive, extensive,
huge, large, roomy, sizable, uncrowded, vast
Antonyms close, confined, cramped, crowd~
ed, limited, narrow, poky, restricted, small

spadework donkey-work, groundwork, la~
bour, preparation

span *n.* **1.** amount, distance, extent, length,
reach, spread, stretch **2.** duration, period,
spell, term ~*v.* **3.** arch across, bridge, cov~
er, cross, extend across, link, range over,
traverse, vault

spank *v.* belt (*Inf.*), cuff, give (someone) a
hiding (*Inf.*), put (someone) over one's knee,
slap, slipper (*Inf.*), smack, tan (*Sl.*), wallop
(*Inf.*), whack

spar *v.* argue, bicker, dispute, exchange
blows, fall out (*Inf.*), have a tiff, lead a cat-
and-dog life, row, scrap (*Inf.*), skirmish,
spat (*U.S.*), squabble, wrangle, wrestle

spare *adj.* **1.** additional, emergency, extra,
free, going begging, in excess, in reserve,
leftover, odd, over, superfluous, supernu~
merary, surplus, unoccupied, unused, un~
wanted **2.** gaunt, lank, lean, macilent
(*Rare*), meagre, slender, slight, slim, wiry
3. economical, frugal, meagre, modest,
scanty, sparing **4. go spare** *Brit. sl.* be~
come angry (distracted, distraught, enraged,
mad (*Inf.*), upset), blow one's top (*Inf.*), do
one's nut (*Brit. sl.*), go mental (*Sl.*), go up
the wall (*Sl.*), have *or* throw a fit (*Inf.*) ~*v.*
5. afford, allow, bestow, dispense with, do
without, give, grant, let (someone) have,

manage without, part with, relinquish **6.** be merciful to, deal leniently with, go easy on (*Inf.*), have mercy on, leave, let off (*Inf.*), pardon, refrain from, release, relieve from, save from
Antonyms *adj.* (*sense 1*) allocated, designat~ ed, earmarked, in use, necessary, needed, set aside, spoken for (*sense 2*) corpulent, fat, flabby, fleshy, generous, heavy, large, plump ~*v.* (*sense 6*) afflict, condemn, damn, destroy, hurt, punish, show no mercy to

spare time free time, leisure, odd mo~ ments, time on one's hands, time to kill

sparing careful, chary, cost-conscious, eco~ nomical, frugal, money-conscious, prudent, saving, thrifty
Antonyms extravagant, lavish, liberal, open-handed, prodigal, spendthrift

spark *n.* **1.** flare, flash, flicker, gleam, glint, scintillation, spit **2.** atom, hint, jot, scintil~ la, scrap, trace, vestige ~*v.* **3.** *Often with* **off** animate, excite, inspire, kick-start, kin~ dle, precipitate, prod, provoke, rouse, set in motion, set off, start, stimulate, stir, touch off, trigger (off)

sparkle *v.* **1.** beam, coruscate, dance, flash, gleam, glint, glisten, glister (*Archaic*), glit~ ter, glow, scintillate, shimmer, shine, spark, twinkle, wink **2.** bubble, effervesce, fizz, fizzle ~*n.* **3.** brilliance, coruscation, dazzle, flash, flicker, gleam, glint, radiance, spark, twinkle **4.** animation, brio, dash, élan, gai~ ety, life, panache, spirit, vim (*Sl.*), vitality, vivacity, zip (*Inf.*)

sparse few and far between, meagre, scanty, scarce, scattered, sporadic
Antonyms crowded, dense, lavish, lush, luxuriant, numerous, plentiful, thick

spartan **1.** abstemious, ascetic, austere, bleak, disciplined, extreme, frugal, plain, rigorous, self-denying, severe, stern, strict, stringent **2.** bold, brave, courageous, dar~ ing, dauntless, doughty, fearless, hardy, he~ roic, intrepid, resolute, unflinching, valor~ ous

spasm **1.** contraction, convulsion, parox~ ysm, throe (*Rare*), twitch **2.** access, burst, eruption, fit, frenzy, outburst, seizure

spasmodic convulsive, erratic, fitful, intermittent, irregular, jerky, sporadic

spate deluge, flood, flow, outpouring, rush, torrent

speak **1.** articulate, communicate, converse, discourse, enunciate, express, make known, pronounce, say, state, talk, tell, utter, voice **2.** address, argue, declaim, deliver an ad~ dress, descant, discourse, harangue, hold forth, lecture, plead, speechify, spiel (*Inf.*), spout **3.** *With* **of** advert to, allude to, com~ ment on, deal with, discuss, make reference to, mention, refer to

speaker lecturer, mouthpiece, orator, public speaker, spieler (*Inf.*), spokesman, spokes~ person, spokeswoman, word-spinner

speak for act for *or* on behalf of, appear for, hold a brief for, hold a mandate for, represent

speaking *adj.* eloquent, expressive, moving, noticeable, striking

speak out *or* **up** **1.** make oneself heard, say it loud and clear, speak loudly **2.** have one's say, make one's position plain, sound off, speak one's mind, stand up and be counted

speak to **1.** accost, address, apostrophize, direct one's words at, talk to **2.** admonish, bring to book, dress down (*Inf.*), lecture, rebuke, reprimand, scold, tell off (*Inf.*), tick off (*Inf.*), warn

spearhead *v.* be in the van, blaze the trail, head, initiate, launch, lay the first stone, lead, lead the way, pioneer, set in motion, set off

special **1.** distinguished, especial, excep~ tional, extraordinary, festive, gala, impor~ tant, memorable, momentous, out of the or~ dinary, red-letter, significant, uncommon, unique, unusual **2.** appropriate, certain, characteristic, distinctive, especial, indi~ vidual, particular, peculiar, precise, spe~ cialized, specific **3.** chief, main, major, par~ ticular, primary
Antonyms common, everyday, general, humdrum, mediocre, multi-purpose, normal, ordinary, routine, run-of-the-mill, undistinctive, undistinguished, unexcep~ tional, unspecialized, usual

specialist *n.* authority, buff (*Inf.*), connois~ seur, consultant, expert, hotshot (*Inf.*), master, maven (*U.S.*), professional, whiz (*Inf.*)

speciality bag (*Sl.*), claim to fame, distinc~ tive *or* distinguishing feature, forte, métier, *pièce de résistance*, special, specialty

species breed, category, class, collection, description, genus, group, kind, sort, type, variety

specific *adj.* **1.** clear-cut, definite, exact, ex~ plicit, express, limited, particular, precise, unambiguous, unequivocal **2.** characteris~ tic, distinguishing, especial, peculiar, spe~ cial
Antonyms approximate, common, general, hazy, imprecise, non-specific, uncertain, un~ clear, vague, woolly

specification condition, detail, item, par~ ticular, qualification, requirement, stipula~ tion

specify be specific about, cite, define, desig~ nate, detail, enumerate, indicate, individu~

alize, itemize, mention, name, particularize, spell out, stipulate

specimen copy, embodiment, example, ex~ emplar, exemplification, exhibit, individual, instance, model, pattern, proof, representa~ tive, sample, type

specious casuistic, deceptive, fallacious, misleading, plausible, sophistic, sophistical, unsound

speck **1.** blemish, blot, defect, dot, fault, flaw, fleck, mark, mote, speckle, spot, stain **2.** atom, bit, dot, grain, iota, jot, mite, modicum, particle, shred, tittle, whit

speckled brindled, dappled, dotted, flecked, freckled, mottled, speckledy, spotted, spotty, sprinkled, stippled

spectacle **1.** display, event, exhibition, ex~ travaganza, pageant, parade, performance, show, sight **2.** curiosity, laughing stock, marvel, phenomenon, scene, sight, wonder

spectacular **1.** *adj.* breathtaking, daring, dazzling, dramatic, eye-catching, fantastic (*Inf.*), grand, impressive, magnificent, marked, remarkable, sensational, splendid, staggering, striking, stunning (*Inf.*) **2.** *n.* display, extravaganza, show, spectacle
Antonyms *adj.* easy, everyday, modest, or~ dinary, plain, run-of-the-mill, simple, unim~ pressive, unostentatious, unspectacular

spectator beholder, bystander, eyewitness, looker-on, observer, onlooker, viewer, watcher, witness
Antonyms contestant, contributor, partak~ er, participant, participator, party, player

spectre apparition, eidolon, ghost, phantom, presence, shade (*Literary*), shadow, spirit, vision, wraith

speculate **1.** cogitate, conjecture, consider, contemplate, deliberate, hypothesize, medi~ tate, muse, scheme, suppose, surmise, theo~ rize, wonder **2.** gamble, have a flutter (*Inf.*), hazard, play the market, risk, take a chance with, venture

speculation **1.** conjecture, consideration, contemplation, deliberation, guess, guess~ work, hypothesis, opinion, supposition, surmise, theory **2.** gamble, gambling, haz~ ard, risk

speculative **1.** abstract, academic, conjec~ tural, hypothetical, notional, suppositional, tentative, theoretical **2.** chancy (*Inf.*), dicey (*Inf., chiefly Brit.*), hazardous, risky, uncer~ tain, unpredictable

speech **1.** communication, conversation, dialogue, discussion, intercourse, talk **2.** address, discourse, disquisition, harangue, homily, lecture, oration, spiel (*Inf.*) **3.** ar~ ticulation, dialect, diction, enunciation, idi~ om, jargon, language, lingo (*Inf.*), parlance, tongue, utterance, voice

speechless **1.** dumb, inarticulate, mum, mute, silent, tongue-tied, unable to get a word out (*Inf.*), wordless **2.** *Fig.* aghast, amazed, astounded, dazed, dumbfounded, dumbstruck, shocked, thunderstruck

speed *n.* **1.** acceleration, celerity, expedi~ tion, fleetness, haste, hurry, momentum, pace, precipitation, quickness, rapidity, rush, swiftness, velocity ~*v.* **2.** barrel (along) (*Inf., chiefly U.S. & Canad.*), belt (along) (*Sl.*), bomb (along), bowl along, burn rubber (*Inf.*), career, dispatch, exceed the speed limit, expedite, flash, gallop, get a move on (*Inf.*), go hell for leather (*Inf.*), go like a bat out of hell (*Sl.*), go like the wind, hasten, hurry, lose no time, make haste, press on, put one's foot down (*Inf.*), quick~ en, race, rush, sprint, step on it (*Inf.*), tear, urge, zoom **3.** advance, aid, assist, boost, expedite, facilitate, further, help, impel, promote
Antonyms *n.* delay, slowness, sluggishness, tardiness ~*v.* crawl, creep, dawdle, delay, hamper, hinder, hold up, retard, slow, take one's time, tarry

speed up accelerate, gather momentum, get moving, get under way, increase, increase the tempo, open up the throttle, put one's foot down (*Inf.*), put on speed
Antonyms brake, decelerate, reduce speed, rein in, slacken (off), slow down

speedy expeditious, express, fast, fleet, fleet of foot, hasty, headlong, hurried, immedi~ ate, nimble, pdq (*Sl.*), precipitate, prompt, quick, quickie (*Inf.*), rapid, summary, swift, winged
Antonyms dead slow and stop, delayed, di~ latory, late, leisurely, lingering, long-drawn-out, plodding, slow, sluggish, tardy, unhur~ ried, unrushed

spell¹ *n.* bout, course, interval, patch, peri~ od, season, stint, stretch, term, time, tour of duty, turn

spell² *n.* **1.** abracadabra, charm, conjura~ tion, exorcism, incantation, sorcery, witch~ ery **2.** allure, bewitchment, enchantment, fascination, glamour, magic, trance

spell³ *v.* amount to, augur, herald, imply, indicate, mean, point to, portend, presage, promise, signify, suggest

spellbound bemused, bewitched, captivat~ ed, charmed, enthralled, entranced, fasci~ nated, gripped, hooked, mesmerized, pos~ sessed, rapt, transfixed, transported, under a spell

spelling orthography

spell out **1.** clarify, elucidate, explicate, make clear *or* plain, make explicit, specify **2.** discern, make out, puzzle out

spend **1.** disburse, expend, fork out (*Sl.*), lay out, pay out, shell out (*Inf.*), splash out

(*Brit. inf.*) **2.** blow (*Sl.*), consume, deplete, dispense, dissipate, drain, empty, exhaust, fritter away, run through, squander, use up, waste **3.** apply, bestow, concentrate, devote, employ, exert, invest, lavish, put in, use **4.** fill, occupy, pass, while away
Antonyms (*senses 1 & 2*) hoard, invest, keep, put aside, put by, save, store

spendthrift 1. *n.* big spender, prodigal, profligate, spender, squanderer, waster, wastrel **2.** *adj.* extravagant, improvident, prodigal, profligate, wasteful
Antonyms *n.* meanie *or* meany (*Inf., chiefly Brit.*), miser, penny-pincher (*Inf.*), Scrooge, skinflint, tight-arse (*Taboo sl.*), tight-ass (*U.S. taboo sl.*), tightwad (*U.S. & Canad. sl.*), ~*adj.* careful, economical, frugal, parsimonious, provident, prudent, sparing, thrifty

spent *adj.* **1.** all in (*Sl.*), burnt out, bushed (*Inf.*), clapped out (*Aust. & N.Z. inf.*), dead beat (*Inf.*), debilitated, dog-tired (*Inf.*), done in *or* up (*Inf.*), drained, exhausted, fagged (out) (*Inf.*), knackered (*Sl.*), played out (*Inf.*), prostrate, ready to drop (*Inf.*), shattered (*Inf.*), tired out, weakened, wearied, weary, whacked (*Brit. inf.*), worn out, zonked (*Inf.*) **2.** consumed, expended, finished, gone, used up

sphere 1. ball, circle, globe, globule, orb **2.** capacity, compass, department, domain, employment, field, function, pale, patch, province, range, rank, realm, scope, station, stratum, territory, turf (*U.S. sl.*), walk of life

spherical globe-shaped, globular, orbicular, rotund, round

spice *n.* **1.** relish, savour, seasoning **2.** colour, excitement, gusto, kick (*Inf.*), pep, piquancy, tang, zap (*Sl.*), zest, zip (*Inf.*)

spike *n.* **1.** barb, point, prong, spine ~*v.* **2.** impale, spear, spit, stick **3.** block, foil, frustrate, render ineffective, thwart

spill *v.* **1.** discharge, disgorge, overflow, overturn, scatter, shed, slop over, spill *or* run over, throw off, upset **2. spill the beans** *Inf.* betray a secret, blab, blow the gaff (*Brit. sl.*), give the game away, grass (*Brit. sl.*), inform, let the cat out of the bag, shop (*Sl., chiefly Brit.*), sing (*Sl., chiefly U.S.*), spill one's guts (*Sl.*), split (*Sl.*), squeal (*Sl.*), talk out of turn, tattle, tell all ~*n.* **3.** *Inf.* accident, cropper (*Inf.*), fall, tumble

spin *v.* **1.** birl (*Scot.*), gyrate, pirouette, reel, revolve, rotate, turn, twirl, twist, wheel, whirl **2.** concoct, develop, invent, narrate, recount, relate, tell, unfold **3.** be giddy, be in a whirl, grow dizzy, reel, swim, whirl ~*n.* **4.** gyration, revolution, roll, twist, whirl **5. (flat) spin** *Inf.* agitation, commotion, flap (*Inf.*), panic, state (*Inf.*), tiz-woz (*Inf.*), tizzy (*Inf.*) **6.** *Inf.* drive, hurl (*Scot.*), joy ride (*Inf.*), ride, turn, whirl

spine 1. backbone, spinal column, vertebrae, vertebral column **2.** barb, needle, quill, rachis, ray, spike, spur

spine-chilling bloodcurdling, eerie, frightening, hair-raising, horrifying, scary (*Inf.*), spooky (*Inf.*), terrifying

spineless chickenshit (*U.S. sl.*), cowardly, faint-hearted, feeble, gutless (*Inf.*), inadequate, ineffective, irresolute, lily-livered, soft, spiritless, squeamish, submissive, vacillating, weak, weak-kneed (*Inf.*), weak-willed, without a will of one's own, yellow (*Inf.*)
Antonyms ballsy (*Taboo sl.*), bold, brave, courageous, gritty, strong, strong-willed

spin out amplify, delay, drag out, draw out, extend, lengthen, pad out, prolong, prolongate, protract

spiral 1. *adj.* circular, cochlear, cochleate (*Biol.*), coiled, corkscrew, helical, scrolled, voluted, whorled, winding **2.** *n.* coil, corkscrew, curlicue, gyre (*Literary*), helix, screw, volute, whorl

spirit *n.* **1.** air, breath, life, life force, psyche, soul, vital spark **2.** attitude, character, complexion, disposition, essence, humour, outlook, quality, temper, temperament **3.** animation, ardour, backbone, balls (*Taboo sl.*), ballsiness (*Taboo sl.*), brio, courage, dauntlessness, earnestness, energy, enterprise, enthusiasm, fire, force, gameness, grit, guts (*Inf.*), life, liveliness, mettle, resolution, sparkle, spunk (*Inf.*), stoutheartedness, vigour, warmth, zest **4.** motivation, resolution, resolve, will, willpower **5.** atmosphere, feeling, gist, humour, tenor, tone **6.** essence, intent, intention, meaning, purport, purpose, sense, substance **7.** *Plural* feelings, frame of mind, humour, mood, morale **8.** apparition, eidolon, ghost, phantom, shade (*Literary*), shadow, spectre, spook (*Inf.*), sprite, vision ~*v.* **9.** *With* **away** *or* **off** abduct, abstract, carry, convey, make away with, purloin, remove, seize, snaffle (*Brit. inf.*), steal, whisk

spirited active, animated, ardent, bold, courageous, energetic, feisty (*Inf., chiefly U.S. & Canad.*), game, have-a-go (*Inf.*), high-spirited, lively, mettlesome, plucky, sparkling, sprightly, spunky (*Inf.*), vigorous, vivacious
Antonyms apathetic, bland, calm, dispirited, dull, feeble, half-hearted, lacklustre, lifeless, low-key, spiritless, timid, token, unenthusiastic, weary

spirits alcohol, firewater, liquor, strong liquor, the hard stuff (*Inf.*)

spiritual devotional, divine, ethereal, ghostly, holy, immaterial, incorporeal, nonmaterial, otherworldly, pure, religious, sacred

Antonyms concrete, corporeal, material, nonspiritual, palpable, physical, substantial, tangible

spit 1. *v.* discharge, eject, expectorate, hiss, spew, splutter, sputter, throw out **2.** *n.* dribble, drool, saliva, slaver, spittle, sputum

spite *n.* **1.** animosity, bitchiness (*Sl.*), gall, grudge, hate, hatred, ill will, malevolence, malice, malignity, pique, rancour, spiteful~ ness, spleen, venom **2. in spite of** despite, (even) though, in defiance of, notwithstand~ ing, regardless of ~*v.* **3.** annoy, discomfit, gall, harm, hurt, injure, needle (*Inf.*), nettle, offend, pique, provoke, put out, put (someone's) nose out of joint (*Inf.*), vex **Antonyms** *n.* benevolence, big-heartedness, charity, compassion, generosity of spirit, goodwill, kindliness, kindness, love, warm- heartedness ~*v.* aid, benefit, encourage, go along with, help, please, serve, support

spiteful barbed, bitchy (*Inf.*), catty (*Inf.*), cruel, ill-disposed, ill-natured, malevolent, malicious, malignant, nasty, rancorous, shrewish, snide, splenetic, venomous, vin~ dictive

splash *v.* **1.** bespatter, shower, slop, slosh (*Inf.*), spatter, splodge, spray, spread, sprin~ kle, squirt, strew, wet **2.** bathe, dabble, paddle, plunge, wade, wallow **3.** batter, break, buffet, dash, plash, plop, smack, strike, surge, wash **4.** blazon, broadcast, flaunt, headline, plaster, publicize, tout, trumpet ~*n.* **5.** burst, dash, patch, spatter~ ing, splodge, touch **6.** *Inf.* display, effect, impact, sensation, splurge, stir **7. make a splash** be ostentatious, cause a stir, cut a dash, go overboard (*Inf.*), go to town, splurge

splash out be extravagant, lash out (*Inf.*), push the boat out (*Brit. inf.*), spare no ex~ pense, spend, splurge

spleen acrimony, anger, animosity, animus, bad temper, bile, bitterness, gall, hatred, hostility, ill humour, ill will, malevolence, malice, malignity, peevishness, pique, ran~ cour, resentment, spite, spitefulness, ven~ om, vindictiveness, wrath

splendid 1. admirable, brilliant, exception~ al, glorious, grand, heroic, illustrious, magnificent, outstanding, rare, remarkable, renowned, sterling, sublime, superb, su~ preme **2.** costly, dazzling, gorgeous, impos~ ing, impressive, lavish, luxurious, magnificent, ornate, resplendent, rich, splendiferous (*Facetious*), sumptuous, su~ perb **3.** boffo (*Sl.*), brill (*Inf.*), chillin' (*U.S. sl.*), cracking (*Brit. inf.*), crucial (*Sl.*), def (*Sl.*), excellent, fantastic (*Inf.*), fine, first- class, glorious, great (*Inf.*), marvellous, mean (*Sl.*), mega (*Sl.*), sovereign, topping (*Brit. sl.*), wonderful **4.** beaming, bright,

brilliant, glittering, glowing, lustrous, radi~ ant, refulgent **Antonyms** beggarly, depressing, disgusting, distressed, drab, dull, ignoble, ignominious, lacklustre, low, mean, mediocre, miserable, ordinary, pathetic, plain, poor, poverty- stricken, rotten, run-of-the-mill, sombre, sor~ did, squalid, tarnished, tawdry, undistin~ guished, unexceptional

splendour brightness, brilliance, ceremony, dazzle, display, éclat, effulgence, glory, gor~ geousness, grandeur, lustre, magnificence, majesty, pomp, radiance, refulgence, re~ nown, resplendence, richness, show, solem~ nity, spectacle, stateliness, sumptuousness **Antonyms** dullness, ignominy, lack~ lustreness, meanness, ordinariness, plain~ ness, poverty, simplicity, sobriety, squalor, tawdriness

splice *v.* braid, entwine, graft, interlace, intertwine, intertwist, interweave, join, knit, marry, mesh, plait, unite, wed, yoke

splinter 1. *n.* chip, flake, fragment, needle, paring, shaving, sliver **2.** *v.* break into smithereens, disintegrate, fracture, shatter, shiver, split

split *v.* **1.** bifurcate, branch, break, break up, burst, cleave, come apart, come undone, crack, disband, disunite, diverge, fork, gape, give way, go separate ways, open, part, pull apart, rend, rip, separate, slash, slit, snap, splinter **2.** allocate, allot, apportion, carve up, distribute, divide, divvy up (*Inf.*), dole out, halve, parcel out, partition, share out, slice up **3.** *With* **on** *Sl.* betray, give away, grass (*Brit. sl.*), inform on, peach (*Sl.*), shop (*Sl., chiefly Brit.*), sing (*Sl., chiefly U.S.*), spill one's guts (*Sl.*), squeal (*Sl.*) ~*n.* **4.** breach, crack, damage, division, fissure, gap, rent, rip, separation, slash, slit, tear **5.** breach, break, break-up, difference, discord, disruption, dissension, disunion, diver~ gence, division, estrangement, partition, rift, rupture, schism ~*adj.* **6.** ambivalent, bisected, broken, cleft, cracked, divided, dual, fractured, ruptured, twofold

split up break up, disband, divorce, go separate ways, part, part company, separate

spoil *v.* **1.** blemish, blow (*Sl.*), damage, de~ base, deface, destroy, disfigure, harm, im~ pair, injure, mar, mess up, ruin, scar, total (*Sl.*), trash (*Sl.*), undo, upset, wreck **2.** baby, cocker (*Rare*), coddle, cosset, indulge, kill with kindness, mollycoddle, overindulge, pamper, spoon-feed **3.** addle, become taint~ ed, curdle, decay, decompose, go bad, go off (*Brit. inf.*), mildew, putrefy, rot, turn **4. spoiling for** bent upon, desirous of, eager for, enthusiastic about, keen to, looking for, out to get (*Inf.*), raring to **Antonyms** (*sense 1*) augment, conserve, en~

hance, improve, keep, preserve, save (*sense 2*) be strict with, deprive, ignore, pay no atten~ tion to, treat harshly

spoils boodle (*Sl., chiefly U.S.*), booty, gain, loot, pickings, pillage, plunder, prey, prizes, rapine, swag (*Sl.*)

spoilsport damper, dog in the manger, kill-joy, misery (*Brit. inf.*), party-pooper (*U.S. sl.*), wet blanket (*Inf.*)

spoken by word of mouth, expressed, oral, phonetic, put into words, said, told, unwrit~ ten, uttered, verbal, viva voce, voiced

spongy absorbent, cushioned, cushiony, elastic, light, porous, springy

sponsor 1. *n.* angel (*Inf.*), backer, god~ parent, guarantor, patron, promoter **2.** *v.* back, finance, fund, guarantee, lend one's name to, patronize, promote, put up the money for, subsidize

spontaneous extempore, free, impromptu, impulsive, instinctive, natural, unbidden, uncompelled, unconstrained, unforced, un~ premeditated, unprompted, voluntary, will~ ing
   Antonyms arranged, calculated, contrived, deliberate, forced, mannered, orchestrated, planned, prearranged, premeditated, pre~ planned, stage-managed, studied

spontaneously extempore, freely, im~ promptu, impulsively, instinctively, off one's own bat, off the cuff (*Inf.*), of one's own accord, on impulse, quite unprompted, voluntarily

sporadic infrequent, intermittent, irregular, isolated, occasional, on and off, random, scattered, spasmodic
   Antonyms consistent, frequent, recurrent, regular, set, steady, systematic

sport *n.* **1.** amusement, diversion, enter~ tainment, exercise, game, pastime, physical activity, play, recreation **2.** badinage, ban~ ter, frolic, fun, jest, joking, josh (*Sl., chiefly U.S. & Canad.*), kidding (*Inf.*), merriment, mirth, raillery, teasing **3.** buffoon, butt, de~ rision, fair game, game, laughing stock, mockery, plaything, ridicule ~*v.* **4.** With **with** amuse oneself, dally, flirt, fool, play, take advantage of, toy, treat lightly *or* cavalierly, trifle **5.** *Inf.* display, exhibit, show off, wear **6.** caper, disport, frolic, gambol, play, romp

sporting fair, game (*Inf.*), gentlemanly, sportsman-like
   Antonyms unfair, unsporting, un~ sportsmanlike

sportive coltish, frisky, frolicsome, full of beans (*Inf.*), full of fun, gamesome, gay, joyous, kittenish, lively, merry, playful, prankish, rollicking, skittish, sprightly

spot *n.* **1.** blemish, blot, blotch, daub, dis~ coloration, flaw, mark, pimple, plook (*Scot.*), pustule, scar, smudge, speck, speckle, stain, taint, zit (*Sl.*) **2.** locality, location, place, point, position, scene, site, situation **3.** *Inf.* bit, little, morsel, splash **4.** *Inf.* difficulty, hot water (*Inf.*), mess, plight, predicament, quandary, tight spot, trouble ~*v.* **5.** catch sight of, descry, detect, discern, espy, iden~ tify, make out, observe, pick out, recognize, see, sight **6.** besmirch, blot, dirty, dot, fleck, mark, mottle, scar, smirch, soil, spatter, speckle, splodge, splotch, stain, sully, taint, tarnish

spotless above reproach, blameless, chaste, clean, faultless, flawless, gleaming, im~ maculate, impeccable, innocent, irre~ proachable, pure, shining, snowy, unblem~ ished, unimpeachable, unstained, unsullied, untarnished, virgin, virginal, white
   Antonyms besmirched, bespattered, blem~ ished, defiled, dirty, filthy, flawed, impure, messy, notorious, reprehensible, soiled, spot~ ted, stained, sullied, tainted, tarnished, un~ chaste, untidy

spotlight *Fig.* **1.** *v.* accentuate, draw atten~ tion to, feature, focus attention on, give prominence to, highlight, illuminate, point up, throw into relief **2.** *n.* attention, fame, interest, limelight, notoriety, public atten~ tion, public eye

spotted dappled, dotted, flecked, mottled, pied, polka-dot, specked, speckled

spouse better half (*Humorous*), companion, consort, helpmate, her indoors (*Brit. sl.*), husband, mate, partner, significant other (*U.S. inf.*), wife

spout *v.* **1.** discharge, emit, erupt, gush, jet, shoot, spray, spurt, squirt, stream, surge **2.** *Inf.* declaim, expatiate, go on (*Inf.*), hold forth, orate, pontificate, rabbit (on) (*Brit. inf.*), ramble (on), rant, speechify, spiel (*Inf.*), talk

sprawl *v.* flop, loll, lounge, ramble, slouch, slump, spread, straggle, trail

spray[1] *v.* **1.** atomize, diffuse, scatter, show~ er, sprinkle ~*n.* **2.** drizzle, droplets, fine mist, moisture, spindrift, spoondrift **3.** aerosol, atomizer, sprinkler

spray[2] *n.* bough, branch, corsage, floral ar~ rangement, shoot, sprig

spread *v.* **1.** be displayed, bloat, broaden, dilate, expand, extend, fan out, open, open out, sprawl, stretch, swell, unfold, unfurl, unroll, widen **2.** escalate, multiply, mush~ room, proliferate **3.** advertise, blazon, broadcast, bruit, cast, circulate, cover, dif~ fuse, disseminate, distribute, make known, make public, proclaim, promulgate, propa~ gate, publicize, publish, radiate, scatter, shed, strew, transmit **4.** arrange, array, cover, furnish, lay, prepare, set ~*n.* **5.** ad~

vance, advancement, development, diffu~
sion, dispersion, dissemination, escalation,
expansion, increase, proliferation, spread~
ing, suffusion, transmission **6.** compass,
extent, period, reach, span, stretch, sweep,
term **7.** *Inf.* array, banquet, blowout (*Sl.*),
feast, repast
Antonyms *v.* (*sense 3*) contain, control, curb,
hold back, hold in, repress, restrain, stifle

spree bacchanalia, beano (*Brit. sl.*), bender
(*Inf.*), binge (*Inf.*), carousal, carouse, de~
bauch, fling, jag (*Sl.*), junketing, orgy, revel,
splurge

sprightly active, agile, airy, alert, animated,
blithe, brisk, cheerful, energetic, frolicsome,
gay, jaunty, joyous, lively, nimble, perky,
playful, spirited, sportive, spry, vivacious
Antonyms dull, inactive, lethargic, seden~
tary, sluggish, torpid, unenergetic

spring *v.* **1.** bounce, bound, hop, jump, leap,
rebound, recoil, vault **2.** *Often with* **from**
arise, be derived, be descended, come, de~
rive, descend, emanate, emerge, grow, issue,
originate, proceed, start, stem **3.** *With* **up**
appear, burgeon, come into existence *or* be~
ing, develop, mushroom, shoot up ~*n.* **4.**
bound, buck, hop, jump, leap, saltation,
vault **5.** bounce, bounciness, buoyancy,
elasticity, flexibility, give (*Inf.*), recoil, re~
silience, springiness **6.** beginning, cause,
fount, fountainhead, origin, root, source,
well, wellspring ~*adj.* **7.** *Of the season*
springlike, vernal

sprinkle *v.* dredge, dust, pepper, powder,
scatter, shower, spray, strew

sprinkling admixture, dash, dusting, few,
handful, scatter, scattering, smattering,
sprinkle

sprint *v.* barrel (along) (*Inf., chiefly U.S. &*
Canad.), dart, dash, go at top speed, hare
(*Brit. inf.*), hotfoot, put on a burst of speed,
race, scamper, shoot, tear, whiz (*Inf.*)

sprite apparition, brownie, dryad, elf, fairy,
goblin, imp, leprechaun, naiad, nymph,
Oceanid (*Greek myth.*), peri, pixie, spirit,
sylph

sprout *v.* bud, develop, germinate, grow,
push, shoot, spring, vegetate

spruce as if one had just stepped out of a
bandbox, dainty, dapper, elegant, natty
(*Inf.*), neat, smart, soigné *or* soignée, trig
(*Archaic or dialect*), trim, well-groomed,
well turned out
Antonyms bedraggled, disarrayed, dishev~
elled, frowsy, messy, rumpled, uncombed,
unkempt, untidy

spry active, agile, alert, brisk, nimble, nippy
(*Brit. inf.*), quick, ready, sprightly, supple
Antonyms awkward, decrepit, doddering,
inactive, lethargic, slow, sluggish, stiff

spur *v.* **1.** animate, drive, goad, impel, in~
cite, press, prick, prod, prompt, stimulate,
urge ~*n.* **2.** goad, prick, rowel **3.** impetus,
impulse, incentive, incitement, inducement,
motive, stimulus **4. on the spur of the**
moment impetuously, impromptu, impul~
sively, on impulse, on the spot, unpremedi~
tatedly, unthinkingly, without planning,
without thinking

spurious artificial, bogus, contrived,
counterfeit, deceitful, ersatz, fake, false,
feigned, forged, imitation, mock, phoney *or*
phony (*Inf.*), pretended, pseudo (*Inf.*), sham,
simulated, specious, unauthentic
Antonyms authentic, bona fide, genuine,
honest, kosher (*Inf.*), legitimate, real, sound,
unfeigned, valid

spurn cold-shoulder, contemn, despise, dis~
dain, disregard, put down, rebuff, reject,
repulse, scorn, slight, snub, turn one's nose
up at (*Inf.*)
Antonyms embrace, grasp, seize, take up,
welcome

spurt **1.** *v.* burst, erupt, gush, jet, shoot,
spew, squirt, surge **2.** *n.* access, burst, fit,
rush, spate, surge

spy *n.* **1.** double agent, fifth columnist, for~
eign agent, mole, nark (*Brit., Aust., & N.Z.*
sl.), secret agent, secret service agent,
undercover agent ~*v.* **2.** *Usually with* **on**
follow, keep under surveillance, keep watch
on, shadow, tail (*Inf.*), trail, watch **3.** catch
sight of, descry, espy, glimpse, notice, ob~
serve, set eyes on, spot

spying *n.* espionage, secret service

squabble **1.** *v.* argue, bicker, brawl, clash,
dispute, fall out (*Inf.*), fight, have words,
quarrel, row, scrap (*Inf.*), spar, wrangle **2.**
n. argument, *bagarre*, barney (*Inf.*), differ~
ence of opinion, disagreement, dispute,
fight, row, scrap (*Inf.*), set-to (*Inf.*), spat, tiff

squad band, company, crew, force, gang,
group, team, troop

squalid broken-down, decayed, dirty, dis~
gusting, fetid, filthy, foul, low, nasty,
poverty-stricken, repulsive, run-down,
seedy, sleazy, slovenly, slummy, sordid, un~
clean, yucky *or* yukky (*Sl.*)
Antonyms attractive, clean, genial, hygien~
ic, in good condition, pleasant, salubrious,
spick-and-span, spotless, tidy, well-kempt,
well looked-after

squalor decay, filth, foulness, meanness,
sleaziness, slumminess, squalidness,
wretchedness
Antonyms beauty, cleanliness, fine condi~
tion, luxury, neatness, order, pleasantness,
splendour

squander be prodigal with, blow (*Sl.*), con~
sume, dissipate, expend, fritter away, frivol
away, lavish, misspend, misuse, run

through, scatter, spend, spend like water, throw away, waste

Antonyms be frugal, be thrifty, economize, keep, put aside for a rainy day, save, store

square *Fig. v.* **1.** *Often with* **with** accord, agree, conform, correspond, fit, harmonize, match, reconcile, tally **2.** *Sometimes with* **up** balance, clear (up), discharge, liquidate, make even, pay off, quit, satisfy, settle **3.** accommodate, adapt, adjust, align, even up, level, regulate, suit, tailor, true (up) **4.** *Sl.* bribe, buy off, corrupt, fix (*Inf.*), rig, suborn ~*adj.* **5.** aboveboard, decent, equitable, ethical, fair, fair and square, genuine, hon~ est, just, kosher (*Inf.*), on the level (*Inf.*), on the up and up, straight, straightforward, upfront (*Inf.*), upright **6.** *Inf.* behind the times, bourgeois, conservative, convention~ al, old-fashioned, out of date, straight (*Sl.*), strait-laced, stuffy ~*n.* **7.** *Inf.* antediluvian, back number (*Inf.*), conservative, die-hard, dinosaur, fuddy-duddy (*Inf.*), old buffer (*Brit. inf.*), (old) fogy, stick-in-the-mud (*Inf.*), traditionalist

Antonyms *adj.* (*sense 6*) fashionable, in vogue, modern, modish, stylish, trendy (*Brit. inf.*), voguish

squash *v.* **1.** compress, crush, distort, flatten, mash, pound, press, pulp, smash, stamp on, trample down **2.** annihilate, crush, humiliate, put down (*Sl.*), put (some~ one) in his (*or* her) place, quash, quell, si~ lence, sit on (*Inf.*), suppress

squashy mushy, pappy, pulpy, soft, spongy, yielding

squawk *v.* **1.** cackle, crow, cry, hoot, screech, yelp **2.** *Inf.* complain, kick up a fuss (*Inf.*), protest, raise Cain (*Sl.*), squeal (*Inf., chiefly Brit.*)

squeak *v.* peep, pipe, shrill, squeal, whine, yelp

squeal *n.* **1.** scream, screech, shriek, wail, yell, yelp, yowl ~*v.* **2.** scream, screech, shout, shriek, shrill, wail, yelp **3.** *Sl.* be~ tray, blab, grass (*Brit. sl.*), inform on, peach (*Sl.*), rat on (*Inf.*), sell (someone) down the river (*Inf.*), shop (*Sl., chiefly Brit.*), sing (*Sl., chiefly U.S.*), snitch (*Sl.*), spill one's guts (*Sl.*), tell all **4.** *Inf.* complain, kick up a fuss (*Inf.*), moan, protest, squawk (*Inf.*)

squeamish **1.** delicate, fastidious, finicky, nice (*Rare*), particular, prissy (*Inf.*), prud~ ish, punctilious, scrupulous, strait-laced **2.** nauseous, qualmish, queasy, queer, sick, sickish

Antonyms bold, brassy, brazen, coarse, earthy, immodest, indifferent, strong-stomached, tough, wanton

squeeze *v.* **1.** clutch, compress, crush, grip, nip, pinch, press, squash, wring **2.** cram, crowd, force, jam, jostle, pack, press, ram,

stuff, thrust, wedge **3.** clasp, cuddle, em~ brace, enfold, hold tight, hug **4.** bleed (*Inf.*), bring pressure to bear on, extort, lean on (*Inf.*), milk, oppress, pressurize, put the screws on (*Inf.*), put the squeeze on (*Inf.*), wrest ~*n.* **5.** clasp, embrace, handclasp, hold, hug **6.** congestion, crowd, crush, jam, press, squash

squint askew, aslant, awry, cockeyed, crooked, oblique, off-centre, skew-whiff (*Inf.*)

Antonyms aligned, even, horizontal, in line, level, perpendicular, plum, square, straight, true, vertical

squire *v.* accompany, attend, companion, escort

squirm agonize, fidget, flounder, shift, twist, wiggle, wriggle, writhe

stab *v.* **1.** bayonet, cut, gore, impale, injure, jab, knife, pierce, puncture, run through, spear, stick, thrust, transfix, wound **2. stab in the back** betray, break faith with, de~ ceive, do the dirty on (*Brit. sl.*), double-cross (*Inf.*), give the Judas kiss to, inform on, let down, play false, sell, sell out (*Inf.*), slander ~*n.* **3.** gash, incision, jab, puncture, rent, thrust, wound **4.** ache, pang, prick, twinge **5. make a stab at** attempt, en~ deavour, essay, give it one's best shot (*Inf.*), have a go (crack (*Inf.*), shot (*Inf.*), stab (*Inf.*)) (*Inf.*), try, try one's hand at, venture

stability constancy, durability, firmness, permanence, solidity, soundness, steadfast~ ness, steadiness, strength

Antonyms changeableness, fickleness, fra~ gility, frailty, inconstancy, instability, un~ predictability, unreliability, unsteadiness

stable abiding, constant, deep-rooted, du~ rable, enduring, established, fast, firm, fixed, immovable, immutable, invariable, lasting, permanent, reliable, secure, sound, staunch, steadfast, steady, strong, sturdy, sure, unalterable, unchangeable, unwaver~ ing, well-founded

Antonyms changeable, deteriorating, errat~ ic, excitable, fickle, frail, inconstant, insecure, irresolute, mercurial, mutable, over-emotional, shaky, shifting, temperamental, uncertain, unpredictable, unreliable, unsta~ ble, unsteady, variable, volatile, wavering

stack **1.** *n.* clamp (*Brit. agriculture*), cock, heap, hoard, load, mass, mound, mountain, pile **2.** *v.* accumulate, amass, assemble, bank up, heap up, load, pile, stockpile

staff *n.* **1.** employees, lecturers, officers, or~ ganization, personnel, teachers, team, workers, workforce **2.** cane, crook, pole, prop, rod, sceptre, stave, wand

stage **1.** *n.* division, juncture, lap, leg, length, level, period, phase, point, step **2.** *v.* arrange, do, engineer, give, lay on, mount,

orchestrate, organize, perform, play, pres~
ent, produce, put on

stagger v. **1.** falter, hesitate, lurch, reel,
sway, teeter, totter, vacillate, waver, wobble
2. amaze, astonish, astound, bowl over
(*Inf.*), confound, dumbfound, flabbergast,
give (someone) a shock, nonplus, over~
whelm, shake, shock, strike (someone)
dumb, stun, stupefy, surprise, take (some~
one) aback, take (someone's) breath away,
throw off balance **3.** alternate, overlap,
step, zigzag

stagnant brackish, motionless, quiet, slug~
gish, stale, standing, still
Antonyms active, clear, flowing, fresh, live~
ly, moving, pure, running, thriving, unpollut~
ed

stagnate decay, decline, deteriorate, fester,
go to seed, idle, languish, lie fallow, rot,
rust, stand still, vegetate

staid calm, composed, decorous, demure,
grave, quiet, sedate, self-restrained, serious,
sober, solemn, steady
Antonyms adventurous, capricious, de~
monstrative, exuberant, flighty, giddy, in~
decorous, lively, rowdy, sportive, wild

stain v. **1.** blemish, blot, colour, dirty, dis~
colour, dye, mark, smirch, soil, spot, tar~
nish, tinge **2.** besmirch, blacken, contami~
nate, corrupt, defile, deprave, disgrace, drag
through the mud, sully, taint ~n. **3.** blem~
ish, blot, discoloration, dye, smirch, spot,
tint **4.** blemish, blot on the escutcheon, dis~
grace, dishonour, infamy, reproach, shame,
slur, stigma

stake[1] n. **1.** pale, paling, palisade, picket,
pole, post, spike, stave, stick ~v. **2.** brace,
prop, secure, support, tether, tie up **3.** *Often
with* **out** define, delimit, demarcate, lay
claim to, mark out, outline, reserve

stake[2] n. **1.** ante, bet, chance, hazard, peril,
pledge, risk, venture, wager **2.** claim, con~
cern, interest, investment, involvement,
share ~v. **3.** bet, chance, gamble, hazard,
imperil, jeopardize, pledge, put on, risk,
venture, wager

stale 1. decayed, dry, faded, fetid, flat, fusty,
hard, insipid, musty, old, sour, stagnant,
tasteless **2.** antiquated, banal, cliché-ridden,
common, commonplace, drab, effete, flat,
hackneyed, insipid, old hat, overused,
platitudinous, repetitious, stereotyped,
threadbare, trite, unoriginal, worn-out
Antonyms crisp, different, fresh, imagina~
tive, innovative, lively, new, novel, original,
refreshing

stalk v. **1.** creep up on, follow, haunt, hunt,
pursue, shadow, tail (*Inf.*), track **2.** flounce,
march, pace, stride, strut

stall v. beat about the bush (*Inf.*), hedge,
play for time, stonewall, temporize

stalwart athletic, beefy (*Inf.*), brawny, dar~
ing, dependable, hefty (*Inf.*), husky (*Inf.*),
indomitable, intrepid, lusty, manly, muscu~
lar, redoubtable, robust, rugged, sinewy,
staunch, stout, strapping, strong, sturdy,
valiant, vigorous
Antonyms faint-hearted, feeble, frail,
infirm, namby-pamby, puny, shilpit (*Scot.*),
sickly, timid, weak

stamina energy, force, grit, indefatigability,
lustiness, power, power of endurance, re~
silience, resistance, staying power, strength,
vigour

stammer v. falter, hem and haw, hesitate,
pause, splutter, stumble, stutter

stamp v. **1.** beat, crush, trample **2.** engrave,
fix, impress, imprint, inscribe, mark,
mould, print **3.** betray, brand, categorize,
exhibit, identify, label, mark, pronounce,
reveal, show to be, typecast ~n. **4.** brand,
cast, earmark, hallmark, imprint, mark,
mould, signature **5.** breed, cast, character,
cut, description, fashion, form, kind, sort,
type

stamp collecting philately

stampede n. charge, flight, rout, rush,
scattering

stamp out crush, destroy, eliminate,
eradicate, extinguish, extirpate, put down,
put out, quell, quench, scotch, suppress

stance 1. bearing, carriage, deportment,
posture **2.** attitude, position, stand, stand~
point, viewpoint

stand v. **1.** be erect, be upright, be vertical,
rise **2.** mount, place, position, put, rank, set
3. be in force, belong, be situated *or* locat~
ed, be valid, continue, exist, halt, hold, ob~
tain, pause, prevail, remain, rest, stay, stop
4. abide, allow, bear, brook, cope with,
countenance, endure, experience, handle,
put up with (*Inf.*), stomach, submit to, suf~
fer, support, sustain, take, thole (*Dialect*),
tolerate, undergo, wear (*Brit. sl.*), weather,
withstand ~n. **5.** halt, rest, standstill, stay,
stop, stopover **6.** attitude, determination,
firm stand, opinion, position, stance, stand~
point **7.** base, booth, bracket, dais, frame,
grandstand, place, platform, rack, rank,
stage, staging, stall, stance (*Chiefly Scot.*),
support, table

standard[1] n. **1.** average, benchmark, canon,
criterion, example, gauge, grade, guide,
guideline, measure, model, norm, par, pat~
tern, principle, requirement, rule, sample,
specification, touchstone, type, yardstick **2.**
Often plural code of honour, ethics, ideals,
moral principles, morals, principles ~adj.
3. accepted, average, basic, customary,
normal, orthodox, popular, prevailing,
regular, set, staple, stock, typical, usual **4.**

approved, authoritative, classic, definitive, established, official, recognized

Antonyms *adj.* abnormal, atypical, exceptional, extraordinary, irregular, singular, strange, unauthorised, uncommon, unconventional, unofficial, unusual

standard[2] *n.* banner, colours, ensign, flag, pennant, pennon, streamer

standardize assimilate, bring into line, institutionalize, mass-produce, regiment, stereotype

stand by 1. back, befriend, be loyal to, champion, defend, stick up for (*Inf.*), support, take (someone's) part, uphold **2.** be prepared, wait, wait in the wings

stand for 1. betoken, denote, exemplify, indicate, mean, represent, signify, symbolize **2.** *Inf.* bear, brook, endure, lie down under (*Inf.*), put up with, suffer, tolerate, wear (*Brit. inf.*)

stand in for cover for, deputize for, do duty for, hold the fort for, replace, represent, substitute for, take the place of, understudy

standing *n.* **1.** condition, credit, eminence, estimation, footing, position, rank, reputation, repute, station, status **2.** continuance, duration, existence, experience ~*adj.* **3.** fixed, lasting, permanent, perpetual, regular, repeated **4.** erect, perpendicular, rampant (*Heraldry*), upended, upright, vertical

standoffish aloof, cold, distant, haughty, remote, reserved, unapproachable, unsociable

Antonyms affable, approachable, congenial, cordial, friendly, open, sociable, warm

stand out attract attention, be highlighted, be prominent (conspicuous, distinct, obvious, striking), be thrown into relief, bulk large, catch the eye, leap to the eye, project, stare one in the face (*Inf.*), stick out a mile (*Inf.*)

standpoint angle, point of view, position, post, stance, station, vantage point, viewpoint

stand up for champion, come to the defence of, defend, side with, stick up for (*Inf.*), support, uphold

stand up to brave, confront, defy, endure, oppose, resist, tackle, withstand

star 1. *n.* celeb (*Inf.*), celebrity, draw, idol, lead, leading man *or* lady, luminary, main attraction, megastar (*Inf.*), name **2.** *adj.* brilliant, celebrated, illustrious, leading, major, paramount, principal, prominent, talented, well-known

stare *v.* gape, gawk, gawp (*Brit. sl.*), gaze, goggle, look, ogle, rubberneck (*Sl.*), watch

stark *adj.* **1.** absolute, arrant, bald, bare, blunt, consummate, downright, entire, flagrant, out-and-out, palpable, patent, pure, sheer, simple, unalloyed, unmitigated, utter **2.** austere, bare, barren, bleak, cold, depressing, desolate, drear (*Literary*), dreary, forsaken, godforsaken, grim, hard, harsh, plain, severe, solitary, unadorned ~*adv.* **3.** absolutely, altogether, clean, completely, entirely, quite, utterly, wholly

stark-naked buck naked (*Sl.*), in a state of nature, in one's birthday suit (*Inf.*), in the altogether (*Inf.*), in the buff (*Inf.*), in the raw (*Inf.*), naked, naked as the day one was born (*Inf.*), nude, stark, starkers (*Inf.*), stripped, unclad, undressed, without a stitch on (*Inf.*)

start *v.* **1.** appear, arise, begin, come into being, come into existence, commence, depart, first see the light of day, get on the road, get under way, go ahead, hit the road (*Inf.*), issue, leave, originate, pitch in (*Inf.*), sally forth, set off, set out **2.** activate, embark upon, engender, enter upon, get going, initiate, instigate, kick off (*Inf.*), kick-start, make a beginning, open, originate, put one's hand to the plough (*Inf.*), set about, set in motion, start the ball rolling, take the first step, take the plunge (*Inf.*), trigger, turn on **3.** begin, create, establish, father, found, inaugurate, initiate, institute, introduce, launch, lay the foundations of, pioneer, set up **4.** blench, flinch, jerk, jump, recoil, shy, twitch ~*n.* **5.** beginning, birth, commencement, dawn, first step(s), foundation, inauguration, inception, initiation, kickoff (*Inf.*), onset, opening, opening move, outset **6.** advantage, edge, head start, lead **7.** backing, break (*Inf.*), chance, helping hand, introduction, opening, opportunity, sponsorship **8.** convulsion, jar, jump, spasm, twitch

Antonyms *v.* (*senses 1, 2 & 3*) abandon, bring to an end, call it a day (*Inf.*), cease, conclude, delay, desist, end, finish, give up, put aside, put off, quit, stop, switch off, terminate, turn off, wind up ~*n.* (*sense 5*) cessation, conclusion, dénouement, end, finale, finish, outcome, result, stop, termination, turning off, wind-up

startle agitate, alarm, amaze, astonish, astound, frighten, give (someone) a turn (*Inf.*), make (someone) jump, scare, shock, surprise, take (someone) aback

startling alarming, astonishing, astounding, extraordinary, shocking, staggering, sudden, surprising, unexpected, unforeseen

starving faint from lack of food, famished, hungering, hungry, ravenous, ready to eat a horse (*Inf.*), sharp-set, starved

state[1] *v.* **1.** affirm, articulate, assert, asseverate, aver, declare, enumerate, explain, expound, express, present, propound, put, report, say, specify, utter, voice ~*n.* **2.** case, category, circumstances, condition, mode, pass, plight, position, predicament, shape, situation, state of affairs **3.** attitude, frame of mind, humour, mood, spirits **4.** ceremony, dignity, display, glory, grandeur, majesty, pomp, splendour, style **5.** *Inf.* bother, flap (*Inf.*), panic, pother, tiz-woz (*Inf.*), tizzy (*Inf.*) **6. in a state** *Inf.* agitated, all steamed up (*Sl.*), anxious, distressed, disturbed, flustered, het up, panic-stricken, ruffled, upset, uptight (*Inf.*)

state² *n.* body politic, commonwealth, country, federation, government, kingdom, land, nation, republic, territory

stately august, ceremonious, deliberate, dignified, elegant, grand, imperial, imposing, impressive, lofty, majestic, measured, noble, pompous, regal, royal, solemn
Antonyms common, humble, lowly, modest, simple, undignified, undistinguished, unimpressive

statement account, announcement, communication, communiqué, declaration, explanation, proclamation, recital, relation, report, testimony, utterance

static changeless, constant, fixed, immobile, inert, motionless, stagnant, stationary, still, unmoving, unvarying
Antonyms active, dynamic, kinetic, lively, mobile, moving, travelling, varied

station *n.* **1.** base, depot, headquarters, location, place, position, post, seat, situation **2.** appointment, business, calling, employment, grade, occupation, position, post, rank, situation, sphere, standing, status ~*v.* **3.** assign, establish, fix, garrison, install, locate, post, set

stationary at a standstill, fixed, inert, moored, motionless, parked, standing, static, stock-still, unmoving
Antonyms changeable, changing, inconstant, mobile, moving, shifting, travelling, unstable, variable, varying, volatile

status condition, consequence, degree, distinction, eminence, grade, position, prestige, rank, standing

stay *v.* **1.** abide, continue, delay, establish oneself, halt, hang around (*Inf.*), hover, linger, loiter, pause, put down roots, remain, reside, settle, sojourn, stand, stay put, stop, tarry, wait **2.** *Often with* **at** be accommodated at, lodge, put up at, sojourn, visit **3.** adjourn, defer, discontinue, hold in abeyance, hold over, prorogue, put off, suspend **4.** *Archaic* arrest, check, curb, delay, detain, hinder, hold, impede, obstruct, prevent ~*n.* **5.** holiday, sojourn, stop, stopover, visit **6.** deferment, delay, halt, pause, postponement, remission, reprieve, stopping, suspension

Antonyms *v.* (*sense 1*) abandon, depart, exit, go, leave, move on, pass through, quit, withdraw

staying power endurance, stamina, strength, toughness

steadfast constant, dedicated, dependable, established, faithful, fast, firm, fixed, immovable, intent, loyal, persevering, reliable, resolute, single-minded, stable, stalwart, staunch, steady, unfaltering, unflinching, unswerving, unwavering
Antonyms capricious, faint-hearted, faltering, fickle, flagging, half-hearted, inconstant, irresolute, uncommitted, undependable, unreliable, unstable, vacillating, wavering

steady *adj.* **1.** firm, fixed, immovable, safe, stable, substantial, unchangeable, uniform **2.** balanced, calm, dependable, equable, having both feet on the ground, imperturbable, level-headed, reliable, sedate, sensible, serene, serious-minded, settled, sober, staid, staunch, steadfast **3.** ceaseless, confirmed, consistent, constant, continuous, even, faithful, habitual, incessant, nonstop, persistent, regular, rhythmic, unbroken, unfaltering, unfluctuating, uninterrupted, unremitting, unvarying, unwavering ~*v.* **4.** balance, brace, secure, stabilize, support **5.** compose *or* calm oneself, cool down, get a grip on oneself, sober (up)
Antonyms *adj.* careless, changeable, faltering, fickle, fluctuating, half-hearted, inconsistent, infrequent, insecure, intermittent, in two minds, irregular, occasional, sporadic, uncommitted, unconscientious, undependable, unpredictable, unreliable, unsettled, unstable, unsteady, vacillating, wavering ~*v.* agitate, shake, tilt, upset, worry

steal 1. appropriate, be light-fingered, blag (*Sl.*), cabbage (*Brit. sl.*), embezzle, filch, half-inch (*Old-fashioned sl.*), heist (*U.S. sl.*), lift (*Inf.*), misappropriate, nick (*Sl., chiefly Brit.*), peculate, pilfer, pinch (*Inf.*), pirate, plagiarize, poach, prig (*Brit. sl.*), purloin, shoplift, snitch (*Sl.*), swipe (*Sl.*), take, thieve, walk *or* make off with **2.** creep, flit, insinuate oneself, slink, slip, sneak, tiptoe

stealing embezzlement, larceny, misappropriation, pilferage, pilfering, plagiarism, robbery, shoplifting, theft, thievery, thieving

stealth furtiveness, secrecy, slyness, sneakiness, stealthiness, surreptitiousness, unobtrusiveness

stealthy clandestine, covert, furtive, secret, secretive, skulking, sly, sneaking, sneaky, surreptitious, underhand

steel *v.* brace, fortify, grit one's teeth, harden, make up one's mind

steep¹ *adj.* **1.** abrupt, headlong, precipitous, sheer **2.** *Inf.* excessive, exorbitant, extor-

tionate, extreme, high, overpriced, stiff, uncalled-for, unreasonable
Antonyms (*sense 1*) easy, gentle, gradual, moderate, slight (*sense 2*) fair, moderate, rea~ sonable

steep² *v.* **1.** damp, drench, imbrue (*Rare*), immerse, macerate, marinate (*Cookery*), moisten, soak, souse, submerge **2.** fill, im~ bue, infuse, permeate, pervade, saturate, suffuse

steer 1. administer, be in the driver's seat, conduct, control, direct, govern, guide, handle, pilot **2. steer clear of** avoid, body-swerve (*Scot.*), circumvent, eschew, evade, give a wide berth to, sheer off, shun

stem¹ 1. *n.* axis, branch, peduncle, shoot, stalk, stock, trunk **2.** *v. Usually with* **from** arise, be caused (bred, brought about, gen~ erated) by, derive, develop, emanate, flow, issue, originate

stem² *v.* bring to a standstill, check, con~ tain, curb, dam, hold back, oppose, resist, restrain, stanch, staunch, stay (*Archaic*), stop, withstand

stench foul odour, mephitis, niff (*Brit. sl.*), noisomeness, pong (*Brit. inf.*), reek, stink, whiff (*Brit. sl.*)

step *n.* **1.** footfall, footprint, footstep, gait, impression, pace, print, stride, trace, track, walk **2.** act, action, deed, expedient, ma~ noeuvre, means, measure, move, procedure, proceeding **3. take steps** act, intervene, move in, prepare, take action, take meas~ ures, take the initiative **4.** advance, ad~ vancement, move, phase, point, process, progression, stage **5.** degree, level, rank, remove **6.** doorstep, round, rung, stair, tread **7. in step** coinciding, conforming, in harmony (agreement, conformity, unison), in line **8. out of step** erratic, incongruous, in disagreement, out of harmony, out of line, out of phase, pulling different ways **9. watch one's step** be discreet (canny, careful, cautious), be on one's guard, have one's wits about one, look out, mind how one goes, mind one's p's and q's, take care, take heed, tread carefully ~*v.* **10.** move, pace, tread, walk

step in become involved, chip in (*Inf.*), intercede, intervene, take action, take a hand

step up accelerate, augment, boost, esca~ late, increase, intensify, raise, speed up, up

stereotype 1. *n.* formula, mould, pattern, received idea **2.** *v.* categorize, convention~ alize, dub, pigeonhole, standardize, take to be, typecast

sterile 1. abortive, bare, barren, dry, empty, fruitless, infecund, unfruitful, unproductive, unprofitable, unprolific **2.** antiseptic, asep~ tic, disinfected, germ-free, sterilized

Antonyms (*sense 1*) fecund, fertile, fruitful, productive, prolific (*sense 2*) contaminated, dirty, germ-ridden, infected, insanitary, un~ hygienic, unsterile

sterilize autoclave, disinfect, fumigate, pu~ rify

sterling authentic, excellent, fine, first-class, genuine, pure, real, sound, standard, sub~ stantial, superlative, true

stern austere, authoritarian, bitter, cruel, drastic, flinty, forbidding, frowning, grim, hard, harsh, inflexible, relentless, rigid, rigorous, serious, severe, steely, strict, un~ relenting, unsparing, unyielding
Antonyms amused, approachable, compas~ sionate, flexible, friendly, gentle, kind, leni~ ent, liberal, permissive, soft, sympathetic, tolerant, warm

stick¹ *v.* **1.** adhere, affix, attach, bind, bond, cement, cleave, cling, fasten, fix, fuse, glue, hold, hold on, join, paste, weld **2.** dig, gore, insert, jab, penetrate, pierce, pin, poke, prod, puncture, spear, stab, thrust, transfix **3.** *With* **out, up,** *etc.* bulge, extend, jut, obtrude, poke, project, protrude, show **4.** *Inf.* deposit, drop, fix, install, lay, place, plant, plonk, position, put, set, store, stuff **5.** be bogged down, become immobilized, be embedded, catch, clog, come to a standstill, jam, lodge, snag, stop **6.** linger, persist, re~ main, stay **7.** *Sl.* abide, bear up under, en~ dure, get on with, stand, stomach, take, tol~ erate **8. stick it out** *Inf.* bear, endure, grin and bear it (*Inf.*), last out, put up with (*Inf.*), see it through, see through to the bitter end, soldier on, take it (*Inf.*), weather **9. stick up for** *Inf.* champion, defend, stand up for, support, take the part *or* side of, uphold

stick² *n.* **1.** baton, birch, cane, crook, pole, rod, sceptre, staff, stake, switch, twig, wand **2.** *Inf.* dinosaur, fuddy-duddy (*Inf.*), (old) fogy, pain (*Inf.*), prig, stick-in-the-mud (*Inf.*) **3.** *Brit. sl.* abuse, blame, criticism, flak (*Inf.*), hostility, punishment

stick to adhere to, cleave to, continue in, honour, keep, persevere in, remain loyal (faithful, true), stick at

sticky 1. adhesive, claggy (*Dialect*), clinging, gluey, glutinous, gooey (*Inf.*), gummy, syr~ upy, tacky, tenacious, viscid, viscous **2.** *Inf.* awkward, delicate, difficult, discomforting, embarrassing, hairy (*Sl.*), nasty, painful, thorny, tricky, unpleasant **3.** clammy, close, humid, muggy, oppressive, sultry, swelter~ ing

stiff 1. brittle, firm, hard, hardened, inelas~ tic, inflexible, rigid, solid, solidified, taut, tense, tight, unbending, unyielding **2.** artificial, austere, ceremonious, chilly, cold, constrained, forced, formal, laboured, man~

nered, pompous, priggish, prim, punctili~
ous, standoffish, starchy (*Inf.*), stilted, un~
easy, unnatural, unrelaxed, wooden **3.** ar~
thritic, awkward, clumsy, creaky (*Inf.*),
crude, graceless, inelegant, jerky,
rheumaticky (*Inf.*), ungainly, ungraceful,
unsupple **4.** arduous, difficult, exacting, fa~
tiguing, formidable, hard, laborious, tough,
trying, uphill **5.** austere, cruel, drastic, ex~
treme, great, hard, harsh, heavy, inexo~
rable, oppressive, pitiless, rigorous, severe,
sharp, strict, stringent **6.** brisk, fresh, pow~
erful, strong, vigorous
Antonyms (*senses 1 & 3*) bendable, ductile,
elastic, flexible, limber, lissom(e), lithe, pli~
able, pliant, supple, yielding (*sense 2*) casual,
easy, informal, laid-back, natural, relaxed,
spontaneous, unceremonious, unofficial

stiffen brace, coagulate, congeal, crystallize,
harden, jell, reinforce, set, solidify, starch,
tauten, tense, thicken

stifle 1. asphyxiate, choke, smother, stran~
gle, suffocate **2.** check, choke back, cover
up, curb, extinguish, hush, muffle, prevent,
repress, restrain, silence, smother, stop,
suppress

still 1. *adj.* at rest, calm, hushed, inert, life~
less, motionless, noiseless, pacific, peaceful,
placid, quiet, restful, serene, silent, smooth,
stationary, stilly (*Poetic*), tranquil, undis~
turbed, unruffled, unstirring **2.** *v.* allay, al~
leviate, appease, calm, hush, lull, pacify,
quiet, quieten, settle, silence, smooth,
smooth over, soothe, subdue, tranquillize **3.**
conj. but, for all that, however, neverthe~
less, notwithstanding, yet **4.** *n. Poetic* hush,
peace, quiet, silence, stillness, tranquillity
Antonyms *adj.* active, agitated, astir, bus~
tling, busy, humming, lively, moving, noisy,
restless, turbulent ~*v.* aggravate, agitate, ex~
acerbate, increase, inflame, rouse, stir up ~*n.*
bustle, clamour, hubbub, noise, uproar

stilted artificial, bombastic, constrained,
forced, grandiloquent, high-flown, high-
sounding, inflated, laboured, pedantic,
pompous, pretentious, stiff, unnatural,
wooden
Antonyms flowing, fluid, free, natural,
spontaneous, unaffected, unpretentious

stimulant analeptic, bracer (*Inf.*), energizer,
excitant, pep pill (*Inf.*), pick-me-up (*Inf.*),
restorative, reviver, tonic, upper (*Sl.*)
Antonyms calmant, depressant, downer
(*Sl.*), sedative, tranquilliser

stimulate animate, arouse, encourage, fan,
fire, foment, goad, impel, incite, inflame,
instigate, prod, prompt, provoke, quicken,
rouse, spur, turn on (*Sl.*), urge, whet

stimulating exciting, exhilarating, galvan~
ic, inspiring, intriguing, provocative, pro~
voking, rousing, stirring, thought-provoking

Antonyms boring, dull, mind-numbing,
unexciting, unimaginative, uninspiring, un~
interesting, unstimulating

stimulus encouragement, fillip, goad, in~
centive, incitement, inducement, provoca~
tion, shot in the arm (*Inf.*), spur

sting *v.* **1.** burn, hurt, pain, smart, tingle,
wound **2.** anger, gall, incense, inflame, in~
furiate, nettle, pique, provoke, rile **3.** *Inf.*
cheat, defraud, do (*Sl.*), fleece, overcharge,
rip off (*Sl.*), skin (*Sl.*), stiff (*Sl.*), swindle,
take for a ride (*Inf.*)

stint 1. *n.* assignment, bit, period, quota,
share, shift, spell, stretch, term, time, tour,
turn **2.** *v.* begrudge, be sparing (frugal,
mean, mingy (*Brit. inf.*), parsimonious)
economize, hold back, save, scrimp, skimp
on, spoil the ship for a ha'porth of tar,
withhold

stipulate agree, contract, covenant, engage,
guarantee, insist upon, lay down, lay down
or impose conditions, make a point of,
pledge, postulate, promise, require, settle,
specify

stipulation agreement, clause, condition,
contract, engagement, precondition, pre~
requisite, provision, proviso, qualification,
requirement, restriction, rider, settlement,
sine qua non, specification, term

stir *v.* **1.** agitate, beat, disturb, flutter, mix,
move, quiver, rustle, shake, tremble **2.** *Of~
ten with* **up** animate, arouse, awaken, ex~
cite, incite, inflame, instigate, kindle, prod,
prompt, provoke, quicken, raise, rouse,
spur, stimulate, urge **3.** affect, electrify, ex~
cite, fire, inspire, move, thrill, touch **4.** be~
stir, be up and about (*Inf.*), budge, exert
oneself, get a move on (*Inf.*), get moving,
hasten, look lively (*Inf.*), make an effort,
mill about, move, shake a leg (*Inf.*) ~*n.* **5.**
activity, ado, agitation, bustle, commotion,
disorder, disturbance, excitement, ferment,
flurry, fuss, movement, to-do, tumult,
uproar
Antonyms *v.* (*senses 2 & 3*) check, curb,
dampen, inhibit, restrain, stifle, suppress,
throw cold water on (*Inf.*)

stirring animating, dramatic, emotive, ex~
citing, exhilarating, heady, impassioned,
inspiring, intoxicating, lively, moving,
rousing, spirited, stimulating, thrilling

stock *n.* **1.** array, assets, assortment, cache,
choice, commodities, fund, goods, hoard,
inventory, merchandise, range, reserve,
reservoir, selection, stockpile, store, supply,
variety, wares **2.** *Animals* beasts, cattle,
domestic animals, flocks, herds, horses,
livestock, sheep **3.** ancestry, background,
breed, descent, extraction, family, forebears,
house, line, lineage, line of descent, parent~
age, pedigree, race, strain, type, variety **4.**

Money capital, funds, investment, property **5. take stock** appraise, estimate, review the situation, see how the land lies, size up (*Inf.*), weigh up ~*adj.* **6.** banal, basic, commonplace, conventional, customary, formal, hackneyed, ordinary, overused, regular, routine, run-of-the-mill, set, standard, staple, stereotyped, traditional, trite, usual, worn-out ~*v.* **7.** deal in, handle, keep, sell, supply, trade in **8.** *With* **up** accumulate, amass, buy up, gather, hoard, lay in, put away, replenish, save, store (up), supply **9.** equip, fill, fit out, furnish, kit out, provide with, provision, supply

stocky chunky, dumpy, mesomorphic, solid, stubby, stumpy, sturdy, thickset

stodgy 1. filling, heavy, leaden, starchy, substantial **2.** boring, dull, dull as ditchwater, formal, fuddy-duddy (*Inf.*), heavy going, ho-hum, laboured, staid, stuffy, tedious, turgid, unexciting, unimaginative, uninspired
Antonyms (*sense 1*) appetizing, fluffy, insubstantial, light (*sense 2*) animated, exciting, fashionable, fresh, interesting, light, lively, readable, stimulating, trendy (*Brit. inf.*), up-to-date

stoical calm, cool, dispassionate, impassive, imperturbable, indifferent, long-suffering, philosophic, phlegmatic, resigned, stoic, stolid

stoicism acceptance, calmness, dispassion, fatalism, forbearance, fortitude, impassivity, imperturbability, indifference, long-suffering, patience, resignation, stolidity

stolid apathetic, bovine, doltish, dozy (*Brit. inf.*), dull, heavy, lumpish, obtuse, slow, stupid, unemotional, wooden
Antonyms acute, animated, bright, emotional, energetic, excitable, intelligent, interested, lively, passionate, sharp, smart

stomach *n.* **1.** abdomen, belly, breadbasket (*Sl.*), gut (*Inf.*), inside(s) (*Inf.*), paunch, pot, potbelly, spare tyre (*Inf.*), tummy (*Inf.*) **2.** appetite, desire, inclination, mind, relish, taste ~*v.* **3.** abide, bear, endure, put up with (*Inf.*), reconcile *or* resign oneself to, submit to, suffer, swallow, take, tolerate

stony *Fig.* adamant, blank, callous, chilly, expressionless, frigid, hard, harsh, heartless, hostile, icy, indifferent, inexorable, merciless, obdurate, pitiless, unfeeling, unforgiving, unresponsive

stoop *v.* **1.** be bowed *or* round-shouldered, bend, bow, crouch, descend, duck, hunch, incline, kneel, lean, squat **2.** *Often with* **to** condescend, deign, demean oneself, descend, lower oneself, resort, sink, vouchsafe ~*n.* **3.** bad posture, droop, round-shoulderedness, sag, slouch, slump

stop *v.* **1.** axe (*Inf.*), be over, break off, bring *or* come to a halt, bring *or* come to a standstill, call it a day (*Inf.*), cease, come to an end, conclude, cut out (*Inf.*), cut short, desist, discontinue, draw up, end, finish, halt, leave off, pack in (*Brit. inf.*), pause, peter out, pull up, put an end to, quit, refrain, run down, run its course, shut down, stall, terminate **2.** arrest, bar, block, break, bung, check, close, forestall, frustrate, hinder, hold back, impede, intercept, interrupt, obstruct, plug, prevent, rein in, repress, restrain, seal, silence, staunch, stem, suspend **3.** break one's journey, lodge, put up, rest, sojourn, stay, tarry ~*n.* **4.** cessation, conclusion, discontinuation, end, finish, halt, standstill **5.** break, rest, sojourn, stay, stopover, visit **6.** bar, block, break, check, control, hindrance, impediment, plug, stoppage **7.** depot, destination, halt, stage, station, termination, terminus
Antonyms *v.* (*senses 1 & 3*) advance, begin, commence, continue, get going, get under way, give the go ahead, go, institute, keep going, keep on, kick off (*Inf.*), proceed, set in motion, set off, start (*sense 2*) assist, boost, encourage, expedite, facilitate, further, hasten, promote, push ~*n.* (*sense 4*) beginning, commencement, kick-off (*Inf.*), start (*sense 6*) boost, encouragement, incitement

stopgap 1. *n.* improvisation, makeshift, resort, shift, substitute, temporary expedient **2.** *adj.* emergency, impromptu, improvised, makeshift, provisional, rough-and-ready, temporary

stoppage 1. abeyance, arrest, close, closure, cutoff, deduction, discontinuance, halt, hindrance, lay-off, shutdown, standstill, stopping **2.** blockage, check, curtailment, interruption, obstruction, occlusion, stopping up

store *v.* **1.** accumulate, deposit, garner, hoard, husband, keep, keep in reserve, lay by *or* in, lock away, put aside, put aside for a rainy day, put by, put in storage, reserve, salt away, save, stash (*Inf.*), stock, stockpile ~*n.* **2.** abundance, accumulation, cache, fund, hoard, lot, mine, plenty, plethora, provision, quantity, reserve, reservoir, stock, stockpile, supply, wealth **3.** chain store, department store, emporium, market, mart, outlet, shop, supermarket **4.** depository, repository, storehouse, storeroom, warehouse **5. set store by** appreciate, esteem, hold in high regard, prize, think highly of, value

storm *n.* **1.** blast, blizzard, cyclone, gale, gust, hurricane, squall, tempest, tornado, whirlwind **2.** *Fig.* agitation, anger, clamour, commotion, disturbance, furore, hubbub, outbreak, outburst, outcry, passion, roar, row, rumpus, stir, strife, tumult, turmoil, violence ~*v.* **3.** assail, assault, beset, char ge, rush, take by storm ~*n.* **4.** assault, at~ tack, blitz, blitzkrieg, offensive, onset, on~ slaught, rush ~*v.* **5.** bluster, complain, fly off the handle (*Inf.*), fume, rage, rant, rave, scold, thunder **6.** flounce, fly, rush, stalk, stamp, stomp (*Inf.*)

stormy blustering, blustery, boisterous, dirty, foul, gusty, inclement, raging, rough, squally, tempestuous, turbulent, wild, windy

story **1.** account, anecdote, chronicle, fictional account, history, legend, narration, narrative, novel, recital, record, relation, romance, tale, urban legend, version, yarn **2.** *Inf.* falsehood, fib, fiction, lie, pork pie (*Brit. sl.*), porky (*Brit. sl.*), untruth, white lie **3.** article, feature, news, news item, re~ port, scoop

stout **1.** big, bulky, burly, corpulent, fat, fleshy, heavy, obese, on the large *or* heavy side, overweight, plump, portly, rotund, substantial, tubby **2.** able-bodied, athletic, beefy (*Inf.*), brawny, hardy, hulking, husky (*Inf.*), lusty, muscular, robust, stalwart, strapping, strong, sturdy, substantial, thickset, tough, vigorous **3.** bold, brave, courageous, dauntless, doughty, fearless, gallant, intrepid, lion-hearted, manly, plucky, resolute, valiant, valorous

Antonyms (*senses 1 & 2*) feeble, flimsy, frail, insubstantial, lanky, lean, puny, skin-and-bones(*Inf.*), skinny, slender, slight, slim(*sense 3*) cowardly, faint-hearted, fearful, irresolute, shrinking, soft, spineless, timid, weak

stouthearted ballsy (*Taboo sl.*), bold, brave, courageous, dauntless, doughty, fearless, great-hearted, gutsy (*Sl.*), heroic, indomitable, intrepid, lion-hearted, plucky, spirited, stalwart, valiant, valorous

stow bundle, cram, deposit, jam, load, pack, put away, secrete, stash (*Inf.*), store, stuff, tuck

straggle drift, lag, loiter, ramble, range, roam, rove, spread, stray, string out, trail, wander

straight *adj.* **1.** direct, near, short, undeviating, unswerving **2.** aligned, erect, even, horizontal, in line, level, perpendicu~ lar, plumb, right, smooth, square, true, upright, vertical **3.** blunt, candid, down~ right, forthright, frank, honest, outright, plain, point-blank, straightforward, unqualified, upfront (*Inf.*) **4.** above board, accurate, authentic, decent, equitable, fair, fair and square, honest, honourable, just, law-abiding, reliable, respectable, trust~ worthy, upright **5.** arranged, in order, neat, orderly, organized, put to rights, shipshape, sorted out, tidy **6.** consecutive, continuous, nonstop, running, solid, successive, sus~ tained, through, uninterrupted, unrelieved

7. *Sl.* bourgeois, conservative, conventional, orthodox, square (*Inf.*), traditional **8.** neat, pure, unadulterated, undiluted, unmixed ~*adv.* **9.** as the crow flies, at once, directly, immediately, instantly **10.** candidly, frank~ ly, honestly, in plain English, point-blank, pulling no punches (*Inf.*), with no holds barred

Antonyms *adj.* (*sense 1*) circuitous, indirect, roundabout, winding, zigzag (*sense 2*) askew, bent, crooked, curved, skewwhiff (*Brit. inf.*), twisted, uneven (*sense 3*) ambiguous, cryptic, equivocal, evasive, indirect, vague (*sense 4*) bent (*Sl.*), crooked (*Inf.*), dishonest, dishon~ ourable, shady (*Inf.*), unlawful (*sense 5*) con~ fused, disorderly, disorganized, in disarray, messy, untidy (*sense 6*) broken, discontinuous, interrupted, non-consecutive (*sense 7*) *Sl.* cool, fashionable, trendy (*Brit. inf.*), voguish

straightaway at once, directly, immedi~ ately, instantly, now, on the spot, right away, straightway (*Archaic*), there and then, this minute, without any delay, with~ out more ado

straighten arrange, neaten, order, put in order, set *or* put to rights, smarten up, spruce up, tidy (up)

straighten out become clear, clear up, correct, disentangle, put right, rectify, regularize, resolve, settle, sort out, unsnarl, work out

straightforward **1.** above board, candid, direct, forthright, genuine, guileless, honest, open, sincere, truthful, upfront (*Inf.*) **2.** clear-cut, easy, easy-peasy (*Sl.*), elementary, routine, simple, uncomplicated, undemand~ ing

Antonyms complex, complicated, confused, convoluted, devious, disingenuous, round~ about, shady, sharp, unclear, unscrupulous

strain[1] *v.* **1.** distend, draw tight, extend, stretch, tauten, tighten **2.** drive, exert, fa~ tigue, injure, overexert, overtax, overwork, pull, push to the limit, sprain, tax, tear, tire, twist, weaken, wrench **3.** bend over backwards (*Inf.*), break one's neck (*Inf.*), bust a gut (*Inf.*), do one's damnedest (*Inf.*), endeavour, give it one's all (*Inf.*), give it one's best shot (*Inf.*), go all out for (*Inf.*), go for broke (*Sl.*), go for it (*Inf.*), knock oneself out (*Inf.*), labour, make an all-out effort (*Inf.*), make a supreme effort, rupture one~ self (*Inf.*), strive, struggle **4.** filter, perco~ late, purify, riddle, screen, seep, separate, sieve, sift ~*n.* **5.** effort, exertion, force, in~ jury, pull, sprain, struggle, tautness, ten~ sion, tensity (*Rare*), wrench **6.** anxiety, burden, pressure, stress, tension **7.** *Often plural* air, lay, measure (*Poetic*), melody, song, theme, tune

Antonyms *v.* (*senses 2 & 3*) idle, loose, pam~ per, relax, rest, slacken, take it easy, yield ~*n.*

(*senses 5 & 6*) ease, effortlessness, lack of ten~ sion, relaxation

strain² *n.* **1.** ancestry, blood, descent, ex~ traction, family, lineage, pedigree, race, stock **2.** streak, suggestion, suspicion, ten~ dency, trace, trait **3.** humour, manner, spirit, style, temper, tone, vein, way

strained artificial, awkward, constrained, difficult, embarrassed, false, forced, la~ boured, put on, self-conscious, stiff, tense, uncomfortable, uneasy, unnatural, un~ relaxed
Antonyms comfortable, natural, relaxed

strait-laced moralistic, narrow, narrow- minded, of the old school, old-maidish (*Inf.*), overscrupulous, prim, proper, prudish, pu~ ritanical, strict, Victorian
Antonyms broad-minded, earthy, immoral, loose, relaxed, uninhibited, unreserved

straits *n.* *Sometimes singular* **1.** crisis, difficulty, dilemma, distress, embarrass~ ment, emergency, extremity, hardship, hole (*Sl.*), mess, panic stations (*Inf.*), pass, per~ plexity, plight, predicament, pretty *or* fine kettle of fish (*Inf.*) **2.** channel, narrows, sound

strand *n.* fibre, filament, length, lock, rope, string, thread, tress, twist, wisp

stranded 1. aground, ashore, beached, cast away, grounded, marooned, wrecked **2.** *Fig.* abandoned, helpless, high and dry, home~ less, left in the lurch, penniless

strange 1. abnormal, astonishing, bizarre, curious, eccentric, exceptional, extraordi~ nary, fantastic, funny, irregular, marvel~ lous, mystifying, odd, oddball (*Inf.*), off- the-wall (*Sl.*), out-of-the-way, outré, peculiar, perplexing, queer, rare, remarkable, rum (*Brit. sl.*), singular, unaccountable, uncan~ ny, uncommon, unheard of, weird, wonder~ ful **2.** alien, exotic, foreign, new, novel, outside one's experience, remote, unex~ plored, unfamiliar, unknown, untried **3.** *Often with* **to** a stranger to, ignorant of, in~ experienced, new to, unaccustomed, un~ practised, unseasoned, unused, unversed in **4.** awkward, bewildered, disoriented, ill at ease, lost, out of place, uncomfortable
Antonyms (*senses 1 & 2*) accustomed, com~ mon, commonplace, conventional, familiar, habitual, ordinary, regular, routine, run-of- the-mill, standard, typical, unexceptional, usual, well-known (*sense 3*) accustomed, fa~ miliar, habitual (*sense 4*) at ease, at home, comfortable, relaxed

stranger alien, foreigner, guest, incomer, new arrival, newcomer, outlander, un~ known, visitor

strangle 1. asphyxiate, choke, garrotte, smother, strangulate, suffocate, throttle **2.** gag, inhibit, repress, stifle, suppress

strap *n.* **1.** belt, leash, thong, tie ~*v.* **2.** bind, buckle, fasten, lash, secure, tie, truss **3.** beat, belt (*Inf.*), flog, lash, scourge, whip

stratagem artifice, device, dodge, feint, in~ trigue, manoeuvre, plan, plot, ploy, ruse, scheme, subterfuge, trick, wile

strategic 1. cardinal, critical, crucial, deci~ sive, important, key, vital **2.** calculated, de~ liberate, diplomatic, planned, politic, tacti~ cal

strategy approach, grand design, manoeu~ vring, plan, planning, policy, procedure, programme, scheme

stray *v.* **1.** deviate, digress, diverge, get off the point, get sidetracked, go off at a tan~ gent, ramble **2.** be abandoned *or* lost, drift, err, go astray, lose one's way, meander, range, roam, rove, straggle, wander ~*adj.* **3.** abandoned, homeless, lost, roaming, va~ grant **4.** accidental, chance, erratic, freak, odd, random, scattered

streak *n.* **1.** band, layer, line, slash, smear, strip, stripe, stroke, vein **2.** dash, element, strain, touch, trace, vein ~*v.* **3.** band, daub, fleck, slash, smear, striate, stripe **4.** barrel (along) (*Inf., chiefly U.S. & Canad.*), burn rubber (*Inf.*), dart, flash, fly, hurtle, move like greased lightning (*Inf.*), speed, sprint, sweep, tear, whistle, whiz (*Inf.*), zoom

stream 1. *n.* bayou, beck, brook, burn, course, creek (*U.S.*), current, drift, flow, freshet, outpouring, rill, river, rivulet, run, rush, surge, tide, tideway, torrent, tribu~ tary, undertow **2.** *v.* cascade, course, emit, flood, flow, glide, gush, issue, pour, run, shed, spill, spout

streamer banner, colours, ensign, flag, gonfalon, pennant, pennon, ribbon, stand~ ard

streamlined efficient, modernized, organ~ ized, rationalized, sleek, slick, smooth, smooth-running, time-saving, well-run

street 1. avenue, boulevard, lane, road, roadway, row, terrace, thoroughfare **2. (right) up one's street** acceptable, com~ patible, congenial, familiar, one's cup of tea (*Inf.*), pleasing, suitable, to one's liking, to one's taste

strength 1. backbone, brawn, brawniness, courage, firmness, fortitude, health, lusti~ ness, might, muscle, robustness, sinew, stamina, stoutness, sturdiness, toughness **2.** cogency, concentration, effectiveness, efficacy, energy, force, intensity, potency, power, resolution, spirit, vehemence, vig~ our, virtue (*Archaic*) **3.** advantage, anchor, asset, mainstay, security, strong point, suc~ cour, tower of strength
Antonyms (*senses 1 & 2*) debility, feebleness, frailty, impotence, infirmity, powerlessness, weakness (*sense 3*) Achilles heel, chink in

one's armour, defect, failing, flaw, short~
coming, weakness

strengthen 1. animate, brace up, consoli~
date, encourage, fortify, give new energy to,
harden, hearten, invigorate, nerve, nourish,
rejuvenate, restore, stiffen, toughen **2.** aug~
ment, bolster, brace, build up, buttress,
confirm, corroborate, enhance, establish,
give a boost to, harden, heighten, increase,
intensify, justify, reinforce, steel, substanti~
ate, support
Antonyms crush, debilitate, destroy, dilute,
enervate, render impotent, sap, subvert,
undermine, weaken

strenuous 1. arduous, demanding, ex~
hausting, hard, Herculean, laborious, tax~
ing, toilsome, tough, tough going,
unrelaxing, uphill **2.** active, bold, deter~
mined, eager, earnest, energetic, persistent,
resolute, spirited, strong, tireless, vigorous,
zealous
Antonyms easy, effortless, relaxed, relax~
ing, undemanding, unenergetic, untaxing

stress *n.* **1.** emphasis, force, importance,
significance, urgency, weight **2.** anxiety,
burden, hassle (*Inf.*), nervous tension, op~
pression, pressure, strain, tautness, tension,
trauma, worry **3.** accent, accentuation,
beat, emphasis ~*v.* **4.** accentuate, belabour,
dwell on, emphasize, harp on, lay emphasis
upon, point up, repeat, rub in, underline,
underscore

stretch *v.* **1.** cover, extend, put forth, reach,
spread, unfold, unroll **2.** distend, draw out,
elongate, expand, inflate, lengthen, pull,
pull out of shape, rack, strain, swell, tight~
en ~*n.* **3.** area, distance, expanse, extent,
spread, sweep, tract **4.** bit, period, run,
space, spell, stint, term, time

strict 1. austere, authoritarian, firm, harsh,
no-nonsense, rigid, rigorous, severe, stern,
stringent **2.** accurate, close, exact, faithful,
meticulous, particular, precise, religious,
scrupulous, true **3.** absolute, complete, per~
fect, total, utter
Antonyms (*sense 1*) easy-going, easy-oasy
(*Sl.*), flexible, laid-back (*Inf.*), lax, mild, mod~
erate, soft, tolerant

strident clamorous, clashing, discordant,
grating, harsh, jangling, jarring, rasping,
raucous, screeching, shrill, stridulant,
stridulous, unmusical, vociferous
Antonyms calm, dulcet, gentle, harmonious,
mellifluous, mellow, quiet, soft, soothing,
sweet

strife animosity, battle, bickering, clash,
clashes, combat, conflict, contention, con~
test, controversy, discord, dissension, fric~
tion, quarrel, rivalry, row, squabbling,
struggle, warfare, wrangling

strike *v.* **1.** bang, beat, box, buffet, chastise,
chin (*Sl.*), clobber (*Sl.*), clout (*Inf.*), clump
(*Sl.*), cuff, deck (*Sl.*), hammer, hit, knock,
lambast(e), lay a finger on (*Inf.*), lay one on
(*Sl.*), pound, punch, punish, slap, smack,
smite, sock (*Sl.*), thump, wallop (*Inf.*) **2.** be
in collision with, bump into, clash, collide
with, come into contact with, dash, hit,
knock into, run into, smash into, touch **3.**
drive, force, hit, impel, thrust **4.** affect,
come to, come to the mind of, dawn on *or*
upon, hit, impress, make an impact on, oc~
cur to, reach, register (*Inf.*), seem **5.** *Some~
times with* **upon** come upon *or* across, dis~
cover, encounter, find, happen *or* chance
upon, hit upon, light upon, reach, stumble
upon *or* across, turn up, uncover, unearth
6. affect, assail, assault, attack, deal a blow
to, devastate, fall upon, hit, invade, set
upon, smite **7.** achieve, arrange, arrive at,
attain, effect, reach **8.** down tools, mutiny,
revolt, walk out

striking astonishing, conspicuous, dazzling,
drop-dead (*Sl.*), extraordinary, forcible, im~
pressive, memorable, noticeable, out of the
ordinary, outstanding, stunning (*Inf.*), won~
derful
Antonyms average, dull, indifferent, undis~
tinguished, unexceptional, unextraordinary,
unimpressive, uninteresting

string *n.* **1.** cord, fibre, twine **2.** chain, file,
line, procession, queue, row, sequence, se~
ries, strand, succession ~*v.* **3.** festoon,
hang, link, loop, sling, stretch, suspend,
thread **4.** *With* **out** disperse, extend, fan
out, lengthen, protract, space out, spread
out, straggle

stringent binding, demanding, exacting,
inflexible, rigid, rigorous, severe, strict,
tight, tough
Antonyms equivocal, flexible, inconclusive,
lax, loose, relaxed, slack, unrigorous, vague

strings *Fig.* catches (*Inf.*), complications,
conditions, obligations, prerequisites, pro~
visos, qualifications, requirements, riders,
stipulations

strip¹ *v.* **1.** bare, denude, deprive, despoil,
dismantle, divest, empty, gut, lay bare, loot,
peel, pillage, plunder, ransack, rob, sack,
skin, spoil **2.** disrobe, unclothe, uncover,
undress

strip² *n.* band, belt, bit, fillet, piece, ribbon,
shred, slip, swathe, tongue

striped banded, barred, striated, stripy

stripling adolescent, boy, fledgling, hobble~
dehoy (*Archaic*), lad, shaver (*Inf.*), young
fellow, youngster, youth

strive attempt, bend over backwards (*Inf.*),
break one's neck (*Inf.*), bust a gut (*Inf.*),
compete, contend, do all one can, do one's
best, do one's damnedest (*Inf.*), do one's
utmost, endeavour, exert oneself, fight, give

it one's all (*Inf.*), give it one's best shot (*Inf.*), go all out (*Inf.*), go for broke (*Sl.*), go for it (*Inf.*), knock oneself out (*Inf.*), labour, leave no stone unturned, make an all-out effort (*Inf.*), make every effort, rupture one~ self (*Inf.*), strain, struggle, toil, try, try hard

stroke *n.* **1.** accomplishment, achievement, blow, feat, flourish, hit, knock, move, movement, pat, rap, thump **2.** apoplexy, at~ tack, collapse, fit, seizure, shock ~*v.* **3.** ca~ ress, fondle, pat, pet, rub

stroll **1.** *v.* amble, make one's way, mooch (*Sl.*), mosey (*Inf.*), promenade, ramble, saunter, stooge (*Sl.*), stretch one's legs, take a turn, toddle, wander **2.** *n.* airing, breath of air, constitutional, excursion, promenade, ramble, turn, walk

strong **1.** athletic, beefy (*Inf.*), brawny, burly, capable, hale, hardy, healthy, Hercu~ lean, lusty, muscular, powerful, robust, sin~ ewy, sound, stalwart, stout, strapping, stur~ dy, tough, virile **2.** aggressive, brave, cou~ rageous, determined, feisty (*Inf., chiefly U.S. & Canad.*), firm in spirit, forceful, hard as nails, hard-nosed (*Inf.*), high-powered, plucky, resilient, resolute, resourceful, self-assertive, steadfast, stouthearted, tena~ cious, tough, unyielding **3.** acute, dedicated, deep, deep-rooted, eager, fervent, fervid, fierce, firm, intense, keen, severe, staunch, vehement, violent, zealous **4.** clear, clear- cut, cogent, compelling, convincing, dis~ tinct, effective, formidable, great, marked, overpowering, persuasive, potent, redoubt~ able, sound, telling, trenchant, unmistak~ able, urgent, weighty, well-established, well-founded **5.** Draconian, drastic, ex~ treme, forceful, severe **6.** durable, hard- wearing, heavy-duty, on a firm foundation, reinforced, sturdy, substantial, well-armed, well-built, well-protected **7.** bold, bright, brilliant, dazzling, glaring, loud, stark **8.** biting, concentrated, heady, highly- flavoured, highly-seasoned, hot, intoxicat~ ing, piquant, pungent, pure, sharp, spicy, undiluted
Antonyms (*senses 1, 2, 3, 4, 5 & 6*) character~ less, delicate, faint-hearted, feeble, frail, inef~ fectual, lacking drive, namby-pamby, puny, slight, spineless, timid, unassertive, uncom~ mitted, unimpassioned, weak (*sense 7*) dull, insipid, pale, pastel, washed-out (*sense 8*) bland, mild, tasteless, vapid, weak

stronghold bastion, bulwark, castle, cita~ del, fastness, fort, fortress, keep, refuge

strong-minded determined, firm, inde~ pendent, iron-willed, resolute, strong-willed, unbending, uncompromising

stroppy awkward, bloody-minded (*Brit. inf.*), cantankerous, destructive, difficult,

obstreperous, perverse, quarrelsome, unco~ operative, unhelpful

structure *n.* **1.** arrangement, configuration, conformation, construction, design, fabric, form, formation, interrelation of parts, make, make-up, organization **2.** building, construction, edifice, erection, pile ~*v.* **3.** arrange, assemble, build up, design, organ~ ize, put together, shape

struggle *v.* **1.** bend over backwards (*Inf.*), break one's neck (*Inf.*), bust a gut (*Inf.*), do one's damnedest (*Inf.*), exert oneself, give it one's all (*Inf.*), give it one's best shot (*Inf.*), go all out (*Inf.*), go for broke (*Sl.*), go for it (*Inf.*), knock oneself out (*Inf.*), labour, make an all-out effort (*Inf.*), make every effort, rupture oneself (*Inf.*), strain, strive, toil, work, work like a Trojan ~*n.* **2.** effort, ex~ ertion, grind (*Inf.*), labour, long haul, pains, scramble, toil, work ~*v.* **3.** battle, compete, contend, fight, grapple, lock horns, scuffle, wrestle ~*n.* **4.** battle, brush, clash, combat, conflict, contest, encounter, hostilities, skirmish, strife, tussle

strut *v.* parade, peacock, prance, stalk, swagger

stub *n.* butt, counterfoil, dog-end (*Inf.*), end, fag end (*Inf.*), remnant, stump, tail, tail end

stubborn bull-headed, contumacious, cross-grained, dogged, dour, fixed, head~ strong, inflexible, intractable, mulish, ob~ durate, obstinate, opinionated, persistent, pig-headed, recalcitrant, refractory, self- willed, stiff-necked, tenacious, unbending, unmanageable, unshakable, unyielding, wilful
Antonyms biddable, compliant, docile, flexible, half-hearted, irresolute, malleable, manageable, pliable, pliant, tractable, vacil~ lating, wavering, yielding

stuck **1.** cemented, fast, fastened, firm, fixed, glued, joined **2.** *Inf.* at a loss, at a standstill, at one's wits' end, baffled, beaten, bereft of ideas, nonplussed, stumped, up against a brick wall (*Inf.*) **3.** *Sl. With* **on** crazy about, for, *or* over (*Inf.*), enthusiastic about, hung up on (*Sl.*), infatuated, keen, mad, obsessed with, wild about (*Inf.*) **4. get stuck into** *Inf.* get down to, make a start on, set about, tackle

stuck-up arrogant, big-headed (*Inf.*), con~ ceited, condescending, haughty, high and mighty (*Inf.*), hoity-toity (*Inf.*), patronizing, proud, snobbish, snooty (*Inf.*), swollen- headed, toffee-nosed (*Sl., chiefly Brit.*), uppish (*Brit. inf.*), uppity (*Inf.*)

stud *v.* bejewel, bespangle, dot, fleck, orna~ ment, spangle, speckle, spot, sprinkle

student apprentice, disciple, learner, ob~ server, pupil, scholar, trainee, undergradu~ ate

studied calculated, conscious, deliberate, intentional, planned, premeditated, pur~ poseful, well-considered, wilful
Antonyms impulsive, natural, spontaneous, spur-of-the-moment, unplanned, unpremedi~ tated

studio atelier, workshop

studious academic, assiduous, attentive, bookish, careful, diligent, eager, earnest, hard-working, intellectual, meditative, reflective, scholarly, sedulous, serious, thoughtful
Antonyms careless, frivolous, idle, inatten~ tive, indifferent, lazy, loafing, negligent, un~ academic, unintellectual, unscholarly

study *v.* **1.** apply oneself (to), bone up on (*Inf.*), burn the midnight oil, cogitate, con (*Archaic*), consider, contemplate, cram (*Inf.*), examine, go into, hammer away at, learn, lucubrate (*Rare*), meditate, mug up (*Brit. sl.*), ponder, pore over, read, read up, swot (up) (*Brit. inf.*) **2.** analyse, deliberate, examine, investigate, look into, peruse, re~ search, scrutinize, survey, work over ~*n.* **3.** academic work, application, book work, cramming (*Inf.*), learning, lessons, reading, research, school work, swotting (*Brit. inf.*), thought **4.** analysis, attention, cogitation, consideration, contemplation, examination, inquiry, inspection, investigation, perusal, review, scrutiny, survey

stuff *v.* **1.** compress, cram, crowd, fill, force, jam, load, pack, pad, push, ram, shove, squeeze, stow, wedge **2.** gobble, gorge, gor~ mandize, guzzle, make a pig of oneself (*Inf.*), overindulge, pig out (*Sl.*), sate, satiate ~*n.* **3.** belongings, bits and pieces, clobber (*Brit. sl.*), effects, equipment, gear, goods and chattels, impedimenta, junk, kit, luggage, materials, objects, paraphernalia, posses~ sions, tackle, things, trappings **4.** cloth, fabric, material, raw material, textile **5.** es~ sence, matter, pith, quintessence, staple, substance **6.** balderdash, baloney (*Inf.*), bosh (*Inf.*), bunk (*Inf.*), bunkum, claptrap (*Inf.*), foolishness, humbug, nonsense, poppycock (*Inf.*), rot, rubbish, stuff and nonsense, tommyrot, tripe (*Inf.*), twaddle, verbiage

stuffing **1.** filler, kapok, packing, quilting, wadding **2.** farce, farcemeat, forcemeat

stuffy **1.** airless, close, fetid, frowsty, fuggy, heavy, muggy, oppressive, stale, stifling, suffocating, sultry, unventilated **2.** conven~ tional, deadly, dreary, dull, fusty, humour~ less, musty, old-fashioned, old-fogyish, pompous, priggish, prim, prim and proper, staid, stilted, stodgy, strait-laced, uninter~ esting
Antonyms (*sense 1*) airy, breezy, cool,

draughty, fresh, gusty, pleasant, well-ventilated

stumble **1.** blunder about, come a cropper (*Inf.*), fall, falter, flounder, hesitate, lose one's balance, lurch, reel, slip, stagger, trip **2.** *With* **on** *or* **upon** blunder upon, chance upon, come across, discover, encounter, find, happen upon, light upon, run across, turn up **3.** falter, fluff (*Inf.*), stammer, stut~ ter

stump *v.* **1.** baffle, bewilder, bring (some~ one) up short, confound, confuse, dumb~ found, flummox, foil, mystify, nonplus, out~ wit, perplex, puzzle, stop, stymie **2.** clomp, clump, lumber, plod, stamp, stomp (*Inf.*), trudge

stump up chip in (*Inf.*), come across with (*Inf.*), contribute, cough up (*Inf.*), donate, fork out (*Sl.*), hand over, pay, shell out (*Inf.*)

stun *Fig.* amaze, astonish, astound, bewilder, confound, confuse, daze, dumbfound, flabbergast (*Inf.*), hit (someone) like a ton of bricks (*Inf.*), knock out, knock (someone) for six (*Inf.*), overcome, overpower, shock, stagger, strike (someone) dumb, stupefy, take (someone's) breath away

stung angered, exasperated, goaded, hurt, incensed, nettled, piqued, resentful, roused, wounded

stunned *Fig.* astounded, at a loss for words, bowled over (*Inf.*), dazed, devastated, dumbfounded, flabbergasted (*Inf.*), gob~ smacked (*Brit. sl.*), numb, shocked, stag~ gered, struck dumb

stunning beautiful, brilliant, dazzling, dev~ astating (*Inf.*), drop-dead (*Sl.*), gorgeous, great (*Inf.*), heavenly, impressive, lovely, marvellous, out of this world (*Inf.*), ravish~ ing, remarkable, sensational (*Inf.*), smash~ ing (*Inf.*), spectacular, striking, wonderful
Antonyms average, dreadful, horrible, me~ diocre, ordinary, plain, poor, rotten, run-of-the-mill, ugly, unattractive, unimpressive, uninspiring, unremarkable

stunt *n.* act, deed, exploit, feat, feature, gest (*Archaic*), *tour de force*, trick

stunted diminutive, dwarfed, dwarfish, lit~ tle, small, tiny, undersized

stupefaction amazement, astonishment, awe, wonder, wonderment

stupefy amaze, astound, bewilder, con~ found, daze, dumbfound, knock senseless, numb, shock, stagger, stun

stupendous amazing, astounding, breath~ taking, brilliant, colossal, enormous, fabu~ lous (*Inf.*), fantastic (*Inf.*), gigantic, huge, marvellous, mega (*Sl.*), mind-blowing (*Inf.*), mind-boggling (*Inf.*), out of this world (*Inf.*), overwhelming, phenomenal, prodigious, sensational (*Inf.*), staggering, stunning (*Inf.*), superb, surpassing belief, surprising, tremendous (*Inf.*), vast, wonderful, wondrous (*Archaic or literary*)

Antonyms average, diminutive, mediocre, modest, ordinary, petty, puny, tiny, unexciting, unimpressive, unremarkable, unsurprising

stupid 1. Boeotian, braindead (*Inf.*), brainless, cretinous, deficient, dense, dim, doltish, dopey (*Inf.*), dozy (*Brit. inf.*), dull, dumb (*Inf.*), foolish, gullible, half-witted, moronic, naive, obtuse, simple, simple-minded, slow, slow on the uptake (*Inf.*), slow-witted, sluggish, stolid, thick, thickheaded, unintelligent, witless, woodenheaded (*Inf.*) **2.** asinine, crackbrained, daft (*Inf.*), futile, half-baked (*Inf.*), idiotic, ill-advised, imbecilic, inane, indiscreet, irrelevant, irresponsible, laughable, ludicrous, meaningless, mindless, nonsensical, pointless, puerile, rash, senseless, short-sighted, trivial, unintelligent, unthinking **3.** dazed, groggy, in a daze, insensate, punch-drunk, semiconscious, senseless, stunned, stupefied

Antonyms astute, brainy, bright, brilliant, clear-headed, clever, intelligent, lucid, on the ball (*Inf.*), prudent, quick, quick on the uptake, quick-witted, realistic, reasonable, sensible, sharp, shrewd, smart, thoughtful, well-thought-out, wise

stupidity 1. asininity, brainlessness, denseness, dimness, dopiness (*Sl.*), doziness (*Brit. inf.*), dullness, dumbness (*Inf.*), feeble-mindedness, imbecility, lack of brain, lack of intelligence, naivety, obtuseness, puerility, simplicity, slowness, thickheadedness, thickness **2.** absurdity, bêtise (*Rare*), fatuity, fatuousness, folly, foolhardiness, foolishness, futility, idiocy, impracticality, inanity, indiscretion, ineptitude, irresponsibility, ludicrousness, lunacy, madness, pointlessness, rashness, senselessness, silliness

sturdy athletic, brawny, built to last, determined, durable, firm, flourishing, hardy, hearty, lusty, muscular, powerful, resolute, robust, secure, solid, stalwart, staunch, steadfast, stouthearted, substantial, thickset, vigorous, well-built, well-made

Antonyms feeble, flimsy, frail, infirm, irresolute, puny, rickety, skinny, uncertain, unsubstantial, weak, weakly

stutter *v.* falter, hesitate, speak haltingly, splutter, stammer, stumble

style *n.* **1.** cut, design, form, hand, manner, technique **2.** fashion, mode, rage, trend, vogue **3.** approach, custom, manner, method, mode, way **4.** *bon ton*, chic, cosmopolitanism, dash, dressiness (*Inf.*), élan, elegance, fashionableness, flair, grace, panache, polish, refinement, savoir-faire,

smartness, sophistication, stylishness, taste, urbanity **5.** affluence, comfort, ease, elegance, gracious living, grandeur, luxury **6.** appearance, category, characteristic, genre, kind, pattern, sort, spirit, strain, tenor, tone, type, variety **7.** diction, expression, mode of expression, phraseology, phrasing, treatment, turn of phrase, vein, wording ~*v.* **8.** adapt, arrange, cut, design, dress, fashion, shape, tailor **9.** address, call, christen, denominate, designate, dub, entitle, label, name, term

stylish à la mode, chic, classy (*Sl.*), dapper, dressy (*Inf.*), fashionable, in fashion, in vogue, modish, natty (*Inf.*), polished, smart, snappy, snazzy (*Inf.*), trendy (*Brit. inf.*), urbane, voguish, well turned-out

Antonyms badly-tailored, naff (*Brit. sl.*), old-fashioned, out-moded, out-of-date, passé, scruffy, shabby, slovenly, tacky, tawdry, unfashionable, unstylish, untrendy (*Brit. inf.*)

suave affable, agreeable, bland, charming, civilized, cool (*Inf.*), courteous, debonair, diplomatic, gracious, obliging, pleasing, polite, smooth, smooth-tongued, sophisticated, svelte, urbane, worldly

subconscious *adj.* hidden, inner, innermost, intuitive, latent, repressed, subliminal, suppressed

Antonyms aware, conscious, knowing, sensible, sentient

subdue 1. beat down, break, conquer, control, crush, defeat, discipline, gain ascendancy over, get the better of, get the upper hand over, get under control, humble, master, overcome, overpower, overrun, put down, quell, tame, trample, triumph over, vanquish **2.** check, control, mellow, moderate, quieten down, repress, soften, suppress, tone down

Antonyms (*sense 2*) agitate, arouse, awaken, incite, provoke, stir up, waken, whip up

subdued 1. chastened, crestfallen, dejected, downcast, down in the mouth, grave, out of spirits, quiet, repentant, repressed, restrained, sad, sadder and wiser, serious, sobered, solemn **2.** dim, hushed, low-key, muted, quiet, shaded, sober, soft, subtle, toned down, unobtrusive

Antonyms bright, cheerful, enthusiastic, happy, lively, loud, strident, vivacious

subject *n.* **1.** affair, business, field of enquiry *or* reference, issue, matter, object, point, question, subject matter, substance, theme, topic **2.** case, client, guinea pig (*Inf.*), participant, patient, victim **3.** citizen, dependant, liegeman, national, subordinate, vassal ~*adj.* **4.** at the mercy of, disposed, exposed, in danger of, liable, open, prone, susceptible, vulnerable **5.** conditional, contingent, dependent **6.** answerable, bound by, captive, dependent, enslaved, inferior, obedient, satellite, subjugated, submissive, subordinate, subservient ~*v.* **7.** expose, lay open, make liable, put through, submit, treat

subjective biased, emotional, idiosyncratic, instinctive, intuitive, nonobjective, person~ al, prejudiced
Antonyms concrete, detached, disinterest~ ed, dispassionate, impartial, impersonal, ob~ jective, open-minded, unbiased

subjugate bring (someone) to his knees, bring to heel, bring under the yoke, con~ quer, crush, defeat, enslave, hold sway over, lick (*Inf.*), master, overcome, over~ power, overthrow, put down, quell, reduce, rule over, subdue, suppress, tame, vanquish

sublime elevated, eminent, exalted, glori~ ous, grand, great, high, imposing, lofty, magnificent, majestic, noble, transcendent
Antonyms bad, commonplace, lowly, mun~ dane, ordinary, poor, ridiculous, worldly

submerge deluge, dip, drown, duck, dunk, engulf, flood, immerse, inundate, overflow, overwhelm, plunge, sink, swamp

submerged drowned, immersed, subaquat~ ic, subaqueous, submarine, submersed, sunk, sunken, undersea, underwater

submission 1. acquiescence, assent, ca~ pitulation, giving in, surrender, yielding **2.** compliance, deference, docility, meekness, obedience, passivity, resignation, submis~ siveness, tractability, unassertiveness **3.** argument, contention, proposal **4.** entry, handing in, presentation, submitting, ten~ dering

submissive abject, accommodating, acqui~ escent, amenable, biddable, bootlicking (*Inf.*), compliant, deferential, docile, dutiful, humble, ingratiating, lowly, malleable, meek, obedient, obeisant, obsequious, pas~ sive, patient, pliant, resigned, subdued, tractable, uncomplaining, unresisting, yielding
Antonyms awkward, difficult, disobedient, headstrong, intractable, obstinate, stubborn, uncooperative, unyielding

submit 1. accede, acquiesce, agree, bend, bow, capitulate, comply, defer, endure, give in, hoist the white flag, knuckle under, lay down arms, put up with (*Inf.*), resign one~ self, stoop, succumb, surrender, throw in the sponge, toe the line, tolerate, yield **2.** commit, hand in, present, proffer, put for~ ward, refer, table, tender **3.** advance, argue, assert, claim, contend, move, propose, pro~ pound, put, state, suggest, volunteer

subnormal cretinous, E.S.N., feeble-minded, imbecilic, mentally defective, mo~ ronic, retarded, simple, slow

subordinate *adj.* **1.** dependent, inferior,

junior, lesser, lower, minor, secondary, subject, subservient **2.** ancillary, auxiliary, subsidiary, supplementary ~*n.* **3.** aide, as~ sistant, attendant, dependant, inferior, jun~ ior, second, subaltern, underling
Antonyms *adj.* central, essential, greater, higher, key, main, necessary, predominant, senior, superior, vital ~*n.* boss (*Inf.*), captain, chief, commander, head, leader, master, prin~ cipal, senior, superior

subordination inferior *or* secondary sta~ tus, inferiority, servitude, subjection, sub~ mission

subscribe 1. chip in (*Inf.*), contribute, do~ nate, give, offer, pledge, promise **2.** acqui~ esce, advocate, agree, consent, countenance, endorse, support

subscription annual payment, contribu~ tion, donation, dues, gift, membership fee, offering

subsequent after, consequent, consequen~ tial, ensuing, following, later, succeeding, successive
Antonyms antecedent, earlier, erstwhile, former, on-time, past, preceding, previous, prior

subsequently afterwards, at a later date, consequently, in the aftermath (of), in the end, later

subservient 1. abject, bootlicking (*Inf.*), deferential, inferior, obsequious, servile, slavish, subject, submissive, sycophantic, truckling **2.** accessory, ancillary, auxiliary, conducive, helpful, instrumental, service~ able, subordinate, subsidiary, useful
Antonyms (*sense 1*) bolshie, bossy, disobedi~ ent, domineering, overbearing, overriding, rebellious, superior, wilful

subside 1. abate, decrease, de-escalate, di~ minish, dwindle, ease, ebb, lessen, let up, level off, melt away, moderate, peter out, quieten, recede, slacken, wane **2.** cave in, collapse, decline, descend, drop, ebb, lower, settle, sink
Antonyms escalate, grow, heighten, in~ crease, inflate, intensify, mount, rise, soar, swell, tumefy, wax

subsidence 1. decline, descent, ebb, settle~ ment, settling, sinking **2.** abatement, de~ crease, de-escalation, diminution, easing off, lessening, slackening

subsidiary aiding, ancillary, assistant, auxiliary, contributory, cooperative, help~ ful, lesser, minor, secondary, serviceable, subordinate, subservient, supplemental, supplementary, useful
Antonyms central, chief, head, key, leading, main, major, primary, principal, vital

subsidize finance, fund, promote, put up the money for, sponsor, support, underwrite

subsidy aid, allowance, assistance, contri~
bution, financial aid, grant, help, stipend,
subvention, support

subsist be, continue, eke out an existence,
endure, exist, keep going, last, live, make
ends meet, remain, stay alive, survive, sus~
tain oneself

subsistence aliment, existence, food, keep,
livelihood, living, maintenance, provision,
rations, support, survival, sustenance,
upkeep, victuals

substance 1. body, element, fabric, ma~
terial, stuff, texture **2.** burden, essence, gist,
gravamen (*Law*), import, main point, mat~
ter, meaning, pith, significance, subject,
sum and substance, theme **3.** actuality,
concreteness, entity, force, reality **4.**
affluence, assets, estate, means, property,
resources, wealth

substantial 1. ample, big, considerable,
generous, goodly, important, large,
significant, sizable, tidy (*Inf.*), worthwhile
2. bulky, durable, firm, hefty, massive, sol~
id, sound, stout, strong, sturdy, well-built **3.**
actual, existent, material, positive, real,
true, valid, weighty
Antonyms (*senses 1 & 2*) feeble, frail, inad~
equate, inconsiderable, infirm, insignificant,
insubstantial, jerry-built, light-weight, mea~
gre, niggardly, poor, rickety, skimpy, small,
weak (*sense 3*) fictitious, imaginary, imagined,
insubstantial, nonexistent, unreal

substantially essentially, in essence, in
essentials, in substance, in the main, large~
ly, materially, to a large extent

substantiate affirm, attest to, authenticate,
bear out, confirm, corroborate, establish,
prove, support, validate, verify
Antonyms confute, contradict, controvert,
disprove, expose, invalidate, negate, prove
false, rebut, refute

substitute *v.* **1.** change, commute, ex~
change, interchange, replace, swap (*Inf.*),
switch **2.** *With* **for** act for, be in place of,
cover for, deputize, double for, fill in for,
hold the fort for, relieve, stand in for, take
over ~*n.* **3.** agent, depute (*Scot.*), deputy,
equivalent, expedient, locum, locum tenens,
makeshift, proxy, relief, replacement, rep~
resentative, reserve, stand-by, stopgap, sub,
supply, surrogate, temp (*Inf.*), temporary
~*adj.* **4.** acting, additional, alternative,
fall-back, proxy, replacement, reserve, sec~
ond, surrogate, temporary

substitution change, exchange, inter~
change, replacement, swap (*Inf.*), switch

subterfuge artifice, deception, deviousness,
dodge, duplicity, evasion, excuse, machina~
tion, manoeuvre, ploy, pretence, pretext,
quibble, ruse, shift, stall, stratagem, trick

subtle 1. deep, delicate, discriminating, in~
genious, nice, penetrating, profound,
refined, sophisticated **2.** delicate, faint, im~
plied, indirect, insinuated, slight, under~
stated **3.** artful, astute, crafty, cunning, de~
signing, devious, intriguing, keen, Machia~
vellian, scheming, shrewd, sly, wily
Antonyms artless, blunt, crass, direct,
downright, guileless, heavy-handed, lacking
finesse, obvious, overwhelming, simple,
straightforward, strong, tactless, unsophisti~
cated, unsubtle

subtlety 1. acumen, acuteness, cleverness,
delicacy, discernment, fine point, intricacy,
nicety, refinement, sagacity, skill, sophisti~
cation **2.** discernment, discrimination,
finesse, penetration **3.** artfulness, astute~
ness, craftiness, cunning, deviousness,
guile, slyness, wiliness

subtract deduct, detract, diminish, remove,
take away, take from, take off, withdraw
Antonyms add, add to, append, increase by,
supplement

suburbs dormitory area (*Brit.*), environs,
faubourgs, neighbourhood, outskirts, pre~
cincts, purlieus, residential areas, suburbia

subversive 1. *adj.* destructive, incendiary,
inflammatory, insurrectionary, overthrow~
ing, perversive, riotous, seditious, treason~
ous, underground, undermining **2.** *n.* de~
viationist, dissident, fifth columnist, insur~
rectionary, quisling, saboteur, seditionary,
seditionist, terrorist, traitor

subvert 1. demolish, destroy, invalidate,
overturn, raze, ruin, sabotage, undermine,
upset, wreck **2.** confound, contaminate,
corrupt, debase, demoralize, deprave, per~
vert, poison, vitiate

succeed 1. arrive (*Inf.*), be successful, come
off (*Inf.*), crack it (*Inf.*), cut it (*Inf.*), do all
right for oneself (*Inf.*), do the trick (*Inf.*),
flourish, gain one's end, get to the top,
make good, make it (*Inf.*), prosper, thrive,
triumph, turn out well, work **2.** be subse~
quent, come next, ensue, follow, result,
supervene **3.** *Usually with* **to** accede, as~
sume the office of, come into, come into
possession of, enter upon, inherit, replace,
take over
Antonyms (*sense 1*) be unsuccessful, col~
lapse, come a cropper (*Inf.*), fail, fall flat, fall
short, flop (*Inf.*), not make the grade, not man~
age to (*sense 2*) be a precursor of, come before,
go ahead of, go before, pave the way, precede

succeeding ensuing, following, next, sub~
sequent, successive
Antonyms antecedent, earlier, former, pre~
ceding, previous, prior

success 1. ascendancy, eminence, fame, fa~
vourable outcome, fortune, happiness, hit
(*Inf.*), luck, prosperity, triumph **2.** best
seller, big name, celebrity, hit (*Inf.*), market

leader, megastar (*Inf.*), sensation, smash hit (*Inf.*), somebody, star, V.I.P., winner
Antonyms collapse, dead duck (*Sl.*), disas~ter, downfall, failure, fiasco, flop (*Inf.*), loser, misfortune, nobody, no-hoper, washout

successful acknowledged, at the top of the tree, best-selling, booming, efficacious, fa~vourable, flourishing, fortunate, fruitful, lucky, lucrative, moneymaking, out in front (*Inf.*), paying, profitable, prosperous, re~warding, thriving, top, unbeaten, victorious, wealthy
Antonyms defeated, failed, ineffective, los~ing, luckless, uneconomic, unprofitable, un~successful, useless

successfully famously (*Inf.*), favourably, in triumph, swimmingly, victoriously, well, with flying colours

succession 1. chain, continuation, course, cycle, flow, order, procession, progression, run, sequence, series, train 2. **in succes~sion** consecutively, one after the other, one behind the other, on the trot (*Inf.*), running, successively 3. accession, assumption, el~evation, entering upon, inheritance, taking over 4. descendants, descent, line, lineage, race

successive consecutive, following, in a row, in succession, sequent, succeeding

succinct brief, compact, compendious, con~cise, condensed, gnomic, in a few well-chosen words, laconic, pithy, summary, terse, to the point
Antonyms circuitous, circumlocutory, dif~fuse, discursive, long-winded, prolix, ram~bling, verbose, wordy

succour 1. *v.* aid, assist, befriend, comfort, encourage, foster, give aid and encourage~ment to, help, minister to, nurse, relieve, render assistance to, support 2. *n.* aid, as~sistance, comfort, help, relief, support

succulent juicy, luscious, lush, mellow, moist, mouthwatering, rich

succumb capitulate, die, fall, fall victim to, give in, give way, go under, knuckle under, submit, surrender, yield
Antonyms beat, conquer, get the better of, master, overcome, rise above, surmount, tri~umph over

sucker butt, cat's paw, dupe, easy game *or* mark (*Inf.*), fool, mug (*Brit. sl.*), nerd *or* nurd (*Sl.*), pushover (*Sl.*), sap (*Sl.*), sitting duck (*Inf.*), victim

sudden abrupt, hasty, hurried, impulsive, quick, rapid, rash, swift, unexpected, un~foreseen, unusual
Antonyms anticipated, deliberate, expected, foreseen, gentle, gradual, slow, unhasty

suddenly abruptly, all at once, all of a sud~den, on the spur of the moment, out of the blue (*Inf.*), unexpectedly, without warning

sue 1. *Law* bring an action against (some~one), charge, have the law on (someone) (*Inf.*), indict, institute legal proceedings against (someone), prefer charges against (someone), prosecute, summon, take (some~one) to court 2. appeal for, beg, beseech, entreat, petition, plead, solicit, supplicate

suffer 1. ache, agonize, be affected, be in pain, be racked, feel wretched, go through a lot (*Inf.*), grieve, have a thin *or* bad time, hurt 2. bear, endure, experience, feel, go through, put up with (*Inf.*), support, sus~tain, tolerate, undergo 3. appear in a poor light, be handicapped, be impaired, deterio~rate, fall off, show to disadvantage 4. *Ar~chaic* allow, let, permit

suffering *n.* affliction, agony, anguish, dis~comfort, distress, hardship, martyrdom, misery, ordeal, pain, torment, torture

suffice answer, be sufficient (adequate, enough), content, do, fill the bill (*Inf.*), meet requirements, satisfy, serve

sufficient adequate, competent, enough, enow (*Archaic*), satisfactory
Antonyms deficient, inadequate, in~sufficient, meagre, not enough, poor, scant, short, sparse

suffocate asphyxiate, choke, smother, stifle, strangle

suffuse bathe, cover, flood, imbue, infuse, mantle, overspread, permeate, pervade, spread over, steep, transfuse

suggest 1. advise, advocate, move, offer a suggestion, prescribe, propose, put forward, recommend 2. bring to mind, connote, evoke, put one in mind of 3. hint, imply, indicate, insinuate, intimate, lead one to believe

suggestion 1. motion, plan, proposal, proposition, recommendation 2. breath, hint, indication, insinuation, intimation, suspicion, trace, whisper

suggestive 1. *With* of evocative, expres~sive, indicative, redolent, reminiscent 2. bawdy, blue, immodest, improper, indecent, indelicate, off colour, provocative, prurient, racy, ribald, risqué, rude, smutty, spicy (*Inf.*), titillating, unseemly

suit *v.* 1. agree, agree with, answer, be ac~ceptable to, become, befit, be seemly, con~form to, correspond, do, go with, gratify, harmonize, match, please, satisfy, tally 2. accommodate, adapt, adjust, fashion, fit, modify, proportion, tailor ~*n.* 3. addresses, appeal, attentions, courtship, entreaty, in~vocation, petition, prayer, request 4. *Law* action, case, cause, industrial tribunal, lawsuit, proceeding, prosecution, trial 5.

clothing, costume, dress, ensemble, habit, outfit **6. follow suit** accord with, copy, emulate, run with the herd, take one's cue from

suitability appropriateness, aptness, fitness, opportuneness, rightness, timeliness

suitable acceptable, applicable, apposite, appropriate, apt, becoming, befitting, con~ venient, cut out for, due, fit, fitting, in character, in keeping, opportune, pertinent, proper, relevant, right, satisfactory, seemly, suited
Antonyms discordant, inapposite, inappro~ priate, incorrect, inopportune, jarring, out of character, out of keeping, unbecoming, unfitting, unseemly, unsuitable, unsuited

suite 1. apartment, collection, furniture, rooms, series, set **2.** attendants, entourage, escort, followers, retainers, retinue, train

suitor admirer, beau, follower (*Obsolete*), swain (*Archaic*), wooer, young man

sulk be in a huff, be put out, brood, have the hump (*Brit. inf.*), look sullen, pout

sulky aloof, churlish, cross, disgruntled, huffy, ill-humoured, in the sulks, moody, morose, perverse, petulant, put out, queru~ lous, resentful, sullen, vexed

sullen brooding, cheerless, cross, dismal, dull, gloomy, glowering, heavy, moody, mo~ rose, obstinate, out of humour, perverse, silent, sombre, sour, stubborn, surly, unso~ ciable
Antonyms amiable, bright, cheerful, cheery, chirpy (*Inf.*), genial, good-humoured, good-natured, pleasant, sociable, sunny, warm, warm-hearted

sullenness glumness, heaviness, ill hu~ mour, moodiness, moroseness, sourness, sulkiness, sulks

sultry 1. close, hot, humid, muggy, oppres~ sive, sticky, stifling, stuffy, sweltering **2.** amorous, come-hither (*Inf.*), erotic, pas~ sionate, provocative, seductive, sensual, sexy (*Inf.*), voluptuous
Antonyms (*sense 1*) cool, fresh, invigorating, refreshing

sum aggregate, amount, entirety, quantity, reckoning, score, sum total, tally, total, to~ tality, whole

summarily arbitrarily, at short notice, ex~ peditiously, forthwith, immediately, on the spot, peremptorily, promptly, speedily, swiftly, without delay, without wasting words

summarize abridge, condense, encapsulate, epitomize, give a rundown of, give the main points of, outline, précis, put in a nutshell, review, sum up

summary 1. *n.* abridgment, abstract, com~ pendium, digest, epitome, essence, extract, outline, précis, recapitulation, résumé, re~ view, rundown, summing-up, synopsis **2.** *adj.* arbitrary, brief, compact, compendious, concise, condensed, cursory, hasty, laconic, perfunctory, pithy, succinct

summit acme, apex, crest, crown, crowning point, culmination, head, height, peak, pin~ nacle, top, zenith
Antonyms base, bottom, depths, foot, lowest point, nadir

summon 1. arouse, assemble, bid, call, call together, cite, convene, convoke, invite, rally, rouse, send for **2.** *Often with* **up** call into action, draw on, gather, invoke, mobi~ lize, muster

sumptuous costly, dear, de luxe, expen~ sive, extravagant, gorgeous, grand, lavish, luxurious, magnificent, opulent, plush (*Inf.*), posh (*Inf., chiefly Brit.*), rich, ritzy (*Sl.*), splendid, splendiferous (*Facetious*), superb
Antonyms austere, basic, cheap, frugal, in~ expensive, meagre, mean, miserly, plain, shabby, wretched

sum up 1. close, conclude, put in a nut~ shell, recapitulate, review, summarize **2.** estimate, form an opinion of, get the meas~ ure of, size up (*Inf.*)

sun 1. *n.* daystar (*Poetic*), eye of heaven, Helios (*Greek myth*), Phoebus (*Greek myth*), Phoebus Apollo (*Greek myth*), Sol (*Roman myth*) **2.** *v.* bake, bask, sunbathe, tan

sunburnt bronzed, brown, brown as a ber~ ry, burnt, like a lobster, peeling, red, ruddy, scarlet, tanned

sundry assorted, different, divers (*Archaic*), miscellaneous, several, some, varied, vari~ ous

sunk all washed up (*Inf.*), done for (*Inf.*), finished, lost, on the rocks, ruined, up the creek without a paddle (*Inf.*)

sunken 1. concave, drawn, haggard, hollow, hollowed **2.** at a lower level, below ground, buried, depressed, immersed, lower, re~ cessed, submerged

sunless bleak, cheerless, cloudy, dark, de~ pressing, gloomy, grey, hazy, overcast, sombre

sunny 1. bright, brilliant, clear, fine, lumi~ nous, radiant, summery, sunlit, sunshiny, unclouded, without a cloud in the sky **2.** *Fig.* beaming, blithe, buoyant, cheerful, cheery, chirpy (*Inf.*), genial, happy, joyful, light-hearted, optimistic, pleasant, smiling
Antonyms cloudy, depressing, doleful, down in the dumps, dreary, dreich (*Scot.*), dull, gloomy, miserable, morbid, murky, overcast, rainy, shaded, shadowy, sunless, unsmiling, wet, wintry

sunrise aurora (*Poetic*), break of day, cock~

crow, dawn, daybreak, daylight, dayspring (*Poetic*), sunup

sunset close of (the) day, dusk, eventide, gloaming (*Scot. or poetic*), nightfall, sundown

superb admirable, boffo (*Sl.*), breathtaking, brill (*Inf.*), chillin' (*U.S. sl.*), choice, excellent, exquisite, fine, first-rate, gorgeous, grand, magnificent, marvellous, mega (*Sl.*), of the first water, splendid, splendiferous (*Facetious*), superior, topping (*Brit. sl.*), unrivalled, world-class
Antonyms awful, bad, disappointing, dreadful, inferior, mediocre, pathetic, poor quality, run-of-the-mill, terrible, third-rate, uninspired, woeful

supercilious arrogant, condescending, contemptuous, disdainful, haughty, high and mighty (*Inf.*), hoity-toity (*Inf.*), imperious, insolent, lofty, lordly, overbearing, patronizing, proud, scornful, snooty (*Inf.*), stuck-up (*Inf.*), toffee-nosed (*Sl., chiefly Brit.*), uppish (*Brit. inf.*), vainglorious
Antonyms deferential, generous, humble, meek, modest, obsequious, self-effacing, submissive, unassuming, unpretentious, warmhearted

superficial 1. exterior, external, on the surface, peripheral, shallow, skin-deep, slight, surface **2.** casual, cosmetic, cursory, desultory, hasty, hurried, inattentive, nodding, passing, perfunctory, sketchy, slapdash **3.** empty, empty-headed, frivolous, lightweight, shallow, silly, trivial **4.** apparent, evident, ostensible, outward, seeming
Antonyms complete, comprehensive, deep, detailed, earnest, exhaustive, in depth, major, penetrating, probing, profound, serious, substantial, thorough

superficiality emptiness, lack of depth, lack of substance, shallowness, triviality

superficially apparently, at first glance, externally, on the surface, ostensibly, to the casual eye

superfluous excess, excessive, extra, in excess, left over, needless, on one's hands, pleonastic (*Rhetoric*), redundant, remaining, residuary, spare, superabundant, supererogatory, supernumerary, surplus, surplus to requirements, uncalled-for, unnecessary, unneeded, unrequired
Antonyms called for, essential, imperative, indispensable, necessary, needed, requisite, vital, wanted

superhuman 1. herculean, heroic, phenomenal, prodigious, stupendous, valiant **2.** divine, paranormal, preternatural, supernatural

superintend administer, control, direct, handle, inspect, look after, manage, overlook, oversee, run, supervise

superintendence care, charge, control, direction, government, guidance, inspection, management, supervision, surveillance

superintendent administrator, chief, conductor, controller, director, governor, inspector, manager, overseer, supervisor

superior *adj.* **1.** better, grander, greater, higher, more advanced (expert, extensive, skilful), paramount, predominant, preferred, prevailing, surpassing, unrivalled **2.** a cut above (*Inf.*), admirable, choice, de luxe, distinguished, excellent, exceptional, exclusive, fine, first-class, first-rate, good, good quality, high calibre, high-class, of the first order, world-class **3.** airy, condescending, disdainful, haughty, lofty, lordly, patronizing, pretentious, snobbish, stuck-up (*Inf.*), supercilious ~*n.* **4.** boss (*Inf.*), chief, director, manager, principal, senior, supervisor
Antonyms *adj.* (*senses 1 & 2*) average, inferior, less, lesser, lower, mediocre, not as good, ordinary, poorer, second-class, second-rate, substandard, unremarkable, worse ~*n.* assistant, dogsbody, inferior, junior, lackey, minion, subordinate, underling

superiority advantage, ascendancy, excellence, lead, predominance, pre-eminence, preponderance, prevalence, supremacy

superlative *adj.* consummate, crack (*Sl.*), excellent, greatest, highest, magnificent, matchless, of the first water, of the highest order, outstanding, peerless, supreme, surpassing, transcendent, unparalleled, unrivalled, unsurpassed
Antonyms appalling, average, dreadful, easily outclassed, inferior, ordinary, poor, rotten, run-of-the-mill, undistinguished, unexceptional, uninspired, unspectacular

supernatural abnormal, dark, ghostly, hidden, miraculous, mysterious, mystic, occult, paranormal, phantom, preternatural, psychic, spectral, supranatural, uncanny, unearthly, unnatural

supersede annul, displace, oust, overrule, remove, replace, set aside, supplant, supplement, suspend, take over, take the place of, usurp

supervise administer, be on duty at, be responsible for, conduct, control, direct, handle, have *or* be in charge of, inspect, keep an eye on, look after, manage, oversee, preside over, run, superintend

supervision administration, auspices, care, charge, control, direction, guidance, instruction, management, oversight, stewardship, superintendence, surveillance

supervisor administrator, boss (*Inf.*), chief, foreman, gaffer (*Inf., chiefly Brit.*), inspector, manager, overseer, steward, superintendent

supervisory administrative, executive, managerial, overseeing, superintendent

supplant displace, oust, overthrow, remove, replace, supersede, take over, take the place of, undermine, unseat

supple bending, elastic, flexible, limber, lis~ som(e), lithe, loose-limbed, plastic, pliable, pliant
Antonyms awkward, creaky (*Inf.*), firm, graceless, inflexible, rigid, stiff, taut, unbend~ ing, unsupple, unyielding

supplement 1. *n.* added feature, adden~ dum, addition, add-on, appendix, codicil, complement, extra, insert, postscript, pull~ out, sequel **2.** *v.* add, augment, complement, extend, fill out, reinforce, supply, top up

supplementary accompanying, additional, add-on, ancillary, auxiliary, complemen~ tary, extra, secondary, supplemental

suppliant 1. *adj.* begging, beseeching, craving, entreating, imploring, importunate, on bended knee **2.** *n.* applicant, petitioner, suitor, supplicant

supplication appeal, entreaty, invocation, petition, plea, pleading, prayer, request, so~ licitation, suit

supply *v.* **1.** afford, cater to *or* for, come up with, contribute, endow, fill, furnish, give, grant, minister, outfit, produce, provide, purvey, replenish, satisfy, stock, store, victual, yield ~*n.* **2.** cache, fund, hoard, quantity, reserve, reservoir, source, stock, stockpile, store **3.** *Usually plural* equip~ ment, food, foodstuff, items, materials, ne~ cessities, provender, provisions, rations, stores

support *v.* **1.** bear, bolster, brace, buttress, carry, hold, hold up, prop, reinforce, shore up, sustain, underpin, uphold **2.** be a source of strength to, buoy up, cherish, en~ courage, finance, foster, fund, keep, look af~ ter, maintain, nourish, provide for, strengthen, subsidize, succour, sustain, take care of, underwrite **3.** advocate, aid, assist, back, boost (someone's) morale, champion, defend, espouse, forward, go along with, help, promote, second, side with, stand be~ hind, stand up for, stick up for (*Inf.*), take (someone's) part, take up the cudgels for, uphold **4.** attest to, authenticate, bear out, confirm, corroborate, document, endorse, lend credence to, substantiate, verify **5.** bear, brook, countenance, endure, put up with (*Inf.*), stand (for), stomach, submit, suffer, thole (*Dialect*), tolerate, undergo ~*n.* **6.** abutment, back, brace, foundation, lin~ ing, pillar, post, prop, shore, stanchion, stay, stiffener, underpinning **7.** aid, ap~ proval, assistance, backing, blessing, cham~ pionship, comfort, encouragement, espousal, friendship, furtherance, help, loyalty, moral support, patronage, promotion, protection, relief, succour, sustenance **8.** keep, liveli~ hood, maintenance, subsistence, sustenance, upkeep **9.** backbone, backer, comforter, mainstay, prop, second, stay, supporter, tower of strength
Antonyms *v.* (*sense 2*) live off, sponge off (*senses 3, 4 & 5*) challenge, contradict, deny, go against, hinder, hold out against, oppose, re~ fute, reject, stab in the back, turn one's back on, undermine, walk away from ~*n.* (*senses 7 & 9*) antagonist, burden, denial, encumbrance, hindrance, impediment, opposition, refuta~ tion, rejection, undermining

supporter adherent, advocate, ally, apolo~ gist, champion, co-worker, defender, fan, follower, friend, helper, henchman, patron, protagonist, sponsor, upholder, well-wisher
Antonyms adversary, antagonist, challeng~ er, competitor, foe, opponent, rival

supportive caring, encouraging, helpful, reassuring, sympathetic, understanding

suppose 1. assume, calculate (*U.S. dialect*), conjecture, dare say, expect, guess (*Inf., chiefly U.S. & Canad.*), imagine, infer, judge, opine, presume, presuppose, surmise, take as read, take for granted, think **2.** believe, conceive, conclude, conjecture, consider, fancy, hypothesize, imagine, postulate, pre~ tend

supposed 1. accepted, alleged, assumed, hypothetical, presumed, presupposed, pro~ fessed, putative, reputed, rumoured **2.** *With* **to** expected, meant, obliged, ought, required

supposedly allegedly, at a guess, avowedly, by all accounts, hypothetically, ostensibly, presumably, professedly, purportedly, theo~ retically
Antonyms absolutely, actually, certainly, in actuality, in fact, really, surely, truly, un~ doubtedly, without a doubt

supposition conjecture, doubt, guess, guesswork, hypothesis, idea, notion, postu~ late, presumption, speculation, surmise, theory

suppress 1. beat down, check, clamp down on, conquer, crack down on, crush, drive underground, extinguish, overpower, over~ throw, put an end to, quash, quell, quench, snuff out, stamp out, stop, subdue, trample on **2.** censor, conceal, contain, cover up, curb, hold in *or* back, keep in check, keep secret, muffle, muzzle, repress, restrain, si~ lence, smother, stifle, withhold
Antonyms encourage, foster, further, incite, inflame, promote, rouse, spread, stimulate, stir up, whip up

suppression check, clampdown, crack~ down, crushing, dissolution, elimination, extinction, inhibition, prohibition, quash~ ing, smothering, termination

suppurate discharge, fester, gather, matu~ rate, ooze, weep

supremacy absolute rule, ascendancy, dominance, domination, dominion, lordship, mastery, paramountcy, predominance, pre~ eminence, primacy, sovereignty, supreme authority, sway

supreme cardinal, chief, crowning, culmi~ nating, extreme, final, first, foremost, greatest, head, highest, incomparable, lead~ ing, matchless, paramount, peerless, pre~ dominant, pre-eminent, prevailing, prime, principal, sovereign, superlative, surpass~ ing, top, ultimate, unsurpassed, utmost
Antonyms least, least successful, lowest, most inferior, most minor, most subordinate, most trivial, poorest, worst

sure 1. assured, certain, clear, confident, convinced, decided, definite, free from doubt, persuaded, positive, satisfied **2.** ac~ curate, dependable, effective, foolproof, honest, indisputable, infallible, never-failing, precise, reliable, sure-fire (*Inf.*), tried and true, trustworthy, trusty, undeni~ able, undoubted, unerring, unfailing, un~ mistakable, well-proven **3.** assured, bound, guaranteed, ineluctable, inescapable, inevi~ table, irrevocable **4.** fast, firm, fixed, safe, secure, solid, stable, staunch, steady
Antonyms distrustful, dodgy (*Brit., Aust., & N.Z. inf.*), doubtful, dubious, fallible, iffy (*Inf.*), insecure, sceptical, touch-and-go, unassured, uncertain, unconvinced, undependable, un~ easy, unreliable, unsure, untrustworthy, vague

surely assuredly, beyond the shadow of a doubt, certainly, come what may, definitely, doubtlessly, for certain, indubitably, inevi~ tably, inexorably, undoubtedly, unquestion~ ably, without doubt, without fail

surface *n.* **1.** covering, exterior, façade, face, facet, outside, plane, side, skin, superficies (*Rare*), top, veneer **2. on the surface** apparently, at first glance, osten~ sibly, outwardly, superficially, to all ap~ pearances, to the casual eye ~*adj.* **3.** ap~ parent, exterior, external, outward, superficial ~*v.* **4.** appear, come to light, come up, crop up (*Inf.*), emerge, materialize, rise, transpire

surfeit 1. *n.* excess, glut, overindulgence, plethora, satiety, superabundance, super~ fluity **2.** *v.* cram, fill, glut, gorge, overfeed, overfill, satiate, stuff
Antonyms *n.* dearth, deficiency, insufficiency, lack, scarcity, shortage, short~ ness, want

surge 1. *v.* billow, eddy, gush, heave, rise, roll, rush, swell, swirl, tower, undulate, well forth **2.** *n.* billow, breaker, efflux, flood, flow, gush, intensification, outpour~

ing, roller, rush, swell, uprush, upsurge, wave

surly bearish, brusque, churlish, crabbed, cross, crusty, curmudgeonly, grouchy (*Inf.*), gruff, ill-natured, morose, perverse, sulky, sullen, testy, uncivil, ungracious
Antonyms agreeable, cheerful, cheery, gen~ ial, good-natured, happy, pleasant, sunny

surmise 1. *v.* come to the conclusion, con~ clude, conjecture, consider, deduce, fancy, guess, hazard a guess, imagine, infer, opine, presume, speculate, suppose, suspect **2.** *n.* assumption, conclusion, conjecture, deduc~ tion, guess, hypothesis, idea, inference, no~ tion, possibility, presumption, speculation, supposition, suspicion, thought

surmount conquer, exceed, master, over~ come, overpower, overtop, pass, prevail over, surpass, triumph over, vanquish

surpass beat, best, eclipse, exceed, excel, go one better than (*Inf.*), outdo, outshine, out~ strip, override, overshadow, top, tower above, transcend

surpassing exceptional, extraordinary, in~ comparable, matchless, outstanding, phe~ nomenal, rare, supreme, transcendent, un~ rivalled

surplus 1. *n.* balance, excess, remainder, residue, superabundance, superfluity, sur~ feit **2.** *adj.* excess, extra, in excess, left over, odd, remaining, spare, superfluous, unused
Antonyms *n.* dearth, deficiency, deficit, insufficiency, lack, paucity, shortage, short~ fall ~*adj.* deficient, falling short, inadequate, insufficient, lacking, limited, scant, scanty, scarce

surprise *v.* **1.** amaze, astonish, astound, be~ wilder, bowl over (*Inf.*), confuse, disconcert, flabbergast (*Inf.*), leave open-mouthed, non~ plus, stagger, stun, take aback **2.** burst in on, catch in the act *or* red-handed, catch napping, catch unawares *or* off-guard, come down on like a bolt from the blue, discover, spring upon, startle ~*n.* **3.** amazement, astonishment, bewilderment, incredulity, stupefaction, wonder **4.** bolt from the blue, bombshell, eye-opener (*Inf.*), jolt, revelation, shock, start (*Inf.*)

surprised amazed, astonished, at a loss, caught on the hop (*Brit. inf.*), caught on the wrong foot (*Inf.*), disconcerted, incredulous, nonplussed, open-mouthed, speechless, startled, taken aback, taken by surprise, thunderstruck, unable to believe one's eyes

surprising amazing, astonishing, astound~ ing, extraordinary, incredible, marvellous, remarkable, staggering, startling, unexpec~ ted, unlooked-for, unusual, wonderful

surrender *v.* **1.** abandon, cede, concede, de~ liver up, forego, give up, part with, relin~

quish, renounce, resign, waive, yield **2.** capitulate, give in, give oneself up, give way, lay down arms, quit, show the white flag, submit, succumb, throw in the towel, yield ~*n.* **3.** capitulation, delivery, relinquishment, renunciation, resignation, submission, yielding
Antonyms *v.* defy, fight (on), make a stand against, oppose, resist, stand up to, withstand

surreptitious clandestine, covert, fraudulent, furtive, secret, sly, sneaking, stealthy, unauthorized, underhand, veiled
Antonyms blatant, conspicuous, frank, honest, manifest, obvious, open, overt, unconcealed, undisguised

surround 1. close in on, encircle, enclose, encompass, envelop, environ, fence in, girdle, hem in, ring **2.** *Military* besiege, invest (*Rare*), lay siege to

surrounding nearby, neighbouring

surroundings background, environment, environs, location, milieu, neighbourhood, setting

surveillance care, control, direction, inspection, observation, scrutiny, superintendence, supervision, vigilance, watch

survey *v.* **1.** contemplate, examine, eye up, inspect, look over, observe, recce (*Sl.*), reconnoitre, research, review, scan, scrutinize, study, supervise, view **2.** appraise, assess, estimate, eye up, measure, plan, plot, prospect, size up, take stock of, triangulate ~*n.* **3.** examination, inquiry, inspection, overview, perusal, random sample, review, scrutiny, study

survive be extant, endure, exist, hold out, keep body and soul together (*Inf.*), last, live, live on, outlast, outlive, pull through, remain alive, subsist

susceptibility liability, predisposition, proneness, propensity, responsiveness, sensitivity, suggestibility, vulnerability, weakness

susceptible 1. *Usually with* **to** disposed, given, inclined, liable, open, predisposed, prone, subject, vulnerable **2.** alive to, easily moved, impressionable, receptive, responsive, sensitive, suggestible, tender
Antonyms immune, incapable, insensible, insusceptible, invulnerable, resistant, unaffected by, unmoved by, unresponsive

suspect *v.* **1.** distrust, doubt, harbour suspicions about, have one's doubts about, mistrust, smell a rat (*Inf.*) **2.** believe, conclude, conjecture, consider, fancy, feel, guess, have a sneaking suspicion, hazard a guess, speculate, suppose, surmise, think probable ~*adj.* **3.** dodgy (*Brit., Aust., & N.Z. inf.*), doubtful, dubious, fishy (*Inf.*), iffy (*Inf.*), open to suspicion, questionable
Antonyms *v.* accept, be certain, be confident

of, believe, buy (*Sl.*), have faith in, know, swallow (*Inf.*), think innocent, trust ~*adj.* above suspicion, innocent, reliable, straightforward, trustworthy, trusty

suspend 1. append, attach, dangle, hang, swing **2.** adjourn, arrest, cease, cut short, debar, defer, delay, discontinue, hold off, interrupt, lay aside, pigeonhole, postpone, put off, shelve, stay, withhold
Antonyms (*sense 2*) carry on, continue, reestablish, reinstate, restore, resume, return

suspense 1. anticipation, anxiety, apprehension, doubt, expectancy, expectation, indecision, insecurity, irresolution, tension, uncertainty, wavering **2. in suspense** anxious, in an agony of doubt, keyed up, on edge, on tenterhooks

suspension abeyance, adjournment, break, breaking off, deferment, delay, disbarment, discontinuation, interruption, moratorium, postponement, remission, respite, stay

suspicion 1. bad vibes (*Sl.*), chariness, distrust, doubt, dubiety, funny feeling (*Inf.*), jealousy, lack of confidence, misgiving, mistrust, qualm, scepticism, wariness **2. above suspicion** above reproach, blameless, honourable, like Caesar's wife, pure, sinless, unimpeachable, virtuous **3.** conjecture, guess, gut feeling (*Inf.*), hunch, idea, impression, notion, supposition, surmise **4.** glimmer, hint, shade, shadow, *soupçon,* strain, streak, suggestion, tinge, touch, trace

suspicious 1. apprehensive, distrustful, doubtful, jealous, leery (*Sl.*), mistrustful, sceptical, suspecting, unbelieving, wary **2.** dodgy (*Brit., Aust., & N.Z. inf.*), doubtful, dubious, fishy (*Inf.*), funny, irregular, of doubtful honesty, open to doubt *or* misconstruction, queer, questionable, shady (*Inf.*), suspect
Antonyms (*sense 1*) believing, credulous, gullible, open, trustful, trusting, unsuspecting, unsuspicious (*sense 2*) above board, beyond suspicion, not open to question, open, straight, straightforward, unquestionable, upright

sustain 1. bear, carry, keep from falling, keep up, support, uphold **2.** bear, bear up under, endure, experience, feel, suffer, undergo, withstand **3.** aid, assist, comfort, foster, help, keep alive, nourish, nurture, provide for, relieve **4.** approve, confirm, continue, keep alive, keep going, keep up, maintain, prolong, protract, ratify **5.** endorse, uphold, validate, verify

sustained constant, continuous, nonstop, perpetual, prolonged, steady, unremitting
Antonyms broken, discontinuous, intermittent, irregular, periodic, spasmodic, sporadic

sustenance **1.** aliment, comestibles, daily bread, eatables, edibles, food, nourishment, provender, provisions, rations, refection, refreshments, victuals **2.** livelihood, main~ tenance, subsistence, support

swagger **1.** v. bluster, boast, brag, bully, gasconade (Rare), hector, hot-dog (Chiefly U.S.), parade, prance, show off (Inf.), strut, swank (Inf.) **2.** n. arrogance, bluster, brag~ gadocio, display, gasconade (Rare), ostenta~ tion, pomposity, show, showing off (Inf.), swank (Inf.), swashbuckling

swallow v. **1.** absorb, consume, devour, down (Inf.), drink, eat, gulp, ingest, swig (Inf.), swill, wash down **2.** Often with up absorb, assimilate, consume, engulf, envel~ op, overrun, overwhelm, use up, waste **3.** choke back, hold in, repress **4.** Inf. accept, believe, buy (Sl.), fall for

swamp n. **1.** bog, everglade(s) (U.S.), fen, marsh, mire, morass, moss (Scot. & north~ ern English dialect), quagmire, slough ~v. **2.** capsize, drench, engulf, flood, inundate, overwhelm, sink, submerge, swallow up, upset, wash over, waterlog **3.** beset, besiege, deluge, flood, inundate, overload, over~ whelm, snow under

swampy boggy, fenny, marish (Obsolete), marshy, miry, quaggy, waterlogged, wet

swanky de luxe, exclusive, expensive, fan~ cy, fashionable, flash, flashy, glamorous, glitzy (Sl.), gorgeous, grand, lavish, luxuri~ ous, ostentatious, plush (Inf.), plushy (Inf.), posh (Inf., chiefly Brit.), rich, ritzy (Sl.), showy, smart, stylish, sumptuous, swank (Inf.), swish (Inf., chiefly Brit.)
Antonyms discreet, humble, inconspicuous, low-key, low-profile, modest, subdued, unas~ suming, unostentatious, unpretentious

swap, swop v. bandy, barter, exchange, interchange, switch, trade, traffic

swarm n. **1.** army, bevy, concourse, crowd, drove, flock, herd, horde, host, mass, multi~ tude, myriad, shoal, throng ~v. **2.** congre~ gate, crowd, flock, mass, stream, throng **3.** With with abound, be alive (infested, over~ run), bristle, crawl, teem

swarthy black, brown, dark, dark- complexioned, dark-skinned, dusky, swart (Archaic), tawny

swashbuckling bold, daredevil, dashing, flamboyant, gallant, mettlesome, roisterous, spirited, swaggering

swastika fylfot

swathe bandage, bind, bundle up, cloak, drape, envelop, enwrap, fold, furl, lap, muffle up, sheathe, shroud, swaddle, wrap

sway v. **1.** bend, fluctuate, incline, lean, lurch, oscillate, rock, roll, swing, wave **2.** affect, control, direct, dominate, govern, guide, induce, influence, persuade, prevail on, win over ~n. **3.** ascendency, authority, clout (Inf.), command, control, dominion, government, influence, jurisdiction, power, predominance, rule, sovereignty **4.** hold sway predominate, prevail, reign, rule, run

swear **1.** affirm, assert, asseverate, attest, avow, declare, depose, give one's word, pledge oneself, promise, state under oath, take an oath, testify, vow, warrant **2.** be foul-mouthed, blaspheme, curse, cuss (Inf.), imprecate, take the Lord's name in vain, turn the air blue (Inf.), utter profanities **3.** With by depend on, have confidence in, rely on, trust

swearing bad language, blasphemy, curs~ ing, cussing (Inf.), foul language, impreca~ tions, malediction, profanity

sweat n. **1.** diaphoresis (Medical), exuda~ tion, perspiration, sudor (Medical) **2.** Inf. agitation, anxiety, distress, flap (Inf.), panic, strain, worry **3.** Inf. backbreaking task, chore, drudgery, effort, labour, toil ~v. **4.** break out in a sweat, exude moisture, glow, perspire **5.** Inf. agonize, be on pins and needles (Inf.), be on tenterhooks, chafe, fret, lose sleep over, suffer, torture oneself, wor~ ry **6. sweat it out** Inf. endure, see (some~ thing) through, stay the course, stick it out (Inf.)

sweaty clammy, drenched (bathed, soaked) in perspiration, glowing, perspiring, sticky, sweating

sweep v. **1.** brush, clean, clear, remove **2.** career, flounce, fly, glance, glide, hurtle, pass, sail, scud, skim, tear, zoom ~n. **3.** arc, bend, curve, gesture, move, movement, stroke, swing **4.** compass, extent, range, scope, span, stretch, vista **5.** draw, lottery, raffle, sweepstake

sweeping **1.** all-embracing, all-inclusive, bird's-eye, broad, comprehensive, extensive, global, radical, thoroughgoing, wide, wide- ranging **2.** across-the-board, blanket, exag~ gerated, indiscriminate, overdrawn, over~ stated, unqualified, wholesale
Antonyms constrained, limited, minor, modest, narrow, qualified, restricted, token, trifling, unimportant

sweet adj. **1.** cloying, honeyed, luscious, melting, saccharine, sugary, sweetened, syrupy, toothsome, treacly **2.** affectionate, agreeable, amiable, appealing, attractive, beautiful, charming, cute, delightful, engag~ ing, fair, gentle, kind, likable or likeable, lovable, sweet-tempered, taking, tender, unselfish, winning, winsome **3.** beloved, cherished, darling, dear, dearest, pet, pre~ cious, treasured **4.** aromatic, balmy, clean, fragrant, fresh, new, perfumed, pure, redo~ lent, sweet-smelling, wholesome **5.** dulcet,

euphonic, euphonious, harmonious, mellow, melodious, musical, silver-toned, silvery, soft, sweet-sounding, tuneful **6. sweet on** enamoured of, gone on (*Sl.*), head over heels in love with, infatuated by, in love with, keen on, obsessed *or* bewitched by, taken with, wild *or* mad about (*Inf.*) ~*n.* **7.** afters (*Brit. inf.*), dessert, pudding, sweet course **8.** *Usually plural* bonbon, candy (*U.S.*), confectionery, sweetie, sweetmeats
Antonyms *adj.* (*sense 1*) acerbic, acetic, acid, bitter, savoury, sharp, sour, tart, vinegary (*senses 2, 3 & 4*) bad-tempered, disagreeable, fetid, foul, grouchy (*Inf.*), grumpy, hated, ill-tempered, loathsome, nasty, noisome, objectionable, obnoxious, rank, stinking, unappealing, unattractive, unlovable, unpleasant, unwanted (*sense 5*) cacophonous, discordant, grating, harsh, shrill, strident, unharmonious, unmusical, unpleasant

sweeten 1. honey, sugar, sugar-coat **2.** alleviate, appease, mollify, pacify, soften up, soothe, sugar the pill

sweetheart admirer, beau, beloved, boyfriend, darling, dear, flame (*Inf.*), follower (*Obsolete*), girlfriend, inamorata, inamorato, leman (*Archaic*), love, lover, steady (*Inf.*), suitor, swain (*Archaic*), sweetie (*Inf.*), true-love, valentine

sweet-scented ambrosial, aromatic, fragrant, perfumed, sweet-smelling
Antonyms fetid, foul-smelling, malodorous, niffy (*Brit. sl.*), noisome, olid, pongy (*Brit. inf.*), smelly, stinking, stinky (*Inf.*), whiffy (*Brit. sl.*)

swell *v.* **1.** balloon, become bloated *or* distended, become larger, be inflated, belly, billow, bloat, bulge, dilate, distend, enlarge, expand, extend, fatten, grow, increase, protrude, puff up, rise, round out, tumefy, well up **2.** add to, aggravate, augment, enhance, heighten, intensify, mount, surge ~*n.* **3.** billow, rise, surge, undulation, wave **4.** *Inf.* beau, blade (*Archaic*), cockscomb (*Inf.*), dandy, fashion plate, fop, nob (*Sl.*), toff (*Brit. sl.*) ~*adj.* **5.** *Inf.* de luxe, exclusive, fashionable, grand, plush *or* plushy (*Inf.*), posh (*Inf., chiefly Brit.*), ritzy (*Sl.*), smart, stylish
Antonyms *v.* become smaller, contract, decrease, deflate, diminish, ebb, fall, go down, lessen, reduce, shrink, wane ~*adj.* common, grotty (*Sl.*), ordinary, plebeian, poor, run down, seedy, shabby, sordid, tatty, unimpressive, vulgar

swelling *n.* blister, bruise, bulge, bump, dilation, distension, enlargement, inflammation, lump, protuberance, puffiness, tumescence

sweltering airless, baking, boiling, burn-

ing, hot, humid, oppressive, roasting, scorching, steaming, stifling, sultry, torrid

swerve *v.* bend, deflect, depart from, deviate, diverge, incline, sheer off, shift, skew, stray, swing, turn, turn aside, veer, wander, wind

swift abrupt, expeditious, express, fast, fleet, fleet-footed, flying, hurried, nimble, nippy (*Brit. inf.*), pdq (*Sl.*), prompt, quick, quickie (*Inf.*), rapid, ready, short, short-lived, spanking, speedy, sudden, winged
Antonyms lead-footed, lingering, plodding, ponderous, slow, sluggish, tardy, tortoise-like, unhurried

swiftly apace, as fast as one's legs can carry one, (at) full tilt, double-quick, fast, hotfoot, hurriedly, in less than no time, nippily (*Brit. inf.*), posthaste, promptly, pronto (*Inf.*), rapidly, speedily, without losing time

swiftness alacrity, celerity, dispatch, expedition, fleetness, promptness, quickness, rapidity, speed, speediness, velocity

swill *v.* **1.** bend the elbow (*Inf.*), bevvy (*Dialect*), consume, drain, drink (down), gulp, guzzle, imbibe, pour down one's gullet, quaff, swallow, swig (*Inf.*), toss off **2.** *Often with* **out** drench, flush, rinse, sluice, wash down, wash out ~*n.* **3.** hogwash, mash, mush, pigswill, scourings, slops, waste

swimmingly as planned, cosily, effortlessly, like a dream, like clockwork, smoothly, successfully, very well, with no trouble, without a hitch

swindle 1. *v.* bamboozle (*Inf.*), bilk (of), cheat, con, cozen, deceive, defraud, diddle (*Inf.*), do (*Sl.*), dupe, fleece, hornswoggle (*Sl.*), overcharge, pull a fast one (on someone) (*Inf.*), put one over on (someone) (*Inf.*), rip (someone) off (*Sl.*), rook (*Sl.*), skin (*Sl.*), stiff (*Sl.*), sting (*Inf.*), take (someone) for a ride (*Inf.*), take to the cleaners (*Inf.*), trick **2.** *n.* con trick (*Inf.*), deceit, deception, double-dealing, fiddle (*Brit. inf.*), fraud, imposition, knavery, racket, rip-off (*Sl.*), roguery, scam (*Sl.*), sharp practice, sting (*Inf.*), swizz (*Brit. inf.*), swizzle (*Brit. inf.*), trickery

swindler charlatan, cheat, chiseller (*Inf.*), confidence man, con man (*Inf.*), fraud, impostor, knave (*Archaic*), mountebank, rascal, rogue, rook (*Sl.*), shark, sharper, trickster

swing *v.* **1.** be pendent, be suspended, dangle, hang, move back and forth, suspend **2.** fluctuate, oscillate, rock, sway, vary, veer, vibrate, wave **3.** *Usually with* **round** curve, pivot, rotate, swivel, turn, turn on one's heel, wheel ~*n.* **4.** fluctuation, oscillation, stroke, sway, swaying, vibration **5. in full swing** animated, at its height, lively, on the go (*Inf.*), under way

swinging dynamic, fashionable, full of go or pep (*Inf.*), groovy (*Dated sl.*), happening (*Inf.*), hip (*Sl.*), in the swim (*Inf.*), lively, trendy (*Brit. inf.*), up-to-date, up to the minute, with it (*Inf.*)

swirl *v.* agitate, boil, churn, eddy, spin, surge, twirl, twist, whirl

switch *v.* **1.** change, change course, deflect, deviate, divert, exchange, interchange, rearrange, replace by, shift, substitute, swap (*Inf.*), trade, turn aside ~*n.* **2.** about-turn, alteration, change, change of direction, exchange, reversal, shift, substitution, swap (*Inf.*) ~*v.* **3.** lash, swish, twitch, wave, whip

swollen bloated, distended, dropsical, edematous, enlarged, inflamed, oedematous, puffed up, puffy, tumescent, tumid

swoop **1.** *v.* descend, dive, pounce, rush, stoop, sweep **2.** *n.* descent, drop, lunge, plunge, pounce, rush, stoop, sweep

sword **1.** blade, brand (*Archaic*), trusty steel **2. cross swords** argue, come to blows, dispute, fight, spar, wrangle **3. the sword** aggression, arms, butchery, death, massacre, military might, murder, slaying, violence, war

sycophantic all over (someone) (*Inf.*), arse-licking (*Taboo sl.*), bootlicking (*Inf.*), cringing, fawning, flattering, grovelling, ingratiating, obsequious, parasitical, servile, slavish, slimy, smarmy (*Brit. inf.*), time-serving, toadying, unctuous

syllabus course of study, curriculum

symbol badge, emblem, figure, image, logo, mark, representation, sign, token, type

symbolic, symbolical allegorical, emblematic, figurative, representative, significant, token, typical

symbolize betoken, body forth, connote, denote, exemplify, mean, personify, represent, signify, stand for, typify

symmetrical balanced, in proportion, proportional, regular, well-proportioned
Antonyms asymmetrical, disorderly, irregular, lopsided, unbalanced, unequal, unsymmetrical

symmetry agreement, balance, correspondence, evenness, form, harmony, order, proportion, regularity

sympathetic **1.** affectionate, caring, commiserating, compassionate, concerned, condoling, feeling, interested, kind, kindly, pitying, responsive, supportive, tender, understanding, warm, warm-hearted **2.** *Often with* **to** agreeable, approving, encouraging, favourably disposed, friendly, in sympathy with, pro, well-disposed **3.** agreeable, appreciative, companionable, compatible, congenial, friendly, like-minded, responsive, well-intentioned

Antonyms apathetic, callous, cold, cold-hearted, disdainful, disinterested, indifferent, inhumane, insensitive, scornful, steely, uncaring, uncompassionate, uncongenial, unfeeling, uninterested, unmoved, unresponsive, unsympathetic

sympathetically appreciatively, feelingly, kindly, perceptively, responsively, sensitively, understandingly, warm-heartedly, warmly, with compassion, with feeling, with interest

sympathize **1.** bleed for, commiserate, condole, empathize, feel for, feel one's heart go out to, grieve with, have compassion, offer consolation, pity, share another's sorrow **2.** agree, be in accord, be in sympathy, go along with, identify with, side with, understand
Antonyms disagree, disregard, fail to understand, have no feelings for, misunderstand, mock, oppose, reject, scorn

sympathizer condoler, fellow traveller, partisan, protagonist, supporter, well-wisher

sympathy **1.** commiseration, compassion, condolence(s), empathy, pity, tenderness, thoughtfulness, understanding **2.** affinity, agreement, congeniality, correspondence, fellow feeling, harmony, rapport, union, warmth
Antonyms (*sense 1*) callousness, coldness, disdain, hard-heartedness, indifference, insensitivity, lack of feeling *or* understanding *or* sympathy, pitilessness, scorn (*sense 2*) antagonism, disapproval, hostility, opposition, resistance, unfriendliness

symptom expression, indication, mark, note, sign, syndrome, token, warning

symptomatic characteristic, indicative, suggestive

synthesis **1.** amalgamation, coalescence, combination, integration, unification, welding **2.** amalgam, blend, combination, composite, compound, fusion, meld, union

synthetic artificial, ersatz, fake, man-made, manufactured, mock, pseudo (*Inf.*), sham, simulated
Antonyms authentic, genuine, kosher (*Inf.*), natural, real

system **1.** arrangement, classification, combination, coordination, organization, scheme, setup (*Inf.*), structure **2.** fixed order, frame of reference, method, methodology, modus operandi, practice, procedure, routine, technique, theory, usage **3.** definite plan, logical process, method, methodicalness, orderliness, regularity, systematization

systematic businesslike, efficient, methodical, orderly, organized, precise, standardized, systematized, well-ordered

Antonyms arbitrary, cursory, disorderly, disorganized, haphazard, indiscriminate, random, slapdash, unbusinesslike, unme~ thodical, unpremeditated, unsystematic

systematize arrange, classify, dispose, make uniform, methodize, organize, put in order, rationalize, regulate, schematize, standardize, tabulate

T

table *n.* **1.** bench, board, counter, slab, stand **2.** board, diet, fare, food, spread (*Inf.*), vict~uals **3.** flat, flatland, mesa, plain, plateau, tableland **4.** agenda, catalogue, chart, dia~gram, digest, graph, index, inventory, list, plan, record, register, roll, schedule, synop~sis, tabulation ~*v.* **5.** enter, move, propose, put forward, submit, suggest

tableau picture, representation, scene, spectacle

taboo 1. *adj.* anathema, banned, beyond the pale, disapproved of, forbidden, frowned on, not allowed, not permitted, outlawed, pro~hibited, proscribed, ruled out, unacceptable, unmentionable, unthinkable **2.** *n.* anath~ema, ban, disapproval, interdict, prohibi~tion, proscription, restriction
Antonyms *adj.* acceptable, allowed, permit~ted, sanctioned

tabulate arrange, catalogue, categorize, chart, classify, codify, index, list, order, range, systematize, tabularize

tacit implicit, implied, inferred, silent, taken for granted, undeclared, understood, unex~pressed, unspoken, unstated, wordless
Antonyms explicit, express, spelled-out, spoken, stated

taciturn aloof, antisocial, close-lipped, cold, distant, dumb, mute, quiet, reserved, reti~cent, silent, tight-lipped, uncommunicative, unforthcoming, withdrawn
Antonyms blethering, chatty, communica~tive, forthcoming, garrulous, loquacious, open, outgoing, prattling, sociable, talkative, unreserved, verbose, voluble, wordy

tack *n.* **1.** drawing pin, nail, pin, staple, thumbtack (*U.S.*), tintack **2.** approach, bearing, course, direction, heading, line, method, path, plan, procedure, tactic, way ~*v.* **3.** affix, attach, fasten, fix, nail, pin, staple **4.** baste, stitch **5.** add, annex, ap~pend, attach, tag

tackle *n.* **1.** accoutrements, apparatus, equipment, gear, implements, outfit, para~phernalia, rig, rigging, tools, trappings **2.** block, challenge, stop ~*v.* **3.** apply oneself to, attempt, begin, come *or* get to grips with, deal with, embark upon, engage in, essay, get stuck into (*Inf.*), have a go at (*Inf.*), have a stab at (*Inf.*), set about, take on, try, turn one's hand to, undertake, wade into **4.** block, bring down, challenge, clutch, confront, grab, grasp, halt, intercept, seize, stop, take hold of, throw

tact address, adroitness, consideration, deli~cacy, diplomacy, discretion, finesse, judg~ment, perception, savoir-faire, sensitivity, skill, thoughtfulness, understanding
Antonyms awkwardness, clumsiness, gau~cherie, heavy-handedness, indiscretion, in~sensitivity, lack of consideration, lack of dis~cretion, tactlessness

tactful careful, considerate, delicate, diplo~matic, discreet, judicious, perceptive, pol~ished, polite, politic, prudent, sensitive, subtle, thoughtful, understanding
Antonyms awkward, clumsy, gauche, in~considerate, indiscreet, insensitive, tactless, tasteless, thoughtless, undiplomatic, unsub~tle, untoward

tactic 1. approach, course, device, line, ma~noeuvre, means, method, move, ploy, policy, scheme, stratagem, tack, trick, way **2.** *Plu~ral* campaign, generalship, manoeuvres, plans, strategy

tactical adroit, artful, clever, cunning, dip~lomatic, foxy, politic, shrewd, skilful, smart, strategic
Antonyms blundering, clumsy, gauche, im~politic, inept

tactician brain (*Inf.*), campaigner, coor~dinator, director, general, mastermind, planner, strategist

tactless blundering, boorish, careless, clumsy, discourteous, gauche, harsh, impo~lite, impolitic, imprudent, inconsiderate, indelicate, indiscreet, inept, injudicious, in~sensitive, maladroit, rough, rude, sharp, thoughtless, uncivil, undiplomatic, unfeel~ing, unkind, unsubtle
Antonyms considerate, diplomatic, discreet, polite, subtle, tactful

tail *n.* **1.** appendage, conclusion, empennage, end, extremity, rear end, tailpiece, train **2.** file, line, queue, tailback, train **3.** *Of hair* braid, pigtail, plait, ponytail, tress **4.** *Inf.* arse (*Taboo sl.*), ass (*U.S. & Canad. taboo sl.*), backside (*Inf.*), behind (*Inf.*), bottom, bum (*Brit. sl.*), buns (*U.S. sl.*), butt (*U.S. & Canad. inf.*), buttocks, croup, derrière (*Euphemistic*), jacksy (*Brit. sl.*), posterior, rear (*Inf.*), rear end, rump **5. turn tail** cut and run, escape, flee, hook it (*Sl.*), make off, retreat, run away, run for it (*Inf.*), run off, scarper (*Brit. sl.*), show a clean pair of heels, skedaddle (*Inf.*), take off (*Inf.*), take to one's heels ~*v.* **6.** *Inf.* dog the footsteps of, follow, keep an eye on, shadow, stalk, track, trail

tail off *or* **away** decrease, die out, drop, dwindle, fade, fall away, peter out, wane
Antonyms grow, increase, intensify, wax

tailor 1. *n.* clothier, costumier, couturier, dressmaker, garment maker, outfitter, seamstress **2.** *v.* accommodate, adapt, adjust, alter, convert, cut, fashion, fit, modify, mould, shape, style, suit

taint *v.* **1.** adulterate, blight, contaminate, corrupt, dirty, foul, infect, poison, pollute, soil, spoil **2.** besmirch, blacken, blemish, blot, brand, damage, defile, disgrace, dishonour, muddy, ruin, shame, smear, smirch, stain, stigmatize, sully, tarnish, vitiate ~*n.* **3.** black mark, blemish, blot, blot on one's escutcheon, defect, demerit, disgrace, dishonour, fault, flaw, shame, smear, smirch, spot, stain, stigma **4.** contagion, contamination, infection, pollution
Antonyms *v.* clean, cleanse, decontaminate, disinfect, purify

take *v.* **1.** abduct, acquire, arrest, capture, carry off, catch, clutch, ensnare, entrap, gain possession of, get, get hold of, grasp, grip, have, help oneself to, lay hold of, obtain, receive, secure, seize, win **2.** abstract, appropriate, blag (*Sl.*), cabbage (*Brit. sl.*), carry off, filch, misappropriate, nick (*Sl., chiefly Brit.*), pinch (*Inf.*), pocket, purloin, run off with, steal, swipe (*Sl.*), walk off with **3.** book, buy, engage, hire, lease, pay for, pick, purchase, rent, reserve, select **4.** abide, bear, brave, brook, endure, go through, pocket, put up with (*Inf.*), stand, stomach, submit to, suffer, swallow, thole (*Scot.*), tolerate, undergo, weather, withstand **5.** consume, drink, eat, imbibe, ingest, inhale, swallow **6.** accept, adopt, assume, enter upon, undertake **7.** do, effect, execute, have, make, perform **8.** assume, believe, consider, deem, hold, interpret as, perceive, presume, receive, regard, see as, think of as, understand **9.** be efficacious, do the trick (*Inf.*), have effect, operate, succeed, work **10.** bear, bring, carry, cart, convey, ferry, fetch, haul, tote (*Inf.*), transport **11.** accompany, bring, conduct, convoy, escort, guide, lead, usher **12.** attract, become popular, captivate, charm, delight, enchant, fascinate, please, win favour **13.** call for, demand, necessitate, need, require **14.** deduct, eliminate, remove, subtract **15.** accept, accommodate, contain, have room for, hold **16.** *Sl.* bilk, cheat, con (*Inf.*), deceive, defraud, do (*Sl.*), dupe, fiddle (*Inf.*), gull (*Archaic*), pull a fast one on (*Inf.*), stiff (*Sl.*), swindle ~*n.* **17.** catch, gate, haul, proceeds, profits, receipts, return, revenue, takings, yield
Antonyms add, avoid, decline, dismiss, dodge, eschew, fail, flop (*Inf.*), free, give, give back, give in, give way, hand over, ignore, let go, put, refuse, reject, release, restore, return, scorn, send, spurn, surrender, yield

take back 1. disavow, disclaim, recant, renege, renounce, retract, unsay, withdraw **2.** get back, recapture, reclaim, reconquer, regain, repossess, retake **3.** accept back, exchange, give one a refund for

take down 1. make a note of, minute, note, put on record, record, set down, transcribe, write down **2.** depress, drop, haul down, let down, lower, pull down, remove, take off **3.** demolish, disassemble, dismantle, level, raze, take apart, take to pieces, tear down **4.** deflate, humble, humiliate, mortify, put down (*Sl.*)

take in 1. absorb, assimilate, comprehend, digest, grasp, understand **2.** comprise, contain, cover, embrace, encompass, include **3.** accommodate, admit, let in, receive **4.** *Inf.* bilk, cheat, con (*Inf.*), cozen, deceive, do (*Sl.*), dupe, fool, gull (*Archaic*), hoodwink, mislead, pull the wool over (someone's) eyes (*Inf.*), stiff (*Sl.*), swindle, trick

takeoff 1. departure, launch, liftoff **2.** *Inf.* caricature, imitation, lampoon, mocking, parody, satire, send-up (*Brit. inf.*), spoof (*Inf.*), travesty

take off 1. discard, divest oneself of, doff, drop, peel off, remove, strip off **2.** become airborne, leave the ground, lift off, take to the air **3.** *Inf.* abscond, beat it (*Sl.*), decamp, depart, disappear, go, hit the road (*Sl.*), hook it (*Sl.*), leave, set out, slope off, split (*Sl.*), strike out **4.** *Inf.* caricature, hit off, imitate, lampoon, mimic, mock, parody, satirize, send up (*Brit. inf.*), spoof (*Inf.*), take the piss (out of) (*Taboo sl.*), travesty

take on 1. employ, engage, enlist, enrol, hire, retain **2.** acquire, assume, come to have **3.** accept, address oneself to, agree to do, have a go at (*Inf.*), tackle, undertake **4.** compete against, contend with, enter the lists against, face, fight, match oneself against, oppose, pit oneself against, vie with **5.** *Inf.* break down, get excited, get upset, give way, make a fuss

takeover change of leadership, coup, incorporation, merger

take to 1. flee to, head for, make for, man, run for **2.** become friendly, be pleased by, be taken with, conceive an affection for, get on with, like, warm to **3.** have recourse to, make a habit of, resort to

take up 1. adopt, assume, become involved in, engage in, start **2.** begin again, carry on, continue, follow on, go on, pick up, proceed, recommence, restart, resume **3.** absorb, consume, cover, extend over, fill, occupy, use up

taking *adj.* **1.** attractive, beguiling, captivating, charming, compelling, delightful,

enchanting, engaging, fascinating, fetching (*Inf.*), intriguing, likable *or* likeable, pleas~ ing, prepossessing, winning **2.** *Inf.* catch~ ing, contagious, infectious ~*n.* **3.** *Plural* earnings, gain, gate, income, pickings, pro~ ceeds, profits, receipts, returns, revenue, take, yield
Antonyms (*sense 1*) abhorrent, loathsome, offensive, repulsive, unattractive, unpleasant

tale 1. account, anecdote, *conte,* fable, fiction, legend, narration, narrative, novel, relation, report, romance, saga, short story, spiel (*Inf.*), story, urban legend, yarn (*Inf.*) **2.** cock-and-bull story (*Inf.*), fabrication, falsehood, fib, lie, rigmarole, rumour, spiel (*Inf.*), tall story (*Inf.*), untruth

talent ability, aptitude, bent, capacity, en~ dowment, faculty, flair, forte, genius, gift, knack, parts, power

talented able, artistic, brilliant, gifted, well-endowed

talk *v.* **1.** articulate, chat, chatter, communi~ cate, converse, crack (*Scot.*), express one~ self, gab (*Inf.*), give voice to, gossip, natter, prate, prattle, rap (*Sl.*), say, speak, spout, utter, verbalize, witter (*Inf.*) **2.** chew the rag *or* fat (*Sl.*), confabulate, confer, have a confab (*Inf.*), hold discussions, negotiate, palaver, parley **3.** blab, crack, give the game away, grass (*Brit. sl.*), inform, reveal information, shop (*Sl., chiefly Brit.*), sing (*Sl., chiefly U.S.*), spill one's guts (*Sl.*), spill the beans (*Inf.*), squeak (*Inf.*), squeal (*Sl.*), tell all ~*n.* **4.** address, discourse, disquisi~ tion, dissertation, harangue, lecture, ora~ tion, sermon, speech **5.** blather, blether, chat, chatter, chitchat, conversation, crack (*Scot.*), gab (*Inf.*), gossip, hearsay, jaw (*Sl.*), natter, rap (*Sl.*), rumour, tittle-tattle **6.** col~ loquy, conclave, confab (*Inf.*), confabulation, conference, congress, consultation, dialogue, discussion, meeting, negotiation, palaver, parley, seminar, symposium **7.** argot, dia~ lect, jargon, language, lingo (*Inf.*), patois, slang, speech, words

talkative big-mouthed (*Sl.*), chatty, effusive, gabby (*Inf.*), garrulous, gossipy, long-winded, loquacious, mouthy, prolix, ver~ bose, voluble, wordy
Antonyms quiet, reserved, reticent, silent, taciturn, tight-lipped, uncommunicative, un~ forthcoming

talker chatterbox, conversationalist, lectur~ er, orator, speaker, speechmaker

talking-to criticism, dressing-down (*Inf.*), lecture, rap on the knuckles, rebuke, repri~ mand, reproach, reproof, row, scolding, slating (*Inf.*), telling-off (*Inf.*), ticking-off (*Inf.*), wigging (*Brit. sl.*)
Antonyms acclaim, approbation, commen~ dation, encouragement, praise

tall 1. big, elevated, giant, high, lanky, lofty, soaring, towering **2.** *Inf.* absurd, embel~ lished, exaggerated, far-fetched, implausible, incredible, overblown, preposterous, steep (*Brit. inf.*), unbelievable **3.** *Inf.* demanding, difficult, exorbitant, hard, unreasonable, well-nigh impossible
Antonyms (*sense 1*) fubsy (*Archaic or dia~ lect*), short, small, squat, stumpy, tiny, wee (*sense 2*) accurate, believable, easy, plausible, realistic, reasonable, true, unexaggerated

tally *v.* **1.** accord, agree, coincide, concur, conform, correspond, fit, harmonize, jibe (*Inf.*), match, parallel, square, suit **2.** com~ pute, count up, keep score, mark, reckon, record, register, total ~*n.* **3.** count, mark, reckoning, record, running total, score, to~ tal **4.** counterfoil, counterpart, duplicate, match, mate, stub
Antonyms (*sense 1*) clash, conflict, contra~ dict, differ, disagree

tame *adj.* **1.** amenable, broken, cultivated, disciplined, docile, domesticated, gentle, obedient, tractable **2.** fearless, unafraid, used to human contact **3.** compliant, docile, manageable, meek, obedient, spiritless, subdued, submissive, unresisting **4.** bland, boring, dull, flat, humdrum, insipid, lifeless, prosaic, tedious, unexciting, uninspiring, uninteresting, vapid, wearisome ~*v.* **5.** break in, domesticate, gentle, house-train, make tame, pacify, train **6.** break the spirit of, bridle, bring to heel, conquer, curb, dis~ cipline, enslave, humble, master, repress, subdue, subjugate, suppress **7.** mitigate, mute, soften, soft-pedal (*Inf.*), subdue, tem~ per, tone down, water down
Antonyms *adj.* aggressive, argumentative, exciting, feral, ferocious, frenzied, hot, inter~ esting, lively, obdurate, savage, stimulating, strong-willed, stubborn, undomesticated, un~ manageable, untamed, wild ~*v.* arouse, incite, intensify, make fiercer

tamper 1. alter, damage, fiddle (*Inf.*), fool about (*Inf.*), interfere, intrude, meddle, mess about, monkey around, muck about (*Brit. sl.*), poke one's nose into (*Inf.*), tinker **2.** bribe, corrupt, fix (*Inf.*), get at, influence, manipulate, rig

tangible actual, concrete, corporeal, definite, discernible, evident, manifest, ma~ terial, objective, palpable, perceptible, physical, positive, real, solid, substantial, tactile, touchable
Antonyms abstract, disembodied, ethereal, immaterial, impalpable, imperceptible, in~ discernible, insubstantial, intangible, theo~ retical, unreal

tangle *n.* **1.** coil, confusion, entanglement, jam, jungle, knot, mass, mat, mesh, ravel, snarl, twist, web **2.** complication, entangle~ ment, fix (*Inf.*), imbroglio, labyrinth, maze,

mess, mix-up ~v. **3.** coil, confuse, entangle, interlace, interlock, intertwist, interweave, jam, kink, knot, mat, mesh, ravel, snarl, twist **4.** *Often with* **with** come into conflict, come up against, contend, contest, cross swords, dispute, lock horns **5.** catch, drag into, embroil, enmesh, ensnare, entangle, entrap, implicate, involve
Antonyms (*sense 3*) disentangle, extricate, free, straighten out, unravel, untangle

tangled 1. entangled, jumbled, knotted, knotty, matted, messy, scrambled, snarled, tousled, twisted **2.** complex, complicated, confused, convoluted, involved, knotty, messy, mixed-up

tantalize baffle, balk, disappoint, entice, frustrate, keep (someone) hanging on, lead on, make (someone's) mouth water, pro~ voke, taunt, tease, thwart, titillate, torment, torture

tantamount as good as, commensurate, equal, equivalent, synonymous, the same as

tantrum bate (*Brit. sl.*), fit, flare-up, hyster~ ics, ill humour, outburst, paddy (*Brit. inf.*), paroxysm, storm, temper, wax (*Inf., chiefly Brit.*)

tap[1] 1. *v.* beat, drum, knock, pat, rap, strike, touch **2.** *n.* beat, knock, light blow, pat, rap, touch

tap[2] *n.* **1.** faucet (*U.S.*), spigot, spout, stop~ cock, valve **2.** bung, plug, spile, stopper **3.** bug (*Inf.*), listening device **4. on tap a.** *Inf.* at hand, available, in reserve, on hand, ready **b.** on draught ~v. **5.** bleed, broach, drain, draw off, open, pierce, siphon off, unplug **6.** draw on, exploit, make use of, milk, mine, put to use, turn to account, use, utilize **7.** bug (*Inf.*), eavesdrop on, listen in on

tape *n.* **1.** band, ribbon, strip ~v. **2.** bind, seal, secure, stick, wrap **3.** record, tape-record, video

taper 1. come to a point, narrow, thin **2.** *With* **off** decrease, die away, die out, dwin~ dle, fade, lessen, reduce, subside, thin out, wane, weaken, wind down
Antonyms (*sense 2*) grow, increase, intensi~ fy, step up, strengthen, swell, widen

target 1. aim, ambition, bull's-eye, end, goal, intention, mark, object, objective **2.** butt, quarry, scapegoat, victim

tariff 1. assessment, duty, excise, impost, levy, rate, tax, toll **2.** bill of fare, charges, menu, price list, schedule

tarnish 1. *v.* befoul, blacken, blemish, blot, darken, dim, discolour, drag through the mud, dull, lose lustre *or* shine, rust, smirch, soil, spot, stain, sully, taint **2.** *n.* blacken~ ing, black mark, blemish, blot, discolora~ tion, rust, smirch, spot, stain, taint

Antonyms *v.* brighten, enhance, gleam, pol~ ish up, shine

tarry abide, bide, dally, dawdle, delay, dwell, hang around (*Inf.*), linger, lodge, loiter, lose time, pause, remain, rest, sojourn, stay, take one's time, wait
Antonyms hasten, hurry, move on, rush, scoot, step on it (*Inf.*)

tart[1] 1. pastry, pie, tartlet **2.** call girl, fallen woman, *fille de joie*, floozy (*Sl.*), harlot, hooker (*U.S. sl.*), loose woman, prostitute, scrubber (*Brit. & Aust. sl.*), slag (*Brit. sl.*), slut, streetwalker, strumpet, trollop, whore, woman of easy virtue, working girl (*Fa~ cetious sl.*)

tart[2] 1. acerbic, acid, acidulous, astringent, bitter, piquant, pungent, sharp, sour, tangy, vinegary **2.** acrimonious, astringent, barbed, biting, caustic, crusty, cutting, harsh, mordacious, mordant, nasty, scath~ ing, sharp, short, snappish, testy, trenchant, vitriolic, wounding
Antonyms (*sense 1*) honeyed, sugary, sweet, syrupy, toothsome (*sense 2*) agreeable, de~ lightful, gentle, kind, pleasant

task *n.* **1.** assignment, business, charge, chore, duty, employment, enterprise, exer~ cise, job, labour, mission, occupation, toil, undertaking, work **2. take to task** bawl out (*Inf.*), blame, blast, carpet (*Inf.*), cen~ sure, chew out (*U.S. & Canad. inf.*), criti~ cize, give a rocket (*Brit. & N.Z. inf.*), lam~ bast(e), lecture, read the riot act, repri~ mand, reproach, reprove, scold, tear into (*Inf.*), tear (someone) off a strip (*Brit. inf.*), tell off (*Inf.*), upbraid ~v. **3.** assign to, charge, entrust **4.** burden, exhaust, load, lumber (*Brit. inf.*), oppress, overload, push, saddle, strain, tax, test, weary

taste *n.* **1.** flavour, relish, savour, smack, tang **2.** bit, bite, dash, drop, morsel, mouthful, nip, sample, sip, *soupçon*, spoon~ ful, swallow, titbit, touch **3.** appetite, bent, desire, fancy, fondness, inclination, leaning, liking, palate, partiality, penchant, predi~ lection, preference, relish **4.** appreciation, cultivation, culture, discernment, discrimi~ nation, elegance, grace, judgment, percep~ tion, polish, refinement, sophistication, style **5.** correctness, decorum, delicacy, discretion, nicety, politeness, propriety, re~ straint, tact, tactfulness ~v. **6.** differentiate, discern, distinguish, perceive **7.** assay, nib~ ble, relish, sample, savour, sip, test, try **8.** have a flavour of, savour of, smack **9.** come up against, encounter, experience, feel, have knowledge of, know, meet with, par~ take of, undergo
Antonyms *n.* bawdiness, blandness, blue~ ness, coarseness, crudeness, disinclination, dislike, distaste, hatred, impropriety, indeli~ cacy, insipidity, lack of discernment, lack of

judgment, loathing, mawkishness, obscenity, tackiness (*Inf.*), tactlessness, tastelessness, unsubtlety ~*v.* fail to achieve, fail to discern, miss, remain ignorant of

tasteful aesthetically pleasing, artistic, beautiful, charming, cultivated, cultured, delicate, discriminating, elegant, exquisite, fastidious, graceful, handsome, harmonious, in good taste, polished, refined, restrained, smart, stylish
Antonyms brash, flashy, garish, gaudy, inelegant, loud, objectionable, offensive, showy, sick, tacky (*Inf.*), tasteless, tawdry, twee, uncultured, unrefined, vulgar

tasteless 1. bland, boring, dull, flat, flavourless, insipid, mild, stale, tame, thin, uninspired, uninteresting, vapid, watereddown, weak **2.** cheap, coarse, crass, crude, flashy, garish, gaudy, graceless, gross, impolite, improper, indecorous, indelicate, indiscreet, inelegant, low, naff (*Brit. sl.*), rude, tacky (*Inf.*), tactless, tawdry, uncouth, unseemly, vulgar
Antonyms (*sense 1*) appetizing, delectable, delicious, flavoursome, savoury, scrumptious (*Inf.*), tasty (*sense 2*) elegant, graceful, refined, tasteful

tasty appetizing, delectable, delicious, flavourful, flavoursome, full-flavoured, good-tasting, luscious, palatable, sapid, savoury, scrumptious (*Inf.*), toothsome, yummy (*Sl.*)
Antonyms bland, flavourless, insipid, tasteless, unappetizing, unsavoury

taunt 1. *v.* deride, flout, gibe, guy (*Inf.*), insult, jeer, mock, provoke, reproach, revile, ridicule, sneer, take the piss (out of) (*Taboo sl.*), tease, torment, twit, upbraid **2.** *n.* barb, censure, cut, derision, dig, gibe, insult, jeer, provocation, reproach, ridicule, sarcasm, teasing

taut 1. flexed, rigid, strained, stressed, stretched, tense, tight **2.** *Nautical* in good order, neat, orderly, shipshape, spruce, tidy, tight, trim, well-ordered, well-regulated
Antonyms (*sense 1*) loose, relaxed, slack

tavern alehouse (*Archaic*), bar, boozer (*Brit., Aust., & N.Z. inf.*), hostelry, inn, pub (*Inf., chiefly Brit.*), public house, taproom, watering hole (*Facetious sl.*)

tawdry brummagem, cheap, cheap-jack (*Inf.*), flashy, gaudy, gimcrack, glittering, meretricious, naff (*Brit. sl.*), plastic (*Sl.*), raffish, showy, tacky (*Inf.*), tasteless, tatty, tinsel, tinselly, vulgar
Antonyms elegant, graceful, plain, refined, simple, stylish, tasteful, unflashy, unostentatious, well-tailored

tax *n.* **1.** assessment, charge, contribution, customs, duty, excise, imposition, impost, levy, rate, tariff, tithe, toll, tribute **2.** burden, demand, drain, load, pressure, strain, weight ~*v.* **3.** assess, charge, demand, exact, extract, impose, levy a tax on, rate, tithe **4.** burden, drain, enervate, exhaust, load, make heavy demands on, overburden, push, put pressure on, sap, strain, stretch, task, try, weaken, wear out, weary, weigh heavily on **5.** accuse, arraign, blame, charge, impeach, impugn, incriminate, lay at one's door
Antonyms (*sense 5*) acquit, clear, exculpate, exonerate, vindicate

taxing burdensome, demanding, enervating, exacting, heavy, onerous, punishing, sapping, stressful, tiring, tough, trying, wearing, wearisome
Antonyms easy, easy-peasy (*Sl.*), effortless, light, unburdensome, undemanding

teach advise, coach, demonstrate, direct, discipline, drill, edify, educate, enlighten, give lessons in, guide, impart, implant, inculcate, inform, instil, instruct, school, show, train, tutor

teacher coach, dominie (*Scot.*), don, educator, guide, guru, handler, instructor, lecturer, master, mentor, mistress, pedagogue, professor, schoolmaster, schoolmistress, schoolteacher, trainer, tutor

team *n.* **1.** band, body, bunch, company, crew, gang, group, line-up, posse (*Inf.*), set, side, squad, troupe **2.** pair, span, yoke ~*v.* **3.** *Often with* **up** band together, cooperate, couple, get together, join, link, unite, work together, yoke

tear *v.* **1.** claw, divide, lacerate, mangle, mutilate, pull apart, rend, rip, rive, run, rupture, scratch, sever, shred, split, sunder **2.** barrel (along) (*Inf., chiefly U.S. & Canad.*), belt (*Sl.*), bolt, burn rubber (*Inf.*), career, charge, dart, dash, fly, gallop, hurry, race, run, rush, shoot, speed, sprint, zoom **3.** grab, pluck, pull, rip, seize, snatch, wrench, wrest, yank ~*n.* **4.** hole, laceration, mutilation, rent, rip, run, rupture, scratch, split

tearful 1. blubbering, crying, in tears, lachrymose, sobbing, weeping, weepy (*Inf.*), whimpering **2.** distressing, dolorous, harrowing, lamentable, mournful, pathetic, pitiable, pitiful, poignant, sad, sorrowful, upsetting, woeful

tears 1. blubbering, crying, distress, lamentation, mourning, pain, regret, sadness, sobbing, sorrow, wailing, weeping, whimpering, woe **2. in tears** blubbering, crying, distressed, sobbing, visibly moved, weeping, whimpering

tease aggravate (*Inf.*), annoy, badger, bait, bedevil, bother, chaff, gibe, goad, guy (*Inf.*), lead on, mock, needle (*Inf.*), pester, plague (*Inf.*), provoke, rag, rib (*Inf.*), ridicule, take the piss (out of) (*Taboo sl.*), tantalize, taunt, torment, twit, vex, wind up (*Brit. sl.*), worry

technique 1. approach, course, fashion, manner, means, method, mode, modus operandi, procedure, style, system, way **2.** address, adroitness, art, artistry, craft, craftsmanship, delivery, execution, facility, knack, know-how (*Inf.*), performance, proficiency, skill, touch

tedious annoying, banal, boring, deadly dull, drab, dreary, dreich (*Scot.*), dull, fatiguing, ho-hum (*Inf.*), humdrum, irksome, laborious, lifeless, long-drawn-out, mind-numbing, monotonous, prosaic, prosy, soporific, tiring, unexciting, uninteresting, vapid, wearisome
Antonyms enjoyable, enthralling, exciting, exhilarating, imaginative, inspiring, interesting, quickly finished, short, stimulating

tedium banality, boredom, deadness, drabness, dreariness, dullness, ennui, lifelessness, monotony, routine, sameness, tediousness, the doldrums
Antonyms challenge, excitement, exhilaration, fascination, interest, liveliness, stimulation

teem abound, be abundant, bear, be crawling with, be full of, be prolific, brim, bristle, burst at the seams, overflow, produce, pullulate, swarm

teeming abundant, alive, brimful, brimming, bristling, bursting, chock-a-block, chock-full, crawling, fruitful, full, numerous, overflowing, packed, replete, swarming, thick
Antonyms deficient, lacking, short, wanting

teenage adolescent, immature, juvenile, youthful

teenager adolescent, boy, girl, juvenile, minor, youth

teetotaller abstainer, nondrinker, Rechabite

telegram cable, radiogram, telegraph, telex, wire (*Inf.*)

telegraph *n.* **1.** tape machine (*Stock Exchange*), teleprinter, telex **2.** cable, radiogram, telegram, telex, wire (*Inf.*) ~*v.* **3.** cable, send, telex, transmit, wire (*Inf.*)

telepathy mind-reading, sixth sense, thought transference

telephone 1. *n.* blower (*Inf.*), handset, line, phone **2.** *v.* buzz (*Inf.*), call, call up, dial, get on the blower (*Inf.*), give (someone) a bell (*Brit. sl.*), give (someone) a buzz (*Inf.*), give (someone) a call, give (someone) a ring (*Inf., chiefly Brit.*), give someone a tinkle (*Brit. inf.*), phone, put a call through to, ring (*Inf., chiefly Brit.*)

telescope *n.* **1.** glass, spyglass ~*v.* **2.** concertina, crush, squash **3.** abbreviate,

abridge, capsulize, compress, condense, consolidate, contract, curtail, cut, shorten, shrink, tighten, trim, truncate
Antonyms (*sense 3*) amplify, draw out, elongate, extend, flesh out, lengthen, protract, spread out

television gogglebox (*Brit. sl.*), idiot box (*Sl.*), receiver, small screen (*Inf.*), telly (*Brit. inf.*), the box (*Brit. inf.*), the tube (*Sl.*), TV, TV set

tell *v.* **1.** acquaint, announce, apprise, communicate, confess, disclose, divulge, express, impart, inform, let know, make known, mention, notify, proclaim, reveal, say, speak, state, utter **2.** authorize, bid, call upon, command, direct, enjoin, instruct, order, require, summon **3.** chronicle, depict, describe, give an account of, narrate, portray, recount, rehearse, relate, report **4.** comprehend, discern, discover, make out, see, understand **5.** differentiate, discern, discriminate, distinguish, identify **6.** carry weight, count, have *or* take effect, have force, make its presence felt, register, take its toll, weigh **7.** calculate, compute, count, enumerate, number, reckon, tally

telling considerable, decisive, effective, effectual, forceful, forcible, impressive, influential, marked, potent, powerful, significant, solid, striking, trenchant, weighty
Antonyms easily ignored, inconsequential, indecisive, ineffectual, insignificant, lightweight, minor, negligible, slight, trivial, unimportant

temper *n.* **1.** attitude, character, constitution, disposition, frame of mind, humour, mind, mood, nature, temperament, tenor, vein **2.** bad mood, bate (*Brit. sl.*), fit of pique, fury, gall, paddy (*Brit. inf.*), passion, rage, tantrum, wax (*Inf., chiefly Brit.*) **3.** anger, annoyance, heat, hot-headedness, ill humour, irascibility, irritability, irritation, passion, peevishness, petulance, resentment, surliness **4.** calm, calmness, composure, cool (*Sl.*), coolness, equanimity, good humour, moderation, self-control, tranquillity ~*v.* **5.** abate, admix, allay, assuage, calm, lessen, mitigate, moderate, mollify, palliate, restrain, soften, soft-pedal (*Inf.*), soothe, tone down **6.** anneal, harden, strengthen, toughen
Antonyms *n.* (*sense 3*) contentment, goodwill, pleasant mood (*sense 4*) agitation, anger, bad mood, excitability, foul humour, fury, grumpiness, indignation, irascibility, irritation, pique, vexation, wrath ~*v.* (*sense 5*) aggravate, arouse, excite, heighten, intensify, provoke, stir (*sense 6*) soften

temperament 1. bent, cast of mind, character, complexion, constitution, disposition, frame of mind, humour, make-up, mettle, nature, outlook, personality, quality, soul, spirit, stamp, temper, tendencies, tendency **2.** anger, excitability, explosiveness, hot-headedness, impatience, mercurialness, moodiness, moods, petulance, volatility

temperamental 1. capricious, easily upset, emotional, erratic, excitable, explosive, fiery, highly strung, hot-headed, hypersensitive, impatient, irritable, mercurial, moody, neurotic, passionate, petulant, sensitive, touchy, volatile **2.** congenital, constitutional, inborn, ingrained, inherent, innate, natural **3.** erratic, inconsistent, inconstant, undependable, unpredictable, unreliable
Antonyms calm, constant, cool-headed, dependable, easy-going, even-tempered, level-headed, phlegmatic, reliable, stable, steady, unexcitable, unflappable, unperturbable

temperance 1. continence, discretion, forbearance, moderation, restraint, self-control, self-discipline, self-restraint **2.** abstemiousness, abstinence, prohibition, sobriety, teetotalism
Antonyms crapulence, excess, immoderation, intemperance, overindulgence, prodigality

temperate 1. agreeable, balmy, calm, clement, cool, fair, gentle, mild, moderate, pleasant, soft **2.** calm, composed, dispassionate, equable, even-tempered, mild, moderate, reasonable, self-controlled, self-restrained, sensible, stable **3.** abstemious, abstinent, continent, moderate, sober
Antonyms excessive, extreme, harsh, immoderate, inclement, inordinate, intemperate, prodigal, severe, torrid, uncontrolled, undisciplined, unreasonable, unrestrained, wild

tempest 1. cyclone, gale, hurricane, squall, storm, tornado, typhoon **2.** commotion, disturbance, ferment, furore, storm, tumult, upheaval, uproar
Antonyms (*sense 2*) calm, peace, quiet, serenity, stillness, tranquillity

tempestuous 1. agitated, blustery, boisterous, breezy, gusty, inclement, raging, squally, stormy, turbulent, windy **2.** agitated, boisterous, emotional, excited, feverish, flaming, furious, heated, hysterical, impassioned, intense, passionate, stormy, turbulent, uncontrolled, violent, wild
Antonyms (*sense 2*) calm, peaceful, quiet, serene, still, tranquil, undisturbed, unruffled

temple church, holy place, place of worship, sanctuary, shrine

temporarily briefly, fleetingly, for a little while, for a moment, for a short time, for a short while, for the moment, for the nonce, for the time being, momentarily, pro tem

temporary brief, ephemeral, evanescent, fleeting, fugacious, fugitive, here today and gone tomorrow, impermanent, interim, momentary, passing, pro tem, *pro tempore*, provisional, short-lived, transient, transitory
Antonyms durable, enduring, eternal, everlasting, long-lasting, long-term, permanent

tempt 1. allure, appeal to, attract, coax, decoy, draw, entice, inveigle, invite, lead on, lure, make one's mouth water, seduce, tantalize, whet the appetite of, woo **2.** bait, dare, fly in the face of, provoke, risk, test, try
Antonyms (*sense 1*) deter, discourage, dissuade, hinder, inhibit, put off

temptation allurement, appeal, attraction, attractiveness, bait, blandishments, coaxing, come-on (*Inf.*), decoy, draw, enticement, inducement, invitation, lure, pull, seduction, snare, tantalization

tempting alluring, appetizing, attractive, enticing, inviting, mouthwatering, seductive, tantalizing
Antonyms off-putting (*Brit. inf.*), unappetizing, unattractive, undesirable, uninviting, untempting

tenable arguable, believable, defendable, defensible, justifiable, maintainable, plausible, rational, reasonable, sound, viable
Antonyms indefensible, insupportable, unjustifiable, untenable

tenacious 1. clinging, fast, firm, forceful, immovable, iron, strong, tight, unshakable **2.** retentive, unforgetful **3.** adamant, determined, dogged, firm, immovable, inflexible, intransigent, obdurate, obstinate, persistent, pertinacious, resolute, staunch, steadfast, stiff-necked, strong-willed, stubborn, sure, unswerving, unyielding **4.** coherent, cohesive, solid, strong, tough **5.** adhesive, clinging, gluey, glutinous, mucilaginous, sticky
Antonyms (*sense 3*) changeable, flexible, irresolute, vacillating, wavering, yielding

tenacity 1. fastness, firmness, force, forcefulness, power, strength **2.** firm grasp, retention, retentiveness **3.** application, determination, diligence, doggedness, firmness, inflexibility, intransigence, obduracy, obstinacy, perseverance, persistence, pertinacity, resoluteness, resolution, resolve, staunchness, steadfastness, strength of purpose, strength of will, stubbornness **4.** coherence, cohesiveness, solidity, solidness, strength, toughness **5.** adhesiveness, clingingness, stickiness
Antonyms (*sense 1*) looseness, powerlessness, slackness, weakness

tenancy 1. holding, lease, occupancy, occupation, possession, renting, residence **2.** incumbency, period of office, tenure, time in office

tenant holder, inhabitant, leaseholder, les~ see, occupant, occupier, renter, resident

tend[1] **1.** be apt, be biased, be disposed, be inclined, be liable, be likely, gravitate, have a leaning, have an inclination, have a ten~ dency, incline, lean, trend **2.** aim, bear, be conducive, conduce, contribute, go, head, influence, lead, make for, move, point

tend[2] attend, care for, cater to, control, cul~ tivate, feed, guard, handle, keep, keep an eye on, look after, maintain, manage, min~ ister to, nurse, nurture, protect, see to, serve, take care of, wait on, watch, watch over
Antonyms disregard, ignore, neglect, over~ look, shirk

tendency 1. bent, disposition, inclination, leaning, liability, partiality, penchant, pre~ dilection, predisposition, proclivity, prone~ ness, propensity, readiness, susceptibility **2.** bearing, bias, course, direction, drift, drive, heading, movement, purport, tenor, trend, turning

tender[1] **1.** breakable, delicate, feeble, frag~ ile, frail, soft, weak **2.** callow, green, im~ mature, impressionable, inexperienced, new, raw, sensitive, unripe, vulnerable, wet behind the ears (*Inf.*), young, youthful **3.** affectionate, amorous, benevolent, caring, compassionate, considerate, fond, gentle, humane, kind, loving, merciful, pitiful, sentimental, softhearted, sympathetic, tenderhearted, warm, warm-hearted **4.** emotional, evocative, moving, poignant, ro~ mantic, touching **5.** complicated, danger~ ous, difficult, risky, sensitive, ticklish, touchy, tricky **6.** aching, acute, bruised, inflamed, irritated, painful, raw, sensitive, smarting, sore
Antonyms advanced, brutal, cold-hearted, cruel, elderly, experienced, grown-up, hard, hard-hearted, inhuman, insensitive, leathery, mature, pitiless, seasoned, sophisticated, strong, tough, uncaring, unkind, unsympa~ thetic, worldly, worldly-wise

tender[2] *v.* **1.** extend, give, hand in, offer, present, proffer, propose, put forward, sub~ mit, suggest, volunteer ~*n.* **2.** bid, estimate, offer, proffer, proposal, submission, sugges~ tion **3.** currency, medium, money, payment, specie

tenderness 1. delicateness, feebleness, fra~ gility, frailness, sensitiveness, sensitivity, softness, vulnerability, weakness **2.** callow~ ness, greenness, immaturity, impression~ ableness, inexperience, newness, rawness, sensitivity, vulnerability, youth, youthful~ ness **3.** affection, amorousness, attachment, benevolence, care, compassion, considera~ tion, devotion, fondness, gentleness, hu~ maneness, humanity, kindness, liking, love,

mercy, pity, sentimentality, softheartedness, sympathy, tenderheartedness, warm~ heartedness, warmth **4.** ache, aching, bruising, inflammation, irritation, pain, painfulness, rawness, sensitiveness, sensi~ tivity, smart, soreness
Antonyms (*sense 3*) cruelty, hardness, harshness, indifference, insensitivity, un~ kindness

tense *adj.* **1.** rigid, strained, stretched, taut, tight **2.** anxious, apprehensive, edgy, fidgety, jittery (*Inf.*), jumpy, keyed up, nervous, on edge, overwrought, restless, strained, strung up (*Inf.*), twitchy (*Inf.*), un~ der pressure, uptight (*Inf.*), wired (*Sl.*), wound up (*Inf.*), wrought up **3.** exciting, moving, nerve-racking, stressful, worrying ~*v.* **4.** brace, flex, strain, stretch, tauten, tighten
Antonyms *adj.* boring, calm, collected, cool-headed, dull, easy-going, flaccid, flexible, limp, loose, pliant, relaxed, self-possessed, se~ rene, unconcerned, uninteresting, unruffled, unworried ~*v.* loosen, relax, slacken

tension 1. pressure, rigidity, stiffness, straining, stress, stretching, tautness, tight~ ness **2.** anxiety, apprehension, edginess, hostility, ill feeling, nervousness, pressure, restlessness, strain, stress, suspense, the jitters (*Inf.*), unease
Antonyms (*sense 2*) calmness, peacefulness, relaxation, restfulness, serenity, tranquillity

tentative 1. conjectural, experimental, in~ definite, provisional, speculative, uncon~ firmed, unsettled **2.** backward, cautious, diffident, doubtful, faltering, hesitant, timid, uncertain, undecided, unsure
Antonyms (*sense 1*) conclusive, decisive, definite, final, fixed, resolved, settled (*sense 2*) assured, bold, certain, confident, unhesitating

tenuous 1. doubtful, dubious, flimsy, insignificant, insubstantial, nebulous, ques~ tionable, shaky, sketchy, slight, weak **2.** at~ tenuated, delicate, fine, gossamer, slim
Antonyms (*sense 1*) significant, solid, sound, strong, substantial

tepid 1. lukewarm, slightly warm, warmish **2.** apathetic, cool, half-arsed, half-assed (*U.S. & Canad. sl.*), half-hearted, indifferent, lukewarm, unenthusiastic
Antonyms (*sense 2*) animated, eager, enthu~ siastic, excited, keen, passionate, vibrant, zealous

term *n.* **1.** appellation, denomination, desig~ nation, expression, locution, name, phrase, title, word **2.** duration, interval, period, season, space, span, spell, time, while **3.** course, session **4.** bound, boundary, close, conclusion, confine, culmination, end, finish, fruition, limit, terminus ~*v.* **5.** call, denominate, designate, dub, entitle, label, name, style

terminal *adj.* **1.** bounding, concluding, extreme, final, last, limiting, ultimate, utmost **2.** deadly, fatal, incurable, killing, lethal, mortal ~*n.* **3.** boundary, end, extremity, limit, termination, terminus **4.** depot, end of the line, station, terminus
Antonyms (*sense 1*) beginning, commencing, first, initial, introductory, opening

terminate abort, axe (*Inf.*), bring *or* come to an end, cease, close, complete, conclude, cut off, discontinue, end, expire, finish, issue, lapse, put an end to, result, run out, stop, wind up
Antonyms begin, commence, inaugurate, initiate, instigate, introduce, open, start

termination abortion, cessation, close, completion, conclusion, consequence, cut-off point, discontinuation, effect, end, ending, expiry, finale, finis, finish, issue, result, wind-up
Antonyms beginning, commencement, inauguration, initiation, opening, start

terminology argot, cant, jargon, language, lingo (*Inf.*), nomenclature, patois, phraseology, terms, vocabulary

terminus **1.** boundary, close, end, extremity, final point, goal, limit, target, termination **2.** depot, end of the line, garage, last stop, station

terms **1.** language, manner of speaking, phraseology, terminology **2.** conditions, particulars, premises (*Law*), provisions, provisos, qualifications, specifications, stipulations **3.** charges, fee, payment, price, rates **4.** footing, position, relations, relationship, standing, status **5. come to terms** be reconciled, come to an agreement, come to an understanding, conclude agreement, learn to live with, reach acceptance, reach agreement

terrible **1.** bad, dangerous, desperate, extreme, serious, severe **2.** *Inf.* abhorrent, abysmal, awful, bad, beastly (*Inf.*), dire, dreadful, duff (*Brit. inf.*), foul, frightful, godawful (*Sl.*), hateful, hideous, loathsome, obnoxious, obscene, odious, offensive, poor, repulsive, revolting, rotten (*Inf.*), shitty (*Taboo sl.*), unpleasant, vile **3.** appalling, awful, dread, dreaded, dreadful, fearful, frightful, gruesome, harrowing, hellacious (*U.S. sl.*), horrendous, horrible, horrid, horrifying, monstrous, shocking, terrifying, unspeakable
Antonyms (*sense 1*) harmless, insignificant, mild, moderate, paltry, small (*sense 2*) admirable, brilliant, delightful, excellent, fine, great, magic, noteworthy, pleasant, remarkable, super, superb, terrific, very good, won-

derful (*sense 3*) calming, comforting, encouraging, reassuring, settling, soothing

terribly awfully (*Inf.*), decidedly, desperately, exceedingly, extremely, gravely, greatly, much, seriously, thoroughly, very

terrific **1.** awesome, awful, dreadful, enormous, excessive, extreme, fearful, fierce, gigantic, great, harsh, horrific, huge, intense, monstrous, severe, terrible, tremendous **2.** *Inf.* ace (*Inf.*), amazing, boffo (*Sl.*), breathtaking, brill (*Inf.*), brilliant, chillin' (*U.S. sl.*), cracking (*Brit. inf.*), excellent, fabulous (*Inf.*), fantastic (*Inf.*), fine, great (*Inf.*), jim-dandy (*Sl.*), magnificent, marvellous, mean (*Sl.*), outstanding, sensational (*Inf.*), smashing (*Inf.*), sovereign, stupendous, super (*Inf.*), superb, topping (*Brit. sl.*), very good, wonderful
Antonyms appalling, awful, bad, calming, comforting, dreadful, encouraging, harmless, hideous, insignificant, lousy (*Sl.*), mediocre, mild, moderate, paltry, reassuring, rotten, settling (*Inf.*), shocking, soothing, terrible, uninspired, unpleasant

terrified alarmed, appalled, awed, dismayed, frightened, frightened out of one's wits, horrified, horror-struck, intimidated, panic-stricken, petrified, scared, scared shitless (*Taboo sl.*), scared stiff, scared to death, shit-scared (*Taboo sl.*), shocked, terror-stricken

terrify alarm, appal, awe, dismay, fill with terror, frighten, frighten out of one's wits, horrify, intimidate, make one's blood run cold, make one's flesh creep, make one's hair stand on end, petrify, put the fear of God into, scare, scare to death, shock, terrorize

territory area, bailiwick, country, district, domain, land, patch, province, region, sector, state, terrain, tract, turf (*U.S. sl.*), zone

terror **1.** alarm, anxiety, awe, consternation, dismay, dread, fear, fear and trembling, fright, horror, intimidation, panic, shock **2.** bogeyman, bugbear, devil, fiend, monster, scourge

terrorize **1.** browbeat, bully, coerce, intimidate, menace, oppress, strong-arm (*Inf.*), threaten **2.** alarm, appal, awe, dismay, fill with terror, frighten, frighten out of one's wits, horrify, inspire panic in, intimidate, make one's blood run cold, make one's flesh creep, make one's hair stand on end, petrify, put the fear of God into, scare, scare to death, shock, strike terror into, terrify

terse **1.** aphoristic, brief, clipped, compact, concise, condensed, crisp, elliptical, epigrammatic, gnomic, incisive, laconic, neat, pithy, sententious, short, succinct, summary, to the point **2.** abrupt, brusque, curt, short, snappy

Antonyms ambiguous, chatty, circumlocu~
tory, confused, discursive, lengthy, long-
winded, polite, rambling, roundabout, vague,
verbose, wordy

test 1. *v.* analyse, assay, assess, check, ex~
amine, experiment, investigate, prove, put
to the proof, put to the test, research, try,
try out, verify, work over **2.** *n.* analysis,
assessment, attempt, catechism, check,
evaluation, examination, investigation, or~
deal, probation, proof, research, trial

testament 1. last wishes, will **2.** attesta~
tion, demonstration, earnest, evidence,
exemplification, proof, testimony, tribute,
witness

testicles balls (*Taboo sl.*), bollocks *or* bal~
locks (*Taboo sl.*), cojones (*U.S. taboo sl.*),
family jewels (*Sl.*), nuts (*Taboo sl.*), rocks
(*U.S. taboo sl.*)

testify affirm, assert, asseverate, attest, bear
witness, certify, corroborate, declare, de~
pone (*Scots Law*), depose (*Law*), evince, give
testimony, show, state, swear, vouch, wit~
ness
Antonyms belie, contradict, controvert,
disprove, dispute, gainsay (*Archaic or liter~
ary*), oppose

testimonial certificate, character, com~
mendation, credential, endorsement, rec~
ommendation, reference, tribute

testimony 1. affidavit, affirmation, attesta~
tion, avowal, confirmation, corroboration,
declaration, deposition, evidence, informa~
tion, profession, statement, submission,
witness **2.** corroboration, demonstration,
evidence, indication, manifestation, proof,
support, verification

text 1. body, contents, main body, matter **2.**
wording, words **3.** *Bible* paragraph, pas~
sage, sentence, verse **4.** argument, matter,
motif, subject, theme, topic **5.** reader, ref~
erence book, source, textbook

texture character, composition, consistency,
constitution, fabric, feel, grain, make, qual~
ity, structure, surface, tissue, weave

thank express gratitude, say thank you,
show gratitude, show one's appreciation

thankful appreciative, beholden, grateful,
indebted, obliged, pleased, relieved
Antonyms thankless, unappreciative, un~
grateful

thankless 1. fruitless, unappreciated, un~
profitable, unrequited, unrewarding, useless
2. inconsiderate, unappreciative, ungra~
cious, ungrateful, unmindful, unthankful
Antonyms (*sense 1*) fruitful, productive,
profitable, rewarding, useful, worthwhile
(*sense 2*) appreciative, grateful, thankful

thanks 1. acknowledgment, appreciation,
Brownie points, credit, gratefulness, grati~

tude, recognition, thanksgiving **2. thanks
to** as a result of, because of, by reason of,
due to, owing to, through

thaw defrost, dissolve, liquefy, melt, soften,
unfreeze, warm
Antonyms chill, congeal, freeze, harden, so~
lidify, stiffen

theatrical 1. dramatic, dramaturgic, melo~
dramatic, scenic, Thespian **2.** actorly, ac~
tressy, affected, artificial, camp (*Inf.*), cer~
emonious, dramatic, exaggerated, hammy
(*Inf.*), histrionic, mannered, ostentatious,
overdone, pompous, showy, stagy, stilted,
unreal
Antonyms (*sense 2*) natural, plain, simple,
straightforward, unaffected, unassuming,
unexaggerated, unpretentious, unsophisti~
cated

theft embezzlement, fraud, larceny, pilfer~
ing, purloining, rip-off (*Sl.*), robbery, steal~
ing, swindling, thievery, thieving

theme 1. argument, burden, idea, keynote,
matter, subject, subject matter, text, thesis,
topic **2.** leitmotiv, motif, recurrent image,
unifying idea **3.** composition, dissertation,
essay, exercise, paper

theological divine, doctrinal, ecclesiastical,
religious

theorem deduction, dictum, formula, hy~
pothesis, principle, proposition, rule, state~
ment

theoretical abstract, academic, conjectural,
hypothetical, ideal, impractical, notional,
pure, speculative
Antonyms applied, experiential, factual,
practical, realistic

theorize conjecture, formulate, guess, hy~
pothesize, project, propound, speculate,
suppose

theory 1. assumption, conjecture, guess,
hypothesis, presumption, speculation, sup~
position, surmise, thesis **2.** philosophy,
plan, proposal, scheme, system
Antonyms certainty, experience, fact, prac~
tice, reality

therapeutic ameliorative, analeptic, ben~
eficial, corrective, curative, good, healing,
remedial, restorative, salubrious, salutary,
sanative
Antonyms adverse, damaging, destructive,
detrimental, harmful

therapy cure, healing, remedial treatment,
remedy, treatment

therefore accordingly, as a result, conse~
quently, ergo, for that reason, hence, so,
then, thence, thus, whence

thesis 1. composition, disquisition, disser~
tation, essay, monograph, paper, treatise **2.**
contention, hypothesis, idea, line of argu~
ment, opinion, proposal, proposition, theo~

ry, view **3.** area, subject, theme, topic **4.** assumption, postulate, premise, proposition, statement, supposition, surmise

thick *adj.* **1.** broad, bulky, deep, fat, solid, substantial, wide **2.** close, clotted, coagulat~ ed, compact, concentrated, condensed, crowded, deep, dense, heavy, impenetrable, opaque **3.** abundant, brimming, bristling, bursting, chock-a-block, chock-full, covered, crawling, frequent, full, numerous, packed, replete, swarming, teeming **4.** blockheaded, braindead (*Inf.*), brainless, dense, dim- witted (*Inf.*), dopey (*Inf.*), dozy (*Brit. inf.*), dull, insensitive, moronic, obtuse, slow, slow-witted, stupid, thickheaded **5.** dense, heavy, impenetrable, soupy **6.** distorted, guttural, hoarse, husky, inarticulate, indis~ tinct, throaty **7.** broad, decided, distinct, marked, pronounced, rich, strong **8.** *Inf.* buddy-buddy (*Sl., chiefly U.S. & Canad.*), chummy (*Inf.*), close, confidential, devoted, familiar, friendly, hand in glove, insepa~ rable, intimate, matey *or* maty (*Brit. inf.*), on good terms, pally (*Inf.*), palsy-walsy (*Inf.*), well in (*Inf.*) **9. a bit thick** excessive, over the score (*Inf.*), too much, unfair, un~ just, unreasonable ~*n.* **10.** centre, heart, middle, midst
Antonyms (*sense 1*) narrow, slight, slim, thin (*sense 2*) clear, diluted, runny, thin, watery, weak (*sense 3*) bare, clear, devoid of, empty, free from, sparse, thin (*sense 4*) articulate, brainy, bright, clever, intellectual, intelligent, quick-witted, sharp, smart (*sense 5*) clear, thin (*sense 6*) articulate, clear, distinct, sharp, shrill, thin (*sense 7*) faint, slight, vague, weak (*sense 8*) antagonistic, distant, hostile, un~ friendly

thicken cake, clot, coagulate, condense, congeal, deepen, gel, inspissate (*Archaic*), jell, set
Antonyms dilute, thin, water down, weaken

thickset 1. beefy (*Inf.*), brawny, bulky, bur~ ly, heavy, muscular, powerfully built, stocky, strong, stubby, sturdy, well-built **2.** closely packed, dense, densely planted, sol~ id, thick
Antonyms angular, bony, gangling, gaunt, lanky, rawboned, scraggy, scrawny, weedy (*Inf.*)

thick-skinned callous, case-hardened, hard-boiled (*Inf.*), hardened, impervious, insensitive, stolid, tough, unfeeling, unsus~ ceptible
Antonyms concerned, feeling, sensitive, tender, thin-skinned, touchy

thief bandit, burglar, cheat, cracksman (*Sl.*), crook (*Inf.*), embezzler, housebreaker, lar~ cenist, mugger (*Inf.*), pickpocket, pilferer, plunderer, purloiner, robber, shoplifter, stealer, swindler

thieve blag (*Sl.*), cabbage (*Brit. sl.*), cheat, embezzle, filch, half-inch (*Old-fashioned sl.*), knock off (*Sl.*), lift (*Inf.*), misappropriate, nick (*Sl., chiefly Brit.*), peculate, pilfer, pinch (*Inf.*), plunder, poach, purloin, rip off (*Sl.*), rob, run off with, snitch (*Sl.*), steal, swindle, swipe (*Sl.*)

thin *adj.* **1.** attenuate, attenuated, fine, nar~ row, threadlike **2.** delicate, diaphanous, filmy, fine, flimsy, gossamer, see-through, sheer, translucent, transparent, unsubstan~ tial **3.** bony, emaciated, lank, lanky, lean, light, macilent (*Rare*), meagre, scraggy, scrawny, skeletal, skinny, slender, slight, slim, spare, spindly, thin as a rake, under~ nourished, underweight **4.** deficient, mea~ gre, scanty, scarce, scattered, skimpy, sparse, wispy **5.** dilute, diluted, rarefied, runny, watery, weak, wishy-washy (*Inf.*) **6.** feeble, flimsy, inadequate, insufficient, lame, poor, scant, scanty, shallow, slight, superficial, unconvincing, unsubstantial, weak ~*v.* **7.** attenuate, cut back, dilute, di~ minish, emaciate, prune, rarefy, reduce, refine, trim, water down, weaken, weed out
Antonyms (*sense 1*) heavy, thick (*sense 2*) bulky, dense, heavy, strong, substantial, thick (*sense 3*) bulky, corpulent, fat, heavy, obese, stout (*sense 4*) abundant, adequate, plentiful, profuse (*sense 5*) concentrated, dense, strong, thick, viscous (*sense 6*) adequate, convincing, strong, substantial

thing 1. affair, article, being, body, circum~ stance, concept, entity, fact, matter, object, part, portion, something, substance **2.** act, deed, event, eventuality, feat, happening, incident, occurrence, phenomenon, pro~ ceeding **3.** apparatus, contrivance, device, gadget, implement, instrument, machine, means, mechanism, tool **4.** aspect, detail, facet, factor, feature, item, particular, point, statement, thought **5.** *Plural* baggage, be~ longings, bits and pieces, clobber (*Brit. sl.*), clothes, effects, equipment, gear, goods, im~ pedimenta, luggage, odds and ends, para~ phernalia, possessions, stuff **6.** *Inf.* attitude, bee in one's bonnet, fetish, fixation, hang-up (*Inf.*), *idée fixe*, mania, obsession, phobia, preoccupation, quirk

think *v.* **1.** believe, conceive, conclude, con~ sider, deem, determine, esteem, estimate, guess (*Inf., chiefly U.S. & Canad.*), hold, im~ agine, judge, reckon, regard, suppose, sur~ mise **2.** brood, cerebrate, chew over (*Inf.*), cogitate, consider, contemplate, deliberate, have in mind, meditate, mull over, muse, ponder, reason, reflect, revolve, ruminate, turn over in one's mind, weigh up **3.** call to mind, recall, recollect, remember **4.** antici~ pate, envisage, expect, foresee, imagine, plan for, presume, suppose **5. think better of** change one's mind about, decide against, go back on, have second thoughts about, reconsider, repent, think again, think twice about **6. think much of** admire, attach im~ portance to, esteem, have a high opinion of, hold in high regard, rate (*Sl.*), respect, set store by, think highly of, value **7. think nothing of** consider unimportant, have no compunction about, have no hesitation about, regard as routine, set no store by, take in one's stride ~*n.* **8.** assessment, con~ sideration, contemplation, deliberation, look, reflection

thinkable conceivable, feasible, imaginable, likely, possible, reasonable, within the bounds of possibility
Antonyms absurd, impossible, inconceiv~ able, not on (*Inf.*), out of the question, unlike~ ly, unreasonable, unthinkable

thinker brain (*Inf.*), intellect (*Inf.*), mahat~ ma, mastermind, philosopher, sage, theo~ rist, wise man

thinking 1. *n.* assessment, conclusions, conjecture, idea, judgment, opinion, out~ look, philosophy, position, reasoning, theo~ ry, thoughts, view **2.** *adj.* contemplative, cultured, intelligent, meditative, philo~ sophical, ratiocinative, rational, reasoning, reflective, sophisticated, thoughtful

think over chew over (*Inf.*), consider, con~ sider the pros and cons of, contemplate, give thought to, mull over, ponder, reflect upon, turn over in one's mind, weigh up

think up come up with, concoct, contrive, create, devise, dream up, imagine, impro~ vise, invent, manufacture, trump up, visu~ alize

thin-skinned easily hurt, hypersensitive, quick to take offence, sensitive, soft, sus~ ceptible, tender, touchy, vulnerable
Antonyms callous, hard, heartless, insensi~ tive, obdurate, stolid, thick-skinned, tough, unfeeling

third-rate bad, cheap-jack, chickenshit (*U.S. sl.*), duff (*Brit. inf.*), indifferent, inferior, low-grade, mediocre, of a sort *or* of sorts, poor, poor-quality, ropy *or* ropey (*Brit. inf.*), shoddy

thirst *n.* **1.** craving to drink, drought, dry~ ness, thirstiness **2.** appetite, craving, de~ sire, eagerness, hankering, hunger, keen~ ness, longing, lust, passion, yearning, yen (*Inf.*)
Antonyms (*sense 2*) apathy, aversion, disin~ clination, dislike, distaste, loathing, revulsion

thirsty 1. arid, dehydrated, dry, parched **2.** athirst, avid, burning, craving, desirous, dying, eager, greedy, hankering, hungry, itching, longing, lusting, thirsting, yearning

thorn 1. barb, prickle, spike, spine **2.** affliction, annoyance, bane, bother, curse, hassle (*Inf.*), irritant, irritation, nuisance,

pest, plague, scourge, torment, torture, trouble
Antonyms (*sense 2*) balm, benefaction, blessing, comfort, manna, solace, succour

thorny 1. barbed, bristling with thorns, bristly, pointed, prickly, sharp, spiky, spi~ nous, spiny **2.** awkward, difficult, harass~ ing, hard, irksome, problematic(al), sticky (*Inf.*), ticklish, tough, troublesome, trying, unpleasant, upsetting, vexatious, worrying

thorough *or* **thoroughgoing 1.** all-embracing, all-inclusive, assiduous, careful, complete, comprehensive, conscientious, efficient, exhaustive, full, in-depth, inten~ sive, leaving no stone unturned, meticulous, painstaking, scrupulous, sweeping **2.** abso~ lute, arrant, complete, deep-dyed (*Usually derogatory*), downright, entire, out-and-out, outright, perfect, pure, sheer, total, unmiti~ gated, unqualified, utter
Antonyms careless, cursory, half-hearted, haphazard, imperfect, incomplete, lackadai~ sical, partial, sloppy, superficial

thoroughbred *adj.* blood, full-blooded, of unmixed stock, pedigree, pure-blooded, purebred
Antonyms crossbred, crossed, half-breed, hybrid, mongrel, of mixed breed

thoroughfare access, avenue, highway, passage, passageway, road, roadway, street, way

thoroughly 1. assiduously, carefully, com~ pletely, comprehensively, conscientiously, efficiently, exhaustively, from top to bot~ tom, fully, inside out, intensively, leaving no stone unturned, meticulously, pains~ takingly, scrupulously, sweepingly, through and through, throughout **2.** absolutely, completely, downright, entirely, perfectly, quite, totally, to the full, utterly, without reservation
Antonyms carelessly, cursorily, half-heartedly, haphazardly, imperfectly, incom~ pletely, in part, lackadaisically, partly, slop~ pily, somewhat, superficially

though 1. *conj.* albeit, allowing, although, despite the fact that, even if, even suppos~ ing, even though, granted, notwithstanding, tho' (*U.S. or poetic*), while **2.** *adv.* all the same, for all that, however, nevertheless, nonetheless, notwithstanding, still, yet

thought 1. brainwork, cerebration, cogita~ tion, consideration, contemplation, delib~ eration, introspection, meditation, musing, reflection, regard, rumination, thinking **2.** assessment, belief, concept, conception, conclusion, conjecture, conviction, estima~ tion, idea, judgment, notion, opinion, thinking, view **3.** attention, consideration, heed, regard, scrutiny, study **4.** aim, de~ sign, idea, intention, notion, object, plan, purpose **5.** anticipation, aspiration, dream, expectation, hope, prospect **6.** dash, jot, lit~ tle, small amount, *soupçon*, touch, trifle, whisker (*Inf.*) **7.** anxiety, attentiveness, care, compassion, concern, kindness, re~ gard, solicitude, sympathy, thoughtfulness

thoughtful 1. attentive, caring, consider~ ate, helpful, kind, kindly, solicitous, unselfish **2.** astute, canny, careful, cautious, circumspect, deliberate, discreet, heedful, mindful, prudent, wary, well-thought-out **3.** contemplative, deliberative, in a brown study, introspective, lost in thought, medi~ tative, musing, pensive, rapt, reflective, ru~ minative, serious, studious, thinking, wist~ ful
Antonyms cold-hearted, extrovert, flippant, heedless, impolite, inconsiderate, insensitive, irresponsible, neglectful, rash, selfish, shal~ low, superficial, thoughtless, uncaring, un~ thinking

thoughtless 1. impolite, inconsiderate, in~ discreet, insensitive, rude, selfish, tactless, uncaring, undiplomatic, unkind **2.** absent~ minded, careless, foolish, heedless, ill-considered, imprudent, inadvertent, inat~ tentive, injudicious, mindless, neglectful, negligent, rash, reckless, regardless, remiss, silly, slapdash, slipshod, stupid, unmindful, unobservant, unthinking
Antonyms attentive, considerate, consid~ ered, diplomatic, intelligent, prudent, smart, tactful, thoughtful, unselfish, well-advised, well-thought-out, wise

thrash 1. beat, belt (*Inf.*), birch, cane, chas~ tise, clobber (*Sl.*), drub, flagellate, flog, give (someone) a (good) hiding (*Inf.*), hide (*Inf.*), horsewhip, lambast(e), leather, lick (*Inf.*), paste (*Sl.*), punish, scourge, spank, take a stick to, tan (*Sl.*), whip **2.** beat, beat (some~ one) hollow (*Brit. inf.*), blow out of the wa~ ter (*Sl.*), clobber (*Sl.*), crush, defeat, drub, hammer (*Inf.*), lick (*Inf.*), maul, overwhelm, paste (*Sl.*), rout, run rings around (*Inf.*), slaughter (*Inf.*), tank (*Sl.*), trounce, wipe the floor with (*Inf.*) **3.** flail, heave, jerk, plunge, squirm, thresh, toss, toss and turn, writhe

thrashing 1. beating, belting (*Inf.*), caning, chastisement, drubbing, flogging, hiding (*Inf.*), lashing, pasting (*Sl.*), punishment, tanning (*Sl.*), whipping **2.** beating, defeat, drubbing, hammering (*Inf.*), hiding (*Inf.*), mauling, pasting (*Sl.*), rout, trouncing

thrash out argue out, debate, discuss, have out, resolve, settle, solve, talk over

thread *n.* **1.** cotton, fibre, filament, line, strand, string, yarn **2.** course, direction, drift, motif, plot, story line, strain, tenor, theme, train of thought ~*v.* **3.** ease, inch, loop, meander, pass, pick (one's way), squeeze through, string, wind

threadbare 1. down at heel, frayed, old, ragged, scruffy, shabby, tattered, tatty, used, worn, worn-out **2.** clichéd, cliché-ridden, common, commonplace, conven~ tional, corny (*Sl.*), familiar, hackneyed, overused, stale, stereotyped, stock, tired, trite, well-worn
Antonyms (*sense 1*) brand-new, good, new, smart, unused, well-preserved (*sense 2*) differ~ ent, fresh, new, novel, original, unconven~ tional, unfamiliar, unusual

threat 1. commination, intimidatory re~ mark, menace, threatening remark, warn~ ing **2.** foreboding, foreshadowing, omen, portent, presage, warning, writing on the wall **3.** danger, hazard, menace, peril, risk

threaten 1. endanger, imperil, jeopardize, put at risk, put in jeopardy **2.** be imminent, be in the air, be in the offing, forebode, foreshadow, hang over, impend, loom over, portend, presage, warn **3.** browbeat, bully, cow, intimidate, lean on (*Sl.*), make threats to, menace, pressurize, terrorize, warn
Antonyms defend, guard, protect, safeguard, shelter, shield

threatening 1. bullying, cautionary, com~ minatory, intimidatory, menacing, mina~ tory, terrorizing, warning **2.** baleful, for~ bidding, grim, inauspicious, ominous, sin~ ister
Antonyms (*sense 2*) auspicious, bright, com~ forting, encouraging, favourable, promising, propitious, reassuring

threesome triad, trilogy, trine, trinity, trio, triple, triplet, triplex, triptych, trium~ virate, triune, troika

threshold 1. door, doorsill, doorstep, door~ way, entrance, sill **2.** beginning, brink, dawn, inception, opening, outset, start, starting point, verge **3.** lower limit, mini~ mum
Antonyms (*sense 2*) close, decline, end, finish, twilight

thrift carefulness, economy, frugality, good husbandry, parsimony, prudence, saving, thriftiness
Antonyms carelessness, extravagance, prodigality, profligacy, recklessness, squan~ dering, waste

thriftless extravagant, improvident, impru~ dent, lavish, prodigal, profligate, spend~ thrift, unthrifty, wasteful
Antonyms careful, economical, frugal, provident, prudent, sparing, thrifty

thrifty careful, economical, frugal, parsimo~ nious, provident, prudent, saving, sparing
Antonyms extravagant, free-spending, gen~ erous, improvident, prodigal, spendthrift, wasteful

thrill *n.* **1.** adventure, buzz (*Sl.*), charge (*Sl.*), flush of excitement, glow, kick (*Inf.*), pleas~

ure, sensation, stimulation, tingle, titilla~
tion **2.** flutter, fluttering, quiver, shudder,
throb, tremble, tremor, vibration ~*v.* **3.**
arouse, electrify, excite, flush, get a charge
(*Sl.*), get a kick (*Inf.*), glow, move, send (*Sl.*),
stimulate, stir, tingle, titillate **4.** flutter,
quake, quiver, shake, shudder, throb, trem~
ble, vibrate
Antonyms (*sense 1*) boredom, dreariness,
dullness, ennui, monotony, tedium

thrilling 1. electrifying, exciting, gripping,
hair-raising, rip-roaring (*Inf.*), riveting,
rousing, sensational, sexy (*Inf.*), stimulat~
ing, stirring **2.** quaking, shaking, shivering,
shuddering, trembling, vibrating
Antonyms boring, dreary, dull, monoto~
nous, quiet, staid, tedious, uninteresting, un~
moving

thrive advance, bloom, boom, burgeon, de~
velop, do well, flourish, get on, grow, grow
rich, increase, prosper, succeed, wax
Antonyms decline, droop, fail, languish,
perish, shrivel, stagnate, wane, wilt, wither

thriving blooming, booming, burgeoning,
developing, doing well, flourishing, going
strong, growing, healthy, prosperous, suc~
cessful, wealthy, well
Antonyms ailing, bankrupt, failing, impov~
erished, languishing, on the rocks, poverty-
stricken, unsuccessful, withering

throb 1. *v.* beat, palpitate, pound, pulsate,
pulse, thump, vibrate **2.** *n.* beat, palpita~
tion, pounding, pulsating, pulse, thump,
thumping, vibration

throng 1. *n.* assemblage, concourse, con~
gregation, crowd, crush, horde, host, jam,
mass, mob, multitude, pack, press, swarm
2. *v.* bunch, congregate, converge, cram,
crowd, fill, flock, hem in, herd, jam, mill
around, pack, press, swarm around, troop
Antonyms *v.* break up, disband, dispel, dis~
perse, scatter, separate, spread out

throttle *v.* **1.** choke, garrotte, strangle,
strangulate **2.** control, gag, inhibit, silence,
stifle, suppress

through *prep.* **1.** between, by, from end to
end of, from one side to the other of, in and
out of, past **2.** as a consequence *or* result of,
because of, by means of, by virtue of, by
way of, using, via, with the help of **3.** dur~
ing, in, in the middle of, throughout **4.**
With **with** at the end of, done, finished,
having completed, having had enough of
~*adj.* **5.** completed, done, ended, finished,
terminated, washed up (*Inf.*) ~*adv.* **6.**
through and through altogether, com~
pletely, entirely, fully, thoroughly, totally,
to the core, unreservedly, utterly, wholly
Antonyms *adv.* moderately, more or less,
partially, partly, somewhat, to some extent

throughout all over, all the time, all

through, during the whole of, everywhere,
for the duration of, from beginning to end,
from end to end, from start to finish, from
the start, over the length and breadth of,
right through, the whole time, through the
whole of

throw *v.* **1.** cast, chuck (*Inf.*), fling, heave,
hurl, launch, lob (*Inf.*), pitch, project, pro~
pel, put, send, shy, sling, toss **2.** *Inf.* aston~
ish, baffle, confound, confuse, disconcert,
dumbfound, faze, put one off one's stroke,
throw off, throw one off one's stride, throw
out **3.** bring down, dislodge, fell, floor, hurl
to the ground, overturn, unseat, upset ~*n.*
4. cast, fling, heave, lob (*Inf.*), pitch, pro~
jection, put, shy, sling, toss **5.** *Inf.* attempt,
chance, essay, gamble, hazard, try, venture,
wager

throw away 1. axe (*Inf.*), bin (*Inf.*), cast
off, chuck (*Inf.*), discard, dispense with,
dispose of, ditch (*Sl.*), dump (*Inf.*), get rid
of, jettison, junk (*Inf.*), reject, scrap, throw
out **2.** blow (*Sl.*), fail to exploit, fritter
away, lose, make poor use of, squander,
waste
Antonyms (*sense 1*) conserve, keep, pre~
serve, rescue, retain, retrieve, salvage, save

throw off 1. abandon, cast off, discard,
drop, free oneself of, rid oneself of, shake
off **2.** elude, escape from, evade, get away
from, give (someone) the slip, leave behind,
lose, outdistance, outrun, shake off, show a
clean pair of heels to **3.** confuse, disconcert,
disturb, faze, put one off one's stroke, throw
(*Inf.*), throw one off one's stride, unsettle,
upset

throw out 1. bin (*Inf.*), cast off, chuck
(*Inf.*), discard, dismiss, dispense with, ditch
(*Sl.*), dump (*Inf.*), eject, evict, expel, get rid
of, give the bum's rush (*Sl.*), jettison, junk
(*Inf.*), kick out (*Inf.*), kiss off (*Sl., chiefly
U.S. & Canad.*), oust, reject, relegate, scrap,
show one the door, throw away, turf out
(*Brit. inf.*), turn down **2.** confuse, discon~
cert, disturb, put one off one's stroke, throw
(*Inf.*), throw one off one's stride, unsettle,
upset **3.** diffuse, disseminate, emit, give off,
put forth, radiate

thrust *v.* **1.** butt, drive, elbow *or* shoulder
one's way, force, impel, jam, plunge, poke,
press, prod, propel, push, ram, shove, urge
2. jab, lunge, pierce, stab, stick ~*n.* **3.**
drive, lunge, poke, prod, push, shove, stab
4. impetus, momentum, motive force, mo~
tive power, propulsive force

thud *n./v.* clonk, clump, clunk, crash, knock,
smack, thump, wallop (*Inf.*)

thug assassin, bandit, bruiser (*Inf.*), bully
boy, cutthroat, gangster, heavy (*Sl.*), hooli~
gan, killer, mugger (*Inf.*), murderer, robber,
ruffian, tough

thumb *n.* **1.** pollex **2. all thumbs** butterfingered (*Inf.*), cack-handed (*Inf.*), clumsy, ham-fisted (*Inf.*), inept, maladroit **3. thumbs down** disapproval, negation, no, rebuff, refusal, rejection **4. thumbs up** acceptance, affirmation, approval, encour~ agement, go-ahead (*Inf.*), green light, O.K. or okay (*Inf.*), yes ~*v.* **5.** hitch (*Inf.*), hitch~ hike **6.** *Often with* **through** browse through, flick through, flip through, glance at, leaf through, riffle through, run one's eye over, scan the pages of, skim through, turn over **7.** dog-ear, finger, handle, mark **8. thumb one's nose at** be contemptuous of, cock a snook at, deride, flout, jeer at, laugh at, laugh in the face of, mock, ridi~ cule, show contempt for, show disrespect to

thumbnail *adj.* brief, compact, concise, pithy, quick, short, succinct

thump 1. *n.* bang, blow, clout (*Inf.*), clunk, crash, knock, punch, rap, smack, thud, thwack, wallop (*Inf.*), whack **2.** *v.* bang, batter, beat, belabour, chin (*Sl.*), clobber (*Sl.*), clout (*Inf.*), crash, deck (*Sl.*), hit, knock, lambast(e), lay one on (*Sl.*), pound, punch, rap, smack, strike, thrash, throb, thud, thwack, wallop (*Inf.*), whack

thumping colossal, elephantine, enormous, excessive, exorbitant, gargantuan, gigantic, great, huge, humongous *or* humungous (*U.S. sl.*), impressive, mammoth, massive, monumental, terrific, thundering (*Sl.*), ti~ tanic, tremendous, whopping (*Inf.*) **Antonyms** inconsequential, insignificant, meagre, measly (*Inf.*), negligible, paltry, petty, piddling (*Inf.*), trifling, trivial

thunder *n.* **1.** boom, booming, cracking, crash, crashing, detonation, explosion, pealing, rumble, rumbling ~*v.* **2.** blast, boom, clap, crack, crash, detonate, explode, peal, resound, reverberate, roar, rumble **3.** bark, bellow, declaim, roar, shout, yell **4.** curse, denounce, fulminate, rail, threaten, utter threats

thundering decided, enormous, excessive, great, monumental, remarkable, unmitigat~ ed, utter

thunderous booming, deafening, ear-splitting, loud, noisy, resounding, roaring, tumultuous

thunderstruck aghast, amazed, astonished, astounded, bowled over (*Inf.*), dazed, dumb~ founded, flabbergasted (*Inf.*), floored (*Inf.*), flummoxed, gobsmacked (*Brit. sl.*), knocked for six (*Inf.*), left speechless, nonplussed, open-mouthed, paralysed, petrified, rooted to the spot, shocked, staggered, struck dumb, stunned, taken aback

thus 1. as follows, in this fashion (manner, way), like so, like this, so, to such a degree **2.** accordingly, consequently, ergo, for this reason, hence, on that account, so, then, therefore

thwart baffle, balk, check, defeat, foil, frus~ trate, hinder, impede, obstruct, oppose, out~ wit, prevent, stop, stymie **Antonyms** aggravate, aid, assist, encourage, exacerbate, facilitate, hasten, help, intensify, support

tick[1] *n.* **1.** clack, click, clicking, tap, tapping, ticktock **2.** *Brit. inf.* flash, half a mo (*Brit. inf.*), instant, jiffy (*Inf.*), minute, moment, sec (*Inf.*), second, shake (*Inf.*), split second, trice, twinkling, two shakes of a lamb's tail (*Inf.*) **3.** dash, mark, stroke ~*v.* **4.** clack, click, tap, ticktock **5.** check off, choose, in~ dicate, mark, mark off, select **6. what makes someone tick** drive, motivation, motive, *raison d'être*

tick[2] account, credit, deferred payment, the slate (*Brit. inf.*)

ticket 1. card, certificate, coupon, pass, slip, token, voucher **2.** card, docket, label, marker, slip, sticker, tab, tag

tickle *Fig.* amuse, delight, divert, entertain, excite, gratify, please, thrill, titillate **Antonyms** annoy, bore, bother, irritate, pester, trouble, vex, weary

ticklish awkward, critical, delicate, difficult, nice, risky, sensitive, thorny, touchy, tricky, uncertain, unstable, unsteady

tick off 1. check off, mark off, put a tick at **2.** *Inf.* bawl out (*Inf.*), berate, carpet (*Inf.*), censure, chew out (*U.S. & Canad. inf.*), chide, give a rocket (*Brit. & N.Z. inf.*), haul over the coals (*Inf.*), lecture, read the riot act, rebuke, reprimand, reproach, reprove, scold, take to task, tear into (*Inf.*), tear (someone) off a strip (*Brit. inf.*), tell off (*Inf.*), upbraid

tide 1. course, current, ebb, flow, stream, tideway, undertow **2.** course, current, di~ rection, drift, movement, tendency, trend

tide over aid, assist, bridge the gap, help, keep one going, keep one's head above wa~ ter, keep the wolf from the door, see one through

tidings advice, bulletin, communication, gen (*Brit. inf.*), greetings, information, intelli~ gence, latest (*Inf.*), message, news, report, word

tidy *adj.* **1.** businesslike, clean, cleanly, me~ thodical, neat, ordered, orderly, shipshape, spick-and-span, spruce, systematic, trig (*Archaic or dialect*), trim, well-groomed, well-kept, well-ordered **2.** *Inf.* ample, con~ siderable, fair, generous, good, goodly, handsome, healthy, large, largish, respect~ able, sizable, substantial ~*v.* **3.** clean, groom, neaten, order, put in order, put in trim, put to rights, spruce up, straighten

Antonyms (*sense 1*) careless, dirty, dishev~
elled, disordered, disorderly, filthy, in disar~
ray, messy, scruffy, sloppy, slovenly, un~
businesslike, unkempt, unmethodical, un~
systematic, untidy (*sense 2*) inconsiderable,
insignificant, little, small, tiny (*sense 3*) dirty,
dishevel, disorder, mess, mess up

tie *v.* **1.** attach, bind, connect, fasten, inter~
lace, join, knot, lash, link, make fast, moor,
rope, secure, tether, truss, unite **2.** bind,
confine, hamper, hinder, hold, limit, re~
strain, restrict **3.** be even, be neck and
neck, draw, equal, match ~*n.* **4.** band,
bond, connection, cord, fastening, fetter,
joint, knot, ligature, link, rope, string **5.**
affiliation, affinity, allegiance, bond, com~
mitment, connection, duty, kinship, liaison,
obligation, relationship **6.** encumbrance,
hindrance, limitation, restraint, restriction
7. dead heat, deadlock, draw, stalemate **8.**
Brit. contest, fixture, game, match
Antonyms free, loose, release, separate,
undo, unfasten, unhitch, unknot, untie

tier bank, echelon, file, layer, level, line, or~
der, rank, row, series, storey, stratum

tie-up association, connection, coordination,
hook-up, liaison, link, linkup, relation, re~
lationship, tie-in

tie up **1.** attach, bind, pinion, restrain,
tether, truss **2.** lash, make fast, moor, rope,
secure **3.** engage, engross, keep busy, occu~
py **4.** bring to a close, conclude, end, finish
off, settle, terminate, wind up, wrap up
(*Inf.*)

tight **1.** close, close-fitting, compact, con~
stricted, cramped, fast, firm, fixed, narrow,
rigid, secure, snug, stiff, stretched, taut,
tense **2.** hermetic, impervious, proof,
sealed, sound, watertight **3.** harsh, inflex~
ible, rigid, rigorous, severe, stern, strict,
stringent, tough, uncompromising, unyield~
ing **4.** close, grasping, mean, miserly, nig~
gardly, parsimonious, penurious, sparing,
stingy, tight-arse (*Taboo sl.*), tight-arsed
(*Taboo sl.*), tight as a duck's arse (*Taboo
sl.*), tight-ass (*U.S. taboo sl.*), tight-assed
(*U.S. taboo sl.*), tightfisted **5.** dangerous,
difficult, hazardous, perilous, precarious,
problematic, sticky (*Inf.*), ticklish, tough,
tricky, troublesome, worrisome **6.** close,
even, evenly-balanced, near, well-matched
7. *Inf.* bevvied (*Dialect*), blitzed (*Sl.*), blotto
(*Sl.*), bombed (*Sl.*), drunk, flying (*Sl.*), half
cut (*Brit. sl.*), half seas over (*Brit. inf.*), in~
ebriated, in one's cups, intoxicated, legless
(*Inf.*), lit up (*Sl.*), out of it (*Sl.*), out to it
(*Aust. & N.Z. sl.*), paralytic (*Inf.*), pickled
(*Inf.*), pie-eyed (*Sl.*), pissed (*Taboo sl.*), plas~
tered (*Sl.*), smashed (*Sl.*), sozzled (*Inf.*),
steamboats (*Sl.*), steaming (*Sl.*), stewed (*Sl.*),
stoned (*Sl.*), three sheets in the wind (*Sl.*),
tiddly (*Sl., chiefly Brit.*), tipsy, under the

influence (*Inf.*), wasted (*Sl.*), wrecked (*Sl.*),
zonked (*Sl.*)
Antonyms (*sense 1*) lax, loose, relaxed, slack,
spacious (*sense 2*) loose, open, porous (*sense 3*)
easy, easy-going, generous, lax, lenient, liber~
al, relaxed, soft, undemanding (*sense 4*) abun~
dant, extravagant, generous, lavish, munifi~
cent, open, prodigal, profuse, spendthrift
(*sense 5*) easy (*sense 6*) easy, landslide, over~
whelming, runaway, uneven (*sense 7*) sober

tighten close, constrict, cramp, fasten, fix,
narrow, rigidify, screw, secure, squeeze,
stiffen, stretch, tauten, tense
Antonyms ease off, let out, loosen, relax,
slacken, unbind, weaken

till[1] cultivate, dig, plough, turn over, work

till[2] cash box, cash drawer, cash register

tilt *v.* **1.** cant, heel, incline, lean, list, slant,
slope, tip **2.** attack, break a lance, clash,
contend, cross swords, duel, encounter,
fight, joust, overthrow, spar ~*n.* **3.** angle,
cant, inclination, incline, list, pitch, slant,
slope **4.** *Medieval history* clash, combat,
duel, encounter, fight, joust, lists, set-to
(*Inf.*), tournament, tourney **5. (at) full tilt**
for dear life, full force, full speed, headlong,
like a bat out of hell (*Sl.*), like the clappers
(*Brit. inf.*)

timber beams, boards, forest, logs, planks,
trees, wood

time *n.* **1.** age, chronology, date, duration,
epoch, era, generation, hour, interval, peri~
od, season, space, span, spell, stretch, term,
while **2.** instance, juncture, occasion, point,
stage **3.** allotted span, day, duration, life,
life span, lifetime, season **4.** heyday, hour,
peak **5.** *Music* beat, measure, metre,
rhythm, tempo **6. all the time** always, at
all times, constantly, continually, continu~
ously, ever, for the duration, perpetually,
throughout **7. at one time a.** for a while,
formerly, hitherto, once, once upon a time,
previously **b.** all at once, at the same time,
simultaneously, together **8. at times** every
now and then, every so often, from time to
time, now and then, occasionally, once in a
while, on occasion, sometimes **9. behind
the times** antiquated, dated, obsolete, old-
fashioned, old hat, outdated, outmoded, out
of date, out of fashion, out of style, passé,
square (*Inf.*) **10. for the time being** for
now, for the moment, for the nonce, for the
present, in the meantime, meantime, mean~
while, pro tem, temporarily **11. from time
to time** at times, every now and then,
every so often, now and then, occasionally,
once in a while, on occasion, sometimes **12.
in good time a.** early, on time, with time
to spare **b.** quickly, rapidly, speedily, swift~
ly, with dispatch **13. in no time** apace, be~
fore one knows it, before you can say Jack

Robinson, in an instant, in a trice (flash, jiffy, moment), in two shakes of a lamb's tail (*Inf.*), quickly, rapidly, speedily, swiftly **14. in time a.** at the appointed time, early, in good time, on schedule, on time, with time to spare **b.** by and by, eventually, one day, someday, sooner or later, ultimately **15. on time** in good time, on the dot, punctually **16. time and again** frequently, many times, often, on many occasions, over and over again, repeatedly, time after time ~*v.* **17.** clock, control, count, judge, measure, regulate, schedule, set

timeless abiding, ageless, ceaseless, changeless, deathless, endless, enduring, eternal, everlasting, immortal, immutable, imperishable, indestructible, lasting, permanent, persistent, undying
Antonyms ephemeral, evanescent, momentary, mortal, passing, temporal, temporary, transitory

timely appropriate, at the right time, convenient, judicious, opportune, prompt, propitious, punctual, seasonable, suitable, well-timed
Antonyms ill-timed, inconvenient, inopportune, late, tardy, unseasonable, untimely

timetable agenda, calendar, curriculum, diary, list, order of the day, programme, schedule

timid afraid, apprehensive, bashful, cowardly, coy, diffident, faint-hearted, fearful, irresolute, modest, mousy, nervous, pusillanimous, retiring, shrinking, shy, timorous
Antonyms aggressive, arrogant, ballsy (*Taboo sl.*), bold, brave, confident, daring, fearless, fierce, forceful, forward, presumptuous, self-assured, self-confident, shameless, unabashed

timorous afraid, apprehensive, bashful, cowardly, coy, diffident, faint-hearted, fearful, frightened, irresolute, mousy, nervous, pusillanimous, retiring, shrinking, shy, timid, trembling
Antonyms assertive, assured, audacious, bold, confident, courageous, daring, fearless

tinge *n.* **1.** cast, colour, dye, shade, stain, tincture, tint, wash **2.** bit, dash, drop, pinch, smack, smattering, *soupçon*, sprinkling, suggestion, touch, trace ~*v.* **3.** colour, dye, imbue, shade, stain, suffuse, tinge, tint

tingle 1. *v.* have goose pimples, itch, prickle, sting, tickle **2.** *n.* goose pimples, itch, itching, pins and needles (*Inf.*), prickling, quiver, shiver, stinging, thrill, tickle, tickling

tinker *v.* dabble, fiddle (*Inf.*), meddle, mess about, monkey, muck about (*Brit. sl.*), play, potter, toy

tinsel *adj.* brummagem, cheap, flashy,

gaudy, meretricious, ostentatious, pinchbeck, plastic (*Sl.*), sham, showy, specious, superficial, tawdry, trashy

tint *n.* **1.** cast, colour, hue, shade, tone **2.** dye, rinse, stain, tincture, tinge, wash **3.** hint, shade, suggestion, tinge, touch, trace ~*v.* **4.** colour, dye, rinse, stain, tincture, tinge **5.** affect, colour, influence, taint, tinge

tiny diminutive, dwarfish, infinitesimal, insignificant, Lilliputian, little, microscopic, mini, miniature, minute, negligible, petite, pint-sized (*Inf.*), puny, pygmy *or* pigmy, slight, small, teensy-weensy, teeny-weeny, trifling, wee
Antonyms colossal, enormous, extra-large, gargantuan, giant, gigantic, great, huge, immense, mammoth, massive, monstrous, titanic, vast

tip[1] 1. *n.* apex, cap, crown, end, extremity, head, peak, point, summit, top **2.** *v.* cap, crown, finish, surmount, top

tip[2] *v.* **1.** cant, capsize, incline, lean, list, overturn, slant, spill, tilt, topple over, upend, upset **2.** *Brit.* ditch (*Sl.*), dump, empty, pour out, unload ~*n.* **3.** *Brit.* dump, midden (*Dialect*), refuse heap, rubbish heap

tip[3] *n.* **1.** baksheesh, gift, gratuity, perquisite, *pourboire* **2.** *Also* **tip-off** clue, forecast, gen (*Brit. inf.*), hint, information, inside information, pointer, suggestion, warning, word, word of advice ~*v.* **3.** remunerate, reward **4.** *Also* **tip off** advise, caution, forewarn, give a clue, give a hint, suggest, tip (someone) the wink (*Brit. inf.*), warn

tipple 1. *v.* bend the elbow (*Inf.*), bevvy (*Dialect*), drink, imbibe, indulge (*Inf.*), quaff, swig, take a drink, tope **2.** *n.* alcohol, booze (*Inf.*), drink, John Barleycorn, liquor, poison (*Inf.*)

tippler bibber, boozer (*Inf.*), drinker, drunk, drunkard, inebriate, soak (*Sl.*), sot, sponge (*Inf.*), toper

tirade abuse, denunciation, diatribe, fulmination, harangue, invective, lecture, outburst, philippic

tire 1. drain, droop, enervate, exhaust, fag (*Inf.*), fail, fatigue, flag, jade, knacker (*Sl.*), sink, take it out of (*Inf.*), wear down, wear out, weary, whack (*Brit. inf.*) **2.** aggravate (*Inf.*), annoy, bore, exasperate, get on one's nerves (*Inf.*), harass, hassle (*Inf.*), irk, irritate, piss one off (*Taboo sl.*), weary
Antonyms (*sense 1*) energize, enliven, exhilarate, invigorate, liven up, pep up, refresh, restore, revive

tired 1. all in (*Sl.*), asleep *or* dead on one's feet (*Inf.*), clapped out (*Aust. & N.Z. inf.*), dead beat (*Inf.*), dog-tired (*Inf.*), done in (*Inf.*), drained, drooping, drowsy, enervated, exhausted, fagged (*Inf.*), fatigued, flagging, jaded, knackered (*Sl.*), ready to drop,

sleepy, spent, weary, whacked (*Brit. inf.*), worn out, zonked (*Sl.*) **2.** *With* **of** annoyed with, bored with, exasperated by, fed up with, irked by, irritated by, pissed off with (*Taboo sl.*), sick of, weary of **3.** clichéd, conventional, corny (*Sl.*), familiar, hack~ neyed, old, outworn, stale, stock, thread~ bare, trite, well-worn
Antonyms energetic, enthusiastic about, fond of, fresh, full of beans, innovative, keen on, lively, original, refreshed, rested, wide-awake

tireless determined, energetic, indefatigable, industrious, resolute, unflagging, untiring, unwearied, vigorous
Antonyms drained, exhausted, fatigued, flagging, tired, weak, weary, worn out

tiresome annoying, boring, dull, exasperat~ ing, flat, irksome, irritating, laborious, mo~ notonous, tedious, trying, uninteresting, vexatious, wearing, wearisome
Antonyms exhilarating, inspiring, interest~ ing, refreshing, rousing, stimulating

tiring arduous, demanding, enervative, ex~ acting, exhausting, fatiguing, laborious, strenuous, tough, wearing, wearying

tissue 1. fabric, gauze, mesh, structure, stuff, texture, web **2.** paper, paper hand~ kerchief, wrapping paper **3.** accumulation, chain, collection, combination, concatena~ tion, conglomeration, fabrication, mass, network, pack, series, web

titbit *bonne bouche*, choice item, dainty, delicacy, goody, juicy bit, morsel, scrap, snack, treat

titillate arouse, excite, interest, provoke, stimulate, tantalize, tease, thrill, tickle, turn on (*Sl.*)

titillating arousing, exciting, interesting, lewd, lurid, provocative, sensational, stimulating, suggestive, teasing, thrilling

titivate doll up (*Sl.*), do up (*Inf.*), make up, prank, preen, primp, prink, refurbish, smarten up, tart up (*Brit. sl.*), touch up

title *n.* **1.** caption, heading, inscription, la~ bel, legend, name, style **2.** appellation, de~ nomination, designation, epithet, handle (*Sl.*), moniker *or* monicker (*Sl.*), name, nickname, nom de plume, pseudonym, so~ briquet, term **3.** championship, crown, lau~ rels **4.** claim, entitlement, ownership, pre~ rogative, privilege, right ~*v.* **5.** call, desig~ nate, label, name, style, term

titter chortle (*Inf.*), chuckle, giggle, laugh, snigger, tee-hee, te-hee

titular honorary, in name only, nominal, puppet, putative, so-called, theoretical, to~ ken
Antonyms actual, effective, functioning, real, true

toady 1. *n.* apple polisher (*U.S. sl.*), ass-kisser (*U.S. & Canad. taboo sl.*), bootlicker (*Inf.*), brown-noser (*Taboo sl.*), crawler (*Sl.*), creep (*Sl.*), fawner, flatterer, flunkey, grov~ eller, hanger-on, jackal, lackey, lickspittle, minion, parasite, spaniel, sycophant, truck~ ler, yes man **2.** *v.* be obsequious to, bow and scrape, brown-nose (*Taboo sl.*), butter up, crawl, creep, cringe, curry favour with, fawn on, flatter, grovel, kiss (someone's) ass (*U.S. & Canad. taboo sl.*), kiss the feet of, kowtow to, lick (someone's) boots, pander to, suck up to (*Inf.*)
Antonyms (*sense 2*) confront, defy, oppose, rebel, resist, stand against, withstand

toast[1] *v.* brown, grill, heat, roast, warm

toast[2] *n.* **1.** compliment, drink, health, pledge, salutation, salute, tribute **2.** darling, favourite, heroine ~*v.* **3.** drink to, drink (to) the health of, pledge, salute

together *adv.* **1.** as a group, as one, cheek by jowl, closely, collectively, hand in glove, hand in hand, in a body, in concert, in co~ operation, in unison, jointly, mutually, shoulder to shoulder, side by side **2.** all at once, as one, at one fell swoop, at the same time, concurrently, contemporaneously, en masse, in unison, simultaneously, with one accord **3.** consecutively, continuously, in a row, in succession, one after the other, on end, successively, without a break, without interruption **4.** *Inf.* arranged, fixed, or~ dered, organized, settled, sorted out, straight, to rights ~*adj.* **5.** *Sl.* calm, com~ posed, cool, stable, well-adjusted, well-balanced, well-organized
Antonyms (*sense 1*) alone, apart, indepen~ dently, individually, one at a time, one by one, separately, singly

toil 1. *n.* application, donkey-work, drudg~ ery, effort, elbow grease (*Inf.*), exertion, graft (*Inf.*), hard work, industry, labour, pains, slog, sweat, travail **2.** *v.* bend over backwards (*Inf.*), break one's neck (*Inf.*), bust a gut (*Inf.*), do one's damnedest (*Inf.*), drag oneself, drudge, give it one's all (*Inf.*), give it one's best shot (*Inf.*), go for broke (*Sl.*), go for it (*Inf.*), graft (*Inf.*), grind (*Inf.*), grub, knock oneself out (*Inf.*), labour, make an all-out effort (*Inf.*), push oneself, rupture oneself (*Inf.*), slave, slog, strive, struggle, sweat (*Inf.*), work, work like a dog, work like a Trojan, work one's fingers to the bone
Antonyms (*sense 1*) idleness, inactivity, in~ dolence, inertia, laziness, sloth, torpor

toilet 1. ablutions (*Military inf.*), bathroom, bog (*Sl.*), can (*U.S. & Canad. sl.*), closet, convenience, crapper (*Taboo sl.*), geňts (*Brit. inf.*), john (*Sl., chiefly U.S. & Canad.*), khazi (*Sl.*), ladies' room, latrine, lavatory, little boy's room (*Inf.*), little girl's room

(*Inf.*), loo (*Brit. inf.*), outhouse, *pissoir,* powder room, privy, urinal, washroom, wa~ ter closet, W.C. **2.** ablutions, bathing, dressing, grooming, toilette

token *n.* **1.** badge, clue, demonstration, ear~ nest, evidence, expression, index, indica~ tion, manifestation, mark, note, proof, rep~ resentation, sign, symbol, warning **2.** keep~ sake, memento, memorial, remembrance, reminder, souvenir ~*adj.* **3.** hollow, mini~ mal, nominal, perfunctory, superficial, symbolic

tolerable 1. acceptable, allowable, bearable, endurable, sufferable, supportable **2.** ac~ ceptable, adequate, all right, average, fair, fairly good, fair to middling, good enough, indifferent, mediocre, middling, not bad (*Inf.*), O.K. *or* okay (*Inf.*), ordinary, pass~ able, run-of-the-mill, so-so (*Inf.*), unexcep~ tional
Antonyms (*sense 1*) insufferable, intolerable, unacceptable, unbearable, unendurable (*sense 2*) awful, bad, dreadful, rotten

tolerance 1. broad-mindedness, charity, forbearance, indulgence, lenity, magnanim~ ity, open-mindedness, patience, permissive~ ness, sufferance, sympathy **2.** endurance, fortitude, hardiness, hardness, resilience, resistance, stamina, staying power, tough~ ness **3.** fluctuation, play, swing, variation
Antonyms (*sense 1*) bigotry, discrimination, intolerance, narrow-mindedness, prejudice, sectarianism

tolerant 1. broad-minded, catholic, chari~ table, fair, forbearing, latitudinarian, liber~ al, long-suffering, magnanimous, open~ minded, patient, sympathetic, unbigoted, understanding, unprejudiced **2.** complai~ sant, easy-going, easy-oasy (*Sl.*), free and easy, indulgent, kind-hearted, lax, lenient, permissive, soft
Antonyms authoritarian, biased, bigoted, despotic, dictatorial, dogmatic, illiberal, in~ tolerant, narrow-minded, prejudiced, repres~ sive, rigid, sectarian, stern, strict, tyrannical, uncharitable

tolerate abide, accept, admit, allow, bear, brook, condone, countenance, endure, in~ dulge, permit, pocket, put up with (*Inf.*), re~ ceive, sanction, stand, stomach, submit to, suffer, swallow, take, thole (*Scot.*), turn a blind eye to, undergo, wink at
Antonyms ban, disallow, disapprove, forbid, outlaw, preclude, prohibit, veto

toleration 1. acceptance, allowance, condo~ nation, endurance, indulgence, permissive~ ness, sanction, sufferance **2.** freedom of conscience, freedom of worship, religious freedom

toll¹ *v.* **1.** chime, clang, knell, peal, ring, sound, strike **2.** announce, call, signal, summon, warn ~*n.* **3.** chime, clang, knell, peal, ring, ringing, tolling

toll² 1. assessment, charge, customs, de~ mand, duty, fee, impost, levy, payment, rate, tariff, tax, tribute **2.** cost, damage, in~ road, loss, penalty

tomb burial chamber, catacomb, crypt, grave, mausoleum, sarcophagus, sepulchre, vault

tombstone gravestone, headstone, marker, memorial, monument

tome book, title, volume, work

tomfoolery 1. buffoonery, childishness, clowning, fooling around (*Inf.*), foolishness, horseplay, idiocy, larks (*Inf.*), messing around (*Inf.*), shenanigans (*Inf.*), silliness, skylarking (*Inf.*), stupidity **2.** balderdash, baloney (*Inf.*), bilge (*Inf.*), bosh (*Inf.*), bunk (*Inf.*), bunkum *or* buncombe (*Chiefly U.S.*), claptrap (*Inf.*), hogwash, hooey (*Sl.*), inan~ ity, nonsense, poppycock (*Inf.*), rot, rubbish, stuff and nonsense, tommyrot, tosh (*Sl., chiefly Brit.*), trash, twaddle
Antonyms demureness, gravity, heaviness, reserve, sedateness, seriousness, sobriety, solemnity, sternness

tone *n.* **1.** accent, emphasis, force, inflection, intonation, modulation, pitch, strength, stress, timbre, tonality, volume **2.** air, ap~ proach, aspect, attitude, character, drift, ef~ fect, feel, frame, grain, manner, mood, note, quality, spirit, style, temper, tenor, vein **3.** cast, colour, hue, shade, tinge, tint ~*v.* **4.** blend, go well with, harmonize, match, suit

tone down dampen, dim, mitigate, moder~ ate, modulate, play down, reduce, restrain, soften, soft-pedal (*Inf.*), subdue, temper

tongue 1. argot, dialect, idiom, language, lingo (*Inf.*), parlance, patois, speech, talk, vernacular **2.** articulation, speech, utter~ ance, verbal expression, voice

tongue-tied at a loss for words, dumb, dumbstruck, inarticulate, mute, speechless, struck dumb
Antonyms articulate, chatty, effusive, gar~ rulous, loquacious, talkative, verbose, vol~ uble, wordy

tonic analeptic, boost, bracer (*Inf.*), cordial, fillip, livener, pick-me-up (*Inf.*), refresher, restorative, roborant, shot in the arm (*Inf.*), stimulant

too 1. also, as well, besides, further, in ad~ dition, into the bargain, likewise, moreover, to boot **2.** excessively, exorbitantly, ex~ tremely, immoderately, inordinately, over-, overly, unduly, unreasonably, very

tool *n.* **1.** apparatus, appliance, contraption, contrivance, device, gadget, implement, in~ strument, machine, utensil **2.** agency, agent, intermediary, means, medium, vehi~

cle, wherewithal **3.** cat's-paw, creature, dupe, flunkey, hireling, jackal, lackey, min~ ion, pawn, puppet, stooge (*Sl.*) ~*v.* **4.** chase, cut, decorate, ornament, shape, work

top *n.* **1.** acme, apex, apogee, crest, crown, culmination, head, height, high point, me~ ridian, peak, pinnacle, summit, vertex, zen~ ith **2.** cap, cork, cover, lid, stopper **3.** first place, head, highest rank, lead **4. blow one's top** *Inf.* blow up (*Inf.*), do one's nut (*Brit. sl.*), explode, fly into a temper, fly off the handle (*Inf.*), go spare (*Brit. sl.*), have a fit (*Inf.*), lose one's temper, see red (*Inf.*), throw a tantrum **5. over the top** a bit much (*Inf.*), excessive, going too far, im~ moderate, inordinate, over the limit, too much, uncalled-for ~*adj.* **6.** best, chief, crack (*Inf.*), crowning, culminating, domi~ nant, elite, finest, first, foremost, greatest, head, highest, lead, leading, pre-eminent, prime, principal, ruling, sovereign, superi~ or, topmost, upper, uppermost ~*v.* **7.** cap, cover, crown, finish, garnish, roof, tip **8.** ascend, climb, crest, reach the top of, scale, surmount **9.** be first, be in charge of, com~ mand, head, lead, rule **10.** beat, best, better, eclipse, exceed, excel, go beyond, outdo, outshine, outstrip, surpass, transcend **Antonyms** *n.* base, bottom, foot, nadir, underneath, underside ~*adj.* amateurish, bottom, incompetent, inept, inferior, least, lower, lowest, second-rate, unknown, unranked, worst ~*v.* be at the bottom of, fail to equal, fall short of, not be as good as

topic issue, matter, point, question, subject, subject matter, text, theme, thesis

topical 1. contemporary, current, news~ worthy, popular, up-to-date, up-to-the-minute **2.** local, parochial, regional, re~ stricted

topmost dominant, foremost, highest, lead~ ing, loftiest, paramount, principal, supreme, top, upper, uppermost **Antonyms** base, basic, bottom, bottommost, last, lowest, undermost

topple 1. capsize, collapse, fall, fall head~ long, fall over, keel over, knock down, knock over, overbalance, overturn, tip over, totter, tumble, upset **2.** bring down, bring low, oust, overthrow, overturn, unseat **Antonyms** (*sense 1*) ascend, build, mount, rise, tower

topsy-turvy chaotic, confused, disarranged, disorderly, disorganized, inside-out, jum~ bled, messy, mixed-up, untidy, upside-down **Antonyms** neat, ordered, orderly, organized, shipshape, systematic, tidy

torment *v.* **1.** afflict, agonize, crucify, dis~ tress, excruciate, harrow, pain, rack, tor~ ture **2.** aggravate (*Inf.*), annoy, bedevil, bother, chivvy, devil (*Inf.*), harass, harry,

hassle (*Inf.*), hound, irritate, nag, persecute, pester, plague, provoke, tease, trouble, vex, worry ~*n.* **3.** agony, anguish, distress, hell, misery, pain, suffering, torture **4.** affliction, annoyance, bane, bother, harassment, has~ sle (*Inf.*), irritation, nag, nagging, nuisance, pain in the neck (*Inf.*), persecution, pest, plague, provocation, scourge, thorn in one's flesh, trouble, vexation, worry **Antonyms** *v.* comfort, delight, ease, encour~ age, make happy, put at ease, reassure, soothe ~*n.* bliss, comfort, ease, ecstasy, encourage~ ment, happiness, joy, reassurance, rest

torn *adj.* **1.** cut, lacerated, ragged, rent, ripped, slit, split **2.** divided, in two minds (*Inf.*), irresolute, split, uncertain, undecided, unsure, vacillating, wavering

tornado cyclone, gale, hurricane, squall, storm, tempest, twister (*U.S. inf.*), typhoon, whirlwind, windstorm

torpor accidie, acedia, apathy, dormancy, drowsiness, dullness, inactivity, inanition, indolence, inertia, inertness, languor, lazi~ ness, lethargy, listlessness, numbness, pas~ sivity, sloth, sluggishness, somnolence, stagnancy, stupor, torpidity **Antonyms** animation, energy, get-up-and-go (*Inf.*), go, liveliness, pep, vigour

torrent cascade, deluge, downpour, effusion, flood, flow, gush, outburst, rush, spate, stream, tide

tortuous 1. bent, circuitous, convoluted, crooked, curved, indirect, mazy, meander~ ing, serpentine, sinuous, twisted, twisting, winding, zigzag **2.** ambiguous, complicated, convoluted, cunning, deceptive, devious, indirect, involved, mazy, misleading, roundabout, tricky **Antonyms** (*sense 2*) candid, direct, honest, ingenuous, open, reliable, straightforward, upright

torture 1. *v.* afflict, agonize, crucify, dis~ tress, excruciate, harrow, lacerate, martyr, pain, persecute, put on the rack, rack, tor~ ment **2.** *n.* affliction, agony, anguish, dis~ tress, hell, laceration, martyrdom, misery, pain, pang(s), persecution, rack, suffering, torment **Antonyms** (*sense 1*) alleviate, comfort, con~ sole, ease, mollify, relieve, salve, solace, soothe (*sense 2*) amusement, bliss, delight, en~ joyment, happiness, joy, pleasure, well-being

toss *v.* **1.** cast, chuck (*Inf.*), fling, flip, hurl, launch, lob (*Inf.*), pitch, project, propel, shy, sling, throw **2.** agitate, disturb, jiggle, jog~ gle, jolt, rock, roll, shake, thrash, tumble, wriggle, writhe **3.** heave, labour, lurch, pitch, roll, wallow ~*n.* **4.** cast, fling, lob (*Inf.*), pitch, shy, throw

tot[1] *n.* **1.** ankle-biter (*Aust. sl.*), baby, child, infant, little one, mite, rug rat (*Sl.*), sprog

(*Sl.*), toddler, wean (*Scot.*) **2.** dram, finger, measure, nip, shot (*Inf.*), slug, snifter (*Inf.*), toothful

tot² *v.* add up, calculate, count up, reckon, sum (up), tally, total

total 1. *n.* aggregate, all, amount, entirety, full amount, mass, sum, totality, whole **2.** *adj.* absolute, all-out, arrant, complete, comprehensive, consummate, deep-dyed (*Usually derogatory*), downright, entire, full, gross, integral, out-and-out, outright, per~ fect, sheer, sweeping, thorough, thorough~ going, unconditional, undisputed, undivid~ ed, unmitigated, unqualified, utter, whole **3.** *v.* add up, amount to, come to, mount up to, reach, reckon, sum up, tot up
Antonyms *n.* individual amount, part, sub~ total ~*adj.* conditional, fragmentary, incom~ plete, limited, mixed, part, partial, qualified, restricted, uncombined ~*v.* deduct, subtract

totalitarian authoritarian, despotic, dicta~ torial, monolithic, one-party, oppressive, tyrannous, undemocratic
Antonyms autonomous, democratic, egali~ tarian, popular, self-governing

totality 1. aggregate, all, entirety, every~ thing, sum, total, whole **2.** completeness, entireness, fullness, wholeness

totally absolutely, completely, comprehen~ sively, consummately, entirely, fully, per~ fectly, quite, thoroughly, unconditionally, unmitigatedly, utterly, wholeheartedly, wholly
Antonyms incompletely, in part, partially, partly, somewhat, to a certain extent

totter falter, lurch, quiver, reel, rock, shake, stagger, stumble, sway, teeter, tremble, walk unsteadily, waver

touch *n.* **1.** feel, feeling, handling, palpation, physical contact, tactility **2.** blow, brush, caress, contact, fondling, hit, pat, push, stroke, tap **3.** bit, dash, detail, drop, hint, intimation, jot, pinch, smack, small amount, smattering, *soupçon*, speck, spot, suggestion, suspicion, taste, tincture, tinge, trace, whiff **4.** direction, effect, hand, influence **5.** ap~ proach, characteristic, handiwork, manner, method, style, technique, trademark, way **6.** ability, adroitness, art, artistry, command, craft, deftness, facility, flair, knack, mas~ tery, skill, virtuosity **7.** acquaintance, awareness, communication, contact, corre~ spondence, familiarity, understanding ~*v.* **8.** brush, caress, contact, feel, finger, fondle, graze, handle, hit, lay a finger on, palpate, pat, push, strike, stroke, tap **9.** abut, adjoin, be in contact, border, brush, come together, contact, converge, graze, impinge upon, meet **10.** affect, disturb, get through to, get to (*Inf.*), have an effect on, impress, influence, inspire, make an impression on,

mark, melt, move, soften, stir, strike, upset **11.** be a party to, concern oneself with, consume, deal with, drink, eat, get involved in, handle, have to do with, partake of, use, utilize **12.** *With* **on** allude to, bring in, cov~ er, deal with, mention, refer to, speak of **13.** bear upon, concern, have to do with, interest, pertain to, regard **14.** be a match for, be in the same league as, be on a par with, come near, come up to, compare with, equal, hold a candle to (*Inf.*), match, paral~ lel, rival **15.** arrive at, attain, come to, reach

touchiness bad temper, crabbedness, fret~ fulness, grouchiness (*Inf.*), irascibility, irri~ tability, peevishness, pettishness, petulance, surliness, testiness, tetchiness, ticklishness

touching affecting, emotive, heartbreaking, melting, moving, pathetic, piteous, pitiable, pitiful, poignant, sad, stirring, tender

touchstone criterion, gauge, measure, norm, par, standard, yardstick

touch up 1. finish off, perfect, put the finishing touches to, round off **2.** brush up, enhance, fake (up), falsify, give a face-lift to, gloss over, improve, patch up, polish up, renovate, retouch, revamp, titivate, white~ wash (*Inf.*)

touchy bad-tempered, captious, crabbed, cross, easily offended, grouchy (*Inf.*), grumpy, irascible, irritable, oversensitive, peevish, pettish, petulant, querulous, quick-tempered, ratty (*Brit. & N.Z. inf.*), splenetic, surly, testy, tetchy, thin-skinned, ticklish
Antonyms affable, cheerful, easy-going, ge~ nial, good-humoured, imperious, indifferent, insensitive, light-hearted, pleasant, sunny, sweet, thick-skinned, unconcerned

tough *adj.* **1.** cohesive, durable, firm, hard, inflexible, leathery, resilient, resistant, rig~ id, rugged, solid, stiff, strong, sturdy, tena~ cious **2.** brawny, fit, hard as nails, hard~ ened, hardy, resilient, seasoned, stalwart, stout, strapping, strong, sturdy, vigorous **3.** hard-bitten, pugnacious, rough, ruffianly, ruthless, vicious, violent **4.** adamant, cal~ lous, exacting, firm, hard, hard-boiled (*Inf.*), hard-nosed (*Inf.*), inflexible, intractable, merciless, obdurate, obstinate, refractory, resolute, severe, stern, strict, stubborn, un~ bending, unforgiving, unyielding **5.** ardu~ ous, baffling, difficult, exacting, exhausting, hard, intractable, irksome, knotty, labori~ ous, perplexing, puzzling, strenuous, thorny, troublesome, uphill **6.** *Inf.* bad, hard cheese (*Brit. sl.*), hard lines (*Brit. inf.*), hard luck, lamentable, regrettable, too bad (*Inf.*), unfortunate, unlucky ~*n.* **7.** bravo, bruiser (*Inf.*), brute, bully, bully boy, heavy

(*Sl.*), hooligan, rough (*Inf.*), roughneck (*Sl.*), rowdy, ruffian, thug

Antonyms accommodating, benign, civi~ lized, compassionate, considerate, delicate, easy, easy-peasy (*Sl.*), flexible, flimsy, fragile, gentle, humane, indulgent, kind, lenient, merciful, mild, simple, soft, sympathetic, ten~ der, unexacting, weak

tour *n.* **1.** excursion, expedition, jaunt, jour~ ney, outing, peregrination, progress, trip **2.** circuit, course, round ~*v.* **3.** explore, go on the road, go round, holiday in, journey, sightsee, travel round, travel through, visit

tourist excursionist, globetrotter, holiday~ maker, journeyer, sightseer, traveller, trip~ per, voyager

tournament 1. competition, contest, event, match, meeting, series **2.** *Medieval* joust, the lists, tourney

tow *v.* drag, draw, haul, lug, pull, trail, trawl, tug

towards 1. en route for, for, in the direc~ tion of, in the vicinity of, on the road to, on the way to, to **2.** about, concerning, for, re~ garding, with regard to, with respect to **3.** almost, close to, coming up to, getting on for, just before, nearing, nearly, not quite, shortly before

tower *n.* **1.** belfry, column, obelisk, pillar, skyscraper, steeple, turret **2.** castle, citadel, fort, fortification, fortress, keep, refuge, stronghold ~*v.* **3.** ascend, be head and shoulders above, dominate, exceed, loom, mount, overlook, overtop, rear, rise, soar, surpass, top, transcend

toxic baneful (*Archaic*), deadly, harmful, le~ thal, noxious, pernicious, pestilential, poi~ sonous, septic

Antonyms harmless, invigorating, non~ poisonous, nontoxic, safe, salubrious

toy *n.* **1.** doll, game, plaything **2.** bauble, gewgaw, knick-knack, trifle, trinket ~*v.* **3.** amuse oneself, dally, fiddle (*Inf.*), flirt, fool (about *or* around), play, sport, trifle, wanton

trace *n.* **1.** evidence, indication, mark, rec~ ord, relic, remains, remnant, sign, survival, token, vestige **2.** bit, dash, drop, hint, iota, jot, shadow, soupçon, suggestion, suspicion, tincture, tinge, touch, trifle, whiff **3.** foot~ mark, footprint, footstep, path, slot, spoor, track, trail ~*v.* **4.** ascertain, detect, deter~ mine, discover, ferret out, find, follow, hunt down, pursue, search for, seek, shadow, stalk, track, trail, unearth **5.** chart, copy, delineate, depict, draw, map, mark out, outline, record, show, sketch

track *n.* **1.** footmark, footprint, footstep, mark, path, scent, slipstream, slot, spoor, trace, trail, wake **2.** course, flight path, line, orbit, path, pathway, road, track, tra~ jectory, way **3.** line, permanent way, rail,

rails **4. keep track of** follow, keep an eye on, keep in sight, keep in touch with, keep up to date with, keep up with, monitor, oversee, watch **5. lose track of** lose, lose sight of, misplace ~*v.* **6.** chase, dog, follow, follow the trail of, hunt down, pursue, shadow, stalk, tail (*Inf.*), trace, trail

track down apprehend, bring to light, cap~ ture, catch, dig up, discover, expose, ferret out, find, hunt down, run to earth, sniff out, trace, unearth

tracks 1. footprints, impressions, imprints, tyremarks, tyreprints, wheelmarks **2. make tracks** beat it (*Sl.*), depart, disappear, get going, get moving, go, head off, hit the road (*Sl.*), leave, set out, split (*Sl.*), take off (*Inf.*) **3. stop in one's tracks** bring to a standstill, freeze, immobilize, petrify, rivet to the spot, stop dead, transfix

tract[1] area, district, estate, expanse, extent, lot, plot, quarter, region, stretch, territory, zone

tract[2] booklet, brochure, disquisition, dis~ sertation, essay, homily, leaflet, monograph, pamphlet, tractate, treatise

tractable 1. amenable, biddable, compliant, controllable, docile, governable, manage~ able, obedient, persuadable, submissive, tame, willing, yielding **2.** ductile, fictile, malleable, plastic, pliable, pliant, tensile, tractile, workable

Antonyms defiant, headstrong, obstinate, refractory, stiff-necked, stubborn, unruly, wilful

traction adhesion, drag, draught, drawing, friction, grip, haulage, pull, pulling, pur~ chase, resistance

trade *n.* **1.** barter, business, buying and selling, commerce, dealing, exchange, traffic, transactions, truck **2.** avocation, business, calling, craft, employment, job, line, line of work, métier, occupation, pro~ fession, pursuit, skill **3.** deal, exchange, interchange, swap **4.** clientele, custom, customers, market, patrons, public ~*v.* **5.** bargain, barter, buy and sell, deal, do busi~ ness, exchange, have dealings, peddle, traffic, transact, truck **6.** barter, exchange, swap, switch

trader broker, buyer, dealer, marketer, merchandiser, merchant, purveyor, seller, supplier

tradesman 1. dealer, merchant, purveyor, retailer, seller, shopkeeper, supplier, vendor **2.** artisan, craftsman, journeyman, skilled worker, workman

tradition convention, custom, customs, es~ tablished practice, folklore, habit, institu~ tion, lore, praxis, ritual, unwritten law, usage

traditional accustomed, ancestral, conven~
tional, customary, established, fixed, folk,
historic, long-established, old, oral, time-
honoured, transmitted, unwritten, usual
Antonyms avant-garde, contemporary,
ground-breaking, innovative, modern, new,
novel, off-the-wall (*Sl.*), original, revolution~
ary, unconventional, unusual

traffic *n.* **1.** coming and going, freight,
movement, passengers, transport, transpor~
tation, vehicles **2.** barter, business, buying
and selling, commerce, communication,
dealing, dealings, doings, exchange, inter~
course, peddling, relations, trade, truck ~*v.*
3. bargain, barter, buy and sell, deal, do
business, exchange, have dealings, have
transactions, market, peddle, trade, truck

tragedy adversity, affliction, bummer (*Sl.*),
calamity, catastrophe, disaster, grievous
blow, misfortune
Antonyms fortune, happiness, joy, prosper~
ity, success

tragic anguished, appalling, awful, calami~
tous, catastrophic, deadly, dire, disastrous,
dismal, doleful, dreadful, fatal, grievous,
heartbreaking, heart-rending, ill-fated, ill-
starred, lamentable, miserable, mournful,
pathetic, pitiable, ruinous, sad, shocking,
sorrowful, unfortunate, woeful, wretched
Antonyms agreeable, beneficial, cheerful,
comic, fortunate, glorious, happy, joyful,
lucky, satisfying, worthwhile

trail *v.* **1.** dangle, drag, draw, hang down,
haul, pull, stream, tow **2.** chase, follow,
hunt, pursue, shadow, stalk, tail (*Inf.*),
trace, track **3.** bring up the rear, dawdle,
drag oneself, fall behind, follow, hang back,
lag, linger, loiter, straggle, traipse (*Inf.*) **4.**
dangle, droop, extend, hang, straggle ~*n.* **5.**
footprints, footsteps, mark, marks, path,
scent, slipstream, spoor, trace, track, wake
6. beaten track, footpath, path, road, route,
track, way **7.** appendage, stream, tail, train

train *v.* **1.** coach, discipline, drill, educate,
guide, improve, instruct, prepare, rear, re~
hearse, school, teach, tutor **2.** exercise, im~
prove, prepare, work out **3.** aim, bring to
bear, direct, focus, level, line up, point ~*n.*
4. chain, concatenation, course, order, pro~
gression, sequence, series, set, string, suc~
cession **5.** caravan, column, convoy, file,
procession **6.** appendage, tail, trail **7.** at~
tendants, cortege, court, entourage, follow~
ers, following, household, retinue, staff,
suite

trainer coach, handler

training **1.** coaching, discipline, education,
grounding, guidance, instruction, schooling,
teaching, tuition, tutelage, upbringing **2.**
body building, exercise, practice, prepara~
tion, working-out

trait attribute, characteristic, feature, idio~
syncrasy, lineament, mannerism, peculiar~
ity, quality, quirk

traitor apostate, back-stabber, betrayer, de~
ceiver, defector, deserter, double-crosser
(*Inf.*), fifth columnist, informer, Judas, mis~
creant, quisling, rebel, renegade, snake in
the grass (*Inf.*), turncoat
Antonyms defender, loyalist, patriot, sup~
porter

traitorous apostate, disloyal, double-
crossing (*Inf.*), double-dealing, faithless,
false, perfidious, renegade, seditious,
treacherous, treasonable, unfaithful, untrue
Antonyms constant, faithful, loyal, patriot~
ic, staunch, steadfast, true, trusty

trajectory course, flight, flight path, line,
path, route, track

trammel **1.** *n.* bar, block, bond, chain,
check, clog, curb, fetter, handicap, hin~
drance, impediment, obstacle, rein, shackle,
stumbling block **2.** *v.* bar, block, capture,
catch, check, clog, curb, enmesh, ensnare,
entrap, fetter, hamper, handicap, hinder,
impede, net, restrain, restrict, snag, tie
Antonyms *v.* advance, assist, expedite, fa~
cilitate, foster, further, promote, support

tramp *v.* **1.** footslog, hike, march, ramble,
range, roam, rove, slog, trek, walk, yomp **2.**
march, plod, stamp, stump, toil, traipse
(*Inf.*), trudge, walk heavily **3.** crush, stamp,
stomp (*Inf.*), trample, tread, walk over ~*n.*
4. bag lady (*Chiefly U.S.*), bum (*Inf.*), der~
elict, dosser (*Brit. sl.*), down-and-out, drifter,
hobo (*Chiefly U.S.*), vagabond, vagrant **5.**
hike, march, ramble, slog, trek **6.** footfall,
footstep, stamp, tread

trample **1.** crush, flatten, run over, squash,
stamp, tread, walk over **2.** do violence to,
encroach upon, hurt, infringe, ride rough~
shod over, show no consideration for, vio~
late

trance abstraction, daze, dream, ecstasy,
hypnotic state, muse, rapture, reverie, spell,
stupor, unconsciousness

tranquil at peace, calm, composed, cool,
pacific, peaceful, placid, quiet, restful, se~
date, serene, still, undisturbed, unexcited,
unperturbed, unruffled, untroubled
Antonyms agitated, busy, confused, dis~
turbed, excited, hectic, restless, troubled

tranquillity ataraxia, calm, calmness, com~
posure, coolness, equanimity, hush, imper~
turbability, peace, peacefulness, placidity,
quiet, quietness, quietude, repose, rest,
restfulness, sedateness, serenity, stillness
Antonyms agitation, commotion, confusion,
disturbance, excitement, noise, restlessness,
turmoil, upset

tranquillize calm, compose, lull, pacify,

quell, quiet, relax, sedate, settle one's nerves, soothe
Antonyms agitate, confuse, distress, disturb, harass, perturb, ruffle, trouble, upset

tranquillizer barbiturate, bromide, downer (*Sl.*), opiate, red (*Sl.*), sedative

transact accomplish, carry on, carry out, conclude, conduct, discharge, do, enact, execute, handle, manage, negotiate, perform, prosecute, see to, settle, take care of

transaction 1. action, affair, bargain, business, coup, deal, deed, enterprise, event, matter, negotiation, occurrence, proceeding, undertaking **2.** *Plural* affairs, annals, doings, goings-on (*Inf.*), minutes, proceedings, record

transcend eclipse, exceed, excel, go above, go beyond, leave behind, leave in the shade (*Inf.*), outdo, outrival, outshine, outstrip, outvie, overstep, rise above, surpass

transcendence, transcendency ascendancy, excellence, greatness, incomparability, matchlessness, paramountcy, preeminence, sublimity, superiority, supremacy

transcendent consummate, exceeding, extraordinary, incomparable, matchless, peerless, pre-eminent, second to none, sublime, superior, transcendental, unequalled, unique, unparalleled, unrivalled

transcribe 1. copy out, engross, note, reproduce, rewrite, set out, take down, transfer, write out **2.** interpret, render, translate, transliterate **3.** record, tape, tape-record

transcript carbon, carbon copy, copy, duplicate, manuscript, note, notes, record, reproduction, transcription, translation, transliteration, version

transfer 1. *v.* carry, change, consign, convey, displace, hand over, make over, move, pass on, relocate, remove, shift, translate, transmit, transplant, transport, transpose, turn over **2.** *n.* change, displacement, handover, move, relocation, removal, shift, transference, translation, transmission, transposition

transfix 1. engross, fascinate, halt *or* stop in one's tracks, hold, hypnotize, mesmerize, paralyse, petrify, rivet the attention of, root to the spot, spellbind, stop dead, stun **2.** fix, impale, pierce, puncture, run through, skewer, spear, spit, transpierce
Antonyms (*sense 1*) bore, fatigue, tire, weary

transform alter, change, convert, make over, metamorphose, reconstruct, remodel, renew, revolutionize, transfigure, translate, transmogrify (*Jocular*), transmute

transformation alteration, change, conversion, metamorphosis, radical change, renewal, revolution, revolutionary change,

sea change, transfiguration, transmogrification (*Jocular*), transmutation

transgress be out of order, break, break the law, contravene, defy, disobey, do *or* go wrong, encroach, err, exceed, fall from grace, go astray, go beyond, infringe, lapse, misbehave, offend, overstep, sin, trespass, violate

transgression breach, contravention, crime, encroachment, error, fault, infraction, infringement, iniquity, lapse, misbehaviour, misdeed, misdemeanour, offence, peccadillo, sin, trespass, violation, wrong, wrongdoing

transgressor criminal, culprit, delinquent, evildoer, felon, lawbreaker, malefactor, miscreant, offender, sinner, trespasser, villain, wrongdoer

transient brief, ephemeral, evanescent, fleeting, flying, fugacious, fugitive, here today and gone tomorrow, impermanent, momentary, passing, short, short-lived, short-term, temporary, transitory
Antonyms abiding, constant, durable, enduring, eternal, imperishable, long-lasting, long-term, permanent, perpetual, persistent, undying

transit *n.* **1.** carriage, conveyance, crossing, motion, movement, passage, portage, shipment, transfer, transport, transportation, travel, traverse **2.** alteration, change, changeover, conversion, shift, transition **3. in transit** during passage, en route, on the journey, on the move, on the road, on the way, while travelling ~*v.* **4.** cross, journey, move, pass, travel, traverse

transition alteration, change, changeover, conversion, development, evolution, flux, metamorphosis, metastasis, passage, passing, progression, shift, transit, transmutation, upheaval

transitional changing, developmental, fluid, intermediate, passing, provisional, temporary, transitionary, unsettled

transitory brief, ephemeral, evanescent, fleeting, flying, fugacious, here today and gone tomorrow, impermanent, momentary, passing, short, short-lived, short-term, temporary, transient
Antonyms abiding, enduring, eternal, everlasting, lasting, long-lived, long-term, permanent, perpetual, persistent, undying

translate 1. construe, convert, decipher, decode, interpret, paraphrase, render, transcribe, transliterate **2.** elucidate, explain, make clear, paraphrase, put in plain English, simplify, spell out, state in layman's language **3.** alter, change, convert, metamorphose, transfigure, transform, transmute, turn **4.** carry, convey, move, remove,

send, transfer, transplant, transport, trans~
pose

translation 1. construction, decoding,
gloss, interpretation, paraphrase, rendering,
rendition, transcription, transliteration,
version **2.** elucidation, explanation, para~
phrase, rephrasing, rewording, simplifica~
tion **3.** alteration, change, conversion,
metamorphosis, transfiguration, transfor~
mation, transmutation **4.** conveyance,
move, removal, transference, transposition

translator interpreter, linguist, metaphrast,
paraphrast

transmission 1. carriage, communication,
conveyance, diffusion, dispatch, dissemina~
tion, remission, sending, shipment, spread,
transfer, transference, transport **2.** broad~
casting, dissemination, putting out, relay~
ing, sending, showing **3.** broadcast, pro~
gramme, show

transmit 1. bear, carry, communicate, con~
vey, diffuse, dispatch, disseminate, forward,
hand down, hand on, impart, pass on, re~
mit, send, spread, take, transfer, transport
2. broadcast, disseminate, put on the air,
radio, relay, send, send out

transparency 1. clarity, clearness, di~
aphaneity, diaphanousness, filminess,
gauziness, limpidity, limpidness, pellucid~
ity, pellucidness, sheerness, translucence,
translucency, transparence **2.** apparentness,
distinctness, explicitness, obviousness,
patentness, perspicuousness, plainness,
unambiguousness, visibility **3.** candidness,
directness, forthrightness, frankness, open~
ness, straightforwardness **4.** photograph,
slide
Antonyms (*sense 1*) ambiguity, cloudiness,
murkiness, obscurity, opacity, unclearness,
vagueness

transparent 1. clear, crystal clear, crystal~
line, diaphanous, filmy, gauzy, limpid, lu~
cent, lucid, pellucid, seethrough, sheer,
translucent, transpicuous **2.** apparent, as
plain as the nose on one's face (*Inf.*), dis~
tinct, easy, evident, explicit, manifest, obvi~
ous, patent, perspicuous, plain, recogniz~
able, unambiguous, understandable, undis~
guised, visible **3.** candid, direct, forthright,
frank, open, plain-spoken, straight,
straightforward, unambiguous, unequivocal
Antonyms ambiguous, cloudy, deceptive,
disingenuous, hidden, muddy, mysterious,
opaque, thick, turbid, uncertain, unclear,
vague

transpire 1. *Inf.* arise, befall, chance, come
about, come to pass (*Archaic*), happen, oc~
cur, take place, turn up **2.** become known,
be disclosed, be discovered, be made public,
come out, come to light, emerge

transplant displace, relocate, remove, re~
settle, shift, transfer, uproot

transport *v.* **1.** bear, bring, carry, convey,
fetch, haul, move, remove, run, ship, take,
transfer **2.** banish, deport, exile, sentence to
transportation **3.** captivate, carry away,
delight, electrify, enchant, enrapture, en~
trance, move, ravish, spellbind ~*n.* **4.** con~
veyance, transportation, vehicle **5.** carriage,
conveyance, removal, shipment, shipping,
transference, transportation **6.** cloud nine
(*Inf.*), enchantment, euphoria, heaven, rap~
ture, seventh heaven **7.** bliss, delight, ec~
stasy, happiness, ravishment
Antonyms (*sense 6*) blues (*Inf.*), depression,
despondency, doldrums, dumps (*Inf.*), melan~
choly

transpose alter, change, exchange, inter~
change, move, rearrange, relocate, reorder,
shift, substitute, swap (*Inf.*), switch, trans~
fer

transverse athwart, crossways, crosswise,
diagonal, oblique

trap *n.* **1.** ambush, gin, net, noose, pitfall,
snare, springe, toils **2.** ambush, artifice,
deception, device, ruse, stratagem, subter~
fuge, trick, wile ~*v.* **3.** catch, corner, en~
mesh, ensnare, entrap, snare, take **4.** am~
bush, beguile, deceive, dupe, ensnare, in~
veigle, trick

trapped ambushed, at bay, beguiled, caught,
cornered, cut off, deceived, duped, en~
snared, in a tight corner, in a tight spot,
inveigled, netted, snared, stuck (*Inf.*), sur~
rounded, tricked, with one's back to the
wall

trappings accoutrements, adornments,
decorations, dress, equipment, finery,
fittings, fixtures, fripperies, furnishings,
gear, livery, ornaments, panoply, parapher~
nalia, raiment (*Archaic or poetic*), things,
trimmings

trash 1. balderdash, balls (*Taboo sl.*), bilge
(*Inf.*), bosh (*Inf.*), bull (*Sl.*), bullshit (*Taboo
sl.*), bunkum *or* buncombe (*Chiefly U.S.*),
cobblers (*Brit. taboo sl.*), crap (*Sl.*), drivel,
eyewash (*Inf.*), foolish talk, garbage (*Inf.*),
guff (*Sl.*), hogwash, hokum (*Sl., chiefly U.S.
& Canad.*), horsefeathers (*U.S. sl.*), hot air
(*Inf.*), inanity, moonshine, nonsense, pap,
piffle (*Inf.*), poppycock (*Inf.*), rot, rubbish,
shit (*Taboo sl.*), tommyrot, tosh (*Sl., chiefly
Brit.*), tripe (*Inf.*), trumpery, twaddle **2.**
dreck (*Sl., chiefly U.S.*), dregs, dross, gar~
bage, junk (*Inf.*), litter, offscourings, refuse,
rubbish, sweepings, waste
Antonyms (*sense 1*) logic, reason, sense,
significance

trashy brummagem, catchpenny, cheap,
cheap-jack (*Inf.*), chickenshit (*U.S. sl.*),
crappy (*Sl.*), flimsy, inferior, meretricious,

of a sort *or* of sorts, poxy (*Sl.*), rubbishy, shabby, shoddy, tawdry, thrown together, tinsel, worthless
Antonyms A1 *or* A-one (*Inf.*), excellent, exceptional, first-class, first-rate, outstanding, superlative

traumatic agonizing, damaging, disturbing, hurtful, injurious, painful, scarring, shocking, upsetting, wounding
Antonyms calming, healing, helpful, relaxing, therapeutic, wholesome

travel *v.* **1.** cross, go, journey, make a journey, make one's way, move, proceed, progress, ramble, roam, rove, take a trip, tour, traverse, trek, voyage, walk, wander, wend **2.** be transmitted, carry, get through, move ~*n.* **3.** *Usually plural* excursion, expedition, globetrotting, journey, movement, passage, peregrination, ramble, tour, touring, trip, voyage, walk, wandering

traveller **1.** excursionist, explorer, globetrotter, gypsy, hiker, holiday-maker, journeyer, migrant, nomad, passenger, tourist, tripper, voyager, wanderer, wayfarer **2.** agent, commercial traveller, rep, representative, salesman, travelling salesman

travelling *adj.* itinerant, migrant, migratory, mobile, moving, nomadic, peripatetic, restless, roaming, roving, touring, unsettled, wandering, wayfaring

traverse **1.** bridge, cover, cross, cut across, go across, go over, make one's way across, negotiate, pass over, ply, range, roam, span, travel over, wander **2.** balk, contravene, counter, counteract, deny, frustrate, go against, hinder, impede, obstruct, oppose, thwart **3.** check, consider, examine, eye, inspect, investigate, look into, look over, pore over, range over, review, scan, scrutinize, study

travesty **1.** *n.* burlesque, caricature, distortion, lampoon, mockery, parody, perversion, send-up (*Brit. inf.*), sham, spoof (*Inf.*), take-off (*Inf.*) **2.** *v.* burlesque, caricature, deride, distort, lampoon, make a mockery of, make fun of, mock, parody, pervert, ridicule, send up (*Brit. inf.*), sham, spoof (*Inf.*), take off (*Inf.*)

treacherous **1.** deceitful, disloyal, double-crossing (*Inf.*), double-dealing, duplicitous, faithless, false, perfidious, recreant (*Archaic*), traitorous, treasonable, unfaithful, unreliable, untrue, untrustworthy **2.** dangerous, deceptive, hazardous, icy, perilous, precarious, risky, slippery, slippy (*Inf. or dialect*), tricky, unreliable, unsafe, unstable
Antonyms dependable, faithful, loyal, reliable, safe, true, trustworthy

treachery betrayal, disloyalty, double-cross (*Inf.*), double-dealing, duplicity, faithlessness, infidelity, perfidiousness, perfidy, stab in the back, treason
Antonyms allegiance, dependability, faithfulness, fealty, fidelity, loyalty, reliability

tread *v.* **1.** hike, march, pace, plod, stamp, step, stride, tramp, trudge, walk **2.** crush underfoot, squash, trample **3.** bear down, crush, oppress, quell, repress, ride roughshod over, subdue, subjugate, suppress **4.** **tread on someone's toes** affront, annoy, bruise, disgruntle, get someone's back up, hurt, hurt someone's feelings, infringe, injure, irk, offend, vex ~*n.* **5.** footfall, footstep, gait, pace, step, stride, walk

treason disaffection, disloyalty, duplicity, lese-majesty, mutiny, perfidy, sedition, subversion, traitorousness, treachery
Antonyms allegiance, faithfulness, fealty, fidelity, loyalty, patriotism

treasonable disloyal, false, mutinous, perfidious, seditious, subversive, traitorous, treacherous, treasonous
Antonyms dependable, faithful, loyal, patriotic, reliable, trustworthy

treasure *n.* **1.** cash, fortune, funds, gold, jewels, money, riches, valuables, wealth **2.** apple of one's eye, darling, gem, jewel, nonpareil, paragon, pearl, precious, pride and joy, prize ~*v.* **3.** adore, cherish, dote upon, esteem, hold dear, idolize, love, prize, revere, value, venerate, worship **4.** accumulate, cache, collect, garner, hoard, husband, lay up, salt away, save, stash (away) (*Inf.*), store up

treasury **1.** bank, cache, hoard, repository, store, storehouse, vault **2.** assets, capital, coffers, exchequer, finances, funds, money, resources, revenues

treat *n.* **1.** banquet, celebration, entertainment, feast, gift, party, refreshment **2.** delight, enjoyment, fun, gratification, joy, pleasure, satisfaction, surprise, thrill ~*v.* **3.** act towards, behave towards, consider, deal with, handle, look upon, manage, regard, use **4.** apply treatment to, attend to, care for, doctor, medicate, nurse **5.** buy for, entertain, feast, foot *or* pay the bill, give, lay on, pay for, provide, regale, stand (*Inf.*), take out, wine and dine **6.** be concerned with, contain, deal with, discourse upon, discuss, go into, touch upon **7.** bargain, come to terms, confer, have talks, make terms, negotiate, parley

treatise disquisition, dissertation, essay, exposition, monograph, pamphlet, paper, study, thesis, tract, work, writing

treatment **1.** care, cure, healing, medication, medicine, remedy, surgery, therapy **2.** action towards, behaviour towards, conduct, dealing, handling, management, manipulation, reception, usage

treaty agreement, alliance, bargain, bond, compact, concordat, contract, convention, covenant, entente, pact

trek 1. *n.* expedition, footslog, hike, journey, long haul, march, odyssey, safari, slog, tramp **2.** *v.* footslog, hike, journey, march, plod, range, roam, rove, slog, traipse (*Inf.*), tramp, trudge, yomp

tremble 1. *v.* oscillate, quake, quiver, rock, shake, shake in one's shoes, shiver, shud~ der, teeter, totter, vibrate, wobble **2.** *n.* os~ cillation, quake, quiver, shake, shiver, shudder, tremor, vibration, wobble

tremendous 1. appalling, awesome, awful, colossal, deafening, dreadful, enormous, fearful, formidable, frightful, gargantuan, gigantic, great, huge, immense, mammoth, monstrous, prodigious, stupendous, terrible, terrific, titanic, towering, vast, whopping (*Inf.*) **2.** *Inf.* ace (*Inf.*), amazing, boffo (*Sl.*), brill (*Inf.*), brilliant, chillin' (*U.S. sl.*), cracking (*Brit. inf.*), excellent, exceptional, extraordinary, fabulous (*Inf.*), fantastic (*Inf.*), great, incredible, jim-dandy (*Sl.*), marvellous, mean (*Sl.*), sensational (*Inf.*), sovereign, super (*Inf.*), terrific (*Inf.*), top~ ping (*Brit. sl.*), wonderful
Antonyms appalling, average, awful, di~ minutive, dreadful, little, mediocre, minus~ cule, minute, ordinary, rotten, run-of-the-mill, small, so-so, terrible, tiny

tremor 1. agitation, quaking, quaver, quiv~ er, quivering, shake, shaking, shiver, trem~ ble, trembling, trepidation, vibration, wob~ ble **2.** earthquake, quake (*Inf.*), shock

trench channel, cut, ditch, drain, earthwork, entrenchment, excavation, fosse, furrow, gutter, pit, trough, waterway

trenchant 1. acerbic, acid, acidulous, acute, astringent, biting, caustic, cutting, hurtful, incisive, keen, mordacious, mor~ dant, penetrating, piquant, pointed, pun~ gent, sarcastic, scathing, severe, sharp, tart, vitriolic **2.** driving, effective, effectual, em~ phatic, energetic, forceful, potent, powerful, strong, vigorous **3.** clear, clear-cut, crisp, distinct, distinctly defined, explicit, salient, unequivocal, well-defined
Antonyms (*sense 1*) appeasing, kind, molli~ fying, soothing (*sense 3*) ill-defined, indistinct, nebulous, obscure, unclear, vague, woolly

trend *n.* **1.** bias, course, current, direction, drift, flow, inclination, leaning, tendency **2.** craze, fad (*Inf.*), fashion, look, mode, rage, style, thing, vogue ~*v.* **3.** bend, flow, head, incline, lean, run, stretch, swing, tend, turn, veer

trepidation agitation, alarm, anxiety, ap~ prehension, blue funk (*Inf.*), butterflies (*Inf.*), cold feet (*Inf.*), cold sweat (*Inf.*), con~ sternation, dismay, disquiet, disturbance,

dread, emotion, excitement, fear, fright, jit~ ters (*Inf.*), nervousness, palpitation, pertur~ bation, quivering, shaking, the heebie-jeebies (*Sl.*), trembling, tremor, uneasiness, worry
Antonyms aplomb, calm, composure, confidence, coolness, equanimity, self-assurance

trespass *v.* **1.** encroach, infringe, intrude, invade, obtrude, poach **2.** *Archaic* offend, sin, transgress, violate, wrong ~*n.* **3.** en~ croachment, infringement, intrusion, inva~ sion, poaching, unlawful entry, wrongful entry **4.** breach, crime, delinquency, error, evildoing, fault, infraction, iniquity, injury, misbehaviour, misconduct, misdeed, mis~ demeanour, offence, sin, transgression, wrongdoing

trespasser 1. infringer, interloper, intrud~ er, invader, poacher, unwelcome visitor **2.** *Archaic* criminal, delinquent, evildoer, malefactor, offender, sinner, transgressor, wrongdoer

tress braid, curl, lock, pigtail, plait, ringlet

triad threesome, trilogy, trine, trinity, trio, triple, triplet, triptych, triumvirate, triune

trial *n.* **1.** assay, audition, check, dry run (*Inf.*), examination, experience, experiment, probation, proof, test, testing, test-run **2.** contest, hearing, industrial tribunal, judi~ cial examination, litigation, tribunal **3.** at~ tempt, crack (*Inf.*), effort, endeavour, go (*Inf.*), shot (*Inf.*), stab (*Inf.*), try, venture, whack (*Inf.*) **4.** adversity, affliction, burden, cross to bear, distress, grief, hardship, hard times, load, misery, ordeal, pain, suffering, tribulation, trouble, unhappiness, vexation, woe, wretchedness **5.** bane, bother, drag (*Inf.*), hassle (*Inf.*), irritation, nuisance, pain in the arse (*Taboo inf.*), pain in the neck (*Inf.*), pest, plague (*Inf.*), thorn in one's flesh, vexation ~*adj.* **6.** experimental, ex~ ploratory, pilot, probationary, provisional, testing

tribe blood, caste, clan, class, division, dyn~ asty, ethnic group, family, gens, house, people, race, seed (*Chiefly biblical*), sept, stock

tribulation adversity, affliction, bad luck, blow, bummer (*Sl.*), burden, care, cross to bear, curse, distress, grief, hardship, hassle (*Inf.*), heartache, ill fortune, misery, mis~ fortune, ordeal, pain, reverse, sorrow, suf~ fering, trial, trouble, unhappiness, vexation, woe, worry, wretchedness
Antonyms blessing, bliss, ease, good for~ tune, happiness, joy, pleasure, rest

tribunal bar, bench, court, hearing, indus~ trial tribunal, judgment seat, judicial ex~ amination, trial

tribute 1. accolade, acknowledgment, ap~

plause, commendation, compliment, enco~
mium, esteem, eulogy, gift, gratitude, hon~
our, laudation, panegyric, praise, recogni~
tion, respect, testimonial **2.** charge, contri~
bution, customs, duty, excise, homage, im~
post, offering, payment, ransom, subsidy,
tax, toll
Antonyms (*sense 1*) blame, complaint, con~
demnation, criticism, disapproval, reproach,
reproof

trick *n.* **1.** artifice, canard, con (*Sl.*), deceit,
deception, device, dodge, feint, fraud, gim~
mick, hoax, imposition, imposture, ma~
noeuvre, ploy, ruse, scam (*Sl.*), sting (*Inf.*),
stratagem, subterfuge, swindle, trap, wile **2.**
antic, cantrip (*Scot.*), caper, device, feat,
frolic, gag (*Inf.*), gambol, jape, joke, juggle,
legerdemain, leg-pull (*Brit. inf.*), practical
joke, prank, put-on (*Sl.*), sleight of hand,
stunt **3.** art, command, craft, device, exper~
tise, gift, hang (*Inf.*), knack, know-how
(*Inf.*), secret, skill, technique **4.** character~
istic, crotchet, foible, habit, idiosyncrasy,
mannerism, peculiarity, practice, quirk,
trait **5. do the trick** *Inf.* be effective *or* ef~
fectual, have effect, produce the desired re~
sult, work ~*v.* **6.** bamboozle (*Inf.*), cheat,
con (*Inf.*), deceive, defraud, delude, dupe,
fool, gull (*Archaic*), have (someone) on,
hoax, hoodwink, impose upon, kid (*Inf.*),
mislead, pull the wool over (someone's)
eyes, put one over on (someone) (*Inf.*), stiff
(*Sl.*), sting (*Inf.*), swindle, take in (*Inf.*), trap

trickery cheating, chicanery, con (*Inf.*), de~
ceit, deception, dishonesty, double-dealing,
fraud, funny business, guile, hanky-panky
(*Inf.*), hoax, hokum (*Sl., chiefly U.S. &
Canad.*), imposture, jiggery-pokery (*Inf.,
chiefly Brit.*), monkey business (*Inf.*), pre~
tence, skulduggery (*Inf.*), swindling
Antonyms artlessness, candour, directness,
frankness, honesty, openness, straight~
forwardness, uprightness

trickle 1. *v.* crawl, creep, dribble, drip, drop,
exude, ooze, percolate, run, seep, stream **2.**
n. dribble, drip, seepage

tricky 1. complicated, delicate, difficult,
knotty, problematic, risky, sticky (*Inf.*),
thorny, ticklish, touch-and-go **2.** artful,
crafty, cunning, deceitful, deceptive, devi~
ous, foxy, scheming, slippery, sly, subtle,
wily
Antonyms (*sense 1*) clear, easy, obvious,
simple, straightforward, uncomplicated
(*sense 2*) above board, artless, direct, genuine,
honest, ingenuous, open, sincere, truthful

trifle *n.* **1.** bagatelle, bauble, child's play
(*Inf.*), gewgaw, knick-knack, nothing, play~
thing, toy, triviality **2.** bit, dash, drop, jot,
little, pinch, spot, touch, trace ~*v.* **3.** amuse
oneself, coquet, dally, dawdle, flirt, fritter,

idle, mess about, palter, play, toy, wanton,
waste, waste time

trifling empty, footling (*Inf.*), frivolous, idle,
inconsiderable, insignificant, measly, mi~
nuscule, negligible, nickel-and-dime (*U.S.
sl.*), paltry, petty, piddling (*Inf.*), puny,
shallow, silly, slight, small, tiny, trivial,
unimportant, valueless, worthless
Antonyms considerable, crucial, important,
large, major, serious, significant, vital,
weighty

trigger *v.* activate, bring about, cause, elicit,
generate, give rise to, produce, prompt,
provoke, set in motion, set off, spark off,
start
Antonyms bar, block, hinder, impede, in~
hibit, obstruct, prevent, repress, stop

trim *adj.* **1.** compact, dapper, natty (*Inf.*),
neat, nice, orderly, shipshape, smart, soigné
or soignée, spick-and-span, spruce, tidy, trig
(*Archaic or dialect*), well-groomed, well-
ordered, well turned-out **2.** fit, shapely,
sleek, slender, slim, streamlined, svelte,
willowy ~*v.* **3.** barber, clip, crop, curtail,
cut, cut back, dock, even up, lop, pare,
prune, shave, shear, tidy **4.** adorn, array,
beautify, bedeck, deck out, decorate, dress,
embellish, embroider, garnish, ornament,
trick out **5.** adjust, arrange, balance, dis~
tribute, order, prepare, settle ~*n.* **6.** adorn~
ment, border, decoration, edging, embel~
lishment, frill, fringe, garnish, ornamenta~
tion, piping, trimming **7.** condition, fettle,
fitness, form, health, order, repair, shape
(*Inf.*), situation, state **8.** clipping, crop, cut,
pruning, shave, shearing, tidying up, trim~
ming **9.** array, attire, dress, equipment,
gear, trappings
Antonyms (*sense 1*) disarrayed, disorderly,
messy, scruffy, shabby, sloppy, ungroomed,
unkempt, untidy

trimming 1. adornment, border, braid,
decoration, edging, embellishment, festoon,
frill, fringe, garnish, ornamentation, piping
2. *Plural* accessories, accompaniments, ap~
purtenances, extras, frills, garnish, orna~
ments, paraphernalia, trappings **3.** *Plural*
brash, clippings, cuttings, ends, parings,
shavings

trinity threesome, triad, trilogy, trine, trio,
triple, triplet, triptych, triumvirate, triune

trinket bagatelle, bauble, bibelot, gewgaw,
gimcrack, kickshaw, knick-knack, nothing,
ornament, piece of bric-a-brac, toy, trifle

trio threesome, triad, trilogy, trine, trinity,
triple, triplet, triptych, triumvirate, triune

trip *n.* **1.** errand, excursion, expedition, for~
ay, jaunt, journey, outing, ramble, run,
tour, travel, voyage **2.** bloomer (*Brit. inf.*),
blunder, boob (*Brit. sl.*), error, fall, false
move, false step, faux pas, indiscretion,

lapse, misstep, slip, stumble ~*v.* **3.** blunder, boob (*Brit. sl.*), err, fall, go wrong, lapse, lose one's balance, lose one's footing, make a false move, make a faux pas, miscalculate, misstep, slip, slip up (*Inf.*), stumble, tumble **4.** catch out, confuse, disconcert, put off one's stride, throw off, trap, unsettle **5.** go, ramble, tour, travel, voyage **6.** caper, dance, flit, frisk, gambol, hop, skip, spring, tread lightly **7.** *Inf.* get high (*Inf.*), get stoned (*Sl.*), take drugs, turn on (*Sl.*) **8.** activate, engage, flip, pull, release, set off, switch on, throw, turn on

tripe balderdash, balls (*Taboo sl.*), bilge (*Inf.*), bosh (*Inf.*), bull (*Sl.*), bullshit (*Taboo sl.*), bunkum *or* buncombe (*Chiefly U.S.*), claptrap (*Inf.*), cobblers (*Brit. taboo sl.*), crap (*Sl.*), drivel, eyewash (*Inf.*), foolish talk, garbage (*Inf.*), guff (*Sl.*), hogwash, hokum (*Sl., chiefly U.S. & Canad.*), horsefeathers (*U.S. sl.*), hot air (*Inf.*), inanity, moonshine, nonsense, pap, piffle (*Inf.*), poppycock (*Inf.*), rot, rubbish, shit (*Taboo sl.*), tommyrot, tosh (*Sl., chiefly Brit.*), trash, trumpery, twaddle

triple 1. *adj.* threefold, three times as much, three-way, tripartite **2.** *n.* threesome, triad, trilogy, trine, trinity, trio, triplet, triumvirate, triune **3.** *v.* increase threefold, treble, triplicate

triplet threesome, triad, trilogy, trine, trinity, trio, triple, triumvirate, triune

tripper excursionist, holiday-maker, journeyer, sightseer, tourist, voyager

trite banal, bromidic, clichéd, common, commonplace, corny (*Sl.*), dull, hack, hackneyed, ordinary, pedestrian, routine, run-of-the-mill, stale, stereotyped, stock, threadbare, tired, uninspired, unoriginal, worn
Antonyms exciting, fresh, interesting, new, novel, original, out-of-the-ordinary, uncommon, unexpected, unfamiliar

triumph *n.* **1.** elation, exultation, happiness, joy, jubilation, pride, rejoicing **2.** accomplishment, achievement, ascendancy, attainment, conquest, coup, feat, hit (*Inf.*), mastery, sensation, smash (*Inf.*), smash-hit (*Inf.*), success, *tour de force*, victory, walkover (*Inf.*) ~*v.* **3.** *Often with* **over** best, carry the day, come out on top (*Inf.*), dominate, flourish, get the better of, overcome, overwhelm, prevail, prosper, subdue, succeed, take the honours, thrive, vanquish, win **4.** celebrate, crow, drool, exult, gloat, glory, jubilate, rejoice, revel, swagger
Antonyms (*sense 2*) catastrophe, defeat, disaster, failure, fiasco, flop (*Inf.*), washout (*Inf.*) (*sense 3*) come a cropper (*Inf.*), fail, fall, flop (*Inf.*), lose

triumphant boastful, celebratory, cock-a-hoop, conquering, dominant, elated, exult-

ant, glorious, jubilant, proud, rejoicing, successful, swaggering, triumphal, undefeated, victorious, winning
Antonyms beaten, defeated, embarrassed, humbled, humiliated, shamed, unsuccessful

trivia details, minutiae, petty details, trifles, trivialities
Antonyms basics, brass tacks (*Inf.*), core, essentials, fundamentals, nitty-gritty (*Inf.*), rudiments

trivial chickenshit (*U.S. sl.*), commonplace, everyday, frivolous, incidental, inconsequential, inconsiderable, insignificant, little, meaningless, minor, negligible, nickel-and-dime (*U.S. sl.*), paltry, petty, puny, slight, small, trifling, trite, unimportant, valueless, worthless
Antonyms considerable, crucial, essential, important, profound, serious, significant, uncommon, unusual, vital, weighty, worthwhile

triviality 1. frivolity, inconsequentiality, insignificance, littleness, meaninglessness, negligibility, paltriness, pettiness, slightness, smallness, triteness, unimportance, valuelessness, worthlessness **2.** detail, no big thing, no great matter, nothing, petty detail, technicality, trifle
Antonyms (*sense 1*) consequence, essential, importance, rudiment, significance, value, worth

troop *n.* **1.** assemblage, band, bevy, body, bunch (*Inf.*), company, contingent, crew (*Inf.*), crowd, drove, flock, gang, gathering, group, herd, horde, multitude, pack, posse (*Inf.*), squad, swarm, team, throng, unit **2.** *Plural* armed forces, army, fighting men, men, military, servicemen, soldiers, soldiery ~*v.* **3.** crowd, flock, march, parade, stream, swarm, throng, traipse (*Inf.*)

trophy award, bays, booty, cup, laurels, memento, prize, souvenir, spoils

tropical hot, humid, lush, steamy, stifling, sultry, sweltering, torrid
Antonyms arctic, chilly, cold, cool, freezing, frosty, frozen, parky (*Brit. inf.*)

trot *v.* **1.** canter, go briskly, jog, lope, run, scamper ~*n.* **2.** brisk pace, canter, jog, lope, run **3. on the trot** *Inf.* consecutively, in a row, in succession, one after the other, without break, without interruption

trot out bring forward, bring up, come out with, drag up, exhibit, recite, rehearse, reiterate, relate, repeat

trouble *n.* **1.** agitation, annoyance, anxiety, bummer (*Sl.*), disquiet, distress, grief, hardship, hassle (*Inf.*), heartache, irritation, misfortune, pain, sorrow, suffering, torment, tribulation, vexation, woe, worry **2.** agitation, bother (*Inf.*), commotion, discontent, discord, disorder, dissatisfaction, disturbance, hassle (*Inf.*), row, strife, tumult,

unrest **3.** ailment, complaint, defect, dis~
ability, disease, disorder, failure, illness,
malfunction, upset **4.** bother, concern, dan~
ger, difficulty, dilemma, dire straits, hassle
(*Inf.*), hot water (*Inf.*), mess, nuisance, pest,
pickle (*Inf.*), predicament, problem, scrape
(*Inf.*), spot (*Inf.*), tight spot **5.** attention,
bother, care, effort, exertion, inconvenience,
labour, pains, struggle, thought, work ~*v.*
6. afflict, agitate, annoy, bother, discom~
pose, disconcert, disquiet, distress, disturb,
faze, fret, grieve, harass, hassle (*Inf.*), in~
convenience, pain, perplex, perturb, pester,
plague, sadden, torment, upset, vex, worry
7. be concerned, bother, burden, discom~
fort, discommode, disturb, impose upon, in~
commode, inconvenience, put out **8.** exert
oneself, go to the effort of, make an effort,
take pains, take the time
Antonyms *n.* agreement, comfort, content~
ment, convenience, ease, facility, good for~
tune, happiness, harmony, peace, pleasure,
tranquillity, unity ~*v.* appease, avoid, be
unharassed, calm, dodge, ease, mollify, please,
relieve, soothe

troublemaker *agent provocateur*, agitator,
firebrand, incendiary, instigator, meddler,
mischief-maker, rabble-rouser, stirrer (*Inf.*),
stormy petrel
Antonyms appeaser, arbitrator, conciliator,
pacifier, peace-maker

troublesome 1. annoying, arduous, both~
ersome, burdensome, demanding, difficult,
harassing, hard, importunate, inconvenient,
irksome, irritating, laborious, oppressive,
pestilential, plaguy (*Inf.*), taxing, tiresome,
tricky, trying, upsetting, vexatious, weari~
some, worrisome, worrying **2.** disorderly,
insubordinate, rebellious, recalcitrant, re~
fractory, rowdy, turbulent, uncooperative,
undisciplined, unruly, violent
Antonyms agreeable, calming, congenial,
disciplined, eager-to-please, easy, obedient,
pleasant, simple, soothing, undemanding,
well-behaved

trough 1. crib, manger, water trough **2.** ca~
nal, channel, depression, ditch, duct, flume,
furrow, gully, gutter, trench, watercourse

trounce beat, blow out of the water (*Sl.*),
clobber (*Sl.*), crush, defeat heavily *or*
utterly, drub, give a hiding (*Inf.*), give a
pasting (*Sl.*), hammer (*Inf.*), lick (*Inf.*), make
mincemeat of, overwhelm, paste (*Sl.*), rout,
run rings around (*Inf.*), slaughter (*Inf.*),
tank (*Sl.*), thrash, walk over (*Inf.*), wipe the
floor with (*Inf.*)

troupe band, cast, company

trouper actor, artiste, entertainer, perform~
er, player, theatrical, thespian

truancy absence, absence without leave,
malingering, shirking, skiving (*Brit. sl.*)

truant *n.* **1.** absentee, delinquent, deserter,
dodger, malingerer, runaway, shirker,
skiver (*Brit. sl.*), straggler **2.** *adj.* absent,
absent without leave, A.W.O.L., missing,
skiving (*Brit. sl.*) *v.* **3.** absent oneself, bob
off (*Brit. sl.*), desert, dodge, go missing, ma~
linger, play truant, run away, shirk, skive
(*Brit. sl.*), wag (*Dialect*)

truce armistice, break, ceasefire, cessation,
cessation of hostilities, intermission, inter~
val, let-up (*Inf.*), lull, moratorium, peace,
respite, rest, stay, treaty

truck *n.* **1.** commercial goods, commodities,
goods, merchandise, stock, stuff, wares **2.**
barter, business, buying and selling, com~
merce, communication, connection, contact,
dealings, exchange, relations, trade, traffic
~*v.* **3.** bargain, barter, buy and sell, deal,
do business, exchange, have dealings, nego~
tiate, swap, trade, traffic, transact business

truculent aggressive, antagonistic, bad-
tempered, bellicose, belligerent, combative,
contentious, cross, defiant, fierce, hostile,
ill-tempered, itching *or* spoiling for a fight
(*Inf.*), obstreperous, pugnacious, scrappy
(*Inf.*), sullen, violent
Antonyms agreeable, amiable, civil, cooperative, gentle, good-natured, peaceable,
placid

trudge 1. *v.* clump, drag oneself, footslog,
hike, lumber, march, plod, slog, stump,
traipse (*Inf.*), tramp, trek, walk heavily,
yomp **2.** *n.* footslog, haul, hike, march, slog,
traipse (*Inf.*), tramp, trek, yomp

true *adj.* **1.** accurate, actual, authentic, bona
fide, correct, exact, factual, genuine, legiti~
mate, natural, precise, pure, real, right,
truthful, valid, veracious, veritable **2.**
confirmed, constant, dedicated, devoted,
dutiful, faithful, fast, firm, honest, honour~
able, loyal, pure, reliable, sincere, staunch,
steady, true-blue, trustworthy, trusty, un~
swerving, upright **3.** accurate, correct, ex~
act, on target, perfect, precise, proper,
spot-on (*Brit. inf.*), unerring ~*adv.* **4.** hon~
estly, rightly, truthfully, veraciously, veri~
tably **5.** accurately, correctly, on target,
perfectly, precisely, properly, unerringly **6.**
come true become reality, be granted, be
realized, come to pass, happen, occur
Antonyms (*sense 1*) abnormal, artificial,
atypical, bogus, counterfeit, erroneous, fake,
false, fictional, fictitious, illegitimate, imagi~
nary, inaccurate, incorrect, made-up, make-
believe, phoney *or* phony (*Inf.*), pretended,
self-styled, spurious, unofficial, untrue, un~
truthful (*sense 2*) deceitful, disloyal, faithless,
false, treacherous, unreliable, untrue, un~
trustworthy (*sense 3*) askew, awry, erroneous,
inaccurate, incorrect, untrue

truism axiom, bromide, cliché, common~ place, platitude, stock phrase, trite saying

truly 1. accurately, authentically, beyond doubt, beyond question, correctly, exactly, factually, genuinely, in actuality, in fact, in reality, in truth, legitimately, precisely, re~ ally, rightly, truthfully, veraciously, veri~ tably, without a doubt **2.** confirmedly, con~ stantly, devotedly, dutifully, faithfully, firmly, honestly, honourably, loyally, sin~ cerely, staunchly, steadily, with all one's heart, with dedication, with devotion **3.** ex~ ceptionally, extremely, greatly, indeed, of course, really, to be sure, verily, very
Antonyms (*sense 1*) doubtfully, falsely, fraudulently, inaccurately, incorrectly, mis~ takenly

trumped-up concocted, contrived, cooked-up (*Inf.*), fabricated, fake, false, falsified, invented, made-up, manufactured, phoney *or* phony (*Inf.*), untrue
Antonyms actual, authentic, bona fide, genuine, real, sound, true, veritable

trumpery *n.* **1.** balderdash, balls (*Taboo sl.*), bilge (*Inf.*), bosh (*Inf.*), bull (*Sl.*), bull~ shit (*Taboo sl.*), bunkum *or* buncombe (*Chiefly U.S.*), claptrap (*Inf.*), cobblers (*Brit. taboo sl.*), crap (*Sl.*), drivel, eyewash (*Inf.*), foolishness, foolish talk, garbage (*Inf.*), guff (*Sl.*), hogwash, hokum (*Sl., chiefly U.S. & Canad.*), horsefeathers (*U.S. sl.*), hot air (*Inf.*), idiocy, inanity, moonshine, nonsense, pap, piffle (*Inf.*), poppycock (*Inf.*), rot, rub~ bish, shit (*Taboo sl.*), stuff, tommyrot, tosh (*Sl., chiefly Brit.*), trash, tripe (*Inf.*), twaddle **2.** bagatelle, bauble, gewgaw, kickshaw, knick-knack, toy, trifle, trinket ~*adj.* **3.** brummagem, cheap, flashy, meretricious, nasty, rubbishy, shabby, shoddy, tawdry, trashy, trifling, useless, valueless, worthless

trumpet *n.* **1.** bugle, clarion, horn **2.** bay, bellow, call, cry, roar **3. blow one's own trumpet** boast, brag, crow, sing one's own praises, vaunt ~*v.* **4.** advertise, announce, broadcast, crack up (*Inf.*), extol, noise abroad, proclaim, publish, shout from the rooftops, sound loudly, tout (*Inf.*)
Antonyms *v.* conceal, hide, hush up, keep secret, make light of, play down, soft pedal (*Inf.*)

trump up concoct, contrive, cook up (*Inf.*), create, fabricate, fake, invent, make up, manufacture

truncate abbreviate, clip, crop, curtail, cut, cut short, dock, lop, pare, prune, shorten, trim
Antonyms drag out, draw out, extend, lengthen, prolong, protract, spin out, stretch

truncheon baton, club, cudgel, staff

trunk 1. bole, stalk, stem, stock **2.** body, torso **3.** proboscis, snout **4.** bin, box, case, casket, chest, coffer, crate, kist (*Scot. & northern English dialect*), locker, portman~ teau

truss *v.* **1.** bind, bundle, fasten, make fast, pack, pinion, secure, strap, tether, tie ~*n.* **2.** beam, brace, buttress, joist, prop, shore, stanchion, stay, strut, support **3.** *Medical* bandage, support **4.** bale, bundle, package, packet

trust *n.* **1.** assurance, belief, certainty, cer~ titude, confidence, conviction, credence, credit, expectation, faith, hope, reliance **2.** duty, obligation, responsibility **3.** care, charge, custody, guard, guardianship, pro~ tection, safekeeping, trusteeship ~*v.* **4.** as~ sume, believe, expect, hope, presume, sup~ pose, surmise, think likely **5.** bank on, be~ lieve, count on, depend on, have faith in, lean on, pin one's faith on, place confidence in, place one's trust in, place reliance on, rely upon, swear by, take at face value **6.** assign, command, commit, confide, consign, delegate, entrust, give, put into the hands of, sign over, turn over
Antonyms *n.* distrust, doubt, fear, incredu~ lity, lack of faith, mistrust, scepticism, suspi~ cion, uncertainty, wariness ~*v.* be sceptical of, beware, disbelieve, discredit, distrust, doubt, lack confidence in, lack faith in, mis~ trust, suspect

trustful, trusting confiding, credulous, gullible, innocent, naive, optimistic, simple, unguarded, unsuspecting, unsuspicious, unwary
Antonyms cagey (*Inf.*), cautious, chary, dis~ trustful, guarded, on one's guard, suspicious, wary

trustworthy dependable, ethical, honest, honourable, level-headed, mature, princi~ pled, reliable, reputable, responsible, right~ eous, sensible, staunch, steadfast, to be trusted, true, trusty, truthful, upright
Antonyms deceitful, dishonest, disloyal, ir~ responsible, treacherous, undependable, un~ ethical, unprincipled, unreliable, untrust~ worthy

trusty dependable, faithful, firm, honest, re~ liable, responsible, solid, staunch, steady, straightforward, strong, true, trustworthy, upright
Antonyms dishonest, irresolute, irrespon~ sible, undependable, unfaithful, unreliable

truth 1. accuracy, actuality, exactness, fact, factuality, factualness, genuineness, legiti~ macy, precision, reality, truthfulness, va~ lidity, veracity, verity **2.** candour, constan~ cy, dedication, devotion, dutifulness, faith, faithfulness, fidelity, frankness, honesty, integrity, loyalty, naturalism, realism, uprightness **3.** axiom, certainty, fact, law,

maxim, proven principle, reality, truism, verity
Antonyms deceit, deception, delusion, dis~honesty, error, fabrication, falsehood, falsity, fiction, inaccuracy, invention, legend, lie, make-believe, myth, old wives' tale, untruth

truthful accurate, candid, correct, exact, faithful, forthright, frank, honest, literal, naturalistic, plain-spoken, precise, realistic, reliable, sincere, straight, straightforward, true, trustworthy, upfront (*Inf.*), veracious, veritable
Antonyms deceptive, dishonest, fabricated, false, fictional, fictitious, inaccurate, incor~rect, insincere, lying, made-up, untrue, un~truthful

try *v.* **1.** aim, attempt, bend over backwards (*Inf.*), break one's neck (*Inf.*), bust a gut (*Inf.*), do one's best, do one's damnedest (*Inf.*), endeavour, essay, exert oneself, give it one's all (*Inf.*), give it one's best shot (*Inf.*), go for broke (*Sl.*), go for it (*Inf.*), have a go (crack (*Inf.*), shot (*Inf.*), stab (*Inf.*), whack (*Inf.*)) (*Inf.*), knock oneself out (*Inf.*), make an all-out effort (*Inf.*), make an at~tempt, make an effort, rupture oneself (*Inf.*), seek, strive, struggle, undertake **2.** ap~praise, check out, evaluate, examine, ex~periment, inspect, investigate, prove, put to the test, sample, taste, test **3.** afflict, annoy, inconvenience, irk, irritate, pain, plague, strain, stress, tax, tire, trouble, upset, vex, weary **4.** adjudge, adjudicate, examine, hear ~*n.* **5.** attempt, crack (*Inf.*), effort, endeav~our, essay, go (*Inf.*), shot (*Inf.*), stab (*Inf.*), whack (*Inf.*) **6.** appraisal, evaluation, ex~periment, inspection, sample, taste, test, trial

trying aggravating (*Inf.*), annoying, arduous, bothersome, difficult, exasperating, fatigu~ing, hard, irksome, irritating, stressful, taxing, tiresome, tough, troublesome, up~setting, vexing, wearisome
Antonyms calming, easy, no bother, no trouble, painless, simple, straightforward, undemanding

try out appraise, check out, evaluate, ex~periment with, inspect, put into practice, put to the test, sample, taste, test

tsar, czar autocrat, despot, emperor, head, leader, overlord, ruler, sovereign, tyrant

tuck *v.* **1.** fold, gather, insert, push ~*n.* **2.** fold, gather, pinch, pleat **3.** *Inf.* comestibles, eats (*Sl.*), food, grub (*Sl.*), nosebag (*Sl.*), nosh (*Sl.*), scoff (*Sl.*), tack (*Inf.*), victuals, vittles (*Obs. or dialect*)

tuck in 1. bed down, enfold, fold under, make snug, put to bed, swaddle, wrap up **2.** chow down (*Sl.*), eat heartily, get stuck in (*Inf.*)

tug 1. *v.* drag, draw, haul, heave, jerk, lug,

pull, tow, wrench, yank **2.** *n.* drag, haul, heave, jerk, pull, tow, traction, wrench, yank

tuition education, instruction, lessons, schooling, teaching, training, tutelage, tu~toring

tumble 1. *v.* drop, fall, fall end over end, fall headlong, fall head over heels, flop, lose one's footing, pitch, plummet, roll, stumble, topple, toss, trip up **2.** *n.* collapse, drop, fall, flop, headlong fall, plunge, roll, spill, stum~ble, toss, trip

tumble-down crumbling, decrepit, dilapi~dated, disintegrating, falling to pieces, ram~shackle, rickety, ruined, shaky, tottering
Antonyms durable, firm, solid, sound, sta~ble, sturdy, substantial, well-kept

tumour cancer, carcinoma (*Pathology*), growth, lump, neoplasm (*Medical*), sarcoma (*Medical*), swelling

tumult ado, affray (*Law*), agitation, alterca~tion, bedlam, brawl, brouhaha, clamour, commotion, din, disorder, disturbance, ex~citement, fracas, hubbub, hullabaloo, out~break, pandemonium, quarrel, racket, riot, row, ruction (*Inf.*), stir, stramash (*Scot.*), strife, turmoil, unrest, upheaval, uproar
Antonyms calm, hush, peace, quiet, repose, serenity, silence, stillness

tumultuous agitated, boisterous, clamor~ous, confused, disorderly, disturbed, excit~ed, fierce, hectic, irregular, lawless, noisy, obstreperous, passionate, raging, restless, riotous, rowdy, rumbustious, stormy, tur~bulent, unrestrained, unruly, uproarious, violent, vociferous, wild
Antonyms calm, hushed, peaceful, quiet, restful, serene, still, tranquil

tune *n.* **1.** air, melody, melody line, motif, song, strain, theme **2.** agreement, concert, concord, consonance, euphony, harmony, pitch, sympathy, unison **3.** attitude, de~meanour, disposition, frame of mind, mood **4. call the tune** be in charge (command, control), call the shots (*Sl.*), command, dic~tate, govern, lead, rule, rule the roost **5. change one's tune** change one's mind, do an about-face, have a change of heart, re~consider, take a different tack, think again ~*v.* **6.** adapt, adjust, attune, bring into har~mony, harmonize, pitch, regulate
Antonyms (*sense 2*) clashing, conflict, con~tention, disagreement, discord, discordance, disharmony, disunity, friction

tuneful catchy, consonant (*Music*), easy on the ear (*Inf.*), euphonic, euphonious, har~monious, mellifluous, melodic, melodious, musical, pleasant, symphonic
Antonyms cacophonous, clashing, discord~ant, dissonant, harsh, jangly, tuneless, unme~lodious

tuneless atonal, cacophonous, clashing, discordant, dissonant, harsh, unmelodic, unmelodious, unmusical
Antonyms harmonious, melodious, musical, pleasing, sonorous, symphonic, tuneful

tunnel 1. *n.* burrow, channel, hole, passage, passageway, shaft, subway, underpass **2.** *v.* burrow, dig, dig one's way, excavate, mine, penetrate, scoop out, undermine

turbulence agitation, boiling, commotion, confusion, disorder, instability, pandemonium, roughness, storm, tumult, turmoil, unrest, upheaval
Antonyms calm, peace, quiet, repose, rest, stillness

turbulent 1. agitated, blustery, boiling, choppy, confused, disordered, foaming, furious, raging, rough, tempestuous, tumultuous, unsettled, unstable **2.** agitated, anarchic, boisterous, disorderly, insubordinate, lawless, mutinous, obstreperous, rebellious, refractory, riotous, rowdy, seditious, tumultuous, unbridled, undisciplined, ungovernable, unruly, uproarious, violent, wild
Antonyms (*sense 1*) calm, glassy, peaceful, quiet, smooth, still, unruffled

turf 1. clod, divot, grass, green, sod, sward **2. the turf** horse-racing, racecourse, racetrack, racing, the flat

turmoil agitation, bedlam, brouhaha, bustle, chaos, commotion, confusion, disarray, disorder, disturbance, ferment, flurry, hubbub, noise, pandemonium, row, stir, strife, trouble, tumult, turbulence, upheaval, uproar, violence
Antonyms calm, peace, quiet, repose, rest, serenity, stillness, tranquillity

turn *v.* **1.** circle, go round, gyrate, move in a circle, pivot, revolve, roll, rotate, spin, swivel, twirl, twist, wheel, whirl **2.** change course, change position, go back, move, return, reverse, shift, swerve, switch, veer, wheel **3.** arc, come round, corner, go round, negotiate, pass, pass around, take a bend **4.** adapt, alter, become, change, convert, divert, fashion, fit, form, metamorphose, mould, mutate, remodel, shape, transfigure, transform, transmute **5.** become rancid, curdle, go bad, go off (*Brit. inf.*), go sour, make rancid, sour, spoil, taint **6.** appeal, apply, approach, go, have recourse, look, resort **7.** nauseate, sicken, upset **8.** apostatize, bring round (*Inf.*), change one's mind, change sides, defect, desert, go over, influence, persuade, prejudice, prevail upon, renege, retract, talk into **9.** construct, deliver, execute, fashion, frame, make, mould, perform, shape, write **10. turn tail** beat a hasty retreat, bolt, cut and run (*Inf.*), flee, hook it (*Sl.*), run away, run off, show a clean pair of heels, take off (*Inf.*), take to one's heels ~*n.* **11.** bend, change, circle, curve, cycle, gyration, pivot, reversal, revolution, rotation, spin, swing, turning, twist, whirl **12.** bias, direction, drift, heading, tendency, trend **13.** bend, change of course, change of direction, curve, departure, deviation, shift **14.** chance, crack (*Inf.*), fling, go, opportunity, period, round, shift, shot (*Inf.*), spell, stint, succession, time, try, whack (*Inf.*) **15.** airing, circuit, constitutional, drive, excursion, jaunt, outing, promenade, ride, saunter, spin (*Inf.*), stroll, walk **16.** affinity, aptitude, bent, bias, flair, gift, inclination, knack, leaning, propensity, talent **17.** cast, fashion, form, format, guise, make-up, manner, mode, mould, shape, style, way **18.** act, action, deed, favour, gesture, service **19.** bend, distortion, twist, warp **20.** *Inf.* fright, scare, shock, start, surprise **21. by turns** alternately, in succession, one after another, reciprocally, turn and turn about **22. to a turn** correctly, exactly, just right, perfectly, precisely

turn down 1. diminish, lessen, lower, muffle, mute, quieten, reduce the volume of, soften **2.** abstain from, decline, rebuff, refuse, reject, repudiate, say no to, spurn, throw out
Antonyms (*sense 1*) amplify, augment, boost, increase, raise, strengthen, swell, turn up (*sense 2*) accede, accept, acquiesce, agree, receive, take

turn in 1. go to bed, go to sleep, hit the sack (*Sl.*), retire for the night **2.** deliver, give back, give up, hand in, hand over, return, submit, surrender, tender

turning bend, crossroads, curve, junction, side road, turn, turn-off

turning point change, climacteric, crisis, critical moment, crossroads, crux, decisive moment, moment of decision, moment of truth

turn-off branch, exit, side road, turn, turning

turn on 1. activate, energize, ignite, kick-start, put on, set in motion, start, start up, switch on **2.** balance, be contingent on, be decided by, depend, hang, hinge, pivot, rest **3.** assail, assault, attack, fall on, lose one's temper with, round on **4.** *Sl.* arouse, arouse one's desire, attract, excite, please, stimulate, thrill, titillate, work up **5.** *Sl.* get high (*Inf.*), get stoned (*Sl.*), take drugs, trip (*Inf.*) **6.** *Sl.* expose, get one started with, inform, initiate, introduce, show
Antonyms (*sense 1*) cut out, put out, shut off, stop, switch off, turn off

turnout 1. assemblage, assembly, attendance, audience, congregation, crowd, gate, number, throng **2.** amount produced, output, outturn (*Rare*), production, production quota, productivity, turnover, volume, yield **3.** array, attire, costume, dress, equipage, equipment, gear (*Inf.*), get-up (*Inf.*), outfit, rigout (*Inf.*)

turn out 1. put out, switch off, turn off, unplug **2.** bring out, fabricate, finish, make, manufacture, process, produce, put out **3.** axe (*Inf.*), banish, cashier, cast out, deport, discharge, dismiss, dispossess, drive out, drum out, evict, expel, fire (*Inf.*), give one the sack (*Inf.*), give the bum's rush (*Sl.*), kick out (*Inf.*), kiss off (*Sl., chiefly U.S. & Canad.*), oust, put out, relegate, sack (*Inf.*), show one the door, throw out, turf out (*Brit. inf.*), unseat **4.** clean out, clear, discharge, empty, take out the contents of **5.** become, come about, come to be, come to light, crop up (*Inf.*), develop, emerge, end up, eventuate, evolve, happen, prove to be, result, transpire (*Inf.*), work out **6.** accoutre, apparel (*Archaic*), attire, clothe, dress, fit, outfit, rig out **7.** appear, assemble, attend, be present, come, gather, go, put in an appearance, show up (*Inf.*), turn up

turnover 1. business, flow, output, outturn (*Rare*), production, productivity, volume, yield **2.** change, coming and going, movement, replacement

turn up 1. appear, arrive, attend, come, put in an appearance, show (*Inf.*), show one's face, show up (*Inf.*) **2.** appear, become known, be found, bring to light, come to light, come to pass, come up with, crop up (*Inf.*), dig up, disclose, discover, expose, find, pop up, reveal, transpire, unearth **3.** amplify, boost, enhance, increase, increase the volume of, intensify, make louder, raise **Antonyms** (*sense 2*) disappear, evaporate, fade, hide, vanish (*sense 3*) diminish, lessen, lower, reduce, soften, turn down

tussle 1. *v.* battle, brawl, contend, fight, grapple, scrap (*Inf.*), scuffle, struggle, vie, wrestle **2.** *n. bagarre*, battle, bout, brawl, competition, conflict, contention, contest, fight, fracas, fray, punch-up (*Brit. inf.*), scrap (*Inf.*), scrimmage, scuffle, set-to (*Inf.*), shindig (*Inf.*), shindy (*Inf.*), struggle

tutor 1. *n.* coach, educator, governor, guardian, guide, guru, instructor, lecturer, master, mentor, preceptor, schoolmaster, teacher **2.** *v.* coach, direct, discipline, drill, edify, educate, guide, instruct, lecture, school, teach, train

tutorial 1. *n.* individual instruction, lesson, seminar **2.** *adj.* coaching, guiding, instructional, teaching

TV gogglebox (*Brit. sl.*), idiot box (*Sl.*), receiver, small screen (*Inf.*), television, television set, telly (*Brit. inf.*), the box (*Brit. inf.*), the tube (*Sl.*), TV set

twaddle 1. *n.* balderdash, balls (*Taboo sl.*),

bilge (*Inf.*), blather, bosh (*Inf.*), bull (*Sl.*), bullshit (*Taboo sl.*), bunkum *or* buncombe (*Chiefly U.S.*), chatter, claptrap (*Inf.*), cobblers (*Brit. taboo sl.*), crap (*Sl.*), drivel, eyewash (*Inf.*), foolish talk, gabble, garbage (*Inf.*), gobbledegook (*Inf.*), gossip, guff (*Sl.*), hogwash, hokum (*Sl., chiefly U.S. & Canad.*), horsefeathers (*U.S. sl.*), hot air (*Inf.*), inanity, moonshine, nonsense, pap, piffle (*Inf.*), poppycock (*Inf.*), rigmarole, rot, rubbish, shit (*Taboo sl.*), tattle, tommyrot, tosh (*Sl., chiefly Brit.*), trash, tripe (*Inf.*), trumpery, verbiage, waffle (*Inf., chiefly Brit.*) **2.** *v.* blather, chatter, gabble, gossip, prattle, rattle on, talk nonsense, talk through one's hat, tattle, waffle (*Inf., chiefly Brit.*)

tweak *v./n.* jerk, nip, pinch, pull, squeeze, twist, twitch

twig branch, offshoot, shoot, spray, sprig, stick, withe

twilight *n.* **1.** dimness, dusk, evening, gloaming (*Scot. or poetic*), half-light, sundown, sunset **2.** decline, ebb, last phase ~*adj.* **3.** crepuscular, darkening, dim, evening **4.** declining, dying, ebbing, final, last **Antonyms** climax, crowning moment, dawn, daybreak, height, morning, peak, sunrise, sunup

twin 1. *n.* clone, corollary, counterpart, double, duplicate, fellow, likeness, lookalike, match, mate, ringer (*Sl.*) **2.** *adj.* corresponding, double, dual, duplicate, geminate, identical, matched, matching, paired, parallel, twofold **3.** *v.* couple, join, link, match, pair, yoke

twine *n.* **1.** cord, string, yarn **2.** coil, convolution, interlacing, twist, whorl **3.** knot, snarl, tangle ~*v.* **4.** braid, entwine, interlace, interweave, knit, plait, splice, twist, twist together, weave **5.** bend, coil, curl, encircle, loop, meander, spiral, surround, twist, wind, wrap, wreathe

twinge bite, gripe, pain, pang, pinch, prick, sharp pain, spasm, stab, stitch, throb, throe (*Rare*), tic, tweak, twist, twitch

twinkle *v.* **1.** blink, coruscate, flash, flicker, gleam, glint, glisten, glitter, scintillate, shimmer, shine, sparkle, wink ~*n.* **2.** blink, coruscation, flash, flicker, gleam, glimmer, glistening, glittering, light, scintillation, shimmer, shine, spark, sparkle, wink **3.** flash, instant, jiffy (*Inf.*), moment, second, shake (*Inf.*), split second, tick (*Brit. inf.*), trice, twinkling, two shakes of a lamb's tail (*Inf.*)

twinkling 1. blink, coruscation, flash, flashing, flicker, gleam, glimmer, glistening, glittering, scintillation, shimmer, shining, sparkle, twinkle, wink **2.** flash, instant, jiffy (*Inf.*), moment, second, shake (*Inf.*), split second, tick (*Brit. inf.*), trice, twinkle, two shakes of a lamb's tail (*Inf.*)

twirl *v.* **1.** gyrate, pirouette, pivot, revolve, rotate, spin, turn, turn on one's heel, twiddle, twist, wheel, whirl, wind ~*n.* **2.** gyration, pirouette, revolution, rotation, spin, turn, twist, wheel, whirl **3.** coil, spiral, twist

twist *v.* **1.** coil, corkscrew, curl, encircle, entwine, intertwine, screw, spin, swivel, twine, weave, wind, wrap, wreathe, wring **2.** contort, distort, screw up **3.** rick, sprain, turn, wrench **4.** alter, change, distort, falsify, garble, misquote, misrepresent, pervert, warp **5.** squirm, wriggle, writhe **6. twist someone's arm** bully, coerce, force, persuade, pressurize, talk into ~*n.* **7.** coil, curl, spin, swivel, twine, wind **8.** braid, coil, curl, hank, plug, quid, roll **9.** change, development, revelation, slant, surprise, turn, variation **10.** arc, bend, convolution, curve, meander, turn, undulation, zigzag **11.** defect, deformation, distortion, flaw, imperfection, kink, warp **12.** jerk, pull, sprain, turn, wrench **13.** aberration, bent, characteristic, crotchet, eccentricity, fault, foible, idiosyncrasy, oddity, peculiarity, proclivity, quirk, trait **14.** confusion, entanglement, kink, knot, mess, mix-up, ravel, snarl, tangle **15. round the twist** *Brit. sl.* barmy (*Sl.*), batty (*Sl.*), bonkers (*Sl., chiefly Brit.*), crazy, cuckoo (*Inf.*), daft (*Inf.*), insane, loopy (*Inf.*), mad, not all there, not right in the head, nuts (*Sl.*), nutty (*Sl.*), nutty as a fruitcake (*Sl.*), off one's rocker (*Sl.*), off one's trolley (*Sl.*), out to lunch (*Inf.*), up the pole (*Inf.*)
Antonyms hold stationary, hold steady, hold still, straighten, uncoil, unravel, unroll, untwist, unwind

twister cheat, chiseller (*Inf.*), con man (*Inf.*), crook (*Inf.*), deceiver, fraud, rogue, swindler, trickster

twit[1] *v.* banter, berate, blame, censure, deride, jeer, make fun of, scorn, taunt, tease, upbraid

twit[2] airhead (*Sl.*), ass, berk (*Brit. sl.*), blockhead, charlie (*Brit. inf.*), chump (*Inf.*), clown, dickhead (*Sl.*), dipstick (*Brit. sl.*), divvy (*Brit. sl.*), dope (*Inf.*), dork (*Sl.*), dweeb (*U.S. sl.*), fool, fuckwit (*Taboo sl.*), geek (*Sl.*), gonzo (*Sl.*), halfwit, idiot, jerk (*Sl., chiefly U.S. & Canad.*), juggins (*Brit. inf.*), nerd *or* nurd (*Sl.*), nincompoop, ninny, nitwit (*Inf.*), numskull *or* numbskull, oaf, pillock (*Brit. sl.*), plank (*Brit. sl.*), plonker (*Sl.*), prat (*Sl.*), prick (*Derogatory sl.*), schmuck (*U.S. sl.*), silly-billy (*Inf.*), simpleton, twerp *or* twirp (*Inf.*), wally (*Sl.*)

twitch 1. *v.* blink, flutter, jerk, jump, pluck, pull, snatch, squirm, tug, yank **2.** *n.* blink, flutter, jerk, jump, pull, spasm, tic, tremor, twinge

two-edged ambiguous, ambivalent, backhanded, double-edged, equivocal

two-faced deceitful, deceiving, dissembling, double-dealing, duplicitous, false, hypocritical, insincere, Janus-faced, perfidious, treacherous, untrustworthy
Antonyms artless, candid, frank, genuine, honest, ingenuous, sincere, trustworthy

tycoon baron, big cheese (*Sl., old-fashioned*), big noise (*Inf.*), capitalist, captain of industry, fat cat (*Sl., chiefly U.S.*), financier, industrialist, magnate, merchant prince, mogul, plutocrat, potentate, wealthy businessman

type 1. breed, category, class, classification, form, genre, group, ilk, kidney, kind, order, sort, species, stamp, strain, subdivision, variety **2.** case, characters, face, fount, print, printing **3.** archetype, epitome, essence, example, exemplar, model, norm, original, paradigm, pattern, personification, prototype, quintessence, specimen, standard

typhoon cyclone, squall, storm, tempest, tornado, tropical storm

typical archetypal, average, characteristic, classic, conventional, essential, illustrative, in character, indicative, in keeping, model, normal, orthodox, representative, standard, stock, true to type, usual
Antonyms atypical, exceptional, out of keeping, out of the ordinary, singular, uncharacteristic, unconventional, unexpected, unique, unrepresentative, unusual

typify characterize, embody, epitomize, exemplify, illustrate, incarnate, personify, represent, sum up, symbolize

tyrannical absolute, arbitrary, authoritarian, autocratic, coercive, cruel, despotic, dictatorial, domineering, high-handed, imperious, inhuman, magisterial, oppressive, overbearing, overweening, peremptory, severe, tyrannous, unjust, unreasonable
Antonyms democratic, easy-going, lax, lenient, liberal, reasonable, tolerant, understanding

tyranny absolutism, authoritarianism, autocracy, coercion, cruelty, despotism, dictatorship, harsh discipline, highhandedness, imperiousness, oppression, peremptoriness, reign of terror, unreasonableness
Antonyms democracy, ease, laxity, leniency, liberality, mercy, relaxation, tolerance, understanding

tyrant absolutist, authoritarian, autocrat, bully, despot, dictator, Hitler, martinet, oppressor, slave-driver

U

ubiquitous all-over, ever-present, every~ where, omnipresent, pervasive, universal

ugly 1. hard-favoured, hard-featured, homely (*Chiefly U.S.*), ill-favoured, misshapen, no oil painting (*Inf.*), not much to look at, plain, unattractive, unlovely, unprepossess~ ing, unsightly **2.** disagreeable, disgusting, distasteful, frightful, hideous, horrid, mon~ strous, objectionable, obscene, offensive, repugnant, repulsive, revolting, shocking, terrible, unpleasant, vile **3.** baleful, dan~ gerous, forbidding, menacing, ominous, sinister, threatening **4.** angry, bad-tempered, dark, evil, malevolent, nasty, spiteful, sullen, surly
Antonyms agreeable, attractive, auspicious, beautiful, friendly, good-humoured, good-looking, good-natured, gorgeous, handsome, likable *or* likeable, lovely, peaceful, pleasant, pretty, promising

ulcer abscess, boil, fester, gathering, gum~ boil, peptic ulcer, pustule, sore

ulterior concealed, covert, hidden, personal, secondary, secret, selfish, undisclosed, un~ expressed
Antonyms apparent, declared, manifest, ob~ vious, overt, plain

ultimate *adj.* **1.** conclusive, decisive, end, eventual, extreme, final, furthest, last, ter~ minal **2.** extreme, greatest, highest, maxi~ mum, most significant, paramount, super~ lative, supreme, topmost, utmost **3.** basic, elemental, fundamental, primary, radical ~*n.* **4.** culmination, epitome, extreme, greatest, height, peak, perfection, summit, the last word

ultimately after all, at last, basically, even~ tually, finally, fundamentally, in due time, in the end, sooner or later

ultramodern advanced, ahead of its time, avant-garde, futuristic, modernistic, neoter~ ic (*Rare*), progressive, way-out (*Inf.*)

umbrage anger, chagrin, displeasure, grudge, high dudgeon, huff, indignation, of~ fence, pique, resentment, sense of injury
Antonyms amity, cordiality, goodwill, har~ mony, pleasure, understanding

umbrella 1. brolly (*Brit. inf.*), gamp (*Brit. inf.*) **2.** aegis, agency, cover, patronage, protection

umpire 1. *n.* adjudicator, arbiter, arbitra~ tor, judge, moderator, ref (*Inf.*), referee **2.** *v.* adjudicate, arbitrate, call (*Sport*), judge, mediate, moderate, referee

umpteen a good many, a thousand and one, considerable, countless, ever so many, mil~ lions, n, numerous, very many

unabashed blatant, bold, brazen, confident, unawed, unblushing, unconcerned, un~ daunted, undismayed, unembarrassed
Antonyms abashed, embarrassed, humbled, mortified, shame-faced, sheepish

unable impotent, inadequate, incapable, in~ effectual, no good, not able, not equal to, not up to, powerless, unfit, unfitted, unqualified
Antonyms able, adept, adequate, capable, competent, effective, potent, powerful

unabridged complete, full-length, uncon~ densed, uncut, unexpurgated, unshortened, whole

unacceptable disagreeable, displeasing, distasteful, improper, inadmissible, insup~ portable, objectionable, offensive, undesir~ able, unpleasant, unsatisfactory, unwelcome
Antonyms acceptable, agreeable, delightful, desirable, pleasant, pleasing, welcome

unaccompanied a cappella (*Music*), alone, by oneself, lone, on one's own, solo, un~ escorted

unaccomplished 1. incomplete, un~ achieved, uncompleted, undone, unfinished, unperformed **2.** inexpert, lacking finesse, uncultivated, unskilful, unskilled

unaccountable 1. baffling, incomprehen~ sible, inexplicable, inscrutable, mysterious, odd, peculiar, puzzling, strange, unexplain~ able, unfathomable, unintelligible **2.** aston~ ishing, extraordinary, uncommon, unheard-of, unusual, unwonted **3.** clear, exempt, free, not answerable, not respon~ sible, unliable
Antonyms (*sense 1*) accountable, compre~ hensible, explicable, intelligible, understand~ able

unaccustomed 1. *With* **to** a newcomer to, a novice at, green, inexperienced, not given to, not used to, unfamiliar with, unprac~ tised, unused to, unversed in **2.** new, out of the ordinary, remarkable, special, strange, surprising, uncommon, unexpected, unfa~ miliar, unprecedented, unusual, unwonted
Antonyms (*sense 1*) experienced, given to, habituated, practised, seasoned, used to, well-versed (*sense 2*) accustomed, familiar, or~ dinary, regular, usual

unaffected[1] artless, genuine, honest, in~ genuous, naive, natural, plain, simple, sin~ cere, straightforward, unassuming, unpre~

tentious, unsophisticated, unspoilt, unstud~
ied, without airs
Antonyms affected, assumed, designing, de~
vious, insincere, mannered, pretentious,
put-on, snobbish, sophisticated

unaffected² aloof, impervious, not
influenced, proof, unaltered, unchanged,
unimpressed, unmoved, unresponsive,
unstirred, untouched
Antonyms affected, changed, concerned,
disrupted, hard-hit, influenced, interested,
responsive, sympathetic, touched

unafraid confident, daring, dauntless, fear~
less, intrepid, unfearing, unshakable
Antonyms afraid, alarmed, anxious, fearful,
frightened, scared

unalterable fixed, fixed as the laws of the
Medes and the Persians, immovable, im~
mutable, invariable, permanent, steadfast,
unchangeable, unchanging
Antonyms alterable, changeable, changing,
flexible, mutable, variable

unanimity accord, agreement, assent, cho~
rus, concert, concord, concurrence, consen~
sus, harmony, like-mindedness, one mind,
unison, unity
Antonyms difference, disagreement, dis~
cord, disunity, division, variance

unanimous agreed, agreeing, at one, com~
mon, concerted, concordant, harmonious, in
agreement, in complete accord, like-minded,
of one mind, united
Antonyms differing, discordant, dissident,
disunited, divided, schismatic, split

unanimously by common consent, nem.
con., unitedly, unopposed, with one accord,
without exception, without opposition

unanswerable 1. absolute, conclusive, in~
contestable, incontrovertible, indisputable,
irrefutable, unarguable, undeniable **2.** in~
soluble, insolvable, unascertainable, unex~
plainable, unresolvable

unanswered disputed, ignored, in doubt,
open, undecided, undenied, unnoticed,
unrefuted, unresolved, unsettled, up in the
air, vexed

unappetizing distasteful, insipid, off-
putting (*Brit. inf.*), tasteless, unappealing,
unattractive, uninteresting, uninviting, un~
palatable, unpleasant, unsavoury, vapid
Antonyms agreeable, appealing, appetizing,
attractive, interesting, palatable, savoury,
tasty, toothsome

unapproachable 1. aloof, chilly, cool,
distant, frigid, offish (*Inf.*), remote, re~
served, standoffish, unfriendly, unsociable,
withdrawn **2.** inaccessible, out of reach,
out-of-the-way, remote, un-get-at-able (*Inf.*),
unreachable
Antonyms (*sense 1*) affable, approachable,
congenial, cordial, friendly, sociable

unarmed assailable, defenceless, exposed,
helpless, open, open to attack, unarmoured,
unprotected, weak, weaponless, without
arms
Antonyms armed, equipped, fortified, pro~
tected, ready, strengthened

unasked 1. gratuitous, spontaneous, un~
bidden, undemanded, undesired, uninvited,
unprompted, unrequested, unsought, un~
wanted **2.** off one's own bat, of one's own
accord, voluntarily, without prompting

unassailable 1. impregnable, invincible,
invulnerable, secure, well-defended **2.** ab~
solute, conclusive, incontestable, incontro~
vertible, indisputable, irrefutable, positive,
proven, sound, undeniable
Antonyms (*sense 2*) debatable, doubtful, du~
bious, inconclusive, uncertain, unfounded,
unproven, unsound

unassertive backward, bashful, diffident,
meek, mousy, retiring, self-effacing, timid,
timorous, unassuming
Antonyms aggressive, assertive, confident,
feisty (*Inf., chiefly U.S. & Canad.*), forceful,
overbearing, pushy (*Inf.*)

unassuming diffident, humble, meek,
modest, quiet, reserved, retiring, self-
effacing, simple, unassertive, unobtrusive,
unostentatious, unpretentious
Antonyms assuming, audacious, conceited,
ostentatious, overconfident, presumptuous,
pretentious

unattached 1. autonomous, free, inde~
pendent, nonaligned, unaffiliated, uncom~
mitted **2.** a free agent, available, by oneself,
footloose and fancy-free, not spoken for, on
one's own, single, unengaged, unmarried
Antonyms (*sense 1*) affiliated, aligned, at~
tached, committed, dependent, implicated,
involved

unattended 1. abandoned, disregarded, ig~
nored, left alone, not cared for, unguarded,
unwatched **2.** alone, on one's own, unac~
companied, unescorted

unauthorized illegal, unapproved, uncon~
stitutional, under-the-table, unlawful, unof~
ficial, unsanctioned, unwarranted
Antonyms authorized, constitutional, law~
ful, legal, official, sanctioned, warranted

unavailing abortive, bootless, fruitless, fu~
tile, idle, ineffective, ineffectual, of no avail,
pointless, to no purpose, unproductive, un~
successful, useless, vain
Antonyms effective, fruitful, productive,
rewarding, successful, useful, worthwhile

unavoidable bound to happen, certain,
compulsory, fated, ineluctable, inescapable,
inevitable, inexorable, necessary, obliga~
tory, sure

unaware heedless, ignorant, incognizant,
oblivious, unconscious, unenlightened, un~

informed, unknowing, unmindful, unsus~
pecting
Antonyms attentive, aware, conscious, in~
formed, knowing, mindful

unawares 1. aback, abruptly, by surprise,
off guard, on the hop (*Brit. inf.*), suddenly,
unexpectedly, unprepared, without warning
2. accidentally, by accident, by mistake, in~
advertently, mistakenly, unconsciously, un~
intentionally, unknowingly, unwittingly
Antonyms deliberately, forewarned, know~
ingly, on purpose, on the lookout, prepared,
wittingly

unbalanced 1. asymmetrical, irregular,
lopsided, not balanced, shaky, unequal, un~
even, unstable, unsymmetrical, wobbly **2.**
barking (*Sl.*), barking mad (*Sl.*), crazy, de~
mented, deranged, disturbed, eccentric, er~
ratic, insane, irrational, loopy (*Inf.*), luna~
tic, mad, *non compos mentis*, not all there,
not the full shilling (*Inf.*), off one's trolley
(*Sl.*), out to lunch (*Inf.*), touched, unhinged,
unsound, unstable, up the pole (*Inf.*) **3.** bi~
ased, inequitable, one-sided, partial, parti~
san, prejudiced, unfair, unjust
Antonyms (*sense 1*) balanced, equal, even,
stable, symmetrical

unbearable insufferable, insupportable, in~
tolerable, oppressive, too much (*Inf.*), unac~
ceptable, unendurable
Antonyms acceptable, bearable, endurable,
supportable, tolerable

unbeatable indomitable, invincible, more
than a match for, unconquerable, unstop~
pable, unsurpassable

unbeaten 1. triumphant, unbowed, unde~
feated, unsubdued, unsurpassed, unvan~
quished, victorious, winning **2.** new, un~
touched, untried, untrodden, virgin

unbecoming 1. ill-suited, inappropriate,
incongruous, unattractive, unbefitting,
unfit, unflattering, unsightly, unsuitable,
unsuited **2.** discreditable, improper, in~
decorous, indelicate, offensive, tasteless,
unseemly
Antonyms (*sense 2*) becoming, decent, deco~
rous, delicate, proper, seemly

unbelief atheism, disbelief, distrust, doubt,
incredulity, scepticism
Antonyms belief, credence, credulity, faith,
trust

unbelievable astonishing, beyond belief,
far-fetched, implausible, impossible, im~
probable, inconceivable, incredible, out~
landish, preposterous, questionable, stag~
gering, unconvincing, unimaginable, un~
thinkable
Antonyms authentic, believable, credible,
likely, plausible, possible, probable, trust~
worthy

unbeliever agnostic, atheist, disbeliever,
doubting Thomas, infidel, sceptic

unbelieving disbelieving, distrustful,
doubtful, doubting, dubious, incredulous,
sceptical, suspicious, unconvinced
Antonyms believing, convinced, credulous,
trustful, undoubting, unsuspicious

unbend 1. be informal, calm down, chill
out (*Sl., chiefly U.S.*), cool it (*Sl.*), ease up,
let it all hang out (*Sl.*), let oneself go, let up,
lighten up (*Sl.*), loosen up, relax, slacken,
slow down, take it easy, unbutton (*Inf.*),
unwind **2.** put straight, straighten, uncoil,
uncurl

unbending 1. aloof, distant, formal,
inflexible, reserved, rigid, stiff, uptight
(*Inf.*) **2.** firm, hard-line, intractable, reso~
lute, severe, strict, stubborn, tough, un~
compromising, unyielding
Antonyms (*sense 1*) approachable, at ease,
flexible, friendly, outgoing, relaxed, sociable

unbiased disinterested, dispassionate,
equitable, even-handed, fair, impartial, just,
neutral, objective, open-minded, unpreju~
diced
Antonyms biased, bigoted, partial, preju~
diced, slanted, swayed, unfair, unjust

unbidden 1. free, spontaneous, unforced,
unprompted, voluntary, willing **2.** unasked,
uninvited, unwanted, unwelcome

unbind free, loosen, release, set free, unbri~
dle, unchain, undo, unfasten, unfetter, un~
loose, unshackle, untie, unyoke
Antonyms bind, chain, fasten, fetter, re~
strain, shackle, tie, yoke

unblemished flawless, immaculate, im~
peccable, perfect, pure, spotless, unflawed,
unspotted, unstained, unsullied, untar~
nished
Antonyms blemished, flawed, imperfect,
impure, stained, sullied, tarnished

unborn 1. awaited, embryonic, expected, *in
utero* **2.** coming, future, hereafter, latter,
subsequent, to come

unbosom admit, confess, confide, disbur~
den, disclose, divulge, get (something) off
one's chest (*Inf.*), get (something) out of
one's system, lay bare, let out, reveal, spill
one's guts about (*Sl.*), tell, unburden
Antonyms conceal, cover up, guard, hold
back, suppress, withhold

unbounded absolute, boundless, endless,
immeasurable, infinite, lavish, limitless,
unbridled, unchecked, unconstrained, un~
controlled, unlimited, unrestrained, vast
Antonyms bounded, confined, constrained,
curbed, limited, restricted

unbreakable armoured, durable, inde~
structible, infrangible, lasting, nonbreak~

able, resistant, rugged, shatterproof, solid, strong, toughened
Antonyms breakable, brittle, delicate, flimsy, fragile, frangible

unbridled excessive, intemperate, licentious, rampant, riotous, unchecked, unconstrained, uncontrolled, uncurbed, ungovernable, ungoverned, unrestrained, unruly, violent, wanton

unbroken 1. complete, entire, intact, solid, total, unimpaired, whole 2. ceaseless, constant, continuous, endless, incessant, progressive, serried, successive, uninterrupted, unremitting 3. deep, fast, profound, sound, undisturbed, unruffled, untroubled 4. unbowed, unsubdued, untamed
Antonyms (*sense 1*) broken, cracked, damaged, fragmented, in pieces, shattered (*sense 2*) erratic, fitful, intermittent, interrupted, irregular, occasional, off-and-on, uneven

unburden 1. disburden, discharge, disencumber, ease the load, empty, lighten, relieve, unload 2. come clean (*Inf.*), confess, confide, disclose, get (something) off one's chest (*Inf.*), lay bare, make a clean breast of, reveal, spill one's guts about (*Sl.*), tell all, unbosom

uncalled-for gratuitous, inappropriate, needless, undeserved, unjust, unjustified, unnecessary, unprovoked, unwarranted, unwelcome
Antonyms appropriate, deserved, just, justified, necessary, needed, provoked, warranted

uncanny 1. creepy (*Inf.*), eerie, eldritch (*Poetic*), mysterious, preternatural, queer, spooky (*Inf.*), strange, supernatural, unearthly, unnatural, weird 2. astonishing, astounding, exceptional, extraordinary, fantastic, incredible, inspired, miraculous, prodigious, remarkable, singular, unheard-of, unusual

unceasing ceaseless, constant, continual, continuing, continuous, endless, incessant, never-ending, nonstop, perpetual, persistent, unending, unfailing, unremitting
Antonyms fitful, intermittent, irregular, occasional, periodic, spasmodic, sporadic

uncertain 1. ambiguous, chancy, conjectural, doubtful, iffy (*Inf.*), incalculable, indefinite, indeterminate, indistinct, questionable, risky, speculative, undetermined, unforeseeable, unpredictable 2. ambivalent, doubtful, dubious, hazy, in two minds, irresolute, unclear, unconfirmed, undecided, undetermined, unfixed, unresolved, unsettled, unsure, up in the air, vacillating, vague 3. changeable, erratic, fitful, hesitant, iffy (*Inf.*), inconstant, insecure, irregular, precarious, unpredictable, unreliable, vacillating, variable, wavering

Antonyms certain, clear, clear-cut, decided, definite, firm, fixed, known, positive, predictable, resolute, settled, sure, unambiguous, unhesitating, unvarying, unwavering

uncertainty ambiguity, bewilderment, confusion, dilemma, doubt, dubiety, hesitancy, hesitation, inconclusiveness, indecision, irresolution, lack of confidence, misgiving, mystification, perplexity, puzzlement, qualm, quandary, scepticism, state of suspense, unpredictability, vagueness
Antonyms assurance, certainty, confidence, decision, predictability, resolution, sureness, trust

unchangeable changeless, constant, fixed, immovable, immutable, inevitable, invariable, irreversible, permanent, stable, steadfast, strong, unalterable
Antonyms changeable, inconstant, irregular, mutable, shifting, unstable, variable, wavering

unchanging abiding, changeless, constant, continuing, enduring, eternal, immutable, imperishable, lasting, permanent, perpetual, unchanged, unfading, unvarying

uncharitable cruel, hardhearted, insensitive, mean, merciless, stingy, unchristian, unfeeling, unforgiving, unfriendly, ungenerous, unkind, unsympathetic
Antonyms charitable, feeling, friendly, generous, kind, merciful, sensitive, sympathetic

uncharted not mapped, strange, undiscovered, unexplored, unfamiliar, unknown, unplumbed, virgin

unchaste depraved, dissolute, fallen, immodest, immoral, impure, lewd, loose, promiscuous, unvirtuous, wanton
Antonyms chaste, decent, innocent, modest, moral, pure, virtuous

uncivil bad-mannered, bearish, boorish, brusque, churlish, discourteous, disrespectful, gruff, ill-bred, ill-mannered, impolite, rude, surly, uncouth, unmannerly
Antonyms civil, courteous, mannerly, polished, polite, refined, respectful, well-bred, well-mannered

uncivilized 1. barbarian, barbaric, barbarous, illiterate, primitive, savage, wild 2. beyond the pale, boorish, brutish, churlish, coarse, gross, philistine, uncouth, uncultivated, uncultured, uneducated, unmannered, unpolished, unsophisticated, vulgar

unclean contaminated, corrupt, defiled, dirty, evil, filthy, foul, impure, nasty, polluted, scuzzy (*Sl., chiefly U.S.*), soiled, spotted, stained, sullied, tainted
Antonyms clean, faultless, flawless, pure, spotless, unblemished, unstained, unsullied

unclear ambiguous, bleary, blurred, confused, dim, doubtful, faint, fuzzy, hazy, ill-defined, indefinite, indeterminate, indiscernible, indistinct, indistinguishable, misty, muffled, obscure, out of focus, shad~ owy, undefined, unintelligible, vague, weak **Antonyms** clear, defined, determinate, dis~ cernible, distinct, distinguishable, evident, intelligible

uncomfortable 1. awkward, causing dis~ comfort, cramped, disagreeable, hard, ill-fitting, incommodious, irritating, painful, rough, troublesome **2.** awkward, confused, discomfited, disquieted, distressed, dis~ turbed, embarrassed, ill at ease, out of place, self-conscious, troubled, uneasy **Antonyms** (*sense 2*) at ease, comfortable, easy, relaxed, serene, untroubled

uncommitted floating, free, free-floating, neutral, nonaligned, nonpartisan, not in~ volved, (sitting) on the fence, unattached, uninvolved

uncommon 1. bizarre, curious, few and far between, infrequent, novel, odd, out of the ordinary, peculiar, queer, rare, scarce, singular, strange, unfamiliar, unusual **2.** distinctive, exceptional, extraordinary, in~ comparable, inimitable, notable, note~ worthy, outstanding, rare, remarkable, sin~ gular, special, superior, unparalleled, un~ precedented **Antonyms** (*sense 1*) common, familiar, fre~ quent, regular, routine, usual (*sense 2*) aver~ age, banal, commonplace, everyday, hum~ drum, mundane, ordinary, run-of-the-mill

uncommonly 1. hardly ever, infrequently, not often, occasionally, only now and then, rarely, scarcely ever, seldom **2.** exception~ ally, extremely, particularly, peculiarly, re~ markably, strangely, unusually, very

uncommunicative close, curt, guarded, reserved, reticent, retiring, secretive, short, shy, silent, taciturn, tight-lipped, unforth~ coming, unresponsive, unsociable, with~ drawn **Antonyms** chatty, communicative, forth~ coming, garrulous, loquacious, responsive, talkative, voluble

uncompromising decided, die-hard, firm, hard-line, inexorable, inflexible, intransi~ gent, obdurate, obstinate, rigid, steadfast, stiff-necked, strict, stubborn, tough, un~ bending, unyielding

unconcern aloofness, apathy, detachment, indifference, insouciance, lack of interest, nonchalance, remoteness, uninterestedness

unconcerned 1. aloof, apathetic, cool, de~ tached, dispassionate, distant, incurious, indifferent, oblivious, uninterested, unin~ volved, unmoved, unsympathetic **2.** blithe, callous, carefree, careless, easy, insouciant, nonchalant, not bothered, relaxed, serene, unperturbed, unruffled, untroubled, unwor~ ried

Antonyms (*sense 1*) avid, curious, eager, in~ terested, involved (*sense 2*) agitated, anxious, concerned, distressed, perturbed, uneasy, worried

unconditional absolute, arrant, categori~ cal, complete, downright, entire, explicit, full, out-and-out, outright, plenary, positive, thoroughgoing, total, unlimited, unqualified, unreserved, unrestricted, utter **Antonyms** conditional, limited, partial, qualified, reserved, restricted

uncongenial antagonistic, antipathetic, disagreeable, discordant, displeasing, dis~ tasteful, incompatible, not one's cup of tea (*Inf.*), unharmonious, uninviting, unpleas~ ant, unsuited, unsympathetic **Antonyms** affable, agreeable, compatible, congenial, genial, harmonious, pleasant, pleasing, sympathetic

unconnected 1. detached, disconnected, divided, independent, separate **2.** discon~ nected, disjointed, illogical, incoherent, ir~ relevant, meaningless, nonsensical, not re~ lated, unrelated **Antonyms** (*sense 2*) coherent, connected, in~ telligible, logical, meaningful, related, rel~ evant

unconquerable 1. indomitable, invincible, unbeatable, undefeatable, unyielding **2.** en~ during, ingrained, innate, insurmountable, inveterate, irrepressible, irresistible, over~ powering

unconscionable 1. amoral, criminal, un~ ethical, unfair, unjust, unprincipled, un~ scrupulous **2.** excessive, exorbitant, ex~ travagant, extreme, immoderate, inordinate, outrageous, preposterous, unreasonable

unconscious 1. blacked out (*Inf.*), coma~ tose, dead to the world (*Inf.*), insensible, knocked out, numb, out, out cold, senseless, stunned **2.** blind to, deaf to, heedless, igno~ rant, in ignorance, lost to, oblivious, un~ aware, unknowing, unmindful, unsuspect~ ing **3.** accidental, inadvertent, unintended, unintentional, unpremeditated, unwitting **4.** automatic, gut (*Inf.*), inherent, innate, instinctive, involuntary, latent, reflex, re~ pressed, subconscious, subliminal, sup~ pressed, unrealized **Antonyms** (*sense 1*) alert, awake, aware, conscious, responsive, sensible (*sense 3*) cal~ culated, conscious, deliberate, intentional, planned, studied, wilful

uncontrollable beside oneself, carried away, frantic, furious, irrepressible, irre~ sistible, like one possessed, mad, strong, ungovernable, unmanageable, unruly, vio~ lent, wild

uncontrolled boisterous, furious, lacking self-control, out of control, out of hand, rampant, riotous, running wild, unbridled,

unchecked, uncurbed, undisciplined, un~
governed, unrestrained, unruly, unsubmis~
sive, untrammelled, violent
Antonyms contained, controlled, disci~
plined, restrained, subdued, submissive

unconventional atypical, bizarre, bohe~
mian, different, eccentric, far-out (*Sl.*),
freakish, idiosyncratic, individual, indi~
vidualistic, informal, irregular, noncon~
formist, odd, oddball (*Inf.*), offbeat, off-the-
wall (*Sl.*), original, out of the ordinary,
outré, uncustomary, unorthodox, unusual,
wacko (*Sl.*), way-out (*Inf.*)
Antonyms conventional, normal, ordinary,
orthodox, proper, regular, typical, usual

unconvincing dubious, feeble, fishy (*Inf.*),
flimsy, hard to believe, implausible, im~
probable, inconclusive, lame, questionable,
specious, suspect, thin, unlikely, unpersua~
sive, weak
Antonyms believable, conclusive, convinc~
ing, credible, likely, persuasive, plausible,
probable

uncoordinated all thumbs, awkward,
bumbling, bungling, butterfingered (*Inf.*),
clodhopping (*Inf.*), clumsy, graceless,
heavy-footed, inept, lumbering, maladroit,
ungainly, ungraceful

uncounted countless, infinite, innumer~
able, legion, multitudinous, myriad, num~
berless, unnumbered, untold

uncouth awkward, barbaric, boorish,
clownish, clumsy, coarse, crude, gawky,
graceless, gross, ill-mannered, loutish, lub~
berly, oafish, rough, rude, rustic, uncivi~
lized, uncultivated, ungainly, unrefined,
unseemly, vulgar
Antonyms civilized, courteous, cultivated,
elegant, graceful, refined, seemly, well-
mannered

uncover 1. bare, lay open, lift the lid, open,
show, strip, take the wraps off, unwrap **2.**
blow wide open (*Sl.*), bring to light, dis~
close, discover, divulge, expose, lay bare,
make known, reveal, unearth, unmask
Antonyms clothe, conceal, cover, cover up,
drape, dress, hide, keep under wraps, sup~
press

uncritical easily pleased, indiscriminate,
undiscerning, undiscriminating, unexact~
ing, unfussy, unperceptive, unselective, un~
thinking
Antonyms critical, discerning, discrimi~
nating, fastidious, fussy, perceptive, selective

undeceive be honest with, correct, dis~
abuse, disillusion, enlighten, open
(someone's) eyes (to), put (someone) right,
set (someone) straight, shatter (someone's)
illusions

undecided 1. ambivalent, dithering
(*Chiefly Brit.*), doubtful, dubious, hesitant,

in two minds, irresolute, swithering (*Scot.*),
torn, uncertain, uncommitted, unsure, wa~
vering **2.** debatable, iffy (*Inf.*), indefinite, in
the balance, moot, open, pending, tentative,
unconcluded, undetermined, unsettled, up
in the air, vague
Antonyms certain, committed, decided,
definite, determined, resolute, resolved, set~
tled, sure

undecipherable crabbed, cryptic, hiero~
glyphic, illegible, impenetrable, incompre~
hensible, indecipherable, indistinct, undis~
tinguishable, unreadable, unrecognizable

undefended defenceless, exposed, naked,
open to attack, unarmed, unfortified, un~
guarded, unprotected, vulnerable, wide
open
Antonyms armed, defended, fortified,
guarded, protected

undefiled chaste, clean, clear, flawless, im~
maculate, impeccable, pure, sinless, spot~
less, squeaky-clean, unblemished, unsoiled,
unspotted, unstained, unsullied, virginal
Antonyms blemished, defiled, flawed, im~
pure, sinful, soiled, spotted, stained, sullied

undefined 1. formless, hazy, indefinite, in~
distinct, shadowy, tenuous, vague **2.** im~
precise, indeterminate, inexact, unclear,
unexplained, unspecified
Antonyms (*sense 2*) clear, defined, definite,
determinate, exact, explicit, precise, specified

undemonstrative aloof, cold, contained,
distant, formal, impassive, reserved, re~
strained, reticent, stiff, stolid, unaffection~
ate, uncommunicative, unemotional, unre~
sponsive, withdrawn
Antonyms affectionate, demonstrative,
emotional, expressive, friendly, outgoing,
overemotional, unreserved, warm

undeniable beyond (a) doubt, beyond
question, certain, clear, evident, incontest~
able, incontrovertible, indisputable, indubi~
table, irrefutable, manifest, obvious, patent,
proven, sound, sure, unassailable, undoubt~
ed, unquestionable
Antonyms debatable, deniable, doubtful,
dubious, questionable, uncertain, unproven

under *prep.* **1.** below, beneath, on the bot~
tom of, underneath **2.** directed by, governed
by, inferior to, junior to, reporting to, sec~
ondary to, subject to, subordinate to, sub~
servient to **3.** belonging to, comprised in,
included in, subsumed under ~*adv.* **4.** be~
low, beneath, down, downward, lower, to
the bottom
Antonyms (*senses 1 & 4*) above, over, up,
upper, upward

underclothes lingerie, smalls (*Inf.*),
underclothing, undergarments, underlinen,
underthings, underwear, undies (*Inf.*), un~
mentionables (*Humorous*)

undercover clandestine, concealed, confi~ dential, covert, hidden, hush-hush (*Inf.*), intelligence, private, secret, spy, surrepti~ tious, underground
Antonyms manifest, open, overt, plain, un~ concealed, visible

undercurrent 1. crosscurrent, rip, rip current, riptide, tideway, underflow, under~ tow **2.** atmosphere, aura, drift, feeling, flavour, hidden feeling, hint, murmur, overtone, sense, suggestion, tendency, ten~ or, tinge, trend, undertone, vibes (*Sl.*), vi~ brations

undercut 1. sacrifice, sell at a loss, sell cheaply, undercharge, underprice, undersell **2.** cut away, cut out, excavate, gouge out, hollow out, mine, undermine

underdog fall guy (*Inf.*), little fellow (*Inf.*), loser, victim, weaker party

underestimate belittle, hold cheap, mini~ mize, miscalculate, misprize, not do justice to, rate too low, sell short (*Inf.*), set no store by, think too little of, underrate, under~ value
Antonyms exaggerate, inflate, overdo, over~ estimate, overrate, overstate

undergo bear, be subjected to, endure, ex~ perience, go through, stand, submit to, suf~ fer, sustain, weather, withstand

underground *adj.* **1.** below ground, below the surface, buried, covered, subterranean **2.** clandestine, concealed, covert, hidden, secret, surreptitious, undercover **3.** alter~ native, avant-garde, experimental, radical, revolutionary, subversive ~*n.* **the under~ ground 4.** the metro, the subway, the tube (*Brit.*) **5.** partisans, the Maquis, the Resist~ ance

undergrowth bracken, brambles, briars, brush, brushwood, scrub, underbrush, underbush, underwood

underhand clandestine, crafty, crooked (*Inf.*), deceitful, deceptive, devious, dishon~ est, dishonourable, fraudulent, furtive, se~ cret, secretive, sly, sneaky, stealthy, sur~ reptitious, treacherous, underhanded, un~ ethical, unscrupulous
Antonyms above board, frank, honest, hon~ ourable, legal, open, outright, principled, scrupulous

underline 1. italicize, mark, rule a line un~ der, underscore **2.** accentuate, bring home, call *or* draw attention to, emphasize, give emphasis to, highlight, point up, stress
Antonyms (*sense 2*) gloss over, make light of, minimize, play down, soft-pedal (*Inf.*), under~ rate

underling flunky, hireling, inferior, lackey, menial, minion, nonentity, retainer, serv~ ant, slave, subordinate, understrapper

underlying 1. concealed, hidden, latent, lurking, veiled **2.** basal, basic, elementary, essential, fundamental, intrinsic, primary, prime, radical, root

undermine 1. dig out, eat away at, erode, excavate, mine, tunnel, undercut, wear away **2.** debilitate, disable, impair, sabo~ tage, sap, subvert, threaten, weaken
Antonyms (*sense 2*) buttress, fortify, pro~ mote, reinforce, strengthen, sustain

underprivileged badly off, deprived, des~ titute, disadvantaged, impoverished, in need, in want, needy, poor

underrate belittle, discount, disparage, fail to appreciate, misprize, not do justice to, set (too) little store by, underestimate, under~ value
Antonyms exaggerate, overestimate, overprize, overrate, overvalue

undersized atrophied, dwarfish, miniature, pygmy *or* pigmy, runtish, runty, small, squat, stunted, teensy-weensy, teeny-weeny, tiny, underdeveloped, underweight
Antonyms big, colossal, giant, huge, mas~ sive, oversized, overweight

understand 1. appreciate, apprehend, be aware, catch on (*Inf.*), comprehend, con~ ceive, cotton on (*Inf.*), discern, fathom, fol~ low, get, get the hang of (*Inf.*), get to the bottom of, grasp, know, make head or tail of (*Inf.*), make out, penetrate, perceive, re~ alize, recognize, savvy (*Sl.*), see, take in, tumble to (*Inf.*), twig (*Brit. inf.*) **2.** assume, be informed, believe, conclude, gather, hear, learn, presume, suppose, take it, think **3.** accept, appreciate, be able to see, commis~ erate, show compassion for, sympathize with, tolerate

understanding *n.* **1.** appreciation, aware~ ness, comprehension, discernment, grasp, insight, intelligence, judgment, knowledge, penetration, perception, sense **2.** belief, conclusion, estimation, idea, interpretation, judgment, notion, opinion, perception, view, viewpoint **3.** accord, agreement, common view, gentlemen's agreement, meeting of minds, pact ~*adj.* **4.** accepting, compas~ sionate, considerate, discerning, forbearing, forgiving, kind, kindly, patient, perceptive, responsive, sensitive, sympathetic, tolerant
Antonyms *n.* (*sense 1*) ignorance, incompre~ hension, insensitivity, misapprehension, misunderstanding, obtuseness (*sense 3*) aloof~ ness, coldness, disagreement, dispute ~*adj.* inconsiderate, insensitive, intolerant, obtuse, rigid, strict, unfeeling, unsympathetic

understood 1. implicit, implied, inferred, tacit, unspoken, unstated **2.** accepted, as~ sumed, axiomatic, presumed, taken for granted

understudy *n.* double, fill-in, replacement, reserve, stand-in, sub, substitute

undertake 1. agree, bargain, commit one~ self, contract, covenant, engage, guarantee, pledge, promise, stipulate, take upon oneself **2.** attempt, begin, commence, embark on, endeavour, enter upon, set about, tackle, take on, try

undertaker funeral director, mortician (*U.S.*)

undertaking 1. affair, attempt, business, effort, endeavour, enterprise, game, opera~ tion, project, task, venture **2.** assurance, commitment, pledge, promise, solemn word, vow, word, word of honour

undertone 1. low tone, murmur, subdued voice, whisper **2.** atmosphere, feeling, flavour, hint, suggestion, tinge, touch, trace, undercurrent, vibes (*Sl.*)

undervalue depreciate, hold cheap, look down on, make light of, minimize, mis~ judge, misprize, set no store by, underesti~ mate, underrate
Antonyms exaggerate, overestimate, over~ rate, overvalue

underwater submarine, submerged, sunk~ en, undersea

under way afoot, begun, going on, in mo~ tion, in operation, in progress, started

underwear lingerie, smalls (*Inf.*), under~ clothes, underclothing, undergarments, underlinen, underthings, undies (*Inf.*), un~ mentionables (*Humorous*)

underweight emaciated, half-starved, puny, skin and bone (*Inf.*), skinny, under~ nourished, undersized

underworld 1. criminal element, crimi~ nals, gangland (*Inf.*), gangsters, organized crime **2.** abode of the dead, Hades, hell, in~ fernal region, nether regions, nether world, the inferno

underwrite 1. back, finance, fund, guaran~ tee, insure, provide security, sponsor, sub~ sidize **2.** countersign, endorse, initial, sign, subscribe **3.** agree to, approve, consent, O.K. *or* okay (*Inf.*), sanction

undesirable disagreeable, disliked, dis~ tasteful, dreaded, objectionable, obnoxious, offensive, out of place, repugnant, (to be) avoided, unacceptable, unattractive, un~ pleasing, unpopular, unsavoury, unsuitable, unwanted, unwelcome, unwished-for
Antonyms acceptable, agreeable, appealing, attractive, desirable, inviting, pleasing, popular, welcome

undeveloped embryonic, immature, in~ choate, in embryo, latent, potential, pri~ mordial (*Biol.*)

undignified beneath one, beneath one's dignity, improper, inappropriate, indeco~

rous, inelegant, infra dig (*Inf.*), lacking dig~ nity, unbecoming, ungentlemanly, unlady~ like, unrefined, unseemly, unsuitable
Antonyms appropriate, becoming, deco~ rous, dignified, elegant, proper, refined, seemly, suitable

undisciplined disobedient, erratic, fitful, obstreperous, uncontrolled, unpredictable, unreliable, unrestrained, unruly, un~ schooled, unsteady, unsystematic, un~ trained, wayward, wild, wilful
Antonyms controlled, disciplined, obedient, predictable, reliable, restrained, steady, trained

undisguised blatant, complete, evident, explicit, genuine, manifest, obvious, open, out-and-out, overt, patent, thoroughgoing, transparent, unconcealed, unfeigned, un~ mistakable, utter, wholehearted
Antonyms concealed, covert, disguised, feigned, hidden, secret

undisputed accepted, acknowledged, be~ yond question, certain, conclusive, freely admitted, incontestable, incontrovertible, indisputable, irrefutable, not disputed, rec~ ognized, sure, unchallenged, uncontested, undeniable, undoubted, unquestioned
Antonyms deniable, disputed, doubtful, du~ bious, inconclusive, questioned, uncertain

undistinguished commonplace, everyday, indifferent, mediocre, no great shakes (*Inf.*), nothing to write home about (*Inf.*), ordi~ nary, pedestrian, prosaic, run-of-the-mill, so-so (*Inf.*), unexceptional, unexciting, un~ impressive, unremarkable
Antonyms distinguished, exceptional, ex~ citing, extraordinary, impressive, notable, outstanding, remarkable, striking

undisturbed 1. not moved, quiet, uninter~ rupted, untouched, without interruption **2.** calm, collected, composed, equable, even, motionless, placid, sedate, serene, tranquil, unagitated, unbothered, unfazed (*Inf.*), un~ perturbed, unruffled, untroubled
Antonyms (*sense 1*) confused, disordered, interfered with, interrupted, moved, muddled (*sense 2*) agitated, bothered, busy, disturbed, excited, flustered, nervous, perturbed, trou~ bled, upset

undivided combined, complete, concentrat~ ed, concerted, entire, exclusive, full, solid, thorough, unanimous, undistracted, united, whole, wholehearted

undo 1. disengage, disentangle, loose, loos~ en, open, unbutton, unfasten, unlock, untie, unwrap **2.** annul, cancel, invalidate, neu~ tralize, nullify, offset, reverse, wipe out **3.** bring to naught, defeat, destroy, impover~ ish, invalidate, mar, overturn, quash, ruin, shatter, subvert, undermine, upset, wreck

undoing 1. collapse, defeat, destruction,

disgrace, downfall, humiliation, overthrow, overturn, reversal, ruin, ruination, shame **2.** affliction, blight, curse, fatal flaw, misfortune, the last straw, trial, trouble, weakness

undone incomplete, left, neglected, not completed, not done, omitted, outstanding, passed over, unattended to, unfinished, unfulfilled, unperformed
Antonyms accomplished, attended to, complete, done, finished, fulfilled, performed

undoubted acknowledged, certain, definite, evident, incontrovertible, indisputable, indubitable, obvious, sure, undisputed, unquestionable, unquestioned

undoubtedly assuredly, beyond a shadow of (a) doubt, beyond question, certainly, definitely, doubtless, of course, surely, undeniably, unmistakably, unquestionably, without doubt

undreamed of astonishing, inconceivable, incredible, miraculous, undreamt, unexpected, unforeseen, unheard-of, unimagined, unsuspected, unthought-of

undress 1. *v.* disrobe, divest oneself of, peel off (*Sl.*), shed, strip, take off one's clothes **2.** *n.* disarray, dishabille, nakedness, nudity

undue disproportionate, excessive, extravagant, extreme, immoderate, improper, inordinate, intemperate, needless, overmuch, too great, too much, uncalled-for, undeserved, unnecessary, unseemly, unwarranted
Antonyms appropriate, due, fitting, justified, necessary, proper, suitable, well-considered

unduly disproportionately, excessively, extravagantly, immoderately, improperly, inordinately, out of all proportion, overly, overmuch, unjustifiably, unnecessarily, unreasonably
Antonyms duly, justifiably, moderately, ordinately, properly, proportionately, reasonably

undying constant, continuing, deathless, eternal, everlasting, immortal, imperishable, indestructible, inextinguishable, infinite, perennial, permanent, perpetual, sempiternal (*Literary*), undiminished, unending, unfading
Antonyms ephemeral, finite, fleeting, impermanent, inconstant, momentary, mortal, perishable, short-lived

unearth 1. dig up, disinter, dredge up, excavate, exhume **2.** bring to light, discover, expose, ferret out, find, reveal, root up, turn up, uncover

unearthly 1. eerie, eldritch (*Poetic*), ghostly, haunted, nightmarish, phantom, spectral, spooky (*Inf.*), strange, uncanny, weird **2.** ethereal, heavenly, not of this world,

preternatural, sublime, supernatural **3.** abnormal, absurd, extraordinary, ridiculous, strange, ungodly (*Inf.*), unholy (*Inf.*), unreasonable

uneasiness agitation, alarm, anxiety, apprehension, apprehensiveness, disquiet, doubt, dubiety, misgiving, nervousness, perturbation, qualms, suspicion, trepidation, worry
Antonyms calm, composure, cool, ease, peace, quiet, serenity

uneasy 1. agitated, anxious, apprehensive, discomposed, disturbed, edgy, ill at ease, impatient, jittery (*Inf.*), nervous, on edge, perturbed, restive, restless, troubled, twitchy (*Inf.*), uncomfortable, unsettled, upset, wired (*Sl.*), worried **2.** awkward, constrained, insecure, precarious, shaky, strained, tense, uncomfortable, unstable **3.** bothering, dismaying, disquieting, disturbing, troubling, upsetting, worrying
Antonyms at ease, calm, comfortable, relaxed, tranquil, unfazed (*Inf.*), unflustered, unperturbed, unruffled

uneconomic loss-making, nonpaying, non-profit-making, nonviable, unprofitable
Antonyms economic, money-making, productive, profitable, remunerative, viable

uneducated 1. ignorant, illiterate, unlettered, unread, unschooled, untaught **2.** benighted, lowbrow, uncultivated, uncultured
Antonyms (*sense 1*) educated, informed, instructed, literate, schooled, taught, tutored

unemotional apathetic, cold, cool, impassive, indifferent, listless, passionless, phlegmatic, reserved, undemonstrative, unexcitable, unfeeling, unimpressionable, unresponsive
Antonyms demonstrative, emotional, excitable, feeling, passionate, responsive, sensitive

unemployed idle, jobless, laid off, on the dole (*Brit. inf.*), out of a job, out of work, redundant, resting (*of an actor*), workless

unending ceaseless, constant, continual, endless, eternal, everlasting, incessant, interminable, never-ending, perpetual, unceasing, unremitting

unendurable insufferable, insupportable, intolerable, more than flesh and blood can stand, unbearable
Antonyms bearable, endurable, sufferable, supportable, tolerable

unenthusiastic apathetic, blasé, bored, half-arsed, half-assed (*U.S. & Canad. sl.*), half-hearted, indifferent, lukewarm, neutral, nonchalant, unimpressed, uninterested, unmoved, unresponsive
Antonyms ardent, eager, enthusiastic, excited, interested, keen, passionate

unenviable disagreeable, painful, thank~

less, uncomfortable, undesirable, unpleas~ant

Antonyms agreeable, attractive, desirable, enviable, pleasant

unequal 1. different, differing, disparate, dissimilar, not uniform, unlike, unmatched, variable, varying **2.** *With* **to** found wanting, inadequate, insufficient, not up to **3.** asym~metrical, disproportionate, ill-matched, ir~regular, unbalanced, uneven

Antonyms (*sense 1*) equal, equivalent, iden~tical, like, matched, similar, uniform

unequalled beyond compare, incompa~rable, inimitable, matchless, nonpareil, paramount, peerless, pre-eminent, second to none, supreme, transcendent, unmatched, unparalleled, unrivalled, unsurpassed, without equal

unequivocal absolute, certain, clear, clear-cut, decisive, definite, direct, evident, explicit, incontrovertible, indubitable, manifest, plain, positive, straight, unam~biguous, uncontestable, unmistakable

Antonyms ambiguous, doubtful, equivocal, evasive, indecisive, noncommittal, vague

unethical dirty, dishonest, dishonourable, disreputable, illegal, immoral, improper, shady (*Inf.*), underhand, under-the-table, unfair, unprincipled, unprofessional, un~scrupulous, wrong

Antonyms ethical, honest, honourable, le~gal, moral, proper, scrupulous, upright

uneven 1. bumpy, not flat, not level, not smooth, rough **2.** broken, changeable, fitful, fluctuating, intermittent, irregular, jerky, patchy, spasmodic, unsteady, variable **3.** asymmetrical, lopsided, not parallel, odd, out of true, unbalanced **4.** disparate, ill-matched, one-sided, unequal, unfair

Antonyms (*sense 1*) even, flat, level, plane, smooth

uneventful boring, commonplace, dull, ho-hum (*Inf.*), humdrum, monotonous, or~dinary, quiet, routine, tedious, unexcep~tional, unexciting, uninteresting, un~memorable, unremarkable, unvaried

Antonyms eventful, exceptional, exciting, interesting, memorable, momentous, re~markable

unexceptional common or garden (*Inf.*), commonplace, conventional, insignificant, mediocre, normal, ordinary, pedestrian, run-of-the-mill, undistinguished, unimpres~sive, unremarkable, usual

Antonyms distinguished, exceptional, im~pressive, notable, noteworthy, outstanding, remarkable, significant, unusual

unexpected abrupt, accidental, astonish~ing, chance, fortuitous, not bargained for, out of the blue, startling, sudden, surpris~ing, unanticipated, unforeseen, unlooked-for, unpredictable

Antonyms anticipated, awaited, expected, foreseen, normal, planned, predictable

unfailing 1. bottomless, boundless, cease~less, continual, continuous, endless, inex~haustible, never-failing, persistent, unflag~ging, unlimited **2.** certain, constant, de~pendable, faithful, infallible, loyal, reliable, staunch, steadfast, sure, tried and true, true

Antonyms (*sense 2*) disloyal, fallible, incon~stant, uncertain, unfaithful, unreliable, un~sure, untrustworthy

unfair 1. arbitrary, biased, bigoted, dis~criminatory, inequitable, one-sided, partial, partisan, prejudiced, unjust **2.** crooked (*Inf.*), dishonest, dishonourable, uncalled-for, unethical, unprincipled, unscrupulous, unsporting, unwarranted, wrongful

Antonyms (*sense 2*) ethical, fair, honest, just, principled, scrupulous

unfaithful 1. deceitful, disloyal, faithless, false, false-hearted, perfidious, recreant (*Archaic*), traitorous, treacherous, treason~able, unreliable, untrustworthy **2.** adulter~ous, faithless, fickle, inconstant, two-timing (*Inf.*), unchaste, untrue **3.** distorted, erro~neous, imperfect, imprecise, inaccurate, in~exact, unreliable, untrustworthy

Antonyms (*sense 1*) constant, faithful, loyal, steadfast, true, trustworthy (*sense 3*) accurate, exact, perfect, precise, reliable

unfamiliar 1. alien, curious, different, little known, new, novel, out-of-the-way, strange, unaccustomed, uncommon, unknown, un~usual **2.** *With* **with** a stranger to, inexperi~enced in, unaccustomed to, unacquainted, unconversant, uninformed about, uninitiat~ed in, unpractised in, unskilled at, unversed in

Antonyms accustomed, acquainted, aver~age, common, commonplace, conversant, everyday, experienced, familiar, knowledge~able, normal, unexceptional, well-known, well-versed

unfashionable antiquated, behind the times, dated, obsolete, old-fashioned, old hat, out, outmoded, out of date, out of fash~ion, passé, square (*Inf.*), unpopular

Antonyms à la mode, fashionable, modern, popular, stylish, trendy (*Brit. inf.*)

unfasten detach, disconnect, let go, loosen, open, separate, uncouple, undo, unlace, un~lock, untie

unfathomable 1. bottomless, immeasur~able, unmeasured, unplumbed, unsounded **2.** abstruse, baffling, deep, esoteric, impen~etrable, incomprehensible, indecipherable, inexplicable, profound, unknowable

unfavourable 1. adverse, bad, contrary, disadvantageous, hostile, ill-suited, infelici~

tous, inimical, low, negative, poor, unfortu~
nate, unfriendly, unsuited **2.** inauspicious,
inopportune, ominous, threatening, un~
lucky, unpromising, unpropitious, unsea~
sonable, untimely, untoward
Antonyms (*sense 1*) amicable, approving, fa~
vourable, friendly, positive, warm, well-
disposed

unfeeling 1. apathetic, callous, cold, cruel,
hardened, hardhearted, heartless, inhuman,
insensitive, pitiless, stony, uncaring, un~
sympathetic **2.** insensate, insensible, numb,
sensationless
Antonyms (*sense 1*) benevolent, caring, con~
cerned, feeling, gentle, humane, kind, sensi~
tive, sympathetic

unfinished 1. deficient, half-done, imper~
fect, incomplete, in the making, lacking,
unaccomplished, uncompleted, undone,
unfulfilled, wanting **2.** bare, crude, natural,
raw, rough, sketchy, unpolished, unrefined,
unvarnished
Antonyms (*sense 2*) finished, flawless, per~
fected, polished, refined, smooth, varnished

unfit 1. ill-equipped, inadequate, incapable,
incompetent, ineligible, no good, not cut out
for, not equal to, not up to, unprepared,
unqualified, untrained, useless **2.** ill-
adapted, inadequate, inappropriate, ineffec~
tive, not designed, not fit, unsuitable, un~
suited, useless **3.** debilitated, decrepit, fee~
ble, flabby, in poor condition, out of kelter,
out of shape, out of trim, unhealthy
Antonyms (*senses 1 & 2*) able, acceptable, ca~
pable, competent, equipped, qualified, ready,
suitable (*sense 3*) fit, healthy, in good condi~
tion, strong, sturdy, well

unflappable calm, collected, composed,
cool, impassive, imperturbable, level-
headed, not given to worry, self-possessed,
unfazed (*Inf.*), unruffled
Antonyms excitable, flappable, hot-headed,
nervous, temperamental, twitchy (*Inf.*), vola~
tile

unflattering 1. blunt, candid, critical,
honest, uncomplimentary, warts and all **2.**
not shown in the best light, not shown to
advantage, plain, unattractive, unbecoming,
unprepossessing

unflinching bold, constant, determined,
firm, immovable, resolute, stalwart,
staunch, steadfast, steady, unfaltering, un~
shaken, unshrinking, unswerving, unwa~
vering
Antonyms cowed, faltering, scared, shaken,
shrinking, wavering

unfold 1. disentangle, expand, flatten, open,
spread out, straighten, stretch out, undo,
unfurl, unravel, unroll, unwrap **2.** *Fig.*
clarify, describe, disclose, divulge, explain,
illustrate, make known, present, reveal,

show, uncover **3.** bear fruit, blossom, de~
velop, evolve, expand, grow, mature

unforeseen abrupt, accidental, out of the
blue, startling, sudden, surprise, surprising,
unanticipated, unexpected, unlooked-for,
unpredicted
Antonyms anticipated, envisaged, expected,
foreseen, intended, predicted

unforgettable exceptional, extraordinary,
fixed in the mind, impressive, memorable,
never to be forgotten, notable, striking

unforgivable deplorable, disgraceful, inde~
fensible, inexcusable, shameful, unjustifi~
able, unpardonable, unwarrantable
Antonyms allowable, excusable, forgivable,
justifiable, pardonable, venial

unfortunate 1. adverse, calamitous, disas~
trous, ill-fated, ill-starred, inopportune, ru~
inous, unfavourable, untoward **2.** cursed,
doomed, hapless, hopeless, luckless, out of
luck, poor, star-crossed, unhappy, unlucky,
unprosperous, unsuccessful, wretched **3.**
deplorable, ill-advised, inappropriate, infe~
licitous, lamentable, regrettable, unbecom~
ing, unsuitable
Antonyms (*senses 1 & 3*) appropriate, oppor~
tune, suitable, tactful, timely (*sense 2*) auspi~
cious, felicitous, fortuitous, fortunate, happy,
lucky, successful

unfounded baseless, fabricated, false,
groundless, idle, spurious, trumped up,
unjustified, unproven, unsubstantiated,
vain, without basis, without foundation
Antonyms attested, confirmed, factual,
justified, proven, substantiated, verified

unfrequented deserted, godforsaken, iso~
lated, lone, lonely, off the beaten track, re~
mote, sequestered, solitary, uninhabited,
unvisited

unfriendly 1. aloof, antagonistic, chilly,
cold, disagreeable, distant, hostile, ill-
disposed, inhospitable, not on speaking
terms, quarrelsome, sour, surly, uncongen~
ial, unneighbourly, unsociable **2.** alien,
hostile, inauspicious, inhospitable, inimical,
unfavourable, unpropitious
Antonyms affable, amiable, auspicious,
congenial, convivial, friendly, hospitable,
propitious, sociable, warm

unfruitful barren, fruitless, infecund, infer~
tile, sterile, unproductive, unprofitable,
unprolific, unrewarding
Antonyms abundant, fecund, fertile, fruit~
ful, productive, profuse, prolific, rewarding

ungainly awkward, clumsy, gangling,
gawky, inelegant, loutish, lubberly, lum~
bering, slouching, uncoordinated, uncouth,
ungraceful
Antonyms attractive, comely, elegant,
graceful, pleasing

ungodly 1. blasphemous, corrupt, de~

praved, godless, immoral, impious, irreli~
gious, profane, sinful, vile, wicked **2.** *Inf.*
dreadful, horrendous, intolerable, outra~
geous, unearthly, unholy (*Inf.*), unreason~
able, unseemly

ungovernable rebellious, refractory, un~
controllable, unmanageable, unrestrainable,
unruly, wild

ungracious bad-mannered, churlish, dis~
courteous, ill-bred, impolite, offhand, rude,
uncivil, unmannerly
  Antonyms affable, civil, courteous, gra~
cious, mannerly, polite, well-mannered

ungrateful heedless, ingrate (*Archaic*),
selfish, thankless, unappreciative, unmind~
ful, unthankful
  Antonyms appreciative, aware, grateful,
mindful, thankful

unguarded 1. careless, foolhardy, heedless,
ill-considered, impolitic, imprudent, incau~
tious, indiscreet, rash, thoughtless,
uncircumspect, undiplomatic, unthinking,
unwary **2.** defenceless, open to attack, un~
defended, unpatrolled, unprotected, vulner~
able **3.** artless, candid, direct, frank, guile~
less, open, straightforward
  Antonyms (*sense 1*) cagey (*Inf.*), careful,
cautious, diplomatic, discreet, guarded, pru~
dent, wary

unhappy 1. blue, crestfallen, dejected, de~
pressed, despondent, disconsolate, dispirit~
ed, down, downcast, gloomy, long-faced,
melancholy, miserable, mournful, sad, sor~
rowful **2.** cursed, hapless, ill-fated, ill-
omened, luckless, unfortunate, unlucky,
wretched **3.** awkward, clumsy, gauche, ill-
advised, ill-timed, inappropriate, inept, in~
felicitous, injudicious, malapropos, tactless,
unsuitable, untactful
  Antonyms (*sense 1*) cheerful, chirpy (*Inf.*),
content, exuberant, genial, good-humoured,
happy, joyful, light-hearted, overjoyed, over
the moon (*Inf.*), satisfied (*senses 2 & 3*) apt, be~
coming, fortunate, lucky, prudent, suitable,
tactful

unharmed in one piece (*Inf.*), intact, safe,
safe and sound, sound, undamaged, unhurt,
uninjured, unscarred, unscathed, un~
touched, whole, without a scratch
  Antonyms damaged, harmed, hurt, im~
paired, injured, scarred, scathed

unhealthy 1. ailing, delicate, feeble, frail,
infirm, in poor health, invalid, poorly (*Inf.*),
sick, sickly, unsound, unwell, weak **2.** del~
eterious, detrimental, harmful, insalubri~
ous, insanitary, noisome, noxious, un~
wholesome **3.** bad, baneful (*Archaic*), cor~
rupt, corrupting, degrading, demoralizing,
morbid, negative, undesirable
  Antonyms (*senses 1 & 2*) beneficial, fit, good,

healthy, robust, salubrious, salutary, well,
wholesome (*sense 3*) desirable, moral, positive

unheard-of 1. little known, obscure, un~
discovered, unfamiliar, unknown, unre~
garded, unremarked, unsung **2.** inconceiv~
able, never before encountered, new, novel,
singular, unbelievable, undreamed of, un~
exampled, unique, unprecedented, unusual
3. disgraceful, extreme, offensive, outland~
ish, outrageous, preposterous, shocking,
unacceptable, unthinkable

unheeded disobeyed, disregarded, forgot~
ten, ignored, neglected, overlooked, unfol~
lowed, unnoticed, unobserved, untaken
  Antonyms heeded, noted, noticed, obeyed,
observed, regarded, remembered

unhesitating 1. implicit, resolute, stead~
fast, unfaltering, unquestioning, unre~
served, unswerving, unwavering, whole~
hearted **2.** immediate, instant, instanta~
neous, prompt, ready, without delay
  Antonyms (*sense 1*) diffident, hesitant, ir~
resolute, questioning, tentative, uncertain,
unsure, wavering

unhinge 1. confound, confuse, craze, de~
range, disorder, distemper (*Archaic*), drive
out of one's mind, madden, unbalance, un~
settle **2.** detach, disconnect, disjoint, dis~
lodge, remove

unholy 1. base, corrupt, depraved, dishon~
est, evil, heinous, immoral, iniquitous, ir~
religious, profane, sinful, ungodly, vile,
wicked **2.** *Inf.* appalling, awful, dreadful,
horrendous, outrageous, shocking, unearth~
ly, ungodly (*Inf.*), unnatural, unreasonable
  Antonyms (*sense 1*) devout, faithful, godly,
holy, pious, religious, saintly, virtuous

unhoped-for beyond one's wildest dreams,
incredible, like a dream come true, out of
the blue, surprising, unanticipated, unbe~
lievable, undreamed of, unexpected, unim~
aginable, unlooked-for

unhurried calm, deliberate, easy, easy-
going, leisurely, sedate, slow, slow and
steady, slow-paced
  Antonyms brief, cursory, hasty, hectic,
hurried, quick, rushed, speedy, swift

unidentified anonymous, mysterious,
nameless, unclassified, unfamiliar, un~
known, unmarked, unnamed, unrecognized,
unrevealed
  Antonyms classified, familiar, identified,
known, marked, named, recognized

unification alliance, amalgamation, coales~
cence, coalition, combination, confedera~
tion, federation, fusion, merger, union,
uniting

uniform *n.* **1.** costume, dress, garb, habit,
livery, outfit, regalia, regimentals, suit
~*adj.* **2.** consistent, constant, equable, even,
regular, smooth, unbroken, unchanging,

undeviating, unvarying **3.** alike, equal, identical, like, same, selfsame, similar
Antonyms *adj.* (*sense 2*) changeable, chang~ ing, deviating, inconsistent, irregular, un~ even, variable

uniformity 1. constancy, evenness, homo~ geneity, invariability, regularity, sameness, similarity **2.** drabness, dullness, flatness, lack of diversity, monotony, sameness, te~ dium

unify amalgamate, bind, bring together, combine, confederate, consolidate, federate, fuse, join, merge, unite
Antonyms alienate, disconnect, disjoin, disunite, divide, separate, sever, split

unimaginable beyond one's wildest dreams, fantastic, impossible, inconceiv~ able, incredible, indescribable, ineffable, mind-boggling (*Inf.*), unbelievable, un~ heard-of, unthinkable

unimaginative banal, barren, common~ place, derivative, dry, dull, hackneyed, life~ less, matter-of-fact, ordinary, pedestrian, predictable, prosaic, routine, tame, uncrea~ tive, uninspired, unoriginal, unromantic, usual
Antonyms creative, different, exciting, fresh, ground-breaking, imaginative, innova~ tive, inventive, original, unhackneyed, un~ usual

unimpassioned calm, collected, composed, controlled, cool, dispassionate, impassive, moderate, rational, sedate, temperate, tran~ quil, undemonstrative, unemotional, un~ moved

unimpeachable above reproach, beyond criticism, beyond question, blameless, faultless, impeccable, irreproachable, per~ fect, unassailable, unblemished, unchal~ lengeable, unexceptionable, unquestionable
Antonyms blameworthy, faulty, imperfect, reprehensible, reproachable, shameful

unimpeded free, open, unblocked, un~ checked, unconstrained, unhampered, un~ hindered, unrestrained, untrammelled
Antonyms blocked, checked, constrained, hampered, hindered, impeded, restrained

unimportant immaterial, inconsequential, insignificant, irrelevant, low-ranking, mi~ nor, nickel-and-dime (*U.S. sl.*), not worth mentioning, nugatory, of no account, of no consequence, of no moment, paltry, petty, slight, trifling, trivial, worthless
Antonyms essential, grave, important, ma~ jor, significant, urgent, vital, weighty

uninhabited abandoned, barren, desert, deserted, desolate, empty, unoccupied, un~ populated, unsettled, untenanted, vacant, waste

uninhibited 1. candid, frank, free, free and easy, informal, instinctive, liberated, natu~ ral, open, relaxed, spontaneous, unre~ pressed, unreserved, unselfconscious **2.** free, unbridled, unchecked, unconstrained, uncontrolled, uncurbed, unrestrained, un~ restricted
Antonyms bashful, careful, checked, con~ strained, controlled, curbed, demure, ham~ pered, inhibited, modest, restrained, self- conscious, shy, uptight (*Inf.*)

uninspired banal, commonplace, dull, humdrum, indifferent, ordinary, prosaic, stale, stock, unexciting, unimaginative, un~ inspiring, uninteresting, unoriginal
Antonyms brilliant, different, exciting, im~ aginative, inspired, interesting, original, out~ standing

unintelligent braindead (*Inf.*), brainless, dense, dozy (*Brit. inf.*), dull, empty-headed, foolish, gormless (*Brit. inf.*), obtuse, slow, stupid, thick, unreasoning, unthinking
Antonyms bright, clever, intelligent, sharp, smart, thinking

unintelligible double Dutch (*Brit. inf.*), il~ legible, inarticulate, incoherent, incompre~ hensible, indecipherable, indistinct, jum~ bled, meaningless, muddled, unfathomable
Antonyms clear, coherent, comprehensible, intelligible, legible, lucid, understandable

unintentional accidental, casual, fortui~ tous, inadvertent, involuntary, unconscious, undesigned, unintended, unpremeditated, unthinking, unwitting
Antonyms conscious, deliberate, designed, intended, intentional, premeditated, volun~ tary, wilful

uninterested apathetic, blasé, bored, dis~ tant, impassive, incurious, indifferent, list~ less, unconcerned, uninvolved, unrespon~ sive
Antonyms alert, concerned, curious, enthu~ siastic, interested, involved, keen, responsive

uninteresting boring, commonplace, drab, dreary, dry, dull, flat, ho-hum (*Inf.*), hum~ drum, mind-numbing, monotonous, tedious, tiresome, unenjoyable, uneventful, unex~ citing, uninspiring, wearisome
Antonyms absorbing, compelling, enjoy~ able, exciting, gripping, inspiring, interest~ ing, intriguing, stimulating

uninterrupted constant, continual, con~ tinuous, nonstop, peaceful, steady, sus~ tained, unbroken, undisturbed, unending

uninvited not asked, not invited, unasked, unbidden, unwanted, unwelcome

uninviting disagreeable, offensive, off- putting (*Brit. inf.*), repellent, repulsive, un~ appealing, unappetizing, unattractive, undesirable, unpleasant, untempting, unwelcoming
Antonyms agreeable, appealing, appetizing,

attractive, desirable, inviting, pleasant,
tempting, welcoming

union 1. amalgam, amalgamation, blend,
combination, conjunction, fusion, junction,
mixture, synthesis, uniting **2.** alliance, as~
sociation, Bund, coalition, confederacy,
confederation, federation, league **3.** accord,
agreement, concord, concurrence, harmony,
unanimity, unison, unity **4.** coition, coitus,
copulation, coupling, intercourse, marriage,
matrimony, nookie (*Sl.*), rumpy-pumpy (*Sl.*),
the other (*Inf.*), wedlock

unique 1. lone, one and only, only, single,
solitary, sui generis **2.** incomparable, in~
imitable, matchless, nonpareil, peerless,
unequalled, unexampled, unmatched, un~
paralleled, unrivalled, without equal

unison accord, accordance, agreement, con~
cert, concord, cooperation, harmony, una~
nimity, unity
Antonyms disagreement, discord, dishar~
mony, dissension, dissidence, dissonance

unit 1. assembly, detachment, entity, group,
section, system, whole **2.** component, con~
stituent, element, item, member, module,
part, piece, portion, section, segment **3.**
measure, measurement, module, quantity

unite 1. amalgamate, blend, coalesce, com~
bine, confederate, consolidate, couple, fuse,
incorporate, join, link, marry, meld, merge,
unify, wed **2.** ally, associate, band, close
ranks, club together, cooperate, join forces,
join together, league, pool, pull together
Antonyms break, detach, disunite, divide,
divorce, part, separate, sever, split

united 1. affiliated, allied, banded together,
collective, combined, concerted, in partner~
ship, leagued, pooled, unified **2.** agreed, in
accord, in agreement, like-minded, of like
mind, of one mind, of the same opinion,
one, unanimous

unity 1. entity, integrity, oneness, single~
ness, undividedness, unification, union,
wholeness **2.** accord, agreement, assent,
concord, concurrence, consensus, harmony,
peace, solidarity, unanimity, unison
Antonyms disagreement, discord, disunity,
division, factionalism, heterogeneity, ill will,
independence, individuality, in-fighting,
multiplicity, separation, strife

universal all-embracing, catholic, common,
ecumenical, entire, general, omnipresent,
total, unlimited, whole, widespread, world~
wide

universality all-inclusiveness, complete~
ness, comprehensiveness, entirety, general~
ity, generalization, totality, ubiquity

universally always, everywhere, in all
cases, in every instance, invariably, uni~
formly, without exception

universe cosmos, creation, everything,
macrocosm, nature, the natural world

unjust biased, inequitable, one-sided, par~
tial, partisan, prejudiced, undeserved, un~
fair, unjustified, unmerited, wrong, wrong~
ful
Antonyms equitable, ethical, fair, impartial,
just, justified, right, unbiased

unjustifiable indefensible, inexcusable,
outrageous, unacceptable, unforgivable, un~
just, unpardonable, unwarrantable, wrong

unkempt bedraggled, blowzy, disarranged,
disarrayed, dishevelled, disordered, frowzy,
messy, rumpled, scruffy, shabby, shaggy,
slatternly, sloppy (*Inf.*), slovenly, sluttish,
tousled, uncombed, ungroomed, untidy
Antonyms neat, presentable, soigné *or* soi~
gnée, spruce, tidy, trim, well-groomed

unkind cruel, hardhearted, harsh, inconsid~
erate, inhuman, insensitive, malicious,
mean, nasty, spiteful, thoughtless, uncaring,
uncharitable, unchristian, unfeeling, un~
friendly, unsympathetic
Antonyms benevolent, caring, charitable,
considerate, generous, kind, soft-hearted,
sympathetic, thoughtful

unknown 1. alien, concealed, dark, hidden,
mysterious, new, secret, strange, unrecog~
nized, unrevealed, untold **2.** anonymous,
nameless, uncharted, undiscovered, unex~
plored, unidentified, unnamed **3.** humble,
little known, obscure, undistinguished, un~
familiar, unheard-of, unrenowned, unsung
Antonyms (*sense 3*) celebrated, distin~
guished, familiar, known, recognized, re~
nowned, well-known

unladylike coarse, ill-bred, impolite, indeli~
cate, rude, uncivil, ungracious, unmanner~
ly, unrefined
Antonyms civil, delicate, gracious, ladylike,
mannerly, polite, refined, seemly

unlamented unbemoaned, unbewailed, un~
deplored, unmissed, unmourned, unregretted,
unwept

unlawful actionable, against the law,
banned, criminal, forbidden, illegal, illegiti~
mate, illicit, outlawed, prohibited, un~
authorized, under-the-table, unlicensed

unlettered ignorant, illiterate, uneducated,
unlearned, unschooled, untaught, untutored
Antonyms educated, learned, literate,
schooled, taught, tutored

unlike contrasted, different, dissimilar, dis~
tinct, divergent, diverse, ill-matched, in~
compatible, not alike, opposite, unequal,
unrelated
Antonyms compatible, equal, like, matched,
related, similar

unlikely 1. doubtful, faint, improbable, not
likely, remote, slight, unimaginable **2.** im~

plausible, incredible, questionable, unbe~
lievable, unconvincing

unlimited 1. boundless, countless, endless,
extensive, great, illimitable, immeasurable,
immense, incalculable, infinite, limitless, un~
bounded, vast **2.** absolute, all-encompassing,
complete, full, total, unconditional, uncon~
strained, unfettered, unqualified, unrestrict~
ed
Antonyms (*sense 1*) bounded, circumscribed,
confined, constrained, finite, limited, re~
stricted

unload disburden, discharge, dump, empty,
lighten, off-load, relieve, unburden, unlade,
unpack

unlock free, let loose, open, release, unbar,
unbolt, undo, unfasten, unlatch

unlooked-for chance, fortuitous, out of the
blue, surprise, surprising, unanticipated,
undreamed of, unexpected, unforeseen,
unhoped-for, unpredicted, unthought-of

unloved disliked, forsaken, loveless, ne~
glected, rejected, spurned, uncared-for,
uncherished, unpopular, unwanted
Antonyms adored, beloved, cherished,
liked, loved, popular, precious, wanted

unlucky 1. cursed, disastrous, hapless,
luckless, miserable, unfortunate, unhappy,
unsuccessful, wretched **2.** doomed, ill-fated,
ill-omened, ill-starred, inauspicious, omi~
nous, unfavourable, untimely
Antonyms (*sense 1*) blessed, favoured, fortu~
nate, happy, lucky, prosperous

unmanageable 1. awkward, bulky, cum~
bersome, difficult to handle, inconvenient,
unhandy, unwieldy **2.** difficult, fractious,
intractable, obstreperous, out of hand, re~
fractory, stroppy (*Brit. sl.*), uncontrollable,
unruly, wild
Antonyms (*sense 2*) amenable, compliant,
docile, easy, manageable, submissive, trac~
table, wieldy

unmannerly badly behaved, bad-mannered,
discourteous, disrespectful, ill-bred, ill-
mannered, impolite, misbehaved, rude, un~
civil, uncouth
Antonyms civil, courteous, mannerly, po~
lite, respectful, well-behaved, well-bred,
well-mannered

unmarried bachelor, celibate, maiden, sin~
gle, unattached, unwed, unwedded, virgin

unmask bare, bring to light, disclose, dis~
cover, expose, lay bare, reveal, show up,
uncloak, uncover, unveil

unmatched beyond compare, consummate,
incomparable, matchless, paramount, peer~
less, second to none, supreme, unequalled,
unparalleled, unrivalled, unsurpassed

unmentionable disgraceful, disreputable,
forbidden, frowned on, immodest, indecent,

obscene, scandalous, shameful, shocking,
taboo, unspeakable, unutterable

unmerciful brutal, cruel, hard, heartless,
implacable, merciless, pitiless, relentless,
remorseless, ruthless, uncaring, unfeeling,
unsparing
Antonyms beneficent, caring, feeling, hu~
mane, merciful, pitying, sparing, tender-
hearted

unmindful careless, forgetful, heedless, in~
attentive, indifferent, lax, neglectful, negli~
gent, oblivious, remiss, slack, unheeding
Antonyms alert, attentive, aware, careful,
heedful, mindful, regardful, watchful

unmistakable blatant, certain, clear, con~
spicuous, decided, distinct, evident, glaring,
indisputable, manifest, obvious, palpable,
patent, plain, positive, pronounced, sure,
unambiguous, unequivocal
Antonyms ambiguous, dim, doubtful,
equivocal, hidden, mistakable, obscure, un~
certain, unclear, unsure

unmitigated 1. grim, harsh, intense, op~
pressive, persistent, relentless, unabated,
unalleviated, unbroken, undiminished,
unmodified, unqualified, unredeemed, un~
relieved **2.** absolute, arrant, complete, con~
summate, deep-dyed (*Usually derogatory*),
downright, out-and-out, outright, perfect,
rank, sheer, thorough, thoroughgoing, utter

unmoved 1. fast, firm, in place, in posi~
tion, steady, unchanged, untouched **2.** cold,
dry-eyed, impassive, indifferent, unaffected,
unfeeling, unimpressed, unresponsive,
unstirred, untouched **3.** determined, firm,
inflexible, resolute, resolved, steadfast,
undeviating, unshaken, unwavering
Antonyms (*sense 1*) shifted, touched, trans~
ferred (*sense 2*) affected, concerned, im~
pressed, moved, persuaded, stirred, swayed,
touched (*sense 3*) adaptable, flexible, shaken,
wavering

unnatural 1. aberrant, abnormal, anoma~
lous, irregular, odd, perverse, perverted,
unusual **2.** bizarre, extraordinary, freakish,
outlandish, queer, strange, supernatural,
unaccountable, uncanny **3.** affected,
artificial, assumed, contrived, factitious,
false, feigned, forced, insincere, laboured,
mannered, phoney *or* phony (*Inf.*), self-
conscious, stagy, stiff, stilted, strained,
studied, theatrical **4.** brutal, callous, cold-
blooded, evil, fiendish, heartless, inhuman,
monstrous, ruthless, savage, unfeeling,
wicked
Antonyms (*senses 1 & 2*) normal, ordinary,
typical (*sense 3*) genuine, honest, natural, sin~
cere, unaffected, unfeigned, unpretentious
(*sense 4*) caring, humane, loving, warm

unnecessary dispensable, expendable, in~
essential, needless, nonessential, redundant,

supererogatory, superfluous, surplus to re~
quirements, uncalled-for, unneeded, unre~
quired, useless
Antonyms essential, indispensable, neces~
sary, needed, required, vital

unnerve confound, daunt, demoralize, dis~
arm, disconcert, discourage, dishearten,
dismay, dispirit, faze, fluster, frighten, in~
timidate, psych out (*Inf.*), rattle (*Inf.*),
shake, throw off balance, unhinge, unman,
upset
Antonyms arm, brace, encourage, hearten,
nerve, steel, strengthen, support

unnoticed disregarded, ignored, neglected,
overlooked, undiscovered, unheeded, unob~
served, unperceived, unrecognized, unre~
marked, unseen
Antonyms discovered, heeded, noted, no~
ticed, observed, perceived, recognized, re~
marked

unobtrusive humble, inconspicuous, keep~
ing a low profile, low-key, meek, modest,
quiet, restrained, retiring, self-effacing,
subdued, unassuming, unnoticeable, unos~
tentatious, unpretentious
Antonyms assertive, blatant, bold, con~
spicuous, eccentric, eye-catching, getting in
the way, high-profile, noticeable, obtrusive,
outgoing, prominent

unoccupied 1. empty, tenantless, unin~
habited, untenanted, vacant 2. at leisure,
disengaged, idle, inactive, unemployed

unofficial informal, personal, private, un~
authorized, unconfirmed, wildcat

unorthodox abnormal, heterodox, irregu~
lar, off-the-wall (*Sl.*), unconventional, un~
customary, unusual, unwonted
Antonyms conventional, customary, estab~
lished, orthodox, sound, traditional, usual

unpaid 1. due, not discharged, outstanding,
overdue, owing, payable, unsettled 2. hon~
orary, unsalaried, voluntary

unpalatable bitter, disagreeable, displeas~
ing, distasteful, horrid, offensive, repug~
nant, unappetizing, unattractive, uneatable,
unpleasant, unsavoury
Antonyms agreeable, appetizing, attractive,
eatable, palatable, pleasant, pleasing, sa~
voury, tasteful

unparalleled beyond compare, consum~
mate, exceptional, incomparable, matchless,
peerless, rare, singular, superlative, un~
equalled, unique, unmatched, unpreceden~
ted, unrivalled, unsurpassed, without equal

unpardonable deplorable, disgraceful, in~
defensible, inexcusable, outrageous, scan~
dalous, shameful, unforgivable, unjustifiable

unperturbed calm, collected, composed,
cool, placid, poised, self-possessed, tranquil,

undismayed, unfazed (*Inf.*), unflustered,
unruffled, untroubled, unworried
Antonyms anxious, dismayed, flustered,
perturbed, ruffled, troubled, worried

unpleasant abhorrent, bad, disagreeable,
displeasing, distasteful, horrid, ill-natured,
irksome, nasty, objectionable, obnoxious,
repulsive, troublesome, unattractive, unlik~
able *or* unlikeable, unlovely, unpalatable
Antonyms agreeable, congenial, delicious,
good-natured, likable *or* likeable, lovely, nice,
pleasant

unpopular avoided, detested, disliked, not
sought out, out in the cold, out of favour,
rejected, shunned, unattractive, undesir~
able, unloved, unwanted, unwelcome
Antonyms desirable, favoured, liked, loved,
popular, wanted, welcome

unprecedented abnormal, exceptional,
extraordinary, freakish, new, novel, origi~
nal, remarkable, singular, unexampled,
unheard-of, unparalleled, unrivalled, un~
usual

unpredictable chance, changeable, doubt~
ful, erratic, fickle, fluky (*Inf.*), iffy (*Inf.*), in~
constant, random, unforeseeable, unreliable,
unstable, variable
Antonyms certain, constant, dependable,
foreseeable, predictable, reliable, stable,
steady, unchanging

unprejudiced balanced, even-handed, fair,
fair-minded, impartial, just, nonpartisan,
objective, open-minded, unbiased, uninflu~
enced
Antonyms biased, bigoted, influenced,
narrow-minded, partial, prejudiced, unfair,
unjust

unpremeditated extempore, impromptu,
impulsive, offhand, off the cuff (*Inf.*), spon~
taneous, spur-of-the-moment, unplanned,
unprepared

unprepared 1. half-baked (*Inf.*), ill-
considered, incomplete, not thought out,
unfinished, unplanned 2. caught napping,
caught on the hop (*Brit. inf.*), surprised,
taken aback, taken off guard, unaware, un~
ready, unsuspecting 3. ad-lib, extempora~
neous, improvised, off the cuff (*Inf.*), spon~
taneous

unpretentious homely, honest, humble,
modest, plain, simple, straightforward, un~
affected, unassuming, unimposing, unob~
trusive, unostentatious, unspoiled
Antonyms affected, assuming, brash, con~
ceited, flaunting, inflated, obtrusive, ostenta~
tious, pretentious, showy

unprincipled amoral, corrupt, crooked, de~
ceitful, devious, dishonest, immoral, tricky,
unconscionable, underhand, unethical, un~
professional, unscrupulous
Antonyms decent, ethical, honest, honour~

able, moral, righteous, scrupulous, upright, virtuous

unproductive 1. bootless, fruitless, futile, idle, ineffective, inefficacious, otiose, un~ availing, unprofitable, unremunerative, un~ rewarding, useless, vain, valueless, worth~ less **2.** barren, dry, fruitless, sterile, unprolific
Antonyms (*sense 1*) effective, fruitful, profitable, remunerative, rewarding, useful, worthwhile (*sense 2*) abundant, fertile, fruit~ ful, productive, prolific

unprofessional 1. improper, lax, negli~ gent, unethical, unfitting, unprincipled, un~ seemly, unworthy **2.** amateur, amateurish, cowboy (*Inf.*), incompetent, inefficient, in~ experienced, inexpert, slapdash, slipshod, untrained
Antonyms (*sense 2*) adept, competent, efficient, experienced, expert, professional, skilful

unpromising adverse, discouraging, doubtful, gloomy, inauspicious, infelicitous, ominous, unfavourable, unpropitious

unprotected defenceless, exposed, helpless, naked, open, open to attack, pregnable, un~ armed, undefended, unguarded, unshel~ tered, unshielded, vulnerable
Antonyms defended, guarded, immune, protected, safe, secure, shielded

unqualified 1. ill-equipped, incapable, in~ competent, ineligible, not equal to, not up to, unfit, unprepared **2.** categorical, down~ right, outright, unconditional, unmitigated, unreserved, unrestricted, without reserva~ tion **3.** absolute, arrant, complete, consum~ mate, deep-dyed (*Usually derogatory*), downright, out-and-out, outright, thorough, thoroughgoing, total, utter

unquestionable absolute, beyond a shad~ ow of doubt, certain, clear, conclusive, definite, faultless, flawless, incontestable, incontrovertible, indisputable, indubitable, irrefutable, manifest, patent, perfect, self~ evident, sure, undeniable, unequivocal, un~ mistakable
Antonyms ambiguous, doubtful, dubious, inconclusive, questionable, uncertain, un~ clear

unravel 1. disentangle, extricate, free, separate, straighten out, undo, unknot, un~ tangle, unwind **2.** clear up, explain, figure out (*Inf.*), get straight, get to the bottom of, interpret, make out, puzzle out, resolve, solve, suss (out) (*Sl.*), work out

unreadable 1. crabbed, illegible, undeci~ pherable **2.** badly written, dry as dust, heavy going, turgid

unreal 1. chimerical, dreamlike, fabulous, fanciful, fictitious, illusory, imaginary, make-believe, phantasmagoric, storybook, visionary **2.** hypothetical, immaterial, im~ palpable, insubstantial, intangible, mythi~ cal, nebulous **3.** artificial, fake, false, insin~ cere, mock, ostensible, pretended, seeming, sham
Antonyms authentic, bona fide, genuine, real, realistic, sincere, true, veritable

unrealistic 1. half-baked (*Inf.*), impracti~ cable, impractical, improbable, quixotic, romantic, starry-eyed, theoretical, unwork~ able **2.** non-naturalistic, unauthentic, un~ lifelike, unreal
Antonyms (*sense 1*) practical, pragmatic, probable, realistic, sensible, unromantic, workable

unreasonable 1. excessive, exorbitant, ex~ tortionate, extravagant, immoderate, steep (*Inf.*), too great, uncalled-for, undue, unfair, unjust, unwarranted **2.** arbitrary, biased, blinkered, capricious, erratic, headstrong, inconsistent, opinionated, quirky **3.** absurd, far-fetched, foolish, illogical, irrational, mad, nonsensical, preposterous, senseless, silly, stupid
Antonyms (*sense 1*) fair, just, justified, mod~ erate, reasonable, temperate, warranted (*sense 2*) fair-minded, flexible, open-minded (*sense 3*) logical, rational, sensible, wise

unrefined 1. crude, raw, unfinished, un~ polished, unpurified, untreated **2.** boorish, coarse, inelegant, rude, uncultured, unso~ phisticated, vulgar

unregenerate 1. godless, impious, profane, sinful, unconverted, unreformed, unrepent~ ant, wicked **2.** hardened, intractable, obdu~ rate, obstinate, recalcitrant, refractory, self-willed, stubborn
Antonyms (*sense 1*) converted, godly, pious, reformed, regenerate, repentant, virtuous

unrelated 1. different, dissimilar, not kin, not kindred, not related, unconnected, un~ like **2.** beside the point, extraneous, inap~ plicable, inappropriate, irrelevant, not ger~ mane, unassociated, unconnected

unreliable 1. disreputable, irresponsible, not conscientious, treacherous, undepend~ able, unstable, untrustworthy **2.** deceptive, delusive, erroneous, fake, fallible, false, im~ plausible, inaccurate, mistaken, specious, uncertain, unconvincing, unsound
Antonyms (*sense 1*) conscientious, depend~ able, regular, reliable, responsible, stable, trustworthy (*sense 2*) accurate, infallible

unrepentant abandoned, callous, hardened, impenitent, incorrigible, not contrite, obdu~ rate, shameless, unregenerate, unremorse~ ful, unrepenting
Antonyms ashamed, contrite, penitent, re~ morseful, repentant, rueful, sorry

unreserved 1. demonstrative, extrovert, forthright, frank, free, open, open-hearted,

outgoing, outspoken, uninhibited, unre~ strained, unreticent **2.** absolute, complete, entire, full, total, unconditional, unlimited, unqualified, wholehearted, without reser~ vation
Antonyms demure, inhibited, modest, re~ served, restrained, reticent, shy, undemon~ strative

unresolved doubtful, moot, open to ques~ tion, pending, problematical, unanswered, undecided, undetermined, unsettled, un~ solved, up in the air, vague, yet to be de~ cided

unrest 1. agitation, disaffection, discontent, discord, dissatisfaction, dissension, protest, rebellion, sedition, strife, tumult, turmoil, upheaval **2.** agitation, anxiety, disquiet, distress, perturbation, restlessness, trepida~ tion, uneasiness, worry
Antonyms calm, contentment, peace, re~ laxation, repose, rest, stillness, tranquillity

unrestrained abandoned, boisterous, free, immoderate, inordinate, intemperate, natu~ ral, unbounded, unbridled, unchecked, un~ constrained, uncontrolled, unhindered, un~ inhibited, unrepressed
Antonyms checked, constrained, frustrated, hindered, inhibited, repressed, restrained

unrestricted 1. absolute, free, free-for-all (*Inf.*), freewheeling (*Inf.*), open, unbounded, uncircumscribed, unhindered, unlimited, unregulated **2.** clear, open, public, unob~ structed, unopposed

unrivalled beyond compare, incomparable, matchless, nonpareil, peerless, supreme, unequalled, unexcelled, unmatched, unpar~ alleled, unsurpassed, without equal

unruly disobedient, disorderly, fractious, headstrong, insubordinate, intractable, lawless, mutinous, obstreperous, rebellious, refractory, riotous, rowdy, turbulent, un~ controllable, ungovernable, unmanageable, wayward, wild, wilful
Antonyms amenable, biddable, docile, gov~ ernable, manageable, obedient, orderly, trac~ table

unsafe dangerous, hazardous, insecure, perilous, precarious, risky, threatening, treacherous, uncertain, unreliable, un~ sound, unstable
Antonyms certain, harmless, reliable, safe, secure, sound, stable, sure

unsaid left to the imagination, tacit, unde~ clared, unexpressed, unspoken, unstated, unuttered, unvoiced

unsatisfactory deficient, disappointing, displeasing, inadequate, insufficient, me~ diocre, not good enough, not up to par, not up to scratch (*Inf.*), pathetic, poor, unac~ ceptable, unsuitable, unworthy, weak

Antonyms acceptable, adequate, passable, pleasing, satisfactory, sufficient, suitable

unsavoury 1. distasteful, nasty, objection~ able, obnoxious, offensive, repellent, repug~ nant, repulsive, revolting, unpleasant **2.** disagreeable, distasteful, nauseating, sick~ ening, unappetizing, unpalatable
Antonyms appetizing, palatable, pleasant, savoury, tasteful, tasty, toothsome

unscrupulous conscienceless, corrupt, crooked (*Inf.*), dishonest, dishonourable, exploitative, immoral, improper, knavish, roguish, ruthless, unconscientious, uncon~ scionable, unethical, unprincipled
Antonyms ethical, honest, honourable, moral, principled, proper, scrupulous, upright

unseasonable ill-timed, inappropriate, in~ opportune, mistimed, out of keeping, un~ suitable, untimely

unseat 1. throw, unhorse, unsaddle **2.** de~ pose, dethrone, discharge, dismiss, displace, oust, overthrow, remove

unseemly discreditable, disreputable, im~ proper, inappropriate, indecorous, indeli~ cate, in poor taste, out of keeping, out of place, unbecoming, unbefitting, undignified, unrefined, unsuitable
Antonyms acceptable, appropriate, becom~ ing, decorous, fitting, proper, refined, seemly, suitable

unseen concealed, hidden, invisible, lurk~ ing, obscure, undetected, unnoticed, unob~ served, unobtrusive, unperceived, veiled

unselfish altruistic, charitable, devoted, disinterested, generous, humanitarian, kind, liberal, magnanimous, noble, self- denying, selfless, self-sacrificing

unsettle agitate, bother, confuse, discom~ pose, disconcert, disorder, disturb, faze, fluster, perturb, rattle (*Inf.*), ruffle, throw (*Inf.*), throw into confusion (disorder, uproar), throw off balance, trouble, unbal~ ance, unnerve, upset

unsettled 1. disorderly, insecure, shaky, unstable, unsteady **2.** changeable, changing, inconstant, uncertain, unpredictable, vari~ able **3.** agitated, anxious, confused, dis~ turbed, flustered, on edge, perturbed, res~ tive, restless, shaken, tense, troubled, un~ easy, unnerved, wired (*Sl.*) **4.** debatable, doubtful, moot, open, undecided, undeter~ mined, unresolved **5.** due, in arrears, out~ standing, owing, payable, pending **6.** unin~ habited, unoccupied, unpeopled, unpopulat~ ed

unshakable absolute, constant, firm, fixed, immovable, resolute, staunch, steadfast, sure, unassailable, unswerving, unwaver~ ing, well-founded

Antonyms insecure, shaky, uncertain, un~
sure, wavering, wobbly

unshaken calm, collected, composed, im~
passive, unaffected, unalarmed, undaunted,
undismayed, undisturbed, unfazed (*Inf.*),
unmoved, unperturbed, unruffled

unsheltered exposed, open, out in the
open, unprotected, unscreened, unshielded

unsightly disagreeable, hideous, horrid, re~
pulsive, revolting (*Inf.*), ugly, unattractive,
unpleasant, unprepossessing
Antonyms agreeable, attractive, beautiful,
comely, handsome, pleasing, prepossessing,
pretty

unskilled amateurish, cowboy (*Inf.*), inex~
perienced, uneducated, unprofessional,
unqualified, untalented, untrained
Antonyms adept, expert, masterly, profes~
sional, qualified, skilled, talented

unsociable chilly, cold, distant, hostile, in~
hospitable, introverted, reclusive, retiring,
standoffish, uncongenial, unforthcoming,
unfriendly, unneighbourly, unsocial, with~
drawn
Antonyms congenial, convivial, friendly,
gregarious, hospitable, neighbourly, out~
going, sociable

unsolicited free-will, gratuitous, sponta~
neous, unasked for, uncalled-for, unforced,
uninvited, unrequested, unsought, unwel~
come, voluntary, volunteered

unsophisticated 1. artless, childlike,
guileless, inexperienced, ingenuous, inno~
cent, naive, natural, unaffected, untutored,
unworldly 2. plain, simple, straightforward,
uncomplex, uncomplicated, uninvolved,
unrefined, unspecialized 3. genuine, not
artificial, pure, unadulterated
Antonyms (*sense 2*) advanced, complex,
complicated, elegant, esoteric, intricate, so~
phisticated

unsound 1. ailing, defective, delicate, de~
ranged, diseased, frail, ill, in poor health,
unbalanced, unhealthy, unhinged, unstable,
unwell, weak 2. defective, erroneous, falla~
cious, false, faulty, flawed, ill-founded, il~
logical, invalid, shaky, specious, unreliable,
weak 3. flimsy, insecure, not solid, rickety,
shaky, tottering, unreliable, unsafe, unsta~
ble, unsteady, wobbly
Antonyms (*sense 3*) reliable, safe, solid,
sound, stable, steady, strong, sturdy, substan~
tial

unspeakable 1. beyond description, be~
yond words, inconceivable, indescribable,
ineffable, inexpressible, overwhelming, un~
believable, unimaginable, unutterable,
wonderful 2. abominable, appalling, awful,
bad, dreadful, evil, execrable, frightful, hei~
nous, hellacious (*U.S. sl.*), horrible, loath~

some, monstrous, odious, repellent, shock~
ing, too horrible for words

unspoiled, unspoilt 1. intact, perfect,
preserved, unaffected, unblemished, un~
changed, undamaged, unharmed, unim~
paired, untouched 2. artless, innocent,
natural, unaffected, unassuming, unstudied,
wholesome
Antonyms (*sense 1*) affected, blemished,
changed, damaged, harmed, impaired, imper~
fect, spoilt, touched

unspoken 1. assumed, implicit, implied,
left to the imagination, not put into words,
not spelt out, tacit, taken for granted, un~
declared, understood, unexpressed, unspo~
ken, unstated 2. mute, silent, unsaid, unut~
tered, voiceless, wordless
Antonyms (*sense 1*) clear, declared, explicit,
expressed, spoken, stated

unstable 1. insecure, not fixed, precarious,
rickety, risky, shaky, tottering, unsettled,
unsteady, wobbly 2. capricious, changeable,
erratic, fitful, fluctuating, inconsistent, in~
constant, irrational, temperamental, unpre~
dictable, unsteady, untrustworthy, vacillat~
ing, variable, volatile
Antonyms (*sense 2*) consistent, constant,
level-headed, predictable, rational, reliable,
stable, steady, trustworthy

unsteady 1. infirm, insecure, precarious,
reeling, rickety, shaky, tottering, treacher~
ous, unsafe, unstable, wobbly 2. change~
able, erratic, flickering, flighty, fluctuating,
inconstant, irregular, temperamental, unre~
liable, unsettled, vacillating, variable, vola~
tile, wavering

unsubstantial 1. airy, flimsy, fragile, frail,
inadequate, light, slight, thin 2. erroneous,
full of holes, ill-founded, superficial, tenu~
ous, unsound, unsupported, weak 3.
dreamlike, fanciful, illusory, imaginary,
immaterial, impalpable, visionary

unsubstantiated open to question, unat~
tested, unconfirmed, uncorroborated, unes~
tablished, unproven, unsupported
Antonyms attested, confirmed, corroborat~
ed, established, proven, substantiated, sup~
ported

unsuccessful 1. abortive, bootless, failed,
fruitless, futile, ineffective, unavailing, un~
productive, useless, vain 2. balked, defeat~
ed, foiled, frustrated, hapless, ill-starred,
losing, luckless, unfortunate, unlucky
Antonyms (*sense 1*) flourishing, fruitful,
productive, prosperous, remunerative, suc~
cessful, thriving, useful, worthwhile (*sense 2*)
fortunate, lucky, triumphant, victorious,
winning

unsuitable improper, inapposite, inappro~
priate, inapt, incompatible, incongruous,
ineligible, infelicitous, out of character, out

of keeping, out of place, unacceptable, un~ becoming, unbefitting, unfitting, unseason~ able, unseemly, unsuited

Antonyms acceptable, apposite, appropri~ ate, apt, compatible, eligible, fitting, proper, suitable

unsung anonymous, disregarded, neglected, unacclaimed, unacknowledged, uncelebrat~ ed, unhailed, unhonoured, unknown, un~ named, unrecognized

unsure 1. insecure, lacking in confidence, unassured, unconfident **2.** distrustful, doubtful, dubious, hesitant, in a quandary, irresolute, mistrustful, sceptical, suspicious, unconvinced, undecided

Antonyms assured, certain, confident, con~ vinced, decided, persuaded, resolute, sure

unsurpassed consummate, exceptional, incomparable, matchless, nonpareil, para~ mount, peerless, second to none, superla~ tive, supreme, transcendent, unequalled, unexcelled, unparalleled, unrivalled, with~ out an equal

unsuspecting confiding, credulous, gul~ lible, inexperienced, ingenuous, innocent, naive, off guard, trustful, trusting, uncon~ scious, unsuspicious, unwarned, unwary

unswerving constant, dedicated, devoted, direct, firm, resolute, single-minded, staunch, steadfast, steady, true, undevi~ ating, unfaltering, unflagging, untiring, un~ wavering

unsympathetic apathetic, callous, cold, compassionless (*Rare*), cruel, hard, harsh, heartless, indifferent, insensitive, soulless, stony-hearted, uncompassionate, uncon~ cerned, unfeeling, unkind, unmoved, un~ pitying, unresponsive

Antonyms caring, compassionate, con~ cerned, kind, pitying, sensitive, supportive, sympathetic, understanding

untamed barbarous, feral, fierce, not bro~ ken in, savage, unbroken, uncontrollable, undomesticated, untameable, wild

untangle clear up, disentangle, explain, ex~ tricate, solve, straighten out, unravel, un~ snarl

Antonyms complicate, confuse, enmesh, entangle, jumble, muddle, puzzle, snarl, tangle

untenable fallacious, flawed, groundless, illogical, indefensible, insupportable, shaky, unreasonable, unsound, unsustainable, weak

Antonyms justified, logical, rational, rea~ sonable, sensible, supported, unarguable, uncontestable, valid, verifiable, well-ground~ ed

unthinkable 1. absurd, illogical, impos~ sible, improbable, not on (*Inf.*), out of the question, preposterous, unlikely, unreason~ able **2.** beyond belief, beyond the bounds of possibility, implausible, inconceivable, in~ credible, insupportable, unbelievable, un~ imaginable

unthinking 1. blundering, inconsiderate, insensitive, rude, selfish, tactless, thought~ less, undiplomatic **2.** careless, heedless, impulsive, inadvertent, instinctive, me~ chanical, negligent, oblivious, rash, sense~ less, unconscious, unmindful, vacant, wit~ less

Antonyms (*sense 2*) careful, conscious, de~ liberate, heedful, mindful, sensible, witting

untidy bedraggled, chaotic, cluttered, disar~ rayed, disorderly, higgledy-piggledy (*Inf.*), jumbled, littered, messy, muddled, muddly, mussy (*U.S. inf.*), rumpled, shambolic, slat~ ternly, slipshod, sloppy (*Inf.*), slovenly, topsy-turvy, unkempt

Antonyms methodical, neat, orderly, pre~ sentable, ship-shape, spruce, systematic, tidy, well-kept

untie free, loosen, release, unbind, unbridle, undo, unfasten, unknot, unlace

untimely awkward, badly timed, early, ill-timed, inappropriate, inauspicious, incon~ venient, inopportune, mistimed, premature, unfortunate, unseasonable, unsuitable

Antonyms appropriate, auspicious, con~ venient, fortunate, opportune, seasonable, suitable, timely, welcome, well-timed

untiring constant, dedicated, determined, devoted, dogged, incessant, indefatigable, patient, persevering, persistent, staunch, steady, tireless, unfaltering, unflagging, un~ remitting, unwearied

untold 1. indescribable, inexpressible, un~ dreamed of, unimaginable, unspeakable, unthinkable, unutterable **2.** countless, in~ calculable, innumerable, measureless, myriad, numberless, uncountable, uncount~ ed, unnumbered **3.** hidden, private, secret, undisclosed, unknown, unpublished, unrecounted, unrelated, unrevealed

untouched 1. intact, safe and sound, un~ damaged, unharmed, unhurt, uninjured, unscathed, without a scratch **2.** dry-eyed, indifferent, unaffected, unconcerned, unim~ pressed, unmoved, unstirred

Antonyms (*sense 2*) affected, concerned, im~ pressed, moved, softened, stirred, touched

untoward 1. annoying, awkward, disas~ trous, ill-timed, inconvenient, inimical, ir~ ritating, troublesome, unfortunate, vexa~ tious **2.** adverse, contrary, inauspicious, inopportune, unfavourable, unlucky, un~ timely **3.** improper, inappropriate, indeco~ rous, out of place, unbecoming, unfitting, unseemly, unsuitable

untrained amateur, green, inexperienced, raw, uneducated, unpractised, unqualified, unschooled, unskilled, untaught, untutored

Antonyms educated, experienced, expert, qualified, schooled, skilled, taught, trained

untroubled calm, composed, cool, peaceful, placid, sedate, serene, steady, tranquil, unagitated, unconcerned, undisturbed, un~ fazed (*Inf.*), unflappable (*Inf.*), unflustered, unperturbed, unruffled, unstirred, unwor~ ried
Antonyms agitated, anxious, concerned, disturbed, flustered, perturbed, ruffled, trou~ bled, worried

untrue 1. deceptive, dishonest, erroneous, fallacious, false, inaccurate, incorrect, ly~ ing, misleading, mistaken, sham, spurious, untruthful, wrong 2. deceitful, disloyal, faithless, false, forsworn, inconstant, perfidious, traitorous, treacherous, two-faced, unfaithful, untrustworthy 3. deviant, distorted, inaccurate, off, out of line, out of true, wide
Antonyms (*sense 1*) accurate, correct, fac~ tual, right, true (*sense 2*) constant, dependable, faithful, honest, honourable, loyal, truthful, virtuous

untrustworthy capricious, deceitful, devi~ ous, dishonest, disloyal, fair-weather, faith~ less, false, fickle, fly-by-night (*Inf.*), not to be depended on, slippery, treacherous, tricky, two-faced, undependable, unfaithful, unreliable, untrue, untrusty
Antonyms dependable, faithful, honest, loy~ al, reliable, reputable, steadfast, true, trust~ worthy, trusty

untruth 1. deceitfulness, duplicity, falsity, inveracity (*Rare*), lying, mendacity, perjury, truthlessness, untruthfulness 2. deceit, fab~ rication, falsehood, falsification, fib, fiction, lie, pork pie (*Brit. sl.*), porky (*Brit. sl.*), pre~ varication, story, tale, trick, whopper (*Inf.*)

untruthful crooked (*Inf.*), deceitful, decep~ tive, dishonest, dissembling, false, fibbing, hypocritical, lying, mendacious
Antonyms candid, honest, sincere, true, truthful, veracious

unusual abnormal, atypical, bizarre, curi~ ous, different, exceptional, extraordinary, notable, odd, out of the ordinary, phenom~ enal, queer, rare, remarkable, singular, strange, surprising, uncommon, unconven~ tional, unexpected, unfamiliar, unwonted
Antonyms average, banal, commonplace, conventional, everyday, familiar, normal, routine, traditional, typical, unremarkable, usual

unutterable beyond words, extreme, inde~ scribable, ineffable, overwhelming, unim~ aginable, unspeakable

unvarnished bare, candid, frank, honest, naked, plain, pure, pure and simple, simple, sincere, stark, straightforward, unadorned, unembellished

unveil bare, bring to light, disclose, divulge, expose, lay bare, lay open, make known, make public, reveal, uncover
Antonyms cloak, conceal, cover, disguise, hide, mask, obscure, veil

unwanted *de trop*, going begging, outcast, rejected, superfluous, surplus to require~ ments, unasked, undesired, uninvited, un~ needed, unsolicited, unwelcome, useless
Antonyms desired, necessary, needed, useful, wanted, welcome

unwarranted gratuitous, groundless, inde~ fensible, inexcusable, uncalled-for, unjust, unjustified, unprovoked, unreasonable, wrong

unwary careless, hasty, heedless, impru~ dent, incautious, indiscreet, rash, reckless, thoughtless, uncircumspect, unguarded, unwatchful
Antonyms cautious, chary, circumspect, discreet, guarded, prudent, wary, watchful

unwavering consistent, dedicated, deter~ mined, immovable, resolute, single-minded, staunch, steadfast, steady, undeviating, unfaltering, unflagging, unshakable, un~ shaken, unswerving, untiring

unwelcome 1. excluded, rejected, unac~ ceptable, undesirable, uninvited, unpopular, unwanted, unwished for 2. disagreeable, displeasing, distasteful, thankless, undesir~ able, unpleasant
Antonyms acceptable, agreeable, desirable, pleasant, pleasing, popular, wanted, welcome

unwell ailing, ill, indisposed, in poor health, off colour, out of sorts, poorly (*Inf.*), sick, sickly, under the weather (*Inf.*), unhealthy
Antonyms fine, healthy, robust, sound, well

unwholesome 1. deleterious, harmful, insalubrious, junk (*Inf.*), noxious, poison~ ous, tainted, unhealthy, unnourishing 2. bad, corrupting, degrading, demoralizing, depraving, evil, immoral, maleficent, per~ verting, wicked 3. anaemic, pale, pallid, pasty, sickly, wan
Antonyms (*sense 1*) beneficial, germ-free, healthy, hygienic, salubrious, sanitary, wholesome (*sense 2*) edifying, moral

unwieldy 1. awkward, burdensome, cum~ bersome, inconvenient, unhandy, unman~ ageable 2. bulky, clumsy, hefty, massive, ponderous, ungainly, weighty

unwilling averse, demurring, disinclined, grudging, indisposed, laggard (*Rare*), loath, not in the mood, opposed, reluctant, resist~ ant, unenthusiastic
Antonyms amenable, compliant, disposed, eager, enthusiastic, inclined, voluntary, will~ ing

unwind 1. disentangle, slacken, uncoil, undo, unravel, unreel, unroll, untwine, un~ twist 2. calm down, let oneself go, loosen up, quieten down, relax, sit back, slow down, take a break, take it easy, wind down

unwise asinine, foolhardy, foolish, ill-advised, ill-considered, ill-judged, impolitic, improvident, imprudent, inadvisable, inane, indiscreet, injudicious, irresponsible, rash, reckless, senseless, short-sighted, silly, stupid
Antonyms discreet, judicious, politic, prudent, responsible, sensible, shrewd, wise

unwitting 1. ignorant, innocent, unaware, unconscious, unknowing, unsuspecting **2.** accidental, chance, inadvertent, involuntary, undesigned, unintended, unintentional, unmeant, unplanned
Antonyms (*sense 2*) conscious, deliberate, designed, intended, intentional, knowing, meant, planned, witting

unworldly 1. abstract, celestial, metaphysical, nonmaterialistic, religious, spiritual, transcendental **2.** green, idealistic, inexperienced, innocent, naive, raw, trusting, unsophisticated **3.** ethereal, extraterrestrial, otherworldly, unearthly

unworthy 1. *With* **of** beneath the dignity of, improper, inappropriate, out of character, out of place, unbecoming, unbefitting, unfitting, unseemly, unsuitable **2.** base, contemptible, degrading, discreditable, disgraceful, dishonourable, disreputable, ignoble, shameful **3.** ineligible, not deserving of, not fit for, not good enough, not worth, undeserving
Antonyms (*sense 3*) commendable, creditable, deserving, eligible, fit, honourable, meritorious, worthy

unwritten 1. oral, unrecorded, vocal, word-of-mouth **2.** accepted, conventional, customary, tacit, traditional, understood, unformulated

unyielding adamant, determined, firm, hardline, immovable, inexorable, inflexible, intractable, obdurate, obstinate, relentless, resolute, rigid, staunch, steadfast, stiff-necked, stubborn, tough, unbending, uncompromising, unwavering
Antonyms adaptable, compliant, compromising, cooperative, flexible, movable, tractable, yielding

upbringing breeding, bringing-up, care, cultivation, education, nurture, raising, rearing, tending, training

upgrade advance, ameliorate, better, elevate, enhance, improve, promote, raise
Antonyms decry, degrade, demote, denigrate, downgrade, lower

upheaval cataclysm, disorder, disruption, disturbance, eruption, overthrow, revolution, turmoil, violent change

uphill *adj.* **1.** ascending, climbing, mounting, rising **2.** arduous, difficult, exhausting, gruelling, hard, laborious, punishing, Sisyphean, strenuous, taxing, tough, wearisome
Antonyms (*sense 1*) descending, downhill, lowering

uphold advocate, aid, back, champion, defend, encourage, endorse, hold to, justify, maintain, promote, stand by, stick up for (*Inf.*), support, sustain, vindicate

upkeep 1. conservation, keep, maintenance, preservation, repair, running, subsistence, support, sustenance **2.** expenditure, expenses, oncosts (*Brit.*), operating costs, outlay, overheads, running costs

uplift *v.* **1.** elevate, heave, hoist, lift up, raise **2.** advance, ameliorate, better, civilize, cultivate, edify, improve, inspire, raise, refine, upgrade ~*n.* **3.** advancement, betterment, cultivation, edification, enhancement, enlightenment, enrichment, improvement, refinement

upper 1. high, higher, loftier, top, topmost **2.** elevated, eminent, greater, important, superior
Antonyms bottom, inferior, junior, low, lower

upper-class aristocratic, blue-blooded, highborn, high-class, noble, patrician, top-drawer, well-bred

upper hand advantage, ascendancy, control, dominion, edge, mastery, superiority, supremacy, sway, whip hand

uppermost 1. highest, loftiest, most elevated, top, topmost, upmost **2.** chief, dominant, foremost, greatest, leading, main, paramount, predominant, pre-eminent, primary, principal, supreme
Antonyms bottom, bottommost, humblest, least, lowermost, lowest, lowliest, slightest

uppish affected, arrogant, cocky, conceited, high and mighty (*Inf.*), hoity-toity (*Inf.*), overweening, presumptuous, putting on airs, self-important, snobbish, stuck-up (*Inf.*), supercilious, toffee-nosed (*Sl., chiefly Brit.*), uppity (*Inf.*)
Antonyms diffident, humble, lowly, meek, obsequious, servile, unaffected, unassertive

upright 1. erect, on end, perpendicular, straight, vertical **2.** *Fig.* above board, conscientious, ethical, faithful, good, high-minded, honest, honourable, incorruptible, just, principled, righteous, straightforward, true, trustworthy, unimpeachable, virtuous
Antonyms (*sense 1*) flat, horizontal, lying, prone, prostrate, supine (*sense 2*) corrupt, devious, dishonest, dishonourable, unethical, unjust, untrustworthy, wicked

uprising disturbance, insurgence, insurrection, mutiny, outbreak, putsch, rebellion, revolt, revolution, rising, upheaval

uproar *bagarre*, brawl, brouhaha, clamour,

commotion, confusion, din, furore, hubbub, hullabaloo, hurly-burly, mayhem, noise, outcry, pandemonium, racket, riot, ruckus (*Inf.*), ruction (*Inf.*), rumpus, turbulence, turmoil

uproarious 1. clamorous, confused, disor~ derly, loud, noisy, riotous, rowdy, tempes~ tuous, tumultuous, turbulent, wild **2.** con~ vulsive (*Inf.*), hilarious, hysterical, killing (*Inf.*), rib-tickling, rip-roaring (*Inf.*), screamingly funny, side-splitting, very fun~ ny **3.** boisterous, gleeful, loud, rollicking, unrestrained
Antonyms (*sense 1*) inaudible, low-key, or~ derly, peaceful, quiet, still (*sense 2*) morose, mournful, sad, serious, sorrowful, tragic

upset *v.* **1.** capsize, knock over, overturn, spill, tip over, topple over **2.** change, disor~ der, disorganize, disturb, mess up, mix up, put out of order, spoil, turn topsy-turvy **3.** agitate, bother, discompose, disconcert, dis~ may, disquiet, distress, disturb, faze, fluster, grieve, hassle (*Inf.*), perturb, ruffle, throw (someone) off balance, trouble, unnerve **4.** be victorious over, conquer, defeat, get the better of, overcome, overthrow, triumph over, win against the odds ~*n.* **5.** defeat, reverse, shake-up (*Inf.*), sudden change, surprise **6.** bug (*Inf.*), complaint, disorder, disturbance, illness, indisposition, malady, queasiness, sickness **7.** agitation, bother, discomposure, disquiet, distress, disturb~ ance, hassle (*Inf.*), shock, trouble, worry ~*adj.* **8.** capsized, overturned, spilled, tipped over, toppled, tumbled, upside down **9.** disordered, disturbed, gippy (*Sl.*), ill, poorly (*Inf.*), queasy, sick **10.** agitated, bothered, confused, disconcerted, dismayed, disquieted, distressed, disturbed, frantic, grieved, hassled (*Inf.*), hurt, overwrought, put out, ruffled, troubled, worried **11.** at sixes and sevens, chaotic, confused, disar~ rayed, disordered, in disarray *or* disorder, messed up, muddled, topsy-turvy **12.** beat~ en, conquered, defeated, overcome, over~ thrown, vanquished

upshot conclusion, consequence, culmina~ tion, end, end result, event, finale, issue, outcome, payoff (*Inf.*), result, sequel

upside down 1. bottom up, inverted, on its head, overturned, upturned, wrong side up **2.** *Inf.* chaotic, confused, disordered, higgledy-piggledy (*Inf.*), in confusion (chaos, disarray, disorder), jumbled, muddled, topsy-turvy

upstanding 1. ethical, good, honest, hon~ ourable, incorruptible, moral, principled, true, trustworthy, upright **2.** firm, hale and hearty, hardy, healthy, robust, stalwart, strong, sturdy, upright, vigorous
Antonyms (*sense 1*) bad, corrupt, dishonest, false, immoral, unethical, unprincipled, un~

trustworthy (*sense 2*) delicate, feeble, frail, infirm, puny, unhealthy, weak

upstart arriviste, nobody, *nouveau riche*, parvenu, social climber, status seeker

up-to-date all the rage, current, fashion~ able, happening (*Inf.*), in, in vogue, modern, newest, now (*Inf.*), stylish, trendy (*Brit. inf.*), up-to-the-minute, with it (*Inf.*)
Antonyms antiquated, dated, *démodé*, obso~ lete, old fashioned, outmoded, out of date, pas~ sé

urban city, civic, inner-city, metropolitan, municipal, oppidan (*Rare*), town

urbane civil, civilized, cosmopolitan, cour~ teous, cultivated, cultured, debonair, el~ egant, mannerly, polished, refined, smooth, sophisticated, suave, well-bred, well- mannered
Antonyms boorish, clownish, discourteous, gauche, impolite, rude, uncivilized, uncouth, uncultured

urbanity charm, civility, courtesy, culture, elegance, grace, mannerliness, polish, refinement, sophistication, suavity, worldli~ ness

urchin brat, gamin, guttersnipe, mudlark (*Sl.*), ragamuffin, street Arab (*Offens.*), waif, young rogue

urge *v.* **1.** appeal to, beg, beseech, entreat, exhort, implore, plead, press, solicit **2.** ad~ vise, advocate, champion, counsel, insist on, push for, recommend, support **3.** compel, constrain, drive, egg on, encourage, force, goad, hasten, impel, incite, induce, insti~ gate, press, prompt, propel, push, spur, stimulate ~*n.* **4.** compulsion, desire, drive, fancy, impulse, itch, longing, thirst, wish, yearning, yen (*Inf.*)
Antonyms *v.* (*senses 1 & 2*) caution, deter, discourage, dissuade, remonstrate, warn ~*n.* aversion, disinclination, distaste, indisposi~ tion, reluctance, repugnance

urgency exigency, extremity, gravity, hur~ ry, imperativeness, importance, importun~ ity, necessity, need, pressure, seriousness, stress

urgent 1. compelling, critical, crucial, im~ mediate, imperative, important, instant, not to be delayed, pressing, top-priority **2.** clamorous, earnest, importunate, insistent, intense, persistent, persuasive
Antonyms apathetic, casual, feeble, half- hearted, lackadaisical, low-priority, minor, perfunctory, trivial, unimportant, weak

urinate leak (*Sl.*), make water, micturate, pass water, pee (*Sl.*), piddle (*Inf.*), piss (*Ta~ boo sl.*), spend a penny (*Brit. inf.*), tinkle (*Brit. inf.*), wee (*Inf.*), wee-wee (*Inf.*)

usable at one's disposal, available, current, fit for use, functional, in running order, practical, ready for use, serviceable, utilizable, valid, working

usage **1.** control, employment, handling, management, operation, regulation, run~ ning, treatment, use **2.** convention, custom, form, habit, matter of course, method, mode, practice, procedure, regime, routine, rule, tradition, wont

use *v.* **1.** apply, avail oneself of, bring into play, employ, exercise, exert, find a use for, make use of, operate, ply, practise, profit by, put to use, turn to account, utilize, wield, work **2.** act towards, behave towards, deal with, exploit, handle, manipulate, mis~ use, take advantage of, treat **3.** consume, exhaust, expend, run through, spend, waste ~*n.* **4.** application, employment, exercise, handling, operation, practice, service, treatment, usage, wear and tear **5.** advan~ tage, application, avail, benefit, good, help, mileage (*Inf.*), point, profit, service, usefulness, utility, value, worth **6.** custom, habit, practice, usage, way, wont **7.** call, cause, end, necessity, need, object, occasion, point, purpose, reason

used cast-off, hand-me-down (*Inf.*), nearly new, not new, reach-me-down (*Inf.*), second-hand, shopsoiled, worn
Antonyms brand-new, fresh, intact, new, pristine, unused

used to accustomed to, at home in, attuned to, familiar with, given to, habituated to, hardened to, in the habit of, inured to, tol~ erant of, wont to

useful advantageous, all-purpose, beneficial, effective, fruitful, general-purpose, helpful, of help, of service, of use, practical, profitable, salutary, serviceable, valuable, worthwhile
Antonyms inadequate, ineffective, unben~ eficial, unhelpful, unproductive, useless, vain, worthless

useless **1.** bootless, disadvantageous, fruit~ less, futile, hopeless, idle, impractical, inef~ fective, ineffectual, of no use, pointless, profitless, unavailing, unproductive, un~ workable, vain, valueless, worthless **2.** *Inf.* hopeless, incompetent, ineffectual, inept, no good, stupid, weak
Antonyms (*sense 1*) advantageous, effective, fruitful, practical, productive, profitable, useful, valuable, workable, worthwhile

use up absorb, burn up, consume, deplete, devour, drain, exhaust, finish, fritter away, run through, squander, swallow up, waste

usher *n.* **1.** attendant, doorkeeper, escort,

guide, usherette ~*v.* **2.** conduct, direct, es~ cort, guide, lead, pilot, show in *or* out, steer **3.** *Usually with* **in** bring in, herald, inaugu~ rate, initiate, introduce, launch, open the door to, pave the way for, precede, ring in

usual accustomed, common, constant, cus~ tomary, everyday, expected, familiar, fixed, general, habitual, normal, ordinary, regu~ lar, routine, standard, stock, typical, wonted
Antonyms exceptional, extraordinary, new, novel, off-beat, out of the ordinary, peculiar, rare, singular, strange, uncommon, unexpec~ ted, unhackneyed, unique, unorthodox, un~ usual

usually as a rule, as is the custom, as is usual, by and large, commonly, for the most part, generally, habitually, in the main, mainly, mostly, most often, normally, on the whole, ordinarily, regularly, routinely

utility advantageousness, avail, benefit, con~ venience, efficacy, fitness, point, practical~ ity, profit, service, serviceableness, use, usefulness

utilize appropriate, avail oneself of, employ, have recourse to, make the most of, make use of, profit by, put to use, resort to, take advantage of, turn to account, use

utmost *adj.* **1.** chief, extreme, greatest, highest, maximum, paramount, pre~ eminent, supreme **2.** extreme, farthest, final, last, most distant, outermost, remot~ est, uttermost ~*n.* **3.** best, greatest, hardest, highest, most

Utopia bliss, Eden, Erewhon, Garden of Eden, heaven, ideal life, paradise, perfect place, seventh heaven, Shangri-la

Utopian **1.** *adj.* airy, chimerical, dream, fanciful, fantasy, ideal, idealistic, illusory, imaginary, impractical, perfect, romantic, visionary **2.** *n.* Don Quixote, dreamer, idealist, romanticist, visionary

utter[1] *v.* **1.** articulate, enunciate, express, pronounce, put into words, say, speak, ver~ balize, vocalize, voice **2.** declare, divulge, give expression to, make known, proclaim, promulgate, publish, reveal, state

utter[2] *adj.* absolute, arrant, complete, con~ summate, deep-dyed (*Usually derogatory*), downright, entire, out-and-out, outright, perfect, sheer, stark, thorough, thorough~ going, total, unmitigated, unqualified

utterly absolutely, completely, entirely, ex~ tremely, fully, perfectly, thoroughly, totally, to the core, wholly

V

vacancy 1. job, opening, opportunity, posi~ tion, post, room, situation **2.** absent-mindedness, abstraction, blankness, inan~ ity, inattentiveness, incomprehension, in~ curiousness, lack of interest, vacuousness **3.** emptiness, gap, space, vacuum, void

vacant 1. available, disengaged, empty, free, idle, not in use, to let, unemployed, unen~ gaged, unfilled, unoccupied, untenanted, void **2.** absent-minded, abstracted, blank, dreaming, dreamy, expressionless, idle, in~ ane, incurious, thoughtless, unthinking, vacuous
Antonyms (*sense 1*) busy, engaged, full, in~ habited, in use, occupied, taken (*sense 2*) ani~ mated, engrossed, expressive, lively, reflective, thoughtful

vacuum emptiness, free space, gap, noth~ ingness, space, vacuity, void

vagabond 1. *n.* bag lady (*Chiefly U.S.*), beggar, bum (*Inf.*), down-and-out, hobo (*U.S.*), itinerant, knight of the road, mi~ grant, nomad, outcast, rascal, rover, tramp, vagrant, wanderer, wayfarer **2.** *adj.* desti~ tute, down and out, drifting, fly-by-night (*Inf.*), footloose, homeless, idle, itinerant, journeying, nomadic, rootless, roving, shiftless, vagrant, wandering

vagary caprice, crotchet, fancy, humour, megrim (*Archaic*), notion, whim, whimsy

vagrant 1. *n.* bag lady (*Chiefly U.S.*), beg~ gar, bird of passage, bum (*Inf.*), hobo (*U.S.*), itinerant, person of no fixed address, rolling stone, tramp, wanderer **2.** *adj.* itinerant, nomadic, roaming, rootless, roving, unset~ tled, vagabond
Antonyms *adj.* established, fixed, purpose~ ful, rooted, settled

vague amorphous, blurred, dim, doubtful, fuzzy, generalized, hazy, ill-defined, impre~ cise, indefinite, indeterminate, indistinct, lax, loose, nebulous, obscure, shadowy, un~ certain, unclear, unknown, unspecified, woolly
Antonyms clear, clear-cut, definite, distinct, exact, explicit, lucid, precise, specific, well-defined

vaguely absent-mindedly, dimly, evasively, imprecisely, in a general way, obscurely, slightly, through a glass darkly, vacantly

vagueness ambiguity, impreciseness, in~ exactitude, lack of preciseness, looseness, obscurity, undecidedness, woolliness
Antonyms clarity, clearness, definition, ex~ actness, obviousness, preciseness, precision

vain 1. arrogant, bigheaded (*Inf.*), cocky, conceited, egotistical, inflated, narcissistic, ostentatious, overweening, peacockish, pleased with oneself, proud, self-important, stuck-up (*Inf.*), swaggering, swanky (*Inf.*), swollen-headed (*Inf.*), vainglorious **2.** abor~ tive, empty, fruitless, futile, hollow, idle, nugatory, pointless, senseless, time-wasting, trifling, trivial, unavailing, unimportant, unproductive, unprofitable, useless, worth~ less **3. be vain** have a high opinion of one~ self, have a swelled head (*Inf.*), have one's head turned, think a lot of oneself, think oneself it (*Inf.*), think oneself the cat's whiskers *or* pyjamas (*Sl.*) **4. in vain** boot~ less, fruitless(ly), ineffectual(ly), to no avail, to no purpose, unsuccessful(ly), useless(ly), vain(ly), wasted, without success
Antonyms (*sense 1*) bashful, humble, meek, modest, self-deprecating (*sense 2*) fruitful, profitable, serious, successful, useful, valid, worthwhile, worthy

valedictory *adj.* farewell, final, parting

valiant bold, brave, courageous, dauntless, doughty, fearless, gallant, heroic, indomi~ table, intrepid, lion-hearted, plucky, re~ doubtable, stouthearted, valorous, worthy
Antonyms cowardly, craven, fearful, shrinking, spineless, timid, weak

valid 1. acceptable, binding, cogent, conclu~ sive, convincing, efficacious, efficient, good, just, logical, powerful, sound, substantial, telling, weighty, well-founded, well-grounded **2.** authentic, bona fide, genuine, in force, lawful, legal, legally binding, le~ gitimate, official
Antonyms (*sense 1*) baseless, bogus, falla~ cious, false, illogical, sham, spurious, unac~ ceptable, unfounded, unrealistic, unrecog~ nized, untrue, weak (*sense 2*) illegal, inopera~ tive, invalid, unlawful, unofficial

validity 1. cogency, force, foundation, grounds, point, power, soundness, strength, substance, weight **2.** authority, lawfulness, legality, legitimacy, right

valley coomb, cwm (*Welsh*), dale, dell, de~ pression, dingle, glen, hollow, strath (*Scot.*), vale

valour boldness, bravery, courage, derring-do (*Archaic*), doughtiness, fearlessness, gallantry, heroism, intrepidity, lion-heartedness, spirit
Antonyms cowardice, dread, fear, timidity, trepidation, weakness

valuable *adj.* **1.** costly, dear, expensive,

high-priced, precious **2.** beneficial, cher~
ished, esteemed, estimable, held dear, help~
ful, important, prized, profitable, service~
able, treasured, useful, valued, worthwhile,
worthy ~*n.* **3.** *Usually plural* heirloom,
treasure(s)
Antonyms *adj.* (*sense 1*) cheap, cheapo (*Inf.*),
chickenshit (*U.S. sl.*), crappy (*Sl.*), inexpen~
sive, worthless (*sense 2*) insignificant, point~
less, silly, trifling, trivial, unimportant,
useless, worthless

value *n.* **1.** cost, equivalent, market price,
monetary worth, rate **2.** advantage, benefit,
desirability, help, importance, merit, profit,
serviceableness, significance, use, useful~
ness, utility, worth **3.** *Plural* code of be~
haviour, ethics, (moral) standards, princi~
ples ~*v.* **4.** account, appraise, assess, com~
pute, estimate, evaluate, price, put a price
on, rate, set at, survey **5.** appreciate, cher~
ish, esteem, hold dear, hold in high regard
or esteem, prize, regard highly, respect, set
store by, treasure
Antonyms *n.* (*sense 2*) insignificance,
unimportance, uselessness, worthlessness
~*v.* disregard, have no time for, hold a low
opinion of, underestimate, undervalue

valued cherished, dear, esteemed, highly
regarded, loved, prized, treasured

valueless miserable, no good, of no earthly
use, of no value, unsaleable, useless,
worthless

vanguard advance guard, cutting edge,
forefront, forerunners, front, front line,
front rank, leaders, spearhead, trailblazers,
trendsetters, van
Antonyms back, rear, rearguard, stern, tail,
tail end

vanish become invisible, be lost to sight, die
out, disappear, disappear from sight *or*
from the face of the earth, dissolve, eva~
nesce, evaporate, exit, fade (away), melt
(away)
Antonyms appear, arrive, become visible,
come into view, materialize, pop up

vanity **1.** affected ways, airs, arrogance,
bigheadedness (*Inf.*), conceit, conceitedness,
egotism, narcissism, ostentation, preten~
sion, pride, self-admiration, self-love, show~
ing off (*Inf.*), swollen-headedness (*Inf.*),
vainglory **2.** emptiness, frivolity, fruitless~
ness, futility, hollowness, inanity, point~
lessness, profitlessness, triviality, unpro~
ductiveness, unreality, unsubstantiality,
uselessness, worthlessness
Antonyms (*sense 1*) humility, meekness,
modesty, self-abasement, self-deprecation
(*sense 2*) importance, value, worth

vanquish beat, blow out of the water (*Sl.*),
clobber (*Sl.*), conquer, crush, defeat, get the
upper hand over, lick (*Inf.*), master, over~

come, overpower, overwhelm, put down,
put to flight, put to rout, quell, reduce, re~
press, rout, run rings around (*Inf.*), subdue,
subjugate, tank (*Sl.*), triumph over, undo,
wipe the floor with (*Inf.*)

vapour breath, dampness, exhalation, fog,
fumes, haze, miasma, mist, smoke, steam

variable capricious, chameleonic, change~
able, fickle, fitful, flexible, fluctuating, in~
constant, mercurial, mutable, protean,
shifting, temperamental, uneven, unstable,
unsteady, vacillating, wavering
Antonyms constant, firm, fixed, settled, sta~
ble, steady, unalterable, unchanging

variance **1.** difference, difference of opin~
ion, disagreement, discord, discrepancy,
dissension, dissent, divergence, inconsist~
ency, lack of harmony, strife, variation **2.**
at variance at loggerheads, at odds, at sixes
and sevens (*Inf.*), conflicting, in disagree~
ment, in opposition, out of harmony, out of
line
Antonyms (*sense 1*) accord, agreement, con~
gruity, correspondence, harmony, similarity,
unison

variant **1.** *adj.* alternative, derived, differ~
ent, divergent, exceptional, modified **2.** *n.*
alternative, derived form, development,
modification, sport (*Biol.*), variation

variation alteration, break in routine,
change, departure, departure from the
norm, deviation, difference, discrepancy,
diversification, diversity, innovation,
modification, novelty, variety
Antonyms dullness, monotony, sameness,
tedium, uniformity

varied assorted, different, diverse, hetero~
geneous, manifold, miscellaneous, mixed,
motley, sundry, various
Antonyms homogeneous, repetitive, simi~
lar, standardized, uniform, unvarying

variety **1.** change, difference, discrepancy,
diversification, diversity, many-sidedness,
multifariousness, variation **2.** array, as~
sortment, collection, cross section, inter~
mixture, medley, miscellany, mixture,
multiplicity, range **3.** brand, breed, catego~
ry, class, kind, make, order, sort, species,
strain, type
Antonyms (*sense 1*) homogeneity, invari~
ability, monotony, similarity, similitude,
uniformity

various assorted, different, differing, dis~
parate, distinct, divers (*Archaic*), diverse,
diversified, heterogeneous, manifold, many,
many-sided, miscellaneous, several, sundry,
varied, variegated
Antonyms alike, equivalent, matching,
same, similar, uniform

varnish *v.* adorn, decorate, embellish, gild,
glaze, gloss, japan, lacquer, polish, shellac

vary alter, alternate, be unlike, change, de~ part, differ, disagree, diverge, diversify, fluctuate, intermix, modify, permutate, re~ order, transform

varying changing, different, distinct, distin~ guishable, diverse, fluctuating, inconsistent
Antonyms consistent, fixed, monotonous, regular, settled, unchanging, unvarying

vast astronomical, boundless, colossal, el~ ephantine, enormous, extensive, gigantic, ginormous (*Inf.*), great, huge, humongous *or* humungous (*U.S. sl.*), illimitable, immeas~ urable, immense, limitless, mammoth, mas~ sive, measureless, mega (*Sl.*), monstrous, monumental, never-ending, prodigious, sweeping, tremendous, unbounded, unlim~ ited, vasty (*Archaic*), voluminous, wide
Antonyms bounded, limited, microscopic, narrow, negligible, paltry, puny, small, tiny, trifling

vault¹ *v.* bound, clear, hurdle, jump, leap, spring

vault² *n.* **1.** arch, ceiling, roof, span **2.** cata~ comb, cellar, crypt, mausoleum, tomb, undercroft **3.** depository, repository, strongroom ~*v.* **4.** arch, bend, bow, curve, overarch, span

vaulted arched, cavernous, domed, hemi~ spheric

vaunt boast about, brag about, crow about, exult in, flaunt, give oneself airs about, make a display of, make much of, parade, prate about, show off, talk big about (*Inf.*)

veer be deflected, change, change course, change direction, sheer, shift, swerve, tack, turn

vegetate **1.** be inert, deteriorate, exist, go to seed, idle, languish, loaf, moulder, stag~ nate, veg out (*Sl., chiefly U.S.*) **2.** burgeon, germinate, grow, shoot, spring, sprout, swell
Antonyms (*sense 1*) accomplish, develop, grow, participate, perform, react, respond

vehemence ardour, eagerness, earnestness, emphasis, energy, enthusiasm, fervency, fervour, fire, force, forcefulness, heat, im~ petuosity, intensity, keenness, passion, verve, vigour, violence, warmth, zeal
Antonyms apathy, coolness, indifference, inertia, lethargy, listlessness, passivity, stoi~ cism, torpor

vehement ardent, eager, earnest, emphatic, enthusiastic, fervent, fervid, fierce, flaming, forceful, forcible, impassioned, impetuous, intense, passionate, powerful, strong, vio~ lent, zealous
Antonyms apathetic, calm, cool, dispas~ sionate, half-hearted, impassive, lukewarm, moderate

vehicle *Fig.* apparatus, channel, means,

means of expression, mechanism, medium, organ

veil **1.** *v.* cloak, conceal, cover, dim, disguise, hide, mantle, mask, obscure, screen, shield **2.** *n.* blind, cloak, cover, curtain, disguise, film, mask, screen, shade, shroud
Antonyms *v.* disclose, display, divulge, ex~ pose, lay bare, reveal, uncover, unveil

veiled concealed, covert, disguised, hinted at, implied, masked, suppressed

vein **1.** blood vessel, course, current, lode, seam, stratum, streak, stripe **2.** dash, hint, strain, streak, thread, trait **3.** attitude, bent, character, faculty, humour, mode, mood, note, style, temper, tenor, tone, turn

venal bent (*Sl.*), corrupt, corruptible, crook~ ed (*Inf.*), dishonourable, grafting (*Inf.*), mercenary, prostituted, purchasable, rapa~ cious, simoniacal, sordid, unprincipled
Antonyms honest, honourable, incorrupt~ ible, law-abiding, principled, upright

vendetta bad blood, blood feud, feud, quar~ rel

veneer *n. Fig.* appearance, façade, false front, finish, front, gloss, guise, mask, pre~ tence, semblance, show

venerable august, esteemed, grave, hon~ oured, respected, revered, reverenced, sage, sedate, wise, worshipped
Antonyms callow, discredited, disdained, disgraced, dishonourable, disreputable, green, ignominious, immature, inexperi~ enced, inglorious, scorned, young, youthful

venerate adore, esteem, hold in awe, hon~ our, look up to, respect, revere, reverence, worship
Antonyms deride, dishonour, disregard, ex~ ecrate, mock, scorn, spurn

veneration adoration, awe, deference, es~ teem, respect, reverence, worship

vengeance **1.** an eye for an eye, avenging, lex talionis, reprisal, requital, retaliation, retribution, revenge, settling of scores **2.** **with a vengeance a.** forcefully, furiously, vehemently, violently **b.** and no mistake, extremely, greatly, to the full, to the utmost, with no holds barred
Antonyms (*sense 1*) absolution, acquittal, exoneration, forbearance, forgiveness, mercy, pardon, remission

venial allowable, excusable, forgivable, insignificant, minor, pardonable, slight, trivial

venom **1.** bane, poison, toxin **2.** acidity, acrimony, bitterness, gall, grudge, hate, ill will, malevolence, malice, maliciousness, malignity, rancour, spite, spitefulness, spleen, virulence
Antonyms (*sense 2*) benevolence, charity,

compassion, favour, goodwill, kindness, love, mercy

venomous 1. baneful (*Archaic*), envenomed, mephitic, noxious, poison, poisonous, toxic, virulent **2.** baleful, hostile, malicious, malignant, rancorous, savage, spiteful, vicious, vindictive, virulent
Antonyms (*sense 1*) harmless, nonpoisonous, nontoxic, nonvenomous (*sense 2*) affectionate, benevolent, compassionate, forgiving, harmless, loving, magnanimous

vent 1. *n.* aperture, duct, hole, opening, orifice, outlet, split **2.** *v.* air, come out with, discharge, emit, empty, express, give expression to, give vent to, pour out, release, utter, voice
Antonyms *v.* bottle up, curb, hold back, inhibit, quash, quell, repress, stifle, subdue

ventilate *Fig.* air, bring out into the open, broadcast, debate, discuss, examine, make known, scrutinize, sift, talk about

venture *v.* **1.** chance, endanger, hazard, imperil, jeopardize, put in jeopardy, risk, speculate, stake, wager **2.** advance, dare, dare say, hazard, make bold, presume, stick one's neck out (*Inf.*), take the liberty, volunteer **3.** *With* **out, forth,** *etc.* embark on, go, plunge into, set out ~*n.* **4.** adventure, chance, endeavour, enterprise, fling, gamble, hazard, jeopardy, project, risk, speculation, undertaking

verbal literal, oral, spoken, unwritten, verbatim, word-of-mouth

verbally by word of mouth, orally

verbatim exactly, precisely, to the letter, word for word

verbose circumlocutory, diffuse, garrulous, long-winded, periphrastic, pleonastic, prolix, tautological, windy, wordy
Antonyms brief, brusque, concise, curt, quiet, reticent, short, succinct, terse, untalkative

verbosity garrulity, logorrhoea, long-windedness, loquaciousness, prolixity, rambling, verbiage, verboseness, windiness, wordiness

verdict adjudication, conclusion, decision, finding, judgment, opinion, sentence

verge 1. *n.* border, boundary, brim, brink, edge, extreme, limit, lip, margin, roadside, threshold **2.** *v.* approach, border, come near

verification authentication, confirmation, corroboration, proof, substantiation, validation

verify attest, attest to, authenticate, bear out, check, confirm, corroborate, prove, substantiate, support, validate
Antonyms deny, discount, discredit, dispute, invalidate, nullify, undermine, weaken

vernacular 1. *adj.* colloquial, common, indigenous, informal, local, mother, native, popular, vulgar **2.** *n.* argot, cant, dialect, idiom, jargon, native language, parlance, patois, speech, vulgar tongue

versatile adaptable, adjustable, all-purpose, all-round, flexible, functional, handy, many-sided, multifaceted, protean, resourceful, variable
Antonyms fixed, inflexible, invariable, limited, one-sided, unadaptable

versed accomplished, acquainted, competent, conversant, experienced, familiar, knowledgeable, practised, proficient, qualified, seasoned, skilled, well informed, well up in (*Inf.*)
Antonyms callow, green, ignorant, inexperienced, new, raw, unacquainted, unfledged, unpractised, unschooled, unskilled, unversed

version 1. account, adaptation, exercise, interpretation, portrayal, reading, rendering, side, translation **2.** design, form, kind, model, style, type, variant

vertical erect, on end, perpendicular, upright
Antonyms flat, horizontal, level, plane, prone

vertigo dizziness, giddiness, lightheadedness, loss of equilibrium, swimming of the head

verve animation, brio, dash, élan, energy, enthusiasm, force, get-up-and-go (*Inf.*), gusto, life, liveliness, pep, punch (*Inf.*), sparkle, spirit, vigour, vim (*Sl.*), vitality, vivacity, zeal, zip (*Inf.*)
Antonyms apathy, disdain, half-heartedness, indifference, inertia, lack of enthusiasm, languor, lethargy, lifelessness, reluctance, torpor

very *adv.* **1.** absolutely, acutely, awfully (*Inf.*), decidedly, deeply, eminently, exceedingly, excessively, extremely, greatly, highly, jolly (*Brit.*), noticeably, particularly, profoundly, really, remarkably, superlatively, surpassingly, terribly, truly, uncommonly, unusually, wonderfully ~*adj.* **2.** actual, appropriate, exact, express, identical, perfect, precise, real, same, selfsame, unqualified **3.** bare, mere, plain, pure, sheer, simple

vessel 1. barque (*Poetic*), boat, craft, ship **2.** container, pot, receptacle, utensil

vest *v.* **1.** *With* **in** *or* **with** authorize, be devolved upon, bestow, confer, consign, empower, endow, entrust, furnish, invest, lodge, place, put in the hands of, settle **2.** apparel, bedeck, clothe, cover, dress, envelop, garb, robe

vestibule anteroom, entrance hall, foyer, hall, lobby, porch, portico

vestige evidence, glimmer, hint, indication,

relic, remainder, remains, remnant, resi~
due, scrap, sign, suspicion, token, trace,
track

vestigial imperfect, incomplete, nonfunc~
tional, rudimentary, surviving, undeveloped
Antonyms complete, developed, functional,
perfect, practical, useful

vet v. appraise, check, check out, examine,
give (someone or something) the once-over
(*Inf.*), investigate, look over, pass under re~
view, review, scan, scrutinize, size up (*Inf.*)

veteran 1. n. master, old hand, old stager,
old-timer, past master, past mistress, pro
(*Inf.*), trouper, warhorse (*Inf.*) **2.** adj. adept,
battle-scarred, expert, long-serving, old,
proficient, seasoned
Antonyms n. apprentice, beginner, fresh~
man, initiate, neophyte, novice, recruit, tyro

veto 1. v. ban, boycott, disallow, forbid, give
the thumbs down to, interdict, kill (*Inf.*),
negative, prohibit, put the kibosh on (*Sl.*),
refuse permission, reject, rule out, turn
down **2.** n. ban, boycott, embargo, interdict,
nonconsent, prohibition
Antonyms v. approve, endorse, O.K. or okay
(*Inf.*), pass, ratify ~n. approval, endorsement,
go-ahead (*Inf.*), ratification

vex afflict, aggravate (*Inf.*), agitate, annoy,
bother, bug (*Inf.*), displease, distress, dis~
turb, exasperate, fret, gall, get on one's
nerves (*Inf.*), grate on, harass, hassle (*Inf.*),
irritate, molest, nark (*Brit., Aust., & N.Z.
sl.*), needle (*Inf.*), nettle, offend, peeve (*Inf.*),
perplex, pester, pique, plague, provoke, put
out, rile, tease, torment, trouble, upset,
worry
Antonyms allay, appease, comfort, console,
gratify, hush, mollify, please, quiet, soothe

vexation 1. aggravation (*Inf.*), annoyance,
displeasure, dissatisfaction, exasperation,
frustration, irritation, pique **2.** bother,
difficulty, hassle (*Inf.*), headache (*Inf.*), irri~
tant, misfortune, nuisance, problem, thorn
in one's flesh, trouble, upset, worry

vexatious afflicting, aggravating (*Inf.*), an~
noying, bothersome, burdensome, disagree~
able, disappointing, distressing, exasperat~
ing, harassing, irksome, irritating, nagging,
plaguy (*Archaic*), provoking, teasing, tor~
menting, troublesome, trying, unpleasant,
upsetting, worrisome, worrying
Antonyms agreeable, balmy, calming, com~
forting, pleasant, reassuring, relaxing, sooth~
ing

vexed 1. afflicted, aggravated (*Inf.*), agitat~
ed, annoyed, bothered, confused, displeased,
distressed, disturbed, exasperated, fed up,
hacked (off) (*U.S. sl.*), harassed, irritated,
miffed (*Inf.*), nettled, out of countenance,
peeved (*Inf.*), perplexed, pissed off (*Taboo
sl.*), provoked, put out, riled, ruffled, tor~

mented, troubled, upset, worried **2.** con~
tested, controversial, disputed, moot, much
debated

viable applicable, feasible, operable, practi~
cable, usable, within the bounds of pos~
sibility, workable
Antonyms hopeless, impossible, impracti~
cable, inconceivable, out of the question, un~
thinkable, unworkable

vibrant 1. aquiver, oscillating, palpitating,
pulsating, quivering, trembling **2.** alive,
animated, colourful, dynamic, electrifying,
full of pep (*Inf.*), responsive, sensitive,
sparkling, spirited, vivacious, vivid

vibrate fluctuate, judder (*Inf.*), oscillate,
pulsate, pulse, quiver, resonate, reverber~
ate, shake, shiver, sway, swing, throb,
tremble, undulate

vibration juddering (*Inf.*), oscillation, pul~
sation, pulse, quiver, resonance, reverbera~
tion, shaking, throb, throbbing, trembling,
tremor

vice 1. corruption, degeneracy, depravity,
evil, evildoing, immorality, iniquity,
profligacy, sin, turpitude, venality, wicked~
ness **2.** blemish, defect, failing, fault, im~
perfection, shortcoming, weakness
Antonyms (*sense 1*) honour, morality, virtue
(*sense 2*) attainment, gift, good point, strong
point, talent

vicinity area, district, environs, locality,
neck of the woods (*Inf.*), neighbourhood,
precincts, propinquity, proximity, purlieus

vicious 1. abandoned, abhorrent, atrocious,
bad, barbarous, corrupt, cruel, dangerous,
debased, degenerate, degraded, depraved,
diabolical, ferocious, fiendish, foul, heinous,
immoral, infamous, monstrous, profligate,
savage, sinful, unprincipled, vile, violent,
wicked, worthless, wrong **2.** backbiting,
bitchy (*Inf.*), cruel, defamatory, malicious,
mean, rancorous, slanderous, spiteful, ven~
omous, vindictive
Antonyms complimentary, docile, friendly,
gentle, good, honourable, kind, playful, tame,
upright, virtuous

viciousness 1. badness, corruption, cruel~
ty, depravity, ferocity, immorality, profli~
gacy, savagery, wickedness **2.** bitchiness
(*Sl.*), malice, rancour, spite, spitefulness,
venom
Antonyms (*sense 2*) gentleness, goodness,
goodwill, graciousness, kindness, mercy, vir~
tue

victim 1. casualty, fatality, injured party,
martyr, sacrifice, scapegoat, sufferer **2.**
dupe, easy prey, fall guy (*Inf.*), gull (*Archa~
ic*), innocent, patsy (*Sl., chiefly U.S. &
Canad.*), sitting duck (*Inf.*), sitting target,
sucker (*Sl.*)

Antonyms (*sense 1*) survivor (*sense 2*) assail~
ant, attacker, culprit, guilty party, offender

victimize 1. discriminate against, have a
down on (someone) (*Inf.*), have it in for
(someone) (*Inf.*), have one's knife into
(someone), persecute, pick on **2.** cheat, de~
ceive, defraud, dupe, exploit, fool, gull (*Ar~
chaic*), hoodwink, prey on, swindle, take
advantage of, use

victor champ (*Inf.*), champion, conquering
hero, conqueror, first, prizewinner, top dog
(*Inf.*), vanquisher, winner
Antonyms also-ran, dud (*Inf.*), failure, flop
(*Inf.*), loser, vanquished

victorious champion, conquering, first,
prizewinning, successful, triumphant, van~
quishing, winning
Antonyms beaten, conquered, defeated,
failed, losing, overcome, unsuccessful, van~
quished

victory conquest, laurels, mastery, success,
superiority, the palm, the prize, triumph,
win
Antonyms defeat, failure, loss

victuals bread, comestibles, eatables, eats
(*Sl.*), edibles, food, grub (*Sl.*), meat, nosebag
(*Sl.*), nosh (*Sl.*), provisions, rations, stores,
supplies, tack (*Inf.*), viands, vittles (*Obso~
lete*)

view *n.* **1.** aspect, landscape, outlook, pano~
rama, perspective, picture, prospect, scene,
spectacle, vista **2.** range *or* field of vision,
sight, vision **3.** *Sometimes plural* attitude,
belief, conviction, feeling, impression, judg~
ment, notion, opinion, point of view, senti~
ment, thought, way of thinking **4.** contem~
plation, display, examination, inspection,
look, recce (*Sl.*), scan, scrutiny, sight, sur~
vey, viewing **5. with a view to** in order to,
in the hope of, so as to, with the aim *or* in~
tention of ~*v.* **6.** behold, check, check out
(*Inf.*), clock (*Brit. sl.*), contemplate, examine,
explore, eye, eyeball (*U.S. sl.*), gaze at, get a
load of (*Inf.*), inspect, look at, observe, recce
(*Sl.*), regard, scan, spectate, stare at, survey,
take a dekko at (*Brit. sl.*), watch, witness **7.**
consider, deem, judge, look on, regard,
think about

viewer observer, one of an audience, on~
looker, spectator, TV watcher, watcher

viewpoint angle, frame of reference, per~
spective, point of view, position, slant,
stance, standpoint, vantage point, way of
thinking

vigilant alert, Argus-eyed, attentive, careful,
cautious, circumspect, keeping one's eyes
peeled *or* skinned (*Inf.*), on one's guard, on
one's toes, on the alert, on the lookout, on
the qui vive, on the watch, sleepless,
unsleeping, wakeful, watchful, wide awake

vigorous active, brisk, dynamic, effective,
efficient, energetic, enterprising, flourish~
ing, forceful, forcible, full of energy, hale,
hale and hearty, hardy, healthy, intense,
lively, lusty, powerful, Ramboesque, red-
blooded, robust, sound, spanking, spirited,
strenuous, strong, virile, vital, zippy (*Inf.*)
Antonyms apathetic, effete, enervated, fee~
ble, frail, inactive, indolent, lethargic, lifeless,
spiritless, torpid, weak, weedy (*Inf.*), wimpish
or wimpy (*Inf.*), wishy-washy

vigorously all out, eagerly, energetically,
forcefully, hammer and tongs, hard, like
mad (*Sl.*), lustily, strenuously, strongly,
with a vengeance, with might and main

vigour activity, animation, balls (*Taboo sl.*),
brio, dash, dynamism, energy, force, force~
fulness, gusto, health, liveliness, might,
oomph (*Inf.*), pep, power, punch (*Inf.*), ro~
bustness, snap (*Inf.*), soundness, spirit,
strength, verve, vim (*Sl.*), virility, vitality,
zip (*Inf.*)
Antonyms apathy, feebleness, fragility,
frailty, impotence, inactivity, inertia,
infirmity, lethargy, sluggishness, weakness

vile 1. abandoned, abject, appalling, bad,
base, coarse, contemptible, corrupt, de~
based, degenerate, degrading, depraved,
despicable, disgraceful, evil, humiliating,
ignoble, impure, loathsome, low, mean,
miserable, nefarious, perverted, shocking,
sinful, ugly, vicious, vulgar, wicked, worth~
less, wretched **2.** disgusting, foul, horrid,
loathsome, nasty, nauseating, noxious, ob~
scene, offensive, repellent, repugnant, re~
pulsive, revolting, sickening, yucky *or* yuk~
ky (*Sl.*)
Antonyms agreeable, chaste, cultured, deli~
cate, genteel, honourable, lovely, marvellous,
noble, pleasant, polite, pure, refined, right~
eous, splendid, sublime, upright, worthy

vilify abuse, asperse, bad-mouth (*Sl., chiefly
U.S. & Canad.*), berate, calumniate, debase,
decry, defame, denigrate, disparage, knock
(*Inf.*), malign, pull to pieces (*Inf.*), revile,
rubbish (*Inf.*), run down, slag (off) (*Sl.*),
slander, smear, speak ill of, traduce, vili~
pend (*Rare*), vituperate
Antonyms adore, commend, esteem, exalt,
glorify, honour, praise, revere, venerate

villain 1. blackguard, caitiff (*Archaic*),
criminal, evildoer, knave (*Archaic*), liber~
tine, malefactor, miscreant, profligate, rap~
scallion, reprobate, rogue, scoundrel,
wretch **2.** antihero, baddy (*Inf.*) **3.** devil,
monkey, rascal, rogue, scallywag (*Inf.*),
scamp
Antonyms (*senses 2 & 3*) angel, goody, hero,
heroine, idol

villainous atrocious, bad, base, blackguard~
ly, criminal, cruel, debased, degenerate, de~
praved, detestable, diabolical, evil, fiendish,
hateful, heinous, ignoble, infamous, inhu~
man, mean, nefarious, outrageous, ruffian~
ly, scoundrelly, sinful, terrible, thievish,
vicious, vile, wicked
Antonyms angelic, good, heroic, humane,
moral, noble, righteous, saintly, virtuous

villainy atrocity, baseness, crime, criminal~
ity, delinquency, depravity, devilry, in~
iquity, knavery, rascality, sin, turpitude,
vice, wickedness

vindicate 1. absolve, acquit, clear, defend,
do justice to, exculpate, excuse, exonerate,
free from blame, justify, rehabilitate **2.** ad~
vocate, assert, establish, maintain, support,
uphold
Antonyms (*sense 1*) accuse, blame, condemn,
convict, incriminate, punish, reproach

vindication apology, assertion, defence, ex~
culpating, exculpation, excuse, exoneration,
justification, maintenance, plea, rehabilita~
tion, substantiation, support

vindictive full of spleen, implacable, mali~
cious, malignant, rancorous, relentless, re~
sentful, revengeful, spiteful, unforgiving,
unrelenting, vengeful, venomous
Antonyms forgiving, generous, magnani~
mous, merciful, relenting, unvindictive

vintage 1. *n.* collection, crop, epoch, era,
generation, harvest, origin, year **2.** *adj.*
best, choice, classic, mature, prime, rare,
ripe, select, superior, venerable

violate 1. break, contravene, disobey, dis~
regard, encroach upon, infract, infringe,
transgress **2.** abuse, assault, befoul, de~
bauch, defile, desecrate, dishonour, invade,
outrage, pollute, profane, rape, ravish
Antonyms (*sense 1*) honour, obey, respect,
uphold (*sense 2*) defend, honour, protect, re~
spect, revere, set on a pedestal

violation 1. abuse, breach, contravention,
encroachment, infraction, infringement,
transgression, trespass **2.** defilement, des~
ecration, profanation, sacrilege, spoliation

violence 1. bestiality, bloodshed, blood~
thirstiness, brutality, brute force, cruelty,
destructiveness, ferocity, fierceness, fight~
ing, force, frenzy, fury, murderousness,
passion, rough handling, savagery, strong-
arm tactics (*Inf.*), terrorism, thuggery, ve~
hemence, wildness **2.** boisterousness, pow~
er, raging, roughness, storminess, tumult,
turbulence, wildness **3.** abandon, acuteness,
fervour, force, harshness, intensity, sever~
ity, sharpness, vehemence

violent 1. berserk, bloodthirsty, brutal,
cruel, destructive, fiery, flaming, forcible,
furious, headstrong, homicidal, hot-headed,
impetuous, intemperate, maddened, mania~
cal, murderous, passionate, powerful, rag~
ing, Ramboesque, riotous, rough, savage,
strong, tempestuous, uncontrollable, un~
governable, unrestrained, vehement, vi~
cious, wild **2.** blustery, boisterous, devas~
tating, full of force, gale force, powerful,
raging, ruinous, strong, tempestuous, tu~
multuous, turbulent, wild **3.** acute, agoniz~
ing, biting, excruciating, extreme, harsh,
inordinate, intense, outrageous, painful, se~
vere, sharp
Antonyms calm, composed, gentle, mild,
peaceful, quiet, rational, sane, serene,
unruffled, well-behaved

virgin 1. *n.* damsel (*Archaic*), girl, maid
(*Archaic*), maiden (*Archaic*), vestal, virgo
intacta **2.** *adj.* chaste, fresh, immaculate,
maidenly, modest, new, pristine, pure,
snowy, uncorrupted, undefiled, unsullied,
untouched, unused, vestal, virginal
Antonyms *adj.* contaminated, corrupted,
defiled, dirty, impure, polluted, spoiled, used

virile forceful, lusty, macho, male, manlike,
manly, masculine, potent, Ramboesque,
red-blooded, robust, strong, vigorous
Antonyms camp (*Inf.*), effeminate, emascu~
late, feminine, impotent, unmanly, weak,
weedy (*Inf.*), wimpish *or* wimpy (*Inf.*)

virility machismo, manhood, masculinity,
potency, vigour
Antonyms effeminacy, femininity, impo~
tence, softness, unmanliness, weakness

virtual essential, implicit, implied, in all but
name, indirect, potential, practical, tacit,
unacknowledged

virtually as good as, effectually, for all
practical purposes, in all but name, in ef~
fect, in essence, nearly, practically, to all
intents and purposes

virtue 1. ethicalness, excellence, goodness,
high-mindedness, incorruptibility, integrity,
justice, morality, probity, quality, rectitude,
righteousness, uprightness, worth, worthi~
ness **2.** advantage, asset, attribute, credit,
good point, good quality, merit, plus (*Inf.*),
strength **3.** chastity, honour, innocence,
morality, purity, virginity **4. by virtue of**
as a result of, by dint of, by reason of, in
view of, on account of, owing to, thanks to
Antonyms (*sense 1*) corruption, debauchery,
depravity, dishonesty, dishonour, evil, im~
morality, sin, sinfulness, turpitude, vice
(*sense 2*) drawback, failing, frailty, short~
coming, weak point (*sense 3*) promiscuity,
unchastity

virtuosity brilliance, craft, éclat, expertise,
finish, flair, mastery, panache, polish, skill

virtuoso 1. *n.* artist, genius, grandmaster,
maestro, magician, master, master hand,
maven (*U.S.*) **2.** *adj.* bravura (*Music*), bril~
liant, dazzling, masterly

virtuous 1. blameless, ethical, excellent, exemplary, good, high-principled, honest, honourable, incorruptible, moral, praise~worthy, pure, righteous, squeaky-clean, upright, worthy **2.** celibate, chaste, clean-living, innocent, pure, spotless, virginal
Antonyms (*sense 1*) corrupt, debauched, de~praved, dishonest, evil, immoral, sinful, un~righteous, vicious, wicked (*sense 2*) impure, loose, promiscuous, unchaste

virulent 1. baneful (*Archaic*), deadly, infec~tive, injurious, lethal, malignant, perni~cious, poisonous, septic, toxic, venomous **2.** acrimonious, bitter, envenomed, hostile, malevolent, malicious, rancorous, resentful, spiteful, splenetic, venomous, vicious, vin~dictive
Antonyms (*sense 1*) harmless, innocuous, nonpoisonous, nontoxic (*sense 2*) amiable, be~nign, compassionate, kind, magnanimous, sympathetic, warm

visible anywhere to be seen, apparent, clear, conspicuous, detectable, discernible, dis~coverable, distinguishable, evident, in sight, in view, manifest, not hidden, noticeable, observable, obvious, palpable, patent, per~ceivable, perceptible, plain, to be seen, un~concealed, unmistakable
Antonyms concealed, hidden, impercep~tible, invisible, obscured, unnoticeable, un~seen

vision 1. eyes, eyesight, perception, seeing, sight, view **2.** breadth of view, discernment, farsightedness, foresight, imagination, in~sight, intuition, penetration, prescience **3.** castle in the air, concept, conception, day~dream, dream, fantasy, idea, ideal, image, mental picture, pipe dream **4.** apparition, chimera, delusion, eidolon, ghost, halluci~nation, illusion, mirage, phantasm, phan~tom, revelation, spectre, wraith **5.** dream, feast for the eyes, perfect picture, picture, sight, sight for sore eyes, spectacle

visionary *adj.* **1.** dreaming, dreamy, ideal~istic, quixotic, romantic, starry-eyed, with one's head in the clouds **2.** chimerical, de~lusory, fanciful, fantastic, ideal, idealized, illusory, imaginary, impractical, prophetic, speculative, unreal, unrealistic, unwork~able, utopian ~*n.* **3.** daydreamer, Don Quixote, dreamer, enthusiast (*Archaic*), idealist, mystic, prophet, romantic, seer, theorist, utopian, zealot
Antonyms *adj.* actual, mundane, pragmatic, real, realistic, unimaginary ~*n.* cynic, pessi~mist, pragmatist, realist

visit *v.* **1.** be the guest of, call in, call on, drop in on (*Inf.*), go to see, inspect, look (someone) up, pay a call on, pop in (*Inf.*), stay at, stay with, stop by, take in (*Inf.*) **2.** afflict, assail, attack, befall, descend upon, haunt, smite, trouble **3.** *With* **on** *or* **upon**

bring down upon, execute, impose, inflict, wreak ~*n.* **4.** call, sojourn, stay, stop

visitation 1. examination, inspection, visit **2.** bane, blight, calamity, cataclysm, catas~trophe, disaster, infliction, ordeal, punish~ment, scourge, trial

visitor caller, company, guest, visitant

visual 1. ocular, optic, optical **2.** discern~ible, observable, perceptible, visible
Antonyms (*sense 2*) imperceptible, indis~cernible, invisible, out of sight, unnoticeable, unperceivable

visualize conceive of, conjure up a mental picture of, envisage, imagine, picture, see in the mind's eye

vital 1. basic, cardinal, essential, fundamen~tal, imperative, indispensable, necessary, radical, requisite **2.** critical, crucial, deci~sive, important, key, life-or-death, significant, urgent **3.** animated, dynamic, energetic, forceful, full of the joy of living, lively, sparky, spirited, vibrant, vigorous, vivacious, zestful **4.** alive, animate, genera~tive, invigorative, life-giving, live, living, quickening
Antonyms (*sense 1*) dispensable, inessential, nonessential, unnecessary (*sense 2*) minor, trivial, unimportant (*sense 3*) apathetic, le~thargic, listless, uninvolved (*sense 4*) dead, dying, inanimate, moribund

vitality animation, brio, energy, exuberance, go (*Inf.*), life, liveliness, lustiness, pep, ro~bustness, sparkle, stamina, strength, vigour, vim (*Sl.*), vivaciousness, vivacity
Antonyms apathy, inertia, lethargy, list~lessness, sluggishness, weakness

vitriolic *Fig.* acerbic, acid, bitchy (*Inf.*), bit~ter, caustic, destructive, dripping with mal~ice, envenomed, sardonic, scathing, venom~ous, virulent, withering

vituperation abuse, billingsgate, blame, castigation, censure, fault-finding, flak (*Inf.*), invective, obloquy, rebuke, repri~mand, reproach, scurrility, tongue-lashing, vilification
Antonyms acclaim, approval, commenda~tion, eulogy, flattery, praise, tribute

vituperative abusive, belittling, calumnia~tory, censorious, defamatory, denunciatory, derogatory, harsh, insulting, malign, op~probrious, sardonic, scurrilous, withering

vivacious animated, bubbling, cheerful, chirpy (*Inf.*), ebullient, effervescent, frolic~some, full of life, gay, high-spirited, jolly, light-hearted, lively, merry, scintillating, sparkling, sparky, spirited, sportive, sprightly, upbeat (*Inf.*), vital
Antonyms boring, dull, languid, lifeless, listless, melancholy, spiritless, unenthusias~tic

vivacity animation, brio, ebullience, effer~
vescence, energy, gaiety, high spirits, life,
liveliness, pep, quickness, sparkle, spirit,
sprightliness
Antonyms apathy, ennui, fatigue, heavi~
ness, inertia, languor, lethargy, listlessness,
weariness

vivid 1. bright, brilliant, clear, colourful,
glowing, intense, rich **2.** distinct, dramatic,
graphic, highly-coloured, lifelike, memo~
rable, powerful, realistic, sharp, sharply-
etched, stirring, strong, telling, true to life
3. active, animated, dynamic, energetic, ex~
pressive, flamboyant, lively, quick, spirited,
striking, strong, vigorous
Antonyms colourless, cool, drab, dull, life~
less, nondescript, ordinary, pale, pastel, quiet,
routine, run-of-the-mill, sombre, unclear, un~
memorable, unremarkable, vague

vixen *Fig.* ballbreaker (*Sl.*), fury, harpy,
harridan, hellcat, scold, shrew, spitfire, ter~
magant (*Rare*), virago, Xanthippe

vocabulary dictionary, glossary, language,
lexicon, wordbook, word hoard, words,
word stock

vocal *adj.* **1.** articulate, articulated, oral, put
into words, said, spoken, uttered, voiced **2.**
articulate, blunt, clamorous, eloquent, ex~
pressive, forthright, frank, free-spoken,
noisy, outspoken, plain-spoken, strident,
vociferous
Antonyms (*sense 2*) inarticulate, quiet, re~
served, reticent, retiring, shy, silent, uncom~
municative

vocation business, calling, career, employ~
ment, job, life's work, life work, métier,
mission, office, post, profession, pursuit,
role, trade

vociferous clamant, clamorous, loud, loud-
mouthed (*Inf.*), noisy, obstreperous, outspo~
ken, ranting, shouting, strident, uproarious,
vehement, vocal
Antonyms hushed, muted, noiseless, quiet,
silent, still

vogue *n.* **1.** craze, custom, *dernier cri*, fash~
ion, last word, mode, style, the latest, the
rage, the thing (*Inf.*), trend, way **2.** accept~
ance, currency, fashionableness, favour,
popularity, prevalence, usage, use ~*adj.* **3.**
fashionable, in, modish, now (*Inf.*), popular,
prevalent, trendy (*Brit. inf.*), up-to-the-
minute, voguish, with it (*Inf.*)

voice *n.* **1.** articulation, language, power of
speech, sound, tone, utterance, words **2.**
decision, expression, part, say, view, vote,
will, wish **3.** agency, instrument, medium,
mouthpiece, organ, spokesman, spokes~
person, spokeswoman, vehicle ~*v.* **4.** air,
articulate, assert, come out with (*Inf.*), de~
clare, divulge, enunciate, express, give ex~

pression *or* utterance to, put into words,
say, utter, ventilate

void *adj.* **1.** bare, clear, drained, emptied,
empty, free, tenantless, unfilled, unoccu~
pied, vacant **2.** *With* **of** destitute, devoid,
lacking, without **3.** dead, ineffective, inef~
fectual, inoperative, invalid, nonviable, nu~
gatory, null and void, unenforceable,
useless, vain, worthless ~*n.* **4.** blank,
blankness, emptiness, gap, lack, opening,
space, vacuity, vacuum, want ~*v.* **5.** dis~
charge, drain, eject, eliminate (*Physiology*),
emit, empty, evacuate **6.** abnegate, cancel,
invalidate, nullify, rescind
Antonyms *adj.* (*sense 1*) abounding, com~
plete, filled, full, occupied, replete, tenanted

volatile airy, changeable, erratic, explosive,
fickle, flighty, gay, giddy, inconstant, lively,
mercurial, sprightly, temperamental, unset~
tled, unstable, unsteady, up and down (*Inf.*),
variable, whimsical
Antonyms calm, consistent, constant, cool-
headed, dependable, inert, reliable, self-
controlled, settled, sober, stable, steady

volition choice, choosing, determination,
discretion, election, free will, option, pref~
erence, purpose, resolution, will

volley *n.* barrage, blast, bombardment,
burst, cannonade, discharge, explosion, fu~
sillade, hail, salvo, shower

volubility fluency, garrulity, gift of the gab,
glibness, loquaciousness, loquacity

voluble articulate, blessed with the gift of
the gab, fluent, forthcoming, glib, loqua~
cious, talkative
Antonyms hesitant, inarticulate, reticent,
succinct, taciturn, terse, tongue-tied, un~
forthcoming

volume 1. aggregate, amount, body, bulk,
capacity, compass, cubic content, dimen~
sions, mass, quantity, total **2.** book, publi~
cation, title, tome, treatise

voluminous ample, big, billowing, bulky,
capacious, cavernous, copious, full, large,
massive, prolific, roomy, vast
Antonyms inadequate, insufficient, scanty,
skimpy, slight, small, tiny

voluntarily by choice, freely, lief (*Rare*), of
one's own accord, of one's own free will, on
one's own initiative, willingly, without be~
ing asked, without prompting

voluntary discretional, discretionary, free,
gratuitous, honorary, intended, intentional,
optional, spontaneous, uncompelled, uncon~
strained, unforced, unpaid, volunteer, will~
ing
Antonyms automatic, conscripted, forced,
instinctive, involuntary, obligatory, uninten~
tional

volunteer *v.* advance, let oneself in for

(*Inf.*), need no invitation, offer, offer one's services, present, proffer, propose, put forward, put oneself at (someone's) disposal, step forward, suggest, tender
Antonyms begrudge, deny, keep, refuse, retain, withdraw, withhold

voluptuous 1. epicurean, hedonistic, licentious, luxurious, pleasure-loving, self-indulgent, sensual, sybaritic **2.** ample, buxom, curvaceous (*Inf.*), enticing, erotic, full-bosomed, provocative, seductive, shapely, well-stacked (*Brit. sl.*)
Antonyms (*sense 1*) abstemious, ascetic, celibate, rigorous, self-denying, Spartan

voluptuousness carnality, curvaceousness (*Inf.*), licentiousness, opulence, seductiveness, sensuality, shapeliness

vomit *v.* barf (*U.S. sl.*), belch forth, be sick, bring up, chuck (up) (*Sl., chiefly U.S.*), chunder (*Sl., chiefly Aust.*), disgorge, do a technicolour yawn (*Sl.*), eject, emit, heave, puke (*Sl.*), regurgitate, retch, sick up (*Inf.*), spew out *or* up, throw up (*Inf.*), toss one's cookies (*U.S. sl.*), upchuck (*U.S. sl.*)

voracious avid, devouring, gluttonous, greedy, hungry, insatiable, omnivorous, prodigious, rapacious, ravening, ravenous, uncontrolled, unquenchable
Antonyms moderate, sated, satisfied, self-controlled, temperate

vote *n.* **1.** ballot, franchise, plebiscite, poll, referendum, right to vote, show of hands, suffrage ~*v.* **2.** ballot, cast one's vote, elect, go to the polls, opt, return **3.** *Inf.* declare, judge, pronounce, propose, recommend, suggest

vouch *Usually with* **for** affirm, answer for, assert, asseverate, attest to, back, certify, confirm, give assurance of, go bail for,

guarantee, stand witness, support, swear to, uphold

vouchsafe accord, cede, condescend to give, confer, deign, favour (someone) with, grant, yield

vow 1. *v.* affirm, consecrate, dedicate, devote, pledge, promise, swear, undertake solemnly **2.** *n.* oath, pledge, promise, troth (*Archaic*)

voyage *n.* crossing, cruise, journey, passage, travels, trip

vulgar 1. blue, boorish, cheap and nasty, coarse, common, crude, dirty, flashy, gaudy, gross, ill-bred, impolite, improper, indecent, indecorous, indelicate, low, nasty, naughty, off colour, ribald, risqué, rude, suggestive, tasteless, tawdry, uncouth, unmannerly, unrefined **2.** general, native, ordinary, unrefined, vernacular
Antonyms aristocratic, classical, decorous, elegant, genteel, high-brow, polite, refined, sophisticated, tasteful, upper-class, well-mannered

vulgarity bad taste, coarseness, crudeness, crudity, gaudiness, grossness, indecorum, indelicacy, lack of refinement, ribaldry, rudeness, suggestiveness, tastelessness, tawdriness
Antonyms decorum, gentility, good breeding, good manners, good taste, refinement, sensitivity, sophistication, tastefulness

vulnerable accessible, assailable, defenceless, exposed, open to attack, sensitive, susceptible, tender, thin-skinned, unprotected, weak, wide open
Antonyms guarded, immune, impervious, insensitive, invulnerable, thick-skinned, unassailable, well-protected

W

wad ball, block, bundle, chunk, hunk, lump, mass, plug, roll

wadding filler, lining, packing, padding, stuffing

waddle rock, shuffle, sway, toddle, totter, wobble

wade 1. ford, paddle, splash, walk through **2.** *With* **through** drudge, labour, peg away, plough through, toil, work one's way **3.** *With* **in** *or* **into** assail, attack, get stuck in (*Inf.*), go for, launch oneself at, light into (*Inf.*), set about, tackle, tear into (*Inf.*)

waffle 1. *v.* blather, jabber, prate, prattle, rabbit (on) (*Brit. inf.*), verbalize, witter on (*Inf.*) **2.** *n.* blather, jabber, padding, prating, prattle, prolixity, verbiage, verbosity, wordiness

waft 1. *v.* bear, be carried, carry, convey, drift, float, ride, transmit, transport **2.** *n.* breath, breeze, current, draught, puff, whiff

wag 1. *v.* bob, flutter, nod, oscillate, quiver, rock, shake, stir, vibrate, waggle, wave, wiggle **2.** *n.* bob, flutter, nod, oscillation, quiver, shake, toss, vibration, waggle, wave, wiggle

wage 1. *n. Also* **wages** allowance, compensation, earnings, emolument, fee, hire, pay, payment, recompense, remuneration, reward, stipend **2.** *v.* carry on, conduct, engage in, practise, proceed with, prosecute, pursue, undertake

wager 1. *n.* bet, flutter (*Brit. inf.*), gamble, pledge, punt (*Chiefly Brit.*), stake, venture **2.** *v.* bet, chance, gamble, hazard, lay, pledge, punt (*Chiefly Brit.*), put on, risk, speculate, stake, venture

waggle 1. *v.* flutter, oscillate, shake, wag, wave, wiggle, wobble **2.** *n.* flutter, oscillation, shake, wag, wave, wiggle, wobble

waif foundling, orphan, stray

wail 1. *v.* bawl, bemoan, bewail, cry, deplore, grieve, howl, keen, lament, ululate, weep, yowl **2.** *n.* complaint, cry, grief, howl, keen, lament, lamentation, moan, ululation, weeping, yowl

wait 1. *v.* abide, bide one's time, cool one's heels, dally, delay, hang fire, hold back, hold on (*Inf.*), linger, mark time, pause, remain, rest, stand by, stay, tarry **2.** *n.* delay, entr'acte, halt, hold-up, interval, pause, rest, stay
Antonyms (*sense 1*) depart, go, go away, leave, move off, quit, set off, take off (*Inf.*)

waiter, waitress attendant, server, steward, stewardess

wait on *or* **upon** attend, minister to, serve, tend

waive abandon, defer, dispense with, forgo, give up, postpone, put off, refrain from, relinquish, remit, renounce, resign, set aside, surrender
Antonyms claim, demand, insist, maintain, press, profess, pursue, uphold

waiver abandonment, abdication, disclaimer, giving up, relinquishment, remission, renunciation, resignation, setting aside, surrender

wake¹ *v.* **1.** arise, awake, awaken, bestir, come to, get up, rouse, rouse from sleep, stir **2.** activate, animate, arouse, awaken, enliven, excite, fire, galvanize, kindle, provoke, quicken, rouse, stimulate, stir up ~*n.* **3.** deathwatch, funeral, vigil, watch
Antonyms (*sense 1*) catnap, doze, drop off (*Inf.*), hibernate, nod off (*Inf.*), sleep, snooze (*Inf.*), take a nap

wake² aftermath, backwash, path, slipstream, track, trail, train, wash, waves

wakeful 1. insomniac, restless, sleepless, unsleeping **2.** alert, alive, attentive, heedful, observant, on guard, on the alert, on the lookout, on the qui vive, unsleeping, vigilant, wary, watchful
Antonyms (*sense 2*) asleep, dormant, dozing, dreamy, drowsy, heedless, inattentive, off guard, sleepy

waken activate, animate, arouse, awake, awaken, be roused, come awake, come to, enliven, fire, galvanize, get up, kindle, quicken, rouse, stimulate, stir
Antonyms be inactive, doze, lie dormant, nap, repose, sleep, slumber, snooze (*Inf.*)

walk *v.* **1.** advance, amble, foot it, go, go by shanks's pony (*Inf.*), go on foot, hike, hoof it (*Sl.*), march, move, pace, perambulate, promenade, saunter, step, stride, stroll, traipse (*Inf.*), tramp, travel on foot, trek, trudge **2.** accompany, convoy, escort, take ~*n.* **3.** constitutional, hike, march, perambulation, promenade, ramble, saunter, stroll, traipse (*Inf.*), tramp, trek, trudge, turn **4.** carriage, gait, manner of walking, pace, step, stride **5.** aisle, alley, avenue, esplanade, footpath, lane, path, pathway, pavement, promenade, sidewalk, trail **6.** area, arena, calling, career, course, field, line, métier, profession, sphere, trade, vocation

walker footslogger, hiker, pedestrian, ram~ bler, wayfarer

walkout industrial action, protest, stoppage, strike

walk out 1. flounce out, get up and go, leave suddenly, storm out, take off (*Inf.*) **2.** down tools, go on strike, stop work, strike, take industrial action, withdraw one's la~ bour **3.** *With* **on** abandon, chuck (*Inf.*), des~ ert, forsake, jilt, leave, leave in the lurch, pack in (*Inf.*), run away from, throw over **Antonyms** (*sense 3*) be loyal to, defend, re~ main, stand by, stay, stick with, support, uphold

walkover breeze (*U.S. & Canad. inf.*), cake~ walk (*Inf.*), child's play (*Inf.*), cinch (*Sl.*), doddle (*Brit. sl.*), duck soup (*U.S. sl.*), easy victory, picnic (*Inf.*), piece of cake (*Inf.*), pushover (*Sl.*), snap (*Inf.*)
Antonyms drudgery, effort, grind (*Inf.*), la~ bour, ordeal, strain, struggle, trial

wall 1. divider, enclosure, panel, partition, screen **2.** barricade, breastwork, bulwark, embankment, fortification, palisade, para~ pet, rampart, stockade **3.** barrier, block, fence, hedge, impediment, obstacle, ob~ struction **4. go to the wall** *Inf.* be ruined, collapse, fail, fall, go bust (*Inf.*), go under **5. drive up the wall** *Sl.* aggravate (*Inf.*), an~ noy, dement, derange, drive crazy (*Inf.*), drive insane, exasperate, get on one's nerves (*Inf.*), infuriate, irritate, madden, piss one off (*Taboo sl.*), send off one's head (*Sl.*), try

wallet case, holder, notecase, pocketbook, pouch, purse

wallow 1. lie, roll about, splash around, tumble, welter **2.** flounder, lurch, stagger, stumble, wade **3.** bask, delight, glory, in~ dulge oneself, luxuriate, relish, revel, take pleasure
Antonyms (*sense 3*) abstain, avoid, do with~ out, eschew, forgo, give up, refrain

wan 1. anaemic, ashen, bloodless, cadaver~ ous, colourless, discoloured, ghastly, livid, pale, pallid, pasty, sickly, washed out, wax~ en, wheyfaced, white **2.** dim, faint, feeble, pale, weak
Antonyms (*sense 1*) blooming, bright, flourishing, glowing, healthy, roseate, rosy, rubicund, ruddy, vibrant

wand baton, rod, sprig, stick, twig, withe, withy

wander *v.* **1.** cruise, drift, knock about *or* around, meander, mooch around (*Sl.*), per~ egrinate, ramble, range, roam, rove, strag~ gle, stravaig (*Scot. & northern English dia~ lect*), stray, stroll, traipse (*Inf.*) **2.** depart, deviate, digress, divagate (*Rare*), diverge, err, get lost, go astray, go off at a tangent, go off course, lapse, lose concentration, lose

one's train of thought, lose one's way, swerve, veer **3.** babble, be delirious, be in~ coherent, ramble, rave, speak incoherently, talk nonsense ~*n.* **4.** cruise, excursion, me~ ander, peregrination, ramble, traipse (*Inf.*)
Antonyms (*sense 2*) comply, conform, fall in with, follow, run with the pack, toe the line

wanderer bird of passage, drifter, gypsy, itinerant, nomad, rambler, ranger, rolling stone, rover, stroller, traveller, vagabond, vagrant, voyager

wandering drifting, homeless, itinerant, migratory, nomadic, peripatetic, rambling, rootless, roving, strolling, travelling, vaga~ bond, vagrant, voyaging, wayfaring

wane *v.* **1.** abate, atrophy, decline, decrease, die out, dim, diminish, draw to a close, drop, dwindle, ebb, fade, fade away, fail, lessen, sink, subside, taper off, weaken, wind down, wither ~*n.* **2.** abatement, atro~ phy, decay, declension, decrease, diminu~ tion, drop, dwindling, ebb, fading, failure, fall, falling off, lessening, sinking, subsid~ ence, tapering off, withering **3. on the wane** at its lowest ebb, declining, dropping, dwindling, dying out, ebbing, fading, less~ ening, obsolescent, on its last legs, on the decline, on the way out, subsiding, tapering off, weakening, withering
Antonyms *v.* blossom, brighten, develop, expand, grow, improve, increase, rise, strengthen, wax ~*n.* advancement, develop~ ment, expansion, growth, increase, rise, strengthening, waxing

want *v.* **1.** covet, crave, desire, eat one's heart out over, feel a need for, hanker after, have a fancy for, have a yen for (*Inf.*), hope for, hunger for, long for, need, pine for, re~ quire, thirst for, wish, yearn for **2.** be able to do with, be deficient in, be short of, be without, call for, demand, fall short in, have need of, lack, miss, need, require, stand in need of ~*n.* **3.** appetite, craving, demand, desire, fancy, hankering, hunger, longing, necessity, need, requirement, thirst, wish, yearning, yen (*Inf.*) **4.** absence, dearth, de~ fault, deficiency, famine, insufficiency, lack, paucity, scantiness, scarcity, shortage **5.** destitution, indigence, need, neediness, pauperism, penury, poverty, privation
Antonyms *v.* be sated, detest, dislike, enjoy, hate, have, loathe, own, possess, reject, spurn, surfeit ~*n.* abundance, adequacy, comfort, ease, excess, luxury, plenty, sufficiency, sur~ plus, wealth

wanting 1. absent, incomplete, lacking, less, missing, short, shy **2.** defective, deficient, disappointing, faulty, imperfect, inadequate, inferior, leaving much to be desired, not good enough, not up to expec~ tations, not up to par, patchy, poor, sketchy, substandard, unsound

Antonyms adequate, complete, enough, full, replete, satisfactory, saturated, sufficient

wanton adj. **1.** abandoned, dissipated, dissolute, fast, immoral, lecherous, lewd, libertine, libidinous, licentious, loose, lustful, of easy virtue, promiscuous, rakish, shameless, unchaste **2.** arbitrary, cruel, evil, gratuitous, groundless, malevolent, malicious, motiveless, needless, senseless, spiteful, uncalled-for, unjustifiable, unjustified, unprovoked, vicious, wicked, wilful **3.** careless, devil-may-care, extravagant, heedless, immoderate, intemperate, lavish, outrageous, rash, reckless, unrestrained, wild ~n. **4.** Casanova, debauchee, Don Juan, gigolo, harlot, lech or letch (Inf.), lecher, libertine, loose woman, profligate, prostitute, rake, roué, scrubber (Brit. & Aust. sl.), slag (Brit. sl.), slut, strumpet, tart (Inf.), trollop, voluptuary, whore, woman of easy virtue ~v. **5.** debauch, dissipate, revel, riot, sleep around (Inf.), wench (Archaic), whore **6.** fritter away, misspend, squander, throw away, waste

Antonyms (sense 1) overmodest, priggish, prim, prudish, puritanical, rigid, strait-laced, stuffy, Victorian (sense 2) called-for, excusable, justified, legitimate, motivated, provoked, warranted (sense 3) cautious, circumspect, guarded, inhibited, moderate, prudent, reserved, restrained, temperate

war **1.** n. armed conflict, battle, bloodshed, combat, conflict, contention, contest, enmity, fighting, hostilities, hostility, strife, struggle, warfare **2.** v. battle, campaign against, carry on hostilities, clash, combat, conduct a war, contend, contest, fight, make war, strive, struggle, take up arms, wage war

Antonyms n. accord, armistice, cease-fire, co-existence, compliance, co-operation, harmony, peace, peace-time, treaty, truce ~v. call a ceasefire, co-exist, co-operate, make peace

war cry battle cry, rallying cry, slogan, war whoop

ward **1.** area, district, division, precinct, quarter, zone **2.** apartment, cubicle, room **3.** charge, dependant, minor, protégé, pupil **4.** care, charge, custody, guardianship, keeping, protection, safekeeping

warden administrator, caretaker, curator, custodian, guardian, janitor, keeper, ranger, steward, superintendent, warder, watchman

warder, wardress custodian, gaoler, guard, jailer, keeper, prison officer, screw (Sl.), turnkey (Archaic)

ward off avert, avoid, beat off, block, deflect, fend off, forestall, keep at arm's length, keep at bay, parry, repel, stave off, thwart, turn aside, turn away

Antonyms accept, admit, allow, embrace, permit, receive, take in, welcome

wardrobe **1.** closet, clothes cupboard, clothes-press **2.** apparel, attire, clothes, collection of clothes, outfit

warehouse depository, depot, stockroom, store, storehouse

wares commodities, goods, lines, manufactures, merchandise, produce, products, stock, stuff

warfare armed conflict, armed struggle, arms, battle, blows, campaigning, clash of arms, combat, conflict, contest, discord, fighting, hostilities, passage of arms, strategy, strife, struggle, war

Antonyms accord, amity, armistice, cessation of hostilities, conciliation, harmony, peace, treaty, truce

warily cagily (Inf.), carefully, cautiously, charily, circumspectly, distrustfully, gingerly, guardedly, suspiciously, vigilantly, watchfully, with care

Antonyms carelessly, hastily, heedlessly, irresponsibly, rashly, recklessly, thoughtlessly, unwarily

wariness alertness, attention, caginess (Inf.), care, carefulness, caution, circumspection, discretion, distrust, foresight, heedfulness, mindfulness, prudence, suspicion, vigilance, watchfulness

Antonyms carelessness, heedlessness, inattention, mindlessness, negligence, oblivion, recklessness, thoughtlessness

warlike aggressive, bellicose, belligerent, bloodthirsty, combative, hawkish, hostile, inimical, jingoistic, martial, militaristic, military, pugnacious, sabre-rattling, unfriendly, warmongering

Antonyms amicable, conciliatory, friendly, nonbelligerent, pacific, peaceable, peaceful, placid, unwarlike

warm adj. **1.** balmy, heated, lukewarm, moderately hot, pleasant, sunny, tepid, thermal **2.** affable, affectionate, amiable, amorous, cheerful, congenial, cordial, friendly, genial, happy, hearty, hospitable, kindly, likable or likeable, loving, pleasant, tender **3.** animated, ardent, cordial, earnest, effusive, emotional, enthusiastic, excited, fervent, glowing, heated, intense, keen, lively, passionate, spirited, stormy, vehement, vigorous, violent, zealous **4.** irascible, irritable, passionate, quick, sensitive, short, touchy **5.** Inf. dangerous, disagreeable, hazardous, perilous, tricky, uncomfortable, unpleasant ~v. **6.** heat, heat up, melt, thaw, warm up **7.** animate, awaken, excite, get going, interest, make enthusiastic, put some life into, rouse, stimulate, stir, turn on (Sl.)

Antonyms adj. aloof, apathetic, chilly, cold, cool, distant, freezing, half-hearted, hostile,

icy, phlegmatic, remote, stand-offish, uncar~
ing, unenthusiastic, unfriendly, unwelcoming
~*v.* alienate, chill, cool, cool down, depress,
freeze, sadden

warm-blooded ardent, earnest, emotional,
enthusiastic, excitable, fervent, impetuous,
lively, passionate, rash, spirited, vivacious

warm-hearted affectionate, compassion~
ate, cordial, generous, kind-hearted, kindly,
loving, sympathetic, tender, tender-hearted
Antonyms callous, cold, cold-hearted, hard,
hard-hearted, harsh, heartless, insensitive,
mean, merciless, unfeeling, unsympathetic

warmonger belligerent, hawk, jingo, mili~
tarist, sabre-rattler

warmth **1.** heat, hotness, warmness **2.** ani~
mation, ardour, eagerness, earnestness, ef~
fusiveness, enthusiasm, excitement, ferven~
cy, fervour, fire, heat, intensity, passion,
spirit, transport, vehemence, vigour, vio~
lence, zeal, zest **3.** affability, affection,
amorousness, cheerfulness, cordiality, hap~
piness, heartiness, hospitableness, kindli~
ness, love, tenderness
Antonyms aloofness, apathy, austerity,
chill, chilliness, cold, cold-heartedness, cold~
ness, coolness, hard-heartedness, hostility,
iciness, indifference, insincerity, lack of en~
thusiasm, remoteness, sternness

warn admonish, advise, alert, apprise, cau~
tion, forewarn, give fair warning, give no~
tice, inform, make (someone) aware, notify,
put one on one's guard, summon, tip off

warning **1.** *n.* admonition, advice, alarm,
alert, augury, caution, caveat, foretoken,
hint, notice, notification, omen, premoni~
tion, presage, sign, signal, threat, tip, tip-
off, token, word, word to the wise **2.** *adj.*
admonitory, cautionary, monitory, omi~
nous, premonitory, threatening

warrant *n.* **1.** assurance, authority,
authorization, carte blanche, commission,
guarantee, licence, permission, permit,
pledge, sanction, security, warranty ~*v.* **2.**
affirm, answer for, assure, attest, avouch,
certify, declare, guarantee, pledge, secure,
stand behind, underwrite, uphold, vouch for
3. approve, authorize, call for, commission,
demand, deserve, empower, entail, entitle,
excuse, give ground for, justify, license, ne~
cessitate, permit, require, sanction

warrantable accountable, allowable, de~
fensible, justifiable, lawful, necessary, per~
missible, proper, reasonable, right
Antonyms indefensible, reasonable,
uncalled-for, undue, unjustifiable, unneces~
sary, unwarrantable, wrong

warrior champion, combatant, fighter,
fighting man, gladiator, man-at-arms, sol~
dier

wary alert, attentive, cagey (*Inf.*), careful,

cautious, chary, circumspect, distrustful,
guarded, heedful, leery (*Sl.*), on one's guard,
on the lookout, on the qui vive, prudent,
suspicious, vigilant, watchful, wide-awake
Antonyms careless, foolhardy, imprudent,
negligent, rash, reckless, remiss, unguarded,
unsuspecting, unwary

wash *v.* **1.** bath, bathe, clean, cleanse, laun~
der, moisten, rinse, scrub, shampoo, show~
er, wet **2.** *With* **away** bear away, carry off,
erode, move, sweep away, wash off **3.** *Inf.*
bear scrutiny, be convincing, be plausible,
carry weight, hold up, hold water, stand up,
stick **4. wash one's hands of** abandon,
accept no responsibility for, give up on,
have nothing to do with, leave to one's own
devices ~*n.* **5.** ablution, bath, bathe, clean~
ing, cleansing, laundering, rinse, scrub,
shampoo, shower, washing **6.** ebb and flow,
flow, roll, surge, sweep, swell, wave **7.** coat,
coating, film, layer, overlay, screen, stain,
suffusion

washed out **1.** blanched, bleached, col~
ourless, etiolated, faded, flat, lacklustre,
mat, pale **2.** all in (*Sl.*), clapped out (*Aust.*
& N.Z. inf.), dead on one's feet (*Inf.*), dog-
tired (*Inf.*), done in (*Inf.*), drained, drawn,
exhausted, fatigued, haggard, knackered
(*Sl.*), pale, spent, tired-out, wan, weary,
worn-out, zonked (*Sl.*)
Antonyms (*sense 2*) alert, chirpy, energetic,
full of pep (*Inf.*), lively, perky, refreshed,
sprightly, zippy (*Inf.*)

washout **1.** disappointment, disaster, dud
(*Inf.*), failure, fiasco, flop (*Inf.*), mess **2.**
failure, incompetent, loser
Antonyms (*sense 1*) conquest, feat, success,
triumph, victory, winner

waspish bad-tempered, cantankerous, cap~
tious, crabbed, crabby, cross, crotchety
(*Inf.*), fretful, grumpy, ill-tempered, iras~
cible, irritable, liverish, peevish, peppery,
pettish, petulant, ratty (*Brit. & N.Z. inf.*),
snappish, splenetic, testy, tetchy, touchy,
waxy (*Inf., chiefly Brit.*)
Antonyms affable, agreeable, cheerful,
easy-going, genial, good-humoured, good-
natured, jovial, pleasant

waste *v.* **1.** blow (*Sl.*), dissipate, fritter
away, frivol away (*Inf.*), lavish, misuse, run
through, squander, throw away **2.** atrophy,
consume, corrode, crumble, debilitate, de~
cay, decline, deplete, disable, drain, dwin~
dle, eat away, ebb, emaciate, enfeeble, ex~
haust, fade, gnaw, perish, sap the strength
of, sink, undermine, wane, wear out, wither
3. despoil, destroy, devastate, lay waste,
pillage, rape, ravage, raze, ruin, sack, spoil,
total (*Sl.*), trash (*Sl.*), undo, wreak havoc
upon ~*n.* **4.** dissipation, expenditure, ex~
travagance, frittering away, loss, lost op~
portunity, misapplication, misuse, prodi~

gality, squandering, unthriftiness, waste~ fulness **5.** desolation, destruction, devasta~ tion, havoc, ravage, ruin **6.** debris, dregs, dross, garbage, leavings, leftovers, litter, offal, offscourings, refuse, rubbish, scrap, sweepings, trash **7.** desert, solitude, void, wasteland, wild, wilderness ~*adj.* **8.** left~ over, superfluous, supernumerary, unused, unwanted, useless, worthless **9.** bare, bar~ ren, desolate, devastated, dismal, dreary, empty, uncultivated, uninhabited, unpro~ ductive, wild **10. lay waste** depredate (*Rare*), despoil, destroy, devastate, pillage, rape, ravage, raze, ruin, sack, spoil, wreak havoc upon
Antonyms *v.* build, conserve, defend, devel~ op, economize, husband, increase, preserve, protect, rally, restore, save, strengthen ~*n.* economy, frugality, good housekeeping, sav~ ing, thrift ~*adj.* arable, developed, fruitful, habitable, in use, necessary, needed, produc~ tive, utilized, verdant

wasteful extravagant, improvident, lavish, prodigal, profligate, ruinous, spendthrift, thriftless, uneconomical, unthrifty
Antonyms economical, frugal, money-saving, parsimonious, penny-wise, provident, sparing, thrifty

wastrel 1. prodigal, profligate, spendthrift, squanderer **2.** drone, good-for-nothing, idler, layabout, loafer, loser, malingerer, ne'er-do-well, shirker, skiver (*Brit. sl.*), waster

watch *v.* **1.** check, check out (*Inf.*), clock (*Brit. sl.*), contemplate, eye, eyeball (*U.S. sl.*), gaze at, get a load of (*Inf.*), look, look at, look on, mark, note, observe, pay atten~ tion, peer at, regard, see, stare at, take a dekko at (*Brit. sl.*), view **2.** attend, be on the alert, be on the lookout, be vigilant, be wary, be watchful, keep an eye open (*Inf.*), look out, take heed, wait **3.** guard, keep, look after, mind, protect, superintend, take care of, tend ~*n.* **4.** chronometer, clock, pocket watch, timepiece, wristwatch **5.** alertness, attention, eye, heed, inspection, lookout, notice, observation, supervision, surveillance, vigil, vigilance, watchfulness

watchdog 1. guard dog **2.** custodian, guardian, inspector, monitor, protector, scrutineer

watcher looker-on, lookout, observer, on~ looker, spectator, spy, viewer, witness

watchful alert, attentive, circumspect, guarded, heedful, observant, on one's guard, on the lookout, on the qui vive, on the watch, suspicious, vigilant, wary, wide awake
Antonyms careless, inattentive, reckless, thoughtless, unaware, unguarded, unmindful, unobservant, unwary

watchfulness alertness, attention, atten~ tiveness, caution, cautiousness, circum~ spection, heedfulness, vigilance, wariness
Antonyms carelessness, heedlessness, inat~ tention, indiscretion, irresponsibility, ne~ glect, recklessness, thoughtlessness

watchman caretaker, custodian, guard, se~ curity guard, security man

watch out be alert, be careful, be on one's guard, be on the alert, be on (the) watch, be vigilant, be watchful, have a care, keep a sharp lookout, keep a weather eye open, keep one's eyes open, keep one's eyes peeled *or* skinned (*Inf.*), look out, mind out, watch oneself

watch over defend, guard, keep safe, look after, preserve, protect, shelter, shield, stand guard over

watchword 1. countersign, magic word, password, shibboleth **2.** battle cry, byword, catch phrase, catchword, maxim, motto, rallying cry, slogan

water *n.* **1.** Adam's ale *or* wine, aqua, H_2O **2. hold water** bear examination *or* scruti~ ny, be credible (logical, sound), make sense, pass the test, ring true, work **3. of the first water** excellent, of the best, of the best quality, of the finest quality, of the highest degree, of the highest grade ~*v.* **4.** damp, dampen, douse, drench, flood, hose, irrigate, moisten, soak, souse, spray, sprinkle **5.** add water to, adulterate, dilute, put water in, thin, water down, weaken

water down 1. add water to, adulterate, dilute, put water in, thin, water, weaken **2.** adulterate, mitigate, qualify, soften, tone down, weaken
Antonyms (*sense 1*) fortify, purify, strength~ en, thicken

waterfall cascade, cataract, chute, fall, force (*Northern English dialect*), linn (*Scot.*)

watertight 1. sound, waterproof **2.** air~ tight, firm, flawless, foolproof, impregnable, incontrovertible, sound, unassailable
Antonyms defective, flawed, leaky, ques~ tionable, shaky, tenuous, uncertain, unsound, weak

watery 1. aqueous, damp, fluid, humid, liq~ uid, marshy, moist, soggy, squelchy, wet **2.** rheumy, tear-filled, tearful, weepy **3.** adul~ terated, dilute, diluted, flavourless, insipid, runny, tasteless, thin, washy, watered-down, waterish, weak, wishy-washy (*Inf.*)
Antonyms concentrated, condensed, dense, fortified, solid, strong, thick

wave *v.* **1.** brandish, flap, flourish, flutter, move to and fro, oscillate, quiver, ripple, shake, stir, sway, swing, undulate, wag, waver, wield **2.** beckon, direct, gesticulate, gesture, indicate, sign, signal ~*n.* **3.** billow, breaker, comber, ridge, ripple, roller, sea

surf, swell, undulation, unevenness **4.** cur~
rent, drift, flood, ground swell, movement,
outbreak, rash, rush, stream, surge, sweep,
tendency, trend, upsurge

waver 1. be indecisive, be irresolute, be
unable to decide, be unable to make up
one's mind, blow hot and cold (*Inf.*), dither
(*Chiefly Brit.*), falter, fluctuate, hesitate,
hum and haw, seesaw, shillyshally (*Inf.*),
swither (*Scot.*), vacillate **2.** flicker, fluc~
tuate, quiver, reel, shake, sway, totter,
tremble, undulate, vary, wave, weave, wob~
ble
Antonyms be decisive, be determined, be of
fixed opinion, be resolute, determine, resolve,
stand firm

wax *v.* become fuller, become larger, devel~
op, dilate, enlarge, expand, fill out, get big~
ger, grow, increase, magnify, mount, rise,
swell
Antonyms contract, decline, decrease, di~
minish, dwindle, fade, lessen, narrow, shrink,
wane

way 1. approach, course of action, fashion,
manner, means, method, mode, plan, prac~
tice, procedure, process, scheme, system,
technique **2.** access, avenue, channel,
course, direction, highway, lane, path,
pathway, road, route, street, thoroughfare,
track, trail **3.** elbowroom, opening, room,
space **4.** distance, journey, length, stretch,
trail **5.** advance, approach, journey, march,
passage, progress **6.** characteristic, conduct,
custom, habit, idiosyncrasy, manner, na~
ture, personality, practice, style, trait,
usage, wont **7.** aspect, detail, feature, par~
ticular, point, respect, sense **8.** aim, ambi~
tion, choice, demand, desire, goal, pleasure,
will, wish **9.** *Inf.* circumstance, condition,
fettle, shape (*Inf.*), situation, state, status
10. forward motion, headway, movement,
passage, progress **11. by the way** by the
bye, en passant, incidentally, in paren~
thesis, in passing **12. give way a.** break
down, cave in, collapse, crack, crumple, fall,
fall to pieces, give, go to pieces, subside **b.**
accede, acknowledge defeat, acquiesce, back
down, concede, make concessions, with~
draw, yield **13. under way** afoot, begun,
going, in motion, in progress, moving, on
the go (*Inf.*), on the move, started

wayfarer bird of passage, globetrotter,
Gypsy, itinerant, journeyer, nomad, rover,
traveller, trekker, voyager, walker, wan~
derer

wayfaring *adj.* drifting, itinerant, journey~
ing, nomadic, peripatetic, rambling, roving,
travelling, voyaging, walking, wandering

waylay accost, ambush, attack, catch, hold
up, intercept, lie in wait for, pounce on, set
upon, surprise, swoop down on

wayward capricious, changeable, contrary,
contumacious, cross-grained, disobedient,
erratic, fickle, flighty, froward, headstrong,
inconstant, incorrigible, insubordinate, in~
tractable, mulish, obdurate, obstinate, per~
verse, rebellious, refractory, self-willed,
stubborn, undependable, ungovernable, un~
manageable, unpredictable, unruly, wilful
Antonyms complaisant, compliant, depend~
able, good-natured, malleable, manageable,
obedient, obliging, predictable, reliable, sub~
missive, tractable

weak 1. anaemic, debilitated, decrepit, deli~
cate, effete, enervated, exhausted, faint, fee~
ble, fragile, frail, infirm, languid, puny,
shaky, sickly, spent, tender, unsound, un~
steady, wasted, weakly **2.** cowardly, impo~
tent, indecisive, ineffectual, infirm, irreso~
lute, namby-pamby, pathetic, powerless,
soft, spineless, timorous, weak-kneed (*Inf.*)
3. distant, dull, faint, imperceptible, low,
muffled, poor, quiet, slight, small, soft **4.**
deficient, faulty, inadequate, lacking, pa~
thetic, poor, substandard, under-strength,
wanting **5.** feeble, flimsy, hollow, inconclu~
sive, invalid, lame, pathetic, shallow, slight,
unconvincing, unsatisfactory **6.** defenceless,
exposed, helpless, unguarded, unprotected,
unsafe, untenable, vulnerable, wide open **7.**
diluted, insipid, milk-and-water, runny,
tasteless, thin, under-strength, waterish,
watery, wishy-washy (*Inf.*)
Antonyms able, capable, conclusive, con~
vincing, effective, energetic, firm, flavour~
some, forceful, hardy, healthy, hefty, intoxi~
cating, invulnerable, mighty, obvious, potent,
powerful, safe, secure, solid, strong, substan~
tial, tasty, tough, trustworthy, uncontro~
vertible, valid, well-defended

weaken 1. abate, debilitate, depress, di~
minish, droop, dwindle, ease up, enervate,
fade, fail, flag, give way, impair, invalidate,
lessen, lower, mitigate, moderate, reduce,
sap, sap the strength of, soften up, temper,
tire, undermine, wane **2.** adulterate, cut,
debase, dilute, thin, thin out, water down
Antonyms boost, enhance, grow, improve,
increase, invigorate, revitalize, strengthen

weakling coward, doormat (*Sl.*), drip (*Inf.*),
jellyfish (*Inf.*), jessie (*Scot. sl.*), milksop,
mouse, sissy, wet (*Brit. inf.*), wimp (*Inf.*)

weakness 1. debility, decrepitude, enerva~
tion, faintness, feebleness, fragility, frailty,
impotence, infirmity, irresolution, power~
lessness, vulnerability **2.** Achilles heel,
blemish, chink in one's armour, defect,
deficiency, failing, fault, flaw, imperfection,
lack, shortcoming **3.** fondness, inclination,
liking, partiality, passion, penchant, predi~
lection, proclivity, proneness, soft spot
Antonyms advantage, aversion, dislike,
forte, hardiness, hatred, health, impregnabil~

ity, loathing, potency, power, stamina, strength, strong point, sturdiness, validity, vigour, virtue, vitality

wealth 1. affluence, assets, big bucks (*Inf.*, *chiefly U.S.*), big money, capital, cash, es~ tate, fortune, funds, goods, lucre, means, megabucks (*U.S. & Canad. sl.*), money, opu~ lence, pelf, possessions, pretty penny (*Inf.*), property, prosperity, resources, riches, substance, tidy sum (*Inf.*), wad (*U.S. & Canad. sl.*) **2.** abundance, bounty, copious~ ness, cornucopia, fullness, plenitude, plenty, profusion, richness, store
Antonyms dearth, deprivation, destitution, indigence, lack, need, paucity, penury, pover~ ty, scarcity, shortage, want, wretchedness

wealthy affluent, comfortable, filthy rich, flush (*Inf.*), in the money (*Inf.*), loaded (*Sl.*), made of money (*Inf.*), moneyed, on Easy Street (*Inf.*), opulent, prosperous, quids in (*Sl.*), rich, rolling in it (*Sl.*), stinking rich (*Sl.*), well-heeled (*Inf.*), well-off, well-to-do
Antonyms broke (*Inf.*), deprived, destitute, dirt-poor (*Inf.*), down and out, flat broke (*Inf.*), impoverished, indigent, needy, penniless, poor, poverty-stricken, short, skint (*Brit. sl.*), without two pennies to rub together (*Inf.*)

wear *v.* **1.** bear, be clothed in, be dressed in, carry, clothe oneself, don, dress in, have on, put on, sport (*Inf.*) **2.** display, exhibit, fly, show **3.** abrade, consume, corrode, deterio~ rate, erode, fray, grind, impair, rub, use, wash away, waste **4.** bear up, be durable, endure, hold up, last, stand up **5.** annoy, drain, enervate, exasperate, fatigue, get on one's nerves (*Inf.*), harass, irk, pester, tax, undermine, vex, weaken, weary **6.** *Brit. sl.* accept, allow, brook, countenance, fall for, permit, put up with (*Inf.*), stand for, stom~ ach, swallow (*Inf.*), take ~*n.* **7.** employ~ ment, mileage (*Inf.*), service, use, useful~ ness, utility **8.** apparel, attire, clothes, cos~ tume, dress, garb, garments, gear (*Inf.*), habit, outfit, things **9.** abrasion, attrition, corrosion, damage, depreciation, deteriora~ tion, erosion, friction, use, wear and tear
Antonyms (*sense 9*) conservation, mainte~ nance, preservation, repair, upkeep

wear down 1. abrade, be consumed, con~ sume, corrode, erode, grind down, rub away **2.** chip away at (*Inf.*), fight a war of attri~ tion against, overcome gradually, reduce, undermine

weariness drowsiness, enervation, exhaus~ tion, fatigue, languor, lassitude, lethargy, listlessness, prostration, tiredness
Antonyms drive, energy, freshness, get-up-and-go (*Inf.*), liveliness, stamina, vigour, vi~ tality, zeal, zest

wearing exasperating, exhausting, fatigu~

ing, irksome, oppressive, taxing, tiresome, tiring, trying, wearisome
Antonyms easy, effortless, light, no bother, painless, refreshing, stimulating, undemand~ ing

wearisome annoying, boring, bothersome, burdensome, dull, exasperating, exhausting, fatiguing, humdrum, irksome, mind-numb~ ing, monotonous, oppressive, pestilential, prosaic, tedious, troublesome, trying, un~ interesting, vexatious, wearing
Antonyms agreeable, delightful, enjoyable, exhilarating, interesting, invigorating, pleas~ urable, refreshing, stimulating

wear off 1. abate, decrease, diminish, dis~ appear, dwindle, ebb, fade, lose effect, lose strength, peter out, subside, wane, weaken **2.** abrade, disappear, efface, fade, rub away
Antonyms grow, increase, intensify, mag~ nify, persist, reinforce, step up, strengthen, wax

wear out 1. become useless, become worn, consume, deteriorate, erode, fray, impair, use up, wear through **2.** enervate, exhaust, fag out (*Inf.*), fatigue, frazzle (*Inf.*), knacker (*Sl.*), prostrate, sap, tire, weary
Antonyms (*sense 2*) buck up (*Inf.*), energize, invigorate, pep up, perk up, refresh, revital~ ize, stimulate, strengthen

weary *adj.* **1.** all in (*Sl.*), asleep *or* dead on one's feet (*Inf.*), clapped out (*Aust. & N.Z. inf.*), dead beat (*Inf.*), dog-tired (*Inf.*), done in (*Inf.*), drained, drooping, drowsy, ener~ vated, exhausted, fagged (*Inf.*), fatigued, flagging, jaded, knackered (*Sl.*), ready to drop, sleepy, spent, tired, wearied, whacked (*Brit. inf.*), worn out, zonked (*Sl.*) **2.** ardu~ ous, enervative, irksome, laborious, taxing, tiresome, tiring, wearing, wearisome **3.** bored, browned-off (*Inf.*), discontented, fed up, impatient, indifferent, jaded, sick (*Inf.*), sick and tired (*Inf.*) ~*v.* **4.** burden, debili~ tate, drain, droop, enervate, fade, fag (*Inf.*), fail, fatigue, grow tired, sap, take it out of (*Inf.*), tax, tire, tire out, wear out **5.** annoy, become bored, bore, exasperate, have had enough, irk, jade, make discontented, plague, sicken, try the patience of, vex
Antonyms *adj.* amused, energetic, excited, exciting, forebearing, fresh, full of beans (*Inf.*), full of get-up-and-go (*Inf.*), invigorated, invig~ orating, lively, original, patient, refreshed, refreshing, stimulated ~*v.* amuse, enliven, excite, interest, invigorate, refresh, revive, stimulate

weather *n.* **1.** climate, conditions **2. under the weather a.** ailing, below par, ill, in~ disposed, nauseous, not well, off-colour, out of sorts, poorly (*Inf.*), seedy (*Inf.*), sick **b.** crapulent, crapulous, drunk, flying (*Sl.*), groggy (*Inf.*), hung over (*Inf.*), inebriated, intoxicated, one over the eight (*Sl.*), the

worse for drink, three sheets in the wind (*Inf.*), under the influence (*Inf.*) ~*v.* **3.** expose, harden, season, toughen **4.** bear up against, brave, come through, endure, get through, live through, make it (*Inf.*), overcome, pull through, resist, ride out, rise above, stand, stick it out (*Inf.*), suffer, surmount, survive, withstand
Antonyms (*sense 4*) cave in, collapse, fail, fall, give in, go under, succumb, surrender, yield

weave 1. blend, braid, entwine, fuse, incorporate, interlace, intermingle, intertwine, introduce, knit, mat, merge, plait, twist, unite **2.** build, construct, contrive, create, fabricate, make, make up, put together, spin **3.** crisscross, move in and out, weave one's way, wind, zigzag **4. get weaving** *Inf.* get a move on, get going, get one's finger out (*Brit. inf.*), get under way, hurry, make a start, shake a leg (*Sl.*), start

web 1. cobweb, spider's web **2.** interlacing, lattice, mesh, net, netting, network, screen, tangle, toils, weave, webbing

wed 1. become man and wife, be married to, espouse, get hitched (*Sl.*), get married, join, make one, marry, splice (*Inf.*), take as one's husband, take as one's wife, take to wife, tie the knot (*Inf.*), unite **2.** ally, blend, coalesce, combine, commingle, dedicate, fuse, interweave, join, link, marry, merge, unify, unite, yoke
Antonyms (*sense 2*) break up, disunite, divide, divorce, part, separate, sever, split

wedding espousals, marriage, marriage ceremony, nuptial rite, nuptials, wedlock

wedge 1. *n.* block, chock, chunk, lump, wodge (*Brit. inf.*) **2.** *v.* block, cram, crowd, force, jam, lodge, pack, ram, split, squeeze, stuff, thrust

wedlock marriage, matrimony

weed out dispense with, eliminate, eradicate, extirpate, get rid of, remove, root out, separate out, shed, uproot

weekly by the week, every week, hebdomadal, hebdomadally, hebdomadary, once a week

weep bemoan, bewail, blub (*Sl.*), blubber, boohoo, complain, cry, greet (*Scot. or archaic*), keen, lament, moan, mourn, shed tears, snivel, sob, ululate, whimper, whinge (*Inf.*)
Antonyms be glad, celebrate, delight, exult, joy, rejoice, revel, triumph

weigh 1. have a weight of, measure the weight of, put on the scales, tip the scales at (*Inf.*) **2.** apportion, deal out, dole out, measure **3.** consider, contemplate, deliberate upon, evaluate, examine, eye up, give thought to, meditate upon, mull over, ponder, reflect upon, study, think over **4.** be

influential, carry weight, count, cut any ice (*Inf.*), have influence, impress, matter, tell **5.** bear down, burden, oppress, prey

weigh down bear down, burden, depress, get down, oppress, overburden, overload, press down, trouble, weigh upon, worry
Antonyms alleviate, ease, hearten, help, lift, lighten, refresh, relieve, unburden

weight *n.* **1.** avoirdupois, burden, gravity, heaviness, heft (*Inf.*), load, mass, poundage, pressure, tonnage **2.** ballast, heavy object, load, mass **3.** burden, load, millstone, oppression, pressure, strain **4.** greatest force, main force, onus, preponderance **5.** authority, bottom, clout (*Inf.*), consequence, consideration, efficacy, emphasis, impact, import, importance, influence, moment, persuasiveness, power, significance, substance, value ~*v.* **6.** add weight to, ballast, charge, freight, increase the load on, increase the weight of, load, make heavier **7.** burden, encumber, handicap, impede, oppress, overburden, weigh down **8.** bias, load, unbalance

weighty 1. burdensome, cumbersome, dense, heavy, hefty (*Inf.*), massive, ponderous **2.** consequential, considerable, critical, crucial, forcible, grave, important, momentous, portentous, serious, significant, solemn, substantial **3.** backbreaking, burdensome, crushing, demanding, difficult, exacting, onerous, oppressive, taxing, worrisome, worrying
Antonyms (*sense 2*) frivolous, immaterial, incidental, inconsequential, insignificant, minor, petty, trivial, unimportant

weird bizarre, creepy (*Inf.*), eerie, eldritch (*Poetic*), far-out (*Sl.*), freakish, ghostly, grotesque, mysterious, odd, outlandish, queer, spooky (*Inf.*), strange, supernatural, uncanny, unearthly, unnatural
Antonyms common, mundane, natural, normal, ordinary, regular, typical, usual

welcome *adj.* **1.** acceptable, accepted, agreeable, appreciated, delightful, desirable, gladly received, gratifying, pleasant, pleasing, pleasurable, refreshing, wanted **2.** at home, free, invited, under no obligation ~*n.* **3.** acceptance, entertainment, greeting, hospitality, reception, salutation ~*v.* **4.** accept gladly, bid welcome, embrace, greet, hail, meet, offer hospitality to, receive, receive with open arms, roll out the red carpet for, usher in
Antonyms (*sense 1*) disagreeable, excluded, rebuffed, rejected, unacceptable, undesirable, unpleasant, unwanted, unwelcome (*sense 3*) cold shoulder, exclusion, ostracism, rebuff, rejection, slight, snub (*sense 4*) exclude, rebuff, refuse, reject, slight, snub, spurn, turn away

welfare advantage, benefit, good, happiness,

health, interest, profit, prosperity, success, wellbeing

well¹ adv. **1.** agreeably, capitally, famously (*Inf.*), happily, in a satisfactory manner, nicely, pleasantly, satisfactorily, smoothly, splendidly, successfully **2.** ably, adeptly, adequately, admirably, conscientiously, correctly, effectively, efficiently, expertly, proficiently, properly, skilfully, with skill **3.** accurately, attentively, carefully, closely **4.** comfortably, flourishingly, prosperously **5.** correctly, easily, fairly, fittingly, in all fairness, justly, properly, readily, rightly, suitably **6.** closely, completely, deeply, fully, intimately, personally, profoundly, thoroughly **7.** approvingly, favourably, glowingly, graciously, highly, kindly, warmly **8.** abundantly, amply, completely, considerably, fully, greatly, heartily, highly, substantially, sufficiently, thoroughly, very much **9. as well** also, besides, in addition, into the bargain, to boot, too **10. as well as** along with, at the same time as, in addition to, including, over and above ~*adj.* **11.** able-bodied, fit, hale, healthy, hearty, in fine fettle, in good health, robust, sound, strong, up to par **12.** advisable, agreeable, bright, fine, fitting, flourishing, fortunate, good, happy, lucky, pleasing, profitable, proper, prudent, right, satisfactory, thriving, useful **Antonyms** adv. badly, coldly, disapprovingly, gracelessly, ham-fistedly, inadequately, incompetently, incorrectly, ineptly, inexpertly, poorly, slightly, sloppily, somewhat, unfairly, unjustly, unkindly, unskilfully, unsympathetically, vaguely, wrongly ~*adj.* ailing, below par, feeble, frail, going badly, ill, improper, infirm, poorly, run-down, sick, sickly, under-the-weather, unfitting, unsatisfactory, unsuccessful, unwell, weak, wrong

well² n. **1.** fount, fountain, pool, source, spring, waterhole **2.** bore, hole, pit, shaft **3.** fount, mine, repository, source, wellspring ~*v.* **4.** exude, flow, gush, jet, ooze, pour, rise, run, seep, spout, spring, spurt, stream, surge, trickle

well-balanced 1. graceful, harmonious, proportional, symmetrical, well-proportioned **2.** judicious, level-headed, rational, reasonable, sane, sensible, sober, sound, together (*Sl.*), well-adjusted **Antonyms** (*sense 2*) erratic, insane, irrational, neurotic, unbalanced, unreasonable, unsound, unstable, volatile

well-bred 1. aristocratic, blue-blooded, gentle, highborn, noble, patrician, well-born **2.** civil, courteous, courtly, cultivated, cultured, gallant, genteel, gentlemanly, ladylike, mannerly, polished, polite, refined, sophisticated, urbane, well-brought-up, well-mannered **Antonyms** (*sense 2*) bad-mannered, base,

coarse, discourteous, ill-bred, rude, uncivilized, uncouth, uncultured, vulgar

well-fed 1. healthy, in good condition, well-nourished **2.** chubby, fat, fleshy, plump, podgy, portly, rotund, rounded, stout

well-groomed dapper, neat, smart, soigné *or* soignée, spruce, tidy, trim, well-dressed, well turned out

well-known celebrated, familiar, famous, illustrious, notable, noted, popular, renowned, widely known

well-nigh all but, almost, just about, more or less, nearly, next to, practically, virtually

well-off 1. comfortable, flourishing, fortunate, lucky, successful, thriving **2.** affluent, comfortable, flush (*Inf.*), loaded (*Sl.*), moneyed, prosperous, rich, wealthy, well-heeled (*Inf.*), well-to-do **Antonyms** (*sense 2*) badly off, broke (*Inf.*), destitute, dirt-poor (*Inf.*), down and out, flat broke (*Inf.*), hard up (*Inf.*), impoverished, indigent, needy, on the rocks (*Inf.*), penniless, poor, poverty-stricken, short, without two pennies to rub together (*Inf.*)

well-thought-of admired, esteemed, highly regarded, of good repute, reputable, respected, revered, venerated **Antonyms** abhorred, derided, despised, disdained, reviled, scorned, spurned

well-to-do affluent, comfortable, flush (*Inf.*), loaded (*Sl.*), moneyed, prosperous, rich, wealthy, well-heeled (*Inf.*), well-off **Antonyms** bankrupt, broke (*Inf.*), destitute, hard up (*Inf.*), indigent, insolvent, needy, poor, ruined

wet *adj.* **1.** aqueous, damp, dank, drenched, dripping, humid, moist, moistened, saturated, soaked, soaking, sodden, soggy, sopping, waterlogged, watery, wringing wet **2.** clammy, dank, drizzling, humid, misty, pouring, raining, rainy, showery, teeming **3.** *Brit. inf.* effete, feeble, foolish, ineffectual, irresolute, namby-pamby, nerdy *or* nurdy (*Sl.*), silly, soft, spineless, timorous, weak, weedy (*Inf.*) **4. wet behind the ears** *Inf.* born yesterday, callow, green, immature, inexperienced, innocent, naive, new, raw ~*n.* **5.** clamminess, condensation, damp, dampness, humidity, liquid, moisture, water, wetness **6.** damp weather, drizzle, rain, rains, rainy season, rainy weather **7.** *Brit. inf.* drip (*Inf.*), milksop, weakling, weed (*Inf.*), wimp (*Inf.*) ~*v.* **8.** damp, dampen, dip, douse, drench, humidify, irrigate, moisten, saturate, soak, splash, spray, sprinkle, steep, water **Antonyms** *adj.* arid, bone-dry, dried, dry, fine, hardened, parched, set, sunny ~*n.* dryness, dry weather, fine weather ~*v.* dehydrate, desiccate, dry, parch

wharf dock, jetty, landing stage, pier, quay

wheedle butter up, cajole, charm, coax, court, draw, entice, flatter, inveigle, per~ suade, talk into, worm

wheel *n.* **1.** circle, gyration, pivot, revolu~ tion, roll, rotation, spin, turn, twirl, whirl **2. at the wheel** at the helm, driving, in charge, in command, in control, in the driving seat, steering ~*v.* **3.** circle, gyrate, orbit, pirouette, revolve, roll, rotate, spin, swing, swivel, turn, twirl, whirl

wheeze *v.* **1.** breathe roughly, catch one's breath, cough, gasp, hiss, rasp, whistle ~*n.* **2.** cough, gasp, hiss, rasp, whistle **3.** *Brit. sl.* expedient, idea, plan, ploy, ruse, scheme, stunt, trick, wrinkle (*Inf.*) **4.** *Inf.* anecdote, chestnut (*Inf.*), crack (*Sl.*), gag (*Inf.*), joke, old joke, one-liner (*Sl.*), story

whereabouts location, position, site, situation

wherewithal capital, equipment, essen~ tials, funds, means, money, ready (*Inf.*), ready money, resources, supplies

whet **1.** edge, file, grind, hone, sharpen, strop **2.** animate, arouse, awaken, enhance, excite, incite, increase, kindle, pique, pro~ voke, quicken, rouse, stimulate, stir **Antonyms** (*sense 2*) blunt, dampen, deaden, depress, dull, numb, smother, stifle, subdue, suppress

whiff *n.* **1.** aroma, blast, breath, draught, gust, hint, niff (*Brit. sl.*), odour, puff, scent, smell, sniff ~*v.* **2.** breathe, inhale, puff, smell, smoke, sniff, waft **3.** *Brit. sl.* hum (*Sl.*), niff (*Brit. sl.*), pong (*Brit. inf.*), reek, stink

whim caprice, conceit, craze, crotchet, fad (*Inf.*), fancy, freak, humour, impulse, no~ tion, passing thought, quirk, sport, sudden notion, urge, vagary, whimsy

whimper **1.** *v.* blub (*Sl.*), blubber, cry, grizzle (*Inf., chiefly Brit.*), mewl, moan, pule, snivel, sob, weep, whine, whinge (*Inf.*) **2.** *n.* moan, snivel, sob, whine

whimsical capricious, chimerical, crotch~ ety, curious, droll, eccentric, fanciful, fan~ tastic, fantastical, freakish, funny, mischie~ vous, odd, peculiar, playful, quaint, queer, singular, unusual, waggish, weird

whine *n.* **1.** cry, moan, plaintive cry, sob, wail, whimper **2.** beef (*Sl.*), complaint, gripe (*Inf.*), grouch (*Inf.*), grouse, grumble, moan ~*v.* **3.** beef (*Sl.*), bellyache (*Sl.*), bleat, carp, complain, cry, gripe (*Inf.*), grizzle (*Inf., chiefly Brit.*), grouch (*Inf.*), grouse, grumble, kvetch (*U.S. sl.*), moan, sob, wail, whimper, whinge (*Inf.*)

whip *v.* **1.** beat, birch, cane, castigate, flagellate, flog, give a hiding (*Inf.*), lam~ bast(e), lash, leather, lick (*Inf.*), punish,

scourge, spank, strap, switch, tan (*Sl.*), thrash **2.** exhibit, flash, jerk, produce, pull, remove, seize, show, snatch, whisk **3.** *Inf.* dart, dash, dive, flit, flounce, fly, rush, shoot, tear, whisk **4.** *Inf.* beat, best, blow out of the water (*Sl.*), clobber (*Sl.*), conquer, defeat, drub, hammer (*Inf.*), lick (*Inf.*), out~ do, overcome, overpower, overwhelm, rout, run rings around (*Inf.*), take apart (*Sl.*), thrash, trounce, wipe the floor with (*Inf.*), worst **5.** agitate, compel, drive, foment, goad, hound, incite, instigate, prick, prod, provoke, push, spur, stir, urge, work up **6.** beat, whisk ~*n.* **7.** birch, bullwhip, cane, cat-o'-nine-tails, crop, horsewhip, knout, lash, rawhide, riding crop, scourge, switch, thong

whipping beating, birching, caning, casti~ gation, flagellation, flogging, hiding (*Inf.*), lashing, leathering, punishment, spanking, tanning (*Sl.*), the strap, thrashing

whirl *v.* **1.** circle, gyrate, pirouette, pivot, reel, revolve, roll, rotate, spin, swirl, turn, twirl, twist, wheel **2.** feel dizzy, reel, spin ~*n.* **3.** birl (*Scot.*), circle, gyration, pirou~ ette, reel, revolution, roll, rotation, spin, swirl, turn, twirl, twist, wheel **4.** confusion, daze, dither (*Chiefly Brit.*), flurry, giddiness, spin **5.** flurry, merry-go-round, round, se~ ries, succession **6.** agitation, bustle, com~ motion, confusion, flurry, hurly-burly, stir, tumult, uproar **7.** **give (something) a whirl** *Inf.* attempt, have a bash (crack (*Inf.*), go (*Inf.*), shot (*Inf.*), stab (*Inf.*), whack (*Inf.*)) (*Inf.*), try

whirlwind **1.** *n.* dust devil, tornado, water~ spout **2.** *adj.* hasty, headlong, impetuous, impulsive, lightning, quick, quickie (*Inf.*), rapid, rash, short, speedy, swift **Antonyms** (*sense 2*) calculated, cautious, considered, deliberate, measured, prudent, slow, unhurried

whisk *v.* **1.** brush, flick, sweep, whip, wipe **2.** barrel (along) (*Inf., chiefly U.S. & Canad.*), burn rubber (*Inf.*), dart, dash, fly, hasten, hurry, race, rush, shoot, speed, sweep, tear **3.** beat, fluff up, whip ~*n.* **4.** brush, flick, sweep, whip, wipe **5.** beater

whisky barley-bree (*Scot.*), bourbon, John Barleycorn, malt, rye, Scotch, usquebaugh

whisper *v.* **1.** breathe, murmur, say softly, speak in hushed tones, utter under the breath **2.** gossip, hint, insinuate, intimate, murmur, spread rumours **3.** hiss, murmur, rustle, sigh, sough, susurrate (*Literary*), swish ~*n.* **4.** hushed tone, low voice, mur~ mur, soft voice, undertone **5.** hiss, murmur, rustle, sigh, sighing, soughing, susurration *or* susurrus (*Literary*), swish **6.** breath, fraction, hint, shadow, suggestion, suspi~ cion, tinge, trace, whiff **7.** *Inf.* buzz, dirt

(*U.S. sl.*), gossip, innuendo, insinuation, re~ port, rumour, word

Antonyms (*sense 1*) bawl, bellow, clamour, roar, shout, thunder, yell

white 1. ashen, bloodless, ghastly, grey, pale, pallid, pasty, wan, waxen, wheyfaced **2.** grey, grizzled, hoary, silver, snowy **3.** clean, immaculate, impeccable, innocent, pure, spotless, squeaky-clean, stainless, un~ blemished, unsullied

Antonyms (*senses 2 & 3*) black, blackish, blemished, dark, dirty, impure, soiled, stained, tarnished

white-collar clerical, executive, nonmanu~ al, office, professional, salaried

whiten blanch, bleach, blench, etiolate, fade, go white, pale, turn pale

Antonyms blacken, colour, darken

whitewash 1. *n.* camouflage, concealment, cover-up, deception, extenuation **2.** *v.* camouflage, conceal, cover up, extenuate, gloss over, make light of, suppress

Antonyms *v.* disclose, expose, lay bare, re~ veal, uncover, unmask, unveil

whittle 1. carve, cut, hew, pare, shape, shave, trim **2.** consume, destroy, eat away, erode, reduce, undermine, wear away

whole *adj.* **1.** complete, entire, full, in one piece, integral, total, unabridged, uncut, undivided **2.** faultless, flawless, good, in one piece, intact, inviolate, mint, perfect, sound, unbroken, undamaged, unharmed, unhurt, unimpaired, uninjured, unmutila~ ted, unscathed, untouched **3.** able-bodied, better, cured, fit, hale, healed, healthy, in fine fettle, in good health, recovered, robust, sound, strong, well ~*adv.* **4.** in one, in one piece ~*n.* **5.** aggregate, all, everything, lot, sum total, the entire amount, total **6.** en~ semble, entirety, entity, fullness, piece, to~ tality, unit **7. on the whole a.** all in all, all things considered, by and large, tak~ ing everything into consideration **b.** as a rule, for the most part, generally, in gener~ al, in the main, mostly, predominantly

Antonyms *adj.* ailing, broken, cut, damaged, diseased, divided, fragmented, ill, incomplete, in pieces, partial, sick, sickly, under-the-weather, unwell ~*n.* bit, component, con~ stituent, division, element, fragment, part, piece, portion

wholehearted committed, complete, dedi~ cated, determined, devoted, earnest, em~ phatic, enthusiastic, genuine, heartfelt, hearty, real, sincere, true, unfeigned, unqualified, unreserved, unstinting, warm, zealous

Antonyms cool, grudging, half-hearted, in~ sincere, qualified, reserved, unreal

wholesale 1. *adj.* all-inclusive, broad, comprehensive, extensive, far-reaching, in~

discriminate, mass, sweeping, wide-ranging **2.** *adv.* all at once, comprehensively, exten~ sively, indiscriminately, on a large scale, without exception

Antonyms *adj.* confined, discriminate, lim~ ited, partial, restricted, selective

wholesome 1. beneficial, good, healthful, health-giving, healthy, helpful, hygienic, invigorating, nourishing, nutritious, salu~ brious, salutary, sanitary, strengthening **2.** clean, decent, edifying, ethical, exemplary, honourable, improving, innocent, moral, nice, pure, respectable, righteous, squeaky-clean, uplifting, virtuous, worthy

Antonyms blue, corrupt, degrading, dirty, dishonest, evil, filthy, immoral, lewd, obscene, pernicious, pornographic, putrid, rotten, tasteless, trashy, unhealthy, unhygienic, un~ principled, unwholesome

wholly 1. all, altogether, completely, com~ prehensively, entirely, fully, heart and soul, in every respect, one hundred per cent (*Inf.*), perfectly, thoroughly, totally, utterly **2.** exclusively, only, solely, without excep~ tion

Antonyms (*sense 1*) incompletely, in part, moderately, partially, partly, relatively, slightly, somewhat

whoop cheer, cry, halloo, holler (*Inf.*), hoot, hurrah, scream, shout, shriek, yell

whore *n.* **1.** brass (*Sl.*), call girl, cocotte, courtesan, demimondaine, demirep (*Rare*), fallen woman, *fille de joie*, harlot, hooker (*U.S. sl.*), hustler (*U.S. & Canad. sl.*), lady of the night, loose woman, prostitute, scrubber (*Brit. & Aust. sl.*), slag (*Brit. sl.*), street~ walker, strumpet, tart (*Inf.*), trollop, woman of easy virtue, woman of ill repute, working girl (*Facetious sl.*) ~*v.* **2.** be on the game (*Sl.*), hustle (*U.S. & Canad. sl.*), prostitute oneself, sell one's body, sell oneself, solicit, walk the streets **3.** fornicate, lech *or* letch (*Inf.*), sleep around (*Inf.*), wanton, wench (*Archaic*), womanize

wicked 1. abandoned, abominable, amoral, atrocious, bad, black-hearted, corrupt, de~ based, depraved, devilish, dissolute, egre~ gious, evil, fiendish, flagitious, foul, guilty, heinous, immoral, impious, iniquitous, ir~ religious, maleficent, nefarious, scandalous, shameful, sinful, unprincipled, unrighteous, vicious, vile, villainous, worthless **2.** arch, impish, incorrigible, mischievous, naughty, rascally, roguish **3.** acute, agonizing, awful, crashing, destructive, dreadful, fearful, fierce, harmful, injurious, intense, mighty, painful, severe, terrible **4.** bothersome, difficult, distressing, galling, offensive, troublesome, trying, unpleasant **5.** *Sl.* adept, adroit, deft, expert, masterly, mighty, outstanding, powerful, skilful, strong

Antonyms benevolent, ethical, good, harm~

less, honourable, innocuous, mannerly, mild, moral, noble, obedient, pleasant, principled, virtuous, well-behaved, wholesome

wide *adj.* **1.** ample, broad, catholic, compre~ hensive, distended, encyclopedic, expanded, expansive, extensive, far-reaching, general, immense, inclusive, large, sweeping, vast **2.** away, distant, off, off course, off target, re~ mote **3.** dilated, distended, expanded, fully open, outspread, outstretched **4.** ample, baggy, capacious, commodious, full, loose, roomy, spacious ~*adv.* **5.** as far as possible, completely, fully, right out, to the furthest extent **6.** astray, nowhere near, off course, off target, off the mark, out

Antonyms *adj.* closed, confined, constricted, cramped, limited, narrow, restricted, shut, strict, tight ~*adv.* barely, narrowly, partially, partly

wide-awake 1. conscious, fully awake, roused, wakened **2.** alert, aware, heedful, keen, observant, on one's toes, on the alert, on the ball (*Inf.*), on the qui vive, vigilant, wary, watchful

Antonyms (*sense 2*) distracted, dreamy, heedless, inattentive, negligent, oblivious, preoccupied, unaware, unobservant

wide-eyed credulous, green, impression~ able, ingenuous, innocent, naive, simple, trusting, unsophisticated, unsuspicious, wet behind the ears (*Inf.*)

widen broaden, dilate, enlarge, expand, ex~ tend, open out *or* up, open wide, spread, stretch

Antonyms compress, constrict, contract, cramp, diminish, narrow, reduce, shrink, tighten

wide-open 1. fully extended, fully open, gaping, outspread, outstretched, splayed, spread **2.** at risk, defenceless, exposed, in danger, in peril, open, susceptible, unpro~ tected, vulnerable **3.** anybody's guess (*Inf.*), indeterminate, uncertain, unpredictable, unsettled, up for grabs (*Inf.*)

widespread broad, common, epidemic, ex~ tensive, far-flung, far-reaching, general, pervasive, popular, prevalent, rife, sweep~ ing, universal, wholesale

Antonyms confined, exclusive, limited, lo~ cal, narrow, rare, sporadic, uncommon

width breadth, compass, diameter, extent, girth, measure, range, reach, scope, span, thickness, wideness

wield 1. brandish, employ, flourish, handle, manage, manipulate, ply, swing, use **2.** ap~ ply, be possessed of, command, control, ex~ ercise, exert, have, have at one's disposal, hold, maintain, make use of, manage, pos~ sess, put to use, utilize

wife better half (*Humorous*), bride, helpmate, helpmeet, her indoors (*Brit. sl.*), little wom~

an (*Inf.*), mate, old lady (*Inf.*), old woman (*Inf.*), partner, significant other (*U.S. inf.*), spouse, (the) missis *or* missus (*Inf.*), woman (*Inf.*)

wild *adj.* **1.** feral, ferocious, fierce, savage, unbroken, undomesticated, untamed **2.** free, indigenous, native, natural, unculti~ vated **3.** desert, deserted, desolate, empty, godforsaken, trackless, uncivilized, unculti~ vated, uninhabited, unpopulated, virgin **4.** barbaric, barbarous, brutish, ferocious, fierce, primitive, rude, savage, uncivilized **5.** boisterous, chaotic, disorderly, impetu~ ous, lawless, noisy, riotous, rough, rowdy, self-willed, turbulent, unbridled, uncon~ trolled, undisciplined, unfettered, ungov~ ernable, unmanageable, unrestrained, un~ ruly, uproarious, violent, wayward **6.** blus~ tery, choppy, furious, howling, intense, raging, rough, tempestuous, violent **7.** di~ shevelled, disordered, straggly, tousled, un~ kempt, untidy, windblown **8.** at one's wits' end, berserk, beside oneself, crazed, crazy, delirious, demented, excited, frantic, fren~ zied, hysterical, irrational, mad, maniacal, rabid, raving **9.** extravagant, fantastic, flighty, foolhardy, foolish, giddy, ill-considered, impracticable, imprudent, mad~ cap, outrageous, preposterous, rash, reck~ less **10.** *Inf.* agog, avid, crazy (*Inf.*), daft (*Inf.*), eager, enthusiastic, excited, mad (*Inf.*), nuts (*Sl.*), potty (*Brit. inf.*) ~*adv.* **11. run wild a.** grow unchecked, ramble, spread, straggle **b.** abandon all restraint, cut loose, go on the rampage, kick over the traces, rampage, run free, run riot, stray ~*n.* **12.** *Often plural* back of beyond (*Inf.*), desert, middle of nowhere (*Inf.*), uninhabit~ ed area, wasteland, wilderness

Antonyms *adj.* advanced, broken, calm, careful, controlled, disciplined, domesticated, friendly, genteel, gentle, lawful, logical, mild, ordered, orderly, peaceful, polite, practical, quiet, realistic, restrained, self-controlled, tame, thoughtful, unenthusiastic, uninterest~ ed, well-behaved, well-thought-out (*senses 2 & 3*) civilized, cultivated, farmed, inhabited, planted, populated, urban

wilderness 1. desert, jungle, waste, waste~ land, wild **2.** clutter, confused mass, confu~ sion, congeries, jumble, maze, muddle, tan~ gle, welter

wildlife flora and fauna

wile 1. artfulness, artifice, cheating, chican~ ery, craft, craftiness, cunning, fraud, guile, slyness, trickery **2.** *Usually plural* artifice, contrivance, device, dodge, imposition, lure, manoeuvre, ploy, ruse, stratagem, subter~ fuge, trick

wilful 1. adamant, bull-headed, determined, dogged, froward, headstrong, inflexible, in~ tractable, intransigent, mulish, obdurate,

obstinate, persistent, perverse, pig-headed, refractory, self-willed, stiff-necked, stubborn, uncompromising, unyielding **2.** conscious, deliberate, intended, intentional, purposeful, volitional, voluntary, willed
Antonyms (*sense 1*) biddable, complaisant, compromising, docile, flexible, good-natured, obedient, pliant, tractable, yielding (*sense 2*) accidental, involuntary, uncalculated, unconscious, unintentional, unplanned, unwitting

will *n.* **1.** choice, decision, determination, discretion, option, prerogative, volition **2.** declaration, last wishes, testament **3.** choice, decision, decree, desire, fancy, inclination, mind, pleasure, preference, wish **4.** aim, determination, intention, purpose, resolution, resolve, willpower **5.** attitude, disposition, feeling **6. at will** as one pleases, as one thinks fit, as one wishes, at one's desire (discretion, inclination, pleasure, whim, wish) ~*v.* **7.** bid, bring about, cause, command, decree, determine, direct, effect, ordain, order, resolve **8.** choose, desire, elect, opt, prefer, see fit, want, wish **9.** bequeath, confer, give, leave, pass on, transfer

willing agreeable, amenable, compliant, consenting, content, desirous, disposed, eager, enthusiastic, favourable, game (*Inf.*), happy, inclined, in favour, in the mood, nothing loath, pleased, prepared, ready, so-minded
Antonyms averse, disinclined, grudging, indisposed, loath, not keen, reluctant, unenthusiastic, unwilling

willingly by choice, cheerfully, eagerly, freely, gladly, happily, of one's own accord, of one's own free will, readily, voluntarily, with all one's heart, without hesitation, with pleasure
Antonyms grudgingly, hesitantly, involuntarily, reluctantly, unwillingly

willingness agreeableness, agreement, consent, desire, disposition, enthusiasm, favour, goodwill, inclination, volition, will, wish
Antonyms aversion, disagreement, disinclination, hesitation, loathing, reluctance, unwillingness

willpower determination, drive, firmness of purpose *or* will, fixity of purpose, force *or* strength of will, grit, resolution, resolve, self-control, self-discipline, single-mindedness
Antonyms apathy, hesitancy, indecision, irresolution, languor, lethargy, shilly-shallying (*Inf.*), torpor, uncertainty, weakness

wilt 1. become limp *or* flaccid, droop, sag, shrivel, wither **2.** diminish, dwindle, ebb,

fade, fail, flag, languish, lose courage, melt away, sag, sink, wane, weaken, wither

wily arch, artful, astute, cagey (*Inf.*), crafty, crooked, cunning, deceitful, deceptive, designing, fly (*Sl.*), foxy, guileful, intriguing, scheming, sharp, shifty, shrewd, sly, tricky, underhand
Antonyms above-board, artless, candid, dull, guileless, honest, ingenuous, naive, simple, straightforward

win *v.* **1.** achieve first place, achieve mastery, be victorious, carry all before one, carry the day, come first, conquer, finish first, gain victory, overcome, prevail, succeed, take the prize, triumph **2.** accomplish, achieve, acquire, attain, bag (*Inf.*), catch, collect, come away with, earn, gain, get, net, obtain, pick up, procure, receive, secure **3.** *Often with* **over** allure, attract, bring *or* talk round, carry, charm, convert, convince, disarm, induce, influence, persuade, prevail upon, sway ~*n.* **4.** *Inf.* conquest, success, triumph, victory
Antonyms *v.* fail, fall, forfeit, lose, miss, suffer defeat, suffer loss ~*n.* beating, defeat, downfall, failure, loss, washout (*Inf.*)

wince 1. *v.* blench, cower, cringe, draw back, flinch, quail, recoil, shrink, start **2.** *n.* cringe, flinch, start

wind¹ 1. *n.* air, air-current, blast, breath, breeze, current of air, draught, gust, zephyr **2.** *Inf.* clue, hint, inkling, intimation, notice, report, rumour, suggestion, tidings, warning, whisper **3.** babble, blather, bluster, boasting, empty talk, gab (*Inf.*), hot air, humbug, idle talk, talk, verbalizing **4.** breath, puff, respiration **5.** *Inf.* flatulence, flatus, gas **6. get** *or* **have the wind up** *Inf.* be afraid (alarmed, frightened, scared), fear, take fright **7. in the wind** about to happen, approaching, close at hand, coming, imminent, impending, in the offing, near, on the cards (*Inf.*), on the way **8. put the wind up** *Inf.* alarm, discourage, frighten, frighten off, scare, scare off

wind² ** *v.* **1. coil, curl, encircle, furl, loop, reel, roll, spiral, turn around, twine, twist, wreathe **2.** bend, curve, deviate, meander, ramble, snake, turn, twist, zigzag ~*n.* **3.** bend, curve, meander, turn, twist, zigzag

wind down cool off, decline, diminish, dwindle, lessen, reduce, relax, slacken, subside, taper off, unwind
Antonyms accelerate, amplify, escalate, expand, heat up, increase, intensify, magnify, step up

winded breathless, gasping for breath, out of breath, out of puff, panting, puffed, puffed out

windfall bonanza, find, godsend, jackpot, manna from heaven, stroke of luck

Antonyms bad luck, disaster, infelicity, misadventure, mischance, misfortune, mishap

winding 1. *n.* bend, convolution, curve, meander, turn, twist, undulation **2.** *adj.* anfractuous, bending, circuitous, convoluted, crooked, curving, flexuous, indirect, meandering, roundabout, serpentine, sinuous, spiral, tortuous, turning, twisting

Antonyms *adj.* direct, even, level, plumb, smooth, straight, undeviating, unswerving

wind up 1. bring to a close, close, close down, conclude, end, finalize, finish, liquidate, settle, terminate, tie up the loose ends (*Inf.*), wrap up **2.** *Inf.* excite, make nervous, make tense, put on edge, work up **3.** *Inf.* be left, end one's days, end up, find oneself, finish up

Antonyms (*sense 1*) begin, commence, embark on, initiate, instigate, institute, open, start

windy 1. blowy, blustering, blustery, boisterous, breezy, gusty, inclement, squally, stormy, tempestuous, wild, windswept **2.** boastful, bombastic, diffuse, empty, garrulous, long-winded, loquacious, meandering, pompous, prolix, rambling, turgid, verbose, wordy **3.** *Sl.* afraid, chicken (*Sl.*), chickenshit (*U.S. sl.*), cowardly, fearful, frightened, nervous, scared, timid

Antonyms (*sense 1*) becalmed, calm, motionless, smooth, still, windless (*sense 2*) modest, quiet, reserved, restrained, reticent, shy, taciturn, unforthcoming (*sense 3*) bold, brave, courageous, daring, fearless, gallant, unafraid, undaunted

wing *n.* **1.** organ of flight, pennon (*Poetic*), pinion (*Poetic*) **2.** arm, branch, cabal, circle, clique, coterie, faction, group, grouping, schism, section, segment, set, side **3.** adjunct, annexe, ell, extension ~*v.* **4.** fly, glide, soar **5.** fleet, fly, hasten, hurry, race, speed, zoom **6.** clip, hit, nick, wound

wink *v.* **1.** bat, blink, flutter, nictate, nictitate **2.** flash, gleam, glimmer, sparkle, twinkle ~*n.* **3.** blink, flutter, nictation **4.** flash, gleam, glimmering, sparkle, twinkle **5.** instant, jiffy (*Inf.*), moment, second, split second, twinkling

wink at allow, blink at, condone, connive at, disregard, ignore, overlook, pretend not to notice, put up with (*Inf.*), shut one's eyes to, tolerate, turn a blind eye to

winkle out dig out, dislodge, draw out, extract, extricate, force out, prise out, smoke out, worm out

winner champ (*Inf.*), champion, conquering hero, conqueror, first, master, vanquisher, victor

winning 1. alluring, amiable, attractive, bewitching, captivating, charming, cute, delectable, delightful, disarming, enchanting, endearing, engaging, fascinating, fetching, likable *or* likeable, lovely, pleasing, prepossessing, sweet, taking, winsome **2.** conquering, successful, triumphant, victorious

Antonyms (*sense 1*) disagreeable, irksome, offensive, repellent, tiresome, unappealing, unattractive, uninteresting, unpleasant

winnings booty, gains, prize(s), proceeds, profits, spoils, takings

winnow comb, cull, divide, fan, part, screen, select, separate, separate the wheat from the chaff, sift, sort out

wintry 1. brumal, chilly, cold, freezing, frosty, frozen, harsh, hibernal, hiemal, icy, snowy **2.** bleak, cheerless, cold, desolate, dismal

Antonyms balmy, bright, mild, pleasant, summery, sunny, tepid, warm

wipe *v.* **1.** brush, clean, dry, dust, mop, rub, sponge, swab **2.** clean off, erase, get rid of, remove, rub off, take away, take off ~*n.* **3.** brush, lick, rub, swab

wipe out annihilate, blot out, blow away (*Sl., chiefly U.S.*), destroy, efface, eradicate, erase, expunge, exterminate, extirpate, kill to the last man, massacre, obliterate, take out (*Sl.*)

wiry 1. lean, sinewy, strong, tough **2.** bristly, kinky, stiff

Antonyms (*sense 1*) fat, feeble, flabby, fleshy, frail, podgy, puny, spineless, weak

wisdom astuteness, circumspection, comprehension, discernment, enlightenment, erudition, foresight, insight, intelligence, judgment, judiciousness, knowledge, learning, penetration, prudence, reason, sagacity, sapience, sense, smarts (*Sl., chiefly U.S.*), sound judgment, understanding

Antonyms absurdity, bêtise (*Rare*), daftness (*Inf.*), folly, foolishness, idiocy, injudiciousness, nonsense, senselessness, silliness, stupidity

wise 1. aware, clever, clued-up (*Inf.*), discerning, enlightened, erudite, informed, intelligent, judicious, knowing, perceptive, politic, prudent, rational, reasonable, sagacious, sage, sapient, sensible, shrewd, sound, understanding, well-advised, well-informed **2. put wise** *Sl.* alert, apprise, clue in *or* up (*Inf.*), inform, let (someone) into the secret, notify, tell, tip off, warn

Antonyms daft (*Inf.*), foolish, injudicious, rash, silly, stupid, unintelligent, unwise

wisecrack 1. *n.* barb, funny (*Inf.*), gag (*Inf.*), jest, jibe, joke, pithy remark, quip, sardonic remark, smart remark, witticism **2.** *v.* be facetious, jest, jibe, joke, quip, tell jokes

wish *v.* **1.** aspire, covet, crave, desiderate,

desire, hanker, hope, hunger, long, need, set one's heart on, sigh for, thirst, want, yearn **2.** bid, greet with **3.** ask, bid, command, desire, direct, instruct, order, require ~*n*. **4.** aspiration, desire, hankering, hope, hunger, inclination, intention, liking, longing, thirst, urge, want, whim, will, yearning **5.** bidding, command, desire, order, request, will
Antonyms (*sense 4*) aversion, disinclination, dislike, distaste, loathing, reluctance, repulsion, revulsion

wistful contemplative, disconsolate, dreaming, dreamy, forlorn, longing, meditative, melancholy, mournful, musing, pensive, reflective, sad, thoughtful, yearning

wit 1. badinage, banter, drollery, facetiousness, fun, humour, jocularity, levity, pleasantry, raillery, repartee, wordplay **2.** card (*Inf.*), comedian, epigrammatist, *farceur*, humorist, joker, punster, wag **3.** acumen, brains, cleverness, common sense, comprehension, discernment, ingenuity, insight, intellect, judgment, mind, nous (*Brit. sl.*), perception, practical intelligence, reason, sense, smarts (*Sl., chiefly U.S.*), understanding, wisdom
Antonyms dullness, folly, foolishness, gravity, humourlessness, ignorance, lack of perception, obtuseness, seriousness, silliness, sobriety, solemnity, stupidity

witch crone, enchantress, magician, necromancer, occultist, sorceress

witchcraft enchantment, incantation, magic, necromancy, occultism, sorcery, sortilege, spell, the black art, the occult, voodoo, witchery, witching, wizardry

withdraw 1. draw back, draw out, extract, pull out, remove, take away, take off **2.** abjure, disavow, disclaim, recall, recant, rescind, retract, revoke, take back, unsay **3.** absent oneself, back out, cop out (*Sl.*), depart, detach oneself, disengage, drop out, fall back, go, leave, make oneself scarce (*Inf.*), pull back, pull out, retire, retreat, secede
Antonyms (*senses 1 & 3*) advance, forge ahead, go on, move forward, persist, press on, proceed, progress

withdrawal 1. extraction, removal **2.** abjuration, disavowal, disclaimer, recall, recantation, repudiation, rescission, retraction, revocation **3.** departure, disengagement, exit, exodus, retirement, retreat, secession

withdrawn 1. aloof, detached, distant, introverted, quiet, reserved, retiring, shrinking, shy, silent, taciturn, timorous, uncommunicative, unforthcoming **2.** hidden, isolated, out-of-the-way, private, remote, secluded, solitary

Antonyms boisterous, bustling, busy, easily accessible, extrovert, forward, friendly, gregarious, open, outgoing, sociable

wither 1. blast, blight, decay, decline, desiccate, disintegrate, droop, dry, fade, languish, perish, shrink, shrivel, wane, waste, wilt **2.** abash, blast, humiliate, mortify, put down, shame, snub
Antonyms (*sense 1*) bloom, blossom, develop, flourish, increase, prosper, succeed, thrive, wax

withering 1. blasting, blighting, devastating, humiliating, hurtful, mortifying, scornful, snubbing **2.** deadly, death-dealing, destructive, devastating, killing, murderous, slaughterous

withhold 1. check, conceal, deduct, hide, hold back, keep, keep back, keep secret, refuse, repress, reserve, resist, restrain, retain, sit on (*Inf.*), suppress **2.** *With* **from** forbear, keep oneself, refrain, stop oneself
Antonyms (*sense 1*) accord, expose, give, grant, hand over, let go, release, relinquish, reveal

withstand 1. bear, brave, combat, confront, cope with, defy, endure, face, grapple with, hold off, hold out against, oppose, put up with (*Inf.*), resist, stand up to, suffer, take, take on, thwart, tolerate, weather **2.** endure, hold *or* stand one's ground, hold out, remain firm, stand, stand fast, stand firm
Antonyms capitulate, falter, give in, give way, relent, succumb, surrender, weaken, yield

witness *n.* **1.** beholder, bystander, eyewitness, looker-on, observer, onlooker, spectator, viewer, watcher **2.** attestant, corroborator, deponent, testifier **3. bear witness a.** depone, depose, give evidence, give testimony, testify **b.** attest to, bear out, be evidence of, be proof of, betoken, confirm, constitute proof of, corroborate, demonstrate, evince, prove, show, testify to, vouch for ~*v.* **4.** attend, be present at, look on, mark, note, notice, observe, perceive, see, view, watch **5.** attest, authenticate, bear out, bear witness, confirm, corroborate, depone, depose, give evidence, give testimony, testify **6.** countersign, endorse, sign

wits 1. acumen, astuteness, brains (*Inf.*), cleverness, comprehension, faculties, ingenuity, intelligence, judgment, nous (*Brit. sl.*), reason, sense, smarts (*Sl., chiefly U.S.*), understanding **2. at one's wits' end** at a loss, at the end of one's tether, baffled, bewildered, in despair, lost, stuck (*Inf.*), stumped

witticism bon mot, clever remark, epigram, one-liner (*Sl.*), play on words, pleasantry,

pun, quip, repartee, riposte, sally, witty re~
mark

witty amusing, brilliant, clever, droll, epi~
grammatic, facetious, fanciful, funny, gay,
humorous, ingenious, jocular, lively, origi~
nal, piquant, sparkling, waggish, whimsical
Antonyms boring, dull, humourless, stupid,
tedious, tiresome, unamusing, uninteresting,
witless

wizard 1. conjurer, enchanter, mage (*Ar~
chaic*), magician, magus, necromancer, oc~
cultist, shaman, sorcerer, thaumaturge
(*Rare*), warlock, witch **2.** ace (*Inf.*), adept,
buff (*Inf.*), expert, genius, hotshot (*Inf.*),
maestro, master, maven (*U.S.*), prodigy,
star, virtuoso, whiz (*Inf.*), whizz kid (*Inf.*),
wiz (*Inf.*)

wizened dried up, gnarled, lined, sere (*Ar~
chaic*), shrivelled, shrunken, withered,
worn, wrinkled
Antonyms bloated, plump, rounded,
smooth, swollen, turgid

wobble *v.* **1.** quake, rock, seesaw, shake,
sway, teeter, totter, tremble, vibrate, waver
2. be unable to make up one's mind, be un~
decided, dither (*Chiefly Brit.*), fluctuate,
hesitate, shillyshally (*Inf.*), swither (*Scot.*),
vacillate, waver ~*n.* **3.** quaking, shake,
tremble, tremor, unsteadiness, vibration

woe adversity, affliction, agony, anguish,
burden, curse, dejection, depression, disas~
ter, distress, gloom, grief, hardship, heart~
ache, heartbreak, melancholy, misery, mis~
fortune, pain, sadness, sorrow, suffering,
trial, tribulation, trouble, unhappiness,
wretchedness
Antonyms bliss, elation, felicity, fortune,
happiness, joy, jubilation, pleasure, prosper~
ity, rapture

woeful 1. afflicted, agonized, anguished,
calamitous, catastrophic, cruel, deplorable,
disastrous, disconsolate, dismal, distressing,
doleful, dreadful, gloomy, grieving, griev~
ous, harrowing, heartbreaking, heart~
rending, lamentable, miserable, mournful,
pathetic, piteous, pitiable, pitiful, plaintive,
sad, sorrowful, tragic, unhappy, wretched
2. abysmal, appalling, awful, bad, deplor~
able, disappointing, disgraceful, dreadful,
duff (*Brit. inf.*), feeble, godawful (*Sl.*), hope~
less, inadequate, lousy (*Sl.*), mean, miser~
able, paltry, pathetic, pitiable, pitiful, poor,
rotten (*Inf.*), shitty (*Taboo sl.*), shocking,
sorry, terrible, wretched
Antonyms (*sense 1*) carefree, cheerful,
chirpy (*Inf.*), contented, delighted, glad, hap~
py, jolly, joyful, jubilant, light-hearted (*sense
2*) abundant, ample, bountiful, enviable, ex~
tensive, generous, lavish, luxurious, profuse,
prosperous

wolf *n.* **1.** *Fig.* devil, fiend, killer, merce~

nary, pirate, predator, robber, savage, shark
2. *Inf.* Casanova, Don Juan, lady-killer, lech
or letch (*Inf.*), lecher, Lothario, philanderer,
seducer, womanizer ~*v.* **3.** *With* **down** bolt,
cram, devour, gobble, gollop, gorge, gulp,
pack away (*Inf.*), pig out (*Sl.*), scoff (*Sl.*),
stuff
Antonyms *v.* bite, nibble, nip, peck, pick at

woman 1. bird (*Sl.*), chick (*Sl.*), dame (*Sl.*),
female, gal (*Sl.*), girl, lady, lass, lassie (*Inf.*),
maid (*Archaic*), maiden (*Archaic*), miss, she,
wench (*Facetious*) **2.** chambermaid, char
(*Inf.*), charwoman, domestic, female serv~
ant, handmaiden, housekeeper, lady-in-
waiting, maid, maidservant **3.** *Inf.* bride,
girl, girlfriend, ladylove, mate, mistress, old
lady (*Inf.*), partner, significant other (*U.S.
inf.*), spouse, sweetheart, wife
Antonyms (*sense 1*) bloke (*Brit. inf.*), boy,
chap (*Inf.*), gentleman, guy (*Inf.*), lad, laddie,
male, man

womanizer Casanova, Don Juan, lady-
killer, lech *or* letch (*Inf.*), lecher, Lothario,
philanderer, seducer, wolf (*Inf.*)

womanly female, feminine, ladylike, ma~
tronly, motherly, tender, warm

wonder *n.* **1.** admiration, amazement,
astonishment, awe, bewilderment, curiosity,
fascination, stupefaction, surprise, wonder~
ment **2.** curiosity, marvel, miracle, nonpa~
reil, phenomenon, portent, prodigy, rarity,
sight, spectacle, wonderment ~*v.* **3.** ask
oneself, be curious, be inquisitive, conjec~
ture, cudgel one's brains (*Inf.*), doubt, in~
quire, meditate, ponder, puzzle, query,
question, speculate, think **4.** be amazed
(astonished, awed, dumbstruck), be
flabbergasted (*Inf.*), boggle, gape, gawk,
marvel, stand amazed, stare

wonderful 1. amazing, astonishing, as~
tounding, awe-inspiring, awesome, extraor~
dinary, fantastic, incredible, marvellous,
miraculous, odd, peculiar, phenomenal, re~
markable, staggering, startling, strange,
surprising, unheard-of, wondrous (*Archaic
or literary*) **2.** ace (*Inf.*), admirable, boffo
(*Sl.*), brill (*Inf.*), brilliant, chillin' (*U.S. sl.*),
cracking (*Brit. inf.*), excellent, fabulous
(*Inf.*), fantastic (*Inf.*), great (*Inf.*), jim-dandy
(*Sl.*), magnificent, marvellous, mean (*Sl.*),
outstanding, sensational (*Inf.*), smashing
(*Inf.*), sovereign, stupendous, super (*Inf.*),
superb, terrific, tiptop, topping (*Brit. sl.*),
tremendous
Antonyms abominable, appalling, average,
awful, bad, common, commonplace, depress~
ing, dire, dreadful, frightful, grim, hellacious
(*U.S. sl.*), indifferent, lousy (*Sl.*), mediocre,
miserable, modest, ordinary, paltry, rotten,
run-of-the-mill, terrible, uninteresting, un~
pleasant, unremarkable, usual, vile

wont 1. *adj.* accustomed, given, in the habit of, used **2.** *n.* custom, habit, practice, rule, use, way

wonted 1. accustomed, given, habituated, in the habit of, used **2.** accustomed, com~ mon, conventional, customary, familiar, frequent, habitual, normal, regular, usual

woo chase, court, cultivate, importune, pay court to, pay one's addresses to, pay suit to, press one's suit with, pursue, seek after, seek the hand of, seek to win, solicit the goodwill of, spark (*Rare*)

wood 1. *Also* **woods** coppice, copse, forest, grove, thicket, trees, woodland **2. out of the wood(s)** clear, home and dry (*Brit. sl.*), in the clear, out of danger, safe, safe and sound, secure **3.** planks, timber

wooded forested, sylvan (*Poetic*), timbered, tree-clad, tree-covered, woody

wooden 1. ligneous, made of wood, of wood, timber, woody **2.** awkward, clumsy, gauche, gawky, graceless, inelegant, mala~ droit, rigid, stiff, ungainly **3.** blank, colour~ less, deadpan, dull, emotionless, empty, ex~ pressionless, glassy, lifeless, spiritless, un~ emotional, unresponsive, vacant **4.** inflex~ ible, obstinate, rigid, stiff, unbending, un~ yielding **5.** dense, dim, dim-witted (*Inf.*), dozy (*Brit. inf.*), dull, dull-witted, obtuse, slow, stupid, thick, witless, woodenheaded (*Inf.*) **6.** dull, muffled
Antonyms (*senses 2 & 4*) agile, comely, el~ egant, flexible, flowing, graceful, lissom(e), nimble, supple

wool 1. fleece, hair, yarn **2. dyed in the wool** confirmed, diehard, fixed, hardened, inflexible, inveterate, settled, unchangeable, uncompromising, unshakable **3. pull the wool over someone's eyes** bamboozle (*Inf.*), con (*Sl.*), deceive, delude, dupe, fool, hoodwink, kid (*Inf.*), lead (someone) up the garden path (*Inf.*), pull a fast one (on some~ one) (*Inf.*), put one over on (*Sl.*), take in (*Inf.*), trick

woolgathering absent-mindedness, ab~ straction, building castles in the air, day~ dreaming, dreaming, inattention, musing, preoccupation, reverie
Antonyms alertness, attention, awareness, concentration, heed, observation, thought~ fulness, vigilance, watchfulness

woolly *adj.* **1.** fleecy, flocculent, hairy, made of wool, shaggy, woollen **2.** blurred, clouded, confused, foggy, fuzzy, hazy, ill-defined, indefinite, indistinct, muddled, nebulous, unclear, vague
Antonyms (*sense 2*) clear, clear-cut, definite, distinct, exact, obvious, precise, sharp, well-defined

word *n.* **1.** brief conversation, chat, chit~ chat, colloquy, confab (*Inf.*), confabulation, consultation, discussion, talk, tête-à-tête **2.** brief statement, comment, declaration, ex~ pression, remark, utterance **3.** expression, locution, name, term, vocable **4.** account, advice, bulletin, communication, communi~ qué, dispatch, gen (*Brit. inf.*), information, intelligence, intimation, latest (*Inf.*), mes~ sage, news, notice, report, tidings **5.** com~ mand, go-ahead (*Inf.*), green light, order, signal **6.** affirmation, assertion, assurance, guarantee, oath, parole, pledge, promise, solemn oath, solemn word, undertaking, vow, word of honour **7.** bidding, command, commandment, decree, edict, mandate, or~ der, ukase (*Rare*), will **8.** countersign, password, slogan, watchword **9. in a word** briefly, concisely, in a nutshell, in short, succinctly, to put it briefly, to sum up ~*v.* **10.** couch, express, phrase, put, say, state, utter

wordplay punning, puns, repartee, wit, witticisms

words 1. lyrics, text **2.** altercation, angry exchange, angry speech, argument, barney (*Inf.*), bickering, disagreement, dispute, falling-out (*Inf.*), quarrel, row, run-in (*Inf.*), set-to (*Inf.*), squabble

wordy diffuse, discursive, garrulous, long-winded, loquacious, pleonastic, prolix, ram~ bling, verbose, windy
Antonyms brief, concise, laconic, pithy, short, succinct, terse, to the point

work *n.* **1.** drudgery, effort, elbow grease (*Facetious*), exertion, grind (*Inf.*), industry, labour, slog, sweat, toil, travail (*Literary*) **2.** business, calling, craft, duty, employment, job, line, livelihood, métier, occupation, office, profession, pursuit, trade **3.** assign~ ment, chore, commission, duty, job, stint, task, undertaking **4.** achievement, compo~ sition, creation, handiwork, *oeuvre*, opus, performance, piece, production **5.** art, craft, skill, workmanship **6. out of work** idle, jobless, on the dole (*Brit. inf.*), on the street, out of a job, unemployed ~*v.* **7.** drudge, ex~ ert oneself, labour, peg away, slave, slog (away), sweat, toil **8.** be employed, be in work, do business, earn a living, have a job **9.** act, control, direct, drive, handle, man~ age, manipulate, move, operate, ply, use, wield **10.** function, go, operate, perform, run **11.** cultivate, dig, farm, till **12.** fash~ ion, form, handle, knead, make, manipulate, mould, process, shape **13.** be agitated, con~ vulse, move, twitch, writhe **14.** *Often with* **up** arouse, excite, move, prompt, provoke, rouse, stir **15.** accomplish, achieve, bring about, carry out, cause, contrive, create, ef~ fect, encompass, execute, implement **16.** force, make one's way, manoeuvre, move, progress **17.** *Inf.* arrange, bring off, con~

trive, exploit, fiddle (*Inf.*), fix (*Inf.*), handle, manipulate, pull off, swing (*Inf.*)
Antonyms *n.* (*sense 1*) ease, leisure, relaxa~ tion, rest (*sense 2*) entertainment, hobby, holi~ day, play, recreation, retirement, spare time, unemployment (*sense 3*) child's play (*Inf.*) ~*v.* (*sense 7*) have fun, mark time, play, relax, skive (*Brit. sl.*), take it easy (*sense 10*) be bro~ ken, be out of order (*sense 15*) counteract, nul~ lify, prevent, reverse (*sense 16*) remain

workable doable, feasible, possible, practi~ cable, practical, viable
Antonyms hopeless, impossible, impracti~ cal, inconceivable, unattainable, unthinkable, unworkable, useless

workaday common, commonplace, every~ day, familiar, humdrum, mundane, ordi~ nary, practical, prosaic, routine, run-of- the-mill
Antonyms atypical, different, exciting, extraordinary, rare, special, uncommon, un~ familiar, unusual

worker artisan, craftsman, employee, hand, labourer, proletarian, tradesman, wage earner, working man, working woman, workman

working *n.* **1.** action, functioning, manner, method, mode of operation, operation, run~ ning **2.** *Plural* diggings, excavations, mine, pit, quarry, shaft ~*adj.* **3.** active, employed, in a job, in work, labouring **4.** functioning, going, operative, running **5.** effective, prac~ tical, useful, viable

workman artificer, artisan, craftsman, em~ ployee, hand, journeyman, labourer, me~ chanic, operative, tradesman, worker

workmanlike, workmanly adept, care~ ful, efficient, expert, masterly, painstaking, professional, proficient, satisfactory, skilful, skilled, thorough
Antonyms amateurish, botchy, careless, clumsy, cowboy (*Inf.*), incompetent, slap-dash, slipshod, unprofessional, unskilful

workmanship art, artistry, craft, crafts~ manship, execution, expertise, handicraft, handiwork, manufacture, skill, technique, work

work out 1. accomplish, achieve, attain, win **2.** calculate, clear up, figure out, find out, puzzle out, resolve, solve, suss (out) (*Sl.*) **3.** arrange, construct, contrive, devel~ op, devise, elaborate, evolve, form, formu~ late, plan, put together **4.** be effective, flourish, go as planned, go well, prosper, prove satisfactory, succeed **5.** come out, de~ velop, evolve, go, happen, pan out (*Inf.*), re~ sult, turn out **6.** do exercises, drill, exer~ cise, practise, train, warm up **7.** add up to, amount to, come to, reach, reach a total of

works 1. factory, mill, plant, shop, work~ shop **2.** canon, *oeuvre*, output, productions,

writings **3.** actions, acts, deeds, doings **4.** action, guts (*Inf.*), innards (*Inf.*), insides (*Inf.*), machinery, mechanism, movement, moving parts, parts, workings

workshop 1. atelier, factory, mill, plant, shop, studio, workroom, works **2.** class, discussion group, seminar, study group

work up agitate, animate, arouse, enkindle, excite, foment, generate, get (someone) all steamed up (*Sl.*), incite, inflame, instigate, move, rouse, spur, stir up, wind up (*Inf.*)

world 1. earth, earthly sphere, globe **2.** everybody, everyone, humanity, human~ kind, human race, man, mankind, men, the public, the race of man **3.** cosmos, creation, existence, life, nature, universe **4.** heavenly body, planet, star **5.** area, domain, envi~ ronment, field, kingdom, province, realm, sphere, system **6.** age, days, epoch, era, pe~ riod, times **7. for all the world** exactly, in every respect, in every way, just as if, just like, precisely, to all intents and purposes **8. on top of the world** *Inf.* beside oneself with joy, cock-a-hoop, ecstatic, elated, ex~ ultant, happy, in raptures, on cloud nine (*Inf.*), overjoyed, over the moon (*Inf.*) **9. out of this world** *Inf.* excellent, fabulous (*Inf.*), fantastic (*Inf.*), great (*Inf.*), incredible, indescribable, marvellous, superb, unbe~ lievable, wonderful

worldly 1. carnal, earthly, fleshly, lay, mundane, physical, profane, secular, sublu~ nary, temporal, terrestrial **2.** avaricious, covetous, grasping, greedy, materialistic, selfish, worldly-minded **3.** blasé, cosmopoli~ tan, experienced, knowing, politic, sophisti~ cated, urbane, well versed in the ways of the world, worldly-wise
Antonyms (*sense 1*) divine, ethereal, heav~ enly, immaterial, noncorporeal, spiritual, transcendental, unworldly (*sense 2*) moral, nonmaterialistic, unworldly (*sense 3*) ingenu~ ous, innocent, naive, unsophisticated, un~ worldly

worldwide general, global, international, omnipresent, pandemic, ubiquitous, uni~ versal
Antonyms confined, insular, limited, local, narrow, national, parochial, provincial, re~ stricted

worn 1. frayed, ragged, shabby, shiny, tat~ tered, tatty, the worse for wear, threadbare **2.** careworn, drawn, haggard, lined, pinched, wizened **3.** exhausted, fatigued, jaded, played-out (*Inf.*), spent, tired, tired out, wearied, weary, worn-out

worn-out 1. broken-down, clapped out (*Brit., Aust., & N.Z. inf.*), decrepit, done, frayed, moth-eaten, on its last legs, ragged, run-down, shabby, tattered, tatty, thread~ bare, used, used-up, useless, worn **2.** all in

(*Sl.*), clapped out (*Aust. & N.Z. inf.*), dead *or* out on one's feet (*Inf.*), dog-tired (*Inf.*), done in (*Inf.*), exhausted, fatigued, fit to drop, jiggered (*Dialect*), knackered (*Sl.*), played-out, prostrate, spent, tired, tired out, weary, zonked (*Sl.*)
Antonyms (*sense 2*) fresh, refreshed, relaxed, renewed, rested, restored, revived, strengthened

worried afraid, anxious, apprehensive, bothered, concerned, distracted, distraught, distressed, disturbed, fearful, fretful, frightened, ill at ease, nervous, on edge, overwrought, perturbed, tense, tormented, troubled, uneasy, unquiet, upset, wired (*Sl.*)
Antonyms calm, fearless, peaceful, quiet, tranquil, unafraid, unconcerned, unfazed (*Inf.*), unworried

worry *v.* **1.** agonize, annoy, badger, be anxious, bother, brood, disquiet, distress, disturb, feel uneasy, fret, harass, harry, hassle (*Inf.*), hector, importune, irritate, make anxious, perturb, pester, plague, tantalize, tease, torment, trouble, unsettle, upset, vex **2.** attack, bite, gnaw at, go for, harass, harry, kill, lacerate, savage, tear ~*n.* **3.** annoyance, bother, care, hassle (*Inf.*), irritation, pest, plague, problem, torment, trial, trouble, vexation **4.** annoyance, anxiety, apprehension, care, concern, disturbance, fear, irritation, misery, misgiving, perplexity, torment, trepidation, trouble, unease, vexation, woe
Antonyms *v.* be apathetic, be unconcerned, be unperturbed, calm, comfort, console, solace, soothe ~*n.* calm, comfort, consolation, peace of mind, reassurance, serenity, solace, tranquillity

worsen aggravate, damage, decay, decline, degenerate, deteriorate, exacerbate, get worse, go downhill (*Inf.*), go from bad to worse, retrogress, sink, take a turn for the worse
Antonyms ameliorate, better, enhance, improve, mend, recover, rectify, upgrade

worship 1. *v.* adore, adulate, deify, exalt, glorify, honour, idolize, laud, love, praise, pray to, put on a pedestal, respect, revere, reverence, venerate **2.** *n.* adoration, adulation, deification, devotion, exaltation, glorification, glory, homage, honour, laudation, love, praise, prayer(s), regard, respect, reverence
Antonyms *v.* blaspheme, deride, despise, disdain, dishonour, flout, mock, revile, ridicule, scoff at, spurn

worst *v.* beat, best, blow out of the water (*Sl.*), clobber (*Sl.*), conquer, crush, defeat, gain the advantage over, get the better of, lick (*Inf.*), master, overcome, overpower, overthrow, run rings around (*Inf.*), subdue,

subjugate, undo, vanquish, wipe the floor with (*Inf.*)

worth 1. aid, assistance, avail, benefit, credit, desert(s), estimation, excellence, goodness, help, importance, merit, quality, usefulness, utility, value, virtue, worthiness **2.** cost, price, rate, valuation, value
Antonyms (*sense 1*) futility, insignificance, paltriness, triviality, unworthiness, uselessness, worthlessness, wretchedness

worthless 1. chickenshit (*U.S. sl.*), futile, ineffectual, insignificant, inutile, meaningless, measly, miserable, nickel-and-dime (*U.S. sl.*), no use, nugatory, paltry, pointless, poor, poxy (*Sl.*), rubbishy, trashy, trifling, trivial, unavailing, unimportant, unusable, useless, valueless, wretched **2.** abandoned, abject, base, contemptible, depraved, despicable, good-for-nothing, ignoble, useless, vile
Antonyms consequential, decent, effective, fruitful, honourable, important, noble, precious, productive, profitable, significant, upright, useful, valuable, worthwhile, worthy

worthwhile beneficial, constructive, expedient, gainful, good, helpful, justifiable, productive, profitable, useful, valuable, worthy
Antonyms inconsequential, pointless, trivial, unimportant, unworthy, useless, vain, valueless, wasteful, worthless

worthy 1. *adj.* admirable, commendable, creditable, decent, dependable, deserving, estimable, excellent, good, honest, honourable, laudable, meritorious, praiseworthy, reliable, reputable, respectable, righteous, upright, valuable, virtuous, worthwhile **2.** *n.* big shot (*Inf.*), bigwig (*Inf.*), dignitary, luminary, notable, personage
Antonyms *adj.* demeaning, disreputable, dubious, ignoble, undeserving, unproductive, untrustworthy, unworthy, useless ~*n.* member of the rank and file, nobody, pleb, punter (*Inf.*)

wound *n.* **1.** cut, damage, gash, harm, hurt, injury, laceration, lesion, slash **2.** anguish, distress, grief, heartbreak, injury, insult, offence, pain, pang, sense of loss, shock, slight, torment, torture, trauma ~*v.* **3.** cut, damage, gash, harm, hit, hurt, injure, irritate, lacerate, pierce, slash, wing **4.** annoy, cut (someone) to the quick, distress, grieve, hurt, hurt the feelings of, mortify, offend, pain, shock, sting, traumatize

wrangle 1. *v.* altercate, argue, bicker, brawl, contend, disagree, dispute, fall out (*Inf.*), fight, have words, quarrel, row, scrap, spar, squabble **2.** *n.* altercation, angry exchange, argy-bargy (*Brit. inf.*), *bagarre*, barney (*Inf.*), bickering, brawl, clash, contest, controversy, dispute, falling-out (*Inf.*), quarrel, row, set-to (*Inf.*), slanging match (*Brit.*), squabble, tiff

wrap 1. *v.* absorb, bind, bundle up, cloak, cover, encase, enclose, enfold, envelop, fold, immerse, muffle, pack, package, roll up, sheathe, shroud, surround, swathe, wind **2.** *n.* cape, cloak, mantle, shawl, stole
Antonyms *v.* disclose, open, strip, uncover, unfold, unpack, unwind, unwrap

wrapper case, cover, envelope, jacket, packaging, paper, sheath, sleeve, wrapping

wrap up 1. bundle up, enclose, enwrap, giftwrap, pack, package **2.** dress warmly, muffle up, put warm clothes on, wear something warm **3.** *Sl.* be quiet, be silent, button it (*Sl.*), button one's lip (*Sl.*), hold one's tongue, put a sock in it (*Brit. sl.*), shut one's face (*Brit. sl.*), shut one's mouth (*Sl.*), shut one's trap (*Sl.*), shut up **4.** *Inf.* bring to a close, conclude, end, finish off, polish off, round off, terminate, tidy up, wind up

wrath anger, choler, displeasure, exaspera~ tion, fury, indignation, ire, irritation, pas~ sion, rage, resentment, temper
Antonyms amusement, contentment, de~ light, enjoyment, gladness, gratification, hap~ piness, joy, pleasure, satisfaction

wrathful angry, beside oneself with rage, displeased, enraged, furious, incensed, in~ dignant, infuriated, irate, on the warpath (*Inf.*), raging, wroth (*Archaic*)
Antonyms amused, calm, contented, de~ lighted, glad, gratified, happy, joyful, pleased, satisfied

wreath band, chaplet, coronet, crown, fes~ toon, garland, loop, ring

wreathe adorn, coil, crown, encircle, en~ fold, entwine, envelop, enwrap, festoon, intertwine, interweave, surround, twine, twist, wind, wrap, writhe

wreck *v.* **1.** blow (*Sl.*), break, cock up (*Brit. sl.*), dash to pieces, demolish, destroy, dev~ astate, fuck up (*Offens. taboo sl.*), mar, play havoc with, ravage, ruin, screw up (*Inf.*), shatter, smash, spoil, total (*Sl.*), trash (*Sl.*), undo **2.** founder, go *or* run aground, run onto the rocks, shipwreck, strand ~*n.* **3.** derelict, hulk, shipwreck, sunken vessel **4.** desolation, destruction, devastation, dis~ ruption, mess, overthrow, ruin, undoing
Antonyms *v.* build, conserve, create, fulfil, make possible, preserve, reconstruct, salvage, save ~*n.* conservation, creation, formation, fulfilment, preservation, restoration, salvage, saving

wreckage debris, fragments, hulk, pieces, remains, rubble, ruin, wrack

wrench *v.* **1.** force, jerk, pull, rip, tear, tug, twist, wrest, wring, yank **2.** distort, rick, sprain, strain ~*n.* **3.** jerk, pull, rip, tug, twist, yank **4.** sprain, strain, twist **5.** ache,

blow, pain, pang, shock, upheaval, uprooting **6.** adjustable spanner, shifting spanner, spanner

wrestle battle, combat, contend, fight, grap~ ple, scuffle, strive, struggle, tussle

wretch 1. asshole (*U.S. & Canad. taboo sl.*), asswipe (*U.S. & Canad. taboo sl.*), bad egg (*Old-fashioned inf.*), bastard (*Offens.*), black~ guard, bugger (*Taboo sl.*), cocksucker (*Ta~ boo sl.*), cur, good-for-nothing, miscreant, mother (*Taboo sl., chiefly U.S.*), mother~ fucker (*Taboo sl., chiefly U.S.*), outcast, profligate, rascal, rat (*Inf.*), rogue, rotter (*Sl., chiefly Brit.*), ruffian, scoundrel, scum~ bag (*Sl.*), shit (*Taboo sl.*), son-of-a-bitch (*Sl., chiefly U.S. & Canad.*), swine, turd (*Taboo sl.*), vagabond, villain, worm **2.** poor thing, unfortunate

wretched 1. abject, brokenhearted, cheer~ less, comfortless, crestfallen, dejected, de~ plorable, depressed, disconsolate, dismal, distressed, doleful, downcast, forlorn, fu~ nereal, gloomy, hapless, hopeless, melan~ choly, miserable, pathetic, pitiable, pitiful, poor, sorry, unfortunate, unhappy, woebe~ gone, woeful, worthless **2.** calamitous, de~ plorable, inferior, miserable, paltry, pathet~ ic, poor, sorry, worthless **3.** base, con~ temptible, crappy (*Sl.*), despicable, low, low-down (*Inf.*), mean, paltry, poxy (*Sl.*), scurvy, shabby, shameful, vile
Antonyms admirable, carefree, cheerful, contented, decent, enviable, excellent, flourishing, fortunate, great, happy, jovial, light-hearted, noble, prosperous, splendid, successful, thriving, untroubled, wonderful, worthy

wriggle *v.* **1.** jerk, jiggle, squirm, turn, twist, wag, waggle, wiggle, writhe **2.** crawl, slink, snake, twist and turn, worm, zigzag **3.** crawl, dodge, extricate oneself, manoeu~ vre, sneak, talk one's way out, worm ~*n.* **4.** jerk, jiggle, squirm, turn, twist, wag, wag~ gle, wiggle

wring 1. coerce, extort, extract, force, screw, squeeze, twist, wrench, wrest **2.** dis~ tress, hurt, lacerate, pain, pierce, rack, rend, stab, tear at, wound

wrinkle¹ 1. *n.* corrugation, crease, crinkle, crow's-foot, crumple, fold, furrow, gather, line, pucker, rumple **2.** *v.* corrugate, crease, crinkle, crumple, fold, furrow, gather, line, pucker, ruck, rumple
Antonyms *v.* even out, flatten, iron, level, press, smooth, straighten, unfold

wrinkle² device, dodge, gimmick, idea, plan, ploy, ruse, scheme, stunt, tip, trick, wheeze (*Brit. sl.*)

writ court order, decree, document, sum~ mons

write author (*Nonstandard*), commit to pa~

per, compose, copy, correspond, create, draft, draw up, indite, inscribe, jot down, pen, put down in black and white, put in writing, record, scribble, set down, take down, tell, transcribe

write off 1. cancel, cross out, disregard, forget about, give up for lost, score out, shelve **2.** *Inf.* crash, damage beyond repair, destroy, smash up, total (*Sl.*), trash (*Sl.*), wreck

writer author, columnist, essayist, hack, lit~ térateur, man of letters, novelist, penman, penny-a-liner (*Rare*), penpusher, scribbler, scribe, wordsmith

writhe contort, distort, jerk, squirm, strug~ gle, thrash, thresh, toss, twist, wiggle, wriggle

writing 1. calligraphy, chirography, hand, handwriting, penmanship, print, scrawl, scribble, script **2.** book, composition, docu~ ment, letter, opus, publication, title, work **3.** belles-lettres, letters, literature

wrong *adj.* **1.** erroneous, fallacious, false, faulty, inaccurate, incorrect, in error, mis~ taken, off beam (*Inf.*), off target, out, un~ sound, untrue, wide of the mark **2.** bad, blameworthy, criminal, crooked, dishonest, dishonourable, evil, felonious, illegal, illicit, immoral, iniquitous, reprehensible, sinful, under-the-table, unethical, unfair, unjust, unlawful, wicked, wrongful **3.** funny, im~ proper, inappropriate, inapt, incongruous, incorrect, indecorous, infelicitous, malap~ ropos, not done, unacceptable, unbecoming, unconventional, undesirable, unfitting, un~ happy, unseemly, unsuitable **4.** amiss, askew, awry, defective, faulty, not working, out of commission, out of order **5.** inside, inverse, opposite, reverse ~*adv.* **6.** amiss, askew, astray, awry, badly, erroneously, inaccurately, incorrectly, mistakenly, wrongly **7. go wrong a.** come to grief (*Inf.*), come to nothing, fail, fall through, flop (*Inf.*), miscarry, misfire **b.** boob (*Brit. sl.*), err, go astray, make a mistake, slip up (*Inf.*), **c.** break down, cease to function, conk out (*Inf.*), fail, go kaput (*Inf.*), go on the blink (*Sl.*), go phut (*Inf.*), malfunction,

misfire **d.** err, fall from grace, go astray, go off the straight and narrow (*Inf.*), go to the bad, lapse, sin ~*n.* **8.** abuse, bad *or* evil deed, crime, error, grievance, immorality, inequity, infraction, infringement, iniquity, injury, injustice, misdeed, offence, sin, sin~ fulness, transgression, trespass, unfairness, wickedness **9. in the wrong** at fault, blameworthy, guilty, in error, mistaken, off beam (*Inf.*), off course, off target, to be blamed ~*v.* **10.** abuse, cheat, discredit, dis~ honour, harm, hurt, ill-treat, ill-use, impose upon, injure, malign, maltreat, misrepre~ sent, mistreat, oppress, take advantage of **Antonyms** *adj.* accurate, appropriate, apt, becoming, commendable, correct, ethical, fair, fitting, godly, honest, honourable, just, laudable, lawful, legal, moral, praiseworthy, precise, proper, righteous, rightful, seemly, sensible, square, suitable, true, upright, vir~ tuous ~*adv.* accurately, correctly, exactly, precisely, properly, squarely, truly ~*n.* de~ cency, fairness, favour, good, good deed, goodness, good turn, high-mindedness, hon~ esty, lawfulness, legality, morality, propriety, virtue ~*v.* aid, do a favour, help, support, treat well

wrongdoer criminal, culprit, delinquent, evildoer, lawbreaker, malefactor, miscreant, offender, sinner, transgressor, trespasser (*Archaic*), villain

wrongful blameworthy, criminal, dishon~ est, dishonourable, evil, felonious, illegal, illegitimate, illicit, immoral, improper, rep~ rehensible, under-the-table, unethical, un~ fair, unjust, unlawful, wicked
Antonyms ethical, fair, honest, honourable, just, lawful, legal, legitimate, moral, proper, rightful

wry 1. askew, aslant, awry, contorted, crooked, deformed, distorted, off the level, skewwhiff (*Brit. inf.*), twisted, uneven, warped. **2.** droll, dry, ironic, mocking, mordacious, pawky (*Scot.*), sarcastic, sar~ donic
Antonyms (*sense 1*) aligned, even, level, smooth, straight, unbent

X.Y.Z

Xmas Christmas, Christmastide, festive season, Noel, Yule (*Archaic*), Yuletide (*Archaic*)

X-rays Röntgen rays (*Old name*)

yank *v./n.* hitch, jerk, pull, snatch, tug, wrench

yardstick benchmark, criterion, gauge, measure, par, standard, touchstone

yarn *n.* **1.** fibre, thread **2.** *Inf.* anecdote, cock-and-bull story (*Inf.*), fable, story, tale, tall story

yawning cavernous, chasmal, gaping, vast, wide, wide-open

yearly annual, annually, every year, once a year, per annum

yearn ache, covet, crave, desire, eat one's heart out over, hanker, have a yen for (*Inf.*), hunger, itch, languish, long, lust, pant, pine, set one's heart upon

yell 1. *v.* bawl, holler (*Inf.*), howl, scream, screech, shout, shriek, squeal **2.** *n.* cry, howl, scream, screech, shriek, whoop
Antonyms *v.* mumble, murmur, mutter, say softly, whisper

yelp cry, yammer (*Inf.*), yap, yip (*Chiefly U.S.*), yowl

yes man ass-kisser (*U.S. & Canad. taboo sl.*), bootlicker (*Inf.*), bosses' lackey, company man, crawler (*Sl.*), creature, minion, sycophant, timeserver, toady

yet 1. as yet, so far, thus far, until now, up to now **2.** however, nevertheless, notwithstanding, still **3.** additionally, as well, besides, further, in addition, into the bargain, moreover, over and above, still, to boot **4.** already, just now, now, right now, so soon

yield *v.* **1.** afford, bear, bring forth, bring in, earn, furnish, generate, give, net, pay, produce, provide, return, supply ~*n.* **2.** crop, earnings, harvest, income, output, produce, profit, return, revenue, takings ~*v.* **3.** abandon, abdicate, admit defeat, bow, capitulate, cave in (*Inf.*), cede, cry quits, give in, give up the struggle, give way, knuckle under, lay down one's arms, part with, raise the white flag, relinquish, resign, resign oneself, submit, succumb, surrender, throw in the towel **4.** accede, agree, allow, bow, comply, concede, consent, go along with, grant, permit
Antonyms *v.* appropriate, attack, combat, commandeer, consume, counterattack, defy, grab, hold on to, hold out, keep, lose, maintain,

oppose, reserve, resist, retain, seize, struggle, use, use up ~*n.* consumption, input, loss

yielding 1. accommodating, acquiescent, biddable, compliant, docile, easy, flexible, obedient, pliant, submissive, tractable **2.** elastic, pliable, quaggy, resilient, soft, spongy, springy, supple, unresisting
Antonyms (*sense 1*) dogged, headstrong, mulish, obstinate, opinionated, perverse, stiff-necked, stubborn, tenacious, wilful

yoke *n.* **1.** bond, chain, coupling, ligament, link, tie **2.** bondage, burden, enslavement, helotry, oppression, serfdom, service, servility, servitude, slavery, thraldom, vassalage ~*v.* **3.** bracket, connect, couple, harness, hitch, join, link, tie, unite

yokel boor, bucolic, clodhopper (*Inf.*), (country) bumpkin, country cousin, countryman, hayseed (*U.S. & Canad. inf.*), hick (*Inf., chiefly U.S. & Canad.*), hillbilly, hind (*Obsolete*), peasant (*Inf.*), rustic

young *adj.* **1.** adolescent, callow, green, growing, immature, infant, in the springtime of life, junior, juvenile, little, unfledged, youthful **2.** at an early stage, early, fledgling, new, newish, not far advanced, recent, undeveloped ~*n.* **3.** babies, brood, family, issue, litter, little ones, offspring, progeny
Antonyms *adj.* adult, advanced, aged, developed, elderly, experienced, full-grown, grown-up, mature, old, ripe, senior, venerable ~*n.* adult, grown-up, parent

youngster boy, cub, girl, juvenile, kid (*Inf.*), lad, lass, pup (*Inf., chiefly Brit.*), teenager, teenybopper (*Sl.*), urchin, young adult, young hopeful, young person, young shaver (*Inf.*), young 'un (*Inf.*), youth

youth 1. adolescence, boyhood, early life, girlhood, immaturity, juvenescence, salad days, young days **2.** adolescent, boy, kid (*Inf.*), lad, shaveling (*Archaic*), stripling, teenager, young man, young shaver (*Inf.*), youngster **3.** teenagers, the rising generation, the young, younger generation, young people
Antonyms adult, adulthood, age, grown-up, later life, manhood, maturity, OAP, old age, pensioner, senior citizen, the aged, the elderly, the old, womanhood

youthful 1. boyish, childish, girlish, immature, inexperienced, juvenile, pubescent, puerile, young **2.** active, fresh, spry, vigorous, young at heart, young looking
Antonyms adult, aged, ageing, ancient,

careworn, decaying, decrepit, elderly, grown-up, hoary, mature, old, over the hill, senile, senior, tired, waning, weary

zeal ardour, devotion, eagerness, earnest~ness, enthusiasm, fanaticism, fervency, fer~vour, fire, gusto, keenness, militancy, pas~sion, spirit, verve, warmth, zest
Antonyms apathy, coolness, indifference, passivity, stoicism, torpor, unresponsiveness

zealot bigot, enthusiast, extremist, fanatic, fiend (*Inf.*), maniac, militant

zealous afire, ardent, burning, devoted, eager, earnest, enthusiastic, fanatical, fer~vent, fervid, impassioned, keen, militant, passionate, rabid, spirited
Antonyms apathetic, cold, cool, half-hearted, indifferent, lackadaisical, lacklustre, languorous, listless, low-key, sceptical, torpid, unenthusiastic, unimpassioned

zenith acme, apex, apogee, climax, crest, height, high noon, high point, meridian, peak, pinnacle, summit, top, vertex
Antonyms base, bottom, depths, lowest point, nadir, rock bottom

zero 1. cipher, naught, nil, nothing, nought **2.** bottom, lowest point *or* ebb, nadir, noth~ing, rock bottom

zero hour appointed hour, crisis, moment of decision, moment of truth, turning point, vital moment

zest 1. appetite, delectation, enjoyment, gusto, keenness, relish, zeal, zing (*Inf.*) **2.** charm, flavour, interest, kick (*Inf.*), pi~quancy, pungency, relish, savour, smack, spice, tang, taste
Antonyms abhorrence, apathy, aversion, disinclination, distaste, indifference, lack of enthusiasm, loathing, repugnance, weariness

zing animation, brio, dash, energy, go (*Inf.*), life, liveliness, oomph (*Inf.*), pep, pizzazz *or* pizazz (*Inf.*), spirit, vigour, vitality, zest, zip (*Inf.*)

zip 1. *n. Fig.* brio, drive, energy, get-up-and-go (*Inf.*), go (*Inf.*), gusto, life, liveliness, oomph (*Inf.*), pep, pizzazz *or* pizazz (*Inf.*), punch (*Inf.*), sparkle, spirit, verve, vigour, vim (*Sl.*), vitality, zest, zing (*Inf.*) **2.** *v.* bar~rel (along) (*Inf., chiefly U.S. & Canad.*), burn rubber (*Inf.*), dash, flash, fly, hurry, rush, shoot, speed, tear, whiz (*Inf.*), zoom
Antonyms apathy, indifference, inertia, la~ziness, lethargy, listlessness, sloth, sluggish~ness

zone area, belt, district, region, section, sec~tor, sphere

zoom *v.* barrel (along) (*Inf., chiefly U.S. & Canad.*), burn rubber (*Inf.*), buzz, dash, dive, flash, fly, hare (*Brit. inf.*), hum (*Sl.*), hurtle, pelt, rip (*Inf.*), rush, shoot, speed, streak, tear, whirl, whiz (*Inf.*), zip (*Inf.*)